The Dictionary of

BRITISH ARTISTS
1880-1940

An Antique Collectors' Club Research Project
listing 41,000 artists.
Compiled by J. Johnson and A. Greutzner

Antique Collectors' Club

Reprinted 1980

This book has been published with financial assistance from the Arts Council of Great Britain.

The illustrations on the dust jacket are a selection of 19th and 20th century paintings reproduced by courtesy of David Messum (Fine Paintings) Ltd., London and Beaconsfield, Bucks.

ISBN 0 902028 36 7

Printed in England by
Baron Publishing, Church Street, Woodbridge, Suffolk.

THE ANTIQUE COLLECTORS' CLUB

The Antique Collectors' Club, formed in 1966, pioneered the provision of information on prices for collectors. The Club's monthly magazine *Antique Collecting* was the first to tackle the complex problems of describing to collectors the various features which can influence prices. In response to the enormous demand for this type of information the *Price Guide Series* was introduced in 1968 with **The Price Guide to Antique Furniture** (new edition 1978), a book which broke new ground by illustrating the more common types of antique furniture, the sort that collectors could buy in shops and at auctions, rather than the rare museum pieces which had previously been used (and still to a large extent are used) to make up the limited amount of illustrations in books published by commercial publishers. Many other price guides have followed, all copiously illustrated, and greatly appreciated by collectors for the valuable information they contain, quite apart from prices.

Club membership, which is open to all collectors, costs £8.95 per annum. Members receive free of charge *Antique Collecting,* the Club's magazine (published every month except August), which contains well-illustrated articles dealing with the practical aspects of collecting not normally dealt with by magazines. Prices, features of value, investment potential, fakes and forgeries are all given prominence in the magazine.

In addition members buy and sell among themselves; the Club charges a nominal fee for introductions but takes no commission. Since the Club started many thousands of antiques have been offered for sale privately. No other publication contains anything to match the long list of items for sale privately which appears monthly.

The presentation of useful information and the facility to buy and sell privately would alone have assured the success of the Club, but perhaps the feature most valued by members if the ability to make contact with other collectors living nearby. Not only do members learn about the other branches of collecting but they make interesting friendships. The Club organises weekend seminars and other meetings.

As its motto implies, the club is an amateur organisation designed to help collectors to get the most out of their hobby: it is informal and friendly and gives enormous enjoyment to all concerned.

For Collectors — By Collectors — About Collecting

The Antique Collectors' Club, Woodbridge, Suffolk.

COMPILERS' NOTES AND ACKNOWLEDGEMENTS

The *Dictionary of British Artists 1760-1893* by Algernon Graves provided the first detailed listing of exhibiting artists. Until the publication of Christopher Wood's *Dictionary of Victorian Painters,* second edition (October 1977), it remained the most complete listing of artists working during the period. The method of compilation was to select some sixteen London exhibitions and from the catalogues arrange the artists in alphabetical order, indicating the number of pictures exhibited at each location. In addition the town of residence was given and a single word description of their "speciality" was provided. The resulting publication was a very useful basic work giving primary information on some 21,000 artists.

The absence of comparable information for the subsequent period has been a noticeable gap in art reference literature and so it was decided to provide what amounts to a much improved continuation of Graves. Whereas Graves confined himself to London, it was decided to extend the scope to the regions and, as can be seen from the list of forty-seven galleries, this has produced a dictionary far more representative of British art, as not every artist chooses to exhibit in London. In addition, more commercial galleries were included.

Thanks to the courtesy of the proprietors of the Art Trade Press Limited, we have sole rights to make use of the editions of "Who's Who in Art" which covered the period, and thus we had access to a mine of information on artists of the period. To this was added a number of contemporary sources listed in the bibliography, together with newspaper reports etc. The result has been to produce a listing of some 41,000 artists which we hope will provide a good basic research document for anyone wishing to gain information about an artist. We have not followed Graves's example in giving a "speciality". Our work on *The Royal Society of British Artists 1824-1893* made it clear that short descriptions of an artist's "speciality" can be positively misleading.

We have endeavoured to include all regular exhibitions from 1880-1940. However in some cases, such as the Royal Hibernian Academy's Annual Exhibitions of 1890 and 1891 and the Nottingham Society of Artists Exhibitions of 1883 and 1905-7, copies of catalogues could not be traced. There were many more galleries which we would have liked to include. For example, in the case of the Royal West of England Academy, thirty-one of the catalogues for the period had been destroyed during the second world war, and to search out and find other sources of these catalogues would have proved too time-consuming and costly. It was therefore regretfully decided to omit such galleries from our list.

The inclusion of a star after an artist's name indicates that a work by him or her has fetched more than £100 at auction in the period 1970-1975. This is not an attempt to provide valuations of an artist's work, but merely to provide an indication of contemporary opinion as to its desirability to collectors, investors, home furnishers etc. This information has been obtained by reference to the excellent publications of Art Sales Index Ltd., who list full details and exact prices at auction of the thousands of pictures of all periods that pass through all the major salerooms and many of the minor ones as well. We have no hesitation in recommending these first-rate publications which are published with remarkable speed after the sales and also appear in convenient annual form. To anyone seriously interested in the market value of paintings, they are indispensable. Current rates of subscription can be obtained from Art Sales Index Ltd., Pond House, Weybridge, Surrey, England.

Only those artists, including foreigners and architects, who exhibited at the galleries listed during the years 1880-1940 have been included in this dictionary; to have mentioned other artists, however important, would have made the book unending.

In an effort to be concise and to keep this volume to a manageable size, relevant information has been recorded as briefly as possible. Arrangement of names is alphabetical.

Where birth and/or death dates are not known, the first and last year of exhibiting has been used prefixed by Exh. (exhibited). The date an artist became a member of a Society is to be found before the address. It was felt to be of value to include works executed or exhibited between 1880-1940 that were purchased by the Chantrey Bequest, which was founded by the considerable fortune left by the sculptor Sir Francis Chantrey R.A. (1781-1841) for the acquisition of works of art executed in Britain. The date of execution of exhibition of the works has only been included if this varies by any great degree from the purchase date. Full addresses have usually been given only when no other address appeared in the catalogues; where several changes occurred the dates of change appear after the various towns of residence.

The following example and explanation are included to clarify the construction of entries.

Example

HARTRICK, Archibald Standish* 1864-1950

Painter and illustrator. b. Madras, India. Married Lily Blatherwick q.v. N.E.A. 1894, A.R.W.S. 1910, R.W.S. 1922. "The Penitents' Bench" (1904). Purchased by Chantrey Bequest 1934. Add: London 1885 and 1892; Helensburgh N.B. 1887. † B 1, BA 1, BG 1, CHE 3, FIN 6, G 2, GI 81, GOU 24, I 72, L 33, LEI 8, M 13, NEA 68, RA 29, RBA 2, RE 1, RHA 16, ROI 5, RSA 21, RWS 229, WG 36.

Explanation

HARTRICK, Archibald Standish

* (At least one picture has sold in one of the major Auction Galleries from 1970-75 as listed by the Art Sales Index for more than £100.)

Born 1864, died 1950. Painter and illustrator. Born in Madras, India. Married Lily Blatherwick who also has an entry in this book. Became a member of the New English Art Club in 1894, an Associate Member of the Royal Society of Painters in Watercolours in 1910 and a full member of the R.W.S. in 1922. "The Penitents' Bench" dated 1904 was purchased by the Chantrey Bequest in 1934. His address was recorded in the catalogues as London 1885-86, Helensburgh 1887-91 and London from 1892 onwards. † (Separation of the main entry from the list of galleries and the total works exhibited.) One work exhibited at the Royal Society of Artists, Birmingham, one work exhibited at the Beaux Arts Gallery, one work exhibited at the Baillie Gallery, etc. etc.

We are conscious that we will inevitably have left out a number of artists and should most grateful for information on these and also of birth and death dates where missing so that they may be included in subsequent editions.

The publishers and ourselves are most grateful to the Arts Council for their financial contribution towards the publication of this book. As the economics of publishing become harder, works of this magnitude are likely to become impossible without a degree of patronage. We should also like to thank all those people and societies — too many to mention by name — who have given their support, assistance, knowledge and patience to this project.

LIST OF GALLERIES AND SOCIETIES WITH THEIR ABBREVIATIONS

AB Abbey Gallery
AG Agnew & Sons Gallery
ALP Alpine Club Gallery
AR Arlington Gallery
B Royal Society of Artists, Birmingham
BA Beaux Arts Gallery
BAR Barbizon House
BG Baillie Gallery
BK Brook Street Art Gallery
BRU Bruton Galleries
CAR Carfax & Co. Gallery
CG Colnaghi & Co. Galleries
CHE Chenil and New Chenil Galleries
CON Connell & Sons Gallery
COO Cooling & Sons Gallery
D Dudley Gallery and New Dudley Gallery
DOW Dowdeswell Galleries
FIN Fine Art Society
G Grosvenor Gallery
GI Glasgow Institute of the Fine Arts
GOU Goupil Gallery
I International Society
L Walker Art Gallery, Liverpool
LEF Lefevre Gallery
LEI Leicester Gallery
LS London Salon
M Manchester City Art Gallery
N Nottingham Museum and Art Gallery
NEA New English Art Club
NG New Gallery
NSA Nottingham Society of Artists
P Royal Society of Portrait Painters
RA Royal Academy
RBA Royal Society of British Artists
RCA Royal Cambrian Academy
RE Royal Society of Painter-Etchers and Engravers
RED Redfern Gallery
RHA Royal Hibernian Academy
RI Royal Institute of Painters in Water Colours
RID Ridley Art Club
RMS Royal Miniature Society
ROI Royal Institute of Oil Painters
RP Royal Society of Portrait Painters
RSA Royal Scottish Academy
RSW Royal Scottish Society of Painters in Water Colours
RWS Royal Society of Painters in Water Colours
SWA Society of Women Artists
TOO Arthur Tooth & Sons Gallery
WG Walker's Gallery, London

GENERAL ABBREVIATIONS

A	Associate
A.A.	Architectural Association
Add.	Address
b.	Born
c.	Circa
C.I.	Channel Islands
d.	Died
Exh.	Exhibited
H	Honorary
I.O.M.	Isle of Man
I.O.W.	Isle of Wight
Junr.	Junior
L.C.C.	London County Council
N.B.	North Britain
Nr.	Near
P	President
q.v.	Quod vide
R.A.M.C.	Royal Army Medical Corps
Rd.	Road
R.F.A.	Royal Field Artilery
R.I.B.A.	Royal Institute of British Architects
Senr.	Senior
Sq.	Square
St.	Saint or Street
Terr.	Terrace
V & A	Victoria and Albert Museum
V.A.D.	Voluntary Aid Detachment
V.P.	Vice President

SELECTED BIBLIOGRAPHY

Art Sales Index 1970-75
British 19th Century Marine Painting by Denys Brook-Hart
British Sculpture and Sculptors of Today by M.H. Spielmann
A Dictionary of Artists 1760-1893 by Algernon Graves
Dictionary of National Biography
Dictionary of Victorian Painters by Christopher Wood
History of the Old Water Colour Society
Royal Academy Exhibitors 1769-1904 by Algernon Graves
Royal Society of British Artists 1824-1893 A.C.C. Research Project
Tate Gallery Collection — Catalogue of Works
Who's Who in Art
The Williams Family of Painters by Jan Reynolds

INTRODUCTION

In 1907 a reviewer of the art world for the *Studio Magazine* saw nothing but a sleepy complacency. "The whole of modern art is affected by this somnolence, and a drowsy inclination to let things stay as they are is one of the most disappointing peculiarities of the artists of the present day."[1]

In the first years of the twentieth century the Royal Academy was accused, even by its friends, of a lack of energy, of a deadening similarity between summer exhibitions and an overt hostility to change. The Royal Hibernian Society failed to convince that Irish art could pull out of its listless decline. The same old faces were to be seen at the annual exhibitions of the Royal Scottish Academy. Throughout the British art market money that should have been supporting living artists was being gambled away on "speculative Old Masters". Only the most established painters could be sure of exhibitions in commercial galleries.

How much more depressing was this "sleepy mellowness" when independent groups and established institutions had, at the beginning of our period, genuinely tried to revitalise British art. With the death of that ossified animal painter, Francis Grant, and the election of the more cosmopolitan and tolerant Frederick Leighton as President, it was hoped that the Royal Academy would be more sympathetic to the young, less restrictive in its practices, and less insular in its attitudes. The attendances at the 1879 Summer Exhibition were a record, nearly 400,000 visitors. There was certainly enough interest to create a market for illustrated records of the chief works at Burlington House. Henry Blackburn's *Academy Notes*, the *Pall Mall Gazette Extras*, Cassell's and Judd's publications took black and white photographs, often from sketches specially drawn by the artist, to those who could not get to London.

The Royal Society of British Artists, itself formed as a radical alternative to the Academy in 1823, had become largely moribund by the 1880s and enlisted the services of James Whistler as member and then President (1886) to widen the aesthetic scope of its exhibitions.

New societies and clubs sprang up from the 1880s to foster specialised branches of art, such as the Society of Painter-Etchers in 1880, the Society of Portrait Painters in 1891 and the Arts and Crafts Exhibition Society in 1888. The opening of the Tate Gallery (1897-9), the Whitechapel Art Gallery (1899) and the Wallace Collection (1900) broadened the scope of art on show in London, while new art galleries opened in Liverpool (1877), Manchester (1882), Leicester and Aberdeen (1885) and Leeds (1888). As well as conserving modern works of art, many institutions organised exhibitions during the year at which living artists could sell their works, the Royal Manchester Institution, the Royal Birmingham Society of Artists, and the Glasgow Institute of the Fine Arts, for example.

The most significant coalescing of extra-Academic forces was largely brought about, not by government or municipal authority, but by the initiative of private individuals: for instance, Sir Coutts Lindsay's financing of the Grosvenor Gallery (1877-1890). The Grosvenor allowed painters such as Whistler, Albert Moore, G.F. Watts and particularly Edward Burne-Jones to show their works annually without suffering the prejudices of unsympathetic juries and hanging committees. The Grosvenor permitted invited artists to hang their works together in blocks, in mutual support, and undertook to treat individual works with "tender understanding".[2] In 1877 Burne-Jones was given the entire south wall of the West Gallery for his paintings. The Royal Academy, on the evidence of W.P. Frith's *The Private View at the Royal Academy* (1883), hung accepted works from floor to ceiling. It was not unusual for a young or controversial artist such as John Brett or John Everett Millais in the 1860s, and Frank Brangwyn in the 1890s, to find his work available only to the spectator with opera glasses. Even in 1898 a critic complained that, "With us in England, an exhibition wall is a thing to be veneered — veneered with painted canvases in gold frames. It is not accepted as a background and discreetly used as such for the display of a few good things."[3]

As Whistler put it, "We want clean spaces round our pictures. We want them to be seen. The British Artists must cease to be a shop."[4] He offered an approach to exhibiting even more radical than that of the Grosvenor with its Palladian portal and rich silk hangings. He reduced the distractions of yawning space in the upper gallery with a hanging velarium and created sympathetic wall surfaces with hangings of white felt, muslin, or green canvas. Nothing was left to chance. His exhibition at Dowdeswell's rooms in Bond Street (1884) was arranged on a theme of flesh colour and grey, with frames of three shades of metallic grey, walls painted accordingly and attendants dressed "en suite".

Apart from the New Gallery, formed in 1888 when Comyns Carr and Charles Hallé broke away from the management of the Grosvenor,[5] the most exciting development in the promotion of progressive British painting was the New English Art Club, which started exhibiting in 1886 at the Marlborough Gallery in Pall Mall, and which was a focus for the new talent that emerged in opposition to the Royal Academy. The Club at its inception was a curious blend of Newlyn *plein-air* painters (La Thangue and Stanhope Forbes), the Glasgow Boys (George Henry, John Lavery) who reacted against the "Gluepotism" of their elders in the Royal Scottish Academy, and that group which were in 1889 to exhibit as the London Impressionists (Sickert, Wilson Steer and Fred Brown). Although the Impressionists soon asserted their influence to the exclusion of the others, the N.E.A.C. remained, at least in the 1890s to the young artist like Roger Fry, "the best place to exhibit in England."[6]

One major agent for the dissemination of contemporary British art was the International Society of Sculptors, Painters and Gravers initiated by Whistler in 1898 at the Knightsbridge Skating Rink. The younger British generation of painters, Charles Shannon, William Rothenstein and William Nicholson, could be seen in the company of contemporary European artists, Monet, Rodin, Lautrec and Toorop, in uncluttered and sensitively decorated surroundings. The International Society did not see these reforms purely in cosmopolitan terms; in 1906 they put on "the most representative show of modern art in the provinces"[7] at the Cartwright Memorial Hall in Bradford.

Sadly, the Royal Academy had not fulfilled the promise of Leighton's early years. Despite his attempts at objectivity Leighton encouraged a school of decorative classicism at the Summer shows and failed to effect a compromise with more dynamic elements outside the Academy, notably Madox Brown, G.F. Watts and Burne-Jones. By 1897 attendances at the Summer exhibition had dropped to 250,000. Leighton had been succeeded by Millais, briefly, then by the irascible and rigid Edward Poynter. Leighton's own very individual style had infected a whole new generation of figure painters such as Harold Speed, Herbert Draper, Henrietta Rae and Herbert Schmalz. The Press and opinion critical of restrictive practices forced the Government to set up a Select Committee in 1904 to examine the Academy's administration of the Chantrey Bequest and apparent refusal to purchase works from outside its ranks. Evidence given by that mainstay of the *status quo*, William Blake Richmond, revealed a vituperative detestation of modern French painting. This augured badly for those young painters who were looking to the continent for a liberation in style and subject matter, and who wished to pursue careers through the London galleries.

The Report of the Select Committee did much to undermine the Academy's authority, already weakened by large retrospective shows of nineteenth century art in Glasgow (1901) and Wolverhampton (1902) which had emphasised how vital were the forces that existed beyond Burlington House. The Franco-British Exhibition (1908) at Shepherds Bush allowed a sizeable contribution from outsiders William Rothenstein, William Orpen, Adrian Stokes and E.A. Hornel.

The resurgence of the British art world in the 1880s had failed elsewhere; the Grosvenor Gallery closed in 1890, the New Gallery after 1909 was transformed, significantly, into a cinema. The Royal Society of British Artists had panicked at the notoriety that Whistler's name had attracted and asked for his resignation in 1888, returning to their comfortable and moribund state. The N.E.A.C. whose rebellion had, it was rumoured, been plotted in pipe and slippers, had developed hardened arteries by 1907 and was to degenerate into a reactionary and repressive force in British art. But this "unusually somnolent condition"[8] that Wyndham Lewis remembered was rudely shattered by that extraordinary series of exhibitions stimulated in London and outside by Roger Fry's exhibition, "Manet and the Post-Impressionists", held in 1910 at the Grafton Gallery in London. It was assembled at great speed and was drawn from the galleries of the Paris dealers mainly, Vollard, Druet and Kahnweiler. Because of the *ad hoc* nature of the preparations, there was a heavy reliance on what was then available, a large number of Cézannes, of Gauguins (37 in all), over twenty Van Goghs, but little adequate coverage of Seurat and Signac. The intensity of the public and critical reception must have shocked even Fry. To a public already disturbed by labour unrest, trouble in Ulster and Suffragettes, the exhibition seemed to add yet further anarchy. Accusations of indecency, pornography and fraud were hurled at Fry and his committee. But the most fruitful aspect of the exhibition was the liberating effect it had on the young generation of painters, on Vanessa Bell and Duncan Grant, for example.[9] Mark Gertler judged in retrospect that the entry of "Cézanne, Gauguin, Matisse, etc., upon my horizon was equivalent to the impact of the scientists of this age upon a simple student of Sir Isaac Newton."[10]

Fry had recorded in 1911 that things had moved in England with prodigious rapidity.[11] His exhibition had done much to wake the sleeper into an awareness of, or reaction against, one vital and original element in contemporary European art, particularly the art of Cézanne, Van Gogh and Gauguin. Two years later, at the "Second Post-Impressionist Exhibition", at the same gallery, there was enough British response to the first show to enable Fry to show Cézanne, Picasso, Braque and Matisse in the company of a British group which included Vanessa Bell, Frederick Etchells, Spencer Gore, Wyndham Lewis and Stanley Spencer. The impact of Fry's Post-Impressionist shows was reinforced by the Stafford Gallery's exhibition of Gauguin and Cézanne (1911), and compounded by Frank Rutter's "Post Impressionist and Others" exhibition at the Doré Gallery (1913).

Another generative influence on the creation of what can be called the first British *avant-garde* since the Pre-Raphaelite generation of the 1840s was Italian Futurism as promoted by Marinetti and seen in shows at the Sackville Gallery (1912) and the Doré Gallery (1914). Marinetti's frenetic and bombastic performances of his own poetry and declamations of his manifestos showed to the British *avant-garde* how artists could make themselves noticed by a generally indifferent public, although no one followed his example of appearing on the music halls. The paintings to which British audiences were directed by Marinetti, such as Carlo Carra's *Funeral of the Anarchist Galli*, (shown at the Sackville Gallery in 1912), celebrated speed, dynamism and violence in a vivid mesh of interpenetrating planes and staccato linear rhythms. The pace of innovation quickened with other readily available influences such as Picasso's 1912 show at the Stafford Gallery.

In contrast with the dormant art world of 1900-1910 and the unpropitious decade of the 1920s, the period between the first Post-Impressionist exhibition and the departure of British artists for the War was anarchic in its groupings and regroupings, its fusion and fracture of personalities and styles. Countless groups emerged only to dissolve when loyalties shifted and stylistic allegiances changed. So Grant could exhibit with the Friday Club, the Grafton Group, at the Omega workshop, at the London Group and even, after Fry's quarrel with Lewis, with the Vorticists. Lewis began to show with the N.E.A.C. and with the Camden Town Group, then at Fry's Second Post-Impressionist exhibition, at the Omega workshops, the Rebel Art Centre and finally at his own Vorticist show in 1915.

"These new masses of unexplored arts and facts are pouring into the vortex of London. They cannot help bringing about changes as great as the Renaissance changes . . .", wrote Ezra Pound.[12] How were these masses to be sorted and distributed to a fascinated but bewildered public? In May 1910 a group including Roger Fry, Clive Bell, Robert Ross and D.S. MacColl formed the Contemporary Art Society to insinuate into public collections works by contemporary artists. Early purchases of Jacob Epstein, Walter Sickert and Augustus John were seen between 1910-1914 in loan exhibitions to Manchester, Leeds,

Bradford and Aberdeen. Within the space of four years the Whitechapel Art Gallery had given two major surveys of contemporary art to the East End of London: "Twenty Years of British Art" (1890-1910), showing the earlier generation of Wilson Steer and William Nicholson, and "Twentieth Century Art. A Review of Modern Movements", concentrating on the new generation of Duncan Grant, Vanessa Bell, Roger Fry, Spencer, Wadsworth, Lewis and Sickert. Exhibitions in Liverpool (1913), Leicester (1913) and Brighton (1913/4) extended the pull of the Vortex beyond London.

But it was in the network of smaller London galleries and transient art societies that the forces of modern art intensified their experiments. The Allied Artists' Association, organised by Frank Rutter, gave the young artist the chance from 1908 to show work without the intervention of dealers or a selecting jury. However, many dealers were willing to take a risk, aesthetic and financial, in a way that would have seemed inconceivable in the nineteenth century. Instead of hedging bets in a mixed show, commercial gallery owners in the early years of this century tended to countenance, even encourage, the one-man show, for example Bevan and J.D. Fergusson at the Baillie Gallery (1905), or Sickert at Merrill's Stafford Gallery (1911). The outstanding gallery in this respect was the Carfax in Bury Street, St. James's, opened in the 1890s by John Fothergill, with Robert Ross as director, Sickert's brother Robert as manager, and William Rothenstein as adviser. Here the British public saw for the first time one-man shows by Augustus John (1899), Ambrose McEvoy (1907), Paul Nash (1912) and Duncan Grant (1920), and the three exhibitions of the Camden Town Group (1911, twice, and 1912). "Ross", it was said, "has never been known to have an uninteresting exhibition."

John Knewstub's Chenil Gallery (financed largely by William Orpen and established near the Chelsea Town Hall) mounted the first exhibition of J.D. Innes (1910/1) and David Bomberg (1914), as well as work by Mark Gertler (1910) and Eric Gill (1911). Also identified with progressive modern art was William Marchant's Goupil Gallery; from 1906 it was his stated policy to "represent the modern school in England", ranging from John Lavery (1908) to Charles Ginner and Harold Gilman (1914) and the London Group from 1914 to 1916. At the Alpine Gallery the paraphernalia of mountaineering was cleared away from 1910 for Fry's Friday Club and Grafton Group shows, and at the Doré Gallery (the scene of periodic conversions in the 1880s before Gustave Dore's gigantic canvases of the life of Christ), could be seen the second and final Futurist exhibition (1914) and the first and only Vorticist exhibition (1915).

It is some measure of the optimism generated after the "Manet and the Post-Impressionists" exhibition that Fry was offered the wall space of the Grafton Gallery during the autumn of each year. He foresaw "a general secession exhibition of non-academic art"[13] but the general instability of the groupings, and suspicions of Fry's motives, prevented its realisation.

With the setting up of the Omega workshops in July 1913 in premises at 33 Fitzroy Square, Fry realised outside a commercial gallery his ideal in creating a centre for young and progressive artists to meet and work in comparative financial security. The Omega provided that element of mutual support Fry felt was so vital for the development of British art. Artists like Grant and Bell, Gaudier and Nina Hamnett, Lewis and Bomberg, worked in the complex of showroom, design studios and artists' workshops. "It will embrace the making of 'character' furniture which will reflect the artistic feeling of the age", read the prospectus.

But Lewis and Fry were, as artists and theoreticians, radically different, and long-concealed hostility and suspicion finally caused the secession of Lewis's group in October 1913 when an argument broke out as to who exactly had been commissioned to design a "Post-Impressionist" room at the Ideal Home Exhibition.[14] In March 1914 Lewis's "little gang" of Roberts, Wadsworth, Hamilton, Dismorr, Saunders and Etchells, formed themselves into the Rebel Art Centre, not far from the Omega, at 38 Great Ormond Street. From here Lewis and the group, in June 1914, announced themselves officially to the nation as the Vorticists, and, in their periodical BLAST (No. 1, July 1914), and their exhibition at the Doré Gallery in 1915, promoted a brilliant individual synthesis of Futurism and Cubism.[15] Vorticism was a vital British abstract art which, with its emphasis on contour and solidity, avoided the heady vulgarity of Futurism while constructing a universe considerably tougher than the fragile, crystal world of the Cubists. Unfortunately, the development of the group was overtaken by a bigger blast, the blast of war.

The outbreak of the war in August 1914 caused a halt in the momentum of modern British art. Of the group around Wyndham Lewis, for example, Gaudier, T.E. Hulme and C.R. Nevinson had joined up by September 1914. Bomberg, Hamilton, Lewis and Wadsworth were in the forces by early 1916. Attendances at art exhibitions generally dropped; the Royal Academy Summer show of 1915 was seen by only 130,000 people. By 1916 all male classes at the Schools had been closed. Rooms at Burlington House were occupied by the British Red Cross or used for rifle storage. In many people's minds experimental art was synonvmous with the unpatriotic, with sinister foreign subversion of British culture. At the London Group exhibition at the Goupil Gallery in 1915, Mark Gertler's *Eve* was disfigured with a label marked "made in Germany".[16] Jacob Epstein's *Rock Drill* aroused similar passions at the London Group exhibitions of 1915 and 1916, so much so that the Group (formed in 1914 as a broadening of the Camden Town Group to include the Vorticists and others) were forced to move in 1917 to Ambrose Heal's Mansard Gallery when Marchant refused to let conscientious objectors or sympathisers with the enemy use the walls of the Goupil

With the departure, and, in some cases, death of the participants of the London art vortex, Roger Fry continued as best he could with the exhibitions and activities at the Omega Workshops and with a courageous showing of "New Movements in Art" in 1917 at the Royal Birmingham Society of Artists, and at Heal's Mansard Gallery, relying primarily on his own, Clive Bell's and Montague Shearman's collections. These included works by Brancusi, Gertler, Hamnett and Grant. The stark, horrifying face of the war itself was brought home in Nevinson's first one-man show at the Leicester Gallery (1916) and Paul Nash's show of drawings made on the Ypres Salient, at the Goupil Gallery (1917). Many artists, among them Augustus John, Henry Lamb, Lewis, Orpen and Rothenstein, were specially employed as War Artists by the Ministry of Information or seconded to the Canadian War Memorials scheme. This resulted after the Armistice in two major exhibitions in 1919 at the Royal Academy, "War Pictures" and "Canadian War Memorials".

There is much evidence to suggest that the Nineteen-twenties was a period of recuperation in the art world, of a slow, cautious process of reappraisal. In 1924 Lewis wrote, "We know that the individual survives today by retrenchment of the personality . . . so that no one shall feel hot through any one else's proximity or receive an electric shock."[17] Paul Nash noted "a marked reaction to naturalism and impressionism; there was a great deal of important talk about the modern Constables and Cromes, and a revival of the English tradition . . ."[18] The intensely exciting art of the pre-war period was associated in the public mind with the anarchy and anxiety of political and social upheaval of those years. After the war many of the central figures in the visual arts themselves retired into varieties of exile, David Bomberg left for Palestine in 1923, both Wadsworth and Roberts abandoned their early experiments and Nevinson retreated into a mannered, touchy conservatism. Initially, the "Seven and Five Society", with their preoccupation with subject matter, looked like a retrogressive group dedicated to reviving the English tradition and standing out against Fry's aesthetic. Lewis accused the Group, formed in 1919, of "abusing the living movements still developing on the continent of Europe." Reviewing the art scene after the war, Lewis found the R.A. shows "a large stagnant mass of indescribable beastliness", the N.E.A.C. "a large and costive society . . . choked with successive batches of Slade talent . . . a constipated mass of art school dogmas." The London Group, a "now rather swollen institution" was obviously going the same way.[19] His own characteristically aggressive response was the formation of Group X, an attempt to rekindle the embers of pre-war Vorticism. To those who had then been summoned to his standard, Etchells, Dismorr, Hamilton, Roberts and Wadsworth, he added Frank Dobson, William Turnbull and

E. McKnight Kauffer. Lewis was committed to the belief that "the experiments undertaken all over Europe during the last ten years should be utilised directly and developed, and not be lightly abandoned . . ."[20] Yet a revival did not prove feasible. The Group X did not meet again, and Lewis, having shown his "Tyros and Portraits" at the Leicester Gallery in 1921, was not to exhibit publicly until his collection of portraits at the Lefevre eleven years later. He "went underground" from 1923 to the early 1930s, going back to essentials in an analysis of "the things we have been taught to live by", in political, literary and satirical tracts for the times.

The Royal Academy, under the guidance of Aston Webb, and then Frank Dicksee, had absorbed the ginger groups of the 1880s, Lavery, Henry, Rothenstein, Orpen and Stott. As Frank Rutter observed, looking back from 1940, "It is not surprising . . . that many pictures seen in the Academies of the 'twenties bore a general family resemblance to paintings seen at the New English in earlier days".[21] The influence of these erstwhile rebels did much to lighten and cheer up the decorations in Burlington House, but, on the evidence of Walter Judd's "Royal Academy Illustrated", failed to raise general standards beyond the trite and derivative, despite some good work shown by Augustus John, Gerald Kelly and William Orpen. The Academy Summer Exhibitions remained an essential part of the London Season and, once visited, were easily forgotten. They only occupied the public mind when established masters and ex-rebels were slighted. Charles Sims's portrait of George V (1924) endowed the monarch, much to his disgust and the public's amusement, with spindly legs in a balletic posture. In 1935 Stanley Spencer's *St. Francis* was rejected for anatomical inaccuracy and *The Dustman* because it was daft. In 1938 Lewis's portrait of T.S. Eliot offended the Academy, that "snobbish commercial symbol of British indifference to the arts of painting, sculpture, architecture and design".[22] Even the conservative *Art Review for 1938* admitted that the constitution of the R.A. needed a drastic overhaul.[23]

Nor was the situation more hopeful in other established art societies between the wars. Critical reactions in 1938 can be taken as representative. Herbert B. Grimsditch found nuggets at the Royal Institute of Painters in Water-Colours, "but it was necessary to turn over a good deal of rubble". Better was the Royal Society of Painters in Water-Colours, under its President, Russell Flint, with notable works by Maxwell Armfield, Ethelbert White and Leonard Squirell. The Ridley Art Club of 1938 was again "a queer mixture of amateurs and professionals". At the Society of Women Artists the gallant Grimsditch remarked on the "extremes of performance". The "Complete Works of Christopher Wood" were at the Redfern, Epstein at the Leicester, Wadsworth's "nautical bric-a-brac" at Tooth's and Lamorna Birch's landscapes of New Zealand at the Greatorex. There were one-man shows presented by William Nicholson, Philip Connard, Paul Nash, Sickert and Lewis. Shows at the Royal Society of Painter-Etchers reflected the prodigious amount of talent thrown up by the revival of wood engraving, John Farleigh, Robert Austin and Stephen Gooden, for instance. At the Society of Wood Engravers could be seen Eric Gill, David Jones and Eric Ravilious.

Yet, where were young and progressive artists between the wars to find a regular and trustworthy outlet for their work? What factors were operating in the 1920s to change attitudes as, once again, the British artist was asked to respond to the Modern Movement?

At its exhibitions between the wars the London Group failed to sustain the dynamic of its early shows. As early as 1920, after a dozen exhibitions, it was described as a cluster of "elderly amateurs". Roger Fry had joined the Group in 1917, spearheading an infiltration of the Bloomsbury coterie, in the form of Duncan Grant and Vanessa Bell in 1919. The exhibitions of the 1920s were given their character by new members, Matthew Smith, Bernard Meninsky, John Farleigh and Frank Dobson. Although the reputation of the London Group continued in the more conservative quarters to be of "a group of the extreme left", it proved too heterogeneous an assembly for the more radical of its members, Paul Nash, Barbara Hepworth and Henry Moore, though it did continue to show experimental work of Bomberg, Piper, Moynihan and Hitchens, together with the more traditional styles of Adrian Allinson and C. Maresco Pearce. The *Art Review of 1937* awarded the year's booby prize without any question to Rodrigo Moynihan "who showed three canvases, each called *Painting,* and each consisting simply of a mass of white and dull red pigment, without the slightest attempt either at design or representation. He asked £100 for the three, too!"[24] The critic greatly preferred their previous show in March that year when at least the wild men were "in an inner room by themselves, so that one could avoid them if one wished." The exhibitions reflected in the late 1930s the reaction to the extremes of Constructivism and Surrealism, in the social realism of the Euston Road painters, William Coldstream and Victor Pasmore. Although no one could pretend they consistently fostered the spirit of experimental art, the London Group did organise the first open-air exhibition of sculpture in Britain on Selfridge's roof garden in 1930, which included works by Barbara Hepworth, Maurice Lambert and Henry Moore.

Roger Fry's London Artists' Association, formed in 1926, offered to a specified number of artists a fixed stipend in exchange for first options on exhibited works. The "Seven and Five Society" was teased away from its introspective preciosity by the arrival of Ben Nicholson in 1924, Winifred Nicholson (1925) and Christopher Wood (1926).

In comparison with the period 1910-1914 there were admittedly fewer galleries willing to cultivate progressive art in Britain. However, the Mayor Gallery in Sackville Street, London, staged the first one-man shows by Matthew Smith (1926), and Ivon Hitchens (1925), the Warren Gallery the first major show for Moore in 1928. The success of Heal's Mansard Gallery, Percy Moore Turner's Independent Gallery in Grafton Street, and Frank Rutter's Adelphi Gallery, with its shows of work by Bomberg, Lewis, Wadsworth and Ben Nicholson, compensated for the loss of Rutter's huge and influential Allied Artists' Association (1920). In the atmosphere of public indifference and professional caution, John Knewstub's New Chenil Gallery (1924-26) looked positively foolhardy. Citing the closure of the Grosvenor and the New, the disappearance of the Doré, the Grafton and the Dudley, Knewstub chose to interpret the evidence as proof that London needed a big, new art centre. He expanded the Chenil Gallery into adjoining premises to provide more gallery space, and facilities for musical and literary clubs as well as an art school, a restaurant, a cafe and a library. The new building was ready in 1925. In 1926 Knewstub staged Gwen John's first one-man show and went bankrupt.

In the same year as the New Chenil closed Dudley Tooth announced that he was no longer to be associated with "academic works by dead masters of the British school", and evidence of his identification with living art came in that year with his Wadsworth show, and later, with his sponsoring of Stanley Spencer.

One neglected aspect of the period had recently been emphasised, Oliver Brown's wide-ranging series of exhibitions at the Leicester Gallery. Kenneth Clark has paid tribute to "that lovable institution", three small and unpretentious rooms off Leicester Square that introduced his generation to modern art in the 1920s and the 1930s. Brown had joined the Phillips brothers in the running of the gallery in 1903, and supervised early shows of Dulac (1908) and Clausen (1909). In 1919, with the help and advice of Michael Sadler, he began a series of one-man shows at the Leicester with paintings by Matisse. There followed comprehensive exhibitions of Picasso (1921), Van Gogh (1923), Gauguin (1924) and Cézanne (1925). He also showed living British artists, Lewis (1921), Wadsworth (1928) and a posthumous Gore exhibition (1928).

The luxury of reflecting in quiet seclusion on the pre-war revolution in European art became more and more difficult by the end of the 1920s as the impact of Surrealism and abstract constructivism made itself felt, culminating in the two seminal exhibitions of 1936, "Abstract and Concrete" at the Lefevre Gallery and the International Surrealist Exhibition of London at the New Burlington Galleries.

The credit for the crystallisation of the talents of the younger British painters of the 1930s must go to Paul Nash, who had realised at Tooth's 1931 "Recent Tendencies in British Painting" that a focus of activities was needed and, in 1933, helped to found Unit 1 with Herbert Read as spokesman. The group used the Mayor Gallery as a base for operations. Their 1934 exhibition at the Mayor revealed two distinct expressions of what the group called "a truly contemporary spirit", the surrealist tendencies of Nash, Moore and Edward Burra, and the abstract constructivism of Hepworth, Wadsworth and Ben Nicholson. Despite this dichotomy there was at least a coherent policy towards art, design and architecture as interrelated fields of experimental activity.[25]

It is perhaps indicative of the revitalised condition of the arts in the 1930s that Zwemmer's Gallery, probably the most adventurous in London, within the space of three years gave John Nash his first one-man show (1933), exhibited Salvador Dali in 1934, and staged the "Objective Abstractions" exhibition of work by Rodrigo Moynihan, Geoffrey Tibble and Ceri Richards, among others. In 1935 the Zwemmer gave shelter to the "7 and 5" (as they now called themselves); after the death of Christopher Wood in 1930, and the admission of Moore and Hepworth in the same year, the Society turned decisively to abstraction, which had rather alarmed their usual venue, the Leicester Gallery.

The momentum of what Barbara Hepworth called "this robust and inspiring wave of imaginative and creative energy" was maintained by Nicolette Gray's 1936 exhibition at the Lefevre of abstract painting, sculpture and constructions by Calder, Gabo, Giacometti, Hepworth, Moholy-Nagy, Mondrian, Nicholson and Moore, and by the "Constructive Art" show at the London Gallery in 1937.

Contacts across the Channel were as fruitful as they had been during the period from 1910-14. In 1932 Nicholson and Hepworth visited Picasso, Brancusi and Arp, and, the next year, joined the "Abstract-Création" group in Paris. In 1937 they were with Braque, Miro and Calder at Varengeville, near Dieppe. The traffic of visitors and distinguished exiles going in the opposite direction gave Britain a potentially spectacular opportunity to learn at first hand of the productions of the Modern Movement, and of its egalitarianism, and internationalist and collectivist concerns. The most immediate public contact with the Constructivist aspect of the Modern Movement was, significantly, the Penguin Pool at London Zoo (1933-35), designed by Bertholt Lubetkin, who settled in Britain in 1930, an authentic witness of the Constructivist turmoil in Russia after the Revolution. After Hitler's rise to power in Germany, Gropius, Breuer and Moholy-Nagy all came to England. They left, disillusioned, in 1937, for the greater understanding and tolerance they anticipated in America. Ironically, the same year, Leslie Martin, Ben Nicholson and Naum Gabo brought out "Circle, International Survey of Constructive Art", maintaining that a "new cultural unity is slowly emerging out of the fundamental changes which are taking place in our present day civilisation".[26]

The virtual indifference of the British public to British abstraction of the 1930s is in marked contrast to the reception accorded to Surrealism, which, with its intensity of vision and obsessive interpretation of the object, struck many familiar chords. The International Surrealist Exhibition was probably the most comprehensive attempt to regulate the exhibition environment since Whistler's experiments in the 1880s. The exhibition of sixty artists from fourteen different countries was complemented by lectures, events and performances. A young girl with a floral head, and wearing a white satin dress, wandered through the vast spaces of the New Burlington Galleries with a false leg in one hand and a raw pork chop in the other. It stimulated audience participation; a kipper was hung from Miro's *Object 228.* Over 20,000 people visited the show and there was sufficient interest generated to encourage E.L.T. Mesens to take over the London Gallery which, until the outbreak of war, was the major centre of Surrealist activity, publications and exhibitions. The London, Mayor and Guggenheim galleries, because of their espousal of the Surrealist cause, were affectionately known as "the little Bethels of Cork Street".

The outbreak of war in 1939 halted the momentum of creative activity, dispersed forces and prevented further contacts with the continent of Europe. British art entered yet again into a period of isolation and introspective retreat, which it found difficult to escape from in the late 1940s.

The period covered by this dictionary, 1880-1940, was one of phenomenal change both socially and artistically, but one constant concern was how the national School should react to the influence of foreign art. Is there such a thing in the twentieth century as a British tradition? Have we sufficient confidence in its authenticity to defend it against the taunts of the Internationalists? If we have in our isolation "slipped back", as Fry, for one, often maintained, can we catch up? Throughout our period the debate continued. Stubborn proclamations of self-sufficiency alternated with paranoid self-deprecation, but always seemingly in a vacuum of basic national indifference. As Lewis wrote in 1937, "It is important to understand what an odd place England is to be an artist in, especially a painter. The English experience little response to artistic stimulus. In their bones they *are* the 'Philistines' Matthew Arnold said they were. They have heard that they are 'civilised' and that civilised people are fond of art. So they make the necessary arrangements for the unavoidable presence of fine arts in their midst."[27]

Chris Mullen

FOOTNOTES

1. *The Studio* June 1907 p.50.
2. See *The Portfolio* 1877 p.98.
3. *The Studio* June 1902 p.90.
4. E.R. and J. Pennell *The Life of James McNeill Whistler* (2 vols.) vol. 1 p.62.
5. See Mrs. J. Comyns-Carr, *Reminiscences* undated, chapter XII.
6. D. Sutton *The Letters of Roger Fry* (2 vols.) London 1972, vol. 1 p.156.
7. *The Studio* December 1905 p.261.
8. *Vogue* September 1956, W. Lewis *The Vorticists* p.221.
9. See I. Dunlop *The Shock of the New*, London 1972, chapter 4.
10. *The Studio* September 1932, Anon *Mark Gertler* quoted in J. Woodeson *Mark Gertler* 1972 p.94.
11. Fry *Letters* vol. 1 p.343.
12. E. Pound *Affirmations VI* p.411 quoted in W.C. Wees, *Vorticism and the English Avant Garde* Manchester 1972 p.11.
13. Fry *Letters* p.98.
14. See Q. Bell and S. Chaplin *The Ideal Home Rumpus, Apollo* October 1964 pp.284-291.
15. See R. Cork *Vorticism and Abstract Art in the First Machine Age* (2 vols.) London 1975 and forthcoming.
16. Woodeson *Mark Gertler* Chapter 22 *Hunnish Indecency*.
17. *The Criterion* May 1924 p.477 W. Lewis *Art-Chronicle*.
18. *The Listener* July 5, 1933 quoted in exhibition catalogue *Paul Nash* A Northern Arts exhibition, 1971.
19. W. Lewis *Foreword* exhibition catalogue, Group X, Mansard Gallery, quoted in W. Michel *Wyndham Lewis* London 1971 p.436.
20. W. Lewis *Foreword*.
21. F. Rutter *Modern Masterpieces* London 1940 p.237.
22. W. Lewis *Wyndham Lewis the Artist, from Blast to Burlington House* London 1939 p. 373.
23. *Art Review . . . during the year 1938* p.13, see H.B. Grimsditch *Art exhibitions of the Year*.
24. *Art Review . . . during the Year 1937* p.23.
25. Exhibition catalogue *Isokon* University of East Anglia 1975, see A. Grieve *Isokon* p.2.
26. J.L. Martin, B. Nicholson, N. Gabo (eds.) *Circle, International Survey of Constructive Art* (1937, 1971 Faber and Faber reprint) *Editorial*.
27. W. Lewis *Blasting and Bombardiering* 1937 pp.212, 213.

SELECT BOOKLIST

S.N. Behrman *Duveen* New York 1952
T. Bodkin *Hugh Lane and his Pictures* Dublin 1956
O. Brown *Exhibition: Memoirs* London 1968
D. Copper *The Courtauld Collection* London 1954
I. Dunlop *The Shock of the New* London 1972
J. Duveen *Thirty Years of British Art*, Studio Special Number, London 1930
Exhibition catalogue, *London Group 1914-1964* London, Tate Gallery 1964
Exhibition catalogue *British Art and the Modern Movement* Welsh Arts Council 1962
Exhibition catalogue *A Man of Influence: Alex Reid* Scottish Arts Council 1968
R. Gimpel *Diary of an Art Dealer* London 1966
C. Hassall *Edward Marsh, Patron of the Arts* London 1959
S.C. Hutchinson *The History of the Royal Academy 1768-1968* London 1968
J. Maas *Gambart, Prince of the Victorian Art World* London 1975
R. Morphet *British Painting 1910-1945* London, Tate Gallery 1967
B.L. Reid *John Quinn and his friends* New York 1968
G. Reitlinger *The Economics of Taste* London 3 vols. 1961
J. Rothenstein *Modern English Painters* London 2 vols. 1952, 1956
F. Rutter *Art in my Time* London 1933
A.B. Saarinen *The Proud Possessors . . . Some Adventurous American Art Collectors* New York 1958
M. Sadleir *Michael Ernest Sadler, A Memoir by his Son* London 1949
D. Sutton (ed.) *The Letters of Roger Fry* (2 vols.) London 1972
A. Thornton *Fifty Years of the New English Art Club* London 1935

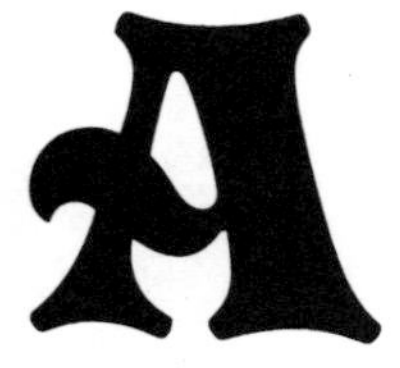

AARENS, B Exh. 1932
† L 2.

AARON, Miss P.M. Exh. 1938
17 Silver Birch Road, Erdington, Birmingham. † B 1.

AARY, Max Exh. 1908
11 Rue Baour Lormian, Toulouse, France. † LS 5.

ABA-NOVAK, Vilmos b. 1894
b. Hungary. Exh. 1935. † RSA 2.

ABBE, van See V

ABBEMA, Madame Louise* 1858-1927
French portrait painter. Exh. 1906. Add: 47 Rue Lafitte, Paris. † L 1.

ABBEY, Miss Anne J. Exh. 1908-10
126 Bradford Road, Huddersfield, Yorks. † L 6.

ABBEY, Edwin Austin 1852-1911
b. Philadelphia d. London. Painter and illustrator of historical subjects. Studied Pennsylvania 1880. Visited Continent several times. Painted the official picture of the Coronation of Edward VII. R.I. 1883, A.R.A. 1896, R.A. 1898, A.R.W.S. 1895. Add: Chelsea and Morgan Hall, Fairford, Glos. † AG 1, B 3, GI 2, L 7, M 4, NG 1, RA 23, RI 4, RSA 1, RWS 1.

ABBINETT, Miss A. Exh. 1882-86
Page Moss, Roby, Liverpool. † L 4.

ABBOTT, Miss Dora Exh. 1886-88
Sculptor. 5 Seymour Place, Fulham, London. † RA 2.

ABBOTT, Edwin Exh. 1886-88
274 Swan Arcade, Bradford, Yorks. † L 3, M 1, RA 1, RSA 1.

ABBOTT, Mrs. E.T. Exh. 1919
6 Pembroke Square, Kensington, London. † SWA 2.

ABBOTT, G.J. Exh. 1938
14a St. Austin's Drive, Carlton, Nottingham. † N 2.

ABBOTT, Miss J. Exh. 1919-20
Crossways Cottage, Ospringe, Kent. † SWA 3.

ABBOTT, John 1884-1956
Oil painter after retirement from Indian Civil Service 1932. Studied art under F. Hodge. Add: Tongue Ghyll, Grasmere Westmorland. † NEA 1, RA 3, ROI 6.

ABBOTT, J.A. Exh. 1902
71 Upper Parliament Street, Nottingham. † N 1.

ABBOTT, Mrs. J.K. Exh. 1918
7 Aubert Park, Highbury, London. † LS 3.

ABBOTT, Miss Nellie Exh. 1889-1910
Northampton. † B 6, L 7, SWA 3.

ABBOTT, Miss Phyllis Exh. 1917-22
London. † P 3, RMS 1, ROI 11, SWA 2.

ABBOTT, Stewart Exh. 1880-82
9 Agnes Street, Glasgow. † GI 2.

ABBOTT, Sidney John Exh. 1915-27
London. † CHE 1, L 1, P 3, RA 1.

ABBOTT, W.B. Exh. 1883-89
Edinburgh 1883; Dundee 1888. † RI 1, RSA 3.

ABDEY, Herbert E. Exh. 1928-29
58 High Street, Harrow-on-the-Hill, Middlesex. † L 1, RA 2.

ABDO, Alexander b. 1865
Painter of fantasies, symbolic and romantic landscapes. Studied art privately. Add: Southall 1908, 1915; London 1913; Ashford 1914. † L 21, LS 2, RA 6, RCA 2.

ABELL, William A. Exh. 1917-40
Watercolour painter. Add: Glasgow. † GI 12, RSW 2.

ABELOOS, Victor Exh. 1901-14
Brussels 1901; Canterbury, Kent 1911-14. † GI 1, L 1, LS 3, RA 1, RCA 6.

ABELSON, Evelyn, nee Levy b. 1886
Oil painter, studied art at Heatherley's. Exh. 1921-40. S.W.A. 1939. Add: London. † COO 3, G 1, GOU 8, NEA 2, RA 5, RBA 22, ROI 16, SWA 17.

ABERCROMBIE, Miss M.C. Exh. 1887-92
23 Upper Wimpole Street, London. † B 3, L 3, NG 1, P 1, RI 3.

ABERCROMBY, Lady Exh. 1888
17 Charles Street, Berkeley Square, London. † D 2.

ABERCROMBY, Mrs. Jessie Exh. 1880-1893
Edinburgh. † RSA 6.

ABERCROMBY, John B. Exh. 1880-1923
Edinburgh, Midlothian and Aberdeen. † GI 15, L 2, RA 2, RCA 1, RHA 2, RSA 95, RSW 1.

ABERIGH-MACKAY, Miss Mary Exh. 1904-6
Falkland House, Long Melford, Suffolk. † L 1, RI 1.

ABERIGH-MACKAY, Miss Patty Exh. 1905-6
Sketching tour in the Kashmir Valley. Add: Falkland House, Long Melford, Suffolk. † L 2, RA 1.

ABINGER, Lord Exh. 1932
Inverlochy Castle, Fort William. † RSA 1.

ABLETT, Thomas Robert 1849-1945
Landscape and figure painter. Art master Bradford Grammar School. Founder and Art Director of Royal Drawing Society 1888. H.R.I. 1932. Add: Bradford 1880; Ilkley 1882; London 1891; Croydon 1921. † G 2, L 1, RA 6, RBA 6, RI 40, ROI 17, RSA 1.

ABLETT, William Albert 1877-1936
b. Paris. Add: Paris 1901-1908. † NG 4, RA 3.

ABORN, John Exh. 1885-1915
Landscape, seascape and genre painter. R.B.A. 1896. Add: Dolwydelelan, N. Wales 1885; Milford, Surrey 1892. † NG 1, RA 18, RBA 35, ROI 13.

ABOT, Miss Esperanze Exh. 1909
† LS 3.

ABRAHAM, Frank Exh. 1887
Oak House. Regent Street, Stoke-on Trent. † RI 1.

ABRAHAM, J. Fell Exh. 1908
53 Bidston Road, Oxton, Cheshire. † L 2.

ABRAHAM, Miss Lilian Exh. 1880-88
Lisle Street, London. † B 2, L 3, RBA 2, RI 3, SWA 5.

ABRAHAM, R.J.* Exh. 1882-1909
Stoke-on-Trent 1880; London 1891. † BG 1, L 10, M 2, NG 1, P 1, RA 6, RI 4, ROI 1.

ABRAHAMS, Miss Enid Exh. 1931-40
Hampstead, London. † NEA 9, RA 10, RBA 14, ROI 4. SWA 1.

ABRAHAMSON, Miss Bessie Exh. 1925
Technical School, Newry. † RHA 1.

ABRAM, Miss Winifred M Exh. 1928 and 1934
19 The Pryors, Hampstead, London. † RA 2.

ABRAMS, Lucien Exh. 1905
9 Rue Falquiere, Paris. † B 1.

ABRAN, Miss Marthe Exh. 1897
38 Cathcart Road, London. † RA 1.

ABSOLON, Constance L. Exh. 1880-84
96 Portsdown Road, London. † SWA 6.

ABSOLON, John* 1815-1895
Landscape, marine, figure and genre painter and illustrator. Studied art at British Museum. Spent a year in Paris. Began painting miniatures then turned to watercolours. Employed as a theatrical scene-painter at Covent Garden. R.I. 1838. R.O.I. 1883. Add: London. † B 4, L 7, M 4, RBA 11, RI 58, ROI 5.

ABSOLON, Louis Exh. 1880-88
London. † B 1, D 2, L 1, RBA 3, RI 5.

ACATOS, Miss H. Exh. 1919
206 The Grove, London. † SWA 1.

ACHESON, Miss Anne Cranford b. 1882
b. Portadown, N. Ireland. Sculptor. Studied Belfast School of Art and Royal College of Art, London. Exh. 1910-40. C.B.E. 1918, S.W.A. 1923. Add: London. † G 2, GI 4, I 1, L 8, M 1, P 8, RA 25, RBA 2, RHA 4, RI 5, RMS 5, SWA 17.

ACHILLE-FOULD, Mlle. Georges 1865-1919
French. Exh. 1901-6. Add: 20 Boulevard de Courcelles, Paris. † L 5, L 7.

ACKERMANN, Arthur Gerald* b. 1876
Exh. 1893-1940. Watercolour painter. Studied at Heatherley's, Westminster and R.A. Schools. Commissioned in R.A.F. 1916. R.I. 1914. Add: London 1893, 1907, 1920; Lewes, Sussex 1901; Sutton, Surrey 1905; Croydon 1915. † CHE 1, FIN 117, GI 2, GOU 2, L 12, LEI 181, M 1, RA 52, RBA 9, RI,139, ROI 12, TOO 1, WG 29.

ACKERMANN, Miss K. Exh. 1906
c/o Miss Glossop, Wellington, Cape Colony, S.A. † RA 1.

ACKLAND, Miss Judith Exh. 1927-38
Watercolour landscape painter. b. Bideford, Devon: Studied Bideford Art School and Regent St. Polytechnic (bronze medal for figure composition). Add: Bideford, Devon. † AB 21, RA 4, SWA 4.

ACKRELL, W. Exh. 1898-99
34 Alma Square, St. John's Wood, London. † RA 2.

ACKROYD, Miss L. Exh. 1928 and 1932
532 Dialstone Lane, Stockport, Cheshire. † L 2, RBA 1.

ACLAND, Miss M.A. Exh. 1916-18
London 1916; Exeter 1918. † I 2, NEA 3, RA 1.

ACLAND, Rt. Rev. Richard Dyke Exh. 1938
Watercolour painter. Bishop of Bombay. † WG 3.

ACOSTA, A del A. y. Exh. 1909
c/o G.F. Coleman, 27 Crosby Road, Seaforth, Liverpool. † L 1.

ACOSTA, Joaquin M. Exh. 1912
c/o J. Espinar, 10 Victoria Street, Liverpool. † L 1.

ACRAMAN, Miss Mary Catherine Exh. 1884-1910
London. † RID 18, SWA 1.

ACRET, John F. Exh. 1884-1902
Hampstead, London. † M 1, P 2, RA 9, RBA 2 RMS 1.

ACWORTH, Mrs. Exh. 1911
† ALP 2.

ADA, Florence Exh. 1880-85
Landscape painter. Add: 8 Lonsdale Road, Barnes, London. † SWA 9.

ADAIR, Miss Exh. 1883-86
Laurel Bank, Stranraer. † RSA 2.

ADAIR, John Exh. 1898-1905
Glasgow. † GI 5.

ADAM, Alexander Exh. 1933-35
Paisley 1933; Glasgow 1935. † GI 2.

ADAM, Benno* Exh. 1883
† FIN 1.

ADAM, Miss C.C. Exh. 1885-86
Glasgow. † GI 1, RSA 1.

ADAM, Miss Camilla de Bels Exh. 1897-99
Liverpool. † L 3.

ADAM, Charlotte E. Exh. 1893-96
Dunblane 1893; Glasgow 1894. † GI 4, RSA 1.

ADAM, Mrs. C. Law Exh. 1903-40
Watercolour painter and silver-worker. Add: Blackwater, Hants. from 1903 and Camberley, Surrey from 1929. † B 2, BG 6, GOU 1, I 12, L 3, LS 6, RA 6, RID 16, SWA 5.

ADAM, C. Moffat Exh. 1896
Biscary House, Biscary, Cornwall. † L 2.

ADAM, Mrs. C. Moffat Exh. 1910-19
London 1910; Cornwall 1914; Salcombe, Devon 1914. † LS 9.

ADAM, David Livingstone 1883-1924
b. Glasgow, d. Chicago. Add: Glasgow 1908-9. † GI 3.

ADAM, Emil* Exh. 1883
† FIN 1.

ADAM, Mrs. Elizabeth C. Exh. 1933-40
Edgbaston, Birmingham. † B 11.

ADAM, Miss E.C. Law Exh. 1899
16 Vicarage Gate, London. † SWA 1.

ADAM, Miss Ethel Lucy Exh. 1919-35
Painter and stained glass designer. Studied under F. Spenlove-Spenlove. Add: Quarry Down, Hythe, Kent.† B 1, D 3, L 4, RCA 16.

ADAM, Joseph* Exh. 1880-85
Father of Joseph Denovan A. q.v. Add: Harrow Road, London 1880; Edinburgh 1885. † GI 10, RA 1, RSA 13.

ADAM, Joseph Denovan 1842-1896
Animal and landscape painter, specialised in painting highland cattle. Studied under his father Joseph A. q.v., and South Kensington. A.R.S.A. 1884, R.S.A. 1892. Add: Edinburgh 1880. Settled at Craigmill, Stirling in 1888 where he founded a school of animal painting. † DOW 99, FIN 1, GI 37, L 7, M 2, NG 4, RA 14, RBA 2, RHA 1, RI 1, RSA 75, RSW 46, TOO 1.

ADAM, J. Denovan, jun. Exh. 1900-31
Edinburgh, Callander and Glasgow. † GI 55, RSA 22.

ADAM, Miss Jean Miller Exh. 1935-40
Glasgow. † GI 3, SWA 2.

ADAM, Miss K.M. Exh. 1897-1900
London 1897; Eastbourne 1900. † GI 2, SWA 1.

ADAM, Matthew Exh. 1904-22
Paisley. † GI 9, L 2, RSA 5.

ADAM, Patrick William* 1854-1930
Painter of landscapes and interiors, pastelier. Studied under George Paul Chalmers and William MacTaggert, won Maclaine Walters medal for best painting from life. A.R.S.A. 1883, R.S.A. 1897. Add: Edinburgh 1880; Rosslyn, Midlothian 1892; Ardilea, North Berwick 1902. † FIN 2, GI 42, GOU 29, L 29, M1, RA 47, RHA 20, RSA 164.

ADAM, R.H. Exh. 1920
Caundhu, Kidderminster. † B 4.

ADAM, Stephen 1858-1910
Artist in stained glass. Add: Glasgow. † GI 18, RA 3, RSA 11, RSW 1.

ADAM, Stephen, jun. Exh. 1907-11
105 Bath Street, Glasgow. † GI 3.

ADAM, William Exh. 1880-1917
Glasgow. † GI 33, RSA 3.

ADAM-LAURENS, Mme. Nanny Exh. 1886-87
7 Rue de Brea, Paris. † GI 3.

ADAMS, Miss A. Exh. 1899
80 Eastgate, Stafford. † B 1.

ADAMS, Alfred b. 1884
Landscape painter. b. Birmingham. Exh. 1907-40. R.B.S.A. 1939. Lived in and around Birmingham. † B 64.

ADAMS, Arthur Christopher b. 1867
Miniature pastel portrait painter. b. Southampton. Exh. 1905-35. Studied Reading University. Married to Minnie Walters Anson q.v. A.R.M.S. 1909, R.M.S. 1915. Add: Reading 1905; Parkstone, Dorset 1921; Streatham Common, London 1929. † L 28, LS 7, RA 16, RMS 106.

ADAMS, Albert George Exh. 1880-87
Land and seascape painter. Add: Peckham and East Dulwich, London. † D 6, RA 2.

ADAMS, Miss B. Exh. 1912
Beckenham, Kent. † SWA 2.

ADAMS, Beale Exh. 1897-1921
R.B.A. 1902. Add: St. Ives, Cornwall 1897, 1906 and 1919; Ilfracombe 1903 and 1911. † B 5, L 2, RBA 35, ROI 3.

ADAMS, Bernard Exh. 1916-39
Landscape and portrait painter. Studied Westminster School of Art, Antwerp Academy, Allan Fraser scholarship. R.O.I. 1924, R.P. 1920. Add: Tring, Herts. and Chelsea, London. † CHE 1, I 2, LEI 3, P 71, RA 2, RI 1, ROI 44.

ADAMS, Miss Beatrice T. Exh. 1907-16
Sheffield. † L 4, LS 3, RA 3.

ADAMS, Miss Cecilia Exh. 1913-16
1 Marlborough Crescent, Bedford Park, London. † L 1, RA 3.

ADAMS, Cole A. Exh. 1882-1902
London. † RA 4.

ADAMS, Cuthbert Harry Exh. 1931-38
99 Park Hill Road, Harborne, Birmingham. † B 7.

ADAMS, Charles James* b. 1859
b. Gravesend. Studied Leicester School of Art. Mulready gold medal for life drawing. Art teacher Leicester School of Art. Exh. 1881-1919. Add: Leciester 1881; Upper Sydenham 1895; Horsham, Surrey 1897; Billingshurst, Sussex 1900; Midhurst 1901; Guildford 1904; Farnham, Surrey 1905. † B 27, D 71, L 37, M 10, N 3, RA 37, RBA 8, RHA 1, RI 30, ROI 9.

ADAMS, Caroline M. Exh. 1893-94
9 Westbourne Square, London. † L 2.

ADAMS, Douglas* 1853-1920
Landscape painter of mainly Scottish subjects. Add: London. † B 22, G 3, GI 7, I 6, L 35, M 19, NG 32, RA 32, RBA 7, RHA 3, ROI 10, TOO 11.

ADAMS, Ernest D. b. 1884
b. Margate. Painter and etcher. Studied Regent St. Polytechnic. Exh. 1938-40. Add: Nr. Banbury, Oxon. 1938-40. † B 1. RBA 4.

ADAMS, Miss Elinor Proby Exh. 1908-38
b. Sudbury, Suffolk. Painter, art critic and reviewer. Studied Slade School of Art, British Institute Scholarship. Add: Newport, Salop. 1908; Coulsdon, Surrey 1915; Sevenoaks, Kent 1920. † ALP 1, GOU 1, I 2, L 5, LS 8, M 1, NEA 5, RA 5, RCA 2, RI 1.

ADAMS, Frank Exh. 1923-35
Landscapes in watercolour and crayon. † G 1, WG 106.

ADAMS, George Gammon 1821-1898
Sculptor. Exh. 1880-95. Add: London. † G 1, M 2, RA 5, RBA 2.

ADAMS, Hervey b.1903
b. London. Landscape painter. Exh. 1932-39. Studied under Bernard Adams. Principal Cotswold School of Landscape Painting. Art master Berkhamstead School 1937-40. R.B.A. 1931. Add: Minchinhampton, Glos. 1932-36; Chesham, Bucks. 1937-39. † BK 47, COO 3, FIN 62, L 1, P 1, RA 6, RBA 44.

ADAMS, Harry Clayton* Exh. 1906-8
Ewhurst Hill, Nr. Guildford, Surrey. † LS 5. ROI 1.

ADAMS, Henry Percy 1866-1930
Architect. Exh. 1888, 1901-7. Add: Ipswich 1888; London 1901-7. † RA 13, RSA 2.

ADAMS, Harry William 1868-1947
Landscape painter. Studied Julians, Paris 1895-6. Visited Switzerland. Worked for 8 years as decorative designer at Royal Worcester Porcelain Works. "Winter Sleep" purchased by Chantrey Bequest 1900. R.B.A. 1912, R.B.S.A. 1919. Born and lived in Worcester. † B 43, L 5, M 1, NG 3, RA 38, RBA 78, RCA 18.

ADAMS, Iris Exh. 1939
The Windmill, Cholesbury, Chesham, Bucks. † RBA 2.

ADAMS, Miss J. Exh. 1905
Bushey, Herts. † SWA 1.

ADAMS, Miss Janie Exh. 1906-8
London 1906, Conway, Wales 1907. † B 1, RCA 3.

ADAMS, John Exh. 1931
Poole Pottery, Poole, Dorset. † B 1.

ADAMS, Miss Joan Clayton Exh. 1890-95
Ewhurst Hill, Nr. Guildford, Surrey. † RA 1 ROI 3.

ADAMS, John Clayton* 1840-1906
Landscape painter. Add: Ewhurst Hill, Nr. Guildford, Surrey. † B 3, DOW 2, G 3, L 18, M 1, NG 8, RA 64, RBA 13, RI 7, ROI 32, TOO 31.

ADAMS, James L. Exh. 1880
Britannia Buildings, Leeds. † RA 1.

ADAMS, J. Seymour* Exh. 1883-88
194 New North Road, Islington, London. † B 4, L 1, M 5, RA 1, RHA 2, RSA 1.

ADAMS, J. Talbot Exh. 1880-1911
London 1880; Sutton, Surrey 1900. † BRU 3, M 4, RA 3, RBA 2, RHA 2.

ADAMS, Miss Katharine (Mrs. Webb) b. 1862
Bookbinder. Exh. 1908-9. Add: Islip, Oxford 1908. † NG 2.

ADAMS, Miss Lilian Exh. 1892-1911
Liverpool 1892; France 1898 and 1911; Handsworth, Birmingham 1908. † B 1, L 2, RA 2.

ADAMS, Mrs. Laura G. Exh. 1916-40
Miniature painter. Add: Monkseaton, Northumberland and Whickham, Co. Durham. † L 6, RA 4.

ADAMS, Leo W. Exh. 1900
Rosedale, Elmdon Road, Acock's Green, Birmingham. † B 1.

ADAMS, Miss M. Exh. 1925
Kingswood, Frodsham, Cheshire. † L 1.

ADAMS, Miss Mary Exh. 1906
Arlunfa Studio, Victoria Drive, Deganwy, N. Wales. † RCA 2.

ADAMS, Monica Exh. 1919
† I 1.

ADAMS, Maurice Bingham 1849-1933
Architect and author: designed London School of Economics; Editor of "Building News". Exh. 1880-1919. Add: London. † RA 26, RHA 4.

ADAMS, M.E. Exh.1929
† AB 2.

ADAMS, Miss M.E. Exh. 1883
Grosvenor Road, Handsworth, Birmingham. † B 1.

ADAMS, Miss M.L. Exh. 1888-91
37 Campbell Street, Greenock. † GI 3, ROI 1, RSA 1.

ADAMS, Mary S. Exh. 1938
Red Roofs, Farnham Common, Bucks. † RBA 1, SWA 1.

ADAMS, Mrs. Nancy Exh. 1935-37
The Studio, Pierpont Street, Worcester. † B 2.

ADAMS, Ronald F. Exh. 1896
Clifton, Ashbourne, Derbys. † B 1.

ADAMS, S. Exh. 1884-91
Dublin. † D 6, TOO 1.

ADAMS, Dr. Thomas Exh. 1938
1 Gordon Square, London. † GI 1.

ADAMS, Wilfred Exh. 1933-37
Cardiff. † RCA 3.

ADAMS, William Exh. 1921
3 Scotts Street, Glasgow. † GI 1, L 1.

ADAMS, William Dacres Exh. 1888-1940
Lechlade, Glos. 1888 and 1896; Bushey, Herts. 1892; London 1907. † COO 4, FIN 123, GI 3, I 1, L 7, LEI 45, P 1, RA 20, RID 42, ROI 4.

ADAMS, W. Danes Exh. 1900-9
Wallingford, Berks. 1900; London 1905. † GI 2, I 1, L 2, NEA 1, NG 3, RA 7, RSA 1.

ADAMS, W.F. Exh.1882-85
Heatley, Nr. Warrington, Lancs. † B 1, L 1, M 2.

ADAMS, W. Naseby Exh. 1913-20
Liverpool 1913; London 1920. † L 1, RA 1.

ADAMS, W.R. Exh. 1928
14 Oakbank Terrace, Glasgow. † GI 1.

ADAMS-ACTON, Gladstone Murray b.1886
Architect. Studied art South Kensington and the Continent. Exh. 1909-15. Son of John A.A. q.v. Add: London. † RA 3.

ADAMS-ACTON, John 1830-1910
Sculptor. Studied R.A. Schools, gold medal for original composition also two silver medals; awarded Travelling Scholarship. Spent his professional life in Italy and England. Exh. 1880-92. Add: London 1880-92. d. Isle of Arran. † G 1, RA 25, RBA 5.

ADAMS-SMITH, Mary R. Exh. 1928
† AB 1.

ADAMSON, A. Exh. 1910-11
c/o W.F. Malcolm & Co., 36 Leadenhall Street, London. † L 2, RA 2.

ADAMSON, Miss Dorothy d. 1934
Animal painter. Exh. 1915-34. R.I. 1929. R.O.I. 1929. Add: Cheshire; Wales; Dorchester and Bushey, Herts. Died in her 30s. † ALP 1, B 4, GI 3, I 2, L 42, RA 19, RCA 8, RI 30, ROI 30, RSA 3, SWA 2.

ADAMSON, David Comba Exh. 1887-1902
Cambuslang by Glasgow 1887; Paris 1891. † GI 5, L 2, M 3, RA 2, ROI 2, RSA 3.

ADAMSON, George Worsley b. 1913
Painter and illustrator. Exh. 1933-40. b. New York. Add: Wigan. † L 2, RA 3.

ADAMSON, Miss H.V. Exh. 1905-8
Kemptown. † SWA 2.

ADAMSON, John Exh. 1890-1918
R.B.A. 1901. Add: London. † B 1, L 12, M 1, RA 12, RBA 57, RI 2, ROI 5.

ADAMSON, John Exh. 1882-83
Edinburgh 1882; Colinton, N.B. 1883. † RSA 2.

ADAMSON, Miss Lorna Exh. 1911-21
London. † GI 1, L 7, RA 4.

ADAMSON, Miss M. Exh. 1923
85 Totteridge Road, High Wycombe, Bucks. † L 1.

ADAMSON, S. Exh. 1908
42A Chepstow Villas, Bayswater, London. † L 1.

ADAMSON, Sydney Exh. 1911-14
278 Boulevard Raspail, Paris. † BG 44, L 2, RSA 1.

ADAMSON, Sarah Gough Exh. 1911-39
Mrs. Walker, painter and embroiderer. b. Manchester. Studied Edinburgh College of Art. Add: Edinburgh 1911; Hemel Hempstead, Herts. 1917; London 1918. † GI 5, I 1, L 12, RA 3, RHA 1. RSA 29, RSW 3, SWA 2.

ADAMSON, T. Exh. 1888-89
Paris 1888; Edinburgh 1889. † RSA 3.

ADAMSON, Thomas A. Exh. 1884-86
Glasgow 1884; Merchiston 1886. † GI 1, RSA 2.

ADAMSON, Travers P.M. Exh. 1895
8 Wynell Road, Forest Hill, London. † M 1.

ADAMSON, Miss Una Duncan Exh. 1929-39
100 Handside Lane, Welwyn Garden City, Herts. † GI 3, RSA 3, RSW 6.

ADAMSON, W.M. Exh. 1885-86
1 St. James's Square, London. † RSA 3.

ADAN, Emile Louis* b. 1839
b. Paris. Exh. 1913. Add: 75 Rue de Courcelles, Paris. † L 2.

ADCOCK, Allan A. Exh. 1915-35
Carlton, Notts. 1915; Burton Joyce, Notts. 1922; Gedling, Notts. 1926. † N 20.

ADCOCK, Miss Constance A. Exh. 1892-95
Blyth, Coleshill, Birmingham. † B 3.

ADCOCK, J. Wilton Exh. 1886-91
Franklin Chambers, Cranby Street, Leicester. † N 5.

ADCROFT, Frank Exh. 1932-40
3 Mitchell Street, Rutherglen. † GI 8.

ADDAMS, Clifford Exh. 1901-19
Figure painter. Add: Paris 1901. London 1904. † GI 16, GOU 6, I 13, L 2, NEA 5, P 1, RHA 1.

ADDAMS, Inez Exh. 1901-27
Married Clifford A. q.v. Add: Paris 1901; London 1903; Esher, Surrey 1927. † GI 3, I 14, L 1, LS 3, P 4, RA 2.

ADDAMS, Miss I.B. Exh. 1912
Two Gables, Meadway, Hendon, London. † RA 1.

ADDELSHAW, H.P. Exh. 1938
† M 1.

ADDENBROOKE, Miss Rosa Exh. 1891-92
3 Park Villas, London Road, Salisbury. † RA 1, RBA 1.

ADDERTON, Charles William B. 1866
Watercolour painter. Exh. 1884-1937. Add: Ockbrook, Nr. Derby 1884, 1902; Scarborough, Yorks. 1894; Nottingham 1920. † B 1, GI 1, M 1, N 226, RA 7, RBA 3, RI 11.

ADDEY, Joseph Poole Exh. 1880-1914
Londonderry, Co. Wicklow, Rathgar, Dublin, Cork 1880; Surbiton, Surrey 1911; Kingston-on-Thames, Surrey 1914. † L 2, RA 1, RHA 125.

ADDEY, Mrs. Louisa Exh. 1883-1902
Londonderry, Dublin, Wicklow, Cork. † RHA 7.

ADDIS, E. Exh. 1884
14 Dame Agnes Street, Nottingham. † N 1.

ADDISON, Alfred H. Exh. 1936
100 Perry Rise, Forest Hill, London. † RA 1.

ADDISON, G.H.M. Exh. 1883
Adelaide, Australia. † RA 1.

ADDISON, Herbert W. Exh. 1922-39
University College Hall, London 1922. † GOU 25, NEA 1.

ADDISON, William Grylls d. 1904
Landscape painter and watercolourist. Exh. 1880-1900. Add: London 1880-83 and 1891-96; Odiham, Hants. 1884-90; Goudhurst, Kent 1897. † D 21, G 1, L 1, M 2, RA 7, RBA 2, RI 3, ROI 3.

ADDY, Alfred Exh. 1896-1903
Bradford, Yorks. 1896; Harrogate, Yorks. 1903. † GI 1, RA 1.

ADEMOLLO, Prof. Cav. Carlo 1825-1911
Exh. 1886. Figline, Val d'Arno, Florence, Italy. † GI 1.

ADENEY, Mrs. Noel Gilford Exh. 1930-39
Painter and textile designer. Studied Slade School of Art. m. Bernard A. q.v. Member London Group 1930. † COO 3, GOU 1, LEI 2.

ADENEY, William Bernard 1878-1966
Painter and textile designer. Exh. 1900-39. Studied Slade School, R.A. Schools 1892-96; Julians, Paris 1897; Board of Studies 1921. Head of Design School L.C.C. Central School of Arts and Crafts 1930. Founder Member London Group 1913 and President 1918-32. Add: Tunbridge Wells, Kent 1900; Manchester 1903. † CHE 4, COO 3, G 3, GOU 6, LEI 18, LS 13, M 1, RA 1.

ADEY, Miss Virginia G. Exh. 1880-94
Lyndhurst, Hants., 1880; Godalming, Surrey 1882; Bishop's Waltham, Hants. 1894. † B 1, D 4, L 1, RBA 2, SWA 1, TOO 1.

ADIE, Miss Edith Helena Exh. 1892-1921
Watercolour painter of gardens. Studied South Kensington Art School, Westminster and Slade School. Teacher of painting in Bordigher, Italy. Add: London 1892 and 1904; Dublin 1902. † BG 3, D 12, FIN 138, LS 6, M 1, RA 4, RBA 4, RHA 11 RI 2, SWA 1.

ADIN, Miss Christine Catherine b. 1884
Embroideress and stage designer. Exh. 1926-39. Add: Whalley Range, Manchester. † L 1, M 2, RCA 7.

ADIN, Charles Waldo 1854-1930
Landscape painter. Studied Manchester School of Art. Travelled in Persia. Add: Hume, Manchester 1885; Chorley, Lancs. 1897; Chorlton cum Hardy, Manchester 1905. † L 33, M 8, RA 6, RCA 9, ROI 7.

ADKINS, Arthur Montressor Exh. 1901-14
Leyton, Essex 1901; Wanstead, Essex 1907. † RA 1, RBA 1, ROI 5.

ADKINS, Miss H.S. Exh. 1911-14
Brighton, Sussex and Mansfield, Notts. † N 1, RA 1.

ADKINS, J.S. Exh. 1906-10
London. † RA 3.

ADLAM, F. Arnold Exh. 1898-1900
7 Marine Terrace, Criccieth, N. Wales. † RBA 2.

ADLER, Jules* b. 1865
Exh. 1901-23. Add: Paris, France. † L 2, RA 1.

ADLINGTON, Miss E.C. Exh. 1893-96
St. Paul's Studios, Colet Gardens, W. Kensington, London. † RA 1, RBA 1, RI 1.

ADNAMS, Miss Marion Exh. 1927-35
22 Otter Street, Derby. † B 4.

ADSHEAD, Charles T. Exh. 1925
Architect. Add: 14 St. Ann's Square, Manchester. † RA 1.

ADSHEAD, Miss Eveline Exh. 1891-94 and 1937
Flower painter. Studied Slade School and in studio of Arthur Wasse. Add: 4 Powis Square, Brighton, Sussex. † B 2, COO 2, M 1.

ADSHEAD, Joseph* Exh. 1883-85
2 Essex Street, Manchester. † M 5, RSA 1.

ADSHEAD, Miss Kathleen Winny Exh. 1922
† RMS 1.

ADSHEAD, Miss Mary b. 1904
Decorative painter. Exh. 1923-40. Studied Slade School of Art. Daughter of Stanley Davenport A. q.v. N.E.A. 1930. Add: London. † ALP 1, BA 6, G 1, GOU 72, L 3, LEF 1, M 1, NEA 42, RA 9, SWA 2.

ADSHEAD, Stanley Davenport 1868-1946
Town planner. Professor of Civic Design, Liverpool, and later of London University. Add: 46 Gt. Russell Street, London, 1903. † RA 11.

ADURKAR, Vasudeow S. Exh. 1939
c/o Windsor and Newton, Rathbone Place, London. † RA 1.

ADYE, Gen. Sir John Miller 1819-1900
Varied military career ending as Governor of Gibraltar 1882-86. Illustrated volume of Autobiographical Reminiscences. Add: 92 St. Georges Square, London 1888. † RI 2.

AFFLECK, Andrew F. Exh. 1904-29
Etcher. Add: Prestwick 1904, Pas de Calais, France 1905; Edinburgh 1907; London 1922. † CON 99, GI 20, L 13, LS 5, RA 3, RSA 10.

AFFLECK, William b. 1869
b. Rochdale. Studied South Kensington, Heatherleys and Lambeth School of Art. Exh. 1890-1932. Add: Camberwell, London 1890; Leppoc Road, Clapham 1895. † B 15, D 40, L 40, M 2, NG 7, RA 28, RBA 5, RI 27, ROI 2.

AGAR, Eileen* b. 1904
Surrealist painter. Exh. 1937-39. b. Buenos Aires. Member London Group 1933. † COO 2, LEI 2.

AGAR, Ethel Exh. 1911-12
Mrs. K. Betty. 8 Bickenhall Mansions, London. † LS 6.

AGARD, Charles Exh. 1902-3
† BG 6.

. GAZARIAN, Mrs. J.M.L. Exh. 1934-38
London. † RCA 3, RHA 3, ROI 4, RSA 4.

AGNEW, Miss Constance Exh. 1897-1909
Edinburgh. † GI 2, RA 2, RSA 8.

AGNEW, Ethel A.S. Exh. 1902-1933
Watercolour painter and wool pictures. Add: Liverpool 1902; London 1906, Wirrall, Cheshire 1929. † L 7, NG 1, RCA 1.

AGNEW, Eric Munro b. 1887
Painter and designer. b. Kirkcaldy, Scotland. Studied Glasgow School of Art and Slade. Exh. 1924-39. Add: London. † COO 1, GOU 1, RA 11, RBA 2.

AGNEW, Mrs. Harriet Exh. 1880-85
Glasgow. † GI 11, RSA 4.

AGNEW, Mrs. P.R. Exh. 1915-22
Ashfield, Heswall, Cheshire. † L 2.

AGOSTINI, Miss Angelina Exh. 1917-20
London. † RA 2, SWA 1.

AGOSTINI, Miss B. Exh. 1906
Kensington, London. † SWA 1.

AHLEFELDT, Countess Ingegerd Exh. 1930-39
Danish painter. Studied Chinese paintings as a child and 3 years at Slade School. † AG 50, WG 196.

AHMAD, L. Sultan Exh. 1920
† M 9.

AICKMAN, W.A. Exh. 1899-1911
34 Gresham Street, London. † RA 6.

AIDE, Hamilton Exh. 1894
Landscape painter. † GOU 89.

AIKEN, John Macdonald Exh. 1905-40
Painter and etcher. Studied Gray's School of Art, Aberdeen and Royal College of Art, London. A.R.E. 1924; A.R.S.A. 1923; R.S.A. 1937. Born and lived in Aberdeen. † G 2, GI 49, L 13, P 6, RA 25, RE 19, RI 8, RSA 127, RSW 2.

AIKEN, Mrs. Mary Exh. 1938
Jeakes House, Rye, Sussex. † RA 2.

AIKMAN, G.M. Exh. 1881-89
23 Buccleuch Place, Edinburgh. † RSA 11.

AIKMAN, George W. 1830-1905
Painter and engraver. A.R.S.A. 1880. Born and lived in Edinburgh. † B 6, GI 28, L 8, M 6, RA 5, RE 2, RHA 2, RSA 144, RSW 19.

AIKMAN, L.J. Exh. 1881-89
Middlefield, Partick, Glasgow. † GI 6.

AIKMAN, Mrs. P.H. Exh. 1891-93
5 Queen Margaret Crescent, Hillhead, Glasgow. † GI 2.

AIKMAN, William* Exh. 1888-1924
Stained glass designer. Add: Edinburgh 1888; London 1891. † GI 2, RA 26, RSA 33.

AILCHISON, J.W. Exh. 1911
† BRU 1.

AIMER, James Exh. 1905
Viewfield, Melrose, N.B. † RSA 1.

AIMERS, J.J.F. Exh. 1936
69 Highfield Road, Dublin. † RHA 1.

AINGER, Miss E. Caroline M. Exh. 1931
7 North Park Terrace. † RSA 1.

AINSCOUGH, Miss Hilda Beatrice Exh. 1925-27
Sculptor. Studied RA Schools and Paris. Add: 47a Boundary Road, London. † P 2, RA 1.

AINSLIE, Miss Kitty F. Exh. 1921
Childwall Vicarage, Liverpool. † L 1.

AINSLIE, R. St. John d. 1908
Exh. 1895-1908. Add: Wedbergh, Yorks. 1895; Dawlish, Devon 1903; Sherborne, Dorset 1906. † L 8, RBA 1.

AINSWORTH, Edgar Exh. 1928-39
Etcher. Add: Royal College of Art, London 1928; Fawcett Street, London 1929. † GOU 1, M 2, NEA 1, RA 2.

AIRD, Charles d. 1927
Exh. 1904-27. Add: Kilmarnock, N.B. † GI 24, L 6, RA 1, RSA 12.

AIRD, Miss Edith d. by 1920
Miniature painter. Exh. 1894-1904. R.M.S. 1896. Add: Moseley, Birmingham 1894; London 1896. † B 1, P 2, RA 12, RI 1, RMS 48, SWA 3.

AIRD, Reginald James Mitchell b. 1890
Portrait painter and decorative artist. Exh. 1914-39. Studied South Kensington under Sir Arthur Cope, R.A. and Watson Nicoll, Paris, Spain and Belgium. Head of Department of Textile Design, Regional College of Art, Bradford, 1939. † GI 3, I 10, LS 3, P 1, RA 2.

AIRY, Miss Anna b. 1882
Painter and etcher. Studied Slade School 1899-1903 under Prof. Fred Brown, Wilson Steer, Henry Tonks and Sir W. Russell, R.A; Melville Nettleship prize 3 consecutive years. Married Geoffrey Buckingham Pocock q.v. A.R.E. 1908; R.E. 1914; R.I. 1918; R.O.I. 1909; R.P. 1913; Add: Hampstead, London 1905; Playford, Ipswich, Suffolk 1934. † BG 2, CAR 38, FIN 135, G 7, GI 47, GOU 13, I 19, L 76, LS 5, M 2, NEA 7, P 13, RA 61, RE 59, RI 51, ROI 39.

AIRY, A.L. Exh. 1904-10
Woodbridge, Suffolk 1904; London 1907; Worthing 1910. † L 1, RA 2.

AIRY, Mrs. Enid Exh. 1930
† L 2.

AIRY, Jack L. Exh. 1936-39
Landscape painter. Add: St. Margaret's Cross, Hawkhurst, Kent. † NEA 4, RA 1, RBA 1.

AISHTON, Frances Exh. 1887
27 Palace Road, Upper Norwood, London. † SWA 2.

AITCHESON, Jessie G.A. Exh. 1901
74 Gt. King Street, Edinburgh. † RSA 1.

AITCHISON, A.W. Exh. 1902
Brieryhill, Hawick, N.B. † RSA 1.

AITCHISON, Miss G. Exh. 1901-3
104 Banbury Road, Oxford. † SWA 3.

AITCHISON, George 1825-1910
Architect. A.R.A. 1881, R.A. 1898. Add: 150 Harley Street, London. † RA 36.

AITCHISON, Dr. Leslie Exh. 1932-39
Birmingham. † B 8.

AITCHISON, Mary Exh. 1911
† BRU 1.

AITCHISON, Miss M.E. Exh. 1897-1903
100 Banbury Road, Oxford. † SWA 8.

AITCHISON, Martin H.H. Exh. 1939-40
7 Hintlesham Avenue, Edgbaston, Birmingham. † B 2, RBA 2.

AITCHISON, Miss W.H. Exh. 1900
104 Banbury Road, Oxford. † SWA 1.

AITKEN, Agnes Exh. 1894-96
17 Crown Terrace, Dowanhill, Glasgow. † GI 1, RSW 1.

AITKEN, Mrs. Emily Exh. 1933-39
3 Steele's Studios, Haverstock Hill, London. † RA 3, ROI 12, SWA 3.

AITKEN, Mrs. Elizabeth M. Exh. 1923-40
Blackheath, London. † P 1, RA 2, RCA 1, RHA 2, ROI 4, RSA 5, SWA 2.

AITKEN, E.V. Exh. 1886
Glenburnie Road, Werter Road, Putney, London. † RE 1.

AITKEN, Miss Gladys M. Exh. 1915
Gullane, Port St. Mary, I.O.M. † L 1.

AITKEN, Geo. Shaw Exh. 1880-1910
Architect. Add: Dundee 1880; Edinburgh 1898. † RSA 8.

AITKEN, James Exh. 1884-1933
Painted on the Continent. Add: Southport, Lancs. 1884; N. Wales 1889; Manchester 1896; Egremont, Cheshire 1898; Liverpool 1902; Gullane, Port St. Mary, I.O.M. from 1911. † B 3, L 75, M 3, RA 7, RCA 29, RI 1, RSA 2.

AITKEN, James Alfred* d. 1897
Landscape painter. A.R.H.A. 1871 (resigned 1890), R.S.W. 1878. Add: Glasgow. † AG 1, DOW 5, G 2, GI 46, RHA 13, RSA 39, RSW 67.

AITKEN, J.D. Exh. 1887-88
114 Argyle Street, Glasgow. † GI 1, L 1.

AITKEN, John Ernest 1881-1957
Watercolour landscape painter. Studied Manchester, Liverpool and Wallasey Schools of Art and under his father James A. q.v. Painted on the Continent. R.S.W. 1929. Add: Egremont, Cheshire 1907; Gullane, Port St. Mary, I.O.M. 1911. † AR 2, B 11, FIN 1, GI 4, L 70, M 2, RA 9, RCA 70, RI 33, RSA 3, RSW 42.

AITKEN, Miss Janet Macdonald Exh. 1893-1940
Portrait and landscape painter. Studied Glasgow School of Art and Colarossi's, Paris. Add: Glasgow 1893; Troon, Ayr 1931. † BG 42, GI 55, L 6, RBA 1, RSA 33, RSW 26, SWA 3.

AITKEN, Katherine D. Exh. 1894
571 Sauchiehall Street, Glasgow. † GI 1.

AITKEN, Mrs. Melita Exh. 1931
650 Linden Avenue, Victoria, B.C. Canada. † RA 1.

AITKEN, Miss Pauline b. 1893
Sculptor. Studied Manchester School of Art, Chelsea Polytechnic and R.A. Schools. Add: London. † L 19, M 2, RA 10, RCA 6, RMS 2, RSA 7, SWA 1

AITKEN, Miss R. Exh. 1915
13 Westholm, Garden Suburb, Hampstead, London. † RA 1.

AITKEN, William Exh. 1928-32
10 Lorne Terr. Larbert. † GI 6, L 1, RSA 11.

AITKINSON, R. Exh. 1885
14 Rue St. Michel, Antwerp, Belgium. † RSA 2.

AKED, George D. Exh. 1929-33
London. † NEA 1, RA 2.

AKERBERG, Knut Exh. 1927
64 Via Della Robbia, Florence, Italy. † RSA 1.

AKERBERG, Mrs. Verna Exh. 1923-28
Switzerland 1923, Corstorphine, Edinburgh 1928. † RSA 4.

AKERBLADH, Alexander b. 1886
Landscape and portrait painter. Exh. 1916-40. b. Sweden. Studied architecture Glasgow School of Art 1900, Art at St. John's Wood School 1916 and in Munich 1917. Add: London. † FIN 59, GI 1, I 4, L 4, NEA 3, P 18, RA 18, RI 6, ROI 13.

AKERMAN, Miss Lilian Exh. 1909-13
Seaton, Devon 1909; Barnes, Surrey 1913. † LS 9.

AKERS-DOUGLAS, Hon. Mrs. Amy Exh. 1918-19
35 Kensington Square, London. † I 3, RA 1.

AKHURST, Miss Hilda O. Exh. 1932-33
Landscape painter. Add: Bournemouth 1932; London 1933. † RA 2.

AKKERINGA, Johann* b. 1864
Exh. 1910. Dutch, b. Formosa. Add: Amsterdam. † L 1.

ALABASTER, Miss Annie Exh. 1884
Park Road, Moseley, Birmingham. † B 1.

ALABASTER, C. Exh. 1883
357 Moseley Road, Birmingham. † B 1.

ALABASTER, Mrs. L. Exh. 1884-85
351 Moseley Road, Birmingham. † B 3.

ALABASTER, Patricia Emma Exh. 1887-88
nee Fahey. The Grange, 51 Shepherds Bush Green, London. † RI 4.

ALAIS, Alfred Clarence Exh. 1881
Engraver. 11 Devonport Road, Shepherds Bush, London. † RA 1.

ALAPHILIPPE, Camille Exh. 1912
9 Cite Canrobert (32 Rue Cambronne), Paris. † L 1.

ALARCON. Exh. 1911
† BRU 1.

ALASONIERE, F. Exh. 1882
c/o M.P. Delarue, 122 Boulevard Street, Germain, Paris. † RA 6.

ALASTAIR Exh. 1914
† LEI 31.

ALBA, Gaston Exh. 1913
19 Rue du Depart, Paris. † RSA 1.

ALBAN, T. Exh. 1914
115 Gt. Portland Street, London. † RA 1.

ALBANESI, Eva Exh. 1918
† I 1.

ALBANO, Salvatore Florenti 1841-1893
Italian sculptor. Exh. 1881-88. Add: Via Del Mandorlo, Florence, Italy. † RA 6.

ALBERMARLE, Lord Exh. 1917-33
Landscapes and character sketches. Add: 39 Belgrave Square, London. † RA 1, WG 93.

ALBERT, Madame Annie Stewart Miles
See MILES.

ALBERT, Ernest Exh. 1891
40 Kilmain Road, Dawes Road, Fulham, London. † RA 1.

ALBERT, Mrs. Lilian Exh. 1904-39
Miniature painter. N.S.A. 1914; R.M.S. 1929. Add: London 1904 and 1933; Nottingham 1908; Torquay, Devon 1925. † B 1, L 19, N 9, NEA 1, P 5, RA 4, RMS 20, RSA 5.

ALBERT, William Exh. 1913-22
Nottingham 1913, Torquay 1922. † L 2.

ALBERTIS, T. Exh. 1888
† FIN 1.

ALBINO, H.H. Exh. 1932
The Manor House, Bourton-on-the-Water, Glos. † B 1.

ALBISETTI, N. Exh. 1909
22 Avenue de Saint Ouen, Paris, France. † L 1.

ALBRECHT, Mendal Exh. 1884-87
72 Bolton Road, Pendleton, Manchester. † M 1, RHA 1.

ALBRECHT, Miss V.E. Exh. 1914
Roundhay, Leeds. † SWA 1.

ALBRIGHT, Miss F. Amy Exh. 1923
17 Wilfield Place, Dingle, Liverpool. † L 1.

ALBRIGHT, Mrs. W.A. Exh. 1923
29 Frederick Road, Birmingham. † B 2.

ALCALA-GALIANO, A. Exh. 1903
chez M. Blanchet, Rue Saint Benoit, Paris. † L 1.

ALCOCK, Miss Beatrice Exh. 1886-1915
Manchester 1886, Ashton-on-Mersey 1892; Birkdale, Lancs. 1914; Southport, Lancs. 1915. † M 5.

ALCOCK, Frederick Exh. 1887-1910
Nr. Liverpool 1887, Oxton, Cheshire 1907. † L 11.

ALCOCK, J. Exh. 1897
1 Park Terrace, Waterloo, Liverpool. † L 1.

ALCOCK, Matte Exh. 1926
† M 3.

ALCOCK, S. Exh. 1883
3 Richmond Villas, Park Hill, Stoke-on-Trent. † RE 1.

ALDA, J.G.* Exh. 1909
50 Tavistock Square, London. † RA 1.

ALDE, Pietri Exh. 1884
The Avenue, 76 Fulham Road, London. † L 1.

ALDEN, G.W. Exh. 1930
Wood engraver. † RED 1.

ALDEN, Phyllis Exh. 1930-36
† COO 2, RED 1.

ALDER, J.S. Exh. 1918
1 Arundel Street, Strand, London. † RA 3.

ALDER, Miss R. Exh. 1910-16
Batheaston, Somerset 1910, Bathfield Lodge, Bath 1914. † L 3, RA 6.

ALDER, Miss W.C. Exh. 1899
c/o Mrs. Fraser, 34 Balliol Road, Bootle. † L 1.

ALDERLEY, Miss Doris Exh. 1912
Vale Farm, Bowdon, Cheshire. † L 3.

ALDERSON, Miss Eileen W.M. Exh. 1929
11 Thorne Road, Doncaster. † L 2.

ALDERSON, Miss Isabel Exh. 1905
Villa Edouard, St. Survan, Ille et Vilaine, France. † B 1.

ALDERSON, James S. Exh. 1905-06
97 Clifton Road, Rugby. † B 2.

ALDERSON, Miss Violet M. Exh. 1901-21
France 1901 and 1905; Bushey, Herts. 1903; Jersey 1913. † B 3, L 2, RCA 2, SWA 5.

ALDHAM, Miss Fannie Exh. 1909
9 Rue Dupin, Paris. † L 1.

ALDIN, Cecil Charles Windsor 1870-1935
Sporting and topographical painter and illustrator. Studied at South Kensington under Frank Calderon. b. Slough, d. Reading. R.B.A. 1898. Add: London 1897; Henley-on-Thames, Oxon 1905. † AB 19, FIN 171, L 1, RA 2, RBA 12, RMS 4.

ALDIS, A.E. Exh. 1885
Newcastle Chambers, Nottingham. † N 2.

ALDIS, E. Exh. 1885
Newcastle Chambers, Nottingham. † N 2.

ALDOM, H.C. Exh. 1896-1902
London. † RA 1, ROI 1.

ALDRED, Miss Laura Exh. 1882-86
Limehurst, Didsbury. † M 6.

ALDRICH, Miss Lorna M. Exh. 1933-35
Portrait painter. 136 Hayes Lane, Bromley, Kent. † RA 4.

ALDRIDGE, Frederick James* 1850-1933
Marine and landscape painter. Lived Worthing. † B 1, D 156, L 3, M 2, NG 1, RA 3, RBA 18, RHA 2, RI 7, ROI 8.

ALDRIDGE, J. Exh. 1904
† TOO 2.

ALDRIDGE, John Arthur Malcolm b. 1905
Landscape painter, designer and illustrator. Exh. 1931-40. Visited Europe. Lived Essex. † LEF 10, LEI 119, RED 1.

ALDWINKLE, Thomas W. Exh. 1890
2 East India Avenue, London. † RA 1.

ALDWORTH, Miss Jane D.S. d. 1913
London 1889; Dorking, Surrey 1899. † LS 9, RA 1, RHA 5, RID 31.

ALEC-TWEEDIE, Mrs. Ethel Brilliana d. 1940
Travelled widely. Presented many of her drawings to Australia and New Zealand. † RED 58.

ALEXANDER, Alexander Exh. 1901-15
Edinburgh. † RSA 8.

ALEXANDER, Miss Ann Dunlop Exh. 1917-40
Watercolour painter. Studied Glasgow School of Art. Add: Glasgow. † GI 19, L 1, RSA 5.

ALEXANDER, A.O. Exh. 1907
Riverdale, West Didsbury, Manchester. † L 1.

ALEXANDER, Miss Camilla Exh. 1931
Old Wilsley, Cranbrook, Kent. † RA 1.

ALEXANDER, Charles Exh. 1893-95
Alderley, Wooton-under-Edge, 1893, London 1895. † L 1, NG 1, RA 3.

ALEXANDER, Miss or Mrs. C.A. Exh. 1885
16 Gloucester Place, London. † SWA 1.

ALEXANDER, Douglas Exh. 1935-38
c/o Victor Waddington Galleries, South Anne Street, London. † RHA 2.

ALEXANDER, Ella Exh. 1890-94
15 Queen's Crescent, Glasgow. † GI 3.

ALEXANDER, Miss Elizabeth Hean Exh. 1893-1936
Glasgow. † GI 15, L 5, RSA 1, RSW 1.

ALEXANDER, Edwin* 1870-1926
Painter of landscapes and nature. Son of Robert A. q.v. Studied in Paris 1891. Visited Egypt 1892-96. Many of his pictures painted on silk, linen or textured paper. "Peacock and Python" purchased by Chantry Bequest 1905. A.R.S.A. 1902; R.S.A. 1913; R.S.W. 1911; A.R.W.S. 1899; R.W.S. 1910. Add: Slateford, Nr. Edinburgh, Musselburgh and Inveresk. † FIN 3, GI 15, L 24, LEI 2, M 4, RA 2, RSA 102, RSW 42, RWS 49.

ALEXANDER, E. Martin b. 1881
Sculptor in bronze. Add: Slateford, Nr. Edinburgh 1923; London 1925; Henley-on-Thames, Oxon 1936. † GI 4, RA 9, RSA 18.

ALEXANDER, Mrs. Edith Meta Exh. 1908-25
London 1908; Killiney, Ireland 1915; St. Ives, Cornwall 1921. † LS 3, RA 1, RHA 9.
ALEXANDER, Mrs. F.E. Exh. 1913
Walberswick, Southwold, Suffolk. † L 1, RA 2.
ALEXANDER, George* Exh. 1902-40
Sculptor. Add: Glasgow 1902; London 1905. † GI 5, L 1, RA 7, RSA 1.
ALEXANDER, Guy Bevan b. 1882
Painter and etcher. b. Yorkshire. Studied Chelsea Art School under Sir William Orpen, A.E. John and Ambrose McEvoy. Served R.N. China War 1900 and 1914-19. Add: Goudhurst, Kent 1908; London 1910. † AB 3, CHE 1, L 1, LS 4, NEA 10, P 4, RCA 1, RHA 6, ROI 2.
ALEXANDER, George Edward b. 1865
Landscape painter. b. Chippenham, Wilts. Self taught. Add: London 1897; Farnham, Surrey 1907; Churt, Surrey 1923. † I 1, LS 8, RA 11, RCA 1, RHA 15, RI 9, RSA 5 WG 228.
ALEXANDER, G.L. Exh. 1903-11
London. † RA 4.
ALEXANDER, Miss Hebe Exh. 1898-1902
Lidwells, Goudhurst, Kent. † D 3, L 1, RA 1, SWA 8.
ALEXANDER, Herbert 1874-1946
Landscape and figure painter. Studied Herkomer's and Slade School. Served with Army in India and Mesopotamia. A.R.W.S. 1905; R.W.S. 1928 Add: Cranbrook, Kent 1893. † BG 1, D 9, DOW 2, FIN 1, GI 2, L 4, M 8, RA 3, ROI 3, RSW 2, RWS 71, WG 3.
ALEXANDER, Lady Jane Exh. 1886
Ty Henharger Place, St. Albans. † D 1.
ALEXANDER, Jean Exh. 1904-5
Hailes Cottage, Slateford, Nr. Edinburgh. † RSA 2.
ALEXANDER, John Exh. 1880-92
Glasgow. † GI 4, M 1, RSA 2.
ALEXANDER, James B. Exh. 1894-1906
Glasgow. † GI 5.
ALEXANDER, Miss Jean Dryden Exh. 1934-40
London 1934; Priests Cottage, Brentwood, Essex 1938. † NEA 3, RA 4.
ALEXANDER, J.M. Exh. 1883
58 Chatham Street, Liverpool. † L 1.
ALEXANDER, J. Scott Exh. 1893
4 Seyton Avenue, Langside, Glasgow. † GI 1.
ALEXANDER, James Stuart Carnegie b. 1900
Watercolour landscape painter. Add: Selkirk 1921; c/o Aitken Dott and Son, Edinburgh 1928. † GI 3, L 6, M 1, RA 5, RI 8, RSA 13, RSW 30.
ALEXANDER, J.W. Exh. 1899
31 Boulevard Berthier, Paris. † RSA 1.
ALEXANDER, L. Exh. 1894-1909
Glasgow. † GI 23, L 2, RSA 5.
ALEXANDER, Miss Lena Exh. 1905-36
Mrs. Lees Duncan. Glasgow 1905; Edinburgh 1919; London 1924; Kirkcudbright 1936. † GI 20, L 6, RA 1, RSA 16, SWA 1.
ALEXANDER, Miss Margaret Exh. 1913-28
Carshalton 1913; Milford, Surrey 1920. † AB 3, D 10, G 2, SWA 4.
ALEXANDER, Miss Marion Exh. 1887-97
Swifts, Cranbrook, Kent 1887; London 1895. † G 1, M 2, NG 3, ROI 2, SWA 3.
ALEXANDER, Russell Exh. 1923-35
Watercolour painter, Add: 43 Old Town, Clapham, London. † NEA 3, RA 5, RSA 4.
ALEXANDER, Robert 1840-1923
Animal painter. A.R.S.A. 1878; R.S.A. 1888; R.S.W. 1889, resigned 1907. Add: Edinburgh 1880; Midlothian 1882; Slateford 1888. † DOW 1, GI 10, L 1, RA 2, RSA 125, RSW 4.
ALEXANDER, Miss R.A. Exh. 1887
66 Inverness Terrace, Hyde Park, London. † D 3.
ALEXANDER, Robert G.D. Exh. 1896-1940
Watercolour landscape painter. Add: London 1896; Priests Cottage, Brentwood, Essex 1911; Clapham, London 1936. † D 18, G 43, GOU 5, NEA 15, RA 10.
ALEXANDER, Miss Sally Exh. 1927-40
Links Lodge, Musselburgh 1927; Edinburgh 1929. † GI 1, RSA 12, RSW 11.
ALEXANDER, W. Exh. 1885
61 Osmaston Street, Derby. † N 1.
ALEXANDER, William* Exh. 1889-98
Watercolour painter. Add: Salisbury, Wilts. † RA 4.
ALEXANDER, W.J. Exh. 1932
38 Argyll Street, Coventry. † B 2.
ALEXANDRE, Louis b. 1867
Painter and sculptor in wood. b. and studied in Paris. Came to London 1914. † RA 3.
ALFORD, Agnes Exh. 1881
12 Oxford Terrace, Hyde Park, London. † RBA 1.
ALFORD, Leonard C. Exh. 1885-1920
Marine painter. Lived Southampton. † B 2, RA 4, RCA 1, RHA 8.
ALFORD, William Exh. 1895
Portrait painter. 7 Sydenham Rise, Forest Hill, London. † RA 1.
ALFRED, Miss Rose Exh. 1931-40
Sculptor. Add: London. † RA 2.
ALGER, Vivian C. Exh. 1882-88
Landscape and coastal painter. Add: London 1882: Bedford 1888. † L 4, RA 8.
ALGIE, Miss Jessie Exh. 1885-1925
Flower painter. Add: Glasgow 1885, Stirling N.B. 1904; Elie N.B. 1916; Kirn, Dunoon 1919. † B 2, BG 22, FIN 15, GI 53, L 24, M 2, NG 1, RA 11, RHA 8, RI 1, ROI 6, RSA 19, RSW 3, SWA 4.
ALGIE, Miss Lucie Exh. 1908
Stirling, N.B. † SWA 2.
ALINGTON, Gervase Exh. 1910
Killard, West Malvern. † B 1.
ALISON, David b. 1882
Painter of portraits and interiors. Studied Glasgow School of Art. R.P. 1917; A.R.S.A. 1916; R.S.A. 1922. Add: Dysart, N.B. 1905, Edinburgh 1909. † GI 72, L 6, M 2, P 42, RA 31, RSA 95, RSW 7.
ALISON, Henry Y. Exh. 1913-39
Dysart, Fifeshire 1913; Glasgow 1921. † GI 54, RA 1, RSA 37.
ALISON, James P. Exh. 1900-10
Bridge Street, Hawick, N.B. † GI 3, RSA 1.
ALISON, J.T. Exh. 1885
Rosehill, Dalkeith. † RSA 1.
ALISON, Mrs. M. Exh. 1925-26
7 Bedford Park, Edinburgh. † L 3.
ALISON, Mrs. M.L. Exh. 1917-18
20 Cockerton Road, Wandsworth Common, London. † RA 2.
ALISON, Thomas Exh. 1880-1913
Rosehill, Dalkeith. † GI 8, RSA 54, RSW 2.
ALISON, Walter Exh. 1939
27 Kirk Wynd, Kirkcaldy. † RSA 1.
ALLAN, Alexander d. 1972
1 Windsor Terrace, Monifieth 1939. † RA 2, RSA 4.
ALLAN, Andrew Exh. 1888-1940
Ayrshire 1888, Glasgow 1892; Cathcart 1904. † GI 73, L 77, NG 1, RSA 34, RSW 15.
ALLAN, Archibald Russell Watson b. 1878
Studied Glasgow School of Art, Paris at Julians and Colarossi's. A.R.S.A. 1932; R.S.A. 1938. Add: Gartocharn by Balloch 1899; Balfron, N.B. 1903; Milngavie 1913 and 1924; Stirling 1921 and 1929. † GI 76, L 4, RSA 32, RSW 1.
ALLAN, C. Exh. 1880
19 St. James's Terrace, Hillhead, Glasgow. † D 1.
ALLAN, Miss Christina Exh. 1884-1900
London 1884. † G 1, GI 1, L 1, RHA 1, RI 5, SWA 1.
ALLAN, Miss Clara Exh. 1890-97
Buxley, Foots Cray, Kent. † SWA 3.
ALLAN, Miss Eva D. Exh. 1922-27
Sculptor. 82 Vincent Square, London. † G 2, RA 3, SWA 1.
ALLAN, Miss Eliza Spence Exh. 1886-98
1 Grosvenor Terrace, Glasgow. † GI 7, RSA 1.
ALLAN, Miss Graham Exh. 1893-95
227 West George Street, Glasgow. † GI 4, RSA 1.
ALLAN, George A. Exh. 1923-25
London. † RA 2.
ALLAN, H. Exh. 1913
Park Cottage Studio, Pelham Street, South Kensington, London. † L 1, RA 1.
ALLAN, H. Exh. 1890-1905
Glasgow 1890; Killin, N.B. 1905. † GI 26, RSA 4.
ALLAN, Henry d. 1912
A.R.H.A. 1895; R.H.A. 1901. Add: Co. Down, 1889; Dublin 1893. † L 5, RHA 109.
ALLAN, Hugh Exh. 1880-98
79 West Regent Street, Glasgow. † GI 43, RSA 10, RSW 3.
ALLAN, John Exh. 1930-36
Coatbridge, Nr. Glasgow. † GI 3.
ALLAN, J.A.O. Exh. 1927
25 Union Terrace, Aberdeen. † RSA 1.
ALLAN, J.K. Exh. 1921
166 Buchanan Street, Glasgow. † RSA 1.
ALLAN, Miss Julian Phelps b. 1892
Sculptor. "Marjorie" purchased by Chantry Bequest 1929. S.W.A. 1935. Add: London. † RA 10, RBA 3, RMS 1, SWA 4.
ALLAN, Miss Jessie R. Exh. 1889-1923
Glasgow. † GI 26, L 2, RSA 9, RSW 3.
ALLAN, J.W.A. Exh. 1915-19
Leith. † RSA 3.
ALLAN, K.G. Exh. 1888
1 Grosvenor Terrace, Glasgow. † GI 1.
ALLAN, Mrs. Margaret Exh. 1897-1940
Glasgow. † GI 18, RSA 2.
ALLAN, Ronald b. 1900
Portrait and figure painter. Studied Manchester School of Art. Add: Stamford Lodge, Heaton Moor, Nr. Stockport. † B 3, D 3, RA 1, RCA 2, RSW 2.
ALLAN, Rosemary b. 1911
Studied Slade School. Exh. 1937. Add: Lechlade and London. † NEA 1.
ALLAN, Robert Weir* 1852-1942
Landscape and marine painter and etcher. Studied Julians Paris. Toured India 1891-92, Japan 1907 and sketched frequently on the Continent. N.E.A. 1886, R.S.W. 1880, A.R.W.S. 1887, R.W.S. 1896, V.P.R.W.S. 1908-10. Add: Glasgow 1880, London 1882. † AG 2, AR 2, B 2, BA 8, CON 2, D 13, DOW 1, FIN 42, G 8, GI 121, I 6, L 114, M 27, NEA 3, NG 25, RA 83, RBA 2, RHA 1, RI 13, ROI 38, RSA 89, RSW 166, RWS 403, TOO 4, WG 3.

ALLAN, Ugolin Exh. 1893-1902
65 West Regent Street, Glasgow. † GI 11, L 1, RSA 2, RSW 2.

ALLAN, Miss Van. Quiller Exh. 1912
London. † L 5, RA 6.

ALLAN, Wilkie Exh. 1892
Albert Studios, Shandwick Place, Edinburgh † RSA 1.

ALLAN, W.H. Exh. 1889
107 King's Park Place, Glasgow. † GI 1.

ALLAN, William J. Exh. 1909-28
Edinburgh 1909, Leith, 1920. † GI 1, RSA 1.

ALLAN, W.M. Exh. 1888
8 Somerville Place, Glasgow. † GI 2.

ALLARDYCE, Archibald M'N. Exh. 1929
3 Waverley Gardens, Crossmyloof, Glasgow. † GI 1.

ALLARDYCE, Miss J.K. Exh. 1899
8 Clydesdale Road, Colville Gardens. † RBA 1.

ALLARDYCE, Miss Mary R. Exh. 1891
8 Clydesdale Road, Colville Square, W. † RA 1.

ALLBERRY, H. Exh. 1937
3 Neville Road, Rathgar, Dublin. † RHA 1.

ALLBON, Charles Frederick 1856-1926
Watercolour and black and white artist and etcher. A.R.E. 1887-1911. Add: Crouch End, Essex 1885; Clapham, London 1887. † RA 6, RE 47.

ALLBON, Miss Henrietta Exh. 1933
Chestnut Cottage, Chingford Green, London. † RA 1.

ALLCHIN, Harry Exh. 1881-1904
London 1881 and 1903, Mass. U.S.A. 1902. † D 1, L 1, NG 1, RA 5, ROI 1.

ALLCHIN, J. Herbert Exh. 1885-86
Sutton Vallence, Nr. Staplehurst, Kent. † D 1, RE 5.

ALLCOTT, Walter Herbert 1880-1951
Landscape and watercolour painter. Oil portrait painter. Studied Birmingham School of Art. Toured Italy. R.B.S.A. 1921. Add: Birmingham 1902, Chipping Campden, Glos. 1920; Haslemere, Surrey 1929. † AR 2, B 105, COO 2, FIN 124, L 8. RA 13, RCA 2, RI 4.

ALLDRIDGE, Mrs. Belinda Exh. 1880-85
20 Newman Street, Oxford Street, London. † B 1, SWA 3.

ALLDRIDGE, Emily Exh. 1880
c/o W. Chandler Roberts Esq., Royal Mint, London. † SWA 2.

ALLEN, Arthur Bayliss b. 1889
Painter, architect and sculptor. Add: Egypt, 1914; Bromley, Kent 1922; Beckenham, Kent 1926. † NEA 2, RA 6, RED 1.

ALLEN, Annie C. Exh. 1881-83
London. † RBA 2.

ALLEN, Miss A.K. Exh. 1905
Greenstead Hall, Halstead, Essex. † D 2.

ALLEN, Arthur W. Exh. 1886
Studios, Brook Green. † B 1, RBA 1.

ALLEN, Basil Elsden b. 1886
Designer and craftsman in metals. Head of metal work department. Royal College of Art and Head of design department. Central School of Arts and Crafts, Birmingham. Add: 4 The Mall, Church Street, London 1927. † L 1.

ALLEN, Miss Beatrice E. Exh. 1900
Villa Road, Handsworrth, Birmingham. † B 1.

ALLEN, Miss Constance Exh. 1893
5 Strowan Terrace, Trinity, Edinburgh. † GI 1.

ALLEN, Cecil J. Exh. 1923-39.
Watercolour landscape painter. Add: Nottingham. † N 19.

ALLEN, Charles John b.1862
Sculptor. Studied Lambeth School of Art under Frith, R.A. Schools. (4 silver medals). Vice-principal and teacher of sculpture Liverpool City School of Art. Add: London 1888; Liverpool 1895. † B 2, GI 8, L 31, RA 31, RSA 1.

ALLEN, Charles W. Exh. 1912-29
Watercolour painter and architect. Add: Nottingham. † N 6.

ALLEN, Miss Daphne Constance b. 1899
Painter and illustrator. Exh. 1914. Add: London. † SWA 10.

ALLEN, Miss Doris I. Exh. 1933
Camborne, Langley Park Road, Sutton, Surrey. † ROI 1.

ALLEN, Miss E. Exh. 1934
Watercolour painter. † COO 2.

ALLEN, Miss E. Clifford Exh. 1887
25 Claremont Street, Belfast. † RHA 1.

ALLEN, Ernest C.P. Exh. 1927-37
Architect. Add: London. † RA 2.

ALLEN, Mrs. Elsie Glenn. Exh. 1940
140 Cromwell Road, London. † RBA 2, ROI 1, SWA 1.

ALLEN, E.J. Milner Exh. 1884-1908
Architect. Add: London. † RA 3.

ALLEN, Ernest Lupton b. 1870
Painter and teacher. Studied National Art Training School, Royal College of Art. Travelling scholarship 1895. Julians, Paris. Appointed Headmaster Redditch School of Art 1897. † LS 1, RA 1.

ALLEN, Miss Eileen M. Exh. 1934
Penarth. † RCA 1.

ALLEN, Miss E.P. Exh. 1938-40
Watercolour painter. † AR 2, RI 3.

ALLEN, Mrs. E.R. Exh. 1904-6
1 Auburn Place, Plymouth, Devon. † D 2, SWA 1.

ALLEN, Frederick E. Exh. 1915-37
Etcher. M. to Dora Bradley q.v. Add: Birkenhead 1915, Neston, Wirral, Cheshire 1924; Lancaster 1931; Bude 1934; Launceston 1937. † L 34, RA 2, RCA 10.

ALLEN, Gordon b.1885
Architect. Studied art A.A. and abroad. 1st prize "Daily Mail" house design 1927. Exh. 1927-34. Add: 435 Strand, London 1927. † RA 8.

ALLEN, George Maule. Exh. 1880
St. John's, Putney Hill, London. † RBA 1.

ALLEN, George P. Exh. 1910-22
Architect. Add: London 1910, Bedford 1922. † RA 3.

ALLEN, Miss Geraldine Whitacre Exh. 1890-3
8 Pilgrims Lane, Hampstead, London. † RBA 1, ROI 1.

ALLEN, Mrs. Hugh Exh. 1893-4
4 Whitehall Park, Highgate, London. † RI 2,SWA 1.

ALLEN, Henry Epworth b. 1894
Studied Sheffield School of Art. R.B.A. 1934. b. and lived Sheffield. † L 7, M 3, RA 20, RBA 36.

ALLEN, Hervey R. Exh. 1936
Sculptor. Eastweald, Tenterden, Kent. † RA 1.

ALLEN, John Edsall 1862-1944
Principal of St. Martins School of Art 1891-1927. Add: 20 Lanhill Road, Elgin Avenue, London 1901. † RA 1.

ALLEN, J.F. Exh. 1928-40
Small Heath, Birmingham 1928; S. Yardley, Birmingham 1938. † B 15, GI 1, L 2.

ALLEN, J.F. Newham Exh. 1891-94
Whalley Range, Manchester. † L 1, M 2.

ALLEN, John M. Exh. 1885
Ruvigny Gardens, Putney, London. † RA 2.

ALLEN, J.S. Exh. 1925
Sandon Studios, School Lane, Liverpool. † L 1.

ALLEN, John Whitacre. Exh. 1886-1901
Hogarth Club, London 1886; Clevedon, Somerset 1901. † D 5, RI 1.

ALLEN, Miss K. Exh. 1902-19
Croydon 1902; Lee, London 1915. † RA 2, SWA 9.

ALLEN, Miss K.O. Exh. 1891
The Limes, Shirley. † B 1.

ALLEN, Miss K. Saywell. Exh. 1936-40
Nuneaton 1936; London 1939. † NEA 3, RA 4.

ALLEN, Miss Lilian. Exh. 1903-15
The Hawthorns, Gateacre, Nr. Liverpool. † L 61.

ALLEN, L.A. Exh. 1925
18 Evelyn Road, Sparkhill, Birmingham.† B 1.

ALLEN, Miss L. Jessie Exh. 1881-86
London. † RBA 7.

ALLEN, Miss M. Exh. 1880-94
Dublin 1880 and 1887; Manchester 1884 and 1889. † B 1, L 3, M 1, RHA 24.

ALLEN, Marie Exh. 1889-1906
Taunton, Somerset 1889; St. Albans 1899; London 1903. † RBA 2, SWA 9.

ALLEN, Miss Marion Exh. 1905-21
471 Gillott Road, Edgbaston, Birmingham. † B 5.

ALLEN, Mrs. M.B. Exh. 1920
50 Paulton Square, Chelsea, London. † NEA 1.

ALLEN, Mary C.R. Exh. 1914
Cilrhiu, Narbeth, S. Wales. † LS 3.

ALLEN, Maxwell J. Exh. 1934-35
30 Conway Road, Sparkbrook. † B 2.

ALLEN, P.K. Exh. 1906
4 Lundhurst Gardens, Tunbridge Wells. † RA 1.

ALLEN, R.A. Exh. 1883
3 The Grove, Handsworth, Birmingham. † B 1.

ALLEN, Theophilus Exh. 1890-1912
Architect. 3 Duke Street, Adelphi, London. † RA 3.

ALLEN, T.E. Exh. 1914
38 Grange Road West, Birkenhead. † L 1.

ALLEN, Thomas Leslie b. 1892
Painter and art critic "Nottingham Journal". Studied under Arthur Spooner, R.B.A. A.N.S.A. 1930; N.S.A. 1936. Add: Mapperley, Notts. 1926; West Bridgford, Notts. 1928. † N 22.

ALLEN, Thomas William b. 1855
Landscape painter. London 1880 and 1886; Woking, Surrey 1885; Milford, Surrey 1894. † B 7, D 2, G 1, GI 4, L 9, LS 6, M 2, RA 19, RBA 14, RCA 2, RHA 9, ROI 5.

ALLEN, Miss Violet M. Exh. 1902-40
Miniature portrait painter. Add: Bristol 1902; Haslemere, Surrey 1914; Brighton 1940. † RA 7, SWA 1.

ALLEN, W. Exh. 1897
5 Charles Street, Barnes, London. † GI 2.

ALLEN, William F. Exh. 1939
1a Newark Parade, Watford Way, London. † ROI 1.

ALLEN, W. Godfrey Exh. 1934
New panelling and stalls, Chapel of St. Michael and St. George, St. Pauls Cathedral. Add: Surveyors Office, St. Pauls Cathedral, London. † RA 1.

ALLEN, William Herbert b. 1863
Landscape painter. Studied Royal College of Art (gold, silver and bronze medals and travelling scholarship). Principal of Farnham School of Art 1888. Director of the Study and Teaching of Art in the Farnham District for Surrey. C.C. 1904-27. R.B.A. 1904. Worked in France and Italy. Add: Farnham, Surrey 1904; Wylye, Wilts. 1933. † B 7, COO 2, D 5, L 5, M 1, RA 15, RBA 310, RI 2.

ALLEYNE, Miss Mabel b. 1896
Illustrator and engraver. b. Southampton. Studied RA Schools. Add: 33 Park Road, Forest Hill, London, 1923. † NEA 1, RA 7, RED 2, RHA 68.

ALLFREE, Geoffrey S. d. c.1918
Watercolour landscape painter. Exh. 1911-18, R.B.A. 1916. Add: London. † BG 38, I 2, LS 3, NEA 2, RBA 18.

ALLFREY, E.W. Exh. 1898-1939
London 1898, Oxford 1902. † AR 1, COO 2, RA 8.

ALLI, Mme. Aino Sofia b. 1879
Landscape, portrait and miniature painter. b. Uleaborg, Finland. Add: Helsingfors, Finland 1927; London 1935. † RA 1, RI 9.

ALLINGHAM, Mrs. Helen* 1848-1926
nee Paterson. Watercolour painter of rustic scenery and gardens. b. Burton-on-Trent. Studied Birmingham School of Design and RA Schools 1867. Short sketching tour of Italy 1868. A.R.W.S. 1875, R.W.S. 1890. Add: London 1880 and 1890; Witley, Surrey 1882. † AG 37, B 5, FIN 659, L 11, LEI 22, M 11, RWS 140, TOO 9.

ALLINGHAM, W.J. Exh. 1902
c/o Clifford and Co., 2 Haymarket, London. † RA 1.

ALLINSON, Adrian Paul* b. 1890
Painter and sculptor. Studied medicine which he abandoned for art. Studied art Slade School; 1910-12, Paris and Munich. Stage designer to Beecham Opera Co. Art master at Westminster Technical Institute. Member London Group 1914. R.B.A. 1933,R.O.I. 1936. Add: London. † BK 2, COO 6, FIN 40, GI 5, GOU 6, I 5, L 6, LEI 26, LS 9, M 4, NEA 10, RA 30, RBA 18, RED 48, ROI 18, RSA 1.

ALLINSON, Alfred P. Exh. 1915
CHE 39.

ALLINSON, Garlies W. Exh. 1935-36
Hillside, Burnham, Bucks. † AR 2, RA 1, ROI 2.

ALLINSON, Mrs. Hannah P. Exh. 1893
4 Spanish Place, Manchester Square, London. † RHA 1.

ALLISON, Andrew Exh. 1911
7 Amos Street, Liverpool. † L 1.

ALLISON, Miss Annie Exh. 1914-19
Watercolour flower painter. Studied Hull School of Art and Royal College of Art. Add: Wellington Road, Bridlington, Yorks. † RA 7.

ALLISON, Cecil C. Exh. 1932-38
Municipal Art School, St. Helens, Lancs. † L 1, NEA 1, RA 2.

ALLISON, F.D. Exh. 1918
12 Belsize Park Gardens, London. † ROI 1.

ALLISON, Miss Helen Exh. 1937-38
Cardiff 1937, Exeter 1938. † RCA 2.

ALLISON, Miss Jeanie Exh. 1895
122 George Street, Edinburgh. † RSA 1.

ALLISON, John Exh. 1935-38
Cardiff. † RCA 8.

ALLISON, John William d. 1934
Figure and portrait painter. Studied Royal College of Art (travelling scholarship). Art master; Principal of Putney School of Art and Portsmouth Municipal School of Art; Board of Education art examination assessor; H.M. Inspector of Schools of Art. R.B.A. 1901. Add: Wimbledon, London 1900; Penzance 1901; Southsea, Hants. 1907. † RA 1, RBA 17, RI 2.

ALLISON, Robert Exh. 1926-40
Glasgow. † GI 7.

ALLISON, Sir Richard John b.1869
Architect. Exh. 1914-25. Studied Lambeth School of Art. Principal work New Science Museum, South Kensington. Chief architect H.M. Office of Works. Add: London. † RA 7.

ALLISTON, Norman Exh. 1928-29
D 3.

ALLNATT, Miss Kathleen Exh. 1923
92 Clarence Gate Gardens, London. † RA 1.

ALLNUTT, Miss Emily Exh. 1902-31
Portrait, miniature and landscape painter. Studied Slade School and Paris. S.W.A. 1917. Add: Windsor 1902; Gerrard's Cross, Bucks. 1915; St. Ives, Cornwall 1926. † D 2, L 3, RA 2, RMS 1, ROI 1, SWA 20.

ALLNUTT, Miss Mabel Exh. 1888-91
Thames Street, Windsor. † B 1, RBA 1.

ALLON, Miss M. Exh. 1912-13
SWA 4.

ALLONGE, Auguste 1833-1898
French painter. Exh. 1883. 83 Rue N-D des Champs, Paris. † GI 1.

ALLOTT, Fred W. Exh. 1884-86
Huddersfield. † RHA 3.

ALLOUARD, Emile Henri 1844-1929
French sculptor. Exh. 1907-13. Add: Paris. † L 7, RSA 3.

ALLPORT, Miss Curzon Louise Exh. 1898-1929
Portrait and landscape painter. Add: London. † GOU 33, I 14, L 20, LS 8, P 7, RA 9, RHA 4, RID 51, ROI 3.

ALLPORT, Harvey. Exh. 1888-91
Landscape painter. Studied Royal College of Art. H.M. Inspector of Schools, Board of Education 1900-26. Add: 2 Milner Street, Cadogan Square, London. † L 3, M 1, RA 1, RBA 3.

ALLPORT, Howard Exh. 1908-9
1 Broughton Road, Handsworth, Birmingham. † B 2.

ALLPORT, Miss Lily Exh. 1890-1902
London. † M 1, RA 2, RBA 1, RHA 1, RID 24, ROI 4.

ALLSEBROOK, A.P. Exh. 1900-1
Wollaton, Nottinghamshire. † N 2.

ALLSOP, George Norbury b. 1911
Painter and wood engraver. Add: Malvern Link, Worcestershire 1940. † RA 1.

ALLSOP, H.B. Exh. 1933
11 Gerald Road, Worthing, Sussex. † L 1.

ALLSOP, Harry S. Exh. 1931-37
Portrait and landscape painter. Add: Cuthford, Kilmaurs, Ayrshire. † GI 6, RSA 2.

ALLSOP, Miss Sarah Exh. 1916-20
Morley Park Farm, Nr. Belper, Derbyshire. † N 5.

ALLWOOD, Miss Elizabeth Exh. 1905-28
37 Swinton Grove, Chorlton-on-Medlock, Manchester. † L 4, M 6. RCA 2.

ALLWOOD, Enid Exh. 1925
Western House, The Park, Nottingham. † N 1

ALLWOOD, Miss Kate Exh. 1892
Youlgrave, Bakewell. † N 2.

ALLWOOD, Victor Exh. 1931-32
29 Jephcott Road, Alum Rock. † B 5.

ALMA-TADEMA, Miss Anna* 1865-1943
Landscape, flower and genre painter. Daughter of Sir Lawrence A-T q.v. Add: Grove End Road, St. John's Wood, London. † B 1, BG 2, FIN 1, G 4, GI 3, L 6, NG 20, RHA 1, RI 2, TOO 3.

ALMA-TADEMA, Sir Lawrence* 1836-1912
b. Holland. Studied Academy of Fine Arts Antwerp 1852 under Leys. Moved to London 1870. Awarded Royal Gold Medal 1906 by R.I.B.A. for his promotion of architecture in painting. "A favourite Custom" purchased by Chantrey Bequest 1909. A.R.A. 1876, R.A. 1879, H.R.B.A. by 1880, R.E. 1881, H.R.E., H.R.M.S. 1896, H.R.O.I. 1898, R.P. 1892, H.R.S.A. 1897, R.S.W. 1882, H.R.S.W. 1906, A.R.W.S. 1873, R.W.S. 1875. Lived London. † AG 12, B 26, CAR 1, FIN 8, G 21, GI 12, I 1, L 28, M 9, NG 31, P 11, RA 52, RBA 1, RCA 1, RE 1, RHA 2, RMS 1, ROI 3, RSA 7, RSW 4, RWS 6, TOO 20.

ALMA-TADEMA, Lady Laura Theresa* 1852-1909
Painter of children, portraits and domestic scenes. Nee Epps, second wife of Sir Lawrence A-T q.v. and mother of Anna A-T q.v. H.S.W.A. 1880. Add: London. † B 3, FIN 3, G 7, GI 3, L 2, M 6, NG 19, RA 21, RHA 2, ROI 1, RSA 4, TOO 2.

ALMENT, Miss Lizzie Exh. 1881-1916
47 Carysfort Avenue, Blackrock, Dublin. † RHA 56.

ALMENT, Miss Mary M. Exh. 1880-1908
47 Carysfort Avenue, Blackrock, Dublin and Dawson Street, Dublin. † RHA 53.

ALMOND, J. Exh. 1929
147 Huddleston Road, London. † L 1, RA 1.

ALMOND, William Douglas 1868-1916
Genre and historical painter. R.B.A. 1890, R.I. 1897, R.O.I. 1896. Add: London. † B 1, FIN 1, GI 9, L 7, M 1, RA 11, RBA 36, RI 19, ROI 39, RSA 1.

ALSINA Exh. 1911
BRU 1.

ALSOP, Frederick Exh. 1883
Milngavie, by Glasgow. † RA 1.

ALSOP, John Exh. 1889-90
Airy Bank, Milngavie. † GI 4.

ALSOP, J.J. Exh. 1894-1940
Married Julia Clutterbuck q.v. R.B.A. 1899. Add: London 1894 and 1911; Birmingham 1907; Northampton 1909; Harpenden, Herts. 1924; Chepstow, Mon. 1937. † B 10, I 6, L 1, LS 5, P 1, RA 2, RBA 97, RI 2, ROI 2.

ALSOP, Rodney H. Exh. 1926-30
Australian. c/o C.A. Farey, 19 Bedford Square, London. † RA 4.

ALSTON, Miss Charlotte M. Exh. 1887-1914
Flower Painter. Add: London. † B 1, BG 1, D 3, FIN 1, RA 3, RBA 10, RI 2, SWA 4.

ALSTON, Edward Constable Exh. 1887-1931
Portrait painter. Instructor in School of Drawing and painting, Royal College of Art. Add: London. † L 10, NEA 5, NG 1, RA 9, RBA 1, ROI 1.

ALSTON, Mrs. E.M. Exh. 1921-30
The Close, Aston-under-Hill, Glos. † B 3, NEA 1.

ALSTON, M.E. Exh. 1884
Great Bromley Hall, Colchester. † SWA 1.

ALTHAUS, Fritz B. Exh. 1881-1914
Marine painter. Add: London 1881; Exeter 1892; Leeds 1908. † B 18, D 2, G 1, GI 4, GOU 3, L 17, M 6, NEA 1, RA 18, RBA 17, RHA 2, RI 20, ROI 8, RSA 3.

ALTINI, Fabi Exh. 1880
Via di San Niccolo da Solentino, Rome. † NG 1, RSA 1.

ALTON, Miss Bryanna Exh. 1895-99
Elim, Grosvenor Road, Dublin. † L 2, RHA 8.

ALTON, J. Poe Exh. 1895
Elim, Grosvenor Road, Dublin. † RHA 3.

ALTREE, Miss F. Exh. 1918
16 Birkbeck Road, South Ealing, London. † RA 1.

ALTSON, Abbey Exh. 1894-1917
Portrait painter. R.B.A. 1896. Add: London. † CON 2, GI 2, LS 8, RA 9, RBA 14.

ALTSON, Daniel Meyer b. 1881
Decorative and portrait painter, etcher. b. Middlesbrough. Studied Melbourne National Gallery (scholarship at 16), Ecole des Beaux Arts and Colarossi's, Paris. Exh. 1925-29. Add: Graham House, 123 Ladbroke Road, London. † RA 4.

ALTSON, Ralph b. 1908
Portrait and decorative painter. Son of Abbey A. q.v. Studied Regent St. Polytechnic (Scholarship and medals). Add: London. † RA 5.

ALVAREZ, R.B. Exh. 1905
8 Rue Victor Cousin, Paris. † RA 1.

ALVERY, Miss L. Exh. 1885
1A King Street, St. James's, London. † G 1, L 1.

ALVIS, Miss Harriet Exh. 1896-97
c/o Mr. A. Steele, Edward Street, Brighton. † RA 2.

ALWORTH, F.P. Exh. 1921
Hazelwood Cottage, Sandcross Lane, Reigate. † RI 1.

AMAN, F.T. Exh. 1902
City Engineer's Dept., Dale Street, Liverpool. † L 1.

AMAN-JEAN, Edmond Francois* b. 1860
Born and lived France. Exh. 1895-1925. † GOU 2, I 10, L 4, P 2.

AMARAL, Luciano Exh. 1923-31
London 1923; Welwyn Garden City, Herts. 1931. † NEA 3, RA 2.

AMARAL, Maria Luiza Exh. 1925-29
72 Eccleston Square, London. † NEA 1, SWA 1.

AMARASEKARA, A.C.G.S. Exh. 1936-40
Watercolour painter. Add: Colombo, Ceylon, 1936. † RA 2, RI 3, ROI 2.

AMARASEKARA, D.S. Exh. 1938-40
† RI 2, ROI 2.

AMATO, Luigi Exh. 1939-40
Oil and pastel painter. Add: c/o Messrs. Bourlet and Son, 17 Nassau Street, London. † AR 59, RBA 1.

AMBLER, B.W. Exh. 1925
775 Chester Road, Birmingham. † B 1.

AMBLER, C. Exh. 1912-14
Buckhurst Hill, Essex. † RA 2.

AMBLER, Miss Esther Exh. 1891
43 Soho Road, Handsworth, Staffordshire. † RI 1.

AMBLER, Louis b. 1862
Architect. Exh. 1890-1929. b. Nr. Bradford. Studied RA. Architectural School. Add: London. † RA 10.

AMBROS, R. Exh. 1890-98
† TOO 12.

AMBROSE P. Exh. 1912-16
Landscape painter. A.N.S.A. 1912. Add: West Bridgford, Nottingham. † N 25.

AMBROSE, Thomas Exh. 1903
23 Junction Road, Sheffield. † B 1, RCA 2.

AMEDEE-WETTER, Henri Exh. 1907
7 Rue Hegesippe-Moreau, Paris. † L 1.

AMEN, Mlle. Jeanne Exh. 1903
63 Rue de Prony, Paris. † L 1.

AMENDOLA, Giambattista 1848-87
Italian sculptor. b. Salerno. d. Naples. Add: London 1880. † G 7, M 1, RA 5.

AMES, Victor Exh. 1895-1917
London. † L 4, LS 10, NG 4, RA 1, ROI 4.

AMHERST, Sybil Exh. 1880-96
Didlington Hall, Brandon. † SWA 3.

AMICI, Signor Oreste Exh. 1905
3 St. Alphonsus Road, Dublin. † RHA 1.

AMISANI, Guiseppi Exh. 1927-31
16 Via Brera, Milan, Italy. † AR 58, P 1.

AMOORE, Miss Beth Exh. 1893-1940
Watercolour painter, enameller and jewellery engraver. Studied S. Kensington School of Art, Westminster and Slade. Art teacher Sydenham High School. A.S.W.A. 1916, S.W.A. 1917. Add: London. † AB 8, D 15, L 1, RCA 13, RI 1, SWA 57.

AMOORE, Miss G.F. Exh. 1916
Droxford, Courthorpe Road, Wimbledon, London. † L 1, RA 1.

AMOUR, Miss Elizabeth Isobel b. 1885
Mrs G.P.H. Watson. Painter and potter. Signs work E.A. Bough. Founder of "Bough Pottery" Edinburgh. Married G.P.H. Watson q.v. Add: Balerno, Midlothian 1937; Edinburgh 1938. † RSA 6.

AMPHLETT, Miss Kate Exh. 1884-90
Landscape painter, London. † B 1, RA 4, RBA 30.

AMSCHEWITZ, John Henry* 1882-1942
Portrait painter, mural decorator, illustrator, etcher and cartoonist. b. Ramsgate. Studied R.A. Schools (prize for mural decoration). R.B.A. 1914. Add: London 1905; Johannesburg 1938. † BG 39, FIN 73, L 6, M 2, NEA 4, P 9, RA 16, RCA 4, RBA 125, ROI 12.

AMSON, John Exh. 1925
40 Third Avenue, Fazakerley, Liverpool. † L 2.

AMYOT, Mrs. Cathinca (Catherine) Exh. 1880-1900
nee Engelhart. Add: Diss, Norfolk 1880; London 1883. † GI 8, L 3, M 1, RA 7, RBA 2, ROI 1, SWA 1, RSA 2.

ANCILL, Joseph Exh. 1918-40
Glasgow. † GI 5, RSA 4.

ANCILOTTE, Torello Exh. 1890
† GI 1.

ANCRUM, Miss Marion Exh. 1885-1919
Mrs. G. Turnbull. Edinburgh. † GI 2, RSA 5, RSW 15.

ANCRUM, Miss Mary Exh. 1887-98
Edinburgh. † GI 7, RA 1, RHA 2, RSA 10.

ANDERS, E. Exh. 1887-88
157 New Bond Street, London. † GI 1, M 1.

ANDERSON, A. Exh. 1882-84
Bedford 1882; Islington, London 1884. † D 5, M 4, RBA 4, RI 1.

ANDERSON, A. Exh. 1881
8 Rosehill Place, Edinburgh. † RSA 1.

ANDERSON, Miss Anne Exh. 1932-37
Illustrator, etcher and watercolour painter. Add: Little Audrey, Burghfield Common, Berks. † RA 1, RBA 7, SWA 1.

ANDERSON, A.G.S. Exh. 1935
Glenthorne, Lenton Avenue, The Park, Nottingham. † N 1.

ANDERSON, Mrs. A.L.H. Exh. 1923
The Homestead, Wildhem, Andover. † L 1.

ANDERSON, Miss C. Exh. 1888
17 Stonegate, York. † L 1.

ANDERSON, Charles Exh. 1881
Sculptor. Add: 48 Dale Road, Kentish Town, London. † RA 1.

ANDERSON, Charles Exh. 1889-94
Landscape painter. Nottingham. † N 13.

ANDERSON, Charles Goldsborough Exh. 1887-1917
Portrait painter. London. † L 8, LS 6, M 2, NG 3, RA 19, RBA 1, ROI 2.

ANDERSON, C.J. Exh. 1915
26 John Street, Liverpool. † L 1.

ANDERSON, C.L. Exh. 1889
St. James Gate, Dublin. † RHA 1.

ANDERSON, Miss C.M. Exh. 1904
13 Roland Gardens. † SWA 1.

ANDERSON, Christina S. Exh. 1890-96
Glasgow. † GI 3, RI 1, RSA 1.

ANDERSON, David Exh. 1880-81
Fishing scenes. Add: Belgrave House, Kings Road, London. † RBA 2.

ANDERSON, David Exh. 1882-83
Glasgow. † GI 2, RSA 1.

ANDERSON, D.C. Exh. 1883
101 St. Vincent Street, Glasgow. † GI 2.

ANDERSON, D.L. Exh. 1889-92
Glasgow 1889; Temple-by-Gorebridge 1891. † GI 1, RSA 2.

ANDERSON, D.M. Exh. 1909-25
Bourhouse, Dunbar, N.B. † L 2, RSA 2.

ANDERSON, Miss Daisy M.G. Exh. 1935-37
57 St. Vincent Crescent, Glasgow. † GI 4.

ANDERSON, Miss Ellen Exh. 1890-1901
York 1890; Scarborough 1901. † NG 1, RA 1.

ANDERSON, E.D. Exh. 1891-1900
Palewell, London. † D 3, P 1.

ANDERSON, Edward Edgar Exh. 1884-1904
London 1884; Whitby, Yorks. 1903. R.B.A. 1903. † B 1, L 10, P 1, RA 8, RBA 6, RHA 1, ROI 1.

ANDERSON, Miss Elspeth M. Exh. 1928-35
Auchengower, Cove, Dumbartonshire. † GI 5, L 2, RSA 3.

ANDERSON, Florence Exh. 1928
Watercolour painter. † BA 73.

ANDERSON Miss F. Olive Exh. 1911-13
Frampton Hall, Boston, Lincs. † L 1, RHA 2.

ANDERSON, Mrs. G. Exh. 1896-97
Ripley House, Freshfield. † L 3.

ANDERSON, Mrs. Georgina Exh. 1936-37
Pangbourne, Berks. † RCA 3.

ANDERSON, G.G. Exh. 1892-1917
Landscape and portrait painter and pastelier. Add: Glasgow. † GI 44, RSA 4, RSW 3.

ANDERSON, George L. Exh. 1891-98
Watercolour painter. Middleboro Street, Coventry. † L 1, RA 4.

ANDERSON, Henry Exh. 1911
51 Woodville Terrace, Everton, Liverpool. † L 1.

ANDERSON, Miss Ida Katherine Exh. 1904-38
Miniature painter. Studied Glasgow School of Art. Add: Glasgow 1904; Knockderry Cove, Dumbartonshire 1913. † GI 16, L 4, RA 1, RSA 3.

ANDERSON, J. Exh. 1885
4 Exchange Street, Manchester. † L 1, M 2.

ANDERSON, Mrs. J. Exh. 1899
Wood Lane Cottage, Falmouth, Cornwall. † RA 1.

ANDERSON, Miss J. Exh. 1920-22
The Manor House, Brondesbury, London. † L 1. SWA 4.

ANDERSON, James Exh. 1883-1907
Balerno Cottage, Bishopton, Glasgow 1884. † GI 9, L 4, RSA 2.

ANDERSON, Miss Janet Exh. 1913-35
Wooler, Northumberland 1913; Limpsfield, Surrey 1935. † RI 1, RSA 2.

ANDERSON, John* Exh. 1880-91
Landscape painter. Coventry 1880; London 1881; Glasgow 1887. † B 2, GI 5, RA 2 RBA 1, RE 3.

ANDERSON, Just Exh. 1925
Copenhagen, Denmark. † L 15.

ANDERSON, James Bell 1886-1938
Portrait, still life and landscape painter. Studied Allan Fraser Art College, Arbroath under George Harcourt, A.R.A.; Edinburgh School of Art and with Jean Paul Laurens in Paris at Julians. His first studio in Glasgow in 1910 was devoted entirely to portraiture. A.R.S.A. 1932, R.S.A. 1938. Add: Glasgow. † GI 74, L 2, LS 3, RA 3, RSA 45, RSW 2.

ANDERSON, Miss J.C. Exh. 1894
Woodlands, Hadley Wood, Herts. † L 1, RA 1.

ANDERSON, Mrs. Jean D. Exh. 1916-39
London. † LS 3, RA 4, RBA 3, RSA 1.

ANDERSON, John Farquharson Exh. 1880-82
Camden Town, London 1880; Plaistow 1881; Dundee 1882. † RBA 3, RSA 3.

ANDERSON, James H. Exh. 1880-93
Paris 1880; London 1882. † GI 8, ROI 2.

ANDERSON, Miss Jessie J. Exh. 1881-85
Ava Lodge, Helensburgh. † GI 11.

ANDERSON, Miss J. McG. Exh. 1883-86
22 James Street, Pilrig, Edinburgh. † RSA 2.

ANDERSON, J. Macvicar Exh. 1896
Architect. 6 Stratton Street. † RA 1.

ANDERSON, Mrs. J.P. Exh. 1897
R.M.S. 1897. Glentaskie, Strathmiglo, Fife. † RMS 4.

ANDERSON, J.S. Exh. 1928
193 Waterloo Road, Wolverhampton. † B 1.

ANDERSON, John Silvey Exh. 1886-90
Watercolour painter. Add: Dorking. † M 2, RA 1, RBA 2, RI 4.

ANDERSON, Miss Kay b. 1902
Painter and etcher. Studied Liverpool School of Fine Arts; Royal College of Art under Prof. W. Rothenstein. Add: Bootle 1924; Caterham, Surrey 1927; London 1931. † L 5, NEA 1, RA 1.

ANDERSON, Mrs. K.B. Exh. 1880-81
10 Southpark Terrace, Glasgow. † G 2.

ANDERSON, L. Exh. 1896
† TOO 1.

ANDERSON, L. Florence Exh. 1886-96
112 Raleigh Street, Nottingham. † N 5.

ANDERSON, Mrs. L.T. Exh. 1902
26 Smith Street, Hillhead, Glasgow. † RSA 1.

ANDERSON, Martin – "Cynicus" 1854-1932
Caricaturist. Add: Dychmont Villa, Cambuslang, Glasgow, 1880. † RSA 1.

ANDERSON, Miss Mary Exh. 1902
31A Clanricarde Gardens, Bayswater, London. † ROI 2.

ANDERSON, Mrs. Millicent Exh. 1908-30
58 Shrewsbury Road, Birkenhead. † L 5, RA 1.

ANDERSON, Miss Minnie Exh. 1888-1909
Dunbar 1888; Greenock 1898. † GI 13, RSA 2.

ANDERSON, Margaret D. Exh. 1893
Mayfield, Largs, N.B. † GI 1.

ANDERSON, Madeleine E. Exh. 1937
† NEA 1.

ANDERSON, Mabel M. Exh. 1910
Crompton Manor House, Strafford, Beds. † LS 3.

ANDERSON, Nina Exh. 1889-98
Greenock 1889; Edinburgh 1898. † GI 1, RSA 2.

ANDERSON, Miss Nora V. Exh. 1915
Knockderry Cove, Dumbartonshire. † L 1.

ANDERSON, Percy 1850-1928
Portrait painter, stage and costume designer. Add: London. † L 1, P 1, RI 1, WG 66.

ANDERSON, Robert 1842-85
Coastal painter. A.R.S.A. 1879. Add: Edinburgh. † AG 4, DOW 1, GI 8, RA 1, RSA 45, RSW 18.

ANDERSON, Robert Exh. 1897-1903
Edinburgh. † RSA 10.

ANDERSON, Rev. R.P.R. Exh. 1940
† RSW 2.

ANDERSON, Sir Robert Rowland 1834-1921
Architect. A.R.S.A. 1876-83, H.R.S.A. 1896. Add: Edinburgh. † GI 4, RA 4, RSA 37.

ANDERSON, S. Exh. 1880-85
† TOO 9.

ANDERSON, Mrs. Sophie* 1823-c.1898
Landscape, portrait and genre painter. b. Paris. Left France for America 1848, married Walter A. q.v. Settled in England 1854. Moved to Italy about 1871 due to ill health but returned to England and settled in Falmouth 1894. † B 11, G 7, GI 2, L 9, M 4, RA 1, RBA 1, RHA 1, ROI 2.

ANDERSON, Stanley b. 1884
Painter and line engraver. Studied Bristol Municipal School of Art 1908; British Institute Engraving Scholarship 1909; Royal College of Art under Frank Short 1909-11; Goldsmith's under Lee-Hankey. A.R.A. 1934, R.A. 1941, A.R.E. 1910, R.E. 1923. Add: Bristol 1906; London 1909. † BA 1, CG 78, CHE 3, CON 4, FIN 1, G 1, GI 12, I 14, L 18, NEA 2, RA 81, RE 97, RHA 13, RSA 5.

ANDERSON, Thomas Alexander Exh. 1930
Painter, poster designer and wood engraver. Studied Glasgow School of Art, special award for portrait painting, diploma 1927. Second master Doncaster School of Arts and Crafts. Add: Paisley 1930. † GI 1.

ANDERSON, Trevor N. Exh. 1892-1902
Edinburgh. † GI 7, L 1, RA 2, RSA 4, RSW 2.

ANDERSON, T.R. Exh. 1891
c/o Smith, 4 Upper Gilmore Place, Edinburgh. † RSA 3.

ANDERSON, Walter Exh. 1881-87
Maried to Sophie A. q.v. Add: Villa Castello, Capri, Italy. † B 2, GI 1, L 3, RA 2.

ANDERSON, Will. Exh. 1880-95
Landscape painter. Add: London. † B 17, L 11, M 10, RA 6, RBA 26, RHA 3, RI 2, ROI 15.

ANDERSON, Miss Winifred Exh. 1903-16
Miniature painter. Add: Farnham, Surrey 1903. † RA 3, RMS 3.

ANDERSON, W.H. Exh. 1937
c/o Bourlet, London. † RCA 1.

ANDERSON, W.H. Exh. 1896-97
Ripley House, Freshfield, Lancs. † L 3.

ANDERSON, W.J. Exh. 1891-97
Glasgow. † GI 10.

ANDERSON, William S. Exh. 1917-30
Hexham, Northumberland 1917; Glasgow 1930. † GI 9, RSA 9, RSW 1.

ANDERSON-COATES, Mrs. Dorothy Exh. 1935
Bournemouth, Dorset. † RCA 2.

ANDERSON-KNOOP, Miss D. Exh. 1923
Hillside, Bentick Road, Altrincham, Cheshire. † RI 1.

ANDERSSON, Mrs. Georgina Exh. 1924-40
Hoylake, Cheshire 1924; Pangbourne, Berks 1935; Whitchurch, Oxon 1938. † L 4, NEA 2, RHA 1, ROI 5, RSA 2.

ANDERSSON, William H. Exh. 1924-37
Hoylake, Cheshire 1924; Pangbourne, Berks 1937. † L 3, RA 1.

ANDERTON, Francis S. c.1867-1909
R.B.A. 1904. The Cottage, Holland Park Road, London. † L 3, NG 7, RA 1, RBA 12, ROI 1.

ANDERTON, Miss F.W. Exh. 1928-29
The Mansion House, Ormskirk, Lancs. † L 3.

ANDERTON, Miss Lavenna Exh. 1927-30
45 Moor Street, Ormskirk, Lancs. † L 4.

ANDERTON, Miss M.M. Exh. 1899
Studio, Claremont Buildings, Newcastle-on-Tyne. † SWA 1.

ANDERTON, Richard b. 1890
Architect. Studied Harris School of Art, Preston; London School of Town Planning. Exh. 1932. Add: 6 Kenilworth Gardens, Blackpool. † RA 1.

ANDERTON, Tom Exh. 1921-28
Lancaster 1921; Preston 1922. † L 4, M 1.

ANDRADE, Miss Kate L. Exh. 1893-1929
London. † I 1, RBA 2, ROI 3, SWA 1.

ANDRE, Albert* Exh. 1901-28
c/o Messrs. Durant Ruel, 16 Rue Lafitte, Paris 1901. † CHE 1, GOU 4, I 1.

ANDRE, E.G. Exh. 1901
Rue du Bac, 6 Charenton, Seine, France. † L 1.

ANDRE, R. Exh. 1892-1903
Melrose, Bushey, Herts. † B 6, L 1.

ANDREA, F.A. Exh. 1898-99
4 Trafalgar Studios, Manresa Road, London. † L 2.

ANDREAE, Conrad R. b. 1871
Watercolour painter. Studied Slade School (1st class certificate for figure painting): Julians, Paris. Exh. 1926-40. Add: Tindharia, Withdean, Brighton. † L 4, RA 5.

ANDREOTTI, Frederigo Exh. 1881-91
London. † GI 2, L 4, M 7, RA 7.

ANDREW, Miss Catherine Exh. 1918-24
Hampstead, London 1918; Birkenhead 1921. † L 4, RA 2, RMS 1.

ANDREW, D. Exh. 1903-6
248 West George Street, Glasgow. † GI 2.

ANDREW, J.V.H. Exh. 1924
Milwick Vicarage, Stafford. † B 1.

ANDREW, Miss M. Exh. 1898
24 Waldeck Road, Ealing, London. † SWA 1.

ANDREW, Miss M.I. Bruce Exh. 1891
Dovecot, Musselburgh. † RSA 1.

ANDREWS, Arthur Henry b. 1906
Portrait and landscape painter, etcher and wood engraver. Studied Hornsey School of Art and Royal College of Art. Headmaster Batley School of Arts and Crafts; Head of Design Department, Derby School of Art. Son of H.B.A. q.v., married Sushila Singh q.v. Add: 64 Medway, Southgate, London 1929. † L 1, M 2, RA 3, RED 1.

ANDREWS, Cecily Exh. 1922-26
Windyridge, Clifton Road, Chesham Bois, Bucks. † RA 1. SWA 1.

ANDREWS, Cyril Bruyn Exh. 1921
Painter and art writer. † LS 3.

ANDREWS, Charlotte J. Exh. 1898
Newlyn Road, Melrose, N.B. † RSA 1.

ANDREWS, Mrs. Charlotte M. Exh. 1932-35
Harrow-on-the-Hill, Middlesex. † NEA 1, RA 2, RBA 1.

ANDREWS, Miss C.M.P. Exh. 1917
40 Coleherne Court, London. † RA 1.

ANDREWS, Doris Godfrey Exh. 1910-25
Mrs. Sampson. Nottingham 1910; Bournemouth 1913; London 1920; Sidmouth, Devon 1925. † L 2, N 12, RA 6, RI 2.

ANDREWS, Douglas Sharpus b. 1885
Watercolour painter and illustrator. Studied Brighton School of Art 1901-6; Royal College of Art 1906-10. Principal Derby School of Art 1919-20; Headmaster City of Bath School of Art; Principal Sheffield College of Art 1926-28; Principal of Leeds College of Art 1929. † I 4, L 4, RA 19.

ANDREWS, Miss E. Exh. 1914
West Hill Drive, Mansfield. † N 1.

ANDREWS, Mrs. Edith Alice Exh. 1900-40
nee Cubitt. Garden and flower painter and illustrator. Studied Goldsmith's College; 1909; Add: Brockley, London 1900; Sandwich, Kent 1909; High Wycombe, Bucks. 1914; Penbury, Kent 1931. † B 1, L 6, RA 11, RI 4.

ANDREWS, Mrs. Eva Allan Exh. 1894-97
98 Clifton Road, Clapham Park, London. † RID 3.

ANDREWS, Miss Elizabeth C. Exh. 1902-38
Member London Group 1927. Add: Eastbourne 1909; Amberley, Sussex 1922. † L 1, LEI 1, NEA 1, RMS 1.

ANDREWS, Miss Eleanor F. Exh. 1909-30
Claughton, Birkenhead 1909; Hoylake, Cheshire 1916; Oxton, Birkenhead 1923. † L 27.

ANDREWS, Miss Eddie J. Exh. 1897-1902
London. † L 1, RA 1, RI 1.

ANDREWS, Edward William Exh. 1884-98
Miniature painter and etcher. R.M.S. 1899. Add: London 1884 and 1890; Kings Langley, Herts. 1886. † L 2, M 1, P 1, RA 3, RE 4, RI 1, RMS 3.

ANDREWS, Felix Emile b. 1888
Landscape painter. Studied Sidcup School of Art; R.A. Schools. Exh. 1919-24. Add: Brook Studio, Amberley, Sussex. † I 2, L 2, RA 1, RI 3.

ANDREWS, George Henry* 1816-1898
Watercolour painter. A.R.W.S. 1856; R.S.W. 1878. Add: London. † L 5, RSW 38.

ANDREWS, H.B. Exh. 1929
64 Medway, Southgate, London. † L 1.

ANDREWS, John Exh. 1885-87
25 Broadhurst Gardens, Hampstead, London. † B 2, M 1, RI 1.

ANDREWS, Joseph b. 1874
Landscape painter, born and lived in Birkenhead. † L 73, RA 6, RCA 14.

ANDREWS, Miss Kathleen H. Exh. 1921
Glentee, Grosvenor Road, Ripley, Derbys. † N 1.

ANDREWS, Mrs. Lilian b. 1878
nee Rusbridge, married to Douglas Sharpus A. q.v. Landscape and animal painter and designer. Studied Brighton School of Art (bronze medal for design). Teacher Brighton School of Art. Add: Brighton 1912; Bath 1920; Sheffield 1927; Leeds 1929. † I 2, RA 22.

ANDREWS, L. Gordon b. 1885
Studied Battersea Polytechnic 1900-3; Clapham School of Art 1903-4; Regent Street Polytechnic 1906; Birmingham School of Art 1908; West Bromwich School of Art 1909. Add: 115 Monkhams Lane, Woodford Green, Essex 1937. † RBA 1.

ANDREWS, Margaret Exh. 1913
† GOU 2.

ANDREWS, M.G. Exh. 1884-89
19 Russell Street, Dublin. † RHA 11.

ANDREWS, Miss P. Exh. 1902-8
Belfast. † SWA 10.

ANDREWS, Mrs. Peggy Exh. 1939
† NEA 2.

ANDREWS, Percy M. Exh. 1914-22
London. † RA 2.

ANDREWS, R. Exh. 1901
51 Westbourne Street, Walsall, Staffs. † RA 1.

ANDREWS, Robert Exh. 1896
69 Abingdon Villas, Kensington, London. † RHA 2.

ANDREWS, Sofy Exh. 1931
† GOU 1.

ANDREWS, Miss Sybil, Exh. 1922-38
Painter, etcher and lino-cut artist. Add: London and Woolpit, Suffolk. † GOU 4, I 1, RBA 5, RED 51, RSA 1.

ANDREWS, Miss Sarah A. Exh. 1918-26
Sundays Well, Cork. † RHA 2.

ANDREWS, Vera Exh. 1939-40
Foxwold, Southbourne-on-Sea, Hants. † RBA 2, SWA 1.

ANDREWS, V.M. Exh. 1909
12 Grosvenor Street, Liscard, Cheshire. † L 1.

ANDROS, Icilius Exh. 1904
† D 1.

ANDROUTZOS, Count Nicholas Exh. 1901
c/o J.W. Godward, 410 Fulham Road, London. † N 2.

ANEILL, Joseph Exh. 1929
117 York Drive, Hyndland, Glasgow. † GI 2.

ANELAY, Henry Exh. 1880-82
Landscape painter. Eyre Cottage, The Grove, Upper Sydenham. † D 3, RBA 1.

ANGEL, Mrs. Andrea Exh. 1925
"Samarkand". Add: 53 Ledbury Road, London. † L 4.

ANGEL, John b. 1881
Sculptor. Studied R.A. Schools. Add: Exeter 1912; London 1913. † GI 3, L 6, RA 18, RSA 2.

ANGEL, R.J. Exh. 1889-1914
Liverpool 1889; Birkenhead 1890; London 1914. † L 3, RA 1.

ANGELI, Von* See V

ANGELL, A.J. Exh. 1914
114 Rosebank Avenue, Sunbury, Nr. Harrow. † RA 1.

ANGELL, Miss Ethel Elizabeth Exh. 1931-35
Flower and landscape painter and teacher. Studied Nuneaton Art School. Add: Ansley Common, Nuneaton. † B 2, RA 1, ROI 1.

ANGELL, Mrs. F. Exh. 1894-96
236 Portsdown Road, Maida Vale, London. † RBA 1, SWA 1.

ANGELL, Frank Exh. 1889-91
150 Elgin Avenue, Maida Vale, London. † D 3, L 3, M 2, RBA 3, RI 1.

ANGELL, Helen Cordelia 1847-84
Fruit, flower and bird painter. Received her first lessons in art from her brother William S. Coleman. Flower painter in Ordinary to Queen Victoria 1879; R.I. 1875-78, R.W.S. 1879. Add: London 1880. † AG 3, BG 2, FIN 3, L 1, RSW 21.

ANGELL, Maude Exh. 1888-1924
Flower painter. Add: London. † B 5, FIN 1, NG 2, RA 18, RBA 4, RI 7, RMS 1.

ANGELL, Robert Exh. 1917-20
Architect. Keith House, 133 Regent Street, London. † RA 2.

ANGEREN, Van See V.

ANGERVILLE, Sem Exh. 1905
11 Place Vintimille, Paris. † L 1.

ANGLADA-y-CAMARASA, Hermenegildo Exh. 1901-37
Paris. † BA 1, I 10, L 13.

ANGLE, Beatrice Exh. 1885-1905
Sculptor. London. † L 8, RA 16, RI 1, SWA 2,

ANGLEY, H.J. Exh. 1883-87
Painter and etcher. R.E. 1885-89. Add: London. † L 4, RA 6, RBA 6, RE 5, RI 6.

ANGUS, Miss Dorothy Exh. 1925
School of Art, Aberdeen. † L 1.

ANGUS, Miss Margaret Exh. 1929-31
Nuneaton 1929; Alfriston, Sussex 1930. † NEA 3, RA 1.

ANGUS, Miss May Exh. 1887-88
2 Nelson Square, Blackfriars Road, London. † ROI 2.

ANGUS, Maria L. Exh. 1888-1912
London 1888; Chorley Wood, Herts. 1912. † L 7, LS 11, M 2, RA 10, RBA 3, RHA 1, RI 10, ROI 1, SWA 8.

ANGUS, Stanley Exh. 1932-38
Etcher. 47 Old Bond Street, London. † BK 3, CON 7, FIN 3, RA 1.

ANITCHKOFF, Alexandre Exh. 1922
Russian landscape painter. Add: c/o Allan Beeton, Esq., 2 Adamson Road, South Hampstead, London. † I 2, RA 2.

ANKER, Albert* c.1831-1910
Swiss genre painter. † GI 1, TOO 4.

ANLEY, H.T. Exh. 1907
Homelands, Leonard Stanley, Stonehouse, Glos. † L 5.

ANNADALE, E.A. Exh. 1896
† RSW 1.

ANNEAR, Miss G. Mary Exh. 1934-38
Miniature portrait painter. Add: London. † RA 2.

ANNENBERG, Miss Sadie Exh. 1919
Portrait painter. Add: 25 Rutland Park Mansions, Willesden Green, London. † RA 1.

ANNESLEY, Mabel Exh. 1930
Wood engraver. † RED 2.

ANNETT, Mrs. E.L. Exh. 1914
Ivy Lea, Rock Park, Rock Ferry, Cheshire. † L 1.

ANNISON, E.S. Exh. 1910-11
36 Fairlawn Grove, Chiswick, London. † L 2, RA 1.

ANNS, Kenneth b. 1881
Architect and painter. Studied Croydon School of Art; St. Martins School of Art and under Walter Sickert. Exh. 1921-22. Add: London. † RI 3.

ANQUETIN, G. Exh. 1898-1904
Paris. † I 1, P 1.

ANREP, Van See V.

ANROOY, Van See V.

ANSDELL, Richard* 1815-1886
Sporting, animal and historical painter. Collaborated with W.P. Frith, John Phillip and Thomas Creswick. b. Liverpool. d. Farnborough, Hants. A.R.A. 1861; R.A. 1870. Add: London 1881. † B 4, FIN 1, L 4, M 1, RA 19, TOO 1.

ANSDELL, Mrs. Sylvia G. Exh. 1820-22
London. † RA 2.

ANSELL, Miss Alice M. Exh. 1892-1901
London. † RBA 1, RI 1, SWA 6.

ANSELL, Miss Maud Exh. 1889-1901
St. George, Portland Road, Southsea. † RBA 5.

ANSELL, William Henry 1872-1959
Architect and etcher. Studied Architectural Association and Royal College of Art. b. Nottingham. A.R.E. 1909. Add: Derby 1897; London 1906 and 1922; Richmond, Surrey 1919. † L 6, N 2, RA 15, RE 23.

ANSON, Arthur M. Exh. 1931
56 Cheapside, London. † RA 1.
ANSON, C.I. Exh. 1881
6 South Crescent, Store Street, Russell Square, London. † RSA 2.
ANSON, Edwin Exh. 1883
221 Bordesley Green, Birmingham. † B 1.
ANSON, Miss Gladys M. Exh. 1928
58 Newlands Park, Sydenham, London. † RA 1.
ANSON, Minnie Walters b. 1875
Portrait, flower and miniature painter. Studied Lambeth School of Art, (seven medals including 2 gold for flower painting) Married to Arthur Christopher Adams q.v. A.R.M.S. 1928, R.M.S. 1933. Add: London 1909 and 1929; Parkstone, Dorset 1917. † L 3, RA 9, RMS 45.
ANSON, Peter Frederick b. 1889
Landscape painter, pencil portrait artist and illustrator. Studied Architectural Association 1908-10. b. Portsmouth. Add: Glasgow 1926; Portsmouth 1928; Gravesend, Kent 1931; Northfleet. Kent 1933: Banffshire 1938. † B 2, GI 2, GOU 3, L 4, M 2, NEA 3, RA 2, RHA 7, RSA 15, RSW 2.
ANSON, Richard F. Exh. 1919-25
Tenby, S. Wales 1919; Glasgow 1924; London 1925. † L 2, LS 3, RSA 3.
ANSTED, Alexander Exh. 1888-93
Etcher. 3 Ranelagh Villas, Grove Park, Chiswick, London. † RA 4.
ANTHONY, George A. Exh. 1923
† G 1.
ANTHONY, Mark 1817-1887
Landscape painter. b. Manchester. Began studying medicine at 13. Studied art Paris 1834-40. Travelled France and Spain. Add: The Lawn, Hampstead Heath, London 1882. † G 1, L 5, RA 2.
ANTIGNA, M. Exh. 1910
Les Troenes, Montigny-sur-Loing, Seine et Marne, France. † L 1.
ANTILL, Amy E. Exh. 1938
† M 2.
ANTISELL, T.C. Exh. 1881
72 Lower Mount Street, Dublin. † RHA 3.
ANTOINE, P.J. Exh. 1886-88
Chorlton-upon-Medlock 1886; Manchester 1887. † M 4.
ANTONI, Louis F. Exh. 1914
12 Boulevard Bon Accueil, Alger., Algerie. † RSA 1.
ANTONIN-CARLES, Jean Exh. 1882-1913
French Sculptor. Add: Paris. † GI 3, RA 3.
ANTONIO, Zona Exh. 1883
44 Via Flaminia, Rome, Italy. † L 1.
ANTRIM, Angela Christina, Countess of b. 1911
Sculptor, painter and cartoonist. nee Sykes. b. Sledmerê, Yorks. Studied Brussels 1927-32 and British School in Rome. Exh. 1937. † RED 16.
ANTROBUS, A. Lizzie Exh. 1882-84
Fernwood, New Oscott, Birmingham. † B 4, RBA 1.
ANTROBUS, Mrs. E. Exh. 1880-84
3 Harewood Square, London. † SWA 2.
ANTROBUS, Miss Jane M.E. Exh. 1896
Eaton Hall, Congleton, Cheshire. † RA 1.
ANTROBUS, Phyllis Mary b. 1905
Watercolour painter and pen and ink artist. 31 Elsmere Avenue, Sefton Park, Liverpool 1926. † L 9.
ANWYL-DAVIES, T. Exh. 1937
149 Harley Street, London. † RA 1.

ANZINO, G.P. Exh. 1907-11
Wahroonga, Nepean Street, Roehampton. † NG 1, RA 3.
"APE" See PELLEGRINI
APEL, Miss Marie Exh 1909-14
6 Oakley Studios, Chelsea, London. † L 1, LS 10, P 1, RA 1.
APLETRE, Mrs. E.M. Exh. 1914
14 Wellesley Terrace, Prince's Park, Liverpool. † L 1.
APOL, Armand Exh. 1909
45 Rue de Ligne, Brussels. † L 1.
APOL C. Exh. 1886
117 New Bond Street, London. † M 3.
APOL, Louis* Exh. 1882-94
The Hague, Holland. † GI 2.
APOLLONI, A. Exh. 1897
53B Via Margutta, Rome, Italy. † L 1.
APPELBEE, Horace, R. Exh. 1889-97
Architect. Add: London. † RA 3.
APPERLEY, George Owen Wynne. b. 1884
Figure and landscape painter. Self taught. R.I. 1912. b. Ventnor, I.O.W. Add: Bushey, Herts 1905 and 1919; St. Leonards-on-Sea 1907; London 1908; Granada, Spain 1920. † GI 1, L 13, LEI 136, LS 9, NG 1, RA 13, RI 85, RSA 4. RSW 1, WG 169.
APPLEBAUM, M. Exh. 1911-12
11 Mayville Road, Allerton Road, Liverpool. † L 8.
APPLEBEY, Wilfred Crawford b. 1889
Painter and etcher. Studied Glasgow School of Art, one bursary and four scholarships. b. Dudley, Worcs. Add: Glasgow 1912. † FIN 7, GI 48, L 3, RSA 14.
APPELBY, Ernest W. Exh. 1885-1907
Portrait and figure painter. Add: London. † G 1, L 7, M 2, RA 16, RBA 11, ROI 12, TOO 1.
APPLEBY, G.W. Exh. 1888
5 Langham Chambers, Portland Place, London. † G 1.
APPLEGATE, Dido Exh. 1932-33
10 Glebe Place, Chelsea, London 1933. † SWA 2.
APPLEGATE, Miss K.E. Exh. 1910-13
7 Percy Place, Bath. † L 8.
APPLETON, A. Exh. 1929
† GOU 1.
APPLETON, Honor C. Exh. 1914
Illustrator. 3 Ventnor Villas, Hove, Sussex. † RA 1.
APPLETON, Herbert D. Exh. 1883-90
157 Wool Exchange, Coleman Street. † RA 3.
APPLETON, Miss Rosa D. Exh. 1888-1902
Withington, Manchester. † L 2, M 4.
APPLETON, Thomas G. Exh. 1886-1905
Bushey, Herts 1886; Shalford, Surrey 1889; Gt. Missenden, Bucks 1904. † RA 12.
APPLETON, W.L. Exh. 1886-95
Didsbury, Manchester 1886; Withington, Manchester 1891. † M 4.
APPLEYARD, Charles F.W. Exh. 1929
4 Cambridge Street, Cleethorpes, Lincs. † L 2.
APPLEYARD. Miss Florence J. Exh. 1888-98
41 Canning Street, Liverpool. † L 7.
APPLEYARD, Fred 1874-1963
Landscape and portrait painter. Studied Scarborough School of Art and Royal College of Art. "A Secret" purchased by Chantry Bequest 1915. b. Middlesborough. Add: London 1900 and 1918; Itchen Stoke, Alresford, Hants 1910 and 1923. † GI 5, L 13, M 1, RA 41.
APTHORPE, Henry Campion Exh. 1909
† LS 3.

ARBUTHNOT, Gerald Exh. 1926
19 Upper Wimpole Street, London. † GOU 1, NEA 1, RBA 2, RI 2.
ARBUTHNOT, Malcolm 1874-1967
Painter and sculptor. London 1918; Jersey 1938; Carbis Bay, Cornwall 1940. † D 2, FIN 75, GOU 2, I 1, LS 1, NEA 3, RA 1, RBA 5, RCA 2, RHA 6, RI 9, ROI 12, RSA 5, RSW 2.
ARBUTHNOTT, Miss E.C. Exh. 1930
10 Wilbraham Place, London. † RA 1.
ARCH, Miss Dorothy C. Exh. 1913-25
17 Southdale Road, Wavertree, Liverpool. † L 7.
ARCHAMBAULT, Miss A. Margaretta. Exh. 1921-30
† RMS 6.
ARCHDALL, Miss L. Exh. 1902-4
Clarisford, Killaloe, Co. Clare, Ireland. † RSA 2.
ARCHER, Miss A. Exh. 1896
32 Colville Street, Nottingham. † N 2.
ARCHER, Miss Ada Exh. 1890-91
3 Palace Gate Mansions, London. † D 8, SWA 2.
ARCHER, Miss Ann Exh. 1882
7 Cromwell Place, South Kensington, London. † RSA 1.
ARCHER, Miss Edith Exh. 1901-21
Portrait painter. London 1901; Eastbourne 1916. † BRU 1, L 4, RA 7, RMS 1, SWA 5.
ARCHER, Edward Exh. 1884-91
Littleford Lodge, Gt. Malvern. † B 2, G 3, L 1, M 2, NG 5, RA 1, ROI 5, TOO 3.
ARCHER, Edward P. Exh. 1936
Architect. 29 Bedford Road, London. † RA 1.
ARCHER, Ethel Stoney Exh. 1937
Cheltenham, Glos. † COO 44, SWA 1.
ARCHER, Frederick G. Exh. 1937
Cork Art Club, 25 Patrick Street, Cork, Ireland. † RHA 1.
ARCHER, Frank Joseph b. 1912
Painter and etcher. Studied Eastbourne School of Art 1928-32; Royal College of Art 1934-38; British School in Rome 1938-39; A.R.E. 1940. Add: Eastbourne 1940. † RA 4, RE 4.
ARCHER, Fred W. Exh. 1882-85
Hayfield, Liscard, Cheshire. † L 3.
ARCHER, Mrs. Hilary Exh. 1938
Foxrock Villa, Foxrock, Co. Dublin. † RHA 1.
ARCHER, Miss Heather L. Exh. 1940
Foxrock Villa, Foxrock, Co. Dublin. † RHA 1.
ARCHER, James* 1824-1904
Scottish painter. Studied Trustees Academy Edinburgh under Sir Wm. Allan. Settled in London 1862. A.R.S.A. 1850; R.S.A. 1858; Hon. Ret. R.S.A. 1896. Add: London 1880 and 1895; Milford, Surrey 1893; Haslemere, Surrey 1899. † B 2, G 1, GI 6, L 3, M 5, RA 34, RBA 1, RSA 46.
ARCHER, Miss Janet Exh. 1881-1916
London 1881; Watford, Herts 1893 and 1912; Bushey Herts 1906. † B 4, D 3, L 6, M 2, RA 6, RBA 7, RI 2, ROI 8, SWA 20.
ARCHER, Miss Jane E. Exh. 1893
32 Colville Street, Nottingham. † N 1.
ARCHER, James I. Exh. 1899
28 London Street, Edinburgh. † RSA 1.
ARCHER, J. Wallace Exh. 1904
34 St. Andrew Square, Edinburgh. † RSA 1.
ARCHER, Miss Lilian Exh. 1929-33
Flower painter. 7 Temple Grove, Golders Green, London. † RI 2.

ARCHER, Miss Mary G. Exh. 1885-1929
London. † GOU 1, L 1, P 1, RID 107, SWA 2.

ARCHER, Miss Olive E.P. Exh. 1923
Airfield, Donnybrooke. † RHA 1.

ARCHIBALD, Gordon R. Exh. 1929-40
Watercolour painter. Add: Stepps, Lanarks 1929; Aberdeen 1940. † GI 12, RSA 10.

ARCHIBALD, John S. Exh. 1929
1440 St. Catherine Street West, Montreal, Canada. † GI 2.

ARCHIBALD, Miss Phyllis M. See CLAY.

ARCOS, Santiago Exh. 1903-04
11 Rue Chateaubriand, Paris. † L 2.

ARDEN, Miss Beatrice M. Exh. 1923-32
14 Bentley Road, Liverpool. † L 16.

ARDEN, Edward See TUCKER.

ARDERN, W. Exh. 1932
† L 1.

ARDIZZONE, Edward Jeffrey Irving b. 1900
Watercolour painter, lithographer and illustrator. b. Haipong, China. Came to England 1905. Studied Westminster School of Art under Bernard Meninsky 1920-21. Official war artist 1940-45. Add: London 1927. † L 3, LEI 1, NEA 2.

ARDRON, Miss Annette Exh. 1906-22
London 1906, Stanmore, Middlesex 1911. † GOU 1, RA 2, RHA 1.

ARENDT, D.M. Exh. 1935
24 Palace Court, London. † RA 1.

ARENDZEN, Rev. L. Andrew Exh. 1921-30
Portrait painter. St. Mary's Rectory, Grantham, Lincs. † N 11.

ARENDZEN, Petrus J. Exh. 1890-99
Etcher. Add: London. † RA 7.

ARGENTA, C. Exh. 1881
Sculptor. 16 Bury Street, Chelsea, London. † RA 1.

ARGENTI, Antonio Exh. 1883
Milan, Italy. † M 1.

ARGLES, Alice Exh. 1880
Barnack Rectory, Stamford. † D 1.

ARGYLE, Miss B. Exh. 1888
56 West Cromwell Road, Kensington, London. † L 2.

ARGYLE, G.E. Exh. 1924-31
A.N.S.A. 1922. Add: Nottingham. † N 5.

ARGYLL, George, The Duke of Exh. 1882-88
Inverary Castle, Inverary. † G 1, RSA 2.

ARGYLE, Duchess of
See Louise, H.R.H. Princess

ARHTZENIUS, F. Exh. 1905
27 van Lennepwey, The Hague. † I 1.

ARKELL, Laura Exh. 1887
Portrait painter. Stratton, Swindon, Wilts. † RBA 1.

ARKWRIGHT, Miss Edith Exh. 1884
Portrait painter. 4 Denmark Terrace, Brighton. † RA 1.

ARKWRIGHT, Miss Olive K.M. Exh. 1929-31
Watercolour coastal and river painter. Add: Sheringham, Norfolk. † AB 4, SWA 2.

ARKWRIGHT, Susan A. Exh. 1890-91
Leeds. † D 4.

ARMADALE, E.A. Exh. 1895
Bielside, Dunbar, N.B. † GI 2.

ARMEL-BEAUFILS, Jean M. Exh. 1925
Rue Auguste Vitu 6, Paris. † L 1.

ARMES, Thomas W. Exh. 1928-33
Landscape painter. Add: Charmouth, Dorset 1928; Crowborough, Sussex 1929; Burgh Heath, Surrey 1931. † RA 6, REA 6.

ARMFELT, Count Exh. 1938
† P 1.

ARMFIELD, Maxwell* 1882-1972
Painter and decorative artist and writer. Studied Birmingham School of Art, Colarossi, Paris and Italy. A.R.W.S. 1937, R.W.S. 1941. Add: Birmingham 1901; Ringwood, Hants 1903 and 1924; London 1907, 1912, 1915 and 1927; Minchinhampton, Glos. 1911; Stroud, Glos. 1914; Lymington, Hants. 1923. † B 16, BG 4, CAR 79, FIN 7, G 1, GI 5, I 2, L 12, LEI 109, LS 3, NEA 25, P 7, RA 37, RHA 2, RSA 1, RWS 28.

ARMFIELD, Miss M.J. Exh. 1906
Ringwood, Hants. † NEA 1.

ARMINGTON, Caroline Helena b. 1875
Etcher. Married to Frank M.A. q.v. Add: 8 Rue de la Grande Chaumiere, Paris, 1910-12. † L 10.

ARMINGTON, Frank M. b. 1876
Etcher. A.R.E. 1910. Add: Paris 1910-14. † L 9, RE 8.

ARMITAGE, Alfred Exh. 1891-94
Shipley, Yorks. 1891; Penzance 1892. † M 1, NG 1, RA 1, RBA 2.

ARMITAGE, C. Liddall Exh. 1891
43 Blenheim Crescent, Notting Hill, London. † RBA 1.

ARMITAGE, C. de W. Exh. 1903-5
39 Grosvenor Street, London. † RA 2.

ARMITAGE, E. Exh. 1914
Slainte Studio, Anhalt Road, Albert Bridge, London. † LS 3.

ARMITAGE, Edward 1817-1896
Historical painter. Studied under Paul Delaroche in Paris 1837. Won many prizes and competitions. Appointed lecturer and professor of painting to R.A. 1875. Took active part in the movements for the restoration of Fresco painting in England and in the decoration of the Houses of Parliament with historical scenes. Died of apoplexy and exhaustion following pneumonia. A.R.A. 1867; R.A. 1872. Add: London 1881. † B 1, GI 2, L 6, M 2, RA 26, RHA 2.

ARMITAGE, F. Willett Exh. 1922
Lyndale, Grange Street, Bixton, Huddersfield. † L 1.

ARMITAGE, Capt. Harry d. 1934
The Grange, N. Berwick, 1901. † LS 1, RCA 3, RHA 7.

ARMITAGE, Jean Exh. 1919-35
Painter, miniaturist and colour woodcut artist. Studied J.D. Batten and Byam Shaw School. Add: Summer Lodge, Camberley, Surrey 1919. † COO 3, I 1, M 2, RI 3, RMS 2, ROI 1.

ARMITAGE, Mrs. M.M.E. Exh. 1914
Longstone Grange, Nr. Bakewell. † RA 1.

ARMITAGE, Robert Linnell b. 1898
Painter and etcher. Studied Manchester Municipal School of Art. Lived Cheshire 1931. † L 2, RCA 8, RHA 2, RSA 3.

ARMITAGE, Thomas Liddall Exh. 1891
43 Blenheim Crescent, Notting Hill, London. † L 1, M 1, RA 1.

ARMITAGE, William 1857-194?
Animal and bird painter and watercolour landscapes. N.S.A. 1891; V.P.N.S.A. 1908-17. Add: Nottingham 1889, 1903 and 1913; Carrington, Notts. 1897, Duffield, Derbys. 1908; Bushey, Herts. 1922; Gorey, Jersey 1925. d. Jersey during German occupation. † B 3, L 12, M 1, N 161, RA 5, RBA 1, RCA 7, RI 3.

ARMITAGE, William J. Exh. 1889
Farnley House, Chelsea, London. † RA 1.

ARMOUR, A.J.R. Exh. 1907
37 Caird Drive, Partick, Glasgow. † GI 1.

ARMOUR, George Denholm 1864-1949
Sporting painter, illustrator, contributor to Punch from 1894. Studied R.S.A. Life School Edinburgh. Add: Edinburgh 1882; London 1891, 1897; Welwyn, Herts. 1894; Devizes, Wilts. 1902; Chippenham, Wilts. 1911; Purton, Wilts. 1912; Corsham, Wilts. 1923; Malmesbury, Wilts. 1928; Yeovil, Somerset 1935; Sherborne, Dorset 1938. † B 2, FIN 66, GI 34, L 21, LEI 219, NG 2, P 1, RA 16, RSA 63, RSW 2.

ARMOUR, Hazel Exh. 1914-40
Mrs. Kennedy. Sculptor. Studied Edinburgh College of Art and Paris. Add: Edinburgh 1914; London 1937. † GI 20, L 3, RA 8, RSA 29, SWA 2.

ARMOUR, James W. Exh. 1906-32
Liscard, Cheshire 1906; Wallasey, Cheshire 1921. † L 6.

ARMOUR, Miss Marion Exh. 1912-26
Haleburns, Altrincham, Cheshire. † M 7.

ARMOUR, Mrs. Mary* b. 1902
Nee Steel. Milngavie 1928. † GI 14, L 1, RSA 21.

ARMOUR, William Exh. 1929-40
R.S.W. 1941. Add: Milngavie. † GI 3, RSA 24, RSW 5.

ARMS, John Taylor 1887-1953
American Etcher. Studied Massachusetts Institute of Technology and Boston. A.R.E. 1934. Add: Fairfield, Conn. U.S.A. † FIN 14, GI 2, RA 9, RE 24.

ARMSTEAD, Miss Charlotte W. Exh. 1885-97
52 Circus Road, London. † B 3, L 4, M 2, RA 3.

ARMSTEAD, Henry Hugh 1828-1905
Sculptor. Came to sculpture through painting and silversmithery. Produced many racing cups. Studied RA Schools. At age 34 turned completely to sculpture. Among his works are the carved panels in the "Queens Robing Room" at the Palace of Westminster, the four bronze statues "Chemistry", "Astronomy", "Medicine" and "Rhetoric" of the Albert Memorial. "Remorse" purchased by Chantry Bequest 1903; A.R.A. 1875; R.A. 1879. Add: Bridge Place, Eccleston Bridge, Belgrave Road, London 1880. † L 1, M 1, RA 43.

ARMSTEAD, Hugh Wells b. 1865
Landscape painter and sculptor. Son of Henry A. q.v. Studied St. John's School of Art and in his father's studio. Lecturer on artistic anatomy of animals at Calderon's School of Animal Painting and on artistic comparative anatomy City and Guilds School of Art 1932. Add: Hindhead, Surrey 1934; Seaton, Devon 1938. † RA 2.

ARMSTEAD, Miss Lottie Exh. 1885
52 Circus Road, London. † RA 2.

ARMSTRONG, A. Exh. 1882-83
c/o Haskard, Florence, Italy. † M 2, RHA 2.

ARMSTRONG, Miss Alice Exh. 1899
114 Denbigh Street, Belgravia, London. † SWA 3.

ARMSTRONG, A.E. Exh. 1933
† RSW 1.

ARMSTRONG, Alixe Jean Shearer b. 1894
Nee Shearer. Flower and portrait painter and illustrator. Studied Malerinnenschule, Karlsruhe and Slade School. Add: Carbis Bay, Cornwall 1927; St. Ives, Cornwall 1928. † AB 1, ALP 1, GOU 2, L 2, NEA 2, RA 9, RBA 7, ROI 7, RSA 1.

ARMSTRONG, Caroline (Carr) Exh. 1881-1922
Portrait, landscape and miniature painter. Studied St. John's Wood 1878; R.A. Schools. R.M.S. 1905. Lived London. † BRU 1, L 7, LS 25, M 3, RA 13, RMS 46, ROI 1, SWA 7.
ARMSTRONG, Charles b. 1864
Landscape painter. Studied Royal College of Art, Julians, Paris. Examiner for 11 years at South Kensington; Headmaster Peterborough School of Art; Headmaster City of London School of Art. Exh. 1901-2. † D 2, RHA 2.
ARMSTRONG, Capt. E. Exh. 1900-2
c/o H.S. Hopwood, Hinderwell, R.S.O. Yorks. † RI 2.
ARMSTRONG, Ernest A. Exh. 1911-23
Landscape painter. Add: 18 Savile Row, London. † NEA 3.
ARMSTRONG, Miss Elizabeth Adela
See Forbes.
ARMSTRONG, Mrs. F. Exh. 1939
Culloden, Edwinstowe, Mansfield, Notts. † N 2.
ARMSTRONG, Miss Fanny Exh. 1883-1899
Landscape painter. Add: Elm Lodge, Iffley, Oxford. † B 1, L 5, M 2, RBA 1, RI 1, SWA 7.
ARMSTRONG, Francis Abel William Taylor 1849-1920
Landscape painter. R.B.A. 1896. Add: 42 St. Michael's Hill, Bristol. 1894. † FIN 126, RBA 34.
ARMSTRONG, Mrs. G.F. Exh. 1881
† RHA 2.
ARMSTRONG, H.B.J. Exh. 1927-38
Landscape painter. † AB 14, WG 13.
ARMSTRONG, J. Exh. 1880-81
51 Cockburn Street, Edinburgh. † RSA 2.
ARMSTRONG, James Exh. 1911
23 Blantyre Road, Sefton Park, Liverpool. † L 1.
ARMSTRONG, John Exh. 1882
95 Bridge Street, Manchester. † M 1, RA 1.
ARMSTRONG, John Exh. 1882-87
Warmington, Nr. Sandbach. † L 3, M 15.
ARMSTRONG, John* b. 1893
Fantasy painter and stage designer. Studied St. John's Wood School for 2 years. Exh. 1933-40. † L 1, LEF 59, LEI 78, RSA 2, TOO 7.
ARMSTRONG, James C. Exh. 1934-40
Drumfinn, Stirling Drive, Bearsden. † GI 6, RSA 1.
ARMSTRONG, L.E. Exh. 1893
44 Canonbury Park South, London. † B 1.
ARMSTRONG, Miss Oliver Exh. 1925
49 Wellington Road, Dublin. † RHA 1.
ARMSTRONG, Miss Phyllis M. Exh. 1927
Rosebank, Windsor Avenue, Belfast. † L 4.
ARMSTRONG, Snowden Exh. 1918
† RSA 1.
ARMSTRONG, Miss S.A. Exh. 1881-87
8 Leeson Park, Dublin. † L 1, RHA 14.
ARMSTRONG, Sylvia Lake Exh. 1938-39
Culloden, Edwinstowe, Mansfield, Notts. † N 4.
ARMSTRONG, Thomas* 1832-1911
Decorative figure painter. Studied under Ary Scheffer in Paris. Appointed Director of Art at South Kensington Museum 1881. Add: London 1880, Abbot's Langley, Herts 1901. † G 7, M 1, NG 1.
ARMSTRONG, T.R. Exh. 1921
116 Fortune Green Road, London. † RI 1.
ARMSTRONG, Walter Exh. 1898-99
Glencaird, Ayr. † GI 4
ARMSTRONG, William* Exh. 1887-96
Glasgow. † GI 7.
ARNAVIELLE, Jean* Exh. 1908-9
5 Rue d'Alencon, Paris. † LS 8.
ARNDT, F. Exh. 1885
† RA 1.
ARNOLD, Miss A.K. Exh. 1914
1 Launceston Place, Kensington, London. † RA 2.
ARNOLD, Annie Merrylees see Merrylees
ARNOLD, Mrs. Annie Russell Exh. 1901-39
Miniature painter. Add: London. † RA 3, RMS 1.
ARNOLD, Bernard Exh. 1927-38
R.B.S.A. 1932. Add: Edgbaston, Birmingham. † B 38.
ARNOLD, Mrs. E. Exh. 1883-85
London. † D 3, RI 1.
ARNOLD, Miss E. Leslie Exh. 1931-32
London 1931; Manchester 1932. † RA 1, RSA 1.
ARNOLD, Miss E.M. Exh. 1910
33 Manor Park, Lee, London. † RA 1.
ARNOLD, Gordon C. Exh. 1930-38
Liverpool 1930; Bromborough, Wirral 1938. † L 3, RA 2.
ARNOLD, Harry Exh. 1882-1910
London 1882 and 1888, Chichester 1886. † D 2, L 7, M 2, NEA 1, RA 15, RBA 3, RI 8, ROI 2.
ARNOLD, Mrs. L.A. Exh. 1887-1927
Sculptor. Add: Ware, Herts. † RA 8, SWA 3.
ARNOLD, Miss Madge Exh. 1925-31
Sculptor and painter. Studied Walter Donnes Lise School and Regent Street Polytechnic. Add: Ware, Herts 1925; Hove, Sussex 1931. † ALP 1, RA 1, RBA 4, RMS 2, ROI 2, SWA 1.
ARNOLD, Miss May Exh. 1898-1911
Miniature portrait painter. London 1898; Horsham, Sussex 1909. † L 3, P 5, RA 12, RHA 1, RMS 2.
ARNOLD, Marguerite S. Exh. 1936
† P 1.
ARNOLD, Miss Nancy Exh. 1916-27
Pook Hill, Witley, Godalming. † L 1, RA 1, ROI 3, SWA 4.
ARNOLD, Miss Patience Exh. 1925-39
Lytham St. Annes, Lancs. † L 14, M 1, RBA 4, RCA 5.
ARNOLD, Reginald Ernest* 1853-1938
Sculptor and painter. R.B.A. 1909. Add: London 1880 and 1922; West Byfleet, Surrey 1919. † D 2, L 5, RA 24, RBA 47, ROI 16.
ARNOLD, T. Exh. 1888
10 Basinghall Street, London. † RSA 1.
ARNOLD, Miss V.F. Exh. 1905-9
Gwynedd, Deganwy, Llandudno. † RCA 2.
ARNOLD-FORSTER, Margaret Exh. 1939
† NEA 2.
ARNOLD-FOSTER, W.E. Exh. 1908-35
Landscape painter and pastellier. † AG 1, CG 35, G 3, GOU 120, NEA 3.
ARNOT, Miss Jessia A. Exh. 1881-82
22 Windsor Terrace, Glasgow. † GI 1, RSA 2.
ARNOTT, Miss A.A. Exh. 1917-19
1 Roseneath Place, Edinburgh. † RSA 3.
ARNOTT, Adam C. Exh. 1937
Benlea, Hendry Road, Kikcaldy. † RSA 1.
ARNOTT, Miss A.J. Exh. 1931
14 Hans Crescent, London. † RA 1.
ARNOTT, James Exh. 1880-81
49 Victoria Street, Kirkcaldy. † RSA 2.
ARNOTT, J.A. Exh. 1939
24 Duke Street, Edinburgh. † RSA 1.
ARNOTT, James Alex Exh. 1897-1907
Edinburgh. † GI 1, RSA 5.
ARNOTT, James George McLellan Exh. 1880-1902
Dumfries 1880 and 1886; Antwerp 1881; London 1883. † B 9, GI 9, RA 1, RSA 9.
ARNTZENIUS, Floris* Exh. 1904-06
The Hague, Holland. † FIN 8, I 2.
ARONSON, Miss Meta Exh. 1883
Queen's College, Wood Green, London. † RA 1.
ARONSON, Naoum Exh. 1908-13
Paris. † L 6, LS 19.
AROSA, Mdlle. Marguerite Exh. 1882-87
5 Rue Prony, Paris. † GI 3.
ARPA, Jose b. 1868
Exh. 1890. † TOO 1.
ARPESANI, Miss Lina Exh. 1925
Sculptor. c/o Beaux Arts Gallery, Bruton Place, London. † L 1, RA 3.
ARRINGTON, Miss M.L. Exh. 1898
4 Rue de Chevreuse, Paris. † B 1.
ARROLL, James Exh. 1883-1909
Henelsburgh, Dumbartonshire 1883; Garelochhead, 1889. † GI 23, L 2, RSA 10, RSW 1.
ARROLL, Richard Hubbard b. 1853
Painter and pen and ink artist. Add: Helensburgh, Dumbartonshire 1886; Glasgow 1893; Bridge of Weir, Ren. 1919; Ayr 1925. † GI 16, RSA 2.
ARROWSMITH, Miss M.N. Exh. 1929
2 Glen Park Road, Wallasey. † L 1.
ARROWSMITH, William A. Exh. 1920
15 Ferndale Road, Sefton Park, Liverpool. † RCA 1.
ART, Berthe Exh. 1896-98
Watercolour painter. 28 Rue Blanche, Brussels. † RA 4.
ARTHUR, Miss Emily Exh. 1903
11 Beaumont Gardens, Kelvinside, Glasgow. † L 1.
ARTHUR, Eric Stafford b. 1894
Landscape and portrait painter. Studied Liverpool School of Art and Royal College of Art. Assistant master Gt. Yarmouth School of Art. Exh. 1919-33. Add: West Kirby, Cheshire. † L 6.
ARTHUR, J. Exh. 1919
137 West Regent Street, Glasgow. † RSA 1.
ARTHUR, Miss Jean Exh. 1913-14
Lamshaw, Stewarton, N.B. † L 2, RSA 1.
ARTHUR, Miss J.D. Exh. 1909
LS 3.
ARTHUR, John M. Exh. 1924-26
4 Graham Street, Airdrie. † GI 1, RSA 1.
ARTHUR, Newman G. Exh. 1895
8 St. Anne's Villa, Notting Hill, London. † ROI 1.
ARTHUR, Reginald* Exh. 1880-96
Historical, figure and portrait painter. Add: London. † L 7, RA 9, RHA 1, ROI 2.
ARTHUR, Sydney Watson b. 1881
Animal and landscape painter. Exh. 1919-32. Add: Hillside, Bettws-y-Coed, N. Wales. † RCA 41.
ARTHUR, Miss Winifred Exh. 1885-1910
Liverpool 1885 and 1891; London 1889. † B 18, GI 2, L 50, M 1, RA 4, ROI 2.
ARTHURSON, Miss Annie Exh. 1925-26
Bidston, Cheshire 1925, Liverpool 1926. † L 3.

ARTINGSTALL, W. Exh. 1882-95
Bettws-y-Coed, Wales 1882; Manchester 1883. † L 1, M 19.

ARTOT, Paul Exh. 1921
19 Avenue Maurice, Brussels. † RSA 6.

ARTUS, Charles Exh. 1926-30
Paris. † GI 4, RSA 5.

ARTZ, David Adolf Constant* 1837-1890
Dutch. Add: The Hague, Holland. † GI 5, M 4, RSA 2, TOO 7.

ARUNDEL, Mrs. Annie S. Exh. 1900-4
Southport, Lancs. † L 4, RHA 1.

ARUNDEL, James b. 1875
Oil painter. Studied Bradford. Exh. 1933-38. Add: North Summercotes, Lincs. † BA 32, L 3, RA 1.

ARUNDEL, Miss Margaret Exh. 1931-40
Kings Heath, Birmingham 1931; Leamington Spa 1938; Swansea 1940. † B 4.

ARUS, R. Exh. 1883
† GI 1.

ASBURY, Miss Dorothy Exh. 1936-37
Chalfont St. Giles, Bucks. † RCA 2.

ASCOUGH, Miss J. Marie Exh. 1882-84
Handsworth, Birmingham. † B 3.

ASCROFT, William Exh. 1886
Landscape and genre painter. Add: 35 Queen's Road, Chelsea, London. † RA 1.

ASENBAUM, Miss Exh. 1890
† SWA 2.

ASH, Albert Edward Exh. 1880-86
Watercolour landscape painter. Add: 4 Bull Street, Birmingham. † B 5, D 2, RA 1, RBA 3, RSA 1.

ASH, Miss Chrissie Exh. 1886-1924
Landscape painter. London. † B 3, L 4, M 3, RA 5, RBA 5, SWA 23.

ASH, Elizabeth Exh. 1885
7 St. Mary's Terrace, Paddington, London. † SWA 1.

ASH, John Willstead Exh. 1887-1902
Leicester 1887; Birmingham 1894; Dudley, Worcs. 1897. † B 7, N 1.

ASH, Thomas Morris Exh. 1882-91
Landscape painter. Birmingham. † B 20, L 3, M 3, RBA 3, RHA 7, RSA 1.

ASHBEE, Miss Agnes Exh. 1892
53 Bedford Square, London. † RI 1.

ASHBEE, Charles Robert c. 1863-1942
Architect and town planner. Add: London and Campden, Glos. † RA 13.

ASHBEE, Miss J. Felicity Exh. 1935-39
Portrait painter. Add: Godden Green, Sevenoaks, Kent. † COO 1, RA 3.

ASHBURN, Miss Alice Exh. 1912
41 Clarendon Road, Whalley Range, Manchester. † M 1.

ASHBURNER, George Exh. 1881
54 Pembridge Villas, London. † RE 1.

ASHBURNER, William F. Exh. 1900-32
London 1900; Ewell, Surrey 1932. † L 5, NG 1, RA 4, RI 9, RSA 3.

ASHBURY, Miss D. Exh. 1937
Harewood, Chalfont St. Giles, Bucks. † B 1.

ASHBY, Miss B. Exh. 1939
65 Rosemary Hill Road. † B 1.

ASHBY, Mrs. Dorothy Exh. 1924
The Cottage, Jockey Road, Sutton Coldfield. † B 1.

ASHBY, Miss Evelyn Exh. 1915-40
Watercolour landscape painter. Add: Redhill, Surrey 1915; Guildford 1923. † AR 2, COO 2, RBA 3, RI 1.

ASHBY, Miss Mabel Exh. 1896-1900
Staines 1896; London 1898. † L 1, NG 1, RA 1, RI 4.

ASHBY, Margaret E. b. 1860
Watercolour landscape painter and teacher. Studied Croydon School of Art and under F. Calderon. Add: Redhill, Surrey 1915; Winscombe, Somerset 1921 and 1925; Reigate, Surrey 1924. † COO 2, L 5, RI 3.

ASHBY-STERRY, John Exh. 1892
† P 1.

ASHCROFT, Miss Constance Exh. 1926-27
66 Knowsley Road, Cressington Park, Liverpool. † L 2.

ASHCROFT, W. Exh. 1882
26 Lomond Road, Liverpool. † L 1.

ASHE, J.W.L. Exh. 1880-84
Painter of Devon and Cornish Coastal scenes. Add: London 1880; Bexley Heath 1882. † RA 6, RBA 2, ROI 1.

ASHENDEN, Edward James b. 1896
Decorative designer, heraldic and commercial artist. Studied Putney School of Art and Royal College of Art. Art master Wandsworth Technical Institute; designer at H.M. Pavilion Wembley; director of Studio, A Century of Progress Exhibition, Chicago 1930-33. Add: 69 Westover Road, Wandsworth Common, London 1923. † L 1, RA 2, RI 1.

ASHER, Florence May b. 1888
Landscape and figure painter and etcher. Studied RA Schools 1913-18 (silver medal and Landseer scholarship). A.R.B.A. 1923, R.B.A. 1926. Add: Nottingham 1910; London 1917; Sevenoaks, Kent 1924; Langton Maltravers, Dorset 1937; Petersfield, Herts 1939. † GI 1, GOU 19, I 3, L 3, N 17, NEA 2, RA 2, RBA 64, SWA 9.

ASHER, John E. Exh. 1935
Sculptor. 75 Station Road, Hepthorne Lane, Chesterfield. † RA 1.

ASHFORD, C.E. Exh 1882-83
The Dingle, Blossomfield, Solihull. † B 2.

ASHFORD, Miss Ellen Edith Exh. 1897-99
306 Hagley Road, Edgbaston, Birmingham. † B 4.

ASHFORD, Miss E.M. Exh. 1882-1904
Edgbaston, Birmingham 1882 and 1894. Add: Bromsgrove, Birmingham 1886; Cleve Prior, Nr. Evesham 1900. † B 27.

ASHFORD, Faith Exh. 1939-40
36 Matlock Road, Caversham, Reading. † NEA 2.

ASHFORD, G.H. Exh. 1892-1932
Sparkhill, Birmingham. † B 14, L 2.

ASHFORD, H. Leonard Exh. 1927-29
19 Downton Avenue, London. † D 11, RBA 2.

ASHFORD, Miss Ida See BIGGS

ASHFORD, Mrs. Olive Exh. 1935
The Priory, Aldeby, Beccles, Suffolk. † RA 1.

ASHLEY, Miss Dorothy Exh. 1922-33
Merrow, Nr. Guildford, Surrey. † D 4, L 2, RMS 1.

ASHLEY, H.V. Exh. 1904
10 Gray's Inn Square, London. † RA 1.

ASHLEY, John Exh. 1940
Bangor, N. Wales. † RCA 1.

ASHLEY, Miss Sophie Exh. 1894
51 Blenheim Terrace, Abbey Road, London. † RA 1.

ASHLIN, George C. Exh. 1880-1903
Architect. A.R.H.A. 1879, R.H.A. 1885. Add: Dublin. † RHA 34.

ASHLIN, Miss M.B. Exh. 1887-88
3 Slatey Road, Claughton, Liverpool. † L 2.

ASHMORE, Miss Sybil M. Exh. 1901-26
Portrait painter. Add: Ross-on-Wye, Herefordshire 1901; London 1918. † GOU 80, I 25, L 12, P 8, D 1, G 3, RA 10, RHA 7.

ASHMORE, W.L. Exh. 1938
15 Fenton Drive, Bulwell Hall, Bulwell, Notts. † N 1.

ASHTON, Miss Amy Exh. 1894
Bosden House, Hazel Grove, Nr. Stockport. † M 1.

ASHTON, Gertrude Annie See LAUDER

ASHTON, James Exh. 1882
Harcourt House, Nr. Teignmouth, Devon. † L 1.

ASHTON, James* Exh. 1911
Sydney Art School, Queen Victoria Market, Sydney, N.S.W. † RA 1.

ASHTON, John William (Will)* 1881-1935
Landscape and sea painter. b. York. Son of James A. artist. Studied under Julius Olsson, Algernon Talmage and Julians, Paris. Wynee Art prize, Sydney 1908. Member of Art advisory board to Government of Australia. R.O.I. 1915. Add: St. Ives, Cornwall 1904; Adelaide, Australia 1915 and 1929; Port Said, Egypt 1926. d. Sydney, Australia. † GOU 1, I 1, L 5, RA 35, RBA 1, ROI 35.

ASHTON, Robert F. Exh. 1937
19 Inman Road, Craven Park, London. † RA 1.

ASHTON, Ralph Exh. 1897
8 Camden Studios, Camden Street, London. † L 1, NG 1.

ASHTON, S. Exh. 1918
15 Hemstal Road, West Hampstead, London. † RA 1.

ASHTON, Stanley Exh. 1903
60 Palatine Road, West Didsbury, Manchester. † B 2.

ASHTON, William Exh. 1899-1901
Claughton, Cheshire 1899; Oxton, Cheshire 1901. † L 4, RA 2, ROI 1.

ASHURST, Maurice Exh. 1938
† M 1.

ASHWELL, Mrs. A.M. Exh. 1926-29
The Cottage, The Park, Buxton. † B 2, L 2.

ASHWELL, Lawrence Tom Exh. 1883-1905
Landscape painter. Add: London 1883; Warlingham, Surrey 1892. † RA 4, RBA 17, ROI 12.

ASHWORTH, Mrs. A.E. Exh. 1932
72 Stoneleigh Avenue, Coventry. † B 1.

ASHWORTH, Bartram Exh. 1909-1930
Liverpool 1909 and 1929; Bromborough, Cheshire 1915. † L 18.

ASHWORTH, Miss B. Exh. 1891
Horefield Hall, Wilmslow, Cheshire. † M 1.

ASHWORTH, Miss Ethel M. Exh. 1914-29
A.N.S.A. 1915. Add: Ruddington Hall, Notts. † N 39.

ASHWORTH, Miss Gertrude Exh. 1919
Beachfield, Court Yard, Eltham, London. † RA 1.

ASHWORTH, Ronald C. Exh. 1913-30
Willaston, Cheshire 1913; Birkenhead 1919; Wallasey 1928. † L 11.

ASHWORTH, Susan A. Exh. 1880-84
Haverstock Hill, London. † D 2, SWA 2.

ASHWORTH, T. Arnold Exh. 1908
14 Castle Street, Liverpool. † L 1.

ASHWORTH, W. Exh. 1914
Oakdene, All Saints Road, Ipswich, Suffolk. † RA 1.

ASHWORTH, Walter Exh. 1935
Sculptor. 72 Stoneleigh Avenue, Coventry. † RA 1.

ASKEW, Mrs. E. Exh. 1919
62 Drewstead Road, London. † SWA 1.

ASKEW, Felicity Katherine Sarah b. 1894
Painter and sculptor. Studied under Max Kruse, F. Calderon and Ernesto Bazzaro. Exh. 1921-25: Add: Castle Hills, Berwick-on-Tweed. † GOU 4, L 7.

ASKEW, Miss R.J. Exh. 1908-9
† LS 6.

ASKEW, Richard J. Exh. 1885-87
Shere, Nr. Guildford, Surrey. † RI 3.

ASPA, Rosario Exh. 1882-95
Leamington, Warwicks. † B 5, L 1, RA 1, RI 1.

ASPDEN, Ruth Spencer b. 1909
Painter and etcher. Studied Blackburn School of Art 1927-33 and Royal College of Art 1933-37. A.R.E. 1937. Add: London. † RA 10, RE 13.

ASPIN, L. Wilson Exh. 1910-12
Bradford. † L 4.

ASPINALL, George S. Exh. 1881-89
Landscape painter. Add: Lee, London 1881; Dorking, Surrey 1882; Blackheath, London 1885. † B 2, D 2, FIN 1, L 4, RA 2, RBA 7, RI 1, ROI 1.

ASPINWALL, Reginald Exh. 1889-1908
Landscape and coastal painter. Add: Lancaster. † B 1, L 13, M 5, RA 7, RBA 1, RCA 24, RI 5.

ASPREY, Miss Minnie Exh. 1893-1901
Merton, Surrey 1893; Scorrier, R.S.O., Cornwall 1898; London 1901. † L 1. RA 2, RHA 9, ROI 2.

ASSAFREY, Miss Alma G.M. Exh. 1913
134 Bath Street, Glasgow. † L 1.

ASSELIN, Maurice* Exh. 1913-29
French artist. Add: c/o Allied Artists' Association, 67 Chancery Lane, London 1913; Paris 1929. † CAR 38, GI 1, GOU 8, LS 6.

ASSENBAUM, Miss Fanny Exh. 1880-93
Landscape painter. S.W.A. 1880. Add: Munich 1880. † B 1, L 2, SWA 13.

ASSER, Richard Charles b. 1896
Landscape painter. Studied St. John's Wood School. Add: Ashley, Felstead, Essex 1923. † RA 3.

ASSMUS, Robert* b. 1837
German. Exh. 1887. † M 1.

ASTE, Miss A. Mildred Exh. 1906-8
Dunsford, Leigham Court Road, Streatham, London. † L 3.

ASTLE, M.J. Exh. 1911-20
Attewell House, Draycott, Nr. Derby. † N 8.

ASTLEY, The Hon. Mrs. S. Exh. 1914-22
38 Half Moon Street, London. † D 1, RA 2.

ASTON, Charles Reginald* 1832-1908
Landscape, coastal and genre painter. R.I. 1882. Add: Birmingham 1880; Leamington 1883; Crowborough, Sussex 1890; Torquay 1891; Oxford 1900. † B 35, D 16, L 3, M 2, RI 104, ROI 3.

ASTON, Evelin Winifred Exh. 1924-40
Mrs. Leigh. Painter and sculptor. Studied Birmingham School of Arts and Crafts and under B. Fleetwood-Walker. Teacher of modelling at the Royal Institute for the Blind, Birmingham. Add: Erdington, Birmingham. † B 8, RBA 1, RCA 2, ROI 3, RSA 1.

ASTON, Florence L.O. Exh. 1880
3 Dean's Yard, Westminster, London. † SWA 1.

ASTON, Gertrude F. Exh. 1880-81
Watercolour landscape painter. Add: 6 Elgin Road, Harrow Road, London. † SWA 3.

ASTON, Miss L.H. Exh. 1885
Eastnor Villa, Redford Road, Leamington, Warwicks. † B 1.

ASTON, Miss T. Exh. 1880-90
Flower painter. Add: 6 Elgin Road, Harrow Road, London. † SWA 9.

ASTON, Miss W.M. Exh. 1920-21
Tennal House, Harborne, Birmingham. † B 3.

ATCHE-LEROUX, Mdme. J. Exh. 1909
10 Place des Vosges, Paris. † L 1.

ATCHERLEY, Miss Ethel Exh. 1894-1905
Watercolour painter. Add: Eccles, Lancs. 1894; Church Stretton, Shrops. 1905. † B 4, GI 1, L 9, M 4, NG 1, RA 3, RBA 6, RI 4.

ATHERTON, Bessie M. Exh. 1930-32
† L 2.

ATHERTON, James Exh. 1914-33
Watercolour painter. Add: 63 Etterby Street, Stanwix, Carlisle. † RA 3. RI 1.

ATHERTON, John Smith Exh. 1911-39
Painter and engraver. Self taught. Add: Todmorden 1911; Hebden Bridge 1916; Grassington, Yorks. 1920. † B 2, GI 2, GOU 6, L 19, M 1, RA 18, RI 2, RSA 3.

ATHOLL-WHYTE, K.R. Exh. 1940
36 Elgin Avenue, London. † RA 1.

ATKIN, Miss Constance Exh. 1909
8 Douglas Road, Nottingham. † N 1.

ATKIN, Ernest H. Exh. 1910-26
Landscape painter. A.N.S.A. 1911. Add: Nottingham 1910; Sherwood, Notts. 1911. † N 48.

ATKIN, Francis Exh. 1884-1916
A.N.S.A. 1908, N.S.A. 1911. Add: Nottingham. † N 16.

ATKIN, Gabriel Exh. 1919
122 Cheyne Walk, Chelsea, London. † LS 1.

ATKIN, Miss Grace Exh. 1914-16
London. † LS 6.

ATKIN, Miss Laura Julia Exh. 1890
Exchange, Market Place, Nottingham † N 1.

ATKIN, Royal H. Exh. 1933
Landscape painter. Add: 33 Heatherdale Avenue, Birkley, Huddersfield. † RA 1.

ATKINS, Miss Alban F.T. Exh. 1938-39
Ends, Sheep Street, Burford, Oxon. † RA 1, RSA 3.

ATKINS, Miss Alice H. Exh. 1908-33
Rock Ferry, Liverpool 1908; Frodsham, Cheshire 1909. † L 8.

ATKINS, C. Exh. 1917
26 Albert Road, Glasgow. † GI 1.

ATKINS, Miss C. Exh. 1918
1 Spring Terrace, Dolphin's Barn, Dublin. † RHA 2.

ATKINS, Catherine J. Exh. 1880-1916
Genre painter. Add: 210 Holland Road, Kensington, London. † B 26, D 9, G 3, L 11, M 10, NG 3, RA 4, RBA 5, RHA 37, RI 6, RSA 1, SWA 18.

ATKINS, Eric Exh. 1940
45 Glenburne Road, London. † RA 1.

ATKINS, Edward Exh. 1894-1901
Decorative artist. Add: London † RA 4.

ATKINS, Emmeline Exh. 1880-96
210 Holland Road, Kensington, London. † B 9, D 3, M 1, RA 2, RBA 2, RHA 16, RI 1, SWA 8.

ATKINS, Miss Hylda M. Exh. 1921-27
Landscape painter and etcher. Add: British School in Rome 1921; London 1924. † BA 32, GI 1, L 1, SWA 1, WG 39.

ATKINS, Mrs. J.A. Exh. 1890
Surbiton, Surrey. † D 2.

ATKINS, J.Haddon Exh. 1899-1905
Rock Ferry, Liverpool. † L 9.

ATKINS, Miss Kathleen Exh. 1930-33
Painter and etcher. Add: 213 Stanley Park Road, Carshalton, Surrey. † RA 5.

ATKINS, Miss M.A. Exh. 1917-19
London. † SWA 5.

ATKINS, Mary Elizabeth (Elise) Exh. 1897-1940
Landscape, flower and interior painter. Studied Slade School. Add: London. † AB 2, BA 2, BG 9, CHE 2, G 2, GOU 7, FIN 3, I 16, L 3, LS 19, M 3, NEA 36, NG 1, P 2, RA 39, RBA 4, RED 1, RHA 2, RID 11, ROI 7, RSA 1, SWA 10.

ATKINSON, Miss Alice Exh. 1909
51 Falkland Road, Egremont, Cheshire. † L 1.

ATKINSON, Amy B. Exh. 1884-1916
Landscape and figure painter. Add: Fakenham Rectory, Norfolk 1884; York 1889; Frensham, Surrey 1894; London 1897. † B 2, BG 3, DOW 1, GI 4, I 11, L 7 LS 3, M 1, NEA 4, NG 2, P 4, RA 6, RBA 8, RHA 2, RID 57, ROI 12, SWA 12.

ATKINSON, Arthur G. Exh. 1880-98
Sculptor. Add: London 1880; Kew 1881; Richmond, Surrey 1898. † L 2, RA 12.

ATKINSON, A. Spence Exh. 1905-10
Liverpool. † L 2.

ATKINSON, B.W. Exh. 1886-30
Egremont, Cheshire 1886; Isle of Man 1896. † B 2, L 38, RA 1.

ATKINSON, Charles Exh. 1880-85
The Avenue, Datchet, Windsor. † G 3, L 1.

ATKINSON, Mrs. C. Exh. 1890
Belmont House, Hoddesdon. † SWA 1.

ATKINSON, Charles Gerrard b. 1879
Portrait, landscape and architectural painter. Add: Felbridge, Surrey 1932; Blue Anchor Bay, Somerset 1935. † B 5, RCA 4.

ATKINSON, Miss C.J. Exh. 1929
Hillside, Woolton, Nr. Liverpool. † L 2.

ATKINSON, Emily Exh. 1885-1889
Brigg, Edinburgh. † RSA 3.

ATKINSON, Emma Exh. 1880
Hilldyke, Boston, Lincs. † SWA 2.

ATKINSON, Frank Exh. 1891-93
Engraver. Add: London. † RA 2.

ATKINSON, G. Exh. 1909-13
30 Buckleigh Road, Streatham Common, London. † RA 2.

ATKINSON, George b. 1880
Painter and etcher. Studied Royal College of Art, Paris and Munich. Headmaster Metropolitan School of Art, Dublin. A.R.H.A. 1912, R.H.A. 1916. Add: London 1909; Dublin 1910. † L 3, RA 2, RHA 41.

ATKINSON, Helen D. Exh. 1884
Watercolour still-life painter. Add: 28 St. Oswald's Road, West Brompton, London. † SWA 2.

ATKINSON, Herbert D. Exh. 1882-90
Wallingford, Berks. 1882; Beckenham, Kent 1889, Liverpool 1890. † B 1, L 4, RBA 1, ROI 1.

ATKINSON, Mrs. Hilda Goffey Exh. 1887-1932
nee Goffey. Add: Blundellsands, Nr. Liverpool 1901; Upton-on-Severn 1926. † B 1, L 59, LS 3, RA 1, RCA 2, RI 1, SWA 2.

ATKINSON, John c. 1924
Newcastle-on-Tyne 1896-1904 and 1914; Slights, Yorks. 1901; Glaisdale, Yorks. 1910. † L 6, M 2, RA 10, RI 6, RSA 9.

ATKINSON, Miss J. Exh. 1882-85
The Laurels, Sale, Manchester. † M 3.

ATKINSON, Miss J. Exh. 1930-33
Hillside, Woolton, Liverpool. † L 5.

ATKINSON, Miss J.N. Exh. 1897
1 Welleswood Park, Torquay. † SWA 2.

ATKINSON, Kate E. Exh. 1880-81
Landscape painter. Add: 54 Culford Road, London. † SWA 5.

ATKINSON, Lawrence* 1873-1931
Painter and sculptor. b. Manchester, d. Paris. Add: Swiss Cottage, London 1913. † LS 3.

ATKINSON, Miss Mabel Exh. 1912-16
85 Broadhurst Gardens, South Hampstead, London. † LS 12.

ATKINSON, Miss Marguerite Exh. 1921-23
9 St. George's Court, Gloucester Road, London. † L 1, SWA 4.

ATKINSON, Maud Tindal* Exh. 1906-37
Painter and miniaturist. Add: London. † B 3, COO 1, L 4, RA 15.

ATKINSON, Robert Exh. 1891
Portrait painter. Add: 75 Cookridge Street, Leeds. † B 1, RA 2.

ATKINSON, Robert b. 1883
Architect. Studied Nottingham School of Art (Tite prizeman 1905). Director of Education Architectural Association, Schools of Architecture. Add: Nottingham 1905; Carshalton, Surrey 1908; London 1909. † GI 3, RA 42, RSA 7.

ATKINSON, R. Frank Exh. 1899-1909
Liverpool 1899; London 1902. † RA 11.

ATKINSON, Miss Sara Exh. 1880-84
Dublin. † RHA 8.

ATKINSON, Mrs. Sheela A.C. Exh. 1918
97 Stephen's Green, Dublin. † RHA 2.

ATKINSON, Miss Sophia Exh. 1905
21 Windsor Terrace, Newcastle-on-Tyne. † RI 1.

ATKINSON, Thomas Lewis b. 1817
Engraver. b. Salisbury. Add: London 1880-89. † RA 15.

ATKINSON, W. Ansell Exh. 1909-11
Southport, Lancs. † L 4, M 1.

ATMORE, Mrs. V. Exh. 1930
† RMS 1.

ATTENBOROUGH, Miss Gladys
Exh. 1908-12
Holbrook, Bedford. † RA 1, RCA 1.

ATTENBOROUGH, Miss M.A.
Exh. 1922-26
60 Scott's Lane, Shortlands, Kent. † NEA 6, SWA 6.

ATTINGER, Miss Exh. 1887
22 King Henry's Road, London. † RHA 1.

ATTLEE, Miss Della Exh. 1886-97
Flower painter. Add: London 1886; Rose Hill, Dorking, Surrey 1887. † RA 7, RBA 1, ROI 9.

ATTLEE, Kathleen May Exh. 1886-98
Flower painter. Add: Rose Hill, Dorking, Surrey. † L 2, RA 6, RBA 2, ROI 10.

ATTLEE, Miss Mabel Exh. 1890
Fair Croft, Cobham, Surrey. † RA 1, RBA 1.

ATWELL, Mabel Lucie Exh. 1924
Mrs. H.C. Earnshaw. Illustrator. S.W.A. 1925. Add: Roland Gardens, London. † SWA 2.

ATWOOD, Clare 1866-1962
Portrait, interior, still-life and decorative flower painter. Studied Westminster and Slade School. N.E.A. 1912, A.S.W.A. 1900. b. Richmond, Surrey. Add: Kew 1893; London 1895; Tenterden, Kent 1940. † BG 5, CHE 3, COO 1, FIN 3, G 7, GI 12, I 7, L 10, LS 6, M 3, NEA 108, NG 3, RA 16, RHA 2, RI 1, RID 15, RSA 4, SWA 19.

AUBER, H. van den See V

AUBINIERE, de l' See D

AUBLET, Albert* b. 1851
French painter. 75 Boulevard Bineau, Neuilly sur Seine, France, 1884. † RA 6.

AUBREY, H. Exh. 1880
23 Church Road, Southgate Road, Islington, London. † RHA 1.

AUBREY, John Exh. 1938-40
London 1938; Fochabers, Morayshire 1940. † RA 2.

AUBRY, Emile* b. 1880
b. Algeria. Add: 11 Rue d'Assas, Paris VI, 1923; † RSA 1.

AUBURTIN, Jean Francis b. 1866
French watercolour painter. Exh. 1913-23. Add: Paris. † FIN 5, L 1, RSW 1.

AUCHINVOLE, Miss Gladys M. Exh. 1929
Lownsniel, Kilmalcolm, Renfrewshire. † RSA 1.

AUCKLAND, Lady Exh. 1888
Edenthorpe, Doncaster, Yorks. † D 1.

AUDLEY, Caroline b. 1864
Painter and pastelier. Studied Liverpool, Rome, Florence and Venice. Add: Fairfield 1887; Llandudno Junction 1918; Colwyn Bay 1920. † B 1, L 35, RCA 13.

AUDLEY, Miss Edith J. Exh. 1900-4
29 Trafalgar Road, Birkdale, Southport. † L 2, M 1.

AUDLEY, John Exh. 1890
Moss Lane, Aintree, Liverpool. † L 1.

AUDLEY, William C. Exh. 1910
7 Prospect Vale, Fairfield, Liverpool. † L 1.

AUDREE, T.H. Exh. 1884
Paris. † L 1.

AUDRY, Miss Eleanor B.E. Exh. 1926-29
10 Woodfield Road, King's Heath, Birmingham. † B 9.

AUDSLEY, Miss Mary C. Exh. 1936
Sculptor. Add: Church Stile House, Cobham, Surrey. † RA 1.

AUERBACH, Arnold b. 1898
Sculptor, painter and etcher. Studied Liverpool City School of Art, Paris and Switzerland. Add: Liverpool 1915; London 1922. † L 27, RA 4.

AUERBACH, Erna Exh. 1938
† BK 31.

AUGER, Miss Ethel Exh. 1923
† RMS 1.

AUGER, J.W. Exh. 1899
8 Laurel Road, Fairfield, Liverpool. † L 1.

AUGLEY, H.J. Exh. 1886
21 Bowness Road, Calford Bridge, Woking. † RHA 1.

AULD, John Exh. 1882-91
Landscape and figure painter. Add: Blackheath, London. † GI 2, M 1, RA 1, RBA 2.

AULTON, Margaret Exh. 1920-25
Etcher and illustrator. b. Littlebridge, Herefords. Add: 18 Bridge Street, Birmingham 1920. † B 12.

AUMONIER, Mrs. Emmeline Exh. 1928-32
Miniature painter. Married to John S.A. q.v. † RMS 2.

AUMONIER, James* 1832-1911
Pastoral landscape and animal painter. Studied Birkbeck Institute, Marlborough House and South Kensington School. Purchased by Chantry Bequest – "Sheep washing in Sussex" 1889 and "The Black Mountains" 1905. N.E.A. 1887, A.R.I. 1876, R.I. 1879, R.O.I. 1909. Add: London 1880 and 1888; Steyning, Sussex 1887. † B 35, DOW 59, FIN 2, G 4, GI 36, GOU 177, I 1, L 24, LEI 61, M 55, NEA 2, NG 2, RA 42, RBA 11, RCA 1, RHA 10, RI 119, ROI 79, TOO 2.

AUMONIER, John S. Exh. 1903-40
Flower and landscape painter. Add: London. † B 1, BG 2, GI 1, LS 9, M 3, RA 8, RI 3, ROI 17.

AUMONIER, Miss Louise Exh. 1880-1901
Flower painter. Add: London. † D 2, FIN 2, G 1, GI 5, L 3, M 2, RA 5, RBA 5, RHA 8, RI 18, ROI 14, SWA 2.

AUMONIER, Miss Minnie Exh. 1918-21
Flower painter. 40 Lambolle Road, South Hampstead, London. † RA 1, SWA 3.

AUMONIER, Miss Nancy Exh. 1903-6
Flower painter. 7 Antrim Mansions, London. † B 1, BG 1, RI 1.

AUMONIER, Stacey J. Exh. 1902-13
Coastal and landscape painter. Add: London. † GOU 37, I 3, RA 3, RI 3, ROI 4.

AUMONIER, William Exh. 1889-90
Architectural sculptor. Add: 1 New Inn Yard, Tottenham Court Road, London. † RA 2.

AURELI, Giuseppi* Exh. 1890
Rome. † D 1.

AUSTEN, John Exh. 1919-30
Decorative illustrator. A.R.B.A. 1919, R.B.A. 1921, Add: London 1917, New Romney, Hants. 1930 † I 3, RA 1, RBA 21.

AUSTEN, Mrs. Roberts Exh. 1886
The Royal Mint, London. † G 1.

AUSTEN, Winifred Marie Louise
Exh. 1899-1940
Mrs. Oliver Frick. Bird and animal painter and etcher. Studied under Mrs. Jopling and at Zoological Gardens. A.R.E. 1907, R.E. 1922, R.I. 1933, A.S.W.A. 1902, S.W.A. 1905. Born Ramsgate. Add: London 1899, Yeovil, Somerset 1918, Dorking, Surrey 1920, Woodbridge, Suffolk 1922, Ufford, Suffolk 1924, Orford, Suffolk 1927. † AB 1, ALP 1, BA 4, CG 1, FIN 22, G 4, L 9, LEI 57, M 2, RA 45, RE 72, RED 1, RHA 7, RI 24, SWA 18.

AUSTIN, A. Exh. 1882
105 Mount Pleasant, Liverpool. † L 1.

AUSTIN, Arthur J. Exh. 1884-88
Birmingham. † B 2.

AUSTIN, Emily Exh. 1880-88
Flower painter. Add: London. † B 1, D 6, L 1, RA 1, SWA 11.

AUSTIN, Frank Exh. 1901-11
Glasgow. † GI 5.

AUSTIN, Frederick George b. 1902
Painter and etcher. Studied Leicester College of Art and Royal College of Art. A.R.E. 1930. Signed work "Austin Frederick". Add: Hammersmith, London 1929. † BA 3, RA 16, RE 39.

AUSTIN, Mrs. Frances M. Exh. 1895-1908
Kings Heath, Birmingham 1895, Knowle, Warwicks. 1904. † B 11.

AUSTIN, Hubert James Exh. 1887-96
The Knoll, Lancaster. † L 1, RI 1.

AUSTIN, Horace J.M. Exh. 1928-31
Architect. Add: Hammersmith, London 1928, Isleworth, Middlesex 1931. † RA 3.

AUSTIN, Miss I. Exh. 1888
107 Mount Pleasant, Liverpool. † L 1.

AUSTIN, Miss Joan Exh. 1936
17 Beech Road, Bournville. † B 1.

AUSTIN, Miss Joyce M. Exh. 1936-37
7 Linden Avenue, Kidderminster. † B 3.

AUSTIN, L. Magnus Exh. 1938
51 Towngate Street, Poole, Dorset. † RA 1.

AUSTIN, Miss R. Exh. 1918
Finchley Road, London. † SWA 1.

AUSTIN, R.C. Exh. 1899-1900
London. † RA 2.

AUSTIN, Robert Sargent 1895-1973
Painter, etcher and engraver. "Le Bain de Pied" purchased by Chantry Bequest 1930. A.R.A. 1939, A.R.E. 1921, R.E. 1928, A.R.W.S. 1930, R.W.S. 1934. b. Leicester, lived London, died Norfolk. † B 2, BA 9, CG 71, CHE 3, FIN 22, GI 24, L 2, NEA 2, RA 49, RE 70, RED 1, RHA 1, RSA 4, RWS 57.

AUSTIN, W. Exh. 1902
7 St. Jude's Terrace, Inchicore Road, Dublin. † RHA 1.

AUSTIN-CARTER, Miss M. Exh. 1902-14
Miniature painter. R.M.S. 1905. Lived Torquay. † L 2, NG 1, RMS 29.

AUSTRIAN, Ben Exh. 1903
c/o H. Graves & Co. 6 Pall Mall, London. † L 2.

AUTANT, Mdlle. M.F. Exh. 1910
2 Rue Emile Menier (XVIe), Paris. † L 1.

AUTY, Charles Exh. 1881-1919
Watercolour painter. Add: London 1881, Blackpool 1888; Port Erin, Isle of Man 1898. † D 1, GI 2, GOU 3, L 8, M 1, RA 1, RBA 4, RHA 1, RI 3, RSA 1.

AVELINE, F. Exh. 1905
1 Bolton Studios, Redcliffe Road, South Kensington, London. † RA 1.

AVELING, Stephen Exh. 1900
Restoration House, Rochester, Kent. † RBA 1.

AVERY, Miss Edith E. Exh. 1887
Sunnyside, Norfolk Road, Edgbaston, Birmingham. † B 1.

AVEZ-DELIT, Mrs. Julia Exh. 1909
110 Rue Caulain Court, Paris. † L 1.

AVIAT, Jules Charles b. 1844
Rue Felbuza 9, Paris, 1900. † L 2.

AVIS Exh. 1892
57 Elm Park Gardens, London. † B 2.

AVY, J.M. Exh. 1912-13
126 Boulevard du Montparnasse, Paris. † FIN 2, L 1.

AWDRY, Miss Eleanor B.E. Exh. 1930-36
10 Woodfield Road, Kings Heath, Birmingham. † B 4, RA 1.

AWDRY, Miss M.F. Exh. 1919
Cromwell Cottage, Courtfield Gardens, London. † SWA 2.

AWDRY, Margaret Jane b. 1854
Painter and jeweller. Studied Municipal School of Art, Birmingham. Art teacher and teacher at School for Jewellers and silversmiths, Birmingham. Add: Birmingham 1887; Clevedon, Somerset 1918. † B 15, L 43, RMS 3.

AXENTOWEIZ, Theodore Exh. 1894
8 St. Leonard's Terrace, Chelsea, London. † NG 1.

AXFORD, Miss Edith Exh. 1905-11
Maycourt, Campden Road, South Croydon. † L 8, RA 3, RMS 1, RSA 2.

AYERS, Rev. G.F. Exh. 1931-38
Watercolour painter. † WG 13.

AYERS, Lottie Mary Pimm Exh. 1913-24
Modeller, embroiderer and decorative artist. Studied St. Martins School of Art (gold, silver and bronze medals). Add: London. † LS 6, RA 2.

AYERST, Miss Eva Exh. 1895-97
22 Blomfield Road, Maida Hill, London. † NG 2.

AYLES, C. Nunn Exh. 1897-1913
Glasgow 1897; Ayr 1904. † GI 9.

AYLES, Mrs. Ellen Exh. 1893
Portrait painter. Add: 2 The Gardens, Tilbury, Essex. † RA 1.

AYLIFF, Miss C. Exh. 1917
Walton on Thames. † SWA 1.

AYLING, Amy Exh. 1884
Flower painter. Add: 2 Clarendon Road, Wallington, Surrey. † SWA 1.

AYLING, Albert W. d. c.1905
Landscape and portrait painter. Add: London 1880 and 1888; Liverpool 1884; Conway, North Wales 1889; Llandudno, Wales 1900. † B 1, D 1, L 49, M 6, RA 4, RBA 4, RCA 128, RHA 4, RI 4.

AYLING, George b. 1887
Marine and landscape painter. Studied Putney School of Art 1912. Lived London. † AR 3, L 8, RA 10, RI 13, ROI 12.

AYLING, Joan b. 1909
Miniature painter. A.R.M.S. 1932. Add: Chipping Campden, Glos. 1927; London 1934. † B 6, L 1, RA 11, RMS 23.

AYLING, R.S. Exh. 1898-1915
Westminster, London. † RA 6.

AYLMER, Caroline M. Exh. 1885-93
Donaden Castle, Kilcock, Ireland. † D 1, SWA 2.

AYLMER, George R. Exh. 1897-99
Religious painter. Add: London. † RA 2.

AYLWARD, Mrs. Annie Exh. 1899
38 Abbey Road, St. John's Wood, London. † L 2.

AYLWARD, James de V Exh. 1895-1917
Liverpool 1895; London 1897. † GI 1, L 33, M 1, RA 9, RBA 2, RCA 1, RI 1, RMS 1, ROI 15.

AYLWARD, John J. Exh. 1935-36
27 Dawson St. Dublin. † RHA 2.

AYNE, Louis A. Exh. 1889
8 Place de l'Hotel de Ville, Paris. † GI 1.

AYNSLEY-COOK, T. Exh. 1902
New Empire Theatre, Lime Street, Liverpool. † L 1.

AYOUB, Mrs. K. Exh. 1911
29 Brook Green, London. † RA 1.

AYOUB, Moussa Exh. 1903-38
Portrait painter. Add: London. † I 1, L 7, P 8, RA 9.

AYRE, George Oliver Exh. 1924
14 Downham Road, Tranmere. † L 2.

AYRE, Miss Minnie Exh. 1886
Flower painter. Add: 4 Brunswick Square, London. † RBA 1, RI 1.

AYRES, Arthur James John b. 1902
Sculptor. Studied RA Schools and British School in Rome (silver and bronze medals and Landseer scholarship). Add: London 1927. † GI 1, L 2, RA 10, RSA 3.

AYRES, C. Harold Exh. 1933
† RSW 2.

AYRES, Miss Joyce Exh. 1933
The Guare, Peaslake, Surrey. † RA 1.

AYRTON, Madame Annie Exh. 1881-89
N.E.A. 1887. Add: Paris. † GI 3, NEA 3, RA 6.

AYRTON, Antony M. Exh. 1933-40
Landscape and portrait painter. Add: London. † GOU 1, RA 4, RSA 4.

AYRTON, Miss Eileen Exh. 1934-39
Belfast. † RHA 3.

AYRTON, Maxwell Exh. 1899-1939
Architect. Add: London. † NEA 1, RA 14, RSA 1.

AYRTON, Oliver Exh. 1888-90
London 1888 and 1890; Paris 1889. † G 1, L 3, M 1, RA 1.

AYRTON, William Exh. 1889-1904
Tenby, Pembs. 1889; Chester 1890; Beccles, Suffolk 1892. † L 5, M 5, RA 4.

AYSCOUGH, Anthony Exh. 1938-40
† LEF 14.

AZEMA, Louis Exh. 1923
2 Rue de Pas de la Mule, Paris 111e. † RSA 2.

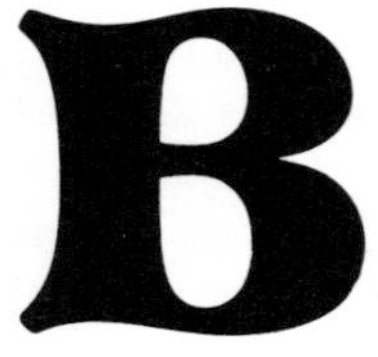

BABB, Charlotte E. c.1830-1906
Figure painter. One of the earliest lady students at R.A. schools. Add: Clapham, London 1885. † B 2, L 1, M 2, RHA 5, ROI 1, SWA 1.

BABB, Henry R. Exh. 1900-16
21 Portland Square, Plymouth. † B 1, L 3, M 3, RA 2, RI 3.

BABB, J. Staines Exh. 1890-1904
Landscape painter. Add: London. † L 19, RA 5, RHA 6.

BABB, Stanley Nicholson 1873-1957
Sculptor. Studied RA schools (gold medal and travelling scholarship). A.R.M.S. 1930; R.M.S. 1932. Add: London. † GI 13, L 14, RA 60, RI 7, RMS 15, ROI 1, RSA 6.

BABBAGE, Herbert Ivan 1875-1916
Died on active service. Exh. 1908 and 1916. Add: St. Ives, Cornwall. † RA 2.

BACARISAS, Gustavo Exh. 1897
Spanish painter. Add: 33 Via Margutta, Rome. † L 1, RA 1.

BACCANI, Attilio Exh. 1880-90
Portrait painter. Add: London. † G 1, L 3, RA 4.

BACCANI, Miss Halia Exh. 1885-1906
Portrait painter. Add: London. † G 1, NG 6.

BACH, Mrs. Alice Exh. 1889-98
A.S.W.A. 1889. Add: London. † RI 3, RMS 1, SWA 3.

BACH, Edward Exh. 1880-93
Figure and still life painter. Add: Kensington, London. † B 15, L 6, M 4, RA 6, RHA 32, ROI 1.

BACH, Guido R.* 1828-1905
Portrait and genre painter. A.R.I. 1865; R.I. 1868; R.O.I. 1883. Add: London, 1880. † AG 7, B 6, GI 5, L 4, M 1, RA 2, RI 38, ROI 15.

BACH, Mrs. Madeline Exh. 1902-33
Miniature painter and potter. Studied Royal Female School of Art; Royal College of Art. Add: 36 Cranbrook Road, Chiswick, London. † B 2, L 3, M 2, RA 1, RI 27, RMS 3.

BACH, Miss M.G. Exh. 1903
534 High Road, Chiswick, London. † L 2.

BACHELOR, Philip H. Wilson Exh. 1921-35
Etcher, dry point and watercolour artist. Add: 31 Kensington Court, London. † FIN 58, L 2, RA 4, RI 3.

BACHER, Otto Henry 1856-1909
American book illustrator and etcher. R.E. 1881. Exh. 1881-82. Add: Venice. † RA 1, RE 20.

BACHMAN, Alfred Exh. 1905
30 Romanstrasse, Munich. † I 2.

BACKHOUSE, James E. Exh. 1886-91
Hurworth Grange, Darlington. † RI 5.

BACKHOUSE, Margaret J. Exh. 1880-85
Nee Holden. Portrait and figure painter. S.W.A. 1880. Add: Whitley Villas, Caledonian Road, London. † RA 2, SWA 6.

BACON, Miss Audrey W. Exh. 1940
33 Southtown Road, Great Yarmouth, Norfolk. † RA 1.

BACON, Charles Exh. 1884
Sculptor. Studied R.A. Schools. Add: Bolton Studios, The Boltons, London. † RA 1.

BACON, Elwyn Exh. 1927-30
Lithographer. Add: Bramhall, Cheshire 1927; London 1928. † AB 1, L 4.

BACON, Mrs. Helen See McALPIN, Helen Emmeline.

BACON, Miss Honor Exh. 1935-40
Marico, South Canterbury. † RI 6.

BACON, Henry Lynch Exh. 1919-21
Portrait painter and illustrator. Studied Royal College of Art. † RA 4.

BACON, John Henry Frederick* 1866-1914
Domestic and genre painter. A.R.A. 1903. Add: London. † B 8, GI 3, L 18, M 2, P 2, RA 75, RHA 1, RI 1, ROI 2.

BACON, Miss Katharine P. Exh. 1920-23
16 Dukes Avenue, Chiswick, London. † RA 1, ROI 2.

BACON, Marjorie May b. 1902
Painter and engraver. Studied Norwich School of Art and Royal College of Art. Add: London 1927 and 1935; Gt. Yarmouth 1930; Newbury, Berks. 1932. † ALP 1, RA 14.

BACON, Percy C.H. Exh. 1885-90
Stained glass artist. Add: London. † RA 3.

BACON, Sewell Exh. 1927-30
Landscape and still life painter. Add: Gate House, Northwood, Middlesex. † L 6, RA 3, ROI 1.

BACON, Miss V.C.P. Exh. 1923
110 Foxhall Road, Nottingham. † N 1.

BACON, W.E. Exh. 1883
Landscape painter. Add: Pentre-dw, Bettws-y-coed, Wales. † RA 1.

BADCOCK, Mrs. E.B. Exh. 1907-13
London. † RA 8.

BADCOCK, Miss Isabel Baynes Exh. 1886-1929
Landscape painter. Add: Ripon, Yorks. 1886; Wells, Somerset 1901; Bures, Suffolk 1929. † M 1, RA 7, RBA 1, RI 1, RID 50.

BADCOCK, Miss K.S. Exh. 1889-90
Animal painter. Add: Ripon, Yorks. † RBA 2.

BADCOCK, Miss Leigh Exh. 1887-93
Landscape painter. Add: London 1887; Tunbridge Wells, Kent 1893. † RBA 6, RI 1, SWA 4.

BADCOCK, O.M. Exh. 1896
108 Tottenham Court Road, London. † RBA 1.

BADDELEY, T.F.J. Exh. 1933-38
Dolgarroc, Conway, Wales. † RCA 5.

BADELEY, Sir Henry John Fanshawe b. 1874
Etcher, engraver and illustrator. A.R.E. 1911; R.E. 1914. b. Elswick, Lancs. Lived London. † RA 28, RE 74, RMS 3.

BADENOCK, Miss M.J.D. Exh. 1892-1911
Lee, Kent 1892; London 1897. † B 7, GI 1, L 1, RA 1.

BADEN-POWELL, Frank Smyth 1850-1933
Painter and sculptor. Older brother of Lord B.P. q.v. Lived St. George's Place, Hyde Park Corner, London. † B 5, G 1, L 9, M 2, P 1, RA 12.

BADEN-POWELL, Lord, Robert Stephenson Smyth c. 1858-1941
Founder of Boy Scout Movement. Contributed War sketches to the Graphic. † BRU 116, COO 2, L 1, RA 1.

BADGER, F. Exh. 1932
Cunard Building, Liverpool. † L 1.

BADGER, G.W. Jun. Exh. 1887
Oxford Road, Moseley, Birmingham. † B 2.

BADHAM, E. Leslie d. 1944
Studied Clapham School of Art, South Kensington and Slade Schools. R.B.A. 1899; R.I. 1937; R.O.I. 1940. Add: London 1896; St. Leonards on Sea, Sussex 1905; Hastings 1930. † GOU 3, L 1, M 2, NEA 1, RA 38, RBA 159, RCA 1, RHA 34, RI 23, ROI 5, RSA 1.

BADMIN, Stanley Roy* b. 1906
Watercolour landscape painter and etcher. Studied Camberwell School of Art, Royal College of Art. A.R.E. 1931; R.E. 1935; A.R.W.S. 1932; R.W.S. 1935. Add: London. † FIN 137, GI 3, L 6, NEA 9, RA 17, ROI 13, RWS 55.

BADNALL, Miss Gertrude Exh. 1895-1914
London. † L 2, RA 2.

BAER, Fritz* Exh. 1904
New Passing B., Munich. † GI 1.

BAER, Guy b. 1897
Landscape painter. b. Switzerland. Settled England 1934. Exh. 1936. † TOO 27.

BAERLEIN, Mrs. Dorothy A. Exh. 1932-38
Miniature painter. Add: Northwick, Cheshire 1932; Croxley Green, Herts. 1938. † L 2, RA 1, RI 3.

BAERTSOEN, Albert Exh. 1890-1918
Landscape painter. Add: London 1890; France 1901. † I 10, RBA 2.

BAES, Firmin Exh. 1909-21
Avenue Moliere, Brussels. † GI 1, L 1, RSA 1.

BAGALLAY, Margaret Exh. 1905-10
London 1905; Dover 1906; Bushey, Herts. 1910. † L 1, SWA 2.

BAGARDE, Van den See V

BAGG, Mdlle. L. Exh. 1910
2 Rue Pierre Charron, Paris. † L 1.

BAGGALLAY, Frank T. Exh. 1880-1906
Architect. Add: Beckenham, Kent 1880; London 1891. † RA 5.

BAGGALLY, Osborn J. Exh. 1891-99
Sculptor. Add: London. † D 9, RA 3.

BAGLEY, G.S. Exh. 1923
71 North Road, West Bridgford, Notts. † N 4.

BAGLEY, S.D. Exh. 1886
6 Guest Street, Hockley, Birmingham. † B 1.

BAGNOLD, Enid H. Exh. 1915-16
Portrait and figure painter. Add: Warren Wood, Shooter's Hill, London. † I 3, NEA 3.

BAGOT, Miss Lucy Exh. 1916
Portrait painter. Add: 28 St. Andrew's Mansions, Dorset Street, London. † NEA 1.

BAGSHAW, Miss Edna Exh. 1920
437 Mansfield Road, Nottingham. † N 2.

BAGSHAW, Edward Exh. 1914
Hazeldene, The Drive, Roundhay, Leeds. † L 1.

BAGSHAW, Edwin* Exh. 1891-1927
Landscape painter. A.N.S.A. 1914. Add: Nottingham. † N 13.

BAGSHAW, Miss Madeline Exh. 1924-28
Brightside, Harper's Lane, Bolton, Lancs. † L 2.

BAGSHAWE, Mrs. F. Exh. 1881
5 Warrior Square, Leonards on Sea. † SWA 1.

BAGSHAWE, Joseph Richard 1870-1909
Marine painter. Grandson of Clarkson Stanfield R.A. R.B.A. 1904. Add: London 1897; Whitby, Yorks. 1903. † FIN 1, GI 3, L 6, M 1, RA 15, RBA 41, RMS 1, ROI 1.

BAGSHAWE, William Wyatt Exh. 1915
c/o E. Schwabe, 43 Cheyne Walk, London. † NEA 1.

BAGWELL, Miss Lilla Exh. 1911-12
Clonmel, Ireland. † SWA 2.

BAIER, Mrs. Ruth Exh. 1909-30
56 Carter Street, Liverpool. † L 4.

BAIKIE, Mrs. Constance N. Exh. 1914
24 Netherley Road, Trinity, Edinburgh. † L 1.

BAIL, Franck A. Exh. 1904-23
29 Quai Bourbon, Paris. † GI 1, L 3, RSA 1.

BAIL, Joseph Claude 1862-1921
French Artist. Exh. 1901-4. Add: Rue Legendre 22, Paris. † L 2.

BAIL, Miss M. Exh. 1920
28 Waterloo Road, Dublin. † RHA 2.

BAILDON, Miss Marion J. Exh. 1892
8 Tavistock Road, Westbourne Park, London. † GI 1.

BAILEY, Mrs. Ada Exh. 1925-40
42 Upper Grosvenor Road, Handsworth Wood. † B 27.

BAILEY, Arthur Exh. 1884
Watercolour painter. Add: 8 Castle Street, Holborn, London. † RBA 2.

BAILEY, Arthur Exh. 1930-36
Landscape painter. Add: London 1930; Chislehurst, Kent 1936. † RA 2.

BAILEY, Alfred Charles b. 1883
Watercolour landscape painter. Studied Brighton School of Art and under Louis Grier. Add: St. Ives, Cornwall 1909-19. † GOU 48, I 1, LS 24, RED 6.

BAILEY, Albert E.* Exh. 1890-1904
Landscape painter. Add: Northampton 1890; Leicester 1904. † RA 31. RBA 7.

BAILEY, C. Collins Exh. 1937
9 Pelham Crescent, Beeston, Notts. † N 5.

BAILEY, Miss Constance E. Exh. 1909
Portland House, Eccles Old Road, Pendleton, Manchester. † B 1.

BAILEY, Miss D.E. Exh. 1901-7
Invergloy, Invernessshire. † D 7.

BAILEY, Mrs. D. Thomas Exh. 1931-36
199 Lozells Road, Handsworth, Birmingham. † B 2.

BAILEY, Miss Edith M. Exh. 1911-13
Landscape painter. † ALP 8.

BAILEY, Miss Elfrida Ormrod Exh. 1909-40
Watercolour painter. Add: Faircoft, Cobham, Surrey. † AR 1, COO 2, LS 5, RI 2, SWA 9.

BAILEY, Ethel Porter Exh. 1908-27
Portrait painter. Add: London. † RA 11, ROI 1, SWA 1.

BAILEY, Fred E. Exh. 1919
† L 1.

BAILEY, G. Exh. 1908
7 Carteret Street, Westminster, London. † RA 1.

BAILEY, Gervase Exh. 1900
Married to Ruby Winifred B. q.v. Add: 43 Sinclair Road, Kensington Park, London. † RA 1.

BAILEY, George William b. 1880
Landscape painter. Studied Chelsea School of Art 1903-4, Victoria and Albert Museum. Curator of the Museum of Spalding Gentlemen's Society 1920. Add: 3 Westlode Street, Spalding, Lincs. † RCA 2, RSA 3.

BAILEY, Harold Exh. 1900-3
Architect. Newark on Trent, Notts. † RA 4.

BAILEY, Harold Exh. 1920
Architectural drawing — war memorial screen. Add: 5 St. John Street, Bedford Row, London. † RA 1.

BAILEY, Harold Exh. 1920-32
Birmingham. † B 31.

BAILEY, Henry Exh. 1880-1907
Landscape and genre painter. Add: London 1880; Mistley, Essex 1899; Gt. Baddow, Chelmsford, Essex 1904. † D 16, G 2, L 8, M 6, RA 12, RBA 28, RHA 15, RI 11.

BAILEY, Miss H.D. Exh. 1897-99
The Hill, Sandiacre. † N 3.

BAILEY, Miss Ivy Exh. 1936-40
Flower painter. Add: 24 Black Lion Lane, London. † RA 3.

BAILEY, J.J. Exh. 1923-37
Handsworth, Birmingham 1923; Sutton Coldfield 1937. † B 13.

BAILEY, Mrs. J. Thomas Exh. 1929
199 Lozells Road, Handsworth, Birmingham. † B 1.

BAILEY, John William d. 1914
Miniature painter. Add: London. † RA 3, RMS 2.

BAILEY, K.W. Exh. 1937-40
91 Eastwood Road, Cannon Hill, Birmingham. † B 4.

BAILEY, Miss Lottie Exh. 1902
33 Portland Road, Edgbaston, Birmingham. † B 1.

BAILEY, Miss M. Exh. 1894-98
Stanley Road, Teddington. † SWA 4.

BAILEY, Mrs. Mildred B. Exh. 1895
Portrait painter. Add: 78 Mount View, Stroud Green, London. † RA 1.

BAILEY, M.F. Exh. 1931
† NEA 1.

BAILEY, M.S. Exh. 1887
Architect. Add: School Board for London, Victoria Embankment, London. † RA 1.

BAILEY, Robert B. Exh. 1904-06
8 Rudolph Terrace, Bushey, Herts. † RA 2.

BAILEY, R.H. Exh. 1911
Montrose, Grove Hill, Woodford, Essex. † D 3.

BAILEY, Ruby Winifred Exh. 1894-1921
Nee Levick. Sculptor. Studied Royal College of Art (2 gold medals, British Institute scholarship and Princess of Wales scholarship). Married Gervase B. q.v. Add: London. † I 1, L 2, RA 28, RID 5.

BAILEY, Thomas J. Exh. 1886-1904
Architect. Add: School Board Victoria Embankment, London. † RA 9.

BAILEY, W. Exh. 1899
Ferncliffe, Derngate, Northampton. † RBA 1.

BAILEY, Wellesley Exh. 1901-36
Edinburgh 1901 and 1936; London 1904; Watford, Herts. 1905. † RSA 8, RSW 1.

BAILEY, William G. Exh. 1889
Stained glass artist. Add: 56 Bolingbroke Grove, Wandsworth Common, London. † RA 1.

BAILEY, William H. Exh. 1881
Landscape painter. Add: Eldon Cottage, Cookham, Berks. † RBA 1.

BAILIE, Mrs. A.E. Exh. 1939-40
34 Brook Street, London. † ROI 2.

BAILLERGEAU, Y. Exh. 1915
89 Rue Vaugirard, Paris. † GI 1.

BAILLIE, Charles Cameron Exh. 1925-31
Glasgow. † GI 4, RSA 1.

BAILLIE, Douglas G. Exh. 1909-21
Paisley 1909; Johnstone, Renfrewshire 1920. † GI 4, RSA 1.

BAILLIE, Mrs. Hilda Exh. 1933
c/o Alexandra College, Dublin. † RHA 3.

BAILLIE, Lady Isabel Exh. 1897-1921
Miniature painter. Add: Polkemmet, Whitburn, Scotland 1897 and 1929; Dinard, France 1898. † RMS 2, RSA 3.

BAILLIE, James Exh. 1900
1 Queensferry Street, Edinburgh. † RSA 1.

BAILLIE, John Exh. 1898-1903
New Zealand Landscapes. Add: London. † BG 36, RBA 3.

BAILLIE, J.T. Exh. 1905
34 St. Andrew Square, Edinburgh. † RSA 1.

BAILLIE, Richard Exh. 1931-32
Deanwood, Pencaitland. † RSA 3.

BAILLIE, Mrs. S.L. Exh. 1908
Barnwell Rectory, Oundle, Northants. † D 3.

BAILLIE, William Exh. 1900-13
Glasgow. † GI 5, RSA 1.

BAILLIE, William b. 1905
Painter and teacher. Studied Glasgow School of Art. Add: 49 Church St. Larkhall, Lanarkshire. † GI 3, RSA 12.

BAILLIE, William Carlisle Exh. 1887-1920
Edinburgh. † GI 3, RSA 6.

BAILLON, Miss M. Exh. 1899
Musters Road, West Bridgford, Notts. † N 1.

BAILWARD, Constance Exh. 1926
† GOU 72.

BAILWARD, Miss M.B. Exh. 1887-91
Landscape painter. Add: 3 Cheyne Walk, Chelsea. † D 15, G 1, L 1, M 2, N 4, RA 1, RBA 1, RI 2.

BAILY, D. Theodor M. Exh. 1928
Isle of Caldy, Nr. Tenby, S. Wales. † RCA 2.

BAILY, Henry J. Exh. 1880
Sculptor. Add: Rowden Abbey, Bromyard. † RA 1.

BAIN, Alex Exh. 1886-90
Stockport, Lancs. † M 2.

BAIN, Alex M. Exh. 1928-32
Woodside, Mauchline. † GI 3.

BAIN, George Exh. 1880-1929
Edinburgh 1880 and 1913, London 1903, Kirkcaldy 1912 and 1921. † GI 1, L 1, RSA 13, RSW 1.

BAIN, Miss Jean Exh. 1912-17
38 York Place, Edinburgh. . † RSA 5, RSW 1.

BAIN, John D. Exh. 1938-39
Cremona, Simpson Crescent, Bathgate. † RSA 2, RSW 2.

BAIN, Marcel A. Exh. 1903-5
18 Rue de St. Petersburg, Paris. † L 2.

BAIN, Walter Exh. 1902
61 Wallace Street, Stirling, N.B. † RSA 1.

BAINBRIDGE, Arthur Exh. 1884
Northcourt, Torquay, Devon. † RI 1.

BAINBRIDGE, Adeline E. Exh. 1890-1900
78 Oxford Terrace, London. † D 3.

BAINBRIDGE, Mrs. A.M. Exh. 1908-9
100 Fellows Road, South Hampstead, London. † RA 2.

BAINBRIDGE, Miss E.M. Exh. 1892
20 Campden Grove, Kensington, London. † L 1.

BAINBRIDGE, Miss L.F. Exh. 1908-10
Sutton, Surrey. † SWA 2.

BAINES, A.C. Exh. 1883
Saxon Villas, Lincoln. † B 2.

BAINES, Blanche Cowper Exh. 1883-93
Hampstead, London. † B 2, D 2, GI 1, L 1, NEA 1, SWA 1.

BAINES, F.R. Exh. 1883
The Elms, Coventry Road, Birmingham. † B 1.

BAINES, Thomas Exh. 1914-38
Portrait painter. Add: Putney, London 1914; Birmingham 1935. † B 1, P 1, RA 3.

BAINSMITH, Henry Exh. 1890-92
Sculptor. Add: Park Studio, Cochrane Street, St. John's Wood, London. † L 2, RA 3, RBA 2.

BAINTON, Kate Exh. 1901
Bewholme, Hull. † RSA 1.

BAIRD, Clarance b. 1895
Interior and figure painter. Studied Liverpool School of Art. Add: 19 Harbord Road, Waterloo, Liverpool 1919 and 1923, Dalkey; Nr. Dublin 1922. † L 8, RCA 10, RHA 2.

BAIRD, Miss D. Exh. 1915-18
Congleton, Cheshire. † RA 2.

BAIRD, Miss Dorothy P. Exh. 1936-37
49 Allesley Old Road, Coventry. † B 4.

BAIRD, Edwin Exh. 1940
39 Bridge Street, Montrose, Angus. † RA 1.

BAIRD, Edward M'Ewan. Exh. 1932-39
Portrait painter. Add: 121 High Street, Montrose N.B. † RA 1, RSA 6.

BAIRD, James Exh. 1882-88
Glasgow. † GI 3, RHA 1.

BAIRD, Johnstone Exh. 1910-30
Painter and etcher. Studied Glasgow School of Art 1900. Naval architect with Admiralty 1917-19. Travelled widely on the continent. Add: London. † AB 1, CON 22, L 1, RSA 2.

BAIRD, Miss Nina Exh. 1904-9
Urie, Stonehaven, N.B. † RA 6.

BAIRD, Nathaniel Hughes John* b. 1865
Portrait and landscape painter. R.O.I. 1897. Add: Kelso 1880; Edinburgh 1881; Dawlish, Devon 1882; Topsham, Devon 1918; Horsham, Sussex 1921; Rockmell, Nr. Lewes, Sussex 1925; Henley on Thames, Oxon 1934. † B 2, GI 11, L 18, M 1, NG 1, RA 32, RBA 3, RI 29, ROI 60, RSA 20.

BAIRD, Robert Exh. 1880-81
Edinburgh. † GI 1, RSA 2.

BAIRD, William* Exh. 1881-87
Landscape painter. Add: 115 High Street, Portobello. † DOW 4, RSA 5.

BAIRD, William Baptiste* b. 1847
Domestic genre painter. b. Chicago. Add: 3 Rue Odessa, Paris 1882-99. † B 4, GI 10. L 4, RA 17, ROI 1.

BAIRNSFATHER, E.H. Exh. 1932-35
London 1932; Godalming, Surrey 1935. † RBA 3, SWA 1.

BAIRSTOW, F. Exh. 1919
† I 1.

BAIRSTOW, Mrs. Nancy Exh. 1924-37
Miniature painter. b. Wolstanton, Staffs. Add: London 1926. † L 7, RA 10, RI 35, RMS 9.

BAKEL, Van See V

BAKER, Miss A. Exh. 1890
7 Austin Terrace, Egremont, Cheshire. † L 2.

BAKER, Annette Exh. 1889-1928
Mrs. W.D. Gloag. Flower painter. Add: London. † M 3, NEA 1, P 1, RA 8, RBA 7, ROI 4, SWA 6.

BAKER, Arthur Exh. 1889
Sporting painter. Add: 36 Upper Grosvenor Road, Tunbridge Wells. † RBA 1.

BAKER, Arthur Exh. 1881-95
Architect. Add: Kensington, London. † RA 3, RCA 16.

BAKER, Miss Alice E.J. Exh. 1880-84
Portrait painter. Add: 4 Hyde Park Square, London. † D 1, RA 2.

BAKER, A.G. Exh. 1933
Crossthorne, Berks. † SWA 1.

BAKER, A.L. Exh. 1923
† SWA 2.

BAKER, Miss A.M. Exh. 1915
Reston Oatlands Park, Weybridge. † RA 1.

BAKER, Arthur P. Exh. 1882-86
Edinburgh. † L 1, RSA 3.

BAKER, Alfred Rawlings b. 1865
Portrait and landscape painter. Studied Hartley School of Art, Southampton; Julians, Paris. Add: Southampton 1885; Belfast 1891. † L 1, NG 5, RA 11, RBA 1, RHA 15, RI 2, WG 87.

BAKER, Alice S. Exh. 1922-24
† SWA 2.

BAKER, Blanche Exh. 1886-1927
Watercolour landscape painter. Studied Bristol Academy. A.S.W.A. 1895. Add: Bristol 1880; London 1890. † ALP 31, B 3, BG 4, L 19, M 2, NG 17, RA 17, RBA 1, RHA 3, RI 10, RSW 1, SWA 9.

BAKER, Col. Bernard GranvilleExh. 1914-30
Military painter. Add: London 1914; Beccles, Suffolk 1929. † L 2, LS 3.

BAKER, Cyril Exh. 1940
Sculptor. Add: 20 Walwyn Avenue, South Bromley, Kent. † RA 1.

BAKER, Miss C.A. Exh. 1907-14
Chester 1907; London 1914. † L 2.

BAKER, Miss C.E. Exh. 1912-15
Ascham St. Vincents, Eastbourne. † RA 2.

BAKER, Charles H. Collins b. 1880
Landscape painter and author. ("Lely and Stuart Portrait Painters" 1912, "Crome" 1921 "Dutch XVIIth Century Painting" 1926 etc) Keeper and secretary National Gallery; Head of Research in Art History, Huntingdon Library, California. N.E.A. 1921 (Hon. Sec. 1921-25). Add: London 1907-32. † G 6, GOU 3, LS 4, M 1, NEA 31, RA 2.

BAKER, C.M. Exh. 1909
40 Mapperley Road, Nottingham. † N 2.

BAKER, Caroline M. Exh. 1921-40
London. † GI 1, L 1, RA 2, RCA 2, RHA 1, ROI 3, RSA 11, SWA 1.

BAKER, Miss E. Exh. 1902-3
3 Tennyson Mansions, Cheyne Row, London. † SWA 3.

BAKER, Edmund Exh. 1898-1902
16 Albert Place, Stirling, N.B. GI 1, RSA 4.

BAKER, Ethelwyn Exh. 1932-33
Sculptor and watercolour painter. b. Belfast. Add: 3 Cockloft Studios, St. John's Wood, London. † L 2, RA 2, RBA 1.

BAKER, Evangeline Exh. 1890-1915
Domestic Painter. Add: London 1890; Coldingham, Berwicks 1892; Kirriemuir, Forfar 1895; Glasgow 1897. † GI 29, L 10, M 1, RBA 9, RI 1, RSA 33.

BAKER, E.H. Exh. 1895-96
Nottingham. † N 2.

BAKER, Emily W. Exh. 1904-31
Married Oliver B. q.v. Add: Coleshill, Warwicks 1904, Stratford on Avon 1906. † B 5, L 1, RCA 12, RI 1.

BAKER, Frances Exh. 1897-1921
Mrs. Kennedy Cahill. Add: Rosses Point, Co. Sligo 1900; Dublin 1916. † I 2, L 2, LS 5. NEA 5, RA 2. RHA 21, ROI 1.

BAKER, Frank Exh. 1920-40
Watercolour landscape painter. Add: 80 Stanford Avenue, Brighton, Sussex. † B 3, D 2, L 1, RA 1.

BAKER, Frederick W. Exh. 1881-1900
Coastal and landscape painter. Add: London 1881; The Lizard, Cornwall 1898. † B 14, D 2, GI 1, RA 19, RBA 7, RHA 11, RI 3, ROI 14.

BAKER, Geoffrey Alan* b. 1881
Landscape painter. Studied Canterbury Art School and Royal College of Art. Principal Bournemouth Art School. Add: Faversham, Kent 1908; Brighton 1911; Christchurch, Hants 1916. † RA 8.

BAKER, Gladys Marguerite b. 1889
Portrait painter and decorator. Studied St. John's Wood School, R.A. School. S.W.A. 1932. Add: London. † I 2, L 1, RA 5, RBA 4, RI 10, SWA 34.

BAKER, Sir Herbert 1862-1946
Architect. A principal architect to Imperial War Graves Commission; collaborating architect for New Delhi for Gov. of India; Architect to Gov. of Kenya; Architect to Bank of England. Among works: Groote Schuur Rhodes Memorial, Cape Town; reconstruction of Bank of England. . A.R.A. 1922, R.A. 1932. Add: London and Owletts, Cobham, Kent. † GI 14, RA 48, RSA 14.

BAKER, Herbert Exh. 1880-1929
Landscape painter. N.S.A. 1882, V.P.N.S.A. 1908-17. Add: Basford, Notts. 1880; Ruddington, Notts. 1912. † N 154.

BAKER, H.E. Exh. 1900-39
Landscape painter. A.N.S.A. 1932. Add: Sandiacre, Derbys. † N 31.

BAKER, Miss H. Isabel Exh. 1892
95 Colmore Row, Birmingham. † B 2.

BAKER, Miss Julia Exh. 1900-10
27 Holywood Road, Fulham Road, London. † RA 2, RMS 1.

BAKER, J.W. Exh. 1918-33
6 Warwick Drive, Liscard, Cheshire. † L 15.

BAKER, Leonard Exh. 1884
22 Albert Place, Stirling. † RSA 1.

BAKER, Leślie Exh. 1883-87
Dublin. † RHA 3.

BAKER, Miss Lily A. Exh. 1899
173 Rathgar Road, Dublin. † RHA 1.

BAKER, Miss L.B. Exh. 1914
15 Eldon Road, Kensington, London. † RA 1.

BAKER, Mrs. L. de C. Exh. 1902
30 Liverpool Road, Thornton Heath, Surrey. † SWA 1.

BAKER, Miss L.H. Exh. 1883
Augustus Road, Edgbaston, Birmingham. † B 1.

BAKER, Miss Lilian L. Exh. 1899-1905
3 Ninian Road, Cardiff. † L 1, RCA 2, SWA 3.

BAKER, Mary b. 1897
Watercolour painter and illustrator of children's books. Add: Runcorn, Cheshire 1926; Leominster, Herefords 1933. † L 4, RCA 4.

BAKER, Miss M.A.E. Exh. 1924-35
Flower painter. Add: Stourbridge 1926; Bournemouth, Hants. 1935. † B 4, RA 1.

BAKER, Muriel Isabella Exh. 1908-1923
nee Alexander, married Charles H. Collins. B. q.v. Add: London. † BG 1, G 3, LS 5, NEA 4.

BAKER, Mabel O. Exh. 1913-19
Portrait painter. Add: Weybridge, Surrey. † RA 5.

BAKER, Miss M.S. Exh. 1908
70 bis Rue Notre Dame des Champs, Paris. † RA 2.

BAKER, N. Exh. 1882
104 Eversley Street, Liverpool. † L 1.

BAKER, Miss Normanhurst Exh. 1899
Upper Teddington, Middlesex. † SWA 1.

BAKER, Oliver b. 1856
Landscape painter. Son of Samuel Henry B. q.v. R.B.S.A. 1884, R.E. 1881. Add: Edgbaston, Birmingham 1880; Coleshill, Birmingham 1904; Stratford on Avon 1906. † B 108, GI 1, L 45, BG 4, RA 7, RBA 2, RCA 75, RE 25, ROI 1, RSW 2.

BAKER, Percy Bryant b. 1881
Sculptor. London 1908. † L 2, LS 7, RA 21.

BAKER, Robert P. b. 1886
Sculptor. London 1912-15. † RA 5.

BAKER, Richard S. Exh. 1898-1927
Cork. † RHA 4.

BAKER, Sidney. Exh. 1881-83
Woody landscape painter. Add: 28 Alma Square, London. † M 2, RBA 6, RHA 1.

BAKER, Miss Silvia Exh. 1928-37
10 Alfred Place, London. † NEA 5, RBA 2, RED 2.

BAKER, Mrs. Sophia Exh. 1906-7
3 Haling Park Road, South Croydon. † RA 2, RMS 1.

BAKER, Samuel Henry* 1824-1909
Landscape painter and watercolourist. Studied Birmingham School of Design; the Birmingham Society and with J.P. Pettitt. R.B.S.A. 1868, R.E. 1882. Add: 101 Gough Road, Edgbaston, Birmingham. † B 146, GI 2, L 26, M 4, NG 2, RA 4, RBA 7, RCA 12, RE 17, RI 8, ROI 6, RSW 1.

BAKER, S. Howard Exh. 1932-36
Glasgow. † GI 2.

BAKER, Thomas Exh. 1882
Fruit painter. Royal Art Gallery, Weymouth, Dorset. † L 2, RA 1.

BAKER, T.E. Exh. 1893
St. Margaret's Cottage, Coldingham, N.B. † GI 1.

BAKER, Violet S. Exh. 1913-15
London 1913; Oxford 1915. † RA 3.

BAKER, W. Moseley Exh. 1883-1936
Landscape painter. Add: Birmingham. † AB 1, B 20.

BAKER, W.R. Exh. 1882-1924
Liverpool. † L 3.

BAKEWELL, Esther M. Exh. 1885-93
Landscape and figure painter. Add: Hampstead, London. † B 3, GI 1, M 2, RA 2, RBA 3, RID 5, SWA 3.

BAKEWELL, Henrietta Exh. 1880-95
Landscape and flower painter. Add: South Hill Park, Hampstead, London. † B 7, L 4, M 1, RI 1, ROI 1, SWA 2.

BAKEWELL, Miss J. Exh. 1917
Streatham Hill, London. † SWA 2.

BAKEWELL, W. Exh. 1902
Architect. 38 Park Square, Leeds. † RA 3.

BAKST, Leon* 1866-1924
Russian painter and stage designer. Studied Moscow and Paris. Designed for Diaghilev. † FIN 277, I 68.

BALACEANO, Alexandra S. Exh. 1935
Sculptor. 7 Joubert Mansions, Jubilee Place, London. † RA 1.

BALAY, J.D. Exh. 1883
19 Rue de Sevres, Ville d'Avray, Seine-et-Oise, France. † GI 1.

BALDING, Alfred Exh. 1887-95
Windsor Villa, Wisbech, Cambs. † RI 1, ROI 2.

BALDOCK, Charles E.M. Exh. 1890-1903
N.S.A. 1897. Add: Nottingham 1890; Cropwell Bishop, Nr. Nottingham 1900. † N 33, RA 1.

BALDOCK, James Walsham* d. c.1897
Animal and sporting painter. N.S.A. 1882. Add: Worksop, 1880; Nottingham 1884. † D 1, L 1, M 1, N 69, RBA 5, RI 6.

BALDREY, Samuel H. Exh. 1897-99
Coastal and landscape painter. Add: 52 Portsdown Road, Maida Vale, London. † RA 3, RBA 1.

BALDRY, Alfred Lys b. 1858
Landscape painter and art critic ("Birmingham Daily Post" and the "Globe"). b. Torquay, Devon. Studied Royal College of Art and under Albert Moore. Add: London 1885; Marlow, Bucks. 1912. † B 11, GI 1, GOU 5, L 9, M 7, NEA 18, NG 11, RBA 3, RI 9, ROI 2.

BALDRY, Miss Grace* Exh. 1897
Portrait painter. 53 Moscow Road, Bayswater, London. † RA 1.

BALDRY, Harry. Exh. 1887-90
Portrait painter. Add: London. † B 1, G 1, M 1, RA 6, TOO 1.

BALDWIN, Archibald Exh. 1894-1900
Landscape painter. Add: Manchester 1894; Walmer, Kent 1900. † L 1, M 3, RA 3.

BALDWIN, Miss A. Josephine Exh. 1909
34 Jewry Street, Winchester. † B 1.

BALDWIN, Mrs. Edith Brake Exh. 1913-40
6 Phillimore Terrace, London 1913; Church Stretton, Yorks. 1939. † I 13, L 1, RI 3, ROI 2, SWA 5.

BALDWIN, Frank S. Exh. 1930-39
Stained glass artist. Add: 29 Minster Road, Sundridge Park, Bromley, Kent. † RA 2.

BALDWIN, Frederick William b. 1899
Pencil, pen and watercolour artist. Self taught. Add: Westhall, Nr. Halesworth, Suffolk 1934. † RA 8, RBA 2.

BALDWIN, Henry C. Exh. 1898
10 Netherall Gardens, Hampstead, London. † RA 1.

BALDWIN, J. Brake 1885-1916
Studied Heatherleys. Add: 6 Phillimore Terrace, Kensington, London 1911. † I 4, RA 1, ROI 3.

BALDWIN, Lane Exh. 1929-36
Stained glass artist. Add: Willesden, London 1929; Greenford, Middlesex 1933. † RA 4.

BALDWIN, M. Brake Exh. 1933-38
Mrs. J.L. Lochhead. Add: 6 Phillimore Terrace, London. † SWA 2.

BALDWIN, P. Brake Exh. 1940
Rose Cottage, Little Stretton, Church Stretton, Yorks. † SWA 1.

BALDWIN, Robert Exh. 1924
Stained glass artist. Add: 20 Droop Street, Queen's Park, London. † RA 3.

BALDWIN, R.W. Exh. 1936
Watercolour landscape painter. † FIN 2.

BALDWIN, W.H. Exh. 1885
8 South Parade, Manchester. † M 1.

BALDWIN, William Wallis
Exh. 1884-87 and 1928
Architect. Add: Queen Anne's Grove, Bush Hill Park, Enfield, Middlesex 1884. † D 2, L 3, M 3, RA 2.

BALDWIN, W.X. Exh. 1889
Bryn Tawel, Dolwyddelen, N. Wales. † M 1.

BALDWIN-GRIFFITH, M. Exh. 1929
† NEA 1.

BALDWYN, Charles H.C. Exh. 1887-1905
Bird painter. Add: Worcester. † L 3, RA 14, RBA 2, RI 3.

BALE, Alice M.E.* Exh. 1933
Portrait painter. Add: c/o Rivercourt, Maldon, Essex. † RA 1.

BALE, Edwin 1838-1923
Domestic and figure and landscape painter. A.R.I. 1876, R.I. 1879, R.O.I. 1883. Add: London † AG 6, B 6, L 10, M 6, P 1, RA 29, RI 70, ROI 6, TOO 1.

BALE, T.C.* Exh. 1886
c/o W.H. Stone, 1 Park Avenue, Slade Lane, Levenshulme. † M 2.

BALFOUR, Andrew Exh. 1901-5
110 Mains Street, Blythwood Square, Glasgow. † GI 4.

BALFOUR, J. Lawson Exh. 1892-1909
Domestic painter. Add: London 1899 and 1900; Bangor, Co. Down, Ireland 1899. † RA 1, RBA 2, RI 1, ROI 1.

BALFOUR, Maxwell Exh. 1901-5
Landscape and figure painter. Add: 118 Cheyne Walk, Chelsea, London. † NEA 3, P 1, RA 2.

BALFOUR, Robert S. Exh. 1897-1905
London. † RA 6.

BALFOUR-BROWNE, Miss Eileen F.
Exh. 1931-33
Wood engraver. Add: Larkhill, Abingdon, Berks. † RA 3.

BALFOUR-BROWNE, Vincent b. 1880
Watercolour sporting painter. Add: Dumfries; and London. Exh. 1907-36. † FIN 269.

BALFOUR-MELVILLE, B. Exh. 1908-25
Pilrig House, Edinburgh. † RSA 1, RSW 1.

BALL, A.C. Exh. 1908
Ithaca, Grove Park Road, Mottingham, Kent. † RA 2.

BALL, Arthur E. Exh. 1880-85
Landscape painter. Add: Putney, Surrey 1880; Richmond, Surrey 1885. † AG 1, D 1, RA 5, RBA 2, RE 2.

BALL, Arthur J. Exh. 1915-28
Wilford, Notts. 1915; Nottingham 1919; Sherwood, Notts. 1923. † N 17

BALL, Charles E. Exh. 1914-18
Staines, Middlesex 1914; Torquay, Devon 1918. † LS 14.

BALL, Miss Christine M. Exh. 1929-35
84 Haywood Road, Mapperley, Notts. † N 4.

BALL, Miss Ethel Exh. 1917-40
Sculptor. Add: 28 Waterloo Road, Dublin. † G 1, RA 1, RHA 57, RMS 1, RSA 1.

BALL, E.C. Exh. 1886
Laurel House, Heald Place, Rusholme. † M 1.

BALL, Fred Hammersley Exh. 1908-38
A.N.S.A. 1908, N.S.A. 1910, V.P.N.S.A. 1931. Add: Hillcrest, Haywood Road, Mapperley, Notts. † N 76, RA 4.

BALL, F.J. Exh. 1910-11
73 Melbourne Street, Derby. † N 3.

BALL, Gertrude Exh. 1926-40
Watercolour landscape painter and wood engraver. b. Auckland, New Zealand. Studied Regent Street Polytechnic. Add: London. † RA 8, RBA 1, SWA 5.

BALL, G.L. Meyer Exh. 1897
4 Nella Villas, Grove Road, Windsor. † NG 1.

BALL, Henry Exh. 1919-39
Nottingham. † N 55.

BALL, Mrs. Hylda Exh. 1916
† LS 3.

BALL, Joseph Exh. 1894
Architect. Add: 15 Clement's Inn, Strand, London. † RA 1.

BALL, Joseph Lancaster Exh. 1885 and 1912
Architect. R.B.S.A. 1923. Add: Warwick Chambers, Corporation Street, Birmingham. † RA 3.

BALL, John P. Exh. 1909-14
6 Cheapside, Liverpool. † L 3.

BALL, Miss K. Exh. 1901
Stanley Road, Hoylake, Cheshire. † L 1.

BALL, Miss Lois Exh. 1912-15
Sedgley House, The Park, Nottingham. A.N.S.A. 1915. † N 14.

BALL, Miss Mary Exh. 1925
Western House, The Park, Nottingham. † N 1.

BALL, Maude Mary b. 1883
Miniaturist and oil painter. Studied R.H.A. and Dublin Metropolitan School of Art. Add: 28 Waterloo Road, Dublin. † RCA 1, RHA 47.

BALL, Percival Exh. 1880-82
Sculptor, London. † RA 5.

BALL, Robert b. 1918
11 Norton Crescent, Birmingham 1937-40. † B 8, NEA 1.

BALL, Tom b. 1888
Watercolour landscape and marine painter. Add: High Street, Budleigh Salterton, Devon 1922-30. † B 8.

BALL, Wilfred Williams 1853-1917
Watercolour landscape and marine painter and etcher. Travelled Continent and Egypt. Died from heat-stroke in Khartoum. R.B.A. 1899, R.E. 1882. Add: Putney 1880; London 1881 and 1906; Godalming, Surrey 1899; Lymington, Hants. 1911. † AB 4, AG 165, D 8, DOW 1, FIN 620, G 9, GI 3, L 3, LEI 163, M 4, NG 23, RA 58, RBA 18, RE 63, RI 16, RID 2.

BALLACHEY, Mary E. Exh. 1885-1904
Flower painter. Add: Dereham, Norfolk 1885; Melton Constable, Norfolk 1893; Norwich 1900; Oxford 1901. † M 3, RI 1, SWA 13.

BALLANCE, Marjorie H. Exh. 1921-29
Painter and woodcut artist. Add: St. Ives, Cornwall 1921; Petersfield, Hants 1928; Cheltenham 1929. † B 14, L 3.

BALLANCE, Percy des Carrieres b.1899
Watercolour landscape painter. b. Birmingham. Add: St. Ives, Cornwall 1919; Naunton, Glos. 1927; Wells, Somerset 1932. † B 3, CG 32, L 1, RA 5, RI 7, ROI 2.

BALLANTINE, James Exh. 1900-2
42 George Street, Edinburgh. † RSA 3.

BALLANTINE, Mary Exh. 1920-39
Married Robert Wilkie q.v. Add: Edinburgh 1920; Glasgow 1927. † GI 1, RSA 11.

BALLANTINE, Miss O. Exh. 1919
121 Victoria Park Road, London. † SWA 1.

BALLANTYNE, Miss Edith Exh. 1880-87
Domestic Painter. Add: London. † L 2, RA 3, RBA 2, RSA 5.

BALLANTYNE, Jean Exh. 1902-11
Mrs. A. Lowis. Add: London. † L 2, RA 4, RSA 6.

BALLANTYNE, John* 1815-1897
Portrait and historical genre painter. Studied Edinburgh. Teacher at Trustee's Academy, Edinburgh. A.R.S.A. 1841, R.S.A. 1860. Add: London 1880; Melksham, Wilts. 1886. † RA 5, RBA 1, RSA 5, RSW 1.

BALLANTYNE, John d. c.1920
Edinburgh 1898 and 1905; Glasgow 1900. † GI 2, RSA 6, RSW 2.

BALLANTYNE, R.M. Exh. 1880-85
London Hill, Harrow. † RA 5.

BALLANTYNE, Thomas Exh. 1897
86 York Street, Westminster, London. † RA 1.

BALLARD, Miss Exh. 1893
Philipburn, Selkirk, N.B. † D 1.

BALLARD, Miss Alice E. Exh. 1897
Ravenscroft Park, High Barnet. † RA 2.

BALLARD, Miss Frances H. Exh. 1934-35
Portrait painter. Add: 10 The Avenue, Orpington, Kent. † RA 3.

BALLARD, Mrs. Freda Mary Exh. 1923
† D 4.

BALLARD, Miss Helen Exh. 1936-38
Miniature painter. Add. 78 Redcliffe Gardens, London. † RA 2, RMS 2, RSA 1.

BALLARD, Miss M.H. Exh. 1891
The Hollies, Flixton. † M 1.

BALLARD, Dr. P.B. Exh. 1923-28
Sutton Court Road, London. † D 14, RI 7.

BALLARDIE, J. de Caynoth Exh. 1887-88
14 West Princes Street, Glasgow. † GI 1, RSA 1.

BALLAVOINE, Jules Frederic Exh. 1882
French painter. † M 1.

BALLEMENT, Miss D. Exh. 1902
Greenock, N.B. † RSA 1.

BALLEMENT, L. Alexandra Exh. 1900-2
Greenock. N.B. † GI 2, L 1, RSA 1.

BALL-HUGHES, Georgina Exh. 1889
Miniature portrait painter. Add: 5 Lyndhurst Road, Hampstead, London. † RA 1.

BALLIN, Auguste* Exh. 1881-99
Landscape and marine painter and etcher. R.E. 1881. Add: St. Andresse, Boston Road, Brentford, Essex. † GI 3, L 14, RA 3, RBA 2, RE 18, RHA 3, ROI 5.

BALLIN, John Exh. 1880-81
Engraver. Add: 141 Holland Road, Kensington, London. † RA 3.

BALLINGALL, Alex Exh. 1880-1909
Edinburgh. † AG 1, GI 1, RI 1, RSA 73.

BALLINGALL, John Exh. 1896-99
Largs, N.B. † RSA 3.

BALLOCH, W.C. Exh. 1938-39
Landscape painter. Add: 11 Haywood Road, Mapperley, Nottingham. † N 5.

BALMAIN, Kenneth Field b. 1890
Landscape painter and photographer. Studied Edinburgh College of Art and R.S.A. Life School. Served R.A.F. 1914-19. Add: Edinburgh 1913; North Berwick 1919. † RSA 10.

BALMER, Clinton Exh. 1901-9
Liverpool. † L 9.

BALMET, Louis Exh. 1909
7 Rue de Nemours, Paris. † L 1.

BALMFORD, Hurst b. 1871
Portrait and landscape painter. Studied Royal College of Art and Julians, Paris. Headmaster Morecambe School of Art. Add: Garstang, Lancs. 1914; St. Ives, Cornwall 1926. † L 3, RA 8, RCA 1, RSA 1.

BALMFORD, Mary A. Exh. 1932
West Kensington, London. † SWA 1.

BALMFORTH, Miss Phyllis Exh. 1913-16
Devon Villa, Eaton Street, Liscard, Cheshire. † L 5.

BALSHAW, Fred Exh. 1888-1914
Landscape painter. Bolton 1888 and 1901; Manchester 1896. † FIN 4, L 11, M 6, RA 3, RHA 3.

BALSHAW, Florence E. Exh. 1912-40
Abergele, Wales 1912; Colwyn Bay 1921; Ton-y-Pandy, Wales 1935. † L 2, RCA 9.

BALSTON, Tom Exh. 1938
Oil and watercolour painter. † RED 60.

BALY, Miss Evelyn P. Exh. 1928-32
London. † L 2, RA 2, RBA 1, ROI 2.

BALY, Miss Gladys M. Exh. 1903
6 Queen's Mansions, Brook Green, London. † RA 1.

BALYDON, Miss Freda Exh. 1914
Queen's Road, Richmond, Surrey. † RHA 1.

BAMBOROUGH, J. Exh. 1885
7 Dick Place, Edinburgh. † RSA 1.

BAMBRIDGE, Arthur L. Exh. 1891-95
Portrait painter. Add: 57 Bedford Gardens, Kensington, London. † L 1, RA 4, RID 4, ROI 1.

BAMFORD, Miss Annie Exh. 1896-1910
54 Trafalgar Road, Egremont, Cheshire. † L 6.

BAMFORD, Alfred Bennett Exh. 1880-1933
Architectural painter. Add: London 1880 and 1899; Romford 1893; Chelmsford 1906; Chester 1927. † D 6, L 10, RA 9, RBA 3, RHA 11, RI 11, ROI 8.

BAMFORD, D. Exh. 1910
9 Clifford's Inn, London. † RA 1.

BAMFORD, Miss E.M. Exh. 1911
54 Trafalgar Road, Egremont, Cheshire. † L 1.

BAMLER, J.F. Exh. 1921
Landscape painter. Add: Derby Road, Heanor, Notts. † N 1.

BANBURY, William b. 1871
Sculptor and craftsman in metal, wood and stone. b. Leicester. Add: Aberdeen 1908. † RA 6, RSA 13.

BANCROFT, Chris L. Exh. 1923-33
Glan Conway, Wales. † L 3, RCA 10.

BANCROFT, Elias Mollineaux d.1924
Landscape painter. Married to Louisa Mary B. q.v. Add: Manchester 1880. † B 10, FIN 1, L 16, LS 7, M 56, NG 1, RA 19, RBA 10, RCA 93, RI 6, ROI 14.

BANCROFT, John H. Exh. 1925-39
Rustic landscape painter. Add: Derby 1925; Burton Joyce, Notts. 1936. † N 11.

BANCROFT, Louisa Mary Exh. 1895-1939
Flower and miniature painter. nee Heald. Married Elias Mollineaux B. q.v. Add: Manchester 1895; Whitby 1938. † COO 4 L 3, M 13, RCA 67, RMS 1.

BAND, Mrs. Amy L. See COOKE

BAND, George M. Exh. 1927-38
17 Kingsway, Wallasey, Cheshire. † L 1, M 1.

BAND, W.D. Exh. 1930
† L 1.

BANES, Fred M. Exh. 1881
24 Spencer Road, Holloway, London. † RA 1.

BANESS, Mrs. Mary Exh. 1904-5
Hillside, Mells Road, Bath. † D 2.

BANFORD, James Exh. 1937
48 Springfield Road, Glasgow. † GI 1.

BANFORD, L. Exh. 1884
c/o Fowler, 19 Manchester Terrace, Kilburn, London. † D 1.

BANGS, Arthur Exh. 1935
154 Lincoln Road, Bush Hill Park, Enfield. † RBA 2.

BANHOF, Frederick Exh. 1900-12
London. † L 1, M 1, RI 1.

BANISTER, Barbara Gillian Exh. 1930-35
Designer, jeweller, silversmith and enameller. Studied Royal College of Art. † RMS 3.

BANISTER, Frederick Exh. 1890-1907
Outer Temple, London. † RA 2.

BANKART, George P. Exh. 1907-19
London 1907; Richmond, Surrey 1919. † RA 3.

BANKES, William Exh. 1909-37
Served Army First World War. Add: Liverpool. † L 8, RCA 10.

BANKS, A.L. Exh. 1904-5
Royal Institution, Edinburgh. † RSA 2.

BANKS, Miss Annie P. Exh. 1937
20 Spottiswoode Road, Edinburgh. † RSA 1.

BANKS, Constance Exh. 1884
Ravensdene, Scarborough. † SWA 1.
BANKS, Catherine A.* Exh. 1886-1907
nee Eggar. Add: London. † D 6, L 2, RA 1, RI 2.
BANKS, Edmond G. Exh. 1881-90
Landscape painter. Add: Glasgow 1881; Kentish Town, London 1889. † RA 1, RI 2, RSA 1.
BANKS, Edward H. Exh. 1932-40
Architect. Add: Purley, Surrey 1932; Coulsdon, Surrey 1930. † RA 6.
BANKS, George Exh. 1909
31 Synod Hall, Edinburgh. † RSW 1.
BANKS, Harry Exh. 1916-21
Watercolour painter. Add: Thorncombe, Chard, Somerset; and 1 Royal York Crescent, Clifton, Bristol. † L 5, RA 3, RI 2.
BANKS, H.J. Exh. 1923
Lebanon Villa, George Street, Lozells. † B 1.
BANKS, John Exh. 1938
† GI 1.
BANKS, Miss L.J. Exh. 1882-83
48 Grange Loan, Edinburgh. † RSA 2.
BANKS, Miss M.E. Exh. 1920
Portrait miniature painter. Add: 13 Mount Nod Road, Streatham, London. † RA 1.
BANKS, Mrs. Stanley Exh. 1908
The Haven, 276 Portland Street, Southport, Lancs. † L 2.
BANKS, Thomas J.* Exh. 1880
Landscape painter. Add: Goathland via York. † RBA 1.
BANKS, Violet b. 1896
Painter and pottery decorator. Studied Edinburgh College of Art. Add: Edinburgh 1918 and 1928; Kirkcaldy 1920. † GI 1, L 1, RSA 6, RSW 9.
BANKS, William Exh. 1880-89
Edinburgh. † RSA 13.
BANKS, William Lawrence d. 1893
Talwynedd, Llanfairpwllgwyngyll, Anglesea. † D 1, RCA 38.
BANMANN, Miss A. Hilda Exh. 1894
Mrs. C. Kohn. Add: 20 Mulgrave Street, Liverpool. † L 2.
BANNATYNE, Annie M. Exh. 1888
15 Lansdowne Crescent, Edinburgh. † RSA 1.
BANNATYNE, J.G. Exh. 1888
c/o W.A. Smith, 22 Mortimer Street, London. † GI 3, RI 1.
BANNATYNE, John James* 1836-1911
Landscape and watercolour painter. R.S.W. 1878. Add: London 1880; Glasgow 1891. † B 2, D 33, DOW 4, GI 84, L 8, M 8, RA 5, RBA 9, RI 13, ROI 10, RSA 4, RSW 70, TOO 1.
BANNATYNE, Miss Mary Exh. 1880-81
9 Nicoll Road, Harlesden, London. † SWA 2.
BANNER, Alex Exh. 1880-90
Art teacher. Add: Glasgow. † GI 2.
BANNER, Alf Exh. 1882-1911
Birmingham 1882 and 1889; London 1887; Kidderminster 1911. † B 54, M 1, RHA 2.
BANNER, Delmar Harmood b. 1896
Landscape, portrait and figure painter. Studied Regent Street Polytechnic 1919-27. b. Freiburg im Breisgau. Add: London 1925; Wadhurst, Sussex 1933. † L 1, P 2, RA 3, RI 5.
BANNER, E.H. Exh. 1890
26 North John Street, Liverpool. † L 1.
BANNER, Miss Florence E. Exh. 1908-22
c/o R. Jackson and Sons, 3 Slater Street, Liverpool. † L 6.
BANNER, Hugh Harmood b. 1865
Painter and etcher. Son of Alex B. q.v. Studied Glasgow School of Art and City of London School. Add: Glasgow 1887; Maxweltown, Dumfries 1906; Carlisle 1928. † GI 2, L 4, P 1.
BANNER, W.W. Exh. 1883
Raleigh House, Bristol Road, mingham. † B 1.
BANNERMAN, Charles Exh. 1933
47 Baker Street, Aberdeen. † SA 1.
BANNERMAN, Mrs. Frances Exh. 1880-91
Figure painter. Add: Beaumont Rise, Gt. Marlow, Bucks. † L 4, RA 3, RBA 3.
BANNERMAN, Hamlet Exh. 1880-91
Landscape and figure painter. N.E.A. 1889-90. Add: London 1880; Gt. Marlow 1890. † L 5, RA 9, RBA 16.
BANNIN, Miss Kate Exh. 1887-90
Sculptor. Add: London. † L 1, RA 3, RBA 3.
BANNISTER, F.W. Exh. 1934-40
41 Dunsford Road, Bearwood. † B 4.
BANNISTER, Isabel Exh. 1922-35
Painter and miniaturist. Add: Richmond, Surrey. † RI 39, SWA 2.
BANNISTER, W.E. Exh. 1919
3 Merrylee Wood, Newlands, Glasgow. † GI 1.
BANNON, Mrs. H.W. Exh. 1898
1 Hyde Park Terrace, London. † D 2.
BANTING, John F. Exh. 1921
Member London Group 1927. † LS 3.
BARAGWANATH, F. Exh. 1909-12
138 Fleet Street, London. † RA 3.
BARALLE, Mlle. Marie Exh. 1903-5
Route de Chatillon 57, Grand Montrouge, Seine, France. † L 3.
BARBASON, M. Exh. 1888
Figure painter. Add: c/o J.C. Cooper, 15 George Street, Euston Road, London. † RBA 1.
BARBER, Miss Exh. 1911
Clapham Park, London. † SWA 1.
BARBER, Miss A.C. Exh. 1920-29
London. † D 7, L 1, SWA 1.
BARBER, Alfred R.* Exh. 1880-1908
Animal painter. Add: Colchester. † B 9, L 3, RBA 6, ROI 13.
BARBER, Charles Burton* 1845-1894
Sporting and animal painter. R.O.I. 1883. Add: Titchfield Road, North Gate, Regents Park, London. † FIN 2, G 1, L 3, M 2, RA 13, ROI 13, TOO 8.
BARBER, C.W. Exh. 1908-14
London. † RA 5.
BARBER, Miss Dorothy M. Exh. 1933
22 Kent Gardens, Ealing, London. † RA 1.
BARBER, Joseph Moseley* Exh. 1880-89
Landscape and genre painter. Add: London. † L 5, RBA 13, RHA 2, RI 2, ROI 6.
BARBER, Marion Exh. 1886
1 Carlton Villas, Wellesley Road, Colchester. † SWA 1.
BARBER, Reginald* Exh. 1882-1908
Figure painter. Add: Ulverston, Lancs. 1882; Manchester 1885. † B 2, D 8, FIN 3, GI 3, L 15, M 34, RA 8, RHA 1, RI 3.
BARBER, Thomas Stanley Exh. 1891
36 Riverdale Road, Highbury, London. † M 1.
BARBER, W. Exh. 1890
George Street, Halifax, Yorks. † RA 1.
BARBER, W.T. Scott Exh. 1880-98
Miniature portrait painter. R.M.S. 1896. Add: London 1880; Clifton, Bristol 1893; Careggi, Florence 1894. † L 1, RA 24, RMS 2, RSA 3.
BARBOSA, A.E.T. Exh. 1923-33
18A Croxteth Road, Liverpool. † L 5.
BARBOSA, Miss M. Exh. 1920-23
18A Croxteth Road, Liverpool. † L 7.
BARBOUR, Miss Margaret S. Exh. 1925
Pitlochry, Scotland. † RSW 1.
BARBROOK, Miss L.H. Exh. 1917
Crowborough, Sussex. † SWA 1.
BARBUDO* Exh. 1886-91
† TOO 7.
BARCH, Bernard M. Exh. 1929
School of Architecture, Liverpool University. † L 1.
BARCLAY, Miss Ada Exh. 1880-1914
Edinburgh 1880; London 1910. † B 1, LS 3, RA 1, RSA 14.
BARCLAY, A.P. Exh. 1880
Landscape painter. Add: 35 St. Julian's Road, Kilburn, London. † D 1.
BARCLAY, A. Patterson. Exh. 1934-35
Edinburgh. † RSA 2.
BARCLAY, Miss A.R. Exh. 1896
West End Lane, Hampstead, London. † SWA 3.
BARCLAY, David Exh. 1896-1905
Glasgow. † GI 9, RSA 4.
BARCLAY, Miss D.C. Exh. 1917
Harestone Heights, White Hill, Caterham, Surrey. † RA 1.
BARCLAY, Edgar* 1824-c.1913
Landscape and genre painter. Studied Dresden and Rome. R.O.I. 1883; R.E. 1885. Add: London. †, B 7, G 51, L 17, M 5, NG 44, RA 26, RE 20, ROI 33, TOO 4.
BARCLAY, Miss Gwen Exh. 1928-32
35 Clapham Road, Anfield, Liverpool. † L 4.
BARCLAY, G.H. Exh. 1880-85
Edinburgh. † RSA 3.
BARCLAY, H. Exh. 1905
245 St. Vincent Street, Glasgow. † GI 3.
BARCLAY, Mrs. Hubert Exh. 1923
Watercolour landscape painter (Japan, Canada, Europe, Middle East and India). † BK 71.
BARCLAY, Helen Lee Exh. 1938-40
101 East Claremont Street, Edinburgh. † GI 1, RSA 3.
BARCLAY, James Exh. 1899
245 St. Vincent Street. Glasgow. † GI 1.
BARCLAY, J. Edward Exh. 1884-88
Landscape painter. Add: London. † RBA 1, ROI 1.
BARCLAY, John Maclaren 1811-1886
Portrait painter. A.R.S.A. 1863, R.S.A. 1871. Treasurer 1884-86. Add: 11 Forres Street, Edinburgh 1880. † GI 1, RSA 30.
BARCLAY, John R.* Exh. 1921-25
28 Albany Street, London. † RSW 3.
BARCLAY, John Rankine b. 1884
Painter and etcher. Studied Edinburgh and Continent (Carnegie travelling scholarship and Guthrie award). Add: Edinburgh 1909; St. Ives, Cornwall 1937. † GI 8, RA 1, RSA 52, RSW 2.
BARCLAY, Miss Maben Exh. 1922-27
5 Randolph Place, Edinburgh. † RSA 3, RSW 1.
BARCLAY, Miss Millicent Exh. 1905-14
32 Wellington Road, Dublin. † RHA 13.
BARCLAY, Miss Rachel Exh. 1911-16
Garden and landscape painter. Add: Carenver, Stracey Road, Falmouth, Cornwall. † WG 98.

BARCLAY, William Exh. 1881-98
Dundee. † RSA 5.
BARCLAY, William James Exh. 1880
Bonvil, Cupar, Fife. † RSA 1.
BARDEN, Mrs. Dora Exh. 1892-1910
Sallymount Terrace, Dublin. † RHA 9.
BARDILI, Beatrice Exh. 1909
† LS 3.
BARDILL, Ralph William 1876-1935
Landscape and coastal painter. Studied Julians, Paris. Add: St. Helens, Lancs. 1896; Glan Conway, N. Wales 1919. † FIN 2, L 74, RA 3, RCA 132, RI 2.
BARDON, Jean Exh. 1909
† LS 3.
BARDSLEY, Geo. Exh. 1905
7 King's Road, Alexandra Park, Manchester. † L 1.
BARDSWELL, Miss Emily Exh. 1884
Landscape painter. Add: Ellerslie, Thornton Hill, Wimbledon, London. † L 1.
BARE, Henry Bloomfield Exh. 1884-1911
Decorative painter. Add: Liverpool. † L 32, RA 1.
BARE, Miss Ruth Exh. 1902-6
Liverpool. † L 7.
BARET, Madame D. Exh. 1888
40 Rue d'Anjou, Paris. † L 2.
BARFIELD, Kenneth C. Exh. 1914-29
Whetstone, Nr. Leicester 1914; Liverpool 1920. † L 11.
BARFIELD, Lawrence Exh. 1880-81
Leicester. † N 2.
BARFIELD, Thomas Charles b. 1858
Painter and modeller. Studied Leicester School of Art, RA Schools and Antwerp. Art master Leicester School of Art; Chief Art Instructor Leicester County Council. Add: Leicester 1880; Rugby 1901; Hinckley 1921. † B 3. N 5, RA 1, RI 2.
BARGER, Miss Margaret Exh. 1937
48 St. Albans Road, Edinburgh. † RSA 1.
BARGMAN, F.J. Exh. 1904-8
The Brambles, Cliftonville, Dorking. † B 1, RA 3.
BARHAM, Miss Sybil Exh. 1910
The Priests House. Bromsgrove. † B 1.
BARHAM-HARRIS, Mrs. H. Exh. 1919-20
7 Carlisle Studios, 296 King's Road, London. † RA 1, SWA 2.
BARILLOT, Leon* Exh. 1883-1907
Paris. † FIN 1, GI 4, L 2.
BARING, Miss B.R. Exh. 1891
Rostrevor, Co. Down, Ireland. † L 1.
BARING, Miss Daphne Exh. 1921-23
26A Bryanston Square, London. † G 1, NEA 2.
BARING, Lady Emma Exh. 1888
Landscape painter. Add: 4 Hamilton Place, Piccadilly, London. † RI 1.
BARING, Col. F. Exh. 1881
† G 1.
BARISON, G.* Exh. 1889
25 Queen Anne Street, London. † B 1.
BARK, Miss C. Exh. 1892
Stanley Park, Litherland, Liverpool. † L 1.
BARK, Miss Edith A. Exh. 1882-1924
Stanley Park, Litherland, Liverpool 1882; Waterloo, Liverpool 1919. † L 26.
BARK, Miss Florence Exh. 1910-12
Walton, Liverpool 1910; Colby, I.O.M. 1912. † L 4.
BARK, Miss L. Exh. 1890-92
Stanley Park, Litherland, Liverpool. † L 5.
BARKAS, H. Dawson d. 1924
Watercolour landscape painter. Add: Reading 1901. † D 4, FIN 62, RA 15, RI 2.
BARKAS, Miss M.B. Exh. 1919
Thornwood, Kew Road, Richmond. † SWA 1.

BARKE, Benjamin John b. 1885
Silversmith. Teacher Coventry School of Art, 1929-40. Add: 7 Earlsdon Avenue, Coventry 1931. † B 5.
BARKER, A.C. Exh. 1908
43 Mill Lane, Liscard, Cheshire. † L 1.
BARKER, Adeline Margery Exh. 1917-38
Landscape, portrait and figure painter. Studied Blackheath Art School and Goldsmiths Art School. Add: 38 Shooter's Hill Road, Blackheath, London. † GI 3, L 3, P 3, RA 12, RCA 1, SWA 8.
BARKER, Anthony Raine Exh. 1908-39
Painter, etcher, lithographer and wood engraver. Add: Harrow 1908; London 1910; Patterdale, Sidcup, Kent 1919. † FIN 1, GI 1, I 10, L 118, LEI 73, M 2, NEA 1, RA 27, RID 1, RSA 2, WG 19.
BARKER, Mrs. Clarissa Exh. 1898-99
Mrs. J.L. Sculptor. 30 Chepstow Villas, Bayswater, London. † L 1, RA 2.
BARKER, Miss Clarissa Exh. 1885-87
Flower painter. Add: Dolgelly, Wales 1885; London 1887. † L 2, RBA 4.
BARKER, Miss Constance D. Exh. 1925
Broadclose, St. Mark's Road, Bath. † L 1.
BARKER, Cicely Mary b. 1895
Watercolour painter of fairies and flowers. Studied Croydon School of Art. Add: The Waldrons, Croydon, Surrey 1913. † RI 1, SWA 11.
BARKER, E. Conyers Exh. 1933
† RSW 2.
BARKER, Miss E.M. Exh. 1912
Carlton in the Willows, Notts. † N 1.
BARKER, Miss E.S. Exh. 1913-17
Mrs. Norman Hope. Add: London. † I 1, RA 1, RI 1, RSW 1, SWA 7.
BARKER, Mrs. E. St. Barbe Exh. 1933-39
5 Hyde Park Place, London. † ROI 6, SWA 1.
BARKER, Ernest William Exh. 1917-18
11 Rathmines Park, Dublin. † RHA 2.
BARKER, Miss F. Exh. 1882
Trent Lodge, Withingham. † M 1.
BARKER, Miss F. Exh. 1887-90
Lenton Boulevard, Nottingham. † N 3.
BARKER, George Exh. 1892-1908
Birmingham. † B 13, RHA 4.
BARKER, H.S. Exh. 1923-27
112 Grosvenor Square, Handsworth, Birmingham. † B 5.
BARKER, J.* Exh. 1931
Watercolour landscape painter. † RED 1.
BARKER, John E. Exh. 1928-33
Watercolour landscape painter. Add: 73 Bath Street, Ilkeston, Derbys. † N 11.
BARKER, John Edward 1889-1953
Oil painter. Studied Bath School of Art and the old Camden School of Art. Exh. 1938. † M 1.
BARKER, J. Lockhart Exh. 1898-1930
Liverpool 1898; Birkenhead 1928. † L 25.
BARKER, Miss Joan M. Exh. 1936-39
Portrait and figure painter. Add: Vaud Studio, 72 St. James's Street, Nottingham. † N 13.
BARKER, James Thomas b. 1884
Figure and landscape painter and stage designer. Studied under Buxton Knight. Producer, designer and owner of the Bijou Marionette Theatre. Add: Oak Cottage, Mill End, Rickmansworth, Herts. 1913-29. † D 1, LS 7, RA 1.
BARKER, Miss Marion Exh. 1883-98
Figure painter. Add: Manchester. † L 3, M 14, RA 1.
BARKER, Miss Margaret Dorothy b. 1907
"Any Morning" purchased by Chantrey Bequest 1929. Add: 22 Castlands Road, Catford, London 1929. † NEA 2.

BARKER, Madeline Graham Exh. 1918-31
Portrait and figure painter. Add: Wimbledon, London. † I 3, RA 9, RMS 2, ROI 1.
BARKER, May H. Exh. 1884-1909
Figure, black and white and relief artist. Add: London.† L 7, LS 3, RA 8, RBA 1, RE 2, SWA 1.
BARKER, Miss M.J. Exh. 1892
6 Gardiner's Row, Dublin. † RHA 2.
BARKER, Miss Nancy C. Exh. 1926
15 Delamere Street, London. † NEA 1.
BARKER, Raymond Turner Exh. 1916
11 Buckingham Street, Strand, London. † RA 1.
BARKER, S.R. Exh. 1910
9 Pennard Mansions, Goldhawk Road, London. † RA 1.
BARKER, Theodore Exh. 1909-16
West Kirby, Cheshire 1909; Liscard, Cheshire 1910; Pendleton, Manchester 1911, Egremont, Cheshire 1912. † L 6.
BARKER, Thomas Jones* 1815-1882
Historical and battle painter. Studied under Horace Vernet in Paris. Add: London 1880.. † GI 1.
BARKER, Wright* Exh. 1885-1935
Figure painter. R.B.A. 1896. Add: Bradford 1885; Edwinstone, Nr. Mansfield, Notts. 1888; Ollerton, Newark, Notts. 1893 and 1905; London 1903; Harrogate, Yorks. 1915. † B 1, L 4, M 1, N 5, NG 1, RA 22, RBA 28, RSA 1.
BARKER, W.D. d. 1889
Landscape painter. Add: Plascock, Trefriw, N. Wales. † D 1, L 21, RCA 14.
BARKHAM, Miss Kathleen A.M. Exh. 1933-40
Miniature portrait painter. Add: Rhianva College, Hunstanton, Norfolk. † RA 7, RMS 1.
BARKIS, Miss Annie Exh. 1880-88
Coldstream, N.B. † RSA 6, SWA 1.
BARKWORTH, Ethel Exh. 1889-93
Figure painter. Add: 3 Ilchester Gardens, Bayswater, London. † RID 8.
BARKWORTH, Miss Emma L. Exh. 1891
Landscape painter. Add: Larchwood, Tunbridge Wells, Kent. † RI 1.
BARKWORTH, Walter T. Exh. 1884-98
Oil landscape painter. Add: Tunbridge Wells, Kent 1884; Dorking, Surrey 1893; London 1898. † B 2, ROI 8.
BARLACH, Ernst 1870-1938
German sculptor. Exh. 1936. † RSA 3.
BARLING, Elsie M. Exh. 1921-25
† GOU 1, I 1, LS 3.
BARLOW, Doris E. Exh. 1936-38
Landscape painter and wood engraver. Add: Mapperley, Nottingham 1936; Nottingham 1938. † N 3.
BARLOW, Miss Edith Mary Exh. 1918-25
Portrait and landscape painter. Travelled N. Africa. Add: Studio, 44 Redcliffe Road, London. † I 2, L 3, WG 23.
BARLOW, Miss Florence E. Exh. 1882-88
Watercolour bird, animal and flower painter. Add: 55 Loughborough Park, Brixton, London. † D 4, L 2, RA 2, RBA 6.
BARLOW, Miss G.B. Exh. 1934
Western Bank, Derby. † RBA 1.
BARLOW, Hannah Bolton Exh. 1880-91
Sculptor. Add: 55 Loughborough Park, Brixton, London. † D 7, L 6, RA 11, RBA 10, SWA 2.
BARLOW, Miss J.E.M. Exh. 1893
21 Philbeach Gardens, London. † D 5.
BARLOW, J.H. Exh. 1915-26
44 Rodney Street. Liverpool. † L 9.

BARLOW, John Noble* 1861-1917
Landscape and sky painter. R.B.A. 1896, R.O.I. 1916. b. Manchester. Add: 9 Barnoon Terrace, St. Ives, Cornwall 1893-1917. † B 5, L 3, M 2, NG 1, RA 28, RBA 7, ROI 10.

BARLOW, Mary, b. 1901
Animal and landscape painter. Studied Southport Art School. † L 1, RCA 4.

BARLOW, Myron Exh. 1898-1911
Paris 1898; Pas de Calais 1901. † L 2, NG 1, ROI 2.

BARLOW, Miss M.G. Exh. 1911
2 Woodlane Terrace, Falmouth, Cornwall. † L 4.

BARLOW, Mrs. N. Exh. 1919
Ladies' Army and Navy Club, London. † SWA 1.

BARLOW, Robert Exh. 1938
Watercolour painter. † WG 2.

BARLOW, Sibyl Margaret d. 1933
Sculptor. b. Essex. Add: London 1922. † I 2, RA 4, RSA 1.

BARLOW, T.H. Exh. 1902-33
Liverpool. † L 9.

BARLOW, Thomas Oldham 1824-1889
Engraver. Studied Manchester School of Design. Articled to Messrs. Stephenson and Royston, Manchester engravers. Engraved many of Millais works. b. Oldham. Moved to London 1847. In 1891 Oldham Corporation acquired an almost complete collection of his engravings. A.R.A. 1873, R.A. 1881. † RA 17.

BARLOW, W. Tillot Exh. 1894-1903
23 Finsbury Circus, London. † RA 4.

BARMAN, L. Exh. 1898-1909
27 University Avenue, Glasgow. † GI 3, L 2.

BARMAN, Mrs. L. Exh. 1917-19
10 University Gardens, Glasgow. † GI 4.

BARNARD, Mrs. Exh. 1895
43 Barkston Gardens, South Kensington, London. † RI 3.

BARNARD, Catherine (Kate) Exh. 1881-1926
Landscape and flower painter. nee Locking. Married J. Langton B. q.v. Add: Chertsey, Surrey 1881; London 1890 and 1900; West Drayton, Middlesex 1895. † B 2, BG 7, D 16, L 6, RA 12, RBA 9, RI 11, ROI 2, SWA 2.

BARNARD, Miss Elinor Exh. 1907-11
London. † L 7, NG 1, RA 3, RI 1.

BARNARD, Mrs. Elizabeth Exh. 1884-1911
Flower and garden painter. Add: London 1884; Farnham, Surrey 1908. † B 1, L 1, LS 12, RA 4, RBA 2, RI 1, ROI 2.

BARNARD, Emily Exh. 1884-1911
Portrait and figure painter. S.W.A. 1885. Add: London 1884. † L 3, M 1, P 1, RA 6, RMS 2, SWA 105.

BARNARD, Edgar K. Exh. 1930-31
Painter of Czechoslovakian landscape. Add: 85 Warwick Road, Earls Court, London. † RA 2.

BARNARD, Frank Exh. 1881-92
Landscape painter. Add: London. † B 2, D 1, RBA 1, RSA 1.

BARNARD, Frederick 1846-1896
Humorous artist and illustrator. Studied Heatherley's and under Jean Bonnat in Paris. Contributed to Punch from 1863 and to London Illustrated News. Died from suffocation in fire at friend's house in Wimbledon. R.B.A. 1882, R.O.I. 1883. Add: London. † B 1, GI 5, L 4, NG 1, RA 6, RBA 3, ROI 5.

BARNARD, George Exh. 1883-91
Landscape painter Studied under J.D. Harding. Add: London 1883; Dorking, Surrey 1889; Broadway, Worcs. 1891. † M 2, NG 1, RI 1, ROI 1.

BARNARD, Miss Gertrude Exh. 1892-93
Flower painter. Add: Putney, London 1892; Bushey, Herts. 1893. † M 1, RBA 1, ROI 1.

BARNARD, Gilbert Exh. 1909-14
East Grinstead 1910; Haslemere, Surrey 1912; Basingstoke, Hants. 1913. † LS 14.

BARNARD, Gwen b. 1912
Studied Chelsea School of Art. Add: London 1938. † GOU 1, ROI 2.

BARNARD, G.B. Exh. 1933-36
Towcester. † SWA 2.

BARNARD, Harold T.B. Exh. 1921-36
London. † RA 3.

BARNARD, J. Langton b. 1853
Domestic genre painter. Married to Catharine B. q.v. Exh. to 1906. Add: Chertsey, Surrey 1880; London 1890; West Drayton, Middlesex 1892. † L 10, M 8, NEA 7, RA 24, RBA 17, RHA 3, ROI 19.

BARNARD, Margaret Exh. 1922-39
Figure painter. Add: Glasgow 1922; Kelso 1923; London 1933. † GI 2, NEA 1, RA 2, RBA 1.

BARNARD, Mary B. Exh. 1894-1913
Mrs. McGregor Whyte. Flower painter. Add: Norbiton, Surrey 1894; London 1898; Glasgow 1902; Oban 1910. † B 1, GI 13, L 4, M 1, NG 2, RA 2, RBA 3, ROI 1, RSA 6.

BARNARD, Miss N. Exh. 1895-96
14 Abingdon Villas, Kensington, London. † SWA 2.

BARNARD, Philip Augustus Exh. 1880-84
Miniature portrait painter. Add: 131 Regent Street, London. † RA 2.

BARNARD, Mrs. William Exh. 1880-81
Figure painter. Add: 3 Douglas Villas, Marischal Road, Lewisham. † RBA 2, SWA 11.

BARNARD, Walter Saunders Exh. 1880-97
Miniature portrait painter. R.M.S. 1897. Add: London. † RA 5, RMS 4.

BARNE, George b. 1882
Member London Group 1922. b. Bristol. Exh. 1921. † G 1.

BARNES, Archibald George b. 1887
Portrait painter. Studied St. John's Wood School of Art and R.A. Schools. R.I. 1924, R.O.I. 1925, R.P. 1924. Add: London. † BA 1, COO 1, FIN 80, G 1, GI 11, I 5, L 13, P 15, RA 20, RI 3, ROI 10.

BARNES, A.W.H. Exh. 1920-38
Glasgow 1920; London 1930; Cambridge 1932. † GI 13, L 3, RL 1, RSA 2, RSW 2.

BARNES, Ellen Exh. 1884-85
Watercolour landscape painter. Add: 8 St. Annes Villas, Notting Hill, London. † SWA 3.

BARNES, E.C.* d. c.1882
Painter of domestic scenes and interiors, especially children. R.B.A. 1864. Add: London. † RA 1, RHA 1.

BARNES, Frederick D. Exh. 1904-15
London 1904; Tonbridge 1908; Tunbridge Wells, Kent 1915. † B 1, RA 5.

BARNES, Gustave Adrian 1878-1921
Painter. Curator of Adelaide Art Gallery, S. Australia. Add: London 1908. † RA 1.

BARNES, H. Exh. 1906
Bank Chambers, West Hartlepool. † RA 1.

BARNES, Miss Helen Exh. 1883
Palschell House, Dartmouth Park Avenue, Liverpool. † L 1.

BARNES, Herbert G. Exh. 1895-98
63/64 Gt. Brunswick Street, Dublin. † RHA 3.

BARNES, Harry Jefferson Exh. 1938-40
Royal Masonic Senior School, The Avenue, Bushey, Herts. † NEA 5, RBA 3.

BARNES, Isabella Exh. 1890-1935
Landscape and portrait painter. Studied Royal College of Art and Lambeth School of Art. Arts and Crafts teacher at Eversley, Folkestone. Add: London. † B 1, I 1, RA 3, RBA 1, RI 5, RID 4, ROI 4, SWA 20, WG 19.

BARNES, Miss J. Exh. 1906
Chelsea, London. † SWA 1.

BARNES, James d. c.1923
Figure painter. Add: Liverpool. † L 131, M 2, RA 2.

BARNES, John b. 1913
21 Endwood Court Road, Handsworth, Birmingham 1936. † B 5.

BARNES, Joseph Exh. 1901-4
Asholme House, Keswick, Cumberland. † D 2, L 1, RCA 1.

BARNES, Joseph H. Exh. 1881-87
Figure painter. Add: Harley Villa, 28 Shaftesbury Road, Hammersmith, London. † B 7, L 8, M 4, RA 2, RBA 3, RHA 6, RI 5.

BARNES, Mrs. Louie Exh. 1882-1928
Moseley, Birmingham. † B 12, RSA 1.

BARNES, Marie Exh. 1885
Fruit painter. Add: 120 Huddleston Road, Tufnell Park, London. † SWA 1.

BARNES, Miss Muriel Exh. 1928-29
Crewe. † RCA 2.

BARNES, Marian L. Exh. 1890-1913
Watercolour flower painter. Add: Lewisham, London 1890 and 1907; Margate 1906 and 1909; Blackheath, London 1912. † B 1, L 1, RA 22, RBA 19, RHA 4, RI 22, SWA 18.

BARNES, Robert Exh. 1880-93
Domestic and figure painter. A.R.W.S. 1876. Add: Redhill, Surrey 1880; Brighton 1893. † B 2, GI 1, L 6, M 2, RA 10, RHA 1, RSW 19.

BARNES, Robert Henry Exh. 1924-40
Mythical figure painter. Add: Lee, London 1924; East Croydon, Surrey 1928; Cheam, Surrey 1939. † GI 1, L 2, RA 10, RBA 3.

BARNES, Miss R.M. Exh. 1906-20
Highfield, Queens Park Road, Caterham. † SWA 2.

BARNES, Samuel J.* Exh. 1882-97
Landscape painter. Add: Moseley Wake Green, Nr. Birmingham 1882; Moseley, Birmingham 1890. † B 10, L 2, M 2, RA 2, RHA 3, RSA 5.

BARNES, Miss Winifred b. 1898
Watercolour painter, miniaturist and commercial designer. Studied Municipal School of Art, Brighton. Add: Brighton 1923; St. Ives, Cornwall 1929. † L 1, M 1, RI 7.

BARNES, W.H.L. Exh. 1887
Ridgfield, Manchester. † M 1.

BARNES, William Rodway Exh. 1885-1919
Landscape painter. Add: Worcester 1885; Codnor, Derbys. 1917. † B 4, L 2, LS 9, M 2, ROI 2.

BARNESBY, A.J. Exh. 1913-22
Derby. † N 15.

BARNETT Exh. 1890
† TOO 1.

BARNETT, Miss Annie Exh. 1891-1914
Fence Avenue, Macclesfield, Cheshire. † L 5, M 1, RA 1, RCA 1.

BARNETT, Miss Alice May See Cook

BARNETT, Bion Exh. 1931-35
Tree and landscape painter. Add: Ajaccio, Corsica 1931; Paris 1932. † RA 6.

BARNETT, Dame Henrietta b. 1851
nee Rowland. Sea, sky and coastal painter. Founder and trustee Whitechapel Art Gallery 1883. Add: South Square, Hampstead Garden Suburb, London 1923. † RA 3.

BARNETT, Henry b. 1916
Landscape painter. Studied Cheltenham Art School and RA Schools. Add: 91 Prestbury Road, Cheltenham 1936. † RA 3.

BARNETT, Henry Exh. 1909-29
West Bridgford, Nottingham. † N 28.

BARNETT, James D. Exh. 1881-92
Landscape painter. Crouch End, Hornsey. † DOW 2, M 2, RBA 5.

BARNETT, Miss Mary Exh. 1932-35
Miniature painter. Add: Hampstead, London. † RA 4.

BARNETT, Miss M.A. Exh. 1882-83
68 Ranelagh Road, Dublin. † RHA 3.

BARNETT, Mrs. M.A. Exh. 1919-27
London. † SWA 5.

BARNETT, Walter Durac b. 1876
Marine, landscape and portrait painter. Studied Wrexham School of Art, Lambeth 1896-1900 (medal and scholarship) and Westminster. Served with Artists Rifles 1914-18. Add: London 1905. † CHE 1, GOU 12, I 1, L 5, M 1, NEA 1, P 7, RA 4, ROI 8.

BARNEWALL, Miss V.M. Exh. 1914-24
London 1914 and 1921; Harrogate, Yorks. 1916. † I 2, L 3, P 1, RHA 5, SWA 1.

BARNEY, Mrs. A. Exh. 1900
153 Avenue Victor Hugo, Paris. † RA 1.

BARNEY, Emily F.H. Exh. 1887-88
Park Avenue, Sandymount, Dublin. † RHA 2.

BARNHAM, Denis b. 1920
Landscape painter. Add: Inglesby, Marlborough Road, Hampton, Middlesex 1938. † RA 2, ROI 1.

BARNISH, Frederick Jardine Exh. 1910
Golden Square, Warrington. † L 3.

BARNISH, Leonard Exh. 1907-33
Birkenhead and Liverpool. † L 10.

BARNS, Mrs. M.D. Exh. 1925
3 Keats Grove, London. † RI 1.

BARNITT, Miss Mary Dyson Exh. 1907-40
Liverpool 1907 and 1913; London 1911; Hoylake, Cheshire 1921. † L 45, M 1, RCA 22.

BARNS-GRAHAM, Miss W. Exh. 1938
5 Alva Street, Edinburgh. † RSA 1.

BARNSLEY, A.E. Exh. 1917
Sapperton, Cirencester, Glos. † RSA 2.

BARNSLEY, J.M. Exh. 1885-86
Paris. † GI 2.

BARNSLEY, Sidney H. c.1865-1926
Architect and craftsman. Add: London 1891; Cirencester, Glos. 1917. † RA 1, RSA 1.

BARNWELL, Alice G.C. Exh. 1931-40
Black and white and watercolour animal painter. Add: Birmingham. † B 21, RA 1, RBA 4, RCA 7, RHA 3, RSA 2.

BARNWELL, Miss E. Exh. 1906-7
Kenilworth. † SWA 2.

BARON, Miss H.M. Exh. 1888
Villa Sainte Rose, Petit Juas, Cannes, Alpes Maritimes, France. † B 1.

BARONI, Paolo Exh. 1904-6
37 Via Bonaccio, Milan. † GI 3.

BARR, Alan Exh. 1912-21
Portrait painter. Served army 1914-18. Add: London. † I 8, P 3, RA 3, ROI 2.

BARR, Agnes C. Exh. 1884-1905
Glasgow. † GI 10, M 1.

BARR, A. Crawford Exh. 1896-98
Glasgow. † RSW 2.

BARR, Miss A.J. Exh. 1897
Mrs. Kingsbury. Add: 12 King Street, Covent Garden, London. † RBA 1.

BARR, George Exh. 1927-40
Glasgow. † GI 16.

BARR, Harry Exh. 1918
49 Anthony Street, St. Georges, London. † LS 3.

BARR, Miss Helen Exh. 1887
Douglas Gardens, Uddington, N.B. † GI 1.

BARR, James Exh. 1881-92
21 Rose Street, Garnet Hill, Glasgow. † GI 4, RSA 2.

BARR, James Exh. 1931-38
Glasgow. † GI 8, RSA 6.

BARR, Miss Robina Exh. 1919-38
Sculptor. Studied Glasgow School of Art. Add: 26 Holyrood Crescent, Glasgow. † GI 19, L 7.

BARR, Tom Exh. 1903-26
Rutherglen, N.B. 1903; Glasgow 1925. † GI 3.

BARR, William 1867-1933
Paisley 1897; Glasgow 1914. b. Glasgow. d. San Francisco. † GI 17, L 6, RSA 3, RSW 3.

BARRA de See "D"

BARRABLE, Mrs. Exh. 1880
Portrait painter. Add: 2 Hanover Street, Hanover Square, London. † RA 1.

BARRABLE, George Hamilton Exh. 1880-90
Interior and domestic genre painter. Add: London. † B 3, G 1, GI 3, L 4, M 2, RA 7, RBA 4, RHA 1, ROI 3.

BARRABLE, Miss Millie Exh. 1883-86
Miniature painter. Add: London. † RA 3.

BARRACLOUGH, James P. d. 1942
Portrait painter. R.O.I. 1922. Add: London 1915. † L 1, P 7, RA 12, ROI 65.

BARRADALE, Isaac Exh. 1880-88
Leicester. † RA 2.

BARRAN, Elaine b. 1892
Landscape painter. Add: Shadwell Grange, Moor Allerton, Nr. Leeds and Madehurst Lodge, Arundel, Sussex. † FIN 46, L 2, RA 16, RBA 8, RI 2, SWA 4.

BARRAN, Miss Eliza Exh. 1903-17
24 Queen's Gate, London. † D 2, L 2, SWA 2.

BARRAN, Miss Gwen Exh. 1918-19
24 Queen's Gate, London. † RI 1, SWA 4.

BARRAN, Miss Louisa Exh. 1903-4
London 1903; Roundhay, Leeds 1904. † D 1, L 3.

BARRATT, Alfred Warsop Exh. 1880-81
Figure and still life painter. N.S.A. 1881. Add: Fern Cottage, Woodthorpe, Notts. † N 4.

BARRATT, Miss Dorothy R. Exh. 1922-26
Nottingham. † N 9.

BARRATT, Evangeline Exh. 1933-39
Watercolour landscape painter. Add: Letchworth, Herts 1933; Guildford 1939. † RA 1, RBA 7, RI 2, SWA 8.

BARRATT, Reginald 1861-1917
Watercolour landscape painter. Travelled India, Middle East and Europe. A.R.W.S. 1901; R.W.S. 1912. Add: London. † B 2, FIN 38, L 5, LEI 49, M 3, NG 22, RA 28, RI 11, RSW 88.

BARRATT, Miss S. Grace Exh. 1935-38
The Glen, South View, Letchworth, Herts. † RBA 7, RI 2, RSA 1.

BARRAU, Exh. 1907
chez M. Strauss, 39 Rue Paradis, Paris. † L 1.

BARRAUD, Allan F. Exh. 1880-1908
Landscape painter and etcher. Add: Watford. † D 5, L 1, RA 40, RBA 4, ROI 1.

BARRAUD, Mrs. Blanche Exh. 1900-3
23 Gaisford Street, London. † RI 3, SWA 1.

BARRAUD, Cyril H. Exh. 1912-34
Etcher and watercolour painter. Add: Sidcup, Kent 1912; London 1934. † FIN 1, L 2, RA 4.

BARRAUD, Charles James Exh. 1880-95
Landscape and coastal painter. Add: London 1880; Wool, Dorset 1892. † D 13, L 6, M 2, RA 7, RBA 5, RI 3.

BARRAUD, Francis* 1856-1924
Genre and portrait painter. ("His Master's Voice"). Add: London 1880 and 1890; Liverpool 1888. † B 1, D 3, L 13, M 3, RA 12, RI 4, ROI 17.

BARRAUD, Francis P. Exh. 1882-1900
Watercolour landscape painter. Add: London. † B 2, DOW 6, L 7, M 6, RA 1, RBA 9, RI 4.

BARRAUD, G. Exh. 1924
† FIN 1.

BARRAUD, Noel Exh. 1919
The White Lea, Dawlish, Devon. † RI 1.

BARRAUD, Ronald b. 1906
Architect and painter. Studied Welsh School of Architecture 1925-28. Add: Saddle Gate, Wollaton, Notts. 1939. † N 2.

BARREE, Mrs. E.M. Exh. 1914
28 Castleton, Mumbles, Glam. † L 3, RA 1.

BARRES, Miss M. Exh. 1931-32
25 Belle Walk, Moseley. † B 4.

BARRET, C. Exh. 1913
† TOO 1.

BARRETT, Arthur Exh. 1911-12
37 Croft Down Road, Highgate, London. † LS 6.

BARRETT, Miss Dora Exh. 1939
Sculptor. Highlands, Kinsbourne Green, Harpenden, Herts. † RA 1.

BARRETT, Duncan Exh. 1938
Dry point artist. 53 Lavenham Road, Southfields, London. † RA 1.

BARRETT, Mrs. E.J. Exh. 1908-9
Longdale, 60 Harold Road, Upper Norwood, London. † LS 8.

BARRETT, F.F. Exh. 1909
† LS 3.

BARRETT, Miss F. Gould Exh. 1925-27
Watercolour painter. 21 St. Georges Square, London. † RI 1, WG 82.

BARRETT, Harry Exh. 1881-83
Sculptor. Campbell Cottage, Mottingham, Kent. † RBA 9.

BARRETT, Jerry 1814-1906
Historical and genre painter. Add: 15 Avenue Road, Regent's Park, London 1880. † B 9, L 4, M 4, RA 4, RBA 3, ROI 7.

BARRETT, John* Exh. 1883
Landscape painter. Add: 8 Stoddon Terrace, Plymouth, Devon. † RA 1.

BARRETT, Miss Kathleen Exh. 1900-31
90 Ennis Road, Plumstead Common, London. † GI 1, RA 2.

BARRETT, Lionel Exh. 1900
Architect. 23 Sheepcote Road, Harrow, Middlesex. † RA 1.

BARRETT, Mrs. M. Exh. 1880-84
Flower painter. Add: 15 Avenue Road, Regent's Park, London. † D 1, SWA 1.

BARRETT, Marcella A.E. Exh. 1905-12
18 Lower Pembroke Street, Dublin. † RHA 6.

BARRETT, Miss Mary E. Exh. 1926
3 Hatfield Road, Ainsdale, Southport, Lancs. † L 1.

BARRETT, Miss Meriel Lambart Exh. 1934-37
Hollywood House, Palmerston Road, Dublin. † RHA 10.

BARRETT, M.M. Exh. 1940
Heckmondwicke. † RCA 1.

BARRETT, Miss N. Exh. 1881
† RHA 1.

BARRETT, Oliver O'Connor b. 1908
Sculptor and poet. Add: 100 Icknield Way, Letchworth, Herts. 1933. † RA 2.

BARRETT, Sydney Exh. 1900-1
Stockport 1900; Manchester 1901. † RCA 2.

BARRETT, Miss Theresa Exh. 1909-14
Hampstead Road, London 1909; Milton Farm, Steventon, R.S.O. 1910. † D 5, RCA 1.

BARRETT, Thomas* Exh. 1880-1909
Landscape painter and etcher. N.S.A. 1881; A.R.E. 1887. Add: Sherwood Rise, Nottingham. † L 2, N 20, RA 11, RBA 1, RE 37.

BARRETT, Thomas Francis. Exh. 1906-34
Painter, sculptor and black and white artist. Add: S.E. London 1906; Weybridge, Surrey 1933; Walton on Thames 1934. † L 1, LS 8, RA 7, RCA 1.

BARRETT, Miss Violet E. Exh. 1897-99
39 Linden Grove, Nunhead. † SWA 4.

BARRIAS, Felix Joseph 1822-1907
French artist. Add: 34 Rue de Bruxelles, Paris 1885. † GI 1.

BARRIBAL, William H. Exh. 1919-38
Figure and studio interior painter. Add: 6 St. Paul's Studios, Barons Court, London. † AR 1, COO 10, L 1, RA 1.

BARRIE, F.H. Exh. 1882-85
Old Trafford, Manchester. † M 4.

BARRIE, Muirhead Exh. 1900
136 Wellington Street, Glasgow. † RSA 2.

BARRILOT, M.L. Exh. 1883
33 Ovington Square, Brompton. † L 1.

BARRINGTON, Lady Kennett Exh. 1890
65 Albert Hall Mansions, London. † SWA 2.

BARRINGTON, Maud Exh. 1880-83
Glendruid, Cabinteely, Ireland 1880; Chapel St. Lynn, Norfolk 1883. † RHA 5.

BARRINGTON, Russell Exh. 1884
Liverpool. † L 2.

BARRINGTON, Rutland Exh. 1898-1919
London 1898; East Hagbourne, Berks. 1919. † RBA 2, ROI 5.

BARRINGTON-WARD, Susan Exh. 1939
† NEA 2.

BARRON, Miss Exh. 1903
Studio, 115 Gower Street, London. † SWA 2.

BARRON, A.J. Exh. 1885
Still life painter. Add: Roebury, St. Ann's Hill, Chertsey. † SWA 1.

BARRON, Miss E.J. Exh. 1888-89
The Homestead, East Dulwich Road, London. † GI 2, RSA 2.

BARRON, Mrs. Gladys Exh. 1905-35
nee Logan. Painter and sculptor. b. India. Studied under Gertrude Bayes and St. John's Wood School of Art. Add: London 1905; Oaklands, Inverness 1925. † B 2, L 38, RA 8, RSA 12.

BARRON, Miss M. Exh. 1903
Taplow House, Bucks. † SWA 2.

BARRON, Miss Maude Exh. 1912
Landscape painter. Add: The Old House, Shute End, Wokingham, Berks. † NEA 2.

BARRON, Miss O.M. Exh. 1902-3
Taplow House, Bucks. † RA 1, SWA 1.

BARRON, Phyllis Exh. 1910-14
Member London Group 1916. Add: Hillingdon, Uxbridge 1910; Hampstead, London 1914. † LS 3, NEA 3.

BARRON, Miss W. Exh. 1880-82
St. Andrews. † GI 1, RSA 1.

BARRON, W.A. Exh. 1885
Linkfield House, Portobello. † RSA 1.

BARROR, Miss Grace Exh. 1932-40
Metropolitan School of Art, Dublin 1932; Donnybrook, Dublin 1937. † RHA 7.

BARROS, de See D

BARROW, Edith Isabel d. 1930
Landscape and flower painter. Studied Goldsmiths Institute (scholarship), South Kensington (silver and bronze medals). Add: London 1887; Coombe Martin, Devon 1907. † AB 3, B 3, BG 1, L 6, LS 3, RA 35, RBA 12, RI 8, ROI 2, SWA 4, WG 32.

BARROW, E.R. Exh. 1910
Lennox House, Norfolk Street, London. † RA 1.

BARROW, Mrs. Fanny Exh. 1904
Fretherne, Bays Hill, Cheltenham, Glos. † RA 1.

BARROW, G. Exh. 1913
62 Kennington Oval, London. † RA 1.

BARROW, Miss Jane Exh. 1890-97
176 Brecknock Road, London. † M 1, RA 1, RBA 3, ROI 2, SWA 2.

BARROW, Maurice F. Exh. 1938
538 Aspley Lane, Nottingham. † N 1.

BARROW, Miss S.V. Exh. 1903-6
Gloucester Place, London. † B 1, D 3, RHA 1.

BARROW, W.H. Exh. 1888
Marine painter. Add: Braybrooke Road, Hastings, Sussex. † ROI 3.

BARROWS, Miss Ethel M. Exh. 1910
66 Harborne Road, Edgbaston. † B 1.

BARROWS, H. Exh. 1886
14 South Street, Huddersfield. † L 1.

BARRY, Miss A.F. Exh. 1907
Beckenham, Kent. † SWA 1.

BARRY, Charles* b. 1823
Architect. Exh. 1880-96. Add: Westminster Chambers, Victoria Street, London. † RA 3.

BARRY, Claude Francis b. 1883
Painter and etcher. R.B.A. 1912. Add: Windsor 1906; St. Ives, Cornwall 1911 and 1940; London 1922. † I 1, L 6, LS 13, NEA 1, RA 17, RBA 78, ROI 2, RSA 5.

BARRY, Desmond Exh. 1888
Landscape painter. Add: 60 Sunnyside Road, Upper Holloway, London. † RBA 1.

BARRY, Dick Exh. 1883
Landscape painter. 32 Queen's Road, Regent's Park, London. † RBA 3.

BARRY, Miss Edith M. Exh. 1891-1901
Portrait painter. Add: Sparrow's Herne House, Bushey, Herts. † B 2, FIN 2, L 1, RA 3, SWA 2.

BARRY, Miss Hope Exh. 1881-83
London. † L 1, SWA 1.

BARRY, J.C. Exh. 1900-1
Birmingham † B 2.

BARRY, Matthew Exh. 1923-39
Dublin. † RHA 38.

BARRY, Miss Moyra A. Exh. 1908-40
Rathmines, Dublin. † RHA 70.

BARRY, Miss M.E. Exh. 1893
Edgefield Mount, Melton Constable. † SWA 2.

BARRY, Vyvyan Exh. 1919
Watercolour figure painter. Add: 5 The Mews, Heathview Gardens, Putney Heath, London. † RA 1.

BARRY, William Exh. 1883-88
10 Picardy Place, Edinburgh. † RSA 6.

BARRY, W. Gerard Exh. 1888
Ballyadam, Carrigtwo Hill, Co. Cork. † RA 1.

BARSBY, Percy J. Exh. 1929-36
Watercolour landscape and dry point artist. Add: Attenborough, Notts. 1929; Long Eaton, Notts. 1935. † N 4.

BARSLEY, H.P. Exh. 1905
6 Colquitt Street, Liverpool. † L 1.

BARSTOW, E. Exh. 1891-94
25 Brownlow Hill, Liverpool. † L 3.

BARSTOW, H. Exh. 1886-93
25 Brownlow Hill, Liverpool. † L 7.

BARSTOW, Montagu Exh. 1891-1919
Watercolour domestic and figure painter. Add: London 1891; Bearstead, Kent 1916. † D 1, L 5, M 1, RA 2, RI 9.

BARTELS, Von* See V

BARTELS, Elizabeth Clayton Exh. 1932-36
Watercolour landscape and flower painter; woodcut artist; teacher. Studied Newcastle on Tyne, Cardiff, London and Newlyn, Cornwall. Add: Alcuin Hall, Bingley, Yorks. † COO 1, RI 2, SWA 4.

BARTER, E.G. Exh. 1931-32
50 Wroughton Road, Battersea, London. † RBA 2.

BARTER, John Exh. 1882-1903
Liverpool 1882; Barmouth, Merioneth 1899. † L 7.

BARTER, Miss L. Exh. 1906
47 Franconia Road, Clapham Park, London. † RA 1.

BARTH, C.W. Exh. 1890
c/o Messrs. Smith and Leppard, 77 Mortimer Street, London. † GI 1.

BARTH, Wilhelm Exh. 1889
15 Stratford Place, London. † RA 1.

BARTHALOT, Marius Exh. 1923
Avenue de Wagram 35, Paris. † L 1.

BARTHOEL, Paul Exh. 1904
133 New Bond Street, London. † RA 1.

BARTHOLD, Manuel b. 1874
b. New York. Add: 65 Avenue Niel, Paris 1923. † L 1, RA 1.

BARTHOLOME, Paul Albert 1848-1928
French sculptor and painter. H.F.R.A. 1921; H.R.S.A. 1911. † GI 3, I 6, L 1, RA 1, RSA 10.

BARTHOLOMEW, Miss Betty Exh. 1927-31
Edinburgh. † RSA 6.

BARTHOLOMEW, Miss F.M. Exh. 1896
Kirkby Lonsdale, Lancs. † SWA 3.

BARTHOLOMEW, Harry Exh. 1890
132 Abbey Road, London. † ROI 1.

BARTHOLOMEW, Miss Isabelle E. Exh. 1928-30
53B Aigburth Road, Liverpool. † L 3.

BARTHOLOMEW, Mrs. L.I. Exh. 1915-20
Norwood, London. † RA 2, SWA 5.

BARTHOLOMEW, Mrs. Zou-Zou Exh. 1937-40
Miniature portrait painter. Add: Pewsey, Wilts. 1937; R.A.F. Andover, Hants. 1940. † RA 3.

BARTIOLI, Frank Exh. 1886
13 Downshire Hill, London. † RI 3.

BARTLAM, Miss Millie Exh. 1913-15
Brown Fields, Longton, Staffs. † L 3.

BARTLE, Miss Amy B. Exh. 1929-31
Liverpool 1929; Hull 1931. † L 5, RCA 2.

BARTLETT, Arthur E. Exh. 1890-1916
Architect. Studied under Sir Reginald Blomfield, R.A. Schools and the A.A. (travelling student). Add: London. † RA 9.

BARTLETT, Charles William Exh. 1885-1928
Landscape and figure painter. Add: London 1885; Beer, Devon 1903; Edinburgh 1913; Honolulu 1921. † B 7, BG 1, CON 1, FIN 4, G 2, GI 8, L 23, M 15, NG 13, RA 15, RBA 3, RI 1, ROI 5.

BARTLETT, Editha E. Exh. 1928-39
8 Gainsborough Studios, Bedford Park, London. † RA 1, ROI 1, SWA 9.

BARTLETT, George A. Exh. 1895-98
Fulham, London. † RBA 1, RHA 1, RI 1, ROI 3, RSA 1.

BARTLETT, Henry F. Exh. 1934-35
32 Winchester Avenue, London. † RBA 2.

BARTLETT, J. Exh. 1899
Architect. 8 Bream's Buildings, Chancery Lane, London. † RA 1.

BARTLETT, Josephine Hoxie Exh. 1887-1899
Landscape painter. Add: Edinburgh. † GI 10, L 1, RA 1, RID 1, RSA 12.

BARTLETT, Nancy Exh. 1937-39
Landscape painter. Add: Brooklyn Road, Cheltenham, Glos. † RA 2.

BARTLETT, Paul Wayland 1865-1925
American sculptor. Add: Paris 1913. † GI 3.

BARTLETT, Miss Violet A. Exh. 1898-1905
The Thatch, Stansted, Essex. † ROI 2.

BARTLETT, William Henry* b. 1858
Landscape, interior and domestic painter. Studied under Gerome in Paris. R.B.A. 1879. Add: London 1880 and 1905; Langley, Bucks. 1901; Donegal, Ireland 1911; Farleigh, Kent 1913; Ventnor, I.O.W. 1924. † B 6, FIN 56, G 15, GI 10, L 41, M 19, NG 26, RA 45, RBA 13, RHA 3, RI 1, ROI 61.

BARTON, Miss Exh. 1894
52 Lower Sloane Street, London. † L 2.

BARTON, Alice Exh. 1914-38
Mrs. H.E. Add: Aberdovey, Wales. † B 4, LS 9, RCA 2.

BARTON, Miss A.G. Exh. 1932-33
62 St. Alban's Road, Moseley. † B 3.

BARTON, Miss C.A. Exh. 1883
Walbrook House, Wincanton. † G 1.

BARTON, Cranleigh Harper b. 1890
Watercolour landscape and architectural painter. Born and educated in New Zealand. Became barrister before taking up art. Add: London 1925-27. † L 1, NEA 2, RI 1.

BARTON, Eleanor Exh. 1935
Figure painter. Add: 47 Wynnstay Gardens, London. † COO 1.

BARTON, Ernest Exh. 1897
† GI 1.

BARTON, Miss Eleanor G. Exh. 1898-1906
Figure painter. Wimbledon Park, London 1898; Bushey, Herts. 1906. † RA 4.

BARTON, J.W. Exh. 1903
42 Burnley Road, Ainsdale, Southport. † L 1.

BARTON, Matilda Exh. 1888-89
Mrs. W. Miniature portrait painter. Add: London. † RA 2.

BARTON, Mary Georgina Exh. 1895
Landscape painter. Studied Westminster School of Art and Rome. A.S.W.A. 1909; S.W.A. 1911. Born Dundalk, Ireland. Lived London and Bracknell, Berks. † D 3, FIN 149, L 4, LS 17, M 1, RBA 4, RHA 4, RI 1, RID 4, SWA 120.

BARTON, Rose M. d. 1929
Oil and watercolour painter. A.R.W.S. 1893; R.W.S. 1897; A.S.W.A. 1886. Add: Dublin and London. † BG 1, D 24, FIN 1, G 2, GI 5, L 7, RA 17, RBA 1, RHA 9, RI 16, RSW 3, RWS 77, SWA 20.

BARTSCH, E. Exh. 1892
Landscape painter. Add: 10 Hamilton Terrace, Hyde Vale, Greenwich. † RBA 1.

BARWELL, Miss Eva Exh. 1913-22
Holmwood, Kenilworth. † LS 6, RI 1, ROI 1.

BARWELL, Miss Emily H. Exh. 1895-1903
Egbaston, Birmingham 1895; London 1898. † B 1, L 2, RA 1, ROI 1.

BARWELL, Frederick Bacon* c. 1831-1922
Genre painter. Inspector of Schools of Art. Add: London 1880; Mumbles, Swansea 1892. † B 2, RA 5, ROI 7.

BARWELL, Henry George c. 1829-1898
Watercolour landscape painter. Add: Norwich, Norfolk 1881. † D 1, RI 9.

BARWICK, Miss M. Exh. 1901-2
Kirkby-in-Furness, Lancs. † L 2, RSA 1.

BARZAGHI, A. Exh. 1889
16 Addison Road, London. † G 1.

BARZAGHI-CATTANEO, Antoine Exh. 1890-95
c/o Swiss Consul, Liverpool 1890; Dublin 1893. † L 2, RHA 5.

BAS, Le* See L

BASCHET, Marcel Exh. 1905-26
17 Quai Voltaire, Paris. † L 3, RA 1.

BASCOMBE, Miss V.B.E. Exh. 1896
37 Grange Park, London. † SWA 1.

BASEBE, Athelstane Exh. 1882-99
Miniature painter. Add: 199 Brompton Road, South Kensington, London 1882; Watford 1899. † RA 2.

BASEBE, C.E. Exh. 1880-82
Miniature painter. Add: London. † RA 3.

BASEBE, Ernest Exh. 1886
Miniature painter. Add: c/o J.B. Smith, 117 Hampstead Road, London. † RA 1.

BASEBE, Ernest Exh. 1921-22
Westmead, Shelford, Cambs. † B 1, RCA 1.

BASEBE, Harold E. Exh. 1881
Miniature portrait painter. Add: 31 Miranda Road, Upper Holloway, London. † RA 1.

BASELEER, Richard* Exh. 1909
Quai Van Dyck 7, Antwerp. † L 1.

BASHAM, Miss Mary E. Exh. 1891
Haverhill, Suffolk. † D 2.

BASHFORD, Elizabeth Exh. 1917-21
London. † LS 8, NEA 2.

BASIL, Antony Exh. 1932
Sculptor. Add: 100 Tottenham Court Road, London. † RA 1.

BASKETT, Charles E.* d. c.1929
Still life painter and etcher. Art master. A.R.E. 1892. Add: Colchester, Essex 1883; Felixstowe, Suffolk 1913. † L 2, M 3, RA 22, RBA 3, RE 38, RHA 1.

BASKETT, Charles Henry 1872-1953
Etcher and aquatinter. Son of Charles E.B. q.v. Studied Colchester School of Art, Lambeth School of Art and charcoal drawing under Frank Mura. Principal Chelmsford School of Art. A.R.E. 1911; R.E. 1918. Add: Chelmsford, Essex 1910; Gt. Baddow, Essex 1927; Southampton 1940. † CG 15, D 4, FIN 2, GI 3, I 12, L 60, M 2, NEA 1, RA 21, RE 65, RHA 1, RSA 4.

BASKETT, Mrs. Florence M. Exh. 1918-19
Baddow Road, Chelmsford, Essex. † RA 6.

BASS, Miss M.F. Exh. 1912-21
9 Grosvenor Road, Muswell Hill, London. † RA 1, SWA 1.

BASSETT, George Exh. 1880-84
c/o A. Rayner, 26 Francis Street, Tottenham Court Road, London. † B 1, RHA 5.

BASSFORD, Margaret Exh. 1908-10
Hopnas, Tamworth, Staffs. † LS 4.

BAST, Earnulf Exh. 1933
Kunstuernes Hus, Oslo. † RSA 2.

BASTABLE, J. Exh. 1928-30
30 Eastdale Road, Wavertree, Liverpool. † B 1, L 2.

BASTERT, Nicolas* b. 1854
Dutch artist. Add: Amsterdam. Exh. 1895-1908. † GI 3, I 1.

BASTET, J. Exh. 1898
Rue des Artistes 36, Paris. † L 1.

BASTIAN, Moncha Exh. 1908-10
c/o Allied Artists' Association, 67 Chancery Lane, London. † LS 6.

BASTIEN, Alfred* Exh. 1909
14 Chausse de Roodebeck, Brussels. † L 1.

BASTIEN-LEPAGE, E. Exh. 1911-19
39 bis Rue de Clezy, Neuilly-sur-Seine, France. † GI 1, L 1.

BASTIEN-LEPAGE, Jules 1848-1884
French portrait and rustic painter. Add: Dieudonne's Hotel, 11 Ryder Street, London 1880. † G 9, GI 1, RA 1.

BASTIN, A.D.* Exh. 1883-1907
Figure painter. Add: London 1883; West Worthing, Sussex 1899. † B 13, L 10, M 1, RA 1, RBA 3, ROI 1.

BASTOW, Basil Exh. 1926-39
Watercolour landscape painter. A.N.S.A. 1931. N.S.A. 1934. Add: Nottingham. † N 51, RCA 3.

BATALHA-REIS, V.C. Exh. 1930
† P 1.

BATCHELER, Miss Mary H. Exh. 1896-1903
Sevenoaks, Kent. † B 3, L 2, RA 1, ROI 1.

BATCHELOR, Arthur Exh. 1909-10
Ormesby, Gt. Yarmouth, Norfolk. † LS 6.

BATCHELOR, Betty Exh. 1930
Hill Wootton House, Nr. Warwick. † NEA 1.

BATCHELOR, Bernard W.R. Exh. 1937-40
Watercolour painter. Add: 27 Corringham Road, Wembley Park, Middlesex. † RA 2, RI 2, RSA 2.

BATCHELOR, Miss E.M. Exh. 1904
127 Cheyne Walk, London. † SWA 2.

BATCHELOR, Frederick Exh. 1908-15
Architect. A.R.H.A. 1901. Add: Dublin. † RHA 5.

BATCHELOR, Miss Kate Exh. 1883-84
Flower painter. Add: 11 King's Parade, Clifton, Bristol. † L 1, ROI 3.

BATE, Miss E. Spence Exh. 1893-1908
Glasgow 1893; London 1900. † GI 3, L 1, M 1, RA 1, RBA 2, RSA 1, SWA 5.

BATE, Howard Edward Davis b. 1894
Sculptor and carver. Studied Plymouth 1914, Torquay 1915, Regent Street Polytechnic 1917, R.A. Schools 1920. Add: 65 Beverley Drive, Edgware, Middlesex 1937. † RA 3.

BATE, H. Francis 1853-1950
Landscape, figure and portrait painter. Studied South Kensington (scholarship) and Antwerp Academy of Arts under Charles Verlat. N.E.A. 1887 (Hon. Sec. 1888-1919 and Hon. Treas. 1886-1919) Add: Antwerp 1883; London 1885. † B 1, G 4, GI 1, GOU 5, L 2, LS 1, M 1, NEA 25, RBA 3.

BATE, Inez Exh. 1900
c/o Mr. Whistler, 9 Rue des Fourneaux, Paris. † GI 2.

BATEMAN, Arthur Exh. 1939
Landscape painter. Add: Victoria Road, Morley, Leeds. † RA 1.

BATEMAN, Miss Annie Exh. 1909 and 1928
Sefton Park, Liverpool 1909; Glan Conway 1928. † L 3, RCA 1.

BATEMAN, Arthur B. Exh. 1913-38
Landscape painter. Add: West Kirby, Lancs. 1913; Birmingham 1919; Southsea, Hants. 1930; Bolton, Lancs. 1933; Eaglescliffe, Co. Durham, 1934. † B 2, GOU 2, L 7, M 1, RA 2, RSA 2.

BATEMAN, B. Arthur Exh. 1885-94
Portrait and figure painter. Add: Reigate, Surrey 1885; Penzance, Cornwall 1886. † GI 1, L 1, RA 3, RBA 3, ROI 2.

BATEMAN, Charles E. Exh. 1904-18
Architect. R.B.S.A. 1912. Add: London 1904; Birmingham 1905. † RA 10.

BATEMAN, Miss Dorothy Exh. 1911
28 Garston Old Road, Cressington, Liverpool. † L 1.

BATEMAN, Harry Exh. 1937-40
† P 2, RI 2.

BATEMAN, Herbert J. Exh. 1907-16
London. † RA 3.

BATEMAN, Henry Mayo b. 1887
Black and white artist and caricaturist. b. N.S.W. Australia. Studied Westminster and New Cross Art Schools and under Charles Van Havenmaet. Exh. 1911-33. Add: Reigate Heath, Surrey 1933. † BK 96, CHE 2, LEI 198, RA 1.

BATEMAN, H.W. Exh. 1911
Parkstone, Nightingale Lane, Clapham, London. † RI 1.

BATEMAN, James* 1893-1959
Painter and wood engraver. b. Kendal. Studied Leeds School of Art 1910-14, Royal College of Art 1914-19, Slade School 1919-21. Painting master Cheltenham School of Art and visiting master Hammersmith School of Art. Purchased by Chantrey Bequest "Pastoral" 1929, "Commotion in the Cattle Ring" 1936 and "Cattle Market" 1938. A.R.A. 1935, R.A. 1942, A.R.B.A. 1929, R.B.A. 1930. A.R.E. 1931. † BAR 3, COO 1, FIN 16, L 5, M 2, NEA 8, RA 27, RBA 15, RE 7, RHA 1, RSA 2.

BATEMAN, Mrs. M.A. Exh. 1932-38
Flower and landscape painter. Visited Malaya. Add: Ecclesbourne Hall, Idridgehay, Derby. † ROI 1, WG 37.

BATEMAN, Robert b. c.1841
Figure painter. Entered R.A. Schools 1865. Add: London 1882 and 1900; Broseley, Salop 1898. † G 11, L 1, BG 4, RA 2.

BATEMAN, Samuel Exh. 1900
17 South Place, Reading Road, Henley on Thames. † RA 1.

BATES, A.R. Exh. 1939
24 Essex Road, Leicester. † N 2.

BATES, C.B. Exh. 1885-86
89 Fellowes Road, South Hampstead, London. † L 2.

BATES, David* c.1841-1921
Landscape and nature painter. Add: Malvern, Worcs. 1880; Birmingham 1891; Sutton Coldfield 1894; Moseley, Birmingham 1898; Cheltenham Glos. 1907; Teddington, Middlesex 1909. † B 42, FIN 2, G 5, L 7, M 4, NG 18, RA 19, RBA 1, RCA 2, ROI 10, TOO 5.

BATES, Dewey 1851-1899
Landscape and figure painter. b. Philadelphia, U.S.A. Add: London 1880; Cookham Dean, Berks. 1886; died Rye, Sussex. † L 3, M 1, P 1, RA 3, RBA 5, RI 4, ROI 5.

BATES, Miss F. Exh. 1900
53 York Road, Edgbaston, Birmingham. † B 1.

BATES, Frederick b. 1867
Portrait, religious and landscape painter. Studied Paris, Antwerp and Brussels. Travelled Middle East. Add: Stockport 1885; Manchester 1891-95. † M 12.

BATES, Geo Exh. 1883-88
Birmingham. † B 4.

BATES, Harry 1850-1899
Sculptor. Apprenticed carver to Messrs. Bridley and Farmer 1869-79. Studied Lambeth School of Art, R.A. Schools (gold medal and travelling studentship) and Paris under Rodin. Purchased by Chantrey Bequest "Pandora" 1891. A.R.A. 1892, Add: Paris 1884; London 1885. † BG 1, G 3, GI 3. L 3, NG 4. RA 36.

BATES, Mrs. Helen Exh. 1923
Miniature painter. Add: 68 Regent Road, Leicester. † RA 2.

BATES, Henry Edward Exh. 1926-39
Wood engraver. Add: Nottingham. † B 10, L 3, N 23, RA 1.

BATES, Henry W. Exh. 1882-88
Landscape painter. Add: 21 King Street, Leicester. † D 5, L 4, RA 1, RBA 3, RI 1.

BATES, John Exh. 1891
1 Temple Chambers, Broad Street, Corner, Birmingham. † B 2.

BATES, J.A. Exh. 1908-36
Landscape painter. Add: Leicester. † N 24.

BATES, Mrs. Jessey Fairfax Exh. 1896-1928
Malvern, Worcs. 1896; Witham, Essex 1907; Leebotwood, Salop 1920; Dolwyddelen, Caerns 1926. † B 2, L 1, RA 1, RCA 3.

BATES, Leo Fison Exh. 1931
Portrait painter. Add: 5 Brook Green Studios, West Kensington, London. † RA 1, RSA 2.

BATES, Maxwell Exh. 1939
Landscape painter. Add: 88 Holland Road, London. † RA 1.

BATES, Marjorie Christine Exh. 1910-34
Figure and landscape painter. Studied Nottingham School of Art and under Jean Paul Laurens, Paris. N.S.A. 1918. Add: The Grange, Wilford, Notts. † N 40, RA 4.

BATES, Robert William Exh. 1924-28
Landscape painter. Studied Newcastle on Tyne School of Art. Add: The Cottage, Lane Ends, Romily, Cheshire. † RCA 5.

BATES, William S. Exh. 1899
Architect. 59 Clarence Road, Clapton, London. † RA 2.

BATESON, Edith Exh. 1891-1937
Sculptor and painter. b. Cambridge. Studied R.A. Schools (3 silver medals). Add: London 1891 and 1913; Much Hadham, Herts. 1896; Ware, Herts. 1902; Robin Hood's Bay, Yorks. 1908; Bushey, Herts. 1915; Storrington, Sussex 1930. † B 2, GI 1, I 6, L 6, LS 6, NG 2, RA 5, RBA 4, RI 2, ROI 3.

BATH, A.B. Exh. 1924-29
Walsall, Staffs. † B 9.

BATHE, de See D

BATHER, E. Walcot Exh. 1932-38
London. † RA 2.

BATHGATE, Miss Ellen Exh. 1886-89
Edinburgh. † RA 1, RSA 6.

BATHGATE, George Exh. 1880-89
Figure painter. Add: Edinburgh 1880 and 1885; Munich 1884; London 1886. † B 3, L 6, RA 4, RBA 1, RSA 11.

BATHGATE, Miss Hattie E. Exh. 1911-14
Brooklyn, Cressington Park, Liverpool. † L 3.

BATHURST, Charles J. Exh. 1903-40
Painter and lithographer. A.R.B.A. 1939. R.B.A. 1940. Add: London. † I 4, NEA 17, RA 13, RBA 12.

BATHURST, R.H. Exh. 1937-39
† P 2.

BATLEY, Henry William Exh. 1881-94
Etcher. R.E. 1881-88. Add: Putney, London 1881; W. Kensington, London 1891. † L 3. RA 14, RE 18.

BATLEY, Marguerite E. Exh. 1889-1900
Portrait and figure painter. Add: Croydon 1889; Bushey, Herts. 1896; London 1898. † B 1. L 4. P 1, RA 6.

BATLEY, Mrs. Mabel Terry See LEWIS

BATLEY, Walter Daniel b. 1850
Landscape painter. Studied Ipswich, South Kensington and R.A. Schools. Add: Ipswich 1880; Felixstowe 1922. † L 2, M 2, RA 23, RBA 2, RI 1, ROI 1.

BATMAN, L. Exh. 1904
21 University Gardens, Glasgow. † L 1.

BATSCHE, Julius Exh. 1882-83
Sculptor. Add: London. † RA 2.

BATSON, Rev. A. Wellesley Exh. 1890-96
London 1890; Nottingham 1896. † G 1, N 1.

BATSON, Frank Exh. 1890-1926
Landscape painter. Add: Hungerford, Berks. 1890; Penzance, Cornwall 1904, Nottingham 1908. † AG 2, L 1, N 42, RA 5, RBA 1, RI 1, ROI 1.

BATT, Arthur* Exh. 1880-93
Domestic painter. Add: Lyndhurst, Hants. 1888. † G 4, GI 16, L 13, RA 4, RBA 13, ROI 7, RSA 1.

BATTEN, Mrs. E.M. Exh. 1922
† NEA 2.

BATTEN, John Dickson 1860-1932
Painter, illustrator and colour print and fresco artist. b. Plymouth. Studied Slade School under Legros. Barrister-at-Law Inner Temple 1884. Introduced to England the Japanese method of cutting and printing from wood-blocks. Add: Cambridge 1882; London 1886. † BG 2, G 2, GI 3, I 1, L 14, M 5, NG 15, RA 9, RE 2.

BATTEN, Mark Exh. 1939
Sculptor. Add: Alciston, Berwick, Sussex. † RA 1.

BATTEN, Mark Wilfred b. 1905
Painter. Studied Beckenham School of Art and Chelsea School of Art. b. Kickcaldy. Add: Beckenham, Kent 1929. † NEA 2.

BATTEN, S. Exh. 1885
15 Airlie Gardens, Campden Hill, London. † RE 1.

BATTERBURY, Thomas Exh. 1899-1918
London. † RA 2.

BATTERSBY, A. Exh. 1883
Liverpool. † L 1.
BATTERSBY, Louise Emilie Exh. 1912
9 Stanger Road, Norwood, London. † LS 3.
BATTERSBY, T. Exh. 1929-33
27 Alexandra Road, St. Annes on Sea. † L 3.
BATTHYANY, Count Gyular b. 1892
London. Exh. 1935. † RSA 2.
BATTIE, Charles A. Exh. 1899-1910
New Scotland Yard, London 1899; Woking, Surrey 1904. † RA 5.
BATTINE, Mrs. Margaret Exh. 1897-98
† D 1, P 2.
BATTLE, Marguerite Exh. 1930
† P 1.
BATTY, E. Exh. 1885
140 Hampstead Road, London. † B 2.
BATY, du See D
BATY, Miss Eleanor Exh. 1919-38
Miniature painter. Add: Newcastle on Tyne. † L 2, RA 5, RMS 2.
BAUBRY, Madame Vaillant Exh. 1881
137 Avenue Malakoff, Paris. † SWA 1.
BAUDRY, A. Exh. 1890
59 Rue de Grenelle, Paris. † N 2.
BAUER, H. Exh. 1930
† GOU 1.
BAUER, Miss Lucette Exh. 1935-36
Sculptor. Add: Studio C2, 416 Fulham Road, London. † RA 2.
BAUER, Marius Alexander Jacques* 1864-1932
Dutch painter and etcher. Add: c/o E.J. Van Wirsselingh, London 1898; Haarlem, Holland 1905. † CG 50, FIN 63, GI 6, I 47, L 4, NEA 7, RSA 9.
BAUERKELLER, Miss Rose Exh. 1914
8 Parsonage Road, Withington, Manchester. † L 1.
BAUERLE, Amelia M. d. 1916
Changed name to Bowerley c.1909. Painter of children, illustrator and etcher. A.R.E. 1900. Add: London 1897. † B 1, BG 1, DOW 65, L 28, RA 13, RBA 1, RE 46, RI 4, RID 30, SWA 1.
BAUERLE, Carl* 1831-1912
Figure painter. Add: London. † B 7, G 1, GI 22, L 7, M 13, RA 11, RBA 15, RHA 5.
BAUGH, Miss L. Exh. 1937-38
25 Victoria Road, Harborne. † B 2.
BAUGNIES, E. Exh. 1883
100 Boulevard Malsherbes, Paris. † GI 2.
BAUGNIES, J. Exh. 1905-6
23 Avenue de Villiers, Paris. † NG 2.
BAUHOF, Frederick Exh. 1903-13
Landscape painter. Add: London 1903 and 1910; Paris 1908. † BG 25, GI 2, L 1, RA 4.
BAUMANN, Miss A. Hilda Exh. 1890
9 Cornwall Terrace, London. † ROI 1.
BAUMANN, Miss Ida Exh. 1892
Portrait painter. Add: The Studio, 7 Chelsea Embankment, London. † P 1, RA 2.
BAUMANN, Miss Pauline Exh. 1929-40
Etcher, lithographer and wood engraver. Add: 46 Lexington Street, Golden Square, London. † L 1, RA 7, RED 1.
BAUMER, Alan E. Exh. 1937-40
Landscape painter. Add: 16 Gardnor Mansions, London. † RA 3.
BAUMER, Lewis Christopher Edward b. 1870
Watercolour portrait painter, etcher, black and white, Punch artist and illustrator. Studied Royal College of Art, St. John's Wood School of Art and R.A. Schools. R.I. 1921. Add: London. † COO 6, FIN 222, GI 1, L 25, P 20, RA 41, RBA 1, RI 59, ROI 2.
BAUMGARTEN, Miss C. Exh. 1906
6 Elers Road, Ealing, London. † RA 1.
BAUMGARTNER, Peter* b. 1834
German artist. Add: Munich 1882. † RSA 1.
BAURE, Albert Exh. 1913
15 bis, Boulevard Lannes, Paris. † L 2.
BAURE, P.A. Exh. 1902
Foissy-sur-Vanne, Yonne, France. † L 1.
BAWDEN, Edward b. 1903
Watercolour painter, illustrator and theatre designer. b. Braintree, Essex. Studied Cambridge School of Art, Royal College of Art (travelling scholarship in design). Add: London 1930. † LEI 40, NEA 1, RED 1.
BAX, Mrs. Vera Exh. 1940
Pembroke Gardens, London. † ROI 2.
BAXANDALL, D. Kighley Exh. 1934-37
Cardiff 1934, Whitchurch, Glam. 1937. † RCA 3.
BAXANDALL, Miss G.M. Exh. 1928-32
73 Martin's Lane, Wallasey. † L 4.
BAXENDALE, Miss Annie E. Exh. 1925-29
Claremont, Mayfield St. Atherton, Manchester. † L 8.
BAXENDALE, Peter Exh. 1933
† CON 1.
BAXENDALE, Ralph G. Exh. 1931
1 Tanfield Road, Blowers Green, Dudley. † B 2.
BAX-IRONSIDE, Lady E.A. Exh. 1914-27
Flower and landscape painter. S.W.A. 1915. Add: Eastry, Kent 1914; London 1919. † RA 4, SWA 23.
BAXTER, Alfred E. Exh. 1932-33
Watercolour painter. Add: Chelsea Arts Club, Church Street, London. † RA 1, RBA 2, RI 2.
BAXTER, Charles H. Exh. 1897-1930
Claughton, Lancs. 1897; St. Ives, Cornwall 1904; Winchelsea, Sussex 1907. † B 5, D 2, L 18.
BAXTER, David A. Exh. 1901-26
Landscape painter. Add: Liverpool 1901 and 1916; Ramsey, I.O.M. 1911; Peel, I.O.M. 1922; Oxford 1926. † D 1, L 55, RA 1, RCA 2.
BAXTER, Miss D.M. Exh. 1933
7 Mellor Road, Birkenhead. † L 2.
BAXTER, D.W. Exh. 1939
Messrs. Johnston and Baxter, 114 Seagate, Dundee. † RSA 1.
BAXTER, Mrs. E. Exh. 1888
Invereighty, Forfar. † RSA 1.
BAXTER, Frank b. 1865
Sculptor. Studied in Paris, under D. Puech and J. Dampt. Add: Rainhill, Lancs. 1895; Paris 1896; Liverpool 1898; London 1902. † GI 7, I 1, L 8, LS 8, NG 2, RA 5.
BAXTER, F. Fleming b. 1873
Sculptor and painter. Add: London 1902. † I 2, L 2, NG 3, RA 5, RID 1.
BAXTER, Frederick T. Exh. 1910-27
Aston Manor, Birmingham 1910; Handsworth, Birmingham 1916; Fairbourne, Merioneth 1927. † B 3, L 3, LS 3, RHA 2.
BAXTER, Herbert Exh. 1889
Castle Townsend, Skibbereen, Co. Cork. † NEA 1.
BAXTER, J. Exh. 1889
18 Cuthbert Buildings, Clayton Square, Liverpool. † L 1.
BAXTER, John Exh. 1886-87
13 Union Street, Edinburgh. † RSA 2.
BAXTER, John Frederick Douglas Exh. 1909-29
Landscape painter. Add: London. † NEA 1, LS 9.
BAXTER, Miss Lucy Exh. 1893-94
The Tower, Rainhill. † L 3.
BAXTER, Leslie Robert b. 1893
Portrait and landscape painter, lithographer and engraver. Studied Brighton School of Art, Assistant at Manchester School of Art. Add: Brighton 1922; Wolverhampton 1924; Adlington, Cheshire 1928; Styal, Manchester 1931. † B 3, L 4, M 3, RA 4.
BAXTER, Miss Margaret Exh. 1928-40
1 Woodhall Drive, Cardonald. † GI 7.
BAXTER, Miss M.D. Exh. 1896-1905
Claughton, Lancs. † L 8, RI 1.
BAXTER, Miss Muriel F. Exh. 1927
134 Meadowpark Street, Dennistoun, Glasgow. † L 1.
BAXTER, Miss Nora E. Exh. 1918-20
47 Gt. Russell Street, London. † I 1, L 1, ROI 1.
BAXTER, Miss Nelly M. Exh. 1925
35 Beaconsfield Road, Cannon Hill, Birmingham. † B 1.
BAXTER, Thomas Tennant b. 1894
Portrait, landscape and animal painter. Studied Slade School. N.E.A. 1920. Add: London 1917; Apsley Guise, Bletchley, Bucks. 1940. † ALP 1, CG 2, CHE 2, COO 2, FIN 3, G 3, GI 1, GOU 2, I 23, NEA 82, P 5, RA 5.
BAXTER, William C. Exh. 1897
Comrie Cottage, Hamilton, N.B. † GI 1.
BAXTER, W.H. Exh. 1884-86
Nottingham. † N 4.
BAY, Mrs. Celia Hansen b. 1875
nee Spurling. Landscape and flower painter. Studied Royal College of Art (Royal Exhibitioner and Queen's prizeman). Add: London 1896; Carlisle 1900; Wirksworth, Derby 1926. † L 1, RA 4.
BAYES, Alfred Walter* 1832-1909
Landscape and figure painter and etcher. A.R.E. 1890, R.E. 1900. Add: London. † B 68, D 26, GI 28, L 31, M 24, NG 2, RA 23, RBA 38, RE 60, RHA 10, RI 35, ROI 30.
BAYES, Gertrude Exh. 1899-1921
nee Smith. Sculptor. Married Gilbert W.B. q.v. Flower and landscape painter. Add: London 1899 and 1911; Hornsea, Yorks. 1907. † B 3, L 10, RA 11, RID 4.
BAYES, Gilbert W. 1872-1953
Sculptor and designer of monuments. Studied City and Guilds, Finsbury, R.A. Schools 1896 (gold medal 1899 and travelling scholarship) Paris and Italy. "Sigurd" purchased by Chantrey Bequest 1910. R.I. 1918, H.R.I. 1922. Add: London. † B 23, D 2, G 1, GI 49, GOU 4, I 3, L 48, M 3, NG 10, P 21, RA 120, RBA 5, RI 40, RMS 5, RSA 21.
BAYES, Jessie Exh. 1901-39
Religious painter, illuminator and mural decorator. A.R.M.S. 1905, R.M.S. 1906, H.R.M.S. 1935. Add: London. † B 2, BG 79, FIN 3, L 26, NG 8, RA 14, RI 6, RID 18, RMS 84, RSA 2.

BAYES, Walter John 1869-1956
Painter, illustrator, poster and theatrical scenery designer. Headmaster Winchester School of Art. Lecturer on perspective to R.A. and Slade Schools. Art critic to "Athenaeum". Son of Alfred Walter B. q.v. Founder member London Group 1913; A.R.W.S. 1900. Add: London. † B 12, BA 1, BG 5, CAR 90, CHE 3, FIN 69, G 4, GI 3, GOU 166, I 5, L 30, LEI 100, LS 6, M 4, NEA 20, NG 1, RA 29, RBA 23, RED 2, RI 11, RSA 6, RSW 73, ROI 16.

BAYFIELD, Fanny Jane Exh. 1887-97
Flower painter. Add: Norwich 1887 and 1897; London 1889. † L 1, RA 3, RBA 2, SWA 1.

BAYFIELD, Kenneth C. Exh. 1924
16 Rutland Avenue, Sefton Park, Liverpool. † L 1.

BAYLDON, Miss F. Exh. 1910-16
100 Queen's Road, Richmond, Surrey. † L 2, RA 5.

BAYLES, Miss Oliver Marian Exh. 1929
Watercolour landscape painter. Add: 70 Macdonald Road, Walthamstow, London. † RA 1.

BAYLEY, Alma Elliott Exh. 1928-38
Portrait and watercolour landscape painter. Add: 3 Devonshire Gardens, London. † AB 3, NEA 4, RA 2

BAYLEY, Barbara Exh. 1931-36
Flower painter. Add: London. † GOU 1, RA 1, SWA 1.

BAYLEY, Ernest Exh. 1926
Etcher, architectural illustrator and perspective artist. Studied R.A. Schools. Add: 108 Beverstone Road, Thornton Heath. † RA 1

BAYLEY, Miss E.M. Exh. 1908-10
The Long Cottage, Knaresborough, Yorks. † L 8, RA 1.

BAYLEY, Lancelot Exh. 1914-28
Nenagh, Ireland. 1914; Houth, Ireland 1919; Bray, Ireland 1926. † RHA 31.

BAYLEY, Margaret Bell Exh. 1920-35
Mrs. Percy Price. Miniature painter. Add: London 1920 and 1929; Clacton, Essex 1923; Eastbourne, 1933. † RA 4, RI 19.

BAYLEY, Marguerite E. Exh. 1929-40
Wood engraver and colour woodcut artist. Add: 5 Hanover House, Royal Breeds Place, Hastings. † AB 2, NEA 7, RA 3. RBA 5, RED 1, SWA 3.

BAYLEY, Thomas b. 1893
Sculptor. Studied Chester School of Art, Royal College of Art (travelling scholarship in Sculpture 1923). Master School of Arts and Crafts, Cheltenham, Glos. Served First World War as Gunner R.F.A. in France, Egypt and Palestine. Add: London. † RA 2, RBA 7.

BAYLIF, Charlotte M.A. Exh. 1885
Figure painter. Add: 177 Finsborough Road, Kensington, London. † SWA 1.

BAYLIFF, M. Exh. 1936
54 Chester Terrace, London. † SWA 1.

BAYLIS, William H. Exh. 1890-97
Carver and sculptor. Add: 38 Mount Ararat, Richmond, Surrey. † RA 2.

BAYLISS, C.E. Exh. 1925-31
Birmingham 1925; West Bromwich 1928. † B 7.

BAYLISS, Elise Exh. 1890-95
Painter and illustrator. Married to Sir Wyke B. q.v. Add: 7 North Road, Clapham Park, London. † RBA 4.

BAYLISS, Edwin Butler b. 1874
Industrial landscape, portrait and poster painter. R.B.S.A. 1920. Add: Tettenhall, Wolverhampton 1897. † B 88, GI 1, L 4, RA 9, ROI 3.

BAYLISS, Margaret E. Exh. 1928-38
Newlands, Boswell Road, Sutton Coldfield. † B 13.

BAYLISS, Miss M.J. Exh. 1885-92
Wednesday 1885; Gt. Barr, Birmingham 1892. † B 3.

BAYLISS, Sir Wyke 1835-1906
Painter, mainly churches, and architect. b. Mandalay, India. R.B.A. 1865, P.R.B.A. 1888-1906, H.R.M.S. 1897. Add: 7 North Road, Clapham Park, London. † B 20, D 1, DOW 39, GI 5, L 42, M 21, RBA 228, RHA 1, RI 1, ROI 1, TOO 2.

BAYLY, Miss H. Exh. 1896
113 Via San Gallo, Florence, Italy. † SWA 3.

BAYLY, Miss Eliza Exh. 1880
Landscape painter. Add: Oxford Cottage, Wandle Road, Upper Tooting, London. † SWA 2.

BAYLY, Gertrude Emily b. 1875
Flower painter and miniaturist on ivory. Add: Cliftonville, Margate 1902. † B 2, COO 12, L 4, NG 1, SWA 3.

BAYNE, B.R. Exh. 1917
Arden, Oval Waye, Gerrard's Cross. † RA 1.

BAYNE, Miss Ethel Exh. 1905
19 Langdale Gardens, Hove, Sussex. † RI 1.

BAYNE, J. Exh. 1892-1908
Bridge of Allan, Glasgow 1892; Edinburgh 1895; Burntisland, N.B. 1908. † GI 2, RSA 4.

BAYNES, Miss Angela Exh. 1938-40
Oxford 1938; Farnham, Surrey 1939. † NEA 1, RA 3, RBA 2.

BAYNES, Rt. Rev. Arthur Hamilton Exh. 1882-1936
Landscape painter. Assistant Bishop of Birmingham. Add: Nottingham 1882; Birmingham 1927. † AB 12, N 5, WG 14.

BAYNES, Miss Cicely M. Exh. 1901-5
Buxton, Derbys. 1901; London 1904; Bath 1905. † L 2, RCA 2.

BAYNES, Miss D. Exh. 1905
† SWA 1.

BAYNES, Keith Stuart b. 1887
Landscape painter. Studied Slade School 1912-14. Member London Group 1919. Add: London. † AG 150, BA 2, CHE 3, G 3, GI 1, GOU 7, I 4, L 3, LEF 33, LEI 18, LS 6, NEA 7, RED 2, RSA 1, TOO 1.

BAYNES, Minnie L.E. Exh. 1914
Fern Villa, Sidmouth, Devon. † LS 3.

BAYNES, Mrs. Rosalind Exh. 1922-24
Miniature painter. Add: Florence, Italy. † RA 6.

BAYNTON, George T. Exh. 1922
Sculptor. Add: 16 Lea Bridge Road, Clapton, London. † RA 1.

BAYNTON, H. Exh. 1883
6 Queen Street, Coventry. † B 1.

BAYZAUD, Mrs. M. Exh. 1917
25 Lee Park, Blackheath, London. † RA 1.

BAZELEY, F. Exh. 1905-15
Shepherd's Bush, London 1905; West Drayton, Middlesex 1915. † RA 1, RI 1.

BAZZANI, Luigi* b. 1836
Italian artist. c/o Squire, 293 Oxford Street, London 1883. † RI 1.

BEACH, Alice Exh. 1898-1940
Landscape painter. A.S.W.A. 1922. Add: London. I 3, L 14, RA 11, RBA 3, RI 14, RID 4, ROI 18, SWA 41.

BEACH, A.J. Exh. 1889
c/o Mr. Sykes, The Studios, 2A Sheriff Road, West Hampstead, London. † M 2.

BEACH, Ernest George* b. 1865
Portrait, figure and landscape painter and lithographer. Lecturer on art. Worked in Holland, Belgium and France. Add: London 1888; Dover 1907; Hythe, Kent 1908. † GI 4, GOU 2, L 8, LS 1, NEA 8, RA 10, RI 4, ROI 3.

BEACH, Miss Winifred V. Hicks Exh. 1919
Portrait painter. Add: 24 Devonshire Terrace, London. † RA 1.

BEACHCROFT, T.S. Exh. 1880
Medina, Western Road, Putney, London. † RBA 1.

BEACON, Charles Exh. 1897-1926
Sculptor. Add: London 1897; Bushey, Herts. 1913. † GI 9, L 3, NG 7, RA 10, RI 1, ROI 2.

BEADLE, Edith Exh. 1887
Flower painter. Add: 6 Queen's Gate Gardens, South Kensington, London. † SWA 1.

BEADLE, James Prinsep Barnes* b. 1863
Military, landscape and animal painter. b. Calcutta. Studied Slade School under Legros, and Beaux Arts. R.B.A. 1909. Add: 17B Eldon Road, Victoria Road, London. † B 17, BG 1, FIN 45, G 12, L L 31, LEI 1, M 8, NG 18, P 1, RA 49, RBA 6, RHA 5, ROI 1.

BEADLE, Oliver Exh. 1936
Studied Heatherleys and Paris at Julians and Academie de la Grande Chaimiere. † WG 37.

BEADLE, Suzanne Exh. 1935-40
Portrait and figure painter. Add: London. † P 4, RA 3, RSA 1.

BEADLEY, Frank Exh. 1886-88
56 Highbury Hill, London. † B 3.

BEADON, Mrs. Joanna Exh. 1908
King and Co. 9 Pall Mall, London. † LS 5.

BEADON, Mrs. Marjory Exh. 1909-33
Landscape painter. Add: Salisbury, Wilts. 1909; Edinburgh 1910; Faringdon, Berks. 1929. † L 1, RA 3, RBA 1, RSA 1, WG 3.

BEAL, Annie L. Exh. 1880-1916
Figure painter. Visited Australia. Add: London. †B 13, GI 1, L 4, M 4, RA 6, RBA 2, RHA 1, ROI 1.

BEALE, E. Exh. 1884
35 Albany Street, Regents Park, London. † M 1.

BEALE, Evelyn Exh. 1904-38
Sculptor and potter. Studied Slade School. Add: Edinburgh 1904; North Shields 1907; Portobello, Midlothian 1909; Rothesay, N.B. 1910; Glasgow 1918. † GI 36, L 3, RSA 18, RSW 1.

BEALE, Edward H. Exh. 1933-35
Watercolour landscape painter. Add: Rockhurst, Burwash, Sussex. † RA 2.

BEALE, Sarah Sophia* Exh. 1880-1909
Genre, portrait and marine painter. Add: London 1880; Oxford 1908. † B 2, D 4, L 4, M 3, RA 3, RBA 2, RHA 2, RI 1, ROI 1, SWA 5.

BEAMER, M.E. Exh. 1893
46 Carlton Road, Birkenhead. † L 1.

BEAMISH, Miss J.E. Exh. 1905-27
Ballymodan House, Bandon, Co. Cork. † RE 3, RHA 51.

BEAN, Ainslie Exh. 1880-86
Urban and landscape painter. Add: London. † L 3, M 2, RBA 4, RHA 2, RI 3.

BEAN, Miss Florence Exh. 1909-12
Welling, Kent. † SWA 3.

BEANLANDS, Mrs. Sophie T. see PEMBERTON

BEAR, George Telfer b. 1874
Oil painter. Studied Glasgow School of Art. Spent some years in Canada. Add: Glasgow 1905 and 1927; Kirkcudbright 1922. † BAR 7, GI 54, RSA 21.

BEARD, Miss Ada Exh. 1885-96
Flower painter. Add: Clapham Common, London. † L 1, RA 7.

BEARD, A.E. Exh. 1933
7a Grove Park Road, Weston super Mare. † B 1.

BEARD, A.F. Exh. 1914
54 Deansgate, Manchester. † RCA 1.

BEARD, Miss C.M. Exh. 1888-90
Thickthorne, Kenilworth. † B 2, L 1.

BEARD, F. Exh. 1929
23 Nevern Place, London. † NEA 1.

BEARD, Miss Freda M. Exh. 1920
Portrait painter. Add: 23 Merton Road, Kensington, London. † RA 2.

BEARD, Miss Kate Exh. 1911-24
Miniature painter. Add: 45 Warrington Road, Harrow, Middlesex. † RA 2, RHA 2.

BEARD, Katharine L. Exh. 1885-1919
Flower painter and black and white artist. Add: London. † M 1, RBA 3, ROI 6, SWA 1.

BEARD, Miss M. Exh. 1882-83
15 South Hill Road, Liverpool. † L 2.

BEARD, Mary Exh. 1935
33 Grove Road, London. † SWA 2.

BEARDS, Harold William b. 1895
Portrait painter. Humorous artist and illustrator. Studied Wolverhampton School of Art and Regent Street Polytechnic. Add: Thorpe Bay, Essex 1937. † B 2, P 1.

BEARDSLEY, Aubrey 1872-1898
Black and white artist and illustrator. Worked in an architect's office and as a clerk with Guardian Insurance Co. Did many designs for Oscar Wilde's works. Died in France of consumption. N.E.A. 1894. † GI 3, P 1, NEA 6.

BEARDSLEY, Davis H. d. c.1926
Landscape painter. Add: Ilkeston, Derbys. 1909. † N 37.

BEARE, Josias Crocker b. 1881
Architectural and landscape watercolour painter and architect. Add: Newton Abbot, Devon. 1921. † L 9, RA 2, RCA 57, WG 68.

BEARE, Miss N.M. Exh. 1898
Rydal Mount, Ableside Avenue, Streatham. London. † RBA 1.

BEARNE, Mrs. Edward see CHARLTON, Catharine

BEARNE, Edward* Exh. 1880-1901
Landscape and rustic genre painter. Visited continent. Add: London 1880, Dunster, Som. 1893. † B 4, D 4, M 12, RA 10, RI 10.

BEASLEY, Miss Jessie M. Exh. 1908-15
25A Prince Alfred Road, Wavertree, Liverpool. † L 4.

BEATER, George P. Exh. 1888-1910
17 Lower Sackville Street, Dublin. † RHA 2, RSA 1.

BEATIE, Robert Exh. 1901-2
Oakdene, Mostyn Avenue, Llandudno. † B 1, RCA 1.

BEATON, Allan Exh. 1920
† RHA 3.

BEATON, Cecil* b 1904
Designer, illustrator, photographer and writer. Exh. 1927 and 1938. † COO 32, RED 2.

BEATON, Penelope d. 1963
Watercolour painter. Add: Edinburgh 1925. † GI 4, L 1, RSA 17, RSW 1.

BEATON, Robert J. Exh. 1898
5 Livingston Terrace, Ibrox, N.B. † GI 1.

BEATON, Wilson Exh. 1894-1902
Glasgow. † GI 10.

BEATRICE, H.R.H. Princess Exh. 1883-85
Watercolour landscape painter. H.R.I. 1882. † RI 3.

BEATSON, C. Exh. 1904
67 Nethergreen Road, Sheffield. † RA 1.

BEATT, Mrs. M. Ethel Exh. 1927-33
Bank of Ireland, Bandon. † RHA 6.

BEATTIE, Alex B. Exh. 1927
50 Mile End Avenue, Aberdeen. † GI 1.

BEATTIE, Thos. Exh. 1913
Dean Studios, Edinburgh. † RSA 1.

BEATTIE, William Exh. 1882-91
Crosshill, Glasgow 1882; Cambuslang 1891. † GI 3, RSA 2.

BEATTIE, William Fras. Exh. 1912-14
Edinburgh. † RSA 2.

BEATTIE, William Hamilton Exh. 1880-96
Architect. Edinburgh. † RA 1, RSA 6.

BEATTIE-CROZIER, Auriol Exh. 1933
† COO 1.

BEATTY, Miss Kathleen J. Exh. 1903-5
6 Novara Terrace, Bray. † RHA 2.

BEATY-POWNALL, David Herman b. 1904
Architect. Studied A.A. (Holloway scholarship). Add: 61 Oakley Street, London 1927. † L 1, RI 1.

BEAUCHAMP, E. Exh. 1920
Sculptor. 14 Cheltenham Terrace, Chelsea, London. † RA 1.

BEAUCHAMP, Earl Exh. 1915
13 Belgrave Square, London. † RA 1.

BEAUDUIN, Jean* 1851-1916
Exh. 1916. † CON 1.

BEAUFEREY, Mlle Berthe Exh. 1909
1 Rue Demour, Paris. † L 1.

BEAUFILS, A.E.J. Exh. 1912
2 Rue Mizon, Paris. † L 1.

BEAUFRERE, Adolphe b. 1876
French etcher. Exh. 1921-26. † FIN 95.

BEAULANDS, Mrs. S. Exh. 1916
Wickhurst Manor, Sevenoaks, Kent. † RA 1.

BEAUMONT, Mrs. Exh. 1900
31 Hydethorpe Road, Balham, London. † NG 1.

BEAUMONT, Annie Exh. 1882-1910
Liverpool 1882; Bebington, Cheshire 1886; Oxton, Cheshire 1888; Birkenhead 1898. † L 20, RCA 1.

BEAUMONT, C.W. Exh. 1907-10
Outer Temple, 222 Strand, London. † RA 3.

BEAUMONT, Miss E. Exh. 1916-17
13 Glaithwaite Road, Lewisham, London. † I 1, L 2, RA,1.

BEAUMONT, Miss Elfreda G. Exh. 1934
Rimpton, Nr. Yeovil, Som. † RA 1.

BEAUMONT, F. Exh. 1901
6 Castle Street, Liverpool. † L 3.

BEAUMONT, Frederick Samuel b. 1861
Portrait and landscape painter. Studied R.A. Schools (silver medal) and Julians, Paris R.I. 1916. Add: London 1884 and 1917, Wimborne, Dorset 1895. † G 3, L 21, NG 3, P 13, RA 25, RBA 1, RI 2, ROI 2, RSA 2.

BEAUMONT, Miss Gertrude Exh. 1919-28
The Crescent, Horsham, Sussex. † L 3.

BEAUMONT, Miss H. Exh. 1916
13 Glaithwaite Road, Lewisham. † L 1.

BEAUMONT, Ivor Exh. 1914-38
Mural painter, designer and illuminator. Add: London 1914, School of Art, Belfast 1919-38. † L 3, RSA 17.

BEAUMONT, Jerold Exh. 1893-94
5A Woodsome Road, Highgate, London. † ROI 2.

BEAUMONT, Leonard b. 1891
Painter, etcher, lino and wood-cut artist. Add: 18 Bents Green Road, Ecclesall, Sheffield. † GI 2, L 11, RED 1.

BEAUMONT, Mrs. M. Exh. 1916
23 Prospect Road, Surbiton, Surrey. † RA 1.

BEAUMONT, William Exh. 1901
Figure painter. Add: St. John's Parsonage, St. John's Wood Road, London. † NEA 1.

BEAUMONT, Miss Winifred Exh. 1900
† P 1.

BEAUPRE, de See D

BEAURY-LAUREL, Mme Amelie Exh. 1921
Galerie Montmartre 27, Paris. † L 1.

BEAUVAIS, Arnold b. 1886
Landscape painter, illustrator and poster designer. Studied under his father and at Bolt Court Art School where he later taught. Exh. 1935. † AR 1.

BEAUVALET, Mlle Jeanne Exh. 1904
88 Rue de Rivoli, Paris. † L 1.

BEAVIS, Maud Exh. 1881
38 Fitzroy Square, London. † RBA 1.

BEAVIS, Minnie S. Exh. 1896-99
Mrs. J.W. The Laurels, Albemarle Road, Beckenham, Kent. † RBA 3, SWA 3.

BEAVIS, Richard* 1824-1896
Landscape and coastal painter. Born Exmouth, Devon. Studied R.A. Schools 1846. Travelled Continent and Middle East. A.R.I. 1867, R.I. 1871, A.R.W.S. 1882, R.W.S. 1892. Add: London 1880. † B 9, BG 1, FIN 1, G 7, GI 7, L 17, M 18, NG 5, RA 17, RI 4, ROI 18, RWS 54, TOO 73.

BEAZLEY, C.M. Exh. 1939-40
72 West Street, Marlow, Bucks. † B 1, RBA 1, RHA 1, ROI 1, RSA 1.

BEAZLEY, C.N. Exh. 1883
8 Delahay Street, Westminster, London. † RA 1.

BEBB, Minnie Rosa b. 1857
Animal painter. Studied Bath School of Art and Tiverton School of Art. Add: Bristol 1898. † B 2, RCA 1, SWA 3.

BECAGLI, Margueritte G. Exh. 1909
† LS 3.

BECHER, Miss A.E.F. Exh. 1883-84
18 Crawford Square, Londonderry. † RHA 2.

BECHER, Miss Augusta L. Exh. 1894
Sydney House, Sinclair Road, Kensington, London. † RA 1.

BECHTEL, B. Roberts Exh. 1909
† LS 3.

BECK, Angelo Exh. 1884-89
Sculptor of portrait medallions. Add: 29 Granville Square, London. † RA 3.

BECK, Miss Elsie W. Exh. 1922
84 Tettenhall Road, Wolverhampton. † B 1.

BECK, H. Exh. 1910
10 High Street, Burton-on-Trent. † RA 1.

BECK, J.W. Exh. 1880-95
Landscape painter. London. † B 1, FIN 2, G 14, L 5, M 7, NG 11, RWS 2.

BECK, Mrs. Mary C. Exh. 1916-19
Elstree 1916; Guildford, Surrey 1919. † GI 1, L 2, RI 2, ROI 1, SWA 2.

BECK, Wallace Exh. 1924-37
Cheltenham, Glos. † B 10.

BECKER, C.J. Exh. 1906
Philadelphia, U.S.A. † RA 1.

BECKER, G. Exh. 1885
† TOO 2.
BECKER, Harry d. 1928
Painter, etcher and lithographer. Studied Antwerp Academy and in Paris. † ALP 124, B 3, BA 26, GI 1, GOU 2, L 15, LS 7, M 7, NG 2, P 5, RA 15, RBA 10, RED 2, RHA 13, RI 6, RSA 12.
BECKETT, Ernest F. Exh. 1905
391 Smithdown Road, Liverpool. † L 2.
BECKETT, Fannie Exh. 1897-1908
Dublin. † RHA 10.
BECKETT, Geo. F. Exh. 1907-10
97 St. Stephen's Green, Dublin. † RHA 10.
BECKETT, Jessie Exh. 1893
Riverside, Sandymount, Dublin. † RHA 1.
BECKETT, Mary C. Exh. 1896-1925
Huyton 1896; Liverpool 1911. † L 7.
BECKETT, Richard Thomas Exh. 1895-1928
Architect. Add: Hartford, Cheshire 1895; Liverpool 1904; Chester 1915; Mold, Flints. 1926. † L 4, RA 6,RCA 2.
BECKETT, Miss S.H.J. Exh. 1911
Westbourne Grove, London. † SWA 2.
BECKHAM, Miss S. Exh. 1889
51 Hope Street, Liverpool. † L 1.
BECKINGHAM, Arthur Exh. 1881-1920
Landscape and figure painter. A.R.B.A. 1918. Add: London 1881; Houghton, Hunts. 1912. † L 6, M 4, RA 13, RBA 21, ROI 7.
BECKLES, Evelyn Lina b. 1888
Mrs. Linton. Portrait and animal painter. Studied Bushey, Herts. (2 year scholarship). Add: Bushey, Herts. 1907; St. Ives, Cornwall 1915; Bristol 1916. † B 1, RCA 4.
BECKLES, G.H. Exh. 1929
† D 1.
BECKLEY, Mrs. M.I. Exh. 1917-21
2 Rushton Crescent, Wimborne Road, Bournemouth. † LS 11.
BECKWITH, Mrs. E.A. Exh. 1892
Pendarren Cottage, Crickhowell, S. Wales. † B 1.
BECKWITH, H.L. Exh. 1928-29
3 Cook Street, Liverpool. † L 5.
BECKWITH, James Carroll 1852-1917
American portrait painter. Exh. 1892. † L 1, RA 1.
BEDDALL, Kathlyn Exh. 1939-40
18 Old Church Street, London. † NEA 1, SWA 1.
BEDDINGTON, Fred Exh. 1929
The White Cottage, Denham, Bucks. † WG 2.
BEDDINGTON, J. Roy b. 1910
Landscape painter and illustrator. Studied Slade School and Florence. Add: London. † COO 1, GOU 3, NEA 1, RA 4, RBA 1, RCA 2, ROI 1.
BEDDINGTON, Maud Exh. 1895-1922
Painter of children and fairies. Add: London. † BG 3, L 1, NG 5, RA 1.
BEDDOE, Violet Bellingham Exh. 1920-37
Southport, Lancs. 1920; London 1927. † L 2, RA 1, RCA 12.
BEDDOES, Thomas H.W. Exh. 1896-98
Coastal painter. Add: 14 St. John Street, Adelphi, London. † M 1, RA 2, RHA 2.
BEDDOW, Alfred E. Exh. 1904
Southwood, Bickley, Kent. † D 2.
BEDFORD, Celia b. 1904
Portrait and figure painter. Studied Chelsea Polytechnic. Add: London. † GI 1, GOU 1, NEA 17, RA 8, RID 4, RSA 1, SWA 2.
BEDFORD, Dorothy Helen b. 1897
Landscape painter, illustrator, wood-engraver, art teacher. Studied Central School of Arts and Crafts. Add: 20 The Common, Ealing, London. † GI 1, NEA 1, RA 4, RED 2.
BEDFORD, Miss Ellen Exh. 1896
† P 1.
BEDFORD, Ella M. Exh. 1882-1908
Figure, decorative and genre painter. Add: London. † B 15, L 1, M 7, RA 22, RBA 9, RI 1, ROI 2, SWA 2.
BEDFORD, Vice Admiral Sir F. Exh. 1898
56 Lexham Gardens, London. † D 3.
BEDFORD, F. Exh. 1920
36 Murray Road, Northwood, Middlesex. † L 1.
BEDFORD, Francis Donkin b. 1864
Painter and illustrator. Studied South Kensington and R.A. Schools. Articled to Sir Arthur Blomfield. Add: London. † L 2, NEA 8, NG 1, RA 9, RID 35.
BEDFORD, Francis W. d. c.1905
Architectural artist. Add: Leeds and London. † RA 18.
BEDFORD, Herbert Exh. 1908-14
London. † L 7, LS 9, RA 2, RMS 1.
BEDFORD, Helen Catharine b. 1874
Portrait painter. née Carter. Married to Francis Donkin B. q.v. Add: London † BG 3, I 8, L 5, NEA 21, NG 1, P 2, RA 13, RID 54, SWA 1.
BEDFORD, Henry E. Exh. 1892-93
Landscape painter. Add: 10 Lancaster Park, Richmond, Surrey. † RBA 3.
BEDFORD, John B. Exh. 1881-86
Landscape and figure painter. Add: 92 Boundary Road, St. John's Wood, London. † D 4, L 2, M 4, RA 4, RBA 1.
BEDFORD, J.D. Exh. 1909
† BG 1.
BEDFORD, Miss M.C. Exh. 1898
1 Palace Gardens Terrace, London. † SWA 1.
BEDFORD, Oliver Herbert b. 1902
Watercolour painter. Professor Royal Institute of Arts, Rome 1923. Exh. 1938. † FIN 50.
BEDFORD, Percy Exh. 1889-1918
Landscape painter. N.S.A. 1890. Add: Kegworth, Derby. † N 23.
BEDFORD, Richard Percy b. 1883
Painter and sculptor. Keeper Dept. of Architecture and Sculpture, Victoria and Albert Museum 1926-46. Member London Group 1932. Exh. 1939. † COO 1.
BEDGOOD, Miss Jane McG. Exh. 1928
Haworth, Renfrew. † GI 1.
BEDINGFIELD, J. Exh. 1890
Figure painter. Add: 19 Sumatra Road, West Hampstead, London. † L 1.
BEDINGFIELD, Richard Thackeray Exh. 1883-94
Figure painter. Add: 16 St. Augustine's Road, Camden Square, London. † B 13, L 1, RA 2, RHA 10.
BEDINGFIELD, R.W. Exh. 1894-99
Architect, Add: Leicester 1894 and 1896; London 1895. † RA 5.
BEDINI, P.* Exh. 1883
c/o Dowdeswell, 133 New Bond Street, London. † M 1.
BEDNON, A. Exh. 1893
Figure painter. Add: Boulogne-sur-mer, France. † RBA 1.
BEE, John William b. 1883
Landscape painter. Studied Sheffield and under James Moore. Add: 4 Washington Road, Sheffield 1923. † L 1.
BEEBE, Annie A. Exh. 1884-90
Figure painter. Add: London. † L 3, M 1, RA 2, RHA 2.
BEEBE, Dee Exh. 1926
† FIN 2.
BEECH, A.J. Exh. 1888-90
Flower painter. Add: London. † GI 1, L 1, M 2, RA 2, RBA 1, RI 1.
BEECH, Constance E. Exh. 1922-40
Miniature portrait painter. Add: Wolverhampton 1922; London 1931. † B 12, NEA 4, RA 5, RI 2.
BEECH, Miss Chrissie H. Exh. 1907-8
Jesmond Grove, Highfield Road, Edgbaston, Birmingham. † B 3.
BEECH, Ellen Exh. 1927-34
Ufton Fields, Near Alfreton, Derbys. † N 3.
BEECH, Miss Eveline Exh. 1907
Jesmond Grove, Highfield Road, Edgbaston, Birmingham. † B 1.
BEECH, Herbert J.G. Exh. 1893
Watercolour portrait painter. Add: Cardiff. † RA 1.
BEECH, Miss Mary Exh. 1905-9
Maesgwyn, Wrexham. † L 1, RCA 1.
BEECHEY, Ernest A. Exh. 1909
Hilgay, Downham, Norfolk. † L 1.
BEECHEY, Richard Brydges* 1808-1895
Marine painter. Son of Sir William Beechey, R.A. Served in the Royal Navy, rising to rank of Admiral. H.R.H.A. Add: Plymouth 1880, Ryde, I.O.W. 1892. † L 2, RHA 17.
BEEDLE, William J. Exh. 1923-38
Landscape painter. Add: 7 Clova Road, Forest Gate, London. † RA 3.
BEEKES, Bernard Exh. 1937-38
Sculptor and pencil artist. Add: 610 Fulham Road, London. † RA 2.
BEER, Joyce Marion Exh. 1934-40
Landscape painter. Add: Bickley, Kent. † RA 1, SWA 4.
BEERBOHM, Max* 1872-1956
Caricaturist and writer. N.E.A. 1909. Add: London 1909. † BG 8, CAR 53, GOU 3, I 1, LEI 283, NEA 42.
BEERE, Alfred Exh. 1880-81
Sculptor. 17 South Street, Greenwich. † RA 3.
BEERLING, Doris Louisa Annie See FLASHMAN
BEERS, Van See V
BEESE, J. Clifford Exh. 1913
Painter of imaginary landscapes. b. Somerset. Studied Battersea Polytechnic. Add: Staines. † LS 3.
BEESON, Charles Richard b. 1909
Painter and etcher. Studied St. John's Wood and R.A. Schools. (bronze medal for drawing). Add: London 1931. † NEA 1, RA 1, RBA 1.
BEEST, E. Van H.V. Exh. 1886
Bese Villa, Zwolle, Holland. † RI 1.
BEESTON, Arthur Exh. 1880-84
Landscape painter. Add: 13 Lower Belgrave St. London. † D 1, RBA 1.
BEETHOLME, George Law F. Exh. 1880-90
Still life and landscape painter. Add: London. † L 1, RBA 3.
BEETLES, Capt. J.A. Exh. 1934
28 Sutton Passeys Crescent, Wollaton Park, Nottingham. † N 2.
BEETON, Alan Edmund 1880-1942
Figure painter. Studied London and Paris. "Decomposing" purchased by Chantrey Bequest 1931. A.R.A. 1938. Add: London 1911 and 1931, Chickendon, Reading 1923. † G 3, GI 3, L 3, LS 9, RA 17, RHA 1.

BEFANI, Gennaro Exh. 1912-37
2 Passage de Dantzig, Paris. † GI 2, L 2.

BEGBIE, Irene b. 1894
Mrs. Ellissen. Portrait and miniature painter b. Grimsby. Studied Slade School and Calderons Animal Painting School. Add: London 1912, Richmond Hill, Surrey 1926. † L 1, RA 3.

BEGG, H.C. Exh. 1923
† D 2.

BEGG, John Exh. 1890-97
Architectural artist (churches). Add: London. † RA 3.

BEGG, John Exh. 1935
23 Rutland Square, Edinburgh. † RSA 2.

BEGG, James L. Exh. 1896-1909
Mount Vernon, Glasgow 1896 and 1902, London 1897. † GI 7, L 1, RSA 2, RSW 1.

BEGG, Miss J.P. Exh. 1892-1906
Paisley, N.B. 1892, Glasgow 1897. † GI 11, M 1.

BEGG, Robert J. d. 1926
Watercolour painter. Add: Udale House, Christchurch Road, Bournemouth, Hants. 1919. † D 15, RCA 4.

BEGG, Samuel Exh. 1886-91
Painter and black and white artist. Add: London. † RA 3.

BEGLEY, H. Exh. 1881-83
Corballa, Limerick. † RHA 4.

BEGLIOSCHI, J. Exh. 1886
c/o W. Theed, 2A Henrietta Street, Cavendish Square, London. † L 1.

BEHENNA, Kathleen Arthur d. 1920's
Miniature painter. R.M.S. 1896. Add: London 1896 and 1911, France 1903. † LS 3, P 7, RA 2, RMS 28.

BEHN, Prof. Fritz Exh. 1935
Drawings of African big game. † FIN 58.

BEHR, Miss Julia Exh. 1885
South End House, Twickenham. † G 1.

BEHREND, Arthur C. Exh. 1885-1911
Liverpool 1885 and 1906, London 1891 and 1911. † L 23.

BEHREND, George Lionel Exh. 1913-40
Watercolour, landscape and still life painter. A.R.B.A. 1921, R.B.A. 1923. Add: London 1913, Liverpool 1920. † GOU 3, L 8, NEA 28, RA 2, RBA 143, RID 3.

BEIJERS, Miss A. Exh. 1914
Canna Cottage, Avenue Stellenbosch, S. Africa. † RA 1.

BEJAR, de. see D

BEJOT, Eugene 1867-1931
French painter and etcher. Born and lived in France. A.R.E. 1899, R.E. 1908. † CON 135, FIN 23, GI 3, L 6, RA 6, RE 126.

BEKEN, Annie Exh. 1898-1933
Watercolour painter. Studied Royal College of Art (silver medal). Art teacher with L.C.C. Assistant at Hornsey and Clapton Schools of Art. Add: London. † AB 2, L 2, LS 15, RA 4.

BEKERATH, Von. see V

BELASCO, Dorothy Exh. 1922-31
Landscape painter. † CG 1, G 5.

BELCHER, Arthur H. d. c.1924
Architect. Add: London. † RA 7, RI 3.

BELCHER, Miss E. Beatrice Exh. 1885
7 Brunswick Square. † RA 1.

BELCHER, George 1875-1947
Painter and etcher. Artist for "Punch", "Tatler" and "Vanity Fair". A.R.A. 1931. Add: London. † CHE 4, FIN 111, GI 13, I 31, L 7, LEI 99, M 3, NEA 1, RA 60, RSA 11.

BELCHER, Miss H. Exh. 1914
c/o J.B. Smith, 117 Hampstead Road, London. † RA 1.

BELCHER, John 1841-1913
Architect. A.R.A. 1900, R.A. 1909. Add: London. † GI 8, RA 98, RSA 5.

BELCHER, Miss Lena Exh. 1915-25
Birkenhead 1915, Liverpool 1920. † L 4.

BELDAM, George W. Exh. 1898-1916
Brentwood, Middlesex 1898, Ealing 1916. † D 2, RA 1.

BELFORD, Mrs. H. Exh. 1880
8 St. Philip's Terrace, Stratford Road, Kensington, London. † SWA 1.

BELFORD, Kate A. Exh. 1880-87
Landscape and figure painter. Add: 4 Christchurch Road, Hampstead, London. † D 10, L 1, RBA 2, RI 4, SWA 13.

BELFRAGE, Miss Elaine Exh. 1937-39
Edinburgh. † RSA 3.

BELFRAGE, J.H. Exh. 1904-5
Architect. 9 Trafalgar Square, Chelsea, London. † RA 1, RSA 1.

BELGRAVE, Dacres T.C. Exh. 1880-90
Watercolour landscape painter. Add: Shooter's Hill, London 1880, Bracknell, Berks. 1889. † B 3, D 1, GI 1, L 14, RA 1, RBA 1, RE 8, RHA 2, RI 3.

BELGRAVE, Percy Exh. 1880-96
Landscape painter. N.E.A. 1887. Add: London. † D 3, G 2, L 8, M 1, NEA 1, NG 1, RA 40, RBA 20, RI 3, ROI 1.

BELGRAVE, William Exh. 1890-97
Landscape painter. Add: London. † L 1, RA 5, ROI 2.

BELK, Mrs. Minnie E. Exh. 1911-21
Portrait painter. Add: Huyton 1911, Liverpool 1921. † L 7, RA 2.

BELL, Mrs. A. Exh. 1921-22
Saxes Plat, Rudgwick, Sussex. † RA 1, RI 1.

BELL, Ada Exh. 1880-1907
Mrs. Frank Whalley. Flower and landscape painter. A.S.W.A. 1889. Add: London 1880, East Sheen, Surrey 1904, Barnes, Surrey 1905, Rudgwick, Sussex 1907. † B 4, D 4, FIN 2, G 10, L 16, M 7, NG 1, RA 16, RBA 15, RI 17, ROI 13, SWA 15, TOO 12.

BELL, Alfred Exh. 1890-95
Watercolour painter. Add: Bayford House, Rosslyn Park, Hampstead, London. † RA 2.

BELL, Ann Exh. 1890-1900
London 1890, Liverpool 1897. † B 2, ROI 1, SWA 1.

BELL, Arthur Exh. 1932-40
Etcher. Add: Parkstone, Dorset, 1932, Cheltenham, Glos. 1940. † RA 5.

BELL, Alex Carlyle Exh. 1880-93
Landscape painter. Add: London 1880, Sterling 1893. † D 20, GI 2, L 4, RA 3, RBA 4, RI 16, ROI 8, RSA 5.

BELL, Ann C. Beatson Exh. 1896-1901
Edinburgh. † RSA 5.

BELL, Agnes E. Exh. 1897-98
London 1897, Liverpool 1898. † L 1, M 1, SWA 2.

BELL, Arthur George* 1849-1916
Landscape and genre painter. N.E.A. 1886. Add: London 1880 and 1897, Christchurch, Hants. 1895. † AG 1, BG 1, D 3, FIN 9, G 1, GI 17, GOU 1, L 17, M 7, NEA 8, NG 14, RA 45, RBA 45, RHA 2, RI 51, ROI 70, RSA 6, TOO 3.

BELL, Asahel P. Exh. 1881-82
Architect. Add: 32 Winter's Buildings, Manchester. † RA 2.

BELL, Mrs. Berthe R. Exh. 1934-37
Landscape painter. Add: Pucknowle, Constitution Hill Road, Parkstone, Dorset. † RA 3.

BELL, Charles Exh. 1881-90
Architect. Add: London. † RA 4.

BELL, Mrs. C.J. Exh. 1897
92 Falkner Street, Liverpool. † L 1.

BELL, Col. D. Exh. 1898-1923
London. † D 3.

BELL, David Exh. 1939-40
Portrait painter. Add: London. † NEA 3, RA 1.

BELL, Dora Exh. 1902
3 Campden Hill Square, London. † SWA 2.

BELL, Dorothea Foster Exh. 1938
Landscape painter. Visited continent. Add: Henley-on-Thames. † RA 2.

BELL, Dorothy J. Exh. 1919-23
Sculptor. Add: London. † I 1, RA 1, RMS 1.

BELL, Eleanor Exh. 1880-86
Figure painter. Add: Munich, Germany 1880, London 1885. † RA 1, RBA 5, RHA 1.

BELL, Edith A. Exh. 1896-1912
Sculptor. Add: London. † L 2, NG 2, RA 11.

BELL, Miss E.H. Exh. 1881
Cuba Cottage, West Broughty Ferry. † RSA 1.

BELL, Edward Ingress Exh. 1880-1908
Architect. Add: Epsom, Surrey, 1880, London 1882. † RA 9.

BELL, Mrs. E.M. Exh. 1893
9 Glebe Crescent, Stirling. † GI 1.

BELL, Eric Sinclair b. 1884
Architect and etcher. Studied Stirling, Glasgow School of Art. London and Aberdeen. Architectural apprenticeship under Sir J.J. Burnet, R.A. Add: Stirling, 1918. † GI 1, I 2, RSA 2.

BELL, Flora Exh. 1896-1908
London 1896, Beckenham, Kent 1908. † NG 1, RI 1, ROI 1, SWA 1.

BELL, Frederick Cyril Exh. 1938
Landscape and figure painter. Add: 6 Peel Street, Langley Mill, Notts. † N 3.

BELL, Miss Florence M. Exh. 1900-21
62 Wellington Road, Dublin. † L 1, RHA 10.

BELL, George b. 1878
Landscape painter. Official war artist First World War. b. Melbourne. Add: London 1908. † GOU 2, L 4, LS 11, NEA 1, P 1, RA 2, ROI 2.

BELL, Graham 1910-1943
b. South Africa. Came to England 1931. Founder of the Euston Road School 1937-39. "Dover Front" painted in 1938 purchased by Chantrey Bequest 1967. Killed while serving with R.A.F. † LEF 1, LEI 1.

BELL, Mrs. Gladys Kathleen M. Exh. 1910-39
Miniature painter. Married to Reginald B. q.v. Studied Cope and Nichols' School of Art. A.R.M.S. 1914, R.M.S. 1927, Add: London. † L 10, RA 23, RI 18, RMS 110, SWA 1.

BELL, Mrs. H. Exh. 1893-1902
Liscard, Cheshire 1893, New Brighton, Cheshire 1896, Liverpool 1900, Edgbaston, Birmingham 1901. † B 9, L 17, M 3.

BELL, Henry A. Exh. 1889
27 Petherton Road, Highbury, New Park, London. † ROI 1.

BELL, Harold Fraser. Exh. 1880-92
Lasswade, Midlothian 1880, Edinburgh 1881. † G 1, GI 7, RSA 21.
BELL, Henry Jobson Exh. 1887-1916
Landscape painter. Add: Edinburgh. † GI 11, L 2, M 1, RA 6, RSA 20.
BELL, Miss Helen P. Exh. 1934
85 Castlemilk Crescent, Glasgow. † RSA 2.
BELL, Miss Ida Exh. 1906
Bromeholme, Rudgwick, Sussex. † L 1.
BELL, Iris C.M. Exh. 1919-40
Miniature portrait painter. Add: Warminster, Wilts. 1919; Mousehole, Penzance, Cornwall 1932. † RA 6.
BELL, Jeanne Exh. 1929-40
Sculptor. Add: London. † GI 1, L 2, RA 8, RMS 14.
BELL, Joan Exh. 1925
Black and white artist. Add: Hill House, Bromley, Kent. † RA 1.
BELL, J. Brownbridge Exh. 1885
15 Summerhall Place, Edinburgh. † RSA 2.
BELL, John Clement b. 1860
Stained glass artist and landscape painter. Studied Slade School (silver medal). Add: London 1890. † B 1, NEA 2, RA 10, RI 1, RSA 1.
BELL, John D. Exh. 1880-1900
Landscape and marine painter. R.S.W. 1878 (resigned 1902). Add: Edinburgh. † DOW 2, GI 25, RSA 42, RSW 70.
BELL, Jos. Jno. Exh. 1883-1908
Roslin, Midlothian 1883; Lasswade, Midlothian 1897. † GI 6, RSA 10.
BELL, John M. Exh. 1894-1940
Birkenhead 1894, Glasgow 1907. † GI 34, L 3, RSA 6, RSW 2.
BELL, James Torrington Exh. 1934-40
Landscape painter. Add: Woodlands, Carnoustie, Angus. † GI 1, RA 10, RCA 3, RSA 3.
BELL: John T. Scott Exh. 1925-32
28 Bothwell Street, Edinburgh. † RSA 13.
BELL, Kate F. Exh. 1898-1900
3 Newton Place, Glasgow. † GI 2.
BELL, Lawrence Exh. 1921-22
13A Heath Street, Hampstead, London. † GI 2.
BELL, Lizzie Exh. 1895-96
3 Westbourne Gardens, Glasgow. † GI 2.
BELL, Miss Louie Exh. 1905
97 Newsham Drive, The Brook, Liverpool. † L 2.
BELL, Laura Anning 1867-1950
Mme Richard-Troncy. Married Robert Anning B. q.v. Portrait painter. Add: Paris 1911-12; London 1919. † FIN 38, GI 1, L 8, P 1, RA 11, RID 5, SWA 3.
BELL, Lucy Hilda d. c.1925
Miniature, landscape and still life painter. R.M.S. 1898. Add: London. † L 13, NG 1, RA 14, RBA 4, RI 7, RMS 64, SWA 19.
BELL, Lilian Russell Exh. 1899-1933
Wallasey, Cheshire 1899; London 1910. † L 58.
BELL, L.S. Exh. 1899
70 South Woodside Road, Glasgow. † GI 1.
BELL, Mary Alexandra see EASTLAKE
BELL, Miss Maud Anna Exh. 1906-11
7 Albert Road, Regents Park, London. † LS 9, RA 1.
BELL, Michael C. Farrar Exh. 1934-37
Stained glass artist. Add: 24 Church Walk, Hampstead, London. † RA 4.
BELL, M.H. Exh. 1883
Kew, Surrey. † L 2.

BELL, Mrs. Mona H. Exh. 1903-20
Liscard, Cheshire 1903; Wallasey, Cheshire 1920. † L 9.
BELL, Mary Montgomerie Exh. 1901-3
72 Great Kind Street, Edinburgh. † RA 1, RSA 3.
BELL, Norman Martin b. 1907
24 Hertford Drive, Wallasey, Cheshire 1924. † L 5, M 3.
BELL, Miss Olive Exh. 1906
19 Cowley Street, Westminster, London. † RI 1.
BELL, Ophelia Gordon b. 1915
Sculptor and painter. Studied Regent Street Polytechnic 1932-36. Add: London 1935. † GI 1, RA 4, RSA 4.
BELL, Pauline Exh. 1898
8 Granville Road, Finchley, London. † RBA 1.
BELL, Peggy Exh. 1930-38
Portrait painter. Add: London. † L 2, P 1, RA 2.
BELL, Percy F.H. Exh. 1887-93
Figure painter. Add: 3 Maitland Villa, Bath Road, Hounslow, Middlesex. † B 1, RA 1, RBA 3, ROI 2.
BELL, Quentin* b. 1910
Still life painter. Son of Vanessa B. q.v. Exh. 1937-40. † AG 1, LEF 4.
BELL, Reginald b. 1886
Stained glass artist and mural decorator. Son of John Clement B. q.v. married to Gladys Kathleen B. q.v. Studied Cope and Nichols' School of Art. Add: London. † L 1, RA 35.
BELL, Robert Anning* 1863-1933
Painter, modeller for coloured relief, black and white illustrator and designer of stained glass and mosaic. Studied Westminster and R.A. Schools. Head of design section Glasgow School of Art. Professor of Design, Royal College of Art, and instructor in painting and design, University College Liverpool. Purchased by Chantrey Bequest "The Listener" 1906, "Mary in the House of Elizabeth" 1918 and "Her Son" 1934. N.E.A. 1888, A.R.A. 1914, R.A. 1922, A.R.W.S. 1901, R.W.S. 1904, Member Society of 25. Married to Laura Anning B. q.v. Add: London 1880 and 1915, Liverpool 1895, East Hagbourne, Berks. 1902, Glasgow 1913. † B 2, BA 1, BG 1, D 1, FIN 255, G 4, GI 14, GOU 6, I 12, L 59, LEI 52, M 7, NEA 23, NG 2, RA 59, RBA 5, RHA 3, RID 25, ROI 4, RSA 11, RSW 6, RWS 97.
BELL, Robert Clifton Exh. 1882-83
Landscape painter. Add: Wandle House, East Moulsey, Surrey. † RBA 3.
BELL, Robert Grant Exh. 1909
39 Howe Street, Edinburgh. † RSA 1.
BELL, Robert Purvis 1841-1931
Painter of portraits and Scottish domestic scenes. Studied Royal Scottish Academy. A.R.S.A. 1880, Edinburgh 1889. † GI 3, RSA 45.
BELL, Miss Sidney Exh. 1889-99
Ware, Herts. 1889; London 1899. † B 1, RBA 1.
BELL, Sibyl N. Exh. 1937
16 Redcliffe Street, London. † SWA 1.
BELL, Thomas Blakemore Exh. 1933-38
Miniature painter. Add: 108 Harlow Terrace, Harrogate, Yorks. † RA 1, RMS 1.
BELL, Thomas Currie Exh. 1892-1925
Edinburgh 1892 and 1904; London 1898. † GI 4, L 1, LS 2, RA 1, RSA 21.

BELL, Thomas S. Exh. 1908-10
Tayside, Gordon Terrace, Craigie, Ayr. † GI 1.
BELL, Vanessa* 1879-1961
Painter and designer. nee Stephen. Sister of Virginia Woolf. Married Clive Bell. Studied under Sir Arthur Cope and at R.A. Schools. "Helen Dudley" painted c.1915 purchased by Chantrey Bequest 1969. Member London Group 1919. Add: London. † AG 29, ALP 6, BA 4, CHE 5, COO 27, FIN 1, G 5, GI 3, GOU 1, L 2, LEF 53, LEI 22, LS 2, M 5, NEA 2, NG 1, RED 1, RHA 1, RSA 3, SWA 2, TOO 1.
BELL, Walter Exh. 1936-37
Industrial landscape painter. Add: 32 Button Lane, Sheffield. † RA 2.
BELL, Miss Winifred Exh. 1928
20 Eccleston Street, Prescot. † L 1.
BELL, William Charles c.1821-1904
Miniature painter. Enamel painter to Queen Victoria for 50 years. Add: Barnes, Surrey 1880; London 1891. † RA 5, RMS 1.
BELL, William H. d. c.1902
Landscape painter. Add: Edinburgh 1885; London 1891 and 1895; Dumfries 1892. † GI 1, NEA 29, RA 1, RID 28, ROI 1, RSA 5.
BELL, Miss W.M. Exh. 1914
c/o J.A. Doudney, 120 Chancery Lane, London. † RA 1.
BELLAMY, Violet Exh. 1917-36
Miniature portrait painter. Add: London. † RA 9.
BELLANGER-ADHEMAR Exh. 1906
151 Boulevard Periere, Paris. † L 1.
BELLARDIE, J. de C. Exh. 1913
c/o L. Sylvester, 158 Fenchurch Street, London. † RI 1.
BELLCOUR, Berne Exh. 1937
† CON 1.
BELLE, de See D
BELLEI, Gaetano* Exh. 1882-83
London. † M 1, RA 1.
BELLENGER, A. Exh. 1881
Wood engraver. Add: London. † RA 1.
BELLENGER, G. I Exh. 1881
33 Avenue de l'Opera, Paris † RHA 1.
BELLEROCHE, Albert* 1864-1944
Painter and lithographer. Studied under Carolus Duran. N.E.A. 1894. b. Swansea. Add: Paris 1894; Rustington, Sussex 1921. † L 2, NEA 13.
BELLES, Miss C.M. Exh. 1918
66 Elsham Road, Kensington, London. † RI 1.
BELLHOUSE, Richard Taylor Exh. 1880-94
Urban and architectural painter. Add: Bruges, Belgium 1880; London 1882. † D 4, L 1, M 3, RBA 6, RI 2.
BELLI, Enrico Exh. 1880-84
Portrait painter. Add: London. † RA 1, RBA 3.
BELLIN, Arthur Exh. 1880-88
Marine and landscape painter. Add: London 1880; Sark, C.I. 1889. † B 1, G 1, L 2, M 3, RA 4, RBA 2, RHA 1, ROI 1.
BELLIN, P. Exh. 1890
Thorne Lodge, Rawcliffe Road, Walton. † L 1.

BELLIN-CARTER, Leslie b. 1878
Landscape painter. Studied under F.G. Stevens 1890, Slade School 1894. Art master Eton 1912-14, Wellington College 1914-38; Examiner in Art Civil Service Commission 1923-41, Central Welsh Board 1924-43, University of Cambridge 1931, University of London 1932. Grandson of Samuel Bellin. † RID 6.

BELLIS, Alan Waddington b. 1883
Architect, watercolour painter, modeller and metal worker. b. Manchester. Studied Leeds College of Art, Royal College of Art (travelling scholarship 1910) and Italy. Master at Ipswich School of Art. Add: Ipswich 1926. † RA 15

BELLIS, Frank Exh. 1887-88
Architect. Add: Chester 1887; Mold, Flints 1888. † L 1, RA 1.

BELLOC, Emma Exh. 1895-1911
Portrait painter. Add: London. † B 2, L 2, M 1, P 3, RA 2, RID 5, ROI 2.

BELLOT, Herbert Exh. 1883-84
2 Royal Avenue, Chelsea, London. † RA 1, RI 1.

BELLOT, Mrs. Julia Cecilia Exh. 1882-94
Figure painter. 2 Royal Avenue Chambers, Chelsea, London. † B 6, D 1, L 4, RA 1, ROI 1.

BELLOWS, Albert Fitch* 1829-1883
American etcher. R.E. 1881. Add: New York 1881. † RE 7.

BELLOWS, Miss E.C. Exh. 1892
c/o Miss Hoffman, 20 Stanley Road, Bootle. † L 1.

BELMONT, Aloysius Exh. 1898
Urban landscape painter (Tangiers). c/o Thomas and Co., 29 Bolsover Street, London. † RA 1.

BELNET, G. Exh. 1911
179 Avenue du Maine, Paris. † L 1.

BELOE, Miss Agnes C. Exh. 1899-1901
Brook Hall, Halesworth, Suffolk. † SWA 3.

BELOE, Miss H.A. Exh. 1916
5 South Street, Thurloe Square, London. † RA 2.

BELPER, Lord Exh. 1884-1903
Landscape painter. Add: Kingston Hall, Derby. † N 22.

BELSHAW, Frank Exh. 1880-84
Landscape painter. N.S.A. 1882. (Sec. 1881) Add: 13 Sherwin Street, Nottingham. † M 1, N 20, RA 1, RBA 2.

BELSKIE, Abraham Exh. 1925
120 Naburn Street, Glasgow. † GI 1.

BELT, Richard C. c.1851-1920
Sculptor. Add: London. Exh. 1880-85. † G 2, RA 12.

BELTON, Leslie F. Exh. 1935
150 Thornhill Road, Streetly. † B 2.

BELTRAND, Jacques b. 1874
French artist. Add: 69 Boulevard Pasteur, Paris, 1913. † L 1.

BENARD, A. Exh. 1898
† P 1.

BENATAR, Molly Exh. 1920-40
Miniature and watercolour painter. Add: London. † L 2, RA 2, RI 7.

BENBOW, Miss Amy S. Exh. 1900-4
21 Dalton Road, Liscard, Cheshire. † L 5.

BENDALL, Claude Exh. 1920-25
London. † L 4.

BENDALL, Miss Mabel E. Exh. 1914
The Hill, Sutton Coldfield, Warwicks. † L 6.

BENDER, Arthur A. Exh. 1922
34 Poulton's Square, London. † ROI 2.

BENDIXEN, Elna Exh. 1935-36
Painter of exotic eastern subjects. Spent honeymoon in forest near Bangkok. Studied Paris 1919. Retired to East 1929. † AR 43, WG 28.

BENECKE, Amy M. Exh. 1885-1905
London 1885; Dorking 1895. † B 2, D 1, L 5, M 2, RI 2.

BENECKE, Margaret Exh. 1907-29
Landscape and interior painter. Add: Eastbourne 1907. † AB 3, NEA 3.

BENEDITO-VIVES, Manuel 1875-c.1931
Spanish artist. Add: Madrid 1908-10. † L 1, RHA 3.

BENEDUCE, Giuseppe Exh. 1931-32
5 Craiglockhart Avenue, Edinburgh. † GI 1, RSA 2.

BENET, R. Exh. 1937
Flower painter. † BA 1.

BENETT, Newton 1854-1922
Landscape painter. Add: London 1880; Lyndhurst, Hants. 1882; Lyme Regis, Dorset 1890; Wallingford, Berks. 1894. † D 59, FIN 104, G 7, L 2, LS 7, M 8, NG 35, RA 15, RBA 1, RI 12, RSW 5, WG 6.

BENETTER, T.T. Exh. 1885
Norway. † RSA 1.

BENGER, Berenger 1868-1935
Landscape painter. b. Tetbury, son of W. Edmund B. q.v. Studied Antwerp. Travelled Europe, Scandinavia and S. Africa (where he died). A.R.B.A. 1925, R.B.A. 1927. Add: Liverpool 1884; Llandudno 1888; Chepstow, Mon. 1892; Uckfield, Sussex 1894; Crowborough, Sussex 1898; Fittleworth, Sussex 1908; Pulborough, Sussex 1916. † AG 1, D 12, L 58, LS 7, M 7, RA 39, RBA 57, RCA 73, RI 10, WG 169.

BENGER, W. Edmund c.1841-1915
Landscape painter. Father of Berenger B. q.v. Add: Llandudno 1882; Liverpool 1883; Uckfield, Sussex 1895; Crowborough, Sussex 1900; Fiddleworth, Sussex 1908. † B 2, GI 1, L 13, LS 10, M 4, RA 4, RI 4.

BENHAM, Miss Jessie Exh. 1887-93
Marine painter. Add: 344 Campden Road, London. † RA 2, ROI 1.

BENHAM, Miss Maude Exh. 1894-1903
Miniature painter. Add: London. † RA 2, RMS 6, SWA 7.

BENHAM, Thomas C.S. Exh. 1881-1911
Landscape, portrait and genre painter. Add: 344 Camden Road, London 1881; Walberswick, Southwold, Suffolk 1904. † B 15, DOW 3, G 2, L 1, M 3, P 1, RA 30, RHA 2, RI 2, ROI 19, TOO 6.

BENISON, Miss Janet Exh. 1903
35 Winstanley Road, Waterloo. † L 1.

BENISON, Sheila Exh. 1938
† M 2.

BENLLIURI, Jose* Exh. 1890
Rome. † D 1.

BENN, Miss C. Exh. 1933
3 Cheltenham Avenue, Liverpool. † L 2.

BENNER, Jean Exh. 1887
Flower painter. Add: 72 Boulevard de Clichy, Paris. † RA 1.

BENNER, William Roger b. 1884
Painter and black and white artist. A.N.S.A. 1920, N.S.A. 1927. Add: Nottingham 1912; West Bridgford, Notts. 1915; Basford, Notts. 1917; Sherwood, Notts. 1925. † N 80.

BENNET, Lord Exh. 1885-91
Miniature portrait painter. Add: London. † RA 30.

BENNET, Miss D.M. Exh. 1916
44 Cawston Road, Highgate, London. † RA 1.

BENNETEAU, Felix Exh. 1927
Sculptor. Add: 5 Rue de Bagneux, Paris. † L 1, RA 1

BENNETT, A. Exh. 1924
† FIN 2.

BENNETT, Alfred* Exh. 1880
Landscape painter. Add: 27 Gaisford Street, Camden Town, London. † RBA 1.

BENNETT, Alfred J. Exh. 1912-23
Painter and etcher. Add: Thornton Heath, Surrey 1912; Knebworth, Herts. 1917. † FIN 1, G 2, I 14, NEA 1, RA 1, ROI 1, WG 75.

BENNETT, Miss A. Sterndale Exh. 1907-15
Landscape and flower painter. Add: London. † BG 50, L 2, NEA 1, RA 2.

BENNETT, Charles Exh. 1924
† RMS 1.

BENNETT, Clara Exh. 1882-89
Manchester 1882; Buxton, Derbys. 1885. † M 9.

BENNETT, Charles Bell Exh. 1892-1912
Glasgow 1892; Bridge of Allan N.B. 1909. † GI 1, L 2, RSA 1.

BENNETT, Miss D. le B. Exh. 1919
Stammerham Farm, Halbrook, Horsham. † SWA 19.

BENNETT, E. Exh. 1887
Burton Villa, Burton Road, Withington. † M 1.

BENNETT, Edward Exh. 1923
17 Guernsey Road, Stonycroft, Liverpool. † L 1.

BENNETT, Miss Ethel G. Exh. 1895-1908
Portrait artist. Bushey Heath, Herts. 1895; Herne Hill, London. 1904. † L 4, RA 5.

BENNETT, Edmund J. Exh. 1893
24 Darnley Road, Gravesend, Kent. † RA 1.

BENNETT, Emily J. Exh. 1892
Netherwood, Langside, Glasgow. † GI 1.

BENNETT, Miss E.M. Exh. 1917
Nancybury, Tewin, Welwyn. † RA 1.

BENNETT, Florence E. Exh. 1899-1934
Miniature painter. R.M.S. 1901. Add: Wimbledon 1899; London 1903. † B 3, L 13, P 2, RA 10, RMS 40.

BENNETT, Frank Moss* b. 1874
Painter, decorator and designer of costume figures. Studied Slade School, St. John's Wood School of Art and R.A. Schools (gold medal and travelling studentship). Add: Chislehurst, Kent 1898; Croydon, Surrey 1899; London 1905-28. † B 4, D 26, L 8, RA 31, RI 4, ROI 8.

BENNETT, F.W. Exh. 1932
† L 1.

BENNETT, Miss Georgina Exh. 1903-5
St. Cross, Bournemouth. † D 2, SWA 4.

BENNETT, Gladys R. Exh. 1923-29
Landscape painter. Add: Roehampton, Surrey. † D 5, GOU 1, RA 1.

BENNETT, H. Exh. 1880
Landscape painter. Add: Ashdale, Forest Hill. † D 2. RBA 2.

BENNETT, Harold Exh. 1930-32
† L 3.

BENNETT, Miss Harriet M. Exh. 1882-92
Watercolour painter. Add: Ashdale, Forest Hill, London. † D 1, RA 3, RI 2.

BENNETT, Mrs. Honor Sterndale c.1876-1975
Watercolour flower painter. Add: Okenwood, Wateringbury, Kent 1933. † RA 3, RBA 1, RI 4, SWA 1.

BENNETT, Isabel Exh. 1880-89
4 Upton Grove, Southgate Road, Islington. † B 1, RHA 15.

BENNETT, Miss Jennie Exh. 1890
Rustic painter. Add: West View, Vickers Street, Nottingham. † N 1.

BENNETT, J.A. Exh. 1882-85
Figure painter. Add: 66 N. Corridor, Royal Exchange, Manchester. † B 1, M 2, RA 1.

BENNETT, J. Gilchrist Exh. 1937-38
113 West Regent Street, Glasgow. † GI 2.

BENNETT, J. Lovett Exh. 1880-86
Parsonstown, Ireland 1880 and 1885; Paris 1884. † RBA 1, RHA 13.

BENNETT, John W. Exh. 1925
Sutherland House, Markinch, Fife. † RSA 1.

BENNETT, Miss Kate Exh. 1888
Ashdale, Forest Hill, London. † RI 1.

BENNETT, Miss L.J. Exh. 1889
Park Villas, West Dulwich, London. † B 1.

BENNETT, Miss Margie Exh. 1895
Oakhill Park, Liverpool. † L 1.

BENNETT, Mrs. Marian Exh. 1900-11
Handsworth, Birmingham. † B 13, RCA 1.

BENNETT, Mary* Exh. 1880
Landscape painter. Add: 4 Springfield Villas, Kilburn, London. † SWA 1.

BENNETT, Miss Mary Exh. 1931
Miniature painter. Add: 140 Alexandra Road, London. † RA 1.

BENNETT, Miss M.E. Exh. 1921
6 Duke's Lane, Kensington, London. † RID 4.

BENNETT, Miss M.L. Exh. 1932
26 Humber Road, Wolverhampton. † B 1.

BENNETT, Mrs. Margery M. Exh. 1915-37
Miniature painter. Add: London 1915 and 1922; Tunbridge Wells, Kent 1918; Brighton 1924. † RA 9, RI 1, RMS 2, WG 2.

BENNETT, Miss Mildred R. Exh. 1906-8
115 Ebury Street, London. † L 2, SWA 3.

BENNETT, Miss Norah Exh. 1926-27
Whalley Range, Manchester. † L 3.

BENNETT, R.S. Exh. 1889
Miniature painter. Add: Delia Cottage, St. Mark's, Cheltenham, Glos. † RA 1.

BENNETT, S.A. Exh. 1900
9 Fulham Park Gardens, London. † RA 1.

BENNETT, Septimus A. Exh. 1900-1
Sculptor. London. † RA 2.

BENNETT, S.E. Exh. 1880
Ashdale, Forest Hill, London. † D 1.

BENNETT, T. Campbell Exh. 1882-1906
Stourbridge 1882; Tavistock, Devon 1887. † B 6.

BENNETT, W. Exh. 1919
Moorcroft, Weston-in-Gordano, Portishead. † GI 1.

BENNETT, William* Exh. 1881-88
Landscape painter. Add: London. † B 2, D 13, GI 4, L 3, M 2, RBA 4, RCA 5, RHA 9, RI 2, TOO 2.

BENNETT, William B. Exh. 1900-13
Landscape and figure painter, 138 Alcert Cottages, Bushey, Herts. † FIN 1, L 1, RA 20, RI 1.

BENNETT, Winifred S. Exh. 1915-20
Bothe Hall, Sawley, Nr. Derby. † N 2.

BENNETTE, H.W.P. Exh. 1913
42 Hamilton Square, Birkenhead. † L 3.

BENNETTE, W.R. Exh. 1910-13
Birkenhead 1910; Liverpool 1912. † L 9.

BENNEY, Ernest Alfred Sallis b. 1894
Painter and designer. Studied Bradford School of Arts and Crafts and Royal College of Art. Headmaster of Northwich School of Art 1918-22; Headmaster of Salisbury School of Art 1922-25; County Director of Art and Education for Gloucestershire and Principal of Cheltenham School of Art 1925-29; Principal of Brighton School of Art and Director of Art Education in Brighton 1929-34. R.B.A. 1936. † COO 1, GI 1, NEA 2, RA 10, RBA 30, RI 4, ROI 1.

BENNIE, Miss Laura J. See LOUDON

BENNIE, Maggie M. Exh. 1897
Airlie, Bridge of Weir, N.B. † GI 2.

BENOIS, Alexandre* 1870-1960
Russian painter and stage designer. Exh. 1937. † RED 2, TOO 60.

BENOIS, Mrs. Nadia* b. 1896
Painter and black and white artist. b. Petersburgh, Russia. Add: London 1924. † AG 1, BA 2, GI 1, GOU 25, L 2, LEF 1, LEI 2, M 2, NEA 12, RED 10, SWA 1, TOO 68.

BENON, Alfred Exh. 1938
Sculptor. Add: 147 Rue Broca, Paris. † RA 1.

BENSA, Francesco Exh. 1880
Flower painter. Add: 21 Via Montebello, Florence, Italy. † RA 1.

BENSLYN, William T. Exh. 1921-29
London. † RA 3.

BENSON, Annette M. Exh. 1931-40
Watercolour painter. Add: 32 Wood Lane, Highgate, London. † NEA 2, RSA 2, RI 3, SWA 3.

BENSON, Miss Charlotte E. d. c.1892
42 Fitzwilliam Square, Dublin. † RHA 11.

BENSON, Miss D. Exh. 1921
10 Leonard Place, Kensington, London. † RA 1.

BENSON, Mrs. Dorothy M. Exh. 1935-36
City Hospital, Edinburgh. † RSW 3.

BENSON, Eugene* 1839-1908
Figure painter. b. U.S.A. Add: Rome 1880; Venice 1888 (where he died). † G 36, L 8, M 2, NG 11, RA 5, RHA 2, ROI 2.

BENSON, Miss Eva E. Exh. 1915-20
Sculptor. Add: London. † L 3, GI 4, RA 5, RSA 1, SWA 2.

BENSON, Mrs. E.J. Exh. 1920
Mrs. T. Sculptor. Add: 22 Jacoba Street, Fairview, Johannesburg, S. Africa. † RA 1.

BENSON, F. Exh. 1912
The Den, Hampton Hill, London. † RA 1.

BENSON, Miss Florence Exh. 1908-12
Maes-y-Porth, Conway. † RCA 2.

BENSON, Frank Weston* 1862-1951
American painter and etcher. † FIN 13, GI 2, L 1, RA 1.

BENSON, Henrietta Exh. 1881-86
Flower and figure painter. Add: West Street, Hertford. † L 2, RI 1, SWA 3.

BENSON, H.C. Exh. 1910
London Road, Hatfield, Herts. † RA 1.

BENSON, James Exh. 1910
187 Bothwell Street, Glasgow. † GI 2.

BENSON, May K. Exh. 1880-1906
Flower, figure and bird painter. Add: Hertford 1880, Dublin 1886 and 1892; Bushey, Herts. 1890; Bath 1906. † B 3, RA 1, RBA 6, RHA 96, ROI 1, RSA 3, SWA 1.

BENSON, Miss Nellie Exh. 1897-1903
Painter and miniaturist. Add: 78 Kensington Gardens Square, London. † L 1, RA 7, RMS 2, SWA 8.

BENSON, Mrs. R. de G. Exh. 1899-1905
Miniature painter. Add: Pulverbach, Shrewsbury. † L 6, RMS 3.

BENSTED, Hubert Exh. 1886
Maidstone, Kent. † RA 1.

BENSUSAN-BUTT, John Gordon b. 1911
Landscape painter. Add: Colchester. † GOU 3, NEA 2, RED 1.

BENT, John D. Exh. 1940
Figure painter. Add: 81 Cambridge Gardens, London. † RA 1.

BENT, Miss Mary E. Exh. 1930-34
46 Russell Road, Moseley. † B 3.

BENTHALL, Anne T. Exh. 1919
† I 2.

BENTHAM, A.W. Exh. 1893-1906
London. † NG 1, RI 1.

BENTHAM, Miss F.M. Exh. 1892-1925
Preston, Lancs. † GI 1, L 20, M 1.

BENTHAM, Percy George b. 1883
Sculptor. Studied City and Guilds, London School of Art; R.A. Schools and Paris. Add: London 1915-30. † L 5, LS 3, RA 13.

BENTHAM, R.H. Exh. 1887-89
5 Avenham Place, Preston, Lancs. † M 3.

BENTINCK, Lady Henry Cavendish Exh. 1899-1902
Underley Hall, Kirkby Lonsdale and Grosvenor Place, London. † NG 2, RA 1.

BENTLEY, Alfred d. 1923
Painter and etcher. A.R.E. 1908, R.E. 1913. Add: London 1908. † FIN 8, GI 2, I 1, L 10, NEA 1, RA 22, RE 55, RID 16, RSA 3.

BENTLEY, Charles Edward Exh. 1886-1922
Dolgelly, N. Wales 1886; Shrewsbury 1890; Tal-y-Cafn, N. Wales 1897; Liverpool 1911. † B 2, L 52, LS 5, M 4, RA 2, RCA 88.

BENTLEY, Mrs. Edith Exh. 1894
Esher, Surrey. † L 2.

BENTLEY, Edward d. c.1882
Flower and nature painter. Add: Crayford Hill, Bexley Heath, Kent. † RBA 4.

BENTLEY, Miss Ethel M. Exh. 1911
113 William Street, Heywood. † RCA 1.

BENTLEY, F.L. Exh. 1891
Broad Oak, 9 Morton Green, Eccles, Nr. Manchester. † M 1.

BENTLEY, Henry G. Exh. 1919
13 Chepstow Place, London. † RA 1.

BENTLEY, Joseph Herbert b. 1886
Portrait painter. Studied Lincoln School of Art, Royal Academy, Antwerp. R.B.A. 1896. Add: Lincoln 1886; Sheffield 1895-1922. † B 1, L 8, P 5, RA 19, RBA 11.

BENTLEY, J.H.N. Exh. 1885
Bridge Street, Haywood, Manchester. † M 1.

BENTLEY, Lilian Exh. 1922
† GOU 1.

BENTLEY, Miss Susan J. Exh. 1888-1922
Dolgelly, N. Wales 1888; Shrewsbury 1891; Tal-y-Cafn, N. Wales 1897; Liverpool 1915. † B 1, L 28, LS 3, RA 1, RCA 3.

BENTLEY, W. Exh. 1902-4
† TOO 2.

BENTON, D. Exh. 1881-83
Rome, Italy. † B 4, L 3, RHA 4.

BENTON, Edward Exh. 1930
Manchester. † RCA 1.

BENTON, Miss Gertrude Exh. 1909-10
102 Holly Road, Handsworth, Birmingham. † B 2.

BENTON, George Bernard b. 1872
Landscape and figure painter and illustrator. Studied Birmingham School of Art (1st class honours for design), Art Master, Repton School, Bromsgrove School and Birmingham Municipal School of Art. Add: Birmingham 1898; Streetly 1935. † B 11, RA 5.

BENTON, Mrs. Julia Exh. 1883-85
Domestic painter. Add: 20 Ladbroke Road, Notting Hill, London. † RA 2, RBA 3.

BENTON, Miss Julia S. Exh. 1895
Westfield, Shortlands, Kent. † L 2.

BENTZ, Frederick Exh. 1880-89
Landscape painter. Add: Edinburgh 1880; Antwerp 1883; Manchester 1886. † B 1, GI 4, L 4, M 5, RA 5, RBA 1, RHA 1, ROI 1, RSA 8.

BENUZZI, Edwin Exh. 1888-89
Painter of Venetian scenes. Add: Hampstead, London. † RBA 6.

BENWELL, Francis Churchill Exh. 1908
5 Trebovir Road, Kensington, London. † LS 3.

BENWELL, Joseph Austin Exh. 1880-86
Painter of Middle Eastern scenes. Add: London. † B 2, L 3, M 4, RA 1, RBA 11, RHA 1, RI 2.

BENYON, Mrs. Exh. 1911
Islip House, Thrapston, Northants. † LS 3.

BEN-ZVI, Zeev Exh. 1938
Sculptor. Add: 23a Clifton Gardens, London. † GI 2, RA 1.

BENZY, de See D

BERAUD, Jean* Exh. 1882-1913
134 New Bond Street, London 1882; 3 Rue du Boccador, Paris 1913. † L 1, RA 1.

BERBIERS, J.L. Exh. 1939-40
89 Balliol Road, Bootle, Liverpool. † B 1, RCA 3.

BERCHMANS, E. Exh. 1909
111 Avenue Rogier, Brussels. † L 1.

BERCKMANS, Carlo Exh. 1917
2 Anglesea Avenue, Blackrock, Dublin. † RHA 1.

BERE, de la See D

BERENS, A.H. Exh. 1888
Figure painter. Add: 68 Great Cumberland Place, Hyde Park, London. † RA 1.

BERESFORD Exh. 1939
Salisbury. † GOU 1.

BERESFORD, A. Edgar Exh. 1910-36
Bedford 1910; London 1924. † RA 5.

BERESFORD, Mrs. Alfreda E. Exh. 1928-39
Miniaturist and sculptor. Studied West Ham Technical School and Central School for Arts and Crafts (King Prize for sculpture). Add: Snaresbrook, Essex 1928; Bournemouth, Hants. 1938. † B 3, L 7, P 1, RA 2, RBA 1, RHA 2, RI 22, RMS 8, RSA 20.

BERESFORD, Miss C.M. Exh. 1880-92
Portrait and figure painter. S.W.A. 1880. Add: Rome 1880; London 1887. † B 4, D 19, G 1, GI 4, L 4, RBA 3, RHA 3, RI 1, SWA 69.

BERESFORD, Daisy Radcliffe Exh. 1904-38
Portrait, landscape and interior painter. nee Clague. Married Frank Ernest B. q.v. Studied Heatherleys, R.A. Schools (3 silver and 2 bronze medals). Art Class Teacher's Certificate at age of 13. Art Mistress' Certificate at age 16. Add: London. † RA 12, SWA 1.

BERESFORD, Frank Ernest b. 1881
Painter of portraits, landscapes, interiors (mainly Dutch) and decorative panels. Studied Derby School of Art 1895-1900; St. John's Wood School of Art 1900-1; R.A. Schools 1901-6; Art Master's Certificate at age 18; British Institute Scholarship; first award for art to a foreigner from the Imperial Japanese Government 1909. Add: London. † AB 1, P 3, RA 12, RI 3, ROI 3.

BERESFORD, George C. Exh. 1900-1
Sculptor. 1 Haverstock Hill, London. † RA 2

BERESFORD, John M Exh. 1908-10
23 Rue le Verrier, Paris. † LS 10.

BERG, Oscar Exh. 1883
Sculptor. Add: Primrose Hill Studios. † RA 1.

BERG, Von See V

BERGEN, George Exh. 1937
Landscape and portrait painter. † AG 2, GOU 36, LEF 45, LEI 1, M 1, TOO 1.

BERGERE, Eck Exh. 1882
16 Avenue Trudaine, Paris. † RHA 2.

BERGERET, Denis P.* c.1843-1910
French flower painter. Add: Paris 1884-93 † GI 17.

BERGH, Van den See V

BERGH, Van der See V

BERGHMAN, Miss M.L. Exh. 1919
Portrait painter. Add: 4 Berkeley Place, Cheltenham, Glos. † RA 1.

BERGHOLZ, Richard Exh. 1901
Place Michel, 4-5 log 46, St. Petersburg, Russia. † RI 1

BERGIER, Alfred Exh. 1930
† RI 1.

BERGIN, Miss Isabella C. Exh. 1881-82
Combre House, Dalkey, Ireland. † RHA 4.

BERGSON, Miss Mina Exh. 1885-88
Black and white artist. Add: London. † RA 3.

BERKELEY, Edith Exh. 1880-97
Figure and landscape painter. nee Savill. Married Stanley B. q.v. R.E. 1884. Add: London 1880; Ham Common, Surrey 1887; Esher, Surrey 1890. † B 9, D 3, G 1, GI 3, L 12, M 5, RA 13, RBA 7, RE 3, RI 11, ROI 3.

BERKELEY, Isabel Exh. 1884-1914
Barnes, Surrey 1884; Ringwood 1910. † B 5, L 1, LS 20, RMS 1, RSA 1, SWA 1.

BERKELEY, Stanley 1855-1909
Animal, sporting and historical battle painter. R.E. 1884. Add: London 1880; Ham Common, Surrey 1887; Esher, Surrey 1889. † B 10, D 7, G 1, L 28, M 11, RA 23, RBA 13, RE 11, RHA 1, RI 9, ROI 5, RSA 6.

BERMEJO, Miss B. Exh. 1930-31
6 Kenilworth Place, Francis Road, Edgbaston, Birmingham. † B 3.

BERNABO, Miss B. Exh. 1884-1900
Liverpool. † L 5, M 1.

BERNAMONT, Mlle. Clarisse Exh. 1907-10
21 Rue de Vieux Colombier, Paris. † L 2.

BERNARD, Joseph* Exh. 1930
24 Avenue Victor Hugo, Boulogne sur Seine, France. † RSA 3.

BERNARD, Margaret Exh. 1883-1924
Landscape painter. Add: Bath 1883; Wimborne, Dorset 1888; Sway, Hants. 1905. † AG 3, B 2, D 116, RA 5, RI 7, SWA 2, WG 33.

BERNARD, Maude Exh. 1939
† COO 39.

BERNARD, Oliver P. Exh. 1934
London. † GI 3.

BERNARD, Pierre Magran Exh. 1913
† RSA 1.

BERNAU, Charlotte A. Exh. 1884-1907
Pencil portrait artist. Add: London 1884; Croydon, Surrey 1892; Whyteleafe, Surrey 1902. † D 1, RA 9, RI 1, RMS 1.

BERNE, Miss E.B. Exh. 1918
Moorcroft, Henley-on-Thames, Oxon. † RA 1.

BERNERS, Lord Exh. 1927-31
Landscape painter. † GOU 14, LEF 38.

BERNERS, Mrs. Ralph Exh. 1924
Landscape painter (Kashmir etc.). † WG 60.

BERNERS-WILSON, Miss Nancie Exh. 1935
The Hardwick, Abergavenny. † RA 2.

BERNEY, Miss Mary A. Exh. 1898
5 Lansdown Terrace, Leamington. † B 1.

BERNHARD-SMITH, Miss M.I. Exh. 1913
59 Albany Mansions, Albert Bridge, London. † LS 3.

BERNHARDT, Carl W.W. Exh. 1882
43 Museum Street, Bloomsbury. † RA 1.

BERNIE, Rex Exh. 1889
36 Tite Street, Chelsea, London. † B 1.

BERNIER, George Exh. 1896-1909
Brussels. † GI 2, L 1.

BERNINGER, Edmund* Exh. 1882
Munich. † RA 1.

BERNSTAMM, L.B. Exh. 1903
69 Rue de Douai, Paris. † L 1.

BERNSTEIN, Miss E. Betty Exh. 1923
Norfolk Court, 7 Belsize Grove, London. † RI 2.

BERRIDGE, Harold Exh. 1933
Architect. Add: 8 Worcester Gardens, Sutton, Surrey. † RA 1.

BERRIDGE, Miss Mary Exh. 1933-35
18 Weston Road, Folkestone, Kent. † RA 1, RSA 2, SWA 1.

BERRIDGE, W.S. Exh. 1902
13 Collingwood Avenue, Muswell Hill, London. † ROI 1.

BERRIE, John Archibald Alexander b. 1887
Portrait and landscape painter. Studied Liverpool School of Art, Bushey, Herts., London and Paris. Travelled widely on the continent. Add: Liverpool. † L 69, RA 5, RCA 51, WG 26.

BERRILL, Mrs. Mary Exh. 1901-3
Green Keys, South Woodford. † SWA 3.

BERRINGTON, Adrian Exh. 1911-13
London. † L 5, LS 3.

BERRINGTON, J.A. Exh. 1920-22
5 St. Andrews Road, Birkenhead. † L 2, NG 3.

BERRINGTON, William b. 1873
Landscape painter. Add: 85 Enid Street, Liverpool 1912-33. † L 20.

BERRY, Berry Francis Exh. 1880-98
Figure and domestic painter. Add: London. † D 2, L 4, NG 7, RA 3, RBA 3, RI 7.

BERRY, B.T. Exh. 1883
Brockham Green, Betchworth, Surrey. † L 1.

BERRY, Dorothy E. Exh. 1926-32
Miniature portrait painter. Add: Innellan, Portland Road, Swinton, Manchester. † L 4, RA 7.

BERRY, Kathleen A. Exh. 1927-32
15 Lyndhurst Road, Wallasey, Cheshire. † L 3.

BERRY, Miss L. Exh. 1907
84 Broadhurst Gardens, South Hampstead, London. † RA 1.

BERRY, Maude Exh. 1885
Flower painter. Add: 27 Southampton Buildings, Chancery Lane, London. † SWA 1.

BERRY, Mary Elizabeth Exh. 1885-1933
Portrait, landscape and Scottish interior painter. Add: London 1885; Leith 1888; Edinburgh 1899. † GI 5, M 1, RA 1, RSA 11, RSW 6.

BERRY, N. Exh. 1929-30
179 Ravenslea Road, London. † NEA 3.

BERRY, Winifred Exh. 1940
Flower painter. Add: 52A Cromwell Road, London. † RA 1.

BERRY, Wilfred E. Exh. 1937-39
Landscape and figure painter. Add: Nottingham. † N 9.

BERRY, William H. Atkin Exh. 1884-1907
Architect. Add: London. † L 2, RA 18.
BERSON, Adolph Exh. 1914
88 Boulevard Periere, Paris. † RSA 1.
BERSTECHER, Harry b. 1893
Painter and etcher. R.S.W. 1926. Add: Glasgow 1917 and 1924; Pittenweem, Fife 1923. † AG 2, GI 34, RSA 6, RSW 40.
BERTHA, Julia Exh. 1881-83
Landscape painter. Add: Cookham, Berks. 1881; New Cross, London 1883. † B 2, M 1, RBA 2.
BERTHELEMY, P.E. Exh. 1883
13 Rue Berthe, Montmartre, Paris. † GI 1.
BERTIE, Amy Exh. 1881-82
Flower painter. Add: 2 Wildman Street, Nottingham. † N 2.
BERTIE, Fanny Exh. 1887-90
Interior and figure painter. Add: Munich. † M 1, SWA 6.
BERTIE, Marion A. Exh. 1886-95
Flower and tree painter. Add: London. † L 1, RA 1, RBA 1.
BERTIER, Ch. Exh. 1913
French landscape painter. † ALP 3.
BERTIER, C.A. Exh. 1886
c/o G. Sinclair, 40 King Street, Soho, London. † RA 1.
BERTIERI, Pilade* b. 1874
Portrait painter. b. Turin. Studied Royal Academies of Art, Turin and Bergamo. Add: London 1908; Paris 1924. † FIN 1, I 6, L 18, NG 1, P 2, RA 5, ROI 2.
BERTINOT, G. Exh. 1886
Engraver. Add: Paris. † RA 1.
BERTIOLI, Frank Exh. 1884-89
Figure and interior painter. Add: 13 Downshire Hill, Hampstead, London. † L 2, RBA 1, RHA 1, RI 7.
BERTOGLIO, Victor Exh. 1940
Landscape painter. Add: 5 Prospect Road, New Barnet, Herts. † RA 1.
BERTON, E. Exh. 1880-81
Domestic painter. Add: 1 Acacia Villas, Upper Richmond Road, Putney, London. † RBA 2.
BERTOUCH, de see D
BERTRAM, Abel* b. 1871
French artist. Add: 10 Rue Seveste, Paris 1913. † L 1.
BERTRAM, Frederick H. Exh. 1896-1907
Marine Painter. Add: 57 Bedford Gardens, London. † L 1, RA 5, RBA 1, ROI 1.
BERTRAM, H.T. Exh. 1882-1906
Glasgow. † GI 7.
BERTRAM, Miss Marion Exh. 1884
203 Euston Road, London. † B 1, G 1, M 1.
BERTRAM, R.J.S. Exh. 1908
10 Percy Avenue, Cullercoats, Northumberland. † RA 1.
BERTRAND, James* Exh. 1883-87
11 Place Pigalle, Paris. † GI 3.
BERTRAND, Marie Exh. 1884
53 Warwick Road, Kensington, London. † SWA 2.
BESCH, Miss L. Exh. 1889
40 Dale Road, London. † RI 1.
BESCHE, Lucien Exh. 1883-85
Miniature portrait painter. Add: London 1883; Stoke-on-Trent 1885. † RA 2.
BESNARD, Miss Charlotte Exh. 1881
Sculptor. Add: 33 Ovington Square, Brompton, London. † RA 1.
BESNARD, Paul Albert* 1849-1934
French painter and etcher. H.F.R.A. 1921, H.R.S.A. 1911. Add: London 1881; Paris 1893. † CG 1, FIN 22, GI 5, GOU 3, I 7, L 7, M 1, P 6, RA 7, RSA 6.
BESNAU, Auguste Exh. 1895
c/o W. Lomax, 75 Oxford Street, Manchester. † M 1.
BESNON, A. Exh. 1893
Coastal painter. Add: Boulogne-sur-mer, France. † RBA 1.
BESSEDE, H.R. Exh. 1925
† GOU 1.
BESSELL, Miss E.S. Exh. 1915-16
13 Bellevue Road, Upper Tooting, London. † L 1, RA 2.
BESSO, Amalia Exh. 1914
Lyceum Club, Piccadilly, London. † LS 2.
BEST, Ailwyn Exh. 1938
6 Milbourne Grove, London. † RA 1.
BEST, Miss A.H. Exh. 1894
37 Lilyville Road, Fulham, London. † SWA 1.
BEST, Eleanor d. 1958
Landscape and flower painter. Studied Slade School. Add: London. † AB 4, CHE 1, G 6, GI 3, GOU 11, I 12, M 1, NEA 37, P 2, RA 19, RBA 6, RHA 1, RSA 3, SWA 6.
BEST, Mrs. Eva Exh. 1897-1900
141 Handsworth Wood Road, Birmingham. † B 4.
BEST, Miss E.A. Exh. 1912
120 Whitaker Road, Derby. † N 1.
BEST, E. Marjorie Exh. 1916-39
Rock Ferry, Cheshire 1916; Neston, Cheshire 1920; London 1930. † L 8, NEA 1, ROI 1.
BEST, F.G.S. Exh. 1880-83
London. † D 1, RBA 1.
BEST, Gladys b. 1898
Watercolour painter. b. Chiswick. Studied Royal Albert Memorial College, Exeter. Art teacher Cheltenham Ladies' College. Add: Topsham, Devon 1928. † COO 2, RA 5, RBA 5, RCA 2, RI 8, RSA 3, SWA 2.
BEST, George Hollings Exh. 1888-1905
Rustic landscape painter. Add: Scratton, North Devon 1888; Chichester, Kent 1899; London 1905. † RA 2, ROI 2.
BEST, Halstead Exh. 1935-39
Leeds Buildings, 20 Clifton Street, Blackpool. † RA 3.
BEST, John Hollis Exh. 1907-40
Birmingham. † B 41.
BESTWICK, Miss M. Exh. 1913
66 Curzon Street, Long Eaton, Nottingham. † N 1.
BESWICK, Frank Exh. 1881-1929
Landscape painter. Add: Chester 1881 and 1889; Liverpool 1886; Southport 1888 and 1891; Deganwy, North Wales 1925. † B 2, L 5, RA 1, RCA 6.
BESWICK, Mrs. Florence E. Exh. 1935-39
London. † RBA 2, ROI 1, SWA 3.
BESWICK, Miss Jessie Exh. 1908-13
Queen's Park, Chester. † L 12.
BESWICK, Mrs. Lilian Exh. 1933
Prestatyn, North Wales. † RCA 1.
BETHEL, Alfred Exh. 1937-38
Landscape and portrait painter. Add: 23 Barnston Road, Nottingham. † N 5.
BETHELL, Miss Kay Exh. 1939-40
Portrait painter. Add: London. † RA 4.
BETHELL, Miss V.S. Exh. 1884
† G 1.
BETHELL, W. Wood Exh. 1882
7 Queen Anne's Gate, Westminster, London. † RA 1.
BETHLEM, J. Exh. 1914-17
London. † RA 2.
BETHUNE, Mrs. Evelyn Exh. 1903-18
45 Bryanston Square, London. † L 42, LS 3, NG 6.
BETTERIDGE, H.W.G. Exh. 1923-39
D 6, RI 2.
BETTESWORTH, Walter Ambrose Exh. 1906
34 Osborne Road, Forest Gate, London. † L 1.
BETTS, Edwin Maurice b. 1885
Painter and etcher. Studied Leicester College of Art (King's Prize for design). Art Master Nottingham High School and Rugby School. A.N.S.A. 1929, N.S.A. 1930. Add: Nottingham 1919. L 1, N 46.
BETTS, Ida 1871-1951
Watercolour flower painter. Add: Kings Langley, Herts. 1898; Abbots Langley, Herts. 1900; Salisbury, Wilts. 1919; Newbury, Berks. 1932. † B 1, BG 2, RA 1, RBA 1, RI 9.
BETTS, Miss Mordaunt Exh. 1904-5
37 Cavendish Square, London. † L 3.
BETTS, Mrs. Mordaunt Exh. 1904-5
37 Cavendish Square, London. † L 3.
BETTS, W.V. Exh. 1919
630 Radford Road, Old Basford, Nottingham. † N 1.
BETTS-BROWN, Edith Marion Exh. 1906
6 Passage Montbrun, Montrouge, Paris. † RSA 1.
BETTY, E. Kimmis Exh. 1912
81 Bickenhall Mansions, London. † LS 3.
BEURDELEY, Jacques b. 1874
French etcher. Add: 11 Rue de Courcelles, Paris 1909-10. † L 3.
BEURDEN, van see V
BEUTTER, A. Exh. 1913
Danesfield, Stanley Road, Hoylake, Cheshire. † L 1.
BEVAN, D.J. Exh. 1936
The Pines, Goathland, Yorks. † RSA 1.
BEVAN, Eric Owen Exh. 1937
9 Vernon Road, Edgbaston, Birmingham. † B 2.
BEVAN, E. Roland Exh. 1923-39
Sculptor and metalworker. London. † GI 2, RA 19.
BEVAN, I. Exh. 1908-15
Rochester, Kent 1908; Bedford 1915. † RA 4.
BEVAN, John jnr. Exh. 1899
Architect. 23 Berkeley Square, Clifton, Bristol. † RA 1.
BEVAN, Mrs. Marjorie Exh. 1937
9 Vernon Road, Edgbaston, Birmingham. † B 2.
BEVAN, Petman B.H. Exh. 1937
† P 1.
BEVAN Mrs. Robert see de KARLOWSKA
BEVAN, Robert Polhill* 1865-1925
Landscape painter. Studied Winchester School of Art and Julien's Paris. Travelled France and Poland. Married Stanislava de Karlowska q.v. N.E.A. 1923, Founder Member London Group 1913. "Horse Sale at the Barbican" purchased by Chantrey Bequest, 1934. Add: London, 1910. † CAR 55, CON 29, G 1, GI 5, GOU 28, LS 28, NEA 28.
BEVER, van de la see V
BEVERIDGE, D. Alston Exh. 1914-33
Architect. 36 Dale Street, Liverpool. † L 11, RA 2, RSA 2.
BEVERIDGE, D. Drysdale Exh. 1901
c/o A. Brown Esq., 15 Leopold Place, Edinburgh. † GI 1.
BEVERIDGE, Erskine Exh. 1904-39
Glasgow 1904 and 1913; Helensburgh 1912; Edinburgh 1919. † GI 11, L 5, M 2, ROI 4, RSA 31, RSW 4.

BEVERIDGE, James b. 1864
Landscape painter. Glasgow 1889; Dorchester, Oxon 1921. † GI 78, L 1, M 1, RA 2, RSA 11, RSW 3.
BEVERIDGE, Miss Kühne Exh. 1896
Sculptor. 66 Avenue Wagram, Paris. † L 2, NG 1, RA 2.
BEVERIDGE, Miss Millicent Exh. 1908-14
Kirkcaldy, N.B. 1908, Paris 1914. † LS 5, RSA 1.
BEVERIDGE, T.J. Exh. 1940
248 West George Street, Glasgow. † GI 1, RSA 1.
BEVERIDGE, William Exh. 1915-19
12 Barnes Street, Barrhead, Glasgow. † GI 6.
BEVERLEY, William Roxby* c1814-1889
Marine and landscape painter. b. Richmond, Surrey. Began his artistic career by painting scenery at the theatres managed by his father. Became principal artist to Theatre Royal, Manchester 1842, and to Princess's, London 1846. In 1847 joined the Lyceum. Scenic director Covent Garden, 1854-84. † D 3, GI 1, RA 1.
BEVERLY, S. Exh. 1938
22 Old Burlington Street, London. † RA 1.
BEVERS, Miss Maud Exh. 1899
Flower painter. 46 Broad Street, Oxford. † RA 1.
BEVES, Mrs. Helen C. Exh. 1900
8 Holly Village, Highgate, London. † L 1, RA 1.
BEVIS, L. Cubitt Exh. 1921-25
6 Margravine Studios, Baron's Court, London. † GOU 5, NEA 2, ROI 1.
BEWERS, W. Herbert Exh. 1907-21
Manchester 1907; Newton Mearns, Renfrewshire 1911. † GI 1, L 4, LS 3, RSW 1.
BEWLAY, Doris Gertrude b. 1901
Landscape and garden painter. Studied Antwerp and Sunderland. Add: Carleton Hall, Holmbrook, Cumberland 1925. † L 2.
BEWLAY, Ernest C. Exh. 1922-36
Architect. 68 Wellington Road, Edgbaston, Birmingham. † B 7.
BEWLEY, Margaret Amy b. 1899
Watercolour and pencil artist. Studied Liverpool School of Art and Press Art School, London. Add: 27 Lyndhurst Road, Wallasey, Cheshire 1925. † L 2.
BEWLEY, Miss M.W. Exh. 1899
16 Beacon Hill, Camden Road, London. † RBA 1.
BEWSEY, John C. Exh. 1906-22
Stained glass artist. London. † RA 9, RSA 3.
BEWSHER, Miss Sarah Exh. 1881
Watercolour painter. Add: 102 Finsborough Road, London. † SWA 2.
BEYERSDORFF, von see V
BEYFUS, C.E. Exh. 1890
34 Russell Square, London. † GI 1.
BEYFUS, Edie Exh. 1889
4 Somerset Place, Glasgow. † GI 2.
BEYLE, Pierre Marie* 1838-1902
French artist. Exh. 1885-86. † GI 3.
BEYNON, C.M. Exh. 1889-91
Landscape painter. London. † RID 15.
BEZNIER, L. Exh. 1910
Rue de la Reforme 4, Brussels. † L 1.
BIANCHI, Dominique Exh. 1903
15 Rue Edouard Jacques, Paris. † L 2.
BIANCHI, Ronie Exh. 1883
15 Ferndale Park, Tunbridge Wells, Kent. † M 1.
BIANCO, Pamela b. 1906
Figure and fairy painter. Exh. 1919-20. † LEI 136.
BIBBY, A.C. Exh. 1920
6 Arkles Road, Anfield, Liverpool. † L 1.
BIBBY, Eric Exh. 1919-22
Birkenhead 1919; New Brighton, Cheshire 1922. † L 6.
BIBBY, Mrs. E. Hartley Exh. 1930-35
Conway, Wales. † RCA 2.
BIBBY, Miss Noelle Hartley Exh. 1929-30
Plas-y-Koe, Conway, Wales. † RCA 2.
BIBBY, W. Cardwell Exh. 1887-98
Fachwell, St. Asaph, N. Wales. † L 8.
BICKERSTAFF, Miss Renée Exh. 1930
17 Newington Street, Antrim Road, Belfast. † RHA 1
BICKHAM, Kate Exh. 1897-98
55 Moseley Street, Manchester. † D 3, SWA 2.
BICKHAM, Miss S. Exh. 1889
51 Hope Street, Liverpool. † L 1.
BICKLEY, H.M. Exh. 1883
Landscape painter. St. John's, Woking, Surrey. † RBA 1.
BICKNELL, Phyllis Ellen b. 1877
nee Lovibond. Watercolour painter. Studied under Arthur G. Bell and Durham University. Add: Newcastle-on-Tyne, 1900. † ALP 4, RI 1.
BIDDER, Fred W. Exh. 1892-93
92 Goldsmith Street, Nottingham. † N 5.
BIDDER, Ida Exh. 1893-1929
Mrs. Elna Kitson Clark. Landscape and portrait painter. Add: London 1893; Leeds 1906. † RID 29.
BIDDER, M. Joyce Exh. 1931-40
Sculptor. A.R.M.S. 1935. 202 Worple Road, Wimbledon, London. † RA 5, RMS 15.
BIDDLE, Miss E. Exh. 1912
Brighton, Sussex. † SWA 2.
BIDDLE, Edith Exh. 1891-95
School of Art, Birmingham 1891. † B 2.
BIDDLE, Miss Florence Exh. 1934
† COO 1.
BIDDLE, Laurence* b. 1888
Flower painter. Add: Brighton, Sussex 1914; London 1932. † FIN 9, RA 1, RBA 1, ROI 1.
BIDDLE, R.J. Exh. 1880-82
Marine painter. Add: 3 Adelphi Terrace, Strand, London. † RBA 4.
BIDDLE, Winifred Percy Exh. 1901-19
Painter and teacher. Studied Lambeth School of Art. Add: Kingston-on-Thames, Surrey. † D 1, L 1, LS 1, RA 3, RI 2, SWA 3.
BIDDLECOMBE, Walter* Exh. 1883-95
Landscape and figure painter. Add: Southampton 1883; Marseilles, France 1895. † L 2, RA 1, RBA 2, RHA 1.
BIDDULPH, A.M. Exh. 1900
38 Tedworth Square, Chelsea, London. † L 1.
BIDDULPH, Mrs. D. Wright Exh. 1910-14
The Chalet, Petworth, Sussex. † LS 9.
BIDDULPH, Edith Exh. 1892-95
Regents Park, London. † B 3, GI 1, RA 1, RBA 2, RI 1.
BIDDULPH, Miss Freda Exh. 1910-36
London. † I 3, LS 7, RBA 11, RSA 1, SWA 5.
BIDDULPH, General Sir Michael A. Exh. 1890
Landscape painter. Add. Biarritz, France. † RBA 2.
BIDDULPH, The Hon. Violet Exh. 1909-37
London 1909; Petersham, Surrey 1913; Cirencester, Glos. 1934. † I 4, LS 5, RSA 2, SWA 6.
BIDDULPH-PINCHARD, C.H. Exh. 1921-35
9 Staple Inn, Holborn, London. † RA 4.
BIDLAKE, William H. Exh. 1888-1937
Architect and architectural artist. R.B.S.A. 1902; Add: Birmingham 1888; Wadhurst, Sussex 1930. † B 14, RA 12.
BIEL, Miss A. Exh. 1880
112 New Bond Street, London. † RHA 1.
BIELENBERG, Alma C. Exh. 1919
† I 1.
BIELER, Ernest* Exh. 1910-11
106 Rue Deufert Rochereau (XIVe), Paris. † L 2.
BIEMME, de See D
BIENVENUE, Ferdinand Exh. 1907
3 Rue Neuve Popincourt, Paris. † L 2.
BIENVETU, G. Exh. 1911-12
c/o T. McLean, 7 Haymarket, London. † L 3.
BIESBROECK, van See V
BIEVRE, de See D
BIGELOW, Olive Exh. 1923-24
Portrait painter. 44 Gloucester Square, London. † L 2, RA 2.
BIGGAR, Miss Helen Exh. 1935
62b Northwoodside Road, Glasgow. † GI 1.
BIGGE, John Exh. 1931-33
† LEF 24, TOO 3.
BIGGE, Mrs. Ruth Selby Exh. 1914
Landscape painter. Add: 5 Phene Street, Chelsea, London. † NEA 1.
BIGGERSNIFF, Edward Exh. 1935-38
Sculptor. Add: 102 Moordown, Shooters Hill, London. † RA 2.
BIGGS, Miss Constance M. Exh. 1927
Sculptor. Add: 2 Breams Buildings, Chancery Lane, London. † RA 1.
BIGGS, Ernest John b. 1896
Wood-engraver and commercial artist. Studied Birmingham School of Art. Add: 2 High Street, Barnet, Herts. 1927. † RBA 2.
BIGGS, Ida Ashford Exh. 1911-32
nee Ashford. Miniature painter. Studied Slade School and Newlyn, Penzance. Add: Putney 1911; Wimbledon 1914; Shanklin I.o.W. 1915; London 1919 and 1932; N. Foreland, Kent 1930. † L 14, P 1, RA 6, RI 4, RMS 2.
BIGGS, John R. b. 1909
Painter, designer and wood-engraver. Add: 19 Hampden Street, Derby. 1930. † RA 1, RCA 2, RED 2.
BIGGS, Lilian Blanche Exh. 1912-25
Painter, miniaturist, modeller and teacher. Queen's Prize S. Kensington at age 15, Art Teachers Certificate at age 18. Add: Park Cottage, Thames Ditton, Surrey. † LS 9, RA 3, RMS 1, SWA 1.
BIGGS, Mary I. Exh. 1924-40
24 Salisbury Road, Moseley, Birmingham. † B 7.
BIGLAND, Alf Exh. 1882
8 Exchange Buildings, Liverpool. † L 1.
BIGLAND, Mary B. Exh. 1880-98
3 Pierremont Crescent, Darlington, Co. Durham. † B 1, D 4, L 6, RI 2, SWA 5.
BIGLAND, Percy c1858-1926
Portrait painter. N.E.A. 1886, R.P. 1891. Add: Liverpool 1882; London 1885; Beaconsfield, Bucks. 1924. † B 19, G 3, GI 1, L 47, M 15, NEA 2, NG 24, P 68, RA 38, RBA 4, RHA 1, RID 33, ROI 4, RSA 1.
BIGNALL, P. Exh. 1912
11 Ben Street, Nottingham. † N 2.
BIGOT, Raymond Exh. 1913
Watercolour bird painter. † FIN 6.

BIGWOOD, Maud Exh. 1910-22
3 Sundial House, High Street, Kensington, London. † I 1, LS 3, RA 6.

BILBAO, Gonzalo* Exh. 1899-1907
Seville, Spain. † GI 1, L 1, RA 1.

BILBAO-Y-MARTINEZ, J. Exh. 1905-6
Seville, Spain. † I 1, L 1.

BILBIE, James Lees d. 1945
Landscape painter. Assistant curator Nottingham Castle 1904-31. Founder member N.S.A. † B 3, L 1, M 2, N 68, RA 2.

BILBIE, J.P. Exh. 1903
Vernon Road, Basford, Nottingham. † N 2.

BILBO, Jack Exh. 1939
Figure painter. † AR 34.

BILIBIN, Alexander Exh. 1931-39
† GOU 3.

BILINSKA, Anna 1857-1893
Polish portrait painter. Add: London 1888; Paris 1892. † L 1, RA 2.

BILL, Miss M.F. Exh. 1909-13
London. † L 4, RA 4, RMS 2.

BILLE, de See D

BILLE, Jacques Exh. 1926-27
Flower painter. 3 Rue Lecourbe, Paris. † RA 4.

BILLET, Pierre* 1837-1922
French artist. Exh. 1884-1907. † GI 1, TOO 2.

BILLIN, Douglas H. Exh. 1938
† M 1.

BILLIN, Edward S. b. 1911
Wood-engraver and watercolour painter. Sheffield. † M 3, RA 2.

BILLING, Arthur Exh. 1886
Architect. Bank Chambers, Tooley Street, London. † RA 1.

BILLING, Clara Exh. 1910-39
Mrs. Jones. Painter and sculptor. Studied Manchester School of Art, Royal College of Art and Paris. A.S.W.A. 1927. Add: London 1910; Blewbury, Berks. 1914. † I 4, L 5, LS 8, RA 1, ROI 1, SWA 12.

BILLING, Miss May Exh. 1926-27
A.S.W.A. 1927. Blewbury, Berks. † L 4, SWA 1.

BILLINGE, Miss W.J. Ophelia Exh. 1905-14
14 Mount Carmel Chambers, Duke's Lane, Kensington, London. † L 1, SWA 5.

BILLINGHURST, Alfred John b. 1880
Portrait and landscape painter. Studied Slade School 1899-1902, Goldsmith's Institute 1900 (King's Prize), Julien's Paris 1902, Ecole des Beaux Arts, Paris 1903. A.R.B.A. 1923, R.B.A. 1925. Add: London. † CHE 1, COO 2, L 1, LS 11, P 5, RA 1, RBA 118, RI 5, RID 3, ROI 7.

BILLINGHURST, Mrs. M.A. Exh. 1884
West View, Caterham Valley, Surrey. † D 2.

BILLINGSLEY, J. Exh. 1887-1932
Birmingham. † B 43.

BILLINGTON, J.R. Exh. 1905-8
Chorley Road, Wingates, Westhoughton, Nr. Bolton, Lancs. † RCA 4.

BILLOTTE, Rene* 1846-1915
French artist. 29 Boulevard Berthier, Paris. Exh. 1894-99. † G 1, GI 1, NG 1.

BILLSON, G.F. Exh. 1934-38
Flower and still life painter. 304 Alfred Street, Nottingham. † N 5.

BILLYEALD, Arthur Exh. 1882-87
Landscape painter. Radcliffe Cottage, Catford Bridge, London. † RA 1, RBA 2.

BILSON, John Exh. 1903-17
Architect. Studied A.A., R.I.B.A., Ashpitel prizeman 1877. Add: Hull. † RA 8.

BILTON, A. Exh. 1893
Brookleigh, Gunnersbury, London. † RI 1.

BINDER, Oscar Exh. 1903
38 Bramshill Gardens, Highgate, London. † RA 1.

BINDLEY, Frank* Exh. 1880-87
Figure painter. Galway, Ireland 1880, London 1883. † B 1, RA 1, RBA 5.

BINDON, George Exh. 1886-93
Sculptor. London 1886, Lichfield, Staffs. 1892. † RA 4.

BINET, Mlle. Alice Exh. 1923
Avenue Mozart 78, Paris. † L 1.

BINET, Victor 1849-1924
French painter. 16 Avenue Troudaine, Paris, 1882-86. † RA 1, RHA 3.

BINFIELD, Miss F. Exh. 1886-87
London. † B 2.

BINGE, F. Exh. 1894
152 Rue de la Consolation, Brussels. † G 1.

BINGGUELY-LEJEUNE, Ginette Exh. 1937-40
nee Lejeune. Sculptor. Studied under Jean George Achard, Paris and under Charles Doman, London. Add: Purley, Surrey 1937. † GI 2, RA 1, RBA 5.

BINGHAM, Miss Alice Exh. 1936-37
Flower painter. 175 Adelaide Road, London. † RA 1, RSA 1.

BINGHAM, W. Mary Exh. 1938-39
Figure and rustic landscape painter. 9 Third Avenue, Sherwood Rise, Nottingham. † N 4.

BINGLEY, Edgar Exh. 1883-1929
Birmingham. † B 21.

BINGLEY, James George c1841-1920
Watercolour landscape painter. Wallington, Surrey 1880, Cocking, Midhurst, Surrey 1884. † AG 11, D 4, RA 10, RI 3, ROI 2.

BINKS, Roland Harvey Exh. 1923
32 Silverdale Avenue, Tudbrook, Liverpool. † L 1.

BINMORE, Thomas Exh. 1938
Torquay, Devon. † RCA 1.

BINNEY, Edwin Exh. 1900-13
Liverpool 1900, Anglesey, N. Wales 1913. † L 3.

BINNEY, Hibbert Exh. 1893-1921
Sculptor. R.B.A. 1913. Add: Snaresbrook, Essex 1893, London 1894. † B 2, L 2, M 1, RA 10, RBA 20, RID 3.

BINNEY, Lilias Exh. 1935-39
15 Royal Avenue, London. † RI 1, SWA 2.

BINNEY, Mrs. Max Exh. 1932-40
15 Royal Avenue, London. † COO 2, RBA 1, RI 2.

BINNEY, R.K. Exh. 1912
25 New Cavendish Street, London. † RA 1.

BINNING, Alexander Exh. 1916
25 Temple Place, Anniesland, N.B. † GI 1.

BINNING, Alfred Bathurst Exh. 1921-38
Glasgow. † GI 3.

BINNS, Mrs. Charlotte A. Exh. 1919
† L 1.

BINNS, Dan Exh. 1930-40
Mount Pleasant, Glusburn, Keighley, Yorks. † B 2, RI 1, RSA 1.

BINNS, Elizabeth Jane* Exh. 1880-1911
Flower and still life painter. Diglis House, Worcester. † B 4, L 2, M 1, RA 5, RBA 5, ROI 1, SWA 18.

BINNS, Frances Rachael Exh. 1880-86
Landscape painter. Add: London. † L 1, RA 5, RBA 4.

BINNS, Henry W. Exh. 1916-40
Architect. Add: London. † RA 3.

BINNS, Miss Muriel Exh. 1916-17
22 Blomfield Court, Maida Vale, London. † ROI 1, SWA 1.

BINNY, Graham Exh. 1895-1919
Watercolour painter. R.S.W. 1909. Edinburgh. † GI 4, L 2, RHA 3, RSA 15, RSW 5.

BINSTEAD, Miss Augusta Exh. 1913
Sea View, Novara Avenue, Bray, Co. Wicklow. † RHA 1.

BINYON, Brightwen Exh. 1887-95
Architect. Ipswich, Suffolk. † RA 4.

BINYON, Helen b. 1904
Wood and line engraver and illustrator. Studied Royal College of Art. Artist at College of Arms. Exh. 1931. † NEA 2.

BINYON, Miss M.S. Exh. 1916
Haydon Ridge, Bushey, Herts. † RA 1.

BION, Cyril W. Exh. 1924-35
Landscape painter. Homeleigh, Carew Road, Wallington, Surrey. † RA 2, WG 31.

BIQUARD. Armand Exh. 1904
171 Stanhope Street, Regent's Park, London. † RA 1.

BIRABONGSE of SIAM, Prince Exh. 1936-40
Sculptor. London. † RA 4.

BIRCH, A. Exh. 1884-95
Salford, Lancs. † M 22.

BIRCH, Alison Exh. 1925-33
Walton-le Dale, Nr. Preston, Lancs. 1925; Fairford, Glos. 1927. † L 3, SWA 2.

BIRCH, Anna Exh. 1891-1907
Landscape painter. London. † GI 6, L 3, M 10, RA 1, RBA 7, ROI 3, SWA 5.

BIRCH, A.F. Exh. 1907-8
London. † L 2.

BIRCH, Charles Bell 1832-1893
Sculptor. Studied Berlin and R.A. Schools (2 medals). Principal assistant to John Henry Foley for ten years. A.R.A. 1880. Add: London. † G 3, GI 3, L 5, P 1, RA 37.

BIRCH, Mrs. C.M. Exh. 1906-8
Married to Lionel B. q.v. La Pietra, Newlyn, Penzance. † RA 2.

BIRCH, David b. c.1895
Landscape and portrait painter and illustrator. Studied Epsom School of Art and Goldsmiths College of Art. Principal Epsom School of Art 1930. † RA 3, ROI 3.

BIRCH, Downard* 1827-1897
Landscape painter. Lived for many years in Italy. Add: Bettws-y-Coed, N. Wales 1882. † L 5, M 4, RA 1.

BIRCH, Effie Exh. 1887
Landscape painter. Alpine Street, Old Basford, Nottingham. † N 1.

BIRCH, Miss Everilda Exh. 1929
Sculptor. Add: 289 Cambridge Road, Bethnal Green, London. † RA 1.

BIRCH, Miss F. Exh. 1887-88
2 Clarges Street, Piccadilly, London. † L 1, M 1.

BIRCH, Mrs. G.A. Exh. 1908
29 Egerton Road, Greenwich, London. † RA 1.

BIRCH, George H. Exh. 1886
Devereux Chambers, Temple, London. † RA 2.

BIRCH, Geraldine R. b. 1883
Mrs. W. Galloway Duncan. Etcher. Add: 15 Thomas Street, Dundee 1910. † LS 3.

BIRCH, John Exh. 1880-86
Architect. Add: 8 John Street, Adelphi, London. † RA 5.

BIRCH, Joan H. Exh. 1934
Landscape painter. Add: Lamorna, Penzance, Cornwall. † RA 1.

BIRCH, Lionel Exh. 1898-1916
Landscape painter. Newlyn, Penzance 1898 and 1907; Florence, Italy 1905; Wimple, Devon 1911; Ottery St. Mary, Devon 1912. † B 3, M 1, RA 15.

BIRCH, Miss Nellie Exh. 1903
23 Oxford Street, Wavertree, Liverpool. † L 1.

BIRCH, Roger Exh. 1911-33
Landscape painter. Add: Quenington, Nr. Fairfield, Glos. 1933. † BRU 1, RA 1.

BIRCH, Sarah Exh. 1884-1905
Figure painter. London 1884 and 1894; Brighton 1890; Ightham, Kent 1905. † L 2, M 1, NG 6, P 1, RA 12, RBA 3, ROI 1.

BIRCH, Samuel John Lamorna* 1869-1955
Landscape painter. b. Egremont. Worked in the mills, Manchester and Lancaster and painted in his spare time. Short study in Paris 1906. Worked with Stanhope Forbes at Newlyn. "St. Ives, Cornwall" purchased by Chantrey Bequest 1938. A.R.A. 1926, R.A. 1934, R.W.S. 1914. Add: Broughton, Lancs. 1889; Manchester 1892; St. Buryan, Cornwall 1898; Lamorna, Penzance, Cornwall 1903. † ALP 1, B 6, CHE 7, CON 1, DOW 2, FIN 445, G 2, GI 61, GOU 22, I 18, L 118, M 40, NG 1, RA 146, RHA 1, RI 8, RSA 6, RSW 1, RWS 287, TOO 1, WG 34.

BIRCH, T.C. Exh. 1915-16
130 Thatto Heath Road, St. Helens, Lancs. † L 3.

BIRCH, Miss Veril Exh. 1934-36
Sculptor. London. † RA 1, SWA 3.

BIRCHALL, Miss Alice Exh. 1910-19
Crank Hall, St. Helen's, Lancs. † L 6.

BIRCHALL, Emma Exh. 1880-81
Flower painter. The Ferns, Green Lanes, London. † SWA 3.

BIRCHALL, Florence L. Exh. 1925-28
Collaborated with her husband James T. B. q.v. Add: Heywood Street, Moss Side, Manchester. † L 32, M 3.

BIRCHALL, James T. Exh. 1908-28
Collaborated with his wife Florence L. B. q.v. Add: Heywood Street, Moss Side, Manchester. † L 34.

BIRCHALL, Miss M. Exh. 1933
13 Waltham Road, Manchester. † L 2.

BIRCHALL, Thomas T. Exh. 1926
† M 3.

BIRCHALL, William Minshall b. 1884
Marine painter. b. Cedar Rapids, Iowa, U.S.A. Add: Liscard, Cheshire 1914. † L 6.

BIRCKDALE, Miss Eleanor Fortescue Exh. 1918
55 Holland Park Road, Kensington, London. † RWS 1.

BIRD, Mrs. Exh. 1917-19
St. Fagan's Rectory, Nr. Cardiff, Wales. † SWA 6.

BIRD, Miss A. Exh. 1907
15 Holland Villas Road, Kensington, London. † NG 1.

BIRD, Alice A. Exh. 1883-87
17 Crofton Road, Camberwell, London. † M 2, SWA 2.

BIRD, Charles Exh. 1892-1907
A.R.E. 1892. London. † RA 1, RE 29.

BIRD, Constance Exh. 1901-33
Watercolour landscape painter and miniaturist. 4 Riversdale Road, Aigburth, Liverpool. † L 63, RA 2, SWA 4.

BIRD, Clarance Arthur Exh. 1896-1914
Portrait painter. Add: London. † B 1, LS 19, RA 2, RBA 1.

BIRD, Cyril Kenneth b. 1887
Black and white humorous and poster artist. Signs work "Fougasse" Art Editor of Punch 1937. Married to Mary Holden B. q.v. Add: Morar, Inverness-shire 1926. † FIN 151, RSA 6.

BIRD, D. Exh. 1910
7 Brazenose Street, Manchester. † RA 1.

BIRD, Eric L. Exh. 1923
34 Bedford Square, London. † RA 1.

BIRD, George Frederick b. 1883
Portrait painter. Studied R.A. Schools (Landseer Scholarship). Add: West Wickham, Kent 1905; London 1910. † L 4, P 8, RA 17.

BIRD, Harrington* b. 1846
Animal painter. Studied R.A. Schools. Director of Art to Board of School Commission, Quebec, Canada. Add: London 1885-93. † B 1, L 1, RA 3, RBA 1.

BIRD, Henry Exh. 1927-28
Sculptor. Add: Hampden Club, London. † RA 2.

BIRD, John R. Exh. 1884
10 Morrison Street, Kingston, Surrey. † GI 1.

BIRD, Leslie Pern Exh. 1930-31
† GOU 3.

BIRD, Margaret Exh. 1891-92
Figure painter. Add: Newlyn, Penzance, Cornwall 1891; Haywards Heath, Sussex 1892. † B 1, DOW 2, L 2, RA 3, RBA 2.

BIRD, Maud B.S. Exh. 1938
Married to Walter Herbert Allcott q.v. Add: Glenwood Bindery, Haslemere, Surrey. † B 1.

BIRD, Mary Holden Exh. 1923-36
Landscape painter and etcher. nee Caldwell. Married Cyril Kenneth B. q.v. Add: Morar, Inverness-shire 1924; London 1933. † FIN 258, L 3, RA 4, RSA 7, RSW 10.

BIRD, N.M. Exh. 1928
† D 2.

BIRD, Samuel Exh. 1880-94
Coastal and genre painter. Add: London. † B 3, L 1, M 2, NG 9, RA 3, RBA 1, TOO 1.

BIRD, William Exh. 1897-1919
Figure and portrait painter and miniaturist. Add: London. † P 1, RA 12, RI 1.

BIRKBECK, Geoffrey 1875-1954
Watercolour painter. b. Norwich. R.B.A. 1903, R.S.W. 1939. Add: London 1898 and 1932; Norwich 1910. † CAR 42, D 3, FIN 105, GI 1, GOU 107, I 1, L 1, RBA 4, RI 8, RSW 3, WG 41.

BIRKENHEAD, Margaret, Countess of Exh. 1940
nee Furneaux. Add: Charlton, Banbury, Oxon. † SWA 2.

BIRKENRUTH, Adolphus b. 1863
Landscape and figure painter. b. Grahamstown, South Africa. Studied London and Paris. Add: London 1883. † CAR 32, G 1, I 10, L 3, P 3, RA 13, RBA 9, RI 4, RID 37, ROI 12.

BIRKENRUTH, P. Exh. 1884
8 Exchange Buildings, Liverpool. † L 2.

BIRKIN, Miss V. Exh. 1915
Lamcote, Radcliffe-on-Trent, Notts. † N 1.

BIRKMYER, James B. Exh. 1880-98
Landscape painter. Add: Mount Radford, Exeter. † RA 8, RBA 3, RHA 2.

BIRKS, Edwin Exh. 1926-38
† M 2.

BIRKS, H. Maurice Exh. 1927
7 Park Range, Victoria, Manchester. † RCA 1.

BIRKS, M.C. Exh. 1908
† P 1.

BIRLEY, Hilda F. Exh. 1930
Queens College, Birmingham and Glenwood, Leamington, Warks. † B 3.

BIRLEY, Hugh H. Exh. 1929
Landscape painter. † AB 2.

BIRLEY, Oswald b. 1880
Portrait and figure painter. Studied Cambridge, Dresden, Paris and St. John's Wood School of Art. R.O.I. 1909, R.P. 1912. Add: St. Asaph, Cornwall 1899; Paris 1904; London 1905. † AG 27, B 2, CG 1, CHE 1, G 14, GI 5, I 14, L 29, LS 3, P 101, RA 59, RHA 5, ROI 11, RSA 15.

BIRNAGE, Sidney W. Exh. 1938
Architect. Add: 11 Carrington Street, Glasgow. † GI 2.

BIRNBAUM, H.B. Exh. 1914
21 Avenue Road, London. † RA 1.

BIRNBAUM, M. Exh. 1906
Mrs. A. Add: 53 Marlborough Hill, London. † RA 1.

BIRNIE, Rix Exh. 1885-87
Domestic figure painter. Pupil of Whistler. Add: London. † RBA 6.

BIRRELL, E. Martin Exh. 1896
7 Polworth Grove, Edinburgh. † GI 1.

BIRRELL, Mrs. James see Dalyell, Amy

BIRSE, Miss Isobel Exh. 1940
16 Alexander Street, Hamilton. † GI 1, RSA 1.

BIRSS, Charles Exh. 1894-1914
Edinburgh. † RSA 11, RSW 4.

BIRT, Herbert W. Exh. 1891-92
Sculptor. Add: 26 Harcourt Terrace, South Kensington, London. † L 1, RA 3.

BIRTLES, Henry Exh. 1880-1905
Landscape and animal painter. Add: Birmingham 1880 and 1901; Alcester, Warwickshire 1892. † B 28, D 5, DOW 3, L 12, M 2, RA 1, RBA 4, RHA 1, RI 10, ROI 8.

BIRTLES, Mrs. M. Exh. 1903
39 Oakfield Road, Stroud Green. † SWA 1.

BIRTWHISTLE, Cecil H. b. 1910
Landscape painter. Son of James Leonard B. q.v. Studied Sheffield College of Art 1924-29, Royal College of Art and South Kensington. † GI 1, RA 3.

BIRTWHISTLE, James Leonard Exh. 1932-35
Landscape and figure painter. Add: 85 Washington Road, Sheffield. † RA 6.

BIRTWHISTLE, W. Exh. 1890
Skipton-in-Craven, Yorkshire. † D 4.

BISBING, Henry Singlewood 1849-1933
American artist. Exh. 1886-91. Add: Paris. † TOO 3.

BISCOMB, Marjorie Exh. 1938-40
Wood-engraver and lino-cut artist. Add: Chester. † M 2, RA 2.

BISEAU, de see D

BISEI, Professor Unno Exh. 1910
Tokyo. † BG 28.

BISEO, Cesare* c.1843-1909
Italian painter. Exh. 1891. † AG 1.

BISH, R.D. Exh. 1924-28
Landscape painter. Add: 1 Thackeray Street, Nottingham. † N 6.

BISH, Stanley H. Exh. 1924-35
Landscape painter. N.S.A. 1929. Add: 1 Thackeray Street, Nottingham 1924; Credling, Notts. 1930. † N 36, RCA 5, ROI 1.

BISHOP, A.M. Exh. 1930
† P 1.
BISHOP, Dorothy Exh. 1938
4 Abinger Road, Bedford Park, London. † RBA 1.
BISHOP, Miss D.L. Exh. 1923
26 Vicarage Road, Wednesbury. † B 1.
BISHOP, Edward Exh. 1930
Wood-engraver. † RED 1.
BISHOP, Frederick A. Exh. 1905-39
Landscape and figure painter. Add: London. † L 3, RA 8, RI 3, ROI 8.
BISHOP, Henry 1868-1939
Landscape painter. Studied Slade School, Paris, Brussels and Pittsburg. Travelled also in Middle East. N.E.A. 1929, A.R.A. 1932, R.A. 1939, R.O.I. 1912. "Shakespeare's Cliff, Dover" purchased by Chantrey Bequest 1933. † BAR 2, BG 37, CG 1, CHE 3, DOW 2, FIN 3, GI 9, GOU 79, I 23, L 3, LEI 41, M 2, NEA 30, P 1, RA 66, RBA 1, RHA 3, ROI 13, RSA 5.
BISHOP, Miss J.M. Exh. 1883-85
41 South Hill Road, Liverpool. † L 4.
BISHOP, Miss Mabel Exh. 1897-98
A.S.W.A. 1899. Add: London. † NG 1, SWA 1.
BISHOP, Marjorie A. Exh. 1930
† P 1.
BISHOP, Maude E. Exh. 1935-40
Stained glass artist. Add: Kingston-upon-Thames, Surrey. † RA 3.
BISHOP, W.B. Exh. 1918
North Dene, The Park, Beckenham, Kent. † RI 1.
BISHOP, Walter Follen* 1856-1936
Landscape painter. Studied Liverpool School of Art and Julien's Paris. R.B.A. 1889. Add: London 1880 and 1920; Liverpool 1883 and 1906; Trefriw, Carnarvonshire 1905; Australia 1928; South Africa 1930; St. Helier, Jersey 1934. † B 39, D 2, GI 1, L 147, LS 1, M 9, RA 33, RBA 128, RCA 77, RI 37, ROI 5.
BISHOP, William James 1805-1888
102 Queen's Road, Everton, Liverpool. † L 12.
BISHOPP, George Exh. 1884-85
Still life painter. Add: 20 Newman Street, London. † RBA 1, ROI 1.
BISHOPP, Patience E. Exh. 1887-1906
Ashford, Kent. † D 16, RA 1, RBA 1.
BISI, Emilio Exh. 1894
Sculptor. Add: Via Borgonuovo 6, Milan. † RA 1.
BISPHAM, Henry Collins 1841-1882
American painter. d. Rome. † GI 1, RA 1.
BISSCHOP, Christoffe 1828-1904
Dutch painter. Add: The Hague, Holland. Exh. 1882-90. † GI 1, M 1, TOO 3.
BISSCHOP, Mrs. Kate Exh. 1880-1901
nee Swift. Figure painter. Married to Christoffe B. q.v. H.S.W.A. 1880. Add: London 1880; The Hague, Holland 1887. † RA 1, SWA 3.
BISSCHOP-ROBERTSON, Mrs. Suze Exh. 1905-9
116 Westerbaenstraat, The Hague, Holland. † LS 9.
BISSELL, Osmond Hick b. 1906
Painter, designer and wood-engraver. Studied Kidderminster School of Art 1924-28, Birmingham College of Art 1928-29. Vice Principal School of Arts and Crafts, York 1929. Add: York 1933. † RA 1.
BISSEN, Vilhelm Exh. 1890
Sculptor. Add: 131 Vestarvoldjade, Copenhagen. † RA 2.
BISSET, Douglas Robertson b. 1908
Sculptor. Studied Glasgow School of Art 1930-33, Royal Danish Academy 1933, British School Rome 1934-35. Teacher Brighton School of Art 1939 and Leeds College of Art 1939. † GI 8, RA 1.
BISSET, Miss Helen K. Exh. 1916-19
Edinburgh. † RSA 5.
BISSETT, Miss Carmel Exh. 1929-35
Clareville House, Harold's Cross Road, Dublin. † RHA 5.
BISSILL, George William b. 1896
Landscape painter. Studied Nottingham School of Art. Worked in the coal mines for 7 years, came to London and worked as a pavement artist in 1922. "Landscape, Layton" purchased by Chantrey Bequest 1940. † BK 1, M 4, N 2, NEA 1, RA 1, RED 58, TOO 2.
BISSON, Edouard b. 1856
French artist. 71 Boulevard Berthier, Paris 1911-12. † L 1, RA 1.
BITHELL, Phyllis Muriel Exh. 1932-35
Saltney, Flints. † RCA 5.
BITTINGER, Charles b. 1879
American artist. Add: Paris 1905-6. † I 1, L 1.
BIVEL, Farnard Exh. 1930
Paris. † GI 2.
BJERG, Johannes Exh. 1934
Frederiksholms Kanal 28, Copenhagen. † RSA 3.
BJORCK, Professor Oscar b. 1860
Portrait painter. Add: Valhallonagen 104, Stockholm, Sweden. Exh. 1924-25. † RA 3.
BLAANW, Miss Frances C. Exh. 1909
Heathlands, Grove Road, Bournemouth, Hants. † B 1.
BLAAS, de See D.
BLABEY, Miss A. Exh. 1920-25
The Priory, Watergate Lane, Woolton, Liverpool. † L 6.
BLABEY, Daniel Exh. 1923
The Priory, Watergate Lane, Woolton, Liverpool. † L 1.
BLACK, Andrew d. 1916
Marine painter. R.S.W. 1885. Add: Glasgow. † DOW 3, GI 100, L 8, M 4, RA 8, RSA 16, RSW 56.
BLACK, Arthur John* 1855-1936
Landscape and figure painter and mural and scenery painter. Studied under Benjamin Constant in Paris. N.S.A. 1881, R.O.I. 1917, H.R.O.I. 1932. Add: Nottingham 1880; Beeston, Notts. 1884; London 1890; Wimborne, Dorset 1931. † BG 1, L 6, M 1, N 27, NEA 2, NG 8, RA 36, RI 6, ROI 54.
BLACK, Ann Spence d. 1947
Flower painter. R.S.W. 1917. Add: Edinburgh 1896. † AR 2, BG 6, GI 38, L 2, M 5, RSA 72, RSW 95.
BLACK, Annie Taylor Exh. 1902-4
122 Cheyne Walk, Chelsea, London. † GI 2, L 3, RSA 1, SWA 2.
BLACK, Duncan B. Exh. 1935
Glendaenel, Portmore, Park Road, Weybridge, Surrey. † RBA 1.
BLACK, Dorothea Foster 1891-1951
Painter and lino-cut artist. Signs work "Dorrit Black". b. Adelaide, Australia. Studied Sydney Art School and Paris. Exh. 1930-35. † RED 7.
BLACK, Edwin Exh. 1880-94
Watercolour landscape and figure painter. Add: London. † D 6, L 1, RA 3, RBA 1, RHA 4, RI 3.
BLACK, Emma L. Exh. 1881-1936
Mrs. J.D.K. Mahomed. Portrait and figure painter. Add: London 1881; Elgin, N.B. 1902. † B 2, L 8, M 1, P 2, RA 8, RBA 4, RI 4.
BLACK, Mrs. E.R. Exh. 1927
† D 2.
BLACK, Francis Exh. 1891-1938
Marine and coastal painter. R.B.A. 1895, Hon. Sec. R.B.A. 1915-18. Add: London 1891, 1921 and 1933; Chesham Bois, Bucks. 1917 and 1929; Selsey, Sussex 1928 and 1931. † L 3, N 1, NG 3, RA 2, RBA 203, RCA 2.
BLACK, Hugh Exh. 1885
30 Steven Street, Glasgow. † GI 1.
BLACK, Lilian M. Exh. 1906-10
Liverpool. † L 17.
BLACK, Montague Birrell b. 1889
Poster artist and illustrator. Add: 40 Marlfield Road, West Derby, Liverpool 1912. † L 1.
BLACK, Margaret L. Exh. 1893
Watercolour painter. Add: 40 South Hill Park, Hampstead, London. † RA 1.
BLACK, Miss Norah Exh. 1923-32
Kingston-on-Thames, Surrey 1923; London 1932. † D 1, RCA 1, RI 1, SWA 2.
BLACK, Nellie Bryce Exh. 1937-40
Sculptor. Add: London. † RA 2.
BLACK, N.I. Exh. 1908
24 Hess Hasse, Munich, Germany. † RA 1.
BLACK, Philip Exh. 1916-19
138 Crown Street, Liverpool. † L 4.
BLACK, Mrs. Rose Exh. 1936
Watercolour painter. † WG 22.
BLACK, Reuben Nathan b. 1899
Landscape painter. Studied Newport Technical Institute. Add: Newport, Mon. 1922. † RCA 3.
BLACK, Sam b. 1913
Studied Glasgow School of Art 1932-36. Add: Longcraigs, Overton Drive, West Kilbride 1937. † GI 4, RSA 2.
BLACK, Miss Sarah Anne Exh. 1880-1900
145 Capel Street, Dublin. † RHA 48.
BLACK, Tom Exh. 1880-1907
Partick, Glasgow. † GI 15.
BLACK, T.S. Exh. 1928-34
Landscape painter. A.N.S.A. 1928, N.S.A. 1934. Add: Melville House, Elm Bank, Nottingham. † N 17, RCA 5.
BLACK, William Exh. 1909-1928
Portrait and landscape painter. Add: London. † AB 6, LS 3, RI 1.
BLACK, W. Milne Exh. 1908-12
20 Dixon Avenue, Crosshill, Glasgow. † GI 4.
BLACK, W.S. Exh. 1881-97
Edinburgh. † M 1, RSA 11.
BLACKBAND, William Thomas Exh. 1931-32
Metal worker and jeweller. Headmaster Birmingham School for Jewellers and Silversmiths. R.B.S.A. 1926. Add: Solihull 1931. † B 12.
BLACKBOURN, J.F. Exh. 1881
90 Gower Street, Bedford Square, London. † RA 1.
BLACKBURN, Arthur Exh. 1890-91
Landscape painter. Add: Leeds. † RA 2.
BLACKBURN, Miss Edith Exh. 1887-89
8 Carlton Mount, Allerton Road, Higher Tranmere, Cheshire. † L 2.
BLACKBURN, Joyce Keble Exh. 1930
32 Hinstock Road, Handsworth Wood, Birmingham. † B 1.
BLACKBURN, R. Exh. 1905-10
Liverpool. † L 11.

BLACKBURN, Miss Winifred Exh. 1905-13
West Kirby, Cheshire and Liverpool. † L 16.

BLACKBURN, William H. Exh. 1927-29
9 Barnston Street, Birkenhead. † L 3.

BLACKBURNE, E.R. Ireland Exh. 1890-1901
Landscape painter. Add: Newlyn, Penzance, Cornwall 1890; Lilliput, Dorset 1900. † DOW 2, L 4, M 4, RA 8.

BLACKBURNE, Helena Exh. 1880-99
Figure painter. Add: London. † B 13, D 3, L 3, M 2, RA 14, RBA 5, RHA 1, RI 7, ROI 2.

BLACKBURNE, Miss M. Ireland Exh. 1925
Hale Hall, Liverpool. † L 1.

BLACKDEN, Hugh C. Exh. 1898-99
Landscape and coastal painter. Merlewood, Bournemouth, Hants. † L 1, M 1, RA 1, RBA 2, ROI 1.

BLACKDEN, M.W. Exh. 1890-91
c/o J.B. Smith, 117 Hampstead Road, London. † L 1. RA 1.

BLACKER, Elva Joan Exh. 1931-39
Portrait painter and miniaturist. Add: Sutton, Surrey. † COO 61, RA 3, RI 21, RMS 4, RSA 3.

BLACKER, Miss Louisa Exh. 1884-89
Cappoquin, Ireland 1884; Newbridge, Ireland 1888. † RHA 8, SWA 1.

BLACKER, Miss L.E. Exh. 1895-1912
35 Evelyn Mansions, Carlisle Place, London. † RA 1, RI 1.

BLACKHAM, Dorothy Isabel b. 1896
Painter, poster and lino-cut artist and teacher. Studied R.H.A. Schools and Goldsmiths College. Add: Dublin. † RHA 55.

BLACKHAM, G. Warren Exh. 1882-1906
Birmingham 1882; Sutton Coldfield, Warwicks. 1885. † B 16, L 1.

BLACKHAM, J. Exh. 1905
44 Heathfield Road, King's Heath, Birmingham. † L 1, M 1.

BLACKIE, Agnes H. Exh. 1887-90
Holydean, St. Boswells, Edinburgh. † RSA 2.

BLACKING, Lt. W.H.R. Exh. 1916
8th London Regt., B.E.F., France. † RA 1.

BLACKLOCK, C. d. c.1893
Landscape painter. Add: St. James' Square, Manchester. † L 1, M 35.

BLACKLOCK, Nellie b. 1889
Watercolour flower painter. Married to W. Kay B. q.v. Add: Walberswick, Suffolk 1915; Leicester 1920; London 1926. † L 4, RA 6, RI 4.

BLACKLOCK, Thomas Bromley* 1863-1903
Landscape, child and fairy tale painter. Studied Edinburgh. Add: Edinburgh. † GI 28, L 5, M 1, RA 2, RSA 81.

BLACKLOCK, William Kay* Exh. 1897-1921
Sunderland 1897; London 1898 and 1909; School of Art, Edinburgh 1902; Walberswick, Suffolk 1912; St. Ives, Hunts. 1918; Leicester 1919. † B 9, GI 12, L 15, LS 5, M 2, RA 16, RI 13, RSA 19, ROI 6.

BLACKMAN, Audrey b. 1907
Sculptor. Add: Wick Cottage, Westleigh Avenue, London 1938. † RA 1.

BLACKMAN, Walter Exh. 1880-1902
Landscape and figure painter. Add: London. † B 7, G 1, GI 9, L 18, M 2, RA 7, RBA 3, ROI 3, RSA 1, TOO 6.

BLACKMORE, Katie Exh. 1913-39
Figure painter. A.R.B.A. 1922, A.S.W.A. 1924, R.B.A. 1925. Add: London and Alassio, Italy 1923; Southsea, Hants. 1925; Stroud, Glos. 1931; Hove, Sussex 1935. † CAR 35, D 9, G 1, L 1, RA 4, RBA 99, RI 11, RID 4, SWA 7.

BLACKSTONE, F.E. Exh. 1884
2 Caroline Street, Bedford Square, London. † D 1.

BLACKWOOD, Lady A. Exh. 1880-81
Landscape painter. Add: Boxmoor House, Boxmoor, Herts. † RBA 1, RSA 1.

BLACKWOOD, Miss Cecilia G. Exh. 1896-1905
4 Brunswick Square, London. † GI 1, SWA 6.

BLADEN, Alfred Exh. 1925-29
Studied Wolverhampton School of Arts and Crafts and Royal College of Art. Add: Wolverhampton. † B 2.

BLADEN, Thomas W. Exh. 1887
Stained glass artist. Add: 62 Sherbrooke Road, Fulham, London. † RA 1.

BLADES, Daisy Exh. 1889-94
Miniature painter. Add: Folkestone 1889 and 1891; London 1890. † NG 2, RA 2.

BLADON, C. Exh. 1920-26
Wallasey, Cheshire 1920 and 1925; Liverpool 1921. † L 5.

BLADON, Mrs. Ethel B. Exh. 1931
Ty Gwyn, Llanbedr, Merioneth. † B 1.

BLADON, T. Murray Bernard b. 1864
Landscape and portrait painter. Studied Birmingham School of Art. Art Master Birmingham School of Arts and Crafts 1896. R.B.S.A. 1918. Add: Birmingham 1888; Lanbedr, Merioneth 1930. † B 142, L 2.

BLAGDEN, Miss Exh. 1906-13
Broughton-in-Furness, Lancs. † SWA 4.

BLAIKIE, Jeanie Exh. 1899
Bridge House, Hawick, Roxburghshire. † GI 1.

BLAIKLEY, Alexander 1816-1903
Portrait and figure painter. b. Glasgow. Add: London 1880. † GI 1, RSA 6.

BLAIKLEY, Ernest b. 1885
Painter and etcher. Studied Slade School and London University College School. Keeper of Pictures, Imperial War Museum 1919. Exh. 1919-39. † I 6, RA 4, RBA 5, RI 4, RSA 4.

BLAIKLEY, Edith S. Exh. 1880
Flower painter. Add: 6 Courtland Terrace, The Mall, Kensington, London. † RBA 1.

BLAIKLEY, Miss J.S. Exh. 1908-10
13 Elsworthy Terrace, London. † RI 2.

BLAIN, James Exh. 1906-40
Kilmarnock, N.B. 1906; Glasgow 1936. † GI 5, RSA 1, RSW 1.

BLAIN, Mlle. Marthe Exh. 1909
17 Rue d'Ourches, St. Germain en Laye, France. † L 2.

BLAIN, Miss R.F. Exh. 1902
Park View, Bushey, Herts. † L 1.

BLAIR, Andrew Exh. 1883-85
Bruce Street, Dunfermline. † L 1, RI 1, RSA 8.

BLAIR, Miss B. Exh. 1889-93
Staplehurst, Kent 1889; Goudhurst, Kent 1890. † D 4, L 1, SWA 1.

BLAIR, Doris V. Exh. 1938-40
Painter and etcher. Add: Belfast 1938; London 1940. † P 2, RA 2, RHA 8, RSA 1.

BLAIR, E. Scott Exh. 1884
4 St. Catherine's Place, Edinburgh. † RSA 2.

BLAIR, Miss Frances M. Exh. 1925-37
Edinburgh. † GI 5, L 7, RSA 9, RSW 9.

BLAIR, Gabriel Exh. 1905-6
59 Cross Lane, Newton-le-Willows. † L 2.

BLAIR, Gorrie McLeich Exh. 1885
8 Hillside Street, Edinburgh. † RSA 1.

BLAIR, John* Exh. 1880-1920
Edinburgh. † D 1, GI 10, L 5, M 1, RHA 2, RI 3, RSA 83, RSW 4.

BLAIR, Janet T.R. Exh. 1899-1913
Glasgow. † GI 1, L 5.

BLAIR, Miss K.M. Exh. 1931-32
Daljarock, The Thrupp, Nr. Stroud, Glos. † B 2.

BLAIR, William Charles d. c.1887
Kincardine-on-Forth 1882 and 1886; Paris 1883; Madeira 1884. † GI 3, L 1, RSA 8.

BLAKE, Miss Bessie Mary Exh. 1900-19
Miniature painter. Add: 5 Philbeach Gardens, Earl's Court, London. † RA 6, RHA 1.

BLAKE, Charles John Exh. 1908
4 Greenhill Terrace, Weymouth, Dorset. † B 1.

BLAKE, Dorothea Frances b. 1895
Landscape, portrait and figure painter. b. Greenock. Studied Byam Shaw and Vicat Cole School of Art and R.A. Schools (silver and bronze medals). Add: London 1921. † L 1, NEA 4, P 3, RA 3, ROI 2.

BLAKE, Mrs. Elizabeth Exh. 1931-33
London 1931, Virginia Water 1933. † ROI 2.

BLAKE, E.C.H. Exh. 1884
Architect. Add: 12 Buckingham Street, Strand, London. † RA 1.

BLAKE, Eileen Mary b. 1878
Landscape, interior and child painter, and black and white artist. Studied Birmingham Art School. Add: Woodcote, Cotton Lane, Moseley, Birmingham. † B 35, L 3, RCA 1, RI 4, ROI 2, SWA 1.

BLAKE, Frederick Donald b. 1908
Painter and etcher and industrial designer. Studied Camberwell School of Art and Crafts, Goldsmiths College and Brixton School of Building. † RBA 1, ROI 1.

BLAKE, Mrs. Frances M. Exh. 1881
Figure painter. Add: 6 South Bank Terrace, Stratford Road, Kensington, London. † SWA 1.

BLAKE, Geraldine B. Exh. 1906-19
Mrs. Thomas. Sculptor. Add: Ashford, Kent 1906; Hereford 1918. † L 1, RA 3.

BLAKE, Henry 1848-1933
Watercolour landscape painter. † ALP 59.

BLAKE, Joseph Exh. 1895
37 Spencer Road, Acton, London. † RHA 1.

BLAKE, J. Elliott Exh. 1884
Rome. † SWA 1.

BLAKE, John R. Exh. 1909
44 Belmont Avenue, Donnybrook, Dublin. † RHA 4.

BLAKE, Leonard Exh. 1880-93
Figure painter and miniaturist. Add: London. † FIN 2, L 1, RA 2, RI 2.

BLAKE, Louisa Exh. 1885-86
4 Coburg Place, Bayswater, London. † L 1, M 1, RA 2, ROI 1.

BLAKE, Miss M.B. Exh. 1887-90
Liverpool. † L 2, M 1.

BLAKE, Stacey Exh. 1891-1939
Landscape painter. A.N.S.A. 1924, N.S.A. 1925, V.P.N.S.A. 1926. Add: Nottingham. † L 2, N 93.

BLAKE, Vernon 1875-1930
Painter and sculptor. Studied Paris and Florence. Travelled Middle and Far East. Teacher at British Academy, Rome. Add: London 1908-9. † LS 5.

BLAKELEY, John Harold b. 1887
Painter and etcher. Add: 5 Hazel Grove, Blackpool 1922. † L 5, RA 1.

BLAKELOCK, Katherine Percy Exh. 1894-1914
Arbroath, Scotland 1894; Carnoustie 1904; Buxton, Derbys. 1909; London 1913. † LS 15, RHA 9, RI 2.

BLAKEMAN, Charles Exh. 1936
17 Graham Street, Edinburgh. † RSA 1.

BLAKENEY, Charlotte See WARD

BLAKER, Hugh d. 1936
Landscape and figure painter. Studied Antwerp and Paris. Curator Holbourne Art Museum, Bath. R.B.A. 1913. Add: Worthing 1897; Bath 1909; Isleworth, Middx. 1913. † I 24, LS 8, NEA 2, P 3, RA 1, RBA 24.

BLAKESLEY, Alicia Exh. 1893-1912
Landscape and figure painter. Add: London 1893; Wallingford, Berks. 1905. † B 2, BG 47, GI 1, RA 1, RBA 3, ROI 1, SWA 13.

BLAKISTON, Miss C. Exh. 1936-37
Flower and landscape painter. † WG 39.

BLAKISTON, Evelyn Exh. 1899-1907
Portrait painter. Add: London 1889, Edgbaston, Birmingham 1907. † L 5, NG 1, P 5, RA 2.

BLAKISTON, Ralph Exh. 1894-1909
Liverpool. † L 11, RCA 4.

BLAMEY, Henwood Exh. 1905-34
Landscape painter. Add: The Orchard, Beer, Axminster, Devon. † RA 13.

BLAMEY, Norman Exh. 1938-40
Figure and urban landscape painter. Add: London. † RA 5.

BLAMPEY, Frederick Exh. 1923-24
Figure painter. Add: The Studio, 422 Archway Road, Highgate, London. † RA 2.

BLAMPIED, Clifford George b. 1875
Watercolour Alpine and Italian landscape painter. Born and lived St. Helier, Jersey, C.I. † ALP 3, LS 3.

BLAMPIED, Edmund b. 1886
Painter, etcher, lithographer and clay modeller. b. Jersey, C.I. R.B.A. 1938, A.R.E. 1920, R.E. 1921. Add: London 1922; St. Aubin, Jersey, C.I. 1939. † BK 2, CHE 2, CON 4, FIN 49, GI 10, L 16, LEI 119, RA 6, RBA 11, RE 49, RHA 1, RSA 1, RSW 1.

BLANC, Frank Edward Belcombe b. 1890
Architect. Studied Edinburgh College of Art. Son of Hippolyte Jean B. q.v. Add: 25 Rutland Square, Edinburgh 1915-25. † RSA 10.

BLANC, Hippolyte Jean 1844-1917
Architect. A.R.S.A. 1892, R.S.A. 1896, Treasurer R.S.A. 1907. Add: Edinburgh. † GI 1, RA 6, RHA 12, RSA 82.

BLANC, Paul Exh. 1925
Etcher. † FIN 2.

BLANCH, Miss Lesley Stuart b. 1904
Painter, commercial artist and journalist. Add: London 1928. † SWA 1.

BLANCHARD, Auguste 1819-1898
Engraver. Add: Rue de la Victoire, Paris. † RA 8.

BLANCHARD, F.L. Exh. 1936-40
† RI 5.

BLANCHE, Jacques Emile* 1862-1942
Portrait painter, art critic and writer. Studied Paris and London. b. Paris, dual French/English nationality. N.E.A. 1887, R.P. 1905. † FIN 3, GI 6, GOU 15, I 38, L 14, LEI 37, M 1, NEA 25, NG 5, P 21, RA 7, RBA 5, ROI 1, RSA 11.

BLANCHE, Norman H. Exh. 1936-38
Portrait painter. † P 4.

BLAND, Benjamin Exh. 1911-14
Kendal, Westmorland. † L 1, RCA 4.

BLAND, C.F. Exh. 1926
† M 1.

BLAND, Emily Beatrice 1864-1951
Landscape and flower painter. Studied Lincoln School of Art and Slade School. N.E.A. 1926. Purchased by Chantrey Bequest "Stripped Camellias" 1929 and "Yachts at Lymington" 1939. Add: London. † BA 9, BG 30, BK 1, CG 1, CHE 5, D 6, FIN 77, G 6, GI 6, GOU 64, I 10, L 14, LEI 272, LS 14, M 9, NEA 108, NG 10, RA 60, RBA 3, RED 83, RHA 7, RID 70, ROI 2, SWA 18, TOO 31.

BLAND, Kenneth W. Exh. 1939
Architect. Add: 94 Eastdean Avenue, Epsom, Surrey. † RA 1.

BLAND, Sydney Josephine b. 1883
Watercolour painter. b. York. Studied Heatherley's 1920-22 and Goldsmiths College 1922-23. Add: London 1935. † P 2, RI 2, SWA 2.

BLAND, William Exh. 1936
Engraver. † RED 1.

BLANDY, Miss L. Exh. 1884
Thorpe House, Cornwall Gardens, London. † D 1.

BLANT, Le See L

BLASHFIELD, Edwin Howland* c.1849-1936
Historical and figure painter. Add: Paris 1880; London 1886-87. † B 2, GI 2, L 2, RA 2, RSA 2.

BLASHKI, M. Evergood Exh. 1910-15
Landscape painter. c/o Bank of Australasia, Threadneedle Street, London. † I 6, NEA 1.

BLATCHFORD, Conway b. 1873
Landscape and marine painter and modeller. Studied Bristol Municipal School of Art (silver medal) and Royal College of Art. Head Master Halifax School of Art and Principal of Newton Abbot School of Art, Devon. Add: London 1906; Heywood, Lancs. 1907; Halifax 1908; Newton Abbot, Devon 1923 † D 1, RA 2, RCA 1.

BLATCHFORD, M. Exh. 1885
Flower painter. † DOW 1.

BLATCHFORD, Mrs. Winifred Exh. 1939
† RMS 1.

BLATHERWICK, Charles d. c.1895
Watercolour landscape painter. Dunaivon, Helensburgh, N.B. † D 2, DOW 1, G 2, GI 14, M 2, RA 3, RI 1, ROI 2, RSA 6, RSW 31.

BLATHERWICK, Lily d. 1934
Flower and pastoral painter. Married Archibald Standish Hartrick q.v. R.S.W. 1878, A.S.W.A. 1886, S.W.A. 1898. Dunaivon, Helensburgh, N.B. 1880; London 1897. † AR 2, BG 4, CHE 3, D 1, DOW 4, G 4, GI 61, GOU 4, I 58, L 7, M 7, NEA 37, NG 4, RA 25, RBA 1, RI 4, ROI 12, RSA 13, RSW 161, SWA 33, WG 4.

BLAXLAND, Cicely J. Exh. 1919
Landscape painter. Fordwich, Brunstead Road, W. Bournemouth, Hants. † RA 1.

BLAYLOCK, Thomas Todd 1876-1929
Painter, etcher and woodcut engraver. b. Langholm, Dumfries. Studied Royal College of Art. Add: London 1899; Leek, Staffs. 1907; Poole, Dorset 1913; Salisbury, Wilts. 1928. † L 56, RA 6, RBA 1.

BLAYMIRES, Charles H. Exh. 1933
108 Golden Hillock Road, Small Heath, Birmingham. † B 1.

BLAYMIRES, Robert W. Exh. 1933
2 Weston Avenue, Aston Brook Street, Birmingham. † B 1.

BLAY-Y-FABREGA, Miguel b. 1866
Spanish sculptor. Passage St. Ferdinand, Neuilly-sur-Seine, France 1902. † L 1.

BLEADON, Mary Exh. 1880-84
Figure and domestic painter. 114 Kensington Park Road, London. † D 4, RBA 3.

BLEAKLEY, Alex Exh. 1884
51 Hamilton Square, Birkenhead. † L 1.

BLEASE, W. Lyon Exh. 1912-20
Liverpool. † L 7.

BLECKMANN, Wilhelm Cristiaan Constant Exh. 1908
2B Wilhelmina Straat, The Hague, Holland. † LS 4.

BLENA, Luis Exh. 1923
c/o Miss F. Linden, 14 Bertram Road, Liverpool. † L 1.

BLENKARN, May A. Exh. 1897-1904
Laurel Bank, Dacre Hill, Rock Ferry, Cheshire. † L 4.

BLENKIRON, Edith b. 1904
Landscape painter. Married Rowland Hilder q.v. b. Northumberland. Studied Goldsmiths College. Add: Blackheath, London 1933. † RA 2.

BLENNER, Carl John* b. 1864
American artist. Add: France 1886; London 1902. † B 1, L 1.

BLES, David* 1821-99.
Dutch artist. The Hague, Holland 1890. † M 3.

BLETSOE, Miss M. Exh. 1904
25 Rosetti Mansions, London. † SWA 1.

BLIECK, Maurice Exh. 1918-20
Chelsea, London 1918; Brussels 1920. † GI 2.

BLIGH, Charles E. Exh. 1938
Landscape painter. Amersham-on-Hill, Bucks. † RA 1.

BLIGH, Dorothy Exh. 1938
† BA 2.

BLIGH, Jabez Exh. 1880-91
Nature and still life painter. Add: Shorne, Gravesend. † B 1, M 2, RA 9, RBA 2, RI 6.

BLIGH, The Hon. Noel G. Exh. 1930-37
Landscape painter. London. † BA 40, RA 2, RBA 3.

BLIGHT, Miss Julia Exh. 1894
16 Barnard Road, Claughton, Birkenhead. † L 1.

BLIGNY, A. Exh. 1883
† GI 1.

BLIND, Rudolf Exh. 1884-88
Figure painter. London. † RA 1, ROI 1.

BLINKS, Thomas* 1860-1912
Sporting and animal painter. London. † B 1, L 12, M 1, RA 29, RBA 4, ROI 4, TOO 68.

BLISS, Miss Ada Exh. 1890
32 Talbot Street, Southport, Lancs. † L 1.

BLISS, Douglas Percy b. 1900
Painter and engraver. b. Karachi, India. Studied Royal College of Art. R.B.A. 1939. Add: London 1930. † GI 2, L 3, LEF 44, M 1, NEA 9, RA 24, RBA 6, RSA 12.

BLISS, Miss E.J. Exh. 1936-38
31 Market Street, Tamworth, Staffs. † B 6.

BLISS, Miss Phyllis Exh. 1930
65 Sancroft Street, London. † RSA 2.

BLOCH, Julius Exh. 1930
Etcher. † FIN 3.

BLOCH, Martin* 1883-1954
Landscape painter. Exh. 1939. † LEF 35.

BLOCK, Louis d. 1909
Painter of fruit. London. † B 3, D 42, FIN 3, L 6, LS 4, M 9, RA 1, RBA 1, RI 23, ROI 2.

BLOCK, Marcel Exh. 1903
88 Rue de la Pompe, Paris. † L 1.

BLOCKMAN, Walter Exh. 1885
c/o Carlile, 5 Dorset Street, Baker Street, London. † RSA 2.

BLOFELD, Miss L.C. Exh. 1913-23
Chipping Norton, Oxon 1913; London 1920. † D 1, SWA 2.

BLOIS, Flavia Exh. 1937-38
Portrait painter. Cranley Place, London. † P 2, SWA 1.

BLOMBERG, Stig. b. 1901
Swedish artist. Add: Stockhold 1933. † RSA 2.

BLOMEFIELD, Eardley W. Exh. 1880-1900
Landscape painter. London 1880; Mansfield, Notts. 1883 and 1896; St. Ives, Cornwall 1890. † B 5, DOW 2, GI 1, L 8, M 3, RA 5, RBA 1, ROI 7.

BLOMFIELD, Arthur Conran c. 1863-1935
Architect to the Bank of England. Went into partnership with his father Sir Arthur William B. q.v. in 1890. Add: London. † RA 34.

BLOMFIELD, Alfred W. Exh. 1934-38
Architect. London. † RA 6.

BLOMFIELD, Sir Arthur William 1829-1899
Ecclesiastical architect. Architect to the Bank of England 1883. A.R.A. 1888, Hon. member of the Danish Academy 1888, Knighted 1889. Add: London and Broadway, Worcs. † RA 33.

BLOMFIELD, C. Geoffrey Exh. 1923-37
Architect. 12 Alipur Road, Delhi, India. † RA 4.

BLOMFIELD, Charles James c.1856-1920
Architect and painter. Son of Sir Arthur William B. q.v. Add: London. † LEI 4, RA 15.

BLOMFIELD, Sir Reginald 1856-1942
Architect and author. A.R.A. 1905, R.A. 1914, Knighted 1919. Among his works are the Menin Gate Memorial at Ypres and Lady Margaret Hall, Oxford. Add: London. † L 5, RA 114, RSA 11.

BLOMMERS, Bernandes Johannes* 1845-1914
Dutch painter and etcher. President of the Dutch Academy. H.R.S.W. 1897. † AG 1, B 6, FIN 5, GI 6, M 1, RA 2, RSA 2, RSW 11.

BLOMVIL-CAMPLING, A.T. Exh. 1931
Seething, Brooke, Norwich. † RA 1.

BLONDAT, M. Exh. 1910-11
6 Rue Mornay, Paris. † GI 1, L 1, RA 1.

BLOOM, Miss Violet Exh. 1904-6
London. † RI 1, SWA 2.

BLOOMER, Hiram Reynolds b. 1845
Landscape painter. b. New York, U.S.A. N.E.A. 1887. Add: London and Cookham Dean, Berks. 1880-90. † G 4, L 1, M 1, NEA 1, NG 3, RA 7, RBA 5, ROI 3, RSA 2.

BLOOMFIELD, Evelyn E. Exh. 1906-8
32 Walpole Street, London. † L 2, LS 5, RHA 2.

BLOOR, D. Smith Exh. 1880-82
Sculptor. London. † D 1, RA 3, RBA 1.

BLORE, Burton Exh. 1885
Figure painter. 38 Howland Street, Fitzroy Square. London. † RBA 1.

BLORE, Kate du Plessis Exh. 1922
nee Hockly. S. African landscape and portrait painter and miniaturist. Studied Herkomer's School, Bushey, Herts. Add: Grahamstown, S. Africa. † RA 1.

BLOSSOM, Joseph B. Exh. 1894-9
Waterloo, Lancs. 1894; Liverpool 1899. † L 2.

BLOUNT, Miss Edith Exh. 1905-17
Dublin. † RHA 7.

BLOW, Detmar Exh. 1924
31 Upper Grosvenor Street, London. † RA 1.

BLOW, Percival C. Exh. 1900
7 London Road, St. Albans, Herts. † RA 1.

BLOXAM, Joan Mary Exh. 1907-28
Landscape painter, black and white artist, miniaturist, lithographer and art teacher. Studied Cope and Nichols School of Art, John Hassals School of Art and the Central School of Arts and Crafts (4 medals for drawing and painting). Add: London. † B 3, L 5, LS 3, RA 3, RBA 2, RHA 14, RMS 2, SWA 2, WG 37.

BLOXAM, Mary A. Exh. 1894
Flower painter. 1 Grosvenor Hill, Wimbledon, London. † RA 1.

BLOXAM, O.A. Exh. 1920
The Malt Cottage, Bourne End, Bucks. † NEA 1.

BLOXCIDGE, Eunice E. Exh. 1896-1925
School of Art, Birmingham 1896; Coleshill 1897; Sutton Coldfield, Warwicks 1925. † B 5, SWA 2.

BLOXHAM, Miss E. Exh. 1896
60 Elsham Road, Kensington, London. † SWA 1.

BLOXHAM, Miss M.C. Exh. 1894-96
16 Bolingbroke Road, London. † SWA 2.

BLOYE, William J. Exh. 1930-40
Sculptor. R.B.S.A. 1931. Add: Golden Hillock Road, Small Heath, Birmingham. † B 1, RA 4.

BLUETT, Duncan C. Exh. 1910
Landscape painter. 7 Doughty Street, London. † NEA 1.

BLUFF, Mrs. Eleanor K. Exh. 1935-36
Miniature painter of dogs. Sandy Acres, Nine Mile Ride, Finchampstead, Berks. † RA 2.

BLUHM, H. Faber Exh. 1880-81
Landscape painter. Add: 38 Lee Park, Lee, London. † RA 4, RBA 1.

BLUM, Ludvik Exh. 1933-38
Landscape painter. Visited M. East. 5 Belsize Park Gardens, London. † FIN 5, RA 2.

BLUM, Robert 1857-1903
American figure painter. Exh. 1882-88 Add: New York. † GI 1, L 1, RA 1.

BLUM, Willy b. 1908
Painter and sculptor. 19 Southwell Road, Lowdham, Notts., 1939. † N 4.

BLUMAN, Miss A. Exh. 1905
46 Sunderland Road, Forest Hill, London. † D 4.

BLUME, Miss R. Exh. 1909
6 Talbot Square, Hyde Park, London. † RA 1.

BLUMENTHAL, Herman 1905-1942
German sculptor. Exh. 1936. † RSA 1.

BLUNDELL, Alfred Richard b. 1883
Landscape painter, etcher and sculptor. Add: Hawstead, Suffolk 1918; Icklingham, Suffolk 1923. † ALP 1, L 4, M 2, NEA 2, RA 4.

BLUNDELL, E.P. Exh. 1888-89
25 Magdala Street, Liverpool. † L 2.

BLUNDELL, Mrs. Fred Exh. 1927
Rydal, Aughton, Nr. Ormskirk, Lancs. † L 3.

BLUNDELL, Mrs. Grace E.M. Exh. 1893-98
Portrait painter and miniaturist. R.M.S. 1897. Add: London 1893 and 1896; Staines, Middx. 1895; Englefield Green, 1898. † M 1, NG 4, RA 3, RMS 2.

BLUNDELL, Josephine Exh. 1902-14
The Manor House, Blandford, Dorset. † D 1, L 1, LS 6, SWA 4.

BLUNDELL, Margaret Leah b. 1907
Mural painter, wood-engraver and commercial artist. Studied Cheltenham and Liverpool Schools of Art. Add: Oxton, Birkenhead 1928. † L 11.

BLUNDELL, Phyllis M. Exh. 1910-35
Mrs. Quirk. Sculptor. London. † L 20, RA 3, RHA 2, RSA 1, SWA 1.

BLUNDSTONE, Ferdinand Victor b. 1882
Sculptor. b. Switzerland. Studied London Technical Art School, R.A. Schools (gold medal and Travelling studentship, Landseer Scholarship). Travelled Europe and M. East. Add: London 1907 and 1909; Stockport, Lancs. 1908. † GI 1, L 1, M 1, RA 35, RSA 2.

BLUNT, Lady Anne Exh. 1880
St. James's Street, Buckingham Gate, London. † G 3.

BLUNT, Arthur Cadogan c.1861-1934
Painter, black and white artist and designer. Glebe Studios, Glebe Place, London 1889-90. † G 1, RI 1, ROI 1.

BLUNT, John Silvester b. 1874
Landscape painter. R.B.A. 1912. Add: Thornton Heath, Sussex 1905; Watford 1911; London 1920; Potters Bar 1924. † B 3, D 1, G 1, L 3, M 1, RA 1, RBA 173, RHA 2.

BLUNT, Miss M.A. Exh. 1906
Beechcroft, Beaconsfield, Bucks. † L 1.

BLUNT, Sybil Allan b. 1880
Painter, etcher and black and white artist. Studied Byam Shaw School of Art and Edinburgh School of Art. Add: Edinburgh 1911; Winchester, Hants. 1923. † CHE 3, COO 2, GOU 2, I 6, L 3, M 2, NEA 3, P 1, RA 4, RSA 3, WG 4.

BLYTH, Alan Exh. 1921-40
Flower, landscape and portrait painter. London 1921; Diss, Norfolk 1933. † L 1, NEA 7, P 8, RA 9, RI 1, ROI 16, WG 67.

BLYTH, Dora Exh. 1904-10
nee Fenton. Miniature painter. Sutton-on-Hull 1904; Pendleton, Manchester 1905; Hull 1906. † L 5, M 1, RA 13, RMS 2.

BLYTH, Mrs. E. Exh. 1880-84
Glentraugh, Santon, Isle of Man. † L 4, RSA 5.

BLYTH, Miss Elinor Exh. 1902
Hatfield, Herts. † RI 1.

BLYTH, M. Exh. 1933
Clifton Hill, London. † SWA 1.

BLYTH, Robert Henderson 1919-1970
38 Auldhouse Road, Glasgow 1937. † GI 3, RSA 5.

BOADLE, William Barnes 1840-1916
Portrait painter. b. Dublin. Add: Liverpool. † L 85, P 1, RA 4, RCA 5.

BOAG, A. Exh. 1886
3 Bank Street, Greenock. † GI 1.

BOAK, Robert Creswell b. 1875
Landscape and portrait painter and etcher. Studied Londonderry School of Art, Royal College of Art, Paris and Rome. Assistant art master and art master in schools in London, Portsmouth and Southsea, Hants. 1900-17. Add: Belfast 1928. † RCA 27, RHA 17.

BOAKE, Miss S. Exh. 1881-82
153 Leinster Road, Dublin. † RHA 3.

BOARD, Miss Ada Constance Exh. 1918-21
1 Lucknow Avenue, Nottingham. † N 5.

BOARD, Ernest* 1877-1934
Portrait and figure painter, stained glass artist and mural painter. Studied Royal College of Art and R.A. Schools. R.O.I. 1906. Add: London 1902 and 1919; Bristol 1915; Albury, Surrey 1928. † B 2, GI 2, L 12, M 1, NG 1, P 3, RA 18, ROI 4.

BOARD, Edwin John b. 1886
Landscape and marine painter. Bristol. Exh. 1916. † RA 1.

BOARD, George Exh. 1930
Landscape painter. † LEF 1.

BOARD, Mrs. Inez Exh. 1939
† RI 1.

BOARDER, Hubert A. Exh. 1919
66 Thornton Avenue, Chiswick, London. † RA 1.

BOARDMAN, J.A.C. Exh. 1896
Limehurst, Dumfries. † GI 1.

BOAST, Herbert Exh. 1937
Landscape painter. Brighton, Sussex. † RA 1.

BOBERG, Ferdinand Exh. 1881-96
Etcher. A.R.E. 1894. Add: London 1888; Stockholm 1894. † RA 1, RE 3.

BOBOVNIKOFF, Mrs. Emily b. 1876
Figure, interior and flower painter. Studied Lambeth School of Art, and Colarossi's, Paris. Add: Mentone, France 1914. † RA 1.

BOCKER, Wilhelmine Exh. 1905
Prospect Road, Moseley, Birmingham. † L 1.

BODARD, Pierre Exh. 1909
95 Rue de Vaugirard, Paris. † L 1.

BODDINGTON, Mrs. Emily Exh. 1907-10
Trepied, Etaples, Pas de Calais, France. † B 2, L 1, RHA 2.

BODDINGTON, Miss Edith M. Exh. 1904
49 Park Road, Moseley. † B 1.

BODDINGTON, Henry Exh. 1908-14
c/o Allied Artists' Assocn. London 1908; Pas-de-Calais, France 1913. † LS 23.

BODDINGTON, Henry Jnr. Exh. 1922
26 Old Burlington Street, London. † RA 1.

BODDINGTON, J.S. Exh. 1886-92
Chester 1886; Northwich, Cheshire 1889. † GI 1, L 1, M 7.

BODDY, Florence E. Exh. 1898
109 Ashted Row, Birmingham. † B 2.

BODDY, Percy C. Exh. 1915 and 1933
Architect. London. † RA 2.

BODDY, William J. c.1831-1911
Landscape and architectural painter. Add: Acomb, York. † GI 7, L 6, M 2, RA 3, RBA 2, RI 4, RSW 1.

BODE, Ottilie Exh. 1886-99
Flower painter. London. † RI 1, SWA 1.

BODEN, Dorothy A. Exh. 1923-28
Landscape painter. Nuthall Rectory, Nottingham. † N 14.

BODEN, George A. 1888-1956
Painter, black and white and lino-cut artist. Studied Lincoln School of Art, Colarossi's, Paris; Academie des Beaux Arts, Antwerp; Camberwell School of Art and John Hassall's Poster School, Kensington. Add: Lincoln 1911-38. † GI 2, M 1, RA 3, RBA 3, RI 4.

BODEN, J.B. Exh. 1893
Landscape painter. 50 Prince's Street, Derby. † N 1.

BODEN, William Exh. 1882-1918
Burton-on-Trent 1882 and 1904; Worksop, Notts. 1899. † B 15, L 8, N 4, RA 1, RBA 1, ROI 2.

BODGER, Frederick A. Exh. 1911-14
Leytonstone, Essex 1911; London 1912. † LS 12.

BODICHON, Barbara Leigh 1827-1891
nee Smith. Landscape painter and watercolourist. Married to a French diplomat. Travelled widely in Canada, America, Europe and N. Africa. One of the founders of Girton College. Add: Hawkhurst, Sussex 1880, London 1883. † D 4, SWA 2.

BODILLY, Frank Exh. 1884-86
Landscape painter. London. † L 1, RA 2.

BODILLY, Miss L. Exh. 1924
St. Ives, Cornwall. † SWA 1.

BODINGTON, Bryan William b. 1911
Portrait and glass painter. b. Cirencester, Glos. Studied Slade School. Add: Leighton Buzzard, Beds. 1931. † P 1, RA 4.

BODINGTON, Philip E. Exh. 1920-33
Landscape painter. Add: Cheltenham 1920; Alresford, Hants. 1928; Winchester 1929; London 1932. † RA 1, RBA 5, RCA 1, RSA 1.

BODKIN, Frederick E. Exh. 1880-1930
Landscape painter. London 1880, 1885 and 1893, Guildford, Surrey 1884; Tenterden, Kent 1888. † D 5, GI 5, L 2, RA 22 RBA 4, RI 12, ROI 10.

BODLEY, Elaine Exh. 1939
Landscape and still life painter. † COO 43.

BODLEY, George Frederick 1827-1907
Architect. A.R.A. 1882, R.A. 1902. b. Hull. Add: London. † RA 31.

BODLEY, Josselin* b. 1893
Landscape painter. Studied Paris. Served in Belgium First War, wounded 1915. Exh. 1934-38. † BA 33, LEI 89, M 2.

BODMER, Karl* 1809-1893
Swiss painter. Went to U.S.A. 1832. Add: Barbizon, France 1882. † GI 2.

BODTKER, Miss Maria Exh. 1910
Flower and landscape painter. Add: c/o Bourlets, London. † BG 42, L 1.

BODYCOTE, Nellie L. Exh. 1936
Miniature portrait painter. S. Shields, Co. Durham. † RA 1.

BOEGEWITZ, Miss Dana L. Exh. 1924-29
Riverslie, Crosby Road, Seaforth, Liverpool. † L 9.

BOEHM, Gustave Exh. 1939
Landscape and architectural painter. † COO 49.

BOEHM, Sir Joseph Edgar 1834-1890
Sculptor. b. Vienna of Hungarian nationality. Came to England 1848 (took British nationality 1865). Studied Italy, Paris and Vienna. Lecturer on Sculpture at R.A. Sculptor in ordinary to Queen Victoria. A.R.A. 1878, R.A. 1882, Knighted 1889. Add: London. † D 1, G 17, NG 4, RA 40.

BOEKBINDER, James M. Exh. 1887-1900
London. † RA 6.

BOELTZIG, Reinhold Exh. 1908-10
Steglitz, Berlin. † L 1, LS 4, RA 1.

BOERS, J.A.A. Exh. 1908
Paris. † L 1.

BOESCH, August Exh. 1888
Sculptor. Zurich, Switzerland. † RA 1.

BOEZKO, Jean Exh. 1908-9
London 1908; Budapest 1909. † D 3.

BOGER, A.C. Exh. 1904-6
Mrs. D. Anderton House, Millbrook, Cornwall. † RA 3.

BOGGIANI, Guido Exh. 1885
Lake Maggiore, Italy. † B 2.

BOGGIS, Miss N.A. Exh. 1912
St. Mary's Vicarage, Barnstaple, Devon. † D 2.

BOGGS, Frank Meyers* 1855-1926
American artist. Exh. 1884-95. Add: Paris. † M 1, TOO 4.

BOGIE, A.M. Exh. 1887
London. † SWA 1.

BOGIE, Miss M. Exh. 1880
6 Danube Street, Edinburgh. † RSA 2.

BOGLE, William Lockhart d. 1950
Portrait and figure painter. Dusseldorf, Germany 1881; Glasgow 1884; Bushey, Herts. 1886; London 1889-97. † B 1, GI 6, L 6, M 6, NG 6, P 4, RA 20, RBA 6, RSA 6.

BOGUE, Miss I.M. Exh. 1919
Sunnybrae, Kirtleton Avenue, Weymouth. † SWA 1.

BOGUE, Thomas H. Exh. 1882-84
Edinburgh. † RSA 3.

BOHM, A.R. Exh. 1887
Park Lodge, Broughty Ferry, N.B. † RSA 2.

BOHM, Max 1868-1923
American landscape painter. Exh. 1898-1909. Add: Etaples, Pas de Calais, France 1898, London 1906. † GI 1, GOU 2, I 2, L 3, LS 2, RA 3, WG 2.

BOHMFIELD, A. Exh. 1880
Landscape painter. Add 51 Havil Street, Peckham Road, London. † RA 1.

BOILOT, Alfred Exh. 1906
41 Rue de Richelieu, Paris. † L 1.

BOIS, du See D

BOIS, Dorothy G. Exh. 1915-22
Flower painter. Add: Godalming, Surrey 1915; London 1919; Lymington, Hants. 1921; Blackmore, Hants. 1922. † L 1, RA 1, RI 1, SWA 9.

BOIS, Miss Sara Ann Exh. 1897
22 Lyndhurst Road, Peckham, London. † SWA 2.

BOISSEAU, E. Alfred* Exh. 1898
Landscape painter. Add: Rue des Volontaires 16, Paris. † L 1.

BOISSIERE, Madame Louis Galtier Exh. 1910-12
29 Rue Vaneau, Paris. † L 1.

BOISSONNADE, Henri Exh. 1913
5 Rue Benouville, Paris. † RSA 1.

BOJIDAR, Mons. Exh. 1889
63 Rue Jouffroy, Paris. † L 2.

BOKELMANN, Christian Ludwig 1844-1894
German painter. Add: 2 Marienstrasse, Dusseldorf, Germany. † RA 1.

BOLAM, F.S. Exh. 1938-39
† GOU 4.

BOLAM, Sidney Exh. 1934
† GOU 2.

BOLAND, Miss Gwendolen Exh. 1922
Watercolour landscape painter. † BK 3.

BOLCHERBY, Harold Exh. 1931-39
R.B.A. 1931. Danbury, Essex 1931; Little Baddow, Essex 1936. † RBA 35.

BOLD, Miss Isabel Exh. 1911-28
Briars Hey, St. Helens, Lancs. 1911; London 1927. † L 49.

BOLD, John b. 1895
Painter and black and white artist. Add: 21 Colley Street, Stretford, Manchester 1928. † L 1, M 1.

BOLDERO, T.R. Exh. 1919
6 Crane Street, Greenwich, London. † LS 3.

BOLDINI, Jean (Giovanni)* c.1845-1931
Italian portrait painter. Add: Paris 1891; London 1903-9. † I 4, NG 2, P 7.

BOLGER, Miss Mollie Exh. 1935
Metropolitan School of Art, Dublin. † RHA 1.

BOLINGBROKE, Minna Exh. 1888-1926
Painter and etcher. Married Charles John Watson q.v. A.R.E. 1893, R.E. 1899-30. Add: Eaton, Norwich 1888; London 1895. † FIN 1, L 2, M 1, RA 44, RBA 1, RE 66, RI 7.

BOLIVAR, de See D

BOLT, Fred E. Exh. 1909
37 Upper Belmont Road, Bristol. † L 1.

BOLT, Miss Marion Exh. 1886
Church Villa, Sunbury. † RI 1.

BOLTON, Miss Ada Exh. 1891-1903
Painter of church interiors. Add: 1 Osborn Terrace, Clapham, London. † RA 3, RBA 2.

BOLTON, Miss Ada Exh. 1928
94 Queen's Park Road, Blackburn, Lancs. † L 2.

BOLTON, Agnes Exh. 1937-38
Miniature portrait painter. Add: London. † RA 2, RMS 1.

BOLTON, Miss Alice Exh. 1900
37 Warwick Road, Maida Vale, London. † L 1.

BOLTON, Albert J. Exh. 1891-92
Architect. Add: 55 Lincoln's Inn Fields, London. † RA 3.

BOLTON, Arthur Thomas c.1873-1954
Architect. Curator of Sir John Soane's Museum. Add: London. † RA 20.

BOLTON, Francis A. Exh. 1933
Moor Court, Oakamoor, N. Staffs. † RI 1.

BOLTON, H.E. Exh. 1889-1915
Donnybrook, Dublin. † RHA 37.

BOLTON, Miss H.E. Exh. 1905-19
Nethercote, Old Colwyn, N. Wales. † RCA 8.

BOLTON, Miss Ida M. Exh. 1897-1905
Still life painter. Add: Leicester 1897; Leeds 1903. † B 3, N 9, RA 3.

BOLTON, James H. Exh. 1930
Architect. Add: 10 Lincoln's Inn Fields, London. † RA 1.

BOLTON, J.N. d.c.1909
Donnybrook, Dublin 1892; Warwick 1899. † B 3, RA 1, RHA 47.

BOLTON, Miss K. Exh. 1896
22 Westbourne Gardens, London. † SWA 1.

BOLTON, Mrs. Louisa Exh. 1881-96
Miniature painter. R.M.S. 1896. Add: Shepton Mallet, Som. 1881; Cardiff 1885. † RA 16, RMS 6.

BOLTON, Miss Minnie Exh. 1926-37
72 Margaret Grove, Harborne, Birmingham. † B 30.

BOLTON, Mrs. Pauline Exh. 1906-8
Sylvan House, Donnybrook, Dublin. † RHA 3.

BOLTON, Miss Rina Exh. 1900-3
67 Kirby Road, Leicester. † B 2, N 12.

BOLTON, Miss Rosa I. Exh. 1911
27 Prince's Avenue, Liverpool. † L 3.

BOLTON, R. Freda Exh. 1888
Moor Court, Nr. Cheadle, Staffs. † GI 2.

BOLTON, William Treacher Exh. 1880-81
Landscape and flower painter. Add: 5 Highbury Terrace, London. † RA 1, RBA 2.

BOLVEY, E.R.C. Exh. 1884
c/o Rowney, 52 Rathbone Place, London. † D 1.

BOMBAY, Bishop of
See ACLAND, Richard Dyke

BOMBERG, David* 1890-1957
Landscape and figure painter. Studied Slade School and attended evening classes by Walter Bayes and Sickert. Visited Paris and Palestine 1924 and made expedition to Petra. Founder member London Group 1913. A collection of his work is in the Tate. Add: London 1913 and 1933; Alton, Hants. 1920. † CG 1, CHE 6, COO 1, G 2, GOU 1, L 2, LEI 58, NEA 12.

BOMBLED, M.* Exh. 1882-93
Paris. † GI 3, RHA 1.

BOMFORD, Miss Lorna Exh. 1912-13
Hillersdon House, Dover. † L 2.

BOMFORD, L.G. Exh. 1880-81
9 Lanark Villas, Maida Vale, London. † D 1, RSA 1.

BOMPARD, Maurice* Exh. 1903-25
167 Boulevard Periere, Paris. † L 3.

BOMPIANI, Augusto* Exh. 1883-90
† D 1, L 1.

BOMPIANI, Prof. Roberto* 1821-1908
Italian portrait and figure painter. Add: Rome 1882. † RA 1.

BONANNI, Prof. V.C. Exh. 1903-10
Sculptor. Add: London. † L 2, LS 6, M 2, NG 11, RA 1.

BON-ARMAND, Madame Ada Exh. 1913
Landscape painter. † ALP 3.

BONAS, J.P. Exh. 1932
143 Markby Road, Handsworth, Birmingham. † B 1.

BONAVIA, Miss A.C. Exh. 1896
17 Netherwood Road, London. † SWA 1.

BONAVIA, Hilda Exh. 1939
† GOU 2, NEA 2.

BONCQUET, Henry Exh. 1906
72 Rue de Hennin, Brussels. † GI 2.

BOND, Miss Ada Exh. 1888-90
Birkenhead. † L 4.

BOND, Miss Amy Exh. 1893-97
Birkenhead. † L 5.

BOND, Amy Exh. 1938-39
Mrs. Wensley Bond. † RMS 5.

BOND, Arthur J.F. b. 1888
Painter and etcher. b. Devonport. Add: St. Margarets on Thames 1912; Twickenham, Middlesex 1913; Barnes, Surrey 1918; Richmond, Surrey 1937. † RA 4.

BOND, Miss C.D. Exh. 1894
† SWA 1.

BOND, Dorothy Elizabeth Exh. 1911-36
Nee Harrison. Miniature painter. A.R.M.S. 1925, Windsor 1911; Cheltenham, Glos. 1921. † COO 3, RA 17, RMS 24.

BOND, Miss Edith F. Exh. 1912
Castlelyons, Fermoy, Co. Cork, Ireland. † RHA 1.

BOND, Mrs. G.M. Exh. 1939
† RI 1.

BOND, H. Exh. 1888
Porlock, Somerset. † B 1.

BOND, Hargreaves Exh. 1883-1911
Liverpool 1883 and 1905; Bootle, Lancs. 1897; Hoylake, Cheshire 1901. † L 31.

BOND, J.H. Exh. 1882
Mersey Bank, Egremont, Liverpool. † L 3.

BOND, Miss J.M. Exh. 1913
Maida Vale, London. † SWA 1.

BOND, Kenneth Exh. 1912-33
Leicester 1912; St. Helens, Lancs. 1925; Moretonhampstead, Devon 1933. † L 3, N 1.

BOND, Lawrence H. Exh. 1936
Grantham, Lincs. † N 1.

BOND, Miss Mildred B. Exh. 1884-85
† ROI 3.

BOND, Miss S. Exh. 1892-98
Birkenhead. † L 7.

BOND, Thomas J. Exh. 1919-33
Ormskirk, Lancs. 1919, Liverpool 1929. † L 10, RI 2.

BOND, William H. Exh. 1896-1907
Marine painter. Add: Brighton. † B 1, L 3, RA 10, RBA 1.

BOND, William Joseph J.C.* 1833-1926
Marine painter. Apprenticed to a Liverpool picture dealer and restorer. Add: Liverpool 1883-1901. † L 19, M 1, RHA 6.

BONDOUX, Georges Exh. 1905
9 Rue Bochard de Saron, Paris. † L 2.

BONE, Mrs. Annie M. Exh. 1906-36
Miniature portrait painter. Add: King's Bench Walk, Temple, London. † GI 2, RA 3.

BONE, Freda C. Exh. 1928-32
Underwood, Helensburgh, Dumbartonshire. † GI 2, RSA 2.

BONE, Gavin Exh. 1936-38
Landscape painter. Add: c/o Colnaghi, New Bond Street, London. † NEA 1, RA 1.

BONE, Herbert A. 1853-1931
Painter and designer of tapestries. Exh. 1880-1905. Add: London. † B 6, L 3, M 4, RA 13, RBA 1, RI 1, ROI 1.

BONE, J. Craigie Exh. 1911-14
45 Marchmont Road, Edinburgh. † RSA 5.

BONE, Miss Margery Exh. 1930
Landscape painter. Add: Montrose, Harpendon Road, St. Albans, Herts. † RA 1.

BONE, Sir Muirhead* 1876-1953
Painter and etcher. Studied Glasgow School of Art. Official war artist 1916-18. Official Admiralty artist 1939-46. Trustee National Gallery, Tate Gallery and Imperial War Museum. N.E.A. 1902. Knighted 1937. Collection of his work in the Tate. Add: Glasgow 1897; Ayr 1900; London 1902; Petersfield, Hants. 1913. † AB 2, AG 14, BA 67, BK 1, CAR 62, CG 290, CHE 3, CON 3, FIN 71, G 158, GI 50, GOU 18, I 10, L 64, M 59, NEA 188, RA 17, RED 1, RSA 77, RSW 3, TOO 10.

BONE, Phyllis Mary b. 1894
Sculptor. Studied Edinburgh College of Art and Paris. A.R.S.A. 1940. Add: Edinburgh. † GI 43, L 14, RA 4, RSA 39.

BONE, Stephen 1904-1958
Painter, illustrator, wood engraver and writer. Son of Sir Muirhead B. q.v. Married Mary Adshead q.v. Studied Slade School 1922-24. N.E.A. 1932. Add: Steep, Petersfield, Hants. 1920; London 1926; Civil Defence Camouflage Establishment, Leamington Spa. Warwicks. 1940. † BAR 3, CG 7, FIN 44, G 10, GI 2, GOU 30, LEF 30, M 3, NEA 47. RA 12, RED 52, RHA 1, TOO 3.

BONE, William Drummond Exh. 1929-40
Ayr. † GI 5, RSA 12.

BONEY, William H. Exh. 1888
Architect. Add: Cholmeley Lodge, Highgate, London. † RA 1.

BONHAM-CARTER, Madge Exh. 1927-31
Mrs. C. Sculptor. Add: London. † L 1, RA 4.

BONHEUR, Rosa* 1822-1899
French animal painter. H.R.I. 1866. Exh. 1882-94. † RI 3.

BONIMANN, James Exh. 1895
38 Cambridge Gardens, Edinburgh. † RSA 2.

BONIN, A. Exh. 1916
Mentone Villas, Clarendon Road, Ashford, Middlesex. † NEA 1.

BONN, Mme. Julie Exh. 1911-13
Feldburgh Strasse, Dresden, Germany. † GI 1, RHA 4.

BONNALLO, William Exh. 1884-89
Landscape painter. Add: 65 Fisher Street, Scotholme, Hyson Green, Notts. † N 2.

BONNAR, Mrs. Exh. 1896
7 Fingal Place, Edinburgh. † RSA 1.

BONNAR, J.A.T. Exh. 1885-89
Edinburgh 1885; Musselburgh 1887. † RSA 12.
BONNAR, M.C. Exh. 1900
The Abbot's House, Dunfermline. † GI 1.
BONNAR, Thomas Exh. 1893-99
Edinburgh. † RSA 17.
BONNAR, Thomas Kershaw Exh. 1897
58 George Street, Edinburgh. † RSA 1.
BONNARD, Pierre* 1867-1947
French painter. Studied Julians and Ecole des Beaux Arts, Paris. Exh. 1925-32. † BA 1, GI 3, GOU 2, L 1, RED 12, RSA 2.
BONNAT, Leon Joseph Florentin 1833-1922
French landscape and portrait painter. H.F.R.A. 1906. Exh. 1891-1905. † L 2, P 3, RA 1.
BONNEAU, Florence Mary Exh. 1880-1904
Mrs. Cockburn. Landscape and figure painter. Studied Heatherley's. Add: Bayswater, London 1881; Wembley, Middlesex 1904. † † L 2, RBA 2, SWA 9.
BONNEFOY, M. Exh. 1883
c/o Graphic, 190 Strand, London. † M 1.
BONNER, Albert E. Exh. 1905
18 Holland Street, Kensington, London. † LS 5.
BONNER, Lady Eveleen Exh. 1897-1929
Landscape and coastal painter. Add: London. † RID 53, SWA 2.
BONNER, Horace T. Exh. 1886
108 High Street, Lewisham, London. † RA 1.
BONNETAIN Exh. 1906
† I 1.
BONNETON, G.E. Exh. 1908
63 Rue Pascal, Paris. † L 1.
BONNEY, Charles Henry Exh. 1887-98
Landscape painter. Add: Rugeley, Staffs. † B 7, D 4, M 2, RA 3, RBA 2.
BONNOR, J.H.M. Exh. 1912
57 Moscow Road, Bayswater, London. † RA 2.
BONNOR, Rose D. Exh. 1895-1916
Portrait painter. Add: London. † L 8, M 1, RA 13, ROI 1.
BONSEY, Mrs. Hilda E. Exh. 1924-40
Painter and etcher. Add: Bristol 1924; Wootton Bassett, Wilts. 1926; St. Ives, Hunts. 1931; Epsom, Surrey 1938; Chertsey, Surrey 1940. † B 2, GOU 1, NEA 1, RA 3, ROI 1.
BONSOR, G.E. Exh. 1882-83
11 Devere Gardens, Kensington, London. † B 3.
BONTEMS, O.J. Exh. 1910-29
Landscape and rustic painter. Add: 11 King Street, Leicester. † N 18.
BONTOR, Mrs. F.G. Exh. 1921
10 Hitson Road, Barnes, London. † L 1.
BONUS, Miss I. Sarum Exh. 1919
Radcliffe Road, Croydon. † SWA 1.
BONVIN, Francois* 1817-1887
French artist. Exh. 1885. † GI 1.
BOOBBYER, Daniel Exh. 1894-1900
18 Castle Gate, Nottingham. † N 2.
BOODLE, Charles Edward b. 1861
Watercolour painter. Exh. 1893-94. Add: Bath. † B 3.
BOODLE, Walter* Exh. 1891-1908
Landscape painter. Add: Bath. † B 18, GI 2, L 3, M 1, RA 8, RHA 2.
BOODLE, W.B. Exh. 1888
28 Church Street, Liverpool. † L 4.
BOOKER, Miss J.M. Exh. 1909
London. † SWA 1.
BOOKER, Louisa E. Exh. 1886-1930
Landscape painter. Add: Nottingham. † N 4.

BOOLE, Miss Millicent A. Exh. 1889
8 Friend's Road, E. Croydon, Surrey. † SWA 1.
BOON, E.M. Exh. 1927
8 Ranpurly Avenue, Bangor, Co. Down, Ireland. † L 2.
BOON, de See D
BOON, Jan Exh. 1913
Etcher. † FIN 7.
BOONZAIER, Gregoire* Exh. 1936-37
Landscape painter. Add: London. † NEA 1, RA 3, RBA 1, ROI 2.
BOOSE, Van See V
BOOT, Leonard Exh. 1930-40
Aston, Birmingham 1930; Erdington, Birmingham 1937. † B 5.
BOOT, William Henry James* 1848-1918
Landscape, interior and genre painter and illustrator. Art editor of the "Strand". b. Nottingham. Studied Derby School of Art. Travelled in Europe and N. Africa. R.B.A. 1884, V.P.R.B.A. 1895-1914, R.I. 1909. Add: London. † B 12, L 7, RA 14, RBA 179, RHA 4, RI 47, ROI 3.
BOOTH, Miss A.L. Exh. 1882
56 Roe Lane, Southport, Lancs. † M 1.
BOOTH, Charles Exh. 1882-92
Figure painter. Add: Gower Street, London. † L 2, RA 1, RBA 1, RI 1.
BOOTH, Constance Gore Exh. 1898-1907
Married to Comte Casimir Dunun Markiewicz q.v. Add: London 1898; Rathgar, Dublin 1904. † RHA 5, SWA 1.
BOOTH, Douglas Exh. 1934
Etcher. Add: 26 College Street East, Crosland Moor, Huddersfield. † RA 1.
BOOTH, Evelyn Exh. 1893-1909
Landscape inter. Add: Folkestone, Kent 1893; Exeter, Devon 1904. † RA 1, RBA 1, SWA 5.
BOOTH, Miss Ethel G. Exh. 1899-1904
Holme Bank, Osborne Road, Levenshulme, Manchester. † L 2.
BOOTH, George Exh. 1883-85
Russian Drive, Green Lane, Liverpool. † L 4.
BOOTH, Gerald B. Exh. 1936
Adlington, Nr. Ashford, Kent. † RA 1.
BOOTH, Hilda Exh. 1908-16
Knutsford, Cheshire 1908; Flixton, Lancs. 1911; Manchester 1916. † L 7, M 3, RCA 1.
BOOTH, Mrs. H. Gore Exh. 1884
Sculptor. Add: Seaside House, Helensburgh. † GI 3, RA 1.
BOOTH, Herbert W. Exh. 1884
Architect. Add: 24 George's Street, Halifax, Yorks. † RA 1.
BOOTH, Isabella Gore Exh. 1883-89
Helensburgh 1883; Manchester 1889. † GI 2, M 3, RSA 1.
BOOTH, John Exh. 1911-16
Flixton, Lancs. 1911; Manchester 1916. † L 4.
BOOTH, James William b. 1867
Figure and rustic painter. Add: Manchester 1886; Scalby, Nr. Scarborough, Yorks. 1902 and London. † B 2, L 3, M 13, RA 24, RCA 174.
BOOTH, Miss Lydia Grace Exh. 1924-30
Elmhurst, Aigburth, Liverpool. † L 8.
BOOTH, Mrs. Margaret Exh. 1911-33
Miniature portrait painter. Add: London. † RA 5.
BOOTH, Miss Sclater Exh. 1881-84
74 St. George's Square, London. † G 3.
BOOTH, Sidney Kenmare Exh. 1914
Bebington, Cheshire. † L 2.
BOOTH, S. Lawson* d. 1928
Roe Lane, Southport, Lancs. 1890-1921. † B 19, L 2, M 1, RCA 132.

BOOTH, Thomas S. Exh. 1904-12
Liverpool. † L 3.
BOOTH, W. Hunton Exh. 1913
Royal Insurance Bdgs., 9 North John Street, Liverpool. † L 1.
BOOTHBY, Miss Beatrice Exh. 1899-1918
London. † SWA 13.
BOOTHBY, Miss Florence Exh. 1886-1917
London. † D 3, SWA 24.
BOOTHROYD, Miss Janet Exh. 1897-1902
London 1897, Northampton 1898. † L 4, RBA 5, RI 2, SWA 2.
BOOTHROYD, Miss M. Exh. 1926
44 Leyland Road, Southport, Lancs. † L 1.
BOOTT, Elizabeth b. 1846
American still-life and flower painter. Exh. 1885. Add: Paris. † RA 2.
BOOTY, Henry R. Exh. 1882-83
Landscape painter. Add: 23 Lansdowne Road, Kensington Park, London. † RA 1, RBA 1.
BOQUET, Jules Exh. 1882-84
Amiens, France 1882; Paris 1884. † GI 2.
BORASTON, William P. Exh. 1928-33
115 Royston Street, Liverpool. † L 9.
BORCHARDT, Hans Exh. 1900
33 Kaulbachstrasse, Munich, Germany. † GI 2.
BORDES, Ernest 1852-1914
French artist. Add: 87 Rue Ampere, Paris 1910. † RA 1.
BOREEL, Wendela b. 1895
Painter and etcher. A.R.E. 1923. b. France. Add: London and Bray-on-Thames. † I 2, L 4, LS 5, NEA 1, RA 2, RE 22, RED 42, SWA 2, WG 52.
BORG, Carl Oscar* b. 1879
b. Sweden. Add: Paris 1913. † RA 1.
BORGLUM, John Gutzon Mothe 1867-1941
American sculptor. R.B.A. 1902. Carved the huge figures of Washington, Jefferson, Lincoln and Roosevelt on the mountains in Dakota, U.S.A. Add: London 1896-1904. † L 2, P 1, RA 3, RBA 4, ROI 3.
BORLAND, Miss M.E. Exh. 1883-88
Castle Douglas, N.B. † GI 3.
BORLASE, Miss E. Exh. 1905-10
The Coombe, Penzance, Cornwall. † B 4.
BORNE, Daisy Theresa b. 1906
Sculptor and teacher of sculpture. Studied London and U.S.A. Add: 6 Briar Walk, Putney, London 1932. † RA 2, SWA 1.
BORRADAIL, Miss Constance V. Exh. 1887-88
London. † M 2.
BORRADAILE, Miss Rosamund Exh. 1924-27
London and The Beeches, Barcombe, Sussex. † NEA 3, P 2, ROI 2.
BORRADAILE, Miss Viola Exh. 1924-40
Sculptor. Add: The Beeches, Barcombe, Sussex and London. † NEA 1, RA 2, ROI 2.
BORRER, Mrs. Dawson Exh. 1880-95
Landscape painter. Add: Altamont, Carlow, Ireland. † RHA 23, SWA 2.
BORRETT, Miss A.L. Exh. 1890-95
3 South Row, Blackheath, London. † RI 1, SWA 3.
BORRILL, J.H. Exh. 1938-40
† RI 5.
BORROW, Miss Lucy E. Exh. 1896-97
Newlands, Twyford, Winchester. † ROI 1, SWA 2.
BORROW, William H. Exh. 1880-1901
Marine and coastal painter. Add: Hastings. † B 2, L 2, M 2, RA 14, RBA 2, RHA 2, ROI 14, TOO 2.

BORROWMAN, Charles Gordon 1892-1956 Figure, animal and landscape painter. b. Edinburgh. Commissioned Indian Army 1912. Add: Punjab, India and Edinburgh. † GI 5, L 1, RSA 18, RSW 21.
BORROWS, Henry Exh. 1884-89 Huddersfield. † L 1, RA 4.
BORROWS, Janet Charlotte Exh. 1923-25 Figure and portrait painter. Add: Portland House, Portland Road, West Bridgford, Notts. † N 6.
BORTHWICK, Alfred Edward 1871-1955 Landscape and portrait painter, etcher and stained glass artist. b. Scarborough, Yorks. Studied Juliens, Paris, Antwerp and Edinburgh School of Art. A.R.B.A. 1927, R.B.A. 1930, A.R.E. 1909, A.R.S.A. 1928, R.S.A. 1939, R.S.W. 1911, P.R.S.W. 1932. Add: Edinburgh and London. † AR 2, CHE 1, G 1, GI 33, L 8, NEA 7, P 6, RA 7, RBA 24, RE 16, RI 1, RSA 88, RSW 93.
BORTHWICK, Miss G.R. Exh. 1927 Daughter of Alfred Edward B. q.v. Add: 8 Merchiston Crescent, Edinburgh. † RSW 1.
BORTHWICK, Miss Marjorie E. Exh. 1933-40 Daughter of Alfred Edward B. q.v. Add: 8 Merchiston Crescent, Edinburgh. † GI 7, RSA 1, RSW 14.
BORTHWICK, Miss Norma Exh. 1897 13 Markham Square, Chelsea, London. † RHA 2.
BORTIGNONI, Guiseppe* Exh. 1883-84 Figure painter. Add: 40A Barclay Road, Walham Green, London. † L 1, M 1, RA 2.
BORTOLOZZI, M. Exh. 1891 † DOW 1.
BORTON, Mrs. Muriel Exh. 1938 Palace Gate, London. † RA 1.
BORWITZ, Von See V
BOS, Van der See V
BOSC, du See D
BOSCH, Ernst* b. 1834 German artist. Exh. 1882. † M 1.
BOSCH-REITZ, S.C. Exh. 1890-93 Figure painter. Add: St. Ives, Cornwall; London and Amsterdam. † DOW 1, L 1, M 1, NG 1, RA 1.
BOSCHEN, R.T. Exh. 1932-33 76 Aughton Street, Liverpool. † L 4.
BOSCHER, G. Exh. 1882 64 Rue des Rabuissons, Amiens, France. † GI 1.
BOSDET, H.T. Exh. 1885 Portrait painter. Add: 81 Charlotte Street, Fitzroy Square, London. † RA 1.
BOSE, Fanindra Nat d. 1926 Sculptor. A.R.S.A. 1925. Add: Edinburgh. † GI 2, RA 4, RSA 22.
BOSKAMP, Hans Exh. 1928 † RED 2.
BOSLEY, Miss Sylvia E. Exh. 1932 Sculptor. Add: 304 Goldhawk Road, London. † RA 2.
BOSS, Marcus Arthur b. 1891 Portrait painter. Studied Birkbeck School of Art and Heatherleys 1908-11 and R.A. Schools 1911-16. Add: London. † I 8, P 2, RI 5, ROI 3.
BOSSANYI, Ervin b. 1891 Figure painter and stained glass artist. Studied Hungarian Royal School of Arts and Crafts, Juliens, Paris, and Camden School of Art. Exh. 1935. † BA 24.
BOSSHARD, Rodolphe Theophile* b. 1889 French painter. Exh. 1929. † GI 1.
BOSSIERE, Mlle. Exh. 1914 Rue du Dome, Paris. † RA 2.
BOSTOCK, Miss Exh. 1905 SWA 1.
BOSTOCK, O. Exh. 1914-29 Landscape painter. Add: 17 Dyron Street, Ilkeston, Derbys. † N 9.
BOSTON, The Lady Exh. 1893 Hedsor, Maidenhead, Berks. † SWA 2.
BOSTON, George F.S. Exh. 1886-1904 Liverpool 1886; Liscard, Cheshire 1903. † L 3.
BOSTON, Eric James b. 1899 Figure and landscape painter. Studied under Orthon Friesz, Paris. Add: Thame, Oxon. † GOU 8, L 1.
BOSTON, Miss M.A. Exh. 1937 162 Windmill Lane, Smethwick, Worcs. † B 1.
BOSTON, Thomas Exh. 1884-86 Glasgow. † GI 2.
BOSWELL, George A. Exh. 1929-33 256 West George Street, Glasgow. † GI 3.
BOSWELL, Jean Exh. 1939 † GOU 1.
BOSWELL, Reginald A. Exh. 1929 Sculptor. Add: 3 Rossetti Studios, Flood Street, Chelsea, London. † RA 1.
BOSWELL, W.C. Exh. 1910-15 West Bridgford, Notts. 1910; Nottingham 1911. † N 11.
BOSWORTH, Miss Fanny Exh. 1908 Yardley House, Yardley, Worcs. † B 1.
BOSWORTH-SMITH, Gladys Exh. 1939 133A Sloane Street, London. † SWA 2.
BOTCHERBY, Harold Llewellyn b. 1907 Still-life, figure and landscape painter. Studied Heatherleys and R.A. Schools; John Crompton Scholarship 1930. R.B.A. 1932. Visiting master of Drawing Chelmsford School of Art. Add: Banbury, Essex and London. † BK 26, RA 3, RBA 11.
BOTERENBROOD, J. Exh. 1936 † RSA 2.
BOTHAMS, Walter Exh. 1882-1914 Figure and domestic painter. Add: London 1882; Salisbury 1886; Malvern, Worcs. 1913. † D 16, DOW 2, I 7, L 10, RA 19, RBA 1, RI 7, ROI 1.
BOTHAMS, William Exh. 1896 Churchfields, Salisbury, Wilts. † L 1.
BOTT, Miss Kathleen M. Exh. 1929-32 Wulfruna Gardens, Richmond Road, Wolverhampton. † B 6.
BOTTOM, de See D
BOTTOMLEY, Albert Ernest b. 1873 Landscape and architectural painter and teacher. Studied under Edwin Tindall. A.R.B.A. 1919, R.B.A. 1921. Add: Leeds 1898; Guildford, Surrey 1904; Reigate 1907. † B 4, BA 8, CHE 6, GI 3, GOU 26, L 1, NEA 10, RA 24, RBA 136, RCA 57, RHA 1, RI 7, ROI 15, RSA 3.
BOTTOMLEY, B.G. Exh. 1889 14 Juno Street, Newton Heath, Manchester. † M 3.
BOTTOMLEY, Edwin 1865-c.1929 Landscape and animal painter. Add: Oldham, Lancs. 1885; Conway, N. Wales 1890; Huddersfield 1902; Whitby, Yorks. 1906; Knaresborough 1915; Harrogate 1927. † L 1, M 7 RCA 64.
BOTTOMLEY, Edith G. Exh. 1891-1900 Paris 1891; Earls Court, London 1892. † B 2, L 3, M 7, SWA 1.
BOTTOMLEY, Frederic 1883-1960 Landscape painter. Studied Slade School. Add: St. Ives, Cornwall 1931-39. † B 2, RA 5, ROI 2.
BOTTOMLEY, Miss Harriet Exh. 1903-8 Chapel House, Ormskirk, Lancs. † L 3.
BOTTOMLEY, J. Mitchell Exh. 1895-1902 Architect. Add: 28 Albert Road, Middlesborough, Yorks. † RA 4.
BOTTOMLEY, John William 1816-1900 Sporting and animal painter. Studied Munich and Dusseldorf. Add: London. † GI 1.
BOTTOMLEY, Reginald Exh. 1883-95 Figure painter. Add: Paris 1883 and 1895; London 1892. † L 4, RA 4.
BOTTOMLEY, R.O. Exh. 1882-86 Oldham, Lancs. † M 9.
BOUCHARD, Henri Louis b. 1875 French sculptor. Exh. 1912 and 1930. Add: Paris. † RSA 2.
BOUCHAUD, R. Exh. 1913 5 Rond Point Bugeaud, Paris. † L 1.
BOUCHER, Alfred Exh. 1925 2 Passage de Dantzig, Paris. † RSA 1.
BOUCHER, B.W. Exh. 1901-8 74 Bismark Street, Leicester. † N 4.
BOUCHER, Mlle. J. Exh. 1938 Clissold, Witton Road, Malvern, Worcs. † B 1.
BOUCHER, Jean Marie b. 1870 French sculptor. Exh. 1913. † GI 1.
BOUCHER, M.C. Exh. 1892 76A Westbourne Grove, Bayswater, London. † B 1.
BOUCHER, Mrs. Mary L.S. Exh. 1904-12 London 1904; Lymington, Hants. 1912. † P 1. RCA 3.
BOUCHER, William Henry d. 1906 Etcher and cartoonist. A.R.E. 1890. Father of Frank Bowcher q.v. † RA 8, RE 14.
BOUCHET, A. Exh. 1883 70 Rue de Tocqueville, Paris. † L 1.
BOUCHETTE, A. Exh. 1888-89 Figure and domestic painter. Add: London. † B 1, M 1, RBA 2.
BOUCHIER, Mrs. E.M. Exh. 1889 Still-life painter. Add: 101 St. George's Square, London. † SWA 1.
BOUCHOR, Joseph Felix* b. 1853 French artist. Exh. 1910-13 † L 2.
BOUCNEAU, Victor E. Exh. 1888-93 Sculptor. Add: London. † D 2, L 2, RA 2, RBA 1.
BOUFFLERS, de See D
BOUGH, E.A. See AMOUR, Elizabeth Isobel
BOUGHTON, George Henry* 1833-1905 Figure, landscape, genre and sporting painter. b. Norwich. Lived for some years in America. Studied Paris. A.R.A. 1879, R.A. 1896, R.I. 1879, R.O.I. 1887. Add: West House, Campden Hill Road, London. † AG 1, B 13, FIN 62, G 17, GI 7, L 25, LEI 2, M 23, NG 35, RA 58, RI 7, RSA 1, TOO 8.
BOUGHTON-LEIGH, Dora Exh. 1903-40 Landscape and figure painter and etcher. Studied Paris. A.S.W.A. 1916. Add: Paris 1903; Burford, Oxon. 1908; London 1910. † BG 18, GOU 5, I 1, L 4, LS 14, NEA 1, RA 4, RBA 2, RHA 1, RI 1, SWA 62.
BOUGHTON-LEIGH, Maude c.1881-1945 Portrait painter. Add: London. † B 1.
BOUGUEREAU, William Adolphe* 1825-1905 French painter. Exh. 1884-1904. Add: Paris. † B 1, GI 2, L 3, RA 10, RSA 2.
BOUILLETTE, Edgard Exh. 1901-13 French painter. Add: 49 Rue Lafitte, Paris. † ALP 2, L 1.
BOUILLON, Leon Exh. 1886-87 39 Rue des Batignolles, Paris. † M 3.
BOUIS, J.V. Exh. 1923-32 356 Rue Paradis, Marseilles, France. † RI 19.

BOUJINSKY, de See D
BOULDERSON, B. Exh. 1884
† ROI 1.
BOULDS, John H. Exh. 1933-39
Birmingham. † B 9.
BOULLEMIER, Antonin Exh. 1881-82
Miniature portrait painter. Add: Penkhull Road, Stoke-on-Trent, Staffs. † RA 3.
BOULNOIS, W. Allen Exh. 1880
Architect. Add: 6 Waterloo Place, London. † RA 1.
BOULTON, Doris Exh. 1916-40
Etcher and wood engraver. A.R.E. 1918. Exhibited as Doris Boulton-Maude from 1939. Add: Wolstanton, Staffs. 1916; London 1916; Gt. Baddow, Essex 1935. † I 3, L 4, NEA 9, RA 15, RBA 1, RE 8, RED 2, SWA 2.
BOULTON, F.A. Exh. 1925-26
136 Lightwoods Road, Bearwood, Berks. † B 2.
BOULTON, Miss C.B. Exh. 1883-84
Landscape painter. Add: Wem, Salop. 1883; Totteridge, Herts. 1884. † L 1, RI 1.
BOULTON, J. Exh. 1920-21
6 Lord Street, Smallthorne, Stoke-on-Trent, Staffs. † L 2.
BOULTON, Miss L.M. Exh. 1920-38
Stourbridge, Worcs. † B 5.
BOUMPHERY, Pauline b. 1886
nee Firth. Sculptor. Add: Hartford, Cheshire 1925; Sandiway, Cheshire 1928 and London. † GI 4, L 7, RA 10.
BOURCHIER, Edward H. Exh. 1884
32 St. George Street, Westminster, London. † RA 1.
BOURDELLE, Emile Antoine* 1861-1929
French sculptor and painter. Exh. 1905-28. Add: Paris. † GI 4, I 5, RA 3, RSA 13.
BOURDILLON, Frank W.* Exh. 1882-93
Landscape and figure painter. N.E.A. 1887. Add: Dorking, Surrey 1884; Newlyn, Penzance 1890 and London. † B 7, DOW 2, G 2, L 12, M 7, NEA 2, RA 9, RBA 6, RHA 2, ROI 6, RSA 1.
BOURDIN, Mrs. Exh. 1884-85
Fruit painter. c/o 76 Elm Park Road, Chelsea, London. † SWA 4.
BOURDON, J.L. Exh. 1907-8
151 bis, Rue de Grenelle, cite Wegrier, Paris. † L 2.
BOURGAIN, G. Exh. 1883
Landscape painter. Add: 116 New Bond Street, London. † RA 1.
BOURGES, Madame Exh. 1883
Rue de l'Eglise, a Auveis sur Oise, France. † L 1.
BOURGOGNE, Pierre Exh. 1888
32 Rue de Brancas, Sevres, Seine et Oise, France. † B 2.
BOURHILL, James E. Exh. 1880-87
Edinburgh. † RSA 7.
BOURKE, J. Michael Exh. 1933-40
Dublin. † RHA 31.
BOURKE, Miss Patita Exh. 1937-38
Ashfield, Beau Parc, Co. Meath, Ireland. † RHA 3.
BOURKE, Thomas Exh. 1939-40
London. † RHA 5.
BOURKE, Tom Exh. 1910-17
98 Pembroke Road, Dublin. † RHA 6.
BOURNE, Miss E. Fox Exh. 1897-1901
London 1897; St. Albans, Herts. 1900. † NEA 1, RBA 8.
BOURNE, E. Grace Exh. 1905
2 Tennison Road, South Norwood, Middlesex. † B 1.
BOURNE, Miss H. Exh. 1889-90
Flower painter. Add: Quarry Road, Hastings, Sussex. † SWA 2.
BOURNE, Herbert Exh. 1881-85
Engraver. 98 South Hill Park, Hampstead, London. † RA 4.
BOURNE, John C. Exh. 1883-85
Landscape painter. Add: Twickenham, Middlesex. † B 2, RI 1.
BOURNE, John Frye b. 1912
Portrait painter. Add: Colwyn Bay, Wales 1927; London 1932; Harpenden, Herts. 1933. † P 1, RA 3, RCA 3.
BOURNE, The Rev. J. Hawforth Exh. 1929
Broome House, Polzeath, Wadebridge, Cornwall. † B 2.
BOURNE, Kate E. Exh. 1881
Still-life painter. Add: 98 South Hill Park, Hampstead, London. † SWA 1.
BOURNE, Miss Muriel See WHEELER
BOURNE, Norah Brereton Exh. 1907-27
Miniature painter. A.R.M.S. 1914. Add: London 1907; Worthing, Sussex 1926. † B 3, L 16, RA 12, RHA 1, RI 8, RMS 10.
BOURNE, Olive Grace b. 1897
Painter, commercial and wood-cut artist. Studied Croydon School of Art. R.A. Schools (Armitage medal 1923). Add: 44 Farnley Road, S. Norwood, London 1923. † L 2, RA 4.
BOURNE, Phyllis Exh. 1920-23
Miniature portrait painter. Add: 53 Oxford Gardens, N. Kensington, London. † L 2, RA 2, RI 4, SWA 1.
BOURNE, Samuel d. c.1912
Landscape painter. P.N.S.A. 1880-1912. Add: Nottingham. † M 4, N 169, RBA 1, RI 5.
BOURNE, W.H. Exh. 1902
Architect. Add: 94 Northgate, Darlington. † RA 1.
BOUSFIELD, Miss Agnes A. Exh. 1913-14
Terrace House, St. Ives, Cornwall. † D 2, SWA 4.
BOUSFIELD, Miss Harriet Mary See HAMILTON
BOUSTEAD, Mrs. L. Exh. 1921
70 Ashley Gardens, Victoria, London. † SWA 1.
BOUTCHER, C.G. Exh. 1909-11
40 Gt. James Street, Bedford Row, London. † RA 2.
BOUTCHER, Harold W. Exh. 1893-94
10 Pembroke Studios, Pembroke Gardens, London. † L 2, P 1.
BOUTFLOWER, Margaret B. Exh. 1925
1 Woodfield Road, Redland, Bristol. † SWA 1.
BOUTIBONNE, Charles Edouard* 1816-1897
Hungarian artist. Add: 26 Rue de Laval, Paris. † GI 1.
BOUTIGNY, Paul Emile 1854-1929
French artist. Add: 18 Avenue de Villiers, Paris. † RHA 2.
BOUTKER, Miss Maria Exh. 1910
c/o Bourlet and Sons, 17 Nassau Street, London. † B 3.
BOUTWOOD, Charles Edward Exh. 1881-89
Landscape painter. Add: London. † B 2, L 3, RA 4, RBA 1, RHA 4, ROI 2.
BOUVAL, Maurice Exh. 1907
11 Impasse du Maine, Paris. † L 1.
BOUVET, Henry Exh. 1904
20 Rue Galvani, Paris. † L 1.
BOUVIER, Augustus Jules c.1825-1881
Figure painter. b. London of French descent. Studied R.A. Schools 1841, France and Italy. A.R.I. 1852, R.I. 1865. Add: London 1880. † RI 2.
BOUVIER, Miss Agnes Rose See NICHOLL
BOUVIER, C. Exh. 1901
13 Rue des Beaux Arts, Paris. † NG 1.
BOUVIER, Gustavus Arthur Exh. 1880-88
Figure and genre painter. Add: London. † B 4, D 6, GI 7, L 1, M 3, RA 1, RBA 10.
BOUVIER, Joseph* Exh. 1881-88
Genre and historical painter. Add: London. † B 2, RA 1, RBA 1.
BOUWENS, Amata Exh. 1889-97
Mrs. T. Watercolour portrait and figure painter. Add: London 1889; Staines, Middlesex 1895; Shepperton, Middlesex 1897. † L 3, RA 9, RI 1, SWA 2.
BOVENSCHEN, Mrs. M.A. Exh. 1919-38
Landscape and still life painter. Add: London. † NEA 1, SWA 5, WG 155.
BOVILL, Constance Exh. 1888
Dorking, Surrey. † D 1.
BOVILL, Miss D.A. Exh. 1911
Maybury, Sea View, Isle of Wight. † RA 1.
BOVILL, Percy C. Exh. 1883-1907
Landscape and figure painter. Add: London 1883 and 1891; Mevagissey, Cornwall 1890; Ruan Minor, Cornwall 1898; Looe, Cornwall 1903; Bournemouth 1907. † L 12, RA 11, RBA 6, ROI 6.
BOWCHER, Alfred W. Exh. 1886-89
Sculptor. Add: Oakley Cottage Studio, Upper Cheyne Row, Chelsea, London. † B 1, L 2, NG 2.
BOWCHER, Frank b. 1864
Sculptor and medal engraver. Son of William Henry Boucher q.v. Studied National Art Training College, South Kensington (National scholar 1885). Add: London. † GI 2, L 7, RA 35, RMS 7.
BOWDAGE, Miss Eileen J. Exh. 1929
Vrondeg, Denbigh, N. Wales. † L 1.
BOWDEN, Miss E.B. Exh. 1919
18 Emperors Gate, London. † SWA 1.
BOWDEN, F. Exh. 1915
12 John Street, Adelphi, London. † RI 1.
BOWDEN, Mrs. Mary Exh. 1880-1919
Flower painter. Add: London. † I 1, L 2, M 5, RA 5, RHA 1, ROI 4, SWA 3.
BOWDEN, Mrs. Vera Exh. 1913-21
Figure and portrait painter. Add: Nottingham 1913 and 1920; London 1919; Skegness, Lincs. 1921. † N 34.
BOWDEN, Miss Violet Exh. 1904-10
740 Fulham Road, London. † L 5, RA 2, RI 4.
BOWDEN-SMITH, Daisy Beatrice b. 1882
Nee Porter. Watercolour painter and miniaturist. b. India. Studied Juliens, Paris. Add: Charmouth, Dorset 1925; Brockenhurst, Hants. 1926. † RA 2, RMS 1.
BOWDEN-SMITH, Miss L.M. Exh. 1921
Cedarcote, Petersfield, Hants. † B 2.
BOWE, Francis Domonic 1892-c.1930
Sculptor, etcher and painter. Studied Metropolitan School of Art, Dublin. Add: Dublin. † RHA 24.
BOWEN, Augusta M. Exh. 1898-1925
Still life painter. Add: Tenby, S. Wales. † BRU 1, L 4, RA 6, RBA 1, RHA 1.
BOWEN, Eva Exh. 1882
37 Queenboro Terrace, Kensington Gardens, London. † D 1.
BOWEN, Elizabeth Constance Cole Exh. 1895
Bowen's Court, Mallow, Co. Cork, Ireland. † RHA 2.
BOWEN, E.F.S. Exh. 1910
c/o Allied Artists Association, London. † LS 3.

BOWEN, Georgina C. Exh. 1911
Mrs. Eynon Bowen. † RMS 1.

BOWEN, Miss G.T. Exh. 1915-16
Mrs. Hemsley. Add: Headingley, Leeds. † L 2, RA 1.

BOWEN, Hugh Exh. 1896-1903
Portrait painter. Add: London. † L 2, RA 2, RBA 1.

BOWEN, Miss Helen S.L. Exh. 1914
84 Church Street, Campden Hill, Kensington, London. † LS 3.

BOWEN, Josephine Exh. 1880
Still life painter. Add: Stourbridge School of Art, Worcs. † SWA 1.

BOWEN, Lota d. c.1934
Landscape painter. Travelled Europe. A.S.W.A. 1901, S.W.A. 1902. Add: London. † ALP 6, B 18, D 7, GI 7, L 22, LS 8, M 3, NG 4, RA 20, RBA 12, RHA 3, RI 6, ROI 4, SWA 173.

BOWEN, Miss Mary Exh. 1885
Avon House, Warwick. † B 1.

BOWEN, Owen* b. 1873
Landscape and still life painter. Studied under Gilbert Foster. R.O.I. 1917. Add: Leeds. † B 1, FIN 4, GI 1, L 101, M 6, NG 1, RA 55, RCA 195, RHA 5, RI 4, ROI 103, RSA 4.

BOWEN, Ralph Exh. 1884-1915
Figure painter. Add: Worcester 1884; Nottingham 1908. † B 1, N 14, RA 1.

BOWEN, Stella Exh. 1936-39
London. † GOU 1, RBA 2, SWA 1.

BOWER, Miss C.C. Exh. 1934
Still life painter. † COO 2.

BOWER, Lady Dorcas Mona Exh. 1926-39
Nee Blackett. Studied in Germany. Lady Mayoress of London 1924-25. Add: Chislehurst 1926. † RHA 1, RI 13, ROI 3, SWA 2.

BOWER, Ethel Alice Chivers See HARRIS

BOWER, Mrs. L.S. Exh. 1916
3 Barnoon Terrace, St. Ives, Cornwall. † RA 1.

BOWER, Philip Exh. 1931
Pencil artist. Add: 9A Joubert Mansions, Jubilee Place, Chelsea, London. † GOU 1, RA 1.

BOWER, Miss Rose Exh. 1922-24
Sculptor. Add: 9 St. Albans Road, London. † RA 1, SWA 2.

BOWER, W.J. Exh. 1928
103 Park Road, Liverpool. † L 1.

BOWERLEY, Miss Amelia See BAUERLE

BOWERLEY, Marta Caroline Exh. 1925-38
Illuminator, illustrator and writer. Studied under Graily Hewitt. Add: London. † ALP 11, L 2, SWA 2, WG 197.

BOWERMAN, Bernard J.W. b. 1911
88 Tyndall Road, London 1935. † RBA 1.

BOWERS, Albert Edward Exh. 1880-93
Landscape painter. Add: Kew, Surrey 1880; London 1889, Richmond, Surrey 1890. † GOU 3, RA 1, RBA 17, RI 5, ROI 2.

BOWERS, Stephen Exh. 1880-91
Landscape painter. Add: 2 Mortlake Terrace, Kew, Surrey. † D 1, RBA 9, RI 1.

BOWES, Miss C. Exh. 1937
102 Queens Gate, London. † ROI 1.

BOWES, Miss Constance Exh. 1890-92
Flower painter. Add: 7 Rue de Bassano, Paris. † L 2, RA 1.

BOWES, Miss Elfrida Exh. 1923-24
Liverpool. † L 2.

BOWES, John b. 1899
Painter and black and white artist. Add: Southport, Lancs. 1928. † GI 1, L 1, M 1, RCA 2, RI 4, ROI 7, RSA 1.

BOWIE, Jessie Exh. 1884
17 Woodside Place, Glasgow. † GI 2.

BOWIE, John Dick 186-?-1914
Landscape and portrait painter. Studied R.S.A., Paris, Haarlem and Madrid. R.P. 1905, A.R.S.A. 1903. Add: Edinburgh and London. † GI 59, L 6, M 3, NG 3, P 32, RA 10, RSA 133.

BOWIE, Thomas Taylor Exh. 1931-37
16 Cadzow Place, Edinburgh. † RSA 6.

BOWKER, Alfred Exh. 1926-35
The Malms, Shawford, Hants. † L 1, RA 3.

BOWKER, Margaret Exh. 1938-39
Flower painter. Add: 11 Severn Road, Sheffield, Yorks. † GOU 1, M 1, RA 1.

BOWKETT, Miss Jessie Exh. 1880-81
Figure and domestic painter. Add: 2 Leamington Villas, Acton, London. † GI 1, RBA 2, RHA 3, RSA 1, SWA 1.

BOWKETT, Jane Maria* Exh. 1880-91
Figure and domestic painter. Married to Charles Stuart q.v. Add: London. † B 12, GI 7, L 12, M 7, RA 3, RBA 9, RHA 9, ROI 3, RSA 3.

BOWKETT, Leila Exh. 1880-83
Figure painter. Add: London. † B 3, GI 1, M 1, RBA 4, RHA 10, RSA 6, SWA 1.

BOWKETT, Miss Nora Exh. 1896-1902
Stonor, Henley-on-Thames 1896; London 1898. † B 2, RA 1, RHA 7.

BOWLBY, Mrs. A. Exh. 1884-85
Watercolour landscape painter. Add: London. † RI 1, SWA 2.

BOWLER, Annie Elizabeth b. 1860
Portrait painter and miniaturist. Studied Lambeth School of Art, R.A. Schools and Paris. Add: London. † M 3, RA 22.

BOWLER, Ellen Annie Exh. 1884-1900
Figure and flower painter. Add: 21 Pembroke Square, Kensington, London. † B 2, L 4, RI 3, SWA 19.

BOWLER, Henry Alexander* 1824-1903
Landscape and genre painter. Headmaster Stourbridge School of Art 1851-55. Professor of Perspective at the R.A. 1861-99. † RI 2.

BOWLES, Charles W. Exh. 1913-28
Architect. Add: London and Sevenoaks, Kent 1922. † RA 7.

BOWLES, Ida A. Exh. 1902-9
Landscape painter. Add: St. Helens, Bideford, Devon. † LS 2, SWA 3.

BOWLES, William Leslie Exh. 1920-23
Sculptor. Add: 3 Radnor Studios, Radnor Street, Chelsea, London. † RA 2.

BOWLEY, Miss May Exh. 1890-92
Decorative painter and designer. Add: Burnt Ash Hill, Lee, 1890; Hampstead, London 1892. † RA 3.

BOWLING, Charles Dawson Exh. 1899-1918
Landscape painter. Add: Grantham, Lincs. 1899; Peterborough 1902 and 1917; Wolverton, Bucks. 1906; Oxford 1911; Royston, Herts. 1914. † N 12, RA 7, RI 9.

BOWLLER, Marjorie E. Exh. 1936
Sculptor. Add: 14 Kelham Lane, Newark, Notts. † N 1.

BOWLS, Mrs. Exh. 1923
5 Sunnyside, Prince's Park, Liverpool. † L 3.

BOWMAN, Alfred George Exh. 1880-1908
Landscape and figure painter. Add: Croydon 1880 and 1889; Red Hill, Surrey 1888; Sydenham, Kent 1890; West Wickham, Kent 1897. † L 1, RA 11, RBA 1, TOO 1.

BOWMAN, Gertrude Exh. 1887-1919
London. † L 1, SWA 1.

BOWMAN, G.G. Exh. 1913-17
11 Victoria Square, Newcastle on Tyne. † RSA 4.

BOWMAN, H. Ernest Exh. 1882-1920
Landscape painter. Add: London 1882 and 1903; Dorking, Surrey 1892. † D 3, NG 1, RA 8, RI 6, ROI 9.

BOWMAN, James Exh. 1884
21 South Apsley Place, Glasgow. † GI 1.

BOWMAN, John Exh. 1892-1915
Landscape painter. N.S.A. 1908. Add: Nottingham 1892; Whitby 1906; Elstree, Herts. 1909. † L 2, N 32, RA 5, ROI 7.

BOWMAN, Maria Exh. 1881
Middleton-by-Youlgreave, nr. Bakewell, Derbys. † N 1.

BOWMAN, Maude Exh. 1913
Landscape painter. † ALP 3.

BOWMAN, Margaret H. Exh. 1892-1921
Portrait painter and woodcut artist. Studied R.A. Schools, Paris and Glasgow School of Art. Add: Leytonstone, Essex 1892; Skelmorlie, Renfrewshire 1895 and 1919; London 1915. † GI 16, I 4, L 2, P 2, RA 2, RI 1, RSA 5, ROI 5.

BOWMAN, Nora b. 1896
Nee Conybeare. Landscape and figure painter. Studied Slade School and under William Thomas Wood. A.R.B.A. 1923, R.B.A. 1931. Add: London and c/o Director of Education, Jerusalem. Exh. 1923-38. † RBA 48, SWA 1.

BOWMAN, Thomas S.* Exh. 1921-26
London 1921; Edinburgh 1926. † RA 1, RSA 2.

BOWN, Albert Charles Exh. 1930-40
Landscape painter. Add: Leatherhead, Surrey 1930; Bridport, Dorset 1935. † CG 32, FIN 7, RA 6, RI 2.

BOWNESS-BURTON, W. Exh. 1913
15 Spring Bank, Preston, Lancs. † RCA 1.

BOWRING, H.G. Exh. 1920-29
c/o Mrs. Cook, 30 Clarence Road, Harborne, Birmingham. † B 5.

BOWRING, W. Arminger Exh. 1921-22
Portrait and figure painter. R.O.I. 1922. Add: London. † L 2, P 1, RA 1, ROI 6.

BOWRON, Miss L. Exh. 1903
38 Abingdon Mansions, Kensington, London. † SWA 1.

BOWSER, Rosa M. Exh. 1889
Flower painter. Add: London. † RA 1.

BOWYER, Alan J. Exh. 1929-31
17 Gartmoor Gardens, Wimbledon Park, London. † ROI 4.

BOWYER, Ellen Exh. 1887-1916
Mrs. R.M. Marsh. Landscape painter. A.S.W.A. 1890. Add: Bath, Som. 1887; London 1888; Mountraith, Dublin 1897. † B 3, G 1, L 5, M 2, NG 4, RA 3, RHA 31, RI SWA 8.

BOWYER, Elsie Clara Exh. 1928-40
Nee Briggs. Portrait, landscape and flower painter. Studied Lambeth Art School, Weybridge Technical and Kingston Art School. Add: Weybridge, Surrey. † L 1, RA 5, SWA 4.

BOWYER, Hilda Exh. 1930-40
Miniature portrait painter. Daughter of John B. q.v. Add: London. † RA 4.

BOWYER, John b. 1872
Studied Croydon School of Art (three Queen's prizes for architecture, modelling and design). Principal Putney School of Art 1901-32. Exh. 1906. † ROI 2.

BOWYER, Miss Mary Exh. 1905
29 Oxford Terrace, Hyde Park, London. † L 1.

BOWYER, Myrtle Exh. 1940
Chestnut Lodge, Webridge, Surrey. † SWA 1.

BOWYER, Miss Marjorie D. Exh. 1929-30
Betley House, Lyth Hill Road, nr. Shrewsbury, Salop. † RCA 2.

BOWYER, Samuel* Exh. 1887-88
3 Acacia Road, Dulwich, London. † L 2.

BOX, du See D

BOX, Alfred Ashdown Exh. 1883-1938
Landscape painter and musician. Add: Birmingham. † B 42.

BOXALL, D'Auvergne Exh. 1928-29
Landscape and figure painter. Add: 14 Clifton Gardens, Maida Vale, London. † NEA 1, RA 1, RI 2, ROI 2.

BOXER, Mrs. E.A.L. Exh. 1939
† RMS 2.

BOXER, P.N. Exh. 1911-14
151 Burnt Ash Hill, Lee, London. † RA 3.

BOXSIUS, Daisy b. 1885
Watercolour painter and illuminator. Nee Tuff. Married Sylvan G.B. q.v. Studied Camden School of Art and Central School of Arts and Crafts. Teacher of design and lettering L.C.C. School of Photo engraving and lithography. Add: Muswell Hill, London. † RA 6, RBA 2, SWA 1.

BOXSIUS, Sylvan G. b. 1878
Portrait and landscape painter, illustrator and engraver. Married to Daisy B. q.v. Studied Royal College of Art (gold ana silver medals). Art supervisor L.C.C. School of Photo-engraving and lithography. Add: London. † RA 6, RBA 12, RED 2.

BOY, Alfred Exh. 1882
59 Belgrave Road, Edgbaston, Birmingham. † B 1.

BOYAJIAN, Miss Isabelle C. Exh. 1908-9
25 London Road, South Hampstead, London. † LS 8.

BOYAJIAN, Miss Z.C. Exh. 1912-29
Landscape painter and illustrator. Add: 33 Marlborough Hill, St. John's Hill, London. † AB 57, LS 6.

BOYCE, Miss Dorothea Exh. 1892-93
Sculptor. Add: The Art College, Wimbledon. † L 1, RA 1.

BOYCE, George Price* 1826-1897
Landscape painter and watercolourist. Trained as an architect. A.R.W.S. 1864, R.W.S. 1877. Add: London. † L 6, RWS 18.

BOYCE, Hubert Rann Exh. 1931-40
655 Stratford Road, Sparkhill, Birmingham. † B 4.

BOYCE, W.S. Exh. 1888
11 Hunter Street, Paisley. † GI 2.

BOYD, A. Exh. 1880
Landscape painter. Add: 92 Cheyne Walk, Chelsea, London. † RA 1.

BOYD, Miss Alix Exh. 1934
† COO 2.

BOYD, Miss Alice M. Exh. 1914
66 Merrion Square, Dublin. † RHA 1.

BOYD, Miss Ann M. Exh. 1927-33
Wadhurst, Sussex. † D 1, RI 4, RSA 1.

BOYD, Arthur M. Exh. 1891
Landscape painter. Add: c/o Commercial Bank of Australia, London. † RA 1.

BOYD, Miss A. S. Exh. 1896-98
Corstorphine, Midlothian. † SWA 6.

BOYD, Alexander Stuart* 1854-1930
Landscape and genre painter and illustrator. Contributor to "Punch" and on staff of "Graphic" and "Daily Graphic". R.S.W. 1885. Add: Glasgow 1880; London 1891; Auckland, N.Z. 1920. † DOW 3, GI 62, L 4, RA 7, RI 1, RSA 11, RSW 66.

BOYD, Mrs. C. Agnes Exh. 1912
Ballymacool, Letterkenny. † RHA 1.

BOYD, Donald Exh. 1935-36
3 Hazlitt Street, Bilsland Drive, Glasgow. † GI 1, RSA 1.

BOYD, Dr. D. D. Exh. 1885
Hertford College, Oxford. † RI 1.

BOYD, Miss Emma Exh. 1918-21
Belfast 1918; Guernsey, C.I. 1921. † RHA 7.

BOYD, Elizabeth Frances Exh. 1896-1935
Painter and wood-cut artist. Add: Dublin 1896; London 1907; Rye, Sussex 1923. † COO 2, GI 2, I 11, L 1, LS 20, RA 1, RHA 3, RSA 1.

BOYD, Emma M. Exh. 1891
Mrs. A. M. Figure painter. Add: c/o Commercial Bank of Australia, London. † L 1, RA 1.

BOYD, Miss E. S. Exh. 1899-1916
Holywood, Co. Down 1899; Southsea, Hants. 1908. † L 5, RHA 19.

BOYD, George Exh. 1889-93
99 Portland Street, Kilmarnock. † GI 4.

BOYD, Miss Hylda A. Exh. 1928
Garville Avenue, Rathgar, Ireland. † RHA 1.

BOYD, James Exh. 1893-1905
Hamilton, Lanarks. 1893; Strathaven, Lanarks. 1894. † GI 7, RSA 2.

BOYD, Janet A. Exh. 1897
Miniature painter. Add: Whitley, Northumberland 1895; Leamside, Durham 1896. † L 1, RA 3, RMS 16, SWA 3.

BOYD, John S. Exh. 1938
264 Bath Street, Glasgow. † GI 1.

BOYD, Katherine M. Exh. 1908-20
Dublin 1908; Howth, Dublin 1920. † P 1, SWA 13.

BOYD, M. Exh. 1880
Gairneyfield, Corstorphine, Edinburgh. † RSA 1.

BOYD, Miss M. Exh. 1906-7
35 Ovington Street, Chelsea, London. † RA 1, RMS 1.

BOYD, M.A. Exh. 1891-93
Dublin. † D 6.

BOYD, Miss Mary S. Exh. 1935-37
14 Belford Mews, Edinburgh. † GI 4, RSA 5.

BOYD, Percy Exh. 1933-40
Dublin. † RHA 8.

BOYD, Miss Sophia Exh. 1883
41 Moray Place, Edinburgh. † RSA 2.

BOYD, Stuart 1887-1916
Landscape and figure painter. Son of Alexander Stuart B. q.v. Add: London. † FIN 42, GI 7, GOU 1, L 3, LS 8, NEA 10, RA 2, ROI 1.

BOYD, Theodore Penleigh Exh. 1912
Landscape painter. Harbour Studio, St. Ives, Cornwall. RA 1.

BOYD, Walter Scott Exh. 1883-99
Figure painter. Add: Birmingham 1883; Dolgelly, Wales 1899. † B 8, RA 4, ROI 1.

BOYD, William Wilson Exh. 1883-1900
Glasgow. † GI 6, RSW 1.

BOYD-BARRETT, J. Exh. 1923
87 Merrion Square, Dublin. † RHA 1.

BOYD-EDKINS, Miss Roslyn Exh. 1937
† NEA 1.

BOYDELL Bertha Stanfield b. 1899
nee White. Sculptor. Studied Henley School of Art 1916-20, Goldsmith's 1920-22. Add: Kingston Hill, Surrey. † RA 1, RMS 2.

BOYDELL, Creswick Exh. 1889-1916
Landscape painter and watercolourist. Add: Liverpool. † B 2, L 60, RA 3, RCA 23.

BOYDELL, J. Exh. 1883
Llanbedr, Tal-y-Bont, N. Wales. † L 1.

BOYE, Abel Exh. 1912
Villa Chaptal, 25 Levallois Perret (Seine) France. † L 1.

BOYER, Charles Exh. 1938
Urban landscape painter. Add: Small Heath, Birmingham. † RA 1.

BOYER, Pierre Exh. 1909
Chez Messrs. Pasquini et Cie, 43 Avenue de Wagram, Paris. † L 1.

BOYES, Miss G. H. Exh. 1906
West Hill House, Beverley, Yorks. † RA 2.

BOYES, Sidney T. Exh. 1907-31
Sculptor. Add: Aberdeen 1907; London 1910; Bexley Heath, Kent 1931. † L 1, RA 11, RSA 1.

BOYLE, Lady A. Exh. 1901
Fairlie, Argyllshire. † D 2.

BOYLE, Alice Exh. 1932-39
Landscape painter. Add: London. † COO 10, NEA 3, RA 2, RBA 1.

BOYLE, Cerise b. 1875
The Hon. Mrs. Robert B. nee de Crespigney. Watercolour painter of horses, landscapes, gardens and miniatures of children. Studied Westminster under Cope and Nichol and three years with Frank Calderon. Travelled Europe and Middle East. Add: Fareham, Hants. 1916. † ALP 26, COO 1, RA 2, WG 71.

BOYLE, Eleanor Exh. 1880-81
The Hon. Mrs. Richard. Add: Huntercombe, Maidenhead. † G 3.

BOYLE, George A.* Exh. 1884-99
Landscape and figure painter. Add: London. † RA 4, RBA 9, ROI 1.

BOYLE, Harry Exh. 1913
Marine painter. † WG 47.

BOYLE, James A. Exh. 1908
51 Gardner Street, Partick, N.B. † GI 1.

BOYLE, John J. 1851-1917
American sculptor. Add: New York 1913. † RA 2.

BOYLE, Miss Kathleen Exh. 1923-26
Wood engraver. Add: 16 Onslow Square, London. † GI 1, NEA 5, P 2, RA 1.

BOYLE, M. Exh. 1885
Methven, Perth. † RSA 1.

BOYLE, Miss O. Exh. 1895
28 Avonmore Gardens, Kensington, London. † SWA 1.

BOYLE, R. B. junr. Exh. 1881
20 Upper Gloucester Street, Dublin. † RHA 2.

BOYNS, Bessie Exh. 1891
Coastal painter. Add: Boswedden, St. Just, Cornwall. † RBA 1.

BOYNTON, Mrs. Winifred A. Exh. 1938-39
Portrait painter. Add: West Bridgford, Notts. † N 2.

BOYS, Justyn J. Exh. 1909
† LS 1.

BOYTON, Charles Exh. 1933
519 Finchley Road, London.† RBA 2.

BOZNANSKA, de see D

BOZZALLA, Guiseppe Exh. 1911
† ALP 1.

BOZZI, Giovanni Exh. 1895-1900
Edinburgh. † L 1, RSA 11.

BOZZI, Jean Louis Exh. 1901-12
French artist. Add: Paris 1901; Seine et Oise 1912. † RSA 3.

BOZZI, Lorenzo Exh. 1896
233 bis, Faubourg St. Honore, Paris † RSA 1.

BRABAZON, Hercules Brabazon* 1821-1906
Watercolour landscape, marine and still life painter. b. Paris. Studied in Rome for 3 years. Travelled Europe, Middle East, N Africa and India. N.E.A. 1891. Collection of his work in Tate Gallery. Add: London 1891; Battle, Sussex 1904. † AG 2, FIN 1, GOU 145, I 20, M 6, NEA 99.

BRABY Newton* Exh. 1898-1911
Domestic and portrait painter. Add: Teddington, Middlesex 1898; London 1907; Kingston on Thames, Surrey 1910. † B 3, LS 9, NG 4, RA 13.

BRACE, Alan Exh. 1911-29
London. † RA 5.

BRACE, Eleanor Exh. 1881-1916
Flower, still life, interior and landscape painter. Add: Brighton 1881; London 1889; Reigate, Surrey 1891. † B 1, D 66, G 4, GI 2, L 3, LS 16, M 1, RA 1, RBA 7, RI 1, ROI 3, SWA 23.

BRACE, Miss M. R. Exh. 1926-29
Collaborated with Miss K. Pilsbury q.v. Add: London. † L 8.

BRACH, Mlle. M. Exh. 1904
76 Rue de Rome, Paris. † L 1.

BRACHER, Mrs. Dorothy Exh. 1936-37
Maidstone, Kent. † SWA 2.

BRACH-SCHREINDAL, Mrs. Bertha Exh. 1914
Grafenau im berge Wald, Low Bavaria. † LS 3.

BRACKEN, A. Exh. 1885
Figure painter. Add: Via delle Port Nouve, Florence, Italy. † RA 1.

BRACKEN, Arthur Exh. 1928-33
Kendal. † L 2.

BRACKENBURY, Mrs. Amy H. Exh. 1913-27
12 Eversley Park, Chester. † L 13.

BRACKENBURY, Miss Georgina A. Exh. 1891-1907
Portrait painter. Add: London. † GI 2, NG 6, P 1, RA 3, ROI 1.

BRACKENBURY, Miss Marie V.C. Exh. 1899-1907
2 Campden Hill Square, London. † NG 5, RBA 2.

BRACKENBURY, Olive Exh. 1914-17
8 Belsize Square, London. † L 2, LS 9.

BRACKMAN, Robert Exh. 1930
Etcher. † FIN 3.

BRACONNOT, Augustin Exh. 1887-88
Sculptor. Add: 23 Oakley Crescent, Chelsea, London. † RA 2.

BRACQUEMOND, Felix Henri Exh. 1833-1917
French etcher. H.R.E. 1891. † FIN 14, RA 3.

BRADBURY, A.A. Exh. 1885
Derby Club, Derby. † N 1.

BRADBURY, Miss A.H. Exh. 1894
Nightingale Lane, London.† SWA 1.

BRADBURY, Arthur Royce Exh. 1913-40
Portrait, landscape and marine painter, etcher and teacher. Studied at St. John's Wood School of Art and R.A. Schools. Served as a cadet in Mercantile Marine before taking up art; served 2nd Royal Inniskilling Fusiliers 1915-16, Dorset Regiment 1917-18. Add: Bournemouth 1913; Parkstone, Dorset 1925. † L 1, RA 13, RBA 6, RI 15, ROI 5, WG 52.

BRADBURY, Eric 1881-1954
Sculptor and designer. Studied Lambeth School of Art (3 silver and 1 bronze medal). Add: Clapham, London 1912-29. † L 9, RA 9.

BRADBURY, Evelyn Exh. 1934
nee Mate. Married to Arthur Royce B. q.v. Add: Bournemouth, Hants. † RA 1.

BRADBURY, Miss E. Louise Exh. 1899-1926
Teacher Manchester Municipal School of Art 1905. Add: Manchester. † L 4, M 2, SWA 2.

BRADBURY, Maurice Exh. 1931-40
Wolverhampton. † B 10.

BRADDELL, D. Exh. 1905
5 Holland Park Avenue, London. † RA 1.

BRADE, Daniel Exh. 1883-94
Architect. Add: Kendal 1883; London 1891. † L 1, RA 4.

BRADEN, Karl Exh. 1886-91
Landscape painter. Add: Castle Place, Lewes, Sussex. † D 1, RA 1, RBA 1, RI 1.

BRADFIELD, Mrs. Elsie M. Exh. 1923-25
† RMS 2.

BRADFIELD, Nancy Exh. 1935-40
Etcher and wood engraver. Add: London. † RA 6.

BRADFORD, Miss C. Exh. 1900
10 Birdhurst Road, South Croydon, Surrey. † RI 1.

BRADFORD, Dorothy E. Exh. 1921-39
Painter and etcher. Studied Slade School. Add: London and Cambridge. † G 4, NEA 12, RA 11.

BRADFORD, May Sutherland Exh. 1901-9
Landscape painter. Add: London. † I 3, L 31, M 1, NEA 2, NG 3, RA 1, ROI 4, SWA 2.

BRADFORD, P. Exh. 1888
Wentworth, Parkett Road, Liscard, Cheshire. † L 1.

BRADLEY, A.E. Exh. 1924
3 Oak Street, Wolverhampton. † B 1.

BRADLEY, Basil* 1842-1904
Landscape and genre painter and watercolourist. Studied Manchester School of Art. A.R.W.S. 1867, R.W.S. 1881. Add: London 1880 and 1891, Marlow, Bucks. 1885; Blackpool 1903. † B 2, D 2, FIN 1, L 17, M 13, RA 10, RBA 1, RWS 28, TOO 2.

BRADLEY, Miss Constance Exh. 1927-38
Figure painter. Add: 71 Campden Street, London. † RA 2, RBA 3, ROI 9.

BRADLEY, Cuthbert Exh. 1908-29
The Lodge, Folkingham, Lincs. † LS 3, N 12.

BRADLEY, Miss C.F. Exh. 1881
32 Kenilworth Square, Rathgar, Ireland. † RHA 1.

BRADLEY, C.S. Exh. 1901-9
Oxted, Surrey 1901; Shoreham, Sussex 1909. † D 6, RI 1.

BRADLEY, Donald Exh. 1910
145 Upper Richmond Road, Putney, London. † RA 1.

BRADLEY, Dorothy E. Exh. 1899-1933
(Dora). Married Frederick E. Allen q.v. Add: New Brighton, Cheshire 1899; Liscard Cheshire 1908; Bentham, Lancs. 1922. † L 49, RCA 8

BRADLEY, Miss Ellen Exh. 1939-40
Stourbridge † RCA 2.

BRADLEY, Florence Exh. 1929-39
Painter and black and white artist. Add: Leeds 1929; Hampstead, London 1937. † B 2, RBA 1, SWA 3.

BRADLEY, Frank Exh. 1935
Manchester. † RCA 1.

BRADLEY, Miss G.E. Exh. 1922
Montrose, Dudley Park Road, Acock's Green, Birmingham. † B 1.

BRADLEY, Gertrude M. Exh. 1897-1900
London 1897, and 1899, Bushey, Herts. 1898. † L 1, RA 2, SWA 1.

BRADLEY, James Exh. 1882-83
The Limes, Timperley, Manchester. † M 1, ROI 1.

BRADLEY, J.H. Exh. 1896
16 Harold Road, Birmingham. † B 1.

BRADLEY, John Henry* b. 1832
Landscape and topographical painter and watercolourist. Add: Florence 1880-8. † D 4, L 4, RBA 2, RE 15, ROI 2.

BRADLEY, J.M. Exh. 1887
5 Edgar Street, Worcester. † B 1.

BRADLEY, Miss J.R. Exh. 1934
18 Greenwood Drive, Kirkby-in-Ashfield, Notts. † N 1.

BRADLEY, Marshall Exh. 1897
31 Old Queen Street, Westminster, London. † RSA 2.

BRADLEY, Mildred M. Exh. 1929
12 Woodley Road, Rock Ferry, Cheshire. † L 1.

BRADLEY, Patricia Exh. 1936
Sculptor. Add: The Turret Studio, Castle View, the Newarke, Leicester. † N 2.

BRADLEY, R. Exh.1902
† BG 1.

BRADLEY, Susan B. Exh. 1880-87
Flower painter. Add: Crewkerne, Somerset. † D 5, RSA 4, SWA 12.

BRADLEY, T.R. Exh. 1893-96
Birmingham 1893; Liverpool 1895. † B 6.

BRADLEY, William* Exh. 1880-89
Watercolour landscape painter. Add: Bourne End, Bucks. † D 22, L 8, M 8, RA 4, RBA 11, RHA 1 RI 6.

BRADLEY, Will A. Exh. 1901
5 Cook Street, Liverpool. † L 1.

BRADLEY, Warre Squire Exh. 1911-12
24A Earl's Court Gardens, London. † LS 6.

BRADNEY, W.J. Exh. 1939
Ounsdale Road, Wombourne, Staffs. † B 2.

BRADSHAW, Constance H. Exh. 1898-1940
Landscape painter. Studied Spenlove School of Art. A.R.B.A. 1919, R.B.A. 1920, R.O.I. 1933, A.S.W.A. 1912, S.W.A. 1916. Acting P.S.W.A. 1936-39. Add: Rostherne, Buckley, Kent. † GI 3, GOU 1, L 1, NEA 1, RA 9, RBA 133, ROI 28, SWA 96.

BRADSHAW, E. Exh. 1890
6 Buckingham Buildings, Hillhead, Glasgow. † GI 1.

BRADSHAW, Florence Exh. 1889-93
Landscape and figure painter. Add: 12 Westgate Terrace, London. † B 3, RBA 2.

BRADSHAW, Frank Exh. 1940
Landscape painter. Add: 17 Waverly Place, Bradford, Yorks. † RA 1.

BRADSHAW, G.E. Exh. 1922-24
24 Teversal Avenue, Nottingham. † N 5.

BRADSHAW, George Fagan b. 1887
Marine painter and black and white artist. b. Belfast. Lieut. Comm. in R.N. until 1921. Add: St. Ives, Cornwall 1923. † AB 2, ALP 1, B 3, L 1, RA 10, RSA 1.

BRADSHAW, Harold Chalton 1893-1943
Architect. Studied Liverpool University and British School at Rome (Rome scholarship in Architecture 1913). Add: Liverpool 1912; London 1920. † L 4, RA 9.

BRADSHAW, J. Champion Exh. 1891-1912
Isle of Man 1891; Stalybridge, Manchester 1907. † L 1, M 10.

BRADSHAW, J.J. Exh. 1906
108 City Road, London. † RA 1.

BRADSHAW, Kathleen Marion Exh. 1929-33
nee Slatter. Married to George Fagan B. q.v. Flower and portrait painter. Add: St. Ives, Cornwall. † RA 1, ROI 1.

BRADSHAW, Miss Muriel Exh.1921-28
Ormskirk, Lancs. 1921; Southport, Lancs. 1923. † L 8, RA 2.

BRADSHAW, Miss Ora Exh. 1939
Youghal, Co. Cork, Ireland. † RHA 2.

BRADSHAW, Raymond Exh. 1939
† P 1.

BRADSHAW, Miss R.M.S. Exh. 1912-19
Dollymount, Dublin 1912; Ballyardle, Co. Down 1919. † RHA 6.

BRADSHAW, Violet Hamilton Exh. 1921-25
Landscape painter. Studied Slade School. Visited West Indies. † CHA 37, GOU 1, NEA 1.

BRADSTREET, Miss S. Exh. 1887
Sculptor. Add: c/o Canon Atkinson, The Close, Winchester, Hants. † RA 1.

BRADY, Alice Exh. 1881
Faucett Street, Sunderland. † GI 1.

BRADY, Emmet* Exh. 1896-1928
Painter and etcher. Studied South Kensington and Paris; Owen Jones medal and two National silver and two bronze medals. Assistant master Glasgow School of Art. Art Master Kelvinside Academy Glasgow. Add: Helensburgh 1896; Glasgow 1901. † GI 31, L 1, LS 2, RHA 6, RSA 10, RSW 3.

BRADY, Kathleen H. Exh. 1897-99
Miniature portrait painter. Add: London 1897; Spalding, Lincs. 1899. † RA 1, RBA 2.

BRADY, Miss Katharine M. Exh. 1929
21 Westbourne Gardens, Kelvinside, Glasgow. † GI 2.

BRADY, Richard Exh. 1939
4 Tower Avenue, Rathgar, Dublin. † RHA 1.

BRAECKE, Pierre b. 1859
Belgian sculptor. Exh. 1914-31. Add: Brussels. † GI 2, RSA 3.

BRAGA, E. Exh. 1883
Milan. † RA 1.

BRAGG, Gerard Exh. 1912-29
Etcher and lithographer. Assistant to F.V. Burridge; teacher Liverpool City Art School. Add: Wavertree, Liverpool. † L 21, RA 1.

BRAGG, Miss Gwendy Exh. 1927-32
Albemarle Street, London. † GOU 1, NEA 5.

BRAGG, Lady G.M. Exh. 1927-29
Albemarle Street, London. † SWA 4.

BRAGG, J. Exh. 1883-88
Hampstead Mount, Handsworth, Birmingham. † B 7.

BRAGGER, Charles Exh. 1880
Portrait and landscape painter. Add: 39B Old Bond Street, London. † AG 1, RA 1.

BRAILSFORD, Alfred b. 1888
Sculptor. b. Carmarthen. Studied Bournemouth Municipal College. Add: Southbourne, Hants. 1931; Bournemouth 1937. † RA 6.

BRAIN, Miss Constance Exh. 1891-1900
London. † L 1, RA 1, RI 2.

BRAIN, F. Exh. 1883
The Mount, Freshwater, Isle of Wight. † RHA 1.

BRAINE, Alice Exh. 1901-16
R.M.S. 1901. Add: London. † L 2, M 9, RA 6, RMS 32.

BRAITH, Anton* Exh. 1885-92
† TOO 2.

BRAITHWAITE, C. Exh. 1892
Bradyll House, Ulverston, Lancs. † L 1.

BRAITHWAITE, Charles d. 1941
Landscape painter. Studied Government School of Art Belfast and Royal Cambrian Academy. Head of Art department Methodist College, Belfast. Add: Belfast. A.R.H.A. 1914. Exh. 1912-29. † RHA 21.

BRAITHWAITE, Florence Exh. 1884
Landscape painter. Add: London. † SWA 1.

BRAITHWAITE, Miss Mary E. Exh. 1909-23
Brook House, Long Melford, Suffolk. † L 5, LS 3, RI 1.

BRAITHWAITE, R.W. Exh. 1890
165 Embden Street, Hulme, Lancs. † M 1.

BRAITHWAITE, Sam Hartley b. 1883
Landscape painter and etcher. b. Egremont, Cumberland. Studied Bournemouth Municipal School of Art. Exh. 1932-37. Add: Bournemouth. † FIN 9, RA 2.

BRAITHWAITE, W. Exh. 1912-16
Leeds. † RA 1, RI 1.

BRAITHWAITE, William Exh. 1892
Landscape painter. Add: 24 Lamberta Cottages, Upper Talbot Street, Nottingham. † N 1.

BRAKELL, Miss Mildred Exh. 1926-32
18a Slater Street, Liverpool. † L 6.

BRAKSPEAR, Harold Exh. 1897
Architect. Add: Corsham, Wilts. † RA 1.

BRAMAH, Bruce Exh. 1937-38
Percy Drive, Giffnock, Glasgow. † GI 2.

BRAMALL, Edwin Exh. 1940
Figure painter. Add: 2 Simmons Street, Chelsea, London. † RA 2.

BRAMANTI, Carlo Exh. 1900-2
c/o T. Sadler, 2 Coram Street, London. † B 1, L 1.

BRAMHAM, John W. Exh. 1937
Landscape painter. Add: West Stockwith, Doncaster, Yorks. † RA 1.

BRAMLEY, Frank* 1857-1915
Portrait, flower and genre painter. N.E.A. 1886, A.R.A. 1894, R.A. 1911. "A Hopeless Dawn" purchased by Chantry Bequest 1888. Add: Lincoln, France and Venice 1880; Newlyn, Penzance, Cornwall 1885 and 1891; Porlock, Devon 1889; Droitwich, Worcs. 1896 and 1899; Grasmere, Westmorland 1897 and 1900; Woodhall Spa, Lincs. 1898. † AG 1, B 7, BG 3, CAR 1, DOW 1, GI 6, L 22, LEI 48, M 8, NEA 2, NG 1, RA 66, RBA 4, RCA 1, RHA 1, ROI 5, RSA 3, TOO 8.

BRAMLEY, Linda Exh. 1937-40
Paddock Wood, Kent 1937; London 1939; New Maldon, Surrey 1940. † B 4, NEA 1, ROI 1, SWA 1.

BRAMLEY, William Exh. 1900-32
Domestic painter. R.B.A. 1905. Add: Peckham, London 1900; New Wanstead, Essex 1901; Woodford, Essex 1907. † B 1, RA 8, RBA 74.

BRAMLEY-MOORE, Millicent Exh. 1899-1914
Mrs. Harris. Urban painter. A.R.E. 1899. Add: London 1899; Hertford 1900; Horsham, Sussex 1914. † LS 3, RA 3, RE 10.

BRAMMER, Leonard Griffith b. 1906
Etcher and lithographer. Travelling scholarship School of Engraving. Principal Longton School of Art 1932-38. A.R.E. 1932. Add: London 1930; Stoke-on-Trent 1930; Stockton Brook, Staffs. 1935. † L 3, RA 10, RE 25.

BRAMPTON, Herbert Exh. 1896
Bedford Villa, Havelock Place, Hanley, Staffs. † B 1, RA 1.

BRAMPTON, Miss Lorna P. Exh. 1914
The Chantry, Elstree, Herts. † LS 3.

BRAMWELL, Mrs. Bridget C. Exh. 1939-40
A.S.W.A. 1940. Add: Ditchling, Sussex. † GOU 2, SWA 4.

BRAMWELL, Dorothy Exh. 1934-37
13 Mount Carmel Chambers, Duke's Lane, London. † RI 1, ROI 2, RSA 3, SWA 1.

BRAMWELL, Edward G. Exh. 1898-1914
Sculptor. Add: London. † L 3, RA 7.

BRAMWELL, Mrs. H. Exh. 1915-23
Beech Hill, Scout Lane, Sherwood, Notts. † N 3.

BRAMWELL, J.S. Exh. 1915-33
c/o Joseph Pearce, Liverpool 1915; 117 Adelaide Road, London 1932. † L 6, RSA 2.

BRAMWELL, James S. Exh. 1916-29
Liverpool. † L 33.

BRANCKER, Miss Ada Exh. 1926
The Shanty, Mossley Hill, Liverpool. † L 1

BRANCUSI, Constantin* 1876-1957
Rumanian sculptor. Exh. 1913-25. Add: Paris. † CHE 5, LS 6.

BRAND, Carlotta Exh. 1934
† GOU 1.

BRAND, J.A. Exh. 1899
Architect. Add: 34 Gresham Street, London. † RA 1.

BRAND, Jane C. Exh. 1890-1903
Faulds Park, Baillieston, N.B. † GI 8.

BRAND, Walter b. 1872
Architect and black and white artist. b. Ipswich. Add: Leicester 1924. † B 11.

BRANDARD, Miss Annie Caroline Exh. 1880-84
Nature painter. Add: 2 Albion Grove, Barnsbury, London. † RA 2. SWA 1.

BRANDARD, Miss Emily Marion Exh. 1885-89
Landscape painter. Add: 2 Albion Grove, Barnsbury, London. † RE 2, SWA 2.

BRANDARD, Edward Paxman Exh. 1884-85
Landscape painter and etcher. Add: 2 Albion Grove, Barnsbury, London. † RA 1, RE 2, RI 1.

BRANDLING, Vincent F. Exh. 1902
Animal painter. Add: Urbino, Bushey, Herts. † RA 1.

BRANDON, C. Exh. 1939
† NEA 1.

BRANDON, Dolly Exh. 1891
Landscape painter. Add: Swiss Cottage, London. † RBA 1.

BRANDON, Henry Exh. 1904
3 Blenheim Drive, Partick, Glasgow † GI 2.

BRANDON, Prof. Raoul Exh. 1912
279 Boulevard Raspail, Paris. † RSA 3.

BRANDON-JONES, Mrs. Anne 1878-1968
nee Brandon. Flower and landscape painter and embroideress. Studied under her husband, Philip B-J. q.v. Add: The Poplars Berkhamsted, Herts. 1934. † P 1, RA 1 RBA 2, ROI 1.

BRANDON-JONES, Noel b. 1911
Architect. Son of Anne and Philip B-J. q.v. Add: c/o Cowley-Voysey, 14 Gray's Innsquare, London 1933. † RA 1.

BRANDON-JONES, Philip 1876-194[illegible]
Watercolour painter and teacher. Studied Slade School. Married to Anne B-J. q.v. Add: The Poplars, Berkhamsted, Herts 1931. † RA 1.

BRANDRETH, Miss Finetta Exh. 1930-3[illegible]
Landscape painter. Add: 1 Hemstal Road London. † COO 1, NEA 1, P 1.

BRANDT, Mrs. Muriel* Exh. 1938-4[illegible]
Bailey, Co. Dublin 1938; Sutton, Co. Dublin 1940. † RHA 7.

BRANDT, Paul Exh. 1901
Mount Pleasant, Waterloo, Liverpool. † L 1.

BRANDT, Richard F.W. Exh. 1897
56 Landwehr Strasse, Munich. † NG 1.

BRANEGAN, J.F. Exh. 1884
26 Francis Street, Tottenham Court Road, London. † RHA 2.

BRANFORD, Maribel Exh. 1885
Still life painter. Add: 36 Talgarth Road, West Kensington, London. † SWA 2.

BRANFORT, Miss Beth Exh. 1920-21
Miniature portrait painter. Add: 5 Carlyle Mansions, The Mall, Kensington, London. † RA 1, RI 2, SWA 1.

BRANGWYN, Frank* 1867-1956
Painter, etcher, lithographer and mural painter. b. Bruges. Studied under William Morris at age 15 before going to sea. A.R.A. 1904, R.A. 1919, R.B.A. 1890, P.R.B.A. 1913, A.R.E. 1904, R.E. 1907, H.R.M.S. 1918, R.O.I. 1893, H.R.S.A. 1914, R.S.W. 1917, A.R.W.S. 1921. "The Poulterer's Shop" purchased by Chantrey Bequest 1916. Add: London 1884. † B 4, BA 7, BAR 85, BG 2, COO 1, FIN 478, G 4, GI 42, GOU 5, L 38, M 4, NEA 1, NG 9, RA 46, RBA 34, RE 8. RHA 4, RI 1, ROI 8, RSA 27, RSW 8, RWS 6, TOO 4.

BRANGWYN, Leslie Maurice Leopold b. 1896
Etcher and wood engraver. Add: 29 Heather Road, London 1940. † RA 1.

BRANNAN, Edward Eaton 1886-1957
b. Nottingham. Studied Grimsby Art School and under H. Rollett. Add: Cleethorpes, Lincs. 1929. † L 1.

BRANSCOMBE, Charles H. Exh. 1891
Bournemouth. † ROI 1.

BRANSCOMBE, J.E.M. Exh. 1909
151 Gloucester Road, London. † RA 1.

BRANSGROVE, Percival Exh. 1917-35
London. † RA 3.

BRANSON, Clive Exh. 1931-38
Portrait and landscape painter. Add: 62A Cheyne Walk, London. † LEF 7, RA 2.

BRANSON, Edith May Olive Exh. 1908-28
Landscape painter. Add: London 1908; France 1924. † CHE 1, GI 2, GOU 1, I 4, L 13, LS 20, NEA 15, RA 4, RHA 4, RI 2, RSA 2, SWA 1.

BRANSON, Mrs. Juliet Exh. 1886-96
Landscape painter. Add: London. † L 2, M 1, RA 3, RBA 2.

BRANSON, Miss J. M. Exh. 1931
74 Arden Road, Birchfield, Birmingham. † B 2.

BRANSTON, Eva M. Exh. 1892-1910
Landscape painter. Add: Beckenham, Kent 1892; South Kensington, London 1894. † B 2, L 2, M 3, RA 2, RBA 5, ROI 9.

BRANWHITE, Charles Brooke* 1851-1929
Landscape painter. Studied under his father Charles B. A.R.W.S. and at South Kensington School of Art. Add: Redland, Bristol. † B 32, GI 14, L 33, M 2, RA 7, RBA 5, RCA 10, RI 14, ROI 2.

BRAQUE, Georges* 1882-1963
French painter. Exh 1925-34. † CHE 3, RSA 2.

BRAQUEMONDE, Exh. 1923
† FIN 1.

BRASSINGTON, S. Exh. 1912-15
29 William St. Long Eaton, Notts. † N 5.

BRAUER, Miss Evelyn Exh. 1899
St. John's Road, Knutsford, Cheshire. † L 1.

BRAUER, Miss E.A. Exh. 1912
8 Cranbourne Road, Stockport, Lancs. † M 1.

BRAUN, Leopold Exh. 1914
Landscape and figure painter. † BG 48.

BRAUN, Veronique Exh. 1935-37
Painter and etcher. † RED 3.

BRAUNEROVA, Mlle. Zdenka Exh. 1908
10 Vsehrdova, Praga11, Bohemia, Austria. † LS 5.

BRAUX de see D

BRAVIERI, C.T. Exh. 1920
7 Abingdon Mansions, Kensington, London. † RHA 1.

BRAY, Miss Jessamine S. Exh. 1927-29
Sculptor. Add: 9 Thurlow Park Road, Dulwich, London. † GI 2, L 2, RA 1, RMS 2.

BRAY, Phyllis Exh. 1930-40
Still life, figure and landscape painter. Member London Group 1933. † BA 1, COO 6, GOU 1, LEF 50, LEI 3, SWA 1.

BRAY, Walter Exh. 1914-20
London and Gerrards Cross, Bucks. † GI 3, L 8, RA 2.

BRAYOVITCH, Yanko b. 1889
Sculptor. b. Yugoslavia. Studied High Academy of Sculpture, Vienna. Add: London 1933-35. † GI 1, RA 3, RSA 1.

BRAYSHAW, Miss Marjorie Exh. 1921-29
56 Manor Road, Wallasey, Cheshire. † L 4.

BRAZIL, Amy Exh. 1889-1940
Watercolour landscape painter. Studied Heatherleys, London, Ecole des Beaux Arts, Brussels, and Paris. Travelled and worked in Europe and Middle East. Add: Bolton-le-Moors 1889; Conway, N. Wales 1892; Manchester 1893; Tal-y- Cafn, N. Wales 1910; Warwick 1914; Coventry 1917. † B 9, M 21, RCA 7, WG 108.

BRAZIL, Miss Angela Exh. 1893-1925
Watercolour landscape painter. Add: 15 Cross Street, Manchester. † M 5, WG 18.

BREACH, E.R.* Exh. 1880-86
Sporting painter. Add: London. † RBA 9.

BREADING, Miss Ivy V. Exh. 1927-37
21 Ranelagh Gardens, London. † L 3, RMS 3, SWA 3.

BREAKELL, Mary Louise Exh. 1880-1912
Figure painter. Add: Manchester 1880; London 1894. † B 8, BRU 3, GI 2, L 12, LS 12, M 17, RA 10, RBA 6, RCA 1, ROI 5, RSA 1, SWA 3.

BREAKSPEARE, John Exh. 1899
Alma Villas, Springfield Road, Kings Heath, Birmingham. † B 1.

BREAKSPEARE, William* Exh. 1856-1914
Genre painter and illustrator. Studied in Paris. R.B.A. 1883, R.B.S.A. 1884, R.O.I. 1896. Add: London 1882 and 1889; Manchester 1887. † B 15, DOW 98, FIN 5, G 6, L 3, M 5, RA 21, RBA 18, RI 1, RMS 1, ROI 52.

BREAL, Aug Exh. 1912-14
Figure and landscape painter. Add: Imperial 21, Sevilla, Spain. † BG 32, I 4, L 2, RHA 2.

BREALEY, William Ramsden b. 1889
Portrait painter and commercial artist. Studied Sheffield Technical School of Art and Royal College of Art. A.R.B.A. 1921, R.B.A. 1922. R.O.I. 1921. Add: Hanwell, Middlesex 1919; London 1923. † GI 1, L 5, P 6, RA 3, RBA 21, ROI 19, RSA 1.

BREANSKI, de see D

BREARD, Henri Exh. 1912
11 Boulevard de Clichy, Paris † L 2.

BREAREY, Fred N. Exh. 1882-88
Edinburgh. † RSA 2.

BREBNER, Elizabeth Margaret Exh. 1884-1925
Flower painter. Add: Edinburgh 1884 and 1904; London 1896 and 1906. † GI 13, L 2, LS 8, RA 5, RSA 21, SWA 3.

BRECHOT, Emile C. Exh. 1920
Sculptor. Add: Greenbank, Burley, Brockenhurst, Hants. † L 2, RA 1.

BREDA, Miss E.M.K. Exh. 1932
Inchory, Barnshot Road, Colinton, Edinburgh. † RSA 2.

BREDALL, Miss Mary see KOOP

BREDBURG, Madame Mira Exh. 1892
13 Mecklenburg Square, London. † NG 1.

BREDEN, Albert C. Exh. 1887-95
Architect. Add: London. † RA 5.

BREDT, Max Exh. 1883
Munich. † L 1.

BREE, de see D.

BREEDEN, W.L. Exh. 1882-1920
Birmingham. † B 3.

BREENGAN, John Exh. 1889-1902
Edinburgh. † RSA 2.

BREITENBACH, Franz Schmid Exh. 1892-93
Munich,Germany. † RHA 2.

BREITNER, Georg Hendrik* Exh. 1857-1923
Dutch painter. Add: Amsterdam. † GI 5, L 1, RSA 1.

BRELING, Heinrich* b. 1849
German artist. † TOO 2.

BRELY, de la see D.

BREMAECKER, de see D.

BREMER, G.C. Exh. 1936
† RSA 1.

BREMER, Miss M. Leonore Exh. 1903-6
Figure painter. London. † RA 2.

BREMNER, Lizzie Exh. 1885-91
11 Scotland Street, Edinburgh. † RSA 6.

BREMNER, Taylor Exh. 1939-40
62 Watson Street, Aberdeen. † RSA 5.

BRENAN, G.A. Exh. 1880-83
51 Camden Street, Dublin. † RHA 30.

BRENAN, James 1837-1907
Headmaster Dublin Metropolitan School of Art. A.R.H.A. 1876, R.H.A. 1878. Add: Sundays Well, Cork 1880; Dublin 1892. † L 3, RHA 62, RSA 4.

BRENAN, Jill Exh. 1939
Cape Cottage, Tonbridge, Kent. † RBA 1.

BRENAN, James Butler d. 1889
A.R.H.A. 1861, R.H.A. 1871. Add: Cork. † RHA 8.

BRENAN, Mrs. J.T. Exh. 1910
Chislehurst, Kent. † SWA 1.

BREND, Marjorie Exh. 1910-29
Mrs. A.F. Spencer. Landscape painter. Add: London. † LS 12, NEA 13, RA 5.

BRENDEL, Albert Heinrich* 1827-1895
German painter. Exh. 1883. † FIN 1.

BRENNAN, Dermott Exh. 1927
19 Ard Righ Road, Dublin. † RHA 2.

BRENNAN, Edward F. Exh. 1933
Cleethorpes, Lincs. † RCA 2.

BRENNAN, E.J. Exh. 1880-84
Ranelagh, Dublin. † RHA 29.

BRENNAN, Fitzjohn Exh. 1885-87
Landscape painter. Add: 76 Park Road, Haverstock Hill, London. † B 1, GI 3, M 3, RA 4.

BRENNAN, James M. Exh. 1935-40
Landscape painter and architect. Add: Dublin. † RHA 12.

BRENNAN, Peter J. Exh. 1938-40
Sculptor. Add: National College of Art, Kildare Street, Dublin. † RHA 5.

BRENNAND, Janet Exh. 1905-24
Mrs. Marsh. Painter, illuminator and decorative figure worker. Studied RA Schools and Royal College of Art. Add: London 1905; Kings Lynn 1923. † RA 5, ROI 1.

BRENNER, Victor David 1871-1924
Sculptor. b. Russia. d. New York. Add: Paris 1906. † RA 1.

BRENNIR, Carl* d. c1924
Landscape painter. N.S.A. 1908. Add: Nottingham 1887. † B 10, M 2, N 74, RA 1.

BRENTA, B. Exh. 1886
† TOO 2.

BRENTNALL, F. Exh. 1913
Roseberry Villas, Denby Lane, Loscoe, Derbys. † N 1.

BRENTNALL, M. Annie Exh. 1884-85
Cocker House, Eastwood, Notts. † N 4.

BRERETON, Miss Annie Exh.1906
8 St. James's Square, Holland Park, London. † RHA 1.

BRESLAU, Marie Louise Catherine* 1856-1927
Portrait and figure painter. Add: c/o W. Cox, Pall Mall, London 1882; Paris 1893. † P 2, RA 1, RHA 1.

BRESSLERN-ROTH, Norbertine b. 1891
nee Roth. Animal painter, miniaturist and woodcut artist. Studied Vienna and Munich. Add: Graz. Exh. 1925-39. † BA 5, FIN 189, GI 3, RHA 11.

BRET, Paul Marie Leonce b. 1902
French painter. Exh. 1928 and 1939. † TOO 59.

BRETHERICK, C.F. Exh. 1890-91
3 Cleveland Terrace, Darwen, Lancs. † M 2.

BRETON, le see L.

BRETON, Emile 1831-1902
French artist. Add: Courrieres, Pas de Calais, France 1884. † GI 1.

BRETON, Miss E.M. Exh. 1903-4
Leek, Staffs. 1903 Stafford 1904. † B 3. L 1.

BRETON, Jules* 1827-1906
French genre painter. Add: Paris 1882; Courrieres, Pas de Calais 1884. † GI 4.

BRETT, Dorothy Eugenie b. 1883
Portrait and figure painter. Add: London 1915-22. Went to U.S.A. 1930's. † G 3, NEA 8.

BRETT, Miss F.M. Exh. 1881
Rosemount, Booter's Town, Ireland. † RHA 2.

BRETT, Miss G.W. Exh. 1909-20
2 Maryland Street, Liverpool. † L 10.

BRETT, H.F. Exh. 1918
Swanton Villa, Stradbrooke Road, Ipswich. † RA 2.

BRETT, Miss Helen M. Exh. 1928-32
Landscape painter. Add: Gretton Villas, Malone, Belfast. † RHA 3.

BRETT, John* c1831-1902
Marine and landscape painter. Visited Europe. A.R.A. 1881. "Britannia's Realm" purchased by Chantry Bequest 1880. Add: London. † B 20, BG 1, D 4, FIN 52, GI 1, L 8, M 23, RA 75, RBA 3, RHA 1, TOO 24.

BRETT, N.C. Exh. 1908
43 Catherine Street, Chester. † L 1.

BRETT, Rosa Exh. 1880-81
Landscape, animal and still life painter. Sister of John B. q.v. Add: London. † RA 1, SWA 2.

BRETTELL, Irene R. Exh. 1932-39
Mrs. J.P. Steephill Cove, Junction Road, Stourbridge, Worcs. † B 5.

BRETT-GARDNER, Miss E. Exh. 1937
56 Kenilworth Road, Leamington Spa. † B 1.

BREUER, Theodore A. Exh. 1901
Flower painter. 51 Boulevard Saint Jacques, Paris. † RA 1.

BREUN, John Ernest d. 1921
Portrait painter. R.B.A. 1896. Add: 4 Greek Street, Soho Square, London. † GI 1, L 26, M 6, RA 13, RBA 70, RHA 4, RI 7, ROI 16.

BREUNING, Von, see V

BREWER, Amy Cobham* Exh. 1886-96
Sculptor and fairy painter. Add: Newark, Notts. 1886; Bushey, Herts. 1892. † FIN 2, L 6, M 1, N 3, NG 1, RA 4, SWA 1.

BREWER, Mrs. C. Cecil Exh. 1906-13
Landscape and interior painter. Add: Gray's Inn Square, London. † RA 3, RID 6.

BREWER, Florence Lucas Exh. 1890-1939
nee Lucas. Married to James Alphege B. q.v. Watercolour painter. Add: London. † RI 6, SWA 1.

BREWER, Miss Hilda Exh. 1906
Elmwood, Harrogate, Yorks. † RCA 1.

BREWER, Henry Charles b. 1866
Decorative and watercolour painter and etcher. Son of Henry William B. q.v. Studied Westminster School of Art 1914. Add: London. † FIN 186, L 10, RA 22, RI 105.

BREWER, Henry William* d. 1903
Architectural and interior painter. Add: London. † RA 15.

BREWER, J. Exh. 1938
Warn Hill, Newmarket, Suffolk. † B 1.

BREWER, John Exh. 1938-40
† RI 3.

BREWER, James Alphege Exh. 1909-38
Painter and etcher. Son of Henry William B. q.v. Add: London. † RA 1, RCA 33, RI 7.

BREWER, Leonard 1875-1935
Painter and etcher. Add: Whalley Range, Manchester. † L 23, M 2, RCA 77.

BREWER, Miss Mary Exh. 1909
7 Park Road East, Birkenhead. † L 2.

BREWER, Miss Maud Exh.1888-1901
Watercolour painter. Add: Sevenoaks, Kent. † RI 7, ROI 2, SWA 2.

BREWILL, Arthur W. Exh. 1891-96
Architect. Add: Angel Row, Nottingham. † N 4, RA 3.

BREWS, Edith Ruby Exh. 1932-33
Mrs. D. Barlow. Figure painter. Add: Letcham Park, Surrey 1932; London 1933. † RA 3.

BREWSTER, Gordon W. Exh. 1916-17
Dublin. † RHA 3.

BREWTNALL, Edward Frederick* 1846-1902
Landscape and figure painter. R.B.A. 1882 R.O.I. 1883. Add: London 1880 and 1890, Dorking, Surrey 1885. † B 7, FIN 2, G 2, GI 3, L 23, M 21, RA 11, RBA 5, ROI 32, RWS 52.

BREZE, de see D

BRIAULT, Sydney Graham 1887-1955
Portrait painter and illustrator. Studied Evening classes at Regent Street Polytechnic 1900 and at St. Martin's School of Art. Add: Walthamstow, London 1918. † RA 1.

BRICARD, Francois Xavier Exh. 1912-16
French artist. Add: Paris 1912; St. Leonard's on Sea 1916. † L 2, RA 2.

BRICE, Miss A.M. Exh. 1897
Sunnyland, Northampton. † B 1, L 1.

BRICE, Ed. E. Exh. 1924
Maythorne, Park Road, Braunton, N. Devon. † B 1.

BRICE, Edward Kington b. 1860
Domestic and mythological painter. Studied Birmingham School of Art. R.B.S.A. 1920. Add: Manchester 1887; Tewkesbury, Glos. 1920. † B 47, L 1, M 4, RA 1, RCA 4.

BRICE, Mrs. R. Exh. 1898
81 St. Giles Street, Northampton. † L 1.

BRICHTA, F.F. Exh. 1888-9
Edinburgh. † GI 8, L 1, RSA 14.

BRIDGE, Miss Annie Exh. 1889-9
Flower painter. Add: 56 South Hill Park Hampstead, London. † RBA 1, SWA 3.

BRIDGE, Aline S. Exh. 1909-1
c/o Allied Artist Association, Londo 1909. Uplyme, Devon, 1911, Paris 1913 † GI 2, L 4, LS 6, RSA 2.

BRIDGE, Elizabeth Exh. 194
17 Powis Gardens, London. † SWA 2.

BRIDGE, Emily J. Exh. 1887-9
Sussex Road, Southsea, Hants. † B 1 SWA 1.

BRIDGE, Florence Exh. 1895-9
62 Claremont Road, Forest Gate, Essex † RBA 2.

BRIDGE, G. Exh. 190
7 Mitcham Park, Surrey. † L 1.

BRIDGE, Henry E. Exh. 1909-1
1 Lower Leeson Street, Dublin. † LS 3 RHA 17.

BRIDGE, Miss Irene Norah Exh. 1931-3
Flower painter. Add: 39 Bedford Gardens London. † NEA 5, RA 1, RBA 2.

BRIDGE, J. Exh. 1890-9
Shrewsbury. † B 2.

BRIDGE, R.S. Exh. 1926-3
Landscape painter. Add: Nottinghham † N 26.

BRIDGE, Vera Ermyntrude Cyprian b.190
Mrs. Osborne. Landscape and child painte and decorative artist. b. Mauritius. Studie at Torquay, Reading and Slade School Exh. 1931. † RI 1.

BRIDGE, W. Exh. 188
Glenville Place, Brighton Road, Birming ham. † B 1.

BRIDGEMAN, Miss Audrey O.W. Exh. 1933-3
Figure painter. Add: Holly Knoll, Chur Farnham, Surrey. † RA 2, RBA 1.

BRIDGES, Miss Amy F. Exh. 190
Miniature painter. Add: Mount Sanford Southborough. † RA 1.

BRIDGES, Miss Clara Exh. 1907-
Warkton Rectory, Kettering. † D 3 RHA 2, SWA 3.

BRIDGES, E.H. Exh. 190
47 Palin Street, New Basford, Notts † N 1.

BRIDGES, Miss Fidelia 1834-192
American painter. Add: 10 Carleton Road Tufnell Park, London. † D 1, RA 1.

BRIDGES, Tom Exh. 193
Landscape painter. Visited West Indies Europe and Australia. † FIN 55.

BRIDGEWATER, Miss Marjorie L. Exh. 1918-2
Portrait and landscape painter. Add London. † ALP 1, RA 4.

BRIDGEWATER, Miss Rosemary Exh. 194
Flower painter. Add: 112 Old Brompto Road, London. † RA 1.

BRIDGFORD, Miss E. Exh. 189
7 Clyde Road, Didsbury, Lancs. † M 1.

BRIDGFORD, Miss F. Exh. 189
Westfield, Bowden, Cheshire. † M 1.

BRIDGFORD, J. Hargrave Exh. 1880-8
3 Lower Merrion Street, Dublin † RHA 7.

BRIDGMAN, Frederick Arthur* 1847-192
Landscape, historical and figure painter. b Alabama, U.S.A. Studied Paris. Travelle Middle East and N. Africa. Add: Pari 1880; Eure, France 1925. † B 16 FIN 233, GI 8, L 11, M 10, RA 35 RBA 2, ROI 14, TOO 2.

BRIDGMAN, May Exh. 1901-27
R.M.S. 1901. Add: Waltham Cross, H erts. 1901; Herne Hill 1905; Bath, Som. 1925. † NG 1, RA 8, RMS 73.

BRIDGMAN, Rose B. Exh. 1911-12
26 Barrack Street, Bridport, Dorset. † LS 6.

BRIDGWATER, Alan 1903-1962
Sculptor. Add: Woodhouse Farm, Tennel Lane. Harborne, Birmingham, 1936. † B 4, RA 1.

BRIDGWATER, H.M. Exh. 1892-1914
Landscape and domestic painter. Married to Harry Scott B. q.v. Add: Bushey, Herts. 1892 and 1914; Rochester, Kent 1902; London 1911. † B 1, FIN 2, L 8, NG 1, RA 7, RI 6.

BRIDGWATER, Harry Scott Exh. 1888-1934
Painter and etcher. b. Dudley. Add: Bushey Herts. 1888; London 1907; Rickmansworth, Herts. 1934. † B 1, FIN 6, G 4, I 2, L 5, M 1, RA 26, RHA 1, RI 1.

BRIDGWATER, Phyllida ScottExh. 1911-27
Watercolour painter. Daughter of H.M. and Harry Scott B. q.v. Add: London 1911 and 1927; Bridgwater, Som. 1913; Bushey, Herts. 1915; Peterhead, Aberdeen 1920. † I 1, L 4, RI 8.

BRIDLE, Arthur J. Exh. 1913
Highland Road, Summersdale, Chichester. † LS 2.

BRIDLE, Kathleen Exh. 1921-39
Landscape, figure and flower painter. Add: Holyhead, Anglesey 1921 and 1926; London 1925; Enniskillen, Ireland 1930. † RHA 32.

BRIDON, Mrs. Mary see GOWLAND

BRIDSON, Thomas Arthur Exh. 1926
Portrait painter. Add: 86 All Saints Road, Wolverhampton. † B 1.

BRIDSON, T.R. Exh. 1907-18
London. † RA 2.

BRIELMAN, J.A. Exh. 1887
16 Rue de Chabrol, Paris. † GI 2.

BRIEN, Miss Norah A. Exh. 1906
Wilton House, Wilton Place, Dublin. † RHA 1.

BRIEN, Stanislaus Exh. 1930-31
Lino-cut artist. † RED 4.

BRIERLEY, Argent Exh. 1914
41 Queen's Avenue, Blackhall. † RSA 1.

BRIERLEY, Ben C. Exh. 1885-91
Rochdale, Lancs. † L1, M 5.

BRIERLEY, C.L. Exh. 1897-98
Architect. Add: 180 Brecknock Road, London. † RA 2.

BRIERLEY, Walter Henry c1862-1926
Architect. Designed improvements to Newmarket and York race courses. Add: York. † RA 24.

BRIERLY, Sir Oswald Walters 1817-1894
Marine painter and watercolourist. b. Chester. Studied at Sass's Academy, London and Naval architecture and rigging at Plymouth. Travelled round the world 1841-51. Appointed marine painter to Queen Victoria 1874 and curator of the Painted Hall at Greenwich 1881. A.R.W.S. 1872, R.W.S. 1880. Knighted 1885. Add: Londonn. † L 3, M 1, RWS 18.

BRIGDEN, F.H. Exh. 1933
† RSW 4.

BRIGDEN, Miss Margaret E. Exh. 1902-4
Miniature portrait painter. Add: Brighton 1902; Surbiton, Surrey 1904. † L 3, RA 3.

BRIGG, Miss Edith Exh. 1905
† SWA 1.

BRIGG, Miss N. Exh. 1904
† P 1.

BRIGGS, Miss A.M. Exh. 1916-18
Sutton in Ashfield, Notts. 1916-18, West Bridgford, Notts. 1917. † N 7.

BRIGGS, Miss Barbara Exh. 1911-22
Beachfield, Sandal Magna, Wakefield, Yorks. † B 1, L 6, RSA 1, SWA 3.

BRIGGS, Ernest Edward 1866-1913
Figure and landscape painter and watercolourist. R.I. 1906. "A flood on the Ken at Earlstoun Linn" purchased by Chantry Bequest 1913. Add: London and Ambleside 1888; Dunkeld, Perthshire 1911. † B 20, FIN 59, L 33, RA 41, RBA 8, RHA 1, RI 53. RSA 2.

BRIGGS, Miss E. Irlam Exh. 1892-1901
Portrait, landscape and mural fresco painter and modeller. Studied Wimbledon Art College, St. John's Wood School, RA Schools and Juliens, Paris. Add: Parkstone, Dorset. † L 1, M 2, RA 5.

BRIGGS, Miss Frances Exh. 1904-5
5 Gloucester Terrace, Regent's Park, London. † NG 2.

BRIGGS, Miss F.M. Exh. 1897-1900
3 Dalebury Road, Trinity Road, Upper Tooting, London. † RBA 3.

BRIGGS, George Exh. 1883-1922
Liverpool 1883 and 1904; Bootle, Lancs. 1894. † L 12.

BRIGGS, Miss Jessie Exh. 1896
3 Dalebury Road, Upper Tooting, London. † RBA 1.

BRIGGS, John Exh. 1885-89
Landscape painter. Add: Edinburgh 1885, London 1889. † L 1, RA 1, RSA 8.

BRIGGS, John Exh. 1925
College of Art, Edinburgh. † RSA 1.

BRIGGS, Nan C. Exh. 1894-99
Edinburgh. † GI 6, RSA 3.

BRIGGS, Robert A. Exh. 1884-1910
Architect. Add: London. † GI 2, RA 34, RHA 1.

BRIGHOUSE, Mona Exh. 1915-16
Mrs. S. McLoughlin. Add: Liverpool. † L 4.

BRIGHT, A. Exh. 1920-33
Formby, Lancs. 1920; Aughton, Lancs. 1932. † L 11.

BRIGHT, Alfred Exh. 1929
The Red Cottage, West Adderbury, Banbury, Oxon. † L 1.

BRIGHT, Beatrice Exh. 1895-1928
Seascape and portrait painter. Studied under Sir Arthur Cope. A.S.W.A. 1897. Add: London. † B 2, GI 1, L 25, NG 1, P 6, RA 23, ROI 10, SWA 57.

BRIGHT, Constance M. Exh. 1905-37
A.S.W.A. 1916; S.W.A. 1921. Add: London. † B 1, L 1, P 1, RA 5, RI 2, ROI 10, SWA 49.

BRIGHT, Archdeacon H. Exh. 1931-34
† WG 8.

BRIGHT, Henry* Exh. 1883-1911
2 Park Place, Giggshill, Thames Ditton, Surrey. † B 1, M 3, RI 1.

BRIGHT, Miss Lilian Exh. 1925-28
Collaborated with her sister Ruth B. q.v. Add: 56 Lethbridge Road, Southport, Lancs. † L 3.

BRIGHT, Miss Ruth Exh. 1924-27
Collaborated with her sister Lilian B. q.v. Add: 56 Lethbridge Road, Southport, Lancs. † L 6.

BRIGHT, Miss S. Exh. 1885-87
Still life painter. Add: 12 Sussex Villas, Kensington, London. † L 2, SWA 2.

BRIGHT, Tyndall Exh. 1895
Briarley, Mersey Road, Liverpool. † L 1.

BRIGHT, W. Frank Exh. 1895
Architect. Add: 26 Sudbourne Road, Brixton, London. † RA 1.

BRIGHTWELL, Miss Beatrice Exh. 1897-99
112 Gough Road, Edgbaston, Birmingham. † B 4.

BRIGHTWELL, G. Exh. 1881-1901
Domestic painter. Add: 8 Victoria Road, Finsbury Park, London. † B 10, RBA 1.

BRIGHTWELL, Helen b. 1876
Miniaturist, enameller and jewellery maker. Studied Birmingham School of Art (3 silver national medals, Queen's prize, John Henry Chamberlain bronze medal for figure design). Add: Harborne, Birmingham 1921-33. † B 14.

BRIGHTWELL, L.R. Exh. 1926-38
Animal painter and etcher. Studied Lambeth School of Art and the Zoological Gardens. Served in France during First War. † AB 1, AR 3, BK 5, CON 20, L 1.

BRIGHTWELL, Miss Mary E. Exh. 1936
107 Handsworth Wood Road, Birmingham. † B 1.

BRIGHTWELL, Miss Nellie Exh. 1897-1913
Edgbaston, Birmingham. † B 4, L 10.

BRILL, Reginald b. 1902
Portrait and figure painter. Studied Slade School; Prix de Rome for painting 1927. Painted and exhibited in Cairo 1930 at invitation of Egyptian Government. Add: London 1928. † LEI 25, M 2, RA 2.

BRIMONT, de See D

BRINDLE, Fred Exh. 1923-24
Landscape painter. Add: 150 Worsley Road, Farnworth, Nr. Bolton, Lancs. † RCA 3.

BRINDLE, Miss Mary Exh. 1923
The Lodge Farm, Pleasington, Nr. Blackburn. † L 1.

BRINDLEY, Charles A. Exh. 1888-98
Domestic watercolour painter. Add: Surbiton. † RA 4, RI 3.

BRINDLEY, John Angell James Exh. 1884-1909
Landscape painter. Add: London. † B 1, GOU 9, LS 8, NEA 8, RA 2, RBA 8, RI 5.

BRINDLEY, Maud Mary Exh. 1905-9
Married to John Angell James B. q.v. Add: Downshire Hill House, Hampstead, London. † LS 8, RI 1, SWA 6.

BRINDLEY, William Exh. 1881-82
Sculptor. Add: Westminster Bridge Road, London. † RA 4.

BRINKLEY, R. Exh. 1880-86
Glasgow. † GI 4.

BRINKMAN, J. Exh. 1936
† RSA 1.

BRINKWORTH, F. Muriel Exh. 1936-40
Westbury, Wilts. † RI 1, SWA 4.

BRINSON, J. Paul d. 1927
Watercolour landscape painter. R.B.A. 1901. Add: West Woodlands, Reading, Berks. † B 23, D 130, GI 13, I 1, L 17, LS 3, RA 6, RBA 199, RI 5.

BRINTON, Mrs. Annie Exh. 1901
25 Clarence Road, Birkdale, Southport, Lancs. † L 2.

BRINTON, Edith D. Exh. 1885-1929
Landscape, portrait and figure painter. Add: London. † M 1, RA 8, RBA 1, RID 70, ROI 1, SWA 1.

BRISAY, de See D

BRISCO, Miss Evelyn Exh. 1940
Miniature portrait painter. Add: Mignon Studio, 8 Nevern Place, London. † RA 1.

BRISCOE, Arthur John Trevor 1873-1943 Marine painter and etcher. b. Birkenhead. Studied Slade School. A.R.E. 1930, R.E. 1933, R.I. 1934. Add: London 1895 and 1926; Maldon, Essex 1898; Orford, Suffolk 1901; Colchester 1920; Walton on the Naze, Essex 1938. † BK 2, CON 4, FIN 635, GI 1, L 14, NEA 14, RA 19, RBA 5, RE 26, RED 1, RI 28.

BRISCOE, Ernest Edward b. 1882 Watercolour painter and illustrator. Add: London 1910; Caterham, Surrey 1926. † M 1, RA 3, RI 1.

BRISCOE-IRONSIDE, Henry Exh. 1908 Auna, Lago Maggiore, Italy. † LS 1.

BRISLEY, Ethel C. Exh. 1908-40 Portrait painter and miniaturist. A.R.M.S. 1920. Add: Bexhill-on-Sea 1908; Streatham 1915; London 1919. † RA 40, RMS 9, SWA 3.

BRISLEY, Joyce Lankester Exh. 1918-23 Illustrator and writer of children's books, ("Milly Molly Mandy"). Studied Lambeth School of Art. Add: 90 Baron's Court Road, London. † RA 6.

BRISLEY, Nina Kennard Exh. 1919-22 Illustrator, poster designer and writer of children's books. Studied Lambeth School of Art. Add: 90 Baron's Court Road, London. † RA 3.

BRISSAUD, Jacques Exh. 1909-10 c/o Allied Artists Association, London. † LS 6.

BRISSOT, Frank Exh. 1881 Animal painter. Add: London. † AG 2.

BRISTOW, Christopher Exh. 1930-39 Architect of telephone exchanges. Add: Office of Works, Storey's Gate, London. † RA 16.

BRISTOW, Miss Dorothy M. Exh. 1907-15 Ivy Lodge, 150 Tulse Hill, London. † RI 3, SWA 2.

BRISTOW, Florence Exh. 1914-36 Mrs. Rowley B. Add: London 1914 and 1917; Chislehurst, Kent 1916. † I 4, LS 10, NEA 2, RBA,1, SWA 1.

BRISTOW, Frederick Page Exh. 1910-11 69 Brailsford Road, Lower Tulse Hill, London. † , LS 6.

BRISTOW, George L. Exh. 1883-92 2 Cedars Road, Clapham Common, London. † RI 8, ROI 1.

BRISTOW, Miss Lily Exh. 1889-1905 Flower and landscape painter. Add: 2 Cedars Road, Clapham Common, 1889 and 1899; Bushey, Herts. 1894; Haslemere, Surrey 1905. † B 1, RA 2, RBA 2, ROI 7, SWA 1.

BRISTOWE, Beatrice M. Exh. 1893-1904 Portrait painter. Add: London. † B 1, RA 3, SWA 1.

BRISTOWE, Ethel Susan Graham Exh. 1899-1934 Mrs. Sydney B. Nee Paterson. Flower painter. Add: Bookham, Surrey. † D 30, WG 46.

BRISTOWE, Mrs. John Syer Exh. 1884-85 Watercolour landscape painter. Add: London. † SWA 3.

BRISTOWE, Nicholas Exh. 1937-40 Landscape painter. Add: London. † LEF 30, NEA 5, RA 1.

BRISTOWE, Mrs. S.C. Exh. 1894 Old Avenue House, Weybridge, Surrey. † GI 2.

BRITTAIN, Miss Alice Exh. 1926-29 Bangor, Co. Down, Ireland 1926; Belfast 1928. † L 17.

BRITTAIN, Isabel Exh. 1891 5 Trafalgar Square, Scarborough. † D 1.

BRITTAIN, Miss Katherine Exh. 1921-22 Liverpool. † L 3.

BRITTAN, Charles Edward b. 1870 Moorland watercolour painter. Studied under his father. Add: Yelverton, Devon 1907; Horrabridge, Devon 1928. † RA 2, RI 1.

BRITTAN, H.W. Exh. 1913 146 St. James's Road, Croydon, Surrey. † RA 1.

BRITTEN, William Edward Frank b. 1857 Decorative and figure painter. Add: London 1880 and 1915; Glasgow 1911. † B 1, G 17, GI 3, L 6, M 2, NG 33, RA 9.

BRITTENDEN, Dora E. Exh. 1887 Flower painter. † SWA 1.

BRIZAC, Paul Exh. 1911 Landscape painter. † BRU 2.

BRO, Cyril Exh. 1920-22 The Laburnums, Castleton, Derbys. † B 3, RCA 1.

BROAD, John Exh. 1890-1900 Sculptor. Add: Wandsworth Common, London. † RA 5.

BROAD, Kenneth Stephen Exh. 1922-35 Watercolour painter and wood engraver. Studied Westminster School of Art. Add: Croydon, Surrey. † COO 1, L 1, RA 1.

BROAD, Sydney M. Exh. 1904 Landscape painter. Add: 6 The Parade, Cardiff. † RA 1.

BROADBENT, A. Exh. 1901-19 Sculptor. Add: 5 Fulham Studios, Walham Green, London. † GI 2, L 4, RA 18, ROI 2.

BROADBENT, Miss Constance H. Exh. 1914-19 The Hollies, Latchford, Warrington. † L 4.

BROADBENT, Frank Exh. 1882-85 22 Holland Street, Fairfield, Liverpool. † L 3, M 1, RA 1.

BROADBRIDGE, Alma Exh. 1880-94 Landscape and figure painter. Add: London 1880 and 1884; Hayward's Heath, Sussex 1882; Brighton 1883 and 1888. † B 10, G 1, L 5, M 3, RA 6, RBA 4, RHA 7, RID 3, ROI 3, SWA 7.

BROADHEAD, Ebenezer Exh. 1938 Cumbernauld, Dumbartonshire. † GI 2.

BROADHEAD, Marion E. Exh. 1904-37 Portrait painter and miniaturist. Studied London School of Art, Paris. A.R.M.S. 1906, R.M.S. 1910. Add: Manchester 1903; Harrow 1916; Macclesfield and London 1918. † L 22, M 23, NG 3, RA 29, RMS 59, SWA 1.

BROADHEAD, W. Smithson Exh. 1923-40 Portrait and horse painter. Add: London. † RA 6.

BROADHOUSE, Laurence J. Exh. 1936 Landscape painter. Add: London. † RA 1.

BROADLEY, Mrs. Kathleen Exh. 1913-14 Tracton Park, Cork, Ireland. † RHA 5.

BROATCH, A. Exh. 1889 Keswick. † M 1.

BROATCH, Miss A. Exh. 1890 4 Brunswick Square, London. † SWA 1.

BROCAS-CLAY, Mrs. Muriel J. Exh. 1913-19 The Folly, East Haddon, Northants. † LS 9.

BROCK, Caroline E. Exh. 1939 Watercolour landscape and flower painter. † AR 2.

BROCK, Charles Edmund 1870-1938 Portrait painter and illustrator. Brother of Henry Mathew and Richard Henry B. q.v. R.I. 1909. Add: Cambridge 1891. † GI 1, L 6, RA 7, RI 8, ROI 3, RSA 1.

BROCK, Miss D.S. Exh. 1932 61 Wickham Road, Beckenham, Kent. † RBA 1, SWA 1.

BROCK, Edmond Exh. 1903-38 Portrait painter. Add: Brondesbury, London 1903; Mayfield, Sussex 1907; St John's Wood, London 1919. † ALP 40, GI 3, L 10, RA 63, RI 3.

BROCK, Miss Ellen Exh. 1883-84 Figure painter. Add: The Hermitage, Guernsey, C.I. † D 1, M 1, RBA 2.

BROCK, Miss Edith M. Exh. 1905-15 Birmingham. † B 8, RA 5.

BROCK, Fannie Exh. 1883-93 Flower painter. Add: London. † RBA 1 SWA 1.

BROCK, Henry Mathew b. 1875 Painter and black and white artist. Brother of Charles Edmund and Richard Henry B q.v. R.I. 1906. Add: Cambridge. † B 5 GI 4, L 16, RA 12, RI 48, RSA 3.

BROCK, Richard Henry* Exh. 1897-1915 Brother of Charles Edmund and Henry Mathew B. q.v. Landscape painter. Add: Cambridge. † B 18, L 19, M 1, RA 8 RBA 3, RI 8, ROI 1.

BROCK, Sir Thomas 1847-1922 Sculptor. b. Worcester. Studied under John Henry Coley, RA Schools 1867 (gold medal 1869). On Foley's death Brock was commissioned to complete his unfinished works. Among his works is the Queen Victoria Memorial outside Buckingham Palace. A.R.A. 1883, R.A. 1891, H.R.B.A 1909, H.R.S.A. 1911. Knighted 1911. "A Moment of Peril" purchased by Chantry Bequest 1881. Add: 30 Osnaburgh St Regent's Park, London. † GI 3, L 7 RA 89, RI 1, ROI 2, RSA 8.

BROCK, T.A. Exh. 1904 Arundine House, Madingley Road, Cambridge. † RA 1.

BROCK, William b. 1874 Landscape and animal painter. Son of Sir Thomas B. q.v. Studied RA Schools and Ecole des Beaux Arts (gold medallist) Add: 30 Osnaburgh St. London 1897 and 1905; Eure, France 1904. † FIN 45, L 3 RA 11.

BROCKBANK, Albert Ernest b. 1862 Landscape painter. Studied Liverpool School of Art, London and Paris. R.B.A 1890. Add: Liverpool. † B 7, L 192 M 21, RA 26, RBA 35, RCA 47, RI 26.

BROCKBANK, Miss G.M. Exh. 1929 Sunny Brow, Heswall, Wirral. † L 2.

BROCKBANK, Miss Lily H. Exh. 188 Brockhurst, Didsbury. † M 1.

BROCKBANK, Marie Elizabeth b. 188 Painter and miniaturist. b. Settle, Yorks Studied Slade School. A.R.M.S. 1913 R.M.S. 1919. Add: Southport, Lancs 1905, Carnforth, Lancs. 1915. † B 6 GI 8, L 28, LS 26, M 9, RA 14, RCA 2 RMS 52, RSA 4, SWA 1.

BROCKELL, Jeanie F. Exh. 188 Animal portrait painter. Add: 4 Pembridge Gardens, London. † RA 1.

BROCKETT, Macfarlane Exh. 1910-2 29 Gibson St. Hillhead, Glasgow. † GI 5 L 9.

BROCKHURST, Gerald Leslie* b. 1890
Painter and etcher. Studied Birmingham School of Art, RA Schools 1907 (Landseer Studentship, Armitage medal, British Institute Studentship and gold medal). A.R.A. 1928, R.A. 1937, R.E. 1921, R.P. 1923. Add: London 1913, 1927 and 1930, Leighton Buzzard 1926; Withingham, Sussex 1929. † AB 4, AG 1, ALP 4, BA 7, BK 2, CG 10, CHE 86, CON 3, FIN 93, G 18, GI 12, L 13, LEI 3, M 1, P 23, RA 62, RE 36, RED 1, RHA 1, RSA 6, TOO 10.

BROCKIE, John Exh. 1908
54 Longland Road, Liscard, Cheshire. † L 1.

BROCKLEBANK, Miss A. Sylvia Exh. 1905
The Hollies, Woolton, Liverpool. † L 1.

BROCKLEBANK G. Exh. 1902-4
c/o Wm. Heatree, Havering, Tunbridge Wells, Kent 1902; 34 Bubbling Wee Road, Shanghai 1904. † L 2.

BROCKLEBANK, Rev. J.W.R.Exh. 1905-26
Landscape painter. Visited South Africa. Add: Heswall, Cheshire 1905; Warminster, Wilts. 1906. † AR 63, L 5.

BROCKLESBURY, Horace b. 1866
Landscape and seascape painter. Add: Elstree, Herts. 1902; Radlett, Herts. 1917. † M 1, RA 2.

BROCKMAN, Charles H. Drake Exh. 1880-1904
Landscape painter. Add: London 1880; Bruges, Belgium 1904. † D 2, L 1, M 2, RA 6, RBA 16, RI 1, ROI 5.

BROCKMAN, Nancy Exh. 1931-40
Landscape, figure and portrait painter. Add: London. † COO 15, NEA 5, RA 8, RBA 3.

BROCKMAN, Walter Exh. 1885
Figure painter. † ROI 2.

BROCKSMIT, Frederika H. Exh. 1908-11
19 Vollenhovenstraat, Rotterdam. † LS 9.

BROCQUY, le See L

BRODERICK, Muriel Alice 1910-1954
Etcher, designer and art teacher. Add: 14 Littledown Avenue, Queen's Park, Bournemouth. † RA 1.

BRODERSON, Miss Marie Exh. 1910-21
Liverpool. † L 2.

BRODIE, A.K. Exh. 1898
Interior painter. Add: 15 Rutland Square, Edinburgh. † RA 1.

BRODIE, C.E. Exh. 1884
37 Raeburn Place, Edinburgh. † RSA 1.

BRODIE, C.H. Exh. 1917
77 Park Lane, Croydon, Surrey. † RA 1.

BRODIE, Mrs. Douglas Exh. 1907
43 Elm Park Gardens, London. † RMS 1.

BRODIE, Gertrude Exh. 1902-21
Illustrator. A.S.W.A. 1916. Add: Epsom, Surrey 1902; London 1917; Settle, Yorks. 1921. † RA 1, RID 4, SWA 2.

BRODIE, Mrs. Grace I. Exh. 1887-1903
Aldridge Lodge, Nr. Walsall, Staffs. † B 3, RMS 2.

BRODIE, Miss Jessie A. Exh. 1880-92
Edinburgh. † RSA 15.

BRODIE, John Lamont Exh. 1881-83
Portrait, Landscape, coastal and historical painter. Add: Lander House, Wimbledon. † M 1, RA 1.

BRODIE, Miss Isabel Exh. 1940
57 Dahousie Street, Glasgow. † GI 1.

BRODIE, Mrs. Kate S. Exh. 1891-1900
Glasgow 1891 and 1895; Edinburgh 1892. † GI 9, RSA 11.

BRODIE, Margaret Exh. 1880
46 Chalcot Terrace, Primrose Hill, London. † SWA 1.

BRODIE, Nellie Exh. 1912
Mowbray, Bickley, Kent. † GI 1, L 2.

BRODIE, William 1815-1881
Sculptor. Studied Trustees School, Edinburgh, and Rome. A.R.S.A. 1852, R.S.A. 1859, Secretary R.S.A. 1876-1881. Add: St. Helens, Cambridge Street, Edinburgh. † GI 6, RA 3, RSA 13.

BRODMEIER, Miss Blanche Exh. 1903-5
5 John Dalton Street, Manchester. † L 1, M 1, RCA 1.

BRODRIBB, Francis A. Exh. 1936-40
Watercolour urban landscape painter. Add: Chapel Row, Bucklebury, Berks. † COO 10, RBA 1, RI 1.

BRODRIBB, Gladys Minola Exh. 1927-40
Pencil artist and etcher. Add: Yattendon, Berks. 1927; Reading, Berks. 1934. † COO 43, L 3, RA 1, RBA 1.

BRODRICK, T.L. Exh. 1933
12 Frognal Gardens, London. † L 3.

BRODRICK, William Exh. 1881
Domestic painter. Add: Littleshill, Chudleigh, Devon. † RA 1.

BRODSKY, Horace* b. 1855
Landscape and figure painter. b. Australia. Travelled Europe and U.S.A. Member London Group 1914. Add: Herne Hill, Kent and London. Exb. 1911-31. † ALP 28, GI 1, GOU 6, LS 18.

BROM, J. Exh. 1907
Drift 15, Utrecht, Holland. † RA 1.

BROMAN, Mrs. M. Clifford Exh. 1929-32
Flower painter. Add: 44 Queen's Gate Gardens, London. † RA 3.

BROMET, Mary Pownall Exh. 1889-1932
nee Pownall, Mrs. Alfred B. Sculptor. Studied Paris 1897 and Rome 1900. S.W.A. 1909. Add: Knutsford, Cheshire 1889; Birkenhead 1891; Paris 1897; Rome 1900; Watford, Herts. 1906. † B 4, GI 7, L 16, LS 10, M 3, RA 16, SWA 2.

BROMHEAD, Frank H. Exh. 1928
Architect. Add: Market Place, Chesterfield, Derbys. † RA 1.

BROMHEAD, Horatio K. Exh. 1897-1915
243 St. Vincent Street, Glasgow. † GI 2.

BROMILOW, John G. Exh. 1886
Stained glass artist. Add: 3 Titchborne Street, Edgware Road, London. † RA 1.

BROMLEY, Albert N. Exh. 1890-1922
Architect. N.S.A. 1917. Add: Nottingham. † N 3, RA 3.

BROMLEY, Alice Louisa Maria Exh. 1880-93
nee Atkinson. Married Valentine Walter B. (1848-1877). Landscape painter. Add: London. † B 7, G 3, GI 11, M 2, NG 3, RBA 6, RI 7, ROI 3, SWA 9, TOO 4.

BROMLEY, C. Shailor Exh. 1882-85
Landscape and fruit painter. Add: London 1882; Rochford, Essex 1885. † RBA 8.

BROMLEY, Clough W. Exh. 1880-1904
Landscape and flower painter and engraver. Add: London. † B 2, D 1, DOW 1, FIN 1, L 12, M 11, RA 15, RBA 12, RHA 2, RI 2, ROI 7.

BROMLEY, F. Exh. 1885
Penzance, Cornwall. † L 1.

BROMLEY, H.T. Exh. 1883-1938
Birmingham 1883; London 1938. † B 5, L 1, ROI 1.

BROMLEY, John Mallard* Exh. 1880-1904
Landscape painter. R.B.A. 1888. Add: London 1880 and 1888; Rochford, Essex. 1885; St. Ives, Cornwall 1897. † B 2, DOW 30, G 2, L 14, M 7, RA 17, RBA 87, RI 11, ROI 4.

BROMLEY, Miss L. Exh. 1909-13
128 Wilberforce Road, Leicester. † N 3.

BROMLEY, William* Exh. 1880-88
Historical and genre painter. Grandson of William B. the engraver 1769-1842, and father of Valentine B. 1848-1877. R.B.A. 1860. Add: London. † B 6, L 2, RBA 37.

BROMLEY, Walter Louis Exh. 1880-82
Watercolour painter. Add: London. † D 1, RBA 3.

BROMLEY-MARTIN, Miss Annora Exh. 1898-1905
Ham Court, Upton-on-Severn, and London. † B 1, L 5, M 1, NG 2.

BRONNE, Clive R. Exh. 1933
Kirdale, Waltham, Lincs. † RBA 2.

BROOK, Arthur B. Exh. 1933
Portrait painter. Add: Newlands, Clarence Road, Hale, Cheshire. † RA 2.

BROOK, Caroline W. Exh. 1883-88
Mrs. T. Domestic and figure painter. Add: Stoke Newington 1883; Hampstead, London 1884. † B 2, L 5, M 2, RA 2, RBA 8, ROI 2, SWA 2.

BROOK, Miss Helen Exh. 1926-36
Landscape painter. † BA 1, NEA 1.

BROOK, J. Exh. 1930
Victoria, London. † SWA 1.

BROOK, Marian Burnham Exh. 1880-89
Portrait and figure painter. Add: Clifton Villa, Albert Road, Peckham, London. † B 3, L 1, RA 3, RHA 6.

BROOKBANK, W.H. Exh. 1883-87
Landscape painter. Add: 12 Lyme Street, London. † RBA 1, RI 1.

BROOKE, Miss Angel S. Exh. 1905
14 Herbert Street, Dublin. † RHA 2.

BROOKE, Arthur S. Exh. 1894-1900
Landscape painter. Add: Yvorne sur Aigle, Vaud, Switzerland. † RID 11.

BROOKE, Miss B.R.P. Exh. 1914
20 Gladhow Gardens, Kensington, London. † LS 3.

BROOKE, E.F. Exh. 1922-26
Rockside, Carlton, Nottingham. † N 4.

BROOKE, Miss E.F. Exh. 1898-1903
Craven Hill Gardens, London. † L 1, SWA 2.

BROOKE, Edmund W. Exh. 1890-91
Landscape and portrait painter. Add: 16 Rue de la Grande Chaumiere, Paris. † RA 2.

BROOKE, F. William Exh. 1886-99
Landscape painter. Add: London 1886; Saxmundham, Suffolk 1887; St. Ives, Cornwall 1896. † B 2, L 6, M 1, RA 3, RBA 6, RI 1.

BROOKE, G.W. Exh. 1892
Figure painter. † FIN 1.

BROOKE, Helen E. Exh. 1908-9
34 de Vere Gardens, Kensington, London. † LS 8.

BROOKE, John Exh. 1883
Etcher. Add: 27 Allen Terrace, Chelsea, London. † RA 1.

BROOKE, John Exh. 1889-97
Architect. Add: 18 Exchange Street, Manchester. † RA 9.

BROOKE, John W. Exh. 1886-1923
Portrait painter. Add: 32 Basinghall Street, Leeds. † B 5, GI 2, GOU 1, L 25, M 2, P 3, RA 12, RSA 1.

BROOKE, Leonard Leslie c.1863-1940
Portrait and figure painter and illustrator (e.g. Nonsense songs of Edward Lear). Add: London 1887 and 1911; Harwell, Berks. 1899. † B 2, BG 121, L 13, LEI 1, M 1, NG 21, P 7, RA 12, RI 1, RSW 1.

BROOKE, M. Exh. 1885
Burnham, Berks. † RHA 1.

BROOKE, Percy Exh. 1894-1916
Blackburn, Lancs. 1894 and 1902; Staithes, Yorks 1898. † L 4, RA 3, RBA 1, RI 2.

BROOKE, The Rev. Stopford A. **Exh. 1897-1905**
1 Manchester Square, London. † NG 7, RHA 1.

BROOKER, Miss Catherine P. **Exh. 1881-1915**
Portrait and figure painter. Add: London. † P 1, RA 3, RBA 1, RI 2, SWA 1.

BROOKER, Harry* Exh. 1880-1908
Domestic, genre and child painter. Add: London. † RA 3, RBA 2.

BROOKER, Peter b. 1900
Figure painter. Studied Slade School. Assistant teacher Slade School. Add: London. † GOU 7, NEA 7.

BROOKES, G.L. Exh. 1939-40
Harborne, Birmingham 1939, Kings Lynn, Norfolk 1940. † B 1, RCA 4.

BROOKES, Hubert M. Exh. 1933-38
Hall Green, Birmingham. † B 5.

BROOKES, Kenneth b. 1897
Watercolour painter, illustrator and poster artist. Add: London 1934; Harrow, Middlesex 1938. † AR 1, RI 7.

BROOKES, May Exh. 1933
Flower painter. b. Australia. Travelled widely. † WG 56.

BROOKES, R.W. Exh. 1884
Sculptor. Add: 3 Ravenswood Terrace, Balham, London. † RA 1.

BROOKES, Warwick Exh. 1880
† AG 1.

BROOK-HANSEN, Theo Exh. 1896
Figure painter. Add: London 1896. Went to Australia c. 1904. † L 1, RA 2.

BROOKING, Mrs. F.F. Exh. 1896
5 St. Stephen's Crescent, Bayswater, London. † SWA 1.

BROOKMAN, Vera E. Exh. 1932-35
Portrait painter. Add: London 1932; Southsea, Hants. 1935. † RA 2.

BROOKS, Miss Alice L. Exh. 1903-37
309 Burbury St. Lozells, Birmingham. † B 6.

BROOKS, Andrew W. Exh. 1931
100 Morley Road, Ward End, Birmingham. † B 1.

BROOKS, Cecil Exh. 1902-14
Architect. Add: Harpenden, Herts 1902; London 1914. † RA 2.

BROOKS, Christian Exh. 1937
† P 2.

BROOKS, Edith M. Exh. 1938
Four Winds, Cornwallis Avenue, Tonbridge, Kent. † M 1, RBA 2.

BROOKS, Frank 1854-1937
Portrait and landscape painter. Son of Henry B. q.v. Add: Salisbury 1880; London 1890; Lyndhurst, Herts 1926. † L 1, LS 8, NG 1, RA 22, RBA 1, RI 3, RMS 14, ROI 2.

BROOKS, Miss F.C. **Exh. 1882-84**
London. † GI 1, RSA 1.

BROOKS, H. Exh. 1882
The Poplars, Shipton, Abingdon, Berks. † M 2.

BROOKS, Henry Exh. 1891
Figure and landscape painter. Father of Frank B. q.v. Add: Salisbury. † B 1, RA 2, RI 1.

BROOKS, Henry Jamyn Exh. 1890-1909
Portrait painter. Add: London. † LS 3, NG 2, RA 4.

BROOKS, Miss Iris Exh. 1925-31
Stained glass artist. Add: 162 Dibble Road, Smethwick. † RA 6.

BROOKS, Ivan Exh. 1937
† NEA 1.

BROOKS, Jacob b. 1877
Landscape, portrait and figure painter and poster designer. Studied Birmingham School of Art, Antwerp Academy and Cape Town. Add: Birmingham. † B 36, GI 1, L 3, RA 4, RI 1.

BROOKS, James 1825-1901
Architect. Add: 35 Wellington Street, Strand, London. † RA 26.

BROOKS, John C.V. Exh. 1938-39
Landscape painter. Add: Four Winds, Cornwallis Avenue, Tonbridge, Kent. † NEA 1, RA 1, RBA 1.

BROOKS, J. Martin Exh. 1887
Architect. Add: 35 Wellington Street, Strand, London. † RA 1.

BROOKS, Kathleen Exh. 1917-26
Portrait painter, miniaturist and church decorator. Studied RA Schools. Add: Eagle Cottage, High Street Hornsey, London. † RA 5, RHA 7.

BROOKS, Louie b. 1900
Birmingham 1926; Codsall, nr. Wolverhampton 1929. † B 7, M 1.

BROOKS, Maria Exh. 1880-90
Portrait and figure painter. Add: London. † B 5, FIN 1, G 4, GI 3, L 14, M 6, RA 13, RBA 18, RHA 2, ROI 3, RSA 1, SWA 1.

BROOKS, Marjorie b. 1904
Mrs. W.G. Holford. Landscape and figure painter. Studied L.C.C. Central School and RA Schools (gold medal and Edward Stott travelling studentship 1927, bronze medals for design, decoration and figure painting). Add: Hornsey, London 1928; Liverpool 1935. † L 1, M 1, RA 5.

BROOKS, Maie L. Exh. 1907-33
Portrait and figure painter and miniaturist. Studied under M. Durant. Add: Hampstead, London. † AB 2, B 5, L 30, P 10, RA 3.

BROOKS, Romaine Exh. 1905-11
Figure painter and etcher. Add: 32 Tite Street, Chelsea, London. † GOU 17, I 2.

BROOKS, Samuel Exh. 1883
Figure painter. Add: 35 Howland Street, Fitzroy Square, London. † RA 1.

BROOKS, T. Exh. 1882
3 St. Helens Terrace, Alexandra Park, Hastings. † L 1.

BROOKS, Thomas* 1818-1891
Genre painter. Studied under H.P. Briggs, R.A. (1791-1844). Add: Kensington, London. † GI 1, RA 2.

BROOKS-TAYLOR, Mrs. M. Exh. 1914
Kenilworth, Neath, Wales. † LS 2.

BROOM, Miss F. Exh. 1901
c/o Countess of Ranfurly, Government House, Wellington, New Zealand. † RI 1.

BROOM, Marion Exh. 1925-39
Flower, landscape and interior painter and operatic singer. Add: High Wycombe, Bucks. † AB 2, AR 2, B 12, COO 8, GI 2, L 11, RA 1, RCA 3, RHA 1, RI 2, ROI 3, SWA 1.

BROOME, Angela Exh. 1905
Mrs. Ralph. Add: The Gables, Lansdown Road, Cheltenham. † B 1.

BROOME, S. Exh. 1884
Elmhurst, Batheaston, Bath. † SWA 1.

BROOMFIELD, George Henry b. 1891
Painter and figure designer. Studied Royal College of Art (King's prize winner). Add: Manchester 1925. † L 4, M 4, RCA 1.

BROOMHALL, Samuel Exh. 1885-1930
Liverpool. † L 14.

BROPHY, A. Finn Exh. 1895-98
Miniature painter and enamellist. Add: 11 Rathbone Place, London. † NG 1, RA 3.

BROPHY, N.A. Exh. 1880-83
Limerick. † RHA 8.

BROQUET, Leon Exh. 1913
Marcilly sur Seine, France. † L 1.

BROTCHIE, James Rainy 1909-1956
Studied Glasgow School of Art (prizeman 1930-31). Assistant curator art department Kelvingrove Art Gallery 1932-36. Son of Theodore Charles Ferdinand B. q.v. Add: Glasgow 1938 and 1940; Edinburgh 1939. † GI 1, RSA 4.

BROTCHIE, Theodore Charles Ferdinand b.1876
Painter and writer. b. Ceylon. Studied Edinburgh School of Art. Director The Art Galleries, Glasgow 1920. Exh. 1915-27. † GI 21.

BROTHERS, Alf Exh. 1882-93
Manchester. † M 16.

BROTHERS, K.E.A. Exh. 1901
6 Rye Hill Park, Peckham Rye. † RBA 2.

BROUCKERE, de See D

BROUET, Auguste b. 1872
French etcher. † FIN 17.

BROUET, L. Exh. 1923
Etcher. † FIN 8.

BROUGH, Alan b. 1890
Sculptor. Studied Manchester School of Art (Primrose bronze medal). Add: The Studio, Wilmslow, Cheshire 1926. † L 1, M 2.

BROUGH, Miss C. **Exh. 1883-84**
Clarendon Terrace, Dundee. † RSA 2.

BROUGH, Mrs. M. Bartlam Exh. 1920-30
Portrait painter. Add: London 1920; Longton, Staffs. 1923. † L 5, RA 1.

BROUGH, Robert 1872-1905
Portrait painter. Died in a rail accident aged 32. R.P. 1900, A.R.S.A. 1904. Add: Edinburgh 1893; Kirkcaldy 1894; Aberdeen 1895; London 1897. † GI 12, I 3, L 10, M 4, NG 13, P 19, RA 7, RSA 24.

BROUGH, Winifred M. Exh. 1911-22
London. † RA 1, SWA 2.

BROUGHTON, Miss B.H. Exh. 1895
Elstowe, nr. Guildford, Surrey. † SWA 2

BROUGHTON, Emily J. Exh. 1880-82
Figure painter. Add: 27 Moreton Terrace Pimlico, London. † D 1, RA 1, RBA 1.

BROUGHTON, Miss Isabel Exh. 1891-1909
Moseley, Birmingham. † B 9.

BROUGHTON, P. Exh. 191
171 Griffin Road, Plumstead, London † RA 1.

BROUGIER, Adolph Exh. 1903-1
R.B.A. 1905. Add: London. † B 1, L 1 RA 11, RBA 38.

BROUILLET, Pierre Aristide Andre 1857-191
French artist. Add: Paris 1901. † L 2.

BROUN-MORISON, Guy E. Exh. 1901-1
R.O.I. 1904. Add: London 1901; Pari 1905; Errol, N.B. 1911. † I 5, L 1 ROI 21.

BROUNCKER, Ista Exh. 194
† COO 1.

BROW, Miss W.D. Exh. 1917-1
34 Miskin Road, Dartford, Kent † SWA 5.

BROWN, A. Exh. 188
Mound, Edinburgh. † RSA 2.

BROWN, Anthony Exh. 1936-3
† M 3, RED 1.

BROWN, Mrs. Anthony Exh. 1910-1
Beckenham, Kent. † SWA 4.

BROWN, Mrs. A.A. Exh. 193
1 Branksome Close, Norwich, Norfolk † ROI 1.

BROWN, Annie Beatrice d. 193
nee Derbyshire. Married Samuel John Milton B. q.v. Add: Wallasey, Cheshire 1928. † L 4.

BROWN, A.E. Exh. 1892
Etcher and black and white artist. Add: Westfield View, Mansfield, Notts. † N 2.

BROWN, Miss Alice G. Exh. 1889-92
Figure and domestic painter. Add: Bryn-Hyfryd, Harrow-on-the-Hill, Middlesex. † RA 6, RID 1.

BROWN, Alexander Kellock 1849-1922
Landscape painter. R.I. 1878, A.R.S.A. 1892, R.S.A. 1908, R.S.W. 1878. Add: Glasgow. † B 3, D 1, DOW 2, G 3, GI 115, I 6, L 54, M 24, NG 5, RA 31, RBA 6, RI 20, ROI 5, RSA 121, RSW 125, TOO 2.

BROWN, Mrs. A.L. Exh. 1902
Chieveley, Boldmere Road, Erdington, Birmingham. † B 1.

BROWN, Miss A.M. Exh. 1884
173 Berners Street, Birmingham. † B 1.

BROWN Mrs. A.T. Exh. 1902
Barnbarroch, Whamp Hill, Scotland. † SWA 2.

BROWN, Anne Werge Exh. 1904
Cottesmore, Brighton, Sussex. † GI 1.

BROWN, Anna Wood Exh. 1908-21
Figure painter. Add: Paris 1908; c/o Rowley Gallery, London 1921. † BG 2, LS 5, NEA 1.

BROWN, Miss B. Exh. 1908
Mrs. Boese. Add: Lyceum Club, Piccadilly, London. † RA 1.

BROWN, Miss Bessie Exh. 1885
Stanhope House, Park Road, Wandsworth, London. † G 1.

BROWN, Miss Betty Exh. 1925-32
32 Croxteth Road, Sefton Park, Liverpool. † L 3.

BROWN, Beatrice A.M. Exh. 1884-1901
Sculptor. Add: Beckenham, Kent 1884; London 1893; Worcester 1900. † B 3, G 5, GI 1, L 4, RA 6, RBA 1.

BROWN, Benjamin B. Exh. 1901-19
50 Dick Place, Edinburgh. † RSA 9.

BROWN, Miss B. May Exh. 1918-40
Watercolour painter. Add: St. Andrews 1918; London 1936. † GI 5, RSA 19, RSW 20.

BROWN, Cecil b. 1902
Architect and painter. Add: London 1940. † RA 1.

BROWN, Cecil Exh. 1888-1925
Sculptor. Add: London and Newbury, Berks. 1906; Godalming, Surrey 1908; Bedford 1921. † B 1, GI 16, L 19, M 12, NG 2, RA 23, RHA 1, ROI 1, RSA 3.

BROWN, Charlotte Exh. 1909
LS 3.

BROWN, Cormack Exh. 1885-87
26 Castle Street, Edinburgh. † RSA 4.

BROWN, Colin C. Exh. 1939-40
Portobello 1939; Corstorphine 1940. † RSA 2.

BROWN, Mrs. Constance E. Exh. 1924-40
Watercolour landscape and flower painter and teacher. Married to Harry V. q.v. A.S.W.A. 1927. Add: Cambridge. † GI 1, L 2, RA 14, RHA 4, SWA 19.

BROWN, Charles H. Exh. 1936-38
Watercolour landscape, fruit and flower painter. Add: Gedling, Notts. † N 3.

BROWN, Charles Sidney Exh. 1889-95
Edinburgh. † GI 3, RSA 9, RSW 2.

BROWN, C. Tim Exh. 1938
Sculptor. Add: London. † GI 1, RA 2.

BROWN, Celia V. Exh. 1927-34
Mrs. G. Boelens. Landscape and figure painter. Visited Europe, N. Africa and Ceylon. A.N.S.A. 1930, N.S.A. 1934. Add: Greystones, Attenborough, Notts. † COO 36, N 16.

BROWN, Miss D. Exh. 1917
Rothes, Moray. † SWA 2.

BROWN, D. Burns Exh. 1906-28
Sculptor. Add: London. † L 1, RA 17, ROI 1.

BROWN, Davina F. Exh. 1904-38
Pollokshields, N.B. 1904; Glasgow 1913. † GI 65, L 2.

BROWN, Denise L. Exh. 1934-40
Etcher. Add: London. † RA 6.

BROWN, E. Exh. 1889-90
Liverpool. † L 3.

BROWN, Edward b. 1869
Watercolour landscape painter. b. Ancaster, Lincs. Studied Slade School. R.B.A. 1904. Add: Bedford. † B 5, D 21, L 1, M 2, RA 6, RBA 93, RI 5.

BROWN, Elizabeth Exh. 1931-36
† NEA 3.

BROWN, Evelyn Exh. 1928-40
Hamilton, N.B. 1928; Ayr 1940. † GI 6, RSW 1.

BROWN, Edward Archibald Exh. 1900-3
Fruit painter. Add: Hertford. † RA 4.

BROWN, Miss Ella A. Exh. 1895-1902
Miniature portrait painter. Add: Bryn-Hyfryd, Harrow, Middlesex 1895; Kingston-on-Thames, Surrey 1900; York 1902. † RA 4, RCA 1, RHA 1, RMS 3.

BROWN, Miss E.B. Exh. 1907
7 Montague Road, Richmond, Surrey. † RA 1.

BROWN, Mrs. E.C. Austen Exh. 1903-31
Landscape painter and lino cut artist. Married Thomas Austen B. q.v. A.R.B.A. 1926, R.B.A. 1928. Add: London 1903; Etaples, de Calais, France 1913. † GOU 1, I 3, L 29, NG 11, RBA 23, RED 3, RID 1, ROI 1, RSA 2.

BROWN, Miss Ella G. Exh. 1887-88
Bird painter. Add: 14 Agnew Street, Lytham, Lancs. † RA 2, RSA 1.

BROWN, E. Hilda Exh. 1894-1927
Flower and landscape painter. Add: Nottingham 1894 and 1909; Alfreton, Notts. 1899; Ruddington, Notts. 1902; Sneinton, Notts. 1917. † N 56, SWA 2.

BROWN, E.M. Exh. 1899
19 Douglas Crescent, Edinburgh. † RSA 1.

BROWN, E.M. Exh. 1884
The Bank, Malvern, Worcs. † M 1.

BROWN, Ethel M. Exh. 1898-1911
Loughborough, Leics. 1898; London 1900; Leeds 1909. † B 1, L 4, N 1, SWA 2.

BROWN, Miss Eva M. Exh. 1927-32
Rawlings Well, Marlborough, Wilts. † B 4, SWA 2.

BROWN, Mrs. E.M.B. Exh. 1915
1 Belsize Grove Mansions, Belsize Grove, Hampstead, London. † RA 1.

BROWN, Miss Estelle T. Exh. 1922-26
Westholme, Hough Green, Widnes. † L 9.

BROWN, Miss E.W. Exh. 1928
17 Bracondale, Norwich, Norfolk. † L 4.

BROWN, Prof. Frederick* 1851-1941
Landscape, genre and portrait painter. b. Chelmsford. Studied Royal College of Art 1868-77 and Paris. Taught Westminster School of Art 1877-92. Professor Slade School 1892-1918. Founder member of N.E.A. 1886 (also compiled rules). Purchased by Chantrey Bequest "Portrait of the Painter" 1933 and "The Ivy Arch" 1940. Add: London and Richmond, Surrey. † AG 1, B 4, CHE 4, D 3, G 5, GI 8, GOU 57, L 15, M 4, NEA 146, RA 13, RBA 15, RED 1, RHA 2, ROI 3, RSA 2.

BROWN, Frances Emily Exh. 1903-8
Mrs. Shelton. Miniature painter. Add: Kingston-on-Thames 1903; Claygate, Surrey 1907; Cobham 1908. † LS 5, RA 2.

BROWN, F. Gregory 1887-1941
Landscape painter, illustrator, metal work and poster designer. R.B.A. 1914, R.O.I. 1917. Add: London. † I 16, L 2, RA 2, RBA 34, ROI 4.

BROWN, F.H. Exh. 1933
82 Rutland Street, Manchester. † L 2.

BROWN, Ford Maddox* 1821-1893
Landscape, historical, biblical and romantic genre painter. b. Calais. Studied Bruges, Ghent and Antwerp under Baron Wapper 1837-39; Paris 1841-44 and Rome. A collection of his works is in the Tate Gallery. Add: Manchester 1882; London 1891. † B 1, GI 2, L 4, M 7.

BROWN, Frederick May Exh. 1906-13
3 The Terrace, Alcombe, Taunton, Somerset. † GI 3, L 2, RA 1.

BROWN, Mrs. F.T. Exh. 1929
18 Mather Avenue, Mossley Hill, Liverpool. † L 1.

BROWN, George Exh. 1888-1911
Tranmere 1888; Aberdeen 1892; Paisley 1893; Glasgow 1895. † GI 8, L 2, RSW 2.

BROWN, Gerald Exh. 1919
Memorial architect. Add: 3 Suffolk Road, Barnes, Surrey. † RA 1.

BROWN, G. Allan Exh. 1913-33
Lower Bebington, Cheshire 1913; Liverpool 1933. † L 14.

BROWN, Prof. Gerard Baldwin 1849-1932
Author; Professor of Ancient History. R.S.A. 1911; Watson-Gordon Professor of Fine Art, University of Edinburgh 1880-1930. Exh. 1882-83. † L 1, RSA 1.

BROWN, George Henry Alan b. 1862
Portrait and figure painter. b. at sea. Studied Liverpool School of Art. Add: Liverpool and Bebington. Exh. 1894-1928. † L 89.

BROWN, G. Lunell Exh. 1883-84
Figure painter. Add: 6 Hillmarten Road, Camden Road, London. † RA 1, RHA 1.

BROWN, Major General G.R. Exh. 1887
5 Pittville Crescent, Cheltenham, Glos. † B 2.

BROWN, G.T. Exh. 1908
c/o A. Kelman, 215 St. Vincent Street, Glasgow. † RA 1.

BROWN, H. Exh. 1912
School of Art, Falmouth, Cornwall. † RA 1.

BROWN, Mrs. Hannah b. 1886
Landscape painter. Studied Italy 1926-37. Add: Villa le Pozzarelle, Via del Bargellino, Fiesole, Italy 1930. † RA 1.

BROWN, Harold Exh. 1938
37 Denorrton Park, Belfast, Ireland. † RHA 1.

BROWN, Harry Exh. 1912-38
Landscape and flower painter, and teacher. Add: Cambridge. † L 4, RA 9.

BROWN, Miss Helen Exh. 1883-1903
Watercolour flower painter. Add: Forest Gate, London 1883 and New Barnet, Herts. 1903. † RA 3, RI 5.

BROWN, Henrietta Exh. 1902
127 Pevril Avenue, Shawlands, Glasgow. † GI 2.

BROWN, H.B. Exh. 1894-95
† TOO 4.

BROWN, Hugh Boycott b. 1909
Landscape painter and black and white artist. Art Master Masonic Junior School, Bushey, Herts. Exh. 1933-37. † RBA 4, RI 1, ROI 2.

BROWN, Henry Harris* b. 1864
Portrait painter. R.P. 1900. Add: Northampton 1889; London 1891. † B 2, FIN 1, GI 9, I 1, L 19, M 5, NG 28, P 174, RA 55, RBA 1, RHA 10.

BROWN, H.J. Exh. 1881-85
Kingstown, Ireland 1881; London 1885. † RHA 13.

BROWN, Henry James Stuart 1871-1941
Etcher and watercolour painter. Add: Cambuslang, N.B. 1896; Lochwinnoch, Renfrews. 1915; Glasgow 1925; Torpichen, Linlithgowshire 1928. † CG 113, GI 3, RA 1, RSA 8, RSW 1.

BROWN, Henry K. Exh. 1880
3 Abbey Street, Norton Park, Edinburgh. † RSA 1.

BROWN, Helen Paxton Exh. 1901-40
Glasgow 1901; Kirkcudbright 1929. † GI 34, L 12, RSA 18, RSW 1.

BROWN, H.W. Jennings d. c.1887
Eastbourne, Sussex 1880; Dundee 1885; Edinburgh 1886. † RHA 1, RSA 23.

BROWN, Mrs. Isabella Exh. 1891-94
Edinburgh. † RSA 3.

BROWN, James Exh. 1886
143 Huddersfield Road, Oldham, Lancs. † M 1.

BROWN, James Exh. 1910-13
London 1910; Richmond, Surrey 1912. † LS 6, NEA 1.

BROWN, James Exh. 1928
48 Benview Street, Firhill, Glasgow. † GI 1.

BROWN, Miss Jean Exh. 1883-93
10 The Elms, Liverpool. † B 2, GI 2, L 3.

BROWN, John Exh. 1930-35
London 1930; Grimsby, Lincs. 1934. † RBA 2, RCA 2.

BROWN, John Exh. 1936-37
Woodhey, Dalmeny Road, Hamilton. † RSA 1, RSW 2.

BROWN, Joseph Exh. 1881-86
Engraver. Add: 61 Dartmouth Road, Forest Hill, London. † RA 7.

BROWN, Joseph d. 1923
Birmingham 1884 and 1905; Edinburgh 1885. † B 1, GI 4, RSA 23.

BROWN, John Alfred Arnesby 1866-1955
Landscape painter. Studied Nottingham and under Herkomer at Bushey, Herts. Married Mia Arnesby B. q.v. P.N.S.A. 1913, A.R.A. 1903, R.A. 1915, R.B.A. 1896, H.R.B.A. 1937. Knighted 1939. Purchased by Chantrey Bequest, "Morning" 1901, "Silver Morning" 1910 and "The Line of the Plough" 1919. Add: Pelham Crescent, The Park, Nottingham; St. Ives, Cornwall and The White House, Haddiscoe, Norwich, Norfolk. † B 11, BA 2, BAR 6, BK 1, CHE 1, DOW 2, FIN 10, G 6, GI 15, GOU 6, L 36, LEI 47, M 17, N 18, NG 8, RA 139, RBA 6, RHA 7, RSA 4, TOO 1.

BROWN, Mrs. J.C. Exh. 1937-38
3 Newnham Road, Edgbaston, Birmingham. † B 2.

BROWN, Miss Jessie C. Exh. 1937
c/o James McClure, Glasgow. † GI 1.

BROWN, J.E. Exh. 1901
4 Greek Street, Soho, London. † L 1.

BROWN, John George* 1831-1913
Domestic painter. Add: London 1880. † RA 2.

BROWN, Miss J.H. Exh. 1903
20 Glebe Road, Bromley, Kent. † SWA 1.

BROWN, J. Hullah Exh. 1914
Sandroyd Place, Cobham, Surrey. † LS 2.

BROWN, J.H.O. Exh. 1883
Orangefield, Ayr. † GI 1.

BROWN, John Lewis* 1829-1890
Paris. † GI 3.

BROWN, J. Michael Exh. 1880-1906
Landscape painter. Add: Edinburgh. † B 1, GI 31, L 17, M 1, RA 5, RBA 3, RHA 2, RSA 80, RSW 4.

BROWN, Miss J.M. Exh. 1886
2 Erldon Street, Edinburgh. † RSA 1.

BROWN, J.P. Exh. 1881
2 The Studios, London. † GI 2.

BROWN, J.R. Exh. 1886-99
Liverpool. † L 22, M 1.

BROWN, J.R. Exh. 1893
Southcliffe, North Malvern, Worcs. † B 2.

BROWN, J.S.C. McEwan Exh. 1922-30
Watercolour landscape painter. Studied in studio of sculptor J. Warrington Hogg. Lived near Christchurch, Hants. † WG 548.

BROWN, J. Taylor Exh. 1893-1940
Stewarton, Ayrshire. † GI 57, L 12, M 7, RSA 8.

BROWN, Miss J.W. Exh. 1882-83
18 Elizabeth Street, Liverpool. † L 3.

BROWN, Kellock 1856-1934
Sculptor. "Ju-Jitsu" purchased by Chantrey Bequest 1924. Add: Glasgow. † GI 89, L 6, RA 8, RSA 35, RSW 1.

BROWN, Kate C. Exh. 1893-94
Free St. Andrew's Manse, Kirkintilloch. † GI 2.

BROWN, Miss Kathleen R.H. Exh. 1921-29
Edinburgh. † RSA 3.

BROWN, Rev. L.G. Exh. 1920-26
St. James's Rectory, Wednesbury. † B 7, RCA 1.

BROWN, Miss L. Henrietta Exh. 1883-87
Sculptor. Add: 1A Phillimore Gardens, London. † L 13, RBA 1, SWA 1.

BROWN, Miss L.J. Exh. 1881-82
Bell's Mills House, Dean, Edinburgh. † RSA 2.

BROWN, M. Exh. 1889-95
Edinburgh. † GI 9, RSA 10, RSW 1.

BROWN, Miss Margaret Exh. 1881
Flower painter. Add: 2 Heathfield Gardens, Hampstead Heath, London. † D 1.

BROWN, Miss Margaret Exh. 1919
Portrait painter. Add: Athol House, Sidcup, Kent. † RA 1.

BROWN, Maynard Exh. 1883-1902
Historical and figure painter. Add: Nottingham 1883; London 1884. † RA 6, ROI 2.

BROWN, Miss Molly Exh. 1923
Ardcaien, Naas, Ireland. † RHA 1.

BROWN, Morse Exh. 1933
Carmarthen School of Art, S. Wales. † RBA 1.

BROWN, Mia Arnesby d. 1931
nee Edwards. Married John Alfred Arnesby B. q.v. Portrait and figure painter. b. Monmouthshire. Studied Herkomer School, Bushey, Herts. Add: Nottingham, St. Ives, and Haddiscoe, Norwich, Norfolk. † GI 1, GOU 4, L 3, M 1, N 1, NG 2, RA 36, ROI 1, SWA 2.

BROWN, Miss M. Baldwin Exh. 1884-1913
Edinburgh 1884; Nottingham 1913. † N 2, RSA 1.

BROWN, Miss M. Cooper Exh. 1896-1920
Landscape painter. Add: 96 South Hill Park, Hampstead, London. † L 1, LS 4, NG 1, RA 8, RBA 2, RI 4, ROI 8.

BROWN, Miss Margaret E. Exh. 1904-5
Handsworth, Birmingham. † B 3.

BROWN, Meta G. Napier Exh. 1903-6
Edinburgh. L 14, RSA 2.

BROWN, Margaret H. Exh. 1902-40
Musselburgh 1902; Liverpool 1912; Edinburgh 1913. † L 4, RSA 2, RSW 7.

BROWN, M. Hilda Exh. 1896
2 Sand Park, Shaldon, Teignmouth, Devon. † B 1.

BROWN, Mabel J. Exh. 1918-30
College of Art, Edinburgh 1918; Blundellsands, Liverpool 1929. † L 4, RSA 1.

BROWN, Mortimer, J. 1874-1966
Sculptor. "Shepherd Boy" purchased by Chantrey Bequest 1912. Add: London. † RA 26, RI 2, ROI 1.

BROWN, Margaret K. Exh. 1906
152A Renfrew Street, Glasgow. † GI 1.

BROWN, Marion Miller Exh. 1893-1938
Musselburgh 1893; Edinburgh 1895 and 1926; High Wycombe, Bucks. 1925. † GI 10, L 1, RSA 16, RSW 1.

BROWN, May Marshall b. 1887
nee Robertson. Married William Marshall B. q.v. Landscape and figure painter, etcher and teacher. Studied Royal Institute Edinburgh and Edinburgh College of Art. R.S.W. 1936. Add: Edinburgh. † GI 21, L 2, RSA 62, RSW 44.

BROWN, Mildred M.M. b. 1898
Painter and fan designer. Studied Preston, Blackburn, Liverpool and Manchester. Add: Manchester 1921; Marples, Cheshire 1922; Cheadle, Cheshire 1928. † L 17.

BROWN, Margaret T. Exh. 1910
Denney, Selkirk, N.B. † RSA 1.

BROWN, Miss Nana Exh. 1938-40
18 Howard Street, Kilmarnock. † GI 1, RSA 2.

BROWN, Miss Nellie Exh. 1894-1905
Watercolour painter. Add: The Studios, 57A Abbey Road, London. † L 2, RA 3, RMS 1, SWA 1.

BROWN, Miss N.F. Exh. 1920
Newhouse, Stirling. † GI 1.

BROWN, Nellie Gertrude Exh. 1931-40
Painter and black and white artist. Studied Wolverhampton School of Art. Add: Wolverhampton. † B 5, RA 1.

BROWN, Miss P. Exh. 1893
95 Colmore Row, Birmingham. † B 2.

BROWN, Peploe Exh. 1882-90
London. † G 11, L 3, ROI 2, RSA 2.

BROWN, Percy 1871-1935
Studied Birmingham School of Art 1885-89, Royal College of Art 1889-92. Principal Mayo School of Art and curator Museum, Lahore, India 1899-1909. Principal Govt. School of Art, Calcutta 1909-37. Exh. 1895. † B 1.

BROWN, Percy b. 1911
Sculptor and potter. Studied Royal College of Art. Teacher of sculpture Leicester College of Art. Add: London 1934; Leicester 1937. † RA 5.

BROWN, Peter Exh. 1935
18 Campview, Bonnyrigg, Dalkeith. † RSA 1.

BROWN, R. Exh. 1928
15 Bernard Street, Carrington, Notts. † N 2.

BROWN, Reginald Exh. 1930-37
Painter and etcher. Add: London 1930 Shoreham by Sea, Sussex 1937. † RA 2

BROWN, Robert Exh. 1901
98 Washington Street, Boston, U.S.A. † RSA 1.

BROWN, Mrs. Rachael Cassels Exh. 1905-31
Rockferry, Cheshire 1905; Liverpoo 1920. † L 15, NEA 3.

BROWN, R.M. Exh. 192
61 Whitworth Road, South Norwood London. † RA 1.

BROWN, Reginald Victor b. 189
Painter, designer and lecturer. Studied i Italy. Add: Manchester. † L 6, M 1 RCA 2.

BROWN, Robert William Exh. 1909-40
Dunning, Perthshire 1909; Ayr 1936. † GI 3, LS 3, RI 1.

BROWN, Samuel Exh. 1884-85
Highfield Terrace, Didsbury. † M 4.

BROWN, S.G. Exh. 1914
32 Girdler's Road, Brook Green, London. † RA 1.

BROWN, Samuel John Milton b. 1873
Marine painter. Studied Liverpool School of Art 1888-1900. Add: Liverpool 1894; Caerwys, Flints. 1937. † B 1, L 95, RCA 15, RI 1.

BROWN, Thea Exh. 1936
Figure and landscape painter. † COO 4.

BROWN, Thomas Exh. 1880
3 Castle Terrace, Edinburgh. † RSA 2.

BROWN, Tom Exh. 1907
202 Parliamentary Road, Glasgow. † GI 1.

BROWN, T.A. Exh. 1931
6 Allandale Road, Leicester. † N 3.

BROWN, Thomas Austen* 1857-1924
Landscape and domestic genre painter, etcher and woodcut artist. Studied R.S.A. Schools. Spent many summers abroad painting. R.I. 1888, A.R.S.A. 1889. Add: Edinburgh, London and Trepied, Etaples France. † AG 1, B 8, FIN 42, G 11, GI 34, GOU 4, I 11, L 46, LEI 56, M 17, NG 19, P 5, RA 31, RHA 1, RI 13, ROI 9, RSA 99.

BROWN, T. Bryant Exh. 1906-9
Wokefield Cottage, Mortimer, Berks. † L 2, RA 1.

BROWN, Thomas Harry b. 1881
Landscape painter, wood engraver and teacher. Studied Manchester. Add: Manchester 1915. † L 5, M 1, RCA 2.

BROWN, Thomas P. Exh. 1897-98
14 Mains Street, Glasgow. † GI 1, RSW 1.

BROWN, Thomas Stirling Exh. 1902-15
Shelford, Cambs. 1902; Woodbridge, Suffolk 1903; Drumchapel, Nr. Glasgow 1909; Glasgow 1911. † B 6, GI 2, L 7, RA 2, ROI 6, RSA 2.

BROWN, Violet Mary See COPESTICK

BROWN, Mrs. W. Exh. 1902-6
Pleyden, Sussex 1902; Manchester 1903. † B 1, M 3.

BROWN, Wegmuller Exh. 1886
3 Stanley Terrace, Norbiton. † D 1.

BROWN, William Exh. 1883-84
London. † D 1, GI 1.

BROWN, William Exh. 1893
151 New City Road, Glasgow. † GI 1.

BROWN, William Exh. 1940
63 Clouston Street, Glasgow. † GI 2.

BROWN, William Beattie* 1831-1909
Landscape painter. A.R.S.A. 1871, R.S.A. 1884. Add: Edinburgh. † GI 60, L 9, M 6, RA 8, RHA 4, RI 2, ROI 3, RSA 170.

BROWN, William Beattie Junr. Exh. 1898-1915
Served in armed forces World War 1. Add: Edinburgh 1898 and 1906. London 1920. † RSA 20.

BROWN, William Chalmers Exh. 1939-40
Edinburgh. † RSA 1, RSW 1.

BROWN, W.E. Exh. 1880-81
Chelsea, London. † D 3, RBA 3.

BROWN, William Fulton d. 1905
Watercolour painter. R.S.W. 1894. Add: Glasgow. † GI 31, L 4, RI 3, RSA 20, RSW 29.

BROWN, William Marshall* 1863-1936
Figure and landscape painter. Studied Royal Institute Edinburgh and R.S.A. Life School (Chelmers Bursary and Stewart prize). Bronze medal for anatomical studies at South Kensington. A.R.S.A. 1909, R.S.A. 1928, R.S.W. 1929. Add: Edinburgh. † AR 2, GI 78, L 19, RA 2, RCA 3, RSA 171, RSW 45.

BROWN, Winifred Sawley Exh. 1921-22
Lodore, Broughton Park, Manchester. † L 1, RCA 1.

BROWN, W. Talbot Exh. 1881-1909
Architect. Add: Wellingborough, Northants. † RA 3.

BROWN, W. Todd Exh. 1894-1920
Landscape painter. Add: London 1894; Weston Turville, Nr. Aylesbury, 1911. † GI 1, I 2, NEA 1, RA 1, RBA 3, ROI 3.

BROWNE, Archibald* Exh. 1912-24
Canadian landscape painter. † BA 1, GOU 38.

BROWNE, Alan Charlson b. 1903
Watercolour landscape painter. b. Blackpool. Studied Liverpool School of Art and School of Art, Christchurch, New Zealand. Add: Appley Bridge, Lancs. 1930. † L 3, RCA 7.

BROWNE, Alfred J. Warne d. 1915
Landscape and marine painter. Add: London 1884 and 1909; Ruan Minor, Cornwall 1895; Lower Shiplake, Oxon 1913. † DOW 3, FIN 57, L 4, RA 20, RI 5, ROI 2, TOO 2, WG 25.

BROWNE, Ben Exh. 1922
Watercolour landscape painter of scenes in Burma and Kashmir. † WG 83.

BROWNE, Charles Francis* Exh. 1890-1904
Paris 1890; Kirkcudbright 1904. † GI 2.

BROWNE, Clive Richard b. 1901
Landscape painter. Add: Habrough, Lincs. 1927; Waltham, Lincs. 1932. † B 6, RA 1, RBA 6, RCA 1, RHA 5, ROI 12, RSA 3.

BROWNE, Emilie A. Exh. 1881-94
Beech Lawn, Leamington, Warwicks. † B 6, GI 1.

BROWNE, Miss E. Warne Exh. 1939
Lino-cut artist. Add: Blewbury, Didcot, Berks. † RA 1.

BROWNE, Florence Crichton Exh. 1885-89
Sculptor. Add: 7 Cumberland Terrace, Regent's Park, London. † G 1, RBA 3, RSA 1.

BROWNE, Geoffrey E. Exh. 1906-22
Landscape painter. Add: Paris 1906; London 1914. † I 1, RA 2, RI 1.

BROWNE, George Elmer* Exh. 1909
Paris. † RSW 1.

BROWN, Gordon Frederick 1858-1932
Painter and illustrator. Son of Hablot Knight B. ("Phiz"). R.B.A. 1891, R.I. 1896. Add: London 1886 and 1911; South Hayling, Hants. 1908; Richmond, Surrey 1916. † B 2, GI 5, L 17, LS 5, M 1, RA 17, RBA 26, RI 132, ROI 4.

BROWNE, George H.* Exh. 1880-85
Marine and landscape painter. Add: 14 Royal Place, Greenwich. † D 4, RA 1.

BROWNE, Sir George Washington 1853-1939
Architect. H.R.A. 1924, H.R.M.S. 1931, A.R.S.A. 1892, R.S.A. 1902, P.R.S.A. 1930. Treasurer R.S.A. 1917-24, R.S.W. 1933, Knighted 1927. Add: Edinburgh. † GI 9, RA 1, RSA 60.

BROWNE, H. Exh. 1913
† TOO 2.

BROWNE, Harold Exh. 1899-1902
N.S.A. 1908. Add: Nottingham. † N 18.

BROWNE, Hamilton Exh. 1886
Allington House, Lewin Road, Streatham. † RI 1.

BROWNE, Mrs. Heitland Exh. 1885-86
Portrait painter and enamel on copper artist. Add: London. † RBA 3.

BROWNE, Mme Henriette* 1829-1901
Nee de Saux. H.R.I. 1867. Add: Paris. † RI 5.

BROWNE, Harry E.J.* Exh. 1891-1917
Figure and landscape painter. Add: London. † DOW 1, GI 4, L 11, NG 2, RA 11, RI 13, ROI 23.

BROWNE, H. Needham Exh. 1910-13
Served Armed Forces World War 1. Add: London 1910; Horsmonden, Kent 1912. † L 3.

BROWNE, Irene M. Exh. 1908-36
Sculptor. Studied Chelsea Polytechnic School of Art. A.R.M.S. 1923, R.M.S. 1929, A.S.W.A. 1927. Add: Sutton, Surrey 1908; London 1911; Horeham Road, Sussex 1932. † GI 1, I 1, L 21, RA 10, RHA 1, RMS 33.

BROWNE, James Loxham Exh. 1890-1905
Landscape and figure painter. Add: Woodbine Cottage, The Vale, Hampstead, London. † L 7, M 1, RA 20, RBA 3, RI 1.

BROWNE, J. Lennox Exh. 1885-1902
Landscape painter. Add: London. † D 1, DOW 1, L 1, RA 2, RBA 2, RI 9.

BROWNE, James R. Exh. 1888-89
c/o V. Smith, Springfield Place, Barnsley, Yorks. † L 1, M 1, RHA 2.

BROWNE, K.M. Exh. 1936-39
London. † GI 1, RSA 1.

BROWNE, Montague Exh. 1884-1902
Leicester 1884; Birkenhead 1902. † L 2, N 3.

BROWNE, Nassau Blair d. 1940
Landscape and animal painter. A.R.H.A. 1901, R.H.A. 1903. Add: Dublin 1894, 1904 and 1932; Kilkenny 1895; Fareham, Hants. 1925. † RHA 122.

BROWNE, Nina Jemmett Exh. 1894-1916
Watercolour painter, coloured wax and black and white artist. b. Cheltenham, Glos. Studied South Kensington. Add: London 1894; Oxford 1909. † L 2, RA 12, RI 1.

BROWNE, Peter C. Exh. 1900
7 Laurel Terrace, Edinburgh. † RSA 1.

BROWNE, Thomas Exh. 1920
Stained glass artist. Add: 36 Church Lane, Smethwick, Birmingham. † RA 1.

BROWNE, Tom 1872-1910
Figure painter and illustrator. R.B.A. 1898, R.I. 1901, R.M.S. 1900. Add: 15 Sherwin Street, Nottingham and Wollaton, Hardy Road, Westcombe Park, Blackheath, London. † B 3, BRU 86, FIN 23, GI 9, L 14, M 2, N 57, RA 9, RBA 86, RI 35, RMS 1.

BROWNE, Mrs. Willcocks Exh. 1934
† COO 1.

BROWNING, Miss A.E. Exh. 1919
† SWA 2.

BROWNING, Mrs. A.G. Exh. 1933
34 Mimosa Road, Liverpool. † L 1.

BROWNING, Amy Katherine b. 1882
Portrait and flower painter. Married Thomas Cantrell Dugdale q.v. Studied Royal College of Art and Paris. R.O.I. 1915, S.W.A. 1922. Add: London 1906 and 1919; Ampthill, Beds. 1912. † BA 5, CHE 5, COO 1, GI 5, I 3, L 4, M 1, NEA 10, P 6, RA 52, RHA 1, RID 3, ROI 78, RSA 1, SWA 48.

BROWNING, B.A. Exh. 1929-34
Landscape painter. † AB 3, WG 6.

BROWNING, Miss Colleen* Exh. 1937
Figure painter. Add: Chimneys, Amesbury, Wilts. † RA 2.

BROWNING, Charles William Exh. 1914-21
Hampstead, London. † LS 17.

BROWNING, Miss E.A. Exh. 1884-85
Yew Bank, Sale, Manchester. † M 2.

BROWNING, George Exh. 1880-83
Rathmines, Ireland. † RHA 6.
BROWNING, Hugh L. Exh. 1932-37
Flower and urban landscape painter. Add: London. † RA 3.
BROWNING, Miss M. Exh. 1908
9 Cadogan Square, London. † RA 1.
BROWNING, Robert Barrett* 1846-1912
Painter and sculptor. Son of Robert and Elizabeth B. Studied in Antwerp and Paris. Add: London 1880-89. † G 14, GI 1, L 1, M 8, RA 8.
BROWNLIE, Jeanie H. Exh. 1893
Springbank, Lenzie, Nr. Glasgow. † GI 1.
BROWNLIE, James Miller Exh. 1895-1921
Strathbungo 1895; Glasgow 1908. † GI 12, L 4, RSA 1, RSW 2.
BROWNLIE, Miss L. Exh. 1883
North Road, Parrhead, Glasgow. † GI 1.
BROWNLIE, R.A. Exh. 1887-91
Coastal and figure painter. Add: Glasgow. † DOW 4, GI 7, L 3, NEA 2, RSA 5, RSW 5.
BROWNLOW, Charles S. Exh. 1937
Sporting painter. † AR 141.
BROWNLOW, Charles V. Exh. 1892
Engraver. Add: Earlsmead Road, South Tottenham, London. † RA 1.
BROWNRIGG, Ann Exh. 1935
Landscape and flower painter. † COO 35.
BROWNRIGG, Dorothy Exh. 1935
Landscape and flower painter. † COO 14.
BROWNRIGG, Miss E.J.D. Exh. 1902-4
Portrait painter. Add: Portrush, Co. Antrim, Ireland. † RA 2.
BROWNSCOMBE, Miss Jennie Exh. 1900
Figure painter. Add: 12 Haymarket, London. † RA 1.
BROWNSWORD, Harold b. 1885
Sculptor. Studied Hanley School of Art and Royal College of Art 1908-13. Sculpture teacher 1914-38; Headmaster Regent St. Polytechnic 1938. Add: London. † GI 3, L 7, RA 29, RI 1.
BROWNSWORD, Harry A. Exh. 1882-96
Landscape and figure painter. N.S.A. 1888, R.B.A. 1894. Add: Nottingham. † N 23, RA 3, RBA 12.
BROWTON, Miss Jessie M. Exh. 1933
Figure painter. Add: 50 Manor Road, Stoke Newington, London. † RA 1.
BROXTON, Thomas b. 1871
Landscape, marine and figure painter. Add: Liverpool. † L 11.
BROZIK, de See D
BRUCE, Mrs. Carmichael Exh. 1883-84
Watercolour flower painter. Add: London. † RBA 2, RI 3.
BRUCE, Mrs. Edith Exh. 1936-39
23 Regent Terrace, Penzance, Cornwall. † B 2, GI 3, RSA 1.
BRUCE, Eleanor Exh. 1885
42 Brunswick Road, Brighton. † GI 1.
BRUCE, Eldred H. Home Exh. 1919-39
Edinburgh 1919; Penzance, Cornwall 1937. † B 2, RSA 1.
BRUCE, Miss Frances M. Exh. 1933
Sculptor. Add: Woodberrie Knoll, Loughton, Essex. † RA 1.
BRUCE, Miss Harriet C. Exh. 1880-99
Watercolour landscape painter. Add: Edinburgh and Lochgilphead, Argyllshire. † B 1, D 2, GI 10, L 6, M 2, RBA 4, RI 5, RSA 27, SWA 3.
BRUCE, Janna Exh. 1920-40
Pook Hill Cottage, Wormley, Nr. Godalming, Surrey 1920; London 1940. † RA 1, SWA 1.
BRUCE, John Exh. 1880
9 St. Bernard's Row, London. † RSA 1.
BRUCE, John S. Exh. 1936
690 Rutherglen Road, Glasgow. † GI 1.
BRUCE, Miss Kathleen See SCOTT
BRUCE, Margaret Exh. 1939
Wood engraver. Add: London. † RA 1.
BRUCE, Martin B. Exh. 1885-99
Landscape painter. R.B.A. 1898. Add: Edinburgh 1885; Elgin 1892; London 1894. † B 11, GI 5, NEA 7, NG 1, RA 2, RBA 22, ROI 2, RSA 7.
BRUCE, P. Ross Exh. 1899-1915
Greenock, N.B. † GI 3, RSA 5.
BRUCE, William Blair* c. 1858-1906
Canadian painter. Add: Barbizon, France 1882; Paris 1898. † L 3, RA 3.
BRUCE-JOY, Albert 1842-1924
Sculptor. b. Dublin. Studied South Kensington RA Schools and under John Foley. A.R.H.A. 1890, R.H.A. 1893. Add: London and Shottermill, Haslemere, Surrey. † B 7, G 1, GI 10, L 28, M 16, RA 75, RHA 26.
BRUCK-LAJOS, L.* Exh. 1889-91
Figure painter. Add: 192 Alexandra Road, St. John's Wood, London. † L 1.
BRUCKMAN, William L. b. 1866
Landscape painter. b. The Hague. Add: London 1904; Gt. Bardfield, Essex 1917. † D 2, FIN 58, GI 14, GOU 16, I 70, L 6, M 2, RA 3, RHA 14, RI 1, RSA 3.
BRUEN, Gerald Exh. 1936-40
Landscape and portrait painter. Add: Dublin. † RHA 12.
BRUETON, Frederick Exh. 1882-1909
Figure and coastal painter. Add: Birmingham 1882; Bideford, Devon 1889; Brighton 1897; Bridgwater, Som. 1906; Paignton, Devon 1909. † B 33, L 4, RA 4, RBA 1.
BRUFORD, Marjorie Frances b. 1902
Portrait painter. b. Eastbourne. Studied Newlyn and Paris. Signs "Midge/Bruford". Add: Paul, Penzance 1924 and 1930; Newlyn 1927; Mousehole, Penzance 1928. † GOU 1, L 2, NEA 2, RA 14, SWA 2.
BRUGAIROLLES, Victor* Exh. 1906
83 Rue Ampere, Paris. † L 1.
BRUGGEMANN, Hans Exh. 1880
Landscape painter. Add: 54 Parliament Street, London. † RA 1.
BRUGNOLI, Emanuele* Exh. 1891
Landscape painter. Carman Palazzo, Foscarini, Italy. † RSA 2.
BRUHL, Louis Burleigh 1862-1942
Landscape painter. b. Baghdad. R.B.A. 1897. Add: London 1890; Romford, Essex 1891; Watford, Herts. 1916. † AR 1, D 183, FIN 52, GI 1, L 30, RA 20, RBA 290, RCA 129, RI 46, ROI 19, WG 169.
BRUHL, Rev. Leopold H. Exh. 1906-11
Mundon Vicarage, Maldon, Essex. † D 12, RCA 1.
BRUMM, Mrs. Laura Exh. 1902-20
Birkdale, Southport, Lancs. 1902; London 1917. † L 9, LS 6, RA 1.
BRUN, Alexandre Exh. 1882-94
Landscape painter. Add: 134 New Bond Street, London 1882; Paris 1884. † GI 1, RA 1.
BRUN, Edouard Exh. 1913
† ALP 3.
BRUN le See L
BRUNDRIT, Reginald Grange 1883-1960
Landscape and figure painter. b. Liverpool. Studied Slade School and under John M. Swan. A.R.A. 1931, R.A. 1938, R.O.I. 1923. Purchased by Chantrey Bequest "Fresh Air Stubbs" 1938 and "Nutwith Common, Masham" 1940. Add: London 1906; Skipton, Yorks. 1911. † BK 2, CHE 2, GI 15, I 2, L 12, M 1, NEA 1, P 1, RA 85, ROI 7, RSA 2.
BRUNELLESCHI, Umberto* Exh. 1911
Italian painter. † GOU 2.
BRUNERY, Francois* Exh. 1901-13
Paris 1901, c/o W.J. Checkley, Hampstead, London 1913. † L 6, RA 1, TOO 1.
BRUNET, Jean Exh. 1901
6 Rue Danton, Levallois Perret, Seine, France. † L 1.
BRUNET, J. Emile Exh. 1928
49 Rue Claude Bernard, Paris. † RSA 1.
BRUNET-DEBAINES, Alfred b. 1845
French etcher. R.E. 1882. Add: London 1881-88. † GI 3, RA 5, RE 2.
BRUNSKILL, B.A.S. Exh. 1911
16 Cintra Park, Upper Norwood, London. † RA 1.
BRUNTON, Annie Exh. 1884-1902
Mrs. A.D. R.M.S. 1897. Add: Brighouse, Yorks. 1884; 25 Clarence Road, Birkdale, Southport, Lancs. 1886. † B 2, L 9, M 1, RMS 6, RSA 1, SWA 1.
BRUNTON, Arthur D.* Exh. 1902-8
25 Clarence Road, Birkdale, Southport, Lancs. † L 2, RCA 1.
BRUNTON, Miss D.C. Exh. 1916-21
7 Victoria Terrace, Terenure Road, Dublin. † RHA 5.
BRUNTON, Elizabeth York Exh. 1906-36
Painter and colour woodcut engraver. Studied Edinburgh College of Art and Paris. Add: Inveresk, N.B. 1906; Edinburgh 1911. † GI 19, L 5, RSA 15, RSW 2.
BRUNTON, Florence Exh. 1907-17
Mrs. Lynch. Add: Southend-on-Sea, Essex 1907; Westcliffe-on-Sea, Essex 1913. † D 1, L 2, M 1, RH 4, ROI 2.
BRUNTON, John Exh. 1880-84
Edinburgh 1880; Liverpool 1881. † RSA 3.
BRUNTON, Mary Campbell Exh. 1885-1933
Glasgow 1885; Connel, Argyll 1930. † GI 35, L 1, M 1, P 1, RSA 11.
BRUNTON, Miss Mabel M. Exh. 1916-26
Leeds 1916; Kircudbright 1926. † RCA 2.
BRUNTON, Violet 1878-1951
Mrs. Angless. Miniature painter. b. Brighouse, Yorks. Daughter of Arthur D. and Annie B. q.v. Studied Southport School of Art, Liverpool School of Art and Royal College of Art (silver and bronze medals). R.M.S. 1924. Add: Birkdale, Southport, Lancs. 1903; London 1923. † AR 70, GI 1, L 9, RA 27, RMS 72.
BRUNTON, Winifred Mabel 1880-1959
Nee Newbury. Miniature portrait and landscape painter. Studied South Africa and Slade School. R.B.A. 1912, A.R.M.S. 1912, R.M.S. 1916. Add: London 1912; Cairo, Egypt 1932. Signs work W.M.N.B. † L 20, RA 11, RBA 54, RMS 103.
BRUSCHI, Domenico Exh. 1884
c/o Dudley Gallery, London. † D 2.
BRUTEY, Robert S. Exh. 1888-1900
Landscape painter. Add: Teignmouth, Devon 1888; Milford on Sea, Wales 1893; Bettws-y-Coed, Wales 1894; Lee on Solent, Hants. 1899. † L 1, RA 4.
BRUTNELL, Elizabeth Exh. 1888-95
Still life and decorative painter. Add: 120 Forest Road West, Nottingham. † N 4.
BRUTTON, William M. Exh. 1894-1902
Architect. Add: London. † RA 2.
BRUYCKER, de See D
BRUYER, Georges b. 1883
French artist. Add: Reading 1909; Asnieres, France 1910. † L 2, RA 1.

BRUYN, de See D

BRUZZI, Stefano J.* Exh. 1883
Figure and landscape painter. Add: 60 Bedford Gardens, Kensington, London. † M 1, RA 2.

BRYAN, Miss Exh. 1885
Birkenhead. † SWA 1.

BRYAN, Miss Doris Exh. 1934
Cardiff. † RCA 2.

BRYAN, D. Margaret Exh. 1922-38
Painter and illustrator. Add: West Bridgford, Notts. † N 25, RSA 1.

BRYAN, Mrs. Hugh Exh. 1898-1900
Landscape painter. Add: Oxton Hall, Notts. 1898; London 1900. † N 3, NEA 1.

BRYAN, H. Dare Exh. 1899-1907
Architect. Add: 38 College Green, Bristol. † RA 7.

BRYAN, Stanley C. Exh. 1937
† P 1.

BRYAN, Thomas D. Exh. 1907-8
Liverpool. † L 3.

BRYANS, Alice Maude Exh. 1912
126 Cheyne Walk, Chelsea, London. † LS 3.

BRYANT, Annie b. 1874
Nee Smith. Landscape and flower painter. b. Port Adelaide, Australia. Studied Adelaide School of Design. Add: The Rectory, Clyst St. Lawrence, Nr. Exeter 1931. † RBA 2, RCA 6, ROI 7, RSA 1, SWA 1.

BRYANT, Charles David Jones 1883-1937
Marine painter. b. N.S.W. Australia. Studied under W. Lister Lister and Julius Olsson. Official artist to the Australia Imperial Forces on the Wester Front 1917. Visited the Mandated Territory of New Guinea as official artist, Commonwealth Govt. 1923. R.B.A. 1923, R.O.I. 1917. Add: London 1910. † AR 4, I 3, L 5, RA 15, RBA 30, RI 6, ROI 52.

BRYANT, Miss F.E. Exh. 1886
22 Bromley Common, Kent. † SWA 1.

BRYANT, Gerard Exh. 1934-35
Flower painter. Add: Hook, Nr. Surbiton, Surrey. † COO 6.

BRYANT, H.C.* Exh. 1880
Domestic and figure painter. Add: 12 Cumberland Street, Portsea. † RBA 3.

BRYANT, Miss R. Exh. 1905
† SWA 1.

BRYCE, Alexander Joshua Caleb b. 1868
Portrait and landscape painter. Studied Glasgow, Manchester and Paris. R.B.A. 1914. Add: Glasgow 1894; Manchester 1900; London 1908; Witham, Essex 1936. † CG 2, CHE 2, G 6, GI 3, I 6, L 4, M 8, P 9, RA 9, RBA 180, RI 1, ROI 13, RSA 3.

BRYCE, Helen Bryne Exh. 1918-31
Painter and poster artist. Studied St. John's Wood School of Art. Add: Harrow, Middlesex 1918; Burford, Oxon 1920. † ALP 16, GOU 1, M 1, RA 5, ROI 3, SWA 1.

BRYCE, Mrs. T.H. Exh. 1890
3 London Terrace, Kelvinside, Glasgow. † GI 1.

BRYCE, V. Exh. 1915
Block J, No. 2 Albany, Piccadilly, London. † RA 1.

BRYCE, W. Snodgrass Exh.1889-1936
Paisley 1889; West Kilbride 1927. † GI 31, L 1, M 1, RSA 9, RSW 1.

BRYCE, W.T.P. Exh. 1933
40 Melville Street, Edinburgh. † RSA 1.

BRYDALL, Robert Exh. 1880-1907
Glasgow 1880; London 1906. † GI 66, RA 1, RSA 15, RSW 3.

BRYDALL, Mrs. Robert Exh. 1899-1901
8 Newton Terrace, Glasgow. † GI 3.

BRYDEN, Andrew F. Exh. 1910-16
147 Bath Street, Glasgow. † GI 3.

BRYDEN, Miss L. Exh. 1903
65 Dyke Road, Brighton, Sussex. † L 1.

BRYDEN, Olivia Mary Exh. 1918-23
Portrait and decorative painter. Studied The Grande Chaumiere Academie and Colarossi's, Paris; Central School of Arts and Crafts and Westminster School of Art, London. Add: London. † G 1, SWA 2.

BRYDEN, Robert b. 1865
Sculptor, etcher and teacher. Studied Royal College of Art, RA Schools, Belgium, France, Italy, Spain and Egypt. A.R.E. 1891, R.E. 1899. Add: London 1891, Ayr, N.B. 1895. † GI 30, I 1, L 10, RA 1, RSA 36, RE 155.

BRYDON, Arthur M'Kenzie Exh. 1906
c/o Wm. Leiper, 121 W. George Street, Glasgow. † GI 1.

BRYDON, Charles Exh. 1880-1901
Edinburgh 1880; Linlithgow, N.B. 1900. † GI 3, RSA 34, RSW 1.

BRYDON, John McK. d. 1901
Architect (e.g. Government Offices, Whitehall). Add: London. † GI 7, RA 27.

BRYDON, M.L. Exh. 1890
15 Dalhousie Street, Glasgow. † GI 1.

BRYGOO, Raoul L. Exh. 1930-38
Landscape painter. Add: Villa les Rosiers, Wissant, Pas de Calais, France. † RA 2, RSA 1.

BRYMER, William 1855-1925
Canadian painter. b. Greenock, Scotland. Hon R.M.S. 1916. Royal Canadian Academician. Add: c/o Jackson, Middleton Junction, Manchester 1884-85. † L 1, M 1, ROI 1.

BRYNMOR-JONES, Florence Exh. 1898-1904
Mrs. D. Miniature painter. Add: 27 Bryanston Square, London. † RA 5.

BRYSON, Alice M. Exh. 1925-40
Landscape painter. Add: London 1925 and 1931; Sidmouth, Devon 1929; Crawley, Winchester, Hants. 1937. † M 2, RA 17, RHA 20, RID 2, SWA 1.

BRYSON, F.W. Exh. 1938
† M 1.

BRYSON, John M. Exh. 1932-34
3 Edward Place, Steps, Glasgow. † GI 1, RSA 1.

BRYSON, Nathaniel Exh. 1905-10
8 Leith St. Terrace, Edinburgh. † GI 1, RSA 2.

BUCCI, Anselmo b. 1887
Italian artist. 39 Rue Caulaincourt, Paris, 1911. † L 2.

BUCCIARELLI, Daniel Exh. 1880-1902
Figure painter. Add: Dublin 1880; London 1885 and 1888 and Rome 1881, 1887 and 1889. † L 3, RHA 76, RI 1, RSA 1.

BUCHAN, Wm. Hamilton Exh. 1899
43 Summer Street, Aberdeen. † RSA 1.

BUCHANAN, A. Exh. 1915-21
Glasgow. † GI 3.

BUCHANAN, Allan Exh. 1880-95
Glasgow. † GI 12, RSA 2.

BUCHANAN, Archibald Exh. 1886-95
Edinburgh. † RSA 2.

BUCHANAN, A.M. Exh. 1919-28
93 Willowbrae Avenue, Edinburgh. † RSA 1, RSW 1.

BUCHANAN, Alexander N. Exh. 1929-34
42 St. George's Road, Palmers Green, London. † RA 1, RI 2.

BUCHANAN, Alexander S. Exh. 1902-14
Figure painter. Add: Southgate, London 1902; 42 St. George's Road, Palmers Green, London 1912. † RA 6.

BUCHANAN, David R. Exh. 1933-40
42 St. George's Road, Palmers Green, London. † RA 1, RI 6, ROI 3.

BUCHANAN, Elspeth b. 1915
Painter and teacher. Add: 2 Learmouth Terrace, Edinburgh. † GI 2, RSA 3, SWA 1.

BUCHANAN, Miss Etta Exh. 1932
Firgrove, Bridge of Allan. † RSA 1.

BUCHANAN, Miss Elizabeth Helen Exh. 1908
75 Lamb's Conduit Street, London. † LS 2.

BUCHANAN, Mrs. E. Oughtred Exh. 1933-40
Landscape painter. Add: 2 Learmouth Terrace, Edinburgh. † GI 2, RA 2, RBA 1, ROI 2, RSA 7, SWA 4.

BUCHANAN, Inez Exh. 1903-19
Miniature painter. A.R.M.S. 1910, R.M.S. 1911. Add: London. † L 3, P 1, RA 28, RMS 28.

BUCHANAN, Ida M. Exh. 1911-12
98 Piccadilly, London. † LS 6.

BUCHANAN, James b. 1889
Landscape painter. Studied Glasgow School of Art. Add: Ferness, Largs 1937. † GI 2, RSW 3.

BUCHANAN, Jan Exh. 1936-38
† NEA 3.

BUCHANAN, Miss Janet Exh. 1910-11
26 Arundel Avenue, Sefton Park, Liverpool. † L 5.

BUCHANAN, John C. Exh. 1932
Kilmacolm, Renfrewshire. † GI .

BUCHANAN, J.P. Exh 1890-91
Figure and landscape painter. Add: Eastbourne 1890; Malvern Link, Worcs. 1891 † NG 1, RBA 2.

BUCHANAN, James W. Exh. 1933
Landscape painter. Add: 34 Fitzwilliam Square, Dublin. † RHA 2.

BUCHANAN, Mary Exh. 1910-36
Sculptor. Add: Cardell, Paisley 1910 and 1914; Paris 1912; Chipstead, Surrey 1926. † GI 7, I 2, RA 3, RSA 4, SWA 3.

BUCHANAN, P. Exh. 1883
4 Victoria Street, Nottingham. † RHA 1.

BUCHANAN, Peter* Exh. 1880-1911
Landscape painter. Add: Glasgow 1880; Putney, London 1885; Bowness-on-Windermere 1891; Trefriw, N. Wales 1905. † GI 34, RA 2, RCA 1, RSA 6.

BUCHANAN, Robert J.M. d. c. 1925
6 Rodney Street, Liverpool. † L 21, RCA 5, RI 1.

BUCHANAN, W.C. Exh. 1881
6 Sutherland Crescent, Helensburgh. † RSA 1.

BUCHANAN, W.E. Exh. 1939
Watercolour landscape painter. † AR 2.

BUCHANNAN, Mabel Exh. 1912-39
Miniature painter. A.R.M.S. 1920, R.M.S. 1928. Add: 42 Coltart Road, Liverpool. † L 56, RA 9. RCA 17. RMS 57.

BUCHEL, Charles A. Exh. 1895-1935
Portrait painter. Add: London. † BRU 2, G 1, L 10, P 4, RA 20, RBA 3, ROI 7, RSA 2.

BUCHEL, Eduard Exh. 1892
Etcher. Add: 12C Schumann Strasse, Dresden. † RA 1.

BUCHER, E. Exh. 1910
80 Rue de St. Dominique (VIIe), Paris. † L 3.

BUCHS, J. Exh. 1910
125 Rue du Ranelagh, Paris. † L 1.

BUCK, Albert Exh. 1927-39
Landscape painter. Add: London 1927; Ilford, Essex 1932. † RA 3, RI 3.

BUCK, Anne Lillias Exh. 1900-25
Miniature painter. Add: Weston-super-Mare, Som. 1900; Edinburgh 1925. † L 1, RA 1, RSA 5.

BUCK, Ida Exh. 1898-1901
Landscape painter. Add: Rome. † D 2, RA 1, RI 2, SWA 2.

BUCK, John Sandford b. 1896
Landscape painter and black and white artist. Studied at Bristol. Add: Holborn House, Brains Green, Blakeney, Glos. † B 5.

BUCK, Miss L. Margaret Exh. 1892-94
8 Lower Brook Street, Ipswich. † ROI 3.

BUCKELL, Francis W. Ashton Exh. 1900-3
Architect. London. † RA 2.

BUCKELS, Alec Exh. 1923-35
Etcher and illustrator. A.R.E. 1924. Add: London. † RA 9, RE 4, RSA 2.

BUCKERIDGE, Charles E. Exh. 1882-83
Landscape painter. Add: 4 Duke Street, Portland Place, London. † RA 1, RBA 2.

BUCKHILL, Mrs. B.M. Exh. 1905
c/o Miss J. Knowles, 54 Deansgate, Manchester. † M 1.

BUCKHURST, Phyllis E. Exh. 1937-38
196 St. Helen's Road, Hastings, Sussex. † RA 1, ROI 2.

BUCKINGHAM, A. Exh. 1886-95
24 New Street, Dorset Square, London. † SWA 3.

BUCKINGHAM, Ethel Exh. 1893-1901
Mrs. C. Havers. Miniature painter. Add: Bushey, Herts. 1893; Norwich 1900. † RA 3, RI 1.

BUCKINGHAM & CHANDOS, The Duchess of Exh. 1919-23
18 Cadogan Square, London. † SWA 2.

BUCKLAND, Arthur Herbert* b. 1870
Painter and illustrator. Studied Royal College of Art and Juliens, Paris. R.B.A. 1894. Add: Taunton, Som. 1893; Paris 1894; London 1895; Barnet, Herts. 1911. † B 1, L 5, RA 19, RBA 11, RI 17, ROI 22.

BUCKLAND, Betty Exh. 1925
† GOU 1.

BUCKLAND, Mrs. E.A. Exh. 1896-98
London. † RBA 1, SWA 4.

BUCKLAND, Herbert T. Exh. 1898-99
Architect. Queen's College, Birmingham. † RA 4.

BUCKLAND, J. Henry Exh. 1910-29
Landscape painter. 112 Ewart Road, Nottingham. † N 32.

BUCKLAND, Miss L. Exh. 1898
95 Jermyn Street, London. † L 1.

BUCKLE, Miss H. Exh. 1913
41 Kingscourt Road, Streatham, London. † RA 1.

BUCKLE, Miss Mary Exh. 1896
41 Deronda Road, London. † SWA 2.

BUCKLER, Muriel Kathleen b. 1898
Landscape and figure painter and teacher. Studied Portsmouth School of Art. Add: 8 Powerscourt Road, Portsmouth. † RA 5, RBA 9.

BUCKLER, Miss Phyllis M. Exh. 1928
29 Reginald Terrace, Leeds. † L 3.

BUCKLES, Alex Exh. 1936-39
† RE 5.

BUCKLEY, A. Exh. 1886
Kingston on Thames. † D 1.

BUCKLEY, Miss A.E. Exh. 1931-32
Davenport, Cheshire. † RCA 2.

BUCKLEY, E.F.C. Exh. 1910
22 Balcombe Street, Dorset Square, London. † RA 1.

BUCKLEY, Mrs. Eva M. Exh. 1912
The Quimba, Freshfield Road, Formby, Lancs. † L 1.

BUCKLEY, Miss Florence Exh. 1930-38
Manchester. † RCA 5.

BUCKLEY, Herbert Exh. 1929-39
Landscape painter. Add: 3 Elm Park Road, Chelsea, London. † NEA 3, RA 3.

BUCKLEY, H. Blanche Exh. 1886-1914
Miniature painter. Add: Kingston-on-Thames 1886; London 1899. † D 1, L 2, NG 3, RA 20.

BUCKLEY, Miss Lena See GEORGE

BUCKLEY, R.F. Exh. 1933
Lamorna Bramcote Drive, West Beeston, Notts. † N 3.

BUCKLEY, William Howard Exh. 1929-40
Painter and etcher. Add: Thornton Heath, Surrey 1929; Worthing, Sussex 1934; Lancing, Sussex 1938; Lydney, Glos. 1940. † L 3, RA 9.

BUCKMAN, Edwin c. 1841-1930
Domestic painter and watercolourist. Art tutor to Queen Alexandra and a member of the original staff of the "Graphic". R.B.S.A. 1890, A.R.W.S. 1877. Add: London 1880, and 1910, Newquay, Cornwall 1897. † B 7, L 10, M 11, RA 2, RBA 1, RWS 27.

BUCKMAN, Percy b. 1865
Portrait and landscape painter, miniaturist and etcher. Studied RA Schools. Art Master at Goldsmiths College of Art, A.R.M.S. 1919, R.M.S. 1921. Add: London 1886 and 1924, Lewisham 1908. † B 13, L 19, RA 39, RBA 1, RI 21, RMS 72, ROI 2, RSA 1.

BUCKMAN, Dr. Robert J. Exh. 1892-95
Liverpool. † L 3.

BUCKMASTER, Dorothy Mary Exh. 1940
Nee Dyer, Flower painter. Married Martin A.B. q.v. Add: 17 Coleherne Mansions, London. † RA 1.

BUCKMASTER, Martin A. b. 1862
Flower, still life and coastal painter. Studied Royal College of Art, Paris and Italy. Art Master Tonbridge School and examiner in art to University of Oxford, Cambridge and London. Exh. 1890-96. † RA 1, RBA 3, RI 1.

BUCKNALL, A.H. Exh. 1885-88
14 Rye Hill Park, Peckham Rye. † RHA 1, ROI 1.

BUCKNALL, Miss Constance C. Exh. 1911
13 Whatley Road, Clifton, Bristol. † RA 1.

BUCKNALL, Ernest Pile* b. 1861
Landscape painter. b. Liverpool. Studied Lambeth and S. Kensington (Queen's prize for perspective 1876). Add: Peckham Rye 1885; Reigate 1887; Tunbridge Wells 1890; Chelmsford 1911; Clifton 1919. † FIN 1, G 2, L 3, LS 4, M 1, RA 41, RBA 3, RE 1, RI 17, ROI 4, TOO 6.

BUCKNALL, William Exh. 1885-87
Architect. Add: 212 South Lambeth Road, London. † RA 3.

BUCKNELL, Leonard H. Exh. 1928-36
Architect. London. † RA 6.

BUCKNER, A.E. Exh. 1893
54 Roslea Drive, Dennistown. † GI 1.

BUCKNER, F.S. Exh. 1881-86
Edinburgh. † GI 1, RSA 3.

BUCKNILL, Julia B. Exh. 1905-28
Portrait painter. Add: Epsom, Surrey 1905; London 1921. † L 4, RA 8, RMS 2.

BUCKNILL, Miss Mabel Exh. 1898
Saunderton Lodge, Malvern. Worcs. † B 2.

BUCKTON, Eveleen Exh. 1900-40
Landscape painter. A.R.E. 1937. Add: London 1900 and 1911; Haslemere, Surrey 1902. † AR 94, GI 1, I 1, L 6, NEA 17, RA 20, RCA 3, RE 21, RI 3, RSA 2.

BUDAY, George b. 1907
Painter, wood engraver and cutter. b. Hungary A.R.E. 1938. Add: London 1939. † RA 2, RE 10.

BUDD, A. Exh. 1933
† COO 1.

BUDD, Barbara Nellie b. 1855
Illuminator, embroiderer, designer and teacher. Studied Camberwell School of Arts and Crafts and Royal College of Art. Add: London 1928. † L 4.

BUDD, Miss C.C. Exh. 1884-87
20 Southernhay, Exeter, Devon. † L 5.

BUDD, Herbert Ashwin 1881-1950
Portrait and domestic painter. Studied Royal College of Art 1903-8. Teacher St. Martin's School of Art 1929-49, Hornsey School of Art 1930-49. R.O.I. 1922. Married Helen Mackenzie q.v. Add: London. † CHE 5, GI 5, I 8, L 3, M 3, NEA 8, P 27, RA 31, ROI 76.

BUDDEN, Prof. Lionel B. Exh. 1924-30
Architect. Add: School of Architecture, Liverpool University. † L 4, RA 1.

BUDGE, Miss May Exh. 1890-1918
Ashlands, Ashton-on-Mersey 1890; Conway, N. Wales 1918. † M 1, RCA 2.

BUDGEN, Frank Spencer Curtis Exh. 1912-24
Painter and sculptor. Add: St. Ives, Cornwall 1912. † GOU 4, ROI 2.

BUDGETT, Miss S.E. Exh. 1880-84
22 Mortimer Street, London. † RHA 1, ROI 1.

BUEHR, Karl Albert b. 1866
German artist. Add: London 1909; Paris 1912. Emigrated to U.S.A. † L 1, RA 1, RSA 1.

BUFFET, Paul Exh. 1908-13
Neuilly-sur-Seine, France 1908; Paris 1913. † L 2.

BUHLER, E. Exh. 1889
Landscape painter. Add: 3 Kensington Mansions, London. † RA 1.

BUHLER, Robert b. 1916
Portrait, urban and landscape painter. Studied London and Zurich. Add: London 1939. † RBA 1.

BUHOT, Felix Hilaire 1847-1898
French etcher. R.E. 1881. Add: Paris. Exh. 1881-85. † GI 4, L 3, RE 21.

BUHRER, Albert Exh. 1917-27
Painter and caricaturist ("Tell"). Add: London. † CHE 47, FIN 1, I 14, NEA 2.

BUHRER, Conrad Exh. 1882-1930
Sculptor. Add: Paris 1882; London 1889-1905 and 1922-30. † GI 1, NEA 3, NG 3, RA 6.

BUKOVAC, Blaise Exh. 1890-92
5 Eagle Place, Piccadilly, London 1890; c/o le Doux, Liverpool 1892. † L 2, RA 1.

BUKOVAC, Prof. Vlacho* Exh. 1910-13
Academy of Art, Prague 1910; Prague, Bohemia 1913. † L 1, RA 2.

BULAND, Jean Eugene 1852-1926
French artist. Add: 1 Rue Michelet, Paris 1886. † M 1.

BULCOCK, Percy 1877-1914
Burnley 1899; Liverpool 1907. † L 32, RA 2.

BULFIELD, Joseph Exh. 1895
Concarneau, Finistere, France. † RA 1.

BULKELEY, The Lady Magdalen Exh. 1929-38
Watercolour painter, painter on glass and lacquer artist. Daughter of the Earl of Hardwicke. Add: Beaumaris, Anglesey. † RCA 4.
BULKELEY-JOHNSON, Miss G. Exh. 1889-1915
Landscape and flower painter. Add: London. † RID 28.
BULKELEY-JOHNSON, Vivian Exh. 1936
Figure painter. Add: 4 South Street, London. † RA 1.
BULKLEY, Helen M. Exh. 1909-29
Brimpton, Reading 1910; St. Agnes, Cornwall 1928. † L 7, LS 12.
BULL, Mrs. Agnes R. Exh. 1913-15
St. Andrews, Southborough, Tunbridge Wells. † D 7.
BULL, Chloe King Exh. 1940
4 Grove End Gardens, London. † SWA 2.
BULL, Mrs. F.M. Exh. 1934
† COO 2.
BULL, Miss G.M. Exh. 1901
14 Rutland Terrace, Stanford, Lincs. † N 1.
BULL, Mrs. Jeanne M. Exh. 1922-25
Etcher. Add: New Barnet, Herts. 1922; Findon, Worthing, Sussex 1925. † RA 1, SWA 1.
BULL, Miss M. Exh. 1912
London. † SWA 2.
BULL, Miss Mary L. Exh. 1882-86
Pakenel Lodge, Burns Street, Nottingham. † N 7.
BULL, Nora Exh. 1885-1904
Portrait painter. Add: Richmond Hill, Surrey 1885; Wimbledon 1889. † L 1, RA 5, RID 22.
BULL, Norma Exh. 1940
Etcher. Add: c/o Commonwealth Bank, Australia House, London. † RA 1.
BULL, P.C. Exh. 1922-23
† G 3.
BULL, Rene Exh. 1911
Figure and military painter. † BRU 73.
BULL, William Carter Exh. 1893
Landscape painter. Add: Bracklyn, Bournevale Road, Streatham. † RBA 1.
BULLEID, Anna Eleanor b. 1872
Mrs. Arthur B. Landscape and flower painter. Add: Dymboro, Midsomer Norton, Somerset. † L 5, RA 6, RI 4, SWA 3, WG 63.
BULLEID, George Lawrence 1858-1933
Painter of Greek and Roman subjects. A.R.W.S. 1889. Add: London, Glastonbury, Bath and Bristol. † B 26, G 14, L 46, M 8, RA 14, RHA 1, RI 3, ROI 3, RSW 1, RWS 113.
BULLEN, Eliza M. Exh. 1880
Watercolour landscape painter. Add: British Museum. † RBA 1.
BULLER, Mrs. F. Manningham Exh. 1917-23
Chester Street, London. † SWA 12.
BULLEY, Georgina E. Exh. 1880-1920
Sculptor and painter. Add: London. † NG 2, RA 14, RBA 1, RI 2, SWA 8.
BULLEY, S. Marshall Exh. 1895-1905
West Down, Hindhead, Haslemere, Surrey. † L 8, RA 2, RBA 2.
BULLICK, Mrs. Esme Exh. 1927
Embroiderer of pictures in silk. Add: Chester Aye, Whitchurch, Salop. † L 1, RCA 2.
BULLIMORE, J.L. Valentine Exh. 1939
† RMS 1.
BULLINGSTEY, J. Exh. 1902
7 Tillingham Street, Sparkbrook, Birmingham. † B 2.

BULLIS, Miss Ina J. Exh. 1898
15 Pond Place, Chelsea, London. † RI 1.
BULLOCH, Archibald E. Exh. 1909-37
Architect. (With H.M. Office of Works 1937). Add: London. † RA 2.
BULLOCK, Beatrice S. Exh. 1910-40
14 Kingsleigh Road, Handsworth Wood, Birmingham. † B 30, RBA 4.
BULLOCK, Charles H. Exh. 1927
65 Alderson Road, Wavertree, Liverpool. † L 1.
BULLOCK, Edith Exh. 1886-1911
Landscape painter. Add: Manchester 1885; Bowdon, Cheshire 1897. † L 5, M 31, RBA 3, RCA 2, ROI 3, SWA 1.
BULLOCK, E.H. Exh. 1911
3 Raymond Buildings, Gray's Inn, London. † RA 1.
BULLOCK, James Exh. 1882
138 Parade, Leamington, Warwicks. † B 1.
BULLOCK, J.E. Exh. 1917
83 Westcombe Park Road, Blackheath, London. † RA 1.
BULLOCK, Miss Mary Exh. 1935-39
Flower painter. Add: Watch Bell Corner, Rye, Sussex. † RA 4.
BULLOCK, Miss Maud Exh. 1889
Derby House, Colchester, Essex. † SWA 1.
BULLOCK, Ralph Exh. 1927-28
Portrait painter, and teacher. Add: Armstrong College, Newcastle on Tyne. † RA 2.
BULLOT, P.L. Exh. 1908
1 Florence Villas, Holmesdale Road, Highgate, London. † RA 1.
BULLOUGH, Miss D.E. Exh. 1927-30
Brooklyn, Claremont Road, Wallasey, Cheshire. † L 4, RCA 1.
BULMAN, Henry Herbert 1871-1929
Flower and landscape painter and black and white artist. A.R.B.A. 1919, R.B.A. 1922. Add: London. † NEA 3, RA 19, RBA 65, RI 9.
BULMER, Herbert Ernest Exh. 1901-14
Artist and teacher. Add: Bootle, Lancs. † L 2.
BUNBURY, H. St. Pierre c.1883-1916
25 Mount Park Crescent, Ealing, London. † RA 1.
BUNCE, Kate Elizabeth 1858-1927
Decorative and figure painter. Studied Birmingham School of Art. Add: Priory Road, Edgbaston, Birmingham 1887-1912. † B 19, FIN 2, L 9, M 3, NG 4, RA 4.
BUNCE, Myra L. Exh. 1880-1910
Landscape painter. Add: Priory Road, Edgbaston, Birmingham. † B 25, L 2, RA 2, RI 1, SWA 1.
BUNCEY, de See D
BUNDY, Edgar* 1862-1922
Historical and genre painter and watercolourist. b. Brighton. Self-taught. A.R.A. 1915, R.B.A. 1891, R.I. 1891, R.O.I. 1892. "The Morning of Sedgemoor" purchased by Chantrey Bequest 1905. Add: London. † B 17, GI 15, L 52, LEI 2, M 8, RA 62, RBA 5, RCA 6, RHA 4, RI 66, ROI 62, RSA 1.
BUNKELL, Miss Alice Exh. 1885
15 Alexandra Villas, Finsbury Park, London. † RA 2.
BUNKER, Joseph Exh. 1883-1903
Fruit painter. Add: Bath. † L 2, RA 2, RI 4.
BUNN, Miss Fanny Exh. 1896-1921
Sculptor. Add: School of Art, Birmingham 1896; West Bromwich 1900. † B 11, L 9, NG 1, RA 3.
BUNN, George Exh. 1897-98
12 Old Bond Street, London. † GI 3, RHA 1, RSA 1.

BUNNEY, John Wharlton 1826-1882
Painter of Venetian scenes. Add: Fondamenta, San Biagio, Venice. † FIN 17, RA 1.
BUNNEY, William B. Exh. 1880
Domestic painter. Add: 18 Featherstone Buildings, Holborn, London. † RBA 1.
BUNNY, Rupert Charles Wolston* b. 1864
Landscape and figure painter. b. Victoria, Australia. R.B.A. 1895. Add: London and Paris. † BG 27, FIN 18, I 1, L 4, LS 5, M 4, NG 2, RA 18, RBA 38, RI 3, ROI 6, RSA 4.
BUNSEN, de See D
BUNT, Bertha Exh. 1913-36
Mrs. Ingle. Landscape painter. Add: London 1913; Broadway, Worcs. 1929; Guildford, Surrey 1936. † COO 3, I 1, L 1, RA 9, WG 3.
BUNT, Emma Exh. 1911-13
Mrs. T. Add: South Croydon 1911; Falmouth, Cornwall 1912. † L 1, RA 1, SWA 2.
BUNTING, May Exh. 1900-10
Walsall, Staffs 1900; Streetley 1905. † B 7.
BUNTING, Margaret G. Exh. 1928-35
Portrait painter. Add: Sidcup, Kent. † COO 4, P 2, SWA 1.
BUNTING, Thomas Exh. 1880-91
Aberdeen 1880 and 1886; Glasgow 1884. † GI 6, RSA 18.
BURBRIDGE, John Exh. 1894
48 Bolton Road, London. † L 1.
BURBRIDGE, Miss K. Exh. 1898-99
30 Church Hill, Leamington, Warwicks. † B 2.
BURBRIDGE, W. Exh. 1933
54 Crantock Street, Newquay, Cornwall. † L 1.
BURBURY, A. Dorothy Exh. 1904-6
17 Upper Phillimore Gardens, Kensington, London. † D 2, RA 1.
BURCHELL, William F. Exh. 1909-37
Landscape painter. A.N.S.A. 1910; N.S.A. 1911. Add: Nottingham 1909; West Bridgford, Notts. 1934. † N 54, RA 3.
BURCHETT, Arthur Exh. 1880-1913
Landscape painter. Add: Willoughby Lodge, Hampstead, London. † D 2, M 2, RA 6, RBA 2, RI 2.
BURD, Miss A.C. Exh. 1884-85
Newport House, Shrewsbury. † B 3.
BURDEKIN, Miss Mary L. Exh. 1896-98
Figure painter. Add: London. † RA 1, ROI 1, SWA 1.
BURDETT, Mrs. E.A. Exh. 1933-35
London. † RI 9.
BURDETTE, Hattie E. Exh. 1931
† RMS 2.
BURDIDGE, Exh. 1880
41 Belgrave Road, London. † RSA 2.
BURDITT, Thomas H. Exh. 1922
Architect. Add: 10 Grafton Street, London. † RA 1.
BURDY, Mdlle. Jeanne A. Exh. 1904-25
Paris. † L 3.
BURDY, Mlle. Marguerite V. Exh. 1924
6 Rue Durg, Paris XVIIe, France. † L 1.
BURFIELD, James M.* Exh. 1880-83
Domestic and figure painter. Add: Steyning, Sussex. † RA 1, RBA 3.
BURFORD, Miss Mary Exh. 1935-38
38 Corser Street, Dudley, Worcs. † B 4.
BURFORD, Roger d'Este Exh. 1928
Painter and author. Add: London and Rothley, Leics. † NEA 2.
BURGER, Ferd. Alb. Exh. 1907
Augsburg, Germany. † B 2.
BURGERS, Henricus Jacobus* 1834-1899
Dutch artist. Add: 17 Rue de Rochefoucauld, Paris 1882. † GI 2.

BURGES, Miss J. Exh. 1915-17
London. † RA 2, RI 1.

BURGES, William 1828-1881
Architect. A.R.A. 1881. Add: London. † RA 1.

BURGESS, Arthur Exh. 1883-84
Landscape painter. Add: 73 Montpelier Road, Peckham, London. † RBA 3, ROI 2.

BURGESS, Arthur James Wetherall* 1879-1956
Marine painter. Studied Sydney, N.S.W. Australia and St. Ives, Cornwall. Official naval artist for Commonwealth of Australia 1918; Art Editor, Brassey's Naval and Shipping Annual. R.I. 1916, R.O.I. 1913. Add: London. † B 2, GI 3, L 16, RA 53, RBA 5, RHA 11, RI 124, ROI 117.

BURGESS, Cecil S. Exh. 1935
University of Alberta, Edmonton, Alberta, Canada. † RSA 1.

BURGESS, Miss D.M. Exh. 1910-13
Landscape painter. Add: 10 Portsdown Road, Maida Vale, London. † NEA 1, RA 1, SWA 1.

BURGESS, Edward Exh. 1880-88
Architect. Add: London. † RA 7.

BURGESS, Emma Exh. 1880-1902
Leicester 1880; Buxton, Derbys. 1884. † B 1, D 7. L 1, M 3, SWA 4.

BURGESS, Miss Ethel K. Exh. 1901-7
Figure painter. Add: 5 Radnor Studios, Radnor Street, Chelsea, London. † L 4, RA 4.

BURGESS, Eliza Mary b. 1873
Portrait painter. Studied Walthamstow and Royal Female School of Art. A.R.M.S. 1910, R.M.S. 1913. Add: Walthamstow 1900; Kensington, London 1930. † COO 1, D 3, L 22, RA 30, RHA 1, RI 13, RMS 89, RSA 32, RSW 4, SWA 11.

BURGESS, Miss Florence Exh. 1885-90
Painter and sculptor. Add: London. † RA 3, RBA 1, RI 2.

BURGESS, Frederick Exh. 1882-97
Landscape painter. Add: Leicester 1882; Tunbridge Wells 1884; London 1887; Malvern 1891; Reading, Berks. 1897. † B 11, D 59, L 1, M 1, RA 1, RBA 10, RHA 2, RI 3.

BURGESS, John Bagnold* 1830-1897
Painter of Spanish Subjects. Studied under Sir William Charless Ross, J.M. Leigh and at RA Schools. Visited Spain annually for 30 years. A.R.A. 1877, R.A. 1888. Add: London. † B 3, GI 3, L 14, M 4, P 2, RA 35, RHA 1, TOO 24.

BURGESS, James G. Exh. 1887-1905
Helensburgh and Edinburgh. † GI 3, RSA 4, RSW 2.

BURGESS, J.H. Exh. 1880
Belfast, Ireland. † RHA 3.

BURGESS, Miss J.M. Exh. 1907-21
Shenfield, Brentwood, Essex. † L 1, RA 3, RMS 2, SWA 1.

BURGESS, Miss M. Exh. 1889-1905
Mrs. Fletcher. Add: Warrington, Cheshire 1889; Whitley, Cheshire 1893. † L 18, M 9.

BURGESS, Mrs. Muriel Exh. 1912-39
London. † RA 3, ROI 23.

BURGESS, Percival William Exh. 1908-9
Station Road, Addlestone, Surrey. † LS 4.

BURGESS, Walter William d. 1908
Etcher. R.E. 1883. Add: London. † L 7, RA 19, RE 92.

BURGKAN, Mlle. Berthe Exh. 1902
Rue Boissonade 12, Paris. † L 1.

BURGOYNE, Lorna Exh. 1917-37
Painter, illustrator and miniaturist. A.R.M.S. 1932, R.M.S. 1937, S.W.A. 1930. Add: London 1917; Ontario, Canada 1937. † ALP 32, I 1, L 10, RA 17, RCA 2, RED 36, RMS 40, ROI 7, RSA 7, SWA 3.

BURKE, Augusta c. 1838-1891
Landscape, genre and historical painter. R.H.A. 1871; Dublin 1880; London 1883 and 1890; Florence, Italy 1889. † B 5, GI 1, L 4, M 2, RA 4, RHA 80, ROI 14.

BURKE, Mrs. A.C. Exh. 1880
Landscape painter. Add: St. Stephens Avenue, Shepherd's Bush, London. † SWA 2.

BURKE, Mrs. Elizabeth Kinross Exh. 1937-38
Landscape and figure painter. Add: Waterford, Ireland. † RHA 2.

BURKE, Harold Arthur 1852-1942
Figure and landscape painter. Studied South Kensington School of Art, RA Schools, Beaux Arts, Paris. R.B.A. 1899, V.P.R.B.A. 1916-18. Add: London. † BG 1, RA 3, RBA 104.

BURKE, Robert Exh. 1932-35
Painter and decorator. Add: 24 Redcross Street, Grantham, Lincs. † N 1, RA 2, RSA 1.

BURKE, Robert Exh. 1937-39
Landscape painter. Add: Waterford, Ireland. † RHA 4.

BURKE, Thomas Exh. 1938-40
Portrait and figure painter. Add: London. † P 1, RA 2.

BURKE, Violet Exh. 1906-10
Alresford, Hants. 1906; Alton, Hants. 1910. † D 2.

BURKINSHAW, Charles D. Exh. 1909-12
Liverpool. † L 2.

BURKINSHAW, S. Exh. 1884-1901
Liverpool. † L 11.

BURLEIGH, Averil Mary* d. 1949
Painter and illustrator. Studied Brighton School of Art. Married Charles H.H. q.v. R.I. 1929, A.R.W.S. 1939, A.S.W.A. 1922. Add: 7 Wilbury Crescent, Hove, Sussex. † FIN 108, G 1, GI 4, GOU 2, I 10, L 13, LS 4, M 2, NEA 3, RA 49, RHA 10, RI 66, ROI 4, RSA 1, RWS 11, SWA 65.

BURLEIGH, Mrs. B. Exh. 1910
4 Victoria Road, Clapham Common, London. † RA 1.

BURLEIGH, Charles H.H. d. 1956
Flower and landscape painter. R.O.I. 1915. Add: Brighton 1896; 7 Wilbury Crescent, Hove, Sussex 1905. † BA 1, FIN 4, I 2, LS 8, RA 26, RBA 1, RHA 3, RI 15, ROI 93.

BURLEIGH, Veronica b. 1909
Landscape, figure and portrait painter. Studied Slade School (scholarship 1929). Daughter of Charles H.H. and Averil May B. q.v. Add: 7 Wilbury Crescent, Hove, Sussex. † GOU 1, NEA 2, RA 14, RI 8, ROI 2, SWA 1.

BURLEY, David William b. 1901
Landscape and seascape painter. Commercial and lino-cut artist. Studied Goldsmiths School of Art. Add: 12 Devonshire Road, London 1924. † L 1, RA 2, RI 1.

BURLIN, Paul 1886-1969
American painter and illustrator. Add: Paris 1925. † CHE 2.

BURLISON, Frances B. Exh. 1899-1920
Sculptor and decorative artist. Studied Slade School. Add: London. † I 16, L 12, NG 2, P 1, RA 14, RMS 5, SWA 2.

BURMAN, Francis Exh. 1892-1909
Birmingham. † B 3, RCA 1.

BURMAN, Miss Hester Exh. 1922-25
Kalmia, Hill Village Road, Four Oaks, Sutton Coldfield, Warwicks. † B 4.

BURMAN, John Exh. 1886-99
Domestic painter. Add: Sutton, Surrey 1886; Epsom 1899. † RA 2, RBA 1.

BURMAN-MORRALL, Harry Exh. 1936
Portrait painter. Add: St. Mary House, York Road, Hoxby, Yorks. † RA 1.

BURMAN-MORRALL, William b. 1890
Sculptor, modeller and mural decorator. Studied York, Sunderland and Royal College of Art (King and Queen's prizeman, gold and silver medallist). Headmaster Exeter School of Art. Add: 80 Howell Road, Exeter 1919. † RA 3.

BURN, Mrs. Alice See GATES

BURN, Gerald Maurice* b. 1862
Painter and etcher. Studied London University College School, Royal College of Art, Cologne, Dusseldorf, Antwerp and Paris. Add: London 1881; Belfast 1899; Amberley, Sussex 1911. † L 3, M 2, RA 5, RBA 4.

BURN, Miss Hilda M. Exh. 1920-30
Painter, designer and pottery worker. Add: 6 Murrayfield Road, Edinburgh. † COO 21, GI 1, L 7.

BURN, Rodney Joseph b. 1899
Landscape and figure painter. Studied Slade School. N.E.A.C. 1926. Add: London. † BA 47, GOU 38, L 1, M 5, NEA 63, RA 3, RED 2.

BURNABY-ATKINS, Miss Violet Exh. 1898-1902
Sevenoaks, Kent 1898; Lichfield, Staffs 1902. † RI 3.

BURNAGE, Robert Exh. 1933-39
42 Jessica Road, London. † RI 3.

BURNAND, Eugene Charles Louis* 1850-1921
Swiss painter of Religious subjects. Add: Switzerland 1898 and 1912; Paris 1910. † DOW 40, L 10, RA 4.

BURNAND, Geoffrey Norman b. 1912
Painter, mural decorator and theatrical designer. Studied Farnham School of Art 1929-31, RA Schools 1931-32, Rome British School 1933-35. † NEA 1, RA 2.

BURNAND, Victor Wyatt 1868-1940
Portrait and landscape painter and illustrator. Studied Royal College of Art and Paris. Art Master Royal College of Art. R.B.A. 1895, A.R.M.S. 1916. Add: London 1895; Farncombe, Godalming, Surrey 1897; Guildford, Surrey 1912. † AR 2, COO 2, I 1, L 5, RA 13, RBA 30, RHA 1, RMS 11.

BURNARD, George Exh. 1884
Sculptor. Add: 151A Stanhope Street, Euston Road, London. † RA 1.

BURNARD, George Arthur b. 1864
Sculptor. Son of George B. q.v. Assistant art master Birkbeck College; Art Master Wellingborough Technical Institute and Grammar School; Art Master Canton Secondary School, Cardiff. Exh. 1893-97. † L 1, RA 2.

BURNARD, Thomas Exh. 1886
Sculptor. Add: London. † RA 1.

BURNE, Ada Dora Exh. 1880-1902
Nee Milne. Flower and landscape painter. Add: London 1880 and 1901; Woking, Surrey 1900. † D 5, RBA 2, SWA 28.

BURNE, Winifred b. 1877
Painter and lithographer. Studied Birkenhead School of Art, Liverpool University School of Architecture and Munich. Add: Birkenhead 1899; Liverpool 1910; Heswall, Cheshire 1912; Carbis Bay, Cornwall 1914. † L 10, LS 18.

BURNE-JONES, Sir Edward Coley* 1833-1898
Painter, designer and watercolourist. Visited Italy. Partner in firm of Morris and Co. A.R.A. 1885, (resigned 1893). R.B.A. 1890, H.R.B.A. 1893, A.R.W.S. 1864, R.W.S. 1865. Created Baronet 1894. Large collection of his works in Tate Gallery. Add: London. † AG 8, B 6, G 21, GI 12, L 11, M 6, NG 89, RA 2, RBA 5, RCA 1, RSW 2, RWS 1.

BURNE-JONES, Sir Philip c. 1862-1926
Portrait painter. Son of Sir Edward B.J. q.v. and nephew of Sir Edward Poynter q.v. Add: London. † B 5, GI 2, L 5, LEI 1, M 3, NG 70, P 4, RA 20, ROI 5, RSA 1, TOO 1.

BURNET, B.C. Exh. 1901
62 Doughty Street, London. † RBA 1.

BURNET, Edith
See HUGHES, Edith Burnet

BURNET, John James 1857-1938
Architect. A.R.A. 1921, R.A. 1925, A.R.S.A. 1893, R.S.A. 1914. Knighted 1914. Add: Glasgow and London. † GI 36, L 2, RA 29, RSA 55.

BURNET, Miss M.F. Exh. 1920
Woolaston Lodge, Halfway House, Nr. Shrewsbury. † RCA 1.

BURNET, W.B.C. Exh. 1908-16
Landscape painter. Add: London 1908; Sidcup, Kent 1917. † LS 26, NEA 3.

BURNETT, Arthur Exh. 1922
15 Ferndale Road, Sefton Park, Liverpool. † L 1.

BURNETT, Miss Alice M. Exh. 1916-28
Miniature painter. Add: 40 Shooter's Hill, Blackheath, London. † RA 3.

BURNETT, Cecil Ross 1872-1933
Portrait, figure and landscape painter. Studied Blackheath, Westminster and RA Schools (Turner gold medal and 1st medal for portrait painting). Principal, Sidcup School of Art. R.I. 1909. Add: Blackheath 1895 and 1903; Lee 1896; Pimlico 1898. † GI 11, I 3, L 1, LS 6, M 2, P 1, RA 18, RBA 10, RI 129, ROI 20, RSW 2.

BURNETT, David Duguid Exh. 1919-40
Edinburgh 1919; Colinton 1934. † RSA 9, RSW 13.

BURNETT, Eleanor Exh. 1883-1925
Landscape painter. Add: 27 South Road, Devonshire Park, Birkenhead. † L 31.

BURNETT, Frank Exh. 1885-89
67 West Regent Street, Glasgow. † GI 4.

BURNETT, G.R. Exh. 1887-93
160 Cromwell Road, London. † D 20.

BURNETT, Miss Isabel Exh. 1897
Montague House, Erdington, Birmingham. † B 1.

BURNETT, Miss J.S. Exh. 1896
52 Filey Avenue, Upper Clapton, London. † RBA 1.

BURNETT, James Walton b. 1874
Landscape and marine painter and naval architect. Studied Liverpool School of Art and Liverpool University. Add: Liverpool 1904; c/o Cammell Laird and Co. Birkenhead 1919. † L 36, RCA 5.

BURNETT, Miss Lorna Exh. 1929
Stoke Rectory, Coventry. † B 1.

BURNETT, L.E. Exh. 1899
Moncrieff House, St. Andrews. † RSA 1.

BURNETT, R. Exh. 1931
Lino-cut artist. † RED 3.

BURNETT, Miss S.J. Exh. 1936-37
Bushey, Herts. 1936; Whitchurch, Salop 1937. † RCA 2.

BURNETT, Thomas Stuart 1853-1888
Sculptor. A.R.S.A. 1883. Add: Edinburgh. † GI 16, RA 5, RSA 49.

BURNETT, Miss Winnie Stuart Exh. 1908-12
17 Luton Place, Edinburgh. † RSA 5.

BURNEY, Henry B. Exh. 1915-36
Flower and still life painter. Add: London. † FIN 2, RA 8.

BURNIE, D.B. Exh. 1890-93
Edinburgh. † GI 2, RSA 3.

BURNIER, Richard* 1826-1884
Domestic painter. b. The Hague. Add: Dusseldorf 1880. † FIN 1, M 1, RA 1, RHA 1.

BURNIP, Mrs. Juliet E. Exh. 1914-22
Flower painter. Add: 13 Loughborough Road, Nottingham. † L 1, N 12.

BURNS, Agnes A. Exh. 1880-90
Rhoda Villa, Ibrox, Glasgow. † GI 6.

BURNS, Alexander S. Exh. 1937-40
Watercolour painter. Add: Norwood, Stonehaven, Kincardingshire. † GI 2, RSA 6.

BURNS, Balfour Exh. 1884-90
Landscape painter. Add: Streatham, London. † RA 6.

BURNS, Cecil Exh. 1927
Architecture. Add: 5 Calverley Terrace, Tunbridge Wells, Kent. † RA 1.

BURNS, Cecil Lawrence c. 1863-1929
Portrait and figure painter. Principal Camberwell School of Arts and Crafts 1897-99. Principal Bombay School of Art 1899-1918. N.E.A. 1887, R.B.A. 1899. † FIN 2, L 3, M 1, NEA 1, NG 1, RA 9, RBA 13, ROI 1.

BURNS, James Exh. 1919-23
Kirriemuir, Stourcliffe Avenue, Bournemouth. † L 1, RA 1, RI 2.

BURNS, Joseph Exh. 1927
153 Slatefield Street, Glasgow. † GI 1.

BURNS, Jean Douglas b. 1903
Painter and engraver. Studied Glasgow School of Art. Add: Cumbernauld House, Cumbernauld, Dumbartonshire. † GI 2, L 2, RED 1, RSA 5, SWA 1.

BURNS, Miss L. Exh. 1908-11
London. † L 1, RA 9.

BURNS, Leonard Exh. 1924
Landscape painter. Add: Landhurst Cottage, Hartfield, Sussex. † RA 1.

BURNS, Leonard B. Exh. 1880-82
Landscape painter. Add: Carshalton Road, Sutton, Surrey. † RBA 2.

BURNS, L. Clarence Exh. 1885-88
Constance Villas, Upper Tooting, London. † RA 1, ROI 10.

BURNS, Margaret Delisle b. 1888
Nee Hanray. Painter and etcher. Studied Slade School. Travelled widely. Add: London. † GI 2, GOU 9, I 1, L 3, NEA 2, SWA 1.

BURNS, Robert b. 1869
Landscape and figure painter, illustrator and designer. Studied Paris. Sketching trip to Morocco. Director of Painting Edinburgh College of Art. A.R.S.A. 1902. † AG 1, B 2, GI 36, I 2, L 8, LEI 43, M 4, RA 1, RHA 2, RSA 68, RSW 6.

BURNS, Thomas Jones b. 1888
Sculptor. Studied Edinburgh School of Art and Royal College of Art. Add: West Bryson Road, Edinburgh. † RSA 14.

BURNS, William Exh. 1934
116 Glencroft Road, Glasgow. † RSA 1.

BURNSIDE, Mrs. Alice M. Exh. 1917-21
A.N.S.A. 1917. Add: Tollerton Hall, Nottingham. † N 9.

BURNSIDE, Cameron b. 1887
Landscape painter. Add: London 1905; Paris 1913. † L 2, RA 8, RI 1.

BURNSIDE, C.W. Exh. 1903
55 Lower Sackville Street, Dublin, Ireland. † RHA 1.

BURR, A.G. Exh. 1940
16 Chestnut Road, Quinton, Worcs. † B 3.

BURR, Alexander Hohenlohe 1835-1899
Genre and historical painter. Studied under John Ballantyne in Edinburgh. Brother of John B. q.v. R.O.I. 1883. Add: London. † GI 3, L 3, M 2, RA 6, RBA 5, ROI 10, TOO 3.

BURR, Frances Violet Exh. 1928-30
Landscape painter. Add: Highcroft, Bramber, Sussex. † RA 2.

BURR, Horace Exh. 1885-99
Figure painter. Add: London 1885; St. Albans, Herts. 1899. † G 1, M 2, RA 1, RBA 2.

BURR, John* 1836-1893
Genre painter. Studied at Trustees Academy Edinburgh. R.B.A. 1875, R.O.I. 1883. Brother of Alexander Hohenlohe B. q.v. Add: London. † B 2, FIN 1, G 5, GI 4, L 6, M 5, RA 2, RBA 15, ROI 14, RSA 2, RWS 9, TOO 4.

BURRA, Edward* 1905-1976
Watercolour painter and wood engraver. Studied Chelsea Polytechnic 1921-23 and a year at the Royal College of Art. Travelled widely. Add: Rye, Sussex. † LEI 68, NEA 1, RED 2, TOO 5.

BURRAS, Caroline Agnes b. 1890
Miniature and landscape painter, illuminator and art teacher. Studied and taught at Leeds College of Art. Add: Horsforth, Nr. Leeds 1918; Southampton 1930. † L 15, RA 8, RCA 1, RMS 7.

BURRAS, James Exh. 1882
St. Mary's College, Beverley, Yorks. † M 1.

BURRELL, Mlle. E.M. Exh. 1887
11 Boulevard de Clichy, Paris. † GI 1.

BURRELL, Miss G.V. Exh. 1916
Connaught Hospital (Sisters Quarters), Aldershot, Hants. † RA 1.

BURRELL, Mrs. H. Theonine Exh. 1897-1920
Portrait painter. A.S.W.A. 1905. Add: Neville Cottage, Newcastle-on-Tyne. † RA 10, RBA 1, SWA 3.

BURRELL, Mrs. Louie
See LUKER, Louise, H.

BURRELL-SMITH, Miss C. Exh. 1893-94
30 Pembroke Road, London. † SWA 2.

BURRIDGE, Mrs. Eleanor Exh. 1898
6 Blackburne Terrace, Liverpool. † L 1.

BURRIDGE, Frederick Vango c. 1869-1945
Painter and etcher. Studied under Frank Short. Principal LCC School of Arts and Crafts 1912-30. A.R.E. 1895, R.E. 1898. Add: London 1895 and 1931; Liverpool 1897. † AB 1, CAR 5, CON 3, GI 2, L 31, RA 31, RE 74.

BURRINGTON, Arthur A. 1856-1924
Figure and domestic painter. R.I. 1896. R.O.I. 1894. Add: France and London. † B 15, FIN 67, L 18, LEI 75, M 8, RA 19, RBA 7, RI 107, ROI 20.

BURROUGHES, Miss Dorothy Mary L. Exh. 1921-39
Painter, illustrator, poster and lino-cut artist. Studied Slade School, Heatherleys and in Paris. A.R.B.A. 1923, R.B.A. 1925. Add: London. † FIN 59, LS 3, RBA 28, SWA 9.

BURROUGHS, A. Leicester Exh. 1881-1916
Figure and portrait painter. R.B.A. 1895. Add: London. † L 2, P 1, RA 15, RBA 9, RI 1, ROI 9, RSA 1.

BURROUGHS, Miss E. May Exh. 1915-16
24 Redcliffe Road, London. † I 1, L 2.

BURROUGHS, Miss Gladys T. Exh. 1929
Barn Hays, Gt. Crosby, Liverpool. † L 1.

BURROUGHS, Miss Mary A. Exh. 1895-99
41 Rodney Street, Liverpool. † L 2.

BURROUGHS-FOWLER, Walter c. 1861-1930
Landscape, decorative and poster painter. R.B.A. 1912. Add: Chesham Bois, Bucks. 1912; London 1915. † GI 11, RA 4, RBA 18, WG 43.

BURROW, Agnes Eliza Exh. 1880-85
Illustrative painter. Add: Kensington, London. † SWA 4.

BURROW, Miss C.F. Severn Exh. 1899-1903
Landscape and portrait painter. Add: Malvern, Worcs. 1897; London 1899. † B 4, RA 3.

BURROW, Frank Exh. 1926
† M 2.

BURROWS, Alan Exh. 1926
† M 1.

BURROWS, Mrs. Edward Exh. 1921-24
Watercolour, pastoral and portrait painter. † WG 89.

BURROWS, Miss Helen Exh. 1929
Lynwood, Church Rd. Haydock, Lancs. † L 1.

BURROWS, Ione See MACDONALD

BURROWS, Miss K.R. Exh. 1913
6 Bertram Road, Sefton Park, Liverpool. † L 1.

BURROWS, Thomas Exh. 1934-38
Landscape and poster painter. Add: 10 Greenway Road, Runcorn, Cheshire. † M 2, RI 1.

BURROWS, T.S. Exh. 1926
14 Bailey Street, Netherfield, Nottingham. † N 1.

BURROWS, W.F. Exh. 1911-32
London. † L 1, RA 1, RBA 3.

BURROWS, Walter T. Exh. 1912
Woodlands, Atherton, Manchester. † L 1.

BURSCOUGH, Miss M.M. Exh. 1927
50 Pitt Street, Blackburn, Lancs. † L 1.

BURT, Charles Thomas* 1823-1902
Landscape painter. b. Wolverhampton. Studied under Samuel Lines and David Cox. Add: London 1880; Birmingham 1885. † B 39, G 2, RA 10, ROI 2, TOO 5.

BURT, Miss Lily Exh. 1902
Pinewood, Stoke Pogis, Slough, Bucks. † L 1.

BURT, Maria E. See SIMPSON

BURT, Robert Douglas Exh. 1921-37
Edinburgh 1921; Walsall, Staffs. 1922; Taunton, Som. 1935. † B 8, ROI 4, RSA 1.

BURT, Revell N. Exh. 1885-92
Lichfield, Staffs. 1885; Chathill, Northumberland 1886; Birmingham 1888. † B 9.

BURT, Miss Sydney Exh. 1890
19 Portland Road, Edgbaston, Birmingham. † B 1.

BURTON, Andrew Exh. 1938
Portrait painter. Add: Chumleigh Street, London. † RA 1.

BURTON, Alice Mary b. 1893
Portrait and flower painter. b. France. Studied Byam Shaw and Vicat Cole Schools of Art, Regent Street Polytechnic School of Art (bronze and silver medals). R.B.A. 1932. Add: Aberdovey, N. Wales 1913; Tunbridge Wells 1920; London 1921. † COO 8, G 1, I 1, L 2, LS 1, P 8, RA 8, RBA 52, ROI 12.

BURTON, Arthur P. Exh. 1894-1914
Portrait and figure painter. Add: Chelsea, London. † B 1, L 2, M 1, NG 1, RA 20, RHA 1, RI 2.

BURTON, Beryl Hope Exh. 1916-35
Nee Bartlett. Portrait and miniature painter. Studied Herkomer's School of Art, and Bushey, Herts. Add: Litcham Rectory, Norfolk. † RA 2, RMS 5.

BURTON, Miss Clare Exh. 1897-1903
Humbrook House, Charlton Kings, Cheltenham, Glos. † B 5, L 1, M 3.

BURTON, Miss Eileen Exh. 1933
28 Rose Hill, Iffley, Oxford. † RBA 1.

BURTON, Miss Emily Exh. 1898-1901
Sandhurst, Arnside, via Carnforth, Lancs. † L 4.

BURTON, Elizabeth Eaton Exh. 1935
Painter of Japanese subjects. † AR 73.

BURTON, Miss Eileen G. Exh. 1910-20
Miniature painter. Add: St. Saviours Vicarage, St. Albans, Herts. 1910; London 1911. † RA 5.

BURTON, Ernest St. John Exh. 1916-22
Landscape painter. Add: Melville, Howard Road, Bournemouth, Hants. † RI 1, ROI 4.

BURTON, Frederic Exh. 1924-27
3 Mandeville House, Grey Street, London. † L 2, RMS 4.

BURTON, Miss Frances M. Exh. 1927-38
Landscape painter. Add: Orston Hall, Notts. † N 2.

BURTON, Sir Frederick William* 1816-1900
Landscape painter and watercolourist. Director of the National Gallery, 1874-94. A.R.H.A. 1837, R.H.A. 1939, H.R.W.S. 1897, Knighted 1894. Add: London 1882. † G 1.

BURTON, Henry Exh. 1883-84
20 Charlotte Street, Fitzroy Square, London. † B 1, RI 2.

BURTON, Mrs. H.A. Exh. 1886-92
Birkenhead. † D 2, L 10, RI 1.

BURTON, H.M. Exh. 1908-9
A.N.S.A. 1908. Plumtree Park, Notts. † N 9.

BURTON, Harry M. Exh. 1932
Figure painter. Add: 3 Pembroke Studios, Pembroke Gardens, London. † RA 1.

BURTON, H.W. Exh. 1909
5 Bloomsbury Square, London. † RA 1.

BURTON, Miss Irene Exh. 1913-40
66 Leam Terrace, Leamington Spa. Warwicks. † B 7, L 16, SWA 1.

BURTON, Jackson Exh. 1935
Urban landscape painter. † AR 4.

BURTON, John Exh. 1884-88
Portrait painter. Add: 50 Portland Road, Nottingham. † N 5.

BURTON, J.E. Exh. 1913
11 Bank Plain, Norwich, Norfolk. † RA 1.

BURTON, Mrs. J.M. Exh. 1888
2 Alexandra Road, Birkenhead. † D 2.

BURTON, James S. Exh. 1904-5
24 Victoria Crescent, Eccles, Lancs. † M 2.

BURTON, L. Exh. 1937
Flower and garden painter. † COO 6.

BURTON, Mungo* 1799-1882
Portrait painter. A.R.S.A. 1845. Add: Edinburgh. † RSA 1.

BURTON, Miss M.R. Hill Exh. 1884-98
Figure and landscape painter. Add: Edinburgh 1884 and 1898; Hawthornden, Midlothian 1893; London 1896. † D 1, GI 8, L 2, M 1, NG 1, RA 2, ROI 3, RSA 22, RSW 2.

BURTON, Miss Nina Exh. 1889
7 Avenue Road, Regents Park, London. † SWA 2.

BURTON, Norah Exh. 1938
Pastellier. † WG 33.

BURTON, Nancy Jane d. 1972
Animal painter and watercolourist and teacher. b. Invernesshire. Studied Glasgow School of Art. R.S.W. 1932. Add: Glasgow 1916; Tyndrum, Perthshire 1921; Aberfoyle 1938. † GI 45, L 3, RSA 27, RSW 38.

BURTON, Rose Exh. 1881-85
Edinburgh. † B 1, GI 5, RSA 7.

BURTON, S.R. Exh. 1906-12
Chelmsford, Essex 1906; London 1911. † RA 4.

BURTON, William Exh. 1887
Cassiobury Villa, New Barnet, Herts. † RA 2.

BURTON, William Paton 1828-1883
Landscape painter. b. India. d. Aberdeen. Travelled continent and middle east. R.B.A. 1883. Add: Witley, Surrey 1880. † D 8, G 1, GI 8, L 1, M 1, RA 5, RBA 9, RI 1, RSA 1.

BURTON, William Shakespeare* 1824-1916
Historical painter. Studied RA Schools. Add: Bognor, Sussex 1894; London 1899. † AG 1, B 2, L 1, NG 1, RA 1.

BURTON, W.W. Exh. 1883
Ennis, Ireland. † RHA 1.

BURT-SMITH, E.H. Exh. 1930-32
The Beulah, Meadfoot Road, Torquay, Devon. † B 3.

BURT-SMITH, Mrs. Ruth Exh. 1930-35
The Beulah, Meadfoot Road, Torquay, Devon. † B 9, L 1.

BURWOOD, Miss A.L. Exh. 1926-32
120 Sycamore Road, Smethwick, Staffs. † B 4, L 3.

BURWOOD, Miss L.D. Exh. 1917
67 Crouch Street, Colchester, Essex. † RA 1.

BURY, Adrian b. 1893
Watercolour painter poet and writer on art. Studied London, Paris and Rome. Nephew of Sir Alfred Gilbert R.A. Add: London 1930. † FIN 3, P 1, RA 3.

BURY, Gaynor Elizabeth b. 1890
Landscape and interior painter. Studied RA Schools (Creswick prize and silver medal). Add: Farnham, Surrey 1914; Bournemouth, Hants. 1923. † L 1, RA 1, ROI 4, SWA 1.

BURY, Miss M. Exh. 1909-11
Scriveton Rectory, Nottingham. † N 3.

BURY, M.S. Exh. 1932
† L 1.

BURY, Viscount Exh. 1883
65 Prince's Gate, London. † D 2.

BUSBY, R.A. Exh. 1884
16 Lord Street, Liverpool. † L 1.

BUSCH, G.H. Exh. 1883
c/o Nicholet, Mellor's Buildings, Liverpool. † L 1.

BUSCH, Mrs. H.M. Exh. 1892-93
3 Portman Mansions, London. † RI 1, SWA 1.

BUSH, Miss A. Exh. 1891-92
48 Park Village East, Regent's Park, London. † L 1, M 1.

BUSH, Miss Ella Shepard Exh. 1930
† RMS 1.

BUSH, Flora Exh. 1899-1929
Nee Hyland. Married Reginald Edgar James B. q.v. Watercolour flower painter. Studied Royal College of Art. Painting teacher Bristol Municipal School of Art. Add: Bristol. † B 1, L 4, RA 2, RE 1, RI 1.

BUSH, F. Thwaites Exh. 1938
Architect. Add: New Scotland Yard, London. † RA 1.

BUSH, Harry 1883-1957
Landscape and flower painter. Studied Regent Street Plytechnic and West Lambeth. R.O.I. 1931. Add: 19 Queensland Avenue, Merton Park, Wimbledon, London. † BAR 1, GI 1, L 4, RA 20, ROI 7, RSA 1.

BUSH, Miss K.E. Exh. 1893-94
67 Belsize Park, London. † SWA 2.

BUSH, Mrs. Noel Laura See NISBET

BUSH, Phyllis Madeleine Hylie b. 1896
Painter and etcher. Daughter of Reginald Edgar James and Flora B. q.v. Studied Bristol Municipal School of Art and Royal West of England Academy School of Architecture. Add: Bristol, 1915. † RA 1.

BUSH, Reginald Edgar James b. 1869
Painter and etcher. Studied Royal College of Art, Paris and Italy (travelling scholarship Royal College of Art, British Institute Scholarship for etching); on staff of Royal College of Art; Principal Bristol Municipal School of Art 1895-1934. A.R.E. 1898, R.E. 1917. † L 4, RA 1, RE 73.

BUSHBY, A.C. Exh. 1940
30 Alcester Road South, Birmingham. † B 1.

BUSHBY, Miss Mary I. Exh. 1919-22
10 Drayton Gardens, London. † SWA 5.

BUSHBY, Thomas Exh. 1898-1914
Landscape painter. Add: Victoria Lodge, Currock, Carlisle. † L 3, RA 4, RCA 14, RI 3, RSA 1.

BUSHILL, Miss A.N. Exh. 1891
Sunny Side, Spencer Road, Coventry. † B 1.

BUSIERE, Louis Exh. 1925
Etcher. Add: 40 Due Denfert-Rochereau, Paris. † RA 1.

BUSK, Bridget A.M. Exh. 1937-38
64 St. James Court, London. † NEA 1, ROI 1.

BUSK, Miss E.M. Exh. 1882-89
Portrait painter. Add: 32 Harley Street, London. † L 1, RA 10.

BUSK, Mrs. Mary Exh. 1926-28
Watercolour weather and landscape painter. † WG 115.

BUSK, William Exh. 1889-92
Figure and portrait painter and teacher. Add: Horsham, Sussex 1889; Dorchester, Dorset 1892. † RA 3.

BUSKENS, J. Exh. 1917
46 Windsor Terrace, Glasgow. † GI 1.

BUSKIRK, Van See V

BUSS, Arthur E. Exh. 1929-35
Stained Glass Artist. Add: 9 Lutwyche Rd. Catford, London. † RA 4.

BUSS, Hugh Exh. 1928
Still life and portrait painter. Add: 75 Trumpington St. Cambridge. † RA 2.

BUSSELL, Freda M. Exh. 1922
† SWA 1.

BUSSELL, Miss Grace V. Exh. 1918-28
Stoke on Trent, Staffs. 1918; Moseley, Birmingham 1920; London 1923; Eastbourne 1928. † B 1, RA 3.

BUSSEY, Leonard O. Exh. 1932-37
Landscape painter. Add: The Green, Horsforth, Nr. Leeds, Yorks. † RA 2, RCA 1.

BUSSEY, Reuben* d. c.1892
Figure and landscape painter. Add: Nottingham. † N 23.

BUSSIERE, Gaston* Exh. 1909
5 Rue Falguiere, Paris, France. † RA 1

BUSSY, Charles Exh. 1911
Flower painter. † BRU 2.

BUSSY, Jane Simone Exh. 1935
Still life, fruit and flower painter. † LEF 24.

BUSSY, Simon* 1870-1954
Landscape and portrait painter and pastellier. Add: France and London. † CAR 54, GI 1, GOU 68, I 20, L 2, NEA 8, P 1.

BUSTARD, W. Exh. 1915
1 Beechmore Road, Battersea, London. † RA 1.

BUTCHART, Theresa North See COPNALL

BUTCHER, Dorothy Joan Exh. 1936-38
Landscape painter. Add: Woodsetts House, Worksop, Notts. † N 6.

BUTCHER, Enid Constance Exh. 1927-33
Engraver and illustrator. Studied Chelsea School of Art and Royal College of Art. Add: Fairfield, Furze Hill, Kingswood, Surrey. † GI 1, L 2, RA 6.

BUTCHER, Miss F. Exh. 1889
George Road, Edgbaston, Birmingham. † B 1.

BUTCHER, George Exh. 1882
63 New Spring Street, Birmingham. † B 2.

BUTCHER, John Exh. 1934-36
10 Ravenscroft Park, Barnet, Herts. † RI 3.

BUTCHER, May Exh. 1922
† SWA 1.

BUTCHER, Miss Nellie Exh. 1894-95
8 George Road, Edgbaston, Birmingham. † B 2.

BUTLER, Alice Exh. 1891-1910
Mrs. Cecil B. Add: Milestown, Castlebellingham, Ireland. † D 5, RHA 1.

BUTLER, Alice Caroline b. 1909
Watercolour painter, black and white artist and miniaturist. b. Bromley, Kent. Studied St. Albans School of Art. Add: Malmsbury, Wilts. 1933. † RA 1.

BUTLER, Alfred M. Exh. 1894
Architect. Add: 16 Finsbury Circus, London. † RA 1.

BUTLER, A.S. George b. 1888
Architect, painter and author. Studied at Architectural Association. Add: London 1929. † RA 1.

BUTLER, Clehorow Caroline Exh. 1881-83
Sculptor. Add: 186 Euston Road, London. † RA 3.

BUTLER, Charles Ernest* b. 1864
Portrait, figure and landscape painter. b. St. Leonards on Sea. Studied St. John's Wood School of Art and RA Schools. Add: London. † L 1, LS 12, RA 22.

BUTLER, Miss Diana Exh. 1928-29
Boulogne sur Seine, France, 1928; London 1929. † NEA 5.

BUTLER, E. Exh. 1880-81
58 North King's Street, Dublin, Ireland. † RHA 3.

BUTLER, Edmund Exh. 1931-34
22 Avenue Road, Leamington, Warwicks. † B 6.

BUTLER, Miss E. Gertrude Exh. 1905-7
Balsall Heath, Birmingham 1905; Warwick 1907. † B 4.

BUTLER, E.S. Exh. 1881-92
Ireland. † RHA 3.

BUTLER, Lady Elizabeth Southerden 1846-1933
Nee Thompson. Military painter. Studied South Kensington 1866, Rome and under Guiseppe Belluci in Florence. R.I. 1874, H.S.W.A. 1880. Add: Plymouth 1881; Aldershot 1895; Dover 1896; Capetown, S.A. 1898; Devonport 1902; Bansha, Co. Tipperary, Ireland 1911; Flax Bourton, Som. 1922. † B 1, D 1, FIN 1, GI 3, L 9, M 4, NG 1, RA 19, RHA 3, SWA 2.

BUTLER, E.T. Exh. 1880-88
Nr. Glasgow. † B 1, GI 6.

BUTLER, Frank Exh. 1922-37
Chelsea, London 1922; Bewdley, Glos. 1937. † B 2, L 1, RA 1.

BUTLER, Miss F.E. Exh. 1907-11
Finchley, London 1907; Rugby 1911. † L 3, RA 5, RMS 3.

BUTLER, George* Exh. 1936-39
Landscape painter. Add: Chipperfield, Herts. † GOU 1, RA 1, ROI 1.

BUTLER, George Edmund* b. 1872
Painter and etcher. Studied Lambeth School of Art, Juliens, Paris and Antwerp Academy. Official artists, New Zealand Expeditionary Force; Art master Clifton College, Bristol. Add: Dunedin, N.Z. 1904; Aylesbury, Bucks. 1907; Bristol 1909, 1914; Westbury on Trym, Glos. 1911; Ipswich 1923. † GI 1, L 1, LS 9, RA 12, RHA 1, RSA 2.

BUTLER, Mrs. Grace F. Exh. 1929-35
Blackmore, Essex 1929; Ongar, Essex 1935. † B 3.

BUTLER, Hester Exh. 1910-28
Portrait painter. Studied London School of Art and Brussels Academy. Add: Gazeley Vicarage, Newmarket, Suffolk 1910; Harting, Petersfield, Hants. 1928. † RA 2.

BUTLER, H. Exh. 1908-19
R.B.A. 1914. Add: Liverpool 1908; London 1914. † I 1, L 1, RBA 40.

BUTLER, Henry Exh. 1938-40
† RI 2.

BUTLER, Herbert E. Exh. 1881-1921
Landscape and figure painter. Add: London 1881; Polperro, Cornwall 1902. † I 1, L 7, M 1, RA 14, RBA 3, RI 1.

BUTLER, H. John Exh. 1928-35
138 High Street, Bushey, Herts. † B 3, RCA 5.

BUTLER, Miss Josephine Exh. 1910
71 Iverna Court, Kensington, London. † ROI 1.

BUTLER, J.D. Exh. 1902-6
Architect. Add: New Scotland Yard, London. † RA 2.

BUTLER, J. Stacy Exh. 1899
Landscape painter. Add: The Studio, Danbury, Essex. † RA 1.

BUTLER, Miss Maud Exh. 1914
7 Craven Road, Harlesden, London. † LS 3.

BUTLER, Miss May Exh. 1914
c/o C.H. West, 117 Finchley Road, London. † L 1.

BUTLER, Miss Mina Exh. 1907
Takabrot, Sutton Court Road, Chiswick, London. † B 1.

BUTLER, Mabel A. Exh. 1896-1915
Landscape painter. Add: Florence 1896; London 1900. † D 1, RA 3, RBA 1.

BUTLER, Mildred Anne 1858-1941
Watercolour painter. Studied Westminster School of Art under Frank Calderon and Norman Garstin. A.R.W.S. 1896. "Morning Bath" purchased by Chantrey Bequest 1896. Add: Kilmurry, Thomastown, Co. Kilkenny 1888; Wellington, New Zealand 1935. † B 8, D 24, DOW 2, FIN 5, G 1, L 35, LEI 90, M 2, NG 15, RA 25, RBA 1, RHA 4, RI 35, RWS 198, SWA 89.

BUTLER, M.E. Exh. 1888-89
Doveridge Place, Walsall, Staffs. † B 2.

BUTLER, Mary E. Exh. 1880-1912
Watercolour landscape painter. Visited South Africa. Add: London 1880; Wrexham, N. Wales 1887; Brixton, Devon 1890. † D 8, DOW 2, FIN 2, M 6, RA 9, RI 17, WG 26.

BUTLER, Mrs. Nina H. Exh. 1884
Flower painter. Add: 1 Castletown Road, West Kensington, London. † RBA 1.

BUTLER, Ottywell Exh. 1894-1916
Dublin, Ireland 1894; London 1916. † RHA 3.

BUTLER, Richard Exh. 1880-86
Landscape painter. Add: 3 Knole Road, Sevenoaks, Kent. † M 1, RA 3.

BUTLER, Robert Exh. 1934
Landscape painter. † COO,2.

BUTLER, Rupert Exh. 1929-38
Watercolour landscape painter. Add: Marlborough, Wilts. 1938. † RBA 1, WG 106.

BUTLER, Ruth Exh. 1936
Figure and portrait, landscape and still life painter. † COO 35.

BUTLER, Prof. Rudolf Maximilian 1872-1943
Architect. Professor of Architecture, National University of Ireland. A.R.H.A. 1927, R.H.A. 1938. Add: Dublin, Ireland. † GI 4, RA 5, RHA 26.

BUTLER, Mrs. R.P. Exh. 1931-36
Wool, Dorset. † RCA 2.

BUTLER, Miss S.A. Exh. 1890
Figure painter. Add: c/o J. Butler, Tetbury, Glos. † RA 2.

BUTLER, Theodore, Earl* Exh. 1909-10
Eure, France 1908; Allied Artists Assoc. London 1910. † LS 9.

BUTLER, T.T. Exh. 1902-3
Moor Lea, Woodley Road, Leeds, Yorks. † RCA 3.

BUTLER, Violet Victoria Exh. 1914-37
Nee Kaul. Miniature painter and teacher A.R.M.S. 1916. Add: London 1914 and 1922; Wealdstone, Middlesex 1918; Harrow, Middlesex 1933. † L 13, RA 18, RMS 2.

BUTLER, William Exh. 1894
Buckingham House, Clay Hill, Bushey, Herts. † RA 1.

BUTLER-JOHNSON, M. Exh. 1900-02
St. George's Lodge, Nr. Ashby de la Zouch, Leics. † N 3.

BUTLIN, Oona H. Exh. 1889-91
Landscape painter. Add: Rock House, Ealing, London. † RID 10.

BUTSON, Nora Exh. 1891-1911
Portrait painter. Add: Henley on Thames 1891; Maidenhead 1903; Devizes, Wilts. 1906. † B 1, L 1, RA 2, RBA 2, RCA 1, RHA 11, RMS 1, ROI 3, SWA 13.

BUTT, C.F. Exh. 1912
17 Chichester Street, Westbourne Square, London. † RA 1.

BUTT, Cecily Vivien b. 1886
Watercolour painter and decorative artist. b. Oxshott, Surrey. Studied Byam Shaw and Vicat School of Art. Add: London 1913. † ALP 1, B 1, D 7, L 8, P 3, RA 1, RBA 1, RI 5, ROI 3.

BUTT, Miss F.E. Exh. 1930
Landscape painter. † WG 13.

BUTT, J. Acton Exh. 1883-91
Birmingham. † B 9, ROI 4.

BUTT, James Henry Exh. 1906-22
St. Donats, Old Colwyn, N. Wales. † LS 9, RCA 5.

BUTT, Miss Olive Exh. 1918-19
21 Clyde Road, Dublin, Ireland. † RHA 3.

BUTT, Miss Winifred Exh. 1915
Limnerslee Studios, Belvedere Road, Prince's Park, Liverpool. † L 1.

BUTTAR, Edward James b. 1873
Landscape and interior painter. Add: London 1913; Cricklade, Wilts. 1922. † ALP 1, GI 27, I 7, NEA 3, RA 26.

BUTTBERG, Albert V. Exh. 1934
Portrait painter. Add: 184 Iverson Road, London. † RA 1.

BUTTBERG, Miss Victorine Exh. 1933-38
Edinburgh. † RSA 4.

BUTTERFIELD, Clement Exh. 1896
34 Abbey Gardens, St. John's Wood, London. † RA 1.

BUTTERFIELD, Miss Dorothy Exh. 1933-40
Etcher. Add: Northdown, Chalfton St. Peter, Bucks. † RA 1, RBA 14, RI 4, SWA 8.

BUTTERFIELD, Francis b. 1905
Studied Bradford School of Art. Add: London 1934. † LEI 36, RED 1.

BUTTERFIELD, Tom C. Exh. 1905-18
Keighley, Yorks. † GI 4.

BUTTERTON, Mary Exh. 1889
Landscape painter. Add: 62 South Lambeth Road, London. † RBA 2.

BUTTERWORTH, Miss Alice Exh. 1925-26
Harrow Street, Higher Crumpsall, Manchester. † RCA 2.

BUTTERWORTH, Charles Exh. 1887-1919
Engraver. Add: London. † L 23, RA 5, RHA 1.

BUTTERWORTH, George Exh. 1880-81
24 Canterbury Road, Croydon, Surrey. † D 2.

BUTTERWORTH, Miss H.M. Exh. 1888
Sweet Briar Hall Studio, Nantwich, Cheshire. † L 1.

BUTTERWORTH, Mrs. Margaret Exh. 1894-1910
Miniature painter. R.M.S. 1897. Add: London. † RA 1, RMS 15.

BUTTERWORTH, Walter Exh. 1938
† M 1.

BUTTERWORTH, Miss W.M. Exh. 1901
Miniature painter. Add: 53 Pulteney Street, Bath. † RA 1.

BUTTERY, Horace A. Exh. 1923-27
Landscape painter. Add: 14 Templewood Avenue, Hampstead, London. † RA 1, TOO 1.

BUTTERY, Walter F.S. Exh. 1935-36
Albion House, Ferring, Nr. Worthing, Sussex. † NEA 2, RBA 1.

BUTTON, Mrs. Freda M. Exh. 1924-29
Clifton, Bristol 1924; Nailsea, Som. 1929. † L 5.

BUTTON, Miss Kate Exh. 1881-1908
Flower painter. Add: Clevedon, Som. † NG 1, RBA 1.

BUTTON, Maud Ireland Exh. 1910-17
Figure painter. R.O.I. 1917. Add: Boscoville, Uxbridge, Middlesex. † I 3, L 8, LS 3, NEA 2, ROI 9.

BUTTS, Mrs. G. Exh. 1883
Villa Strohl Teru. Rome, Italy. † L 1.

BUXTON, Alfred 1883-1963
Sculptor and decorative carver. Studied RA Schools (gold medal and travelling studentship for sculpture 1909). Served Royal Flying Corps 1916-19. Add: London. † RA 9.

BUXTON, Miss Amy L. Exh. 1893-94
Elm Cottage, Wimbledon Common, London. † M 1, ROI 4.

BUXTON, A.S. Exh. 1919-22
Ravenscroft, Mansfield, Notts. † N 7.

BUXTON, Cedric Exh. 1920-21
1 Travis Place, Broomshall, Sheffield. † L 3.

BUXTON, Robert Hugh b. 1871
Sporting, portrait and landscape painter and wood carver. Studied Herkomer's School, Bushey, Herts and Slade School. Add: Wimbledon Common 1894; London 1904. † BRU 1, FIN 138, L 3, M 1, RA 19, RI 2, ROI 5.

BUXTON, William Exh. 1891
Architect. Add: Imperial Buildings, Ludgate Circus, London. † RA 1.

BUXTON, Winifred Exh. 1898-1901
Fritton, Gt. Yarmouth, Norfolk. † D 6, SWA 1.

BUXTON, William Graham Exh. 1885-93
Landscape and figure painter. Add: London. † B 3, M 6, RA 1, RBA 5, ROI 1.

BUYS, Ir. J.W.E. Exh. 1936
† RSA 2.

BUYSSE, Georges* Exh. 1906-8
Landscape painter. † GOU 1, I 2.

BUZZARD, Mary C. Exh. 1897-1926
Sculptor. Married A. Bertram Pegram q.v. Studied Wimbledon College of Art 1897. Add: Wimbledon 1897; Brighton 1904; Reigate, Surrey 1906; London 1914. † GI 3, L 4, RA 12, SWA 1.

BUZZARGA, G. Exh. 188
University College, Gower Street, London. † NG 1.

BYARD, Arthur Exh. 1919-2
44 Stanley Gardens, Hampstead, London. † LS 4.

BYARD, Miss Florence Exh. 1890-9
Flower painter. Add: 4 Warrington Street Oakley Square, London. † RA 1, ROI 1

BYATT, Edwin 1888-194
Landscape and flower painter. R.I. 1933 Add: Wandsworth Common 1925; Ewell Surrey 1935. † L 1, RA 21, RI 29, ROI 2

BYERLEY, Miss Mabel Exh. 192
† RMS 1.

BYERS, Sidney C. Exh. 193
† P 1.

BYGATE, Joseph E. Exh. 189
Landscape painter. Add: 17 Sherbrook Road, Fulham, London. † RBA 1.

BYLANDT, de See

BYLES, William Hounsom* Exh. 1890-191
Landscape, portrait and figure painte R.B.A. 1901. Add: Chichester and Lon don. † B 1, L 9, LEI 1, NG 11, P 1, RA RBA 57, ROI 2.

BYRD, Miss E.M. Exh. 1911-1
Limnerslee Studios, Belvidere Road Prince's Park, Liverpool. † L 12.

BYRDE, Mrs. T. Exh. 191
4 Rock Park, Rock Ferry, Cheshire † L 1.

BYRNE, B.H. Exh. 191
† I 1.

BYRNE, Claude Exh. 188
5 Ormond Terrace, Rathmines, Dubli † RHA 1.

BYRNE, Mrs. Cornelia Exh. 191
2 Summer Hill Terrace, St. Luke's, Cor † RHA 1.

BYRNE, D. Exh. 188
Miniature portrait painter. Add: 76 Sh Street, Brighton, Sussex. † RA 1.

BYRNE, Herbert J. Exh. 19
115 Main Street, Newton Mearns, N Glasgow. † GI 1.

BYRNE, Miss J.H. Exh. 1891-
12 Norma Road, Waterloo, Nr. Liverpo † L 2.

BYRNE, P.J. Lyons Exh. 18
303 Strand, London. † RHA 1.

BYRNE, William Exh. 1881-
Landscape painter. Add: London 188 1885 and 1887; Liverpool 1883; Glasg 1886. † B 2, GI 1, L 7, M 1, RA RBA 1.

BYRNE, W.H. Exh. 1883-
Dublin. † GI 1, RHA 3.

BYRON, Robert Exh. 1934
Illustrations of a Journey in Persia and Afghanistan. † WG 26.

BYSE, Mrs. Fanny Exh. 1902-11
Sculptor. Add: 23 Valentine, Lausanne, Switzerland. † RA 2, RBA 1.

BYWATER, Elizabeth Exh. 1880-94
Flower painter. Add: 5 Hanover Square, London. † B 3, D 5, G 4, L 5, M 3, P 1, RA 21, RBA 7, RI 3, SWA 25.

BYWATER, Katherine D.M. Exh. 1883-96
Domestic painter. S.W.A. 1886. Add: 5 Hanover Square, London. † B 4, L 4, M 2, RA 9, RBA 1, SWA 20.

BYWATER, Marjorie b. 1905
Painter and illustrator. Studied Ealing School of Arts and Crafts and Royal College of Art. Add: 24 Waldegrove Road, Ealing, London 1933. † RA 1.

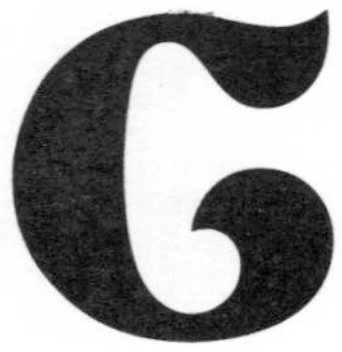

CABIANCA, Vincenzo* 1827-1902
Italian landscape painter. Add: Rome. † B 1, D 6, G 1, L 3, NG 1, RA 7, RI 5, RSA 2.

CABEANCHI, Igenio Exh. 1890
31 Rue Bayen, Paris. † GI 1.

CABIE, Louis* Exh. 1912
74 Avenue de Villiers, Paris. † RA 2.

CABRERA, Miss Ada Exh. 1889
Animal painter. Add: Wentworth, Ascot. † SWA 1.

CABUCHE, Millicent Eugenie
See CROOM-JOHNSON

CACCIA, Mrs. Anne Exh. 1937-39
Portrait and figure painter. Add: 106 Grosvenor Road, London. † P 2, RA 1, SWA 1.

CACCIA, Carlo Exh. 1895-99
Sculptor. Add: London. † NG 4, RA 1.

CACHEMAILLE-DAY, N.F. Exh. 1938-39
Architect. Add: 26 Dorset Street, London. † RA 3.

CACKETT, Leonard 1896-c.1965
Studied Tottenham Polytechnic School of Art, Bolt Court and Hackney Institute. Add: London 1939. † ROI 3.

CADBURY, Agnes Exh. 1882
Ashover, Chesterfield, Derbys. † M 1.

CADBY, Walter F. Exh. 1894-1904
Portrait and flower painter. N.E.A. 1896. Add: London. † I 3, L 6, NEA 14.

CADDICK, Miss Bessie Exh. 1897
Dorset House, Wellington Road, Edgbaston, Birmingham. † B 1.

CADDICK, Richard Exh. 1933
† L 1.

CADELL, Agnes Morison Exh. 1914-28
Landscape and figure painter. Travelled Africa, Malta and the Continent. Sister to Florence St. John C. q.v. Add: 20 Murrayfield Drive, Edinburgh. † ALP 35, LS 2, RA 1, RSA 3.

CADELL, Francis Campbell Bolleau*
1883-1937
Landscape, interior and figure painter. Studied RSA Schools, Juliens, Paris 1899-1903 and Munich 1907. Visited continent often. A.R.S.A. 1931, R.S.A. 1937, R.S.W. 1935. Add: Edinburgh. † BAR 13, BG 64, GI 62, I 30, L 15, LEI 41, RSA 77, RSW 12.

CADELL, Florence St. John Exh. 1900-40
Landscape and figure painter. Travelled widely. Sister of Agnes Morison C. q.v. Add: Edinburgh 1900; St. Adrian's Crail, Fife 1929; Coldbridge, Edinburgh 1932; Cumberland 1937. † ALP 52, GI 4, L 1, LS 2, P 1, RSA 15, RSW 1.

CADELL, Gilbert Laurie Exh. 1930-40
Murrayfield, Edinburgh 1930; London 1940. † RSA 12, RSW 9.

CADELL, H.M. Exh. 1925
The Grange, Linlithgow. † RSA 1.

CADELL, Miss I.M. Exh. 1900-40
Edinburgh. † RSA 4, RSW 4.

CADENHEAD, James 1858-1927
Painter, etcher and lithographer. Studied RSA Schools, Paris under Carolus Duran 1882. N.E.A. 1887, A.R.S.A. 1902, R.S.A. 1921, R.S.W. 1893. Add: Edinburgh and Aberdeen. † BG 2, CON 5, GI 27, L 9, M 5, NEA 3, RSA 148, RSW 60, TOO 1.

CADIX, A. Exh. 1882
29 Delamere Terrace, London. † L 1.

CADMAN, Alfred Exh. 1909-10
c/o Allied Artists' Association, London. † LS 4.

CADMAN, Miss D. Exh. 1914-16
Bleanofow, Harlesden Road, London. † LS 6.

CADMAN, or CODMAN, W.C. Exh. 1881
Architect. † RA 1.

CADNESS, H. Exh. 1886 and 1926
Textile designer and teacher. Add: Manchester. † M 2.

CADNESS, Miss Mildred M. Exh. 1912-13
43 Bamford Road, Didsbury, Manchester. † L 6.

CADNEY, Miss Marjorie F. Exh. 1918
† RMS 1.

CADOGAN, Herbert Exh. 1933
Cardiff. † RCA 1.

CADOGAN, Sidney Russell d. 1911
Landscape painter. Add: London and Seven Oaks, Kent. † B 1, G 5, M 4, NG 19, RA 11, ROI 3.

CADWALADER, William Exh. 1905-11
18 Marine Terrace, Criccieth, N. Wales. † BRU 1, L 1.

CADWALLADER, Miss Winefred
Exh. 1895-1904
20 Alfred Place West, South Kensington, London. † RBA 1, RI 1, SWA 15.

CADZOW, James b. 1881
Painter and etcher. Studied Edinburgh College of Art. Art master Dundee High School. Add: Broughty Ferry, Dundee. † GI 32, I 2, L 23, RSA 32.

CAESAR, Miss Evelyn Exh. 1933-35
Landscape painter. Add: The Gables, Upper Hale, Farnham, Surrey. † RA 3.

CAETANI, Lelia Exh. 1937
Landscape and figure painter. † LEF 40.

CAFE, James Watt b. 1857
Architectural and interior painter and etcher. Brother of Thomas Watt C. q.v. Studied King's College, London. Add: 46 Clifton Hill, St. John's Wood, London. † B 5, D 71, L 2, M 2, RA 8, RBA 2, RHA 1, RI 9, RSA 2.

CAFE, Thomas Watt 1856-1925
Architectural and interior and figure painter. Brother of James Watt C. q.v. Studied King's College London and RA Schools. R.B.A. 1896. Add: 46 Clifton Hill, St. John's Wood, London. † B 2, GI 2, L 5, M 1, RA 19, RBA 25, ROI 2, RSA 1.

CAFFERATA, Miss B.J. Exh. 1896-1915
Nottingham 1896; Grantham, Lincs. 1911. † N 9.

CAFFERATA, Miss D. Exh. 1913-15
Grantham, Lincs. † N 3.

CAFFIERI, Hector* 1847-1932
Landscape painter and watercolourist. Studied in Paris under Bonnat and J. Lefebvre. R.B.A. 1876, R.I. 1885, R.O.I. 1894. Add: London 1880 and 1889; Cookham, Berks. 1887; Boulogne, France 1903. † AG 3, B 25, D 6, G 2, GI 24, L 26, M 15, NG 1, P 1, RA 38, RBA 58, RI 148, ROI 17, RSA 1, RSW 2.

CAFFIN, Miss Mary Exh. 1898
Broadway, Worcs. † NG 1.

CAFFIN, Miss Maud Exh. 1888-89
Sculptor. Add: Broadway, Worcs. † RBA 2.

CAFFREY, Miss Mary Exh. 1911-25
Airfield House, Andersonstown, Belfast. † RHA 4.

CAFFYN, Walter Wallor* d. 1898
Landscape painter. Add: 1 South Villas, Vincent Road, Dorking, Surrey. † RA 10, RBA 8, ROI 5.

CAGNA, A. Exh. 1910
9 Rue Bocard de Saron, Paris. † L 1.

CAHILL, J. Exh. 1881-86
197 Gt. Brunswick Street, Dublin. † RHA 3.

CAHILL, Mrs. Kennedy
See BAKER, Frances

CAHILL, Richard S. Exh. 1881-1900
Figure painter. Add: Keswick, Cumberland 1881; London 1885. † B 5, L 5, M 3, RHA 12, RI 3.

CAILLE, Leon* 1836-1907
French Artist. Exh. 1883. † GI 1.

CAIN, Charles William b. 1893
Etcher. Studied Camberwell School of Art. 1915 served with Artists Rifles in Near East. Worked in a studio in Baghdad for a year after the war. On his return to England studied Royal College of Art. Add: London 1921; Beckenham, Kent 1925. † CHE 1, FIN 7, GI 3, L 8, RA 21, RSA 4.

CAINE, Miss Muriel Exh. 1919-25
Birkenhead 1919; Bebington, Cheshire 1924. † B 2, L 5, RCA 6.

CAINE, Miss Mary Hall Exh. 1935
London. † RCA 1.

CAINE, Osmund b. 1914
Painter and lithographer. Add: 7 Thyra Grove, Nottingham 1938. † B 3, N 8.

CAIRATI, Gerolamo Exh. 1905
62 Goethestrasse, Munich, Germany. † I 2.

CAIRD, Andrew J. Exh. 1926-32
Carlisle. † RSA 7.

CAIRD, Miss Rorie Exh. 1918-19
13 Charlotte Square, Edinburgh. † RSA 4.

CAIRNEY, John Exh. 1883-1906
Glasgow and Bearsden. † GI 38, RHA 5, RSA 7.

CAIRNCROSS, Charles Exh. 1900-9
Edinburgh. † GI 1, L 1, RSA 4.

CAIRNES, W.S. Exh. 1887
Seafield, Malahide, Dublin. † RHA 3.

CAIRNS, Hugh Exh. 1890-91
Glasgow. † GI 2.

CAIRNS, H.S. Exh. 1883-86
17 Rue Bleue, Paris. † RHA 8.

CAIRNS, James Exh. 1935-39
75a Hanover Street, Edinburgh. † RSW 4.

CAIRNS, James D. Exh. 1909-11
63 George Street, Edinburgh. † RSA 2.

CAIRNS, Robert D. Exh. 1905-40
Dumfries 1905; Bearsden 1931. † GI 8, RSA 1.

CAKE, Miss Dorothy F. Exh. 1935-38
Cragdarroch, Cove on Clyde, Dumbartonshire. † B 3, GI 2, RSW 1.

CALABRINE, L.A. Exh. 1938
c/o J. Bourlet & Sons, London. † RBA 1.

CALABRINI, Marquis Exh. 1939
18 via Adelaide, Ristori, Rome. † RSA 1.

CALBET, Antoine* Exh. 1912
† GOU 1.

CALDECOTT, Randolph* 1846-1886
Illustrator and watercolourist. Studied Manchester Art School and Slade School. Contributor to "Punch" and the "Graphic" and "London Society". R.I. 1882, R.O.I. 1883, b. Chester. Add: London 1880 and 1883; Sevenoaks, Kent 1882. Died Florida U.S.A. † B 2, BG 3, FIN 2, G 4, GI 2, L 8, M 7, RA 1, RI 6, ROI 5.

CALDER, Miss Edith Exh. 1900
Gorse Hill, New Brighton, Cheshire. † L 1

CALDER, Mrs. Fanny Dove Hamel
See LISTER

CALDER, W.Y. Exh. 1893-94
209 St. Vincent Street, Glasgow. † GI 2.

CALDERINI, Marco* Exh. 1892
Sura, Lago Maggiore, Italy. † GI 2.

CALDERON, Abelardo Alvarez Exh. 1880-94
Figure painter. Add: 9 Elm Tree Road, St. John's Wood, London. † RA 2, RBA 1.

CALDERON, Charles Exh. 1886
Sculptor. Add: c/o Lucas, 31 New Bond treet, London. † RA 1.

CALDERON, Elwyn Exh. 1897-98
Portrait painter. Add: London. † RA 2.

CALDERON, Fred Exh. 1896
Burlington House, Piccadilly, London. † RA 2.

CALDERON, Philip Hermogenes 1833-1898
Domestic, portrait and historical painter. b. Poitiers. Studied at J.M. Leigh's Art School, London and under Picot in Paris. 1887 elected keeper of the Royal Academy and managed the RA Schools. A.R.A. 1864, R.A. 1867. "Renunciation" purchased by Chantrey Bequest 1891. Add: London. † AG 1, B 1, FIN 2, G 6, GI 2, L 10, M 7, NG 1, P 2, RA 35, RBA 2.

CALDERON, William Frank 1865-1943
Portrait, landscape, figure and sporting painter. Son of Philip Hermogenes C. q.v. Studied Slade School. Founder and Principal of the School of Animal Painting 1894-1916. R.O.I. 1891. Add: London 1883 and 1890; Midhurst, Surrey 1889; Charmouth, Dorset 1922. † B 9, FIN 8, G 1, GI 1, L 22, M 10, NG 1, P 10, RA 61, RBA 3, RHA 6, ROI 9.

CALDERSMITH, M. Exh. 1940
York Studio, Piazza Chambers, Covent Garden, London. † SWA 2.

CALDERWOOD, Mrs. A.L.R. Exh. 1933-40
35 Harriet Street, Glasgow. † GI 6, RSW 4.

CALDERWOOD, Miss Dorothy Exh. 1930
† L 1.

CALDERWOOD, Miss Winifred D. Exh. 1929-30
83 Hampton Road, Forest Gate, London. † L 3.

CALDERWOOD, William Leadbetter b. 1865
Portrait painter. Studied Edinburgh College of Art. Travelled and worked in U.S.A., Italy and Spain. Add: Edinburgh. † GI 2, L 1, P 1, RSA 12.

CALDOW, Hugh Exh. 1919
61 Exeter Drive, Partick, Glasgow. †, GI 1.

CALDWELL, Miss Charlotte Exh. 1913
Elderlie, Albion Street, New Brighton, Cheshire. † L 1.

CALDWELL, Edmund* d. 1930
Landscape and animal painter. Add: London 1881 and 1898; Swanley, Kent 1887; Guildford, Surrey 1890. † D 2, GI 1, L 4, M 1, RA 9, RBA 4, RHA 1, RI 22, ROI 6.

CALDWELL, Miss Jean M. Exh. 1926
Metropolitan School of Art, Kildare Street, Dublin. † RHA 1.

CALDWELL, Miss Lizzie Exh. 1900
82 Dixon Avenue, Crosshall, Glasgow. † GI 1.

CALDWELL, Mary E. Exh. 1887
Bushey, Herts. † GI 1.

CALDWELL, Tom R. Exh. 1904
Still life painter. Add: 22 Marlborough Terrace, Mansfield, Notts. † N 1.

CALDWELL, W. Exh. 1880-1900
Edinburgh 1880; Glasgow 1900. † G 1, GI 2, RSA 23.

CALEY, Miss Elsie M. Exh. 1929
Landscape painter. Add: Langley Dale, Grove Avenue, Nottingham. † N 1.

CALKIN, Lance b. 1859
Portrait and domestic painter. Studied Slade School and RA Schools. R.B.A. 1884, R.O.I. 1895. Add: London. † ALP 1, B 6, G 4, GI 1, L 9, M 11, NG 22, P 6, RA 30, RBA 14, ROI 27.

CALLAHAN, James E. Exh. 1895-98
19 Lucretia Road, Kennington, London. † RA 2.

CALLARD, J. Percy Exh. 1882-89
Landscape and domestic painter. Add: London. † G 1, L 2, M 1, RA 1, RBA 3, ROI 2.

CALLARD, Miss Lottie Exh. 1883-94
Domestic painter. Add: London. † GI 1, L 4, RA 4, RBA 1, ROI 4.

CALLARD, Miss Liebie Exh. 1915-23
Sculptor. Add: London. † L 2, RA 3.

CALLCOTT, C. Exh. 1881-83
Dublin 1881; London 1883. † RHA 4.

CALLCOTT, Frederick T. Exh. 1880-1914
Sculptor. Add: London. † D 1, G 1, L 16, M 3, NG 1, RA 21, RBA 5.

CALLCOTT. Mrs. Florence See NEWMAN

CALLCOTT, William J. Exh. 1881-96
Marine painter. Add: London. † B 2, RA 4, RHA 1, RI 2.

CALLEAR, Miss Agnes Exh. 1934-40
Corlatt, Frankfort Avenue, Rathgar. † RHA 10.

CALLENDER, Bessie Exh. 1931-37
Sculptor and pencil artist. Studied Art Students League, New York. Add: London. † GI 1, L 1, RA 5.

CALLIAS, de See D

CALLOT, Georges Exh. 1901
Domestic painter. c/o R.J. Stannard, 30 Gt. Russell Street, London. † RA 1.

CALLOW, G.S. Exh. 1883
Hotel Street, Leicester. † L 1.

CALLOW, William* 1812-1908
Landscape, architectural and marine painter. Taught in Paris and appointed drawing master to the family of Louis Philippe. A.R.W.S. 1838, R.W.S. 1848. Add: Gt. Missenden, Bucks 1880. † B 5, CON 1, FIN 2, GI 3, L 10, M 9, RWS 298, WG 119.

CALLOWHILL, J. Exh. 1881-82
Spetchley Road, Worcester. † B 1, RHA 1.

CALLOWHILL, Scott Exh. 1882
London Road, Worcester. † B 3.

CALLUM, Frances E. Exh. 1910-13
Landscape and miniature portrait painter and teacher. Studied Leeds School of Art. Add: 30 Kensington Terrace, Leeds 1910. † L 5.

CALLWELL, Anette Exh. 1882-87
Landscape, figure and coastal painter. Add: London. † D 2, G 1, RA 3, RBA 2, ROI 1.

CALLWELL, Winifred O. Exh. 1922
† SWA 2.

CALOSCI, Arturo Exh. 1889-90
25 Queen Ann Street, London. † B 1, RBA 1.

CALTHROP, Claude Andrew* 1845-1893
Genre and historical painter. Studied under John Sparks. Lived in Paris for a time. Add: London 1880. † B 5, GI 2, L 4, M 3, RA 22, RHA 1, TOO 3.

CALTHROP, Dion Clayton d. 1937
Painter and theatrical scenery and costume designer. Exh. 1900-3. Add: London. † BG 1, RA 2, ROI 1.

CALTHROP, Gladys Exh. 1938
Theatrical designer. † RED 11.

CALTHROP, Mable Exh. 1881-98
London. † RA 3, SWA 1.

CALUWAERS, Jean Joseph Exh. 1916
78 Elms, Clapham Park, London. † RSA 6.

CALUWE, de See D

CALVELY, J. Exh. 1885
Fountain Cottage, Cheetwood, Manchester. † M 1

CALVERLEY, William Exh. 1929
52 Palatine Road, Blackburn, Lancs. † L 1.

CALVERT, Edith L. Exh. 1886-93
Flower painter. Add: London. † RBA 2, SWA 3.

CALVERT, Edwin Sherwood* 1844-1898
Landscape painter. Often painted in N. France. R.S.W. 1878. Add: Glasgow 1880 and 1889; London 1884. † B 3, D 1, DOW 3, GI 31, L 17, M 1, NG 6, RA 14, RBA 1, RHA 3, RI 1, RSA 17, RSW 36.

CALVERT, Frederick Exh. 1900-9
Figure painter. London. † RA 2.

CALVERT, Jane Gordon Exh. 1931-34
Miniature painter. Studied Ablett School, Dublin. Add: Wetmore, Onibury, Salop. † RA 4, RI 4.

CALVERT, L. Delepierre Exh. 1883-85
Sculptor. Add: London. † D 1, RA 1.

CALVERT, Samuel* Exh. 1882-85
Manchester. † M 3.

CALVERT, S.S. Exh. 1882
1 Doune Terrace, Kelvinside, Glasgow. † GI 1.

CALVES, Madame G. Exh. 1881-82
16 Avenue Trudaine, Paris. † RHA 3.

CALVES, Leon George Exh. 1911
Animal painter. † BRU 1.

CALVET, Henri Exh. 1909-10
c/o Allied Artists' Association, London. † LS 6.

CALVI, Pietro Exh. 1880-83
Sculptor. Add: Milan, Italy. † RA 3.

CAMBIER, Juliette Exh. 1922
† GOU 1.

CAMBIER, Louise Exh. 1922
† GOU 1.

CAMBIER, Louis G.* Exh. 1903
12 Avenue Jeanne, Brussels. † L 1.

CAMBIER, Nestor Exh. 1916-31
Portrait painter. Add: Henley on Thames, Oxon. † RA 3.

CAMBOS, J.J. Exh. 1907
16 Impasse di Maine, Paris. † L 1.

CAMERON, Alexander Exh. 1921-29
Seton House, Jedburgh 1921; Port Helen, Islay 1929. † GI 1, RSA 3.

CAMERON, Adeline A. Exh. 1888-1907
Married to Hugh C. q.v. Add: London 1880; c/o Lloyds Bank, Hereford 1903. † D 10, RSA 1.

CAMERON, Miss A.E. Exh. 1880
Milton House, Sunderland. † RSA 1.

CAMERON, Miss A.J. Exh. 1938
45 Victoria Street, Aberdeen. † RSA 1.

CAMERON, Alexander K. Exh. 1889
42 Dundas Street, Glasgow. † GI 2.

CAMERON, C. Exh. 1933
Washington, U.S.A. † SWA 1.

CAMERON, Mrs. Campbell Exh. 1882
38 Via Degli, Rome, Italy. † G 2.

CAMERON, C.E. Exh. 1922
27 Cooper Street, Doncaster, Yorks. † B 1.

CAMERON, Duncan* Exh. 1880-1908
Landscape painter. Add: Edinburgh. † GI 18, L 5, M 6, RA 14, RBA 5, RHA 3, RSA 85.

CAMERON, D.G. Exh. 1898
c/o A.W. Collie, 39B Old Bond Street, London. † NG 2.

CAMERON, Miss Doreen M. Exh. 1929-32
Sundown, Meols Drive, Hoylake, Cheshire. † L 3.

CAMERON, Sir David Young* 1865-1945
Painter, etcher and illustrator. Studied Glasgow and Edinburgh. Official artist World War I for Canadian Government. Trustee National Gallery of Scotland and National Gallery of London. A.R.A. 1916, R.A. 1920, A.R.E. 1889, R.E. 1895, R.O.I. 1902, A.R.S.A. 1904, R.S.A. 1918, R.S.W. 1906, H.R.S.W. 1934, A.R.W.S. 1904, R.W.S. 1915. Knighted 1924. Brother of Katharine C. q.v. Add: Edinburgh 1886; Glasgow 1887; Kippen, Stirlingshire and London 1900. † AB 1, AG 9, B 1, BA 17, BAR 34, BK 4, CG 14, CON 134, FIN 206, G 23, GI 56, GOU 8, I 24, L 92, LEI 14, M 19, NEA 2, NG 3, RA 71, RE 139, RHA 4, RI 4, ROI 8, RSA 80, RSW 10, RWS 33, TOO 23.

CAMERON, E. Josephine Exh. 1912-14
30 Lansdowne Crescent, Glasgow. † GI 2, L 1.

CAMERON, George C. Exh. 1939
15 The Oval, Clarkston. † RSA 3.

CAMERON, Mrs. Hardinge Exh. 1916-17
London 1916; Oxford 1917. † LS 6.

CAMERON, Hugh* 1835-1918
Portrait and genre painter. Studied under Scott Lauder at the Trustees Academy 1852. R.O.I. 1883, A.R.S.A. 1859, R.S.A. 1869, R.S.W. 1878, H.R.S.W. 1916. Add: Kensington, London 1880; Lower Largo, Fife 1889; Edinburgh 1894. † G 9, GI 20, L 1, RA 11, RBA 1, ROI 8, RSA 88, RSW 9, RWS 1.

CAMERON, H. Armstrong Exh. 1901-23
Served in forces World War I. Add: Largo, Fife 1901; Edinburgh 1907. † L 1, RSA 12, RSW 2.

CAMERON, Isa Exh. 1938
† P 1.

CAMERON, Isabel Armstrong Exh. 1908
45 George Square, Edinburgh. † RSA 1.

CAMERON, J. Exh. 1888-89
15 Hill Street, Garnet Hill, Glasgow. † GI 2.

CAMERON, John Exh. 1912-22
Portrait painter. Add: 16 Wellington Square, Chelsea, London. † I 2, L 1, RA 2.

CAMERON, John Exh. 1888-1931
Etcher and dry point artist. Add: Inverness 1917; Corstorphine 1918. † B 11, GI 4, L 5, RHA 2, RSA 16.

CAMERON, J. Bruce Exh. 1902-38
Glasgow 1902; Milngavie, N.B, 1912. † GI 31, RSA 16.

CAMERON, Julia F. Exh 1880-1900
Flower and landscape painter. Add: London. † GI 1, RBA 2, RI 1, SWA 4.

CAMERON, John Jackson Exh. 1901-8
Illustrator. 296 King's Road, Chelsea, London. † LS 2, RA 1.

CAMERON, John P. Exh. 1899
135 Rue de Soeres, Paris. † RSA 1.

CAMERON, Mrs. Jessie T. Exh. 1896
8 Merchiston Place, Edinburgh. † RSA 1.

CAMERON, Katharine* 1874-1965
Mrs. Arthur Kay, sister of David Young C. q.v. Landscape and flower painter and etcher. Studied Glasgow School of Art 1898 and Colarossi's, Paris. A.R.E. 1920, R.S.W. 1897. Add: Glasgow 1893; Stirling 1910; Edinburgh 1928. † AR 2, BAR 26, BG 7, CON 56, FIN 47, G 7, GI 76, I 6, L 58, RA 18, RE 39, RSA 107, RSW 130, SWA 1, WG 153.

CAMERON, Miss L.T. Exh. 1914-20
London. † L 1, SWA 1.

CAMERON, Miss Lou V. Exh. 1932-37
Meiklehill, Kirkintilloch. † GI 5.

CAMERON, Mary Exh. 1889-97
Dublin. † RHA 2.

CAMERON, Mary d. 1921
Mrs. Cameron Millar. Painter of Spanish scenes. Add: Edinburgh. † GI 16, L 12, P 1, RA 2, RSA 53, RSW 2, SWA 1.

CAMERON, Sister M. Gertrude Exh. 1926-39
Miniature painter and illuminator. Studied illuminating at the British Museum. Add: Franciscan Convent, Bocking, Braintree, Essex. † RI 38.

CAMERON, Margaret Kerr Exh. 1899
8 Merchiston Place, Edinburgh. † RSA 1.

CAMERON, Marion L. Exh. 1932-34
Strathaven, Lanarkshire 1932; Glasgow 1934. † GI 2, RSA 1.

CAMERON, Margaret P. Exh. 1897-1902
140 Govan Street, Glasgow. † GI 1, RSA 1.

CAMERON, P. Exh. 1882-83
Limner's Club, Ridgefield, Manchester. † M 3.

CAMERON, Robert Exh. 1883-92
Edinburgh. † RSA 3.

CAMERON, Robert Christie Exh. 1938 40
130 Drumfrochar Road, Glasgow. † GI 1, RSW 1.

CAMERON, R. Macfarlane Exh. 1893
24 George Street, Edinburgh. † RSA 3.

CAMERON, S. Exh. 1934
12 Holland Road, Sutton. † SWA 1.

CAMERON, Samuel R. Exh. 1921-39
Sculptor. Add: London 1921; Nottingham 1939. † L 1, N 2, RA 6, RSA 8.

CAMERON, Miss T. Exh. 1887
18 Kensington Court Place, London. † L 1.

CAMERON, Miss Una Exh. 1929-39
Painter and wood engraver. Add: London. † AB 1, L 2, RHA 5, RSA 18.

CAMERON, W. Otway Exh. 1907
4 Earlston Road, Liscard, Cornwall. † L 1.

CAMINO, A.C. Exh. 1881
16 Avenue Trudaine, Paris. † RHA 1.

CAMM, Florence 1874-1960
Stained glass and decorative artist and cartoonist. In partnership with brothers Robert and Walter Herbert C. q.v. in firm founded by father Thomas William C. q.v. Studied Birmingham School of Art. Add: Smethwick, Birmingham 1905 and 1936; Warley Wood, Nr. Birmingham 1922. † B 2, L 8, RA 43, RSA 2.

CAMM, James F.P. Exh. 1892-1902
Birmingham 1892; Edinburgh 1902. † RHA 1, RSA 1.

CAMM, Miss N Exh. 1913-15
Harleston House, Quorn. † N 6.

CAMM, Robert 1878-1954
Stained glass artist. In partnership with sister Florence C. q.v. and brother Walter Herbert C. q.v. in firm founded by father Thomas William C. q.v. Studied Birmingham School of Art. Add: Smethwick 1920; Warley Wood, Nr. Birmingham 1931. † RA 13, RSA 1.

CAMM, Thomas William d. 1914
Stained glass artist. Father of Florence, Robert and Walter Herbert C. q.v. Add: Smethwick, Birmingham 1885. † B 2, RA 4, RHA 1.

CAMM, Walter Herbert b. 1876
Stained glass artist. In partnership with sister Florence and brother Robert C. q.v. In firm founded by father Thomas William C. q.v. Studied Birmingham and West Bromwich Schools of Art. Add: Smethwick, Birmingham 1907. † B 3, L 4, RA 47, RSA 3.

CAMMACK, Robert Exh. 1916
Dublin. † RHA 23.

CAMMACK, Robert A. Exh. 1899
56 Rathmines Road, Dublin. † RHA 1.

CAMMARANO, Mio Exh. 188
14 Piazza Barberini, Rome. † RSA 1.

CAMOIN, Charles* b. 187
French artist. Exh. 1924-28 † GOU 9.

CAMP, Isabella Exh. 188
Portrait painter. Add: 167 High Street Watford, Herts. † D 1, RBA 1.

CAMP, Robert C. Exh. 189
Pen and ink artist. Add: 2 Agnes Terrace Dame Agnes Street, Nottingham. † N 1.

CAMPBELL, A. Exh. 189
41 Howland Street, London. † B 1.

CAMPBELL, Alice C.T. Exh. 188
Flower painter. Add: 30 Richmon Terrace, Earl's Court, London. † SWA 1

CAMPBELL, Arthur Exh. 193
Landscape painter. Add: Belfast Telegrap Belfast, Ireland. † RHA 1.

CAMPBELL, A. Mellon Exh. 192
2 Upper Cliff Road, Gorleston on Se Norfolk. † L 1.

CAMPBELL, Mrs. Barbara Exh. 1936-3
Figure painter. Add: London. † NEA 1 RA 2, RBA 2, ROI 1, SWA 1.

CAMPBELL, Mrs. Beatrice Exh. 1925-3
Figure and portrait painter. Add: Clonar Kimmage Road, Terenure, Irelan † RHA 14.

CAMPBELL, Christopher b. 190
Painter, etcher and stained glass artis Studied Dublin Metropolitan School of Ar Add: 17 Brian Road, Clontarf, Dubli Ireland 1929. † RHA 48.

CAMPBELL, Lady Constance Exh. 189
Argyll. † D 1.

CAMPBELL, Lady Colin d. 191
Painter and art critic. Add: Londo 1880-99. † RBA 1, SWA 6.

CAMPBELL, Mrs. Corbett Exh. 1886-8
Edinburgh 1886; London 1888. † GI RSA 1.

CAMPBELL, Colin Cairness Clinton b. 189
Portrait and flower painter. Studied Ne York, Byam Shaw School and Slade Schoo Add: London 1927 and 1936; Argyll 193 Aldington, Kent 1938. † D 1, GI 1 GOU 2, RSA 7.

CAMPBELL, C.H. Exh. 191
The Moors, Pangbourne, Berks. † L RA 1.

CAMPBELL, Charles William d. 18
Engraver. Add: Tubs-Hill, Sevenoaks, Ke 1887. † RA 1.

CAMPBELL, D. Exh. 1891-
Glasgow. † GI 4.

CAMPBELL, Mrs. Douglas Exh. 19
16 Cheniston Gardens, Kensington, Lo don. † D 1.

CAMPBELL, Miss D.H. Exh. 19
12 Dene Mansions, West Hampste London. † RA 1.

CAMPBELL, Eleanora Exh. 18
149 Warrender Park Road, Edinburg † GI 1, RSA 1.

CAMPBELL, Mrs. E.C. Exh. 18
3 Marchhall Crescent, Edinburg † RSA 1.

CAMPBELL, Miss F.M. Exh. 1908-
Oakley House, Abingdon, Berks. † LS

CAMPBELL, George E. Exh. 1934-
Sculptor. Add: London. † RA 9, RBA RSA 3.

CAMPBELL, Mrs. H. Exh. 19
† P 1.

CAMPBELL, Hay Exh. 1892-
Bayswater, London. † B 3, P 2, RBA RSA 1.

CAMPBELL, Hugh Exh. 19
20 Union Street, Greenock. † RSW 1.

CAMPBELL, Miss Helen McD. Exh. 1935-40
Portrait painter. Add: 4 Joubert Studios, Jubilee Place, London. † NEA 1, P 5, RA 3, SWA 1.

CAMPBELL, I. Exh. 1912
Mrs. S. Williams. Add: Cowley Rectory, Nr. Cheltenham, Glos. † RA 1.

CAMPBELL, Ian Exh. 1926-40
Portrait painter. Add: Oban 1926; Glasgow 1930; Dollar, Clackmannanshire 1937. † GI 8, RA 2, RSA 8.

CAMPBELL, Ina Exh. 1916-22
Mrs. E.J. Unthoff. Add: 1 St. James Street, Glasgow. † GI 4, RSA 2.

CAMPBELL, James* 1828-1903
Genre and landscape painter. Studied RA Schools 1851. Add: 165 Northbrook Street, Prince's Road, Liverpool 1883. † L 3.

CAMPBELL, James Exh. 1880-96
Glasgow. † GI 8, RSA 1.

CAMPBELL, Miss Jane Exh. 1883
1 Park Circus, Ayr. † RSA 1.

CAMPBELL, Jean Exh. 1913-33
London 1913; East Grinstead, Sussex 1933. † L 30, LS 3, RA 1, RMS 4.

CAMPBELL, Jenny b. 1887
Mrs. R. Hipkins. Landscape painter. Visited New Zealand. Add: Ayr 1913; London 1928. † AB 23, GI 2, I 3.

CAMPBELL, John Exh. 1893-1907
Cathcart, Glasgow. † GI 4.

CAMPBELL, John Exh. 1930-37
Glasgow. † GI 2.

CAMPBELL, John Exh. 1930
28 Finchley Road, London. † RA 1.

CAMPBELL, John Exh. 1880-89
27 Mountjoy Square, Dublin, Ireland. † RHA 14.

CAMPBELL, J.A. Exh. 1886-1909
Glasgow. † GI 18, RSA 15.

CAMPBELL, Miss J.C. Exh. 1881
Sauchie House, Crieff, N.B. † RSA 1.

CAMPBELL, J.F. Exh. 1913
19 Wilton Road, Muswell Hill, London. † RA 1.

CAMPBELL, John Hay Exh. 1937-38
30 Cadzow Street, Hamilton. † GI 1,, RSA 1.

CAMPBELL, John Hodgson Exh. 1880-1906
Landscape and domestic painter. . Add: Edinburgh 1880; Newcastle-on-Tyne 1884. † L 1, RA 5, RI 7, RSA 11.

CAMPBELL, Laurence 1911-1964
Painter, sculptor and black and white artist. Studied Dublin Metropolitan School of Art. A.R.H.A. 1938, R.H.A. 1939, Keeper R.H.A. 1939. Add: Dublin 1930 and 1940; Stockholm, Sweden 1937; Paris 1939. † RHA 52.

CAMPBELL, Miss M. Exh. 1881-88
13 Derby Street, Trinity, Edinburgh. † RSA 13.

CAMPBELL, Miss Mabel Exh. 1928-29
Miniature portrait painter. Add: 22 Beaufort Mansions, London. † L 3, RA 2, RI 3.

CAMPBELL, Miss Mariot Exh. 1920-24
Milano, Vico Road, Dalkey, Nr. Dublin, Ireland. † RHA 3.

CAMPBELL, Molly Exh. 1915-37
Painter and etcher. Studied Goldsmith's College and Crystal Palace School of Art (scholarship) A.R.E. 1920. Add: Upper Norwood, London. † I 2, L 2, NEA 18, RA 8, RE 32, SWA 4.

CAMPBELL, Miss Muriel Exh. 1894-97
Painter and etcher. Add: London. † RA 2, SWA 1.

CAMPBELL, Miss M.A. Exh. 1926
26 Vicarage Avenue, Derby. † N 2.

CAMPBELL, Miss M.C. Exh. 1935-37
The Zephyrs, Red Hill, Worcs. †, B 1, SWA 3.

CAMPBELL, Miss Mary E. Exh. 1913-32
12 Wesley Avenue, Liscard, Wallasey, Cheshire. † L 18, RCA 4.

CAMPBELL, Miss Margaret M. Exh. 1936-38
33 Granville Street, Glasgow. † RSA 1, RSW 4.

CAMPBELL, Patrick Maitland Exh. 1919-28
Edinburgh. † RSA 1, RSW 1.

CAMPBELL, Phillys Vere Exh. 1911
Watercolour painter. † BG 20.

CAMPBELL, Rosella Exh. 1935
Flower painter. † BA 1.

CAMPBELL, Rowland Exh. 1937-39
c/o Robert Sielle, 14 Buckingham Street, London. † GOU 1, RA 1, ROI 1.

CAMPBELL, Robert A. Exh. 1940
Columba, 95 Colchester Road, Ipswich, Suffolk † RSA 2.

CAMPBELL, Roy B. Exh. 1932-38
82 Cambridge Terrace, London. † GI 3, RSA 1.

CAMPBELL, Reginald Henry b.1877
Portrait painter. Studied RSA Schools (Maclaine-Watter's Medal 1899, Keith Bursary, Chalmers Jervise Prize). Add: Edinburgh 1896; London 1917. † GI 7, RA 1, RSA 19.

CAMPBELL, Miss R.M. Exh. 1921-22
Airos, Sydenham Hill, London. † SWA 2.

CAMPBELL, Thomas Exh. 1901-40
Paisley and Glasgow. † L 5, GI 31, RSA 3.

CAMPBELL, Miss T.C. Exh. 1880
1 Erskine Place, Edinburgh. † RSA 2.

CAMPBELL, W.W. Exh. 1940
Ashfield, Lanarks. † GI 1.

CAMPI, G.* Exh. 1882
c/o Searle, Crediton, Devon. † M 2.

CAMPION, Howard Exh. 1880-83
Landscape painter. Visited USA. Add: London. † G 2, M 4, RA 3, RBA 7, RHA 4.

CAMPION, Sarai M. Exh. 1880-82
Mrs. Howard C. Landscape painter. Travelled on the Continent. Add: London. † B 2, RA 1, RBA 1, SWA 2.

CAMPOTOSTO*, Henry d.1910
Rustic genre painter. b. Brussels. Add: London 1882; Bletchingley, Surrey 1892. † B 6, RHA 1.

CAMPOTOSTO, Octavia Exh. 1882-92
Sister of Henry C. q.v. Add: 7 Kensington Gardens, London. † B 2, RHA 1.

CAMPRIANI, A. Exh. 1882
1 St. John's Wood Studios, London. † L 1.

CAMUS, Jean M. Exh. 1909
Rue St. Simon, Paris, France. † L 1.

CAMWELL, Alice Mabel Exh. 1908-36
Gold and silversmith, teacher of metalwork and jewellery making. Studied Birmingham Central School of Art (1 gold and 4 silver medals for jewellery design). Add: Walsall 1908; Selly Oak, Birmingham 1936. † B 10, L 26.

CAN, Miss E.M. Exh. 1906
Buckingham Palace Road, London. † SWA 1.

CANCHOIS, Henri Exh. 1883-90
Flower and still life painter. Add: London. † B 2, M 1, RBA 9, RHA 1, ROI 1.

CANDEL, W.P. Exh. 1888
† FA 1.

CANDIDA Exh. 1920
† SWA 4.

CANDLER, Mrs. Edith Benedicta Exh. 1911-13
Landscape painter. † ALP 12.

CANDOW, William Exh. 1924-33
Edinburgh 1924; Stirling 1928. † GI 1, RSA 4.

CANE, Edith Exh. 1880-84
Landscape painter. Add: 11 Lowndes Street, London. † SWA 7.

CANE, du See D

CANE, Herbert Collins Exh. 1883-91
Animal painter. Add: London. † B 4, L 2, M 3, RA 3, RI 5.

CANE, Percy S. Exh. 1929
2 Westminster Palace Gardens, London. † RA 1.

CANN, Annie Mary b. 1866
Watercolour painter and pastellier. Studied Wallasey School of Art. Add: 23 Penkett Road, Wallasey, Cheshire, 1924-33. † L 5.

CANN, Miss F.L. Exh. 1928-29
19 Warwick Drive, Wallasey, Cheshire. † L 2.

CANN, Gwendolen Exh. 1930
† P 1.

CANNEEL, E. Exh. 1915
30 Crockerton Road, Upper Tooting, London. † RA 1.

CANNELL, W. Otway See McCANNELL

CANNEY, Miss Grace E. Exh. 1929
Watercolour painter. Add: 33 St. Paul's Hill, Winchester, Hants. † RA 2.

CANNICCI, Niccolo* Exh. 1883
Figure and landscape painter. Add: 60 Bedford Gardens, Campden Hill, London. † RA 1.

CANNIECIONI, Leon Exh. 1923
18 Rue de Moulin de Beurre, Paris. † RSA 1.

CANNING, Miss Constance P. Exh. 1907-8
Bridge End, Warwick. † B 1, L 1.

CANNING, Miss Florence Exh. 1906-10
London. † B 2, LS 7, SWA 2.

CANNING, J. Exh. 1925
Flixton, Manchester. † RCA 1.

CANNING, Lilian Exh. 1917-36
Landscape painter. Add: London. † AB 2, B 5, L 2, RI 1, SWA 5.

CANNING, W. Exh. 1885
42 John Dalton Street, Manchester. † M 1.

CANNON, Edith Margaret Exh. 1892-1903
Portrait and miniature painter. Add: 7 Windsor Road, Ealing, London. † L 3, M 2, RA 1, RCA 1, RMS 1, ROI 5.

CANNON, H.W. Exh. 1890
Decorative designer. Add: 41 Fitzroy Square, London. † RBA 1.

CANNON, Thomas Exh. 1894
Sculptor. Add: 134 Akerman Road, N. Brixton, London. † RA 1.

CANNON, Walter Exh. 1908-13
156 Melforth Road, Thornton Heath, Surrey. † D 12.

CANONICA, Pietro b. c. 1870
Italian sculptor. Add: Torino 1903; Turin 1904; London 1905-06. † L 2, NG 1, RA 6.

CANTI, Horace R. Exh. 1894
Dorset Villa, Sutton, Surrey. † RBA 1.

CANTON, Susan Ruth Exh. 1880-1920
Sculptor. Add: London. † BRU 1, L 26, M 2, RA 22, RBA 8, RMS 1, SWA 8.

CANTRILL, J. Exh. 1883-93
100 Oxford Street, Manchester. † M 2.

CANTRILL, Mrs. Jean Exh. 1924-40
London 1924; Coleshill, Birmingham 1939. † B 3, SWA 1.

CANZIANI, Estella 1887-1964
Portrait and landscape painter, illustrator and decorator. Daughter of Louisa Starr, q.v. Studied Arthur Cope and Erskine Nichols' School, South Kensington and RA Schools. A.R.B.A. 1919, R.B.A. 1930. Add: London. † ALP 1, BG 54, L 5, NG 3, P 12, RA 23, RBA 14, RI 5, RID 2, RMS 3, RSA 1, SWA 6, WG 256.

CANZIANI, Mrs. Louisa Starr See STARR

CAPARN, I.J. Exh. 1884
Winthorpe Road, Newark on Trent, Notts. † N 1.

CAPARN, W.J. Exh. 1882-95
Landscape painter. Add: Benefield Road, Oundle, Northants 1882; London 1895. † B 2, D 4, GI 1, L 1, RBA 1, RHA 1, RI 3.

CAPEL-CURE, Mrs. H.M. Exh. 1914
Ladies Athenaeum Club, 32 Dover Street, London. † D 3.

CAPEY, Reco 1895-1961
Painter, carver and lacquer-work artist. Studied and taught Royal College of Art. Add: Stoke-on-Trent, 1915; London 1926. † FIN 3, GI 1, L 14, NEA 2, RA 5.

CAPMANY, Ramon b. 1899
or Capmany de Montaner. Landscape painter. b. Barcelona. Exh. 1937. † BA 1.

CAPON, Arthur Exh. 1921-40
Solihull, Warwicks. † B 22.

CAPON, Robert Exh. 1930
† L 1.

CAPON, R.M. Exh. 1903-04
49a Rodney Street, Liverpool. † L 2.

CAPPER, Miss Annie Exh. 1893
Huyton Park, Huyton, Lancs. † L 1.

CAPPER, Miss Edith* Exh. 1880-1908
Landscape painter. Add: London. † B 1, D 3, G 1, L 3, M 2, RA 2, RI 3, SWA 1.

CAPPER, Stewart Henbest 1859-1925
Royal Canadian Academician. Add: Edinburgh 1892-95. † GI 4, RSA 5.

CAPPON, Thomas Martin Exh. 1895-1915
Architect. Add: Dundee. † D 3, RA 5, RSA 1.

CAPSTICK, George T. Exh. 1910
Sandon Studios, Liberty Buildings, Liverpool. † L 1.

CAPUTO, Ulisse* b. 1872
Italian artist. Add: 17 Rue Boissonade, Paris 1907-13. † L 3, LS 8.

CARBONERO, Jose Moreno b. 1860
Spanish artist. Add: Marques del Riscall, Madrid, Spain 1906. † RA 1.

CARDEN, Lilian E. Exh. 1898-1902
Flower painter. Married Louis Ginnett q.v. Add: Brighton, Sussex. † RA 2.

CARDEN, Victor Exh. 1888
13 Fitzroy Street, London. † ROI 1.

CARDER, Arthur A. Exh. 1903-04
Architect. Add: 4 The Chase, Clapham Common, London. † RA 2.

CARDER, Frederick Exh. 1893
Sculptor. Add: Ivydene, John Street, Wordsley, Staffs. † RA 1.

CARDER, Frederick Exh. 1905
Stenben Glass Works, Corning, New York. † L 1.

CARDEW-CREE, Miss A. Exh. 1898-1905
Bushey, Herts. 1898; Sheffield 1901. † B 5, L 5, SWA 1.

CARDON, Claude* Exh. 1892-1915
Domestic painter. Add: London 1892 and 1908; Manchester 1901. † L 2, M 3, RA 9, RBA 1.

CARDOSO, Amadeo de Sousa 1887-1918
Portuguese painter. Add: 1 Villa Lowat, 38 bis Rue Boulevard, Paris 1914. † LS 3.

CARDWELL, Miss F.M. Exh. 1887-90
Landscape painter. Add: 11 Cromwell Place, London. † D 2, SWA 5.

CARELLI, Conrad H.R. b. 1869
Landscape painter and watercolourist. Studied Juliens, Paris 1889. Son of Gabriel C. q.v. Add: London. † B 2, L 3, NG 2, RA 1, RBA 4, RI 5.

CARELLI, Gabriel Exh. 1880-89
Interior painter. Add: London 1880 and 1884; Kenilworth 1882. † D 1, L 6, M 2, RA 1.

CAREW, Berta b. 1878
Mrs. Frank Carew. American miniature painter. A.R.M.S. 1921. Add: Pine Forge, Pennsylvania, U.S.A. 1921-22. † RMS 8.

CAREY, Miss A.S. Exh. 1881-84
6 Belhaven Terrace, Glasgow. † G 1, GI 2.

CAREY, Mrs. Charles Exh. 1881-84
Coastal painter. Add: Beaumont, Guernsey, C.I. † SWA 2.

CAREY, Charles William 1862-1943
Keeper of the Picture Gallery and art master at Royal Holloway College from 1887. Picture restorer. Studied South Kensington, Heatherleys, British Museum, St. John's Wood School of Art, Colarossi's Paris and RA SChools 1881. Add: London 1882. † RBA 1.

CAREY, Henrietta Exh. 1880-81
Still Life Painter. Add: The Park, Nottingham. † N 2.

CAREY, Joseph W. Exh. 1915-35
Watercolour landscape painter. Add: Belfast. † RHA 25.

CAREY, Miss Margery H. Exh. 1907-11
Lea Copse, Burgess Hill, Sussex. † B 2, M 1, RA 1.

CAREY, P. Norman Exh. 1914-21
Figure and portrait painter. Add: Nottingham 1914, Sherwood, Notts 1918, Castle Donington, Leics. 1921. † N 26.

CAREY, Miss Violet M. Exh. 1894-95
Portrait artist. Add: 39 Belsize Avenue, Hampstead, London. † RA 2.

CARFRAE, John Alex Exh. 1897-1921
3 Queen Street, Edinburgh. † RSA 4.

CARFRAE, Miss M. Exh. 1891-92
Edinburgh. † GI 2, RSA 1.

CARGILL, Miss A. Exh. 1899
Miniature portrait painter. Add: 26 Harrington Road, South Kensington, London. † RA 1.

CARGIN, Agnes R. Exh. 1908-09
Fortrose, Greystones, Co. Wicklow, Ireland. † GI 2, L 1, RHA 1.

CARIN, Miss Marie Exh. 1889
Miniature painter. Add: 51 Rue Palikao, Lille, France. † RA 3.

CARLANDI, Mrs. L. Haverty Exh. 1925-30
Portrait painter. Add: 5 Via Maria Christina, Rome, Italy. † RHA 4.

CARLANDI, Onorato b. 1848
Landscape painter. Add: Rome and London 1880-1921. † D 2, FIN 226, L 2, NG 1, RA 11, RHA 2, RI 7, WG 61.

CARL-ANGST, A. Exh. 1909
39 Boulevard St., Jacques, Paris. † L 1.

CARLAW, Miss E. Exh. 1883-87
385 Sauchiehall Street, Glasgow 1883; West George Street, Glasgow 1885. † GI 4, RSA 1.

CARLAW, John d. 1934
Landscape painter. R.S.W. 1885. Add: 385 Sauchiehall Street, Glasgow 1880; West George Street, Glasgow 1885; Helensburgh 1892 and 1895; Edinburgh 1894. † DOW 3, GI 46, RA 14, RHA 4, RSA 13, RSW 63.

CARLAW, Miss Lizzie Exh. 1883-84
385 Sauchiehall Street, Glasgow. † GI 2.

CARLAW, William Exh. 1880-89
385 Sauchiehall Street, Glasgow 1880; West George Street, Glasgow 1885. † D 1, GL 19, RHA 4, RI 1, RSA 2, RSW 33.

CARLEBUR, Francois* Exh. 1883-93
Marine Painter. Add: Dordrecht, B303, Holland. † RHA 14.

CARLES, Domingo Exh. 1937
† BA 3.

CARLESS, Frank Exh. 1904-05
Morley, Northiam, Sussex. † D 3.

CARLIER, Camille Marie Louise Exh. 1913
French painter. † ALP 2.

CARLILL, Mary Exh. 1895-98
Miniature painter. Married to Stephen B.C. q.v. R.M.S. 1898. Add: Kings Langley, Herts 1895; Collingham, Yorks. 1897; Natal, South Africa 1898. † L 2, NG 1, RA 3, RMS 2.

CARLILL, Stephen B. Exh. 1888-97
Figure and portrait painter. Add: Cottingham, Hull, Yorks. 1888; Kings Langley, Herts. 1895. † NG 3, RA 5, RI 1.

CARLIN, C.A. Exh. 1923-31
Figure and portrait painter. Add: Nottingham 1923; Chaddesden, Nr. Derby 1926. † N 4.

CARLINE, George 1855-1920
Flower, figure and landscape painter. R.B.A. 1904. Add: Lincoln 1886; London 1887, 1917; Repton, Derbys 1899; Oxford 1903. † B 7, DOW 59, GI 1, L 4, M 2, P 1, RA 10, RBA 52, RI 14, ROI 3, RSA 3.

CARLINE, Hilda Exh. 1920-40
Landscape painter. Daughter of George F.C. q.v. Married Stanley Spencer q.v. Add: London. † BA 1, GOU 5, NEA 8, RA 6.

CARLINE, Richard Cotton b. 1896
Landscape, figure and marine painter. Son of George F.C. q.v. Studied Paris and Slade School; Assistant Ruskin Drawing School and temporary Ruskin Master of Drawing, Oxford University. Travelled widely. Member London Group 1921. Add: London 1918. † COO 4, . G 1, GOU 148, LEI 2, LS 9, M 39, NEA 3.

CARLINE, Sydney William 1888-1929
Landscape and portrait painter and medallist. Son of George F.C. q.v. Studied Slade School and Paris. Ruskin master of Drawing, Oxford University. Travelled Middle East. Add: Oxford 1911; London 1920. † G 1, GI 1, GOU 86, LS 9, M 45, NEA 16, RA 4.

CARLING, Miss C. Exh. 1885
8 Grosvenor Road, Birkdale, Southport, Lancs. † L 1.

CARLISLE, 9th Earl of,
See HOWARD, George James

CARLISLE, Anne Exh. 1938
Portrait, figure and landscape painter. † RED 32.

CARLISLE, Cecilia b. 1882
Nee Sacret. Portrait and miniature painter and medallion artist. Studied Torquay, Glasgow and Liverpool. Add: Birkenhead 1927-28. † L 3, RA 1.

CARLISLE, G.B. Exh. 1933-38
Watercolour painter. † WG 11.

CARLISLE, John Exh. 1880-1916
Landscape painter. Travelled in Italy. Add: London. † B 1, D 190, L 4, RA 3, RBA 7, RI 10, TOO 1, WG 62.

CARLISLE, Mary Helen d. 1925
Painter of landscapes and gardens and figures b. South Africa. d. New York. Add: London 1890. † B 1, D 4, GI 1, L 12, NG 3, RA 6, RBA 2, WG 40.

CARLOPEZ Exh. 1911
Figure painter. † GOU 5.
CARLOS, Ernest S. Exh. 1901-15
Figure and military painter. Add: 42 Foxley Road, North Brixton, London. † RA 8.
CARL-ROSA, Mario* Exh. 1891
17 Rue Cauchois, Paris. † GI 1.
CARLYLE, Miss Exh. 1887
44 Esplanade, Greenock. † GI 2.
CARLYLE, Florence Exh. 1896-1921
Figure painter. Add: London 1896 and 1921; Crowborough, Sussex 1914. † L 1, RA 8.
CARLYLE, Fred W. Exh. 1933
502 Duke Street, Glasgow. † RSA 1.
CARLYON, Cecily K. Exh. 1916-35
Landscape painter. A.S.W.A. 1932. Add: Exeter, Devon. † RA 1, RBA 1, RI 3, SWA 12.
CARMICHAEL, C.H.R. Exh. 1928
116 Princes Road, Liverpool. † L 1.
CARMICHAEL, Daniel Exh. 1912
34 Causewayside, Paisley, Glasgow. † GI 1.
CARMICHAEL, Duncan Exh. 1891
1 Cromwell Grove, West Kensington, London. † RA 1.
CARMICHAEL, Frank J. Exh. 1923-29
Portrait painter. Add: Leicester. † L 5, P 3, RA 1, RSA 1.
CARMICHAEL, Lady Gibson Exh. 1904
Miss Mary Helen Elizabeth Nugent. Married Sir Thomas Gibson Carmichael (1st Baron of Stirling). Travelled widely. Add: Balerno, Italy 1901. † RSA 2.
CARMICHAEL, Herbert See SCHMALZ
CARMICHAEL, Stewart b. 1867
Portrait painter, decorator and architect. Studied Dundee, Antwerp, Brussels and Paris. Add: Dundee. † GI 6, L 4, RSA 71.
CARNDUFF, D. M'Queen Exh. 1918
1 Johnston Street, Paisley. † GI 1.
CARNE, Richard A. Exh. 1880
27 Mecklenburgh Square, London. † RA 1.
CARNEGIE, Miss I.F. Exh. 1883-97
Dublin, Ireland. † L 7, RHA 22.
CARNEGIE, Rachel b. 1901
Mrs. D. Chayton. Portrait painter and etcher. Studied Slade School and Chelsea Polytechnic. Add: London 1929; Northallerton, Yorks. 1936. † P 3, RA 2, RHA 4.
CARNEVALE, Giuseppe Exh. 1889
Sculptor. Add: 10 Piazza Turreta del Monte, Tome, Italy. † RA 1.
CARNIEL, R. Exh. 1914
69 Rue Froidevaux, Paris, France. † LS 3.
CARNOCK, J.J. Exh. 1886
7 Richmond Hill, Clifton, Bristol. † M 3.
CARO-DELVAILLE, Henry* 1876-1928
French artist. Add: Paris 1905. † I 1.
CAROE, Mrs. G. Exh. 1934
18 Markham Square, London. † NEA 1.
CAROE, William Douglas c. 1858-1938
Architect to the Ecclesiastical Commission. Add: London. † GI 4, L 20, RA 102, RSA 3.
CAROLUS-DURAN, Emile Auguste* 1838-1917
French portrait painter and teacher. Elected Academie des Beaux Arts 1904. Exh. 1883-1909. Add: Paris. † B 2, GI 2, NG 1, P 7, RA 12.
CARON, Alexandre Exh. 1912-18
Paris. † L 3, RA 1.
CARPENTER, Alfred A. Exh. 1899-1900
Decorative and tapestry artist. Add: 64 Charlotte Street, Fitzroy Square, London. † RA 2.
CARPENTER, A.R. Exh. 1882-88
Burlington Chambers, Birmingham. † B 8.
CARPENTER, Miss Betty Exh. 1924-27
91 Shrewsbury Road, Birkenhead. † L 5.
CARPENTER, Dora Exh. 1880-84
Domestic Painter. Add: Brighton and London. † L 1, RA 1, RBA 2.
CARPENTER, H. Barrett Exh. 1890-1903
Painter and teacher. Add: Liverpool 1890; Rochdale, Lancs. 1903. † L 5, M 2, ROI 1.
CARPENTER, J. Lant Exh. 1880-1901
Landscape painter. N.S.A. 1890; Castle Connington, Leics. 1880; Matlock Bank, Derbys. 1899; Newark, Notts. 1900. † N 69, RA 3, RBA 2.
CARPENTER, O.R. Exh. 1890
14 Burlington Chambers, New Street, Birmingham. † B 1.
CARPENTER, William 1818-99
Figure, portrait, historical and mythological painter. Lived in London until 1862 when he went to Boston, U.S.A. Travelled with the Punjab Irregular Force to Afghanistan in 1855. Exh. 1885. † G 1.
CARPENTER, William John Exh. 1884-93
Figure painter. Add: London. † D 2, GOU 3, L 4, RA 1, RBA 9, RHA 1, RI 4, ROI 1.
CARPENTIER, Evariste* b. 1845
Belgian artist. Add: Paris 1884; Brabant, Belgium 1896. † GI 3.
CARPENTIER, Felix Exh. 1888
Flower painter. Add: c/o M.P. Lehuraux, 6 Dareville Road, Denmark Hill, London. † RBA 1.
CARPENTIER, Modeste Exh. 1913
31 Rue de l'Abbaye, a Henin-Lietard, Pas de Calais, France. † RSA 1.
CARPMAEL, Mrs. Cecilia Exh. 1898-1930
Flower, figure and landscape painter. Add: Bromley, Kent 1898; London 1905. † I 2, L 15, LS 15, NEA 4, RA 10, RMS 1, ROI 2.
CARR, Allan Exh. 1939
† NEA 1.
CARR, Alwyn C.E. Exh. 1905-22
Silversmith. Served with forces during World War 1. Add: London. † NG 1, RA 2.
CARR, Mrs. A. Fortescue Exh. 1885
Watercolour flower painter. Add: 3 Grove Place, Pont Street, London. † SWA 1.
CARR, Mrs. Anita M. Exh. 1908-39
Landscape and portrait painter. Add: Pulborough, Sussex 1908 and 1938; Esher, Surrey 1911. † COO 2, NG 1, RA 4, SWA 3.
CARR, A. Michael Exh. 1939
† GOU 4.
CARR, Bessie Exh. 1883-90
Figure and portrait painter. Add: Paris 1883; Worthing 1885 and 1890; London 1887. † RA 3, RBA 2.
CARR, Bernard James Exh. 1910-23
Landscape and seascape painter and etcher. Studied Sheffield College of Arts and Crafts and Juliens, Paris. Art Critic with the "Sheffield Daily Telegraph". Add: Sheffield. † L 2, RCA 1, RHA 3.
CARR, David 1847-1920
Figure painter. Add: London 1880, 1882 and 1895; Paris 1881; Beer, Devon 1891. † B 10, D 4, FIN 1, G 9, GI 15, L 6, M 21, NG 32, RA 6, RI 7, ROI 14, TOO 1.
CARR, Dorothy Comyns Exh. 1901-34
Landscape and flower painter. Add: London 1901; Newcastle on Tyne 1934. † L 2, NEA 4, NG 8, RA 1, RI 1, ROI 1, SWA 3.
CARR, Ellis Exh. 1884
† ROI 1.
CARR, Edith M. 1875-1949
Portrait and miniature painter and church decorator. Studied Croydon School of Art and Academie Delecluse, Paris. A.S.W.A. 1930, S.W.A. 1933. Add: Croydon 1907 and 1914; London 1912. † L 4, RA 20, RMS 5, SWA 6.
CARR, Mrs. G. Exh. 1901-16
Sculptor. Add: London. † L 3, RA 6.
CARR, Henry Exh. 1907-29
Liverpool. † L 15.
CARR, Henry Marvell b. 1894
Landscape and portrait painter. Studied Leeds College of Art and Royal College of Art. Add: Leeds 1922; Westerham, Kent 1927; London 1935. † L 1, NEA 17, P 2, RA 17, RBA 3.
CARR, Mrs. Laura Exh. 1894-1902
Boyton House, Beckenham, Kent. † RBA 6, ROI 1, SWA 16.
CARR, Lyell* 1857-1912
American painter. Add: New York 1890. † RA 1.
CARR, Miss Mabel Exh. 1898-99
Ringstead, The Grove, Wandsworth, London. † SWA 3.
CARR, Sydney H. Exh. 1894
Bratoft, Penzance, Cornwall. † GI 1.
CARR, Terence Exh. 1929-37
Architect. Add: Kensington, London 1929; Woking, Surrey 1930. † RA 3.
CARR, Thomas Exh. 1907-9
Carlisle, Cumberland 1907; Bushey, Herts. 1908. † B 5, NG 1, RA 2, RCA 1, RSA 4.
CARR, Thomas b. 1909
Landscape painter. Add: c/o Contemporary Pictures, 16 South Leinster Street, Dublin, Ireland 1940. † RHA 1.
CARRE, Joseph S.M. Exh. 1900-14
Sculptor. Add: London 1900; Dublin 1909. † RA 1, RHA 13.
CARRERE, F. Cuillon Exh. 1913
11 Rue des Sablons, Paris 16e. † LS 3.
CARRICK, Alexander Exh. 1910-40
Sculptor. Studied Royal College of Art. A.R.S.A. 1918, R.S.A. 1929. Add: Edinburgh. † GI 14, L 3, P 2, RA 6, RSA 46.
CARRICK, Ethel Exh. 1903-39
Landscape, figure and flower painter. Married Emanuel Phillips Fox q.v. Travelled widely. Add: Ealing 1903; Paris 1906; London 1918. † ALP 8, COO 67, I 2, LS 5, RA 5, RI 2, ROI 8, SWA 2.
CARRICK, Edward Anthony b. 1904
Painter, etcher, engraver and illustrator. Son of Edward Gordon Craig q.v. Studied in Italy 1917-26. Add: London 1930. † RED 5.
CARRICK, E. Jean Exh. 1938
Laburnum Cottage, Thistlewaite, York. † RBA 2.
CARRICK, James Exh. 1933
25 Wellington Square, Ayr. † RSA 1.
CARRICK, Robert* 1849-1904
Landscape and genre painter. A.R.I. 1848, R.I. 1850, R.O.I. 1883. Add: London. † B 1, L 2, RA 1, RI 37, ROI 19.
CARRICK, William Arthur Laurie b. 1879
Landscape and seascape painter. Studied and practised architecture but gave up for health reasons. Add: Pollokshields, Glasgow 1905; Biggar, Lanarks 1913; Symington, Lancs. 1918; Findhorn, Forres 1937. † GI 32, L 9, RSA 10, RSW 13.
CARRIE, de SEE D

CARRIER-BELLEUSE, Louis Robert 1848-1913
French artist. Exh. 1885-98. Add: Paris. † GI 1, L 1.

CARRIER-BELLEUSE, Pierre* 1851-1933
French painter and illustrator. Exh. 1903-13. Add: Paris. † I 1, L 2, LS 1.

CARRIERE, A.F. Exh. 1905
† P 1.

CARRIERE, Eugene* 1849-1906
French artist. Exh. 1903-6. Add: Paris. † I 5, P 3.

CARRINGTON, Adeline Exh. 1914-29
Flower painter. A.S.W.A. 1925. Add: London 1914; Northam, Devon 1923; Ightham, Sevenoaks, Kent 1925. † LS 3, RA 1, SWA 9.

CARRINGTON, Dora Exh. 1914-16
Landscape, figure and flower painter. Add: London. † NEA 3.

CARRINGTON, Dorothy Exh. 1921
† G 1.

CARRINGTON, Donald P. b. 1907
Portrait painter. Add: Stoneygate, Leicester 1937. † RA 4.

CARRINGTON, Edith Exh. 1881
Flower painter. Add: 4 Spencer's Belle Vue, Bath, Som. † SWA 1.

CARRINGTON, James Yates 1857-1892
Landscape and genre painter. Add: London. † B 3, G 3, GI 4, L 4, M 9, RA 11, RBA 6, RE 5, ROI 4, TOO 1.

CARRINGTON, Louis Exh. 1880-88
Landscape and coastal painter. Add: London 1880; Dorking, Surrey 1884. † B 3, M 1, RBA 5, RI 4, ROI 2.

CARRINGTON, Mrs. Patty Exh. 1883-87
Watercolour painter. Add: St. Cloud, Nr. Worcester. † RI 3.

CARROLL, Colin R. d. c. 1899
Landscape painter. A.R.E. 1895. Add: 8 Cavendish Road, Blundellsands, Liverpool. † L 24, RA 1, RE 19.

CARROLL, F.J. Exh. 1913
242 Stanley Road, Kirkdale, Liverpool. † L 1.

CARROLL, G.E. Exh. 1887
Beaconsfield Road, Parkgate, Liverpool. † L 1.

CARROLL, Miss Jane de la Cour Exh. 1883-1906
Sculptor. Add: London. † I 1, RA 1.

CARROLL, J. Rawson Exh. 1888
176 Gt. Brunswick Street, Dublin. † RHA 2.

CARROLL, Jessie R. Exh. 1899
8 Cavendish Road, Blundellsands, Liverpool. † L 1.

CARROLL, William Exh. 1895
Miniature portrait painter. Add: 4 West Hampstead Studios, Sherriff Road, London. † RA 1.

CARRUTHERS, Frank J.C. Exh. 1890-96
Architect. Add: Edinburgh 1890; Dumfries 1896. † RA 1, RSA 1.

CARRUTHERS, George P. Exh. 1897-1930
Landscape painter. Add: Leeds 1897; London 1928. † RA 3.

CARRUTHERS, Ivy Exh. 1940
† COO 1.

CARRUTHERS, James Exh. 1909-11
Glasgow. † GI 2, L 1.

CARRUTHERS, Mrs. J.R. Exh. 1896
View Park, Partick, Glasgow. † GI 1.

CARRUTHERS, The Hon. Mrs. Mary b. 1878
Berner Hall, Kings Lynn, Norfolk 1939. † B 1, RBA 1, RSA 3.

CARRUTHERS, Victoria M. Exh. 1892-94
82 Langside Road, Crosshill, Lanarks. † GI 2.

CARSE, A. Duncan Exh. 1904-38
Figure and decorative painter. Add: London 1904; Knebworth, Herts. 1922; Crowthorne, Berks. 1925. † FIN 8, L 3, LS 1, RA 13.

CARSLAKE, Mary b. 1904
Lettering and woodcut artist and illuminator. Studied Birmingham School of Art. Add: Edgbaston, Birmingham 1927; Alvechurch, Worcs. 1929. † B 17, M 1.

CARSLAW, Evelyn J.L. Exh. 1908
25 Sandyford Place, Glasgow. † GI 1.

CARSON, A.S. Exh. 1880
Portrush, Co. Antrim, Ireland. † RHA 1.

CARSON, W.M. Exh. 1884-95
Glasgow. † L 1, GI 18

CARSTAIRS, H. Exh. 1931
Lino-cut artist. † RED 1.

CARSTAIRS, J. Exh. 1931
Lino-cut artist. † RED 1.

CARSTAIRS, J.L. Exh. 1926
20 Landsdowne Crescent, Glasgow. † GI 1.

CARSTAIRS, Stewart Exh. 1925
c/o M. Knoedler & Co. 15 Old Bond Street, London. † L 1.

CARSTENSEN, A.R. Exh. 1899
c/o Chapman Bros. 251 King's Road, London. † B 2.

CARSTENSEN, Thelma Exh. 1930-39
Landscape painter and etcher. Add: Hornsey, London. † GOU 44, NEA 9, RA 3, RBA 1.

CARSTON, Norman Exh. 1892
Newlyn, Penzance, Cornwall. † RSA 1.

CARSWELL, Mary F. Exh. 1882-85
61 Sardinia Place, Glasgow. † GI 1, RSA 3.

CARTE, Miss D.M. Exh. 1902
13 Upper Woburn Place, Tavistock Square, London. † L 2.

CARTE, Miss Rose Exh. 1885
63 King's Road, Chelsea, London. † G 1.

CARTER, Albert Clarence b. 1894
Sculptor and goldsmith. Studied Lambeth and Central Schools, and as a goldsmith's apprentice. Add: London 1923; Reading, Berks. 1930. † RA 3.

CARTER, Ann G. Exh. 1930
Wood engraver. † RED 1.

CARTER, Amy Joyce Exh. 1895-97
Miniature portrait painter. R.M.S. 1896. Add: London. † RA 2, RMS 5.

CARTER, Miss Austen M. Exh. 1880-1911
Watercolour painter. R.M.S. 1898. Add: London 1880; Torquay, Devon 1898. † B 1, L 3, M 1, RI 5, RMS 19, RSA 2, SWA 14.

CARTER, Miss Christian Exh. 1910-19
Miniature portrait painter. Add: The Cottage Falconer Road, Bushey, Herts. † L 2, RA 8.

CARTER, David Exh. 1883
† ROI 3.

CARTER, Doreen Exh. 1913-35
Nee Bellamy. Figure painter. Add: Sheffield, 1913; London 1929. † N 2, NEA 1, P 2, RA 1, RI 1, ROI 1, SWA 1.

CARTER, D. Broadfoot Exh. 1905-10
Illustrator and designer. Studied Glasgow School of Art and Paris. Settled in London as a professional lithographer. Add: Glasgow 1905. † GI 5.

CARTER, Donald Maynard Exh. 1934-40
Wood engraver. Add: 44 Arodene Road, Brixton Hill, London 1934; Kensington, London 1940. † NEA 2, RA 1, RBA 5.

CARTER, Miss Emily Exh. 1886
Still life painter. Add: 13 Alfred Place, Thurloe Square, London. † SWA 1.

CARTER, Mrs. Eric Exh. 1895-1901
Chadhill Cottage, Edgbaston, Birmingham. † B 5.

CARTER, Miss E. Ellin Exh. 1910-28
Leatherworker. Add: London 1910 and 1928; Brighton 1911. † ALP 26, LS 9, RCA 1.

CARTER, Mrs. E.L. Exh. 1888-91
Sunbury on Thames, Middlesex. † D 5.

CARTER, Mrs. Eva L. Exh. 1911-16
1 Wylam Road, Newcastle on Tyne. † RCA 5.

CARTER, Miss Florence Exh. 1882-83
5 St. Mary's Street, Manchester. † L 1, M 4.

CARTER, Frederick b. 1885
Painter, engraver and writer ("The Dragon of the Alchemists" 1926). Studied London, Paris and Antwerp. A.R.E. 1910, ceased 1916, re-elected 1922. Add: London 1908 and 1928; Pontesbury, Salop 1922; Liverpool 1925. † BG 49, CHE 2, I 15, L 11, NEA 3, RA 10, RE 37, ROI 8.

CARTER, Frank (Francis) Thomas b. 1853
Landscape painter. Add: 18 Nun Street, Newcastle on Tyne 1887 and 1908; Gateshead, Yorks. 1907. † B 13, GI 12, L 7, M 12, NG 1, RA 18, RBA 6, RCA 11, RHA 25, ROI 6, RSA 11.

CARTER, Frank (Francis) W. 1870-1933
Portrait, landscape and interior painter. Son of Hugh C. q.v. Studied Slade School. R.O.I. 1905. Add: 12 Clarendon Road, Notting Hill, London. † B 3, GOU 53, I 5, L 3, LS 11, M 1, NEA 18, NG 2, P 11, RA 9, RID 68, ROI 90.

CARTER, G. Christopher Exh. 1897-98
Architect. Add: 51 Aynhoe Road, Brook Green, London. † RA 2.

CARTER, Miss Gertrude H. Exh. 1902
Miniature portrait painter. Add: The Grange, Howden, Yorks. † RA 1.

CARTER, Miss Hilda Exh. 1901
67 Upper Leeson Street, Dublin, Ireland. † RHA 1.

CARTER, Hugh* 1837-1903
Domestic painter. Father of Frank W.C. q.v. N.E.A. 1899, A.R.I. 1871, R.I. 1875, R.O.I. 1883. Add: 12 Clarendon Road, Notting Hill, London. † B 2, FIN 2, L 13, M 4, NEA 32, P 4, RA 16, RI 74, ROI 55.

CARTER, H.B. Exh. 1937
Marine painter. † CON 1.

CARTER, H. Rogers Exh. 1931-33
Prestatyn, Wales. † RCA 3.

CARTER, Henry William* Exh. 1880-95
Domestic painter. Add: 3 King Edward Road, Hackney, London. † L 1, RA 2, RBA 4.

CARTER, James Exh. 1882
65 St. Thomas Street, Portsmouth, Hants. † B 2.

CARTER, Joseph Exh. 1920-40
Landscape painter. R.B.S.A. 1935. Add: Birmingham. † B 101, RA 5.

CARTER, J. Coates Exh. 1887-1911
Architectural artist. Add: Cardiff 1887; Prestbury, Glos. 1911. † RA 15.

CARTER, John F. Exh. 1936
Animal painter. Add: 10 Nevern Road, Earls Court, London. † RA 1.

CARTER, L. Exh. 1912
Ashington, Sussex. † RA 1.

CARTER, Miss Mabel Exh. 1892-94
The Cottage, Bexley, Kent. † ROI 3.

CARTER, Mrs. Mary Exh. 1925-26
The Liverpool Society of Handloom Weavers, 50a Lord Street, Liverpool. † L 3.

CARTER, Molly Exh. 1930
Portrait painter. Add: 49 Hugh Street, London. † P 1.

CARTER, Margaret E. Exh. 1895-1924
Portrait painter. Add: London 1895; Leamington Spa, Warwicks 1924. † B 2, RA 1.

CARTER, Miss Mary E. Exh. 1884-90
Watercolour flower painter. Add: 17 Tufnell Park Road, London. † RBA 1, SWA 2.

CARTER, Mary F. Exh. 1932
Sculptor. Add: Kennett Hall, Newmarket, Suffolk. † RA 1.

CARTER, Norman St. Clair b. 1875
Australian artist. Add: c/o C.H. West, 117 Finchley Road, London 1914. † RA 1.

CARTER, P. Youngman Exh. 1928-34
Etcher. Add: London 1928; Wakes Colne, Essex 1933. † RA 4.

CARTER, Rosa Exh. 1889-1935
Miniature painter. Add: London. † GI 2, L 2, RA 6, RBA 2, RI 31, RMS 1, SWA 3.

CARTER, R.F. Exh. 1887
37 Springfield Road, St. John's Wood, London. † RI 1.

CARTER, Richard Harry c.1840-1911
Landscape painter. Add: Truro, Cornwall 1882; Falmouth, Cornwall 1884; London 1891; Petersfield, Hants. 1894; Plymouth 1896; Lands End, Cornwall 1908. † B 10, DOW 1, G 2, L 13, M 1, RA 7, RI 19, ROI 4, TOO 11.

CARTER, Robert Radcliffe b. 1867
Landscape painter. Principal of Walsall Municipal School of Art. R.B.S.A. 1929. Add: Liverpool 1894; Walsall, Staffs 1906; Edgware, Middlesex 1930. † B 40, GI 1, L 5, M 1, RA 1, RI 3.

CARTER, Sam Exh. 1935-37
Landscape, figure and still life painter. Add: 61 Brook Lane, King's Heath, Birmingham. † B 3, LEF 4.

CARTER, Samuel jnr. Exh. 1880-88
9 Coleherne Terrace, Richmond Road, London. † RBA 3, ROI 3.

CARTER, Sydney* Exh. 1894-1936
Landscape and figure painter. Add: Loughton, Essex 1894; Scarborough, Yorks. 1919; Johannesburgh, South Africa 1933. † L 1, RA 10, RBA 5, RCA 3, RHA 67. ROI 3.

CARTER, Samuel John* 1835-1892
Animal and sporting painter. b. Swaffham, Norfolk. Studied Norwich. R.O.I. 1883. Add: 10 Richmond Terrace, Richmond Road, London 1880. † FIN 2, G 1, RA 12, ROI 12.

CARTER, Thomas Exh. 1886-1900
Sculptor. Add: Cheltenham, Glos. 1886; London 1900. † G 1, RA 3.

CARTER, Truda Exh. 1931
Poole, Dorset. † B 1.

CARTER, Vernet Exh. 1891-1915
Engraver. Son of Samuel John C. q.v. Add: London. † L 1, RA 7.

CARTER, William* 1863-1939
Portrait and animal painter. b. Swaffham, Norfolk. Son of Samuel John C. q.v. Studied RA Schools (71 awards). R.B.A. 1884, R.P. 1917. "The Refectory Table" purchased by Chantrey Bequest 1937. Add: London. † G 4, L 3, LS 2, NEA 2, NG 3, P 27, RA 72, RBA 6, ROI 2, RSA 1.

CARTER, W. Allan Exh. 1887-92
Architect. Add: Edinburgh. † RSA 10.

CARTER, Walter Dyke 1894-c. 1965
London. † RA 1, RCA 2.

CARTER, W. Hesterson Exh. 1921-22
Rose Bank, The Mount, Shrewsbury. † L 2.

CARTER W.J.B. Exh. 1880
Portrait painter. Add: 69 Wimpole Street, Cavendish Square, London. † RA 1.

CARTERET, de See D

CARTLEDGE, William b. 1891
Portrait, landscape and flower painter. Studied Manchester School of Art and Slade School (University of London Diploma in Fine Art). Sketched in India. Assisted Art master Liverpool City School of Art; Headmaster Pudsey School of Arts and Crafts, Yorks. Add: Manchester 1908; Pudsey, Yorks. 1928. † ALP 1, AR 102, CHE 1, GOU 2, M 6, RA 2, RCA 5, RI 1.

CARTLIDGE, Geo. Exh. 1900-1
Portrait painter. Add: 14 Snow Hill, Hanley, Staffs. † RA 2.

CARTMEL, Miss Alice Exh. 1909-14
232 Warbreck Moor, Aintree, Liverpool. † L 4.

CARTWRIGHT, Lady Exh. 1930-38
Aynho Park, Banbury, Oxon. † B 6.

CARTWRIGHT, Frederick William Exh. 1881-1900
Landscape, portrait and rustic genre painter. Add: Dulwich 1881; London 1893. † D 7, DOW 12, RA 3, RBA 1, RI 9.

CARTWRIGHT, Miss Jane Exh. 1928-34
Wood engraver. Add: Glenmore, Sutton Courtenay, Nr. Abingdon, Berks. † GOU 1, NEA 4, RBA 3, RED 1, ROI 1, SWA 1.

CARTWRIGHT, Mrs. Lucette Exh. 1937-38
Sculptor. Add: London. † RA 2.

CARTWRIGHT, Mrs. M.H. Exh. 1908-29
Whitehall, Himley, Nr. Dudley, Worcs. † B 6.

CARTWRIGHT, Miss Rose Exh. 1883-88
London. † G 5, M 1, NG 1.

CARTWRIGHT, William Exh. 1887-99
Chudleigh, Devon 1887; Harborne, Birmingham 1899. † B 3.

CARTWRIGHT, W.W. Exh. 1932
† L 1.

CARUS-WILSON, C.D. Exh. 1925-27
12 Ann Street, Edinburgh. † RSA 5.

CARVER, Constance E. Exh. 1915-20
Mrs. Reeve. Portrait painter. Add: Leicester. † L 3, RA 4.

CARVER, E.F. Exh. 1921
6 Clarendon Terrace, Brighton, Sussex. † B 1.

CARVER, Grace E. Exh. 1920-3?
Mrs. J. Robertson Carver. Flower painter. Add: Mobberley, Cheshire 1920, Sutton Courtenay, Berks. 1932. † COO 4, L 6, M 1, RI 4, SWA 5.

CARVER, Nora L. Exh. 1938
2 Sussex Square, Brighton, Sussex. † RA 1.

CARVER, Miss Sarah Exh. 1940
Chester. † RCA 1.

CARVILL, George B. Exh. 1897-98
Architect. Add: 1 Brondesbury Road, London. † RA 1.

CARVIN, A.J.C. Exh. 1910
37 Rue Robert de Luzarches, Amiens, France. † L 1.

CARWARDINE, Mary E. Exh. 1882-88
Landscape painter. Add: 6 Rudall Crescent, Hampstead, London. † L 1, RBA 8, RI 4, SWA 3.

CARY, Lucy Winifred See MACDONALD

CASADAVANT, Theodora Exh. 1909
† LS 2.

CASAS, Ramon 1867-1932
Spanish painter. † P 1.

CASCELLA, Michele Exh. 1929
Landscape painter. † BA 52.

CASCIANI, Antonio Exh. 1887-89
Dublin. † RHA 3.

CASCIARO, Guiseppe* Exh. 1911
Naples, Italy. † RSA 1.

CASE, Miss Anne Exh. 1896
Llandulas, Abergele, Wales. † L 1.

CASE, H.F. Exh. 1930-34
Beechwood, Old Lane, Eccleston Park, Prescot, Lancs. † L 2, RCA 1.

CASE, Mary Exh. 1884
Elmside, Surbiton, Surrey. † D 1.

CASE, Miss N. Exh. 1906-10
Berkhamsted 1906; London 1907; Lambourne, Berks. 1910. † RA 3.

CASELLA, Miss Ella Exh. 1884-1913
Wax sculptor. Add: 1 Wetherby Road, South Kensington, London. † G 12, L 2, NG 23, RA 45, RMS 2.

CASELLA, Miss Julia Exh. 1885
1 Wetherby Road, South Kensington, London. † G 2.

CASELLA, Miss Nelia Exh. 1884-1930
Wax sculptor. Add: 1 Wetherby Road, South Kensington, London. † G 5, L 6, NG 30, RA 59, RMS 6.

CASEY, Miss N. Exh. 1915
San Remo, Mornington Road, Chingford, Essex. † RA 1.

CASEY, W. Exh. 1913
† CG 1.

CASH, John Exh. 1885-1909
Architect. Add: Harlesden, Middlesex 1885; London 1896. † RA 12, RI 1.

CASH, Mrs. S.E. Exh. 1930-40
Four Winds, Boars Hill, Oxford. † SWA 9.

CASHEL, Miss A.L. Exh. 1888-1902
Higher Tranmere 1888; Wavertree, Essex 1889; Oxton 1890; Hoylake, Cheshire 1896. † L 6.

CASHEL, Miss Mary Exh. 1892
44 Upper Park Road, Haverstock Hill, London. † RI 1.

CASHEN, M. Exh. 1880-83
3 Salus Rathgar Avenue, Dublin, Ireland. † RHA 3.

CASHMORE, Francis Milton Exh. 1917-26
Architect. Add: London. † RA 12.

CASHMORE, M. Exh. 1914
26 Englands Lane, Hampstead, London. † RA 1.

CASINI, Miss Cornelie Exh. 1894
Sculptor. Add: c/o Miss Cohen, 21 Hamilton Terrace, St. John's Wood, London. † RA 1.

CASLEY, Leonard Exh. 1924
Pentreath, The Lizard, Cornwall. † B 2.

CASLEY, William Exh. 1891-1912
The Lizard, Cornwall, 1891; Liverpool 1912. † L 3, RI 3.

CASPARI, Mrs. Agnes Exh. 1897-1912
Liverpool. † L 12.

CASS, Miss Margaret Exh. 1890
6 Tregunter Road, South Kensington, London. † ROI 1.

CASS, Miss Maud L. Exh. 1931
3 Grundy Street, Alfreton Road, Nottingham. † N 1.

CASSAMAIO, Signorini Exh. 1881
c/o J.N. Perks, 19 Elgin Gardens, Brixton Road, London. † RA 1.

CASSATT, Mary* 1844-1926
American painter. Settled and died in Paris. † GOU 1, I 17.

CASSE, J. Exh. 1905-6
10 Rue de Bouvines, Lille, France. † RA 2.

CASSELLS, William Exh. 1893
Watercolour landscape painter. Add: Bellview Villa, Bishopbriggs, Glasgow. † GI 1, RA 1, RSW 1.

CASSIDY, John b. 1860
Sculptor. b. Co. Meath, Ireland. Studied Manchester School of Art. Add: Manchester. Exh. 1889-1926. † B 3, L 8, LS 17, M 42, NG 13, RA 7, RCA 23, RHA 6.

CASSIE, Miss May Exh. 1940
4 Learmonth Gardens, Edinburgh. † RSA 1.

CASSIERS, Henri b. 1858
Belgian landscape painter. Add: Rue de l'Abbaye 16, Brussels. † FIN 10, GI 3.

CASSON, Alfred Joseph* Exh. 1933
Canadian Associate Academician. Add: Toronto, Canada. † RSW 4.

CASSON, Bernard Exh. 1925-40
Landscape painter. Add: The Vicarage, Croft, Leics. † B 1, GOU 5, NEA 8.

CASSON, Randal Exh. 1937
Landscape painter. Add: Little Heath, Bassett, Southampton. † RA 1.

CAST, Jesse Dale Exh. 1919-39
Landscape and architectural painter. Add: London. † M 1. NEA 7, P 2, RA 10, RHA 1, ROI 1.

CASTAING, Henri J. Exh. 1909-10
Paris 1909; London 1910. † L 2.

CASTAN, E. Exh. 1880-1911
Landscape painter. Add: 13 Rue Rombale, Paris. † BRU 1, M 1, RSA 1.

CASTEL, Gaston Exh. 1914
218 Avenue du Maine, Paris. † RSA 4.

CASTELEIN, Ernest 1881-1945
Belgian portrait painter. Settled in London. Died after being attacked in his studio. Exh. 1925. † L 1.

CASTELLANETA, Miss E. Exh. 1896-1902
c/o Robson, Albert Galleries, Edinburgh. † GI 1, L 5, RSA 1.

CASTELLI, Alessandro* Exh. 1883-85
Domestic painter. Add: Birmingham. † B 5.

CASTELLOW, C. Exh. 1911
Forest Hill, Roundhay, Leeds, Yorks. † RA 2.

CASTELLOW, Mrs. Ethel M. Exh. 1929-30
14 The Avenue, Roundhay, Leeds, Yorks. † L 2.

CASTELUCHO, Claudio 1870-1927
Spanish artist. Add: 22 Rue Boissonade, Paris 1905. † I 2.

CASTIGLIONI, G. Exh. 1900
Boulevard de Cluchy, II, Paris. † L 1.

CASTLE, Florence E. b. 1867
Portrait, landscape and still life painter, illustrator. Studied Lambeth School of Art and Paris. Add: Peckham Rye 1891; East Dulwich 1894; Maidstone, Kent 1899; Kensington, London 1902-1938. † L 2, RA 6, RBA 7, ROI 3, SWA 1.

CASTLE, Horace F. Exh. 1909-19
Artist and teacher. Add: Coalbrookdale, Salop 1909; London 1910; Bolton, Lancs. 1914. † L 1, RA 2.

CASTLE, Sydney E. Exh. 1903-22
Architect. Add: London. † L 1, RA 5.

CASTLE, Thomas Charles Herbert Exh. 1882-1927
Portrait and landscape painter. Add: Birkenhead 1882; London 1890; Liverpool 1897; Bushey, Herts. 1910. † L 39, RA 3, RBA 1.

CASTRO, de See D

CASWALL, Edith E. Exh. 1912-34
Landscape and flower painter. Travelled on the Continent. Add: London. † BA 65, COO 2, L 2, RA 3, RI 7, SWA 3.

CASWELL, Leslie Exh. 1940
Sculptor. Add: 9 Pendrell Road, London. † RA 1.

CASWELL, Mrs. Frank Exh. 1900
8 King Street, Manchester. † M 2.

CASWELL, W.F. Exh. 1882-1911
Birmingham. † B 35, L 1.

CATANI, Ugo Exh. 1905-11
18 Kensington Court Place, Kensington, London. † BRU 1, L 4, RA 2.

CATANIA, Francesco Exh. 1912
Maltese artist. Add: c/o Allied Artists Association Ltd., London. † LS 3.

CATARGI, Gheorghe Exh. 1936-37
Figure painter. Add: Bucharest, Rumania. † RA 2.

CATCHPOLE, Neil M. Exh. 1932-37
Greenock. † GI 2, RSA 1, RSW 2.

CATCHPOLE, Frederick T. Exh. 1897-1940
Landscape and figure painter. R.B.A. 1913. Add: 183 King's Road, Chelsea, London. † CHE 1, D 1, GI 1, GOU 2, I 2, L 1, LS 8, NEA 1, RA 11, RBA 94, RI 9, ROI 4.

CATCHPOOL, H. Exh. 1881-82
Hillside, Crouch End Hill, London. † D 1, RBA 1.

CATHCART, Mariette Exh. 1885-86
117 Adelaide Road, Primrose Hill, London. † M 2.

CATHER, Miss Jessie Exh. 1884
The Hermitage, Limavady, Co. Derry, Ireland. † RHA 1.

CATHIE, Mrs. A.E. Exh. 1891
39 South View, Hustler Street, Bradford, Yorks. † M 1.

CATHIE, Miss Ellen Exh. 1921-30
Portrait painter. Add: London. † L 2, RA 3.

CATLEY, Agatha B. Exh. 1895
22 Grattan Road, Kensington, London. † NG 1.

CATLIN, Christopher Herbert Henry b. 1902
Painter and taxi driver. A.R.B.A. 1940. Add: Fulham 1937. † RBA 5.

CATLING, Isobel Exh. 1930-31
† GOU 3.

CATLING, Reginald B. Exh. 1935
1 Coulter Road, London. † RI 1.

CATLOW, George Sprawton Exh. 1884-1916
Landscape and coastal painter. A.N.S.A. 1908. Add: Leicester. † B 2, L 3, N 13, RA 7, RI 2.

CATOR, Diana J. Exh. 1935-37
Painter and engraver. Add: London. † RED 1, SWA 5.

CATSTREE, Miss M.R. Exh. 1896
South View, 127 Golden Hillock Road, Birmingham. † B 1.

CATTERALL, Frederick W. Exh. 1902-5
Architect. Add: 33 Windley Square, Preston, Lancs. † RA 3.

CATTERALL, Mary Exh. 1883-90
Flower painter. Add: 10 Mount Ephraim, Tunbridge Wells, Kent. † L 1, SWA 6.

CATTERMOLE, Charles 1832-1900
Figure painter. R.B.A. 1876, A.R.I. 1862, R.I. 1870, R.O.I. 1883. Add: London. † B 6, GI 2, L 20, RBA 62, RI 44, ROI 3.

CATTERMOLE, Leonardo Exh. 1881-86
Figure and historical painter. Add: London. † G 7.

CATTERMOLE, Lance b. 1898
Painter and teacher. Grandson of George C. A.R.A. Studied Central School of Arts and Crafts 1922-23 and Slade School 1923-26. Add: London 1938; Worthing 1940. † P 1, RA 1, RBA 3, ROI 4.

CATTERNS, Edward R. Exh. 1880-1907
Portrait painter. Add: 122 Wellington Street, Glasgow. † GI 33, L 1, RA 1, RSA 6, RSW 1.

CATTLE, Mrs. M.A. Exh. 1902
2 East Circus Street, Nottingham. † N 1.

CATTLEY, Emily F. Exh. 1905-7
30 Peel Street, Princes Park, Liverpool. † L 2.

CATTO, R. Exh. 1921
Via Constantino, 12, Naples, Italy. † RA 1.

CAUER, Ludwig Exh. 1892-95
Sculptor. Add: Chelsea, London 1892; Berlin 1895. † L 2, NG 3, RA 7.

CAULBY, W.F. Exh. 1901
10 Aubrey Walk, Campden Hill, London. † I 3.

CAULDWELL, Leslie Griffen b. 1861
American landscape and figure painter. Add: Paris 1887 and 1891; New York 1888. † L 4, RA 2, RBA 3.

CAULDWELL, Hugo Exh. 1926
Landscape painter. Add: 7 Torrington Square, London. † RA 1.

CAULFIELD, Hon. Rachel Exh. 1904-39
Miniature portrait painter. Add: London 1904 and 1936; Cheam, Surrey 1920. † L 2, RA 12, RMS 2.

CAULFIELD, Sidney B. Exh. 1903-8
Architect. Add: London. † RA 2.

CAULFIELD, Vivian Exh. 1901
Portrait painter. Add: 22 King Henry's Road, London. † RA 1.

CAULKIN, Ferdinand Edward Harley b. 1888
Landscape and figure painter. Studied Handsworth School of Art and Birmingham School of Landscape Art. Add: Birmingham. † B 22.

CAUS, Emile Exh. 1894
Astene, Belgium. † GI 2.

CAUSER, William Sidney 1876-1958
Landscape painter. Studied Wolverhampton School of Art. R.B.S.A. 1930, R.I. 1936. Add: Wolverhampton 1921; London 1926. † B 68, FIN 30, GI 3, L 4, LEI 3, M 1, NEA17, RA 20, RI 34, RSA 6.

CAUTLEY, Ivo Ernest b. 1893
Landscape, figure, portrait and still life painter. Add: Dublin, Ireland. † RHA 10.

CAUTY, Horace Henry 1846-1909
Historical and genre painter. Curator of RA Schools. R.B.A.1879. Add: Gordon Place, London 1880; Sutton, Surrey 1892. † B 6, D 1, L 7, M 10, RA 24, RBA 73, RHA 2, RI 1, ROI 1.

CAUTY, Horace Robert Exh. 1880-93
Landscape painter. Add: Gordon Place, London 1880; Sutton, Surrey 1891. † B 2, M 3, RA 1, RBA 59, RI 1.

CAUVY, Leon Exh. 1906
205 bis, Boulevard Raspail, Paris. † L 2.

CAVE, Aylwin Osborn Exh. 1907-19
Architect. b. Witham, Essex. Add: London 1907; Letchworth, Herts. 1909. † RA 3.

CAVE, Mrs. Ina Exh. 1934
Maer Lake House, Bude, Cornwall. † RBA 1.

CAVE, Miss Louise Catherine See DYKE

CAVE, Mrs. Walter See COCHRANE, Jessica M.

CAVE, Walter Frederick b. 1863
Architect and painter. Studied Bristol School of Art and RA Schools. Married Jessica M. Cochrane q.v. Add: London 1889 and 1926; Birkenhead 1922. † L 3, RA 17, RSA 3.
CAVE, William Wilfred Exh. 1908-32
Figure and landscape painter. Signs work Wilfrid Cave. Studied Slade School. Add: Birkenhead and London 1908; Cheltenham 1932. † L 4, LS 7, NEA 1, RA 1.
CAVEN, Miss E.M. Exh. 1910-21
Cleveland, Westminster Road, Leicester. † N 3. SWA 1.
CAVEN, Mary Exh. 1937
Watercolour portrait and flower miniature painter. Studied Heatherleys, London, Florence and Paris. Travelled widely. WG 62.
CAVENAGH, Miss K. Exh. 1927
78 Carless Avenue, Harborne, Birmingham. † B 1.
CAVERS, Joan Exh. 1938-40
Portrait painter. Add: 59 Edwardes Square, London. † RA 1, SWA 1.
CAW, James Lewis b. 1864
Landscape painter. Studied Glasgow, Edinburgh and abroad. Curator of the Scottish National Portrait Gallery 1895. Director of National Galleries of Scotland 1907. Add: Ayr 1884; Edinburgh 1890. † GI 20, NEA 3, RSA 29, RSW 3.
CAWKER, Maud Exh. 1896
16 Meadow Studios, Bushey, Herts. † RA 1.
CAWLWOOD, James Exh. 1885-99
Landscape painter. Add: Nottingham 1885; West Bridgford, Notts. 1899. † N 6.
CAWOOD, Herbert Harry b. 1890
Sculptor and modeller. Studied Sheffield Technical School of Art, RA Schools (silver and bronze medals). Add: London 1920. † RA 5.
CAWSTON, Arthur Exh. 1880-84
Architect. Add: London. † RA 3.
CAWTHRA, Hermon b. 1886
Sculptor. Studied Salts Art School, Shipley, Yorks 1904, Leeds School of Art 1907-9, Royal College of Art 1909-11, RA Schools 1912-16. Add: London. † GI 3, L 5, RA 52.
CAY, Isabella Exh. 1883-1913
Edinburgh 1883; Paris 1905; Venice 1913. † GI 3, L 4, LS 12, RA 1, RSA 9.
CAY, W.D. Exh. 1885
107A Prince's Street, Edinburgh. † RSA 3.
CAYLEY, Gwladys E. Exh. 1925
6 Watery Lane, Merton, Wimbledon, London. † SWA 1.
CAYRON, Jules b. 1868
French artist. Add: 31 Boulevard Berthier, Paris 1902. † L 1.
CAYZER, Alice A. Exh. 1895
Aigburth, Liverpool. † L 1.
CAZALET, Miss A.T. Exh. 1907-16
Neva, Westgate-on-Sea. Thanet. † RA 5, RMS 1.
CAZIN, Michel d. 1901
French landscape painter. Teacher at South Kensington. Add: Paris 1899. † RA 1.
CECIL, Fred Exh. 1905
Elmbank, Rainford Road, St. Helens, Lancs. † L 4.
CECIL, Miss Maria Exh. 1896
119 Wood Street, Liverpool. † L 1.
CECIL, Maud Exh. 1936
Landscape and portrait painter. † FIN 43.
CECIL, Miss V. Exh. 1882
Tower View, Liscard, Cheshire. † L 1.
CECILE, Alma Exh. 1916-19
18 Berlin Road, Catford. † I 2, NEA 2.
CEDERLAND, Gustaf Exh. 1909
† LS 3.
CEI, Cipriano* Exh. 1897
Figure painter. Add: c/o Henry Mitchell, Augustus Road, Edgbaston, Birmingham. † B 2.
CELOS, Julian Exh. 1915
Landscape and figure painter and etcher. † GOU 45.
CENTER, Edward K. b. 1903
Landscape, portrait and figure painter. Studied Grey's School of Art, Aberdeen and Allan Fraser Art College, Arbroath. Add: Ditchling, Sussex 1939. † ROI 2.
CERFOLA Exh. 1891-92
c/o A. Nelson, 19 Hanover Street, Edinburgh. † RSA 2.
CERIA Edmond* b. 1884
French artist. Add: c/o Glaerie Marcel Bernheim, 2 bis rue de Caumartin, Paris 1929. † GI 1.
CERNY, V.J. Exh. 1931
Watercolour landscape painter. Add: Czechoslovakia. † WG 41.
CESARE, Cavaliere Exh. 1887
Sculptor. Add: Fantacchetti, Florence, Italy. † RA 1.
CESBRON, Achille Exh. 1909
13 Rue Jacquemont, Paris. † L 1.
CETNER de See D
CEUNIS, Gerard Exh. 1930-31
Italian landscape and interior painter. Add: Salve, Gosmore Road, Hitchin, Herts. † RA 2.
CHABANIAN, Arsene Exh. 1905-9
Turkish artist. Add: Paris 1905. † I 1, L 1.
CHABAS, Maurice* Exh. 1906-9
French artist. Add: 3 Villa Sainte Foy, Neuilly-sur-Seine, France. † L 3.
CHABAS, Paul Exh. 1920-25
Portrait painter. Add: 23 Boulevard Berthier, Paris. † L 1, RA 1.
CHABAUD, Auguste Elisee* b. 1882
French painter. Exh. 1914. † ALP 1.
CHADBURN, G. Haworth Exh. 1891-1919
Landscape and portrait painter. R.B.A. 1902. Add: Sutton, Surrey 1891; London 1901 and 1909; Kings Langley, Herts. 1903. † RA 10, RBA 13.
CHADBURN, Miss M.E. Exh. 1917-40
London 1917; Bushey, Herts. 1938; Sidley, Sussex 1940. † B 3, RCA 2, SWA 4.
CHADEL, Jules Exh. 1927
c/o Redfern Gallery, 27 Old Bond Street, London. † GI 2.
CHADWICK, Ernest Albert b. 1876
Watercolour landscape and flower painter and wood engraver. Son of John William C. q.v. Studied Birmingham Municipal School of Art. R.B.S.A. 1912, R.I. 1939. Add: Hampton-in-Arden, Warks. 1897; Solihull 1915; Henley-in-Arden 1932. † B 180, BG 4, FIN 1, L 45, RA 17, RCA 79, RI 25, WG 151.
CHADWICK, Mrs. E.L. Exh. 1902
St. Ives, Cornwall. † RHA 1.
CHADWICK, Miss Emma L. Exh. 1890
7 Rue Scribe, Paris. † ROI 2.
CHADWICK, F.B. Exh. 1892
26 Bedford Gardens, Campden Hill, London. † NEA 1.
CHADWICK, Henry Daniel Exh. 1880-96
Figure painter. Add: London 1880 and 1886; Bromley, Kent 1885. † L 4, M 2, RA 11, RBA 1, RHA 1.
CHADWICK, John William Exh. 1882-96
Wood engraver. Father of Ernest Albert C. q.v. Add: Birmingham 1882; Hampton-in-Arden, Warks. 1896 † B 6.
CHADWICK, Marion Exh. 1880-81
Flower painter. Add: Park Cottage, East Sheen, London. † RSA 2, SWA 2.
CHADWICK, Miss Mary Exh. 1884-98
Stameen, Drogheda, Ireland 1884; Bath 1897. † RHA 9.
CHADWICK, Tom Exh. 1934-38
Painter and engraver. Add: London. † GI 1, NEA 2, RA 1, RBA 16, RED 2, ROI 1.
CHADWICK, W.H. Exh. 1905
17 Masham Street, Armley, Leeds, Yorks. † RCA 1.
CHAFFANEL, E. Exh. 1910
71 Rue Caulaincourt, Paris. † L 1.
CHAFFAULT, du See D
CHAHINE, Edgar* b. 1874
French painter and etcher. b. Constantinople. A.R.E. 1900-8. Exh. 1900-24. † FIN 28, I 12, L 10, RE 26.
CHAIGNEAU, Jean Ferdinand* 1830-1906
French artist. Add: Paris. Exh. 1884-89. † D 1, L 1, RE 1.
CHAIKIN, Benjamin Exh. 1939
Architect. Add: c/o W. Warman, Woodcote, Priory Avenue, Petts Wood, Kent. † RA 1.
CHALCRAFT, H.T. Exh. 1909
48 Bishopgate Street, Within, London. † RA 1.
CHALDECOTT, Mrs. Ursula Exh. 1932-39
Landscape painter. Add: Kirkby Lonsdale, Lancs. † GOU 3, L 1, M 1, RA 2, SWA 2.
CHALK, Brenda M. Exh. 1899
Sunset, Redhill, Surrey. † B 1.
CHALK, Miss Hilda Exh. 1899-1902
Figure painter. Add: Brighton 1899; London 1902. † RA 1, RBA 2, RI 1, ROI 1, SWA 3.
CHALKER, Cissie Exh. 1890-1902
Mrs. Jack Fison. Miniature painter. R.M.S. 1897. Add: Bellevue House, New Bridge Hill, Bath, Som. 1890; Thetford, Norfolk 1897. † L 1, RA 12, RMS 14.
CHALKER, Miss Sophia Exh. 1888-89
Miniature painter. Add: Bellevue House, New Bridge Hill, Bath, Som. † RA 1, RBA 3.
CHALLANDS, Miss Beatrice M. Exh. 1898-1921
Landscape painter. Add: The Park, Nottingham. † N 11.
CHALLENER, Miss May Exh. 1897-99
61 Bowyer Road, Saltley, Birmingham. † B 6.
CHALLENGER, J. Exh. 1893
Landscape painter. Add: Lyon Studio, Richmond Road, Twickenham, Middlesex. † RBA 1.
CHALLICE, Annie Jane Exh. 1881-1908
Domestic painter. Add: London. † B 5, GI 1, L 2, NG 1, RA 3, RBA 2, RCA 1, RHA 4, SWA 5.
CHALLISS, Charles A. Exh. 1899
Landscape painter. Add: Northolt Road, Harrow, Middlesex. † RA 1.
CHALLONER, Miss Molly Exh. 1927-31
15 Framlington Place, Newcastle-on-Tyne. † L 4, RMS 4.
CHALMERS, Lady Elizabeth Exh. 1894-1939
nee Graham. Flower painter. Add: Grasmere, Westmorland 1894; Linlithgow, N.B. 1907; Bathgate, N.B. 1914; London 1929. † AR 37, L 2, RBA 1, RID 3, RSA 5, SWA 3, WG 56.

CHALMERS, Miss Evelyn Caroline Exh. 1909-36
Portrait and figure painter. Add: Aldbar Castle, Brechin, N.B. 1909; Bridge of Dun, Montrose 1929. † LS 6, RA 3, RSA 7.
CHALMERS, G. Exh. 1880-81
25 Hayburn Crescent, Glasgow. † RSA 2.
CHALMERS, Hector c.1849-1943
Scottish artist. Add: Edinburgh. † GI 68, RHA 2, RSA 176. RSW 5.
CHALMERS, Isabel M. Exh. 1928-29
Figure painter. A.N.S.A. 1930. Add: 1 Devonshire Avenue, Beeston, Notts. † N 2.
CHALMERS, James Exh. 1885-1913
Glasgow. † GI 10.
CHALMERS, John Exh. 1880-93
Glasgow. † GI 3, RSA 7.
CHALMERS, Jean Jamieson Exh. 1880-90
19 Union Street, Edinburgh. † RSA 15.
CHALMERS, Miss Mary H. Exh. 1880-82
Figure painter. Add: 6 Collingham Road, London. † RBA 2, RSA 4.
CHALMERS, P.M. Exh. 1888-1921
Glasgow. † GI 39, RA 2, RSA 8.
CHAMBERLAIN, D. Exh. 1887-1912
Glasgow. † GI 8, RSW 3.
CHAMBERLAIN, Frank Exh. 1904
78 Fulham Road, Sparkhill, Birmingham. † B 1.
CHAMBERLAIN, Frederick Exh. 1907
23 Herbert Street, West Bromwich. † B 1.
CHAMBERLAIN, Joseph Exh. 1925-26
Landscape painter and pen and ink artist. b. Lambourne, Berks. Studied Heatherleys 1925. Add: London 1925. Add: London 1925; Marlborough, Wilts. 1926. † RA 1, ROI 1.
CHAMBERLAIN, Ronald Exh. 1938
91 Davies Road, West Bridgford, Nottingham. † N 2.
CHAMBERLAIN, Samuel b.1895
Painter, etcher, illustrator and writer. b. U.S.A. Studied Ecole des Beaux Arts, Paris, Royal College of Art (John Simon Guggenheim Fellowship holder 1926). Add: Paris. Exh. 1928-30. † BA 3, L 4, RA 1.
CHAMBERLIN, Amy Gertrude Exh. 1894-1935
nee Rowney. Miniature painter. Studied Heatherleys. Add: London. † L 52, M 9, RA 9, RI 32, RMS 1, SWA 8.
CHAMBERLIN, Miss Irene Exh. 1927
Watercolour landscape painter. Add: 26 Radmoor Road, Loughborough, Leics. † N 1.
CHAMBERLIN, William Benjamin Exh. 1880-95
Landscape and interior painter. R.S.W. 1881. Add: Brighton. † DOW 5, RA 1, RI 1, RSA 29, RSW 9.
CHAMBERS, Miss Ada C. Exh. 1899-1900
c/o Mrs. Hopgood, Granville Mansions, Uxbridge Road, London. † GI 2, RHA 1.
CHAMBERS, Alice May Exh. 1881-94
Figure painter. Add: London. † B 2, L 4, M 3, NG 1, RA 9, RI 3.
CHAMBERS, Admiral Bertram Mordant 1866-1945
Watercolour painter and writer. Studied Chelsea Polytechnic. Exh. 1928. Add: London. † RBA 6.
CHAMBERS, Coutts L. Exh. 1883-90
Paris 1883, Venice 1886, London 1887. † G 10.
CHAMBERS, Mrs. Dorothy Exh. 1920-21
87 Wentworth Road, Harborne, Birmingham. † B 4.
CHAMBERS, Miss D.G. Exh. 1901-5
Park Road, Clarence Gate, London. † D 4, SWA 3.
CHAMBERS, Miss Evelyn F. Exh. 1898
Clarence Gate, London. † SWA 1.
CHAMBERS, Mrs. E. Joan Exh. 1935-40
Landscape and figure painter. Add: Gove Cottage, Newtown, Waterford, Ireland. † RHA 6.
CHAMBERS, Miss E.R. Bromhall Exh. 1903
† RMS 1.
CHAMBERS, Frederick Exh. 1886-1914
Landscape painter. Add: Gypsy Hill 1886; Upper Norwood 1908. † B 1, LS 22, RA 1, RBA 1, RCA 1, RHA 1, ROI 1.
CHAMBERS, Florence E. Exh. 1913-35
Southport, Lancs. 1913; Tirril, nr. Penrith, Cumberland 1935. † L 1, RA 3, RSA 1.
CHAMBERS, Frank Pentland b. 1900
Architect and sculptor. Studied RA Schools; Essays Medal R.I.B.A. 1925; Commonwealth Fund Fellowship, Harvard University U.S.A. 1927. Exh. 1928. Add: London. † L 2, RA 1.
CHAMBERS, H. Exh. 1891-93
61 Manchester Road, Bolton, Lancs. † L 2, M 1.
CHAMBERS, Miss H.C. Exh. 1890
16 Lorne Road, Oxton. † L 1.
CHAMBERS, H.M. Exh. 1894-1902
Liverpool. † B 3, L 5.
CHAMBERS, Mrs. H.V. Exh. 1933
Southampton. † RCA 1.
CHAMBERS, John Exh. 1886-1915
Brixton 1886, North Shields 1888. † RI 3.
CHAMBERS, J.S. Claud Exh. 1923-24
16 Yeoman's Row, Brompton Road, London. † NEA 2, RSA 1.
CHAMBERS, L.R. Exh. 1909
9 Rue Dupin, Paris. † L 2.
CHAMBERS, Miss Maud Exh. 1897
37 Rosary Gardens, South Kensington, London. † NG 1.
CHAMBERS, Miss M.A. Exh. 1912
8 Kensington Crescent, London. † RA 1, SWA 2.
CHAMBERS, Miss Mary Helen Brook Exh. 1905-18
Berkhamsted, Herts. 1905; Kings Langley, Herts. 1909. † LS 8, RA 4, RHA 8.
CHAMBERS, Mrs. Nora Exh. 1898-1905
Miniature portrait painter. Add: Currabinny, Epsom 1898; London 1901. † B 2, GI 2, L 4, NG 3, P 3, RA 2, RHA 2, RI 1, RSA 1.
CHAMBERS, Paul B. Exh. 1894-96
Architect. Add: Ship Street Chambers, Brighton, Sussex. † RA 2.
CHAMBERS, Miss R. Exh. 1905
42 Pembroke Square, London. † RA 1.
CHAMBERS, W. Exh. 1880
36 Howston Street, Glasgow. † GI 1.
CHAMBERS, William Exh. 1906
4 Trafalgar Studios, Manresa Road, Chelsea, London. † B 1, NG 1.
CHAMBERS, Winifred Exh. 1899-1908
London 1899 and 1908; Etaples, Pas de Calais, France 1906. † GI 1, L 1, LS 5, RA 2, ROI 1, SWA 4.
CHAMBERS, W.T. Bradley Exh. 1919-39
Architectural and landscape painter. Add: West Bridgford, Notts. 1919 and 1928; Sherwood, Notts. 1926. † N 25.
CHAMBRE, Olive Exh. 1901-24
Slane, Co. Meath 1901; Monkstown, Co. Dublin, Ireland 1924. † RA 1, SWA 1.
CHAMIER, Barbara Dorothy b. 1885
Figure, portrait and miniature painter and restorer. b. Faizazad, India. Studied King's College. Add: London 1904; East Grinstead 1928. † GI 1, L 4, RA 16, SWA 2.
CHAMIER, Hilda Exh. 1936
Watercolour landscape painter. † WG 64.
CHAMIER, Mrs. Lena M. Exh. 1908-9
c/o Percy Young, 131 Gower Street, London. † LS 7.
CHAMNEY, Catherine Rosabelle Exh. 1922-34
Landscape painter. b. India. Add: Royston, The Avenue, Bushey, Herts. 1922. † D 20, L 5, RBA 2, RCA 6, RI 3, SWA 1.
CHAMPCOMMUNAL, Joseph Exh. 1908-16
French painter and engraver. Add: Paris 1908; Holland Park, London 1916. † GI 1, LS 8, NEA 3.
CHAMPION, Edward C. Exh. 1883
Domestic painter. Add: 11 Clapham Road, London. † RBA 3.
CHAMPION, Mrs. H. Exh. 1880-85
Watercolour figure painter. Add: 14 Minford Gardens West, Kensington, London. † D 7, L 5, M 5, RBA 8, RI 4, SWA 11.
CHAMPION de CRESPIGNY see De Crespigny
CHAMPNEYS, Amian L. Exh. 1903
Architect. Add: Hall Oak, Frognal, Hampstead, London. † RA 1.
CHAMPNEYS, Basil 1842-1935
Architect (e.g. Manchester Cathedral). Add: London. † GI 2, RA 42.
CHAMPNEYS, May Exh. 1889
nee Drummond. Married Basil C. q.v. Add: Manor Farm, Frognal, Hampstead, London. † RHA 1.
CHANCE, Julie C. Exh. 1896-98
Mrs. W. Animal painter. Add: Frimley, Surrey 1896; Kemendyne, Guildford, Surrey 1898. † NG 2, RA 3, RSA 1.
CHANCE, Jane Linnell c.1857-1941
Portrait painter. Founder of the Camden School of Art. Exh. 1888. Add: London. † ROI 1.
CHANCE, Miss Lilian Exh. 1901-5
London 1901, Shrewsbury 1905. † B 4.
CHANCE, Walter Maxwell Exh. 1907-39
Landscape and miniature painter. Add: Hazelwell, nr. Birmingham 1907; Sherwood, Notts. 1910 and 1921; Bushey, Herts. 1911; London 1935. † B 5, N 17, RA 2, RMS 2.
CHANCELLOR, Mrs. Beresford Exh. 1927
Figure and landscape painter. Travelled on the continent. † COO 31.
CHANCELLOR, H.S. Exh. 1896-1907
Figure painter. Add: Dalkey, Co. Dublin 1896; London 1901; Dublin 1906. † M 1, NEA 3, RHA 11.
CHANDLER, E. Exh. 1926
† M 2.
CHANDLER, G.W. Exh. 1914
80 Rue Vaneau, Paris. † RA 2.
CHANDLER, Miss Margaret Exh. 1933
Portrait painter. Add: Three Arts Club, 19a Marylebone Road, London. † RA 1.
CHANDLER, Roland M. Exh. 1934
Landscape painter. Add: 38 Mayfield Avenue, Orpington, Kent. † RA 2.
CHANDLER, Rose M. Exh. 1882-96
Flower, bird and landscape painter. Add: Haslemere, Surrey 1882; Shere, Guildford Surrey 1890; London 1895. † D 5, L 4 RBA 4, RI 9, SWA 16.
CHANDLER, W.F. Exh. 1911-12
Kensington, London. † RA 2.

CHANDLER, W.P. Exh. 1915
Calabar, Malone Avenue, Belfast, Ireland. † RHA 1.

CHANDLER-THOMSON, Kate Exh. 1929-40
Miniature portrait and landscape painter. A.R.M.S. 1932, R.M.S. 1935. Add: London. † RA 2, RHA 9, RMS 36, SWA 1, WG 80.

CHANDLEY, Miss H.J. Exh. 1914-19
Nottingham 1914; Rolleston, Notts. 1915. † N 7.

CHANDOR, Douglas Exh. 1923
Portrait painter. Add: 132 Sloane Street, London. † RA 1.

CHANET, Henri Exh. 1883
Portrait painter. Add: Paris and c/o Maclean, Haymarket, London. † RA 1.

CHANLER, Albert b. 1880
Painter and etcher. Studied Glasgow School of Art and Royal Institute, Edinburgh. Add: Glasgow 1897; Edinburgh 1907; London 1931. † GI 1, RBA 2, RSA 1.

CHANLER, Robert Winthrop 1872-1930
American painter. Exh. 1925. † CHE 2.

CHANNER, Cecilia Alfreda Exh. 1880-94
Domestic, landscape and interior painter. Add: London. † B 3, D 5, GI 1, L 3, RA 4, RBA 6, RE 3, RI 6, ROI 2, SWA 9.

CHANNER, Miss C.C. Exh. 1928
Lace-maker and embroiderer. Add: 29 Abingdon Street, Northampton. † L 4.

CHANNING, Mrs. Julia Georgiana Exh. 1904-21
Landscape painter. Add: 62 Fellows Road, Hampstead, London. † LS 33, RA 1.

CHANT, James John Exh. 1880-83
Engraver. Add: The Limes, Epsom, Surrey. † RA 5.

CHANTEAU, A. and G. Exh. 1914
The Amazing Twins. Portrait drawings. † BK 27.

CHAPEL, Miss Helen Exh. 1901-29
Caenlochan, Arbroath, N.B. 1901 and 1929. † RSA 6.

CHAPEL, Miss Jeannie K. Exh. 1900-1
Caenlochan, Arbroath, N.B. † RSA 2.

CHAPLIN, Mrs. Annie Exh. 1883
Figure painter. Add: 10 Earl's Court Square, South Kensington, London. † RA 1.

CHAPLIN, Arthur* Exh. 1905-9
9 Rue Poulletier, Ile St. Louis, Paris. † I 2, L 1.

CHAPLIN, Adrienne L. Exh. 1904
Miniature painter. Add: Deal, Kent 1904; London 1930. † RA 1, RBA 1.

CHAPLIN, Alice M. Exh. 1880-1906
Sculptor. Add: London. † G 14, L 16, NG 12, RA 18, RI 2.

CHAPLIN, C. Exh. 1906
† TOO 1.

CHAPLIN, Charles H.A. Exh. 1939-40
Etcher. Add: 19 Highfield Way, Rickmansworth, Herts. † RA 2.

CHAPLIN, Miss D. Exh. 1903-4
Penywern Road, London. † SWA 3.

CHAPLIN, Florence Exh. 1882
8 Upper Cheyne Row, Chelsea, London. † RBA 1.

CHAPLIN, Miss Florence Eleanor see SHEPARD

CHAPLIN, Rosamund Exh. 1911
Broughton, Asley Hall, Leicester. † LS 2.

CHAPLIN, Miss Sybil Exh. 1895
122 Lisson Grove, London. † NG 1.

CHAPLIN, Walter H. Exh. 1899-1933
Birkenhead. † L 23.

CHAPMAN, Anna Exh. 1928
Landscape painter. † AB 2.

CHAPMAN, Annie Hamilton Exh. 1897-1900
Miniature painter. R.M.S. 1898. Add: Walpole House, St. Margaret's, Middlesex. † B 6, GI 1, M 1, RA 1, RMS 9.

CHAPMAN, Miss A.J. Exh. 1892-97
30 Inverleith Row, Edinburgh. † GI 6, RSA 2.

CHAPMAN, Miss A.M. Exh. 1902
Animal painter. † BG 1.

CHAPMAN, Miss Berna Exh. 1940
Still life painter. Add: c/o Contemporary Pictures, 16 South Leinster Street, Dublin. † RHA 2.

CHAPMAN, C.E. Exh. 1916
Pine Croft, Lyndhurst, Hants. † RA 1.

CHAPMAN, Mrs. Catherine J. Exh. 1894
Flower painter. Add: 3 Springdale, Cheshunt, Herts. † RA 1.

CHAPMAN, Carleton Theodore* 1860-1925
American painter. Exh. 1905. Add: 58 West 57th Street, New York, U.S.A. † I 4.

CHAPMAN, Miss Elsie Exh. 1908
115 Hampton Road, Southport, Lancs. † LS 5.

CHAPMAN, Ernest J. Exh. 1892
Stained glass artist. Add: 6 Red Lion Square, London. † RA 1.

CHAPMAN, Elizabeth Maria Exh. 1896-1938
Painter and lithographer. Studied portrait painting under Reginald Barker at the Manchester School of Art and lithography under Leslie Ward at Bournemouth. Add: Manchester. † L 9, M 5.

CHAPMAN, Miss F. Exh. 1887
Fairholme, Crosby. † L 1.

CHAPMAN, H. Ascough Exh. 1902-11
Architect. Add: Prudential Buildings, Park Row, Leeds, Yorks. † RA 2.

CHAPMAN, John Watkins* Exh. 1880-1903
Genre painter and engraver. Add: London. † AG 4, B 14, GI 10, L 17, M 7, RA 6, RBA 21, RHA 4, RI 10, ROI 10, RSA 9, TOO 2.

CHAPMAN, Laura Exh. 1880-83
Burghill, Hereford. † GI 7, RSA 1.

CHAPMAN, Louisa G. Exh. 1900-12
Flower painter. Add: 62 South Street, Greenwich. † LS 3, RA 3, RBA 1.

CHAPMAN, Max b. 1911
Exh. 1934. † COO 2.

CHAPMAN, M.D. Exh. 1929
Broughton House, Nr. Preston, Lancs. † L 1.

CHAPMAN, Miss M.J. Exh. 1913
9 Rue Falguiere, Paris. † RA 1.

CHAPMAN, Norman B. Exh. 1930-32
Landscape painter. Add: 31 Umfreville Road, London. † NEA 4, RA 3.

CHAPMAN, R. Hamilton Exh. 1881-1903
Landscape painter. Add: Cookham, Berks. 1881; London 1882 and 1897; Cookham Dene, Berks. 1884; Thames Ditton, Surrey 1889; Shrewsbury 1895. † L 5, RA 12, RBA 21, RI 5, ROI 2.

CHAPMAN, Stephen H. Exh. 1938-40
† NEA 5, P 1.

CHAPMAN, W. Exh. 1890
Agnew Villa, Helensburg, N.B. † GI 1.

CHAPPEL, Mrs. Edward (A.) Exh. 1886-1914
London. † L 1, RA 1, SWA 1.

CHAPPEL, Edward Exh. 1892-1933
Landscape painter. R.O.I. 1920. Add: London 1892; Cros de Cagnes, France 1928. † AB 44, CHE 1, B 4, FIN 2, G 10, GI 3, GOU 35, I 10, L 16, LS 30, M 4, RA 34, RBA 1, ROI 51, RSA 2, TOO 10.

CHAPPELL, William Exh. 1880-82
Figure painter. Add: 219 Stanhope Street, Hampstead Road, London. † D 1, RBA 3, RHA 2.

CHAPPELL, William Exh. 1938
Costume designer. † RED 3.

CHAPPELLE, Miss Annie E. Exh. 1900-5
Thomond Cottage, Glenarm Avenue, Drumcondra, Dublin, Ireland. † RHA 6.

CHAPPLE, T.W. Exh. 1914-15
323 Glossop Road, Sheffield, Yorks. † L 2.

CHAPUY, Andre Exh. 1908-11
French artist. Add: Paris and c/o Allied Artists Association, London. † LS 8.

CHARAVEL, Paul* Exh. 1938
Paris. † GI 1.

CHARBONNIER, Theodore Exh. 1894
Sculptor. Add: Barnstaple, Devon. † M 1, RA 1.

CHARD, Elsie Exh. 1914-28
Sculptor. A.S.W.A. 1920. Add: London. † ALP 1, L 6, RA 5, SWA 7.

CHARDE, Hugh C. Exh. 1886-1936
Portrait and landscape painter. Studied Cork, Antwerp and Paris. Principal Cork School of Art. Add: Cork, Ireland. † RHA 46.

CHARDON, Francis E. Exh. 1897
Landscape painter. † DOW 88.

CHARLES, Miss Agnes E. Exh. 1931-40
Portrait and landscape painter. Add: Tunbridge Wells, Kent 1931 and 1940; London 1939. † RA 5.

CHARLES, Catherine L. Exh. 1928-37
Edinburgh. † L 2, RSA 8.

CHARLES, Charles S. Exh. 1896-1902
Hampstead, London. † RBA 1, RI 2, ROI 1.

CHARLES, H.W.W. Exh. 1888-92
2 Blacket Place, Edinburgh. † GI 2, RSA 5.

CHARLES, James* 1851-1906
Portrait, landscape and rustic genre painter. Studied Heatherleys, RA Schools 1872 and Academie Julien, Paris. Visited Italy 1891 and 1905. N.E.A. 1886. Add: London 1880; Harting, nr. Petersfield, Hants. 1888; Bosham, Chichester, Sussex 1889. † G 8, GI 3, I 2, L 23, M 16, NEA 29, NG 27, RA 45, RBA 1, RHA 1.

CHARLES, Miss Lucie Exh. 1932-35
Painter and sculptor. Add: Metropolitan School of Art, Dublin, Ireland. † RHA 17.

CHARLES, Miss M.C. Exh. 1916
Incegarth, Moor Park, Great Crosby, Liverpool. † L 1.

CHARLES, Miss Sheila b. 1918
Figure painter. Daughter of Robert Charles Peter q.v. Add: London 1939. † RA 1.

CHARLESWORTH, Alice Exh. 1894-1907
Portrait painter. Add: Nutfield Court, Surrey. † D 33, L 2, M 2, RA 8, RBA 3, SWA 15.

CHARLESWORTH, Eleanor b. 1891
Landscape and flower painter. Studied Slade School. Add: 38 Clarendon Road, Holland Park, London 1929. † BK 31, GOU 1, NEA 1, RA 3, RSA 3, RHA 2, RI 7, ROI 24, RSA 1, RSW 1, SWA 10.

CHARLESWORTH, Sam Exh. 1900
Prescott, Uffculme, Cullompton, Devon. † B 1.

CHARLET, Franz* 1862-1928
Belgian figure painter. Exh. 1888-1913. † FIN 2, GOU 2, ROI 1.

CHARLEY, Constance S. Exh. 1889-1901
Sutton, Surrey 1889; London 1901. † SWA 2.

CHARLEY, Thelma Exh. 1938
† M 1.

CHARLIER, Charles Henri Exh. 1909
† LS 2.

CHARLOT, Louis* b. 1878
French artist. Exh. 1923-25. † GOU 6.

CHARLTON, Mrs. A. Exh. 1920-22
Liverpool. † L 2.

CHARLTON, Alan Bengall b. 1913
b. North Shields. Exh. 1938. † M 1.

CHARLTON, Catherine Exh. 1880-90
Landscape painter. Married Edward H. Bearne q.v. Add: London. † G 3, M 1, RA 6, ROI 4, SWA 2.

CHARLTON, Evan Exh. 1930-37
Portrait painter. Add: 17 Bath Street, Finsbury, London. † NEA 4.

CHARLTON, Mrs. Edith M. Exh. 1894-1914
Miniature portrait painter. Add: London 1894; Farnborough, Kent 1914. † RA 10, RSA 2.

CHARLTON, Edward William b. 1859
Landscape painter. A.R.E. 1892, R.E. 1907. Add: Ringwood, Hants 1890; Lymington, Hants. 1899. † L 20, RA 22, RE 171, ROI 1.

CHARLTON, Miss G. Exh. 1901
Portrait painter. Add: 16 Milton Chambers, Cheyne Walk, Chelsea, London. † NEA 1.

CHARLTON, George J. b. 1899
Figure and landscape painter. Studied Slade School 1914. On staff of Slade School from 1919; Examiner for University of London General School Examinations from 1931; Examiner for Board of Education Art Examination from 1932. N.E.A. 1926. Add: London. † G 4, GOU 7, L 4, M 1, NEA 71, RED 42.

CHARLTON, H. Exh. 1921
92 St. Donatt's Road, London. † RA 1.

CHARLTON, H.V. d. 1916
Killed in action in World War I. Add: 6 William Street, Albert Gate, London 1912. † RA 1.

CHARLTON, John* 1849-1917
Portrait, sporting and military painter. Studied Newcastle School of Art and South Kensington. R.B.A. 1882, R.O.I. 1887, R.P. 1897. Add: Cullercoats, Newcastle-on-Tyne and London. † B 18, GI 4, I 1, L 26, M 6, NG 5, P 48, RA 56, RBA 13, ROI 11, RSA 1.

CHARLTON, Mrs. John Exh. 1901
† RMS 3.

CHARLTON, Miss Louisa Exh. 1897
Flower painter. Add: 10 Stoke Road, Shelton, Stoke-on-Trent. † RA 1.

CHARLTON, Miss Rosalie Exh. 1929
Sandburne, Keswick. † L 1.

CHARLTON, William Henry Exh. 1889-1912
Landscape painter. Add: Causey House, Gosforth, Newcastle-on-Tyne. † GI 7, I 1, L 2, RA 2, RSA 2.

CHARLTON, Watson Exh. 1907-21
London 1907, Grimsby 1921. † L 1, RI 1.

CHARNLEY, Miss D. Exh. 1921-33
West Kirby, Cheshire 1921; Hoylake, Cheshire 1922. † L 184.

CHARNLEY, Miss Edith Exh. 1929
1 Brenk Avenue, Aintree, Liverpool. † L 1.

CHARNLEY, Miss E.H. Exh. 1898-1911
Liverpool 1891; Huyton 1901; West Kirby, Cheshire 1911. † L 5.

CHARNOCK, Charles H. Exh. 1910-11
Crewe 1910, Manchester 1911. † L 2, M 2.

CHAROL, Mrs. Dorothea Exh. 1937
Sculptor. Add: 130 Westbourne Terrace, London. † RA 1.

CHAROUX, Siegfried 1896-1967
Sculptor. Studied Academy of Fine Arts, Master Classes, Vienna. Add: 65 Holland Park Road, London 1940. † RA 2.

CHARPENTIER, Felix Maurice 1858-1925
French sculptor. Exh. 1911-13. Add: Paris. † RSA 3.

CHARPENTIER, Georges* Exh. 1923
Boulevard Raspail 234, Paris. † L 1.

CHARPENTIER, Leon Exh. 1891-92
1 Rue Houdon, Place Pigalla, Paris. † GI 2.

CHARPIN, Albert* 1842-1924
French artist. Add: 59 Avenue de Courbevoie, Asnieres, France 1913. † L 1.

CHARRETON, Victor Leon Jean Pierre* b. 1864
French artist. Exh. 1907 and 1913. Add: Paris. † L 2.

CHARRINGTON, Charlotte E. Exh. 1913
Charlwood, Surrey. † D 1.

CHARRINGTON, Miss M.L. Exh. 1897-1910
Sutton, Surrey 1897; Leatherhead, Surrey 1910. † SWA 2.

CHART, D.D. Exh. 1930-31
Linocut artist. † RED 2.

CHART, Louie M. Exh. 1925
Edinburgh. † L 1.

CHARTERS, Isabella M. Exh. 1894-1900
69 Princes Street, Leicester. † L 2, N 5, SWA 1.

CHARTERIS, Miss Exh. 1888
16 Grosvenor Square, Chelsea, London. † G 1.

CHARTERIS, Hon. Capt. F.W. Exh. 1880-83
49 Gt. Cumberland Place, London. † D 2, G 6, RI 1, RSA 2.

CHARTERIS, Lady Louisa Exh. 1880-1910
Landscape painter. Add: 49 Gt. Cumberland Place, London. † D 1, FIN 40, G 6.

CHARTIER, Henri Georges Jacques 1859-1924
French artist. Add: Rue de la Tombe, Issore 83, Paris. † L 1.

CHARTIER, Paul Louis Exh. 1909-10
c/o Allied Artist Association, London. † LS 6.

CHARTRAN, Theobald 1849-1907
French miniature portrait painter. Add: London 1881; Paris 1883. † G 5, M 2, P 2, RA 5.

CHASE, Miss Emily Exh. 1899
18 Hall Road, Handsworth, Birmingham. † B 2.

CHASE, Emmie Emilie Exh. 1907-32
nee Martin. Signs work E. Gordon Chase. Landscape and figure painter. Add: London 1907, 1919 and 1928; Reading, Berks. 1910; Farnham, Surrey 1921. † GI 1, GOU 1, L 6, RI 3, ROI 10, RSA 1, SWA 16.

CHASE, Frank M. Exh. 1880-98
Landscape and coastal painter. Add: London. † L 1, M 6, RA 7, RBA 10, RI 6.

CHASE, Harry Exh. 1940
Landscape painter. Son of Emmie Emilie C. q.v. Add: 36 Acacia Road, London. † RA 1.

CHASE, Jessie Exh. 1884-90
Flower painter. A.S.W.A. 1886. Add: Haddon Lodge, Quex Road, Kilburn, London. † L 1, RI 1, SWA 17.

CHASE, John Exh. 1908
Hotel Foyot, 33 Rue de Tournon, Paris. † LS 1.

CHASE, Marian Emma 1844-190
Flower painter. A.R.I. 1875, R.I. 1879 Add: London. † B 2, L 11, LEI 1, M 1 RHA 14, RI 146, ROI 1, SWA 4.

CHASE, Powell Exh. 1892-190
Watercolour figure painter. Add: London † B 1, RA 4, RBA 2.

CHASE, Miss Una Exh. 190
Figure painter. Add: 14 Church Street Chelsea, London. † NEA 1.

CHASE, William Arthur 1878-194
Portrait and flower painter. Studie London City and Guilds School of Ar Regent Street Polytechnic (2 silver, bronze medal). Painted in Italy and America. Add: Bristol 1910; Londo 1912; Didcot, Berks. 1925. † B 2 CON 39, FIN 3, I 4, RA 7, RI 4.

CHASE, William Merritt* 1849-191
American painter. Exh. 1901-5. Add: New York, U.S.A. † I 7.

CHATER, J. Exh. 1886-190
Argyle House, Peckham Rye 1886; Ventnor, I.O.W. 1909. † LS 1, M 2.

CHATFIELD, Mrs. Exh. 190
The Argord, Monmouth. † SWA 1.

CHATROUSSE, Emile Exh. 188
Sculptor. Add: 253 Boulevard d'Enfe Paris. † RA 1.

CHATTEL, du See

CHATTERIS, Vere Exh. 191
† I 1.

CHATTERTON, Miss Norah S. Exh. 1936-3
Landscape painter. Add: Kilgarron, Enniskerry, Co. Wicklow, Ireland. † RHA 5.

CHATTOCK, Miss Mabel E. See HAYE

CHATTOCK, Richard Samuel 1825-190
Landscape painter and etcher. R.E. 188 Add: 15 Lancaster Road, Belsize Park London 1880; Newbury, Berks. 189 Solihull, Birmingham 1901. † B 2 FIN 11, L 3, RA 8, RE 29, RI 1.

CHAUSSE, de See

CHAUVEL, Theophile Narcisse 1831-191
French etcher. Exh. 1886-97. Add: Pari † RA 5.

CHAUVIN, Enid Exh. 194
Landscape painter. Visisted China and th Continent. Add: 73 Ivor Court, Gloucest Place, London. † RA 2, SWA 1.

CHAVAGNAT, Mdlle A. Exh. 190
11 Rue Chanzy, Nanterre, Seine, Pari † RA 1.

CHAVALLIAUD, Leon Exh. 1893-191
Sculptor. Add: London 1893; Reim France 1912. † L 1, NG 1, RA 6.

CHAWNER, Harold Exh. 1908-1
Aigburth, Liverpool 1908; New Ferry Cheshire 1910. † L 2.

CHEADLE, Henry* b. 185
Landscape painter. Studied Birmingha School of Art and South Kensingto (silver and bronze medals). Add: Birmingham. † B 105, L 4, RCA 16.

CHECA y Sanz, Ulpiano* 1860-191
Spanish artist. Exh. 1904-10. Add: 23 Rue du Faubourg, St. Honore, Pari † L 2.

CHEDSON, Charles R. Exh. 189
1 Crosshall Street, Liverpool. † L 2.

CHEEK, Doris M. Exh. 194
38 The Grove, Osterley. † RA 1.

CHEESEMAN, Miss D. Exh. 190
37 Hotham Road, Putney, Londo † RA 1.

CHEESEMAN, Thomas Gedge Exh. 1890-192
Domestic painter. Add: Highbury, Londo 1890; Battersea, London 1908. † RA ROI 1.

CHEESMAN, Florence Edith Exh. 1897-1923
Painter and etcher. b. Westwell, Kent. Studied King's College School of Art, Chelsea School of Art. Official artist to Gold Coast Government and Government of Southern Rhodesia. Visited Middle East. Add: Tonbridge, Kent 1897; London 1908. † L 2, LS 4, RA 2, SWA 4, WG 95.

CHEESMAN, Harold Exh. 1940
Landscape painter. Add: 78 Cambridge Road, Ilford, Essex. † RA 2.

CHEESMAN, William c.1841-1910
Landscape and figure painter. Add: Esher, Surrey 1890; Surbiton 1903. † RA 2.

CHEESWRIGHT, Ethel S. Exh. 1896-1913
R.M.S. 1897. Add: Croydon, Surrey 1896; Sark, C.I. 1901 and 1912, Oxford 1908. † RMS 20, SWA 2.

CHEETHAM, Mrs. C. Roche Exh. 1927-39
Cannes, France 1927; London 1932. † B 2, GOU 2, NEA 1, RBA 1, RCA 1, ROI 2, SWA 8.

CHEFFETZ, Asa Exh. 1929
American engraver. Add: 484 White Street, Springfield, Mass. U.S.A. † RA 1.

CHELIUS, Adolf Exh. 1892
Landscape painter. Add: 75 Theresien Strasse, Munich, Germany. † RA 1.

CHELL, John Arthur b. 1879
Painter, decorative and poster artist. Studied Wolverhampton and Birmingham Schools of Art. Add: Barn Cottage, Church Walk, Penn Fields, Wolverhampton, 1926-37. † B 10.

CHELMINSKI, Jan V.* 1851-1925
Military painter. b. Warsaw. Add: London 1882; Paris 1915. † FIN 38, M 1, NG 3, P 2, RA 6, ROI 8.

CHELMSFORD, Lady Exh. 1938
Landscape painter. † FIN 57.

CHELONI, M. Exh. 1882
c/o C. Loughi, 27 New Broad Street, London. † RA 1.

CHEREAU, Claude* Exh. 1913-14
Paris. † LS 4.

CHERRILL, Nelson K. Exh. 1904-5
Landscape painter. Add: Fleur d'Orient, Lausanne, Switzerland. † D 3, RA 1.

CHESHIRE, Francis Exh. 1886-1906
Birmingham 1886 and 1905; Seaford, Sussex 1889. † B 4, L 12.

CHESHIRE, John K.C. Exh. 1907-11
Springbank, Bewdley, Worcs. † B 1, LS 2.

CHESHOLM, H.J. Exh. 1888
Grant Road, Knotty Ash, Liverpool. † L 1.

CHESSA, Charles Exh. 1907
127 Rue Boucicaut, Fontenay aux Roses, France. † L 3.

CHESSER, John Exh. 1888
1 Chalmers Street, Edinburgh. † RSA 1.

CHESSHIRE, Miss E. Exh. 1912
Chorley Wood, Herts. † SWA 1.

CHESTER, Amy Exh. 1887
Blenheim House, Caversham, Berks. † SWA 1.

CHESTER, Miss Catherine Exh. 1924
Flower painter. Add: c/o Grove House, Peel Street, Nottingham. † N 3.

CHESTER, Frederick Exh. 1883-89
66 Courtfield Gardens, South Kensington, London. † B 2, M 3, RA 1, ROI 2, TOO 1.

CHESTER, George 1813-1897
Landscape painter. Add: 10 St. Albans Road, Kensington, London. † B 2, L 1, M 1, NG 1, RA 9, RBA 1, ROI 11, RSA 1.

CHESTER, Luke Barzillai b. 1865
Landscape painter. Add: 4 Holly Road, Northampton 1910-23. † LS 9, RA 1, ROI 7.

CHESTERS, S. Exh. 1885
Portrait painter. Add: Rydal Villa, Avenue Road, Scarborough, Yorks. † RA 1.

CHESTERTON, Frank S. Exh. 1903-15
Architect. Add: 51 Cheapside, London. † RA 8.

CHESTERTON, Maurice Exh. 1921-25
Watercolour landscape painter. Add: 28 Willifield Way, London. † ALP 41, RA 1.

CHESTON, Charles Sidney 1882-1960
Landscape painter and etcher. Studied Slade School. Married Evelyn C. q.v. N.E.A. 1917, A.R.E. 1929, A.R.W.S. 1929, R.W.S. 1937. Add: London 1911; Axminster, Devon 1924. † AG 49, BA 2, BAR 4, CG 89, CHE 4, CON 2, FIN 12, G 4, GI 2, GOU 2, L 4, M 3, NEA 128, RA 24, RE 10, RHA 6, RWS 72, WG 2.

CHESTON, Evelyn 1875-1929
nee Davy. Married George Sidney C. q.v. Landscape painter. N.E.A. 1909. Add: Studland, Dorset 1907; London 1910; Axminster, Devon 1924. † CG 2, CHE 2, G 7, GOU 3, I 5, M 1, NEA 98.

CHETTLE, Elizabeth M. Exh. 1883-1917
Architectural landscape, figure and flower painter. Add: London 1883; Sharnbrook, Bedford 1889; Dormansland, Surrey 1912. † FIN 67, L 10, LS 3, NG 1, RA 9, RBA 1, ROI 1, SWA 1.

CHETTLE, James Patchell b. 1871
Landscape painter. Studied Manchester Academy. R.B.A. 1935. Exh. 1926-39. Add: The Cottage, Davenport Park, Stockport, Lancs. † L 5, M 2, RBA 31, RCA 1, RSA 1.

CHETWOOD, Henry J. Exh. 1912-21
Architect. Add: 5 Bedford Row, London. † RA 2.

CHETWOOD-AIKEN, Edward Hamilton b. 1867
Landscape and flower painter. Exh. 1912-26. Add: Combe Dingle, Westbury-on-Tryn, Bristol. † L 2, LS 6, RA 1, RE 2.

CHETWOOD-AIKEN Walter C. d. c. 1899
Landscape and decorative painter. Add: London and Paris 1894; Stoke Bishop 1898. † L 1, RA 4, RBA 1, ROI 1.

CHETWYND, Miss F. Exh. 1921
97 Clarence Gate Gardens, London. † RA 2.

CHETWYND, Ida Exh. 1892-99
Figure painter. Add: London. † NG 1, RBA 1.

CHETWYND, Katie F. Exh. 1892
Figure painter. Add: 18 Walton Place, London. † RBA 1.

CHEVALIER, le See L

CHEVALIER, E.J. Exh. 1905
151 Rue de Grenelle, Paris. † L 1.

CHEVALIER, Miss Lena Exh. 1931
"Gorse", Budleigh Salterton, Devon. † RBA 1.

CHEVALIER, Nicholas* 1828-1902
Figure and landscape painter. b. Leningrad. Add: London 1880. † FIN 1, L 1, M 1, RA 10, RI 3.

CHEVALIER, Robert Magnus* Exh. 1880-1911
Landscape painter. Visited the Middle East Add: 76 Westbourne Grove, London. † B 8, D 3, G 1, GI 15, L 4, M 13, NG 1, RA 7, RBA 17, RHA 3, RI 6, ROI 6.

CHEVIOT, Lilian* Exh. 1894-1902
Animal and figure painter. Studied Calderon's School of Animal Painting and Walter Donne's Life School. Add: Thorpe, East Molesey, Surrey. † B 2, RA 2, RBA 4.

CHEWETT, A.R. Exh. 1915
Reveley Lodge, Bushey Heath, Herts. † L 1, RA 1.

CHEWETT, J. Exh. 1929
26 Stanhope Gardens, London. † NEA 1.

CHEWTON, Miss M.G. Exh. 1905
† SWA 1.

CHEYNE, Ian Alec Johnson 1895-1955
Wood-cut artist. Studied Glasgow School of Art. Add: Glasgow. † B 2, COO 3, GI 9, L 1, RED 3, RSA 9, RSW 1.

CHEYNE, Leo Exh. 1909
† LS 2.

CHEYNEY, S. Emma Exh. 1889-1906
Flower painter. Add: Denmark House, Red Hill, Surrey. † L 1, RA 1, RBA 2, RI 4, RMS 2, ROI 5, SWA 19.

CHIALIVA, Luigi* 1842-1914
Swiss painter. Exh. 1880-1911. Add: Paris and Ecouen, France. † AG 11, FIN,1, L 4, M 2, RI 1, RSA 1.

CHICHESTER, E.B. Exh. 1911
23 Morpeth Mansions, London. † LS 3.

CHICHESTER, Miss H. Exh. 1914-23
Culverleigh, Tiverton, Devon. † D 5.

CHIDSON, C. Exh. 1884-86
Liverpool. † L 4.

CHIERICI, Gaetano* Exh. 1880
Florence, Italy. † RA 1.

CHILD, A.E. Exh. 1908-11
24 Upper Pembroke Street, Dublin, Ireland. † RHA 2.

CHILD, Annie M. Exh. 1884-86
Domestic painter. Add: 39 Bickerton Road, Dartmouth Park Hill, London. † SWA 4.

CHILD, Charles Koe c.1867-1935
Landscape painter. Studied Westminster School of Art and Slade School. Senior Assistant to Henry Tonks at Slade School. N.E.A. 1927. Hon. Sec. N.E.A. 1925-28. Add: London. † NG 3, ROI 2.

CHILD, Miss Elizabeth Exh. 1929
Carrickmines Rectory, Co. Dublin, Ireland. † RHA 2.

CHILD, Ethel M. Exh. 1904-40
Miniature painter. Add: Abergele, N. Wales 1904; Mountnessing, Essex 1909; Meopham, Kent 1911; London 1915; Wormley, Herts. 1917; Tunbridge Wells, Kent 1929; Crowborough, Sussex 1937. † B 5, L 19, LS 30, M 1, RA 3, RCA 23, RHA 9, RI 13, RSA 11.

CHILD, Howard Exh. 1892
Greenwood Road, Acock's Green, Birmingham. † B 1.

CHILD, Miss J. Heather Exh. 1933-34
† RMS 2.

CHILD, Miss Louie Exh. 1892-93
175 Heathfield Road, Handsworth, Birmingham. † B 4.

CHILD, Miss M.F. Exh. 1923-24
"Kelvinside", Quantock Road, Weston-super-Mare. Som. † B 7.

CHILDE, Ellen E. Exh. 1885
Watercolour fruit painter. Add: 129 Fulham Road, London. † SWA 1.

CHILDERS, Mrs. E. Exh. 1908-10
Mrs. Hugh. Add: 6 Hereford Square, London. † RA 2.

CHILDERS, Miss Louise Exh. 1885
117 Piccadilly, London. † RI 2.

CHILDERS, Milly Exh. 1890-1921
Figure, portrait, interior and landscape painter. Add: London. † L 3, LS 9, NEA 2, NG 6, RA 8, RBA 3, RID 39.

CHILDERSTONE, Henry M. Exh. 1899-1935
Portrait and figure painter. Add: Kew Gardens, Surrey 1899; London 1905; Cherry Hinton, Cambs. 1906; Bedford 1931. † L 1, RA 4.

CHILDS, Ada E. Exh. 1880
57 Ellington Street, Arundel Square, London. † SWA 1.

CHILDS, Charles M. Exh. 1938-39
Architect of employment exchanges. Add: H.M. Office of Works. Add: Story's Gate, London. † RA 6.

CHILDS-CLARKE, Miss Sophia Exh. 1889
Still life painter. Add: Thorverton Vicarage, Devon. † RA 1.

CHILTON, G.W. Exh. 1914
Woodhay, Gamon's Lane, Watford, Herts. † RA 1.

CHILTON, Margaret Isabel Exh. 1909-40
Stained glass artist. Add: Bristol 1909; Westbury-on-Trym, Bristol 1913; Glasgow 1918; Edinburgh 1924. † L 2. RA 2, RI 1, RSA 25.

CHILVERS, Herbert Exh. 1908-38
Landscape painter. A.N.S.A. 1911, N.S.A. 1913. Add: 53 Caledon Road, Sherwood, Notts. † N 61.

CHILVER-STAINER, C.A. Exh. 1922-25
A.R.B.A. 1922. Add: Bournemouth 1922; Winchmore Hill, London 1924. † RBA 11.

CHING, Cyril Exh. 1900
3 Friar's Stile Road, Richmond, Surrey. † B 1.

CHIPARUS, D. Exh. 1930
† RSA 1.

CHIPP, Herbert Exh. 1880-86
Belfast, Ireland 1880; London 1882. † B 4, D 1, L 1, RHA 1, RI 2.

CHIPPERFIELD, Phyllis Ethel b. 1887
Painter and miniaturist. Studied Hammersmith and Central Schools of Art. Add: London 1911; Epsom 1918; Birmingham 1934.
† L 9, RA 12, RI 1.

CHIRICO, de See D

CHIRM, Miss Edith Exh. 1892-93
Birmingham. † B 2.

CHISHOLM, Annie Exh. 1881-1903
Miniature portrait painter. R.M.S. 1898. Add: London. † M 1. RA 1, RI 2, RMS 1, RSA 4.

CHISHOLM, Archibald Exh. 1924-29
Landscape painter. Add: Cookham Dean, Berks. 1924; Liverpool 1927. † CHE 1, I 1, L 3, M 1, RA 1, ROI 2.

CHISHOLM, A. Douglas Exh. 1913
20 Greasby Road, Liscard, Cheshire. † L 1.

CHISHOLM, A. MacLeod Exh. 1911
11Ravenscourt Road, Birkenhead. † L 1.

CHISHOLM, David John Exh. 1919
1 Mayfield Road, Edinburgh. † RSA 1.

CHISHOLM, Miss E. Grace Exh. 1932-35
Redhurst, Coatbridge. † GI 2, RSA 2.

CHISHOLM, Helen Exh. 1887
Haslemere, Surrey. † RI 1.

CHISHOLM, John M.A. Exh. 1917-25
Edinburgh. † GI 1, RSA 4, RSW 2.

CHISHOLM, Peter Exh. 1897-1922
Portrait and landscape painter. Principal Douglas School of Art, I.O.M. Add: North Shields 1897; London 1903; Douglas, I.O.M. 1921. † L 5, RA 1, RSA 6.

CHISHOLM, Robert Fellowes Exh. 1881-1914
Architect. Add: India 1881; Southsea, Hants. 1908. † LS 12, RA 7.

CHISHOLM, T.A. Exh. 1911
c/o Garnet & Sons, Sankey Street, Warrington, Lancs. † L 2.

CHISWELL, Miss Naomi K. Exh. 1912-31
Miniature portrait painter. Add: Royston, Thames Ditton, Surrey. † RA 6, RMS 1.

CHITTENDEN, Enid Exh. 1909-10
London 1909; Weybridge, Surrey 1910. † SWA 2.

CHITTENDEN, Mrs. Edwige N. Exh. 1931
Still life painter. Add: 19 Chichester Road, East Croydon, Surrey. † RA 1.

CHITTY, Mrs. Adeline Exh. 1932
Flower painter. Add: Belmont, Ightham, Kent. † RA 1.

CHITTY, Cyril Exh. 1912-29
Flower painter. Add: Belmont, Ightham, Kent and London. † LS 9, P 1, RA 1. RID 3.

CHITTY, Lily Frances b. 1893
Watercolour and line artist. Prehistoric research worker, draughtswoman to the Bronze Age Committee of the British Association. Studied Shrewsbury School of Art. Exh. 1923-24. Add: Yockleton Rectory, Nr. Shrewsbury. † RCA 2.

CHIU, Teng-Hiok b. 1903
Portrait and landscape painter. b. Amoy, China. Studied Museum of Fine Arts, Boston, Mass. U.S.A. and RA Schools (Landseer Scholarship 1925-27, Creswick prize 1926, and silver and bronze medals). A.R.B.A. 1927. Add: London 1924. † ALP 1, FIN 1, GOU 2, L 4, M 2, NEA 1, RA 5, RBA 75, RCA 2, ROI 13, RSA 1.

CHOCARNE-MOREAU, Paul Charles* b. 1855
French artist. Add: 96 Avenue des Ternes, Paris, France 1904. † L 1.

CHOFU, Omura Exh. 1920
Japanese painter. Add: c/o Dicksee & Co., 7 Duke Street, St. James's, London. † L 1, RA 2.

CHOLMELEY, Mrs. Sylvia Exh. 1929-34
Landscape, interior and flower painter. Add: 19 Hamilton Terrace, London. † COO 5, RA 1, WG 2.

CHOLMONDELEY, Lettice Exh. 1937-38
Fairholm, Larkhall, Nr. Hamilton. † RSA 4.

CHOPPING, Richard Exh. 1939
† GOU 2.

CHORLEY, Adrian William Herbert b. 1906
Landscape painter and etcher. b. East Bergholt, Suffolk. Studied Byam Shaw School and Royal College of Art. Add: London 1924. † L 2, NEA 1, RA 12, RI 2, ROI 7.

CHORLTON, H.C.D. Exh. 1887-1926
Didsbury, Manchester 1887; Bramhall 1911. † M 5.

CHOULER, Miss M. Exh. 1916
Lawn Bank, North Hill, Highgate, London. † RA 1.

CHOWNE, Gerard 1875-1917
Flower painter. N.E.A. 1905. Died of wounds at Salonika. Add: London 1899 and 1909; Liverpool 1905. † AG 2, BG 11, CAR 47, GOU 32, I 1, LEI 2, LS 4, NEA 66, P 4, RHA 4.

CHRETIEN, Madame L.C. Exh. 1905-11
French artist. Add: Meaux, France 1905; Paris 1911. † L 2.

CHRIMES, Miss A. Exh. 1889-93
Warrington, Lancs. 1889; Chorlton-cum-Hardy 1893. † M 2, NG 1.

CHRISTEN, Miss C. Exh. 1883
† L 1.

CHRISTEN, Rodolphe c.1859-1906
Teacher and lecturer. Add: Aberdeen 1892; Dublin 1898. Died Aberdeen. † GI 1, RHA 1.

CHRISTIAN, Barbara Exh. 1923-40
Landscape painter and wood engraver. Married Harry Watson q.v. Add: London. † GOU 1, L 1, RA 22, ROU 2, SWA 6.

CHRISTIAN, C. Exh. 1889
Tenterfield House, Putney Hill, London. † L 1.

CHRISTIAN, Clara J. d. 1906
Mrs. MacCarthy. Landscape, interior and still life painter. Visited Italy 1904. Add: Dublin 1885 and 1902; London 1898. † GI 2, L 4, NEA 10, P 1, RA 3, RBA 1 RHA 15, SWA 4.

CHRISTIAN, Gertrude Exh. 1884-88
Watercolour flower painter. Add: 8 Coulson Terrace, Penzance, Cornwall † RI 1, SWA 7.

CHRISTIAN, J.H. Exh. 1884-85
64 Carter Street, Liverpool † L 2.

CHRISTIE, Alexander b. 1901
Landscape, interior and portrait painter. b Aberdeen. Studied Gray's School of Ar Aberdeen and RA Schools (Bryne Scholar ship, Robert Brough Studentship, Scottish Educ. Dept. Travelling Studentship 1926) Add: London 1928. † GI 1, P 9, RA 7 RSA 4.

CHRISTIE, Archibald H. Exh. 1888-190
Figure and landscape painter. R.B.A 1898. Related to Robert C. q.v. Add: 1 Hamilton Terrace, St. John's Wood London. † L 7, RA 2, RBA 4, ROI 5 RSA 4.

CHRISTIE, Arthur S. Exh. 1938-4
2 Argyle Place, Rothesay. † GI 3, RSW 5

CHRISTIE, Miss Clyde Exh. 1904-2
Portrait painter, illustrator and illumina tor. Add: Glasgow 1904; London 1917 † GI 14, L 5, RA 1.

CHRISTIE, Constance M. Exh. 1900-1
Colwyn, N. Wales. † RCA 14.

CHRISTIE, Ella Exh. 188
31 College Bounds, Old Aberdeen † RSA 1.

CHRISTIE, Ernest Exh. 1886-193
Landscape painter. Related to Henry C q.v. Add: Redhill, Surrey 1886; Caterham Valley, Surrey 1904; Dorking, Surrey 1927. † L 2, LS 27, RA 6, RBA 8, ROI 3

CHRISTIE, Faraday Exh. 189
Landscape painter. Add: Broadstairs Kent. † RA 1.

CHRISTIE, Herbert Exh. 193
Landscape painter. Add: 7 Langthorn Crescent, Grays, Essex. † RA 1.

CHRISTIE, Henry C. Exh. 1881-190
Sculptor. Related to Ernest C. q.v. Add Redhill, Surrey 1881; London 188 Caterham Valley 1900. † GI 1, L 2 RA 12, RBA 1.

CHRISTIE, James Elder* 1847-191
Figure and portrait painter. Studie Paisley School of Art and South Kensing ton. Visited Paris. N.E.A. 1887. Add London 1880; Glasgow 1894. † B 2 G 11, GI 84, L 30, M 16, NEA 33, NG P 3, RA 21, RBA 5, ROI 1, RSA 13.

CHRISTIE, Jean Lyal Exh. 1922-3
Watercolour painter. Married James Gra q.v. Add: Edinburgh. † L 2, RSA RSW 9.

CHRISTIE, Lily Wrangel Exh. 1898-192
nee Wrangel. Married Robert C. q. Portrait, domestic and still life painte Add: London. † L 2, LS 7, M 1, P RA 12, RBA 3, ROI 3, SWA 3.

CHRISTIE, Mrs. Mabel Exh. 1937
111 Randolphe Road, Glasgow. † GI 1.
CHRISTIE, Miss Mamie M. Exh. 1932
18 Baxter Park Terrace, Dundee. † RSA 2.
CHRISTIE, Mary Macdonald Exh. 1934
Mrs. A. Thorburn. Add: "Sylt", Mill Lane, Northfield, Warwicks. † B 4.
CHRISTIE, Miss R. Exh. 1924
8 Gordon Terrace, Bangor, Wales. † RCA 1.
CHRISTIE, Reka Exh. 1916-21
10 Sydenham Villas, Bray, Co. Wicklow, Ireland. † RHA 8.
CHRISTIE, Robert Exh. 1901-3
170 Leith Walk, Edinburgh. † RSA 3.
CHRISTIE, Robert Exh. 1887-1926
Landscape and figure painter. R.B.A. 1894. Married Lily Wrangel C. q.v. Related to Archibald C. q.v. Add: London. † GI 2, I 4, L 6, M 11, P 3, RA 20, RBA 41, ROI 7, RSA 5.
CHRISTIE, Miss Vera Exh. 1893-1904
Portrait painter. Add: 16 York Street Chambers, Bryanston Square, London. † NG 1, P 8, RA 2, SWA 2.
CHRISTIE, Winefred Exh. 1901-8
181 Morningside Road, Edinburgh. † GI 2, RSA 10.
CHRISTISON, James Exh. 1905
22 Fettes Row, Edinburgh. † RSA 1.
CHRISTMAS, E.W.* d. 1918
Landscape painter. R.B.A. 1909. Travelled Australia and New Zealand. Died Honolulu. Add: London 1909. † L 1, RA 4, RBA 34, RI 1, ROI 2.
CHRISTOL, F. Exh. 1931
† GOU 1.
CHRISTOPHERSON, Jose Exh. 1935-36
20 Harrington Road, London. † SWA 2.
CHRISTY, Beatrice Exh. 1937-39
Wood engraver. Add: 27 Roxborough Park, Harrow-on-the-Hill, Middlesex. † RA 6.
CHRISTY, Miss Eva Exh. 1898
West Hampstead, London. † SWA 1.
CHRISTY, Josephine Exh. 1888-1906
Figure and landscape painter. Add: Boynton Hall, Chelmsford, Essex. † B 3, D 25, L 4, M 1. RA 2, RBA 2, RI 1.
CHRISTY, Susannah Exh. 1905-9
Flower painter. † BG 2, SWA 1.
CHRYSTAL, Arthur Exh. 1926-40
Edinburgh. † GI 2, RSA 10.
CHUBB, H.P.B. Exh. 1938
† WG 4.
CHUBB, Ralph Nicholas 1892-1960
Figure and landscape painter. Art master Bradfield College. Captain in King's Own Scottish Borderers World War I. Add: London 1920; Newbury, Berks. 1925. † ALP 34, CHE 1, GOU 9, I 1, L 2, NEA 3, RA 1.
CHUCKS, S.T. Exh. 1935
Landscape painter. † AR 1.
CHUGHTAI, M.A. Rahman Exh. 1937
Figure painter. Add: Chabuk Sawaran, Lahore, India. † RA 1.
CHURCH, Miss E.M. Exh. 1880-85
3 South Park Terrace, Hillhead, Glasgow. † GI 3.
CHURCH, Frederick Stuart* 1842-1924
American artist. R.E. 1881-87. Exh. 1881-84. Add: c/o Cassell & Co. Ludgate Hill, London. † L 1, RE 10.
CHURCH, H.G. Exh. 1931
Stockport, Lancs. † RCA 1.
CHURCH, Katharine D. b. 1910
Portrait, landscape and still life painter. Studied Brighton School of Art, Slade School and RA Schools. Add: London 1932; Marlborough, Wilts. 1940. † LEF 67, NEA 1, P 1, RA 3, RBA 3, RED 2.
CHURCHER, G.P. Exh. 1886-95
Landscape painter. Add: Oxford. † RBA 1, RHA 2.
CHURCHILL, Miss Elizabeth E. Exh. 1897
91 Cromwell St., Stretford, Nr. Manchester. † M 1.
CHURCHILL, Miss J.P. Exh. 1916
West End House, Poole, Dorset. † RA 1.
CHURCHILL, Miss Lallah Exh. 1930
Sculptor. Add: The Crown and Thistle, Abingdon, Berks. † RA 1.
CHURCHILL, Miss Mary Exh. 1887
Holmby House, Eastnor Grove, Leamington, Warwicks. † B 1.
CHURCHILL, Rt. Hon. Sir Winston Spencer* 1874-1965
Exh. 1919 and 1935. "The Loup River, Alpes Maritimes" painted 1930 now in the Tate Gallery. † LEI 1, P 1.
CHURLEY, Arthur Frank b. 1866
Pen and ink artist. Add: Birmingham 1924-35. † B 30.
CHURNSIDE, T.E. Exh. 1901-5
16 Laygate Terrace, South Shields. † GI 2, RCA 1, RHA 1.
CHURTON, Mary A. Exh. 1884-1904
Landscape and interior painter. Add: 45 Buckingham Place, Brighton, Sussex. † D 1, RBA 1, SWA 9.
CHUTE, Desmond Macready Exh. 1914
Portrait painter. Add: 2 Fitzroy Square, London. † NEA 1
CHUTNEY, Jesus Exh. 1929
† NEA 1.
CHUYSENAAR, Alfred Exh. 1891
Portrait painter. † P 1.
CIAMBERLANDI, Albert Exh. 1921
28 Boulevard de la Cambre, Brussels. † RSA 1.
CIANCIANAINI, F. Exh. 1911-13
Paris. † L 4.
CIAPELLI, G.L. Exh. 1884-89
The Lizard, Cornwall 1884; Florence 1888; London 1889. † ROI 3, RSA 1.
CIAPPA, Giovanni Exh. 1894
95 Bath St., Glasgow. † GI 1.
CIARDI, Beppi (Giuseppi)* 1875-1932
Italian artist. Exh. 1905-11. Add: Venice, Italy. † GI 6, I 2.
CIARDI, Emma* 1879-1933
Italian landscape and figure painter. Exh. 1914-34. † FIN 164, GI 1, LEI 80, RSA 2.
CIARDI, Guglielmo 1843-1917
Italian artist. Exh. 1882-1911. Add: Venice, Italy. † GI 4, I 1, M 7.
CIARDIELLO, Michelle Exh. 1885-1901
Domestic painter. Add: London. † B 2, GI 4, L 2, M 2, RBA 2.
CIMA, Luigi Exh. 1891-92
Italian artist. Add: Venice, Italy 1891. † RSA 2.
CIPPICO, Countess May Exh. 1929
24 Ilchester Place, London. † GI 1.
CIPRIANI, Giulio Exh. 1931
Sculptor. Add: Via del Romito 27, Florence, Italy. † GI 1, RA 2.
CIPRIANI, Nazareno Exh. 1888-92
Italian landscape painter. Add: Rome, Italy. † RA 3, RI 5.
CIREL, F.L. Exh. 1933-38
Cardiff, Wales. † RCA 8.
CITTADINI, Tito Exh. 1930
Spanish artist. † L 2.
CLACK, Arthur Baker Exh. 1924-33
Landscape painter. Add: London. † BA 116, COO 2, L 1, M 1, RA 3.
CLACK, Estcourt J. Exh. 1931-40
Sculptor. Add: London. † GI 1, L 1, RA 8.
CLACK, Thomas Exh. 1881-91
Landscape and domestic painter. Add: London. † D 2, RA 2.
CLACY, Ellen* Exh. 1880-1916
Domestic painter. Add: London 1880; Rugby, Warwicks. 1902; Worcester 1905; Liverpool 1909. † B 9, D 1, G 1, GI 3, L 60, M 2, RA 18, RHA 1.
CLAGUE, Daisy Radcliffe See BERESFORD
CLAIRIN, Pierre-Eugene* Exh. 1929
c/o Galerie Marcel Bernheim, 2 bis Rue de Caumartin, Paris. † GI 1.
CLANAHAN, Miss Cecilia Exh. 1923-26
The Wood, Hale, Cheshire. † L 2, RCA 2.
CLANCY, Mrs. Carmel Exh. 1937-40
Portrait painter. Add: 59 Strand Road, Sandymount, Dublin, Ireland. † RHA 2.
CLAPHAM, Frederick D. Exh. 1899-1910
Architect. Add: Eltham, Middlesex 1899; London 1910. † RA 2.
CLAPHAM, Mary Exh. 1885
Landscape painter. Add: 210 Adelaide Road, London. † ROI 1, SWA 1.
CLAPHAM, Miss Winifred E. Exh. 1913-23
Portrait and figure painter. Add: Manor Croft, Thames Ditton, Surrey 1913; London 1923. † L 4, RA 5.
CLAPP, Elizabeth Anna b. 1885
Sculptor, decorative artist and teacher. Studied Brighton School of Art and Regent Street Polytechnic. Add: Eastbourne 1915; London 1920. † GI 30, L 10, RA 9, RSA 10.
CLAPPERTON, Annie A. Exh. 1890
Drumslea, Greenock. † GI 1.
CLAPPERTON, Thomas John b. 1879
Sculptor. b. Galashiels. Studied Glasgow School of Art and RA Schools (gold medal and travelling studentship for sculpture). Add: London. † GI 13, L 6, RA 24, RSA 16.
CLAPPON, T.M. Exh. 1893
† GI 2.
CLARA, Jose b. 1878
Spanish sculptor. Add: Villa Malakoff, 39 Avenue Malakoff, Paris 1910. † L 1.
CLARE, Miss Bertha Exh. 1927-29
Liverpool. † L 2.
CLARE, J.F. Leigh Exh. 1906-11
Artists Club, Aberle St., Liverpool. † L 9.
CLARE, Miss Margaret E. Exh. 1914
352 Crow Lane West, Newton le Willows, Lancs. † L 3.
CLARE, Oliver* Exh. 1883-1908
Fruit and flower painter. Add: London 1883; Birmingham 1886. † B 18, GI 2, L 3, M 6, RA 1, RCA 4.
CLARE, Sidney B. Exh. 1906
Nursery Road, Southgate, London. † L 1.
CLARE, Vincent* Exh. 1888-97
Fruit and flower painter. Add: Fern Cottage, Nursery Road, Southgate, London. † L 3.
CLARENBACH, Maximilien* b. 1880
German landscape painter. Add: Bockum bei Kaiserswerth, 1905. † I 1.
CLAREBOUT, Miss Valerie Exh. 1933
Sculptor. Add: 37 Elms Road, Clapham Common, London. † RA 1.
CLARENCE, Arderne Exh. 1908-37
Landscape painter. Add: London 1908; Bournemouth 1935. † L 1, LS 3, RA 6.

CLARIDGE, George b. 1868
Landscape and still life painter. b. Bow Brickhill, Bucks. 32 years in Regular and Territorial Army. Studied Wrexham Art School. Add: Holywell, N. Wales 1923. † RCA 4.

CLARK, A.D. Exh. 1904
15 Ossian Road, Stroud Green, London. † L 1.

CLARK, Alec D. Exh. 1903
Architect. Add: 30 Brymner St., Greenock, N.B. † RA 1.

CLARK, Miss A. Marian Exh. 1900-3
Aborfield, Weybridge, Surrey. † B 2, GI 2, L 4, NEA 1, RI 1.

CLARK, Agnes Wilson Exh. 1899-1912
Mrs. Finlay. Add: Rutherglen, N.B. 1899; Newton, N.B. 1904; Pollokshields 1908; Bridge of Weir 1909; Wemyss Bay 1912. † GI 23, RSA 2.

CLARK, Mrs. Brodie Exh. 1889-1929
Domestic and still life painter. Add: Syon Park House, Brentford, Middlesex. † RID 16.

CLARK, Christopher 1875-1942
Military and historical painter and illustrator. Lieut. R.N.V.R. 1917-18. R.I. 1905. Add: London. † L 1, RA 6, RI 40.

CLARK, Charles Herbert b. 1890
Etcher. Studied Liverpool School of Art. Add: Liverpool. † L 44, RA 1.

CLARK, C. Macdonald Exh. 1881
Figure painter. Add: Gainsborough House, Bournemouth. † RA 1.

CLARK, Charles W. Exh. 1914-30
Architect. Add: Metropolitan Offices, Baker St., London. † RA 2.

CLARK, Dixon Exh. 1889-1902
Animal painter. Add: Blaydon-on-Tyne 1889; Whickham, Nr. Newcastle on Tyne 1907. † BG 1, L 1, M 1, RA 8, RSA 2.

CLARK, Dixon, junr. Exh. 1919
Figure painter. Add: 50 West Street, Gateshead. † RA 1.

CLARK, Miss Dorothy M. Exh. 1903
Miniature portrait painter. Add: 19 Cavendish Street, St. John's Wood, London. † RA 1.

CLARK, Ernest E. Exh. 1904-30
Landscape, seascape and interior painter. Served in forces World War I. Add: Derby. † N 14.

CLARK, Mrs. E. Kitson See BIDDER, Ina

CLARK, Edward Owen Exh. 1900
Designer. Add: 76 Finsbury Pavement, London. † RA 2.

CLARK, Falconer Exh. 1888
Watercolour rustic figure painter. Add: Rosehill, Dorking, Surrey. † GOU 7, RI 2.

CLARK, G. Exh. 1887
Ellesdon House, Bexley Heath, Kent. † B 3.

CLARK, Miss G.C. Exh. 1914-18
Newcastle House, Park Terrace, Nottingham. † N 2.

CLARK, G.F. Scotson Exh. 1909-12
London. † GOU 2, L 1.

CLARK, G.J. D'arcy Exh. 1937-38
† NEA 2.

CLARK, Hardy Exh. 1894
40 Lorne Grove, Urmston, Manchester. † M 1.

CLARK, Harriet Exh. 1902-3
Landscape painter. Add: Sunnycroft, Pinner, Middlesex. † L 1, RA 1.

CLARK, Harry Exh. 1890
5 Cannon Road, Liverpool. † L 1.

CLARK, H. Fuller Exh. 1903
Architect. Add: 30 John Street, Bedford Row, London. † RA 1.

CLARK, Harriett R. Exh. 1910-33
Figure and flower painter. Add: Ripley, Derbys. 1910; Nottingham 1912. † N 32.

CLARK, Henry Taprell Exh. 1881-82
Landscape painter. Add: Kegworth Rectory, Derby. † N 2.

CLARK, James Exh. 1884-1909
Glasgow. † GI 36, L 2, RSA 4.

CLARK, James Exh. 1898
124 George Street, Edinburgh. † RSA 1.

CLARK, James Exh. 1913-29
Edinburgh. † RSA 9.

CLARK, James* 1858-1943
Landscape, figure and fresco painter, illustrator and designer. Art Examiner for Cambridge examinations and the Government Board of Education. N.E.A. 1886, R.I. 1903, R.O.I. 1891. Add: London 1881 and 1887; West Hartlepool 1882. † B 8, FIN 42, GI 2, L 27, M 3, NEA 2, NG 7, P 6, RA 53, RBA 11, RI 101, ROI 50.

CLARK, Jane Exh. 1884-90
9 Wilton Crescent, Glasgow. † GI 9, RSA 1.

CLARK, Joseph* 1834-1926
Domestic and biblical painter. Studied under J.M. Leigh. Purchased by Chantrey Bequest "Early Promise" 1877 and "A Mother's Darling" 1885. b. near Dorchester. Add: London 1880, 1889 and 1903; Hazelbury, nr. Crewkerne, Som. 1887; Winchester 1897; Harrow, Middlesex 1899. † B 8, D 4, G 2, GI 4, L 7, M 3, RA 58, RHA 1, RI 1, ROI 63.

CLARK, Joseph Benwell Exh. 1880-94
Rustic painter. Collaborated with V.M. Hamilton q.v. Add: 22 King Henry's Road, Chalk Farm, London. † G 5, RA 8, RBA 3, RE 2, ROI 3.

CLARK, John Cosmo 1897-c.1967
Landscape and coastal painter. Son of James Clark, R.I. q.v. Studied Goldsmith's College School of Art 1914-18, Academie Julien, Paris 1918-19, RA Schools 1919-21. Add: London. † GI 1, L 4, LEI 3, NEA 4, P 1, RA 10, RBA 3, RI 1, ROI 1.

CLARK, James H. Exh. 1930-40
Sculptor. A.R.S.A. 1935. Add: Edinburgh. † GI 3, RA 1, RSA 25.

CLARK, James N.C. Exh. 1931-37
Peterhead, Aberdeen 1931; Troon, Ayr 1937. † GI 1, RSA 1.

CLARK, Miss J.S. Exh. 1918
Mrs. Robinson. Add: 39 Eskdale Terrace, Whitby Bay, Yorks. † RA 2.

CLARK, John Stewart Exh. 1899-1937
Miniature painter. Related to Dixon C. q.v. Add: Whickham, Nr. Newcastle-on-Tyne 1899; Gateshead-on-Tyne 1908; Whitby Bay, Yorks. 1918; Mitcham, Surrey 1937. † L 12, RA 13, RMS 4.

CLARK, Joseph Southall Exh. 1896
Kingsgate Road, Winchester, Hants. † ROI 2.

CLARK, J. Wait Exh. 1890-1901
Landscape painter. Add: North Shields, 1890; South Shields 1901. † L 2, RA 1.

CLARK, Louisa Campbell Exh. 1887-91
Miniature portrait painter. Add: London. † RA 3.

CLARK, Mary Brodie Exh. 1889-1932
Fruit and figure painter. Add: Brentford, Essex 1889; London 1932. † L 2, RA 2, RBA 1, SWA 3.

CLARKE, Miss M.G. Exh. 1903
Haslemere, Bourne Hall Road, Bushey, Herts. † SWA 1.

CLARK, Miss M. Hay Exh. 1907
2 Glencoe Road, Bushey, Herts. † B 1.

CLARK, Philip Lindsey b. 1889
Sculptor. Son of Robert Lindsey C. q.v. Studied City Guilds Art Schools, Kennington (silver medal for life modelling) and RA Schools (Landseer scholarship). Served in forces World War I. Add: London 1920. † GI 4, L 5, RA 17, RBA 3, RSA 3.

CLARK, Roland Exh. 1929
Etcher. † CON 1.

CLARK, Miss R. Cresswell Exh. 1927-29
Sculptor. Add: London. † L 2, RA 1.

CLARK, Rose E. Exh. 1896-1906
Tufnell Park, London. † B 5, GI 3, L 1, RA 1, RSA 1, SWA 1.

CLARK, Robert Lindsey d. c.1926
Sculptor. Father of Philip Lindsey C. q.v. Exh. 1893-1924. Add: Cheltenham. Glos. † B 1, L 1, RA 4.

CLARK, R.P. Exh. 1883-84
6 Thistle Place, Edinburgh. † RSA 2.

CLARK, S.* Exh. 1910
50 West Street, Gateshead-on-Tyne. † RA 1.

CLARK, Thomas Exh. 1882-84
Liverpool. † L 2.

CLARK, Thomas G. Exh. 1929
87 Winchester Road, Higham's Park, London. † NEA 1.

CLARK, Mrs. Walter C. Exh. 1893-98
Orleans House, Sefton Park, Liverpool. † L 3.

CLARK, Winifred E. Exh. 1919-26
Miniature painter. Add: 35 Arlington Road, West Ealing, London. † RA 4, RMS 1.

CLARK, W.F. Exh. 1936-38
47 Mulberry Road, Bournville. † B 4.

CLARK, W.F.C. Exh. 1884-90
Watercolour landscape painter. Add: St. John's Wood, London 1884; Rosehill, Dorking, Surrey 1888. † L 1, RBA 2, RI 7.

CLARK, William N. Exh. 1934-37
86 Milton Road West, Edinburgh. † RSA 1, RSW 3.

CLARKE, Ada Exh. 1892-98
Landscape, figure and flower painter. Add: 6 Kidbrook Grove, Blackheath, London. † L 2, RA 1, RBA 4, SWA 1.

CLARKE, A.C. Exh. 1924
Landscape painter. Add: Costock Rectory, Loughborough, Leics. † N 1.

CLARKE, Alice Clementine Exh. 1903-19
Brasted, Kent 1903; London 1909. † LS 21, RCA 2, RHA 3, SWA 5.

CLARKE, Miss A.D. Exh. 1912-4
London. † RA 3, SWA 5.

CLARKE, A.F. Graham Exh. 188
Rhayadar, Wales. † ROI 1.

CLARKE, Mrs. Avril le Gros Exh. 1916-36
Painter and engraver. Add: Rye Cottage Hickling, Norfolk. † NEA 1, RED 1.

CLARKE, A. Noel Exh. 1928-2
Landscape painter. Add: Hambleton, 2 Albert Road, West Bridgford, Notts † N 2.

CLARKE, A.T. Exh. 1890-9
The Vale, Chelsea, London. † RI 2.

CLARKE, Bethia d. 195
Domestic and landscape painter. Studie Westminster and Paris. Add: Eastbourn 1892; London 1895. † B 2, BG 2, GI 10 I 3, L 21, M 1, NG 1, P 2, RA 11, RBA 8 ROI 8, SWA 32.

CLARKE, Bramford Exh. 191
97 Bexley Road, Erith, Kent. † LS 3.

CLARKE, Miss C.M. Exh. 1914-1
117 Inwood Road, Hounslow, Middlese † LS 6, RA 1.

CLARKE, Miss D. Exh. 1908
Skegby Lodge, Nr. Mansfield, Notts. † N 1.

CLARKE, David* Exh. 1880-81
Landscape painter. Add: 19 Wollaton Street, Nottingham. † N 2.

CLARKE, Derek Exh. 1939
Landscape painter. Add: Noan, Thurles, Co. Tipperary, Ireland. † RHA 1.

CLARKE, Dora Exh. 1916-38
Sculptor. Studied Slade School. Add: Harrow, Middlesex 1916; London 1923. † G 1, GI 4, I 1, L 2, NEA 2, RA 14.

CLARKE, Derek H. Exh. 1935
Figure painter. Add: Old Pound House, Datchworth, Knebworth, Herts. † RA 1.

CLARKE, Eddie Exh. 1907
Westfield, Heaton Norris, Stockport, Lancs. † RCA 1.

CLARKE, Edward Exh. 1880
Architect. Add: 6 Adam Street, Adelphi, London. † RA 2.

CLARKE, Miss Emma Exh. 1911
23 Stamford Villas, Bury St. Edmunds, Suffolk. † LS 3.

CLARKE, Edward Francis C. Exh. 1881-87
Painter and architect. Add: London. † D 4, L 1, RBA 7, RI 6, RSA 3.

CLARKE, Miss Ethel M. Exh. 1897
Endwood Court, Handsworth, Birmingham. † B 1.

CLARKE, Eva M. Exh. 1911-35
Cutnall Green, Nr. Droitwich, Worcs. 1911; Selly Park, Birmingham 1934. † B 2. RCA 2.

CLARKE, Evelyn Percival Exh. 1899-1906
Landscape and portrait painter. Add: London. † M 3, NG 3, P 10, RA 3, ROI 1, SWA 1.

CLARKE, Fannie Exh. 1885
Leslie House, Lenton Road, The Park, Nottingham. † N 1.

CLARKE, F.B. Exh. 1925
† RMS 1.

CLARKE, Florence Hill Exh. 1912-19
London. † LS 16.

CLARKE, Gertrude C. Exh. 1909-36
Burton-on-Trent 1910; Edgbaston, Birmingham 1914; Dublin 1920; Leamington Spa, Warwick 1936. † B 2, LS 3, RA 2, RHA 2.

CLARKE, George Row Exh. 1880-89
Watercolour architectural painter. Add: 27 Gt. James Street, Bedford Row, London. † RA 1, RBA 8.

CLARKE, George Somers d.1882
Architect. Pupil of Sir Charles Barry. Add: 20 Cockspur Street, Pall Mall, London 1881. † RA 2.

CLARKE, Harry 1891-1931
Stained glass and decorative artist and illustrator. Studied Metropolitan School of Art, Dublin 1910. A.R.H.A. 1924, R.H.A. 1925. Add: 33 North Frederick Street, Dublin, Ireland. † FIN 3, I 2, RHA 32.

CLARKE, H. Chatfield Exh. 1896-1903
Architect. Add: 63 Bishopsgate, St. Within, London. † RA 4.

CLARKE, Helen E. Exh. 1880
Landscape painter. Add: Burton Road, Derby. † SWA 1.

CLARKE, H.G. Exh. 1899
Billington, Burton-on-Trent. † N 1.

CLARKE, Harry Harvey b. 1869
Landscape painter. b. Northampton. Studied and taught Leicester College of Art. N.S.A. 1911. Exh. 1899-1940. Add: Leicester. † B 5, L 2, N 13, RA 15, RBA 1, ROI 4.

CLARKE, H.M. Exh. 1891-1900
Riverslea, Orrell Road, Liscard, Cheshire. † B 1, L 5.

CLARKE, Mrs. H. Saville Exh. 1886-97
Coastal painter. A.S.W.A. 1886. Add: London. † NG 4, SWA 4.

CLARKE, H.W. Exh. 1924-25
60 Stockwell Road, Handsworth, Birmingham. † B 2.

CLARKE, Ida Wilson Exh. 1884-99
Sculptor. Married Paul Hardy q.v. Add: London 1884; St. Mary Cray, Kent 1889; Bexley Heath, Kent 1890; Cobham, Surrey 1899. † G 1, L 1, NG 3, RA 6.

CLARKE, John Exh. 1884-1912
19 Castle Street, Liverpool. † L 3, RA 2.

CLARKE, Jessie B. Exh. 1891-1926
Folkestone, Kent 1891; London 1913. † D 4, LS 5, M 2.

CLARKE, John Daniel b. 1880
Architect. b. Cambridge. Add: Eastbourne 1913-33. † RA 8.

CLARKE, Miss J.E. Exh. 1889-1904
Landscape and figure painter. Add: London 1889; Rose Hill, Dorking, Surrey 1903. † L 2, RID 2, SWA 2.

CLARKE, John Moulding b. 1889
Painter and etcher. b. Bolton le Sands, Lancaster. Studied Slade School, RA Schools and Royal College of Art. Add: Matlock, Derbys. 1924; Preston, Lancs. 1926 and 1934; Pinner, Middlesex 1929; Welwyn Garden City, Herts. 1932. † B 3, GI 1, L 3, M 3, RA 2, RCA 7.

CLARKE, Joseph William b. 1898
Watercolour painter. Studied Chester School of Art 1915-17. Lecturer in Art, Chester College 1923. Exh. 1935. Add: Chester. † RCA 1.

CLARKE, K. Exh. 1926
† M 3.

CLARKE, Kate Exh. 1884-1902
Landscape painter. Add: London 1884; Chislehurst, Kent 1902. † RBA 1, SWA 3.

CLARKE, Miss Lizzie Exh. 1894-1907
Cork, Ireland. † RHA 15.

CLARKE, Mrs. Lucy Jackson Exh.1908-19
London. † LS 20.

CLARKE, L.J. Graham Exh. 1880-92
Landscape painter. Add: Glanrhos, Rhayader, Wales. † L 1, RA 7, RBA 1, RCA 5, ROI 1.

CLARKE, L.K. Exh. 1928
† AB 1.

CLARKE, Miss Margaret Exh. 1921-23
Sculptor. Add: 20 Kimbolton Avenue, Nottingham. † N 4.

CLARKE, Mrs. Margaret d. 1961
Portrait and flower painter. A.R.H.A. 1926, R.H.A. 1927. Add: Dublin, Ireland. † RHA 50.

CLARKE, Maurice b. 1875
Watercolour landscape painter and chalk and pencil portrait artist. Studied Birmingham Municipal School of Art. Assistant Art master Repton School 1909 and Art master Harrow School 1922. † B 4, P 2, RA 11, RI 2, WG 39.

CLARKE, Mary C. Exh. 1880-90
Domestic painter. Add: Westfield, Bromley, Kent. † B 1, RA 1, SWA 4.

CLARKE, Marian Eagle Exh. 1908-27
Mrs. Richard N. Coulson. Watercolour landscape painter. Travelled widely. Add: Edinburgh 1908; Airthrey, Ayr 1921. † RSA 3, RSW 1, WG 65.

CLARKE, Minnie Ellen Exh. 1892-1936
Miniature and flower painter and pastellier. Studied Lambeth and Paris. A.R.M.S. 1924. Add: London. † GI 2, L 32, LS 6, RA 2, RBA 1, RCA 10, RI 2, RMS 43, ROI 3, SWA 17.

CLARKE, Miss Pollie Exh. 1891-1903
Domestic painter. Add: 1 Meadow Studios, Bushey, Herts. † L 3, M 1, RA 3, SWA 4.

CLARKE, Mrs. Polly Hill Exh. 1930-40
Sculptor. Add: 3 Edith Grove, Chelsea, London. † RA 6, SWA 1.

CLARKE, Miss Phyllis N. Exh. 1926-32
9 Mount Road, New Brighton, Cheshire. † L 3, RCA 2.

CLARKE, Richard E. Exh. 1909-36
Scarborough, Yorks. † L 9, LS 12, RA 6, RBA 2, RI 2.

CLARKE, Somers 1841-1926
Architect. Exh. 1881-90. Add: London. † RA 2.

CLARKE, S.C. Exh. 1933-39
Nottingham 1933; Wilford, Notts. 1939. † N 3.

CLARKE, Mrs. Theresa Exh. 1926-40
Erdington, Birmingham 1926; Edgbaston, Birmingham 1938. † B 22.

CLARKE, T.A. Exh. 1927-38
20 Glen Eldon Road, Lytham St. Annes, Lancs. † L 4, M 1, RCA 4.

CLARKE, Thomas Flowerday Exh. 1932-40
Landscape painter. Studied Heatherleys and Central School of Arts and Crafts. Add: 22 Blenheim Park Road, South Croydon. † COO 1, RA 6, ROI 4.

CLARKE, Thomas Shields 1860-1920
American painter and sculptor. Exh. 1906. Add: Hotel Cecil, London. † L 1.

CLARKE, W. Exh. 1881-88
Dublin, Ireland. † RHA 8.

CLARKE, W. Gilbert Exh. 1889-1929
Landscape painter. N.S.A. 1908. Add: Nottingham. † L 2, N 38.

CLARKE, W.H. d. c.1924
Rustic and figure painter. Add: London 1911; Milngavie, N.B. 1913; Kirkcudbright 1916. † GI 33, L 2, RSA 17, RSW 2.

CLARKE, W. Lee Exh. 1903
Architectural painter. Add: 29 West Bank, Stamford Hill, London. † RA 1.

CLARK-KENNEDY, Miss G.M. Exh. 1909-21
Ewhurst Rectory, Guildford 1909; Cambridge 1919. † L 1, RA 7.

CLARKSON, George H. Exh. 1903-23
Sculptor. Add: Sunderland. † RA 10.

CLARKSON, Marion F. Exh. 1891-1901
Domestic painter. Add: London. † L 2, RA 5.

CLARKSON, Penelope Flint Exh. 1916-28
Still life painter. Add: 43 Holland Road, Kensington, London. † G 1, GI 3, I 3, L 4, M 1, NEA 8, RA 7, ROI 7.

CLARKSON, Robert Exh. 1880-1914
Landscape painter. Add: Picklington, Yorks. 1880; Scarborough, Yorks, 1886. † GI 1, L 1, RA 4, RBA 1, RHA 17, RSA 4.

CLARKSON, Tom P. Exh. 1899
Architect. Add: 7 South Square, Gray's Inn, London. † RA 1.

CLARKSON, William H. Exh. 1893-1940
Landscape and figure painter. A.R.B.A. 1928. R.B.A. 1930. Add: London 1893; Godalming, Surrey 1901; Littlehampton, Sussex 1924. † L 43, NEA 12, RA 13, RBA 41, RHA 3, ROI 1.

CLARSON, Miss Marie Exh. 1899
The Mount, Tamworth, Staffs. † B 1.

CLAUDE, Eugene* Exh. 1886
France. † GI 1.

CLAUDE, J. Exh. 1908
2 Finborough Road, South Kensington, London. † RA 1.

CLAUDE, Jean Maxime c.1834-1904
French painter. Exh. 1883. † FIN 1, M 1.

CLAUDEL, Camille Exh. 1886
French sculptor. Add: Paris. † RA 1.

CLAUDET, Mary H. Exh. 1881
Landscape painter. Add: 10 Oak Hill Park, Hampstead, London. † SWA 4.

CLAUS, Emile* 1849-1924
Belgian landscape painter. Exh. 1895-1920. Add: Astene, Belgium, 1895; London 1917. † GI 3, GOU 5, I 5, L 5, RSA 1.

CLAUS, Prof. Fritz Exh. 1935
Sculptor. Add: Feldmannstrasse 134; Saarbrucken, Germany. † RA 1.

CLAUSE, William Lionel 1887-1946
Figure and landscape painter. b. Middleton, Lancs. Studied Slade School. N.E.A. 1929. Hon. Treas. N.E.A. 1933-35. Add: London. †, CG 58, CHE 10, FIN 12, GOU 14, I 1, L 4, M 3, NEA 73, P 2, RA 2, ROI 2, RSA 2.

CLAUSEN, Agnes M. Exh. 1882-84
Nee Webster. Married George C. q.v. Domestic painter. Add: Childwick Green, St. Albans, Herts. † L 2, RBA 2, RI 2.

CLAUSEN, Miss Catherine Exh. 1929
Flower painter. † FIN 2.

CLAUSEN, Charles Exh. 1926
Flower painter. † CG 1.

CLAUSEN, C.G. Exh. 1883
Childwick Green, St. Albans, Herts. † L 1.

CLAUSEN, Miss Elenore M. Exh. 1886-90
Flower painter. Add: 10 Mimosa Street, Fulham, London. † B 3, G 1, NEA 1, RBA 1.

CLAUSEN, Sir George* 1852-1944
Landscape, figure, portrait and still life painter. Studied Royal College of Art and South Kensington and in Paris under Bastien-Lepage. Visited Holland and Belgium. Professor of Painting RA Schools. A.R.A. 1895, R.A. 1908, H.R.B.A. 1923, A.R.I. 1878, R.I. 1879, R.O.I. 1883, R.S.W. 1926, A.R.W.S. 1889, R.W.S. 1898. Knighted 1927. Purchased by Chantrey Bequest "The Girl at the Gate" 1890, "The Gleaners Returning" 1908, "The Road, Winter Morning" 1923, "A Dancer" 1929 and "My Back Garden" 1940. Add: London. † AG 1, B 1, BA 26, BAR 195, BG 3, CAR 4, CG 6, FIN 69, G 75, GI 35, GOU 11, L 46, LEI 113, M 46, NG 5, NEA 16, P 8, RA 196, RBA 5, RED 5, RHA 27, RI 12, ROI 5, RSA 21, RSW 13, RWS 214, TOO 2.

CLAUSEN, Katharine Frances 1886-1936
Mrs. O'Brien. Portrait figure and landscape painter. Daughter of Sir George C. q.v. Studied RA Schools. A.R.W.S. 1931. Add: London. † BA 55, FIN 3, G 5, GI 3, GOU 5, L 29, M 2, NEA 19, RA 30, RHA 32, RSW 2, RWS 66, SWA 6.

CLAUSEN, William 1855-1882
Decorative artist. Add: 20 Walham Grove, Fulham, London. † RA 2.

CLAUSTON, Mrs. T.S. Exh. 1902
11 Braid Road, Morningside, Edinburgh. † RSA 1.

CLAXTON, Miss A. Exh. 189
28 Bath Road, Chiswick, London † SWA 1.

CLAXTON, F. Exh. 1880-89
Domestic painter. Add: London. † SWA 3.

CLAY, Sir Arthur Temple Felix Bt. 1842-1928
Historical, domestic, landscape and portrait painter. Add: Shere, Guildford, Surrey 1882; Gomshall, Guildford, Surrey 1883; London 1889. † FIN 47, G 5, L 4, M 2, NG 13, RA 13, RHA 1, RI 1, ROI 9.

CLAY, Beryl M. b. 1889
Ambleside, Westmorland 1921; London 1936. † NEA 4, RBA 8, RSA 9, SWA 3.

CLAY, Elizabeth C. Fisher Exh. 1927-38
Nee Fisher. Landscape and flower painter. b. Dedham, Mass. U.S.A. Studied Boston Art Museum; New York School of Art,, Henri School of Art, New York City; Paris under Robert Henri (scholarship from Clease School of Art, Madrid and Henri School of Art, Madrid). Add: Halifax, Yorks. † M 1, NEA 1, RA 2, RCA 2, SWA 1.

CLAY, Miss E.M. Exh. 1880-81
The Front, Litherland Park, Nr. Liverpool. † L 1.

CLAY, Julia M. Exh. 1880-81
c/o Dr. Sigestwood, Royal Hospital, Chelsea, London. † D 3.

CLAY, J.N. Angus Exh. 1930
† L 1.

CLAY, Maud Hogarth Exh. 1908-14
Plymouth, Devon. † B 2, L 1, LS 5, RA 1, SWA 2.

CLAY, Phyllis Archibald Exh. 1902-37
Nee Archibald. Sculptor. b. Tunbridge Wells. Studied Glasgow School of Art. Add: Glasgow 1902, Paris 1909, London 1911, Bletchingley, Surrey 1930. † GI 37, I 8, L 5, LS 1, RA 6, RSA 11, SWA 3.

CLAY, Patricia Thomson Exh. 1925-40
Edinburgh 1925 and 1928; Florence, Italy 1926. † L 1, RSA 18, RSW 24.

CLAY, Miss Stella Exh. 1931-35
Landscape and portrait painter. Add: Chelmsford, Essex 1931; Tadworth, Surrey 1935. † COO 4, NEA 1, RA 3.

CLAYDON, Lifford Exh. 1924
Watercolour architectural painter. Add: 20 Boscombe Road, Uxbridge Road, London. † RA 1.

CLAYES, des See D

CLAYS, Paul Jean 1819-1900
Belgian coastal painter. Add: Paris 1884. † G 1, M 1, TOO 1.

CLAYSON, Cuthbert Exh. 1880-91
Landscape painter. N.S.A. 1881. Add: Nottingham. † N 12.

CLAYTON, Albert Exh. 1933
Watercolour landscape painter. Add: 2 Elm Hall Gardens, Wanstead, Essex. † RA 1.

CLAYTON, A.A. Exh. 1922-38
Beeston, Notts. 1922; Long Eaton, Notts. 1936. † N 32.

CLAYTON, Mrs. Elsie M. Exh. 1935
Pencil artist. Add: 2 Elm Hall Gardens, Wanstead, Essex. † RA 1.

CLAYTON, Faith Exh. 1910-11
Glengariff, Kew Road, Surrey. † LS 6.

CLAYTON, F.R. Exh. 1923-25
Landscape painter. Add: 19 Friar Lane, Nottingham. † N 5.

CLAYTON, G.H. Exh. 1903
46a Everton Crescent, Liverpool. † L 3.

CLAYTON, H. Exh. 1911-32
Landscape painter. Add: Nottingham. † N 22.

CLAYTON, Harold* Exh. 1931-32
Painter and engraver. Add: 19 Greenhill Crescent., Harrow-on-the-Hill, Middlesex. † RA 3.

CLAYTON, James Exh. 1914
6 Glover Street, Birkenhead. † L 3.

CLAYTON, J. Essex Exh. 1885
145 Fellowes Road, London. † RA 1.

CLAYTON, J. Hughes Exh. 1891-1929
Liverpool 1891 and 1916; Cemaes Bay, Anglesea 1907; Wallasey, Cheshire 1928. † L 42.

CLAYTON, John Exh. 1898-1910
Medallist. Add: London. † LS 3, RA 2.

CLAYTON, Miss Kathleen Exh. 1898
5 Bersted, Bognor, Sussex. † SWA 3.

CLAYTON, Miss Katherine M. Exh. 1923-33
London. † GI 1, L 16, RA 1.

CLAYTON, Miss Mary Anna Exh. 1884-85
Flower painter. Add: 22 High Croft Villas, Duke Road Drive, Brighton, Sussex. † RBA 1, ROI 3.

CLAYTON, Percy Exh. 1902
39 Wellclose Terrace, Leeds, Yorks. † RCA 1.

CLAYTON, Thomas Exh. 1900
65 King's Road, Rochdale, Lancs. † L 1.

CLEASBY, Ethel A. Exh. 1914-26
Miniature portrait painter. Add: Leaholm, Waterden Road, Guildford, Surrey. † RA 10.

CLEAVER, James b. 1911
Figure painter. Add: 28 Redcliffe Gardens, London, 1939. † RA 1.

CLEAVESMITH, Edmund Exh. 1880-84
Landscape and coastal painter. Add: 10 Figtree Lane, Sheffield, Yorks. † B 1, L 2, RBA 8, RI 5.

CLEEVE, Mrs. H.L. Exh. 1896
Highfield, Frant. Sussex. † SWA 2.

CLEGG, Ernest Exh. 1939
32 Duchess Road, Edgbaston, Birmingham. † B 2.

CLEGHORN, G. Exh. 1881
78 Waterford Road, Fulham, London † D 1.

CLELAND, A.H. Exh. 188
16 India Street, Edinburgh. † RSA 1.

CLELAND, Peter Exh. 1880-1901
Edinburgh. † GI 1, RSA 28.

CLELAND, William H. Exh. 1892-1917
Landscape painter. Add: London 1892 and 1917; Banstead, Surrey 1894 † NG 1, RA 3.

CLELLAND, David Exh. 1932-3
Rear of 120 Union Street, Larkhall † GI 2, RSA 2.

CLEMENS, Benjamin d. 195
Sculptor. Among his works the sculptur on Africa House, Kingsway, London. Add London. † GI 5, I 2, L 1, RA 30, RSA 2

CLEMENS, Matt. H. Exh. 1895-9
Figure and landscape painter. Add Bushey, Herts. 1895; London 1896 Truro, Cornwall 1897. † RA 3.

CLEMENT, Mrs. Exh. 192
Society of Handloom Weavers, Melvill Chambers, Lord Street, Liverpool. † L 1

CLEMENT, Mrs. Dorothea Exh. 193
Sculptor. Add: 12 Stanley Crescent London. † L 1, RA 1.

CLEMENT, W.M. Exh. 191
King Edward Street, Ruislip, Middlesex † LS 3.

CLEMENTS, Astell Maude Mary b. 187
Miniature and watercolour painte Studied Canterbury, Maidstone and Bat Schools of Art. Add: Harbledown, Canterbury 1918. † RA 5.

CLEMENTS, Miss Elizabeth Exh. 193
Sculptor. Add: "Clonsillah", Antri Road, Belfast, Ireland. † RA 1.

CLEMENTS, Miss G.D. Exh. 188
c/o Drexel, Harjes & Co., Paris. † L 4.

CLEMENTS, G.H. Exh. 188
14 Chalk Farm Road, Haverstock Hil London. † RBA 1.

CLEMENTS, Stella Exh. 1914-2
Miniature portrait painter and black an white artist. Lived and painted in S America. Add: London 1914. † RA 2.

CLEMINSHAW, M. Isabella Exh. 1887-1913
Landscape painter. Add: Belvedere, Kent 1887; London 1888 and 1913; Cannes, France 1904. † B 1, D 16, L 2, RA 1, RBA 3, RHA 3.

CLENCH, Miss N. Exh. 1898
44 Longridge Road, Earl's Court, London. † L 1.

CLENNELL, Miss Beatrice E. Exh. 1902-6
87 Downs Road, Clapton, London. † RCA 1, SWA 2.

CLERCK, de See D

CLERK, H.E. Exh. 1922-23
† D 6.

CLERY, Pierre Edward Exh. 1887
5 Rue Littres, Paris, France. † GI 2.

CLEVELAND, C.B. Exh. 1910
5 John Street, Adelphi, London. † RA 2.

CLEVERLEY, Charles F. Exh. 1893-1907
Figure painter. R.B.A. 1901. Add: London 1893; Ripley, Surrey 1905. † L 2, M 2, NG 5, RA 3, RBA 10, ROI 2.

CLIBBORN, Mrs. J.S. Exh. 1923-33
10 Ashburton Avenue, Oxton, Birkenhead. † L 11.

CLIBBORN, R. Exh. 1902-23
Liverpool and White House, Templemore Road, Oxton, Birkenhead. † L 24.

CLIFF, Thomas James b. 1873
Sculptor. Studied Heatherleys and City and Guilds. Add: London 1910; Becontree, Essex 1927. † LS 3, RA 2.

CLIFFE, H.H. Exh. 1887-95
Lower Broughton, Manchester. † M 6.

CLIFFORD, Edward* 1844-1907
Portrait and biblical genre painter. Studied Bristol and RA Schools. Add: Kensington, London 1891. † NG 55, RA 1.

CLIFFORD, Edward C. 1858-1910
Figure painter. R.B.A. 1896, R.I. 1899. Add: London. † L 10, M 3, RA 10, RBA 2, RI 31, ROI 6.

CLIFFORD, Mrs. E.M.J. Exh. 1940
Light House, Chart Road, Sutton Valence, Kent. † RBA 2, ROI 1.

CLIFFORD, Henry Exh. 1884
1 Lansdowne Place, Blackheath, London. † RI 1.

CLIFFORD, Henry Charles b. 1861
Landscape painter. R.B.A. 1912. Add: London 1890; Birkenhead 1922. † L 2, RA 10, RBA 77, ROI 7.

CLIFFORD, H.E. Exh. 1884-1909
196 St. Vincent Street, Glasgow. † GI 23, RHA 1.

CLIFFORD, Harry Percy* Exh. 1895-1938
Painter and black and white artist. R.B.A. 1898. Add: London. † B 1, L 15, RA 11, RBA 107, RI 6.

CLIFFORD, Miss Joyce Exh. 1929
Durham Wharf, Hammersmith Terrace, London. † L 1.

CLIFFORD, Maurice Exh. 1890-95
Domestic and figure painter. Add: London. † L 2, M 2, RA 2, ROI 6.

CLIFFORD, May Exh. 1916-28
Flower and still life painter. Add: London. † L 2, NEA 2, RA 3, RBA 2, WG 101.

CLIFFORD, Robin b. 1907
92 Margarets Street, Rochester, Kent 1940. † NEA 1.

CLIFFORD, R.R. Exh. 1940
Chart Road, Sutton Valence, Kent. † ROI 1.

CLIFFORD, Thomas Exh. 1937-38
Landscape and figure painter. Add: 14 Eden Terrace, Sandycove, Co. Dublin, Ireland. † RHA 6.

CLIFT, Stephen Exh. 1883-88
Landscape and figure painter. Add: Geneva 1883; London 1885. † D 4, L 1, RA 1, RBA 2, RHA 2.

CLIFT, Miss Winifred I. Exh. 1922-35
Miniature painter. Add: Esher, Surrey. † RA 1, SWA 3.

CLIFTON, Matthew Leonard b. 1908
Commercial and industrial artist. Studied Camberwell School of Art. Teacher Beckenham School of Art and Hammersmith School of Arts and Crafts. Add: 53 Oxford Gardens, London 1931. † ROI 1.

CLIFTON, R.W. Exh. 1889-90
George Street, Edinburgh. † RSA 2.

CLIFTON, William Exh. 1882-85
Landscape painter. Add: Clarence Cottage, Woolwich. † D 2, RA 1, RI 2.

CLILVERD, Graham Barry b. 1883
Painter and etcher. Studied Central Arts, London. Served R.F.A. and R.E. (camouflage section) 1915-18. Add: London 1926. † ALP 1, CON 14, L 3, RA 11, RBA 4, RCA 2, RED 1, RHA 1, RSA 1.

CLIMIE, Mrs. Barbara Exh. 1938
Lowndes Street, Glasgow. † GI 1.

CLINCH, Mrs. A.C. Exh. 1919-30
Figure painter. A.N.S.A. 1917. Add: Mapperley, Nottingham. † N 13.

CLINK, Edith L. Exh. 1895-1913
Miniature painter. A.R.M.S. 1890. Add: London 1895; Littlehampton, Sussex 1903. † GI 2, L 1, RA 23, RBA 1, RMS 3, ROI 1.

CLINK, Miss Isabelle Exh. 1897-98
Portrait painter. Add: London. † L 1, RA 1.

CLINK, Miss Matilda J. Exh. 1891
Flower painter. Add: Osborn House, Holland Park Terrace, Kensington, London. † RA 1.

CLINKSKILL, Miss L.S. Exh. 1884-89
Glasgow. † GI 10, RSA 1.

CLINT, Alfred* 1807-1883
Landscape, marine and portrait painter and etcher. R.B.A. 1843, Sec. R.B.A. 1848, P.R.B.A. 1879, R.I. 1833. Add: 54 Lancaster Road, London 1880. † RBA 6.

CLINTON, Miss D.V. Exh. 1917
Hampstead, London. † SWA 2.

CLITHEROE, John Exh. 1934
St. Helens, Lancs. † RCA 1.

CLOAKE, Miss B. Exh. 1918
Stotfold, Bromley, Kent. † RA 1.

CLOGSTOUN, Ina Exh. 1902-6
Flower and landscape painter. † BG 1, FIN 110.

CLOSE, Mrs. Exh. 1884-87
82 St. Stephen's Green, Dublin, Ireland. † L 1, RHA 4.

CLOSE, Clarkson Exh. 1913
The Poplars, Newton Park, Leeds, Yorks. † L 1.

CLOSE, Miss Edith M Exh. 1902
† RMS 1.

CLOSE, Miss Gladys Mary Exh. 1916-30
Portrait painter. Add: 81 Dartmouth Road, Brondesbury, London. † RA 3.

CLOSE, Samuel P. d. 1926
A.R.H.A. 1891. Add: Belfast, Ireland. † RHA 20.

CLOUGH, Colin Exh. 1923-28
Glan Conway, N. Wales 1923; Bettws-y-coed 1924. † L 1, RCA 14.

CLOUGH, Miss Florence K. Exh. 1901-31
Figure painter. Add: Margate, Kent. † RA 2, SWA 2.

CLOUGH, Miss Nellie Exh. 1914-20
The Hollies, Glan Conway, N. Wales. † RCA 7.

CLOUGH, Tom Exh. 1882-1939
Landscape and figure painter. Add: Hulme, Lancs. 1882; Bolton, Lancs. 1890; Glan Conway, N. Wales 1895; Bettws-y-coed, Wales 1924. † B 1, L 19, M 2, RA 14, RBA 3, RCA 116, RI 10.

CLOUSEN, Miss E.M. Exh. 1887
10 Mimosa Street, Fulham, London. † B 1.

CLOUSTON, Miss Nancy Exh. 1927-28
Wimbledon, London. † SWA 3.

CLOUSTON, Robert S. d. 1911
Engraver. Add: Edinburgh 1880; Beesley, Herts. 1886; Watford, Herts 1888. † GI 2, N 5, RA 8, RSA 18.

CLOVER, Miss Annette Exh. 1901
Westfield, Bidston Road, Birkenhead. † L 3.

CLOW, Miss D. Exh. 1902
6 South Cliff Street, Tenby, Wales. † SWA 1.

CLOW, Florence Exh. 1882-87
Flower painter. Add: 11 Upper Hamiton Terrace, London. † B 1, L 1, RA 1, RBA 4, RHA 2, ROI 1, SWA 4.

CLOWER, Agnes Exh. 1925-29
Flower painter. Add: Nottingham Road, Ripley Derby. † N 4.

CLOWES, Rollo Exh. 1903
Architect. Add: 47 Palewell Park, East Sheen, London. † RA 1.

CLOWES, William Exh. 1922
26a Green Street, Macclesfield, Cheshire. † L 1.

CLOWSER, Miss A. Exh. 1900
7 Prince of Wales Terrace, Kensington, London. † L 1.

CLOY, James Exh. 1883
Glasgow. † GI 1.

CLUER, Percy D. Exh. 1901
Landscape painter. Add: c/o Mrs. Woodward, The Cross Path, Radlett, Herts. † RA 1.

CLUFF, Elsie M. Exh. 1891-1904
Architectural painter. Add: Walthamstow, London 1891; Ballyboy, Co. Meath, Ireland 1904. † B 7, RA 3, RBA 1, RHA 2, RI 1, SWA 1.

CLULOW, Miss Freda See MARSTON

CLUNAS, Miss Laura B.S. See FIDLER

CLUNAS, W.R. Exh. 1887
c/o A. Scott, 78 Princes Street, Edinburgh. † D 4.

CLUTTERBUCK, Julia E. d. 1932
Painter and etcher. Married J.J. Alsop, q.v. A.R.E. 1916. Add: Harpenden, Herts. 1909 and 1924; London 1918; Chepstow, Mon. 1929. † GI 1, I 5, L 11, RA 5, RE 20, RSA 1.

CLUTTERBUCK, Madeleine Exh. 1887-90
Hardenhuish Park, Chippenham, Wilts. † D 2, SWA 1.

CLUTTERBUCK, Mrs. Margery Exh. 1934
Portrait painter. Add: 63 Walliscote Road, Weston-super-Mare, Som. † RA 1.

CLUTTON-BROCK, Evelyn Alice b.1876
Landscape and portrait painter. Studied Slade School and Chelsea Polytechnic. Add: Godalming, Surrey 1912; London 1929. † ALP 5, GOU 3, NEA 5, RA 1, RED 1, SWA 3.

CLUYSENAAR, Andre Exh. 1909-15
17 Avenue Hamoir, Uccle, Brussels. † L 2, RSA 1.

CLUYSENAAR, John G. Exh. 1924-29
Sculptor. Add: c/o Bourlet, 17 Nassau Street, London. † GI 1, I 2, L 2, RA 4.

CLYDE, Helen F. Exh. 1932-39
Glasgow. † GI 3, RSA 4.

CLYDE, Dr. William M. Exh. 1939
7 Beechwood Terrace, Dundee. † RSW 2.

COAD, Kathleen E. Exh. 1894-1910
Miniature painter. Add: London. † L 4, LS 3, M 2, RA 4, RMS 2, SWA 1.
COAD, Richard Exh. 1885-87
Architect. Add: 3 Duke Street, Adelphi, London. † RA 5.
COAKLEY, J.J. Exh. 1881
7 Camden Quay, Cork, Ireland. † RHA 1.
COATE, W.H. c.1890-1917
Architect. Killed in action. Add: St. Matthews Vicarage, Luton, Beds. 1909. † RA 1.
COATES, Lady Celia Exh. 1907
Dublin Castle, Ireland. † RHA 1.
COATES, Dorothy Marie Anderson Exh. 1924-26
nee Knoop. Miniature painter. Studied under Mrs. E. Palmer, R.M.S. Add: Waterloo, Liverpool 1924; Bournemouth, Hants. 1925. † RI 4.
COATES, Miss E. Exh. 1923
Mrs. A.E. Banks. Add: 1 Weld Road, Birkdale, Lancs. † L 1.
COATES, E. Davies Exh. 1933
Wood engraver. Add: 81 Chamberlayne Road, Kensal Rise, London. † RA 1.
COATES, F. Exh. 1912
The Mount Studio, Private Road, Sherwood, Notts. † N 1.
COATES, George James 1869-1930
Portrait and mural painter. War artist. b. Melbourne, Australia. Studied National Gallery, Melbourne (gold medal and travelling scholarship and Juliens, Paris. R.O.I. 1915, R.P. 1915. Add: Paris 1898; London 1902. † CHE 5, GI 1, I 23, L 8, LS 7, M 1, P 37, RA 20, ROI 27, RSA 1.
COATES, John W. Exh. 1900-23
26 Cornwall Road, Bradford, Yorks. † L 6.
COATES, Kate Bedford Exh. 1890-93
Belford Lodge, Lewin Road, Streatham, London. † RI 1, SWA 2.
COATS, Alice Margaret b. 1905
Painter, engraver and woodcut artist. Studied Birmingham Central School and Slade School. Add: 37 Radnor Road, Handsworth, Birmingham 1928. † B 7, GI 1, M 1, RBA 1, RED 1, RSA 2.
COATS, Janie H. Exh. 1889
Ellangowan, Paisley, Scotland. † GI 2.
COATS, Jessie Exh. 1889-90
Ferndean, Castle Head, Paisley, Scotland. † GI 4.
COATS, Mary Exh. 1899
Painter and ceramic painter. Studied Paisley School of Art, Glasgow School of Art and America (china painting). Head mistress West Public School, Paisley. Add: Glenview, Barterholm, Paisley, Scotland 1899. † GI 1.
COBB, Alfred F. Exh. 1880-89
Watercolour landscape and coastal painter. Add: London 1880; New Hampton, Middlesex 1889. † D 8, RBA 8.
COBB, Mrs. Emily J. Exh. 1890
Miniature painter. Add: 4 St. Luke's Road, Westbourne Park, London. † RA 1.
COBB, H.T. Exh. 1882-86
Ashton-under-Lyne, Manchester. † M 5.
COBB, James W. Exh. 1902
Architect. Add: 24a Regent Street, London. † RA 1.
COBBAN, Rose C. Exh. 1936
Portrait painter. Add: The Blue House, Ditchling, Sussex. † RA 1.
COBBE, Bernard* Exh. 1883-85
Domestic and figure painter. Add: London. † B 2, RBA 1.
COBBE, Miss Ethel L. Exh. 1901-12
20 St. George's Road, Eccleston Square, London. † L 12, M 2, RA 4, RMS 1.
COBBETT, Miss A.D. Exh. 1928
35 Queen's Road, Richmond, Surrey. † RBA 2.
COBBETT, Edward John* 1815-1899
Genre and landscape painter. R.B.A. 1856. Add: London 1880; Addlestone, Surrey 1885. † B 7, GI 7, L 1, M 2, RA 1, RBA 97, TOO 1.
COBBETT, Hilary Dulcie b. 1885
Watercolour painter. Daughter of William V.H.C. q.v. Studied Richmond, Surrey. A.S.W.A. 1937. Add: 35 Queen's Road, Richmond, Surrey 1928. † AB 2, COO 2, RA 5, RBA 2, RI 14, ROI 17, SWA 14.
COBBETT, Phoebe Exh. 1880-82
Domestic painter. Add: 20 Oakley Square, St. Pancras, London. † RBA 5, SWA 1.
COBBETT, William V.H. Exh. 1887-1901
Landscape and architectural painter. Add: 15 Cardigan Road, Richmond, Surrey. † D 22, L 2, M 1, RBA 6.
COBDEN-SANDERSON, Thomas James c.1848-1922
Printer and bookbinder. Founder of the Dover Press. Add: The Doves Bindery, 15 Upper Mall, Hammersmith, London 1908. † NG 1.
COBELY, William Henry Exh. 1892-1903
Landscape painter. Add: London. † B 1, M 4, RA 1.
COBHAM, Anne Exh. 1934-36
116A Holland Road, London. † COO 5.
COBLENZ, R. Exh. 1926-27
17 Primrose Hill, Port Sunlight, Cheshire. † L 3.
COBLEY, Miss Florence Exh. 1888-96
London. † M 1, RBA 1, ROI 2.
COBLEY, H.H. Exh. 1886
Grove Cottage, Tettenhall Wood, Wolverhampton. † RHA 1.
COCHRAN, Miss Annie Exh. 1897
Ainsdale, Southport, Lancs. † L 1.
COCHRAN, John Exh. 1929
37 Whitby Street, Parkhead, Glasgow. † GI 1.
COCHRAN, Kate Exh. 1919
24 Lawrence Road, Hove, Sussex. † I 1.
COCHRAN, Robert d. 1914
Watercolour painter. R.S.W. 1910. Add: Paisley, nr. Glasgow 1895. † GI 19, L 1, RSA 5, RSW 13.
COCHRAN, William Exh. 1883
12 St. James Street, Paisley Road, Glasgow. † GI 1.
COCHRANE, Miss Eileen Exh. 1905
Arnold House, South Farnborough, Hants. † RA 1.
COCHRANE, Helen Lavinia b. 1868
nee Shaw. Watercolour landscape and figure painter. b. Bath. Studied Liverpool School of Art, Munich and Westminster. Director of Military hospitals in France and Italy 1915-18. R.I. 1932. Add: Newcastle-on-Tyne 1894; London 1925; Prov. di Spezia, Italy 1926. † D 2, FIN 306, L 8, RA 8, RBA 1, RI 41, SWA 3.
COCHRANE, Jessica M. Exh. 1887-1903
Married to Walter F. Cave, q.v. Add: London. † NG 2, SWA 2.
COCHRANE, John S. Exh. 1913-15
9 Finnart Street, Greenock. † GI 1, RSA 3.
COCHRANE, Miss M. Exh. 1912
Oakleigh, Ryde, I.o.W. † RA 1.
COCHRANE, Robert Exh. 1893-1901
17 Highfield Road, Rathgar, Dublin, Ireland. † RHA 4.
COCHRANE, R.G. Exh. 1926
47 Queensborough Gardens, London. † RSW 1.
COCK, Edward Charles Loveland Exh. 1906-34
Landscape painter. Add: London. † BRU 3, G 1, GI 1, I 1, LS 8, NG 3, RA 3, RI 1, ROI 3.
COCKBURN, Miss A. Exh. 1904-7
Abbottsdene, Richmond, Surrey. † RI 2, SWA 6.
COCKBURN, Alexander Exh. 1906
120 West Campbell Street, Glasgow. † GI 1.
COCKBURN, Miss E.G. Exh. 1924
Milton Mount College, Crawley, Sussex. † SWA 1.
COCKBURN, John Exh. 1889
13 Dean Street, Edinburgh. † RSA 1.
COCKBURN, Laelia Armine Exh. 1913-40
Animal painter. Studied Kemp-Welch School, Bushey, Guthrie award at RSA 1925. R.S.W. 1924. Add: North Berwick 1913; Crianlarich 1919; Edinburgh 1924 and 1932; Ottery St. Mary, Devon 1928; Currie, Midlothian 1930; Balerno, Midlothian 1936. † GI 37, L 8, RA 2, RI 1, ROI 3, RSA 77, RSW 51, SWA 1.
COCKBURN, Miss Mabel Exh. 1895-1901
Portrait painter. Add: London. † RA 2.
COCKBURN, Miss Mary Exh. 1938
Urban landscape painter. Add: 29 Grafton Road, London. † RA 1.
COCKBURN, Miss Maud Lee Exh. 1894-1920
Miniature painter. Add: London 1894; Godalming, Surrey 1920. † RA 3, RMS 4.
COCKBURN, W. Laughland Exh. 1909-38
Maryton, Oldhall, Paisley, Scotland. † GI 8, L 2, RSA 5.
COCKERAM, Miss Bertha Exh. 1914
The Hutch Studio, St. Ives, Cornwall. † LS 3.
COCKERELL, Miss Catherine b. 1903
298 Norton Way, Letchworth, Herts. 1925-27. † L 16.
COCKERELL, Christabel A. Exh. 1884-1910
Domestic painter. Married Sir George J. Frampton q.v. Add: London. † L 8, NG 6, RA 10, RBA 1, ROI 1.
COCKERELL, Edward A. Exh. 1883
Landscape painter. Add: Ravenswing House, Stamford Hill, London. † RBA 1.
COCKERELL, Lady Kinsford Exh. 1922-37
Flower painter. Add: 3 Shaftesbury Road, Cambridge. † FIN 2, G 1, GI 1, RI 1, SWA 1.
COCKERELL, Louis Exh. 1890-1908
Figure and landscape painter. Add: Birmingham 1890; London 1900. B 6, L 1, NG 14, RA 2.
COCKERELL, Samuel Pepys b. 1844
Painter and sculptor. Add: London 1880-1907. † G 1, L 11, M 2, NG 13, RA 24, RBA 2, ROI 1.
COCKERHAM, J.W. Exh. 1893-97
Heatherley, Yorks. 1893; Bingley, Yorks. 1896. † L 3.
COCKERILL, Alice M. Exh. 1884-1921
Flower and fruit painter. Add: 20 Granby Street, Mornington Crescent, London. † L 3, LS 27, RA 1, SWA 4.
COCKRAM, George 1861-1950
Watercolour landscape painter. b. Birkenhead. Studied Liverpool School of Art 1884 and Paris 1889. R.I. 1913. "Solitude" purchased by Chantrey Bequest 1892. Add: Liverpool 1882; Conway, North Wales 1890; Anglesey 1895. † B 11, GI 8, L 139, LS 3, M 22, RA 46, RBA 3, RCA 149, RI 158.

COCKRILL, R. Scott Exh. 1924
Architect. Add: 12 Norfolk Street, Strand, London. † RA 1.

COCKS, Bertram H. Exh. 1938-39
† RMS 2.

COCROFT, Miss Ella M. Exh. 1904-5
Figure painter. Add: 26 Victoria Street, London. † L 1, RA 2.

COCQ, le see L

COCTEAU, Jean* 1889-1963
French writer, dramatist, critic and illustrator. Exh. 1914. † FIN 1.

CODD, John Exh. 1883-1911
Architect. Add: St. John's Wood, London 1883; Ventnor, I.o.W. 1911. † RA 5.

CODD, Walter Exh. 1935-39
Flower painter. Add: Grantham, Lincs. † N 9.

CODDINGTON, Hillary Exh. 1891-99
West Hampstead, London 1891; Blackburn, Lancs. 1893. † D 3, L 3, ROI 1, SWA 2.

CODNER, Maurice Frederick b. 1888
Portrait painter. R.P. 1937. Add: 26 Temple Fortune Hill, London. † GI 2, L 2, P 24, RA 16, ROI 4, RSA 2.

CODRINGTON, Isabel Exh. 1918-35
Painter and etcher. b. Devon. Studied RA Schools (2 medals). Add: Wistler's Wood, Woldingham, Surrey. † CG 25, COO 5, FIN 47, G 15, GOU 9, L 9, P 4, RA 15, RHA 2, RI 1, RSA 4, SWA 1.

COE, Mrs. Sarah E. Exh. 1936
Portrait painter. Add: c/o J. Bryce Smith Ltd. 117 Hampstead Road, London. † RA 1.

COENRACTS, Ferd. Exh. 1884
† GI 1.

COESSIN, Exh. 1887
52 Boulevard Sanes, Paris, France. † M 1.

COEURET, A. Exh. 1911
Figure painter. † GOU 2.

COFFEY, Alfred Exh. 1937
Landscape painter. Visited Australia. Add: c/o J. Bourlet, Nassau Street, London. † RHA 1.

COFFEY, George d. 1916
Professor of antiquities R.H.A. Exh. 1905-7. Add: 5 Harcourt Terrace, Dublin, Ireland. † RHA 5.

COFFEY, Miss L.T. Exh. 1898-1901
Dublin, Ireland. † RHA 4.

COFFEY, Miss Mary Exh. 1894
24 Grove Street, Liverpool. † L 1.

COFFIN, Miss N.P. Exh. 1914
Seacroft, Exmouth, Devon. † RA 1.

COFFIN, T.W. Exh. 1901
Maldon Crescent, London. † RI 1.

COGAN, Hubert Exh. 1934-38
Figure and landscape painter. Add: 3 Prince Arthur Terrace, Leinster Square, Rathmines, Dublin, Ireland. † RHA 3.

COGAN, Maurice F. Exh. 1936-39
Portrait and landscape painter. Studied Metropolitan School of Art, Dublin 1936. Add: 4 Glenbeigh Road, North Circular Road, Dublin, Ireland 1938. † RHA 9.

COGAN, Maurice O'Brien Exh. 1933-40
Figure and landscape painter. Add: 3 Prince Arthur Terrace, Leinster Square, Rathmines, Dublin, Ireland. † RHA 6.

COGEN, Felix Exh. 1880-85
Brussels 1880; Paris 1885. † GI 1, RHA 1, RSA 1.

COGGER, Florence J. Exh. 1927-35
Watercolour flower and figure painter. Add: Kingston Hill, Surrey. † AB 1, L 2, RA 5, RHA 1, RI 6, RSA 1, SWA 1.

COGGHE, Remy Exh. 1887-89
Figure painter. Add: Roubaix, France. † L 1, RA 2.

COGGIN, Clarence Exh. 1892-96
Architectural painter. Add: 8 Roland Mansions, South Kensington, London. † RA 2.

COGGIN, Mrs. Jeannie Exh. 1892
Architectural painter. Add: Roland Mansions, South Kensington, London. † RA 1.

COGHILL, Sir Egerton Bushe, Bt. 1853-1921
Landscape and figure painter. Son of Sir John Joscelyn C. q.v. Studied Dusseldorf and Paris. N.E.A. 1887. Add: Castletowns End, Skibbereen, Cork. † L 3, NEA 3, RHA 22.

COGHILL, Sir John Joscelyn 1826-1905
Irish painter. Exh. 1880. Add: Glenbarrahane, Co. Cork. † RHA 1.

COGIE, Henry George b. 1875
Painter, etcher and wood engraver. Assistant master Belfast School of Art. Headmaster School of Arts and Crafts, Battersea Polytechnic. Add: Belfast 1908; London 1912; Newton Ferrers, Devon 1939. † GOU 3, L 1, RA 6, RBA 2, RED 1, RHA 5.

COGILL, Emily Exh. 1894-1925
St. Ives, Cornwall 1894; Surbiton, Surrey 1897; Seaton, Devon 1925. † RA 2, RBA 1, SWA 14.

COGNIET, Marcel Exh. 1911
Landscape painter. † BRU 85.

COGSWELL, Miss G. Exh. 1916-18
6 Buckley Road, Brondesbury, London. † RA 3.

COGSWELL, Gerald Exh. 1897-1915
Architect. Add: London. † L 5, RA 6.

COGSWELL, W.G. Exh. 1909-11
St. John, 28 Theobalds Road, London. † L 1, RA 2.

COGSWELL, Rev. Canon W.H.L. Exh. 1910-13
The Rectory, Wallasey, Cheshire. † L 4.

COHEN, Lady Exh. 1933
Landscape painter. † COO 2.

COHEN, A. Dorothy Exh. 1917-38
Flower and figure painter. Add: London. † COO 3, I 6, L 2, RA 13, RI 3, ROI 2, SWA 2.

COHEN, Ellen Gertrude Exh. 1884-1905
Figure and domestic painter. Add: London. † B 4, L 5, M 5, P 1, RA 14, RBA 3, RI 11, ROI 3, SWA 5.

COHEN, Hannah Exh. 1934-36
Domestic painter. † LEF 3.

COHEN, Miss H.T. Exh. 1889
Hawkesmoor, Fallowfield, Manchester. † M 1.

COHEN, Isaac Michael 1884-1951
Portrait painter. b. Ballarat, Australia. Studied Melbourne (travelling scholarship 1905, National Gallery of Victoria) and Paris. R.O.I. 1921, R.P. 1928. Add: London 1908. † BA 1, CHE 3, GI 1, I 1, L 10, P 45, RA 40, RHA 2, ROI 34, RSA 6, WG 96.

COHEN, Lewis 1857-1915
Anglo-American painter. b. London. d. New York. Add: London 1896-1903. † M 1, RA 3, ROI 5.

COHEN, Lucy Exh. 1886-87
Landscape painter. Add: 5 Great Stanhope Street, Mayfair, London. † SWA 4.

COHEN, Minnie Agnes* b. 1864
Painter and pencil artist. b. Eccles. Studied RA Schools and Paris. Add: Manchester 1889; Axminster, Devon 1895; London 1897; Watford, Herts. 1935. † B 8, L 4, LS 5, M 2, RA 16, RBA 1, RI 2, ROI 6, WG 74.

COHN, Miss Ola b. 1892
Born Bendigo, Australia. Add: 1 Coleherne Road, London 1929. † RBA 1, SWA 1.

COIGNARD, Louis* Exh. 1887
Brussels, Belgium. † M 1.

COIGNARD, W. Exh. 1888
4 Exchange Street, Manchester. † B 1.

COIT, Adela Exh. 1939-40
Landscape painter. Add: Birling Gap, nr. Eastbourne. † BA 40, NEA 1, RA 1.

COIT, Margaret Exh. 1917-19
Sculptor. Add: London. † I 1, RA 3.

COKE, Alfred Sacheveral Exh. 1881-92
Historical and figure painter. R.O.I. 1883. Add: London 1881; Totland Bay, I.o.W. 1889. † L 3, RA 7, RBA 1, ROI 12.

COKE, Dorothy Josephine b. 1897
Painter and teacher. Studied Slade School 1914-18. N.E.A. 1920, A.R.W.S. 1935, R.W.S. 1941. Add: London 1918; Rottingdean, Sussex 1938. † G 1, NEA 68, RA 6, RWS 30, SWA 1.

COLAHAN, Colin b. 1897
Landscape and figure painter. Born Melbourne, Australia. Add: London 1922 and 1936; Paris 1926. † AR 45, LEF 19, NEA 1, P 1, RA 2, RBA 3, ROI 5.

COLAM, Mrs. Cecilia Exh. 1926-27
Peppermill House, Craigmillar, Edinburgh. † GI 2.

COLAROSSI, Ernest Exh. 1889
Sculptor. Add: 14 Masborough Road, West Kensington, London. † RA 1.

COLAROSSI, Philip or Filippo Exh. 1884-88
Sculptor. Add: 14 Marlborough Road, Brook Green, London 1884; Paris 1885. † G 1, RA 2.

COLBERT, Miss G. Exh. 1932
15 Brunts Street, Mansfield, Notts. † N 1.

COLBORNE, Miss T.E. Exh. 1909-11
London 1909, Southampton 1911. † L 2, RA 1, RHA 2.

COLBORNE, Vera Exh. 1909
† LS 3.

COLBOURN, Lillian Victoria E. b. 1898
b. Epworth, Lancs. Studied Bury School of Art, Lancs. Exh. 1932. † L 1.

COLBY, Joseph Exh. 1886
Figure painter. Add: 76 Grafton Street, Fitzroy Square, London. † RA 1.

COLBY, Miss Josephine W. Exh. 1901
Woodcroft, Gateacre, Liverpool. † L 4.

COLCHESTER, Charles E. Exh. 1881
Ventnor, I.o.W. † RE 1.

COLCUTT, B.H. Exh. 1907
36 Park Avenue, Willesden Green, London. † RA 1.

COLDMAN, Winifreda E. Exh. 1936
Sculptor. Add: Northmount, Whetstone, London. † RA 1.

COLDSTREAM, William b. 1908
Landscape and portrait painter. b. Belford, Northumberland. Studied Slade School 1926-29. Founder of Euston Road School 1937. Member London Group 1933. "Man with a Beard" purchased by Chantrey Bequest 1940. Add: London 1928. AG 1, COO 4, LEF 7, LEI 1, NEA 2, RHA 1.

COLDWELL, Edward W. Exh. 1923-24
Architect. Add: 83 Pall Mall, London. † RA 3.

COLDWELL, Miss Muriel Exh. 1903-5
Kingsland Grove, Shrewsbury. † B 1, SWA 1.

COLE, Alfred Benjamin Exh. 1880-86
Landscape painter. Add: London 1880; Reading, Berks. 1886. † B 1, L 2, M 2, RA 1, RBA 8, ROI 1.

COLE, Alice Gertrude Exh. 1928-40
Watercolour painter. Studied Shrewsbury School of Art. Add: Glynne Villa, Bell Vue Road, Shrewsbury. † B 19, RCA 7.
COLE, Alphaens Philemon* b. 1876
American painter. Studied in Paris at Juliens 1893-1903 and Ecole des Beaux Art. Add: London 1902-12. † B 6, L 3, LS 6, M 1, NEA 1, RA 7.
COLE, Alan S. Exh. 1901-7
20 Alfred Place West, London. † NG 10.
COLE, Blanche Vicat Exh. 1890-1901
Domestic painter. Add: London 1890; Fowey, Cornwall 1901. † ROI 8.
COLE, Chisholm d. c.1902
Landscape painter. Add: Church House, Llanbedr, Conway, Wales. † L 16, RA 6, RCA 60.
COLE, Cyril Exh. 1919-29
London. † GOU 1, I 1, RI 1, ROI 2.
COLE, Miss D. Exh. 1907
Kings Ride, Richmond, Surrey. † RA 1.
COLE, Ernest Exh. 1915-19
Figure painter. † CG 1, I 3, LEI 5.
COLE, Ethel Kathleen b. 1892
Landscape painter, black and white and poster artist, illustrator, lithographer and teacher. Studied Slade School. Born Beccles, Suffolk. Add: Clifton, Bristol 1917; Brighton 1918; London 1919. † G 3, NEA 10, RA 3.
COLE, F. Exh. 1930
† LEI 2.
COLE, F.A.P. Exh. 1902
† P 1.
COLE, Frederick W. Exh. 1937-39
Stained glass artist. Add: Sanderstead, Surrey. † RA 2.
COLE, George* 1810-1883
Portrait, landscape and animal painter. Painted posters of wild animals for Wombwell's Menagerie. R.B.A. 1851. Add: London 1880. † B 1, RA 3, RBA 15, TOO 2.
COLE, George Vicat* 1833-1893
Landscape painter. Son of George C. q.v. b. Portsmouth. A.R.A. 1870, R.A. 1880. "The Pool of London" purchased by Chantrey Bequest 1888. Add: Little Campden House, Kensington, London. † B 2, M 1, RA 27, RI 1, TOO 16.
COLE, Herbert Exh. 1898-1900
Illustrator. Add: London. † RA 2.
COLE, Henry Alexander Exh. 1909-33
Watercolour landscape painter. Studied Liverpool School of Art. Add: The Homestead, Vyner Road, Bidston, Birkenhead. † L 13.
COLE, James* Exh. 1880-85
Domestic painter. Add: Grove Lodge, Acton, London. † B 2, GI 5, RBA 16, RI 1.
COLE, John* b. 1903
Landscape painter. Son of Rex Vicat C. q.v. A.R.B.A. 1929, R.B.A. 1930, R.O.I. 1935. Add: London. † BAR 35, GI 4, L 8, M 1, NEA 6, RA 25, RBA 70, RID 4, ROI 45.
COLE, J.F. Exh. 1884
c/o Cassell & Co., Ludgate Hill, London. † L 1.
COLE, John H. d. c.1895
Landscape painter. Add: Llanbedr, Conway, Wales. † L 4, RA 1, RCA 69.
COLE, Miss L. Exh. 1889-1913
Gateshead, Northumberland 1889; Whitley, Newcastle 1892; Hinderwell, Yorks. 1911. † L 1, M 1, RA 2.
COLE, Miss Mabel Exh. 1897
66 Eaton Place, London. † SWA 2.
COLE, Monica A. Exh. 1929
Sculptor. Add: 52 Wood Lane, Spring Grove, Osterley. † RA 1.
COLE, Maud Lowry Exh. 1884-1909
Still life painter. Add: Wimbledon 1884; 66 Eaton Place, London 1897. † SWA 4.
COLE, Miss Nesbit Exh. 1899
66 Eaton Place, London. † RSA 1.
COLE, Philip Tennyson Exh. 1880-1930
Portrait and domestic painter. Add: Grove Lodge, Acton, London 1880; Barnes, Surrey 1882; London 1885; St. Leonards-on-Sea 1927. † GI 2, I 6, L 1, LS 7, NG 2, P 2, RA 8, RBA 13, RI 3.
COLE, Philip William 1884-1964
Watercolour painter, stained glass artist and metal worker. Studied Hastings School of Art, Royal College of Art 1909-13. R.B.A. 1932. Add: Tilekiln, Fairlight, Sussex 1926. † RA 12, RBA 46.
COLE, Robert Langton 1858-1928
Architect. Exh. 1896-1902. Add: 23 Throgmorton Street, London. † RA 2.
COLE, Rex Vicat 1870-1940
Landscape painter. Son of George Vicat C. q.v. Studied St. John's Wood School of Art. R.B.A. 1900, R.O.I. 1929. † B 6, BG 4, COO 2, DOW 49, GI 5, L 27, M 3, RA 70, RBA 73, RHA 2, RI 3, ROI 54, RSA 3.
COLE, Timothy 1852-1931
Wood engraver. Born London. Died Poughkeepsie, U.S.A. Exh. 1905-10. Add: New York 1905; Belgium 1907. † GI 1, I 27, G 8.
COLE, Thomas William b. 1857
Painter, etcher and teacher. Studied Shrewsbury School of Art and Royal College of Art (silver medal). Add: London 1886; Slough, Bucks. 1922. † RA 8, RBA 4, RI 2.
COLE, Violet Vicat b. 1890
Portrait and landscape painter. Born Caversham, Oxon. Studied at Sir Arthur A. Cope's School and in Italy and Holland. Art mistress Hastings Grammar School. Add: St. Leonards-on-Sea 1926; Henley-on-Thames, Oxon 1940. † RA 1, ROI 6.
COLE, W. Exh. 1889
83 Oxford Street, Liverpool. † L 2.
COLEBROOK, Miss M.F. Exh. 1932
† RMS 1.
COLECLOUGH, F.T. Exh. 1936
12 Holly Road, Handsworth, Birmingham. † B 1.
COLEMAN, Amelia Exh. 1880
Flower painter. Add: 18 Southampton Street, London. † SWA 1.
COLEMAN, Charles Caryl 1840-1928
Landscape painter. Born Buffalo, U.S.A. Died Capri, Italy. Add: London 1883 and 1896; Capri, Italy 1887. † G 3, L 1, NG 7, ROI 1.
COLEMAN, Frank Exh. 1880-92
Domestic painter. Add: Bradford, Yorks. 1880; Ilkley, Yorks. 1891. † AG 13, D 1, L 2, RA 5, RBA 11, RSA 3.
COLEMAN, G. Exh. 1884
† TOO 1.
COLEMAN, Mrs. Gertrude Exh. 1881
75 Elm Park, Brixton. † RBA 1.
COLEMAN, Mrs. Gladys Exh. 1936
Golders Green, London. † SWA 1.
COLEMAN, G.B. Exh. 1927-32
Sospel, West Heath Road, London. † RA 1, RBA 3.
COLEMAN, Henry Exh. 1882-1909
Landscape painter. Add: Rome, Italy 1882; London 1889. † D 2, NG 2, RA 1, TOO 1.
COLEMAN, Helen Cordelia See ANGELL
COLEMAN, J. Exh. 1925-27
92 Willows Road, Cannon Hill, Birmingham. † B 2.
COLEMAN, J.A. Exh. 1894-1903
c/o G.C. Ashlin, 7 Dawson Street, Dublin, Ireland. † RHA 6, TOO 1.
COLEMAN, Miss Millicent Exh. 1928-30
199 Piccadilly, London. † L 5.
COLEMAN, Ronald I. Exh. 1933
Urban landscape painter. Add: 22 Denton Road, Hornsey, London. † RA 1.
COLEMAN, Rose Rebecca Exh. 1880-84
Figure painter. S.W.A. 1880. Add: 18 Southampton Street, Fitzroy Square, London. † SWA 2, TOO 2.
COLEMAN, Simon b. 1916
Duleek, Co. Meath, Ireland 1940. † RHA 2.
COLEMAN, T.H.D.W. Exh. 1939
48 Kingsley Road, Birmingham. † B 1.
COLEMAN, William Stephen* 1829-1904
Etcher and illustrator. b. Horsham, Sussex. Add: 3 St. John's Wood Studios, Queen's Terrace, London. † DOW 1, TOO 31.
COLENUTT, Fabian Exh. 1891
Hillside Park Road, Ryde, I.o.W. † B 1.
COLERIDGE, F.G. Exh. 1880-1914
Landscape painter. Add: Twyford, Berks. † D 253, FIN 10, L 5, NG 1, RBA 2, RI 1, WG 125.
COLERIDGE, Hon. Gilbert 1859-1953
Sculptor and author. Married Marion C. q.v. Son of Lord Coleridge, Lord Chief Justice of England. Brother of Stephen C. q.v. Exh. 1931. Add: Haverfield House, Kew Green, Surrey. † RA 1.
COLERIDGE, Marion d. 1917
Portrait painter. nee Darroch. Married Hon. Gilbert C. q.v. Exh. 1891-1906. Add: 11 Roland Gardens, London. † GI 1, RID 15.
COLERIDGE, Maud Exh. 1893-1903
Miniature portrait painter. Add: London. † GI 2, L 5, NG 1, P 8, RA 2, SWA 3.
COLERIDGE, Hon. Stephen 1854-1936
Landscape painter. Son of Lord Coleridge, Lord Chief Justice of England, brother of Gilbert C. q.v. Exh. 1886-1910. Add: 7 Egerton Mansions, South Kensington, London. † ALP 51, B 11, L 5, M 5, RA 1, RBA 13.
COLES, Miss Amy Exh. 1887-93
Offchurch, Leamington, Warwicks. † B 4.
COLES, Annie J. Exh. 1889-1914
Figure and landscape painter. Add: Elmfield, Streatham, Surrey 1889; Pinner, Middlesex 1900; Shenley Hill, Herts. 1909; Radlett, Herts. 1912. † B 1, L 2, RA 1, RID 68, SWA 3.
COLES, Frank A. Exh. 1889-1921
Landscape painter. Add: Elmfield, Streatham, Surrey 1889; Pinner, Middlesex 1900; Horsted Keynes, Sussex 1912; East Moseley, Surrey 1921. † B 1, L 5, RA 1, RID 100.
COLES, Fanny Louisa Exh. 1916-19
York House, Poole Road, Bournemouth. † RI 5.
COLES, F.R. Exh. 1882-89
The Hermitage, Tongueland, Kirkcudbright. † RSA 3.
COLES, Godfrey Clement Exh. 1916
† NEA 2.
COLES, Katharine M. Exh. 1889-1929
Landscape and portrait painter. Add: Elmfield, Streatham, Surrey 1889; Pinner, Middlesex 1900; Shenley Hill, Herts. 1909; Radlett, Herts. 1912. † RID 81.
COLES, Walter Exh. 1894
Architect. Add: 31 Bath Road, Exeter, Devon. † RA 1.

COLES, William C. Exh. 1881-1914
Landscape and coastal painter. Add: Devizes, Wilts. 1881; Winchester, Hants. 1892. † B 3, D 1, GI 1, GOU 12, I 1, L 2, M 2, NEA 25, RA 4, RBA 1.

COLEY, Alice Maria b. 1882
Miniature, watercolour portrait and landscape painter. Add: The Craft Rooms, Queen's College, Paradise Street, Birmingham 1916. † B 15, L 2, RA 6, RMS 2.

COLEY, Hilda May Exh. 1920-24
Botanical and flower painter. Born Bristol. Studied Liverpool School of Art. Add: Four Oaks, Warwicks. 1920; Reigate, Surrey 1924. † B 6, L 1.

COLEY, W.H. Exh. 1924-32
26 Amesbury Road, Moseley, Birmingham. † B 8.

COLIN, Frank Exh. 1928
41 John Dalton Street, Manchester. † RCA 2.

COLIN, Georges Exh. 1912
1 Boulevard Davoust, Paris, France. † L 1.

COLIN, Gustave Henri* 1828-1911
French artist. Add: 17 Rue Victor Masse, Paris, France 1904. † L 1.

COLIN, Paul Emile* b. 1877
French artist. Add: 48 Boulevard de la Republique, Noisy le See, Seine, Paris, France 1908-11. † L 25.

COLIN-LIBOUR, Madame U. Exh. 1883-1913
35 Fentiman Road, Clapham Road, London 1883; Paris 1913. † L 1,RA 1.

COLLARD, John Exh. 1918
† I 2.

COLLCUTT, Grace Marion Exh. 1899-1929
Landscape painter. Daughter of Thomas Edward C. q.v. Add: London 1908; Brighton 1925. † AB 52, BG 7, GOU 9, L 4, LS 8, RA 2, SWA 1.

COLLCUTT, Thomas Edward c.1840-1924
Architect (e.g. Imperial Institute and Savoy Hotel). Add: London. † GI 3, RA 31, RSA 3.

COLLE, de see D

COLLENS, Miss Mary E. Exh. 1921-30
25 Joliffe Street, Princes Park, Liverpool. † L 2.

COLLES, Alexander Exh. 1882-1938
Landscape and portrait painter. Studied R.H.A. Schools. Add: Dublin, Ireland. † LS 12, RHA 79.

COLLES, Elizabeth Orme Exh. 1896-1922
Portrait painter. Add: Manchester. † L 10, M 2, RCA 2.

COLLES, Lille Exh. 1880
2 Mill Street, Kilkenny, Ireland. † RHA 2.

COLLET, Ruth Salaman Exh. 1938-39
Portrait, figure and landscape painter. Add: London. † GOU 43, RA 1.

COLLETT, Sophie E. Exh. 1889-98
Miniature painter. Add: Bury St. Edmunds, Suffolk 1889; Chelsea, London 1891. † L 2, M 2, RA 9, RMS 1.

COLLETT-MASON, William Exh. 1938
† P 1.

COLLEY, Andrew Exh. 1891-1910
Landscape and figure painter. Add: Newcastle-on-Tyne 1891; London 1904. † I 2, L 6, LS 7, M 1, NEA 3, NG 4, RA 7.

COLLEY, A.H.D. Exh. 1886
48 King Street, Manchester. † M 2.

COLLEY, Miss F. Exh. 1890
23 Marlborough Hill, London. † M 1.

COLLEY, Miss Jessie Exh. 1891-92
Rudgrave Place, Egremont, Cheshire. † L 2.

COLLEY, Tom Exh. 1882-86
3 John Street, Bowdon, Cheshire. † M 2.

COLLEY, W.F. Exh. 1930-37
Painter and lithographer. Add: 141 Sladefield Road, Ward End, Birmingham. † B 2, NEA 2, RED 1.

COLLIE, George Exh. 1922-40
Portrait painter. A.R.H.A. 1933. Add: Dublin, Ireland. † RHA 92.

COLLIE, Miss K. Exh. 1895-1910
Liverpool. † GI 1, L 25, RA 1, RCA 1, RMS 4.

COLLIE, W.S.G. Exh. 1906-19
16 Burnbank Gardens, Glasgow. † GI 3.

COLLIER, Alexander Exh. 1880-1908
Landscape painter. Add: London 1880; Bushey, Herts. 1892. † B 1, D 2, GI 1, RA 7, RBA 2, RI 2, RSW 1.

COLLIER, Amy Exh. 1881
Carthamartha, Callington, Cornwall. † SWA 1.

COLLIER, Arthur Bevan* Exh. 1880-99
Landscape painter. Add: Carthamartha, Callington, Cornwall, and London. † B 3, L 4, M 2, RA 4, RBA 19.

COLLIER, Ada L. Exh. 1908-25
Etaples, France 1908; Fittleworth, Sussex 1916; Petworth, Surrey 1917; Crick, Nr. Rugby 1925. † GI 1, I 1, L 17, LS 13, RI 2, RSA 1.

COLLIER, Bernard C. Exh. 1880-88
Figure painter. Add: London 1880; Canterbury 1887. † L 2, M 1, RA 2, RBA 3, RHA 2.

COLLIER, Christine C. Exh. 1923-35
Landscape and flower painter. Add: London 1923; South Brent, Devon 1930. † COO 2, NEA 6.

COLLIER, Emily E. Exh. 1881-1901
Shortlands, Kent 1880; Reigate, Sussex 1885. † D 2, RBA 2, RI 2, SWA 1.

COLLIER, Mrs. E.M. Exh. 1901-20
A.S.W.A. 1905. Add: Acton and Chiswick Polytechnic, Bedford Park, London 1901; Kew Gardens, London 1906; Gunnersbury 1919. † I 2, L 2, RA 3, SWA 8.

COLLIER, F.S. Exh. 1937
Animal painter. Add: c/o Mrs. F.S. Collier, Shottery, Killiney, Co. Dublin, Ireland. † RHA 2.

COLLIER, Imogen Exh. 1899-1904
Landscape and animal painter. Add: Foxhams, Horrabridge, Devon. † RA 2.

COLLIER, Iris D. Exh. 1914-39
Portrait painter. Add: London 1914 and 1919, Crewe, Cheshire 1915. † I 1, L 10, P 1, RA 1, SWA 1.

COLLIER, John Exh. 1935-37
Interior painter. Add: Bottesford, Notts. † N 3.

COLLIER, Hon. John* 1850-1934
Figure, portrait and landscape painter. Son of Robert P.C. q.v. Studied Slade School Paris under J.P. Laurens and in Munich. Married Marian C. q.v. R.O.I. 1909, R.P. 1891. "The Last Voyage of Henry Hudson" purchased by Chantrey Bequest 1881. Add: London. † ALP 1, AR 93, B 21, FIN 2, G 29, GI 14, L 81, LEI 52, M 27, NG 48, P 165, RA 130, RBA 3, RHA 4, RI 5, ROI 67.

COLLIER, Joyce See KILBURN

COLLIER, James A. Exh. 1933
12 Ashbourne Road, Derby. † B 1.

COLLIER, Miss Lilian Exh. 1880-83
Carthamartha, Callington, Cornwall. † B 1, L 2, SWA 2.

COLLIER, L.C. Exh. 1923-35
Painter and wood carver. Add: Old Basford, Notts. 1923; Woodthorpe, Notts. 1930; Nottingham 1931. † N 8.

COLLIER, Marian d. 1887
Portrait, figure and flower painter. Nee Huxley. Married Hon. John C. q.v. Add: London. † D 1, G 6, GI 2, L 3, M 4, RA 3, RBA 1.

COLLIER, Mary Exh. 1881
Flower painter. Nee Hardcastle. Married eldest son of Sir Robert P.C. q.v. Add: 7 Chelsea Embankment, London. † D 1.

COLLIER, Hon. Sir Robert Porrett 1817-1886
Landscape painter of alpine scenes. Judge and 1st Lord Monkswell (1885). Father of Hon. John C. q.v. R.B.A. 1879. Add: London. Died Grasse, France. † ALP 1, G 6, M 2, RA 4, RBA 9.

COLLIER, Robert William Exh. 1881
Holyport House, Shortlands, Kent. † RA 1.

COLLIER, Thomas* 1840-1891
Watercolour landscape painter. Studied Manchester School of Art. A.R.I. 1870, R.I. 1872, R.O.I. 1883. Add: Etherow, Hampstead Hill Gardens, London. † B 3, FIN 1, L 2, RA 1, RHA 1, RI 10, ROI 8, TOO 10.

COLLIN, Agnes B. Exh. 1921
Enamel artist. Add: 20 Paulton's Sq., Chelsea, London. † RA 1.

COLLIN, Alberic Exh. 1931
36 Avenue Van Put, Antwerp, Belgium. † GI 3, RSA 8.

COLLIN, Miss F.S. Exh. 1928
28 Eaton Terrace, London. † L 1.

COLLING, James Kellaway Exh. 1883
Architect. Add: 6 Salisbury St., Strand, London. † RA 1.

COLLINGBOURNE, Laura M. Exh. 1923-24
Trafalgar Rd., Beeston, Notts. † N 2.

COLLINGHAM, G. Exh. 1880-81
7 Devonshire Terrace, Kensington, London. † D 3.

COLLINGRIDGE, Mrs. J. Exh. 1888
Brooklet, Winchmore Hill, London. † ROI 1.

COLLINGRIDGE, John Exh. 1903
Landscape painter. Add: Domus, Brentwood, Essex. † RA 1.

COLLINGRIDGE, Ruth Exh. 1912-21
Landscape painter. Add: The Cottage, Brentwood, Essex. † D 2, GOU 2, SWA 2.

COLLINGS, Albert Henry* d. 1947
Portrait and figure painter. R.B.A. 1897. R.I. 1913. Add: London. † AR 9, COO 4, FIN 3, L 10, P 5, RA 29, RBA 98, RI 90, ROI 4.

COLLINGS, Charles John 1848-1931
Landscape painter. b. Devon. Add: Chudleigh, Devon 1887; London 1898. Emigrated to Canada c. 1910. † B 2, DOW 103, GI 2, L 1, RA 5, ROI 3.

COLLINGS, Ernest Henry Roberts Exh. 1909-25
Black and white artist. Add: London. † GOU 4, LS 24, RSA 2.

COLLINGS, John Exh. 1902
98 Kurwick's Lane, Sparkbrook, Birmingham. † B 1.

COLLINGS, Robert Exh. 1883
Portrait painter. Add: 1 Berkeley Gardens, Kensington, London. † RBA 1.

COLLINGWOOD, Miss Barbara Exh. 1911-17
Lanehead, Coniston, Lancs. 1911; London 1916. † I 1, L 2, RA 3.

COLLINGWOOD, Miss Dorothy Exh. 1909-11
Lanehead, Coniston, Lancs. † L 3.

COLLINGWOOD, Ellen Exh. 1880
Fruit painter. Add: 73 St. James Rd. London. † SWA 1.

COLLINGWOOD, Mrs. E.M.D. Exh. 1884-1924
Miniature painter. Add: Gillhead, Windermere 1884; Lanehead, Coniston, Lancs. 1901. † L 4, M 1, RA 4, RI 1.

COLLINGWOOD, Lily Exh. 1882
29 Maitland Park Villas, Haverstock Hill, London. † D 1.

COLLINGWOOD, William 1819-1903
Watercolour landscape painter. Born Greenwich. Studied under J.D. Harding and Samuel Prout. A.R.I. 1846, R.I. 1848, (resigned 1854), A.R.W.S. 1855, R.W.S. 1884. Add: Liverpool 1880; Greenwich 1885 and 1890; Hastings, Sussex 1886; Bristol 1891. Died Bristol. † L 25, M 3, RWS 151.

COLLINGWOOD, William Gershom c. 1854-1932
Landscape painter. Travelled widely. Add: Gillhead, Windermere 1886; London 1890; Coniston, Lancs. 1894. † ALP 4, BRU 108, D 2, G 1, L 9, M 1, NG 3, RA 10, RBA 4, RI 13.

COLLINS, Archibald 1853-1922
Figure, landscape and fruit painter. b. Worcester. Add: London 1880 and 1896; Cowley, Oxford 1894. Died Australia. † L 6, RBA 8, RHA 2, ROI 8.

COLLINS, Arthur Exh. 1909
Fir Grange, Weybridge, Surrey. † RI 1.

COLLINS, Arthur Leslie Exh. 1907-11
Woodside, Knockholt, Kent. † B 1, L 2, LS 5, RA 3.

COLLINS, Miss Albina M. Exh. 1910
Gladstone St., Clonmel, Co. Tipperary, Ireland. † RHA 1.

COLLINS, Charles* d. 1921
Figure, rustic, genre painter. R.B.A. 1895, Father of George Edward C. q.v. Add: Dorking, Surrey. † B 2, D 9, G 1, L 6, M 7, RA 32, RBA 225, RCA 36, RI 18, ROI 18.

COLLINS, D. Lincoln Exh. 1880-82
Landscape painter. Add: Gravesend 1880; London 1882. † D 4.

COLLINS, George Edward b. 1880
Nature painter and etcher. Son of Charles C. q.v. Studied Epsom School of Art and Lambeth. Art Master King Edward VI School, Guildford 1911-47. R.B.A. 1905. Add: Dorking, Surrey 1903; Gomshall, Guildford 1926. † BK 57, D 4, L 2, RA 14, RBA 81, RCA 108, RI 12.

COLLINS, G.W. Exh. 1914
46 Lincoln's Inn Fields, London. † RA 1.

COLLINS, Hugh Exh. 1880-92
Portrait painter. Add: Dundee 1880; Edinburgh 1884. † GI 2, RA 2, RSA 28.

COLLINS, Horace W. Exh. 1903
Architect. Add: Walreddon, Redruth, Cornwall. † RA 1.

COLLINS, Miss Jennett Exh. 1881-1900
Domestic painter. Add: Broughton Ferry, N.B. 1881; Edinburgh 1884. † GI 2, RA 2, RSA 16.

COLLINS, John Exh. 1886-1923
Birmingham. † B 6.

COLLINS, J.E. Exh. 1883
80A Brook St., Grosvenor Square, London. † B 1.

COLLINS, Miss M. Exh. 1935-40
South Cottage, Chequers Hill, Amersham, Bucks. † RI 6, ROI 4.

COLLINS, Miss M. Exh. 1886
28 Harcourt St., Dublin, Ireland. † B 1.

COLLINS, Maria Exh. 1885-89
Landscape painter. Add: 38 Moray Place, Edinburgh. † RA 1, RSA 8.

COLLINS, Mary Exh. 1895
Flower painter. Add: Sunnyside, Epsom, Surrey. † RA 1.

COLLINS, Marcus Evelyn c. 1861-1944
Architect. Add: 105 Old Broad St., London 1934. † RA 1.

COLLINS, Margaret E. Exh. 1890
Sunnyside. Child's Hill, Hendon. † B 2.

COLLINS, Miss Mary E. Exh. 1929
18 Sunnyside, Princes Park, Liverpool. † L 1.

COLLINS, Ormond E. Exh. 1914-27
Landscape painter. R.B.S.A. 1921. Add: London 1914; Stechford, Birmingham 1927. † RA 5.

COLLINS, Roland A.F. Exh. 1937-40
Architectural watercolour landscape painter. Add: London. † NEA 1, RA 6.

COLLINS, T. Exh. 1882-93
Vicarage Road, Birmingham. † B 14.

COLLINS, W. Exh. 1886-89
1 St. Oswald's Terrace, Fulford, Yorks. † B 5, L 2, M 4.

COLLINS, William B. Exh. 1929-32
Landscape painter. Add: 21 Sheldon Avenue, London. † RA 1, RBA 2.

COLLINS, W.R. Exh. 1897-99
London. † L 1, RBA 1.

COLLINS, William Wiehe 1862-1951
Landscape painter. Studied Lambeth School of Art 1884-85, Juliens, Paris 1886-87. Travelled on the continent. R.I. 1898. Add: London 1883; Wareham, Dorset 1902 and 1913; Corfe Castle, Dorset 1907; Holford, Bridgwater, Som. 1922. † AB 39, B 11, FIN 75, GI 2, I 1, L 15, LEI 79, LS 5, M 4, NG 2, RA 11, RBA 10, RHA 1, RI 158, RID 41, ROI 9, WG 426.

COLLINSON, Miss Bessie Exh. 1901
23 Avondale Road, Southport, Lancs. † L 1.

COLLINSON, Frank G. Exh. 1893
Architect. Add: c/o Collinson & Lock, 76 Oxford St., London. † RA 1.

COLLINSON, George F. Exh. 1899
Architect. Add: 2 Broad St. Buildings, London. † RA 1.

COLLINSON, Harold Exh. 1914-39
Etcher. Etching master Nottingham Municipal School of Art. A.N.S.A. 1923, N.S.A. 1925. Add: 8 Holme Road West, Bridgford, Notts. † N 62, RBA 1, RCA 4.

COLLINSON, Hugh b. 1909
Urban landscape painter. Add: 64 Westerfield Road, Ipswich, Suffolk 1931. † RA 1.

COLLINSON, James* 1825-1881
Domestic painter. Studied RA Schools R.B.A. 1860. Member of the Pre-Raphaelite Brethren. Add: St. Servan, France and Camberwell, London 1880. † RBA 3.

COLLINSON, Robert* b. 1832
Genre painter. Add: 20 Hereford Square, South Kensington, London 1880-91. † B 9, D 1, GI 4, M 9, RA 7, RBA 2, RCA 3, ROI 6.

COLLISON, Harry Exh. 1909-36
Portrait and landscape painter. Practised as a barrister until ill health forced him to travel outside England. Studied under J.M. Swan and Frank Brangwyn. Add: London. † I 1, L 3, LS 3, NEA 2, RA 6, WG 91.

COLLISTER, Alfred James Exh. 1895-1939
R.B.A. 1899. Add: London 1895; Clymping, Nr. Littlehampton, Sussex 1932. † I 18, L 1, RBA 181, RI 3.

COLLS, Mrs. Clara Exh. 1901
Landscape painter. Add: Beaconwood, Barnt Green, Worcs. † B 1, RA 1.

COLLS, Harry* Exh. 1882-1902
Marine painter. Add: Barnes, Surrey. † B 3, BG 1, G 1, L 3, RA 4, RBA 1, ROI 2.

COLLS, Miss Kate Exh. 1894-1907
Landscape painter. Add: 26 Park Crescent, Portland Place, London. † L 3, NG 2, RA 8, ROI 4, SWA 9.

COLLS, Marjory E. Exh. 1939
Glenfield, Cringleford, Norwich, Norfolk. † SWA 1.

COLLUM, Katie Exh. 1887
Landscape painter. Add: 30 Fulham Place, Paddington, London. † SWA 1.

COLLYER, A. Exh. 1891
183 Lodge Lane, Liverpool. † M 1.

COLLYER, Eric John Exh. 1924-37
Landscape and portrait painter. A.N.S.A. 1931, N.S.A. 1936. Add: Mapperley, Notts. † N 6.

COLLYER, E.N. Exh. 1905-17
Purley, Surrey. † RA 5, RSA 5

COLLYER, Herbert Hood b. 1863
Watercolour landscape and seascape painter. A.N.S.A. 1931, N.S.A. 1936. b. Leicester. Add: Nottingham 1895-1939. † B 4, L 16, N 26, RCA 5.

COLLYER, Miss Kate Winifred See WALKER

COLLYER, Margaret Exh. 1893-1910
Domestic and figure painter. Add: London. † B 4, RA 14, ROI 2, SWA 1.

COLLYER, Mildred H. Exh. 1894-1931
Flower, portrait and figure painter. Add: London. † I 1, L 4, M 1, RA 7, RED 4, RI 1, RMS 2.

COLLYNS, Miss Enid A.L. Exh. 1936-37
Miniature portrait painter. Add: Glenburn, Tonbridge, Kent. † RA 3.

COLMAN, Samuel* 1832-1920
American painter. Exh. 1881-84. Add: c/o Cassell & Co., Ludgate Hill, London. † L 1, RE 5.

COLOM, Juan Exh. 1937-38
Landscape painter. Add: 67 Welbourne Road, London. † BK 31, GI 1, RA 1.

COLOMB, Wellington Exh. 1884
c/o J.B. Spence, Dublin, Ireland. † L 1.

COLOMBEL, G. Exh. 1884
c/o Morgan, 7 North Bank, St. John's Wood, London. † GI 1.

COLQUHOUN, Amalie Exh. 1936
Portrait and landscape painter. † AR 18.

COLQUHOUN, Archibald Exh. 1925-36
Portrait and landscape painter. Add: Paris 1925; London 1936. † AR 35, P 1, ROI 3.

COLQUHOUN, Annie Trew Exh. 1893-1927
Londonderry, Ireland 1893; London 1921. † RI 1, SWA 8.

COLQUHOUN, Miss Campbell Exh. 1888
Chartwell, Westerham, Kent. † D 1.

COLQUHOUN, Miss Ithell Exh. 1930-35
Figure and flower and mural painter. Add: London 1930 and 1934; Paris 1932; Athens 1933. † NEA 2, RA 1, RBA 1, RCA 1, RHA 1, RSA 2.

COLQUHOUN, Robert* 1914-1962
Studied Glasgow School of Art and in Italy, France, Holland, and Belgium. Add: 4 New Mill Road, Kilmarnock, Ayrshire 1940. † RSA 2.

COLSON, Julia b. 1867
Painter and etcher. Studied London, Paris and Venice. Add: London 1898 and 1930; Beckenham, Kent 1925. † B 1, GI 1, I 1, L 2, RA 1, RBA 4, RCA 11, RHA 5, ROI 4, RSA 1, SWA 3.

COLSTON, John Exh. 1893
486 Victoria Road, Crosshill, Glasgow. † GI 1.

COLTART, Alan H. Exh. 1928
c/o R. Jackson & Sons, 18 Slater Street, Liverpool. † L 1.

COLTART, G.A. Exh. 1881-82
24 Windsor Street, Edinburgh. † GI 3.

COLTHURST, Annie Cape d. c. 1930
Landscape, portrait and still life painter. b. Ireland. Studied Pau, Paris and London. Add: London 1902-29. † BG 46, I 1, L 2, LS 17, P 1, RA 1, RHA 43, WG 60.

COLTHURST, Francis Edward b. 1874
Landscape, figure and portrait painter. Studied Taunton and National Art Training School (silver and bronze medals). Painted in Spain, Morocco, Italy and Holland. Teacher of drawing and painting, Regent Street, Polytechnic. Add: Taunton, Som. 1903; London 1904. † B 5, L 3, RA 12.

COLTMAN, Abe T. Bewick Exh. 1931-40
29 Wheeler's Lane, Brixham, S. Devon. † B 14.

COLTMAN, Hilda Exh. 1912-19
Landscape painter. Add: Hartfield, Sussex 1913; London 1914. † ALP 35, I 11, LS 16.

COLTON, William Robert 1867-1920
Sculptor. Studied RA Schools and Paris. A.R.A. 1903, R.A. 1919. Purchased by Chantrey Bequest "The Girdle" 1899 and "The Springtime of Life" 1903. Add: London. † B 1, GI 5, L 12, M 2, NG 8, RA 58, RI 4, RSA 6.

COLUCCI, Guido Exh. 1913
9 Rue Campagne Premiere, Paris. † L 4.

COLUMBANO, Exh. 1901-2
94 Alegria, Lisbon, Portugal. † GI 2, I 2.

COLVILLE, Miss E. Exh. 1880-86
Flower painter. Add: St. Stephen's Square, Bayswater, London. † D 2, L 3, RBA 1, SWA 7.

COLVILLE, Helen Exh. 1900-40
Landscape and flower painter. Add: Co. Dublin, Ireland. † B 2, RHA 20, SWA 4.

COLVIN, Meta Exh. 1881-88
Glasgow 1881; Kilcreggan 1887. † GI 6, RSA 1.

COLVIN, Sir Sidney 1845-1927
Slade Professor of Fine Art, Cambridge 1873-85; Director Fitzwilliam Museum 1876-84. Keeper of Prints and Drawings, British Museum 1884-1912. R.E. 1911. Exh. 1915. Add: 35 Palace Gardens Terrace, London. † RE 3.

COLWELL, Frederick Exh. 1939
Landscape painter. Add: 27 St. Peter's Square, London. † RA 1.

COLWELL, Mrs. M.J. Exh. 1905
41 Thames St., Windsor, Berks. † B 1.

COLYER, Miss C. Exh. 1924-38
Landscape and animal painter. Add: East Boldre, Brockenhurst, Hants. † RCA 18.

COMBA, J. Exh. 1886
28 Duke Street, London. † M 2.

COMBE, Rev. A. Exh. 1934-40
Birmingham. † B 14.

COMBER, Miss B. Exh. 1890-94
Leighton Park Gate, Cheshire. † L 3.

COMBER, Miss Mary E. Exh. 1886-1910
Warrington, Cheshire 1886; Hoylake, Cheshire 1909. † B 2, L 9, RI 1.

COMBES, Alice H. Exh. 1885-1912
Watercolour landscape painter. Travelled widely. † ROI 1, WG 113.

COMBES, Edward 1839-1895
Landscape painter. R.I. 1885. Add: Sydney, Australia 1884; London 1885 and 1892; Richmond, Surrey 1890. † D 1, RA 1, RI 11, ROI 4.

COMBES, Frank Exh. 1936
Landscape painter. † RED 1.

COMBES, Grace Emily Exh. 1880-87
Flower and bird painter. Add: 15 Harpur St., Queen's Square, London. † RBA 5, RI 3, SWA 1.

COMERELL, Mrs. L. Heertjes Exh. 1930-32
Still life painter. Add: 2 Linnell Close, London. † GOU 3, RA 1, RBA 1, ROI 1.

COMERRE, Leon Francois* 1850-1916
French portrait painter. Add: London 1892; Paris 1897. † GI 1, P 4, RA 1.

COMERY, Harry Exh. 1909-17
A.N.S.A. 1909, N.S.A. 1910. Add: Trent, Nr. Nottingham. † N 15.

COMFORT, Arthur Exh. 1893-1935
Painter and wood engraver. Add: London 1893; Leeds 1899; Hawes, Yorks. 1904; Harrogate 1906; Halifax 1927. † RA 23, RI 1, RSA 2.

COMFORT, Charles Fraser* b. 1900
Canadian artist. b. Edinburgh. Exh. 1933. Add: Toronto. † RSW 3.

COMMON, Violet M. Exh. 1893-1921
London. † D 10, L 11, RA 2, RCA 6, RSA 1, SWA 1.

COMMUNAL, J. Exh. 1913
† ALP 3.

COMPER, John Ninian 1864-1960
Architect and designer. Exh. 1903-28 Add: London. † RA 2, RSA 9.

COMPTON, Annie F. Exh. 1923
White Hall, South Norwood Hill, London. † RI 1.

COMPTON, Edward Harrison* b. 1881
Landscape and architectural painter and pencil artist. Born Feldafing, Bavaria. Studied under his father Edward Theodore C. q.v. and at the L.C.C. School of Arts and Crafts. Add: Bavaria 1904 and 1909; London 1906. † FIN 5, L 1, RA 10.

COMPTON, Edward Theodore* Exh. 1880-1914
Landscape painter. Add: Feldafing, Bavaria and London. † ALP 11, B 2, D 7, FIN 54, GI 4, L 16, M 1, RA 26, RBA 1, RHA 5, RI 11, RSA 1.

COMPTON, Henry Eugene Exh. 1907-33
Landscape and coastal painter. A.R.B.A. 1919, R.B.A. 1921. Add: London. † FIN 53, I 9, LS 20, RA 8, RBA 38, ROI 2.

COMPTON-SMITH, Cecilia Exh. 1931-37
Line engraver and illustrator. Add: London. † NEA 1, RA 2, RCA 1, RSA 1.

COMRIE, Minnie M. Exh. 1898
220 Langside Road, Crosshill, Glasgow. † GI 1.

COMYN, Denis F. Exh. 1938
Portrait painter. Add: 23 Serpentine Avenue, Ball's Bridge, Dublin, Ireland. † RHA 1.

COMYN, Heaton Exh. 1905-26
Architect. Add: London. † RA 4.

CONAN, Miss Florence Exh. 1895-97
Roseneath, Sandymount, Dublin, Ireland. † RHA 3, RSA 1.

CONAN, J.C. Exh. 1892-94
Roseneath, Sandymount, Dublin, Ireland. † RHA 2.

CONANT, Amy L.E. Exh. 1885
Watercolour landscape painter. Add: Lyndon, Oakham, Rutland. † RBA 1.

CONBY, Frederick Exh. 1925
15 Prussia Street, Cork, Ireland. † RHA 1.

COND'AMIN, Henry* Exh. 1894
Interior painter. Add: 23 Rue Oudinot, Paris, France. † RA 1.

CONDER, Charles* 1868-1909
Landscape and portrait watercolour painter on silk. b. London. Spent early years in India and Australia. Studied Melbourne and Sydney. Went to Paris 1890, London 1895. N.E.A. 1900. A collection of some of his works are in Tate Gallery. † AG 2, B 1, CAR 21, I 23, L 3, LEI 75, M 1, NEA 17, NG 1, P 1, RA 1, RID 6, ROI 1.

CONDER, E. Lauriston Exh. 1887
Architectural artist. Add: 21 Parliament Street, London. † RA 1.

CONDER, Helen E. Exh. 1900-11
Portrait and landscape painter. Studied Herkomer's School. Drawing mistress at Francis Holland School. R.M.S. 1900. Add: London. † L 5, NG 2, RA 1, RMS 27.

CONDER, Helen Louise Exh. 1889-1921
Landscape and miniature painter. R.M.S. 1898. Add: London. † L 5, NG 2, RA 9, RBA 7, RI 9, RMS 46, SWA 15.

CONDER, Josiah Exh. 1885
Architectural painter. Add: Tokio, Japan. † RA 3.

CONDER, Roger T. Exh. 1883
Interior painter. Add: 2 Wyndham Crescent, Junction Road, London. † RA 1.

CONDIE, Robert Hardie Exh. 1937
10 Cookston Road, Brechin, Angus. † RSA 1.

CONGREVE, Eleanor Exh. 1905-10
Landscape painter. Add: Acton Lodge, Leamington, Warwicks. † B 2, BG 24.

CONINCK, de See D

CONN, James Exh. 1909-12
Wellington Villa, Dalry, N.B. † GI 2.

CONN, Thomas Exh. 1905-40
Dalry, Ayrshire. † GI 18, RSA 6.

CONN, W.H. Exh. 1934-35
Landscape and figure painter. Add: Twickenham Street, Belfast, Ireland. † RHA 4.

CONNAH, J. Douglas Exh. 1894
Figure painter. Add: 8 Margravine Gardens, Kensington, London. † RA 1.

CONNARD, Philip* b. 1875
Painter and designer. Studied South Kensington and under Constant and Laurens in Paris. Art master Lambeth School of Art. N.E.A. 1909, A.R.A. 1918, R.A. 1925, R.I. 1927, A.R.W.S. 1933. Add: London. † AG 5, BA 7, BAR 37, CG 3, CHE 4, FIN 14, G 9, GI 14, GOU 59, I 19, L 28, LEI 56, LS 5, M 2, NEA 92, P 4, RA 111, RED 1, RHA 1, ROI 1, RSA 9, RSW 1, RWS 56.

CONNAUGHT, H.R.H. Princess Patricia of See RAMSAY

CONNELL, Miss D.M. Exh. 1909
50 Grove End Road, London. † RA 1.

CONNELL, Frank J. Exh. 1939
6 Ainslie Place, Edinburgh. † RSA 1.

CONNELL, Miss G. Exh. 1885
St. Mark's Rectory, Longsight, Manchester. † M 1.

CONNELL, Janet Exh. 1890-1908
Miniature painter. Add: London. † B 2, NG 1, RA 7, RMS 3.

CONNELL, Lt. Col. J.C.W. Exh. 1929-40
Landscape painter. Add: London. † L 1, RA 1, RBA 8, RSA 2.

CONNELL, J. Minton Exh. 1880-82
2 Lower Abbey St., Dublin, Ireland. † RHA 8.

CONNELL, Miss L. Exh. 1912-13
London. † SWA 5.

CONNELL, L.S. Exh. 1885
22 Inverleith Row, Edinburgh. † RSA 1.

CONNELL, M. Christine Exh. 1885-1907
Domestic painter. Add: London. † B 4, L 3, M 2, NG 3, RA 6, RBA 8, ROI 7, SWA 2.

CONNER, Essie Exh. 1903
Figure painter. Add: 18 Glyn Mansions, Addison Bridge, London. † RA 1.

CONNER, William Tait Exh. 1895-1901
121 West Regent Street, Glasgow. † GI 4.

CONNING, George J. Exh. 1890
31 Manor Road, Stamford Hill, London. † RA 1.

CONNOLLY, Michael Exh. 1885-1917
Figure painter. Add: London. † RA 7.

CONNOR, Arthur Bentley Exh. 1903-18
Portrait painter. Add: London 1903; Penarth, S. Wales 1915; Weston super Mare, Som. 1918. † P 6, RA 5

CONNOR, Charles Exh. 1917-24
Figure painter. Add: 1 Lower Crescent, Harpfields, Stoke on Trent, Staffs. † RA 2.

CONNOR, Miss Gwen Exh. 1920-28
Liverpool. † L 14.

CONNOR, Jerome 1876-1943
Irish American sculptor. Exh. 1929-38. Add: 2 North Circular Road, Dublin, Ireland. † RA 5, RHA 15.

CONNOR, Joseph Thomas b. 1874
Watercolour landscape painter. Born Hobart, Tasmania. Exh. 1928. Add: Hobart, Tasmania. † RA 1.

CONOLLY, Miss Ellen Exh. 1880-85
London. † B 1, D 1, GI 1, L 1, M 1, RA 5, RHA 3, RSA 2.

CONOR, William d. 1968
Portrait and figure painter. Studied Belfast School of Art, London and Paris. A.R.H.A. 1938, R.O.I. 1932. Exh. 1918-40. Add: Belfast, Ireland. † G 3, GI 19, GOU 6, P 7, RA 11, RHA 48, ROI 24.

CONQUEST, Alfred Exh. 1880-1904
Landscape and coastal painter. Add: Pont Aven, Finisterre, France 1880; Woodford, Essex 1884; Hastings, Sussex 1904. † B 8, G 4, L 5, M 7, RA 10, RBA 11, RHA 1, ROI 1.

CONRAD, L. Exh. 1906
192 Alexandra Road, St. John's Wood, London. † RA 1.

CONRADE, Alfred Charles Exh. 1911-33
Painter and modeller. b. Leeds. Studied at Academy of Dusseldorf, Paris and Madrid. Chief artist White City 1911-14. Add: 25 Lorn Road, Brixton, London. † D 43, RA 9.

CONSTABLE, Miss A.E. Exh. 1913-19
Ardtully, Kilgaravan, Co. Kerry, Ireland. † RHA 10.

CONSTABLE, Blanche 1882-1956
Watercolour painter and designer. Born Malton, Yorks. Studied Bradford School of Art. Art mistress and head of department, Varndean Secondary School, Brighton. Exh. 1922. † I 1.

CONSTABLE, Douglas J. Exh. 1908-9
12 Bedford Gardens, Campden Hill, London. † LS 7

CONSTABLE, Miss E. Exh. 1908
68 Evelyn Gardens, London. † NG 1.

CONSTABLE, Mrs. E.M. Exh. 1912-17
Ardtully, Kilgarvan, Co. Kerry, Ireland. † RHA 10.

CONSTABLE, E.P. Exh. 1880
31 Norfolk Terrace, Westbourne Grove, Bayswater, London. † GI 1.

CONSTABLE, H. Golding Exh. 1914-18
Ardtully, Kilgarvan, Co. Kerry, Ireland. † RHA 5.

CONSTABLE, Jane Bennett b. 1865
Landscape and figure painter. Studied under F. Calderon and Walter Donne. Add: Balmyle, Blairgowrie, N.B. 1888-1930. † D 19, L 8, RSA 4, SWA 7.

CONSTABLE, James Lawson b. 1890
Landscape and portrait painter. Studied Glasgow School of Art. Add: Glasgow 1920; Chantinghall Rd., Hamilton 1924. † GI 14, L 1, RSA 9.

CONSTABLE, Mrs. Margaret Exh. 1932
Nee Taylor. Married James Lawson C. q.v. Add: Chantinghall Road, Hamilton. † GI 1.

CONSTABLE, Miss Ranson Exh. 1935
Landscape of Iceland. † WG 16.

CONSTABLE, Roddice
See PENNETHORNE

CONSTABLE, Sally C. Exh. 1891-1914
Landscape and figure painter. Add: London 1891; Dorking, Surrey 1908. † RA 1, RBA 1, SWA 5.

CONSTABLE, William George b. 1887
Studied Slade School 1919-23. Assistant Director National Gallery; Director of Courtauld Institute of Art (London University); Slade professor of Fine Art, Cambridge. Curator of Paintings at Boston Museum of Fine Art, U.S.A. Exh. 1919. † I 1.

CONSTANT, Benjamin* 1845-1902
French portrait and figure painter. Member of Academie des Beaux Arts. Add: Paris. † FIN 21, GI 1, L 6, M 4, NG 2, P 1, RA 10, RHA 3, TOO 4.

CONSTANTIN, Battista Exh. 1905
Venice, Italy. † I 1.

CONSTANTINE, G.H. b. 1878
13 Ratcliffe Road, Sharrow, Sheffield, Yorks. 1913. † L 3.

CONSTANTINE, Harry C. Exh. 1937
Architect. Add: 82 Mortimer Street, London. † RA 1.

CONSTANTINIDES, D.L. Exh. 1901-12
Glasgow 1901; London 1912. † GI 1, LS 1, RA 1.

CONTI, Tito* b. 1842
Italian figure painter. Exh. 1880-84. Add: London. † RA 3.

CONVERS, Louis 1860-1915
French sculptor. Add: 47 Rue Poncelet, Paris, France 1901-2. † GI 3, L 3.

CONWAY, Miss Frederica Exh. 1929-35
23 Howitt Road, Belsize Park, London. † RI 12.

CONWAY, Harold Edward b. 1872
Flower painter. b. Wimbledon. Studied Slade School and Juliens, Paris. Add: Burford, Oxon, 1915-23. † GOU 1, RA 8, RI 5, ROI 1.

CONWAY, James b. 1891
Portrait, landscape and still life painter. Studied Metropolitan School of Art, Dublin 1927-30. Fireman with Dublin Fire Brigade. Add: Dublin, Ireland. † RHA 14.

CONWAY, L. Russell b. 1882
Painter and etcher and illustrator. Studied Slade School. Exh. 1922. Add: Stisted, nr. Braintree, Essex. † RI 2.

CONWAY, Philip Exh. 1914-19
Still life painter. Add: Richmond, Surrey 1914 and 1918; Ashford, Kent 1916. † LS 3, NEA 5.

CONYERS, Agnes Exh. 1913-22
Dublin 1913; Kilkee, Co. Clare, Ireland 1918. † RHA 19.

COOBAN, Miss F.M. Exh. 1899-1901
Liverpool. † L 3.

COODE, Helen Hoppner Exh. 1880-82
Figure painter. Add: Guildford, Surrey 1880; London 1882. † M 1, RBA 1.

COODE, Miss W.K. Exh. 1920
37 Westmoreland Road, London. † SWA 1.

COOK, Ambrose B. Exh. 1886
Domestic painter. Add: 332 Goldhawk Road, Hammersmith, London. † RBA 1.

COOK, Alice May 1876-1960
nee Barnett. Miniature painter and illustrator. Studied St. John's Wood School and RA Schools. A.R.M.S. 1921, R.M.S. 1930. Add: London. † D 3, L 11, RA 38, RHA 2, RMS 77, RSA 4, SWA 4.

COOK, C.A. Exh. 1882
11 Lansdowne Place, Blackheath, London. † D 1.

COOK, de see D

COOK, Miss Evelyn Exh. 1897-98
22 Evesham Road, London. † SWA 3.

COOK, Emily Annie Exh. 1880-1909
Flower and figure painter. Add: London. † B 1, L 3, M 1, RA 14, RBA 10, RMS 1, ROI 4, SWA 16.

COOK, Ethel Isabel Exh. 1895-1938
Woodside, New Road, Solihull, nr. Birmingham. † B 14.

COOK, Ethel M. Exh. 1902
Miniature painter. Add: 17 Keppel Street, Russell Square, London. † RA 1.

COOK, Ebenezer Wake* 1843-1926
Watercolour landscape painter. Studied under N. Chevalier. Lived in London. † B 9, D 35, FIN 372, L 16, RA 32, RBA 3, RI 10, TOO 2.

COOK, Miss Frances Exh. 1931
9 Netherhall Gardens, Hampstead, London. † RBA 1.

COOK, Frederick Exh. 1883-91
Landscape painter. Add: London. † RBA 3, RI 1.

COOK, Sir Francis Ferdinand Maurice, Bt. b. 1907
Flower painter. Studied under Harold Speed 1926-32; Sir J. Arnsby Brown 1932-34 and S.J. Lamorna Birch 1935-36. A.R.B.A. 1938. Exh. 1936-40. Add: London. † RA 2, RBA 12.

COOK, Fanny Louisa Exh. 1881
Figure painter. Add: 17 Keppell Street, Russell Square, London. † SWA 2.

COOK, George Edward Exh. 1880-1905
Landscape and coastal painter. Add: London. † B 1, G 8, GI 1, M 1, NG 4, RA 14, RBA 3, RHA 1, RID 15, ROI 16.

COOK, George Frederick Exh. 1880-97
Flower, still life and figure painter. Add: London. † RA 5, RBA 11.

COOK, Geoffrey W. Exh. 1933
Architect. Add: 35 Whitehorn Avenue, Yiewsley, Middlesex. † RA 1.

COOK, H. Exh. 1880-83
Landscape painter. Add: Holland Park Road Studios, Kensington, London. † G 5, RA 1.

COOK, Helen A. Exh. 1909-12
Carrick House, Earlsferry, N.B. † GI 1, RSW 1.

COOK, Herbert Moxon Exh. 1881-1926
Landscape and coastal painter. Add: Manchester 1881 and 1914; Isle of Arran 1889 and 1898; London 1890 and 1899; Liverpool 1904; Kenilworth 1907. † AG 2, B 13, D 4, GI 15, L 20, M 32, RA 5, RBA 6, RCA 4, RHA 1, RI 10, ROI 1, RSA 6, WG 64.

COOK, Henry S. Exh. 1890
Figure painter. Add: 185 Hampstead Road, London. † RA 1.

COOK, Hilda V. Exh. 1909-28
Miniature portrait painter. Add: Ashford, Middlesex 1909; Tetsworth, Oxon. 1921; Stradhampton, Oxon. 1928. † L 9, RA 13, RSA 3.

COOK, Jack Exh. 1934-37
Nuthall, Notts. 1934; Bilborough, Notts. 1937. † N 4.

COOK, James Exh. 1905
Englethwaite, Castlehead, Paisley, Scotland. † GI 1.

COOK, Joseph Exh. 1931
Etcher. Add: 7 Muirfield Road, Inverness. † RSA 5.

COOK, J.A. Exh. 1883
9 Amor Road, Hammersmith, London. † G 2.

COOK, James B. Exh. 1917-40
Kilbirnie, N.B. 1917; Glasgow 1921; Motherwell 1938. † GI 10, L 3, RSA 4.

COOK, J.H. Exh. 1887
12 St. George's Crescent, Liverpool. † L 1.

COOK, John Kingsley Exh. 1930-39
Figure and landscape painter. Add: Woodford Green, Essex 1930; London 1938. † RA 6.

COOK, Miss Lena Exh. 1906-7
11 Quarry Road, Wandsworth, London. † RI 2, SWA 1.

COOK, L.B. Exh. 1910-15
London 1910 and 1914; Paris 1913. † ,RA 4.

COOK, Miss L.S. Exh. 1881
Smallbridge Vicarage, Rochdale, Lancs. † G 1.

COOK, Mrs. M. Exh. 1932-36
Mrs. Samuel C. Add: Vanderbilt Hotel, Cromwell Road, London. † RBA 2, SWA 2.

COOK, Mark b. 1868
Born Oxford. Exh. 1899-1932. Add: Chester. † B 1, L 12.

COOK, Margaret C. Exh. 1897-1913
Painter and illustrator. Add: Union Bank House, Ardrossan, Ayrshire 1897 and 1908; London 1906. † BG 36, GI 6, RA 1, RBA 1, RSA 6.

COOK, Nelly E. Exh. 1887-1906
Flower and figure painter. Add: London 1887; West Bromwich 1906. † B 3, M 2, RA 7, RBA 1, RI 1, RMS 1, SWA 2.

COOK, Stanley L.A. Exh. 1935
81 Boldmere Road, Eastcote, Middlesex. † ROI 1.

COOK, Theodore Exh. 1883-95
Figure painter. Add: London 1883; St. Ives 1894. † L 2, RA 6, RBA 4, RE 1, ROI 3.

COOK, Rev. Thomas Exh. 1917-21
Levern Manse, Nitshill, N.B. † GI 4.

COOK, Tess S. Exh. 1939-40
Stanhope Court Hotel, London. † GOU 4, RBA 2.

COOK, Mrs. Tillie S. Exh. 1928
Bailey's Hotel, London. † SWA 1.

COOK, Miss Winifred A. Exh. 1896-1930
Claughton 1896; Oxton, Birkenhead 1899. † L 11.

COOK, Walter F. Exh. 1894-1933
Figure and portrait painter. Add: London. † RA 10.

COOK, Walter J.R. Exh. 1934-40
Polmont, Stirlingshire 1934; Edinburgh 1936. † RSA 6.

COOKE, A. Exh. 1902
86 Cambridge Street, Leicester. † N 2.

COOKE, Arthur Claude b. 1867
Figure painter. Born Luton, Beds. Studied RA Schools. Add: London 1890 and 1892; Luton 1891; Radlet, Herts. 1915. † B 12, L 12, RA 21, RBA 3, ROI 1.

COOKE, Arthur H. Exh. 1929-39
Marine and landscape painter. Add: Leicester. † N 26.

COOKE, A.J. Exh. 1899-1900
Leicester. † N 4.

COOKE, Arthur J. Exh. 1882
Designer. Add: 11 St. Julians Road, Kilburn, London. † RA 1.

COOKE, Amy L. Exh. 1888-1933
Mrs. W.D. Band. Add: Liscard, Cheshire 1888; Wallasey, Cheshire 1920. † L 44, RI 2.

COOKE, Miss A. Maud Exh. 1928
The Brooklands, Crewe. † L 1.

COOKE, Betty Exh. 1933
Portrait painter. † COO 2.

COOKE, Caroline Exh. 1884
8 Wellington Road, Oxton, Liverpool. † L 1.

COOKE, Charles Exh. 1883
1 Trafalgar Road, Moseley, Birmingham. † B 1.

COOKE, Charles Allan b. 1878
Portrait painter. Born Southsea. Studied London School of Art and under Philip de Laszlo. Exh. 1910-20. Add: London. † RI 2, ROI 1.

COOKE, C.H. Exh. 1883-84
7 Grosvenor Park Road, Walthamstow, Essex. † M 2.

COOKE, C.H. Exh. 1909-11
Tudor Street, Sutton-in-Ashfield, Notts. † N 3.

COOKE, Charles W. Exh. 1918-19
Portrait painter. Add: 8 Hereford Road, South Ealing, London. † RA 2.

COOKE, Miss Dorothy Exh. 1922-25
Figure painter. Add: "Dunvegan", Carbis Bay, Cornwall. † B 5, RA 1.

COOKE, Edith M. Exh. 1931
Still life painter. Add: 118 Hunger Hill Road, Nottingham. † N 1.

COOKE, Miss Ellen Miller Exh. 1885-93
Flower painter. Add: Balham 1885; Hereford 1892. † B 18, L 3, RA 5, RBA 2, ROI 2, SWA 5.

COOKE, Evelyn M. Exh. 1889-1921
Figure and landscape painter. Add: London. † RID 22.

COOKE, Ernest O. d. 1937
Landscape, flower and bird painter. Add: Lenton, Notts. 1884; Nottingham 1889; Elton, Notts. 1895; Plumtree, Notts. 1903. † L 2, N 135, RA 3.

COOKE, Mrs. F.H. Exh. 1907
The Parsonage, Dalkeith, N.B. † RSA 1.

COOKE, Miss Frances L. Exh. 1898-1900
Studio, Ancient High House, Stafford. † B 2, RCA 1, RHA 1.

COOKE, Fred W. Exh. 1892-1912
Landscape painter. Add: Nottingham. † N 2.

COOKE, George Ernest Exh. 1880-81
Royal Circus, Lothian Road, Edinburgh. † RSA 4.

COOKE, George R. Exh. 1881-84
Landscape and coastal painter. Add: Clovelly, Devon. † M 1, RBA 4.

COOKE, Helen Exh. 1933
Landscape painter. † COO 1.

COOKE, Hildegarde Gratton Exh. 1921-26
Figure, portrait and landscape painter. Add: 20 Molesworth Street, Dublin, Ireland. † RHA 8.

COOKE, Mrs. Hythe Exh. 1889-90
Landscape painter. Add: Southampton. † SWA 3.

COOKE, Miss H.M. Exh. 1882-86
Aughton Aprings, nr. Ormskirk, Lancs. † B 2, L 6, M 6.

COOKE, Ida Exh. 1939-40
Portrait painter. Add: 1 Park Hill Court, King's Road, London. † COO 1, NEA 1, ROI 1.

COOKE, Iris Exh. 1933-34
Sculptor. Add: 5 Alexander Street, London. † B 2, L 1, RA 1.

COOKE, Isaac* 1846-1922
Landscape painter. R.B.A. 1896. Add: Liscard, Cheshire 1880 and 1883; Wallasey, Cheshire 1883 and 1910. † AG 1, L 131, M 4, RA 9, RBA 60, RHA 1, RI 23, RSW 1.

COOKE, John Exh. 1885-1927
Portrait and landscape painter. Add: Balham 1885; 2 Trafalgar Studios, Manresa Road, Chelsea, London 1890. † B 1, GI 2, L 12, NEA 7, NG 4, P 3, RA 39, RBA 6, RHA 2, ROI 3.

COOKE, John Percy Exh. 1892-1939
Portrait and landscape painter. Studied RA Schools (silver medal). Add: Wolverhampton 1892; Altrincham, Cheshire 1895; Southport, Lancs. 1906; London 1910; Brixham, Devon 1912. † B 16, L 1, LS 11, M 2, RCA 1.

COOKE, Miss L. Exh. 1884
Flower painter. Add: Art Studio, Duke Street, Bath, Somerset. † L 1, RI 1.

COOKE, Miss Mollie Exh. 1912-20
Portrait painter. Add: 125 Cheyne Walk, Chelsea, London. † RA 8.

COOKE, Miss M.H. Exh. 1884-85
28 Tolmer's Square, Hampstead Road, London. † B 2, RHA 1.

COOKE, M. Jervis Exh. 1884
Watercolour landscape painter. Add: Stanley Villa, Paignton, South Devon. † SWA 2.

COOKE, Miss Netta Exh. 1899-1900
72 Hill Rise, Richmond, Surrey. † RMS 3.

COOKE, Miss Nina Exh. 1898
Riverdale, Richmond, Surrey. † RMS 1.

COOKE, Miss O.M. Exh. 1921
Orchard Studio, Newlyn, Penzance, Cornwall. † L 3, RA 2.

COOKE, Samuel N. Exh. 1933-35
Architect. Add: Sun Building, Bennetts Hill, Birmingham. † RA 2.

COOKE, Thomas Etherington Exn. 1891-95
Landscape and coastal painter. Add: Glasgow. † GI 1, RSA 1.

COOKE, Vivian G. Exh. 1935-39
Figure and landscape painter. Add: St. Anne's, Sheen Gate Gardens, London. † RA 2, RBA 2, SWA 2.

COOKE, William Cubitt b. 1866
Landscape and flower painter, black and white artist and teacher. Studied Heatherleys and Westminster. Add: London. † RA 11, RBA 4, RI 9.

COOKE, William Edward Exh. 1880-87
Figure and landscape painter. Add: Loughborough 1880 and 1886; Derby 1885. † N 8, RA 2, RBA 2, ROI 3.

COOKE-COLLIS, Mrs. Silvia Exh. 1936-37
Landscape painter. Add: Ballymacmoy House, Killavullen, Co. Cork, Ireland. † RHA 2.

COOKESLEY, Margaret Murray* d. 1927
Landscape and figure painter. Visited Middle East. A.S.W.A. 1899. Add: London 1884, and 1893, Rockbourne, nr. Salisbury 1891, Bath 1915. † L 31, M 1, NG 6, RA 24, RI 18, ROI 39, RSA 1, SWA 9, TOO 1.

COOKSEY, Arthur W. Exh. 1892
Architect. Add: St. Helier, Brownswood Park, London. † RA 1.

COOKSEY, Miss E.G. Exh. 1899
5 Mount St., Liverpool. † L 1.

COOKSEY, May Louise Greville* b. 1878
Ecclesiastical artist, landscape and figure painter and etcher. Born Birmingham. Studied Leamington and Liverpool Schools of Art. (silver and bronze medal and travelling scholarship in Italy). Art mistress at South Kensington. Add: Liverpool 1899; Freshfield, Lancs. 1921. † B 5, GI 1, I 4, L 147, RA 8, RCA 1, RI 1.

COOKSON, Ethel M. Exh. 1897
Forebridge, Stafford. † B 1.

COOL, de See D

COOLEY, Victor Exh. 1920-35
Landscape painter. Add: London. † RA 3.

COOLING, John Albert 1860-1931
Portrait painter and art specialist and dealer. Studied South Kensington, RA Schools, National Gallery and British Museum. Add: 8 Fitzroy St., London 1880. † RA 1.

COOMBE, Miss L.E. Exh. 1888
Richmond Gardens, Holland Park, London. † B 2.

COOMBE, Miss Mary Exh. 1915-26
Miniature portrait painter. Add: St. Peter St., Tiverton, Devon. † RA 9.

COOMBER, W. Scott Exh. 1927-31
Landscape painter. Add: 41 Upper O'Connell St., Dublin, Ireland. † RHA 5.

COOMBES, C.W. Exh. 1912-14
152 Willifield Way, Golder's Green, London. † RA 3.

COOMBS, Miss Amy A. Exh. 1891
27 Portland Crescent, Plymouth Grove, Manchester. † M 1.

COOMBS, Miss Elsie M. Exh. 1924-36
Cadnant Park, Conway, Wales. † RCA 7.

COOMBS, G.J. Exh. 1917
15 Richmond Mount, Headingley, Leeds, Yorks. † RA 1.

COOMBS, Jessie Exh. 1880-85
Flower painter. Add: Villa Frederico, Capri, Italy 1880; Bagna di Lucca, Italy 1881. † SWA 8.

COONAN, M. Exh. 1910-25
Liverpool. † L 2.

COOP, Mrs. E. Exh. 1939-40
Colwyn Bay, Wales. † RCA 3.

COOP, Harold 1890-1930
Etcher and black and white artist. Studied Lincoln School of Art (silver medal and 1st class honours for design). On the staff Sheffield College of Arts and Crafts and Lincoln School of Art. Add: Lincoln 1913; Sheffield 1922. † L 2, N 7, RA 6.

COOP, Hubert b. c. 1875
Landscape and coastal painter. Studied Birmingham and Wolverhampton. R.B.A. 1897. Add: Birmingham 1895; Conway, Wales 1899; Lowestoft 1912; Bideford, Devon 1920. † B 20, FIN 4, L 39, RA 19, RBA 24, RCA 8, RI 3.

COOP Katherine E. Exh. 1929-30
7 Waverley Rd., Sefton Park, Liverpool. † L 4.

COOP, Wallace Exh. 1911-13
Liverpool 1911; Birkenhead 1913. † L 4.

COOPE, Clifford Exh. 1935-40
Birmingham. † B 4, RCA 2, ROI 1.

COOPER, Mrs. Exh. 1896
42 Inverness Terrace, London. † SWA 1.

COOPER, Miss Exh. 1903
Colosseum Terrace, Regents Park, London. † SWA 2.

COOPER, Ada Exh. 1899-1904
Flower painter. Add: Nottingham and London. † N 3.

COOPER, Alick Exh. 1880-93
Figure and domestic painter. Add: 103 Gower Street, London. † B 1, D 3, L 1, M 1, RBA 9, RCA 4, RHA 1, RI 1, ROI 4.

COOPER, Arthur Alfred b. 1883
Painter and illustrator. Studied Gt. Yarmouth, London and Manchester. Art Director and Curator Art Gallery Merthyr Tydfil 1915-20, Principal Wolverhampton School of Art 1920-46. Exh. 1922. † B 1.

COOPER, Alexander Davis Exh. 1880-89
Landscape, portrait and genre painter. Add: 103 Gower St., London. † B 1, GI 2, M 1, RA 6, RBA 4, RHA 9.

COOPER, Alfred Egerton b. 1883
Portrait and landscape painter. Studied Bilston School of Art, Royal College of Art. Served with Artists Rifles World War 1. A.R.B.A. 1921, R.B.A. 1923. Exh. 1911-40. Add: London. † CG 1, CHE 4, FIN 6, GI 2, GOU 1, I 1, L 6, LEI 12, M 1, NEA 5, P 10, RA 22, RBA 110, RI 2, ROI 3, RSA 1.

COOPER, Annie G. Exh. 1914-28
Portrait painter. Add: West Bridgford, Notts. 1914; London 1923. † L 3, N 5, RA 1.

COOPER, Alfred Heaton 1864-1929
Landscape painter. Father of William Heaton C. q.v. Add: Heaton, Bolton-le-Moors 1885 and 1889; London 1886; Southport, Lancs. 1897; Ambleside, Westmoreland 1898 and 1913; Coniston, Lancs. 1901; Ulverston, Lancs. 1908. † GOU 3, L 24, M 3, RA 15, RI 7, ROI 1.

COOPER, A.J. Campbell Exh. 1922
Landscape painter. Add: "Ashby", Duck's Hill, Northwood, Middlesex. † RA 1.

COOPER, Miss A.S. Exh. 1930
55 Elphinstone Road, Hastings, Sussex. † GI 1.

COOPER, A.W. Exh. 1880-1901
Domestic painter. Add: 7 Manor Road, Twickenham, Middlesex. † B 4, D 3, DOW 3, FIN 1, RA 6, RBA 1, RI 3, ROI 4.

COOPER, Miss B. Exh. 1902
c/o C. Jordan, Inner Circle, Regent's Park, London. † RA 1.

COOPER, Miss B.N. Exh. 1916-17
Culland Hall, Brailsford, Derby. † L 1, SWA 2.

COOPER, Miss B.R. Exh. 1905
2 Walden Terrace, Clapton, London. † RA 1.

COOPER, Catherine Constance Exh. 1903-10
Miniature painter. Add: The Vicarage, Robin Hood's Bay, Yorks. † L 2, LS 6, RA 1, SWA 4.

COOPER, Colin Campbell* b. 1856
American painter. Add: 44 Titchfield Street, Oxford Street, London 1895. † NEA 1.

COOPER, Claude H. Exh. 1881
Animal painter. Add: The Towers, Sneinton, Notts. † N 1.

COOPER, C.J. Harold Exh. 1898-1903
Architect. Add: London. † RA 8.

COOPER, Daisy Exh. 1922-25
Portrait painter. Add: Peckham, London 1922; Birchington, Kent 1925. † RA 2.

COOPER, David H. D'Oyly Exh. 1936-38
Landscape painter. Add: St. Columba's College, Nr. Rathfarnham, Ireland. † NEA 1, RHA 6.

COOPER, Sir Edwin 1874-1942
Architect. A.R.A. 1930, R.A. 1937. Knighted 1923. Exh. 1913-40. Add: 4 Verulam Buildings, Grays Inn Square, London. † GI 2, RA 44, RSA 9.

COOPER, Mrs. Emma Exh. 1880-1905
Portrait, landscape, bird and flower painter and miniaturist. S.W.A. 1880. Add: London. D 4, L 7, M 1, RA 8, RBA 2, RHA 1, RI 18, RID 39, SWA 47.

COOPER, Enid Exh. 1918
Landscape painter. b. Manchester. Studied under her father George Gordon Byron C. q.v. Add: The Birches, Bowdon, Cheshire. † RA 1.

COOPER, Edith A. Exh. 1884-89
Flower and portrait painter. Add: 140 Portsdown Road, Maida Vale, London. † G 1, M 1, RA 2, ROI 2, SWA 6.

COOPER, Frank B. Exh. 1894-95
Architect. Add: Leicester 1894; Bolton-le-Moors 1895. † RA 2.

COOPER, Fred L. Exh. 1928-38
Glasgow 1928; Rutherglen 1935. † GI 5, L 1.

COOPER, Florence M. Exh. 1886-1935
Miniature portrait painter. Add: London. † L 9, NG 9, P 2, RA 9, RI 27, RMS 6, SWA 1.

COOPER, George Exh. 1881-1901
Landscape painter. Add: 1 Osborne Villas, Putney, London 1881, Charmouth, Dorset 1901. † M 2, NG 1, RA 2, RBA 6.

COOPER, George Exh. 1920-40
Ladywood, Birmingham 1920; Edgbaston, Birmingham 1934. † B 57.

COOPER, Gerald Exh. 1928-40
Landscape and figure painter. Add: Chelsea, London 1928; Wimbledon, London 1933; East Horsley, Surrey 1940. † L 2, NEA 5, RA 9.

COOPER, G.F.V. Exh. 1913-14
44 Stanhope Gardens, Highgate, London. † LS 6.

COOPER, George Gordon Byron d. 1933
Landscape and portrait painter. Studied Manchester Academy of Fine Arts. Add: Manchester 1881; Knutsford, Cheshire 1894; Dunham Massey, Cheshire 1897; Mobberley, Cheshire 1902; Bowdon, Cheshire 1904. † ALP 1, D 4, L 10, LS 5, M 67, RA 31, RBA 1, RI 4.

COOPER, George Warren Exh. 1886-94
Architect. Add: 7 John St., Bedford Row, London. † RA 2.

COOPER, Herbert Exh. 1884-85
27 Molesworth Street, Dublin. † RHA 2.

COOPER, Hugh Exh. 1896
9 Elder Park Street, Govan, Glasgow. † RSW 1.

COOPER, H.A. Exh. 1925
Glencairn, Albemarle Road, Woodthorpe, Nottingham. † N 1.

COOPER, Herbert F.T. Exh. 1894-1904
Architect. Add: London 1894; Bexley Heath, Kent 1904. † RA 5.

COOPER, Hercelia S. Exh. 1929-30
Hastings, Sussex. † GI 1, NEA 1.

COOPER, John Exh. 1922-39
Landscape painter. b. Bolton, Lancs. Studied Slade School. Member London Group 1930. Add: 7 Camden Studios, Camden Street, London. † AG 9, G 1, GOU 24, LEF 59, LEI 3, M 1, NEA 9, TOO 2.

COOPER, James Albert Exh. 1909-10
84 Lordship Lane, East Dulwich, London. † LS 4.

COOPER, J.C. Exh. 1912
Euclid, Bothwell Road, Hamilton, N.B. † GI 1.

COOPER, J.E. Exh. 1922-26
Landscape painter. Add: 52 Victoria Road, Sherwood, Nottingham. † N 4.

COOPER, John H. Exh. 1887-96
Liverpool 1887; Edinburgh 1896. † L 1, RSA 1.

COOPER, John Paul 1869-1933
Gold and silversmith and watercolour painter. Designed Sword of Honour presented to Earl Haig and the Casket for Ellen Terry's ashes. Add: London 1898; Castle Bromwich 1904; Hunton, Nr. Miadstone, Kent 1908; Westerham, Kent 1916. † I 18, L 93, NG 2, RMS 5, WG 58.

COOPER, James Robert Exh. 1897-1906
Manchester 1897; Southport, Lancs. 1906. † L 1, M 2, RA 1.

COOPER, Kate Exh. 1916-28
Watercolour and miniature painter. Studied Herkomer's. Add: Robin Hood's Bay, Yorks. 1916; Bushey, Herts. 1921. † L 2, RA 2, SWA 5.

COOPER, Kathleen Mary Exh. 1924-38
Flower and figure painter. Add: 9 Gedling Grove, Nottingham. † N 19.

COOPER, Miss Lydia Exh. 1891-99
Landscape and figure painter. Add: London. † N 1, RA 1, RBA 2, ROI 2, SWA 1.

COOPER, Margaret Exh. 1899
Mrs. H.F.T. Architect. Add: 10 Flanders Road, Bedford Park, London. † RA 1.

COOPER, Miss M.A. Exh. 1897-1900
18 Carisbrooke Road, St. Leonard's on Sea, Sussex. † RBA 1, SWA 3.

COOPER, M.B. Exh. 1921
† LS 3.

COOPER, Mary Cuthbert Exh. 1880-84
Sculptor. Add: London. † RA 8.

COOPER, Mabel Edith Exh. 1898-1904
Twyford, Berks. 1898; Bath, Som. 1900. † B 1, D 5, L 2.

COOPER, Miss M.F. Exh. 1897
The Towers, Sneinton, Notts. † N 1.

COOPER, Mrs. Marie S. Exh. 1886-97
West Bromwich. † B 5.

COOPER, Mary U. Exh. 1884-86
Flower painter. Add: 14 Queen Square, London. † SWA 2.

COOPER, Norman Exh. 1935
50 Blakes Lane, New Malden, Surrey. † ROI 1.

COOPER, Miss Olive Exh. 1937
Prestatyn, Wales. † RCA 1.

COOPER, Phyllis M. b. 1895
London. † L 6, RI 6, RMS 1.

COOPER, Robert Exh. 1880-84
Glasgow. † GI 3, RSA 3.

COOPER, Richard T. Exh. 1926-30
Urban landscape and figure painter. Add: 21 Warwick Crescent, London. † P 1, RA 1.

COOPER, Stephany* Exh. 1931-40
Figure, still life and landscape painter. Add: Iver, Bucks. † COO 8, NEA 5, RA 4, RBA 8, ROI 1.

COOPER, Suzanne Exh. 1936-38
Landscape painter. Add: Woking, Surrey. † RED 3, SWA 2.

COOPER, S.J. Exh. 1886-1903
Manchester 1886; Thornholme, Timperley, Cheshire 1892. † M 5.

COOPER, T.E. Exh. 1904-14
Architect. Add: 11 Gray's Inn Square, London. † RA 6.

COOPER, Thomas George* Exh. 1880-98
Landscape, pastoral and rustic painter. Son of Thomas Sidney C. q.v. Add: 42 Chepstow Villas, Bayswater, London. † AG 2, B 6, L 4, M 3, RA 15, RE 1, RI 13, ROI 13, RSA 1, TOO 1.

COOPER, Thomas Sidney* 1803-1902
Animal and landscape painter. Studied RA Schools. Taught in Brussels 1827-1931 A.R.A. 1845, R.A. 1867, R.I. 1833. Several examples of his work in the Tate. Add: 42 Chepstow Villas, Bayswater, London and Vernon Holme, Harbledown, Canterbury, Kent. † AG 40, B 11, FIN 2, GI 6, L 25, M 19, RA 103, RHA 2, ROI 15, TOO 16.

COOPER, Winifred Exh. 1905-29
Figure and landscape painter. Married William Otway McCannell q.v. Add: Guildford 1905; Stockport 1913; St. Albans 1915; Halifax 1921. † B 2, GOU 144, L 8, LS 3, RA 1.

COOPER, W.F. White Exh. 1886
Architect. 19 Berkeley Square, London. † RA 1.

COOPER, William Heaton b. 1903
Landscape painter. Studied under his father Alfred Heaton C. q.v. and RA Schools 1924-27. Married Ophelia Gordon Bell q.v. Add: Ambleside, Westmoreland 1922 and 1931; London 1924; Grasmere 1933. † FIN 3, GOU 2, L 1, RA 6, RBA 3.

COOPER, W.J. Exh. 1880-83
Painter and etcher. Add: London. † D 1, RBA 4, RE 2.

COOPER, William R. Exh. 1896-1903
Landscape painter. London. † RA 1, RBA 1.

COOPER, W. Savage* Exh. 1880-1926
Landscape and figure painter. Add: Canterbury 1880; London 1882; Althorne, Essex 1916. † B 3, L 7, M 4, RA 38, RBA 9, RHA 2, RI 3.

COOPER, William Sidney* Exh. 1880-1923
Landscape painter. Father of Thomas George C. q.v. Add: London 1880 and 1890; Pangbourne, Berks. 1886; Herne Bay, Kent 1892. † B 13, D 3, L 5, M 7, RA 13, RBA 21, RI 4, ROI 8, RSA 1, TOO 1.

COOPER-BAILEY, Jessie b. 1901
Nee Thompson. Miniature painter. Studied King Edward VII School of Art, Newcastle; Byam Shaw and Vicat Cole Schools of Art and RA Schools. Add: The Knoll, Duchy Rd., Harrogate, Yorks. 1932. † RA 1, RMS 1.

COOTE, Miss L. Exh. 1906
Wandsworth, London. † SWA 1.

COOTE, Mrs. Maxwell Exh. 1895
Ross, Tullamore, King's County, Ireland. † RHA 1.

COOTE-LAKE, B. Exh. 1938
c/o Rowley Gallery, 140 Church St., London. † RBA 2.

COOTE-LAKE, E.F. Exh. 1938-40
Crouch Hill, London 1938; Ware, Herts. 1940. † RBA 2.

COPE, Sir Arthur Stockdale 1857-1940
Portrait painter. Son of Charles West C. q.v. R.P. 1900, A.R.A. 1899, R.A. 1910, Knighted 1919. Add: London 1880; Treniffle, Nr. Launceston, Cornwall 1935. † B 11, G 1, GI 4, L 28, M 9, NG 2, P 12, RA 271, RI 1, ROI 10.

COPE, Charles West* 1811-1890
Painter, illustrator, engraver and fresco painter. Born Leeds. Studied at Sass's Academy 1927, RA Schools 1928, Paris, Italy and Munich. A.R.A. 1843, R.A. 1848, R.E. 1881. Professor of painting at R.A. 1867-75. Won prize in competition for decoration of Houses of Parliament 1843 and did several frescos for the House of Lords. Add: Kingsland, Herefords. 1880; Maidenhead, Berks. 1881. † L 1, RA 7, RE 5.

COPELAND, A.B. Exh. 1883-85
37 Quai des Grands Augustines, Paris, France. † B 3.

COPELAND, A.J. Exh. 1882
Landscape painter. Add: Dellfield, Watford, Herts. † RBA 1.

COPELAND, M. Banyon Exh. 1922-29
Mrs. Anderson. Flower and portrait painter. Born El Paso, Texas, U.S.A. Add: London. † RA 4.

COPEMAN, Constance Gertrude b. 1864
Painter and etcher. Studied Liverpool School of Art (silver medal and Queen's Prize winner) A.R.E. 1897. Add: Liverpool. † B 19, GI 1, L 128, M 17, NG 1, RA 6, RCA 25, RE 37.

COPESTICK, Ernest Exh. 1927
6 Napier Terrace, Mutley, Plymouth, Devon. † B 2.

COPESTICK, Violet Mary Exh. 1928-30
Nee Brown. Miniature flower painter, embroiderer and leather worker. Studied Central School of Arts and Crafts, Plymouth. Add: 6 Napier Terrace, Mutley, Plymouth, Devon. † B 3, D 4, L 1.

COPINGER, Mrs. W.F. Exh. 1909
Florence, Italy. † SWA 1.

COPLAND, J. Exh. 1901-21
Studio, Dundrennan, Kirkcudbright, N.B. † GI 5, RSA 13.

COPLEY, H.J. Exh. 1914
97 Morton Terrace, Gainsborough, Lincs. † I 1.

COPLEY, John 1875-1950
Painter, lithographer and etcher. Studied Manchester School of Art and RA Schools. Married Ethel Leontine Gubain, q.v. R.B.A. 1932. Add: Longfield, Kent 1908; Hampstead, London 1921. † CG 139, CHE 2, GI 6, GOU 106, I 12, L 20, LS 29, M 2, NEA 1, RA 5, RBA 40, RSA 26.

COPNALL, Edward Bainbridge b. 1903
Painter and sculptor. Born Cape Town, S.A. Studied Goldsmith's College and RA Schools. Add: Horsham, Surrey 1924; Slinfold, Nr. Horsham 1928; London 1933. † ALP 1, GOU 1, L 10, NEA 1, P 2, RA 6, RBA 2, ROI 1, RSA 2.

COPNALL, Frank T. b. 1870
Portrait painter. b. Ryde, I.O.W. Studied Ryde and Finsbury Park Colleges. Exh. 1894-1937. Add: Liverpool. † I 2, L 104, M 2, P 15, RA 52, RCA 2.

COPNALL, Theresa North b. 1882
Née Butchart. Married Frank T.C. q.v. Portrait and flower painter. Studied Slade School, Herkomer's and Brussels. Add: Barrow-in-Furness 1908; Liverpool 1915; Hoylake, Cheshire 1922. † B 1, GI 2, L 26, RA 7, RBA 3, RCA 2, ROI 1, RSA 4, SWA 2.

COPPARD, C. Law Exh. 1880-91
Landscape painter. Add: 58 London Rd., Brighton, Sussex. † RBA 1, TOO 11.

COPPER, André C. Exh. 1904-11
Etcher. Add: Brixton, London 1904; Paris 1911. † L 1, RA 1.

COPPER, S.J. Exh. 1894
Thornholm, Timperley, Cheshire. † L 1.

COPPING, Harold 1863-1932
Illustrator. Studied RA Schools and Paris (Landseer scholarship). Visited Palestine, Egypt and Canada. Add: London 1881 and 1804; Selhurst 1889; Sevenoaks, Kent 1902. † L 5, M 4, RA 18, RBA 2, RI 6.

COPSEY, Helen Dorothy b. 1888
Figure and flower painter. Add: 4 Middleton Rd., London 1933. † NEA 1, RA 4, RBA 2, SWA 3.

CORABOEUF, Jean Alexander Exh. 1911
French artist. Add: 16 Rue de la Grande Chaumiere, Paris, France. † L 1.

CORAH, William J. Exh. 1883-1917
Landscape painter. Add: Liverpool 1883; Nr. Conway 1885 and 1895; Amlwch, Anglesey 1892; Llandudno, Wales 1894. † B 5, L 25, LS 3, RA 1, RBA 2, RCA 77, RHA 2.

CORAM, James H. Exh. 1902
Architect. Add: 11b Featherstone Buildings, Holborn, London. † RA 1.

CORBAN, Myra Exh. 1887
17 Ailesbury Rd., Dublin, Ireland. † RHA 1.

CORBAUX, Louisa 1808-1884/88
Painter and lithographer. R.I. 1837. Add: 2 Lansdowne Terr., Brighton, Sussex. † RI 3.

CORBET, Edith Exh. 1891-1916
Landscape and figure painter. Married Matthew Ridley C. q.v. Add: London. † GI 1, L 20, N 31, RA 33, ROI 3.

CORBET, Matthew Ridley* 1850-1902
Landscape and portrait painter. Studied Slade School and RA Schools and under Giovanni Costa in Rome. A.R.A. 1902, R.M.S. 1896. Purchased by Chantrey Bequest "Morning Glory" 1894 and "Val d'Arno: Evening" 1901. Add: London. † BG 1, G 31, GI 1, L 18, M 12, NG 39, RA 32, RI 2.

CORBET, William Exh. 1880
6 Royal Park Terr., Edinburgh. † RSA 1.

CORBETT, Alfred E. Exh. 1902
Architect. Add: 78 Cross St., Manchester. † RA 3.

CORBETT, Christina Exh. 1904
1 George St., Carlisle. † RHA 1.

CORBETT, Julian S. Exh. 1882
3 King's Bench Walk, Temple, London. † RE 1.

CORBETT, Mary Exh. 1898-1905
Painter and illustrator. Add: London. † NEA 13.

CORBETT, S.B. Exh. 1882-89
Landscape painter. Add: Cheadle Hulme, Cheshire 1882; Levenshulme, Cheshire 1889. † L 2, M 8, SWA 3.

CORBIN, Rosa H. Exh. 1887-89
Landscape painter. Add: 23 Lodge Rd., Southampton. † RA 1, RSA 1.

CORBIN, Thomas James b. 1906
Painter and etcher. Studied Croydon School of Art 1922-27 and Royal College of Art 1927-30. Add: Chellaston, Caterham Valley, Surrey 1929. † L 3, RA 1.

CORBIN, William Henry Exh. 1932
Ringwood, Hants. † RCA 1.

CORBINEAU, A.C. Exh. 1881
16 Avenue Trudaine, Paris, France. † RHA 1.

CORBLET, C.J. Exh. 1911
355a, Clapham Rd., London. † RA 1.

CORBOULD, Alfred Chantrey d. 1920
Painter and illustrator and "Punch" artist. R.B.A. 1893. Add: 8 Pembroke Rd., Kensington, London. † B 1, L 3, RA 2, RBA 7, RHA 10, RI 8, ROI 2.

CORBOULD, Edward Henry* 1815-1905
Watercolour painter and illustrator. Studied at Sass's Academy and RA Schools. Appointed instructor of historical painting to the Royal Family 1851-72. R.I. 1838. Add: London and Sutton, Surrey. † G 1, GI 1, L 9, M 3, RHA 1, RI 42, ROI 1.

CORBOULD, Walter Edward Exh. 1887-1916
Figure painter. Add: Liverpool 1887 and 1905; London 1889 and 1910. † L 19, M 1, RA 2, RI 3.

CORBOULD-ELLIS, Eveline M. Exh. 1896-1932
Miniature portrait painter. R.M.S. 1896. S.W.A. 1919. Add: London 1896; Goring-on-Thames, Oxon 1909 and 1926; Stevenage, Herts. 1910; Reading, Berks. 1931. † GI 1, L 10, M 1, NG 12, P 5, RA 21, RMS 79, SWA 6.

CORBYNPRICE, Frank Exh. 1882-84
Watercolour landscape painter. Add: 159 Winstan Rd., Stoke Newington, London. † D 2, RBA 2.

CORCORAN, Jessie R. Exh. 1880-84
Flower and figure painter. Add: 5 Wallace Rd., Canonbury, London. † L 1, SWA 4.

CORDEN, Victor Milton b. 1860
Landscape and military painter and teacher. Studied London. Add: Datchet, Nr. Windsor 1885; London 1887; Newbury, Berks. 1899. † B 28, D 3, LS 12, RA 1, WG 71.

CORDER, Miss Rosa Exh. 1882
91 Southampton Row, Russell Sq., London. † G 1.

CORDERY, John H. Exh. 1915-23
Romford, Essex 1915; Boscombe, Hants. 1919; West Southbourne, Hants. 1920. † D 14, RCA 5.

CORDEUX, Thomas F. Exh. 1901-2
Coastal painter. Add: Bushey Heath, Herts. † B 1, RA 3.

CORDIER, Mdme. A. Delville Exh. 1881-83
Miniature painter on ivory. Add: Paris, France 1881; London 1883. † M 2, RA 2, RHA 5.

CORDINGLEY, George Richard Exh. 1893-96
Landscape painter. Add: 9 Addison Rd., Bedford Park, Turnham Green. † RA 2.

CORDNER, Miss J. Exh. 1881
3 Lakeland's Park, Terenure, Ireland. † RHA 1.

CORDOBA, de See D

CORE, F. Exh. 1906
3 Shrewsbury Rd., Bayswater, London. † RA 1.

CORELLI, Augusto 1853-1910
Italian painter. Add: London 1881; Rome 1890. † D 1, L 1, RA 1, RBA 1.

CORELLI, Conrad R.H. Exh. 1893
c/o Oscar Andrese, Ethick Lodge, Langley Park, Sutton, Surrey. † B 1.

COREY, Mrs. Linda W. Exh. 1904-23
Miniature portrait painter. Add: Twickenham, Middlesex 1904; Marlow, Bucks. 1923. † RA 2.

CORFE, Beatrice O. Exh. 1910-13
93 Cheesehill St., Winchester, Hants. † RA 2, SWA 3.

CORFE, Philip Exh. 1923-26
8 Kensington Crescent, London. † RI 4.

CORFE, Roger Exh. 1935-40
Landscape painter and etcher. Add: London 1935; Maidstone, Kent 1940. † RA 2, ROI 2.

CORFIELD, Evelyn L. Exh. 1932
Miniature portrait painter. Add: Elmwood Cottage, Mearse Lane, Barnt Green, Birmingham. † RA 1.

CORFIELD, Rose M. Exh. 1905-8
London. † D 6, SWA 3.

CORGIALEGNO, F. Exh. 1906
85 Rue Notre Dame des Champs, Paris, France. † L 1.

CORGIALEGNO, M. Exh. 1909
90 Rue d'Assas, Paris, France. † L 2.

CORIN, Edwin P. Exh. 1912-21
c/o Allied Artists' Assn. London 1912, Paris 1913. † LS 12.

CORINTH, Lovis* 1858-1925
German painter. Exh. 1902. † P 1.

CORK, Miss A. Exh. 1894
Sutton, Surrey. † SWA 1.

CORK, Miss N.E. Exh. 1900
60 Alexandra Road, London. † RI 2.

CORKER, C.H. Exh. 1909
96 Leopold Road, Kensington, Liverpool. † L 1.

CORKERY, Daniel Exh. 1917-22
1 Auburn Villas, Ashburton, Cork, Ireland. † RHA 8.

CORKHILL, D.H. Exh. 1914
40 Berry Street, Liverpool. † L 1.

CORKHILL, Mrs. L. Exh. 1882-86
The Cliff, Poplar Road, Oxton, Liverpool. † L 4.

CORKLING, May Exh. 1880
Flower painter. Add: 17 St. Edmund's Terrace, Regent's Park, London. † G 1, SWA 2.

CORKRAN, Henriette L. d. 1911
Figure painter. Add: London. † B 3, L 1, LS 10, NEA 2, RA 18, RI 1, RMS 1, ROI 1, SWA 10.

CORLETTE, Hubert C. Exh. 1895-1930
Architect and architectural artist. Add: London 1895 and 1929; Liverpool 1927. † L 1, RA 25.

CORMACK, Minnie Exh. 1892-1919
nee Everett. Miniature portrait painter and engraver. Add: London 1892; Dorking, Surrey 1915; Selsey-on-Sea, Sussex 1918; Salcombe, Devon 1919. † L 1, RA 16.

CORMAND, J.D. Exh. 1883
Auckland Villa, Rosement Road, Richmond, Surrey. † L 1.

CORMODY, Miss G.E. Exh. 1907-10
Seacombe, Cheshire; Liscard, Cheshire 1910. † L 2.

CORMON, Fernand Anne Piestre* 1845-1924
French portrait painter. Exh. 1891-1909. Add: Paris. † L 1, P 4.

CORNELISSEN, Marie d. 1921
Figure and domestic painter. Married John Seymour Lucas q.v. Add: London. † B 7, L 7, M 7, RA 45, RBA 11, ROI 7, SWA 1.

CORNELL, Henry b. 1884
Served with Royal Sussex Regiment for 13 years. b. Brighton. Began painting c.1934. Exh. 1939. † LEI 39.

CORNER, Dulcie Exh. 1933
Landscape painter. Add: Llangattock-juxta-Usk Rectory, Abergavenny, Wales. † RA 1.

CORNER, George E. Exh. 1886-91
Figure and coastal painter. Add: Art Club Studios, Blackheath, London. † RBA 10.

CORNER, John Exh. 1885-87
5 Claremont Terrace, Edinburgh. † RSA 3.

CORNET, Jas Exh. 1889
Dalmuir, Nr. Glasgow. † GI 1.

CORNEY, F.W. Exh. 1893
Maiden Lane, Club Moor, Liverpool. † L 1.

CORNISH, E. Philip Exh. 1905-26
Landscape painter. Add: London. † LS 12, RA 3.

CORNISH, Katherine E. Exh. 1890-1911
London. † LS 3, SWA 1.

CORNISH, Margaret M. Exh. 1899-1917
London 1899; Hucclecote, Glos. 1911; Purley, Surrey 1917. † NEA 1, RA 5, RHA 7, ROI 5, SWA 1.

CORNISH, William Permeanus Exh. 1880-1917
Figure and landscape painter. Add: London. † L 8, RA 9, RBA 7, RI 4.

CORNOCK, Charlotte Mary Exh. 1919-32
Landscape painter. Studied Brighton School of Art and under Bertram Priestman. Art mistress, Sydenham High School. Add: Sydenham, London. † GI 1, I 2, RA 5.

CORNWALLIS, Brownell d. 1916
Figure painter. Exh. 1911-15. Died on foreign service. † I 2, NEA 1.

CORNWELL, Dean b. 1892
American painter and illustrator. Add: 76 Fulham Road, London 1926-30. † RA 2.

COROE, W.D. Exh. 1893
35 New Bond Street, London. † GI 1.

CORONNE, Henri b. 1822
French artist. Add: Fontenay, Sous Bois, France 1883. † GI 1.

CORRIE, Miss Jessie E. Exh. 1898-1910
Itchen Abbas, Alresford, Hants. † RMS 2, SWA 1.

CORRIE, Miss M. Exh. 1912
Alresford, Hants. † SWA 1.

CORRODI, Hermann* 1844-1905
Italian landscape and figure painter. Add: Rome, Italy 1880-81. † G 1, RA 1, RBA 2, RSA 2.

CORRY, Berta M. Exh. 1898
8 Eaton Square, London. † RI 1.

CORRY, Eileen Exh. 1918
Ulster Bank, Tuam, Co. Galway, Ireland. † RHA 1.

CORRY, Emily D. Exh. 1920-40
nee Workman. Painter, pencil and poster artist, and lithographer. Studied Belfast and Germany. Add: Redroofs, Newtownbreda, Belfast, Ireland. † RA 1, RCA 12, RHA 5, ROI 2, RSA 2, SWA 1.

CORRY, H. Lowry Exh. 1903-6
15 Warwick Square, London. † RA 2.

CORSELLIS, Elizabeth b. 1907
Painter and etcher. Studied Chelsea Polytechnic. Add: Hampstead, London 1928-31. † NEA 2, RA 2.

CORSON, Margaret A. Exh. 1921-23
45 Frederick Street, Edinburgh. † RSA 3, RSW 2.

CORTE, Aurelio Della Exh. 1910-17
London. † LS 6, RA 1.

CORTISSOS, Charles Exh. 1882
142 Abbey Foregate, Shrewsbury. † M 1.

CORY, Mrs. G. Exh. 1928-29
Campsea Ash Rectory, Wickham Market, Suffolk. † L 2.

CORYNDON, Lady Phyllis Mary Exh. 1930-34
nee Worthington. Married in 1909 to Sir Robert C. Governor of Kenya and High Commissioner of Zanzibar. † RMS 7.

COSOMATI, Mrs. Eileen Exh. 1929
Sculptor. Add: Cockloft Studios, 33 Cochrane Street, St. John's Wood, London. † GI 1, RA 1.

COSSAAR, Jan C.W.* Exh. 1906-29
Landscape and figure painter. Add: c/o Messrs. Wallis & Son, New Bond Street, London 1929. † GI 1, GOU 39, I 1, LS 5.

COSSINGTON-SMITH, Grace* Exh. 1929-32
Born Australia. Studied Sydney, Winchester and Germany. Add: c/o Redfern Gallery, Old Bond Street, London. † NEA 1, SWA 2, WG 38.

COSTA, A. Exh. 1884-89
Italian artist. Add: Rome 1884; Paris 1889. † G 1, M 2.

COSTA, da See D

COSTA, Professor Giovanni* 1827-1903
Italian landscape and portrait painter. Add: London 1880; Rome 1890. † BG 1, FIN 19, G 16, L 11, M 2, NG 40, RA 3.

COSTA, St. Jean Exh. 1887
Nr. Monaco, France. † M 1.

COSTANTINI, Virgil Exh. b. 1882
Portrait and figure painter. b. Italy. Studied Royal Academy, Venice. R.I. 1923. Add: Paris 1909; London 1923. † FIN 1, G 1, GI 1, L 9, RA 1, RI 10, ROI 2, RSA 3.

COSTEKER, Jane Exh. 1885-90
Monton, Eccles, Manchester. † B 2, L 2, M 9, ROI 2.

COSTELLO, Jensine b. 1886
Portrait painter. b. Norway. Studied Heatherleys. Add: Ilford, Essex 1935; London 1937. † P 3, ROI 5, SWA 1.

COTARD-DUPRE,**
Mdme. Therese Marthe Francois Exh. 1911
Figure painter. Add: 11 Rue des Bouchers, Saint Quentin (Aisne) France. † L 1.

COTES, Archibald Exh. 1895
15 Claremont Road, Seaforth, Lancs. † I 1

COTES, John C.C. Exh. 1913
Point Neptune, Fowey, Cornwall. † LS 3.

COTESWORTH, Lillias E. Exh. 1885-1907
Flower and figure painter. Add: Kingsworthy, Winchester, Hants. 1885; London 1907. † M 9, RA 1, RBA 1, ROI 4, RSA 1.

COTMAN, Frederick George* 1850-1920
Landscape, portrait, historical and genre painter. b. Ipswich, Suffolk. Studied RA Schools 1868. Nephew of John Snell C. R.I. 1882, R.O.I. 1883. Add: London 1880; Lowestoft, Suffolk 1897; Hemingford Grey, St. Ives, Hunts. 1908; Felixstowe, Suffolk 1916. † AG 1, B 6, D 3, DOW 52, FIN 37, G 6, GI 5, L 10, M 6, RA 26, RBA 3, RI 132, ROI 80, RSA 7, WG 3.

COTTAM, A. Exh. 1887-89
Elder Croft, Essex Road, Watford, Herts. † D 4.

COTTAM, Edith Exh. 1886-92
Wightwick House, Higher Broughton, Manchester. † M 3.

COTTAM, Ellen Exh. 1887-92
Manchester 1887; London 1892. † M 4, RBA 1.

COTTEE, Mabel Winifred b. 1905
Watercolour painter. Studied Nottingham College of Art 1924-34. Add: 43 Albert Grove, Nottingham 1934. † N 5.

COTTELL, Miss M.H. Exh. 1912-17
Illustrator and modeller. Add: 27 Victoria Road, Kensington, London. † RA 3.

COTTER, Miss K. Exh. 1881-91
Albert Gallery, Shandwick Place, Edinburgh. † RSA 5.

COTTER, Ruth Salaman Exh. 1938
56B North Hill, London. † SWA 1.

COTTERILL, Miss A.M. Exh. 1905
Ellacombe, Beeches Road, West Bromwich. † B 1.

COTTERILL, Ethel Exh. 1928
16 Clarendon Road, Leeds, Yorks. † M 2.

COTTERILL, Reginald Thomas b. 1885
Sculptor and painter. Studied Royal College of Art. Head of Sculpture Leeds College of Art. Principal York School of Arts and Crafts. Exh. 1927. Add: 16 Clarendon Road, Leeds. † L 1.

COTTET, Charles* 1863-1925
French landscape painter. Exh. 1901-23. Add: Paris. † GI 1, GOU 4, I 34, L 4.

COTTON, Ernest W. Exh. 1900
Echelhurst, Anderton Park Road, Moseley, Birmingham. † B 2.

COTTON, George J. Exh. 1936-40
Bedford. † RCA 4.

COTTON, John b. 1844
Landscape painter. Studied and practised architecture until 1890. Add: Oxford 1901; Leamington, Warwicks 1904. Add: 53 Gladstone Road, Sparkbrook, Birmingham 1908. † B 31, RCA 5.

COTTON, J.W. Exh. 1912
St. Ives, Cornwall. † L 2, RA 2.

COTTON, Marietta Exh. 1891-1927
Mrs. Leslie C. American. Portrait and figure painter. Add: London 1891 and 1909; Munich, Germany 1892. † P 1, RA 6.

COTTON, Miss Pamela Exh. 1938
Portrait painter. Add: Mount Alverno, Dalkey. † RHA 1.

COTTON, Violet Laura Caroline b. 1867
Mrs. Sidney C. nee Reed. Still life flower and landscape painter. Studied North Audley Street Art School. Exh. 1908-35. Add: London. † BG 1, ROI 7, WG 30.

COTTRELL, Henry J. Exh. 1882-1924
Birmingham 1882; Smethwick, Birmingham 1922. † B 8, L 1.

COTTRELL, Mrs. Lily Exh. 1940
86 Lasswade Road, Liberton, Dalkeith. † RSA 1.

COTTRELL, Wellesley Exh. 1882-1913
Landscape painter. Add: Birmingham 1882; Glan Conway, Wales 1900. † B 72, L 1, NG 38, RA 5, RCA 10.

COUCHMAN, Florence A. Exh. 1884-90
Interior and architectural painter. Add: 7 Pendlebury Road, Tottenham, London. † B 1, G 1, L 1, RA 1, RBA 5, RI 2.

COUGHTRIE, James Billington Exh. 1881-1914
Landscape painter. Add: London. † LS 20, RBA 1.

COUGHTRIE, Miss Kate Ruskin Exh. 1904-17
Figure painter. Add: London. † LS 5, NG 3, RA 4.

COUGNARD, Miss Augusta Exh. 1886-92
Miniature painter. Add: London 1886; Paris 1892. † RA 3, RBA 1.

COULBORN, May Exh. 1894-97
Glasgow 1894; Beckenham, Kent 1896. † GI 3, L 2.

COULDERY, Horatio Henri* b. 1832
Animal painter. Exh. 1880-1910. Add: Addington Grove, Lower Sydenham, London. † B 51, D 5, FIN 1, L 2, M 6, RA 11, RBA 25, RHA 3, ROI 7, TOO 1.

COULDERY, Thomas W. Exh. 1882-1898
Domestic painter. Add: London 1882; Pulborough, Sussex 1890; Chichester 1893; Brighton 1897. † B 3, D 3, L 5, M 7, RA 3, RBA 3, RI 8.

COULDREY, Oswald Exh. 1927-40
26 Victoria Road, Abingdon, Berks. † D 2, RI 3.

COULDWELL, Miss A.M. Exh. 1907-10
Garforth, Nr. Leeds, Yorks. † L 5, RA 1.

COULIN, Mdme. Marie E. Exh. 1913
47 Rue de la Procession, Paris, France. † L 1.

COULING, Arthur Vivian b. 1890
Painter and etcher. b. Shantung, China. Studied Edinburgh College of Art. Exh. 1922-40. Add: Edinburgh. † GI 12, L 1, RSA 28.

COULON, James Exh. 1892
Flower painter. Add: 473 Fulham Road, London. † RA 1.

COULON, John Exh. 1889
Figure painter. Add: Grosvenor Studios, Vauxhall Bridge, London. † RBA 1.

COULSON, Henry Major b. 1880
Painter and etcher. b. South Shields. Exh. 1921-37. Add: Southport, Lancs. † L 9, RSA 8.

COULSON, Miss Phyllis Exh. 1924-25
Waldon, Cadnant Park, Conway, Wales. † RCA 4.

COULSON, Raymond Exh. 1924-25
68 Corringham Road, London. † L 3.

COULSON, Richard C. Exh. 1929
Architect. Add: New Court, Temple, London. † RA 2.

COULTER, Ethel G. Exh. 1889-97
Landscape painter. Add: Faversham, Kent. † L 1, RBA 4, RI 1, SWA 2.

COULTER, Marie T. Exh. 1936-40
Portrait painter. Add: 70 Somerset Road, Wimbledon, London. † RA 2.

COULTER, William Exh. 1880-89
Flower painter. Add: London 1880; Godalming, Surrey 1882. † M 2, RA 1, RBA 1, RHA 2, RSA 1.

COULTHURST, Charles Exh. 1909
† LS 1.

COUPER, Miss Exh. 1901
Camberley, Surrey. † L 1.

COUPER, May Coventry Exh. 1896-1905
3 Charlotte Square, Edinburgh. † RSA 1, RSW 1.

COUPER, William b. 1853
American sculptor. Exh. 1885. Add: 6 Via Dante da Castiglione, Florence, Italy. † RA 3.

COUPER, W.N. Exh. 1890
37 Lansdowne Crescent, Glasgow. † GI 1.

COURANT, Maurice August Francois* 1847-1925
French seascape painter. Exh. 1880. Add: London. † AG 1.

COURLANDER, Mrs. Elsa Exh. 1929
Decorative flower painter. † WG 42.

COURSE, John L. Exh. 1922-27
21 Blackstock Road, Finsbury Park, London. † RA 2.

COURT, Miss Ada L. Exh. 1897
Snargate Street, Dover, Kent. † SWA 2.

COURT, Catherine Payn Exh. 1886-91
Flower painter. Add: 88 Talbot Road, Bayswater, London. † RBA 2, ROI 2.

COURT, Emily G.* Exh. 1905-40
Landscape, figure and flower painter. b. Newport, Essex. Studied Slade School. R.O.I. 1915, S.W.A. 1927. Add: London 1905 and 1916; Bedford 1915. † AB 3, CON 1, G 1, GI 3, GOU 2, I 14, L 1, M 1, NEA 2, RA 31, RHA 19, ROI 66, SWA 22.

COURT, Sidney A. Exh. 1932
3 Buckthorne Road, London. † RI 1.

COURTAULD, Catherine Exh. 1909-10
Oakhill, Heron's Gate, Rickmansworth, Herts. † LS 2.

COURTAULD, J.B. Exh. 1931
† GOU 2.

COURTENEY, E.J. Exh. 1890
115 Eversleigh Road, Lavender Hill, London. † B 1.

COURTENS, Hermann Exh. 1923
108 Rue de Liedekerke, St. Josse, Brussels. † L 1.

COURTIN, C. Exh. 1880-82
16 Avenue Trudaine, Paris, France. † RHA 10.

COURTNEY, Miss D.A. Exh. 1910-21
9 Chenies Street, Glasgow. † G 1, GI 3.

COURTNEY, Frederick E. b. 1901
b. Menston in Wharfedale. Exh. 1930. † L 1.

COURTNEY, Miss J. Exh. 1918
Bromley, Kent. † SWA 2.

COURTOIS, Gustave b. 1852
French portrait painter. Exh. 1893-98. Add: Paris 1893; London 1898. † GI 1, P 3.

COURTRAY, Charles Exh. 1884
Engraver. Add: c/o Messrs. Virtue, 294 City Road, London. † RA 1.

COURVOISIER, Jules Exh. 1928
† M 1.

COUSENS, Hal S. Exh. 1905
6 Berkeley Road, Tunbridge Wells, Kent. † L 1.

COUSIN, Mlle. Adrienne Exh. 1906
33 Rue Etienne Marcel, Paris, France. † L 1.

COUSINS, Samuel 1801-1887
Mezzotint engraver. A.R.A. 1835, R.A. 1855. Add: 24 Camden Square, London 1880. † RA 1.

COUSTON, A.S. Exh. 1884
265 High Street, Kirkaldy. † RSA 1.

COUTEUX, le See L

COUTTS, Gordon Exh. 1885
224 Sauchiehall Street, Glasgow. † GI 1.

COUTTS, Gordon* b. 1880
Landscape and figure painter. Teacher at various art schools in Australia. Exh. 1917-30. Add: London. † GI 3, L 1, P 4, RA 5.

COUTTS, Hubert d. 1921
Watercolour landscape painter. R.I. 1912. Add: Elterwater, Ambleside 1880, Windermere 1886. † B 5, D 10, GI 3, L 77, M 8, RA 74, RI 55, RSA 11.

COUTTS, J. Exh. 1880-89
Edinburgh. † GI 6.

COUTTS, J.H. Exh. 1881
Church Road, Buckie, Banffshire. † RHA 1.

COUTTS, W.G. Exh. 1885
London. † RSA 1.

COUVER, Van See V.

COVELLI, G. Exh. 1915-16
3 Bolton Studios, Redcliffe Road, London. † RA 2.

COVENTRY, Frederick Halford b. 1905
Painter, mural, poster and glass painter and engraver. Studied Wellington Technical College, New Zealand 1922-25; Julia Ashton Art School, Sydney 1926-28; Grosvenor School of Art 1929. Add: 12 Westbourne Grove Terrace, London 1932. † RA 4.

COVENTRY, Gertrude Mary b. 1886
Mrs. E. Robertson. Portrait, Landscape and coastal painter. Daughter of Robert McGown C. q.v. Add: Glasgow 1904; Inveresk, N.B. 1915; Bangor, Wales 1922. † B 1, GI 47, RA 1, RCA 5, RSA 20.

COVENTRY, Robert McGown 1855-1914
Landscape, portrait and coastal painter. Studied in Paris. A.R.S.A. 1906; R.S.W. 1889. Add: Glasgow. † DOW 6, GI 82, M 3, NEA 1, RA 5, RSA 27, RSW 65.

COVERLEY-PRICE, A. Victor b. 1901
Landscape painter. b. Winchester, Hants. Add: London 1924; The Hague, Holland 1939. † RA 2, RBA 2, RI 5.

COVILLOT, Edouard Exh. 1911
3 Cavendish Mansions, Clapton Square, London. † LS 2.

COWALL, A.B. Exh. 1932-33
3 Coningsby Road, Anfield, Liverpool. † L 2.

COWAN, A. Exh. 1889
Edenarroch, Ayr. † GI 1.

COWAN, Rev. Arthur A. Exh. 1927-40
Watercolour painter. Add: Inverleith Manse, Inverleith Gardens, Edinburgh. GI 5, RSA 1, RSW 12, WG 5.

COWAN, Mrs. A.D. Exh. 1929
72 Bedford Street, Liverpool. † L 5.

COWAN, Edith C. Exh. 1891
Portrait artist. Add: 31 Belsize Park Gardens, Hampstead, London. † RA 1.

COWAN, Georgina Exh. 1904-27
Watercolour painter. Add: Edinburgh. † RSA 4, RSW 5.

COWAN, James Exh. 1881-99
Glasgow. † GI 9, RSA 3.

COWAN, Jessie B. Exh. 1897
7 East Fettes Avenue, Edinburgh. † RSA 1.

COWAN, Janet D. Exh. 1882-94
Domestic and figure painter. Add: London. † L 4, M 2, P 2, RBA 3, ROI 2, SWA 1.

COWAN, Mrs. Jean Hunter d. c.1967
nee Hore. Add: Edinburgh 1935. † RSA 5, RSW 4.

COWAN, J.L. Exh. 1895-98
136 Wellington Street, Glasgow. † GI 2.

COWAN, Jessie R. Exh. 1911-27
Birkenhead 1911; London 1924; Bombay, India 1925. † L 8, RI 3.

COWAN, Mabel G. Exh. 1923-37
Landscape, interior and flower painter Add: Kingston Hill, Surrey 1923; London 1924 and 1929; Sidmouth, Devon 1927. † GI 3, RA 7, SWA 3.

COWAN, Miss M.M. Exh. 1920
14 Elm Park Road, Finchley Church End, London. † L 1.

COWAN, Ralph Exh. 1926-40
46 West Princes Street, Glasgow. † GI 4.

COWAN, William Exh. 1907-25
Glasgow 1907; Douglas, I.O.M. 1921. † GI 4, L 2.

COWAN, Wilson d. c.1918
Served Royal Flying Corps, World War I. Add: Corstorphine 1911; Edinburgh 1914. † GI 1, RSA 6.

COWAN-DOUGLAS, Lilian Horsburgh b. 1894
Watercolour landscape and flower painter. b. Calgary, Mull. Studied Edinburgh College of Art. Exh. 1930-40. Add: Corbet Tower, Kelso. † GI 5, RSA 17, RSW 21.

COWARD, C. Brenda Exh. 1910-25
Flower painter. Add: 10 Melbury Road, Kensington, London. † RA 2.

CORDEROY, Kate E. Exh. 1905-19
Miniature painter. Add: The Retreat, Hillside Road, New Bushey, Herts. † L 3, RA 17.

COWDEROY, William Exh. 1883-84
Figure painter. Add: Gordon House, Prince of Wales Road, London. † RBA 4.

COWELL, C.H. Exh. 1890
Carlisle Studios, King's Road, Chelsea, London. † NG 1.

COWELL, Mrs. Eva Exh. 1897-1925
Portrait painter. Married to George J.C. q.v. Add: Maida Hill, London 1897; Saxmundham, Suffolk 1901; Leiston, Suffolk 1911; Aldeburgh, Suffolk 1925. † L 4, NG 8, P 1, RA 1, SWA 1.

COWELL, Miss Fan Exh. 1903-8
Leeds, Yorks. † L 9, RA 1.

COWELL, G.H. Sydney Exh. 1884-1906
Figure painter. Add: London. † B 1, M 1, RA 5, RBA 2, ROI 3.

COWELL, George J. Exh. 1886-1914
Sculptor. Add: London 1886; Saxmundham, Suffolk 1903; Leiston, Suffolk 1914. † L 4, NG 9, RA 14.

COWELL, Lilian b. 1901
Landscape painter, modeller and embroideress. Studied Laird School of Art, Birkenhead. Exh. 1923-32. Add: Mayfield, Frankley, Cheshire. † L 10.

COWELL, Miss May F. Exh. 1909-12
21a Exchange Buildings, Liverpool. † L 7.

COWEN, Miss L. Exh. 1881
154 North Strand Road, Dublin, Ireland. † RHA 3.

COWEN, Lionel J.* Exh. 1880-88
Figure painter. R.B.A. 1888. Add: 41 Broadhurst Gardens, Finchley Road, London. † G 1, L 4, M 1, RA 4, RBA 4, TOO 1.

COWEN, Pyzer Exh. 1923
16a Soho Square, London. † NEA 2.

COWEN, Walter Exh. 1926-29
15 North John Street, Liverpool. † L 6.

COWERN, Raymond Teagne Exh. 1932-40
Painter and etcher. A.R.E. 1935, A.R.W.S. 1940. Add: Handsworth, Birmingham 1932; London 1933. † B 26, GI 3, RA 16, RE 26, RSA 6, RWS 4.
COWHAM, Hilda Exh. 1911-30
Watercolour painter, etcher and illustrator. Married Edgar Lander q.v. Studied Lambeth School of Art. First woman to draw for "Punch". Add: London. † GI 9, L 16, LS 17, RA 3, SWA 2, WG 50.
COWHAM, Hilda G. Exh. 1898-1901
Landscape and domestic painter. Add: Chelsea, London. † RA 2.
COWIE, G.M. Exh. 1883
1 London Street, Edinburgh. † RSA 1.
COWIE, James Exh. 1880-84
Edinburgh. † RSA 9.
COWIE, James Exh. 1916-40
Landscape and portrait painter. A.R.S.A. 1937. Add: Glasgow 1916 and 1927, Bothwell, 1924, Arbroath 1936. † GI 26, L 1, M 2, NEA 3, RA 4, RSA 44.
COWIE, Mrs. Nancy Exh. 1921
c/o Stevenson, 571 Sauchiehall Street, Glasgow. † GI 1, RSA 3.
COWIE, Richard K. Exh. 1939-40
50 Burnt Ash Hill, London. † RHA 1, RI 1.
COWIESON, Agnes M. Exh. 1882-1940
Domestic painter. Add: Edinburgh. † GI 46, L 7, RA 8, RSA 73, RSW 3.
COWLAND, Mary G. Exh. 1926-35
Landscape painter. Add: Hillden, Horeham Road, East Sussex. † AR 35, RA 1.
COWLES, Geoffrey Clement Exh. 1916-40
Landscape, figure and flower and mythology painter. Add: London. † CHE 5, NEA 13, RA 4.
COWLEY, Charles George Exh. 1880-92
Landscape and figure painter. Add: Burton Joyce, Nottingham 1880; Nottingham 1892. † N 4.
COWLEY, Frank Exh. 1909-14
Borough Green, Sevenoaks, Kent 1909; West Malling, Kent 1913; Gravesend 1914. † LS 9, RA 1.
COWLEY, Irene Exh. 1940
Burmont, Woodford Road, South Woodford, London. † RBA 1.
COWLEY, John Exh. 1885-1902
Moss-side, Manchester. † L 1, M 10.
COWLEY, Miss Sarah Exh. 1903
Flower painter. Add: 12 Stamford Avenue, Brighton, Sussex. † RA 1.
COWLISHAW, Thomas Exh. 1891-1901
Painter and designer. Add: Tonge, Ashby-de-la-Zouch, Leics. † N 5, RA 1.
COWLMAN, Emma L. Exh. 1913-16
Watercolour landscape painter and poster designer. Sister of John E.C. q.v. Studied Regent Street Polytechnic. Add: 78 Hencroft Street, Slough, Bucks. † I 5, L 2.
COWLMAN, John E. Exh. 1908-25
Landscape painter. Add: 78 Hencroft Street, Slough, Bucks. † G 5, I 5, L 1, RA 1, ROI 1, RSA 2.
COWPER, Frank Exh. 1899
5 Thelsford Crescent, Alcester Road, Moseley, Birmingham. † B 1.
COWPER, Frank Cadogan* 1877-1958
Portrait, historical, fantasy and mural painter. Studied St. John's Wood School of Art, RA Schools and under Edwin Abbey. A.R.A. 1907, R.A. 1934, R.P. 1921, A.R.W.S. 1904, R.W.S. 1911. Purchased by Chantrey Bequest "St. Agnes in Prison receiving from Heaven the Shining White Garment" 1905 and "Lucretia Borgia reigns in the Vatican in the Absence of Pope Alexander VI" 1914. Add: London. † B,1, FIN 1, G 1, GI 2, L 35, M 1, P 3, RA 123, ROI 1, RWS 15.
COWPER, Gertrude J. Exh. 1900-5
Miniature portrait painter. Add: London. P 1, RA 3, RMS 2, SWA 3.
COWPER, Jas. R. Exh. 1911-13
Doonbank, Helensburgh, N.B. † GI 3.
COWPER, J.S. Exh. 1898
10 Augusta Street, Moseley, Birmingham. † B 1.
COWPER, Lawrence Exh. 1926
13 Bowden Street, Litherland, Liverpool. † L 2.
COWPER, Max Exh. 1893-1911
Figure painter. Add: Dundee 1893; Edinburgh 1894; London 1901. † GI 4, L 1, RA 8, RSA 3.
COWPER, Richard Exh. 1882-84
Landscape painter. Add: 3 The Residences, South Kensington, London. † D 4, RI 1, ROI 1.
COWPER, Mrs. Richard Exh. 1889
Landscape painter. Add: Copped Hill, Totteridge, Herts. † SWA 1.
COWPER, Thomas Exh. 1891-1906
Figure, flower and portrait painter. Add: London. † L 5, M 2, NG 1, P 1, RA 11, ROI 8.
COWPER, W.H. Exh. 1885-92
7 Scotland Street, Edinburgh. † GI 5, RSA 16.
COX, A. Exh. 1908-12
A.N.S.A. 1908. Add: Homewood, Gedling, Notts. † N 5.
COX, Miss A. Exh. 1891
1 Osbourne Terrace, Woodchurch Road, Oxton, Liverpool. † L 1.
COX, Annie H. Exn. 1882-99
Birmingham. † B 15.
COX, Albert J. Exh. 1885-1909
Landscape painter. Add: London. † BG 1, GOU 3, RA 1, RBA 1, RI 4.
COX, Miss Adela Leader Exh. 1898-1907
Flower painter. Add: Rose Hill, Dorking, Surrey 1897; London 1913. † L 3, RA 3, RI 1, SWA 16.
COX, Arthur L. Exh. 1934
Mezzotint engraver. Add: c/o 12 Rudolph Road, Bushey, Herts. † RA 1.
COX, Alfred Wilson Exh. 1885
Landscape painter. Add: Sherwood House, Beeston, Nottingham. † RA 1.
COX, Mrs. B. Exh. 1894-96
Portrait painter. Add: London 1894; Glasgow 1896. † GI 2, L 1, RA 1.
COX, Bertram Exh. 1893-1901
Portrait painter. Add: London. † RBA 2.
COX, C. Exh. 1899
50a Trinity Square, Borough, London. † RHA 2.
COX, Charles Arthur Exh. 1880-1930
Painter, black and white and crayon artist. Son of Charles Hudson C. q.v. Artist correspondent for 35 years to the "Graphic" and "Daily Graphic". Studied Birkenhead and Antwerp. Add: Birkenhead 1880; Liverpool 1897; Bootle 1928. † D 2, L 102, RBA 1, RCA 5, RI 1.
COX, Charles Edward Exh. 1880-1901
Still life and landscape painter. Add: London. † RA 7, RBA 14, ROI 2.
COX, Charles Hudson 1829-1901
Landscape painter. Father of Charles Arthur C. q.v. Born Liverpool. Died Texas, U.S.A. Add: Shrewsbury Road, Birkenhead 1880. † D 3, L 21, RI 1, ROI 5.
COX, Charles T. d. 1914
Exh. 1898-1912. Add: Birmingham. † B 22.
COX, C.V. Exh. 1939-40
40 Green Lanes, Erdington, Birmingham. † B 3.
COX, David junr.* 1809-1885
Landscape painter. Studied under his father David C. (1783-1859). A.R.I. 1841, R.I. 1845 (resigned 1846), A.R.W.S. 1848. Add: Chester House, Mount Ephraim Road, Streatham, London 1880. † GI 1, RWS 25.
COX, Dorothy C. Exh. 1938-40
Miniature portrait painter. Add: 42 Herberton Road, Bournemouth, Hants. † RA 3.
COX, Dorothy M. b. 1882
Mrs. Llewellyn Lewis. Landscape and miniature portrait painter. R.M.S. 1901. Add: London 1898 and 1908; Croydon 1905; Shoreham-by-Sea 1925. † B 2, FIN 2, G 2, GI 1, L 5, P 1, RA 7, RHA 4, RI 5, RMS 13, SWA 4, WG 65.
COX, Ernest Exh. 1909-38
Landscape painter. Add: Nottingham. † N 56.
COX, Elija Albert b. 1876
Landscape painter and commercial artist. Travelled on the Continent. R.B.A. 1915, R.I. 1921, R.O.I. 1924. Add: London. † FIN 4, GI 3, I 2, L 2, RA 12, RBA 49, RI 7, RSA 3.
COX, Ernest B. Exh. 1930
† L 1.
COX, Miss E.B. Exh. 1884-1929
Derby 1884; Liverpool 1920. † B 1, L 8.
COX, Ethel Mary Exh. 1921-28
Watercolour painter. Studied Cheltenham School of Art. Add: Connellmore, Cheltenham, Glos. † B 6, L 1, RHA 4.
COX, Everard Morant Exh. 1884-85
Domestic painter. Add: London. † RA 2.
COX, Miss Eileen R. Exh. 1926-28
Earledon, Eccleston Park, Prescot, Lancs. † L 3.
COX, Frank E.* Exh. 1880-95
Landscape painter. Add: London. † B 14, D 6, FIN 1, G 1, GI 10, L 7, M 8, RA 16, RBA 1, RHA 1, RI 8, ROI 2.
COX, F. Russell Exh. 1925-33
Solihull. † B 3.
COX, Garstin* 1892-1933
Landscape painter. Studied Camborne Art School, Newlyn and St. Ives. Add: Camborne, Cornwall 1912; The Lizard, Cornwall 1928. † L 2, RA 4.
COX G.A. Exh. 1905
33 Newhall Street, Birmingham. † RA 1.
COX, Gertrude Florence Mary Exh. 1880-1930
Painter and etcher. Studied Exeter School of Art. Add: London 1880; Exeter 1929. † L 1, SWA 6.
COX, Rev. Sir George W. Exh. 1888-89
Landscape painter. Add: Scrayingham Rectory, York 1888; London 1889. † RI 2.
COX, Harold Exh. 1921-28
Flower painter. Add: Cheltenham 1921; Warwick 1923 and 1928; Dunstable, Beds. 1926. † B 3, L 6, RA 1.
COX, Henry Exh. 1882
256 Arkwright Street. Nottingham. † N 1.
COX, Mrs. H.M. Exh. 1929
46 Poplar Road, Oxton, Birkenhead. † L 2.
COX, J.C. Exh. 1881-86
Beechwood, Nr. Dundee 1881; Lochee, N.B. 1884. † GI 4, L 5, RHA 3, RSA 11.
COX, Jane Wells Exh. 1880-86
Landscape and flower painter. Add: London. † D 5, RBA 6, SWA 1.
COX, Miss Kathleen Exh. 1930-33
Sculptor. Add: Howth, 1930; Dublin 1931. † RHA 17.
COX, Kenyon 1856-1919
American mural and portrait painter. Member of the American National Academy. Exh. 1882. † FIN 1.

COX, Mrs. K.W. Exh. 1889
25 Wyndham Road, Birmingham. † B 1.
COX, L. Exh. 1918
"Solon", Bushey, Herts. † RA 1.
COX, Leonard C. Exh. 1900-9
Landscape painter. Add: Tunbridge Wells, Kent 1900; Battle, Sussex 1909. † L 1, RA 3.
COX, Louisa E. Exh. 1880-88
Miniature painter. Add: 11 St. James Street, Nottingham. † N 18, RA 7.
COX, Marion Exh. 1898-1912
Adyar Studio, Bedford Park, London. † RI 1, SWA 5.
COX, Martin Exh. 1924
116 Addison Road, King's Heath, Birmingham. † B 1.
COX, Michael Exh. 1914
Adyar Studio, Bedford Park, London. † LS 3.
COX, Mary Constance Exh. 1892-1935
Watercolour landscape, seascape, figure and animal painter and teacher. Born Rochdale. Studied Manchester School of Art, Dresden, Paris and the British Academy, Rome. Add: Manchester 1892; Malvern, Worcs. 1927. † AB 1, B 3, L 3, M 3, RBA 2.
COX, Minnie Paton Exh. 1910-21
Rock Ferry, Cheshire 1910; Hoylake, Cheshire 1920. † L 11, RSA 2.
COX, Miss N. Exh. 1904
Thirkleby, Fair View Road, Birkenhead. † L 1.
COX, Norman Exh. 1909
† LS 3.
COX, Richard G. Exh. 1935
Architect. Add: 60a High Street, Acton, London. † RA 1.
COX, Thomas Exh. 1882-1925
Birmingham. † B 9.
COX, Trena Exh. 1916-29
Stained glass artist. Add: Birkenhead 1916; Chester 1924. † L 13, RA 2.
COX, Thomas V. Exh. 1920-38
Erdington, Birmingham. † B 12.
COX, Miss Valerie Exh. 1939
Sculptor. Add: L'Hermitage, Beaumont, Jersey, C.I. † RA 1.
COX, Walter Exh. 1888-94
Etcher. Add: London 1891 and 1893; Penbridge, Herefords. 1892. † M 1, RBA 1, ROI 3.
COX, Wilson Exh. 1881-86
Landscape painter. Add: Nottingham 1881; Liverpool 1886. † L 2, M 1, RBA 3.
COX, W.A. Exh. 1910
34 Ennis Road, Finsbury Park, London. † RA 1.
COXETER, Miss Constance Exh. 1894
Landscape painter. Add: 111 Southwood Lane, Highgate, London. † RA 1.
COXETER, Harold Exh. 1929
Hoe, Gomshall, Surrey. † L 1.
COXETER, Lucy Gee Exh. 1896-1930
Mrs. H. nee Gee. Portrait painter. Add: London. † L 1, RA 6, SWA 1.
COXHEAD, Olive Lydia Exh. 1915-17
Painter and woodcut artist. Add: 7 Essex Villas, Kensington, London. † NEA 7.
COXON, Ernest James Exh. 1898-1910
Figure painter. Add: London. † L 2, LS 6, RA 1.
COXON, Miss E.M. Exh. 1923
2 Stoke Lane, Gedling, Notts. † N 2.
COXON, Raymond James b. 1896
Painter, lithographer and writer. Married Edna Ginesi q.v. Studied Leeds School of Art and Royal College of Art. Member London Group 1931. Exh. 1928-40. Add: London. † BA 2, BK 1, COO 7, GOU 7, L 4, LEI 42, M 2, RED 1.

COYLE, A.H. Exh. 1913
Baroda, India. † RA 2.
COYNERS, Miss A. Exh. 1920
Clifton Terrace, Kilkee, Co. Clare, Ireland. † RHA 2.
COZE, de la See D
CRABBE, Herbert G. Exh. 1885-91
Landscape painter. Add: Heatherlee, Beckenham, Kent. † D 1, L 2, RA 4, RBA 7, RI 2.
CRABTREE, Miss Mary Exh. 1900-23
Redhill, Surrey 1906; Tadworth, Surrey 1919. † RA 3, RI 2, SWA 6.
CRACE, John Gregory d. 1919
Decorative artist. Add: 38 Wigmore Street, London. † L 3, RA 3.
CRACE, Lewis Paxton Exh. 1881-86
Decorative artist. Add: 58 Wigmore Street, London. † RA 4.
CRACKNELL, C. Exh. 1939
† GOU 1.
CRACOWSKI, B. Exh. 1926
† M2.
CRADDOCK, Mrs. A.B. Exh. 1929
42 Shamrock Road, Cloughton, Birkenhead. † L 1.
CRADDOCK, Gladys M. Bettney Exh. 1930-33
Sandown, Upton, Wirral, Cheshire. † L 2.
CRADDOCK, J.W. Exh. 1906-8
63 Upper George Street, Kingstown, Ireland. † RCA 1, RHA 1.
CRADOCK, Hannah Exh. 1939
Landscape painter. Add: Sandhutton, Thirsk, Yorks. † RA 1.
CRAFT, Percy Robert* 1856-1934
Figure, landscape and coastal painter. Studied Heatherley's and Slade School (gold and silver medallist). R.B.A. 1898. Add: London 1880, 1900 and 1910; Newlyn, Penzance, Cornwall 1890; Buckden, Hunts. 1902. † B 19, BG 1, DOW 3, GI 5, L 28, M 5, NG 1, RA 39, RBA 64, RCA 65, RE 1, ROI 27, RSA 1.
CRAFTON, Richard Exh. 1880-82
Landscape and coastal painter. Add: Stanstead, Bishops Stortford, Herts. † RBA 5.
CRAGGS, John Exh. 1905
Bridge Street, Haverfordwest, Wales. † L 1.
CRAIG, Ailsa Exh. 1927-29
3 Foremount Terrace, Downshill, Glasgow. † L 3.
CRAIG, Alex A. Exh. 1889
7 Holland Place, Glasgow. † GI 1.
CRAIG, Mrs. Clara L. Exh. 1912-38
Glasgow. † GI 1, L 2.
CRAIG, David Exh. 1934-39
Flower painter. Add: Marlborough Studios, Finchley Road, London. † NEA 1, RA 1, RCA 1.
CRAIG, Donald Exh. 1938-40
Figure and landscape painter. Add: Links Cottage, Queen's Park, South Drive, Bournemouth. † RA 3.
CRAIG, Mrs. Elizabeth Exh. 1937
Marlborough Studios, Finchley Road, London. † RSW 2.
CRAIG, Mrs. Ethel Exh. 1917-37
26 Belmont Drive, Giffnock, Glasgow. † GI 2, RSA 2.
CRAIG, Miss Ethel Exh. 1932-40
Still life and landscape painter. Add: Belmont Drive, Giffnock, Glasgow. † GI 9, RA 2, RSA 11.
CRAIG, Edward A. See CARRICK
CRAIG, Edward Gordon* 1872-1966
Painter, theatrical designer and wood engraver. Son of Ellen Terry. Father of Edward A. Carrick, q.v. Exh. 1902-38. Add: London and Florence, Italy, † BG 105, GI 12, LEI 86, RED 1, RHA 2.

CRAIG, Miss E. Helen Exh. 1904-24
Colebrook, Longton Avenue, Upper Sydenham, London. † L 1, LS 3, RCA 1, SWA 4.
CRAIG, Miss Effie M. Exh. 1926
Portrait painter. Add: 30 Tite Street, Chelsea, London. † RA 1.
CRAIG, Frank 1874-1918
Painter and black and white war artist. R.O.I. 1906. "The Heretic" purchased by Chantrey Bequest 1906. Add: Hampstead, London 1892; Hindhead, Surrey 1903; Ewhurst, Surrey 1909; Shottermill, Surrey 1914. † GI 3, I 10, L 5, M 1, RA 49, RBA 2, ROI 8, RSA 4.
CRAIG, F. Barrington (Barry) Exh. 1925-40
Portrait and landscape painter. Add: London. † BA 1, COO 1, GOU 1, NEA 7, P 4, RA 10, RI 2, RSA 1, TOO 3.
CRAIG, Miss Graham Exh. 1931-34
Etcher. Add: Liverpool 1931 and 1934. Royal College of Art, London 1933. † GI 1, L 3, RA 1.
CRAIG, Jean Exh. 1897
7 Ardgowan Terrace, Glasgow. † GI 1.
CRAIG, J. Humbert* d. 1944
Landscape painter. A.R.H.A. 1925, R.H.A. 1928. Exh. 1915-40. Add: Bangor, Co. Down 1915; Belfast, Ireland 1928. † FIN 242, GI 21, RA 3, RHA 124, ROI 6, RSA 1.
CRAIG, Miss Muriel Exh. 1925-29
Liverpool. † L 6.
CRAIG, Nellie P. Exh. 1902-18
Flower painter. Add: Canterbury 1902; London 1918. † RA 2.
CRAIG, Robert Exh. 1887-89
Craegest, Dalkeith, N.B. † GI 1, RSA 5.
CRAIG, W. Wood Exh. 1907-13
5 Maurice Place, Edinburgh. † GI 3.
CRAIGMILE, Mrs. Exh. 1904-15
10 Melrose Terrace, Liscard, Cheshire. † L 16.
CRAIGMILE, William Exh. 1905-13
Leek, Staffs. 1905; Banchory, Aberdeen 1907; Conway, Wales 1912. † LS 8, RCA 2.
CRAIG-WALLACE, Robert Exh. 1929-40
Painter and etcher. Add: 5 Westercraigs, Dennistoun, Glasgow. † GI 23, RA 1, RSA 15.
CRAIK, Anna R. Exh. 1899-1900
2 West Halkin Street, London. † SWA 2.
CRAINE, Miss Catherine G Exh. 1905
14 Richmond Terrace, Liverpool. † L 1.
CRAINE, Miss Frances G. Exh. 1902-8
14 Richmond Terrace, Liverpool. † L 3.
CRAISTER, Miss A. Exh. 1908
28 Spencer Place, Leeds, Yorks. † RA 1.
CRAISTER, Mrs. Walter Exh. 1892
21 Tadema Road, Chelsea, London. † RI 1.
CRAKE, Cicely Exh. 1893
The Art College, South Wimbledon, London. † RA 1.
CRAKE, Frances Exh. 1927
† D 1.
CRAKE, W.V. Exh. 1906
Highlands Cottage, St. Leonards on Sea. † L 1.
CRAMER, Mrs. A. Van Rensselaer Exh. 1897-99
R.M.S. 1898. Add: London. † RMS 4, SWA 1.
CRAMER, Belle Exh. 1917-39
Landscape, figure, flower and still life painter. Studied Edinburgh School of Art. Add: London. † COO 72, GOU 33, LS 9, M 1, NEA 8, P 1, ROI 3, SWA 6.
CRAMM, Von see V

CRAMP, H. Exh. 1910
King Street, Huthwaite, Nr. Mansfield, Notts. † N 1.

CRAMPTON, Maude M. Exh. 1896
Miniature portrait painter. Add: 2 North Parade, Queen Anne's Place, Bootham, Yorks. † RA 1.

CRANBALL, J. Exh. 1901
Beacon Banks, Easingwold, Yorks. † I 2.

CRANE, Miss E.G. Exh. 1920
207 West Derby Road, Liverpool. † L 1.

CRANE, H.W. Exh. 1912
The Barracks, Tullamore, Ireland. † RHA 1.

CRANE, J. Exh. 1886-89
12 Chapel Street, Lancaster. † L 1, M 1.

CRANE, Lancelot Exh. 1908-14
Son of Walter C. q.v. Visited Egypt 1911. Add: 13 Holland Street, Kensington, London. † NG 1, RA 4.

CRANE, Lionel F. Exh. 1898-1921
Architect. Son of Walter G q.v. Add: London. † NG 8, RA 13.

CRANE, Thomas Exh. 1890-1900
Landscape painter. Add: London. † L 1, RA 2.

CRANE, Walter* 1845-1915
Painter, illustrator and designer. b. Liverpool. Principal Royal College of Art 1898-99. R.I. 1882 (resigned 1886), R.O.I. 1883, A.R.W.S. 1888, R.W.S. 1899. Add: London. † B 11, CAR 31, D 4, DOW 47, FIN 122, G 59, GI 13, I 10, L 29, LEI 56, LS 5, M 17, NG 39, P 1, RBA 9, RHA 1, RI 13, ROI 6, RSA 2, RWS 110.

CRANE, Mrs. Walter 1846-1914
Expert on art needlework. Add: 13 Holland Street, Kensington, London. † SWA 1.

CRANFIELD, Sydney W. Exh. 1899-1922
Architect. Add: London. † RA 8.

CRANK, Adolphe Exh. 1907
181 Avenue du Maine, Paris. † L 1.

CRANSHAW, Lionel T. Exh. 1897
Warmsworth House, Doncaster, Yorks. † M 1.

CRANSTON, Andrew Exh. 1933-39
63 Kintore Road, Glasgow. † RSW 7.

CRANSTOUN, James H. Exh. 1880-93
Landscape painter. Add: 3 Athole Street, Perth. † RSA 17.

CRANTON, Margaret Exh. 1937-40
Miniature portrait painter. Add: Stoke Green nr. Slough 1937; London 1940. † COO 4, NEA 2, RA 2.

CRANWELL, Miss Mia Exh. 1920
† RMS 1.

CRAPELLI, G.L. Exh. 1885
23 Moray Place, Edinburgh. † RSA 1.

CRAPPER, Edith B. Exh. 1916-39
Miniaturist. A.R.M.S. 1923, R.M.S. 1927. Add: 27 Bolingbroke Grove, Wandsworth Common, London. † L 7, RMS 27.

CRASKE, Leonard b. 1882
Sculptor. Add: Rutland House, Albert Bridge Road, London 1915. † RA 1.

CRASKE, Olive Exh. 1923-24
Landscape and interior painter. Add: Burseldon, Southampton 1923; Oulton Broad, Lowestoft, Suffolk 1924. † RA 2.

CRASTER, J. Exh. 1892-93
Wellington, Penicuik, Midlothian. † GI 3.

CRAWCOUR, W.H. Exh. 1901-2
90 Musters Road, West Bridgford, Notts. † N 2.

CRAWFORD, Alex Hunter Exh. 1892-1911
Edinburgh. † RSA 12.

CRAWFORD, C.P. Exh. 1891-93
3 Westminster Terrace, Ibrox, Glasgow. † GI 3.

CRAWFORD, David Exh. 1887
George Villa, Kilmalcolm, Glasgow. † GI 1.

CRAWFORD, Miss Doreen Exh. 1926
"Cloreen", University Road, Belfast, Ireland. † RHA 2.

CRAWFORD, David William Exh. 1899-1912
12 Carlton Street, Edinburgh. † RSA 4.

CRAWFORD, Mrs. Emily* Exh. 1880-1906
Portrait, figure and landscape painter. Add: London 1880 and 1886; Glanmire, Co. Cork, Ireland 1882; Chiddingfold, Surrey 1900. † RA 1, RHA 1, SWA 18.

CRAWFORD, Edmund Thornton 1806-1885
Landscape and coastal painter. Studied at Trustees Academy, Edinburgh. Often visited Holland. Foundation Associate R.S.A. 1926. One of nine artists who withdrew after the first meeting. Admitted R.S.A. by Hope and Cockburn Award 1929. Resigned 1932. Re-elected A.R.S.A. 1939. R.S.A. 1948. Add: Loanhead, Edinburgh 1882. † GI 1, RSA 2.

CRAWFORD, Hugh Adana Exh. 1931-40
A.R.S.A. 1939. Add: Glasgow. † GI 12, RSA 12.

CRAWFORD, John Exh. 1886
39 Cranston Street, Glasgow. † GI 2.

CRAWFORD, J.M. Exh. 1904-15
Glasgow 1904; Torrance 1914. † GI 5, RSW 3.

CRAWFORD, John T. Exh. 1938
31 Jacks Road, Saltcoats. † RSA 1.

CRAWFORD, Julia T. Exh. 1937-38
c/o Robert Sielle Esq. 14 Greenwell Street, London. † RBA 1, RSA 1.

CRAWFORD, Jennie W. Exh. 1888-90
Hayfield, Rutherglen, Glasgow. † GI 4.

CRAWFORD, Kate Exh. 1889-92
Figure painter. Add: 12 Norland Place, Notting Hill, London. † RID 11.

CRAWFORD, Peter Exh. 1905-11
Glasgow. † GI 10.

CRAWFORD, Robert C. Exh. 1880-1924
Landscape, marine and flower painter. Add: Glasgow. † GI 114, L 2, M 1, RA 15, RSA 6, RSW 3.

CRAWFORD, Richard Goldie Exh. 1898-1916
Portrait and figure painter. Add: London 1898; Jersey, C.I. 1907. † L 2, LS 2, M 1, RA 4, ROI 2.

CRAWFORD, R.P. Exh. 1915
26 North John Street, Liverpool. † L 1.

CRAWFORD, Susan F. d. c. 1918
Etcher. A.R.E. 1893. Add: Glasgow. † BRU 81, GI 61, L 30, M 3, RA 3, RE 104, RHA 3, RSA 51, RSW 1.

CRAWFORD, Tom Exh. 1888
3 Dundas Terrace, Crosshill, Glasgow. † GI 1.

CRAWFORD, Thomas Hamilton Exh. 1891-1933
Watercolour painter and mezzotint engraver. Studied Glasgow and Edinburgh. R.S.W. 1887. Add: Glasgow 1891; London 1893; Hemel Hempstead, Herts. 1909; Berkhamstead, Herts. 1919. † DOW 4, FIN 2, GI 21, L 4, RA 25, RE 2, RI 3, RSA 3, RSW 27.

CRAWFORD, W. Exh. 1909
Synod Hall, Edinburgh. † RSA 2.

CRAWFORD, William Caldwell Exh. 1898-1936
Craiglockhart, N.B. 1898; Edinburgh 1906; East Lothian 1920; Loanhead, Midlothian 1924. † GI 9, L 2, RSA 29, RSW 3.

CRAWFORTH, Harold Exh. 1935
107 Gillshill Road, Hull. † RA 1.

CRAWHALL, Joseph* 1861-1913
Animal and landscape painter and teacher. b. Morpeth. Studied in London and briefly under Aime Morot in Paris (1882). Add: Newcastle on Tyne 1882; Easingwold, Yorks. 1903. † G 2, GI 11, I 18, L 12, M 1, NEA 9, RA 2, RSA 22, RSW 22.

CRAWLEY, Miss Elsie C. Exh. 1900
Blythewood, Solihull, Birmingham. † B 1.

CRAWLEY-BOEVEY, Francis H. Exh. 1910
Barrow Green Court, Oxted, Surrey. † LS 3.

CRAWSHAW, Dagmar M. Exh. 1934
9 Gloucester Avenue, Blackpool. † GI 1.

CRAWSHAW, Ella Burnett Exh. 1938-40
Miniature portrait painter. Add: Epsom, Surrey. † RA 6, RMS 1.

CRAWSHAW, Mrs. Frances b. 1876
nee Fisher. Second wife of Lionel Townsend C. q.v. Flower painter. Studied Westminster School of Art, Scarborough School of Art and Milan. Add: Whitby, Yorks. 1931; Edinburgh 1935; Droitwich 1937. † B 5, GI 2, RA 1, RBA 1, ROI 7, RSA 8, RSW 7, SWA 6.

CRAWSHAW, Lionel Townsend Exh. 1905-40
Painter and etcher. Qualified as a solicitor before taking up Art. Studied Dusseldorf, Karlsruhe and Paris. R.S.W. 1923. Add: Doncaster 1905; Edinburgh 1925; Whitby, Yorks. 1932; Droitwich, Worcs. 1938. † AR 2, B 6, GI 17, L 9, LS 12, NEA 4, RA 13, RI 9, ROI 16, RSA 37, RSW 75, WG 134.

CRAWSHAW, Miss Margaret Exh. 1913
5 Langdale Terrace, Whitby, Yorks. † L 1.

CRAWSHAY, Miss C. Exh. 1890
34 Brook Street, London. † L 1.

CREALOCK, John d. 1959
Landscape and portrait painter. Studied Juliens, Paris. R.P. 1919. Add: Paris 1902; London 1904. † B 6, CHE 1, COO 2, GI 1, GOU 10, I 7, L 24, LS 5, NEA 1, NG 1, P 59, RA 8, RHA 8, ROI 6.

CREAMER, Julia Exh. 1898-1922
Mrs. H. Landscape, figure and still life painter. Add: London. † BG 2, GOU 8, I 6, L 3, NEA 6, RA 1, RI 2, ROI 2, SWA 9.

CREAMER, May Exh. 1916-24
Sculptor. Add: London. † I 1, NEA 2, RA 3.

CREBASSA, P.E. Exh. 1910
50 Rue Vereingelorix, Paris, France. † L 1.

CREEBBIN, W. Exh. 1886-88
Liverpool. † L 4.

CREDLAND, W.R. Exh. 1886
Free Library, King Street, Manchester. † M 1.

CREE, Miss F. Exh. 1888-93
Ingleside, Lenzie, Glasgow. † GI 3.

CREE, Janet b. 1910
Figure and portrait painter. "The Oriental Portrait" purchased by Chantrey Bequest 1933. Add: London. † COO 11, RA 6.

CREED, Miss Mercy Exh. 1925
† RMS 1.

CREED, R. Exh. 1914
5 Verulam Buildings, Gray's Inn, London. † RA 1.

CREESER, Miss Exh. 1905
Oundle, Northants. † L 1.

CREGAN, Betty Exh. 1922-33
Miniature painter. Add: Clonskeagh Castle, Dublin 1922; Monkstown 1933. † RHA 4.

CREGEEN, Bertha M. Exh. 1893-96
Portrait painter. Add: Brockley, London. † RA 4.

CREGEEN, Emily A. Exh. 1885-1908
Portrait painter. Add: Forest Hill, London 1885; Brockley, London 1890; Sidcup, Kent 1908. † B 7, L 4, RA 1, ROI 1, RSA 1.

CREGEEN, Nessy Exh. 1885-92
Portrait painter. Add: Forest Hill, London 1885; Brockley, London 1890. † B 7, L 2, M 1, RA 2.

CREIGHTON, Mary Exh. 1909-11
124 Cheyne Walk, Chelsea, London. † L 1, LS 4, P 1.

CREKAY, G. Exh. 1883
Brussels, Belgium. † GI 1.

CRESPEL, Mdme. Henrietta Exh. 1913
† FIN 1.

CRESPIGNY, de see D

CRESSWELL, A.T. Exh. 1913
East Leake, Loughborough, Leics. † N 1.

CRESSWELL, Miss C.W.B. Exh. 1881
Walton Lodge, Crieff, N.B. † RSA 1.

CRESWELL, Emily Grace b. 1889
Miniature portrait painter. Studied Leicester, Harrogate and Leamington Schools of Art and under S.A. Lindsey in London. A.R.M.S. 1935 Add: Leamington Spa, Warwicks. 1926; London 1933. † B 4. RI 11, RMS 26.

CRESWELL, Frances Exh. 1893
Morning Cross, Hereford. † D 1, SWA 1.

CRESWELL, Henrietta Exh. 1888-98
Flower painter. Add: Winchmore Hill, London. † B 2, GI 8, L 3, M 2, RA 1, RBA 7, RHA 3, RI 5, RSA 2, SWA 9.

CRESWELL, Harry Bulkeley 1869-1960
16 Gt. Marlborough Street, London 1912. † RA 1.

CRESWELL, Herbert Osborn 1860-1919
Architect. Add: London. † RA 17.

CRESWELL, John J. Exh. 1901
Architect. Add: 77 Victoria Street, Grimsby. † RA 1.

CRESWICK, A. Exh. 1906
13 Wellington Square, Chelsea, London. † RA 1.

CRESWICK, Benjamin Exh. 1884-1910
Sculptor, and teacher. R.B.S.A. 1914. Add: London 1884; Liverpool 1886; Manchester 1888; Sutton Coldfield 1890 and 1905; Birmingham 1902. † B 25, L 11, RA 4.

CRESWICK, John Exh. 1922
46 Torphihen Street, Edinburgh. † RSA 1.

CRESWICK, Mortimer Exh. 1882-89
Landscape painter. Add: Llanbedr, Tal-y-bont, Wales, 1882; Liverpool 1889. † L 2, RA 1.

CRETIUS, Prof. Konstantin Franz 1814-1901
Historial figure painter. Add: Royal Academy of Arts, Berlin, Germany 1883. † RA 1.

CREW, Miss G. Exh. 1913-14
Manor House, Higham Ferrers, Northants. † D 4, SWA 2.

CREW, Dr. Helen C. Exh. 1938-40
41 Mansionhouse Road, Edinburgh. † RSA 1, RSW 3.

CREWE, Mrs. Bessie Exh. 1920-28
Cae Coch, Trefriw, Wales. † RCA 7.

CREWE, C.W. Exh. 1920-31
Cae Coch, Trefriw, Wales, † RCA 6.

CREWE, Miss Esther Exh. 1927
Gatley, Dee Bank, Chester. † L 1.

CREYKE, Miss B. Exh. 1901-2
Sewerby, Bridlington, Yorks. 1901; Congleton, Cheshire 1902. † L 3, RI 1.

CRIBB, Joseph Exh. 1928
† GOU 1.

CRIBB, Preston 1876-1937
Illustrator, etcher and cartoonist. Studied Portsmouth and London. Add: 41 Lakey Lane, Hall Green, Birmingham 1920. † B 34, RA 1, RBA 2, RCA 2, ROI 1.

CRIBBES, George O. Exh. 1929-38
16 Springvalley Terrace, Edinburgh. † GI 1, RSA 17.

CRICHTON, A. Exh. 1930-34
College of Art, Belfast, Ireland. † GI 3.

CRICHTON, Edward J. Exh. 1932-37
Edinburgh. † RSA 3.

CRICHTON, James Angus Exh. 1901
34 York Place, Edinburgh. † RSA 1.

CRICHTON, M. Hewan Exh. 1910-22
Sculptor. Add: Birmingham 1910; Bromsgrove, Worcs. 1920. † B 1, RA 2, RSA 5.

CRICHTON, N.S. Exh. 1888-89
Landscape painter. Add: Manningham, Bradford and Leeds, Yorks. † RBA 3.

CRICK, Montague Exh. 1898-1904
Landscape and portrait painter. Add: Norwich, Norfolk. † RA 3.

CRICKMAY, George A. Exh. 1890
Architect. Add: 17 Parliament Street, Westminster, London. † RA 1.

CRICKMER, Courtenay M. Exh. 1909-40
Architect. Add: 1 Lincoln's Inn Fields, London. † RA 12.

CRIDDLE, Mrs. May Ann Exh. 1880
Addlestone, Weybridge, Surrey. † RWS 2.

CRIDLAND, Miss Helen Exh. 1886-1909
Figure painter. Add: Bushey, Herts. † B 3, L 1, NG 1, RA 8, ROI 3.

CRIGHTON, H.A. Exh. 1880-82
Glasgow. † GI 4, RSA 2.

CRIGHTON, Mrs. Louisette Exh. 1932
Twickenham Park, Middlesex. † SWA 1.

CRILLY, Miss Margaret Exh. 1913
6 St. John's Terrace, Clontarf, Dublin, Ireland. † RHA 4.

CRILLEY, Mrs. R. Exh. 1895-98
Fethard, Co. Tipperary, Ireland. † RHA 2.

CRIPPIN, Miss C.M. Exh. 1883-92
44 Wincheap, Canterbury, Kent. † L 6.

CRIPPS, George R. Exh. 1919-20
Gorphwysfa, Llanrwst, Wales. † L 1, RCA 2.

CRISP, Frank E.F. d. 1915
St. John's Wood, London 1906. Probably died on active service. † L 4, RA 5, RSA 1.

CRISP, Miss L.M. Exh. 1908-12
Hampstead, London 1908; Geneva, Switzerland 1912. † L 7, RA 3, RMS 2.

CRIPSE, E. Neale Exh. 1895
Eastworth House, Chertsey, Surrey. † M 1.

CRISPE, Leila Constance Exh. 1885-87
Flower painter. Add: 4 Cheapside, London. † RBA 1, ROI 2.

CRISTALL, Miss Anna Exh. 1888-1904
Portrait painter. Add: London. † B 1, RA 1.

CRISTALL, Walter Exh. 1925-40
Landscape painter. Add: 15 Nassington Road, Hampstead, London. † AG 6, NEA 13, RA 2, RBA 3, RSA 1.

CRITCHLEY-SALMONSON, A. Exh. 1893
1 Rochebury Street, St. Helier, Jersey, C.I. † B 2.

CRITTENDEN, Dora E. Exh. 1884-87
Flower painter. Add: 31 Cantlowes Road, Camden Square, London. † RA 1, SWA 4.

CROALL, Annie A. Exh. 1886
Southfield, Libberton, Lanark. † RSA 1.

CROASDALE, P. Exh. 1952
† L 3.

CROCHEPIERRE, Andre Antoine b. 1860
French artist. Exh. 1901-5. Add: Chemin de Galaup, Villenauve sur Lot, France. † L 3.

CROCKER, A.C. Exh. 1885-86
Bury Green, Cheshunt, Herts. † RI 3.

CROCKER, Barbara b. 1910
Painter, illustrator and lithographer. Studied Slade School. Add: 21 Cromer Villas Road, London 1932. † SWA 1.

CROCKET, Douglas G. Exh. 1901-9
Landscape painter. Add: London 1901; Barcombe, Lewes, Sussex 1905. † RA 4.

CROCKET, Henry Edgar 1870-1926
Landscape, figure and portrait painter. A.R.W.S. 1905, R.W.S. 1913. Add: London 1894; Barcombe, Lewes, Sussex 1908; Bournemouth 1920. † B 1, BG 3, GI 3, L 9, M 1, RA 14, RI 3, ROI 4, RWS 49.

CROCKETT, Dora Exh. 1920-39
Countess Eric Lewenhayst. Flower, landscape and portrait painter. Add: London. † GOU 72, L 1, P 2, RA 2, RBA 1, RI 1, ROI 3.

CROCKFORD, Gertrude Exh. 1881-86
Sculptor. Add: 190 Camden Road, London. † D 2, G 1, L 4, RA 1, RBA 10.

CROEBAR, Paul O. Exh. 1913
9 Palmerston Place, Edinburgh. † RSA 1.

CROEGAERT, Georges* Exh. 1886
Figure painter. Add: 51 Rue Gabrielle, Paris, France. † ,M 2.

CROFT, Arthur Exh. 1889-93
Landscape painter. Add: London 1889; Wadhurst, Sussex 1890. † RA 6.

CROFT, Marion Exh. 1881-86
Watercolour figure painter. S.W.A. 1880. Add: 58 Finchley Road, St. John's Wood, London. † B 1, D 6, SWA 6.

CROFT, Marjorie b. 1889
nee Hall. Painter, etcher and wood engraver. Add: Penshurst, Kent 1927; London 1928. † NEA 15, RA 2, RBA 6, SWA 1.

CROFTON, Mrs. Caldwell
See MILMAN, Helen

CROFTON, Hon. Mrs. Marcus Exh. 1932
Flower painter. Add: Ahascragh, Co. Galway, Ireland. † RHA 2.

CROFTON, Mrs. W.S. Exh. 1898
Johnstown House, Kilternan, Co. Dublin, Ireland. † RHA 1.

CROFTS, Anna Exh. 1898
71 Eccles Street, Dublin, Ireland. † RHA 1.

CROFTS, Ernest* 1847-1911
Illustrator and painter of battle scenes. b. Leeds, Yorks. A.R.A. 1878, R.A. 1896. Add: London. † B 1, GI 1, L 7, M 4, RA 40, ROI 1, TOO 8.

CROFTS, James N. Exh. 1884-97
5 Harrington Street, Liverpool. † L 14.

CROFTS, Mrs. M.H. Exh. 1918-28
West Kirby, Cheshire. † L 9, RHA 2, RSA 2.

CROFTS, Stella Rebecca 1898-1964
Painter and animal sculptor. Studied L.C.C. Central School of Arts and Crafts 1916-22, Royal College of Art 1922-23. A.R.M.S. 1925, A.S.W.A. 1925, S.W.A. 1927. Add: West Kirby, Cheshire 1925; Ilford, Essex 1926; Billericay, Essex 1932. † L 11, RA 2, RMS 53.

CROFTS, William Exh. 1891
33 Princess Court, Bury, Lancs. † L 1.

CROIL, Gladys M. Exh. 1912
Coastal painter. Add: 381 Union Street, Aberdeen. † NEA 1.

CROISTER, Mrs. Walter Exh. 1890
21 Tadema Road, West Brompton, London. † RI 1.

CROKE, Lewis Edmund b. 1875
Pastel artist, etcher and lithographer. Studied L.C.C. Central School of Art. Exh. 1923-32. Add: London. † B 12, D 12, GI 1, L 12, RCA 5.

CROKER, Emily Exh. 1910-17
Glenasmoil, Grosvenor Road, Rathgar, Dublin, Ireland. † RHA 7.

CROMBIE, Allan B. Exh. 1900
Union Chambers, Dumfries. † RSA 1.

CROMBIE, David A. Exh. 1882-89
Edinburgh. † RSA 2.

CROMBIE, Ethel Exh. 1902-23
Clifton, York 1902; Bootham, York 1911. † GI 8, L 17, RCA 15, RHA 12, RI 1, RSA 6.

CROMBIE, Elizabeth E. Exh. 1888-97
Flower painter. Add: 2 Breakspear Road, St. John's Wood, London. † GI 2, RA 3, RI 3.

CROMBIE, Mrs. Frances A. Exh. 1936-37
11 Cranworth Street, Glasgow. † RSW 2.

CROMBIE, Miss Harley B. Exh. 1934
Miniature portrait painter. Add: 158 Holland Road, London. † RA 1.

CROME, J.S. Exh. 1927-34
Landscape painter. Add: Elwinstan, Kingsway, Woking, Surrey. † COO 2, RBA 1.

CROME, Vivian* Exh. 1882-94
Birmingham. † B 18.

CROMIE, Robert Exh. 1936
Architect. Add: 6 Cavendish Square, London. † RA 1.

CROMPTON, Beatrice M. Exh. 1914-16
Corporation Street, Warrington, Lancs. † L 6.

CROMPTON, Miss Cecilia Exh. 1917-25
Animal painter. Add: Stanton by Dale, Nr. Nottingham. † N 12.

CROMPTON, Miss C.C. Exh. 1922-29
"Shap", Westmorland. † L 2.

CROMPTON, Edward Exh. 1893-1921
Sculptor. Add: Shirley, Southampton 1893; Edinburgh 1909. † L 2, RA 2, RSA 10.

CROMPTON, Gertrude b. 1874
Mrs. Hall. Watercolour painter. Studied Westminster School of Art and Paris. Exh. 1897-1927. Add: London 1897; East Clevedon, Somerset 1923; Fowey, Cornwall 1927. † D 3, GOU 3, RI 1, SWA 11.

CROMPTON, John c.1855-1927
Landscape and figure painter. Principal of Heatherley's School of Art 1888-1908. Exh. 1882-86. Add: Hartham Road, Camden Road, London. † B 2, D 1, L 3, M 3, RBA 5, ROI 1.

CROMPTON, James Shaw 1853-1916
Watercolour figure painter. R.I. 1898. Add: Hartham Road, Camden Road, London 1882; Haverstock Hill, London 1897. † AG 4, B 8, D 2, FIN 1, L 34, M 9, RA 2, RBA 10, RI 49.

CROMPTON, Mabel Ann Elizabeth Exh. 1901-30
Landscape, flower, figure and portrait painter and miniaturist. Studied Southport School of Art and Royal College of Art. Assistant teacher Southport School of Art; Supervisor of Art, Brandon, Manitoba, Canada. Add: Southport, Lancs. 1901-15. !† L 16, M 5, RA 1, RCA 8.

CROMPTON, Oswald Exh. 1899-1932
A.R.M.S. 1911, R.M.S. 1914. Add: London 1899; Sunderland 1908; Croydon, Surrey 1920. † L 7, RA 2, ROI 1, RMS 8.

CROMPTON, Vernon Exh. 1919
Architect. Add: 6 John Street, London. † RA 1.

CROMPTON, William E.V. Exh. 1902
Architect. Add: 6 John Street, Bedford Row, London. † RA 1.

CROMPTON-STANSFIELD, Miss E.A. Exh. 1893
Eshott Hall, Shipley, Yorks. † SWA 1.

CRONE, H. Exh. 1914
10 Gt. Ormond Street, London. † RA 1.

CRONK, Edwin Evans Exh. 1881
Architect. Add: 23 Cockspur Street, Charing Cross, London. † RA 1.

CRONYN, Hugh Verschoyle b. 1905
Painter and wood engraver. b. Vancouver, Canada. Add: London 1940. † COO 1, LEF 3.

CROOK, A.W. Exh. 1884
Architect. Add: 37 Carlton Road, Maida Vale, London. † RA 1.

CROOK, Frederick Exh. 1939
† GOU 1.

CROOK, John Exh. 1887
18 Nicholas Street, Dublin, Ireland. † RHA 1.

CROOK, Thomas Mewburn b. 1869
Sculptor. Studied Manchester Technical School and Royal College of Art (3 silver and 5 bronze medals). Assistant modelling master Royal College of Art 1894-95. Modelling master and anatomy lecturer Manchester School of Art 1896-1905. R.B.A. 1910, H.R.I. 1918. Add: Manchester 1897; London 1907-40. † GI 11, L 13, M 12, NG 3, RA 31, RBA 6, RI 12, ROI 4.

CROOKE John Exh. 1890-98
Landscape painter. Add: Newlyn, Penzance, Cornwall 1890; London 1896. † DOW 1, G 1, L 1, M 1, NG 1, RA 2.

CROOKE, Muriel Elise b. 1901
Painter and etcher. Add: 3 Warren Drive, Wallasey, Cheshire. † ALP 1, L 14, RA 2, RCA 3, RHA 1, RSA 2.

CROOKE, Stephen J. Exh. 1937-39
† ROI 2.

CROOKENDEN, Irene M. 1880-1957
Flower painter. Add: Southsea, Hants. 1912; London 1936. † GOU 1, L 2, RA 1, RCA 4, SWA 1.

CROOKES, H. Exh. 1911-24
Landscape and portrait painter. Add: Nottingham. † N 10.

CROOKS, James Exh. 1939
† GOU 1.

CROOKS, Samuel Exh. 1882-83
197 Canongate, Edinburgh. † RSA 2.

CROOKSHANK, Miss M. Exh. 1920
Ardglas, Dundrum, Co. Dublin, Ireland. † RHA 1.

CROOM-JOHNSON, Millicent Eugene (Ena) b. 1903
nee Cabuche. Miniature painter. A.R.M.S. 1923. Add: Putney 1922; Windsor, Berks. 1928; Datchet, Berks. 1931; Westcliffe-on-Sea, Essex 1933. † L 8, RA 11, RMS 45.

CROPP, Miss E. Exh. 1914
46a Pelham Street, Kensington, London. † RA 1.

CROPSEY, Jaspar Francis* 1823-1900
American landscape and seascape artist. Add: Hastings-upon-the-Hudson. New York. U.S.A. 1889. † L 1.

CROSBEE, Mrs. W.G. Exh. 1927
21 Claremont Crescent, Edinburgh. † RSA 1.

CROSBIE, L. Stanley Exh. 1911-24
Architect. Add: London. † RA 5.

CROSBIE, William Exh. 1937
7 Lindsay Place, Glasgow. † RSA 2.

CROSBY, G. Exh. 1916-21
Leamington Spa, Warwicks. 1916 and 1921; London 1917. † RA 3.

CROSBY, Miss G.D. Exh. 1920-23
3 Union Street, Liverpool 1920; Birkenhead 1923. † L 5.

CROSBY, J. Lionel Exh. 1940
Flower painter. Add: 7 St. Margaret's Square, Cherry Hinton Road, Cambridge. † RA 1.

CROSBY, Percy b. 1891
American painter, lithographer and cartoonist. Exh. 1935. † AR 115.

CROSFIELD, Miss Gertrude Exh. 1897-99
14 Bedston Road, Oxton, Birkenhead. † L 2.

CROSFIELD, Miss H. Exh. 1895-97
46 Bedston Road, Oxton, Birkenhead. † L 2.

CROSFIELD, Miss L. Exh. 1892-94
46 Bedston Road, Oxton, Birkenhead. † L 2.

CROSFORD, Miss Agnes M. Exh. 1896
Ivydene, Brentford, Essex. † B 3.

CROSHER, Miss S.A.G. Exh. 1937
30 Blairgowrie Road, Cardonald, Glasgow. † RSA 1.

CROSLAND, Enoch Exh. 1880-90
Landscape painter. N.S.A. 1882. Add: Nottingham 1880; Whatstandwell, Derbys. 1883; Duffield, Derbys. 1886. † B 1, N 60, RA 4, RBA 1.

CROSLEY, Edith A. Exh. 1880-94
Landscape and figure painter. Add: London 1880; Newark, Notts. 1885. † L 1, N 1, RA 1, RBA 7, ROI 1, SWA 4.

CROSLEY, Gladys D. Exh. 1922-26
Queen's Hotel, Park Entrance, Birkenhead. † L 2.

CROSNIER, Jules Exh. 1902-3
Landscape painter. Add: 8 Exhibition Road, South Kensington, London. † L 2, RA 2.

CROSS, A. Campbell Exh. 1897
22 Oakley Crescent, Chelsea, London. † RA 1.

CROSS, Alfred W. Exh. 1881-1912
Architect. Add: London 1881 and 1903; Hastings 1885. † RA 10.

CROSS, Frederick A. Exh. 1933
† RSW 2.

CROSS, F. Henry Exh. 1928-29
Landscape painter. Add: Nottingham. † N 2.

CROSS, Miss Gwendoline Exh. 1927-39
Bristol. † L 4, RA 1, RBA 1, SWA 4.

CROSS, J. Exh. 1898-1939
Grantham, Lincs. † N 10.

CROSS, Joseph Exh. 1883-96
Landscape painter. Add: Preston, Lancs. † L 14, RA 2.

CROSS, Kenneth M.B. Exh. 1934-39
Architect of Public Baths. Add: 45 New Bond Street, London. † RA 7.

CROSS, Max Exh. 1896-98
Landscape painter. Add: 13 Eglantine Road, Wandsworth, London. † RA 1, RI 1.

CROSS, Odo Exh. 1926
Landscape, flower and portrait painter. † ALP 27.

CROSS, Thomas B. Exh. 1894-96
Landscape painter. Add: Royal Avenue, Scarborough, Yorks. † RA 2, ROI 1.

CROSS, T.G. Exh. 1933
St. Leonard's, Grafton Drive, Upton, Wirral, Cheshire. † L 1.

CROSSE, Edward Exh. 1923-33
London. † RI 17.

CROSSE, Edwin Reeve Exh. 1888-1912
Landscape, figure and portrait painter. Add: Headingley, Leeds, Yorks. 1888 and 1896; Bushey, Herts. 1890. † RA 7.

CROSSE, Thomas Warren 1851-1938
Watercolour painter. Studied law which he gave up for art and studied at Slade School. Add: 3 Garden Studios, Manresa Road, Chelsea. † RBA 4, WG 24.

CROSSKEY, L.R. Exh. 1882
28 George Road, Edgbaston, Birmingham. † B 1.

CROSSKEY, Miss R.M. Exh. 1920
54 Portland Road, Edgbaston, Birmingham. † B 2.

CROSSLAND, E.H. Exh. 1882-85
Liverpool. † L 2.

CROSSLAND, H.S. Exh. 1913
24 New Market Street, Blackburn, Lancs. † L 1.

CROSSLAND, James Henry b. 1852
Landscape painter. Add: Belper 1884; South Langrigge, Windermere 1889; Broughton-in-Furness 1903; Ambleside 1924. † B 15, L 5, M 4, N 15, RA 10, RBA 1, RCA 24.

CROSSLAND, William Henry Exh. 1881-84
Architect. Add: Egham, Surrey 1881; London 1884. † RA 5.

CROSSLEY, Miss Clare Exh. 1928-31
26 Mallord Street, London. † NEA 3.

CROSSLEY, Cuthbert b. 1883
Painter and etcher. Add: Halifax, Yorks. † AB 6, B 10, GI 2, L 8, RA 6, RBA 3, RI 6, RSA 12.

CROSSMAN, Mrs. M.P. Exh. 1929
17 Hougomont Avenue, Waterloo, Liverpool. † L 1.

CROSSTHWAITE, Miss Edith Exh. 1907
Quinta das Maravillias, Madeira. † L 1.

CROSTON, J.A. Exh. 1932
† L 1.

CROSTON, Frank Exh. 1928-30
23 Falkner Square, Liverpool. † L 4.

CROUCH, Alice L. Exh. 1907-8
West Kirby, Cheshire. † L 2.

CROUCH, A. Rutledge Exh. 1936
† RI 1.

CROUCH, Henry A. Exh. 1905-8
Architect. Add: 19 Gray's Inn Square, London. † RA 2.

CROUDACE, Mrs. E.H. Exh. 1880-81
Figure, portrait and landscape painter. Add: 2 Stow House, North End, Hampstead, London. † SWA 4.

CROUEE, de la See D

CROUSE, M. Exh. 1907
Ashley Villa, Dane Road, Sale, Cheshire. † L 1.

CROW, Margaret G. Exh. 1897
Domestic Painter. Add: 21 Penywern Road, Earl's court, London. † RA 1.

CROW, Richard W. Exh. 1928
53 Greville Road, Emscote, Warwick. † B 2.

CROWDY, Constance E. Exh. 1899-1919
Nr. Kingsbridge, Devon. † L 4, LS 3, RCA 3, SWA 1.

CROWDY, Rose Exh. 1895
Figure painter. Add: 1 Higher Terrace, Torquay, Devon. † RA 1.

CROWE, A. Casmeh Exh. 1912
228 Castillain Mansions, Maida Vale, London. † LS 2.

CROWE, Miss A.K. Exh. 1895
4 New Brighton, Monkstown, Co. Dublin, Ireland. † RHA 1.

CROWE, Mrs. Constance Exh. 1922-27
Sculptor. Add: 12 Kensington Court Place, London. † RA 1, SWA 1.

CROWE, Eyre* 1824-1910
Historical, domestic and portrait painter. Studied under Paul Delaroche. Visited Rome 1843. Secretary to Thackeray and accompanied him on a lecture tour of America in 1852. A.R.A. 1876. Add: London. † L 13, M 7, RA 62.

CROWHURST, Julia M. Exh. 1897-1940
Miniature portrait painter. Add: London. † GI 1, L 2, RA 4, RI 2, RMS 1.

CROWLE, Mark Exh. 1886
66 Green Lanes, Stoke Newington, London. † D 1.

CROWSON, Mrs. F.J. Exh. 1916
19 Portland Street, Newark-on-Trent, Notts. † N 1.

CROWTHER, H.A. Exh. 1905
51 Birmingham Road, West Bromwich. † B 1.

CROWTHER, Miss H.V. Exh. 1889
Ramsden House, Slaithwaite, Nr. Huddersfield. † M1.

CROWTHER, John Exh. 1886-1902
Landscape painter. Add: London 1886 and 1890; Reading, Berks. 1889. † D 2, RA 7, RBA 1 RI 5.

CROWTHER, Mrs. Margaret Exh. 1925-36
Miniature portrait painter. Add: York. † L 8, RA 2, RCA 2, RHA 1, RSA 3.

CROWTHER, W.E. Exh. 1924-40
267 Barcley Road, Warley Woods 1925; Edgbaston, Birmingham 1934. † B 22.

CROXFORD, Agnes McIntyre Exh. 1897-1910
Mrs. Freeman Smith. Add: Brentford, Essex 1897; London 1902. † B 25.

CROXFORD, Grace Marie Exh. 1912-30
Mrs. G.D. Butterworth. b. Hastings. Daughter of William Edward C. q.v. Studied under Lionel Heath. Add: Newquay, Cornwall. † RA 7, RMS 3.

CROXFORD, Thomas Swainson Exh. 1880-84
Landscape painter. Add: Brentford, Essex. † RA 2, RBA 2, ROI 2.

CROXFORD, William Edward Exh. 1882-97
Landscape and marine painter. Add: Brentford, Essex 1882; St. Leonards-on-Sea 1886; Hastings 1889; St. Ives, Cornwall 1892; Newquay, Cornwall 1894. † FIN 6, L 1, RA 5, RBA 6, RI 6.

CROZIER, Miss Anne Jane Exh. 1882-1908
Figure and landscape painter. Add: Manchester. † M 11, RA 1, RCA 10, RI 4.

CROZIER, Lt. F.R. Exh. 1919
87 Clifton Hill, St. John's Wood, London. † RA 1.

CROZIER, George d. 1915
Landscape painter. Add: London 1880; Tal-y-bont, Conway, Wales 1882; Bolton-le-Sands, Carnforth, Lancs. 1893. † L 2, M 28, RA 2, RCA 88, RI 1.

CROZIER, Ivor D. Exh. 1927
53 Wake Green Road, Moseley, Birmingham. † B 1.

CROZIER, Miss M.J. Exh. 1897
826 Stockport Road, Manchester. † M 1.

CROZIER, Robert Exh. 1882
Domestic painter. Add: 47 Sidney Street, Manchester. † RA 1.

CROZIER, William d. 1931
A.R.S.A. 1930. Add: Edinburgh. † GI 10, L 2, RSA 41, RSW 3.

CRUICKSHANK, Amy W. Exh. 1897
Clevedon, Somerset. † RMS 1.

CRUICKSHANK, Catherine Gertrude Exh. 1882-89
Miniature portrait painter. Add: London. † RA 9.

CRUICKSHANK, Doris M.L. Exh. 1926-27
St. Leonard's. Banff 1926; Glasgow 1927. † GI 3, RSA 2.

CRUICKSHANK, F. Exh. 1880-81
Edinburgh. † RSA 2.

CRUICKSHANK, George Exh. 1921
Norwood, Linlithgow. † RSA 1.

CRUICKSHANK, Mary Exh. 1929-30
Landscape painter. Add: Maingerton, Foxrock, Co. Dublin, Ireland. † RHA 4.

CRUICKSHANK, William Exh. 1880-86
Still life, fruit, bird, game and genre painter. Add: London. † L 6, RBA 15.

CRUIKSHANK, Alfred G. Exh.1913
35 Hartley Road, Leytonstone, Essex. † LS 3.

CRUIKSHANK, Dora Exh. 1884-1911
Figure, flower and landscape painter. Add: London. † RI 1, SWA 6.

CRUIKSHANK, Mrs. Elizabeth Exh. 1938-40
2 Park Circus, Glasgow. † GI 3.

CRUIKSHANK, George* c.1842-1909
Still life painter on ivory. Add: Edinburgh. † GI 4, RSA 18.

CRUIKSHANK, Grace Exh. 1884-94
Miniature painter. Add: London. † RA 4, RI 2. SWA 1.

CRUIKSHANK, Miss H. Exh. 1913
4 Rue de Chevreuse, Paris, France. † RA 2.

CRUIKSHANK, Ronald Exh. 1933
7 Ardmillan Terrace, Edinburgh. † RSA 1.

CRUIKSHANK, R.A. Exh. 1887-1904
Kilmun, Nr. Greenock and Glasgow. † GI 9, L 10, RBA 2, RSA 4.

CRUM, Paul see PETTIWARD Roger

CRUMP, Arthur Exh. 1896-99
10 Clissold Road, London. † ROI 1.

CRUMP, Gerda Exh. 1901-5
London 1901; Richmond, Surrey 1905. † D 5, SWA 1.

CRUTTWELL, Grace Exh. 1903-40
Portrait painter. Add: Bushey, Herts. 1903; St. Andrews 1918; Frome, Somerset 1919; Rhyl 1937. † RA 1, RCA 7, RSA 4.

CRUTTWELL, Maud Exh. 1889-94
Domestic painter. Add: London. † RA 1, ROI 14, SWA 2.

CRUTTWELL, W.H.G. Exh. 1907-15
Oxford Lodge, St. Leonard's Road, Surbiton, Surrey. † P 1, RA 5.

CUBBIN, Miss I. Exh. 1920-28
Cliftonville, Breck Road, Wallasey, Cheshire. † L 56.

CUBBON, Thomas W. Exh. 1888-1903
51 Hamilton Square, Birkenhead. † L 6.

CUBITT, Charlotte Exh. 1880
Mrs. L. Sculptor. Add: 22 Hill Street, Berkeley Square, London. † RA 1.

CUBITT, Miss Edith Alice See ANDREWS

CUBITT, James Exh. 1883-90
Architect. Add: 3 Broad Street Buildings, London. † RA 5.

CUBLEY, Gertrude Exh. 1887-1903
Landscape painter. Married to H. Hadfield C. q.v. Add: Montpellier, Matlock Bath, Derbys. † B 2, M 2, N 7.

CUBLEY, H. Hadfield Exh. 1882-1904
Landscape painter. Add: Newark, Notts. 1882; Wolverhampton 1884; Montpellier, Matlock Bath, Derbys. 1887. † B 22, GI 4, L 5, M 2, N 34, RA 3, RBA 3, ROI 3, RSA 2.

CUBLEY, William Harold 1816-1896
Landscape painter. Add: Newark, Notts. 1880 and 1894; Wolverhampton 1885. † B 1, N 17, RBA 1.

CUCUEL, Edward b. 1879
American artist. Add: Klarstrasse 5, Munich, Bavaria 1924. † L 1.

CUENOT, Henry Exh. 1913
† ALP 1.

CUFF, Miss Kathleen R. Exh. 1908-19
Preston Bank, Chorley, Lancs. † B 1, L 8.

CULL, Alma Burlton Exh. 1906-27
Marine painter. Add: Chiswick, London 1906; Harrow-on-the-Hill, Middlesex 1908. † ALP 98, B 2, BRU 1, L 1, LS 12, RA 3, RI 6.

CULL, James Allanson Exh. 1880-86
Figure painter. Add: Thornton Heath, Surrey and London. † D 2, L 1, RA 2, RI 1, RSA 1.

CULLEN, Alex Exh. 1891-1929
Architect. Add: Motherwell, Edinburgh and Hamilton. † GI 33, RA 2, RSA 13.

CULLEN, Alexander Exh. 1925-38
88 Cadzow Street, Hamilton, N.B. † GI 16.

CULLEN, Frederick Exh. 1880-1911
Landscape, figure and portrait painter. N.S.A. 1890. Add: Nottingham 1880; Gerrard's Cross, Bucks. 1895. † L 1, N 24, NG 2, RA 5.

CULLEN, Mrs. G.M. Exh. 1905
† SWA 1.

CULLEN, John Exh. 1906
461 Albert Road, Langside, Glasgow. † RI 3.

CULLEN, Nora H. Exh. 1933-40
Mrs. J.B. Flower painter. Add: Sevenoaks, Kent. † RA 1, RBA 3, RI 6, ROI 10, SWA 7, WG 60.

CULLEN, W. Exh. 1884-87
3 Cumberland Place, North Circular Road, Dublin, Ireland. † RHA 4.

CULLIN, Isaac* Exh. 1881-89
Figure and portrait painter. Add: Kensington, London. † L 1, RA 4.

CULLUM, Annie Exh. 1898
Figure painter. Add: Oaklands, Chingford, Essex. † RA 1.

CULMER, Miss A. Exh. 1919
Speldhurst, Faversham, Kent. † SWA 1.

CULPEPER, Nellie C. Bishop Exh. 1885-1917
Figure painter. Add: Wraysbury, Bucks. 1885; London 1902; Barnet, Herts. 1911; Watton, Norfolk 1917. † I 1, LS 3, RA 3, SWA 2.

CULVER, Fred Exh. 1890-94
Landscape and river painter. Add: London. † RA 1, RBA 10, RI 1.

CULVERT, Edith Exh. 1887
† SWA 1.

CULVERWELL, Celia P. Exh. 1886-1926
Dublin, Ireland. † D 11, RHA 32.

CULVERWELL, Josephine Exh. 1887-1926
Dublin, Ireland. † D 11, RHA 38.

CUMBERBATCH, Mrs. Exh. 1884
Landscape painter. Add: 25 Cadogan Place, London. † SWA 3.

CUMBERBATCH, Edward b. 1877
Exh. 1923-32. Add: 3 Tonge Park Avenue, Bolton, Lancs. † L 1, RCA 2.

CUMBERLAND, Miss Olive Exh. 1908
The Lynchet, Luton, Beds. † B 1.

CUMBERLEGE, Mrs. Phyllis L. Exh. 1931-35
Miniature portrait painter. Add: 129 The Grove, Ealing, London. † RA 4.

CUMMING, Miss Ann Exh. 1938
46 Clarence Drive, Glasgow. † GI 1.

CUMMING, Mrs. Belle Skeoch Exh. 1938-40
31 Buckingham Terrace, Edinburgh. † GI 2, RSA 2, RSW 2.

CUMMING, Miss C.F. Exh. 1882-83
Glencairn House, Crieff. † RSA 3.

CUMMING, Constance H. Exh. 1895-1910
Miniature painter. Add: Dedham, Essex 1895; Bushey, Herts. 1897 and 1910; Ipswich, Suffolk 1898. † RA 8, RMS 4.

CUMMING, Jane Ferguson Exh. 1889
1 Bath Place, Portobello, Midlothian. † RSA 1.

CUMMING, James M. Exh. 1919-20
Figure painter. Add: Kilncroft, Helensburgh, N.B. † GI 1, RA 1, RSA 3.

CUMMING, Miss L.M. Exh. 1928
30 High Street, Tarporley, Cheshire. † L 1.

CUMMING, Marion Gordon Exh. 1907-20
Miniature painter. Add: Wimbledon, London. † RA 3.

CUMMING, R.J. Exh. 1892-1909
Dalmuir, N.B. 1892; Glasgow 1902; Lenzie, N.B. 1904; Bridge of Allan, N.B. 1907. † GI 16, RSA 1.

CUMMING, W. Skeoch Exh. 1885-1906
Figure and military painter. Add: Edinburgh. † L 1, NG 1, RA 2, RSA 48.

CUMMINGS, Erskine S. Exh. 1913-20
Architect. Add: London. † RA 2.

CUMMINGS, Lawrence Exh. 1933
Flower painter. † FIN 2.

CUMMINGS, Miss Margaret Exh. 1919
Miniature painter. Add: 29 Ella Road, Crouch End, London. † L 1, RA 1.

CUMMINGS, V.J. Exh. 1905
9 Werter Road, Putney, London. † RA 2.

CUMMINS, Jennie Exh. 1885
Coastal and Canadian landscape painter. Add: 185 High Road, Lee. † SWA 3.

CUNARD, Mrs. William (L) Exh. 1890-1907
95 Eaton Square, London. † RBA 15, ROI 2.

CUNARD, W.S. Exh. 1890-93
Landscape painter. Add: London 1890; Tilehurst, Berks. 1891; Pangbourne, Berks. 1892. † RBA 13.

CUNDALL, Charles Ernest* 1890-1971
Landscape and portrait painter, pottery and stained glass artist. b. Lancashire. Spent part of his childhood in the Philippines and Austrália. Studied Manchester School of Art, Royal College of Art, Slade School, Paris and Italy. Also visited Sweden and Russia. Designer under Gordon Forsyth at Pilkington Pottery Co. N.E.A. 1924, A.R.A. 1937, R.P. 1934. Purchased by Chantrey Bequest "Bank Holiday, Brighton" 1933 and "Building in Berkeley Square" 1938. Exh. 1918-40. Add: Chelsea, London. † AG 1, BA 1, BK 2, CG 65, CHE 5, CON 2, FIN 4, G 44, GI 6, GOU 13, I 1, L 12, LEI 42, M 23, NEA 81, P 11, RA 60, RHA 1, RSA 3, RWS 34.

CUNDELL, Helena b. 1893
nee Scott. Sculptor. Studied Slade School. Add: 3 Acacia Gardens, London 1929. † RA 2.

CUNDELL, Naomi Exh. 1883-92
Flower and domestic painter. Add: Reading, Berks. 1883; Malvern, Worcs. 1891. † B 3, RA 1, RBA 1, SWA 10.

CUNDELL, Nora Lucy Mowbray 1889-1948
Painter and writer. Studied Slade School and Westminster. Add: London 1914; Dorney, Bucks. 1932. † BA 2, CHE 6, G 9, GOU 17, I 2, M 3, NEA 19, RA 16, RSA 1, SWA 5.

CUNDY, Alice Langford see SPEAIGHT

CUNEO, Cyrus* 1878-1916
Painter and illustrator. b. San Francisco, U.S.A. R.O.I. 1908. Add: Paris 1900; London 1902. † GI 5, L 6, RA 13, RHA 9, ROI 16.

CUNEO, Nell Marion Exh. 1893-1940
nee Tenison. Married Cyrus C. q.v. Figure painter. Studied Cope and Nicoll School, London 1879 and Paris. S.W.A. 1918. Add: London 1893 and 1937; St. Ives, Cornwall 1925. † GOU 1, L 1, RA 11, RBA 1, RHA 1, ROI 1, SWA 46.

CUNEO, Terence T.* Exh. 1936-39
47A Priory Road, London. † ROI 5.

CUNINGHAM, Miss F. Exh. 1913
Queen Alexandra's House, Kensington Gore, London. † RA 1.

CUNINGHAM, Oswald Hamilton b. 1883
Painter and etcher, black and white artist and illustrator. Studied Dublin Metropolitan School of Art and Slade School. Add: Dublin, Ireland 1920; London 1922. † L 2, RA 4, RHA 12.

CUNINGHAM, Vera d. 1955
Figure and portrait painter. Member London Group 1927. Exh. 1937-40. † COO 8, LEI 2.

CUNLIFFE, Mrs. A.M. Exh. 1906
Windlesham Hall, Bagshot, Surrey. † B 1.

CUNLIFFE, R.H. Exh. 1911
5 Birch Street, Accrington, Lancs. † RA 2.

CUNNINGHAM, A.W. Exh. 1883-86
Edinburgh. † GI 2, RSA 1.

CUNNINGHAM, Mrs. Georgina Exh. 1888-93
1 Keswick Road, Putney, London. † GI 2, RA 1.

CUNNINGHAM, Jane Exh. 1886-97
Glasgow. † GI 8, RSA 1.

CUNNINGHAM, Jessie C. Exh. 1880
Ettrick Road, Edinburgh. † RSA 1.

CUNNINGHAM, Miss M.D. Exh. 1905
Higher Tranmere College, Birkenhead. † L 1.

CUNNINGHAM, Miss M.L.D. Exh. 1891-92
Liberton House, Midlothian. † RSA 2.

CUNNINGHAM, Miss S.S. Exh. 1886-99
Flower painter. Add: Pollokshields 1886; Glasgow 1892. † GI 5, NEA 1, RSA 5.

CUNNINGHAM, T.E. Exh. 1892
16 Spittal Street, Edinburgh. † RSA 1.

CUNNINGHAM, Victor Exh. 1916-24
Portrait painter. Add: Reading, Berks. † RA 2.

CUNNINGTON, Anna Exh. 1938
† NEA 1.

CUNYNGHAM, Helen Dick Exh. 1888
Caskilben, Aberdeen. † RSA 1.

CUNYNGHAM, Mrs. V. Dick Exh. 1939
† RI 1.

CUNYNGHAME, Eleanor A. Blair Exh. 1903
18 Rothesay Place, Edinburgh. † RSA 1.

CURLING, Gladys Spencer Exh. 1925-39
Hitchin, Herts. 1925; Walmer, Deal, Kent 1939. † SWA 3.

CURNOCK, James Jackson* 1839-1892
Landscape painter. Add: 7 Richmond Hill, Clifton, Bristol. † B 22, D 4, DOW 4, FIN 1, L 24, M 11, RA 7, RBA 16, RCA 25, RHA 2, RI 17

CURNOW, Millicent Exh. 1933-40
47 Cambridge Road, King's Heath, Birmingham. † B 13.

CURPHEY, D.A. Exh. 1912
Cronk-e-Thatcher, Colby, I.o.M. † L 1.

CURPHY, William Exh. 1889-93
48 Bank Road, Bootle, Lancs. † L 5.

CURR, Amy Exh. 1892-93
Seafield, Aberdeen. † GI 4.

CURR, James B.S. Exh. 1934
7 Wellmeadow Street, Paisley. † GI 1.

CURREY, Ada Exh. 1881-90
Landscape painter. Add: Weybridge Heath, Surrey. † B 1, RI 2, SWA 10.

CURREY, Esme Mary Evelyn Exh. 1908-40
Painter and etcher. b. London. Studied Melbourne, Slade and Goldsmith's College. A.R.E. 1937, A.R.M.S. 1929. Add: London. † B 3, C 5, L 1, NEA 2, RA 8, RBA 4, RE 10, RHA 1, RMS 24.

CURREY, Fanny W. Exh. 1880-99
Figure, flower, landscape and interior painter. S.W.A. 1886. Add: Lismore, Ireland. † B 4, D 22, FIN 6, G 8, GI 1, L 11, M 8, NG 14, RA 20, RBA 3, RHA 15, RI 19, ROI 12, SWA 29.

CURREY, W.F. Exh. 1916
65 Park Mansions, Knightsbridge, London. † RI 1.

CURRIE, Exh. 1918
† I 1.

CURRIE, Andrew Exh. 1881
Darnick by Melrose, Scotland. † GI 1.

CURRIE, Enid M. Exh. 1925
26 Lansdown Place, Cheltenham, Glos. † B 4.

CURRIE, Isabella Exh. 1885
16 Roxburgh Street, Edinburgh. † RSA 1.

CURRIE, James Exh. 1880-87
Sculptor. Add: 240 Oxford Street, London. † RA 2.

CURRIE, Jessie Exh. 1897-1916
Watercolour painter. Add: London. † RA 3, RI 1.

CURRIE, John* Exh. 1914-15
5 John Dickie Street, Kilmarnock. † GI 2.

CURRIE, Mrs. John Exh. 1919
45 West Street, Newcastle. † NEA 1.

CURRIE, J.C. Exh. 1934-37
35 West Graham Street, Glasgow. † GI 6.

CURRIE, John S. c.1884-1914
Figure painter. N.E.A. 1914. Add: Dublin, Ireland 1909; London 1912. † ALP 1, CHE 35, GOU 4, NEA 7, RA 2, RHA 4.

CURRIE, Maud Exh. 1912-16
Edinburgh. † GI 2, RSA 1.

CURRIE, Robert Exh. 1881-85
Etcher. Add: Bridge of Earn, Perthshire. † RA 1, RE 2.

CURRIE, Sidney d. 1930
Landscape painter. R.B.S.A. 1921. Add: Birmingham 1882; Worcester 1901; Hereford 1906; Edgbaston, Birmingham 1909; Churchdown, Glos. 1928. † B 122, GI 2, L 4, M 3, RA 1, RBA 1, RCA 6.

CURRIE, William Exh. 1938
52 Murchiston Street, Greenock. † GI 2.

CURRY, Harry S. Exh. 1932-35
Landscape and interior painter. Add: Ipswich, Suffolk. † RA 3.

CURSITER, Stanley 1887-1976
Landscape and figure painter and lithographer. Studied Edinburgh School of Art and RA Schools. Director of National Galleries of Scotland 1930. A.R.S.A. 1927, R.S.A. 1938, R.S.W. 1914. Served with Scottish Rifles in France World War I. Exh. 1909-40. Add: Edinburgh. † BAR 2, CG 1, G 2, GI 30, L 28, RA 9, RHA 6, RI 1, RSA 69, RSW 45.

CURTICE, George M. Exh. 1885-88
Sculptor. Add: London. † RA 3.

CURTIS, Annie Exh. 1880
Thurlow House, Hampstead, London. † SWA 1.

CURTIS, Miss A.N. Exh. 1886-87
Ebberly, Greenock. † GI 2.

CURTIS, Dora Exh. 1899-1901
Figure painter. Add: 67 Frith Street, Soho, London. † NEA 2.

CURTIS, Miss E. Exh. 1880-87
Greenbank, Greenock. † GI 5.

CURTIS, Elizabeth b. 1873
American figure, landscape and portrait painter. Exh. 1931. † ALP 46.

CURTIS, E.M. Exh. 1887
27 Bentinck Street, Greenock. † GI 1.

CURTIS, E.M. Emmie Exh. 1894
19 Lascon Place, Alfred Street North, Nottingham. † N 1.

CURTIS, George D. Exh. 1882-98
Landscape painter. Add: Fulham Place, Higher Broughton, London. † FIN 2, G 1, L 9, M 9, NEA 5, RA 7, RSA 1.

CURTIS, Gertrude M. Exh. 1905-14
Landscape painter. Add: London. † I 3, L 5, LS 15, NEA 1, RA 6, ROI 2.

CURTIS, Nora Exh. 1932-40
Figure painter and illustrator. Add: London. † RA 1, ROI 1.

CURTIS, Miss R.F. Exh. 1887-91
Flower painter. Add: 37 Springfield Road, St. John's Wood, London. † RBA 2, RI 1, SWA 1.

CURTIS, Ralph Wormsley 1854-1922
Landscape and coastal painter. Add: London 1882; Venice 1883; Lucerne, Switzerland 1886. † G 1, M 2, RA 1.

CURTOIS, Ella R. Exh. 1884-1913
Sculptor. Sister of Mary Henrietta Dering C. q.v. Add: Lincoln 1884 and 1893; Paris 1885; Lands End, Cornwall 1913. † L 1, RA 3, SWA 2.

CURTOIS, Mary Henrietta Dering d. 1929
Landscape and portrait painter. Sister of Ella R.C. q.v. Studied Lincoln School of Art, Juliens, Paris and London. Add: Lincoln 1886; London 1896; Little Missenden, Bucks. 1909. † B 2, L 1, LS 24, N 7, NG 1, P 1, RA 4, SWA 13.

CURTOVICH, Oride Exh. 1892
Landscape painter. Add: Atelier's Passage, Smyrna. † RA 2.

CURWEN, A.E. Exh. 1906
16 Falconer Road, Bushey, Herts. † RA 1.

CURWEN, Clare Winifred Exh. 1924-34
Flower painter. Add: London. † L 2, RA 1, ROI 1, SWA 1.

CURWEN, Edward Exh. 1922-30
Glasgow 1922; Rutherglen 1923; Greenock 1927. † GI 4, RSA 1.

CURWEN, Robert Exh. 1929
207 Breck Road, Liverpool. † L 1.

CURZON, Stanley B. Exh. 1915
99 Upper Parliament Street, Liverpool. † L 1.

CUSHING, Alice Whitlia Exh. 1905-7
Oxford 1905; Llanfairfechan, Wales 1907. † L 1, RHA 3.

CUSSONS, Mrs. K.B. Exh. 1882-87
Flower painter. Add: Southport, Lancs. 1882; Liverpool 1884. † B 3, L 1, M 6, SWA 4.

CUST, Emmeline Mary Elizabeth b. 1867
nee Welby. Mrs. Henry C. Signs work "Nina Cust". Sculptor and author. Add: Grantham, Lincs. 1893; London 1897-1927. † L 1, NG 3, RA 2.

CUTFIELD, Mrs Emily Mary Exh. 1908-13
St. Leonards-on-Sea, Sussex 1908; Farnham, Surrey 1913. † LS 4, RA 1.

CUTHBERT, Diana M. Exh. 1940
† NEA 1.

CUTHBERT, Mrs. Gwen Exh. 1923
Illustrator. Add: 38 Bingham Terrace, Dundee. † RSA 1.

CUTHBERT, J.S. Exh. 1884
101 Cheyne Walk, Chelsea, London. † L 1.

CUTHBERT, Margot Lindsey b. 1893
nee Spring. b. Tiverton, Devon. Add: 28 Northcote Road, St. Margaret's on Thames 1925. † L 2, RA 1.

CUTHBERTSON, Alice Exh. 1880-87
Landscape and flower painter. Add: Rome 1880; London 1886. † RSA 1, SWA 4.

CUTHBERTSON, David P. Exh. 1940
3 Wilmot Street, Glasgow. † GI 1, RSW 2.

CUTHBERTSON, J. Exh. 1887-93
Kilmarnock. † GI 4.

CUTHBERTSON, Kenneth J. Exh. 1920-40
Inveresk, Midlothian 1920; Edinburgh 1922; Corstorphine 1929. † GI 3, L 3, RSA 17, RSW 16.

CUTHBERTSON, Thomas D. Exh. 1930-34
Goldsmith. R.B.S.A. 1932. Add: 30 Colmore Road, King's Heath, Birmingham. † B 10.

CUTHBERTSON, Mrs. W. Exh. 1891-1914
Edinburgh. † GI 2, RSA 6.

CUTHBERTSON, William A. Exh 1920
Elmhurst, St. Peter's Road, Croydon, Surrey. † RA 1.

CUTHILL, Walter M. Exh. 1929-33
4 Magdala Mews, Edinburgh. † RSA 3.

CUTLER, Miss C. Exh. 1919-23
Mrs. Lilly. Add: London. † NEA 1, LS 3, WG 36.

CUTLER, Cecil E. Exh. 1886
Springfield, Putney, London. † L 1, RBA 1.

CUTLER, Ernest J.H. Exh. 1887
Landscape painter. Add: 12 Hermitage Villas, Highgate Rise, London. † RBA 2.

CUTLER, Thomas William Exh. 1880-1901
Architect. Add: 5 Queen Square, Bloomsbury, London. † RA 11.

CUTTING, Harry F. Exh. 1896-1901
Painter and etcher. Add: Beccles, Suffolk 1896; London 1899; Wyvenhoe, Essex 1901. † RA 3, RBA 1.

CUTTS, John T. Exh. 1885-86
6 Renshaw Street, Liverpool. † D 1, RI 1.

CUYER, Monsieur E. Exh. 1882
16 Avenue Trudaine, Paris, France. † RHA 1.

CUZNER, Miss A. Exh. 1938
92 Carless Avenue, Harborne, Birmingham. † B 5.

CUZNER, Bernard b. 1877
Jeweller. R.B.S.A. 1931. Collaborated with his wife Ethel C. q.v. Add: Bourneville, Birmingham 1903; King's Norton, Birmingham 1931; 92 Carless Avenue, Harborne, Birmingham 1936. † B 21, L 74, NG 3.

CUZNER, Ethel Exh. 1920-31
Jeweller. Collaborated with her husband Bernard C. q.v. Add: Birmingham. † B 3, L 33.

CUZNER, Miss F.S. Exh. 1932
342 Selby Oak Road, King's Norton, Birmingham. † B 1.

"CYNICUS" see ANDERSON, Martin

CYNWALL-JONES, Hilda M. Exh. 1929
Lark Hill, Conway, Wales. † L 1.

CYRIAX, Miss Tony Exh. 1914-15
Figure painter. Add: 23 Abergare Gardens, Hampstead, London. † NEA 7.

CYRLAS-WILLIAMS, J. Exh. 1928
29 Gt. Western Road, London. † RBA 2.

CZEDEKOWSKI, Boleslaw Jan b. 1885
Polish figure painter. Add: 63 Avenue de Breteuil, Paris, France 1928. † GI 3, L 2, RA 10, RSA 1.

CZERNY, Waclar L. Exh. 1911
c/o Allied Artists Association, London. † LS 2.

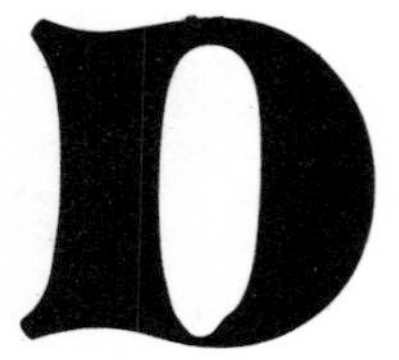

DABIS, Anna Exh. 1888-95
Sculptor. Add: London. † RA 10.

DABO, Leon* b. 1863
American painter. Exh. 1908-10. Add: c/o Goupil Gallery, Regent Street, London. † GOU 2, LS 11.

DABO, Theodore Scott b. 1877
American artist. Add: 8 Rue de la Grande Chaumiere, Paris, France 1909. † GI 1.

D'ACHE, Caran See POIRE, Emmanuel

DACKENHAUSEN, Von See V

DA COSTA, Miss H. Exh. 1909-13
Bromborough, Cheshire 1909; Willaston, Cheshire 1913. † L 16

DA COSTA, H.W. Exh. 1886
15 Impasse Helene, Avenue de Clichy, Paris, France. † GI 1.

DA COSTA, John 1867-1931
Portrait painter. Studied for 3 years in Paris. R.O.I. 1905, R.P. 1912. Add: Newlyn, Penzance, Cornwall 1880; London 1898 and 1910; Clanfield, Oxon 1908. † DOW 1, G 4, GI 7, I 4, L 13, M 5, NG 1, P 25, RA 30, RHA 3, RID 19, ROI 18, RSA 2.

DACRE, Susan Isabel Exh. 1880-1929
Landscape and figure painter. Add: Manchester 1880 and 1886; London 1883 and 1907. † B 1, L 6, M 27, NEA 15, NG 3, P 3, RA 8, RSA 4, SWA 1, WG 58.

DADD, Frank* 1851-1929
Painter and illustrator. Studied South Kensington School of Art and RA Schools. Worked for "Illustrated London News" 1878-84 and "Graphic" from 1884. R.I. 1884, R.O.I. 1888. "Gold Lace has a charm for the Fair" purchased by Chantrey Bequest 1908. Add: London 1880; Wallington, Surrey 1905; Teignmouth, Devon 1920. † B 9, D 3, FIN 9, GI 8, L 19, M 8, RA 9, RI 56, ROI 27.

DADD, G. Exh. 1914-15
Add: South London. † RA 2.

DADD, Marjory Exh. 1917-26
Miniature portrait painter. Add: Wallington, Surrey 1917; Croydon 1920; Purley, Surrey 1923. † RA 9.

DADD, Philip J.S. d. 1916
Painter and illustrator. Killed in action World War 1. Exh. 1905-14. Add: Hornsey, London. † BK 1, L 4, RA 4, RI 5, ROI 1.

DADD, Stephen T. Exh. 1880-1912
Figure painter. Add: South London. † D 2, L 2, M 1, RA 1, RBA 1, RI 12, ROI 1, TOO 2.

DADE, Ernest b. 1868
Marine painter. b. London. Studied Juliens, Paris. N.E.A. 1887. Add: London 1886 and 1917; Scarborough, Yorks. 1889. † D 2, DOW 38, I 1, L 1, NEA 2, RA 19, RBA 2, RI 2.

DADSLEY, Albert Exh. 1919
The Grange, Roscoe, Nr. Cadnor, Derbys. † LS 1.

D'AETH, Mrs. Eleanor Hughes Exh. 1896-97
Miniature portrait painter. R.M.S. 1897. Add: Eythorn House, Nr. Dover, Kent. † RA 3, RMS 2.

DAEYE, Hippolyte* 1873-1952
Belgian painter. Add: 8 Mayfield Road, Sanderstead, Surrey. † I 9, L 1, NEA 2.

DA FANO, Mrs. Dorothea Natalie Sophia See LANDAU

DAFFARN, Miss Alice Exh. 1886-87
Haselmere, Surrey. † ROI 2.

DAFFARN, William George Exh. 1880-1908
Landscape and genre painter. Add: London. † B 6, GI 3, L 8, M 5, RA 36, RBA 5, RI 2, ROI 2.

DAFFIN, Miss O. Exh. 1915
Dunraven, Cliftonville Road, Belfast, Ireland. † RA 1.

DAFTERS, G.E. Exh. 1939
66 Grandison Road Clapham Common, London. † RBA 1.

DAGLEY, C.L. Exh. 1920
5 Marlborough Park, Central Belfast, Ireland. † B 1.

DAGLISH, Eric Fitch b. 1894
Wood engraver, and writer. Exh. 1921-37. Add: Haddenham, Bucks. † NEA 2, RED 10.

DAGNAN-BOUVERET, Pascal Adolphe Jean* 1852-1929
French painter. H.F.R.A. Exh. 1886-1917. Add: Neuilly-sur-Seine, France. † L 3, M 1, NG 1, RA 4, RSA 4, TOO 4.

DAGOBERT, F. Exh. 1880
Landscape painter. Add: 6 Albert Mansions, Victoria Street, London. † RBA 1.

DAHL, Hans Andreas* 1849-1910
Norwegian artist. Add: Dunstanburgh, Vineyard Hill Road, Wimbledon Park, London, 1908-10. † LS 9.

DAIN, Alice Exh. 1915-16
10 Rock Lane, Rock Ferry, Cheshire. † L 2.

DAIN, Beatrice Exh. 1915-33
Rock Ferry, Cheshire 1915; Colwyn Bay, Wales 1929; Birkenhead 1932. † L 11, RCA 9.

DAIN, E.L. Exh. 1916-33
10 Rock Lane, Rock Ferry, Cheshire. † L 10, RCA 5.

DAINTETH, R. Exh. 1902-4
49 Sankey Street, Warrington, Lancs. † L 2.

DAINTREY, Adrian Maurice b. 1902
Portrait, figure, landscape and mural painter. Studied Slade School and Paris. Add: London. † AG 2, ALP 8, BK 2, CG 1, COO 31, G 1, GOU 1, L 1, LEI 1, NEA 4, RED 8.

DAINTREY, Alice S. Exh. 1880-1913
Figure and flower painter. Add: Petworth, Sussex. † L 1, LS 6, SWA 3.

D'AJURIA, Mrs. Gregoria Exh. 1897-99
R.M.S. 1898. Add: New York, U.S.A. † RMS 7.

DAKERS, Robert A. Exh. 1913-24
Haddington, East Lothian 1913; Edinburgh 1920; Alnwick, Northumberland 1924. † RSA 28.

DAKERS, W.S. Exh. 1921
12 Charterhouse Square, London † RA 1.

DAKHYL, Gertrude Exh. 1928
Landscape painter. † AB 3.

DAKIN, Mrs. A. Winifred Exh. 1916-29
Landscape and figure painter. Add: Willowmere Curzon Park, Chester. † L 4, RID 4.

DAKIN, Isaac Exh. 1885-88
Stockport Road, Manchester. † M 2.

DAKIN, Joseph Exh. 1880-1914
Landscape and figure painter. Add: Redhill, Surrey 1880; London 1896; Folkestone 1909. † D 1, L 5, LS 18, RA 5, RBA 5, RHA 8, RI 1, ROI 1.

DAKIN, Mrs. Mary D. Exh. 1929-38
Portrait and miniature painter. Add: 13 Bigwood Road, Hampstead Garden Suburb, London. † RA 4.

DAKIN, Rose Mabel Exh. 1905-32
Mrs. C.A. Gayer Phipps. Sculptor and miniature portrait painter. Studied Manchester School of Art (King's prize) and under Stanhope Forbes at Newlyn, Cornwall. A.R.M.S. 1910, R.M.S. 1919. Add: Grappenhall, Cheshire 1905 and 1915; London 1911 and 1917; Melbourne, Australia 1924; Dartmouth 1928. † L 23, M 5, RA 5, RHA 6, RMS 33.

DAKIN, Sylvia Concanen Exh. 1892-1922
Landscape painter. Travelled widely on the continent and the Middle East. Add: London. † L 4, RBA 3, RID 53, SWA 3, WG 66.

DALAL, Maneck Exh. 1930
† GOU 1.

DALBY, Arthur 1900-1961
Engraver. Studied Liverpool School of Art and Royal College of Art. H.M. Inspector of Art Schools from 1934. Add: Liverpool 1922; London 1928. † L 3, RA 1.

DALBY, Edwin Exh. 1887
Architect. Add: 13 St. Michael's Road, Bowes Park, London. † RA 1.

DALBY, Harry S. Haylock Exh. 1909-26
Rydal Lodge, Breckside Park, Liverpool. † L 5.

DALE, Constance M.M. Exh. 1898-1906
Figure painter. Add: St. Mary's, Weston super Mare, Somerset. † B 3, D 3, L 1, RA 1, RBA 1, SWA 3.

DALE, Mrs. Edith E. Exh. 1937-38
Birmingham. † B 2.

DALE, Emily L. Exh. 1902-3
Miniature painter. Add: The Knoll, Peppard, Henley on Thames, Oxon. † RA 5, RMS 1.

DALE, Mrs. E.O. Exh. 1925-29
Cheeshyre, The Vicarage, Hythe, Kent. † B 1, L 1, SWA 1.

DALE, Gertrude 1851-1927
Nee Brown. Miniature painter. A.R.M.S. 1912, R.M.S. 1913. Add: London 1890 and 1908; Marlborough, Wilts. 1907. † B 1, L 9, RA 6, RMS 10, ROI 1, SWA 1.

DALE, Mrs. Harriet Exh. 1904
345 Park Road, Dingle, Liverpool. † L 2.

DALE, Henry Sheppard 1852-1921
Painter and etcher. A.R.E. 1909. Add: Scarborough 1880 and 1883; London 1881; Taunton, Somerset 1893; Rye, Sussex 1900. † D 4, FIN 1, L 8, M 1, RA 5, RBA 1, RE 17, RI 2.

DALE, J.L. Exh. 1909
1 Cathcart Studios, Redcliffe Rd., London. † RA 1.

DALE, Muriel Exh. 1924
6 Christchurch Road, Oxton, Birkenhead. † L 3.

DALE, Miss M.H. Exh. 1910-13
The Lawn, Archer's Road, Southampton. † L 10, RA 1.

DALE, Paul Exh. 1886
16 Balliol Chambers, 15 Stanley Street, Liverpool. † L 1.

DALE, Thomas Lawrence 1884-1959
Architect. Add: London 1927; Oxford 1934. † RA 4.

DALE, Violet Exh. 1928
† GOU 1.

DALGETY, Miss K. Exh. 1933-35
6 Brookbridge Road, Tuebrook, Liverpool. † I 3, L 1.

DALGLEISH, Lizzie Exh. 1901
108 Woodlands Road, Glasgow. † GI 1.

DALGLIESH, Helen L. Exh. 1930-38
Flower painter. A.N.S.A. 1935. N.S.A. 1936. Add: West Bridgford, Notts. † N 6, RA 6.

DALGLIESH, Margaret Exh. 1909-17
Folkestone, Kent 1909; London 1917. † L 1, LS 4, RA 1.

DALGLIESH, Theodore Irving 1855-1941
Painter and etcher. Studied under Legros. N.S.A. 1886, R.E. 1881 (Hon. Retd. 1926). Add: London 1880, 1888 and 1922; Nottingham 1881; Folkestone, Kent 1890; Hythe, Kent 1914. † L 5, N 33, RA 18, RBA 1, RE 125.

DALGLISH, Andrew Adie Exh. 1880-1904
Glasgow 1880; Pollokshields, Glasgow 1892. † G 12, GI 19, RSA 2, RSW 5.

DALGLISH, Elsa N. Exh. 1904-24
Landscape painter. Travelled on the continent. Add: 16 West Cromwell Road, London. † BA 35, SWA 1.

DALGLISH, O.A. Exh. 1890
21 Princess Street, Pollokshields, Glasgow. † GI 2.

DALGLISH, William c. 1890-1909
Landscape painter. Add: 26 Renfield Street, Glasgow. † GI 60, L 3, RA 1, RI 3, RSA 17, RSW 6.

D'ALHEEM, Jean* Exh. 1892-93
18 Avenue de Villiers, Paris. † RHA 9.

DALISON, Miss Exh. 1919
Guild of Irish Ladies, Red Lodge, Millfield, Folkestone, Kent. † SWA 1.

DALL, John Exh. 1897-1904
Glasgow. † GI 5, RSA 1.

DALLACHY, John E.W. Exh. 1930
Architect. Add: 173 Bath Street, Glasgow. † GI 2.

DALLAS, Alexander A.K. Exh. 1925-39
Edinburgh 1925; Leith 1932. † RSA 2, RSW 5.

DALLAS, Anne Chassar Exh. 1926-40
Landscape and figure painter. Travelled on the continent. Add: London. † GOU 1, NEA 7, RED 48.

DALLAS, Hilda Exh. 1912-18
London. † LS 18, RA 1, SWA 2.

DALLEVES, R. Exh. 1910
Sion, Valais, Switzerland. † L 1.

DALLEY, Winifred L. Exh. 1889-94
Flower, figure and landscape painter. Add: 78 Ladbroke Grove, Notting Hill, London. † RID 16.

DALLIN, Miss H.I. Exh. 1907
Oxford. † SWA 1.

DALLMEYER, E. Rose Exh. 1898-1901
Landscape painter. Add: Kensington, London. † L 2, RA 3, ROI 1, SWA 12.

D'ALMEIDA, W.B. Exh. 1885
London. † ROI 1.

DALOBBE, F.A. Exh. 1904
27 Rue d'Alesia, Paris, France. † L 1.

DALOU, Aime Jules 1838-1902
French sculptor. Exh. 1902. † RSA 1.

DALSTON, Anne Exh. 1932-35
Sculptor. Add: London. † RA 1, ROI 1, SWA 1.

D'ALTENA, Comte Charles de Borchgrave Exh. 1931
Sculptor. Add: 90 Rue d'Arlon, Brussels. † RA 3.

DALTON, Miss A.E. Exh. 1893
Woodlands Grove, Rock Ferry, Liverpool. † L 1.

DALTON, Miss C. Exh. 1885
Dennistoun, Greenock. † RSA 2.

DALTON, C.W. Exh. 1920
4 Royston Terrace, Edinburgh. † RSA 1.

DALTON, Miss Helen Exh. 1903
Wyke Lodge, Winchester, Hants. † RI 1.

DALTON, Ironside W. Exh. 1932
40 de Vere Gardens, London. † RBA 2.

DALTON, John William Exh. 1886-1930
Liverpool 1886; Wolverhampton 1899; Rock Ferry, Cheshire 1926. † B 3, L 6, M 1.

DALTON, L. Masters Exh. 1928-36
† WG 58.

DALTON, Miss M. Exh. 1905-14
A.R.M.S. 1912. Add: Hampstead, London. † B 1, L 5, NG 2, RA 5, RMS 7.

DALTON, T.M. Exh. 1889
Pareara, Guildford, Surrey. † B 4, M 1.

DALTON, William B. b. 1868
Sculptor, pottery artist and decorator. Studied Royal College of Art (travelling scholarship 1894) and Italy. Principal L.C.C. School of Arts and Crafts, Camberwell. Exh. 1931-36. Add: Garrow Longfield, Kent. † RA 4.

DALY, Miss A. Exh. 1903-5
Grange House, Rathfarnham, Co. Dublin, Ireland. † RHA 3.

DALY, Mrs. Brian Exh. 1906-8
1 Cambridge Road, Battersea Park, London. † NG 9.

DALY, Herbert J. Exh. 1918-28
Dublin 1918; Paris 1927. † RHA 13.

DALY, William Edward b. 1879
Landscape painter. Studied Manchester School of Art and Paris. Principal Kidderminster School of Art. Add: Knockeen, Chester Rd., Kidderminster, 1930. † RA 1.

DALYELL, Amy d. 1962
Mrs. James Birrell. Landscape painter. R.S.W. 1914. Add: Edinburgh from 1901. † AR 2, GI 6, L 1, RSA 27, RSW 53.

DALYELL, Miss Gladys Exh. 1912-19
10 Merchiston Crescent, Edinburgh. † GI 1, RSA 8, RSW 1.

DALZELL, Alexander C. Exh. 1935-39
Landscape painter. Add: Warwick Square, London. † L 1, M 1, RA 5.

DALZIEL, Caroline A. Exh. 1906-10
Edinburgh. † GI 3, L 1, RSA 2.

DALZIEL, Edward 1817-1905
Painter, illustrator and wood engraver. 5th son of Northumberland artist Alexander D. Came to London 1839 and with his brother George founded firm of "Brothers Dalziel". Father of E. Gilbert D. q.v. and Edward Gurden D. q.v. Add: Hampstead 1898. † ROI 1.

DALZIEL, E. Gilbert 1853-1930
2nd son of Edward D. q.v. Studied South Kensington, Slade School and under "Brothers Dalziel". Add: Hampstead, London 1882. † D 2.

DALZIEL, Edward Gurden* 1849-1888
Figure and landscape painter. Eldest son of Edward D. q.v. Add: Hampstead, London 1882. † L 2, M 3, RA 1, RI 2.

DALZIEL, Herbert Exh. 1881-1902
Flower, figure and landscape painter. N.E.A. 1887. Add: 7 Oppidan's Road, Primrose Hill, London 1881; Ewell, Nr. Dover 1895. † B 1, D 2, G 1, L 8, M 9, NEA 3, NG 4, RA 10, RBA 24, RHA 7, RI 1, ROI 10.

DALZIEL, James Exh. 1880
Landscape painter. Add: 39 George Street, Portman Square, London. † RA 1.

DALZIEL, John Exh. 1940
35 Commercial Road, Barrhead, Renfrewshire. † GI 1.

DALZIEL, Nan Exh. 1923-31
Glasgow 1923; Paris 1931. † GI 6, L 1, M 1, RSA 2.

DALZIEL, Owen* Exh. 1880-1908
Landscape, figure and marine painter. N.E.A. 1888. Add: 7 Oppidan's Road, Primrose Hill, London 1880; Ewell, Nr. Dover 1895; Herne Bay 1900. † B 7, D 1, G 2, L 2, M 7, NEA 2, RA 17, RBA 23, RI 1, ROI 14.

DALZIEL, Thomas Bolton Gilchrist 1823-1906
Landscape and figure painter and wood engraver. 7th son of Northumberland artist Alexander D. Joined "Brothers Dalziel" 1860. Add: 7 Oppidan's Road, Primrose Hill, London, 1881. † M 2, RHA 2.

DALZIEL, Thomas J. Exh. 1884
Architect. Add: 35 George Street, Hampstead Road, London. † RA 1.

D'AMATO, Gennaro Exh. 1899
Urban landscape painter. Add: 198 Strand, London and Genoa, Italy. † M 1, RA 1.

DAMERON, Emile* Exh. 1880-93
Paris, France. † GI 6, RHA 6.

DAMIANOS, V. Exh. 1936
† RI 1.

DAMME, Van See V

DAMOYE, Pierre Emmanuel* 1847-1916
French artist. Add: London 1883; Paris 1890. † GI 9.

DAMPT, Jean Auguste b. 1854
French sculptor. Exh. 1921. Add: 17 Rue Campagne Premiere, Paris, France. † RSA 2.

DAMSEY, H. Exh. 1902
1 Sussex Villas, Kensington, London. † L 1, M 1.

DANA, William Parsons Winchester* 1833-1927
American marine painter. b. Boston, U.S.A. died London. Add: 57 Onslow Gardens, London 1898. † B 1.

DANBY, Geo. F. Exh. 1901
Architect. Add: 10 Park Row, Leeds, Yorks. † RA 1.

DANBY, John C. Exh. 1881-82
River and coastal painter. Add: Chertsey, Surrey 1881; Beckenham, Kent 1882. † RBA 2.

DANBY, Thomas* c. 1818-1886
Landscape painter. Studied under his father Francis D., A.R.A. Travelled on the continent. R.H.A. 1860, A.R.W.S. 1867, R.W.S. 1870. Add: 11 Park Road, Haverstock Hill, London. † AG 1, GI 1, L 5, RA 2, RWS 22.

DANDIE, Alex Exh. 1925
105 Joppa Road, Portobello, Nr. Edinburgh. † RSA 1.

DANENBERG, Alice Exh. 1928
† ALP 7.

D'ANETHAN, Mlle. Exh. 1885
76 Bedford Gardens, Campden Hill, London. † M 1.

DANFORD, Charles G. Exh. 1883-91
Harpenden, Herts 1883; Banchory, Aberdeenshire 1885; Cookham Dean, Berks. 1891. † B 1, D 4, GI 1, RI 3.

DANFORD, E.R. Exh. 1908-10
St. John's Chamber, Newland, Northampton. † RA 2.

DANGERFIELD, Agnes Exh. 1894
Miniature portrait painter. Add: 40 Central Hill, Upper Norwood, London. † RA 1.

DANGERFIELD, Mrs. Margaret Exh. 1926-27
Ickneild House, Streetly, Beds. † B 5.

DANIEL, Doris Exh. 1924-35
37 Woodlands Road, Aigburth, Liverpool. † I 7, L 16.

DANIEL, Emily D. Exh. 1915-23
37 Underley Street, Smithdown Road, Liverpool. † L 18.

DANIEL, Henry Wilkinson Exh. 1909-36
Painter and etcher. Studied Slade School. Art master Trinity College, Glenalmond and Governor Allan-Fraser Art College, Hospitalfield, Arbroath. Add: London 1908; Playden, Sussex 1912; Cramond Bridge, Midlothian 1916; Arbroath 1927. † GI 8, GOU 4, I 1, L 1, P 3, RA 6, ROI 2, RSA 30, RSW 5.

DANIEL, J.A. Exh. 1903
4 Warwick Studios, Kensington, London. † NG 1.

DANIEL, Kate Exh. 1928
50 Grove Street, Liverpool. † L 1.

DANIELL, Frank Exh. 1889-1921
Portrait painter. Add: London 1889 and 1916; Colchester 1895. † L 2, LS 9, P 7, RA 18, ROI 1.

DANIELL, Mrs. Henry Exh. 1887
Landscape painter. Add: Worcester House, Oxford. † SWA 1.

DANIELL, Mary Bampfylde Exh. 1898-1903
R.M.S. 1898; Kensington, London 1898; Bourton on the Hill, Morton in Marsh, Glos. 1903. † P 1, RMS 9.

DANIELL, Madeline Hurst Exh. 1884-87
1 Marlborough Crescent, Bedford Park, London. † SWA 2.

DANIELLS, R.W. Exh. 1938
† M 1.

DANIELS, Mrs. Amy Exh. 1889
Landscape painter. Add: 33 Mimosa Street, Fulham, London. † RA 1.

DANIELS, Edith M. Exh. 1911
Lightpill, Stroud, Glos. † LS 3.

DANIELS, George b. 1854
Church decorator, stained glass artist and miniaturist. Exh. 1884-1917. Add: London. † RA 11.

DANIELS, Leonard Exh. 1939
† GOU 1.

DANIELS, William* Exh. 1923
16A Broughton Street, Edinburgh. † RSA 1.

DANIELS, Winifred Exh. 1918-28
Portrait and figure painter. Add: West Croydon, Surrey 1918; London 1927. † ALP 1, I 1, NEA 1, P 1, RA 1.

DANIELSEN, Anna G. Exh. 1927-31
Edgbaston, Birmingham 1927; Cranleigh, Surrey 1930. † B 10.

DANITRY, Miss A. Exh. 1894
4 King Street, Kensington, London. † M 1.

DANKS, Harold S. Exh. 1920-40
Stained glass artist. Add: London. † RA 6.

DANKS, Walter* Exh. 1882-1918
Landscape painter. A.N.S.A. 1908. Add: Nottingham 1882 and 1889; Sneinton Dale, Notts. 1885. † N 59.

DANN, A.C. Exh. 1928-35
Liverpool. † L 3, RI 1.

DANN, Edith Exh. 1929
Western House, The Ropewalk, Nottingham. † N 1.

DANNAT, William Turner* 1853-1929
Portrait, figure and still life painter. b. U.S.A. d. Paris. R.B.A. 1885. Exh. 1885-93. Add: Paris. † GI 3, RA 1, RBA 9.

DANNATT, Annie M. Exh. 1909-11
Corner House, Westcombe Park, Blackheath, London. † LS 9, SWA 1.

DANSEY, Herbert Exh. 1903
c/o Jas. Clark, 18 Greenhill Gardens, Edinburgh. † RSA 1.

DANTE, F. Exh. 1884
Sculptor. Add: 13 Beaumont Road, West Kensington, London. † RA 1.

DANVERS, Mrs. Margaret Exh. 1894-1923
London. † D 7, SWA 22.

DANYELL, Alice Johnson Exh. 1889-1908
London. † LS 3, SWA 4.

DANYELL, Miss C.J. Exh. 1890
c/o Smith and Uppord, 77 Mortimer Street, London. † B 1.

DANYELL, Herbert (Berto) Exh. 1890-93
Florence and Kensington, London. † B 1, G 1, L 2, M 2, RI 1, RSA 1.

DA PORZO, C. Exh. 1882
c/o W.M. Wyllie, 70 Carlton Hill, London. † D 1.

DA POZZO, Guiseppe Exh. 1883-1910
Interior, figure and landscape painter. Add: Prov. D'Udine, Italy 1883; Rome 1885. † B 4, L 8, M 5, RA 2, RBA 1, RHA 20, RI 1.

DARBON, William Exh. 1886
Mount Batten, Plymouth, Devon. † RI 1.

DARBOUR, Margaret Mary Exh. 1904-38
Coastal, landscape, portrait and flower painter. Add: Basses, Pyrenees 1904; Dordogne, France 1917. † COO 48, RA 3.

DARBY, Anne Exh. 1927
Blackheath, London. † SWA 1.

DARBY, Rev. John Henry b. 1880
Watercolour painter. Add: Hednesford, Staffs 1922; St. Marks Vicarage, Ocker Hill, Tipton, Staffs. 1924. † B 27, WG 12.

DARBYSHIRE, A. Exh. 1886-93
Brazenose Street, Manchester. † M 4.

D'ARCY, J.W. Exh. 1901
29 Balfour Road, Nottingham. † N 2.

DARCY, Laura Exh. 1881-1905
Figure painter. Add: London. † L 3, M 1, RA 8, RBA 4, RI 3.

D'ARCY, Louise F. Exh. 1888-1912
4 Mount Tallant Avenue, Terenure, Dublin, Ireland. † RHA 25.

D'ARCY, Marianne Exh. 1887-1911
4 Mount Tallant Avenue, Terenure, Dublin, Ireland. † RHA 26.

D'ARCY, Miss M.E.H. Exh. 1890
16 Vanbrugh Park Road, London. † SWA 1.

D'ARCY, Will Exh. 1902-31
Landscape painter. Add: Nottingham 1902; West Bridgford, Notts. 1913. † N 26.

D'AREILLE, Luke Exh. 1889
1 Rue de Triomphe, Paris, France. † GI 1.

DARIEN, Henry Exh. 1889-1909
113 Boulevard St. Michel, Paris, France. † L 3.

DA RIOS, Luigi 1844-1892
Italian figure painter. Add: c/o Joy, Queen Anne Street, London. † B 1, GI 2, L 4, M 2, RA 2, RE 1, RI 4, ROI 2.

DARKING, Harry Fred Exh. 1936-39
Landscape, figure and portrait painter. Add: Sherwood, Nottingham. † N 5.

DARLEY, Mrs. Cherry Exh. 1936
Etcher. Add: Roden Lodge, Shawbury, Salop. † RA 1.

DARLEY, J.F. d. 1932
Landscape and figure painter. R.B.A. 1901. Add: London 1886; Addlestone, Surrey 1898. † B 1, L 1, RBA 66, ROI 1.

DARLING, Norman P. Exh. 1936
Landscape painter. Add: 86 St. Andrews Road, Southsea, Hants. † RA 1.

DARLINGTON, Frances Exh. 1900-9
Sculptor. Studied Slade School and South Kensington. Add: Kensington, London 1900; Harrogate, Yorks. 1903; Ilkley in Wharfedale, Yorks. 1909. † L 5, NG 1, RA 5, SWA 1.

DARLINGTON, Fred Exh. 1938
† M 1.

DARLINGTON, K. Mary Exh. 1900
The Grange, Halewood, Liverpool. † L 1.

DARMESTETER, Helena Arsene Exh. 1884-1916
Portrait and figure painter. Add: Paris, 1884 and 1908; London 1890. † B 1, G 5, LS 21, M 3, P 1, RA 4, ROI 2.

DARNELL, Dorothy Exh. 1904-22
Miniature painter. A.S.W.A. 1915, S.W.A. 1916. Add: Kensington, London. † L 1, RA 1, SWA 6.

DARNELL, E.A. Exh. 1889
Gorgelfield Trinity, Edinburgh. † RSA 1.

DARNEY, Lilian D. Exh. 1891-1909
Miniature portrait painter. Add: Kinghorn N.B. 1891; Colinton, Midlothian 1894; Witney, Oxon 1909. † GI 2, RA 3, RSA 6.

DARNLEY, The Dowager Duchess of, Exh. 1928-30
Watercolour painter. † WG 158.

DARRAGH, William Exh. 1899
45 Atlantic Avenue, Belfast, Ireland. † RHA 3.

DARRIEUX, C.R. Exh. 1913
57 Rue d'Assas, Paris, France. † RSA 1.

DARRY, Dorothy Helen b. 1899
Jeweller, metalworker, embroiderer and designer. Exh. 1920-29. Add: 26 Adding-ham road, Mossley Hill, Liverpool. † L 8.

DART, Maud D. Exh. 1912-32
Watercolour painter and etcher. Add: Aigburth Drive, Liverpool 1912; London 1930. † B 4, L 28, RCA 11.

DARTON, William Exh. 1887-89
Mount Batten, Plymouth, Devon. † L 1, RI 1.

DARVALL, Frank Exh. 1881
c/o Mr. Smithers, 95 Leadenhall Street, London. † G 1.

DARVALL, Henry* Exh. 1880-89
Figure and landscape painter. Add: London 1880; Venice, Italy 1882. † B 1, D 3, FIN 1, G 1, L 3, RA 4, RBA 1.

DARWIN, Elinor Mary Exh. 1899-1929
Nee Monsell. b. Limerick, Ireland. Portrait and figure painter, illustrator, painter on silk and fans, and wood cut artist. Studied Slade School (Slade scholarship 1896). Add: London 1899 and 1919; Cambridge 1917; Downe, Kent 1929. † ALP 8, BG 2, I 4, M 1, NEA 19, RA 1, RHA 10.

DARWIN, Mrs. G.H. Exh. 1913-18
Creskeld, Arthington, Leeds, Yorks. † LS 15.

DARWIN, Robin* Exh. 1929-39
Landscape and figure painter. † AG 73, BK 1, NEA 4, RED 50.

DASH, Miss H.B. Exh. 1913-22
Surbiton, Surrey 1913; Chelsea, London 1915. † G 1, L 5, RA 4, RI 1, SWA 6.

DASHWOOD, Miss Alice Exh. 1890-1903
London. † SWA 9.

DASHWOOD, Cuthbert W.L. Exh. 1908-21
Yarmouth, I.O.W. † LS 26.

DASHWOOD, Miss S.A. Exh. 1897
59 Oakley Street, Chelsea, London. † RBA 1.

DASTUGNE, Maxime Exh. 1884
French artist. Add: 15 Rue Boissonade, Paris, France. † GI 1.

DAUBENY, Mrs. A. Exh. 1934-35
c/o Elands Art Gallery, Exeter, Devon. † B 2.

DAUBIGNY, Karl* 1846-1886
French miniature painter. Add: Avenue Frochot 15, Paris, France 1882-84. † GI 3.

DAUCHEZ, Andre b. 1870
French landscape painter. Exh. 1901-12. Add: Paris, France. † GOU 1, I 1, L 4.

DAUDETEAU, L.U.R. Exh. 1884
Rue de Trussac, Vannes, Morbihan, France. † GI 1.

DAUM, Johannes M. (Jan) Exh. 1915-29
Etcher. A.R.E. 1923. Add: Brook Green, London 1915; Amberley, Sussex 1925. † RA 8, RE 18.

DAUNCEY, Lt. Col. Thursby Exh. 1914-15
Junior Carlton Club, London. † LS 3, RA 1.

DAUNT-HEARD, Geoffrey Exh. 1909
† LS 3.

DAVENPORT, Claudia Mary Exh. 1886-90
Figure painter. Add: Oxford 1886; Ludlow, Salop 1890. † D 4, SWA 1.

DAVENPORT, Cyril Talbot Exh. 1883-99
Landscape painter. Add: London 1883; Hawkhurst, Kent 1892. † B 1, D 7, RBA 1.

DAVENPORT, Mrs. Enid Exh. 1921
37 Montgomery Terrace, Mount Florida, Glasgow. † GI 1.

DAVENPORT, Hayward M. Exh. 1898-1904
Landscape and coastal painter. Add: The Cheal, Twickenham, Middlesex. † D 2, FIN 1, RA 3.

DAVENPORT, Leslie b. 1905
Landscape painter. Exh. 1931-39. Add: Hillingdon, Middlesex. † GOU 1, NEA 1, RED 1.

DAVEY, Edith Exh. 1915-16
57 New Fillebrooke Road, Leytonstone, Essex. † L 2, RA 1.

DAVEY, Edith Mary Exh. 1910-37
Portrait painter, miniaturist and black and white artist. Studied Lincoln School of Art and Royal College of Art. Add: London 1910. † L 8, RA 21, RI 44, RMS 8, SWA 1.

DAVEY, Edward O. Exh. 1901-4
Landscape painter. Add: 40 Wellesley Road, Croydon, Surrey. † RA 3.

DAVEY, Florence Exh. 1881
Watercolour flower painter. Add: Aldrid Villa, Station Road, Horsham, Sussex. † RBA 2.

DAVEY, Fred Exh. 1922-32
3 Clifton Hill, Brighton, Sussex. † B 10.

DAVEY, Mildred C. Exh. 1889-1907
Landscape, flower and tree painter. Add: London. † L 1, NG 5, RID 12.

DAVEY, William T. Exh. 1882-84
Engraver. Add: 1 Denmark Villas, Mill Hill Road, Acton, London. † RA 3.

DAVID, Agnes Exh. 1910-14
Aberdeen. † GI 4, RA 6, RSA 5.

DAVID, E. Exh. 1885-86
Paris, France. † GI 2.

DAVID, F.M. Exh. 1891
Sculptor. Add: St. James's Club, Montreal, Canada. † RA 1.

DAVID, Mrs. Vere Exh. 1923
Friar Park, Henley on Thames, Oxon. † RI 1.

DAVIDGE, William R. Exh. 1929-39
Architect. Add: 5 Victoria Street, London. † RA 2.

DAVIDS, Arlette Exh. 1935
Flower painter. † FIN 72.

DAVIDS, Miss A.E. Exh. 1880-83
23 Upper Grosvenor Place, Tunbridge Wells, Kent. † G 1, ROI 1, SWA 2.

DAVIDSON, Alexander* d. 1887
Domestic painter. Add: 65 West Regent Street, Glasgow. † D 1, GI 46, L 3, M 1, RA 1, RBA 2, RSA 15, RSW 26.

DAVIDSON, Allan Douglas* 1873-1932
Figure and portrait painter. Son of Thomas D. q.v. Studied St. John's Wood, RA Schools (silver and bronze medals) and Juliens, Paris. Teacher L.C.C. Central School of Arts and Crafts. R.B.A. 1901, A.R.M.S. 1920, R.O.I. 1920. Add: London 1892; Walberswick, Suffolk 1925. † GI 1, L 7, LEI 6, M 1, RA 25, RBA 96, RED 2, RMS 5, ROI 55.

DAVIDSON, A. Murray Exh. 1904-5
Liverpool. † L 3.

DAVIDSON, A.W. Exh. 1905-21
Landscape, figure and flower painter. A.R.B.A. 1919. Add: Newlyn, Penzance 1905; South Brent, Devon 1907; Garelockhead, Scotland 1914; London 1920. † BG 35, GI 1, GOU 4, L 7, RBA 19, RI 4, RID 12, RSA 1.

DAVIDSON, A. Williamson Exh. 1890-1903
Edinburgh 1890; Berwick on Tweed 1903. † GI 4, RSA 9, RSW 2.

DAVIDSON, Bessie* b. 1879
Australian artist. Exh. 1912-14. Add: Paris. † RSA 5.

DAVIDSON, Charles Exh. 1896-97
Terrace Buildings, Paisley, Scotland. † GI 3.

DAVIDSON, Caroline E. b. 1838
52 Gloucester Terrace, Hyde Park, London 1898. † D 2.

DAVIDSON, Charles Grant 1824-1902
Watercolour landscape painter. A.R.I. 1847, R.I. 1849 (resigned 1853), A.R.W.S. 1855, R.W.S. 1858. Add: London and St. Buryan, Penzance 1880; Trevina, Falmouth 1884 and 1898; Perranporth, Cornwall 1898. † B 1, D 8, DOW 60, FIN 2, GI 4, L 13, M 9, RA 2, RI 3, ROI 3, RWS 211, TOO 8.

DAVIDSON, Charles James Exh. 1880
24 Caledonian Crescent, Edinburgh. † RSA 1.

DAVIDSON, Charles Lamb b. 1897
Cartoonist, stained glass designer and interior decorator. b. Brechin, Forfarshire. Studied Glasgow School of Art (Haldane travelling scholarship 1920). Married J. Nina Miller, q.v. Add: Glasgow. † GI 4, RSA 1.

DAVIDSON, Charles Topham b. 1848
Landscape and coastal painter. Son of Charles Grant D. q.v. Add: London 1883 and 1892; Trevina, Falmouth 1887; King's Langley, Herts. 1898; Swanage, Dorset 1910. † D 66, G 2, L 7, LS 6, M 3, RA 15, RBA 23, RHA 1, RI 25, ROI 2.

DAVIDSON, Daniel Pender* 1885-1933
Portrait, landscape and decorative painter. Studied Glasgow School of Art, Brussels and Munich. Add: Glasgow 1915; Milngavie, N.B. 1916; London 1918. † L 6, RA 1.

DAVIDSON, Miss E. Exh. 1886
Rose Cottage, Broughty Ferry, Nr. Dundee. † RSA 1.

DAVIDSON, Edward M. Exh. 1901-2
Dundee. † GI 2.

DAVIDSON, George Exh. 1903-10
Landscape painter. Add: Aberdeen. † GI 8, LS 5, RA 3, RSA 4.

DAVIDSON, Ian W. Exh. 1937-39
33 Gladstone Place, Aberdeen. † RSA 3.

DAVIDSON, Miss J. Exh. 1889
† L 1.

DAVIDSON, James Exh. 1880-82
Edinburgh. † GI 1, RSA 2.

DAVIDSON, Jennie Exh. 1897-1904
18 Merchiston Terrace, Edinburgh. † GI 1, RSA 7.

DAVIDSON, Jo b. 1883
American sculptor. Add: 6 Rue Leconte-de-Lisle, Paris 1927. † RA 1.

DAVIDSON, John Exh. 1918
6 Adie Road, Hammersmith, London. † ROI 1.

DAVIDSON, John Exh. 1881-95
Edinburgh. † RSA 11.

DAVIDSON, James S. Exh. 1884-89
20 Clarendon Street, Partick, Glasgow. † GI 3.

DAVIDSON, Miss J.T. Exh. 1884-87
11 Rue Casimir Perier, Paris 1884; Glasgow 1887. † GI 2, L 1.

DAVIDSON, Jessie Y. Exh. 1885-92
Figure painter. Add: Liverpool 1885; Kensington, London 1892. † GI 2, L 7, RA 1.

DAVIDSON, Lilian Lucy* d. 1954
Figure and landscape painter and etcher. A.R.H.A. 1940. Exh. 1914-20. Add: Dublin, Ireland. † RHA 75.

DAVIDSON, Miss M. Exh. 1911
93 Boulevard St. Michel, Paris, France. † RSA 1.

DAVIDSON, Mrs. Marianne Exh. 1940
34 Cambridge Gardens, Edinburgh. † RSA 1.

DAVIDSON, Mary C. d. 1950
Watercolour painter. R.S.W. 1936. Exh. 1906-36. Add: Edinburgh. † GI 6, L 1, RA 1, RSA 24, RSW 44.

DAVIDSON, Miss M.D. Exh. 1899
3 Garden Road, St. John's Wood, London. † L 1.

DAVIDSON, Nora Exh. 1926-27
Figure painter. Add: "Coniston", Robinson Road, Mapperley, Notts. † N 2.

DAVIDSON, Peter Wylie Exh. 1906-40
Goldsmith, leatherworker and decorative artist. b. Bridge of Allan, Scotland. Studied Glasgow School of Art, London and Paris. Add: Glasgow. † GI 9, L 5, RSA 3.

DAVIDSON, Robert G. Exh. 1903-8
Edinburgh. † RSA 3.

DAVIDSON, Sara M. Exh. 1880
Dean Park, Balerno, Edinburgh. † RSA 1.

DAVIDSON, Taffy Exh. 1923-35
8 Thisle Street, Aberdeen. † RSA 4.

DAVIDSON, Thomas Exh. 1890
5 Spring Gardens, Kelvinside, Glasgow. † GI 1.

DAVIDSON, Thomas* Exh. 1880-1908
Historical and genre painter. Father of Allan Douglas D. q.v. Add: Hampstead, London 1880; Walberswick, Suffolk 1908. † B 12, D 1, GI 11, L 11, M 4, RA 12, RBA 26, RHA 6, ROI 24, TOO 3.

DAVIDSON, T. Furlong Exh. 1893
76 Montgomerie Street, Kelvinside, Glasgow. † GI 2.

DAVIDSON, T.G. Exh. 1905-11
London. † RA 4.

DAVIDSON, Thomas L. Exh. 1923
Ellenlea, Brechin. † GI 1.

DAVIDSON, William b. 1875
Architect and decorative artist. Teacher of architecture Edinburgh College of Art. Writer on architecture, sculpture and decorative art. Exh. 1901-32. Add: Edinburgh. † GI 6, RA 3, RSA 33, RSW 7.

DAVIDSON, W. Armstrong Exh. 1907-12
Collaborated with Kate W. Thomson, q.v. Add: 93 Hope Street, Glasgow. † L 10.

DAVIDSON, W.D. Exh. 1913-19
Brechin, N.B. † GI 3.

DAVIDSON, Walter R. Exh. 1900-13
Architect. Add: London. † RA 4, RSA 3.

DAVIDSON, William W. Exh. 1909-11
Dublin, Ireland. † RHA 3.

DAVIE, Emma Exh. 1895-97
17 Cintra Road, Upper Norwood, London † RBA 3.

DAVIE, James William b. 1889
Painter and etcher. Studied Glasgow, London and Paris. Add: Grangemouth, N.B. † GI 3, L 4, P 2, RSA 10.

DAVIEL, Leon Exh. 1893-1930
Portrait and figure painter and wood engraver. Add: London. † CHE 1, I 3, NEA 1, NG 1, P 10, RA 12, ROI 1.

DAVIES, A. Exh. 1890
73 Elizabeth Street, Cheetham, Manchester. † M 1.

DAVIES, A. Exh. 1909
Miniature painter. Add: Sanford Villa, College Road, Cheltenham, Glos. + RA 1.

DAVIES, Alice Exh. 1915-21
College Hall, Byng Place, London. † NEA 3.

DAVIES, Arthur B. Owen* 1862-1928
American painter. b. U.S.A. d. Florence, Italy. Exh. 1904 and 1925. † CHE 4, NEA 1.

DAVIES, Arthur Edward b. 1893
Landscape painter. Studied Metropolitan School of Art, Dublin, Ireland. Exh. 1932-40. Add: Studio 50, Park Lane, Norwich, Norfolk. † RA 4, RBA 4, RCA 9, RSA 6.

DAVIES, Aimee M. Exh. 1904-14
Miniature painter. Add: London. † RA 7, RCA 1.

DAVIES, Benedict Exh. 1935-39
Figure painter. Add: 72 Wallingford Avenue, Kensington, London. † RA 2.

DAVIES, C. Blanche Exh. 1898-1920
Hay, Herefords. 1898; Birmingham 1901. † B 9.

DAVIES, Charlotte J. Exh. 1880-84
Landscape painter. Add: c/o Mylne, Amwell, Ware, Herts. † SWA 9.

DAVIES, David* b. 1864
Landscape and coastal painter. Studied Malbourne and Juliens, Paris. R.O.I. 1920. Add: St. Ives, Cornwall 1898; Lelant, Cornwall 1899; London 1906; Charlton Kings, Cheltenham, Glos. 1924. † NEA 2, RA 6, RI 5, RID 15, ROI 7.

DAVIES, Dorothy Exh. 1905-40
nee Prickett. Watercolour landscape painter. Studied under Sir A. Cope and Chelsea Polytechnic. Visited Australia. Add: Gt. Yarmouth, Norfolk 1905; Heston, Middlesex 1921. † AR 73, RBA 2, RCA 1, SWA 4, WG 78.

DAVIES, D. Gorozwy Exh. 1901-36
Liverpool. † L 7, RCA 3.

DAVIES, Miss E. Exh. 1913
31 West Lodge, West Acton, London. † RA 1.

DAVIES, Edward* 1841-1920
Landscape painter and watercolourist. R.I. 1896. Add: Leicester. † B 4, BG 2, D 3, I 1, L 18, N 4, RA 29, RBA 1, RI 171, ROI 7.

DAVIES, Ernest Exh. 1928-31
Still life painter. Add: London. † GI 1, RA 1, ROI 4.

DAVIES, Ethel Exh. 1896-1924
Figure painter. Married to George H. Hughes, q.v. Add: Liverpool 1896, Welford on Avon 1909; Tewkesbury 1920. † B 2, L 33, RA 5, RCA 4, RI 2.

DAVIES, E.J. Exh. 1921
135 Corporation Street, Stafford. † ROI 1.

DAVIES, Edgar W. Exh. 1893-1910
Manchester 1893; London 1900. † B 1, L,4, M 1, NG 4, RA 1, RBA 4.

DAVIES, Fred L. Exh. 1925
43 Ronald Road, Newport, Mon. † RCA 2.

DAVIES, George Exh. 1886-93
Landscape painter. Add: Leicester. † L 4, RBA 2, RI 8.

DAVIES, Gladys R. Exh. 1937-38
† P 2.

DAVIES, Gerald Stanley c. 1846-1927
Painter and writer on art. Add: London 1885; Charterhouse, Godalming 1886. † RBA 2, RE 1.

DAVIES, Hilda Eynon Exh. 1928
Flower and figure painter. Add: 62 Westbourne Road, Forest Hill, London. † RA 2.

DAVIES, John Exh. 1887
3 Osborne Road, Liverpool. † L 1.

DAVIES, J.E. Exh. 1932-40
Erdington, Birmingham 1932; Olton, Birmingham 1936. † B 9.

DAVIES, James Hey* b. 1844
Landscape painter. Studied Manchester, RA Schools, Sweden and France. Add: Manchester 1882-1926. † GI 1, L 1, M 33, NEA 2, RA 5, RBA 6, RCA 16, ROI 1, RSA 3.

DAVIES, Leonard Exh. 1929-31
Landscape painter. Add: "Overdale", Newland Sherborne, Dorset. † B 1, RA 2.

DAVIES, Miss M. Exh. 1888-90
60 King Street, Manchester. † L 2.

DAVIES, Mary Exh. 1912-13
4 Pelham Grove, Liverpool. † L 2.

DAVIES, Miss M.E. Exh. 1891
Vyrnwy Bank, Llanymynech, Salop. † M 3.

DAVIES, Marie Gertrude Exh. 1923-31
Flower painter. Studied Municipal School of Art, Manchester (Lady Whitworth scholarship 1912. Board of Education scholarship 1914-17). Art teacher Mexborough Secondary School, Yorks. and St. Anne's High School, St. Anne's on Sea, Lancs. Add: 17 Rossall Road, Ansdell, Lytham, Lancs. † L 3, RA 2, RCA 3.

DAVIES, Minnie M. Exh. 1882-1903
Mrs. C. Dean. Miniature portrait painter. Add: London 1882; Manchester 1896. † D 3, L 11, M 1, RA 3, RBA 2, RI 2.

DAVIES, Margaret Sydney Exh. 1934-35
Newton, Mon. † RCA 10.

DAVIES, Rita M. Exh. 1917
Clyndwr, Cornwall Road, Sutton, Surrey. † RCA 1.

DAVIES, Sidney Exh. 1918
44 St. Stephens Green, Dublin, Ireland. † RHA 6.

DAVIES, Tom Exh. 1895-1929
Liverpool 1895; Bidston, Birkenhead 1898. † L 25.

DAVIES, T. Anwyl Exh. 1934
c/o Bourlet and Son, Nassau Street, London. † ROI 1.

DAVIES, Ursula M. Exh. 1881-88
Landscape painter. Add: Harlech, Wales 1881; 38 Willes Road, Leamington, Warwicks. 1883. † B 4, L 1, M 1, SWA 5.

DAVIES, William Exh. 1883-88
Portrait sculptor. Add: London. † L 2, M 2, RA 4.

DAVIES, W.J. Exh. 1903
Architect. Add: Thornton Dene, Sidcup, Kent. † RA 1.

DAVIES-COLLEY, Frances Exh. 1895-96
Figure painter. Add: 36 Harley Street, London. † L 2, NEA 2.

DAVIES-COLLEY, Margaret Exh. 1904
Borough Pulborough, Sussex. † L 2.

DAVIES-COLLEY, Susan Exh. 1935-40
Landscape and portrait painter. Add: London. † NEA 1, P 2, RA 3, RI 3.

D'AVIGDOR, Estelle Exh. 1890-96
Miniature portrait painter. Add: London. † FIN 1, M 2, P 2, RA 6.

DAVIS, A. Exh. 1914
206 Verdant Lane, Hither Green, Kent. † RA 1.

DAVIS, Anna Exh. 1889-1937
88 Fulham Road, London. † L 1, ROI 1.

DAVIS, Arthur Alfred* Exh. 1881-84
Figure and landscape painter. Add: London. † RBA 2.

DAVIS, Arthur H. Exh. 1893-94
The Haven, Lansdowne Road, Bournemouth, Hants. † ROI 2.

DAVIS, Arthur Joseph 1878-1951
Architect. Studied Ecole des Beaux Arts, Paris 1896-1900. A.R.A. 1934, R.A. 1942. Exh. 1934-39. Add: 1 Old Burlington Street, London. † RA 5.

DAVIS, A. Saville Exh. 1931
c/o Messrs. Bourlet, Nassau Street, London. † RCA 1.

DAVIS, C. Exh. 1890-91
St. Ives, Bushey Grove Road, Watford, Herts. † B 2, DOW 2, L 1.

DAVIS, Celia Exh. 1889-93
Landscape painter. Add: York. † M 1, RA 1, RBA 1, SWA 3.

DAVIS, Cyril Exh. 1922-35
Figure and flower painter. Add: London. † RA 3.

DAVIS, Charles H. Exh. 1891
c/o H.G. Murcott, 6 Endell Street, Long Acre, London. † RA 4.

DAVIS, Miss C.L. Exh. 1880-98
Landscape painter. Add: London. † SWA 24.

DAVIS, David Exh. 1881-87
Sculptor. Add: 16 Mansfield Road, Gospel Oak, London. † RA 6.

DAVIS, Doris A. Exh. 1919-28
Miniature painter and etcher. Add: Brockley, South London 1919; Bickley, Kent 1928. † GI 1, I 1, RA 3.

DAVIS, Miss E. Exh. 1903-11
Albert Road, Aston, Birmingham. † B 10.

DAVIS, Mrs. Eileen Exh. 1907-38
London. † I 4, L 8, RA 1, RI 4, SWA 7.

DAVIS, Edith Florence b. 1898
Mrs. T.W. Ridge. Watercolour portrait and miniature painter. Studied at Goldsmith's College. Add: 33 Carholme Road, Forest Hill, London 1927-40. † RA 4.

DAVIS, Ethel H. Exh. 1897
7 Pembridge Crescent, London. † RA 1.

DAVIS, Frederick Exh. 1880-92
Watercolour landscape painter. Add: Kentish Town, London 1880; Tufnell Park, London 1890. † D 1, L 4, RA 3, RBA 4.

DAVIS, Frederick Coulson b. 1891
Painter, etcher, wood carver and teacher. Studied South Kensington and Royal College of Art. Add: 46 Penge Road, Upton Park, Essex 1914. † RA 1.

DAVIS, Fanny Elton Exh. 1880-81
Grove House, West End, Hammersmith, London. † SWA 3.

DAVIS, Flórence M. Exh. 1902-6
Leicester 1902; Bramley, Leeds 1906. † B 4, L 1.

DAVIS, Frederick William 1862-1919
Figure painter. R.B.A. 1892, R.B.S.A. 1892, R.I. 1897. Add: 39 Temple Row, Birmingham and Hampstead Row, Handsworth, Birmingham. † B 21, L 1, RBA 19, RI 10.

DAVIS, Gertrude Exh. 1889-98
Belfast 1889; Dublin 1898. † GI 1, RHA 2.

DAVIS, G.G.M. Exh. 1884
† ROI 1.

DAVIS, Miss H. Exh. 1915
Leicester Road, Hinckley. † RA 1.
DAVIS, Hilda Exh. 1937-40
Mrs. Cyril Davis. Studied Grosvenor School of Modern Art 1935-39. Add: London. † GOU 1, NEA 3, RBA 1, ROI 2, SWA 4.
DAVIS, Horace Exh. 1939
Landscape painter. Add: 5 Cooper Road, Westbury-on-Trym, Bristol. † RA 1.
DAVIS, H. Brandon Exh. 1920-21
Doone Gate, Southam Road, Hall Green, Birmingham. † B 4.
DAVIS, Henry William Banks* 1833-1914
Landscape and animal painter and sculptor. A.R.A. 1873, R.A. 1877. Purchased by Chantrey Bequest "Returning to the Fold" 1880 and "Approaching Night" 1899. Add: London 1880; Rhayader, Radnor, Wales 1910. † AG 1, B 5, CAR 1, D 2, FIN 61, G 1, L 13, M 13, NG 3, RA 125, TOO 25.
DAVIS, Joseph Bernard b. 1861
Landscape painter and illustrator. b. Bowness on Windermere. Add: London 1890 and 1926, Gerrard's Cross 1911. † B 8, GI 10, L 14, LS 3, RA 14, RBA 3, RCA 8, RI 14, ROI 2, RSA 2, RSW 1.
DAVIS, John J.* Exh. 1883-84
Landscape painter. Add: 108 Gordon Road, Peckham, London. † RA 1, RBA 4.
DAVIS, J.J.M. Exh. 1887
19 Arnott Street, Dublin, Ireland. † RHA 3.
DAVIS, J. Pain Exh. 1882-1910
Ronaleyn, Trefriew, N. Wales 1882 and 1894, Regents Park, London 1887. † M 2, RCA 44.
DAVIS, Mrs. J.S.C. Exh. 1923-30
M.S. Davis. Flower and landscape painter. † WG 114.
DAVIS, Kathleen Exh. 1892-94
108 Upper Tulse Hill, London. † NG 2, ROI 5.
DAVIS, Laurence Exh. 1899-1901
Figure painter. Add: 5 Highbury Grove, London. † RA 2, RBA 1.
DAVIS, Louis Exh. 1897-1911
A.R.W.S. 1898. Add: Ewelme, Pinner, Middlesex. † I 2, L 1, NG 1, RWS 19.
DAVIS, Lucien* b. 1860
Portrait, landscape and figure painter. b. Liverpool. Brother of William Paul D. q.v. and Valentine D. q.v. Studied RA Schools. Principal artist for social events for 20 years with "Illustrated London News". Art master Ignatius College, London. R.I. 1893. Add: London 1885 and 1920, Lightwater, Bagshot, Surrey 1911, Enfield Chase, Middlesex 1932. † FIN 1, GI 3, L 16, M 2, P 1, RA 37, RI 99, ROI 9.
DAVIS, Lena M. Exh. 1891-92
Figure painter. Add: 9F Hyde Park Mansions, London. † RBA 2.
DAVIS, Lady Mary 1866-1941
nee Halford. Painter and decorative artist. Add: London 1880; Canterbury, Kent 1929. † FIN 1, G 3, GOU 10, I 21, L 3, LEI 50, RA 1, RID 94, ROI 3.
DAVIS, Magdalene A. Exh. 1935-38
Woodcut artist. Add: 14 Dix's Field, Exeter, Devon. † COO 3, SWA 1.
DAVIS, Miriam J. Exh. 1881-1920
Mrs. Imano. Domestic and figure painter. Add: London. † B 2, G 1, L 11, LS 32, M 4, NG 3, RA 12, RBA 23, ROI 5, SWA 15.
DAVIS, Miss N. Exh. 1892-1902
Birmingham. † B 20.

DAVIS, N. Denholm Exh. 1899-1939
Portrait and figure painter. N.S.A. 1908, V.P.N.S.A. 1923. Add: London and Nottingham. † B 1, L 2, N 193, RA 13.
DAVIS, Owen W. Exh. 1881-84
Architect. Add: London. † RA 3.
DAVIS, P. Exh. 1903
17 Lenton Road, The Park, Nottingham. † N 1.
DAVIS, Miss P.M. Exh. 1914
Oakhurst, The Park, Nottingham. † N 1.
DAVIS, Philip W. Exh. 1931-39
Painter and etcher. Add: 30 Bedford Gardens, London. † RA 2, RBA 1.
DAVIS, Stanley Exh. 1926
Landscape painter. Add: 3 Brook Green Studios, Dunsany Road, London. † RA 1.
DAVIS, Stuart G. Exh. 1893-1917
Figure painter. Add: London. † B 2, GI 1, L 2, M 1, NG 10, RA 20, RI 2, RMS 1, ROI 1.
DAVIS, Stanley R. Exh. 1909
† LS 3.
DAVIS, Thomas Exh. 1880
Watercolour landscape painter. Add: 74 Widmore Road, Bromley, Kent. † RBA 1.
DAVIS, T.P. Exh. 1886
Portrait painter. Add: Ightham, Kent. † RBA 1.
DAVIS, Valentine 1854-1930
Landscape painter. Brother of Lucien D. q.v. and William Paul D. q.v. Studied under his father. R.B.A. 1890. Add: London. † B 22, GI 49, L 21, M 9, NG 6, RA 36, RBA 162, RHA 1, RI 28, RMS 4, ROI 16.
DAVIS, William A. Exh. 1890
Sculptor. Add: 16 Connaught Road, Finsbury Park, London. † RA 1.
DAVIS, William D. Brokman Exh. 1930-37
Painter and etcher. Add: Leek, Staffs. † RA 3, RBA 1, RCA 2, RSA 2.
DAVIS, W.H. Exh. 1893
Domestic painter. Add: 23 Carlton Crescent, Southampton. † RBA 1.
DAVIS, William Paul Exh. 1883-1917
Figure painter. Brother of Lucien and Valentine D. q.v. Add: London. † L 5, RA 7, RBA 7, RI 1.
DAVIS, W.T. Exh. 1888-90
2 Lauderdale Road, Maida Vale, London. † L 1. ROI 1.
DAVISON, Miss A. Scott Exh. 1894-97
23 Park Place, East Sunderland. † L 6, RI 3, SWA 4.
DAVISON, Eleanor Exh. 1880-81
Landscape painter. Add: 10 Margaret Street, Cavendish Square, London. † D 1, SWA 7.
DAVISON, F.C. Exh. 1935-39
R.B.A. 1935. Add: The Studio, 8 High Street, Gosport, Hants. † NEA 2, RBA 20.
DAVISON, Miss G.D. Exh. 1911-16
Portrait painter. Add: 48 Lupus Street, St. George's Square, London. † I 1, LS 6, NEA 4, P 1, RA 1, ROI 1.
DAVISON, Miss Ivy Exh. 1933
Landscape painter. † COO 1.
DAVISON, John Exh. 1917
348 Rectory Road, Gateshead-on-Tyne. † RHA 1.
DAVISON, Miss M. Exh. 1893-94
23 Park Place East, Sunderland. † L 2, SWA 1.
DAVISON, Mrs. Munro Exh. 1897
142 Stroud Green Road, London. † RA 1.
DAVISON, Minnie D. See SPOONER
DAVISON, Miss M.L. Exh. 1916
57 Cavendish Road, Brondesbury, London. † RA 1.

DAVISON, Nora Exh. 1881-1900
Landscape and coastal painter. Add: London. † AG 2, D 19, FIN 2, G 3, L 1, NG 8, RA 2, RBA 15, SWA 23.
DAVISON, R. Exh. 1886
1 Carlisle Place, London. † RI 1.
DAVISON, Thomas Exh. 1892-1904
Architect. Add: London. † RA 9.
DAVISON, Thomas Raffles Exh. 1881-1922
Architect. Add: Manchester 1881; London 1883; Woldingham, Surrey 1904. † RA 19, RHA 12.
DAVISON, William Henry b. 1904
Designer and commercial artist. Studied Bolt Court L.C.C. School of Photo-Engraving. Add: 246 Odessa Road, London 1927. † RI 1.
DAVISON, W. Rupert Exh. 1904-17
Architect. Add: Woldingham, Surrey and London. † RA 5.
DAVISS, Mrs. Jessica Exh. 1898-1911
Miniature painter. Add: Clapham, London 1898; Cosham, Hants. 1911. † BRU 1, RA 2.
DAVY, Barbara Exh. 1910-14
Landscape painter. Add: London. † NEA 5.
DAVY, Henry Exh. 1886-1901
19 Milton Place, Halifax, Yorks. † B 1, L 3, M 1.
DAVY, Kate Exh. 1887
Flower painter. Add: Ford Park, Plymouth, Devon. † SWA 1.
DAVY, Phyllis Exh. 1895-96
St. Helens, Highfield Road, Rathgar, Dublin, Ireland. † RHA 3.
DAWBARN, Graham Exh. 1935
Architect. Add: 43 Grosvenor Road, Waterloo, Liverpool. † RA 1.
DAWBARN, Joseph Yelverton Exh. 1887-1933
Painter and barrister. Studied under Fleury 1890-94. Add: Liverpool. † B 3, I 1, L 33, M 2, RA 12, RCA 4, RI 9.
DAWBER, Sir Edward Guy c.1860-1938
Architect and painter. A.R.A. 1927. Add: Bourton-on-the-Hill, Moreton-in-Marsh, Glos. 1888; London 1885 and 1895. † COO 2, GI 7, L 6, RA 71, RBA 2, RI 26, RID 4, RSA 8, RWS 1.
DAWBER, Florence M. Exh. 1921-32
52 Queen's Drive, Walton, Liverpool. † L 14.
DAWE, Fred, G. Exh. 1908
22 Aberdeen Road, Wealdstone, Middlesex. † L 1.
DAWE, Jessie Exh. 1905
242 Gt. Clowes Street, High Broughton. † M 1.
DAWE, P.H. Exh. 1931
Toronto, Canada. † RCA 2.
DAWE, William E. Exh. 1929
Still life painter. Add: 9 Elsinore Road, Forest Hill, London. † RA 1.
DAWES, Harry R. Exh. 1896
12 Oxford Terrace, Hyde Park, London. † RI 1.
DAWES, Rev. J.W. Exh. 1898
All Saints Vicarage, St. Domingo Grove, Liverpool. † L 1.
DAWES, Marjorie Lilian See THOMAS
DAWKINS, Laura N. Exh. 1894-1910
Coventry. † B 13, L 11.
DAWKINS, Mary C.S. Exh. 1896
Interior painter. Add: 41 Oakley Crescent, Chelsea, London. † RA 1.
DAWNAY, Helen Exh. 1921-23
Flower and figure painter. Add: Brampton House, Northampton. † RA 4.

DAWNEY, D. Exh. 1940
Figure painter. † COO 2.

DAWNEY, O.F. Exh. 1905
58 Criffel Avenue, Streatham, London. † RA 1.

DAWS, Frederick Thomas b. 1878
Painter and sculptor. Studied Lambeth School of Art. Add: Kent House Road, Beckenham, Kent. † GI 1, L 5, RA 12, RBA 6, ROI 1.

DAWSON, Alfred* Exh. 1881-94
Landscape painter and etcher. Younger brother of Henry Thomas D. q.v. Add: Chiswick, London. † B 2, RA 3, RBA 1, RE 1, ROI 2.

DAWSON, Amy Exh. 1889-91
Flower, fruit and portrait painter. Add: London. † RBA 3.

DAWSON, Archibald C. d. 1938
Sculptor. A.R.S.A. 1937. Add: Glasgow. † GI 16, RSA 16.

DAWSON, Mrs. A.R. Exh. 1895
Landscape painter. Add: "Ingleside", Magdala Road, Nottingham. † N 1.

DAWSON, Mrs. B. Exh. 1885
Fruit and flower painter. Add: The Mount, Hampstead, London. † SWA 2.

DAWSON, Bryon Exh. 1928-33
Decorative painter. Add: Newcastle-on-Tyne. † RA 2, RSA 3.

DAWSON, B. James Exh. 1936-40
Portrait painter. Add: 27 Edith Grove, London. † RA 4.

DAWSON, Miss C. Exh. 1896
43 Magdala Road, Nottingham. † N 1.

DAWSON, Charles Frederick Exh. 1909-33
Painter and designer. Studied Shipley School of Art, Bradford, Manchester and Newlyn, Cornwall. Married to Mary Elizabeth D. q.v. Headmaster of Bingley, Nelson and Accrington Schools of Art. Add: 7 Eaton Bank, Accrington. † I 1, L 12, M 1, RA 2.

DAWSON, Mrs. D.M. Exh. 1927-29
Oak Leigh, The Woodlands, Ledsham, Cheshire. † L 3.

DAWSON, E. Exh. 1929
104 West George Street, Glasgow. † GI 1.

DAWSON, Ethel Exh. 1930
L 1.

DAWSON, Edith Brearey Exh. 1895-1919
Painter and metal worker. Collaborated with her husband Nelson D. q.v. in metalwork. Add: London. † BG 2, I 2, L 20, LEI 9, NEA 2, RA 16.

DAWSON, Miss Elsie May See ROBSON

DAWSON, Gladys b. 1909
Painter, black and white artist, writer and illustrator of children's books. Studied Heatherley's. Add: Old Colwyn, Denbighshire 1930-40. † RCA 21, SWA 2.

DAWSON, George A. Exh. 1931-35
196 Clarkston Road, Glasgow. † GI 2, RSW 2.

DAWSON, Grace Munro Exh. 1929-36
The Mount, Dixon's Green, Dudley, Worcs. † B 6.

DAWSON, H. Hardwick Exh. 1929-32
Architect. Add: Milton Chambers, Milton Street, Nottingham. † N 2.

DAWSON, Miss H.M.W. Exh. 1933
5 Hague Road, West Didsbury, Manchester. † L 1.

DAWSON, Henry Thomas* Exh. 1882-96
Marine painter. Elder brother of Alfred D. q.v. Add: Salcombe, Devon. † B 5, L 2, TOO 11.

DAWSON, J. Allan* Exh. 1893-1936
Edinburgh. † GI 14, L 1, M 1, RA 1, RSA 26, RHA 1.

DAWSON, Mabel Exh. 1880-81
59 Westbourne Park Road, London. † D 2.

DAWSON, Mabel 1887-1965
Bird and animal painter, decorative panel and embroidery artist. Studied Edinburgh College of Art. R.S.W. 1917. Add: Edinburgh. † AR 2, GI 41, L 10, RA 1, RSA 78, RSW 95.

DAWSON, Madge Exh. 1911
22 Forest Drive, Leytonstone, London. † RA 1.

DAWSON, Marion Exh. 1904-40
Landscape and figure painter. Nursed in Russia and Salonika World War I. Add: London. † GOU 4, I 1, L 13, LS 10, M 1, NEA 2, P 3, RA 13, ROI 11, SWA 4.

DAWSON, Mary Elizabeth Exh. 1916-33
nee Bell. Watercolour and decorative painter and embroiderer. Married Charles Frederick D. q.v. Add: 7 Eaton Bank, Accrington, Lancs. † L 13, M 4, RA 5.

DAWSON, Matthew J. Exh. 1903
Architectural landscape painter. Add: 33 Ossington Street, Bayswater, London. † RA 1.

DAWSON, Montague J.* 1895-1973
Marine painter. Born at sea the son of an English Merchant Marine Captain. Add: London 1917; Milford-on-Sea, Hants. 1933. † CON 2, L 3, RA 7.

DAWSON, Nelson 1859-1941
Coastal and landscape painter, metalworker and etcher. Collaborated with his wife Edith Brearey D. q.v. in metalwork. N.E.A. 1887, R.B.A. 1890, A.R.E. 1910, R.E. 1915, A.R.W.S. 1921. Add: London. † ALP 4, B 16, BG 1, CG 1, CHE 1, DOW 1, FIN 6, G 6, GI 18, GOU 7, I 46, L 67, LEI 67, LS 11, M 8, NEA 21, NG 32, RA 39, RBA 49, RE 48, RI 7, RID 27, RSA 1, RSW 2, RWS 75.

DAWSON, Philip Exh. 1906-12
Liverpool. † L 3.

DAWSON, Percy A. Exh. 1903
Architect. Add: 11 Park Valley, The Park, Nottingham. † N 1.

DAWSON, P. Norman b. 1902
Mural painter, decorator and pottery artist. Studied Royal College of Art (prizes for design and travelling scholarship in decorative painting), Paris, Rome and Florence. Studied etching and engraving under Sir Frank Short. Member London Group 1933. Exh. 1937-39. † COO 2, LEI 2.

DAWSON, Rhoda Exh. 1919-39
Landscape painter. Daughter of Nelson and Edith D. q.v. Add: London. † I 1, NEA 4, RA 2, RSA 1.

DAWSON, Rev. Roy Exh. 1908
9 Ramsay Gardens, Edinburgh. † RSA 1.

DAWSON, Robert Arthur Exh. 1900-33
Decorative designer and painter. Studied Royal College of Art. Assistant master Royal College of Art, Municipal School of Art, Belfast, Professor of Design Queen's University and Examiner in art at Irish Secondary School. Principal Municipal School of Art, Manchester. Add: London 1900; Belfast 1904; Holywood, Co. Down 1906; Manchester 1919. † L 2, RA 2, RHA 20.

DAY, Miss Exh. 1926
Landscape painter. † WG 41.

DAY, Barclay Exh. 1881
† GI 1.

DAY, Cicely E. Exh. 1894-96
Landscape painter. Add: 52 Lower Sloane Street, Chelsea, London. † RID 3.

DAY, Dorothy Exh. 1939
2 Windsor Road, Dublin, Ireland. † RHA 1.

DAY, E. Exh. 1885-86
Brooklands, Trafalgar Road, Moseley, Birmingham. † B 4.

DAY, Miss E. Exh. 1912
11 Cambridge Park, Twickenham, Middlesex. † RA 1.

DAY, Mrs. Ella B. Exh. 1907
85 Lower Leeson Street, Dublin, Ireland. † RHA 1.

DAY, Eva G. Exh. 1926-39
Church Street, Warwick. † B 15, RI 2, RSA 1.

DAY, Miss F.G. Exh. 1905
Blenheim, Dewsbury, Yorks. † RA 1.

DAY, Frances S. Exh. 1916-38
Miniature and flower painter. Add: Dublin, Ireland. † B 2, RHA 9.

DAY, George H.J. Exh. 1909-38
Painter, etcher and sculptor. Add: London. † CHE 2, I 3, L 1, NEA 6, RA 11.

DAY, Gladys Muriel Exh. 1908-13
Greystones, Co. Wicklow, Ireland 1908; Chester 1913. † L 3, RHA 1.

DAY, G.R. Exh. 1926
11 Marldon Road, King's Heath, Birmingham. † B 1.

DAY, Henry D. Exh. 1903
Architect. Add: Railway Approach, Godalming, Surrey. † RA 1.

DAY, Miss H.E. Exh. 1882
Trinity Road, Birmingham. † B 1.

DAY, Miss K.M. Exh. 1936-39
895 Stratford Road, Hall Green, Birmingham. † B 8.

DAY, Lily Exh. 1898-1921
Bootle 1898; Liverpool 1903; Dyserth, Wales 1911; Prestatyn, Wales 1921. † L 44.

DAY, Mrs. Louisa Exh. 1929
Flower and still life painter. Add: 4 College Road, Isleworth, Middlesex. † ROI 1.

DAY, Miss L.F. Exh. 1895-96
London. † SWA 2.

DAY, Lewis Foreman c.1855-1910
Decorative artist. Add: 13 Mecklenburgh Square, London. † GI 2, RA 4.

DAY, Mrs. Mary Exh. 1909
Tavistock Road, London. † SWA 1.

DAY, Miss M.B. Exh. 1893-94
Cork Street Hospital, Dublin, Ireland. † RHA 4.

DAY, Mrs. Mary S. Exh. 1913
St. Peters Rectory, Sandwich, Kent. † D 2.

DAY, Nicholas Exh. 1932
Portrait painter. Add: 17 Castletown Road, London. † RA 1.

DAY, Winifred Exh. 1924
School of Arts, Lowestoft, Suffolk. † L 1.

DAY, William C. Exh. 1933-35
Sculptor. Add: London. † RA 2.

DAY, William Cave* 1862-1924
Domestic and figure painter. R.B.A. 1904. Add: Dewsbury 1890; Harrogate 1898; St. Ives, Cornwall 1920. † FIN 1, L 17, M 7, NG 1, RA 10, RBA 120, ROI 6.

DAY, William Inglis Exh. 1938
Bruce Street, Dunbarton. † GI 2.

DAY, W. Percy Exh. 1905-22
Figure painter. Add: Luton, Beds. 1905; London 1922. † GI 2, L 1, RA 9.

DAYDI-VALENZUELA, Francisco Exh. 1914
Riverside House, Strand-on-the-Green. † LS 2.

DAYKIN, Gilbert Exh. 1929-39
79 Sycamore Street, Church Warsop, Mansfield, Notts. † N 8.

DAYMAN, Francis S. Exh. 1883-1938
Landscape painter. Add: Ashley Court, Tiverton, Devon. † D 4, L 13, RA 1, RCA 2, RI 19, RSA 2.

DEACON, Allan Exh. 1895-1914
Portrait painter. Add: Paris 1895; St. Ives, Cornwall 1901. † GI 1, L 8, RA 9.

DEACON, A.O. Exh. 1880-88
Landscape painter. Add: Derby 1880; Ilkeston, Derbys. 1886. † B 1, N 13.

DEACON, Charles Ernest Exh. 1902-24
Painter and architect. Add: Liverpool. † RA 2.

DEACON, Charles Ernest d. c.1965
Landscape, seascape and flower painter. Studied Richmond School of Art. Son of Charles Ernest D. q.v. Add: 36 Palewell Park, East Sheen, London 1934. † RBA 1, RI 1.

DEACON, Dora Exh. 1894-1939
Landscape painter. Add: Loughton, Essex. † AR 1, COO 2, D 9, RI 3.

DEACON, Henry D. Exh. 1880
Landscape painter. Add: Harcourt Villa, Cardiff, and Bristol. † D 1, RBA 1.

DEACON, Monica Stuart Exh. 1925-30
Wallasey, Cheshire 1925; Liverpool 1929. † L 7.

DEACON, Percy Exh. 1931
6 Moat Avenue, Green Lane, Coventry. † B 1.

DEACON, T.V. Exh. 1923-24
South Cottage, Parkgate, Cheshire. † L 4.

DEACON, Miss V. Exh. 1885
Fairlight House, York Road, Eastbourne. † RI 1.

DEAKES, Mrs. Olive M. Exh. 1937-38
A.S.W.A. 1938; S.W.A. 1939. Add: Lower Farm, Kingston Blount, Oxon. † RA 1, SWA 5.

DEAKIN, Andrew Exh. 1882
The Hollies, Soho Park, Birmingham. † RE 2.

DEAKIN, Jane Exh. 1880-1908
Landscape and figure painter. A.S.W.A. 1884. Add: Watford, Herts. 1880; Chalfont St. Peter, Bucks. 1881; Birmingham 1887. † B 12, L 1, M 3, RI 1, SWA 34.

DEAKIN, Mabel G. Exh. 1914-32
Sculptor. Add: Dewhurst, Egerton, Bolton, Lancs. † GI 1, L 1, LS 1, RA 3.

DEAKIN, Peter* Exh. 1884
Landscape painter. Add: Chalfont St. Peter, Bucks. † B 1, L 1.

DEAKINS, Cyril Edward b. 1916
Painter, etcher and wood engraver. Studied Hornsey School of Art. Add: 114 High Road, New Southgate, London 1938. † RA 3.

DEAL, William J. Exh. 1939
† RI 1.

DEALY, Jane M. Exh. 1880-1931
Lady Lewis. Genre painter and illustrator of children's books. R.I. 1887. Add: Blackheath, London. † B 1, D 5, DOW 6, FIN 1, L 9, M 5, RA 21, RBA 5, RI 46, ROI 2.

DEAN, Arthur Exh. 1899
42 Grange Road, West Kirby, Cheshire. † L 1.

DEAN, Mrs. C. see DAVIES, Minnie M.

DEAN, Christopher Exh. 1895-99
Glasgow 1895; Marlow, Bucks. 1898. † GI 3, RSA 2.

DEAN, Dora Exh. 1881
Westra, Highland Road, Upper Norwood, London. † SWA 1.

DEAN, Frank b. 1865
Landscape painter. Studied Slade School and Paris. Travelled in Middle East and India. R.B.A. 1895. Add: Leeds 1887, 1896 and 1910; London 1890 and 1902; Arundel, Sussex 1898; Harpenden, Herts. 1899; Baldock, Herts. 1904. † B 3, FIN 129, L 18, M 6, NEA 3, NG 1, RA 26, RBA 16, RCA 2, RI 8, ROI 6, RSA 1.

DEAN, J.R.M. Exh. 1932
† L 1.

DEAN, Samuel Exh. 1895-1938
Birkenhead 1895; Glan Conway, Wales 1913. † L 19, RCA 24.

DEAN, Stanmore Exh. 1894-1902
180 West Regent Street, Glasgow. † GI 14, I 1, L 2, RSA 1.

DEANE, Miss Exh. 1890
Bolton Studios, Redcliffe Road, London. † G 1.

DEANE, Dorothy Exh. 1907-13
Newlands, Surbiton, Surrey 1907; Earl's Court, London 1913. † D 2, LS 3, RA 2.

DEANE, Emmeline Exh. 1881-1919
Miniature painter. Add: Bath 1881; Box, Wilts. 1892; London 1894. † L 1, LS 9, NG 4, RA 7, RMS 1, SWA 1.

DEANE, F. Exh. 1902
† BG 1.

DEANE, Miss L. Exh. 1884-91
Landscape painter. Add: Zion Hill, Bath. † B 5, D 2, L 2, M 2, RI 1, SWA 1.

DEANE, Mrs. M. Exh. 1921
Sea View House, Parkgate, Cheshire. † L 1.

DEANE, Miriam Exh. 1902-27
Liverpool 1902 and 1925; London 1909. † B 1, GI 2, I 3, L 13, LS 20.

DEANE, Sir Thomas Manby 1851-1933
Architect. Son of Sir Thomas Newenham D. q.v. A.R.H.A. 1898, R.H.A. 1910. Add: Dublin 1893; London 1906. Exh. 1893-1914. † GI 3, RA 4, RHA 4.

DEANE, Sir Thomas Newenham c.1828-1899
Architect. Father of Sir Thomas Manby D. q.v. A.R.H.A. 1861, R.H.A. 1864. Add: 3 Upper Merrion Street, Dublin. † RA 2, RHA 24.

DEANE-BURDETT, Ethel Exh. 1928-38
Flower and landscape painter. † COO 13, NEA 1.

DEANES, Edward Exh. 1880-1912
Figure and portrait painter. Add: London. † RA 12, RHA 4, RMS 1.

DEANES, H. Christabelle Exh. 1887-1911
Miniature portrait painter. Add: London. † RA 5.

DEARDEN, Fred Exh. 1901-39
Landscape painter. Add: The Fosse (North), Leicester. † N 24, RA 1.

DEARDEN, H. Exh. 1914
3 Oakley Street, Chelsea, London. † RA 1.

DEARE, Margaret Exh. 1884-97
Landscape and figure painter. Add: Englefield Green, Surrey 1884; Milford-on-Sea, Hants. 1897. † B 7, M 2, RBA 3.

DEARING, Rose Exh. 1930
24 Burnsall Street, London. † GI 1.

DEARLE, John Henry 1860-1932
Decorative artist and designer of stained glass and tapestries etc. Studied West London School of Art. Pupil, partner and art director with Wm. Morris & Co. Add: Regents Park, London 1880; Pirbright, Woking, Surrey 1887; Ramsgate, Kent 1902. † B 16, D 6, G 1, GI 2, L 1, M 6, RA 13, RI 11, ROI 2.

DEARNLEY, Miss Exh. 1903-4
12 Spellow Lane, Liverpool. † L 2.

DEARNLEY, A. b. 1904
Portrait sculptor. Add: 55 Southfield Road, London 1932. † RA 6, RSA 1.

DEARSLEY, Olive M. Exh. 1935-38
Figure painter. Add: Sutton, Surrey 1935; Normandy, nr. Guildford, Surrey 1938. † RA 2.

DEAS, Frank Exh. 1898-1908
Edinburgh. † GI 3, RSA 6.

DEAS, Kenneth Exh. 1890-92
London. † G 1, GI 1, L 1, ROI 2.

DEAS, William b. 1876
Landscape and interior painter. Add: Airds Cottage, Forgandenny, Perthshire 1925. † L 1, RBA 2, RI 2, RSA 5, RSW 20.

DEASE, Gerald Exh. 1899-1912
Watercolour landscape painter. Add: Turbetson, Coole, Co. Westmeath, Ireland. † NG 4, RHA 2, RI 3, WG 56.

DEASY, Lucila C. Exh. 1933-34
Painter and wood engraver. Add: Cnocna-Tatre, Carrighorig, Birr. † RHA 6.

DE BARRA, Eamonn Exh. 1935
Landscape painter. Add: Cork Art Club, 25 Patrick Street, Cork, Ireland. † RHA 1.

DE BARROS, Henrique M. Exh. 1927-34
Portrait painter. Add: 10 Portsdown Road, London. † RA 2.

DE BATHE, Miss D. Exh. 1910
50 Grove End Road, London. † RA 1.

DE BEAUPRE, A. Bastien Exh. 1884
Figure painter. Add: 13 Rue de Filles du Calvaire, Paris. † RA 1.

DE BEJAR, P.A. Exh. 1909-15
Portrait painter. Add: London. † RA 2.

DE BELLE, Charles Exh. 1900-11
Dublin 1900; Glasgow 1907; Kilbride, N.B. 1909; London 1911. † RA 1, RHA 1, RSA 3.

DE BENGY PUYVALLEE, Georges Exh. 1890-96
Sculptor. Add: Paris. † NG 1, RA 1.

DEBENHAM, Alison Exh. 1940
Landscape painter. † COO 2.

DEBENHAM, A.E. Exh. 1925
† GOU 1.

DEBENHAM, Miss K.M.H. Exh. 1929-33
London. † SWA 2.

DE BERTOUCH, Baron Rudolf Exh. 1908
7 Hereford Square, London. † B 1.

DE BIEMME, G. Exh. 1916
c/o Mrs. Vickery, Castletownhend, Ireland. † RHA 8.

DE BIEVRE, Marie Exh. 1883-84
61 Rue de Livourne, Quatre Louise, Brussels. † GI 3.

DEBILLEMONT-CHARDON, Gabrielle Exh. 1897-1913
Miniature portrait painter. R.M.S. 1898. Add: Paris. † L 24, NG 2, P 5, RA 7, RMS 56.

DE BISEAU, A. Exh. 1880-83
Landscape painter. Add: London 1880; Brussels 1881. † RA 1, RHA 5.

DE BLAAS, Eugene* Exh. 1882-1907
Figure painter. Add: Venice, Italy. † FIN 1, L 2, NG 1, RA 11, TOO 17.

DE BLAAS, Giulio 1888-1934
Portrait painter. Add: c/o Chapman Bros., 241 King's Road, Chelsea, London 1929. † RA 1.

DEBLOIS, Charles E. Exh. 1888
Figure painter. Add: 5 Haymarket, London. † RA 1.

DE BOCK, Theophile Emile Achile* 1851-1904
Dutch landscape painter. Exh. 1882-94. Add: The Hague, Holland. † GI 3, GOU 70, M 3.

DE BOLIVAR, Gabriella Exh. 1908-9
25 Victoria Road, Eccles Old Road, Manchester. † L 1, M 1.

DE BOON, H. Exh. 1883
20 Mortimer Street, Regent Street, London. † RHA 1.

DE BOTTON, John Exh. 1939
185 Queen's Gate, London. † RA 1.

DE BOUFFLERS, Mme Fanny Exh. 1928
Round House, Magazines Lane, New Brighton, Cheshire. † L 2.

DE BOUJINSKY Exh. 1938
Stage designer. † RED 2.

DE BOZNANSKA, Olga Exh. 1904-22
Paris, France. † I 14, L 1, RSA 1.

DE BRAUX, Genevieve Exh. 1911-19
Hampstead, London. † LS 26.

DE BREANSKI, Alfred* Exh. 1880-1919
Landscape and river painter. Brother of Gustave D. q.v. R.B.A. 1890. Add: Cookham, Berks. 1880; Greenwich 1883; London 1887. † B 9, D 9, G 1, GI 6, I 4, L 11, M 2, RA 24, RBA 80, RCA 8, RHA 2, RI 3, ROI 12, TOO 12.

DE BREANSKI, Gustave* Exh. 1880-92
Marine painter. Brother of Alfred D. q.v. Add: Cookham, Berks 1880; Lee, Kent 1884; Bromley, Kent 1887; Brockley, London 1890. † B 4, GI 1, L 4, M 4, RA 6, RBA 40, RHA 7, ROI 3, TOO 2.

DE BREE, Anthony Exh. 1882-1913
Interior painter. Add: London. † L 1, LS 9, M 3, RBA 8, ROI 3.

DE BREMAECKER, Eugene J. Exh. 1908-29
Sculptor. Add: Brussels. † GI 6, L 5, LS 6, RA 4.

DE BREZE, Louis Exh. 1908-9
110A Inverson Road, West Hampstead, London. † LS 6.

DEBRIE, Gustav Exh. 1910
54 Rue Lhomond, Paris. † L 1.

DE BRIMONT, G. Exh. 1886
25 Boulevard du Mont Parnasse, Paris. † M 1.

DE BRISAY, Marguerite Exh. 1892-93
Sculptor. Add: 11 Bradmore Road, Oxford. † RA 2.

DE BROUCKERE, Mlle. Jeanne Exh. 1903
Regensburgerstrasse, Berlin. † NG 4.

DE BROZIK, V. 1851-1901
Czechoslovakian artist. Director of Fine Arts, Prague. Add: Paris 1892. † B 2.

DE BRUYCKER, Jules* b. 1870
Belgian etcher. Add: 8 Fitzroy Street, London 1918. † I 1, RA 1.

DE BRUYN, Joseph Exh. 1880-94
Sculptor. Add: London. † L 6, RA 5, RBA 1.

DE BUNCEY, Phillippe Exh. 1927
29 Rue Coperine, Paris. † GI 1.

DE BUNSEN, Lady Exh. 1926-36
43 Ennismore Gardens, London. † RI 14.

DE BYLANDT, A.* Exh. 1882-86
Landscape painter. Add: 29 Bolsover Street, London. † B 5, M 3, RBA 2.

DE BYLANDT, Comtesse Amelie Exh. 1895-97
c/o Mrs. Miller, 13A Summer Place, Onslow Crescent, London. † RHA 3.

DE CALLIAS, Suzanne Exh. 1909-10
35 Rue Marbeuf, Paris. † L 2.

DE CALUWE, M. Exh. 1891-1910
6 Princes Road, Liverpool. † L 2.

DECAMPS, A. Exh. 1886
c/o A.H. Rigg, 94 Manningham Lane, Bradford, Yorks. † M 1.

DE CARRIE, Mrs. Ana Exh. 1901
Portrait painter. Add: 13 Blomfield Road, Maida Hill, London. † RA 1.

DE CARTERET, Doris H. b. 1897
Landscape painter. Studied at Byam Shaw and Vicat Cole School of Art 1915-19. Add: London 1926; Seaford, Sussex 1934; Arundel, Sussex 1937. † RA 1, RBA 9, RID 4, ROI 16, RSA 2.

DE CARTERET, Miss Malet Exh. 1903
Beaumont, Jersey, C.I. † SWA 1.

DE CASTRO, Harry M. Exh. 1880-92
Landscape painter. Add: London 1880; Mortlake, Surrey 1892. † L 2, M 1, RA 4, RBA 5.

DE CASTRO, Miss Mary Beatrice b. 1870
Landscape and miniature portrait painter. Studied South Kensington, Slade School, Colarossi's, Paris and under Mme Debillemont-Chardon. Add: Mortlake, Surrey 1893; London 1898; Reigate, Surrey 1928. † P 1, RA 2, RMS 6.

DECELLE, Edmond Carl b. 1889
American landscape painter. Add: Camberwell, London 1912-14. † LS 3, NEA 2, RA 1.

DE CETNER, A. Exh. 1881-83
Palazzo Ressenico, Venice, Italy. † RSA 6.

DECHAUME, C. Geoffroy Exh. 1910-25
Landscape and figure painter. Add: 31 Upper Grosvenor Street, London 1925. † CAR 20, RA 1.

DE CHAUSSE, Mlle Cecile Exh. 1901
W.G. Padgett. † RMS 2.

DE CHIRICO, Giorgio* b. 1888
Italian painter. Exh. 1921-38. † GI 2, GOU 1, LEF 31, RED 4.

DECKER, Elizabeth Exh. 1899-1904
Painter and etcher. A.R.E. 1900 (membership ceased 1904). Add: 4 Parkfield Road, Liverpool. † L 18, RE 16.

DE CLERCK, Jan Exh. 1915
† I 2.

DE COLLE, Signor Exh. 1922
United Arts Club, Dublin. † RHA 1.

DE CONINCK, Pierre Louis Joseph* 1828-1910
25 Rue Voiture, Amiens, France 1904. † L 1.

DE CONINCK, Mlle R. Exh. 1904
25 Rue Voiture, Amiens, France. † L 1.

DE COOK, C. Exh. 1881
16 Avenue Trudaine, Paris. † RHA 1.

DE COOL, Mme Delphine Exh. 1880-81
Enamel miniature painter. Add: 89 Rue de Rennes, Paris. † RA 4.

DE COOL, Gabriel Exh. 1909
15 Avenue Duquesne, Paris, France. † L 1.

DECORCHEMONT Exh. 1927
c/o E. Trower & Co. Ltd., Brown's Arcade, 92 Regent Street, London. † L 6.

DE CORDOBA, Mathilde J. d. 1912
American artist. Add: 138 Boulevard du Montparnasse, Paris 1909. † L 1.

DE CRESPIGNY, Rose Champion Exh. 1891-1929
nee Cooper-Key. Landscape painter. Add: Lyndhurst, Hants. 1891; London 1914. † D 2, LS 14, RBA 2, RID 62, ROI 1, SWA 8.

DEEGAN, Philip Exh. 1930
Landscape and figure painter. Add: 32 Fitzroy Avenue, Drumcondra, Ireland. † RHA 5.

DE EGUSQUIZA, Rogelio Exh. 1898-1900
A.R.E. 1898, membership ceased 1902. Add: 32 Rue Copernic, Paris. † RE 8.

DEELEY, Geoffrey H. Exh. 1935-39
Sculptor. Add: 19 Arch Hill Road, Netherton, Dudley, Worcs. † GI 1, RA 4.

DEERING, Miss F. Exh. 1884-87
The Bank, Tipton, Staffs. † B 2.

DEES, J.A. Exh. 1911-15
Newcastle-on-Tyne 1911; Gateshead-on-Tyne 1915. † RA 2, RI 1.

DEEVAR, Isa M. Exh. 1888
West Lodge, Dingwall. † RSA 1.

DEFAUX, Alexandre* 1826-1900
French artist. Add: Paris. † RHA 24.

DE FLEURY, J.V.* Exh. 1892-93
Landscape painter. Add: 53 Islington Row, Birmingham. † B 2.

DEFRIES, Lily Exh. 1886-1915
Landscape and flower painter. A.S.W.A. 1914, S.W.A. 1915. Add: London 1886; Orpington, Kent 1912. † BG 2, G 1, L 4, LS 13, RA 4, ROI 4, SWA 8.

DE FRISTON, Adrian Exh. 1925-28
Parkstone, Dorset 1925; Bournemouth 1928. † B 1, L 2, RA 1.

DEGAS, Hilaire Germain Edgar* 1834-1917
French painter and sculptor. H.R.S.A. 1911. Exh. 1888-1915. Add: Paris. † GI 1, GOU 1, I 8, NEA 6, RSA 3.

DE GAVERE, Cornelia b. 1877
Born Java. Exh. 1912-14. Add: London 1912 and 1914; Holland 1913. † LS 8, RA 1.

DE GERNON, Mrs. Emma Exh. 1894
The Studios, Chiniston Gardens, Kensington, London. † RHA 1.

DE GERNON, V. Exh. 1881-1909
Dublin, Ireland 1881 and 1907; Kensington, London 1893. † RHA 18.

DE GESNE, G. Exh. 1882
Paris, France. † GI 1.

DE GIGUEFELT, W. Exh. 1882
16 Avenue Trudaine, Paris. † RHA 1.

DE GIOVANNI, Cavaliere G. Exh. 1881
Sculptor. Add: 38 Wellington Street, Camden Town, London. † RA 1.

DE GLEHN, Jane Erin Exh. 1905-40
Formerly Von Glehn. Nee Emmet. Married Wilfred Gabriel D.G. q.v. Portrait and landscape painter. Add: 73 Cheyne Walk, London. † CHE 2, FIN 2, G 2, GOU 2, I 5, L 14, LS 5, NEA 7, NG 7, P 21, RA 21, RHA 11.

DE GLEHN, Wilfred Gabriel 1870-1951
Formerly Von Glehn. Landscape, portrait and marine painter. Married Jane Erin D.G. q.v. Studied South Kensington and Ecole des Beaux Arts, Paris. N.E.A. 1900, R.P. 1904, A.R.A. 1923, R.A. 1932. Add: London. † BA 2, BAR 56, CAR 39, CHE 6, COO 1, FIN 8, G 2, GI 29, GOU 128, I 17, L 57, LEI 46, LS 5, M 12, NEA 94, NG 20, P 53, RA 125, RHA 21, RSA 3.

DE GRINEAU, Bryan Exh. 1939
Colour landscape drawings of the Caribbean. † WG 50.

DE GRIVAL, Marie J.G. Exh. 1893-1909
Kensington, London 1893; Paris 1909. † GI 1, L 1, RI 3.

DE GROOT, Maurice Exh. 1908
6 Trafalgar Studios, Manresa Road, London. † LS 5.

DE HAAS, Johannes Hubertus Leonhardus* 1832-1908
Belgian Painter. Exh. 1886. Add: 117 New Bond Street, London. † M 2.

DE HALPERT, Dorothea or Doris Exh. 1916-19
25 Ashley Place, London. † I 1, NEA 3.

DE HEM, Louise Exh. 1909
11 Rue Darwen (ar. Brugmann) Brussels, Belgium. † L 1.

DE HOOG, Bernard* b. 1867
Dutch painter. Exh. 1907-37. † CON 2, L 2, RA 1.

DE HORMANN, Theodore* Exh. 1890
Figure painter. Add: 10 Seilerstatt, Vienna, Austria. † RA 2.

DE HOUGHTON, Miss Exh. 1883-87
78 Warwick Sq., London. † B 1, G 5, L 2.

DE HOZE, Miss J.M. Martinez Exh. 1909
12 Hobart Place, London. † L 1.

DE HUSSEY, Mme Mabel Exh. 1909
33 Rue de la Faisanderie, Paris. † L 1.

DEIKER, Johannes Exh. 1883
Animal painter. † FIN 1.

DEJEAN, Louis Exh. 1930
6 bis Rue St. James, a Neuilly sur Seine, France. † RSA 2.

DE JEANSON, Alfred Exh. 1913
2 Rue Gaillard, Paris. † L 1.

DE JERSEY, L. Exh. 1916
12 Arthur Avenue, Lenton, Nottingham. † N 2.

DE JONG, P. de Josselin Exh. 1891
† P 2.

DE JONGH, Tinus* Exh. 1933
Landscape painter Visited Africa. † AR 29.

DE JONGHE, Gustave* c.1828-1893
Belgian artist. Exh. 1884. † GI 1.

DE KAPPAY, A.J. Exh. 1914
c/o Agnew & Sons, 43 Old Bond Street, London. † RA 1.

DE KARLOWSKA, Stanislawa 1876-1952
Landscape and figure painter. Married Robert P. Bevan q.v. Member London Group 1914. Exh. 1908-40. Add: 14 Adamson Road, Hampstead, London. † COO 8, G 1, GOU 13, LEI 2, LS 38, NEA 2.

DE KAROLIS, Adolphe Exh. 1916
c/o A. Stiles & Sons, 617 Fulham Road, London. † GI 2.

DE KERCKHOVE, Paul V. Exh. 1917-19
Sculptor. Add: London. † RA 5.

DE KERVILY, le Serrac Exh. 1913-14
140 bis Rue de Rennes, Paris. † LS 6.

DE KEYSER, J. Exh. 1883
Sculptor. Add: 14 Rue de la Poterie, Brussels, Belgium. † RA 1.

DEKKERT, Eugene Exh. 1899-1938
Landscape and coastal painter. Add: Glasgow 1899 and 1904; St. Monans, N.B. 1903 and 1907. † BRU 33, GI 27, I 14, L 8, M 3, RSA 12, RSW 3.

DE KLERK, M. Exh. 1936
† RSA 2.

DE KOSSAK, A. Exh. 1907
51A Conduit Street, London. † RA 1.

DE KURNATOWSKA, Cecile Exh. 1912
2 Rue Antoine Dubois, Paris. † RSA 1.

DE KUSEL, Irma Exh. 1909-11
Portrait painter. † BRU 3, LS 3.

DE KUZMIK, Livia Exh. 1927
Sculptor. Add: Karva, Zupa Nitra, Slovensko, Europe. † RA 2.

DE LA BERE, Stephen Baghot Exh. 1904-15
Figure and landscape painter. Studied Westminster School of Art. R.I. 1908. Add: London 1904 and 1915; Bishops Stortford, Herts. 1913. † BRU 81, D 4, FIN 75, GOU 9, L 3, RA 2, RI 11.

DE LABILLIERE, May Exh. 1897
Portrait artist. Add: Harrow-on-the-Hill, Middlesex. † RA 1.

DE LA BRELY, A. Exh. 1883-84
Landscape and figure painter. Add: c/o Ludovici, 20 Mornington Road, Regents Park, London. † GI 1, M 1, RBA 4, ROI 1.

DELACHAUX, Leon* Exh. 1905-13
20 Rue Durantin, Paris. † L 4, RSA 1.

DELACOUR, Clovis Exh. 1896-1906
Sculptor. Add: London. † B 4, I 1, L 4, RA 3.

DE LA COZE, F.M. Exh. 1932-40
Landscape and figure painter. Travelled on continent, Middle East, India and South Africa. Add: Midhurst, Sussex 1932; Hayling Island 1934. † AR 110, RBA 2, RCA 5, ROI 1.

DE LACROIX, Madame Exh. 1880
Miniature painter. Add: 15 Shrewsbury Road, St. Stephens Square, Bayswater, London. † RA 1.

DE LA CROUEE, H. Exh. 1885
20 Bolton Studios, Redcliffe Road, London. † RI 1.

DE LACY, Charles John* Exh. 1885-1918
Landscape, coastal and naval portrait painter and black and white artist. Studied Lambeth and South Kensington. Special press artist and correspondent to "Illustrated London News", "Graphic" etc. Also artist to the Admiralty and Port of London Authority. Add: London. † L 4, M 2, RA 4, RBA 13.

DELAFIELD, Margaret* Exh. 1921-39
Flower, portrait and miniature painter. A.R.M.S. 1921, A.S.W.A. 1936. Add: London. † L 11, RA 8, RHA 3, RMS 24, RSA 4, SWA 14.

DE LAFONTAINE, H.P. Cart Exh. 1923-38
Architect. Add: London. † RA 8.

DE LAFONTINELLA, Rene Exh. 1898
Landscape painter. Add: 12 Clarendon Road, Notting Hill, London. † NEA 1.

DE LA FONTINELLE, Jean Exh. 1930
150 Avenue du Roule, Neuilly sur Seine, France. † RA 1.

DE LA GANDARA, Antonio 1862-1917
French painter. Exh. 1895-1909. Add: Paris. † P 4.

DE LAGERBERG, Miss Brita see WARD

DELAGRANGE, Leon Exh. 1906
14 Rue Fontaine, Paris. † L 1.

DELAHOGUE, A.E.G. Exh. 1911
† BRU 4.

DELAHUNT, Jennie b. 1877
Sculptor and modeller. Studied Manchester Municipal School of Art (medallist and scholarship winner). Art teacher Lancaster School of Art and Girls' Grammar School. Exh. 1904-19. Add: Lancaster. † L 1, M 1, RA 2.

DE LALAING, Jacques 1858-1917
Sculptor and painter. H.R.S.A. 1914. Add: 43 Rue Ducale, Brussels, Belgium. † L 1, RA 2, RSA 8.

DELAMBRE, L.P. Exh. 1882
13 Avenue de Rondpoint, Lilas, France. † GI 2.

DE LANDRE, Helen R. Exh. 1909
1 Gardenville, Chapelizod, Co. Dublin. † RHA 3.

DE LANNOY, Mme Florence Exh. 1923-36
88 Lyncombe Hill, Bath. † GI 2, L 12, RCA 3, RSA 2.

DELANOY, Jacques* Exh. 1887
Still life painter. Add: 89 Rue des Marnis, Paris. † GI 2.

DELAON, Paul E.V. Exh. 1914
43 Rue de Seine, Paris. † RSA 2.

DE LA RIVA-MUNOZ Exh. 1904
233 Faubourg St. Honore, Paris. † NG 1.

DELAROCHE, Paul C. Exh. 1907
6 Rue des Beaux Arts, Paris. † L 1.

DE LA ROSA, M. Exh. 1883-88
† TOO 5.

DELASALLE, Mlle. Exh. 1902
3 Rue Jean Baptiste Dumas, Paris. † NG 1.

DE LASSENCE, Paul* Exh. 1911
7 Rue de Bagneux, Paris. † L 2.

DE LASZLO, Philip Alexius (Fulop)* 1869-1937
Portrait painter. b. Hungary. Naturalised British subject. Studied Budapest, Munich and Paris. H.R.B.A. 1907, P.R.B.A. 1930, R.P. 1913. Add: Budapest 1901; Vienna 1902; London 1907. † AG 29, ALP 1, B 5, DOW 40, FIN 4, GI 25, I 16, L 46, M 2, NG 1, P 14, RA 4, RBA 38, RHA 13, RSA 18.

DE LATENAY, Gaston Exh. 1909
147 Avenue de Villiers, Paris. † L 2.

DELATRE, Pauline Exh. 1908
87 Rue Lepic, Paris. † L 1.

DE L'AUBINIERE, Georgina M. Exh. 1880-1905
Figure and landscape painter. Add: London 1880 and 1890; Addiscombe, Surrey 1881; Paris 1882; Cornwall 1902. † B 7, G 1, M 3, NG 2, RA 10, RI 1, ROI 1.

DELAUNAY, Jules Elie* 1828-1891
French figure painter. Add: 134 New Bond Street, London 1882. † RA 2.

DELAUNOIS, Alfred N. Exh. 1905-15
Landscape and figure painter. Add: Liege. † FIN 5, I 9.

DELAUNOIS, Eugene Exh. 1905
63 Rue de Bogards, Liege. † I 2.

DE LAUTOUR, Amelia Cate Exh. 1925-31
Sculptor. b. Scotland. Studied Bournemouth School of Art, Central School of Arts and Crafts. Add: London. † L 6, RA 3, RMS 1, SWA 1.

DELAYE, Charles Exh. 1886
7 Passage Menelmontant, Paris. † M 1.

DELBOS, C.E. Exh. 1908-12
Snowdon, Woldingham, Surrey 1908 and 1912; Downside Abbey, Bath 1910. † GI 2, GOU 1, L 1, NEA 1, ROI 1.

DELBOS, Julius M. b. 1879
Landscape painter. Add: Bowden College, Cheshire 1906; Great Yarmouth, Norfolk 1912; Uppingham, Rutland 1916; London 1926. † D 5, GI 1, L 1, RA 6.

D'ELBOUX, Elise b. 1870
Painter and pen and ink artist. Studied Royal College of Art; Juliens, Paris; Camden School of Art and Chelsea School of Art. Art mistress Royal College of Art 1897-1901. Exh. 1902-20. Add: London. † L 7.

DEL CAMPO, Frederico* Exh. 1909
c/o W. Graham, Isola di Capri, Italy. † B 1.

DE LEEUW, A. Exh. 1881-96
London. † RHA 12.

DELEEVAULT, Pierre Exh. 1888
259 Union Street, Aberdeen. † GI 1.

DE LESSEPS, Charles V. Exh. 1912
7 Rue Lalo, Paris. † L 1.

DE LEUVILLE, Marquis Exh. 1886
2 The Albany, Piccadilly, London. † RHA 1, RSA 2.

DE L'HOPITAL, Rene* Exh. 1907-29
Portrait painter. Add: London. † L 1, LS 3, NG 1, RA 1.

DE LIERRES, Etienne Exh. 1924
95 Avenue de Versailles, Paris. † L 1.

DE LISLE, Fortunee Exh. 1897-1910
Miniature painter. Add: London. † L 8, LS 4, NG 9, P 3, RA 5, RBA 2, SWA 4.

DE LISLE, Georgina Lucy Exh. 1897-1933
Painter, etcher and miniaturist. Studied Lambeth, Westminster, Juliens, Paris. A.S.W.A. 1932. Add: Wimbledon, London. † L 7, LS 6, P 2, RA 5, RBA 1, RMS 3, ROI 2, SWA 2.

DELITZ, Leo Spiridion b. 1880
Figure and landscape painter. b. Yugoslavia. Studied Vienna and Munich. Add: 23 Greville Road, London 1939. † RA 2.

DELL, A.S. Exh. 1889
30 Castle Street, Liverpool. † L 1.

DELL, Ethelene Eva Exh. 1885-1923
Figure painter. Add: South London. † B 22, D 58, L 3, LS 16, M 8, RA 2, RBA 1, RI 7, ROI 2, SWA 2.

DELL, Henry L. Exh. 1894-1910
Figure and landscape painter. Add: London 1894; Petersfield, Hants. 1904; Midhurst, Surrey 1908. † B 1, BG 30, D 6, L 4, M 1, RA 8, RBA 2, RI 3.

DELL, John H.* 1830-1888
Landscape and rustic genre painter. Add: 5 Montern Road, New Malden, Surrey. † B 2, M 1, RBA 5.

DELL, Rose Exh. 1881
Flower painter. Add: The Lodge, Upper Tooting Park, London. † SWA 1.

DELL'ACQUA, G. Exh. 1880
83 Rue due Prince Royal, Brussels. † RHA 1.

DELLEANY, Greta Exh. 1913-40
Etcher. A.R.E. 1919. Add: Tottenham, N. London 1913; Harrow, Middlesex 1931. † L 8, RA 16, RE 19.

DELLENBAUGH, Frederick Samuel b. 1853
American artist. Add: Concarneau, Finistere 1884. † GI 1.

DELLER, Lawrence Exh. 1906-14
Lichfield, Staffs. 1906; London 1914. † B 1, LS 3.

DELLSCHAFTE, Margarethe Exh. 1911-13
Highbury Grove, N. London. † SWA 3.

DELMAR, Frances Exh. 1900
76 Fulham Road, London. † RBA 1.

DELMEGE, Miss C. Exh. 1889
13 Royal Terrace, East Kingstown, Dublin. † RHA 1.

DELMUE, Maurice August b. 1878
c/o E.J. Van Wisselingh, 14 Grafton Street, London 1913. † RA 1.

DELOBBE, Francois Alfred b. 1835
French artist. Add: 27 Rue d'Alesia, Paris 1901-5. † L 5.

DE LORIOL, Miss M. Exh. 1900
Villa Gros, Route D'Antibes, Cannes, France. † SWA 2.

DE LORME, Mlle. M.A.R. Exh. 1907
277 bis, Rue St. Jacques, Paris. † L 1.

DELPECH, P.C.F. Exh. 1908
41 Rue de Villiers, Neuilly sur Seine, France. † L 1.

DELPY, Hippolyte Camille* 1842-1910
French landscape painter. Add: 17 Rue Hegesippe, Morcan, Paris 1901. † I 1, L 2.

DELRENNE, Edmond Exh. 1915-16
c/o Dermond O'Brien, P.R.H.A., Dublin. † RHA 4.

DELUG, Alois b. 1859
Landscape painter. Add: 3 Neureutherstrasse, Munich 1896. † RA 1.

DELVILLE, Jean* Exh. 1902-4
Glasgow. † GI 1, RSA 1.

DELVIN, J. Exh. 1901
282 Rue de Royghem, Ghent, Belgium. † I 1.

DE LYNDEN, Baroness Frideswith Exh. 1926
Portrait, figure, landscape and religious painter. † BA 87.

DE LYNDEN, Baron R.A. Exh. 1923
Portrait painter. † WG 16.

DE LYONCOURT, Baron H. Exh. 1880-84
Landscape painter. Add: 1 Albion Road, St. John's Wood, London. † RA 1, RHA 4.

DE MAINE, Miss A.E. Exh. 1881-97
Landscape painter. Add: Bolton Abbey, Skipton, Yorks. 1881; St. Moritz, Switzerland 1896. † D 1, RHA 1, RI 1, SWA 6.

DE MAINE, George Exh. 1888
4 Burnaby Street, Chelsea, London. † NEA 1.

DE MAINE, George Frederick b. 1892
Landscape painter. b. Keighley, Yorks. Add: London 1921; Bushey Heath, Herts. 1936. † ALP 1, RA 7.

DE MAINE, Henry (Harry) b. 1880
Exh. 1904-39. Add: Liverpool. † L 8, NEA 1, RI 2, RSW 2.

DE MARCILLY, Millet Exh. 1889
Sculptor. Add: c/o Lady Colin Campbell, 67 Carlyle Mansions, London. † RA 1.

DE MARTINO, Eduardo* c.1834-1912
Marine painter. Add: 1 St. John's Wood Studios, Queen's Terrace, London 1897. † FIN 72, L 1.

DE MATTOS, Ethel M. Exh. 1918-26
Flower painter. Add: London. † G 3, GOU 11, I 8, L 1, RA 1, SWA 2.

DE MATTOS, Henry Teixeira Exh. 1891-98
Sculptor. Add: London. † L 4, RA 3.

DE MAURINGNY, E. Exh. 1891
12 Hawthorn Grove, Heaton Chapel, Manchester. † L 1.

DE MEESTER, R. Exh. 1918
13 Kensington Palace Gardens, London. † RA 1.

DE MELLANVILLE, G. Exh. 1912
22 Rue de Tourlaque, Paris. † L 1.

DE MERBITZ, Marguerite Exh. 1895-1906
Miniature painter. R.M.S. 1896. Add: 11 Rue de Penthievre, Paris. † L 1, RA 11, RMS 9.

DE MERIC, Rosalie Exh. 1938
† NEA 1.

DE MESTRE, R. Exh. 1930
† L 1.

DE METZ, Lanfant Exh. 1882
16 Avenue Trudaine, Paris. † RHA 4.

DE MIGL, Arpad Exh. 1904
45 Avenue de Villiers, Paris. † L 1.

DE MIRMONT, Mme. R. Exh. 1905
8 Boulevard de Courcelles, Paris. † L 1.

DE MOLEYNS, Maj. Gen. Townsend Aremberg c.1838-1926
Exh. 1895-1913. Add: London. † D 59.

DE MONARD, L. Exh. 1910
3 Rue Dutot, Paris. † L 1.

DE MONIGOT, B.H. Exh. 1923
† P 1.

DEMONT, Adrien Louis 1851-1928
French artist. Exh. 1898-1913 † GI 1, NG 2, RSA 1.

DE MONT, Rene Exh. 1925-30
Landscape painter. London. † NEA 7, RA 1.

DEMONT-BRETON, Virginie b. 1859
Married Adrien Louis D. q.v. Add: Montgeron, Seine et Oise, France 1898. † NG 2.

DE MONTHOLON, J. Exh. 1887
20 Rue des Martyrs, Paris. † GI 1.

DE MONTMORENCY, Lily Exh. 1895-1904
Landscape and figure painter. A.S.W.A. 1898. Add: Streatham, London 1895; Bushey, Herts. 1898. † L 1, RA 2, RID 29, SWA 7.

DE MONTMORENCY, Miles Fletcher b. 1893
Landscape and figure painter. Married to Rachel Marion de M. q.v. Studied Dover School of Art 1910-11, Byam Shaw and Vicat Cole School of Art 1912-13, RA Schools 1914-15. Served Army 1915-19. R.B.A. 1935. Add: London. † ALP 1, COO 9, GOU 1, I 4, RA 12, RBA 28, ROI 1, WG 5.

DE MONTMORENCY, Rachel Marion Exh. 1920-38
nee Tancock. Married Miles Fletcher de M. q.v. Landscape painter and stained glass artist. Add: London. † COO 9, RA 11, RSA 1, WG 2.

DE MONTRAVEL, Violet Exh. 1900-2
56 Woodstock Rd., Bedford Park, Chiswick, London. † B 1, SWA 3.

DE MONVEL, Barnard Boutet* b. 1884
French artist. Add: 11 Passage de la Visitation, Paris, 1911. † L 1.

DE MONVEL, Louis Maurice Boutet 1851-1913
French painter. Exh. 1890-1902. Add: Paris. † GOU 36, FIN 1, P 5, RA 2, RSA 1.

DE MORGAN, Mrs. Evelyn See PICKERING

DEMPSEY, Charles W. Exh. 1880
16 Cheyne Row, Chelsea, London. † RBA 1.

DEMPSEY, John Exh. 1934
Sculptor. 43 Parnell Rd., Dublin. † RHA 2.

DEMPSTER, Elizabeth S. Exh. 1935-39
Edinburgh. † RSA 5.

DEMPSTER, F. John Exh. 1937-38
Portrait painter. "Glenmoor", Moor Rd., Bestwood, Notts. † N 2.

DEMPSTER, Miss Margaret See NISBET

DEMPSTER, M.J. Exh. 1884-1910
Flower painter. Add: Stirling and Edinburgh. † BG 5, GI 7, L 2, RSA 2.

DE MUNKACSY, Michel* 1844-1900
Hungarian painter. Exh. 1880-84. Add: London and Paris. † GI 1, RA 2.

DE NAGY, Segismund b. 1872
Rumanian landscape painter. Exh. 1925. † TOO 42.

DE NATHUSENS, Miss S. Exh. 1887
77 Rue Norre Dame des Champs, Paris. † L 1.

DENBY, W. Neville Exh. 1890-1926
87 Camp St. Broughton, Manchester. † M 7.

DENCH, W.J. Exh. 1921
37 Fitzwilliam Place, Dublin. † RHA 1.

DENDY, G. Exh. 1895-99
† TOO 2.

DE NEER, Pav. Exh. 1889
111 Chaussee d'Alemberg, Neele, Belgium. † B 2.

DENET, Charles Exh. 1900
2 Rue Jouffroy, Paris. † GI 1.

DE NEUVILLE, Claud Exh. 1880-83
Oxford. † D 1, FIN 1.

DENHAM, F.C. Exh. 1920-28
13 Cranbrook Park, Wood Green, London. † L 6.

DENHAM, Henry James b. 1893
Painter, illustrator and black and white artist. Exh. 1934-39. Add: Beckenham, Kent 1935; West Wickham, Kent 1939. † COO 2, RA 1, RI 2.

DENHOFF, Anna Exh. 1939
† GOU 1.

DENHOLM, James Exh. 1885-94
Dunbar. † L 1, RSA 2.

DENHOLM, Robert Exh. 1897-1927
Etcher. Add: Edinburgh 1897; Chorley Wood, Herts. 1907. † ALP 44, BK 22, L 3, RA 1, RSA 7.

DENING, Charles Frederick William b. 1876
Architect and artist. Exh. 1929-40. Add: Gaunt House, Orchard St., Bristol. † RI 11, ROI 4.

DENIS, Esther Exh. 1897-1908
Dublin 1897 and 1905; Belfast 1901; Bristol 1904. † B 1, L 1, RA 1, RHA 17.

DENIS, Maurice* 1870-1943
French painter and engraver. Exh. 1912-37. † GOU 12, L 1, RED 1, RSA 3.

DENISON, Miss C. Exh. 1905
4 Headingley Terr., Leeds, Yorks. † RA 1.

DENISON, Ethel M. Exh. 1898
Sculptor. Clarendon Rd., Leeds, Yorks. † RA 1.

DENISON, H. Exh. 1906
4 Headingly Terr., Leeds, Yorks. † RA 1.

DENISON, J. Exh. 1882
† G 1.

DENISON, Lucy Exh. 1880-81
Landscape and coastal painter. London. † SWA 3.

DENISON, Stephen b. 1909
Landscape painter. Self taught. Add: Ramsgill, nr. Harrogate, Yorks. 1939. † RA 1.

DENISON-PENDER, Lady Exh. 1907-11
6 Grosvenor Crescent, London. † L 7.

DE NITTIS, J. Exh. 1880-83
Paris. † G 2, GI 1.

DENLEY, Mary Exh. 1889
Stained glass artist. 7 Endlesham Rd., Balham, London. † RA 1.

DENMAN, John L. Exh. 1933
Architect. Olways, Hurstpierpoint, Sussex. † RA 1.

DENMAN-JONES, Gladys b. 1900
Portrait, landscape and miniature painter. Studied Slade School. Add: The Logs, Chagford, Devon 1926. † RI 9.

DENNE, Charlotte Exh. 1932
Etcher. c/o Barclays Bank Ltd. 15 Gt. Portland St., London. † RA 1.

DENNIS, Ada See GANDY

DENNIS, Alfred Exh. 1901
Landscape painter. 49 Ravenscourt Gardens, Hammersmith, London. † RA 1.

DENNIS, Ada L. Exh. 1897-1934
Portrait, landscape and seascape painter. b. Chester. Studied Juliens, Paris. R.O.I. 1917. Add: Chester 1897; London 1910 and 1921; Bishop's Stortford, Herts. 1917. † I 2, L 17, M 1, P 2, RA 4, RCA 1, RI 6, ROI 53, SWA 3.

DENNIS, Kathleen Exh. 1893
Rathmore, Naas, Ireland. † RHA 2.

DENNIS, L. Exh. 1906
Crowborough, Sussex. † RA 1.

DENNIS, James Morgan b. 1891
American etcher. Exh. 1936. † FIN 2.

DENNIS, W. Exh. 1913-22
A.N.S.A. 1908. Add: Nottingham 1913; Hyson Green, Nottingham 1922. † N 21.

DENNIS, W.S. Exh. 1934-37
55 Gristhorpe Rd., Selly Oak, Birmingham. † B 3.

DENNISON, Christabel Exh. 1909-19
The Sheiling, Grance Rd., Bushey, Herts. † I 6, LS 8.

DENNISS, Jacqueline Exh. 1933
Flower painter. Kirk Style, West End, Nr. Southampton. † RA 1.

DENNISTOUN, Mrs. R. Exh. 1880
Helensburgh. † GI 1.

DENNISTOUN, William Exh. 1880-84
Landscape painter. Isola di Capri, Italy. † D 4, GI 1, RI 1, RSA 3.

DENNY, Thomas J. Exh. 1932-34
Architect. 111 Clarence Rd., Clapham Park, London. † RA 2, RSA 1.

DENNYS, Joyce Exh. 1918-21
Figure painter. 117 Warwick Rd., London. † RID 7.

DENT, Clara W. Exh. 1891-1902
Wolverhampton 1891; Cheltenham 1902. † RCA 2, RSA 1.

DENT, G.H.M. Exh. 1902
Pitville Gates, Cheltenham, Glos. † RCA 1.

DENT, Miss M.R. Exh. 1921
7 Rosemount Rd., Bournemouth. † RA 1.

DENT, Rupert Arthur Exh. 1884-1909
Animal and figure painter. Add: Wolverhampton 1884; London 1887; Edinburgh 1889; Cheltenham, Glos. 1897. † B 1, GI 3, L 13, RA 6, RCA 4, RHA 17, RI 2, ROI 1, RSA 5.

DENT, Robert Stanley Gorrell b. 1909
Painter and etcher. Studied Newport School of Arts and Crafts and Royal College of Art. Assistant master Cheltenham School of Art 1935. A.R.E. 1935. Add: Newport, Mon. 1932 and 1936; London 1935. † COO 4, RA 9, RE 20, RSA 7.

DENTON, Annie Exh. 1921-23
Handsworth, Birmingham 1921; Boscombe, Hants. 1923. † B 2.

DENTON, Emily Bailey Exh. 1887
Flower painter. Orchard Court, Stevenage, Herts. † SWA 1.

DENTON, Miss M.E. Exh. 1929
Bilton, Rugby. † B 1.

DENTY, John H. Exh. 1919
Miniature portrait painter. 209 Willesden Lane, London. † RA 1.

DENVIL, Mlle A.B. Exh. 1905
3 Rue Vallier, Levallois-Perret, Seine, France. † L 1.

DENYER, Alfred Exh. 1882-99
Landscape painter. Bedford. † RBA 17.

DE PARIS, Alphonse G. Exh. 1933
Figure painter. 12 Observatory Gardens, London. † RA 1.

DE PENNE, Charles Olivier* 1831-1897
French sporting painter. Exh. 1880. † AG 2.

DEPEW, Agnes V. Exh. 1939
2 Stanley Studios, Park Walk, London. † RBA 1, SWA 1.

DE PIENKOWSKI, Ignacey b. 1877
Polish artist. 8 Rue de la Grande Chaumiere, Paris 1908. † LS 3.

D'EPINAY, Count Charles Adrian Prosper 1836-1914
Sculptor. Exh. 1881. Add: Rome. † RA 1.

D'EPINAY, Marie b. 1870
Portrait painter. Daughter of C.A. Prosper D'E. q.v. Studied Rome and Paris. Exh. 1907-17. Add: Paris. † FIN 24, RA 1.

DE POIX, Hugh Exh. 1913-38
Landscape painter. A.R.B.A. 1927, R.B.A. 1929. Add: Broome Place, Nr. Bungay, Suffolk 1913; London 1928. † COO 16, P 4, RA 1, RBA 58.

DE POTT, Liza Exh. 1914
90 Rue de Tram, Watermael, Brussels. † RSA 1.

DE PRESALE, Mme Mario Exh. 1928
27 Rue George Sand, Paris. † GI 1, RSA 1.

DE PURY, Baron Edmond Jean* 1845-1911
Swiss figure painter. 3 Rue du Musee, Neuchatel, Suisse 1891. † L 1, RA 1.

DERAIN, Andre* 1880-1954
French painter. Exh. 1914-37. † ALP 1, CHE 13, GOU 5, RED 3.

DE RENAULT, Lex Exh. 1898-1908
Portrait and figure painter. Add: London. † GI 1, RA 6, RBA 2.

DE RICCI, Miss L. Exh. 1884
Moulsey House, Hampton Court, London. † RHA 1.

DERING, Arthur R. Exh. 1889
Landscape painter. 28 Upper Berkeley St., Portman Sq., London. † RA 1.

D'ERLANGER, Catherine Exh. 1918
Baroness Marie Rose Antoinette Catherine D'E. Daughter of Marquis de Rochegude. Studied under Walter Sickert and Juliens, Paris. † I 1.

D'ERLANGER, Robin c. 1896-1934
Painter and decorative artist. Exh. 1918-19. † I 7.

D'ERLANGER, Baron Rodolphe 1872-1932
Landscape and portrait painter. Son of Catherine D'E. q.v. and Baron Emile D'E. Lived in Tunisia for many years. Exh. 1922-31. † ALP 60, GI 2, I 1, L 7, P 5, RA 1, RHA 4, ROI 10.

DERMOTT, Marie Exh. 1918-26
Mrs. Pons. Miniature painter. Add: 24 Old Park Ave., London. † RA 5, SWA 3.

DE ROBECK, Lady Exh. 1937
Marine painter. † WG 16.

DE ROC-B'HIAN, Aufray Exh. 1882
Etcher. c/o M.P. Delarue, 122 Bould, St. Germain, Paris. † RA 3.

DE ROME, Adam Exh. 1911
74 Stramongate, Kendal, Westmoreland. † LS 3.

DE ROMER, Anna Exh. 1931
Watercolour painter. b. Poland. † BA 42.

DE ROSALES, E.O. Exh. 1909-13
Paris 1909; Chelsea, London 1913. † I 1, L 3.

DE ROUSSADO, Marguerite Exh. 1907-10
Liverpool. † L 7.

DE ROZSNYAY, Calman V.H. Exh. 1900
Figure painter. 25 Hornton St., Kensington, London. † NEA 1.

DERREUX, Charles Exh. 1882
16 Avenue Trudaine, Paris. † RHA 3.

DERRICK, Clara Exh. 1901-2
39 Sydenham Hill, Cotham, Bristol. † B 2, L 3.

DERRICK, Freda Exh. 1921
5 Culworth St., St. John's Wood, London. † L 1.

DERRICK, Thomas C. 1885-1954
Illustrator, mural decorator and lecturer on Art. Instructor in decorative painting Royal College of Art. b. Bristol. Add: London 1909; Hungerford, Berks. 1920; Bucklebury, Nr. Reading, Berks. 1930. † FIN 14, G 1, I 4, NEA 1, RA 6.

DERRICK, W.M. Exh. 1890-91
Weston Super Mare 1890; Redland, Bristol 1891. † B 3.

DERRICOURT, Marjorie J. Exh. 1931-34
Figure painter. 162 Stoney Lane, Sparkhill, Birmingham. † B 3, RA 2.

DERRY, Mrs. Anne Exh. 1903
Miniature portrait painter. Add: The Ingle Nook, Streatham Park, London. † RA 1.

DERRY, Constance M. Exh. 1899
Miniature portrait painter. Add: Woodlands, Tooting Common, London. † RA 1.

DERRY, Miss E.K. Exh. 1886
Figure painter. Add: Coombe Field, Maldon, Surrey. † RA 1.

DERRY, Mrs. J. Exh. 1903
285 Derby Rd., Lenton, Notts. † N 1.

DERRY, Miss Mary Exh. 1897-99
Interior painter. 8 Darnley Rd., Royal Crescent, London. † RA 1, RBA 1.

DE RUDDER, Isidore Exh. 1892
76 Rue Dehennin, Brussels. † GI 2.

DE RUILLE, Comte Geoffroy Exh. 1911
233 Rue du Faubourg. Saint Honore, Paris. † L 1.

DERUJINSKY, Gleb W. b. 1888
Sculptor. b. Smolensk, Russia. Studied Fine Art Academy, Petrograd, Juliens, Paris and Colarossi's, Paris. Add: 39 West 67th Street, New York, U.S.A. 1929. † RA 1.

DE RUYTER, Victor Exh. 1900-1
Harringay, Middlesex 1900; Isleworth, Middlesex 1901. † RBA 1, ROI 1.

DE SACHEZ, Henri Exh. 1880-82
26 Maida Vale, London 1880; Paris 1882. † RHA 3.

DE SAEDELEER, Valerius* b. 1869
Belgian artist. Exh. 1918. † I 2.

DE SAEGHER, Rodolphe Exh. 1908-9
16 Rue Guillaume Tell, Gand, Belgique. † LS 6.

DE ST. CROIX, Miss I. d'A. Exh. 1880
Flower painter. 3 Hastings Terr., Jersey, C.I. † SWA 1.

DE ST. DALMAS, F. Emeric Exh. 1880
Landscape painter. 50 Hauteville, Guernsey, C.I. † RA 1.

DE SAINT-MARCEAUX, Rene 1845-1915
French sculptor. Exh. 1896-1912. Add: Paris. † NG 2, RSA 1.

DE SALINELLES, B. Exh. 1913
Landscape painter. † ALP 3.

DE SANCTIS, Guglielmo Exh. 1881
Portrait painter. Via Margutta, Rome. † RA 1.

DESANGES, Louis William b. 1822
Historical and portrait painter. b. Bexley, Kent. Travelled Continent and India. Add: 16 Stratford Place, London 1882-87. † B 2, RA 2.

DE SATUR, Edmond Byrne* Exh. 1880-85
Domestic painter. 1 Clifton Villas, Highgate Hill, London. † L 2, M 1, RA 9, RHA 3, ROI 4.

DE SATUR, Frances Exh. 1881-84
Landscape painter. Clifton Villas, Highgate Hill, London. † M 2, RA 5.

DE SAULLES, George William 1862-1903
Sculptor. b. Birmingham. Add: London 1897. † B 8, L 1, RA 14.

DE SAUSMAREZ, Maurice b. 1915
Exh. 1938-40. † NEA 6.

DE SAUTY, A. Exh. 1914
30 Glebe Place, Chelsea, London. † RA 1.

DESBOIS, Jules b. 1851
French sculptor. Exh. 1905-28. Add: Paris. † GI 3, I 2, RSA 9.

DESBOROUGH, Montague W. Exh. 1896
Landscape painter. 21 Pinfold Rd., Streatham, London. † RA 1.

DESBOUTIN, Marcellin Gilbert 1823-1902
French artist. c/o Edward Bella, 113 Charing Cross Rd., London 1894. † NEA 1.

DESCH, Th. A. Exh. 1905
15 Rue Hegesippe-Moreau, Paris. † L 1.

DE SCHAMPHELEER, Edmond* Exh. 1886-94
Landscape painter. 30 Rue du Marteau, Brussels. † RHA 6.

DESCHAMPS, Louis Henri 1846-1902
French artist. c/o Miss Halked, Lime St. Studio, Sevenoaks, Kent. Exh. 1894-95. † GI 1, RBA 1.

DES CLAYES, Alice b. 1891
Animal agricultural and sporting painter. b. Aberdeen. Associate Royal Canadian Academy. Exh. 1915-26. Add: 156 Holland Park Ave., London. † BA 2, GI 1, L 1, RA 5.

DES CLAYES, Berthe* Exh. 1905-27
Landscape and figure painter. b. Aberdeen. Add: London. † BA 5, L 5, P 1, RA 3, RI 2, ROI 1.

DES CLAYES, Gertrude* Exh. 1905-27
Landscape and portrait painter. b. Aberdeen. Add: 156 Holland Park Ave., London. † BA 7, BG 2, GI 1, L 8, RA 7, ROI 2.

DE SEGRAIS, John Exh. 1940
Architect. 57 Rusper Court, Clapham Rd., London. † RA 1.

DESFONTAINES, Henri Bellery Exh. 1894
67 Rue du Theatre, Paris. † G 1.

DESHAYES, Charles Felix Edouard b. 1831
16 Avenue Trudaine, Paris 1882. † RHA 2.

DE SIEDLECKA, Viga Exh. 1910
c/o Allied Artists Assn. 67 Chancery Lane, London. † LS 3.

DESIGNOLLE, P. Exh. 1913
Landscape painter. † ALP 3.

DE SILVA, Josephine Exh. 1915-28
Liverpool. † L 9.

DE SISTERE, Mons. Exh. 1882
16 Avenue Trudaine, Paris. † RHA 1.

DE SLOOVERE, G. Exh. 1912
11 Boulevard Phillippe le Bon, Bruges, Belgium. † RA 1.

DE SMET, Leon* b. 1881
Belgian painter. Studied under Jean Delvin at Ghent. Add: London 1915. † G 1, GI 1, GOU 1, I 9, L 3, LEI 106, NEA 7, RA 1.

DESMOND, Creswell Hartley b. 1877
Painter and sculptor. Add: Boldre, Lymington, Hants. 1903 and 1911; Bushey, Herts. 1906. † L 7, M 1, RA 17, ROI 3.

DESMOND, Nerine* Exh. 1938
† NEA 1.

DESMOULIN, F. Exh. 1910
57 Rue Ampere (XVIIe) Paris. † L 1.

DE SMOURS, The Marchesa Maris T. Dusmet Exh. 1919
† I 1.

DE SOISSONS, Louis b. 1890
Architect. Studied RA Schools and Ecole des Beaux Arts (Tite prizeman 1912 and Jarvis Rome scholar 1913). Architect to Welwyn Garden City 1920. Add: Welwyn Herts. 1921, St. James's London 1924. † GI 10, RA 17, RSA 1.

D'ESPAGNAT, Georges* b. 1870
French artist. Exh. 1901-28. † CHE 1, GOU 3, I 1.

DESPIAN, Charles 1874-1946
French sculptor. Studied under Rodin. Add: 2 Rue d'Arceuil, Paris 1930. † RSA 2.

DESPIE, Mdme. Iva Exh. 1927
Sculptor. Add: Kralje Petre 17, Sarajevo, Jugoslavia. † RA 2.

DESPREZ, Lilian Exh. 1898-1901
Miniature portrait painter. Streatham, London. † L 1, RA 2, RMS 1.

D'ESSEO, Miss Elizabeth Exh. 1927-28
† RMS 4.

DESSERTENNE, Jacques M. Exh. 1913
25 Rue Humboldt, Paris. † L 1.

DESSOUREAUX, Laurent* Exh. 1880
16 Avenue Trudaine, Paris. † RHA 1.

DE STEIGER, Isabel Exh. 1881-1926
Figure and flower painter. Add: London 1882; Liverpool 1891 and 1920; Edinburgh 1895; Birmingham 1903; Rock Ferry, Cheshire 1909. † B 7, L 29, M 7, RA 1, RBA 1, RHA 6, ROI 1, RSA 4, SWA 3.

D'ESTIENNE, Henri b. 1872
French painter. Exh. 1905-12. Add: 48 Avenue Daumesnil, Paris. † GOU 2, L 3.

DESTREE, Johannes Josephus* Exh. 1885
Dutch painter. Add: 23 Buitenhoff. The Hague, Holland. † GI 1, L 1.

DESTREM, C. Exh. 1886
127 Rue Notre Dame des Champs, Paris. † M 1.

DE STREUVE, Ellen Exh. 1939-40
c/o S.F. Pitman Esq. 2 Oakwood Court, Kensington, London. † P 1, RBA 2, ROI 2, SWA 1.

DE STROBL, Sigismund Exh. 1933-37
Sculptor. 51 Prince's Sq., London. † L 1, RA 8, RSA 1.

DESVALLIERES, Gaston Oliver b. 1861
French artist. 14 Rue St. Marc, Paris 1904-08. † I 2.

DESVIGNES, Emily Exh. 1881
62 Doughty St., Mecklenburgh Sq., London. † SWA 1.

DESVIGNES, Louis Exh. 1912
26 Rue de Sevigne, Paris. † RHA 1.

DE SYANKOWSKI, B. Exh. 1902-5
Paris 1902; Munich 1905. † NG 1, RSA 1.

DE TEISSIER, H.P. Exh. 1881
Landscape painter. 29 Pembroke Gardens, Kensington, London. † D 2.

DE TEISSIER, Rose Exh. 1881-89
Landscape painter. Add: Kensington, London 1881; Leatherhead, Surrey 1889. † SWA 2.

DE TERRY, Fernando Exh. 1897
c/o T.M. Deane, Esq., 5 Ely Place, Dublin. † RHA 1.

D'ETIOLLES, Mdme. le Roy Exh. 1899-1912
Paris. † GI 1, L 5, M 1, RSA 2.

DETMAR, Lionel G. Exh. 1904-6
Architect. Hazeldean, Sutton, Surrey. † RA 3.

DETMOLD, Charles Maurice* 1883-1908
Painter, etcher and illustrator. Collaborated with his brother Edward Julius D. q.v. A.R.E. Jan-Nov 1905. Add: Hampstead, London. † FIN 53, GI 5, I 1, NEA 1, RA 5, RE 7, RI 2.

DETMOLD, Edward Julius* b. 1883
Painter, etcher and illustrator. Collaborated with his brother Charles Maurice D. q.v. A.R.E. Jan-Nov 1905. Exh. 1897-1935. Add: London. † AG 1, AR 68, BG 43, BK 46, CHE 1, FIN 115, GI 2, I 1, NEA 2, RA 5, RI 14.

DETMOLD, Henry E. Exh. 1880-1902
Landscape, figure and marine painter. N.E.A. 1886. Add: Paris 1881 and 1900; London 1883; Hastings 1892; St. Leonards 1898. † B 23, DOW 3, G 1, GI 14, L 15, M 25, NEA 1, RA 16, RBA 22, RHA 4, RI 1, ROI 6.

DE TOMMASI, Publio* b. 1849
Italian artist. 53B Via Margutta, Rome 1902. † L 1.

DE TREY, Marianne Exh. 1931
52 British Grove, London. † SWA 1.

DETTI, Cesar Auguste* 1847-1914
Italian painter. Paris 1883; London 1889. † AG 1, M 2, RA 1.

DETTMAR, Mrs. E.E. Exh. 1913
Westwood, Pinner, Middlesex. † RA 1.

DEUCHAR, C.R. Exh. 1885
22 Morningside Place, Edinburgh. † RSA 1.

DEUCHARS, Louis Exh. 1898-1925
Landscape painter. Add: Godalming, Surrey 1898; Guildford 1899; Inverness 1901; London 1903 and 1908; Hughendon, Bucks. 1906; Edinburgh 1908 and 1920; Leith 1918. † GI 5, L 5, NG 20, P 1, RA 6, RSA 20, RSW 1

DEULLY, Eugene Auguste Francois b. 1860
French painter. Villa Rubens, 9 Impasse du Maine, Paris 1904. † COO 1, L 2.

DEUSKAR, Gopal D. Exh. 1935-39
Figure and landscape painter. London. † RA 4.

DEUTMANN, F. Exh. 1891-92
Landscape painter. 122 Loampit Vale, Lewisham, London. † PBA 1, ROI 1.

DEUTSCH, Ludwig* b. 1855
Austrian painter. Paris 1901-11. † L 4.

DEVAS, Anthony 1911-1959
Portrait, figure and flower painter. Studied Slade School 1927-30. "Mrs. Wilson" purchased by Chantrey Bequest 1939. Add: London 1935; Walton on Thames 1938. † COO 3, LEF 6, NEA 3, RBA 1, RED 1.

DE VASCONCELLOS, Josephina Alys b. 1904
Sculptor. Studied Regent St. Polytechnic, Paris under Bourdelle and Florence under Andreotti. Add: Manchester 1926; London 1929; Wadhurst, Sussex 1938; Ambleside, Westmoreland 1939. † GI 1, L 1, RA 5, RSA 2.

DE VASSELOT, Anatole Marquet Exh. 1882-83
Sculptor. 7 Rue Talma, Passy, Paris. † GI 1, RA 1.

DE VEGA, Pedro* Exh. 1884-85
Urban landscape painter. 6 Bridge St., Cambridge. † RA 2, ROI 1.

DEVENISH, Miss H. Exh. 1910
Bath. † SWA 1.

DEVENPORT, Annie Exh. 1920-32
Sculptor. 7 Annandale Ave., Clontarf, Ireland. † RHA 17.

DE VERE, Aroldo du Chene Exh. 1909-10
14 Trafalgar Studios, Manresa Rd., Chelsea, London. † LS 6.

DEVEREUX, A. Exh. 1925
Fingal House, Clontarf, Ireland. † RHA 1.

DEVEREUX, Mrs. Blanche I. Exh. 1900
34 Rosemont Rd., Acton, London. † B 1, SWA 1.

DEVERILL, G. Exh. 1899
9 Maud St. New Bashford, Notts. † N 1.

DEVERILL, G. Exh. 1928
12 Victor Terrace, Burnham Street, Sherwood, Nottingham. † N 1.

DE VESCI, Viscountess Exh. 1908
33 Portman Square, London. † NG 2.

DE VIGNE, Paul 1843-1901
Belgian sculptor. Add: Brussels. † GI 4, RA 2.

DE VILLE, Vickers d. 1925
Landscape and figure painter. R.B.S.A. 1917. Add: Wolverhampton. † B 19, FIN 1, GI 18, L 1, RA 20, RSA 11, ROI 2.

DEVINE, Catherine Exh. 1891-94
Miniature portrait painter. Glebe Place, Chelsea, London. † D 8, RA 3, RSA 1, TOO 1.

DE VLAMINCK, Maurice 1876-1958
French painter. Exh. 1924-38. † BA 2, GOU 8, RED 1.

DEVLIN, May Exh. 1922-36
Mrs. Alex F. Dale. Watercolour painter. Studied Glasgow School of Art. Art Mistress at Bearsden Academy. Add: Dumbarton 1922; London 1934; Glasgow 1935. † GI 7, RSA 5, RSW 7.

DEVLIN, W.J. Exh. 1908-16
Architect. Add: London 1908; Aberdeen 1916. † RA 2, RSA 1.

DEVREESE, G. Exh. 1909-23
Brussels. † GI 1, L 4, RA 1, RSA 7.

DEW, Miss M.W. Exh. 1905-12
Kensington Gore, London 1905; Hoddesdon, Herts. 1908. † SWA 5.

DE WALDEN, Lord Howard Exh. 1938
Landscape and portrait painter. † GOU 60.

DEWAR, Alex C. Exh. 1884
34 Marchmont Crescent, Edinburgh. † RSA 1.

DEWAR, Miss I.M. Exh. 1887-91
West Lodge, Dingwall, N.B. † RSA 4.

DEWAR, J.S. Exh. 1881-89
Glasgow. † GI 6, RSA 3.

DEWAR, Miss L. Exh. 1901
St. Heliers, Hampton Wick, Middlesex. † SWA 1.

DEWAR, Margaret de Courcy Lewthwaite Exh. 1901-40
Painter, enameller, metal worker. Born Kandy, Ceylon. Studied Glasgow School of Art and Central School of Arts and Crafts, London. Teacher of enamelling at Glasgow School of Art. Travelled widely. Add: Glasgow 1901; Edinburgh 1930. † GI 15, L 14, RSA 11, RSW 6.

DEWAR, William Jesmond Exh. 1903
Figure and landscape painter. Add: Lyndhurst, Blenheim Park, South Croydon, Surrey. † RA 2.

DEWAR-MILLS, John Exh. 1940
5 Kingsbridge House, Beaconsfield Road, London. † RA 1.

DE WARVILLE, F. Brissot Exh. 1882
Animal painter. 134 New Bond Street, London. † RA 1.

DEWE, Miss Ellen Exh. 1895
Burghfield, nr. Reading, Berks. † L 1.

DEWE, Miss Nellie Exh. 1893-94
39 Alma Square, St. John's Wood, London. † B 1, L 1, ROI 2.

DEWHURST, H. Exh. 1886
43 Shrewsbury Street, Old Trafford, Manchester. † M 1.

DEWHURST, J.P. Exh. 1891
Healy, Rochdale, Lancs. † M 1.

DEWHURST, Ronald Exh. 1928-34
Figure and still life painter. 47 Markeaton Street, Derby. † N 10.

DEWHURST, Wynford* b. 1864
Landscape painter. Studied under Gerome in Paris. R.B.A. 1901. Add: Leighton Buzzard, Beds. 1898 and 1907; Wiesbaden, Germany 1901; Tunbridge Wells 1909; Hampstead, London 1917. † AG 1, BG 72, FIN 44, G 1, GI 4, L 7, LS 16, M 10, NEA 2, RA 8, RBA 74.

DE WITT, Gerard Exh. 1923-29
Painter and etcher. Add: Dublin 1925; South Kensington, London 1929. † FIN 2, GOU 1, L 1, RHA 6.

DEWS, P. Exh. 1888-96
Birkenhead 1888; Rock Ferry, Cheshire 1891. † L 13.

DEWSBURY, Lilian Exh. 1901
Allestree, Duchy Road, Harrogate, Yorks. † RSA 1.

DEXTER, A.H. Exh. 1901
3 Holles Crescent, The Park, Nottingham. † N 2.

DEXTER, Mrs. G. Exh. 1938
31 Elmside, Onslow Village, Guildford, Surrey. † ROI 1.

DEXTER, Gordon Exh. 1937-38
141 Carlton Avenue East, Wembley, Middlesex. † ROI 4.

DEXTER, James Henry b. 1912
Landscape and still life painter and designer. Studied Leicester College of Art. Exh. 1933-37. Add: 77 Farringdon Street, Leicester. † NEA 4. RA 1.

DEXTER, Phyllis C.F. Exh. 1922-23
Lowdham, Notts. 1922; Sherwood, Notts. 1923. † N 4.

DEXTER, Robert Amos Exh. 1910
49 Bridge Road West, Battersea, London. † LS 3.

DEXTER, Tom E. Exh. 1913-30
Stained glass artist. Add: 27 Waldeck Road, Carrington, Nottingham. † N 16, RA 3.

DEXTER, Walter 1876-1958
Landscape, interior, portrait and still life painter, and illustrator. b. Wellingborough, Northants. Studied Birmigham School of Art. R.B.A. 1905. Add: Kings Lynn, Norfolk 1901 and 1913; Kensington, London 1904; Felixstowe, Suffolk 1909. † B 13, BRU 1, L 5, RA 6, RBA 31, RI 1, ROI 1.

DEXTER, W.J. Exh. 1920-32
Illuminator. Nottingham. † N 8.

DEY, James Exh. 1901-21
Edinburgh 1908; Corstorphine, N.B. 1902. † RSA 5.

DEY, Mukul Chandra b. 1895
Etcher, drypoint and decorative artist. Studied Slade School, Royal College of Art (Bengal Government Scholarship for 3 years). Principal Government School of Art, Calcutta, Keeper Government A.G. Calcutta, Officer in Charge of Art Section and Trustee Indian Museum, Calcutta; formerly member of the Advisory Committee for Mural Decoration at New Delhi, India House, London. Add: Kensington, London 1922. † CON 3, G 4, L 1, NEA 5, RA 1.

DEYKIN, Henry Cotterill b. 1905
Portrait and landscape painter. Studied Slade School and Birmingham School of Art. Add: Olton, nr. Birmingham 1933; Leamington Spa, Warwicks. 1936. † RA 4.

DE ZIELINSKA, Angele Exh. 1909
c/o 25 Hale Road, Liscard, Cheshire. † L 1.

DHARVILLE, Laure Exh. 1909
† LS 1.

D'HAUTEVILLE, Paul Grand Exh. 1927
Landscape painter. † WG 47.

D'HAVELOOSE, Marnix Exh. 1909-15
Ixelles, Brussels 1909; London 1915. † GI 4, I 6, L 2, RSA 2.

D'HERBOIS, Miss L. Collot Exh. 1930
Barston, nr. Hampton-in-Arden. † B 1, NEA 1.

DIAMONDSTEIN, Bushka Exh. 1917-20
Sculptor. London. † I 1, RA 4.

DIAZ, Robert Exh. 1893-96
128 West Graham Street, Glasgow. † GI 1, RSW 1.

DIBBLEE, Bessie M. Exh. 1908-27
Handforth, Manchester 1908; Wilmslow, Cheshire 1912; London 1927. † G 2, I 5, L 1, LS 10, SWA 1.

DIBDEN, Miss Marian Alice see MONTFORD

DIBDIN, Mrs. Charles Exh. 1926-28
3 Sandheys, Parkgate, Cheshire. † L 1, RCA 1.

DIBDIN, Edward Rimbault b. 1853
Artist, lecturer and writer. Studied Edinburgh Trustees Academy. Art Critic "Liverpool Courier" 1887-1904; Curator Walker Art Gallery 1904-16; Director in Europe for Canadian National Exhibition, Toronto from 1911; Organiser and arranger of Baroda Art Gallery 1919-21. H.R.M.S. 1916. Married Sarah Beatrice D. q.v. Add: Liscard, Cheshire 1884; Liverpool 1922; London 1926. † G 1, L 15, RCA 11, RMS 3.

DIBDIN, Sara Beatrice b. 1874
nee Guthrie. Painter and metal worker. Studied Glasgow School of Art and Munich. 2nd wife of Edward Rimbault D. q.v. Add: Glasgow 1893; Liverpool 1913; London 1926. † GI 1, L 101, M 1, RA 1, RCA 26, ROI 5, RSA 1, RSW 2.

DIBDIN, Thomas Colman* 1810-1893
Landscape and architectural painter. London. † M 1, RBA 2, RHA 4.

DICEY, Frank Exh. 1880-88
Figure painter. R.O.I. 1883. Add: London. † B 4, G 10, GI 8, L 9, M 8, RA 7, RBA 4, RI 1, ROI 12.

DICHMONT, James Exh. 1933
† RSW 1.
DICK, A. Exh. 1908
20 Tower Street, Selkirk. † RSA 1.
DICK, Catherine M. Exh. 1914-35
1 Brandon Mansions, Queen's Club Gardens, London. † L 7, RA 5, RI 33.
DICK, Mrs. Dorothy J. Exh. 1911-20
nee Swan. Sculptor. Married Stewart D. q.v. Add: London. † GI 1, L 2, LS 11, RA 3, RSA 1, SWA 1.
DICK, Mrs. Edith A. Exh. 1907-11
44 Holland Street, Kensington, London. † LS 2, NG 1, SWA 1.
DICK, Miss E.E. Exh. 1934
Watercolour animal painter. † COO 2.
DICK, Eliza Izzett Exh. 1880-82
17 Elm Row, Edinburgh. † GI 3, RSA 2.
DICK, Isabel Elizabeth Exh. 1925-28
Flower painter. Studied London and France. Travelled and sketched a great deal abroad. Add: Studio F, 29 Notting Hill Gate, London. † RA 1, SWA 1, WG 34.
DICK, Jean Exh. 1919-25
1 Glebe Road, Wallasey, Cheshire. † L 4.
DICK, John Exh. 1905
36 James Street, Perth. † GI 1.
DICK, Jessie Alexandra Exh. 1920-40
Painter and teacher. Studied Glasgow School of Art. Signs work "J. Alix Dick". Add: Dunoon 1920; Glasgow 1928. † GI 19, L 1, RE 1, RSA 14, RSW 2.
DICK, J.T. Exh. 1892-96
Glasgow. † GI 3.
DICK, Norman A. Exh. 1936
16 Blythwood Square, Glasgow. † RSA 2.
DICK, Reginald T. Exh. 1900-1
Coastal landscape painter. Add: Cliff Cottage, Newlyn, Cornwall. † L 3.
DICK, Stewart b. 1874
Artist and lecturer. Studied Edinburgh School of Art. Lecturer in art to Oxford, London and Bristol Universities; Official Lecturer at the National Gallery, London 1919-26. Exh. 1908-14. Add: Sevenoaks, Kent 1908; London 1914. † BG 1, NEA 1, RA 1.
DICK, T.S. Exh. 1880
18 Berkeley Street, Glasgow. † GI 1.
DICK, Sir William Reid 1879-1961
Sculptor. Studied Glasgow School of Art and London. Kings sculptor in Ordinary for Scotland 1938; Trustee of Royal Academy; member of Royal Fine Art Commission 1928; member of Mint Advisory Committee; Trustee of Tate Gallery 1934-41. A.R.A. 1921, R.A. 1928, H.R.S.A. 1939. "Androdus" purchased by Chantrey Bequest 1919. Add: Glasgow 1906; London 1908. † GI 51, I 9, L 32, P 3, RA 108, RI 3, RSA 31, RSW 2.
DICKENS, Miss F.M. Exh. 1926-28
Cearns House, Cearns Road, Oxton, Birkenhead. † L 3.
DICKENSON, John Exh. 1882
1 Oxford Street, Newcastle. † RSA 4.
DICKER, Alice M. Exh. 1888-89
Figure painter. 205 The Grove, Denmark Hill, London. † RA 2, RBA 1, ROI 1, SWA 1.
DICKER, Hamilton Exh. 1929-30
Figure painter. 31 Howland Street, London. † LEF 4, NEA 2.
DICKER, Mabel G. Exh. 1909-11
Landscape painter. 7 Macauley Road, Clapham, London. † L 1, RA 4, SWA 2, WG 44.
DICKES, W. Exh. 1881
7 Loughborough Park, London. † D 1.
DICKESON, Agnes Exh. 1889
Flower painter. 7 Harold Terrace, Dover, Kent. † SWA 1.

DICKEY, Edward Montgomery O'Rourke b. 1894
Painter and wood engraver. b. Belfast. Studied Westminster School of Art. Professor of Fine Art and Director of King Edward VII School of Art, Armstrong College, Newcastle-on-Tyne; member London Group 1920. Add: London 1916; Dublin 1921; Burgess Hill, Sussex 1923; Oundle, Northants. 1924; Newcastle-on-Tyne 1928; Richmond, Surrey 1934. † BA 43, FIN 3, G 2, L 3, LEI 38, LS 6, M 12, NEA 14, RA 8, RCA 1, RHA 1.
DICKIE, Miss Janet A. Exh. 1925-26
Burnbank, Yoker, nr. Glasgow. † GI 2.
DICKIE, Miss K.M. Exh. 1923-29
Jeweller. Holywood, Co. Down 1923; Edinburgh 1929. † L 15.
ICKIE, Rev. William Exh. 1896-1928
Lynwood, Partick Hill, Glasgow. † L 1, RSW 2.
DICKIN, Miss P. Exh. 1920
Hampton-in-Arden. † B 1.
DICKINS, Miss C. Exh. 1917
Park Side Farm, Wollaton, Notts. † N 1.
DICKINS, Mrs. Constance Exh. 1900-13
Landscape painter. A.N.S.A. 1908. Add: Lenton, Notts. 1900 and 1909; West Bridgford, Notts. 1903. † B 2, LS 6, M 1, N 10, RHA 1, ROI 1, RSA 1.
DICKINS, Charles Bumpus b. 1871
Liverpool 1904; Liscard, Cheshire 1905-7. † L 4.
DICKINS, Miss Emily Exh. 1903
Glencairn, Manor Road, Coventry. † B 1.
DICKINS, Frank Exh. 1886
Fruit painter. Arkendale, Putney Hill, London. † B 1, RBA 1.
DICKINSON, Arthur Exh. 1882
Landscape painter. London 1881; Wreckin, Wellington, Salop. 1882. † D 2, RA 2.
DICKINSON, Annie Josephine b. 1863
Figure, landscape and flower painter. Studied London and Paris. Head of Crafts School in Yugoslavia. Add: London 1885; Painswick, Glos. 1920 and Belgrade. † RA 2, RID 67, SWA 12.
DICKINSON, Miss Dulcie Exh. 1907
China Cottage, Storr's Park, Windermere † L 1.
DICKINSON, F.P. Exh. 1913
Croyden Villa, West Parade, Lincoln. † N 2.
DICKINSON, Henry R. Exh. 1881-97
Landscape painter. 190 Strand, London. † RA 2.
DICKINSON, John Exh. 1880-87
Portrait and miniature painter. London. † RA 10.
DICKINSON, J. Reed Exh. 1881-89
Figure and portrait painter. 141 The Grove, Hammersmith, London. † D 1, L 2, M 2, RA 1.
DICKINSON, Lilian Exh. 1880-83
Portrait painter. Roseneath House, Cathnor Road, Shepherd's Bush, London. † RA 3, SWA 1.
DICKINSON, Lowes Cato* 1819-1908
Portrait painter. All Souls Place, Portland Place, London. † RA 19.
DICKINSON, Miss M. Exh. 1911
160 Cromwell Road, London. † L 1, RA 1.
DICKINSON, Mary Exh. 1936-40
Portrait and figure painter. 7 Rossetti Studios, Flood Street, Chelsea, London. † NEA 1, P 3, RBA 1, RCA 4, RHA 1, ROI 4, RSA 5, SWA 1.
DICKINSON, Miss M.A. Exh. 1916-34
12 North Road, St. Helens, Lancs. † L 4, RCA 1.

DICKINSON, Page L. Exh. 1907-13
13 South Frederick Street, Dublin. † RHA 4.
DICKINSON, Mrs. S S. Exh. 1889-90
Landscape painter. Bramblebury, Wandsworth Common, London. † RID 5.
DICKINSON, T. Exh. 1919
129 Brucefield Avenue, Dunfermline. † RSA 1.
DICKSEE, Miss E. Exh. 1917
Starborough House, Rugby. † RA 2.
DICKSEE, Sir Francis Bernard* 1853-1928
Portrait, figure and landscape painter. Son of Thomas Francis D. q.v. Studied RA Schools. A.R.A. 1881, R.A. 1891, P.R.A. 1924, H.R.E. 1925, R.I. 1891, H.R.M.S. 1925, H.R.O.I. 1898, R.P. 1926, H.R.S.A. Knighted 1925. "Harmony" purchased by Chantrey Bequest 1877 and "The Two Crowns" 1900. Add: London. † AG 2, B 4, FIN 2, G 1, GI 5, L 31, M 12, P 2, RA 152, RHA 2, RI 6, ROI 2, RSA 1, TOO 2.
DICKSEE, Herbert Thomas 1862-1942
Painter and etcher. Son of John Robert D. q.v. Studied Slade School (medals for painting and drawing from life, Slade scholarship). Drawing master at City of London School. R.E. 1885. Add: London. † B 1, FIN 52, GI 1, L 44, M 4, RA 95, RBA 1, RE 143, RI 2, ROI 1.
DICKSEE, John Robert* 1817-1905
Portrait and genre painter. Father of Herbert Thomas D. q.v. and brother of Thomas Francis D. q.v. Head Drawing master of City of London School. Add: London. † B 24, GI 15, L 12, M 21, RA 11, RBA 1, RHA 21, RI 1.
DICKSEE, Margaret Isabel* 1859-1903
Landscape and figure painter. Daughter of Thomas Francis D. q.v. and sister of Francis Bernard D. q.v. Add: London. † L 4, RA 18, RBA 2, RWS 1.
DICKSEE, Thomas Francis* 1819-1895
Portrait and historical genre painter. Studied under H.P. Briggs. Father of Francis and Margaret D. q.v. Add: London. † B 6, G 1, GI 3, L 4, M 2, RA 20, ROI 1.
DICKSON, Adelaide C. Exh. 1889-1908
Landscape and flower painter. Edinburgh 1889; London 1903. † BG 1, L 3, RA 2, RSA 2.
DICKSON, A.N. Exh. 1903
23 Radcliffe Road West Bridgford, Notts. † N 1.
DICKSON, Miss E.G. Exh. 1881-1902
Edinburgh 1881 and 1900; Glasgow 1883. † GI 3, RSA 8.
DICKSON, Frank 1862-1936
Figure and flower painter. R.B.A. 1896; Chester 1889; Stratford on Avon 1897; London 1905. † B 11, L 1, M 2, RA 8, RBA 51, RHA 5, ROI 8.
DICKSON, H. Exh. 1894
87 Canfield Gardens, London. † L 1.
DICKSON, Miss Jeanie Exh. 1880-86
Edinburgh. † GI 8, RSA 17.
DICKSON, L. Exh. 1889
56 Grove St., Liverpool. † L 1.
DICKSON, Lalia C. Exh. 1936-40
Edinburgh. † RSA 5, RSW 1.
DICKSON, L.M. Exh. 1889
Mount Pleasant, Belfast. † RHA 1.
DICKSON, Margaret Exh. 1932-35
17 Dunard Road, Rutherglen. † GI 2.
DICKSON, Nell Gwenllian P. 1891-1967
Mrs. Ian D. Landscape painter. Studied under W.G. Collingwood 1910 and A. Seaby 1911. Add: Norwich 1934. † RA 1, RCA 2, RSA 4, SWA 1.

DICKSON, Thomas Elder b. 1899
Studied Glasgow School of Art. Exh. 1932-40. Add: 12 Bank Terrace, Corstorphine. † RSA 9, RSW 3.
DICKSON, William Exh. 1898
Maybank, Blairgowrie, N.B. † RSA 2.
DICKSON, William Exh. 1881-1908
Landscape painter. London 1881; Tadley, Basingstoke, Hants. 1895. † L 1, M 1, NG 2, RA 12, RBA 1, RID 20.
DICKSON, W.P. Exh. 1897-1912
Landscape and portrait painter. London. † L 5, M 1, RA 8.
DICKSON, W.T.G. Exh. 1883
Westfield House, Partick Hill, Glasgow. † GI 1.
DIDIER, Jules* 1831-1892
French artist. 104 Maida Vale, London 1880. † RHA 1.
DIDIER, M. Exh. 1882
16 Avenue Trudaine, Paris 1882. † RHA 2.
DIEHL, Arthur* Exh. 1889
Landscape painter. 28 York Street, Baker Street, London. † RA 1.
DIELMAN, Ernest b. 1893
American sculptor. c/o D. Barnham Esq., Marlborough Road, Hampton, Middlesex 1938. † RA 1.
DIELMAN, Fred Exh. 1884
c/o Cassell & Co., Ludgate Hill, London. † L 1.
DIELMAN, Marguerite Exh. 1909
26 Rue de Marteau, Brussels. † L 1.
DIEN, Achille Exh. 1890
3 Rue des Beaux Arts, Paris. † GI 2.
DIERCKX, Pierre Jacques* b. 1855
Belgian artist. Anvers, Belgium 1898; Antwerp 1903. † GI 1, L 1.
DIEY, Yves Exh. 1938
Figure painter. † CG 12.
DIGBY, George Exh. 1888-89
Landscape painter. London 1888; Ilfracombe, Devon 1889. † GI 1, L 1, RA 6, RBA 2, ROI 1.
DIGBY, Grace 1895-c.1965
Landscape painter. Shillingford, Oxon 1920; Edgbaston, Birmingham 1922. † B 12, L 1, RA 1, RCA 1.
DIGBY, Mrs. Violet M. Exh. 1938
nee Kidd. b. Plymouth. Studied Slade School and Beaux Arts, Paris. Add: London. † RCA 2.
DIGGLE, Jane Chadderton b. 1882
Watercolour painter and poster artist. Studied Heatherleys and Central School of Arts and Crafts. Add: London 1920; Tenterden, Kent 1936. † L 3, P 1, RA 1, RI 3, SWA 11.
DIGGLES, Miss Ethel Exh. 1884
Brookfield, Eccles, Manchester. † M 1.
DIGGLES, Miss G.E. Exh. 1882-84
Eccles, Manchester. † M 3.
DI GIORGIO, Ettore Exh. 1916
c/o A. Stiles & Sons, 617 Fulham Road, London. † GI 1.
DIGNAM, Mary Ella* Exh. 1926-33
Canadian painter. nee Williams. Studied Paris, Holland and Italy. † AR 38, GI 1, L 1, ROI 1.
DIGNAM, Michael J.H. Exh. 1912-16
Dublin. † RHA 9.
DILKS, Elsie Exh. 1904-10
Leicester 1904 and 1908; Birmingham 1905. † B 10.
DILKS, N. Exh. 1923
8 Alpine Terrace, Hunt Street, Nottingham. † N 1.
DILL, Ludwig* b. 1848
German artist. Munich, Germany 1893. † GI 2, I 3.
DILLAYE, Blanche d. 1931
American artist. 1334 Chestnut Street, Philadelphia, U.S.A. 1884. † L 3.
DILLENS, Julien 1849-1905
Belgian sculptor. Brussels 1894. † G 1, RSA 1.
DILLON, Arthur Exh. 1897-98
22 Lawrence Road, Clontarf, Ireland. † RHA 2.
DILLON, Frank* 1823-1909
Topographical painter. Studied under James Holland. Travelled on the continent, Middle and Far East. R.I. 1882, R.O.I. 1883. Add: 13 Upper Phillimore Gardens, Kensington, London. † B 12, D 4, GI 3, L 15, M 5, NG 20, RA 18, RHA 10, RI 78, ROI 33.
D'ILLZACH, Ringel Exh. 1893-94
57 Rue du Point du Jour, Paris. † GI 8.
DIMANT, David Exh. 1909
† LS 3.
DIMELOW, Amy Beatrice Caroline Exh. 1906-10
Sculptor and painter. Studied Manchester School of Art. Add: 149 Palatine Road, West Didsbury, Manchester. † L 4, M 3.
DIMITRIADES, C. Exh. 1912
1 St. Pauls Studios, Baron's Court, London. † RA 2.
DIMMA, Ada C.G. Exh. 1891-94
59 The Common, Upper Clapton, London. † ROI 4.
DIMMACH, J.N. Exh. 1884
Gravelly Hill, Birmingham. † B 1.
DIMMOCK, Miss D.M. Exh. 1929
Raikerwood Road, Skipton, Yorks. † L 1.
DIMMOCK, Jane Exh. 1882
† B 1.
DIMOND, Lynden Exh. 1940
Flower painter. East Grinstead, Sussex. † NEA 1, RA 1.
DINET, Etienne b. 1861
French artist. c/o Barlow, Stakehill, Chaddarton, Lancs. 1884. † M 1.
DINGLE, Thomas junr. Exh. 1880-89
Landscape painter. Plymouth, Devon 1880; Newton Ferrers, nr. Plympton, Devon 1889. † RBA 6.
DINGLEY, H.J. Exh. 1888-91
Dunoon, N.B. † GI 3.
DINGLEY, H.T. Exh. 1883-85
8 Hampden Terrace, Mount Florida, Glasgow. † GI 6, RHA 3, RSA 2.
DINGLI, Edward Caruana b. 1876
Portrait and genre painter. Studied Malta and Rome. Served with Malta Artillery World War 1. Director Malta Government School of Art. Add: 6 Strada Magazhini Floriana, Malta 1927. † RA 1.
DINGWALL, Miss H.C. Exh. 1883
The Glennan, Helensburgh, N.B. † GI 1.
DINGWALL, Miss Isabella Exh. 1883-90
The Glennan, Helensburgh, N.B. † GI 2.
DINGWALL, John Exh. 1896
The Glennan, Helensburgh, N.B. † RSA 1.
DINKEL, Ernest Michael b. 1894
Painter and designer. Studied Royal College of Art (Owen-Jones travelling scholarship for colour decoration). A.R.W.S. 1939. "The Deluge" purchased by Chantrey Bequest, 1929. Add: London. † L 1, NEA 5, RA 13, RCA 2, RWS 11.
DINSDALE, John Exh. 1884-89
32 Torriano Avenue, Camden Road, London. † RI 2.
DIRCKX, Anton Exh. 1913
† GOU 1.
DISCART, T.B. Exh. 1909
37 Rue de la Charite, Brussels. † L 1.
DISCART, T.C. Exh. 1886
† TOO 2.
DISLEY, John Exh. 1929
6 Hallville Road, Mossley Hill, Liverpool. † L 1.
DISMORR, Jessica 1885-1939
b. Gravesend. Studied in Paris 1910-13. Member London Group 1926. † COO 1, LEI 2.
DISMORR, J.S. Exh. 1893-1914
Gravesend, Kent 1893; Harrow, Middlesex 1912; Chelsea, London 1913; West Byfleet, Surrey 1914. † LS 8, RI 2.
DISTON, J. Exh. 1885
21 Raeberry Street, Glasgow. † RSA 1.
DITCHFIELD, Arthur 1842-1888
Painter, watercolourist and traveller. Add: 12 Taviton Street, Gordon Square, London. † D 6, L 1, RA 2, RI 4.
DITTMAR, Emilie Exh. 1880-85
Flower painter. Stamford, Lincs. 1880; Halliford on Thames, Shepperton, Surrey 1881. † SWA 4.
DIVER, Mrs. Annie K. Exh. 1917-21
London 1917 and 1919; Hove, Sussex 1918. † LS 12.
DIX, Arthur J. Exh. 1898-1915
Stained glass artist. London. † RA 7.
DIX, Ben Exh. 1918
Studio, 57 Broadhurst Gardens, London. † LS 3.
DIX, Mrs. Dorothy Exh. 1922-31
Landscape painter. 66 Ellerton Road, Wandsworth Common, London. † RA 1, SWA 2.
DIX, Eulabee b. 1879
American miniature portrait painter. A.R.M.S. 1906. Add: London 1906. † FIN 22, L 1, RA 1, RMS 2.
DIX, G.W. Exh. 1929
66 Ellerton Road, London. † RBA 1.
DIXEY, Frederick Charles Exh. 1881-1914
Marine painter. London 1881; Richmond, Surrey 1891. † D 128, L 1, RA 1, RBA 4, RHA 2, RI 5, ROI 3, TOO 5
DIXEY, Miss May Exh. 1883
11 The Hawthorns, Churchend, Finchley, London. † RHA 1.
DIXON, Mrs. Exh. 1934
Landscape painter. † COO 2.
DIXON, Alfred 1842-1919
Domestic painter. Father of Charles D. q.v. Add: London. † L 2, M 1, RA 9, RBA 6, ROI 3, RSA 1.
DIXON, Anna d. 1959
Landscape and figure painter. Studied RSA Schools. R.S.W. 1917. Add: Edinburgh. † AR 2, GI 62, L 4, M 1, RA 2, RSA 94, RSW 98.
DIXON, Annie d. 1901
Miniature painter. London. † RA 61.
DIXON, Arthur A. Exh. 1893-1920
Figure painter. London 1893, Horsham, Sussex 1901; Petworth, Sussex 1905; Berkhamsted, Herts. 1911. † B 13, GI 2, L 9, M 1, NG 1, RA 16, RBA 9, RHA 2, RI 8, ROI 1, RSA 1.
DIXON, A.E. Exh. 1905-6
65 King's Street, Manchester. † RA 2.
DIXON, Arthur P. Exh. 1884-1917
Edinburgh. † GI 26, L 2, RSA 57, RSW 1.
DIXON, A.W.L. Exh. 1902
82 Goldsmith Street, Nottingham. † N 2.
DIXON, Charles* 1872-1934
Marine painter. Son of Alfred D. q.v. R.I. 1900. Add: London 1889; Itchenor, Chichester, Sussex and London 1917. † B 1, D 4, GI 2, L 23, M 1, RA 52, RI 170, ROI 4, WG 171.
DIXON, Mrs. Charles Exh. 1908
Westbourne, Edgbaston, Birmingham. † B 1.

DIXON, Clive MacDonnell Exh. 1907-11
Gt. Ayton, R.S.O. Yorks. 1907; Stokesley, Yorks. 1911. † L 2, RA 5.

DIXON, Dudley Exh. 1924-40
Landscape painter. 265 King's Road, London. † D 1, RA 1, RCA 5, RHA 5, ROI 8, RSA 5, WG 19.

DIXON, Dorothy A. Exh. 1919-24
Miniature portrait painter. Whatcroft Hall, Northwich, Cheshire. † L 1, RA 3, RI 1, RMS 1.

DIXON, Mrs. Dorothea M. Exh. 1934-38
Landscape painter. Temple Road, Dublin. † RHA 2.

DIXON, Miss E. Exh. 1919-21
42 Lilybank Gardens, Glasgow. † GI 2, L 1.

DIXON, Emily Exh. 1882-97
Flower and landscape painter. Hull 1882; Chelsea, London 1889. † L 4, M 1, N 1, RA 2, RBA 2, RSA 1, SWA 5.

DIXON, Ella Hepworth Exh. 1880-83
Landscape and flower painter. 6 St James's Terrace, Regents Park, London. † RBA 1, SWA 3.

DIXON, Emily J. Exh. 1897-1910
Interior painter. Middle Gate, Newark, Notts. † N 12.

DIXON, Edna M. Exh. 1931-40
Portrait painter. 5 Dowanside Road, Glasgow. † GI 10, RA 1, RSA 5.

DIXON, Edith R. Exh. 1882-84
Birmingham. † B 2.

DIXON, Frederick Clifford b. 1902
Painter and etcher. Studied Derby School of Art and Royal College of Art. Add: Derby 1925 and 1930; London 1927. † ALP 1, L 3, M 2, N 5, NEA 3, RA 4.

DIXON, G. Calvert Exh. 1926
Flower painter. 71 Alexandra Road, Erith, Kent. † CG 1, RA 1.

DIXON, George Scholefield b. 1890
Portrait painter, illustrator and commercial artist. Add: Leeds 1910; London 1924; West Drayton, Middlesex 1929. † L 16, RA 5.

DIXON, Harry 1861-1942
Sculptor, painter, etcher and illustrator. Studied West London School of Art, Heatherleys and Juliens, Paris. R.B.A. 1902. "Lions" purchased by Chantrey Bequest 1891. Add: London 1881 and 1904; Shoreham, Kent 1898; Knockholt, Kent 1902. † AR 1, GI 5, I 3, L 12, M 2, NEA 1, NG 11, RA 29, RBA 7, RI 2, ROI 8.

DIXON, Henry Exh. 1923-34
Portrait painter. London. † GOU 2, NEA 1, RA 6.

DIXON, Hodgkin Exh. 1904-25
Landscape and figure painter. b. Southport, Lancs. Studied Slade School. Add: London 1904; Liscard, Cheshire 1913. † L 5, RA 4.

DIXON, J. Exh. 1898
Brougham Chambers, Wheeler Gate, Nottingham. † N 1.

DIXON, Joan Exh. 1932
Park House, Reigate, Surrey. † RA 1, ROI 1.

DIXON, John Exh. 1880-87
Marine painter. Surbiton, Surrey 1880; London 1881. † D 3, RBA 4, RI 1.

DIXON, John Exh. 1935-39
Newport, Mon. † RCA 10.

DIXON, John b. 1869
Flower and miniature portrait painter. Studied Newcastle on Tyne, St. John's Wood and RA Schools. Add: Morpeth, Northumberland. † L 1, RA 7.

DIXON, Joyce Deighton Exh. 1919-40
London. † B 2, GI 1, L 1, RCA 13, RHA 1, ROI 9, RSA 2, SWA 8.

DIXON, John L. Exh. 1927-30
Portrait and landscape painter. Metropolitan School of Art, Dublin 1927; Kilmainham, Dublin 1930. † RHA 4.

DIXON, John M. Exh. 1925
Landscape painter. Ladycross Cottage, Milford, Godalming, Surrey. † RA 1.

DIXON, John Percy Exh. 1892-1900
Architectural artist. Nottingham. † N 9.

DIXON, Martin Exh. 1932
Sculptor. Studied Dublin School of Art. Add: 124 Rock Road, Booterstown, Co. Dublin 1932. † RHA 1.

DIXON, Mary Exh. 1901-4
Miniature portrait painter. Nr. Bolton, Lancs. 1901; Harlow, Essex 1904. † L 1, RA 1.

DIXON, M.E. Exh. 1892-94
Thornton Lodge, Hooton, Cheshire. † L 2.

DIXON, Nellie Gertrude Exh. 1900-32
Painter and etcher. Southport, Lancs. † L 24, RA 2, RCA 7.

DIXON, Percy* 1862-1924
Landscape and coastal painter. R.I. 1915. Add: Bournemouth, Hants. 1880 and 1899; London 1888. † AR 92, B 39, D 14, DOW 59, L 2, M 1, RA 17, RBA 17, RHA 1, RI 85, RSW 1.

DIXON, Sean Exh. 1933-38
Landscape painter. Kilmainham, Dublin 1933; Rialto, Dublin 1938. † RHA 4.

DIXON, T.A. Exh. 1885
1 Frankfort Place, Upper Rathmines, Dublin. † RHA 1.

DIXON, William F. Exh. 1884-89
Stained glass artist. 18 University Street, Gower Street, London. † RA 6.

DOBBIE, Christina Exh. 1887-98
Glasgow. † GI 5.

DOBBIE, Isa Exh. 1896
Laurel Bank, Ayr. † GI 1.

DOBBIE, John Exh. 1920-35
Glasgow. † GI 10, RSA 5.

DOBBIN, Alfred W. Exh. 1911
Frankfort, Cork. † RHA 2.

DOBBIN, Ethel F. Exh. 1910
Sidney Lodge, Bray, Co. Wicklow. † RHA 2.

DOBBIN, Ethel M. Exh. 1924-39
Etcher, illustrator and Christmas Card designer. Studied Nottingham School of Art. N.S.A. 1924. Add: 6 Colville Street, Nottingham. † L 1, N 22.

DOBBIN, John Exh. 1880-84
Landscape and interior painter. Add: London. † GI 1, RBA 1.

DOBBIN, Lady Kate Exh. 1894-1940
Watercolour landscape and flower painter. Add: Cork, Ireland. † FIN 3, RHA 93.

DOBBS, Frank Exh. 1898
28 Westwick Gardens, West Kensington, London. † ROI 1.

DOBBS, Fred J. Exh. 1932-37
Penarth, Glam. † RCA 4.

DOBBS, Mrs. H.E. Exh. 1885-97
Dublin. † RHA 5.

DOBBS, Mrs. Sara Exh. 1909-15
31 Lower Beechwood Avenue, Ranelagh, Dublin. † RHA 5.

DOBELL, C.O. Exh. 1914-17
Staines, Middlesex 1914; Twickenham, Middlesex 1917. † LS 6.

DOBELL, William Exh. 1933
Figure painter. 34 Alexander Street, Bayswater, London. † RA 1.

DOBIE, Beatrix Charlotte* b. 1887
Mme. Rene Vernon. Landscape, portrait, animal and marine painter. b. Whangarei, New Zealand. Studied Calderon's School of Animal painting, South Kensington. Served with Red Cross 1914-18. Add: London 1925. † I 4, RCA 2, SWA 2.

DOBIE, James Exh. 1885-1923
Etcher. London. † RA 41, RSA 1.

DOBIE, Miss M. Exh. 1883
1 Buchanan Terrace, Paisley. † GI 1, L 1.

DOBINSON, Adeline M. Exh. 1929-33
157 St. Andrews Road, St. Annes on Sea, Lancs. † L 5.

DOBLE, Frank Sellar b. 1898
Landscape and still life painter and decorative designer. Exh. 1924-32. Add: Gt. Crosby, nr. Liverpool. † L 11.

DOBREE, Edwin de S. Exh. 1889
Landscape painter. New Club, Jersey, C.I. † L 1, RA 1.

DOBSON, Alfred Exh. 1893-1900
Domestic painter. London. † RA 1, RBA 1.

DOBSON, Cowan b. 1893
Portrait painter. b. Bradford. Son of Henry John D. q.v. A.R.B.A. 1919. Add: Edinburgh 1913; Galloway 1918; London 1919 and 1929; Glasgow 1920. † FIN 30, GI 35, L 5, P 15, RA 9, RBA 18, RCA 6, RSA 23, RSW 6.

DOBSON, Mrs. D.M. Exh. 1937
Landscape painter. 32 Millicent Road West Bridgford, Nottingham. † N 2.

DOBSON, Edmund A. Exh. 1883-89
Figure and landscape painter. Hampstead, London 1883; Petworth, Sussex 1885. † RA 5, RBA 5.

DOBSON, Miss E.E. Exh. 1916
16 Verulam Street, Liverpool. † L 1.

DOBSON, Frank* 1887-c.1965
Sculptor and painter. Studied from age of 14 in the studio of Sir William Reynolds Stephens; Scholarship to Hospitalfield School of Art, Arbroath; City and Guilds School, London and Newlyn. Member London Group 1922. Exh. 1916-39. Add: London. † AG 38, BK 2, CHE 11, COO 1, GOU 4, L 1, LEI 145, NEA 2, RA 6, RED 14, RHA 2, RSA 9, TOO 3.

DOBSON, Henry John* 1858-1928
Genre painter. Father of Cowan D. q.v. R.S.W. 1890. Add: Edinburgh 1880, 1899, 1919 and 1921; Bradford 1892; Peebles 1898; Dalry, Kirkcudbrightshire 1915. † DOW 1, GI 48, L 3, RA 6, RBA 4, RCA 54, RI 2, RSA 62, RSW 55.

DOBSON, Henry Raeburn b. 1901
Portrait and figure painter. Studied Edinburgh College of Art. Add: Edinburgh 1918; London 1929. † L 4, P 4, RA 6, RCA 23, RSA 6, RSW 5.

DOBSON, Mrs. Joanna L. Herbert
See HERBERT

DOBSON, Margaret Stirling Exh. 1905-36
Painter and etcher. Studied Edinburgh College of Art. A.R.E. 1917. Add: Edinburgh 1905; London 1912. † AB 5, I 4, L 3, RA 5, RE 12, RI 1, RSA 4.

DOBSON, Robert Exh. 1889-1901
Birkenhead 1889; Liverpool 1898. † L 5, M 1.

DOBSON, William Charles Thomas*
1817-1898
Religious, historical, genre and portrait painter. b. Hamburg, Germany. Studied RA Schools, Italy and Germany. A.R.A. 1860, R.A. 1871, A.R.W.S. 1870, R.W.S. 1875, H.R.B.A. 1883. Add: Hampstead, London 1880; Petworth, Sussex 1884. † AG 1, B 4, L 8, RA 19, RBA 3, RWS 10, TOO 3.

DOBSON, W.E. Exh. 1899-1910
Architect. London. † RA 4.
DOBSON, Walter E. Exh. 1913
Nutbourne, Pulborough, Sussex. † NEA 1.
DOBSON, W.L. Exh. 1884-1913
Glasgow. † GI 3.
DOCHARTY, Alexander Brownlie* Exh. 1880-1940
Landscape painter. Glasgow 1880 and 1899; Rugden by Maybole, Ayrshire 1893. † CON 24, GI 155, L 7, M 3, NEA 2, RA 12, RSA 19, RSW 5.
DOCHARTY, James L.C. d. c.1915
134 Bath Street, Glasgow. † GI 79, RSA 9, RSW 3.
DOCKER, Edward Exh. 1883-1908
Domestic painter. Birmingham 1883; Newlyn, Penzance 1890; Leamington, Warwicks 1892; Etaples, Calais, France 1896; Letchworth, Herts. 1907. † B 21, DOW 1, L 3, M 2, RA 4, ROI 3.
DOCKERILL, Margaret Exh. 1900-4
Miniature portrait painter. 5 Meadow Studios, Bushey, Herts. † L 4, RA 10, RMS 1, RSA 2.
DOCKERY, Susanna Exh. 1895-1901
Mrs. T. Landscape painter. Witley, Surrey 1895; Guildford, Surrey 1901. † D 8, RA 1, RI 3.
DOCKRAY, S.M. Louisa Exh. 1887
Figure painter. Stoke Headington, Oxford. † SWA 1.
DOCKREE, Mark Edwin* Exh. 1880-90
Landscape painter. St. John's Wood, London 1880; Rickmansworth, Herts. 1883. † RA 6, RBA 5, ROI 1.
DODD, Arthur C.* Exh. 1880-91
Sporting and figure painter. Tunbridge Wells, Kent 1880; London 1881. † B 14, D 3, G 3, GI 2, L 10, M 12, RA 8, RBA 34, RHA 3, ROI 5.
DODD, Charles Tattershall Exh. 1892-1929
Landscape painter. Tunbridge Wells, Kent. † L 1, RA 16, RI 2, ROI 1.
DODD, Francis* 1874-1949
Painter and etcher. b. Holyhead. Studied Glasgow and Italy. N.E.A. 1904 (Hon. Sec. N.E.A. 1919-21 and Hon. Treas. N.E.A. 1919-20) A.R.A. 1927, R.A. 1935, R.P. 1909, A.R.W.S. 1923, R.W.S. 1929. "A Smiling Woman" (1904) purchased by Chantrey Bequest 1924 and "In the Parlour" 1938. Add: Glasgow 1892; Manchester 1897; London 1905. † AG 5, BA 13, BK 4, CG 4, CHE 1, CON 42, FIN 7, GI 12, GOU 2, I 1, L 46, M 64, NEA 248, P 21, RA 77, RSA 16, RSW 2, RWS 124.
DODD, Miss M. Exh. 1918
171 Ivydale Road, Nunhead, London. † RA 1.
DODD, Phyllis Exh. 1920-40
Figure and landscape painter. Chester 1920; London 1927. † L 11, NEA 1, P 3, RA 12.
DODD, Ruth A. Exh. 1896
The Grove, King's Norton, Birmingham. † B 1.
DODD, R. Fielding Exh. 1931-39
Architect. 21 Turl Street, Oxford. † RA 18, RSA 2.
DODD, T.W. Exh. 1890-97
Liverpool. † L 9.
DODD, William b. 1908
Watercolour painter. Studied Kendal Art School 1926-33. Add: 15 Cliff Terrace, Kendal 1934. † L 2, RSA 3.

DODDS, Albert Charles 1888-1964
Landscape and portrait painter. Studied Edinburgh College of Art and RSA Life School (Carnegie travelling scholarship 1914). Visiting master Edinburgh Academy. A.R.S.W. 1937. Add: Leith 1909; Edinburgh 1913. † G 3, GI 12, L 2, RSA 44, RSW 24.
DODDS, W. Exh. 1881-1910
Roxburgh, Galashiels. † GI 3, RBA 1, ROI 3, RSA 13, RSW 2.
DODGSON, Catharine Exh. 1923-40
nee Spooner. Mrs. Campbell D. Landscape and figure painter. 22 Montagu Street, London. † CG 36, NEA 2, RA 9, SWA 3.
DODGSON, Eveline Exh. 1923-26
London. † NEA 3.
DODGSON, John* 1890-1969
Studied Slade School 1914-15. Exh. 1923-33. Add: London. † L 2, NEA 3.
DODMAN, Frank E. Exh. 1932-39
Etcher. Add: Altrincham, Cheshire 1932; Blackhall, Nr. Edinburgh 1935; Hale, Cheshire 1938. † B 2, L 3, M 2, RA 2, RSA 7.
DODS, Andrew Exh. 1925-39
Edinburgh. † RSA 17.
DODS, John W. Exh. 1893-1900
Sculptor. Add: St. Mary's Place, Dumfries. † GI 12, RA 1, RSA 4.
DODS, R.S. Exh. 1918
Royal Assurance Buildings, Sydney, New South Wales. † RSA 1.
DODSHON, G.M. Exh. 1892
15 Great Coram Street, Brunswick Square, London. † RSA 1.
DODSON, Miss A.C. Exh. 1910
45 Freehold Street, Liverpool. † L 1.
DODSON, D. or G. Exh. 1894-95
† TOO 2.
DODSON, George J. Exh. 1899
Landscape painter. Add: 23 Clapham Road, London. † RA 1.
DODSON, John Gordon b. 1882
Studied Norwich and Bournemouth Schools of Art, Heatherleys and the Victoria and Albert Museum. Exh. 1924-26. Add: Monchurch, Ipswich Road, Norwich. † L 1, RI 1.
DODSON, Sarah Paxton Ball 1847-1906
Landscape painter. b. Philadelphia, U.S.A. Add: Brighton 1891. Died Brighton. † B 1, GI 2, GOU 83, L 2, M 1.
DODS-WITHERS, Isobelle Ann 1876-1939
Landscape painter. nee Dods. Married Alfred Withers q.v. Studied Edinburgh and London. R.O.I. 1929, S.W.A. 1935. Member of Society of 25 artists. Add: Dunbar 1899; London 1903. † B 1, BA 1, BG 2, FIN 3, GOU 1, I 16, L 9, LEI 30, M 2, NG 6, RA 17, RHA 1, ROI 31, RSA 3, SWA 4.
DOEG, Robert E. Exh. 1903
4 Craighall Terrace, Musselburgh, N.B. † RSA 1.
DOERING, Miss A. Exh. 1885
14 Princes Gardens, Hyde Park, London. † SWA 1.
DOGGET, Miss G. Exh. 1913-15
53 Peele Street, Dingle, Liverpool. † L 2.
DOGGET, Miss M. Exh. 1910-16
Liverpool. † L 6.
DOGGETT, Ruth T. Exh. 1915-38
Landscape painter. Member London Group 1920. Add: London. † FIN 44, LEI 2, LS 3, NEA 1, RBA 3, ROI 13.
DOIDGE, Sarah A. Exh. 1880-1901
Landscape painter. Add: London 1880 and 1886; Birkenhead 1882. † L 1, RBA 1, SWA 14.

DOIGNEAU, Edouard Exh. 1906
2 Villa Niel, Paris. † L 1.
DOLBY, Harry H. Exh. 1923
Rydal Lodge, Breckside Park, Liverpool. † L 1.
D'OLIER, Florence Exh. 1912-22
Knocklina, Bray, Ireland. † RHA 6.
DOLLAR, Peter Exh. 1885-92
Architect. Add: 44 Great Marlborough Street, London. † RA 4.
DOLLMAN, Guy Exh. 1929-39
Landscape and flower painter. Add: London. † AR 1, COO 1, RA 3, RI 2, ROI 11.
DOLLMAN, Herbert P.* Exh. 1880-1905
Domestic painter. Add: London. † D 3, L 5, M 8, RA 6, RBA 7, RI 3, ROI 3.
DOLLMAN, John Charles* 1851-1934
Historical genre painter and black and white artist. b. Brighton. Studied RA Schools. R.I. 1886, R.O.I. 1887, A.R.W.S. 1906, R.W.S. 1913. Add: London 1880; Hove House, Newton Grove, Bedford Park, London 1884. † B 22, D 4, FIN 49, GI 4, L 27, M 25, RA 55, RHA 1, RI 19, ROI 24, RSA 1, RWS 176, TOO 1.
DOLLMAN, Kate Exh. 1887
14 Alma Road, Canonbury, London. † SWA 1.
DOLLMAN, Mary Exh. 1910-23
Hove House, Newton Grove, Bedford Park, London. † RI 3, TOO 40.
DOLLMAN, Ruth Exh. 1905-28
Landscape and flower painter. Add: Hove House, Newton Grove, Bedford Park, London. † B 2, FIN 69, LEI 112, RA 11, RI 14, RWS 6.
DOLLOND, W. Anstey Exh. 1880-1911
Landscape painter. Add: London 1880; Totteridge, Herts. 1897; Deal, Kent 1898. † L 4, M 1, RA 6, RBA 3, RI 7, TOO 1.
DOLTON, Phyllis Eileen Exh. 1922
† GOU 1.
DOMAN, Charles Leighfield J. b. 1884
Decorative and architectural sculptor. Studied Nottingham Municipal School of Art, triple gold, silver and bronze medallist (national competition), 1st national scholarship in sculpture (1906), travelling scholarship in sculpture at R.C.A. (1908). British Institute scholarship for sculpture 1908. Add: London. † GI 1, RA 29, RBA 1.
DOMBROWSKI, C.V. Exh. 1930
† L 1.
DOMERGUE, Jean Gabriel* b. 1889
French portrait and decorative artist. Studied Ecole des Beaux Arts, Paris. Add: 14 Rue de Chabrol, Paris. † BK 39, RA 1, RSA 2.
DOMINGO, F. Exh. 1892
† P 2.
DOMINGO, Roberto b. 1883
Spanish painter. Exh. 1914. † BG 56.
DOMINIUS, A. Exh. 1882-83
Rome. † D 2, L 2.
DOMMETTE, Doris Jane Exh. 1926-40
Portrait painter. Add: London. † RA 2.
DON, C.B. Exh. 1885-86
Landscape and figure painter. Add: c/o Mr. Meadows, 59 Gracechurch Street, London. † D 2, RBA 5.
DONALD, Adam T. Exh. 1934
Dundonald Arms, Culross, nr. Dunfermline. † RSA 1.
DONALD, David Exh. 1897-1917
Landscape painter. Add: Streatham, London 1897; Tilford, nr. Farnham, Surrey 1912; Reigate, Surrey 1917. † BRU 1, GI 1, RA 9, RBA 2.

DONALD, Emily Exh. 1886
Still life painter. Add: 92 Anerley Park, Anerley, London. † RBA 1.

DONALD, J.M. Exh. 1888-94
8 Leslie Place, Edinburgh. † GI 1, RSA 1.

DONALD, Mary Exh. 1886
9 Whitehouse Terrace, Edinburgh. † RSA 1.

DONALD, Tom 1853-1883
Glasgow. † GI 12, RSA 7, RSW 18.

DONALD, W. Exh. 1897-98
63 West Bank Road, Birkenhead. † L 3.

DONALD-SMITH, Helen Exh. 1884-1929
Portrait and landscape painter. b. Scotland. Studied Kensington, Paris and Herkomer's, Bushey, Herts. A.S.W.A. 1893. Add: Kensington, London. † B 2, BG 66, D 5, G 3, L 13, NG 15, P 2, RA 10, RBA 4, RI 20, RID 97, ROI 20, RSA 3, SWA 20.

DONALDSON, Andrew B.* 1840-1919
Historical, religious and landscape painter. R.B.A. 1875. Add: London 1880; Lyndhurst, Hants. 1907. † B 34, D 15, G 5, GI 11, L 18, M 30, NG 36, RA 12, RBA 16, RHA 17, RI 16, ROI 2.

DONALDSON, A.F. Exh. 1933
The Sheiling, Heather Dene Road, West Kirby, Lancs. † L 1.

DONALDSON, David A. Exh. 1934-40
54 Lavelle Drive, Cliftonville, Coatbridge. † GI 2, RSA 6.

DONALDSON, Mrs. D.J. Exh. 1917-18
Lower Franklands, Pangbourne, Berks. † RA 3.

DONALDSON, Miss E. Exh. 1909
19 Imperial Buildings, Old Millgate, Manchester. † L 3.

DONALDSON, Mrs. F. Irene Exh. 1922-33
Miniature painter. A.R.M.S. 1928. Add: The Elms, Peartree Avenue, Southampton. † L 3, RA 16, RMS 13.

DONALDSON, H. Exh. 1887-91
Edinburgh. † GI 3, RSA 5.

DONALDSON, Isobel Exh. 1916-36
Sculptor. Sister of Mary D. q.v. Add: Kensington, London. † G 1, L 2, RA 21, SWA 2.

DONALDSON, John Exh. 1884-1912
St. Vincent Street, Glasgow. † GI 2, RI 1.

DONALDSON, J.B. Exh. 1890-1917
Liverpool. † L 32.

DONALDSON, John G. Exh. 1916
8 Newbridge Avenue, Sandymount, Dublin. † RHA 1.

DONALDSON, James H. Exh. 1883-1938
Flower and still life painter. Add: Scarborough, Yorks. 1883; Pont Aven, Finisterre, France 1889; Milford, Surrey 1908; Leith 1938. † BG 1, LS 5, P 1, RA 2, RBA 1, RI 1, RSA 2.

DONALDSON, Margaret Exh. 1905-36
Glasgow 1905; Killearn, N.B. 1911; Blanefield, Stirlingshire 1929. † GI 7, RSW 1.

DONALDSON, Mary Exh. 1905-37
Portrait and figure painter. Sister of Isobel D. q.v. Add: London. † LS 6, NEA 2, RA 19.

DONALDSON, N. Exh. 1898
5 Crown Terrace, Dowanhill, N.B. † GI 1.

DONALDSON, R.H. Exh. 1883-86
Edinburgh. † GI 1, RSA 8.

DONALDSON, Virginia Exh. 1899
5 Crown Terrace, Glasgow. † RSA 1.

DONALDSON, William b. 1882
Architectural sculptor. Studied Inverness, Glasgow and Edinburgh. Teacher of modelling Glasgow School of Art. Add: Edinburgh. † GI 1, L 1, RSA 3.

DONAS, Mlle. M. Exh. 1915-16
Dublin. † RHA 6.

DONCASTER, Gertrude Exh. 1923-24
Nottingham 1923; Sandiacre, nr. Nottingham 1924. † N 2.

DONDERS, Mrs. Exh. 1890
c/o Sir Wm. Bowman, Joldwynds, Dorking, Surrey. † NG 1.

DONE, Miss E. Exh. 1886-87
College Green, Worcester. † B 2.

DONGHI, Eileen Exh. 1929-40
14 Via Camilla, San Francisco d'Albaro, Genoa, Italy. † RCA 2, ROI 1, RSA 1.

DONGWORTH, Winifred Cecile b. 1893
Watercolour and miniature portrait painter. Interior decorator and colour scheme artist. Studied Brighton Municipal Art School, Putney Art School and RA Schools. Add: Putney 1914; London 1917. † RA 8, RMS 1.

DONILO Exh. 1911
† GOU 3.

DONKERSLEY, Miss M. Stroyan Exh. 1902-21
Wood View, Almonsbury, Huddersfield. † B 1, L 11.

DONKIN, Alice Emily Exh. 1880-1909
Landscape and figure painter. Add: Windsor, Berks. 1880; London 1882; Englefield Green, Surrey 1891. † D 5, G 1, L 1, LS 13, M 1, NG 1, RA 6, RBA 2, RI 2, SWA 4.

DONKIN, John Exh. 1880
Watercolour landscape painter. Add: 17 Argyll Road, Kensington, London. † RBA 1.

DONKIN, Winifred H. d. c.1925
Miniature animal painter. A.R.M.S. 1921. Add: Walthamstow, Essex. † L 3, RA 5, RMS 8, RSA 1.

DONN, Dennis L. Exh. 1938
† NEA 2.

DONN, Isadore S. Exh. 1895
5 St. John's Wood Studios, Queen's Terrace, London. † M 1.

DONN, Robert Exh. 1902-6
1 Westfield Lane, Dundee. † RSA 3.

DONNAN, Robert Exh. 1888-1937
Painter, etcher, applied art designer and potter. Studied South Kensington and l'Academie Delecluse, Paris. Art master Allan Glens School, Glasgow. Add: Glasgow 1888; Milngavie, N.B. 1911. † GI 36, L 1, RSA 6.

DONNAY, A. Exh. 1915
† I 3.

DONNE, Anna Exh. 1884-85
Landscape, interior and flower painter. Add: 31 Campden Grove, Kensington, London. † SWA 4.

DONNE, Benjamin John Morefield Exh. 1889-1901
Landscape painter. Add: Seaton, Devon 1891; Colyford, Devon 1896. † D 13, DOW 78, L 1, NG 1, RA 2, RI 2.

DONNE, Donisthorpe Exh. 1895-1905
Putney 1895; Chichester 1905. † D 5, RBA 1.

DONNE, D.A. Exh. 1906
Collingwood, Spring Grove, Isleworth, Middlesex. † D 2.

DONNE, Mrs. E.M.A. Exh. 1901
Merifield, Exmouth, Devon. † D 1.

DONNE, Col. H.R.B. Exh. 1906-39
Landscape painter. Add: London. † ALP 19, AR 2, COO 2, D 9, RI 1.

DONNE, J.M. Exh. 1880-88
Landscape painter. Add: Kensington, London. † B 2, D 24, DOW 134, G 15, L 3, NG 1, RA 3, RBA 4, RI 9.

DONNE, Rose Exh. 1884
Landscape and flower painter. Add: 31 Campden Grove, Kensington, London. † D 1, SWA 2.

DONNE, Mrs. Walter Exh. 1910-21
London 1910 and 1916; Thirsk, Yorks. 1914. † RA 3, RCA 1, RI 2, SWA 4, WG 68.

DONNE, Winifred Exh. 1916-22
"Skylark", Shoreham on Sea, Sussex. † G 2, I 5, RI 1.

DONNE, Walter J. b. 1867
Landscape painter. R.O.I. 1905. Scarborough 1885; London 1890; Shoreham on Sea, Sussex 1923. † B 2, GI 9, I 7, L 19, M 5, NEA 4, NG 4, P 5, RA 42, RBA 4, RHA 5, RI 12, RID 72, ROI 12.

DONNELLY, Gerald Exh. 1936-38
Landscape painter. Dublin. † RHA 3.

DONNELLY, Maj.-Gen. Sir John F.D. 1834-1902
Landscape painter. London. † NG 28, RA 1.

DONNELLY, M. Exh. 1880-81
12 Adelaide Road, London. † RHA 2.

DONNER, Edgar P. Exh. 1893
Etcher. 78 Tierney Road, Streatham Hill, London. † RA 1.

DONNISON, Miss P. Exh. 1886-90
7 Angel Park Gardens, Brixton, London. † B 6, GI 5, L 2.

DONNISON, T.E. Exh. 1882
Rock Ferry, Cheshire. † L 1.

DONNITHORNE, Miss Vere Exh. 1908-12
London. † LS 3, RA 3.

DONOGHUE, John 1853-1903
Sculptor. 21 Bolton Studios, London. † RA 2.

DONOHUE, A. Exh.1901-8
Liverpool. † L 4.

DONOVAN, Amy G. Exh. 1936-38
Torquay, Devon. † NEA, RBA 1, RCA 1.

DONOVAN, Miss P. Exh. 1930-40
Figure and flower painter. Ballymore, Camolin, Co. Wexford. † L 2, RHA 19.

DOO, George Thomas 1800-1886
Historical engraver to Queen Victoria. A.R.A. 1856, R.A. 1857. Add: 4 Chancellor Road, West Dulwich 1880. † RA 1.

DOODY, Laura Exh. 1900-2
Birmingham. † B 2.

DOOIJEWAARD, Jacob* Exh. 1906
Figure Painter. Holland. † I 1.

DOOLIN, Walter G. Exh. 1880-1901
Dublin. † RHA2.

DOON, J.A. Exh. 1890
27 Carnarvon Street, Glasgow. † GI 2.

DOPPING-HEPENSTAL, Haidie Exh. 1893-96
Derrycassan, Granard, Co. Longford. † RHA 3.

DORAN, Mrs. Exh. 1881-90
12 Windsor Terrace, W. Glasgow. † GI 2.

DORAN, Miss A.M. Exh. 1920-30
6 St. James Road, Liverpool. † L 15.

DORAN, Christopher M. Exh. 1937-40
Landscape painter. c/o Waddington Galleries, South Anne Street, Dublin. † RHA 7.

DORBEC-CHARVOT, Mme. Exh. 1909
51 Rue de Maubeuge, Paris. † L 1.

DORE, Miss G. Exh. 1908
Pinner Hill, Pinner, Middlesex. † RA 1.

DOREY, J.A. Exh. 1920-40
Birmingham. † B 31.

DORIGNAC, George 1879-1925
French artist. 2 Passage de Dantzig, Paris. † RSA 1.

DORING, Adolf G. Exh. 1897
Etcher. Villa Douzette, Barth a/d Ostsee, Germany. † RA 1.

DORING, Marguerite Exh.1922-35
Decorative painter. Sally Lun, Rottingdean, Brighton, Sussex. † G 2, RA 1.

DORMAN, Dorothy Exh. 1926-27
13 Westercraigs, Dennistoun, Glasgow. † GI 3.

DORMAN, Frances Exh. 1926-30
13 Westercraigs, Dennistoun, Glasgow. † GI 3, RSA 2.

DORMER, Lord Exh. 1890-91
Grove Park, Warwick. † L 2.

DORMER. Mrs. E.H. Exh. 1905
Nightingale Place, Nr. Polegate, Sussex. † L 1.

DORMER, Hon. Louise Exh. 1891
Grove Park, Warwick. † ROI 1.

DORNBERGER, C.T. Adam Exh. 1889
30 North Fort Street, Leith. † RSA 1.

DORNOIS, A. Exh. 1882-83
50 Rue de Lille, Paris. † GI 3.

DORPH, Mrs. B. Exh. 1905
11 Hardorffsrej, Copenhagen. † I 1.

DORPH, N.V. Exh. 1905
11 Hardorffsrej, Copenhagen. † I 1.

DORR, F. Exh. 1930
† L 1.

DORR, Harry Exh. 1936
Landscape painter. c/o W.F. Watson, 15 Harlaxton Street, Leicester. † N 1.

DORRIEN-SMITH, Anne Exh. 1935
Watercolour painter. † WG 21.

DORRIEN-SMITH, Charlotte Exh. 1911
Watercolour landscape painter. † WG 19.

DORRIEN-SMITH, Cicely Exh. 1911
Watercolour landscape painter. † WG 25.

DORRIEN-SMITH, Gwendolen Exh. 1911-37
Watercolour landscape painter. † ALP 25, WG 97.

DORRIEN-SMITH, Innis Exh. 1911-35
Watercolour landscape painter. † WG 85.

DORRIEN-SMITH, Mary L.H. Exh. 1896-1901
Mrs. Theo D-S. R.M.S. 1896, Hon. Sec. R.M.S. 1896-96. Add: Chalfont St. Peter, Bucks 1896; Rickmansworth, Herts 1901. † L 1, RA 1, RMS 8.

DORRINGTON, Cissie Exh. 1906-12
Gt. Grosby, Liverpool. † L 4, RCA 5.

DOTT, Mrs. David Exh. 1894
Windsor Cottage, Musselburgh. † RHA 1.

DOTT, Jessie W. Exh. 1882-1918
Edinburgh. † RSA 8.

DOUBLEDAY, Matthew Exh. 1881-1900
Landscape painter. N.S.A. 1881, Council Member N.S.A. 1886. Add: Old Radford, Notts. 1881; West Bridgford, Notts. 1889. † N 19.

DOUBLEDAY, William Exh. 1882-1933
Architect, Birmingham. † B 4, RA 2.

DOUBTING, James 1841-1904
Landscape and animal painter. Warmley, Nr. Bristol 1882. † L 1.

DOUCET, Henri* d. 1916
Landscape painter. Add: c/o Allied Artists Association, Chancery Lane, London 1913. † ALP 3, LS 6.

DOUCET, Lucien Exh. 1888-92
6 Rochefoucald, Paris. † D 2, P 1.

DOUDNEY, Eric John b. 1905
Sculptor. St. Margarets on Thames 1935; Teddington, Middlesex 1937. † RA 5.

DOUGALL, Margaret S. Exh. 1927-31
Glasgow. † GI 4.

DOUGAN, S. Eric Exh. 1937-38
Sculptor. 76 Hawton Road, Newark, Notts. † N 3.

DOUGHERTY, Paul* Exh. 1925
† CHE 2.

DOUGHERTY, Parke Curtis b. 1867
American artist. Exh. 1906-9. Add: Paris. † I 1, LS 6.

DOUGHTY, Eleanor Exh. 1890-96
Flower painter. 8 Philbeach Gardens, Earls Court, London. † RA 1, RBA 7, SWA 1.

DOUGHTY, Miss F.G. Exh. 1932-37
A.R.M.S. 1933. Add: Merriecroft, Cranbrook, Kent. † RMS 13.

DOUGHTY, Gilbert S. Exh. 1901-3
Architect. Royal Insurance Buildings, Nottingham. † RA 3.

DOUGLAS, Miss A Exh. 1892
The Ghyll, Applethwaite, Keswick. † L 1.

DOUGLAS, Alex Exh. 1899
40 Main Street, Bridgend, Perth. † RSA 1.

DOUGLAS, Anna Exh. 1898-1910
Portrait and landscape painter. Married to James D. q.v. Add: Edinburgh 1898; Chilworth, Surrey 1901; London 1902; Tayport, N.B. 1905. † GI 1, RA 2, RSA 5.

DOUGLAS, Anne Exh. 1902-11
Kensington, London. † L 5, RA 2, RSA 2.

DOUGLAS, Andrew A. 1870-1934
Cattle and landscape painter. Studied Edinburgh (bronze medallist and Queen's prizeman). A.R.S.A. 1920, R.S.A. 1933. Add: Edinburgh. † GI 78, L 13, M 3, RA 20, RSA 119, RSW 1.

DOUGLAS, A.E. Exh. 1881-82
Warren Point, Ireland. † RHA 10.

DOUGLAS, Alice, M. Exh. 1907-21
Rathgar, Dublin 1907; Handsworth, Birmingham 1921. † B 2, RHA 9.

DOUGLAS, Bessie Exh. 1901
Ashlea, Bellahouston, N.B. † GI 1.

DOUGLAS, C. Exh. 1891
266 St. Vincent Street, Glasgow. † GI 1.

DOUGLAS, Dan Exh. 1884
135 Caledonian Road, Glasgow. † GI 1.

DOUGLAS, Miss E. Exh. 1911-13
Dorset House, Bexhill, Surrey. † L 1, RA 1, RMS 1.

DOUGLAS, Edward Exh. 1931-33
Still life and portrait painter. 105 Moyne Road, Rathmines, Dublin. † RHA 3.

DOUGLAS, Edwin* 1848-1914
Sporting and animal painter and engraver. b. Edinburgh. Studied R.A. Schools. Add: Shere, Nr. Guildford, Surrey 1880; Wothing, Sussex 1889; Findon, Sussex 1891. † B 3, FIN 1, GI 3, L 3, M 3, RA 22, ROI 14.

DOUGLAS, Elsie Exh. 1909
† BG 1.

DOUGLAS, Ena Exh. 1930-32
Still life and figure painter. Dublin. † RHA 10.

DOUGLAS, Edward A.S.* Exh. 1880-92
Sporting painter. Barnes, Surrey. † B 1, L 2, RA 10.

DOUGLAS, George Exh. 1887
272 Causewayside, Edinburgh. † RSA 1.

DOUGLAS, Georgina Exh. 1885
Bellevue Bank, Helensburgh. † GI 1.

DOUGLAS, Gordon Exh. 1892-93
64 Dee Street, Aberdeen. † L 1, RHA 3.

DOUGLAS, George Cameron Exh. 1908-9
41 Reform Street, Dundee, N.B. † LS 8.

DOUGLAS, Hope Toulmin b. 1883
nee Smith. Minature painter. Studied Calderon's School of Animal painting (scholarship 1899); Frank Brangwyn's Life School and under Alyn Williams. A.R.M.S. 1912, R.M.S. 1913. Add: Dulwich Common, London 1902; Redruth, Cornwall 1910; Lutterworth, Leics. 1918; Colyton, Devon 1930; Leeds 1931; Settle, Yorks. 1933; † B 2, L 14, RA 10, RMS 64.

DOUGLAS, H.K. Exh. 1883
98 Brecon Road, Merthyr, Wales. † L 1.

DOUGLAS, H.R. Exh. 1885-1900
Belfast. † L 1, RHA 1.

DOUGLAS, Isabel Exh. 1899-1902
Blair Villa, Lenzie, N.B. † GI 2.

DOUGLAS, Isobella H.L. Exh. 1938-39
53 Frederick Street, Edinburgh. † RSA 2.

DOUGLAS, J. Exh. 1890
105 Byars Road, Partick. † GI 1.

DOUGLAS, James Exh. 1881-1907
Landscape painter. R.S.W. 1900, Struck off 1907. Add: Edinburgh 1881 and 1898; Applethwaite, Keswick 1893, Chilworth, Surrey 1901; London 1902; Tayport, N.B. 1906. † GI 4, L 3, RA 4, RSA 71, RSW 13.

DOUGLAS, John b. 1867
Landscape and figure painter. Studied Glasgow School of Art. Add: Glasgow 1899; Kilmarnock 1904 and 1906; Tayport N.B. 1905; Ayr 1925. † GI 13, L 1, RSW 3.

DOUGLAS, John Exh. 1881-1902
Architect. 6 Abbey Square, Chester. † L 2, RA 7, RCA 7.

DOUGLAS, John Hamilton Exh. 1911-32
Grammar School, Margate 1911; London 1932. † B 1, LS 12, RBA 1.

DOUGLAS, Jessie Ogsten Exh. 1894-1925
Figure painter. Belfast. † B 6, CON 3, FIN 1, GI 23, L 20, LS 2J, RA 2, RHA 8, RI 6. RSA 1, SWA 5.

DOUGLAS, J. Olive Exh. 1939
Rhyl, Wales. † RCA 2.

DOUGLAS, J.P. Exh. 1908
32 Grosvenor Road, Westcliff on Sea, Essex. † B 1.

DOUGLAS, Mrs. Mabel M. Exh. 1904-37
Minature portrait painter. Add: St. Ives, Cornwall. † RA 22.

DOUGLAS, Marion MacQ. Exh. 1927-36
Portrait painter. Add: Crawley Down, Sussex 1927; Felbridge, Sussex 1936. † P 2, RA 1, ROI 2, RSA 1

DOUGLAS, M.W. Exh. 1939
† RI 1.

DOUGLAS, R. Exh. 1937
167 West Graham Street, Glasgow. † GI 1.

DOUGLAS, Rose Exh. 1893-98
St. Paul's, London 1893; St. George's Lodge, Winchester 1895. † D 9, L 1, M 1, RBA 1, RI 3.

DOUGLAS, R. Smeaton Exh. 1900-12
St. Andrews, N.B. 1900; Ayr 1905. † GI 5, RSA 8.

DOUGLAS, Miss S.B. Exh. 1900-2
22 Drummond Place, Edinburgh. † RSA 3.

DOUGLAS, Sholto Johnstone Exn. 1899-1920
Portrait painter. London. † ALP 39, GI 3, L 8, LS 2, NEA 6, NG 6, P 4, RA 13, RSA 9.

DOUGLAS, William Exh. 1935
10 Polwarth Crescent, Edinburgh. † RSA 1.

DOUGLAS, Winifred Exh. 1935
Watford, Herts. † RCA 1.

DOUGLAS, Sir William Fettes* 1822-1891
Portrait, interior, landscape and historical genre painter. Took up painting after 10 years as a Bank clerk in Edinburgh. Self taught. Visited Italy 1857. A.R.S.A. 1851, R.S.A. 1854, P.R.S.A. 1882-91. Knighted 1882. Curator of National Gallery of Scotland 1877-82. Add: Edinburgh. † G 1, RSA 28, RSW 2.

DOUGLAS-HAMILTON, R. Exh. 1888
5 Kensington Studio, Kelso Place, London. † ROI 1.

DOUGLAS-IRVINE, Lucy Christina b. 1874
Cattle and barn interior painter and pencil artist. Studied Glasgow School of Art and Kemp-Welch School of Painting. Exh. 1923-33. Add: Pittenweem, Fife and Edinburgh. † L 1, RCA 2, RHA 2, RSA 1, RSW 3.

DOUGLASS, Richard Exh. 1882-90
Landscape painter. Park Village East, Regent's Park, London. † G 1, RBA 4, RI 6, RSA 1.

D'OUSELEY, Miss Sophie see MEREDITH

D'OUSEY, Miss S. Exh. 1885-86
78 Frithville Gardens, Uxbridge Road, London. † B 1, M 1.

DOUTON, Isabel F. d. c.1925
Minature portrait painter. A.R.M.S. 1905. Add: Cheltenham, Glos. 1893; London 1904. † B 1, L 12, NG 3, RA 19, RMS 60.

DOUX, le see L

DOVASTON, Margaret* Exh. 1908-13
R.B.A. 1910. Add: 14 Madeley Road, Ealing, London. † RA 1, RBA 11, WG 49.

DOVER, Henry T. Exh. 1918-21
12 Abercorn Place, St. John's Wood, London † LS 9.

DOW, Alexander Warren 1873-1948
Landscape and still life painter, etcher and art critic. Studied under Norman Garstin, Frank Brangwyn, Heatherleys and in France. R.B.A. 1919. Add: London. † AB 2, D 48, I 5, L 20, LS 9, M 1, NEA 2, RA 2, RBA 181, RHA 4, RI 4, ROI 8, RSA 2.

DOW, David S. Exh. 1880-1905
Perth 1880; Edinburgh 1898. † RSA 16.

DOW, Harold James b. 1902
Sculptor. London. † RA 10, RMS 1.

DOW, James William Exh. 1880-85
10 Claremont Place, Edinburgh. † RSA 3.

DOW, Lumley Exh. 1893-94
21 Pembridge Road, Notting Hill, London. † ROI 2.

DOW, Mary Exh. 1885
Beech Grove, Moffat, Edinburgh. † RSA 1.

DOW, Mary Exh. 1885-92
Glasgow. † GI 9.

DOW, Thomas Millie 1848-1919
Landscape and flower painter. Studied in Paris. N.E.A. 1887, R.O.I. 1903, R.S.W. 1885. Add: Kirkcaldy 1880 and 1889; Dysart, Fifeshire 1885; Glasgow 1888 and 1893; St. Ives, Cornwall 1897. † B 1, BG 3, DOW 3, G 3, GI 45, I 9, L 17, M 9, NEA 7, RBA 4, ROI 4, RSA 24, RSW 24.

DOWALL, Mrs. H.M. Exh. 1939
c/o Rowley Gallery, 140 Kensington Church Street, London. † SWA 1.

DOWD, John Exh. 1897
13 Venus Street, Liverpool. † L 1.

DOWD, James H. 1884-1956
Painter and etcher. Sheffield 1912; London 1918. † AB 40, COO 35, GI 4, I 4, L 7, P 10, RA 11, RMS 1, RSA 1.

DOWD, Roland Hall b. 1896
Landscape painter, etcher, illustrator, poster designer and teacher. Add: 3 Bank of Liverpool Chambers, Lord Street, Southport, Lancs. 1924. † L 1, RCA 3.

DOWDALL, Edward Exh. 1898-99
Figure and landscape painter. Add: Newman Street, London. † RA 1, RBA 1.

DOWDEN, Anna Exh. 1908-11
Edinburgh. † RHA 1, RSA 1.

DOWELL, Charles R. d. 1935
R.S.W. 1933. St. Vincent Street, Glasgow. † GI 76, L 2, RSA 14, RSW 21.

DOWER, Mrs. A. Lavender Exh. 1929
35 Lowndes Street, London. † RBA 1.

DOWIE, Adeline M. Exh. 1906-11
Liverpool. † L 4, RSA 1.

DOWIE, Beatrice M. Exh. 1900-13
Landscape painter. London 1900; Chilworth, Surrey 1913. † B 1, BG 17, SWA 7.

DOWIE, Miss G.M. Exh. 1895
c/o Wm. Lomax, Oxford Street, Manchester. † M 1.

DOWIE, Miss Lucy Exh. 1890
36 Percy Street, Liverpool. † L 1.

DOWIE, Sybil M. Exh. 1889-1922
Portrait and landscape painter. Brighton 1889; London 1896 and 1921; Chilworth, Surrey 1911. † B 7, BG 31, L 4, LS 3, P 4, RA 5, RID 69 SWA 14.

DOWLING, J.J. Exh. 1893
Victoria House, Foxrock, Co. Dublin. † RHA 1.

DOWLING, Robert* 1827-1886
Landscape, figure and historical painter. 27 Colehorne Road, Radcliffe Square, West Brompton, London. † B 2, D 4, GI 1, L 5, RA 3, RBA 2, RHA 1.

DOWLING, Sidney W. Exh. 1901
34 Church Road, Richmond, Surrey. † B 1.

DOWLING, William Exh. 1940
Landscape painter. 99 St. Declan Road, Dublin. † RHA 3.

DOWN, Vera Emily b. 1888
Landscape and figure painter, etcher and teacher. Studied Grosvenor Life School under Walter Donne, Paris and Central School of Art. Add: London 1919; Woldingham, Surrey 1931. † L 2, RA 7, RBA 6, RI 8, RID 4, ROI 2, SWA 10, WG 25.

DOWNARD, Ebenezer Newman* Exh. 1880-92
Landscape and genre painter. Add: 2 Theresa Terrace, Hammersmith, London. † AG 1, D 1, GI 5, RA 8, RHA 1, ROI 1, TOO 1.

DOWNES, Annabel Exh. 1885-90
Figure painter. 19 Upper Phillimore Place, Kensington, London. † B 1, G 1, L 2, RA 6, RBA 1, RI 3.

DOWNES, Ada E. Exh. 1893
Urban landscape painter. Add: 18 High Street, Notting Hill Gate, London. † RBA 1.

DOWNES, Gertrude M. Exh. 1885-86
Animal painter. 26 Bridge West, Battersea, London. † SWA 3.

DOWNES, J.V. Exh. 1929-37
Architect. Dublin. † RHA 5.

DOWNES, Miss L.A. Exh. 1915-17
Newstead House, Carlton, Nottingham. † N 2.

DOWNES, Miss Sarah J. Geale Exh. 1894-1904
Dublin. † RHA 10, SWA 1.

DOWNES, Thomas Price Exh. 1880-87
Portrait painter. London † RA 2.

DOWNES, Miss W.D. Exh. 1921
"Capelulo", Penmaenmawr, N. Wales. † RCA 1.

DOWNEY, Alfred James Exh. 1909-35
Painter, engraver and illustrator. London. † L 5, RA 18, RMS 1.

DOWNEY, Thomas Exh. 1935
Figure painter. † AR 2.

DOWNIE, Helen Exh. 1895-97
nee Cochran. Married Partrick D. q.v. Add: Paisley, Glasgow. † GI 5, L 1, RSA 1.

DOWNIE, John C. Exh. 1933
Sculptor. Add: 16 Frankfurt Road, Herne Hill, London. † RA 1.

DOWNIE, Miss J.F. Exh. 1911
Raglan, Waterloo, Liverpool. † L 1.

DOWNIE, John Patrick* d. 1945
Landscape painter. R.S.W. 1903. Glasgow 1887-1940. Died 4th April. † GI 118, L 14, M 1, NEA 4, P 2, RSA 24, RSW 51, RWS 2.

DOWNIE, Patrick b. 1945
Landscape and coastal painter. Studied Paris. R.S.W. 1902. Add: Greenock 1883; Paisley 1888; Glasgow 1897 and 1916; Skelmorlie, N.B. 1903; Largs, N.B. 1908; Kilbride 1913. Died 16th May. † AR 2, GI 133, L 36, M 7, RA 16, RBA 3, RI 4, RSA 54, RSW 126.

DOWNING, Charles Palmer Exh. 1880-99
Portrait painter. London. † GI 2, L 3, P 1, RA 22, ROI 5.

DOWNING, Delapoer* Exh. 1885-1902
Figure painter. London. † B 1, L 1, M 1, RA 7, RBA 2, ROI 10.

DOWNING, Edith E. Exh. 1890-1910
Sculptor. London. † GI 3, L 7, RA 9, SWA 10.

DOWNING, George Henry b. 1878
Landscape painter, art teacher, lecturer and writer. Studied Portsmouth. A.R.B.A. 1919, R.B.A. 1921. Ech. 1917-38. Add: 102 Frensham Road, Southsea, Hants. † AB 3, RA 3, RBA 146.

DOWNING, H.P. Burke Exh. 1904-32
Architect. Studied R.A. Schools. Add: Merton, Surrey 1904; 12 Little College Street, Westminster, London 1905. † RA 35, RSA 3.

DOWNING, J.E. Exh. 1913-14
Tresco, Avenue Road, Falmouth, Cornwall. † RA 2.

DOWNING, Mary M.B. Exh. 1893-1905
London. † B 1, L 1, RCA 5, SWA 23.

DOWNING, Miss R. Exh. 1928-29
The Walk, Beccles, Suffolk. † L 2.

DOWNING, T.W. Exh. 1882-1910
Birmingham. † B 11.

DOWNS, Edgar b. 1876
Animal painter. Studied Munich Academy of Arts (silver medal). R.O.I. 1920. Add: Nayland, nr. Colchester, Essex 1903; London 1907; Littlehampton, Sussex 1923-31. † CHE 1, D 13, L 4, RA 17, RCA 2, RI 1, ROI 37.

DOWNTON, John Exh. 1936-40
Portrait and figure painter. Sevenoaks, Kent 1936; Cambridge 1940. † RA 7.

DOWNTON, Mrs. W.H. Exh. 1918
The Nunnery, Diss, Norfolk. † RA 1

DOWSE, Fred W.H. Exh. 1880
Windmill House, Edinburgh. † RSA 1.

DOWSON, Elinor Exh. 1899-1913
A.S.W.A. 1909. Chelsea, London 1899; Hartfield, Sussex 1913. † LS 5, NG 1, SWA 3.

DOWSON, Nancy Exh. 1925
Landscape painter. Danehurst, Northdown Way, Margate, Kent. † RA 1, SWA 1.

DOWSON, Russell Exh. 1880-1911
Landscape and coastal painter. Travelled on the continent. Add: London 1880 and 1901; Eton, Bucks 1881. † AG 7, B 15, D 29, FIN 77, G 4, L 5, M 2, RA 7, RBA 5, RI 9, ROI 12.

DOXEY, W.H. Exh. 1914-26
93 Rumford Street,C on M. Manchester. † LS 2, M 2.

DOXFORD, James B. 1899
Painter and black and white artist. Studied Durham University and Newcastle on Tyne. Principal Bridgwater Art and Technical School 1932-38. Principal Barnstaple Art and Technical School 1938-44. Exh. 1939-40. † RA 2.

DOYLE, Alice F. Exh. 1905-14
56 George Street, Limerick, Ireland. † RHA 8.

DOYLE, Bertha Exh. 1907-8
26 Blenheim Terrace, Leeds, Yorks. † B 1, L 4.

DOYLE, Bentinck Cavendish Exh. 1885-1928
Sea and flower painter. Studied Slade School and Paris under Carolus Duran. Add: London 1885; Worthing, Sussex 1916. † B 5, L 3, RA 1, ROI 2.

DOYLE Charles Altamont* 1832-1893
Fantasy painter and illustrator. Brother of Richard D. q.v. and father of Sir Arthur Conan D. Add: 23 George Square, Edinburgh. † RSA 1.

DOYLE, Honor Camilla b. 1888
Portrait, landscape and furniture painter and poet. b. Norwich. Studied Slade School. Add: London 1911, Rickmansworth, Herts. 1916. † AB 1, NEA 7.

DOYLE, Henry Edward 1827-1892
Director of National Gallery of Ireland. A.R.H.A. 1872, R.H.A. 1874. Exh. 1884. † RHA 1.

DOYLE, Harcourt M. Exh. 1940
Stained glass artist. 46 Mortimer Road, London. † RA 1.

DOYLE, J. Francis Exh. 1884-1912
Architect. 4 Harrington Street, Liverpool. † L 4, RA 13.

DOYLE, Richard* 1824-1883
Fantasy painter, caricaturist and illustrator. Contributor to "Punch" 1843-50. Brother of Charles A.D. q.v. Add: 7 Finborough Road, Fulham Road, London. † G 18, L 2.

DOYLE, William F. d. 1891
A.R.H.A. 1869. Add: Dublin. † RHA 10.

DOYLE-JONES, Francis W. d. 1938
Sculptor. Exh. 1903-36. Add: London. † GI 1, I 4, L 3, RA 30, RHA 15.

D'OYLEY, A. Exh. 1881
20 Mortimer Street, Regent Street, London. † RHA 1.

D'OYLY, Constance F. Exh. 1896-1913
Portrait and figure painter. 15 Onslow Studios, 183 King's Road, London. † D 4, LS 14, P 1.

D'OYLY, Mabell Exh. 1932-37
Flower, landscape and still life painter and engraver. 10 South Eaton Place, London. † COO 25, SWA 3.

DRABBLE, Dorothy G. Exh. 1900-8
Landscape painter. Woodside, Sundridge, Sevenoaks, Kent. † B 4, LS 5, RA 1, SWA 3.

DRABBLE, J.D. Exh. 1880
Landscape and shell painter. 1 Pembridge Square, Bayswater, London. † RBA 2.

DRABBLE, R. Exh. 1881-85
Landscape painter. London 1881; Sevenoaks, Kent 1885. † RA 2.

DRACOPOLI, N.F. Exh. 1886-89
Edgbaston, Birmingham 1886; Antibes, France 1889. † B 3.

DRAGE, E. Alice Exh. 1889-1900
Portrait painter. Surbiton, Surrey 1889; Beckenham, Kent 1900. † SWA 5.

DRAGE, Mrs. Gilbert Exh. 1904
North Place, Hatfield, Herts. † NG 1.

DRAGE, J. Henry Exh. 1882-1905
Landscape and figure painter. Croydon, Surrey 1882; Eastbourne 1901. † L 2, M 1, NG 13, RA 7, RI 8.

DRAGE, Mildred Frances Exh. 1882-92
Landscape and figure painter. Hatfield, Herts. † L 4, M 3, NG 4, RA 3, RBA 1, ROI 1.

DRAKE, Charles E. Exh. 1904-10
Figure painter. London † LS 6, RA 1.

DRAKE, Elizabeth 1866-1954
Painter, miniaturist, lithographer and teacher. Studied Rochester and Westminster Art Schools and Colarossi's, Paris. Travelled in South Africa. Add: Rochester, Kent 1897; London 1904; Bristol 1909. † B 3, L 1, LS 3, RA 2, RI 1, RWS 3, SWA 2.

DRAKE, J.W. Exh. 1915
20 Shakleton Road, Southall, Middlesex. † L 1, RA 1.

DRAKE, Wilfred b. 1879
Designer and stained glass artist. Studied Teignmouth School of Art. Served 1st Battalion Somerset Light Infantry 1916-19. Add: London 1923-31. † RA 3.

DRAKEFORD, Mrs. A. Exh. 1927-28
24 St. James Road, Liverpool. † L 6.

DRANE, Herbert Cecil Exh. 1890-1905
Rustic painter. Oakbank, Dorking, Surrey. † L 3, NG 9, RA 1, RBA 11, RHA 2, ROI 6.

DRAPER, Amy G. Exh. 1892-1904
Mrs. Sumner. Landscape and portrait painter. N.E.A. 1894. Add: Bromley, Kent 1892; London 1893; Farnham, Surrey 1903. † GI 1, L 3, M 3, NEA 21, NG 8, P 3, RBA 4, RID 23, ROI 1.

DRAPER, Charles F. Exh. 1880-1910
Landscape and marine painter. London 1880; Eastbourne 1899; Dublin 1908. † M 1, RA 2, RBA 3, RHA 4, RI 3.

DRAPER, Herbert James* 1864-1920
Landscape and figure painter. Studied St. John's Wood School of Art, R.A. Schools 1884 (Gold medal and travelling studentship), Juliens, Paris and in Rome 1890-91. "The Lament for Icarus" purchased by Chantrey Bequest 1898. Add: Bromley, Kent 1887, London 1892. † ALP 3, B 5, BG 1, GI 5, L 44, LEI 131, M 3, NG 10, P 4, RA 61, RBA 1, RHA 2, ROI 3.

DRAPER, Miss May Exh. 1910
26 Grosvenor Road, Rathmines, Dublin. † RHA 1.

DRAPER, Ralph Exh. 1940
17 Maxwell Avenue, Garrowhill, Ballieston, Edinburgh. † GI 1, RSA 1,.

DRAPER, Robert N. Exh. 1887
10 Leinster Street, Dublin. † RHA 1.

DRAYTON, Miss F.S. Exh. 1895-1901
West Hill House, Sutton Common, Surrey. † B 3, L 5, ROI 4, SWA 2.

DRAYTON, Hilda Exh. 1913
12 Paulton Square, Chelsea, London. † LS 3.

DRAYTON-TAYLOR, Mrs. Emily Exh. 1930
† RMS 2.

DRESCHFELD, Mrs. Julius Exh. 1891
325 Oxford Road, Manchester. † M 1.

DRESSER, Arthur Exh. 1890
Figure painter. Springfields, Bexley Heath, Kent. † RA 1.

DRESSER, Mrs. A.R. (or J.R.) Exh. 1889
Figure painter. Springfields, Bexley Heath, Kent. † RA 1.

DRESSER, G.C. Exh. 1928
35 Cleveland Terrace, Darlington, Co. Durham. † RI 1.

DRESSLER, Ada Exh. 1889-1913
Landscape and flower painter. Add: London 1889 and 1902; Dublin 1901; Southsea, Hants 1907. † B 1, GOU 2, L 5, NG 4, RA 2, RBA 1, SWA 5.

DRESSLER, Conrad 1856-1940
Sculptor. Studied Royal College of Art. Set up pottery in Birkenhead with Harold Rathbone. Add: London 1883 and 1904; Birkenhead 1894; Gt. Marlow, Bucks 1899. † B 1, G 7, GI 1, I 7, L 51, M 2, NG 21, RA 26, RBA 6, RHA 1, RI 1.

DREW, Mrs. Exh. 1897
20 St. Petersburg Place, Bayswater, London. † NG 1

DREW, Mrs. A. Exh. 1895
38 Rue du Luxembourg, Paris. † M 1.

DREW, Diana Exh. 1930-31
Lino cut artist. † RED 3.

DREW, Miss D.A.H. Exh. 1896-98
Bletchingley, Surrey. † SWA 6.

DREW, Herbert J. Exh. 1900-24
Miniature painter. R.B.A. 1905. London. † L 1, RA 7, RBA 37.

DREW, J. Exh. 1889-91
4 Crown Circus, Glasgow. † GI 3.

DREW, Jacob Exh. 1931
Engraver. 71 West Cromwell Road, London. † RA 1.

DREW, Joan Harvey Exh. 1899-1900
Designer and embroiderer. Studied Westminster School of Art. Add: Bletchingley, Surrey. † D 2, SWA 2.

DREW, Mary Exh. 1880-1901
Figure and nature painter. London 1880; Seaford, Sussex 1901. † B 3, L 5, M 2, RA 23, RBA 13, RHA 2, ROI 10, SWA 7.

DREW, Miss M.H. Exh. 1906
Westcott, Surrey. † SWA 1.

DREW, Mrs. Nell Exh. 1912
32 Comely Bank, Edinburgh. † RSA 1.

DREW, Pamela b. 1910
Milnethorpe, Westmorland 1935; Rathvilly, Eire 1936. † RBA 1, RI 1, ROI 3.

DREW, Sylvia Exh. 1894-1921
Landscape and figure painter. Bletchingley, Surrey 1894; Dorking, Surrey 1904; Chilworth, Surrey 1910. † D 31, I 2, L 6, LS 8, RA 8, RBA 3, RI 4, RID 41, SWA 6.

DREW, Sir Thomas 1838-1910
Architect. A.R.H.A. 1870, R.H.A. 1871, P.R.H.A. 1900, H.R.B.A. 1907, H.R.M.S. 1901, H.R.S.A. 1907. Add: Dublin. † RA 2, RHA 32, RSA 4.

DREWE, Alfred Exh. 1887
Architect. 28/29 St. Swithin's Lane, London. † RA 1.

DREWE, Mrs. Perak (F) Exh. 1913-16
70 Lansdowne Road, Bournemouth. † L 11, RCA 2, RHA 6.

DREWE, P.R. Exh. 1923
65 Milton Road, Waterloo, Liverpool. † L 1.

DREWE, Reginald Frank Knowles b. 1878
Figure and landscape painter and art master. b. Faringdon, Berks. Exh. 1918-40. Add: 28 Castle Street, Berkhamsted, Herts. † LS 3, RA 4, RCA 2.

DREWITT, F.D. Exh. 1914-15
14 Palace Gardens Terrace, Kensington, London. † L 1, RA 2.

DREWRY, Miss M.F. Exh. 1906-10
3 Windmill Hill, Hampstead, London. † L 1, RA 2.

DREYDORFF, J.G. Exh. 1905-8
St. Anne on Sluis, Holland. † I 2.

DREYFUS, Raoul Henri Exh. 1909-12
Paris. † L 2.

DRIAN Exh. 1937-39
† WG 107.

DRIFFIELD, Mrs. E.B. Exh. 1915
Gosbenton, Carr's Crescent, Formby, Liverpool. † L 1.

DRING, Mrs. Elizabeth see ROTHWELL

DRING, William b. 1904
Landscape and figure painter. Studied Slade School 1922-25 (Slade Scholarship, 1st prize in drawing and painting of figure and head, 2nd prize for composition). Teacher of drawing and painting at Southampton School of Art. Married Elizabeth Rothwell, q.v. Add: London 1928; Winchester, Hants 1935. † AG 12, GOU 14, L 3, M 1, NEA 9, RA 11, RSA 1.

DRINKWATER, Agnes M. Exh. 1898
4 Merridale Crescent, Wolverhampton. † B 2.

DRINKWATER, George Carr 1880-1941
Architect and portrait and figure painter. Oxford rowing blue 1902 and 1903. Served South African campaign 1900, yeomanry 1914-19. R.B.A. 1912. Add: London. † I 1, L 1, P 3, RA 5, RBA 5, ROI 5.

DRINKWATER, H.C. Exh. 1905-8
Grosvenor Lodge, Wrexham 1905; London 1908. † L 2, RHA 1.

DRITTLER, Mrs. F. Exh. 1895-1900
48 Charlotte Road, Edgbaston, Birmingham. † B 3, SWA 1.

DRIVER, Miss G. Exh. 1885-86
Victoria Grove, Heaton Chapel. † L 3, M 3.

DRIVER, Sydney Amos b. 1865
Landscape and animal painter. Studied St. Martins School of Art, Lambeth and Slade School. Exh. 1928. Add: Ingleside, Ardleigh, Nr. Colchester, Essex. † M 1.

DRIVIER, Leon Ernest b. 1878
French sculptor. 14 Rue Guilleminot, Paris 1930. † RSA 2.

DRON, James A. Exh. 1892-1929
Glasgow. † GI 14, RSA 1, RSW 1.

DRUCE, Miss Elsie d. c.1965
Painter, etcher and wood engraver. b. Weybridge. Add: Sevenoaks, Kent 1905; London 1924. † AB 7, GI 2, GOU 4, I 11, L 13, LS 23, NEA 3, RA 6, ROI 3, SWA 8.

DRUCE, Miss Helen Exh. 1884-95
Landscape painter. London † B 4, D 17, L 4, M 4, RA 1, RBA 1, RI 2, SWA 14.

DRUCE, Mrs. John Exh. 1890-1918
Landscape painter. Bishops Down, Tunbridge Wells, Kent 1890; Goudhurst, Kent 1905. † RID 43.

DRUCKER, Amy Julia Exh. 1899-1939
Painter, etcher, miniaturist, lithographer, woodcut engraver and teacher. Studied St. John's Wood, Lambeth and Paris. Add: London. † B 5, BG 3, G 1, GI 1, GOU 4, I 11, L 6, LS 9, P 5, RA 13, RHA 1, RI 3, RMS 1, ROI 1, SWA 3.

DRUERY, Henry Exh. 1881-88
Architect. 12 Potter's Fields, Tooley Street, London † D 1, RA 1,.

DRUITT, Emily Exh. 1881-86
Landscape, figure and interior painter. 8 Strathmore Gardens, Kensington, London. † RBA 1, ROI 2, SWA 3.

DRUMAUX, Mlle. Angelina Exh. 1906
20 Rue du Vertbois, Liege, Belgium. † L 1.

DRUMMOND, Arthur* Exh. 1890-1901
Figure painter. London 1890; Guildford, Surrey 1896. † B 2, M 1, RA 5, ROI 4.

DRUMMOND, Mrs. A. Exh. 1886-1900
London 1886; Edinburgh 1900. † D 9, RSA 1.

DRUMMOND, Cecil H. Exh. 1934
Landscape painter. 31 Wydehurst Road, Addiscombe, Croydon, Surrey. † RA 1.

DRUMMOND, David Exh. 1911
Drymen, Stirlingshire. † LS 2.

DRUMMOND, Frances Exh. 1896-1925
Landscape and flower painter. Oxford. † FIN 6, L 15, LS 7, RA 15, RBA 1, RI 12, SWA 10.

DRUMMOND, G.E. Exh. 1892
Landscape painter. † FIN 1.

DRUMMOND, H. Exh. 1880
Landscape and coastal painter. 122 St. Paul's Road, Camden Town, London. † RBA 1.

DRUMMOND, Julian E. Exh. 1892-1903
Landscape and coastal painter. London 1892; Brighton 1896. † L 2, RA 4, RBA 1, RI 5.

DRUMMOND, J. Nelson Exh. 1882-96
Landscape painter. Manchester 1882; Leatherhead, Surrey 1884; Greenhithe, Kent 1888; London 1890. † D 1, L 4, M 2, RA 4, RBA 1.

DRUMMOND, Malcolm C.* 1880-1945
Figure painter. Founder member London Group 1913. Exh. 1910-39. Add: London. † CAR 8, GOU 56, LS 15, NEA 1, RED 3.

DRUMMOND, Mrs. Margaret L. Exh. 1936-40
High Trees, The Common, Gerrards Cross. † SWA 4.

DRUMMOND, P.G. Exh. 1926
105 Canning Street, Liverpool. † L 1.

DRUMMOND, Rosabella Exh. 1895-1904
R.M.S. 1898, London 1895 and 1900; Oxford 1899. † L 1, RMS 21, SWA 4.

DRUMMOND, R.R. Exh. 1926
† M 1.

DRUMMOND-FISH, Capt. G. Exh. 1906-38
Portrait and landscape painter. Studied Liverpool School of Art. Travelling scholarship to Paris, Brussels and Antwerp. Served World War 1. Add: Hoylake 1906; Dublin 1918; Dalkey Co. Dublin 1925. † L 1, RCA 3, RHA 12, RI 1, WG 468.

DRURY, Elizabeth Exh. 1919-31
Portrait, figure and still life painter. † CHE 1, G 3, GOU 4, I 2, LEI 2.

DRURY, Edward Alfred Briscoe 1850-1944
Sculptor and painter. Studied Oxford National Art Training School and Paris under Dalou. A.R.A. 1900, R.A. 1903, R.I. 1918. "Griselda" purchased by Chantrey Bequest 1896. Add: London. † B 2, BG 1, G 4, GI 23, I 3, L 21, M 3, NG 18, P 11, RA 96, RBA 4, RI 5, ROI 6, RSA 15.

DRURY, Mildred Exh. 1922
Landscape and flower painter. † BK 16.

DRURY, Paul Dalou b. 1903
Painter and etcher. Son of Edward Alfred Briscoe D. q.v. Studied Westminster and Goldsmith's College 1920-25, B.I. Scholarship in Engraving 1924. Married Enid Solomon q.v. A.R.E. 1926, R.E. 1932. Add: Lancaster Lodge, Lancaster Road, Wimbledon, London. † ALP 1, BA 5, CHE 3, FIN 14, GI 2, NEA 1, P 7, RA 28, RE 27, RHA 2.

DRURY, T. Exh. 1885
4 Church Street, Liverpool. † L 1.

DRUZBACKA, Anna Exh. 1884
Figure painter. Warsaw. † SWA 2.

DRYHURST, S. Exh. 1938-39
176 Alfred Road, Birmingham. † B 3.

DRYSDALE, George Exh. 1913-39
Ecclesiastical architect. London. † RA 9, RSA 1.

DRYSDALE, Jeannie T. Exh. 1881-1900
Figure, landscape, flower and coastal painter. London. † NEA 4, RA 2, RBA 4.

DRYSDALE, Mary b. 1912
Architect. Studied Edinburgh College of Art. Exh. 1932. Add: Heathersett, Crieff, Perthshire. † RSA 2.

DUASSUT, Curtius Exh. 1889-1930
Landscape painter. Hampstead, London 1889; Ealing, London 1892; Amersham, Bucks. 1898; Stamford Hill, London 1899; Chelmsford, Essex 1901; Herne Bay, Kent 1907; Tonbridge, Kent 1909. † B 1, D 64, GI 5, L 60, M 6, RA 36, RBA 27, RI 13, ROI 5.

DUB, Jaroslav b. 1878
Bohemian painter. Studied Prague. Add: Llys Mon, Sea Bank Road, Rhyl 1940. † RCA 1.

DU BATY, Mlle. L.M. Rallier Exh. 1906
1 Rue Humboldt, Paris. † L 1.

DUBE, Mme. Mattie b. 1861
Fish painter. b. Florence. Add: 59 Avenue de Saxe, Paris 1891. † RA 1.

DU BOIS, Paul b. 1859
Sculptor. Studied L'Academie des Beaux Arts, Brussels. Exh. 1914-31. Add: 57 Avenue de Longchamps, Brussels. † GI 4, L 1, RSA 10.

DU BOSC, Miss E. Exh. 1888
† D 3.

DUBOURG, Victoria* Exh. 1882-99
Flower painter. 26 Golden Square, London. † B 14, D 5, DOW 14, FIN 4, G 2, GI 15, L 4, M 1, RA 10, RBA 4, RI 29, SWA 4.

DU BOX, E.E. Exh. 1886
46 Emperor's Gate, London. † D 1.

DUBRET, Henri Exh. 1907
1 Rue d'Hauteville, Paris. † L 7.

DUBSON, Leo Exh. 1927
† RMS 2.

DU CANE, Ella Exh. 1893-1910
Flower painter. 41 Eaton Place, London. † D 2, FIN 64, RBA 1, RI 1.

DUCE, George Raymond Exh. 1937-40
226 Ferry Road, Edinburgh. † RSA 3.

DU CHAFFAULT, Comtesse M.L. Exh. 1899
5 Avenue d'Eylau, Paris. † RA 1.

DU CHATTEL, Fredericus J. Exh. 1884-95
Landscape painter. The Hague, Holland. † GI 1, M 7, RA 1.

DUCHENNE, M. Exh. 1880
16 Avenue Trudaine, Paris. † RHA 1.

DUCIE, Pietro Exh. 1886-87
Carrara, Italy. † RHA 2.

DUCKETT, Lady Exh. 1880-84
Bird painter. Newington, Wallingford, Berks. † SWA 4.

DUCKWORTH, Mrs. A.M. Exh. 1883-87
Thorn Cottage, Bacup 1883; Oxton, Birkenhead 1887. † B 1, L 2, M 6.

DUCKWORTH, C. Exh. 1883
3 Summer Place, Inverleith Row, Edinburgh. † RSA 1.

DUCLOS, Mlle. Janine Exh. 1927
French painter. 212 Boulevard Pereire, Paris. † RA 1.

DUDENEY, Wilfred E. b. 1911
Sculptor. b. Leicester. Add: Staines, Middlesex 1937; Dublin 1939 † RA 2, RHA 1.

DUDGEON, Miss B. Exh. 1907-12
The Spring House, Ewell, Surrey. † RI 1, SWA 1.

DUDGEON, Emilia Dorothea Maria b. 1866
Miniature painter, black and white decorative artist. Married Philip Eustace Stretton q.v. Studied Calderon's School of Animal painting, National Gallery and National Portrait Gallery. Add: London 1893; Cranbrook, Kent 1900; Sea View, I.o.W. 1907. † NG 12, RA 1, ROI 1.

DUDLEY, Ambrose Exh. 1912-19
Landscape painter. 31 Lansdowne Road, Notting Hill, London. † RA 2.

DUDLEY, Arthur Exh. 1890-1907
Fruit, flower and fish painter. London 1890 and 1906; Bath 1901. † B 1, L 11, RA 13, RBA 6, RI 5.

DUDLEY, Carol R. Exh. 1937-38
† RSW 4.

DUDLEY, F.G.W. Exh. 1908
Architect. 11 Peter's Street, St. Albans, Herts. † RA 1.

DUDLEY, F.H. Exh. 1886-1918
Liverpool 1886 and 1900; Liscard, Cheshire 1899; Conway 1917; Trefriw, Wales 1918. † L 8, RCA 2.

DUDLEY, Miss J. Exh. 1904
29 Grosvenor Terrace, York. † SWA 2.

DUDLEY, O. Exh. 1905
23 Linden Gardens, London. † RA 1.

DUDLEY, Robert* Exh. 1880-93
Landscape painter. 31 Lansdowne Road, Notting Hill, London. † AG 2, B 10, D 1, GI 1, L 12, M 4, RA 14, RI 6.

DUDLEY, Mrs. Ruth M. Exh. 1923-32
Landscape, portrait and miniature painter. Royal Dockyard, Woolwich, London 1923; Ventnor, I.O.W. 1932. † RI 5.

DUDLEY, Samuel J. Exh. 1900-5
Wombourn, nr. Wolverhampton. † B 3.

DUDLEY, Tom Exh. 1889-92
Grosvenor Terrace, York. † B 2, M 1.

DUDLEY, William Harold b. 1890
Landscape and portrait painter. Studied Royal College of Art. Art master Cheltenham New Central School and School of Arts and Crafts; lecturer St. Anne's on Sea Summer School 1921, Headmaster Newport School of Art, Monmouth. Add: Cheltenham 1920; Newport, Mon. 1929. † B 6, GI 1, RA 16, RCA 4.

DUDNEY, Wilfred E. Exh. 1933
Sculptor. 1 Harley Studios, Cresswell Place, London. † RA 1.

DUENES, Marie Exh. 1897
Mdme d'Alheim. Figure painter. 18 Impasse du Maine, Paris. † RA 1.

DUESBURY, Lillie Exh. 1895-96
West Parade, Hull, Yorks. † RBA 2, RSA 1.

DUEZ, Ernest Ange* 1843-1896
French artist. Paris. † G 2, GI 1, RHA 1.

DUFF, George b. 1888
Portrait painter. 1381 Argyle Street, Glasgow. † GI 2, L 1, RSA 6, RSW 1.

DUFF, Heather Mary Abercromby Exh. 1902
Watercolour landscape painter. 11 Eaton Place, London. † SWA 2.

DUFF, John Robert Keitley 1862-1938
Painter, etcher and barrister. Studied Slade School. N.E.A. 1903, A.R.E. 1914, R.E. 1919, R.I. 1913. Member of Society of 25 Artists. Add: Sunningfields, Hendon, London. † FIN 5, GI 2, GOU 143, I 17, L 12, M 3, NEA 26, NG 8, RA 24, RBA 9, RE 61, RI 113, RID 9, ROI 3, WG 24.

DUFF, Marjory F. Exh. 1884-86
Landscape painter. London. † RA 1, SWA 1.

DUFF, Neil C. Exh. 1906-14
Glasgow. † GI 7, RSA 2.

DUFF, T.J. Exh. 1883
14 Nelson Street, Dublin. † RHA 1.

DUFFES, Honor Exh. 1915-20
Mrs. Arthur P. 24 Queen Street, Edinburgh. † B 2, GI 2, L 2, RSA 3.

DUFFEY, Caroline B. Exh. 1910
30 Fitzwilliam Place, Dublin. † RHA 1.

DUFFEY, Miss M. Exh. 1933
II Prescot Street, New Brighton, Cheshire. † L 1.

DUFFIELD, Agnes M. Exh. 1897-1903
London. † D 1, SWA 11.

DUFFIELD, Mary Ann 1819-1914
nee Rosenberg. Married William D. (1816-1863). Flower painter and watercolourist. R.I. 1861. Add: London. † B 4, DOW 3, L 2, M 1, RBA 2, RI 163, RWS 1.

DUFFIELD, William L. Exh. 1880
Landscape and figure painter. Probably son of Mary Ann D. q.v. Add: 4 Upper Phillimore Gardens, Kensington, London. † RBA 1.

DUFFIN, Margaret R. Exh. 1929-38
Landscape painter. Belfast. † RCA 1, RHA 7.

DUFFIN, Miss O. Exh. 1915-17
Belfast 1915; Eastbourne 1916. † L 2, RA 2.

DUFFY, Daniel J. b. 1878
Landscape, portrait and still life painter. Studied Glasgow School of Art and Italy. Add: Glasgow 1909; Coatbridge 1924. † GI 36, L 4, RA 5, RBA 1, RHA 2, ROI 8, RSA 5.

DUFFY, E. Exh. 1938
151 Jervoise Road, Weoley Castle. † B 1.

DUFFY, Patrick Vincent 1836-1909
Landscape painter. Studied at the Royal Dublin Society Schools. A.R.H.A. 1860, R.H.A. 1860. Keeper of R.H.A. 1871-1909. Add: Dublin. † L 7, RBA 2, RHA 226.

DUFOUR, Silvain Exh. 1909
9 Rue de Jouy, Paris. † L 1.

DU FRENES, R. Hirth Exh. 1882-91
Munich 1882; Oberbayern, Bavaria 1891. † M 1, RHA 8.

DUFRENOY, George Leon b. 1871
Exh. 1912. † GOU 1.

DUFY, Raoul* 1877-1953
French painter. Exh. 1936-38. † BA 1, LEF 1, RED 5.

DUGALD-SMITH, Ellen Barbara Exh. 1897-98
c/o Mr. Solomon, High Street, Watford, Herts. † L 2.

DU GARDIER, Raoul Exh. 1907-27
Paris. † L 3.

DUGDALE, Thomas Cantrell 1880-1952
Figure and potrait painter, decorator and designer. b. Blackburn. Studied Royal College of Art and Juliens, Paris. A.R.A. 1936, R.O.I. 1910, R.P. 1923. Add: London 1902; Iken, Suffolk. † ALP 1, CHE 5, G 4, GI 22, GOU 8, I 24, L 16, LEI 58, M 10, NEA 15, P 78, RA 78, RED 1, RHA 1, ROI 20, RSA 4.

DUGGAN, Mary E. Exh. 1912-20
Blackheath, London 1912; Minehead, Som. 1920. † LS 3, SWA 1.

DUGGINS, James Edward b. 1881
Landscape, figure and miniature painter. Studied under Algernon Talmage at St. Ives 1904-5. A.R.B.A. 1927, R.B.A. 1929. Exh. 1901-35. Add: Leamington, Warwicks. † B 12, L 3, LS 3, RA 2, RBA 56, RI 1.

DUGUID, Christine C. Exh. 1920-29
15 Holland Road, Wallasey, Cheshire. † L 51, RCA 7.

DUGUID, John Exh. 1931-34
Marine painter. † GOU 6.

DUHAMEL, Mlle. Jeanè A.M. Exh. 1911-13
London 1911; Paris 1913. † L 1, RA 1.

DUIGAN, Sydney Mary Exh. 1916-32
Landscape painter. Bedford 1927. † I 1, RID 4, SWA 7.

DUJARDIN, Edouard Exh. 1884
Sculptor. 28 Gairloch Road, Camberwell, London. † RA 1.

DUJSIN, Cata Exh. 1937
Portrait and landscape painter. † COO 30.

DUKE, Alfred* d. c.1905
Manchester 1893; Disley Nr. Manchester 1903. † B 2, L 3, M 16.

DUKE, Constance Exh. 1885-94
Lake House, Salisbury, Wilts. † D 4, RBA 1, SWA 3.

DUKE, Cecil R. Exh. 1927-38
Landscape painter. † AB 8, WG 15.

DUKE, George Exh. 1900
Peacock Cross, Hamilton, N.B. † GI 1.

DUKE, W. Medleycott Exh. 1888
Urban landscape painter. 11 Portsea Place, Connaught Square, London. † RBA 1.

DUKES, William J. Exh. 1908-36
Landscape painter. Newcastle under Lyme, Staffs. 1908; Stoke on Trent, Staffs. 1909. † B 5, RA 4, RCA 3.

DULAC, Edmund* 1882-1953
Portrait painter, illustrator, caricaturist, decorator, stage and medal designer and lecturer. b. Toulouse, France. Studied Toulouse Art School and Juliens, Paris. Settled in England 1906. Add: London. † FIN 1, I 11, L 3, LEI 401, RI 1, RID 3.

DULEY, Edward Exh. 1933-35
Architect. 9 Hanover Square, London. † RA 2.

DULUARD, Hippolyte Francoise Leon Exh. 1905-16
French artist, Paris. † CON 2, L 6, RA 1.

DUMAS, Ada Exh. 1918-39
Figure painter. Southersea, Hants. † GI 1, GOU 15, L 2, RA 2.

DUMAS, Mlle. A. Dick. Exh. 1903-11
2 Cite Gaillard, Paris. † L 3, RA 4.

DUMAS, Hector Exh. 1909
28 Rue Vernier, Paris. † L 1.

DU MAURIER, George Louis Palmella Busson 1834-1896
Black and white artist, illustrator and novelist. b. Paris. Studied under Gleyre in Paris 1856/7 and under De Keyser and Van Lerins in Antwerp 1857-60. Joined staff of "Punch" 1864. A.R.W.S. 1881. Add: London. † FIN 472, L 2, M 2, NG 4, RA 17, RWS 11.

DU MAURIER, Jeanne Exh. 1936-39
S.W.A. 1939. London. † RBA 2, SWA 6.

DUMBELL, Alice Ruth b. 1855
nee Morrish. Painter and miniaturist. Exh. 1895-1926. Add: Liverpool. † L 16.

DUMBLETON, Betram Walter b. 1896
Figure, portrait and landscape painter. b. South Africa. Studied Regent Street Polytechnic and Juliens, Paris. Add: London 1920, Chichester, Sussex 1932. † COO 2, M 1, NEA 1, RA 13.

DUMBRECK, Kate Exh. 1893
Craigholm, Colinton, Midlothian. † GI 1.

DUMENIL, Pierre Exh. 1911
18 Rue de l'Arrivee, Paris. † RI 2.

DUMMETT, Joan Katherine b. 1905
Sculptor and pastellier. Studied under Jules Van Biesbroeck. Add: Reading, Berks 1927; London 1930. † L 1, RA 4, RMS 1.

DU MONT, August Neven d. c.1910
Portrait painter. R.P. 1900. Add: Bournemouth, Hants and South Kensington, London 1897. † GI 2, I 17, L 6, P 25, RA 1, RSA 3.

DUMONT, Cesar A. Exh. 1894
c/o W. Goodman, 44 Richmond Road, Shepherds Bush, London. † RA 1.

DUMONT, Eugenie A. Exh. 1894
c/o W. Goodman, 44 Richmond Road, Shepherds Bush, London. † M 1.

DUMONT, Henry Courselles Exh. 1889-90
c/o Mr. Wright, 8 Berkley Road, London. † RI 2, RBA 1.

DUMONT-SMITH, Robert Exh. 1939
119 Cherry Orchard Road, East Croydon, Surrey. † RBA 1.

DU MOULIN-BROWN, Rev. F.S. Exh. 1932
The Oratory, Birmingham. † B 2.

DUN, John* Exh. 1880-1908
Figure and landscape painter. Add: Edinburgh. † G 1, GI 17, L 1, RA 1, RSA 64.

DUNBAR, Evelyn 1906-1960
Landscape and figure painter. Exh. 1931-40. † GOU 2, NEA 4.

DUNBAR, Miss H.C. Exh. 1907-14
Sydenham, London. † RA 4.

DUNBAR N.M. Exh.1880-81
207 Sauchiehall Street, Glasgow. † GI 3.

DUNBAR, R. Brassey Exh. 1886-1912
Glasgow. † GI 12.

DUNBAR, Lady Sophia Exh. 1880-1904
Landscape and flower painter. Duffur, Elgin, Scotland. † GI 2 RSA 6, SWA 5.

DUNBREEK, Miss K. Exh. 1886
Teviotside House, Hawick, Yorks. † RSA 1.

DUNCALFE, Mrs. R. Exh. 1918
4 Brunel Terrace, Derby Road, Nottingham. † N 1.

DUNCAN, Miss Exh. 1904
25 Priory Road, London. † SWA 1.

DUNCAN, Allan Exh. 1880-87
Landscape and coastal painter. 36 Upper Park Road, Haverstock Hill, London. † B 4, D 4, L 4, M 3, RA 1, RBA 4, RI 6.

DUNCAN, Ann Exh. 1930-37
Figure, portrait, landscape and still life painter. Married to John McK. D. q.v. Add: London 1930; Mousehole, Penzance 1937. † FIN 30, P 1, RA 3.

DUNCAN, Alexander C.W. Exh. 1884-1932
Landscape painter. Glasgow 1884; Colinsburgh, Fife 1908. † GI 68, L 3, RA 2, RSA 9, RSW 3.

DUNCAN, Alice E. Exh. 1890
142 Sinclair Road, W. Kensington, London. † RI 1.

DUNCAN, Betty Exh. 1914
44 St. Stephen's Green, Dublin. † RHA 1.

DUNCAN, C. Exh. 1912
Davaar, Darlton, Notts. † N 1.

DUNCAN, Charles Exh. 1880-85
Edinburgh. † GI 2, RSA 15.

DUNCAN, David b. 1868
Painter and etcher. Studied Dunfermline and Edinburgh. Exh. 1897-1940. Add: Grieve Street, Dunfermline. † GI 27, L 12, RED 1, RSA 22, RSW 1.

DUNCAN, Dorothy Exh. 1909-38
Mrs. John D. Kensington, London 1909; Arbroath 1937. † ROI 3, RSA 3.

DUNCAN, D.M. Exh. 1880-82
6 Springfield Road, Glasgow. † GI 2.

DUNCAN, E. Exh. 1937
Landscape painter. † CON 1.

DUNCAN, Edward* 1803-1882
Marine and landscape painter, watercolourist and engraver. R.I. 1833 (resigned 1847). A.R.W.S. 1848, R.W.S. 1849. Add: Haverstock Hill, London. † AG 10, RA 6, RBA 4, RI 7, RWS 7.

DUNCAN, Emily Exh. 1881-1917
Landscape painter. London 1881 and 1898; Maindenhead, Berks 1896; Farnham Common, Bucks 1913. † D 1, GI 2, L 5, LS 13, M 1, RA 12, RBA 2, RHA 7, RI 4, ROI 12, SWA 6.

DUNCAN, Miss E.A. Exh. 1940
2 Coningsby Place, Alba. † GI 1.

DUNCAN, E.G. Exh. 1892
60 Wigmore Street, London. † NG 1.

DUNCAN, Fanny Exh. 1880-89
Figure painter. Paris. † D 1, L 2, M 1, RA 4, ROI 1.

DUNCAN, Frederick Exh. 1932
Flower painter. † COO 33.

DUNCAN, Gideon Exh. 1887-89
45 Dumbarton Road, Glasgow. † GI 5.

DUNCAN, George B. Exh. 1936-38
Landscape painter. 36 Gt. Ormond Street, London. † RA 2, ROI 4.

DUNCAN, George W. Exh. 1897-1904
Glasgow. † GI 3.

DUNCAN, James Exh. 1888-1901
Helensburgh 1888; Milngavie, N.B. 1901. † GI 4.

DUNCAN, John Exh. 1917-38
Watercolour painter of birds. Glasgow. † BK 49, GI 3, RSA 1.

DUNCAN, John* 1866-1945
Legendary, historical and decorative painter and illustrator. Studied London, Antwerp and Dusseldorf. A.R.S.A. 1910, R.S.A. 1923, R.S.W. 1930. Add: Glasgow 1890; Edinburgh 1893 and 1905; Dundee 1898. † AR 2, FIN 21, GI 20, L 17, NG 1, RA 5, RSA 85, RSW 47.

DUNCAN, James Allan Exh. 1895-97
Glasgow. † GI 2, RSA 1.

DUNCAN, J.C. Exh. 1889
8 Clydeview Terrace, Glasgow. † RSA 1.

DUNCAN, J.C. Exh. 1901
Ashwell Street, Netherfield, Notts. † N 1.

DUNCAN, John McKirdy Exh. 1921-37
Landscape and portrait painter. Married to Ann D. q.v. Add: London 1921, Mousehole, Penzance Cornwall 1933. † I 1, L 2, P 2, RA 14, RI 1.

DUNCAN, James S.R. Exh. 1914
Bonnington, Milngavie, N.B. † GI 1.

DUNCAN, Lawrence Exh. 1882-91
Landscape painter. 5 Langham Chambers, All Souls Place, London. † M 2, RA 3, RBA 1.

DUNCAN, Lilias L. Exh. 1925
Piemans Way, Taplow, Bucks. † SWA 1.

DUNCAN, Miss M. Exh. 1904-25
Pollokshields, N.B. 1904; Glasgow 1907. † GI 7, L 5, RSA 8.

DUNCAN, Margaret Exh. 1914-16
73 Harrow View, Harrow, Middlesex. † RA 2.

DUNCAN, Mary 1885-c.1967
Painter and etcher. Studied Slade School and Paris. Add: Dublin 1910; Bushey, Herts 1922, Paul, Nr. Penzance, Cornwall 1927; Mousehole, Nr. Penzance 1936. † B 2, GI 2, GOU 1, I 1, L 8, M 8, NEA 3, RA,10 RCA 2, RHA 65, ROI 4, RSA 12.

DUNCAN, Muriel Exh. 1896
3 Crosfield Road, Belsize Park, London. † RA 1.

DUNCAN, Nina Exh. 1928
† GOU1.

DUNCAN, Una Exh. 1913-17
Dublin 1913; Galway 1917. † RHA 2.

DUNCAN, Walter Exh. 1880-1906
Figure painter. A.R.W.S. 1874. Add: London 1880; Kingston on Thams, Surrey 1896; Norbiton, Surrey 1902. † AG 1, B 1, FIN 1, G 2, L 1, LEI 1, M 1, NG 3, RA 2 RBA 2, RI 1, ROI 1, RWS 82.

DUNCANSON, Mrs. A.J. Exh. 1901
16 Deane Road, Liverpool. † L 1.

DUNDAS, Mrs. Exh. 1881
Landscape and coastal painter. 16 Charles Street, St. James, London. † SWA 5.

DUNDAS, Agnes Exh. 1884
Bird painter. Hawthornden, Clarendon Road, Putney, London. † SWA 1.

DUNDAS, Douglas Exh. 1929
Landscape painter. 14 Clifton Gardens, London. † RA 1.

DUNDAS, Faith Exh. 1907
32 Clarendon Road, Bedford. † B 1.

DUNDAS, George Exh. 1928
Painswick, Stroud, Glos. † NEA 1.

DUNDAS, Georgina Exh. 1898-1922
Landscape and figure painter. Abinger Hammer, Dorking 1898; West Bromwich 1899; London 1909. † B 3, BK 17, GI 3, M 1, RBA 1.

DUNHAM, Miss A. Exh. 1890
† SWA 1.

DUNHAM, Peter Browning b. 1911
Landscape painter. 232 Stockingstone Road, Luton, Beds. 1940. † RA 1.

DUNINGTON, A.* Exh. 1885
150 Queen's Walk, Nottingham. † N 6.

DUNKERLEY, C.L. Exh. 1936-38
† WG 9.

DUNKERLEY, F.B. Exh. 1910
Architect. 17 St. Ann's Square, Manchester. † RA 2.

DUNKLEY, Blanche Exh. 1901
The Rockery, North Road, Calpham, London. † RI 1.

DUNKLEY, Edward Lowther Exh. 1899-1924
Sculptor. Walthamstow, Essex 1899; Hackney, London 1904. † RA 6.

DUNLOP, Miss Exh. 1894-95
II Kearsland Terrace, Hillhead, Glasgow. † GI 2.

DUNLOP, Denis Cheyne b.1892
Sculptor. Studied St. Martins and Central School of Arts and Crafts. Add: Hornchurch, Essex 1909; London 1933. † D 3, RA 1.

DUNLOP, Gilbert P. Exh. 1939
1 Blackness Avenue, Dundee. † RSA 1.

DUNLOP, Hazel B. Exh. 1935-40
Portrait painter. Studied Slade School. A.S.W.A. 1939. Married Francis E. Hodge q.v. Add: 76 Fulham Road, London. † P 3, ROI 2, SWA 8.

DUNLOP, H.W.D. Exh. 1887
Lucan, Nr. Dublin. † RHA 1.

DUNLOP, Mrs. Irene Exh. 1927-39
Miniature portrait painter. A.R.M.S. 1938. Add: London 1927; Lane End, Bucks. 1939. † RA 1, RMS 13.

DUNLOP, Jessie I. Exh. 1933-35
Mrs. Wilson. Lathan Sona, Kinpurnie Road, Oldhall, Paisley. † L 1. RSA 2.

DUNLOP, J.K. Exh. 1880
16 Hope Street, Edinburgh. † RSA 1.

DUNLOP, James M. Exh. 1900-15
Glasgow. † GI 2, RSA 2.

DUNLOP, John R. Exh. 1908
34 Tait Street, Carlisle. † B 1.

DUNLOP, Miss Margaret I. Exh. 1910-11
Bristol. † SWA 2.

DUNLOP, Mrs. Marguerite I. Exh. 1931
Miniature portrait painter. Huntingfield, Faversham, Kent. † RA 1.

DUNLOP, Marion Wallace Exh. 1902-5
Portrait and figure painter. London. † GI 1, NEA 1, RA 4, SWA 2.

DUNLOP, Ronald Ossory* b. 1894
Landscape, portrait, flower and still life painter. b. Dublin. Studied Manchester School of Art and Wimbledon School of Art. N.E.A. 1937, A.R.A. 1939, R.B.A. 1930. Member London Group 1931. "Lifeboat, Walberswick" purchased by Chantrey Bequent 1937 and "Rosalind Iden as Ophelia" 1940. Add: London 1929; Leatherhead, Surrey 1938. † AG 4, BA 6, BAR 2, BK 51, CG 1, COO 11, GI 4, GOU 32, L 3, LEF 60, LEI 2, M 1, NEA 18, RA 13, RBA 70, RED 286, RHA 1, RSA 1, TOO 6.

DUNLOP, Mrs. R.R.B. Exh. 1912-21
Glasgow 1912; Helensburgh 1920. † GI 3, RA 3.

DUNMORE, The Earl of Exh. 1894
Watercolour painter, Indian and Far Eastern landscapes. † FIN 71.

DUNMORE, Miss L. Exh. 1885
7 Yew Tree Road, Edgbaston, Birmingham. † B 1.

DUNMORE, S. Exh. 1882
7 Yew Tree Road, Edgbaston, Birmingham. † B 1.

DUNN, A. Exh. 1882
Castle Hill, Wylam on Tyne. † RA 1.

DUNN, A. Exh. 1907
The Woodhouse, Branksome, Bournemouth. † RA 1.

DUNN, A.C. Exh. 1923
9 Denman Drive, Newsham Park, Liverpool. † L 1.

DUNN, Constance Exh. 1883-85
Flower painter. 34 Belgrave Street, St. John's Wood, London. † RBA 1, ROI 1, SWA 1.

DUNN, Mrs. Eva G. Exh. 1922
† D 3.

DUNN, Mrs. H. Exh. 1912-21
8 Westmount Road, Eltham. † SWA 7.

DUNN, Henry Treffry 1838-1899
Figure and interior painter. b. Truro. Studied Heatherley's. Studio assistant to D.G. Rossetti for 20 years. Add: Vale Cottage, King's Road, Chelsea, London 1882. † L 1.

DUNN, Issac Exh. 1881
61 Pigott Street, Birmingham. † RE 1.

DUNN, Ian G.D. Exh. 1939
c/o Watson, 34 Marchmont Crescent, Edinburgh. † RSA 1.

DUNN, John Exh. 1886-94
Architect. 1 John Street, St. James Square, London. † RA 5.

DUNN, James Bow 1861-1931
Architect. A.R.S.A. 1918, R.S.A. 1931. Add: Edinburgh. † GI 3, RSA 46.

DUNN, Joyce V. Exh. 1929
19 Huntley Gardens, Glasgow. † GI 1.

DUNN, Miss M.E. Exh. 1895
Thorpe Lodge, Newark, Notts. † N 1.

DUNN, Mrs Nellie Exh. 1903.
8 West Mount Road, Eltham, London. † SWA 1.

DUNN, Normand R. Exh. 1937
† RSW 1.

DUNN, Olaf Exh. 1932
Portrait painter. 8 Westmount Road, Eltham, London. † RA 1.

DUNN, Miss P. Exh. 1896-97
42 Athole Gardens, Glasgow. † GI 3.

DUNN, Patrick S. Exh. 1880-1918
Glasgow. † GI 5, RSW 1.

DUNN, S.F. Exh. 1885
13 Glengyle Terrace, Edinburgh. † RSA 2.

DUNN, Thomas F. Exh. 1896-1912
Garngilloch House, Cumbernauld 1896; Theatre Royal, Glasgow 1908. † GI 3.

DUNN, William Exh. 1896-1927
Landscape painter. Add: Helensburgh, N.B. 1896; New Romney, Kent 1920. † GI 18, L 10, M 4, RHA 2, RSA 8.

DUNN, William E. Exh. 1893-97
Galston, Ayreshire 1893; Glasgow 1897. † GI 4, L 1, RSW 1.

DUNNE, J.J. Exh. 1881
Goldsmith Street, Dublin. † RHA 2.

DUNNE, Kathleen Plunkett Exh. 1906-14
Brittas, Clonaslee, Queen's County, Ireland. † RCA 1, RHA 5, ROI 1, SWA 1.

DUNNETT, Miss J. Florrie Exh. 1936-37
52 Argyle Square, Wick. Caithness. † RSA 3.

DUNNETT, Oswald Exh. 1904-14
Tunbridge Wells, Kent. † L 1, LS 12, RA 3, RI 1, ROI 4.

DUNN-GARDNER, Violet Exh. 1891-98
Figure and landscape painter. London. † D 2, NEA 1, P 2, RA 2, ROI 7.

DUNNILL, Mrs. M. Exh. 1912-14
Nottingham 1912; Woodthorpe, Notts. 1914. † N 14.

DUNNING, Agnes Exh. 1890
Flower painter. Higham House, Farm Avenue, Streatham, London. † RBA 1.

DUNNING, Rev. Geo. C. Exh. 1928-29
Landscape and lino-cut artist. Yewtree, Kendal, Westmorland. † AB 2, L 3.

DUNNING, John R. Exh. 1892-1914
London 1892; St. Albans, Herts. 1896. † NG 1, RA 2, RBA 3, RI 4. ROI 3.

DUNNING, John Thomson 1851-1931
Figure and landscape painter and writer. b. Middlesborough. Studied Heatherley's and Exeter. R.B.A. 1899. Add: London 1889. † B 14, D 3, GI 3, L 4, M 5, RA 2, RBA 76, RHA 17, RI 2, RSA 2.

DUNNINGTON, Albert* Exh. 1886
45 Warwick Street, Manchester. † M 1.

DUNOYER de SEGONZAC, Andre* b. 1884
French painter. Exh. 1925-38. † BA 1, GI 6, GOU 1, RED 2, RSA 3.

DUNPHY, Mrs. E. Wynne Exh. 1929
Lark Hill, Conway, Wales. † L 1.

DUNSMORE, John Ward Exh. 1884-88
Figure painter. Blackheath, London 1884, Hampstead, London 1888. † L 1, RBA 5 ROI 3.

DUNSMORE, William Exh. 1934-40
71 Cartvale Road, Langside, Glasgow. † GI 2, RSA 1.

DUNSMUIR, James Exh. 1885-96
10 Coates Crescent, Edinburgh. † RSA 1, RSW 1.

DUNSTAN, Pauline Exh. 1925
16 Beaufort Road, Edgbaston, Birmingham. † B 2.

DUNTHORN, Mrs. Annie Exh. 1924-25
32 Davey Road, Perry Barr, Birmingham. † B 2.

DUPERELLE, Francois Exh. 1913-14
Savigny sur Orge (Seine et Oise) France. † L 2, LS 3.

DU PLESSIS, H.E. b. 1894
Landscape, interior, figure and still-life painter and journalist. b. South Africa. Member London Group 1929. Exh. 1929-40. Add: London. † AG 29, COO 9, GOU 46, LEI 2, RED 1, RHA 1, TOO 3.

DUPON, A. Exh. 1918
34 Gloucester Road, Teddington, Middlesex. † GI 1, RA 1.

DUPON, Josue b. 1864
Belgian sculptor. 483 Longue Rue d'Argile, Antwerp 1914-15. † L 1, RSA 1.

DU PONT, P. Exh. 1905-13
Etcher. † FIN 10, I 4.

DU PONTET, Clement Exh. 1939
Portrait, flower, still life and landscape painter. Studied Vicat Cole and Byam Shaw School and Slade School. † WG 63.

DU PONTET, Mary Exh. 1929-37
Figure, portrait and bird painter. 26 Danvers Street, Cheyne Walk, London. † COO 8, ROI 2.

DUPRAT Exh. 1911
† BRU 1.

DUPRAY, Henri Louis* 1841-1909
French military painter. Add: Paris. † FIN 1, M 1.

DUPRE, Jules* 1811-1889
French artist. Seine et Oise, France. † GI 2, M 1.

DUPRE, Julien* 1851-1910
French animal painter. 20 Boulevard Flandrin, Paris 1903-4. † L 2.

DUPRE-LAURENCE, Alexandria Exh. 1891
St. Ives, Cornwall. † M 1.

DUPREY, Miss M. Exh. 1916-29
The Corner House, Playden, Sussex. † L 9, RI 1.

DUPUIS, Felix* Exh. 1880-82
Portrait painter. 21 Fitzroy Street, London. † RA 3.

DUPUIS, Mrs. F.J. Exh. 1908
The Vicarage, Car Colston, Notts. † N 1.

DU PUIS, Toon Exh. 1904
The Hague, Holland. † I 1.

DUPUY, Paul Michel b. 1869
French artist. 45 Rue de Levis, Paris 1908-9. † L 1, LS 5.

DURANCAMPS, Rafael Exh. 1937
Spanish landscape and coastal painter. † BA 1.

DURAND, Arthur Exh. 1920
Architect. 22 Orchard Street, Portman Square, London. † RA 1.

DURAND, G. Exh. 1882
† M 2.

DURAND, Miss M. Exh. 1909-14
13 Newcastle Drive, The Park, Nottingham. † N 2.

DURANT, W. Exh. 1890
Meadow Villa, Stratford-on-Avon. † B 2.

DURAS, Mrs. Mary Exh. 1940
Sculptor. Russelvue, London Road, Wendover-Dean, Bucks. † RA 1.

D'URBAN, William Exh. 1886-88
Landscape painter. The Studios, High House, Bushey, Herts. † GI 1, M 1, NG 1, RE 1, ROI 2.

DURDEN, James 1878-1964
Landscape and portrait painter. Studied Manchester School of Art and Royal College of Art. R.O.I. 1927. Add: Claygate, Surrey 1909; London 1910 and 1927; Keswick, Cumberland 1925. † GI 2, L 5, M 3, P 2, RA 29, RI 3, ROI 44.

DURDIN, Chas. Exh. 1892
Tipperary, Ireland. † RHA 1.

DURELL, Amy Clara b. 1865
Mrs. A.C. Eustace. Portrait painter. Studied Lambeth School of Art and RA Schools. Add: London. † D 2, RA 2, RI 3, SWA 2.

DURELLE, Miss M. Exh. 1914
Sloane Street, London. † SWA 3.

DURENNE, Exh. 1924
† GOU 1.

DURHAM, C.J. d. 1889
Figure painter. Taught at Slade School. Add: London. † RBA 1.

DURHAM, Christine N. Exh. 1913
Landscape painter. † ALP 2.

DURHAM, Ida L. Exh. 1935
Figure painter. The Waterworks, Hanworth Road, Sunbury Common, Middlesex. † RA 1.

DURHAM, Mary Edith d. 1944
Portrait painter. Travelled widely. Exh. 1890-1900. Add: London. † RA 3, RI 1, ROI 1, SWA 1.

DURHAM, W.H. Exh. 1890
Miniature portrait painter. 6 Myrtle Grove, Sydenham. † RA 1.

DURNFORD, F. Andrew Exh. 1886
Marine painter. Rosedale, Walton-on-Thames. † RBA 1.

DURRANNI, B. Exh. 1880
Portrait painter. Endsleigh, Streatham, London. † RA 1.

DURRANT, A.M. Exh. 1909-11
Architect. Leverstock Green, Hemel Hempstead, Herts. † RA 3.

DURRANT, Dorothea Exh. 1904-22
Landscape painter. Bushey, Herts 1904; Marlborough, Wilts. 1913. † L 1, RA 2, SWA 2.

DURST, Auguste* Exh. 1883
Puteaux, Paris. † GI 1.

DURST, Austin Exh. 1902
Architect. London. † RA 8, RHA 5, RSA 2.

DURST, Alan Lydiat 1883-1970
Sculptor. Studied Central School of Arts and Crafts and Chatres, France. Teacher of wood carving Royal College of Art 1925-40. Member London Group 1927. Add: London. † GI 2, L 3, RA 3, RMS 2, RSA 5.

DURVERGER Exh. 1884-91
† TOO 2.

DURWARD, Miss J. Exh. 1881-83
1 Clerk Street, Edinburgh. † RSA 2.

DURY, Tony* Exh. 1882-83
Liverpool. † L 2.

DUSEK, Jan V. Exh. 1932-35
Sculptor. London 1932. Czechoslovakia 1935. † RA 4.

DUST, Miss E.R. Exh. 1911-35
Dalham Lodge, Mayfield Road, Whalley Range, Manchester. † L 2, M 2, RCA 15.

DU SUAR, de la CROIX, Le Comte Exh. 1908
81 Avenue Borquet, Paris. † NG 1.

DUTCH, L.H. Exh. 1887
97 Dickenson Road, Rusholme. † M 2.

DUTHIE, A. Louis Exh. 1926
77 Edge Lane Drive, Liverpool. † L 3.

DUTHIE, Arthur L. Exh. 1892-98
Stained glass artist. Chelsea, London 1892 and 1898; Granton, N.B. 1897. † GI 2, RA 1, RSA 2.

DUTHIE, Alexander S. Exh. 1922
Portrait painter. 54 Brook Street, London. † RA 1.

DUTHIE, C.C. Exh. 1880
Flower painter. Clewer, Windsor, Berks. † SWA 1.

DUTHIE, Charlotte C. Exh. 1907-9
The Presbytery, North Berwick. † RSA 4.

DUTHIE, Mary E. Exh. 1887
Landscape painter. Row Doune, Perthshire. † D 2, SWA 3.

DUTHIE, Spottiswood Exh. 1893-1912
Landscape and figure painter. Udney, Aberdeenshire 1893; Aberdeen 1896; Glasgow 1911. † L 4, RA 10, RBA 7, RSA 3.

DUTHIE, William Exh. 1889-94
Ashley Lodge, Aberdeen 1889; London 1892. † GI 2, RSA 5.

DUTHOIT, Elizabeth Emma Exh. 1885
Landscape painter. 184 Highbury New Park, London. † RI 1.

DU TOIT, S. Jane Exh. 1906-7
184 Highbury New Park, London. † B 2.

DUTOIT, Ulysse A. Exh. 1906
Ashdene, Park Street, Scarborough, Yorks. † L 2.

DUTTON, Alfred H. Exh. 1899-1900
102 Wood Street, Liverpool. † L 3.

DUTTON, Bertha Exh. 1884-1900
Still life painter. Bernard House, Addiscombe Road, Croydon, Surrey. † SWA 5.

DUTTON, Blanche Exh. 1934-40
Flower, landscape and still life painter. Add: London. † COO 9, RA 1.

DUTTON, Miss Constance See THOMPSON

DUTTON, Daisy Exh. 1895-1900
Trefriew, N. Wales 1895; Llandudno 1900. † L 2.

DUTTON, Eileen M. Exh. 1932-34
Crewe, Cheshire. † RCA 2.

DUTTON, Harold John b. 1889
Landscape painter. b. Birmingham. A.N.S.A. 1923, N.S.A. 1927. Secretary N.S.A. 1926-30. Add: Beeston, Notts. † B 10, N 91.

DUTTON, I.H. Exh. 1931
† NEA 2.

DUTTON, John Frederick Harrison Exh. 1893-1909
Portrait painter. Chester 1893 and 1895; Bushey, Herts. 1894. † L 4, LS 3, RA 5. RCA 1.

DUTTON, Miss V. Exh. 1925-40
St. Helens, Lancs. † L 10, RCA 6.

DUTTON-GREEN, Miss O. Exh. 1920-24
c/o Bank of Adelaide, Leadenhall Street, London. † SWA 3.

DUVAL, Edward J. Exh. 1880-1916
Landscape painter. Southport, Lancs. 1880; Liverpool 1893; Gt. Marlow, Bucks. 1895; Blackheath 1903; Wimbledon 1906; Richmond, Surrey 1908. † B 1, D 4, L 2, M 6, RA 7, RBA 4, RI 3, RID 23.

DUVAL, John* Exh. 1882
Animal and sporting painter. Ipswich, Suffolk. † L 1, RBA 1.

DUVE, Mrs. M. de W. Exh. 1915-19
London. † ROI 2, SWA 1.

DUVENECK, Frank* 1848-1919
American painter and teacher. R.E. 1881-89. Add: Venice 1881; London 1885. † L 5, RE 19.

DUVERGE, Mme. Yseult K. Exh. 1897-1926
Miniature portrait painter. Surbiton, Surrey 1897; London 1923. † L 5, RA 11, SWA 3.

DUVERGER, Theophile Emmanuel* 1821-c.1901
French artist. Ecouen, Seine et Oise, France. † GI 9, L 4.

DUVOCELLE, Julien A. Exh. 1912-14
9 Rue Bochart de Saron, Paris. † L 1, LS 3.

DUXBURY, G. Carr Exh. 1914-26
Figure painter. Hedge End, Northdown Way, Margate, Kent. † RA 2.

DVORAK, Franz b. 1862
Austrian painter. France 1898; London 1909-12. † L 4, RA 4.

DYAS, Edith Mary Exh. 1920-34
Landscape painter. b. Stockport, Lancs. Married Arthur Netherwood, q.v. Add: Prestbury Studio, Port Hill, Shrewsbury. † B 5, L 5, RCA 7, RI 1, ROI 2.

DYAS, Miss Nancy Exh. 1931
Melcheston, Port Hill, Shrewsbury. † B 2, RCA 2.

DYASON, E.H.* Exh. 1884-86
Marine and landscape painter. 1 Westbourne Terrace, Worthing, Sussex. † D 2, RBA 3.

DYASON, Miss Francis Sanford Exh. 1887-91
7 Boscobel Gardens, London. † B 3.

DYBALL, Sextus Exh. 1893
Architect. 35 Bucklersbury, Cheapside, London. † RA 1.

DYCE, G.S. Exh. 1888
Wellington Club, Grosvenor Place, London. † L 1.

DYCE, James Exh. 1918-19
17 Albany Street, Edinburgh. † RSA 15.

DYCE, J. Stirling* Exh. 1884-98
Landscape and portrait painter. London 1884 and 1890; Henley-on-Thames 1885. † GI 1, RA 5, RID 17, TOO 1.

DYER, A.H. Exh. 1905
Oakleigh, Hoddesdon, Herts. † RA 1.

DYER, Mrs. Bernard Exh. 1892-96
Flower and figure painter. Rowdon, Arkwright Road, Hampstead, London. † RID 5.

DYER, Charles E. Exh. 1882
Architect. 2 John Street, Bedford Row, London. † RA 1.

DYER, Charles F. or G. Exh. 1880
Figure painter. Union Bank, Munich. † RA 1.

DYER, Miss Dudley P. Exh. 1935-39
Landscape and interior painter. London 1935; South Nutfield, Surrey 1939. † RA 2.

DYER, Miss E.A. Exh. 1916
11 Deanery Road, Romford Road, Forest Gate, London. † RA 1.

DYER, Gertrude M. Exh. 1891-96
Flower painter. Gt. Bookham, Leatherhead, Surrey. † RI 3.

DYER, Mrs. Josephine A. Exh. 1940
Miniature portrait painter. Scarvell, Woodlands Avenue, Eastcote, Ruislip, Middlesex. † RA 1.

DYER, Lowell b. 1856
American painter. St. Ives, Cornwall 1890-1921. † DOW 1, G 1, L 1, ROI 1.

DYER, L. Swynnerton Exh. 1909-14
London 1909; Oxton, Salop. 1914. † LS 8, ROI 1.

DYER, Muriel G. Exh. 1894-1924
Flower and landscape painter. Ringwood Hants. 1894 and 1899; London 1898 † RA 15, ROI 4, SWA 10.

DYER, Miss R.M. Exh. 1924
18 Platts Lane, Hampstead, London. † SWA 2.

DYER, Mrs. Theresa Sylvester see STANNARD

DYER-GOUGH, S. Exh. 1920
† NEA 1.

DYKE, Miss Exh. 1888-93
45 Park Street, London. † D 6.

DYKE, David N. Exh. 1929-36
Architect. H.M. Office of Works, Storey's Gate, London. † RA 9.

DYKE, Louise Catherine b. 1874
Nee Cave. Watercolour landscape painter. b. Hanbury, Glos. Studied Westminster. Add: London 1899; Baluchistan, India 1904. † D 2, SWA 2.

DYKES, Andrea Exh. 1939
c/o J.J. Patrickson, 120 Fulham Road, London. † SWA 1.

DYKES, Miss J.A. Exh. 1904-5
8 Grosvenor Place, Bath. † L 2.

DYKES, Miss J.C. Exh. 1928
High Bank, Overton, Warrington, Lancs. † L 1.

DYMOCK, Dorothy Graham Exh. 1928-35
Portrait and landscape painter. Studied Slade School and Westminster. Served as V.A.D. Cook in Red Cross Hospital World War I. A.S.W.A. 1932. Add: London 1928; Bedford 1929; Prestbury, Glos. 1932. † B 1, RA 2, RBA 1, RID,4, ROI 1, SWA 9.

DYMOND, Mrs. V.I. Exh. 1936
Urban landscape painter. 49 Cyril Mansions, London. † RA 1.

DYNE, Musgrave Exh. 1908-21
London. † I 4, L 3, LS 8, RA 4.

DYSON, Ada Exh. 1936
Springfield, The Avenue, Upper Park Road, Broughton Park, Salford, Lancs. † B 1, RCA 2.

DYSON, Mrs. Hilda Exh. 1933-40
411 Hagley Road, Edgbaston, Birmingham. † B 5.

DYSON, Mrs. H.G. Exh. 1927
Brook House, Timperley, Cheshire. † L 3.

DYSON, Irene Beatrice b. 1907
Animal painter, miniaturist and fabric painter. Exh. 1923-35. Add: Brook House, Timperley, Cheshire. † L 14, RA 2.

DYSON, Will 1883-1938
Satirical painter. b. Ballarat, Australia. Exh. 1915-38. Add: London. † LEI 25, RHA 2, RSA 4.

DYSON-SMITH, Charles William Exh. 1919-40
Sculptor. Studied RA Schools, Royal College of Art and Munich. Add: London. † GI 4, L 2, P 3, RA 44, RBA 1, ROI 3, RSA 5.

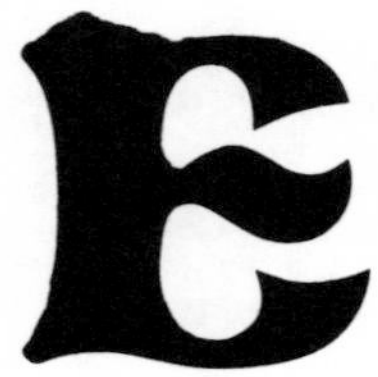

EADES, Hugh R.H. Exh. 1933-36
Architect. Quarry Cottage, Shalford Road, Guildford, Surrey. † RA 2, RSA 4.

EADES, Stanley C. Exh. 1913-29
Etcher. Bristol 1913; London 1921. † L 5, RA 4.

EADIE, Agnes S. Exh. 1901-36
Landscape and miniature painter. London 1901 and 1934; Bournemouth 1927. † B 1, GI 1, I 2, L 14, NEA 1, RA 1, RBA 2, RMS 2, SWA 5.

EADIE, Charles Exh. 1880-91
Hillhead, Glasgow. † GI 6.

EADIE, Ian G.M. Exh. 1936-40
Painter and etcher. 21 Park Road, Fairmuir, Dundee. † P 1, RA 3, RSA 7, RSW 1.

EADIE, John Exh. 1880-94
Glasgow. † GI 8.

EADIE, Kate M. Exh. 1905-32
Stained glass artist, illuminator and jeweller A.R.M.S. 1914, R.M.S. 1919. Add: Moseley, Birmingham. † B 3, L 69, RA 7, RMS 11.

EADIE, Miss K.U. Exh. 1930
51 Oakfield Avenue, Glasgow. † GI 1.

EADIE, Robert* 1877-1954
Portrait and landscape painter, poster artist and lithographer. Studied Glasgow School of Art, Munich and Paris. R.S.W. 1917. Exh. 1912-40. Add: Glasgow. † AR 2, GI 76, L 9, M 1, RA 1, RSA 43, RSW 95.

EADIE, William Exh. 1880-94
Domestic painter. St. John's Wood, London 1880; St. Ives, Cornwall 1888. † DOW 3, G 2, GI 7, L 4, RA 7, RSA 1.

EADON, Miss M. Exh. 1890
Snaith, Yorks. † SWA 2.

EAGIE, E. Exh. 1880-83
47 Park Avenue, Sandymount, Dublin. † RHA 8.

EAGLE, R.H. Exh. 1881-86
19 Brunswick Street, Hillside, Edinburgh. † RSA 4.

EAGLESTON, Mrs. Theodosia Exh. 1898
Cambridge Road, Aldershot, Hants. † SWA 1.

EAGLESTON, V.F. Exh. 1938
69 Antrim Mansions, London. † SWA 2.

EAGLETON, Aileen C. b. 1902
126 Oakwood Court, London 1926. † L 1, SWA 1.

EAGLETON, Miss E. Exh. 1924
Westfield, Mowbray Road, Upper Norwood, London. † SWA 1.

EALES, Mrs. Annie Lord Exh. 1906-12
89 City Road, Manchester. † M 5.

EAMES, Edward A. Exh. 1905
2 Claribel Street, Liverpool. † L 1.

EAMES, Felix Henry b. 1892
Painter and woodcut artist. b. Matlock. Studied Loughborough, Leicester and Liverpool. Add: Glynceiriog, Wrexham 1929. † L 4.

EAMES, John H. Exh. 1934-40
Painter and etcher. London. † RA 3.

EARITH, Mrs. Exh. 1882
32 Merrion Square, Dublin. † RHA 2.

EARL, George* Exh. 1880-95
Sporting and animal painter. Father of Maud E. q.v. Add: Newman Street, London. † M 1, RA 4, TOO 3.

EARL, Maud* d. 1943
Animal painter. Daughter of George E. q.v. Exh. 1884-1914. Add: London. Died in New York. † B 1, FIN 20, L 19, M 1, RA 13.

EARL, Thomas* Exh. 1880-85
Animal painter. 39 Highgate Road, London. † RBA 8.

EARLE, Miss Exh. 1893
Allerton Tower, Woolton. † L 1.

EARLE, Charles c. 1831-1893
Landscape painter and watercolourist. R.I. 1882, R.O.I. 1883. Add: 9 Duke Street, Portland Place, London. † B 7, D 13, FIN 2, G 4, L 24, M 9, NG 6, RA 6, RI 74, ROI 15.

EARLE, Dennis Exh. 1934
Figure painter. 112B Cheyne Walk, London. † RA 1.

EARLE, E.E. Marples Exh. 1931-36
† WG 11.

EARLE, Kate Exh. 1887-1914
Portrait, figure and miniature painter. R.M.S. 1897. Add: London. † G 1, GI 2, L 5, M 2, RA 5, RBA 10, RHA 1, RI 3, RMS 27, ROI 7, RSA 2, SWA 6.

EARLE, Maria T. Exh. 1880
47 Cambridge Terrace, Hyde Park, London. † D 2.

EARLES, F.R. Exh. 1908
4 Wynchcombe Studios, England's Lane, Hampstead, London. † RA 1.

EARLEY, John Exh. 1887-1904
Dublin. † RHA 4.

EARLEY, William Exh. 1903-4
56 South Richmond Street, Dublin. † RHA 7.

EARNSHAW, Miss E. Exh. 1909-14
Domestic painter. Married to John E. Sutcliffe q.v. Add: Bushey, Herts. † RA 2.

EARNSHAW, Frank Exh. 1893
3 Bartholomew Road, London. † D 1.

EARNSHAW, Harold Exh. 1912-26
Watercolour landscape painter. Married Mabel Lucie Atwell q.v. Add: Coulsdon, Surrey. † CHE 1, RI 3.

EARNSHAW, Mrs. Mary Harriot Exh. 1889-1904
Portrait, figure and flower painter. Add: London. † GI 1, L 15, M 1, RA 1, RBA 3, RI 2, RMS 3, ROI 1, SWA 6.

EARP, Henry Exh. 1882-86
Landscape painter. Brighton, Sussex. † L 3, M 2, RI 2.

EARP, Vernon Exh. 1900
Landscape painter. 10 Albert Mansions, Crouch Hill, London. † RA 1.

EARTHROWL, Eliab George b. 1878
Watercolour painter, modeller and etcher. Studied Goldsmith's College (landscape prize). Professor Hammersmith School of Art. A.R.E. 1924. Exh. 1902-39. Add: London. † CON 2, GI 1, L 1, M 1, RA 14, RE 23.

EASOM, Alfred Exh. 1887-97
Portrait painter. N.S.A. 1891. Peoples Hall, Heathcote Street, Nottingham. † N 10.

EASSIE, F. Exh. 1923-34
Dublin. † RHA 8.

EAST, Sir Alfred 1849-1913
Landscape painter and etcher. b. Kettering, Northants. Studied Glasgow School of Art and Ecole des Beaux Arts, Paris. Travelled on Continent, N. Africa and Japan. N.E.A. 1887 A.R.A. 1899, R.A. 1913, R.B.A. 1883, P.R.B.A. 1906, R.E. 1885, R.I. 1887 (resigned 1898) H.R.M.S. 1907, R.O.I. 1888. Knighted 1910. Add: Glasgow 1881; London 1886. † AG 1, B 41, CAR 1, D 10, DOW 76, FIN 147, G 11, GI 41, GOU 9, L 65, LEI 69, M 50, NEA 1, NG 32, RA 108, RBA 66, RE 67, RHA 4, RI 30, ROI 27, RSA 23, TOO 5, WG 3.

EAST, Miss A.M. Exh. 1889-93
Kimberham, Horley, Surrey. † B 7.

EAST, Frances Exh. 1880-85
Flower painter. Prestbury, Cheltenham, Glos. † SWA 3.

EAST, F.J. Exh. 1934-37
Landscape painter. 156 Queen's Drive, Nottingham. † N 4.

EAST, H.S. Exh. 1918
14 Gray's Inn Square, London. † RA 1.

EAST, Kate Exh. 1908-16
Ealing, London. † B 5, RA 2.

EAST, Mrs. M.G. Exh. 1932-35
La Juania, San Remo, Italy. † RCA 1, ROI 3, RSA 1.

EASTAUGH, H.N. Exh. 1923-28
22 Upper Park Fields, Putney, London. † L 4.

EASTERFIELD, Fanny H. Exh. 1882-1913
Landscape, interior and flower painter. Add: Newark on Trent, Notts. † N 10.

EASTHAM, H.S. Exh. 1888-89
23 Langsdale Street, Liverpool. † L 3.

EASTHER, Charlotte D. Exh. 1902-21
Miniature portrait painter. 57 Bedford Gardens, Kensington, London. † LS 3, RA 1.

EASTLAKE, Lady Exh. 1881
† RE 1.

EASTLAKE, Charles Herbert Exh. 1889-1927
Landscape painter. Studied Antwerp and Paris. Travelled widely. R.B.A. 1895. Add: Balham, London 1889; Croydon, Surrey and London 1900. † BG 37, L 1, RA 17, RBA 36, RI 1.

EASTLAKE, Elizabeth R. Exh. 1880-83
Domestic painter. Horrabridge, South Devon 1880; Plymouth 1882. † D 2, L 1, RA 1.

EASTLAKE, Mary Alexandra Exh. 1891-1936
nee Bell. Portrait, figure and landscape painter. b. Canada. Married Charles Herbert E. q.v. Studied Paris. Add: Paris 1891, St. Ives, Cornwall 1895; Croydon, Surrey and London 1900. † BG 31, GI 2, I 2, L 6, RA 17, RBA 1, SWA 11.

EASTMAN, Frank S. Exh. 1902-40
Portrait, figure, landscape and flower painter. Married Maud E. q.v. Add: London. † BRU 1, G 1, L 7, M 1, RA 36, RBA 2, WG 95.

EASTMAN, Maud Exh. 1902-32
nee Mair. Married Frank S.E. q.v. Miniature portrait painter. Add: London. † RA 47, RMS 2, SWA 1, WG 39.

EASTON, Miss Meg H. Exh. 1923-32
Edinburgh. † RSA 1, RSW 5.

EASTON, Reginald Exh. 1880-87
Miniature portrait painter. 35 Ledbury Road, Bayswater, London. † RA 58.

EASTON, William George b. 1879
Painter, illustrator and designer. Studied Bolt Court and Kensington Schools. Exh. 1910-23. Add: South London. † RA 5.

EASTWOOD, Miss A. Exh. 1923-25
Oak Mount, Ramsgreave, Nr. Blackburn, Lancs. † L 4.

EASTWOOD, C.H. Exh. 1901-2
Sandringham Street, Hull, Yorks. † RCA 2.

EASTWOOD, D.C. Exh. 1940
2 Chelsea Court, Embankment Gardens, London. † SWA 1.

EASTWOOD, Francis H. Exh. 1880-1908
Landscape and figure painter. London 1880; Haslemere, Surrey 1908. † D 9, L 3, M 2, RA 8, RBA 7, RI 11.

EASTWOOD, J.H. Exh. 1889-1908
Decorative artist. London. † RA 9.

EASTWOOD, Walter b. 1867
Painter and black and white artist. Studied Heywood School of Art. Exh. 1911-33. Add: Lytham St. Annes, Lancs. † B 15, L 16, RCA 23.

EATON, Charles Warren b. 1857
American landscape painter. Exh. 1890-1906. Add: New York and Soho, London. † G 1, L 1, RA 11, RBA 5, RHA 3, RI 2.

EATON, Ellen M.M. Exh. 1897-1940
Painter and wood engraver. Add: Birchington, Kent 1897; London 1898; Whatmer Hall. Sturry, Nr. Canterbury, Kent 1908. † B 19, G 1, GI 3, L 30, M 1, NEA 12, RA 6, RBA 4, RCA 19, RHA 2, RI 5, RSA 2, RSW 1, SWA 27.

EATON, G.M. Exh. 1911-12
The Summit, Burton Road, Derby. † N 3.

EATON, Helen Exh. 1922
† G 1.

EATON, Mrs. H.E. Exh. 1932
Conway, Wales. † RCA 1.

EATON, Maria Exh. 1890-1937
Miniature portrait painter. Married Ernest Llewellyn Hampshire q.v. Add: Macclesfield 1890; Manchester 1902; London 1905 and 1914; Isle of Man 1913. † L 14, M 19, RA 14, RI 40, SWA 9.

EATON, Marion Exh. 1881-88
Still life painter. Nottingham. † N 4.

EATON, Rose Exh. 1889
47 Tindal Terrace, Walsall Heath, Birmingham. † B 1.

EATON, Stephen O. Exh. 1889
Landscape and flower painter. 17 Fitzroy Street, Fitzroy Square, London. † RA 3.

EAVENS, Mabel Exh. 1910
1193 Burdett Avenue, Kickon, Canada. † L 1.

EAVES, Miss M. Exh. 1921-27
300 Alcester Road, Moseley, Birmingham. † B 2.

EAVESTAFF, S.L. Exh. 1897
2 The Avenue, Brondesbury, London. † RBA 1.

EBBUTT, Thomas Kerr Exh. 1906
98 Hanover Street, Edinburgh. † RSA 1.

EBDY, T.C. Exh. 1888-89
Birkenhead. † L 3.

EBEL, William Augustus Exh. 1884
Decorative artist. 16 Camden Grove, Peckham, London. † RA 1.

EBERT, Paul Exh. 1928
† GOU 1.

EBNER, Louis F. Exh. 1889-90
Landscape painter. London. † L 1, M 1, NG 1, RA 1.

EBNER, M. Exh. 1880-82
16 Avenue Trudaine, Paris. † RHA 4.

ECCLES, Agnes Exh. 1905
Hawkshaw Avenue, Darwen, Lancs. † L 1.

ECCLES, J. Evans Exh. 1881-86
Coastal and figure painter. London 1881; Bury, Lancs. 1884. † M 8, RA 1, RBA 2.

ECCLES, T.E. Exh. 1912-33
60 Castle Street, Liverpool. † L 6.

ECCLESTON, Philip E. Exh. 1937
25 Reston Drive, Glasgow. † GI 1.

ECHAGUE, Antonio Ortiz Exh. 1921
Spanish artist. 5 Rue Teheran, Paris. † RSA 1.

ECHALAY, Mrs. Elizabeth Exh. 1886-88
Landscape painter. London. † D 3, SWA 1.

ECHTLER, Adolf 1843-1914
German artist. 36B Schwanthler Strasse, Munich 1891. † GI 1.

ECKERSLEY, B. Exh. 1932
† L 1.

ECKERSLEY, Mabel T. Exh. 1920
Portrait painter. 28 Wellsway, Bath. † RA 1.

ECKFORD, Miss A.L. Exh. 1902-5
8 Norfolk Square, Hyde Park, London. † SWA 2.

ECKHARDT, Oscar Exh. 1896-1901
R.B.A. 1896. Add: London. † L 1, RBA 18, ROI 1.

ECKHOUT, B. Exh. 1894
43 Laan Copes, The Hague, Holland. † GI 1.

ECKSTEIN, Chas. Alphonse Exh. 1910-12
c/o Allied Artists Association, 67 Chancery Lane, London. † LS 6.

ECKSTEIN, Herbert Exh. 1929-33
14 Victoria Mount, Oxton, Birkenhead. † L 5.

ECKSTEIN, Mrs. Mary Exh. 1929
14 Victoria Mount, Oxton, Birkenhead. † L 1.

ECRLEMEN, O. Exh. 1886
117 New Bond Street, London. † M 2.

EDDINGTON, A.C. Exh. 1911
118 Stanhope Street, London. † L 1, RA 1.

EDDINGTON, William Clark Exh. 1880-85
Landscape painter. Bloomsbury, London 1880; Worcester 1881. † B 1, RA 2, RI 5.

EDDIS, Eden Upton* 1812-1901
Portrait and nature painter. Add: 65 Harley Street, Cavendish Square, London. † RA 5, RHA 1.

EDDISON, Jean b. 1910
Portrait, figure and interior painter. Studied Westminster School of Art and under Keith Henderson. Add: Bedford Gardens, Campden Hill, London 1933. † P 1, RA 1.

EDDISON, Sam Exh. 1891-92
Portrait painter. 49 Cemetery Road, Leeds. † RA 2.

EDE, H.S. Exh. 1922
† NEA 1.

EDE, Mabel B. Exh. 1902-23
Manchester. † L 3, M 1, RCA 4.

EDE, Miss M.H. Exh. 1882-94
Levenshulme, Manchester 1882; Urmston 1884; Didsbury 1894. † L 1, M 4.

EDELFELT, Albert Gustaf Aristide* 1854-1905
Finnish painter. 147 Avenue de Villiers, Paris 1891. † RA 1.

EDELSTEIN, Wilhelmina N.F. Exh. 1920-38
Landscape painter. London. † L 4, RA 3.

EDELSTEN, Alice J. Exh. 1887
Flower painter. 7 Lansdown Terrace, Leamington, Warwicks. † SWA 1.

EDEN, Christopher Exh. 1919
† L 1.

EDEN, C.G. Exh. 1920
19 Highfield Road, Northwood, Middlesex. † NEA 1.

EDEN, Denis William* b. 1878
Figure, historical and nature painter. Son of William E. q.v. Studied under F.G. Stephens, St. John's Wood School and RA Schools. R.O.I. 1906. Add: London 1901, 1907; Newport, Essex 1907; Romsey, Hants. 1911; Abingdon, Berks. 1914; Burford, Oxon 1915; Begbrook, Oxon 1919; Woodstock, Oxon 1924. † B 1, FIN 1, GI 2, L 14, RA 33 ROI 1, RSA 1.

EDEN, Frederick Charles b. 1864
Architect. London. † RA 5, RHA 2, RSA 2.

EDEN, Sir Timothy Bt. Exh. 1924-39
Flower and still life painter. Son of Sir William E. q.v. Add: Windlestone, Ferry Hill, Durham. † ALP 10, RED 1, TOO 36.

EDEN, William Exh. 1880-1906
Landscape painter. Father of Denis E. q.v. Add: Liverpool 1880; London 1885. † D 4, GI 1, L 29, RA 18, RI 11.

EDEN, Sir William Bt. c. 1849-1915
Landscape painter and watercolourist. Travelled widely. Father of Sir Timothy E. q.v. Add: Windlestone, Ferry Hill, Co. Durham. † D 107, GOU 133, I 10, LS 5, NEA 22, NG 1, RI 6.

EDGAR, Alexander Exh. 1906
154 West Regent Street, Glasgow. † GI 1.

EDGAR, David Exh. 1893-1907
Kilmarnock, N.B. † GI 2.

EDGE, Helga V. Exh. 1922-28
Painter and etcher. London 1922; Colchester, Essex 1928. † RA 1, SWA 4.

EDGE, Isabella Exh. 1937
† P 1.

EDGE, Mrs. Lisette Exh. 1921-29
The Station House, Bebington, Birkenhead. † L 4.

EDGE, Nellie Exh. 1898
Ribbleton, Llandudno, Wales. † RCA 1.

EDGE, Miss W. Exh. 1917-18
33 Arkwright Road, Hampstead, London. † RA 3.

EDGECOMBE, Reginald Edward b. 1885
Painter, etcher, black and white artist, designer and craftsman in metal and glass. Studied Birmingham Municipal School of Art. Add: Birmingham. † B 28.

EDGELL, Mrs. Fanny Exh. 1935-36
Miniature painter. Little Stakes, Westerham, Kent. † RA 2, SWA 3.

EDGELOW, Alice Maud Exh. 1889-90
3 Tavistock Square, London. † B 1, M 1, SWA 2.

EDGERLY, Miss M. Exh. 1912-13
London. † L 2, RA 3.

EDGHILL, Ernest G. Exh. 1901-3
Colwyn Bay, N. Wales. † RCA 3.

EDGINGTON, E.W. Exh. 1887-88
Landscape painter. Brook Green Studios, Hammersmith, London. † RA 1, RBA 2.

EDIE, R. Exh. 1923
2 West Regent Street, Glasgow. † L 1.

EDINGER, William H. Exh. 1892-97
Landscape painter. Wanstead, Essex 1892; Snaresbrook, Essex 1896. † RA 1, RI 2, RSW 1.

EDIS, Mary Exh. 1910-40
Portrait and figure painter. London. † GOU 1, I 1, L 1, P 2, RA 3, ROI 7, SWA 8.

EDIS, Robert William Exh. 1880-96
Architect. 14 Fitzroy Square, London. † GI 2, RA 21, RHA 9.

EDLER, John D. Exh. 1936
Sculptor. 10 Wallwood Road, Leytonstone, Essex. † RA 1.

EDMONDS, Alf Exh. 1884-86
13 Hillmarten Road, Holloway, London. † L 3, M 2, RHA 1.

EDMONDS, Mrs. Courtney Exh. 1882-1903
Landscape painter. Exeter, Devon. † B 1, GI 2, L 3, RA 1, RBA 1, RI 4, ROI 1.

EDMONDS, Edith Lilian Exh. 1924-40
nee Barnish. Landscape and still life painter. Studied Liverpool School of Art 1921-22 and Paris, Atelier Delbos 1923-24. Add: Newholme, Woodlands, Conway, Wales. † GOU 1, M 1, RA 1, RBA 1, RCA 17, SWA 10.

EDMONDS, E.M. Exh. 1889-1905
Landscape painter. London. † B 1, NG 37.

EDMONDS, F. Exh. 1885
22 Cloudsley Square, Islington, London. † RHA 1.

EDMONDS, Lilian Exh. 1896-1936
Figure and landscape painter. London 1896; Cambridge 1935. † GOU 3, L 3, LS 16, M 1, NG 1, RA 7, RBA 1, ROI 1, SWA 4.

EDMONDS, Miss M. Alizon Exh. 1934
Etcher. 71 Lowther Road, Bournemouth, Hants. † RA 1.

EDMONDS, Miss Mabel M. Exh. 1907
The Manor House, Islip, Thrapston, Notts. † L 1.

EDMONDS, Paul b. 1873
Painter, sculptor, linocut artist and embroiderer. b. Stroud. Add: London 1927; Brighton 1933. † RA 1, RBA 4, RED 4.

EDMONDS, Stuart Exh. 1925-27
† GOU 5.

EDMONDSON, Robert H. Exh. 1882-95
Landscape and coastal painter. Manchester 1882; Wilmslow, Cheshire 1885; Newton le Willows, Cheshire 1895. † L 1, M 5, RA 1.

EDMONSTON, Agnes Exh. 1885-1921
2 Kilgraston Road, Edinburgh. † D 2, GI 16, L 1, M 5, RSA 52, RSW 4.

EDMONSTON, Anne B.D. Exh. 1880-87
1 Brunstane Villas, Joppa, Edinburgh 1880; 136 George Street, Edinburgh 1883. † RSA 12.

EDMONSTON, Samuel* Exh. 1880-87
1 Brunstane Villas, Joppa, Edinburgh 1880; 136 George Street, Edinburgh 1883. † RSA 28.

EDMUNDS, Herbert Exh. 1910
402 Waterside, Chesham, Bucks. † LS 1.

EDMUNDS, Keith McKay Exh. 1917-22
Figure and portrait painter. R.O.I. 1921. Add: London. † I 1, P 8, RA 5, ROI 8.

EDMUNDS, Nellie Mary Hepburn d. 1953
Portrait and miniature portrait painter. Studied Slade School, University College, London and Westminster School of Art. R.M.S. 1901. V.P.R.M.S. from 1914. H.R.M.S. 1929 (Hon. Sec. 1916-19). Exh. 1896-1940. Add: London. † B 1, L 15, NG 11, RA 87, RI 7, RMS 265, SWA 3.

EDMUNDS, Vernon Exh. 1920-21
370 Moseley Road, Birmingham. † B 2.

EDNIE, Andrew Exh. 1903-5
73 Ashley Terrace, Edinburgh. † GI 1, RSA 3.

EDNIE, John Exh. 1903-10
Edinburgh 1903, 1907; Bishopton, N.B. 1904. † GI 5, RSA 2.

EDNIE, Mrs. Lily R. Exh. 1904-8
Rose Vale, Bishopton, N.B. † GI 1, RSA 1.

EDRIDGE-GREEN, M. Exh. 1896
6 Ravensfield Villas, Hendon, London. † ROI 1.

EDRINGTON, Amy Exh. 1898-1901
Portrait painter. 18 Dancer Road, Fulham, London. † L 1, RA 2, RI 1, RMS 1.

EDSON, Allan* Exh. 1886
Landscape painter. 39 Clifton Gardens, Maida Vale, London. † M 1, RA 2, RBA 2, RSA 1.

EDSTROM, David b. 1873
Sculptor. b. Sweden. c/o Allied Artists Assn. 67 Chancery Lane, London 1910; Stockholm 1913. † I 8, LS 13.

EDWARD, Albert Exh. 1885-86
Landscape painter. 27 Park Lane, London. † RI 1.

EDWARD, Alfred S. 1852-1915
Marine painter. R.B.A. 1894. Add: London 1880; Puckeridge, Herts. 1908. † B 12, D 1, GI 28, NG 4, RA 5, RBA 216, RHA 10, ROI 12, RSA 14.

EDWARD, C. Exh. 1884
Rustic landscape painter. 1 Talgarth Road, W. Kensington, London. † L 1, RA 2, ROI 1.

EDWARD, Maggie W. Exh. 1889
235 Bath Street, Glasgow. † GI 1.

EDWARDES, Clara Exh. 1911-14
Portrait painter. Studied Paris and London. Add: The Tower, 73 Springfield Road, London. † LS 8.

EDWARDES, Hon. Elizabeth Exh. 1880-91
Landscape painter. 67 Mount Street, London. † B 1, D 5, SWA 8.

EDWARDES, Francis A. Exh. 1916-20
Sculptor and enameller. Trentham Park, Trentham, Staffs. † B 1, RA 2.

EDWARDES, May de Montravel 1887 c. 1967
Portrait, figure, historical and miniature painter. Studied Cope and Nicol School of Art, S. Kensington and RA Schools (1907-12). Exh. 1917-35. Add: 175 Cromwell Road, London. † RA 3, RI 6.

EDWARDS, Annie Exh. 1899-1920
Miniature painter. A.R.M.S. 1908, R.M.S. 1909. Add: Stratford on Avon 1899; School of Art, Birmingham 1905; Leamington, Warwicks. 1906. † B 11, L 6, NG 2, RA 14, RMS 9, SWA 4.

EDWARDS, A.C.M. Exh. 1912
337 Birkbeck Chambers, High Holborn, London. † RA 1.

EDWARDS, Miss A.G. Exh. 1893
56 Fellows Road, London. † RI 1.

EDWARDS, Ada L. Exh. 1882-85
4 Goldsmith Square, Nottingham. † N 4.

EDWARDS, Alice M. Exh. 1932-39
Mrs. T.H. Figure and portrait painter. 4 Welby Gardens, Grantham, Lincs. † N 17.

EDWARDS, Arthur Sherwood b. 1887
Painter and sculptor. b. Leicester. Studied Grimsby and Newcastle (bronze medal). Add: Stoke Newington, London 1911; Grimsby, Lincs. 1913; Ashton on Mersey, Cheshire 1922. † GI 1, L 11, M 2, RA 10, RBA 1, RCA 2, RI 1, ROI 1.

EDWARDS, Beryl Exh. 1933-40
Wood engraver. London. † NEA 2, RA 7, RED 1.

EDWARDS, Catherine D. Exh. 1935
13 Dalhousie Street, Brechin, Angus. † RSA 1.

EDWARDS, Cyril Walduck b. 1902
Landscape painter. Studied Regent Street, Polytechnic. R.B.A. 1935, R.I. 1936. Add: London 1926; Upper Wyche, Malvern, Worcs. 1936. † B 2, L 5, RA 7, RBA 27, RCA 2, RI 19, ROI 1, RSA 2.

EDWARDS, Dorothy Exh. 1929
1 Speedwell Road, Birkenhead. † L 1.

EDWARDS, E. Exh. 1894
Halstead Road, Seacombe. † L 1.

EDWARDS, Ellen Exh. 1898
146 Lancaster Road, Notting Hill, London. † ROI 2.

EDWARDS, Emily Exh. 1885
18 Trinita dei Monte, Rome. † SWA 1.

EDWARDS, Ernest Exh. 1913-29
Twickenham Ferry 1913; Liscard, Cheshire 1920. † L 2, LS 6, NEA 2, RI 1.

EDWARDS, Evan Exh. 1928-32
Edinburgh. † RSA 4.

EDWARDS, Miss E. Hewlett Exh. 1912
Tenby, S. Wales. † SWA 1.

EDWARDS, F.E. Pearce Exh. 1906-25
Architect. Bradford 1906; Sheffield 1912. † RA 5.

EDWARDS, Grace Exh. 1902-8
Sculptor. London. † L 1, RA 8.

EDWARDS, Geo Hay Exh. 1900
Landscape painter. Roselea, Lower Common, Putney, London. † RA 1, RBA 2.

EDWARDS, George Henry Exh. 1883-1911
Figure and landscape painter. Add: London. † L 11, RA 10, RBA 8, RI 26, RMS 2, ROI 9.

EDWARDS, H.E. Exh. 1885-87
London 1885; Singlewell, nr. Gravesend, Kent 1886. † B 4.

EDWARDS, Helen M. Exh. 1900
Beach Lawn, Waterloo, Liverpool. † L 1.

EDWARDS, Mrs. Inez C. Stanley Exh. 1901-2
Miniature portrait painter. Sunny bank, Marlow, Bucks. † RA 1, RMS 1.

EDWARDS, James Exh. 1880-88
Landscape painter. N.S.A. 1881. Add: Nottingham. † N 36.

EDWARDS, Jennie Exh. 1927
Portrait painter. 15 Walpole Terrace, Kemp Town, Brighton, Sussex. † RA 1.

EDWARDS, John* Exh. 1880-1909
Landscape painter. N.S.A. 1881. Add: Nottingham 1880; Sneinton Dale, Notts. 1909. † N 31.

EDWARDS, John Exh. 1928
13 Faraday Street, Everton, Liverpool. † L1.

EDWARDS, Miss Jowett Exh. 1938-39
Figure and portrait painter. 2A Mount Ephraim Lane, London. † RA 5.

EDWARDS, John Kelt Exh. 1907-8
28 Egerton Studios, Brompton Road, London. † LS 4, RCA 1.

EDWARDS, Miss J.M. Exh. 1912-18
Clarendon Studio, Wolverhampton. † RA 7.

EDWARDS, Louisa Exh. 1884-86
Flower painter. London. † RBA 3, SWA 1.

EDWARDS, Lionel Dalhousie Robertson* b. 1878
Painter and illustrator. Studied under A. Cope and F. Calderon. R.I. 1927. Add: Conway, Wales 1901 and 1906; London 1903; Abingdon, Berks. 1909; Salisbury, Wilts. 1923. † D 9, L 2, RA 1, RCA 41, RI 38.

EDWARDS, Mrs. L.K. Exh. 1917-28
Landscape painter. 9 Cathcart Studios, Redcliffe Road, London. † AB 2, SWA 2.

EDWARDS, Mrs. L.M. Exh. 1921-23
Honeywood, Carshalton, Surrey. † RI 1, SWA 1.

EDWARDS, Mrs. M. Exh. 1920
5 Brook Road, Walton, Liverpool. † L 2.

EDWARDS, Mabel b. 1884
Mrs. Rahbula. Miniature painter. Studied Copes S. Kensington and RA Schools. (Silver medal 1910.) A.R.M.S. 1916. R.M.S. 1926, A.S.W.A. 1916. Add: Pinner, Middlesex 1907; London 1912, Harrow-on-the-Hill, Middlesex 1916; Ewell, Surrey 1925. † ALP 10, L 15, RA 32, RMS 65, SWA 6.

EDWARDS, Marian Exh. 1880-92
Landscape painter. A.S.W.A. 1880. Add: 3 Jolly Villas, Leytonstone, London. † FIN 1, SWA 15.

EDWARDS, Mia See BROWN

EDWARDS, Miss Muriel Exh. 1920-21
5 Brook Road, Walton, Liverpool. † L 3.

EDWARDS, Mary Ellen b. 1839
Mrs. John C. Staples (formerly Mrs. John Freer). Painter and illustrator. b. Kingston, Surrey. Add: Brighton, Sussex 1880; Shere, Surrey 1889; London 1900; Haywards Heath 1903-8. † D 1, DOW 18, GI 3, L 5, RA 15, RBA 1, ROI 9.

EDWARDS, Miss Mary Spencer See McEVOY

EDWARDS, Mary Stella Exh. 1931-38
Watercolour landscape, coastal and figure painter. † AB 54, SWA 4.

EDWARDS, Nowell M. Exh. 1934-39
Landscape painter. The Deanery, Canterbury, Kent. † RA 2.

EDWARDS, R.G. Exh. 1920-23
5 Brook Road, Walton, Liverpool. † L 16.

EDWARDS, Samuel Arlent b. 1862
Engraver. b. Somerset. 70 The Grove, Hammersmith, London 1887. † RA 1.

EDWARDS, Sidney J. Exh. 1926
Architect. c/o Booty and Edwards, Colombo and Singapore. † RA 1.

EDWARDS, Stanley J. Exh. 1910-14
37 Parkside, Egremont, Cheshire. † L 5.

EDWARDS, T.R.L. Exh. 1885
24 Brunswick Street, London. † M 3.

EDWARDS, W. Exh. 1890
Mount Pleasant Road, Liscard, Cheshire. † L 1.

EDWARDS, W.G. Exh. 1915
7 Favart Road, Fulham, London. † RA 2.

EDWELL, Bernice b. 1880
Miniature and landscape painter. b. Newbury, Berks. Studied Colarossi's, Paris and the Art Society, New South Wales. Add: 18 Darling Street, South Yarra, Victoria, Australia 1921-23. † RA 5.

EDWIN, Eileen Exh. 1930-40
Wood engraver. † NEA 2, RED 1.

EDWIN, Horace Exh. 1881-82
Figure painter. Hackney, London. † RA 2.

EDWIN, J. Exh. 1885-90
Valeview, Battlefield, Langside, Glasgow. † GI 3, RSA 1.

EDWIN, Mrs. Mary Exh. 1892-93
1 Clifton Terrace, S. Norwood, London. † P 1, ROI 1.

EDYE, Miss D. Exh. 1885-86
11 Old Shore, Brighton, Sussex. † L 2.

EDZARD, Kurt Exh. 1935
Sculptor. 8 Trafalgar Studios, Manresa Road, London. † RA 2.

EERELMAN, Otto Exh. 1908
Animal painter. Amsterdam. † GI 1.

EGAN, Emily C. Exh. 1907
13 Montpellier Parade, Monkstown, Co. Dublin. † RHA 2.

EGAN, James Exh. 1892
Stained glass artist. 38 Broad Street, Golden Square, London. † RA 1.

EGAN, Wilfrid B. Exh. 1901-5
4 Margravine Studios, W. Kensington, London † B 1, P 1, RBA 1.

EGERTON, Lady Alexander Exh. 1894-1918
London 1894; Ringwood, Hants 1918. † L 2, LS 1, SWA 2.

EGERTON, John C. Exh. 1899
Portrait painter. 18 Milsom Street, Bath. † RA 1.

EGERTON, Mrs. M. Exh. 1939
9 Royal Avenue, London. † SWA 1.

EGERTON, Will Exh. 1880-81
Landscape painter. 27 King Street, St. James's, London. † RBA 2.

EGESTORFF, Paul Exh. 1938-40
Landscape painter. Clarkeville, Baldoyle, Ireland. † RHA 5.

EGGAR, Catherine A See BANKS

EGGINTON, Frank J. b. 1908
Landscape painter. Son of Wycliffe E. q.v. Add: Teignmouth, Devon 1925; Dunfanaghy, Co. Donegal 1931; c/o Bank of Ireland, Belfast 1938. † FIN 127, GI 2, L 5, RCA 34, RHA 17, RI 5, RSA 1.

EGGINTON, Lucy Exh. 1932-34
Daughter of Wycliffe E. q.v. Add: Teignmouth, Devon. † RCA 5.

EGGINTON, Wycliffe 1875-1951
Landscape painter. b. Birmingham. R.I. 1912. Father of Frank and Lucy E. q.v. Add: Liscard, Cheshire 1895; Wallasey, Cheshire 1907; City School of Art, Liverpool 1909; Newton Abbot, Devon 1910; Teignmouth, Devon 1922. † FIN 832, GI 2, L 56, RA 11, RCA 73, RHA 2, RI 138, WG 34.

EGGISTON, William S. Exh. 1930
R.B.S.A. 1930. 70 Tennyson Road, Small Heath, Birmingham. † B 3.

EGIE, H. Exh. 1883-84
20 Belgrave Road, St. John's Wood, London. † B 2, L 1.

EGLEY, William Maw* 1826-1916
Historical, genre and illustrative painter. Son of William E. (1798-1870) the miniaturist. Add: 26 Bassett Road, Notting Hill, London. † B 12, L 7, M 5, RA 9, RBA 9, RHA 1, RI 2, ROI 6.

EGLIN, Jane M. Exh. 1888
370 Gt. Western Road, Glasgow. † GI 2.

EGNER, Maria* Exh. 1888
Rustic landscape painter. 30 Thurloe Place, S. Kensington, London. † RA 1.

EGREMONT, Maud Exh. 1905-15
Mrs. Burford Thorp. London 1905; Teddington, Middlesex 1915. † L 6.

EGSMOND, F. Exh. 1890
† TOO 1.

EGUSQUIZA, de See D

EHRKE, Julius Exh. 1889-90
Landscape painter. Rosslyn House, Gt. Malvern, Worcs. † RA 2.

EHRLICH, Georg 1897-1966
Sculptor, draughtsman and etcher. Studied Vienna Kunstgewerbeschule 1912-15. Exh. 1940. Add: 15 St. Peter's Square, London. † GI 1, RA 2.

EICHFIELD, Hermann Exh. 1886-88
20 Friedrich Strasse, Munich. † GI 2, RSA 1.

EICKEN, Miss E. von Lutzowski Exh. 1897
Berlin. † SWA 1.

EICKEN, Von See V

EICKHELBERG, W.H.* Exh. 1881
16 Avenue Trudaine, Paris. † RHA 3.

EICKLEBERG, M. Exh. 1881
20 Mortimer Street, Regent Street, London. † RHA 1.

EIJSKENS, Felix Exh. 1912
5 Rue de Bagneux, Paris. † RSA 1.

EKDAHL, Edmund G. Exh. 1918-1921
Landscape painter. 6 Chelsea Manor Studios, Flood Street, London. † RA 3.

EKENGREN, E. Exh. 1914
7 Scarsdale Studios, Stratford Road, Kensington, London. † RA 1.

EKSTRUM, Mons. Exh. 1882
16 Avenue Trudaine, Paris. † RHA 1.

ELAND, John Shenton 1872-1933
Portrait and figure painter. Add: London 1895-1913. Died in New York. † BG 11, L 6, LS 5, M 2, NG 3, P 1, RA 8, RCA 20, RI 2, ROI 4.

ELCOCK, George A. Exh. 1881-92
Landscape and figure painter. London. † D 3, M 3, RBA 5.

ELDER, Arthur John b. 1874
Landscape painter. 101 Cheyne Walk, Chelsea, London. † NEA 1.

ELDER, Clarence Exh. 1920-21
136 Wellington Street, Glasgow. † L 1, RSA 4.

ELDER, Dorothy Gertrude b. 1892
Nee Riley. Animal painter. Add: The Vicarage, Otford, Kent 1925. † RA 1.

ELDER, Ethel Harriet Exh. 1910-15
Figure painter. London. † NEA 11.

ELDER, Miss G. Exh. 1882
5 St. Bernard's Row, Edinburgh. † RSA 1.

ELDER, J. Exh. 1883-1901
Glasgow 1883 and 1901; Cathcart 1893. † GI 6.

ELDER, Miss J. Exh. 1940
† RI 1.

ELDER, James Exh. 1895-97
Muirhead, Chryston. † GI 2, RSW 1.

ELDER, J.F. Exh. 1896-98
33 Monteith Road, Glasgow. † GI 3.

ELDER, Miss Louie Exh. 1894-97
Figure painter. London. † NEA 2.

ELDER, Ralph H. Exh. 1880-85
274 Renfrew Street, Garnet Hill, Glasgow. † GI 5, RSA 3.

ELDERSHAW, John b. 1896
Landscape painter. b. Sydney, Australia. Studied Sydney Art School; L.C.C. Central School and Paris. Add: c/o D. Boxall, 14 Clifton Gardens, London 1927-28. † CHE 2, RA 1.

ELDERTON, Miss V.H. Exh. 1896
3 Upper Berkeley Street, London. † SWA 3.

ELDH, Carl Johan b. 1873
Swedish sculptor. Paris 1903; Stockholm 1932. † GI 4, RSA 3.

ELDRIDGE, Mildred E. b. 1909
Landscape and figure painter. b. Wimbledon. Add: Leatherhead, Surrey 1934; Chirk, N. Wales 1940. † BA 10, GOU 3, NEA 1, RA 11, RBA 1, RCA 2, RHA 2, ROI 1, RSA 4.

ELES, Von See V

ELEY, Miss Frances Exh. 1890
Miniature portrait painter. 23 Baker Street, London. † RA 2.

ELEY, Mary Exh. 1880-1903
Mrs. Gauntlett. Figure and domestic painter. A.S.W.A. 1900. Add: London. † D 10, FIN 1, L 4, M 2, RA 15, RBA 6, RI 8, ROI 1, SWA 22.

ELFVERSTON, Johan B.G. Exh. 1935-38
Sculptor. 18 Lambolle Place, Belsize Park, London. † RA 3.

ELGAR, R. Exh. 1937-38
Selwin House, Batsford, Moreton-in-Marsh, Glos. † NEA 1, ROI 1.

ELGIE, Howard Exh. 1880-81
Landscape painter. c/o Mr. Casey, 52 Stanhope Street, Euston Road, London. † RBA 2.

ELGOOD, Frank M. Exh. 1896-1918
Architect. 98 Wimpole Street, London. † RA 5.

ELGOOD, George Samuel 1851-1943
Painter and architect of gardens. Studied Royal College of Art. Travelled widely. R.I. 1882, R.O.I. 1883. Add: Leicester 1880; Tenterden, Kent 1909. † AB 1, B 10, BG 1, D 3, FIN 881, L 11, LEI 1, M 2, RI 107, ROI 8.

ELGOOD, Thomas Exh. 1903
90 New Walk, Leicester. † B 2.

ELIAS, Miss A. Exh. 1938
17 Chantry Road, Moseley, Birmingham. † B 1.

ELIAS, Alfred* Exh. 1881-1911
Landscape and rustic painter. London 1881; Chorley Wood, Herts. 1906. † G 1, GI 4, GOU 1, L 16, M 6, NG 1, RA 8, RBA 1, RE 1, RI 1, ROI 7, TOO 1.

ELIAS, Annette d. 1921
Landscape and flower painter. A.S.W.A. 1895, S.W.A. 1897. Add: 9 Vicarage Gardens, Kensington, London 1881; Niton, I.O.W. 1912. † B 12, BG 7, D 3, GI 2, L 22, M 4, NEA 2, NG 20, RA 28, RBA 9, RE 3, RI 2, ROI 10, RSA 2, SWA 53.

ELIAS, Arthur E. Exh. 1898-1906
Llanrwst, N. Wales 1898; Dean Close School, Cheltenham 1906. † L 7, RCA 9.

ELIAS, Mrs. Alice S. Exh. 1923
Holt House, Grassendale Park, Liverpool. † L 1.

ELIAS, Emily Exh. 1884-1909
Mrs. Alfred E. Landscape, figure and still life painter. R.M.S. 1898. Add: Paris 1884; Tonbridge, Kent 1892; London 1899; Chorley Wood, Herts. 1906. † L 6, LS 3, RA 5, RMS 17, SWA 9.

ELIASON, Miss Exh. 1894
Prince's Park Terrace, Liverpool. † L 1.

ELIENA, Olga Exh. 1930-39
Flower and landscape painter. 2B West End Mansions, 311 West End Lane, London. † FIN 3, GOU 6, NEA 3, RI 25.

ELIOT, C. Exh. 1906-7
128 Mount Street, Grosvenor Square, London. † RA 4.

ELIOT, Granville Exh. 1891
Figure painter. Woodstock, Slinford, Nr. Horsham, Sussex. † RA 1.

ELIOT, G.H. Exh. 1908
643 Fulham Road, London. † RI 1.

ELIOT, Maurice Exh. 1907
37 Boulevard de Clichy, Paris. † L 1.

ELIOT, Mrs. M.R. Exh. 1937-39
Birmingham. † B 4.

ELKAN, Benno b. 1877
Sculptor. Studied Royal Academy, Munich 1898-1901; Karlsruhe, Baden 1901-4 and Paris 1905-10. Add: 3 Warwick Avenue, London 1935. † RA 8.

ELLEBY, William Alfred Exh. 1883-1903
Landscape painter. Ashbourne, Derbys. † B 6, GI 7, L 5, M 12, N 19, RA 8, RBA 1, RSA 1.

ELLENOR, Laura K. Exh. 1893-1911
Flower, figure and still life painter. 39 Wandle Road, Upper Tooting, London. † L 2, RBA 6, SWA 5.

ELLERBECK, Kate Exh. 1895-1905
Liverpool 1895; Brimfield, Herefords. 1908. † L 2.

ELLERBY, Ethel Exh. 1890-1901
Manchester. † M 9.

ELLERTON-HILL, Frances Exh. 1923-24
† GOU 3.

ELLIDGE, Miss G.A. Exh. 1909-16
Oxton, Birkenhead. † L 17.

ELLINGHAM, S.G. Exh. 1932
22 Bonchurch Road, London. † RI 64.

ELLINGHAM, T.R. Exh. 1907-8
96 Effingham Road, Harringay, London. † D 7.

ELLINGTON, Douglas D. Exh. 1914
78 Rue Dutot, Paris. † RSA 1.

ELLIOT, Dorothy M. Exh. 1915-37
Painter and wood cut artist. Harpenden, Herts. 1915; Lewes, Sussex 1936; Sunderland 1937. † COO 4, I 2, L 1, SWA 1.

ELLIOT, Edward Exh. 1880-1911
Landscape, coastal and figure painter. R.B.A. 1884. Add: Abinger Hammer, Dorking, Surrey 1880; Hethersett, Wymondham, Norfolk 1881; Lowestoft 1895; Norwich 1905. † B 1, BRU 3, D 3, G 1, GI 5, L 14, M 11, RA 27, RBA 29, ROI 12.

ELLIOT, Miss E.M. Exh. 1940
Rowanlea, Clovenfords, Nr. Galashiels. † RSA 2.

ELLIOT, Mrs. L. Exh. 1912-14
63 Church Street, Preston, Lancs. † L 2.

ELLIOT, Mabel Exh. 1909-15
Newton STewart, Wigtown 1909; Barrhill, Ayrs. 1913. † RSA 3, RSW 1.

ELLIOT, M.S. Exh. 1881
34 Regent's Terrace, Edinburgh. † RSA 1.

ELLIOT, Marjorie Scott
See EVANS, Marjorie

ELLIOTT, Aileen Mary b. 1896
Mrs. H. Beale. Painter and etcher. Add: London 1921 and 1927; Lee on Solent, Hants 1922; Wokingham, Berks. 1932. † AR 1, L 4, RA 8, RBA 5, RSA 14, SWA 3.

ELLIOTT, Barbara G. Exh. 1920
Miniature portrait painter. The Corner Cottage, Hadley Green, Barnet, Herts. † RA 1.

ELLIOTT, Charlotte E. Exh. 1898-1903
Liverpool. † L 8, SWA 1.

ELLIOTT, Rev. Edmund Hamilton Exh. 1909-10
Petworth, Sussex. † LS 4.

ELLIOTT, Edward M. Exh. 1920-34
The Croft, Gorway, Walsall, Staffs. † B 20.

ELLIOTT, Miss E.M. Exh. 1889-1924
Walsall, Staffs. † B 23, RCA 32.

ELLIOTT, Frank b. 1858
Portrait, figure and landscape painter. Studied Royal College of Art and RA Schools. Assistant master University College School and Eton College. Add: 13 Langham Street, Portland Square, London 1884. † RA 1.

ELLIOTT, Fanny B. Exh. 1904
12 Westbourne Villas, Headingley, Leeds. † RCA 1.

ELLIOTT, F.J. Exh. 1938-40
Torquay, Devon. † RCA 4.

ELLIOTT, Grace L.M. Exh. 1906-18
Landscape and coastal painter. A.S.W.A. 1915. Add: London. † B 8, L 3, LS 9, RA 5, RI 1, ROI 1, SWA 21.

ELLIOTT, Mrs. Henrietta Exh. 1935
Etcher. Applegarth, Hartley, Longfield, Kent. † RA 1.

ELLIOTT, James Exh. 1882-97
Landscape painter. Manchester 1882; Bettws-y-coed 1887; London 1897. † B 6, GI 1, L 13, M 28, RA 12, RBA 1, ROI 2.

ELLIOTT, Kate E. Exh. 1881-86
Landscape, fruit and flower painter. 21 Hockley, Nottingham. † N 6.

ELLIOTT, Miss L.M. Exh. 1926
West Croft, Uphill Road, Weston-super-Mare. Som. † B 1.

ELLIOTT, Miss P. Exh. 1881-82
Flower Painter. Carrington, Notts. † N 4.

ELLIOTT, R. Exh. 1937
Argyll Cottage, Lee-on-Sea, Hants. † RBA 1.

ELLIOTT, Robert Exh. 1901-9
Dublin. † LS 3, RSA 14.

ELLIOT, Robinson 1814-1894
Religious, portrait, landscape and genre painter. Add: Newcastle on Tyne 1880; South Shields 1884. † RA 3, RI 2.

ELLIOT, Richard H. Exh. 1914
40 Carr Road, Nelson, Lancs. † RA 1.

ELLIOT, William Exh. 1898
22 Lenster Road, Rathmines, Dublin. † RHA 1.

ELLIOTT, William John Exh. 1935
Stained glass artist. 20 Fleetwood Street, Belfast. † RHA 1.

ELLIS, Aline Exh. 1933-40
Watercolour animal and figure painter and sculptor. Ebury Lodge, Little Hadham, Herts. † FIN 74, RA 1.

ELLIS, Arthur Exh. 1880-1918
Landscape, coastal and figure painter. † R.B.A. 1906. Married Lydia C. Louise E. q.v. Add: London 1880; Lewes, Sussex 1905; Seaford, Sussex 1913. † D 1, FIN 1, GI 1, L 2, LS 8, M 1, NEA 2, NG 5, RA 20, RBA 72, RI 8, ROI 6.

ELLIS, Agnes A. Exh. 1880-85
Landscape painter. 6 Bruce Grove, Tottenham, London. † SWA 4.

ELLIS, Alice Blanche Exh. 1880-1916
Flower painter. Hereford 1880; Hounslow, Middlesex 1900. † D 73, L 1, LS 22, RA 2, RBA 10, RI 1, SWA 4.

ELLIS, Annie Edith Exh. 1912-40
Landscape painter. 22 The Parade, Canford Cliffs, Bournemouth, Hants. † L 8, M 3, RA 4, RI 4.

ELLIS, Agnes M. Exh. 1923
Landscape painter. † WG 47

ELLIS, Bert Exh. 1890-92
Landscape and marine painter. London. † RBA 7.

ELLIS, Miss Beatrice E. Exh. 1903-4
Queen's Chambers, John Dalton Street, Manchester. † L 2, RCA 1.

ELLIS, Beryl M.Y. Exh. 1905
Shadingfield Hall, Wangford, Suffolk. † B 1.

ELLIS, Beryl S. Exh. 1937-38
Sculptor. London 1937; Broadstairs, Kent 1938. † RA 3.

ELLIS, Cecil P. Exh. 1907-24
Knotty Ash, Liverpool 1907; Liverpool 1922. † L 7.

ELLIS, C. Wynn d. 1915
Portrait and figure painter. London 1880 and 1908; Bishops Stortford, Herts 1895; Sandown, I.O.W. 1914. † D 3, L 1, NG 3, RA 16, RBA 1, RI 9.

ELLIS, Miss D. Exh. 1916
Beachcliffe Promenade, Hoylake, Cheshire. † L 1.

ELLIS, Dora b. 1902
Portrait and glass painter and teacher. Studied Glasgow School of Art. Add: 62 Gt. George Street, Glasgow 1925-26. † GI 2.

ELLIS, Mrs. Dewi Exh. 1918
79 West Regent Street, Glasgow. † GI 1.

ELLIS, Edwin* 1841-1895
Marine and landscape painter. b. Nottingham. Studied under Henry Dawson. N.S.A. 1885, R.B.A. 1875. Add: London 1880; Manchester 1893. † AG 11, B 4, D 6, FIN 1, G 7, GI 1, L 5, M 19, RA 13, RBA 56, RHA 2, RI 2, RSA 1 TOO 5.

ELLIS, Miss Elsie Exh. 1929
Ashlea Rock Park, Rock Ferry, Cheshire. † L 2.

ELLIS, Ernest Exh. 1903-5
Liverpool. † L 2.

ELLIS, Ethel E. Exh. 1884-85
North End, Hampstead, London. † SWA 2.

ELLIS, Edwin John Exh. 1888-99
Figure painter. London. † D 4, RA 2, ROI 2.

ELLIS, Eleanor Joan b 1904
Mrs. White. Painter and wood engraver. Exh. 1927-32. Add: London. † NEA 2, RBA 1, RED 2, RHA 1.

ELLIS, Mrs. Edith Kate Exh. 1906-25
Portrait painter. Eaglescliffe, Co. Durham 1906; Bedford 1914. † L 1, LS 2, RA 4.

ELLIS, Miss Edith Maud Exh. 1908
37 Prince's Gate, London. † LS 3.

ELLIS, Dr. F.W. Exh. 1932
68 Hagley Road, Edgbaston, Birmingham. † B 1.

ELLIS, H. Exh. 1921
34 Rylett Road, London. † RA 1.

ELLIS, Hilda M. Exh. 1928-29
40 South Castle Street, Liverpool. † L 8.

ELLIS, Horace N. Exh. 1914
† M 1.

ELLIS, Ivy Anne Exh. 1920-39
Wood engraver. Studied Birmingham School of Arts and Crafts. Add: Edgbaston, Birmingham. † B 27.

ELLIS, J. Exh. 1895
Hartley Heaton Chapel. † M 1.

ELLIS, John Exh. 1884
Landscape painter. Clovelly, North Devon. † RBA 1.

ELLIS, John Rogers Exh. 1932-34
68 Hagley Road, Edgbaston, Birmingham. † B 2.

ELLIS, Jeanie Wright Exh. 1917-32
nee Paulin. Portrait and animal painter. Black and white artist. Studied Glasgow School of Art. Sister of George Henry Paulin q.v. Add: Milngavie 1917; Bearsden 1932. † GI 9, RSA 2.

ELLIS, Miss K. Exh. 1886-87
31 Church Street, Harpurley. † M 3.

ELLIS, Miss K.M. Exh. 1899
212 Wellington Road, Handsworth, Birmingham. † B 2.

ELLIS, Miss L. Exh. 1888-89
13 Westbank Road, Devonshire Park, Birkenhead. † L 3.

ELLIS, Lionel b. 1903
Horse and flower painter and wood engraver. Studied Plymouth School of Art 1918-22. Royal College of Art 1922-25 (travelling scholarship 1925), Colarossi's, Paris, Florence and Rome. Painting master, Wimbledon School of Art. Exh. 1927-33. Add: London. † NEA 3, RED 45.

ELLIS, Mrs. Lumley Exh. 1939
Rustic figure painter. † AR 2.

ELLIS, Lydia C. Louise Exh. 1893-1940
nee Pringle. Married Arthur E. q.v. Portrait painter. Studied Paris and London. Add: London 1893; Brighton, Sussex 1909 and 1930; Seaford, Sussex 1916. † L 3, RA 2, RBA 7. RI 5.

ELLIS, Mackenzie Exh. 1924
† GOU 1.

ELLIS, Marian Exh. 1912-40
Painter and lithographer. b. Bridgwater, Som. Studied Central School of Art, London. Add: Southsea, Hants 1912; London 1917. † COO 8, GI 1, M 1, NEA 11, RA 15, RED 1, SWA 2.

ELLIS, Marjorie Exh. 1923
27 Greenherp Road, Liverpool. † L 1.

ELLIS, Paul H.* Exh. 1882-1908
Handsworth, Birmingham 1882; Rhyl, Wales 1908. † B 17, D 2, L 7, M 2, RA 1, RBA 7, RI 2, ROI 5, TOO 10.

ELLIS, Ralph Gordon b. 1885
Inn sign painter. Studied Slade School. Add: Chester 1919; Arundel, Sussex 1926. † G 1, I 1, L 2, NEA 1 RA 2.

ELLIS, Tristram* 1844-1922
Landscape painter and watercolourist. Initially an engineer on the District and Metropolitan Railway. Studied under Bonnat in Paris. Travelled widely. A.R.E. 1887. Add: London 1881; Dorking, Surrey 1900; Barnes, London 1906; † FIN 1, G 23, GOU 59, L 7, M 5, NG 46, RA 33, RE 34, RI 8.

ELLIS, W. Exh. 1882-94
10 Villa Road, Handsworth, Birmingham. † B 20, L 1, RHA 1.

ELLISON, Mrs. Exh. 1882
c/o Dr. Ellison, Windsor, Berks. † RHA 3.

ELLISON, Adeline Exh. 1900-1
Liverpool. † L 2.

ELLISON, A.F. Exh. 1885
Rectory, Queen's Road, Manchester. † M 2.

ELLISON, Miss Edith Exh. 1884-90
Portrait painter. London 1884; Old Vicarage House, Windsor, Berks 1886 † G 2, RA 5, ROI 1.

ELLISON, M.E. Exh. 1911
5 High Street, Bushey, Herts. † L 1.

ELLISON, Thomas b. 1866
Landscape painter. Add: St. Helens, Lancs. 1896, Glan Conway, Wales 1907; Wrexham, Wales 1921; Abergele 1933. † B 1, L 75, M 1, RA 11, RCA 185, RI 6.

ELLISON, W.S. Exh. 1882-1924
Liverpool. † L 4.

ELLISTON, Mrs. Dorothy E. Exh. 1932
Sculptor. Greenwood, Sollershott W., Letchworth, Herts. † RA 2.

ELLWOOD, George Montague 1875-1955
Interior decorator and designer. Studied Camden School of Art, Paris, Vienna, Berlin and Dresden. Joint Editor "Drawing and Design" 1916-24. Design master Camden School of Art. Exh. 1899-1915. Add: London. † L 1, RA 4.

ELLWOOD, Ida F. Exh. 1909
nee Ravaison. Flower painter. Married George Montague E. q.v. † BG 1.

ELMES, Gertrude Exh. 1904
Coleswood, Harpenden, Herts. † D 1, RCA 2.

ELMHIRST, Charles Cutts Exh. 1897-1912
Thorne, Nr. Doncaster, Yorks. † B 2, GI 4, LS 3, RA 1, RBA 3, RCA 7, RHA 2, RI 1.

ELMORE, Alfred W.* 1815-1881
Historical and genre painter. b. Clonakilty, Co. Cork. Studied RA Schools 1832. Lived in Paris 1833-39; Munich 1840 and Rome 1842-45. A.R.A. 1845, R.A. 1857. Add: 1 St. Albans Road, Victoria Road, Kensington, London 1880. † RA 2.

ELMORE, Miss Edith Exh. 1880-87
Flower painter. 1 St. Albans Road, Kensington, London. † RA 6, RBA 2, ROI 2.

ELMORE, Miss Fanny Mary Exh. 1882-84
Fruit painter. 85 Lansdowne Road, London. † B 2.

ELMORE, Richard Exh. 1882-86
Landscape and figure painter. 85 Lansdowne Road, London. † B 1, GI 1, L 4, M 1, RA 1, RHA 1.

ELMQUIST, Hugo Exh. 1898
Sculptor. 9 Rue des Fourneaux, Paris. † RA 1.

ELMSLIE, Miss Essil Exh. 1906-24
Figure and portrait painter. Add: London 1906 and 1919; Hemel Hempstead, Herts 1916. † GOU 1, L 1, LS 8, NEA 27.

ELPHICK, Mrs. A.A. Exh. 1940
Kendal, Westmorland. † RCA 1.

ELPHINSTONE, Archibald Howard 1865-1936
Landscape and seascape apinter. R.B.A. 1905. Add: London. † L 2, NG 1, P 3, RA 11, RBA 110, ROI 3.

ELPHINSTONE, Lucy C. Exh. 1939-40
Still life painter. 12 Grosvenor Place, London. † COO 1, GOU 3, SWA 1.

ELRINGTON, Julia F. Exh. 1900
Leamington, Warwicks. † B 1.

ELRINGTON, Miss I. Exh. 1900
Leamington, Warwicks. † B 1.

ELSE, Joseph b. 1874
Sculptor. Studied Royal College of Art. Modelling master and lecturer on anatomy Belfast School of Art. Principal of City of Nottingham School of Art. N.S.A. 1923, V.P.N.S.A. 1933-35. Add: London 1909 and 1911; Nottingham 1910 and 1918-38. † N 19, RA 18.

ELSLEY, Arthur John* b. 1861
Animal, figure and landscape painter. Exh. 1880-1927. Add: London. † B 2, GI 2, L 11, M 4, RA 51, RBA 6, ROI 13.

ELSON, R. Exh. 1883-84
133 St. George's Road, Peckham, London. † L 1, RI 2.

ELSTOW, William b. 1895
Portrait and subject painter. Studied Bolt Court, Fleet Street and St. Martin's School of Art. Add: 18 Girdlers Road, London 1928. † L 2, RA 1.

ELSWORTH, Alfred Exh. 1903-9
Landscape painter. Ivy House, Meanwood, Leeds. † RA 5.

ELTEN, Van see V

ELTON, Amy Exh. 1931
74 Ellison Road, Streatham Common, London. † RA 1.

ELTON, Gladys Exh. 1925-38
Mrs. Hughes. 3 Oxford Road, Ansdell, Lytham, Lancs. † L 3. M 2. RCA 3.

ELTON, Margery Exh. 1924
† RMS 1.

ELTON, Samuel J. Exh. 1880-84
Landscape and coastal painter. Westbrook Villa, Darlington, Durham. † RA 1, RBA 1.

ELVERY, Miss Beatrice see GLENAVY

ELVERY, Miss D.M. Exh. 1904-6
Rothbury, Foxrock, Co. Dublin. † RHA 3.

ELVERY, Wilfred Exh. 1929
† RMS 1.

ELWELL, Francis Edwin 1858-1922
American sculptor. 62 North Avenue, Cambridge, Mass. U.S.A. 1885. † RA 1.

ELWELL, Francis Kenneth* Exh. 1938-40
Interior and figure painter. Beverley, Yorks. † RA 3.

ELWELL, Frederick William 1870-1958
Portrait and domestic painter. Studied Lincoln School of Art, Royal Academy, Antwerp and Juliens, Paris. Married Mary Dawson E. q.v. A.R.A. 1931, R.A. 1938, R.O.I. 1917, R.P. 1933. "The Beverley Arms Kitchen" purchased by Chantrey Bequest 1919. Add: Paris 1895; Beverley, Yorks 1901. † B 1, GI 11, L 28, P 3, RA 110, RHA 1, ROI 26, RSA 2.

ELWELL, Jerome Exh. 1903
7 Primrose Hill Studios, Fitzroy Road, London. † ROI 1.

ELWELL, Mary Dawson b. 1874
nee Bishop. Landscape and interior painter. Studied under her husband Frederick William E. q.v. A.S.W.A. 1935. Add: The Bar House, Beverley, Yorks. † GI 17, L 6, M 1, RA 45, RBA 1, RSA 1, SWA 19.

ELWES, Cecilia 1874-1952
nee Forsyth. Flower painter. Studied under Stanhope Forbes, Newlyn, Penzance and Switzerland. Add: Bournemouth. † RI 1, ROI 1, RSW 1, SWA 2.

ELWES, Eleanor Mabel Exh. 1903-6
Miniature painter. Lee, London 1903; Gant, Belgium 1906. † B 4, L 3, M 4, NG 1, RA 2, RMS 1.

ELWES, Miss K. Exh. 1912
Moss Close, Manor Road, Bournemouth. † D 1.

ELWES, Mary Exh. 1913-25
Painter of gardens and lecturer. Travelled widely. Add: Woolbeding Rectory, Midburst 1913; Bramshott, Liphook 1925. † L 2, LS 3, RI 1.

ELWES, Simon 1902-1975
Portrait painter. b. Theddingworth, Rugby. Studied Slade School and Paris. R.P. 1934. Exh. 1927-39. Add: London. † GI 2, L 1, P 30, RA 22.

ELWES, W.C Exh. 1885
4 Durham Road, Portobello, Edinburgh. † RSA 3.

ELWIN, Mrs. Emma Exh. 1881
Portrait and still life painter. Add: 70 Field Strasse, Dusseldorf, Germany. † RHA 1.

ELWIN, Fountain Exh. 1887
Sculptor. Bolton Studios, Redcliffe Road, London. † RA 1.

ELWOOD, H.E. Exh. 1884-85
Nottingham. † N 6.

ELWOOD, Marian L. Exh. 1886-91
Flower painter. Beech Avenue, Sherood Rise, Nottingham. † N 13.

ELWORTHY, Miss E. Exh. 1884
Sunnyside, Wellington, Som. † D 1.

ELWORTHY, Miss E.W. Exh. 1915
134 Prince's Road, Liverpool. † L 1.

ELWORTHY, Rona Exh. 1928
Union Bank of Australia, 71 Cornhill, London. † RCA 1.

ELY, Mrs. Gertrude Exh. 1928-35
Flower painter. St. Leonards on Sea, Sussex. † RA 3, RBA 2.

ELY, John Exh. 1885-93
Architect. Manchester. † M 1, RA 1.

ELYAN, Jessica Exh. 1934
596 Clarkston Road, Glasgow. † GI 1.

EMANUEL, Miss D. Exh. 1918
30 Holland Park Avenue, London. † RA 1.

MANUEL, Frank Lewis 1865-1948
Painter, etcher, black and white artist, designer, teacher and writer. Studied University College, London, Slade School and Juliens, Paris. Chief Examiner Royal Drawing Society. Special artist with "Manchester Guardian" for many years. Travelled widely. "A Kensington Interior" purchased by Chantrey Bequest 1912. Exh. 1885-1939. Add: London. † BA 4, D 1, G 2, I 2, L 17, LS 5, M 3, NEA 7, P 1, RA 38, RBA 2, RE 1, RI 2, ROI 3, RSA 1.

EMANUEL, Mrs. F.R. Exh. 1908-15
Sculptor. 24 Westbourne Park Road, London. † L 1, RA 5.

EMBERTON, Joseph Exh. 1930-33
Architect. 136 Regent Street, London. † RA 3.

EMERIS, Frances R. Exh. 1886-89
Flower painter. The Rectory, Upton, St. Leonards, Glos. † RI 1, SWA 1.

EMERSON, C.E. Exh. 1881
20 Queen's Square, Bath. † D 1.

EMERSON, Ernest Exh. 1901-14
Architect. London. † RA 7.

EMERSON, E.C. Bomford Exh. 1895-99
Mrs. D.N. Landscape and coastal painter. Melton House, Belgrave, Leicester. † RID 10.

EMERSON, Robert Jackson b. 1878
Sculptor and teacher. Studied Leicester College of Art. R.B.S.A. 1925. Add: Rothley, Nr. Loughborough 1906; Wolverhampton 1913. † B 34, GI 2, RA 24, RMS 1, ROI 1.

EMERSON, Sybil Exh. 1908
Figure painter. Foxwold, Southbourne on Sea, Christchurch, Hants. † NEA 1.

EMERSON, Thomas H. Exh. 1934-38
Miniature painter. Acomb, Hexham, Northumberland. † M 1, RA 1.

EMERSON, Sir William c.1843-1924
Architect. Exh. 1888-1911. Add: London. † RA 10.

EMERY, Miss L. Exh. 1889-1906
Haywood Lodge, Leamington, Warwick. † B 14, L 1.

EMETT, Agnes Exh. 1905-10
12 Beech Range, Gorton, Manchester. † L 2, M 8.

EMETT, Frederick Rowland Exh. 1930-40
Coastal landscape painter. Birmingham. † B 13, NEA 1, RA 1.

EMILE, Paul Exh. 1911
Landscape painter. The Brook, Hammersmith, London. † LS 3, NEA 2.

EMILE-DOMERGUE, Jean Exh. 1925
Avenue du Main, Paris. † L 1.

EMMERSON, Miss E. Stevenson Exh. 1927-29
Darlington House, Balls Road, Birkenhead. † L 6.

EMMERSON, Henry H.* 1831-1895
Genre painter and illustrator of children's books. Studied Newcastle with William Bell Scott. Add: 16 John Street, Cullercoats, Newcastle on Tyne 1883. † RA 4, ROI 1.

EMMERSON, Jessie M. Exh. 1927
Darlington House, Balls Road, Birkenhead. † L 1.

EMMERSON, Phyllis K. Exh. 1913-25
Chelsea, London 1913; Glasgow 1924. † LS 3, M 1, NEA 1, RSA 1, RSW 5.

EMMETT, Miss E.E. Exh. 1904
64 Washington Square South, New York. † NG 1.

EMMONS, Robert Van Buren Exh. 1928-38
Portrait, figure, landscape and still life painter. London. † AG 27, RA 2, RED 1.

EMMOTT, Lady Constance Exh. 1896-1920
London 1896 and 1912; Barnard Castle 1908; Inveraray, N.B. 1916. † GI 2, M 1, NG 1, RA 2, RSA 3, SWA 2.

EMMS, John* 1843-1912
Sporting and animal painter. London 1880; Lyndburst, Hants 1887. † B 1, BRU 1, D 1, G 2, L 5, M 8, RA 14, RBA 19, RI 2, ROI 3.

EMPTMEYER, Clement Exh. 1883-88
Sculptor. London. † RA 3.

EMSLEY, Alexander Exh. 1927-34
71 Chancellor Street, Partick. † GI 2, RSA 2.

EMSLEY, Walter Exh. 1883-1927
Landscape painter. Manchester 1883 and 1899; Bushey, Herts 1896. † L 8, M 30, RA 5, RCA 8.

EMSLIE, Alfred Edward* 1848-1918
Genre and portrait painter. Brother of John Phillipps E. q.v. Married to Rosalie M. E. q.v. Spent 3 months walking tour Japan. R.P. 1892. A.R.W.S. 1888. Add: London 1880; Otford, Sevenoaks, Kent 1895. † AG 1, B 18, D 3, FIN 82, G 16, GI 1, L 18, LEI 71, M 26, NG 2, RA 54, RBA 11, RI 6, ROI 19, RWS 35.

EMSLIE, John Phillipps 1839-1885
Figure painter. Brother of Alfred Edward E. q.v. Add: 47 Gray's Inn Road, London 1880. † D 3, G 1, RA 1, RBA 2.

EMSLIE, Mrs. Rosalie M. d. c.1932
Miniature painter. Wife of Alfred Edward E. q.v. and mother of Rosalie E. q.v. R.M.S. 1909. Add: London 1887 and 1918; Otford, Sevenoaks, Kent 1895 and 1925. † B 10, G 2, GI 5, I 3, L 35, M 5, NEA 2, NG 27, P 15, RA 106, RBA 8, RI 3, RMS 79, ROI 3, RSW 1, RWS 1.

EMSLIE, Miss Rosalie M. b. 1891
Figure, portrait and landscape painter. Daughter of Alfred Edward and Rosalie M.E. q.v.Studied R.A. Schools. A.R.B.A. 1923, R.B.A. 1926. Add: London 1917 and 1932; Otford, Sevenoaks, Kents 1924. † GOU 5, L 2, RA 8, RBA 54, SWA 9.

ENDER, Miss C. Exh. 1883
Mulberry Cottage, Townsend Lane, Liverpool. † L 1.

ENDERBY, Samuel G. Exh. 1886-1915
Portrait and figure painter. London 1886 and 1895, Boston, Lincs 1890; Newlyn, Penzance 1892. † L 5, M 11, P 5, RA 13.

ENEFER, Miss E. Exh. 1923
† SWA 2.

ENFIELD, Miss Anna Exh. 1894-1905
Figure and still life painter. Bramcote, Nottingham. † L 4, M 1, N 19, RSA 2.

ENFIELD, Frances Exh. 1881
29 Arboretum Street, Nottingham. † N 1.

ENFIELD, Henry* Exh. 1880-1911
Landscape, coastal and figure painter. N.S.A. 1908. Add: London 1880 and 1893; Antwerp 1883; Nottingham 1894. † B 2, L 5, N 18, RA 6, RBA 2.

ENFIELD, Mary P. Exh. 1892-1914
Miniature painter. R.M.S. 1900, A.N.S.A. 1914, N.S.A. 1915. Add: Bramcote, Nr. Nottingham. † L 4, N 6, NG 1, RA 11, RMS 22, RSA 2.

ENGEL, Celia Exh. 1939
Portrait painter. 12 Holland Villas Road, London. † RA 1.

ENGEL, Joseph Exh. 1888
Sculptor. 17 Burton Street, Burton Crescent, London. † RA 3.

ENGELBACH, Florence 1872-1951
nee Neumegen. Portrait and flower painter. b. Spain. Studied Slade School. R.O.I. 1932, A.S.W.A. 1908. Add: Old Benwell, Newcastle 1907; London 1915 and 1936; Northfield, Warwick 1933 and 1939. † BA 46, GOU 6, L 2, LEF 28, LEI 36, NEA 1, RA 6, RHA 1, ROI 21, RSA 2, SWA 11, TOO 2.

ENGLAND, Miss Exh. 1880
Landscape painter. Tan Vale Terrace, Crediton, Devon. † SWA 1.

ENGLAND, Bernard Exh. 1911-12
Cavendish Park, Rock Ferry, Cheshire. † L 4.

ENGLAND, Mrs. Florence Exh. 1937-40
Watercolour painter. Windyridge, Pentire, Newquay 1937; London 1940. † RI 4, RSA 2, RSW 2, SWA 2.

ENGLAND, M. Douglas Exh. 1923-25
2 Onslow Gardens, Muswell Hill, London. † GOU 2, L 3.

ENGLAND, Norah b. 1890
Mrs. A.G.S. Figure and portrait painter. A.R.B.A. 1920; S.W.A. 1922. Exh. 1919-28. Add: 10 Porchester Place, London. † CON 22, I 8, L 3, P 3, RA 3, RBA 7, RI 2, SWA 5.

ENGLEBACK, Lilian Exh. 1906-9
Meadowside, King Charles Road, Surbiton, Surrey. † L 24.

ENGLEFIELD, Arthur Exh. 1891-1904
Portrait, figure and landscape painter. St. Albans, Herts. 1891; Gloucester 1893; Stonehouse, Glos. 1899; Longford, Glos. 1901. † L 2, M 1, P 1, RA 10, RI 1.

ENGLEHEART, Lt. Col. Evelyn L. Exh. 1906-21
Landscape painter. Travelled widely. 6 Charles Street, Berkeley Square, London. † B 2, L 2, LS 3, RI 3, WG 21.

ENGLIER Exh. 1887
9 Rue Cherche, Midi, Paris. † M 1.

ENGLISH, C.W. Exh. 1917
36 Mecklenburgh Square, London. † RA 1.

ENGLISH, E. Exh. 1911
Staple Inn Buildings, London. † RA 2.

ENGLISH, Grace d. 1956
Painter and etcher. Studied Slade School 1912-14, Paris and etching at South Kensington 1921. Add: London. † G 1, I 1, L 2, NEA 11, P 4, RA 16, RCA 1, RHA 3, RSA 5, SWA 6.

ENGLISH, Norman H. Exh. 1930-40
Sutton Coldfield 1930; Wylde Green 1940. † B 4.

ENGLISH, Stanley Sydney Smith b. 1908
Sculptor. 426 Fulham Road, London 1939. † RA 5.

ENGLISH, T.J. Exh. 1885
128 Fulham Road, London. † RE 1.

ENJOLRAS, Delphin* b. 1865
French painter. Exh. 1938. † COO 1.

ENNESS, Augustus William* b. 1876
Landscape painter. A.R.B.A. 1923, R.B.A. 1925. Add: Whitby, Yorks. 1905; London 1915-37. † CHE 2, D 10, FIN 67, GI 4, L 5, M 2, RA 9, RBA 43, RI 2, RID 4, ROI 40, RSA 1, RSW 1.

ENNIS, George Pearce b. 1884
American artist. Exh. 1936. † RI 2.

ENNIS, J. Exh. 1888
Lyndhurst, Hants. † RI 1.

ENNIS, Miss K. Exh. 1920-29
Sandymount, Ireland 1920; Dublin 1921. † RHA 14, RI 3.

ENOCH-WILLIAMS, T. Exh. 1938
† M 1.

ENOCK, Arthur Henry Exh. 1882-1912
Watercolour landscape painter. Birmingham 1882; Dartmouth, Devon 1889 and 1896; Torquay, Devon 1892; Newton Abbott, Devon 1900. † AG 4, B 25, D 1, DOW 2, L 3, LS 3, M 2, RHA 1, RI 13, RSA 2.

ENSOR, Mrs. Henry M. Exh. 1897
1 Lynch's Quay, Queenstown, Ireland. † RMS 1.

ENSOR, James* 1860-1949
Belgian painter. 21 Rampe de Flandre, Ostend. Exh. 1905-15. † I 11.

ENTHOVEN, Julia Exh. 1889-95
Flower painter. The Gable House, Sydenham, Kent. † B 2, RA 1.

ENTWISTLE, Miss Gladys see LINES

ENTWISTLE, Helen Exh. 1906-10
Victoria Park, Manchester 1906; Southport, Lancs. 1908. † L 3, M 10.

ENTWISTLE, Hilda Exh. 1927-29
7 Ormonde Street, Liscard, Wallasey, Cheshire. † L 4.

ENTWISTLE, Mrs. Vivienne Exh. 1924-40
Miniature portrait painter. London. † RA 1, RI 5.

EPINETTE, Mlle. Exh. 1881
Engraver. 6 St. James' Terrace, Regent's Park, London. † RA 1.

EPPS, Miss J. Exh. 1914
95 Upper Tulse Hill, London. † RA 1.

EPPS, Mary C.L. Exh. 1931
Portrait painter. Russetings, Loudwater, Rickmansworth, Herts. † RA 1.

EPRILE, Cecil J. Exh. 1935-39
Architect. 107 Jermyn Street, London. † RA 3.

EPSTEIN, Jacob* 1880-1959
Sulptor and painter. b. New York of Russian-Polish parents. Studied Arts Students League, New York and Juliens, Paris. Became British suject 1907. Founder member London Group 1913. "Nan" (1909) purchased by Chantrey Bequest 1922, "Albert Epstein" in 1934 and "Mrs. Mary McEvoy" (1910) in 1953. Add: London. † BK 2, COO 5, G 2, GI 12, GOU 1, I 3, L 8, LS 8, NEA 1, RA 1, RED 74, RSA 11, RSW 6, TOO 76.

ERIAH, Miss S. Exh. 1890
9 Brondesbury Villas, Kilburn, London. † SWA 1.

ERICHSEN, Miss B. Exh. 1912
6 Strandgade, Copenhagen, Denmark. † LS 5

ERICHSEN, Nelly Exh. 1883-97
Figure and domestic painter. London. † L 4, RA 15, RBA 3, ROI 1, SWA 5.

ERICHSON, Dora Exh. 1908-18
Landscape painter. Paris 1908; London 1916. † LS 11, NEA 2.

ERIKSSON, Christian b. 1858
Swedish sculptor. Maria Prastgardsgata 3, Stockholm. † RSA 2.

ERISTOFF, Princess Maria d. 1934
Russian artist. Exh. 1915-16. † P 3.

ERNI, Hans* b. 1909
Swiss painter. Exh. 1936. † LEF 3.

ERNLE, the Lady Barbara see HAMLEY

ERNST, Max* 1891-1976
Painter and sculptor. Exh. 1926-38. † CHE 8, RED 4.

ERNST, Rudolph* Exh. 1886-1911
Paris. † GI 3, L 6, M 1, TOO 3.

ERSKINE, the Hon. Lady Exh. 1903-25
Watercolour landscape painter. Westwood Lodge, Windlesham, Surrey. † D 1, SWA 2, WG 57.

ERSKINE, Miss C.M. Exh. 1881-1906
Landscape painter. Ackrington, Northumberland 1881; Stamford 1906. † SWA 2.

ERSKINE, Edith E.H. Exh. 1886-87
Flower and landscape painter. 66 Oxford Terrace, Hyde Park, London. † B 3, RA 2, SWA 1.

ERSKINE, Gwladys Exh. 1909-30
Mrs. Frederick Pollock. Hoylake, Cheshire. † L 24.

ERSKINE, Henry Exh. 1884-1929
Glasgow. † GI 11, L 5, RSA 3, RSW 11.

ERSKINE, W.C. Exh. 1881
Landscape painter. 26 Castle Street, Edinburgh. † RSA 2.

ERTZ, Edward Frederick 1862-1954
Painter, etcher and wood engraver. b. Illinois, U.S.A. Studied New York and Paris. Professor of drawing and painting at Academy Delecluse, Paris 1892-99. Married Ethel E. q.v. R.B.A. 1902. Add: Paris 1899; Polperro, Cornwall 1900; Yealmpton, Devon 1904; Slapton, Nr. Kingsbridge, Devon 1911; Pulborough, Sussex 1913. † GI 7, L 12, LS 14, M 1, RA 14, RBA 30, RI 3, ROI 2.

ERTZ, Ethel Horsfall Exh. 1897-1918
nee Horsfall. Miniature painter. Married Edward E. q.v. A.S.W.A. 1912, S.A.W.A. 1919. Add: London 1897, Polperro, Cornwall 1901, Yealmpton, Devon 1905, Slapton, Nr. Kingsbridge, Devon 1908; Pulborough, Sussex 1914. † L 6, M 1, RA 7, RBA 1, RI 1, SWA 11.

ERWOOD, Ada Exh. 1903-4
Portrait painter. London. † RA 2.

ERZIA, Stepan Exh. 1934
Sculptor. Florida 940, Buenos Aires. † RA 1.

ESCHKE, Prof. Hermann Exh. 1881-85
Landscape painter. 11 Apostel Kirche, Berlin. † RA 1, RBA 1.

ESCHKE, Prof. Richard Exh. 1884-89
Landscape and coastal painter. Notting Hill, London 1884; Berlin 1889. † B 1, L 1, RA 1, RBA 2, ROI 1.

ESCOMBE, Anne Exh. 1887
The Grove, Penshurst, Kent. † L 1.

ESCOMBE, Miss E.N. Exh. 1927
3 South Park, Sevenoaks, Kent. † L 2.

ESCOMBE, Jane* Exh. 1882-87
Penshurst, Tonbridge, Kent. † L 2, M 1, ROI 3.

ESCOSURA, Leon Y.* 1840-1901
Spanish painter. 74 Newman Street, Oxford Street, London 1882. † RA 1.

ESCOULA, Jean Exh. 1906
193 Rue de Vaugirard, Paris. † L 1.

ESHELBY, Alan Exh. 1925
Kingsway House, 103 Kingsway, London. † L 3.

ESHELBY, J.D. Exh. 1899
49 Princess Street, Leicester. † N 4.

ESPLIN, Mabel Exh. 1907
39 Smith Street, Chelsea, London. † L 2.

ESPLIN, Tom Exh. 1935
Links Road, Leven. † RSW 1.

ESQUIZA, R.H. Exh. 1880
c/o Spanish Ambassador, London. † G 1.

ESSEN, Van see V

ESSERY, Grace Exh. 1902-5
Tewkesbury 1902, Warwick 1905. † B 5, L 2.

ESSEX, Miss O. Exh. 1929.
20th Century Club, Stanley Gardens, London. † L 3.

ESSEX, Thomas R. Exh. 1888-1911
Sculptor. London. † L 6, RA 10.

ESSON, Miss M. Exh. 1911
52 Hamilton Road, Oxford. † RA 1.

ESTALL, William Charles* Exh. 1880-1926
Landscape painter. Ripley, Surrey 1880; Manchester 1884; Pulborough, Sussex and London 1888. † D 1, G 2, GI 3, L 1, M 5, NEA 16, RA 4, RBA 10, RI 1, ROI 5.

ESTCOURT, Frank Exh. 1935
Stockport, Lancs. † RCA 1.

ESTCOURT, Miss F.J. Exh. 1892-93
Bushey, Herts. † ROI 2.

ESTE, Florence 1860-1926
Watercolour landscape painter. b. U.S.A., died France. Exh. 1913. † FIN 5.

ESTY, Edward Exh. 1916
Glebe Studio, Pulborough, Sussex. † RSA 1.

ETCHEVERRY, Hubert Denis b. 1867
French portrait painter. Exh. 1906 and 1924. Paris. † L 2, RA 1.

ETHELSTON, Edmund Exh. 1889-1902
Landscape and figure painter. 58 Bedford Gardens, Campden Hill, London 1890; Wimborne, Dorset 1901. † RBA 1, RID 10.

ETHERIDGE, Mrs. Florence Payne Exh. 1899-1909
Leamington, Warwicks. 1899; London 1910. † B 1, LS 14, RA 1, RI 1.

ETHERIDGE, Ken Exh. 1934
Ammanford, Carmarthenshire. † RCA 2.

ETHERINGTON, Miss Lilian Mary see REYNOLDS

ETHRIDGE, H.A. Exh. 1882
Landscape painter. c/o G.A. White, Charterhouse. † RBA 1.

EULER, Margaret Ida Exh. 1927-40
Figure and landscape painter. London 1927; Bromley, Kent 1940. † RA 4.

EURICH, Richard Ernst* b. 1903
Figure and landscape painter. Studied Bradford School of Arts and Crafts 1920-24 and Slade School 1924-26. "Antwerp" purchased by Chantrey Bequest 1940. War artist to the Admiralty 1940-45. Add: London 1927. † BK 2, GOU 48, L 4, LEF 1, LEI 1, M 2, NEA 7, RA 5, RED 144, TOO 5.

EUSTACE, Violet b. 1875
Landscape painter. Studied Slade School. b. Wolseley Hall, Staffs. Add: Wokingham, Berks. 1901; Lymington, Hants. 1933. † NEA 6, RBA 1, SWA 5.

EVA, Charles Andrew b. 1867
Figure painter. b. Penzance. Studied Royal College of Art. Acting Principal Hammersmith School of Arts and Crafts. Headmaster LCC School of Art, Hackney. Exh. 1898-1907. Add: 28 Cranbrook Road, Chiswick, London. † RA 2.

EVA, Sofie F. Exh. 1914-23
nee Martin. Enameller. Married Charles Andrew E. q.v. Add: 3 Cleveland Avenue, Chiswick, London. † RA 5.

EVANS, Miss A. Exh. 1916-29
Gwalia, W. Derby, Liverpool. † L 6, RA 1.

EVANS, Alfred Exh. 1904
45 Crane's Buildings, Church Street, Liverpool. † L 1.

EVANS, Alfred Exh. 1919-21
Bryn Crafnant, Trefriw, Wales. † RCA 2.

EVANS, Miss Amy Exh. 1880-83
Flower painter. Maisonette, Crystal Park, London. † D 1, RBA 1.

EVANS, Arthur F. Exh. 1912
16 Cook Street, Liverpool. † L 1.

EVANS, Mrs. Bernard Exh. 1888
1 Mornington Road, Regents Park, London. † RBA 1.

EVANS, Miss B. Hope Exh. 1896
The Spring, Kenilworth, Warwicks. † B 1.

EVANS, Bernard Walter 1843-1922
Watercolour landscape painter. b. Birmingham. R.B.A. 1879, R.I. 1892, H.R.I. 1915. Add: London. † AG 1, B 5, CON 1, DOW 3, L 16, M 2, RA 8, RBA 41, RCA 3, RHA 8, RI 32, RSA 3, WG 6.

EVANS, Miss C. Exh. 1903
20 Apsley Road, Clifton, Bristol. † SWA 2.

EVANS, Charlotte Exh. 1921
1 Castle Esplanade, Nicholas Street, Chester. † L 1.

EVANS, David b. 1895
Sculptor and carver. Studied Manchester School of Art, Royal College of Art and RA Schools (British Institute Scholarship 1921, Landseer Scholarship 1922). Add: London 1921 and 1933; Michigan, U.S.A. 1930; Welwyn Garden City, Herts. 1940. † GI 3, L 5, M 2, RA 26.

EVANS, Edmund 1826-1905
Etcher. Witley, Surrey 1880. † RA 1.

EVANS, Eleanor Exh. 1911
Figure painter. † BRU 1.

EVANS, Ernest Exh. 1898
Architect. 15 Bloomsbury Street, London. † RA 1.

EVANS, E.H. Exh. 1916
61 Heathfield Road, Liverpool. † L 1.

EVANS, Edmund William Exh. 1880-1900
Landscape painter. London 1880 and 1893; High Barnet, Herts. 1891. † RA 14, RBA 5, RHA 3.

EVANS, Frank Exh. 1922
c/o Harrison and Cox, 109 Colmore Row, Birmingham. † B 1.

EVANS, Mrs. F.M. Exh. 1880-81
Maisonette, Crystal Palace Park, London. † D 3.

EVANS, Frederick M.* Exh. 1888-1916
Figure and domestic painter. London 1888 and 1916; Penzance, Cornwall 1895. † B 1, DOW 2, GOU 4, L 7, M 3, RA 12, RI 23.

EVANS, Godfrey Exh. 1899
Coningsby, Belmont Park, Belfast. † RHA 1.

EVANS, Gwendoline Edith Marion b. 1898
Illustrator, animal and portrait painter and wood engraver. Studied Slade School, Westminster Technical Institute and under Walter Sickert and Sylvia Gosse. Exh. 1917-39. Add: London. † CHE 1, COO 30, GOU 24, I 2, NEA 12, RA 2, SWA 1.

EVANS, Gwendolen M. Exh. 1916-28
Landscape painter. Nottingham. † N 11.

EVANS, G.M.P. Exh. 1916
Mrs. Harvey Blake. Bury, Lancs. † L 1.

EVANS, Herbert Davies Exh. 1883-84
Flower painter. 31 Gordon Square, London. † RBA 3.

EVANS, Herbert E. Exh. 1893-1903
Fruit painter. London. † GI 1, RA 3, RBA 5, RI 6, ROI 5, RSW 2.

EVANS, Henry J. Exh. 1935-36
Chesham, Bucks. † RCA 2.

EVANS, Helena M. Exh. 1891-1911
Flower painter. Trevaughan, Carmarthen, Wales. † RBA 1, RI 4, SWA 2.

EVANS, H.P. Exh. 1930
† L 2.

EVANS, John Exh. 1880-92
Landscape painter. 4 Vanbrugh Terrace, Blackheath, London. † B 10, D 20, L 5, M 7, RA 2, RBA 10, RHA 2, RI 16.

EVANS, Mrs. Juliet E. Exh. 1928-39
Edgbaston, Birmingham 1928; Solihull, Warwicks. 1937. † B 18.

EVANS, J.M. Exh. 1895
136 Wellington Street, Glasgow. † GI 1.

EVANS, Kate Exh. 1884
Flower painter. Trosnant, Beulah Hill, Upper Norwood, London. † RA 1.

EVANS, Leslie Exh. 1930-31
Wood engraver and etcher. 276 Green Street, Forest Gate, London. † RA 2.

EVANS, Lena M. Exh. 1890
Flower painter. 38 Gower Street, Bedford Square, London. † RBA 1, SWA 1.

EVANS, Linton W. Exh. 1914
21 Belgrade Road, Tyndall's Park, Clifton, Bristol. † M 1.

EVANS, Miss M. Exh. 1917
Beckenham, Kent. † SWA 2.

EVANS, Miss M. Exh. 1915-29
Gwalia, Sandfield Park, Liverpool. † L 43.

EVANS, Marjorie Exh. 1880-1904
Mrs. A. Scott Elliot. Flower painter. R.S.W. 1891 (resigned 1902). Add: London 1880 and 1897; Greenock 1887; Richmond Hill, Surrey 1892; Aberdeen 1895. † DOW 1, L 1, NG 3, RA 2, RSA 4, RSW 6, SWA 2.

EVANS, Mary Exh. 1892-94
Trevaughan, Carmarthen, Wales. † ROI 3.

EVANS, Maud Exh. 1899-1901
Alpha House, East India Road, London. † L 1, RBA 2.

EVANS, Moira Exh. 1938
52 Hogarth Road, London. † SWA 1.

EVANS, Miss M.A. Exh. 1882-98
Highfield, Wylde Green, Birmingham 1882; Bushey, Herts. 1898. † B 28, L 6, M 1, SWA 6.

EVANS, Molly B. Exh. 1895-96
Domestic painter. The Red House, Bushey, Herts. † RA 1, SWA 3.

EVANS, Miss M.E. Exh. 1889-91
Landscape painter. Friary Cottage, Winchester, Hants. † L 1, RID 10.

EVANS, Myfanwy Lloyd Exh. 1903-8
Bryn Llywd, Menai Bridge, Anglesey, Wales. † L 1, RCA 5.

EVANS, Merlyn Oliver b. 1910
Figure painter. "The Conquest of Time" (1934) purchased by Chantrey Bequest 1966. Add: 15 Abbotsford Avenue, Rutherglen 1929. † GI 1, LEF 7, RSA 2.

EVANS, Miss N.H.P. Exh. 1899-1925
Tenby, Wales. † B 3, L 1.

EVANS, Powys Arthur Lenthall b. 1899
Painter, cartoonist and draughtsman. Studied Slade School, Westminster School and under Walter Sickert and Sylvia Gosse. Add: London. † CG 27, CHE 2, COO 30, GOU 24, M 2, NEA 3.

EVANS, P. Hazelden Exh. 1908-11
New Brighton, Cheshire 1908; Liverpool 1911. † L 3.

EVANS, Rachel Bridget Exh. 1925-31
Painter and wood engraver. Studied Slade School. Add: 11 Gayton Crescent, Hampstead, London. † GOU 17, M 1, NEA 2.

EVANS, Rufus E. Exh. 1904-40
Newcastleton, Roxburghshire, N.B. † GI 1, RSA 8, RSW 15.

EVANS, Sebastian Exh. 1881
Figure painter. Heathfield, Alleyn Park, West Dulwich, London. † RA 1.

EVANS, Samuel H. Exh. 1929
Architect. 17 Buckingham Street, London. † RA 1.

EVANS, Samuel T.G.* 1829-1904
Watercolour painter. Drawing master at Eton. A.R.W.S. 1858, R.S.W. 1897. Add: Eton College, Berks. 1880. † B 3, L 6, RWS 68.

EVANS, T. Exh. 1890
Leanbeds, Conway, Wales. † L 2.

EVANS, Tim Exh. 1893-1923
Liverpool 1893; Birkenhead 1894; Llanbedr, Talycafn, Wales 1897. † L 9, RCA 18.

EVANS, Miss T.P. Exh. 1922-28
4 Poplar Avenue, Grantham Road, Sparkbrook, Birmigham. † B 7.

EVANS, Vincent b. 1896
Painter, etcher and teacher. Studied Swansea School of Art and Royal College of Art. Add: Ystalyfera, Glamorgan 1920; London 1936. † NEA1, RA 5, RCA 1.

EVANS, Wilfred Exh. 1880-1905
Ecclesiastical, interior and still life painter. Add: London. † B 2, D 7, M 1, RBA 9, RHA 2.

EVANS, Will Exh. 1935-40
Swansea, Wales. † RCA 19.

EVANS, William Exh. 1903
75 Ullett Road, Liverpool. † L 1.

EVANS, William Charles Exh. 1886
Architect. 3A Poet's Corner, Westminster Abbey, London. † RA 1.

EVANS, William E. Exh. 1889-1909
Figure and domestic painter. London. † L 2, RA 6, RBA 1, RI 6.

EVANS, W.J. Exh. 1897
36 Clarence Road, Sparkhill, Birmingham. † B 1.

EVANS, Wilfred Muir Exh. 1887-1908
Portrait and figure painter. Bushey, Herts. 1887; Richmond, Surrey 1899; Southwold, Suffolk 1907; London 1908. † FIN 1, M 1, NG 2, RA 6, RID 1, ROI 3.

EVANS, W. Sidney Exh. 1888-1924
Eton College, Berks. 1888; Harborne, Birmingham 1920. † B 7, D 31, G 4, RI 1.

EVANS-HUGHES, Robert b. 1896
Landscape and figure painter. Studied Royal Art Society, Sydney, N.S.W. and LCC School of Art. Add: St. Elmo, Victoria Avenue, Craigydon, Llandudno, Wales. † RCA 7.

EVE, George d. c.1914
Etcher and illustrator. A.R.E. 1894, R.E. 1903. Add: London. † L 6, RA 25, RE 82.

EVE, Miss J.M. Exh. 1885
Blackburn House, Southgate, London. † SWA 2.

EVELYN, Edith Exh. 1886-94
Portrait painter. London. † RA 5, ROI 6, SWA 2.

EVELYN, Henrietta Exh. 1903
Wootton Place, Nr. Dorking, Surrey. † NG 1.

EVELYN, Miss M.A. Exh. 1912
Malvern, Oampit Hill, Lewisham, Kent. † RA 1.

EVELYN-SMITH, Mrs. M. Exh. 1938
† RI 1.

EVELYN-SMITH, Miss M.A. Exh. 1918
48 Sandbourne Road, Brockley, London. † RA 1.

EVERALL, Walter Exh. 1924-32
7 Beaconsfield Street, Liverpool. † L 4.

EVERARD, Miss Alice Exh. 1905
9 Augusta Road, Ramsgate, Kent. † L 1, RA 1.

EVERARD, Bertha Exh. 1911-23
nee King. Landscape painter. b. London. Add: Bonnefoi, E. Transvaal, South Africa 1911; Harpenden, Herts. 1921. † GOU 1, RA 2.

EVERARD, C.S. Exh. 1935-36
Horse Shoe Studio, St. Ives, Cornwall. † B 2.

EVERARD, Mrs. Dorothy Exh. 1936-39
Dragon Studio, Norway Lane, St. Ives, Cornwall. † B 2, P 1, SWA 4.

EVERART, Mme. Martha Exh. 1905
233 bis Rue du Raubourg, St. Honore, Paris. † L 1.

EVERDINGEN, Van see V

EVERETT, Ethel Fanny Exh. 1900-39
Portrait painter of children and illustrator of children's books. Studied RA Schools. Add: Wimbledon 1900; Kensington, London 1915. † AR 1, COO 2, L 1, LS 5, RA 7, RMS 5, SWA 9, WG 96.

EVERETT, E.M. Exh. 1907
3 Underhill Road, London. † D 2.

EVERETT, Mrs. Edith M.L. Exh. 1934
Portrait painter. Chelsea Studios, 416 Fulham Road, London. † RA 1.

EVERETT, Edwin W. Exh. 1880-84
Landscape and figure painter. London 1880; Totton, Southampton 1883. † M 1, RBA 6, RI 1.

EVERETT, Frederic Exh. 1882-90
Landscape and figure painter. 16 Bexley Road, Erith, Kent. † L 1, RA 2, RBA 1.

EVERETT, Herbert Exh. 1900-4
Landscape and coastal painter. 51 Fitzroy Street, London 1900; Enniskerry, Co. Wicklow 1904. † L 1, NEA 1, RHA 4.

EVERETT, John Exh. 1908-36
Marine and landscape painter and etcher. Corfe Castle, Dorset 1908; Broadstone, Dorset 1911; London 1924. † FIN 60, GI 2, GOU 13, I 4, L 9, NEA 8, RSA 4.

EVERETT, Penelope Mary see GOODMAN

EVERGOOD, Miles Exh. 1918-19
5 Turner's Studios, Glebe Place, Chelsea, London. † I 3.

EVERIDGE, Jane Exh. 1912
19 Lovelace Road, Surbiton, Surrey. † RHA 4.

EVERIDGE, Jean Exh. 1909
† P 1.

EVERINGTON, Miss E.A. Exh. 1936
† P 2.

EVERINGTON, Miss K.E. Exh. 1920
One Oak, Bickley, Kent. † SWA 2.

EVERINGTON, P. Exh. 1930-39
Chislehurst, Kent. † SWA 3.

EVERITT, W. Exh. 1905-11
Miniature portrait painter. 55 Baker Street, Portman Square, London. † L 1, NG 2, RA 15.

EVERS, Inez Exh. 1915
c/o Mrs. Edwards, 34 Norfolk Square, London. † L 1.

EVERS, Mrs. Joanna Exh. 1939
Portrait and figure painter. 19 Lansdowne Walk, London. † P 1, RA 1.

EVERS, Miss M. Exh. 1924
9 Eastnor Grove, Leamington Spa, Warwicks. † B 1.

EVERSEN, Jan H.* Exh. 1936-39
Still life painter. Maida Vale, London 1936; The Hague, Holland 1939. † RA 1, ROI 5.

EVERSHED, Dr. Arthur 1836-1919
Landscape painter and etcher. Studied under Alfred Clint. A.R.E. 1891, R.E. 1898, H.R.E. 1914. Add: London 1881; Fishbourne, Chichester, Sussex 1896. † B 2, RA 23, RE 124, RI 2, ROI 4.

EVERSHED, Katherine (Kitty) M.F. Exh. 1913-38
Landscape painter. A.S.W.A. 1933, S.W.A. 1934. Add: 60 South Edwardes Square, London. † B 7, BG 48, GI 2, L 6, RHA 15, RMS 2, RSA 2.

EVERY, Miss A.V. Exh. 1904
18 Montagu Street, Portman Square, London. † L 1.

EVERY, Miss E.M. Exh. 1889-1902
Eggington Hall, Burton-on-Trent 1889; 18 Montagu Street, Portman Square, London 1900. † D 1, RI 1, SWA 1.

EVERY, George H. Exh. 1885-1905
Engraver. London. † RA 9.

EVES, Miss E.M. Exh. 1909-11
Miniature portrait painter. 2 Winchester Avenue, Brondesbury, London. † RA 2.

EVES, Reginald Grenville* 1876-1941
Portrait painter. Studied Slade School. A.R.A. 1934, R.A. 1939, R.B.A. 1909, R.O.I. 1915, R.P. 1913. "Max Beerbohm" purchased by Chantrey Bequest 1937. Add: London. † BA 1, G 5, GI 9, I 1, L 21, LS 2, P 128, RA 101, RBA 67, RED 2, RI 25, ROI 40, RSA 7.

EVILL, Norman Exh. 1905-36
Architect and architectural painter. London. † P 2, RA 16, WG 49.

EVISON, G. Henry Exh. 1890-1923
Illustrator. Add: Bootle 1890; London 1896. † L 5, RA 4.

EWAN, Alfred W. Exh. 1934-36
Dundee 1934; Barry Links, Angus 1936. † RSA 2.

EWAN, Miss F. Exh. 1907
11 Elm Grove, Cricklewood, London. † RA 1.

EWAN, Miss Frances Exh. 1929
St. Ives, Cornwall. † SWA 1.

EWAN, Miss F.A.E. Exh. 1892-94
C on M Manchester 1892; Manchester 1894. † M 3.

EWAN, Marion C. Exh. 1935
13 Warrender Park Crescent, Edinburgh. † RSA 1.

EWAN, R. Exh. 1885-91
75 Bath Street, Glasgow. † GI 2.

EWART, Arthur Exh. 1937-39
Landscape and portrait painter. 124 Cheyne Walk, London. † BK 42, NEA 4, RA 1.

EWART, Charles Exh. 1913
c/o Reynolds, 29 London Street, Edinburgh. † RSA 1.

EWART, David S. b. 1901
Portrait painter. Studied Glasgow School of Art, Italy and France. Exh. 1924-40. Add: Glasgow. † GI 36, L 4, RA 2, RSA 34.

EWEN, Miss Exh. 1892
† FIN 1.

EWEN, A.J.C. Exh. 1907-10
London. † RA 2.

EWERS, H. Exh. 1880
† TOO 1.

EWING, G.E. Exh. 1880
287 Bath Street, Glasgow. † GI 3, RSA 1.

EWING, Hugh M. Exh. 1928-32
114 St. James Court, London. † RCA 3, RSA 4.

EWING, James A. Exh. 1880-98
Glasgow. † GI 31, RSA 8.

EWING, J.G. Exh. 1890-1904
Glasgow 1890; London 1893; St. Andrews 1897. † G 1, GI 5, RSA 2.

EWING, Michael Exh. 1899-1907
265 Kenmure Street, Pollokshields, Glasgow. † GI 4, RSA 5.

EWING, William Exh. 1887-88
363 Essex Road, London. † GI 1, RSA 2.

EXLEY, John R. Exh. 1931-34
Kelbrook, Nr. Calne, Wilts. † RCA 4.

EXLEY, James Robert Granville b. 1878
Painter and engraver. b. Bradford. Studied Royal College of Art and France. 2nd Master and deputy headmaster Ryland Memorial Municipal School of Art 1909, Principal of the Camb. and County School of Arts and Crafts 1909-12 and Headmaster of the City of Hull Municipal School of Art 1912-19. A.R.E. 1905, R.E. 1923. Add: London 1906; Cambridge 1909; Hull 1912; Hessle, Yorks. 1913; London 1920. † CON 55, GI 2, L 2, RA 41, RE 44, RED 22, RI 1.

EYLAND, J.F. Exh. 1903
29 Alcester Road, Moseley, Birmingham. † B 1.

EYLES, Charles b. 1851
Landscape painter. Studied London and Paris. Add: London 1881; Saffron Walden, Essex 1899. † RA 8, RBA 9, ROI 2.

EYNON, Mrs. L.B. Exh. 1920-35
Leamington Spa, Warwicks. † B 3.

EYRE, Amy Exh. 1900
26 Bridge Road West, Battersea, London. † RBA 1.

EYRE, Carmela Rosemary Exh. 1927-30
8 Waterford Road, Oxton, Cheshire. † L 2.

EYRE, John d. 1927
Figure and domestic painter. b. Staffordshire. R.B.A. 1896, R.I. 1917. Add: London 1880; Petworth, Sussex 1918; Cranleigh, Surrey 1923. † AG 2, GI 10, L 15, M 15, RA 25, RBA 173, RHA 3, RI 53, RSW 3.

EYRES, Mrs. Dora Exh. 1911-16
50 High Street, Christchurch, Hants. † B 1, L 6.

EYRES, Emily Exh. 1892-1905
Portrait and domestic painter. Walton-on-Thames 1892; London 1899. † L 1, RA 6.

EYRES, John W. Exh. 1887-89
Landscape painter. Walton-on-Thames. † RA 5.

EYRIE, The Lady Alice Exh. 1886
73 Upper Berkeley Street, London. † G 2.

EYTON, Mrs. Phyllis Exh. 1929
Landscape painter. Old Meadows, Silchester, Nr. Reading, Berks. † RA 1, ROI 2.

EZEKIEL, Sir Moses Jacob 1844-1917
Sculptor. b. U.S.A., died Rome. Exh. 1889-94. Add: Rome. † RA 3.

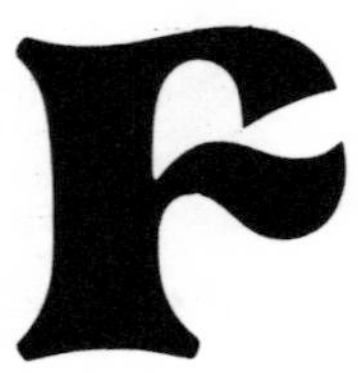

FABBRIOCOTTI, Countess Gabriella Exh. 1931
14 Brook Street, London. † ROI 1.
FABBRUCCI, Aristide Exh. 1880-85
Sculptor. Fulham, London. † G 1, L 2, RA 9.
FABBRUCCI, L. Exh. 1880-84
Sculptor. 14A Hollywood Road, Fulham, London. † L 2, RA 5.
FABIAN, Ernest Exh. 1889
61 Walham Grove, Fulham, London. † RA 1.
FABIAN, Maud Exh. 1906-9
Sculptor. 25 Streatley Road, Brondesbury, London. † L 3, SWA 1.
FACEY, W.H.D. Exh. 1913-23
Landscape painter. † BK 5, CG 2.
FAED, Henrietta Exh. 1880
Russell House, Tavistock Square, London. † SWA 1.
FAED, James* d. 1911
Engraver. Brother of John and Thomas F. q.v. Add: 7 Barnton Terrace, Edinburgh. † D 3. GI 27, RA 16, RSA 53, TOO 4.
FAED, James junr.* c.1847-1920
Landscape painter. Son of James F. q.v. Add: Edinburgh 1880; London 1900. † B 1, BRU 2, GI 36, L 9, M 4, RA 13, RSA 50.
FAED, John* c.1819-1902
Genre and historical and miniature painter. Brother of James and Thomas F. q.v. Studied Edinburgh. A.R.S.A. 1847, R.S.A. 1851, H.R.S.A. 1896. Add: London 1880; Gatehouse-of-Fleet, Galloway 1881. † B 3, GI 5, L 3, M 4, RA 11, RSA 39, TOO 2.
FAED, John Francis Exh. 1882-92
Marine painter. 24A Cavendish Road, St. John's Wood, London 1882; Edgware, Middlesex 1890. † B 1, GI 3, M 2, RA 8, RBA 3, RSA 1.
FAED, Miss S.B. Exh. 1883-84
24A Cavendish Road, St. John's Wood, London. † GI 1, RSA 3.
FAED, Thomas* 1826-1900
Landscape and domestic genre painter. Studied Edinburgh. Brother of John and James F. q.v. A.R.A. 1861, R.A. 1864, H.R.B.A. by 1880, A.R.S.A. 1849, H.R.S.A. 1862. Add: 24A Cavendish Road, St. John's Wood, London. † AG 1, B 2, GI 11, L 7, M 6, RA 34, RI 1, RSA 5, TOO 4.
FAED, William C.* Exh. 1880-97
Figure painter. 7 Barnton Terrace, Edinburgh 1880; West Dulwich, Surrey 1897. † B 2, GI 22, L 1, M 1, RA 3, RBA 1, RSA 40.
FAGAN, Betty Maud Christian d. c.1931
nee Smith. Portrait, figure and flower painter. b. Devizes, Wilts. Studied Lambeth School of Art. Married William Bateman F. q.v. R.O.I. 1912. Add: London 1903. † B 5, CHE 1, FIN 2, G 2, GI 5, GOU 26, I 10, L 10, LS 5, NEA 9, P 13, RA 17, ROI 26, RSA 2, SWA 12.
FAGAN, Geo W. Exh. 1905-6
Astagob, Clonsilla, Co. Dublin. † RHA 5.
FAGAN, Miss Isobel Exh. 1924-31
Stained glass artist. London. † L 4, RA 2.
FAGAN, Louis Alexander 1845-1903
English etcher. b. Naples. d. Florence. Assistant Keeper, Department of Prints and Drawings British Museum. Exh. 1887. Add: London. † RA 2.
FAGAN, William Bateman b. 1860
Sculptor. Married Betty Maud Christian F. q.v. Exh. 1887-1935. Add: London. † B 1, GI 3, I 2, L 4, M 1, RA 12, ROI 1.
FAGERLIN, Ferdinand Julius* 1825-1907
Swedish painter. Dusseldorf, Germany 1882. † L 2, RA 2.
FAGNANI, Nina Exh. 1892
Miniature portrait painter. 14 Rue Lauriston, Paris. † RA 1.
FAHEY, Aelfred Exh. 1902-8
Landscape painter. London 1902; Ockham Court, Surrey 1907. † B 1, GI 1, M 1, NG 2, RA 10, RHA 1, ROI 1.
FAHEY, Edward Henry* 1844-1907
Landscape and figure painter. A.R.I. 1870, R.I. 1876, R.O.I. 1883. Add: 10 Elsham Road, Kensington, London 1880. † B 6, BG 2, FIN 3, G 10, GI 1, L 12, M 6, NG 13, RA 21, RHA 3, RI 132, RID 20, ROI 45.
FAHEY, James 1804-1885
Watercolour landscape, portrait and figure painter. Drawing master at Merchant Taylors School 1856-83. R.I. 1834. Add: London. † G 1, L 1, RI 13.
FAILL, Ina Exh. 1883-85
Glasgow. † GI 3.
FAILL, Miss M.S. Exh. 1883-89
Glasgow. † GI 7.
FAIRBAIRN, Henry Exh. 1880
16 Drumdryan Street, Edinburgh. † RHA 1.
FAIRBAIRN, Hilda d. c.1917
Figure and domestic painter. A.S.W.A. 1902. Add: Henley-on-Thames 1893 and 1898; Bushey, Herts. 1895; London 1902. † D 5, FIN 1, L 5, NG 1, RA 8, ROI 11, SWA 50.
FAIRBAIRN, Henry G. Exh. 1931
Portrait and still life painter. 9 Henslowe Road, East Dulwich, London. † AG 1, RA 1.
FAIRBAIRN, Ida M. Exh. 1923-39
Mrs. Sidney F. Flower, landscape and still life painter. Add: 11 Bolton Gardens, London. † D 1, RBA 2, RID 4, ROI 10, SWA 3.
FAIRBAIRN, J. Clark Exh. 1885
Aberdare. † RSA 1.
FAIRBAIRN, Thomas* Exh. 1880-85
Parkview, Clydesdale Street, Hamilton, N.B. † GI 16, L 6, RSA 13, RSW 32.
FAIRBAIRN, Walter Exh. 1903
9 Spence Street, Edinburgh. † RSA 1.
FAIRBANKS, Frank Perley b. 1875
American painter and architect. b. Boston, Mass. Professor, School of Fine Arts, American Academy in Rome. Exh. 1912-13. Add: Paris. † RA 2.
FAIRBANKS, Nancy Exh. 1908-14
Wells, Somerset 1908; Shanklin, I.o.W. 1910; Kingston-on-Thames, Surrey 1913. † LS 17.
FAIRCLOUGH, Wilfred b. 1907
Etcher and engraver. Studied Royal College of Art 1931-34, British School at Rome 1934-37. A.R.E. 1934. Exh. 1933-40. † B 1, GI 4, L 3, RA 12, RE 26, RED 1, RSA 6.
FAIRFAX, A. Exh. 1881
Fairfax House, Withington, Manchester. † G 1.
FAIRFAX, J.S. Exh. 1886
190 Camden Road, London. † L 1.
FAIRFAX, Mrs. J.S. Exh. 1886
190 Camden Road, London. † L 2.
FAIRFAX, Miss L. Exh. 1892-94
Loweswater Hall, Loweswater, Cumberland. † B 3.
FAIRFAX, Miss Theo Exh. 1916-18
Paddock Studioes, Herkomer Road, Bushey, Herts. † I 1, LS 3, RHA 4, RI 1, SWA 1.
FAIRFIELD, Agnes Exh. 1880-87
Miniature painter. 13 James Street, Birkenhead. † L 11, M 4, RSA 4, SWA 1.
FAIRFOWL, Kathlene M. Exh. 1923-27
c/o Mrs. Duffus, 73 Haymarket Terrace, Edinburgh. † RSA 2.
FAIRHOLME, Mrs. Exh. 1885
Watercolour painter. Elm Tree House, Shrivenham, Berks. † SWA 2.
FAIRHOLME, Miss Adele Exh. 1899-1936
Animal painter. London 1899; Austria 1936. † L 1, M 1, RA 2, ROI 1, RSA 1.
FAIRHOLME, Miss K. Exh. 1894
Kilmacthomas, Ireland. † RHA 1.
FAIRHURST, Enoch b. 1874
Portrait and miniature painter, etcher, poster designer and illustrator. A.R.M.S. 1918. Add: London 1918; Bolton, Lancs. 1924. † L 50, M 3, RA 15, RCA 6, RMS 64, RSA 1.
FAIRHURST, Harry Smith Exh. 1926-29
Architect, painter and etcher. Studied Manchester. Add: 14 Chancery Lane, Manchester. † GI 2, M 3, RA 3.
FAIRHURST, Joseph Exh. 1924-26
17 Greenough Street, Wigan, Lancs. † L 4.
FAIRHURST, Jack Leslie b. 1905
Portrait painter and draughtsman. Studied Camberwell School of Art 1919-23 and Royal College of Art 1923-27. Exh. 1936. † P 1.
FAIRLESS, Miss B. Exh. 1920
Lezayre Road, Ramsey, I.o.M. † L 1.
FAIRLEY, Dorothy M. b. 1898
Wood engraver and etcher. Studied Richmond Art School and Regent Street Polytechnic. Exh. 1921-40. Add: 11 Lion Gate Gardens, Richmond, Surrey. † AB 3, GI 4, L 6, NEA 3, RA 4, RBA 4, ROI 5, RSA 13, SWA 5.
FAIRLEY, James Graham Exh. 1880-1920
Architect. Edinburgh. † GI 7, RA 6, RSA 36.
FAIRLEY, John J. Exh. 1927-29
9 Woodstock Parade, Sandford Road, Dublin. † RHA 5.
FAIRLEY, J. McLellan Exh. 1890-1911
Edinburgh. † RSA 3.
FAIRLEY, Madge B. Exh. 1905-12
Edinburgh. † LS 4, RHA 4, RSA 2, SWA 1.
FAIRLEY, Robert Exh. 1891
7 Minto Street, Edinburgh. † RSA 1.
FAIRLIE, Mrs. Helen see FRANCK
FAIRLIE, Reginald Exh. 1911-37
Architect. A.R.S.A. 1923, R.S.A. 1935. Add: Edinburgh. † GI 7, RA 2, RSA 33.
FAIRLIE, R.N. Exh. 1883-94
Ayr 1883 and 1894; Dollar, Edinburgh 1885. † GI 3, RSA 2.
FAIRMAN, Frances C.* c.1836-1923
Animal painter (especially dogs). A.S.W.A. 1886. Add: Wingham, Kent 1884; London 1894. † B 1, D 33, GI 1, L 9, LS 5, NG 11, P 2, RA 3, RBA 2, RID 48, RSA 2, SWA 170.
FAIRWEATHER, Adam Exh. 1883-96
Blairgowrie 1883; Dundee 1890. † GI 1, RSA 12.

FAIRWEATHER, H.M. Exh. 1916
25 Beeches Avenue, Carshalton, Surrey. † RA 1.

FAIRWEATHER, Ian* b. 1891
Painter of figures and landscapes in China. Exh. 1936-38. † RED 34.

FAITHFUL, Leila (Mrs. G.) b. 1898
nee Reynolds. Portrait painter. Studied Slade School 1923-24 and le Grande Chaumiere, Paris. Exh. 1931-40. Add: London. † GI 1, LEF 2, LEI 51, NEA 7, RA 9, RBA 3, ROI 2.

FALCHETTI, Alberto Exh. 1910-13
Landscape painter. † ALP 5, GOU 2.

FALCHETTI, Giuseppe Exh. 1913
Landscape painter. † ALP 1.

FALCKE, Gladys Exh. 1902-10
Miniature portrait painter. Birmingham. † B 8, L 3, RA 4, RMS 1.

FALCON, Miss B. Exh. 1883
14 Pittsville Lawn, Cheltenham, Glos. † B 1.

FALCON, Miss I. Exh. 1911
Kingsland, Milverton, Somerset. † RA 1.

FALCON, Maud Exh. 1888-90
London. † G 3.

FALCON, Thomas Adolphus b. 1872
Landscape painter and decorator. b. Pudsey, Yorks. R.B.A. 1902. Add: Starcross, Devon 1897; Studland, Wareham, Dorset 1899; Braunton, Devon 1902-40. † B 11, L 26, M 1, P 1, RA 2, RBA 138, RCA 2, ROI 3.

FALCONER, Agnes Trotter b. 1883
Painter of landscapes and boat subjects, and lithographer. Studied Edinburgh College of Art. Lecturer on art at National Gallery of Scotland to Schoolchildren. Exh. 1916-40. Add: 45 Frederick Street, Edinburgh. † B 1, GI 5, L 2, RSA 24.

FALCONER, Miss J. Exh. 1886
Belvidere, Aberdeen. † GI 1.

FALCONER, John M. 1820-1903
Painter and etcher. b. Scotland. R.E. 1881-98. Add: Brooklyn, New York, U.S.A. 1881. † L 4, RE 10.

FALERO, Luis 1851-1896
Spanish painter. 100 Fellowes Road, London 1887-93. † L 3, M 1, RA 8, ROI 3.

FALKENBERG, Exh. 1891
† TOO 1.

FALKINER, Miss Edith Exh. 1900
34 Palmerston Road, Rathmines, Dublin. † RHA 1.

FALKNER, Anne L. Exh. 1893-1933
Landscape painter. Clevelands, Bedford 1893; Chieveley, Berks. 1900; Faringdon, Berks. 1908; St. Ives, Cornwall 1910; London 1930. † BA 37, L 3, LS 8, RA 4, RBA 8, ROI 3, RSA 1, SWA 1.

FALKNER, Harold Exh. 1900-24
Architect. 24 West Street, Farnham, Surrey. † RA 6.

FALKNER, Mary G. Exh. 1899
c/o Miss Irwin, Park House, Knutsford, Cheshire. † RA 1.

FALLON, Robert T. Exh. 1882
Sculptor. 13A Bloomfield Place, Pimlico, London. † RA 1.

FALLON, Sarah W.M. Exh. 1880-95
Figure and domestic painter. Edinburgh 1880; London 1883. † GI 1, RA 1, RBA 5, RSA 8, SWA 7.

FALLON, V.L. Exh. 1931
Linocut artist. † RED 2.

FALLS, R.* Exh. 1893-99
Landscape painter. London 1893; Guernsey, C.I. 1895. † L 1, M 1, NG 4, RBA 1.

FANANI, Luigi Exh. 1930
Sculptor. Via Cimabue, 6, Florence, Italy. † RA 1.

FANE, Gen. Walter Exh. 1883-84
Figure and landscape painter. London. † D 2, RI 2.

FANNER, Alice Maud d. 1930
Mrs. Taite. Landscape and marine painter. Studied Slade School, Richmond School of Art and St. Ives, Cornwall under Julius Olsson. Worked in Paris. Art teacher Richmond School of Art. Visited South Africa. S.W.A. 1918. Add: Putney 1895; Chiswick 1896; Datchet, Bucks. 1901; London 1912; Burnham-on-Crouch, Essex 1914. † B 1, CG 1, FIN 3, G 12, GI 11, GOU 23, I 2, L 20, M 13, NEA 88, RA 42, RBA 4, RCA 2, RHA 26, ROI 6, RSA 1, SWA 18, WG 73.

FANNER, Henry George Exh. 1880-88
Portrait painter. 26 Cavendish Square, London 1880; Glasgow 1888. † D 1, GI 3, RSA 7.

FANO, Mrs. Dorothea Natalie Sophia da see LANDAU

FANSHAW, H. Valentine Exh. 1933
† RSW 1.

FANTACCHIOTTI, Cesare Exh. 1880
Sculptor. Florence. † RA 2.

FANTIN-LATOUR, Henri* 1836-1904
French painter and lithographer. R.O.I. 1883. Add: c/o Mrs. Edwards, 26 Golden Square, London 1880-1902. † B 30, FIN 6, G 11, GI 29, L 25, M 44, NG 6, P 6, RA 63, RBA 3, RHA 2, ROI 52.

FANU, le see L

FARADAY, May Exh. 1907-8
Carshalton House, Withington, Manchester. † M 2.

FARASYN, Edgar b. 1858
Belgian artist. Exh. 1882-95. Add: 2 Rue Schul, Antwerp, Belgium. † GI 3, L 6, M 2, RHA 2.

FAREINI, Mons. Exh. 1882
16 Avenue Trudaine, Paris. † RHA 1.

FAREY, Ada A. Exh. 1909-20
Bellevue Terrace, Skipton in Craven, Yorks. † L 4.

FAREY, Cyril Arthur b. 1888
Architect and watercolour painter. Studied RIBA (Sloane medallion) and RA Schools (gold medal and travelling studentship). Add: London 1911 and 1921; Salisbury, Wilts. 1919. † GI 6, RA 39, RSA 6.

FAREY, Michael A.J. Exh. 1936-40
Architect and painter. Son of Cyril Arthur F. q.v. Add: 83 Albert Road, Regent's Park, London. † RA 2.

FARGUES, Leon Exh. 1903
156 Rue de Faubourg, St. Martin, Paris. † L 4.

FARHALL, Miss Hilda Mary see SARE

FARLEIGH, Elsie b. 1900
Portrait and figure painter. Studied Central School of Arts and Crafts 1917-21. Member London Group 1931. Add: London. † COO 1, LEF 3, LEI 2.

FARLEIGH, John 1900-1965
Painter, wood engraver and illustrator. Studied Central School of Arts and Crafts. Teacher at Rugby School 1922-24, and Central School of Arts and Crafts from 1924. Member London Group 1927. A.R.E. 1937. Add: London. † COO 1, LEI 48, M 2, RE 7, RED 13, RSA 1.

FARLEY, Charles W. Exh. 1935-40
Portrait and urban landscape painter. Add: 64 Queen's Road, Richmond, Surrey. † AR 2, P 1, RA 1, RI 2.

FARLEY, John J. Exh. 1930-32
Portrait and figure painter. Sandford Road, Dublin. † RHA 3.

FARLEY, William Exh. 1936-40
Figure and landscape painter. Hessett, Bury St. Edmunds, Suffolk. † RA 6, RBA 1.

FARLOW, Harry M. Exh. 1929
33 London Street, Edinburgh. † RSA 2.

FARMAN, Mrs. Exh. 1919
† SWA 1.

FARMAN, Miss A.E. Exh. 1894
55 Melbourne Road, Leicester. † B 1, SWA 1.

FARMER, Miss A. Exh. 1917
Chelsea, London. † SWA 2.

FARMER, Corrall Exh. 1893-1929
Landscape painter. Loxwood, New Billinghurst, Sussex. † L 8, LS 3, NG 1, RA 2, RBA 3, RID 2, ROI 8.

FARMER, Emily 1826-1905
Watercolour figure and domestic painter. R.I. 1854. Add: Porchester House, Porchester, Hants. † L 2, RI 21, RSW 1.

FARMER, Miss E.S. Exh. 1911-17
Cockloft Studios, Cochrane Street, St. John's Wood, London. † P 1, RA 1.

FARMER, Florence Exh. 1899-1900
Bromley, Kent. † RBA 2.

FARMER, F. Olga Exh. 1932-39
Portrait and flower painter. A.N.S.A. 1937, N.S.A. 1938. Daughter of Walter F. q.v. Add: Car Colston, East Bridgford, Notts. † N 13, RA 1.

FARMER, Gertrude Exh. 1885-1902
Flower and still life painter. 192 Anerley Road, Anerley 1885; Apsley Guise, Beds. 1900. † SWA 8.

FARMER, Henry Exh. 1923
Flower painter. 7A Belsize Avenue, London. † G 1, RA 1.

FARMER, Henry Exh. 1897
Architect. 17 Bridge Street, Walsall, Staffs. † RA 2.

FARMER, John Exh. 1925-35
Still life painter. Cockloft Studios, 35 Cochrane Street, St. John's Wood, London. † P 1, RA 2, ROI 2.

FARMER, Kathleen Exh. 1925-40
Loxwood, Nr. Horsham, Sussex. † RI 3, SWA 1.

FARMER, Mary Exh. 1886
Poole, Dorset. † ROI 1.

FARMER, Mabel S. Exh. 1932
Marlborough House, Wardle Road, Sale, Cheshire. † RSA 1.

FARMER, Walter Exh. 1897-1932
Landscape, figure and interior painter. N.S.A. 1908, V.P.N.S.A. 1914-17, Treasurer N.S.A. 1914-19. Add: Nottingham 1897; Car Colston, East Bridgford, Notts. 1912. † L 1, N 53, RA 7.

FARMILOE, Edith Exh. 1893-1908
nee Parnell. Painter of children. A.S.W.A. 1905, S.W.A. 1907. Add: London. † SWA 3.

FARNSWORTH, J.T. Exh. 1900
28 Waldeck Road, Nottingham. † N 2.

FARNSWORTH, S. Exh. 1915-16
Painter and illuminator. 9 Hall Street, Chelmsford, Essex. † RA 4.

FARNUM, H. Cyrus Exh. 1896
Landscape painter. 11 Impasse Rousin, Paris. † RA 1.

FARNWORTH, Miss E.M. Exh. 1910
Cheadle Hulme, Cheshire. † L 3.

FARNWORTH, Maria A. Exh. 1904-23
Langho, Nr. Blackburn, Lancs. 1904; Liverpool 1906. † L 17.

FARNWORTH, T. Exh. 1923
168 Brownlow Hill, Liverpool. † L 1.

FARQUHAR, Archibald Exh. 1882
Central Chambers, Birmingham. † B 1.

FARQUHAR, Miss D. Exh. 1914
† P 1.

FARQUHAR, Helen Exh. 1903-23
8 The Mall, Parkhill Road, London. † L 7, RA 4, RI 3.

FARQUHARSON, David* 1840-1907
Landscape painter. b. Blairgowrie. A.R.A. 1905, A.R.S.A. 1882, R.O.I. 1904, R.S.W. 1885. "In a Fog" purchased by Chantrey Bequest 1897 and "Birnam Wood" 1906. Add: Edinburgh 1880; London 1886; Sennen Cove, Penzance, Cornwall 1895. † B 4, GI 28, L 6, M 5, RA 39, RHA 1, ROI 1, RSA 63, RSW 2, TOO 130.

FARQUHARSON, H. Exh. 1912
14 North Audley Street, London. † RA 1.

FARQUHARSON, John Exh. 1885-1905
Edinburgh 1886 and 1891; London 1889. † GI 1, L 1, RSA 16.

FARQUHARSON, Joseph* 1846-1935
Landscape and portrait painter. Studied under Peter Graham and at the Board of Manufacture School, Edinburgh; RSA Life School, and in Paris under Carolus Duran. Visited Middle East. A.R.A. 1900, R.A. 1915, R.O.I. 1887. "A Joyless Winter Day" purchased by Chantrey Bequest 1883. Add: Porchester Gardens, London 1880; Finzean Aboyne, Aberdeenshire 1917. † AG 1, B 15, D 1, FIN 181, G 4, GI 22, L 47, M 18, NG 2, P 2, RA 204, RCA 1, RID 19, ROI 25, RSA 5, TOO 5.

FARQUHARSON, Jean S. Exh. 1924-40
Portrait and figure painter. Radlett, Herts. 1924; Hampstead, London 1930. † GOU 1, NEA 6, RA 3.

FARQUHARSON, Margaret Exh. 1913
Landscape painter. 48 Tedworth Square, Chelsea, London. † NEA 1.

FARR, Emily Exh. 1924
Sandon Hall Gardens, Stafford. † B 1.

FARR, Heather Mary b. 1912
Landscape painter. Studied Slade School and Nottingham School of Art. † Add: Worksop Manor, Worksop, Notts. 1937. † N 5.

FARRALL, J.C. Exh. 1881
Clonmel, Ireland. † RHA 1.

FARRAN, Lulu Exh. 1887-92
Portrait painter. London 1887 and 1890; Gibraltar 1888; Glasgow 1889. † GI 4, L 2, RA 1, RI 4, RSA 1.

FARRAN, Thomas Exh. 1881
Sculptor. Suffolk House, Haygrove Road West, Hampstead, London. † RA 1.

FARRAR, C. Brooke Exh. 1929-40
Landscape and figure painter. A.R.B.A. 1940. Travelled widely. Add: Lynwood, Bedford 1929; South Moulton, Devon 1940. † GOU 40, NEA 4, RA 1, RBA 4, RCA 1, ROI 3, RSA 2.

FARRAR, Mrs. F.E.W. Exh. 1900-38
Miniature painter. London. † GI 5, L 4, M 3, RCA 2, RI 7, RMS 2, RSA 2.

FARRAR, John T. Exh. 1925-28
All Saints Studios, 11 Grosvenor Street, All Saints, Manchester. † L 3.

FARRAR, Miss M.R.H. Exh. 1919
25 Farnaby Road, Bromley, Kent. † SWA 1.

FARRELL, Frederick A. b. 1882
Painter and etcher. Studied Civil engineering before he began to etch. Self taught with advice from Muirhead Bone. Add: Glasgow 1911 and 1917; London 1915. † AB 1, CON 3, FIN 1, GI 43, L 10, RA 3, RSA 1.

FARRELL, James 1821-1891
Sculptor. Studied under his father Terence F. (1798-1896). A.R.H.A. 1880, R.H.A. 1882. Add: Dublin. † L 2, RHA 22.

FARRELL, John Exh. 1880-95
Dublin 1880; Stillorgan 1895. † RHA 4.

FARRELL, Joseph Exh. 1881-96
Dublin 1881; Stillorgan 1895. † RHA 26.

FARRELL, J.J. Exh. 1888
6 Westmoreland Street, Dublin. † RHA 1.

FARRELL, Michael b. 1893
Painter. b. Sligo. Studied Metropolitan Art School, Dublin. Exh. 1921-26. Add: Dublin. † RHA 3.

FARRELL, Sir Thomas d. 1900
Sculptor. H.R.M.S. 1897, R.H.A. 1860, P.R.H.A. 1893. Add: 30 Mountjoy Square, East Dublin. † L 7, RA 1, RHA 50.

FARRELL, William Exh. 1883-1903
Dublin 1883 and 1903; Stillorgan 1895. † RHA 10.

FARREN, Miss Jessie Exh. 1886-96
Miniature portrait painter. Scarborough 1886; Cambridge 1895. † RA 3, RMS 2.

FARREN, Robert Exh. 1880-90
Etcher. Cambridge 1880; Scarborough 1889. † L 1, M 1, RA 4, RE 6.

FARREN, W. Exh. 1880
Etcher. † DOW 1.

FARRER, C.B. Exh. 1940
† COO 1.

FARRER, Fanny Exh. 1898-1904
London. † SWA 6.

FARRER, Henry 1843-1903
Etcher. R.E. 1881-87. b. London. d. New York. U.S.A. Exh. 1881-84. † L 1, RE 12.

FARRER, Thomas Charles 1839-1891
Painter and etcher. R.E. 1885. Add: London. † FIN 3, G 18, L 2, M 6, NG 8, RA 8, RBA 2, RE 30, ROI 6, RSA 1.

FARRER, Reginald Exh. 1917
Watercolour painter of flowers and landscapes of China and Tibet. † FIN 101.

FARRINGTON, Miss R. Exh. 1912
† M 1.

FARROW, William John Exh. 1890-99
Figure and domestic painter. London † RBA 4, ROI 11.

FARTHING, Elsie Exh. 1924
Westfield, Alton, Hants. † SWA 1.

FASHAM, Geo. W. Exh. 1922-32
King's Norton, Birmingham. † B 17.

FASHAM, W.H. Exh. 1925-30
King's Norton, Birmingham 1925; Harborne, Birmingham 1930. † B 12.

FATH, Rene Maurice 1850-1922
French artist. 49 Rue du Mesnil Maisons, Lafitte, Seine et Oise, France 1908. † I 1.

FATHERS, George b. 1898
Urban landscape painter. b. Derby. Add: 59 Redcliffe Road, London 1925. † RA 1.

FAUCONNIER, le See L

FAULCONBRIDGE, Miss H.S. Exh. 1896-1901
94 Noel Street, Nottingham. † N 11.

FAULDS, James Exh. 1896-1938
Glasgow. † GI 36, RSA 1, RSW 1.

FAULKNER, A.L. Exh. 1930-31
Linocut artist. † RED 3.

FAULKNER, B.R. Exh. 1926
† M 1.

FAULKNER, Florence Exh. 1904-40
Miniature painter. Studied Delecluse and Juliens, Paris and Central School of Arts and Crafts, London. A.S.W.A. 1929. Add: Freshfield, Lancs. 1904 and 1913; Bath 1912; London 1920. † L 14, RA 7, RI 39, RMS 11, SWA 8.

FAULKNER, F.M. Exh. 1924-25
17 September Road, The Brook, Liverpool. † L 2.

FAULKNER, John* Exh. 1880-90
Landscape and coastal painter. A.R.H.A. 1861, R.H.A. 1861. Resigned 1870. Add: London. † GI 1, L 3, M 2, RA 4, RBA 2, RHA 4, RI 1, RSA 5.

FAULKNER, Nina Exh. 1892
Miniature portrait painter. 7 Hyde Park Mansions, London. † RA 1.

FAULKNER, Richard b. 1917
Landscape painter. Exh. 1937-40. Add: Denwood, Denorrton Park, Hollywood Road, Belfast. † RHA 8.

FAUNTLEROY, Mrs. C.S. Exh. 1880-85
Domestic and still life painter. Northcomb, Highampton, Devon. † RBA 1, SWA 3.

FAURE, Helene 1878-1932
French miniature painter. 83 Rue de Chaillot, Paris 1910-12. † L 2, RA 1.

FAUSSETT, Mrs. Billie Exh. 1927
Clarence House, Rhyl, N. Wales. † RCA 1.

FAUTRIES, Jean Exh. 1916-17
Portrait painter. 35A St. Georges Road, Hampstead, London. † NEA 4.

FAUX-FROIDURE, Mme. E.J. Exh. 1913
4 Villa Neil, Paris. † L 1.

FAVAI, Gennaro b. 1879
Italian artist. 15 Rue Delambre, Paris 1908. † LS 5.

FAVARGER, H. Exh. 1905
2 Balfour Place, London. † RA 1.

FAVRE, Maurice Exh. 1908-19
Sculptor. Paris. † RA 3.

FAVRETTO, Giacomo Exh. 1886
Landscape painter. c/o G.P. Mendoza, 4A King Street, St. James', London. † RA 1.

FAWCETT, Dorothea M. Exh. 1904
41 Upper Mount Street, Dublin. † RHA 1.

FAWCETT, Emily Addis Exh. 1883-96
Sculptor. London. † L 3, RA 9, RHA 2, SWA 3.

FAWCETT, Miss E.M. Exh. 1923
† NEA 1.

FAWCETT, Mrs. Gertrude Exh. 1916-39
Flower and still life painter. A.S.W.A. 1927. Add: 3 Wilbury Villas, Hove, Sussex. † I 3, LS 3, RA 8, RBA 1, ROI 34, SWA 20.

FAWCETT, Hugh A. Exh. 1924
6 Victoria Road, Stafford. † B 2.

FAWCETT, Major P.H. Exh. 1906
Royal Artillery, Spike Island, Cork, Ireland. † RA 1.

FAWCETT, William Milner 1832-1908
Architect. Add: 1 Silver Street, Cambridge. † RA 5.

FAWKE, Miss A. Exh. 1902
Victoria House, Lord Street, Southport, Lancs. † L 2, RCA 1.

FAWKES, Harriet Exh. 1936
Landscape painter. † COO 3.

FAWKES, Madeline C. (Madge) Exh. 1909-31
Portrait, landscape and flower painter. Studied Paris and under Stanhope Forbes and Newlyn, Penzance. Add: Cheltenham, Glos. 1909; London 1919. † B 1, I 1, RA 10, SWA 5.

FAWKES, Phyllis Exh. 1936-39
c/o K.E. Mackenzie, Esq., British Embassy, Brussels. † SWA 4.

FAWSSETT, Constance Mary Exh. 1898
36 Crockerton Road, Upper Tooting, London. † RHA 1.

FAWSSETT, Miss M.C. Exh. 1904-9
Northdown Avenue, Cliftonville, Margate, Kent. † RCA 5.

FAY, William Exh. 1908-10
Rathgar, Co. Dublin 1908; Dunmow, Essex 1910. † RHA 3.

FAY, W.G. Exh. 1927
c/o F.J. Jay, Dublin. † RHA 1.

FAYA, Reginald Kearsley Exh. 1909
† LS 3.

FAYRER, Ethel Exh. 1901-4
Miniature portrait painter. Macclesfield, Cheshire. † L 6, M 3, RA 2.

FAZAKERLEY, J. Exh. 1908
38 Paradise Street, Liverpool. † L 1.

FAZAKERLEY, M. Campbell Exh. 1921-23
Dunedin, Heswall Hills, Cheshire. † L 3.

FEARN, Cyril R. Exh. 1922-30
Landscape painter. 1 Collin Street, Beeston, Notts. † N 11, RCA 1.

FEARNLEY, John Henry Exh. 1903-10
Upper House, Hopton, Mirfield, Nr. Huddersfield, Yorks. † L 1, LS 4.

FEARNSIDE, E.M. Exh. 1884-85
Swift's Hospital, Dublin. † RHA 2.

FEARNSIDE, R. Kitto Exh. 1923
64 Fulham Road, Sparkhill, Birmingham. † B 1.

FEARON, Miss Ann See WALKE

FEARON, Edith A. Exh. 1903-10
Landscape painter. Dapdune House, Guildford, Surrey. † FIN 1, L 1.

FEARON, Hilda 1878-1917
Figure, domestic and still life painter. Studied Slade School. R.O.I. 1910. Add: London. † B 1, GI 4, GOU 8, I 4, L 8, LS 4, M 1, NEA 1, RA 18, RHA 5, ROI 8.

FEARS, Miss C. Exh. 1940
† RI 1.

FEATHERSTON, Frances Exh. 1884
Sowber Gate, Northallerton, Yorks. † SWA 1.

FEATHERSTON, J. Marianne Exh. 1884
Landscape painter. Sowber Gate, Northallerton, Yorks. † SWA 1.

FEAVER, Christine Exh. 1940
Figure painter. † COO 1.

FEDARB, Mrs. Daphne S. Exh. 1934-40
Landscape painter. Canterbury 1934; London 1937. † COO 1, FIN 11, NEA 2, SWA 3.

FEDARB, Ernest J. Exh. 1928-36
Landscape painter. Canterbury 1928; London 1936. † FIN 53, RBA 4.

FEDDEN, A. Romilly 1875-1939
Landscape painter. Studied Herkomer's, Bushey, Herts. and Juliens, Paris. Served with Army in France World War I. Travelled widely in Europe and North Africa. R.B.A. 1903. Add: Henbury, Glos. 1903; Burford, Oxon 1908; Playden, Rye, Sussex 1913; Chantemesle, par Vetheuil, Seine et Oise, France 1928. † BG 45, FIN 46, G 2, GI 6, GOU 105, L 14, RA 3, RBA 24, WG 432.

FEDDEN, Herbert L. Exh. 1895-1905
Architect. London. † RA 3.

FEDER, Adolph b. 1886
French/Russian painter. Exh. 1935. † BA 21.

FEDOROVITCH, Sophie Exh. 1928-33
Portrait and still life painter. † BA 32, LEI 5.

FEELY, Miss Mary S.O. Exh. 1930
Hoylake, Cheshire. † L 1.

FEENEY, Mrs. Exh. 1912
Clippesly Hall, East Norfolk. † B 2.

FEENEY, Mrs. John Exh. 1905-27
The Moat, Berkswell, Warwicks. † B 5, NG 1.

FEENEY, Peregrine M. Exh. 1882-1912
Landscape and coastal painter. R.B.S.A. 1906. Add: London 1882 and 1906; Croyde, N. Devon 1892; Fleggburgh, Norfolk 1909. † B 54, D 1, L 1, M 3, RA 4, ROI 2.

FEENEY, William P. Exh. 1880-1920
Coastal painter. London. † B 26, GI 6, L 1, RA 2, RBA 8, ROI 1, RSA 1.

FEHDMER, Karl Exh. 1888
† D 1.

FEHR, Henry Charles 1867-1940
Sculptor. Studied City of London School, RA Schools and in the studio of Thomas Brock. "The Rescue of Andromeda" purchased by Chantrey Bequest 1894. Add: Leytonstone, Essex 1887; London 1892. † B 2, GI 3, L 15, M 1, NG 2, RA 42.

FEIBUSCH, Hans b. 1898
Painter and lithographer. Member London Group 1934. Exh. 1937-40. † COO 3, LEF 44, LEI 2, RED 1.

FEILD, E. Maurice Exh. 1929-30
Landscape painter, etcher and wood engraver. † COO 14, WG 29.

FEILDEN, H. Exh. 1913
37 Redcliffe Road, London. † RA 1.

FELBER, Charles Exh. 1921
c/o Ernest Scholl, Drayton Road, Boreham Wood, Herts. † GI 1.

FELCE-HARE, Mrs. C. Exh. 1893
65 Herne Hill Road, Camberwell, London. † SWA 1.

FELDMAN, Louis Exh. 1899
Figure painter. Dusseldorf, Germany. † RA 1.

FELGATE, Miss W. Palmer Exh. 1926
Burton Villa, Haxby Road, York. † L 2.

FELIU, Manel Exh. 1913
16 Rue Olivier de Serres, Paris. † L 1.

FELIX, Leon Pierre b. 1869
French artist. 88 Boulevard Pereine, Paris 1912-13. † GI 1, L 1.

FELKEL, Carl F. b. 1896
Landscape and figure painter. Studied Vienna and Munich. Exh. 1938-40. Add: 70 Holland Park, London. † GOU 51, RA 1.

FELKIN, Mrs. Margaret Exh. 1919-32
Watercolour painter. Travelled in Far East. Add: 55 St. Georges Square, London. † RA 2, RI 1.

FELL, Catharine Exh. 1937
Landscape painter. † COO 2.

FELL, Eleanor d. 1946
nee Mitchell. Painter and etcher. Studied Westminster School of Art and Paris. A.R.E. 1908. Add: London 1899, 1912 and 1921; Brighton 1901; Hove 1903; Shoreham, Sussex 1907; Squirrell's Heath, Essex 1913; Chislehurst, Kent 1916; Worthing, Sussex 1932. † GI 2, I 2, L 7, NEA 12, RA 13, RE 27, RI 1, SWA 3.

FELL, Mrs. Florence Exh. 1933-34
Stained glass artist. 5 Cutler Street, Smethwick, Birmingham. † RA 3.

FELL, Miss Frances E. Exh. 1926-29
17 Liverpool Road, Southport, Lancs. † L 7.

FELL, G.P.R. Exh. 1911
† ALP 1.

FELL, Herbert Granville 1872-1951
Figure and landscape painter. Studied Heatherley's, British Museum, Paris and Brussels. Editor of the "Connoisseur". Add: London. † CHE 2, NG 1, RA 10.

FELL, M. Katharine Exh. 1937-39
Portrait painter. Ulverston, Lancs. 1937; London 1938. † NEA 2, RA 1, ROI 1.

FELL, Phyllis b. 1901
Nee Munday. Miniature painter. Add: Hartley, Plymouth 1936. † RA 5, RMS 1.

FELL, Thomas Exh. 1921
Algave, Bellafurt Road, Port Erin, I.O.M. † L 1.

FELL-CLARK, Pat Exh. 1939-40
Mill Court, Cholsey, Berks. † NEA 1, ROI 1, SWA 1.

FELLER, Frank Exh. 1881-95
Painter and black and white artist. London 1881 and 1895; Kingston on Thames 1887. † RA 3, RBA 2.

FELLOES, Frank Exh. 1896-98
London. † RI 2.

FELLOWES, Emily Exh. 1906-7
Gipsyside, Wokingham, Berks. † D 2.

FELLOWES, Lilah Exh. 1924
Landscape and coastal painter. † WG 91.

FELLOWES, Madelene Exh. 1903-5
Miniature portrait painter. Winchester, Hants. 1903; Brussels 1905. † L 1, RA 2, RMS 1.

FELLOWS, Annie Exh. 1898
49 Hall Road, Handsworth, Birmingham. † B 1.

FELLOWS, George Exh. 1891-1914
Landscape painter. Beeston Fields, Notts. 1891; Loughborough, Leics. 1914. † N 19.

FELTON, Lydia M. Exh. 1890-91
Figure painter. Chiswick, London 1890; Exmouth, Devon 1891. † RBA 3.

FELTONA, Jaques Exh. 1911
Landscape painter. † BRU 1.

FENAILLON, Madeleine Exh. 1912
17 Rue de la Paix, Bois Colombes, France. † L 1.

FENDER, Maggie F. Exh. 1889-92
Landscape painter. Edinburgh 1889; Ayton, N.B. 1891. † GI 2, RA 2, RSA 2.

FENDICK, Miss D. Exh. 1917
47 Gloucester Gardens, Bishop's Road, London. † RA 1.

FENN, Annie S. Manville Exh. 1881-95
Figure painter. A.S.W.A. 1886. Add: Hawkhurst, Kent 1881; Syon Lodge, Isleworth, Middlesex 1895. † RHA 2, SWA 14.

FEBB, Annie S. Manville Exh. 1883-96
Figure painter. 20 Woodstock Road, Bedford Park, London. † L 2, RBA 3, SWA 6.

FENN, Louisa Manville Exh. 1885-95
Figure and flower painter. Bedford Park, London 1885; Syon Lodge, Isleworth 1890. † L 1, M 3, RHA 4, SWA 4.

FENN, W.W. Exh. 1880
Landscape painter. 15 Gt. Marlborough Street, Regent Street, London. † D 1.

FENNELL, Louisa Exh. 1880-94
Westgate, Wakefield, Yorks. † L 2, RBA 3, SWA 3.

FENNELL, Nina Keith Exh. 1897-98
R.M.S. 1897. London. † RI 1, RMS 5.

FENNELL, Mrs. Sylvia Exh. 1913-17
West Wittering, Chichester 1913; Warrington, Lancs. 1917. † L 2, RA 1.

FENNELL, William J. Exh. 1880-1908
Belfast. † RHA 20.

FENNESSY, Emily Exh. 1882-83
Mrs. R.J. Sculptor. 24 Gloucester Road, Regent's Park, London. † RA 2.

FENNING, Miss Marjorie See HOLMES

FENTON, Annie Grace Exh. 1880-90
Figure and domestic painter. Richmond, Surrey 1880; London 1890. † B 4, RA 4, SWA 2.

FENTON, Miss Dora See BLYTH

FENTON, Harold Exh. 1908
Brentwood, Eccles Old Road, Pendleton, Lancs. † L 2.

FENTON, James Exh. 1911-19
Clifton Park, Wormit on Tay 1911; West Newport, Fife 1919. † GI 3.

FENTON, Roxburgh Exh. 1901
14 Thomson Street, Dundee. † GI 2.

FENTON, Rose M. Exh. 1885
Portrait painter. Westcombe Lodge, Hayes, Middlesex. † RA 1.

FENTON, William Exh. 1916
150 Joan Street, Benwell, Newcastle on Tyne. † L 1.

FENWICK, Diana Exh. 1935-36
Bedford. † SWA 2.

FER, Edouard Exh. 1912
11 Avenue de Versailles, Paris. † L 1.

FERGUS, Robert Exh. 1882
Landscape painter. 223 Stanhope Street, Regent's Park, London. † RBA 1.

FERGUSON, Miss A.B. Exh. 1895-98
Ochiltree, Benburb House, Lenzie, N.B. † GI 2, RSW 2.

FERGUSON, Annie M. Exh. 1902
31 George Square, Edinburgh. † RSA 1.

FERGUSON, Charles J. Exh. 1881-99
Architect. Carlisle 1881; London 1887. † RA 19.

FERGUSON, Miss C.M. Exh. 1897-1900
16 Lennox Street, Edinburgh. † SWA 4.

FERGUSON, Charles S.R. Exh. 1895-97
Glasgow. † GI 3.

FERGUSON, Daniel Exh. 1880-96
Glasgow. † GI 27.

FERGUSON, Edith Exh. 1880-1905
nee Marrable, Mrs. Austin F. Flower painter. London 1880; Sidmouth, Devon 1889. † D 5, L 1, M 3, SWA 25.

FERGUSON, Eleanor Exh. 1885-1908
Fruit painter. Hammersmith, London 1885; Dublin 1892. † RBA 1, RHA 4.

FERGUSON, Felicitie Exh. 1937-38
Landscape, coastal and flower painter. Newcastle, Co. Down 1937; London 1938. † RHA 6.

FERGUSON, Mrs. G. Munro Exh. 1889-91
Novar, Argylshire 1889; London 1890. † D 3, RSA 1.

FERGUSON, Hugh Exh. 1933
101 Drumoyne Road, Glasgow. † RSA 1.

FERGUSON, Ian Exh. 1930-33
Edinburgh. † RSA 4.

FERGUSON, Jane Exh. 1882
47 Queensboro Terrace, Kensington, London. † D 1.

FERGUSON, John Knox* Exh. 1880-91
Historical figure painter. Edinburgh. † L 2, RA 2, RSA 20.

FERGUSON, John M. Exh. 1885
Architect. 7 Princess Street, Cavendish Square, London. † RA 1.

FERGUSON, James M. Exh. 1882
Landscape and tree painter. 89 Shepherdess Walk, London. † RBA 1.

FERGUSON, James Matheson Exh. 1932-38
Dalserf 1932; Glasgow 1938. † RSA 2.

FERGUSON, James W. Exh. 1915-40
Stirling 1915; Glasgow 1918. † GI 31, L 6, RSA 24, RSW 3.

FERGUSON, Miss Marion Exh. 1883-1912
Sculptor. London 1883; Dublin 1907. † GI 1, L 1, RA 3, RHA 3, RSA 3.

FERGUSON, Robert J. Exh. 1880-90
Edinburgh. † RSA 6.

FERGUSON, W. Exh. 1912
Knowes Mill, East Linton, Prestonkirk, East Lothian. † L 1.

FERGUSON, William Exh. 1881-1917
Flower painter. Edinburgh. † GI 6, M 1, RA 1, RSA 48, RSW 1.

FERGUSON, William Forbes Exh. 1929-40
Landscape painter. The Knowl, Bearsden, Glasgow. † GI 11, L 2, RA 1, RSA 1, RSW 15.

FERGUSON, W.H. Exh. 1884-89
London 1884; Edinburgh 1885. † RSA 4.

FERGUSON, William J. Exh. 1882-1900
Landscape painter. London. † D 47, L 2, M 1, RBA 2, RI 2.

FERGUSSON, A.C. Exh. 1888
21 University Gardens, Glasgow. † GI 2.

FERGUSSON, Christian Jane Exh. 1922-40
nee Stark. Landscape painter. b. Dumfries. Studied Crystal Palace School of Art and Glasgow School of Art. (two travelling scholarships). Teacher at Glasgow School of Art and Art mistress Glasgow High School for Girls. Add: Dumfries. † GI 29, L 4, M 1, RA 2, RSA 16, RSW 10.

FERGUSSON, Miss Gillon Exh. 1881-1902
31 Chester Street, Edinburgh. † RSA 6.

FERGUSSON, Mrs. Gywenneth Exh. 1938
Miniature portrait painter. 3 Adelaide Crescent, Hove, Sussex. † RA 1.

FERGUSSON, Isa K. Exh. 1892
31 Chester Street, Edinburgh. † RSA 1.

FERGUSSON, James d. 1886
Archaelogical architect and author. 20 Langham Place, London. Exh. 1882-84. † RA 3.

FERGUSSON, John Duncan* 1874-1961
Painter and sculptor. Travelled on the continent and North Africa. R.B.A. 1902. Add: Leith 1897; Edinburgh 1899; Paris 1908. † BA 1, BAR 9, BG 100, CHE 2, CON 32, G 1, GI 14, GOU 5, I 2, L 5, LEF 41, LEI 7, LS 19, RBA 74, RI 4, RSA 8.

FERGUSSON, Nan S. Exh. 1932-37
Southdean, Dumfries 1932; 51 Gilmore Place, Edinburgh 1934. † GI 1, RSA 5.

FERN, Miss E. Exh. 1931-34
c/o Bourlet, London. † RCA 2.

FERNANDES, Joy M.L. Exh. 1935-38
Miniature portrait painter. Whitney on Wye, Herefords. † RA 1, SWA 2.

FERNANDEZ, S. Exh. 1920
10 Victoria Street, Liverpool. † L 1.

FERNBANK, R. Exh. 1938
152 Renfrew Street, Glasgow. † GI 1.

FERNESS, May Exh. 1938
† M 1.

FERNLEY, Edith Helen Exh. 1900-02
Miniature portrait painter. London. † RA 3.

FERRABY, Miss E. Dorrien Exh. 1922-24
Figure painter. A.N.S.A. 1924. Add: 401 Mansfield Road, Nottingham. † N 8.

FERRABY, Dr. H.P. Exh. 1902-14
Landscape painter. A.N.S.A. 1914. Add: Nottingham. † N 20.

FERRAN, George Exh. 1906
Coolikeigh House, Enniskerry, Co. Wicklow. † RHA 1.

FERRARI, C. Exh. 1916
c/o G. Nicali, 22 Sir Thomas Street, Liverpool. † L 1.

FERRARI, Giuseppe Exh. 1880-83
10 Canal Cottages, Bude, Cornwall. † GI 1, L 2, RA 1, RSA 9.

FERRE, M.E. Exh. 1913-14
London. † LS 2, RA 1.

FERRETTI, Paolo Exh. 1900
Corso Vittorio Emmanuele 39, Rome. † NG 2.

FERRI, A. Exh. 1910
c/o 3 Slater Street, Liverpool. † L 1.

FERRIER, Andree G. Exh. 1913
18 Rue de General Appert, Paris. † RSA 1.

FERRIER, C.W. Exh. 1910-11
11 Waterloo Place, London. † RA 3.

FERRIER, George Straton d. 1912
Landscape painter. R.E. 1881-82. R.I. 1898, R.S.W. 1881. Add: Edinburgh. † D 2, DOW 4, GI 30, L 11, RA 4, RE 4, RI 92, RSA 92, RSW 68.

FERRIER, James Exh. 1880-83
Edinburgh. † RSA 7.

FERRIS, Doris Exh. 1920-23
Painter of fairies. 15 Sydenham Avenue, Sydenham, London. † RA 1, RI 1.

FERRIS, E. Exh. 1881-90
Landscape painter. London. † D 2, RA 1, RBA 6.

FERRIS, R. Exh. 1885-1906
Glasgow. † GI 5.

FERRO, Cesare Exh. 1922
Figure painter. 10 Penywern Road, Earl's Court, London. † L 1, RA 2.

FERZI, Miss Francisca Exh. 1916-19
Figure painter. London. † RA 3.

FETCH, Ernest E. Exh. 1905
Architect. 20 John Street, Adelphi, London. † RA 1.

FETCH, Phyllis Eleanor b. 1908
Landscape painter. Daughter of Ernest F. q.v. Studied Teddington School of Art and Royal College of Art, diploma of R.C.A. 1931. Continuation scholarship 1931, British Institution Scholarship 1931. Add: Teddington, Hampton Wick 1933-35. † NEA 1, RA 2.

FEWSTER, Muriel Exh. 1910-14
Landscape painter. 30 St. Leonard's Terrace, Chelsea, London. † GOU 5, L 3, NEA 7.

FFELAN, Joseph A. Exh. 1902-24
Stained glass and decorative artist. London. † RA 7.

FFOLLIOTT, Agnes Exh. 1896
132 Sloane Street, London. † RI 1.

FFOLLIOTT, Anna Exh. 1889
Hollybrook, Boyle, Ireland. † D 3.

FFOLLIOTT, Col. John Exh. 1888-89
Hollybrook, Boyle, Ireland. † D 4.

FFOLLIOTT, Margaret Zaida Exh. 1886-97
Landscape painter. London. † D 1, NG 1, RI 1, SWA 2.

FFOULKES, Charles John b. 1868
Illustrative painter. Studied in Paris under Doucet and Duran. Curator of Armouries Tower of London 1913. Curator of Imperial War Museum 1917. Hon. Adviser to the Admiralty on Heraldry and Design. Add: London 1894 and 1901; Rye, Sussex 1897. † L 1, RA 4, RBA 1.

FIASCHI, G. Exh. 1883-84
c/o Italian Consul, Manchester. † L 1, M 1.

FICKLIN, Alfred Exh. 1884-98
Landscape painter. Norbiton, Surrey. † RBA 1, RI 3.

FICKLIN, George Exh. 1881-85
Landscape and coastal painter. Add: Penge, Kent 1881; Falmouth, Cornwall 1885. † RBA 2, RI 1.

FIDDES, Jane Exh. 1901-3
Hollywood, Monaghan, Ireland 1901; Belfast 1902. † RHA 3.

FIDDIAN, Dorothy b. 1891
Bookbinder. b. Calcutta, India. Studied Acton and Chiswick Polytechnic. Add: 31 Priory Road, London 1926-29. † L 5.

FIDGEON, Vera Exh. 1914-40
nee Laing-Scott. Flower and landscape painter. Add: Liscard, Cheshire 1914; Woking, Surrey 1924. † AR 2, COO 2, L 3, RBA 1, RI 4, ROI 1, SWA 3.

FIDLER, Constance Louise b. 1904
Portrait painter. Studied Liverpool City School of Art and Royal College of Art. Art mistress County School for Girls, Llanelly and Llanelly School of Art 1930-31, Senior art mistress County School for Girls, Twickenham 1931-34; Teacher of Crafts, Victoria Art School, Southport 1936-40. Exh. 1928-40. † M 1, NEA 3, RBA 1.

FIDLER, Fanny Exh. 1900
Teffont Magna, Salisbury, Wilts. † RI 1.

FIDLER, Gideon M. Exh. 1883-1910
Figure and domestic painter. Teffont Magna, Salisbury, Wilts. † B 12, D 1, L 16, LS 6, RA 13, RBA 2, RI 16, ROI 6, RSA 1.

FIDLER, Harry* d. 1935
Figure, rustic and domestic painter. Studied Herkomer's, Bushey, Herts. Married Laura B.S.F. q.v. R.B.A. 1919, R.O.I. 1921. Add: Teffont, Salisbury, Wilts. 1891 and 1898; Bushey, Herts. 1895; Andover, Hants. 1907. † AR 23, B 21, CHE 3, G 2, GOU 12, I 9, L 30, RA 30, RBA 116, RI 6, ROI 24.

FIDLER, Laura B.S. d. 1936
nee Clunas. Portrait and figure painter. Married Harry F. q.v. Add: Bushey, Herts. 1899; Andover, Hants. 1907. † AR 18, G 1, GI 1, L 5, P 3, RA 11, ROI 10, RSA 2, SWA 14.

FIEBIG, Frederick Exh. 1911-14
c/o Allied Artists Association, 67 Chancery Lane, London 1911; Paris 1913. † LS 9.

FIELD, Dick Exh. 1936-39
Landscape and portrait painter. London 1936; Winson, Nr. Cirencester, Glos. 1937. † RA 4.

FIELD, Dorothie S. Exh. 1937-39
Still life and figure painter. Vaud Studio, 72 St. James Street, Nottingham. †, N 10.

FIELD, Edwin Exh.1927-31
41 Dunsford Road, Bearwood, Birmingham; † B 1, M 1.

FIELD, Elizabeth b.1902
Mrs. W.A. Eden. Watercolour painter and wood engraver. Studied Birmingham Central School of Arts and Crafts and Slade School. Add: Wolverhampton 1925; Edgbaston, Birmingham 1928. † B 16, NEA 2.

FIELD, Freke Exh. 1890-94
Portrait and figure painter. Letchmere, Hamps. Surrey 1890; Chelsea, London 1894. † RA 3.

FIELD, Frances A. Exh. 1882-89
Flower painter. 9 Merton Street, Oxford. † D 1, L 1, M 1, RA 1, RBA 3, RI 6.

FIELD, F.H. Exh. 1913
14 The Circus, Greenwich, London. † RA 1.

FIELD, Miss G. Exh. 1911
51 Brunswick Square, Hove, Sussex. † RA 2.

FIELD, Mrs. G.V. Exh. 1932
2B Hartington Road, Buxton, Derbys. † RBA 1.

FIELD, Horace b. 1861
Architect. Studied South Kensington, RA Schools and under John Burnet of Glasgow. Exh. 1886-1930. Add: London. † GI 1, RA 36.

FIELD, Minnie A. Exh. 1886-87
Figure painter. Penrhos., Chislehurst, Kent. † SWA 2.

FIELD, Mrs. Mary F. Exh. 1890-1918
Figure and domestic painter. Hampstead, London 1890; Woking, Surrey 1907. † RA 12, RBA 1, ROI 1, RSA 1, SWA 8.

FIELD, Nora Exh. 1889
Alexandra House, Kensington Gore, London. † ROI 1.

FIELD, Walter 1837-1901
Landscape painter. A.R.W.S. 1880. Add: East Heath Studio, Hampstead, London. † B 1, D 4, FIN 1, L 11, M 1, RA 8, RWS 68.

FIELDEN, Alice Exh. 1914-37
Mrs. Caton-Jones. Landscape, portrait and miniature painter. Studied under Leon Sprinck in London and at Juliens, Paris. Travelled extensively in India, Middle East and East Africa. Add: Tadcaster 1914; Pontesford, Salop 1919. † RA 2, WG 58.

FIELDER, Fanny Exh. 1889
3 Wellington Terrace, Old Trafford, Manchester. † M 1.

FIELDER, Henry Exh. 1880-85
Landscape painter. Linden Cottage, Dorking, Surrey. † RBA 9.

FIELDHOUSE, Mrs. Florence Exh. 1940
Flower painter. 5 Helpston Villas, Clough Road, Rotherham, Yorks. † RA 1.

FIELDHOUSE, Harry Exh. 1927
30 Springwood Avenue, Huddersfield, Yorks. † RCA 2.

FIELDING, Aubrey Exh. 1938-39
42A Linden Gardens, London. † RBA,3.

FIELDING, Dora W. Exh. 1938
† M 1.

FIELDING, Julia Exh. 1935
3 Melrose Avenue, Norbury, London. † SWA 1.

FIELDING, John S. Exh. 1929
Glan Aber Park, Chester. † L 1.

FIELDING-OULD, Rev. F. Exh. 1925-29
Landscape and figure painter. Studied Paris for 3 years. Travelled in Italy. Add: London. † AB 6, WG 162.

FIELDS, H.A. Exh. 1939
62 Sherwood Street, Nottingham. † N 1.

FIENNES-CLINTON, E. Exh. 1912-14
4 Northcote House, Hampstead, London. † LS 9.

FIFE, Miss Violet See HORWOOD

FIGGINS, Miss E.M. Exh. 1889
11 Thorncliffe Grove, Oxford Road, Manchester. † M 1.

FIGGIS, Kathleen E. Exh. 1904-39
Miniature portrait painter. London. † B 1, L 6, P 2, RA 11, RHA 2, RI 3, RMS 9.

FIGGIS, T. Phillips Exh. 1887-1910
Architect. London. † RA 14.

FIGURA, Hans Exh. 1932
Etcher. † RA 6.

FILBY, James Exh. 1908-12
Fenstanton, Hunts. 1908; Ilkley, Yorks. 1910; Esswick, Yorks. 1912. † LS 17.

FILDES, Cdr. Denis Quintin b. 1889
Still life and flower painter. Served Royal Navy. Son of Sir Luke and Lady F. q.v. Exh. 1927-32. Add: Antrobus House, Amesbury, Salisbury, Wilts. † ALP 1, L 3, RA 5, WG 23.

FILDES, Fanny* d. c. 1927
Lady Luke F. nee Woods. Flower, still life and domestic painter. Add: 11 Melbury Road, Holland Park, London. † L 1, P 2, RA 8, ROI 1, TOO 1.

FILDES, Geoffrey Exh. 1924
73 St. George Road, London. † RA 1.

FILDES, Lucy Exh. 1900-09
Miniature painter. 14 School Road, Sale, Nr. Manchester. † L 5, M 7, RA 1.

FILDES, Sir Luke* 1843-1927
Portrait and genre painter and illustrator. b. Liverpool. Studied Mechanics Institute and School of Art, Liverpool, Warrington School of Art and South Kensington 1863. Worked as an illustrator on "Once a Week" and "The Graphic". Painted several Royal Portraits. A.R.A. 1879, R.A. 1887, Knighted 1906. Add: 11 Melbury Road, Kensington, London. † AG 1, B 3, GI 4, L 40, M 12, RA 145, TOO 4.

FILKIN, G.G. Exh. 1882
73 Coventry Road, Birmingham. † B 1.

FILKIN, Mrs. Hetty Exh. 1906
432 Slade Road, Gravelly Hill, Birmingham. † B 1.

FILKINS, Edward W. Exh. 1904-5
Architect. 35 Mead Road, Gravesend, Kent. † RA 2.

FILLINGHAM, Mrs. M. Ethel Exh. 1908-12
Leeds 1908; Grange over Sands 1909. † RCA 5.

FILTON, H. Exh. 1885
Runcorn, Cheshire. † M 3.

FINBERG, Alexander Joseph Exh. 1888-1921
Painter and etcher. London. † D 1, L 1, NEA 2, RA 1, RI 1.

FINCH, Alfred William Exh. 1886-1909
Landscape and figure painter. Mariakerken, Ostend. † LS 3, RBA 4.

FINCH, Edith M. Exh. 1908-38
Landscape and coastal painter. London 1908; Corfe Castle, Dorset 1938. † B 2, BK 42, RA 3, RHA 1, RI 2, SWA 1.

FINCH, H.H. Exh. 1901-11
London 1901; Sutton, Surrey 1910. † GI 8, LS 3.

FINCH, Mrs. J. Mary See SCOTT

FINCH, Miss L.W. Exh. 1895-96
48 Bracondale, Norwich, Norfolk. † SWA 2.

FINCH, Mme. Renee Exh. 1907-16
Portrait and figure painter. Founder Member London Group 1913. Add: London. † I 2, LS 22, NEA 10, RA 1.

FINCH, William Robert b. 1905
Etcher. 80 Richmond Road, Ilford, Essex 1933. † RA 1.

FINCHAM, Hjalmar Exh. 1924
5 Ennismore Avenue, Chiswick, London. † RA 1.

FINCHETT, D.R. Exh. 1885
80 Shakespear Street, Manchester. † M 1.

FINDEN, George C. Exh. 1880
Engraver. 3 Culmore Road, Balham, London. † RA 1.

FINDLATER, Lydia Exh. 1908-27
74 George Street, Edinburgh. † RSA 8, RSW 2.

FINDLAY, Anna R. Exh. 1923-38
Linocut artist. Glasgow. † BA 1, G 1, GI 6, L 7, M 5, RED 4, RSA 7.

FINDLAY, Edith A. Exh. 1885-90
Landscape and interior painter. London. † RA 1, RBA 3, RSA 1, SWA 1.

FINDLAY, Jane Leslie Exh. 1889-91
3 Rothesay Terrace, Edinburgh. † RSA 3.

FINDLAY, Margaret C.P. Exh. 1925-35
Sculptor. 30 Falkland Mansions, Hyndland, Glasgow. † GI 12, L 3, RA 1, RSA 5.

FINDLAY, William Exh. 1888-1929
Portrait painter. Dennistoun, N.B. 1888; Glasgow 1897. † GI 46, RA 1, RSA 13, RSW 2.

FINK, A. Exh. 1883
† G 1.

FINLAY, Alexander* Exh. 1880-93
Figure painter. Glasgow 1880 and 1888; Linlithgow 1887. † GI 25, RA 1.

FINLAY, Anne Exh. 1932-40
Landscape and figure painter. Studied Edinburgh College of Art. A.S.W.A. 1939. Add: 3 Primrose Hill Road, London. † BA 1, GI 1, GOU 3, NEA 5, RA 17, RBA 1, RSA 10, SWA 15.

FINLAY, Helen Exh. 1885-87
5 Colebrook Terrace, Hillhead, Glasgow. † GI 6.

FINLAY, Janetta Exh. 1888
4 Spring Gardens, Kelvinside, Glasgow. † GI 1.

FINLAY, Kirkman J. Exh. 1889
Dolgelly, N. Wales. † RSA 2.

FINLAY, R.H. Exh. 1883
13 Hill Street, Garnet Hill, Glasgow. † GI 1.

FINLAY, S.A. Exh. 1882-85
Liverpool. † L 5.

FINLAY, S.S. Exh. 1933
† RSW 1.

FINLAY, W.R. Exh. 1932-33
Edinburgh. † RSA 2.

FINLAYSON, Clifford Exh. 1932
4 Haymarket Terrace, Edinburgh. † GI 1.

FINLAYSON, James A. Exh. 1940
Kilmeny, Hawick. † RSA 2.

FINLAYSON, John D. Exh. 1904-7
Longniddry, N.B. † NG 1, RSA 2.

FINLAYSON, Kenneth Exh. 1920
28 West End Park Street, Glasgow. † RSA 1.

FINLAYSON, Muriel Exh. 1933
Flower painter. † COO 1.

FINLAYSON, Peter Exh. 1889-93
Glasgow. † GI 5.

FINLAYSON, W.A. Exh. 1882
The Oaks, Johnstone, Glasgow. † GI 2.

FINLEY, Arthur Exh. 1907
Grasmere, Altrincham, Cheshire. † L 1.

FINLINSON, Edith M. Exh. 1893-1923
Portrait painter. Add: Godstone, Surrey 1893; The Art College, Wimbledon 1898. † L 3, M 1, P 2, RA 4, RI 1, ROI 1, SWA 12.

FINN, Herbert John b. 1861
Painter and etcher. Studied S. Kensington, Antwerp and Paris. Add: St. Margarets, N. Devon 1885; London 1886 and 1906; Tunbridge Wells, Kent 1889; Deal, Kent 1891 and 1898; Sandwich, Kent 1894; Folkestone, Kent 1910. † AB 18, B 2, CHE 1, D 13, GI 1, GOU 1, L 14, RA 1, RBA 5, TOO 2.

FINN, Leonard Richard b. 1891
Portrait painter. Son of Herbert John F. q.v. Exh. 1921-25. Add: 8 Chelsea Manor Studios, Flood Street, London. † CHE 1, ROI 4.

FINN, Michael J. Exh. 1929
24 Snowden Road, Birkenhead. † L 2.

FINNEMORE, Charles H. Exh. 1897
29 Ravenstone Road, Hornsey, London. † B 1.

FINNEMORE, Ethelwyn Exh. 1910-23
Elmstone, Green Lane, Northwood, Middlesex. † B 1, D 1, RCA 5.

FINNEMORE, Joseph 1860-1939
Figure painter. Etcher and illustrator. Studied Birmingham and Antwerp. Special artist to the "Graphic". R.B.A. 1893, R.B.S.A. 1901, R.I. 1898. Add: Birmingham 1882; London 1885; Northwood, Middlesex 1900. † B 34, D 30, GI 11, L 22, RA 18, RBA 132, RCA 148, RHA 1, RI 184, ROI 1.

FINNEY, Miss A. Exh. 1891-97
Listowel, Folkestone, Kent. † B 3.

FINNEY, Arthur G. Exh. 1928-33
17 Palace Grove, Bromley, Kent. † NEA 1, RI 5.

FINNEY, H.A. Exh. 1927-34
London. † NEA 4.

FINNEY, James H. Exh. 1902-19
Landscape painter. Nottingham 1902; Mansfield, Notts. 1908; Lenton, Notts. 1918. † N 9.

FINNEY, Mrs. Virginia L. Exh. 1887-96
Portrait painter. 32 Camden Grove, Kensington, London. † NG 1, P 2, RA 2.

FINNIE, John 1829-1907
Landscape painter, etcher and engraver. b. Aberdeen. Headmaster of the Mechanics Institute and School of Art, Liverpool until 1896. R.B.A. 1884, R.E. 1895. Add: Liverpool 1880 and 1906; Llandudno, Wales 1897. † B 26, D 4, GI 4, L 84, M 8, NG 3, RA 33, RBA 18, RCA 56, RE 61, RI 12, ROI 3, RSA 6.

FINNY, Richard Jeffery b. 1909
Painter and pencil artist. Studied Byam Shaw School (school scholarship 1929). Assistant drawing master at the Byam Shaw School of Drawing and painting. Art master at Oundle School. Add: London 1932; Oundle 1934. † RA 1, RHA 5.

FIORCI, Mrs. Josephine Exh. 1931-32
† RMS 2.

FIRKINS, W.A. Exh. 1891-1903
The Willows, Barbourne, Worcester. † B 9, L 6, M 1, RCA 4, RE 1, RHA 3.

FIRTH, Mrs. F. Exh. 1908
Manor Oak Cottage, Frant, Sussex. † RA 1.

FIRTH, F.G. Exh. 1914
17 Aberdeen Grove, Armley, Leeds. † RA 1.

FIRTH, Miss G.M. Exh. 1924-28
Leather and metal worker and jeweller. Add: 34 Corn Market, Derby. † L 11.

FIRTH, Mrs. H.M. Shaw Exh. 1931
Flower painter. 21 Gedling Grove, Nottingham. † N 1.

FIRTH, J. Shaw Exh. 1927-37
Landscape and interior painter. 21 Gedling Grove, Nottingham. † N 4.

FIRTH, Marjorie Exh. 1920-40
Wood engraver. Richmond, Surrey 1920; St. John's Wood, London 1923. † NEA 6, RA 2, RED 1, RHA 1, SWA 1.

FIRTH, S. Exh. 1905-29
Rosehill Terrace, Marsden, Huddersfield. † L 3, RCA 2.

FIRTH, Susannah Exh. 1896-1929
Black and white artist, bookbinder, jeweller and designer. Studied Liverpool University. Add: Kirkby Lonsdale, Lancs. 1896; Liverpool 1907. † L 66, SWA 3.

FISCHER, Adam Exh. 1934
c/o Mrs. Asgar Fischer, Maglemosevej 18, Charlottenlund. † RSA 3.

FISCHER, Carl Exh. 1892
Landscape painter. † FIN 4.

FISCHER, C. le Marie Exh. 1890-91
Landscape painter. High Street, Bushey, Herts. † RBA 1, ROI 2.

FISCHER, Edgar H. Exh. 1903-14
Animal painter. London 1903; Birchington-on-Sea, Kent 1914. † GOU 78, L 2, RA 11, RI 2.

FISCHER, Miss J.M.T. Exh. 1909-16
Liverpool. † L 7.

FISCHER, Mrs. Natalie Exh. 1909-10
32 Vereker Road, West Kensington, London. † LS 6.

FISCHER, Otto Exh. 1911
† M 3.

FISH, Miss A.E. Exh. 1911-12
91 Forest Road, Nottingham. † N 3.

FISH, Anne Hariet Exh. 1913-33
Painter and black and white artist. b. Bristol. Studied London and Paris. Add: London 1913; East Grinstead, Sussex 1933. † FIN 128, LS 3, RA 1.

FISH, C.W. Exh. 1900
Manchester Road, Accrington, Lancs. † L 1.

FISH, Miss G.E. Exh. 1911
91 Forest Road, Nottingham. † N 1.

FISH, G.W. Exh. 1893-94
22 North Road, Devonshire Park, Birkenhead. † L 2.

FISH, N. Hilda Exh. 1909-38
Landscape painter. Nottingham. † N 13.

FISHER, Alexander b. 1864
Sculptor. Exh. 1886-1922. Add: London. † I 3, L 13, LS 7, NG 17, RA 41, RMS 2, ROI 1.

FISHER, Arthur Exh. 1904-12
Nantwich, Cheshire 1904; Shrewsbury 1906; Whitchurch, Salop. 1910. † LS 2, RCA 4.

FISHER, Amy E. Exh. 1880-88
Watercolour, figure, flower and domestic painter. Add: Penge, Kent and Soho Square, London. † D 6, L 1, RA 4, RBA 2, RI 3, SWA 3.

FISHER, Arthur E. Exh. 1891-1900
Watercolour figure painter. London 1891; Freemantle, Southampton 1900. † RA 3.

FISHER, Alfred Hugh 1867-1945
Painter, etcher and author. Studied S. Kensington and Paris. Travelled widely. A.R.E. 1898. Add: London 1887; Amberley, Nr. Arundel, Sussex 1917. † L 33, NEA 7, NG 6, RA 36, RBA 10, RE 105, RED 1, RI 4, ROI 2.

FISHER, Alfred Thomas b. 1861
Landscape painter. b. Plymouth. Add: 23 Kimberley Road, Cardiff 1922-34. † RCA 7.

FISHER, A.W. Exh. 1913
Bryn Estyn, Whitchurch, Salop. † LS 1.

FISHER, Beatrix Exh. 1889-95
Portrait and flower painter. London. † L 1, M 1, NG 2, RBA 6, ROI 1, SWA 2.

FISHER, Benjamin Exh. 1886-1938
Landscape painter. Talcafn, Nr. Conway, Wales. † L 6, RA 1, RCA 169.

FISHER, Charles Exh. 1881-90
Landscape and coastal painter. London 1883; Birmingham 1890. † B 1, RA 1, RBA 2, ROI 3.

FISHER, Catherine E. Exh. 1908-19
Gorsedd, Nr. Holywell. † L 2.

FISHER, Claude Leighton b. 1888
Painter, etcher, modeller and poster designer. Studied Liscard, Wallasey School of Art, Liverpool City School of Art. Art master at Liscard High School and Merchant Taylors School, Crosby, Lancs. Add: Liscard, Cheshire 1908; Liverpool 1930-32. † L 26, RCA 3.

FISHER, D. Exh. 1895
† TOO 1.

FISHER, Daniel Exh. 1881-86
Landscape and figure painter. Milford, Godalming, Surrey 1881; Witley, Godalming 1883. † G 1, M 2, RA 5, RBA 7, ROI 4.

FISHER, David Exh. 1882-84
Callender, N.B. † RSA 3.

FISHER, Don Exh. 1890
Winchester Hill, Stockbridge, Hants. † NG 1.

FISHER, Edgar Exh. 1919-20
31 Gt. King Street, Edinburgh. † GI 1, RSA 1.

FISHER, Mrs. Edith Exh. 1894-1926
Landscape painter. Weybridge, Surrey 1896; Westerham, E. Molesey, Surrey 1917; London 1925. † L 8, RA 4, SWA 2.

FISHER, Elizabeth A. Exh. 1891-1915
Figure painter. Prairie Cottage, Addlestone, Surrey. † B 3, RA 1, RBA 1, RI 1, ROI 4.

FISHER, Edgar H. Exh. 1909-33
Animal painter. London 1909; Wootton Wawen 1933. † B 2, LS 3, RA 1.

FISHER, Ernest W. Exh. 1933
Architect. 10 Old Burlington Street, London. † RA 1.

FISHER, F. Exh. 1922-39
Nottingham. † N 4.

FISHER, Frank Exh. 1885-98
Sculptor. Prairie Cottage, Addlestone, Surrey. † L 3, RA 6, RBA 3, ROI 2.

FISHER, F.C. Exh. 1887-1910
Gainsboro, Lincs. 1887; Burton-on-Trent 1907. † B 5.

FISHER, F.H. Exh. 1894
10 Victoria House, S. Lambeth Road, London. † RBA 1.

FISHER, G. Birkett Exh. 1920-33
Wallasey, Cheshire 1920; Liverpool 1932. † L 19, RCA 2.

FISHER, Miss G.G. Exh. 1892
† FIN 1.

FISHER, Mrs. George M. Exh. 1889-90
Landscape and figure painter. 5 Pitt Street, Camden Hill, London. † RID 8.

FISHER, George P. Exh. 1895-1907
Landscape painter. Fulham, London 1895; Upper Parkstone, Dorset 1907. † D 1, RA 1, RBA 3.

FISHER, G.T. Exh. 1916
23 Launceston Place, Kensington, London. † RA 1.

FISHER, Miss Helena Exh. 1891-1908
Animal painter. The Prairie Cottage, Addlestone, Surrey. † B 4, M 1, RA 7, RBA 2, ROI 8.

FISHER, Horace* Exh. 1883-1930
Landscape, interior and portrait painter. Add: London and Elmfield, Herne Hill 1883-98; Venice 1886-87; Brentford, Essex 1899; Camberley, Surrey 1909. † B 23, L 57, M 39, RA 56, RBA 7, RHA 3, RI 1, ROI 17.

FISHER, James Exh. 1892-98
Stained glass artist. London. † RA 6.

FISHER, Janet Exh. 1891-1925
Landscape, figure and flower painter. Studied Bushey, Herts. A.S.W.A. 1906, S.W.A. 1911. Add: Walton Rectory, Burton-on-Trent 1891; Bushey, Herts. 1892; Storrington, Sussex 1902; London 1906. † B 10, D 32, G 2, GI 1, GOU 27, I 4, L 26, LS 7, RA 12, RBA 3, RI 4, ROI 13, RSA 1, SWA 64.

FISHER, John Exh. 1887-88
Sculptor. Merchant Venturer's School, Bristol. † B 2, M 2, RA 1.

FISHER, Joseph Exh. 1921
12 Newington Green, London. † ROI 1.

FISHER, Joshua b. 1859
Landscape and figure painter and black and white illustrator. Studied Liverpool School of Art. Exh. 1884-1933. Add: Liverpool. † L 90, RCA 24.

FISHER, James A.S. Exh. 1935-40
55 Hillview Crescent, Corstorphine. † RSA 3.

FISHER, Miss J.C. Exh. 1886
24 Bank Street, Hillhead, Glasgow. † GI 2.

FISHER, Joshua Howard Exh. 1921-25
419 Poulton Road, Wallasey, Cheshire. † L 7, RCA 1.

FISHER, J.H. Vignoles Exh. 1884-1939
Landscape painter. London 1884; Shanley Green, Guildford, Surrey 1900; Shackleford, Surrey 1903; Alfriston, Sussex 1932. † AB 32, B 1, BG 33, DOW 182, G 1, I 4, L 2, NEA 1, RA,35, RBA 6, RI 14, ROI 12, TOO 5.

FISHER, Laura Margaret Exh. 1896-1940
Miniature painter. London. † L 2, LS 5, RA 23, RMS 1, ROI 1.

FISHER, Maddison Branch Exh. 1908-11
Portarlington, Queen's County 1908 and 1923; Dublin 1917. † RHA 12.

FISHER, Maud Charlton Exh. 1906
Painter, etcher, miniaturist, illustrator, designer and teacher. Studied Bristol School of Art. Add: Bristol 1906. † RA 1.

FISHER, Margaret D. Exh. 1900
5 Belgrave Mansions, Abbey Road, London. † L 1.

FISHER, Millicent Margaret See PROUT

FISHER, O. Exh. 1909
9 Stamer Street, S. Circular Road, Dublin. † RHA 2.

FISHER, Olive Exh. 1939
† GOU 1.

FISHER, Penelope E.T. Exh. 1933-40
Landscape and portrait painter. The Parsonage, Fleggburgh, Norfolk 1933; London 1937. † AR 43, GOU 2, L 1, RA 1, RI 1, ROI 3.

FISHER, Percy Harland* b. 1867
Portrait and figure painter. Add: Herne Hill, Sussex 1886; London 1895; Camberley, Surrey 1909-30. † B 40, COO 2, L 50, M 11, NG 2, P 3, RA 36, RBA 6, RHA 1, RI 14, ROI 20.

FISHER, Ralph Exh. 1909-22
Deganwy, Wales 1909; Llandudno 1913; Conway 1922. † RCA 18.

FISHER, Mrs. Rosa Exh. 1890-91
59 Broad Street, Birmingham. † B 2.

FISHER, Rebecca A. Exh. 1885-94
Landscape, flower and bird painter. Add: Scarrington House, Aslockton, Notts. † N 14.

FISHER, Robert B. Exh. 1936-38
Hamilton 1936; Glasgow 1938. † GI 1, RSA 1.

FISHER, R.M. Exh. 1881-90
Helensburgh. † GI 8, RSA 4.

FISHER, Mrs. R.M. Exh. 1881
Campbell Street, Helensburgh. † GI 1.

FISHER, R. Stanley Exh. 1920-38
Talycafn, N. Wales 1920; Ty'nygroes, Conway 1930. † RCA 29.

FISHER, Sybil Exh. 1911-27
Landscape and flower painter. Arno Vale, Nottingham. † N 25.

FISHER, S. Melton 1859-1939
Portrait, figure painter. A.R.A. 1917, R.A. 1924, R.I. 1936, R.O.I. 1888, V.P.R.O.I. 1898, R.P. 1900. Member of Society of 25 Artists. "In Realms of Fancy" purchased by Chantrey Bequest 1898. Add: London 1880 and 1894; Venice 1886. † B 22, BG 1, FIN 3, G 6, GI 11, L 70, M 32, NG 26, P 35, RA 188, RBA 3, RHA 2, RID 18, ROI 42, RSA 2.

FISHER, Stefani Melton b. 1891
Portrait painter and wood engraver. Son of S. Melton F. q.v. Studied Byam Shaw and Vicat Cole School of Art and RA Schools. Art master at Byam Shaw and Vicat Cole School and art master at Dulwich College. R.O.I. 1925. Exh. 1922-40. Add: 12 Orme Square, London. † COO 5, GI 1, L 2, RA 35, RCA 2, RI 26, ROI 44, WG 5.

FISHER, Thomas Exh. 1931-37
Metal worker. The Lawns, Tile Cross Road, Marston Green, Birmingham. † B 3.

FISHER, Tyson Exh. 1926-39
Liverpool. † L 2, RCA 1.

FISHER, Thomas Henry b. 1882
Painter, black and white artist and poster designer. Studied Nottingham School of Art. Cartoonist on the "Nottingham Guardian". Signs work Thomas Henry. N.S.A. 1915. Add: Keyworth, Notts. 1909; Plumtree, Notts. 1912. † L 4, N 35.

FISHER, Miss Vaudrey Exh. 1910-19
Miniature painter. London. † RA 4, RI 1.

FISHER, William Exh. 1880-86
Portrait painter. 24 Welbeck Street, London. † G 5, M 1, RA 1, RI 2, ROI 4.

FISHER, W.L.T. Exh. 1928
Tasburgh, Nr. Norwich, Norfolk. † RBA 2.

FISHER, William Mark* 1841-1923
Landscape, genre and portrait painter. b. Boston, U.S.A. Studied at the Lowell Institute, Boston and under George Innes. Went to Paris 1861 and studied under Gleyre and Corot. Came to England 1872. Father of Millicent M. Prout, q.v. N.E.A. 1886, A.R.A. 1911, R.A. 1919, R.I. 1881, R.O.I. 1883. Purchased by Chantrey Bequest "A Vision of the Sea" 1915, "Feeding the Fowls" in 1920 and "Snow Scene" (1894) in 1942. Add: London 1880; Steyning, Sussex 1882; Bourne Road, Bucks. 1885; Stockbridge, Hants. 1889; Newport, Essex 1893; Harlow, Essex 1901. † AG 1, B 6, BA 8, BG 1, D 4, G 28, GI 31, GOU 9, I 13, L 23, LEI 251, LS 3, M 45, NEA 133, NG 23, RA 89, RBA 3, RHA 14, RI 1, ROI 12, RSA 9, TOO 5.

FISHWICK, Miss J. Exh. 1912
The Heights, Rochdale. † L 1.

FISK, S. Exh. 1906
42 Hatherley Street, Princes Road, Liverpool. † L 1.

FISKER, Jessie Exh. 1888
24 Bank Street, Hillhead, Glasgow. † GI 1.

FISON, Miss W.L. Exh. 1907
West Hampstead, London. † SWA 1.

FITCH, Winifred Emily b. 1888
Mrs. Mackenzie. Portrait painter. Studied Hornsey School of Art. Exh. 1912-24. Add: London 1912; Minchinhampton, Glos. 1923. † L 1, RA 1, SWA 1.

FITCHEW, Dorothy Exh. 1910-22
Landscape and figure painter. The Oriels, Widmore, Bromley, Kent. † L 2, RA 7, RI 3, SWA 2.

FITHIAN, Edith Exh. 1894
Portrait painter. Silverdale, Aldenham Road, Bushey, Herts. † RA 1.

FITTON, E. Exh. 1884-1906
Heywood, Manchester. † B 1, L 1, M 3, RCA 4.

FITTON, Hedley 1859-1929
Etcher. A.R.E. 1903, R.E. 1908. Add: Didsbury 1891; Shottermill, Surrey 1898; Haslemere, Surrey 1912. † AB 2, FIN 16, GI 2, L 23, M 1, P 2, RA 8, RE 36, RHA 1.

FITTON, James b. 1899
Painter, lithographer and theatrical designer. b. Oldham. Studied Manchester School of Art and Central School, London. Member of London Group 1934. Exh. 1927-40. Add: 10 Pond Cottages, Dulwich Village, London. † BA 2, COO 2, GI 8, L 1, LEI 1, NEA 4, RA 17, RED 2, TOO 25.

FITTON, Margaret Exh. 1930-40
nee Cook. Married James F. q.v. Painter, sculptor, lithographer and illustrator. Studied London. Add: 10 Pond Cottages, College Road, Dulwich Village, London. † NEA 5, RA 9, SWA 2.

FITZ, M.J. Exh. 1887
The Hollies, Broadgreen Avenue, Croydon, Surrey. † B 3.
FITZ, P.E. Exh. 1886
122 Lowden Road, Herne Hill, Kent. † B 1.
FITZ, William Exh. 1880-91
Landscape and figure painter. London. † D 1, L 1, RA 2, RBA 3,, RHA 5, ROI 2, RSA 2.
FITZCOOK, H. Exh. 1898
23 Wellington Square, Hastings, Sussex. † RA 2.
FITZGERALD, Lady Exh. 1893
8 Hertford Street, Mayfair, London. † NG 1.
FITZGERALD, Mrs. Annie Exh. 1888
Miniature painter. Old Charlton, Kent. † RA 1.
FITZGERALD, Augustine Exh. 1903
11 Avenue Hoche, Paris. † NG 1.
FITZGERALD, Miss Betty
See ROTHENSTEIN
FITZGERALD, Claude J. Exh. 1893-1912
London. † L 1, RA 1, ROI 2.
FITZGERALD, Dorothy b. 1888
Painter and lithographer. Studied RHA Schools. Add: Dublin 1905; London 1911. † FIN 3, L 1, P 6, RA 1, RHA 16, RI 1.
FITZGERALD, Eva Exh. 1906-10
Via Monteleone, 23 Palermo, Sicily. † RHA 1, RI 1.
FITZGERALD, Florence d. 1927
Painter and sculptor. Married W. Follen Bishop q.v. Add: London 1884 and 1922; Liverpool 1890. † B 19, L 94, LS 3, M 1, RA 17, RBA 25, RCA 45, ROI 5, RSA 1.
FITZGERALD, Frederick R.
Exh. 1897-1938
Landscape and marine painter. Cotswold House, Orford Road, Boscombe, Hants. † B 2, BRU 1, L 1, RA 5, RBA 4, RCA 3, RI 10, ROI 12.
FITZGERALD, Hazelwood B. Exh. 1925
Sculptor. 115 Ebury Street, London. † RA 1.
FITZGERALD, J. Exh. 1880-94
4 Henrietta Place, Dalkey, Dublin. † RHA 20.
FITZGERALD, John Anster* 1819-1906
Fairy and figure painter. London. † B 8, D 11, GI 1, L 24, RA 2, RBA 18, RHA 6, RI 20, ROI 10.
FITZGERALD, Michael Exh. 1880-85
Figure painter. London. † D 1, L 1, RA 2, RHA 2.
FITZGERALD, Murroc Exh. 1930-33
Figure, landscape and still life painter. † LEF 17.
FITZGERALD, Peggy Exh. 1938-40
Portrait painter. Titcomb Cottage, Kintbury, Berks. † L 1, NEA 2, RA 2.
FITZHERBERT, Dorothy Exh. 1911
Kingswear, S. Devon. † L 1.
FITZHERBERT, H.G. Exh. 1912-22
Carbis Bay, Cornwall 1912; Exmouth 1921. † ROI 4.
FITZHUGH, Charlotte A. Exh. 1901-3
Uckfield, Sussex 1901; London 1903. † D 2. SWA 1.
FITZJAMES, Anna Maria Exh. 1880-86
Flower and fruit painter. S.W.A. 1880. Add: London. † SWA 14.
FITZJOHN, E. Exh. 1884
76 Park Road, Haverstock Hill, London. † RBA 1, ROI 1.
FITZMAURICE, Elsie Exh. 1898
c/o Miss Pearson, 19 Bolton Studios, Redcliffe Road, London. † RMS 2.
FITZMAURICE, Harrietta Exh. 1888-1911
Cork 1888; London 1898. † GI 2, L 1, LS 9.
FITZMAURICE, R. Exh. 1922
38 Forest Road, Moseley, Birmingham. † B 3.
FITZPATRICK, Fred Exh. 1896-97
Dublin. † RHA 5.
FITZROY, Cyril D. Exh. 1886-95
Landscape and interior painter. London. † RA 4, RBA 1.
FITZSIMONS, W.G. Exh. 1882-1916
Liverpool. † L 42.
FITZWILLIAMS, Joyce Exh. 1936
Portrait painter. c/o Rowley Gallery, Church Street, Kensington, London. † RA 1.
FIX-MASSEAU, Exh. 1911-12
30 Rue de Bruxelles, Paris. † L 2.
FIZELLE, Rah* Exh. 1928
Landscape painter. 14 Clifton Gardens, Maida Vale, London. † GI 1, RA 1.
FLACH, Charles Exh. 1890-92
Portrait and figure painter. Little Bushey, Herts. 1890; Surbiton, Surrey 1892. † FIN 1, RA 3, RBA 1.
FLACK, Edith Mary Exh. 1887-89
Watercolour painter of church interiors. 26 Hartham Road, W. Holloway, London. † RA 1, RBA 1.
FLAMENG, Francois* 1856-1923
French portrait and historical painter. Son of Leopold F. q.v. Add: Paris 1905 and 1911; 9 St. Paul's Studios, Talgarth Road, London 1908. † AG 24, L 3, NG 2.
FLAMENG, Leopold 1831-1911
French engraver. Exh. 1883-98. Add: 29 Boulevard Montparnasse, Paris. † RA 10.
FLAMENG, Marie Auguste 1843-1893
French artist. 47 Rue Ampere, Paris 1882. † GI 1.
FLANAGAN, John P. Exh. 1915-39
Portrait, still life and landscape painter. London. † BA 1, CHE 1, I 1, NEA 3, RA 1.
FLANDERS, Marguerite Exh. 1928-39
nee Sandell. Mrs. Bernard F. Miniature painter and designer. Studied North London School of Art. A.R.M.S. 1929. Add: London 1928, Woodford, Essex 1936. † L 3, RA 2, RMS 33.
FLANDRIN, Jules* b. 1871
French painter. Exh. 1912-23. † GOU 11.
FLANDRIN, Paul Exh. 1885
10 Rue Garanciere, Paris. † GI 1.
FLANEUR, G. Exh. 1903
Etcher. c/o F.C. McQueen, 33 Haymarket, London. † RA 1.
FLASHMAN, Doris Louisa Annie b. 1897
nee Beerling. Miniature painter and pastellier. Studied Dover and Bournemouth Art Schools. Exh. 1927-30. Add: Dover. † RA 3, RMS 1.
FLATHER, Mrs. J. Exh. 1888
Cavendish College, Cambridge. † B 1.
FLATTER, T. Otto Exh. 1937
† P 1.
FLATTERY, Ivy Exh. 1931
Miniature portrait painter. 2 Grove Court, Drayton Gardens, London. † RA 1.
FLAWS, A. Exh. 1885-86
Stockport, Lancs. † M 4.
FLEETWOOD-WALKER, Bernard b. 1893
Portrait and figure painter. Studied Birmingham School of Arts and Crafts, London and Paris. A.R.W.S. 1940. Exh. 1930-40. Add: Birmingham. † P 2, RA 13, RWS 3.
FLEISCHER, P. Exh. 1888
Munich and Edinburgh. † RSA 1.
FLEISCHMANN, Asphodel E. Exh. 1931-39
American landscape painter. Chetwode Manor, Buckingham. † BA 57, GOU 10, NEA 2, SWA 4.
FLEMING, le See L
FLEMING A.G. Exh. 1933-35
50 Ann Street, Edinburgh. † RSW 7.
FLEMING, Desmond J. Exh. 1938-39
Landscape painter. 387 Clontarf Road, Dublin. † RHA 2.
FLEMING, Herbert S. Exh. 1908-39
Architect. Erith, Kent 1908; London 1921. † RA 8.
FLEMING, Ian b. 1906
Painter and etcher. Studied Glasgow School of Art and Paris. Senior Lecturer Glasgow School of Art 1931-47. Exh. 1927-40. Add: Glasgow. † GI 16, M 6, RA 4, RSA 29.
FLEMING, John Exh. 1880-81
1 Scotland Street, Glasgow. † GI 2.
FLEMING, Mrs. J. Arnold Exh. 1932-37
Locksley, Helensburgh. † GI 4.
FLEMING, J. Edith Exh. 1897-1902
Edinburgh 1897 and 1902, Cambeltown, N.B. 1899. † GI 4, RSA 7.
FLEMING, Marion Exh. 1900-33
Southport, Lancs. † L 6.
FLEMING, Marjorie Exh. 1886
† SWA 1.
FLEMING, Mary Exh. 1930
3 Gambier Terrace, Liverpool. † L 1.
FLEMING, Miss M.H. Exh. 1885
c/o W. Bright Esq., Catterick Hall, Withington, Manchester. † M 1.
FLEMING, Violet M. Exh. 1894-1900
29 Windsor Road, Rathmines, Dublin. † RHA 2.
FLEMING, William J. Exh. 1887
Miniature portrait painter. 15 Lovell Terrace, Leeds, Yorks. † RA 2.
FLEMMING, Leila Exh. 1890-1908
Landscape painter. Freshford, Bath 1890; Bradford on Avon, Wilts. 1908. † B 1, L 1, RA 1, RHA 1, RI 1, SWA 4.
FLEMMING-WILLIAMS, C.R. Exh. 1920
Watercolour figure painter. Southernwood, Letchworth, Herts. † RA 1.
FLEMWELL, George Exh. 1892-1910
Flower, landscape and figure painter. Add: Antwerp 1892; Sutton, Surrey 1894. † BG 34, L 2, RA 3.
FLENLEY, Mrs. Dulcie Exh. 1921
c/o R. Jackson & Sons, 3 Slater Street, Liverpool. † L 1.
FLESCH, L. Exh. 1881
16 Avenue Trudaine, Paris. † RHA 1.
FLETCHER, Lady Exh. 1937-40
† NEA 1, RI 2.
FLETCHER, Miss A. Exh. 1882-85
Elmdon, Sellyhill, Birmingham. † B 2.
FLETCHER, Mrs. Agnes E. Exh. 1913-27
Portrait painter. Coolbanagher, Portarlington, Ireland. † RHA 3.
FLETCHER, Annie Gertrude
Exh. 1886-1939
Mrs. Edgar J. Houle. Portrait and ivory miniature painter and bookplate designer. b. Richmond, Surrey. Studied Slade School and in studio of E.C. Alston. R.M.S. 1897. Add: London 1886; Harrow on the Hill, Middlesex 1919. † L 29, NG 3, RA 33, RI 6, RMS 174, SWA 2.
FLETCHER, Archibald Michael b. 1887
Painter, lithographer and decorative artist. Studied York School of Art, Leeds School of Art and Royal College of Art. Art master at St. Martin's School of Art, London and at Birmingham Central School of Art. R.B.S.A. 1931. Add: Warley Woods, Birmingham 1924; Solihull 1934. † B 33, NEA 3, RA 16.

FLETCHER, A.T. Exh. 1882-98
Birmingham. † B 10.

FLETCHER, Sir Banister 1866-1953
Architect and surveyor. Studied R.A. Schools (many prizes and scholarships). Exh. 1926-38. Add: London. † RA 10.

FLETCHER, Benton d. 1944
Watercolour landscape painter. Travelled widely. Exh. 1914. † FIN 38.

FLETCHER, Blandford* Exh. 1880-1918
Landscape and figure painter. London 1880 and 1918; Enfield, Middlesex 1884; Westcott, Dorking, Surrey 1905; Abingdon, Berks 1917. † B 24, FIN 1, GI 3, L 11, M 16, RA 21, RBA 9, RHA 6, RI 1, ROI 5, TOO 84.

FLETCHER, Bramwell Exh. 1920
30 Grove Terrace, Highgate Road, London. † ROI 1.

FLETCHER, B.J. Exh. 1917-25
R.B.A. 1919. Leicester 1917, Central School of Arts and Crafts, Birmingham 1922. † B 1, RBA 10.

FLETCHER, Mrs. Clare Exh. 1909-39
Derby 1909; Mansfield, Notts. 1912; Matlock, Derbys. 1939. † N 11.

FLETCHER, Lady Dorothy Exh. 1939
† GOU 3.

FLETCHER, Miss D.M. Exh. 1913
73 Kremlin Drive, Stoneycroft, Liverpool. † L 2.

FLETCHER, Evelyn Exh. 1880-89
Landscape painter. Court House, Hampton Court, Middlesex. † RBA 1, SWA 6.

FLETCHER, Flitcroft Exh. 1882-86
Landscape painter. 6 Wellesley Road, Croydon, Surrey. † RA 5, RBA 1.

FLETCHER, Fannie Julie Exh. 1914
8 Heath Villas, Vale of Health, Hampstead, London. † LS 3.

FLETCHER, Frank Morley b. 1866
Portrait painter and engraver. London 1888; Reading 1893 and Edinburgh 1911. † I 11, L 2, RA 2, ROI 1, RSA 1.

FLETCHER, George Exh. 1912
53 Pembroke Road, Dublin. † RHA 1.

FLETCHER, Mrs. Grace Exh. 1888
Fruit painter. 11 Rue le Maitre, Puteaux, Seine, Paris. † RA 1.

FLETCHER, G. Stuart Exh. 1931-38
Flower, figure and portrait painter. Sandiacre, Nottingham 1931; Bramcote, Notts. 1938. † N 19.

FLETCHER, Hanslip 1874-1955
Painter and etcher. Exh. 1906-38. Add: London. † BA 8, BAR 1, D 2, G 2, GOU 88, I 19, L 16, LS 8, NEA 7, RA 18, RI 3, RSA 1.

FLETCHER, Lady Helen Exh. 1940
Saxlingham Hall, Norwich, Norfolk. † SWA 2.

FLETCHER, Henry Exh. 1939
† GOU 1.

FLETCHER, Hubert H. Exh. 1898
Sculptor. 41 Melody Road, East Hill, Wandsworth. † RA 1.

FLETCHER, Miss H.M. Exh. 1907
Marlingford Hall, Nr. Norwich, Norfolk. † RA 1.

FLETCHER, Miss H.M. Exh. 1925
14 Charlotte Road, Edgbaston, Birmingham. † B 1.

FLETCHER, Henry M. Exh. 1904-23
Architect. 10 Lincoln's Inn Fields, London. † RA 10.

FLETCHER, H. Murray Exh. 1883-1903
Landscape painter. Stoke Newington, London 1883; Ramsgate, Kent 1896. † D 3, RA 1, RBA 5, RI 1.

FLETCHER, John Exh. 1922-25
Landscape painter. 5 Lime Grove, Long Eaton, Nr. Nottingham. † N 4.

FLETCHER, Joseph Exh. 1916-30
R.B.A. 1920. Southall, Middlesex 1916; London 1919. † RBA 33.

FLETCHER, J.H. Exh. 1884-1912
Painter and illuminator. Gresham Chambers, Nottingham. † N 8, RA 1.

FLETCHER, L. Exh. 1881
Landscape painter. Court House, Hampton Court, Middlesex. † SWA 1.

FLETCHER, Margaret Exh. 1886
Portrait painter. Earls Croome, Oxford. † RA 1.

FLETCHER, Miss Margaret
See LEADBITTER

FLETCHER, Miss P.M. Exh. 1928
15 Fox Road, West Bridgford, Notts. † N 1.

FLETCHER, Rosamund M.B. b. 1914
Sculptor. Studied under Rutherston 1935-37 and Slade School 1937-39. Add: 305 Woodstock Road, Oxford. † RA 5, RBA 1.

FLETCHER, Miss U.R. Exh. 1925
14 Charlotte Road, Edgbaston, Birmingham. † B 2.

FLETCHER, Mrs. Violet Exh. 1930
Stained glass artist. 40 Edith Street, West Bromwich, Staffs. † RA 1.

FLETCHER, Walter Exh. 1939
Coastal painter. 11 Embankment Gardens, Chelsea, London. † RA 1.

FLETCHER, W.J. Exh. 1932
R.A. Mess, Colchester, Essex. † RCA 1.

FLETE, Mrs. Glena Exh. 1935
Llanaudno, Wales. † RCA 2.

FLEURY, de See D

FLEURY, Miss F. Exh. 1886-92
10 Rue Fontaine, Paris. † GI 11, L 1.

FLEURY, H. Exh. 1885-90
Liverpool 1885; Bradford, Yorks. 1890. † L 1, M 1.

FLEUSS, Oswald Exh. 1890-1911
Stained glass artist. London. † RA 9.

FLEWETT, Miss C.N. Exh. 1882-97
Smethwick, Birmingham. † B 10, L 1.

FLEWITT, E. Exh. 1924-31
Landscape and figure painter. Mapperley, Nottingham. † N 12.

FLIGHT, Capt. Claude 1881-1955
Painter, sculptor, wood cut artist and teacher. Editor of "Arts and Crafts Quarterly" and art lecturer for L.C.C. A.R.B.A. 1923, R.B.A. 1925. Add: London 1921-31. † GI 1, L 2, RA 1, RBA 69, RED 110.

FLIGHT, Elizabeth Gill Exh. 1921
Bristol. † RMS 1.

FLINN, Doris K. Exh. 1927-36
Sculptor. Manchester 1927; Bristol 1935. † B 3, GI 1, M 1, RA 1 RSA 4.

FLINT, Miss E.M. Exh. 1938-40
94 Lichfield Street, Walsall, Staffs. † B 4.

FLINT, Francis Murray Russell b.1915
Landscape painter. Son of William Russell F. q.v. Studied Grosvenor School of Modern Art, R.A. Schools and Paris. Add: 80 Peel Street, Campden Hill, London 1937. † RA 5.

FLINT, Francis Wighton Exh. 1888
Painter and designer. Father of William Russell and Robert Purves F. q.v. Add: 5 Rosefield Place, Portobello, N.B. † RSA 1.

FLINT, Robert Purves 1883-1947
Landscape painter and etcher. Son of Francis Wighton F. q.v. Studied Edinburgh College of Art. Served in Army World War I. Wounded in Flanders 1917. R.S.W. 1918., A.R.W.S. 1932., R.W.S. 1937. Add: Portobello, N.B. 1906; Edinburgh 1910; Whitstable, Kent 1923. † AR 1, B 1, FIN 42, G 6, GI 67, I 6, L 18, LEI 50, M 7, RA 4, RHA 13, RSA 33, RSW 72, RWS 82, WG 48.

FLINT, Savile* Exh. 1880-97
Landscape painter. London 1880; Manchester 1897. † G 2, M 5, NG 1, RA 7, RBA 12, RHA 3, ROI 1, RSA 1.

FLINT, William Russell* 1880-1969
Painter, illustrator, medical illustrator and lithographer. Son of Francis Wighton F. q.v. Studied Edinburgh School of Art and at Heatherleys, London. Served World War I in R.N.V.R. and R.A.F. On Staff of "London Illustrated News" 1904-8. A.R.A. 1924. R.A. 1933, A.R.E. 1931, R.E. 1933, R.O.I. 1912, R.S.W. 1913, A.R.W.S. 1914, R.W.S. 1917, P.R.W.S. 1936. Add: Portobello, N.B. 1898; London 1902 and 1925; Edinburgh 1913; Helensburgh 1919. † AG 7, B 6, BA 8, BAR 39, CHE 1, COO 1, FIN 480, G 5, GI 69, GOU 2, I 31, L 114, M 10, RA 123, RE 28, RHA 1, RI 1, ROI 10, RSA 22, RSW 63, RWS 208, TOO 2, WG 45.

FLOCKHART, William Exh. 1885-1913
Architect. London. † GI 2, RA 18, RSA 3.

FLODIN, Hilda Exh. 1906
Figure painter. 107 Avenue du Main, Paris. † NEA 1.

FLOOD, Mrs. A. Exh. 1893-97
Walton on Thames 1893; Cookham, Berks. 1896. † SWA 3.

FLOOD, Alice Exh. 1896-98
2 Church Street, Tewkesbury. † B 4.

FLOOD, Alice Hanford Exh. 1901
Victorian Club, Sacheville Street, Piccadilly, London. † D 1.

FLOOD, Constance W. Exh. 1889-95
Landscape and coastal painter. Crag-y-Barnes, Sidmouth, Devon 1893. † D 1, SWA 7.

FLOOD, J.J. Exh. 1929-31
31 North Frederick Street, Dublin. † RHA 5.

FLOOD-JONES, Constance Exh. 1886-1915
Landscape painter. London. † L 2, NG 1, RA 1, RBA 1, RI 1.

FLORENCE, Henry Louis c. 1844-1916
Architect. Exh. 1891-1902. Add: 3 Verulam Buildings, Gray's Inn, London. † RA 3.

FLORENCE, Mary Sargent 1857-1954
nee Sargent. Decorative mural painter and fresco artist. Studied Slade School and Colarossi's, Paris. N.E.A. 1911. "Suffer Little Children to Come unto Me" (1913) purchased by Chantrey Bequest in 1932, "Pentecost" (1913) in 1932 and "Children at Chess" (1903) in 1949. Add: London 1894; Lord's Wood, Marlow, Bucks. 1911. † L 1, NEA 55, RA 5, SWA 3.

FLORIAN, Ernest Exh. 1907-11
Paris. † L 5.

FLOTOW, Von See V

FLOWER, Miss Exh. 1902
Mallards Court, Stockenchurch, Nr. Wallingford, Berks. † SWA 1.

FLOWER, Alice Exh. 1882-1903
nee Perry. Married Charles Edwin F. q.v. Landscape painter. Add: London. † L 11, RA 1, SWA 2.

FLOWER, Arthur S. Exh. 1893
Architect. 22 Surrey Street, London. † RA 1.

FLOWER, Beatrice Exh. 1927-28
Redhill Cottage, Newbury, Berks. † AB 1, M 1.

FLOWER, Clement Exh. 1899-1908
Portrait and figure painter. Chapel Studio, Bushey, Herts. † RA 4.
FLOWER, Charles Edwin b. 1871
Painter, wood engraver, lithographer and illustrator. Married to Alice F. q.v. b. Merton, Surrey. Studied Royal College of Art. Add: Anerley 1899, Wallingford, Berks. 1907. † B 17, L 7, RA 13, RBA 1.
FLOWER, Edgar Exh. 1890
Landscape painter. Stratford on Avon. † RBA 1.
FLOWER, Mrs. E.B. Exh. 1917
Bay View, Northam, N. Devon. † RA 1.
FLOWER, Marmaduke C. William d. 1910
Portrait and figure painter. Herkomer's first assistant at Bushey School. Add: Leeds 1880; Bushey 1887. † FIN 1, LS 5, RA 21, ROI 1.
FLOWER, Noel E. Exh. 1897-1913
Portrait painter. London. † L 19, NG 1, P 1, RA 7, RMS 1.
FLOWERDEW, Charles E. Exh. 1885
1 Walter Street, Nottingham. † N 1.
FLOWERDEW, Miss M. Exh. 1901-3
57 Langtry Grove, New Bashford, Notts. † N 3.
FLOWERS, Peter 1916-1950
Landscape painter. Studied under Bertram Nicholls. A.R.B.A. 1940. Add: Sunwayes, York Avenue, Hove, Sussex. † RA 2, RBA 7, ROI 3.
FLOYD, Benjamin Exh. 1896
3 Fulham Studios, 452B Fulham Road, London. † L 1.
FLOYD, Donald H. Exh. 1914-40
Landscape painter. Plymouth, Devon, 1914; Caldicot, Nr. Newport, Mon. 1920; Chepstow, Mon. 1932; Tintern, Mon. 1940. † B 2, L 3, RA 11.
FLOYD, F.H. Exh. 1905
4 The Broadway, Newbury, Berks. † RA 1.
FLOYD, Frank P. Exh. 1908
29 Thornton Road, Wimbledon, London. † RA 1.
FLOYD, G.W. Exh. 1932
121 Sneinton Road, Nottingham. † N 1.
FLOYD, H. Exh. 1905
96 bis Rue de la Tour, Paris. † RA 1.
FLOYD, H. Exh. 1917
Highmead, Tilford, Farnham, Surrey. † RA 1.
FLOYD, Harry Exh. 1884-90
Figure painter. Eastbourne 1884; London 1887. † B 1, G 1, L 1, M 1, RA 3.
FLOYD, Henry Exh. 1909
† LS 1.
FLOYD, J. Ashton Exh. 1926
† M 2.
FLUHART, George Exh. 1910
Watercolour painter of American landscapes. † FIN 10.
FLUX, Gladys B. Exh. 1937
Cardiff, Wales. † RCA 1.
FLYNN, Carmel Exh. 1937-40
Landscape and coastal painter. Ardeevin House Dalkey, Co. Dublin. † RHA 11.
FOCARDI, Giovanni Exh. 1883-88
Sculptor. 10 Auriol Road, W. Kensington, London. † G 8, RA 3, RI 2.
FOCARDI, R. Exh. 1881
Etcher. Byerley House, Parchmore Road, Thornton Heath, Surrey. † RA 2.
FOCILLON, V. Exh. 1906-10
c/o Frost and Reed, 8 Clare Street, Bristol. † RA 3.
FOGERTY, J.F. Exh. 1886-95
Architect. Dublin 1886; Shifnel, Salop 1888; Bournemouth, Hants. 1895. † RHA 6.
FOGGIE, David 1878-1948
Figure and portrait painter. Studied Antwerp, Paris, Florence and Holland. Teacher of Drawing at Edinburgh College of Art. A.R.S.A. 1925; R.S.A. 1931; R.S.W. 1918. Add: Leuchars Fife 1905; Dundee 1913; 38 Danube Street, Edinburgh 1924. † AG 2, GI 72, L 6, RA 5, RSA 114, RSW 91.
FOGGIE, Neil Exh. 1935-40
38 Danube Street, Edinburgh 1935; Brookside, Dollar 1938. † GI 2, RSA 8.
FOISTER, John Arthur Exh. 1934-36
Beeston, Notts. 1934; Olton, Warwicks. 1935. † B 3, N 2, RCA 1.
FOLEY, Agnes E. Exh. 1906-21
Liverpool. † L 11.
FOLEY, George C. Exh. 1938-40
28 Mungalhead Road, Falkirk. † RSA 4.
FOLEY, Mrs. Margaret W. Exh. 1904
† RMS 1.
FOLI, Mme Rosita Exh. 1885
49 St. James's Street, London. † ROI 1.
FOLIN, Mlle Anais Exh. 1915
Figure painter. Holbein Studios, 52 Redcliffe Road, London. † NEA 2.
FOLKARD, Elizabeth Exh. 1880-95
Figure and domestic painter. Sister of Julia Bracewell F. q.v. London. † B 3, D 3, DOW 1, L 3, M 1, RA 2, RBA 4, RI 3.
FOLKARD, Edward C.N. Exh. 1932-39
Sculptor. 2 Court Farm Road, Nottingham, Kent. † RA 2.
FOLKARD, Julia Bracewell* 1849-1933
Portrait and domestic painter. A.S.W.A. 1886. Sister of Elizabeth F. q.v. Add: London. † B 22, FIN 10, G 1, L 8, M 18, P 2, RA 19, RBA 1, RHA 2, ROI 9, SWA 11.
FOLLETT, Sydney G. Exh. 1903-7
22 Fountain Hall Road, Edinburgh. † RSA 3.
FOLLIOTT, Miss Exh. 1896
132 Sloane Street, London. † SWA 2.
FOLLIOTT, Miss A. Exh. 1896
132 Sloane Street, London. † SWA 2.
FONCE, Camille Exh. 1896-1909
Engraver. St. James's, London 1896; Bristol 1902; Paris 1909. † L 1, RA 3.
FONTAINE, Prof. Antoine Exh. 1883
† RSA 2.
FONTAINE, Mlle J. Exh. 1911
15 Rue du Louvre, Paris. † L 1.
FONTANA, Miss A. Exh. 1919
† L 1.
FONTANA, Aristide Exh. 1880-85
Sculptor. 180 Buckingham Palace Road, London. † L 1, RA 6, RBA 6, TOO 1.
FONTANA, Mrs, A.J. Exh. 1920
Park Nook, Ullet Road, Liverpool. † L 1.
FONTANA, Giovanni 1821-1893
Sculptor. b. Italy. d. London. Add: London. † L 3, RA 3, RI 1, RSA 2.
FONTVILLE, A. Exh. 1893-97
Landscape painter. London. † RBA 2.
FOOKES, Ursula Exh. 1931-39
Lino cut artist. 71 St. Mary's Mansions, Paddington, London. † RED 3, SWA 2.
FOORD-KELCEY, Mrs. Irene Exh. 1939
Sculptor. 49 Greek Street, Soho, London. † RA 2.
FOOT, Edith Exh. 1905-7
50 Falkland Road, Egremont, Cheshire. † L 2.
FOOT, John Tayler Exh. 1882-86
Medalist. London. † RA 6.
FOOT, Leslie Exh. 1935-38
Portrait painter. The Boltons Studios, Redcliffe Road, London. † P 1, RA 1.
FOOT, Rita Exh. 1907-27
57 Northumberland Road, Dublin. † L4, RHA 6.
FOOT, William Yates Exh. 1880
Landscape painter. Moulsford Vicarage, Nr. Wallingford, Berks. † RBA 1.
FOOTE, Amy Nora Exh. 1914-30
Mrs. Harold N. Flower and portrait painter. Bunbury, Hayling Island, Hants. † AB 1, LS 15, P 2.
FOOTE, Edward K. Exh. 1889-1906
Figure painter. Venice 1889; London 1898. † B 2, RA 1, RI 1.
FOOTE, Robert Exh. 1919-38
Cathcart, Glasgow 1919; Clarkston by Busby 1930. † GI 15.
FOOTNER, Frances Amicia de Biden Exh. 1900-21
Watercolour portrait painter. Studied Liverpool R.A. Schools and abroad. Add: Chester 1900; Bournemouth 1914; Bath 1920. † L 9, NG 3, RA 7.
FOOTTET, Fred Francis c. 1851-1935
Landscape painter and lithographer. R.B.A. 1901. b. Yorkshire. Add: Matlock, Derby 1882; Idridgehay, Derbys. 1884; London 1893. † BA 1, BG 25, BRU 25, G 1, GI 5, GOU 1, I 4, L 34, LS 26, N 9, NEA 1, NG 1, RA 7, RBA 145, RHA 4, ROI 6, RSA 1.
FORAIN, Jean Louis* 1852-1931
French painter, etcher and caricaturist. b. Pheims. Studied Paris. Member Academie des Beaux Arts. Exh. 1901-29. Add: Paris. † BG 3, CHE 6, FIN 2, G 3, GI 2, I 1, L 1, RSA 8.
FORAN, Miss A.C. Exh. 1882
39 Leyland Road, Southport, Lancs. † L 2, M 1.
FORBERG, Ernest Exh. 1898
Portrait painter. Konigliche Kunst Academie, Dusseldorf, Germany. † RA 1.
FORBES, C. Exh. 1906
37 Queen's Gate Gardens, London. † RA 2.
FORBES, Miss D.E. Exh. 1934
82 Floyer Road, Small Heath, Birmingham. † B 1.
FORBES, Ernest Exh. 1911-39
Portrait and landscape painter. A.R.B.A. 1921, R.B.A. 1926, Add: Leeds 1911; Otley, Yorks. 1914; Blackpool 1918; London 1919 and 1935; Rawdon, Nr. Leeds 1924. † ALP 1, GI 1, L 1, LS 4, P 4, RA 12, RBA 21, RCA 2.
FORBES, Elizabeth Adela 1859-1912
nee Armstrong. Rustic genre painter and etcher. b. Ontario, Canada. Founded the Newlyn Art School 1899 with her husband Stanhope Alexander F. q.v. N.E.A. 1886, R.E. 1885-89, A.R.W.S. 1899. Add: London 1883; Newlyn, Penzance, Cornwall 1899. † B 8, D 3, DOW 3, FIN 52, G 5, GI 5, L 37, LEI 25, M 9, NEA 4, NG 6, RA 40, RBA 13, RHA 1, RI 29, ROI 16, SWA 1.
FORBES, Miss E.M. Exh. 1897-98
Alvington, Reigate, Surrey. † B 1, SWA 5.
FORBES, Mrs Feridah Exh. 1925
416 Fulham Road, London. † GI 1.
FORBES, Frances E. Exh. 1893-1914
Bishops Stortford 1893; Little Island, Co. Cork 1905. † RHA 11, SWA 2.
FORBES, Ian Exh. 1938
Architect. 35 Bruton Street, London. † RA 1.
FORBES, Jock Exh. 1930
Watercolour landscape painter. † WG 18.
FORBES, James Edwin Exh. 1898
8 Hermitage Terrace, Edinburgh. † RSA 1.

FORBES, Kenneth K.* b. 1892
Portrait and figure painter. b. Toronto. Add: London 1913; Toronto, Canada 1935. † G 1, L 6, P 5, RA 14, ROI 3.

FORBES, Margaret Exh. 1908-14
219 King's Road, Chelsea, London. † L 3, LS 14.

FORBES, Marie Exh. 1886
15 Stafford Street, Edinburgh. † RSA 1.

FORBES, Marjory Exh. 1939-40
Miniature portrait painter. 10 Grimsdale Lane, Amersham, Bucks. † P 1, RA 1.

FORBES, Maud C. Stanhope Exh. 1903-40
nee Palmer. Still life, landscape and figure painter. 2nd wife of Stanhope Alexander F. q.v. Add: Gorey, Jersey 1903; Newlyn, Penzance 1909 and 1916; Bexhill, Kent 1910. † L 5, RA 20.

FORBES, Patrick Lewis Exh. 1893-1914
Landscape painter. Hampstead, London. † LS 6, RA 11, RBA 3, RI 6.

FORBES, Rachel H. Exh. 1901-25
Portrait and miniature painter. Paris 1901; Kensington, London 1907. † B 1, RA 6, RHA 1, RMS 2.

FORBES, Stanhope Alexander* 1857-1947
Rustic genre, historical and landscape painter. b. Dublin. Studied Lambeth School of Art and R.A. Schools 1874-78 and under Bonnat in Paris for 2 years. Founded the Newlyn Art School with his 1st wife Elizabeth Adela F. q.v. in 1899. Married 2nd wife Maud C.S.F. q.v. N.E.A. 1886, A.R.A. 1892, R.A. 1910. Add: London 1880; Newlyn, Penzance 1899. † AG 1, B 6, DOW 4, FIN 5, G 7, GI 11, L 43, M 14, NG 3, RA 223, RBA 1, RHA 4, ROI 4, RWS 3.

FORBES, Mrs. Ulrica Exh. 1923-36
Pen and wash artist. 19A Marylebone Road, London. † G 1, NEA 4, RA 2, SWA 1.

FORBES, Vivian 1891-1937
Figure, imaginative and decorative painter. Studied Manresa Road Polytechnic and under Glyn Philpot. Exh. 1918-38. Add: London. † BA 2, CG 2, FIN 51, G 5. GI 2, I 6, L 2, RA 12, RED 54, ROI 1.

FORBES, William Exh. 1934
9 Rutland Street, Edinburgh. † RSW 2.

FORBES-DALRYMPLE, Arthur Ewan b. 1912
Painter and pastellier. Studied Heatherley's 1930-32, Goldsmith's College 1932-34. Add: Greville Road, N.W London 1937. Signs work "Forbes". † ROI 2.

FORBES-ROBERTSON, Cecilia Exh. 1917-21
48 Hogarth Road, London. † LS 3, RA 2.

FORBES-ROBERTSON, Eric 1865-1935
Figure and landscape painter. Exh. 1884-1917. Add: London. † G 1, GI 2, LS 15, M 1, P 1, RA 2, RBA 5, ROI 8.

FORBES-ROBERTSON, Janina Exh. 1908-12
18 Batoum Gardens, Shepherds Bush, London. † LS 9.

FORBES-ROBERTSON, Johnston 1822-1903
Portrait painter and writer. Add: 25 Charlotte Street, Bedford Square, London. † G 9, GI 2, M 1, NG 1, RA 4, ROI 3.

FORBES-ROBERTSON, Miss Margaret Exh. 1885-1922
Portrait and miniature painter. 22 Charlotte Street, Bedford Square, London 1885; Cheltenham, Glos. 1922. † L 1, RA 5, SWA 1.

FORBES-ROBERTSON, Philip Exh. 1914-19
London. † LS 11.

FORCE, A. Exh. 1885
6 Rue de Furstenberg, Paris. † RE 5.

FORD, B, Exh. 1887-88
Urban landscape and interior painter. London. † RBA 2, RSA 1.

FORD, Barbara Exh. 1927
Flower painter. Arundel House, Amersham, Bucks. † RA 1, RBA 1, RSA 1.

FORD, Lady Ellen E. Exh. 1897-1910
Sydenham, London 1897; Upper Norwood, London 1900. † B 2, L 1, RBA 1, SWA 11.

FORD, Edward Onslow 1852-1901
Sculptor and painter. Studied painting in Antwerp 1870 and Munich 1871-72. Won competition run by the City of London for a statue to the memory of Rowland Hill. A.R.A. 1888, R.A. 1895. Add: London. † G 14, GI 22, L 34, M 9, NG 12, RA 84, RBA 3, RHA 2, RMS 1, RSA 2.

FORD, Emily S. Exh. 1880-1918
Landscape and figure painter. Adel Grange, Leeds 1880 and London. † G 1, L 2, LS 14, RA 2, RE 3, SWA 4.

FORD, Francis G. Exh. 1931
Architect. 89 Hatton Gardens, London. † RA 1.

FORD, F.H. Exh. 1921-23
153 Ewart Road, Forest Fields, Nottingham. † N 2.

FORD, George Exh. 1939
Architect. H.M. Office of Works, Gt. Westminster House, London. † RA 1.

FORD, George Henry b. 1912
Sculptor. Studied Hornsey School of Art. Add: 70 Cromwell Avenue, Highgate, London 1936-40. † GI 1, RA 2.

FORD, G.M. Exh. 1885-88
1 Vanburgh Place, Leith Links, Edinburgh. † RSA 2.

FORD, Gordon Onslow Exh. 1913-37
c/o Rowley Gallery, 140 Church Street, London. † P 1, RBA 3, RI 1.

FORD, Harriet Mary Exh. 1890-1908
Portrait, figure and decorative painter. b. Ontario, Canada. Studied Ontario School of Art, St. John's Wood School, R.A. Schools, Paris and Italy. Add: St. Ives, Cornwall 1890; San Gimignano, Tuscany 1892; Gt. Marlow, Bucks. 1902. † DOW 1, GI 1, I 1, RBA 1, ROI 3.

FORD, Hugh C. Exh. 1926-39
Amersham, Bucks. † RI 3, ROI 11.

FORD, H.E. Exh. 1889-92
Deganway, N. Wales. † B 4, M 2.

FORD, Henry Justice* 1860-1941
Portrait and landscape painter, and illustrator. Studied Slade School and Herkomer's, Bushey, Herts. Add: London. † BG 130, G 1, L 5, M 1, NG 52, RA 27, ROI 2.

FORD, Harry W. Exh. 1915-23
Architect. 11 Old Queen Street, Westminster, London. † RA 2.

FORD, John Exh. 1936-38
114 Tiverton Road, Bournbrook, Birmingham. † B 2.

FORD, J.A. Exh. 1881-1923
Edinburgh. † GI 39, RSA 79, RSW 2.

FORD, Jessie A. Exh. 1918-36
Miniature painter. London 1919; Stourbridge, Worcs. 1921. † B 7, RA 3.

FORD, Mrs. Marjorie C. Exh. 1922-24
Watercolour painter. Cleveland House, Cherry Orchard, Shrewsbury, Salop. † RA 2, SWA 1.

FORD, R. Exh. 1881
Trafalgar Studios, S.W. London. † GI 1.

FORD, R. Onslow Exh. 1897-1918
62 Acacia Road, St. John's Wood, London 1897; Wendover, Bucks. 1910. † GI 2, L 7, M 1, NG 2, RA 12.

FORD, S. Exh. 1909
Architect. 3 South Square, Gray's Inn, London. † RA 2.

FORD, William B. Exh. 1882-95
Miniature painter and enameller. Trinity Road, Wood Green, Essex. † RA 8, RBA 2.

FORD, W.F. Exh. 1900-13
N.S.A. 1910-16. Nottingham 1900; Carlton, Notts. 1903. † N 14.

FORD, W. Onslow Exh. 1895-1916
Portrait, landscape and still life painter. St. John's Wood, London. † BG 35, GI 3, L 6, M 1, NG 5, RA 22.

FORDATI, F. Helen Exh. 1880-81
Landscape painter. 18 Craven Hill, London. † SWA 4.

FORDE, Edward Exh. 1909
65 West Regent Street, Glasgow. † GI 1.

FORDE, Miss G.M. Exh. 1880-1918
Landscape and figure painter. London. † SWA 13.

FORDHAM, Ethel M. Exh. 1935-40
Still life and flower painter. 57 Cottenham Park Road, Wimbledon, London. † RA 2, ROI 2.

FORDHAM, Montague Exh. 1905
9 Maddox Street, London. † L 4.

FORDRED, Ronald F. Exh. 1929
Coastal painter. 65 Greenvale Road, Eltham Park, London. † RA 1.

FOREL, Alexis Exh. 1886-87
R.E. 1885-89. 6 Rue de Furstenburg, Paris. † RE 12.

FOREMAN, Agnes E. Exh. 1910-39
Figure and flower painter. Pembury, Kent 1910; Crowborough, Sussex 1912. † GOU 2, D 1, L 4, RA 5, RBA 4, RI 2, SWA 7.

FORES, Mary H. Exh. 1888-89
Figure painter. 28 Cavendish Road, London. † L 1, RA 1, SWA 2.

FORESTER, W. Exh. 1890-91
Edinburgh. † RSA 2.

FORESTER, Y.B. Exh. 1884
Trowbridge, Wilts. † ROI 1.

FORESTIER, A. Exh. 1882
Figure painter. 3 Oakfield Road, Penge, Kent. † RBA 1.

FORESTIER, Amedee* Exh. 1903-22
Figure and landscape painter and illustrator. 7 Alleyn Park, W. Dulwich, London. † L 2, RA 8, ROI 2.

FORESTIER, Mrs. Lutita Exh. 1904-5
7 Alleyn Park, W. Dulwich, London. † SWA 3.

FORESTIER, M. Exh. 1906-14
W. Dulwich 1906; London 1908. † LS 3, ROI 4.

FORGE, Frederick L. Exh. 1920
Architect. 3 Crooked Lane, King William Street, London. † RA 1.

FORMILLI, Cesare T.G. Exh. 1887-1913
Decorative artist. Rome 1887; Wentworth Studios, Manresa Road, London 1894; The Boltons, London 1909. † D 2, G 2, L 28, NG 30, RA 12, RHA 2, RI 7, ROI 2.

FORNEROD, R. Exh. 1920-24
† GI 3, RSA 1.

FORRES, Lady Freda Exh. 1926-38
Sculptor. Glenogil, Kirriemuir, Forfarshire and London. † ALP 1, GI 1, RA 5, RSA 1, ROI 5.

FORREST, Archibald Stevenson Exh. 1893-1909
Landscape painter. Forest Gate, Essex 1893; Blackheath 1908. † LS 5, RBA 2.

FORREST, George Topham c.1873-1945
Architect, with L.C.C. 1919-35. New County Hall, London. † RA 10.

FORREST, Norman John b. 1898
Wood sculptor. Edinburgh. † GI 10, RSA 17.

FORREST, Robert Smith Exh. 1908-34
Portrait painter and etcher. Studied Edinburgh. Add: Edinburgh. † RSA 6. RSW 4.

FORRESTER, A. Exh. 1939
Burgh Surveyor, Dalkeith. † RSA 1.

FORRESTER, Alexander Exh. 1881-83
Edinburgh. † RSA 2.

FORRESTER, Anne Exh. 1928
Landscape painter. † AB 3.

FORRESTER, Anna Hardie b. 1875
Miniature and portrait painter. Manchester. † L 1, M 8, RA 1, RMS 1.

FORRESTER, W.K. Exh. 1911-28
16 Newark Street, Walton. Liverpool. † D 1, L 1.

FORROW, Jessie E. Exh. 1904
Still life painter. Pinethrope, Lake, Nr. Sandown, I.O.W. † RA 1.

FORSAITH, Miss A.M. Exh. 1903
The Ferns, Amerland Road, London. † SWA 2.

FORSETH, Einar Exh. 1930
Landscape, figure and portrait painter. † FIN 83.

FORSHALL, Francis S.H. Exh. 1893-99
Portrait and figure painter. Hampstead, London. † L 1, RA 3.

FORSHAW, John Henry Exh. 1935
Miners Welfare Committee, Mines Dept., London. † RSA 1.

FORSTER, Edward Exh. 1933
Urban landscape painter. 34 Fitzwilliam Square, Dublin. † RHA 1.

FORSTER, Francis L.M. Exh. 1891-1900
Figure and landscape painter. N.E.A. 1895. Add: London. † NEA 24.

FORSTER, Miss G.F. Exh. 1933
Oakdene, Rainhill, Lancs. † L 1.

FORSTER, J.D. Exh. 1925
47 Goodison Road, Walton, Liverpool. † L 1.

FORSTER, Joseph Wilson Exh. 1889-1916
Portrait painter. London 1889; Bushey, Herts. 1913. † L 6, M 1, NG 2, P 3, RA 10, RI 1.

FORSTER, John Wycliffe Lowes* b. 1850
Canadian portrait painter. Exh. 1900-11. Add: King Street West, Toronto, Canada. † L 2, LS 1, M 1.

FORSTER, Mary 1853-1885
Landscape painter. Daughter of T.W.B.F. q.v. Died a few months after her marriage to Samuel H.S. Lofthouse q.v. A.R.W.S. 1884, A.S.W.A. 1880. Add: Holt, Wilts. 1880; Lower Halliford on Thames 1884. † D 10, FIN 4, L 2, M 1, RA 3, RI 1, RWS 11, SWA 7.

FORSTER, Maude Exh. 1900
Bellerive, St. Peter's Road, St. Margaret's, Twickenham, Middlesex. † RBA 1, RI 1.

FORSTER, Rose Exh. 1913
Landscape painter. † ALP 1.

FORSTER, T.W.B. Exh. 1881-86
Holt, Trowbridge, Wilts. † D 1, FIN 1, RA 4.

FORSTER, William Exh. 1905
39 Colville Gardens, Bayswater, London. † L 1.

FORSTER-KNIGHT, Mary Exh. 1933
Animal painter. 25 Milverton Crescent, Leamington Spa, Warwicks. † RA 1.

FORSYTH, A. Exh. 1889
6 Roseneath Terrace, Edinburgh. † RSA 1.

FORSYTH, Adam Exh. 1889-92
Landscape painter. London. † RA 1, RI 2.

FORSYTH, Anne Exh. 1932
Market Place, Malton, Yorks. † RSA 2.

FORSYTH, Amelia B. Exh. 1939
90 Springkell Avenue, Glasgow. † RSA 1.

FORSYTH, Miss C. Exh. 1934
27 Grange Loan, Edinburgh. † RSA 1.

FORSYTH, Miss Cecilia See ELWES

FORSYTH, Mrs. Dorothea Exh. 1907-13
Malton, Yorks. † GI 1, RSA 3, RSW 1.

FORSYTH, Gordon Mitchell 1879-1952
Painter, pottery and stained glass artist. Studied Gray's School of Art, Aberdeen and Royal College of Art (travelling scholarship in design). R.I. 1927. Designer at the Pilkington Tile and Pottery Co., Adviser British Pottery Manufacturers Federation; Art Director City of Stoke on Trent School of Art. Exh. 1913/40. Add: Newcastle under Lyme, Staffs. and Stoke on Trent. † AG 2, B 1, FIN 2, G 2, GI 8, L 4, M 2, RA 16, RI 63.

FORSYTH, Miss J. Exh. 1907
Montagu Place, London. † SWA 1.

FORSYTH, James Exh. 1880-89
Architectural sculptor. Father of James Nesfield F. q.v. Add: London. † GI 4, RA 10.

FORSYTH, John Dudley d. 1926
Stained glass designer and pottery artist. Exh. 1895-1925. Add: London. † GI 4, L 1, RA 22.

FORSYTH, James Law Exh. 1931-36
7 Mulberry Road, Glasgow. † GI 1, RSA 1, RSW 1.

FORSYTH, James Nesfield b. 1864
Sculptor. Son of James F. q.v. Studied RA Schools (silver medal) and Paris. Exh. 1889-1927. Add: London. † GI 20, L 13, M 5, P 2, RA 25, RHA 2, RI 1, ROI 2.

FORSYTH, Lilian Exh. 1939
Alandale, Brede, Rye, Sussex. † SWA 1.

FORSYTH, Moira b. 1905
Stained glass and pottery artist. Studied Burslem School of Art and Royal College of Art. Add: London 1929. † RA 12.

FORSYTH, V.N. Exh. 1921
57 Abbey Road, St. John's Wood, London. † RA 1.

FORSYTH, William A. Exh. 1896-1938
Architect. London. † GI 1, RA 3.

FORTESCUE, George A. Exh. 1926
46 Dover Street, London. † RA 2.

FORTESCUE, Mathew Exh. 1916
56 Grosvenor Road, Rathgar, Dublin. † RHA 1.

FORTESCUE, William Banks* d. 1924
Figure and landscape painter. R.B.S.A. 1898. Add: Birmingham 1880; Southport, Lancs. 1887 and 1895; Newlyn, Penzance 1890; St. Ives, Cornwall 1896. † B 71, D 4, DOW 4, GI 18, I 2, L 37, LS 7, M 24, RA 26, RBA 10, RCA 9, RHA 1, RI 1, ROI 14, RSA 1.

FORTESCUE-BRICKDALE, Sir C. Exh. 1887-1911
London. † RA 1, RI 1.

FORTESCUE-BRICKDALE, Eleanor 1871-1945
Painter, stained glass artist and illustrator. Studied Crystal Palace School of Art and RA Schools. R.O.I. 1903, A.R.W.S. 1902, R.W.S. 1919. Add: London. † COO 3, DOW 121, GI 1, L 35, LEI 92, M 1, NG 2, RA 35, RI 1, ROI 3, RWS 66.

FORTESCUE-PICKARD, Mrs. Maud Exh. 1918-39
R.B.A. 1923. Add: London. † RBA 9, RMS 2.

FORTIE, John Exh. 1880
2 South Charlotte Street, Edinburgh. † RSA 1.

FORTUNA, V. Exh. 1887
20 Victoria Park, Dover, Kent. † D 3.

FORTUNE, Euphemia Charlton b. 1885
Landscape painter. b. California. Studied St. John's Wood School of Art, Art Student's League, New York. Add: Edinburgh 1911, 1921-23 c/o Bourlet, London 1933. † GI 1, L 4, RA 4, RSA 6.

FORTUNE, J.D. Exh. 1896
31 Brondesbury Road, London. † B 1.

FORTY, Frank Exh. 1932-40
52 Charlotte Road, Edgbaston, Birmingham 1932 and 1939; Cambridge 1938. † B 11.

FORTY, Gerald C. Exh. 1936-40
52 Charlotte Road, Edgbaston, Birmingham. † B 5.

FORTYE, W.H. Exh. 1880-86
Landscape painter. London. † D 2, RI 5.

FOSBERY, Ernest George b. 1874
Painter and etcher. Studied Ottawa School of Art, Royal College of Art 1890-97 and under Fernand Corman in Paris 1897-98. Add: c/o Mrs. A. Clutterbuck, St. Giles, Harpenden, Herts. 1917. † RA 1.

FOSBERY, Lionel Exh. 1927
Sculptor. 17 Welbeck Mansions, W. Hampstead, London. † RA 1.

FOSBROOKE, Leonard Exh. 1884-1907
Landscape painter. Ravenstone, Ashby de la Zouche, Leics. † L 4, M 5, N 40, RA 7, RBA 1, RI 21.

FOSET, P. Exh. 1882
16 Avenue Trudaine, Paris. † RHA 1.

FOSKEY, Harry Exh. 1895-1903
Figure painter. London. † B 4, GI 2, L 1, M 2, RA 4, RBA 1, RHA 2, RI 2, ROI 1.

FOSS, Harriet Campbell b. 1860
American painter. 43 Avenue Victor Hugo, Paris 1899. † RA 1.

FOSS, J.H. Beart Exh. 1911-38
Architect. London. † RA 2.

FOSSI, A.P. Florence Exh. 1888
† D 1.

FOSTER, A. Exh. 1886
158 Lower Hasting Street, Leicester. † N 1.

FOSTER, Alice Exh. 1904
29 Rathgat Avenue, Dublin. † RHA 2.

FOSTER, Mrs. Annie Exh. 1908
Catethorpe Hall, Rugby, Staffs. † D 2.

FOSTER, Anthony Exh. 1939
Sculptor. Bryants Bottom, Gt. Missenden, Bucks. † RA 1.

FOSTER, Arthur Bell b. 1901
Landscape painter, designer and illustrator. Studied Sheffield School of Art 1924-29. Exh. 1934-40. Add: Moseley, Birmingham. † B 10, RBA 3, RI 1.

FOSTER, A.H. Exh. 1922
One Oak, Penn's Lane, Erdington, Birmingham. † B 1.

FOSTER, Amy H. Exh. 1881-1910
Mrs. R.K. Leather. Landscape and coastal painter. Add: Clifton 1886; London 1892 and 1900; Teignmouth 1893. † D 2, L 2, NG 2, RI 7, RBA 1, RSA 2, SWA 6.

FOSTER, Arthur J. Exh. 1880-1905
Portrait and landscape painter. London. † L 1, M 1, P 2, RA 14, RBA 4, RHA 1, ROI 8.

FOSTER, A.M. Exh. 1910-11
6 Bridge Avenue, Hammersmith, London. † L 4, RA 1.

FOSTER, Alfred Walton Exh. 1914-38
Landscape and portrait painter. Studied and taught Nottingham School of Art. A.N.S.A. 1922, N.S.A. 1927. Add: Nottingham. † N 81.

FOSTER, Beryl Exh. 1938-40
Miniature portrait painter. London. † RA 3.

FOSTER, Catherine Exh. 1931
Lewes, Sussex. † RCA 2.

FOSTER, Cecilia C. Exh. 1897-1911
Birmingham. † B 7, RCA 1.

FOSTER, Mrs. C.E. Exh. 1916
19 Grimston Gardens, Folkestone, Kent. † RA 1.

FOSTER, Mrs. Catherine M. Exh. 1929-40
Watercolour landscape painter. Oaken Lodge, Finchfield Road, Merridale, Wolverhampton. † B 25, RA 2.

FOSTER, Miss C.S. Exh. 1934-39
Landscape painter. † AR 1, COO 2.

FOSTER, Dorothea Exh. 1900-11
Mrs. Reginald Hirst. Figure painter. Halton, Leeds 1900, Dewsbury, 1904. † L 9, RA 3.

FOSTER, Eleanor Exh. 1901
Brynhyfyd, Llanfestiniog, Wales. † RCA 2.

FOSTER, Elsie Exh. 1906
4 Victoria Road, Harborne, Birmingham. † B 1.

FOSTER, Elizabeth G. Exh. 1885
Moredun House, Fettes College, Edinburgh. † RSA 1.

FOSTER, Mrs. E. Rees Exh. 1908-9
Llanberis, N. Wales. † RCA 2.

FOSTER, F. Exh. 1887
23 Upper Rutland Street, Mountjoy Square, Dublin. † RHA 1.

FOSTER, Frank Exh. 1900-3
Architect. 8 Duke Street, Adelphi, London. † RA 2.

FOSTER, Fred Exh. 1880-97
West Hackney, London 1880; Sutton, Surrey 1893; Twickenham, Middlesex 1896. † B 6, RHA 21.

FOSTER, Fanny E. Exh. 1880-84
Landscape painter. Sandringham Road, North Hackney, London. † RHA 4, SWA 1.

FOSTER, Geo. Sherwood Exh. 1894-1904
Landscape painter. Birmingham 1894; Kensington, London 1901. † B 9, RA 4.

FOSTER, Helen Exh. 1880
Landscape painter. 4 Upton Grove, Southgate Road, Islington, London. † RBA 1.

FOSTER, H.E. Exh. 1926-34
Birmingham 1926; The Cliff, Manchester 1932. † B 7.

FOSTER, Helen L. Exh. 1922-30
Landscape painter. Peer Gynt, Grassington, Nr. Skipton, Yorks. † L 4, RA 2.

FOSTER, Herbert Wilson Exh. 1881-1917
Figure painter. Stoke on Trent, Staffs. 1881; Hollywell, N. Wales 1890; School of Art, Nottingham 1893; West Bridgford, Notts 1895. † B 2, L 21, M 5, N 33, RA 19, RHA 1, RI 6, ROI 1.

FOSTER, John Exh. 1881
Landscape painter. Alexandra Street, Sherwood Rise, Nottingham. † N 4.

FOSTER, John Ernest b. 1877
Flower painter. Studied Royal College of Art. Add: Cork 1897; Hull 1907; Dedham, Essex 1929. † L 6, LS 3, M 1, RA 19, RI 5, ROI 3.

FOSTER, John J. Exh. 1923-30
35 Braemar Street, Langside, Glasgow. † GI 5.

FOSTER, J.T. Exh. 1898-1914
Sherwood, Notts. 1898; Nottingham 1914. † N 2.

FOSTER, Kate E. Exh. 1882-89
Landscape painter. Married Walter H.W.F. q.v. Add: 66 Sandringham Road, Dalston, London. † GI 1, M 1, RBA 2, SWA 3.

FOSTER, Mrs. Lucy Exh. 1937-39
† RI 4.

FOSTER, Miss Lys Exh. 1901-4
Liverpool. † L 9.

FOSTER, Myles Birket* 1825-1899
Landscape and rustic painter, illustrator and engraver. b. North Shields. Came to London when aged 5. Contributer to "Illustrated London News". Travelled on the continent. Father of William F. q.v. A.R.W.S. 1860, R.W.S. 1862. Add: The Hill, Witley, Surrey. † AG 186, DOW 59, FIN 3, GI 1, L 7, M 2, RA 1, RE 1, RWS 68, TOO 67.

FOSTER, Marcia Lane b. 1897
Mrs. Jarrett. Wood engraver and illustrator. Studied St. John's Wood School of Art, Central School of Arts and Crafts (silver medal for figure painting 1920-21). Add: 43 Boundary Road, London 1924. † NEA 2.

FOSTER, Mary Melville b. 1890
nee Farrar. Landscape painter. Studied Reading School of Art and under P. Tudor-Hart in Paris. Exh. 1925-39. Add: 14 Iverna Court, Kensington, London. † GOU 4, NEA 1, RA 3, RBA 1, SWA 2.

FOSTER, Nellie Exh. 1905
4 Victoria Road, Harbourne, Birmingham. † B 1.

FOSTER, Ruth Exh. 1918
† I 1.

FOSTER, Mrs. R.A. Exh. 1898-1939
Flower painter. Married to Herbert Wilson F. q.v. A.N.S.A. 1913, N.S.A. 1915. Add: Munster's Road, West Bridgford, Notts. † B 2, L 1, N 157.

FOSTER, Mrs. R.C. Exh. 1894-1909
Rugby 1894; Hillingdon, Middlesex 1909. † D 23, RBA 1.

FOSTER, Sybilla C. Exh. 1881-1921
Landscape painter. Travelled widely. Add: London 1881; Salcombe, S.Devon 1909. † RBA 1, RID 46, RSA 2.

FOSTER, Stanley Mace b. 1884
Sculptor, modeller and silver and goldsmith. Studied Manchester School of Art and Royal College of Art (silver medal). Served R.F.C. and R.A.F. World War I. Headmaster Ryland Memorial School of Art, West Bromwich. Exh. 1913-38. Add: West Bromwich. † B 4, L 4, RA 3.

FOSTER, Thomas O. Exh. 1910-35
Architect. London. † RA 11.

FOSTER, Mrs. Warren Exh. 1906-15
Landscape and figure painter. King John's, Thundersley, Essex. † RID 8.

FOSTER, William 1853-1924
Watercolour landscape, interior, still life and genre painter and black and white illustrator. Son of Myles Birket F. q.v. Fellow of the Zoological Society. Add: The Hill, Witley, Surrey 1880; Weybridge, Surrey 1899. † AG 6, D 31, DOW 28, FIN 78, L 10, M 15, RA 17, RBA 1, RI 10, RSA 3.

FOSTER, William Gilbert* 1855-1906
Landscape and rustic genre painter. b. Manchester. Studied under his father, a Birkenhead portrait painter. Art master Leeds Grammar School for several years. R.B.A. 1893. Add: Headingley, Leeds 1885; Halton, Leeds 1894. † B 3, L 5, M 8, RA 39, RBA 28, ROI 1.

FOSTER, W.H. Exh. 1885-89
London. † G 1, RHA 2.

FOSTER, W.H.P. Exh. 1885
3 Vyse Street, Birmingham. † B 1.

FOSTER, Walter H.W. Exh. 1881-88
Landscape and figure painter. Married Kate E.F. q.v. Add: 66 Sandringham Road, Dalston, London. † B 1, GI 1, L 1, M 1, RA 4, RBA 8, RHA 1.

FOSTER-PEGG, Mrs. Kathleen Exh. 1919
Miniature portrait painter. Edensor Vicarage, Bakewell, Derbs. † RA 1.

FOTHERGILL, Charles Exh. 1880-83
Coastal painter. London 1880; Pulborough, Sussex 1883. † D 1, RBA 3.

FOTHERGILL, C.W. Exh. 1898-1900
Landscape painter. Cranbrook, Kent. † RA 1, RI 1.

FOTHERGILL, George Algernon b. 1868
Watercolour painter, illustrator and writer. Gave up his medical practice to become a professional artist. Served as Medical Officer in charge of 1st Cavalry Brigade 1918-19. Add: Darlington 1901; Balckhall, N.B. 1909; Old Farmhouse, Cramond Bridge, W. Lothian 1913. † D 4, L 11, RSA 17, WG 45.

FOTHERGILL, John Exh. 1908
18 Fitzroy Street, London. † LS 4.

FOTHERGILL, Margery Exh. 1908-12
Mines Avenue, Aigburth, Liverpool. † L 4.

FOTHERGILL, Theodore R. Exh. 1893
71 Portland Place, London. † D 2.

FOTHERINGHAM, Miss A.E. Exh. 1925
7 Beaconsfield Road, Seaforth, Liverpool. † L 1.

FOTHERINGHAM, Clare b. 1890
Watercolour painter. 118 Tonbridge Road, Maidstone, Kent 1940. † RSA 2.

FOTHILL, Mary D. Exh. 1884
Stoke Bishop, Bristol. † D 1.

FOTTRELL, Eileen Exh. 1897
8 North George Street, Dublin. † RHA 1.

FOUALL, G. Exh. 1888
Rue du Val de Grace, Paris. † GI 1.

FOUGASSE, see BIRD, Cyril Kenneth

FOUJITA, Tsugouharu* b.1886
Japanese figure painter. Exh. 1924-38. † COO 2, GOU 1.

FOULD, Mme. Consuelo* Exh. 1898-1904
Rue de Prony 21, Paris. † L 3.

FOULD, G. Exh. 1888
† TOO 1.

FOULGER, Howson Rutherford Exh. 1890
Domestic painter. Queensborough Studios, Queensborough Terrace, London. † M 1, RA 1.

FOULIS, E. Exh. 1885-88
191 Hill Street, Glasgow. † GI 4, RSA 2.

FOULIS, Miss Euphan A. Exh. 1927-38
Elie, Fife 1927; Glasgow 1930. † GI 11, L 1, M 2, RSA 12.

FOULIS, Mrs. H.B. Exh. 1880-89
Edinburgh. † RSA 7.

FOULKES, Hilda R. Exh. 1902-29
Bona Vista, Livingstone Drive, Liverpool. † L 6.

FOULKES, S. Colwyn Exh. 1924-31
Central Chambers, Colwyn Bay, Wales. † L 3, RCA 2.

FOUND, Mrs. Ethel M. Exh. 1937-39
Landscape painter. 2 St. George's Avenue, London. † RA 2.

FOUND, James Arthur Exh. 1907-38
Landscape painter. Hull 1909; Ealing, London 1911. † I 2, L 3, RA 7.

FOUNTAIN, Miss M.D. Exh. 1909
Miniature portrait painter. 63 Middleton Road, Bowes Park, London. † RA 1.

FOUNTAINE, Miss C.L. Exh. 1893
Eaton Lodge, W. Norwich, Norfolk. † SWA 1.

FOUQUERAY, Dominique Charles b. 1871
French artist. 52 Rue Lhomond, Paris 1923. † RSA 1.

FOURACRE, John T. Exh. 1896-1905
16 Portland Square, Plymouth, Devon. † RA 1, RI 1.

FOURNIER, Marcel* Exh. 1913
c/o Allied Artists Assn. 67 Chancery Lane, London. † LS 3.
FOURNIER, Maurice Exh. 1912
17 Rue Mirabeau, Paris. † RSA 2.
FOWERAKER, A. Moulton Exh. 1898-1912
Flower and landscape painter. R.B.A. 1902. Add: Exeter 1898; Carbis Bay Lelant, Cornwall 1901. † B 4, D 1, GI 2, L 4, M 1, RA 1, RBA 52, RI 2, ROI 3, RSA 3.
FOWKE, F.R. Exh. 1884
24 Victoria Road, Fulham Road, London. † RI 1.
FOWKES, C. Roy Exh. 1936-39
Architect. London. † RA 4.
FOWLE, Bertha 1894-1964
Flower, landscape and miniature painter. Studied and taught at Gravesend School of Art. A.R.M.S. 1927. Exh. 1916-39. Add: Gravesend, Kent. † B 16, L 35, RA 11, RI 53, RMS 67, SWA 4.
FOWLER, Agnes Exh. 1891-1907
Flower and landscape painter. Add: London. † D 2, RID 15.
FOWLER, Alec Exh. 1923-34
"Llanber", Walton Road, Altrincham, Cheshire. † RCA 3.
FOWLER, Alfred H. Exh. 1904-30
Birmingham. † B 11.
FOWLER, Alice L. Exh. 1903
Watercolour landscape painter. † WG 57.
FOWLER, Benjamin* Exh. 1882-1908
Landscape painter. Liverpool 1882; Tal-y-bont, Conway 1886; Trefrew, Wales 1889. † B 1, L 32, RCA 82.
FOWLER, Mrs. Beryl Exh. 1924-39
Portrait painter. 14 Framlington Place, Newcastle on Tyne. † L 1, P 3.
FOWLER, Mrs. C.A. Exh. 1912-14
Bournemouth, Hants. † SWA 3.
FOWLER, C. Hodgson Exh. 1884-99
Architect. The College, Durham. † RA 4.
FOWLER, Ethel Exh. 1887-1930
Mrs. Pickering Jones. Tal-y-bont, Conway 1887; Trefrew, Wales 1891; Little Sutton, Cheshire 1895. † L 23.
FOWLER, Mrs. E. Miller Exh. 1894-1923
Flower painter. Hereford 1894 and 1920; Donnington, Spalding, Lincs. 1897; Stoke on Trent 1902. † B 18, L 4, RA 1.
FOWLER, F.H. Exh. 1925-27
14 Framlington Place, Newcastle on Tyne. † L 3.
FOWLER, Frank H. Exh. 1903-7
Landscape painter. Earley, Nr. Reading, Berks. † L 1, WG 53.
FOWLER, Geo Exh. 1892-1902
Edinburgh. † RSA 8.
FOWLER, Howard Exh. 1882-91
Landscape and rustic painter. Staines, Middlesex 1882; Woodbastwick, Norwich 1891. † RA 1, RBA 7, RI 2.
FOWLER, Herbert E. Exh. 1904
72 Goswell Street, Liverpool. † L 1.
FOWLER, H.H. Exh. 1923-32
51 Cottenham Street, Liverpool. † L 3.
FOWLER, Harrison R. b. 1876
Portrait relief and colour print artist and metalworker. Studied Liverpool School of Art. Headmaster Londonderry School of Art. Add: Liverpool 1901 and 1920; Londonderry 1909; Bewdley 1913. † L 33.
FOWLER, Mrs. J. Exh. 1890-95
Liverpool. † L 4.
FOWLER, John W. Exh. 1915-37
London 1915; West Hartlepool 1931. † L 1, RA 1, RSA 5.
FOWLER, Miss L. Exh. 1898-1907
60 Bristol Road, Birmingham. † B 12.
FOWLER, Miss M. Exh. 1885-98
Mrs. Heckle. Southampton 1885; Trefriw, Wales 1892; Menai Bridge, Wales 1894; Llanfairfechan 1895. † L 7, RCA 2.
FOWLER, Munro Exh. 1880-88
Landscape and flower painter. Southampton and London. † D 1, RBA 4, RI 3.
FOWLER, Robert* 1853-1926
Landscape painter and decorative painter of myth and allegory. b. Anstruther. Studied in London. R.I. 1891. Add: Liverpool 1880; London 1904. † AB 1, ALP 1, B 3, BG 27, CHE 1, D 2, G 1, GI 1, GOU 1, I 1, L 114, LS 9, M 5, NG 6, RA 33, RBA 12, RCA 27, RI 49, ROI 12, RSA 1, RSW 3.
FOWLER, Rachel J. Exh. 1881
Flower painter. Woodford, Essex. † RBA 1, SWA 3.
FOWLER, T.B. Exh. 1920-33
69 Lansdown Road, Handsworth, Birmingham. † B 21.
FOWLER, T.P. Exh. 1885-1911
Liverpool. † L 2.
FOWLER, Walter d. 1911
Landscape painter. R.B.A. 1896. Treasurer R.B.A. 1907-10. Add: Richmond, Surrey 1887; Kew, Surrey 1902; London 1909. † B 8, BK 54, L 5, M 3, RA 13, RBA 132, RI 5, ROI 11.
FOX, Allan Exh. 1882-86
Adswood, Stockport, Lancs. † M 4.
FOX, Augustus Exh. 1889
Adswood, Stockport, Lancs. † M 1.
FOX, Mrs. Alice Cheney Exh. 1933-38
Cardiff, Wales. † RCA 7.
FOX, A.F.M. Exh. 1911
Landscape painter. † BG 7.
FOX, Alice L. b. 1870
nee Livingston. Miniature painter. Exh. 1920-24. Add: London. † RA 3, RMS 2, SWA 1.
FOX, Aldeline M. b. 1870
Landscape and flower painter. b. Ireland. Studied Westminster School of Art. A.S.W.A. 1920. Add: Kensington, London 1911; Northease Farm, Nr. Lewes, Sussex 1920; Aldbourne, Wilts. 1924. † GOU 3, I 7, L 8, M 1, NEA 4, RA 4, RBA 4, RHA 13, ROI 3, SWA 14.
FOX, Mrs. Bridell Exh. 1883-87
Landscape and figure painter. 4 Campden Hill Road, Kensington, London. † RA 1, SWA 3.
FOX, Caroline Exh. 1880-99
nee Potchett. Landscape painter. Add: London 1880; St. Leonards on Sea, Sussex 1892. † D 1, RBA 3, RHA 1, SWA 2.
FOX, Charles James b. 1860
Landscape painter. Add: London 1883 and 1896; Derby Dale Nurseries, Derbys. 1894; Buxton, Derbys. 1897; Tamworth, Staffs. 1898; Braunton, Devon 1905; Norton, Herts. 1907. † B 1, GI 2, GOU 1, L 3, NG 1, RA 18, RBA 4, RCA 1, RI 2, ROI 1.
FOX, Mrs. Ethel Carrick see CARRICK
FOX, Emanuel Phillips* 1865-1915
Portrait, figure and landscape painter. b. Melbourne, Australia. Add: St. Ives, Cornwall 1890; St. John's Wood, London 1903 and 1908; Paris 1906. † B 1, DOW 1, GI 1, L 7. P 1, RA 26, ROI 1.
FOX, Ernest R. Exh. 1883-1919
Landscape painter. N.E.A. 1888. Add: Teddington, Middlesex 1883; Strood, Kent 1886; Wingham, Dover, Kent 1891; Hythe, Kent 1917. † ALP 3, B 25, D 1, DOW 2, G 2, GI 1, L 4, LS 12, M 3, NEA 9, RA 17, RBA 2, ROI 4.
FOX, Miss Florence Exh. 1881-1903
Miniature painter. Montrose 1881; London 1886; Epsom, Surrey 1887; Slinfold, Sussex 1903. † L 1, RA 4, RHA 1, RSA 2.
FOX, F.S. Exh. 1939
29 Maitland Road, Woodthorpe, Nottingham. † N 1.
FOX, George* Exh. 1880-89
Figure and domestic painter. 40 Brewer Street, Golden Square, London. † B 2, L 3, M 8, RBA 10, ROI 7.
FOX, George E. Exh. 1880-84
Decorative artist. 4 Campden Hill Road, Kensington, London. † RA 3.
FOX, Henry Exh. 1882
Adswood, Stockport, Lancs. † M 2.
FOX, Henry Charles* b. 1860
Landscape painter. R.B.A. 1889. Exh. 1880-1913. Add: London 1880; Kingston on Thames 1899. † B 7, D 6, GI 3, L 13, M 8, RA 21, RBA 113, RHA 5, RI 6, ROI 13, RSA 1.
FOX, H.T.F. Exh. 1884
Halton, Montrose. † RSA 1.
FOX, J. Exh. 1880
Faskfern Lodge, Esplanade, Bray. † RHA 1.
FOX, Kathleen Exh. 1911-24
Landscape painter. Glasthule Lodge, Glenageary 1911; Paris 1913; Dublin 1914 and 1922; London 1918. † L 6, NEA 3, P 1, RA 3, RHA 54, RSA 1, SWA 4.
FOX, Louisa Bushe Exh. 1905-15
Ben Lomond House, Hampstead, London. † L 9, RA 4, RHA 3, RMS 4, SWA 2.
FOX, Louis H. Exh. 1920-22
Landscape painter. 173 Goldhurst Terrace, Hampstead, London. † GI 2, RA 3.
FOX, Mrs. Minnie Exh. 1912-35
Miniature painter. A.R.M.S. 1914. Add: Kent Hatch, St. Helen's, Hastings 1912; Croydon, Surrey 1935. † RA 4, RMS 5.
FOX, Mabel G. Exh. 1916-20
Miniature painter. London. † RA 2.
FOX, Miss M.H. Exh. 1911
Landscape painter. † ALP 5.
FOX, Nicholas Percy Exh. 1892-1908
Landscape painter. 38 Belsize Road, Hampstead, London. † B 11, NG 1, RA 3, RBA 1, RHA 15, RI 1.
FOX, R. Exh. 1882
4 Victoria Terrace, Rathgar, Ireland. † RHA 1.
FOX, Samuel M. Exh. 1886-87
Sculptor. London. † L 3, RA 2.
FOX, Miss V.S. Exh. 1929
2 Beverley Road, Wavertree, Liverpool. † L 1.
FOX, Mrs. Waller Exh. 1895-1910
2 New Brighton, Monkstown 1895; Edgworthstown, Co. Longford 1906. † RHA 8, SWA 2.
FOX, William Edward b. 1872
Painter and etcher. Studied Slade School. Exh. 1896-1938. Add: 17 Camden Hill Gardens, London. † NEA 14, RA 29, RBA 1, ROI 2.
FOXCROFT, Ellen E. Exh. 1929
8 Briardale Road, Rock Ferry, Birkenhead. † L 3.
FOXELL, Rev. Maurice Frederic b. 1883
Watercolour painter, wood engraver, pastel and lino cut artist. Succentor of St. Paul's Cathedral. Exh. 1927-33. Add: London. † AB 19, WG 10.
FOXLEY, Allen b. 1869
Architect. Add: 1 Lincoln's Inn Fields, London 1922. † RA 1.

FOX-PITT, Douglas 1864-1922
Landscape painter and illustrator. 5th Son of General Fox-Pitt Rivers. Studied Slade School. Edited and illustrated "The Barbarians of Morocco". R.B.A. 1906. Add: London 1893 and 1910; Caterham, Surrey 1908; Brighton 1912. † AB 58, CAR 30, G 2, GOU 2, I 1, LEI 37, LS 10, M 2, NEA 12, RBA 33, RI 9.

FOX-STRANGWAYS, Lady Muriel Exh. 1903
Melbury, Dorchester. † D 2.

FOXWELL, H.S. Exh. 1891-95
Birmingham 1891; Malvern, Worcs. 1895. † B 2.

FOYSTER, Miss E.M. Exh. 1921-95
8 Whalley Road, Whalley Range, Manchester. † L 2.

FRADGLEY, Ellen Exh. 1923-40
Portrait and landscape painter. A.S.W.A. 1927. Add: Burford, Oxon 1923; St. Ives, Cornwall 1924; Southampton 1936; Chilbolton, Hants. 1939. † L 1, ROI 1, SWA 11.

FRAENKEL, Mrs. Else Exh. 1936
Sculptor. 10 Linden Gardens, London. † RA 1.

FRAENK L. Mrs. Hatton
See KING, Lilian Yeend

FRAGGI, Raymond Exh. 1935
Landscape painter. 18 Rue de la Republique, Marseilles, France. † RA 1.

FRAGIACOMO, Pietro 1856-1922
Italian landscape painter. Exh. 1882-1905. Add: Venice. † FIN 3, I 3.

FRAIPOINT, G Exh. 1911
95 Rue de Vaugirard, Paris. † L 1.

FRAMPTON, Alfred Exh. 1881-84
Architect. London. † RA 5.

FRAMPTON, E. Exh. 1917
Beechwood Lodge, Sutton, Surrey. † RA 1.

FRAMPTON, Edward c. 1846-1929
Stained glass artist. Father of Edward Reginald F. q.v. Exh. 1880-94. Add: London. † RA 16.

FRAMPTON, Mrs. E.R. Exh. 1901-20
London. † GI 4, M 1, NG 1, RA 2, RI 2, ROI 3.

FRAMPTON, Edward Reginald* 1872-1923
Landscape, figure and religious painter and sculptor. Son of Edward F. q.v. R.B.A. 1896, R.O.I. 1904. Exh. 1893-1923. Add: London. † B 2, BG 1, FIN 50, G 1, GI 21, I 1, L 28, M 3, NG 11, P 1, RA 35, RBA 12, RI 10, RMS 1, ROI 71.

FRAMPTON, Sir George James 1860-1928
Sculptor. ("Peter Pan" in Kensington Gardens) Studied Lambeth School of Art, RA Schools (gold metal and travelling studentship) and Paris. A.R.A. 1894, R.A. 1902, H.R.B.A. 1907, H.R.I. 1926. Add: London. † B 6, GI 17, I 1, L 25, NG 13, P 3, RA 101, RBA 4, RHA 4, RI 2, RSA 17, RSW 1.

FRAMPTON, Lady George James
See COCKERELL

FRAMPTON, Meredith b. 1894
Landscape and portrait painter. Son of George James F. q.v. A.R.A. 1934. "Portrait of a Young Woman" purchased by Chantrey Bequest 1935. Exh. 1918-39. Add: London. † I 2, L 10, M 1, RA 29.

FRAMPTON, S. Exh. 1894
Beechwood Lodge, Sutton, Surrey. † RBA 1.

FRANCE, Alfred Exh. 1908-9
London. † RI 2.

FRANCE, Charles* Exh. 1887-92
Landscape painter. Huddersfield 1887; Bardon, Nr. Skipton, Yorks. 1888; Tal-y-Bont, Conway, Wales 1889. † L 3, M 2, RA 2.

FRANCE, Dorothy b. 1893
Landscape and flower painter. b. Glan Conway, Wales. Daughter of Charles F. q.v. Studied Harrogate School of Art. Add: Fernside, Forest Moor, Knaresborough, Yorks. 1921. † RCA 1.

FRANCE, George A. Exh. 1931
Sculptor. 43 Perry Rise, Forest Hill, London. † RA 1.

FRANCIA, A. Exh. 1880
Quartier Leopold, Brussels. † RHA 1.

FRANCIS, Miss C. Exh. 1914-33
London. † L 6, RA 1.

FRANCIS, David A. d. c.1931
Sculptor. A.R.S.A. 1927. Add: College of Art, Edinburgh 1915; Youngs St. Lane, North Edinburgh 1924. † GI 10, L 4, RA 2, RSA 32.

FRANCIS, E. Exh. 1900
8 Park Valley, The Park, Nottingham. † N 1.

FRANCIS, Edwin Exh. 1927-32
Wallasey, Cheshire 1927; W. Derby, Liverpool 1929. † L 3.

FRANCIS, Eva Exh. 1887-1924
Flower and figure painter. West Raynham, Norfolk 1887; Southsea, Hants. 1889; Wrexham 1904. † B 16, L 17, M 3, RA 6, RHA 10, RI 11, SWA 1.

FRANCIS, Mrs. E.A. Exh. 1890-99
St. John's Studio, Warwick. † B 5, SWA 1.

FRANCIS, Eric Carwardine b. 1887
Architect. Exh. 1935-37. Add: Taunton. † RA 2.

FRANCIS, E. Joyce Exh. 1928-37
Birmingham. † B 26, RSA 5.

FRANCIS, George Charles b. 1860
Landscape and figure painter. Exh. 1907-31. Add: 13 Robert Street, Hampstead Road, London. † LS 3, M 1, RA 3.

FRANCIS, Helena Exh. 1881
Landscape painter. 36 Belgrave Square, London. † SWA 1.

FRANCIS, Mrs. L. Exh. 1900
13 Bescot Road, Walsall, Staffs. † B 1.

FRANCIS, Miss M Exh. 1884-90
Landscape painter. London 1884; West Raynham, Norfolk 1886; Fakenham, Norfolk 1890. † B 4, GI 1, ROI 2.

FRANCIS, Margery Exh. 1923-40
Birmingham. † B 21, D 2, RSA 2.

FRANCIS, Miss M.C. Exh. 1928
Wessex, Thornton Hough, Cheshire. † L 2.

FRANCIS, Miss M.M. Exh. 1902
183 King's Road, Chelsea, London. † L 1.

FRANCIS, Thomas Edward Exh. 1899-1912
Landscape painter. London. † LS 2, M 1, NEA 3, RA 4, RBA 2.

FRANCIS, Miss V. Exh. 1928
14 Croxteth Road, Princes Park, Liverpool. † L 1.

FRANCK, Helene d. 1916
Mrs. Fairlie. Landscape and figure painter. Exh. from 1884. Add: London. † B 30, D 4, GI 14, L 10, LS 14, M 10, RA 21, RBA 14, RHA 43, RI 1, ROI 14, SWA 16.

FRANCK, J. Ernest Exh. 1906-10
Architect. 11 Pancras Lane, Queen Street, London. † RA 4.

FRANCO, L. Exh. 1883
c/o Smith, 4 Victoria Street, Nottingham. † L 1.

FRANCO, Rudolph Exh. 1911
c/o Allied Artists Asscn. 67 Chancery Lane, London. † LS 3.

FRANCOIS, Gustave* b. 1883
Swiss artist. 10 Rue Michelet, Suresnes, France 1911. † L 1.

FRANCOIS, Joseph Exh. 1909
39 Rue de la Charite, Brussels. † L 1.

FRANK, Alberta Exh. 1880
Interior painter. 14 Chalcot Terrace, London. † SWA 1.

FRANK, Ellen A. Exh. 1889-1912
Mrs. G.A. Landscape and domestic painter. A.S.W.A. 1904. Add: London 1889; Tenby, Wales 1910. † B 2, G 1, L 4, M 3, NG 2, RA 6, RBA 12, RI 19, ROI 15, SWA 47.

FRANK, Hannah Exh. 1930-38
72 Dixon Avenue, Glasgow. † GI 4.

FRANK, Hans* b. 1884
Woodcut artist. b. Vienna. Exh. 1932-35. † BA 1, RED 3.

FRANK, Hilda Exh. 1928-33
6 Sefton Drive, Liverpool. † L 6.

FRANK, Raoul Exh. 1904-6
30 Theresianstrasse, Munich. † GI 1, I 1.

FRANKEL, Otto Exh. 1898
7 Adamson Road, Swiss Cottage, London. † RBA 1.

FRANKLAND, Mrs. F.M. Exh. 1898
Sandfield Cottage, Hoylake, Cheshire. † L 1.

FRANKLIN, D. Ethel Exh. 1930-36
Birmingham 1930; Shirley 1936. † B 3.

FRANKLIN, Jeannette L. Exh. 1909-23
Sculptor. 32 Hyde Park Gardens, London. † L 4, LS 18, RA 2.

FRANKLIN, Matilda Exh. 1883
Landscape painter. The Elms, Harlington. † RBA 1.

FRANKS, Ada Stuart Exh. 1909-12
Gomshall, Surrey 1909; Peaslake, Surrey 1910. † LS 6, SWA 2.

FRANKS, Benjamin Exh. 1904-7
31 Whittall Street, Birmingham. † B 3.

FRANKS, Norah Exh. 1914
St. Brigid's, Clonskea, Ireland. † RHA 2.

FRANKS, Rosalie Exh. 1928
Malahide, Co. Dublin. † RHA 1.

FRANKS, William J. Exh. 1916-20
A.R.B.A. 1919. London. † I 5, RBA 20.

FRANZ, Ettore Roesler Exh. 1880-89
Italian landscape painter. Rome 1880; c/o G. Square, 293 Oxford Street, London 1885. † D 16, L 1, RA 3, RI 6.

FRAPPA, Jose* 1854-1904
French artist. Exh. 1882-92. Paris. † GI 9.

FRASCHERI, Exh. 1882
5 Trafalgar Studios, Kings's Road, Chelsea, London. † M 3.

FRASER, Mrs. A. Exh. 1900
Ganthorpe House, Yorks. † SWA 1.

FRASER, Agnes Exh. 1884-91
London. † D 2, RI 2.

FRASER, Alec Exh. 1903-12
Aberdeen. † GI 15, L 6, M 1, RSA 19.

FRASER, Alexander Exh. 1936
214 Union Street, Aberdeen. † GI 2.

FRASER, Alexander* 1828-1899
Landscape painter. Studied Trustees Academy Edinburgh. A.R.S.A. 1858, R.S.A. 1862. Add: Edinburgh 1880; Musselburgh 1887. † G 1, GI 37, L 2, M 1, RA 1, RBA 5, RSA 99, RSW 3.

FRASER, Alice Exh. 1891
Oakfield, Stevenage, Herts. † RBA 1.

FRASER, Annie Exh. 1880-95
Landscape and figure painter. Edinburgh. † GI 5, L 1, M 2, RSA 21, RSW 2.

FRASER, A. Anderson Exh. 1884-91
Landscape painter. c/o E. Hill, 151 Essex Road, Islington 1884; Bedford 1886. † D 2, L 2, RBA 3.

FRASER, A. Coutts Exh. 1895-1902
Aberdeen 1895; Stonehaven 1899; Newtonhill, Kincardineshire 1902. † GI 7, RSA 11.
FRASER, Alexander R. Exh. 1914-35
Sculptor. London. † GI 3, L 1, RA 8, RSA 2.
FRASER, B. Exh. 1933
c/o S. Longlai, 7 Wilifield Way, Golders Green, London. † RBA 1.
FRASER, C. Gordon Exh. 1895-99
Landscape painter. 2 Wychcombe Studios, England's Lane, Haverstock Hill, London. † L 10, M 1, NG 1, RA 1.
FRASER, Claude Lovat* 1890-1921
Theatrical designer and illustrator. Exh. 1917. Add: 12 Cresswell Gardens, London. † I 2, NEA 2.
FRASER, C. Mary Exh. 1881
Figure and flower painter. Bank House, Newbiggin by Sea, Morpeth, Northumberland. † SWA 2.
FRASER, Dorothea Exh. 1912
Woodlands, Elderslie, N.B. † RA 1.
FRASER, Dorothy Exh. 1906-8
79 West Regent Street, Glasgow. † GI 4, L 1.
FRASER, E Exh. 1884
Glasgow. † GI 1.
FRASER, Edith Exh. 1922
Eastwood Hotel, Lower Leeson Street, Dublin. † RHA 1.
FRASER, Mrs. Elizabeth Exh. 1901
2 Old Bath Street, Southport, Lancs. † L 1.
FRASER, Eric George b. 1902
Painter and etcher. Add: 23 Earl Street, Westminster, London 1924. † RA 1.
FRASER, Mrs. Ella M. Exh. 1885-1924
Landscape and flower painter. London 1885; Red Barns, Formby, Lancs. 1905. † L 5, SWA 2, WG 5.
FRASER, Florence Exh. 1880-1905
Figure painter. Kensington, London 1880; Castleconnell, Co. Limerick 1896. † B 1, M 1, RBA 2, RHA 9, RSA 1, SWA 1.
FRASER, Francis Arthus Exh. 1880-83
Landscape and figure painter. Crawley, Sussex 1880; Upfolds, Holmbury St. Mary, Nr. Dorking 1881; Shere, Surrey 1882. † D 4, L 2, RBA 6.
FRASER, G. Exh. 1908-13
Architect. 20 Castle Street, Liverpool. † L 7, RA 2.
FRASER, George Gordon d. 1895
Landscape and figure painter. Stoke Newington 1880; Bedford 1883; London 1886; Hemingford Abbots, Hunts. 1888; Houghton, Hunts. 1893. † D 2, G 1, L 1, RA 8, RI 1.
FRASER, Gilbert W. Exh. 1930-33
Architect. Wellington Buildings, The Strand, Liverpool. † L 5.
FRASER, Mrs. H.J. Exh. 1885-87
Mrs A. Landscape painter. Fairlea, Headingley, Leeds. † R 11, SWA 1.
FRASER, Herbert Ross Exh. 1909-14
Edingburgh 1909; Hamilton, N.B. 1910. † GI 2, RSA 7.
FRASER, Janet Exh. 1898-1902
Glasgow 1898 and 1902; Lenzie 1900. † GI 4.
FRASER, John* Exh. 1880-1919
Landscape and marine painter. R.B.A. 1889. Add: Stoke Newington 1880; Seaford, Sussex 1887 and London 1891. † B 7, D 11, FIN 60, G 1, L 30, M 7, RA 61, RBA 65, RI 12, ROI 12, RSA 3.
FRASER, John A. Exh. 1889
Landscape painter. 3 St. John's Wood Studios, Queens' Terrace, London. † L 1, RA 1.

FRASER, J.G. Exh. 1893
9 Gt. Queen Street, Westminster, London. † RHA,1.
FRASER, Mrs. Jane Hyde Exh. 1902-39
Forress 1902; Nairn, N.B. 1906. † D 6, RSA 4, RSW 8, SWA 7.
FRASER, John P Exh. 1881-84
Flower, figure and landscape painter. School of Art, Aberdeen 1881; 46 Garden Place, Aberdeen 1882. † RA 2, RSA 4.
FRASER, John Simpson Exh. 1880-93
Edinburgh 1880; Auchmithie, Forfarshire 1887. † GI 2, RI 1, RSA 32.
FRASER, Miss L. Exh. 1893-96
27 Nightingale Place, Woolwich, London. † SWA 3.
FRASER, L.F. Exh. 1931
† GOU 1.
FRASER, Miss M. Exh. 1908
15 Arundel Street, Nottingham. † N 1.
FRASER, Marion Exh. 1929-38
30 Queen's Road, Gt. Crosby, Liverpool. † L 7, M 1.
FRASER, Margaret Lorna Exh. 1924-38
A.S.W.A. 1925. Rutland House, Southend Road, Beckenham, Kent. † NEA 4, SWA 12.
FRASER, Miss M.T. Exh. 1900-2
Nottingham. † N 3.
FRASER, N. Exh. 1893-97
Saffron Hall Mansions, Hamilton, N.B. † GI 3.
FRASER, Mrs. R.A. Exh. 1896-1901
Serpentine South, Blundellsands, Liverpool. † L 4.
FRASER, R.E. Exh. 1881
Barnton Lodge, Davidson's Mains, Edinburgh. † RSA 1.
FRASER, Robert George Exh. 1880-88
Manse, St. Thomas', Leith. † RHA 3, RSA 8.
FRASER, Robert Macdonald b. 1870
Landscape and coastal painter. Studied Liverpool Institute. Exh. 1910-38. Add: Liverpool. † L 50, M 1, RA 7, RCA 2.
FRASER, Rose M. Exh. 1908-16
34 St. Andrews Square, Edinburgh. † GI 1, RSA 13.
FRASER, Robert W. Exh. 1880-1904
Landscape painter. London 1880 and 1889; Bromley, Kent 1887; Hemingford Grey, Hunts. 1888; Soham, Suffolk 1899. † D 23, L 6, M 2, RA 19, RBA 12, RHA 1, RI 22, RSA 3.
FRASER, Sarah Francis Exh. 1881-83
Edinburgh. † GI 1, RSA 5.
FRASER, William Exh. 1897-1906
248 West George Street, Glasgow. † GI 3.
FRASER-TYTLER, Miss K.A. Exh. 1882-95
Edinburgh 1882; Woodhouselee, Midlothian 1885; Milton Bridge, N.B. 1894. † G 1, GI 8, L 10, M 3, RSA 12.
FRASI, Horace C. Exh. 1892-97
Architect. 22 Southampton Buildings, London. † RA 2.
FRATER, Henry Exh. 1899-1912
241 St. George's Road, Glasgow. † GI 2, L 2.
FRATER, Margaret Exh. 1893
44 Dumbarton Road, Glasgow. † GI 1.
FRAYE, Andre* b. 1888
French artist. Exh. 1925-28. † GOU 5.
FRAZER, Charles E. Exh. 1881
Portrait painter. 4 John Street, Hampstead, London. † RA 1.
FRAZER, William Miller* b. 1864
Landscape painter. Studied Edinburgh and Paris. A.R.S.A. 1909, R.S.A. 1924. Exh. 1888-1940. Add: Perth 1888 and 1895; Bridge of Earn, N.B. 1892; Edinburgh 1898. † GI 125, L 13, M 3, RA 3, RBA 1, RHA 6, ROI 1, RSA 182, RSW 1.

FRAZIER, Gertrude B. Exh. 1906-9
Trinity Road, Birchfield, Birmingham. † B 4.
FRAZIER, Laurie Exh. 1904-10
Birchfield, Birmingham 1904; Little Orme, Llandudno 1908. † B 4, L 2, RCA 2.
FREAKE, Mrs. I. Exh. 1881
Cromwell House, London. † SWA 1.
FRECK, Lilian G. Exh. 1904-32
nee Watson. Landscape painter. A.N.S.A. 1912. Add: Sutton Coldfield 1904; West Bridgford, Notts. 1908. † B 2, N 51.
FRECKER, H.E. Exh. 1911
St. Elmo, Staunton Road, Kingston on Thames, Surrey. † RA 1.
FRECKLETON, H.W. Exh. 1908-35
Portrait painter. A.N.S.A. 1913, N.S.A. 1916. Add: Nottingham. † N 9.
FREDERIC, Leon Henri Marie* b. 1856
Belgian artist. Exh. 1894-1921. Add: Brussels. † GI 2, L 2, RSA 3.
FREDERICK, Austin
See AUSTIN, Frederick George
FREDERICKSON, Beatrice Exh. 1894
Briennesstrasse, 45, Munich. † RBA 1.
FREDRIKSEN, Stinius Exh. 1933
Kunstuernes Hus, Oslo. † RSA 2.
FREE, J.A. Exh. 1882-85
306 Pershore Road, Birmingham. † B 4.
FREE, M. Constance Exh. 1915-27
Still life painter. London. † RA 3.
FREEBORN, Mildred Exh. 1913-27
Landscape painter. † FIN 163.
FREEDMAN, Barnett 1901-1958
Painter and lithographer. Studied Royal College of Art 1922-25. Offical war artist 1940. Add: London 1927. † FIN 6, LEI 1, NEA 12.
FREELAND, David Exh. 1933
65 Drygate Street, Larkhill, Edinburgh. † RSA 2.
FREELING, Miss L. Exh. 1897
11 Sussex Gardens, London. † SWA 1.
FREEMAN, Mrs. Agnes Exh. 1936-37
Flower painter. 53A Stanley Gardens, Belsize Grove, London. † RA 2.
FREEMAN, A.W. Exh. 1924-29
Highgate House, Walsall, Staffs. † B 5, GI 3.
FREEMAN, Miss B.G. Exh. 1933
22 Palm Grove, Oxton, Birkenhead. † L 1.
FREEMAN, Dorothy Exh. 1927-38
Landscape, still life, animal and bird painter. Add: 135 Hornsey Lane, London. † NEA 7, RA 7, RID 1, SWA 1.
FREEMAN, Edward Canning Exh. 1939
Portrait and landscape painter. Studied Bushey, Herts. and Byam Shaw School. † WG 18.
FREEMAN, Frank b.1901
Landscape and portrait painter. b. Barbados, West Indies. Trained as a bacteriologist and biologist. Exh. 1928. Add: London. † GOU 2.
FREEMAN, F.R. Exh. 1906-15
Smalleys Chambers, Bolton, Lancs. † RA 3.
FREEMAN, H. Exh. 1905
87 Martin's Lane, Liscard, Cheshire. † L 1.
FREEMAN, John Exh. 1885-89
Landscape painter. Windmill Street, Radford, Nottingham. † N 5.
FREEMAN, J. Kelly Exh. 1894-1901
Dublin. † RHA 8.
FREEMAN, J.R. Exh. 1930
† GOU 1.
FREEMAN, Miss M. Exh. 1913
† M 1.
FREEMAN, Madge Exh. 1927
Figure painter. c/o Rowley Gallery, Church Street, Kensington, London. † RA 1.

FREEMAN, Mary Exh. 1927-29
Flower painter. 5 Queen's Gate Terrace, London. † AR 2, RA 1.
FREEMAN, Miss M.H. Exh. 1922-23
Heewaydin, Preston Lane, Birkenhead. † L 3.
FREEMAN, M. Winefride Exh. 1886-1912
Domestic painter. Falmouth, Cornwall 1886; London 1888, 1895 and 1912; Brighton 1892; Newlyn, Penzance 1897; Bushey, Herts. 1902. † B 5, L 6, M 1, NG 8, RA 11, RI 14, SWA 1.
FREEMAN, P.B. Exh. 1917
6 Gray's Inn Square, London. † RA 1.
FREEMAN, Phyllis J. Exh. 1930
Still life painter. Dial House, Shepperton on Thames. † RA 1.
FREEMAN, Robert Exh. 1916-17
Primrose Mansions, Battersea Park, London. † RI 2.
FREEMAN, Richard Knill. Exh. 1882-94
Architectural painter. Bolton le Moors, Lancs. † L 9, M 3, RA 9, RHA 9.
FREER, H.B. Exh. 1905-15
Rochester 1905; Gravesend 1910; Blackheath 1914. † B 1, L 1, RA 5.
FREESHEL, M.M. Exh. 1903-9
8 Onslow Studios, 183 King's Road, London. † L 4.
FREETH, Hubert Andrew b. 1912
Portrait painter and engraver. Studied Birmingham College of Art (Rome scholarship in engraving 1936), British School at Rome 1936-39. A.R.E. 1937. Exh. 1935-40. † B 27, RA 15, RE 18.
FREETH, James Wilfred b. 1872
Painter, etcher and enameller. Studied West Bromwich School of Art and Royal College of Art. Headmaster Limerick School of Art and Rotherham School of Art. Add: Bromwich 1899; Limerick, Ireland 1901; Rotherham 1914. † B 7, RA 1, RHA 5.
FREETH, Col. W. Exh. 1887
Dudley Gallery, London. † D 3.
FREIFELD, E. Exh. 1938
† NEA 1.
FREIGHT, Miss F.C. Exh. 1904
13 Howdon Road, North Shields. † SWA 1.
FREKE, Mrs. R. Hussey Exh. 1895-1902
Enford, Pewsey, Wilts. 1895; Highworth, Wilts. 1899. † D 18, SWA 2.
FREMIET, Emmanuel 1824-1910
French sculptor. H.F.R.A. Exh. 1904-10. Add: Paris. † L 2, RA 21.
FRENCH, Annie* Exh. 1904-24
Painter and etcher. Glasgow 1904; Tulse Hill, London 1915. † B 4, BG 2, CON 2, G 1, GI 49, I 2, L 31, M 10, RA 28, RHA 3, RI 1, RSA 28, RSW 2.
FRENCH, Cecil Exh. 1902-22
Landscape painter. London. † BG 2, I 2, RA 1, RHA 2.
FRENCH, Christine Exh. 1895-96
5 Raglan Road, Dublin. † RHA 2.
FRENCH, C.H. Exh. 1928-32
Fletcher Close, Walshaw, Bury, Lancs. † RCA 2.
FRENCH, Edith Scrivener Exh. 1881
Landscape painter. The Wymeshead, Kegworth, Derby. † N 1.
FRENCH, Mrs. Helen M.C. Exh. 1896-97
35 Mespil Road, Dublin. † RHA 2.
FRENCH, Miss I. Exh. 1914
Fulham Road, London. † SWA 3.
FRENCH, Miss J. Exh. 1917
Chelsea, London. † SWA 2.
FRENCH, J.J. Exh. 1912
7 Harlescott Road, Nunhead, London. † RA 1.
FRENCH, Jane K. Exh. 1928-30
Portrait painter. 15 Lower Pemb;oke Street, Dublin. † RHA 2.
FRENCH, Miss Jinnie K. Exh. 1899-1907
Miniature painter. 15 Lower Pembroke Street, Dublin. † L 4, RA 8, RHA 3.
FRENCH, Viscount John R. Exh. 1912-23
Military painter. Waltham Cross, Herts. 1912; London 1917. † FIN 30, L 7, RA 2, RI 1.
FRENCH, Margaret Exh. 1900
The Log House, Hindhead, Surrey. † SWA 1.
FRENCH, Mary Exh. 1884-87
Flower and bird painter. 50 Cathcart Road, London. † SWA 4.
FRENCH, Percy 1854-1920
London. † D 16, RHA 1.
FRENCH, P.C. Exh. 1885
Sporting painter. 5 Fitzwilliam Place, Dublin. † RBA 1.
FRENCH, W.P. Exh. 1892-99
Dublin. † RHA 23.
FRENES, du see D
FRENZENY, Paul Exh. 1898
47 Brompton Road, London. † RI 1.
FRERE, Miss Exh. 1880
Portrait painter. Government House, Capetown, South Africa. † SWA 1.
FRERE, Amy Hanbury Exh. 1907-9
45 Unthank Road, Norwich, Norfolk. † LS 8, RA 1.
FRERE, Sir Bartle C. Exh. 1920
Watercolour painter of middle eastern landscapes. † WG 142.
FRERE, Chas.* 1815-1886
French artist. 6 Boulevard de Clichy, Paris 1882. † GI 3, M 1.
FRERE, Eustace Corrie b. 1863
Architect. b. Cape of Good Hope. Studied RA Schools and Atelier Pascal, Paris. Exh. 1907-32. Add: Lincoln's Inn Fields, London. † RA 16.
FRERE, Elizabeth F.T. Exh. 1928-36
Landscape painter. 71 Campden Street, London. † L 1, RA 4, RBA 10, RHA 1, ROI 1, SWA 1.
FRERE, Humphrey Exh. 1898
4 Dudley Street, Wolverhampton. † B 1.
FRERE, Herbert H. Exh. 1893-94
7 Mornington Road, Bow Road, London. † ROI 2.
FRERE, Laurie Exh. 1903-12
Taunton, Somerset 1903; Boxford, Colchester, Essex 1904; Bishops Stortford, Herts. 1912. † B 7, L 7, LS 6, RA 2.
FRERE, Pierre Edouard* 1819-1886
French painter. Ecouen, Seine et Oise, France 1880. † AG 7, GI 5, M 1, RA 7.
FRESHWATER, Miss M.H. Exh. 1916-22
52 Springfield Road, St. John's Wood, London. † L 2, RA 1.
FRETTINGHAM, L. Exh. 1909
19 Trinity Avenue, Lenton, Nottingham. † N 1.
FREW, Alexander Exh. 1883-1905
Landscape and marine painter. Glasgow 1883 and 1897; Helensburgh 1894. † GI 29, I 3, L 7, M 2, NEA 2, RA 8, RSA 3.
FREW, Bessie G. Exh. 1889
7 Lilybank Gardens, Glasgow. † GI 1.
FREYBURG, Frank Proschwitzry* b. 1862
Landscape and portrait painter. Studied RA Schools. Married Monica McIvor q.v. Exh. 1893-1939. Add: Hassocks, Sussex 1893; St. Ives, Cornwall 1907; 75 Holland Park Road, Kensington, London 1913. † I 1, L 3, LS 4, RA 24, ROI 27.
FRIANT, Emile 1863-1932
French artist. 11 Boulevard de Clichy, Paris 1913. † L 6.
FRIDELL, Axel Exh. 1929
Etcher. 85 Oakley Street, Chelsea, London. † RA 1.
FRIDELL, John A. Exh. 1934
Dry point artist. 85 Oakley Street, Chelsea, London. † RA 1.
FRIDLANDER, Ernest D. Exh. 1899-1914
Landscape and figure painter. Coventry. † B 6, BG 14.
FRIDMAN, S. Exh. 1916
† I 1.
FRIEDENSON, Arthur* 1872-1955
Landscape and coastal painter. "Runswick Bay" purchased by Chantrey Bequest 1907. Exh. 1889-1938. Add: Leeds 1889; Runswick, Hinderwell, Yorks. 1906; Wareham, Dorset 1909; Corfe Castle, Dorset 1931. † B 2, FIN 51, GI 18, GOU 28, I 1, L 10, M 3, NEA 2, NG 3, RA 54, ROI 2, RSA 3.
FRIEDENSON, Joseph T. Exh. 1899-1909
Landscape painter. London. † NEA 1, RA 2.
FRIEDENSON, Thomas Exh. 1910-28
Landscape painter. London. † AB 10, BG 32, RA 5, RI 1, ROI 2.
FRIEDLANDER, Gertrude Exh. 1910-12
25 Belsize Park, London. † L 8.
FRIEDRICH, Helen Exh. 1884-85
Flower painter. 5 Denbigh Road, Bayswater, London. † SWA 5.
FRIEND, Alfred Percy Exh. 1929-35
Landscape painter. London 1929; Chatham, Kent 1931; Tonbridge, Kent 1935. † RA 5.
FRIEND, George Taylor Exh. 1913-40
Line and seal engraver. A.R.M.S. 1921. Add: London. † L 9, RA 20, RHA 3, RMS 15, RSA 3.
FRIER, Mrs. A. Exh. 1889-94
Black Forest Villa, Champion Hill, Denmark Hill, London. † L 1, M 2, ROI 2.
FRIER, Harry Exh. 1880-90
Edinburgh 1880; Taunton, Somerset 1890. † GI 1, RSA 8.
FRIER, Jessie Exh. 1880-1912
Landscape and coastal painter. Edinburgh. † GI 9, RSA 35, SWA 7.
FRIER, Mary Exh. 1880-89
Landscape painter. Edinburgh. † GI 1, RSA 20, SWA 2.
FRIER, Maggie E. Exh. 1880
62 Queen Street, Edinburgh. † RSA 1.
FRIER, Robert Exh. 1880-91
Edinburgh. † GI 1, RSA 36.
FRIER, R.H. Exh. 1888-92
Currie, N.B. † RSA 5.
FRIESE, R. Exh. 1892
† TOO 1.
FRIESEKE, Frederick Carl* b. 1874
American artist. 6 Rue Victor Considerant, Paris 1903-22. † GI 1, I 7, L 3, RSA 4.
FRIESZ, Emile Othon* b. 1879
French painter. Exh. 1914-33. † ALP 4, GI 2, GOU 1, L 2.
FRIGOUT, Mrs. Julie Exh. 1885-89
Landscape and nature painter. Brockley, Kent 1885; New Cross, Kent 1888. † L 3, RA 1, RBA 9, RSA 2.
FRIMSTON, Mrs. Ethel Martin Exh. 1911-24
Liverpool. † L 7.
FRIMSTONE, Winifred Exh. 1910-13
13 Hargreaves Road, Sefton Park, Liverpool. † L 5.

FRIPP, Alfred Downing* 1822-1895
Landscape and figure painter. b. Bristol. Younger brother of George Arthur F. q.v. Studied RA Schools and the British Museum. Visited Italy 1850. A.R.W.S. 1844, R.W.S. 1846 (Secretary 1870). Add: London. † AG 4, L 8, RWS 25.

FRIPP, Charles Edwin* 1854-1906
Painter of battle scenes. Son of George Arthur F. q.v. A.R.W.S. 1891. Add: Hampstead, London 1885. Died in Canada. † L 5, M 1, RA 2, RHA 4, RWS 18.

FRIPP, Constance L. Exh. 1883-1900
Landscape painter. A.S.W.A. 1886. Add: Kensington, London 1885; Hampstead, London 1887. † D 5, L 2, RA 1, RBA 1, RI 5, SWA 26.

FRIPP, George Arthur* 1813-1896
Landscape painter. b. Bristol. Brother of Alfred Downing F. q.v. and father of Charles Edwin F. q.v. Studied under J.B. Pyne and Samuel Jackson. Toured the continent 1834. A.R.W.S. 1841, R.W.S. 1845 (Secretary 1848-54). Add: London. † AG 18, CON 1, D 3, DOW 1, FIN 3, L 1, M 4, RWS 102, TOO 6.

FRIPP, Innes b. 1867
Decorative, pictorial and portrait painter and stained glass illustrator. Studied Bristol School of Art, Royal College of Art and Paris. Assistant master Royal College of Art and Lambeth School of Art, Life master South London Technical Art School and Professor of Art at Queen's College, Harley Street. Exh. 1893-1939. Add: London. † D 17, L 5, M 1, NG 2, RA 19, RI 21.

FRIPP, J.W. Exh. 1893
Landscape painter. Holmdale Road, West Hampstead, London. † NG 1.

FRIPP, Paul b. 1890
Painter, black and white artist, metalworker, jeweller and photographer. b. Mansfield, Notts. Studied Leicester School of Art and Royal College of Art. Served as Intelligence officer in Middle East World War I. Director of Art Cheltenham Ladies' College 1921, and Bideford School of Art 1932. † NEA 3, RA 4.

FRIPP, Susan Beatrice d. 1913
nee Lock. Exh. 1906-12. 4 St. James's Terrace, Regent's Park, London. † L 1, RA 5.

FRIPP, S.T. Exh. 1934
† RMS 1.

FRIPP, Tom Exh. 1890-99
Figure and landscape painter. London. † L 2, NG 2, RA 2, RBA 6, RI 1.

FRISENDAHL, Carl Exh. 1912
Hernosand, Sweden. † RSA 1.

FRISTON, de see D

FRISTON, W. Exh. 1882
c/o Wroe, 89 Moss Lane, Manchester. † M 1.

FRISWELL, Harry P. Hain Exh. 1881-1906
Landscape painter. R.B.A. 1897. Add: Bexley Heath, Kent 1881; Tyn-y-Groes, Conway, Wales 1888; East Bergholt, Suffolk 1906. † B 1, L 4, RA 7, RBA 17, ROI 3.

FRITEL, Pierre Exh. 1913
64 Rue Mouton Dubernet, Paris. † L 1.

FRITH, Edgar Silver b. 1890
Sculptor. Son of William Silver F. q.v. Studied Kennington and Lambeth Art Schools and RA Schools. Headmaster, Sculpture Section, Kennington and Lambeth Schools of Art. Exh. 1923-35. Add: London. † L 3, P 1, RA 10.

FRITH, William Powell* 1819-1909
Painter of historical genre and scenes of Victorian life. b. nr. Ripon, Yorks. Studied at Sass's Academy 1835 and RA Schools 1837. A.R.A. 1845, R.A. 1854, H.R.B.A. by 1880. Add: Bayswater, London 1880; Sydenham Rise 1889; St. John's Wood, London 1897. † B 18, CAR 3, G 1, GI 5, L 32, M 24, RA 53, RBA 1, RHA 1, ROI 15, TOO 3.

FRITH, William Silver d. 1924
Sculptor. Father of Edgar Silver F. q.v. Studied Lambeth School 1870 and RA Schools 1872. Modelling master at Lambeth School. Exh. 1884-1912. Add: Herne Hill 1884; London 1892. † RA 12.

FRITSCH, Hans Exh. 1905
3 Terrassenstrasse, Dresden. † I 1.

FROBISHER, Lucy Marguerite Exh. 1916-40
Animal painter. Studied Kemp-Welch School of Painting. Head of the Frobisher School of Painting. Add: Headingley, Leeds 1916; Bushey, Herts. 1921. B 52, D 11, GI 13, I 1, L 10, P 2, RA 1, RCA 94, RI 12, ROI 9, RSA 8, SWA 3.

FROES, Cecily M. Exh. 1923
1 Rodney Street, Liverpool. † L 1.

FROGGATT, H. Exh. 1925-27
Architectural painter. 3 Freiston Street, Hyson Green, Nottingham. † N 3.

FROGGATT, Janet O. Exh. 1925-27
Miniature painter. Illingworth, Pinner, Middlesex. † RA 2, RI 4, RMS 1.

FROLICH, F. Exh. 1890
161 Cromwell Road, South Kensington, London. † RA 1.

FROLICH, L. Exh. 1883
† FIN 1.

FROMENT, E. Exh. 1911
3 Rue de la Redoute, Fontenay aux Roses, France. † L 1.

FROMUTH, Charles Henry b. 1861
American artist. Exh. 1900-24. Add: Concarneau, France 1900; c/o Aitken, Dott and Son, Edinburgh 1922. † GI 3, I 10, RHA 4, RSA 4.

FROOD, Hester b. 1882
Mrs. Gwynne-Evans. Painter and etcher. b. New Zealand. Studied Exeter and Paris. Worked in Italy, France, Holland and Spain. A.R.E. 1920-21. Add: Topsham, Devon 1904; Woodchester, Glos. 1906; Wadhurst, Sussex 1912; Bideford, Devon 1919; Chard, Somerset 1925; Odiham, Hants. 1933. † B 3, CG 49, CON 13, G 5, GI 3, I 4, L 3, M 17, NEA 10, RA 13, RE 4, RED 1, RSA 3.

FROOD, Millie Exh. 1936-40
Hayfield, Hamilton Road, Motherwell. † RSA 3, RSW 1.

FROOMS, H. Lionel Exh. 1910-33
24 Athol Road, Alexandra Park, Manchester. † L 6.

FROST, Agnes Exh. 1926-35
Landscape painter. Waterford 1929; Cork 1935. † RHA 5.

FROST, A.B. Exh. 1880
148 Strand, London. † RHA 1.

FROST, Bertha b. 1877
nee Glazier. Modeller and colour wood-cut artist. b. Rochdale. Daughter of Richard Glazier q.v. Studied Manchester School of Art, Halifax and Rochdale. Lived in Far East. Exh. 1919-35. Add: Didsbury, Manchester 1920. † COO 4, L 3, M 2.

FROST, Lady Dora Exh. 1927-28
Upton Lawn, Chester. † L 1, RCA 1.

FROST, Minnie P. Exh. 1892
Warleys, Walm Lane, Willesden Green, London. † RBA 1.

FROST, R. Exh. 1882
Portrait painter. 53 Winchester Street, London. † RA 1.

FROST, Stella Exh. 1935
Landscape painter. Hazel Brook, Terenure, Dublin. † RHA 2.

FROST, Miss S.L. Exh. 1904-7
9 Cook Street, Liverpool. † L 6, RCA 1.

FROST, William Exh. 1907-16
Derby. † L 1, NG 1.

FRUEN, Helena Maud Exh. 1901-4
London. † L 4, RCA 7, M 1.

FRY, Miss A.J. Exh. 1908-14
London. † LS 3, RA 4.

FRY, A.P. Exh. 1893-1905
18 Hackin's Hey, Liverpool. † L 5.

FRY, Caroline Nottidge Exh. 1880-82
nee Nottidge. Figure painter. Married to Samuel F. q.v. Add: Windmill Hill, Hampstead, London. † B 2, G 1, M 1, RA 4, RHA 1, SWA 2.

FRY, Douglas Exh. 1910
c/o G. Rowney & Co., 10 Percy Street, London. † RA 1.

FRY, Ethne B. Exh. 1935
Flower painter. 14 Cathcart Studios, 33 Redcliffe Road, London. † RA 1, RI 1.

FRY, E.G. Exh. 1924-30
Horsley Hall, Gresford, Nr. Wrexham. † L 1, P 1.

FRY, Ernest H. Exh. 1902-3
Landscape painter. 41 Lansdown Road, London. † L 1, RA 1.

FRY, E. Maxwell Exh. 1921-22
1 Cavendish Gardens, Princes Park, Liverpool. † GOU 2, L 1.

FRY, Edith M. Exh. 1922-29
Landscape and flower painter. 150A Haverstock Hill, London. † AB 2, I 1, P 1, ROI 1, SWA 2.

FRY, Gladys Windsor Exh. 1929-36
nee Hardy-Syms. Watercolour painter and art lecturer. Studied Horsham, Chichester and London. Married Harry Windsor F. q.v. Add: London. † RBA 1, WG 12.

FRY, Helen Exh. 1903-4
Mrs. Roger F. Landscape painter. 22 Willow Road, Hampstead, London. † CAR 1, NEA 2.

FRY, Harry Windsor Exh. 1884-1939
Figure and portrait painter. b. Torquay. Served with Royal Fusiliers 1914-19. R.B.A. 1895. Add: London. † B 4, L 11, M 6, NG 6, P 2, RA 6, RBA 76, RHA 1, RI 3, ROI 3, WG 23.

FRY, Lily Exh. 1895
7 West Bank Road, Fairfield, Liverpool. † L 1.

FRY, Lewis G. 1860-1933
Landscape painter. R.B.A. 1902. Add: Hampstead, London 1895; Limpsfield, Surrey 1900. † AR 64, NEA 1, RA 3, RBA 117.

FRY, Muriel Exh. 1912-30
Liverpool. † L 11.

FRY, Nora Exh. 1920-28
Etcher and illustrator. Huddersfield 1920; Liverpool 1921; London 1928. † L 5, RA 1.

FRY, R.C. Exh. 1912-13
12 Clifford's Inn, London. † RA 2.

FRY, R.D. Exh. 1897-98
53 Butter Market, Ipswich, Suffolk. † RI 2.

FRY, Roger Elliot* 1866-1934
Landscape and figure painter and critic. Slade professor Cambridge. N.E.A. 1893. Member London Group 1917. Add: London 1891, 1903 and 1932; Bristol 1898; Dorking, Surrey 1900; Guildford 1909. † ALP 175, AG 11, CAR 99, CHE 9, DOW 2, GI 3, GOU 18, L 5, LEI 18, LS 3, M 4, NEA 88, RSA 1.

FRY, Samuel Exh. 1882-1905
Sculptor. London. † B 2, L 4, NG 1, RA 19.

FRY, William b. 1865
Landscape, seascape and portrait painter. b. Otley, Yorks. Exh. 1919-31. Add: High Street, Holywood, Co. Down. † RHA 10.

FRY, William H. Exh. 1937-38
Flower and landscape painter. 3 West Elmwood, Belfast. † RHA 2.

FRYER, E.L. Exh. 1882
45 Salisbury Street, Liverpool. † L 1.

FRYER, Katherine Mary b. 1910
Painter and wood engraver. Studied Leeds College of Art 1926-31 (Princess of Wales Scholarship in engraving 1931). Teacher Bath School of Art 1937. Exh. 1936. † RED 1.

FRYER, Rose Exh. 1882
62 St. Mary's Terrace, Paddington, London. † D 1.

FRYER, Stan b. 1906
Painter, pen and ink and commercial artist. b. Manchester. Exh. 1926. † M 1.

FRYER, Wilfred Moody b. 1891
Painter and black and white artist. Studied Bradford School of Art. Exh. 1922-30. Add: Addiscombe, Croydon, Surrey. † L 4, RA 4, RBA 2.

FRYERS, Arthur G. Exh. 1893
Glen Road, Potterhill, Paisley, Glasgow. † GI 1.

FUCHS, Emile 1866-1929
Portrait painter and sculptor. b. Vienna. R.B.A. 1903, R.M.S. 1921. Add: London 1898; New York 1921. † GI 2, I 1, L 58, LS 1, M 1, NG 10, P 2, RA 14, RBA 10, RMS 1.

FUERST, W.R. Exh. 1924
c/o R.H. Morton, 25 York Place, Edinburgh. † GI 1.

FULCHER, Norah Exh. 1895-1921
Portrait painter. Chingford, Essex 1895; Notting Hill, London 1898. † B 14, L 15, NG 1, RA 3, RBA 3, RI 2, SWA 3.

FULFORD-EALES, H.B. Exh. 1928
Landscape painter. † AB 1.

FULLARTON, S.R. Exh. 1891
2 Garscube Terrace, Edinburgh. † RSA 1.

FULLBROOK, Mrs. Rose Exh. 1932-33
Sculptor. 23 Riverside, Sunbury-on-Thames. † GI 1, RA 1.

FULLER, Miss Annice Exh. 1921
Red House, Furzedown College, London. † RHA 1.

FULLER, Arthur P. Exh. 1926-35
Portrait painter. 105 Cowper Road, Hanwell, Middlesex. † L 1, RA 7.

FULLER, Miss B.J. Exh. 1897-1902
London. † L 2, ROI 2, SWA 1.

FULLER, Donald Exh. 1934
Figure painter. 106 Mayfield Avenue, North Finchley, London. † RA 1.

FULLER, Miss Edith Exh. 1893-95
Figure painter. Hollywood, Duppas Hill, Croydon, Surrey. † L 1, NG 3.

FULLER, Edmund G.* Exh. 1888-1916
Landscape and figure painter. R.B.A. 1895. Add: W. Cults, N.B. 1888; London 1891; St. Ives, Cornwall 1892. † B 23, D 3, RA 23, RBA 17.

FULLER, E. Murray Exh. 1932
c/o Bourlet and Sons, 17 Nassau Street, London. † RI 1.

FULLER, Florence A. Exh. 1897-1904
Figure painter. London. † M 1, RA 2, ROI 1.

FULLER, Miss G.F. Exh. 1888-89
Corsham, Wilts. and London. † D 2.

FULLER, Henry Exh. 1940
c/o Mrs. Stewart, 56 Home Street, Edinburgh. † RSA 1.

FULLER, Horace Exh. 1880-86
Watercolour landscape painter. London. † D 1, RA 1, RBA 1, RI 1.

FULLER, Isabella J. Exh. 1884
Landscape painter. Ramsdale Vicarage, Basingstoke, Hants. † SWA 1.

FULLER, Rev. J.F. Exh. 1929-38
Landscape painter. † AB 2, WG 8.

FULLER, Mrs. Kate Sidney Exh. 1889-1909
Flower and portrait painter. Cromwell Road, London 1889; Epsom, Surrey 1900; Wimbledon 1909. † RID 10, SWA 2.

FULLER, Lucy Exh. 1880-84
Croft House, Aston, Wallingford, Berks. † B 1, RSA 3.

FULLER, Miss L.F. Exh. 1910
c/o Chenil & Co., 183 King's Road, Chelsea, London. † RA 1.

FULLER, Leonard John* b. 1891
Portrait, figure and still life painter. Studied Clapham School of Art, RA Schools; national silver and bronze medallist 1912-13. British Institute Scholarship in painting 1913. On Active Service 1914-18. Art teacher St. John's Wood 1922-32. Assistant art teacher Dulwich College 1926-38. Principal St. Ives School of Painting 1938. R.O.I. 1933. Exh. 1919-40. Add: Sutton, Surrey 1919 and 1933; London 1920; Cheam, Surrey 1931; St. Ives, Cornwall 1938. † GI 2, L 2, M 1, P 19, RA 21, RCA 47, RHA 2, ROI 36.

FULLER, Maud Exh. 1924-25
41 Emys Road, Eastbourne. † GOU 2, SWA 1.

FULLER, Miss M.J. Exh. 1896-98
9 Palace Road, Surbiton, Surrey. † SWA 5.

FULLER, Rosa Exh. 1884
Strensham Road, Moseley Road, Birmingham. † B 1.

FULLER, Theresa Exh. 1936
Oxted, Surrey. † SWA 2.

FULLER, W. Exh. 1890
Miall, Grasmere, Oaks Crescent, Wolverhampton. † B 2.

FULLER, William b. 1888
Ornamental sculptor. Studied City and Guilds of London (silver medal for life modelling). Exh. 1924-31. Add: Belmont, Surrey. † GI 2, L 3, RA 1.

FULLER, Capt. W.A. Exh. 1927-34
Sandcroft, Towyn, Merioneth, Wales. † B 10.

FULLER, William G. Exh. 1933-35
Landscape, black and white and linocut artist. 106 Mayfield Avenue, N. Finchley, London. † RBA 4.

FULLER-CLARKE, Beatrice Exh. 1928
† AB 1.

FULLERTON, Miss Jane Exh. 1886
Sculptor. Merksworth House, Paisley, Glasgow. † RA 1.

FULLERTON, J.G. Exh. 1929-32
6 Walmer Terrace, Glasgow. † GI 2, RSW 1.

FULLERTON, Leonard Exh. 1929-40
Aberdeen 1929; Dundee 1931; W. Newport, Fife, 1936. † RSA 10.

FULLERTON, Mrs. S. Exh. 1885-96
Flower painter. 1 Garthland Place, Paisley. † GI 13, L 2, RA 2, ROI 3, RSA 4.

FULLEYLOVE, Mrs. Elizabeth S. Exh. 1892-1908
London. † RI 27, SWA 1.

FULLEYLOVE, John* c.1846-1908
Landscape and architectural painter and illustrator. A.R.I. 1878, R.I. 1879, R.O.I. 1883, V.P.R.O.I. 1906. Add: Leicester 1881; London 1883. † B 10, FIN 407, G 2, L 18, LEI 2, M 11, RA 10, RHA 6, RI 133, ROI 59, TOO 1.

FULLEYLOVE, Joan E. Exh. 1916-30
Stained glass artist. Hampstead, London. † RA 9.

FULLWOOD, Albert Henry* b. 1864
Landscape and architectural painter and etcher. b. Birmingham. Exh. 1882-1926. Add: London. † B 3, BG 1, CHE 94, GI 1, GOU 14, I 8, L 5, LS 5, NEA 8, NG 2, RA 14, RHA 19, ROI 5.

FULLWOOD, Charles Exh. 1888
Landscape painter. 23 Maygrove Road, Brondesbury, London. † RBA 1.

FULLWOOD, John* d. 1931
Landscape painter, etcher and illustrator. Studied Birmingham and Paris. R.B.A. 1891, R.B.S.A. 1891. Add: Penzance, Cornwall 1882; Paris 1883; Twickenham, Middlesex 1884; Richmond, Surrey 1890; Hastings 1894; Slinfold, Sussex 1896; London 1905; Sunbury on Thames 1906. † B 21, D 5, L 8, M 2, NG 2, RA 21, RBA 99, RI 7, ROI 2.

FULTON, David* d. 1930
Landscape, interior and figure painter and engraver. Studied Glasgow School of Art. R.S.W. 1890. Exh. 1880-1929. Add: Glasgow. † D 2, DOW 3, GI 138, L 17, M 7, RA 1, RSA 72, RSW 85.

FULTON, Mrs. Edith Exh. 1909-30
Birkenhead 1909; Port Sunlight, Cheshire 1929; Bromborough, Cheshire 1930. † L 4.

FULTON, Miss E. Duncan Exh. 1912-18
132 West Princes Street, Glasgow. † GI 4, L 3.

FULTON, J.B. Exh. 1905
14 Bedford Row, London. † GI 1, RA 1.

FULTON, Samuel b. 1855
Animal painter (principally dogs). Exh. 1890-1940. Add: Glasgow 1890; Torrance, N.B. 1906; Campsil Glen, N.B. 1915; Kilmacolm 1930. † GI 117, RSA 10, RSW 3.

FUNK, Wilhelm Heinrich b. 1866
b. Hanover, Germany. Add: 12 West 44th Street, New York, U.S.A. 1903. † L 1.

FURBER, Jessie R. Exh. 1908-38
Mezzotint engraver. Whitchurch, Salop. † L 9, RA 3.

FURLONG, Marianne M. Exh. 1891-1900
Flower painter. Woolwich 1891; Plumstead 1900. † L 3, RA 1, RBA 2, RI 6.

FURLONG, R.J. Exh. 1910
38 Albert Edward Road, Liverpool. † L 1.

FURLONGER, Mrs. Mary Exh. 1908
Woodside, Windsor Forest, Berks. † D 2.

FURMAGE, Hal Exh. 1923
Etcher. 10 Fulham Park Gardens, London. † RA 1.

FURMAGE, Louise Exh. 1880-1934
Landscape and flower painter. A.S.W.A. 1908. Add: London. † BG 4, D 5, LS 5, RI 1, SWA 75.

FURNELL, Mrs. Exh. 1893
53 Cambridge Terrace, London. † SWA 1.

FURNER, A. Stanley Exh. 1923
Sculptor. 12 Normandy Avenue, Barnet, Herts. † RA 1.

FURNESS, T.L. Exh. 1926
† M 1.

FURNISS, Harry 1854-1925
Political caricaturist and illustrator. On staff of "Punch" 1884-94. b. Wexford. Add: London 1880. † FIN 463, RA 4, RHA 1.

FURNISS, Marian Elizabeth (May) Exh. 1898-1940
Landscape and figure painter. Married William Shackleton q.v. Add: Epsom, Surrey 1898; London 1916; Skipton, Yorks. 1940. † L 2, LS 6, RA 15, RI 9, ROI 1, SWA 7.

FURNIVALL, Frank Exh. 1925-27
Illustrator, black and white and poster artist. Add: 25 Guildford Road, Brighton. † RA 2.

FURSDON, Mrs. Exh. 1892
Coastal landscape painter. Pool Hall, Menheniot, Cornwall. † RID 1.

FURSE, Charles Wellington* 1868-1904
Portrait and figure painter, lecturer and writer. Studied Slade SChool 1884, Juliens, Paris and Westminster School of Art. Brother of John H.M.F. q.v. Died of Tuberculosis. N.E.A. 1892, R.P. 1891, A.R.A. 1904. "The Return from the Ride" (1902) purchased by Chantrey Bequest 1905. Add: London. † B 3, G 1, GI 2, L 11, M 2, NEA 35, NG 2, P 4, RA 24, RBA 1, ROI 2.

FURSE, John H.M. Exh. 1891-1909
Sculptor. Brother of Charles Wellington F. q.v. Add: London 1891 and 1896; Bushey, Herts. 1892; Netherhampton House, Nr. Salisbury 1905. † GI 2, I 7, L 11, M 1, NG 13, RA 19.

FURSE, John Paul W., Lieut. R.N. Exh. 1933-38
Miniature flower painter. H.M.S. Dolphin, Gosport, Hants. 1933; Alverstone, Hants. 1937; Ashford, Kent 1938. † COO 1, RA 7.

FUSSELL, Alice E. Exh. 1880-1902
Landscape, flower and still life painter. Nottingham. † N 40.

FUSSELL, Mrs. D. Exh. 1916
Hillside House, Kingswood Hill, Nr. Bristol. † RA 1.

FUSSELL, Fred R. Exh. 1889
Pastel landscape artist. 13 Gill Street, Nottingham. † N 1.

FUSSELL, Joseph* Exh. 1880-94
Landscape and seascape painter. Nottingham. † N 15.

FUSSEY, Ada E. Exh. 1880-9
Still life, landscape and flower painte Nottingham. † N 24.

FUSSEY, E.E. Exh. 192
† SWA 1.

FYFE, Elizabeth (Bessie) b. 189
Etcher, engraver and teacher. b. Sydney Australia. Studied Slade School and Centra School of Arts and Crafts. Exh. 1920-27 Add: London. † BA 1, NEA 13, RCA 2 RSA 1.

FYFE, Theodore c.1875-194
Architect. 2 Gray's Inn Square, Londo 1922. † RA 1.

FYFE, William Baxter Collier* 1836-188
Figure painter. b. Dundee. Add: 62 Abbe Road, St. John's Wood, London 1881 † GI 2, RA 1.

FYSON, Mrs. D.R. Exh. 1933-3
Laugherne House, Rushwick, Worcs † RI 2, RCA 2, SWA 1.

FYSON, J.G. Exh. 1908-1
Hackney, London. † RA 2, ROI 1.

FYZEE-RAHAMIN, S. Exh. 1914-3
Indian figure and mythological painte Add: London and Bombay. † L 21, RA 3 RI 5, TOO 43.

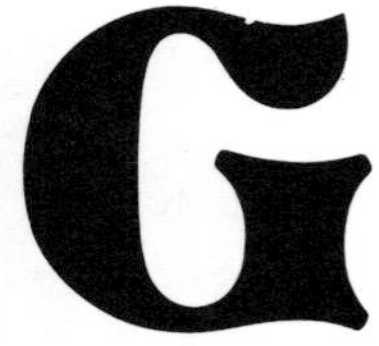

GABAIN, Ethel b. 1883
Painter and lithographer. Married John Copley q.v. R.B.A. 1932, R.O.I. 1935, S.W.A. 1934. Exh. 1906-40. Add: France 1906; London 1908, 1912 and 1932; Bushey, Herts. 1909; Longfield, Kent 1913. † CG 161, CHE 2, COO 8, GI 64, GOU 88, I 27, L 42, M 9, NEA 12, P 12, RA 32, RBA 48, RCA 4, RED 2, RHA 8, ROI 22, RSA 23, SWA 31.

GABBETT, Miss M.C. Exh. 1885-87
24 Stafford Street, Edinburgh. † GI 1, L 1, RHA 2, RSA 3.

GABELL-SMITH, Miss E. Exh. 1922
S.W.A. 1916. † SWA 2.

GABOWITCH, Joseph Exh. 1907-10
75 Rue Vopolna, Warsaw. † L 15.

GABRIEL, Caroline S. Exh. 1937
Painter and lecturer. Studied Slade School 1934-38. † NEA 1.

GABRIEL, C. Wallis Exh. 1882-85
Weston, Bath. † M 1, RA 1.

GABRIEL, Edward Exh. 1904
Architect. 42 Old Broad Street, London. † RA 2.

GABRIEL, Mrs. Emma Exh. 1905-11
Birkenhead. † L 4.

GABRIEL, Edith M. Exh. 1923-40
nee South. Sculptor. Studied Heatherleys, and Paris. Add: 1 The Mall, Parkhill Road, London. † GI 5, L 6, RA 13, RSA 3.

GABRIEL, M. Exh. 1916
1 The Mall, Parkhill Road, London. † RA 1.

GABRIEL, Paul Joseph Constantin* 1828-1903
Dutch painter. Brussels 1884; Scheveningen, Holland 1885. † GI 7.

GABRIELLI, G. Exh. 1880-82
Portrait painter. Walham Grove, Fulham, London. † M 1, RA 1.

GABRIELLI, William Exh. 1901-31
Miniature portrait painter. London. † L 1, RA 4.

GACHET, Mario Exh. 1911
Landscape painter. † ALP 1.

GADD, S. Marianne Exh. 1920-40
Redlands, Bromsgrove, Worcs. †, B 18, L 3, RCA 2.

GADDUM, Mrs. Exh. 1880
† GI 1.

GADDUM, Edith Exh. 1911
Landscape painter. † BG 46.

GADDUM, Miss E.S. Exh. 1887
Withington, Manchester. † D 3.

GADSBY, Miss Tettie Exh. 1905-37
Landscape painter. 25 Burton Street, Loughborough, Leics. † B 2, L 10, N 49, RCA 4.

GADSBY, William H.* 1845-1924
Domestic genre painter. R.B.A. 1876. Exh. 1880-1913. Add: London. † B 1, D 1, L 3, M 1, RA 1, RBA 43, RSA 2.

GAENSSLEN, Otto Robert b. 1876
American artist. 6 Impasse du Maine, Paris 1912. † L 1.

GAFFNEY, Una Exh. 1912-19
Claremont, Charles Berrington Road, Wavertree, Liverpool. † L 8, RA 4.

GAFFRON, H.C. Exh. 1935
Figure painter. † AR 2.

GAGLIARDINI, Julien Gustave* 1847-1927
French artist. 12 Boulevard de Clichy, Paris 1908. † L 1.

GAGNON, Clarence* b. 1881
Canadian artist. 49 Boulevard du Montparnasse, Paris 1906-8. † L 2.

GAHAN, George Wilkie b. 1871
Painter and etcher. b. Newcastle on Tyne. Studied Dundee School of Art. Exh. 1920-22. Add: Dundee. † L 2, RSA 4.

GAIFFE, Mme. Alice Paquelier Exh. 1907
16 Avenue de la Grande Armee, Paris. † L 1, RA 2.

GAILLARD, Lucien Exh. 1905-10
107 Rue la Boetie, Paris. † NG 4, RMS 2.

GAIR, Alice Exh. 1884-1902
Falkirk, N.B. 1884 and 1902; Edinburgh 1901. † GI 16, RSA 20.

GAIR, Frances Exh. 1939-40
A.S.W.A. 1940. The Splatts, Spaxton, Som. † RA 1, SWA 4.

GAIR, James A. Exh. 1931-33
Aberdeen. † GI 1, RSA 1.

GAISSER, Max* b. 1857
Bavarian artist. Exh. 1888-90; † TOO 4.

GAITSKELL, H.E. Hamilton Exh. 1897
7 Holland Park Road, London. † RBA 1.

GALARD, Marte Exh. 1910
c/o Allied Artists Assn. 67 Chancery Lane, London. †, LS 3.

GALBALLY, Cecil Exh. 1940
Portrait and figure painter. 73 Sandford Road, Dublin. † RHA 3.

GALBRAITH, Alex Exh. 1926-30
Glasgow. † GI 4.

GALBRAITH, Miss F.H. Exh. 1914-16
77 St. George's Road, London. † RA 2.

GALBRAITH, Isabel Exh. 1888
15 Lansdowne Crescent, Glasgow. † GI 1.

GALBRAITH, Kate Exh. 1884-92
Glasgow. † GI 7.

GALBRAITH, K.A. Exh. 1890-94
Blairhoyle, Lee, Kent. † GI 2, L 3.

GALBRAITH, K. Alexander Exh. 1910
c/o 3 Slater Street, Liverpool. † L 1.

GALBRAITH, M.S. Exh. 1897
St. Bernard's, Helensburgh. † GI 1.

GALE, Goddard F. Exh. 1924
Belmont, Hartledown, Canterbury, Kent. † L 1.

GALE, James Exh. 1920-33
Wolverhampton. † B 10.

GALE, Mrs. M.E. Exh. 1913
Gotham Rectory, Derby. † N 1.

GALE, Mrs. S. Exh. 1880-86
Flower painter. 17 Park Village West, London. † SWA 8.

GALE, William* 1823-1909
Portrait, figure, historical and biblical genre painter. Studied RA Schools. Travelled on Continent, Middle East and N. Africa. Exh. 1880-1900. Add: London. † B 16, GI 2, L 11, M 6, RA 21, RBA 9, RI 2, ROI 7, RSA 2.

GALEOTA, Leopold Exh. 1912
Appleton Hall, Warrington, Lancs. † L 1.

GALER, Ethel Caroline Hughes Exh. 1901-11
110 Croxted Road, Dulwich, London. † L 2, LS 7, RA 2, RMS 2.

GALI-FABRA, Francis Exh. 1939
† NEA 2.

GALLAGHER, F. O'Neill Exh. 1910
Landscape painter. 48 Rue St. Spire, Corbeil, France. † NEA 1.

GALLAGHER, Muriel Exh. 1930-32
Potrait painter. 28 Recreation Road, Colchester, Essex. † P 3, RCA 1.

GALLAHER, Mabel L. Exh. 1909-40
Watercolour painter and miniaturist. Sutton, Surrey 1909; Bournemouth, Hants 1931. † RA 11, RHA 7, RI 16.

GALLANT, Margaret Exh. 1923-27
Miniature painter. 51 Parrock Street, Gravesend, Kent. † RA 6.

GALLEGOS-Y-ARNOSA, Jose* b. 1859
Spanish sculptor. Exh. 1884-1902. † TOO 39.

GALLET-LEVADE, Mme. Louise E. Exh. 1913.
9 Rue Bochard de Saron, Paris. † L 1.

GALLIE, Miss H.N. Exh. 1916
25 Regent Street, Portobello, Edinburgh. † RSA 1.

GALLIEN, Louise Exh. 1906-10
59 Boulevard Barbes, Paris. † L 4.

GALLIENNE, le see L

GALLIMORE, Samuel Exh. 1881-93
Landscape and portrait painter. Newcastle, Staffs 1881; Huddersfield 1889. † L,3, M 1, RA 4, RI 1.

GALLON, Robert* Exh. 1880-1924
Landscape and coastal painter. Add: 28 Alma Square, St. John's Wood, London. † B 4, L 1, RA 15, RBA 10, RI 11, ROI 12, TOO 14.

GALLOWAY, Denis Exh. 1910
Watercolour figure painter. † FIN 23.

GALLOWAY, Everett Exh. 1918-20
14 Upper Crescent, Belfast. † RHA 3.

GALLOWAY, Gordon Exh. 1906
7 Beech Avenue, Bellahouston. † GI 1.

GALLOWAY, H.G. Exh. 1885
Holyrood Place, Dunfermline. † RSA 2.

GALLOWAY, Isobel Exh. 1925
Minto Manse, Hawick. † RSW 1.

GALLOWAY, Madge Exh. 1896-98
Normanby, Altrincham, Cheshire. † L 1, M 3, RI 1.

GALLOWAY, Mrs. Margaret Exh. 1926
Miniature portrait painter. 21 St. Martin's Square, Chichester. † RA 1.

GALLOWAY, Vincent b. 1894
Portrait painter. Studied Hull College of Art. Director Ferens Art Gallery, Hull. Exh. 1927-37. Add: Grantham, Lincs. 1927; Hull 1930. † N 1, P 2, RBA 1.

GALLOWAY, W. Exh. 1919
44 Wellington Place, Belfast. † RHA 2.

GALLWAY, Miss B.P. Exh. 1890-96
Thirkleby, Thirsk, Yorks. † SWA 4.

GALMUZZI, A. Exh. 1893
7A Upper Charlton Street, Portland Road, London. † L 1.

GALOFRE-Y-GIMENEZ, Baldomero* Exh. 1881-84
Figure and landscape painter. Paris 1881; Rome 1882. † RA 2, RHA 1, TOO 4.

GALPIN, Miss K. Exh. 1898
7 Albert Terrace, Finchley, London. † SWA 2.

GALPIN, Will Dixon Exh. 1882-87
Figure painter. Roehampton 1882 and 1885; Bushey, Herts 1884. † B 3, GI 3, L 3, RA 3, RBA 1.

GALSWORTHY, Frank b. 1863
Flower, garden and landscape painter. Studied Slade School. Exh. 1910-31. Add: Green Lane Farm, Chertsey, Surrey. † BG 71, L 8, WG 150.

GALSWORTHY, Gordon C. Exh. 1893-1917
Landscape and figure painter. London 1893; Steyning, Sussex 1897. † GI 1, L 1, RA 3, RBA 7, ROI 5.

GALT, Alexander M. Exh. 1933-40
Greenock. † ,GI 6, RSA 4, RSW 1.

GALT, John Exh. 1917
225 St. Vincent Street, Glasgow. † GI 1.

GALTER, Pietro Exh. 1892
c/o Leopold Negri, 11 Dale Street, Liverpool. † L 1.

GALTON, Ada Mary Exh. 1899-1928
Watercolour painter and etcher. Studied Slade School. Add: Sylvan Road, Upper Norwood, London. † AB 1, L 2, NG 2, RA 5, RI 7, SWA 3.

GALWAY, Clare Exh. 1896-1914
Osborne House, Seapoint, Dublin. † LS 7, RHA 6.

GALWAY, Mrs. Payne Exh. 1889-91
69 Elizabeth Street, Eaton Square, London. † D 9.

GALZENATI, Chas. Exh. 1912
42 Brunswick Street, Edinburgh. † RSA 1.

GAMBA, V. Exh. 1888
Vell'Allese, Brianza, Italy. † RSA 1.

GAMBARDELLA, Julia Exh. 1899
97 Crayford Road, Tufnell Park, London. † RMS 1.

GAMBIER-PARRY, Major Ernest* c. 1854-1936
Elmcroft, Goring on Thames 1898-99. † B 2, L 2, RA 3.

GAMBLE, James Exh. 1888-92
Sculptor. 24 Richmond Terrace, South Kensington, London. † RA 3.

GAMBLE, J.T. Exh. 1937
Sculptor. 5 Northumberland Street, Nottingham. † N 1.

GAMBODGE, E. Exh. 1881
16 Avenue Trudaine, Paris. † RHA 1.

GAME, Clement Exh. 1907
Portrait painter. c/o C. Thomas, 29 Bolsover Street, London. † NEA 1.

GAMLEN, Madeline F. Exh. 1907-26
Miniature painter. Welwyn, Herts 1907; Princes Risborough 1926. † RA 4.

GAMLEY, Andrew Archer d. 1949
Watercolour painter. b. Johnshaven, Kincardineshire. Studied R.S.A. Schools (First Carnegie travelling scholarship and Keith Prize). R.S.W. 1924. Add: Edinburgh 1896; Pittenweem, Fife 1920; Gullane, East Lothian 1934. † AR 2, GI 44, L 4, RA 1, RSA 83, RSW 80.

GAMLEY, Henry Snell 1865-1928
Sculptor. (Memorial statue to Edward VII at Holyrood). b. Logie Pert, Montrose. Studied Royal Institute Edinburgh. A.R.S.A. 1908; R.S.A. 1920. Add: Edinburgh. † GI 19, L 4, RA 3, RSA 86, RSW 5.

GAMLEY, Miss Lola Exh. 1933-36
18 Craiglockhart Place, Edinburgh. † GI 2.

GAMLEY, Miss L. Vince Exh. 1919-22
7 Montpelier Park, Edinburgh. † RSA 7.

GAMMELL, Mrs. Annie Exh. 1910-14
Lethendy, Tarbock Road, Huyton, Liverpool. † L 7.

GAMMELL Mrs. N. Exh. 1913-21
63 Brown Buildings, Exchange, Liverpool. † L 9, RCA 2.

GAMMELL, Sydney A. Exh. 1909-37
A.R.E. 1913. Tarbock Road, Huyton, Liverpool 1909; St. John Street, Liverpool 1914. † L 19, RCA 1, RE 13.

GAMMON, Reginald b. 1894
Watercolour landscape painter and commercial artist. b. Petersfield, Hants. Exh. 1938-40. Add: Sunnyside Fernhurst, Haslemere. † AR 2, BK 40, NEA 3, RA 2, RBA 3, RI 3.

GAMON, Gilbert P. Exh. 1924
Daisymere, Fairfield, Buxton. † L 3.

GAMSON, G.C. Exh. 1924
29 St. John's Road, Newport, Mon. † B 2.

GANDARA, de la see D

GANDY, Ada d. 1900
nee Dennis. Figure and portrait painter and illustrator. Exh. 1892-98. Add: Brixton, London. † L 2, RA 2, RBA 5.

GANDY, C.J. Exh. 1898
Upton Lodge, Bushey, Herts. † B 2.

GANDY, Herbert* Exh. 1881-1911
Figure and domestic painter. London. † B 12, GI 2, L 9, M 2, RA 21, RHA 2, RI 2, ROI 2.

GANDY, W. Exh. 1910-13
27 Rodenhurst Road, Clapham Park, London. † RA 4.

GANDY, Walton Exh. 1893
Watercolour landscape painter. 34 Loughborough Road, London. † RBA 1.

GANGOOLY, J.P. Exh. 1908-13
171 Lower Circular Road, Calcutta, India. † LS 5.

GANLEY, Bernard Exh. 1932-40
50 Wenlock Road, Handsworth, Birmingham. † B 22.

GANLY, Mrs. Brigid see O'BRIEN

GANLY, Mrs. Eileen Exh. 1939
Flower painter. 24 Fortfield Road, Terenure, Dublin. † RHA 1.

GANSKY, Rene Exh. 1911-12
Figure painter. c/o Goupil Gallery, London. † GOU 2, RHA 1.

GANTZ, N. Margaret Exh. 1939
† NEA 1.

GANZ, Henry F.W. Exh. 1888-1919
Painter and etcher. London. † G 1, I 9, L 6, LS 8, M 1, NEA 2, RA 8, ROI 3.

GARAS, Fredric R. Exh. 1937
Sculptor. 6 Lees Road, Hillingdon, Middlesex. † RA 1.

GARAU, Dolores Exh. 1916
65 West Regent Street, Glasgow. † GI 1.

GARBE, Richard 1876-1957
Sculptor. Studied Central School of Arts and Crafts and R.A. Schools. Teacher of sculpture Central School of Arts and Crafts 1901-29. Professor at Royal College of Art 1929-46. A.R.A. 1929, R.A. 1936. "A Drake" purchased by Chantrey Bequest 1925, "Sea Lion" in 1929 and "Autumn" in 1930. Add: London 1898; Hornchurch, Essex 1908; Westcott, Dorking, Surrey 1933. † B 4, GI 25, L 22, M 1, NG 1, RA 108, RI 1, RMS 11.

GARCIA, Miss Exh. 1904-5
Mon Abri, Cricklewood, London. † NG 2.

GARDELL-ERICSON, Mme. Anna Exh. 1884
19 Rue Lebon Ternes, Paris. † D 3, L 2.

GARDEN, E.C. Exh. 1887
56 Ambler Road, Finsbury Park, London. † RI 1.

GARDEN, James A. Exh. 1927-32
Kirkaldy. † RSA 3.

GARDEN, Louisa E. Exh. 1880-85
Landscape and figure painter. 42 Carlton Hill, St. John's Wood, London. † B 1, SWA 8.

GARDEN, W.F. Exh. 1882-90
Landscape painter. Bedford 1882, London 1885. † DOW 6, RA 11, RI 1.

GARDET, Georges b. 1863
French sculptor. 38 Rue Boileau, Paris 1908-12. † L 1, LS 3, RSA 2.

GARDIER, du see D

GARDINER, Annette Exh. 1901-12
Landscape painter. London. † B 4, GI 6, L 1, LS 5, NEA 2, RA 1.

GARDINER, Annie Exh. 1881
1 Lendel Terrace, Glasgow. † GI 1.

GARDINER, Alfred Clive 1891-1960
Landscape and figure painter. Married Lilian Lancaster q.v. Add: London. † COO 1, I 4, LEI 1, M 2, NEA 12, P 5, RA 7.

GARDINER, Mrs. C.B. Exh. 1920-26
8 Withen's Lane, Liscard, Cheshire. † L 1, P 2.

GARDINER, Edith Exh. 1921-23
† G 4.

GARDINER, Elizabeth Exh. 1890-97
† TOO 3.

GARDINER, Mrs. Elp Exh. 1922-25
Bredon House, Selwyn Gardens, Cambridge. † B 2, NEA 1, SWA 11.

GARDINER, Edwin A. d. 1916
Killed carrying dispatches. Exh. 1908-15. Add: Leicester. † B 2, N 20, RA 1.

GARDINER, Miss E.G. Exh. 1922
† NEA 2.

GARDINER, Gerald b. 1902
Landscape painter and teacher. Studied Royal College of Art and Beckenham School of Art. Add: Farnborough, Kent 1927; Up Hatherley, Nr. Cheltenham, Glos. 1928; Bisley Stroud, Glos. 1936. † COO 3, M 2, NEA 3, RA 16, RSA 2.

GARDINER, Joyce Exh. 1938-40
Figure painter. London 1938; Market Harborough, Leics 1939. † NEA 2, RA 2, RBA 1, RSA 4.

GARDINER, John H. Exh. 1918-25
Portrait painter. London 1918; Little Holland, Clacton on Sea, Essex 1920. † L 1, RA 5.

GARDINER, Kathleen Exh. 1936-39
Painter and engraver. † GOU 1, NEA 1, RED 1.

GARDINER, Mrs. May R. Exh. 1914-19
Kilburn, London. † I 1, SWA 6.

GARDINER, Stanley Horace b. 1887
Landscape painter and teacher (University College, Reading). Studied Allan Fraser Art College, Arbroath. Exh. 1927-39. Add: Lamorna, Nr. Penzance, Cornwall. † FIN 44, L 1, M 2, RA 11, RSA 1.

GARDINER, Vida M. Exh. 1936
7 Leven Terrace, Edinburgh. † RSA 1.

GARDINER, W.S. Exh. 1924
Landscape painter. † FIN 1.

GARDINI, Theophile L. Exh. 1938-40
Landscape painter. Lodge Park, Machynlleth, N. Wales. † B 1, BA 2.

GARDNELO-y-ALDA, J. Exh. 1906-9
Figure painter. Madrid 1906; Chelsea, London 1908. † RA 3.

GARDNER, Lord Exh. 1887-90
Landscape painter. Abinger Common, Dorking 1887; London 1888. † RI 5.

GARDNER, Alexander Exh. 1904
209 St. Vincent Street, Glasgow. † GI 1.

GARDNER, Allan Constant b. 1906
Etcher and stained glass designer. b. Valpariso. Studied Edinburgh College of Art. Add: Edinburgh 1931; Broom Knowe, Kilmacolm 1932; Wandsworth Common, London 1933. † RA 8, RSA 6.

GARDNER, Miss A.M. Exh. 1886-93
Glasgow. † GI 6.

GARDNER, Alex M'Innes Exh. 1904-32
Glasgow. † GI 13.

GARDNER, Delphis. b. 1900
Wood engraver and printer. In partnership with her sister Phyllis G. q.v. in the Asphodel Press. Studied Slade School. Exh. 1927. † ALP 4.

GARDNER, Diana Exh. 1937
10 Campden Hill Gardens, London. † RBA 2.

GARDNER, Dorothy I.E. Exh. 1927
Leighton, Merrilocks Road, Blundellsands, Liverpool. † L 1.

GARDNER, Evelyn Exh. 1893-97
Sea Croft, Blundellsands, Liverpool. † L 4.

GARDNER, Edwin C.* Exh. 1880-88
Landscape and figure painter. London. † L 2, RA 3, RBA 8, RI 2, ROI 1.

GARDNER, Frederick Exh. 1913-39
Figure painter. A.R.B.A. 1919, R.B.A. 1921. Add: London 1913 and 1919; Chesham Bois, Bucks. 1916. † GI 1, RA 3, RBA 10, ROI 3.

GARDNER, Frederick E. C. Exh. 1917-33
Sculptor. London 1917; Leicester 1920; Liverpool 1932. † L 7, RA 6.

GARDNER, G. Exh. 1884-85
Watercolour fruit painter. 31 Senrab Street, Chalres Street, Stepney, London. † RBA 2.

GARDNER, Miss H.A. Exh. 1890-97
West End Chambers, Broad Street Corner, Birmingham. † B 12.

GARDNER, Harry R. Exh. 1897-1933
Architect. Hastings 1897; London 1904 and 1930; Leatherhead, Surrey 1907. † RA 5.

GARDNER, Ivy H. Exh. 1921-40
Kilmory, Gourock 1921; Glasgow 1930. † GI 41, RA 1, RSA 21.

GARDNER, James 1883-1937
Sculptor. b. Belfast M.P. for North Hammersmith 1923-24 and 1926-31. Exh. 1917-19. Add: Fulham, London. † RA 3.

GARDNER , J.L. Exh. 1880-88
Landscape painter. London. † L 3, M 3, RA 5, RBA 2.

GARDNER, J.M. Exh. 1932
† L 1.

GARDNER, Mabel Exh. 1900-3
Melbourne Lodge, Carlton Road, Putney, London. † B 1, SWA 3.

GARDNER, Mary Exh. 1887-95
Dunholme, Skelmorlie. † GI 12, L 1.

GARDNER, Phyllis b. 1890
Painter, wood engraver, carver and printer. In partnership with her sister Delphis G q.v. in the Asphodel Press. Studied Slade School, British Museum and Frank Calderon's School of Animal Paintings. Exh. 1913-27. Add: Tadworth, Surrey 1913; Hampstead, London 1921. † ALP 13, L 1, NEA 3, RMS 3, SWA 5.

GARDNER, R.A. Exh. 1902-17
Flower painter. Bourne Lincs. † RA 3.

GARDNER, Sidney V. Exh. 1891-1927
Landscape and flower painter. N.S.A. 1908. Add: Nottingham 1891 and 1909,; London 1898; St. Albans, Herts. 1907. † N 73, RA 5, RBA 2.

GARDNER, W. Exh. 1930
3 Leyden Gardens, Glasgow. † GI 1.

GARDNER, William Biscombe c.1849-1919
Painter and wood engraver. Add: London 1880 and 1897 ; Dorking, Surrey 1883; Haslemere, Surrey 1891; Tunbridge Wells, Kent 1906. † D 4, G 14, L 3, LS 8, NG 9, RA 44, RI 31, ROI 8, RSW 1.

GARDNER-M'LEAN, G. Exh. 1932-37
Glasgow. † GI 4.

GARDNER-M'LEAN, Mrs. Madge Exh. 1930-40
Glasgow 1930 and 1933, Drumahoe, Londonderry 1931. † GI 2, L 2, RA 1, RSA 1, RSW 3, RWS 1.

GARDOM, Barbara Cronhelm Exh. 1924-31
Painter and teacher. Studied Juliens, Paris, Heatherleys and Slade School. Add: 35 Promenade, Cheltenham, Glos. † RA 5, RMS 1, RSA 1.

GARDON, Felix Exh. 1939
13 Highbury Grange, London. † RBA 1.

GARDYNE, Major A.D.G. Exh. 1906
Castle Hill Barracks, Aberdeen. † RA 1.

GARDYNE, Helen Exh. 1889-96
Glenforsa Aros, N.B. 1889; Tobermory, N.B. 1896. † GI 2, RSA 1.

GARDYNE, T. Bruce Exh. 1880
Middleton, Arbroath. † RSA 1.

GARFORD, Nina B. Exh. 1906-24
Miniature painter. Exmouth, Devon. † RA 3.

GARLAND, Austin b. 1887
Portrait, figure and landscape painter. Studied Liverpool School of Art. Assistant master Liverpool School of Art; 2nd master Dudley School of Arts and Crafts and Headmaster Lincoln School of Art. Exh. 1908-39. Add: Liverpool 1908; Dudley 1920; Lincoln 1921. † B 3, L 5, N 20.

GARLAND, Charles Trevor Exh. 1880-1901
Landscape, portrait, child and genre painter. Add: Rome 1880; London 1881, Trevellyn, Penzance 1892. † B 3, D 4, GI 5, L 8, M 9, RA 19, RBA 6, RI 1, ROI 14.

GARLAND, Dorothy G. Exh. 1909-10
Northfield, Worcs. † B 2.

GARLAND, Henry* Exh. 1880-92
Landscape and genre painte. London 1880; Leatherhead, Surrey 1887. † B 11, L 1, M 4, RA 13, RBA 13, ROI 6, TOO 3.

GARLAND, Louise Exh. 1923-25
38 Hanover Road, Willesden, London. † L 7.

GARLAND, Mary Exh. 1881-1903
Lydney, Glos. † RI 2, RSA 2.

GARLAND, Margaret L. Exh. 1926-34
Painter and mural painter. Studied Royal College of Art. Add: Bathford House, Bath, Som. † M 1, NEA 4, SWA 1.

GARLAND, Valentine Thomas* d. 1914
Animal painter. Winchester 1880 and 1895; London 1885. † B 16, L 1, M 11, RA 20, RBA 12, RI 17, ROI 2, RSA 1.

GARLANT, Edith Exh. 1910-21
London. † LS 15.

GARLICK, John Henry Exh. 1923-29
Watercolour painter. 14 Gt. Orme's Road, Llandudno, Wales. † B 3, RCA 3.

GARLICK, Maud Exh. 1901-16
Cantsfield, Clarence Road, Birkenhead 1901; West Kirby, Lancs. 1910. † L 18.

GARLING, Henry Bayly Exh. 1899
Architect. 25 Clifton Crescent, Folkestone, Kent. † RA 1.

GARMAN, Mabel Exh. 1900-1
Figure and portrait painter. Gt. Barr, Birmingham 1900; Lapley Hall, Nr. Stafford 1901. † L 2, RA 1.

GARNER, A. Exh. 1915
55 Wellington Road, Stockport, Lancs. † L 1.

GARNER, Dorothy Exh. 1938
Dover, Kent. † SWA 1.

GARNER, Edith Mary b. 1881
Painter and etcher. b. Wasperton Hill, Nr. Warwick. Studied Slade School, Paris and Italy. 2nd wife of William Lee-Hankey q.v. R.O.I. 1931. Travelled on Continent and Spain. Add: London 1914 and 1931; Le Touquet, Paris Plage, Pas de Calais, France 1924. † GI 1, I 2, L 1, LS 15, NEA 1, RA 19, RI 8, ROI 38, SWA 5, TOO 5, WG 52.

GARNER, Ethel M. Exh. 1922
† G 1.

GARNER, Harry Exh. 1916
55 Wellington Road, Stockport, Lancs. † L 3.

GARNER, H.F. Exh. 1915-19
19 Charlton Street, Euston Road, London. † I 2, ROI 1.

GARNER, Maud E. Exh. 1919-28
Garston, Liverpool. † L 10, RCA 3.

GARNER, Thomas Exh. 1887-97
Architect. 7 Gray's Inn Square, London. † RA 5.

GARNER-RICHARDS, J.B. Exh. 1929-38
Southmead, Carr's Crescent, Formby, Liverpool. † L 1, M 1.

GARNET, Rhoda M. Exh. 1906-7
332 Kew Road, Kew Gardens, London. † L 2, NG 1.

GARNETT, Mrs. Exh. 1907
Christleton Rectory, Chester. † L 1.

GARNETT, Anne Exh. 1929-32
Highgate, London 1929; Taunton, Som. 1930; Wellington, Som. 1931. † B 4, RCA 2.

GARNETT, Alfred Payne Exh. 1896-1909
Landscape painter. Bushey, Herts. 1896; London 1902 and 1909; Swaffham Prior, Nr. Cambridge 1907. † L 9, LS 5, M 1, NG 2, RA 2, RI 5, ROI 4.

GARNETT, Miss B. Exh. 1882-92
Lewisham 1882; Bloomsbury, London 1892. † B 2, L 2.

GARNETT, Claude Exh. 1934-39
Flower painter. Add: London. † WG 135.

GARNETT, Eve Exh. 1923-40
Landscape painter and illustrator. Studied Chelsea School of Art, R.A. Schools and under Alexander Jamieson. Add: Queensbury Place, S.W. London. † NEA 3, ROI 1, SWA 1.

GARNETT, Eric C.E. Exh. 1922-36
Leintwardine, Herefords. 1922; Parkstone, Dorset 1934; Conington, Nr. Peterborough 1936. † B 6, L 1, RBA 4, RCA 21.

GARNETT, Miss Frances Exh. 1904-14
Miniature painter. Jersey, C.I. † L 1, LS 1, RA 4, SWA 1.

GARNETT, Frederick b. 1878
Illustrator. b. Hengoed, Glam. Studied and taught Manchester School of Art. Exh. 1909-10. Add: Ferndale, The Park, Eccles. † L 2, RCA 1.

GARNETT, Miss F.I. Exh. 1928
18 Thorburn Road, New Ferry, Cheshire. † L 1.

GARNETT, Kate Exh. 1909-24
Hill Cliffe Road, Lower Walton, Warrington, Lancs. 1909; Wallasey, Cheshire 1924. † L 20.

GARNETT, Mewburn Exh. 1925
Landscape painter. † GOU 53.

GARNETT, Ruth Exh. 1893-1919
Portrait and figure painter. London. † L 4, M 1, NG 1, P 4, RA 10, RHA 1, RID 38, ROI 3.

GARNHAM, Kathleen Exh. 1926-34
Landscape painter. 2 Whitehall Court, London. † RI 2, SWA 1, TOO 3.

GARNIER, Geoffrey Sneyd* 1889-c.1971
Engraver. b. Wigan, Lancs. Studied Bushey, Herts., Toronto, Canada and under Stanhope Forbes. Exh. 1923-34. Add: Orchard Cottage, Newlyn, Penzance. † B 12, GI 1, L 9, RA 2, RBA 7, RCA 1, RSA 19.

GARNON, Vincent Exh. 1880
Cafe du Telegraph, Grand Place, Antwerp. † RHA 1.

GARNOT, G. St. F. Exh. 1905
11 Rue Constance, Paris. † L 1.

GARRAD, Miss Dora Exh. 1896-1904
Kingswood Grange, Hockley Heath, Warwicks. † B 2.

GARRAD, Miss Margaret M. Exh. 1896-1902
Kingswood Grange, Hockley Heath, Warwicks. † B 2.

GARRARD, Aspley Cherry Exh. 1936
Watercolour landscape painter. † FIN 3.

GARRARD, Mrs. Bain Exh. 1921
6 Hogarth Road, London. † SWA 1.

GARRARD, Dorothy A. Exh. 1935
† RMS 1.

GARRARD, Capt. Lindsay Exh. 1916-23
Watercolour painter. Ryton House, Lechlade, Glos. † LEI 1, LS 3, WG 39.

GARRARD, Violet Exh. 1909-25
43 Glebe Place, Chelsea, London. † RA 1, WG 30.

GARRATT, Agnes M. Exh. 1891-97
Studio, Shorne Ridgeway, Gravesend, Kent. † B 2, RBA 1, RHA 1, SWA 1.

GARRATT, Arthur Paine b. 1873
Portrait and urban landscape painter. Studied City of London School. Spent several years in U.S.A. Exh. 1899-1919. Add: London. † FIN 28, I 2, L 3, LS 1, P 8, RA 17.

GARRATT, Mrs. Clan Exh. 1910
Buckingham House, Montpelier Road, Twickenham, Middlesex. † L 1, RA 1.

GARRATT, Dorothy A. Exh. 1912-40
Miniature portrait painter. Oxford 1912; Golders Green, London 1937. † RA 5.

GARRATT, Sam Exh. 1900-38
Landscape painter. b. Barwell, Leics. Son of farm labourer, became a bootmaker and studied for 15 years as a night student at Leicester School of Art. Add: Leicester 1900; Burton on Trent 1903; Brecon, Wales 1906. † B 9, L 7, LS 18, N 6, RA 2, RCA 33, RHA 36.

GARRATT, Thomas Exh. 1889-92
Architect. 112 Percy Road, Shepherds Bush, London. † RA 3.

GARRAWAY, George Hervey b. 1846
Figure painter. b. Dominica, W. Indies. Studied Heatherleys School of Art and L'Ecole des Beaux Arts, Paris (prizes for drawing). Exh. 1882-1908. Add: Liverpool 1882; Florence, Italy 1903. † B 7, L 25, M 8, RA 1, RBA 1, RI 1.

GARRETT, Frank G. Exh. 1911-38
Birmingham. † B 23, L 28.

GARRETT, Lucy Exh. 1917-29
Limasol, Glenageary, Co. Dublin. † L 42, RHA 2.

GARRETT, Mrs. Victoria E. Exh. 1920-22
Miniature painter. Bittern Moor, Cleave Hill, Nr. Cheltenham, Glos. † RA 2.

GARRETT, W. Walter Exh. 1939-40
Landscape painter. 19 Castlehill Road, Belfast. † RHA 3.

GARRIDO, Leandro Ramon 1868-1909
French painter. R.O.I. 1903. Add: Paris 1902; Etaples, France 1905; Sleights, Yorks. 1906; Moret sur Loing, France 1907. † GI 6, I 3, L 8, RHA 2, ROI 19.

GARRIDO, T.L. Exh. 1920
† GI 1.

GARROD, Violet Nellie b. 1898
Painter and miniaturist. Studied St. John's Wood School of Art. Add: Weybridge, Surrey 1923; Bournemouth, Hants. 1930-40. † RA 7, RMS 2.

GARROW, Miss J.I. Exh. 1919-25
11 Montgomerie Road, Newlands, Glasgow. † GI 10, L 2, RSA 4, RSW 1.

GARRY, John H. Exh. 1900
Architect. 39 Torrington Square, London. † RA 1.

GARSIDE, Jean Exh. 1930
Wood engraver. † RED 3.

GARSIDE, John b. 1887
Painter, poster, advertising and black and white artist and actor. b. Salford, Lancs. Studied Manchester School of Art; Slade School. Add: Liverpool 1910; London 1919. † L 7, LS 2, RA 2, RBA 4.

GARSIDE, Oswald 1879-1942
Watercolour painter. b. Southport, Lancs. Studied 3 years in Paris and 1½ years in Italy. R.I. 1916. Exh. 1902-40. Add: 1 White Hart Lane, Barnes, London. † B 13, BG 2, L 72, LS 10, M 8, RA 37, RCA 101, RHA 1, RI 140.

GARSTANG, Edith Mary Exh. 1925-27
14 Jermyn Street, Liverpool. † L 4.

GARSTIN, Miss Alethea Exh. 1912-38
Figure and domestic painter. 4 Wellington Terrace, Penzance 1912; London 1936. † ALP 24, G 1, GI 1, I 6, L 3, NEA 2, P 4, RA 27, RI 4, SWA 1.

GARSTIN, Miss H.C. Exh. 1887
Brazantown, Castle Bellingham, Dublin. † RHA 1.

GARSTIN, Norman 1847-1926
Figure and landscape painter. Travelled widely. N.E.A. 1887. Add: Tipperary 1882; Parsonstown, Ireland 1883; Huddersfield 1886; Penzance 1887. † B 28, D 3, DOW 3, FIN 93, G 5, GI 28, I 2, L 34, M 27, NEA 4, RA 40, RBA 12, RCA 2, RHA 33, RI 1, RID 34, ROI 9, RSA 2, WG 204.

GARTH, Margaret F. Exh. 1919
4A Eton Road, Hampstead, London. † LS 3, SWA 2.

GARTSIDE, Fred Exh. 1887
The Studio, 71 Waterloo Street, Glasgow. † GI 1.

GARTSIDE, John S. Exh. 1934
20 Fieldhead Avenue, Bury Road, Rochdale, Lancs. † RBA 1.

GARVEY, Clara Exh. 1887-95
Flower and figure painter. East Dulwich 1887; Camden Square, N.W. London 1890. † RA 2, ROI 5.

GARVIE, Thomas Bowman b. 1859
Portrait, landscape and interior painter. Studied R.A. Schools (1st silver medal for painting) and Juliens, Paris. Exh. 1886-1914. Add: Morpeth, Northumberland 1886; Rothbury, Northumberland 1894. † GI 1, L 2, RA 13, RBA 2, RSA 1.

GARWOOD, Miss A.C. Exh. 1928
Rock Bank, Elmsley Road, Liverpool. † L 2.

GARWOOD, Tirzah Exh. 1930
Wood engraver. † RED 3.

GASCOIGNE, Miss H. Exh. 1902
Uplands, Sherwood, Notts. † N 3.

GASCOYNE, Alexander Exh. 1901-27
Stained glass artist. 7 Shakespeare Street, Nottingham 1901; London 1927. † N 2, RA 27.

GASCOYNE, C. Exh. 1900
Cavendish Hill, Sherwood, Notts. † N 2.

GASCOYNE, C. Exh. 1912-13
6 Gray's Inn Square, London. † RA 2.

GASCOYNE, D. Exh. 1901
Ashleigh, Sherwood, Notts. † N 7.

GASCOYNE, Ethel Slade Exh. 1885-1925
nee King. Portrait, landscape and fan painter. m. George G. q.v. A.S.W.A. 1908. Add: London 1885; Knockholt, Sevenoaks, Kent 1903; Bridgwater, Som. 1910, Glastonbury, Som. 1913; Tunbridge Wells, Kent 1924. † G 1, L 7, RA 31, RE 1, RID 47, ROI 1, SWA 11.

GASGOYNE, George 1862-1933
Painter and etcher. Studied Slade School. m. Ethel Slade G. q.v. R.E. 1885. Add: London and Sittingbourne, Kent 1883; Bridgwater, Som. 1910; Glastonbury, Som. 1912; Tunbridge Wells, Kent 1920. † BI 1, GI 1, L 18, NEA 4, RA 21, RBA 1, RE 60, RID 35, ROI 9, RSA 1.

GASCOYNE, G.F. Exh. 1886
14 Park Street, Nottingham. † N 1.

GASH, Eva Exh. 1933-40
73 Ausley Road, Nuneaton, Warwicks. † B 2, SWA 2.

GASH, Walter Bonner 1869-1928
Portrait, figure and landscape painter. Studied Lincoln School of Art and Academie des Beaux Arts, Anvers. Assistant art master Lincoln School of Art; art master at Wellingborough Technical Institute and Kettering Grammar and High Schools. N.S.A. 1898. Add: Nottingham 1888; Kettering 1896. † L 2, N 39, RA 8.

GASKELL, George Arthur Exh. 1885-1900
Figure and domestic painter. Bradford, Yorks. 1885; Brighton 1894; London 1897. † B 3, L 4, M 3, RA 4, RBA 1.

GASKELL, George Percival 1868-1934
Painter, etcher and engraver. b. Shipley, Yorks. Studied South Kensington, Paris and Italy. Principal Regent Street Polytechnic and Staff lecturer on art history for the London University Extension Board. R.B.A. 1896. A.R.E. 1908. R.E. 1911. Exh. 1895-1934. Add: London. † B 5, FIN 10, GI 2, L 19, M 2, RA 60, RBA 101, RE 81, RHA 3, RI 1, ROI 3, RSA 2.

GASKELL, H.M. Exh. 1911
Landscape painter. † CAR 4.

GASKELL, William J. Clare Exh. 1934-40
Landscape painter and chalk artist. Kew, Surrey 1934; Ashford, Kent 1936. † RA 8.

GASKILL, C. Mildred Exh. 1926
11 Dacey Road, Anfield, Liverpool. † L 1.

GASKIN, Arthur Joseph 1862-1928
Painter, illustrator and pencil portrait artist. Studied and taught Birmingham School of Art. Director of the Jewellers and Silversmiths School, Birmingham. Collaborated with his wife Georgie Evelyn Cave G. q.v. A.R.E. 1927. R.B.S.A. 1905. Add: Wolverhampton 1883; Smallheath, Birmingham 1889, Olton, Warwicks. 1896; Edgbaston, Birmingham 1920. † B 46, BG 36, FIN 34, GI 4, I 1, L 36, M 1, NEA 12, NG 18, RA 3, RBA 8, RE 4, RMS 8.

GASKIN, Georgie Evelyn Cave Exh. 1896-1930
nee France. Married Arthur Joseph G. q.v. Add: Olton, Warwicks. 1896. † B 2, I 1, L 102, NG 8, RMS 9.

GASKIN, Miss J.V. Exh. 1920-28
Mrs. Turner. Daughter of Arthur Joseph and Georgie Evelyn Cave G. q.v. Add: 13 Calthorpe Road, Edgbaston, Birmingham. † B 12.

GASPAR, Jean Exh. 1909-15
16 Rue des Vileton, Arlon, Belgium. † L 3, RSA 2.

GASQ, Paul Exh. 1902
233 Faubourg St. Honore, Paris. † L 1.

GASS, Miss E. Exh. 1902
Studio, Bank of Ireland Chambers, Ann Street, Belfast. † SWA 1.

GASS, John Bradshaw 1855-1939
Architect. Exh. 1880-1910. Add: Bolton, Lancs. † RA 5.

GAST, Bertram Exh. 1888-95
Landscape and decorative painter. Collaborated with Frank G. q.v. Add: Hampstead, London. † RA 5, RBA 7, RI 1.

GAST, B.P. Exh. 1914
The Studio, Vale of Health, Hampstead, London. † RA 1.

GAST, Frank Exh. 1891-96
Landscape and decorative painter. Collaborated with Bertram G. q.v. Add: Hampstead, London. † RA 3, RBA 3.

GASTALDI, Nicholas Exh. 1888-94
4 Dee Villas, South View, Chester. † L 2.

GASTER, H. Exh. 1932-40
Pear Tree Cottage, Knightcote, Bishops Itchington, Leamington Spa, Warwicks. † B 15, P 1.

GASTINEAU, Maria d. 1890
Landscape painter. Daughter of Henry G. (c.1791-1876). Add: 145 Cold Harbour Lane, Camberwell. † SWA 25.

GATACRE, Miss J. Exh. 1881-90
Gatacre's Hall, Bridgnorth, Salop. † B 2, RSA 1.

GATE, Mrs. Edith Exh. 1896-1904
Liscard, Cheshire. † L 5.

GATE, H. L. Exh. 1922-23
A.N.S.A. 1922. 17 Mansfield Grove, Nottingham. † N 9.

GATEHOUSE, Rosalind Exh. 1914-28
Mrs. Pelly. Watercolour painter. Add: Abbot's Grange, Bebington, Cheshire. † B 4, L 14, RA 1, RCA 5.

GATES, Alice Exh. 1892-1929
Mrs. Burn. Landscape painter. Bradford Yorks 1892; South Kensington, London 1900; Painswick, Glos. 1921. † L 14, RID 13.

GATES, Mrs. Nancy Exh. 1931
Domestic painter. 2 Cheyne Walk, London. † RA 1.

GATES, Rev. Sebastian Exh. 1904-7
Painter and sculptor. St. Dominic Priory, Haverstock Hill, London. † M 2, RA 2.

GATES, William Henry Exh. 1888-1935
Painter, sculptor and designer. Studied Royal College of Art. Headmaster at the School of Science and Art, Coalbrookdale, Salop. Author of "The Art of Drawing the Human Figure, Simplified". Add: Wolverhampton 1888, Ironbridge, Salop 1923; Combe Martin, Devon 1933. † B 2, L 2, RA 2, RBA 2, RCA 1, RI 1, RSA 2.

GATIER, Pierre b. 1878
French landscape painter. Exh. 1906-28. 55 Rue des Abbesses, Paris. † L 2, LEF 35.

GATTER, Frank Exh. 1907-27
Sculptor. London. † GI 1, L 3, RA 13.

GATTI, Lady Exh. 1938
† P 2.

GATTI, Miss Ida Exh. 1937-38
40 Aubrey Walk, London. † RI 1, ROI 1.

GATTO, Saverio Exh. 1914
Piazza Cr. B. Vico 39, Naples. † LS 2.

GAUCHER, Emile Exh. 1903
Rue Foure, Nantes, France. † GI 1.

GAUDET, Claire Exh. 1911-14
120 Cheyne Walk, Chelsea, London. † RA 3.

GAUDIER-BRZESKA, Henri* 1891-1915
Sculptor and painter. b. in France. Came to England c.1909. Joined the French army 1914 and was killed in action. Founder Member of London Group 1913. Although he died at an early age a considerable number of his works are in the Tate Gallery including "Horace Brodsky" (1913) pur chased by Chantrey Bequest 1957. Add: Studio 5, 454 Fulham Road, London 1913. † LS 15.

GAUDIN, Felix Exh. 1906
6 Rue de la Chaumiere, Paris. † L 1.

GAUGUIN, Jean Exh. 1934
Nyhavn, 33, Copenhagen. † RSA 4.

GAUJEAN, E. Exh. 1888
Etcher. 45 Rue de Sevres, Paris. † RA 2.

GAUL, August 1869-1921
German sculptor. Exh. 1904. † I 2.

GAULD, David* 1865-1936
Cattle, landscape and decorative portrait painter and stained glass artist. A.R.S.A. 1918, R.S.A. 1924. Add: Glasgow 1886 and 1907; Torrance, N.B. 1906. † CON 6, GI 85, I 1, L 6, M 1, RSA 44.

GAULD, Mrs. David Exh. 1905
23 Belmont Street, Glasgow. † GI 2.

GAULD, John Richardson d. 1962
Landscape, portrait and mural painter and lithographer. b. Gateshead on Tyne. Studied Royal College of Art. Chief Assistant at Huddersfield School of Art. Add: London 1911; Huddersfield 1920; Bolton, Lancs. 1932. † GI 2, GOU 11, I 4, L 4, M 2, RA 4.

GAULDIE, John Lyon Exh. 1935-39
3 Midmar Gardens, Edinburgh. † RSA 2.

GAUNT, Thomas Edward Exh. 1880-92
Figure and domestic painter. London. † B 2, RA 2, RBA 2.

GAUNT, William b. 1900
Painter, writer and art critic. Studied Westminster School of Art 1924-25. Exh. 1930-37. Add: London. † LEF 24, RA 1, RED 63.

GAUNTLETT, F.H. Exh. 1894-95
43 Sprules Road, Brockley, London. † RBA 2.

GAUNTLETT, Gertrude E. Exh. 1880-81
Figure and domestic painter. 96 Bromfelde Road, Clapham, London. † RA 1, RBA 2, SWA 2.

GAUNTLETT, Mrs. Mary see ELEY

GAUNTLETT, Miss S. Exh. 1916-17
60 Duke Street, Grosvenor Square, London. † RA 2, ROI 1.

GAUPP, Gustave Exh. 1884
Portrait painter. 8 Duchess Street, Portland Place, London. † RA 1.

GAUSDEN, Sydney H. Exh. 1919-21
Landscape and figure painter. † I 1, RID 4.

GAUSSENT, Mrs. G.F. Exh. 1890
The Hampstead Conservatoire, Eton Avenue, London. † ROI 1.

GAUTHIER, Mlle. G. Exh. 1909
3 Avenue Lowendall, Paris. † L 1.

GAUTHIER, M.F. Exh. 1905
5 Rue Juliette, Paris. † NG 1.

GAUTIER, Louis Exh. 1885-1913
Paris 1885 and 1912; London 1906. † B 6, L 5, LS 8, NG 2, RE 6, RI 1, RSA 1.

GAVERE, de see D

GAVEY, Edith Exh. 1901-10
Flower painter. Fairlight, Hampton Wick. † RA 2, ROI 1.

GAVIN, Hugh Exh. 1930-40
11 Ardberg Street, Glasgow. † GI 12.

GAVIN, Jessie Exh. 1903-12
Denehurst, Talbot Road, Oxton, Cheshire. † L 17.

GAVIN, Malcolm b. 1874
Portrait painter. Studied South Kensington and R.A. Schools. R.P. 1919, A.R.S.A. 1920. Exh. 1904-34. Add: Edinburgh 1904; London 1930. † GI 9, L 6, P 35, RSA 42.

GAVIN, Robert* 1827-1883
Figure and domestic painter. A.R.S.A. 1854, R.S.A. 1879. Add: Cherry Bank, Newhaven Road, Edinburgh 1880. † GI 3, L 2, RSA 12.

GAWEN, Joseph b. 1825
Sculptor. Studied R.A. Schools 1847. Add: 419 Oxford Street, London 1882. † RA 1.

GAWTHORN, Henry George 1879-1941
Painter, architect, lithographer and commercial artist. b. Northampton. Studied Regent Street Polytechnic and Heatherleys. Exh. 1917-34. Add: London. † P 2, RA 6.

GAY, G. Exh. 1880
Sculptor. 40 Beaufort Street, Chelsea, London. † RA 1.

GAY, Lydia Exh. 1887-1903
Medalist. London 1887 and 1891; Solihull, Warwicks. 1889, Ightham, Sevenoaks, Kent 1894. † L 1, RA 27.

GAY, Rosalie Exh. 1881-89
Flower painter. London 1881; Manchester 1884. † M 2, SWA 4.

GAY, Walter* b. 1856
Interior painter. b. Hingham, Mass. U.S.A. Exh. 1882-1925. Add: Paris. † FIN 5, GI 4, L 4, M 1, RA 4, RSA 2, TOO 1.

GAYDON, William L. Exh. 1936
Wood engraver. 15 Gt. Norwood Street, Cheltenham, Glos. † COO 4, RSA 2.

GAYE, Howard Exh. 1880-91
Architect and watercolour interior painter. London. † D 4, RA 2, RSA 1.

GAYER-ANDERSON. Col. T.G. Exh. 1929-38
Figure painter. London 1929 and 1938; Lavenham, Suffolk 1936. † RA 3.

GAYET, Ernest Exh. 1909
† LS 3.

GAYFORD, Mrs. A.E. Exh. 1921-24
Bowscale, Lindon Avenue, Blundellsands, Liverpool. † B 2, L 1.

GAYLER, Mrs. Ellen A. Exh. 1891-1906
Figure and domestic painter. Bristol 1891; St. John's wood, London 1895. † L 2, M 1, RA 7.

GAYMARD, A. Exh. 1916
Beau Sejour, Bridge Lane, Golders Green, London. † RA 1.

GAYNOR, Mrs. Sophia T. see STERN

GAYTON, Anna M Exh. 1888-1910
Portrait painter and sculptor. London 1888; Much Hadham, Herts. 1890. † LS 4, NG 2, RA 9, RBA 2, RI 1.

GEACH, Oswald Exh. 1908-10
1 White Hart Lane, Barnes, London. † L 5.

GEACH, Portia Exh. 1907-25
Liverpool 1907; Union Bank of Australasia, 71 Cornhill, London 1925. † L 7.

GEAR, A. Handel Exh. 1892-97
Figure painter. London. † L 2, M 1, RA 1.

GEAR, Mabel b. 1900
Decorative painter of birds and animals. b. Ashby Rectory, Suffolk. Studied Colchester School of Art and at Bushey, Herts. Married Ivor I.J. Symes q.v. R.I. 1927, R.O.I. 1925. Add: Babbacombe, Devon 1920 and 1926; Bushey, Herts. 1922; Tadley, Hants. 1929. † GOU 1, L 8, RA 11, RBA 2, RI 10, ROI 25, RSA 1, SWA 3.

GEAR, William b. 1915
Studied Edinburgh College of Art. 5 Randolph Street, East Wemyss, Fife 1934. † RSA 2.

GEARING, Miss M.E. Exh. 1928
Ellerslie, Dutton Broad, Nr. Lowestoft, Suffolk. † L 1.

GEBBIE, Mrs. Ouida Exh. 1930
Miniature portrait painter. The Rookery, Roehampton Lane, Putney, London. † RA 1.

GEBHARTD, Von see V

GEBSATTEL, Baroness S. Exh. 1893
Figure painter. 7 Academie Strasse, Munchen. † RA 1.

GEDDES, Elijah Exh. 1920-28
School of Art, Stafford. † B 9, L 1, RA 1.

GEDDES, Ewan d. 1935
Landscape painter. R.S.W. 1902. Exh. 1884-1935. Add: Edinburgh and Blairgowrie, N.B. † GI 68, L 7, RA 2, RHA 5, RSA 151, RSW 113.

GEDDES, Geo. W. Exh. 1931
31 Rampart Avenue, Glasgow. † GI 1.

GEDDES, Mrs. Lucy B. Exh. 1932-39
Portrait and miniature painter. London. † P 1, RA 2, RMS 2, SWA 1.

GEDDES, Margaret b. 1914
Landscape painter. Studied Westminster School of Art, 1930-36. Add: Westcott, Dorking, Surrey 1935. † NEA 4, RA 1, SWA 7.
GEDDES, R. Smith Exh. 1907
Gowanbrae, Blairgowrie, N.B. † GI 1.
GEDDES, William 1841-1884
Still life painter. Gowanbrae Cottage, Blairgowrie, N.B. † GI 4, RSA 6.
GEDDES, Wilhelmina Margaret Exh. 1914-30
Painter, stained glass, black and white and lino and woodcut artist. Studied Belfast and Dublin. Add: Dublin 1914; Fulham, London 1930. † RHA 4.
GEE, Gilbert Exh. 1940
45 Worcester Lane, Four Oaks, Birmingham. † B 3.
GEE, Jessie A. Exh. 1897-98
4 Belgrave Street, Liscard, Cheshire. † L 2.
GEE, Jos. T. Exh. 1895
Warkden, Nr. Manchester. † L 1.
GEE, Jos. T. Exh. 1923-32
Brooklyn, Cadnant Park, Conway. † RCA 15.
GEE, Lucy see COXETER
GEEN, Mrs. Evelyne Exh. 1917-37
Mrs. B. Watercolour painter. London. † RI 7.
GEERTZ, Julius 1837-1902
German artist. Dusseldorf 1882-86. † RHA 3.
GEETS, Willem Exh. 1884-91
Figure painter. c/o Lefevre, 1A King Street, St. James', London 1884 and 1890; 5 Quai au Sel, Malines, France 1886. † B 4, GI 1, L 2, RA 1.
GEFLOWSKI, E. Edward Exh. 1880-94
Sculptor. London. † G 3, L 9, RBA 4.
GEHRTS, Carl Exh. 1889
Illustrative painter. Dusseldorf, Germany. † L 2, RA 1.
GEIKIE, Lucy Exh. 1901-13
Landscape painter. 10 Chester Terrace, Regents Park, London. † ALP 4, RA 2.
GEISSLER, William H. d. 1963
52 Audley Avenue, Edinburgh 1938. † RSW 1.
GELDART, Mary C. Exh. 1900
15 Park Road, Norbiton, Surrey. † L 1.
GELDART, T.H. Exh. 1883-1905
Liverpool. † L 3.
GELDER, William B. Exh. 1905-22
Landscape painter. Brighouse, Yorks. 1905; Barnet. Herts. 1921. † L 1, RA 5.
GELEE, Mlle. Isabel Exh. 1906
71 Rue Nollet, Paris. † L 2.
GELIBERT, Gaston 1850-1931
French painter. Exh. 1883. † FIN 1.
GELIVERT, Jules 1833-1916
French painter. 47 Rue Denfert. Rochereau. Paris 1883-86. † FIN 1, GI 1, M 1.
GELL, Ada Freeman Exh. 1887-1916
nee Evershed. Sculptor. Brighton 1887; London 1890. † G 3, GI 2, L 13, M 6, RA 19, RBA 1.
GELL, A.G. Exh. 1920-27
Bradford, Yorks. 1920; Chelsea, London 1927. † L 2, M 1.
GELL, F.L. Exh. 1908
5 Sherwin Street, Nottingham. † N 1.
GELLETT, Mrs. Sarah Exh. 1921-28
Miniature painter. The Cottage, Hampton in Arden 1921; Balsall, Nr. Coventry 1922. † B 7.
GELLIBRAND, Paula Exh. 1908-9
27 Longridge Road, Earls Court, London. † LS 3.
GEM, Mrs. M.A. Exh. 1935-39
86 Carless Avenue, Harborne, Birmingham. † B 2.
GEMMEL, David Exh. 1936-40
48 Clermiston Road North, Barnton. † RSA 1.
GEMMELL, J.L. Exh. 1883-85
5 Woodville Place, Govan, Glasgow. † GI 4, RSA 2.
GEMMELL, Marion Exh. 1887-1909
Figure and domestic painter. London 1887 and 1892, Glasgow 1888. † B 2, GI 2, L 5, LS 2, P 1, RI 1, ROI 2, SWA 6.
GEMMELL, Mary Exh. 1881-1903
Flower, figure and domestic painter. London. † B 3, D 1, GI 6, L 10, M 3, NEA 1, RA 5, RBA 2, ROI 3, SWA 2.
GEMMILL, William Exh. 1888
317 St. Vincent Street, Glasgow. † GI 2.
GEMS, Julius A. Exh. 1939
Sculptor. 2 Stratford Studios, London. † RA 1.
GENE, A. Exh. 1890-93
c/o R. Jeffreys, 88 Bold Street, Liverpool. † L 1, M 1.
GENEVER, Ernest Exh. 1925-28
Nene Cottage, Ravenhust Road, Harborne, Birmingham. † B 3.
GENGE, Charles Exh. 1895-1929
Landscape painter. Epping Villa, Elgin Road, Wallington 1895; London 1914. † GOU 8, NEA 5, RBA 1, ROI 1.
GENN, Ellen Exh. 1880
Flower painter. Woodlane, Falmouth, Cornwall. † SWA 1.
GENSEL, Henri Exh. 1913-15
Landscape painter. The Brook, Stamford Brook Road, W. London 1913; Ashford, Middlesex 1915. † LS 3, NEA 3.
GENTILLI, Madge H. Exh. 1936-39
45 Phillimore Gardens, London. † P 2, RBA 1, ROI 4.
GENTLEMAN, Tom Exh. 1921-29
Landscape painter, poster and book designer. Studied Glasgow School of Art. Married to Winifred Murgatroyd q.v. Add: Glasgow 1921; Coatbridge 1925; London 1929. † GI 7, M 1. RSA 2, WG 4.
GENTZ, Ismael Exh. 1913-14
6 Hildebrandstrasse, Berlin. † L 1, LS 3.
GEOFFROI, Charles Louis Exh. 1908-10
Portrait, figure and landscape painter. † CAR 112, DOW 2, GOU 4.
GEOFFROI, Harry Exh. 1884-91
Landscape painter. Malcolm Villa, Alexandra Road, Penzance, Cornwall. † L 1, M 1, RBA 1, RI 1.
GEOFFROY, Jean 1853-1924
French domestic painter. 6 New Compton Street, Soho, London 1890; Paris 1910. † L 1, RA 1.
GEOGHEGAN, Charles Exh. 1880
205 Gt. Brunswick Street, London. † RHA 1.
GEOGHEGAN, H.T. Exh. 1911-14
Eversham, Stillorgan, Co. Dublin. † RHA 9.
GEORGALA, Helen Exh. 1892-1921
Mrs. W.F. Walker. Liverpool. † L 18, SWA 1.
GEORGE, Mrs. A.W. Exh. 1919
A.S.W.A. 1917. 32 Argyll Mansions, Chelsea, London. † SWA 2.
GEORGE, Miss B. Exh. 1901-3
16 Grange Road, Gunnersbury, London. † L 1, SWA 2.
GEORGE, Miss Basille E. Exh. 1939
Sculptor. 40 Lilyville Road, Fulham, London. † RA 1.
GEORGE, Dorothea Exh. 1908
25 Rue Boissonade, Paris. † LS 4.
GEORGE, Miss D. St. J. Exh. 1914-17
32 Argyll Mansions, Chelsea, London. † RA 1, SWA 2.
GEORGE, Sir Ernest 1839-1922
Watercolour painter, etcher and architect. A.R.A. 1910, R.A. 1917, R.B.A. 1889, R.E. 1881-98. Knighted 1912. Add: London. † D 1, FIN 760, RA 43, RBA 19, RE 17, RHA 14, RI 3, RSA 3.
GEORGE, Eric B. b. 1881
Portrait and figure painter. Exh. 1907-34. Add: London. † CHE 1, COO 1, GI 2, GOU 5, I 3, L 4, LS 5, M 1, NEA 10, P 3, RA 11, RHA 1, ROI 1.
GEORGE, Miss Esther H. see JOHNSON, Esther Borough
GEORGE, Florence Exh. 1921
11 Verdun Avenue, Vickerstown, Barrow in Furness, Lancs. † L 1.
GEORGE, Fred W. Exh. 1936-37
37 Salisbury Terrace, Aberdeen. † RSA 2.
GEORGE, Herbert Exh. 1906-39
Landscape painter. Studied South Kensington, Bushey, Herts., Newlyn, Penzance and St. Ives. Add: Hindhead, Surrey 1906; London 1915; Gomshall, Surrey 1926. † AR 2, B 1, COO 1, LS 8, RA 6, RI 1.
GEORGE, Miss H. Chalmers Exh. 1905-8
The Highlands, 89 South Hill Park, Hampstead, London. † LS 4, SWA 1.
GEORGE, Harold K. Exh. 1937
Etcher. 3 Douglas Avenue, Wembley, Middlesex. † RA 1.
GEORGE, Helen Margaret Exh. 1922-40
Painter and sculptor. Studied under Antoine Bourdelle in Paris. A.S.W.A. 1939. Add: Blandford, Dorset 1922 and 1936; London 1928; Paris 1930. † B 2, GOU 12, L 2, M 2, RA 1, RI 1, RSA 2, SWA 11.
GEORGE, Jessie Louise Exh. 1908-18
London. † LS 5, RA 4.
GEORGE, Lena Exh. 1912-25
nee Buckley. Landscape painter. Married W.S.G. q.v. Add: London 1912 and 1925; Delhi, India 1920. † L 3, RA 7.
GEORGE, Millicent Exh. 1912-13
Figure and religious painter. 14 St. Loo Mansions, Cheyne Gardens, Chelsea, London. † NEA 4.
GEORGE, May Butler Exh. 1913-19
Miniature portrait painter. London. † GI 1, L 7, RA 3, RMS 1, RSA 2.
GEORGE, Miss N. Exh. 1893-95
89 South Hill Park, Hampstead, London. † SWA 2.
GEORGE, Peter Exh. 1940
Portrait painter. 16 Court Lane Gardens, Dulwich, London. † RA 1.
GEORGE, Mrs. Rachel Exh. 1912-21
64 Burnley Road, Edenfield, Nr. Manchester. † L 1, M 2.
GEORGE, Richard Exh. 1914-20
64 Burnley Road, Edenfield, Nr. Manchester. † L 1, M 1.
GEORGE, Miss V.M. Exh. 1920
Duncroft, Gedling, Notts. † N 1.
GEORGE, W. Exh. 1907
14 Crescent Avenue, Whitby. † L 2.
GEORGE, Winifred (Wyn) Exh. 1908-39
Landscape and figure painter and pastellier. Add: London 1908; Blandford, Dorset 1912. † ALP 30, B 2, G 1, GI 2, GOU 45, I 2, L 2, LS 8, NEA 1, P 1, SWA 2.
GEORGE, W.S. Exh. 1908-15
Married to Lena G. q.v. Add; London. † RA 4.
GEORGES, Charles E. Exh. 1893-1902
Landscape painter. R.B.A. 1899. Add: London 1893; Surrey 1894; Worcester 1899. † RBA 20.

GEORGES, Frank E. Exh. 1914
School of Art, Albion Street, Lewes, Sussex. † RI 1.

GEORGET, Exh. 1931
† WG 38

GEORGINA, Exh. 1936-37
† NEA 3.

GERANZANI, Cornelio Exh. 1922
Figure painter. Quarto dei Mille, Genoa, Italy. † RA 1.

GERARD, Mme. Lola Exh. 1926
The Wytch Studio, 14 Glyn Mansions, Avonmore Road, London. † L 3.

GERARDDIN, D.D. Exh. 1885
76 Southampton Row, Russell Square, London. † B 1.

GERBER, Pierre* Exh. 1923
2 Rue de Ponthiau, Paris. † RSA 2.

GERE, Charles March* 1869-1957
Landscape and portrait painter and illustrator. Studied and taught Birmingham School of Art. Worked with William Morris and for the Kelmscott Press. N.E.A. 1911, A.R.A. 1933, R.A. 1939, R.B.S.A. 1906, A.R.W.S. 1921, R.W.S. 1927. Add: Leamington, Warwicks. 1890; London 1900; Painswick, Glos. 1902. † AG 15, B 76, BA 1, CAR 63, CHE 1, COO 3, FIN 35, GI 6, GOU 11, I 1, L 19, M 3, NEA 144, NG 49, RA 60, RHA 2, RMS 1, RSW 1, RWS 171, TOO 2, WG 4.

GERE, Miss Margaret 1878-1965
Landscape, portrait and figure painter. N.E.A. 1925. Add: Leamington, Warwicks. 1900; Painswick, Glos. 1902. † B 15, CAR 10, CHE 2, COO 3, FIN 14, L 2, NEA 85, NG 6, RA 1, RHA 1.

GERHARDI, Alexander Exh. 1924-27
Portrait, figure and landscape painter. 13 Bramerton Street, Chelsea, London 1924; Belvedere, Kent 1927. † ALP 14, M 1, RA 1.

GERMAIN, Mlle L.D. Exh. 1908
11 Rue Bosio, Paris. † LS 5.

GERNEZ, Paul Elie* b. 1888
Watercolour painter and pastellier. b. Valenciennes. Studied Ecole des Beaux Arts, Valenciennes. Exh. 1931-39. Add: 7 Bruton Place, London. † BA 68, GI 4, RA 6, RED 1, RSA 1.

GERNON, de see D

GEROME, Jean Leon* 1824-1904
French painter and sculptor. H.F.R.A. Exh. 1883-93. Add: Paris. † GI 1, M 1, RA 2.

GERON, R.W. Exh. 1914
6 Rue Oudinot, Paris. † RSA 1.

GERRARD, A. Horace b. 1899
London. † NEA 7.

GERRARD, Charles Robert 1892-c.1971
Flower, landscape and portrait painter. Studied Lancaster and Royal College of Art. R.B.A. 1931, R.O.I. 1935. Add: London 1926; Sir J.J. School of Art, Bombay 1936. † CG 1, COO 33, L 7, M 1, NEA 7, RA 3, RBA 23, RED 35.

GERRARD, Miss W.M. Exh. 1882-86
Edinburgh. † RSA 3.

GERRING, C. Exh. 1929
2 Collin's Hospitals, Carrington Street, Nottingham. † N 1.

GERSHON, Olive Marie b. 1889
nee Jonas. Interior painter. Studied Juliens and Colarossi's, Paris. Exh. 1931-36. Add: London. † RA 1, ROI 2.

GERSTL, Arnold Exh. 1935
Portrait painter. 32 Hampstead Way, London. † RA 1.

GERTH, Fritz Exh. 1888-92
Sculptor. Rome. † RA 4.

GERTLER, Mark* 1892-1939
Portrait, figure, flower, still life and landscape painter. Studied Slade School 1909. N.E.A. 1912. Member London Group 1915. "The Artist's Mother" (1911) purchased by Chantrey Bequest 1944. Add: London. † ALP 2, AG 4, BA 12, CHE 20, COO 1, GOU 163, L 1, LEI 118, M 2, NEA 24, RED 8, RSA 1, TOO 1.

GERTNER, Chas. M. Exh. 1936
37 Camp Hill Road, Worcester. † B 1.

GERVEX, Henri* 1852-1929
French artist. exh. 1893-1907. Add: 12 Rue Roussel, Paris. † P 1, RA 1.

GERVIS, Ruth Exh. 1927-33
nee Streatfield. Painter, illustrator and teacher. Add: The Vicarage, Eastbourne 1927; Nortons, Sherborne, Dorset 1932. † L 2, RA 1, SWA 2.

GESNE, de see D

GETH-ARTHUR, H. Norman Exh. 1897-99
Field Studio, Hill Farm, Holcombe, Wallingford, Berks. † RA 1, RBA 2.

GETHIN, G. Percy Exh. 1906-10
Painter and etcher. 27 Pilgrim Street, Liverpool. † CAR 5, D 1, L 1.

GETHIN, Col. J.P. Exh. 1907
Bellindoon, Boyle. † D 2.

GETHIN, Percy Francis d. 1916
Painter and etcher. Teacher at Central School of Arts and Crafts. Killed whilst serving with Artists Rifles. Add: London 1899 and 1913. Holywell, Sligo 1904; Liverpool 1908. † B 1, CG 8, L 18, LS 2, NEA 8, RHA 16, RSA 3.

GETHING, Frank Exh. 1938
Landscape painter. 59 Central Avenue, Hucknall, Notts. † N 1.

GETHING, May Exh. 1897-1923
Portrait and miniature painter. Add: Nottingham and London. † GI 2, L 8, N 19, RA 9, RCA 12.

GETHING, W. Exh. 1931
Watercolour landscape painter. † RED 1.

GETTLESON, A.A. Exh. 1910
2 Byron Street, Leeds, Yorks. † L 1.

GEUL, Jo Romein Exh. 1939
Flower, figure and portrait painter. 75 Merrion Square South, Dublin. † RHA 3.

GEVERS, Helene Exh. 1894
Figure painter. 10 Rue Herreyns, Antwerp. † RA 1.

GEYER, Rev. A.H. Exh. 1912
35 Blythswood Drive, Glasgow. † GI 1.

GEYGER, Ernest M. Exh. 1898
Sculptor. 8 Via di. Marignolle, Florence, Italy. † RA 1.

GHENT, Ada Exh. 1896
Llanbedr, Conway, Wales. † L 1.

GHENT, Peter 1857-1911
Landscape painter. Liverpool 1880 and 1905; Conway, N. Wales 1884. † B 1, D 2, G 1, L 60, M 8, RA 21, RBA 1, RCA 81, RI 9, ROI 5.

GHILCHIK, David L. Exh. 1930-39
Figure painter. 39 Hartswood Road, Stamford Brook, London. † L 1, P 1, RA 1, ROI 6.

GHILCHIK, Mrs. Josephine Exh. 1938-40
39 Hartswood Road, London. † P 1, ROI 3, SWA 2.

GHOSLEY, Henry S. Exh. 1935
Landscape painter. Uplands, Portland Avenue, Exmouth, Devon. † RA 1.

GIACCOMETI, P. Exh. 1901
c/o Fisher Unwin, 11 Paternoster Buildings, London. † I 1.

GIACHI, F. Exh. 1888
c/o T. Richardson & Co., 43 Piccadilly, London. † ROI 1.

GIAMPIETRI, Mrs. Amy B.* Exh. 1882-97
nee Butts. Figure painter. A.S.W.A. 1885. Add: Rome 1882; 2 Scarsdale Studios, Stratford Road, Kensington, London 1894. † D 1, L 4, M 6, P 1, RMS 1, SWA 18.

GIAMPIETRI, Settin Exh. 1882-1921
Landscape painter. Rome 1882 and 1907; 2 Scarsdale studios, Stratford Road, Kensington, London 1894. † B 8, D 23, FIN 1, GI 2, L 12, M 5, NG 2, RA 5, RBA 5, RHA 5, RI 1.

GIANNETTI, Raffaelle Exh. 1881-87
Figure painter. Venice 1882; 4A King Street, St. James', London 1885. † RA 4.

GIBB, Chas. Exh. 1900
8 Whitevale Street, Glasgow. † GI 1.

GIBB, Ethel A. Exh. 1912-21
Strathbungo, N.B. 1912; Langside, Glasgow 1916. † GI 7.

GIBB, George Exh. 1895
31 Joppa, Portobello, Edinburgh. † RSA 1.

GIBB, H. Elrington Exh. 1916-27
London. † ROI 3.

GIBB, Henry M. Exh. 1931
23 Kennoway Drive, Glasgow. † RSW 1.

GIBB, Harry Phelan 1870-1948
Figure and landscape painter. Alnwick, Northumberland 1894; Paris 1908. † ALP 90, BG 94, GI 1, LS 12, RED 1, RHA 5, RSA 1.

GIBB, Miss J. Exh. 1915
51 York Street Chambers, Bryanston Square, London. † RA 1.

GIBB, Lewis Taylor Exh. 1918-39
Landscape painter. London 1919; West Mersea, Nr. Colchester, Essex 1931. † GI 15, I 9, L 18, RA 14, RCA 11, RHA 13, RI 2, ROI 27, RSA 16.

GIBB, Robert* 1845-1932
Painter of romantic, historical, portrait and military subjects. Brother of William G. q.v. A.R.S.A. 1880, R.S.A. 1882. Add: Edinburgh. † GI 6, M 2, RA 5, RSA 119..

GIBB, Miss Sadie* Exh. 1913-16
93 Hope Street, Glasgow. † L 19.

GIBB, Stanley Watson b. 1898
Landscape painter, watercolourist, designer and teacher. Studied Scarborough School of Art and Goldsmiths College. Add: 559 Lordship Lane, Dulwich, London 1929. † RA 1.

GIBB, T.H. Exh. 1883-85
Alnwick, Northumberland. † RHA 1, RSA 2, TOO 1.

GIBB, William 1839-1929
Watercolour painter and lithographer. Brother of Robert G. q.v. Add: Glasgow 1880; London 1918. † GI 1, RSA 8.

GIBBERD, Frederick b. 1908
Architect. Studied Birmingham School of Architecture. Add: 11 Clareville Court, London 1940. † RA 3.

GIBBERD, Harry Exh. 1930
78 Bournbrook Road, Selly Oak, Birmingham. † B 1.

GIBBERD, Marion Exh. 1895
Roselands, Coventry. † B 4.

GIBBINGS, H. Exh. 1924-25
Woodside, Halebank, Nr. Widnes, Lancs. † L 2.

GIBBINGS, Robert 1889-1958
Sculptor, wood and copper engraver. Studied under Harry Sculley, in Cork, Slade School (2 years) and Central School of Arts and Crafts, London. Director of the Cockerel Press. Add: Cork 1913; Twyford, Berks. 1924; London 1925. † I 4, L 4, RED 14, RHA 6.

GIBBON, Benjamin b. 1914
Landscape and mural painter. Studied Slade School. Add: Abberton Hall, Pershore, Worcs. 1934-40. † B 3, COO 2, GOU 2, NEA 4, RA 9.

GIBBON, Mrs. Clara E. Exh. 1930-38
36 St. Agnes Road, Moseley, Birmingham. † B 9.

GIBBON, Miss F.A. Exh. 1897
Upper Norwood, London. † SWA 2.

GIBBON, Mrs. Gwendolen Exh. 1907-12
The White Cottage, Galley Hill, Waltham Abbey, Essex. † L 3, LS 4, P 2.

GIBBON, Miss G.I. Exh. 1921-22
Hughenden, Peters Finger, Salisbury, Wilts. † SWA 3.

GIBBON, James Exh. 1905-24
Kensington, London 1905; Waltham Abbey, Essex 1907. † GOU 1, LS 6, P 3, ROI 4.

GIBBON, Michael Exh. 1936
Figure painter. † COO 4.

GIBBON, Sidney Exh. 1935-36
Flower painter. 55 Victoria Street, Newark on Trent, Notts. † N 4.

GIBBON, T. Exh. 1905
6 East Chapel Street, Mayfair, London. † RA 1.

GIBBONS, Angela b. 1896
Mrs. S. Latham. Painter, decorator and fresco painter. Studied Wolverhampton School of Art (from age 12 to 16). Oxford, London and Paris. Served as V.A.D. 1915-18. Exh. 1919-33. Add: Penn, Staffs. † B 11, I 3, L 1, P 1, RA 2, ROI 2, SWA 5.

GIBBONS, Ethel W. Exh. 1899-1922
Liverpool. † B 6, L 34, RCA 9, SWA 4.

GIBBONS, F. Exh. 1912
16 Halstead Road, Somerville, Poulton, Cheshire. † L 1.

GIBBONS, Francis Exh. 1894-1907
Landscape painter. Stourbridge, Worcs. † B 5, RA 1.

GIBBONS, J. Harold Exh. 1905-40
Architect. 4 St. Mary's Parsonage, Manchester 1905; St. John's Wood, London 1913. † RA 21.

GIBBONS, William* Exh. 1880-90
Landscape and figure painter. Nottingham 1880; Beeston, Notts. 1885. † N 11.

GIBBONS, William Exh. 1893-1904
Currock, Carlisle. † D 1, I 1.

GIBBS, Beatrice Exh. 1887-1908
Figure painter. London. † B 4, I 1, L 2, M 1, P 2, RA 7, RBA 1, ROI 5.

GIBBS, Charles Exh. 1880-99
Landscape painter. Dorking, Surrey. † B 3, L 13, M 4, RA 9, RBA 15, RHA 3, ROI 7.

GIBBS, Catherine M. Exh. 1899
Cambridge House, Hill Street, Coventry. † B 1.

GIBBS, Mrs. Dorothy Agnes Exh. 1917-29
Miniature painter. Norwich, Norfolk. † L 2, RA 6, RMS 4.

GIBBS, E. Exh. 1907
11 Montpelier Road, Kentish Town, London. † RA 1.

GIBBS, Edward M. Exh. 1903-12
Architect. 15 St. James' Row, Sheffield. † RA 4.

GIBBS, Evelyn M. Exh. 1926-39
Etcher, painter and wood engraver. A.R.E. 1929. Add: Liverpool 1926; London 1929 and 1933; Rome 1930. † L 5, NEA 5, RA 8, RE 21.

GIBBS, Henry* Exh. 1880-1907
Portrait and landscape painter. London 1880; Handcross, Crawley, Sussex 1896. † GI 7, L 2, M 2, RA 25, RE 2, ROI 2.

GIBBS, Herbert Edward b. 1872
Portrait and landscape painter, and mural decorator. Studied Birmingham School of Art, Herkomer's, Bushey, Herts., and Juliens, Paris. Art master Birmingham School of Art. Add: Birmingham 1898; Stratford-on-Avon 1930. † B 18, L 1, RCA 3.

GIBBS, Isaac Exh. 1881-88
Stained glass artist. 64 Charlotte Street, Fitzroy Square, London. † RA 2.

GIBBS, Miss J. Exh. 1928
The Vicarage, Alderham, Watford, Herts. † B 1.

GIBBS, Joseph Exh. 1891-1906
121 St. Paul's Road, Smethwick, Birmingham. † B 8.

GIBBS, J.B. Exh. 1888-94
Liverpool 1888; Congleton, Cheshire 1903. † L 10, M 1.

GIBBS, P.W. Exh. 1894-1937
Portrait and landscape painter. Studied RA Schools (Creswick prize 1895). Add: London 1894; East Molesey, Surrey 1903. † GI 6, L 3, RA 36.

GIBBS, Rev. Reginald Exh. 1931-33
† WG 8.

GIBBS, Rosemary Exh. 1922
† G 1.

GIBBS, Ruth Exh. 1906-16
10 Lillington, Leamington, Warwicks. † B 1, RA 1.

GIBBS, Robert E. Exh. 1936
Harby, Melton Mowbray, Leics. † N 1.

GIBBS, Snow 1882-c.1970
Portrait and landscape painter. Studied Central School of Arts and Crafts, New York School of Art, Ecole des Beaux Art, Paris (1907-14). Exh. 1916-32. Add: 5 Thurloe Square, London. † L 2, LS 3, RCA 1.

GIBBS, Thomas Binney b. 1870
Portrait and landscape painter and teacher. Studied Liverpool School of Art. Exh. 1901-38. Add: Manchester 1901; London 1915. † BA 54, CHE 2, GOU 20, I 8, L 7, M 12, P 13, RA 18, ROI 5, WG 62.

GIBBS, W.J. Exh. 1907-9
Flower painter. 2 Cherson Terrace, Wood Green, London. † RA 3.

GIBERNE, Edgar Exh. 1880-88
Landscape painter. Epsom 1880; London 1885. † D 12, L 2, RBA 1, RI 3, ROI 1.

GIBNEY, Tom Exh. 1940
Landscape painter. National College of Art, Kildare Street, Dublin. † RHA 1.

GIBNEY, William R. Exh. 1921-25
2 Dargle Terrace, Bray, Ireland. † RHA 5.

GIBOUT, J.V.G. Exh. 1910
Rue de la Vallee 50, Brussels. † L 1.

GIBSON, A. Exh. 1888
Landscape painter. 222 Lenton Sands, Nottingham. † N 1.

GIBSON, Arthur Exh. 1928
Landscape painter. † AB 2.

GIBSON, Albert Arthur Exh. 1909
† LS 3.

GIBSON, Arthur A. Exh. 1894
Architect. Old Bank Chambers, Harrogate, Yorks. † RA 1.

GIBSON, Alex R. Exh. 1912-40
Kilsyth, Glasgow. † GI 13, L 5, RSA 15, RSW 1.

GIBSON, Bessie Exh. 1905-26
Miniature painter. Add: Edinburgh 1905; Paris 1906. † I 4, L 6, RA 14, RMS 2, RSA 1.

GIBSON, Clara Exh. 1898
Hexham on Tyne, Northumberland. † GI 1.

GIBSON, Colin Exh. 1935-38
Figure painter. Lynash, Hill End Road, Arbroath. † RA 1, RSA 2.

GIBSON, Charlotte Ellen b. 1902
Sculptor. b. Cornwall. Studied Regent Street Polytechnic 1925-31, and British School at Rome 1931-32. Teacher of Sculpture Regent Street Polytechnic 1933. Exh. 1926-40. † GI 3, L 1, RA 8, RSA 1.

GIBSON, Edward Exh. 1900
c/o Mr. John Wright, Rocklands, Rock Lane, Rock Ferry, Cheshire. † L 1.

GIBSON, Ellinor Bethell Exh. 1897-1900
R.M.S. 1897. 11 Westbourne Square, London. † RMS 11.

GIBSON, Edith M. Exh. 1882-1918
Landscape, figure and portrait painter. A.S.W.A. 1886. Add: Dublin 1882; London 1883. † B 5, D 3, L 4, M 3, RA 5, RBA 3, RHA 14, RID 26, ROI 2, SWA 27.

GIBSON, Mrs. E.W. Exh. 1920
Strangeways, 25 Duchess Road, Edgbaston, Birmingham. † B 2.

GIBSON, Miss F. Exh. 1896
R.M.S. 1896. Add: The Grange, Lisners Park, Belvedere, Kent. † RMS 1.

GIBSON, George Exh. 1936
1669 N. Crescent Heights Boulevard, California, U.S.A. † GI 1.

GIBSON, G. Selkirk Exh. 1901-2
46 Polwarth Gardens, Edinburgh. † RSA 3.

GIBSON, H. Exh. 1899
369 Oxford Street, London. † RBA 1.

GIBSON, Miss I.M. Exh. 1914-18
Sherwood, St. James Road, New Brighton, Cheshire. † I 2, L 1.

GIBSON, J. Exh. 1920-21
26 Anderson Street, Grimsby, Lincs. † B 2.

GIBSON, James Brown b. 1880
Painter, etcher, lithographer, textile and stained glass designer, sculptor and modeller. Studied Glasgow School of Art. Add: Bearsden, N.B. 1905; Glasgow 1910 and 1931; Milngavie 1921; Killearn 1936. † GI 24, L 3, RSA 20, RSW 3.

GIBSON, J.H.S. Exh. 1901-9
Liverpool. † L 3.

GIBSON, J.J. Exh. 1887
Miniature portrait painter. 2 Shamrock Terrace, Gardiner's Hill, Cork. † RA 1.

GIBSON, James S. Exh. 1889-1910
Architect. London. † RA 4, RSA 1.

GIBSON, Jessie S. Exh. 1917-29
Mrs. Howson. Figure and interior painter. A.S.W.A. 1917, S.W.A. 1918. Add: 8 Cranley Place, S. Kensington, London. † I 1, L 1, RA 3, SWA 23.

GIBSON, Joseph Vincent Exh. 1884-98
Figure and portrait painter. R.M.S. 1896. London. † L 2, RA 4, RMS 2, ROI 1.

GIBSON, Katherine B.S. Exh. 1902
10 Belgrave Crescent, Edinburgh. † RSA 1.

GIBSON, L. Exh. 1889
159 High Street, Notting Hill, London. † M 1.

GIBSON, M. Exh. 1880
38 Burnbank Gardens, Glasgow. † GI 2.

GIBSON, Miss M. Exh. 1881-88
Rose Bank, Doune. † GI 4, RSA 3.

GIBSON, Mary F. Exh. 1894-1916
Belfast 1894; Dublin 1900. † D 2, LS 2, RHA 14, SWA 1.

GIBSON, Mary Gwenillan Exh. 1927-40
Painter and craft worker. Studied Wolverhampton and Birmingham Schools of Art. Teacher of leather work design and bookbinding, Wolverhampton School of Art. Add: 52 Waterloo Road, Wolverhampton. † B 23, L 1, RA 4.

GIBSON, Mary Josephine Exh. 1887-1924
Miniature portrait painter. R.M.S. 1896. London. † L 3, NG 1, RA 69, RMS 18.

GIBSON, Mary S. Exh. 1940
25 Rue Jean Dolent, Paris. † RSA 1.

GIBSON, Miles S. Exh. 1896-1906
131 West Regent Street, Glasgow. † GI 6, RSA 1.

GIBSON, Mrs. N. Exh. 1884-96
Birmingham. † B 8.

GIBSON, Phoebe Exh. 1938
53 Murray Road, Wimbledon, London. † RBA 1.

GIBSON, Mrs. Perle Siedle Exh. 1933-34
Landscape painter. c/o Bourlet, 17 Nassau Street, London 1933; Durban, S. Africa 1934. † RCA 1, RHA 1, RSA 1.

GIBSON, Robert W. Exh. 1880
Architect. 14 Albion Road, Clapham, London. † RA 1.

GIBSON, Vera Exh. 1891-99
1 Princes Street, Cavendish Square, London. † M 1, RBA 1.

GIBSON, Victoria E. Exh. 1887-93
18 College Green, Dublin. † RHA 9.

GIBSON, William Exh. 1925
45 West Nile Street, Glasgow. † GI 1.

GIBSON, William Alfred* 1866-1931
Landscape, coastal and figure painter. Studied National Training College, Glasgow. Add: Glasgow. † FIN 89, GI 101, L 27, M 16, RA 3, RSA 36.

GIBSON, William John Exh. 1938
† GI 1.

GIBTON, Miss G.M. Exh. 1894
6 Gresham Terrace, Kingstown. † RHA 1.

GIDDENS, George Exh. 1880-85
Landscape painter. Hogarth Studios, 64 Charlotte Street, Fitzroy Square, London. † RBA 6, ROI 1.

GIDDENS, Joseph Exh. 1940
Landscape painter. 2 Glebe Road, Barnes, London. † RA 1.

GIDDENS, Philip H. Exh. 1933
Portrait artist. c/o Guaranty Trust Co., 50 Pall Mall, London. † RA 1.

GIDLEY, Jean Exh. 1922-23
c/o Miss Bucton, 34 High Street, Hampstead, London. † RCA 2.

GIELE, Ferdinand Exh. 1918-19
Etcher. 74 Elbourne Road, Tooting Common, London. † RA 1.

GIFFORD, G.P. Exh. 1904
8 Temple Villas, Rathmines, Dublin. † RHA 1.

GIFFORD, M.W. Exh. 1893
Cowley Rectory, Cheltenham, Glos. † RHA 1.

GIFFORD, Robert Swain* 1840-1905
Americal landscape painter. R.E. 1881-89. Exh. 1881-84. Add: New York, U.S.A. † L 1, RA 1, RE 7.

GIGUEFELT, de See D

GIHON, Albert Dakin b. 1866
Americal landscape painter. 59 Avenue de Saxe, Paris 1900. † M 1, RA 1.

GIHON, Clarence Montford 1871-1929
Born U.S.A. Died Paris. Add: Hotel Foyot, 33 Rue de Tournon, Paris 1908. † LS 3.

GIL, A.B. Exh. 1883
† TOO 1.

GILARDI, Pier C. Exh. 1883-95
Figure painter. Paris 1883; London 1884; Accademia Albertina 8, Turin, Italy 1895. † GI 1, RA 1, ROI 3.

GILARDONI, J. Exh. 1914
17 Avenue Emile Deschaud, Paris. † LS 3.

GILBERT, Achille Exh. 1882-84
Etcher. 4 Rue des Grandes Degres, Paris. † G 2, RA 4.

GILBERT, Sir Alfred 1854-1934
Sculptor. Studied S. Kensington and Ecole des Beaux Arts, Paris. Assistant to Sir E.J. Boehm. A.R.A. 1887, R.A. 1892 (resigned 1908, resumed membership 1932). H.R.B.A. 1909, H.R.I. 1893 (resigned 1909, re-elected 1932). Knighted 1932. "Model for Eros on the Shaftesbury Memorial, Piccadilly Circus" (1890) purchased by Chantrey Bequest 1925 and "Ignacy Jan Paderewski" (c. 1900) in 1934. Add: Rome 1882; London 1884 and 1932; Bruges, Belgium 1905. † FIN 19, G 1, GI 6, I 4, L 9, M 1, NG 1, RA 37, RHA 1, RI 1, RSA 7.

GILBERT, Arthur 1819-1895
Landscape painter. b. London. 4th son of Edward "Old" Williams (1782-1855). Changed his name to avoid confusion with other members of the family. Father of Horace Walter and Kate Elizabeth G. q.v. Add: De Tillens House, Limpsfield, Surrey. † L 1, M 1, RA 2, RBA 16, ROI 5, TOO 5.

GILBERT, Miss A.L. Exh. 1932
3 Newstead Grove, Nottingham. † N 1.

GILBERT, Albert Thomas Jarvis d. 1927
Painter, illustrator, poster artist and teacher. Studied Southport, Lancs. R.O.I. 1909. Exh. 1899-1927. Add: London. † I 1, L 2, RA 11, RI 14, ROI 53.

GILBERT, Cass C. 1860-1934
American architect. H.F.R.A. Exh. 1931-32. Add: New York. U.S.A. † RA 5, RSA 4.

GILBERT, Charles Web 1867-1925
Australian sculptor. "The Critic" purchased by Chantrey Bequest 1917. Exh. 1915-18. Add: 5 Netherton Grove, Chelsea, London. † GI 1, L 2, RA 9.

GILBERT, Donald 1900-1961
Sculptor. b. Burcot, Worcs. Son of Walter G. q.v. Studied RA Schools (silver and bronze medals), Royal College of Art, Rome and Florence. R.B.S.A. 1937. Add: Edgbaston, Birmingham 1922; London 1930. † B 20, GI 1, L 3, RA 16, RHA 1, RSA 3.

GILBERT, Miss E. Exh. 1903
67A Upper Tulse Hill, London. † SWA 1.

GILBERT, Ellen Exh. 1880-1903
Watercolour painter. Vanbrugh Park, Blackheath, London. † B 4, RBA 22.

GILBERT, George Exh. 1937
† RMS 1.

GILBERT, George M. Exh. 1936-40
21 Cromwell Street, Glasgow. † GI 6, RSA 4, RSW 5.

GILBERT, Horace Walter* b. 1855
Landscape and figure painter. Only son of Arthur G. q.v. Exh. 1882-85. Add: De Tillens House, Limpsfield, Surrey. † L 2, M 2, RA 2, RBA 3, ROI 4, TOO 1.

GILBERT, Jeannie Exh. 1896
16 Glengyle Terrace, Edinburgh. † RSA 1.

GILBERT, Sir John* 1817-1897
Historical genre painter,illustrator and watercolourist. Contributor to "Illustrated London News". A.R.A. 1872, R.A. 1876, H.R.B.A. by 1880, H.R.S.W. 1884, A.R.W.S. 1852, R.W.S. 1854, P.R.W.S. 1871-97; Knighted 1872. Add: Vanbrugh Park, Blackheath, London. † AG 11, B 2, L 12, M 2, RA 24, RBA 7, RSW 1, RWS 26, TOO 3.

GILBERT, John Exh. 1885-1915
Cork. † RHA 8.

GILBERT, Kate Elizabeth b. 1843
Landscape painter. Daughter of Arthur G. q.v. Married Humphrey Hughes, a schoolmaster. Add: De Tillens House, Limpsfield, Surrey 1880; West Croydon 1885. † RBA 1, SWA 2.

GILBERT, Kate H. Exh. 1890
13 Yew Tree Road, Edgbaston, Birmingham. † B 1.

GILBERT, Miss M. Exh. 1922-40
Edgbaston, Birmingham 1922; Oxted, Surrey 1940. † B 4, L 1, SWA 1.

GILBERT, Minnie F.W. Exh. 1889
Fruit painter. 93 Paris Street, Exeter, Devon. † RA 1.

GILBERT, Michel Gerard Exh. 1939
† GOU 4.

GILBERT, Millicent J. Exh. 1936
Sculptor. South Ascot, Berks. † RA 1.

GILBERT, Miss Oriana Pond Exh. 1880-91
Vanbrugh Park, Blackheath, London. † B 1, RBA 19.

GILBERT, Stephen b. 1910
Flower painter. 11 Meadow Studios, Bushey, Herts. 1936. † RA 1.

GILBERT, V. Exh. 1886
† TOO 1.

GILBERT, Varnee Exh. 1888
Portrait painter. 15 Hartesmere Road, Walham Green, London. † RBA 1.

GILBERT, Victor* Exh. 1880-83
Paris. † GI 2, RHA 3.

GILBERT, Walter 1871-1946
Sculptor, metal worker and designer. Collaborated with Louis Weingartner in several works, e.g. The Gates of Buckingham Palace. Studied Municipal School of Art, Birmingham, S. Kensington, France, Belgium and Germany. Taught art at Rugby and Harrow Schools. Travelled in the U.S.A. and India. Father of Donald G. q.v. Exh. 1930. Add: Kensington, London. † B 1.

GILBERT, W.A. Exh. 1892-95
Fallowfield, Manchester. † M 2.

GILBERT, William H. Exh. 1884-88
Portrait painter. London. † L 1, RBA 1.

GILBERTSON, Alfred Exh. 1895-1930
Liverpool. † L 6.

GILBERTSON, J.J. Exh. 1888-1922
Liverpool 1888; Llanbedr, Talycafn, Wales 1915. † L 9, RCA 11.

GILBERTSON, Mary Exh. 1918-19
7 Hogarth Hill, Hendon, London. † LS 4.

GILCHRIST, Alexander P. Exh. 1921-28
Painter and etcher. London. † GI 4, L 2, RA 2.

GILCHRIST, Herbert H. Exh. 1880-1914
Portrait and figure painter. London 1880 and 1910; Hollingborne, Kent 1906. † B 3, G 3, GI 1, L 2, LS 2, P 6, RA 21, ROI 2.

GILCHRIST, Miss J.A. Exh. 1885-1913
Landscape and coastal painter. St. Kilda, Sidmouth, Devon. † D 66, RI 3, RSA 1, SWA 20.

GILCHRIST, J.D. Exh. 1937
82 Ardshiel Road, Glasgow. † GI 2.

GILCHRIST, Martha M. Exh. 1931-33
8 Herries Road, Maxwell Park, Glasgow. † GI 2, RSA 3.

GILCHRIST, Mary S. Exh. 1883-85
Manse, Shotts., N.B. † RSA 3.

GILCHRIST, Philip Thomson 1865-1956
Landscape and marine painter. Studied under Tom Mostyn. R.B.A. 1906. Add: Manchester 1891; Southport, Lancs. 1900; Sunderland Point, Lancs. 1911. † B 1, GI 2, L 33, M 12, NG 1, RA,7, RBA 39, RHA 2, RSA 3.

GILCHRIST, Miss R.R. Exh. 1919
86 Inverleith Place, Edinburgh. † RSA 1.

GILCHRIST, W.W. Junr. Exh. 1911
† BRU 1.

GILDARD, Robert J. Exh. 1899-1900
23 Marchmont Crescent, Glasgow. † GI 2, RSA 1.

GILDAWIE, James Exh. 1880
31 Broughton Street, Edinburgh. † RSA 1.

GILENA, O. Exh. 1889
c/o W. Severn, Esq., 9 Earls Court Square, London. † D 1.

GILES, Alice B. Exh. 1903
Landscape painter. 166 Lambeth Road, London. † RA 1.

GILES, Albert J. Exh. 1922-40
Landscape painter. 241 Mansel Road, Small Heath, Birmingham. † B 29, RA 1, RCA 2.

GILES, Mrs. Ada M. See SHRIMPTON

GILES, Catherine Exh. 1919-28
London. † I 1, NEA 5.

GILES, Edith Exh. 1891
Landscape painter. 8 Union Road, Tufnell Park, London. † RBA 1.

GILES, Frances S. Exh. 1889
Landscape painter. 60 Nevern Square, London. † SWA 2.

GILES, Godfrey Douglas 1857-1923
Painter of horses, battles and military scenes. b. India and served with the army in India, Afghanistan and Egypt. Studied in Paris. Exh. 1882-1904. Add: London 1882; Newmarket 1904. † G 1, GI 1, L 4, M 2, RA 4, RBA 1, ROI 1, RSA 1.

GILES, John Exh. 1894
Architect. 28 Craven Street, Charing Cross, London. † RA 1.

GILES, Linton Exh. 1940
Figure and landscape painter. Ilford, Essex and Raynes Park, London. † RA 3, RBA 2.

GILES, Margaret M. Exh. 1884-1909
Mrs. Bernard Jenkins. Portrait and figure painter. London. † GI 12, NG 1, RA 21, RBA 1, RID 10.

GILES, William b. 1872
Watercolour painter and colour print artist. b. Reading. Studied Royal College of Art, Paris, Scandinavia, Germany and Italy. Exh. 1899-1933. Add: Reading, Berks. 1899; London 1908. † CHE 4, GI 8, I 4, L 20, LS 8, RA 7, RI 3, ROI 2, RSA 2.

GILFILLAN, Arthur Exh. 1893-1938
Dennistoun, N.B. 1893; Glasgow 1899. † GI 5, RSA 1, RSW 4.

GILFILLAN, James R. Exh. 1928
Drumhart, Eglinton Street, Saltcoats. † GI 1.

GILFILLAN, Miss M.A. Exh. 1913
9 Muswell Avenue, Muswell Hill, London. † L 7.

GILFILLAN, Tom Exh. 1932-40
Saltcoats 1932; Glasgow 1940. † GI 3, RSA 1.

GILFORD, Noel See ADENEY, Noel Gilford

GILKES, Pamela D.M. Exh. 1937
Still life painter. Ames House, 44 Mortimer Street, London. † RA 1.

GILKS, Brian M. Exh. 1930-36
88 Claverton Street, London. † NEA 2.

GILL, Mrs. Betty Gilson Exh. 1924-39
Landscape painter. Northwood, Middlesex 1924; Ryde, I.O.W. 1935. † GOU 1, L 1, RA 1, RI 3, SWA 3.

GILL, Christopher Exh. 1884-86
Decorative designer. London. † RA 2.

GILL, Colin Unwin 1892-1940
Decorative and genre painter. b. Bexley Heath, Kent. Studied Slade School, Rome Scholarship 1913. Official war artist 1919-20. On staff Royal College of Art 1922-25. Add: Cudham, Kent 1913; London 1922. † CG 25, CHE 4, G 5, GI 1, L 1, LEI 1, NEA 24, RA 12.

GILL, Edmund* 1820-1894
Landscape and coastal painter. Add: Linn Villa, Sutton, Surrey 1880. † L 2, M 7, RA 6, RBA 4, RHA 1, ROI 1, TOO 23.

GILL, Elizabeth Exh. 1910
26 Freer Road, Birchfield, Birmingham. † B 2.

GILL, Eric* 1882-1940
Sculptor, wood engraver and draughtsman. b. Brighton. Apprenticed to Architect 1899-1903. Among his works the Stations of the Cross in Westminster Cathedral. A.R.A. 1937. Add: London 1924; High Wycombe, Bucks. 1938. † AG 2, COO 2, GI 4, GOU 83, I 2, L 3, RA 13, RED 28, RHA 1, RSA 12.

GILL, Ernest Exh. 1928-31
Sheffield 1928; South Shields 1931. † GI 2, RSA 3.

GILL, Miss E.A. Exh. 1920-22
310 Franklin Road, King's Norton, Birmingham. † B 3.

GILL, E.M. Exh. 1884-98
Landscape painter. Apps Court, West Molesey, Surrey. † SWA 9.

GILL, F. Exh. 1892
56 Brunswick Road, Liverpool. † M 1.

GILL, Frank Exh. 1882
Warfield, Bracknell, Berks. † GI 2.

GILL, Mrs. F.M. Exh. 1899
29 Trafford Chambers, St. John Street, Liverpool. † L 1.

GILL, Miss Florence M. Exh. 1894-1926
London 1894; Liverpool 1898 and 1902; Watford, Herts. 1901; Milngavie, N.B. 1912; Newcastle-on-Tyne 1920. † GI 2, L 16, RI 1.

GILL, H. Exh. 1882-84
Birmingham. † B 5.

GILL, H.P. Exh. 1914-30
Landscape, figure painter and architect. A.N.S.A. 1921, N.S.A. 1927 (secretary 1923-24). Add: Nottingham. † N 28.

GILL, Harry Pelling d. 1916
Landscape painter. Exh. 1881-82. Add: 18 Bramerton Street, Kings Road, London. † D 1, RBA 3, RHA 1.

GILL, Miss Janet M. Exh. 1926-27
141 Duthie Terrace, Aberdeen. † L 6.

GILL, L.M. Exh. 1907-10
16 Old Buildings, Lincoln's Inn, London. † RA 2.

GILL, Macdonald 1884-1947
Architect and mural painter. Studied Chichester Art School and Central School of Arts and Crafts. Exh. 1913-23. Add: 1 Hare Court, Temple, London. † RA 2.

GILL, Muriel Exh. 1936
Engraver. † RED 1.

GILL, Richard Exh. 1907
5 South View Terrace, Yeadon, Leeds. † RCA 1.

GILL, R.A. Exh. 1880-86
Watercolour landscape painter. 1 Bow Churchyard, London. † D 3, RA 1, RBA 1, RI 1.

GILL, Rosa M.F. Exh. 1880
Landscape painter. Ulverston House, Portinscale Road, Putney, London. † SWA 1.

GILL, Rowland Roy Exh. 1910-40
Painter and etcher. b. Bridport, Dorset. Studied Royal College of Art and Juliens, Paris. Served as Captain in Royal Engineers World War I. A.R.E. 1920. Add: London. † I 2, M 1, NEA 4, RA 14, RE 24.

GILL, Winifrid Exh. 1914
Interior painter. † ALP 1.

GILL, William Exh. 1936-40
Chard Street, Axminster, Devon. † NEA 1, RI 1, ROI 3.

GILLAM, Ernest Exh. 1930-37
Landscape and cattle painter. 56 Leverton Street, Kentish Town, London. † RA 4.

GILLAM, William C.F. Exh. 1899-1910
Architect. 162 North Street, Brighton. † RA 2.

GILLAN, Isabel Joan. b. 1894
nee Clarke. Flower, portrait and landscape painter. b. Southsea, Hants. Studied Norwich School of Art and St. Ives, Cornwall. Exh. 1933-39. Add: Sunrise Cottage, Avenue South, Sheringham, Norfolk. † RA 1, RI 4, SWA 4.

GILLANDERS, J.B. Exh. 1891
17 King's Crescent, Aberdeen. † RSA 1.

GILLARD, W.B. Exh. 1883-84
Chester 1883; Handley, Cheshire 1884. † B 2.

GILLES, Paul Exh. 1912
238 Rue de Vaugirard, Paris. † L 1.

GILLESPIE, Alexander Bryson Exh. 1906-40
Edinburgh 1906; Corstorphine 1939. † GI 11, L 2, RSA 45, RSW 17.

GILLESPIE, Alexander L. Exh. 1888-99
10 Walker Street, Edinburgh. † RSA 3, RSW 2.

GILLESPIE, D. Exh. 1908-17
West Bridgford, Nottingham. † N 4.

GILLESPIE, Dugald H. Exh. 1936-40
4 McAlister Avenue, Airdrie. † GI 7, RSA 1.

GILLESPIE, Ethel C. Exh. 1902-8
London. † M 1, RI 1.

GILLESPIE, Florence Exh. 1906
The Crescent, Boyle, Co. Roscommon. † RHA 2.

GILLESPIE, Floris Mary Exh. 1926-40
Painter and teacher. Sister of Janetta S.G. q.v. Studied Glasgow School of Art. Add: Bonnybridge, Stirlingshire 1926; Stranraer 1930. † GI 12, L 3, RSA 7, RSW 14.

GILLESPIE, H.L. Exh. 1895
4 Oxford Street, Edinburgh. † RSA 1.

GILLESPIE, James Exh. 1903-4
6 Bruntsfield Gardens, Edinburgh. † RSA 2.

GILLESPIE, J. Staff Exh. 1902
53 Bothwell Street, Glasgow. † GI 1.

GILLESPIE, Janetta S. d. 1956
Painter and teacher. Sister of Floris Mary G. q.v. Studied Glasgow School of Art. Exh. 1928-40. Add: Rosarnach, Bonnybridge, Stirlingshire. † GI 15, L 2, RSA 18, RSW 20.

GILLESPIE, Mrs. L. Exh. 1881-82
Netherlea, Dumfries. † GI 2.

GILLET, John Exh. 1886-92
Miniature portrait painter. London. † RA 5.

GILLET, R. Exh. 1883
30 Treborth Street, Princes' Park, Liverpool. † L 2.

GILLETT, Miss D.E.L. Exh. 1911-12
Battersea Park, London. † SWA 3.

GILLETT, Edward Frank 1874-1927
Painter, black and white artist and illustrator. b. Worlingham, Suffolk. On the staff of the "Daily Graphic" 1898-1908, "Black and White" 1908-11 and "Illustrated Sporting and Dramatic" 1910-23. R.I. 1909. Add: St. Albans, Herts. 1909; London 1911; Beccles, Suffolk 1918. † FIN 2, GI 2, L 2, RA 2, RI 46.

GILLETT, M. Louise Exh. 1923-39
† RMS 4, SWA 2.

GILLETT, W.F. Exh. 1881-84
London. † D 3, L 1.

GILLETT, William J. Exh. 1884
Watercolour landscape painter. 1 Upper George Street, Bryanston Square, London. † RBA 2.

GILLI, Alberto M. Exh. 1887
Etcher. Calcographie Royale, Rome. A.R.E. 1887-89. † RA 1.

GILLIARD, Claude b. 1906
Landscape painter. Exh. 1939-40. Add: Charlton Park, Keynsham, Som. † RCA 3.

GILLICK, Ernest George d. 1951
Sculptor. Studied Royal College of Art. Married Mary G. q.v. A.R.A. 1935. Exh. 1904-39. Add: London. † I 1, L 1, RA 33, RSA 1.

GILLICK, Mary G. d. 1965
nee Tutin. Sculptor, medallist. Studied Royal College of Art. Married Ernest George G. q.v. Exh. 1911-40. Add: 14A Cheyne Row, Chelsea, London. † RA 27.

GILLIES, Harold Exh. 1933-40
59 Frognal, Hampstead, London. † ROI 15.

GILLIES, Margaret 1803-1887
Genre and miniature painter. Studied under Frederick Cruickshank and in Paris 1851 under Ary Scheffer. A.R.W.S. 1852. Add: 25 Church Row, Hampstead, London 1880. † G 1, L 1, RSW 7.

GILLIES, Mrs. Margaret* Exh. 1936
Gerrards Cross, Bucks. † SWA 1.

GILLIES, Mrs. Marjorie Exh. 1938-39
Closeburn, Gerrards Cross, Bucks. † RI 1, RSA 1.

GILLIES, W.G. Exh. 1890-1924
West Regent Street, Glasgow. † GI 28, RSA 1.

GILLIES, William George* 1898-1973
Landscape and still life painter. Studied Edinburgh College of Art, Italy and under Andre Lhote in Paris. Exh. 1927-39. Add: Edinburgh. † BAR 6, RSA 7.

GILLIGAN, Barbara b. 1914
Landscape painter. Studied Slade School and under Cedric Morris at the East Anglian School of Art. Exh. 1933. † COO 2.

GILLILAND, Mrs. Annie Moore Exh. 1909-36
Land and seascape painter. Studied under W.L. Wyllie. Became colour blind World War I, and gave up painting. Add: Londonderry. † B 1, LS 3, SWA 1, WG 45.

GILLING, Mrs. Gertrude F. Exh. 1926
Miniature portrait painter. Edenbridge, Broxbourne, Herts. † L 4, RA 1.

GILLIVERY, J.P.M. Exh. 1883
112 Bath Street, Glasgow. † RSA 1.

GILLMAN, Edith J. Exh. 1908
Flower painter. † BG 2.

GILLMAN, Gustave Exh. 1880-81
2 Harrington Mansions, Queens' Gate, London. † D 5.

GILL-MARK, Mary Exh. 1931-38
Landscape painter. 14 Chapel Street, London. † NEA 1, RA 1

GILLOT, Eugene Louis* Exh. 1903-14
Landscape and figure painter. 17 Quai Voltaire, Paris. † FIN 2, I 2, L 5, RSA 1.

GILLOTT, A.H. Exh. 1923-25
Still life painter. The Square, Heanor, Notts. † N 3.

GILLOTT, Kitty Exh. 1920-25
Still life painter. The Square, Heanor, Notts. † N 6.

GILLOTT, T.J. Exh. 1908-13
Upland House, Eastwood, Notts. † L 1, N 8.

GILMAN, Grace Cawedy Exh. 1905-8
Snargate Rectory, Romney Marsh, Kent. † LS 5, P 1.

GILMAN, Harold 1876-1919
Landscape, interior, figure and portrait painter. b. Somerset. Studied Hastings School of Art 1896, Slade School 1897. Founder Member and first President of the London Group 1913. "The Artist's Mother" (c. 1913) purchased by Chantrey Bequest 1943 and "Edwardian Interior" (c. 1900-5) 1956. Commissioned by Canadian Government for the War Memorial Fund at Ottawa. Add: Pangbourne, Berks. 1904; Snargate Rectory, Romney Marsh, Kent 1913; London 1914. † BG 1, CAR 32, GOU 38, LEI 61, LS 26, NEA 13, ROI 1.

GILMER, Arthur Exh. 1914
35 Wellington Place, Belfast. † RHA 2.

GILMORE, Miss A. Exh. 1913
128 Piccadilly, London. † RA 1.

GILMORE, Agnes G. Exh. 1905-8
Baddow Hall, Chelmsford, Essex. † GI 2, L 2, LS 5, RMS 2.

GILMOUR, A. Exh. 1925
Omiha, Swanage, Dorset. † SWA 1.

GILMOUR, Ellen Exh. 1880
Landscape and interior painter. Sandygate, Sheffield. † SWA 2.

GILMOUR, George Fisher Exh. 1940
Studied Kingston on Thames, School of Art. Add: 34 Penrhyn Road, Kingston on Thames. † RBA 2.

GILMOUR, James Exh. 1886-1937
Glasgow 1886, 1911 and 1935; Liverpool 1907 and 1926; Crossmyloof, N.B. 1908. † GI 7, L 5, RSA 1, RSW 3.

GILMOUR, Miss L. Exh. 1894
Newholme, Addlestone, Surrey. † SWA 1.

GILMOUR, Miss Lilian Exh. 1908-32
Blundellsands, Liverpool 1908; Heswall, Cheshire 1911; Liverpool 1922; Hoylake, Cheshire 1930; Hemel Hempstead, Herts. 1931. † B 1, L 23, NEA 1, P 1, RCA 8, SWA 1.

GILMOUR, Miss Margaret Exh. 1880-1907
Glasgow. † GI 11, RSA 1.

GILMOUR, Lady Montrave Exh. 1899
Levon, Fife. † SWA 3.

GILMOUR, Mary A.B. Exh. 1896-1906
8 Ailsa Drive, Langside, N.B. † GI 3, RSW 1.

GILOSSI, G. Exh. 1882-83
Landscape painter. Farnham Common, Slough 1882; Burnham, Bucks. 1883. † RBA 2.

GILPIN-BROWN, Miss L.D. Exh. 1905-10
Elmley Lodge, Leamington, Warwicks. † B 1, L 2.

GILROY, John T. Exh. 1927-40
Landscape, figure and portrait painter. The Cottage, High Park Road, Kew Gardens, London. † FIN 125, M 2, P 5, RA 8, ROI 1.

GILROY, John W. Exh. 1898-1904
Seascape painter. Gas Office Chambers, Granger Street West, Newcastle. † L 1, RA 1.

GILSOUL, Victor* b. 1867
Belgian artist. Exh. 1908-9. 50 Rue de la Vallee, Brussels. † L 1, LS 5.

GIMBRETT, Miss A. Exh. 1909-14
Miniature painter. 30 St. Mark's Road, North Kensington, London. † RA 3.

GIMMI, Wilhelm* Exh. 1928-38
Figure painter. † BA 1, GOU 6.

GIMSON, Ernest W. Exh. 1917
Pinbury, Nr. Cirencester, Glos. † RSA 1.

GIMSON, Miss N.K. Exh. 1929
Springfield House, Chelmsford, Essex. † B 2.

GINESI, Edna b. 1902
Landscape and figure painter and interior decorator. Studied Leeds School of Art and Royal College of Art. Married Raymond Coxon q.v. Member London Group 1933. Exh. 1935-40. Add: London. † BK 1, COO 6, LEI 3, M 1.

GINGER, George Exh. 1935
Figure and interior painter. 25 Shas Road, Acton, London. † RA 1.

GINGER, Phyllis E. Exh. 1938-40
Painter and lithographer. 6 Belsize Square, London. † RA 4.

GINHAM, Percy N. Exh. 1902
Architect. 11 Hart Street, Bloomsbury, London. † A 1.

GINNER, Charles* 1878-1952
Painter and wood engraver. b. Cannes, France. Studied Paris. Went to Buenos Aires 1909. Settled in London 1910. Official War artist World War I. N.E.A. 1920, R.O.I. 1932, A.R.W.S. 1938. Founder Member London Group 1913. "Hartland Point from Boscastle" purchased by Chantrey Bequest 1941. Exh. 1908-39. † BK 1, CAR 8, CHE 2, COO 4, FIN 6, G 1, GI 1, GOU 138, L 4, LEI 37, LS 33, NEA 40, RED 33, ROI 11, RSW 1, RWS 11.

GINNETT, Louis c. 1875-1946
Portrait and interior painter and decorative artist. R.O.I. 1908. Add: London 1906; Ditchling, Sussex 1919. † COO 2, FIN 28, GOU 2, I 1, L 10, LS 4, M 1, NEA 1, RA 30, RHA 1, RI 6, ROI 74.

GIOJA, Edouardo 1862-1937
Portrait painter. 58 Glebe Place, Chelsea, London 1922-23. † L 1, RA 2.

GIOLI, Francesco* Exh. 1880-87
Landscape painter. London. † G 1, L 1, M 1, RA 1, RBA 1.

GIORDANI, Italo Exh. 1921
† GOU 1.

GIORGIO, di See D

GIORSIE, Carlo Exh. 1890
c/o Mrs. Silver, Beechcroft, Oatlands Park, London. † D 1.

GIOVANNI, de See D

GIRALDON, Adolphe 1855-1933
French artist. 167 Renfrew Street, Glasgow and 69 Boulevard St. Jaques, Paris 1905-11. † GI 2, I 2, RSA 1.

GIRARD, A. Exh. 1883
69 Rue de Courcelles, Paris. † GI 1.

GIRARD, Founan Exh. 1883
Paris. † GI 1.

GIRARDET, Eugene* 1853-1908
French artist. Exh. 1883-90. Add: Paris. † GI 12.

GIRARDET, Jules* b. 1865
French artist. Exh. 1883-1904. Add: 12 Rue Pergolise, Paris. † GI 9, L 2.

GIRARDET, Leon 1857-1895
French artist. 7 bis Rue Remont, Versailles, Paris 1883. † GI 1.

GIRARDOT, Ernest Gustave* Exh. 1880-1904
Portrait, figure and domestic painter. R.B.A. 1874. Add: London. † GI 3, L 3, RA 9, RBA 17, RHA 8, RSA 1.

GIRARDOT, G.M.J. Exh. 1908-11
48 Rue Cardinet, Paris. † L 1, LS 4.

GIRARDOT, Henri Exh. 1909
c/o Allied Artists Assn. 67 Chancery Lane, London. † LS 3.

GIRARDOT, Louis Auguste Exh. 1910-12
68 Rue d'Assas, Paris. † L 3.

GIRARDOT, Mrs. Mary J. Exh. 1909-13
A.S.W.A. 1913. Longham, Surrey 1909; London 1911. † B 1, ROI 1, SWA 7.

GIRAUD, Exh. 1924
† GOU 1.

GIRAUDAT, Edgard Exh. 1887
Landscape painter. 62 Avenue du Bois de Boulogne, Paris. † RA 1.

GIRDLESTONE, Lucy Exh. 1886-88
Flower painter. Sunningdale, Berks. † B 3, RBA 2.

GIRDWOOD, Sheila Exh. 1937
9 Elmer Gardens, Edgward, Middlesex. † RA 1.

GIRLANO, F.F. Exh. 1883
c/o Italian Consul, Manchester. † M 1.
GIRLING, Miss D. Exh. 1905-11
28 Warwick Gardens, Kensington, London. † RA 2, SWA 2.
GIRLING, Millicent Exh. 1922-29
4 Garville Road, Rathgar, Dublin. † RHA 12.
GIROD, Alexander Exh. 1924
Figure painter. Les Petits Monts, sur le Locle, Switzerland. † RA 1.
GIRON, Louis F. Exh. 1919-28
5 Charleville Road, North Circular Road, Dublin. † RHA 4.
GIROUST, Rene Exh. 1912
† GOU 2.
GISBORNE, C. Exh. 1901
43 Welbeck Street, Nottingham. † N 1.
GISBORNE, Miss E.M. Exh. 1886
64 Conning Street, Liverpool. † L 1.
GITTENS, Edith Exh. 1883-93
Salisbury Road, Leicester. † D 1, L 1, RI 4, SWA 1.
GITTES, A. Exh. 1933
Figure painter. † RED 1.
GITTINS, Mrs. Addie Exh. 1895
Grassmere, Moseley, Birmingham. † B 1.
GITTINS, Miss D.E. Exh. 1914
Wallasey, Cheshire 1914; Leicester 1915. † L 1, N 2.
GITTLESON, Albert Abram Exh. 1911-40
Portrait, landscape and miniature painter. Teacher and restorer. Born Kovno, Russia. Studied Leeds School of Art, Royal College of Art, under Owen Bowen and abroad. Married Sadie G. q.v. Add: Leeds 1911 and 1921; Dublin 1919; Glasgow 1929. † GI 4, L 1, RA 1, RCA 1, RHA 8, RSA 5.
GITTLESON, Sadie Exh. 1928
nee Michaelson. Married Albert Abram G. q.v. Add: 47 Camphill Avenue, Langside, Glasgow. † GI 1, RSA 1.
GIUDICI, Miss J. Exh. 1928
Park View, Croom's Hill, London. † L 2.
GIULIANI, Amedeo Exh. 1913-15
722 Argyle Street, Glasgow. † GI 4, RSA 1.
GIULIANI, Giulio Exh. 1903
Sunny Croft, Pinner, Middlesex. † L 1.
GIUSTI, Giuseppe Exh. 1900-13
Figure painter. London 1900 and 1912; St. Ives, Cornwall 1910. † I 1, L 3, LS 6, NEA 1, P 1, RA 3, RSA 1.
GIVEN, David Exh. 1891
23 Ann Street, Edinburgh. † RSA 1.
GLACKENS, William Exh. 1925
Figure painter. † CHE 1.
GLADNEY, Graves Exh. 1931
† NEA 2.
GLADSTONE, Miss C. Exh. 1902-7
Woolton Vale, Liverpool. † L 3.
GLADSTONE, Mrs. Grace E. Exh. 1902-7
Landscape painter. Mansfield House, Canning Town, London. † RA 4.
GLADSTONE, Helen Exh. 1898-1904
Woolton Valve, Liverpool. † L 7.
GLADSTONE, Lindsay Exh. 1937-40
Figure painter. Frimley Park, Frimley, Surrey. † RA 4.
GLADWELL, Allen R. Exh. 1908-9
24 Broadgate, Preston, Lancs. † L 2.
GLAISTER, Hilda Exh. 1923
5 Greenfield Road, Old Swan, Liverpool. † L 1.
GLAISTER, K.G. Exh. 1939
† GOU 1.
GLAIZE, Leon Pierre Paul b. 1842
French artist. Exh. 1883-1913. Add: Rue de Vaugirard, Paris. † G 1, L 2.
GLANDFIELD, Garnet R. Exh. 1913
Garland House, Oswestry. † LS 2.
GLANFIELD, Ernest B. Exh. 1919-40
Architect. 6 Raymond Buildings, London. † RA 2.
GLANSDORFF, Hubert Exh. 1909
28 Rue Lens, Brussels. † L 1.
GLASBEY, Edwin H. Exh. 1922-25
Landscape painter. Lane End, Chapeltown, Sheffield. † GI 2, L 6, RA 4.
GLASBY, William Exh. 1900-23
Stained glass artist. London. † LS 5, RA 10.
GLASGOW, Alexander Exh. 1880-84
Figure and domestic painter. 5 Cromwell Crescent, Cromwell Road, W. Kensington, London. † RA 2, RBA 3.
GLASGOW, Edwin b.1874
Painter and pastellier. b. Liverpool. Studied University College, Liverpool and Wadham College, Oxford. Add: Bootle, Lancs. 1896; Snaresbrook, Essex 1902; Newcastle on Tyne 1909; Birmingham 1927. † B 11, L 16, RA 5, RI 7.
GLASGOW, Miss Roberta Exh. 1908-30
Bootle, Lancs. 1908; Oxton, Birkenhead 1914. † L 26.
GLASS, Dodie Exh. 1938
† NEA 2.
GLASS, Douglas Exh. 1939
† LEF 4.
GLASS, Frederick James 1881-1930
Artist and writer. Studied Bristol Municipal School of Art and Royal College of Art. Headmaster of Doncaster, Darlington and Londonderry Schools of Art. Exh. 1916-18. Add: Londonderry. † RHA 9.
GLASS, John d. 1885
A.R.S.A. 1849. Add: 6 Orchardfield Place, Edinburgh. † RSA 17.
GLASS, John Hamilton Exh. 1890-1925
Edinburgh 1890; Pencaitland, N.B. 1905; Musselburgh, N.B. 1915. † GI 3, L 1, RHA 4, RSA 19.
GLASS, Pauline b. 1908
Portrait and still life painter. Studied Lycee Emile Max, Brussels, Academie des Beaux Arts, Brussels and Birmingham College of Art. Add: Birmingham 1937. † B 1, RA 2.
GLASS, William Mervyn Exh. 1910-40
A.R.S.A. 1934. Edinburgh. † GI 20, I 1, L 4, RA 1, RSA 48.
GLASSBY, Robert Edward Exh. 1883-96
Sculptor. Chelsea, London. † G 4, NG 4, RA 9.
GLASSON, Mrs. Jane Exh. 1929-31
Miniature portrait painter. 51 Addison Avenue, London. † RA 2.
GLASSON, Lancelot Myles b. 1894
Portrait and figure painter. Exh. 1925-38. Add: London. † BAR 5, GI 1, L 1, RA 13, RSA 1.
GLAZEBROOK, F.H. Exh. 1922-37
Chester 1922; Newborough, Anglesey 1925; Treaddur Bay, Anglesey 1932. † L 3, RCA 12.
GLAZEBROOK, Hugh de Twenebrokes 1855-1931
Portrait and landscape painter. R.P. 1891. Exh. 1885-1928. Add: London. † B 25, FIN 73, G 4, GI 4, L 17, LS 5, M 12, NG 25, P 104, RA 53, RHA 10.
GLAZIER, H. Exh. 1884-87
Florence House, Stanley, Longsight, Manchester. † M 4.
GLAZIER, Louise M. Exh. 1902-10
Mitcham, Surrey 1902; Bruges, Belgium 1906. † BG 37, L 10.
GLAZIER, Richard Exh. 1883-92
Architect and art master. Father of Bertha Frost q.v. Add: King's Road, Rochdale, Lancs. 1883; Technical School, Manchester 1886. † L 5, M 7.
GLEADOWE, Reginald Morier Yorke 1888-1944
Painter and designer. Studied Slade School. Art Master Winchester College; Lecturer National Gallery; Assistant to Director National Gallery and Slade professor 1928-33. Exh. 1920-29. † CG 40, G 6, M 1, NEA 3.
GLEAVE, Joseph Lea Exh. 1934
29 Royal Terrace, Edinburgh. † RSA 3.
GLEAVE, W.R. Exh. 1903-4
Architect. Nottingham. † N 7.
GLEAVES, P. Exh. 1910
9 Kingswood Road, Fulham, London. † RA 1.
GLEDHILL, D.W. Exh. 1935-40
71 Branstone Road, Burton-on-Trent. † B 6.
GLEDHILL, James Exh. 1884-91
Llanbedr, N. Wales. † L 2, M 5.
GLEDSTANES, Elsie Exh. 1916-40
Portrait, landscape and figure painter. Studied Slade School, Byam Shaw and Vicat Cole School and Paris. A.R.B.A. 1923, R.B.A. 1930, S.W.A. 1935. Add: London. †, COO 9, L 3, P 1, RA 10, RBA 110, RID 3, SWA 14, WG 5.
GLEDSTONE, R. Exh. 1900
North Ferriby, Brough, E. Yorks. † L 2.
GLEHN, de See D
GLEHN, Von See V
GLEICHE, Max Exh. 1909-24
Dublin. † RHA 20.
GLEICHEN, The Countess Feodora 1861-1922
Sculptor. Studied under her father Victor G. q.v. and at the Slade School and in Rome. Sister of Helena G. q.v. R.E. 1884. Add: St. James's Palace, London. † G 7, GI 4, I 3, L 9, LS 2, NG 29, RA 39, RE 11, RI 1, SWA 3.
GLEICHEN, Lady Helena b. 1873
Landscape and animal painter. Daughter of Victor G. q.v. Studied Rollshoven, Westminster and Calderon's School of Animal Painting. R.B.A. 1910. Exh. 1899-1933. Add: St. James's Palace, London. † ALP 56, BA 1, GI 1, GOU 82, LS 5, M 2, NG 3, RA 11, RBA 7, ROI 4, SWA 8.
GLEICHEN, Count Victor 1833-1891
Prince of Hohenloe. Sculptor. Admiral in the Royal Navy. b. Wurtemburg, Germany. d. London. H.R.I. 1884. Add: St. James's Palace, London. † G 21, L 3, RA 18.
GLEN, Graham* Exh. 1897-1915
Edinburgh 1897; Chelsea, London 1915. † GI 5, L 1, M 1, RA 2, RSA 27.
GLEN, John Anderson Exh. 1921-22
8 Bain Street, Cambusland. † GI 5.
GLEN, J. Scott Exh. 1894
30 Lilybank Gardens, Hillhead, Glasgow. † GI 1.
GLENAVY, Lady Beatrice 1883-1970
nee Elvery. Painter, stained glass artist and modeller. Studied Dublin School of Art and Slade School (won Taylor Scholarship 3 times, bronze and silver medals). Teacher Dublin Metropolitan School of Art. A.R.H.A. 1932, R.H.A. 1934. Add: Rothbury, Foxrock, Co. Dublin 1902, Dublin 1932. † RA 2, RCA 2, RHA 48, SWA 1.
GLENDENING, Alfred Junr.* 1861-1907
Landscape, genre and theatrical scenery painter. Studied under his father Alfred Augustus G. q.v. "Haymaking" purchased by Chantrey Bequest 1898. R.B.A. 1890. Add: London. † B 5, BK 17, D 2, DOW 3, L 7, M 4, RA 28, RBA 47, RI 2, ROI 2.

GLENDENING, Alfred Augustus* Exh. 1881-1903
Landscape painter. Father of Alfred G. junr. q.v. Add: London. † D 1, L 8, M 3, RA 22, RBA 4, ROI 3.

GLENN, D. Newsome Exh. 1940
11 Fairfax Road, London. † B 1.

GLENN, William St. John Exh. 1936
6 Chilworth Buildings, Stranmillis Road, Belfast. † RHA 2.

GLENNIE, Arthur* d. 1890
Landscape painter. A.R.W.S. 1837, R.W.S. 1858. Add: 17 Piazza Morgana, Rome. † L 5, RWS 43.

GLENNIE, Miss E.M. Exh. 1906-12
Wimbledon, London. † SWA 4.

GLENNIE, F. Forbes Exh. 1897-1900
Architect. 12 Lansdowne Road, Wimbledon, London. † RA 5.

GLENNIE, George F. Exh. 1880-85
Landscape painter. Bickley, Kent. † D 13, L 2.

GLENNIE, Mrs. G.M. Exh. 1914
Culbleau, Horsell Common, Woking, Surrey. † RA 2.

GLICENSTEIN, Prof. Henry b. 1870
Sculptor. b. Poland. Add: Rome 1905; 112 Haverstock Hill, London 1923. † GI 1, I 8, L 1, RA 4.

GLIDDON, Katie Exh. 1928-37
Flower painter. 32 Kendall Avenue, Sanderstead, Surrey. † NEA 4, RA 2, SWA 7.

GLINDONI, Henry Gillard* 1852-1913
Genre and historical painter. R.B.A. 1879, A.R.W.S. 1883. Add: London. † B 25, L 35, M 8, RA 32, RBA 41, RE 1, ROI 4, RWS 42.

GLISENTI, A. Achille Exh. 1882
Landscape painter. 75 Westbourne Terrace, Hyde Park, London. † RA 1.

GLISSMANN, Hans Exh. 1940
7 Kingsburgh Road, Edinburgh. † RSA 1.

GLOAG, Angela Mary Dundas Exh. 1927-29
Painter, designer, engraver and sculptor. Studied Chelsea Polytechnic, Slade School, Westminster Technical Institute and Rome. Add: London. † RA 1, SWA 2.

GLOAG, H. de T. Exh. 1893-1915
55 Elm Park Gardens, London. † I 1, P 6.

GLOAG, Isabella Lilian* d. 1917
Portrait, figure and still life painter. Studied S. Kensington, Slade School and Paris. R.O.I. 1910. Exh. 1889-1916. Add: London. † B 8, BG 2, FIN 2, GI 6, I 3, L 8, RA 18, RBA 2, RI 18, RID 76, ROI 21, SWA 1.

GLOAG, Mrs. W.D. See BAKER, Annette

GLOUCESTER, H.R.H. The Duchess of b. 1901
Lady Alice Montagu-Douglas-Scott. Daughter of 7th Duke of Buccleuch. R.S.W. 1938. Exh. 1938-39. Add: St. James's Palace, London. † GI 2, RSW 2.

GLOVER, Arthur Exh. 1913-40
Sculptor. London. † RA 12, RSW 1.

GLOVER, Albert A. Exh. 1889
27 Robart's Road, Anfield, Liverpool. † L 1.

GLOVER, Beatrice Exh. 1924-39
Painter and sculptor. Nottingham 1924; Ruddington, Notts. 1938. † N 18.

GLOVER, F.C. Exh. 1935-39
Still life painter. 11 Holme Street, Meadow Lane, Nottingham. † N 4.

GLOVER, Miss Hannah Exh. 1884
9 South End, Croydon, Surrey. † ROI 1.

GLOVER, John Exh. 1891-1900
Dublin. † AG 1, RHA 11.

GLOVER, J. McN. Exh. 1904
Hazelwood, Dumfries, N.B. † RSA 1.

GLOVER, Richard S. Exh. 1923
Landscape painter. Blyth House, Southwold, Suffolk. † RA 1.

GLOVER, Sidney Exh. 1911
Urban landscape painter. † GOU 2.

GLOVER, William Exh. 1880-1900
Glasgow 1880 and 1894; Rutherglen, N.B. 1891; Cumbermauld, N.B. 1898. † GI 24, RSA 4, RSW 34.

GLUCK Exh. 1926
Figure and landscape painter. c/o Fine Art Society Ltd., 138 New Bond Street, London. † GI 1, FIN 44.

GLYDE, Henry G. Exh. 1931-33
Mythological figure painter. Kenton, Middlesex 1931; Totteridge, High Wycombe, Bucks. 1933. † RA 4, RBA 1.

GLYDON, Miss M. Exh. 1882-86
Birmingham. † B 3.

GLYN, Leo C. Exh. 1921
c/o Messrs Chenil & Co. King's Road, Chelsea, London. † RCA 1.

GLYNN, John Exh. 1891-1940
Liverpool 1891; Hoylake, Cheshire 1896; Caldy, Cheshire 1908; Crowborough, Sussex 1924. † L 72, RA 6, RCA 2, RI 18.

GLYNN, Miss L. Exh. 1906-7
Sefton House, Sefton Park, Liverpool. † L 3.

GLYNN, Mrs. M.L. Exh. 1894-1916
Hoylake, Cheshire 1894; Caldy, Cheshire 1909. † L 20.

GLYNN, Thomas Robinson b. 1841
Landscape and interior painter. Exh. 1900-27. Add: Liverpool 1900; St. Asaph, N. Wales 1926. † L 16, RCA 1.

GNISTA, Erik Exh. 1933
Flysta, Petersberg, Spanga, Sweden. † RSA 2.

GOAD, Mrs. Howard Exh. 1926
Landscape painter. † WG 48.

GOAD, Mrs. M. Exh. 1934
219 Knightsbridge, London. † ROI 1.

GOADBY, L.S. Exh. 1884
Henley on Thames. † D 1.

GOADBY, Miss L.S. Exh. 1906-9
Tilehurst, Berks. † SWA 3.

GOARD, W.H. Exh. 1938
† M 1.

GOATER, Miss Ira Exh. 1895-96
Landscape painter. Nottingham. † N 2.

GOBL, Hermann Exh. 1908
Schottenfeldgasse 26, Vienna. † B 6.

GOBLE, Warwick Exh. 1893-1924
Watercolour painter and illustrator. On staff of "Pall Mall Gazette" and "Westminster Gazette". Add: London 1893; Surbiton, Surrey 1923. † FIN 115, L 2, RA 3, WG 95.

GODBOLD, Samuel Berry Exh. 1880
Portrait and figure painter. 60 Gloucester Place, Portman Square, London. † RHA 1.

GODDARD, Diana Exh. 1936
Sculptor and potter. c/o The Turret Studio, Castle View, The Newarke, Leicester. † N 5.

GODDARD, Miss D.M. Exh. 1901-7
London and Bushey, Herts. † RBA 1, SWA 3.

GODDARD, Eliza Exh. 1884-97
Flower painter. Rotten Row, Christchurch, Hants. † RA 1, SWA 2.

GODDARD, Lt. Col. Francis Ambrose D'Oyley b. 1868
Landscape painter. A.R.M.S. 1937. Exh. 1932-40. Add: 45 Warwick Road, London. † AR 31, B 10, RA 1, RMS 16, ROI 3.

GODDARD, George Bouverie 1832-1886
Sporting and animal painter. b. Salisbury. Add: London. † B 3, FIN 1, G 1, L 3, RA 5.

GODDARD, Henry L. Exh. 1899
Architect. 6 Market Street, Leicester. † RA 1.

GODDARD, J. Bedloe Exh. 1880-94
Landscape painter. Christchurch, Hants. † B 4, D 10, RBA 4, RI 2.

GODDARD, Miss K.M. Exh. 1901-3
Alipore, 39 Crockerton Road, Upper Tooting, London. † SWA 5.

GODDARD, Louis Charles Exh. 1901-21
Portrait painter. Stockport, Lancs. 1901; Mansfield, Notts. 1902; Manchester 1913; Wallasey, Cheshire 1920. † B 1, BRU 1, L 4, N 2.

GODDARD, Muriel Exh. 1914
Oban, Bournemouth, Hants. † LS 3, SWA 1.

GODDARD, Rainald W.K. Exh. 1892-99
Architect. 133 Denmark Hill, London. † RA 3.

GODDARD, William Charles Exh. 1885
55 Mornington Road, Regents Park, London. † RI 1.

GODDEN, Charles Edward Victor b. 1901
Dry point, pencil and chalk artist. Studied Portsmouth School of Art 1922-24, Goldsmith's College 1934-39. Exh. 1939. † RA 2.

GODDEN, W. Exh. 1886
Ridgfield, Wimbledon, London. † D 1.

GODDING, Ernest F.G. Exh. 1928-30
9 The Pentagon, Sea Mills, Bristol. † RCA 2.

GODET, Henri Exh. 1907
52 Rue de Rendezvous, Paris. † L 1.

GODET, Julius Exh. 1880-94
Landscape painter. London. † B 8, GI 6, L 2, M 2, RBA 3, RI 1.

GODFREY, Miss Exh. 1881-84
Landscape and flower painter. Brookhouse, Ash, Sandwich, Kent. † SWA 3.

GODFREY, Mrs. Amy Exh. 1902-4
43 St. Michael's Road, Bedford. † B 5, RCA 1.

GODFREY, I.P. Exh. 1931
† NEA 1.

GODFREY, J.K. Exh. 1937
Landscape painter. † COO 3.

GODFREY, Miss Lil Exh. 1897-1908
The Greenway, Cheltenham, Glos. † B 7.

GODFREY, Louis Exh. 1885-92
Engraver. London. † RA 3.

GODFREY, L.M. (Ellen) Exh. 1882
Portrait painter. 31 Emery Street, Cambridge. † RA 1.

GODFREY, Mary C. Exh. 1913-19
Enameller. 34 Twyford Avenue, Acton, London. † RA 4.

GODFREY, Mabel Molesworth Exh. 1913-40
Landscape, interior and still life painter. Studied under Fred Milner, Chelsea and London Schools of Art, and Stratford Studios. Add: The Haven, Mill Street, Houghton, Hunts. † GOU 2, I 1, L 4, LS 12, RA 4, RBA 1, RCA 1, RHA 5, ROI 12, RSA 7, SWA 9.

GODFREY, Phyllis M. Exh. 1920-38
Painter and linocut artist. Dublin 1920; Milltown, Co. Kerry 1924; Glasnevin 1930. † RHA 36.

GODFREY, Walter Hindes b. 1881
Architect and illustrator. Exh. 1930. Add: Queen Anne's Gate, London. † RA 1.

GODGIFT, J. Exh. 1898
Urban landscape painter. Cercle Artistique, Cairo, Egypt. † RA 1.

GODLEE, Miss R.G. Exh. 1896
Landscape painter. 19 Wimpole Street, London. † NEA 1.
GODLEY, Maude Exh. 1897-98
Drominchin, Carrigallen, Co. Leitrim. † RHA 2, SWA,1.
GODMAN, Jessie Harrison Exh. 1893-1936
nee Harrison. Portrait, landscape and miniature painter, etcher and teacher. Studied Royal College of Art. A.R.E. 1893-1920. Add: London 1893; Dowlais, S.Wales 1897; School of Art, Warrington 1898; London 1899 and 1907; Banstead, Surrey 1904. † L 6, RA 7, RE 30, RMS 1.
GODON, Louis Exh. 1888-90
Sculptor. 141 Church Street, Chelsea, London. † G 2, RBA 1.
GODSAL, Mary Exh. 1887-96
Figure painter. London 1887; Crickhowell, S.Wales 1889; Whitchurch, Salop 1892; Bushey, Herts. 1896. † RA 2, ROI 5, SWA 1.
GODSELL, Mary E. Exh. 1880-1901
Domestic and fruit painter. London 1880; Stroud, Glos. 1896. † B 8, D 2, RA 3, RI 2.
GODSON, Ada Charlotte Exh. 1923-35
Watercolour painter and miniaturist. Studied Berlin, Florence, Paris and Sir Arthur Cope's School. Travelled to India, China, Japan, South America and Egypt. Add: Tenbury, Worcs. † B 2, RI 20.
GODSON, J.B. Exh. 1911
27 Paulton's Square, Chelsea, London. † RA 1.
GODWARD, John William* 1861-1922
Genre painter. R.B.A. 1889. Died of suffocation. Exh. 1886-1916. Add: London. † B 2, CON 1, GI 1, L 8, M 2, NG 7, RA 19, RBA 4, ROI 5, TOO 3.
GODWIN, Charlotte Exh. 1901
Grosvenor Studio, Vauxhall Bridge, London. † RBA 1.
GODWIN, Charlotte Exh. 1929
29 Spencer Road, S.W. London. † ROI 1.
GODWIN, E. Exh. 1901-21
Sculptor. London. † B 2, I 1, GI 2, L 1, RA 7, RMS 1.
GODWIN, Frederica Vincentia di. 1934
nee Pearse. Landscape painter. Studied Newbury School of Art. A.S.W.A. 1914. Add: Rotherhithe, Kent 1906; Reigate, Surrey 1917. † L 4, RA 3, RBA 6, RI 2, ROI 11, SWA 39.
GODWIN, Miss G. Exh. 1921
The Studio, Lyndhurst, Maple Road, East Grinstead, Sussex. † SWA 2.
GODWIN, J. Arthur Exh. 1889-93
Landscape painter. 9 Spring Bank, Bradford, Yorks. † L 5, RBA 3.
GODWINN, Marianne d. 1887
The Caricaturist "Jack". Burnt to death. Exh. 1887. Add: 13 Fitzroy Street, London. † D 2.
GODWIN, Mary 1887-1960
Figure, portrait and domestic painter. Member London Group 1914. Exh. 1913-40. Add: London. † CHE 3, COO 11, GI 1, GOU 5, I 3, LEI 2, LS 15, M 1, NEA 24, RA 2, WG 3.
GOEDHART. Jan F.C. Exh. 1931
Figure painter. 182 Eschdoornstraat, The Hague, Holland. † RA 1.
GOETHEM, Van See V
GOETZ, Walter b. 1911
Landscape painter, illustrator and cartoonist. Exh. 1938. † LEF 2.
GOETZE, Leopold Exh. 1907-14
Etcher. 86 Carlton Hill, London. † L 8, RA 11.
GOETZE, Sigismund 1866-1939
Portrait and figure painter. Exh. 1888-1924. Add: London. † B 3, G 1, GI 1, L 25, M 9, P 2, RA 39, RHA 3, ROI 4, RSA 1.
GOFF, Bertha L. Exh. 1899-1905
Sculptor. London. † RA 7.
GOFF, Frederick E.J. Exh. 1891-1900
Landscape painter. Add: London. † GI 13, RA 3, RI 5.
GOFF, Miss M.M. Exh. 1914
Wilmington Lodge, Nr. Dartford, Kent. † L 1, RA 2.
GOFF, Col. Robert Charles 1837-1922
Landscape painter and etcher. R.E. 1887. Add: London 1880; Brighton 1891 and 1907; Florence, Italy 1903; Tunbridge Wells 1906. † B 7, D 22, FIN 306, G 2, L 15, M 2, NEA 2, RA 18, RE 190, RHA 6, RID 17, RI 20, ROI 18.
GOFFEY, Bertha Exh. 1891-1915
94 Hartington Road, Sefton Park, Liverpool. † L 7.
GOFFEY, Harry 1871-1951
Portrait and landscape painter and etcher. Studied Liverpool School of Art, Herkomer's, Bushey, Herts. and Chelsea Polytechnic. Add: Liscard, Cheshire 1894; Bushey, Herts. 1897 and 1902; Liverpool 1898; Berkhamsted, Herts. 1917. † L 27, RA 11.
GOFFEY, Miss Hilda See ATKINSON
GOFFEY, Mrs. T. Exh. 1888-1911
Amalfi, Blundellsands, Liverpool. † L 31.
GOGARTY, Brenda Exh. 1937-38
Sculptor. 15 Ely Place, Dublin. † RHA 4.
GOGGS, Evelyn Dorothy b. 1900
Book-binder, textile designer and wood engraver. b. Edinburgh. Studied Central School of Arts and Crafts. Exh. 1926. Add: 11 Durrington Park Road, London. † L 4.
GOGIN, Alma Exh. 1895-1901
Mrs. Charles G. Domestic painter. Add: Shoreham, Sussex 1895; Brighton 1898. † B 2, RA 2, RBA 1, SWA 2.
GOGIN, Charles b. 1844
Painter and teacher. Studied RA Schools and Paris. N.E.A. 1886. Add: London 1880; Shoreham, Sussex 1892. † B 2, GI 1, L 4, RA 6, RBA 2, RHA 4, RSA 1, WG 204.
GOLD, Hugh A. Exh. 1922
Architect. 14 Bedford Row, London. † RA 1.
GOLDBERG, Michael Exh. 1931-40
Portrait and figure painter. London. † P 1, RA 4.
GOLDBERG, S. Exh. 1940
Lithographer. 130 Gt. Titchfield Street, London. † RA 2.
GOLDEN, Rev. F.S. Exh. 1925-33
Maney Vicarage, Sutton Coldfield, Warwicks. † B 2.
GOLDEN, Grace L. b. 1904
Painter, black and white and poster artist, and wood engraver. Studied Chelsea Art School and Royal College of Art. "Summer Evening, Embankment Gardens" purchased by Chantrey Bequest 1934 and "Free Speech" 1940. Exh. 1927-40. Add: London. † L 2, RA 6, RBA 2.
GOLDEN, James Exh. 1918
29 Belgrave Road, Dublin. † RHA 1.
GOLDEN, Lilla Exh. 1923
† SWA 1.
GOLDEN, Sheila Ann Exh. 1939-40
Sculptor. 29 Belgrave Road, Rathmines, Dublin. † RHA 2.
GOLDFINCH, Nancy Exh. 1935
6 Courtfield Gardens, London. † RBA 1.
GOLDFOOT, Miss J. Exh. 1912
45 Brondesbury Road, Kilburn, London. † RA 1.
GOLDIE, Cyril Exh. 1910-22
33 Washington Street, St. James' Road, Liverpool. † L 6. NEA 1.
GOLDIE, Charles A. Exh. 1901-12
St. Gervan, Ile et Vilaine, France 1901 and 1911; St. Helier, Jersey, C.I. 1908. † B 2, L 2, LS 5. RA 1.
GOLDIE, Charles Frederick Exh. 1934-35
New Zealand painter. c/o T. Bond, 3 Fawcett Street, London. † RA 4.
GOLDIE, Edward Exh. 1880-1903
Architectural artist. London. † RA 11.
GOLDIE, Lancelot Lyttleton b. 1872
Architect, painter and etcher. b. Elvaston, Nr. Derby. Add: Spondon, Nr. Derby 1902; Irongate, Derby 1910; Co. Durham 1917; Bath 1921. † D 3, L 11, N 19, RA 1, RSA 7, WG 76.
GOLDIE, Marjorie H. Exh. 1936
7 Eyre Terrace, Edinburgh. † RSA 1.
GOLDIE, Pat C. Exh. 1882-88
Edinburgh 1882; Lenzie, N.B. 1887. † GI 6, RSA 5.
GOLDIE, William Exh. 1880-88
Edinburgh. † RSA 13.
GOLDING, Bessie Exh. 1907
Colwyn Cottage, Grove Road, Wallasey, Cheshire. † L 1.
GOLDING, S. Exh. 1888
8 Mulgrave Street, Liverpool. † L 1.
GOLDINGHAM, James A. Exh. 1880-81
Figure painter. Holland Park Road, London. † RA 2.
GOLDRICKE, James Exh. 1897-1903
47 Lyon Street, Whitevale 1897; Glasgow 1900. † GI 3, RSA 1.
GOLDSBOROUGH, Francis Exh. 1922-33
18 Bennett's Hill, Birmingham. † B 9.
GOLDSCHMIDT, Alice Exh. 1891
66 Mount Street, Park Lane, London. † D 3.
GOLDSMID, C. Exh. 1884
Figure painter. 32 Nottingham Place, Regents Park, London. † RBA 1.
GOLDSMID, Miss C. Exh. 1885-89
Kensington, London. † B 4.
GOLDSMID, Evelyn J. Exh. 1886
Sculptor. 45 Bryanston Square, London. † RA 1.
GOLDSMITH, Alfred Exh. 1940
Landscape painter. Fairway, Gravesend Road, Wrotham, Kent. † RA 1.
GOLDSMITH, Beatrice Exh. 1925
31 Cheyne Row, Chelsea, London. † SWA 1.
GOLDSMITH, Bessie Exh. 1921-23
Lettering and illuminating artist. A.R.M.S. 1921. Add: Braeside, Park Road, New Barnet, Herts. † L 1, RMS 7.
GOLDSMITH, E.J. Exh. 1912
Allington Rectory, Grantham, Lincs. † N 1.
GOLDSMITH, Francis T.W. Exh. 1906-22
Architect. 1 Verulam Buildings, Grays Inn, London. † RA 3.
GOLDSMITH, George H. Exh. 1937
Architect. 44 Gt. Russell Street, London. † RA 1.
GOLDSMITH, Henry Exh. 1899-1903
Architect. 63 Faulkner Street, Manchester. † RA 3.
GOLDSMITH, Walter H.* Exh. 1880-98
Landscape painter. Maidenhead, Berks. † B 3, D 5, GI 1, L 5, M 2, RA 18, RBA 24, RHA 4, RI 5, ROI 7.
GOLDSTEIN, Von See V
GOLDSTEIN, Morris Exh. 1913-16
Figure painter. London. † NEA 8.

GOLDTHWAIT, Harold Exh. 1895-192?
Landscape painter. Carshalton, Surrey 1895; Norwood Hill, London 1898; Lewes, Sussex 1910; Brighton 1916. † GOU 3, L 2, LS 8, RA 12, RHA 6, ROI 3.

GOLDTHWAIT, Mrs. Sophy Exh. 1915
3 Wallands Crescent, Lewes, Sussex. † L 1.

GOLE, Lydia Exh. 1895
R.M.S. 1897. 26 Woodsome Road, Highgate, London. † RI 1.

GOLLANCZ, Alide Exh. 1926
Landscape and figure painter. † BA 43.

GOLLANCZ, Ruth Exh. 1933
Portrait painter. † COO 1.

GOLLCHER, O.F. Exh. 1921
Via dei Graechi 297, Rome. † RA 2.

GOLLINS, Ormond Edwin b. 1870
Landscape and mural painter. b. Shrewsbury. Second master at Birmingham Municipal School of Art. Add: Birmingham 1896; Stechford, Birmingham 1925; Broadway, Worcs. 1932. † B 26, L 5, RA 1, RHA 1, RI 1, ROI 1.

GOMME, Mrs. Phyllis Exh. 1938
c/o Mrs. A.E. Haswell Miller, Hailes Cottage, Kingsknowe. † RSA 1.

GONIN, Jacques F. Exh. 1930
Portrait and figure painter. 7 Rue Lalo, Paris. † L 3, RA 3.

GONNE, Maude Exh. 1908-9
13 Rue de Passy, Paris. † LS 8.

GONTCHAROVA, Natalie* b. 1881
b. Russia. Exh. 1928. † GOU 3.

GONZALEZ, Madame E.C. Exh. 1883-84
18 Rue Brunel, Paris. † GI 2.

GONZALEZ, Juan Antonio* b. 1842
Spanish figure painter. 18 Rue Brunel, Ternes, Paris 1884. † GI 1.

GOOCH, Edward J. Exh. 1893-1930
Figure painter. Liverpool 1893; Southport, Lancs. 1912. † L 26, RA 1, RCA 3, RWS 3.

GOOD, Charles Stephen b. 1905
Landscape and portrait painter and illustrator. Studied Harrogate School of Art and Royal College of Art. Instructor at Schools of Art, Bury 1928-29, Southport 1930, Derby 1931, L.C.C. 1932 and the Air Ministry 1940. Exh. 1932-36. † P 1, RA 2, RBA 2.

GOOD, Thomas Exh. 1910-27
Edinburgh. † GI 1, L 3, RSA 10.

GOODACRE, Adeline Exh. 1921-30
Sefton Park, Liverpool 1921; New Brighton, Cheshire 1923. † L 6.

GOODACRE, Miss D. Exh. 1923-24
100 Earleston Road, Liscard, Wallasey, Cheshire. † L 3.

GOODACRE, Grace Exh. 1902-28
Mrs. Alfred Grant. Miniature painter. Putney 1902; Northwood 1909. † RA 15, RI 2, RMS 3.

GOODACRE, Mrs. J.A. Exh. 1883
Sunnyside, Clifton Park, Birkenhead. † L 1.

GOODALL, Agnes M. Exh. 1906-9
Watercolour painter of African landscapes. Add: Farnham, Surrey. † FIN 50, SWA 2.

GOODALL, Edward A.* 1819-1908
Landscape and battle painter. Brother of Frederick and Walter G. q.v. Accompanied the Schomburgh Guiana Boundary Expedition 1941. Visited the Crimea 1854 as artist for "Illustrated London News". Also visited Morocco, Spain, Portugal and Italy. A.R.W.S. 1858, R.W.S. 1864. Add: London. † AG 2, B 1, FIN 1, GI 2, L 11, M 1, RA 1, RWS 86, TOO 2.

GOODALL, Florence Exh. 1892
Colnbrook, Grosvenor Road, Gunnersbury. † RBA 1.

GOODALL, Frederick* 1822-1904
Painter of landscapes, genre, biblical and Egyptian subjects. Brother of Edward A. and Walter G. q.v. Won a silver medal at the Society of Arts at the age of 14. A.R.A. 1852. R.A. 1863. R.I. 1867. Add: London. † AG 4, B 14, FIN 54, G 3, GI 4, L 34, M 22, P 2, RA 95, RI 1, ROI 5, TOO 27.

GOODALL, George Exh. 1926
† M 3.

GOODALL, Herbert d. 1907
Figure and landscape painter. London. † I 10, L 2, NEA 8, RBA 6.

GOODALL, J. Edward Exh. 1880-1911
Figure and domestic painter. R.B.A. 1902. Add: London. † D 10, L 7, RA 9, RBA 26, RHA 7, RI 17, ROI 2.

GOODALL, Thomas F.* c. 1857-1944
Landscape, coastal and rustic genre painter. Studied under John Sparkes. N.E.A. 1886. Add: Dulwich 1880; Oulton Broad, Lowestoft 1899. † B 10, D 5, G 4, GI 12, L 16, M 10, NEA 3, NG 6, RA 16, RBA 30, ROI 3.

GOODALL, Walter* 1830-1889
Figure, domestic and coastal painter. Brother of Edward A and Frederick G. q.v. Studied RA Schools. A.R.W.S. 1853, R.W.S. 1861. Add: London. † AG 1, RWS 6.

GOODCHILD, Emily Exh. 1888-97
Portrait painter. Hampstead, London. † B 4, GI 1, L 1, P 4, RA 5.

GOODCHILD, Florence A. Exh. 1907-10
Elmwood Lodge, Long Lane, Finchley, London. † LS 3, RA 3, RMS 1.

GOODCHILD, G. Spiers Exh. 1920
Portrait painter. Hinton, Kohinoor Avenue. Bushey, Herts. † RA 1.

GOODCHILD, John Charles b. 1898
Painter, black and white artist, etcher and lithographer. b. London. Studied School of Arts and Crafts, Adelaide and Central Schoolof Arts and Crafts, London. Teacher of etching at Adelaide School of Arts and Crafts, Australia, and teacher of Drawing at Central School of Arts and Crafts, London. Exh. 1937. † GI 1.

GOODCHILD, J. Howard Exh. 1908
Elmwood Lodge, Long Lane, Finchley, London. † LS 4.

GOODCHILD, Mrs. Lilian Exh. 1940
† RI 1.

GOODDY, R. Exh. 1884
Woodbank, Trefriw, Wales. † L 1.

GOODEN, Stephen 1892-1955
Engraver and illustrator. A.R.A. 1937, A.R.E. 1931, R.E. 1933, R.M.S. 1925. Add: Enfield, Middlesex 1913; London 1920; Bishops Stortford, Herts. 1928; Chesham Bois, Bucks. 1940. † NEA 7, RA 12, RE 23, RMS 20.

GOODENOUGH, Miss S. Exh. 1892-93
Figure painter. 3 Challoner Street, W. Kensington, London. † RID 7.

GOODERHAM, Horace H. Exh. 1934-40
Figure painter. London 1934; New Barnet, Herts. 1939. † GI 2, RA 12.

GOODFELLOW, A. Exh. 1882-93
Manchester. † L 1, M 16.

GOODFELLOW, David Exh. 1929-39
81 Gray Street, Broughty Ferry, Dundee. † RI 1, RSA 2.

GOODFELLOW, Reginald F. Exh. 1939
1b Clareville Grove, London. † RA 1.

GOODHALL, May C. Exh. 1887-1918
Figure and still life painter. Twickenham, Middlesex 1887; 27 Nevern Square, Earls Court, London 1889. † L 2, M 4, RID 50.

GOODHART-RENDEL, Harry Stuart 1887-1959
Architect. Exh. 1910-40. Add: London. † B 2, RA 19.

GOODIER, Arthur Exh. 1883
Watercolour landscape painter. 13 Lady Margaret's Road, Kentish Town, London. † RBA 1.

GOODIN, Walter Exh. 1935-39
Landscape painter. London 1935; Beverley, E. Yorks. 1938. † RA 5.

GOODLIFFE, Herbert Exh. 1925-39
Landscape painter. A.N.S.A. 1929. Add: Nottingham. † N 38.

GOODMAN, Arthur J. Exh. 1902-13
Wigwam Studio, Gedling, Notts. † N 12, P 1.

GOODMAN, George W. Exh. 1930-35
Sculptor. London. † GI 1, RA 6.

GOODMAN, Julia (Mrs. L.) 1812-1906
nee Salaman. Portrait and figure painter. Exh. 1880-88. Add: London. † M 1, RBA 2, SWA 3.

GOODMAN, Miss J.C. Exh. 1901-7
Kingston Hill, Surrey and London. † L 2, RI 1, ROI 1, SWA 2.

GOODMAN, John Reginald b. 1878
Watercolour landscape painter. b. St. Albans, Herts. Studied under Wilfred Ball, Geo. C. Harte, and C. Hook; also in Holland, South Africa and New South Wales. Served in Army World War I. Married to Kathleen Mary G. q.v. Exh. 1901-18. Add: Kensworth Lynch House, Nr. Dunstable, Beds. 1901; Marsham, Norwich 1909; Prees Heath Camp, Salop 1918. † D 20, L 1, RA 1, RI 1.

GOODMAN, Kathleen Mary b. 1879
nee Dix. Painter, miniaturist and pastellier. Studied under E.H. Marten and Frank O. Salisbury. Married John Reginald G. q.v. Exh. 1909-34. Add: Marsham, Norwich 1909; Gt. Missenden, Bucks. 1915; Wellingborough, Northants. 1923. † L 4, RA 7, RCA 2.

GOODMAN, Miss M. Exh. 1900
40 Upper Parliament Street, Liverpool. † L 1.

GOODMAN, Maude* Exh. 1880-1920
Mrs. Scanes. Painter of genre and humorous pictures of children. Add: Kensington, London 1880; Southport, Lancs. 1907. † B 21, G 5, GI 1, L 30, M 21, RA 52, RHA 3, RI 12, ROI 8, SWA 2, TOO 4.

GOODMAN, Penelope Exh. 1933-40
nee Everett. Painter and black and white artist. Studied Blackheath Art School and Slade School. Add: Belvedere, Kent 1933; London 1937. † RHA 1, RI 5, ROI 3, RSA 2, SWA 3.

GOODMAN, Phyllis M. Exh. 1930-31
30 Parkdale, Wolverhampton. † B 10.

GOODMAN, Robert Gwelo* d. 1939
Landscape painter. b. Cape Colony, South Africa. Studied under J.S. Morland. Went to Paris 1896 to continue his study and came to London 1898. Travelled widely. † B 13, FIN 62, GI 3, GOU 22, I 4, L 35, LEI 118, LS 4, M 13, NEA 1, NG 1, RA 36, RBA 19, RHA 1, RI 7, ROI 8, RSA 4.

GOODMAN, Walter b. 1838
Portrait painter. Exh. 1883-1906. Add: London 1883; Brighton 1889; Henfield, Sussex 1906. † L 2, RA 1, RBA 1, ROI 4, RSA 1.

GOODMAN, W.H. Exh. 1885
65 Dearman Road, Sparkbrook, Birmingham. † B 1.

GOODMAN, W.H. Exh. 1930
12 Victoria Road, Harborne, Birmingham. † B 1.

GOODRICH, W.R.E. Exh. 1912
13 Leamington Street, Crooksmoor, Sheffield. † RA 1.

GOODRICKE, Annie P. Exh. 1889
Brooklyn House, 174 Clapham Road, London. † SWA 1.

GOODRUM, Phyllis Exh. 1935-39
6 Watergate, Grantham, Lincs. † N 3.

GOODSIR, Agnes Noyes Exh. 1907-38
Portrait, flower and still life painter. b. Victoria, Australia. Studied Juliens and Colarossi's, Paris. Add: London. † COO 64, LS 8, RA 4, ROI 2.

GOODSON, Hugh Exh. 1931
† WG 29.

GOODWIN, Agnes Exh. 1934
37 Pattison Road, London. † RA 1.

GOODWIN, Albert* 1845-1932
Painter of landscapes and biblical, allegorical and imaginative subjects. Studied under Arthur Hughes and Ford Madox Brown. Accompanied Ruskin on a trip to Italy in 1872. Travelled widely in Europe, India, Egypt and the South Sea Islands. A.R.W.S. 1871, R.W.S. 1881. "Ali Baba and the Forty Thieves" purchased by Chantrey Bequest 1901. Add: Ilfracombe, Devon 1880; Bexhill, Sussex 1906. † AG 5, B 3, D 1, DOW 2, FIN 613, G 1, GOU 3, L 27, LEI 1, M 22, NG 7, RA 83, RBA 1, RWS 300, TOO 1, WG 11.

GOODWIN, A.E. Exh. 1884-86
14 Vernon Street, Derby. † N 2.

GOODWIN, Dorothea Exh. 1904
Nicholas Road, Blundellsands, Liverpool. † L 1.

GOODWIN, Edith Chester Exh. 1916-38
Illuminator. Birmingham. † B 10, RMS 1.

GOODWIN, Edith L.A. Exh. 1901
38 Wellington Buildings, Bow Road, London. † RBA 1.

GOODWIN, Miss E.M. Exh. 1907-14
Miniature painter. Ellerslie Lane, Bexhill, Sussex. † L 4, RA 8, RMS 4.

GOODWIN, Elizabeth Nancie b. 1905
Sculptor, illustrator and black and white artist. Exh. 1924-32. Add: Beechfield, Barnston, Birkenhead. † L 11.

GOODWIN, Frank A. Exh. 1887-1907
Oxton, Birkenhead 1887; New Brighton, Cheshire 1895; Wallasey, Cheshire 1896. † B 3, L 34, RCA 2.

GOODWIN, F.H. Exh. 1915
2 Tenniel Studios, Redcliffe Road, Kensington, London. † RA 1, ROI 1.

GOODWIN, Mrs. Gwendoline Exh. 1922-23
Snaithfield, Ecclesall, Sheffield. † L 3.

GOODWIN, Hamilton Exh. 1888
c/o Mr. Chaplain, 121 Weedington Road, Kentish Town, London. † B 1.

GOODWIN, Harry* d. 1925
Landscape and genre painter. Married to Kate Malleson G. q.v. Add: Brighton, Sussex 1880; Croydon, Surrey 1881; Torquay 1898; Hastings, Sussex 1916. † ALP 4, B 3, D 30, DOW 77, FIN 6, GI 2, L 24, M 21, RA 15, RBA 10, RHA 1, RI 28, ROI 11, RSW 2, WG 50.

GOODWIN, Miss H.M. Exh. 1907-11
243 Boulevard Raspail, Paris. † RA 3.

GOODWIN, Mrs. Jeanie Exh. 1936
Landscape painter. 73 Drayton Gardens, London. † RA 1.

GOODWIN, Kate Malleson Exh. 1880-1900
nee Malleson. Landscape painter. Married Harry G. q.v. Add: Brighton 1880; Croydon, Surrey 1882; Torquay, Devon 1900. † B 1, D 3, DOW 1, L 2, M 1, MG 1, RA 3.

GOODWIN, Mary Exh. 1895
Cappach, Killiney. † RHA 1.

GOODWIN, Mary Exh. 1921
3 Paulton's Square, Chelsea, London. † GI 1.

GOODWIN, Norman Exh. 1927-30
c/o St. George's Gallery, George Street, London. † GI 2, M 2.

GOODWIN, Sidney Exh. 1912-22
Southampton 1912; Dublin 1917. † RHA 15.

GOODWIN, W.S. Exh. 1894-1913
Southampton. † RHA 4.

GOODY, Florence P. Exh. 1886-1901
Figure and domestic painter. Lewisham, London. † B 3, D 3, L 2, M 2, RA 1, RBA 3, RI 3, SWA 6.

GOODYEAR, Alice M. Exh. 1897
36 Metchley Lane, Harborne, Birmingham. † B 1.

GOODYER, Mary Helen Exh. 1881-85
Still life painter. Mosley Street, New Basford, Notts. 1881; Hyson Green, Notts. 1884. † N 6.

GOOLD, Trevor S. Exh. 1922-31
Landscape and flower painter. London. † RA 2.

GOOLD, V. Exh. 1930
Fleet Street, London. † SWA 1.

GORAN, Maitland Exh. 1885
Albert Gallery, Edinburgh. † RSA 1.

GORBATOFF, Konstantin b. 1876
Russian painter. Exh. 1937. † COO 44.

GORDIGIANI, Prof. Michele 1830-1909
Italian portrait painter. Add: c/o Agnews, Old Bond Street, London 1886; Florence 1894. † NG 2, RA 1.

GORDINE, Dora b. 1906
The Hon. Mrs. R. Hare. Sculptor. Paris 1927; London 1933. † GI 1, L 3, LEI 21, RA 8, RSA 2.

GORDON, Miss Exh. 1888
Oat Hall, Hayward's Heath, Sussex. † L 1.

GORDON, Mrs. Exh. 1881
Woodside, Teddington, Middlesex. † SWA 1.

GORDON, Hon. Lady Exh. 1880-81
Landscape painter. 50 Queen's Gate Gardens, London. † SWA 4.

GORDON, A. Exh. 1905-14
Gourock, N.B. 1905; Glasgow 1909. † GI 1, RA 1, RCA 2, RSA 3, RSW 2.

GORDON, Adam Exh. 1922-23
c/o J.F.E. Grundy, 24 Buckingham Street, London. † D 1, RI 2.

GORDON, Alexander Exh. 1890-98
Watercolour interior and rustic painter. Add: Underbank, Largs, N.B. 1890; School of Art, Taunton 1891; West Dulwich 1897; Balham 1898. † B 1, GI 4, RA 4, RBA 2.

GORDON, A. Esme Exh. 1931-40
21 Heriot Row, Edinburgh 1931; 34 Castle Street, Edinburgh 1939. † GI 1, RSA 8, RSW 2.

GORDON, Alexander E. Exh. 1922-34
Garnethill, Glasgow 1922; Wimbledon Park, London 1923; 21 Heriot Row, Edinburgh 1934. † GI 2, RSA 1.

GORDON, Andrew J. Exh. 1887-1901
Architect. London. † RA 3.

GORDON, A.W. Exh. 1889-92
5 Greyfriar's Place, Edinburgh. † RSA 2.

GORDON, Cora Josephine Exh. 1908-40
nee Turner. Painter, wood engraver, etcher and illustrator. b. Buxton. Studied Slade School. Co-author and illustrator with her husband Godfrey Jervis G. q.v. of travel books. A.R.B.A. 1939, R.B.A. 1940. Add: Dublin 1908; Wadhurst, Sussex 1910; London 1916. † COO 26, GOU 2, L 10, LEF 23, LS 23, P 1, RBA 11, ROI 4, SWA 11.

GORDON, Caroline L. Exh. 1914-16
The Red House, Slade End, Wallingford, Berks. † LS 5.

GORDON, Miss E. Exh. 1885
68 Elm Park Road, Chelsea, London. † B 1.

GORDON, Edward Exh. 1880-83
Coltbridge, Edinburgh. † RSA 3.

GORDON, G. Exh. 1908
219 Kings Road, Chelsea, London. † L 1.

GORDON, Hon. George Exh. 1904-8
Sculptor. 5 Turner Studios, Glebe Place, London. † RA 3.

GORDON, G. Hamilton Exh. 1895
Architect. 2 Prince's Mansions, Victoria Street, London. † RA 1.

GORDON, Godfrey Jervis (Jan) 1882-1944
Painter, etcher, lithographer, writer, critic and illustrator. Co-author and illustrator with his wife Cora Josephine G. q.v. of travel books. Art critic with "New Witness" 1916-19, "Observer and Athenaeum" 1919, "Land and Water" 1920 and the "Observer". R.B.A. 1935. Add: London 1908 and 1916; Wadhurst, Sussex 1910; Paris 1911. † GOU 3, L 7, LEF 26, LS 12, NEA 1, RA 2, RBA 34, RI 2, ROI 1.

GORDON, Miss H. Exh. 1903
The Boynes, Shanklin, I.O.W. † D 1.

GORDON, Herbert Lewis Exh. 1930-40
The Gable Cottage, Alton, Hants. 1930; Edinburgh 1933. † GI 3, RSA 5.

GORDON, Hilda May Exh. 1901-29
Figure and landscape painter. Travelled widely. Add: London 1901. † D 6, FIN 79.

GORDON, Miss I. Exh. 1908-12
Alassio, Italy 1908; Paris 1909; Chelsea, London 1910. † L 1, RA 4, RMS 1.

GORDON, James Exh. 1885-89
Edinburgh 1885; Glasgow 1889. † GI 1, RSA 3.

GORDON, James Exh. 1940
c/o Todd, Clerk Street, Edinburgh. † RSA 1.

GORDON, Jan
See GORDON, Godfrey Jervis

GORDON, J.E. Exh. 1918-22
3 Abercromby Place, Edinburgh. † RSA 2, RSW 2.

GORDON, Jack Moire Exh. 1923
47 York Road, Rathmines, Dublin. † RHA 3.

GORDON, John Ross b. 1890
Etcher and watchmaker. Studied Gray's School of Art, Aberdeen. Add: Aberdeen 1924; Edinburgh 1931 and 1937; Wardie 1933. † L 1, RA,1, RSA 6.

GORDON, Mrs. J.W. Exh. 1889
Ellon, Aberdeen. † L 1.

GORDON, Miss Katie Exh. 1897-98
The Close, Salisbury, Wilts. † RI 2.

GORDON, Miss M. Exh. 1921
20 Chesterford Gardens, Hampstead, London. † RA 1.

GORDON, Miss Nora Mary Exh. 1935-40
Portrait painter, miniaturist. Studied St. John's Wood Art School. Add: London 1916; Hatch End, Middlesex 1924; The Gable Cottage, Alton, Hants 1930; Edinburgh 1935. † GI 3, L 1, RA 5, RSA 17.

GORDON, R. Exh. 1883
† TOO 2.

GORDON, R.G. Exh. 1890
Precincts, Canterbury, Kent. † RI 1.

GORDON, Robert James* Exh. 1880-94
Genre painter. R.B.A. 1876. Add: London. † B 5, GI 1, L 16, M 8, RA 12, RBA 44, ROI 1, RSA 2.

GORDON, Samuel Exh. 1900
Landscape painter. 42 Freke Road, London. † RA 1.

GORDON, Thomas Exh. 1884
Architect. 33 Argyll Street, Regent Street, London. † RA 1.

GORDON, Mrs. T.W. Exh. 1890
Manningdown, Farnborough, Hants. † SWA 2.

GORDON, W.R. Exh. 1921-26
17 Bridge Street, Belfast. † RHA 5.

GORDON, William Sinclair Exh. 1920
83 Hill Street, Garnet Hill, Glasgow. † ROI 2.

GORDON-THOMSON, Marian Exh. 1938
Crowborough, Sussex. † SWA 1.

GORE, Elizabeth M. Exh. 1884-97
Landscape painter. Visited U.S.A. Add: Brighton 1884; The Vicarage, Bowdon, Cheshire 1897. † M 1, SWA 1.

GORE, Frederick* Exh. 1936-38
Landscape, figure and interior painter. † COO 7, NEA 1, RED 31.

GORE, Millicent Exh. 1893-1904
Domestic painter. Brookside, Barnes, London. † D 8, L 4, RA 2, RBA 1, RI 2, ROI 2, SWA 6.

GORE, Spencer Frederick* 1878-1914
Landscape and figure painter. Studied Slade School. Taught painting and drawing for 1 year at the L.C.C. Technical Institute. Founder of the Allied Artists Association. Founder Member of the London Group 1913. N.E.A. 1909. "The Gas Cooker" (1913) purchased by Chantrey Bequest 1962. Add: London 1906. † BG 1, CAR 34, LS 23, M 2, NEA 30.

GORE, St. John Exh. 1912
5 Ham Place, London. † LS 3.

GORE, William Crampton 1877-1946
Portrait, landscape and interior painter. b. Ireland. Gave up the practice of medicine to paint. Studied Slade School. Served as Captain in the R.A.M.C., World War I. A.R.H.A. 1916, R.H.A. 1918. Add: Enniskerry, Co. Wicklow 1902; London 1908; Paris 1912; Knocklin, Bray, Co. Wicklow 1920; Montreuil sur Mer, France 1930; Colchester, Essex 1933. † BA 1, FIN 7, GOU 28, I 1, LS 5, NEA 5, RA 2, RHA 113, ROI 7, RSA 1.

GORE, William Henry Exh. 1880-1916
Landscape and figure painter. R.B.A. 1893. Add: London 1880 and 1909; Newbury, Berks. 1905 and 1915. † B 49, G 3, GI 2, L 35, LEI 1, M 7, NG 1, RA 34, RBA 99, RHA 5, RI 23, ROI 14.

GORE-BOOTH, Colum Exh. 1937-40
Landscape painter. London. † RA 2, RI 3, ROI 4.

GORELL, Lord Exh. 1929-40
Watercolour landscape painter. 31 Kensington Square, London. † NEA 2, RA 2, RI 11, RSW 1.

GORELL, Norman Exh. 1922-23
114 West Campbell Street, Glasgow. † GI 3.

GORGES, J.A.H. Exh. 1883-84
15 Royal Terrace, East Kingstown, Dublin. † RHA 2.

GORGES, Miss J.T. Exh. 1895-99
15 Royal Terrace, East Kingstown, Dublin. † RHA 7.

GORHAM, Miss E. Exh. 1907
Merrymount, Bushey, Herts. † RA 1.

GORI, A. Exh. 1920
† L 1.

GORMAN, Amy F. Exh. 1884
The Rectory, Thomastown, Ireland. † RHA 1.

GORMAN, Ernest Hamilton b. 1869
Landscape painter. b. Gosport, Hants. Studied Regent Street Polytechnic, Working Men's College and Goldsmiths. Exh. 1923-33. Add: 14 St. Andrews Road, Lower Bebington, Birkenhead. † L 6.

GOROY, J.T. Exh. 1925-34
50 St. Quentin Avenue, N. Kensington, London. † RI 1, ROI 1.

GORRIE, Helen Exh. 1925-27
The Croft School, Dunfermline. † L 3.

GORRY, James Aloysius b. 1905
Figure painter and picture restorer. Studied RHA Schools. Exh. 1930-31. Add: Balham, London. † RHA 2.

GORSE, J. Exh. 1904
42 Pierrepoint Road, Trent Boulevard, Nottingham. † N 1.

GORST, Bertha b. 1873
Mrs. Aiken. Etcher. b. Thornton Hough. Studied Birkenhead and Liverpool Schools of Art. Exh. 1906-26. A.R.E. 1902-29. Add: Abersoch, North Wales 1897; Birkenhead 1899; Llangollen, Wales 1906. † L 29, RE 12.

GORST, Mrs. H.C. Exh. 1888-1913
Flower and figure painter. Irrawang, Rockferry, Cheshire 1888; Liverpool 1898. † L 27, RBA 2, SWA 1

GORST, Hester Gaskell Exh. 1919-29
† GOU 2, I 1, NEA,1.

GORST, Miss Jessie Elliot Exh. 1889-99
Landscape painter. Irrawang, Rockferry, Cheshire. † L 1, SWA 1.

GORTER, Arnold Marc* b. 1866
Dutch artist. Exh. 1914-15. Add: 30 Pieter de Hoogstraat, Amsterdam. † RA 1, RSA 1.

GORYNSKA, Wiktorya Exh. 1932
Polish colour woodcut artist. † BA 2.

GOS, Albert* 1852-1942
Swiss Alpine landscape painter. Exh. 1883-1911. Add: Geneva, Switzerland. † ALP 6, L 2, M 2, RA 5, RBA 1.

GOSEDA, H. Exh. 1904
c/o H. Dixon, Esq., Dundereck, Pitlochry. † RI 2.

GOSHAWK, Louie G. Exh. 1898-99
Miniature painter. R.M.S. 1890. Add: 18 Carmalt Gardens, Putney, London. † RA 1, RBA 1, RMS 3.

GOSHERON, Muriel Exh. 1925-40
Mrs. Quinton. Miniature painter. A.R.M.S. 1930, R.M.S. 1938. Add: Streatham, London 1926; Bromley, Kent 1931; Beckenham, Kent 1937. † L 5, RA 17, RMS 28.

GOSLETT, H. Exh. 1905
28 Theobalds Road, London. † RA 1.

GOSLETT, Wallis Exh. 1939
† GOU 2.

GOSLING, J. Exh. 1916
21 Colwick Road, Sneinton, Nottingham. † N 1.

GOSLING, James S. Exh. 1909-10
101 Evelyn Road, Sparkhill, Birmingham. † B 3.

GOSLING, Jessie W. Exh. 1897
Fruit painter. Braintree, Essex. † RA 2.

GOSLING, Margaret Exh. 1923
Watercolour painter of pastoral scenes. † WG 35.

GOSLING, M.A. Exh. 1924-25
† GOU 2.

GOSLING, William W.* 1824-83
Landscape and rustic genre painter. R.B.A. 1854. Add: Sycamore Lodge, Wargrave, Henley on Thames. † D 1, RA 2, RBA 22.

GOSNELL, Duncan H. Exh. 1884-1912
Landscape painter. Brockham, Surrey 1884; Goudhurst, Kent 1895. † L 2, RA 11, ROI 3, RSA 3.

GOSS, Horace C. Exh. 1919
Miniature painter. 133 Sutherland Road, Forest Hill, London. † RA 1.

GOSS, Miss Phillippe Exh. 1936-37
Portrait painter. Broomfield Park, Sunningdale, Berks. † RA 2.

GOSSE, Mrs. Edmund Exh. 1880-90
Miss Nellie Epps. Landscape painter. Add: 29 Delamere Terrace, Westbourne Square, London. † G 15, L 2, RBA 1, ROI 2.

GOSSE, Laura Sylvia* 1881-1968
Painter and etcher. Daughter of Mrs. Edmund G. q.v. Studied RA Schools and under Sickert. A.R.B.A. 1928, R.B.A. 1930, A.R.E. 1917, S.W.A. 1935. Founder member London Group 1913. Exh. 1908-40. Add: London. † BA 41, BAR 1, CAR 90, CG 80, CHE 4, CON 2, FIN 1, G 5, GI 1, GOU 42, I 15, L 14, LEF 62, LS 30, NEA 27, RA 16, RBA 59, RE 26, SWA 8, TOO 40.

GOSSEN, F.M. Exh. 1912
14 Elliot Street, Plymouth, Devon. † L 1, RA 1.

GOSSET, Phyllis T. Exh. 1914-19
Mrs. H.H.E. Miniature painter. Broadway, Worcs. † RA 2.

GOSSMAN, Mary Exh. 1940
49 Killermont Road, Bearsden. † GI 1.

GOTCH, Bernard Cecil b. 1876
Watercolour landscape painter. Winchester 1906 and 1930; Southampton 1921; Bath 1928; Oxford 1936-40. † FIN 89, GOU 15, L 4, NEA 2, RA 26, RI 9.

GOTCH, Miss C. Exh. 1893
70 Gower Street, London. † SWA 2.

GOTCH, Caroline Burland Exh. 1880-1902
nee Yates. Landscape and figure painter. Married Thomas Cooper G. q.v. Add: London 1880 and 1891; Newlyn, Penzance 1887; Shottermill, Surrey 1899. † B 9, D 1, DOW 1, FIN 1, G 1, GI 4, L 11, NG 1, RA 7, RBA 6, RHA 2, ROI 2.

GOTCH, Oliver Horsley Exh. 1937
† NEA 1.

GOTCH, Thomas Cooper* 1854-1931
Painter, pastellier and etcher. b. Kettering. Studied Heatherley's, Ecole des Beaux Arts, Antwerp, Slade School and in Paris. Visited Australia 1883 and Italy 1891. Married Caroline Burland G. q.v. N.E.A. 1886, R.B.A. 1885, R.I. 1912, R.P. 1913. "Alleluia" purchased by Chantrey Bequest 1896. Add: London 1880, 1891 and 1906; Newlyn, Penzance 1888 and 1895; Shottermill, Surrey 1899; Trewarveneth, Penzance 1910. † B 23, D 2, DOW 2, FIN 26, G 1, GI 14, L 52, M 19, NEA 3, NG 26, P 12, RA 68, RBA 19, RCA 1, RHA 8, RI 63, ROI 2, TOO 16.

GOTH, Imre Exh. 1938-40
Portrait painter. London. † RA 3.

GOTH, Phyllis Exh. 1930
Wood engraver. † RED 1.

GOTHARD, Fred Exh. 1915
17 Glyn Road, Liscard, Cheshire. † L 3.

GOTT, John William Exh. 1883-1900
Landscape and figure painter. London. † RA 1, RBA 1, RI 2.

GOTTHARDT, C.F. Exh. 1895
5 Marmion Road, Hoylake, Cheshire. † L 1.

GOTTLIEB, Leopold 1883-1934
Portrait painter. Exh. 1909. † P 2

GOTTO, Basil 1866-1954
Sculptor. Studied Paris and RA Schools (Landseer scholarship). Add: St. Albans 1889; London 1891; Twyford, Hants. 1920. † GI 10, L 5, NG 13, RA 41, RI 2, ROI 2.

GOTTSCHALK, Blanche d. c.1931
Miniature painter. R.M.S. 1896. Add: London. † L 21, LS 10, M 1, NG 6, P 1, RA 3, RI 1, RMS 75, ROI 6, SWA 14.

GOTTSCHALK, Miss Etty Exh. 1899
15 Victoria Park, Shipley, Yorks. † RBA 1.

GOUBIE, Jean Richard * 1842-1899
French painter. Exh. 1883. † FIN 1.

GOUDIE, Isobel Turner Maxwell b. 1903
Stained glass artist and potter. Studied Glasgow School of Art. Add: Stirling 1928; Edinburgh 1931. † GI 3, RHA 2, RSA 10.

GOUDIE, John Exh. 1911-17
1 Bank Street, Barrhead, N.B. † GI 4, L 1.

GOUDIE, Zilla H. Exh. 1935-38
Landscape painter. Travelled widely. Add: Radcliffe on Trent, Notts. 1935; Bingham, Notts. 1937. † N 7.

GOUGH, Arthur J. Exh. 1903-12
Landscape painter. Mill Lane Cottage, W. Hampstead, London. † RA 11, RI 4.

GOUGH, Mrs. B.S. Exh. 1901-4
Caer Rhun, Tal y Cafn, Wales. † RCA 2.

GOUGH, Hugh R. Exh. 1884-87
Architect. London. † RA 2.

GOUGH, Mrs. Hugh S. Exh. 1906-33
Government House, St. Heliers, Jersey, C.I. 1906; Llangynog, Oswestry, Salop 1912. † RCA 32, SWA 10.

GOUGH, J. Exh. 1903
44 Hood Street, Sherwood, Notts. † N 3.

GOUGH, J.H. Exh. 1884-86
36 Sherwin Street, Nottingham. † N 4.

GOUGH, Miss Margaret Exh. 1930
95 Harborne Road, Birmingham. † B 3.

GOUGH, Thomas b. 1858
Landscape and portrait painter. b. Manchester. Studied in Paris under Gilbert and La Gandara. Exh. 1903-36. Add: Macclesfield 1903; Bognor, Sussex 1908; Lancing, Sussex 1929. † M 2, RA 3.

GOULBORN, Mrs. M.J. Exh. 1929
Bredon Croft, Alvechurch, Worcs. † B 1.

GOULD, Alexander Carruthers b. 1870
Landscape painter. b. Woodford, Essex. Son of Sir Francis C.G. q.v. R.B.A. 1903. Exh. 1892-1940. Add: Buckhurst Hill, Essex 1892; London 1896; Porlock, Som. 1917. † B 5, CHE,1, G 4, GI 3, I 3, L 10, LS 11, M 8, NEA 6, RA 20, RBA 301, RI 9, ROI 4, WG 24.

GOULD, David* Exh. 1885-1930
Landscape and flower painter. Ambleside 1885; Belfast 1903 and 1928; Lisburn, Nr. Belfast 1918. † GI 1, L 5, M 1, RA 1, RHA 25.

GOULD, Mrs. Elsie Exh. 1925-40
Hampstead, London 1925; Beckenham, Kent 1934; West Worthing, Sussex 1940. † RBA 1, SWA 6.

GOULD, Sir Francis Carruthers 1844-1925
Political caricaturist. Father of Alexander G. q.v. Exh. 1907-24. † BK 165, WG 385.

GOULD, Florence E. Exh. 1897-1901
Miniature portrait painter. Herne Hill 1897; Bath 1898; Hull 1901. † RA 2, RMS 2.

GOULD, George T.S. Exh. 1937-40
Broompark, Ketty Avenue, Bo'ness. † RSA 4.

GOULD, T. Butler Exh. 1912-18
46 Park Street, Southport, Lancs. † L 9, RA 4.

GOULDEN, Mrs. M.O.C. Exh. 1915-39
Landscape painter. London. † AR 45, L 1.

GOULDEN, Richard Reginald 1877-1932
Sculptor. b. Dover. Exh. 1903-32. Add: London. † GI 6, L 2, RA 27, RMS 1.

GOULDING, Frank Exh. 1923-40
Figure painter. London. † RA 3.

GOULDING, Frederick Exh. 1881-83
Etcher. Kingston House, Shepherd's Bush Road, London. † RE 4.

GOULDSMITH, Edmund 1852-1932
Landscape and portrait painter. Studied South Kensington and RA Schools. R.B.A. 1895. Add: Cotham, Bristol 1882; Clifton, Bristol 1901; Bath 1902 and 1911; Tavistock 1905. † B 5, L 2, RA 14, RBA 50, RI 1, ROI 2, RSA 3.

GOUNOD, Jean Exh. 1903
c/o H. Roche, Esq., 29 Brompton Road, London. † ROI 2.

GOUPY, Marcel Exh. 1927
c/o E. Trower & Co. Ltd., Brown's Arcade, 92 Regent Street, London. † L 6.

GOURLIE, Edith Exh. 1881-89
Figure painter. London. † B 1, GI 1, RA 1, ROI 2, RSA 1, SWA 8.

GOURLIE, Norah Dundas Exh. 1914-39
London. † LS 3, SWA 5.

GOURSAT, George 1863-1934
"Sem". French portrait painter and caricaturist. b. Perigneux and lived in Bordeaux, Marseilles and Paris. Visited England often between 1905-10 to sketch at Newmarket races and Cowes Regatta. Exh. 1907. † BG 9.

GOURSE, H.C. Exh. 1906
6 Rue d'Estrees, Paris. † L 1.

GOUT-GERALD, le See L

GOUTHWAITE, Miss A.B. Exh. 1889
31 Rockybank Road, Devonshire Park, Birkenhead. † L 1.

GOVAN, Mary Maitland Exh. 1884-1925
Flower painter. b. Gibraltar. Studied Birkenhead, Antwerp and Edinburgh. Add: Musselburgh 1884; Edinburgh 1886. † B 1, BG 4, GI 21, LS 5, M 1, RA 2, RSA 51, RSW 2.

GOVANE, R. Stewart Exh. 1880-86
Edinburgh 1880; Helensburgh, N.B. 1885. † L 1, RSA 6.

GOVER, Agnes L. Exh. 1884-85
8 Wharfedale Street, Redcliffe Square, London. † SWA 2.

GOVER, Mary Edith Exh. 1886-87
Flower painter. 13 Winchester Road, South Hampstead, London. † RBA 2, RI 1.

GOVIER, L.W. Exh. 1929
3 Grove Hill Road, Handsworth, Birmingham. † B 2.

GOW, Andrew Carrick* 1848-1920
Painter of historical and military subjects, genre and portraits. Keeper of the Royal Academy. A.R.A. 1881, R.A. 1891, A.R.I. 1868, R.I. 1870. "Cromwell at Dunbar" purchased by Chantrey Bequest 1886. Add: London. † AG 14, B 3, CAR 1, FIN 5, GI 2, L 12, M 7, NG 1, RA 84, RHA 1, RSA 1, RSA 1, RSW 1, TOO 8.

GOW, David Exh. 1886-1908
5A Blenheim Villas, St. John's Wood, London 1886; Glasgow 1891. † GI 11, M 2, RI 5, RSA 3.

GOW, Dorothy Willett Exh. 1926-34
nee Willett. Potter and modeller. Studied Central School of Arts and Crafts, London. A.S.W.A. 1928. Add: 42 Drayton Gardens, London. † L 14, RBA 1.

GOW, Dr. James Exh. 1888
Watercolour painter. 1 Waverley Street, Nottingham. † N 1.

GOW, Mrs. James Exh. 1888
Watercolour painter. 1 Waverley Street, Nottingham. † N 1.

GOW, James d. 1886
Genre and historical painter. R.B.A. 1868. Add: London. † GI 2, M 2, RA 1, RBA 19, RSA 1.

GOW, James F. Macintosh Exh. 1881-98
Landscape painter. Edinburgh 1881; Knocke sur Mer, Belgium 1898. † GI 4, M 1, RA 6, RSA 44.

GOW, Lucienne M. Exh. 1933-38
Painter and etcher. Studied Heatherley's School of Art and Paris. Add: 47 Maresfield Gardens, London. † P 2, RBA 1, ROI 9, SWA 3.

GOW, Mary L. 1851-1929
Figure painter. Married Sydney Hall q.v. R.I. 1875, R.M.S. 1900. "Marie-Antoinette" purchased by Chantrey Bequest 1908. Exh. 1880-1927. Add: London. † AG 12, B 1, DOW 2, FIN 1, G 2, GI 5, L 17, M 11, P 1, NG 19, RA 23, RI 9.

GOW, Mabel S. Exh. 1929
29 Hamilton Park Terrace, Glasgow. † RSW 1.

GOW, Robert F. Exh. 1882
Etcher. 21 Homefield Road, Wimbledon, London. † RA 1.

GOWAN, Mary Exh. 1908-33
Miniature painter. London. † L 18, RA 25, RMS 1, RSA 8.

GOWANS, Charles Exh. 1884-85
Woodend, Langside, Glasgow. † GI 3, RSA 1.

GOWANS, George Russell c.1843-1924
Landscape painter. R.S.W. 1893. Exh. 1880-1923. Add: Aberdeen. † GI 22, L 1, RA 3, RBA 1, RI 1, RSA 19, RSW 28.

GOWANS, Miss I. de Grotte Exh. 1881-83
Edinburgh. † RSA 2.

GOWANS, Mrs. Jessie Exh. 1907
119 Broomhill Road, Aberdeen. † GI 1.

GOWER, Francis H. Exh. 1940
Portrait painter. 17 Lancaster Grove, Swiss Cottage, London. † RA 1.

GOWER, N. Exh. 1940
14 Brook Street, London. † SWA 2.

GOWER, Lord Ronald S. 1845-1916
Sculptor. Exh. 1880-97. Add: London. † G 2, RA 3.

GOWERS, W.R. Exh. 1888
Marine painter. 50 Queen Ann Street, Cavendish Square, London. † RA 1.

GOWLAND, Mary Exh. 1908-23
Mrs. Bridon. Liverpool 1908; Treharris, Glam. Wales 1922. † L 31.

GOW-STEWART, Alice M. Exh. 1900-6
Hawkhurst, Kent 1900; Bloomsbury, London 1901. † B 2, SWA 3.

GOYDER, Alice Kirkby b. 1875
Watercolour painter, etcher and dry point artist. Studied Bradford School of Art and London. Exh. 1899-1939. Add: Bradford, Yorks. 1899; Faversham, Kent 1922; Orford, Suffolk 1930. † B 2, L 2, M 2, RA 12, SWA 2.

GRACE, Agnes Exh. 1900
Baddow Hall, Chelmsford, Essex. † L 2.

GRACE, Alfred Fitzwalter* 1844-1903
Landscape and portrait painter. Studied Heatherleys and RA Schools (Turner gold medal). Author of "A Course of Landscape painting" 1881. Married Emily M.G. q.v. R.B.A. 1875. Add: Amberley, Arundel, Sussex 1880; Steyning, Sussex 1889. † B 6, D 2, G 2, GI 8, L 12, M 5, NG 2, RA 38, RBA 46, RI 12, ROI 12, RSA 7, TOO 3.

GRACE, Anna M. Exh. 1880-1910
Miniature portrait, still life and landscape painter. 54 York Road, Brighton. † GI 1, NG 2, RA 2, RBA 8, RMS 2.

GRACE, Charles H. Exh. 1897-98
Rhos Neigr, Ty Croes, R.S.O. Anglesey. † L 3.

GRACE, Emily M. Exh. 1881-88
Miniature painter and enameller. Married Alfred Fitzwalter G. q.v. Add: Amberley, Sussex. † RA 9.

GRACE, Frances Lily Exh. 1880-1909
Figure painter. 54 York Road, Brighton. † P 1, RA 3, RBA 9.

GRACE, Harriette Edith 1860-1932
Figure, landscape and still life painter. Exh. 1880-1900. 54 York Road, Brighton. † B 1, L 1, M 1, RA 11, RBA 8, ROI 1.

GRACE, James Edward* 1851-1908
Painter and illustrator. R.B.A. 1879. Married Mary G. q.v. Add: Milford, Surrey 1880; Bedford Park, London 1898. † AG 1, B 28, D 8, G 15, GI 24, L 29, M 35, NEA 4, NG 63, RA 31, RBA 133, RHA 5, RI 33, RID 41, ROI 30, RSA 10, TOO 10.

GRACE, L.U. Exh. 1905-15
London. † RA 5.

GRACE, Miss M. Exh. 1911
Pen Craig, Enderby, Nr. Leicester. † N 3.

GRACE, Mary Exh. 1881-1907
Landscape painter. Married James Edward G. q.v. Add: Milford, Godalming, Surrey 1881; Bedford Park, London 1898. † NG 13, RBA 2, ROI 3, SWA 1.

GRACE, Millicent Exh. 1899-1908
Daughter of James Edward and Mary G. q.v. Bedford Park, London. † NG 11, ROI 1.

GRACE, Miss M.S. Exh. 1905-8
Gracechurch Street, London. † SWA 6.

GRACEY, Theo T. Exh. 1924-40
Watercolour painter. Belfast. † FIN 3, RHA 55.

GRACHI, F. Exh. 1889
43 Piccadilly, London. † ROI 1.

GRACIE, K. Jean Exh. 1938-40
9 Clevedon Crescent, Glasgow. † GI 3.

GRAEF, Prof. Gustave 1821-1899
German portrait painter. London 1880; Berlin 1881. † G 2, RA 5.

GRAESSLE, Mrs. Beatrice Louise Exh. 1918
† RMS 1.

GRAF, Paul b. 1872
Sculptor. Etaples, Pas de Calais, Paris 1891; Stockholm, Sweden 1892; Glasgow 1902. † GI 5.

GRAFTON, Clare Exh. 1922
Perryfield House, Bromsgrove, Birmingham. † B 1.

GRAHAM, Alexander Exh. 1881-93
Architect. Carlton Chambers, 4 Regent Street, London. † RA 8.

GRAHAM, A.B. Exh. 1881
Hazelbank, Murrayfield, Edinburgh. † RSA 1.

GRAHAM, Alice G. Exh. 1898-1902
Foxhall, Bentley, Hants. † D 1, SWA 2.

GRAHAM, A. Ruth Exh. 1902
The Downs, Altrincham, Cheshire. † M 1.

GRAHAM, Dr. C. Honoria Exh. 1888-91
Sculptor. London. † RA 3.

GRAHAM, Caroline St. C. Exh. 1908-13
Rednock, Dursley, Glos. 1908; Chelsea, London 1912; Newlyn, Penzance 1913. † LS 8, RA 1.

GRAHAM, Delia Exh. 1894-97
116 Rathgar Road, Dublin. † RHA 5.

GRAHAM, Miss Elizabeth See CHALMERS

GRAHAM, Ethel Exh. 1906-8
4 Windsor Road, Rathmines, Dublin. † RHA 2.

GRAHAM, Evelyn Exh. 1927
Belle Vue, Horsforth, nr. Leeds. † L 1.

GRAHAM, E.R.D. Exh. 1897
Huntingstile, Grasmere. † RSA 1.

GRAHAM, Fergus Exh. 1928-37
Landscape, flower and interior painter. 4 Earl's Court Terrace, London. † AR 8, CG 1, LEF 83, RED 32, RA 1.

GRAHAM, Florence E. Exh. 1881-1905
Portrait and figure painter. 15 Cromwell Place, London. † B 1, GI 3, NG 4, P 8, RA 4, RMS 1, ROI 1, RSA 2, SWA 6.

GRAHAM, Frances H. Exh. 1893-94
28 Kirwan Street, Dublin. † RHA 2.

GRAHAM, Frances J. Exh. 1908-16
Miniature painter. Carnethick, Fowey, Cornwall. † RA 12.

GRAHAM, George* b. 1882
Painter and wood engraver. R.I. 1921, R.O.I. 1917, R.S.W. 1927. Exh. 1904-40. Add: Leeds 1904; Redmire, Yorks. 1912; Winchelsea, Sussex 1923. † AG 1, FIN 93, GI 52, I 3, L 35, LS 5, M 1, NEA 2, RA 55, RCA 1, RI 111, ROI 31, RSA 6, RSW 47.

GRAHAM, G.H. Exh. 1889-1914
Glasgow. † GI 10.

GRAHAM, George William Exh. 1880-89
Glasgow. † GI 6, RSA 7.

GRAHAM, J. Exh. 1912
20 Abingdon Court, Kensington, London. † RA 1.

GRAHAM, Mrs. J. Exh. 1923
Selkirk. † RSW 1.

GRAHAM, Ven. John Exh. 1915-31
Landscape painter. Archdeacon of Stoke on Trent. Add: Tretham Vicarage, Staffs. † AB 11, RI 1, RCA 2, WG 3.

GRAHAM, John Exh. 1880-85
Murrayfield 1880; Hawick 1883; Edinburgh 1885. † RSA 5.

GRAHAM, Josephine Exh. 1883-84
Mrs. W.J. † RI 3.

GRAHAM, Jean Douglas Exh. 1889-1904
Flower, figure and landscape painter. London. † L 2, M 2, RA 1, RBA 1, RHA 1, RI 3, SWA 7.

GRAHAM, James Hunter Exh. 1889-93
Figure and landscape painter. Brighton. † RA 3, RBA 1.

GRAHAM, J.L. Exh. 1891
Warrender Park Crescent, Edinburgh. † RSA 1.

GRAHAM, J.L. Exh. 1898
Garfield Cottage, Garfield Road, Chingford, Essex. † ROI 1.

GRAHAM, J.P. Exh. 1883
31 Greenside Street, Edinburgh. † RSA 1.

GRAHAM, Mrs. Lilias Jane Exh. 1883-1900
Miniature and figure painter. Bedford Park, London 1883; Bath 1898. † L 3, RA 2, RBA 1, RSA 3.

GRAHAM, Madge Exh. 1910-36
Flower, figure and landscape painter. Lived in France for many years. † AR 69, BG 51, RSW 1, SWA 2, WG 169.

GRAHAM, Nancy Exh. 1922-37
Landscape painter. Blanefield, Stirlingshire 1922; Polegate, Sussex 1936. † L 1, NEA 1, RA 1, RBA 2, RSA 2, SWA 3.

GRAHAM, Norman Exh. 1898-1915
Landscape painter. Merrow, Guildford 1898; Brook, Godalming, Surrey 1915. † RA 3, RBA 2, ROI 4.

GRAHAM, Peter* 1836-1921
Landscape, cattle and coastal painter. Studied under R.S. Lauder in Edinburgh. A.R.A. 1877, R.A. 1881, A.R.S.A. 1860, H.R.S.A. 1877. Add: London 1880; St. Andrews, N.B. 1909. † AG 4, B 1, GI 4, L 8, M 4, RA 67, RSA 5, TOO 34.

GRAHAM, Reginald Exh. 1937-38
† WG 7.

GRAHAM, Robert Exg. 1896-97
112 Bath Street, Glasgow. † GI 1, RSW 2.

GRAHAM, Robert F. Exh. 1904
Architect. 10 Queen Anne's Gate, London. † RA 1.

GRAHAM, Thomas Exh. 1896-97
63 Comely Bank Avenue, Edinburgh. † RSA 3.

GRAHAM, Thomas Alexander Ferguson 1840-1906
Painter of fishing and country life and portraits. Studied Trustees Academy, Edinburgh 1855. Travelled on the Continent and North Africa. R.O.I. 1883, H.R.S.A. 1883. Add: London and Edinburgh. † B 4, G 7, GI 21, L 23, M 14, NG 3, P 9, RA 26, RBA 1, RI·2, ROI 32, RSA 40.

GRAHAM, William* Exh. 1885
6317 S.S. Gio et Paolo, Venice. † ROI 1.

GRAHAM, W.C. Exh. 1909-11
20 Marlfield Road, West Derby, Liverpool. † L 2.

GRAHAME, H. Exh. 1910-11
1 Hamstone House, Kensington Court Place, London. † RA 2.

GRAHAME, James B. Exh. 1880-82
Landscape painter. 7 West Castle Road, Edinburgh. † GI 2, RSA 8.

GRAHAME, Jessie Ottilie Exh. 1894-1905
Flower painter. c/o Miss Ramsey, 15 Cromwell Crescent, South Kensington, London 1894; c/o R. Jackson & Son, 3 Slater Street, Liverpool 1900. † L 5, RID 11, ROI 1.

GRAHAME, Lewis Exh. 1934
† LEI 1.

GRAHAME-THOMSON, Leslie Exh. 1927-40
Architect. A.R.S.A. 1938. Add: Edinburgh. † RA 2, RSA 28.

GRAHAM-YOOLL, Helen Annie Exh. 1880-98
Figure painter. Pittenweem 1880; Edinburgh 1883. † G 1, RSA 10.

GRAINGER, Edward Exh. 1883-1913
Landscape painter. Dudley, Worcs. 1883; Broadhaven, Pembroke. 1904. † B 38, RA 5.

GRANDY, The Marchioness of see RUTLAND

GRANDGERARD, Lucien Henri* b. 1880
French painter. Exh. 1930. † L 2.

GRANDIDIER, Mrs. Alice Exh. 1932
Southsea, Hants. † RCA 1.

GRANDIS, Andrew Exh. 1939
Landscape painter. Leicester House, Montpelier Row, Twickenham, Middlesex. † RA 1.

GRANDMOULIN, Leandre Exh. 1923
37 Groeselenberg, Uccle, Brussels. † RSA 2.

GRANER-Y-ARRUFI, Luis 1867-1929
Spanish artist. c/o Roses & Co. Barcelona, Spain. † L 1.

GRANET, P. Exh. 1910
129 Rue Borghese, Neuilly sur Seine, France. † L 1.

GRANGE, de la See D

GRANGER, Miss Dorothy Exh. 1914-37
Decorative painter. A.S.W.A. 1929. Add: Wallingford, Berks. 1914; London 1928; Oxford 1935. † L 1, RA 9, SWA 12.

GRANGER, Mrs, Dorothy A. Exh. 1936
Figure painter. 21 Clarendon Road, Southsea, Hants. † RA 1.

GRANGER, E. Exh. 1907
Myrtle Cottage, Newlyn, Penzance. † L 2.

GRANGER, E.B. Exh. 1909
Illustrative painter. Little Milton, Wallingford, Berks. † NEA 1.

GRANGER, F.S. Exh. 1888
Architect. 10 Clinton Street, Nottingham. † N 1.

GRANGER, Genevieve Exh. 1902-11
Medalist. 37 Rue Denfert Rochereau, Paris. † L 2, RA 3, RHA 1.

GRANGER, J. Exh. 1883-84
18 Shaftesbury Terrace, Glasgow. † GI 2.

GRANGER, Lizzie Exh. 1899
38 Carlisle Mansions, London. † RSA 1.

GRANGER, Stephen Exh. 1906
Figure painter. 132 Cheyne Walk, Chelsea, London. † NEA 1.

GRANGER, W. Fraser Exh. 1938-39
Architect. 9 Saville Road, London. † RA 2.

GRANGER-TAYLOR, Mrs. Edith d. 1958
Figure and portrait painter. A.R.B.A. 1924, R.B.A. 1925, S.W.A. 1924, A.R.W.S. 1936 (resigned 1937). Exh. 1920-38. Add: London. † BA 2, CHE 1, COO 5, G 5, GI 2, GOU 7, I 2, L 4, NEA 9, P 11, RA 11, RBA 51, RI 2, RWS 20, SWA 31.

GRANGER-TAYLOR, J. Exh. 1936-38
Landscape painter. R.B.A. 1936. Add: 18 St. Mary Abbot's Terrace, London. † NEA 4, RA 4, RBA 16.

GRANT, A. Exh. 1920
682 Alum Rock Road, Birmingham. † B 1.

GRANT, Alexander Exh. 1880-81
Buckhaven, Fifeshire. † RSA 2.

GRANT, Alice Exh. 1881-1907
Portrait, figure and landscape painter. A.S.W.A. 1894, S.W.A. 1895. Add: London. † B 3, D 1, G 2, L 5, NEA 2, NG 3, P 6, RA 31, RBA 5, RHA 2, RI 8, RID 2, ROI 12, RSA 2, SWA 13.

GRANT, Beryl Exh. 1936-40
Portrait, figure and landscape painter. London. † COO 58, NEA 1, RI 1, SWA 3.

GRANT, Carleton Exh. 1885-99
Landscape painter. R.B.A. 1895, Add: Liverpool 1885; Liscard, Cheshire 1888; Rhyl, Wales 1890; Eton, Bucks. 1892; Gt. Marlow, Bucks. 1895; Windsor 1897; Shanklin, I.O.W. 1899. † B 5, L 10, M 1, RA 10, RBA 24.

GRANT, Constance Exh. 1922-25
Painter and wood engraver. Twickenham, Middlesex 1922; Staines, Surrey 1924. † L 1, RA 4.

GRANT, Duncan* b. 1885
Decorative, portrait, landscape and still life painter and industrial designer. b. Inverness. Studied Westminster School of Art 1902, Italy 1902-3, Paris under Jacques Emile Blanche and Slade School 1907. Member of London Group 1919. "The Kitchen" (1902) purchased by Chantrey Bequest 1959, "The Tub" (1912) in 1965 and "Girl at the Piano" 1940. Exh. 1909-40. † AG 103, ALP 6, 3A 1, BAR 1, BK 1, CAR 1, CHE 7, COO 51, GI 2, GOU 10, L 4, LEF 23, LEI 22, NEA 3, RED 29, RHA 2, RSA 4, TOO 11.

GRANT, D. Marion b. 1912
Stained glass artist. Studied Central School of Arts and Crafts 1931-35. Exh. 1940. Add: Chelsea, London. † RA 1.

GRANT, Edward Exh. 1938
Pollok House, Glasgow. † GI 1, RSW 1.

GRANT, George Exh. 1921
30 Williamsburg, Paisley, Glasgow. † RSA 1.

GRANT, G. Gregor Exh. 1928
Architect. 7 London Road, Tunbridge Wells, Kent. † RA 1.

GRANT, Henry Exh. 1882-93
Figure, portrait and landscape painter. London. † B 3, L 5. RA 2.

GRANT, Ian McDonald b. 1904
Painter and pastelier. Studied Glasgow School of Art 1922-26, Colarossi's, Paris 1927, Royal College of Art 1927-30. Taught Victoria School of Art, Southport, Lancs. 1935 and painting master Manchester School of Art from 1937. Exh. 1929-40. † GI 5, M 3, RA 3, RSA 9.

GRANT, James Exh. 1886
21 West Nile Street, Glasgow. † GI 1, TOO 1.

GRANT, James A. b. 1887
Painter and etcher. Studied under Fred Burridge in Liverpool, Juliens, Paris and London Central Technical School. R.P. 1931, A.R.E. 1928. Add: Liverpool 1906; Hoylake, Cheshire 1909, London 1914. † AB 2, CHE 28, GI 3, I 3, L 21, LEI 3, M 1, NEA 4, P 27, RA 23, RE 18, RHA 1, ROI 2, RSA 3.

GRANT, John A.W. Exh. 1936-39
25 Rutland Square, Edinburgh. † GI 3, RSA 5.

GRANT, Jane E. Exh. 1884-89
Glasgow. † GI 4.

GRANT, J.F.W. Exh. 1909
Architect. Bronte Cottage, Southend Road, Hampstead, London. † RA 1.

GRANT, J.M. Exh. 1920
Archibald Place, Edinburgh. † RSA 1.

GRANT, John P. Exh. 1923-24
Architect. Bute Estate Chambers, Castle Street, Cardiff, Wales. † RA 2, RSA 1.

GRANT, Lewis Exh. 1901
Llanfellyn Cottage, Bushey, Herts. † RA 1.

GRANT, L.J.M. Exh. 1905
Sendhurst Grange, Send, Surrey. † RA 1.

GRANT, Mary c.1830-1908
Sculptor. Studied in Paris, Florence and in London under J.H. Foley. Exh. 1880-92. Add: London. † RA 13, RSA 3.

GRANT, Mary Isabella Exh. 1880-93
Watercolour landscape and figure painter. Hillersdon, Cullompton, Devon. † RBA 5, RI 7.

GRANT, Miss Margaret Ross see HISLOP.

GRANT, Mary R. Exh. 1903-6
Sculptor. 3 West Road Park, Tottenham, London. † RA 1, SWA 3.

GRANT, Nan Exh. 1915-27
Sculptor. b. Birmingham. Studied London and Paris. Add: 16 Canfield Gardens, London. † B 2, I 7, L 3, P 2, RA 4.

GRANT, Peter Exh. 1938-40
Painter and sculptor. National College of Art, Kildare Street, Dublin. † RHA 7.

GRANT, Reginald Exh. 1922
† BK 2.

GRANT, Miss Robina B.I. Exh. 1940
3 Park Terrace, Annan, Dumfries. † RSA 2.

GRANT, Spencer W. Exh. 1903-7
Architect. 63 Finsbury Pavement, London. † RA 2.

GRANT, Thomas F.W. Exh. 1923
Architect. 11 Buckingham Street, Adelphi, London. † RA 1.

GRANT-DUFF, Lily Exh. 1900
Chelsea Embankment, London. † NG 2.

GRANTHAM, G.H. Exh. 1938
Bannaboo, Farnham Common, Bucks. † RSA 1.

GRANT-SUTTIE, Mrs. Isobel Exh. 1932
Cannon Hill Lane, West Wimbledon, London. † GI 1.

GRANVILLE, Evelyn Exh. 1883
Miniature portrait and landscape painter. 15 Beaumont Street, Portland Place, London and RA Schools, Burlington House, London. † RA 1, RBA 1.

GRANZOW, Vladislav Exh. 1908-10
c/o Allied Artists Assn., 67 Chancery Lane, London. † LS 8.

GRAS, Jean P. Exh. 1912
83 Rue de la Tombre Issoire, Paris. † L 1.

GRASETT, Katherine Exh. 1919-22
Tapestry and brocade weaver. Studied School of Art and Handicraft, Vienna and in Stockholm. Proprietor of the London School of Weaving. A.S.W.A. 1935. Add London. † SWA 4.

GRASS, A. Exh. 1890
The Avenue, 76 Fulham Road, London. † NG 1.

GRASSBY, C.B. Exh. 1881-84
227 West Campbell Street, Glasgow. † GI 2.

GRASSEL, Franz* Exh. 1904-13
Munich. † GI 15, L 4.

GRATTON, Anna Exh. 1900-4
London 1900; Chesterfield 1904. † B 1, SWA 1.

GRATTON, Thomas O.W. Exh. 1940
Architect. 93 Douglas Street, Glasgow. † GI 1.

GRATZ, Miss N. Exh. 1909-12
Sculptor. 16 Canfield Gardens, London. † L 5, RA 1.

GRAU-SALA* Exh. 1937
Figure painter. † BA 28.

GRAVELL, William D. Exh. 1894
Architect. 6 Queen Anne's Gate, London. † RA 1.

GRAVELY, Percy Exh. 1886-1904
Landscape and cattle painter. Bushey, Herts. 1886; Lewes, Sussex 1890; Edgbaston, Birmingham 1904. † B 4, L 1, RA 1, RBA 2, ROI 1, RSA 1.

GRAVENEY, William Charles b. 1904
Wood carver, modeller and architectural sculptor. Studied School of Wood Carving, South London Art School. Exh. 1926-40. Add: London. † P 3, RA 7.

GRAVES, Charles A. Exh. 1884
Marine painter. 57 Kenilworth Road, St Leonards-on-Sea, Sussex. † RA 1.

GRAVES, Miss D.M. Exh. 1920-21
London. † SWA 2.

GRAVES, Hon. Henry Richard Exh. 1880-81
Portrait painter. 159 Cromwell Road, London. † RA 2.

GRAVIER, Alexandre Louis Exh. 1882-97
Etcher and engraver. London 1882 and 1889; Brighton 1885. † RA 12.

GRAY, Alice* Exh. 1882-1904
Portrait and figure painter. Edinburgh. † GI 12, L 1, RA 2, RBA 1, RI 1, RSA 29.

GRAY, Bella Exh. 1910
12 Deva Terrace, Chester. † L 1.

GRAY, Claude W. Exh. 1897-1902
Landscape painter. Chelsea, London 1897; Hale, Westmorland 1902. † RA 2.

GRAY, Douglas Stannus 1890-1959
Portrait, landscape and genre painter. Brother of Rosalind Stannus G. q.v. Studied Croydon and RA Schools (Landseer and British Institute Scholarships). War service with London Regiment 1914-19. R.O.I. 1927, R.P. 1934. "Rosalind" purchased by Chantrey Bequest 1926. Exh. 1919-39. Add: Clapham Park, London. † GI 3, I 1. L 3, NEA 1, P 9, RA 34, ROI 26.

GRAY, Ethel 1879-1957
Painter, etcher and craftsman. b. Newcastle-on-Tyne. Studied York, Leeds and Royal College of Art. Art mistress at York and Leeds Schools of Art and Leeds Training College. Add: Oxford 1900; Leeds 1939. † L 1, RA 2, SWA 1.
GRAY, Frances Exh. 1910
12 Deva Terrace, Chester. † L 2.
GRAY, Mrs. F.S. Exh. 1924-33
28 Westcliffe Road, Birkdale, Lancs. † L 4.
GRAY, George Exh. 1880-1909
Landscape painter. Edinburgh 1880; Musselburgh N.B. 1898. † GI 15, RHA 1, RSA 89, RSW 5.
GRAY, G. Kruger Exh. 1919-40
Painter and sculptor. London. † RA 22.
GRAY, Henry Exh. 1885-97
Miniature portrait painter. London. † RA 6.
GRAY, Herbert Exh. 1901
Landscape painter. London. † RA 1.
GRAY, Isabella Exh. 1892-94
1 Warrender Park Crescent, Edinburgh. † RSA 3, RSW 1.
GRAY, Ian Campbell Exh. 1927-38
† GOU 10, RED 1, TOO 55.
GRAY, Jack Exh. 1920-22
43 Briarbank Terrace, Edinburgh. † GI 2, RSA 4.
GRAY, James Exh. 1893-1925
Sculptor. Kilmarnock 1893; Glasgow 1900 and 1920; Milngavie, N.B. 1912 and 1925. † GI 29, RA 1, RSA 16.
GRAY, James d. 1947
Watercolour flower painter. Married Jean Lyal Christie q.v. R.S.W. 1936. Add: Burntisland 1917; Edinburgh 1927. † GI 18, L 8, RA 6, RSA 35, RSW 38.
GRAY, John d. 1957
Landscape painter. R.S.W. 1941. Add. London 1885; Thursley, Nr. Godalming, Surrey 1890; Maiden Newton, Dorset 1899; Blandford, Dorset 1909; Hawick 1910 and 1925; Saxmundham, Suffolk 1917; Broughty Ferry 1937. † B 2, M 2, NG 1, P 2, RA 23, RBA 10, ROI 4, RSA 2, RSW 4.
GRAY, Joseph b. 1890
Painter and etcher. Studied South Shields School of Art. Sketching trips to Russia, Germany, Spain, France and Holland. Served with Black Watch and as war artist to the "Graphic" World War I. Exh. 1919-37. Add: Barnhill, Broughty Ferry, Angus. † BA 1, CON 4, FIN 17, RSA 2.
GRAY, J.C. Exh. 1911
Alexander Place, Downfield, Dundee. † GI 1.
GRAY, Jeannie C. Exh. 1896-1911
Edinburgh 1896 and 1910; Dollar, N.B. 1908. † L 1, RSA 5.
GRAY, John C. Exh. 1929
Tritonville Lodge, Sandymount, Dublin. † RHA 3.
GRAY, J. Crosbie Exh. 1939-40
43 Lamb Street, Glasgow. † GI 1, RSW,1.
GRAY, Jessie Exh. 1881-93
Figure painter. Edinburgh. † GI 4, RA 1, RSA 42.
GRAY, Mrs. Jean Lyal See CHRISTIE
GRAY, John R. Merton Exh. 1907
Cavendish Road, Chorlton-cum-Hardy, Manchester. † M 1.
GRAY, Miss M. Exh. 1889
21 Bolton Studios, Redcliffe Road, London. † L 1, M 1.
GRAY, Mabel Exh. 1906-14
Glasgow. † GI 5.
GRAY, Mrs. Mary Exh. 1910-11
12 Deva Terrace, Chester. † L 3.
GRAY, Maurice Exh. 1913
Landscape painter. 88 Oakley Street, London. † NEA 1.
GRAY, Millicent Etheldreda* b. 1873
Portrait and figure painter and illustrator. Studied Cope and Nicol's School of Art (bronze medal) and RA Schools. Exh. 1899-1929. Add: London. † COO 6, GI 2, L 16, LEI 24, P 9, RA 28, RID 15, ROI 2, SWA 5, WG 1.
GRAY, Monica F. Exh. 1898-1919
Landscape painter. London. † L 4, RA 6, SWA 6.
GRAY, Miss Marion I. Exh. 1936
† RI 1.
GRAY, Norah Neilson d. 1931
Portrait and figure painter and watercolourist. b. Helensburgh. Studied Glasgow School of Art. Spent war years in France. R.S.W. 1914. Exh. 1905-30. Add: Glasgow. † GI 40, I 5, L 10, P 4, RA 7, RSA 27, RSW 55.
GRAY, Ronald 1868-1951
Figure and landscape painter. Studied Westminster School of Art. N.E.A. 1923, A.R.W.S. 1934, R.W.S. 1941. "My Mother" (1908) purchased by Chantrey Bequest 1925. Exh. 1889-1940. Add: London. † CG 26, CHE 3, COO 2, FIN 3, G 5, GI 1, GOU 87, I 2, L 6, M 2, NEA 89, P 9, RA 6, RHA 4, RI 2, RSA 6, RWS 57.
GRAY, R.C. Exh. 1885-86
72 Northumberland Street, Edinburgh. † RSA 7.
GRAY, Rosalind Stannus b. 1892
Painter and miniaturist. Sister of Douglas Stannus G. q.v. Studied Croydon School of Art. Exh. 1928-40. Add: Clapham Park, London. † RA 6, RMS 4.
GRAY, Robert W. Exh. 1898-1911
Liverpool. † L 7.
GRAY, S. Exh. 1883
9 Coleherne Terrace, Richmond Road, South Kensington, London. † RBA 1.
GRAY, Thomas Exh. 1881-1914
Figure and domestic painter. London 1881; Broadwater, Worthing, Sussex 1908. † D 1, L 3, LS 9, RA 2, RBA 9, RI 9, ROI 1.
GRAY, Thomas U. Exh. 1893
Sculptor. Lansdowne Houses, 340 Essex Road, London. † RA 1.
GRAY, William Exh. 1883
1 Morden Road, Blackheath, London. † RI 1.
GRAY, William Exh. 1933-40
22 Berryhill Drive, Giffnock, Glasgow. † GI 6.
GRAY, William Everatt 1892-1957
Sculptor in wood and ivory. Studied Regent Street Polytechnic. Exh. 1939. Add: 6 Somerset Avenue, Surbiton, Surrey. † RA 1.
GRAY, W.H. Exh. 1891-92
4 Percy Terrace, 36 Monkton Street, Ryde, I.o.W. † B 3.
GRAY, W.P. Exh. 1882-1904
7 Cable Street, Liverpool. † L 16.
GRAYSON, Clifford P. Exh. 1883
Marine painter. Concarneau, Finisterre, France. † RBA 1.
GRAYSON, G.E. Exh. 1884
31 James Street, Liverpool. † L 1.
GRAYSON, H. Exh. 1912-13
Royal Liver Building, Liverpool. † L 1, RA 1.
GRAYSON, Stanley b. 1898
Portrait and landscape painter. b. Aylesbury. Studied London and Chelsea Schools of Art. Exh. 1930-40. † NEA 2, RA 3.
GRAYSON, W. Exh. 1894-1930
Liverpool. † L 22.
GRAYSTON, George Exh. 1937
† NEA 1.
GRAZEBROOK, Ellen Lucy Exh. 1894-1909
Hagley, Stourbridge, Worcs. † B 2, LS 3.
GRAZIOSI, Guiseppe Exh. 1916
c/o A. Stiles & Sons, 617 Fulham Road, London. † GI 1.
GREACEN, Edmund* b. 1877
American artist. Giverny Par Vernon, Eure, France 1908-9. † LS 8.
GREASON, R. Exh. 1883
81 Union Street, Southwark, London. † RHA 1.
GREATBACH, Ada Exh. 1901
30 Smallbrook Street, Birmingham. † B 1.
GREATOREX, Eleanor Exh. 1908
c/o Jas. Paterson, 115 George Street, Edinburgh. † RSA 1.
GREATOREX, Kathleen H. Exh. 1895-98
10A Cunningham Place, London. † B 1, SWA 6.
GREATOREX, Miss L. Exh. 1885
20 Princes Road, Manchester. † M 1.
GREATWOOD, Fanny Ethel Exh. 1910-19
Hagley, Nr. Stourbridge, Worcs. 1910; Wallingford, Berks. 1919. † LS 9.
GREAVES, Bailey Exh. 1907
10 Grange Avenue, Leeds. † RCA 2.
GREAVES, Constance Exh. 1934-39
c/o Barclays Bank Ltd., Dyke Road, Brighton. † RCA 2, SWA 1.
GREAVES, Hilda Exh. 1911-12
Bank House, Ecclesfield, Nr. Sheffield. † GI 1, L 2, M 1.
GREAVES, Isabel Exh. 1894
33 Marlborough Place, London. † M 1.
GREAVES, John Exh. 1910-24
Architect. London. † RA 2.
GREAVES, M.E. Exh. 1881
Watercolour still life painter. Mackworth, Derby. † SWA 1.
GREAVES, Walter* 1846-1930
Painter of landscape and river scenes. Pupil and studio assistant to Whistler. "Hammersmith Bridge on Boat Race Day" (c.1862) purchased by Chantrey Bequest 1922, "Old Battersea Bridge" (c.1874) in 1931 and "The Green Dress" (c.1875) in 1931. Add: London. † G 23, GI 3, GOU 112, L 1, M 1.
GREAVES, William* Exh. 1882-1920
Landscape and figure painter. Leeds. † B 2, L 2, M 2, RA 9, RCA 2, ROI 1.
GREEN, Mrs. Alfred Exh. 1880
Fruit painter. Add: Female School of Art. † SWA 1.
GREEN, Arthur Exh. 1920
212 Lozells Road, Birmingham. † B 1.
GREEN, Aveling Exh. 1897-1903
2 Steele's Studios, Haverstock Hill, London. † L 7.
GREEN, Arthur B. Exh. 1935-37
Landscape painter. 105 Kenilworth Court, Putney, London. † RA 2.
GREEN, A.E. Exh. 1880
107 Victoria Street, Westminster, London. † RHA 1.
GREEN, Amy F. Exh. 1936-39
Landscape and figure painter. 56 Northcourt Avenue, Reading, Berks. † COO 51, SWA 3.

GREEN, A. Romney Exh. 1927-29
25 Bridge Street, Christchurch, Hants. † L 9.

GREEN, Annie T.M. Exh. 1896-97
148 Church Hill Road, Handsworth, Birmingham. † B 2.

GREEN, B. Exh. 1909
Rostletop Road, Earby, Nr. Colne, Lancs. † RCA 1.

GREEN, Betty Exh. 1934
Lochend, Bardowie, by Milngavie. † RSA 1.

GREEN, Miss C. Exh. 1912-14
Silsoe Villa, Ealing, London. † RA 4.

GREEN, Charles Exh. 1889
Sculptor. 20 Shrewsbury Road, Sheffield. † RA 1.

GREEN, Charles* 1840-1898
Watercolour painter of genre and historical subjects and illustrator. Brother of H. Towneley G. q.v. A.R.I. 1864, R.I. 1867, R.O.I. 1883. Add: London. † B 4, FIN 3, GI 2, L 4, M 5, RA 6, RI 25, ROI 3.

GREEN, Miss Conyngham Exh. 1928
Burcot, Townsend Road, St. Albans, Herts. † RBA 3.

GREEN, Miss C.J. Exh. 1889
17 Highfield Street, Leicester. † B 1.

GREEN, Christopher Lawrence Exh. 1921
† LS 3.

GREEN, Constance Marjorie Mortimer b. 1888
Landscape painter, architect and etcher. Studied Liverpool City School of Art, Byam Shaw and Vicat Cole School of Art and Cheltenham School of Art. Exh. 1909-33. Add: Birkenhead 1903; Battledown, Cheltenham 1921. † B 10, L 18.

GREEN, Mrs. Dora Exh. 1900-26
152 Chorlton Road, Manchester. † M 2.

GREEN, David Gould 1854-1918
Watercolour landscape painter. R.I. 1898. Add: St. John's Wood, London 1880; Hampstead, London 1894. † AG 7, D 72, G 4, GI 1, L 8, LEI 1, NG 2, RA 17, RBA 23, RHA 4, RI 144. RSA 1, WG 52.

GREEN, Edith Exh. 1900-6
Mrs. David G. 30 Fairfax Road, Hampstead, London. † D 1, RI 3.

GREEN, Mrs. Edridge Exh. 1896
6 Ravensfield Villas, Hendon, London. † ROI 1.

GREEN, Mrs. Evelyn Exh. 1919
8 Bassett Road, London. † RI 2.

GREEN, Miss Ethel A. Exh. 1898-1904
Marlborough House, Woodstock Road, Moseley, Birmingham. † B 8.

GREEN, Mrs. Eliza Goodwin Exh. 1884-86
Hawthorndene, Buckland Road, Maidstone, Kent. † ROI 1, SWA 1.

GREEN, E. Margaret Exh. 1900-3
Mrs. F. Curtis. Miniature portrait painter. 7 Rosetti House Studios, Rosetti Gardens, Chelsea, London. † RA 4, RMS 2.

GREEN, Miss E. West Exh. 1907
West Hayes, Sheepscombe, Stroud, Glos. † B 1.

GREEN, Frank Exh. 1920-21
212 Lozells Road, Birmingham. † B 3.

GREEN, Miss F.E. Exh. 1914
Haddenham, Bucks. † SWA 1.

GREEN, Miss Florence Marjorie Exh. 1935-37
Wood engraver. The Five Winds, Bovey Tracey, Devon. † COO 28, RA 1, RED 1, SWA 2.

GREEN, G. Exh. 1922
124 Gregory Boulevard, Nottingham. † N 1.

GREEN, Geo K. Exh. 1899
42 Blacket Place, Edinburgh. † RSA 1.

GREEN, G.W. Exh. 1920-23
Landscape painter. Kimberley, Notts. † N 13.

GREEN, Herbert M. Exh. 1919
Miniature painter. 98 Ulleswater Road, Southgate, London. † RA 1.

GREEN, H. Taylor Exh. 1937
Watercolour landscape painter. 2 Tower View, Halifax, Yorks. † RA 1.

GREEN, Henry Towneley* 1836-1899
Painter and black and white artist. Brother of Charles G. q.v. A.R.I. 1875, R.I. 1879, R.O.I. 1883. Add: Hampstead, London. † B 2, FIN 1, L 6, M 8, RI 54, ROI 12.

GREEN, H. Vaughan Exh. 1884-87
Watercolour landscape and coastal painter. 108 Fishergate, Preston, Lancs. † B 4, M 4, RBA 3.

GREEN, James Exh. 1882-1901
Grasmere. † L 8, RSA 3.

GREEN, Jenny Exh. 1938-39
Dry point artist. 15 Kingsmead Road South, Oxton, Birkenhead. † M 1, RA 1, RCA 2, RSA 3.

GREEN, Miss J.F. Exh. 1897-1909
London 1897, The Pleasaunce, Bearsted, Kent 1909. † L 1, SWA 4.

GREEN, J.J. Exh. 1928-29
Riverbank Road, Heswall, Cheshire. † L 2.

GREEN, J. Jameson Exh. 1913
19 St. John Street, Liverpool. † L 4.

GREEN, John Kenneth Exh. 1925-40
Portrait and landscape painter and wood cut artist. Southwold, Suffolk 1925; Redcliffe Road, London 1928; Crowthorne, Bucks. 1937. † AR 68, NEA 10, P 10, RA 9, RBA 1.

GREEN, J.W. Exh. 1900
40 Dacre Hill, Rock Ferry, Cheshire. † L 1.

GREEN, L.D. Exh. 1930
† P 1.

GREEN, Leonard James Exh. 1936-39
† P 2.

GREEN, Leonora Kathleen b. 1901
nee Silver. Painter and textile designer. Studied Camberwell School of Arts and Crafts. Exh. 1931-40. Add: 70 Battersea Rise, London. † RA 3.

GREEN, Leslie W. Exh. 1904-6
Architect. 71 Strand, London. † RA 2.

GREEN, Mabel Exh. 1880-89
Landscape and figure painter and black and white artist. London. † L 2, RA 5, RBA 2, ROI 4, SWA 4.

GREEN, Madeline Exh. 1912-40
Figure painter. S.W.A. 1923. Add: The Mall, Ealing, London. † GI 27, I 2, L 7, M 1, RA 30, RHA 1, RSA 1, SWA 30.

GREEN, Mary C. Exh. 1890-1919
Landscape painter. London. † L 12, RA 3, RI 1, SWA 1.

GREEN, Margaret E. Exh. 1911-27
Landscape painter. Manchester 1911; 83 Gunterstone Road, London 1925. † L 1, LS 6, RA 3, ROI 1.

GREEN, M. Helen Exh. 1884-1909
Mrs. J.R. Cohu (1910). Flower painter. Add: St. John's Wood, London 1884; St. Albans, Herts. 1892. † D 39, GI 1, RA 3, RI 3, SWA 2.

GREEN, M.M. Exh. 1888-89
Antwerp 1888; Dublin 1889. † RHA 2.

GREEN, Miss M. Taylor Exh. 1904-13
Figure painter. Tutbury, Burton on Trent 1904; London 1913. † B 3, M 1, RA 2.

GREEN, Miss N.E. Exh. 1934-38
West Bromwich. † B 3.

GREEN, Nathaniel Everett Exh. 1880-96
Landscape painter. 39 Circus Road, St. John's Wood, London. † B 5, D 48, GI 1, L 6, RA 2, RBA 3, RI 12.

GREEN, Reginald Exh. 1911-38
Etcher. A.R.E. 1918. Add: Wimbledon 1911; Cobham, Surrey 1918; West Byfleet, Surrey 1925. † BK 3, CON 8, L 1, RA 5, RE 26, RED 1, RHA 1.

GREEN, Roland Exh. 1929-32
Etcher. Ruskin Studio, 7 New Court, Lincoln's Inn, London. † CON 3, L 2.

GREEN, Richard Crafton b. 1848
Portrait, landscape and flower painter. Studied British Museum and Heatherley's. Exh. 1889-1916. Add: Saffron Walden, Essex 1889; Newport, Essex 1897. † B 5, M 1, RA 17, ROI 1.

GREEN, Miss Tennyson Exh. 1921-40
Portrait and landscape painter and etcher. Studied Slade School. Add: London. † NEA 6, P 1, RA 8, RI 1, SWA 2.

GREEN, Thomas Exh. 1930
The Hollies, Allbatts Road, Brownhills, Nr. Walsall, Staffs. † B 1.

GREEN, T. Frank Exh. 1923
Etcher. 272 Willesden Lane, London. † RA 1.

GREEN, T.H. Exh. 1887-89
London. † B 2.

GREEN, Mrs. W. Exh. 1914
Edgbaston, Birmingham. † SWA 2.

GREEN, Will A. Exh. 1931-33
24 Belle Vue,. Belgrave Road, Birmingham. † B 2.

GREEN, William Curtis b. 1875
Architect (The Dorchester Hotel, London). Studied R.A. Schools. Exh. 1900-32. Add: London. † GI 3, RA 39, RSA 4.

GREEN, William John Exh. 1880-81
Architect. 8 Delahay Street, Westminster, London. † RA 3.

GREENAWAY, Kate 1846-1901
Watercolour painter and illustrator of children's books. R.I. 1889. Add: London. † D 2, FIN 400, RA 4, RI 14.

GREENBANK, Arthur Exh. 1888-1902
Figure painter. London. † B 24, L 4, M 2, RA 5, RBA 5, RCA 4, RI 9, ROI 6.

GREENBERG, Mabel Exh. 1927-33
Portrait and figure painter. Studied Slade School. A.R.B.A. 1928, R.B.A. 1930. Add: 32A Queen's Road, London. † B 4, NEA 5, P 2, RA 2, RBA 42, RED 1, SWA 2.

GREENDALE, Mrs. M.C. Exh. 1901-3
27 Watcombe Circus, Carrington, Notts. † N 5.

GREENE, Alice Exh. 1883-87
Landscape painter. 7 Coverdale, Richmond Hill, Surrey. † B 5, GI 2, L 1, RBA 4, ROI 2.

GREENE, Anthony Exh. 1938
Landscape painter. 19 Redcliffe Gardens, London. † RA 1.

GREENE, C.A.C. Exh. 1910
18 Norfolk Street, Sunderland. † RA 1.

GREENE, Editha Exh. 1893
Millbrook, Mageney, Co. Kildare. † RHA 1.

GREENE, G.M.K. Exh. 1909
Mrs. E. Miniature portrait painter. Cappagh Lodge, Monaghan, Ireland. † RA 1.

GREENE, J. Exh. 1880-86
Mountjoy Square, Dublin 1880; Paris 1885. † RHA 5.

GREENE, J.A. Exh. 1915
49 Blenheim Crescent, Notting Hill, London. † RA 1.

GREENE, J. Blake Exh. 1892-1905
London. † RHA 5.

GREENE, Mary Charlotte b. 1860
Landscape painter. Studied St. John's Wood and R.A. Schools. Principal and owner Garden Studio, Cambridge. Exh. 1892-1919. Add: Harston House, Harston, Cambs. † L 2, LS 9, RA 1, SWA 2.

GREENE, T. Garland Exh. 1933
† RSW 1.

GREENER, Leslie Exh. 1930-31
Linocut artist. † RED 2.

GREENFIELD, Mrs. E. Exh. 1905
Barholm, Chorley Wood, Herts. † I 1.

GREENFIELD, E. Latham Exh. 1886
Landscape painter. 6 Bedford Gardens, Campden Hill, London. † RBA 1.

GREENFIELD, Mrs. E. Latham (C.) Exh. 1883-1905
Landscape and flower painter. Old Palace, Richmond, Surrey 1883; St. Ives, Cornwall 1897. † B 4, G 1, I 1, L 5, M 1, RA 1, RBA 2, ROI 3, SWA 6.

GREENGRASS, W.E. b, 1892
Linocut artist. Exh. 1930-38. † RED 6.

GREENHALGH, J. Exh. 1882-97
Southport, Lancs. † L 12, M 9, RHA 6.

GREENHALGH, Joan Kevan b. 1906
Painter, illustrator and poster statuette artist. Studied at Miss Wright's Studios in Liverpool and under W.C. Penn. Exh. 1923-29. Add: Liverpool. † L 10.

GREENHAM, Peter G. b. 1909
Figure painter. Brother of Robert D.G. q.v. 16 Court Lane Gardens, Dulwich, London 1934. † RA 1.

GREENHAM, Robert Duckworth b. 1906
Painter, etcher, wood engraver and mural decorator. Studied Byam Shaw and Vicat Cole School 1924 and R.A. Schools 1926-29 (Landseer and British Institute scholarships, Creswick prize, silver and bronze medals). R.B.A. 1931, R.O.I. 1933. Exh. 1925-40. Add: London. † BAR 3, CHE 3, M 2, NEA 14, P 9, RA 12, RBA 54, RED 1, ROI 36.

GREENHEAD, Henry T. Exh. 1896-1910
Etcher. 15 Gloucester Road, Regents Park, London. † RA 7.

GREENHILL, Alexander Mcdonald b. 1907
Watercolour landscape painter and etcher. Studied evenings at Glasgow School of Art. Carpet designer for Glasgow Company. Exh. 1927. Add: Hillhead, Glasgow. † RSW 1.

GREENHILL, Miss Harriot Exh. 1900
150 Selhurst Road, South Norwood, London. † SWA 1.

GREENHILL, Mina Exh. 1939
18 Roland Gardens, London. † RA 1.

GREENHILL, Mary Esther Exh. 1880-1909
Figure and domestic painter. London. † B 1, L 4, LS 4, RA 1, RHA 3, SWA 6.

GREENISH, Miss E. Exh. 1918
Bournemouth. † SWA 1.

GREENISH, Emma Exh. 1885
Flower painter. 5 Lyvedon Terrace, Billing Road, Northampton. † SWA 2.

GREENISH, Mrs. Florence E. Exh. 1880-85
Landscape painter. Leeds 1880; Harrogate 1883; 7 Lyvedon Terrace, Northampton 1884. † D 1, RA 1, RBA 1, ROI 2, SWA 2.

GREENLAW, Jean-Pierre Exh. 1936
Urban landscape and figure painter. 46 Gloucester Place, London. † RA 1.

GREENLEES, James Exh. 1880-83
136 Wellington Street, Glasgow 1880; Dunblane 1883. † GI 4, RSA 1.

GREENLEES, Miss Maggie Exh. 1884-85
12 Cunun Place, Grange, Edinburgh. † RSA 3.

GREENLEES, Robert* Exh. 1880-94
Watercolour landscape painter. Glasgow. † DOW 4, GI 44, L 7, RHA 5, RSA 28, RSW 24.

GREENMAN, Edwin Exh. 1931-36
Wood engraver. Studied Beckenham School of Art 1926-29, Royal College of Art 1929-33. Add: Beckenham, Kent. † RA 4.

GREENOUGH, Miss B. Exh. 1899
48 Bloomsbury Street, London. † RMS 1.

GREENOUGH, Richard Exh. 1885
Sculptor. c/o McCracken, 38 Queen Street, London. † RA 1.

GREENSHIELDS, T. Exh. 1939
Westhay, Hawkchurch, Axminster, Devon. † RBA 2.

GREENSLADE, James Thomas Exh. 1886-87
Figure painter. Walthamstow, London. † RA 1, RI 2.

GREENSLADE, Sidney K. Exh. 1893-1924
Architect, London. † RA 16.

GREENSMITH, William H. Exh. 1881-85
Landscape painter. N.S.A. 1881. 21 Sherwin Street, Nottingham. † N 3.

GREENUP, Joseph Exh. 1932-40
Figure painter. R.I. 1936. Add: Chesham Bois, Bucks. 1932; Abbey Road, Hampstead, London 1934. † B 3, P 1, RA 3, RI 20.

GREENWOOD, Beatrice Exh. 1892-1909
Figure and domestic painter. Married Edwin Noble q.v. A.S.W.A. 1903. Add: Willesden Green 1892; Guildford 1903; Chelsea, London 1906. † BG 1, RA 11, RBA 9, ROI 2, SWA 14.

GREENWOOD, Colin H. Exh. 1880-81
Watercolour landscape painter. Fairfield, Mount Ararat, Richmond Hill, Surrey. † RBA 8.

GREENWOOD, Frank Exh. 1924-27
14A Cannon Street, Manchester. † L 3, M 3.

GREENWOOD, Harold Exh. 1929-35
Urban landscape painter. London 1929; Pinner, Middlesex 1935. † RA 2.

GREENWOOD, John Frederic 1885-1954
Etcher and wood engraver. Studied Shipley 1904-7, Bradford 1907-8, Royal College of Art 1908-11. Head of Design School, Leeds College of Art. R.B.A. 1940, A.R.E. 1922, R.E. 1939. Add: Battersea Park, London 1914; Ilkley, Yorks. 1933. † CHE 1, GI 8, L 3, M 2, RA 8, RE 63, RED 3, RHA 3, RSA 3.

GREENWOOD, Mrs. L.D. Exh. 1917
3 Gerard Road, Wester super Mare, Som. † RA 2.

GREENWOOD, Mrs. Maud Exh. 1924-25
Sonning, Sunnyside Avenue, Blackburn, Lancs. † B 1, L 2.

GREENWOOD, Miss M.L. Exh. 1905-14
1 Friar's Terrace, York. † L 3, RA 4, RCA 7, RHA 7, RSA 3.

GREENWOOD, Orlando b. 1892
Figure painter. b. Nelson, Lancs. Studied Goldsmith's College 1913. In 1914 joined the Royal Engineers and resumed his studies in 1919. A.R.B.A. 1920, R.B.A. 1922. Exh. 1920-33. Add: London. † BA 31, FIN 2, G 1, GI 1, GOU 7, L 7, LEI 30, P 1, RA 3, RBA 32, RI 1.

GREENWOOD, Sydney Earnshaw b. 1887
Figure painter. Studied Liverpool, Juliens, Paris and Slade School. Teacher of life drawing, Central School of Arts and Crafts. Add: Liverpool 1912; London 1920-33. † GOU 5, L 2, NEA 3, RA 1.

GREENWOOD, William E. Exh. 1924
Architect. King's Ride, Sheen Road, Richmond, Surrey. † RA 1.

GREENWOOD-SMITH, Miss A.C. Exh. 1918
4 Thirlmere Road, Streatham, London. † RA 1.

GREER, Mrs. Ellen Exh. 1904
Col a More Cottage, Dalkey, Co. Dublin. † RHA 1.

GREEVES, J. Arthur Exh. 1936
Landscape painter. Bernagh, Strandtown, Belfast. † RHA 2.

GREG, Barbara b. 1900
Wood engraver. b. Cheshire. Studied Slade School. A.R.E. 1940. Exh. 1928-40. Add: London. † GI 3, L 6, M 6, RA 7, RE 4, RED 2, RHA 1.

GREGORY, Charles* 1849-1920
Genre and historical painter. A.R.W.S. 1882, R.W.S. 1884. Add: London 1880, Ripley, Surrey 1881, Milford, Godalming, Surrey 1894; Marlow, Bucks. 1940. † B 2, DOW 92, FIN 4, GI 4, L 21, M 7, RA 7, RHA 1, RWS 127.

GREGORY, Christine Exh. 1909-40
Sculptor and potter. Teacher of modelling Hammersmith School of Arts and Crafts from 1918. A.S.W.A. 1919, S.W.A. 1924. Add: London. † GI 1, I 11, L 14, RA 41, RMS 2, SWA 2, WG 2.

GREGORY, Mrs. Cora Exh. 1895-1900
36 Birdhurst Rise, South Croydon, Surrey. † SWA 2.

GREGORY, Daisy Exh. 1910-11
Beresford Road, Wallasey, Cheshire. † L 3.

GREGORY, Edward Exh. 1907-31
Figure and landscape painter. Bradford 1907; London 1910. † GOU 1, L 8, M 4, NEA 9, P 2, RA 4.

GREGORY, Elsie Exh. 1900-33
Mrs. J.A.C. Osborne. Miniature portrait painter. Add: London. † BG 1, I 1, L 25, RA 17, RI 1, RMS 2.

GREGORY, Edward John* 1850-1909
Genre and portrait painter and illustrator. b. Southampton. Studied Royal College of Art and R.A. Schools. Employed on decorating the V & A and worked for the "Graphic" 1871-75. A.R.A. 1883, R.A. 1898, A.R.I. 1891, R.I. 1896, P.R.I. 1898, H.R.M.S. 1896, R.O.I. 1883 (Hon. Retd. 1903), R.S.W. 1900. Add: Maida Vale, London 1880 and 1897; Cookham Dene, Berks. 1889. † B 1, FIN 1, G 12, GI 2, L 10, M 8, RA 29, RCA 1, RI 46, RMS 1, ROI 5, RSA 4.

GREGORY, Edith Marian Exh. 1885-1910
Figure painter. London. † B 9, G 1, L 2, LS 2, P 1, RA 3, ROI 9.

GREGORY, Edward W. Exh. 1891-1911
Urban landscape painter. Derby 1891; London 1898. † B 1, L 3, N 2, RI 1.

GREGORY, Mrs. Mary Isabella Exh. 1896-1914
Halberton Vicarage, Nr. Tiverton, Devon 1896; Exmouth, Devon 1910. † D 40.

GREGORY, Robert Exh. 1912-15
Landscape and figure painter. Coole Park, Gort, Co. Galway. † BG 24, CHE 28, NEA 3.

GREGORY, Sara Exh. 1900-13
Higher Broughton, Manchester 1900; Bolton, Lancs. 1913. † L 1, M 1.

GREGORY, W.H. Syder Exh. 1925-26
Architect. 24 Penywern Road, London. † RA 2.

GREGORY, Wallace J. Exh. 1930-40
Architect. London. † L 1, RA 2.

GREGORY, Yvonne Exh. 1916-38
Mrs. Bertram Park. Miniature painter. 43 Dever Street, London. † RA 9.

GREGSON, Miss D.J. Exh. 1914
Heald House, Leyland. † L 1.

GREGSON, Isabelle B. Exh. 1901-10
Miniature portrait painter. A.R.M.S. 1909. Add: London. † L 7, M 3, NG 2, RA 5, RMS 1.

GREGSON, J. Exh. 1932
† L 1.

GREGSON, Vallance Jean Exh. 1933-38
52 Booth Road, Stackstead, Bacup, Lancs. † L 2, M 1.

GREIFFENHAGEN, Maurice William* 1862-1931
Painter and illustrator. Studied R.A. Schools (Armitage prize). Worked for "The Lady's Pictorial" and "The Daily Chronicle", illustrated the novels of Rider Haggard. Taught Glasgow School of Art 1906. N.E.A. 1886, A.R.A. 1916, R.A. 1922, R.P. 1909. "Women by a Lake" purchased by Chantrey Bequest 1914 and "Dawn" in 1926. Add: London. † B 4, DOW 49, FIN 2, G 1, GI 35, I 5, L 36, M 3, NEA 8, NG 1, P 19, RA 104, RBA 4, ROI 2, RSA 12.

GREIG, Mrs. Catherine H. Exh. 1895-1904
Bird painter. Thuboro House, Holsworthy, N. Devon. † B 1, L 2, RA 1.

GREIG, Mrs. E. Exh. 1911-16
21 Ravenscourt Park, London 1911; Hounslow, Middlesex 1915. † L 13, RA 5, RMS 2.

GREIG, James 1861-1941
Painter and black and white artist and writer. Studied London and Paris. Art critic on the "Morning Post". R.B.A. 1898. Exh. 1897-1907. Add: London. † RBA 67.

GREIG, Miss J.G. Exh. 1884-87
Manse Kinfauns, Flencarse 1884; Murrayfield 1887. † RSA 3.

GREIG, J.M. Exh. 1884
† RSA 1.

GREIG, John Russell* b. 1870
Portrait, figure and landscape painter. Studied Gray's School of Art, Aberdeen, R.S.A. Schools and Paris. Teacher of drawing and painting at Gray's School of Art, Aberdeen. Exh. 1898-1939. Add: Aberdeen 1898 and 1921; Chelsea, London 1906. † GI 8, LS 5, M 1, P 1, RA 2, RSA 35.

GREIG, O. Exh. 1898
6 Rue Boissonade, Boulevard Raspail, Paris. † RBA 2.

GREINER, Dick Exh. 1936
† RSA 1.

GRENET, Edward Exh. 1890-1909
Paris. † GI 1, L 1.

GRENFELL, Francis H. Exh. 1936
Sculptor. Glendower Hotel, Glendower Place, London. † RA 1.

GRESLEY, Daisie Exh. 1887-88
Fruit painter. 69 Elizabeth Street, Eaton Square, London. † D 5, SWA 2.

GRESLEY, Frank Exh. 1881-1920
Landscape painter. Father of Harold G. q.v. N.S.A. 1881. Add: Ockbrook, Nr. Derby 1881, Borrowash, Nr. Derby 1882; Derby 1885; Chellaston, Nr. Derby 1920. † N 9.

GRESLEY, Harold b. 1892
Landscape and figure painter. Son of Frank G. q.v. Studied Derby School of Art 1912, Nottingham School of Art 1919 and Royal College of Art. Assistant art master Repton School. A.N.S.A. 1930, N.S.A. 1936. Exh. 1920-40. Add: Chellaston, Nr. Derby. †, B 2, COO 30, N 18, RA 1, RI 5.

GRESLEY, Mrs. J.B. Exh. 1903
Green Bank, Shottle, Derby. † N 1.

GRESLEY, James S.* Exh. 1880-85
Landscape painter. N.S.A. 1882. Add: Draycott, Nr. Derby 1880; Borrowash, Nr. Derby 1882; Bolton Abbey, Nr. Skipton, Yorks. 1883; Derby 1885. † N 7, RBA 1, RI 1.

GRESLEY, Miss W.M. Exh. 1886-93
Domestic and flower painter. The Close, Lichfield, Staffs. † B 1, RI 1, SWA 3.

GRESTY, Hugh 1899-1958
Landscape painter. b. Nelson, Lancs. Studied Lancashire School of Art and Goldsmith's College. A.R.B.A. 1925, R.B.A. 1927, R.I. 1935. Add: Barrowfield, Lancs. 1922; Greenwich, London 1923, St. Ives, Cornwall 1927. † B 5, GI 2, L 18, RA 20, RBA 48, RCA 4, RI 6, RSA 2.

GREUX, Gustave Exh. 1881
† RE 1.

GREVILLE, Col. the Hon. Alwyn Exh. 1916-27
Sculptor. Chelmsford, Essex 1916; Woodford, Salisbury, Wilts. 1919. † I 1, L 2, RA 3.

GREVILLE, Eveline Exh. 1895-1902
Laleham, Middlesex 1895; Addlestone Surrey 1900. † SWA 8.

GREVILLE, Irwin Exh. 1936
33 London Road, Ewell, Surrey. † ROI 1.

GREW, Miss G. Exh. 1911-14
Breconbrae, Portadown. † RHA 2.

GREW, Thomas Exh. 1891-95
Stained glass artist and architectural decorator. 4 Salisbury Mews, Gloucester Place, London. † RA 4.

GREY, Alfred* d. 1926
Landscape and cattle painter. A.R.H.A. 1869, R.H.A. 1870. Exh. 1880-1924. Add: Lower Sherrard Street, Mountjoy Square, Dublin. † B 4, L 6, RA 1, RHA 368, ROI 3.

GREY, Charles d. 1892
A.R.H.A. 1838, R.H.A. 1845. 1 Lower Sherrard Street, Mountjoy Square, Dublin. † L 2, RHA 27.

GREY, Mrs. Charles Exh. 1935
Flower painter and illustrator. † WG 52.

GREY, C.M. Exh. 1880
1 Lower Sherrard Street, Mountjoy Square, Dublin. † RHA 2.

GREY, Mrs. Edith F. Exh. 1889-1913
Fruit and flower painter. Newcastle on Tyne. † L 2, M 2, RA 16, RBA 1, RI 13, RMS 1, SWA 2.

GREY, Gregor Exh. 1880-1911
1 Lower Sherrard Street, Mountjoy Square, Dublin. † RHA 107.

GREY, George B. Exh. 1882
Hugwy Cottage, Bettws-y-Coed, Wales. † L 1.

GREY, James* d. 1905
Domestic and figure painter. A.R.H.A. 1875, R.H.A. 1875. Add: Dublin. † L 1, RHA 9.

GREY, John Exh. 1880-87
172 West George Street, Glasgow. † GI 26, M 2, RHA 1, RSA 3.

GREY, Mrs. Jane Willis Exh. 1880-96
Domestic and figure painter. London. † D 6, RA 5, RBA 19, RI 8, ROI 4, SWA 1.

GREY, Philip Exh. 1899
130 Whitehead Road, Aston, Birmingham. † RHA 1.

GREY, Mrs. W. Exh. 1898-99
27 Maida Vale, London. † RBA 1, ROI 1.

GREYSMITH, Ralph Glanville 1874-1953
Painter and designer. b. Manchester. Studied Brighton School of Art and Juliens, Paris. Examiner Reading University and Goldsmith's College. Superintendent of Art Institution, Brighton. Head of Department, Training of Art Teachers, School of Art, Brighton. Exh. 1931-40. Add: Hove, Sussex. † RA 3, RBA 1, RI 2.

GRIBBLE, Bernard Finegan* b. 1873
Marine and portrait painter, and architectural artist. Son of Herbert A.G. q.v. Married Eleanor Mabel G. q.v. Studied Belgium, South Kensington and under Albert A. Toft. Marine painter to the Worshipful Company of Shipwrights from 1912. Exh. 1891-1940. Add: London 1891 and 1915; Rickmansworth, Herts. 1910; Parkstone, Dorset 1937. † B 4, GI 22, L 22, NG 25, RA 66, RHA 8, RI 1, RMS 1, ROI 24.

GRIBBLE, Mrs. Eleanor Mabel Exh. 1932-36
nee Clumm. Married to Bernard Finegan G. q.v. Ipswich, Suffolk. † RCA 4.

GRIBBLE, Herbert A. Exh. 1880-82
Architect (Brompton Oratory). Father of Bernard Finegan G. q.v. 10 Alexander Square, Kensington, London. † RA 2.

GRIBBLE, Mrs. Nora Exh. 1883-86
37 Hans Place, London. † RI 2.

GRIBBLE, Vivien d. 1932
Mrs. Douglas Jones. Wood engraver and illustrator. Studied Munich, Slade School and Central School of Arts and Crafts. Exh. 1920. Add: Chelsea, London. † NEA 2.

GRIBBON, Miss A. Exh. 1882-1905
Dublin. † RHA 34.

GRIBBON, C. Edward Exh. 1931-35
Landscape painter. 3 Upper Ely Place, Dublin. † RED 1, RHA 1.

GRICE, Kathleen G. Exh. 1910-14
Woodhey Road, Rock Ferry, Cheshire. † L 8.

GRICE, William Stanley b. 1889
Architect. Studied A.A. and under Sir Ernest George. Exh. 1919-28. Add: London. † GI 3, RA 6.

GRICE, Winifred S. Exh. 1935
Figure and animal painter. Cross House, Bootle, Cumberland. † RA 2.

GRIER, Edmund Wyly b. 1862
Painter and sculptor. b. Melbourne, Australia. Exh. 1886-95. Add: London 1886 and 1892; St. Ives, Cornwall 1889. † DOW 1, GI 1, L 1, P 2, RA 6, RBA 2, ROI 1.

GRIER, Louis Monro* c.1864-1920
Landscape and marine painter. R.B.A. 1906. Add: St. Ives, Cornwall. † B 1, BG 1, DOW 2, G 1, GI 3, L 8, M 7, NG 1, RA 11, RBA 41, RHA 2, RID 41, ROI 8.

GRIERSON, Miss Exh. 1913
Florence. † SWA 1.

GRIERSON, Charles MacIver* 1864-1939
Painter, black and white and pastel artist. b. Queenstown, Ireland. R.I. 1892. Add: London 1885 and 1890; Newlyn, Penzance, Cornwall 1888. † AB 64, B 13, D 11, DOW 1, FIN 1, GI 3, GOU 5, L 17, LEI 1, M 6, P 1, RA 9, RBA 2, RHA 7, RI 81, ROI 7.

GRIERSON, Edith Exh. 1926-33
10 Hill Top Avenue, Cheadle Hulme, Manchester. † L 10, RCA 3.

GRIERSON, Miss E.M. Exh. 1893-95
Avonmore Road, Kensington, London. † SWA 4.

GRIERSON, Miss Hilda Beatrice Corbett
see HARRISSON

GRIERSON, Miss Jean Exh. 1928
Torville, Sedbergh Park, Ilkley, Yorks. † L 1.

GRIERSON, Miss L. Hamilton
Exh. 1935-39
Edinburgh. † GI 1, RSA 7, SWA 2.

GRIERSON, Margaret Exh. 1906-34
Glenville, Blackrock, Co. Dublin 1906; Cranleigh, Surrey 1932. † GI 2, GOU 5, I 2, NEA 2, RHA 11, RSA 6.

GRIERSON, Miss M.M. Exh. 1905
27 Newsham Drive, Liverpool. † L 1.

GRIERSON, Robert Exh. 1890-94
Masonic Chambers, Bangor, Wales. † RCA 8.

GRIERSON, Ronald b. 1901
Linocut artist, textile and embroidery designer. Studied Grosvenor School of Modern Art 1926-29. Exh. 1932-38. † BA 1, RED 2.

GRIESBACH, Julia A. Exh. 1882-83
Miniature portrait painter. 20 Holland Street, Kensington, London. † RA 2.

GRIEVE, Alec d. 1933
Portrait and landscape painter. Studied Dundee, London and Colarossi's. Paris. Add: Dundee 1891, Tayport, Fife 1897. † GI 5, L 2, RA 1, RSA 15.

GRIEVE, George Exh. 1884
18 Cook Street, Liverpool. † L 1.

GRIEVE, John Exh. 1880-84
Edinburgh. † RSA 8.

GRIEVE, Marion Exh. 1880-1911
Glasgow. † GI 43, RSA 9, RSW 1.

GRIEVE, Walter Graham d. 1937
A.R.S.A. 1920, R.S.A. 1929, P.R.S.A. 1931, R.S.A. 1934. Exh. 1895-1938. Add: Edinburgh. † GI 40, L 8, M 1, RSA 101, RSW 11.

GRIFFIN, Amy Exh. 1896-97
Cromwell House, Northampton. † B 3.

GRIFFIN, Anna Exh. 1888-94
Portrait and figure painter. Chelsea, London. † RBA 3, RI 2, SWA 1.

GRIFFIN, Anthony Exh. 1939-40
Cholesbury, Nr. Tring, Herts. 1939; London 1940. † NEA 1, RBA 2.

GRIFFIN, Ella Frances 1898-1953
Portrait and figure painter. Studied Chelsea School of Art 1915-20. Teacher at Chelsea School of Art from 1920. A.S.W.A. 1924. Add: Bushey, Herts. 1900; Watford, Herts 1910; London 1922. † B 3, LS 18, NEA 3, P 1, RA 4, RCA 1, RHA 4, RI 1, ROI 2, SWA 58.

GRIFFIN, Ernest H. Exh. 1922-39
Wolverhampton. † B 4.

GRIFFIN, Miss E.M. Exh. 1912-15
1 Lincoln Drive, Liscard, Cheshire. † L 6.

GRIFFIN, Frank Exh. 1934-39
Landscape painter. Bolton, Lancs. † GOU 54, RCA 1.

GRIFFIN, Fred Exh. 1926-29
Landscape painter and sculptor. 114 Russell Road, Nottingham. † L 1, N 9, RA 1.

GRIFFIN, F.W. Exh. 1938
Torquay, Devon. † RCA 1.

GRIFFIN, Heneage Exh. 1903-4
Hotel Cecil, London. † D 9.

GRIFFIN, James Exh. 1893
42 Patrick Street, Cork. † RHA 1.

GRIFFIN, J.C. Heyness Exh. 1886-88
Watercolour landscape painter. 17 Turret Grove, Clapham, London. † GOU 4, RI 1.

GRIFFIN, Miss J.L. Exh. 1883-85
Landscape and figure painter. London. † L 1, RA 1, SWA 1.

GRIFFIN, Oswald Exh. 1928-39
Northfield, Warwicks. 1928; Brimingham 1935. † B 19.

GRIFFITH, Agnes Exh. 1886
Flower painter. Courts Hill, Haslemere, Surrey. † RBA 1.

GRIFFITH, Annie H. Exh. 1895-97
17 Egypt Street, Liverpool. † L 3.

GRIFFITH, Arthur Troyte Exh. 1905-13
The Priory Gateway, Malvern, Worcs. † B 1, D 2, LS 10.

GRIFFITH, E. Exh. 1884
13 Raymond Street, Chester. † L 1.

GRIFFITH, Mrs. E. Exh. 1938
20 Cantelupe Road, Bexhill on Sea, Sussex. † B 3.

GRIFFITH, Mrs. Emily Exh. 1886-92
Sculptor. London. † L 2, RA 4.

GRIFFITH, Edward Hales b. 1909
Exh. 1927-30. South View, Alexandra Drive, Rock Ferry, Wirral, Cheshire. † L 3.

GRIFFITH, E.O. Exh. 1888-1912
Chester 1888; Rock Ferry, Wirral, Cheshire 1909; Liverpool 1911. † L 5.

GRIFFITH, Frank b. 1889
Landscape and portrait painter. Studied Academie Ranson, Paris and under Sickert in London. Add: Paris 1913; London 1914; Marlborough 1939. † BG 37, G 1, GOU 1, LS 10, P 2, RBA 1.

GRIFFITH, Griff R. Exh. 1889-91
15 Melrose Road, Liverpool. † L 2.

GRIFFITH, Miss H.M. Exh. 1910-16
60 Fitzjohn Avenue, London. † L 1, RA 8.

GRIFFITH, Joan E.G. Exh. 1928-33
Flower painter. Kingswood, Surrey 1921; Chelsea, London 1931. † RA 1, ROI 2, SWA 2.

GRIFFITH, James Milo Ap Exh. 1880-89
Sculptor. London. † L 11, M 1, RA 18.

GRIFFITH, Kate Exh. 1880-90
Bird, flower and fruit painter. Turgiss Rectory, Winchfield, Hants. † D 2, L 5, RA 4, RBA 3, SWA 12.

GRIFFITH, Lillian E. 1877-c.1967
Sculptor and miniature painter. Studied Wimbledon College of Art. Add: Wimbledon 1902; Maesteg, Glam. 1909; Liverpool 1916; Hengoed, Glam. 1924. † L 3, RA 19.

GRIFFITH, Mary E. Exh. 1881-1923
Portrait, landscape and miniature painter. London 1881; Dublin 1915. † RA 1, RBA 2, RHA 7, RMS 1, ROI 2.

GRIFFITH, Miss N. Exh. 1914
Brentwood, Belgrave Street, Liscard, Cheshire. † L 1.

GRIFFITH, Robert G. Exh. 1914
432 Lower Breck Road, Anfield, Liverpool. † L 1.

GRIFFITH, Mrs. V.E.G. Exh. 1894
131 South Circular Road, Dublin. † RHA 1.

GRIFFITH, William Exh. 1882-83
Figure painter. Bromley House, Bromley, Kent. † L 1, RA 1, RBA 2.

GRIFFITH, William Gladwell Exh. 1907-14
45 Frederick Street. Edinburgh. † GI 1, LS 18, RSA 1.

GRIFFITH, Miss W. Wyn Exh. 1919-21
Glencairne, Neston, Cheshire. † L 2.

GRIFFITHS, A. Exh. 1935-36
Cardiff. † RCA 3.

GRIFFITHS, Major Arthur Exh. 1894-1900
Landscape painter. Visited Egypt. Add: 74 South Audley Street, London. † RID 10.

GRIFFITHS, A.R. Exh. 1929-30
8 Carlingford Road, London. † NEA 4.

GRIFFITHS, Brian C. Exh. 1937
Penarth, Glam. † RCA 1.

GRIFFITHS, Blanche M. Exh. 1896
Stained glass artist. 65 Blenheim Terrace, St. John's Wood, London. † RA 1.

GRIFFITHS, C. Exh. 1887
13 Raymond Street, Chester. † L 4.

GRIFFITHS, Cicely Exh. 1921
64 Gloucester Place, London. † SWA 3.

GRIFFITHS, David T. Exh. 1921-25
School of Art, Birkenhead. † L 6.

GRIFFITHS, Miss Erica Exh. 1919-33
Liverpool. † L 5.

GRIFFITHS, Miss E.C. Exh. 1902
200 Sutherland Avenue, London. † SWA 1.

GRIFFITHS, Miss Ena N. Exh. 1923
1 Eastfield Drive, Aigburth, Liverpool. † L 1.

GRIFFITHS, G. Exh. 1886
31 Park Row, Nottingham. † N 1.

GRIFFITHS, Gwenny b. 1867
Portrait painter. b. Swansea. Studied Slade School (landscape prize 1890) and Juliens, Paris. Exh. 1889-1929. Add: London. † B 1, GI 1, L 13, NG 5, P 11, RA 2, RBA 1, RCA 3, SWA 6.

GRIFFITHS, J. Exh. 1939
5 Edgar Avenue, Mansfield, Notts. † N 2.

GRIFFITHS, John 1838-1918
Figure and portrait painter. Add: School of Art, Bombay and c/o Mr. W. Emmerson, 1 Westminster Chambers, London 1880-94. † RA 7.

GRIFFITHS, Leslie Exh. 1930-32
25 Hopton Grove, Billesley, Birmingham. † B 3.

GRIFFITHS, Mat. Exh. 1882-83
80 Soho Street, Liverpool. † L 2.

GRIFFITHS, Miss M. Day Exh. 1901-6
Mertyn, Woodville Road, Ealing, London. † SWA 8.

GRIFFITHS, O.T. Exh. 1938
St. Colmans Avenue, Cosham, Portsmouth. † RBA 2.

GRIFFITHS, Rhys Exh. 1935
Hampstead, London. † RCA 1.

GRIFFITHS, Tom Exh. 1880-1904
Landscape painter. London 1880; Amberley, Arundel, Sussex 1893; Bideford, Devon 1901. † B 2, D 2, GI 9, L 1, M 3, NG 1, RA 19, RBA 8, RHA 3, RI 2, ROI 12.

GRIFFITHS, W.J. Exh. 1892-1908
Stained glass artist. London. † RA 7.

GRIFFITHS, William L. Exh. 1895
Architect. 27 High Street, Newport, Mon. † RA 1.

GRIGG, Edgar P. Exh. 1940
Figure painter. 21 Highfield Grove, Horfield, Bristol. † RA 1.

GRIGG, F.R. Exh. 1890-92
Figure painter. Percy House, North End, Hampstead, London. † B 1, RBA 3.

GRIGGS, Frederick Landseer Maur 1876-1939
Painter, etcher and illustrator. A.R.A. 1922, R.A. 1932, R.B.S.A. 1925, A.R.E. 1916, R.E. 1918. Add: Hitchin, Herts. 1897; Chipping Campden, Glos. 1909. † BA 6, BG 62, CG 3, FIN 58, GI 1, L 7, RA 37, RE 43, RSA 2, TOO 3.

GRIGGS, H.T. Brock Exh. 1930
Etcher. 9 Bramerton Street, Chelsea, London. † RA 1.

GRIGGS, N. Heath Exh. 1930
65 Bromford Lane, Erdington, Birmingham. † B 2.

GRIGOR, Archibald d. 1929
Yoker, N.B. 1912; Scotstoun, Glasgow 1925. † GI 2, L 3, RSA 2.

GRILLET, A. Exh. 1881
22 Rue Vienanse, Passy, Paris. † RHA 2.

GRIMALDI, Argenta L. Exh. 1907-37
Painter and miniaturist. Bournemouth 1907; Broughton, Hants. 1933. † B 2, RA 4.

GRIMBLE, J. Exh. 1939
c/o Mrs. Turpin, Beverley Gardens, Casterton Road, Stamford, Lincs. † N 1.

GRIMES, Robert Exh. 1934
School of Art, Dublin. † RHA 1.

GRIMLEY, Edith M. Exh. 1895-96
Metropolitan Bank, Bennetts Hill, Birmingham. † B 2.

GRIMM, Stanley A 1891-c.1967
Landscape, portrait and figure painter. Studied Riga, Russia 1912. R.O.I. 1935, R.P. 1936. Exh. 1924-40. Add: London. † ALP 34, CHE 1, GI 1, GOU 4, L 3, LEI 3, NEA 4, P 25, RA 3, RED 4, ROI 16.

GRIMMOND, Amelia G.J. Exh. 1889
271 Sauchiehall Street, Glasgow. † GI 1.

GRIMMOND, Mrs. Catharine M. Exh. 1938-40
Landscape painter. 28 Well Walk, Hampstead, London. † RA 2.

GRIMMOND, William Exh. 1880-1914
Figure painter. 271 Sauchiehall Street, Glasgow 1880; Fallowfield, Manchester 1909. † GI 41, L 2, RA 3, RSA 3, RSW 2.

GRIMMOND, William Junr. b. 1884
Painter, illustrator, theatrical and poster designer. b. Manchester. Studied Manchester School of Art. Add: Fallowfield, Manchester 1911; 28 Well Walk, Hampstead, London 1928. † FIN 3, GI 2, L 3, M 1, NEA 20, RA 22, RBA 3, RI 2.

GRIMSDALE, Fred Exh. 1892-1906
Liverpool 1892; Hoylake, Cheshire 1894. † L 14.

GRIMSHAW, Emma Exh. 1892-1904
Belfast 1892; Portrush 1902. † RHA 2, RSA 1.

GRIMSHAW, H.S. Exh. 1914
† M 1.

GRIMSHAW, John Atkinson* 1836-1893
Landscape painter. Knostrop Old Hall, Nr. Leeds. † G 1, L 4, M 1, RA 4, RHA 1, ROI 1, TOO 8.

GRIMSHAW, Miss M. Exh. 1885
Plantation House, Accrington, Lancs. † M 1.

GRIMSHAW, Mary Exh. 1926
South View, Gomersal, Nr. Leeds. † L 1.

GRIMSHAW, W.H. Murphy Exh. 1885-96
Landscape and figure painter. London 1885; Prittlewell Priory, Essex 1892. † L 1, RA 6, RBA 3, RHA 4, ROI 2.

GRIMSHAW, W.M. Exh. 1907
109 Cromwell Road, London. † RA 1.

GRIMSLEY, F.J. Exh. 1888
Landscape painter. 3 Queen's Walk Villas, Nottingham. † N 1.

GRIMSON, N.K. Exh. 1929
† D 3.

GRIMSTONE, James Exh. 1898-1914
Glasgow 1898 and 1905; London 1901. † GI 10.

GRIMSTONE, Mary Exh. 1881-99
Still life and flower painter. London 1881; Harrow, Middlesex 1898. † D 1, L 1, SWA 5.

GRIMWOOD, Hertbert Charles b. 1880
Sculptor. Studied Colchester and in Ireland. Exh. 1928. Add: 2 Hervey Street, Ipswich. Suffolk. † RA 1.

GRINDLEY-FERRIS, Vyvyan Exh. 1935-40
Etcher. A.R.E. 1938. Add: Natal, South Africa 1935; 52 Northgate, Regent's Park, London 1937; Cape Town, South Africa 1939. † RA 5, RE 8.

GRINEAU, de See D

GRINLING, Mrs. Alice G. Exh. 1893
Figure painter. Orm Lodge, Stanmore, Middlesex. † RA 1.

GRINNELL-MILNE, Geo. Exh. 1911-13
23 Ennismore Gardens, London. † D 3.

GRISAR, Jacques Exh. 1919-24
† GOU 3, I 2.

GRISARD, Henri D. Exh. 1907
31 Rue Crozatier, Paris. † L 1.

GRISCHOTTI, N. Margaret Exh. 1936-39
85 Kensington Court, London. † P 3, RBA 1.

GRISHOTTI, Nina M. Exh. 1891
12 Belmont Gardens, Hillhead, Glasgow. † GI 1.

GRISDALE, Miss I.M. Exh. 1928
14 Thornfield Road, Headingley, Leeds. † L 1.

GRISDALE, W.T. Exh. 1915
c/o R. Jackson & Sons, 51 Moorfields, Liverpool. † L 1.

GRISON, Francois Adolphe* 1845-1914
French painter. Exh. 1884-85. Rue Grand, Champigny sur Marne, France. † GI 3.

GRITTON, Miss Toby Exh. 1900-3
Brakenhurst, Redhill, Surrey. † SWA 5.

GRIVAL, de See D

GRIVEAU, Georges b. 1863
French artist. 15 Quai d'Anjou, Paris 1905. † L 1.

GRIVEAU, Lucien Exh. 1906
22 Rue Monsieur le Prince, Paris. † L 1.

GRIXONI, Count Mario Exh. 1914-40
Portrait painter. London. † L 10, P 11, RA 5, RI 10, ROI 4.

GROBE, German b. 1857
German artist. Winkelsfelderstrasse 15, Dusseldorf, Germany 1913. † RA 2.

GROCOCK, George H. Exh. 1892-99
Architect. Bute Estate Office, Cardiff 1892; Times Buildings, Bedford 1898. † RA 3.

GROGAN, Anthony Exh. 1929-31
Portrait painter. School of Art, Dublin. † RHA 3.

GROLL, Jan F. Exh. 1907
17 West Gardens, Tooting, London. † RA 1.

GROLLER, P. M. Exh. 1901
32 Rue de Vaugirard, Paris. † L 1.

GROLLERON, Paul Louis Narcisse* 1848-1901
French painter of military subjects. Exh. 1884-85. † ROI 4, TOO 6.

GRONBERG, Miss Xenia Exh. 1939
Cardiff. † RCA 1.

GRONDARD, Ph. Exh. 1909
85 Rue Ampere, Paris. † L 1.

GRONE, Ferdinand E.* Exh. 1888-1919
Figure and landscape painter. R.B.A. 1903. Add: Colchester 1888; Dulwich, London 1919. † B 12, D 3, L 12, M 7, RA 11, RBA 119, RI 11.

GRONE, Miss R.H. Exh. 1911-12
Richmond Hill, Monkstown, Co. Dublin. † RHA 2.

GRONNO, Arthur Exh. 1926
† M 1.

GRONVOLD, Elsa Exh. 1925-40
Portrait and figure painter. London. † COO 6, L 2, NEA 1, P 3, RA 7, ROI 7.

GROOM, Charles W. Exh. 1889-99
Landscape painter. Wallington, Surrey 1889; Carshalton, Surrey 1890. † B 1, G 1, L 1, NG 2, RA 5, RBA 5, ROI 5.

GROOM, Emerson Exh. 1936-40
Etcher. Merilies Close, Westcliffe on Sea, Essex. † RA 2.

GROOM, Mary Exh. 1930
† RSA 1.

GROOME, William Henry Charles Exh. 1881-1911
Landscape painter. R.B.A. 1901. Add: London. † D 6, G 1, RA 11, RBA 37, RI 13, ROI 2.

GROOT, de See D

GROSCLAUDE-BODENSTEIN, Mme. Exh. 1913
Route d'Antibes, Cannes, France. † LS 2.

GROSE, Miss A. Exh. 1906
51 York Street, Westminster, London. † RA 1.

GROSE, Melicent S. Exh. 1880-1923
Landscape and figure painter. A.S.W.A. 1886. Add: London 1880, 1889 and 1905; Pont Aven, Finisterre, France 1881; Oxford 1900. † B 2, D 5, DOW 2, L 2, M 4, NEA 1, NG 4, RA 1, RBA 11, RI 3, SWA 182.

GROSJEAN, Henry Exh. 1906
4 Rue Poussin, Paris. † L 1.

GROSS, Anthony b. 1905
Painter, etcher and illustrator. Studied Slade School, Juliens, Paris and Madrid. Exh. 1924-39. Add: London. † AG 176, FIN 6, L 4, LEI 81, RA 6.

GROSS, May Exh. 1909-14
Gondville Lodge, Cambridge. † LS 13, SWA 2.

GROSS, Peter Alfred* 1849-1914
American landscape painter. 7 Rue Chaptal, Paris, 1887. † GI 1.

GROSS, Richard Oliver 1882-1964
Sculptor. Exh. 1930. Add: 422 Manukau Road, Auckland, New Zealand. † RA 1.

GROSS, Valentine Exh. 1914
Theatrical portrait painter. † FIN 19.

GROSSE, Prof. Franz Theodor 1829-1891
German portrait painter. Dresden 1886. † G 2, M 2.

GROSSMITH, Weedon d. 1919
Painter, actor and author. Studied Slade School, London University and RA Schools. Exh. 1880-1919. Add: London. † B 3, G 2, L 3, M 4, RA 10, RBA 2, RHA 4, ROI 4.

GROSVENOR, Caroline Exh. 1889-1906
Hon. Mrs. Norman G. Miniature portrait and watercolour landscape painter. Add: Grosvenor Square, London 1889; St. Cross Lodge, Winchester 1902. † L 1, N 16, P 12, RA 6, RI 1.

GROSVENOR, E.H. Exh. 1927-38
Poplars, Church Lane, Normanton, Yorks. † L 2, M 2.

GROTRIAN, Miss Exh. 1937
9 Ashburn Place, London. † ROI 1.

GROUND, Miss C.G. Exh. 1884-1902
Malvern House, Mosely Road, Birmingham. † B 2.

GROVE, A. Exh. 1905-15
15 Clifford's Inn, Fleet Street, London. † RA 2.

GROVE, Annie Exh. 1882-83
Bell House, Northfield, Birmingham. † B 2.

GROVE, Gen. Sir Coleridge Exh. 1890-1919
Landscape painter. London. † RI 1, RID 40, ROI 9.

GROVE, Emma P. Exh. 1885-1913
Landscape and coastal painter. West Dulwich 1885; Richmond Hill, Surrey 1887; The Wardrobe, The Close, Salisbury, Wilts. 1899. † D 15, SWA 11.

GROVE, Florence Exh. 1885-93
Landscape painter. Guildford, Surrey 1885; Beccles, Suffolk 1889; Hampstead, London 1890; Gloucester 1891; Chelsea, London 1893. † D 13, L 1, M 1, SWA 2.

GROVE, Muriel Annie Florence b. 1902
Wood engraver. Studied Central School of Art, Birmingham. Exh. 1927-31. Add: Edgbaston, Birmingham. † B 1, M 1.

GROVE, William Henry Exh. 1908
Onslow Studios, King's Road, Chelsea, London. † LS 5.

GROVER, Miss Exh. 1902
Bassett Wood, Southampton. † SWA 2.

GROVER, Charlotte P. Exh. 1901-2
Elmlands, Watford, Herts. † RMS 1, SWA 1.

GROVER, Dorothy H. Exh. 1901-4
Chelsea, London. † D 2, SWA 1.

GROVER, Oliver Dennett* 1861-1927
American painter. 76 Fulham Road, London 1898. † RA 1.

GROVES, Mrs. Harriet Exh. 1926-27
57 Duke Street, St. Helens, Lancs. † L 2.

GROVES, L. Exh. 1882
32 Seymour Place, Bryanston Square, London. † L 1.

GROVES, Mary Exh. 1883-1917
Figure, domestic and still life painter. London. † B 15, D 3, L 3, LS 8, M 4, RA 8, RBA 6, RI 1, ROI 5, SWA 2.

GROVES, Robert E. d. c.1944
Landscape, figure and coastal painter. Travelled North Africa and Mediterranean. Add: Leicester 1887; Chelsea, London 1893; St. Albans, Herts. 1895. † B 1, GI 9, L 6, RA 14, RBA 2, RI 12, RSW 2.

GROVES, Mrs. Stephen Exh. 1926-34
82 South Croxted Road, London. † RI 16.

GROVES, Thomas Exh. 1881-94
Landscape painter. 2 Lansdowne Terrace, West Street, Leicester. † B 2, L 3, M 2, N 3, RA 2, RBA 1, RI 9.

GROVESANDE, C. Exh. 1885
195 Rue du Crone, Brussels, † L 1.

GRUBB, William Mortimer Exh. 1890-95
5 Osborn Place, Dundee. † RSA 4.

GRUBBE, Lawrence Carrington Exh. 1893-1908
Figure painter. 2 Margravine Gardens, W. Kensington, London 1893; Southwold, Suffolk 1907; Hampstead, London 1908. † LS 5, RA 2.

GRUBBE, Mrs. Marie E. Exh. 1910-20
Miniature painter. Hampstead, London 1910; Southwold, Suffolk 1914. † RA 10.

GRUISEN, Van See V

GRUN, Jules Alexandre* b. 1868
French painter. Exh. 1913-19. Add: 31 Boulevard Berthier, Paris. † GI 2, L 2.

GRUN, Maurice* b. 1860
Landscape painter. Exh. 1899-1904. Add: West Hampstead, London 1899; 192 Alexandra Road, St. John's Wood, London 1902; 144 Mill Lane, West Hampstead, London 1904. † L 2, NG 1, RA 3.

GRUN, Samuel G. Exh. 1901-4
Sculptor. 192 Alexandra Road, St. John's Wood, London 1901; 144 Mill Lane, West Hampstead, London 1903. † RA 3.

GRUNDY, Sir Cuthbert Cartwright c. 1847-1946
Landscape and figure painter. Studied Victoria University, Australia. Joint donor with his brother J.R.G. q.v. of the Blackpool Art Gallery. Governor National Museum of Wales. R.I. 1909, H.R.M.S. 1925. Knighted 1920. Add: Bankfield, Bury, Lancs. 1880; Conway 1893; Blackpool 1899 and 1908; Ambleside 1904 and 1930; Colwyn Bay, Wales 1913. † B 1, D 3, L 17, M 2, RA 7, RCA 87, RHA 2, RI 17, ROI 11, RSA 1.

GRUNDY, J.R.G. d. 1915
Landscape painter. Joint donor with his brother Sir Cuthbert G. q.v. of the Blackpool Art Gallery. Add: Bury, Lancs. 1880; Blackpool, Lancs. 1887; Ambleside 1905. †, L 2, M 2, RA 2, RCA 35, RHA 8, ROI 2, RSA 1.

GRUNER, Elioth* Exh. 1922
Australian painter. c/o P. and D. Colnaghi, 144 New Bond Street, London. † RA 2.

GRUNWALD, Bela Ivanyi Exh. 1935
† RSA 1.

GRUPPE, Charles Paul* b. 1860
Landscape and figure painter. b. Canada. Exh. 1898-1908. Add: Katwyk a Zee, Holland. † FIN 30, GI 2, RSW 1.

GRUT, Henrietta Exh. 1881
Watercolour landscape painter. 9 Newcomen Street, Southwark, London. † SWA 1.

GRUTERING, Anton Exh. 1910
c/o Mrs. V. Zimmerman, Schloss strasse, Bonn, Germany. † L 3, LS 3.

GRUYER-BRIELMAN, Mme. E. Exh. 1909
12 Cite du Retiro, Paris. † L 2.

GRYLLS, Harry Exh. 1937
Architect. 36 Gt. Ormond Street, London. † RA 1.

GRYLLS, Miss H.T. Exh. 1882
3 Fernclough Villas, Plymouth, Devon. † B 1, L 1, M 2.

GRYLLS, Miss Mary Exh. 1921-37
Watercolour figure, flower and landscape painter. Studied Crystal Palace School of Art and under M. Garstin. Add: Ar-lyn, Lelant, Cornwall. † RA 1, SWA 11.

GRYLLS, Thomas J. Exh. 1882-1902
Stained glass artist. 23 Newman Street, Oxford Street, London. † RA 5.

GUACCIMAMI, Alessandro Exh. 1902-3
Italian artist. c/o C.D. Soar, 1 Sussex Villas, Kensington, London. † B 2, RI 1.

GUBBINS, Mrs. Exh. 1883
Yarmouth, I.O.W. † L 1.

GUBBINS, Miss B.E. Exh. 1897-1937
Figure and landscape painter. Dunkathel, Glanmire, Co. Cork. † RHA 36.

GUDGEON, Ralston Exh. 1932-40
Bird and animal painter. R.S.W. 1937. Add: Kilbarchan 1932; Milliken Park, Renfrewshire 1936. † CON 33, FIN 58, GI 11, RSA 5, RSW 9.

GUDMUNDSSON, Eggert Exh. 1937
c/o Royal Danish Consulate, Leith. † RSA 1.

GUENTHER, Miss Gisela Exh. 1933
Sculptor. 32 Schone Aussicht, Wiesbaden, Germany. † RA 1.

GUERARD, H. Exh. 1881
† RE 3.

GUERCIO, B. Claudia Exh. 1923
6B Cathedral Mansions, Huskisson Street, Liverpool. † L 1.

GUERIN, Mrs. A. Lukis Exh. 1880-99
Anna Maria Edmonds. Flower, figure, landscape and decorative painter. A.S.W.A. 1880. Add: Maida Hill, London 1880; Folkestone 1884. † B 5, D 19, L 8, M 2, RA 6, SWA 26.

GUERIN, Charles* b. 1875
French painter. Exh. 1912-21. † GOU 4.

GUERIN, E. Exh. 1937
Quiberon, Brittany. † RCA 1.

GUERIN, Jules b. 1866
American artist. c/o J.P. Downie, 160 Bath Street, Glasgow 1898. † GI 1.

GUERIN, Marie Exh. 1881-84
Figure painter. Paris. † SWA 3.

GUERY, Armand* Exh. 1904
135 bis Rue de Rome, Paris. † L 1.

GUERY, M. Exh. 1886
c/o Rignon and Ralpin, Paris. † M 2.

GUEST, Agnes W. Exh. 1890-93
Landscape painter. London. † RBA 1, RI 1.

GUEST, H.B. Exh. 1909
Broncastell, Conway, Wales. † RCA 4.

GUEVARA, Alvaro 1894-1951
Portrait and figure painter. b. Valparaiso, Chile. Came to England 1908. Studied Slade School (3 years). N.E.A. 1920. Lived in London until 1922 when he returned to Chile. † GOU 1, I 1, LEI 34, NEA 15.

GUFFIE, David Exh. 1907-8
38 Sharon Street, Dalry, Ayrs. † GI 2.

GUIDICI, Jessie Exh. 1925-29
Elmside Studio, Dartmouth Place, London. † L 7.

GUIGNARD, Gaston Exh. 1902-7
25 Boulevard Berthier, Paris. † L 2.

GUILD, Emma Cadwallader b. 1843
Sculptor. b. U.S.A. Exh. 1885-98. Add: London 1885; Hamburg 1891; Berlin 1898. † G 1, L 4, RA 10.

GUILD, J. Horsburgh Exh. 1885-1932
1 Livingstone Place, Edinburgh. † L 1, M 1, RSA 3.

GUILD, Rose M. Exh. 1939
† GOU 1.

GUILFORD, Miss F. Exh. 1929
Kingston on Thames, Surrey. † SWA 1.

GUILLAUME, Albert* b. 1873
French figure painter. Exh. 1910-24. † L 4.

GUILLAUMIN, Armand* 1841-1927
Landscape painter. Exh. 1921-25. † CHE 1, GOU 2.

GUILLEMARD, Mrs. E. Exh. 1906
8 Swan Walk, Chelsea, London. † RA 1.

GUILLEMARD, Miss Mary F. Exh. 1882-83
Figure painter. 5 St. Peter's Terrace, Cambridge. † B 1, RA 1, RBA 1.

GUILLEMET, Jean Baptiste Antoine* 1842-1918
French landscape painter. Exh. 1883-92. 6 Rue Clausel, Paris. † GI 3.

GUILLEMIN, Joseph E. Exh. 1909
12 Rue Chevert, Paris. † L 1.

GUILLEZ, A.E. Exh. 1911
77 Rue de la Chapelle, Paris. † L 1.

GUILLOD, Bessie Exh. 1880-94
Flower painter. Chelsea, London. † B 2, L 5, RA 1, RBA 3, ROI 6, SWA 10.

GUILLON, Alfred Exh. 1887-1905
Concarneau, Finisterre, France 1887; Paris 1905. † B 1, L 1.

GUILLON, E.A. Exh. 1901
Mechain 10, Paris. † L 1.

GUILLONNET, Octave Denis Victor* Exh. 1911
60 Boulevard de Clichy, Paris. † L 1.
GUILLOT, A. Exh. 1907
152 Rue de Vaugirard, Paris. † L 1.
GUIMARAENS, R.A.F. Exh. 1937
Exh. 1937. † NEA 1.
GUINIER, Henri 1867-1927
French artist. Exh. 1907-13. 61 Avenue de Neuilly sur Seine, France. † L 1, RSA 1.
GUINNESS, Bridget Henrietta d. 1931
Mrs. Benjamin G. Exh. 1915-19. † I 3.
GUINNESS, Miss D. Exh. 1902-3
Rathfarnham, Dublin. † SWA 5.
GUINNESS, Elizabeth S. Exh. 1880-95
Figure and domestic painter. London. † B 1, D 3, G 1, L 4, RA 3, RBA 5, RHA 7, SWA,8.
GUINNESS, May Exh. 1897-1911
Rathfarnham, Ireland. † RHA 6.
GUINO, Richard Exh. 1925
7 Rue Daguerre, Paris. † GI 3, RSA 3.
GUIRAND-de-SCEVOLA, Lucien Victor* b. 1871
Figure painter and pastelier. 91 Avenue de Villiers, Paris. † L 1.
GUISTI, Giuseppe Exh. 1904-5
20 Hereford Square, London. † I 2.
GUITERREZ, Miss M. Exh. 1903
c/o Miss Birch, Roland Gardens. London. † SWA 2.
GULICH, John Percival 1864-1898
Landscape and figure painter. R.I. 1897. Add: West Hampstead, London. † D 6, L 1, RA 4, RBA 10, RI 3.
GULL, Claire Exh. 1896-1900
15 Hill Street, Rutland Gate, London. † RMS 4.
GULLAND, Elizabeth d. 1934
Painter, engraver and illustrator. Studied Edinburgh and Herkomer's, Bushey, Herts. Exh. 1880-1910. Add: Edinburgh 1880; Bushey, Herts. 1886. † FIN 5, GI 2, L 6, NG 1, RA 15, ROI 3, RSA 17.
GULLEY, Miss C.B. Exh. 1908-28
Clifton, Bristol. † B 3, L 11, M 1, RA 5.
GULLICK, Thomas John Exh. 1880-84
Miniature painter. 103 New Bond Street, London. † L 1, RBA 1.
GULLIVER, Miss H.G. Exh. 1933
38a Springdale Road, Stoke Newington, London. † L 1.
GULLY, Miss L. Exh. 1923
255 Goldhurst Terrace, West Hampstead, London. † RI 1.
GULSTON, A.S. Exh. 1883
c/o Bourlet, 17 Nassau Street, London. † G 1.
GUMMELL, Miss M. Exh. 1886
45 Gloucester Street, Warwick. † M 1.
GUNDRY, Thomas Exh. 1891
15 Lombard Street, London. † RA 1.
GUNDY, Herbert Exh. 1903
101 Chelsea Gardens, London. † L 1.
GUNN, Dorothy B. Exh. 1928-36
Nargrie, Borgue, Kirkcudbright. † GI 2, RSW 2.
GUNN, David W. Exh. 1927-29
26 East Port, Dunfermline. † L 1, RSA 2.
GUNN, Edward Exh. 1904
Architect. 76 Finsbury Pavement, London. † RA 1.
GUNN, F. Exh. 1937
Portrait painter. †, BA 1.
GUNN, Fred J.T. Exh. 1889-1905
Landscape painter. Edinburgh. † GI 6, L 4, RA 3, RHA 4, RSA 7, RSW 5.
GUNN, Geo. Exh. 1900
103 Bath Street, Glasgow. † GI 1.
GUNN, Herbert James 1893-1964
Portrait and landscape painter. Studied Glasgow, Edinburgh and Juliens, Paris. R.S.W. 1930. Exh. 1909-40.
Add: Glasgow 1909; Chadlington, Oxon 1922; London 1925. † B 1, BAR 41, CG 44, COO 3, FIN 46, G 7, GI 46, GOU 1, L 12, P 14, RA 38, RED,1, RSA 24.
GUNN, Jessie Exh. 1891
15 Glengyle Terrace, Edinburgh. † RSA 1.
GUNN, John H. Exh. 1924-25
15 Ashted Row, Birmingham. † B 2.
GUNN, Maud H. Exh. 1903-13
Flower painter. The Lodge, Stoneygate, Leicester. † N 13.
GUNN, Richard R. Exh. 1901
15 Windsor Street, Glasgow. † GI 1.
GUNN, William Archibald b. 1877
Landscape painter and pastelier. Studied Glasgow School of Art 1897-1901. Exh. 1929-30. Add: Newport, Mon. 1929; York 1930. † L 2.
GUNNELL, Mrs. Margaret F. Exh. 1925
6 Esplanade, Waterloo, Liverpool. † L 2.
GUNNER, Charles Exh. 1936
† RMS 3.
GUNNING, Miss A.H. Exh. 1911
Sand Rock House, Heswall, Cheshire. † L 2.
GUNNINGHAM, Richard Exh. 1939
Highlands, Cranleigh Avenue, Rottingdean, Sussex. † RA 1.
GUNNINGHAM, William Exh. 1893-94
34 Church Street, Liverpool. † L 2.
GUNNIS, Louis J. Exh. 1887-97
Figure and domestic painter. London. † L 1, RA 6.
GUNSTON, Audley J. Exh. 1903-35
Portrait and figure painter. London. † GI 2, RA 16, RI 18.
GUNSTON, E. Leslie Exh. 1925-29
Architect. London. † RA 2.
GUNSTON, Sheelah H. Exh. 1911-16
Figure and interior painter. 5 Grosvenor Gardens, London. † L 1, LS 15, NEA 2.
GUNTER, Miss Ann Exh. 1938
Jordans, Eashing, Godalming, Surrey. † RSA 1.
GUNTER, Arthur Exh. 1904
Porthminster House, Penare Road, Penzance, Cornwall. † L 1.
GUNTHER, Edith Exh. 1910
Portrait and figure painter. Studied under William Orpen. Add: 2 Harley Studios, Cresswell Place, London. † GOU 1, L 1, NEA 2.
GUNTHER, Rudolph Exh. 1904-13
Landscape painter. 50 Park Hill Road, London. † LS 12, M 1, RA 1.
GUNTHER, Reginald J. Exh. 1937-40
Sculptor. Withington, Cheltenham, Glos. † RA 2.
GUNTHORP, Beatrice Exh. 1925-34
nee Hibbitts. Portrait painter. b. Rhyl, N. Wales. Studied RA Schools. Married Cecil G. q.v. Add: London. † RA 3.
GUNTHORP, Cecil Exh. 1926-38
Sculptor. Studied City and Guilds of London Institute and Royal College of Art. Married Beatrice G. q.v. Add: London. † RA 3.
GUNTHORP, Henry Exh. 1885-1903
Sculptor. Herne Hill, London. † L 2, RA 18.
GUNTON, Miss Kit Exh. 1938
Cotham, Bristol. † SWA,1.
GURNEY, Mrs. Exh. 1880
Landscape painter. Sprowston Hall, Norwich. † SWA 2.
GURNEY, Ernest T. Exh. 1900
Landscape painter. 43 Ampthill Square, Hampstead Road, London. † RA 1.
GURR, George A. b. 1911
Watercolour landscape and coastal painter. Studied Leicester College of Art 1932-37. Exh. 1937. Add: 69 Saltersford Road, Leicester. † N 4, NEA 1.
GURSCHNER, Herbert b. 1901
Portrait, landscape and figure painter. Exh. 1929-38. † COO 60, 100.
GUSSOW, Carl* Exh. 1881-82
Figure painter. 26 Maida Vale, London. † M 1, RA 1.
GUTHRIE, Miss A.B. Exh. 1893-94
3 Albert Road, Levenshulme, Manchester. † L 2.
GUTHRIE, Mrs. Anna M.B. Exh. 1908-21
Noness, Colinton, Midlothian. † L 6, RA 1, RSA 15, RSW 1.
GUTHRIE, Mrs. E.M.S. Exh. 1933
Swanston Cottage, Storeton, Cheshire. † L 1.
GUTHRIE, Gale Exh. 1934-35
Still life painter. 38 Rue Mathurin Regnier, Paris. † RA 1, RSA 1.
GUTHRIE, George Davidson b. 1893
Dry point artist. Director of Arthur Guthrie and Sons Ltd. Printers and Publishers, Ardrossan. Exh. 1923-25. Add: Saltcoats, Ayrs. † GI 2, L 2.
GUTHRIE, Helen Exh. 1898-1915
Edinburgh. † GI 1, L 8, RSA 3, RSW 1.
GUTHRIE, Iris Exh. 1911
Elmhurst, Braintree, Essex. † L 1.
GUTHRIE, Sir James* 1859-1930
Portrait and landscape painter. Trustee for National Galleries of Scotland 1906-20. N.E.A. 1889, R.B.A. 1907, H.R.M.S. 1904, H.R.O.I. 1903, R.P. 1893, A.R.S.A. 1892, R.S.A. 1895, P.R.S.A. 1902-19, R.S.W. 1890, H.R.S.W. 1903. Knighted 1903. Add: London 1882; Cockburnspath, Berwicks 1884; Glasgow 1886; Edinburgh 1902; Row, Dumbartonshire 1925. † BAR 1, G 2, GI 57, I 3, L 11, M 1, NEA 5, P 16, RA 3, RHA 2, ROI 2, RSA 135, RSW 1.
GUTHRIE, John Exh. 1880-1905
Landscape painter. 385 Sauchiehall Street, Glasgow. † GI 10, RA 1, RSA 4.
GUTHRIE, James J. 1874-1952
Painter, illustrator, designer, author and hand press printer. b. Glasgow. Father of Robin Craig G. q.v. Add: South Harting, Petersfield, Hants. 1901; Bognor, Sussex 1925. † BG 105, RA 3, RSA 2.
GUTHRIE, Mrs. Kathleen b. 1905
Mrs. C.S. nee Maltby. Flower painter. b. Feltham, Middlesex. Studied Slade School 1921-23., RA Schools 1923-26. Exh. 1926-40. Add: London 1930 and 1939; Steyning, Sussex 1935; Brighton, Sussex 1940. † GOU 1, NEA 3, RA 3, RBA 2.
GUTHRIE, Leonard Rome Exh. 1899-1934
Architect and landscape painter. The Croft, Hairmyres, Lanarks. 1899; London 1911. † GI 10, RA 10, RSA 1.
GUTHRIE, Robin Craig b. 1902
Genre, landscape and portrait painter and teacher. b. Harting, Hants. Son of James J.G. q.v. Studied Slade School. N.E.A. 1931. Exh. 1922-40. Add: London 1923 and 1940; Brighton, Sussex 1934; Bramber, Sussex 1935. † BA 2, FIN 81, GI 1, GOU 83, L 1, M 2, NEA 53, P 5, RA 11, RED 3, RSA 5, TOO 1.
GUTHRIE, Susan Exh. 1929
Landscape and interior painter. † AB 3.
GUTHRIE, Sara Beatrice See DIBDEN

GUTHRIE, T. Jnr. Exh. 1896
† P 1.

GUTHRIE, William Exh. 1880-97
385 Sauchiehall Street, Glasgow. † GI 5.

GUTHRIE, William Exh. 1920-31
Helensburgh, N.B. † GI 13, RSA 6.

GUTHRIE, W.D. Exh. 1881-82
Landscape and flower painter. 17 Richmond Crescent, Barnsbury and Witley, Surrey. † D 2, RA 1, RBA 3.

GUTSCHER, Paul Exh. 1911-14
Watercolour landscape painter. Austria 1911; Rome 1912; London 1914. † L 5, RA 1, RI 6, RSA 2, WG 42.

GUTTERES, Maud Exh. 1901-10
London. † LS 3, SWA 4.

GUTTERIDGE, Herbert Exh. 1919
6 Lady Bay Road, West Bridgford, Nottingham. † N 1.

GUTTMANN, Agnes Exh. 1911
18 Aberdare Gardens, West Hampstead, London. † LS 3.

GUY, Cyril Graham Exh. 1929-38
Landscape painter. R.B.A. 1930. Add: Danehill, Chesswood Road, Worthing, Sussex. † NEA 1, RA 3, RBA 28, RCA 10, RHA 1, ROI 5, RSA 8.

GUY, H.A. Exh. 1897
70 Salisbury Road, Wavertree, Liverpool. † L 2.

GUY, Mary E. Exh. 1889-90
Flower painter. Beech Avenue, Sherwood Rise, Nottingham. † N 2.

GUY, Maurice H. Exh. 1912
22 Monsieur le Prince, Paris. † RSA 1.

GUY, O. Exh. 1885
Warwick House, Somerset Road, Tottenham, London. † M 1.

GUY, Vivian Exh. 1921
Watercolour landscape painter and pastelier. † WG 96.

GUYARD-CHARVET, Mme. A. Exh. 1904
4 Rue Berite, Paris. † L 1.

GUYER, Maude Louise Exh. 1908-10
London. † LS 4, RA 1.

GUYMER, W. Exh. 1921
231 Marton Road, Middlesborough. † B 2.

GUYON, Agnes E. Exh. 1900-10
Landscape, flower, still life painter and lithographer. Studied Slade School, Delecluse's, Paris and St. Ives, Cornwall. Add: Clifton, Bristol. † BG 4. SWA 3.

GUZZONE, Sebastian Exh. 1882-90
Figure painter. Manchester 1882; Rome 1883; Paris 1885. † L 3, M 8, RBA 1.

GWATKIN, Arthur Exh. 1890-99
Landscape painter and frieze designer. Add: Oakdene, Wallingham Station, Surrey 1890; Partick, Glasgow 1896. † L 1, RA 10, RBA 1.

GWATKIN, G.W. Exh. 1894
88 Newgate Street, London. † GI 2.

GWATKIN, Stewart Beauchamp Exh. 1888-93
Figure and still life painter. London. † L 4, M 1, RBA 8, RI 6.

GWENNET, W. Gunn Exh. 1903-40
Landscape painter. London 1903; Richmond, Surrey 1940. † L 3, LS 8, RA 8, RI 4, RSA 2, WG 75.

GWYNNE, Miss I. Exh. 1888
36 Brunswick Gardens, Kensington, London. † D 3.

GWYNNE-DAVIES, W. Exh. 1907
12 Bournbrook Road, Selly Park, Birmingham. † B 1.

GWYNNE-JONES, Allan* b. 1892
Landscape, portrait and still life painter and etcher. Studied Slade School. N.E.A. 1926. Trustee of the Tate Gallery 1939. Exh. 1913-39. Add: London. † AG 3, CG 11, CHE 1, CON 2, FIN 16, G 15, GOU 5, L 2, LEF 1, M 4, NEA 64, RA 1, RCA 3, RED 7, RSA 1, TOO 10.

GYMER, B. Exh. 1918
† I 1.

GYNGELL, Albert E. Exh. 1882-1911
Portrait and figure painter. Worcester 1882; Ditchling, Sussex 1911. † B 14, RA 6, RI 1, ROI 2.

GYNGELL, Edmund Exh. 1893
Portrait painter. Le Marie, Bushey, Herts. † RA 2.

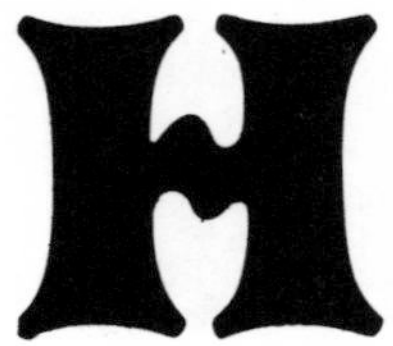

HAAG, Carl* 1820-1915
Landscape, portrait and miniature painter. b. Erlangen, Bavaria. Studied Nuremberg and Munich. Came to England 1847. Travelled widely. R.B.A. 1882, A.R.W.S. 1850, R.W.S. 1853. Exh. 1880-1911. Add: Hampstead, London. † AG 4, FIN 30, G 4, L 6, M 2, RA 2, RBA 3, RWS 56.

HAAGENSEN, F.H. Exh. 1930
Etcher. † AG 25.

HAANEN, Adriana* Exh. 1883
Flower, still life and bird painter. Villa Garda, Oosterbeck, Holland. † RA 1.

HAANEN, Van see V

HAAS, de see D

HAAS, F.H. Exh. 1884
c/o Cassell & Co., Ludgate Hill, London. † L 1.

HAAS, H. Dee Exh. 1911
† BRU 1.

HABERSHON, Ada R. Exh. 1887
70 Brook Street, Grosvenor Square, London. † SWA 1.

HABERT, E. Exh. 1886-87
64 Rue Dulong, Paris. † GI 1, M 1.

HACHFORD, Mary Exh. 1881
Flower painter. 14 North Terrace, Wandsworth, London. † SWA 1.

HACK, Matthew Starmer Exh. 1894-1910
Architect. London. † RA 11.

HACKER, Arthur* 1858-1919
Portrait, genre and historical painter. Studied R.A. Schools and with Bonnat in Paris. Married Lilian Price H. q.v. N.E.A. 1886, A.R.A. 1894, R.A. 1910, R.I. 1918, R.O.I. 1883, R.P. 1891. "The Annunciation" purchased by Chantrey Bequest 1892. Add: London. † AG 1, B 22, CAR 1, G 5, GI 12, L 88, M 20, NG 16, P 42, RA 155, RHA 8, RI 2, ROI 30.

HACKER, A.J. Exh. 1885
† TOO 1.

HACKER, Blanche Exh. 1915-26
Miniature painter. Studied Slade School and Juliens, Paris. A.R.M.S. 1916. Add: Southlands, Harrow on the Hill, Middlesex. † L 12, RA 4, RMS 13, RSA 4.

HACKER, Mrs. Comber Exh. 1932
Salisbury, Wilts. † RCA 1.

HACKER, Lilian Price Exh. 1909-32
Miniature painter. Married Arthur H. q.v. A.R.M.S. 1917, R.M.S. 1919. Add: London 1909 and 1915, Glynde, Sussex 1912, Milford, Surrey 1925. † L 4, RA 15, RMS 6.

HACKER, Miss R. Exh. 1903-4
30 Fellows Road, Hampstead, London. † SWA 3.

HACKETT, Jennie Ashton Exh. 1898-1906
38 Patrick Street, Cork. † RHA 4.

HACKING, Frederic Sidney b. 1873
Painter and modeller. b. Darwen, Lancs. Studied Royal College of Art and Harris Institute, Preston. Exh. 1918-28. Add: 14 Princess Road, Mexborough, Yorks. † RA 2.

HACKING, Joan M. Exh. 1937-38
† P 2.

HACKING, M. Exh. 1935-36
28 Cathcart Road, London. † SWA 2.

HACKING, Patricia W.H. Exh. 1940
Lithographer. Firdene, Balmoral, Belfast, † RA 1, RHA 1.

HACKL, G. Exh. 1891
New Academy, Munich. † GI 1.

HACKMAN, Frederick James Exh. 1908
8 Howard Road, Walthamstow, London. † LS 5.

HACKSTOUN, William Exh. 1896-1916
Landscape painter. Notting Hill, London 1896; Garnethill, Glasgow 1916. † GI 1, NEA 2.

HACON, Jessie Exh. 1886-1904
Interior and architectural painter. London. † RBA 1, RI 2, SWA 9.

HADAMARD, Auguste Exh. 1884
14 Rue Teresa, Paris. † GI 1.

HADAWAY, Mrs. Exh. 1908
Bushey, Herts. † NG 1.

HADAWAY, W.S. Exh. 1902-5
Bushey, Herts. † L 21.

HADCOCK, R. Neville Exh. 1930
Westbrooke, Hexham, Northumberland. † L 2.

HADDAN, Isabella Exh. 1910
36A Brunswick Place, Brighton. † D 1.

HADDAN, Percy Exh. 1900
3 Norfolk Mansions, Lithos Road, South Hampstead, London. † RA 1.

HADDEN, Doris Exh. 1934-38
Sturminster Newton, Dorset. † RMS 3, SWA 1.

HADDEN, Lucy E. Exh. 1903-7
Flixton, Nr. Manchester 1903; Talycafn, Wales 1905. † L 3, RCA 11.

HADDEN, Nellie d. c.1917
Landscape, figure and miniature painter. R.M.S. 1902. Add: Berkhamsted, Herts. 1884; Sunningdale, Berks. 1891 and 1904; Kensington, London 1899. † B 1, GI 1, L 15, N 1, NG 2, RBA 3, RI 6, RMS 21, ROI 5, SWA 26, WG 49.

HADDEN, R. Exh. 1880
6 Upper Barnsbury Street, Islington, London. † RSA 1.

HADDOCK, Ethel Exh. 1884
Flower painter. 7 Windsor Terrace, Bedford. † SWA 1.

HADDON, Arthur Lumley Exh. 1893
Landscape and figure painter. 9 Sutherland Place, London. † RA 1.

HADDON, Arthur Trevor* 1864-1941
Portrait and genre painter and author. Studied Slade School (3 year scholarship, 1883, landscape prize and medal for painting from life, 1885), 1 year in Spain, Herkomer's Bushey, Herts and in Rome 1896-97. R.B.A. 1896. Exh. 1883-1939. Add: London. † D 28, FIN 5, L 11, M 2, NG 1, P 1, RA 19, RBA 178, RHA 4, RI 13, ROI 11, TOO 1.

HADDON, D.W.* Exh. 1884-1911
Birmingham. † B 35, L 1.

HADDON, Isabel Exh. 1898
Odiham Close, Winchfield, Hants. † SWA 1.

HADDON, Mrs. Omy Exh. 1896-99
Birmingham. † B 4.

HADDON, Wilberforce Exh. 1880-82
Watercolour landscape painter. Rose Cottage, Wanstead, Essex. † D 1, RA 1, RBA 2.

HADDOW, Theo Exh. 1916-40
Fairhill, Uddingston, N.B. 1916; Glasgow 1933. † GI 13.

HADEN, Sir Francis Seymour 1818-1910
Painter and etcher. R.E. 1880, P.R.E. 1882, H.R.M.S. 1897. Knighted 1894. Add: London 1880; Alresford, Hants. 1891. † CON 3, DOW 3, FIN 53, LEI 16, RA 3, RE 286, RSA 4.

HADENFELDT, Gertrude Exh. 1907-38
Watercolour painter. R.I. 1929 (resigned 1940). Add: Neasden, London 1907; Huson, Tenterden, Kent 1925 and 1931; c/o Stiles and Sons, Fulham Road, London 1926. † D 2, GI 2, L 4, RA 1, RI 33, SWA 1.

HADFIELD, Charles Alfred Exh. 1881-1911
Figure and portrait painter. London. † BRU 1, L 1, LS 3, RA 1, RBA 2, RI 1.

HADFIELD, Daphne E. Exh. 1935
167 Loughborough Road, West Bridgford, Notts. † N 4.

HADFIELD, H.H. Exh. 1882-87
Pendleton, Manchester. † L 1, M 10.

HADFIELD, T.R. Exh. 1882
9 Woodbine Street, Moss Side, Manchester. † M 1.

HADLAND, J.W. Exh. 1906
Norwood, Beverley, Yorks. † B 1.

HADLEY, W.D. Exh. 1932
Sandycroft, Park Road, Wolverhampton. † B 1.

HAEFLIGER, Paul Exh. 1934
Colour wood cut artist. c/o Bourlet & Sons, 17 Nassau Street, London. † RA 1.

HAEHNEL, Julius Exh. 1881-99
Sculptor. c/o 29 Welbeck Street, London 1881; Schmiedeberg im Birzegebirge, Saxony 1899. † RA 2.

HAEREM, Mrs. Mabel Exh. 1924
Miniature painter. Sandown, Wilmslow, Cheshire. † RA 1.

HAES, Margaret Exh. 1924
45 Kirkley Cliffe, Lowestoft, Suffolk. † L 3.

HAGARTY, A. Exh. 1885
c/o J.F. Jeffs, Wellington Street, Luton, Beds. † B 1.

HAGARTY, Miss Mary S. Exh. 1882-1938
Landscape painter. A.S.W.A. 1915. S.W.A. 1916. Add: Liverpool 1882; London 1896. † B 5, D 3, L 189, RA 26, RBA 5, RI 58, SWA 93.

HAGARTY, Parker b. 1859
Portrait, landscape and figure painter. b. Canada. Studied Liverpool School of Art and Juliens, Paris. Ech. 1882-1934. Add: Liverpool 1882; Cardiff 1890. † B 4, D 2, GI 2, L 131, M 4, RA 24, RCA 142, RI 11, ROI 5, RSA 1.

HAGARTY, Miss W.S. Exh. 1894
Farnham Common, Slough, Bucks. † RI 1.

HAGBORG, Auguste* 1852-1921
5 bis Rue Jardin, Paris 1905. † L 1.

HAGBORG, Otto Exh. 1901-14
London. † RA 2.

HAGEDORN, Karl b. 1889
Painter, cotton print designer and commerical artist. b. Berlin. Came to England 1905 (naturalised 1914). Studied Manchester and Paris. R.B.A. 1935. Add: Manchester 1911 and 1913; Paris 1912; Belsize Park Gardens, London 1931. † FIN 72, L 15, LS 12, M 5, NEA 17, P 1, RA 4, RBA 30, RI 3.

HAGEN, Anny R. Exh. 1938-40
London. † SWA 2.

HAGER, Albert Exh. 1914
5 Avenue de Saturne, Uccle, Brussels. † RSA 2.

HAGER, Miss Dorothy Exh. 1905
4 Lucerne Chambers, Kensington Mall, London. † L 1.

HAGG, Arthur T. b. 1895
Painter and designer. Studied Norwich School of Art 1912 and Westminster School of Art. Exh. 1939. † RI 1.

HAGGAR, Reginald George b. 1905
Watercolour painter and designer. Studied Ipswich Art School 1920-26 and Royal College of Art 1926-29. Art Director. Mintons 1930-35. Head of Stoke Art School 1934-41. Exh. 1935-39. Add: Stoke on Trent, Staffs. † M 2, RA 2, RBA 4, RI 1, RSA 2, RSW 2.

HAGGARD, Miss D.E. Exh. 1932-37
Landscape and portrait painter. Grantham, Lincs. † N 12.

HAGGART, Donald C. Exh. 1881-1912
Sculptor. Glasgow. † G 1, GI 31, RA 3, RSA 4.

HAGGIS, John Alfred b. 1897
Landscape painter and etcher. b. London. Studied Royal College of Art and in Australia. Worked as Australian Boundary rider, station hand, plumbers mate, beekeeper and in insurance. Exh. 1932-38. Add: 1597 Stratford Road, Hall Green, Birmingham. † B 3, L 1, RA 5, RCA 2, ROI 9, RSA 1.

HAGGO, Matthew Exh. 1920
12 Westfield Street, Glasgow. † GI 1.

HAGHE, Louis* 1806-1885
Landscape and historical genre painter and lithographer. b. Tournai, Belgium. Worked with his left hand as his right was deformed. R.I. 1835, P.R.I. 1873, H.P.R.I. 1884. Add: 103 Stockwell Green, Stockwell Road, London. † GI 1, L 3, RHA 1, RI 4.

HAGHE, Mrs. L. Exh. 1880
Flower painter. 103 Stockwell Green, Stockwell Road, London. † RA 1.

HAGREEN, H.W. Owen Exh. 1883-85
Watercolour landscape painter. 16 Thistle Green, South Kensington, London. † RA 2, RI 1.

HAGREEN, Philip Exh. 1918-19
† I 4.

HAGUE, Dick Exh. 1908-16
Deganwy, Llandudno, Wales. † L 8, M 2, RA 3, RCA 24.

HAGUE, Joshua Anderson* 1850-1916
Landscape painter and watercolourist. Studied Manchester Art School. N.E.A. 1887, R.B.A. 1884, R.O.I. 1892. Add: Stockport, Lancs. 1880; Tywyn, Conway, Wales 1885; Deganwy, Llandudno, Wales 1889. † B 11, BG 1, DOW 30, G 8, GI 3, L 66, M 69, NEA 6, NG 23, RA 39, RBA 12, RCA 147, RI 41, ROI 3.

HAGUE, J. Edward Homerville Exh. 1884-1917
Painter and sculptor. Hansfield, Cookham, Berks. 1884; Maidenhead, Berks. 1886; London 1887 and 1903; Fishbourne, Wootton, I.O.W. 1893; Wallingford, Berks. 1917. † B 2, D 4, M 4, NEA 1, NG 5, RA 12, RBA 1, ROI 1.

HAGUE, John Houghton* b. 1842
Figure and landscape painter. Studied Manchester Art School. Master at Oldham School of Art. Exh. 1882-1901. Add: Oldham, Lancs. † L 7, M 15, RA 2.

HAGYARD, A.S. Exh. 1908-9
1 Ebberston Terrace, Hyde Park, Leeds. † L 10.

HAHN, Miss C.M. Exh. 1881
Landscape painter. Ashfield Villa, Upper Tulse Hill, London. † SWA 1.

HAHN, Siegfried Exh. 1938
Landscape painter. 25 Robert Adam Street, London. † RA 1.

HAIG, Axel Herman 1835-1921
Etcher. b. Gotland, Sweden. R.E. 1881. Add: Kilburn, London 1880; Haslemere, Surrey 1892. † B 1, D 4, DOW 3, FIN 126, L 17, RA 27, RBA 1, RE 151, RI 10.

HAIG, Miss C.W. Exh. 1931-33
Miniature painter. Thatched Cottage, Llanwern, Newport, Mon. † RA 1, RMS 1.

HAIG, Elizabeth Exh. 1904-6
2 Rossetti House, Chelsea, London. † RCA 2, RSA 1.

HAIG, Evelyn Cotton Exh. 1886-1908
Figure and miniature portrait painter. R.M.S. 1900. Add: Edinburgh. † GI 17, L 2, NG 1, RA 2, RHA 1, RMS 18, RSA 23.

HAIG, Florence E. Exh. 1886-1929
Portrait and figure painter. A.R.B.A. 1925, R.B.A. 1926, S.W.A. 1923. Add: Edinburgh 1886; London 1911. † GI 4, LS 3, P 8, RA 2, RBA 12, RSA 12, SWA 16.

HAIG, James Exh. 1885
164 Bath Street, Glasgow. † GI 1.

HAIG, Miss Janet Exh. 1932-39
Sculptor. 9 Abercorn Place, London. † RA 2.

HAIG, J. Hermiston Exh. 1887-1919
Glasgow and Chirnside, Berwickshire. † GI 53, RSA 15, RSW 3.

HAIG, Miss V. Exh. 1904
7 Boyn Hill Avenue, Maidenhead, Berks. † SWA 1.

HAIGH, Alfred G.* Exh. 1890-1928
Park Gate, Cheshire 1890; Adderbury, Banbury, Oxon 1928. † L 3.

HAIGH, Elsie Stead Exh. 1935
Huddersfield, Yorks. † RCA 1.

HAIGH, Frank Exh. 1901-8
5 Gloucester Terrace, Hyde Park, London and The Cedars, Pilton, Shepton Mallet, Som. † L 1, RCA 7, ROI 1.

HAIGH, Harold B. Exh. 1934
St. Helens, Lancs. † RCA 2.

HAIGH, L. Exh. 1880-84
Landscape painter. Liverpool. † SWA 3.

HAIGH, Molly Exh. 1940
Flower painter. R.A.F. Officers Hospital, Torquay, Devon. † RA 1.

HAIGH, Miss M.L. Exh. 1939
Malvern Hills, Worcs. † RCA 1.

HAIGH, Norman Exh. 1915
1 Dalton Lees Fold, Kirkheaton, Huddersfield. † RCA 1.

HAIGH, T.W. Exh. 1916
2 Exchange Street East, Liverpool. † L 1.

HAILE, Richard Neville b. 1895
Miniature painter and portrait photographer. b. London. Exh. 1921. Add: 8 York Road, Bognor, Sussex. † RA 1.

HAILE, Samuel 1909-1948
Exh. 1937. † NEA 1.

HAILE, T.S. Exh. 1931
100 Church Lane, London. † RHA 1.

HAILSTONE, Bernard b. 1910
Portrait painter. Studied Goldsmiths College and R.A. Schools. Exh. 1935-40. Add: London. † RA 2, RBA 1.

HAILWOOD, Mary Irene b. 1908
Portrait and figure painter, black and white artist and etcher. Studied Leeds College of Art and Royal College of Art. Exh. 1931-35. Add: Beacon House, Morley, Leeds. † RA 1, SWA 1.

HAINES, Agnes Eliza Exh. 1887-88
35 Cathcart Road, South Kensington, London. † L 1, ROI 1.

HAINES, Clara Exh. 1896-97
Figure painter. 125 Alexandra Road, St. John's Wood, London. † RA 1, SWA 1.

HAINES, K.S. Exh. 1935-39
London. † RBA 1. SWA 3.

HAINES, Robert J. Exh. 1888-1912
Landscape and still life painter. 12 Beaumont Street, Oxford. † RA 8.

HAINES, Miss S. Exh. 1910-21
Cheltenham, Glos. 1910; Weymouth 1918. † L 9, RA 4.

HAINES, Sybil Exh. 1940
58 Stanhope Gardens, London. † NEA 1, RBA 2, RI 2.

HAINES, Vincent Exh. 1881-82
Figure painter. 28 Upper Phillimore Place, Kensington, London. † RBA 2.

HAINES, William Henry 1812-1884
Genre and landscape painter and picture restorer. Often used pseudonym "William Henry". Painted views of Venice in the manner of Canaletto and Guardi which were passed off as originals. Add: London. † B 4, D 3, L 3, M 3, RA 1, RBA 18, RHA 25, ROI 2.

HAINS, Eric P. Exh. 1938
Trewent, Goldthorne Avenue, Penns, Wolverhampton. † B 1.

HAINSSELIN, Henry Exh. 1886
Walton New Road, Nr. Warrington, Lancs. † M 1.

HAINSWORTH, Miss C.M. Exh. 1938-40
Edgbaston, Birmingham 1938; Sale, Cheshire 1940. † B 3.

HAINSWORTH, Thomas b. 1873
Painter and etcher. Studied Halifax Technical College. Exh. 1925-40. Add: Newhaven, Browfoot Gate, Halifax. † L 4, RA 6.

HAIR, George Exh. 1934-35
Penarth, Glam. † RCA 2.

HAITE, George Charles* 1855-1924
Painter, illustrator and writer. b. Bexley. Self taught. R.B.A. 1892, R.I. 1901, R.M.S. 1900, R.O.I. 1907. Add: Bedford Park, London. † AG 1, AR 98, B 21, BG 1, D 31, FIN 1, GI 20, L 62, M 27, RA 32, RBA 212, RCA 4, RHA 3, RI 111, RID 84, RMS 6, ROI 79.

HAITH, Mrs. Kate Exh. 1900-15
Landscape painter. Maritzburg, Natal, South Africa 1900; 176 Church Street, Stoke Newington, London 1915. † RI 6, WG 45.

HAKE, G.D. Gordon b. 1887
Watercolour painter, pencil and crayon artist and architect. Studied Ecole des Beaux Arts Geneva, A.A. London and articled to Sir Robert Ecles. Exh. 1921. Add: 15 St. Mary's Square, London. † RA 1.

HAKE, Miss M.L. Exh. 1887-89
Flower painter. 14 Velwell Villas, Exeter. † RI 4, SWA 1.

HAKE, Mrs. Rose Gordon Exh. 1893-1912
London 1893 and 1903; Axmouth, Coltford, Devon 1899. † D 72.

HAKING, Hilda B. Exh. 1894-97
Flower painter. Alexandra House, Kensington Gore, London. † RA 1, SWA 5.

HAKSTEEN, A. Exh. 1928
Flower and landscape painter. † AB 2.

HALAHAN, Agatha Exh. 1929-33
Flower painter. Drum Manor, Co. Tyrone 1929; Nailards, Amberley, Sussex 1933. † RHA 2.

HALAY, Maurice Exh. 1908-10
c/o Allied Artist Assn. 67 Chancery Lane, London. † LS 11.

HALBRITTER, Sidney C. Exh. 1933
Interior pencil artist. 31 Madeira Road, Cliftonville, Kent. † RA 1.

HALDANE, Mary Exh. 1881-92
Landscape and coastal painter. Milford, Surrey. † G 5, L 2, M 1, RA 1, RBA 23.

HALDANE, Miss M.E. Exh. 1881
17 Charlotte Square, Edinburgh. † RSA 1.

HALE, C.E. Exh. 1900-9
† P 6.

HALE, Ellen D. Exh. 1882
Figure painter. The Cottage, Tite Street, Chelsea, London. † RA 1.
HALE, Edward Matthew 1852-1924
Genre painter. Studied in Paris with Cabanel and Carolus Duran 1873-75. War artist for "Illustrated London News" with Russian Army 1877-78 and in Afghanistan. R.O.I. 1898. Add: London 1881; Godalming, Surrey 1896; Eashing, Surrey 1916. † B 5, G 10, GI 5, L 21, M 9, NG 13, RA 33, RBA 1, RI 3, ROI 75.
HALE, Miss E. Thomas Exh. 1892-1919
Figure painter. London. † B 21, L 9, LS 3, RA 4, RBA 3, RI 9, ROI 10, SWA 14.
HALE, Fred Exh. 1886
Newlyn, Penzance, Cornwall. † ROI 1.
HALE, H. Exh. 1928
6 John Street, Bedford Row, London. † NEA 1.
HALE, Miss J. Exh. 1940
† RI 1.
HALE, Jessie Exh. 1903
Riddesdale, Purley, Surrey. † L 1.
HALE, John Howard 1863-1955
Portrait and landscape painter and craft worker. b. Farnham, Surrey. Studied Westminster School of Art and Royal College of Art. Director of Art and Craft Studies at Bermondsey Hospital for soldiers World War 1, and Director of Art at Blackheath School of Arts and Crafts. A.R.B.A. 1919, R.B.A. 1921. Add: Blackheath 1900; Farnham, Surry 1929. † LS 12, RA 3, RBA 100, RHA 1, ROI 1.
HALE, Kathleen b. 1898
b. Biggar, Peeblesshire. Exh. 1922-37. Add: Rabley Willow, South Mimms, Herts. † G 2, NEA 2, RBA 1.
HALE, M.B. Exh. 1880-83
Flower painter. 10 Raby Place, Bath. † D 3, L 2, RA 1, SWA 6.
HALE, Mary M. Exh. 1940
35 Wentworth Road, Harborne, Birmingham. † B 2.
HALE, Owen Exh. 1884-90
Sculptor. R.B.A. 1889. Add: 46 Gt. Russell Street, London. † RA 4, RBA 4, RI 1, ROI 1.
HALE, William Matthew 1837-1929
Marine and landscape painter. Studied under J.D. Harding and Collingwood Smith. A.R.W.S. 1871, R.W.S. 1881. Add: London 1880; Stoke Bishop, Nr. Bristol 1916. † B 9, BG 2, FIN 5, G 2, GI 3, L 19, M 3, RA 10, ROI 3, RSA 1, RWS 237.
HALE, Walter Stearne Exh. 1895-97
Etcher. A.R.E. 1895-99. Add: New York, U.S.A. † RE 10.
HALEY, Herbert Exh. 1893-99
Flower painter. Dudley Hill, Bradford, Yorks. 1893; Tottenham, London 1899. † RA 2, RBA 1.
HALEY, Henry James* b. 1874
Painter, line and wood engraver. b. Tunbridge Wells. Studied City and Guilds Technical Art School, R.A. Schools and in Paris. Exh. 1901-31. Add: London 1901 and 1922; Enfield, Middlesex 1919. † B 1, NG 1, P 2, RA 14, RI 2, ROI 2.
HALEY, Miss Margaret see REYNOLDS
HALFNIGHT, Richard William*
Exh. 1880-1923
Landscape and coastal painter. b. Sunderland. Add: London 1880 and 1914; Newcastle on Tyne 1901. † B 8, D 4, GI 5, L 17, M 25, RA 8, RBA 32, RI 32, ROI 18, RSA 2, TOO 4.
HALFORD, Miss Constance See REA
HALFORD, George b. 1885
b. Bradford. Exh. 1921-22. Add: Cleeve Prior, Evesham, Worcs. † B 2.
HALFORD, Jane Charlotte Exh. 1900-27
Watercolour landscape painter. b. Leeds. Studied under Edith Gittins. Add: Leicester. † N 7.
HALFPENNY, John C. Exh. 1882-1927
Landscape and figure painter. Liverpool 1882; Freshfield, Liverpool 1884; Rock Ferry, Cheshire 1887; London 1889 and 1897; Croydon, Surrey 1892; Neston, Cheshire 1910; Southampton 1911; Bournemouth 1914. † L 55, M 6, RA 17, RBA 5, RI 8, ROI 1.
HALHED, Miss A.E. Exh. 1890
5 Endsleigh Street, Tavistock Square, London. † SWA 1.
HALHED, Harriet d. 1933
Portrait, figure and domestic painter. Studied under Deschamps. A.S.W.A. 1896. Add: Canterbury, Kent 1884; Sevenoaks, Kent 1890; London 1897; Wokingham, Berks. 1913. † B 2, BG 18, GI 14, I 4, L 14, LS 19, M 1, NG 1, P 24, RA 12, RBA 7, RI 8, ROI 4, RSA 1, SWA 25.
HALKERSTON, Charles d. 1899
Edinburgh. † GI 14, L 1, RSA 63, RSW 2.
HALKET, Thomas Exh. 1887-89
113 West Regent Street, Glasgow. † GI 3.
HALKETT, Miss E. Exh. 1880-92
5 Douglas Crescent, Edinburgh. † RSA 7.
HALKETT, George Roland 1855-1918
Caricaturist and writer. Edinburgh. † BG 14, GI 1, RSA 12.
HALKETT, Helen F. Exh. 1888-89
5 Douglas Crescent, Edinburgh. † RSA 5.
HALKETT, Miss K.E. Exh. 1913-14
Sheepscombe Vicarage, Stroud, Glos. † LS 6.
HALL, van see V
HALL, A. Exh. 1884
3 Raby Place, Bath, Som. † L 2.
HALL, Mrs. A. Exh. 1902
60 Guttridge Street, Coalville, Nr. Leicester. † N 1.
HALL, Ambrose b. 1881
Etcher. Studied City School of Art, Liverpool. Exh. 1919-32. Add: 121 Bedford Road, Rock Ferry, Cheshire. † L 11, RSA 5.
HALL, Amos Exh. 1888
Architect. St. George's Chambers, Greyfriars, Leicester. † RA 1.
HALL, Annie Exh. 1884-98
Interior and architectural painter. Streatham, London 1884 and 1898; Newbury, Berks. 1893. † RBA 2, ROI 1, SWA 4.
HALL, A. Brames Exh. 1881-83
Etcher. R.E. 1881-87. Add: London 1881; Ravenswell, Kingswear, Devon 1883. † RE 5.
HALL, Agatha Catherine see SHORE
HALL, Alfred Ernest Exh. 1933-34
Cardiff. † RCA 2.
HALL, Mrs. Agnes F. Exh. 1939
Tunbarr, Headley, Epsom, Surrey. † RSA 1.
HALL, Miss A.F.G. Exh. 1926-33
19 West Cliff, Preston, Lancs. † B 4, L 5, RCA 2, ROI 1.
HALL, Arthur H. Exh. 1916-40
Painter and etcher. London. † COO 1, LEI 1, RA 1.
HALL, Alner W. Exh. 1927-35
Architect. London. † RA 4.
HALL, Caroline Exh. 1880
Beechwood, Petworth, Sussex. † SWA 1.
HALL, Caroline Exh. 1915
3 Toward Terrace, Sunderland. † L 1.
HALL, Christopher Exh. 1927-29
Figure and still life painter. † GOU 6.
HALL, Clifford b. 1904
Portrait, figure and landscape painter. Studied R.A. Schools (Landseer scholarship) and in Paris. Add: Richmond, Surrey 1926 and 1930; London 1927. † GOU 4, NEA 3, P 2, RA 1, RED 1, ROI 2.
HALL, Compton 1863-1937
Architect and landscape painter. R.B.A. 1919. Add: London 1906; Reigate, Surrey 1915; Litlington, Sussex 1931; Alfriston, Sussex 1935. † RA 2, RBA 125, RI 1.
HALL, Clare C. Exh. 1902-11
The Needles, Howth, Ireland 1902; Coolock, Co. Dublin 1907; Booterstown, Co. Dublin 1909. † RHA 8.
HALL, Miss C.L. Exh. 1889
Witley Manor, Godalming, Surrey. † M 1.
HALL, E. Exh. 1883-88
Albert Chambers, Paradise Street, Birmingham. † B 2.
HALL, Ernest Exh. 1929
Coastal painter. 41 Spalding Road, Nottingham. † N 2.
HALL, Ethel Exh. 1894-1909
Mrs. R.A. Waddilove. Miniature painter. R.M.S. 1896. Add: Croydon, Surrey 1894; Kensington, London 1897; Purley, Surrey 1905. † RMS 74, SWA 12.
HALL, Ethel Exh. 1894-1940
Watercolour landscape and flower painter and pencil artist. Bowden, Cheshire 1894; Altrincham, Cheshire 1920. † B 10, COO 27, L 32, M 7, RA 1, RBA 2, RCA 2, RI 1, SWA 5.
HALL, Eva Exh. 1907-12
St. Brendan's, Coolock, Co. Dublin. † RHA 4.
HALL, Edna Clarke b. 1881
nee Waugh. Watercolour painter, etcher, illustrator, lithographer and pen and ink artist. Studied Slade School (scholarship 1897). Visited the Middle East. Exh. 1899-1939. Add: Thames Ditton, Surrey 1899; London 1902; Harold Wood, Essex 1907. † ALP 4, CHE 2, GI 2, LS 5, NEA 19, RED 255, TOO 1.
HALL, Elsie H. Exh. 1931
87 St. Agatha's Road, Ward End, Birmingham. † B 1.
HALL, Edwin Stanley d. 1940
Architect. Exh. 1914-35. Add: 54 Bedford Square, London. † RA 5.
HALL, Edwin Thomas 1851-1923
Architect. Exh. 1880-1909. Add: London. † RA 12.
HALL, Fairfax Exh. 1937-38
Landscape, figure and still life painter. † RED 39.
HALL, Fred* b. 1860
Landscape and rustic genre painter. Studied Lincoln School of Art and under Verlat at Antwerp Academy. N.E.A. 1888. Exh. 1883-1937. Add: Wragby, Lincs. 1883; Newlyn, Penzance 1884; Liverpool 1899; Westcott, Dorking, Surrey 1901; London 1904; Speen, Newbury, Berks. 1912. † B 14, DOW 1, FIN 60, G 2, GI 7, L 32, M 7, NEA 1, NG 12, P 1, RA 69, RBA 6, RHA 1, RID 15, ROI 6, RSA 4.
HALL, Grahame Exh. 1921-22
Landscape painter. Sutton, Pulborough, Sussex. † RA 3, RSA 1.
HALL, George A. Exh. 1902-13
Architect. 1 Victoria Street, London. † RA 2.
HALL, Miss G.A.L. Exh. 1890
2 Newnham, Cambridge. † SWA 1.

HALL, George Henry* Exh. 1889-90
Flower painter. Paris 1889; London 1890. † G 2.

HALL, George Lowthian 1825-1888
Landscape painter. Menai Bridge, Anglesey. † D 7, L 2.

HALL, G.L. Desmond Exh. 1926
Architect. 1 Victoria Street, London. † RA 1.

HALL, George Wright b. 1895
Portrait and watercolour painter and decorative designer. Studied R.S.A. Schools (Keith prize 1921) and Edinburgh College of Art. Painting master Manchester School of Art. Exh. 1920-40. Add: Edinburgh. † GI 6, L 3, RA 1, RSA 10, RSW 2.

HALL, Gertrude W. Exh. 1913
4 The Avenue, Brondesbury, London. † LS 3:

HALL, Harold Exh. 1928-38
147 Woodchurch Road, Birkenhead. † L 4, RCA 2.

HALL, Henry Exh. 1886
Architect. 19 Doughty Street, London. † RA 1.

HALL, H. Austen Exh. 1915-40
Architect. London. † GI 1, RA 12, RSA 1.

HALL, Harry C. Exh. 1914
School of Arts and Crafts, Swansea. † L 2.

HALL, Hylda G. Exh. 1920-31
Landscape and miniature painter. London. † RA 2.

HALL, Miss H.K. Exh. 1919
44 Kensington Park Road, London. † SWA 1.

HALL, H.R. Exh. 1895-1902
Landscape painter. Blackpool 1895; Broughton in Furness 1902. † B 2, RA 1, RSA 1.

HALL, J. Exh. 1890
71 Sackville Road, West Brighton, Sussex. † RBA 1.

HALL, J. Exh. 1900-4
† TOO 2.

HALL, James Exh. 1909
36 Arnold Street, Liverpool. † L 3.

HALL, Jeanne Exh. 1917-18
The Bank House, Tring, Herts. † RA 1, SWA 2.

HALL, Jessie d. 1915
Animal painter. Studied under Fred Calderon. Died in a cycling accident. A.S.W.A. 1905. S.W.A. 1912. Add: Croydon, Surrey 1893; Seaford, Sussex 1902; Purley, Surrey 1903. † B 13, D 20, L 26, M 1, RA 2, RBA 5, RI 16, ROI 7, SWA 83.

HALL, John Exh. 1882-85
10 South Castle Street, Liverpool. † B 1, GI 1, L 4, M 1.

HALL, J.B. Exh. 1909-15
Dublin. † RHA 2.

HALL, John C. Exh. 1896-1937
Glasgow. † GI 20, RA 1, RSA 1.

HALL, Jean D. Exh. 1928-29
Norwich, Norfolk. † L 8.

HALL, J.P. Exh. 1916
6 Victoria Grove, Kensington, London. † RA 1.

HALL, J.R. Exh. 1888
Landscape painter. 1 Larkdale Street, Nottingham. † N 1.

HALL, Joseph Thomas b. 1886
Textile designer. Studied Leeds School of Art and Royal College of Art. Art master Clitheroe Grammer School and Blackburn Grammar School. Teacher of textile design. Exh. 1932. † L 1.

HALL, Kate A. Exh. 1882-86
Flower painter. Handsworth, Birmingham 1882; Edgbaston, Birmingham 1885. † B 2, M 1, SWA 1.

HALL, Miss K.V. Exh. 1904-6
5 Genoa Road, Anerley. † SWA 3.

HALL, Lilian Exh. 1908-19
Miniature portrait painter. London. † L 1, RA 10.

HALL, Lindsey Bernard 1859-1935
Portrait and figure painter. Director of National Gallery of Victoria from 1892. N.E.A. 1886. Exh. 1882-1923. Add: Liverpool 1882; South Kensington, London 1883. † I 1, L 14, M 2, NEA 6, RA 8, RBA 5, ROI 6.

HALL, Lily Elizabeth b. 1901
Portrait and figure painter and illustrator. Studied Slade School and Chelsea Polytechnic. Exh. 1925-33. Add: 61 Parson's Green Lane, London. † NEA 2, RA 2.

HALL, Louie E. Exh. 1901
c/o J. Stewart, 43 Princes Street, Strathbung, N.B. † GI 1.

HALL, Miss Lilian May Bevis see ROWLES

HALL, Mrs. M. Exh. 1909
7B Canadian Buildings, James Street, Liverpool. † L 4.

HALL, Miss M. Exh. 1931-40
Smethwick, Birmingham. † B 3.

HALL, Mrs. Margaret Exh. 1919
Miniature painter. 11 The Grangeway, Grange Park, London. † RA 1.

HALL, Minnie Exh. 1924
23 Margaret Street, West Bromwich, Staffs. † B 1.

HALL, Margaret Bernadine 1863-1910
Dudlow House, Wavertree, Liverpool 1884. † L 1.

HALL, Mary B. Exh. 1886-88
Flower painter. Penstones, Lancing, nr. Worthing, Sussex. † L 1, RA 1.

HALL, Margaret E. Exh. 1895-1906
The Grange, Hale, Nr. Altrincham, Cheshire. † M 5.

HALL, Mary E. Exh. 1892-94
26 Paradise Street, Birmingham. † B 2.

HALL, Mabel G. Blythe Exh. 1893-1910
Edinburgh 1893; Trefaes, Towyn, Merioneth 1910. † RSA 9.

HALL, Margaret L. Exh. 1896-1905
Miniature painter. R.M.S. 1896. Add: 52 Palace Gardens Terrace, Kensington, London. † RA 1, RMS 81.

HALL, Mildred M. Exh. 1892-1935
Bowden, Cheshire 1892; Arnhall, St. Anne's on Sea, Lancs. 1893. † B 2, L 11, M 5, RCA 2.

HALL, North Exh. 1888-89
Figure painter. 12 Caldervale Road, Clapham Common, London. † RI 1, ROI 1.

HALL, Oliver* 1869-1957
Painter and etcher. Studied Royal College of Art, Lambeth and Westminster School of Art. Travelled in Italy and Spain. A.R.A. 1920, R.A. 1927, A.R.E. 1891, R.E. 1895-1916, A.R.W.S. 1916, R.W.S. 1919, Member of Society of 25 Artists. "Shap Moors" purchased by Chantrey Bequest 1920 and "Vale of Festiniog" in 1936. Add: Brixton, London 1980; West Chiltington, Nr. Pulborough, Sussex 1899 and 1905; Fittleworth, Sussex 1903 and 1906; Sutton, Nr. Pulborough, Sussex 1914. † AG 5, B 1, BA 6, BAR 67, CAR 1, CHE 1, DOW 218, FIN 55, G 21, GI 38, GOU 1, I 46, L 55, LEI 170, M 8, NEA 6, NG 5, RA 108, RBA 4, RE 110, RHA 3, RI 5, ROI 3, RSA 8, RSW 2, RWS 189, WG 9.

HALL, R. Exh. 1904-5
Portrait painter. 43 Avenue Victor Hugo, Paris. † GI 1, RA 2.

HALL, Richard Exh. 1933
Bangor, Wales. † RCA 3.

HALL, Ralph F. Exh. 1910-32
Sculptor. N.S.A. 1933. Add: Sherwood, Notts. 1910; Nottingham 1914. † N 9, RA 2.

HALL, R.H. Exh. 1897
26 Milburn Street, Blackpool. † B 1.

HALL, R.M. Exh. 1926
Landscape painter. † FIN 1.

HALL, R. Newman Exh. 1925
25 Norma Road, Waterloo, Liverpool. † L 1.

HALL, R. Selby Exh. 1930
Lino cut artist. † RED 2.

HALL, S.F. Exh. 1938
120 Perrywood Road, Great Barr, Birmingham. † B 2.

HALL, Sydney Prior 1842-1922
Portrait painter. Married Mary L. Gow, q.v. Exh. 1880-1920. Add: London. † D 1, G 12, L 13, M 4, NG 15, P 8, RA 31, RHA 5, RI 1.

HALL, Thomas Exh. 1880-96
Architect. 8 George Street, Edinburgh. † RA 4, RSA 1.

HALL, T. Hall Exh. 1911-13
Landscape painter. † ALP 6.

HALL, Miss Westralia Exh. 1919-20
Portrait and miniature painter. 78 Broadhurst Gardens, Hampstead, London. † RA 2.

HALL, William d. c.1885
Watercolour landscape painter. Add: Eaton Square, London. † L 2, M 3, RA 3, RBA 1, RI 1.

HALL, W.E. Exh. 1888
2 Cleveland Row, St. James', London. † D 4.

HALL, W. Honnywill* Exh. 1880-90
Landscape painter. London. † RA 2, RBA 15, RHA 4, ROI 3.

HALL, Mrs. W. Honnywill Exh. 1880-86
Flower and landscape painter. Add: London and Birmingham. † D 1, RBA 3, ROI 4.

HALL, William Henry Exh. 1882-1926
Watercolour landscape painter. Birmingham. † B 127, RA 1, RBA 3, RHA 3, ROI 1.

HALL, Walter J. Exh. 1909
21 Birley Street, Bury, Lancs. † L 1.

HALL, W.O.B. Exh. 1916
21 Rathgar Road, Dublin. † RHA 1.

HALL, W. Patrick b. 1906
Landscape painter and chalk artist. Exh. 1928-40. Add: York. † L 2, RA 5.

HALL, Miss Y.G. Exh. 1919
509 Fulham Road, London. † SWA 2.

HALL, Miss Z.M. Exh. 1916-20
Liverpool. † L 4.

HALLAM, Charlotte E. Exh. 1891-1911
18 St. Peter's Road, Handsworth, Birmingham. † B 18, L 1.

HALLAM, E.G. Exh. 1910-16
Southport, Lancs. 1910; Birkdale, Lancs. 1916. † L 4.

HALLAM, H.C. Exh. 1920
23 Brownsville Road, Heaton Moor, Manchester. † L 1.

HALLAM, John Algernon Exh. 1908-36
Painter and architect. Studied Regent Street Polytechnic, L.C.C. School of Arts and Crafts and the A.A. Add: London 1908; Cardiff 1923. † LS 8, NEA 2, RA 3, RCA 4.

HALLAM, Mrs. Jane B. Exh. 1934
Llandudno, Wales. † RCA 1.

HALLAM, J.S. Exh. 1933
† RSW 4.

HALLAM, Miss Lesa Exh. 1908-21
Miniature painter. London. † L 2, RA 10.

HALLAM, Vera Exh. 1918
216 Derby Road, Nottingham. † N 2.

HALLAS, Harold W. Exh. 1928-32
Architectural painter. Huddersfield, Yorks. † L 3, RA 2.

HALLATZ, Emil Exh. 1880-83
Figure painter. 30 Bessborough Street, London. † FIN 2, RSA 1.

HALLAWELL, Mrs. T.A. Exh. 1897
4 Parkside, Hooton, Lancs. † L 1.

HALLE, Charles Edward* 1846-1919
Portrait and decorative figure painter. Son of Charles Halle, the musician. Studied under Baron Marochetti and L. Von. Mottez. Director of the New Gallery 1888-1909. Add: London 1880; Venice 1912. † B 13, BG 1, G 40, GI 9, L 35, M 11, NG 103, P 3, RA 1.

HALLE, Elinor Exh. 1882-1914
Sculptor and enameller. Studied under Legros. R.E. 1884-91. Add: London 1882 and 1892; Ightham, Nr. Sevenoaks, Kent 1891. † G 5, L 24, NG 24, RA 5, RE 4.

HALL-EDWARDS, Major J. Exh. 1920-26
Birmingham. † B 4.

HALLEN, Van See V

HALLER, Miss Lilian P. Exh. 1930
Plymouth, Devon. † L 1.

HALLET, Andre Exh. 1920-21
Landscape painter. † GOU 4, M 1.

HALLETT, Alfred W. Exh. 1937
Figure painter. Upper Norwood, London 1937; Eastbourne, 1939. † RA 2.

HALLETT, Dorothy S. Exh. 1913-30
Animal painter (dogs and cats), miniaturist and illustrator. Studied Academie Grande Chaumiere, Paris. Add: London. † L 3, RA 5, WG 61.

HALLETT, Ellen Kathleen b. 1899
Etcher. 3 Logan Road, Bishopston, Bristol 1934. † RA 1.

HALLETT, Miss W.A. Miller Exh. 1914
Chelsfield, Kent. † SWA 1.

HALLGREEN, Ernst Exh. 1914
Etcher. A.R.E. 1914-21. Add: Grefmagringat 13, Stockholm. † RE 5.

HALLIDAY, Edwin Irvine b. 1902
Portrait and decorative painter and interior decorator. Studied City School of Art, Liverpool, Colarossi's, Paris, Royal College of Art and British School at Rome. Add: Garston, Liverpool 1923; London 1929-40. † L 15, P 12, RA 20, RBA 3.

HALLIDAY, George Exh. 1888-1912
Sculptor. Edinburgh 1888; Sheffield 1899; Moseley, Birmingham 1910. † RA 3, RSA 1.

HALLIDAY, George E. Exh. 1894-1910
Architect. Llandaff, South Wales 1894; Cardiff 1898. † RA 4.

HALLIDAY, J.T. Exh. 1916
14 John Dalton Street, Manchester. † RA 1.

HALLIDAY, Sybil G. Exh. 1935
Sculptor. 45 Earl's Court Square, London. † RA 1.

HALLIDAY, Thomas Symington b. 1902
Etcher, stained glass artist, mural decorator. b. Thornhill, Dumfries. Studied Glasgow School of Art. Art master Prestwich High school. Exh. 1927-40. Add: Ayr 1927; Alloa 1936. † GI 7, L 2, RSA 14, RSW 6.

HALL-JONES, F. Exh. 1918
Parliament Mansions, Victoria Street, London. † RA 1.

HALLMAN, William Wallace Exh. 1909-19
Egremont, Cheshire. † L 5.

HALLOWES, Sidney M. Exh. 1900-8
Landscape painter. Heath Fern Lodge, Heathside, Hampstead, London. † RA 5.

HALLS, Robert Exh. 1893-1909
Miniature portrait painter. London 1893 and 1904; Birkenhead 1903. † L 3, NEA 1, P 7, RA 25, RMS 5.

HALLS, R.H. Exh. 1910
Dyxcroft, Wallands Park, Lewes, Sussex. † RA 1.

HALLWARD, Adelaide Exh. 1909
Painter and illustrator. † DOW 25.

HALLWARD, Ella F.G. Exh. 1898
25 Hogarth Road, London. † NG 1.

HALLWARD, Michael Exh. 1909
Architect. † DOW 2.

HALLWARD, Patience Mary Exh. 1909-40
Painter and lithographer. Add: London 1940. † AR 8, DOW 2, RA 1, RMS 1.

HALLWARD, Reginald 1858-1948
Painter, stained glass artist and decorative designer. Studied Slade School and Royal College of Art. Exh. 1883-1937. Add: London. † AR 69, DOW 139, G 2, L 5, NEA 5, NG 3, RA 11, RBA 1.

HALNON, Frederick James b. 1881
Sculptor. Studied Goldsmith's College 1892 (2 gold medals 1902 and 1903) and under Alfred Drury. Modelling master at Goldsmith's College. Exh. 1904-31. Add: London. † GI 5, L 5, RA 32, RI 1.

HALPERT, de See D

HALSALL, Miss Ella Exh. 1919
† L 1.

HALSE, Miss Emmeline d. 1930
Sculptor. Studied R.A. Schools (3 medals) and Paris. Exh. 1881-1920. Add: 15 Clarendon Road, Notting Hill, London. † GI 22, L 12, M 2, NG 7, RA 31, RMS 1.

HALSE, George Exh. 1880-93
Sculptor. Add: 15 Clarendon Road, Notting Hill, London. † G 1, GI 7, L 7, M 2, RA 6, RBA 3, RHA 2, RSA 4.

HALSEY, Gertrude Exh. 1923-27
Portrait painter and lithographer. London. † RA 2, SWA 2.

HALSTEAD, Samuel Exh. 1894-95
3 Matlock Terrace, Chapeltown Road, Leeds. † L 3.

HALSTED, Evelyn V. Exh. 1939
† GOU 1.

HALSWELLE, Keeley* 1832-1891
Genre and landscape painter and illustrator. Worked for "Illustrated London News". R.I. 1882, R.O.I. 1883, A.R.S.A. 1865. † AG 8, B 3, D 1, DOW 1, FIN 2, G 15, GI 4, L 11, M 11, NG 3, RA 19, RHA 1, RI 23, ROI 13, RSA 14, TOO 24.

HALTON, W. Exh. 1883-84
Adelphi Chambers, Strand, London. † L 1, RHA 1.

HAM, Ada J. Exh. 1885-88
Watercolour flower and fruit painter. Hampstead, London 1885; 58 Merrion Square, Dublin 1888. † L 2, RA 5, RHA 3, RI 2.

HAMAND, Louis Arthur b. 1873
Watercolour painter and black and white artist. Exh. 1922-25. Add: The Dingle, Christchurch Road, Great Malvern, Worcs. † GI 2, NEA 1, RA 2.

HAMBLIN-SMITH, M.I. Exh. 1935
Wood cut artist. † COO 3.

HAMBLY, Arthur Creed b. 1900
Watercolour landscape painter, etcher and illuminator. Studied Newton Abbot School of Art and Bristol Municipal School of Art. Temporary Headmaster of Salisbury School of Art and Headmaster of Camborne and Redruth School of Art. Add: Bristol 1923; Redruth, Cornwall 1927. † D 1, NEA 1, RBA 2, RI 1.

HAMBROUCK, H. Exh. 1918
Southfield House, Newton Mearns, Nr. Glasgow. † GI 1.

HAMDY, Osman 1842-1910
Turkish figure and portrait painter. Director of the Imperial Museums in Constantinople. H.F.R.A. Exh. 1903-9. Add: Constantinople. † L 2, RA 4.

HAMER, H. Adrian Exh. 1930
Wallasey, Cheshire. † L 1.

HAMER, Heather G. Exh. 1934
Black and white artist. † AR 68.

HAMER, John Exh. 1890-91
Urban landscape painter. London. † RBA 2.

HAMERSLEY, Constance Exh. 1930-34
Landscape painter. b. New Zealand. Add: Rycote Park, Wheatley, Oxon. † RA 1, SWA 1.

HAMERTON, Philip Gilbert 1834-1894
Etcher, author and critic. H.R.E. 1880. Exh. 1885. Add: Autun, Saone et Loire, France. † RE 4.

HAMILTON, Mrs. Exh. 1885
Watercolour landscape painter. Queen Anne's Mansions, London. † SWA 2.

HAMILTON, Archibald Exh. 1898-99
Oakthorpe, Windermere. † M 1, RI 1.

HAMILTON, Augusta D. Exh. 1896
Portrait painter. 86 West Cormwell Road, London. † RA 1.

HAMILTON, Alan W.B. Exh. 1908
Glen View, Fleet, Hants. † LS 1.

HAMILTON, Mrs. Baillie Exh. 1889-90
55 Sloane Street, London. † D 4.

HAMILTON, Beth Exh. 1909-16
Ealing, London. † L 2, M 1, RA 5, RHA 1.

HAMILTON, Blanche Douglas Exh. 1891
Pen-y-Bryn, Bryn Road, Swansea. † M 1.

HAMILTON, Cecil Exh. 1916-18
London. † L 2, RA 2.

HAMILTON, Mrs. Charles Exh. 1883-86
Flower and architectural painter. Waterlane House, Headcorn, Kent. † SWA 3.

HAMILTON, C. Winifred Exh. 1907-12
Ardedynn, Kelvinside, Glasgow 1907; 19 Beaufort Gardens, London 1910. † GI 5.

HAMILTON, David Exh. 1882-87
Horsburgh Castle, Peebles, Lancs. † GI 5, RSA 1.

HAMILTON, Dorothy Exh. 1904
6 James Place, Leith. † RSA 1.

HAMILTON, Miss E. Exh. 1896-1916
Barncheith, Hamilton. † D 1, I 1, P 3.

HAMILTON, Edith Exh. 1929
Flower and still life painter. † AB 2.

HAMILTON, Miss E.B. Exh. 1923
Western House, The Park, Nottingham. † N 2.

HAMILTON, Eva Henrietta 1880-1959
Portrait and landscape painter. Studied Slade School and Metropolitan School of Art, Dublin. Sister of Letitia Marion H. q.v. Add: Dunboyne, Co. Meath 1904 and 1909; Dublin 1907 and 1911; Monasterevin 1918; Palmerston, Dublin 1919; Dunsinea, Castle Knock 1935. † FIN 1, GOU 2, L 1, RHA 20.

HAMILTON, Miss F. Exh. 1908
Skene House, Aberdeen. † L 1.

HAMILTON, George Exh. 1882-94
Edinburgh. † RSA 3.

HAMILTON, H. Exh. 1882
c/o G. Worthington, Altrincham, Cheshire. † M 1.

HAMILTON, Harriet Mary b. 1865
Mrs. W.R. nee Bousfield. Portrait and landscape painter. Studied under Matthew White Ridley. Add: Bedford 1889; Nottingham 1897. † N 6, RA 3, RID 39.

HAMILTON, Innes Exh. 1899-1927
Miniature portrait and watercolour painter. 4 Scarsdale Studios, Kensington, London. † NG 3, RA 13, RCA 1, RHA 2.

HAMILTON, Iris A. Exh. 1930-40
Etcher. West Harrow, Middlesex. † L 1, RA 1.

HAMILTON, Ian B.M. Exh. 1929-30
Architect. 16 Old Buildings, Lincoln's Inn, London. † RA 2.

HAMILTON, James* 1855-1894
Figure and landscape painter. A.R.S.A. 1886. Add: Edinburgh. † GI 16, L 1, M 4, RA 1, RSA 44.

HAMILTON, John Exh. 1901-3
4 Castlewood Road, Stamford Hill, London. † D 7.

HAMILTON, John Exh. 1902-7
212 St. Vincent Street, Glasgow. † GI 2.

HAMILTON, J.A. Exh. 1885-91
Edinburgh. † L 2, RSA 32.

HAMILTON, J.C. Exh. 1887
17 Villiers Road, Bushey, Herts. † RI 1.

HAMILTON, John McClure 1853-1936
Portrait painter. b. Philadelphia, U.S.A. Studied Pennsylvania Academy of Fine Arts, Royal Academy, Antwerp and Paris. Settled in London in 1878. N.E.A. 1890, R.P. 1891. † BAR 27, G 4, GI 14, L 20, NEA 3, P 6, RA 8, RBA 1, RHA 2, RI 1, ROI 1, RSA 1, TOO 1.

HAMILTON, J.S. Exh. 1922-31
School of Art, Dundee 1922; Oakhill Road, Aberdeen 1931. † RSA 2.

HAMILTON, J.W. Exh. 1889
6 New Compton Street, Soho, London. † RHA 1.

HAMILTON, James Whitelaw* 1860-1932
Landscape painter. Studied in Glasgow and Paris. N.E.A. 1887, A.R.S.A. 1911, R.S.A. 1922, R.S.W. 1895. Member of the Society of 25 Artists. Add: Helensburgh, N.B. 1882, 1890 and 1895; Glasgow 1888 and 1893; Edinburgh 1894. † BAR 2, GI 120, I 20, L 16, M 3, NEA 6, P 1, RA 10, RHA 1, RSA 113, RSW 75.

HAMILTON, Kathleen Exh. 1885
Figure painter. 28 Pembroke Gardens, London. † ROI 1.

HAMILTON, Kate Exh. 1890-1900
Edinburgh. † RSA 3.

HAMILTON, Letitia Marion* d. c.1965
Landscape painter and enamel-plaque artist. Studied Dublin Metropolitan School of Art, Chelsea Polytechnic and under Sir William Orpen and Frank Brangwyn. A.R.H.A. 1934. Sister of Eva Henrietta H. q.v. Add: Dunboyne, Co. Meath 1909; Dublin 1914; Monasterevin, Co. Kildare 1917, Palmerston, Dublin 1919; Dunsinea, Castle Knock 1935. † FIN 3, GOU 55, I 15, P 1, RA 5, RBA 5, RHA 131, WG 56.

HAMILTON, Lilian V. b. 1865
nee Swainson. Sculptor and medalist. b. Mitcham. Studied Slade School (Slade Scholarship 1884). Married Vereker Monteith H. q.v. A.R.E. 1887, A.R.M.S. 1928. Exh. 1886-1932. Add: London 1886; Cowden, Kent 1928. † G 2, GI 1, I 4, L 3, LS 8, RA 24, RE 26, RMS 11.

HAMILTON, Maggie see PATERSON

HAMILTON, Marjorie Exh. 1913-14
23 Redcliffe Road, London. † D 4, LS 3.

HAMILTON, Mary A. Exh. 1915-24
Newsham Park, Liverpool 1915; Colwyn Bay, Wales 1924. † I 4, L 2, RCA 1.

HAMILTON, Mary Elizabeth Exh. 1898-1936
Landscape painter, bookplate and linocut artist and designer. b. Skene. Studied Byam Shaw School of Art. Add: Skene House, Aberdeen 1898; London 1908; Murtle, Aberdeenshire 1923. † B 1, BA 60, COO 6, D, 2, GI 2, L 20, RA 5, RI 2, RSA 2, SWA 1, WG 3.

HAMILTON, Maud S. Exh. 1898
Designer. Crouch End, London. † RA 1.

HAMILTON, Nora G. Exh. 1919-35
Watercolour painter. Studied under Norman Garstin. Add: Inistioge, Ireland 1919; Clondalkin, Co. Dublin 1921. † RA 1, RHA 4, SWA 2.

HAMILTON, Mrs. Olivia Exh. 1899-1908
R.M.S. 1899. Bromley, Kent 1899; St. John's Wood, London 1901. † L 2, RMS 28.

HAMILTON, Mrs. R. Exh. 1901
The Studio, 32 Wellington Place, Belfast. † RHA 1.

HAMILTON, Mrs. Rachel Exh. 1932
25 Buckingham Terrace, Edinburgh. † RSW 1.

HAMILTON, Robert Exh. 1896-1903
Belfast. † RHA 21.

HAMILTON, R.D. Exh. 1886
331 Strand, London. † B 1.

HAMILTON, Ruth Sargeant Exh. 1924-29
Holywood, Co. Down 1924; Hollywood, Belfast 1925. † L 18.

HAMILTON, Mrs. Stella Exh. 1938
Flower painter. b. Blagdon, Northumberland. † WG 34.

HAMILTON, T. Exh. 1924-28
Artists Club, Eberu Street, Liverpool. † L 4.

HAMILTON, Thomas Crawford Exh. 1880-90
Edinburgh 1880; Glasgow 1886. † GI 11, RSA 5, RSW 10.

HAMILTON, T. Hay Exh. 1906
† I 1.

HAMILTON, T.M. Exh. 1920-23
Font Hill, Palmerston, Co. Dublin. † RHA 7, RI 1.

HAMILTON, Thomas T. Exh. 1886-87
Shepherd's Bush, London 1886; Dangan, Galway 1887. † L 2, RA 1, RHA 1.

HAMILTON, T.W. Exh. 1927
12 Oxford Street, Nottingham. † L 4.

HAMILTON, Vereker Monteith 1856-1931
Military, landscape and figure painter. b. Hafton, Argyll. Studied Slade School (1st landscape prize 1886). Married Lilian V.H. q.v. Collaborated with Joseph Benwell Clark q.v. R.E. 1887. Add: London 1886; Cowden, Kent 1927. † BRU 33, DOW 65, G 5, GI 5, L 2, LS 12, M 4, NG 1, RA 32, RE 6, RHA 2.

HAMILTON, William Exh. 1932
221 Renfrew Street, Glasgow. † GI 2.

HAMILTON, William Exh. 1901
Butterburn Park, Hamilton, N.B. † GI 1.

HAMLEY, Barbara Exh. 1881-99
Mrs. Rowland Prothero, later Lady Ernle. Miniature portrait painter. R.M.S. 1897. Add: London. † D 1, GI 2, L 2, RA 2, RI 6, RMS 8, SWA 4.

HAMLYN, Reginald B. Exh. 1921-28
London 1921; Peverell, Plymouth 1923. † I 1, L 1, RSW 1.

HAMMARSKIOLD, Birgitta Exh. 1921
† LS 3.

HAMMER, Victor Exh. 1933-34
Figure painter. 2B Pembroke Road, London. † RA 3.

HAMMERSHOI, Svend Exh. 1904-31
Landscape painter. Southampton Lodge, Fitzroy Park, Highgate, London 1931. † I 2, RA 1.

HAMMERSLEY, B.J. Exh. 1930-32
10 Minstead Road, Erdington, Birmingham. † B 3.

HAMMERSLEY, Maud Exh. 1922-24
Still life painter. 64 Forest Road, West, Nottingham. † N 13.

HAMMERSLEY-HEENAN, Eileen Exh. 1925
Sculptor. 3 Cockloft Studios, 35 Cochrane Street, London. † RA 1.

HAMMERSTON, Effie Exh. 1926
57 Woodsley Road, Leeds. † L 1.

HAMMICK, Joseph William Exh. 1907-12
34 Mount Ephraim, Tunbridge Wells, Kent. † LS 3, RA 4.

HAMMOND, Arthur Exh. 1912-14
Studio, Bramhall, Cheshire. † L 2, M 9.

HAMMOND, Aubrey b. 1893
Illustrator, black and white artist, stage decorator and poster designer. Studied London School of Art, Byam Shaw School of Art and Juliens, Paris. Instructor in commercial and theatrical art, Westminster School of Art. Exh. 1938. † RED 8.

HAMMOND, Adeline C. Exh. 1922
Sculptor. 89 Pepys Road, New Cross, London. † RA 2.

HAMMOND, Arthur Henry Knighton* 1875-1970
Painter, black and white artist and etcher. b. Arnold, Notts. Studied Nottingham School of Art, Westminster and Paris. Travelled widely. R.I. 1933, R.O.I. 1938, R.S.W. 1940. Add: Arnold, Notts. 1895; London 1901 and 1934; Sherwood, Notts. 1902; Bakewell, Derbys. 1906; France 1926; Alton, Hants. 1933; Ditchling, Sussex 1936. † BA 16, FIN 61, GI 6, L 3, M 2, N 17, NEA 2, P 7, RA 9, RBA 4, RI 45, ROI 13, RSW 1.

HAMMOND, Miss A.V. Exh. 1907-8
17 Elvaston Place, Queen's Gate, London. † ROI 2.

HAMMOND, A. Victor Exh. 1909
c/o Soar & Son, 1 Launceston Place, Kensington, London. † L 1, LS 3.

HAMMOND, Christine M. Demain Exh. 1886-95
Figure and domestic painter. Sister of Gertrude E. Demain H. q.v. Add: London. † RA 6, RBA 2, RI 2, ROI 1.

HAMMOND, Edith Exh. 1925-39
S.W.A. 1935. Add: Flat 3, 95 Fitzjohn's Avenue, Hampstead, London. † L 1, NEA 1, RBA 1, RI 1, SWA 13.

HAMMOND, Miss F.E. Exh. 1912-14
43 Holly Terrace, Hensingham, Whitehaven. † D 5, RBA 4.

HAMMOND, Gertrude E. Demain Exh. 1886-1940
Flower, figure and domestic painter. R.I. 1896. Sister of Christine M. Demain H. q.v. Add: London 1886 and 1929; Stow on the Wold, Glos. 1919; Worthing, Sussex 1932. † L 34, M 6, RA 21, RBA 4, RHA 1, RI 142.

HAMMOND, Horace Exh. 1902-39
Landscape painter and pen and wash artist. Birmingham 1902; Kidderminster 1927; London 1939. † B 16, L 1, RA 1.

HAMMOND, H.B. Exh. 1931
Still life painter. Castlemoate, Swords, Co. Dublin. † RHA,1.

HAMMOND, H. Fauchon Exh. 1939
† NEA 1.

HAMMOND, Hermione F.E. Exh. 1938
Figure painter. 59 South Edwardes Square, London. † RA 1.

HAMMOND, John* b. 1843
Candian landscape painter. St. John's, New Brunswick, Canada. † L 1, M 1, RA 4.

HAMMOND, Miss K. Exh. 1918
Slade Park Cottage, Saltash, Cornwall. † RA 1.

HAMMOND, Miss Kate See SHEPHERD

HAMMOND, Miss K.G. Exh. 1913
Tufnell Park, London. † SWA 1.

HAMMOND, Kathleen M. Exh. 1935
Stained glass artist. 12 Waddon Close, Croydon, Surrey. † RA 1.

HAMMOND, Lucy Exh. 1887-88
Chestnut Cottage, Rocky Lane, Sutton Coldfield, Birmingham. † B 2.

HAMMOND, May Exh. 1914
Millbrook House, Ware, Herts. † LS 3.

HAMMOND, Mildred L. Exh. 1918-37
Landscape and flower painter. London. † NEA 3, RA 3, SWA 1.

HAMMOND, Percy Exh. 1908
20 University Road, Bootle, Lancs. † L 1.

HAMMOND, Percy E.D. Exh. 1896-1901
Stained glass artist. London. † RA 2.

HAMMOND, P.J. Exh. 1882-87
Landscape painter. 70 Friar Gate, Derby. † B 1, N 8.

HAMMOND, R. Gardiner Exh. 1900-11
Architect. 16 Essex Street, Strand, London. † RA 11.

HAMMOND, R.J.* Exh. 1882-1911
Birmingham. † B 40, M 1.

HAMMOND, Thomas William Exh. 1882-1934
Land and seascape painter. N.S.A. 1908-33. V.P.N.S.A. 1928. Add: Nottingham. † B 3, FIN 10, L 38, M 1, N 230, RA 37, RCA 6, RSA 1.

HAMMOND-GRAEME, Lady Exh. 1887
Figure painter. Bucklands, East Cowes, I.O.W. † SWA 1.

HAMMONDS, Miss D.M. Exh. 1925
21 Huskisson Street, Liverpool. † L 1.

HAMNETT, Nina* 1890-1956
Portrait and landscape painter and illustrator. b. Tenby, S. Wales. Studied London School of Art (silver medal). Member of the London Group 1917. Add: London. † ALP 1, CHE 1, GOU 4, L 1, NEA 10, TOO 41.

HAMP, Stanley b. 1879
Architect. Exh. 1908-37. Add: London. † GI 1, RA 18, RSA 13.

HAMPEL, Carl* b. 1891
Landscape, portrait and flower painter. b. Victoria, Australia. Self taught. Exh. 1930-40. Add: London and Maldon, Essex. † B 1, FIN 159, GI 1, RA 3, RBA 2, RSA 1.

HAMPSHIRE, Ernest Llewellyn b. 1882
Landscape painter, etcher and architect. Studied Clapham School of Art, King's College, London (architecture), Central School of Arts and Crafts (etching) and Heatherleys. Exh. 1907-38. † I 6, L 2, RA 13, RI 12, ROI 9.

HAMPSHIRE, J. Exh. 1903-19
Huddersfield. † L 1, RCA 8.

HAMPSHIRE, Miss K.E. Exh. 1926
Westwood, Station Road, Mickleover, Nr. Derby. † N 2.

HAMPSHIRE, Mrs. Maria See EATON

HAMPSON, W. Exh. 1924
Ennerdale, Formby, Lancs. † L 1.

HAMPTON, Herbert 1862-1929
Sculptor and painter. Studied Lambeth, Westminster and Slade Schools, and Cormon's and Juliens in Paris. Add: Hoddesden, Herts. 1886 and 1891; London 1888, 1897 and 1902; Bishops Stortford, Herts. 1893; Reed, Herts. 1901; Bardfield, Nr. Braintree, Essex 1927. † GI 6, I 5, L 17, LS 5, M 1, NG,2, RA 55, RBA 2, RMS 3, ROI 1, RSA 4.

HAMPTON, Herbert G. Exh. 1915-34
Landscape painter. Ealing, London. † RA 7.

HAMPTON, Mary Exh. 1884-85
Landscape painter. 33 Eaton Square, London. † SWA 3.

HAMPTON, W.H.D. Exh. 1922
† I 1.

HAMSHERE, David Exh. 1922-36
Landscape and portrait painter. Waterloo, Liverpool and London. † L 5, NEA 1, P 1, RA 2.

HAMSON, T.D. Exh. 1920-35
28 King Richard Street, Coventry. † B 12.

HANBRIDGE, J.E. Exh. 1880-1908
Crosshill, Glasgow. † GI 28, L 1, RSA 4.

HANBURY, Ada Exh. 1881-87
Flower painter. 16 Chivalry Road, Wandsworth Common, London. † G 2, RA 1, RI 2.

HANBURY, Blanche Exh. 1880-87
Flower and landscape painter. 16 Chivalry Road, Wandsworth Common, London. † D 4, RA 2, RBA 3, RI 2, SWA 1.

HANCOCK, Christine P. Exh. 1934-40
Landscape painter. Hove, Sussex 1934 and 1940; Brighton 1937. † RA 3, RI 3, RSW 2, SWA 3, WG 3.

HANCOCK, E. Exh. 1881
26 Winchester Road, Belsize, London. † SWA 1.

HANCOCK, Elizabeth A. Exh. 1910-25
Still life and flower painter. Stoke Newington, London 1910; Finsbury Park, London 1915. † L 1, RA 5.

HANCOCK, Frederick Exh. 1894
Oak Tree Cottage, Regent Street, Stoke on Trent, Staffs. † L 1.

HANCOCK, George A. Exh. 1922-31
Landscape painter. A.N.S.A. 1927, N.S.A. 1929. Add: Nottingham. † N 10, RA 1.

HANCOCK, George H. Exh. 1913
43 Upper Brook Street, Ipswich, Suffolk. † LS 3.

HANCOCK, Grace Violet Exh. 1912-20
Miniature painter. Alfriston, Surbiton, Surrey. † RA 5, RMS 1.

HANCOCK, H.F. Exh. 1880-81
c/o T. McLean and Co., Haymarket, London. † D 3.

HANCOCK, J. Exh. 1905
45 Bramwell Lane, Porthill, Nr. Burslem, Stoke on Trent, Staffs. † L 1.

HANCOCK, Jennetta Flora Exh. 1919-29
Miniature painter. Studied Heatherleys. Add: Coombe Martin, N. Devon 1919; Torquay, S. Devon 1927. † L 1, RA 1, RI 7.

HANCOCK, K.W. Exh. 1938
Swansea, Wales. † RCA 1.

HANCOCK, Mary Exh. 1939-40
11 Bickley Road, Bickley, Kent. † SWA 2.

HANCOCK, Mildred Exh. 1890-97
Mrs. Welsford. Portrait and figure painter. Nottingham 1890; Harrow on the Hill, Middlesex 1891. † L 1, M 2, N 7, RA 3, RBA 3, RI 1, ROI 3.

HANCOCK, Richard Exh. 1885-1902
Stained glass and mosaic artist. Mortlake 1885; Putney 1896. † RA 3.

HANCOCK, Samuel Harry d. 1932
Landscape, portrait and poster painter. Studied evening classes at Birkbeck College and City and Guilds. Exh. 1910-32. Add: Ilford, Essex. † AR 72, LS 3, RA 5.

HANCOCK, Sarah H. Exh. 1910-14
28 Bergholt Crescent, Stamford Hill, London. † LS 6, RA 1.

HANCOCKS, B. Exh. 1909-16
67 Aston Street, Birmingham. † B 2, RA 2.

HAND, Elmira Exh. 1889-1914
Landscape painter. 64 Elgin Crescent, Notting Hill, London. † RID 39.

HAND, Frederick b. 1880
Studied Brook Green School of Art. Exh. 1936-40. Add: London. † RBA 3, WG 3.

HAND, Miss M.R.K. Exh. 1904
16A Brook Green, Hammersmith, London. † SWA 1.

HANDCOCK Alice B. Exh. 1897-99
Winchester 1897; Newbury, Berks. 1898. † L 1, RHA 2.

HANDFORD, A.S. Exh. 1905
21 Lynton Avenue, West Ealing, London. † RA 1.

HANDFORTH, Thomas Exh. 1929
Etcher. † BA 2.

HANDLER, Blanche Exh. 1906-33
Miniature painter. Balham, London 1906; Croydon, Surrey 1916. † RA 7.

HANDLEY, Miss E.U. Exh. 1896-1907
Stoke Newington, London 1896; Kingston on Thames 1907. † B 1, L 2, RI 4, SWA 5.

HANDLEY, F. Montague Exh. 1880
Sculptor. No. 12 Studio, The Avenue, Fulham Road, London. † RA 3.

HANDLEY, Miss F.W. Exh. 1918
Claremont House School, Brownhill Road, Catford, London. † LS 3.

HANDLEY, G.A. Exh. 1932
11 Carlton Road, Derby. † RI 1.

HANDLEY, Harry Exh. 1906
439 Walton Breck Road, Liverpool. † L 1.

HANDLEY, John S. Exh. 1911-12
Sefton Park, Liverpool. † L 2.

HANDLEY, Susan E. Exh. 1926
48 Milton Road, Waterloo, Liverpool. † L 2.

HANDLEY, Thomas Exh. 1895-96
146 Breck Road, Liverpool. † L 2.

HANDS, Edith Exh. 1911-33
Oxton, Birkenhead 1911; Liverpool 1921. † L 23.

HANDS, Miss H.M. Exh. 1923-33
65 Maitland Park Road, London 1923; Malvern Links, Worcs. 1927; Deganwy, Wales 1931. † RCA 8.

HANDS, Lizzie Exh. 1907-27
Miniature painter. 57 Portsdown Road, Maida Vale, London. † L 2, RA 12, RI 2.

HANHART, Michael Exh. 1880-1900
Landscape and figure painter. Hampstead, London. † D 1, L 2, RA 2, RBA 3.

HANKINS, George Exh. 1880-82
Landscape painter. 2 Bellevue Place, Upper Clapton, London. † RBA 7.

HANKINSON, Miss M.E. Exh. 1927
Rosemore, The Cliff, Higher Broughton, Manchester. † B 1.

HANLEY, Edgar Exh. 1880-83
Figure and still life painter. London. † RA 16, RBA 2.

HANLEY, Mrs. Edmund Exh. 1905-11
Forbury Grove, Kintbury, Hungerford, Berks. † RID 2.

HANLON, E.L. Exh. 1888-97
Innishannon, Co. Cork. † B 1, RHA 1.

HANLON, Miss H.J. Exh. 1886-88
53 Kenilworth Square, Rathmines, Dublin. † RHA 2.

HANLON, John (Jack) Paul b. 1913
Landscape and portrait painter. Exh. 1934-38. Add: Fortrose, Templeoge, Co. Dublin. † RHA 5.

HANLON, Mrs. W. Exh. 1883-89
Innishannon, Co. Cork. † B 2, RHA 6.

HANMER, G.W. Exh. 1910
67 Blenheim Road, Moseley, Birmingham. † B 1.

HANN, Walter Exh. 1883-1904
Landscape painter. London. † RA 3, RHA 1.

HANN, W.T. Exh. 1882-1908
Liverpool. † L 3.

HANNA, Dennis O'Donoghue Exh. 1932-39
Architect. Holywood, Co. Down 1932; Belfast 1933. † RHA 16.

HANNA, Mrs. T. (J) Exh. 1939-40
17 Milverton Road, Knowle, Warwicks. † B 2.

HANNAFORD, Charles A. Exh. 1919-35
A.R.B.A. 1919, R.B.A. 1921. Add: Canterbury 1919; Rye, Sussex 1921; Bushey, Herts. 1925; London 1928. † GI 1, RA 1, RBA 68.

HANNAFORD, Charles E. 1863-1955
Landscape painter. Studied under Stanhope Forbes and in Paris. R.B.A. 1916. Add: The Mumbles, Swansea 1897; Plymouth 1902; East Grimstead, Sussex 1913; London 1916; Stalham, Norwich, Norfolk 1927. † M 1, RA 1, RBA 83, RCA 1, RI 2, WG 120.

HANNAH, Andrew G. Exh. 1906-40
Glasgow 1906; Milngavie, N.B. 1912. † GI 23, RSA 1, RSW 1.

HANNAH, Barbara Exh. 1926
Landscape, figure, flower and portrait painter. † GOU 65.

HANNAH, Mrs. Edith B. Exh. 1931-32
The Whim, Lamancha, Midlothian. † RSA 2.

HANNAH, E.M. Exh. 1906
8 Doune Gardens, Glasgow. † GI 2.

HANNAH, Marjorie J.W. Exh. 1925-33
52 Langdale Road, Sefton Park, Liverpool. † L 9.

HANNAH, S. Crichton Exh. 1887-90
Architect. 51 Walterton Road, St. Peter's Park, London. † RA 3.

HANNAH, W.M. Exh. 1905
25 Honoria Street, Huddersfield. † L 1.

HANNAM, Florence Exh. 1887-1906
Figure painter. London. † L 9, RA 5, RBA 8, ROI 1, SWA 2.

HANNAUX, Emmanuel c. 1857-1934
French sculptor. 11 Rue St. Simon, Paris 1907. † L 1.

HANNAY, Alys M. Exh. 1908-33
Landscape, figure and flower painter. London. † GOU 25, I 6, L 5, LS 5, RA 2, RBA 2, ROI 6, RSA 1, SWA 4.

HANNAY, Mrs. E. Exh. 1882
Stoke Road, Guildford. † D 1.

HANNAY, Elizabeth Exh. 1939
Portrait painter. Studied Florence, Slade School, Walker Art School, Boston, and under Bernard Adams. † WG 37.

HANNAY, E.M. Exh. 1891-1923
Glasgow 1891; Helensburgh, N.B. 1923. † GI 15, RSA 3, RSW 1.

HANNAY, Mrs. H. Exh. 1907-10
Sussex. † SWA 2.

HANNAY, Miss Isa Exh. 1910-20
17 Queensway, Wallasey, Cheshire. † L 6.

HANNAY, Miss Margaret Exh. 1912
Landscape and figure painter. 34 Avenue Road, St. John's Wood, London. † GOU 1, NEA 1.

HANNAY, Mrs. Reine Exh. 1911
Pembroke Road, London. † SWA 1.

HANNAY, Mrs. Winifred Lynton Exh. 1914-35
Portrait and landscape painter. London. † GOU 3, NEA 13, P 1, RA 1, RBA 5.

HANNEY, Clifford Exh. 1926-38
Figure, landscape and marine painter. Studied West Marlands School of Art, Southampton and Queen's Road School of Art, Clifton, Bristol. Assistant master Oldham School of Art and Art Lecturer Cheshire County Training College. Add: Publow, Pensford, Nr. Bristol 1926; Wistaston, Nr. Crewe 1932. † L 1, M 2, RA 1, RBA 1, ROI 1.

HANRAHAN, Joseph Exh. 1905-9
15 Spencer Street, North Strand, Dublin. † RHA 4.

HANRAHAN, Mona M. Exh. 1906-15
Kingstown, Ireland 1906; Limerick 1907. † RHA 8.

HANSARD, Freda Exh. 1899-1901
Figure painter. London. † GI 1, L 1, RA 4.

HANSEN, Christine Exh. 1911-26
Lenzie, Nr. Glasgow 1911; Ben Rhydding, Yorks. 1919. † GI 2, L 7, LS 8, RCA 1, RSA 2.

HANSEN, Hans* 1853-1923
Landscape, interior and figure painter. b. Copenhagen. A.R.S.W. 1893, R.S.W. 1906 (struck off 1913). Add: Edinburgh 1888; London 1899. † GI 23, L 10, M 1, NG 1, RA 13, RBA 13, RHA 2, RI 14, ROI 2, RSA 37, RSW 49.

HANSEN, Miss H.K. Exh. 1932-35
Glasgow. † GI 2, RSA 4.

HANSEN, Sigvard* Exh. 1889-90
Landscape painter. London. † L 2, RA 3.

HANSFORD, Daisy Exh. 1913-16
Painter and etcher. London. † RA 2, RI 1, WG 21.

HANSON, Albert J.* Exh. 1892-95
Australian landscape painter. Euston Square, London 1892; Leominster, Warwicks. 1895. † RBA 23, RI 5, ROI 2.

HANSON, E. Exh. 1893-1901
Accrington, Lancs. † L 1, M 1.

HANSON, Edith Mary Exh. 1913-40
Portrait painter. Born, studied and lived in Edinburgh. † GI 1, P 1, RA 1, RSA 7, RSW 4.

HANSON, Emilie M. Exh. 1921
Brook House, Preston Brook, Cheshire. † L 1.

HANSON, J.S. Exh. 1884
Architect. 27 Alfred Place, South Kensington, London. † L 1.

HANSON, R. Exh. 1940
† COO 1.

HANTON, Peter K. Exh. 1934-36
Architect. H.M. Office of Works, Storey's Gate, London. † RA 3.

HAPPERFIELD, Laura A. Exh. 1904-33
Watercolour flower painter. Bishopston, Bristol 1904; Holland Park, London 1924. † D 2, L 4, RA 4, RI 2, SWA 2.

HARAM, Beatrice Chetwynd Exh. 1894-1907
The Avenue, Surbiton, Surrey. † L 6, SWA 2.

HARBER, William F. Exh. 1899-1905
Architect. London. † RA 5.

HARBORD, Marian D. Exh. 1939
Portrait painter. Pound's Cross, Polperro, Cornwall. † RA 1.

HARBOTT, Miss L.R. Exh. 1930
50 Hornchurch Road, Essex. † L 1.

HARBUTT, Mrs. B. Cambridge (Elizabeth) Exh. 1883-95
Miniature portrait painter. Add: Paragon Art Studios, 15 Bladud Buildings, Bath. † L 2, RA 13, RBA 1.

HARBUTT, Miss O.C. Exh. 1919
The Grange, Bathampton, Som. † SWA 1.

HARCOURT, A. Exh. 1940
Sparrows Hearne, Bushey, Herts. † SWA 1.

HARCOURT, Aletha Exh. 1932-40
Portrait painter. Daughter of George H. q.v. Add: London. † P 12, RA 5.

HARCOURT, Anne Exh. 1932-38
Portrait painter. Daughter of George H. q.v. 34 Dorset Street, London. † P 12, RA 3.

HARCOURT, Clewin b. 1870
Portrait and landscape painter. b. Victoria, Australia. Studied Melbourne National Gallery Art School, Westminster and Academie des Beaux Arts, Antwerp, (silver medal). Exh. 1909-28. Add: London 1909; Bushey, Herts. 1925. † L 1, LS 6, RA 5.

HARCOURT, George 1868-1948
Figure and portrait painter. b. Dunbartonshire. Studied for 3 years with Herkomer. Governor Hospitalfield Art School, Arbroath 1901-9. Married Mary Lascelles H. q.v. and father of Anne, Aletha and Mary E.H. q.v. A.R.A. 1919, R.A. 1926, R.B.A. 1897, R.P. 1912. Add: Bushey, Herts. 1893 and 1909; Hospitalfield, Arbroath 1901. † B 1, FIN 2, G 1, GI 7, L 25, M 7, NG 7, P 45, RA 118, RBA 1, RSA 6.

HARCOURT, Louis Exh. 1887-90
Blackwell, Nr. Bromsgrove, Birmingham. † B 3.

HARCOURT, Miss L.F. Exh. 1888
Vernon, Warren Wood, Shooter's Hill, Kent. † D 3.

HARCOURT, Mary Edeva Exh. 1922-27
Portrait painter. Daughter of George H. q.v. Studied R.A. Schools. Add: High Sparrows, Herne, Bushey, Herts. † RA 2.

HARCOURT, Mary Lascelles Exh. 1892-1922
Landscape, figure and portrait painter. Married George H. q.v. and mother of Anne, Aletha and Mary E. H. q.v. Add: Bushey, Herts. 1893 and 1909; Hospitalfield, Arbroath 1901. † FIN 1, M 1, NG 2, RA 11, RHA 1, RSA 3.

HARD, Miss H.A. Exh. 1888
The Castle, Portstewart, Ireland. † M 1.

HARDCASTLE, Miss B.M. Exh. 1906
28 Well Walk, Hampstead, London. † RI 2.

HARDCASTLE, Mrs. Emily Exh. 1905
12 Gainsborough Gardens, Hampstead, London. † ROI 1.

HARDCASTLE, W.J. Exh. 1906
130 Temple Chambers, London. † RA 1.

HARDEN, Edmund Harris d. c.1880
Painter of historical and biblical genre, figures and landscapes. 6 Hyde Vale Cottages, Greenwich. † B 3, RBA 1.

HARDESTY, Miss E. Exh. 1927
8 Marlowe Road, Wallasey, Cheshire. † L 2.

HARDGRAVE, Charles Exh. 1885-1918
Painter and stained glass artist. Brixton, London 1885; Clapham Common, London 1893. † RA 21.

HARDGRAVE F.M. Exh. 1885
Landscape painter. Forest Moor, Knaresborough, Yorks. † RA 1.

HARDIE, Annie Exh. 1910
2 Queen's Crescent, Glasgow. † GI 1.

HARDIE, Charles Martin* 1858-1917
Landscape and figure painter. Uncle of Martin H. q.v. A.R.S.A. 1886, R.S.A. 1895. Add: Edinburgh. † B 14, BG 28, GI 15, L 5, M 2, RA 13, RHA 2, RI 1, RSA 161.

HARDIE, Martin 1875-1952
Painter and etcher. Studied under Sir Frank Short. Nephew of Charles Martin H. q.v. Keeper of Departments of Painting and Engraving, Illustration and Design at the Victoria and Albert Museum. A.R.E. 1907, R.E. 1920, R.I. 1924, V.P.R.I. 1934, R.S.W. 1934. Exh. 1906-40. Add: London. † AB 2, AG 21, BA 2, BG 20, CG 20, CHE 5, CON 2, FIN 135, G 6, GI 9, GOU 22, L 52, LEF 33, NEA 3, RA 45, RE 95, RI 68, RID 3, RSA 4, RSW 22, WG 423.

HARDIMAN, A. Exh. 1931
Linocut artist. † RED 2.

HARDIMAN, Alfred Frank 1891-1949
Sculptor. Studied Royal College of Art, R.A. Schools and British School of Rome (1924). A.R.A. 1934. Exh. 1915-39. Add: London. † GI 5, L 6, RA 31, RE 2, RI 5, RSA 13.

HARDING, Lord Exh. 1880
South Park, Penshurst, Kent. † D 1.

HARDING, Albert G. Exh. 1938-40
Watercolour landscape painter. Ickenham, Middlesex. † RA 2.

HARDING, Dorothea b. 1898
Miniature and landscape painter. Exh. 1925-26. Add: 6 Kerrison Lodge, Kerrison Road, Ealing, London. † L 3, RA 2.

HARDING, Deborah Neild b. 1903
Potter and pottery teacher. b. Sheffield. Studied Central School of Arts and Crafts, Royal College of Art and in Holland. Exh. 1926-27. Add: Winterbrook, Meadow Way, Letchworth, Herts. † L 15.

HARDING, Emily J. Exh. 1892-1901
Miniature portrait painter. Married Edward William Andrews q.v. Add: London. † L 1, RA 2, RMS 5.

HARDING, E. Paxton Exh. 1929-33
Dorchester House, Boughton, Chester. † L 4.

HARDING, Frank Exh. 1885-90
Figure and domestic painter. 28 Kenninghall Road, Lower Clapton, London. † L 1, RBA 5, ROI 2.

HARDING, Gertrude Conroy Exh. 1903-4
Miniature painter. London 1903; Torquay 1904. † RA 2.

HARDING, H.J. Exh. 1916
17B Abercorn Place, St. John's Wood, London. † RA 1.

HARDING, Mrs. Jannette Exh. 1886
Landscape painter. Bridlington Quay, Yorks. † SWA 1.

HARDING, J.H. Exh. 1911
† M 1.

HARDING, Kate Exh. 1896
Rydal House, Huyton, Lancs. † L 1.

HARDING, Louise Exh. 1905-7
Flat 21, 169 Queen's Gate, London. † L 3, NG 1, RI 2, SWA 2.

HARDING, Mary Exh. 1880-1916
Figure, flower, interior and decorative painter. London 1880; Exeter 1908. † B 1, GI 1, L 10, RA 30, RBA 2, RI 4, ROI 8, SWA 10.

HARDING, Morris d. c.1963
Sculptor. A.R.H.A. 1933, R.H.A. 1932. Add: London 1901; Holywood, Co. Down 1929. † GI 3, L 7, LS 14, RA 15, RHA 29, RSA 1.

HARDING, Miss M.L. Exh. 1913
1 Launceston Place, Kensington, London. † RI 1.

HARDING, Mrs. P. Exh. 1881-1907
Landscape painter. H.S.W.A. 1886. Pentwyn, Monmouth. † SWA 15.

HARDING, Miss Phyllis Exh. 1909
Regent's Park, London. † SWA 1.

HARDING, Samuel A. Exh. 1924-36
Watercolour landscape painter. Travelled widely. Add: Brackenwood, Leatherhead, Surrey. † RA 6, WG 169.

HARDING, W. Exh. 1911-33
1 Rawcliffe Road, Birkenhead. † L 19.

HARDING-BINGLEY, H. Exh. 1939
† RMS 1.

HARDINGE, Ruth Exh. 1926
c/o Kemp and Co., 293 Victoria Street, London. † L 2.

HARDINGE, Mrs. W. Exh. 1887-89
Elmhurst, Shooter's Hill, London. † D 9.

HARDISTY, W. Cecil Exh. 1897-1902
Architect. Queen's Chambers, John Dalton Street, Manchester. † RA 2.

HARDMAN, Miss B. Exh. 1902
4 Princess Royal Park, Scarborough, Yorks. † B 3.

HARDMAN, Mrs. Emma Louise Exh. 1886-1918
nee Shubrook. Flower, portrait, miniature and landscape painter. Married Thomas H. q.v. Sister of Minnie Jane H. q.v. and Laura A. Shubrook q.v. Add: 16 Plimsoll Road, Finsbury Park, London 1886; Hawthorn, Potters Bar, Herts. 1887; Eastcote, Northaw, Potters Bar, Herts. 1897. † BG 1, D 1, L 10, RA 7, RBA 9, RI 4.

HARDMAN, J.H. Exh. 1925
Kynance, Walmley Road, Wylde Green, Birmingham. † B 1.

HARDMAN, Mary G. Exh. 1926-37
Miniature painter. Wigan, Lancs. 1926 and 1930; Southport, Lancs. 1929. † L 9, RA 1.

HARDMAN, Mrs. Minnie Jane b. 1867
nee Shubrook. Portrait and flower painter. Studied R.A. Schools (silver medal). Sister of Emma Louise H. q.v. and Laura A. Shubrook q.v. Add: 63 Plimsoll Road, Finsbury Park, London 1886; Thorntons, Northaw, Potters Bar, Herts. 1900 and Westcott, Northaw, Potters Bar, Herts. 1908. † D 1, L 5, M 2, RA 29, RBA 17, RHA 5, RI 6, RMS 3, ROI 6.

HARDMAN, Thomas Exh. 1885-95
Landscape, figure and rustic painter. Married Emma Louise H. q.v. Add: Highbury 1885; Hawthorn, Potters Bar, Herts. 1886. † B 1, L 4, RA 5, RBA 15, RI 2, ROI 2.

HARDMAN, Winifred Elizabeth Beatrice Exh. 1914-39
Portrait painter, mural decorator and signboard artist. b. Rawtenstall, Lancs. Studied St. John's Wood and R.A. Schools (Armitage bronze medal and silver medal for perspective). Add: London. † GOU 2, I 1, L 3, M 1, NEA 1, RA 10, RED 1, RSA 1.

HARDOUIN, Maurice E. Exh. 1938-39
Architect. 74 Eastdean Avenue, Epsom, Surrey. † RA 2.

HARDS, Charles G. Exh. 1883-98
Figure and domestic painter. London. † D 1, RA 8, RBA 3, RI 7, ROI 2.

HARDSTAFF, George Exh. 1903
36 Lenton Boulevard, Nottingham. † N 2.

HARDWICK, Arthur Jessop Exh. 1902-10
Architect. Eagle Chambers, Kingston on Thames, Surrey. † RA 4.

HARDWICK, John Jessop 1832-1917
Fruit and flower painter. Worked as illustrator for "London Illustrated News" 1858. A.R.S.W. 1882. Add: Thames Ditton, Surrey. † AG 5, B 12, D 6, GI 3, L 16, M 14, RA 27, RBA 4, RHA 2, RSW 221.

HARDWICK, Jane T. Exh. 1908
24 Grove Terrace, Leeds. † L 1.

HARDY, A. Exh. 1882
13 Boundary Road, St. John's Wood, London. † L 2.

HARDY, Albert Exh. 1887-1907
Brondesbury, London 1887; East Dulwich Road, London 1903. † RI 3.

HARDY, Miss A.G. Exh. 1896
Cranbrook, Kent. † RI 1.

HARDY, Ada Muriel b. 1879
Painter, miniaturist and linocut artist. b. Nottingham. Studied Herkomer's, Bushey and Paris. Exh. 1897-1931. Add: Nottingham 1897; Newbury, Berks. 1905; Ringmer, Sussex 1910; Lewes, Sussex 1930. † L 11, N 1, RA 17, RI 2, RMS 3, ROI 1, SWA 2.

HARDY, Cissy Exh. 1906-10
Headingley, Leeds 1906; Selly Park, Birmingham 1908. † B 4.

HARDY, Cicely A. Exh. 1927
18 Howard Place, Edinburgh. † RSA 1.

HARDY, Dorofield Exh. 1882-1920
Figure, landscape, interior and miniature portrait painter. Add: London. † B 7, D 16, L 2, M 3, NG 1, RA 7, RBA 1 RI 11, RMS 8.

HARDY, Dudley 1866-1922
Painter, illustrator and poster designer. b. Sheffield. Studied under his father Thomas Bush H. q.v. and in Dusseldorf, Antwerp and Paris. Worked as an illustrator and cartoonist for many magazines. R.B.A. 1889, R.I. 1897, R.O.I. 1898. Member of Society of 25 Artists. Add: London 1884 and 1916; Paris 1914. † B 1, FIN 6, G 2, GI 4, I 1, L 11, LS 3, M 3, NG 2, P 2, RA 33, RBA 60, RI 54, RMS 3, ROI 15.

HARDY, Edwin George Exh. 1881-86
Architectural and interior sketcher. Add: 17 Brunswick Gardens, Kensington, London. † RA 13.

HARDY, Frank Exh. 1937-38
Landscape painter. 11A Broomhill Road, Bulwell, Nottingham. † N 6.

HARDY, Miss Florence Exh. 1896-1901
Miniature portrait painter. London 1896 and 1899; Walmer, Kent 1897. † RA 2, RMS 6.

HARDY, Mrs. Florence Exh. 1880-1932
nee Small. Mrs. Deric H. Portrait painter. b. Nottingham. Studied Geneva, Berlin and Paris. N.S.A. 1885, A.S.W.A. 1896, S.W.A. 1897. Add: Nottingham 1880; London 1893. † B 3, I 4, L 16, LS 15, M 5, N 72, NG 12, P 7, RA 36, RBA 3, RMS 1, ROI 8, RSA 1, SWA 32.

HARDY, Frederick Daniel* 1826-1911
Genre painter. Studied under Thomas Webster. Brother of George H. q.v. Add: Kensington, London 1880; Cranbrook, Kent 1898. † L 1, M 1, RA 16, TOO 11.

HARDY, Gertrude Exh. 1898
Cranbrook, Kent. † D 1.

HARDY, George* 1822-1909
Genre painter. Brother of Frederick Daniel H. q.v. Add: Cranbrook, Kent 1880; Staplehurst, Kent 1886; Shepherds Bush, London 1892. † RA 5, RSA 1.

HARDY, G. Gordon Exh. 1929-37
Landscape painter. V.P.N.S.A. 1936. Add: South Road, The Park, Nottingham. † N 5.

HARDY, Miss G.M. Exh. 1889
14 Upper Station Road, Finchley, London. † L 1.

HARDY, Heywood* 1842-1933
Animal, sporting and genre painter, etcher and church decorator. Studied Paris and Antwerp. Painted altar piece for Haslar R.N. Hospital Chapel. R.E. 1880, R.O.I. 1883, R.P. 1891, A.R.W.S. 1885. Add: London 1880; Worthing 1918. † BG 1, D 1, DOW 5, FIN 1, G 22, L 12, M 3, NG 19, P 26, RA 30, RE 8, ROI 7, RWS 4, TOO 36.

HARDY, Ida Wilson See CLARKE

HARDY, James Junr.* 1832-1889
Landscape, figure, sporting and still life painter. A.R.I. 1874, R.I. 1877, R.O.I. 1883. Add: Thyra House, Moss Hall. N. Finchley, London, 1880. † RA 3, RI 9, ROI 6, TOO 3.

HARDY J.W. Exh. 1926
45 Rose Avenue, Horsforth, via Leeds. † RCA 1.

HARDY, L. Exh. 1934-35
Radford, Nottingham. † N 4.

HARDY, Lawrence Exh. 1912-26
Sculptor. London 1912 and 1915; Fakenham, Norfolk 1914. † I 5, L 4, LS 17, NEA 2, RA 3.

HARDY, Leo Exh. 1936-40
Landscape painter. Walsall, Staffs. 1936; Westcliffe on Sea, Essex 1940. † NEA 2, RA 3.

HARDY, Margaret E. Exh. 1893
Interior and figure painter. Sisinghurst, Staplehurst, Kent. † RBA 1.

HARDY, Miss Nina Exh. 1890-1929
Painter and miniaturist. London 1890; Windsor, Berks. 1914. † B 3, G 2, L 11, NG 22, P 2, RA 16, ROI 4.

HARDY, Norman H. c. 1864-1914
Painter and etcher. London 1888 and 1898; Herald Office, Sydney, N.S.W. 1896. † D 5, RA 6.

HARDY, Paul Exh. 1890-99
Historical artist. Married Ida Wilson Clarke q.v. Add: Bexley Heath, Kent 1890; Chobham, Surrey, 1899. † L 1, RA 1.

HARDY, Ruth Exh. 1898
† P 1.

HARDY, Thomas Bush* 1842-1897
Marine painter. Travelled on the continent. Father of Dudley H. q.v. R.B.A. 1884. Add: London. † AG 10, DOW 3, FIN 7, G 3, L 6, M 8, RA 21, RBA 44, RHA 1, RI 7, ROI 1, RWS 1, TOO 8.

HARDY, Thomas E. Exh. 1899
Architect. 12 Aberdeen Place, Maida Vale, London. † RA 1.

HARDY, W.H. Exh. 1891-92
Landscape painter. Rockwood, Friern Barnet, Middlesex 1891; London 1892. † RBA 2.

HARE, Augustus J.C. Exh. 1902
Watercolour landscape painter. † LEI 136.

HARE, C.G. Exh. 1908-23
Architect. Gray's Inn Square, London. † RA 15, RSA 3.

HARE, Miss H.M. Exh. 1918-20
Knightsbridge, London. † SWA 2.

HARE, Henry Thomas d. 1921
Architect. Exh. 1890-1920. Add: London. † GI 1, RA 28, RSA 2.

HARE, Julius* Exh. 1886-1927
Landscape and coastal painter. Llanbedr, Conway 1886; Gt. Yarmouth 1887; London 1888; 1902 and 1908; Port St. Mary, I.O.M. 1896; Talycafn, Wales 1904; Capel Curig, Wales 1923. † L 5, M 1, RA 1, RBA 1, RCA 22, RHA 2.

HARE, J.T. Exh. 1914
Duke Street, Adelphi, London. † RA 1.

HARE, Lettice Exh. 1933-38
Figure painter. London. † RA 1, RBA 1.

HARE, Maisie Exh. 1930
2 Brockswood Lane, Welwyn, Herts. † NEA 1.

HARE, Mrs. Margaret Exh. 1904-14
St. Saviour's Vicarage, Herne Hill Road, London. † LS 3, SWA 6.

HARE, Muriel Exh. 1925-39
Painter and wood engraver. London. † COO 3, GOU 1, L 1, RA 2, RBA 1, RHA 2, ROI 5, SWA 2.

HARE, Ruby M. Exh. 1914-18
† I 2, NEA 1.

HARE, St. George* 1857-1933
Genre and portrait painter. Born and studied in Limerick under N.A. Brophy and at Royal College of Art 1875. R.I. 1892, R.O.I. 1892. Add: London. † B 5, BG 1, D 3, FIN 1, G 3, GI 3, L 39, M 10, NG 4, P 1, RA 32, RBA 15, RHA 29, RI 121, ROI 143.

HARE, Thomas Leman 1872-1935
Flower painter and art editor of "Apollo" etc. Exh. 1926. Add: London. † AB 2.

HARE, Walter Exh. 1895-98
16 Royal Terrace East, Kingstown Ireland. † RHA 6.

HAREUX, Ernest Victor 1847-1909
French landscape painter. Exh. 1880-82. Add: 16 Avenue Trudaine, Paris. † RHA 16.

HARFORD, Alfred Exh. 1886-88
Limmeridge, Cromwell Road, Bristol. † B 3, M 1, ROI 1.

HARFORD, W. Exh. 1882-84
36 The Grove, Hammersmith, London. † L 4.

HARGER, W.M. Exh. 1931
† NEA 1.

HARGITT, Edward* 1835-1895
Landscape painter. b. Edinburgh. Studied under Horatio MacCulloch. A.R.I. 1865, R.I. 1867, R.O.I. 1883. Add: Chiswick, London 1880; Broadwater, Worthing, Sussex 1887; Basingstoke, Hants. 1891; Streatham, London 1893. † AG 2, GI 1, L 6, M 6, RA 2, RI 68, ROI 22, TOO 1.

HARGRAVE, Caroline S. Exh. 1910-14
Ingleside, Willes Terrace, Leamington Spa, Warwicks. † B 2, L 2, SWA 3.

HARGRAVE, Ellwood Exh. 1906
Upper Oak Street, Windermere. † L 1, RCA 1.

HARGRAVE, Frank H. Exh. 1886
Landscape painter. The Abbey Plain, Knaresborough, Yorks. † RA 1.

HARGRAVES, J.V. Exh. 1930-39
Landscape painter. Leicester. † N 5.

HARGREAVES, Henry Exh. 1883
Watercolour landscape painter. 177 Romford Road, Stratford, London. † RBA 1.

HARGREAVES, Miss H.E. Exh. 1894
254 Stockport Road, Manchester. † M 2.

HARGREAVES, Isabella S. Exh. 1908-11
The Woodlands, Rock Ferry, Cheshire. † L 2.

HARGREAVES, J. Exh. 1899-1904
Architect. Southport, Lancs. † L 2, RA 2.

HARGREAVES, Mrs. K. Exh. 1908
The Promenade, Southport, Lancs. † L 3.

HARGREAVES, Mrs. Lucy Exh. 1894-1914
Llan-y-Cefn, Ellesmere, Salop. † B 9, L 4, LS 12, M 3, RA 1, RCA 1, RHA 6, RSA 1.

HARGREAVES, William J. Exh. 1935
Foulis Crescent, Juniper Green, Edinburgh. † RSA 1.

HARGREAVES, William Y. Exh. 1895
24 Brougham Place, Edinburgh. † RSA 1.

HARGROVE, Ethel Craven d. 1932
Illustrator and designer. b. York. Studied Lambeth School of Art. Exh. 1917. Add: Sandown, I.O.W. † SWA 2.

HARING, Augustus W. Exh. 1898-1901
Guinevere, Tennyson Road, Small Heath, Birmingham. † B 5.

HARKE, Evelyn Exh. 1899-1909
Landscape and domestic painter. 113 Church Road, Upper Norwood, London. † GI 1, I 1, L 3, LS 3, RA 3, SWA 3.

HARKER, Ethel Exh. 1916-30
Landscape, flower, still life and portrait painter. Studied Chester School of Art. Add: Heswell, Cheshire 1919; Liverpool 1928. † L 12, RCA 3.

HARKER, Gertrude Exh. 1898-1904
Denmark Hill, London 1898; Champion Hill, London 1902. † SWA 9.

HARKNESS, A.* Exh. 1916
18 Hornsey Road, Anfield, Liverpool. † L 1.

HARKNESS, David Exh. 1886-1938
Stockbridge, Perth 1886; Clydebank 1928. † GI 3, RSA 3.

HARLAMOFF, Alexis Alexejewitsch* b. 1849
Russian painter. Exh. 1886. † GI 1.

HARLAND, Miss E. Exh. 1883-84
25 Acomb Street, Greenheys, Manchester. † M 2.

HARLAND, Miss E.P.A. Exh. 1939
Watford, Herts. † RCA 1.

HARLAND, G. Exh. 1908
85 Hawksley Road, Stoke Newington, London. † RA 1.

HARLAND, Mary b. 1863
Figure painter. Exh. 1882-1905. Manchester 1882; London 1903. † L 4, M 5, RA 3, RMS 1.

HARLEY, A. Ernest Exh. 1899-1928
Edinburgh. † GI 3, L 7, RSA 7.

HARLEY, Ethel B. Exh. 1884
Flower painter. 25 Harley Street, London. † SWA 1.

HARLEY, George Wills Exh. 1909
5 Church Street, Slough, Bucks. † LS 3.

HARLEY, Herbert E. Exh. 1884-1908
Interior and figure painter. 2 Monmouth Road, Bayswater, London. † L 1, M 1, RA 13, RBA 5, RHA 1, ROI 18.

HARLEY, H. Vincent Exh. 1890-97
Figure painter. 8 Monmouth Road, Bayswater, London. † ROI 6.

HARLEY, Mrs. Lilian See ROWNEY

HARLEY, Margaret M. Exh. 1900
Redholm, Loughborough, Leics. † RMS 1.

HARLEY, Netty Exh. 1884-1905
Coney Park, Uddingston, Nr. Glasgow 1884; Waterloo, Liverpool 1905. † GI 6, L 1.

HARLEY, Peter Exh. 1880-83
4 Richmond Lane, Edinburgh. † RSA 2.

HARLEY, Primrose b. 1908
Painter and engraver. Studied Juliens, Paris and Chelsea School of Art. Exh. 1933. Add: 3 Stirling Street, Knightsbridge, London. † RA 1, SWA 1.

HARLEY-SMITH, R. Exh. 1932-39
Watercolour painter and architect. West Bridgford, Notts. 1932; Nottingham 1935. † N 12.

HARLIN, Kate Exh. 1888
Figure painter. 7 Hill Street, Birmingham. † RA 1.

HARLING, Helen M. Exh. 1934
Sculptor. 3 Pembroke Studios, Pembroke Gardens, London. † RA 1.

HARLING, W.O. Exh. 1882
Landscape, figure and portrait painter. 57 Freshfield Terrace, Brighton. † L 2.

HARLOCH, Miss G. Exh. 1888
Brookfield, Nantwich, Cheshire. † B 1.

HARLOW, James Exh. 1886-87
Landscape painter. Nottingham 1886; Burton Road, Derby 1887. † N 3.

HARMAN, Rev. A.C. Exh. 1931-38
Watercolour painter. † WG 13.

HARMAN, Miss F. Exh. 1892
8 Alfred Place, Bedford Square, London. † L 1.

HARMAN, Geraldine Exh. 1880-1911
Miniature painter. Sister of Harriette H. q.v. Add: Kilburn, London. † L 16, RA 12, RBA 1, RHA 2, RI 2, RMS 2.

HARMAN, Harriette Exh. 1881-1910
Miniature painter. Sister of Geraldine H. q.v. R.M.S. 1897. Add: Kilburn, London. † B 1, L 13, RA 8, RHA 2, RI 1, RMS 12, SWA 2.

HARMAN, Mabel Exh. 1904
Courtfield Gardens, London. † D 1.

HARMAN, Ruth Exh. 1887
Watercolour painter. Balcombe House, Dartmouth Park Avenue, Highgate, London. † RBA 1.

HARMAR, Miss Fairlie d. 1945
Landscape, figure, interior and portrait painter. b. Weymouth. Studied Slade School. N.E.A. 1917. Exh. 1906-40. Add: Ramridge, Andover, Hants. and London. † BA 5, CG 1, CHE 3, FIN 3, G 6, GI 2, GOU 18, I 10, L 10, M 3, NEA 108, P 13, RA 20, RCA 1.

HARMER, Edith E. Exh. 1908
28 Highfield Hill, Upper Norwood, London. † LS 5.

HARMS, Edith Margaret Exh. 1897-1932
Watercolour landscape and flower painter. Art mistress at Horsham Art School. Add: 23 The Carfax, Horsham, Sussex. † L 4, RA 3, RBA 1, RI 27, SWA 4.

HARMSWORTH, The Hon. Desmond Exh. 1939
Landscape and portrait painter. 13 Hyde Park Gardens, London. † RA 2.

HARMSWORTH, James Sydney Exh. 1903-9
Amberley, Sussex. † L 1, LS 3.

HARMSWORTH, R.A. Exh. 1927-33
Landscape painter. London. † GI 1, RA 1, RCA 1, RSA 1.

HARNACK, John Exh. 1884-90
Landscape painter. London. † D 2, RBA 7.

HARNETT, William Michael b. 1851
American painter. New York 1880 and 32 Hanway Street, London 1885. † RA 1, RHA 1.

HARNON, F.J. Exh. 1914
1 Arran Road, Catford, London. † RA 1.

HARPER, Claudius Exh. 1882-99
Archaelogical landscape painter. London. † B 3, L 4, M 3, NG 11, RA 5, ROI 2, RSA 4.

HARPER, C.G. Exh. 1886
27 Connaught Street, Hyde Park, London. † L 1.

HARPER, Cecily T. Exh. 1890-1902
Church interiors and still life painter. London. † L 4, RA 2, RBA 11, SWA 2.

HARPER, Miss E. Exh. 1908-23
Breaston, Nr. Derby. † N 23.

HARPER, Ernest Exh. 1930-31
170 Grange Road, King's Heath, Birmingham. † B 3.

HARPER, Edward Steel Senr. b. 1854
Portrait and figure painter. Director of Life Academy, Municipal School of Art, Birmingham 1880-1919; art critic for "Birmingham Post". Father of Edward Steel H. junr. q.v. R.B.S.A. 1888. Exh. 1882-1939. Add: Birmingham. † B 88, L 3, M 1, RA 19, RI 1.

HARPER, Edward Steel junr. 1878-1951
Landscape painter. Art master Wolverhampton Grammar School. Son of Edward Steel H. senr. q.v. Exh. 1920-37. Add: 55 Moor Pool Avenue, Harborne, Birmingham. † B 26, L 2, RA 2, ROI 2.

HARPER, F.G. Exh. 1884
Watercolour flower painter. 105 Park Street, Camden Town, London. † RBA 1.

HARPER, F.S. Exh. 1920-28
Birmingham. † B 9.

HARPER, Gertrude Exh. 1886-1900
Watercolour flower painter. Add: Bloemfontein, Barnet Green, Worcester 1900. † B 1, RBA 1.

HARPER, Guy Exh. 1923-37
Birmingham. † B 17.

HARPER, Henry Andrew* 1835-1900
Watercolour landscape and genre painter. Painted in Palestine and Egypt. Add: Guildford, Surrey 1880; London 1881; Offley, Luton, Beds. 1885; Milford on Sea, Hants. 1893; Reigate, 1895. † AG 20, D 18, FIN 570, GI 1, L 13, RA 10, RBA 8, RI 10.

HARPER, Ivy E. d. 1933
85 Wentworth Road, Harborne, Birmingham 1921-31. † B 3.

HARPER, L. Miles Exh. 1935
Watercolour figure painter and illustrator. † COO 31.

HARPER, Marjorie Exh. 1938
33 Cheyne Walk, London. † RBA 2.

HARPER, Miss M.A. Exh. 1938
152 All Saints Road, Kings Heath, Birmingham. † B 1.

HARPER, Malcolm McL. Exh. 1888-1908
Castle Douglas, N.B. † GI 13, M 2, RSA 8.

HARPER, T.J. Exh. 1882-1907
Birmingham. † B 24.

HARPER, Miss V.E. Exh. 1929
35 Moses Street, Princes Park, Liverpool. † L 1.

HARPIGNIES, Henri Joseph* 1819-1916
French landscape painter. Exh. 1881-1911. Add: Paris. † AG 16, GOU 6, RHA 1, RI 2, RSA 1.

HARPSAU, C. Exh. 1891
27 Rossett Street, Rocky Lane, Fulbrook, Liverpool. † L 3.

HARPWOOD, Mrs. M. Exh. 1884
The Avenue, Gipsy Hill, London. † RI 1.

HARRAND, Lucie Exh. 1900-3
Portrait painter. 11 Alwyne Square, Canonbury, London. † L 1, RA 2, SWA 1.

HARRAND, Olga Exh. 1912-19
Miniature painter. 21 Coleridge Road, Crouch End, London. † RA 5.

HARRIES, Leslie S.G. Exh. 1936
† RI 1.

HARRIES-JONES, Mrs. Harriet Exh. 1911
Tan-y-Bryn, Colwyn Bay, Wales. † RCA 1.

HARRILD, Fred b. 1883
Architect. b. Thames Ditton. Studied at the A.A. and under Sir Edwin Lutyens. Add: Totnes, S. Devon 1923 and 1930; Storrington, Sussex 1929; Queen Anne's Gate, London 1933. † RA 15.

HARRINGTON, Mrs. A. Exh. 1895-97
1 Woodchurch Road, Birkenhead. † L 4.

HARRINGTON, Charles Exh. 1912-35
Watercolour landscape and pastoral painter. Brighton 1912; Lewes, Sussex 1921. † B 6, D 3, FIN 4, L 3, M 1, RA 8, RI 7, WG 36.

HARRINGTON, Douglas William b. 1910
Architect. Studied Central School of Arts and Crafts. Add: 31 Craven Street, Strand, London 1931. † RA 1.

HARRINGTON, Emily Exh. 1904-9
Figure painter. Studio, 50 Buckingham Palace Road, London. † LS 8, RA 2, SWA 1.

HARRINGTON, Harry Exh. 1890
Architect. 9 Albert Square, Manchester. † RA 1.

HARRINGTON, Dr. H.N. Exh. 1891-1905
1 Woodchurch Road, Birkenhead. † L 21.

HARRIS, Lady Alice Exh. 1893
Figure painter. Tetworth Park, Ascot, Berks. † RA 1.

HARRIS, Arthur Exh. 1891-95
Landscape painter. Elmbank House, Newport, Fife. † GI 1, RA 1, RSA 6, RSW 1.

HARRIS, Augustine Exh. 1916
21 Villars Street, London Road, Liverpool. † L 3.

HARRIS, Albert E. Exh. 1917
25/1 Rowland Road, Calcutta, India. † RA 1.

HARRIS, Mrs. Alexandrina Robertson Exh. 1925
† RMS 1.

HARRIS, Miss B. St. Clears Exh. 1897
Tyrwhitt Road, St. John's, S.E. London. † RBA 1.

HARRIS, C.C. Exh. 1907
3 Cavendish Road, St. John's Wood, London. † RA 1.

HARRIS, Carlton E. Exh. 1892-98
Eton Wick, Windsor 1892; Broadway, Worcs. 1893; Birmingham 1894. † B 9, RHA 1.

HARRIS, Dorothy M. Exh. 1940
Miniature portrait painter. 29 Carysfort Road, London. † RA 1.

HARRIS, Doris T. Exh. 1916
Chelmsford, Avoca Avenue, Blackrock, Dublin. † RHA 2.

HARRIS, Edwin Exh. 1882-1915
Figure and portrait painter. Birmingham 1882, 1899 and 1914; Penzance 1884; Newlyn, Penzance 1889; Evesham 1901. † B 31, G 1, L 6, M 2, RA 13, RBA 1, RHA 2, ROI 3.

HARRIS, Evelyn Exh. 1938
† M 2.

HARRIS, Lady Ethel Alice Chivers b. 1867
nee Bower. Medalist. b. Wadworth Hall, Doncaster. Studied Royal College of Art (bronze and silver medals). Exh. 1901-22. Add: London. † RA 34.

HARRIS, Edwin Lawson James b. 1891
Landscape painter. Exh. 1912-39. Add: Elm Lea, Littlehampton, Sussex. † AG 2, COO 2, LS 3.

HARRIS, Mrs. Elinor M. Harewood Exh. 1901-4
The Shrubbery, Weston Super Mare, Som. † D 5.

HARRIS, E. Vincent b. 1879
Architect. A.R.A. 1936. Exh. 1906-40. Add: London. † RA 22, RSA 3.

HARRIS, Frederick Exh. 1881-92
Watercolour painter. Lincoln 1881; Stafford 1892. † RA 2.

HARRIS, F.H. Howard Exh. 1882-1901
Birmingham. † B 69.

HARRIS, Hon. Frederick Leverton c. 1865-1926
Figure and landscape painter. Exh. 1922-27. Add: 70 Grosvenor Street, London. † CHE 1, G 1, GOU 68, NEA 2.

HARRIS, George Exh. 1880-81
Figure and portrait painter. 2 Oak Villas, Cantwell Road, Shooters Hill, Woolwich, London. † RA 2.

HARRIS, George Exh. 1919-35
Landscape painter. Leytonstone, E. London 1919; Ilford, Essex 1935. † RA 2.

HARRIS, George F. Exh. 1903-20
Fruit and still life painter. Queen Street, Cardiff. † L 3, RA 3.

HARRIS, G.W. Exh. 1903-16
Liverpool. † L 18.

HARRIS, George Walter* Exh. 1880-93
Fruit painter. New Southgate, London 1880; West Brighton, Sussex 1884; Burgess Hill, Sussex 1885. † RA 4, RBA 2.

HARRIS, Harteric Exh. 1893-94
26 Clark Street, Stapleton Road, Bristol. † B 2.

HARRIS, Henry Alfred b. 1871
Landscape and figure painter and teacher. Studied Hammersmith School of Art and under Sydney Muschamp and William Rainey. Exh. 1920-39. Add: London. † AB 2, D 2, GOU 1, L 3, ROI 2.

HARRIS, Isobella M. Exh. 1898-1912
Flower painter. St. Albans, Herts. 1898; Watford, Herts. 1901. † RA 3, RI 6.

HARRIS, Joseph Exh. 1882
155 Kirkwhite Street, Nottingham. † N 1.

HARRIS, Sir James C. 1831-1904
Landscape painter. H.R.I. 1888. Exh. 1880-1903. Add: British Consulate, Nice, France. † G 5, RA 1, RI 26, ROI 3.

HARRIS, J.E. Exh. 1908-20
Nottingham. † N 5.

HARRIS, Juan Eduardo Exh. 1902
86 Rue Notre Dame des Champs, Paris. † L 1.

HARRIS, J.O. Exh. 1882-84
Lewes, Sussex 1882; Bolton le Moors 1884. † B 1, L 1.

HARRIS, Mrs. K. Foard Exh. 1881-98
Watercolour flower and landscape painter. Brooke House, Fleet, Hants. 1881; Southsea, Hants. 1898. † B 1, D 1, M 3, SWA 11.

HARRIS, Miss Lilian (Lily) Exh. 1929-36
Still life and flower painter. 33 Hall Croft, Beeston, Notts. 1929; Chilwell, Notts. 1932. † N 7.

HARRIS, Mrs. L. (M.) Exh. 1924-28
Watercolour landscape and still life painter. 33 Hall Croft, Beeston, Notts. † N 7.

HARRIS, Lilian E.A. Exh. 1904-21
Miniature painter. London 1904 and 1911; Esher, Surrey 1910; Burford, Oxon 1913. † L 1, LS 19, NEA 4, RA 3.

HARRIS, Louisa H. Exh. 1894-1920
Telford House, Ross, Herefords. 1894; Hastings, Sussex 1909. † B 3, L 1.

HARRIS, Lilias Olive Exh. 1912-34
Miniature portrait painter. 31 Blenheim Road, Bedford Park, London. † L 5, RA 8, RI 9.

HARRIS, M. Exh. 1882
Hoddlesden Vicarage, Darwen, Lancs. † L 1.

HARRIS, Mabel Exh. 1914-33
Watercolour flower, architectural and landscape painter. Linocut artist and designer. Married John Higgins q.v. Add: Ingatestone, Essex 1914; Leytonstone 1929. † L 1, RA 5, SWA 1.

HARRIS, Maude Exh. 1883-1936
Flower, figure and landscape painter. A.S.W.A. 1916. Add: London 1883; Bromley, Kent 1929. † L 7, LS 26, RA 10, RBA 3, ROI 8, SWA 56.

HARRIS, Mrs. Millicent
See BRAMLEY-MOORE

HARRIS, Mary E. Exh. 1889-94
Interior and architectural painter. 48 Highbury New Park, N. London. † RI 1, RSW 1, SWA 3.

HARRIS, Miss M.M. Exh. 1937
Colwyn Bay, Wales. † RCA 1.

HARRIS, Mary Packer b. 1891
Exh. 1919. Ellargowan, Crieff. † RSW 1.

HARRIS, Nicholas Exh. 1930
† NEA 1.

HARRIS, Peter Exh. 1926-33
Landscape painter. 1 Rathmore Terrace, Bray. † RHA 2.

HARRIS, Pamela Exh. 1921-23
Sculptor. 10 Catherine Street, Buckingham Gate, London. † RA 2.

HARRIS, P. Capes Exh. 1914-20
31 Arundel Avenue, Liverpool. † L 8.

HARRIS, Robert Exh. 1882
47 Burns Street, Nottingham. † N 1.

HARRIS, Robert* 1849-1919
Figure painter. b. Conway, Wales. d. Montreal, Canada. President Royal Canadian Academy 1893-1905. Exh. 1882-1906. † L 8, M 1, RA 2, RBA 2, ROI 2.

HARRIS, R. Keith Exh. 1931
Australian landscape painter. 56 Upper Mall, London. † RA 1.

HARRIS, Sophia Exh. 1889-1904
Figure and interior painter. London 1889 and 1895; Rotherham 1894. † L 1, RA 3, ROI 1.

HARRIS, Sarah Eliza b. 1886
Miniature painter. Studied Rochester School of Art. Exh. 1919-29. Add: Rochester, Kent 1919 and 1928; Wimbledon, London 1927. † RA 7, RI 8.

HARRIS, Violet Exh. 1905-23
The Cedars, Alderton, Woodbridge, Suffolk. † B 1, SWA 1.

HARRIS, Vera Furneaux b. 1902
Miniature painter. A.R.M.S. 1933. Add: Linton, Maidstone, Kent 1933; Hawkhurst, Kent 1938. † L 4, RA 3, RMS 31.

HARRIS, William Exh. 1882-1931
Landscape painter. Add: Birmingham 1882 and 1894; Eton Wick, Windsor 1886; Broadway, Worcs. 1893. † B 36, G 1, GI 4, L 4, M 3, RA 3, RBA 2, RHA 7, ROI 5, RSA 1.

HARRISON, Lady Exh. 1881
Watercolour landscape painter. 114 Harley Street, London. † SWA 3.

HARRISON, Miss Exh. 1913
14 North Frederick Street, Dublin. † RHA 1.

HARRISON, Miss A. Exh. 1885
c/o Alfred Parsons, 54 Bedford Gardens, London. † ROI 1.

HARRISON, Alexander Exh. 1885-1908
Figure and landscape painter. N.E.A. 1887, R.O.I. 1888. Add: c/o Messrs Shepherd Bros., King Street, London 1885; Paris 1889. † L 3, M 1, NEA 3, RA 4, RBA 3, ROI 14.

HARRISON, Arthur d. 1922
Painter and architect. R.B.S.A. 1918. Exh. 1903-22. Add: Birmingham. † B 11, RA 1.

HARRISON, Amy Exh. 1927-40
16 Pierremont Crescent, Darlington. † RI 3, SWA 6.

HARRISON, Annie Jane Exh. 1888-1910
Landscape, portrait and miniature painter. Add: Newcastle, Staffs. 1888; London 1892. † FIN 1, L 1, RA 19, RBA 2, RMS 1, ROI 1.

HARRISON, A.W. Exh. 1913-14
The Studio, Newcastle, Staffs. † RCA 3.

HARRISON, Birge* 1854-1929
American landscape painter. Exh. 1888. Add: c/o Drexel, Harges & Co., 31 Boulevard Haussmann, Paris. † RBA 2.

HARRISON, Bernard Exh. 1898-1937
Landscape painter. Paris 1898 and 1904; London 1900. † BG 30, COO 42, FIN 60, M 1, NG 12.

HARRISON, Miss C. Exh. 1890
Haslemere, Surrey. † SWA 2.

HARRISON, Mrs. Cholmeley Exh. 1914-37
Painter and decorative designer. London. † RI 5, SWA 5.

HARRISON, Claude Exh. 1880-95
Landscape painter. N.S.A. 1881. Add: Nottingham. † N 27.

HARRISON, Charles H.* Exh. 1886
Watercolour painter. 5 Seymour Place, Gt. Yarmouth, Norfolk. † RI 2.

HARRISON, Clarence J. Exh. 1929
Etcher. 217 Neville Road, Forest Gate, London. † RA 1.

HARRISON, Darent Exh. 1896-1900
Portrait painter. London. † L 1, M 1, NG 2, RA 4.

HARRISON, David Exh. 1883-90
Liverpool 1883; Carlton upon Medlock 1885; Ashton on Mersey 1890. † L 3, M 2.

HARRISON, Miss Dorothy Elizabeth
See BOND

HARRISON, Eleanor Exh. 1898-99
Minafon, Bettws-y-Coed, Wales 1898; Brynhyfryd, Festiniog, Wales 1899. † RCA 3.

HARRISON, Emily Exh. 1892-94
Flower painter. Birmingham 1892; Fulham, London 1893. † ROI 3.

HARRISON, Mrs. Evelyn Exh. 1920-37
Architectural painter. Hove, Sussex 1920; Bearsted, Kent 1937. † L 1, RA 1, RSA 2, SWA 3.

HARRISON, E.C. Exh. 1885
9 Chester Street, Regent's Park, London. † L 3.

HARRISON, E.D. Exh. 1889-1921
Liverpool 1889; Liscard, Cheshire 1897. † L 17, RA 2.

HARRISON, Miss E.E. Exh. 1901
Sinclair House, Masboro Road, West Kensington Park, London. † SWA 1.

HARRISON, Emma Florence Exh. 1887-91
Figure and domestic painter. 10 Marlboro Road, London. † RA 3.

HARRISON, E.M. Exh. 1884-86
Landscape painter. 115 Gloucester Terrace, London. † SWA 6.

HARRISON, Edward Stroud b. 1879
Painter and printer. Exh. 1906-29. Add: Elgin, N.B. † GI 17, L 23, RSA 47.

HARRISON, Miss F. Exh. 1883
Lindirr, Llandulas, Abergele, Wales. † L 1.

HARRISON, F.E. Exh. 1885
3 Bath Road, Bedford Park, Chiswick, London. † G 2.

HARRISON, F.S. Exh. 1910-11
38 Station Road, Ilkeston, Derbs. † N 2.

HARRISON, George Exh. 1883-1910
Watercolour landscape painter. Bettws-y-Coed, N. Wales. † B 1, L 3, RCA 93.

HARRISON, George Exh. 1920-22
Landscape painter. 9 Tower Place, York. † L 3, RA 1, RSA 1.

HARRISON, George Exh. 1898-1907
50 Rockingham Road, Kettering, Northants. † B 2, N 3.

HARRISON, George Exh. 1933-34
† RCA 2.

HARRISON, Greta Exh. 1923
The Holt, Barnet Green, Worcs. † B 1.

HARRISON, Capt. George A. Exh. 1884-90
London. † G 2, L 5, ROI 1.

HARRISON, Mrs. George A. Exh. 1886
79 Lexham Gardens, Kensington, London. † G 1.

HARRISON, Gerald E. Exh. 1890-1932
Miniature portrait painter. London 1890 and 1918; Brighton 1898; East Grinstead, Sussex 1906; Smeeth, Kent 1922; Mersham, Nr. Ashford, Kent 1923; Charing, Kent 1928. † B 2, L 11, M 4, P 5, RA 13, RBA 2, RHA 3, RMS 6, ROI 1, RSA 8.

HARRISON, Gertrude H. Exh. 1928
Miniature painter. 15 Cambridge Avenue, Lincoln. † RA 2.

HARRISON, George L. Exh. 1881-1904
Domestic and figure painter. London. † RA 7, RBA 2.

HARRISON, Miss G.R. Exh. 1902
123 Trafalgar Roadm Moseley, Birmingham. † B 1.

HARRISON, Harriet Exh. 1880-86
Landscape painter. H.S.W.A. 1880. 115 Gloucester Terrace, London. † SWA 5.

HARRISON, Mrs. Helen G. Exh. 1900-2
3 Napier Road, Edinburgh. † RSA 3.

HARRISON, H.J. Exh. 1882
137 Bury New Road, Manchester. † M 1.

HARRISON, Miss H.K. Exh. 1924-29
8 Lancaster Avenue, Sefton Park, Liverpool. † L 19.

HARRISON, H.R. Exh. 1882-85
84 Shakspeare Street, Ardwick, Lancs. † M 2.

HARRISON, H. St. John Exh. 1921-31
Architect. London. † RA 5.

HARRISON, H. Scott Exh. 1929-32
87 Shandwick Place, Edinburgh. † GI 2, RSA 2.

HARRISON, Miss H.W. Exh. 1939-40
46 St. Oswald's Road, Small Heath, Birmingham. † B 3.

HARRISON, Isabella Exh. 1907
Hagley, Stourbridge, Worcs. † B 1.

HARRISON, Miss I. Frances Exh. 1935-39
Miniature painter. 5 Borthwick Road, Boscombe, Bournemouth. † GI 1, RA 9, RMS 2.

HARRISON, Ida H. Exh. 1904-6
64 Prospect Terrace, Hunslet, Leeds. † RCA 3.

HARRISON, J. Exh. 1938
58 Madeley Road, Sparkhill, Birmingham. † B 2.

HARRISON, Jane Exh. 1911-34
Miniature portrait painter. London 1911; Yarmouth, I.O.W. 1934. † L 1, RA 7.

HARRISON, Jessie See GODMAN

HARRISON, John Exh. 1932
Architect. The Castle, Winchester. † RA 1.

HARRISON, John Exh. 1940
Architect. County Offices, St. Mary's Gate, Derby. † RA 3.

HARRISON, Joseph Exh. 1881
Landscape painter. Headmaster Nottingham Municipal School of Art. N.S.A. 1881. † N 2.

HARRISON, Josephine Exh. 1931
Linocut artist. † RED 1.

HARRISON, John A.C. Exh. 1919-20
Illustrator and engraver. 34 Chatsworth Road, London. † RA 4.

HARRISON, John B. Exh. 1920-35
Watercolour landscape painter. Darlington, Co. Durham. † GI 1, L 5, RA 1, RCA 4, RI 1.

HARRISON, J.C. Exh. 1882-1900
Figure and domestic painter. Kentish Town, London. † B 1, L 4, M 3, RA 2, RBA 12, RI 18.

HARRISON, J.E. Exh. 1895-1907
Glasgow. † GI 3.

HARRISON, John E.K. Exh. 1936-40
Architect. 7 Carteret Street, London. † RA 2.

HARRISON, J.H. Exh. 1887
Runcorn, Liverpool. † L 1.

HARRISON, Rev. J.P. Exh. 1928
Landscape and flower painter. The Rectory, Brendon, Barnstaple, Devon. † AB 2.

HARRISON, John Scott Exh. 1906-33
Liverpool. † L 21, RCA 2.

HARRISON, Joseph S. Exh. 1889-1906
Watercolour landscape painter. London 1889; Leatherhead, Surrey 1904. † L 1, RA 2, RI 5.

HARRISON, John W. Exh. 1886-90
Fruit, flower and still life painter. Orchard House, Stapleford, Notts. † N 7.

HARRISON, L.A. Exh. 1903-9
Portrait and landscape painter. N.E.A. 1904. Add: Cheyne Walk, Chelsea, London. † L 1, M 1, NEA 26.

HARRISON, Miss Leslie A.M. Exh. 1910-24
Liverpool 1910; Wallasey, Cheshire 1924. † L 5.

HARRISON, L.B. Exh. 1882
Figure and landscape painter. c/o Messrs. Thomas & Co., 29 Bolsover Street, Fitzroy Square, London. † FIN 1, RA 1.

HARRISON, Lucy B. Exh. 1899-1923
Portrait painter. Nottingham 1899; Eastwood, Notts. 1908. † N 8.

HARRISON, Mabel Exh. 1907-36
Figure, landscape and still life painter. Travelled in North Africa. Add: Hagley, Stourbridge, Worcs. 1907; Chelsea, London 1934. † B 2, LS 11, NEA 1, RA 4.

HARRISON, Margaret Exh. 1910
Higham, Winchelsea, Sussex. † LS 2.

HARRISON, Maria Exh. 1880-1900
Watercolour flower painter. A.R.W.S. 1847. Add: London 1880; Old Colwyn, Wales 1893. † GI 2, L 4, RA 1, RWS 81, SWA 2.

HARRISON, Mrs. Mary Kent See KENT

HARRISON, Margaret Stewart
Exh. 1890-1904
Figure painter. 2 Corona Road, Lee, London. † L 2, RA 1, SWA 9.

HARRISON, Norah Exh. 1908-20
A.R.M.S. 1917. London 1908; Broadway, Worcs. 1920. † L 3, NG 1.

HARRISON, N.M. Exh. 1896
35 De Crespigny Park, S.E. London. † SWA 2.

HARRISON, Oliver Ormerid Exh. 1905-8
22 Baker Street, London. † LS 4, RA 2.

HARRISON, Richard Exh. 1936
Watercolour bird painter. † FIN 3.

HARRISON, Robert Exh. 1928
c/o R. Jackson and Son, 18A Slater Street, Liverpool. † L 1.

HARRISON, Ronald Exh. 1937
12 Herald Avenue, Glasgow. † GI 1, RSA 1.

HARRISON, Stockdale Exh. 1881
Architect. St. Martin's, East Leicester. † RA 1.

HARRISON, Sarah Cecilia b. 1863
Portrait and miniature painter. b. Co. Down. Studied Slade School (scholarship). Exh. 1886-1933. Add: London 1886 and 1890; Dublin 1889, 1905 and 1910; Hertford 1909. † B 1, GI 1, L 2, M 1, NEA 4, NG 6, P 1, RA 12, RE 1, RHA 52.

HARRISON, Sylvia N. Exh. 1924
5 Lancaster Avenue, Sefton Park, Liverpool. † L 1.

HARRISON, Theodora Exh. 1890-93
Landscape painter. Kensington, London. † RA 1, RBA 3.

HARRISON, Dr. Thomas Exh. 1936
6 Ribblesdale Place, Preston, Lancs. † GI 1.

HARRISON, Thomas Erat Exh. 1880-1913
Sculptor, painter, illustrator and engraver. London. † G 2, L 4, LS 16, RA 18, RHA 1.

HARRISON, Violet E. Exh. 1904-15
Miniature painter. London 1904; Liverpool 1912. † L 13, RA 7, RMS 1.

HARRISON, William Exh. 1893
Architect. 64 Cannon Street, London. † RA 1.

HARRISON, William A.D. Exh. 1896
Portrait painter. 9 St. Paul's Studios, Talgarth Road, West Kensington, London. † RA 2.

HARRISON, William B. Exh. 1909-10
Liverpool. † L 3.

HARRISON, William Henry Exh. 1894-1910
Architect. 66 Victoria Street, Westminster, London. † RA 7.

HARRISS, K. Exh. 1928
16 Roxburgh Avenue, Birkenhead. † L 1.

HARRISS, Thomas James 1901-1930
Painter, etcher and designer. b. Birmingham. Studied Birmingham School of Art and Royal College of Art. Add: 113 Knollys Road, Streatham, London 1928. † RA 2.

HARRISSON, Hilda Beatrice Corbett
Exh. 1910-26
nee Grierson. Landscape painter and pencil portrait artist. b. Liverpool. Studied Ruskin School of Drawing. Add: Hoylake, Cheshire 1910; Church Handborough, Oxford 1926. † L 1, NEA 1.

HARROLD, A. Winifred Exh. 1919-37
Landscape painter. Travelled widely. Add: Newquay, Garston Old Road, Aigburth, Liverpool. † COO 16, L 3.

HARROP, Frederick Samuel 1887-c.1971
b. Stoke on Trent. Add: 69 Oxford Gardens, London 1931. † RBA 1.

HARROP, Miss M.C. Exh. 1927
64 Park Road, St. Anne's on Sea, Lancs. † L 2.

HARROW, Mrs. A.W.S. Exh. 1914
36 Linden Gardens, London. † RA 1.

HARROWAY, Henry G. Exh. 1889-95
Landscape painter. London. † RBA 3.

HARROWER, Jean H. Exh. 1883-86
Whickham Hall, Newcastle on Tyne. † RSA 2.

HARROWINA, Walter Exh. 1885
† L 1.

HARSTEN, Mrs. Georgina Exh. 1901
Miniature portrait painter. Venice, Italy. † RA 1.

HART, Mrs. Anne E. Exh. 1883-94
Watercolour figure painter. London. † D 1, M 3, RA 1, RI 2, SWA 2.

HART, Alfred H. Exh. 1893-1940
Watercolour painter and architect. Studied R.A. Schools (gold medal) and the A.A. (silver medal). Travelling scholarship. Add: London 1893 and 1922; Enfield, Middlesex 1910; Burton Bradstock, Dorset 1939. † RA 23, RI 13, WG 125.

HART, Mrs. C.J. Exh. 1882-83
Altadore, Moseley, Birmingham. † B 2.

HART, Elizabeth Exh. 1898-1921
Landscape painter. A.S.W.A. 1902. Add: Stirling, N.B. 1898; Bushey, Herts. 1899. † GI 5, L 3, RA 3, SWA 27.

HART, Emily* Exh. 1909-10
14 Avenue Hoche, Paris. † L 2.

HART, Mrs. Ernest Exh. 1896-98
Watercolour and pastel landscape painter. Fairlawn, Totteridge, Middlesex. † D 1, DOW 11.

HART, E.B. Exh. 1898-1903
10 Buckingham Terrace, Edinburgh. † RSA 8, RSW 2.

HART, Eric G. Exh. 1933-38
Sculptor. 37 Trinity College, Dublin. † RHA 4.

HART, Frank 1878-1959
Black and white artist, lecturer and writer. b. Brighton. Exh. 1921-39. Add: Firle, Lewes, Sussex 1921; Eastbourne, Sussex 1933. † RA 4, RI 3.

HART, F.J.W. Exh. 1897-1900
Nottingham 1897; Sherwood, Notts. 1900. † N 7.

HART, F. Vincent Exh. 1896
Stained glass artist. c/o Messrs. Cottiers, 4 St. James' Terrace, Regent's Park, London. † L 1, RA 1.

HART, George H. b. 1882
Essex House, Campden, Glos. 1929. † L 6.

HART, Miss G.L. Exh. 1916
27 Wellmeadow Road, Hither Green, London. † L 3, RA 1.

HART, George Overbury* 1868-1933
"Pop". American painter. Exh. 1925. † CHE 2.

HART, Herman Exh. 1883-96
Landscape painter. London. † D 2, NG 1, RBA 1, RI,1.

HART, Horace Exh. 1887-1908
Figure, landscape and interior painter. London. † RA 3, RBA 2.

HART, Henry D'Arcy Exh. 1909-37
Flower painter. 18 Pembridge Gardens, London. † B 1, BG 11, I 3, L 1, NEA 2, RA 26, WG 29.

HART, John J. Exh. 1925-28
Birmingham. † B 3.

HART, J. Lawrence Exh. 1882-1906
Landscape and coastal painter. Edge Hill, Nr. Banbury, Oxon 1882; Rugby 1886; Stratford on Avon 1893; Blockley, Worcs. 1898; Edgbaston, Birmingham 1901. † AG 3, B 23, L 1, M 1, RBA 1, RI 1.

HART, James T. d. 1900
Landscape and portrait painter. N.S.A. 1880. V.P.N.S.A. 1881-98. Add: 13 Wildman Street, Nottingham. † N 28.

HART, Miss M. Exh. 1906
67 Cathcart Studios, Redcliffe Road, London. † RA 1.

HART, Mrs. P. Exh. 1881-82
Belsize Park, London 1881; Nuneaton, Warwicks. 1882. † D 1, M 2.

HART, Percival Exh. 1891
5 Crindan Road, Newport, Mon. † D 1.

HART, Solomon Alexander* 1806-1881
Portrait, historical, biblical, genre and miniature painter. b. Plymouth. Studied R.A. Schools 1823. Professor of Painting R.A. Schools 1855-65. Librarian R.A. Schools 1865. A.R.A. 1935, R.A. 1840. † RA 2.

HART, Thomas Exh. 1880-82
Marine painter. Polbrean, Lizard, Helston, Cornwall. † G 2, L 1.

HART-DYKE, Miss Eleanor Exh. 1884-1927
Landscape painter. London. † GI 2, RI 5, RMS 1, SWA 2, WG 50.

HART-DYKE, Mrs. Millicent Ada Exh. 1905-27
Mrs. R.C. Miniature painter. Studied France and Italy. Add: New Barnet, Herts 1905; Hadley Wood, Herts. 1927. † RA 6, RMS 2.

HARTE, G.C. Exh. 1885-86
Ormsby Lodge, Bedford Park, London. † L 2.

HARTE, Margaret K. Exh. 1888-94
Portrait painter. London. † L 1, M 1, RA 2, RHA 1, SWA 3.

HARTING, Miss A.E. Exh. 1883
Carlton Chambers, Manchester. † L 1.

HARTLAND, Barbara Exh. 1927
Sculptor. 35 Hampstead Lane, Highgate, London. † RA 1.

HARTLAND, Henry Albert* 1840-1893
Watercolour landscape painter. b. Cork, Ireland. Add: Egremont, Cheshire 1880; Dolgelly, N. Wales 1881; Liverpool 1886; London 1887. † AG 1, B 3, D 3, L 16, M 5, RA 9, RBA 1, RI 2.

HARTLEY, Alfred 1855-1933
Painter and etcher. b. Stocken Pelham, Herts. Studied Royal College of Art and Westminster School of Art. Married Nora H. q.v. R.B.A. 1890, A.R.E. 1894, R.E. 1897, R.O.I. 1899. Add: London 1884 and 1908; Gillingham, Dorset 1898; St. Ives, Cornwall 1906 and 1911; Llandrindod Wells, Wales 1931. † AB 1, B 1, FIN 5, G 5, GI 12, I 2, L 30, LEI 43, M 1, NEA 7, NG 27, P 4, RA 65, RBA 34, RE 72, RHA 6, RI 3, ROI 32.

HARTLEY, Miss B. Exh. 1892-94
St. John's Wood, London. † L 3.

HARTLEY, Bernard W. Exh. 1901
Gordon Institute, Stanley Road, Liverpool. † L 1.

HARTLEY, Miss D. Exh. 1916-23
Rempstone Rectory, Loughborough, Leics. † N 9.

HARTLEY, Edgar Exh. 1891
Architectural artist. 59 Bradshawgates, Leigh, Lancs. † RA 1.

HARTLEY, Ernest Exh. 1908
147 Heathcote Road, Gorton, Manchester. † L 1.

HARTLEY, Mrs. Gertrude Exh. 1903
Middleton Road, Morley, Yorks. † RCA 1.

HARTLEY, Hazlewood Carter Exh. 1910-14
Ashgrove House, Harrogate Road, Ecclesfield, Bradford, Yorks. † LS 15.

HARTLEY, Isabella Exh. 1894-1933
Tranmere, Birkenhead 1894; Seacombe, Cheshire 1899; Frankby, Cheshire 1902. † B 2, L 58.

HARTLEY, Jonathan Scott 1845-1912
American sculptor. c/o Deschamps, 1 Old Bond Street, London. † G 1.

HARTLEY, Marie Exh. 1929
Baron Hill, Wetherby, Yorks. † L 2.

HARTLEY, Nora Exh. 1897-1936
Flower and domestic painter. m. Alfred H. q.v. Add: London 1897 and 1934; Gillingham, Dorset 1899; St. Ives, Cornwall 1907; Llandrindod Wells, Wales 1931. † BG 4, D 21, L 3, NG 9, RA 13, RHA 1, RI 1, ROI 11, SWA 1.

HARTLEY, Richard d. 1921
Landscape painter. Exh. 1882-1922. Add: 32 Sandon Buildings, Church Street, Liverpool. † B 4, L 94, RA 4, RCA 2.

HARTLEY, Ridgard Exh. 1893-1924
Zig Zag Road, Liscard, Cheshire 1893; Higher Tranmere 1908; Birkenhead 1916. † L 34, RCA 6.

HARTLEY, William Exh. 1882-1938
Watercolour painter, press and poster designer. Studied Liverpool. Art Editor of the "Star" 1895-1919. Add: Liverpool 1882; London 1889; Coventry 1938. † B 1, L 4, RI 7.

HARTLEY, Winifred Exh 1903
30 Adair House, Oakley Street, Chelsea, London. † RCA 1.

HARTMANN, Rudolf Hans Exh. 1889-90
Sculptor. 36 II. Durer Strasse, Dresden. † L 2, RA 3.

HARTNELL, Katherine Grant Exh. 1911-40
nee Jefferies. Painter and etcher. b. Bristol. Studied Slade School (1st prize for figure painting and figure composition). Add: Bristol 1911; London 1921. † BA 31, GOU 2, L 11, M 2, NEA 11, RA 10, RHA 1, RI 2.

HARTOG, May Exh. 1894-99
Miniature portrait painter. Cork 1894; Westbourne Park, London 1899. † RA 1, RHA 2.

HARTRICK, Archibald Standish* 1864-1950
Painter and illustrator. b. Madras, India. Married Lily Blatherwick q.v. N.E.A. 1894, A.R.W.S. 1910, R.W.S. 1922. "The Penitents' Bench" (1904) purchased by Chantrey Bequest 1934. Add: London 1885 and 1892; Helensburgh, N.B. 1887. † B 1, BA 1, BG 1, CHE 3, FIN 6, G 2, GI 81, GOU 14, I 72, L 33, LEI 8, M 13, NEA 68, RA 29, RBA 2, RE 1, RHA 16, ROI 5, RSA 21, RWS 229, WG 36.

HARTRICK, Mrs. A.S.
See BLATHERWICK, Lily

HARTRY, Miss E. Exh. 1883-1909
Figure painter. 12 Cranbury Place, Southampton 1883; Elsted, Sussex 1907. † B 3, L 2, M 1, RBA 1, ROI 3, RSA 1, SWA 6.

HARTSHORN, Evelyn Exh. 1938-39
Prestatyn, Wales. † RCA 2.

HARTSHORN, William E. Exh. 1889
Landscape painter. 3 Wildman Street, Nottingham. † N 1.

HARTSHORNE, Mrs. Bertram Exh. 1893-98
Chelsea, London. † D 5.

HARTSHORNE, Mrs. Frederica Amelia Exh. 1908
29 St. Margaret's Road, Oxford. † LS 5.

HARTWELL, Charles Leonard 1873-1951
Sculptor and teacher. Studied R.A. Schools and under Onslow Ford. A.R.A. 1915, R.A. 1924, H.R.I. 1918. "A Foul in the Giants' Race" purchased by Chantrey Bequest 1908 and "Dawn" in 1914. Add: London 1900; Bognor Regis, Sussex 1935. † GI 30, L 28, P 6, RA 128, RI 23, ROI 5, RSA 15.

HARTWELL, Mlle. Nina R. Exh. 1911
2 Square Delambre, Paris. † L 1.

HARTWICH, Herman 1853-1926
American artist. Munich 1891-92. † GI 2.

HARTWICK, A.S. Exh. 1887
Burnside Cottage, Lundin Mill, Largo, Fife. † ROI 1.

HARTY, Rose Exh. 1896-1900
5 Trevelyan Terrace, Brighton Road, Rathgar, Dublin. † RHA 7.

HARVARD, Mrs. S.P. Exh. 1882
Wigan Road, Ormskirk, Lancs. † L 1.

HARVEST, Col. Sidney Exh. 1932-35
Landscape painter. 3 Gloucester Mansions, Harrington Gardens, London. † ROI 3.

HARVEY, Mrs. Anna Exh. 1885
Ickwell-Bury, Biggleswade, Beds. † SWA 1.

HARVEY, Agnes Bankier Exh. 1899-1916
Goldsmith and enameller. Studied Glasgow School of Art and London School of of Silversmithing. Instructor of silversmithing at Glasgow School of Art. Add: Gourock, N.B. 1899; Glasgow 1904. † GI 5, RSA 1.

HARVEY, Miss A.E. Exh. 1886
Wellington Road, Bromsgrove. † B 1.

HARVEY, Arthur Edward b. 1893
Designer and craftsman in plaster, wood, pottery and metal. Studied Royal College of Art, Slade School and R.A. Schools. Drawing and design master at Hammersmith School of Arts and Crafts, Wimbledon School of Art and Birmingham Central School of Arts and Crafts. Add: London 1916 and 1919; Enfield, Middlesex 1918; Birmingham 1927. † RA 6.

HARVEY, Alys M. Exh. 1927-31
Hampstead, London. † NEA 1, SWA 1.

HARVEY, Charles Exh. 1924-34
Landscape painter. A.R.B.A. 1928, R.B.A. 1929. Add: Leytonstone, Essex 1924; London 1926. † D 11, L 2, RA 3, RBA 56, RI 6, ROI 15, RSA 1.

HARVEY, Clara Exh. 1893-1903
2 Victoria Road, Leicester. † B 4, N 1.

HARVEY, Edith Exh. 1893-1905
2 Victoria Road, Leicester. † B 8, N 4.

HARVEY, Euphemia Exh. 1889-94
Gowan Brae, Stirling. † B 2, GI 2, RSA 3.

HARVEY, Elsie M. b. 1893
nee Mackrow. Mrs. Rupert H. Portrait painter. Studied Camden School of Art, British and Kensington Museums. Teacher of drawing and painting Camden School of Art 1913-15. A.R.M.S. 1920, R.M.S. 1926. Exh. 1919-39. Add: London 1919; Linton, Cambs. 1925. † L 7, RA 4, RMS 66, SWA 2.

HARVEY, F. Milton Exh. 1936
Architect. 3 Raymond Buildings, Gray's Inn, London. † RA 1.

HARVEY, F.V. Exh. 1913
16 Wick Road, Brislington, Bristol. † L 1.

HARVEY, Gertrude b. 1889
nee Bodinnar. Flower and landscape painter. Self taught. m. Harold H. q.v. Exh. 1915-39. Add: Maen Cottage, Newlyn, Penzance. † FIN 1, GOU 2, I 2, L 1, LEI 39, RA 8, SWA 2.

HARVEY, Henry Exh. 1883-90
Sculptor. 10 The Avenue, 76 Fulham Road, London. † G 2, RA 1.

HARVEY, Harold C.* b. 1874
Portrait and landscape painter. Studied at Penzance with Norman Garstin, Juliens, Colarossi's and under Delecluse, Paris. Married Gertrude H. q.v. Exh. 1898-1940. Add: Penzance 1898; Newlyn, Penzance 1912. † AB 1, BA 1, G 7, GI 5, GOU 5, I 4, L 22, LEI 92, M 2, RA 55, RBA 1, RCA 6, RHA 15, ROI 5, RSA 2.

HARVEY, H.E. Exh. 1893
11 Howe Street, Edinburgh. † RSA 1.

HARVEY, Miss H.E. Exh. 1885
Grange, Waterford, Ireland. † RSA 1.

HARVEY, Herbert Johnson 1884-1928
Painter and etcher. Son of John Rabone H. q.v. Add: 126 Newton Road, Sparkhill, Birmingham 1908; Earl's Court, London 1926. † B 51, L 2, RA 1.

HARVEY, Hilda Mary Exh. 1886-1939
Landscape and still life painter. London 1886, 1918 and 1922; St. Leonard's on Sea 1887; 126 Newton Road, Sparkhill, Birmingham 1920 and 1923; St. Just in Roseland, Cornwall 1935; Yardley, Warwicks. 1939. † B 24, NEA 9, RA 5, RBA 1.

HARVEY, J. Luck Exh. 1935
39 West Hill, Wydenham, London. † RI 1.

HARVEY, J. Martin Exh. 1893
New Inn Hotel, Winchelsea, Sussex. † M 1.

HARVEY, John Rabone d. 1933
Pastoral and portrait painter. Studied Slade School. Father of Herbert Johnson H. q.v. R.B.S.A. 1917. Add: Birmingham 1886; Sparkbrook, Birmingham 1890; Sparkhill, Birmingham 1897. † B 68, L 2, NEA,1, RA 3.

HARVEY, Mrs. Maughan Exh. 1936-38
Hightrees, Park Avenue, Solihull, Warwicks. † B 4.

HARVEY, Marion Rodger Hamilton b. 1886
Animal painter. b. Ayr. N.B. Exh. 1916-40. Add: Glasgow. † CON 2, GI 27, L 19, RSA 4, RSW 1, SWA 2.

HARVEY, Nellie Exh. 1890-1938
Watercolour bird painter. Studied under J. Donovan Adams and under Delecluse in Paris. Add: Gowanbrae, Stirling 1890, 1897 and 1906; Rathmines, Dublin 1896; Munich 1904. † B 2, GI 17, I 1, P 3, RHA 3, RSA 18, RSW 5, SWA 3.

HARVEY, Miss R.B. Exh. 1883
32 George Square, Edinburgh. † GI 1.

HARVEY, R.L. Exh. 1906-7
Lyngarth, Bearsden, N.B. † GI 2.

HARVEY, Seymour Garstin Exh. 1896-1906
Watercolour landscape painter and pencil portrait artist. London. † CAR 29, NEA 2, NG 8, RA 1.

HARVEY, W. Exh. 1932-33
The Hut, 49 Kingsway, Wallasey, Cheshire. † L 2.

HARVEY, Winnie Exh. 1910-13
31 Coniston Drive, Edinburgh. † RSA 4.

HARVEY-BLOOM, Mrs. D. Exh. 1930-38
Linocut artist. London 1932; Carshalton, Surrey 1936. † RBA 12, RED 1, ROI 3.

HARVEY-BLOOM, J. Exh. 1930-40
Landscape painter and linocut artist. R.B.A. 1934. Add: London 1932; Carshalton, Surrey 1935. †, COO 11, RA 3, RBA 42, RED 3, RSA 1.

HARVEY-JONES, Dorothy b. 1898
Watercolour painter and woodcut artist. Studied Hastings Municipal School of Art. Add: 22 Manor Road, Bexhill on Sea, Sussex 1924. † RA 1.

HARWOOD, A. Exh. 1882
Lea Green, Mirfield, Yorks. † L 1.

HARWOOD, E. Exh. 1894
c/o Messrs. Harnell, 4 Southampton Row, London. † RBA 2.

HARWOOD, Edith Exh. 1894-1908
London. † RI 2, SWA 3.

HARWOOD, Henry Exh. 1892-1915
Allerton, Nr. Bradford 1892; Maningham, Yorks. 1908. † B 2, GI 4, L 14, M 6, NEA 2, NG 1, RA 13, RBA 7, RHA 2, RI 2, ROI 1, RSA 1.

HARWOOD, John Hammond b. 1904
Watercolour painter. Studied Harrogate School of Art and Royal College of Art. Exh. 1932-35. Add: Southampton. † NEA 1, RA 2.

HASELDEN, Percy Exh. 1926
32 Warley Mount, Brentwood, Essex. † L 1.

HASELDINE, Lieut. Cyril F.W. Exh. 1913-37
Architect. Beeston, Notts. 1913; Nottingham 1924 and 1927; Applewick, Notts. 1926. † N 36, RA 1.

HASELTINE, Herbert b. 1877
Sculptor. b. Rome. Exh. 1907-35. Add: Paris. † L 2, RA 17.

HASELTINE, William Stanley* 1835-1900
American artist. Add: Palazzo Altiero, Rome 1883. † L 1.

HASKARD, Margaret E. Exh. 1936
Flower painter. 7 Newhall Grove, West Bridgford, Nottingham. † N 1.

HASLAM, A.W. Exh. 1914
Fall House, Heanor, Derbys. † LS 2.

HASLAM, Miss B. Exh. 1913-17
8 Park Hill Road, Croydon, Surrey. † RI 1, SWA 1.

HASLAM, Daniel Exh. 1904-26
Landscape painter. London. † RA 6.

HASLAM, G.M. Exh. 1940
Landscape painter. † COO 2.

HASLAM, Mrs. Vera Exh. 1936-39
Miniature painter. A.R.M.S. 1938. Northwood, Middlesex 1936; Bournemouth, Hants. 1938. † RA 2, RMS 14.

HASLEGRAVE, Adelaide L. Exh. 1901-16
Landscape painter. London. † RA 1, SWA 1.

HASLEHURST, Edward Exh. 1894
Architect. 7A Lawrence Pountney Hill, London. † RA 1.

HASLEHURST, Ernest William 1866-1949
Landscape painter and illustrator. b. Walthamstow, Essex. Studied Slade School and University College, London. R.B.A. 1911, R.I. 1924. Exh. 1888-1940. Add: Burnt Ash Hill, Lee, Kent. † GI 3, L 3, RA 18, RBA 217, RI 93, RID 4.

HASLER, Ida Exh. 1894-95
3 Castle Street, Beaumaris, N. Wales. † L 2.

HASLER, Miss J. Exh. 1885
Pooltock House, Wigan, Lancs. † M 1.

HASLEWOOD, N.A.F. Exh. 1914
2 Darlan Mansions, 580 Fulham Road, London. † LS 3.

HASSALL, Joan b. 1906
Painter, wood engraver and typographer. Daughter of John H. q.v. Studied R.A. Schools. L.C.C. School of Photo-Engraving and Lithography, Bolt Court. A.R.E. 1938. Exh. 1936-40. Add: London. † NEA 7, RA 8, RBA 6, RE 6, RED 1, RHA 5, RI 3, RSA 2.

HASSALL, John b. 1868
Poster designer and illustrator. Studied Antwerp and Paris. Father of Joan H. q.v. R.I. 1901, R.M.S. 1901. Exh. 1894-1940. Add: London 1894 and 1900; Helensburgh, N.B. 1897. † AR,3, B 5, BG 6, D 4, FIN 35, GI 9, L 20, RA 12, RI 80, RMS 1, RSW 1.

HASSAM, Childe* 1859-1935
American painter and etcher. Exh. 1904. Add: New York. † I 2.

HASSARD, Miss H. Tamison Exh. 1920-32
Landscape painter. 4 Kenilworth Square, Dublin. † RHA 5.

HASSELL, Hilary Clements **Exh. 1911-36**
Landscape and coastal painter. Riding Mill, Northumberland 1911; London 1914. † G 2, GOU 16, LS 21, NEA 3, RA 1, RBA 2, RCA 1, RHA 2, ROI 1, SWA 2.

HASSELT, Van See V

HASTIE, Grace H. Exh. 1880-1925
Fruit, flower and landscape painter. A.S.W.A. 1880, S.W.A. 1889. Add: London. † B 47, D 7, G 2, GI 4, L 34, LS 6, M 3, NG 26, RA 18, RBA 7, RHA 2, RI 27, RSA 8, SWA 253.

HASTING, Miss M. Exh. 1884
Lilsden House, Nr. Leeds. † M 2.

HASTINGS, Viscount Exh. 1936
Portrait and landscape painter. † LEF 40.

HASTINGS, Agnes Exh. 1908
23 Cumberland Terrace, London. † B 1.

HASTINGS, Ethel Exh. 1887-89
Figure painter. 1A Berkeley Gardens, London. † L 1, RBA 1, SWA 2.

HASTINGS, George* Exh. 1886
14 Regent Street, Clifton, Bristol. † RSA 1.

ASTINGS, Mrs. Kate Gardiner Exh. 1880-1908
Figure and portrait painter. London. † B 1, D 2, G 8, L 15, M 3, NG 24, RA 5, ROI 1, SWA 6.

ASTINGS, Miss M. Exh. 1904
1 Sidlan Terrace, Bognor, Sussex. † SWA 1.

ASTINGS, Mabel Exh. 1909-19
Westgate on Sea, Thanet 1909; Tunbridge Wells, Kent 1911; Folkestone, Kent 1913; Hindhead, Surrey 1919. † L 3, LS 18, RSA 1.

ASTINGS, Maud Exh. 1896-97
London. † B 2.

ASTINGS, Sybil Hamilton b. 1890
Watercolour landscape and flower painter. b. Wells, Norfolk. Studied under J. Noble Barlow and Norman Garstin and at the Byam Shaw and Vicat Cole School of Art. Exh. 1923-36. Add: The Haven, Woodbridge, Suffolk. † COO 7, L 1, SWA 3, WG 3.

ASTLING, Annie E. Exh. 1882-95
Figure and domestic painter. Sheffield 1882; Manchester 1884; Doncaster 1890. † L 4, M 8, RA 1, RI 4.

ASWELL, F.T. Exh. 1910-16
Chester 1910; Baron's Court, London 1914. † B 1, L 6, RA 1.

ASWELL, Grace B. Exh. 1915-30
5 Midmar Gardens, Edinburgh. † GI 4, RSA 12, RSW 9.

ASWELL, J. Exh. 1908-10
Landscape painter. 2 The Esplanade, Sunderland. † B 2, L 2, NG 1, RA 3, RSA 1.

ASWELL, Jessie Exh. 1885
Interior painter. 17 Canonbury Park North, London. † SWA 1.

ATCH, Edith Exh. 1932-38
A.R.M.A. 1933. Abercorn, Cranston Road, East Grinstead, Sussex. † B 5, L 4, RI 12, RMS 21.

ATCH, Ethel C. Exh. 1894-1940
Flower and figure painter. b. Oxford. Studied Slade School. Lived for some years in Italy. S.W.A. 1935. Add: London 1894 and 1921; Oxford 1907. † AB 97, BA 2, CHE 1, G 1, GOU 6, I 4, L 7, M 1, NEA 24, RA 18, RBA 4, RI 7, SWA 36, WG 76.

ATCHARD, Dora J Exh. 1932
Etcher. 49 St. Matthews Road, Cotham, Bristol. † RA 1.

ATCHARD, O.B. Exh. 1907-9
Architect. Khartoum, Sudan 1907; Bromley, Kent 1909. † RA 2.

ATCHER, Roberta G. Exh. 1928-38
Mrs. J.G. Everett. Sculptor. St. John's Wood, London 1928; Hornchurch, Essex 1935. † RA 4.

ATFIELD, Mrs. C. Hilda Exh. 1916-39
Flower, still life and figure painter. Nottingham 1916; London 1932. † N 4, NEA 1, P 1, RA 2, SWA 3.

ATHAWAY, Arthur J Exh. 1940
Landscape painter. 278 West Wycombe Road, High Wycombe, Bucks. † RA 1.

ATHAWAY, F. Exh. 1892
King's Heath, Birmingham. † B 1.

ATHERELL, William* 1855-1928
Figure and landscape painter and illustrator. Contributor to the "Graphic" and "Harpers". R.I. 1888, R.O.I. 1901. "O Romeo, Romeo, wherefore art thou Romeo?" purchased by Chantrey Bequest 1913. Add: London. † B 1, D 1, GI 5, L 36, M 4, NEA 2, RA 43, RBA 2, RI 68, ROI 4, RSA 1.

HATT, Doris Brabham b. 1890
Painter and wood engraver. Studied Bath School of Art, Goldsmith's College, New Cross School of Art, Royal College of Art and wood cutting in Vienna under Prof. Martin. Add: Bath 1918; Clevedon, Som. 1923; Walton in Gordans, Som. 1931. † I 4, NEA 1, RA 3, SWA 1.

HATTEMORE, Archibald Exh. 1926-30
Still life, landscape and flower painter. 6 Kenmure Road, Hackney, London. † LEF 3, NEA 4.

HATTON, Brian 1887-1916
Received Bronze Medal at the Royal Drawing Society at the age of 8 and a gold star 2 years later. Studied Oxford 1905-6, South Kensington and Juliens, Paris. Travelled to Egypt 1908. Exh. 1911-14. Add: Hereford 1911; London 1912. † P 3, RA 1, ROI 4.

HATTON, Ellen H. Exh. 1890
† G 1.

HATTON, Ella M. Exh. 1930
Hagley House, Nr. Stourbridge, Worcs. † B 1.

HATTON, E.W. Exh. 1882
Portrait painter. 1 St. John's Road, Hornsey Rise, London. † RA 1.

HATTON, Miss Helen Howard
See MARGETSON

HATTON, Irene Exh. 1937
Watercolour painter. Studied Heatherleys. † WG 17.

HATTON, Miss J. Exh. 1910
Kew Gardens, London. † SWA 1.

HATTON, Prof. Richard George
c. 1863-1925
Professor of fine art Armstrong College, Newcastle on Tyne. Exh. 1887-95. Add: Birmingham 1887; Gosforth, Newcastle on Tyne 1892. † B 4.

HATTON, W.H. Exh. 1920-22
Derwent House, Leamington, Warwicks. † B 4.

HATTS, Kenneth Exh. 1940
Landscape painter. 19 Ashridge Crescent, Shooter's Hill, London. † RA 1.

HAUFF, Kenneth Exh. 1939-40
Portrait painter. London. † RA 3.

HAUGH, W. Exh. 1885
22 Newman Street, Oxford Street, London. † RSA 2.

HAUGHTON, Benjamin 1865-1924
Landscape painter. Studied Herkomers, Bushey. Married Janet Mabel H. q.v. R.B.A. 1903. Add: Dawlish, Devon 1892; Bushey, Herts. 1895; Benenden, Kent 1898; Ottery St. Mary, Devon 1906; Barnstaple, Devon 1919. † B 4, FIN 2, L 2, NG 18, RA 20, RBA 18, ROI 1.

HAUGHTON, G. Exh. 1910
151 Gloster Road, London. † LS 2.

HAUGHTON, Janet Mabel b. 1870
Potter (figures modelled in china clay). b. Colne, Lancs. Married Benjamin H. q.v. A.R.M.S. 1926, R.M.S. 1927. Exh. 1925-39. Add: Barnstaple, Devon 1925; Cranbrook, Kent 1931. † L 14, RMS 51.

HAUSER, Natalie Exh. 1898
8 Holland Park Road Studios, London. † L 1.

HAVELL, Alfred C.* c.1855-1928
Sporting and figure painter. Exh. 1884. Add: c/o Scott, 100 Gt. Portland Street, London. † RA 1.

HAVELL, Edmund Junr.* 1819-1894
Figure, portrait and genre painter. Visited the U.S.A. Add: London. † L 2, M 1, RA 11.

HAVELL, Ernest Binfield c.1861-1934
Sculptor. Exh. 1890-91. Add: School of Art. Madras, India. † RA 2.

HAVELL, Mrs. H. Christabelle Exh. 1902-4
Portrait painter. 7 Dilke Street, Chelsea Embankment, London. † RA 1, SWA 3.

HAVENHAND, James Exh. 1893
Sculptor. 22 Milman Street, Bloomsbury, London. † L 1, RA 1.

HAVERFIELD, J.T. Exh. 1880-81
Titley House, Titley, Herefords. † GI 1, RHA 3.

HAVERGAL, Mrs. E. Exh. 1909
Miniature painter. Brent Eleigh Rectory, Lavenham, Suffolk. † RA 1.

HAVERGILL, Mrs. E.M. Exh. 1918
12 Prince's Square, Bayswater, London. † RA 1.

HAVERMAET, Van See V

HAVERMAN, Hendrik Johannes b. 1857
Dutch figure and portrait painter. Exh. 1904-10. Add: Wagenarrideg, The Hague, Holland. † FIN 10, I 1, L 1.

HAVERS, Alice Mary* 1850-1890
Genre and landscape painter. b. Norfolk. Studied South Kensington. Married Frederick Morgan, q.v. H.S.W.A. 1886. Add: London. † B 7, DOW 13, FIN 1, G 3, GI 9, L 12, M 10, RA 17, RBA 3, RHA 1, ROI 1, SWA 4.

HAVERS, Val* d. 1912
Portrait and domestic painter. R.O.I. 1906. Add: London 1898 and 1904; Gomshall, Guildford, Surrey 1901; Wareham, Dorset 1910; Poole, Dorset 1911. † GI 2, L 3, M 1, RA 13, ROI 6.

HAVET, Henri Exh. 1884-88
Paris. † GI 1, RSA 4.

HAVILAND, Francis A. c.1869-1912
Miniature portrait painter. London. † D 2, L 4, RA 20, RMS 2.

HAVILAND, Miss K.M. Exh. 1929-37
Landscape painter. 61 Earl's Avenue, Folkestone, Kent. † AB 4, ROI 2, SWA 7.

HAVINDEN, Ashley Eldrid b. 1903
Painter, commercial artist and industrial designer. Exh. 1939. † LEF 6.

HAWARD, E.A. Exh. 1916
Woodstock Corner, Bedford Park, London. † RA 1.

HAWARD, Mrs. Elsie E. Exh. 1936-40
Watercolour landscape painter. Broad Beech, Belstead Road, Ipswich. Suffolk. † RA 1, RI 6.

HAWARD, Mary Ellen Exh. 1912-40
Watercolour painter, pastelier and pencil artist. Studied Croydon School of Art and Chelsea Polytechnic. Add: Croydon, Surrey 1912; Hove, Sussex 1921; Brighton 1929. † AG 2, B 11, COO 2, D 23, L 5, LS 18, RBA 1, RCA 19, RHA 2, RI 1, RSA 1, SWA 11.

HAWARD, Sidney Exh. 1916
Woodstock Corner, Bedford Park, Chiswick, London. † I 50.

HAWDON, Miss C.A. Exh. 1911-22
Trewarveneth, Paul, Penzance 1911; Kensington, London 1922. † D 2, G 1, RA 1.

HAWEIS, Stephen Exh. 1911-14
Figure and landscape painter. London. † BG 113, I 8, L 1, LS 6, RSA 2.

HAWES, Ada Exh. 1920-30
Portrait painter. London. † L 17, RA 1.

HAWES, Arthur G. Exh. 1890-91
Landscape painter. 121 Queen's Road, Bayswater, London. † M 1, RBA 1, ROI 1.

HAWES, Edward B. Exh. 1905-16
Richmond, Surrey 1905; Chichester 1909; Sutton, Surrey 1913. † L 4.

HAWES, Eva L. Exh. 1919
Miniature painter. 24 Windsor Road, Church End, Finchley, London. † RA 2.

HAWES, Rev. John Cyril b. 1876
Church architect and Catholic Priest. Studied A.A. and L.C.C. School of Arts and Crafts. Add: Richmond, Surrey 1898; Sutton, Surrey 1923. † RA 3.

HAWES, Meredith William b. 1905
Landscape painter and black and white artist. b. Thornton Heath, Surrey. Head of Design Dept. Derby School of Art 1931-33. Vice Principal Hull College of Art 1938-45. Exh. 1929-40. † B 5, RA 13.

HAWKE, Mrs. Exh. 1918
Highgate, London. † SWA 1.

HAWKE, A. Phil Exh. 1926
† M 1.

HAWKE, Miss Ruth Exh. 1908
37 Overstrand Mansions, London. † LS 5.

HAWKER, Miss E.B. Exh. 1910-16
Wimbledon, London 1910; New Malden, Surrey 1913. † RA 5.

HAWKER, Florence Exh. 1889-91
Watercolour painter. 37 Cadogan Place, London. † D 11, RI 1.

HAWKER, Marguerita E. Exh. 1890-95
Watercolour painter. 37 Cadogan Place, London. † D, M 1, RI 1.

HAWKES, Clara M. Exh. 1884-94
Figure painter. Kensington, London. † L 1, RA 2, RBA 1.

HAWKES, C.P. Exh. 1912
Caricaturist. † BG 27.

HAWKES, Mrs. Gertrude M. Exh. 1903-4
New Brighton, Cheshire 1903; Leamington Spa, Warwicks. 1904. † B 1, L 1.

HAWKES, Irene Exh. 1907
22 Abercromby Square, Liverpool. † L 2.

HAWKES, T. Frank Exh. 1932-33
Architect. Lynton, Woodside Avenue, Esher, Surrey. † RA 2.

HAWKESWORTH, J.S. Exh. 1940
c/o Rowley Gallery, Kensington Church Street, London. † RBA 2, RI 2.

HAWKINGS, Frederick J. Exh. 1928-31
Sculptor. 203 Goldhawk Road, London. † RA 3.

HAWKINS, Amy Exh. 1892
39 Pembroke Square, Kensington, London. † RI 1.

HAWKINS, Grace Mary Exh. 1914-29
Portrait painter. Studied under Sir Arthur Cope and R.A. Schools (silver medal). Add: Acton, London and Westgate on Sea, Kent. † L 2, RA 7.

HAWKINS, Henry Exh. 1880-81
Portrait, figure and landscape painter. R.B.A. 1824. Add: 18 Crowndale Road, Camden Town, London. † RBA 2.

HAWKINS, Harold Frederick Weaver b. 1893
Portrait, landscape and figure painter, etcher and linocut artist and teacher. Studied Camberwell School of Art, Westminster School of Art and Royal College of Art. Exh. 1920-26. Add: London. † GOU 14, L 2, NEA 5, RA 3.

HAWKINS, Irene Exh. 1939
† GOU 3.

HAWKINS, Jane Exh. 1882-86
Figure and portrait painter. 5 Walpole Street, Chelsea, London. † B 2, M 3, ROI 3.

HAWKINS, Mrs. Lily Exh. 1932-33
Barnfield, Riverhead, Sevenoaks, Kent. † RBA 3, SWA 2.

HAWKINS, Louise Exh. 1880-89
Landscape painter. 5 Walpole Street, Chelsea, London. † B 2, RBA 2, RI 1, SWA 4.

HAWKINS, L. Welden Exh. 1886-1907
23 Boulevard Gouvion St. Cyr, Paris and the Grafton Galleries, London. † GI 2, M 2.

HAWKINS, M. Exh. 1929
Leighton Manor, Camden, Kent. † L 1.

HAWKINS, Majorie Exh. 1927-29
Sculptor. Little Oaks, Hutton, Essex 1927; London 1928. † RA 3.

HAWKINS, Sheila Exh. 1939
35 Haymarket, London. † GOU 3, SWA 1.

HAWKINS, W.B. Exh. 1921-25
Blundellsands, Nr. Liverpool 1921, Roby, Liverpool 1923. † L 9.

HAWKSLEY, Miss Exh. 1899
60 Porchester Terrace, London. † SWA 1.

HAWKSLEY, Arthur 1842-1915
Landscape painter. London. † B 2, GI 3, L 3, M 6, RA 3, RBA 3, RHA 4, ROI 1.

HAWKSLEY, Dorothy Webster 1884-c.1971
Portrait and figure painter. Studied R.A. Schools (silver medal and Landseer scholarship), and St. John's Wood School of Art (silver medal). R.I. 1917. Exh. 1909-40. Add: London. † FIN 6, G 4, GI 8, I 1, L 34, M 1, P 3, RA 47, RHA 1, RI 57, RID 8, ROI 2, RSA 1, SWA 13.

HAWKSLEY, F. Exh. 1914
38 Bath Road, Bedford Park, London. † LS 3.

HAWKSLEY, Florence Exh. 1881
Figure painter. 14 Phillimore Yard, Kensington, London. † RA 1.

HAWKSLEY, Miss F.E. Exh. 1903
3 Fern Avenue, Hucknall Road, Nottingham. † N 1.

HAWKSLEY, J.W. Exh. 1917
Figure painter. 2 Primrose Hill Studios, London. † NEA 1.

HAWKSWORTH, William Thomas Martin 1853-1935
Watercolour painter. Articled to E.W. Pugin, architect. R.B.A. 1903, R.I. 1934. Add: London 1881, Herne Bay, Kent 1933. † B 5, CHE 2, D 15, G 7, GI 7, GOU 1, L 46, NEA 17, RA 33, RBA 317, RI 18, RSA 2, RSW 2.

HAWLEY, E.H. Exh. 1909
Etcher. 22A Barmouth Road, Wandsworth Common, London. † RA 1.

HAWLEY, Mrs. E.M. d. 1915
Australian artist. Exh. 1908-9. Add: 105 Cheyne Walk, London. † LS 3, RA 1.

HAWLEY, E. Stretton and George Exh. 1905
Figure, landscape, marine and animal painter. † BRU 56.

HAWLEY, H. Denton Exh. 1924-28
† GOU 4.

HAWLEY, Margaret Foote b. 1880
American miniature painter. R.M.S. 1927. Exh. 1926-29. Add: 58 West 57th Street, New York, U.S.A. † RMS 4.

HAWLEY, Mrs. S. Exh. 1904-8
45 Fairfax Road, London. † SWA 7.

HAWORTH, Charles S. 1884-1917
Exh. 1905-14. Liverpool. † L 6.

HAWORTH, Miss E. Fanny Exh. 1880
Still life and landscape painter. 66 Scarsdale Villas, Kensington, London. † SWA 2.

HAWORTH, E. Mary Exh. 1913
69 Manchester Road, Southport, Lancs. † L 2.

HAWORTH, James W. Exh. 1915
17 Andrew Street, Seacombe, Cheshire. † L 1.

HAWORTH, Mrs. Pauline Exh. 1924
Sculptor. 48 Grove End Road, London. † RA 1.

HAWORTH, Peter* Exh. 1933
† RSW 2.

HAWORTH, Mrs. R.F. Exh. 1920-22
Owlscot, Hale, Cheshire. † L 5.

HAWORTH, Zenna Exh. 1933
† RSW 2.

HAWTHORN, Exh. 1882
110 Belgrave Road, Birmingham. † B 1.

HAWTHORN, Charles W. Exh. 1914
51 Boulevard St. Jacques, Paris. † RSA 1.

HAWTHORN, Wilfred Charles 1877-1955
Portrait and landscape painter. Studied Wyggeston Art School, Leicester, Wimbledon School of Art, Juliens, Paris, under Bougereau and Ferrier, Paris (1901) and under Sir Alfred East. Art master Kettering and Wellingborough; specialist teacher of drawing at Poole, Dorset and chief assistant art master Loughborough College of Art. Add: Kettering 1899; Coventry 1925. † B 23, CHE 1, N 7, RA 1.

HAWTHORNE, Elwin Exh. 1930-38
Landscape painter. London. † AG 2, LEF 99.

HAXTON, Elaine* Exh. 1937
c/o B. Cooley, 91 Kensington Garden Square, London. † ROI 1.

HAXTON, W. Exh. 1881
31 Willowbank Crescent, Glasgow. † GI 1, RSA 1.

HAY, le see L

HAY, A. Exh. 1887
4 Charlotte Place, Edinburgh. † RSA 1.

HAY, Adele Exh. 1895-99
Sculptor. North House, Putney, London. † L 1, RA 3.

HAY, Alec John b. 1878
Painter and stained glass artist. b. Aberdeen. Studied Edinburgh College of Art (travelling scholarship). Supervisor of Art at Dunfermline Elementary Schools. Add: Leith 1914, Dunfermline 1929. † RSA 2, RSW 1.

HAY, A.M. Exh. 1884
37 Queensferry Street, Edinburgh. † RSA 2.

HAY, Bernard* Exh. 1882
216 Rue de la Victoria, Brussels. † L 1.

HAY, Charles Exh. 1892-98
Edinburgh. † RSA 2.

HAY, Cecil George Jackson b. 1899
Flower and still life painter. b. Sandgate, Kent. Studied Glasgow School of Art. Exh. 1918-40. Add: Glasgow 1918; London 1922. † CHE 2, G 4, GI 28, GOU 1, RA 12, RSA 9.

HAY, Mrs. Enid d. c.1911
Flower painter. m. James Hamilton H. q.v. Add: Audlem, Cheshire 1908. † BG 1, L 8, LS 16.

HAY, Evelyn Dalrymple Exh. 1888-90
Landscape painter. 108 St. George's Square, London. † D 6, SWA 3.

HAY, Mrs. E.G. Exh. 1918
Herefordshire. † SWA 1.

HAY, George* 1831-1912
Figure painter. A.R.S.A. 1869, R.S.A. 1876. Secretary R.S.A. 1881-1907, H.R.S.A. 1910. Add: Edinburgh. † DOW 2, GI 5, RSA 67.

HAY, Helen Exh. 1933-40
Paisley 1933; Whiteheath, Egglesham 1937. † GI 3, RSA 2.

HAY, James Exh. 1880-1908
Figure and domestic painter. Edinburgh. † B 2, GI 8, L 2, RA 2, RI 4, RSA 12, RSW 1.

HAY, Jessie Exh. 1932-34
59 Lexham Gardens, London. † RBA 1, RI 1.

HAY, John Exh. 1889-92
Aberdeen 1889; Edinburgh 1892. † RSA 2.

HAY, John A.M. b. 1887
Portrait painter. Studied Alan Fraser Art College, Aberdeen. R.P. 1929. Add: London. † GI 1, L 5, P 24, RA 23.

HAY, John C. Exh. 1880
4 Charlotte Road, Edinburgh. † RSA 1.

HAY, James Hamilton 1874-1916
Landscape painter and etcher. b. Birkenhead. m. Enid H. q.v. Member London Group 1914. Add: Birkenhead 1894; Liverpool 1899; Audlem, Cheshire 1908; Heswall, Cheshire 1911; Chelsea, London 1912. † BG 95, GI 8, GOU 125, I 2, L 68, LS 26, M 11, NEA 14, RA 3, RSA 4.

HAY, J.M. Exh. 1889-92
Architect. Liverpool. † L 3.

HAY, James S. Exh. 1907
Caxton Chambers, Bank Street, Kilmarnock, N.B. † GI 1.

HAY, Peter Alexander 1866-1952
Landscape, portrait, figure and still life painter. R.I. 1917, R.S.W. 1891. Add: Edinburgh 1886; London 1893. † AR 2, B 8, DOW 2, GI 33, I 2, L 47, LEI 12, M 1, NG 18, P 24, RA 64, RBA 10, RHA 4, RI 126, RID 4, ROI 13, RSA 27, RSW 136.

HAY, Rhoda M.M. Exh. 1938
3 Windsor Street, Dundee. † RSA 1.

HAY, Ralph W. Exh. 1919-21
George Watson's Boys College, Edinburgh. † RSA 1, RSW 1.

HAY, Thomas Marjoribanks d. 1921
Landscape painter. R.S.W. 1895. Exh. 1882-1920. Add: Edinburgh. † B 2, G 1, GI 23, L 6, M 1, RA 1, RHA 3, RI 12, ROI 2, RSA 88, RSW 59.

HAY, Thomas Wallace Exh. 1884-1903
Decorative painter. London. † RA 4, RBA 2.

HAY, W.A. Exh. 1889
15 Castle Street, Liverpool. † L 1.

HAY, William Hardie b. 1859
Landscape painter. b. Birkenhead. Studied Glasgow School of Art and Paris. Exh. 1887-1933. Add: Glasgow. † GI 97, L 7, NG 1, RSA 13, RSW 5.

HAY, William M.* Exh. 1880-87
Portrait, genre and biblical painter. Fitzroy Square, London. + M 3, RBA 4.

HAY, William Robert b. 1886
Painter, etcher and lettering artist. Studied Westminster School of Art (King's prize for perspective). Exh. 1911-23. Add: London. † L 1, LS 12, RA 1.

HAYBROOK, Auxiliary Fireman Exh. 1940
† LEI 43.

HAYBROOK, Rudolf b. 1898
Portrait and figure painter. Exh. 1938. † BK 41.

HAYCOCK, Augustus Edmonds Exh. 1882-85
Figure and domestic painter. 2 St. George's Square, Primrose Hill, London. † L 1, RA 2, RBA 2, ROI 3.

HAYCRAFT, Lillie Stacpoole Exh. 1888-1900
Mrs. J.B. Figure painter. Edinburgh 1888; Cardiff 1896. † B 2, L 1, RA 1, RSA 5.

HAYDEN, Fred b. 1874
Landscape painter. b. Wolverhampton. Exh. 1921-25. Add: Finchfield, Ombersley Road, Worcester. † B 4.

HAYDN, J.A. Exh. 1933-37
Architectural painter. 26 Barrington Street, Limerick. † RHA 2.

HAYDOCK, Miss M.S. Exh. 1903
44 Tedworth Square, London. † SWA 3.

HAYE, Ia see L

HAYE, J. Macpherson Exh. 1893-96
London. † RI 1, ROI 2.

HAYES, Arthur Exh. 1880-94
Figure painter. London. † L 1, RA 1, RBA 1, ROI 4.

HAYES, A.B. Exh. 1936
† RI 1.

HAYES, Albert E. EXh. 1923
173 Hale End Road, Walthamstow, London. † RI 1.

HAYES, A.M. Exh. 1922
† SWA 1.

HAYES, A.P. Exh. 1929
20 Glenhurst Road, Plymouth, Devon. † L 2.

HAYES, Bret Exh. 1897-1900
Broad Street, Birmingham. † B 4, RHA 9.

HAYES, Miss C. Exh. 1907
19 Heaton Road, Mitcham, Surrey. † RA 1.

HAYES, Claude* 1852-1922
Landscape and portrait painter. b. Dublin. Sone of Edwin H. q.v. Ran away to sea. Spent a year in America. Studied Heatherleys, R.A. Schools (3 years) and under Verlat in Antwerp. R.I. 1886, R.O.I. 1883, R.S.W. 1902-7. Add: London 1880; Addleston, Surrey 1892; Guildford, Surrey 1901; Christchurch, Hants 1909; Woking, Surrey 1913. d. Brockenhust Hants. † AG 1, B 5, BK 242, D 32, FIN 1, G 4, GI 34, L 39, LS 3, M 10, NG 12, RA 76, RBA 28, RHA 4, RI 205, RID 16, ROI 93, RSW 11, WG 282.

HAYES, Charles S. Exh. 1932-36
Lincoln. † N 8, NEA 1.

HAYES, Claude Watford Exh. 1920
St. John Avenue, Boscombe, Hants. † L 1.

HAYES, Edwin* 1819-1904
Marine painter. b. Bristol. Father of Claude H. q.v. A.R.H.A. 1852, R.H.A. 1861, A.R.I. 1860, R.I. 1863, R.O.I. 1883. "Sunset at Sea: from Harlyn Bar, Cornwall" purchased by Chantrey Bequest 1894. Add: London. † B 47, DOW 243, FIN 1, G 9, GI 40, L 39, LEI 2, M 35, NG 56, RA 42, RBA 22, RHA 84, RI 165, ROI 68, RSA 3, RSW 1, TOO 16.

HAYES, Elise Exh. 1902-3
18 Merrion Square, Dublin. † RHA 3.

HAYES, Edith Caroline b. 1860
Painter and wood engraver. b. Southsea, Hants. Studied St. John's Wood and R.A. Schools. Exh. 1888-1912. Add: Paris 1889; Southsea, Hants 1891; San Gimignano, Toscana, Italy 1892; Newlyn, Penzance 1897; Gt. Marlow, Bucks 1912. † DOW 3, M 1, NEA 1, NG 1, RA 2, RHA 2, ROI 6.

HAYES, Ernest C. Exh. 1932-40
Portrait and landscape painter. Dublin 1932; Glasnevin 1935. † RHA 41.

HAYES, Edith D. Exh. 1888-1914
Liverpool 1888; Paris 1898; London 1907; Little Barrington, Burford, Oxon. 1914. † L 4, LS 13, RA 2.

HAYES, Mrs. E. Irene Exh. 1887-98
Domestic and figure painter. Liverpool 1887; Manchester 1890; Southport, Lancs. 1897. † L 2, M 2, RA 1, ROI 1.

HAYES, E.M. Exh. 1880
15 Queensborough Terrace, London. † SWA 1.

HAYES, Frederick William* 1848-1918
Landscape and coastal painter, novelist, playwright and economist. b. Cardiff. Exh. 1880-1917. Add: London. † B 35, L 3, LS 6, M 2, RA 14, RBA 2, RCA 177, RI 4, ROI 3.

HAYES, Gabriel Exh. 1932-40
Painter and linocut artist. Belfast 1932; Metropolitan School of Art, Dublin 1933; Clontarf, Dublin 1935 and 1939; Monkstown, Co. Cork 1938 and 1940. † RHA 22.

HAYES, George Exh. 1884-93
Conway, N. Wales. † M 6, RCA 22.

HAYES, Gerald Exh. 1919-20
Figure painter. 76 Linden Gardens, London. † I 1, RA 1.

HAYES, Mrs. Gladys B. Exh. 1932-34
Portrait, animal and flower painter. London 1932; Virginia Water, Surrey 1933. † RA 3.

HAYES, Gertrude Ellen b. 1872
Painter, etcher and repoussee metal worker. Studied Royal College of Art. Head of Art Centre, Forest Hill and assistant art mistress at Rugby School. m. Alfred Kedington Morgan q.v. A.R.E. 1897. S.W.A. 1922. Exh. 1896-1940. Add: London 1896, Rugby 1908; Harborne, Birmingham 1932. † ALP 1, B 1, CON 10, L 11, M 11, P 1, RA 20, RE 79, RSA 1, SWA 25.

HAYES, Henry Exh. 1900-8
Figure painter. Ilford, Essex 1900; Mitcham, Surrey 1908. † RA 2.

HAYES, Henry Edgar Exh. 1881-86
Figure painter. London. † RBA 2.

HAYES, Miss H.M. Exh. 1918
St. Leonard's on Sea, Sussex. † SWA 2.

HAYES, Irma Exh. 1902
18 Merrion Square, Dublin. † RHA 1.

HAYES, Ivor D. Exh. 1938-40
Landscape painter and wood engraver. Hampstead, London. † GOU 4, NEA 1, RA 2.

HAYES, James Exh. 1898
41 Charlotte Square, Edinburgh. † RSW 2.

HAYES, John Exh. 1897-1902
Landscape painter. Acton, London 1897; Ilford, Essex 1902. † RA 2.

HAYES, Joseph Exh. 1936
10 Sutherland Avenue, Newbiggin by Sea, Northumberland. † RA 1.

HAYES, J. Percy Exh. 1890
Figure painter. Fern Villa, High Road, Chiswick, London. † ROI 2.

HAYES, Lionel Exh. 1902
18 Fox Street, Liverpool. † L 1.

HAYES, Marjorie Exh. 1935-36
Landscape painter. 173 Hale End Road, Walthamstow, London. † RA 1, SWA 1.

HAYES, Mabel E. Exh. 1898-1923
nee Chattock. Add: Newbury, Berks 1898; Birmingham 1899; Highgate, London 1920; Long Wittenham, Nr. Abingdon, Berks. 1921. † B 7.

HAYES, Nellie Angelo Exh. 1884-87
Elm Grove, Ranelagh, Dublin. † RHA 2.

HAYES, Sydney d. c.1923
Flower painter. Exh. 1905-24. Add: 19 Heaton Road, Mitcham, Surrey. † RA 6.

HAYES, S.J. Exh. 1880
Landscape painter. 8 Harold Street, Camberwell, London. † RBA 1.

HAYES, William B. Exh. 1885-92
Landscape and figure painter. Barnet, Herts. 1885; Notting Hill, London 1886. † L 1, M 1, P 1, RA 1, ROI 1.

HAYES, W.F.B. Exh. 1882-84
London. † GI 1, RHA 3, RSA 1.

HAYES, Winifred Yule Exh. 1913-38
nee Yule. SCulptor. b. London. Studied Aberdeen School of Art and Edinburgh College of Art. Add: Edinburgh 1913; London 1927. † GI 2, P 2, RA 14, RSA 1, SWA 2.

HAYES-HAMMOND, Natalie b. 1905
American artist. A.R.M.S. 1928. Exh. 1927-29. Add: Washington, D.C., U.S.A. 1928; New York, U.S.A. 1929.

HAYLES, Edward E. Exh. 1896-1908
London. † RA 2, RI 1.

HAYLEY, Eleanor Exh. 1938
† M 1.

HAYLEY, Mrs. Vera Exh. 1916
24 Prince's Gate, London. † LS 3.

HAYLLAR, Algernon Victor Exh. 1889
Engraver. Castle Priory, Wallingford, Berks. † RA 2.

HAYLLAR, Miss Edith* Exh. 1881-97
Figure and domestic painter. Castle Priory, Wallingford, Berks. † B 10, L 4, M 2, RA 12, RBA 16, ROI 6, TOO 3.

HAYLLAR, James* 1829-1920
Portrait, genre and landscape painter. b. Chichester. Studied with F.S. Cary and at R.A. Schools. Travelled in Italy 1851-53. R.B.A. 1876. Add: Castle Priory, Wallingford, Berks. 1880; Red Holme, Cambridge Road, Bournemouth 1899. † B 24, D 4, L 17, M 14, RA 22, RBA 119, RHA 5, RI 5, ROI 4, TOO 4.

HAYLLAR, Miss Jessica* Exh. 1880-1915
Flower, figure and domestic painter. Castle Priory, Wallingford, Berks. 1880; Red Holme, Cambridge Road, Bournemouth 1899. † B 7, D 1, FIN 1, L 7, M 3, RA 37, RBA 14, ROI 8, TOO 6.

HAYLLAR, Miss Kate Exh. 1883-1900
Figure and domestic painter. Castle Priory, Wallingford, Berks. † RA 12, RBA 6, RI 2, TOO 3.

HAYLLAR, Miss Mary Exh. 1880-85
Figure and domestic painter. Castle Priory, Wallingford, Berks. † D 1, L 3, M 4, RA 5, RBA 15, RI 1.

HAYMAN, Miss C.M. Exh. 1912
52 Brook Green, London. † D 2.

HAYMAN, Miss L. Exh. 1910-11
9 Rue Vineuse, Paris. † LS 3, RA 1.

HAYNE, J.C. Exh. 1900-1
Hornsey Rise Gardens, London. † D 5.

HAYNES, Alice M. Exh. 1903-4
80 Castle Road, Bedford. † B 1, RCA 3, SWA 3.

HAYNES, Arthur S. Exh. 1885-1906
Landscape painter and architect. London. † GI 1, I 4, L 2, M 2, NEA 6, RA 7, RBA 3, ROI 2, RSA 1.

HAYNES, Bessie Exh. 1881-88
Domestic painter. 45 Roden Street, London 1881; Thorne, Cuckfield, Sussex 1888. † ,M 1, RHA 1, SWA 7.

HAYNES, Constance B.H. Exh. 1902-14
Jersey, C.I. † LS 3, SWA 2.

HAYNES, C.E. Exh. 1914
The Grange, Radcliffe-on-Trent, Notts. † N 2.

HAYNES, Edith M. Exh. 1926-38
Morfa, Penmaenmawr, Wales. † RCA 9.

HAYNES, Elsie N. Exh. 1906-35
Birmingham 1906; Sutton Coldfield 1909; Beer, Devon 1935. † B 9, L 1, RA 1, RCA 2, RI 1.

HAYNES, Edward Travanyon Exh. 1881-85
Landscape, portrait and figure painter. London. † RA 3, RBA 1.

HAYNES, Isabel Exh. 1939
† RI 2.

HAYNES, James Dudley Exh. 1925-34
Landscape painter and etcher. Studied painting under F.E. Jackson and etching under Malcolm Osborne, F.L. Emanuel and W.P. Robins. Add: Penlee, West Drayton, Middlesex. † B 1, RA 3.

HAYNES, John William* Exh. 1882
Genre painter. 45 Roden Street, London. † RBA 2.

HAYNES, Miss L. Exh. 1913
The Grange, Radcliffe-on-Trent, Notts. † N 1.

HAYNES, Laura Exh. 1882-87
Coventry 1882 and 1887, Handsworth, Birmingham 1886. † B 1, L 2.

HAYNES, Nancy Exh. 1897
Sunday's Well, Cork. † RI 1.

HAYNES, Neta Exh. 1921
11 Victoria Square, Reading, Berks. † L 1, SWA 1.

HAYNES-WILLIAMS, Miss Ethel Exh. 1886-94
Painter. Wredhern, Maresfield Gardens, Hampstead, London 1886; Shirley Place, Nr. Southampton 1893. † G 5, GI 1, RA 2, RI 1, ROI 11.

HAYNES-WILLIAMS, John* 1836-1908
Genre painter. Studied Worcester and Birmingham. R.B.S.A. 1890, R.O.I. 1883. Add: Wredhern, Maresfield Gardens, Hampstead, London 1880; Shirley Place, Nr. Southampton 1893; Eastbourne 1899. † B 13, G 15, GI 10, L 18, M 8, NG 8, RA 16, RBA 1, RHA 1, RI 3, ROI 33, TOO 1.

HAYNES-WILLIAMS, Miss Nina Exh. 1888
Wredhern, Maresfield Gardens, Hampstead, London. † RI 1.

HAYS, Beatrice Exh. 1888-93
Flower and figure painter. Briar Mount, Caterham Valley, Surrey 1888; Kensington, London 1889. † L 1, RA 3, RBA 2, ROI 4.

HAYS-FFIELD, Mrs. B. Exh. 1938-40
Crooked Walls, Harvington, Nr. Evesham, Worcs. † B 4.

HAYTER, Edith C. Exh. 1889-99
Landscape painter. London. † D 6, L 3, NG 2, ROI 1, SWA 7.

HAYTER-COX, Rev. E. Exh. 1928-31
Landscape painter. † AB 6, WG 3.

HAYTHORNE, Margaret Curtis b. 1893
Painter and wood engraver. Studied Liverpool City School of Art and Central School of Arts and Crafts (Queen's scholarship). Add: Liverpool 1915 and 1929-38; London 1923. † L 9, M 2, NEA 5, RCA 2, RED 5.

HAYWARD, Albert Exh. 1885
Landscape painter. Montpelier Road, St. John's College Park, London. † RA 1.

HAYWARD, Arthur b. 1889
Portrait and figure painter. b. Southport, Lancs. Studied Warrington School of Art and under Stanhope Forbes. Exh. 1920-40. Add: Newlyn, Penzance 1920; St. Ives, Cornwall 1924. † RA 19, ROI 5.

HAYWARD, Alfred Frederick William* b. 1856
Flower painter. b. Ontario, Canada. Studied West London School of Art and R.A. Schools. m. Edith H. q.v. R.O.I. 1903. Exh. 1880-1939. Add: London 1880; Winchester 1890; Northwood, Middlesex 1908; Hemingford Grey, St. Ives, Hunts. 1919. † ,AB 1, B 3, BA 3, BG 6, CG 1, FIN 39, G 4, I 2, L 15, M 5, NG 55, P 1, RA 66, RBA 1, RE 4, RHA 2, ROI 133, RSA 15.

HAYWARD, Alfred Robert 1875-1971
Portrait and landscape painter and decorator. Studied South Kensington and Slade School. N.E.A. 1910, R.O.I. 1928, R.P. 1929. Add: London 1895; Battle, Sussex 1934. † CHE 7, FIN 3, G 16, GI 2, GOU 70, I 33, L 2, LS 5, M 4, NEA 117, P 23, RA 23, RBA 2, RHA 29, RI 1, RID 4, ROI 2, RSA 8.

HAYWARD, Charles Exh. 1880-82
Landscape painter. 21 Bilbie Street, Nottingham. † N 7.

HAYWARD, Charles Foster Exh. 1886-94
Architect. 47 Museum Street, Bloomsbury, London and Hazelbank, Godalming, Surrey. † RA 3.

HAYWARD, C.G. Exh. 1911-14
London. † L 1, RA 4.

HAYWARD, Edith Exh. 1897-1933
nee Burrows. Landscape painter. m. Alfred F.W.H. q.v. Add: Winchester 1897; Northwood, Middlesex 1911; Hemingford Grey, St. Ives, Hunts. 1929. † NG 2, RA 5, RI 2.

HAYWARD, Emily L. Exh. 1887
Portrait artist. 64 Charlotte Street, Fitzroy Square, London. † RA 1.

HAYWARD, Gerald S. Exh. 1880-82
Miniature portrait painter. Holly Village, Highgate, London. † B 2, RA 4.

HAYWARD, Johnson Exh. 1911-25
Flower painter. Godalming, Surrey † BG 3, GI 1, GOU 1, L 5, RA 1, RCA 2, RHA 2, ROI 8, RSA 1.

HAYWARD, Kate Louise Exh. 1887-88
Flower and architectural painter. Highfield House, Wellingore, Grantham, Lincs. † N 4.

HAYWARD, Lucy F. Exh. 1891-1916
Mrs. Pearson H. Miniature and animal painter. Add: Exeter 1891; Teignmouth, Devon 1905. † B 2, L 6, LS 11, RHA 12.

HAYWARD, Mrs. Margaret I'Anson
See I'ANSON

HAYWOOD, Ann Exh. 1931-38
Landscape painter, etcher, designer and teacher. Studied Cheltenham School of Art and Royal College of Art. Add: Farnham, Surrey. † L 1, RA 5, SWA 2.

HAYWOOD, Mrs. Emma Exh. 1885-86
Portrait and landscape painter. 14 The Avenue, Gipsy Hill, London. † RI 1, SWA 1.

HAYWOOD, Emily F. Exh. 1899-1914
Figure and domestic painter. A.N.S.A. 1908. Add: Shrewsbury House, Alexandra Park, Nottingham. † N 8.

HAYWOOD, George Exh. 1904
Portrait painter. Royal College of Art, South Kensington, London. † RA 1.

HAYWOOD, Julia Exh. 1900-1
40 South Street, Park Lane, London. † RI 2, ROI 1.

HAYWOOD, Lily Exh. 1902-5
8 Cottesmore Gardens, Kensington. London. † B 4, L 6, RA 1.

HAYWOOD, Lucretia Exh. 1938
Miniature portrait painter. London Road, Cheltenham, Glos. † RA 1.

HAYWOOD, Leslie S. Exh. 1923-34
Landscape painter. Brighouse, Yorks 1923; Wembley, Middlesex 1934. † L 1, RA 1.

HAYWOOD, W. Exh. 1908-15
Architect. Birmingham. † RA 4.

HAYWORTH, C.S. Exh. 1913
School of Art, Lincoln. † N 2.

HAZARD, Hortense Exh. 1880
Sculptor. Berners Hotel, Berners Street, London. † RBA 1.

HAZARD, Rhona Exh. 1928-30
Linocut artist. Aisne, France. † RED 1, SWA 1.

HAZEL, John T. Exh. 1937
10 Forth Street, Edinburgh. † RSW 1.

HAZELDINE, Miss A. Exh. 1905
Barnfield, Blindley Heath, Surrey. † RA 1.

HAZELDINE, Alfred Exh. 1908-14
7 Avenue de Saturne, Mele, Brussels. † LS 11.

HAZELL, W. Ernest Exh. 1901-19
Architect. 5 Tavistock Square, London. † RA 7.

HAZLEDINE, Charles Henry Exh. 1881-82
Landscape and coastal painter. 8A Holden Street, Radford, Notts. † N 3.

HAZZLEDINE, Margaret R. Exh. 1891
Flower painter. 9 Watcombe Circus, Carrington, Notts. † N 2.

HEAD, Arthur William b. 1861
Landscape, still life and flower painter. Studied under E.H. Holder and at Royal College of Art. Teacher of the drawing and painting of diseases of human eyes for the medical profession. Exh. 1886-1926. Add: London. † L 1, RA 4, RBA 2, RI 1, RMS 1.

HEAD, B.G.* Exh. 1880-90
Figure painter. London. † B 5, L 1, RA 2, RBA 7, ROI 2.

HEAD, Edward Joseph b. 1863
Still life, figure and landscape painter and teacher. Studied Regent Street Polytechnic and Scarborough School of Art. Exh. 1889-1929. Add: Scarborough, Yorks. 1889; London 1893 and 1916; Tenby, S. Wales 1895. † L 5, RA 18, RBA 3.

HEAD, Miss M. Exh. 1913-14
London. † SWA 2.

HEAD, Timothy J. Exh. 1895
Landscape painter. Arundel House, Worcester Park, Surrey. † RA1.

HEADE, Reginald C.W. Exh. 1932-33
Watercolour painter and chalk artist. 433 Strand, London. † RA 1, RI 2.

HEADLAM, Mrs. Horace (Mary) Exh. 1911-40
Painter and illustrator. London. † NEA 4, RA 1.

HEADLAND, Margaret Exh. 1887-92
Flower painter. London. † M 1, RA 4, ROI 5.

HEADLEY, Lorenzo Headley b. 1860
Flower painter. Exh. 1889-1930. Add: Birmingham 1889; Stoke Prior, Bromsgrove 1902. † B 17.

HEAL, Albert V. Exh. 1926
Architect. 11 Gray's Inn Square, London. † RA 1.

HEALD, Josephine Exh. 1927
3 Marine Park Mansions, Wallasey, Cheshire. † L 1.

HEALEY, Arthur Exh. 1928
3 Noel Street, Derby. † NEA 1.

HEALEY, Alfred J. Exh. 1928-29
Architect. 9 Gray's Inn Square, London. † RA 3.

HEALEY, Col. Charles Exh. 1917-39
Watercolour painter. Preston Leys, Bishop's Stortford, Herts. † AR 2, COO 2, RA 1, WG 72.

HEALEY, C.E.H. Exh. 1890
119 Harley Street, London. † RBA 1.

HEALEY, G.F.W. Exh. 1932-35
Watercolour landscape painter. Steep Acre Farm, Chobham, Surrey. † COO 2, RI 6.

HEALEY, William T.J. Exh. 1923-28
Watercolour painter. 50 Thorney Edge Road, Gunnersbury, London. † RI 4.

HEALY, George Peter Alexander* Exh. 1883
Portrait painter. 64 Rue de la Rochefoucauld, Paris. † RA 2.

HEALY, Henrietta Exh. 1924-30
Landscape and architectural painter. Dublin. † RHA 5.

HEALY, Henry Exh. 1938-40
Landscape painter. 4 Thomas Davis Street, Dublin. † RHA 7.

HEALY, John Exh. 1903
13 Adelaide Road, Kensington, Liverpool. † L 1.

HEALY, M. Exh. 1912-14
41 Heytesbury Street, Dublin. † RHA 14.

HEANEY, Alexander J. Exh. 1914-29
Etcher. 13 Downend Road, Fishponds, Bristol. † L 2, RA 7.

HEANLY, Mildred Exh. 1900-34
Miniature painter and pastellier. Studied under Mrs. Louise Jopling and Alexander Jamieson and at University College, Reading. Visited India in 1913 and returned in 1923 to teach art. † P 1, WG 48.

HEAP, Amy E. Exh. 1938
† M 1.

HEAPHY, Archibald C. Exh. 1881-82
Figure painter. Crowthorne, Nr. Wokingham, Berks. 1881; Chelsea, London 1882. † L 1, RBA 1.

HEAPHY, Theodosia Exh. 1883-85
Flower and figure painter. Chelsea, London. † RBA 4, SWA 1.

HEAPS, J.L. Exh. 1897-1901
Long Eaton, Notts. † N 3.

HEAPS, Maud D. Exh. 1913-14
Ben Rhydding, Ilkley, Yorks. † LS 6.

HEARD, Hugh Percy Exh. 1886-1914
Swansea 1886 and 1892; Bideford, Devon 1891, 1896 and 1914, London 1903. † D 2, L 12, RA 2, RBA 2.

HEARD, Jacqueline Exh. 1934
Bridgend, Glam. † RCA 1.

HEARD, Mrs. Marina Mikhaliovna b. 1902
Miniature portrait painter. b. Kiev, Russia. Daughter of H.E. Mous. Mikhail Soukovkine, Chamberlain to H.I.M. Emperor Nicholas II. Studied Paris. Exh. 1931-38. Add: Icklesham, Sussex 1931; Bristol 1938. † RA 2.

HEARD, Nathaniel b. 1872
Landscape and figure painter. b. Holsworthy, Devon. Studied Royal College of Art for 6 years. Headmaster Bath School of Arts and Crafts, Lucknow, India. Established Museum of Arts and Crafts at Lucknow. Exh. 1903. Add: Shipley, Yorks. † B 1.

HEARD, W.C. Exh. 1928
44 Benedict Street, Bootle, Lancs. † L 1.

HEARDEN, Mrs. S.A. Exh. 1881-84
Landscape painter. 6 Douglas Terrace, Broughty Ferry, N.B. † RSA 1, SWA 1.

HEARN, George R.M. Exh. 1900-2
8 Camden Studios, Camden Street, London. † RHA 2.

HEARN, Miss H.M. Exh. 1886-88
Strathmore Lodge, Bush Hill Park, Enfield, Middlesex. † RHA 4.

HEARN, Ila Exh. 1923-28
Pen artist. Croydon, Surrey 1923; London 1927. † L 2, RA 1.

HEARN, Margaret Frances Exh. 1916-18
Heasley, Leawood Road, Bournemouth. † L 1, RA 1.

HEARN, R.F.S. Exh. 1884-86
London 1884; Strathmore Lodge, Bush Hill Park, Enfield, Middlesex 1885. † RHA 4.

HEARN, Victor Exh. 1937-40
Landscape painter. 83 Woodhurst Avenue, Petts Wood, Kent. † RA 2.

HEARNE, Mrs. M.J. Exh. 1897
465 Kinsland Road, London. † RHA 1.

HEASMAN, Ernest Exh. 1896
Decorative designer. 54 Upper Marylebone Street, London. † RA 1.

HEASON, Arthur J. Exh. 1927
Stained glass artist. 10 Flintham Drive, Sherwood, Nottingham. † N 2.

HEASON, Jessie E. Exh. 1937-39
Mrs. G. McIntyre. Figure and animal painter. Add: 634 Wollaton Road, Wollaton, Nottingham. † N 5.

HEATH, Miss Exh. 1884-89
Landscape and architectural painter. The Firs, Clay Hill, Enfield, Middlesex. † SWA 2.

HEATH, A.H. Exh. 1916
The Grange, Whitchurch, Aylesbury, Bucks. † RI 1.

HEATH, Barbara Exh. 1927-28
Textile designer and decorative painter. Studied Woolwich Polytechnic and Victoria and Albert Museum. Add: 194 Greenvale Road, London. † L 4.

HEATH, Cicely Exh. 1907-8
† RMS 2.

HEATH, Ernest Dudley Exh. 1886-1922
Painter and illustrator. Son of Henry Charles and brother of Lionel H. q.v. Studied R.A. Schools. Lecturer on art, University of London Extension 1903-8. Principal, Hampstead Garden Suburb School of Arts and Crafts 1914-26. Lecturer on Principles of Art Teaching, Royal College of Art 1927. † L 6, M 1, RA 12, RBA 2, RMS 1, ROI 4.

HEATH, Miss E.F. Exh. 1890-97
25 Hyde Park Place, London. † SWA 9.

HEATH, Ellen Maurice Exh. 1897-1914
Landscape and coastal painter. 24 Park Dwellings, Hampstead, London. † GOU 75, LS 6, NEA 1, P 4, WG 55.

HEATH, Frank Gascoigne 1873-1936
Landscape and figure painter. b. Purley, Surrey. Studied South Kensington, Croydon, Westminster, Antwerp and Bushey. Served with Royal Fusiliers World War I. Exh. 1899-1935. Add: Newlyn, Penzance, Cornwall 1899; St. Buryan, Cornwall 1912. † I 3, L 14, M 1, NG 1, RA 26, ROI 6.

HEATH, Henry Charles d. c.1898
Miniature painter to Queen Victoria. Father of Ernest Dudley and Lionel H. q.v. Add: London. † B 1, L 4, M 3, RA 67, RHA 1, RI 2, RMS 4.

HEATH, Mrs, Ivor Exh. 1933-38
Cardiff, Wales. † RCA 3.

HEATH, John C.W. Exh. 1940
Etcher. Redcliffe Gardens, London. † RA 2.

HEATH, Lionel b. 1871
Portrait, landscape and miniature painter. Son of Henry Charles and brother of Ernest Dudley H. q.v. Married Maggie F.H. q.v. Studied West London School of Art and Regent Street Polytechnic School of Art. Principal Mayo School of Arts, Lahore and Curator Central Museum Lahore, India. R.M.S. 1897. Exh. 1892-1933. Add: London 1892; Walton-on-Thames, Surrey 1932. † D 2, L 6, M 7, NG 3, RA 47, RMS 78.

HEATH, Marjorie Exh. 1931-35
Portrait painter. West Harrow, Middlesex 1931; Hampstead, London 1935. † RA 2, ROI 1.

HEATH, Maurice Exh. 1923-35
Watercolour and portrait painter. 39 Mexfield Road, East Putney, London. † RA 5, RI 6.

HEATH, Margaret A. Exh. 1886-1914
Figure, domestic and miniature painter. R.M.S. 1896, A.S.W.A. 1902. Add: Manchester 1886; London 1894. † B 3, D 4, L 26, M 4, RA 16, RI 9, RMS 4, ROI 2, SWA 25.

HEATH, Maggie Forsyth Exh. 1907-9
nee Forsyth. Miniature painter. m. Lionel H. q.v. Add: 40 Norland Square, Holland Park, London. † RA 2, RMS 3.

HEATH, Thomas Hastead Exh. 1901-5
Portrait and figure painter. 53 Park Place, Cardiff, Wales. † L 1, RA 3.

HEATH, T.J. Exh. 1883
1 Hatherley Street, Liverpool. † L 1.

HEATH, William Exh. 1899
137 Clapham Road, London. † RBA 1.

HEATH, Mrs. W. Bayley Exh. 1881-90
Landscape and coastal painter. 1 Ilchester Gardens, London. † SWA 8.

HEATHCOTE, Mrs. A. Exh. 1911
Landscape painter. † ALP 2.

HEATHCOTE, Charles H. Exh. 1897
Architect. 6 Princess Street, Manchester. † RA 1.

HEATHCOTE, D.H. Exh. 1896-98
Wollaton, Nr. Nottingham. † N 5.

HEATHCOTE, Mrs. Evelyn Exh. 1880-1904
Watercolour painter and illustrator. Winchester 1883 and 1904; Oxford 1895; London 1896. † D 57, FIN 46, L 1, RI 3, SWA 5.

HEATHCOTE, Fred Exh. 1921-23
22 Arden Road, Birchfield, Birmingham. † B 3.

HEATHCOTE, Freda M. Exh. 1928-39
Landscape and figure painter. Newstead Colliery, Nr. Nottingham 1928; Linby, Nr. Nottingham 1936. † N 8.

HEATHCOTE, Henry A.Y. Exh. 1910
47 Barton Street, West Kensington, London. † LS 3.

HEATHCOTE, Lucy Helena Exh. 1937
Sculptor. 28 Argyll Road, London. † GI 1, RA 1.

HEATHCOTE, Mrs. Margaret Exh. 1880-1913
Watercolour landscape painter. Borodale Gates, Keswick 1880; London 1887. † ALP 1, D 5, SWA 1.

HEATHER, Miss B. Exh. 1885
Rich Terrace, Rusholme, Manchester. † M 1.

HEATHER, Medora Exh. 1931
† NEA 1.

HEATHER, Naomi H. Exh. 1940
Figure painter. Lisduggan Lodge, Waterford. † RHA 2.

HEATHERELL, Jessie Exh. 1887
Marylea, Bearsden, Glasgow. † GI 2.

HEATHERINGTON-BROMILOW, W. Exh. 1912-14
Crouch End, London. † LS 9.

HEATLEY, Lilian Exh. 1904-35
Watercolour painter. Married Harold Swanwick, q.v. Add: Winsford, Cheshire 1904; Middlewich, Cheshire 1907; Polegate, Sussex 1911. † B 1, L 15, RA 1, RCA 27, RI 11.

HEATLIE, William Exh. 1881-90
Cloister Cottage, Melrose. † RSA 11.

HEATON, Ada Exh. 1892
230 St. Andrew's Road, Smallheath, Birmingham. † B 2.

HEATON, Augustus Goodyear 1844-1930
American artist. Exh. 1913-17. Add: Carnegie Hall, New York City, U.S.A. † LS 8.

HEATON, Angela M. Exh. 1940
Sculptor. Chipping Camden, Glos. † GI 1, RA 1.

HEATON, Clement Exh. 1892-1911
Landscape painter, and stained glass artist. 33 Langham Street, London 1892; Watford, Herts. 1894. † ALP 7, RA 3.

HEATON, Dorothy Aspen Exh. 1897
Pinner, Middlesex. † SWA 1.

HEATON, Miss G. Exh. 1928
19 Lenton Road, The Park, Nottingham. † N 3.

HEATON, Hon. Lady Henniker Exh. 1924
87 Cadogan Gardens, London. † RI 4.

HEATON, John Exh. 1884-90
Watercolour landscape painter. Park Cottage, Datchett, Bucks. † M 1, RI 1.

HEATON, J.A. Exh. 1888
Decorative painter. 26 Charlotte Street, Bedford Square, London. † L 1, RA 3.

HEATON, J.M. Exh. 1906
† P 1.

HEATON, Miss L.P. Exh. 1908-11
Watercolour painter. Park Cottage, Datchett, Bucks. † RI 3.

HEATON, Miss M. Exh. 1914
Sheffield. † SWA 1.

HEATON, Margaret Exh. 1923
19 Lenton Road, Nottingham. † N 2.

HEATON, Monica Exh. 1881
Portrait painter. 29 Bloomsbury Square, London. † RA 2.

HEATON, T.M. Exh. 1906
103 Cavendish Street, Keighley, Yorks. † L 2, RA 2.

HEAVEN, Margaret F. Exh. 1923-29
Landscape and architectural painter. Ealing, London. † NEA 1, RA 3.

HEAVISIDE, Frederick Exh. 1911-15
27 Torwood Street, Torquay, Devon. † L 1, LS 2, RHA 4.

HEBBERD, Mrs. Stanley Exh. 1900
Moreton, Dorset. † SWA 1.

HEBBERT, Mrs. J.C. Exh. 1898-1925
London. † B 2, GI 1, I 1, L 7, LS 26, RHA 1, ROI 6, SWA 16.

HEBDEN, Donovan b. 1893
Watercolour painter, poster designer, etcher and wood engraver. b. Yorkshire. Exh. 1929-33. Add: Leigh-on-Sea, Essex. † RA 5, RBA 1, RI 1.

HEBELER, Miss P.M. Exh. 1928-29
60 Castle Street, Edinburgh. † RSA 3.

HEBNER, Frederick Exh. 1913-14
Probus Villa, Clyde Terrace, Marine Town, Sheerness, Kent. † LS 5.

HECHLE, George Exh. 1910-11
38 Linwood Road, Higher Tranmere, Cheshire. † L 3.

HECHLE, Hilda Exh. 1902-38
Painter and illustrator. b. Brassington Hall, Derbys. Studied St. John's Wood and R.A. Schools. A.R.B.A. 1924, R.B.A. 1926, S.W.A. 1929. Add: Colwyn Bay, Wales 1902; London 1913. † ALP 12, COO 9, G 4, GI 2, L 9, RA 8, RBA 96, RCA 2, RI 1, SWA 35.

HECHT, Van der See V

HECHT, Wilhelm Exh. 1883
Etcher. 32 Briennerstrasse, Munich. † RA 2.

HECTOR, Gertrude Mary b. 1888
Designer and craft worker. b. Calcutta, India. Studied Gray's School of Art, Aberdeen and Battersea Art School. Exh. 1916-22. Add: Aberdeen. † L 2, RSA 2.

HECTOR, James A.H. Exh. 1894-1938
Landscape painter. Aberdeen. † GI 9, L 8, RA 2, RSA 24.

HECTOR, Mary Exh. 1896-1908
London. † B 1, L 2, LS 3, RBA 8, RHA 1, SWA 2.

HECTOR, W. Cunningham Exh. 1900-9
164 Bath Street, Glasgow. † GI 11, L 2, RSA 1.

HEDDEGHEM, Van See V

HEDDERLY, Alice N. Exh. 1890-91
Watercolour bird painter. Bulcote, Burton Joyce, Notts. † N 2.

HEDDERWICK, Percy D. Exh. 1880
26 Newton Place, Glasgow. † GI 2.

HEDGER, Ruth Exh. 1932-38
Malton, Yorks. 1932; Goatland, Yorks. 1936. † M 4, RSA 8.

HEDGES, Florence Exh. 1903-21
Sculptor. 130 Elm Park Mansions, Chelsea, London. † GI 1, RA 4, ROI 1.

HEDLEY, Percival Exh. 1905-8
London. † GI 1, L 1, RA 1, RHA 1, RMS 1, RSA 1.

HEDLEY, Ralph* 1851-1913
Genre painter. b. Richmond, Yorks. Studied Newcastle Art School. R.B.A. 1899. Add: 11 New Bridge Street, Newcastle-on-Tyne. † B 2, L 11, M 2, RA 51, RBA 30, RI 10, RSA 5.

HEELEY, Arthur Exh. 1895-97
Leicester 1895, Bude, Cornwall 1896. † L 1, RHA 2, RI 1, ROI 3.

HEEMSKERCK, Van See V

HEFFER, Edward A. Exh. 1885-88
Decorative designer. 6 Victoria Road, Kilburn, London. † L 3, RA 1.

HEFFNER, Karl* b. 1849
German landscape painter. Exh. 1880-88. Add: London. † G 1, GI 1, RA 2.

HEGERTY, Mary Exh. 1890
Egremont, Cheshire. † GI 1.

HEGG, Mme. Teresa 1829-1911
Watercolour flower painter. R.I. 1886. Add: Nice, France 1881; Cannes, France 1890. † BG 1, D 1, RI 49, SWA 9.

HEGGS, W.H. Exh. 1904
Landscape painter. 54 Balfour Road, Nottingham. † N 3.

HEIMAN, Sam Isaac b. 1896
Calligrapher, illuminator, etcher and silversmith. b. Bangor, N. Wales. Studied Royal College of Art and Liverpool School of Art. Exh. 1921-25. Add: 17 Verulam Street, Upper Parliament Street, Liverpool. † L 7.

HEINEMANN, Miss E.J. Exh. 1888
10 Lancaster Gate, London. † B 1.

HEINISCH, C. Exh. 1883
† GI 1.

HEINITZ, Miss A. Exh. 1896-97
99 Charlton Lane, Charlton, Kent. † RBA 2.

HEINTZELMANN, Arthur William b. 1892
American etcher. Exh. 1926-29. † CON 1, FIN 22.

HEITLAND, Mrs. H. Exh. 1892-93
Amberley Art Studios, Crouch Hill, London. † RI 2.

HEITLAND, Miss Ivy Exh. 1894
Amberley Studios, Crouch Hill, London. † RI 1.

HEITLAND, J. Exh. 1893
Amberley Studios, Crouch Hill, London. † RI 1.

HEITLAND, Miss Violet Exh. 1894
Amberley Studios, Crouch Hill, London. † RI 1.

HEITON, Andrew G. Exh. 1884-1909
Architect. 72 George Street, Perth and Darnick, Perth. N.B. † GI 4, RA 1, RSA 5.

HELCK, Peter Exh. 1923
Landscape painter. 5 Brook Green Studios, Dunsany Road, London. † RA 1.

HELCKE, Arnold* Exh. 1880-1911
Landscape and marine painter. R.B.A. 1896. Add: East Molesey, Surrey and Portland Place, London 1880, Herne Bay, Kent 1907. † B 20, D 7, G 8, GI 1, L 18, M 16, NG 15, RA 23, RBA 38, RHA 4, RI 5, ROI 22.

HELCKE, Laura Exh. 1888-90
Cromwell House, Suffolk Road, Bournemouth. † D 1, ROI 1.

HELEY, Joan Exh. 1939-40
c/o Heatherley School of Art, 9 George Street, Baker Street, London. † NEA 1, RBA 1, SWA 1.

HELFRICHT, Emil Exh. 1883
Medalist. 89 Gt. Portland Street, London. † RA 1.

HELION, Joan* b. 1904
French painter. Exh. 1936. † LEF 3.

HELLABY, Richard Sydney b. 1887
Landscape and portrait painter. b. Aukland, New Zealand. Studied Lambeth School of Art, Juliens and Ecole des Beaux Arts, Paris. Exh. 1920-38. Add: London. † GOU 20, I 1, L 1, RA 6, RI 1, ROI 4, WG 58.

HELLEU, Paul Cesar* 1859-1927
Etcher and portrait artist. A.R.E. 1892, R.E. 1897. Exh. 1892-1908. Add: Paris. † L 2, P 1, RE 111.

HELLICAR, Evelyn A. Exh. 1891-1909
Architect. London. † RA 6.

HELLIER, Mrs. G.S. Exh. 1907-8
Thornedene, Homesdale Road, Bromley, Kent. † RA 2.

HELLMER, H.C. Exh. 1910-11
22 St. Anne's Villas, Kensington, London. † L 2, RA 2.

HELLWAG, Rudolph* b. 1867
German landscape painter. Exh. 1901-10. Add: St. Ives, Cornwall 1901; Kensington, London 1903. † GI 1, I 4, M 1, NEA 4, RA 1.

HELMICK, Howard* 1845-1907
American figure painter. R.B.A. 1879, R.E. 1881. Exh. 1880-89. Add: London. † B 1, GI 1, L 3, M 7, RA 9, RBA 8, RE 2, RHA 1, ROI 2.

HELMORE, Rev. Thomas Exh. 1885
Watercolour landscape painter. 72 St. George's Square, London. † RI 1.

HELPS, Bettie Exh. 1936-38
c/o Francis Helps, 13 Holford Square, London 1936; Chelsea, London 1938. † GI 1, RBA 2.

HELPS, Francis Exh. 1910-40
Portrait, figure and landscape painter. A.R.B.A. 1923, R.B.A. 1933. Add: London. † ALP 60, BA 6, I 2, NEA 4, RA 3, RBA 43.

HELSBY, Alfred Exh. 1907-8
Landscape painter. Paris 1907; Acton, London 1908. † BK 100, D 3, RA 1.

HELSBY, Mary Esther Exh. 1909-14
London. † LS 13.

HEM, de See D

HEMING, Richard Exh. 1894
16 Brandon Terrace, Cheltenham, Glos. † B 1.

HEMINGS, Frederick Exh. 1888-89
Architect. 7 Fenchurch Street, London. † RA 3.

HEMINGWAY, A. Exh. 1884
Architectural painter. Rosenstein Villa, Roehampton. † RA 1.

HEMINGWAY, Charles W Exh. 1932-37
Portrait painter. Aberdeen. † GI 2, RA 2, RSA 4.

HEMINGWAY, H. Exh. 1932
† L 1.

HEMM, Gordon d. 1956
Architect and architectural artist. School of Art, Hope St. Liverpool 1920; Mamchester 1940. † L 2, RA 1.

HEMMEL, G. Henry Exh. 1885-1908
Redditch, Worcs. 1885; Cheltenham, Glos. 1890; Langport, Somerset 1891. † B 11, L 10.

HEMMERLE, Alma Exh. 1923-24
† SWA 2.

HEMMING, Alfred Charles Exh. 1927-33
Cardiff, Wales. † M 2, RCA 2.

HEMMING, Alfred O. Exh. 1889-94
Stained glass artist. 47 Margaret Street, Cavendish Square, London. † RA 5.

HEMMING, C.J. Exh. 1882-1910
Birmingham. † B 12, RCA 1.

HEMMING, Edith Exh. 1904-11
Miniature portrait painter. London 1904, Dollar, N.B. 1907. † GI 7, L 6, RA 3, RSA 4.

HEMMING, Fanny Exh. 1885
Landscape painter. 87 Lancaster Gate, Hyde Park, London. † RA 1.

HEMMING, G.P. Exh. 1911
Hill Crest, Willingdon, Sussex. † B 1.

HEMMING, Mary T. Exh. 1885-96
Holme Lodge, Edgbaston, Birmingham. † B 9.

HEMSLEY, H.L. Exh. 1922
159 Musters Road, West Bridgeford, Nottingham. † N 5.

HEMSLEY, Hugh S. Exh. 1906-20
Landscape painter. The Glebelands, Headingley, Leeds. † RA 3.

HEMSLEY, William* 1819-1906
Genre painter. Self taught. R.B.A. 1859. Add: London. † B 16, L 6, M 5, RBA 76, RI 1, ROI 3, TOO 1.

HEMSLEY-THOMPSON, B. Exh. 1936
† NEA 1.

HEMSTED, E. Exh. 1896
c/o Mr. Soar, 1 Sussex Villas, Kensington, London. † ROI 2.

HEMY, Charles Napier* 1841-1917
Landscape and marine painter. Brother of Thomas M.M.H. q.v. Studied Newcastle Art School and Antwerp. A.R.A. 1898, R.A. 1910, R.I. 1884, R.O.I. 1885, A.R.W.S. 1890, R.W.S. 1897. "Pilchards" purchased by Chantrey Bequest 1897 and "London River" in 1904. Add: London 1880; Falmouth, Cornwall 1883. † AG 4, B 22, CAR 2, CON 1, D 2, FIN 1, G 27, GI 23, L 72, M 27, NG 36, RA 126, RCA 5, RHA 1, RI 5, ROI 10, RSA 1, RSW 2, RWS 88, TOO 2.

HEMY, Miss G. Exh. 1905-11
Mrs. Harold de Brath. Daughter of Thomas M.M.H. q.v. Add: London. † RA 2.

HEMY, J. Exh. 1882
High Coniscliffe, Nr. Darlington, Co. Durham. † L 1.

HEMY, P. Napier Exh. 1909-12
Architect. London. † RA 2.

HEMY, Thomas Marie Madawaska 1852-1937
Marine painter. Brother of Charles Napier and father of Miss G.H. q.v. Studied Newcastle Art School and under Verlat in Antwerp. Add: Eske Village, Nr. Durham 1880; London 1883. † B 6, D 2, DOW 1, G 4, GI 6, L 13, M 11, RA 22, RBA 2, RI 15, ROI 9.

HENDERSON, A. Exh. 1888
c/o Miss Stringer, 5 Kensington Park Road, London. † RI 1.

HENDERSON, Anne Exh. 1935-38
Linocut artist. North House, Bearsden, Glasgow. † RED 1, RSA 1.

HENDERSON, Mrs. A.C. Exh. 1888-89
Glasgow 1888; Shandon, Dumbartonshire 1889. † GI 2.

HENDERSON, A. Dorothy Exh. 1905
1 Lansdowne Terrace, Eastbourne. † RSA 1.

HENDERSON, Arthur Edward 1870-1956
Architect and painter. b. Aberdeen. Studied A.A. (bronze medal) and City and Guilds (silver medal); R.I.B.A. Owen Jones travelling studentship; British School at Athens; architect to the British Museum excavations at the Temple of Diana, Ephesus (1905-6). R.B.A. 1902. Add: London 1897 and 1907; Constantinople 1901; Crawley Down, Sussex 1938. † L 3, RA 6, RBA 123.

HENDERSON, A. Graham Exh. 1913-15
Glasgow. † GI 1, RSA 1.

HENDERSON, Mrs. Ann H. Exh. 1934-40
Watercolour painter. Beechwood, Merstham, Surrey. † RA 1, RI 8.

HENDERSON, A.J. Exh. 1889
20 Haddington Place, Edinburgh. † RSA 1.

HENDERSON, A.R. Exh. 1880-95
Glasgow. † GI 15, RSA 4.

HENDERSON, Miss A.S. Exh. 1931-32
Pembridge Gardens Hotel, London. † RI 2.

HENDERSON, Betty Exh. 1924
Sandon Studios, School Lane, Liverpool. † L 3.

HENDERSON, Catherine Exh. 1881-89
17 Belhaven Terrace, Glasgow. † GI 7.

HENDERSON, Dorothea Exh. 1926-31
Watercolour painter. Kenilworth Road, Leamington Spa, Warwicks. † B 7, WG 35.

HENDERSON, Elsie Marion b. 1880
Sculptor, lithographer, charcoal and pencil artist. b. Sussex. Studied Slade School 1903-4 and London Zoological Gardens. Worked for a while in France. Exh. 1902-38. Add: Liverpool 1902; Guernsey, C.I. 1913; London 1922. † G 1, GI 4, GOU 7, I 3, L 2, LEI 49, LS 9, M 1, NEA 7, RA 11, RED 55, RSA 1, SWA 2.

HENDERSON, Miss E.R. Exh. 1925-26
60 Bessborough Road, Harrow, Middlesex. † L 5.

HENDERSON, George L. Exh. 1890
Etcher. 32 King Street, Cheapside, London. † RA 1.

HENDERSON, Hilda Exh. 1921-23
† GOU 3.

HENDERSON, Irene Exh. 1910-12
Chisholme, Hawick, Roxburghshire. † L 4.

HENDERSON, James Exh. 1880-90
47 Gt. King Street, Edinburgh. † L 1, RSA 5.

HENDERSON, James Exh. 1934-39
Edinburgh 1934; Galashiels 1937. † RSA 3.

HENDERSON, James Exh. 1908-9
8 Fitzroy Street, London. † LS 8.

HENDERSON, John d. c. 1924
Probably son of Joseph H. q.v. Exh. 1884-1924 Glasgow. † GI 101, L 5, M 6, RSA 47, RSW 3.

HENDERSON, Joseph* 1832-1908
Landscape, portrait, genre and coastal painter. Studied Trustees Academy, Edinburgh. Father of Joseph Morris H. q.v. and probably father of John H. q.v. A.R.S.W. 1878, R.S.W. 1906. Add: Glasgow. † GI 70, L 3, M 4, RA 8, RBA 4, RI 1, RSA 25, RSW 47, TOO 3.

HENDERSON, J.C. Exh. 1881
21 St. Andrew Square, Edinburgh. † GI 2, RSA 1.

HENDERSON, J.D. Exh. 1891
Fetcham, Leatherhead, Surrey. † D 1.

HENDERSON, J.L. Exh. 1881
113 Gloucester Terrace, Hyde Park, London. † RSA 1.

HENDERSON, Joseph Morris* 1863-1936
Landscape painter. Son of Joseph H. q.v. Studied Glasgow School of Art. A.R.S.A. 1928 R.S.A. 1936. Add: Glasgow 1889; Busby, Lanarks. 1930. † GI 129, L 8, M 6, NG 1, RA 5, RSA 80, RSW 3.

HENDERSON, Keith b. 1883
Landscape and figure painter and illustrator. Studied Slade School and Paris. R.O.I. 1934, R.P. 1912, A.R.S.W. 1930, A.R.W.S. 1930, R.W.S. 1937. Add: London 1904 and 1930; Burleigh, Glos. 1920; Fort William, Inverness 1934; Spean Bridge, Inverness 1939. † B 2, BA 50, BG 27, CHE 2, FIN 104, GI 5, L 13, NEA 7, NG 2, P 21, RA 27, ROI 20, RSA 10, RSW 18, RWS 83.

HENDERSON, Katherine Elizabeth Exh. 1930
21 Rue Paul Berb, Paris. † NEA 1.

HENDERSON, Katharine G. Exh. 1927-39
Applethwaite Lodge, Windermere. † L 2, RMS 4.

HENDERSON, Matthew Exh. 1919-33
Etcher and dry point artist. Glasgow. † GI 10, L 7, RSA 6.

HENDERSON, Madge Exh. 1930-32
North Court, Leamington Spa, Warwicks. † B 2.

HENDERSON, Maud Exh. 1905-27
Figure, landscape and flower painter. London. † BG 21, L 3, RA 2.

HENDERSON, M.A. Exh. 1894
Towerville, Helensburgh. † GI 1.

HENDERSON, M. Beatrice Exh. 1900-05
Bushey, Herts. 1900; Edinburgh 1904; London 1905. † GI 1, RA 1, RSA 6, SWA 1.

HENDERSON, M. Eadie Exh. 1893-94
19 Elmbank Place, Glasgow. † GI 2.

HENDERSON, Mrs. M.H. Exh. 1889
Flower painter. Skipton in Craven, Yorks. † SWA 1.

HENDERSON, Mary Reid Exh. 1909-35
Painter, etcher, illuminator, enameller, embroiderer and metal worker. Studied Glasgow School of Art. Teacher at embroidery continuation classes at Motherwell Technical School. Formerly head teacher of art at Helensburgh and teacher of drawing and metalwork at Stirling. Add: Glasgow. † GI 12, L 5, RSA 4.

HENDERSON, Margaret T. Exh. 1900
19 Princes Square, Strathbungo, N.B. † GI 1.

HENDERSON, Peter L. Exh. 1901
122 George Street, Edinburgh. † RSA 1.

HENDERSON, Ralph Exh. 1911-32
Glasgow 1911; Bootle, Liverpool 1913; Greenock 1929. † GI 4, L 3.

HENDERSON, Robert d. 1904
Miniature painter. Exh. 1883-95. London. † RA 61.

HENDERSON, Richard G. Exh. 1897
345 New City Road, Glasgow. † GI 1.

HENDERSON, Sheila Scott b. 1910
Portrait painter. Studied at the Spenlove School of Painting 1930-35. Exh. 1936-40. Add: The Grange, Walton on the Hill, Tadworth, Surrey. † BK 26, NEA 2, P 2, RA 1, RBA 2, RCA 3, ROI 5, RSA 2.

HENDERSON, Mrs. Violet Exh. 1933-35
Wallington, Surrey 1933; London 1935. † RI 4.

HENDERSON, W. Exh. 1880-81
86 North Frederick Street, Glasgow. † GI 2, RSA 1.

HENDERSON, William Exh. 1880-94
Figure painter. Whitby, Yorks. 1880; Grosmont, Yorks. 1882; Goathland, Yorks. 1887. † B 3, GI 2, RBA 3, RSA 5, ROI 1.

HENDERSON, William Exh. 1886-1914
Mezzotint engraver. Bushey, Herts. 1886; London 1897; Birkenhead 1914. † FIN 2, L 1, RA 9.

HENDERSON, William Exh. 1935-40
Beechwood, Merstham, Surrey. † RI 2.

HENDERSON, W.H. Exh. 1933
The Studio, 11½ Broad Street, Nottingham. † N 1.

HENDLEY, G.E. Exh. 1886
Figure painter. Avondale, Bowes Park, London. † RBA 1.

HENDRIE, Herbert 1887-1946
Landscape painter and stained glass artist. b. Manchester. Studied Royal College of Art (1911) and Slade School. Head of Design School, Edinburgh from 1923. Add: London 1911; Edinburgh 1921. † G 3, GI 1, L 1, NEA 2, RA 17, RSA 2, RSW 4.

HENDRY, Arch Hunter b. 1890
Exh. 1931-32. 11 Leslie Road, Rosyth. † RSW 2.

HENDRY, George E. d. 1916
Landscape and portrait painter. Killed in Flanders, World War 1. Exh. 1901-14. Add: London. † B 1, BRU 17, L 2, LS 7, RA 2.

HENDRY, Miss M. M'Leod Exh. 1935-40
Married Neil Foggie q.v. Add: Edinburgh 1935; Dollar, Clackmannanshire 1939. † RSA 5.

HENDRY, William Exh. 1884
Burrell Square, Crieff. † GI 1.

HENDRY, W. Leslie Exh. 1928-33
21 Broomfield Lane, Hale, Cheshire. † L 6, RCA 3.

HENDY, Miss E.M. Exh. 1906-9
Bushey, Herts. 1906; Lamorna, Penzance 1907. † L 42.

HENEAGE, The Hon. Miss Adela Exh. 1904
Dainton Hall, Lincoln. † N 1.

HENEAGE, Miss E.M. Exh. 1896
The Priory, Old Windsor, Berks. † L 1, RI 1, SWA 2.

HENERSON, Eva M. Exh. 1937
Moor Park, Middlesex. † SWA 2.

HENGELER, Adolf C.* Exh. 1898-99
Arciostrasse 15, Munich. † GI 3.

HENKES, Gerke* Exh. 1883-86
Voorburg, nr. The Hague, Holland 1883; 117 New Bond Street, London 1886. † L 1, M 1, RI 3.

HENKLEY, Henry Exh. 1886
Haslemere, Cazenove Road, London. † RI 1.

HENLE, Paul W. Exh. 1940
Sculptor. Fairfax Road, London. † RA 1.

HENLEY, Alfred* Exh. 1888
Eton Wick, nr, Windsor, Berks. † B 1.

HENLEY, A.W. Exh. 1880-1908
Sherpherd's Bush, London 1880; 17 Brackenbury Road, Hammersmith, London 1905. † G 1, LS 5, RHA 1, RSA 2.

HENLEY, H.W. Exh. 1891-94
Birmingham. † B 3.

HENLEY, Lionel Charles* c.1843-c.1893
Genre painter. Studied in Dusseldorf. R.B.A. 1879. Add: London. † B 8, L 5, RA 3, RBA 95, ROI 4.

HENMAN, Charles Exh. 1892
Architect. 64 Cannon Street, London. † RA 1.

HENMAN, William Exh. 1893-95
Architect. 42 Cherry Street, Birmingham. † GI 1, RA 1.

HENN, Marion R. Exh. 1888-1901
Miniature portrait painter. Manchester 1888; Stockport 1889; London 1898. † B 1, L 3, RA 2, RI 1, RMS 1, SWA 3.

HENNAH, Joseph Edward b. 1897
Landscape and portrait painter and etcher. Exh. 1926-27. Add: 25 Morden Road, Newport, Mon. † RA 2.

HENNELL, Alexander R. Exh. 1900
Architect. 8/9 Essex Street, Strand, London. † RA 1.

HENNELL, Mrs. Harold Exh. 1900
Tenderfield, Forest Hill, London. † SWA 1.

HENNELL, Mrs. M. Exh. 1917
Children's Convalescent Home, Beaconsfield, Bucks. † RA 1.

HENNELL, S.T. Exh. 1914
443 Bank Chambers, High Holborn, London. † RA 1.

HENNELL, Thomas Barclay 1903-1945
Watercolour painter. b. Ridley, Kent. Studied Regent Street Polytechnic. A.R.W.S. 1938. Add: London 1925; Bath 1928; Wrotham, Kent 1938. † GOU 1, NEA 12, RA 4, RWS 27.

HENNEMAN, Valentin Exh. 1902-3
Assebrouck by Bruges, Belgium. † GI 2.

HENNES, Hubert b. 1907
Portrait painter. b. London. Studied at the Working Mens College, N.W. London (Lowes Dickinson travelling scholarship and silver medal 1925). Exh. 1939-40. Add: Leicester. † RA 2.

HENNESSY, Patrick Exh. 1939
Landscape painter. 9 Bridge Street, Arbroath. † RSA 2.

HENNESSY, William John* 1840-1917
Landscape and figure painter. R.O.I. 1902. Add: London 1880; France 1890; Brighton 1894. † B 2, G 19, GI 10, L 15, M 24, NEA 1, NG 21, P 1, RA 4, RHA 6, ROI 8.

HENNIKER, Annie L. Exh. 1897-1925
Figure and domestic painter. London. † B 1, L 2, RA 9, ROI 2.

HENNIKER, Mrs. R. Exh. 1940
172 Craigleith Road, Edinburgh. † RSW 2.

HENNING, Gerhard b. 1880
Swedish sculptor. Danasvej 18, Copenhagen 1934. † RSA 3.

HENNING, Mrs. Olive Cunningham Exh. 1933-38
Landscape and still life painter. Monkstown 1933; Upper Rathmines, Dublin 1938. † RHA 4.

HENNING, Walton G. Exh. 1886-87
Miniature portrait painter. 31 Westcroft Square, Hammersmith, London. † RA 3.

HENNINGSEN, Erik* Exh. 1904
Figure painter. 38 Hailsham Avenue, Streatham Hill, London. † RA 1.

HENRAUX, Mme. Bernieres Exh. 1905-6
60 Avenue Victor Hugo, Paris. † NG 2.

HENRI, Gervex Exh. 1907
12 Rue Roussel, Paris. † L 1.
HENRI, Lucien Exh. 1887
Flower painter. 185 Victoria Street, Sydney. † RA 1.
HENRICI, Maria Exh. 1887
Flower painter, 37 Ennismore Gardens, London. † SWA 1.
HENRIQUES, Ethel Quixano 1868-1936
Landscape, interior and still life painter. b. Manchester. Studied Slade School 1899 and under Bertram Priestman. Lived in London but travelled a few months each year visiting Italy, France, Sicily and various parts of England. † BA 1, CG 22, D 1, G 4, GI 1, GOU 17, I 15, L 10, LS 14, M 3, NEA 9, RA 4, RED 1, RI 5, ROI 27, RSA 1, SWA 7.
HENRIQUES, Rose L. Exh. 1937-40
Figure painter. The Settlement, Berners Street, London. † RA 1, RBA 6.
HENRY, Alice M. Exh. 1884-98
Edinburgh. † RSA 18.
HENRY, Barclay Exh. 1891-1940
Marine painter. Craigmill House, by Stirling 1891; Arrochar, Dumbartonshire 1892. † CON 2, GI 88, RA 1, RSW 2.
HENRY, E. Grace Exh. 1901-40
nee Mitchell, landscape and figure painter. Married Paul H. q.v. Add: London 1901 and 1910; Knapp Hill, Surrey 1904; Belfast 1913; Dublin 1930; Clondalkin 1934; Monkstown, Co. Dublin 1935. † COO 36, FIN 4, L 8, LEI 16, LS 8, RA 3, RHA 13, RMS 1.
HENRY, Edward Lamson* 1841-1919
American painter. 51 West Tenth Street, New York, U.S.A. 1882. † L 2.
HENRY, Francis A. Exh. 1883-87
Landscape and coastal painter. London. † RA 2, RBA 1.
HENRY, George* c. 1859-1943
Landscape, portrait and decorative painter. b. Ayrshire. Studied Glasgow School of Art 1882. Collaborated with E.A. Hornel q.v. and visited Japan with him in 1892. N.E.A. 1887, A.R.A. 1907, R.A. 1920, R.P. 1900, A.R.S.A. 1892, R.S.A. 1902, A.R.S.W. 1900-6. Add: Glasgow 1882; London 1904. † AG 1, G 1, GI 104, GOU 3, I 1, L 14, NEA 2, NG 15, P 20, RA 121, RBA 1, ROI 1, RSA 33, RSW 4.
HENRY, Hilda E. Exh. 1930
Bonehill Cottage, Tamworth, Staffs. † B 1.
HENRY, Miss J. Exh. 1938
163 Holly Road, Handsworth, Birmingham. † B 1.
HENRY, John Exh. 1929-38
Landscape painter. Ranelagh, Dublin 1929; The Creek, Strand Road, Sutton 1936. † RHA 14.
HENRY, James Levin b. 1855
Landscape painter. N.E.A. 1887. Member of the Society of 25 Artists. Exh. 1880-1938. Add: London. † B 1, D 10, FIN 3, G 2, GI 4, GOU 3, I 5, L 27, LEI 35, M 21, NEA 111, RA 85, RBA 12, RHA 2, RI 9, ROI 14, RSA 2.
HENRY, J. McIntyre Exh. 1885-1909
Edinburgh. † GI 1, RSA 19.
HENRY, Jane W. Exh. 1886-95
London. † GI 1, RBA 2.
HENRY, Leonore G. Exh. 1930
† P 2.
HENRY, Paul* b. 1876
Landscape and coastal painter. Married E. Grace H. q.v. A.R.H.A. 1926, R.H.A. 1929. Add: Aigburth, Liverpool 1901; London 1910; Belfast 1913; Dublin 1927; Kilmacanogue, Co. Wicklow 1933. † FIN 7, GOU 9, L 3, LEI 34, LS 7, RA 3, RHA 17.
HENRY, T. Exh. 1891
27 Bolton Studios, Redcliffe Road, London. † D 1.
HENRY, William see HAINES
HENS, Franz Exh. 1893-1915
Antwerp. † GI 1, I 2.
HENSE, S. Exh. 1906
Flower painter. † BG 4.
HENSHALL, Miss D.A. Exh. 1916-32
28 Salisbury Street, Chester. † L 11.
HENSHALL, John Henry* 1856-1928
Figure painter. Studied South Kensington and R.A. Schools. A.R.W.S. 1883, R.W.S. 1897. Add: London 1880; Southport, Lancs. 1895; Pinner, Middlesex 1904; Bosham, Sussex 1917. † B 41, D 9, FIN 1, GI 12, L 79, LEI 56, M 30, RA 72, RBA 5, RI 1, RMS 2, ROI 2, RSW 5, RWS 171.
HENSHAW, Miss A.M. Exh. 1892-94
42 Victoria Street, Birmingham. † B 2.
HENSHAW, C.T.A. Exh. 1892
89 Victoria Street, Smallheath, Birmingham. † B 1.
HENSHAW, Frederick Henry* 1807-1891
Landscape painter. Studied under J.V. Barber. Travelled on the continent, 1837-40. Add: Green Lanes, Birmingham. † B 12.
HENSLEY, F. Lily Exh. 1895-96
Haileybury College, Hertford. † M 2.
HENSLEY, Marie c. 1856-1911
Mrs. Philip H. Flower painter and designer. Exh. 1897-1904. Add: 4 Henrietta Street, Cavendish Square, London 1897; Surbiton Hill, 1904. † B 4, L 8, M 1, NG 2, RA 2, RI 5, SWA 7.
HENSMAN, Miss E.A. Exh. 1891
20 Laurel Road, Fairfield, Liverpool. † L 1.
HENSMAN, Frank H. Exh. 1890
Landscape painter. Holmleigh, Windsor, Berks. † RA 1.
HENSMAN, Juliet Exh. 1890-98
Figure painter. London 1890; Sevenoaks, Kent 1897. † NEA 6.
HENSMAN, Rosa Fryer Exh. 1886-97
Mrs. Wyman. Figure and domestic painter. Add: London. † L 1, M 1, NEA 1, P 3, RA 2, RBA 6, ROI 2, SWA 8.
HENSMAN, Walter Exh. 1880-91
Decorative designer. Blomfield Road, Shepherds Bush, London. † RA 6.
HENSON, Edward Exh. 1880-81
Figure painter. Committee member, N.S.A. 1881. Add: 9 Milton Street, Nottingham. † N 4.
HENSON, Gertrude Exh. 1902-17
Mrs. E.H. Watson. London 1902; Chigwell, Essex 1913. † B 4, L 2, RA 3, RI 1, SWA 6.
HENTON, George Moore c.1861-1924
Landscape and architectural painter. Leicester. † B 1, L 21, M 1, N 31, RA 14, RI 27, ROI 1.
HENTY-CREER, Deirdre Exh. 1940
Landscape painter. b. Sydney, Australia. Add: Garden House, Cornwall Gardens, London. † NEA 1, RA 1.
HEPBURN, Mrs. Blanche Exh. 1891
Figure painter. 3 Nevern Mansions, London. † ROI 1.
HEPBURN, Edith Mary Exh. 1880-87
Landscape and flower painter. Clapham Common, London. † SWA 7.
HEPBURN, Eleanor M. Exh. 1880
Flower painter. 53 Buckingham Road, Brighton. † SWA 1.
HEPBURN, Hugh Exh. 1913-17
12 City Road, Newcastle on Tyne. † I 1, RA 1, RCA 2, RSA 5.
HEPBURN, J. William Exh. 1922-38
Painter and architect. A.R.B.A. 1922, R.B.A. 1924. Add: London. † L 1, RBA 70.
HEPBURN, Sophia Exh. 1886-87
Coastal painter. Heath Edge, Haslemere, Surrey. † SWA 3.
HEPBURN, T.N. Exh. 1908
122 Marchmont Road, Edinburgh. † RSA 1.
HEPPELL, Thomas Daniel b. 1890
Commercial artist. 4 Victoria Terrace, Finsbury Park, London 1921. † RA 1.
HEPPLE, Robert Norman b. 1908
Painter, engraver and sculptor. Studied R.A. Schools, Royal College of Art, and Goldsmiths College; British Institute Scholarship in engraving. Exh. 1928-40. Add: London. † RA 5.
HEPWORTH, Dame Barbara* 1903-1975
Sculptor. b. Wakefield, Yorks. Studied Leeds School of Art 1920, Royal College of Art 1921-24, Florence and Rome 1924-26. Married first John Rattenbury Skeaping q.v. and second Ben Nicholson q.v. Member London Group 1930. Exh. 1928-33. Add: London. Moved to St. Ives in 1939. Died in a fire at her studio. † BA 10, L 1, RSA 3.
HEPWORTH, Dorothy M. Exh. 1916-23
112 New Walk, Leicester. † NEA 1, RA 4.
HEPWORTH, Philip Dalton b. 1888
Architect. Studied at the A.A., Ecoles des Beaux Arts, Paris and the British School at Rome. Exh. 1919-39. Add: London. † GI 17, RA 31, RSA 3.
HEPWORTH, Walter Exh. 1885-86
Landscape and figure painter. Boltons Studios, South Kensington, London. † GI 1, RA 1, RBA 2, RI 1, ROI 1.
HERALD, James W. Exh. 1887-1911
Landscape and coastal painter. Edinburgh 1887; Arbroath 1911. † BG 66, GOU 3, RSA 5, RSW 2.
HERAPATH, Miss H.W. Exh. 1908-10
2 Addison Road, Kensington, London. † RA 2.
HERAPATH, M. Exh. 1908-15
Sculptor. London. † I 1, L 3, RA 8.
HERBERT, A. Exh. 1901-4
† TOO 2.
HERBERT, Amy Exh. 1903-13
Landscape painter. A.N.S.A. 1908. Add: Moira House, Villa Road, Nottingham. † N 22.
HERBERT, A.J. Exh. 1904
18 Trafalgar Road, Twickenham, Middlesex. † B 2.
HERBERT, Alex S. Exh. 1894
12 Derby Street, Glasgow. † GI 1.
HERBERT, Mrs. Beatrice Exh. 1917-40
Flower painter. A.S.W.A. 1918, S.W.A. 1919. Add: 4 Hammersmith Terrace, London. † COO 3, RI 1, SWA 97.
HERBERT, Miss E. Exh. 1909-17
Landscape painter. Leatherhead, Surrey 1909; Tadworth, Surrey 1913; Coulsdon, Surrey 1917. † B 1, RA 5.
HERBERT, Ernest Exh. 1903
Architect. 32 Bedford Row, London. † RA 1.
HERBERT, Ernest Exh. 1908-21
4 Hammersmith Terrace, Hammersmith, London. † LS 36.
HERBERT, Elizabeth C. Exh. 1884
Miniature portrait painter. † RA 1.
HERBERT, Miss G. Exh. 1907-8
Chelsea, London 1907; Dublin 1908. † L 1, RA 1, RHA 2.

HERBERT, H. Exh. 1920
9 Regent Street, Nottingham. † N 3.
HERBERT, James Exh. 1892
71 Comerton Road, Edinburgh. † RSA 1.
HERBERT, Joanna L. Exh. 1902-40
Mrs. Dobson. Glasgow and March Hill, Riddrie, N.B. † GI 14, L 5, RSA 2, RSW 6.
HERBERT, J. Margaret Exh. 1910
Highfield Villas, Gores Lane, Freshfield, Formby, Lancs. † L 2.
HERBERT, John Rogers* 1810-1890
Portrait, historical, genre, biblical and landscape painter. Studied R.A. Schools 1826-28. A.R.A. 1841, R.A. 1846, R.I. 1867. Add: The Chimes, West End Lane, Kilburn, London. † AG 2, B 11, FIN 1, L 1, M 10, RA 34, RI 2.
HERBERT, Margaret Exh. 1937
Watercolour painter. † AR 51.
HERBERT, Mrs. M.L. Exh. 1933-38
c/o Bourlet, London. † RCA 5.
HERBERT, Philip Exh. 1938
Pastel artist. 35 Joyce Avenue, Sherwood, Nottingham. † N 1.
HERBERT, Richard Exh. 1892-1916
Landscape painter. Leatherhead, Surrey. † B 9, RA 3, RBA 3, RI 3, ROI 5.
HERBERT, Sydney d. 1914
Coastal painter. Exh. 1885-99. Add: Carlton Lodge, Cheltenham, Glos. † RCA 2, RI 4.
HERBERT, T. Exh. 1888-89
14 St. Peters Square, Hammersmith, London. † B 2.
HERBERT, Wilfred V. Exh. 1880-91
Figure painter. The Chimes, Kilburn 1880; West Hampstead 1884; Kensington 1891. † B 2, RA 8.
HERBO, Leon* Exh. 1882-1912
Glasgow 1882; Brussels 1896. † GI 2, LS 3.
HERD, J. Grosvenor Exh. 1916-19
Whytebank, Kirkcaldy, N.B. † RSA 4.
HERD, T. Exh. 1883
6 Murdoch Terrace, Edinburgh. † RSA 1.
HERDMAN, Edith Exh. 1882-1908
Liverpool. † B 1, L 9.
HERDMAN, Maud Exh. 1891-97
Portrait painter. Sion House, Co. Tyrone, Ireland. † RA 6, RHA 6.
HERDMAN, Robert* 1829-1888
Portrait, landscape, genre, historical and flower painter. b. Perthshire. Studied Trustees Academy Edinburgh 1852, (Keith prize 1854). Visited Italy 1855. Father of Robert Duddingstone H. q.v. A.R.S.A. 1858, R.S.A. 1863. Add: St. Bernard's, Bruntsfield Crescent, Edinburgh. † GI 10 L 1, RA 8, RSA 41.
HERDMAN, Robert Duddingstone* 1863-1922
Portrait and figure painter. Son of Robert H. q.v. A.R.S.A. 1908. Add: St. Bernard's, Bruntsfield Crescent, Edinburgh. † GI 43, L 24, RA 10, RSA 101, RSW 27.
HERDMAN-SMITH, Robert b. 1879
Painter, etcher, sculptor. b. Liverpool. Studied Leeds, London, Paris, Antwerp and Munich. Travelled and painted on the Continent and in Egypt, India, Australia, New Zealand, South America and Japan. Director of School of Art, Canterbury College, New Zealand University. Exh. 1920-32. Add: Newlyn, Penzance 1920, Wareham, Dorset 1932. † L 5.
HEREFORD, Edgar Exh. 1920-26
London. † L 1, NEA 10.
HEREFORD, Edward W. Exh. 1884-1915
Watercolour painter. Gourock by Greenock 1884; St. Albans, Herts. 1903; Addlestone, Surrey 1906. † D 62, L 2, M 1, RI 2, RSA 1.
HEREFORD, Henry J.R. Exh. 1917-20
Portrait painter. 1 Frognal Gardens, Hampstead, London. † RA 2.
HERING, George Ernest Exh. 1900-14
Marazion, Cornwall 1900; Parkstone, Dorset 1910. † L 1, LS 18.
HERIOT, Mrs. A. Exh. 1904
53 Hans Place, London. † SWA 1.
HERIOT, B. Exh. 1908
† P 1.
HERIOT, C.J.R. Exh. 1926
Flower painter. † AB 1.
HERIOT, Miss E.M. Exh. 1916
5 North Grove, Highgate, London. † RI 1.
HERIOT, Robertine Exh. 1907-27
Landscape painter. London. † GI 1, GOU 10, I 2, L 5, LS 14, NEA 3, ROI 3.
HERKIND, Miss V. Exh. 1896
19 Lancaster Gate, London. † SWA 1.
HERKLOTS, Rev. Gerard A. Exh. 1893
Landscape and coastal painter. St. Saviours Vicarage, Eton Road, Hampstead, London. † RBA 1.
HERKOMER, Bertha Exh. 1889-1915
Figure painter. Watford, Herts. † FIN 2, RA 1, ROI 4.
HERKOMER, Sir Hubert* 1849-1914
Portrait, historical, landscape and figure painter, and engraver. b. Bavaria. Came to England 1857. Studied South Kensington 1866. Contributed to the "Graphic" 1869. Founded and directed the Bushey School of Art 1883-1904. Slade Professor of Fine Arts at Oxford 1885-94. A.R.A. 1879, R.A. 1890, R.B.A. 1908, R.E. 1880, R.I. 1873, R.O.I. 1883, R.P. 1894, A.R.S.W. 1895, A.R.W.S. 1893, R.W.S. 1894. Knighted 1907. "Found" purchased by Chantrey Bequest 1885 and "The Council of the Royal Academy" in 1909. Add: Bushey, Herts. † AG 1, B 16, CAR 1, D 2, DOW 2, FIN 153, G 27, GI 12, L 55, LEI 60, M 27, NG 19, P 23, RA 195, RBA 7, RCA 6, RE 34, RHA 3, RMS 1, ROI 3, RSA 4, RSW 7, RWS 33, TOO 1.
HERKOMER, Herman G. Exh. 1883-1912
Landscape, portrait and figure painter. R.O.I. 1888, R.P. 1891. Add: Bushey, Herts. 1883; Lowndes Square, London 1886. † B 10, G 1, L 12, M 5, NG 15, P 80, RA 22, RBA 4, RHA 1, ROI 41.
HERMAN, Geraldine Exh. 1887
Miniature painter. 45 Victoria Road, Kilburn, London. † SWA 1.
HERMAN, Miss L. Exh. 1895-96
Paris 1895; Glasgow 1896. † L 2.
HERMANN, Hans* Exh. 1900
7 W. Dornberstrasse, Berlin. † GI 2.
HERMANN, H.F. Exh. 1882-87
Liverpool 1882; Lynmouth, North Devon 1883. † L 3.
HERMANN, Louise Exh. 1896
c/o Mr. A.W. Johnson, 62A Westbourne Grove, London. † B 1, GI 1, RI 1.
HERMANN, Paul* Exh. 1909-10
c/o Allied Artists Assoc., 67 Chancery Lane, London. † LS 3.
HERMANS, C. Exh. 1880-94
London 1880; Brussels 1894. † GI 2, M 1, RHA 1.
HERMES, Gertrude b. 1901
Sculptor and wood engraver. b. Bromley, Kent. Studied Leon Underwood's School. Married Blair Hughes Stanton q.v. Member London Group 1935. Exh. 1926-40. Add: London. † COO 3, GI 5, L 3, LEI 1, M 2, RA 7, RED 2, RHA 3, RSA 2.
HERMON, Mrs. Ruth Exh. 1926-27
King's Road, Chelsea, London. † NEA 2, SWA 1.
HERMSTIN, O. Exh. 1880
Landscape painter. c/o Messrs. Colnaghi, London. † RA 1.
HERN, Charles Edward Exh. 1883-93
Landscape and architectural painter. London. † D 41, DOW 91, FIN 4, L 1, M 6, RA 5, RBA 6, RI 8.
HERNE, E. May Exh. 1921-36
Suffolk House, Llandaff, Cardiff, Wales. † L 1, RCA 8.
HERON, A. Harry Exh. 1911-19
Architect. London. † RA 2.
HERON, Ethel Exh. 1902-33
Portrait and still life painter. Studied under Bertram Priestman, and at Academie de la Grande Chaumiere, Paris. Add: Harrogate 1902; London 1933. † L 9, RA 2, SWA 1.
HERON, James Exh. 1880-1919
Edinburgh. † GI 7, RSA 105.
HERON, William Exh. 1883-96
Edinburgh 1883 and 1896; Liverpool 1885. † RSA 8.
HEROYS, B.V. Exh. 1927-30
London. † NEA 2.
HERRD, Alice Exh. 1918
† I 1.
HERRICK, F.C. Exh. 1913
23 Hereford Buildings, Church Street, Chelsea, London. † RA 1.
HERRICK, William Salter Exh. 1880-87
Figure painter. London. † B 2, GI 1, RA 1.
HERRIES, James W. Exh. 1932-40
22 Findhorn Place, Edinburgh. † RSA 4.
HERRIN, Joan Exh. 1930
Wood engraver. † RED 1.
HERRING, Evelyn M. Exh. 1934-40
Landscape painter. c/o Bourlet & Sons, London 1934; St. Ives, Cornwall 1937. † NEA 3, RA 4, SWA 1.
HERRING, John Frederick junr.* c.1815-1907
Sporting and animal painter. Son of J.F.H. senr. (1795-1865). Exh. 1882-83. Add: Fulbourn, Nr. Cambridge. † B 2, TOO 1.
HERRING, Miss K. Exh. 1933
12 Cedar Grove, Prestwich, Manchester. † L 1.
HERRINGHAM, Christina Jane c.1853-1929
nee Powell. Married Sir Wilmot Parker H. Exh. 1894. Add: 13 Upper Wimpole Street, London. † NG 1.
HERRINGTON, Fred W. Exh. 1882-90
Still life painter. London. † RBA 1, RI 1.
HERST, B. Exh. 1911
Landscape painter. † BRU 2.
HERTFORD, Samuel Irvine Exh. 1893-1938
Landscape painter. b. Liverpool. Educated in U.S.A. Studied Liverpool School of Art. Add: Liverpool 1893; London 1907; Bootle, Lancs. 1919; Wallasey, Cheshire 1925. † B 1, L 43, M 1, RA 2, RCA 22.
HERTSLET, Ivy Exh. 1906-7
Ambassadors Court, St. James's Palace, London. † L 4.
HERVEY, Miss Leslie Exh. 1893-1920
Flower, Landscape and figure painter. Bedford 1893; Chieveley, Berks. 1900; Farringdon, Berks. 1908; Shrivenham, Berks. 1919; St. Ives, Cornwall 1911 and 1920. † BA 25, I 1, L 1, LS 7, RA 4, RBA 4, ROI 2.
HERWEGEN, V.M. Exh. 1890
c/o W. Ehrhardt, Hill Crest, Richmond Hill Road, Edgbaston, Birmingham. † B 1.
HERZER, Von See V

HERZMARK, Louis Exh. 1911
26 Queen Street, Cheetham, Manchester. † L 4.

HESELTINE, Arthur Exh. 1896-1915
c/o J. Guthrie, 7 Woodside Place, Glasgow 1896; Marlotte, Seine et Marne, France 1915. † GI 1, I 4, LS 3.

HESELTINE, John Postle c.1843-1929
Etcher. Trustee of the National Gallery from 1893. R.E. 1881. Exh. 1880-1928. Add: London. † DOW 6, RA 21, RE 46.

HESELTINE, Phyllis Exh. 1912-35
Watercolour and portrait painter. b. Essex. Studied Beckenham School of Art and the Spenlove School of Painting. A.S.W.A. 1915. Add: Bromley, Kent 1912; Chislehurst Common, Kent 1925. † P 4, RA 4, RBA 2, RCA 3, RI 1, ROI 1, SWA 16.

HESKETH, E. Exh. 1882
31 Uxbridge Street, Liverpool. † L 1.

HESKETH, Edith Exh. 1928-29
Robbins Bridge Farm, Aughton, Lancs. † L 2.

HESLOP, Arthur Exh. 1914-16
20 Framlington Place, Newcastle-on-Tyne. † L 2, RSA 1.

HESP, Miss A. Exh. 1932-33
28 Princes Street, Bury, Lancs. † L 3.

HESS, Florence Exh. 1924-40
Figure painter. Studied Leeds School of Art. Add: Far Headingley, Leeds 1924; Alwoodley, Leeds 1928. † L 2, M 1, NEA 1, RA 7.

HESSE, H.R.H. The Grand Duchess Victoria Melita 1876-1936
Grand-daughter of Queen Victoria. Exh. 1905. Add: 21 Queensberry Place, South Kensington, London. † L 1, NG 1.

HESTER, Edward Gilbert d. 1903
Engraver. Chiswick, London 1882; Hammersmith, London 1884; St. Albans, Herts. 1891. † RA 21.

HESTER, R. Wallace Exh. 1897-1904
Engraver. Tooting, London 1897; Purley, Surrey 1901. † RA 5.

HETHERINGTON, Eleanor M. Exh. 1938
Hydeneye, Waverley Lane, Farnham, Surrey. † RBA 1, SWA 1.

HETHERINGTON, Ethel M. Exh. 1930
53 Northfield Road, King's Norton, Birmingham. † B 1.

HETHERINGTON, Ivystan Exh. 1880-1915
Landscape painter. R.B.A. 1898. Add: London. † B 2, G 7, L 14, M 11, NG 25, RA 15, RBA 16, ROI 15.

HETHERINGTON, Lilian Exh. 1885
† SWA 1.

HETHERINGTON, Mabel A. Exh. 1930
53 Northfield Road, King's Norton, Birmingham. † B 1.

HETHERINGTON, Walter F. Scott* Exh. 1895-1940
Portrait and miniature painter. b. Liverpool. Add: Formby, Lancs. 1895; London 1902; Trowbridge, Wilts. 1940. † GI 2, L 11, LS 3, RA 4, RMS 1, ROI 2, RSA 1.

HETZE, Paul Exh. 1898-1901
12 Amalienstrasse, Munich. † GI 6.

HEUTH, Margaret A. Exh. 1886
8 York Place, Baker Street, London. † D 1.

HEWARD, Harold Cornelius b. 1881
Landscape and figure painter and black and white illustrator. b. Southsea, Hants. Studied Lambeth School of Art. Exh. 1921-39. Add: 34 Kitts Road, St. Catherine's Park, London. † RA 1, RBA 3, ROI 9.

HEWARD, Leslie J. Exh. 1938
Landscape painter. 32 Outram Road, Croydon, Surrey. † RA 1.

HEWAT, Sybil F. Exh. 1927-29
8 The Pheasantry, Chelsea, London. † L 6, RSA 1.

HEWER (Jack) John Edward b. 1889
Etcher, designer and commercial artist. Exh. 1927. Add: 6 Stanley Road, Halifax, Yorks. † L 2, RCA 2, RSA 1.

HEWETSON, Miss A. Exh. 1886
9 Carlton Street, Edinburgh. † RSA 1.

HEWETSON, Edith Exh. 1893-94
8 St. James' Terrace, Regent's Park, London. † ROI 2.

HEWETSON, Edward Exh. 1889
Architectural artist. 45 Rue de Frejus, Cannes, France. † RA 1.

HEWETSON, Mabel L. Exh. 1925-28
A.S.W.A. 1924. Add: 89 Earl's Court Road, London. † L 9.

HEWETT, Doris Exh. 1910-14
London. † LS 12.

HEWETT, Mrs. F. Exh. 1917-22
Penchester, Shawfield Park, Bromley, Kent. † SWA 4.

HEWETT, Frank Exh. 1903-14
Kingsbridge, South Devon. † M 1, RA 1, RCA 6.

HEWETT, M. Exh. 1937
Lithographer. † RED 2.

HEWETT, Mabel Calton Exh. 1898-1914
Still life, flower and portrait painter. London. † B 13, NEA 2, RA 12.

HEWETT, Miss M.E. Exh. 1890
19 Holland Street, Kensington, London. † SWA 1.

HEWETT, Sir Prescott, Bt. Exh. 1883-89
Watercolour landscape painter. Mayfair, London 1883; Horsham, Sussex 1884. † FIN 2, RSW 4.

HEWETT, Sarah F. Exh. 1880-85
Figure painter. Woodlands Villa, Leamington, Warwicks. † B 1, RI 1, RSA 1.

HEWINS, Alfred J. Exh. 1887-91
Landscape painter. Wolverhampton 1887; Albrighton, Wolverhampton 1888. † B 6, RA 1.

HEWIT, Forrest 1870-1956
Figure and landscape painter. Studied under Sickert. Director of the Calico Printers Association Ltd. R.B.A. 1940. Exh. 1925-40. Add: Overhill, Wilmslow, Cheshire. † COO 1, GOU 3, L 3, M 3, NEA 8, P 1, RA 6, RBA 11, RCA 3, RHA 1, ROI 7, RSA 9.

HEWITT, Miss A. Exh. 1896
Bedford Park, Chiswick, London. † SWA 1.

HEWITT, Alfred E. Exh. 1891-1900
Decorative designer. School of Science and Art, Guernsey, C.I. 1891; St. Andrews, Guernsey, C.I. 1900. † B 4, RA 1.

HEWITT, Alice J. Exh. 1880-88
Figure painter. London 1880; St. Leonards-on-Sea, Sussex 1884. † RBA 1, RHA 1, ROI 1, RSA 1, SWA 1.

HEWITT, Miss A.M. Exh. 1900-3
65 Silverdale, Sydenham, London. † RBA 1, SWA 3.

HEWITT, Beatrice M. Exh. 1884-1902
Portrait painter. London. † L 1, RA 13, RI 5.

HEWITT, Mrs. Beatrice Pauline b. 1907
Landscape and portrait painter and teacher. Studied Slade School and Paris. R.O.I. 1940. Add: St. Ives, Cornwall. † GI 1, I 2, RA 15, RBA 5, ROI 19, SWA 28.

HEWITT, David Exh. 1902-12
St. Helens, Lancs. 1902; Beddgelert, N. Wales 1912. † L 12, RA 2, RCA 2.

HEWITT, Ena Exh. 1898-99
89 Cambridge Gardens, N. Kensington, London. † RMS 2.

HEWITT, Evelyn b. 1882
Miniature painter, pastelier and designer. Studied Goldsmith's College. Add: Blackheath, London 1928; Ufford, Woodbridge, Suffolk 1929. † RA 3, RMS 1.

HEWITT, Mrs. F. Adelaide Exh. 1907-9
Forest Hill, London. † LS 2, SWA 1.

HEWITT, Graily Exh. 1920-39
H.R.M.S. 1920. Phillis Mead, Treyford, Petersfield, Hants. † RMS 17.

HEWITT, H.E. Exh. 1931-35
182 Boundary Road, St. Helens, Lancs. † L 1, RCA 8.

HEWITT, Henry George Exh. 1884-1907
Landscape, flower and figure painter. R.B.A. 1893. Add: London 1884; Godalming, Surrey 1900; Hereford 1902. † B 2, FIN 1, L 3, M 2, RA 7, RBA 36, RHA 1, RI 5, ROI 1.

HEWITT, J. Hall Exh. 1908
16 Lord Street, Liverpool. † L 1.

HEWITT, James S. Exh. 1897
36 Breeze Hill, Bootle, Lancs. † L 1.

HEWITT, M. Exh. 1922-28
21 Greetby Hill, Ormskirk, Lancs. † L 8.

HEWITT, Walter E. Exh. 1901-10
Architect. 22 Buckingham Street, Strand, London. † RA 2.

HEWITT, William H. Muller Exh. 1909
† LS 1.

HEWKLEY, Henry Exh. 1885-1924
Landscape painter. London. † RA 2, RBA 3, RI 12.

HEWKLEY, Marion Edith Exh. 1911-40
Mrs. Sutherland Gill. Miniature painter. Studied Slade School, South Kensington and Paris. A.S.W.A. 1929. Add: London. † L 21, RA 23, RI 25, RMS 6, SWA 4.

HEWLAND, Elsie Dalton b. 1901
Figure painter. Studied Sheffield College of Art 1921-24, R.A. Schools 1926-30. Add: London 1928, Chorley Wood, Herts. 1930, Chalfont St. Giles, Bucks. 1933. † RA 9.

HEWLETT, Allan B. Exh. 1935-36
Landscape painter. 65 Battersea Park Road, London. † RA 2.

HEWLETT, Arthur L. Exh. 1882-1926
Painter and etcher. Manchester 1882 and 1891; Bushey, Herts. 1889 and 1914. † FIN 4, L 3, M 4, RA 5.

HEWLETT, Doris Exh. 1917-24
Beckenham, Kent. † SWA 8.

HEWLETT, Florence K. Exh. 1908-34
Miniature portrait painter. Richmond, Surrey 1908; Sutton, Surrey 1933. † L 1, M 1, RA 5, RMS 3, SWA 1.

HEWLETT, H.B. Exh. 1924-37
Landscape painter. Melton Mowbray, Leics. † N 4.

HEWLINGS, H.H. Exh. 1895
Beechlawn, Terenure, Ireland. † RHA 1.

HEXT, Miss M. Exh. 1899
Steeple Langford, Bath. † SWA 1.

HEY, Cicely b. 1896
Mrs. Tatlock. Portrait and figure painter. b. Farringdon, Berks. Studied Central School of Arts and Crafts. Member London Group 1927. Exh. 1924-39. Add: London. † COO 2, LEF 36, LEI 2, NEA 2.

HEY, L. Muriel Exh. 1929
Firbeck, Grove Road, Ilkley, Yorks. † L 2.

HEY, S. Exh. 1905-12
Glan Conway, N. Wales. † RCA 5.

HEYDEMANN, William b. 1866
Portrait and miniature painter, etcher and picture restorer. Studied R.A. Schools, Amsterdam Academy, Hague Academy and under L. Lowestam. Painter in Ordinary to H.R.H. Prince George of Greece 1907. Exh. 1886-1917. Add: London. † L 16, RA 30, RHA 6, RMS 3, ROI 2, RSA 4.

HEYDEN, Von See V

HEYDENDAHL, Joseph Exh. 1880-88
Figure and military painter. c/o J. Rorke, 54 Parliament Street, London. † D 1, RA 1, RBA 1.

HEYENBROCK, H. Exh. 1909
† LS 2.

HEYERMANS, Jean Arnould* b. 1837
Figure painter. Exh. 1881-99. Add: Antwerp 1881; S. Kensington, London 1898. † B 1, G 3, GI 2.

HEYES, J.F. Exh. 1882
162 Phythian Street, Liverpool. † L 1.

HEYMAN, Aline Exh. 1937-38
† P 2.

HEYMANS, Adriaan Joseph 1839-1921
Belgian painter. Exh. 1905-21. Add: Brussels. † I 4, RSA 2.

HEYNEMAN, Elsa Exh. 1933-38
Still life, flower, fruit and miniature painter. 16 Barrington Road, Crouch End, London. † RA 3.

HEYNEMANN, Julie H. Exh. 1907-13
London. † RA 1, RHA 3.

HEYS, Mary Exh. 1901
Rockmount, Barrhead, N.B. † GI 2.

HEYS, Ward Exh. 1882-1905
14 Ridgefield, Manchester. † L 5, M 28.

HEYSEN, Hans* 1876-c.1971
Watercolour landscape painter. b. Hamburg. Exh. 1922-35. Add: Ambleside, S. Australia 1922. † CG 36, RA 1.

HEYSEN, Nora Exh. 1935
5 Duke's Lane, London. † ROI 1.

HEYWOOD, Brookes d. 1926
Exh. 1926. † B 2.

HEYWOOD, Eleanor Exh. 1932
The Dower House, Ufford, Woodbridge, Suffolk. † RA 1.

HEYWOOD, Tom Exh. 1882-1913
Lyceum, Oldham, Lancs. 1882; Colwyn Bay, Wales 1901. † M 10, RCA 13.

HEYWORTH, Richard b. 1862
Landscape painter. Studied Ecole des Beaux Arts, Paris. R.O.I. 1919 (Hon. Ret. 1940). Add: London 1890, 1914 and 1919; Mumbles, Nr. Swansea 1903; Falmouth, Cornwall 1909; Teignmouth, Devon 1912; Charlton Kings, Nr. Cheltenham, Glos. 1923. † L 4, LS 5, P 2, RA 10, RHA 6, RID 26, ROI 71.

HIBBERD, Freda M. Exh. 1935
5 Colville Villas, Nottingham. † N 2.

HIBBERD, Gladys Mary Exh. 1927-35
Pottery figure artist. Studied Camberwell School of Arts and Crafts. Add: 37 Mayon Road, Forest Hill, London. † L 2, SWA 2.

HIBBERD, Margaret Exh. 1936-39
Portrait and miniature painter. 5 Colville Villas, Nottingham. † N 5.

HIBBERT, Ellen Exh. 1884-1905
Godley, Nr. Manchester 1884; Birkenhead 1895. † L 5, M 1.

HIBBERT, Frederick G. Exh. 1891
May Villa, Chilwell, Notts. † N 1.

HIBBERT, G. Exh. 1889
45 Alford Street, Edge Lane, Liverpool. † L 1.

HIBBERT, G.M. Exh. 1885
287 Prescot Road, Fairfield, Liverpool. † L 1.

HIBBERT, Phyllis I. b. 1903
Flower painter. Exh. 1925-38. Add: 59 Blackpool Road, Ansdell, Lytham, Lancs. † L 14, M 1, RA 1, RCA 2.

HIBBITTS, Miss Beatrice See GUNTHORPE

HICHENS, Margaret Exh. 1898
Guilsborough, Northampton. † SWA 2.

HICK, Allanson b. 1898
Painter and architect. Exh. 1931-40. Add: 82 Albany Street, Spring Bank, Hull. † RA 5, RSA 1.

HICK, A. Crawford Exh. 1897
Architect. Royal Arcade, Newcastle-on-Tyne. † RA 1.

HICK, Edwin M. Exh. 1902-5
Architect. Bath 1902; Barnes, London 1905. † RA 2.

HICK, Mary Exh. 1937-39
London 1937; Maidstone, Kent 1939. † SWA 4.

HICKEY, Rev. Father Ephrem Exh. 1909-14
Franciscan Friary, Forest Gate, London. † LS 3, RHA 6.

HICKIN, G.A. Exh. 1880
Landscape painter. 207 Albert Road, Aston Park, Birmingham. † RA 1.

HICKINGBOTHAM, A.R. Exh. 1939
28 Gorse Rise, Grantham, Lincs. † N 2.

HICKLIN, K. Exh. 1937
Architectural painter. 155 Gerard Street, Derby. † N2.

HICKLING, Edith Exh. 1881
The Park, Nottingham. † N 1.

HICKLING, Edward Albert b. 1913
Landscape, portrait and figure painter. Exh. 1934-39. Add: 56 Wilford Crescent, Nottingham. † N 17.

HICKLING, Miss F.M. Exh. 1885
77 Forest Road West, Nottingham. † N 1.

HICKLING, H.T. Exh. 1900
The Chestnuts, Stratford-on-Avon, Warwicks. † B 1.

HICKMAN, Evelyn Exh. 1890-1914
Landscape painter. St. Leonards-on-Sea, Sussex 1890; Chelsea, London 1909. † I 2, L 3, M 1, RA 1.

HICKMAN, Evelyn A. Exh. 1922
Sculptor. 52 Oakley Street, Chelsea, London. † RA 1.

HICKS, Albert S. Exh. 1885
Domestic painter. Fir Hill, Southend Lane, Lower Sydenham. † RA 1.

HICKS, Evelyn Woodroffe Exh. 1898-1912
London 1898; Wickham, Hants. 1904. † B 4, GI 1, L 7, LS 3, RBA 2, ROI 3, SWA 15.

HICKS, F.E. Exh. 1932
† L 1.

HICKS, Frederick G. d. c.1965
Painter and architect. A.R.H.A. 1929. Exh. 1902-38. Add: Dublin. † RHA 11.

HICKS, George Elgar* 1824-1914
Genre and portrait painter. Abandoned the study of medicine for painting. Studied R.A. Schools 1844. R.B.A. 1889. Add: London. † B 1, D 1, G 3, L 6, M 1, RA 44, RBA 13, ROI 2, RSA 4, TOO 1.

HICKS, Lottie Braxton Exh. 1916-17
3A Perham Road, West Kensington, London. † LS 6.

HICKS, Margaretta Exh. 1903-14
Camden Road, London. † LS 11, SWA 1.

HICKS, Miss Mary Exh. 189-
Bird painter. The Lodge, Copford, Colchester, Essex. † RBA 1.

HICKS, Mrs. Mary C. Exh. 1902-30
Figure and domestic painter. Rock Ferry, Cheshire 1902; Chester 1904; Stockport, Lancs. 1910; Birkenhead 1925. † L 13, M 3, RA 1.

HICKS, Mabel E. Exh. 1932
Miniature portrait painter. 39 Station Road, Harlesden, London. † RA 1.

HICKS, Minnie J. Exh. 1892
Figure and bird painter. Hendon Grove, Hendon, London. † RA 1, RBA 1.

HICKSON, Annie W. Exh. 1886-91
Watercolour flower painter. London. † RA 2, RI 1.

HICKSON, Margaret Exh. 1880-1901
Figure and landscape painter. London. † B 10, D 4, GI 1, L 4, M 3, NG 1, RA 9, RBA 7, RHA 1, RI 4, ROI 3, RSA 1, SWA 18.

HICKSON, Miss M.R. Exh. 1911-12
Hilville, Marlfield Road, Wallasey, Cheshire. † L 5.

HICKSON, Miss M.W.D. Exh. 1913-19
20 Ellerdale Road, Hampstead, London. † L 2, RA 2, SWA 2.

HICKSON, Stanley Exh. 1935
Linocut artist. † RED 1.

HICKSON, S.A. Exh. 1928-35
Long Eaton, Notts. 1928; Nottingham 1934. † N 12.

HIDE, Horace C. Reid Exh. 1901-2
Architect. 17 Gracechurch Street, London. † RA 2.

HIDES' George E. Exh. 1906-7
109 Highfield Road, Saltley, Birmingham. † B 2.

HIER, Van See V

HIGGIN, Miss R.E. Exh. 1883
Ethersall, Roby, Liverpool. † L 1.

HIGGINBOTTOM, William Hugh b. 1881
Landscape painter and lecturer. b. Newcastle-on-Tyne. Studied R.A. Schools and Juliens, Paris. Exh. 1908-26. Add: London. † RA 2, ROI 1.

HIGGINGTON, Miss R.F. Exh. 1927
Wood View, Nailsea, Bristol. † RI 2.

HIGGINS, A.A.W. Exh. 1882
52 Bath Row, Birmingham. † B 1.

HIGGINS, Agatha F. Exh. 1932-33
Watercolour landscape painter. Sudbrook Cottage, Ham Common, Surrey. † RA 2.

HIGGINS, Miss C. Exh. 1880-84
Landscape and figure painter. 53 Via Margutta, Rome. † L 2, RA 1, RBA 1, SWA 3.

HIGGINS, Elsie Exh. 1895-1916
Portrait and landscape painter. R.M.S. 1900. Add: Birkenhead 1895; Rye, Sussex 1899; Shalford, Surrey 1900; Bushey, Herts 1901. † GI 1, L 20, RA 11, RMS 3, SWA 3.

HIGGINS, E.W. Exh. 1888
1 Rosendale Villa, Murdock Road, Handsworth, Birmingham. † B 1.

HIGGINS, Frank Wilfrid b. 1893
Portrait painter. Studied Chester School of Art, London and Italy. Served R.F.C. and R.A.F. in France and Italy World War I. Exh. 1924-40. Add: London. † L 11, RA 1, RHA 1, RSA 1.

HIGGINS, H. Exh. 1931
Liverpool. † RCA 1.

HIGGINS, Henry Exh. 1894-99
247 St. Vincent Street, Glasgow. † GI 2.

HIGGINS, James Exh. 1881-86
95 Bath Street, Glasgow. † GI 2.

HIGGINS, Joseph Exh. 1912-25
School of Art, Cork 1912; Youghal, Co. Cork 1915. † RHA 15.

HIGGINS, John Gray Exh. 1922-33
Landscape and figure painter. Northampton 1928; Gidea Park, Essex 1927; Leytonstone, Essex 1932; Dedham, Essex 1935. † ALP 1, D 20, RA 7.

HIGGINS, Reginald Edward b. 1877
Portrait and decorative painter, poster artist and teacher. Studied St. John's Wood, R.A. Schools and British Museum. R.B.A. 1914, R.O.I. 1922. Exh. 1900-32. Add: London. † G 1, I 1, LS 4, P 5, RA 8, RBA 73, ROI 7.

HIGGINS, Miss S. Exh. 1885
11 Claremont Road, Alexandra Park, Manchester. † M 1.

HIGGINS, Theresa M.L. Exh. 1880-88
Liverpool. † L 4, RSA 1.

HIGGINS, William A.A. Exh. 1891-97
Coastal and landscape painter. 64 Islington Row, Edgbaston, Birmingham. † B 2, RA 4.

HIGGINS, William P. Exh. 1935
Landscape painter. Cork Art Club, 25 Patrick Street, Cork. † RHA 1.

HIGGINSON, George Exh. 1896
c/o J.G. Whitehouse, The Polygon, Bourdon, Cheshire. † NG 1.

HIGGINSON, May Exh. 1888-94
Flower painter. Torquay 1888 and 1892; Cushendun, Co. Antrim 1891; London 1894. † D 2, M 1, NG 1, RA 3, RBA 2, SWA 2.

HIGGINTON, Fay b. 1899
Miniature and watercolour painter. Studied Goldsmith's College. A.R.M.S. 1927. Exh. 1923-36. Add: London 1923; Purley, Surrey 1931. † L 2, RA 12, RI 11, RMS 24.

HIGGS, A.L. Exh. 1922
18 City Road, Birmingham. † B 3.

HIGGS, Miss E. Exh. 1896
57 London Road, Leicester. † SWA 2.

HIGGS, Madeline Exh. 1886-88
Still life painter. Whittingham Lodge, Nr. Barnet, Herts. † RA 1, RHA 1, ROI 1.

HIGHAM, Bernard Exh. 1917-19
Landscape painter. Stratton House, Woodcote Avenue, Wallington, Surrey. † RA 2.

HIGHAM, Beatrice A. Exh. 1898-1900
Miniature portrait painter. R.M.S. 1899. Stratton House, Burnt Ash Road, Lee, London. † RA 2, RMS 5.

HIGHAM, Maud Exh. 1900-8
Finchley Lodge, St. John's Road, Blackheath, London. † RBA 2, RI 4.

HIGHAM, Miss P. Exh. 1883
The Poplars, Sankey, Nr. Warrington, Lancs. † M 1.

HIGHAM, W.H.M. Exh. 1913-16
The Parsonage, Seaman's Orphanage, Newsham Park, Liverpool. † L 5.

HIGHET, Graeme I.C. Exh. 1934-39
Watercolour painter and architect. 21 Tothill Street, Westminster, London. † AR 2, COO 2, RA 1.

HIGHET, Miss K. Exh. 1883-89
Troon, N.B. † GI 1, RSA 1.

HIGHMAN, Peggy Exh. 1933-38
Watercolour painter. Nottingham 1933; Sherwood, Notts. 1934. † N 9.

HIGHMAN, William Exh. 1936-40
Landscape painter. 86 Edgehill Road, Mitcham, Surrey. † RA 4.

HIGHT, A.E. Exh. 1912-14
c/o Robertson & Co., 99 Long Acre, London 1912; Via Segli Artisti 8, Firenze, Italy 1913. † LS 5, M 2, RA 2.

HIGHT, Miss Beryl Exh. 1913-14
Via Segli Artisti 8, Firenze, Italy. † LS 4.

HIGHTON, H. Exh. 1894
Ivy Mount, Oakhill Park, Liverpool. † L 1.

HIGHT-TUMIATI, Mrs. Exh. 1925
c/o C. Robertson & Co., 99 Long Acre, London. † GI 1.

HIGNETT, Miss J. Exh. 1916
Baliol, West Derby, Liverpool. † L 2.

HIGNETT, Reginald A. Exh. 1926-40
Sculptor. Grassendale, Liverpool 1926; London 1927. † GI 1, L 6, RA 10, RSA 2.

HIGUER, Arnold Exh. 1916
5 Sheriff Road, West Hampstead, London. † LS 3.

HIKINS, J.B. Exh. 1885-93
Liverpool. † L 3.

HILDA, Mme. E. Exh. 1902
29 Rue Humboldt, Paris. † L 1.

HILDEBRAND, Adolph S. b. 1847
German sculptor. Francesco di Paola 3, Florence, Italy 1886. † G 1.

HILDER, Dorothy Exh. 1939
9 Avenue Studios, 76 Fulham Road, London. † SWA 1.

HILDER, Rowland* b. 1905
Painter, illustrator and decorator. b. Long Island, U.S.A. Studied Goldsmith's College. m. Edith Blenkiron q.v. Illustration master at Goldsmith's College. R.I. 1938. Exh. 1926-40. Add: London. † NEA 1, RA 23, RHA 1, RI 12.

HILDESHEIM, Herman Exh. 1900-6
Portrait painter. London. † M 1, NEA 5, P 2, RA 1.

HILDESHEIM, Miss H. Gertrude Exh. 1900
Decorative designer. 13 Redington Road, Frognal, Hampstead, London. † RA 1.

HILDESLEY, Joan Exh. 1939
Sculptor. 90 Walton Street, London. † RA 1.

HILDESLEY, P.T. Exh. 1907-15
Wandsworth Common, London. † RA 4.

HILDITCH, Margery Kathleen b. 1899
Miniature and portrait painter. Exh. 1918-27. Add: High Street, Nantwich, Cheshire. † RCA 8.

HILDRED, Edward V. Exh. 1918-22
Miniature painter. Forest Gate, London 1918; Seven Kings, Essex 1921. † RA 4.

HILDYARD, C. Exh. 1928-29
Portrait painter. † AB 6.

HILES, Miss Barbara Exh. 1911-12
Sunningdale Road, New Brighton, Cheshire. † L 2.

HILES, Bartram 1872-1927
Watercolour painter and designer who painted holding his brush in his mouth as he lost his arms in a Bristol tramcar accident. Studied Royal College of Art. Add: London 1893; Clifton, Bristol 1908. † D 3, GI 1, L 1, RA 2, RBA 1, RI 4.

HILES, George Exh. 1892
Landscape painter. 67 Faulden Road, Stoke Newington, London. † RA 1.

HILES, Henry Edward b. 1857
Landscape painter. Studied at the Academie de la Grande Chaumiere and in the studio of E. Phillips Fox, Paris. Exh. 1882-1928. † AG 81, B 13, L 97, M 2, RA 5, RCA 8.

HILEY, F.E. Exh. 1912
20 Cyril Mansions, Battersea Park, London. † RA 1.

HILEY, Maud Exh. 1896-1910
Harborne, Birmingham 1896; Uley, nr. Dursley, Glos. 1910. † B 8.

HILEY, Muriel B.G. Exh. 1929
Sculptor. 23 Southend Lane, London. † RA 1.

HILKEN, A. Kathleen Exh. 1939
† NEA 2.

HILL, Adele Exh. 1903-14
Landscape painter. 8 Dean's Yard, Westminster, London. † B 11, D 17, L 3, RA 2, RHA 5, RI 1, RSA 2, SWA 2.

HILL, Adrian b. 1897
Painter, etcher, black and white artist and illustrator. b. Charlton, Kent. Studied St. John's Wood 1912-14 and Royal College of Art 1919-20. Official war artist 1917-19. Visiting art master Hornsey School of Art. R.B.A. 1926. R.I. 1928, R.O.I. 1931. Exh. 1923-40. Add: London 1923; Haslemere, Surrey 1937; Midburst, Surrey 1940. † BK 45, D 2, FIN 2, GI 2, L 1, NEA 8, RA 28, RBA 101, RHA 1, RI 47, ROI 38.

HILL, Alex Exh. 1888-89
13 Herriot Street, Pollokshields, Lanarks. † GI 3.

HILL, Alfred Exh. 1881-1917
22 George Street, Cork. † RA 1, RHA 8.

HILL, Arthur* Exh. 1880-94
Landscape, genre and portrait painter. R.B.A. 1880. Add: London. † B 4, GI 3, L 3, M 4, RA 6, RBA 16.

HILL, A.C.E. Exh. 1888-1910
Landscape painter. London. † B 3, I 1, L 11, M 2, NG 5, RA 3, RBA 2, ROI 15.

HILL, Anne E.G. Exh. 1886-1912
Moseley, Birmingham. † B 9, L 1, LS 12.

HILL, Arthur G. Exh. 1880-91
Church organ architect. London. † RA 2.

HILL, Agnes Thompson Exh. 1902-29
nee Thompson. Watercolour painter, jeweller, and silversmith. Liverpool 1902; Chorlton on Medlock, Manchester 1903; Manchester 1907. † L 375.

HILL, Mrs. Catherine Exh. 1930
Holmleigh, 116 Langley's Road, Selly Oak, Birmingham. † B 2.

HILL, Clara Exh. 1897-98
Sandringham Villa, Warwick Road, Olton, Warwicks. † B 3

HILL, Lady Caroline Emily Gray 1843-1924
Birkenhead 1883 and 1920; London 1919. † G 4, L 95, LS 8, RCA 1, SWA 1.

HILL, C.F. Exh. 1906-9
Sculptor. Chelsea, London.1906. Borough Green, Kent 1909. † B 1, L 1, RA 2.

HILL, Constance M. Exh. 1884-87
Figure painter. Clifton, Bristol 1884; St. Winnow Vicarage, Lostwithiel, Cornwall 1885. † GI 1, SWA 2.

HILL, Daisy Exh. 1888-98
Sandringham Villa, Olton, Warwicks. † B 3, L 1, M 2.

HILL, Derek* b. 1916
Landscape, figure and portrait painter. Exh. 1938-40. † GI 1, LEF 9, RED 4.

HILL, Dick Exh. 1940
Pencil portrait artist. 50 Westbourne Park Villas, London. † RA 1.

HILL, Dora de Clermont Exh. 1904
Animal painter. Park House, Southwell, Notts. † N 1.

HILL, Mrs. D.O. Exh. 1881-1902
Newington Lodge, Edinburgh. † GI 1, RSA 4.

HILL, Edith Exh. 1883
Sculptor. † RBA 1.

HILL, Ethel Exh. 1899-1901
Northampton 1899; Bath 1901. † B 4.

HILL, Edwin A. Exh. 1894
Architect. Oakfield, Brentwood, Essex. † RA 1.

HILL, Ernest F. Exh. 1897-1940
Landscape painter. Birmingham. † B 61, L 1, RA 1, RI 3.

HILL, Ellen G. Exh. 1880-1921
Figure painter. 27 Thurlow Road, Hampstead 1880; c/o Lady Scott, Westminster, London 1921. † B 1, D 7, L 5, M 2, P 5, RA 7, RI 9, ROI 1.

HILL, E.H. Exh. 1923-26
Higher Tranmere, Birkenhead 1923; Woodhey, Bebington, Cheshire 1925. † L 6.

HILL, E. Stainsby Exh. 1906-7
5 Hesketh Avenue, Didsbury, Manchester. † M 2.

HILL, Frank b. 1881
Watercolour painter, etcher and designer. Studied Putney School of Art and Central School of Arts and Crafts. Exh. 1926-30. Add: 153 Elborough Street, Southfield, London. † L 3, M 1.

HILL, F.E. Exh. 1899
22 New Street, Worcester. † B 1.

HILL, Mme F.E. de Lannoy Exh. 1913-19
38 Syncombe Hill, Bath. † LS 21, SWA 4.

HILL, F.W. Exh. 1912-14
59 Topsham Road, Smethwick, Birmingham. † RA 3.

HILL, G. Noel Exh. 1936
Architect. Town Hall, Manchester. † RA 1.

HILL, Gertrude N. Exh. 1923-26
Miniature portrait painter. 27 Coperscope Road, Beckenham, Kent. † RA 3.

HILL, George S. Exh. 1893-1902
Glasgow. † GI 10.

HILL, Henry Exh. 1900-3
101 Broadhurst Gardens, West Hampstead, London. † RI 2.

HILL, H.D. Exh. 1916
Glenholm, Waterlooville, Hants. † L 1.

HILL, Henry Houghton d. c.1951
Architect. A.R.H.A. 1941. Exh. 1927. Add: George Street, Cork. † RHA 1.

HILL, Mrs. Henrietta M.T. Exh. 1894
Rosedene, Little Park, Enfield, Middlesex. † RHA 1.

HILL, Isa E. Exh. 1925
St. Vigeans, Giffnock, Glasgow. † GI 1.

HILL, James Exh. 1934-36
3 Esplanade, Stirling. † GI 1, RSW 2.

HILL, Joseph Exh. 1936
Architect. 34 Gordon Square, London. † RA 1.

HILL, Justus Exh. 1884-98
Figure and landscape painter. London. † B 10, G 11, L 4, M 1, RA 13, RBA 1, RHA 5, RI 1, ROI 1, RSA 1.

HILL, J. Allen Exh. 1929-38
Landscape painter. Leyland, Lancs. † L 5, RA 1.

HILL, James John* 1811-1882
Landscape, portrait and rustic genre painter. Born and studied in Birmingham. Came to London 1839. Frequently visited Ireland. R.B.A. 1842. Add: Sutton House, West Hill, Highgate, London 1880. † RBA 2, TOO 1.

HILL, J. Raworth Exh. 1940
Architect. 11 Buckingham Gate, london. † RA 1.

HILL, James Stephens 1854-1921
Landscape and flower painter. R.B.A. 1885, R.I. 1898, R.O.I. 1895. Exh. 1880-1920. Add: Hampstead, London. † B 2, BG 3, D 3, GI 9, I 8, L 17, M 16, NG 9, RA 35, RBA 36, RI 39, ROI 62.

HILL, Mrs. Kate E. Exh. 1895-98
Figure painter. 29 Skell Bank, Ripon, Yorks. † L 2, RA 3, RBA 1.

HILL, Kate T. Exh. 1906
Sunnyside House, Forfar, N.B. † GI 2.

HILL, L. Exh. 1939
197 Stoney Lane, Sparkhill, Birmingham. † B 1.

HILL, Sir Leonard Erskine b. 1866
Painter, architect and illustrator. Exh. 1899-1922. Add: Frognal, London 1899; Loughton, Bucks. 1915. † I 8, LS 3, RBA 2, RI 1, ROI 2.

HILL, Lucie M. Exh. 1895-1914
Miniature painter. R.M.S. 1897. Add: 12 Kensington, Bath, Som. † L 26, RA 2, RHA 5, RI 2, RMS 12, RSA 2, SWA 3.

Hill, Mrs. M. Exh. 1934
Highgate, London. † SWA 1.

HILL, Mabel Exh. 1932-38
c/o Bourlet & Sons, London. † P 1, RCA 2, ROI 4.

HILL, Marion Exh. 1931-34
Landscape painter. † COO 2, RMS 1.

HILL, Mary Exh. 1912-28
Miniature painter. 4 Gayton Crescent, Hampstead, London. † D 7, I 1, L 1, RA 3, RI 4.

HILL, Mary de Clermont Exh. 1904
Flower painter. Park House, Southwell, Notts. † N 1.

HILL, Miss M.F. Exh. 1933
La Guardiola, Taormina, Sicily. † RSA 1.

HILL, Miss M.J. Exh. 1926
† RMS 1.

HILL, Miss M.T. Exh. 1928
Henar, Llanrwst, N. Wales. † L 1.

HILL, N. Exh. 1889
Rye, Sussex. † B 2, L 1.

HILL, Miss N. Exh. 1907-29
Liverpool. † L 5.

HILL, Miss N. Exh. 1913-24
156 Hatfield Road, Fleetville, St. Albans, Herts. † L 3.

HILL, Nathaniel d. 1920
Figure painter. A.R.H.A. 1892, R.H.A. 1894. Add: Drogheda 1880; Royal Hibernian Academy, Dublin 1905. † L 3, RHA 25, ROI 7.

HILL, Mrs. Nina Exh. 1927-36
Flower and still life painter. Reigate, Surrey 1927; Westerham, Kent 1933. † L 1, RA 5, RBA 1, RHA 1, RI 12, RSA 2.

HILL, Oliver Exh. 1911-40
Architect. London. † GI 1, RA 29, RSA 10.

HILL, Osbourn Exh. 1927
Watercolour figure painter. c/o Captain M.O. Roberts, Woolsthorpe by Belvoir. † N 2.

HILL, Perry Exh. 1935
Sculptor. Guntsfield, Ditchling, Hassocks, Sussex. † RA 1.

HILL, Phillip Maurice 1892-1952
Marine and landscape painter. Studied London and St. Ives. Add: London and Partridges, Wadhurst, Sussex. † AR 108, GOU 1, NEA 4, RA 1, RBA 11, ROI 12, RSA 1.

HILL, Queenie Exh. 1903
250 Bristol Road, Birmingham. † B 1.

HILL, Roland Exh. 1889-90
Architect. 124 Hurlingham Road, Fulham, London. † RA 2.

HILL, Rowland Exh. 1935-38
Landscape painter. Belfast. † RHA 3.

HILL, Rowland Henry b. 1873
Painter and black and white artist. Studied Halifax School of Art, Bradford Technical College and Herkomer's, Bushey, Herts. Painted on the continent. Exh. 1897-1940. Add: Halifax 1897; Runswick, Hinderwell, Yorks. 1908. † L 14, RA 21.

HILL, Stella Exh. 1898-1905
Olton, Birmingham † B 9, L 1.

HILL, Sarah B. Exh. 1929
Engraver. 135 East 66th Street, New York, U.S.A. † RA 1.

HILL, Thomas* 1829-1908
Portrait and figure painter. Wednesfield, nr. Wolverhampton 1883; Codsall, Wolverhampton 1887; Radford, nr. Stafford 1895; Birmingham 1899. † B 24, GI 4, L 5, M 4, NEA 1, NG 1, RA 7, RHA 4, ROI 5.

HILL, Thomas c.1852-1926
Portrait and landscape painter. Add: London. † B 6, GI 3, L 6, M 1, NG 1, RA 16, RBA 2, RCA 1, ROI 2.

HILL, Vernon b. 1887
Sculptor, etcher, engraver and draughtsman. b. Halifax. Apprenticed to a lithographic artist at the age of 13. Exh. 1908-27. Add: London. † CHE 2, LEI 81, NEA 5, RA 2, RSA 2.

HILL, William J. Exh. 1883-1921
Birmingham. † B 20.

HILL, Wiliam Robert Exh. 1884
Figure painter. Upper Holloway, London. † ROI 2.

HILLER, Eric Exh. 1938
Watercolour landscape painter. † GOU 46.

HILLER, Henry Gustave b. 1864
Stained glass artist, gesso modeller and painter. Studied Manchester School of Art. Exh. 1903-25. Add: Liverpool. † L 19.

HILLIARD, Lawrence Exh. 1881-87
Still life painter. Cowley Rectory, Uxbridge, Middlesex 1881; Coniston, Ambleside 1883. † D 7, L 5, RHA 1, RI 7, ROI 1.

HILLIARD, Maud Exh. 1889-1928
nee Ruault. Watercolour miniature painter and crayon artist. Studied St. John's Wood. Add: London. † RA 1, RID 12.

HILLIARD, William Henry 1836-1905
American painter. Boston, U.S.A. and 50 Boulevard Haussmann, Paris 1880. † RA 1.

HILLIER, Edith Exh. 1880
Landscape painter. 36 Elgin Road, Dublin. † SWA 1.

HILLIER, Herbert Exh. 1923-26
Etcher. † FIN 8.

HILLIER, H.W. Exh. 1912-14
London. † RA 3.

HILLIER, Tristram* b. 1905
Landscape painter. b. Peking. Studied Slade School and in France. Lived in France until 1939/40. † COO 1, LEF 54, TOO 5.

HILLINGFORD, Robert Alexander* 1828-1893
Historical genre and figure painter. Studied in Dusseldorf, Munich and London. Lived in Italy for several years. Add: London. † B 2, GI 2, L 8, M 1, RA 19, RBA 1, ROI 4, TOO 1.

HILLIS, S.E. Exh. 1889
121 Grosvenor Street, Chorlton on Medlock, Manchester. † M 1.

HILLKIRK, Isabel Exh. 1900-8
Southport, Lancs. 1900; Clevedon, Som. 1902; Sidmouth, S. Devon 1908. † L 1, M 9.

HILLS, Laura Coombs Exh. 1922
† RMS 2.

HILLS, W. Noel Exh. 1920-24
Landscape painter. 10 Essex Road, Leyton, London. † D 3, RA 1.

HILL-SNOWE, Lilly Exh. 1885
Figure painter. 3 Holtman Road, Abbey Road, London. † RA 1.

HILSON, Jessie M. Exh. 1898-1900
35 Belmont Road, Jersey, C.I. † L 3, RMS 1, RSA 1.

HILTON, Arthur Cyril b. 1897
Watercolour painter. Self taught. Exh. 1926-32. Add: 32 Borchfields Road, Longsight, Manchester. † L 2, M 1.
HILTON, Dorothy Frances Exh. 1911-14
Toy maker, enamel plaque artist and dog miniaturist. Studied Birmingham, Slade School and under Miss Sawyer, Bushey, Herts. A.R.M.S. 1911. Add: Portinscale, nr. Keswick, Cumberland. † L 4, RA 1, RMS 19.
HILTON, Mrs. Florence Exh. 1936-37
Colwyn Bay, Wales. † RCA 2.
HILTON, G.H. Exh. 1920-39
Stechford, Birmingham 1920; Four Oaks, Birmingham 1931. † B 17.
HILTON, Henry Exh. 1880-88
Landscape painter. Birkenhead 1880 and 1883; Trefriw, nr. Conway, Wales 1881; Liscard, Cheshire 1885; c/o King, Liverpool 1887. † L 2, RA 4, RBA 1, RCA 2.
HILTON, Marie E. Exh. 1889
Still life painter. 76 Bow Road, London. † RA 1.
HILTON, Robert Exh. 1886
Landscape painter. 11 Elm Grove, Cricklewood, London. † RA 1, RBA 2.
HILTON, Roger* b. 1911
Figure painter. Exh. 1937. † AG 1.
HILTON, Stanfield Exh. 1895-97
5 Cook Street, Liverpool. † L 4.
HIME, Harry b. 1863
Landscape, figure and animal painter. b. Donegal. Studied under T.D. Watson. Painter and adviser to H.H. Gaekwar of Baroda. Exh. 1882-1933. Add: Liverpool 1882 and 1886; Bettws-y-Coed, Wales 1885. † L 78, M 3, RA 8, RBA 2, RCA 17, RI 4.
HIMONA, Nicolas d. 1929
Landscape painter. b. Russia of Greek parentage. Exh. 1928. † AR 41.
HIMSWORTH, Joyce Rosemary Exh. 1927-33
Designer and craftsman of ecclesiastical and domestic plate, jeweller and enameller. Studied Sheffield College of Arts and Crafts and in Italy. Teacher of metalwork and jewellery at Chesterfield and district School of Arts and Crafts and at Rotherham School of Art. Add: 31 Chelsea Road, Brincliffe, Sheffield. † L 14.
HINCHLEY, Edith Mary b. 1870
nee Mason, Miniature and portrait painter and illustrator. Studied National Art Training School (silver medal). R.M.S. 1898, H.R.M.S. 1930, S.W.A. 1923. Exh. 1897-1938. Add: London 1897 and 1908; Bangkok, Siam 1906; Buxton, Derbys. 1907. † ALP 1, L 17, M 1, NG 4, RA 29, RBA 1, RHA 1, RI 4, RMS 118, SWA 12.
HINCHLIFF, Major C.H. Exh. 1889-90
Watercolour painter. Worlington House, Instow, nr. Bideford, Devon. † D 2, RI 2.
HINCHLIFF, Woodbine K. Exh. 1895-1913
Landscape, figure and flower painter. A.R.E. 1895. Add: Bushey 1895; Instow, nr. Bideford, Devon 1897; London 1901; Headley, Hants. 1912. † BG 1, L 7, M 2, RA 15, RE 24, RI 2, RID 37, ROI 1.
HINCHCLIFFE, Richard George 1868-1942
Portrait and landscape painter. b. Manchester. Exh. 1894-1940. Add: Liverpool. † L 99, M 3, RA 7, RCA 48.
HINCKLIEFF, Miss M.E. Exh. 1928
Cedar House, Woodthorpe Avenue, Nottingham. † N 2.
HINCKS, H.T. Exh. 1913-38
Stained glass artist. Beeston, Notts. 1913; Nottingham 1926. † N 11.
HINCKS, Mary Exh. 1904
Baron's Down, Dulverton, Som. † B 1.
HIND, Arthur Magyar 1880-1957
Watercolour landscape painter and writer. b. Burton on Trent. Slade Professor of Fine Art, Oxford University 1921-27. Norton Professor of Poetry, Harvard University 1930-31, Keeper of Prints and Drawings British Museum 1933-45. H.R.E. 1932. Exh. 1920-38. † AG 21, CG 28, COO 2, FIN 3, G 7, GOU 33, NEA 7, RA 3, WG 3.
HIND, Ellen Mary Exh. 1887-1900
Flower and figure painter. 25 Dartmouth Park Hill, London. † RA 1, RBA 1, RI 1, SWA 2.
HIND, Frank Exh. 1884-1904
Leamington, Warwicks. 1884 and 1893; Correze, France 1892. † B 8, FIN 1, G 2, GI 1, L 13, M 1, RA 15, RBA 17, ROI 3.
HIND, Gertrude F. Exh. 1904
Landscape painter. 4 Thurlow Road, Hampstead, London. † RA 1.
HINDE, Mrs. E. Exh. 1934-35
9 Arundel Mansions, London. † RBA 3.
HINDE, T. Junr. Exh. 1897-1915
10 Richmond Street, Liverpool. † L 25, RCA 1.
HINDLE, Albert b. 1888
Accrington 1912; London 1916. † I 1, L 1, ROI 1.
HINDLE, Gertrude Exh. 1919-23
26 Maudesly Road, Eltham, London. † LS 3, ROI 2.
HINDLEY, Mrs. Greta Exh. 1925-27
Miniature painter. High Prestwick, Wormley, Godalming, Surrey. † RA 2.
HINDLEY, Godfrey C. Exh. 1880-1910
Figure, flower painter and illustrator. R.O.I. 1898. Add: London. † B 11, D 1, GI 9, L 14, M 4, RA 24, RBA 3, RHA 2, RI 4, ROI 27.
HINDLEY, Helen M. Exh. 1901-15
Figure and portrait painter. London. † B 1, L 1, RA 9, ROI 7.
HINDON, Miss E.L. Exh. 1905-6
Longfield, Gordon Road, Ealing, London. † ROI 3.
HINDS, W.E. Exh. 1909-26
Liverpool. † L 4.
HINE, Esther Exh. 1885
Hurstleigh, Arkwright Road, London. † RI 1.
HINE, George T. Exh. 1890
Architect. Nottingham † RA 1.
HINE, Harry 1845-1941
Landscape painter (formerly Mate in Merchant Service). Son of Henry George H. q.v. Married Victoria H. q.v. R.I. 1879, H.R.I. 1918, R.O.I. 1883. Add: London 1880; St. Albans, Herts. 1884 and 1898; Stevenage, Herts. 1895; Botesdale, Suffolk 1906. † B 5, D 19, DOW 80, FIN 1, GI 3, L 25, LEI 1, M 10, NG 7, RA 2, RBA 1, RHA 1, RI 221, ROI 17, RSW 1.
HINE, Henry George* 1811-1895
Landscape painter and illustrator. On staff of "Punch" 1921-44, and "Illustrated London News". Father of Harry H. q.v. A.R.I. 1863, R.I. 1864, V.P.R.I. 1887. Add: Hampstead, London. † AG 3, FIN 7, L 5, M 2, RI 92.
HINE, Helen Pillans Exh. 1886
12 Tantallon Place, London. † RSA 1.
HINE, J.F. Exh. 1896
c/o Dr. T. Wright, Castle Place, Nottingham. † N 1.
HINE, L. Margaret Exh. 1923-28
Figure and landscape painter. West Bridgeford, Notts. † N 17.
HINE, Muriel Exh. 1928-33
10 Highfield Villas, Kendal. † L 3.
HINE, Thomas C. Exh. 1888-94
Painter of churches and church interiors. Regent Street, Nottingham. † N 5.
HINE, Victoria Exh. 1880-1912
nee Colkett. Landscape painter. Married Harry H. q.v. A.R.E. 1887, R.E. 1896. Add: London 1880; St. Albans, Herts 1881 and 1905; Stevenage, Herts. 1895; Botesdale, Suffolk 1908. † D 6, DOW 56, M 4, NG 2, RBA 2, RE 7, RI 19, SWA 9.
HINE, William Egerton d. 1926
Landscape painter. Art master Harrow School 1892-1922. Add: London 1882; Westcott, Dorking, Surrey 1888; Reigate, Surrey 1891; Harrow 1892; Haslemere, Surrey 1923. † D 1, FIN 81, L 3, M 3, NG 3, RA 14, RBA 3, RI 6, ROI 1.
HINE, Mrs. W. Egerton Exh. 1887-95
Westcott, Dorking 1887; Reigate, Surrey 1890; Harrow 1895. † D 2, L 2, NG 1, RI 1, ROI 2, SWA 1.
HINES, Ada F. Exh. 1901-7
Sale, Cheshire. † L 2, M 10.
HINES, Frederick Exh. 1880-97
Landscape painter. Brother of Theodore H. q.v. Add: London 1880, and 1893; Epping, Essex 1885; Chingford, Essex 1886. † D 14, DOW 19, G 2, GI 10, L 1, M 1, RA 13, RBA 39, RHA 1, RI 3, ROI 2.
HINES, Theodore* Exh. 1880-90
Landscape painter. Brother of Frederick H. q.v. Add: London. † G 1, GI 5, L 1, RA 8, RBA 29, RHA 2, TOO 1.
HINGSTON, Miss D. Exh. 1938
43 Middleton Hall Road, Kings Norton, Birmingham. † B 1.
HINKLEY, F. Exh. 1881
May Villa, Victoria Road, Aston, Birmingham. † RSA 2.
HINKLEY, Helen E. Exh. 1926-28
Midhurst, Sussex. † L 6.
HINLEY, Alfred Exh. 1882-90
Landscape painter. Liverpool 1882; Birmingham 1883. † B 12, RA 1.
HINLEY, Charles Exh. 1890
Oulton Cross, nr. Stone, Staffs. † B 1.
HINSON, Ethel Brooke Exh. 1886-91
Figure painter. Sutton, Beckenham, Kent. † RA 4.
HINTON, Miss M.B. Exh. 1891
23 Calthorpe Road, Edgbaston, Birmingham. † B 2.
HIORNS, Frederick Robert Exh. 1904-40
Architect, watercolour painter, critic and writer. Add: London. † GI 1, RA 5.
HIPKINS, Edith Exh. 1880-98
Fruit and figure painter. 100 Warwick Gardens, Kensington, London. † D 4, G 1, L 3, RA 5, RBA 6, SWA 5.
HIPKINS, Miss E.J. Exh. 1911
52B Russell Road, Kensington, London. † RA 1.
HIPKINS, John Exh. 1897
Etcher. 100 Warwick Gardens, Kensington, London. † RA 1.
HIPKINS, Roland 1895-1951
Landscape painter. b. Bilston, Staffs. Visited New Zealand. Exh. 1920-28. Add: London 1920; Bilston, Staffs. 1921. † AB 33, B 4.
HIPSLEY, John Henry Exh. 1882-1910
Flower painter. Liverpool 1882; London 1883; Hemel Hempstead, Herts. 1891; Birmingham 1899. † B 8, D 1, L 3, RBA 2, RI 2.
HIPWELL, H. Exh. 1936-39
† RI 3.

HIPWELL, Miss M.E. Exh. 1936
23 Beaufort Road, Edgbaston, Birmingham. † B 1.

HIRD, Mrs. Linda Helen Exh. 1910-32
London 1910 and 1927; Folkestone, Kent 1924 and 1932. † L 1, RI 6, RMS 1.

HIRONS, Mrs. E. Exh. 1920-27
49 Highbridge Road, Wylde Green, Birmingham. † B 5.

HIRSCH, Otto Exh. 1892
3 Tanfield Place, Leeds. † L 1.

HIRSHFELD, Mrs. E.B. Exh. 1901
9 Rue Say, Paris. † L 1.

HIRST, Benjamin C.C. Exh. 1936
129 Selly Oak Road, King's Norton, Birmingham. † B 1.

HIRST, Mrs. Dorothy b. 1888
nee Stephenson. Painter and wood engraver. Exh. 1921-33. Add: Holyport House, Holyport, Berks. † GI 8, I 2, M 2, NEA 3, RA 11, RSA 1.

HIRST, Mrs. D.F. Exh. 1913-27
Batley, Yorks. 1913; Collingham Bridge, Yorks. 1915; Cloxwold, Yorks. 1918; Henley-on-Thames 1926. † I 2, L 15, LS 6, RA 5, RI 3, ROI 1.

HIRST, Eve Exh. 1936
Figure painter. Nether Haugh, Rotherham, Yorks. † RA 1.

HIRST, J.H. Exh. 1902
Architect. Town Hall, Hull. † RA 1.

HIRST, Laura Exh. 1882-84
110 Upper Mary Street, Birmingham. † B 2.

HIRST, Miss M. Exh. 1882-1901
Birmingham. † B 22.

HIRST, Norman 1862-1956
Mezzotint engraver. b. Liverpool. Studied Herkomer's, Bushey (2 year painting scholarship). A.R.E. 1931. Add: Bushey, Herts 1890; Parkstone, Dorset 1895; Christchurch, Hants. 1898; Langport, Somerset 1902; Seaford, Sussex 1922. † AG 1, FIN 7, L 14, RA 44, RE 4, RI 1.

HIRST, Sydney G. Exh. 1936-37
Landscape painter. Dublin 1936; Montenotte, Cork 1937. † RHA 3.

HIRSZENBERG, Samuel Exh. 1905-7
20 Smolenska, Cracow, Poland. † L 3.

HISCOCK, L.R. Exh. 1936
Architect. Lloyds Bank Chambers, High Street, Guildford, Surrey. † RA 1.

HISCOX, George Dunkerton 1840-1909
Landscape painter. Beaufort House, The Grove, Slough 1880; Windsor, Berks. 1888; London 1900. † B 12, D 8, L 20, NG 1, RA 19, RBA 19, RHA 24, RI 8, ROI 3.

HISCOX, Miss Laura Exh. 1880-86
Watercolour landscape painter. Beaufort House, The Grove, Slough, Bucks. † D 3, RBA 6, RI 1.

HISLOP, Andrew Exh. 1880-1903
Landscape painter. Glasgow. † G 1, GI 31, RA 1, RSA 12.

HISLOP, Andrew Healey 1887-1954
Painter and etcher. Teacher of drawing Edinburgh College of Art. Married Margaret Ross H. q.v. Exh. 1919-40. Add: Edinburgh. † GI 7, L 1, NEA 1, RSA 54, RSW 6.

HISLOP, Margaret Ross Exh. 1919-40
nee Grant. Painter. Married Andrew Healey H. q.v. Add: West Calder 1919; Edinburgh 1922. † GI 8, RSA 24, RSW 1.

HISLOP, Miss S. Exh. 1881-90
Auchterarder, Edinburgh. † GI 2, RSA 7.

HISLOP, Walter B. Exh. 1912-13
Colinton, N.B. 1912; Edinburgh 1913. † L 1, M 1, RSA 2.

HITCH, Frederick Brook b. 1877
Sculptor. Son of Nathaniel H. q.v. Studied R.A. Schools. Exh. 1906-34. Add: London 1906 and 1913, Ware, Herts. 1912. † L 3, RA 20, RCA 4, ROI 1.

HITCH, J.O. Brook Exh. 1932-33
Architect. 3 Staple Inn, High Holborn, London. † RA 2.

HITCH, Nathaniel Exh. 1884
Sculptor. Father of Frederick Brook H. q.v. Add: 60 Harleyford Road, Kennington, London. † RA 1.

HITCHCOCK, Arthur Exh. 1884
Watercolour painter. 87 Ramsden Road, Balham, London. † RBA 1.

HITCHCOCK, George* 1850-1913
Landscape and figure painter. b. U.S.A. d. Holland. Married Cecil Jay q.v. Add: c/o Gladwell Bros., Gracechurch Street, London 1883; Holland 1891; Paris 1908. † GOU 24, L 10, NG 5, RA 11, RBA 1, RI 2, ROI 1. TOO 1.

HITCHCOCK, Mrs. H.F. Exh. 1908
East Bergholt, Suffolk. † SWA 2.

HITCHCOCK, Kate Exh. 1884-97
Figure painter. 96 Adelaide Road, South Hampstead, London. † B 1, L 2, M 1, RA 2, RBA 5, RI 2, ROI 5, SWA 1.

HITCHCOCK, S. Exh. 1882
30 Gt. Russell Street, London. † D 1.

HITCHCOCK, Miss S.M. Exh. 1919
Northfield, Sherborne, Dorset. † RI 1.

HITCHCOCK, Theodore Charles Basil b. 1892
Painter and teacher. Studied Hornsey School of Art. Exh. 1935-38. Add: 1 Florence Drive, Enfield, Middlesex. † ROI 3.

HITCHENS, Alfred b. 1861
Portrait, figure and landscape painter. Studied South Kensington (2 gold medals), Juliens, Paris and Rome. Father of Ivon H. q.v. Exh. 1884-1919. Add: London 1884 and 1911; Ilkley, Yorks. 1895; Englefield Green, Surrey 1896. † G 2, GI 3, L 17, LS 3, M 1, NEA 1, NG 6, P 2, RA 17, RHA 4, ROI 14, WG 331.

HITCHENS, Ivon* b. 1893
Landscape, still life painter and mural decorator. Son of Alfred H. q.v. Studied St. John's Wood and R.A. Schools. Member London Group 1931. "Coronation" (1937) purchased by Chantrey Bequest 1964. Exh. 1931-40. Add: London. † AG 1, COO 5, L 2, LEF 74, LEI 33.

HITCHINGS, T.C.R. Exh. 1929-34
60 Connaught Road, Roath, Cardiff, Wales. † B 2, RCA 4.

HITCHONS, Ethelwyn M. Exh. 1926
† M 1.

HITZ, Dora Exh. 1887-90
Figure painter. London. † L 1, RA 1.

HJORTH, Bror b. 1894
Swedish sculptor. Add: Gotgatan 71, Stockholm 1933. † RSA 2.

HOAD, Mrs. Agnes Exh. 1922-37
Landscape painter. Beckenham, Kent 1922; Weybridge, Surrey 1930. † D 3, COO 2, RBA 3, RI 7, SWA 13.

HOAD, Betty Exh. 1930-31
Beckenham, Kent. † NEA 1, SWA 2.

HOAD, Mary Exh. 1930-40
Figure painter. Abington High Pin Close, Weybridge, Surrey. † COO 1, GOU 2, NEA 8.

HOAR, Mrs. Amy Exh. 1886
Bantony House, Robertsbridge, Sussex. † D 1.

HOAR, Harold F. Exh. 1932
Architect. 5 Gunnersbury Drive, Ealing, London. † RA 1.

HOARE, Miss D.M. Exh. 1906-7
Bicester, Oxon. † RA 2.

HOARE, Edythe Exh. 1900-5
Park Villa, Holly Walk, Leamington, Warwicks. † B 2, D 2.

HOARE, Edward B. Exh. 1922-23
Architect. 22 Portman Square, London. † RA 2.

HOARE, Miss F.E. Exh. 1915-22
23 Jameson Road, Bexhill-on-Sea, Sussex. † RI 4, SWA 1.

HOARE, George T. Exh. 1888-91
Landscape painter. Burnham House, Clifton Grove, Slough, Bucks. † RA 2, ROI 2.

HOARE, Marjorie d. 1953
Painter and pencil artist. Studied Slade School 1927 and under Franklin White. Exh. 1927-40. Add: The Grange, Barcombe, Nr. Lewes, Sussex. † GOU 1, NEA 9, RA 1, RED 1, RHA 1.

HOBART, Miss Exh. 1901
18 Chapel Street, Belgrave Square, London. † SWA 1.

HOBBIS, Charles Wilfred b. 1880
Silver worker and sculptor. b. Sheffield. Studied Sheffield School of Art and Royal College of Art. Headmaster Norwich School of Art. Exh. 1918. Add: 204 College Road, Norwich, Norfolk. † RA 1.

HOBBISS, Holland W. Exh. 1903-28
Architect. London 1903; 33 Newhall Street, Birmingham 1921. † B 7, RA 1.

Hobbs, Doris Exh. 1912-13
9 Huskisson Street, Liverpool. † L 2.

HOBBS, F.W. Exh. 1932
27 Meersbrook Road, Sheffield. † B 1.

HOBBS, Mrs. J. Exh. 1920
60 Crosby Green, West Derby, Liverpool. † L 1.

HOBBS, Katie Exh. 1889-1900
Flower and landscape painter. Bourton-on-the-Water; Glos. 1889 and 1891; London 1890; High Wycombe, Bucks. 1895. † B 2, M 1, RBA 6, RI 1, ROI 1, SWA 7.

HOBDAY, Col. E.A.P. Exh. 1925
Landscape painter. † GOU 30.

HOBDAY, Winifred A. Exh. 1935-38
Curtis House, Poplar Road, Solihull, Warwicks. † B 7.

HOBDEN, Frank Exh. 1882-1915
Figure and domestic painter. R.B.A. 1901. Add: London 1882; Benfleet, Essex 1907. † B 22, D 6, GI 1, L 9, M 5, RA 10, RBA 104, RI 20, ROI 37.

HOBDEY, William Exh. 1889-92
192 Lloyd Street, Greenheys, Manchester. † M 4.

HOBKIRK, Stuart Exh. 1897-1920
Landscape and figure painter. St. Ives, Cornwall 1897; Tonbridge, Kent 1920. † B 5, GI 5, L 7, M 5, RA 14, RBA 6, RHA 1, ROI 3, RSA 1.

HOBLEY, Edward George 1866-1916
Landscape painter. Art master, Penrith. Exh. 1892-1909. Add: Bradford 1892; Farsley, Nr. Leeds 1893; Penrith, Cumberland 1899. † B 2, L 3, M 3, RA 5, RCA 18.

HOBSON, Miss A.E. Exh. 1918
65 Redcliffe Road, South Kensington, London. † RA 1.

HOBSON, Alice Mary b. 1860
Watercolour painter. Studied under James Orrock, John Fulleylove and Wilmot Pillsbury. R.I. 1881 (resigned 1931). Add: Leicester 1883; Bedford 1896 and 1912; London 1911, 1914 and 1916; Doncaster 1915; Midhurst, Sussex 1918; Chichester 1923; Marazion, Penzance, Cornwall 1928. † B 1, L 4, RA 1, RI 148.

HOBSON, Cecil James 1874-1918
Miniature portrait painter. R.I. 1901, R.M.S. 1896. Add: London. † B 2, D 2, L 3, NG 3, RA 26, RI 24, RMS 47, ROI 1.

HOBSON, Ellen M. Exh. 1884-1914
Landscape painter. 10 Regent's Park Road, London 1884 and 1914; Bedford 1898. † RI 1, SWA 7.

HOBSON, F.W. Exh. 1888-91
Landscape painter. Cottesford Place, Lincoln. † B 1, L 1, RBA 1.

HOBSON, H.E. Exh. 1887
c/o J. Searle, Crediton, Devon. † M 2.

HOBSON, Kenneth b. 1897
Painter, etcher and colour print engraver. Studied Slade School, St. Martins School of Art, Central School of Arts and Crafts, Paris and Rome. Exh. 1922-28. Add: London. † BA 2, BAR 1, D 4, GOU 2, I 3, L 2, NEA 1.

HOBSON, Laurence b. 1872
Architect and painter. Exh. 1896-1928. Add: Rock Ferry, Cheshire 1896; Liscard, Cheshire 1897; Wallasey, Cheshire 1916; Oxton, Birkenhead 1920; Liverpool 1924. † L 49, RCA 3.

HOBSON, Mabel Emily See LEE-HANKEY

HOBSON, Ruth Exh. 1909-13
Admaston, Wellington, Salop. † B 2, L 3, LS 6, RA 1.

HOBSON, Sophie Exh. 1880-87
Mrs. Ernest H. nee Barker. Figure painter. Add: 27 Ainger Road, Primrose Hill, London. † SWA 6.

HOBSON, Viva Mary b. 1895
Miniature portrait painter and old master copyist in miniature. Studied Chelsea School of Art. Exh. 1916-40. Add: London. † L 4, RA 14, RMS 6.

HOBSON, V.W. Exh. 1888
Westbrook Villas, Darlington, Co. Durham. † M 1.

HOCH, Franz Exh. 1904-6
91 Kaulbach Strasse, Munich. † GI 1, I 1.

HOCHARD, Gaston Exh. 1903-10
French artist. 181 Rue de Courcelles, Paris. † I 1, L 4.

HOCK, Daniel Exh. 1890-93
Figure painter. Hundsthurmer Strasse, Vienna. † RA 2.

HOCKEY, James Morey b. 1904
Painter and etcher. R.B.A. 1940, R.O.I. 1940. Add: West Dulwich 1927; New Malden, Surrey 1935. † M 2, NEA 2, RA 1, RBA 2, ROI 2.

HOCKEY, Miss S.F. Exh. 1906-12
Miniature portrait painter. London. † RA 6.

HOCKIN, Olive Exh. 1903-15
Figure painter. Mortimer, Berks. 1904 and 1914; Kensington, London 1908. † L 5, LS 2, RA 4, SWA 6.

HODDER, Albert Exh. 1880-95
Marine and coastal landscape painter. Add: School of Art, Worcester. † L 3, RA 6, RI 2, TOO 1.

HODDER, Mrs. Charlotte Exh. 1883
Flower painter. Married Albert H. q.v. Add: Rainbow Hill, Worcester. † RA 1.

HODDER, C.A. Exh. 1881
Edinburgh. † RHA 1.

HODEBERT, Leon Auguste Cesar Exh. 1887
French artist. 33 Boulevard Beauvoisin, Rouen, France 1887. † GI 2.

HODEL, Ernst Exh. 1930
Landscape painter. † FIN 43.

HODEL, Joseph A. Exh. 1904-28
Park Road, Acton, London 1904; City School of Art, Liverpool 1909. † L 78, RCA 1.

HODGE, Alma Exh. 1882
9 Clifton Gardens, Maida Vale, London. † L 1.

HODGE, Albert Hemstock 1876-1918
Sculptor. Father of Jessie M.M.H. q.v. Add: Glasgow 1897; London 1900. † GI 17, RA 22, RI 1, RSA 6.

HODGE, Miss E.G. Exh. 1886-87
Flower painter. 140 Adelaide Road, London. † ROI 3.

HODGE, Francis Edwin b. 1883
Portrait and figure painter and decorator. b. Devon. Studied Westminster School of Art, Slade School and Paris. Studied and worked under Augustus John and William Orpen. Assitant to Professor Gerald Moira at the Royal College of Art. R.B.A. 1915, R.I. 1931, R.O.I. 1927, R.P. 1929. Exh. 1906-40. Add: London. † CHE 3, COO 4, G 3, GI 1, GOU 7, I 4, L 2, M 2, NEA 19, P 51, RA 30, RBA 16, RI 7, ROI 37, RSA 1.

HODGE, Ina Exh. 1888
Flower painter. West Kensington, London. † RA 1, RBA 1.

HODGE, John Henry Upton b. 1890
Wood and stone carver and potter. Studied Central School of Arts and Crafts, School of Wood Carving. Exh. 1940. Add: 3 Redford Walk, London. † RA 3.

HODGE, Jessie Mary Margaret b. 1901
Painter and mural decorator. Daughter of Albert Hemstock H. q.v. Studied at R.A. Schools (bronze medal for life painting, Landseer scholarship). Exh. 1922-40. Add: London. † GI 8, L 5, RA 12, RMS 2, RSA 8, RSW 2.

HODGE, Miss M.F.P. Exh. 1915-20
Kensington, London 1915; Bath 1920. † ROI 1, SWA 2.

HODGE, Simon Prince b. 1903
Painter and illustrator. b. Glasgow. Studied Glasgow School of Art. President Johannesburg Art Club 1931-32. Exh. 1933-40. Add: 3 The Hollies, Manor Way, Blackheath, London and Johannesburg, South Africa. † RA 4, RI 2.

HODGE, Thomas Exh. 1880
West View, St. Andrews. † RSA 1.

HODGEN, James Exh. 1922-28
Painter and designer. b. Co. Down. Studied Royal College of Art (travelling scholarship). Exh. 1922-28. Add: 10 Albertville Drive, Belfast. † RHA 15.

HODGES, C.M.* 1858-1916
Exh. 1900-15. Add: Bath. † L 4.

HODGES, Ernest Exh. 1888-94
Landscape and figure painter. Ellerslie, Groombridge, Kent. † RA 1, RBA 1, ROI 5.

HODGES, Florence Mary Exh. 1890-93
Landscape painter. b. Durham. Studied Royal Female School of Art, Calderon School of Animal Painting and under Frank Short. Add: London. † L 3. RA 1, SWA 2.

HODGES, Gertrude Martin Exh. 1925-37
Painter and etcher. Cambridge House, Sydenham Park Road, London. † ALP 1, NEA 6, RA 5, RSA 7.

HODGES, Lancelot J. Exh. 1913-25
Figure and landscape painter. A.N.S.A. 1918, N.S.A. 1921. Add: Nottingham. † N 19, RA 1.

HODGES, Phyllis Oldaker Exh. 1927-39
Painter and etcher. Cambridge House, Sydenham Park Road, London. † L 1, NEA 7, RA 7, RHA 8, RI 3, RSA 5.

HODGES, Sydney Exh. 1880-93
Portrait painter. London. † G 2, L 2, RA 11.

HODGES, William E. Exh. 1913-34
Stained glass artist. Hichison Road, Newlands, Peckham Rye, London. † RA 15.

HODGES, W.H. Exh. 1911-23
Landscape painter. A.N.S.A. 1913. Add: Beeston Notts. 1911; Nottingham 1912, West Bridgford, Notts. 1914; Sneinton, Notts. 1916.

HODGES, William Merrett Exh. 1896-1938
Painter, etcher, photographer and art dealer. Add: Birmingham. † B 50, L 16, RA 2. RCA 12.

HODGES, Winifred R. Exh. 1934
Cambridge House, Sydenham Park Road, London. † RSA 1.

HODGES, W. Roberta Exh. 1929-40
Figure and landscape painter. 4 St. Mary Street, St. Andrews, Fife. † NEA 1, RBA 2, RHA 2, RSA 3.

HODGKIN, Eliot b. 1905
Landscape painter. "October" purchased by Chantrey Bequest 1936. Exh. 1934-40. Add: London. † NEA 3, RA 11, RBA 3.

HODGKIN, J. Edward b. 1875
Watercolour painter. No formal art training. Trustee Bowes Museum and Art Gallery, Barnard Castle. A.R.B.A. 1926, R.B.A. 1928. Exh. 1926-39. Add: Darlington, Co. Durham. † L 1, RBA 96, RI 5, WG 63.

HODGKINS, Frances* 1870-1947
Figure, landscape and still life painter. b. New Zealand. No formal art training. Came to England 1900. First woman on the teaching staff at Colarossi's in Paris. Travelled on the continent, N. Africa and Middle East. A.S.W.A. 1909. Member London Group 1940. Several examples of her work are in the Tate Gallery. Add: London 1900, Paris 1902 and 1922, St. Ives, Cornwall 1914. † AG 2, B 5, BG 1, FIN 9, G 1, GI 4, GOU 6, I 83, L 13, LEF 153, LEI 43, LS 6, M 1, NEA 5, RA 5, RED 8, RI 5, RSA 2, RSW 3, SWA 9.

HODGKINSON, G.A. Exh. 1904
1 Claremont, Headingley, Leeds. † RCA 1.

HODGKINSON, Louis Exh. 1909-10
Woodlands, Honley, Huddersfield. † L 2.

HODGKINSON, George Exh. 1897-1904
Urban landscape painter. 9 Glebe Street, Nottingham. † N 3.

HODGSON, Betty Exh. 1934
† RMS 1.

HODGSON, Mrs. Brian Exh. 1889
Alderley Grange, Wooton Under Edge, and Villa Himalaya, Mentone, France. † D 1.

HODGSON, Clara Exh. 1886
St. Kevins, Upper Rathmines, Dublin. † RHA 1.

HODGSON, Mrs. Dora Exh. 1885
Fruit painter. † ROI 1.

HODGSON, Mrs. Dora b. 1891
nee Houghton, Miniature painter. b. Moore, Cheshire. Exh. 1926-35. Add: Hills Barn, Horsham, Sussex. † L 6, RA 10, RMS 4.

HODGSON, Elizabeth K. Exh. 1934-37
Figure and landscape painter. Wokingham, Berks. and London. † RA 2, RBA 2, ROI 1.

HODGSON, Miss E.M. Exh. 1909-13
London. † D 11.

HODGSON, Edward S. Exh. 1922
Landscape and coastal painter. St. Ninians, Finch Lane, Bushey, Herts. † RA 7.

HODGSON, F.W. Exh. 1909
13 Melbourne Road, Carlisle. † L 1.

HODGSON, George d. 1921
Landscape, cartoon and allegorical painter. N.S.A. 1885, V.P.N.S.A. 1908-17. Hon. Sec. N.S.A. 1892, Council member N.S.A. 1887-89 and 1893-94. Add: Nottingham 1881 and 1893; West Bridgford, Notts. 1888; Ruddington, Notts. 1897. † B 3, N 184, RA 4, RBA 2.

HODGSON, G.B. Exh. 1901-25
Egremont, Cheshire 1901; Grange-over-Sands, Lancs. 1911. † L 11.

HODGSON, Dr. Harold Exh. 1910-35
Landscape, coastal and figure painter. The Lindens, Alresford, Hants. † ALP 1, L 10, RA 12, RBA 6, RI 5.

HODGSON, John Evan* 1831-1895
Painter of genre, landscapes, historical and eastern subjects. b. London. Spent his early years in Russia. Studied R.A. Schools 1853. Librarian and professor of painting at the R.A. 1882-1895. A.R.A. 1873, R.A. 1879, R.E. 1881. Add: St. John's Wood, London 1880; Coleshill, Amersham, Bucks. 1890. † AG 4, B 5, D 1, GI 6, L 5, M 5, RA 39, RE 3, ROI 1.

HODGSON, J.J. Exh. 1898-1905
13 Melbourne Road, Carlisle. † L 3, RSW 2.

HODGSON, Louisa Exh. 1934-40
Figure, portrait and landscape painter. 11 Northumberland Terrace, Tynemouth, Northumberland. † RA 8.

HODGSON, M. Exh. 1940
45 Howitt Road, London. † RBA 1.

HODGSON, Miss M. Exh. 1882-85
Lane Grove, Altrincham, Cheshire. † L 1, M 11.

HODGSON, Miss M.L. Exh. 1912-14
London. † RA 2.

HODGSON, T.R. Exh. 1915-16
Liverpool. † L 3.

HODGSON, William J. Exh. 1891-93
Black and white artist. Clovelly, N. Devon 1891; Lawrencekirk, N.B. 1892; Scarborough, Yorks. 1893. † L 2, RA 1.

HODGSON, William Scott b. 1864
Landscape and coastal painter. Self taught. N.S.A. 1908. Exh. 1900-27. Add: Nottingham 1900; Whitby, Yorks. 1907. † B 7, N 62, RA 2.

HODKINSON, Edward Exh. 1885-1902
Architect. Chester. † L 8, RA 5.

HODKINSON, W.E. Exh. 1928
7 Carnarvon Road, Preston, Lancs. † L 4.

HODSON, A. Margaret Exh. 1904
Lyndhurst, Farquhar Road, Edgbaston, Birmingham. † B 1.

HODSON, Mrs. Edith Exh. 1898
7 Hillmarten Road, Camden Road, London. † RI 1.

HODSON, Miss F. Exh. 1903
Hoddesden, Herts. † SWA 1.

HODSON, J. Exh. 1883
49 Park Road, Hampstead, London. † B 2.

HODSON, J.A. Exh. 1907
31 Thorp Street, Peel Green, Patricroft. † M 1.

HODSON, S. Exh. 1882
72 Varna Road, Birmingham. † L 1.

HODSON, Shirley Exh. 1882
Figure painter. 2 Harpur Street, London. † D 1.

HODSON, Samuel John 1836-1908
Landscape and architectural painter and lithographer. Studied R.A. Schools. Worked for the "Graphic" as colour lithographer. R.B.A. 1881, A.R.W.S. 1882, R.W.S. 1890. Add: 7 Hillmarten Road, Camden Road, London. † B 21, FIN 55, L 21, LEI 2, M 12, RA 4, RBA 7, RCA 41, ROI 2, RWS 101.

HOECK, Ebenezer Exh. 1886-1931
Glasgow 1886 and 1915; Bruges, Belgium 1910; Edinburgh 1929. † GI 34, L 1, RSA 2.

HOECKER, Paul* 1854-1910
German artist. Exh. 1890. Add: 24 Nymphenburgher Strasse, Munich. † L 1.

HOEDT, Louis Exh. 1888
Watercolour landscape with cattle painter. † FIN 4.

HOEPFNER, Franz Exh. 1886
Islington, London. † L 1.

HOETERICKX, E. Exh. 1881
Avenue de l'Opera, Paris. † RHA 2.

HOETGER Exh. 1906
† I 1.

HOFF, Van't See V

HOFF, G. Rayner d. 1937
Australian sculptor. Exh. 1920-28. Add: Old Lenton, Nottingham 1920; London 1922. † RA 3, RMS 2.

HOFFBAUER, Charles b. 1875
Exh. 1909. † LS 3.

HOFFIE, William Exh. 1883-1900
Edinburgh. † RSA 14.

HOFFMAN, George S. Exh. 1922
Landscape painter. 8 West Hill Road, London. † RA 1.

HOFFMAN, Henry L. Exh. 1935
Marine painter. 109 Upper Richmond Road, Putney, London. † RA 1.

HOFFMAN, H.W. Exh. 1880
Watercolour landscape painter. 2 Munster Road, Fulham, London. † RBA 1.

HOFLER, Max R.* Exh. 1938-40
Architectural painter. Harrow-on-the-Hill, Middlesex. † RA 1, RI 3, ROI 2.

HOFMANN, Von See V

HOFMANN, E. Daniel Exh. 1937
Architect. 36 Denbigh Street, London. † RA 2.

HOFMANN, Louis Exh. 1928
Etcher. 6 Edith Terrace, Chelsea, London. † RA 1.

HOG, Caroline Maynard Mary Exh. 1905-18
Shepherd's Bush, London 1905; Cranford, nr. Hounslow, Middlesex 1909. † LS 9, SWA 9.

HOGAN, Denis F. Exh. 1909-15
Dublin 1909; Sandymount, Co. Dublin 1915. † RHA 4.

HOGAN, James H. Exh. 1910-36
Painter and stained glass artist. East Dulwich, London 1910; Hammersmith, London 1915. † D 1, RA 13.

HOGAN, Lauriena Exh. 1935
39 Larkfield Road, Richmond, Surrey. † SWA 1.

HOGARTH, E. Exh. 1888
Glebe Street, Cambeltown, N.B. † RSA 1.

HOGARTH, Edith Victoria Exh. 1936-40
Watercolour flower painter. Elmcroft, Gosport, Hants. † RA 1, RHA 1, RI 4, RSA 1, SWA 1.

HOGARTH, Lizzie b. 1879
Landscape and still life painter. Studied under James Hector, Aberdeen and St. Martin's School of Art, London. R.B.A. 1916, S.W.A. 1922. Exh. 1900-40. Add: Aberdeen 1900; London 1913; Sherborne, Dorset 1932. † GI 2, I 1, L 7, RBA 92, ROI 1, RSA 16, SWA 39.

HOGARTH, Mary Henrietta Uppleby c. 1861-1935
Painter, illustrator, etcher and designer. Taught drawing at Wycombe Abbey School. Add: London 1897; High Wycombe, Bucks 1909. † CAR 23, LS 22, NEA 30, SWA 6, WG 46.

HOGE, Frances Exh. 1928
62 Glebe Place, Chelsea, London. † NEA 1.

HOGG, Arthur Exh. 1913-29
Etcher. b. Kendal, Westmorland. Studied South Kensington and Paris. Add: London. † CHE 3, LS 1, RA 9.

HOGG, Hon. A. McGarel Exh. 1896-99
Architect. London. † RA 2.

HOGG, Archibald W. Exh. 1885-1903
Landscape painter. Edinburgh. † RA 1, RHA 3, RSA 45.

HOGG, Edward Albert Exh. 1919-20
Miniature portrait painter. 147 Plashet Grove, Manor Park, London. † L 3, RA 3.

HOGG, Mrs. Edith B. Exh. 1905-19
Miniature painter. Blackburn, Lancs. 1905; Dewsbury, Yorks. 1911; Wolverhampton 1919. † L 7, RA 11.

HOGG, Mrs. Edith J. Exh. 1926-33
Miniature painter. Rexon, Ashburton, S. Devon. † RA 4.

HOGG, Emma M. Exh. 1880
Landscape painter. 33 Lexham Gardens, Cromwell Road, London. † SWA 1.

HOGG, Herbert W. Exh. 1883-85
Sculptor. 4 Compton Street, Derby. † L 1, RA 5.

HOGG, Isobel b. 1887
Sculptor. b. Montreal, Canada. Studied Birmingham and Paris. Exh. 1916-23. Add: 23 Netheravon Road, Chiswick, London. † G 3, L 2, RA 5, RSA 1.

HOGG, Janie Exh. 1892
Flower painter. 36 Upper Talbot Street, Nottingham. † N 1.

HOGG, J.S. Exh. 1914-20
Belfast. † RHA 9.

HOGG, Mary Exh. 1911
Ferncraig, Old Kilpatrick, N.B. † GI 1.

HOGG, Margaret L. Exh. 1927-28
Miniature painter. Rexon, Ashburton. S. Devon. † RA 2.

HOGG, William A. Exh. 1923-40
Abbotsford, Scott Street, Hamilton. † GI 4, RSA 1.

HOGGARTH, Arthur Henry Graham 1882-1964
Watercolour painter and black and white artist. b. Kendal. Contributor to "Punch", Master, then Headmaster of Churcher's College, Petersfield, Hants. Exh. 1909-35. Add: St. Abbs, Kendal and Sandwich, Kent 1909; Petersfield, Hants. 1911. † L 12, RA 10, RI 1.

HOGGATT, William b. 1880
Landscape painter. Studied Juliens, Paris 1899-1901. R.I. 1925. Exh. 1904-40. Add: Caton, nr. Lancaster 1904; Port St. Mary, I.O.M. 1907 and 1909; Lancaster 1908, Port Erin, I.O.M. 1926. † GI 3, L 65, LS 5, M 3, RA 32, RCA 42, RHA 4, RI 45, ROI 1, RSA 2, RSW 1.

HOGGE, Miss M.R. Exh. 1905-13
Blackheath, London 1905; Newbury, Berks. 1906. † RA 2, RHA 1, RMS 1.

HOGLEY, Stephen E. Exh. 1881-93
Landscape painter. Holmfirth, Huddersfield. † M 3, RBA 1.

HOHENLOHE, Prince
see GLEICHEN, Count Victor
HOHENWART, Countess Constance
See MÜNCH
HOHLER, Miss H.E. Exh. 1881
Watercolour landscape painter. Fawkham Manor, Kent. † SWA 1.
HOILE, Millicent Exh. 1903
7 Palace Terrace, Fulham, London. † NG 1.
HOLBROOK, Violet Exh. 1923-25
Embroiderer. 13 Ridding Terrace, Welling Street, Nottingham. † N 2.
HOLCOMBE, Ellen T. Exh. 1912
121 St. Marks Road, North Kensington, London. † LS 3.
HOLDEN, Albert William 1848-1932
Religious and historical painter. Studied R.A. Schools. Professor of Fine Art, King's College, London 1887-1904. Exh. 1881-1915. Add: London. † GI 3, L 2, P 1, RA 6, RBA 12, RHA 1, ROI 7.
HOLDEN, Charles 1875-1960
Architect. Architect with the Imperial War Graves Commission 1918-22. Exh. 1934-40. Add: London. † GI 2, RA 10, RSA 2.
HOLDEN, Charles N. Exh. 1913
128 Wrottesley Road, Harlesden, London. † L 1.
HOLDEN, Evelyn B. Exh. 1890-1907
Hockley Heath, nr. Birmingham 1890; Knowle, nr. Birmingham 1897. † B 20, L 2, RA 1, SWA 3.
HOLDEN, Ethel Lofft Exh. 1885
Figure and landscape painter. 20 Redcliffe Quare, London. † SWA 3.
HOLDEN, G.H. Exh. 1936-38
Son of Harold Henry H. q.v. 14 Charlotte Road, Edgbaston, Birmingham. † B 3.
HOLDEN, G.W.R. Exh. 1911-17
Liverpool 1911; Kingston on Thames, Surrey 1916. † L 1, RA 2.
HOLDEN, Harold Henry b. 1885
Watercolour painter and etcher. b. Settle, Yorks. Studied Skipton School of Art, Leeds School of Art and Royal College of Art. Principal of Cheltenham School of Arts and Crafts 1920, Leeds School of Art 1923 and Birmingham Central School of Arts and Crafts. Director of Art Education, Birmingham 1929. Father of G.H. and John H. q.v. R.B.S.A. 1929. † B 43, COO 1, L 2, RA 19.
HOLDEN, H.L. Exh. 1883
202 Mount Pleasant, Liverpool. † L 1.
HOLDEN, John Hamilton Exh. 1934-40
Watercolour landscape painter. Son of Harold Henry H. q.v. Add: 14 Charlotte Road, Edgbaston, Birmingham 1934; Hove, Sussex 1940. † B 14, RA 3, RBA 2.
HOLDEN, Maud Exh. 1931
Manchester. † RCA 1.
HOLDEN, Mildred Exh. 1904-24
Flower painter. Chorlton cum Hardy, Manchester 1904; Heaton Mersey, Manchester 1922. † B 4, L 13, LS 3, M 4, RA 5, RCA 5, SWA 1.
HOLDEN, Miss M.T. Exh. 1913-16
25 Greenheys Road, Liverpool. † L 4.
HOLDEN, Paul Exh. 1898-1901
London. † RI 2.
HOLDEN, Thomas Exh. 1908-24
Walton, Liverpool 1908; Bootle, Lancs. 1924. † L 2.
HOLDEN, Violet Exh. 1907
† FIN 1.
HOLDEN, W.F.C. Exh. 1920
Landscape painter. The Cottage, Baring Road, Beaconsfield, Bucks. † GI 1, RA 1.
HOLDER, Van see V

HOLDER, C.S. Exh. 1886-89
Liverpool. † L 2.
HOLDER, C. Vincent d. 1916
Exh. 1913-14. Add: London. † RA 2.
HOLDER, Edward Henry* Exh. 1884-1917
Landscape and coastal painter. b. Scarborough. Visited South Africa. Add: London 1884 and 1906; Reigate, Surrey 1893. † B 2, L 2, LS 3, M 5, RA 1, RBA 5, RHA 2, ROI 8, TOO 1.
HOLDER, Reyner Exh. 1938-40
110 Lauriston Place, Edinburgh. † RSA 3.
HOLDERNESS, May Exh. 1908
St. Margaret's, Bushey, Herts. † RI 1.
HOLDICH, Whyte Exh. 1886-87
Landscape painter. Hull. † RBA 1, RHA 4, RI 2, RSA 4.
HOLDING, Casper Exh. 1882
9 Oxford Street, Manchester. † M 2.
HOLDING, Emma Exh. 1883-87
12 Poynter Street, Greenbeys, Manchester. † M 4.
HOLDING, Edgar Thomas 1870-1952
Landscape painter. b. Horncastle, Lincs. A.R.W.S. 1920, R.W.S. 1929. Add: London 1899; Sutton, nr. Pulborough, Sussex 1915. † AG 17, COO 1, FIN 16, G 4, GI 7, GOU 5, I 6, L 15, M 2, RA 39, RBA 1, RHA 5, ROI 1, RSA 1, RWS 209, WG 38.
HOLDING, George Exh. 1882-1911
Manchester 1882; Liscard, Cheshire 1895; Ruabon, nr. Wrexham 1911. † L 17, M 14.
HOLDING, John* Exh. 1881-93
12 Poynter Street, Greenheys, Manchester. † GI 1, L 8, M 23, RHA 1.
HOLDING, Mrs. Mary Exh. 1922
A.S.W.A. 1923. † SWA 3.
HOLDING, May Exh. 1925-26
Daughter of Edgar Thomas H. q.v. Sutton, nr. Pulborough, Sussex. † L 5.
HOLDING, Matthew H. Exh. 1888-91
Architect. Northampton. † RA 2.
HOLDING, Ursula Exh. 1911
Newbury, Berks. † SWA 1.
HOLDSWORTH, H.A.G. Exh. 1912
c/o Allied Artists Assn. 67 Chancery Lane, London. † LS 3.
HOLDSWORTH, Violet M. Exh. 1910-13
Bournemouth 1910; Chelsea, London 1913. † LS 7.
HOLE, Miss A. Exh. 1917
Muswell Hill, London. † SWA 1.
HOLE, Alice Exh. 1886
Figure painter. Bray Vicarage, Maidenhead, Berks. † RA 1.
HOLE, Miss A.F. Exh. 1910
15 Manor Garden, Larkhall Rise, London. † RA 1.
HOLE, Dora Exh. 1913-35
Edinburgh. † RSA 4.
HOLE, Mrs. Ethel (F.R.) Exh. 1899-1918
nee Knight. Portrait painter. West Bridgford, Notts. † N 30.
HOLE, William Brassey 1846-1917
Painter and etcher. R.E. 1885, A.R.S.A. 1878, R.S.A. 1889, R.S.W. 1885. Add: Edinburgh. † B 1, CON 13, FIN 80, GI 18, L 8, M 12, RA 16, RE 52, RHA 1, RSA 111, RSW 11.
HOLEHOUSE, H.R. Exh. 1900
67 Willoughby Street, New Lenton, Notts. † N 1.
HOLEWINSKI, Muriel Gailey Exh. 1916-17
Landscape painter. Newcastle, Staffs. 1916; Brook Green, London 1917. † NEA 2.
HOLFORD, F. Exh. 1911
Fulthorpe House, 5A Warwick Avenue, London. † RA 1.

HOLGATE, Eleanor Exh. 1906-8
38 Wellington Street, St. John's Blackburn, Lancs. † L 1, RCA 2.
HOLGATE, J. Exh. 1882-87
Stamford Bridge Studios, Chelsea Station, Fulham, London. † L 1, RI 1, ROI 1.
HOLGATE, Thomas W. Exh. 1899-1910
Portrait and figure painter. R.B.A. 1904. Add: London. † B 2, L 4, RA 5, RBA 27, ROI 1.
HOLIDAY, Gilbert 1879-1937
Painter and black and white artist. Studied R.A. Schools. Served with the R.F.A. World War 1. Add: London 1903; Seymour House, East Molesey, Surrey 1919. † M 1, RA 6, RI 1, ROI 1, RSA 3.
HOLIDAY, Henry George* 1839-1927
Painter, illustrator (Lewis Carroll's "Hunting of the Snark"), glass maker, enameller and sculptor. Studied Leigh's Academy and R.A. Schools. Travelled on the Continent, India, America and Canada. Founded his own glass works in Hampstead 1890. † G 7, L 20, LS 8, M 5, RA 24, WG 40.
HOLIDAY, Leigh Exh. 1893
31 Balmoral Terrace, Seedley, Manchester. † M 1.
HOLL, Francis 1815-1884
Engraver. Father of Frank H. q.v. Add: Elm House, Godalming, Surrey 1881. † RA 1.
HOLL, Frank* 1845-1888
Portrait and genre painter and illustrator. Son of Francis H. q.v. Studied R.A. Schools 1860 (gold medal 1863). Visited Italy 1869. A.R.A. 1878, R.A. 1883, R.E. 1881, A.R.W.S. 1883. Add: London. Died on a visit to Spain. † B 10, G 20, L 2, M 3, P 1, RA 55, RE 1, RHA 3, RI 1, RSA 3, TOO 8.
HOLL, Mrs. Frank Exh. 1881-82
Watercolour flower painter. 4 Camden Square, London. † RBA 6.
HOLL, G. Exh. 1883-84
1 Horbury Crescent, Notting Hill, London. † D 2.
HOLLAENDER, Alphonse* Exh. 1884-87
Florence, Italy 1884; London 1887. † B 1, GI 1, ROI 1.
HOLLAMS, F. Mabel Exh. 1897-1929
Mrs. C.L. Fox. Figure, animal and flower painter. A.S.W.A. 1899, S.W.A. 1902. Add: Tonbridge, Kent. † L 2, RA 8, SWA 19, WG 66.
HOLLAND, Miss Exh. 1886
Great Easton, Leicester. † N 1.
HOLLAND, Anne J. Exh. 1938-40
London 1938; Cirencester, Glos. 1939. † RBA 3, SWA 3.
HOLLAND, Ada R. Exh. 1887-1914
Portrait and figure painter. Studied Ecole des Beaux Arts, Paris. Married John Shirley-Fox, q.v. Add: London. † L 4, M 2, NEA 2, NG 3, P 6, RA 8, RBA 6, RI 4, ROI 1, RSW 1, SWA 2.
HOLLAND, Miss C. Exh. 1914-21
8 North Mall, Cork 1914; Camberley, Surrey 1921. † RHA 16.
HOLLAND, Mrs. Caroline Clark
Exh. 1916-25
nee Knott. Painter and black and white artist. b. Illinois, U.S.A. Studied U.S.A., Germany, France and England. Add: London. † I 1, RI 2.
HOLLAND, Charlotte F. Exh. 1882-92
Landscape painter. Greville House, Greville Place, Maida Vale, London. † B 1, RBA 2, ROI 1, SWA 1.
HOLLAND, C.M. Exh. 1886
Wrexham, N. Wales. † L 1.

HOLLAND, D. Exh. 1935-40
Painter and linocut artist. 98 Fordwych Road, Hampstead, London. † RA 3, RED 3.

HOLLAND, Edward Exh. 1909-10
Gell-y-Vorwyn, Llanbedr, Talycafn, N. Wales. † L 2.

HOLLAND, Capt. Escourt Exh. 1913-19
Architect. 30 John Street, Bedford Row, London. † L 2, RA 3.

HOLLAND, Mrs. Florence see HUMPHREY

HOLLAND, Miss F.E. Exh. 1904-5
65 Sydney Street, Chelsea, London. † D 3, SWA 2.

HOLLAND, Miss G. Exh. 1884
72 Brook Street, Grosvenor Square, London. † D 1.

HOLLAND, George Herbert Buckingham b. 1901
Portrait, still life and landscape painter. Studied Leicester College of Art, Northampton School of Art and Chelsea Polytechnic. Add: Northampton 1926; London 1935. † ALP 1, P 5, RA 6, ROI 3, RSA 1.

HOLLAND, Grace M. Exh. 1923-38
Sutton Coldfield, Warwicks. 1923; Llandudno, Wales 1925. † B 8, L 6, RCA 21.

HOLLAND, Henry Exh. 1887-90
Figure painter. 33 Howland Street, Fitzroy Square, London. † RI 1.

HOLLAND, Humphrey Exh. 1938
† P 1.

HOLLAND, Miss H.G. Exh. 1907-10
Carnatic Hall, Mossley Hill, Liverpool. † L 3.

HOLLAND, H.R. Exh. 1890
1 Garden Studios, Manresa Road, Chelsea, London. † L 1.

HOLLAND, Henry T. Exh. 1885
Figure painter. 375 City Road, Islington, London. † RBA 1.

HOLLAND, John Exh. 1880-84
Landscape painter. N.S.A. 1881. Add: Gunthorpe on Trent, Notts. 1880; Nottingham 1881. † N 13.

HOLLAND, James Sylvester b. 1905
Painter, lithographer and decorator. b. Gillingham, Kent. Studied Rochester School of Art and Royal College of Art (scholarship). Exh. 1927-33. Add: London. † NEA 1. RA 1.

HOLLAND, Miss K. Exh. 1907
Carnatic Hall, Mossley Hill, Liverpool. † L 2.

HOLLAND, M. Exh. 1914-19
8 North'Mall, Cork. † RHA 5.

HOLLAND, Philip Exh. 1886-87
Still life painter. 6 Larkhall Lane, Clapham, London. † RBA 2.

HOLLAND, Philip Sidney* 1855-1891
Genre, historical and flower painter. London. † B 2, L 5, M 5, RA 3, RBA 3, RI 1.

HOLLAND, Miss S.A. Exh. 1933-34
c/o N.B. of New Zealand, 8 Moorgate, London. † ROI 1, RSA 1, SWA 1.

HOLLAND, Sebastopol Samuel Exh. 1880-1911
Landscape and coastal painter. N.S.A. 1881-1913. Council Member N.S.A. 1884-85. Add: Nottingham. † L 4, M 2. N 49, RA 2, ROI 1.

HOLLAND, Thomas J.B. Exh. 1881
Architectural landscape painter. 21 Carlton Road, Finsbury Park, London. † RA 1.

HOLLEBY, Miss Aileen see WALKER

HOLLEYMAN, Miss M.B. Exh. 1934
52 Welford Road, Shirley, Warwicks. † B 1.

HOLLIDAY, C. Exh. 1890-93
Lansdowne Road, Tottenham, London. † L 7.

HOLLIDAY, Edward Exh. 1880-84
Still life painter. Dean Road, South Croydon, Surrey. † B 1, L 4, M 3, RA 4, RBA 14.

HOLLIDAY, Miss J. Exh. 1905-8
Kensington Gore, London 1905; Harrow, Middlesex 1907. † L 1, LS 3, RA 2.

HOLLIDAY, Miss Lily Exh. 1880-97
Flower and still life painter. Dean Road, South Croydon, Surrey. † B 1, L 1, RBA 11, ROI 1, SWA 5.

HOLLIES, F.N. Exh. 1937
7 Shrubbery Villas, Horseley Road, Tipton, Staffs. † B 1.

HOLLINGDALE, Horatio R.* Exh. 1880-99
Landscape painter. R.B.A. 1888. Add: London. † B 3, L 13, RA 11, RBA 55, ROI 18, TOO 3.

HOLLINGDALE, Richard* Exh. 1893-99
Genre and portrait painter. 1 Rackham Street, Ladbroke Grove Road, London. † RA 8.

HOLLINGS, H.B. Exh. 1923-24
22 Garratt Street, West Bromwich, Birmingham. † B 2.

HOLLINGSHEAD, Albert Exh. 1903-7
Sculptor. London. † L 2, RA 2.

HOLLINGSHEAD, W. Exh. 1889
Decorative designer. 7 Chapter Road, Willesden Grove, London. † RA 1.

HOLLINGSWORTH, Bruce C. Exh. 1939-40
Flower painter. Monkswood, Heathside Park Road, Woking, Surrey. † RA 1, RBA 1.

HOLLINGSWORTH, Ruth Exh. 1906-34
Landscape, still life and flower painter. Studied Slade School and London School of Art. Add: London 1906; Holbrook, Suffolk 1931. † B 36, COO 2, FIN 2, G 2, GOU 6, NEA 4, RA 14, ROI 2, SWA 4.

HOLLINGWORTH, Thomas Exh. 1884-87
Figure painter. Upper Westbourne Park, London. † RHA 5, ROI 1.

HOLLINGWORTH, Miss S.A. Exh. 1914
The Glen, Gurnard, Cowes, I.O.W. † RA 1.

HOLLINS, F. Exh. 1883-91
Manchester. † M 10.

HOLLINS, Henrietta Exh. 1889-1928
Watercolour landscape painter. Pleasley Vale, Mansfield, Notts. † N 7, WG 134.

HOLLINS, H. Plant Exh. 1891-98
Portrait, figure and landscape painter. Chelsea, London. † NEA 2, RA 2, RBA 2.

HOLLINSHEAD, Albert E. Exh. 1908-16
2 Queen's Road, Hartshill, Stoke on Trent. † L 5, LS 4.

HOLLINSHEAD, Joseph b. 1894
Etcher and black and white artist. b. Newcastle under Lyme, Staffs. Studied Royal College of Art (British Institute Scholarship in Etching 1921). Exh. 1923-27. Add: 87 Finborough Road, Earl's Court, London. † NEA 3, P 1.

HOLLIS, Charles T. Exh. 1881-82
Landscape painter. 6 Claremont, Windsor, Berks. † RA 1, RBA 1.

HOLLIS, Miss E. Exh. 1889-95
Hanbury Grange, Sudbury, Derby. † B 10.

HOLLIS, Gerald b. 1908
Landscape, figure and flower painter. 3 Oak Grove, Garstang, Lancs. 1938. † BK 25, RBA 1.

HOLLIS, Julia Exh. 1906-26
Miniature painter. London. † RA 4.

HOLLOND, Miss E.E. Exh. 1917
5 Norfolk Crescent, Hyde Park, London. † RA 1.

HOLLOWAY, Arthur Thomas b. 1870
Landscape painter and heraldic artist. Studied Lambeth School of Art, Heatherley's and R.A. Schools (silver medal for life painting). Teacher of landscape painting, Blackheath School. Exh. 1925. Add: 20 Wisteria Road, Lewisham, London. † L 2, RA 1.

HOLLOWAY, Charles Edward 1838-1897
Landscape and marine painter, engraver and lithographer. Studied at Leigh's Academy. Associated with William Morris in the production of stained glass till 1866. N.E.A. 1893, R.E. 1882, A.R.I. 1875, R.I. 1879. Add: London. † B 3, FIN 1, G 9, GI 2, L 7, M 10, NEA 22, RA 8, RE 10, RI 39, ROI 7.

HOLLOWAY, C.N. Exh. 1902-3
Newcastle Chambers, Angel Row, Nottingham. † N 2.

HOLLOWAY, Edgar Exh. 1940
Royal Masonic School, The Avenue, Bushey, Herts. † RBA 2.

HOLLOWAY, Edgar A. b. 1914
Etcher. London 1934; Barnby Dun, Doncaster 1935; 5th Batt. Wilts Regiment H.Q. Company, Hythe, Kent 1940. † M 5, NEA 1, RA 6, RBA 1, RI 5, RSA 7.

HOLLOWAY, R. Exh. 1925-35
Landscape painter. Mansfield, Notts. † N 3.

HOLLOWAY, W.H. Exh. 1919
† L 2.

HOLLOWOOD, W.J. Exh. 1938
Five Ways Inn, Heath Hays, Stafford. † B 1.

HOLLWAY, Janet Exh. 1887-97
Miniature portrait painter. London 1887 and 1896; Worthing, Sussex 1895. † L 2, P 3, RA 17, RI 2, RSW 2.

HOLLWEY, Eleanor Exh. 1894-1901
Crumlin, Dublin 1894 and 1899; Terenure 1896; Belfast 1901. † RHA 16.

HOLLYER, Eva* Exh. 1889-1902
Figure painter. Liverpool 1889 and 1902; Oxton, Cheshire 1890; Walton, Cheshire 1892 and 1894; Rock Ferry 1893; Little Paxton, St. Neots, Hunts. 1896; Claughton, Cheshire 1898; Birkenhead 1899. † B 2, L 27, M 2, RA 3, RBA 3, RCA 2.

HOLLYER, Maud Exh. 1902-3
Onchan, I.O.M. 1902; Douglas, I.O.M. 1903. † L 2.

HOLMAN, Agnes Gladys b. 1885
Animal and portrait painter, miniaturist illustrator and sculptor. b. Charlton Kings, Glos. Studied St. John's Wood. Worked with the Land Army World War 1. Exh. 1921-31. Add: London. † RI 11.

HOLMAN, Edward Exh. 1934-39
Architect. Sutton Coldfield, Warwicks. 1934; Four Oaks, Birmingham 1936. † B 6.

HOLMAN, Elizabeth Exh. 1927
102 Edgware Road, London. † RBA 2.

HOLMAN, Edwin Charles Pascoe Exh. 1918-39
Watercolour landscape painter. Nottingham 1918; Conway, Wales 1923; Lostwithiel, Cornwall 1924; Steyning, Sussex 1927; Wareham, Dorset 1929; Ringwood, Hants 1935. † B 8, D, 3, L 1, N 3, RCA 17.

HOLMAN, George E. Exh. 1912-22
Flower and fruit painter. Reigate, Surrey. † RA 4, ROI 1.

HOLMAN, Hester M. Exh. 1925-29
Sculptor. London. † L 1, NEA 5, RA 2.

HOLMBOE, Thorolf* b. 1866
Norwegian artist. Exh. 1901-9. Add: 11 Olap Kyrres Gd., Christiania, Norway. † GI 1, I 1, LS 3.

HOLME, C. Geoffrey Exh. 1911-14
R.B.A. 1912. The Gables, Church Crookham, Fleet, Hants. † L 1, RBA 12.

HOLME, Mrs. D. Exh. 1928-30
Forest Road, Meols, Hoylake, Cheshire. † L 4.

HOLME, Miss Dora Exh. 1899-1905
Miniature portrait painter. Bexley Heath, Kent 1899; Winchfield, Hants. 1904. † B 2, RA 7.

HOLME, F.U. Exh. 1885-94
8 Westminster Chambers Crosshall Street, Liverpool. † L 9.

HOLME, George Exh. 1893
8 Westminster Chambers, Crosshall Street, Liverpool. † L 1.

HOLME, Herbert J. Exh. 1909-19
8 Fenwick Street, Liverpool. † L 2.

HOLME, Miss P. Exh. 1888
Cardiston, 88 Shrewsbury Road, Birkenhead. † L 1.

HOLMES, Alice A. Exh. 1894-95
Wyndcliffe, School Road, Moseley, Birmingham. † B 2.

HOLMES, Beatrix Exh. 1917-33
The Briars, Station Road, Thames Ditton, Surrey 1917; London 1929. † L 1, NEA 1, RA 2.

HOLMES, C.B. Exh. 1884-85
10 St. Mary's Parsonage, Blackfriars, Manchester. † M 2.

HOLMES, Sir Charles John* 1868-1936
Landscape painter, etcher and writer. b. Preston. Editor "Burlington Magazine" 1903-9, Slade Professor of Fine Art, Oxford 1904-10, Director, National Portrait Gallery 1909-16, Director National Gallery 1916-28. N.E.A. 1905, A.R.W.S. 1924, R.W.S. 1929. Knighted c.1920. Add: London. † AG 8, BA 1, BAR 4, CAR 87, CG 55, DOW 1, FIN 98, G 116, GI 10, GOU 12, I 3, L 14, M 18, NEA 181, RA 10, RSA 10, RSW 2, RWS 99, TOO 1, WG 3.

HOLMES, Miss E. Exh. 1892
Wyndcliffe, School Road, Moseley, Birmingham. † B 1.

HOLMES, Miss E. Exh. 1926
40 Westbourne Gardens, Glasgow. † GI 1.

HOLMES, Edward* d. c.1893
Landscape, marine and portrait painter. Brother of George Augustus H. q.v. R.B.A. 1889. Add: 62 Cheyne Walk, Chelsea, London. † B 3, G 1, L 7, M 3, RA 6, RBA 67.

HOLMES, Elizabeth Exh. 1895-96
London. † RHA 2.

HOLMES, Elizabeth Exh. 1922-28
Watercolour painter, miniaturist and illustrator. Add: Handfords, Yateley, Hants. † L 1, RA 4, SWA 1.

HOLMES, Frederick Exh. 1924-37
Landscape and figure painter. London. † CHE 4, RA 13, RBA 5.

HOLMES, George Augustus* d. 1911
Genre painter. Brother of Edward H. q.v. R.B.A. 1863. Add: 62 Cheyne Walk, Chelsea, London. † B 26, FIN 1, G 1, L 13, M 4, RA 20, RBA 83, RCA 2, ROI 3, RSA 1.

HOLMES, Henry Exh. 1902-5
Landscape painter. 13 Crosland Terrace, Dewsbury Road, Leeds. † L 2, RA 5, RCA 2.

HOLMES, Iris Exh. 1903-5
Dublin. † RHA 2.

HOLMES, John Exh. 1890-1928
Glasgow. † GI 15.

HOLMES, J.H. Exh. 1888
63 Sandyfauld Street, Glasgow. † GI 1. I.

HOLMES, Kenneth b. 1902
Painter, etcher, draughtsman and engraver. Studied Skipton School of Art 1919-21, Leeds College of Art 1921-23, Central School of Art, Chelsea School of Art and Royal College of Art 1923-27 and Italy 1927-28. Principal Huddersfield School of Art 1932 and Principal Leicester School of Art 1934. m. Marjorie H. q.v. † BK 3, FIN 5, GI 1, L 7, NEA 8, RA 11, RHA 7.

HOLMES, Lily Exh. 1901-14
Colwyn Bay, N. Wales. † RCA 11.

HOLMES, Marcus b. 1880
Painter and etcher. b. Ipswich, Suffolk. Studied Aberdeen Art School, Herkomer's, Bushey, Herts. and Florence. Art master Monmouth School 1907-46. Add: Dovercourt, Essex 1901; Oundle, Northants. 1904; Monmouth 1907. † L 6, LS 9, RCA 4.

HOLMES, Marjorie Exh. 1930-36
nee Fenning. Painter and illustrator. b. Cheltenham, Glos. Studied Royal College of Art. m. Kenneth H. q.v. Add: East Sheen, London 1930; Leicester 1936. † RA 2.

HOLMES, Miss M.A. Exh. 1910-15
Leck, Kirby Lonsdale, Westmorland. † L 6.

HOLMES, Mrs. Mary D. Exh. 1904-13
Flower and landscape painter. Beverley, Yorks. † L 2, RA 4, SWA 1.

HOLMES, Mildred Spaswick Exh. 1920-33
Mrs. G. North. Painter and engraver. b. Liverpool. Studied Sidcup School of Art and R.A. Schools. Add: Aigburth, Liverpool 1920; London 1931. † L 9, NEA 1, RA 2, SWA 1.

HOLMES, Rhoda Exh. 1881-82
Landscape and figure painter. Venice. † D 1, RA 1, RBA 1, RHA 3.

HOLMES, Sir Richard Rivington 1835-1911
Figure and landscape painter. Librarian of Windsor Castle. H.R.M.S. 1905. Exh. 1880-91. Add: Windsor. † G 7, NG 2.

HOLMES, Sophia Exh. 1883-91
Flower painter. Dublin. † D 3, FIN 2, L 1, RA 1, RBA 1, RHA 13, RI 6, SWA 1.

HOLMES, Thomas Exh. 1915
43 Gt. George Street, Liverpool. † L 1.

HOLMES, T.W. Exh. 1892-93
6 Highfield Terrace, Kingston Road, Leeds. † GI 1, L 1.

HOLMS, Archibald Campbell d. 1898
Watercolour painter. R.S.W. 1894. Add: Sandyford, nr. Paisley. † GI 10, RSW 3.

HOLMS, Elfrida Exh. 1919
38 Sardinia Terrace, Hillhead, Glasgow. † GI 1.

HOLMS, Florence Exh. 1884-1936
Landscape painter. London. † GI 2, L 2, M 1, RA 1, SWA 5.

HOLMS, Lisette H.D. Exh. 1884-88
Hope Park, Partick, Glasgow. † GI 6.

HOLMSTROM, Annie Exh. 1911-12
41 Beaufort Road, Kingston on Thames. † N 1, ROI 1.

HOLROYD, Sir Charles 1861-1917
Painter and etcher. b. Leeds. Studied Slade School for 4 years (travelling scholarship) and Italy 2 years. Assistant to Legros at Slade School. Keeper of the Tate Gallery 1898-1906. Director of the National Gallery 1906-19. R.E. 1885, H.R.M.S. 1912. Knighted 1902. Add: Leeds 1884; London 1885 and 1898; Chertsey, Surrey 1895; Richmond, Surrey 1897; Epsom, Surrey 1899; Weybridge, Surrey 1904. † B 1, DOW 2, FIN 4, G 1, GI 3, I 30, L 26, RA 17, RE 229, RI 3, ROI 4, RSA 4.

HOLROYD, Lady Fannie F. d. 1924
Portrait painter. Wife of Sir Charles H. q.v. Exh. 1892-1909. Add: London 1892; Weybridge, Surrey 1909. † NG 1, RA 2.

HOLROYD, John N. Exh. 1929
Miniature painter. 77 Oxford Gardens, London. † RA 1.

HOLROYD, Lilian Exh. 1929
46 St. Annes Road, Lytham, Lancs. † L 1.

HOLROYD, Newman Exh. 1906-14
R.B.A. 1906. Ryde, I.O.W. 1906,; Brading, I.O.W. 1912. † L 1, RA 2, RBA 8.

HOLROYD, T. Exh. 1884
Esplanade House, Harrogate, Yorks. † GI 1.

HOLROYD, W.B. Exh. 1927-28
28 Carrington Street, Birkenhead. † L 2.

HOLROYDE, E. Exh. 1901-21
Watercolour architectural painter. St. Paul's Cray, Kent. † B 12, D 8, L 4, M 3, RA 11, RI 2.

HOLROYDE, James Exh. 1882
St. John Street, Lichfield, Staffs. † L 1.

HOLST, Lauritz* 1848-1934
Marine painter. b. Denmark. Add: Thelwall, nr. Warrington, Lancs. 1883 and 1885; Elsinore, Denmark 1884 and 1891; Kensington, London 1895; Bournemouth, Hants. 1913. † L 11, RA 11, RHA 1.

HOLT, C.F. Exh. 1933
The Cedars, Fairview Road, Birkenhead. † L 1.

HOLT, Miss E. Exh. 1887-1906
Liverpool. † L 9.

HOLT, E.F.* Exh. 1886
64 Sneinton Road, Nottingham. † N 1.

HOLT, Miss F. Exh. 1919
4 Merton Road, London. † SWA 1.

HOLT, Gwynneth b. 1909
Sculptor. Studied Wolverhampton School of Art 1925-30. m. Thomas B. Huxley Jones q.v. Add: Wednesbury 1931; Cults, Aberdeen 1938. † B 3, RA 3.

HOLT, Gertrude M. Exh. 1908-13
14 Elm Park Gardens, London. † L 7, M 1, P 4.

HOLT, Harry Exh. 1922-32
Llandudno 1922; Waterloo, Liverpool 1923. † L 2, RCA 2.

HOLT, Herbert b. 1891
Portrait painter. Studied St. Helen's School of Art, Liverpool and Slade School. Add: Liverpool 1925; London 1937. † L 19, RA 4, RCA,1.

HOLT, H. Guy Exh. 1923-31
Architect. London. † RA 2.

HOLT, Kathleen Exh. 1939
† P 1.

HOLT, Miss L. Exh. 1917-19
Elm Park Gardens, London. † SWA 6.

HOLT, Miss M. Exh. 1902
40 Montague Street, London. † SWA 2.

HOLT, M.A.A. Exh. 1888
Mancetteo, St. Michael's Road, West Cliff, Bournemouth. † GI 1.

HOLT, T. Exh. 1929
64 Rodney Street, Liverpool. † L 1.

HOLT, T.J.W. Exh. 1921-30
New Brighton, Cheshire 1921; Wallasey, Cheshire 1928. † L 9.

HOLT, Will Exh. 1919
† L 1.

HOLTBURN, Amy B. Exh. 1893
c/o H.W. Crosbie, Kinross, Seabank Road, Liscard, Cheshire. † L 1.

HOLTBY, Miss M. Exh. 1893-94
183A King's Road, Chelsea, London. † L 4.

HOLTE, A.B. Exh. 1883-1904
Landscape painter. Llanrwst, N. Wales 1883; Bettws-y-Coed, N. Wales 1884; Leamington, Warwicks. 1885; Warwick 1897. † B 7, RCA 3.

HOLTON, Lucy Emily Exh. 1935-40
Mrs. H.E. Cleeve. Landscape painter. Tanglewood, Ganghill, Guildford, Surrey. † AR 2, RA 2, RI 2.

HOLYOAK, Mrs. E.T. Exh. 1899
22 Market Square, Northampton. † B 2.

HOLYOAKE, P.W. Exh. 1910
School of Art, Kendal, Westmorland. † RA 1.

HOLYOAKE, Rowland* Exh. 1880-1911
Genre, portrait, landscape and interior painter. Son of William H. q.v. Add: London. † B 18, G 1, GI 1, L 32, M 2, RA 28, RBA 57, RHA 1, RI 3, ROI 24.

HOLYOAKE, William 1834-1894
Genre and historical painter. Curator at the R.A. Schools. R.B.A. 1879, V.P.R.B.A. Add: London. † GI 2, L 3, M 4, RA 3, RBA 28, ROI 4.

HOLZAPEL, M. Exh. 1924-25
† GOU 2.

HOLZER, Henry Exh. 1938
† P 1.

HOMAN, Alice Exh. 1886
Christiana, Norway. † RSA 1.

HOMAN, Gertrude Exh. 1886-1905
Figure painter. 4 Regent's Park Road, Gloucester Gate, London. † L 8, M 2, RA 18, RBA 7, ROI 3, SWA 1.

HOMAN, W. McLean Exh. 1918-32
Glasgow 1918; Winchelsea, Sussex 1932. † GI 3, L 3, RSA 8.

HOME, Bruce J. Exh. 1905-7
5 Upper Gray Street, Edinburgh. † RSA 3.

HOME, Mrs. Evelyn E. Milne Exh. 1939
c/o Lady Milne Home, Canonbie. † RSW 2.

HOME, Emily G. Exh. 1900
10 Duchess Road, Clifton, Bristol. † SWA 1.

HOME, Gordon b. 1878
Landscape painter. Epsom, Surrey 1900. † RA 1.

HOME, G.W. Exh. 1921
Crossways, Woldingham, Surrey. † RA 1.

HOME, Janet Exh. 1922-37
Watercolour painter. London 1922; Woldingham, Surrey 1923; Warlingham, Surrey 1924. † COO 2, RA 2, RI 22, SWA 7.

HOME, Jean Mary Milne Exh. 1917-29
Paxton, Berwick on Tweed. † RSW 2.

HOME, Percy Exh. 1926
Landscape painter. † AB 4.

HOME, Robert b. 1865
Landscape and portrait painter, illuminator, stained glass artist and book decorator. Exh. 1882-1928. Add: Edinburgh 1882; Cupar, Fife 1921. † GI 10, RA 2, RSA 46.

HOMEMAN, Miss Exh. 1889
64 Charlotte Street, Fitzroy Square, London. † ROI 1.

HOMER, S.F. Exh. 1938-40
23 Norris Road, Handsworth, Birmingham. † B 4.

HOMER, Winslow* 1836-1910
American painter. Exh. 1882 and 1901. Add: Cullercoats, Newcastle on Tyne. † I 1, RA 1.

HOMERE, S. Exh. 1905-13
Kingham, Chipping Norton, Oxon 1905; Etaples, Pas de Calais, France 1907; Wallingford, Berks. 1913. † L 4, RA 2.

HONAN, Kathleen Exh. 1927-33
14 St. Domingo Vale, Everton, Liverpool. † L 3.

HONAN, Matthew Exh. 1909-14
Architect. 36 Dale Street, Liverpool. † L 12, RA 6.

HONAN, P. Martin Exh. 1899
30 Grosvenor Road, Chester. † L 1.

HONE, Evie* 1894-1955
Painter and stained glass artist. Dower House, Marley, Rathfarnham. † LEI 1, RHA 11.

HONE, Nathaniel Junr.* 1831-1917
Landscape painter. Professor of Painting. R.H.A. A.R.H.A. 1879, R.H.A. 1880. Add: Malahide, Ireland 1880; Raheny, Ireland 1896. † L 4, RHA 156.

HONEY, C. Winifred Exh. 1915-29
Painter. London. † L 2, RA 1, RI 1, ROI 1.

HONEYMAN, Herbert L. Exh. 1910-13
180 West Regent Street, Glasgow. † GI 1, RSA 1.

HONEYMAN, John 1831-1914
Architect. A.R.S.A. 1892, R.S.A. 1896, H.R.S.A. 1905. Add: Glasgow. † GI 12, RA 1, RSA 14.

HONEYMAN, J. Maclaren Exh. 1925
194 West Regent Street, Glasgow. † GI 1, RSA 1.

HONEYWOOD, Lady Exh. 1911
† BRU 1.

HONNOR, Timothy Exh. 1903-6
Architect. 28 Theobalds Road, London. † RA 2.

HONS, T.G. Exh. 1882
The Hague, Holland. † GI 1.

HOOD, Barbara M. Exh. 1897-1900
Park Lane, London. † SWA 3.

HOOD, Eileen Exh. 1916-24
Kenley, Surrey 1916; Stanmore, Middlesex 1917. † GOU 1, RI 2.

HOOD, G.F. Exh. 1928-29
Landscape painter. 3 Violet Road, West Bridgford, Notts. † N 5.

HOOD, W. Geddes Exh. 1917-20
c/o Arnot, 76 Raeburn Place, Edinburgh and Damacre Road, Brechin. † RSA 3, RSW 1.

HOOG, de See D

HOOGTERP, John A. Exh. 1934-36
Architect. P.O. Box 677, Nairobi, Kenya Colony. † RA 3.

HOOK, Allan J. Exh. 1880-1900
Landscape and coastal painter. Son of James Clark H. q.v. Add: Churt, Farnham, Surrey. † B 1, L 2, M 4, RA 20, TOO 1.

HOOK, Bryan Exh. 1880-1923
Landscape, coastal and figure painter and etcher. Son of James Clarke H. q.v. Travelled in Africa. Add: Churt, Farnham, Surrey 1880; Brixham, Devon 1923. † ALP 2, FIN 2, L 4, M 3, RA 45, RI 1, ROI 4.

HOOK, James Clarke* 1819-1907
Landscape, coastal and portrait painter. Studied under John Jackson and at R.A. Schools 1836. Spent 3 years in France and Italy. Father of Allan and Bryan H. q.v. A.R.A. 1850, R.A. 1860, R.E. 1881. "The Stream" purchased by Chantrey Bequest 1885. Add: Churt, Farnham, Surrey. † B 3, BG 1, FIN 10, G 1, GI 3, L 1, M 4, RA 80, RCA 2, RE 4, RSA 2, TOO 12.

HOOK, Samuel Exh. 1882-87
Watercolour landscape painter. London. † RBA 1, RI 1.

HOOK, Una Exh. 1913-22
Churt, Farnham, Surrey 1913 and 1916; Welwyn, Herts. 1917; London 1921. † I 1, L 1, NEA 1, RA 1, RI 2, SWA 6.

HOOKE, R. Exh. 1880-81
41 Donegall Place, Belfast. † RHA 2.

HOOKER, H.G. Exh. 1927-32
8 Liscard Road, Wavertree, Liverpool. † L 6.

HOOKER, S. Margaret Exh. 1922-40
Erdington Secondary School, Birmingham. † B 11.

HOOKHAM, John Exh. 1922-38
Painter and pencil artist. Muswell Hill, London 1922; Cambridge 1934. † RA 3.

HOOLE, A.H. Exh. 1906-10
Architect. 36 Gt. James Street, Bedford Row, London. † RA 3.

HOOLE, Gerald S. Exh. 1918
Mamby, Garelochhead. † GI 1.

HOOPER, Alfred William Exh. 1880-83
Watercolour architectural painter. 68 Ebury Street, London. † D 3.

HOOPER, Mrs. Eglantine Exh. 1922
3 Sunnyside, Princes Park, Liverpool. † L 1.

HOOPER, Francis Exh. 1890-92
Architect. 14 Sackville Street, London. † RA 2.

HOOPER, Mrs. Florence C.L. Exh. 1923
† SWA 1.

HOOPER, George b. 1910
Landscape painter. b. Gorakhpur, India. Exh. 1932-39. Add: 71 Huron Road, London. † NEA 1, RA 1.

HOOPER, Hilda Jessie Exh. 1934
Landscape painter, black and white and pastel artist. Studied R.A. Schools, Cope and Nicol's School and London School of Art. Worked in South Africa, Greece, Italy, France and Switzerland. Art mistress City of London School for Girls. Add: London. † WG 64.

HOOPER, Miss I.F. Exh. 1935
Lansdown, Allerton Drive, Liverpool. † I 8.

HOOPER, Irene L. Exh. 1908-14
Miniature painter. A.R.M.S. 1911. Add: 15 Shepherd Street, Mayfair, London. † L 2, RA 6, RMS 13.

HOOPER, John Horace* Exh. 1885-99
Landscape painter. London. † L 4, RA 6, RHA 3, TOO 8.

HOOPER, Luther 1849-1932
Landscape painter. Stoke Newington, London 1880; East Bergholt, Suffolk 1884; Bentley, Ipswich 1889. † D 6, RA 4, RBA 3, RI 4.

HOOPER, Margaret L. Exh. 1881-1911
Figure and portrait painter. London. † B 2, G 2, L 1, LS 9, M 1, RA 4, RI 1, ROI 6, RSA 5.

HOOPER, Miriam Mabel b. 1872
Watercolour landscape painter. Studied Croydon School of Art and under William Tatton Winter. Exh. 1915-39. Add: Redhill, Surrey. † AR 1, COO 2, L 3, RA 2, RBA 1, RI 9, SWA 1.

HOOPER, Nora Exh. 1900
Rathgowry, Eastbourne. † RBA 1.

HOOPER, William Exh. 1881-1911
Watercolour figure and landscape painter. London 1881; Christchurch, Hants. 1894; Bournemouth, Hants. 1907, Southbourne, Hants. 1911. † D 6, L 1, RA 5, RBA 1, RI 1.

HOOSE, Annie C. Exh. 1929-30
190 North Parade, Meols, Wirral, Cheshire. † L 2.

HOOTON, Miss N.B. Exh. 1910-16
Noel Street, Nottingham. † N 6.

HOOVER, Dorothy Exh. 1933
† RSW 2.

HOPE, Alan Exh. 1938
Architect. National College of Art, Kildare Street, Dublin. † RHA 2.

HOPE, Mrs. Adrian C. d. 1929
nee Troubridge. Portrait and figure painter. Exh. 1893-1901. Add: 34 Tite Street, Chelsea, London. † L 1, NG 5, P 1, SWA 1.

HOPE, A.J. Exh. 1906-17
Architect. London 1906; Bolton, Lancs. 1909. † RA 4.

HOPE, Evelyn Exh. 1933-35
Painter and wood engraver. 135 Hornsey Lane, London. † RA 2.

HOPE, Edith A. Exh. 1907-40
Painter, etcher, lithographer and wood engraver. b. Sydney, Australia. Studied Slade School (2 prizes). R.B.A. 1919. Add: London 1907; Steep, Petersfield, Hants. 1932. † GI 8, GOU 2, I 2, L 27, LS 5, M 6, NEA 1, RA 3, RBA 142, RHA 1, ROI 2, RSA 10, WG 78.

HOPE, Mrs. Ethel H. Exh. 1922
Miniature painter. 40 Downshire Hill, Hampstead, London. † L 1, RA 1.

HOPE, E. Lyn Exh. 1940
Landscape painter. c/o The Victor Waddington Galleries, 28 South Ann Street, Dublin. † RHA 2.

HOPE, Frances Exh. 1884
Landscape painter. Bowdon, Cheshire. † SWA 2.

HOPE, Mrs. Harry Exh. 1919
Barneyhill, Dunbar. † RSA 1.

HOPE, Henrietta Isabella Exh. 1908
7 Drayton Gardens, London. † LS 3.

HOPE, Helen J. Exh. 1898
St. Mary's Isle, Kirkenbright. † D 2.

HOPE, Lady Josephine Exh. 1893-1905
21 Elvaston Place, Queen's Gate, London. † D 10.

HOPE, M. Exh. 1892-93
22 Lower Dominick Street, Dublin. † RHA 3.

HOPE, M. Exh. 1892
Westlea, Helensburgh, N.B. † RSA 1.

HOPE, Miss M. Exh. 1880-88
Edinburgh 1880; Bourmont, Dunbar 1885. † GI 5, RSA 14.

HOPE, Mrs. May Exh. 1920
Highfield, Longton Avenue, Upper Sydenham, London. † L 1.

HOPE, Muriel Hollinger b. 1902
Portrait and landscape painter. b. Manchester. Twin sister of Rosa Somerville H. q.v. Studied Slade School (scholarship and 1st figure painting prize). Exh. 1923-38. Add: London. † GOU 55, M 2, NEA 6, RA 1, ROI 2.

HOPE, Mrs. R. Exh. 1937
Ridge Green Farm, South Nutfield, Surrey. † B 1.

HOPE, Robert* 1869-1936
Portrait, figure and landscape painter. A.R.S.A. 1911, R.S.A. 1925. Add: Edinburgh. † GI 93, L 20, M 3, RA 1, RSA 153, RSW 7.

HOPE, Rosa Somerville b. 1902
Watercolour painter and etcher. b. Manchester. Twin sister of Muriel Hollinger H. q.v. Studied Slade School, Central School of Art (Slade scholarship). On staff of Michaelis School of Fine Art, Cape Town University 1935-38. Senior lecturer in Fine Art, Natal University College, S. Africa from 1938. A.R.E. 1923. † M 4, NEA 17, RA 5, RE 33, RSA 2.

HOPE, Truda Exh. 1937-38
Durrington, Wilts. † SWA 2.

HOPE, William Henry Exh. 1881-1916
Landscape painter. Croydon, Surrey. † B 5, RBA 3, RHA 25.

HOPE-PINKER, Henry Richard 1850-1927
Sculptor. Studied R.A. Schools. Add: Kensington, London. † L 11, RA 48.

HOPGOOD, Maud Exh. 1898-1900
London. † B 3, GI 1, L 1, RBA 1, ROI 1.

HOPITAL, de l' See D

HOPKIN, A.Ll. Exh. 1937
6 Temple Chambers, Broad Street, Birmingham. † B 2.

HOPKIN, Mrs. Frances Exh. 1925
Watercolour painter. Oxton, Notts. † N 1.

HOPKING, Noel Hubert Exh. 1921-40
Watercolour painter. London. † D 6, TRA 2, RI 13.

HOPKINS, A. Exh. 1897-1902
West Bromwich, Birmingham. † B 3.

HOPKINS, Amy Exh. 1893
Portrait painter. Married Everard H. q.v. Add: 9 Pembroke Road, Kensington, London. † RID 2.

HOPKINS, Arthur 1848-1930
Landscape and coastal painter and illustrator. On staff of "Punch" and the "Graphic". A.R.W.S. 1877, R.W.S. 1896. Add: London. † B 41, DOW 48, FIN 76, GI 26, L 47, LEI 2, M 34, RA 32, ROI 2, RSW 235, WG 89.

HOPKINS, A.G. Exh. 1925
149 Lower Kennington Lane, London. † L 4.

HOPKINS, Miss B. Exh. 1909
Miniature portrait painter. Dornie, Westward Ho!, North Devon. † RA 1.

HOPKINS, C. Beresford Exh. 1900
84 Wellesley Street, Shelton, Stoke on Trent. † B 1.

HOPKINS, E. Exh. 1888
13 Barkston Mansions, Barkston Gardens, S. Kensington, London. † M 1.

HOPKINS, Edith Exh. 1910
Verecroft, Glenville Road, Rustington, Nr. Worthing, Sussex. † RHA 2.

HOPKINS, Evan Exh. 1904-6
Redcliffe Square, S. Kensington, London. † D 8.

HOPKINS, Everard d. 1928
Watercolour painter. Artist for "Punch". m. Amy H. q.v. Exh. 1882-1908. Add: London. † GI 1, M 1, RA 1, RI 6.

HOPKINS, Mrs. Edna Boies b. 1878
American artist. m. James R.H. q.v. Exh. 1913. Add: Paris. † L 4.

HOPKINS, Frances Ann 1856-1919
nee Beechey. Landscape and figure painter. Grand-daughter of Sir William Beechey, R.A. Exh. 1880-1918. Add: London. † B 1, D 7, L 2, M 3, RA 7, SWA 9, WG 89.

HOPKINS, Mrs. F.B. Exh. 1933
33 Mayfield Avenue, London. † RI 1.

HOPKINS, Francis Ellice Exh. 1922-32
Portrait and seascape painter. Formerly a sugar planter in Jamaica. Studied Heatherleys and Paris. Add: London. † L 1, RA 1, ROI 3.

HOPKINS, F.R. Exh. 1931-32
Architectural and urban landscape painter. Derby. † N 7.

HOPKINS, Germaine Exh. 1929
c/o Footprints, Durham Wharf, London. † L 1.

HOPKINS, Harold J. Exh. 1938
Coastal painter. 110 Harrow Road, Wollaton Park, Nottingham. † N 1.

HOPKINS, Mme. Isabel P. Exh. 1906
7 Rue Leopold Robert, Paris. † RA 1.

HOPKINS, James R. b. 1878
American artist. Married Edna Boies H. q.v. Exh. 1913. Add: Paris. † L 2.

HOPKINS, Miss L.F. Exh. 1908-10
Eastwood, Notts. † N 4.

HOPKINS, William H.* d. 1892
Landscape, animal and sporting painter. London. † RA 2.

HOPKINSON, Anne Elizabeth Exh. 1880-87
Flower and fruit painter. Kentwood, Blythe Hill, Catford, London. † RA 2, RBA 4, RI 2, SWA 11.

HOPKINSON, Emma Exh. 1885-88
Flower painter. 20 Colville Terrace, Colville Street, Nottingham. † N 2.

HOPKINSON, J.W. Exh. 1933-35
10 Moorcroft Road, Liverpool. † I 8, L 1.

HOPKYNS, F. Molly Exh. 1940
Figure and flower painter. 6A Queen's Terrace, London. † RA 2.

HOPLEY, Muriel Exh. 1909
Lesketh Row, Ambleside. † L 1.

HOPPE, B. Exh. 1884-87
116 New Bond Street, London. † GI 4, M 2.

HOPPE, Ernest O. b. 1878
b. Munich. Studied Munich, Vienna and Paris. Exh. 1918-19. Add: Mulais House, Cromwell Place, London. † I 4.

HOPPE-KINROSS, Mrs. Erna Exh. 1910-20
Landscape, portrait and figure painter. 12 Ormonde Terrace, Regent's Park, London. † BG 57, LS 6, RA 1, RID 4, SWA 1.

HOPPER, Charles W. Exh. 1893-1902
Landscape and figure painter. London. † RA 6.

HOOPER, W. Cuthbert Exh. 1880
Landscape painter. Odiham, Hants. † RA 1, RBA 1.

HOPTON, Miss D.C. Exh. 1912
Homend, Stretton Grandison, Ledbury, Herefords. † D 4.

HOPTON, Gwendoline M. Exh. 1897-1913
Painter and miniaturist. R.M.S. 1897. Kemerton Upper Court, Nr. Tewkesbury, Glos. 1897 and 1900; London 1899. † B 2, RA 3, RMS 9, ROI 5, WG 71.

HOPTON, Mona Exh. 1894-96
92 Falkner Street, Liverpool. † L 5.

HOPTON, Miss W.G. Exh. 1933
17 Frederick Road, Edgbaston, Birmingham. † B 2.

HOPWOOD, Henry Silkstone* 1860-1914
Watercolour painter. A.R.W.S. 1896, R.W.S. 1908. "Industry" purchased by Chantrey Bequest 1894. Add: Manchester 1882; Whitby, Yorks. 1895; London 1898 and 1912; Hinderwell, Yorks. 1900; Montreuil sur Mer, Pas de Calais, France 1909. † B 9, FIN 183, GI 2, L 15, LEI 1, M 20, RA 9, RI 2, RWS 70.

HORDER, P. Morley Exh. 1894-1922
Architect. London. † RA 16.

HORDERN, Agnes Exh. 1913-35
Miniature painter. A.R.M.S. 1926. Add: London 1913, 1918 and 1921; Bushey, Herts. 1915; Appledore, Devon, 1919. † L 7, RA 9, RI 5, RMS 24, SWA 1.

HORLEY, Annie Exh. 1908
Watercolour flower painter. † BG 2.

HORLEY, Margaret Exh. 1895
35 Arundel Avenue, Sefton Park, Liverpool. † M 2.

HORLEY, Ronald b. 1904
Exh. 1937. b. Pinner. † RI 1.

HORLOR, Emma Exh. 1881
Rustic landscape painter. Bristol. † SWA 2.

HORLOR, George W.* Exh. 1890
Animal painter. The Elms, 47 Boston Road, Brentford, Essex. † RA 1.

HORMAN-FISHER, Maud Exh. 1880
Landscape painter. 29 St. Paul's Crescent, Camden Square, London. † D 1.

HORMANN, de See D

HORN, Helena M. Exh. 1924-27
12 Sunnyside, Princes Park, Liverpool. † L 3.

HORN, Marion F. See LUCK

HORNBLOWER, Miss A.L. Exh. 1888-1903
58 Park Road, Birkenhead. † B 7, L 8, M 6.

HORNBLOWER, F.W. Exh. 1883-84
Baltic Buildings, Red Cross Street, Liverpool. † L 4.

HORNBLOWER, George Exh. 1898-1923
Architect. 2 Devonshire Terrace, Portland Place, London. † RA 15.

HORNBLOWER, Winifred b. 1879
Miniature painter. Studied Laird School of Art and London. Exh. 1905-38. Add: 34 Carlton Road, Birkenhead. † B 4, GI 3, L 55, M 1, RA 2, RCA 15.

HORNBUCKLE, John H. Exh. 1934-39
Painter and linocut artist. Nottingham. † N 20.

HORNBY, Miss F.M. Exh. 1889-1920
Liverpool 1889; Ham, Surrey 1898. † L 31.

HORNE, Miss A.R. Exh. 1912
Beulah, Weybridge, Surrey. † RA 1.

HORNE, Barbara Exh. 1938-40
1 Westhall Gardens, Edinburgh. † RSA 2, RSW 2.

HORNE, Frank E. Exh. 1896-1933
Watercolour landscape painter. Keighley, Yorks. 1896; Ripon, Yorks. 1908; Harrow, Middlesex 1911; Grassington, Yorks. 1920 and 1923; Ilkley, Yorks. 1921; Skipton 1922 and 1930; London 1927. † FIN 1, GI 14, GOU 3, L 9, M 1, NEA 1, RA 21, RI 18, RSA 12.

HORNE, Margery Exh. 1898-1901
Mrs. W.E., Hall Place, Shackleford, Surrey. † NG 2.

HORNEL, Edward Atkinson* 1864-1933
Genre and decorative painter. Born in Australia. Came to Britain as a child. Studied at Trustees Academy, Edinburgh and under Verlat at Antwerp. Collaborated with George Henry q.v. and visited Japan with him in 1894. R.O.I. 1904, Member of Society of 25 Artists, declined A.R.S.A. 1901. Add: Kirkcudbright 1883 and 1896; Glasgow 1888. † B 1, BG 2, CON 18, FIN 3, G 2, GI 103, GOU 6, I [illegible] L 43, M 11, NEA 1, NG 2, RA 11, ROI 2, RSA 19, RSW 3.

HORNEMAN, Miss S.R. Exh. 1907
Rotherhithe, London. † SWA 1.

HORNER, Miss Exh. 1905
9 Buckingham Gate, London. † NG 1.

HORNER, Miss C.E. Exh. 1914-19
152 Finborough Road, London. † I 2, L 5, RA 1.

HORNER, Grace Malleson Exh. 1916-33
nee Fearon. Flower painter. b. Kent. Studied London School of Art. Add: London. † I 4, RA 5, SWA 4.

HORNER, Jocelyn Exh. 1927-28
Sculptor. Green Hayes, Halifax. † ALP 1, L 4, RA 1.

HORNER, John Exh. 1881-91
Landscape and figure painter. London. † D 1, RBA 4, RI 1.

HORNETT, C.C. Exh. 1882
The Lodge, Southwood, Bickley, Kent. † M 2.

HORNSBY, Mrs. Exh. 1899
Branscombe, Upper Richmond Road, Putney, London. † SWA 1.

HORNSBY, Anne Louise Exh. 1933
132 Swanhurst Lane, Moseley, Birmingham. † B 1.

HORNUNG, Bertha Exh. 1909-17
Landscape painter. Comptons Lea, Horsham, Sussex. † L 4, NEA 1.

HORNUNG, Kathleen Exh. 1919-25
Oaklands, Horley, Surrey. † I1, L 1.

HORRELL, Charles A. Exh. 1895
Stained glass artist. 9 Arundel Road, Croydon, Surrey. † RA 1.

HORRELL, Fred G. Exh. 1922-23
† D 4.

HORRELL, Mrs. Norah A. Exh. 1910-28
Miniature painter. Worthing, Sussex 1910; Harpenden, Herts. 1926. † RA 9.

HORRIDGE, S. Exh. 1938
† M 1.

HORRIDGE, T. Exh. 1935-36
Landscape and decorative painter. 14 Victoria Road, Nottingham. † N 4.

HORROCKS, Annie Exh. 1898-1903
Poplar Cottage, Penworthan Hill, Preston, Lancs. † L 5.

HORROCKS, Miss E.A. Exh. 1884
28 Rue d'Orleans, Neuilly sur Seine, Paris. † B 1.

HORROCKS, Mrs. F. Exh. 1927-28
Atherton, Manchester. † L 3.

HORSBRUGH, A. Exh. 1926-29
Blanefield 1926; Glasgow 1928. † GI 7.

HORSBRUGH-PORTER, William Eric b. 1905
Landscape and coastal painter. Studied Slade School. Exh. 1932-40. Add: Glenhest, Carrickmines, Co. Dublin. † COO 57, NEA 1, RA 2, RHA 22, ROI 4.

HORSBURGH, Edith M. Exh. 1900
Aberdour House, Aberdour, Fife. † RSA 1.

HORSBURGH, Victor D. Exh. 1901-35
Edinburgh 1901; Toronto, Canada 1935. † RSA 5.

HORSFALL, Charles M. Exh. 1907
c/o L. White King, Roebuck Hall, Co. Dublin. † RHA 1.

HORSFALL, Ernest Exh. 1889-93
Figure painter. 4 Belsize Square, South Hampstead, London. † B 1, L 4, P 1, RBA 1.

HORSFALL, Ethel See ERTZ

HORSFALL, Jesse Exh. 1898-1907
Architect. Todmorden, Yorks. † RA 4.

HORSFALL, Mary Exh. 1903
Painter. 7 Elm Tree Road, St. John's Wood, London. † RA 1.

HORSFIELD, Arthur E. Exh. 1909
82A George Street, Edinburgh. † RSA 2.

HORSFORD, Olive Exh. 1907-40
Miniature painter. London. † L 4, RA 29, RCA 9, RHA 2, RMS 3.

HORSLEY, Miss A.S.C. Exh. 1915
St. Stephen's Lodge, Canterbury, Kent. † RA 1.

HORSLEY, Charles d. 1921
Landscape painter. R.B.A. 1904. Add: Croydon, Surrey 1893; London 1901 and 1913; Beckenham, Kent 1908. † L 1, LS 5, RA 2, RBA 76, ROI 4.

HORSLEY, Mrs. Elizabeth Exh. 1921
Flower painter. 1 Grove Villas, Wilford Grove, Nottingham. † N 1.

HORSLEY, Gerald Callcott Exh. 1882-1915
Architect, architectural and decorative artist. Son of John Callcott H. q.v. Add: London. † GI 4, RA 62.

HORSLEY, Hopkins Horsley Hobday* 1807-1890
Landscape painter. Rugeley, Staffs. 1882; Birchfield, Birmingham 1890. † B 39.

HORSLEY, H.W. Exh. 1916
Amberley House, Norfolk Street, Strand, London. † RA 1.

HORSLEY, John Callcott* 1817-1903
Historical genre painter. Studied R.A. Schools. Father of Gerald C. and Walter C.H. q.v. A.R.A. 1855, R.A. 1864. Add: Willesley, Staplehurst and 1 High Row, Kensington, London. † B 3, GI 3, M 3, RA 27.

HORSLEY, Mrs. L. Exh. 1899
Grove Terrace, Wilford Grove, Nottingham. † N 1.

HORSLEY, Walter Charles* c. 1867-1934
Figure and landscape painter. Exh. 1880-1916. Add: London. † B 4, BG 1, D 2, GI 1, L 12, LEI 1, M 10, RA 45, RI 1, ROI 2.

HORSMAN, W.G. Exh. 1906-7
27A Sackville Street, London. † RA 2.

HORSNELL, Alick G. d. 1916
A.R.E. 1912. Exh. from 1909. Add: London. † L 7, RA 6, RE 17.

HORTH, Frederick J. Exh. 1909-29
Architect. Hornsea, Essex 1909; Hull, Yorks. 1929. † RA 3.

HORTON, A.E. Exh. 1920-26
Newport, Mon. † L 1, RCA 3, RHA 2.

HORTON, Alice M. Exh. 1911
10 Kingsmead Road South, Oxton, Birkenhead. † L 2.

HORTON, Etty Exh. 1892-1905
Landscape painter. London 1892; Hawkhurst, Kent 1903. † B 4, M 1, RA 2, RBA 4, RI 4, SWA 11.

HORTON, George Edward b. 1860
Landscape and marine painter and etcher. Exh. 1891-1938. Add: North Shields 1891; South Shields 1895; London 1916. † FIN 52, GI 1, GOU 1, I 4, L 3, RA 6, RI 4, RSA 9.

HORTON, Percy* 1897-1970
Painter and draughtsman. Studied Brighton Art School 1914-16, Central School of Arts and Crafts 1918-20, Royal College of Art 1922-25. Exh. 1927-40. † GOU 2, M 1, NEA 19, RA 1.

HORTON, Ronald Exh. 1928-39
Landscape painter. London 1928; Loughton, Essex 1939. † NEA 4, RA 2.

HORTON, Sallie Exh. 1908-9
Stapleton, Four Oaks, Birmingham. † B 2.

HORTON, Sarah Elizabeth b. 1865
Painter and illustrator and teacher. b. Australia. Studied Herkomer's, Bushey, Herts. and South Kensington. Add: London 1889 and 1893; Bushey, Herts. 1891; Bath, Som. 1915. † RA 3, RBA 1, RI 4, SWA 7.

HORTON, Winifred M. Exh. 1906-11
19 Westminister Chambers, Crosshall Street, Liverpool. † L 8, RA 1.

HORTON, William Samuel* b. 1865
Figure and landscape painter. b. U.S.A. Exh. 1928. † BA 58.

HORTON, William T. Exh. 1890
Architect. 52 Craster Road, Brixton Hill, London. † RA 1.

HORVATH, Joseph Exh. 1938
Watercolour figure painter. Gyirota Utca 7, Sopron, Hungary. † RA 1.

HORWITZ, Emanuel Henry Exh. 1886-1935
Portrait and landscape painter, etcher, lithographer and pastel artist. Studied Westminster, Juliens, Paris, Munich and Holland. Add: London. † D 3, G 1, GI 5, GOU 4, L 3, M 1, P 3, RA 16, RBA 2, RHA 2, RI 7, RID 29, ROI 4.

HORWITZ, Helena d. 1921
Miniature painter. R.M.S. 1901. Exh. 1889-1920. Add: London. † GI 6, L 6, RA 33, RHA 1, RI 5, RMS 16.

HORWITZ, Herbert A. Exh. 1892-1906
Portrait painter. Studied R.A. Schools. Add: London. † GI 1, L 4, NG 2, RI 10, RBA 1.

HORWITZ, Louise B. Exh. 1892-1914
Miniature portrait painter. 13 Grazebrook Road, Clissold Park, London. † GI 2, RA 15, RMS 4.

HORWOOD, Mrs. Violet Exh. 1894-1929
nee Fife. Landscape painter. Goring on Thames, Reading, Berks. 1894; Westgate on Sea, Kent 1910; Haxby, Yorks. 1914. † RID 33, SWA 2.

HOSACK, Isobel Exh. 1922-35
Mrs. G.D. Grant-Suttie. Sculptor. Add: Crieff 1922; Goring on Thames, Berks. 1935. † RA 1, RSA 1.

HOSBAND, H.H. Exh. 1887-89
Stoke on Trent, Staffs. † B 3.

HOSEL, Erich Exh. 1903
Sculptor. Huasa Allee, 186 Obercassel, Dusseldorf. † RA 1.

HOSKIN, Richard Exh. 1900
Painter. 2 Sherwell Arcade, Plymouth, Devon. † RA 2.

HOSKING, Edith M. Exh. 1916-36
Portrait painter. London. † I 2, L 2, RA 10.

HOSKYNS, Miss G. Exh. 1918
Nairn, N.B. † SWA 2.

HOSKYNS-ABRAHALL, T. Exh. 1936
c/o R. Sielle Esq., 14 Buckingham Street, London. † RBA 2, RI 1.

HOSSACK, Alexander Exh. 1929
Portrait painter. 18 Hall Road, Newlands, London. † RA 1.

HOSSACK, James Wright b. 1895
Landscape, coastal and figure painter. b. Edinburgh. Studied Camberwell School of Arts and Crafts. Exh. 1920-31. Add: 18 Hall Road, Newlands, London. † GOU 4, L2, RA 5.

HOTCHKIS, Anna Mary Exh. 1915-40
Watercolour painter and woodcut artist. Studied Glasgow and Edinburgh. Visited China on a sketching tour 1923. Sister of Isobel H. q.v. Add: Edinburgh. † GI 9, L 1, RSA 11, RSW 10.

HOTCHKIS, Isobel Exh. 1913-40
Watercolour painter. Studied Glasgow School of Art and under Jean Delville, Brussels. Visited South Africa. Add: Edinburgh and Liverpool. † GI 9, L 7, RSA 10, RSW 15.

HOUBLON, Margaret Archer Exh. 1898-1935
Sculptor. London 1898; Bishops Stortford, Herts. 1903; Newbury, Berks. 1931. † L 2, NG 7, RA 2.

HOUCHEN, Harry Exh. 1909-14
Cork 1909; School of Art, Londonderry 1913. † LS 3, RHA 22.

HOUCHIN, Harold R. Exh. 1910-35
Architect. Ruislip, Middlesex 1910; London 1935. † RA 2.

HOUFTON, Miss A.P. Exh. 1909-13
Carr Bank, Mansfield, Notts. † N 4.

HOUFTON, Percy B. Exh. 1906
Furnival Chambers, Chesterfield. † RA 1.

HOUGANT, Miss M.S. Exh. 1889
4 Brunswick Square, London. † RI 1.

HOUGH, Graham G. Exh. 1926-28
Grasscroft, Archway Road, Huyton, Liverpool. † L 4.

HOUGH, T.B. Exh. 1886-87
Surveyor's Department, Municipal Offices, Dale Street, Liverpool. † L 2.

HOUGH, William* Exh. 1880-94
Fruit and still life painter. London. † B 5, D 7, L 5, M 1, RA 11, RI 3, TOO 1.

HOUGHTON, C.A. Exh. 1940
Flint, Wales. † RCA 1.

HOUGHTON, de See D

HOUGHTON, Evelyn Exh. 1931
Figure painter. St. Andrews, Burford, Oxford. † RA 1.

HOUGHTON, Mrs. Elizabeth Ellen Exh. 1886-1910
Stockton Heath, Warrington, Lancs. † L 10, M 3.

HOUGHTON, H.W. Exh. 1926-32
Urban and architectural painter. N.S.A. 1937. Add: Nottingham 1926; Sherwood, Nottingham 1937. † N 25.

HOUGHTON, Mrs. Janet M. Exh. 1927
East Downe House, Nr. Barnstaple, Devon. † RMS 5.

HOUGHTON, J.R. Exh. 1910
Painter. Mill End Studios, Little Easton, Dunmow, Essex. † NEA 1.

HOUGHTON, Philip Exh. 1909-22
London 1909; Ashton on Clun, Salop 1913; Montgomery, N. Wales 1914; Four Marks, Hants. 1920. † L 6, LS 6, RI 1.

HOUGHTON, Sydney C. Exh. 1895
16 Comely Bank Road, Egremont, Cheshire. † L 1.

HOULE, Mrs Annie Gertrude See FLETCHER

HOULGRAVE, A.M. Exh. 1886-93
146 Upper Parliament Street, Liverpool. † B 1, L 3, RHA 1, RSA 1

HOULT, J.H. Exh. 1902
104 Hunger Hill Road, Nottingham. † N 1.

HOUNSELL, Francis William b. 1885
Watercolour landscape painter. Studied Brighton School of Art, Royal College of Art. Served in army in France, Salonika and Palestine World War I. Principal of Derby School of Arts and Crafts; Headmaster of Colchester School of Arts and Crafts; Assistant art master at the Brighton School of Art. Exh. 1930-34. Add: 191 Maldon Road, Colchester, Essex. † RA 5.

HOUNSFIELD, Miss T.M. Exh. 1909-13
Dover 1909; Bromley, Kent 1910. † D 6, L 1, RI 1, SWA 5.

HOURIGAN, Francis Exh. 1937-40
Sculptor. Cork 1937; National College of Art, Kildare Street, Dublin 1940. † RHA 4.

HOUSEMAN, Edith Giffard b. 1875
Watercolour landscape painter, wood engraver and pencil portrait artist. b. Bredwardine, Herefords. Exh. 1906-40. Add: Bagshot, Surrey 1906; Petworth, Sussex 1920. † AR 2, B 46, COO 2, D 28, L 15, LS 3, RA 4, RBA 9, RHA 6, RI 4 RSA 7, SWA 30, WG 30.

HOUSMAN, Clemence Exh. 1903
Wood cut artist. † BG 19.

HOUSMAN, Laurence 1861-1950
Painter and illustrator. Exh. 1894-1906. Add: London. † BG 55, FIN 82, NEA 21.

HOUSTON, Charles Exh. 1881-1936
Glasgow 1881; Dennistoun, N.B. 1892; Cambuslang, N.B. 1898; Rutherglen, N.B. 1908. † GI 55, M 2, RSA 10, RSW 5.

HOUSTON, Frances Exh. 1890
Portrait painter. 115 Rione Amedo, Naples. † RA 1.

HOUSTON, George* b. 1869
Painter and etcher. R.I. 1920, A.R.S.A. 1909, R.S.A. 1925, R.S.W. 1906. Member of Society of 25 Artists. Exh. 1897-1940. Add: West Lynn, Dalry, Ayrshire and Glasgow. † FIN 2, GI 95, I 1, L 16, M 7, RI 3, RSA 70, RSW11.

HOUSTON, James Exh. 1938
Whitehurst, Kilburnie, Ayrshire. † GI 2.

HOUSTON, John Adam* 1812-1884
Historical genre painter and watercolourist. Studied Edinburgh, Paris and Germany. A.R.I. 1874, R.I. 1879, R.O.I. 1883, A.R.S.A. 1842, R.S.A. 1845. Add: London. † B 1, GI 3, L 6, M 1, RBA 3, RI 17, ROI 4, RSA 13.

HOUSTON, J.A.T. Exh. 1902-5
Glasgow. † GI 2.

HOUSTON, John Rennie McKenzie Exh. 1882-1932
Figure and interior painter. Studied Glasgow. Add: Glasgow 1882; Dennistoun, N.B. 1891 and 1900; Cambuslang, N.B. 1898; Rutherglen, N.B. 1907; Edinburgh 1932. † DOW 2, GI 45, RSA 3, RSW 36.

HOUSTON, Mary G. Exh. 1901-4
Painter and decorative artist. London. † RA 5.

HOUSTON, Margaret M. Exh. 1904
Miniature portrait painter. The College, Coleraine, Co. Derry, Ireland. † RA 2.

HOUSTON, Peter D. Exh. 1933-36
38 Burnside Road, Rutherglen, N.B. † GI 2, RSA 2.

HOUSTON, Robert* 1891-1940
Landscape and figure painter. Studied Glasgow School of Art. R.S.W. 1936. Add: Kilbirnie, Ayrs. 1911; Helensburgh, 1921; Glasgow 1929. † CON 1, GI 27, L 7, RA 6, RSA 8, RSW 11.

HOUSTORME-WARD, Mrs. E.M. Exh. 1912
Teversal Grange, Mansfield, Notts. † N 1.

HOUTHUESEN, Albert* b. 1903
Landscape painter. b. Amsterdam. Came to England as a child. "Maes Gwyn Stack Yard" (1935) purchased by Chantrey Bequest 1939. Exh. 1928-40. Add: 20 Constantine Road, London. † NEA 5, RA 2.

HOUY, William Exh. 1883
Kelso. † RSA 1.

HOVE, Van See V

HOVELT, Christine Exh. 1900-5
London. † L 1, NG 3.

HOVENDEN, Ethel L. Exh. 1899-1901
Miniature painter. Glenlea, Thurlow Park Road, West Dulwich, London. † RA 1, RMS 2.

HOVENDEN, Miss M. Exh. 1901
Glenlea, 109 Thurlow Park Road, West Dulwich, London. † SWA 1.

HOVENDEN, Thomas* Exh. 1880
Landscape painter. Pont Avern, Finisterre, France. † RBA 1.

HOW, Beatrice* 1867-1932
Figure painter. b. Devon. Studied Herkomer's, Bushey, Herts. and Paris. "L'Infirmiere" (c. 1914-18) purchased by Chantrey Bequest 1935. Add: Walkington Rectory, Beverley, Yorks. and Paris. † GI 10, I 3, L 11, M 2, RA 2, RSA 2.

HOW, Mrs. Edith J. Exh. 1917
† P 1.

HOW, Miss F. Exh. 1889
Landscape painter. 23 Melville Street, Edinburgh. † SWA 1.

HOW, F. Douglas Exh. 1889-97
Landscape painter. Wakefield, Yorks. † B 7, M 1, RBA 1, RHA 1, RI 1.

HOW, Frances Thalia Exh. 1896-1928
Watercolour painter, jeweller and enameller. London. † I 7, L 4, RA 2, RSA 3, RSW 2.

HOW, Miss L. Exh. 1895
61 Cadogan Square, London. † GI 1.

HOW, R. Exh. 1909
Painter. † BG 1.

HOWARD, A. Exh. 1898-1901
Dudley Road, Grantham, Lincs. † N 3.

HOWARD, Annie Exh. 1883-1900
Miniature portrait painter. London. † L 1, M 1, RA 30.

HOWARD, A.L. Exh. 1915
4 Avenue Studios, 76 Fulham Road, London. † RA 1.

HOWARD, Alice L. Exh. 1880
Landscape painter. Thorn Lea, Morland Road, Croydon, Surrey. † SWA 1.

HOWARD, Beatrice Exh. 1900
Miniature portrait painter. 38 Lincoln's Inn Fields, London. † L 2, RA 1.

HOWARD, Brian Exh. 1922
† I 1.

HOWARD, Catherine Exh. 1888-1901
Landscape and flower painter. 205 Amherst Road, Hackney Downs, London. † L 1, RA 1, RBA 2, RI 1.

HOWARD, Cecil Exh. 1925
† CHE 5.

HOWARD, Charlotte Exh. 1885-94
Mrs. A.J. Lugard. Miniature painter. Forest Hill, London 1885; Beckenham, Kent 1889. † RA 12, RI 4.

HOWARD, Constance M. Exh. 1936-37
Cardiff, Wales. † RCA 2.

HOWARD, Charles T. Exh. 1897-1903
Painter. 149 Dudley Road, Grantham, Lincs. 1897; Peterborough 1903. † L 1, N 22, RA 1.

HOWARD, Evelyn Exh. 1895-1904
4 Baring Place, Exeter 1894; Northam, N. Devon 1902. † B 1, L 1, RI 2, SWA 10.

HOWARD, Elizabeth H. Exh. 1880-81
Landscape painter. Milstead Manor, Sittingbourne, Kent. † D 1, SWA 4.

HOWARD, Mrs. Florence Exh. 1927
22 Temple Gardens, London. † NEA 1.

HOWARD, Francis 1874-1954
Painter and critic. Studied Geneva, Paris, London and Bushey. Exh. 1896-1919. Add: London. † GI 2, I 18, L 5, NG 1, P 2.

HOWARD, George 1843-1911
9th Earl of Carlisle. Landscape painter. Studied South Kensington. Travelled widely. Chairman of the Trustees of the National Gallery for 30 years. H.R.W.S. Add: 1 Palace Green, Kensington, London 1880; Castle Howard, Yorks. 1905. † FIN 1, G 18, L 4, M 4, NG 20, RA 1, RHA 1, RWS 11.

HOWARD, Henry* Exh. 1880-1913
Landscape painter. Stonehouse, Kidderminster. † ALP 5, B 9, L 2, M 1, RA 5, RBA 4.

HOWARD, H.E. Exh. 1927-33
Southport, Lancs. † L 2.

HOWARD, Henry James b. 1876
Etcher, illustrator and Civil Servant. Father of Margaret Maitland H. q.v. Exh. 1935. Add: St. Katharine's, Mulgrave Road, Sutton, Surrey. † RA 1, ROI 1.

HOWARD, Henry M. Exh. 1896-1908
Paris. † L 1, LS 2, NG 1.

HOWARD, H. Wickham Exh. 1890-95
Landscape painter. Chiswick Mall, London. † G 1, NG 1, ROI 7.

HOWARD, J. Exh. 1933
221 Gladstone Street, Sherwood Rise, Nottingham. † N 1.

HOWARD, James Campbell b. 1906
Landscape painter. Self taught. Add: Ilford, Essex 1932; Ewell, Surrey 1936. † RA 2, RCA 1.

HOWARD, John L. Exh. 1922-38
15 Chester Terrace, London. † GOU 3, NEA 6.

HOWARD, L.G. Exh. 1918
Park Chambers, Nassau Street, Dublin. † RHA 2.

HOWARD, Mary E. Exh. 1909-20
Flower painter. 53 Addiscombe Road, Croydon, Surrey. † B 1, BG 1.

HOWARD, Margaret Maitland b. 1898
Portrait and subject painter, illustrator and miniaturist. Daughter of Henry James H. q.v. Studied Byam Shaw and Vicat Cole School and R.A. Schools (5 silver medals). Exh. 1923-40. Add: St. Katharine's, Mulgrave Road, Sutton, Surrey. † COO 2, L 2, NEA 2, P 2, RA 10, ROI 13, SWA 4.

HOWARD, Miss Noel Exh. 1938
51 Queensborough Terrace, London. † SWA 1.

HOWARD, Norman 1899-1955
Painter and illustrator. Studied Camberwell School of Art 1918-20, Westminster School of Art 1920-24. Exh. 1921-25. Add: Putney, London. † GOU 11, I 1, NEA 2, RA 1, ROI 1.

HOWARD, Squire Exh. 1882-95
Manchester. † L 1, M 24.

HOWARD, Stanley G. Exh. 1907-8
26 Berners Street, London. † L 2.

HOWARD, Theodore A. Exh. 1880-1904
Architect. London 1880; St. Matthews Vicarage, The Elms, Liverpool 1902. † L 3, RA 4.

HOWARD, Vernon Exh. 1883-1902
Landscape painter. Boston, Lincs. 1883; Grantham, Lincs. 1894. † L 1, N 20, RA 4, RI 14.

HOWARD, W.C. Exh. 1891-1909
Edinburgh. † RSA 13.

HOWARD-JONES, Ray b. 1903
Landscape and portrait painter. Studied Slade School 1921-24 and Hospitalfield, Arbroath. Exh. 1925-28. Add: Penarth, Glam. † GOU 4.

HOWARD-JONES, Miss Rosemary Exh. 1934-39
Penarth, Glam. † RCA 6.

HOWARD-MERCER, Miss H. Exh. 1937
Decorative painter. 60 Sutton Court, Brighton Road, Sutton, Surrey. † RA 1.

HOWARTH, Albany E. 1872-1936
Watercolour painter, etcher and lithographer. A.R.E. 1910. Add: London 1905; Downhall, Essex 1906; Hutton, Essex 1910; Watford, Herts. 1929. † AG 1, CG 4, FIN 68, I 1, L 19, RA 6, RE 24, RI 2.

HOWARTH, C.S. Exh. 1908-10
Sandringham Road, Waterloo, Liverpool. † L 3.

HOWARTH, Charles Wilfred b. 1893
Painter and illustrator. Studied Sheffield School of Art 1910-12, Birmingham School of Art 1912-14. Exh. 1920-40. Add: Erdington, Birmingham 1920; Coleshill, Birmingham 1927. † B 17, RCA 3.

HOWARTH, Miss F.A Exh. 1884-1903
Watercolour landscape painter. South Croydon, Surrey 1884; South Norwood, London 1902. † D 13, RBA 1, SWA 12.

HOWARTH, Mrs. H.C. Exh. 1886-9
Hoylake, Cheshire. † B 3, GI 1, L 6 RHA 3, RSA 2.

HOWARTH, J.A. Exh. 190
29 Norwood Avenue, Bradford Road Shipley, Yorks. † RA 1.

HOWARTH, J.H. Exh. 1920-21
15 Exchange Buildings, Liverpool. † L 3 RCA 2.

HOWARTH, J.P. Exh. 1894-190
Liscard, Cheshire 1894; Wallasey, Cheshire 1902. † L 3.

HOWARTH, Singleton Exh. 1906
23 Oxford Road, Waterloo, Liverpool. † L 1.

HOWARTH, Will H. Exh. 1897-1908
Liverpool. † L 5.

HOWDEN, May Exh. 1928
10 Moray Place, Edinburgh. † RSA 1.

HOWDEN, Marion A. Exh. 1902-22
Ettrick Road, Edinburgh. † GI 1, RI 1, RSA 4.

HOWE, Miss E. Gambier Exh. 1895-1906
London. † L 6, NG 2.

HOWE, Frank E. Exh. 1922
† I 2.

HOWE, F.T. Exh. 1891
Central Hotel, Edinburgh. † RSA 1.

HOWE, Winifred b. 1880
Flower and landscape and portrait painter. Studied Slade School. Exh. 1907-39. Add: West Horsley, Surrey 1907; London 1933. † BG 1, GOU 32, I 2, NEA 2, P 1, RA 2, ROI 7.

HOWELL, Ada Mary Exh. 1897-1927
Miniature portrait painter. R.M.S. 1897. Add: Eastbourne. † L 2, RA 41, RMS 6.

HOWELL, Miss B. Exh. 1933
Berwen Bank, Barnard's Green Road, Gt. Malvern, Worcs. † L 1.

HOWELL, Constance E. Exh. 1880-93
Flower painter. 14 Pembroke Road, Kensington, London. † B 7, D 5, L 1, M 1, RBA 1, SWA 10.

HOWELL, Dulcie M. Exh. 1933
Collingwood, Harwick Road, Streetly, Warwicks. † B 2, RCA 1.

HOWELL, Ethel Exh. 1913-35
Mrs. Nash. Miniature painter. London 1913; Worcester Park, Surrey 1934. † L 4, RA 9, RMS 1.

HOWELL, Gwen Exh. 1934-37
Miniature portrait painter. London. † B 2, RA 1.

HOWELL, Mary E. Exh. 1910-13
Wellington Road, Nantwich, Cheshire. † RCA 2.

HOWELLS, Miss F.M. Exh. 1916
1 Allerton Road, Mossley Hill, Liverpool. † L 2.

HOWELLS, Howard Exh. 1901
Painter. Lydney, Glos. † RA 1.

HOWELLS, Leonard T. Exh. 1901
Landscape painter. 41 High Street, Lydney, Glos. † RA 1.

HOWES, Edgar Allan b. 1888
Sculptor. b. East Dereham, Norfolk. Studied R.A. Schools (Landseer Scholarship, 4 first prizes and silver medal) and Slade School. Exh. 1918-40. Add: London. † GI 9, L 12, M 1, RA 30, RMS 5, RSA 3.

HOWES, Frank G. Exh. 1938
Figure and urban landscape painter and pencil artist. 51 Perrymead Street, London. † RA 3.

HOWES, Gertrude C. Exh. 1890
Watercolour interior painter. 86 Ber Street, Norwich. † RBA 1.

HOWES, Madeline A. Exh. 1901-4
Victoria Lodge, Donnybrook, Co. Dublin. † RHA 4.

HOWES, Miss P. Exh. 1916
Abbotsford Hotel, Russell Square, London. † RA 1.

HOWES-DOUGLAS, Mrs. Phyllis Exh. 1922-25
Palace Hotel, Bloomsbury, London. † L 5, RA 1, RMS 4, SWA 1.

HOWET, Mlle. Marie Exh. 1938
c/o Bourlet and Sons, Nassau Street, London. † ROI 1, RSA 1.

HOWEY, J.W. Exh. 1923
33 Grange Road, West Hartlepool. † ROI 1.

HOWEY, Mary G.O. Exh. 1907-14
Cradley, Malvern, Worcs. † B 3, LS 18, RHA 5.

HOWEY, Robert L. Exh. 1931-32
Linocut artist. 108 Percy Street, West Hartlepool. † RED 4, RSA 2.

HOWGATE, William Arthur Exh. 1884-1906
Landscape painter. Leeds. † L 3, RA 17, RBA 9, RI 1.

HOWGEGO, Miss E.C. Exh. 1906-9
Miniature portrait painter. London. † RA 1, SWA 2.

HOWIE, Mrs. J. Edith Exh. 1925
Craig-na-Nullie, Strathdon, Aberdeenshire. † RSA 1.

HOWIE, Lily Exh. 1900-13
Mrs. F.H. Miall. Southport, Lancs. 1900; Liverpool 1908. † L 7, RCA 3.

HOWIE, W.H. Exh. 1888-1906
131 West Regent Street, Glasgow. † GI 4.

HOWIESON, Charles T. Exh. 1940
10 Pentland Crescent, Edinburgh. † RSA 1.

HOWITT, Thomas Cecil b. 1889
Architect. Studied A.A. Travelled Italy, Greece, Germany, Austria, U.S.A. and Canada. A.N.S.A. 1929. Exh. 1925-38. Add: Nottingham. † GI 3, RA 9.

HOWITT-LODGE, B. Exh. 1938
† RMS 1.

HOWLAND, Olin Exh. 1930
Figure and still life painter. † COO 24.

HOWLAND, H.S. Exh. 1885
37 Front Street, Toronto, Canada. † RE 2.

HOWLETT, Rosa E. Exh. 1903-28
Landscape painter. Norwich 1903; Slater Street, Liverpool 1904; Bushey, Herts. 1928. † L 3, LS 15, RA 1.

HOWORTH, Amy Exn. 1890-91
Bentley House, Moses Gate, Nr. Bolton, Lancs. † M 2.

HOWORTH, James Exh. 1922-23
Deganwy, Wales 1922; Birkenhead 1923. † L 1, RCA 3.

HOWORTH, J. Pennington Exh. 1896-1906
Liscard, Cheshire 1896; Freshfield, Lancs. 1906. † L 3, RCA 1.

HOWORTH, Lydia Isabel Exh. 1912-28
Mrs. Altham. Miniature painter. A.R.M.S. 1916. Add: Blackpool 1912; St. Anne's on Sea, Lancs. 1913; Kensington, London 1918; Elstree, Herts. 1921; Richmond Hill, Surrey 1928. † L 11, RA 13, RMS 12.

HOWSE, Fanny Exh. 1880-81
Landscape, flower and figure painter. 6 Westbourne Square, Bayswater, London. † SWA 5.

HOWSE, Frederick D. Exh. 1884-94
Figure painter. London. † M 2, NG 1, RA 5, ROI 7.

HOWSE, G. Exh. 1895
† TOO 1.

HOWSE, Kate Exh. 1881
Figure painter. 6 Westbourne Square, Bayswater, London. † RA 1.

HOWSE, Mrs. Rose C. Exh. 1936-40
A.R.M.S. 1938. Add: Ellersleigh, Kilmacolm, Renfrewshire. † GI 2, RMS 8.

HOWSLEY, Alice Exh. 1899-1914
Landscape and portrait painter. 12 Eyre Street, Chesterfield. † N 19.

HOWSON, Joan Exh. 1919-35
Stained glass artist. River Wall, Deodar Road, Putney, London. † L 5, RA 3.

HOWSON, Mrs. Jessie S. See GIBSON

HOY, Winifred K. Exh. 1923
Glencoe, College Road, Crosby, Liverpool. † L 1.

HOYER, Magdalen Z. Exh. 1899-1904
Blundellsands 1899; Waterloo, Liverpool 1902. † L 53.

HOYLAND, Adelaide Exh. 1894-1909
Kendal 1894; Selly Oak, Birmingham 1909. † B 5.

HOYLAND, Miss Hannah See MAYOR

HOYLAND, Henry G. 1894-1948
Portrait and figure painter. Studied Sheffield, London and Paris. On the staff, Sheffield College of Arts 1921-29, Deputy Chief Camouflage Office, Ministry of Home Security 1939-44. A.R.B.A. 1921, R.B.A. 1925. Add: Sheffield 1921; London 1931. † L 4, NEA 1, RA 13, RBA 102, RCA 1, RSA 3.

HOYLAND, Mrs. J.M. Exh. 1939-40
Holland House, Woodbrooke, Selly Oak, Birmingham. † B 6.

HOYLE, F.W. Exh. 1921-22
2 Harold Street, Egremont, Wallasey, Cheshire. † L 14.

HOYLE, Hannah Exh. 1920-26
Wesley Place, Tottington, Lancs. † L 4.

HOYLE, W. Exh. 1911
24 Park Place, Gravesend, Kent. † RA 1.

HOYLE, Winifred Exh. 1904
26 Mauldeth Road, Heaton Mersey, Manchester. † L 1.

HOYLES, B. Exh. 1890-1906
Tal-y-bont, Conway 1890; Victoria House, Colwyn Bay, Wales 1903. † M 1, RCA 26.

HOYLES, W.R. Exh. 1906-29
Victoria House, Conway Road, Colwyn Bay, Wales. † L 1, RCA 13.

HOYTE, Lucy Exh. 1893-95
Landscape painter. 6 Malwood Road, Balham, London. † RBA 3, SWA 3.

HOYTEMA, Van See V

HOYTON, Edward Bouverie Exh. 1924-39
Painter and etcher. R.B.A. 1936. Add: London 1924 and 1933; Axminster, Devon 1929; Chertsey, Surrey 1931; Harrogate, Yorks. 1936; Leeds 1938. † FIN 57, GI 1, L 4, RA 10.

HOYTON, Charles Exh. 1939
† GOU 1.

HOZE, de See D

HOZER, Miss M.A. Exh. 1903
The Pines, Elmfield Road, Bromley, Kent. † SWA 1.

HUARD, Franz Exh. 1882
Figure painter. 3 Lancaster Place, Hill Rise, Richmond, Surrey. † D 1.

HUBBACK, Mary C Exh. 1895-1901
Figure and domestic painter. Rock Ferry, Cheshire 1895 and 1901; Heswall, Cheshire 1899. † L 7, M 1, RA 2, RBA 1.

HUBBALL, Elsie b. 1902
Watercolour painter, embroiderer and leather worker. Studied Wolverhampton School of Art. Exh. 1927-29. Add: 18 Byrne Road, Blakenhall, Wolverhampton. † B 1, L 2.

HUBBARD, E. Hesketh 1892-1957
Painter, etcher, furniture designer and printer. Founder and director of the Forest Press. A.R.B.A. 1923, R.B.A. 1924, R.O.I. 1922. Add: Croydon, Surrey 1914; London 1916, 1920 and 1929; Ringwood, Hants. 1919; Breamore, Hants. 1922. † B 7, BAR 1, CHE 3, CON 31, COO 1, GI 11, GOU 1, L 23, RA 20, RBA 73, RCA 4, RHA 18, RID 4, ROI 124, RSA 19.

HUBBARD, Vera Exh. 1899-1903
12 Beaufort Gardens, London. † SWA 5.

HUBBELL, Henry Salem b. 1870
American artist. Exh. 1902-8. Add: 17 Rue Boissonade, Paris. † I 1, L 1.

HUBER, Carl Rudolf* 1839-1898
Figure and landscape painter. c/o Graphic, 190 Strand, London 1883. † FIN 1, M 1.

HUBER, Ernst* b. 1895
Landscape and figure painter. Exh. 1930. † LEF 24.

HUBERT, A. Exh. 1889
Sculptor. 20 Beaufort Street, Chelsea, London. † RA 2.

HUBERT, H.L. Exh. 1881-85
Sculptor. 20 Beaufort Street, Chelsea, London. † RA 3.

HUBNER, Peter Paul Exh. 1908-13
244 Brecknock Road, London. † LS 9, RA 3.

HUBRICHT, Miss Exh. 1884
c/o L. Alma-Tadema, Regent's Park, London. † B 2.

HUCK, James Exh. 1911-35
Glasgow. † GI 16, L 1, RSA 7, RSW 2.

HUCKER, Ruby Exh. 1932
Watercolour painter. 15 Downside Road, Sutton, Surrey. † RA 1.

HUCKLE, Miss A.H. Exh. 1930-32
54 Priory Road, Hampstead, London. † P 1, ROI 2, SWA 1.

HUCKS, Miss H.M. Exh. 1880
Flower painter. 4 Port Vale Terrace, Hertford. † RBA 1, SWA 1.

HUDDART, M. Exh. 1932
49 St. George's Square, London. † SWA 2.

HUDDLESTON, G. Exh. 1923
† D 1.

HUDSON, Mrs. Exh. 1886
28 Elm Park Road, Chelsea, London. † D 1.

HUDSON, Alfred Exh. 1913
4 Nowell View, Harehills Lane, Leeds. † RCA 2.

HUDSON, Alfred A. Exh. 1881
Architect. Portland Place, Southsea, Hants. † RA 2.

HUDSON, Annie Hope Exh. 1908-39
Landscape, figure and architectural painter. Founder Member London Group 1913. Add: London 1908 and 1922; Wallingford, Bucks. 1910. † BG 2, CAR 23, COO 2, GOU 10, LEI 1, LS 19, NEA 17.

HUDSON, Albert Wilfrid b. 1874
Landscape painter. b. Bingley, Yorks. Studied Juliens, Paris. Exh. 1923-35. Add: Elderslea, Bushey, Herts. 1923; Southampton 1934. † L 2, RA 8, RHA 1.

HUDSON, C.W.S. Exh. 1907
Museum Studio, Cole Park, Twickenham, Middlesex. † RA 1.

HUDSON, Doris E. Exh. 1927-29
25 Hazel Road, Altrincham, Cheshire. † L 2, RSA 1.

HUDSON, Etty Exh. 1882
113 Arlington Road, Camden Town, London. † RHA 1.

HUDSON, Eleanor Erlund b. 1912
Etcher and painter. A.R.E. 1937, A.R.S.W. 1939. Exh. 1935-40. Add: London. † COO 6, RA 13, RE 14, RWS 10.

HUDSON, Edith H. Exh. 1883-91
Landscape and figure painter. 8 Oakroyd Terrace, Bradford, Yorks. † L 2, M 3, RA 2, SWA 1.

HUDSON, Gertrude Exh. 1921
Sculptor. Wellow Vicarage, Newark, Notts. † N 1.

HUDSON, Gynedd Exh. 1912
Painter and illustrator of fables and fairy stories. Studied Municipal School of Art, Brighton. Add: 6 Denmark Villas, Hove, Sussex. † RA 1.

HUDSON, Gerald C. Exh. 1924-30
† P 2.

HUDSON, G.F. Exh. 1926-38
Landscape painter and humorous pen and ink artist. Elstow, Derby Road, Kegworth, Nr. Derby. † N 6.

HUDSON, Grace Mabel Exh. 1918-27
Miniature painter. 28 Sellons Avenue, Harlesden, London. † RA 2, RI 14, RMS 1.

HUDSON, Henry Exh. 1898
Still life painter. Sherborne School, Dorset. † RA 1.

HUDSON, H.D. Exh. 1910
A.N.S.A. 1913. 41 Dryden Street, Nottingham. † N 1.

HUDSON, Henry John Exh. 1881-1910
Portrait, figure and domestic painter. R.P. 1891. Add: London. † B 1, G 2, L 24, M 4, NG 2, P, 84, RA 34, RBA 1, ROI 10, RSA 1.

HUDSON, Miss H.M. Exh. 1911-12
Elderslea, Bushey Heath, Herts. † RA 2.

HUDSON, J. Exh. 1910-16
24 York Place, Portman Square, London. † RA 2.

HUDSON, K.H. Exh. 1911
Tavistock House, 13 Brondesbury Road, London. † LS 3.

HUDSON, Lena Exh. 1889-93
Landscape painter. Castlemede, Florence Road, Southsea, Hants. 1889; Harting Rectory, Petersfield, Hants. 1893. † SWA 2.

HUDSON, Marion B. Exh. 1912-14
69 Anfield Road, Liverpool. † L 2.

HUDSON, Paul Greville Exh. 1908-9
10 Lismore Street, Carlisle. † LS 8.

HUDSON, Robert* d. 1884
Landscape painter. Sheffield. † RSA 2.

HUDSON, Willis K. Exh. 1922-34
Landscape painter. Knowle, Nr. Birmingham 1922; Campden, Glos. 1923; Stow on the Wold, Glos. 1927; Ford, Nr. Cheltenham, Glos. 1934. † B 23, RA 4.

HUDSON, William S. Exh. 1939-40
Landscape painter. 11 Dunollie Road, Kentish Town, London. † LEF 1, RA 1.

HUE-WILLIAMS, Evelyn Exh. 1905
Uplands, Leatherhead, Surrey. † D 2.

HUET, R. Paul Exh. 1882
15 Rue Neuve des Petits Champs, Paris. † GI 2.

HUFFMAN, Mrs. Isobel Mary See KNOX

HUGARD, F. Exh. 1909
c/o M. Georges Petit, 8 Rue de Seze, Paris. † L 1.

HUGER, K. Exh. 1880
Florence, Italy. † RSA 1.

HUGGARD, Mrs. Florence E. Exh. 1895-97
Clonmore, Tralee, Co. Kerry. † RSA 5.

HUGGILL, Henry Percy 1886-1957
Landscape painter and etcher. Studied Royal College of Art 1908-14. Principal Liverpool City School of Art. A.R.E. 1917. Add: London 1912; Liverpool 1920 and 1932; Southport, Lancs. 1924. † L 20, RA 12, RCA 2, RE 12.

HUGGINS, Wilfrid Exh. 1912-38
Bushey, Herts. 1912; Twickenham, Middlesex 1922; Windsor, Berks. 1938. † L 3, RA 5.

HUGGINS, William* 1820-1884
Animal and landscape painter. Studied at Mechanics Institute. Add: Roch House, Christleton, Nr. Chester. † L 3.

HUGHES, Alice Exh. 1890-1903
Figure and portrait painter. Widcombe, Nr. Newport, I.O.W. 1890 and 1903; Edge Hill, Liverpool 1900. † L 2, RA 1, RBA 2, SWA 1.

HUGHES, Amy Exh. 1881-82
Figure painter. Wandle Bank, Wallington, Surrey. † G 1, ROI 1.

HUGHES, Arthur* 1832-1915
Painter and illustrator. Studied under Alfred Stevens and at R.A. Schools 1847. Add: Wandle Park, Wallington, Surrey. † B 2, D 2, FIN 80, G 7, GI 6, L 13, M 15, NG 17, RA 24, RI 3, ROI 12.

HUGHES, Mrs. A.B. Exh. 1907-9
431 Chester Road, Old Trafford, Manchester. † M 5, RCA 3.

HUGHES, Arthur Foord* 1856-1914
Landscape and windmill painter. Studied Heatherleys, Slade School and R.A. Schools. Add: Wallington, Surrey 1880; Thurloe Square, London 1890. † AG 2, G 3, L 19, NG 19, RA 18, RBA 2, RI 4, ROI 1.

HUGHES, Miss B. Exh. 1913
192 Lordship Road, Stoke Newington, London. † RA 1.

HUGHES, Bertha M. Exh. 1902
Alewynd, Bangor, Wales. † RCA 1.

HUGHES, Catherine Exh. 1908-34
Enameller on metal. Studied London and Paris. Add: Bristol. † LS 4, P 2.

HUGHES, Christopher Wyndham 1881-1961
Painter and dry point artist and illustrator. Studied under his father and at the Slade. Art master Marlborough College 1920-40. Mayor of Marlborough 1935. Exh. 1938. † WG 35.

HUGHES, Miss Dickie Exh. 1914
Bella Vista, Rye, Sussex. † LS 1.

HUGHES, Dorothy Exh. 1921-22
31 Selborne Street, Princes Road, Liverpool. † L 2.

HUGHES, Diana M. Exh. 1939-40
Wood engraver. 90 Caversham Road, London. † RA 3.

HUGHES, Dorothy T. Exh. 1936
† RI 1.

HUGHES, E. Exh. 1880
† TOO 1.

HUGHES, Edith Exh. 1913-36
Painter, lithographer and designer. Studied Heatherleys 1913 and under Harold Gilman, Sickert and Ernest Jackson. S.W.A. 1936. Add: London. † GOU 3, RA 1, RCA 1, ROI 3, SWA 20.

HUGHES, Edward 1832-1908
Genre and portrait painter. London. † G 2, RA 8.

HUGHES, Edwin* Exh. 1880-95
Figure and portrait painter. London. † B 4, L 9, M 4, RA 11, ROI 2.

HUGHES, Eleanor b. 1882
Watercolour painter. b. New Zealand. Studied Newlyn, Penzance under Stanhope and Elizabeth Forbes. Married Robert Morson H. q.v. R.I. 1933. Exh. 1905-40. Add: Lamorna, Penzance 1911; London 1914; St. Buryan, Cornwall 1915. † AB 3, G 1, GI 9, GOU 1, I 5, L 6, NEA 7, RA 37, RI 34, SWA 3.

HUGHES, Emily Exh. 1890-95
Woodhouse, Handsworth Wood, Birmingham. † B 5.

HUGHES, Mrs. Ethel See DAVIES

HUGHES, E. Brooke Exh. 1887
29 S. King Street, Dublin. † RHA 1.

HUGHES, Edith Burnet Exh. 1920-29
nee Burnet. Add: Glasgow. † GI 6, RSA 1.

HUGHES, Miss E.H. Exh. 1907
120 Summerville Terrace, Booterstown, Co. Dublin. † RHA 1.

HUGHES, Evan Lloyd Exh. 1925
47 Vulcan Street, Holyhead, Anglesey. † L 1.

HUGHES, Edward Robert* 1851-1914
Historical genre painter. Studied R.A. Schools and under Holman Hunt and his uncle Arthur H. q.v. A.R.W.S. 1891, R.W.S. 1895. Add: London. † B 2, D 7, FIN 1, G 9, L 13, LEI 1, M 4, NG 6, RA 18, RI 32, ROI 3, RSW 7.

HUGHES, Miss F.E. Exh. 1906-18
Shortlands, Kent. † SWA 17.

HUGHES, Miss F.L. Exh. 1884
c/o Pragnell, 22 St. Paul's Churchyard, London. † RI 1.

HUGHES, Frederick W. Exh. 1905
112 Churchill Road, Handsworth, Birmingham. † B 2.

HUGHES, Mrs. Gladys See ELTON

HUGHES, Gwen Exh. 1905-35
Sculptor and miniature painter. Richmond, Surrey 1905 and 1919; Hove, Sussex 1918; Petersham, Surrey 1926. † L 37, M 2, RA 14, RHA 4, RI 36, RMS 7, RSA 16, SWA 1.

HUGHES, Godfrey Exh. 1891-1910
Landscape painter. East Side House, Kew Green, London. † NG 2, RA 2, ROI 1.

HUGHES, George Frederick Exh. 1883
Landscape painter. 79 Lancaster Road, Notting Hill, London. † B 1.

HUGHES, George H.* Exh. 1894-1909
Figure and domestic painter. Married Ethel Davies q.v. Add: Liverpool 1894 and 1905; Oxton, Cheshire, 1903; Welford on Avon, Stratford, Warwicks. 1909. † B 2, L 35, RA 3, RBA 1, RCA 2, RI 1.

HUGHES, Harry Exh. 1898-1916
Interior painter. London. † RA 2, ROI 1.

HUGHES, Henry Exh. 1883
Stained glass artist. 67 Frith Street, Soho Square, London. † RA 2.

HUGHES, Harold E. Exh. 1889
74 Devonshire Road, Liverpool. † L 1.

HUGHES, Henry Harold d. 1940
Landscape painter and archaelogist. Add: Handsworth, Birmingham 1890; Bangor, N. Wales 1892. † B 6, GI 1, RA 1, RCA 20.

HUGHES, Harold J. Exh. 1933-34
134 Heather Road, Small Heath, Birmingham. † B 2.

HUGHES, J. Exh. 1885-91
School Road, Sale, Cheshire. † L 5, M 3, RHA 4.

HUGHES, Miss Jessie Exh. 1899-1908
37 Villa Road, Handsworth, Birmingham. † B 6.

HUGHES, John Exh. 1887
13 Lisle Street, Leicester Square, London. † ROI 1.

HUGHES, John b. 1849
Sculptor. A.R.H.A. 1895, R.H.A. 1900. Exh. 1895-1901. Add: 28 Lennox Street, Dublin. † L 2, RA 3, RHA 8.

HUGHES, Mrs. J.A. Exh. 1890-92
Frankley Lodge, King's Norton, Birmingham. † B 2.

HUGHES, J. Allan Exh. 1886-1928
Stained glass artist and decorative architect. Liverpool 1886 and 1916; London 1903. † L 13, RA 2.

HUGHES, J.J. Exh. 1882-1908
37 Villa Road, Handsworth, Birmingham. † B 67.

HUGHES, John L. Exh. 1922-27
Liverpool. † L 10.

HUGHES, John O. Exh. 1929
67 Arundel Street, Liverpool. † L 2.

HUGHES, J.P. Exh. 1903-5
Sculptor. London. † RA 2.

HUGHES, Leonard Exh. 1888-1924
Portrait painter. Holywell, N. Wales 1888; The Castle, Dyserth, Rhyl, N. Wales 1912. † L 2, RA 2, RCA 39.

HUGHES, Lorna Exh. 1923
102 Queen's Road, Everton, Liverpool. † L 1.

HUGHES, Lily G. Exh. 1906
John Dalton Street, Manchester. † GI 1.

HUGHES, Lily Jones Exh. 1896-1938
Miniature painter. R.M.S. 1896. Add: Bangor, N. Wales 1896; Bushey, Herts. 1897; East Grinstead, Sussex 1900; Rhyl, N. Wales 1902; Penmaenmawr, Wales 1923. † L 17, NG 1, RA 6, RCA 60, RMS 15.

HUGHES, Louisa Margaret See WATTS

HUGHES, Mary Exh. 1890-1940
Miniature painter. Brentford, Essex 1890; Anglesey, 1902 and 1907; London 1916, 1921 and 1934; Chester 1929. † L 12, P 1, RA 6, RCA 3, RI 3, SWA 1.

HUGHES, Melbury Exh. 1885-90
18 Fountain Street, High Tranmere, Cheshire. † G 1, GI 1, M 3, RSA 1.

HUGHES, Millward Exh. 1926-27
45 Beresford Road, Oxton, Birkenhead. † L 2.

HUGHES, Miss M.B. Exh. 1928
90 Penkett Road, Wallasey, Cheshire. † L 1.

HUGHES, Myra Kathleen d. 1918
Etcher. b. Ireland. A.R.E. 1911, A.S.W.A. 1909. Add: London 1898 and 1906; Wexford, Ireland 1899; Hindhead, Surrey 1917. † GOU 2, L 6, RA 15, RE 13, RHA 13.

HUGHES, Miss M.L. Exh. 1884
1 Gt. Charles Place, N. Kensington, London. † M 1.

HUGHES, Mabel Violet Exh. 1901-8
Miniature and landscape painter. b. Everton, Liverpool. Studied Liverpool School of Art, Birkenhead School of Art, Juliens and Studio Delecluse, Paris and Penzance, Cornwall. Add: Oxton, Birkenhead 1901; Prestbury, Nr. Cheltenham, Glos. 1906. † B 1, L 7, RHA 3.

HUGHES, Robert Exh. 1895-98
6 Park Avenue, Chelmsford 1895; Richmond, Surrey 1898. † RI 2.

HUGHES, Mrs. Rose E. Exh. 1910-14
Inchneuk, Row, Dumbartonshire. † D 6, GI 1, L 4, LS 4, RI 9, RSA 2.

HUGHES, Robert Morson 1873-1953
Landscape painter. Studied Lambeth School of Art and South London Technical Art School. Married Eleanor H. q.v. Add: Chelsfield, Kent 1909; Lamorna, Penzance 1910; St. Buryan, Cornwall 1912. † ALP 1, G 4, GOU 1, I 3, L 3, M 2, NEA 2, RA 21. RI 4. ROI 1.

HUGHES, Miss S.E. Exh. 1895-99
Wepre Cottage, Connah's Quay, Flint. † RHA 7.

HUGHES, Talbot* Exh. 1886-1921
Landscape and figure painter. R.O.I. 1903. (Hon. Ret. 1938.) Add: London. † B 2, CON 1, FIN 52, G 5, L 25, M 5, NG 7, RA 38, RBA 1, RHA 1, RI 5, ROI 35.

HUGHES, T. Harold Exh. 1916-38
Glasgow. † GI 9, LEI 1, RSA 2.

HUGHES, Thomas John Exh. 1880-94
Figure and domestic painter. Hampstead, London 1880; Lyneham, Wealdstone, Harrow, Middlesex 1892. † L 2, RBA 6, RI 2, ROI 5, RWS 1.

HUGHES, T. Rowland Exh. 1920-33
Plas Iolyn, Conway, Wales. † RCA 3.

HUGHES, William* 1842-1901
Still life painter. Studied under George Lance and W.H. Hunt. Father of Sir Herbert Hughes-Stanton, q.v. Add: Chelsea, London 1880; Brighton, Sussex 1895. † G 31, L 15, M 5, RA 8, RBA 15, ROI 2.

HUGHES-GOLDEN, C. Exh. 1922
† G 2.

HUGHES-GARBETT, Miss P.C.M. Exh. 1919
33 Royal Park, Clifton, Bristol. † L 2.

HUGHES-STANTON, Blair Rowlands b. 1902
Painter and wood engraver. Studied Byam Shaw School, R.A. Schools and Leon Underwood's School. Son of Sir Herbert H.S. q.v. Married Gertrude Hermes q.v. Exh. 1926-39. Add: London. † COO 2, GI 2, L 3, LEI 2, RED 9, RHA 1.

HUGHES-STANTON, Sir Herbert* 1870-1937
Landscape painter. Studied under his father William Hughes q.v. Father of Blair H-S. q.v. A.R.A. 1913, R.A. 1920, H.R.M.S. 1925, R.O.I. 1901, H.R.O.I. 1922, R.S.W. 1922, A.R.W.S. 1909, R.W.S. 1915, P.R.W.S. 1920. Member of Society of 25 Artists. Knighted 1923. "A Pasturage among the Dunes, Pas de Calais, France" purchased by Chantrey Bequest 1908. Add: London. † B 8, BAR 1, CG 47, DOW 2, FIN 247, G 9, GI 45, GOU 8, I 2, L 61, LEI 121, M 10, NG 10, RA 157, RHA 5, RI 12, ROI 53, RSA 2, RSW 17, RWS 201, WG 24.

HUGH-JONES, Rose K. Exh. 1922-33
Painter. Rhyl 1922; London 1923. † RA 1, RCA 2, SWA 3.

HUGILL, Annie Exh. 1902-40
Landscape painter. Keighley, Yorks 1902 and 1926; Skipton, Yorks 1922. † I 1, L 4, RA 10, RI 7.

HUGILL, Mrs. G.M.W. Exh. 1915-23
Chester 1915; Liverpool 1920; Dyserth, N. Wales 1923. † L 25.

HUGO, Jean* b. 1894
French landscape painter. Exh. 1937. † LEF 50.

HUGHES, Jean Exh. 1898
Rue Perrie Charron, 31 bis, Paris. † L 1.

HUHN, Mathilde Exh. 1907-13
London. † L 1, RA 2, RMS 1.

HUISH, Marcus Bourne d. 1921
Watercolour landscape painter. Editor of "The Art Journal" and founder of "The Years Art". Exh. 1896-1919. Add: London. † FIN 128, RA 2, RI 2.

HULBERT, Miss A. Exh. 1896
Colnehurst, Watford, Herts. † SWA 1.

HULK, Abraham, Senr.* 1818-1897
Marine painter. Studied at the Amsterdam Academy. Visited the U.S.A. Settle in London 1870. Exh. 1890. † RA 2.

HULK, Abraham, Junr.* Exh. 1881-96
Landscape painter. London 1881 and 1891; Dorking, Surrey 1880; Charlwood, Surrey 1889. † L 2, RA 23, RBA 6.

HULK, F. Martinus Exh. 1896-1926
Landscape painter. Brixton Hill, London 1896; St. Margaret's Cliffe, Kent 1926. † L 1, RA 1.

HULK, Frederick William* Exh. 1898-1901
Landscape painter. Church Villa, Shere, Guildford, Surrey. † GI 1, RA 1.

HULK, John F. b. 1855
Animal painter. b. Holland. Exh. 1895. Add: 72 Piccadilly, London. † RA 2.

HULK, William Frederick* Exh. 1880-1900
Landscape and animal painter. London 1880; Shere, Guildford, Surrey 1882. † B 10, D 5, GI 20, L 11, M 3, RA 50, RBA 24, RI 18, ROI 17.

HULL, Clementina M. Exh. 1881-1908
Landscape, figure and flower painter. London. † D 1, G 1, L 12, M 1, NG 2, RA 9, RBA 2, RI 1, SWA 14.

HULL, F.W. Exh. 1903-30
Landscape and still life painter. 8 Ireton Street, Belfast. † L 1, RHA 35.

HULL, George Exh. 1882-1910
Landscape painter. Leicester. † B 2, N 9, RI 1.

HULL, John Pinkerton Exh. 1927
Watercolour painter, etcher and teacher. Studied Leicester School of Art and Central London Technical School. Add: Hampstead, London. † RA 1.

HULL, Mary A. Exh. 1884-1910
Fruit painter. Leicester. † B 3, N 5, RI 3.

HULL, Norman T.S. Exh. 1936
Burton on Trent. † RCA 1.

HULLAND, William Exh. 1885
Engraver. Victoria Road, Farnworth, Lancs. † RA 1.

HULME, Alfred J. Exh. 1905-8
Shrewsbury 1905; Wimbledon 1908. † B 1, LS 5.

HULME, Alice L. Exh. 1882-91
Flower and landscape painter. London. † B 6, L 3, RA 4, ROI 1, SWA 12.

HULME, Frederick J. Exh. 1908-40
Flower painter. London. † NEA 1, RA 13.

HULME, Frederick William* 1816-1884
Landscape painter, illustrator and engraver. b. Swinton, Yorks. Studied under his mother. Add: London. † B 2, L 3, RA 4, ROI 1.

HULME, Jessie Exh. 1884-86
66 Ducie Grove, Oxford Street, Manchester. † M 4.

HULTON, Everard Exh. 1882
Landscape painter. 38 Redcliffe Road, London. † B 2, M 2, RA 1.

HULTON, William d. 1921
Landscape painter. Exh. 1882-1909. Add: London 1882; Venice 1896. † B 5, M 4, NG 1, RA 8, RBA 5, ROI 1.

HULTZ, P. Exh. 1891
1 Livingston Street, Chorlton on Medlock, Manchester. † M 1.

HUMAN, Miss I. Exh. 1903
62 Birdhurst Road, South Croydon, Surrey. † SWA 1.

HUMBERT, Manuel b. 1890
Still life painter. b. Barcelona. Exh. 1937. † BA 1.

HUME, Edith* Exh. 1880-1906
nee Dunn. Genre painter. Married Thomas O.H. q.v. Add: South Harting, Petersfield, Hants. † B 10, D 2, FIN 1, G 1, GI 24, L 11, M 17, RA 19, RBA 5, RI 3, ROI 6, RSA 10, RSW 1, TOO 4.

HUME, J. Henry 1858-1881
Landscape, figure, portrait and flower painter. Brother of Thomas O.H. q.v. Add: South Harting, Petersfield, Hants. † RBA 2.

HUME, Miss K.M. Exh. 1920-33
5 Euston Grove, Birkenhead. † L 6.

HUME, Miss M. Exh. 1917-21
A.S.W.A. 1919. Add: 14 King's Mansions, Chelsea, London. † RA 1, SWA 4.

HUME, Robert Exh. 1884-1937
Landscape and rustic genre painter. R.B.A. 1896. Add: Edinburgh 1884 and 1918; London 1892. † GI 9, L 1, RA 10, RBA 51, RI 7, RSA 45, RSW 5.

HUME, Thomas O.* Exh. 1880-94
Landscape painter. Brother of J. Henry H. q.v. and married Edith H. q.v. Add: South Harting, Petersfield, Hants. † B 6, GI 3, L 4, M 7, RA 5, RBA 9.

HUME-WILLIAMS, Lady L.A. Exh. 1909-40
Watercolour landscape painter. Studied Slade School and Florence. Add: Ewhurst, Surrey and London. † AR 2, B 1, COO 2, D 31, L 2, RA 5, RBA 2, RI 19, SWA 21, WG 105.

HUMMEL, Professor Theodore Exh. 1914
Friedrichstrasse 15, Munich. † GI 2.

HUMMEL, Tessie M. Exh. 1935
Flower painter. 15 Broomhill Park, Belfast. † RHA 1.

HUMMERSTON, Effie b. 1891
Watercolour painter. Studied Leeds School of Art. Exh. 1928. Add: 57 Woodsley Road, Leeds. † L 1.

HUMPHREY, Agnes Ellen Exh. 1886-87
Fruit painter. Redcliffe Cottage, Redcliffe Road, Nottingham. † N 2.

HUMPHREY, Edward J. Exh. 1880-90
Figure, landscape and interior painter. London. † RA 5, RBA 2, RHA 2, RI 4, ROI 5.

HUMPHREY, Florence Exh. 1905-40
Mrs. C.T. Holland. Landscape and figure painter. Add: 4 Briardale Gardens, London. † P 5, RA 1, RI 3, ROI 13.

HUMPHREY, Mrs. Florence Pash See PASH

HUMPHREY, Winifred Exh. 1921-30
Flower and still life painter. Florence, Italy 1921; Beaulieu, Hants. 1922; London 1927; St. Ives, Cornwall 1929. † L 8, RA 3, RCA 1, ROI 2.

HUMPHREYS, Mrs. A.H. Exh. 1914-15
Cambridge 1914; Battersea Park, London1915. † L 1, RA 1.

HUMPHREYS, Aileen Maude Exh. 1930
nee Faulkner. Silver and goldsmith, enameller and jeweller. Studied Central School of Arts and Crafts. Add: London. † RMS 2.

HUMPHREYS, E. Exh. 1883
152 Varna Road, Birmingham. † B 1.

HUMPHREYS, F.W. Exh. 1882-83
16 Wheeley's Road, Birmingham. † B 2.

HUMPHREYS, George Alfred d. 1948
Architect. Exh. 1895-1925. Add: Llandudno, Wales. † RCA 19.

HUMPHREYS, Henry Norman 1905-1955
Landscape and decorative painter. Liverpool 1928 and 1939; Hastings, Sussex 1936. † L 2, RA 2.

HUMPHREYS, Jane K. Exh. 1880-1905
Figure painter. London 1880; Llandudno, Wales 1898. † B 1, L 1, M 1, RBA 2, RCA 5.

HUMPHREYS, Millicent F. Exh. 1929
Brassey Street, Central School, Birkenhead. † L 1.

HUMPHREYS, Mrs. N. Exh. 1930-39
Llandudno, Wales. † RCA 8.

HUMPHREYS, Mrs. N.E. Exh. 1899-1911
Caer-y-Cae, Hoole, Chester. † RCA 6.

HUMPHREYS, Phillip Callon Exh. 1930
145 Elms Road, Clapham Park, London. † B 1, P, 1.

HUMPHREYS, Walter Exh. 1921-25
29A Friars Road, Coventry. † B 1, LS 2.

HUMPHREYS, Winifred O. Exh. 1915-38
Liverpool 1915 and 1923; Craven Arms, Salop 1921. † I 10, L 13, M 1.

HUMPHRIES, James H. Exh. 1927-38
Landscape painter. † AB 13, WG 20.

HUMPHRIES, Miss J.M. Exh. 1937
31 Beech Road, Bournville, Birmingham. † B 2.

HUMPHRIES, Kathleen Exh. 1900
Ravensdale Park, Dundalk, Ireland. † SWA 1.

HUMPHRIS, Mrs. Miriam Exh. 1935
The Grange, Fort William, Invernesshire. † RI 1.

HUMPHRIS, William H. Exh. 1881-1916
Figure and domestic painter. London 1881 and 1896; Bettws-y-Coed, Wales 1886; Falmouth, Cornwall 1889. † B 1, DOW 1, L 8, RA 14, RBA 6, RI 8, ROI 8.

HUMPHRY, C. Exh. 1880
Domestic painter. 48 Delancey Street, Regent's Park, London. † RBA 1.

HUMPHRY, K. Maude Exh. 1883-91
Portrait and figure painter. 26 Princes Square, London. † B 1, M 1, RA 1, RBA 1, SWA 5.

HUNDLEY, Marie Exh. 1880-81
Flower painter. 39 Fortress Terrace, Kentish Town, London. † SWA 3.

HUNDLEY, Philip Exh. 1880
Watercolour figure and landscape painter. 222 Strand, London. † D 1, RBA 1.

HUNGERFORD, Edith Exh. 1913-14
Littlecote, Paignton, Devon. † LS 4.

HUNN, Thomas H. Exh. 1880-1908
Watercolour landscape painter. Godalming, Surrey 1880; Horsham, Sussex 1884; Billingshurst, Sussex 1888; London 1891; New Down Road, Nr. Guildford, Surrey 1898. † D 2, M 6, NG 1, RA 16, RBA 13, RI 5.

HUNT, Miss Exh. 1883
247 Hagley Road, Edgbaston, Birmingham. † B 2.

HUNT, Adelin Exh. 1905
Whitehall, Bathwell. † GI 1.

HUNT, Arthur Ackland Exh. 1881-1913
Figure and domestic painter. London. † B 2, D 9, M 2, RA 6, RE 1, RHA 9, RI 6.

HUNT, Amy Henrietta Exh. 1887-91
Sculptor. 3 Kensington Studios, Stanford Road, Kensington, London. † RA 5, RBA 4, SWA 4.

HUNT, Arthur Hill b. 1874
Miniature painter. Pendennis, Desenfans Road, Dulwich, London. † RA 9, RI 1, RMS 3.

HUNT, Alfred William* 1830-1896
Landscape, painter and watercolourist. Travelled on the continent. A.R.W.S. 1862, R.W.S. 1864. Add: London. † AG 2, B 12, DOW 3, FIN 11, G 2, L 11, M 10, NG 7, RA 12, RE 1, RWS 63.

HUNT, Charles* Exh. 1891-93
Figure painter. 6 Granville Road, Wandsworth, London. † B 1, RA 1.

HUNT, Cecil Arthur b. 1873
Landscape painter. b. Torquay. R.B.A. 1914, A.R.W.S. 1919, R.W.S. 1925. Exh. 1912-40. Add: London. † AG 42, ALP 12, BA 3, CHE 2, FIN 369, G 1, GI 54, GOU 25, I 8, L 22, M 1, RA 51, RBA 59, RHA 1, RI 7, RID 22, ROI 2, RSA 3, RSW 3, RWS 220, WG 24.

HUNT, Clyde du Vernet b. 1861
Sculptor. b. Glasgow. Exh. 1898 and 1920. Add: Hurlingham, London 1898; Paris 1920. † L 1, RA 2.

HUNT, C.H. Exh. 1892
37 Bickerton Road, Upper Holloway, London. † L 1.

HUNT, Miss E. Exh. 1918-19
Tyneholme, Shirley Road, Ripley, Derbys. † N 2.

HUNT, Edgar* Exh. 1902-10
Animal and rustic painter. Southfields, Wandsworth, London 1902; Alresford, Hants. 1906. † B 11, L 1, LS 3.

HUNT, Mrs. Ernest Exh. 1896
Pastel landscape artist. † DOW 40.

HUNT, Lady Ernestine Exh. 1899
Carragh Lake, Co. Kerry. † RHA 2.

HUNT, E. Aubrey* 1855-1922
Landscape painter. R.B.A. 1884. Add: Ripley, Surrey 1880; London 1882 and 1900; Tangier, Morocco 1894; Hemingford Grey, St. Ives, Hunts. 1902; Hastings, Sussex 1912 and 1916; St. Leonards on Sea, Sussex 1916. † B 3, DOW 41, FIN 1, G 1, GI 9, GOU 46, L 3, M 2, NEA 2, NG 2, RA 26, RBA 38, ROI 17, TOO 1.

HUNT, Edward A. Exh. 1906-38
Architect. London 1906 and 1938; Conway, N. Wales 1907; Lowestoft, Suffolk 1910. † B 1, L 1, RA 7.

HUNT, Miss Eva E. Exh. 1885-94
Flower painter. 4 Hyde Vale Villas, Greenwich, London. † B 1, G 3, GI 1, L 6, M 2, RA 5, RBA 18, SWA 4.

HUNT, E.G. Exh. 1910
21 Foregate Street, Stafford. † B 1.

HUNT, E.J.K. Exh. 1916-24
Served with the Machine Gun Corps in France World War I. Add: Seaforth, Liverpool 1916; Gt. Crosby, Lancs. 1924. † L 2.

HUNT, Edith M. Exh. 1905-6
81 Princess Road, Moss-side, Manchester. † M 2.

HUNT, Mrs. Emma W. Exh. 1884-89
Flower painter. 11 Colville Road, Bayswater, London. † RA 4.

HUNT, Miss F.S. Exh. 1889-93
Astrop, Nr. Banbury, Oxon. † B 3, SWA 2.

HUNT, George E. Exh. 1920-38
11 Station Road, Harborne, Birmingham. † L 221, RCA 2, RMS 16.

HUNT, Gladys Holman Exh. 1904-20
Mrs. M. Joseph. Sculptor. Add: 18 Melbury Road, Kensington, London 1904; 15 Lancaster Gate Terrace, London 1920. † NG 3, RA 5.

HUNT, G.J. Exh. 1904-11
3 Lord Street, Liverpool 1904; 7 Regent's Park Terrace, London 1910. † L 1, RA 3.

HUNT, Gerard Leigh b. 1858
Portrait painter and etcher. Exh. 1894-1937. Add: London 1894; Bournemouth, Hants. 1928. † B 12, L 5, LS 3, RA 10, RCA 41.
HUNT, G.P. Holman Exh. 1917
18 Melbury Road, Kensington, London. † RA 1.
HUNT, G. Sydney Exh. 1880-1917
Landscape and portrait painter. London 1880; Leyton, Essex 1897; Leigh on Sea, Essex 1904. † L 1, RA 10, RBA 1.
HUNT, Hannah Exh. 1897
13 Springfield Place, Leeds. † GI 1.
HUNT, Miss Harding F. Exh. 1921
13 Grove Park, Liverpool. † L 1.
HUNT, Henry J. Exh. 1931-33
Stained glass artist. 10 Talbot Road, Bromley, Kent. † RA 2.
HUNT, H.S. Exh. 1893
Figure painter. Rossmore, Eltham Road, Lee, London. † RBA 1.
HUNT, Mrs. James (S.R.) Exh. 1890-1900
Brougham House, Olton, Warwicks. † B 6.
HUNT, Jane Exh. 1882
The Old Bank, Kirby Lonsdale, Westmorland. † M 1.
HUNT, L. Guy Exh. 1911
Almeira, Alhambra Road, Southsea, Hants. † LS 3.
HUNT, L.V. Exh. 1908
34 Queen Street, London. † RA 1.
HUNT, Mrs. Mary Exh. 1895-1901
London. † B 3, GI 2, L 2, M 1, NG 2, RBA 3, RHA 1, ROI 1.
HUNT, Muriel Exh. 1900-6
Southwood, Torquay, Devon. † L 2, RI 1, SWA 4.
HUNT, O. Ward Exh. 1930-31
Wood engraver and lino cut artist. † RED 6.
HUNT, Percy W. Exh. 1883-1927
Wanstead, Essex 1883; Bishops Stortford, Herts. 1927. † L 3.
HUNT, Reginald G. Exh. 1937
Portrait painter. 194 Crowborough Road, Streatham, London. † RA 1.
HUNT, Rhoda H. Exh. 1899-1904
Birmingham 1899; Beckenham, Kent 1904. † B 2, SWA 1.
HUNT, S. Exh. 1886
49 Aberdeen Street, Birmingham. † B 2.
HUNT, Samuel Exh. 1924
136 Church Road, Erdington, Birmingham. † B 2.
HUNT, Sidney Exh. 1931
† LEI 1.
HUNT, Miss S. St. John Exh. 1913-16
Mrs. H. Harrison. London. † RA 7, RMS 1.
HUNT, Thomas 1854-1929
Figure and landscape painter. Studied Glasgow School of Art and Paris. A.R.S.A. 1925, R.S.W. 1885. Add: Glasgow. † AG 1, DOW 2, GI 138, L 20, M 3, RA 22, RI 5, RSA 64, RSW 129.
HUNT, Walter* 1861-1941
Animal painter. "The Dog in the Manger" purchased by Chantrey Bequest 1885. Add: Park View, Granville Road, Wandsworth, London. † B 12, L 3, RA 28, TOO 21.
HUNT, William Exh. 1888-1911
Landscape,figure and still life painter. R.B.A. 1895. Add: Greenwich, London 1888; Kensington, London 1892. † AG 130, B 1, G 2, L 9, M 1, NEA 2, RA 11, RBA 27, RHA 3.
HUNT, Winifred Exh. 1903-4
Sculptor. London. † L 1, RA 2.
HUNT, William G. Exh. 1901-2
Architect. 12 Bedford Gardens, Kensington, London. † RA 2.
HUNT, William Holman* 1827-1910
Figure and religious painter. Studied under Henry Rogers; National Gallery; British Museum and R.A. Schools 1844. Visited the Middle East 1854, 1869 and 1873. Member of the Pre-Raphaelite Brotherhood. H.R.B.A. 1901, A.R.W.S. 1869, R.W.S. 1887. "Claudio and Isabella" (1850) purchased by Chantrey Bequest 1919. Add: London. Buried in St. Paul's Cathedral. † B 12, FIN 1, G 7, GI 4, L 16, M 6, NEA 2, NG 7, RBA 2, RHA 2, RSA 1, RWS 6, TOO 8.
HUNT, William H. Thurlow Exh. 1883-85
Portrait, figure and landscape painter. 160 Camden Road, London. † GI 1, L 2, M 1, RA 4, RBA 5.
HUNT, W.J. Exh. 1914-20
15 Mayfield Grove, Nottingham. † N 5.
HUNTER, Miss Exh. 1885
Landscape painter. 4 Kingsdown Road, Holloway, London. † SWA 2.
HUNTER, Ada Exh. 1886-1907
Watercolour figure and miniature portrait painter. South Kensington, London. † RA 10, RI 5.
HUNTER, Agnes Exh. 1881-1907
Coldstream, N.B. 1881; Rothesay 1884; Cathcart, N.B. 1906. † GI 7, RSA 2.
HUNTER, A.A. Exh. 1940
Newburgh on Tay. † RSW 1.
HUNTER, Blanche F. Exh. 1889-1907
Watercolour painter. 130 Finborough Road, South Kensington, London. † NG 1, RA 3, RI 2.
HUNTER, Bella J. Exh. 1893
9 Hope Street, Edinburgh. † RSW 1.
HUNTER, Colin* 1841-1904
Marine painter. b. Glasgow. Studied under J. Milne Donald. Father of John Young H. q.v. A.R.A. 1884, R.E. 1881, R.I. 1882, R.O.I. 1883, R.S.W. 1879. "Their only Harvest" purchased by Chantrey Bequest 1879. Add: 14 Melbury Road, Kensington, London. † AG 1, B 4, DOW 4, FIN 1, G 1, GI 31, L 15, M 10, NG 12, RA 76, RBA 6, RE 4, RI 1, ROI 3, RSA 3, RSW 2, TOO 2.
HUNTER, Eleanore Exh. 1908-9
Padstow, Cornwall. † B 1, L 2, RSA 1.
HUNTER, Dr. Ewing Exh. 1893-97
Helensburgh, N.B. † GI 3.
HUNTER, George Leslie* 1879-1931
Landscape and portrait painter and illustrator. b. Rothesay. Studied in San Francisco, U.S.A. and Paris. Returned to Scotland 1906. Worked in Italy 1923. Exh. 1915-30. Add: Glasgow. † BAR 7, GI 28, L 8, LEF 52, LEI 28, RSA 13, TOO 1.
HUNTER, Miss G.M.K. Exh. 1916-17
25 Crofton Road, Ealing, London. † RA 2.
HUNTER, G. Sherwood d. c.1920
Landscape and genre painter. R.B.A. 1889. Add: Aberdeen 1880; London 1887; Newlyn, Penzance 1903. † GI 12, L 17, M 1, RA 16, RBA 77, ROI 12, RSA 17.
HUNTER, Harriet B. Exh. 1905-6
12 Randolph Crescent, Edinburgh. † RSA 2.
HUNTER, Isabel Exh. 1881
Anton's Hill, Coldstream, N.B. † SWA 1.
HUNTER, James Brownlee Exh. 1883-1919
Engraver. Edinburgh 1883; Duddingston, Midlothian, N.B. 1908. † RA 3, RSA 18.
HUNTER, John Frederick b. 1893
Metal worker, enameller, stained glass artist, etcher, wood engraver and art inspector. b. Chin-Chow, Manchuria. Studied Dublin Metropolitan School of Art 1920 and Royal College of Art. Add: Royal Inniskilling Fusiliers, Donnybrook 1918; Dublin 1920. † RHA 6.
HUNTER, James Kennedy Exh. 1898-1919
Architect. 51 Sandgate, Ayr. † GI 4, RA 1, RSA 4.
HUNTER, John T. Exh. 1940
47 George Square, Edinburgh. † RSA 1.
HUNTER, John Young 1874-1955
Figure and portrait painter. b. Scotland. Studied R.A. Schools (2 silver medals). Son of Colin H. q.v. Married Mary Young H. q.v. R.B.A. 1914. "My Lady's Garden" purchased by Chantrey Bequest 1899. Add: London 1894 and 1908; Moreton in Marsh, Glos. 1902; Wickhambrook, Suffolk 1904. Went to U.S.A. c.1925. † B 2, FIN 70, GI 15, L 17, LEI 1, M 2, NG 10, P 6, RA 42, RBA 3, RI 1, ROI 2.
HUNTER, Lucy Exh. 1883-88
Figure painter. Add: Belchester, Coldstream, N.B. † RSA 5, SWA 2.
HUNTER, Marshall b. 1905
Portrait painter and teacher b. Glasgow. Studied Edinburgh College of Art and Moray House Training College. Exh. 1931-34. Add: North Lodge, Inveresk, Midlothian. † RSA 2.
HUNTER, Mason 1854-1921
Landscape and coastal painter. A.R.S.A. 1913, R.S .W. 1889. Add: Edinburgh. † D 2, DOW 3, GI 57, L 5, M 4, RBA 1, RHA 3, RI 1, RSA 145, RSW 86.
HUNTER, Mary Ethel d. c.1936
Portrait, landscape and figure painter. b. Yorkshire. Studied Newlyn, Penzance and Paris. Art mistress at St. Albans. Add: Rathmines, Dublin 1902; Ripon, Yorks. 1908; and London. † B 1, GI 1, I 6, LS 10, M 1, NEA 4, P 6, RA 9, RHA 3, ROI 1, SWA 4.
HUNTER, Mary Sutherland b. 1899
Portrait, landscape and interior painter and sculptor. Studied Edinburgh College of Art and R .S.A. Schools (Chalmers Jervise award 1922). Exh. 1923-40. Add: 26 Hermitage Drive, Edinburgh. † GI 3, L 1, RSA 10, RSW 1.
HUNTER, Mary Young* Exh. 1900-14
Watercolour landscape figure and miniature painter. Married John Young H.q.v. A.S.W.A. 1901. Add: London 1900 and 1908; Moreton in Marsh, Glos. 1902; Wickhambrook, Suffolk 1904. † FIN 51, GI 5, L 11, LEI 1, NG 1, P 1, RA 22, ROI 1, SWA 5.
HUNTER, Norman M. Exh. 1919-22
1 Bedford Place, Edinburgh. † RSA 2.
HUNTER, Patty Exh. 1938-40
Alexandria, Dumbartonshire. † GI 6.
HUNTER, Pauline Exh. 1929-40
Landscape and figure painter and black and white artist. Add: Derby 1929; Duffield, Derbys. 1940. † B 4, N 28, RCA 1.
HUNTER, Robert Exh. 1886-89
28 Queen Street, Edinburgh. † RSA 6.
HUNTER, Susan Exh. 1937
Still life painter. Add: 187 Queen's Gate, London. † RA 1.
HUNTER, S.H. Exh. 1914
11 Harringay Park, Crouch End, London. † RA 1.
HUNTER, Stephen W. Exh. 1901
Figure painter. Add: 6 Camden Studios, Camden Street, London. † RA 1.

HUNTER, William Exh. 1913-40
Figure painter. Studied Glasgow School of Art. R.O.I. 1928. Add: Glasgow. † GI 37, L 4, RA 1, ROI 28, RSA 15.

HUNTINGDON, Beatrice M.L. Exh. 1918-40
Married William MacDonald q.v. Add: St. Andrews 1925; 116 Hanover Street, Edinburgh 1930. † I 5, RSA 6.

HUNTINGDON, Francis H. Exh. 1894
Watercolour landscape painter. Add: Mervel Hill, Hambledon, Godalming, Surrey. † RA 1.

HUNTLEY-GORDON, Herbert Exh. 1890-1900
Architect. Add: 123 Cannon Street, London. † RA 13.

HUNTLY, Agnes W. Exh. 1935-39
44 Paulton Square, London. † P 1, ROI 10.

HUNTLY, Miss Nancy See SHEPPARD

HUNTLY, W.B. Exh. 1906-14
London 1906; Grately, Hants. 1913; Assington, Suffolk 1914. † RA 3, RI 2.

HUNTON, Charlotte Exh. 1892-93
Sculptor. Add: Browshill, Torquay, Devon. † L 2, RA 3.

HUNTON, Edith Exh. 1889-90
Browshill, Torquay, Devon. † ROI 2.

HUNTON, Evelyn Exh. 1936
Flower painter. 115 Cromwell Road, South Kensington, London. † RA 1, SWA 1.

HUNTSMAN, Maud Exh. 1897-1910
London. † P 1, RHA 5, ROI 1, SWA 3.

HURD, Margaret McFarlane b. 1902
Painter, etcher, leather and craft worker. b. Bothwell. Studied Harrow School of Art. Exh. 1926-40. Add: Harrow, Middlesex 1926; Grindleford, Derbys. 1932. † AB 6, D 2, GI 12, L 1, RA 3. RCA 5, RSA 12.

HURDMAN, Frederick Exh. 1922
Sculptor. 6 Jubilee Place, Chelsea, London. † RA 1.

HURD-WOOD, Fergus S. Exh. 1897-1935
Figure and miniature painter. Leatherhead, Surrey 1897; London 1901; Benenden, Kent 1935. † L 1, RA 3.

HURFORD, Miss J.E. Exh. 1936
106 Corporation Street, Birmingham. † B 1.

HURLE, Ruth Exh. 1939-40
Portrait and figure painter. Badbury Wick House, Chiseldon, Wilts. † NEA 1, RA 2.

HURLEY, N. Exh. 1911
54 Sackville Gardens, Hove, Sussex. † RA 1.

HURLSTONE, C. Exh. 1920
8 Montague Road, Handsworth, Birmingham. † B 2.

HURNALL, Miss C. Exh. 1901
Borrowdale, Northwood, Middlesex. † SWA 1.

HURREN, Alfreda M. Exh. 1936
Acquatinter. 5 Buxton Road, Willesden Green, London. † RA 1.

HURRY, Agnes Exh. 1901-36
Portrait and miniature painter. London. † RA 26, RMS 2.

HURRY, Leslie S. Exh. 1929
53 High Street, London. † RBA 1.

HURSE, Katie Exh. 1882-93
Torquay, Devon 1882 and 1891; South Norwood, London 1886. † B 15, RHA 7.

HURSE, Mabel Exh. 1905-6
3 Glanmire Terrace, Ranelagh, Co. Dublin. † RHA 2.

HURST, Hal d. c.1938
Portrait painter and etcher. Studied R.A. Schools. R.B.A. 1896, R.O.I. 1900. Founder member R.M.S. 1896, V.P.R.M.S. 1896-1913, H.R.M.S. 1914. Add: London. † L 44, NG 2, RA 19, RBA 112, RHA 2, RI 125, RMS 59, RWS 2.

HURST, Maud D. Exh. 1896-1927
Etcher. Horsham Park, Sussex. † BG 33, I 4, LS 13, SWA 21.

HURST, Phyllis C. Exh. 1909-13
Liverpool 1909; Sheffield 1913. † L 2.

HURT, Mrs. Louis B. (H.M.) Exh. 1886-88
Landscape painter. Ashbourne, Derbys. 1886; Darley Dale, Derbys. 1888. † GI 1, RBA 1.

HURT, Louis Bosworth* b. 1929
Painter of highland landscapes. Ashbourne, Derbys. 1881; Ironbrook, Darley Dale, Derbys. 1888. † B 6, CON 1, GI 22, L 9, M 25, N 10, RA 19, RBA 24, ROI 4, RSA 4.

HUSBAND, Eliza S. Exh. 1889-1913
Edinburgh. † GI 11, M 1, RSA 25, RSW 1.

HUSBAND, Mrs. K. Exh. 1932-33
Rock Mount, Frodsham, Chester. † L 3.

HUSGEN, P. Exh. 1906
72 Eaton Terrace, Kensington, London. † RA 1.

HUSKINSON, Edwin A. Exh. 1914-28
Sculptor. London. † L 1, RA 8.

HUSKINSON, John Exh. 1886-87
Sculptor. N.S.A. 1886. Add: Bingham, Notts. 1886; Chelsea, London 1887. † N 1, RA 2.

HUSKINSON, Thomas L.B. Exh. 1927-38
Landscape, interior and still life painter. Langar Hall, Notts. 1927; Woodstock, Oxon 1936. † BA 77, N 14, RA 4.

HUSKISSON, Miss M. Exh. 1916
32 St. Andrews Road, Southsea, Hants. † L 1.

HUSON, Thomas* 1844-1920
Landscape and genre painter and engraver. R.I. 1883, R.E. 1881. Add: Waterloo, Liverpool 1880; Pen-y-Garth, Bala, Wales 1907. † AG 1, B 5, G 1, GI 2, L 116, M 10, RA 9, RBA 11, RCA 46, RE 26, RI 116, ROI 26.

HUSON, Mrs. T. (J.E.) Exh. 1882-1916
Landscape painter. Waterloo, Liverpool 1882; Pen-y-Garth, Bala, Wales 1907. † L 11, RCA 2.

HUSSEY, de See D

HUSSEY, Mrs. Exh. 1880-93
Landscape painter. S.W.A. 1880. Add: The Close, Salisbury, Wilts. and Maitland House, Church Street, Kensington, London. † SWA 23.

HUSSEY, Miss Agnes Exh. 1880-91
Landscape and figure painter. The Close, Salisbury, Wilts. and Maitland House, Church Street, Kensington, London. † D 17, L 1, M 1, RBA 1, RI 4, SWA 8.

HUSSEY, Barbara Exh. 1937
Landscape painter. † COO 14.

HUSSEY, G.M. Exh. 1884
58 Queen's Gardens, London. † SWA 1.

HUTCHENS, Frank T. Exh. 1908
Etaples sur mer, France. † RA 1.

HUTCHESON, Jessie Exh. 1888-93
Govan 1888; Whiteinch 1893. † GI 3.

HUTCHESON, Miss M. Exh. 1894-96
Albert Road, Crosshill, Glasgow. † GI 2.

HUTCHESON, Walter* d. 1910
Crosshill, Glasgow. † B 1, GI 61, M 1, RHA 2, RSA 15.

HUTCHIN, Joyce Exh. 1927
Fieldside, Bank Avenue, Gt. Meols, Cheshire. † L 1.

HUTCHINGS, Hilda Edith b. 1890
Painter and etcher. Studied Bristol Municipal School of Art. On staff of Bristol Municipal School of Art and art teacher West Ham School of Art. Exh. 1913-40. Add: Redland, Bristol 1913; London 1927 and 1930; New Barking, Essex 1929. † B 1, L 10, RA 9, RI 1, ROI 2.

HUTCHINGS, J. Exh. 1893
Watercolour landscape painter. 12 Cartledge Street, Sandyford, Tunstall, Staffs. † RBA 1.

HUTCHINGS, J. Hanmer Exh. 1911
Arosfa, Deganwy, N. Wales. † B 2.

HUTCHINGS, William Harold Exh. 1910-21
Liverpool. † L 3.

HUTCHINS, Eliza Exh. 1908-26
Rose Cottage, Styal, Handforth, Cheshire 1908; Longsight, Manchester 1913. † L 1, M 4.

HUTCHINS, May Exh. 1926-28
The Craft Rooms, Queen's College, Birmingham. † L 19.

HUTCHINS, Ruth M. Exh. 1918-21
Earl's Court, London. † NEA 1, SWA 3.

HUTCHINSON, Miss Exh. 1881
Landscape painter. 15 Cavendish Square, London. † SWA 1.

HUTCHINSON, Allen Exh. 1883-95
Sculptor. Blurton Vicarage, Stoke on Trent, 1883 and 1886; London 1884. † GI 4, NG 1, RA 6, RHA 1, ROI 1, RSA 2.

HUTCHINSON, Miss A.S. Exh. 1896-1900
70 Wilson Street, Derby. † N 2.

HUTCHINSON, Beryl Exh. 1930-35
Landscape painter. A.N.S.A. 1932. Add: Nottingham. † N 7.

HUTCHINSON, C. Bernard Exh. 1904-7
Architect. 20 Queen Street, Deal, Kent. † RA 5.

HUTCHINSON, Charles E. Exh. 1903-4
Architect. 11 John Street, Bedford Row, London. † RA 2.

HUTCHINSON, Miss D. Mason Exh. 1911-15
The Marfords, Bromborough, Cheshire. † L 13.

HUTCHINSON, Miss E. Exh. 1892
Watercolour painter. West Hill House, Basford, Notts. † N 1.

HUTCHINSON, E.L. Exh. 1882
Figure painter. 14 Onslow Gardens, South Kensington, London. † RBA 1.

HUTCHINSON, F.L. Exh. 1896
Meadow Studios, Bushey, Herts. † ROI 1.

HUTCHINSON, George Exh. 1884-87
31 Cantlowes Road, Camden Square, London. † L 1, RA 2, ROI 1.

HUTCHINSON, Gertrude Kinsey Exh. 1899-1907
Miniature portrait painter. Dublin 1899; London 1900. † L 5, NG 2, RA 9.

HUTCHINSON, G.P. Exh. 1889-1917
Glass worker. London. † B 2, RA 1.

HUTCHINSON, George W.C. Exh. 1881-90
Figure and domestic painter. Add: London 1881; Clifton, Bristol 1889. † RA 3, RBA 4, RHA 1.

HUTCHINSON, Isabel M. Exh. 1897-1901
Portrait painter. London. † RA 1, SWA 1.

HUTCHINSON, James Exh. 1880-81
Lochgoilhead. † GI 3, RSA 1.

HUTCHINSON, Mrs. Jane P. Exh. 1880-85
Landscape painter. 15 Cavendish Square, London. † D 2, RBA 1, SWA 7.

HUTCHINSON, Mary Exh. 1920
Stained glass artist. 17 Queensbury Place, South Kensington, London. † RA 1.

HUTCHINSON, R. Exh. 1883
115 Grafton Street, Dublin. † RHA 1.
HUTCHISON, Doris F. Exh. 1939-40
7 Bellshaugh Road, Glasgow. † GI 1, RSA 1.
HUTCHISON, Emily Exh. 1895-1902
195 Nithsdale Road, Pollokshields. † GI 9.
HUTCHISON, G.J. d. c.1918
Exh. 1915-18. Add: 8 St. Bernard's Crescent, Edinburgh. † GI 4, L 5, RA 6, RSA 4, RSW 1.
HUTCHISON, G.S. Exh. 1933-34
36 St. Peter's Road, St. Albans, Herts. † ROI 3.
HUTCHISON, Ian Exh. 1917
114 Berkeley Street, Glasgow. † GI 1.
HUTCHISON, Isabel Exh. 1896-1901
Birkill, Stirling, N.B. 1896; Glasgow 1899. † GI 5.
HUTCHISON, Isobel W. Exh. 1930-39
Landscape painter. Visited North America and Greenland. Add: Carlowrie, Kirkliston. † COO 21, RSA 9, RSW 5.
HUTCHISON, John 1833-1910
Sculptor. Studied under Robert Scott Lauder in Edinburgh and Alfred Gatley in Rome. Among his work was a colossal bronze statue of John Knox for the Quadrangle of New College, Edinburgh. A.R.S.A. 1862, R.S.A. 1867 (Librarian 1877-1886 and Treasurer 1886-1907). Hon. Ret. R.S.A. 1909. Add: Edinburgh. † GI 1, RA 9, RSA 79.
HUTCHISON, John Exh. 1891-1900
St. Vincent Street, Glasgow. † GI 3.
HUTCHISON, J.H. Exh. 1881
10 Breadalane Terrace, Edinburgh. † RSA 1.
HUTCHISON, Miss K.G. Exh. 1909-15
Birkenhead 1909; Farnham, Surrey 1911. † L 18.
HUTCHISON, Maud Gemmell Exh. 1908-25
Musselburgh, N.B. 1908; Edinburgh 1912. † GI 7, L 2, RSA 11, RSW 4.
HUTCHISON, Robert C. Exh. 1932-38
Edinburgh. † RSA 4.
HUTCHISON, Robert Gemmell* 1860-1936
Landscape, figure and portrait painter. Studied Board of Manufacturers School of Art, Edinburgh. R.B.A. 1896, R.O.I. 1901, A.R.S.A. 1901, R.S.A. 1911, R.S.W. 1895. Add: Edinburgh 1888, 1894 and 1912; London 1885; Manchester 1887; Musselburgh, N.B. 1905. † AR 2, B 1, G 2, GI 111, L 63, M 5, RA 55, RBA 14, RHA 6, RI 6, ROI 52, RSA 184, RSW 118, TOO 1.
HUTCHISON, William Oliphant 1889-c.1971
Portrait and landscape painter. Studied Edinburgh and Paris. A.R.S.A. 1938. Add: Kirkcaldy and Edinburgh 1911-21; London 1922; Glasgow 1932 and 1940; Letheringham, Nr. Woodbridge, Suffolk 1936. † BAR 3, GI 39, I 3, L 13, P 11, RA 25, RBA 2, RSA 63.
HUTH, Frederick d. c.1906
Engraver. Edinburgh. † RA 8, RSA 24.
HUTSON, M. Exh. 1926-27
Watercolour landscape painter. 39 Athorpe Green, Vernon Avenue, Old Basford, Nottingham. † N 4.
HUTSON, Marshall C. Exh. 1931-39
Painter and sculptor. Cork. † RA 1, RHA 15.
HUTTON, Alfred Exh. 1884-86
Landscape painter. London. † RI 4.
HUTTON, Dorothy b. 1889
Flower painter. b. Bolton. Exh. 1914-40. Add: London. † GI 1, L 2, M 1, NEA 9, RA 17.
HUTTON, James Exh. 1893
† GI 1.
HUTTON, John P. Exh. 1913
71 Clerk Street, Edinburgh. † L 1.
HUTTON, Katharina Exh. 1898
Briarfield, Coalbridge, N.B. † GI 1.
HUTTON, Mary Exh. 1892-96
Olton, Warwicks. 1892; Moseley, Birmingham 1896. † B 2.
HUTTON, Philip Exh. 1928
† D 1.
HUTTON, R. Exh. 1884
Landscape painter. 38 The Grove, Ealing, London. † RBA 1.
HUTTON, R.L.* Exh. 1912-17
5 Porthminster Terrace, St. Ives, Cornwall. † D 10, I 1, L 1, ROI 2.
HUTTON, S. Clarke b. 1898
Landscape and figure painter. London. † B 2, D 16, GI 4, L 1, RA 2, RI 4, RED 1, ROI 1.
HUTTON, T.G. Exh. 1895
Watercolour landscape painter. 1 Eldon Square, Newcastle on Tyne. † RA 1.
HUTTON, Thomas S. Exh. 1887-1906
Landscape painter. Glasgow 1887 and 1906; Wavertree, Liverpool 1897; Seacombe, Cheshire 1898; Hoylake, Cheshire 1899. † D 2, GI 1, L 5, M 1, RA 2, RSA 4.
HUTTON, Walter C. Stritch Exh. 1888-1935
Portrait, figure and landscape painter. London 1888; Rome 1894; Bedford 1895; Liverpool 1901; Salisbury, Wilts. 1909, Parkstone, Dorset 1925. † L 7, LEI 1, RA 11, ROI 7.
HUTTULA, Richard Exh. 1880-88
Watercolour painter. Upper Tollington Park, London. † B 2, D 4, L 6, RBA 11, RI 5.
HUXLEY, A. Exh. 1891
8 Erskine Street, Liverpool. † L 1.
HUXLEY, Anne Exh. 1912
39 Cambrian View, Chester. † L 1.
HUXLEY, Mary E. Exh. 1905-6
41 Cheyney Road, Chester. † L 6.
HUXLEY, Nettie Exh. 1885-88
Figure and domestic painter. Marlborough Place, St. John's Wood, London. † G 4, L 1, RA 2, ROI 2.
HUXLEY, W.T. Exh. 1913-20
Liverpool 1913; Birkenhead 1920. † L 2.
HUYBERS, John Exh. 1886-87
Urban landscape painter. N.E.A. 1886. Add: 13 Lisle Street, Leicester Square, London. † NEA 2, RBA 2.
HUYGELEN, Frans Exh. 1914
72 Rue de Bruxelles, Uccle, Brussels. † GI 1.
HUYS, Modeste* b. 1875
Belgian artist. Vive St. Eloi (Wareghem), Fl. Occidentale, Belgium 1914. † RSA 1.
HUYSMANS, Jean Baptiste* Exh. 1882-91
Paris. † GI 14, M 2.
HYAMS, Henry Exh. 1922-33
Architect. Buckfastleigh, Devon 1922; Wandsworth Common, London 1933. † RA 2.
HYAMS, William b. 1878
Watercolour landscape painter. 115 Queen's Park Road, Brighton, Sussex. † RA 2, RI 1.
HYDE, Ann Exh. 1931
Linocut artist. † RED 1.
HYDE, Elizabeth L. Exh. 1893-96
Mrs. Richard H. Landscape, interior and portrait painter. London. † B 4, RA 2, RBA 1, SWA 4.
HYDE, Frank* Exh. 1880-1916
Portrait and figure painter. London 1880; Valetta, Malta 1910; Southsea, Hants. 1912. † B 1, L 5, M 1, RA 4, RBA 1.
HYDE, Mrs. Florence Exh. 1925-37
Landscape painter. Hillbrow, Palmerston Street, Derby. † N 8.
HYDE, Henry James Exh. 1883-92
Figure painter. London. † RBA 1, RI 11, ROI 6.
HYDE, Irene Exh. 1936
† RI 1.
HYDE, Joan Exh. 1936
Engraver. † RED 1.
HYDE, J.S. Exh. 1910
17 Castle Gate, Nottingham. † N 1.
HYDE, Phil Exh. 1904-25
Tuebrook, Liverpool 1904; Liscard, Cheshire 1914. † L 8.
HYDE, William d. 1925
Landscape painter and illustrator. London 1889; Guildford, Surrey 1905. † DOW 64, RA 8.
HYDE, W. Sidney c.1864-1940
Miniature painter and engraver. A.R.M.S. 1922. Add: London. † B 7, L 7, RA 7, RMS 4.
HYERMANS, T. Exh. 1888
40 Rue van Schonebeke, Antwerp. † L 1.
HYETT, A.G. Exh. 1885
Landscape painter. 12 Strathmore Gardens, Kensington, London. † SWA 2.
HYETT, John Edward c.1867-1936
Sculptor. b. Gloucester. Studied Royal College of Art. Married Kathleen H. q.v. Add: London 1904 and 1909; Cheltenham, Glos. 1905 and Sutton on Sea, Lincs. † L 13, RA 20, RI 2.
HYETT, Kathleen Exh. 1912-40
Painter and lithographer. Studied under F.E. Jackson. Married John Edward H. q.v. S.W.A. 1919. Add: S. Croydon, Surrey 1912; London 1914; Sutton on Sea, Lincs. 1919. † I 5, L 4, LS 7, RA 1, SWA 9.
HYETT, Margaret Exh. 1919-29
Landscape painter. Painswick, Glos. † RID 8.
HYLAND, F. Exh. 1894
18 Fitzroy Street, Fitzroy Square, London. † RBA 1.
HYMAN, Louis Exh. 1914-19
26 Bedford Street, Liverpool. † L 2.
HYNDMAN, Arnold Exh. 1921-32
Portrait and landscape painter. London 1921; Southbourne, Hants. 1931. † RA 6, ROI 5.
HYNES, E. Exh. 1921
Portrait painter. 68 Shakespeare Street, Nottingham. † N 2.
HYNES, Gladys Exh. 1911-33
Painter and sculptor. b. Indore, India. Studied under Stanhope Forbes, Newlyn, Penzance and London School of Art. Add: Penzance, Cornwall 1911; London 1914. † G 1, I 4, L 5, LS 3, RA 3, RI 2.
HYSLOP, Theo B. Exh. 1901-16
Landscape painter. London. † RA 3, ROI 1.
HYTCH, Mrs. E. Preston Exh. 1899
Holmleigh, Ashfield Avenue, Kings Heath, Birmingham. † B 2.
HYTCHE, Miss Kezia Exh. 1884-93
Landscape, interior and still life painter. London. † RA 1, RBA 4, RI 1, ROI 2, SWA 5.

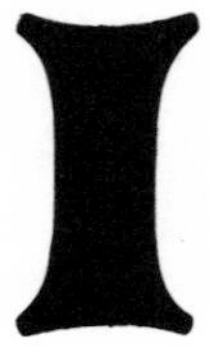

I'ANSON, Charles Exh. 1880-1907
Landscape painter. N.E.A. 1891, R.O.I. 1899. Add: London. † B 9, D 2, G 1, L 14, M 5, NG 3, RA 24, RBA 11, RI 24, ROI 43.

I'ANSON, Edward d. 1888
Architect. 7A Lawrence Pountney Hill, Cannon Street, London. † RA 1.

I'ANSON, Edward B. Exh. 1891-1906
Architect. 7A Lawrence Pountney Hill, Cannon Street. London. † RA 3.

I'ANSON, Margaret Exh. 1907-37
Mrs. Hayward. Miniature painter. Paignton, Devon 1907; Kingston Hill, Surrey 1911; South Croydon 1919; Newport, Essex 1923; Saffron Walden, Essex 1935. † B 5, L 2, RA 7, ROI 1.

IBBERSON, Herbert G. Exh. 1898-1911
Architect. 28 Martin's Lane, Cannon Street. London. † RA 10.

IBBETSON, Ernest Exh. 1903
Figure painter. 12 Myddleton Road, Ilkley, Yorks. † RA 1.

IBBETSON, J.C. Exh. 1926-33
Figure and landscape painter. † L 2, TOO 1.

IBBOTSON, Helena Mary Exh. 1916-36
Enameller, gold and silver worker and teacher. Studied Sheffield College of Arts and Crafts, and London. Add: Sheffield. † B 2, L 23.

IBBOTSON, Marjorie Exh. 1937-39
Sharrow, Sheffield 1937; Edinburgh 1939. † B 1, RSA 1, SWA 1.

IBBS, Edith A. Exh. 1889-1905
Architectural painter. 4 Brunswick Square, London. † SWA 3.

ICHENHAUSEN, Mrs. Natalie Exh. 1891-95
Portrait and figure painter. 1 Langham Chambers, Portland Place, London. † GI 2, L 5, M 2, RA 1, ROI 1.

IEVERS, Mrs. Butler Exh. 1908
2 Anglesea Villas, Ball's Bridge, Dublin. † RHA 1.

IHLEE, Rudolph Exh. 1910-37
Figure and landscape painter. N.E.A. 1919. Add: London 1910; Collieure, Pyrenees Orientales, France 1929. † CAR 35, GOU 17, L 5, LEI 46, M 1, NEA 67, RED 1, RSA 4.

IHLER, Mrs. Ada M. Exh. 1910-21
Malvern House, Llandudno, Wales. † GI 2, LS 14, RCA 7.

ILCHESTER, The Countess of d. 1956
Helen Vane Tempest Stewart. Holland House, Kensington, London. † D 3, RA 1.

ILES, Mrs. Violet Exh. 1921-35
Twyford, Sherbourne Road, Acocks Green, Birmingham. † B 27, RCA 5.

ILIFFE, Charles Exh. 1909-11
5 Yew Tree Avenue, Carrington, Nottingham. † N 8.

ILLES, A. Exh. 1900
66 Doddington Grove, Kennington Park, London. † RI 1.

ILLINGWORTH, Adeline S. Exh. 1896-1935
Painter and etcher. A.R.E. 1904. Add: Chelsea, London. † GI 4, L 12, LS 5, RA 21, RE 60, RHA 7, RSA 5, SWA 4.

ILSLEY, Ethel M. Exh. 1898-1908
15 Dorville Road, Lee, London. † RA 1, ROI 2.

IMAGE, Selwyn c.1849-1930
Watercolour painter, designer and poet. Slade Professor at Oxford 1910 and 1913. Exh. 1912 and 1928. Add: London. † FIN 40, I 2.

IMANO, Mrs. Miriam J. See DAVIS

IMLACH, Agnes C. Exh. 1880-1901
Edinburgh. † RSA 14.

IMLACH, Archibald F. Exh. 1880-92
Edinburgh. † GI 12, L 3, M 1, RSA 36.

IMMS, A.E. Exh. 1921-23
Stoneleigh Road, Handsworth, Birmingham. † B 2.

IMMS, Florence H. Exh. 1910
Oxford Road, Moseley, Birmingham. † B 1.

IMMS, Miss F.M. Exh. 1921
10 Haldon Avenue, Teignmouth, Devon. † B 3.

IMPEY-PEARSE, Mrs. M. Exh. 1894-96
Ardvullen, Kilmallock 1894; Bandon, Co. Cork 1895. † RHA 7.

IMRIE, Archibald Brown b. 1900
Painter, lithographer and commerical artist. Studied Edinburgh College of Art. R.S.A. Life School, Paris and Florence (Carnegie travelling scholarship). Exh. 1922-35. Add: Edinburgh. † GI 1, RSA 17, RSW 1.

INCE, Audrey Exh. 1930-39
Flower and landscape painter. Add: Hampstead, London 1930; Letchworth, Herts. 1932. † AR 1, SWA 3, WG 48.

INCE, Miss A.C. Exh. 1896
21 Baker Street, London. † SWA 1.

INCE, Charles* b. 1875
Landscape painter. R.B.A. 1912, R.I. 1927. Exh. 1909-40. Add: Purley, Surrey 1909; Nyewood, Bognor, Sussex 1924; Fareham, Hants. 1933; Southsea, Hants. 1935; Purbrook, Hants. 1937. † FIN 13, GI 26, GOU 32, L 6, M 2, RA 16, RBA 179, RHA 1, RI 39, ROI 5, RWS 4.

INCE, Evelyn c.1886-1941
Landscape and portrait painter, illustrator and teacher. b. Bhagulpur, India. Studied Byam Shaw and Vicat Cole School (scholarship 1913). Land worker 1917-18. A.R.B.A. 1923, R.B.A. 1926, A.R.W.S. 1937. "Flower Piece" purchased by Chantrey Bequest 1934. Add: London 1915 and 1924; Petworth, Sussex 1921; Letchworth, Herts. 1930. † ALP,1, COO 3, I 2, L 3, M 1, NEA 2, P 2, RA 19, RBA 59, ROI 2, RWS 9, WG 4.

INCE, J. Howard Exh. 1882-1904
Architect. London. † NG 1, RA 7.

INCE, T.M. Exh. 1888
Watercolour landscape painter. † FIN 1.

INCHBOLD, John William* 1830-1888
Landscape painter. b. Leeds. Studied under Louis Haghe and R.A. Schools 1847. Spent his later years mostly abroad in Spain, Italy and Algeria. Add: Switzerland 1882; London 1883. † G 2, L 1, M 4, RA 3.

INCHBOLD, Stanley b. 1856
Landscape painter and architect. Studied Herkomers, Bushey. Travelled on the continent, Middle East, Canada and the U.S.A. Exh. 1884-1919. Add: London 1884; Bushey, Herts. 1891; Eastbourne, Sussex 1894 and 1898; Alfriston, Sussex 1892; Brading, I.O.W. 1917. † B 2, FIN 80, L 7, M 2, RA 9, RBA 1, RI 12.

INCLEDON, Mrs. H. Elsie Exh. 1903
1 Montague Road, Edgbaston, Birmingham. † B 1.

INDUNI, Gottardo Exh. 1887-88
Sculptor. 1 Upper Cheyne Row, Chelsea, London. † RA 2.

INDUNI, Peter Exh. 1933
Sculptor. 4 Fulham Park Gardens, London. † RA 1.

INGALL, Miss E.M. Exh. 1925-40
Erdington, Birmingham 1925; Streetly, Birmingham 1937. † B 21.

INGALL, J. Spence Exh. 1892-97
Landscape and coastal painter. Hinderwell, Yorks. † L 1, M 1, RA 1, RI 1.

INGERSOLL, Ginerva Exh. 1916-19
† I 5.

INGHAM, Charles Frederick b. 1879
Landscape, flower and miniature painter and black and white artist. Studied Royal College of Art. Exh. 1924-31. Add: Rosedene Victoria Terrace, Tadcaster, Yorks. † RCA 13.

INGLE, Leura Exh. 1896-1925
Portrait and miniature painter. London. † RA 7.

INGLES, George Scott b. 1874
Painter, lithographer and wood block printer. b. Hawick. Studied Royal College of Art (travelling scholarship). Vice principal Leicester College of Arts and Crafts. Exh. 1907-33. Add: Tweed House, Fosse Road, Leicester. † GI 5, I 5, L 3, M 2, RA 19, RSA 19.

INGLIS, Alexander Exh. 1932-40
Edinburgh. † RSA 12.

INGLIS, Alice Exh. 1906
Beaufort Street, London. † SWA 2.

INGLIS, Bessie D. Exh. 1927-39
Edinburgh. † RSA 10, RSW 6.

INGLIS, David N. d. 1933
Portrait painter. A.R.H.A. 1919. Add: Selkirk and Edinburgh 1912; Dublin 1917; London 1930. † GI 1, L 1, RHA 25, RSA 4.

INGLIS, Frank Caird Exh. 1900-4
Rock House, Calton Hill, Edinburgh. † RSA 5.

INGLIS, H.V. Exh. 1885-86
Rudgwick, Sussex. † L 1, RHA 3.

INGLIS, James Exh. 1885-91
6 Comely Green Place, Edinburgh. † RSA 8, TOO 2.

INGLIS, Jane d. 1916
Landscape, figure and still life painter. Exh. 1881-1915. Add: London. † B 16, D 26, L 4, LS 7, M 5, NEA 4, RA 9, RBA 6, RI 3, ROI 10, RSA 2, SWA 23.

INGLIS, J.A. Russell Exh. 1882-1901
Edinburgh. † RSA 4.

INGLIS, Johnston J. Exh. 1885-1903
Landscape painter. A.R.H.A. 1892, R.H.A. 1892-1912. Add: Monkstown 1885; Ballsbridge, Dublin 1887 and 1892; London 1890; Donnybrook, Dublin 1896. † B 8, GI 2, L 8, M 2, RA 13, RHA 70, RSA 5.

INGLIS, Jean Winifred b. 1884
Portrait, landscape and still life painter and teacher. Studied Slade School. Exh. 1909-40. Add: London. † GI 1, GOU 4, I 3, L 1, LS 3, NEA 17, P 8, RA 4, RSA 2.

INGLIS, Miss M. Exh. 1906
5 Wentworth Mansions, Hampstead Heath, London. † RA 1.

INGLIS, Miss M. Haddon Exh. 1927
The Little House, Nairn, N.B. † L 1.

INGLIS, Robert Exh. 1899
19 North Coburg Street, Glasgow. † GI 1.

INGLIS, William S.A. Exh. 1910-40
Hawick. † L 1, RSA 18.

INGRAM, Mrs. Exh. 1930-32
8 Thorn Road, Bournville, Birmingham. † B 2.

INGRAM, Alex Exh. 1884
32 Bank Street, Hillhead, Glasgow. † GI 2.

INGRAM, Archibald B. Exh. 1881-87
Watercolour landscape painter. London. † D 1, RBA 1.

INGRAM, Archibald Bennett b. 1903
Sculptor and painter. Son of Charles A.I. q.v. Studied Nottingham School of Art and Royal College of Art (travelling scholarship). Add: Nottingham 1925; London 1927 and 1934; Cranbrook, Kent 1931. † N 10, RA 7, RCA 2.

INGRAM, Charles A. Exh. 1886-1912
Lithographer. Father of Archibald Bennett I. q.v. Add: Carrington, Notts. 1886; Nottingham 1898. † N 8.

INGRAM, Herbert C. Exh. 1900
Architect. 9 Ironmonger Lane, London. † RA 1.

INGRAM, Jane S. Exh. 1928
22 Gt. King Street, Edinburgh. † RSA 1.

INGRAM, Margaret K. Exh. 1883-86
Landscape painter. Add: London 1883; Venice 1884; Aberdeen 1886. † B 3, RBA 2.

INGRAM, William Ayerst 1855-1913
Landscape painter. b. Glasgow. Studied under J. Steeple and A.W. Weedon. Travelled frequently. R.B.A. 1883, R.I. 1907, R.O.I. 1906. Add: London 1880 and 1890; Surbiton, Surrey 1889 and 1896; Falmouth, Cornwall 1894 and 1904. † B 1, D 15, DOW 7, FIN 97, GI 4, GOU 51, L 23, M 7, NG 17, RA 44, RBA 143, RI 53, RID 48, ROI 27, RSW 1, TOO 11.

INGRAM, Walter Rowlands Exh. 1881-94
Sculptor. London. † L 8, RA 24.

INGREY, Mabel Exh. 1918-20
42 Leamington Road Villas, London. † SWA 2.

INJALBERT, Jean Antonin 1845-1933
French sculptor. Exh. 1911-25. Add: Paris. † GI 1, RSA 2.

INMAN, Henry Reid Exh. 1937
† RI 1.

INMAN, Miss M.D. Exh. 1906-8
London. † RA 2.

INNAMORATTI, Lilian Exh. 1937-40
1435 Pershore Road, Birmingham. † B 7.

INNES, Agnes Exh. 1902
Glan Menai, Penmaenmawr, Wales. † RCA 1.

INNES, George B. Exh. 1939
996 Pollokshaws Road, Glasgow. † RSA 1.

INNES, Helen Exh. 1909-14
Landscape painter. 4 Audley Square, London. † L 9, NEA 6, RA 1.

INNES, Henry P. Exh. 1897-99
Figure painter. 318 Holloway Road, London. † RA 2.

INNES, John Exh. 1939
11 Eltringham Gardens, Edinburgh. † RSA 1.

INNES, James Dickson* 1887-1914
Landscape painter. b. Llanelly. Studied Carmarthen School of Art and Slade School. Visited France and Spain 1908-12. Went to Morocco for his health in 1913 and died of consumption at Swanley, Kent. N.E.A. 1911. "The Waterfall" (1910) purchased by Chantrey Bequest 1922. † CAR 4, CHE 29, GOU 2, LS 5, NEA 17.

INNIS, Miss E.F. Brooke Exh. 1897
34 Craven Hill Gardens, London. † SWA 1.

INNIS, Josephine Exh. 1936
c/o Robert Sielle, 14 Buckingham Street, London. † RBA 1.

INNOCENTI, Signor Exh. 1883-1911
Tunbridge Wells, Kent 1883; Paris 1885 and 1888; Neuilly, Seine, France 1887; Rome, Italy 1911. † B 1, M 9, RSA 1.

INSKIP, John Henry d. 1947
Landscape and interior painter and critic. R.B.A. 1894. Exh. from 1886. Add: 19 Esplanade, Scarborough, Yorks. † B 6, L 10, RA 32, RBA 78, ROI 1.

INSTONE, Bernard Exh. 1930-34
Langstone Works, 27 Digbeth, Birmingham. † B 49.

I'ONS, A. Exh. 1910
43 Lamb's Conduit Street, London. † RA 1.

IPSEN, Ernest L. Exh. 1924
† P 1.

IRELAND, Mrs. A.E. Exh. 1882-86
Inglewood, Bowdon, Cheshire. † GI 3, M 1.

IRELAND, Mrs. Beryl Exh. 1938
† RMS 1.

IRELAND, James Exh. 1882-1928
Figure painter. Liverpool 1882; Wallasey, Cheshire 1928. † GI 1, L 57, M 4, RA 5, RI 3.

IRELAND, Mrs. M. Exh. 1929
Brizlincote, Burton on Trent, Staffs. † B 1.

IRELAND, Thomas Exh. 1880-1903
Landscape painter. R.B.A. 1895. Probably father of T. Taylor I. q.v. Add: London. † B 10, G 7, L 12, NG 20, RA 26, RBA 73, RI 13, ROI 16.

IRELAND, T. Tayler Exh. 1894-1921
Landscape painter. Probably son of Thomas I. q.v. Add: London. † B 2, M 1, NG 25, RA 7, RBA 1, RI 17, ROI 5.

IRELAND, William E. Exh. 1928-29
49 Goldsmith Street, Liverpool. † L 2.

IREMONGER, Miss M.H. Exh. 1894-96
London. † L 1, SWA 1.

IROLLI, Vincent* Exh. 1910
c/o Allied Artists Association, 67 Chancery Lane, London. † LS 3.

IRONMONGER, G. Exh. 1939
30 Mirfield Road, Solihull, Warwicks. † B 1.

IRONS, Agnes R. Exh. 1898-1924
13 Glenorchy Terrace, Edinburgh. † GI 1, RSA 15, RSW 1.

IRVINE, Miss Exh. 1898
7 Fosseway, Clifton, Bristol. † SWA 3.

IRVINE, Henrietta Exh. 1924
Landscape and portrait painter. † AR 66.

IRVINE, James 1833-1899
Portrait painter. Studied under Colvin Smith at Brechin and Edinburgh Academy. Add: 51 York Place, Edinburgh 1880; 1 West Maitland Street, Edinburgh 1884; Montrose 1889. † GI 5, RA 1, RSA 30.

IRVINE, Miss L. Pearson Exh. 1906
Elgin Avenue, London. † SWA 1.

IRVINE, Margaret S. Exh. 1930
86 Findhorn Place, Edinburgh. † RSA 1.

IRVINE, Mabel V. Exh. 1936-37
Lady Irvine. The University House, St. Andrews. † RSA 3.

IRVINE, Miss R. Exh. 1908
101 Lansdowne Road, Holland Park, London. † RA 1.

IRVINE, Robert Scott b. 1906
Watercolour painter. Studied Edinburgh College of Art. R.S.A. 1933. Add: 5 Spence Street, Newington, Edinburgh. † GI 5, RSA 7, RSW 18.

IRVING, Mrs. Constance Exh. 1910-36
Flower and landscape painter. Hightown, Liverpool 1910; London 1915. † L 12, RA 1.

IRVING, Miss E.B. Exh. 1882
26 Strehlener Street, Dresden, Germany. † L 1.

IRVING, Edward E. Exh. 1910-32
Oxton, Cheshire 1910; Birkenhead 1915; Liverpool 1923. † L 23, RCA 4.

IRVING, E.O. Bell Exh. 1885
50A Frederick Street, Edinburgh. † RSA 3.

IRVING, Hamilton Exh. 1914
9 Upper Brook Street, London. † LS 1.

IRVING, James Exh. 1880-91
Painter. 17 Sutton Place, Edinburgh. † GI 2, RA 1, RSA 35.

IRVING, Jean Bell Exh. 1884
22 India Street, Edinburgh. † RSA 1.

IRVING, J. Thwaite Exh. 1888-1909
Landscape and figure painter. Witley, Surrey 1888; Milford, Surrey 1890 and 1893; London 1892; Porchester, Fareham, Hants. 1899; Thursley, Surrey 1901. † G 1, L 1, NG 7, RA 1, RBA 4, RI 1, ROI 12.

IRVING, Laurence Henry b. 1897
Landscape painter, illustrator and stage and film designer. Studied Byam Shaw School and R.A. Schools. Art director to Douglas Fairbanks 1928-29. Exh. 1921-37. Add: The Black Windmill, Whitstable, Kent. † FIN 195, GI 3, RA 6.

IRVING, Miss M.E. Exh. 1920-24
Hewell House, Friars Road, Barry Island, Glam. † L 3.

IRVING, V.B. Exh. 1933
† L 1.

IRVING, W. Exh. 1898-1906
Domestic painter. Newcastle on Tyne. † L 2, RA 3.

IRVING, W. Noel Exh. 1902-15
Liverpool 1902; Hightown, Nr. Liverpool 1909; London 1915. † L 10.

IRWIN, Annie L. Exh. 1886-93
Flower painter. 18 Murton Street, Sunderland. † L 1, M 2, RA 1, ROI 2, SWA 2.

IRWIN, Clara Exh. 1891-1916
Dublin 1891; Carnagh, Co. Armagh 1901. † RHA 28.

IRWIN, Miss E. Exh. 1881-82
34 Upper Leeson Street, Dublin. † RHA 1.

IRWIN, Greville b. 1893
Landscape and figure painter. Studied Juliens, Paris 1924, Academie des Beaux Arts, Brussels 1926. R.B.A. 1934. Add: London 1933; Ewell, Surrey 1935; Leamington, Warwicks. 1940. † AR 2, GI 1, NEA 3, RA 4, RBA 33, RI 6, ROI 6.

IRWIN, Jean H. Exh. 1931
5 Dumbreck Road, Glasgow. † RSA 1.

IRWIN, Capt. J.J. Exh. 1889
2nd E.F. Regiment, Newry. † RHA 1.

IRWIN, Madelaine Exh. 1881-1906
Portrait and figure painter. Add: Dublin 1881; Eastbourne 1887; Colchester, Essex 1888. † B 2, D 2, L 4, M 1, RA 10, RBA 2, RHA 3.

IRWIN, Mrs. Maud Exh. 1922-40
Belfast. † RHA 10.

IRWIN, Nora E. Exh. 1936
22 Carpenter Road, Edgbaston, Birmingham. † B 1.

ISAAC, Jessie M. Exh. 1921
Redland, Bristol. † RMS 1.

ISAAC, Lily Exh. 1890-93
3 Mayfield Road, Aigburth, Liverpool. † L 2.

ISAAC, Mary Exh. 1890
Albrighton, Wolverhampton. † B 1.

ISAAC, Miss M.J. Exh. 1908
Redcliffe House, Henley on Thames. † RA 1.

ISAAC, Nellie E. Exh. 1904-21
Miniature painter. 20 Dennington Park Road, West Hampstead, London 1904; Chelsea, London 1921. † L 11, RA 2, SWA 2.

ISAAC, Miss R.A. Exh. 1907-14
20 Dennington Park Road, West Hampstead, London. † L 20.

ISAACS, Edith Exh. 1902-39
Animal painter. The Hollies, Alexandra Mount, Litherland, Liverpool. † B 2, L 43, RCA 33.

ISAACS, Esther Stella See SUTRO

ISAACS, Florence Exh. 1886
Painter. 21 Belsize Park, Hampstead, London. † SWA 1.

ISAACS, Miss G.E. Exh. 1889-94
Glasgow. † GI 5, RSA 1.

ISAACS, Miss L. Exh. 1888
67 West Derby Street, Liverpool. † L 1.

ISAACS, Rose Exh. 1912-38
The Hollies, Alexandra Mount, Litherland, Liverpool. † B 1, L 10, RCA 24.

ISAACS, Winifred Exh. 1900-38
The Hollies, Alexandra Mount, Litherland, Liverpool. † L 74, RCA 41.

ISAACSON, Mrs. H.B. Exh. 1892
Landscape painter. Governor's House, H.M. Prison, Reading, Berks. † RID 1.

ISABEY, Louis Gabriel Eugenie* 1803-1886
French painter. Bois de Chigny, pres Lagny, Seine, France 1883. † RI 3.

ISBELL, W.G.R. Exh. 1886
Landscape painter. 20 Carisbrooke Road, St. Leonards, Sussex. † RBA 1.

ISELIN, Eleanor Exh. 1930
Sculptor. Katonak, New York, U.S.A. † RA 1.

ISHERWOOD, Frank Bradshaw Exh. 1910-11
Frimley Lodge, Frimley Grove, Farnborough, Kent. † D,6.

ISHERWOOD, J. Exh. 1898-99
Mansfield, Notts. † N 3.

ISHERWOOD, Jessie Exh. 1889
13 Howe Street, Edinburgh. † RSA 1.

ISHERWOOD, Miss R.M. Exh. 1886-87
13 Howe Street, Edinburgh. † M 3.

ISHIBASHI, Kazunori 1879-1928
Portrait and Japanese silk painter. b. Matsuye, Japan. Studied R.A. Schools 1905-10. R.O.I. 1917, R.P. 1918. Exh. 1906-27. Add: London. Died in Tokio. † D 3, I 3, L 14, P 10, RA 15, RI 7, ROI 8.

ISLES, Lal Exh. 1916
c/o Isles, Love and Co., Brisbane, Australia. † L 1.

ISRAEL, George Exh. 1940
Landscape painter. 45 Woodgrange Road, London. † RA 1.

ISRAELS, Isaac* 1865-1934
Dutch painter. Son of Josef I. q.v. Exh. 1912-28. Add: The Hague, Holland. † GI 1, RSA 2.

ISRAELS, Josef* 1824-1911
Dutch painter. Father of Isaac I. q.v. H.R.I. 1894, H.R.S.A. 1887, R.S.W. 1894, H.F.R.A. Add: The Hague, Holland. † GI 20, GOU 3, I 5, L 2, M 6, RI 9, RSA 15, RSW 2.

ISRAELS, Miriam b. 1907
Mrs. Franklin. American artist. Exh. 1937-38. † NEA 3.

ITEN, Hans 1874-c.1930
Landscape, flower and still life painter. b. Zurich. Studied School of Art, St. Gall, Switzerland. Exh. 1908-30. Add: Belfast. † FIN 6, GI 8, L 4, RA 3, RHA 48.

IVANOWITCH, Paul* Exh. 1908-29
Portrait painter. Vienna 1908; Acton, London 1929. † L 1, RA 2.

IVATTS, Mrs. L. Leared Exh. 1904-6
12 Augustine's Road, Edgbaston, Birmingham. † B 8.

IVENS, Mary Exh. 1911
Glengariffe, Pittville, Cheltenham, Glos. † B 1.

IVES, John Exh. 1909
29 Millmount Avenue, Drumcondra, Dublin. † RHA 2.

IVES, Miss L. Exh. 1891
Adswood Lane, Stockport, Lancs. † L 1, M 1.

IVEY, Marion Teresa Exh. 1884-88
Portrait and figure painter. Add: The Tower of London, London. † L 1, RA 2, RI 1.

IVIMEY, Fairfax Exh. 1932-39
Landscape painter. The Fort, Newquay, Cornwall. † GI 2, RBA 1, RCA 3, RHA 1.

IVISON, Frederick W. Exh. 1903
Stained glass artist. 102 Savernake Road, Hampstead, London. † RA 1.

IWAI, Takahito Exh. 1922-25
Japanese artist. A.R.B.A. 1923, H.R.B.A. 1925. Add: London. † I 1, RBA 9.

IWILL, Marie Joseph* 1850-1923
French painter. Exh. 1887-1911. Add: 11 Quai Voltaire, Paris. † BRU 30, GI 1, L 2.

IZANT, Herbert Exh. 1880-1900
Landscape painter. Thornton Heath, Surrey 1880; Croydon, Surrey 1895. † NG 5, RA 4, RBA 5, ROI 2.

IZARD, Edwin Exh. 1880-85
Landscape painter. London. † RA 4, RBA 12, RHA 2.

IZARD, Miss Edith A. Exh. 1884-92
Figure and landscape painter. Add: London 1884; Twickenham, Middlesex 1892. † B 1, L 3, RA 1, RBA 1.

IZARD, Mrs. Eleanor W. Exh. 1934-38
Miniature painter. 980 Arundel Drive, Victoria, B.C. Canada. † RA 1, RMS 1.

IZARD, Gertrude M. Exh. 1890-91
Flower painter. 13 St. John's Park, London. † RBA 1.

IZIEDINOFF, George Dondukoff Exh. 1935-39
Miniature painter. A.R.M.S. 1937. Add: London 1935; Paris 1939. † RMS 12, WG 73.

IZOD, Charles Exh. 1936
197 Green Lane, Norbury, London. † RBA 1.

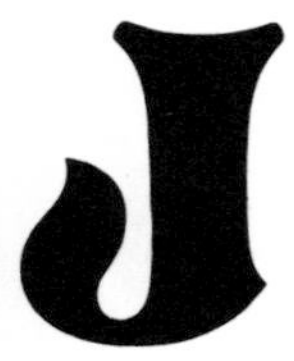

"JACK" See GODWIN, Marianne

JACK, Andrew M. Exh. 1907
Craigmill House, Stirling, N.B. † GI 2.

JACK, G. Exh. 1902-10
Architect. Station Road, Church End, Finchley, London. † RA 3.

JACK, Mrs. Isabel Exh. 1910-30
Boughton, Chester 1910; Earl's Court, London 1930. † L 4.

JACK, John Exh. 1880-91
1 Hermitage Place, Edinburgh. † RSA 11.

JACK, Marion E. Exh. 1898-1912
London 1898 and 1911; Paris 1901; Rye, Sussex 1902. † B 11, LS 6.

JACK, Patti Exh. 1881-97
Landscape painter. Ardmohr, Dunblane, N.B. 1881; St. Andrews 1884. † B 2, GI 3, RA 1, RSA 33.

JACK, Richard* 1866-1952
Portrait, figure, landscape and interior painter. b. Sunderland. Studied York School of Art and South Kensington. A.R.A. 1914, R.A. 1920, R.I. 1917, R.M.S. 1896, R.P. 1900. "Rehearsal with Nikisch" purchased by Chantrey Bequest 1912. Add: Paris 1893; London 1895; Montreal, Canada 1932. † FIN 75, G 1, GI 8, L 40, M 6, NG 12, P 43, RA 154, RI 14, RID 28, RSA 3.

JACKLIN, George William Exh. 1881-1900
Landscape painter. Nottingham 1881; West Bridgford, Notts. 1897. † N 3.

JACKMAN, Kate Exh. 1890
11 Stoke Newington Road, London. † ROI 1, SWA 1.

JACKSON, A. Exh. 1885-87
Bradford 1885; Huddersfield 1886. † B 1, L 3.

JACKSON, Miss A. Exh. 1911
The Manor House, Brentwood, Essex. † RA 1.

JACKSON, Arthur Exh. 1890
2 Milner Street, Cadogan Square, London. † RI 1.

JACKSON, Arthur b. 1911
Painter. b. Rotherham, Yorks. Studied St. Martins School of Art and under Ben Nicholson. Exh. 1934-39. † LEF 8, LEI 3.

JACKSON, A. Blomfield Exh. 1920
Architect. Father of Muriel Blomfield J. q.v. Add: 3 New Square, Lincoln's Inn, London. † RA 1.

JACKSON, A.E. Exh. 1901-2
St. Martin's Chambers, Loseby Lane, Leicester. † N 3.

JACKSON, A.E. Exh. 1927
Architect. Town Hall, Southport, Lancs. † RA 1.

JACKSON, Albert Edward 1873-1952
Painter. Exh. 1897-1901. Add: London. † RA 1, RBA 2.

JACKSON, A. Logan Exh. 1912-29
Glasgow 1912; Milngavie 1929. † GI 2.

JACKSON, Alexander Young* b. 1882
Exh. 1910-35. Add: Surbiton, Surrey 1910; Paris 1912. † L 2, RA 1, RSA 3.

JACKSON, Barry Exh. 1909-20
Wake Green Road, Moseley, Birmingham. † B 4.

JACKSON, B. Leslie Exh. 1913
Croft Lodge, The Park, Newark on Trent, Notts. † N 3.

JACKSON, Cara Exh. 1894-97
Devonshire Square, Bandon, Co. Cork. † RHA 6.

JACKSON, Caroline Exh. 1888-1928
Birkenhead 1888 and 1911; St. Ives, Cornwall 1904 and 1920. † L 29.

JACKSON, Constance Exh. 1912
Lynwood, Ripon, Yorks. † L 1.

JACKSON, Charles d'Orville Pilkington b. 1887
Sculptor. b. Grampound, Cornwall. Studied Edinburgh College of Art and British School at Rome. A.R.B.A. 1922. Exh. 1910-34. Add: Edinburgh. † GI 11, L 6, RA 10, RBA 2, RSA 26.

JACKSON, C.E. Exh. 1912
c/o Knight, 9 Gladstone Terrace, Edinburgh. † RSA 2.

JACKSON, Christine H. Exh. 1930-38
Figure painter. Add: Wallington, Surrey 1930; Carshalton Beeches, Surrey 1934. † RA 3.

JACKSON, Cyril H. Exh. 1903-34
Miniature portrait painter. London. † RA 2.

JACKSON, Miss C.P. Exh. 1890
2 St. James' Terrace, Bushey, Herts. † RBA 1.

JACKSON, C. Randle Exh. 1912-36
Sculptor. Add: Croydon 1912 and 1917; 7th East Surrey Regt. B.E.F. France 1916. † RA 4, ROI 3.

JACKSON, Miss D. Exh. 1937-38
Erdington, Birmingham 1937; Atherstone, Warwicks 1938. † B 2.

JACKSON, Diana Exh. 1901-35
Mrs. Morton. Miniature portrait painter. Add: Addlestone, Surrey 1901; London 1923; Bexhill on Sea, Sussex 1926. † L 7, RA 4, RI 15.

JACKSON, Mrs. E. Exh. 1882
The Rookery, Middleton. † M 1.

JACKSON, Enid Exh. 1900-8
Portrait and figure painter. Add: Birkenhead 1900; St. Ives, Cornwall 1905. † GOU 3, L 11, LS 5, NEA 3.

JACKSON, Evelyn Exh. 1898-1903
Landscape painter. 101 Tulse Hill, London. † L 1, RA 1, RI 2.

JACKSON, Miss E.B.W. Exh. 1889
Ashnest, West Hill, Sydenham, London. † B 1.

JACKSON, Edith C. Exh. 1891-93
Watercolour flower, fruit and bird painter. Add: Nottingham. † N 4.

JACKSON, E. Dudley Exh. 1901-3
40 Dover Street, London. † RI 2.

JACKSON, Emily E. Exh. 1881-84
Landscape and architectural painter. Add: The Rectory, Stoke Newington, London. † RA 3, RBA 1, SWA 2.

JACKSON, Emily F. Exh. 1880-94
Flower painter. Add: Beechwood, Carshalton, Surrey. † B 6, D 11, G 2, GI 5, L 6, M 3, RA 14, RBA 3, RI 7, SWA 17.

JACKSON, Mrs. E.H. Exh. 1901
The Cabin, Blackburn, Lancs. † L 1, SWA 1.

JACKSON, Edward H.T. Exh. 1937
Landscape painter. Add: 19 Mersey Road, Liverpool. † RA 1.

JACKSON, E. Jeaffreson Exh. 1884-87
Architectural painter. Add: 9 Highbury Grove, London. † RA 3.

JACKSON, Edith M. Exh. 1889
Landscape painter. Herkomer's Schools, Bushey, Herts. † RID 1.

JACKSON, Miss F. Exh. 1903
32 Musters Road, West Bridgford, Notts. † N 1.

JACKSON, The Rev. Frederick C. Exh. 1880-84
Marine painter. Add: St. Ruan Rectory, Nr. Helston, Cornwall 1880; Stanmore, Middlesex 1884. † D 1, RA 1.

JACKSON, Francis Ernest 1872-1945
Portrait painter and lithographer. Studied Paris. Instructer in drawing at R.A. Schools. A.R.A. 1944. "Mrs. Beasley" (1936-37) purchased by Chantrey Bequest 1940. Exh. from 1907. Add: London. † COO 6, FIN 1, GI 3, I 12, L 8, M 6, NEA 14, P 1, RA 25, RHA 8, RSA 1.

JACKSON, Frank G. Exh. 1882-1902
Birmingham 1882; Olton, Warwicks. 1900. † B 12.

JACKSON, Frederick Hamilton 1848-1923
Painter, illustrator and designer. Studied R.A. Schools. R.B.A. 1890. Add London. † B 34, D 12, G 1, GI 4, L 5, M 10, NG 3, RA 18, RBA 181, RHA 2, RI 11, ROI 2.

JACKSON, Frederick William* 1859-1918
Landscape and marine painter. Studied Oldham School of Art, Manchester Academy and Paris. Travelled in Italy and Morocco. N.E.A. 1886, R.B.A. 1894. Add: Chadderton, Nr. Manchester 1880; Middleton Junction, Nr. Oldham and Manchester 1882; Hinderwell, Yorks. and Manchester 1905. † B 10, GI,1, GOU 3, L 25, M 65, NEA 10, RA 52, RBA 16, ROI 7.

JACKSON, G.E.V. Exh. 1912
Bottesford Rectory, Notts. † N 1.

JACKSON, Gerald Goddard Exh. 1907-36
Portrait and landscape painter. Add: London 1907 and 1912; Stamford, Lincs. 1910; Penn, Bucks. 1922; Westleton, Suffolk 1924. † I 2, L 4, LS 5, NEA 2, RA 9.

JACKSON, Mrs. Harry Exh. 1926-29
8 Beechbank Road, Liverpool. † L 2.

JACKSON, Hazel Exh. 1935-36
31 Thurloe Square, London. † RSA 4.

JACKSON, Helen d. 1911
Painter and illustrator of children's books. Exh. 1884-1906. Add: 101 Tulse Hill, London. † B 1, L 2, RA 7, RBA 3, RI 4, ROI 1, SWA 9.

JACKSON, Herbert Exh. 1898-1900
University College, Liverpool. † L 3.

JACKSON, Honora Exh. 1912-39
Mrs. Guy J. Miniature portrait painter. Add: Longcroft, Devises, Wilts. † AR 2, L 1, RA 5, RI 1, SWA 9.

JACKSON, Herbert P. Exh. 1890-1901
Landscape and portrait painter. Add: Warwick Road, Earl's Court, London. † L 1, NG 1, P 2, RA 3, RID 5, ROI 1, RSA 1.

JACKSON, H. Sinclair Exh. 1887-96
1 Cyprus Villas, South Avenue, Polstoe Road, Exeter. † M 8.

JACKSON, H.Y. Exh. 1890
Flower painter. Add: Etchingham House, Finchley, London. † RBA 1.

JACKSON, Mrs. H. Yates Exh. 1904
Illustrative painter. Add: 4 Whitehall Court, London. † RA 1.

JACKSON, Joseph Exh. 1887-1901
Preston, Lancs. † L 5.

JACKSON, J.A. Exh. 1921-29
Portrait painter. Add: 9 Wilford Terrace, Waterway Street, Nottingham. † N 31.

JACKSON, James Eyre Exh. 1882-1906
Landscape and figure painter. Add: Heathfield, Sussex 1882; Torquay 1883; Polgate, Sussex 1884; Eastbourne 1906. † M 1, RA 4, RBA 2.

JACKSON, Miss J.M. Exh. 1904
12 Forest Road, Birkenhead. † L 1.

JACKSON, Kate Exh. 1885
29 Tennyson Street, Nottingham. † N 1.

JACKSON, L. Exh. 1885
Landscape painter. Add: 16 Barnsbury Terrace, Windmill Road, Chiswick, London. † RBA 2.

JACKSON, Miss L. Exh. 1887
12 Forest Road, Birkenhead. † L 1.

JACKSON, Lucy J. Exh. 1889-90
Figure, landscape and interior painter. Add: 79 Warwick Road, South Kensington, London. † RID 5.

JACKSON, M. Exh. 1882
3 Wellington Terrace, Taunton, Som. † B 1.

JACKSON, Miss M. Exh. 1937-38
5 Oak Street, Kingswinford, Nr. Dudley, Worcs. † B,2.

JACKSON, Maggie Exh. 1886-88
Landscape painter. Add: 29 Tennyson Street, Nottingham. † N 2.

JACKSON, Marion Exh. 1889-1913
Landscape and portrait painter. Add: London 1889; Pirbright, Surrey 1906. † L 1, RA 1, RID 26.

JACKSON, Mason 1819-1903
Painter and engraver. Editor of the "Illustrated London News" for 35 years. Exh. 1895-97. Add: London. † RBA 1, RI 2.

JACKSON, Matthew Exh. 1900-9
61 Jane Street, Glasgow. † GI 4.

JACKSON, Mildred Exh. 1902-16
Miniature portrait painter. Add: 43 Longridge Road, Earl's Court, London. † I 1, RA 1, RMS 1, SWA 1.

JACKSON, Mrs. Marie Blanche Exh. 1923-37
Portrait, flower and interior painter. b. France. Studied Westminster, Slade School and Juliens, Paris. Add: 11 Cheyne Place, Chelsea, London. † ALP 1, COO 4, L 1, NEA 3, RA 2, RI 1.

JACKSON, Muriel Blomfield b. 1901
Portrait painter, wood engraver and mural decorator. Daughter of A. Bloomfield J. q.v. Studied Central School of Arts and Crafts. Exh. 1923-40. Add: London. † NEA 7, RA 5, RED 5.

JACKSON, Margaret E. Exh. 1904
† RMS 1.

JACKSON, Mary M. Exh. 1894
Blenheim House, Olton, Warwicks. † B 1.

JACKSON, Mrs. Nell Exh. 1937
Grove Road, Hampstead, London. † SWA 1.

JACKSON, Miss Nellie Exh. 1889-93
216 Upper Parliament Street, Liverpool. † L 3.

JACKSON, Nena Exh. 1921-23
† G 7.

JACKSON, R. Exh. 1905-6
Marsh End, Knottingley, Yorks. † RCA 2.

JACKSON, Stanley b. 1917
Painter. Studied St. Martins School of Art. R.B.A. 1940. Exh. 1939-40. Add: 13 Bower Hill, Epping, Essex. † RA 1, RBA 4.

JACKSON, Miss S.A. Exh. 1921-30
Lea End House, Alvechurch, Warwicks. † B 5.

JACKSON, Samuel Phillips* 1830-1904
Landscape and marine painter. b. Bristol. Studied under his father Samuel J. (1794-1869) A.R.W.S. 1853, R.W.S. 1876. Add: Henley on Thames 1880; Clifton, Bristol 1888. † AG 12, B 1, L 13, M 6, RA 2, RWS 217, TOO 2.

JACKSON, Sir Thomas Graham c.1836-1924
Architect (Examination Schools, Oxford). A.R.A. 1892, R.A. 1896. Knighted c.1912. Add: London. † D 3, RA 90.

JACKSON, Therese M. Exh. 1895-99
12 Forest Road, Birkenhead. † L 8.

JACKSON, T.W. Exh. 1882
36 Falkland Road, Egremont, Cheshire. † L 1.

JACKSON, Walter Exh. 1885
2 Kenilworth Terrace, Portland Road, Nottingham. † N 1.

JACKSON, Winifred Exh. 1905-35
Hollywood, Chorlton cum Hardy, Manchester. † RCA 4.

JACKSON, Miss W.H. Exh. 1915-39
Brighton 1915; The Nunnery, Diss, Norfolk 1916. † L 2, RA 3, RI 2.

JACKSON, Miss W.L. Exh. 1900
85 Grosvenor Road, Wavertree, Liverpool. † L 1.

JACKSON, Wilfrid Scarborough b. 1871
Watercolour painter and black and white artist. Studied Heatherleys. Exh. 1924. Add: 17 Edwardes Square, London. † RA 1.

JACKSON, W.W. Exh. 1924-31
23 Upper Grosvenor Road, Handsworth, Birmingham. † B 2.

JACOB, Edith Exh. 1882-1910
Watercolour flower painter. Add: London 1882, 1888 and 1892; Waterloo, Liverpool 1886; Egremont, Cheshire 1887 and 1890. † BG 7, L 5, RA 3, RI 13.

JACOB, Eleanor Exh. 1899-1905
Crane Lodge, Salisbury, Wilts. † SWA 12.

JACOB, Ella Exh. 1881-98
Landscape painter. The Close, Salisbury, Wilts. † SWA 12.

JACOB, G.N. Exh. 1908
c/o F. Batchelor, A.R.H.A., 86 Merrion Square, Dublin. † RHA 2.

JACOB, J.E. Otto Exh. 1905-10
Flower painter. Add: South Woodford, Essex. † BG 2, LS 11, RA 3, RI 1.

JACOB, Jessie M. Exh. 1933
Stained glass artist. 50 Ferne Park Road, Stroud Green, London. † RA 1.

JACOB, L. Exh. 1892-96
Gladstone Street, Waterford, Ireland. † RHA 4.

JACOB, Max Exh. 1922
† GOU 1.

JACOB, W.H. Exh. 1904-8
57 Cooper Street, St. Helens, Lancs. † L 6.

JACOBI, M.M. Exh. 1882
207 Sherlock Street, Birmingham. † B 1.

JACOBS, Helen Mary Exh. 1910-28
Painter and illustrator of childrens books. Studied West Ham Municipal College. Add: Buckhurst Hill, Essex 1910; Winchmore Hill, London 1914. † D 2, RA 5, RI 2.

JACOBS, John E. Exh. 1880-1915
Landscape painter. R.B.A. 1896. Add: London. † RA 9, RBA 27, ROI 1.

JACOBS, J.F. Exh. 1884
Flower painter. Add: 17 Fitzroy Street, London. † RBA 1.

JACOBS, Louisa Exh. 1884-89
Sculptor. London. † RA, RBA 5, ROI 1.

JACOBS, Louise R. Exh. 1910-38
Landscape and flower painter. Add: London 1910; Hull 1923; New Malden, Surrey 1935. † I 1, L 30, P 1, RA 8, RBA 1, RCA 4, RHA 13, ROI 2, RSA 2, SWA 1, WG 42.

JACOBSEN, Susan Exh. 1939
† NEA 2.

JACOBSON, Miss S. Howard Exh. 1880
Flower and fruit painter. Add: 71 Balfour Road, Highbury New Park, London. † SWA 2.

JACOBY, Prof. Louis Exh. 1884-93
Engraver. Add: Berlin 1884; Charlottenburg, Germany 1893. † RA 4.

JACOMB-HOOD, Agnes Exh. 1888-96
Landscape, interior and portrait painter. Add: 25 Bramham Gardens, South Kensington, London. † RBA 1, RID 13.

JACOMB-HOOD, George Percy* 1857-1929
Painter, illustrator, etcher and sculptor. Studied 3 years at Slade School and at L'Ecole des Beaux Arts, Paris. Visited Greece 1896, Delhi 1902, India on the Prince and Princess of Wales' Tour 1905 and George V's tour of 1911 whilst artist correspondent with the "Graphic". Founder Member N.E.A. 1886, R.B.A. 1884, R.E. 1881, R.O.I. 1902, R.P. 1891. Add: London. † B 22, BG 1, FIN 3, G 15, GI 11, L 31, M 12, NEA 4, NG 32, P 17, RA 54, RBA 25, RE 30, RHA 2, RID 4, ROI 22, WG 312.

JACOMIN, Alfred Louis b. 1842
French artist. Exh. 1882-89. St. Germain en Laye, France 1882; Chaton, France 1883. † GI 6.

JACQUE, Charles* 1813-1894
French painter. Exh. 1893. † GI 1.

JACQUES, A. Exh. 1905-6
130 Mill Lane, London. † RA 2.

JACQUES, Charles Exh. 1922-30
21 St. Stephens Square, Bayswater, London. † FIN 1, ROI 1.

JACQUES, J. Exh. 1929
167 Gt. Howard Street, Liverpool. † L 1.

JACQUES, Miss L. Exh. 1914
Clumber Avenue, Mapperley, Nottingham. † N 1.

JACQUET, Achille 1846-1908
French etcher. Exh. 1886-94. Add: Paris. † RA 3.

JACQUET, C. Exh. 1914-15
Brussels, Belgium 1914; Barnet, Herts. 1915. † L 2, LS 3, RA 1, RI 1.

JACQUET, Gustave* 1846-1909
French painter. Exh. 1884-97. Add: c/o Tooth and Sons, 5 Haymarket, London. † G,1, TOO 28.

JACQUET, Jules 1841-1909
French engraver. Exh. 1884-97. Add: Avenue de la Grande Armee, Paris. † RA 2.

JACQUIER, Bernard Exh. 1900
25 Mawson Street, Ardwick Green, Manchester. † M 1.

JACQUIER, Ivy G.M. Exh. 1925
Painter and illustrator. † CHE 2.

JACQUIER, Marcel Exh. 1907-9
100 Rue d'Amsterdam, Paris. † L 3.

JAFFE, Miss L. Exh. 1929-30
41 Parkfield Road, Sefton Park, Liverpool. † L 3.

JAGGARD, Walter R. Exh. 1896-1917
Architect. Add: London 1896 and 1912; Twickenham, Middlesex 1900; New Barnet, Herts. 1909. † RA 8.

JAGGER, Charles Sargeant 1885-1934
Sculptor. A.R.A. 1926. Add: London. † RA 29.

JAGGER, Davis Exh. 1917-40
Figure, portrait and landscape painter. A.R.B.A. 1919, R.B.A. 1921. Add: Chelsea, London. † CHE 4, G 3, GI 2, L 19, M 1, P 15, RA 27, RBA 14, ROI 22, RSA 3.

JAGGER, Edith Exh. 1932-38
Flower painter. Add: 70 Millhouses Lane, Sheffield. † RA 3, RI 3, ROI 7.

JAGGER, E.L. Exh. 1921
Carlton Studio, 4 Andover Place, Maida Vale, London. † L 1.

JAGGER, Mrs. Ethel May Exh. 1933
Cardiff, Wales. † RCA 2.

JAGGER, Wilson Exh. 1900
Still life painter. Add: 39 Mortimer Road, Roath Park, Cardiff, Wales. † RA 1.

JAGGS, Miss Alex Reid Exh. 1929-30
14 Meadowcroft Road, Wallasey, Cheshire. † L 5.

JAHN, A.C.C. Exh. 1898-1901
Municipal School of Art, Wolverhampton. † B 3.

JAHN, Francis Exh. 1901-28
Sculptor. Add: Hanley, Staffs. 1901; Sheffield 1907. † B 3, GI 3, L 4, RA 18.

JAKOBIDES, Georg Exh. 1886
Figure painter. Add: 26 Gothestrasse, Munich. † RA 1.

JALLAND, G.H. Exh. 1901
Figure and domestic painter. † FIN 83.

JAMAR, Armand Exh. 1912-13
74 Rue de la Consolation, Brussels. † L 1, RSA 1.

JAMES, Miss Exh. 1936
Cardiff, Wales. † RCA 1.

JAMES, A. Exh. 1917
Gwavas Studios, Newlyn, Cornwall. † RA 1.

JAMES, Alice Exh. 1884-1930
Miniature painter. R.M.S. 1896. Add: Soho, London 1884; Bath 1887; Clifton, Bristol 1908. † D 3, L 30, NG 1, RA 19, RMS 50.

JAMES, A. Collier Exh. 1931-38
Architect and painter. Add: Derby. † B 5, N 2, RCA 6, RSW 1.

JAMES, Arthur C. Exh. 1888-89
Landscape painter. Add: Eton College, Berks. † RI 4.

JAMES, Alan Gosset 1875-1950
Landscape painter. "Winter on the Windrush" purchased by Chantrey Bequest 1938. Add: London 1911; Naunton, Glos. 1938. † GOU 1, NEA 2, RA 6.

JAMES, Alfred Percy Exh. 1901-8
Figure and religious painter. Add: Derwent House, Blessington Road, Lee, London. † L 1, NG 2, RA 4.

JAMES, C. Exh. 1881
Landscape painter. Add: 14 Arundel Place, Haymarket, London. † RBA 2.

JAMES, Caroline Exh. 1924-34
Miniature painter. Add: 8 Ernall Place, Uplands, Swansea. † RA 2.

JAMES, C. Boucher Exh. 1900-13
Figure and domestic painter. Add: 552 Oxford Street, London and Halsannerry, Bideford, Devon. † B 4, LS 1, M 1, RA 3, RSA 1.

JAMES, C.E. Exh. 1924-29
28 Glebe Place, London. † P 2, ROI 3.

JAMES, Charles Holloway b. 1893
Architect. A.R.A. 1937. Exh. 1927-30. Add. London. † RA 3.

JAMES, Charlotte Isa Exh. 1880-1914
Flower painter. S.W.A. 1880. Add: London. † B 1, L 2, M 2, SWA 39.

JAMES, C.K. Exh. 1911-27
Allerton, Liverpool 1911; Bushey, Herts. 1924. † L 5.

JAMES, Clifford R. Exh. 1919
Colour Mezzotint engraver. Add: Fortfield, Weston super Mare, Som. † L 1.

JAMES, David* Exh. 1883-97
Marine painter. Add: Plymouth 1883; Bowden, Devon 1885; Dalston 1886; London 1892. † B 2, M 1, RA 4.

JAMES, Dora Exh. 1897
Portrait painter. Add: 3 Hamilton Gardens, London. † RA 1.

JAMES, Doris Dixon Exh. 1925-31
Landscape and tree painter. Add: Southsea, Hants. 1925; Cheadle, Staffs. 1927. † B 5, RA 3, RBA 3, RI 2, ROI 4, SWA 1.

JAMES, E. Exh. 1920-25
Redditch, Worcs. † B 6.

JAMES, Miss Edith Exh. 1883-96
Portrait and flower painter. Add: Eton College, Bucks. 1883; London 1885; Paris 1890; Tunbridge Wells, Kent 1891. † B 6, G 1, L 5, M 3, NG 1, RA 3, RBA 2, RID 4, RSA 2, SWA 1.

JAMES, Ernest C. Exh. 1894-1927
Landscape painter. Add: Nottingham 1894; Keyworth, Notts. 1909; Plumtree, Notts. 1919; Wilford, Notts. 1924. † N 10.

JAMES, E. d'O. James Exh. 1885
Landscape painter. Add: c/o 293 Oxford Street, London. † SWA 2.

JAMES, Miss Frances Exh. 1903-27
Tormaston Rectory, Chippenham, Wilts. 1903; Waterford, Ireland 1904; Bray, Co. Wicklow, 1908; Kingstown, Ireland 1911. † B 1, L 2, RHA 18.

JAMES, Fred Exh. 1893
117 Moss Lane, Manchester. † M 1.

JAMES, Francis Edward 1850-1920
Flower and landscape painter. Self taught. Suffered through illness for most of his life. N.E.A. 1888, R.B.A. 1884, A.R.W.S. 1908, R.W.S. 1916. Add: Hastings, Sussex 1883; Tuston, N. Devon 1902; Instow, N. Devon 1903; Torrington, Devon 1913. † AG 1, BA 29, BG 28, D 3, FIN 46, G 1, GI 3, GOU 19, L 17, LEI 123, M 2, NEA 133, RBA 14, RSA 2, RSW 1. RWS 30, TOO 16, WG 2.

JAMES, Frederick George Exh. 1903
Landscape painter. Add: 5 Addington Road, Nottingham. † N 5.

JAMES, Frank James Exh. 1888-90
Landscape painter. Add: London 1888; Weybridge, Surrey 1890. † RA 2, RBA 3.

JAMES, Gilbert Exh. 1886-95
Figure and still life painter. Add: Fairfield, Liverpool 1886; London 1892. † L 4, NEA 2.

JAMES, G.C. Exh. 1913
20 Byron Road, West Bridgford, Notts. † N 1.

JAMES, Henry Exh. 1911
Springfield House, Springfield Street, Lancaster. † L 1.

JAMES, Harry E. Exh. 1882-1912
Landscape and coastal painter. Add: London 1882 and 1892; Mevagissey, Cornwall 1890; Heavitree, Exeter 1894; Upton, Nr. Andover, Hants. 1907. † B 1, D 1, L 14, LS 6, M 1, RA 7, RBA 2, RCA 1, RI 6, ROI 13.

JAMES, Miss J.C. Exh. 1906
Devonshire. † SWA 1.

JAMES, Jeanette E. Exh. 1908-9
11 Holmeside Road, Kew Gardens, London. † LS 4.

JAMES, Jessie Frances Exh. 1921
Landscape painter. Add: 5 Hardy Street, Mount Hooton Road, Nottingham. † N 1.

JAMES, J. King Exh. 1882
1 St. James Road, Birmingham. † B 2.

JAMES, Louisa Exh. 1881
Watercolour landscape painter. Add: 128 Belgrave Road, London. † SWA 1.

JAMES, Laura Gwenllian Exh. 1897-1907
nee Rice. Landscape painter. m. Walter John J. q.v. Add: 1 Courtfield Road, London. † M 1, NG 5, RA 8.

JAMES, Mary Exh. 1880-87
Flower, figure and still life painter. Add: 81 White Lion Street, Islington, London. † SWA 9.

JAMES, Mrs. Margaret Calkin Exh. 1939
Flower and landscape painter. Add: Hornbeams, Winnington Road, London. † RA 1.

JAMES, Marie E. Exh. 1889
Landscape painter. Add: West View, Vickers Street, Nottingham. † N 1.

JAMES, O.F. Exh. 1936
6 Asmuns Place, London. † SWA 1.

JAMES, Percy L. Exh. 1904
Architect. Add: 6 Milton Park, Hornsey Lane, London. † RA 1.

JAMES, Richard S. Exh. 1880-1900
Genre painter. Add: Brixton, London. † RA 13, RBA 6.

JAMES, Hon. Robert St. Nicholas Exh. 1913-14
Flower and still life painter. Add: Richmond, Yorks. † NEA 2.

JAMES, S. Exh. 1882-90
Landscape painter. London. † RA 1, RBA 1.

JAMES, S. Exh. 1924
Still life painter. Add: Grey Street, Newthorpe Common, Newthorpe, Notts. † N 1.

JAMES, Sarah Exh. 1880-93
Figure painter. Add: West Tilbury, Essex. † B 1, D 13, M 1, SWA 15.

JAMES, T.E.L. Exh. 1905-8
27 Chancery Lane, London. † RA 5.

JAMES, Vyvyan Exh. 1915-20
Westways, Beaconsfield, Bucks. † B 3, RI 2, ROI 1.

JAMES, Winifred Exh. 1915-32
Wallasey, Cheshire 1915; Parbold, Lancs. 1926. † L 3, NEA 1.

JAMES, Walter John 1869-1932
Lord Northbourne. Painter and etcher. Studied under Davis Cooper and Frank Short. Trustee of the Wallace Collection. Married Laura Gwenllian J. q.v. A.R.B.A. 1919, R.B.A. 1920, A.R.E. 1909, R.E. 1912. Add: London 1897; Eastry, Kent 1926. † B 1, FIN 48, GI 6, L 2, LS 5, M 1, NG 7, RA 29, RBA 12, RE 29, RHA 3, RID 1.

JAMES, W.R.L. Exh. 1908
309 Ladbroke Grove, London. † RI 1.

JAMESON, Agnes Exh. 1899
9 The Grove, Blackheath, London. † RBA 2, ROI 1.

JAMESON, Cecil Exh. 1910-37
Portrait and landscape painter. R.P. 1921. Add: Hospitalfield, Arbroath, N.B. 1914; London 1920. † FIN 14, GI 2, GOU 1, I 6, L 3, NEA 1, P 82, RA 6, RHA 1, ROI 3, RSA 1.

JAMESON, Mrs. E.M. Exh. 1914-23
Rye, Sussex 1914; Bridgnorth, Salop 1923. † L 2, LS 6.

JAMESON, Frank b. 1899
Figure, portrait and landscape painter and etcher. Exh. 1921-39. Earlier works signed F. Jameson-Smith. Add: 28 Mason Road, Redditch, Worcs. † B 7, RA 2, RBA 3, ROI 3.

JAMESON, Flora H. Exh. 1935
Black and white artist. † WG 8.

JAMESON, Georgina Exh. 1896
Still life painter. Add: 61 Broadhurst Gardens, Hampstead, London. † RA 1.

JAMESON, Col. H.W. Exh. 1913-14
Titness Cottage, Sunninghill, Berks. † D 9.

JAMESON, Mrs. H.W. Exh. 1914-16
Titness Cottage, Sunninghill, Berks. † LS 6.

JAMESON, Mrs. Joan Exh. 1933-38
Flower, figure and landscape painter. Studied at Juliens, Paris. Add: Tourin, Cappoquin, Waterford, Ireland. † GOU 1, LEI 67, RED 1, RHA 3.

JAMESON, J.A.H. Exh. 1883-1923
Donnybrook, Ireland 1883; Bideford, Devon 1888; Kingstown, Ireland 1905; Castle Bellingham, Ireland 1907. † RHA 28.

JAMESON, Mrs. J.B. Exh. 1900
Alexandra Hall, Blackheath, London. † SWA 2.

JAMESON, John Blaxland Exh. 1909-14
Belvedere Cottage, Rye, Sussex. † LS 15.

JAMESON, Kenneth Ambrose b. 1913
Exh. 1939-40. Add: 24 Raglan Road, Edgbaston, Birmingham. † B 1, RBA 1.

JAMESON, Mrs. Lena Exh. 1911-12
Cheltenham, Glos. 1911; London 1912. † LS 7.

JAMESON, Margaret Exh. 1909-20
Mrs. H. Bacon. Flower and portrait painter. Add: London. † L 1, RA 3, SWA 1.

JAMESON, Mrs. Mellor Exh. 1916
Limnerslee Studios, Belvedere Road, Liverpool. † L 3.

JAMESON, Middleton* d. 1919
Landscape, figure and flower painter. Add: Paris 1881; London 1887 and 1903; Etaples, Pas de Calais, France 1888; Glasgow 1896. † B 2, GI 6, L 8, LS 4, RA 18, RI 5, ROI 4, RSA 3.

JAMESON, M.L. Exh. 1930
10 Charlbert Street, London. † NEA 1.

JAMESON, Marcia Maziere Exh. 1895
Balmoral Castle Avenue, Clontarf, Ireland. † RHA 1.

JAMESON, Rosa Exh. 1885-95
Figure and domestic painter. Add: London 1885; Wadhurst, Sussex 1890. † L 5, RA 4, RBA 1, RI 3, ROI 3.

JAMESON, R.P. Exh. 1936
Watercolour coastal painter. † FIN 3.

JAMESON-SMITH, Frank
See JAMESON, Frank

JAMIESON, Alexander* 1873-1937
Landscape and portrait painter. b. Glasgow. Studied Glasgow Haldane Academy School of Art, and Paris. Served in France World War I. Married Biddy MacDonald q.v. R.O.I. 1927. Add: Paris 1899; London 1901 and 1921; Weston Turville, Aylesbury, Bucks. 1920 and 1925. † AG 1, CAR 39, CHE 2, G 2, GI 15, GOU 35, I 27, L 12, LS 13, M 1, NEA 18, P 6, RA 14, ROI 20, RSA 15.

JAMIESON, Mrs. Biddy See MACDONALD

JAMIESON, Hazel D. Exh. 1908
The Dean, Bowness. † RSA 1.

JAMIESON, Isabel Exh. 1880-96
Mrs. A. Flower painter. Add: St. Helens, Lancs. 1880; London 1889. † D 2, L 3, M 1, RA 4, RI 2.

JAMIESON, Mary Exh. 1885-86
Paris 1885; Old Aberdeen 1886. † GI 2.

JAMIESON, P.T. Exh. 1905-16
London. † GI 1, L 1, RA 3.

JAMIESON, Robert Kirkland b. 1881
Landscape painter. b. Lanark. Studied London, Glasgow and Paris. Lecturer on art, Shoreditch Training College for teachers. Headmaster Westminster School of Art 1933-39. Married Dorothea Selous q.v. A.R.B.A. 1922, R.B.A. 1925, R.O.I. 1932. Add: London. † AG 2, COO 1, D 10, GI 4, GOU 5, L 2, NEA 10, RA 11, RBA 101, RED 1, RI 6, ROI 13, TOO 2.

JAMIESON, Mrs. R. Kirkland
See SELOUS, Dorothea

JAMIESON, Sarah Exh. 1890
Flower painter. Add: 33 Magdala Street, Belfast. † RI 1.

JAMIESON, W.H. Exh. 1911-18
A.N.S.A. 1922. Add: Wollaton, Notts. 1911; Mapperley, Nottingham 1918. † N 3.

JANE, Fred T. Exh. 1894
Black and white artist. Add: 12A Edith Terrace, Fulham Road, South Kensington, London. † RA 1.

JANES, C.J. Exh. 1928
40 Farnbridge Road, Maldon, Essex. † NEA 1.

JANES, Margarite Exh. 1916-31
Landscape, coastal and figure painter. Add: London. † GOU 60, I 6, L 3, NEA 4, P 3, RA 2.

JANES, Norman b. 1892
Painter, etcher and wood engraver. b. Egham, Surrey. Studied Slade School, Central School of Arts and Crafts and Royal College of Art. A.R.E. 1921. Exh. 1922-40. Add: London. † BA 10, CHE 3, G 1, GI 3, GOU 3, I 2, M 2, NEA 22, RA 20, RE 43, RED 3, RHA 1.

JANNOCH, Vena Exh. 1898-1922
Flower painter. Add: Dersingham, Kings Lynn, Norfolk 1898; London 1916. † RA 5, RMS 1.

JANSEN, Fritz Exh. 1883-85
Portrait painter. Add: 57 Bedford Gardens, Campden Hill, London. † L 2, RA 1, RI 1, ROI 4.

JANSON, Gunnar b. 1906
Norwegian artist. Exh. 1933. Add: Kunsternes Hus, Oslo. † RSA 2.

JANSON, Sophia Exh. 1881-85
Watercolour landscape painter. Add: The Grove, Park Lane, Croydon, Surrey. † SWA 5.

JANSSENS, Jacques Exh. 1882
10 Avenue Wappers, Antwerp. † GI 1.

JANSSENS, Rene b. 1870
Belgian painter and lithographer. Studied Ecole des Beaux Arts, Brussels. Exh. 1921. Add: 138 Ave Moliere, Brussels. † RSA 2.

JAPP, Miss Exh. 1890
c/o A. Brownlie Doherty, 134 Bath Street, Glasgow. † GI 2.

JAPP, Darsie b. 1883
Landscape painter. N.E.A. 1919. Exh. 1912-21. Add: London. † GOU 1, NEA 10.

JAQUES, Mrs. B. Exh. 1911
Leighton Dene, Hylands Road, Epsom, Surrey. † RA 1.

JAQUES, Charles H.B. Exh. 1919-23
† P 3.

JAQUES, F.W. Exh. 1890-97
Knowle, Warwicks. 1890; Leamington, Warwicks. 1893; Edgbaston, Birmingham 1896. † B 8.

JAQUES, Jules Exh. 1882
Landscape painter. Add: 3 Mawsom Row, Chiswick, London. † RBA 1.

JAQUES, Lilian Exh. 1904
Portrait painter. Add: 76 Francis Street, Leeds. † RA 1.

JAQUET, Cecilia Exh. 1890-1909
Landscape painter. Add: Southwark London. † D 32, G 1, NG 1, RBA 2, RI 1 SWA 8.

JARDALLA, Miss J.G. Exh. 1925-28
5 Adelaide Road, Seaforth, Liverpool. † L 6.

JARDINE, Aeta Exh. 1917-40
Painter. Add: Glasgow 1917 and 1921, Hunters Quay, Argyllshire 1918; London 1929. † GI 6, RA 1, RBA 1, ROI 1, RSA 4, RSW 1.

JARDINE, Mrs. James (E.A.)
Exh. 1885-1913
Landscape painter. A.S.W.A. 1901, S.W.A 1905. Add: London. † ALP 12, D 55, L 2, LS 8, RA 2, RI 1, SWA 58, WG 40.

JARDINE, Jessie Exh. 1927-28
5 Manchester Road, Chorlton cum Hardy, Manchester. † L 4.

JARDINE, Miss Jet S. Exh. 1917-40
Watercolour painter. Add: Helensburgh, N.B. 1917; Hunters Quay, Argyllshire 1918; London 1927. † GI 3, RA 4, RI 5, RSA 5, SWA 2.

JARDINE, Thomas Exh. 1884
29 Brougham Street, Edinburgh. † RSA 1.

JARL, Viggo Exh. 1918
† I 2.

JARMAN, Henry T. Exh. 1899-1938
Landscape and figure painter. Add: Leytonstone, Essex 1899; West Hampstead, London 1914. † L 1, RA 15, RBA 3, RCA 2, RI 12, ROI 4.

JARMAN, Nesta Exh. 1933-38
Portrait and miniature painter. b. Sutton, Surrey. Studied Cardiff School of Art and Heatherleys. Add: 52 Brean Down Avenue, Weston super Mare, Som. † RA 2, RCA 3, RMS 1.

JARVIS, Mrs. A.J. Exh. 1902
Furze Cottage, Eastliss, Hants. † SWA 1.

JARVIS, A.W. Exh. 1902-6
Architect. London. † RA 3.

JARVIS, Elizabeth Scott Exh. 1914-19
Portrait painter. Add: 27 Crescent Lane, Clapham Park, London. † RA 2, RMS 1.

JARVIS, Frank B. Exh. 1937-39
Architectural painter and etcher. Add: 2 Mabel Grove, West Bridgford, Notts. † N 6.

JARVIS, George Exh. 1881-90
Figure and domestic painter. Add: Lancaster Road, Belsize Park, London. † B 2, L 3, M 2, RA 2, RBA 6, RI 1, ROI 3.

JARVIS, Hilda Exh. 1940
Landscape painter. Add: 25 Foxley Road, Thornton Heath, Surrey. † RA 1.

JARVIS, Henry C. 1867-1955
Watercolour landscape painter. Studied Goldsmiths College. Add: London 1904 and 1922; Billinghurst, Sussex 1915; Sevenoaks, Kent 1935. † AB 17, D 18, RA 12, RI 3.

JARVIS, J. Bradford Exh. 1912
Whistler Studios, 8 Fitzroy Street, London. † RA 1.

JARVIS, Matthew Exh. 1880-87
Watercolour landscape painter. Add: Liverpool. † B 1, L 16, M 12, RA 1, RBA 1, RI 2, RSA 1.

JARVIS, Muriel Exh. 1927
† M 1.

JAY, Carrie Exh. 1880-83
Landscape painter. Add: London 1880; Wimbledon 1882; Lee, Kent 1883. † M 1, RBA 2.

JAY, Miss Cecil Exh. 1902-28
Miniature painter. Married 1st George Hitchcock q.v. (d.1913), 2nd O.V. Calder. R.M.S. 1904. Add: Bushey, Herts. 1902; c/o J.W. Payne, Cannon Street, London 1905; Paris 1908; London 1927. † L 9, RA 18, RMS 5.

JAY, Miss F. Exh. 1905-20
2 Geneva Terrace, Peterborough 1905; 9 The Temple, Dale Street, Liverpool 1920. † L 2, RA 4.

JAY, Hamilton Exh. 1880-1913
Landscape and figure painter. Add: London 1880; Abinger Hammer, Dorking, Surrey 1885; South Harting, Nr. Petersfield, Hants. 1887; Yapton, Nr. Arundel, Sussex 1895; Littlehampton, Sussex 1904. † L 3, M 1, NG 1, RA 8, RBA 10, ROI 1.

JAY, J.A.B. Exh. 1880-83
Painter. Add: Beverley, Yorks. 1880; Hertford 1882. † L 3, RA 1.

JAY, Jane Isabella Lee Exh. 1881-1909
Flower, fruit and landscape painter. Add: London. † LS 11, RA 1, RBA 1, RCA 2, SWA 9.

JAY, Leonard Exh. 1938
83 Doveridge Road, Hall Green, Birmingham. † B 6.

JAY, Mrs. M. Langdon Exh. 1926
15 Kremlin Drive, Stoneycroft, Liverpool. † L 1.

JAY, T.G. Exh. 1888
Fairstead, Littledown Street, Bournemouth. † B 2.

JAY, Miss V.R. Exh. 1928-33
7 Thoroton Road, West Bridgford, Notts. † N 2.

JAY, William Samuel* 1843-1933
Landscape painter. R.B.A. 1889. Add: London 1880; Arundel, Sussex 1890; Littlehampton, Sussex 1897. † B 3, G 10, GI 1, L 19, M 14, NG 10, RA 20, RBA 46, ROI 5, TOO 2.

JEAKES, Kingsley Exh. 1934-37
Landscape painter. Add: March Mill House, Henley on Thames. † COO 6.

JEAN, Thomas Exh. 1921
† GOU 1.

JEANNIN, Georges* 1841-1925
French artist. Exh. 1882 and 1901. Add: Paris. † L 1, RHA 1.

JEANNIOT, Pierre George* 1848-1934
French painter and etcher. A.R.E. 1904. Exh. 1904-9. Add: Paris. † L 2, RE 11.

JEANS, Miss D.I. Exh. 1934-39
Winchester House, Sherwood, Nottingham. † N 2.

JEANS, Fanny H. Exh. 1897-98
Gt. Sankey, Warrington, Lancs. † L 2.

JEANS, Rev. T. Jeffery Exh. 1929
5 Chatworth Grove, Whalley Range, Manchester. † L 1.

JEANSON, de See D

JEANSON-VIGOUREUX, Mme. E.L. Exh. 1912
54 Avenue du Maine, Paris. † L 1.

JEAYES, Constance L. Exh. 1930
Interior painter. Add: Lutterworth Road, Nr. White Stone Nuneaton, Warwicks. † RA 1.

JEAYES, Josephine Exh. 1891
7 Victoria Gardens, Southsea, Hants. † D 3.

JEBB, Gertrude Exh. 1902-39
Flower painter. Add: Fairyfield, Gt. Barr, Birmingham. † B 11, RA 1, RI 2.

JEBB, Kathleen Mary b. 1878
Painter, etcher and black and white artist. b. Liverpool. Assistant evening teacher, Municipal School of Art, Bristol. Exh. 1905-30. Add: 49 Westbury Road, Bristol. † B 2, L 28, RA 6, RSA 2.

JEBB, Mrs. Rose Exh. 1927-39
Watercolour painter. Add: London. † RBA 1, SWA 2, WG 38.

JEE, Amy Exh. 1901-3
19 Moody Terrace, Congleton, Cheshire. † L 1, RI 1.

JEEVES, Mrs. Catherine Exh. 1898
Ruswarp Hall, Whitby. † B 1.

JEEVES, Mrs. C.C. Exh. 1888
Victoria Park, Manchester. † M 1.

JEEVES, Louisa Exh. 1884-86
Figure painter. Add: Sun Street, Hitchin, Herts. 1884 and 1886; 27 Brunswick Square, London 1885. † B 1, RBA 1, RHA 2, SWA 1.

JEEVES, S. Gordon Exh. 1925-38
Architect. Add: 16 Hanover Square, London. † RA 9, RSA 2.

JEFFAY, Saul Exh. 1920
c/o Bathgate, 108A West Regent Street, Glasgow. † RSA 1.

JEFFCOCK, Charles Augustine Castleford b. 1872
Landscape painter. b. Wolstanton, Staffs. Studied Keble College, Oxford (Law degree). 4 years technical study at Heatherleys in the winters and under Claude Hayes in the summers. Exh. 1905-34. Add: London 1905 and 1913; Harpenden, Herts. 1912; Brighton 1927; The Haven, Seaview, I.O.W. 1928. † RA 4, RI 4, WG 214.

JEFFCOCK, Robert Salisbury Exh. 1906-11
R.B.A. 1911, A.R.M.S. 1906, R.M.S. 1908. Add: Ringstead, Harpenden, Herts. † L 4, NG 1, RBA 4, RMS 18.

JEFFERIES, Miss B.S. Exh. 1913-28
c/o Mrs. Hitcham, Devereux House, West Cliff, Whitby 1913; Redland, Bristol 1920. † L 3.

JEFFERIES, E.C. Exh. 1887-94
Battlefield, Bromsgrove, Birmingham. † B 4, L 1.

JEFFERIES, Edith S. Exh. 1906-10
Bedford 1906; Bournemouth 1908. † B 2, RCA 7, SWA 2.

JEFFERIES, Mrs. Gladys Exh. 1932
12 Robert Road, Handsworth, Birmingham. † B 2.

JEFFERIES, Hilda E. Exh. 1911-15
7 Logan Road, Bishopston, Bristol. † L 8, RHA 2.

JEFFERIES, Katherine Grant See HARTNELL

JEFFERIES, Miss Star Exh. 1938-40
Bristol. † RCA 2.

JEFFERIES, Wilfred Avalon b. 1907
Domestic painter. b. Bristol. Exh. 1940. Add: 132A High Street, Portsmouth. † RA 1.

JEFFERIS, Miss A.C. Exh. 1896-98
19 Lexham Gardens, London. † SWA 2.

JEFFERSON, Miss Exh. 1894
Strandtown, Belfast. † SWA 2.

JEFFERSON, C.G. Exh. 1880-1902
Glasgow 1880; South Shields 1895. † GI 18, RSA 11.

JEFFERY, Miss Annie Exh. 1884-90
Flower and fruit painter. Add: Gt. Haywards, Haywards Heath, Sussex. † B 2, D 2, M 2, RA 1, RBA 2, ROI 1.

JEFFERY, Elizabeth C. Exh. 1881
Watercolour painter. Add: Rome and 2 Charlton Villas, Old Charlton, Kent. † RBA 1, SWA 1.

JEFFERYS, Miss Bertha Exh. 1889-1901
Flower painter. Add: Hampstead, London. † RBA 2, RI 1, SWA 10.

JEFFERYS, Marcel* 1872-1922
Landscape painter. Exh. 1896-1920. Add: Brussels 1896; Chelsea, London 1917. † GI 1, GOU 5, L 2, NEA 8, RSA 1.

JEFFREY, Edward b. 1898
Exh. 1936-40. † RI 3.

JEFFREY, George Exh. 1895
Architect. Add: c/o H.J. Murcott, 6 Endell Street, Long Acre, London. † RA 1.

JEFFREY, James Hunter b. 1874
Landscape painter and textile designer. Studied at School of Art, Belfast and Royal College of Art. Teacher at Belfast School of Art, Municipal College of Technology and at Bangor Municipal Technical School. Chief designer at Henry Matier and Co. Ltd., Belfast. Exh. 1914-20. Add: Belfast. † RHA 15.

JEFFREY, Rachel S. Exh. 1901
14 Randolph Crescent, Edinburgh. † RSA 2.

JEFFREYS, Anne Exh. 1929
† NEA 1.

JEFFREYS, Mrs. Annie M. Exh. 1912-27
Landscape painter. A.N.S.A. 1922. Add: Nottingham 1912; West Bridgford, Notts. 1915. † N 36.

JEFFREYS, Charles William b. 1869
Royal Canadian Academician. b. Rochester, Kent. Exh. 1933. † RSW 2.

JEFFREYS, Edith Gwyn Exh. 1885-89
Sculptor. Add: London. † RA 9.

JEFFREYS, Gwendoline M. Exh. 1923-27
Miniature painter. Add: Killa Croft, Sketty, Swansea. † RA 2.

JEFFRYES, T. Arnold Exh. 1938
1 Gordon Square, London. † GI 1.

JEFFS, James G. Exh. 1938-40
The Yellow Door Studio, Dumfries. † GI 3.

JEHLY, Jacob Exh. 1891
Portrait painter. Add: c/o C. Healy, Esq., Croxley Green, Rickmansworth and Austria. † RA 1.

JELL, G. Thrale Exh. 1909-24
Architect. Add: London. † RA 6.

JELLAR, S. Exh. 1885
3 Slater Street, Liverpool. † L 1.

JELLETT, Miss Mainie H. Exh. 1918-37
Painter. Add: 36 Fitzwilliam Square, Dublin. † LS 9, RHA 32.

JELLEY, Mrs. Edith M. Exh. 1922-40
Mrs. J.V. Add: Solihull, Warwicks. 1922; Knowle, Warwicks. 1940. † B 52, RI 4.

JELLEY, James Valentine* Exh. 1883-1940
Landscape and flower painter. R.B.S.A. 1891. Add: Birmingham 1883; Hampton in Arden, Warwicks. 1890; Solihull, Warwicks. 1920; Knowle, Warwicks. 1940. † B 172, BG 1, FIN 1, G 1, L 3, RA 44, RI 3.

JELLICOE, J. Exh. 1880-87
Watercolour figure painter. Add: London. † D 1, RBA 1.

JELLICOE, Mary E. Exh. 1909-28
Portrait and landscape painter. Add: London 1909; Brighton 1928. † B 1, L 1, SWA 1.

JEMMETT, Arthur R. Exh. 1889-94
Architect. Add: 47 Alexandra Road, Wimbledon, London. † RA 2.

JEMMETT, Mary Kate Exh. 1904-24
Miniature painter. b. Tunbridge Wells, Kent. Studied Calderons School; under Alyn Williams and at Paris. Add: Feltham, Middlesex 1904; Guildford, Surrey 1915; Folkestone, Kent 1920. † B 10, GI 1, L 12, M 1, RA 1, RCA 6, RHA 3, RI 9, SWA 3.

JENKIN, M.M. (Mrs. B.) Exh. 1910-12
Camden Street, Kensington, London. † GI 3, L 3, RA 3, RSA 4.

JENKINS, Anne Exh. 1880-85
Flower and still life painter. Add: Berners Street, London. † D 3, G 2, RA 6, RBA 4, ROI 1, RSA 3, SWA 1.

JENKINS, Arthur F. Exh. 1905-6
75 Ombersley Road, Birmingham. † B 2.

JENKINS, Arthur Henry b. 1871
Landscape and figure painter. Studied Edinburgh School of Art and Colarossi's, Paris. Art master at King's School, Bruton, Som. Art master Trinity College, Glenalmond and Edinburgh Academy. m. Violet Edgecombe H. q.v. Exh. 1898-1938. Add: Galashiels, N.B. 1898; Edinburgh 1900; Bathampton, Som. 1920; Bath 1928; Newbury, Berks. 1930; Little Bedwyn, Wilts. 1934. † BA 114, GI 9, L 16, RA 16, RCA 5, RSA 40, RSW 3.

JENKINS, Miss A.L. Exh. 1904
The Rectory, Galashiels. † L 1.

JENKINS, Blanche Exh. 1880-1915
Portrait, figure, domestic and flower painter. A.S.W.A. 1886, S.W.A. 1899. Add: London. † B 19, D 1, G 4, GI 5, L 30, M 21, NG 17, P 2, RA 37, RBA 5, RHA 2, ROI 10, RSA 7, SWA 30.

JENKINS, C.H. Exh. 1936
Cardiff. † RCA 1.

JENKINS, David C. d. 1916
Landscape and rustic painter. Add: London 1884; Nottingham 1886; Liverpool 1890. † L 52, M 1, N 10, RA 7, RBA 1, ROI 1.

JENKINS, Miss E.M. Exh. 1909
Miniature portrait painter. Add: 111 Highbury Quadrant, London. † RA 1.

JENKINS, Mrs. Elizabeth T. Exh. 1938
Twitchells End, Jordans, Bucks.

JENKINS, Emily V. Exh. 1889-1906
Interior and architectural painter. Add: 38 St. Margarets Road, Oxford. † B 1, D 2, RBA 1, RI 5.

JENKINS, Frank Lynn 1870-1927
Sculptor. b. Torquay. Collaborated with Gerald Moira q.v. Died in New York. Exh. 1896-1915. Add: London. † GI 1. I 1, L 9, LS 3, RA 23, RI 1.

JENKINS, Joseph John 1811-1885
Watercolour painter and engraver. A.R.I. 1842, R.I. 1843, A.R.W.S. 1849, R.S.W. 1850. Add: St. John's Wood, London. † RSW 14.

JENKINS, Lincoln P. Exh. 1929-39
Painter and wood engraver. Married to Phyllis J. q.v. Add: Southdown Avenue, South Road, Handsworth, Birmingham. † B 29, RA 4.

JENKINS, Miss M. Exh. 1907
Malvern Link, Worcs. † SWA 1.

JENKINS, Myfanwy b. 1908
Miniature painter. Add: 1 Bryn Toe, Mountain Hare, Merthyr Tydfil, Wales. † RA 1.

JENKINS, Mrs. Phyllis Exh. 1929-30
Watercolour landscape painter. Married to Lincoln P.J. q.v. Add: Southdown Avenue, Handsworth, Birmingham. † B 4, RA 1.

JENKINS, Reginald Exh. 1932
WAtercolour landscape painter. Add: 97 Elgin Crescent, London. † RA 1.

JENKINS, Violet Edgecombe Exh. 1900-21
nee Shepherd. Painter and illustrator of childrens books. Married Arthur Henry J. q.v. Add: Methley, Leeds 1900; Edinburgh 1907; Bathampton, Som. 1920. † GI 4, L 12, RA 1, RSA 5, RSW 2.

JENKINS, W. Exh. 1885
230 Marylebone Road, London. † L 1.

JENKINSON, Charlotte F.A. Exh. 1880-89
Landscape painter. Add: Ilfracombe, Devon 1880; Holyport, Maidenhead, Berks. 1889. † G 1, SWA 1.

JENKINSON, J.H. Exh. 1889
Crowborough, Tunbridge Wells, Kent. † D 5.

JENKS, Alfred J. Exh. 1891-1938
Liverpool 1891 and 1909; Rock Ferry, Cheshire 1901; Higher Tranmere, Cheshire 1906. † L 64, RCA 16.

JENKYNS, Mrs. H. Exh. 1884
Landscape painter. Add: Riverside, East Molesey, Surrey. † SWA 2.

JENNENS, Luke Exh. 1880-97
Watercolour figure painter. Add: Fulham, London 1880; Harrow, Middlesex 1881; Fulmer, Bucks. 1897. † RA 3.

JENNINGS, Mrs. Alix Exh. 1927
nee Thomson. Figure painter. b. Carlisle. Add: Pera, Fellows Road, Farnborough, Hants. † RA 1.

JENNINGS, Charles Exh. 1919-35
Landscape painter. Add: Sutton in Ashfield, Notts. † N 31.

JENNINGS, Edward Exh. 1881-88
Watercolour landscape painter. Add: London. † D 1, RA 4, RI 2.

JENNINGS, Emma M. Exh. 1880-84
Architectural painter. Add: 14 Malcolm Road, Penge, Kent. † RBA 1, SWA 4.

JENNINGS, E. Owen b. 1899
Painter, etcher, engraver and illustrator. b. Cowling, Yorks. Studied Skipton School of Art 1917-19, Leeds College of Art 1920-22 and Royal College of Art 1923-36. 2nd master Doncaster School of Art. Add: London 1925; Skipton, Yorks. 1929; Leeds 1930; Tunbridge Wells, Kent 1935. † NEA 1, RA 14.

JENNINGS, Edward W. Exh. 1885
Architectural artist. Add: Heathcliffe, Swansea. † RA 1.

JENNINGS, Frank Exh. 1929
Architect. Add: 39 St. James Street, London. † RA 1.

JENNINGS, F. Nevill Exh. 1902-8
Miniature portrait painter. Add: London. † L 5, LS 5, RA 3.

JENNINGS, Leonard 1877-1956
Sculptor. Studied Lambeth School of Art, Glasgow School of Art and R.A. Schools. Sculptor to Government of India 1907-9 Exh. 1904-39. Add: London. † GI 1, I 1, L 4, NG 1, P 2, RA 30, RI 1.

JENNINGS, Mary Exh. 1885-87
Miniature portrait painter. Add: 33 Brunswick Terrace, Brighton. † RA 2.

JENNINGS, Reginald George 1872-1930
Figure, portrait, landscape and miniature painter. Studied National Art Training School and Westminster School of Art. Instructor in painting at King's College for Women and Instructor in painting and design for Middlesex County Council. Add: London 1906 and 1925; Siena, Italy 1924. † L 1, LS 6, NG 1, RA 3, RI 12, WG 71.

JENNIS, Gurnell C. Exh. 1910-36
Etcher. A.R.E. 1914. Add: London. † CHE 2, I 4, L 7, NEA 1, RA 9, RE 8.

JENNISON, George Exh. 1926-37
28 Park Drive, Grimsby, Lincs. † L 5, RI 1.

JENNY, Mrs. A. Exh. 1925-26
Ingleton, Aigburth Hall Road, Edgbaston, Birmingham. † L 3.

JENSEN, George Exh. 1922-29
Silver worker. Add: 56 Maddox Street, London. † L 248, RA 1.

JENSEN, L. Exh. 1905-6
Nylandsvij 4B, Copenhagen. † RA 2.

JEPHSON, Lady Alfred (Harriet J.) Exh. 1884-1923
Landscape painter. Travelled widely. Add: East Cowes, I.O.W. 1884; London 1888. † D 26, G 2, NG 4, RBA 5, RI 10, SWA 10, WG 64.

JENSON, Alexander George b. 1899
Architect. Studied Liverpool University School of Architecture. Articled to Nicol and Nicol, Birmingham architects 1916-17 and 1919-22. Exh. 1922-25. Add: 20 Carpenter Road, Edgbaston, Birmingham. † B 4

JEPHSON, Ina Exh. 1925
Sibyl Hill, Raheny, Co. Dublin. † GI 1.

JEPHSON, Miss S.H. Exh. 1911
4 Cornwall Gardens, London. † NEA 1.

JEPSON, Sybil F.E. Exh. 1929
Watercolour landscape painter. Add: 10 Highdown Avenue, West Worthing, Sussex. † RA 1.

JERACE, Professor I.L. Exh. 1911
c/o Dudley Galleries, 169 Piccadilly, London. † M 5.

JERDAN, James Exh. 1892-1921
74 George Street, Edinburgh 1892; 12 Castle Street, Edinburgh 1895. † RSA 13.

JERDAN, John Exh. 1896-1938
12 Castle Street, Edinburgh. † RSA 6.

JERMYN, Frederick H. Exh. 1895-96
Dublin. † RHA 3.

JERROLD, Daphne Exh. 1929-31
Flower painter. Add: 18 Rosecroft Avenue, Hampstead, London. † RA 3.

JERROLD, Dorothy Exh. 1908-40
Flower painter. Add: Surbiton, Surrey 1908; 304 Elgin Avenue, London 1916; Charmouth, Dorset 1932. † I 2, LS 6, RA 5, RBA 5, ROI 4, RSA 1, SWA 12.

JERROLD, Phyllis Exh. 1932-38
Flower and portrait painter. Add: 23 Malborough Road, London. † NEA 1, P 1, RA 3, RSA 2, SWA 6.

JERSEY, de See D

JERVIS, Edward de Rosen Exh. 1890-1900
Landscape painter. Add: Roseneath, Sidmouth, Devon 1890; Wallingford, Berks. 1900. † RBA 3.

JERVIS, Miss W. Exh. 1903-4
The Cliff House, Felixstowe, Suffolk. † SWA 3.

JESPER, Charles Frederick Exh. 1920-33
Painter, etcher and black and white artist. Studied Victoria School of Art, Southport, Lancs. Add: 24 Southbank Road, Southport, Lancs. † L 4.

JESSE, Miss Cicely M. Exh. 1907
Myrtle Cottage, Newlyn, Penzance. † L 1.

JESSE, Miss W.T. Exh. 1907-9
Myrtle Cottage, Newlyn, Penzance. † L 3.

JESSEL, Robert Exh. 1932-34
Watercolour painter. † RED 40.

JESSETT, Claude Exh. 1892
Craigland, Bycullah Park, Enfield, Middlesex. † B 1.

JESSON, Henry Exh. 1884
1 Belmont Terrace, Stillorgan, Ireland. † RHA 1.

JESSOP, Effie G. Exh. 1909-15
Sculptor. Cavendish Crescent, The Park, Nottingham 1909; Kensington, London 1913. † L 2, N 2, RSA 2.

JESSOP, Ernest Maurice Exh. 1883-1907
Painter and etcher. Add: London. † BK 35, L 2, RA 3.

JESSOP, Florence M. Exh. 1882-1903
Sculptor, painter and leatherworker. Add: Nottingham. † N 15.

JESSUP, Miss E.M. Exh. 1917
6 Walpole Road, Twickenham, Middlesex. † RA 1.

JETTEL, Eugen* 1845-1901
Landscape painter. c/o Sedelmeyer, Rue Rochefoucauld, Paris, 1884. † GI 1.

JEUNE, le See L

JEVONS, A. Exh. 1889
Ben Venlee, Lockgoilhead, Glasgow. † GI 1.

JEVONS, Mrs. F. Exh. 1882
1 Beresford Road, Birkenhead. † M 1.

JEVONS, George W. Exh. 1891-96
Landscape painter. Add: Liverpool 1891; Roswick St. Martin, Cornwall 1894. † L 7, M 2, NEA 1, RA 2.

JEVONS, Mrs. Louisa E. Exh. 1893-1901
Miniature portrait painter. Add: Durham. † RA 2, RMS 1.

JEVONS, Mary C. Exh. 1880-86
Landscape painter. Add: London 1880; Bridgwater, Som. 1886. † D 3, RI 1.

JEVONS, W. Howard Exh. 1922-40
Newlyn, Barnet Green, Birmingham. † B 14.

JEWELL, Evangeline Exh. 1936
95 High Road, London. † ROI 1.

JEWESBURY, Miss L. Exh. 1916
39 Avonmore Road, Kensington, London. † RA 1.

JEWITT, Clement W. Exh. 1895-1907
Sculptor. Add: London. † B 3, L 1, M 1, RA 4, RBA 1, RI 1.

JEWITT, Edward Holmes Exh. 1881
Stained glass artist. Add: c/o Shrigley and Hunt, Lancaster. † RA 1.

JEWITT, Mrs. S.M.B. Exh. 1918-20
Bank House, Melbourne, Derbys. † N 2.

JEWITT, W.H. Exh. 1882-1910
Manchester 1882; London 1907. † M 1, RA 3.

JEWSON, Norman b. 1884
Architect and craftsman. Studied A.A. articled to H.G. Ibberson 1905-8, pupil and assistant to Ernest W. Gimson, Architect and Craftsman 1908-14, independent practice since 1914. Exh. 1918-36. Add: Sapperton, Cirencester, Glos. † RA 2.

JEX-BLAKE, Evangeline Exh. 1886-1913
Figure painter. Add: Dusseldorf 1886; Alvechurch Rectory, Redditch, Worcs. 1887; The Deanery, Wells, Som. 1893; London 1913. † B 10, D 65, ROI 2.

JEYES, Edith Exh. 1910
6 Lichfield Road, Kew Gardens, Surrey. † B 1.

JILLARD, Hilda K. Exh. 1928
The Bungalow, Park Lane, Kings Lynn, Norfolk. † B 1.

JIMINEZ, Manuel Exh. 1885
Spanish artist. Add: 6 Rue Boissonade, Paris. † GI 1.

JIMINEZ-y-ARANDA, Luis* b. 1845
Spanish painter. Exh. 1884-86. Add: 6 Rue Boissonade, Paris. † GI 5.

JJONAH, See JONES, Langford

JOASS, John J. Exh. 1896-1936
Architect. Add: London. † RA 15, RSA 6.

JOB, E.W. Exh. 1928
103 Gantshill Crescent, Ilford, Essex. † RI 1.

JOBBINS, W.A. Exh. 1890
Holborn Chambers, 14 Broad Street Corner, Birmingham. † B 1.

JOBBINS, William H. Exh. 1881-93
Landscape painter. Add: 4138 Riva degli Schiavoni, Venice. † FIN 3, M 1, RA 2, RI 1, ROI 2.

JOBLING, Mrs. Isa See THOMPSON

JOBLING, Robert* 1841-1923
Genre, river and marine painter. Studied at evening classes at Newcastle School of Art. Married Isa Thompson q.v. Exh. 1883-1911. Add: Newcastle on Tyne. † B 2, L 7, RA 20, RBA 1.

JOBSON, P.A. Exh. 1938
Goatsway, 3 The Meadway, Buckhurst Hill, Essex. † RBA 1.

JOBSON, R.H. Exh. 1940
Presteigne, Wales. † RCA 1.

JOEL, Constance Exh. 1928
Miniature portrait painter. Add: Eversley Lodge, Winchmore Hill, London. † RA 1.

JOEL, Grace J. Exh. 1903-22
Figure and landscape painter. A.S.W.A. 1916. Add: London. † BG 33, GOU 1, L 1, LS 14, P 4, RA 3, ROI 2, RSA 2, SWA 4.

JOETS, Jules* Exh. 1923
97 Rue de Dunkerque, St. Omer, Pas de Calais, France. † RSA 1.

JOHN, Augustus Edwin* 1878-1961
Portrait and decorative painter and etcher. b. Tenby, Wales. Brother of Gwen J. q.v. Studied at Slade School 1894-98. Travelled widely on the continent and spent many of his holidays travelling with gypsies. Professor of painting Liverpool University. Trustee of Tate Gallery. Married Ida Nettleship q.v. Father of Edwin and Vivien J. q.v. N.E.A. 1903, A.R.A. 1921, R.A. 1928 (resigned 1938 and re-elected 1940), R.P. 1926. Hon. Member London Group 1940. "Lord David Cecil" purchased by Chantrey Bequest 1935, "W.B. Yates" (1907) in 1940, "Blue Cineraria" (c.1928) in 1940, "Edward Grove" (1940) in 1957 and "Theodore Powys" (c.1932) in 1958. Add: London 1900 and 1918; Parkstone, Dorset 1915; Fryern Court, Fordingbridge, Salisbury, Wilts. 1935. † AG 12, ALP 117, BA 86, BAR 7, BK 15, CAR 131, CG 47, CHE 377, COO 1, FIN 28, G 26, GI 18, GOU 90, I 12, L 25, LEF 4, LEI 86, LS 1, M 27, NEA 141, P 14, RA 24, RCA 13, RED 41, RHA 10, RSA 21, TOO 85.

JOHN, C. Exh. 1918-20
26 Queen's Road, Bromley, Kent and 2 Milton Road, Highgate, London. † RCA 3.

JOHN, Edwin b. 1905
Watercolour painter. Son of Augustus J. q.v. and Ida Nettleship q.v. Exh. 1937. † BA 50, CON 37.

JOHN, Gwendoline May* 1876-1939
Portrait painter. b. Haverfordwest, Wales. Sister of Augustus J. q.v. Studied Slade School, (Melvill Nettleship Prize for figure composition 1897) and Whistlers School in Paris. Lived in France for most of her life. Several of her works are in the Tate Gallery. Exh. 1900-26. † CAR 3, CHE 48, NEA 12.

JOHN, Vivien b. 1915
Watercolour figure and portrait painter. Daughter of Augustus J. q.v. and Dorelia McNeill. Exh. 1935-38. † COO 14, RED 1.

JOHN, Sir William Goscomb 1860-1952
Sculptor. b. Cardiff, the son of a sculptural carver. Studied Cardiff School of Art, City and Guilds of London School of Art and R.A. Schools (gold medal and travelling studentship 1889). Designed the regalia for Investment of the Prince of Wales at Carnarvon (1911) and George V Silver Jubilee Medal (1935). A.R.A. 1899, R.A. 1909, H.R.I. 1918. Knighted c.1911. "A Boy at Play" purchased by Chantrey Bequest 1896. Exh. from 1886. Add: London. † ALP 1, B 1, GI 17, I 1, L 29, NG 5, P 4, RA 181, RI 8, ROI 3, RSA 11.

JOHNES, Sydney Exh. 1926-33
Liverpool 1926; Birkenhead 1933. † L 2.

JOHNS, Miss A.M. Exh. 1919
15 Beckenham Road, Beckenhan, Kent. † SWA 1.

JOHNS, Cecil Starr Exh. 1909-13
Oak Cottage, Dormans Park, Surrey. † L 2, LS 13.

JOHNS, Edwin Thomas Exh. 1905-39
Watercolour urban landscape painter. Add: Ipswich, Suffolk. † RA 8.

JOHNS, Miss F.B. Exh. 1928-30
19 Palm Hill, Oxton, Birkenhead. † L 6.

JOHNS, Louis A. Exh. 1908
1 Pleasant Street, Blackpool. †, L 2.

JOHNS, Miss O.M. Exh. 1919
15 Beckenham Road, Beckenham, Kent. † SWA 1.

JOHNSON, Alfred Exh. 1881-87
Landscape painter. Add: 1A Ruvigny Gardens, Putney, London. † L 2, RA 1, RBA 4, ROI 3.

JOHNSON, A.C. Exh. 1937-40
7 Ladbrooke Road, Solihull, Warwicks. † B 5.

JOHNSON, A.H. Exh. 1909-28
Landscape painter. Add: 8 Grundy Street. Nottingham. † N 51.

JOHNSON, Mrs. A. Ingram Exh. 1909
3 Park Hill, Ealing, London. † L 1.

JOHNSON, Alfred J. Exh. 1880-85
Figure and domestic painter. London. † D 3, L 2, RA 4, RBA 1, RI 2.

JOHNSON, Alice M. Exh. 1908-10
Still life painter. Add: Duke William Mount, The Park, Nottingham. † N 4.

JOHNSON, Barbara Exh. 1897-1933
Mrs. Wallace Stratton. Flower painter. b. Essex. Daughter of Edward Killingworth J. q.v. Add: Harrow, Middlesex 1897; London 1898. † BA 1, COO 2, L 4, NG 5, P 3, RA 3, ROI 1, WG 141.

JOHNSON, Beatrice Exh. 1938
Tunbridge Wells, Kent. † SWA 2.

JOHNSON, Mrs. Bessie Exh. 1885-1933
nee Percival. Landscape, portrait and figure painter. Studied St. John's Wood School of Art. Add: Trinity College, Oxford 1885; Rugby 1907, Eton College, Windsor 1918. † D 7, I 7, L 1, RA 13, RI 1, RID 9, ROI 2, WG 109.

JOHNSON, Miss Bertha J. Exh. 1901-20
Miniature portrait painter. A.R.M.S. 1907. Add: The Homestead, Hornsey Lane, London. † L 7, NG 2, RA 10, RCA 1, RMS 28, SWA 2.

JOHNSON, Bertha J. (Mrs. A.H.) Exh. 1880-82
Portrait painter. Add: 22 Norham Gardens, Oxford. † D 1, RA 2.

JOHNSON, Bertram V. Exh. 1895
Architect. Add: 50 Queen Anne's Gate, London. † RA 1.

JOHNSON, Mrs. C. Exh. 1881-91
Landscape, flower and still life painter. Add: Nottingham. † N 12.

JOHNSON, Cyrus 1848-1925
Landscape, genre and miniature portrait painter. R.I. 1887, R.O.I. 1887. Add: London. † AG 1, B 7, FIN 1, G 3, L 8, M 1, P 2, RA 39, RBA 6, RHA 3, RI 36, ROI 76, RSW 1.

JOHNSON, Cecil A. Exh. 1904-11
Sculptor. London. † L 3, LS 2, RA 2.

JOHNSON, Charles Edward* 1832-1913
Landscape painter. b. Stockport. Studied R.A. Schools. Conducted a school for landscape painting at Richmond, Surrey. R.I. 1882, R.O.I. 1883. "The Swineherd: Gurth, Son of Beowulph" purchased by Chantrey Bequest 1879. Add: Haverstock Hill, London 1880; Richmond, Surrey 1896. † AG 2, B 27, FIN 2, G 2, GI 22, L 21, M 17, NG 1, RA 54, RBA 1, RHA 1, RI 78, ROI 74, TOO 6.

JOHNSON, Clara L. Exh. 1923-24
Landscape painter. Add: 19 Bingham Road, Sherwood, Notts. † N 6.

JOHNSON, Col. C.R. Exh. 1880-89
Landscape painter. Add: London 1880; Dublin 1885. † RA 11, RBA 1.

JOHNSON, Charles V. Exh. 1894
Architect. Add: 119 Gt. Russell Street, Bloomsbury, London. † RA 2.

JOHNSON, Charles William Exh. 1908-27
Watercolour painter and etcher. b. Birmingham. Studied Birmingham School of Art. Art master at Charterhouse. Add: Charterhouse, Godalming, Surrey. † B 2, L 2, M 1, NEA 2, RA 17.

JOHNSON, Drayton Exh. 1901
Canal Side, Water Tower Street, Chester. † L 1.

JOHNSON, Dorothy A. Exh. 1923-29
Portrait painter. Add: Nottingham. † N 7.

JOHNSON, Edith b. 1902
Miniature portrait painter, illuminator and teacher. b. Leicester. Studied Derby School of Art. Exh. 1923-36. Add: 84 Eden Street, Alvaston, Derby. † L 2, RA 7, RMS 2.

JOHNSON, Eli Exh. 1880-81
Sculptor. Add: 11 High Street, Eccleston Square, London. † RA 1, RHA 2.

JOHNSON, Evelyn Exh. 1900-11
Landscape painter. Add: 4 The Terrace, Richmond, Surrey. † GOU 1, RBA 1.

JOHNSON, Ernest Borough* b. 1866
Painter, etcher, lithographer and pencil artist. b. Shifnal, Salop. Studied Slade School and Herkomer's, Bushey, Herts. Professor of Fine Arts, Bedford College, London University. Headmaster for 15 years of the Art Department Chelsea Polytechnic, teacher of Life Painting and Drawing at the London School of Art and at Byam Shaw and Vicat Cole School of Art. R.B.A. 1896, R.I. 1906, R.O.I. 1903, R.M.S. 1897, R.P. 1937. Married Esther B.J. q.v. Exh. 1886-1940. Add: Bushey, Herts. and Basingstoke, Hants. 1886; London 1897 and 1914; Richmond, Surrey 1909. † B 11, COO 2, DOW 40, FIN 5, G 1, GI 6, GOU 11, I 15, L 8, M 3, NG 8, P 28, RA 50, RBA 55, RI 12, RMS 1, ROI 13, RSA 4.

JOHNSON, Esther Borough Exh. 1896-1940
nee George. Portrait, flower and landscape painter. b. Sutton Maddock, Salop. Studied Birmingham School of Art, Chelsea Art School and Herkomer's, Bushey, Herts. Married Ernest B.J. q.v. Add: Bushey, Herts. 1896; London 1899, 1904 and 1914; Swaffham, Norfolk 1902; Richmond, Surrey 1911. † BA 41, BG 1, CHE 3, GOU 9, I 9, L 12, NG 8, P 17, RA 27, RMS 2, SWA 1.

JOHNSON, Edward Killingworth* 1825-1896
Watercolour landscape and figure painter. Self taught. A.R.W.S. 1866, R.W.S. 1876. Add: Sible Hedingham, Nr. Halstead, Essex 1880, London 1888. † AG 1, B 3, DOW 9, FIN 1, L 19, M 7, RBA 2, RWS 51, TOO 2.

JOHNSON, Franz Exh. 1936
Landscape and figure painter. † FIN 37.

JOHNSON, Frances L. Exh. 1910-11
18 York Avenue, Sefton Park, Liverpool. † L 6.

JOHNSON, G.F. Waldo Exh. 1894-96
London 1894; Salisbury, Wilts. 1896. † B 1, RA 1.

JOHNSON, Gertrude M. Exh. 1897
103 Stirling Road, Edgbaston, Birmingham. † B 1.

JOHNSON, Harry Exh. 1882
12 Ford Street, St. Mary, Nottingham. † N 1.

JOHNSON, Herbert b. 1848
Figure and landscape painter. Exh. 1880-1906. Add: London. † GI 3, L 1, M 7, RA 6, RBA 2, ROI 2.

JOHNSON, Harry John* 1826-1884
Landscape painter. b. Birmingham. Studied Birmingham Society of Arts under Samuel Lines and then William Muller whom he accompanied on the Lycian Expedition to the Levant 1843-44. A.R.I. 1868, R.I. 1870. Add: London. † B 3, L 8, RA 2, RI 27, ROI 8.

JOHNSON, Helen Mary Exh. 1880-81
Figure painter. Add: 106 Gower Street, London. † D 2, SWA 1.

JOHNSON, Helen North Exh. 1897-1935
Flower and landscape painter. Add: Castleknock, Co. Dublin 1897; Booterstown, Ireland 1917. † RHA 56.

JOHNSON, H.W. Exh. 1910
Bank Chambers, Market Harborough, Leics. † RA 1.

JOHNSON, Inez Exh. 1922-40
Miniature painter. A.R.M.S. 1927, R.M.S. 1935. Add: Meopham, Kent 1922; Leicester 1923; 21 South Norwood Hill, London 1924 and 1940; Nottingham 1939. † L 7, N 1, RA 25, RMS 56.

JOHNSON, John Exh. 1883-95
Fernhill, Trefiw, N. Wales. † L 3, RCA 52.

JOHNSON, J.C. Edith Exh. 1881-96
Figure and still life painter. Add: Nottingham 1881; Carrington, Notts. 1888; London 1894. † N 5, RA 1, RI 1.

JOHNSON, J.J. Exh. 1911
Ashleigh Moor, Orleton, Hereford. † LS 2.

JOHNSON, Katharine A. Exh. 1902-25
Flower painter. Add: West Hampstead, London 1902; Hitchin, Herts. 1921. † BG 2, L 5, RA 2, RI 5.

JOHNSON, Miss L. Exh. 1920-23
† SWA 3.

JOHNSON, Miss Laura See KNIGHT

JOHNSON, Lucretia Exh. 1915-17
64 Drakefield Road, Tooting Bec Common, London. † L 1, RA 1.

JOHNSON, Louisa H. Kate Exh. 1894-1912
Landscape, flower and still life painter. Add: Nottingham 1881 and 1897; Carrington, Notts. 1884; Filey, Yorks. 1912. † L 1, N 58, RA 2.

JOHNSON, Mabel Exh. 1883-95
Landscape painter. Add: London. † B 1, RI 1, SWA 1.

JOHNSON, Mrs. Marie Exh. 1896-1908
Landscape painter. Add: Beeston, Notts. 1896; Derby 1904. † N 11.

JOHNSON, Miss Marie Exh. 1902-20
Miniature portrait painter. Add: London. † L 3, RA 15, RMS 2.

JOHNSON, Marjorie Exh. 1914
36 Cardigan Road, Leeds. † L 1.

JOHNSON, Mary Exh. 1893
Shamongate, Kendal, Westmorland. † D 1.

JOHNSON, Mary Exh. 1935
Grinshill, Nr. Shrewsbury. † RSW 2.

JOHNSON, Mary E. Exh. 1891-1903
Landscape and flower painter. Add: Nottingham 1891; Leicester 1901. † N 9.

JOHNSON, Miss M. Labron Exh. 1929
22 Alleray Park Road, Wallasey, Cheshire. † L 1.

JOHNSON, Mrs. M.R. Exh. 1912-14
49 Portsdown Road, Maida Vale, London. † L 1, LS 7, RA 1.

JOHNSON, May S. Exh. 1914-22
Little Island, Co. Cork 1914; Rath Lee, Cork 1915. † RHA 18.

JOHNSON, Norah Exh. 1913-19
Miniature portrait painter. London. † RA 10.

JOHNSON, N.B. Exh. 1938
Landscape painter. Add: The Watch House, Groomsport, Co. Down. † RHA 3.

JOHNSON, Olivia Exh. 1940
† NEA 2.

JOHNSON, Percy F. Exh. 1921
74 Woodchurch Road, Birkenhead. † L 1.

JOHNSON, Mrs. Patty Townsend Exh. 1880-1907
nee Townsend. Landscape and figure painter. S.W.A. 1893. Add: Attleborough Hall, Nuneaton, Warwicks. † D 13, G 1, L 12, M 2, RA 9, RBA 2, RI 31, SWA 31.

JOHNSON, R. Exh. 1912
2a Merivale Road, Putney, London. † RA 1.

JOHNSON, Robin Exh. 1880
Landscape painter. Add: 10 Fitzroy Street, London. † RA 1, RBA 1.

JOHNSON, Miss R.E.W. Exh. 1883-84
Park Avenue, Soho Hill, Birmingham. † B 2.

JOHNSON, Robert J. Exh. 1885-87
Architect. Newcastle on Tyne. † RA 4.

JOHNSON, Mrs. S. Exh. 1905-8
London. † B 6, RA 1, ROI 1, SWA 10.

JOHNSON, Sarah Exh. 1891-92
Watercolour landscape painter. Add: 13 All Saints Street, Nottingham. † N 2.

JOHNSON, Thomas Exh. 1903-11
Architect. Add: Nottingham 1903; West Bridgford, Notts. 1906; London 1907.

JOHNSON, Thomas Crowshaw Exh. 1880
Landscape painter. Add: 28 Leicester Square, London. † RBA 2.

JOHNSON, T.S. Exh. 1919
† L 4.

JOHNSON, Will Exh. 1889
Landscape painter. Add: 274 Swan Arcade, Bradford, Yorks. † RA 1.

JOHNSON, Wynne Exh. 1906-8
Moseley, Birmingham. † B 4.

JOHNSON, Miss W.A. Exh. 1915
19 Corporation Oaks, Nottingham. † N 1.

JOHNSON, William Aloysius b. 1892
Watercolour painter, pencil and crayon artist, etcher and teacher. b. Manchester. Studied Salford School of Art. Travelled on the continent, Africa and North and South America as a boy. Exh. 1926-34. Add: Manchester. † FIN 3, L 6, M 3, RI 1.

JOHNSON, Walter G. Exh. 1905-22
Portrait painter. Add: London 1905; Guildford, Surrey 1922. † L 4, LS 5, RA 6.

JOHNSON, W. Noel Exh. 1887-1914
Landscape painter. Altrincham, Cheshire 1887; Bowden, Cheshire 1890. † B 1, D 6, GI 2, L 8, M 30, RBA 1.

JOHNSON, Walter R.H. Exh. 1922-38
Painter and wood engraver. Add: Liverpool 1922; London 1930. † COO 1, L 2, RA 1.

JOHNSSON, Ivar b. 1885
Sculptor. b. Sweden. Add: Heleneborg, Stockholm 1933. † RSA 3.

JOHNSTON, Alexander* 1815-1891
Historical, genre and portrait painter. Studied Trustees Academy, Edinburgh 1831-34 and R.A. Schools 1836. Add: London. † B 7, GI 6, L 1, M 1, RA 4, RHA 2, ROI 4.

JOHNSTON, Mrs. Alice A.P. Exh. 1925
7 Wester Coates Road, Edinburgh. † RSA 1.

JOHNSTON, Arnrid Banniza b. 1895
Sculptor, carver and modeller. b. Uddevalla, Sweden. Studied Slade School (scholarship, Countessa Feodora Gleichen Memorial Prize 2 years running). Exh. 1917-40. Add: London. † NEA 1, RA 1.

JOHNSTON, Charles S.S. Exh. 1890-91
10A North St. David Street, Edinburgh. † GI 1, RSA 2.

JOHNSTON, Dorothea M.S. Exh. 1914-15
36 Devonshire Road, Claughton, Birkenhead. † L 7.

JOHNSTON, Edward 1872-1944
Illuminator, calligrapher and writer. b. Uruguay. Studied at the British Museum. Teacher of writing and illumination with the London County Council 1899. Teacher at the Royal College of Art. Exh. 1908. Add: London, later moving to Ditchling, Sussex. † L 6, NG 1.

JOHNSTON, Graham Exh. 1917
H.M. Register House, Edinburgh. † RSA 1.

JOHNSTON, Mrs. Hamilton Exh. 1906-10
Cadogan Gardens, London. † SWA 4.

JOHNSTON, Henry Exh. 1896-98
Stirling, Clonee, Co. Meath. † RHA 6.

JOHNSTON, Sir Harry Hamilton c. 1866-1927
Painter and explorer. H.R.W.S. Add: London 1880 and 1903; Tunis 1898; Arundel, Sussex 1907. † B 1, D 2, GI 2, L 3, M 1, RA 16, RWS 13.

JOHNSTON, Hilda R. Exh. 1907-9
9 Greenheys Road, Prince's Gate, Liverpool. † L 4.

JOHNSTON, Helen S. d. 1931
Landscape and figure painter. Glasgow 1916 and 1923; Kirkcudbridge 1917. † GI 28, L 5, RA 5, RSA 23.

JOHNSTON, I. Eva Exh. 1901-10
Glynn, Co. Antrim. † LS 5, RHA 7, SWA 3.

JOHNSTON, Janet Exh. 1880-97
Edinburgh. † GI 1, RSA 18.

JOHNSTON, John Exh. 1888-93
52 Portugal Street, Glasgow. † GI 2, RSA 1.

JOHNSTON, Miss J.G. Exh. 1919
† L 1.

JOHNSTON, J. Humphreys Exh. 1892-93
Landscape painter. Add: 59 Rue de Vaugirard, Paris. † L 3, NEA 2.

JOHNSTON, J. Nicholson Exh. 1883-1907
Architect. Add: London 1883; Yeovil, Som. 1895. † RA 6.

JOHNSTON, Miss J.S. Exh. 1914-22
36 Devonshire Road, Claughton, Birkenhead. † L 13.

JOHNSTON, M.D. Exh. 1939
Watercolour figure painter. † AR 2.

JOHNSTON, Margaret N. Exh. 1887
Balgowrie, Culross. † RSA 1.

JOHNSTON, Maurice O. Exh. 1936
Landscape painter. Add: White Lodge, Bosham, Sussex. † RA 1.

JOHNSTON, N. Exh. 1907-8
Wellwood, Ayr, N.B. † RSA 3.

JOHNSTON, Ninian Exh. 1938
6 Glenbank Road, Lenzie. † GI 2.

JOHNSTON, Phyllis I. Exh. 1917-36
London 1917; Eastbourne 1936. † LS 1, NEA 1, RBA 1.

JOHNSTON, Philip Mainwaring 1865-1936
Architect. Exh. 1885 and 1909. Add: Champion Hill, London. † RA 2.

JOHNSTON, Phyllis St. G. Exh. 1912-14
5 Sanford Parade, Dublin. † RHA 4.

JOHNSTON, Robert B. Exh. 1880-1903
Edinburgh. † GI 8, L 4, M 1, RSA 25.

JOHNSTON, R.F. Exh. 1913-14
1 Brook Street, Hanover Square, London. † RA 4.

JOHNSTON, Ruth J. Exh. 1918-21
Ardoch House, Bearsden 1918; Swansea 1919. † GI 3, RA 1, RSA 1.

JOHNSTON, Stuart b. 1891
Painter and etcher. b. Cupar, Fife. Studied Glasgow School of Art. Exh. 1923-38. Add: Glasgow. † GI 12, L 4.

JOHNSTON, Thomas C. Exh. 1880-86
Edinburgh. † RSA 9.

JOHNSTON, William Exh. 1921-39
Landscape and figure painter. Add: Edinburgh 1921; Glasgow 1928. † GI 9, LEF 5, RSA 5, RSW 3.

JOHNSTON, W.H. Exh. 1883-92
Manchester. † M 3.

JOHNSTON, W. Miles Exh. 1926-38
Landscape, animal and bird painter. Studied Edinburgh College of Art and in America. Add: Edinburgh. † RSA 8.

JOHNSTON, William P.M. Exh. 1914-22
37 Fountainhall Road, Edinburgh. † L 2, RSA 10.

JOHNSTONE, Dorothy b. 1892
Figure painter. Daughter of George Whitton J. q.v. Studied Paris and Florence. Teacher at Edinburgh College of Art 1914-24. Married David M. Sutherland q.v. Exh. 1912-39. Add: Edinburgh 1912; Aberdeen 1931. † GI 20, I 1, L 9, M 1, P 6, RA 3, RSA 56, RSW 1.

JOHNSTONE, Eva Tocque Exh. 1910
Broad Road, Sale, Cheshire. † L 1.

JOHNSTONE, F.J. Exh. 1916-18
47 Ashfield Road, Sneinton, Nottingham. † N 3.

JOHNSTONE, George Whitton 1849-1901
Landscape and portrait painter. b. Glamis, Forfarshire. Studied at the R.S.A. Life School. Father of Dorothy J. q.v. A.R.S.A. 1883; R.S.A. 1895; R.S.W. 1885. Add: Edinburgh. † B 1, DOW 3, GI 37, L 2, RA 13, RSA 103, RSW 28.

JOHNSTONE, Henry James* 1835-1907
Figure painter. b. Birmingham. R.B.A. 1886. Add: London 1881 and 1891; Gt. Marlow, Bucks. 1884; Wadhurst, Sussex 1897. † AG 2, D 12, I 1, L 4, RA 19, RBA 13, TOO 3.

JOHNSTONE, J. Exh. 1910-22
47 Ashfield Road, Sneinton Dale, Nottingham. † N 10.

JOHNSTONE, J.B. Exh. 1882
Glebe Terrace, Dumfries. † RSA 1.

JOHNSTONE, James M. Exh. 1897
Engraver. Add: 42 Deanville Road, Clapham Common, London. † RA 1.

JOHNSTONE, Louis Exh. 1936
† RI 1.

JOHNSTONE, Miss M. Ball Exh. 1915
Belgrano, Hillside Road, Colwyn Bay, Wales. † RCA 1.

JOHNSTONE, Pamela R. Exh. 1939-40
† NEA 2.

JOHNSTONE, Rennie Exh. 1906
21 Hardman Street, Liverpool. † L 1.

JOHNSTONE, William Exh. 1892-1913
Engraver. Edinburgh. † RA 3, RSA 7.

JOLLEY, Martin Gwilt Exh. 1884-1914
Figure and landscape painter. Add: London 1884, 1894 and 1909; Bushey, Herts. 1893; Etaples, Pas de Calais, France 1908. † B 39, DOW,1, L 31, LS 5, M 20, NG 1, P 1, RA 28, RBA 13, RHA 13, RI 2, ROI 10.

JOLLY, Eveline Isabella Exh. 1924-40
Watercolour painter and illuminator. Add: St. George's Lodge, Earlsferry, Elie, Fife. † GI 3, RSA 2, RSW 2.

JOLLY, Stratford D. Exh. 1915-22
Sculptor. 5C Warwick Avenue, Maida Vale, London. † L 1, RA 2.

JOLYET, Phillipe Exh. 1908
Place de la Republique, a Nay, Basses-Pyrenees, France. † L 1.

JONAS, H.E. Exh. 1881-84
31 Wright's Houses, Edinburgh. † RSA 7.

JONAS, Harry M. Exh. 1916-36
Figure and portrait painter. Add: London. † G 1, I 2, RA 4.

JONAS, Lucien Exh. 1912
238 Boulevard Raspail, Paris. † RSA 1.

JONCKHEERE-COX, Mrs. Thirza Exh. 1917-40
Miniature painter. Add: Enfield, Middlesex 1917 and 1934; Observatoire de Lille, Hem, France, Nord 1922. † RA 8.

JONES, Lady Exh. 1930-40
39 Harrington Gardens, London. † RI 14.

JONES, Miss Exh. 1903-6
Normandy House, The Dell, New Ferry, Cheshire. † L 3.

JONES, A. Exh. 1881
Queen's Bays, Dundalk, Ireland. † RHA 2.

JONES, Abel Exh. 1900
29 Mount Street, Liverpool. † L 1.

JONES, Adrian* 1845-1938
Sculptor and painter. b. Ludlow, Salop. Studied under C.B. Birch. Veterinary officer in the Army for 23 years and served in India, the Abyssinian, Boer and Nile Wars. Exh. 1884-1935. Add: London. † BG 1, G 4, GI 7, L 14, LS 4, RA 34, ROI 9.

JONES, Archie Exh. 1882-88
Liverpool. † L 5.

JONES, Agnes A. Exh. 1903-12
Canonbury, London. † L 2, NG 1, RA 2, RMS 2.

JONES, A.E. Exh. 1921-27
Liverpool 1921; Grange over Sands, Lancs. 1927. † L 4.

JONES, A. Edwards Exh. 1910
Windmill Street, Horse Fair, Birmingham. † L 13.

JONES, A. Gwendoline Exh. 1904-13
Flower and fruit painter. Add: Clwyd House, Hartopp Road, Leicester. † N 6.

JONES, Alfred Garth b. 1872
Landscape painter, illustrator and advertisement designer. Studied Westminster School of Art, Slade School, Juliens, Paris and South Kensington. Visiting master in design at Lambeth and Manchester Schools of Art. Exh. 1900-39. Add: London. † CHE 1, NEA 1, RA 5.

JONES, Arthur H. Exh. 1927-29
Liverpool. † L 2.

JONES, Miss A.L. Exh. 1908-14
2 Ethel Road, Seacombe, Cheshire. † L 17.

JONES, Anna M. Exh. 1884-85
Watercolour coastal painter. Add: 19 Norland Square, London. † SWA 4.

JONES, Apphia Mary Exh. 1933-34
21 Bristol Road, Weston super Mare. † RCA 2.

JONES, Agnes Rupert Exh. 1910-13
Add: London. † M 1, RA 3.

JONES, Arthur S. Exh. 1892-1906
Architect. Add: London 1892; Twickenham, Middlesex 1905. † RA 6.

JONES, Albert V. Exh. 1910-31
Oxton, Birkenhead 1910; Claughton, Birkenhead 1918. † L 9, P 1, RCA 3.

JONES, B. Exh. 1929-40
Grendon Common, Atherstone, Warwicks. † B 11.

JONES, Beatrice A. Exh. 1909
† LS 2.

JONES, Bertha C. Exh. 1906-14
Kensington, London 1906; Etaples, Pas de Calais, France 1913; Paris 1914. † LS 6, RCA 1.

JONES, Miss B. Ross Exh. 1937-40
67 Middlemore Road, Northfield, Warwicks. † B 8.

JONES, C. Exh. 1906-8
2 Eaton Villas, Chingford, Essex. † RA 1, RI 1.

JONES, Champion* Exh. 1881-1901
Coastal, landscape, river and figure painter. Add: London. † G 1, RA 9, RBA 12, RI 2.

JONES, Charles* 1836-1892
Animal and landscape painter. b. Nr. Cardiff. Add: London. † B 24, D 1, GI 1, L 7, M 7, RA 1, RBA 19, RCA 22, RHA 14, RI 10, ROI 4, TOO 2.

JONES, C. Agnes Exh. 1893-99
Landscape painter. Add: London. † RBA 9, RHA 3, RI 1, SWA 13.

JONES, Charles Digby Exh. 1880-86
12 Chester Street, Edinburgh. † RSA 3.

JONES, Constance Flood Exh. 1890-1913
Figure painter. Add: London 1890; Beaconsfield, Bucks. 1913. † G 1, RA 1.

JONES, C.H. Exh. 1888
14 St. James Road, Liverpool. † L 1.

JONES, Conway Lloyd Exh. 1880-81
Landscape painter. Add: Beauchamps, Wimborne, Dorset. † D 3, RBA 1.

JONES, Charles Stansfield Exh. 1909
117 Kenilworth Avenue, Wimbledon Park, London. † RCA 1.

JONES, Miss D. Exh. 1928-29
Battersea Bridge Road, London. † SWA 2.

JONES, David Exh. 1890-91
Landscape painter. Add: 41 Wellington Road, Dudley, Worcs. † B 2, RA 1.

JONES, David b. 1895
Painter, wood and copper engraver. Studied at Camberwell and Westminster Schools of Art and under Eric Gill. Exh. 1921-40. Add: Brockley, London. † AG 1, BA 5, GOU 60, L 1, LEI 19, NEA 3, RED 46, TOO 1.

JONES, Doyley Amos Exh. 1926
† M 2.

JONES, Dora C. Exh. 1928-30
St. Bede's Vicarage, Sefton Park, Liverpool. † L 3.

JONES, Dan Rowland b. 1875
Painter, etcher and sculptor. Studied London School of Art, Royal College of Art and Juliens, Paris. Art master at University College of Wales and Chief Examiner in art, Central Welsh Board. Exh. 1921-34. Add: Aberystwyth. † RCA 16.

JONES, E. Exh. 1886
Landscape painter. Add: 7 Stanford Road, Kensington, London. † SWA 1.

JONES, Miss E. Exh. 1917
Upper Tooting, London. † SWA 2.

JONES, Eric b. 1904
Exh. 1930. Add: 37 Hollywood Road, South Kensington, London. † NEA 2.

JONES, Ethel Exh. 1893
Brookhurst, Leamington, Warwicks. † B 1.

JONES, Evan Exh. 1928
13 Lancaster Gardens, Ealing, London. † RI 1.

JONES, Ernest A. Exh. 1927
Sculptor. Add: 125 Hurlingham Road, London. † RA 1.

JONES, E. Blanche Exh. 1914-35
Watercolour painter, etcher and black and white artist. Add: Liverpool 1914; Hough Green, Chester 1920. † L 26, RSA 1.

JONES, E. Buckingham Exh. 1899
7 Highfield Road, Walton, Liverpool. † L 1.

JONES, Miss E.C. Exh. 1887
Figure painter. Add: Harrow, Middlesex. † ROI 1.

JONES, Miss E. Charlotte Exh. 1939
† RI 1.

JONES, Eric C. Exh. 1939-40
28 Chudleigh Road, Erdington, Birmingham. † B 4.

JONES, Miss E.D. Exh. 1912
Fairmount, Denbigh, Wales. † RCA 1.

JONES, Enid E. Exh. 1914-26
53 Belgrave Road, London. † I 3, LS 3, P 2.

JONES, E. Gawan Exh. 1908
The Laurels, Chiswick Lane, London. † RA 1.

JONES, Ethel Gertrude Exh. 1894-1930
Portrait and landscape painter. Studied under Richard Hartby at Liverpool, and Paris. Add: Claughton, Birkenhead 1894; Hoylake, Cheshire 1900. † L 36, RCA 3.

JONES, E.H. Exh. 1887-91
17 St. James' Road, Liverpool. † L 2.

JONES, Ernest Ll. Exh. 1901-23
Painter. Add: London. † B 4, L 4, LS 11, NG 2, RA 1, RCA 16.

JONES, Mrs. E.M. Exh. 1927
13 Sandringham Drive, Sefton Park, Liverpool. † L 1.

JONES, E. Nora Exh. 1890-1917
Miniature portrait painter. R.M.S. 1896. Add: London. † L 17, LS 12, M 1, RA 7, RI 2, RMS 43, SWA 2.

JONES, Ernest Stephen Exh. 1923-36
Sculptor. Add: London. † NEA 2, RA 1.

JONES, Edward T. Exh. 1901-12
Landscape painter. Add: Leeds. † L 2, RA 5, RCA 12.

JONES, Edith Wynne Exh. 1930-36
Flower painter. Add: 13 Ashley Avenue, Gt. Meols, Cheshire. † L 7, RCA 9.

JONES, Emrys Wyn Exh. 1935
Ruthin, Wales. † RCA 1.

JONES, Ernest Yarrow b. 1872
Painter, sculptor and illuminator. b. Liverpool. Studied South Kensington, Westminster, Juliens, Paris and Colarossi's Paris. Exh. 1898-1921. Add: London 1898; Paris 1904; Bagshot, Surrey 1910; Hythe, Kent 1914 and 1918; Reading, Berks. 1917. † I 4, L 9, LEI 39, LS 17, RA 3.

JONES, Frank Exh. 1918-31
Miniature painter. Add: The Studios, Edith Terrace, Chelsea, London. † I 1, RA 4.

JONES, Frederick Exh. 1885
Watercolour landscape painter. Add: 19 Argyll Square, London. † RA 1.

JONES, Frederick Cecil 1891-1956
Painter, etcher and teacher. Studied Bradford College of Art (2 silver and 1 bronze medal). Related to Maud Raphael J. q.v. R.B.A. 1940. "Chimney Stacks and Winding Ways, Whitby" purchased by Chantrey Bequest 1937. Add: Bradford, Yorks. 1912; Leeds 1937. † L 2, RA 16, RSA 12.

JONES, Florence E. Exh. 1903-8
Mrs. H.F. Vaughan. Portrait painter. Add: Kew, Surrey 1903; Northwood, Middlesex 1908. † RA 2.

JONES, Francis E. Exh. 1881
Architect. Add: 20 Cockspur Street, London. † RA 1.

JONES, Frances M. Exh. 1882-85
Figure and domestic painter. Add: c/o G.C. Jones, King's College Chambers, Strand, London. † RBA 6.

JONES, F.R. Exh. 1890-91
198 Lozells Road, Birmingham. † B 3.

JONES, George Exh. 1929
The Shanty, Bromborough, Birkenhead. † L 1.

JONES, Glyn Exh. 1930-34
Landscape and portrait painter. Add: Ilford, Essex 1930; London 1933. † FIN 59, NEA 1, P 1, RA 2, ROI 1, RSA 1.

JONES, Bishop Gresford Exh. 1927
Landscape painter. † AB 2.

JONES, Gwilyn E. Exh. 1923-36
Painter, wood engraver and stained glass artist. A.S.W.A. 1925. Add: Chelsea, London 1923; Rodborough, Stroud, Glos. 1933. † COO 4, NEA 1, RA 4.

JONES, George Kingston Exh. 1896-99
Landscape painter. Add: 28 Lewisham Road, Highgate Road, London. † RA 3.

JONES, G.P. Exh. 1932
Avondale, Hobs Road, Wednesbury, Staffs. † B 1.

JONES, Gwendoline Rhys Exh. 1925
9 Victoria Terrace, Beaumaris, N. Wales. † RCA 1.

JONES, George W. Exh. 1885
Portrait painter. Add: 120 Adelaide Road, London. † RA 1.

JONES, H. Exh. 1887-93
East Wickham House, Welling, Kent. † D 5.

JONES, Harold b. 1904
Etcher, lithographer and illustrator. Studied Royal College of Art 1924-28. Exh. 1927-40. Add: London. † NEA 1, RA 3.

JONES, Harry Exh. 1880-1916
10 Berners Street, Oxford Street, London 1880; 32 Acfold Road, Fulham, London 1908. † D,1, L 1, RA 3.

JONES, Herbert Exh. 1929-36
Landscape painter. Add: Hornchurch, Essex 1929; London 1931. † GI 2, NEA 3, RA 3, RSA 2.

JONES, Sir Horace d. 1887
Architect. Add: Architect's Office, Guildhall, London. † RA 6.

JONES, Mrs. Hilda Blayney Exh. 1923-39
Miniature painter. Add: 41 Beech Avenue, Gatley, Cheshire. † L 9, RA 7, RMS 3.

JONES, Hugh Bolton* 1848-1927
American landscape painter. Exh. 1882-97. Add: London. † B 2, RBA 2.

JONES, H.C. Exh. 1884-97
Liverpool. † L 3.

JONES, H. Conway Exh. 1936-39
Southall, Middlesex. † RCA 4.

JONES, Howel Clayton b. 1897
Painter and illustrator. Studied under Tim Evans. Exh. 1927-40. Add: Llandudno. † NEA 1, RCA 7.

JONES, H. Edward Exh. 1928
Engraver. † ALP 1.

JONES, Harry E. Exh. 1882-1916
Landscape, rustic and figure painter. Add: London 1880; Brentford, Essex 1882; Epsom, Surrey 1891; Marlborough, Wilts. 1905; Fulham, London 1908. † B 2, D 2, L 8, M 2, RA 6, RBA 4, RHA 2.

JONES, Helena E. Exh. 1899-1903
3 Wilmont Terrace, Belfast. † GI 3, RHA 3.

JONES, Henry E. Exh. 1892
17 Gillespie Crescent, Edinburgh. † RSA 1.

JONES, Henrietta G. Exh. 1930
Alderley Edge, Cheshire. † RCA 1.

JONES, Helena G. de Courcy Exh. 1897-1919
Miniature painter. R.M.S. 1898. Add: 6 St. Charles Square, Bayswater, London. † L 2, RA 3, RMS 12.

JONES, Harold Harris b. 1908
Portrait and figure painter. Studied Southport School of Art 1933, Harris Art School, Preston 1934 and under Albert Woods 1935-40. Exh. 1938. Add: 80 Waterloo Road, Aston on Ribble, Preston, Lancs. † RA 1.

JONES, Mrs. H. Mildred Exh. 1924-40
Liverpool 1924; Starcroft, Old Colwyn 1926 and 1939; Tal-y-Cafn, Denbighs 1927. † L 3, RCA 16.

JONES, H. Overton Exh. 1897-1922
Stafford 1897; Little Haywood, Staffs. 1900 and 1912; London 1904; Chorley Wood, Herts. 1908. † B 11, L 19, RA 1, RI 1, RCA 2, RSA 4.

JONES, Mrs. H. Rogers Exh. 1927-28
The Cliffe, Penmaenrhos, Colwyn Bay, Wales. † L 2, RCA 1.

JONES, Mrs. Irving Exh. 1890-92
35 Caird Street, Liverpool. † L 3.

JONES, Ida A. Exh. 1915-30
Tenby, S. Wales 1915; Penally, Pembrokes. 1930. † B 6, L 1.

JONES, Ida S. Exh. 1892-95
Brookhurst, Leamington, Warwicks. † B 3.

JONES, J. Exh. 1938
† NEA 1.

JONES, Jo Exh. 1934-40
c/o Stiles and Sons, 37 Brook Green Road, London 1939; Long Bredy, Dorchester 1940. † GOU 3, RBA 1, SWA 2.

JONES, Joseph Exh. 1881-84
Ashby de la Zouch, Leics. 1881; Stroud, Glos. 1884. † B 1, D 1.

JONES, Josiah Exh. 1905-6
21 Chapel Street, St. Helens, Lancs. † L 2.

JONES, Joyce Exh. 1936
Figure painter. † COO 2.

JONES, J.A. Exh. 1910
4A Heathview Road, Thornton Heath, Surrey. † RA 1.

JONES, Josiah Clinton 1848-1936
Landscape and seascape painter. b. Wednesbury, Staffs. Studied Liverpool School of Art. Add: Liverpool 1882; Llanbedr, Conway, Wales 1885; Tal-y-bont, Conway 1896. † B 1, L 101, M 1, RA 5, RCA 258, RI 1.

JONES, J. Ford Exh. 1887-1933
Liverpool. † B 1, L 140, RCA 7.

JONES, Jessie H. Exh. 1901
Painter. Add: Treton Lodge, Wolverhampton. † RA 1.

JONES, Miss J. Mansell Exh. 1901-10
Fern Glen, Herkomer Road, Bushey, Herts. 1901; Fordbrook, Ealing 1903; Hyde Park, London 1905. † SWA 6.

JONES, Mrs. Kenneth Exh. 1937
Cardiff, Wales. † RCA 1.

JONES, Langford b. 1888
Painter, copper and wood engraver, sculptor and medallist. Studied Royal College of Art. Signs work "Jjonah". Exh. 1922-37. Add: London 1922; Blewbury, Berks. 1932. † B 2, L 2, RA 13, RMS 10.

JONES, Lily Exh. 1891
Flower painter. Add: Woodlands, Sutton Coldfield, Nr. Birmingham. † RA 1.

JONES, Lily Exh. 1933
78 Hagley Road, Edgbaston, Birmingham. † B 1.

JONES, Llewellyn Exh. 1909-23
Seguryn Side, Nr. Llandudno, Wales. † RCA 4.

JONES, Laura Edwards Exh. 1886-1902
Figure and domestic painter. Add: London. † FIN 1, L 5, RA 3, RBA 2, ROI 3, SWA 4.

JONES, Lionel J. Exh. 1892-94
Watercolour urban landscape painter. Add: Kensington, London. † NEA 1, RA 1, RI 1.

JONES, Miss Louie JohnsonExh. 1888-1922
Pystill, Holywell. † B 4, L 5, RCA 4.

JONES, L.N. Exh. 1938
7 Emmanuel Road, Wylde Green, Sutton Coldfield, Warwicks. † B 1.

JONES, Llewellyn Petley Exh. 1935-38
Landscape painter. Add: Beckenham, Kent 1935; Richmond, Surrey 1936; Putney, London 1938. † NEA 1, P 1, RA 2, RBA 3, RHA 1, ROI 3, RSA 1.

JONES, Margaret Exh. 1935-38
Colwyn Bay, Wales. † RCA 4.

JONES, Marion Exh. 1923-34
Portrait and flower painter. b. Bendigo, Australia. Studied Melbourne National Gallery (prizes and scholarship). Add: 1 Carlyle Studios, 296 King's Road, Chelsea, London. † FIN 2, GI 3, L 2, P 3, RA 2, ROI 3, RSA 1, SWA 1.

JONES, Miss Morfudd Exh. 1938
Holywell, Flintshire. † RCA 1.

JONES, Mabel Budgett Exh. 1895-1909
Mrs. Alfred Puleston. Miniature painter. R.M.S. 1896. Add: London. † RA 4, RI 7, RMS 45.

JONES, Mrs. Marion Clayton b. 1872
nee Clarke. Watercolour landscape, flower and miniature painter. Exh. 1908-29. Add: Silverton House, Nr. Exeter. † L 6, RA 11.

JONES, Mary Cecilia Exh. 1907-23
Tunbridge Wells, Kent. † L 1, LS 6, SWA 2.

JONES, Minnie C. Exh. 1890
Livingstone Road, Handsworth, Birmingham. † B 2.

JONES, Margaret E. Exh. 1912-33
Pendleton, Manchester 1912; Wavertree, Liverpool 1920. † L 10.

JONES, Marion E. Exh. 1897-1903
Bradenham, Knighton Park Road, Leicester. † L 1, N 7.

JONES, Miss M.F. Exh. 1885
Figure painter. Add: c/o Mr. G. Conway, 173 Hampstead Road, London. † L 2, RA 1, RBA 1.

JONES, Mary Helen Exh. 1883-90
Portrait painter. Add: 33 Jermyn Street, London. † B 1, RA 1, ROI 1.

JONES, Miss M.J. Exh. 1912-30
9 Wellington Road, Oxton, Birkenhead. † L 19, RCA 1.

JONES, Maud Raphael Exh. 1889-1907
Landscape and rustic painter. b. Bradford. Related to Frederick Cecil J. q.v. Add: Bradford, Yorks. † G 1, GI 1, L 4, M 6, NG 7, RA 22, RI 5.

JONES, Mrs. M. Summer Exh. 1882-1910
Flower painter. Add: 8 Brandeburg Road, Gunnersbury, London. † BG 2, M 5.

JONES, Miss Marguerite S. Exh. 1907-8
Sherborne, Wellesley Road, Chiswick, London. † B 2.

JONES, Nora Exh. 1928
8 Hamilton Place, Chester. † L 1.

JONES, Purcell Exh. 1917
† LEI 40.

JONES, Percy J. Exh. 1932
Portrait painter. Add: Holmwood, Prince's Avenue, Petts Wood, Orpington, Kent. † RA 1.

JONES, Phyllis Jacobine Exh. 1928-31
Sculptor. Add: London. † L 2, RA 3.

JONES, Reginald Exh. 1884-1920
Landscape painter. R.B.A. 1915. Travelled widely. Add: London 1880 and 1905; The Shrublands, Eltham, Kent 1884. † AB 1, AG 2, B 6, BK 129, D 17, DOW 2, G 2, GI 19, L 14, RA 18, RBA 71, RHA 3, RI 20, RID 65, TOO 1, WG 144.

JONES, Mrs. Reginald Exh. 1910-20
Watercolour landscape painter. † BK 10, WG 15.

JONES, Robert Exh. 1906-40
Landscape painter. Add: Elm Grove, Bodhyfryd Road, Llandudno. † RA 2, RCA 42.

JONES, Ronald G. Exh. 1903
Allerton Beeches, Liverpool. † L 1.

JONES, Rowland G. Exh. 1889-1913
Decorative designer. Add: London. † RA 7.

JONES, R.J. Cornewall Exh. 1886
Architect. Add: 44 High Street, Ryde, I.O.W. † RA 1.

JONES, Rosa K. Hesketh Exh. 1903-29
Watercolour painter. Add: Croydon, Surrey. † B 2, D 13, L 1, LS 3, RA 1, RI 2, ROI 2, SWA 5.

JONES, R.M. Exh. 1890
487 Harewood Street, Bradford, Yorks. † NG 1.

JONES, Ronald P. Exh. 1904-29
Architect. Add: London. † L 1, RA 4.

JONES, R.S. Exh. 1932-33
1 Buckland Street, St. Michaels, Liverpool. † L 3.

JONES, Shone Exh. 1935
Sculptor. Add: 12 Wetherall Gardens, Hampstead, London. † RA 2.

JONES, Stanley Exh. 1932
Devonia, Narrow Lane, Blackheath, London. † B 1.

JONES, S. Maurice d. 1932
Rhos Ruabon 1883; Carnarvon, Wales 1887; Liverpool 1923; Llandudno 1928. † L 7, RCA 145.

JONES, Sydney Robert b. 1881
Painter, etcher and designer. Studied Birmingham School of Art. Exh. 1907-38. Add: Birmingham 1907; Warwick 1913; London 1921. † BK 3, CON 40, L 13, RA 10, RI 1.

JONES, Theodore Exh. 1880-89
Watercolour landscape painter. Regent's Park, London. † RA 4, RBA 10, RI 1.

JONES, Tom Exh. 1890
7 Erddy Terrace, Wrexham, Wales. † L 1.

JONES, Sir Thomas Alfred 1823-1893
Portrait painter. Studied at the Royal Dublin Society and R.H.A. Schools. A.R.H.A. 1860, R.H.A. 1861, P.R.H.A. 1869. Knighted 1880. Add: Dublin. † D 1, GI 1, L 4, M 1, RHA 81.

JONES, Thomas Bayliss Huxley b. 1908
Sculptor. Studied Wolverhampton School of Art 1924-29 and Royal College of Art 1929-33 (Travelling scholarship). Teacher of sculpture Gray's School of Art, Aberdeen from 1934. Married Gwynneth Holt q.v. Exh. 1927-40. † B 12, GI 2, L 1, RA 1, RSA 6.

JONES, T. Hampson 1846-1916
Landscape painter. Travelled widely. Add: New Brighton, Cheshire 1880; Liverpool 1884 and 1894; Birkenhead 1890. † L 69, RA 11, RI 3, DOW 48.

JONES, T. Harry Exh. 1881
Grand Hotel, Concarneau, Finisterre, France. † RBA 1.

JONES, Tom H. Exh. 1908-38
Landscape painter. A.N.S.A. 1911, N.S.A. 1917 (secretary 1918-22 and Chairman of Council 1925). Add: Mapperley, Notts. 1908 and 1912; Lenton, Notts. 1910; Nottingham 1921. † N 47, RCA 61.

JONES, Thomas J. Exh. 1901-34
Painter, etcher and sculptor. b. Bideford, Devon. Studied Royal College of Art. Principal of the School of Arts and Crafts, Tunbridge Wells; design master at Wedgwood's School of Art, Burslem, Stoke-on-Trent and head of the Art Department of Borough Polytechnic, London. Add: London 1901 and 1915; Burslem, Staffs. 1904; Tunbridge Wells, Kent 1934. † RA 11.

JONES, Trefor O. Exh. 1924-38
Pen and wash artist. Holyhead 1924; Hampstead Garden Suburb, London 1934. † L 1, RA 3.

JONES, T.R. Exh. 1885
3 Blockett Place, Newcastle-on-Tyne. † L 1.

JONES, Vida Exh. 1893
Mrs. D. Portrait painter. Copse Hill, Wimbledon, London. † RA 1.

JONES, Vivian D. Exh. 1938
c/o Pollock, Kilmarnock. † GI 1.

JONES, Violet Madeline Exh. 1916-29
Figure and portrait painter. London. † CHE 28, GOU 4, NEA 5, RI 2.

JONES, Victor T. Exh. 1894
Landscape painter. 12 Albany Road, South Hampstead, London. † RA 1.

JONES, W. Exh. 1923-24
Portrait painter. Nottingham. † N 3.

JONES, Wallis Exh. 1883-91
Manchester 1883; Birmingham 1886. † B 5, M 1.

JONES, William Exh. 1898
23 Goldsmith Street, Dublin. † RHA 2.

JONES, Winifred Exh. 1926
Flower painter. † AB 4.

JONES, W. Campbell Exh. 1894-1934
Architect. London. † RA 21.

JONES, Wilfred Emmanuel b. 1890
Painter, etcher and mezzotint engraver. Self taught. Add: Liverpool 1913; Solihull, Warwicks. 1940. † B 1, L 2, RCA 1.

JONES, W.H. Exh. 1920
Manaton, Nr. Moretonhampstead, Devon. † B 1.

JONES, Major W.H. Exh. 1918-20
London. † RI 2, ROI 1.

JONES, W.O. Exh. 1882-86
Formby, Lancs. 1882; Southport, Lancs. 1886. † L 2.

JONGERS, Alphonse b. 1872
Portrait painter. b. France. Exh. 1935. Add: Montreal, Canada. † RA 1.

JONGH de See D

JONGHE, de See D

JONNIAUX, Alfred Exh. 1919-39
Portrait painter. London. † L 5, P 8, RA 8.

JONSSON, R. Exh. 1915
Ropewalk Street, Newlyn, Penzance, Cornwall. †, RA 1.

JONZEN, Basil b. 1916
Landscape, portrait and flower painter. Exh. 1933-40. Add: c/o Redfern Gallery, 27 Old Bond Street, London. † NEA 2, RBA 3, RED 163, TOO 1.

JOPLING, Joseph Middleton 1831-1884
Watercolour historical, genre, still life, flower, portrait and landscape painter. Self taught. A.R.I. 1859. Married to Louise J. q.v. Add: London. † G 19, GI 12, L 7, M 9, RA 3, RI 4, RSA 1.

JOPLING, Louise* 1843-1933
nee Goode. Portrait, genre and landscape painter and teacher. Studied under Charles Chaplin. Married 1st Frank Romer (d. 1873) 2nd Joseph M.J. q.v. in 1874. First woman to be elected R.B.A. in 1902; R.P. 1891, S.W.A. 1880. Add: London. † B 20, D 1, FIN 1, G 26, GI 30, I 1, L 38, LS 6, M 17, P 62, RA 45, RBA 70, RHA 6, RI 3, ROI 6, SWA 55.

JORDAN, Florence Exh. 1896-1912
Liverpool 1896; Mobberley, Cheshire 1912. † L 7, RCA 3.

JORDAN, Imelda Exh. 1896
c/o Messrs. Jackson and Son, Slater Street, Liverpool. † L 1.

JORDAN, Miss P. Tiel Exh. 1928
Flower painter. 24 Pierremont Crescent, Darlington. † RA 1.

JORDAN, R. Furneaux Exh. 1932
Architect. 17 Easy Row, Birmingham. † RA 1.

JORDAN, Vera Exh. 1901-4
Liverpool. † L 4.

JORDAN, William b. 1884
Watercolour flower painter. b. Appledore, Devon. Assistant master at Plymouth School of Art. Exh. 1923-26. Add: 7 Springfield Terrace, Westward Ho!, Devon. † FIN 5, L 3, RSA 2.

JORGENSEN, Justus Exh. 1926-27
Figure and flower painter. Paris 1926; London 1927. † RA 2, RBA 2, ROI 1.

JORON, Maurice* Exh. 1912
12 Rue Alfred de Vigny, Paris. † RSA 1.

JOSE, Juliana Exh. 1885
22 Mortimer Street, Regent Street, London. † L 1.

JOSEBURY, L.E. Exh. 1883
Grosvenor Road, Handsworth, Birmingham. † B 1.

JOSEPH, Miss A. Exh. 1903-4
34 Inverness Terrace, London. † SWA 4.

JOSEPH, Mrs. Amy 1876-1961
Urban landscape painter. A.R.B.A. 1940. Add: Squires Mount, Hampstead Heath, London. † GOU 5, NEA 2, P 2, RA 4, RBA 20, RI 7, RSA 1, SWA 7.

JOSEPH, Bail Exh. 1899
198 Strand, London. † M 1.

JOSEPH, Delissa 1859-1927
Architect. Married Lily D.J. q.v. Exh. 1897-1923. Add: London. † RA 9.

JOSEPH, Hope Exh. 1907-36
Portrait and landscape painter, illustrator, poster, woodcut and pottery artist. b. Ajmeer, India. Studied under Stanhope Forbes at Newlyn, Penzance. Add: Zennor, Nr. St. Ives, Cornwall 1907; Paul, Penzance 1908; London 1909 and 1926; Ashtead, Surrey 1920. † GOU 2, L 2, LS 15, M 2, P 1, RA 6, RHA 3, ROI 1, RSA 1, SWA 11.

JOSEPH, Lily Delissa 1864-1940
nee Solomon. Portrait, landscape and interior painter. Studied South Kensington School of Art. Sister of Solomon J. Solomon q.v. Married Delissa J. q.v. "Roofs, High Holborn" purchased by Chantrey Bequest 1937. Exh. 1889-1938. Add: London. † GI 2, L 2, NEA 3, P 8, RA 25, RBA 2, RID 7, ROI 3, SWA 7.

JOSEPH, S. Exh. 1911-12
c/o Lazard Bros. 40 Threadneedle Street, London. † L 5, RA 3.

JOSEPH, W.L. Exh. 1911
1 Park View Mansions, Highgate, London. † LS 1.

JOSEPHI, Isaac J. Exh. 1904
American miniature painter. R.M.S. 1905. Add: 12 St. Dunstan's Road, West Kensington, London. † NG 1, RMS 1.

JOSEPHY, Hetty Exh. 1931-40
Landscape, flower and still life painter. Studied in Yorkshire. Add: Rushmere, Orley Farm Road, Harrow-on-the-Hill, Middlesex. † ROI 6, WG 40.

JOSEY, John William Exh. 1891-92
Engraver. London. † RA 2.

JOSEY, Richard 1841-1906
Mezzotint engraver. Add: London 1880 and 1887; Penn, Bucks. 1883. † RA 14.

JOSHUA, Joan Exh. 1910-20
Miniature portrait painter. 89C King Henry's Road, Hampstead, London. † RA 4, ROI 2.

JOSHUA, Nellie Exh. 1902-11
Painter. London. † RA 5, ROI 9, SWA 2.

JOSLING, H.S. Exh. 1905-6
27 Shaftesbury Avenue, London. † RA 2.

JOSS, Eleanor M. Exh. 1940
1 Succoth Place, Edinburgh. † GI 1, RSA 1, RSW 1.

JOSSET, Lawrence b. 1910
Watercolour portrait painter, etcher and mezzotint engraver. Studied Bromley and Beckenham Schools of Art and Royal College of Art 1932-35. A.R.E. 1936. Exh. 1936-40. Add: Maidstone, Kent 1936; 4 Red Hill, Chislehurst, Kent 1937. † RA 6, RE 23.

JOSSO, Camille P. Exh. 1938
Etcher. † COO 16.

JOUBERT, Felix Exh. 1902-7
London. † NG 4.

JOUBERT, Ferdinand Jean 1810-1884
French engraver. Exh. 1881. Add: 66 Margaret Street, London. † RA 1.

JOUGHIN, Miss S.H. Exh. 1925
Bell Vue, Peel, I.O.M. † L 1.

JOURDAIN, Henri 1864-1931
French artist. Exh. 1909. Add: 4 Rue des Eaux, Paris. † L 1.

JOURDAIN, John Exh. 1907-8
8 Messina Avenue, Hampstead, London. † D 2.

JOURDAN, Adolphe 1825-1889
French artist. Exh. 1881. Add: 16 Avenue Trudaine, Paris. † RHA 2.

JOUVET-NAGRAN, Dominique Exh. 1933
c/o Messrs. Grindley and Palmer, 14 North John Street, Liverpool. † L 1.

JOUVIN, H. Exh. 1893
18 Avenue de Villiers, Paris. † RHA 1.

JOUVRAY, Mlle. M. Exh. 1906-11
47 Rue Blomet, Paris. † L 3.

JOWETT, Ellen Exh. 1912
† M 2.

JOWETT, Frank B. Exh. 1915-38
Mezzotint engraver. Kettering, Northants. 1915; Rhos-on-Sea, Conway 1930. † L 1, RA 1, RCA 14, RI 9, RSW 1.

JOWETT, F.G. Conway Exh. 1931-38
Sculptor. Ash Tree Villa, Codnor Park, Notts. 1931; Codnor, Derbys. 1938. † N 19.

JOWETT, John Marshall Exh. 1900-24
Liscard, Cheshire 1900; New Brighton, Cheshire 1904. † L 26.

JOWETT, Percy Hague 1882-1955
Landscape and flower painter. Studied Harrogate Technical School and Royal College of Art (travelling scholarship in painting). Principal Royal College of Art. N.E.A. 1929, R.W.S. 1938. Exh. 1907-39. Add: London. † BA 1, CHE 8, FIN 1, I 1, L 5, LEF 1, LEI 8, M 1, NEA 77, RA 15, RED 10, RSA 1, RWS 33.

JOWITT, Ruth Exh. 1909
5 Bramerton Street, Chelsea, London. † L 1.

JOWSEY, J. Wilson Exh. 1931-32
10A Cunningham Place, London. † RBA 1, RCA 2.

JOY, George William* 1844-1925
Historical genre and portrait painter. b. Dublin. Studied South Kensington and R.A. Schools and under Jalabert in Paris 1868. Brother of Albert Bruce-Joy q.v. R.O.I. 1896. Exh. 1881-1914. Add: London. † B 9, GI 6, L 25, M 8, NG 6, P 1, RA 41, RHA 8, ROI 21.

JOYCE, Annie G. Exh. 1896-1900
Figure and domestic painter. c/o Mr. Chapman, King's Road, Chelsea, London 1896; Burleigh, Tenbury, Worcs 1897. † B 2, RA 1, RBA 2.

JOYCE, Florence S.K. Weston Exh. 1901-6
Birmingham. † B 5.

JOYCE, Mary Exh. 1880-96
Figure, flower and portrait painter. London. † B 9, L 6, M 3, RA 3, RBA 5, RI 9.

JOYCE, Sydney H. Exh. 1930-40
Landscape painter. London. † NEA 1, RA 13.

JOYNER, Frederick G. Exh. 1933-34
Birmingham. † B 2.

JOYNER, Harry St. John Exh. 1898-1908
London. † LS 5, RBA 3.

JUBB, Mrs. Anne E. Exh. 1922
Miniature portrait painter. Dunelm, Elmhurst Road, Dovercourt, Essex. † RA 1.

JUBIER, F. Exh. 1910
6 Rue Darreau, Paris. † L 1.

JUCKES, Miss M. Exh. 1891
The Quorn House, Rowley Park, Stafford. † B 1.

JUDD, Mrs. A.F. Exh. 1903
Holmfirth, Holmfield Road, Leicester. † N 2.

JUDD, Florence Exh. 1884
Portrait painter. 151 Coningham Road, Uxbridge, Middlesex. † SWA 1.

JUDGE, Eugene Exh. 1940
Painter. c/o Contemporary Pictures, 16 South Leinster Street, Dublin. † RHA 1.

JUDGE, Michael Exh. 1916-17
Dublin. † RHA 2.

JUILLERAT, Marie Exh. 1900-3
c/o Miss M.W. Watson, 7 Grosvenor Crescent, Glasgow and Geneva, Switzerland. † GI 1, RSA 1.

JUKES, Beth Exh. 1935-37
Sculptor. London. † RA 2.

JULIANA, Jose* Exh. 1881-84
Figure painter. London 1881; Rome 1884. † D 3, M 3, RBA 2.

JULYAN, Mary Exh. 1880-1911
Flower painter. Dublin 1880 and 1884; London 1881. † L 1, RBA 1, RHA 22.

JUMEAUX, Dr. B. Exh. 1885
Springfield, Ambleside, Westmorland. † L 1.

JUMP, Mary Victoria b. 1897
Watercolour painter, linocut artist and teacher. Studied Liverpool and Birkenhead Schools of Art. Exh. 1924-38. Add: Bebington, Cheshire. † L 13, M 2.

JUNCK, Ferdinand Exh. 1880-95
Sculptor. St. John's Wood, London. † D 43, L 6, RA 8, RBA 10, RHA 2.

JUNCK, Oscar Alexander Exh. 1882-86
Sculptor. Grosvenor Lodge, Bolton Road, London. † D 2, RA 2.

JUNGMAN, Nico W.* 1872-1935
Landscape and figure painter and restorer. b. Holland. Naturalised British. Exh. 1897-1932. Add: London. † B 2, DOW 203, I 3, L 13, LEI 69, LS 5, M 3, RA 7, RBA 3, RHA 4.

JUNIPER, Muriel Exh. 1938-39
London. † NEA 1, RBA 3, SWA 1.

JUPP, George Herbert b. 1869
Painter and pastel artist. Exh. 1895-1925. Add: London 1895; Maidenhead, Berks. 1896; Bray, Berks. 1915. † RA 13.

JURRES, Johannes Hendrik* b. 1875
Dutch artist. Exh. 1905. Add: Helmerstraat, Amsterdam. † I 2.

JURY, Anne P. Exh. 1929-39
Flower and still life painter. Brooklands, Dunmurray, Co. Antrim. † RHA 7.

JUSTICE, Miss L. Exh. 1881-85
Co. Tyrone, Ireland. † RHA 8.

JUSTIN, Jules Exh. 1885
3 Avenue Trudaine, Paris. † GI 1.

JUTA, Jan Exh. 1924
Painter and illustrator. † ALP 40.

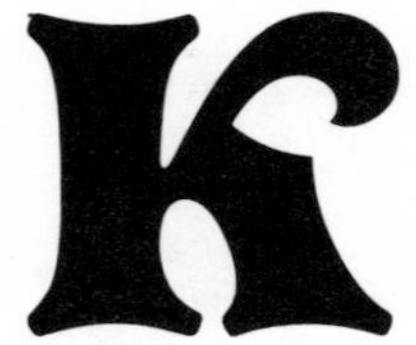

KADAR, Mrs. Livia Exh. 1928
A.R.M.S. 1928. Add: 218 Boulevard Raspail, Paris. † RMS 3.

KAGAN-RUSTCHUK, Mrs. Lottie Exh. 1922-36
Sculptor. Studied Slade School (silver medal). Add: London. † L 4, P 1, RA 5, SWA 1.

KAHLE, von See V

KAIN, Thomas b. 1886
Portrait painter, decorator and lacquer worker. Exh. 1923-28. Add: 15 Old Camden Street, Dublin. † RHA 4.

KAISER, Richard* b. 1868
German artist. Exh. 1900. Add: 40 Grovgenstrasse, Munich. † GI 2.

KALE, Arthur J. Exh. 1905-12
Royston Park, Pinner, Middlesex. † D 7, L 1.

KAMPF, Eugen 1861-1933
Landscape painter. Exh. 1905. Add: 78 Karolingerstrasse, Dusseldorf. † I 1.

KAMPTZ, von see V

KANDINSKY, Wassily* 1866-1944
Painter. b. Moscow. Studied in Munich. Travelled widely on the continent. Exh. 1909-35. † LEF 3, LS 16.

KANE, Agnes A. Exh. 1923
40 Carless Avenue, Harborne, Birmingham. † B 2.

KANE, Clara E. Exh. 1911-13
Melrose Avenue, Brooklands, Surrey. † M 5.

KANE, George M'D. B. Exh. 1915
c/o Rodman & Co. 41 Donegal Place, Belfast. † RSA 2.

KANELBA, Raymond b. 1897
Painter. Studied Warsaw, Academy of Fine Arts Vienna and Paris. Exh. 1936. † LEF 19.

KANT, Janet C. Exh. 1914-17
546 Argyll Street, Glasgow. † GI 6, RSA 4.

KANTCHALOVSKY, Pierre Exh. 1911
c/o Allied Artist Assn., 67 Chancery Lane, London. † LS 3.

KAPE, William Jack b. 1904
Wood carver and designer on wood and metal, lecturer on design. Studied High Wycombe Technical Institute (Bucks. County Art scholarship) and Royal College of Art. Assistant master High Wycombe Technical Institute. Headmaster Bridgwater School of Art and Headmaster Bilston School of Art. Exh. 1935-38. Add: Bilston, Staffs. † B 7.

KAPP, Edmond Xavier* b. 1890
Painter, draughtsman, caricaturist and lighographer. b. London. Studied London, Paris and Rome. Served with B.E.F. 1914-19. Official war artist 1940-41. Exh. 1922-40. Add: London. † CHE 5, COO 1, GOU 10, LEI 67.

KAPP, Helen b. 1901
Painter, illustrator and wood engraver. Studied Slade School and Paris. Exh. 1940. Add: 14 Maitland Park Villas, Hampstead, London. † RA 1.

KAPPARDSKI, S. Exh. 1887
Portrait artist. 36 Ladbroke Road, Bayswater, London. † RA 1.

KAPPAY, de see D

KARL, Jean Exh. 1908-10
37 Rue Davioud, Paris. † L 2.

KARLOWSKA, de see D

KARLSSON, Miss K Exh. 1914
7 Chalcot Crescent, Regent's Park, London. † LS 1.

KARMARKAR, V.P. Exh. 1921
The Studio, Thornton Street, Brixton Road, London. † RA 1.

KAROLIS, de see D

KAROLYI-SZECHENYI, Countess I. Exh. 1939
Portrait and figure painter. † AR 45.

KARPELES, Andree Exh. 1908-11
c/o Allied Artists Assn., 67 Chancery Lane, London. † LS 1.

KARR, Mrs. W. Exh. 1885
67 North Street, St. Andrews, Edinburgh. † RSA 1.

KARSCH, Joachim 1897-1945
German sculptor. Exh. 1936. † RSA 1.

KARUTH, Ethel Exh. 1901-9
Miniature painter and illustrator. A.S.W.A. 1906. Add: London. † L 6, P 1, RA 3, RMS 1.

KASIMIR, Luigi b. 1881
Etcher. 12 Himmelstrasse, Vienna 1914. † RA 2.

KASPER, Ludwig 1893-1943
German sculptor. Exh. 1936. † RSA 1.

KATCHADOURIAN, Sarkis b. 1886
Persian painter. Exh. 1926-28. Add: c/o Fine Art Society, 148 New Bond Street, London. † FIN 118, GI 4, L 61.

KATZ, Michael Exh. 1920-23
Sculptor. c/o Mrs. Compton Mackenzie, Markham House, King's Road, Chelsea, London 1920; Isle of Herm, C.I. 1923. † GI 1, RA 2.

KATZEUSTEIN, Louis Exh. 1882
Manchester. † M 1.

KAUFFER, Edward McKnight* d. 1954
Painter and poster designer. b. U.S.A. Member London Group 1916. Exh. 1917-36. Add: London. † GOU 3, LS 3, NEA 1, TOO 21.

KAUFMAN, Bernard Exh. 1892-1901
Married Lily Skeaping K. q.v. Add: Liverpool. † B 3, L 23, RI 3.

KAUFMAN, Hugo Exh. 1904
† I 1.

KAUFMAN, Joseph Exh. 1896
18 Upper Stanhope Street, Liverpool. † L 1.

KAUFMAN, Leon Exh. 1908-13
91 Rue de Prony, Paris. † L 1, LS 5.

KAUFMAN, Lily Skeaping Exh. 1894-1930
nee Skeaping. Figure, landscape and miniature painter. Studied Liverpool School of Art and on the continent. Teacher of dress design St. Helens School of Art and art teacher at Liverpool Technical Institute. Sister of John Skeaping q.v. Married Bernard K. q.v. Add: Liverpool 1894 and 1912; St. Helens, Lancs. 1910; Prescot, Lancs. 1919. † B 2, L 82, RI 1.

KAUFMANN, H. Exh. 1884
† TOO 1.

KAUFMANN, Miss K.S. Exh. 1933
Beauvallon, Heron Road, Gt. Meols, Cheshire. † L 2.

KAUFMANN, Philipp Exh. 1940
Figure painter. 7 Hill Road, London. † RA 1.

KAUL, Violet Victoria see BUTLER

KAVANAGH, John F. b. 1903
Sculptor. "Russian Peasant" (c. 1935-39) purchased by Chantrey Bequest 1943. Exh. 1934-39. Add: London. † RA 8, RHA 3.

KAVANAGH, Joseph M. d. 1919
Painter. A.R.H.A. 1889, R.H.A. 1892. Add: Dublin 1880 and 1910; Clontarf, Co. Dublin 1883; Blackrock, Co. Dublin 1908. † RA 2, RHA 211.

KAVANAGH, Raymond J. Exh. 1937-40
Architect. Dublin. † RHA 4.

KAY, Alicia Exh. 1905-15
71 Newsham Drive, Liverpool. † L 13.

KAY, Archibald* 1860-1935
Landscape painter. Studied Juliens, Paris. Married Mary Margaret K. q.v. A.R.S.A. 1916, R.S.A. 1931, R.S.W. 1892. Add: Glasgow 1882, 1913 and 1918; Callandar, N.B. 1910 and 1917. † AR 2, B 1, GI 141, L 25, M 3, NG 1, RA 28, RI 3, RSA 102, RSW 82.

KAY, Arthur Exh. 1881
27 Belhaven Terrace, Glasgow. † GI 1.

KAY, Christina Exh. 1889-93
120 Mains Street, Glasgow. † GI 6.

KAY, Dorothy Exh. 1921-40
Far end, Port Elizabeth, South Africa. † RBA 1, RHA 15.

KAY, E. Exh. 1907
9 Richmond Road, Cambridge. † RA 1.

KAY, Mrs. Ethel Exh. 1937
25 Empress Drive, Walney, Barrow in Furness. † RSA 1.

KAY, Grace M. Exh. 1904-5
59 Hamilton Terrace, London. † L 3.

KAY, Harriet M. Exh. 1880-1904
Miniature painter. Edinburgh. † RA 1, RSA 4.

KAY, Miss I.L. Exh. 1910-11
Gillott Road, Edgbaston, Birmingham. † B 1, RA 1.

KAY, James* 1858-1942
Landscape and marine painter. b. Lamlash, Isle of Arran. Studied Glasgow School of Art. A.R.S.A. 1934, R.S.A. 1939, R.S.E. 1897. Add: Glasgow 1884, 1904 and 1911; Pollokshields 1902; Whistlefield, Dumbartonshire 1908 and 1917. † AR 2, CON 32, GI 138, L 28, M 13, RA 3, RSA 67, RSW 155.

KAY, J.I. Exh. 1917-18
10 Cedars Road, Barnes, London. † RA 2.

KAY, Katherine Cameron see CAMERON

KAY, Mary Margaret Exh. 1904-12
nee Thomson. Married Archibald K. q.v. Add: Glasgow 1904; Callander, N.B. 1905. † GI 7.

KAY, Richard Exh. 1883
Landscape painter. Claremont, Quarry Road, Hastings, Sussex. † RBA 1, ROI 1.

KAY, Thomas Edwin Exh. 1930-36
Ganton, Wellclose Terrace, Whitby, Yorks. † GOU 3, NEA 2.

KAY, Violet McNeish 1914-1971
Painter. Studied Glasgow School of Art. Exh. 1935-40. Add: 12 Ruskin Terrace, Glasgow. † GI 9, RSW 10.

KAY, William Exh. 1927-31
Firwood, Coed Mor Drive, Prestatyn, Flints. † RCA 3.

KAY, William H. Exh. 1887-91
Bolton 1887 and 1891, Chorlton on Medlock, 1889. † L 1, M 3.

KAYE, Mrs. Dorothy Exh. 1922
Rothbury, Foxrock, Co. Dublin. † RHA 2.

KAYE, D.K. Martin Exh. 1924
Architect. 99 Boston Avenue, Southend on Sea, Essex. † RA 1.

KAYE, Mary Exh. 1931-38
Etcher, illustrator, engraver and pencil artist. Add: 19 Thorngrove Road, Upton Park, London. † B 1, RA 3.
KAYE, Violet L. Exh. 1898
Manor House, Stretton on Dunsmore, Rugby, Warwicks. † B 1.
KEAN, Miss C. Exh. 1922
Three Arts Club, 19A Marylebone Road, London. † NEA 2.
KEANE, Mariella Exh. 1940
140 Sutherland Avenue, London. † NEA 1, RBA 2, SWA 1.
KEARLEY, Hon. Mark H. Exh. 1931-32
Flower and architectural painter. Nicolai Platz, Munich 1931; Uxbridge, Middlesex 1932. † RA 2.
KEARNE, J. Hamilton Exh. 1906-13
Sutton, St. Helens, Lancs. 1906; Penketh, Lancs. 1913. † L 5, RCA 4.
KEARNE, L Exh. 1889
Castle Hill, Bassenthwaite, Keswick. † B 1.
KEARNE, Mrs. Lindsay Exh. 1890-95
Portrait and landscape painter. Grantham, Lincs. 1890; Brampton, Huntingdon 1895. † N 2, RBA 1.
KEARNEY, Eloise Guest Exh. 1919-33
London 1919; Upper Basildon, Pangbourne, Berks. 1933. † L 4, RI 2.
KEARNS, Mrs. Grace D. Exh. 1899-1902
Claughton, Birkenhead 1899; Parkgate, Cheshire 1902. † L 3.
KEARY, Maud Exh. 1925-27
15 Cheyne Walk, London. † SWA 2.
KEARY, Sidney J.B. Exh. 1896-98
Burlington, Malvern Link, Worcs. † B 2.
KEASBEY, Henry Turner b. 1882
American artist. Exh. 1909. † LS 3.
KEAST, H. Exh. 1909-13
Sculptor. Putney, London. † RA 3, RCA 3.
KEATES, Henry T. Exh. 1889
Architect. 23 Crawfurd Street, London. † RA 1.
KEATES, John Gareth b. 1915
Painter. Studied Liverpool College of Art 1933-38 and Central School of Art, London. Exh. 1937. † M 2.
KEATING, Christopher Exh. 1935-40
Landscape painter. Ballinavary House, Macmine, Co. Wexford and Dun Mona, Four Oaks, Birmingham. † B 5, RHA 7.
KEATING, Miss H. Exh. 1923
14 Cranmer Street, Nottingham. † N 3.
KEATING, John b. 1889
Figure and portrait painter. Studied Dublin Metropolitan School of Art (Orpen painting prize and Taylor scholarship). A.R.H.A. 1918, R.H.A. 1924. Exh. 1915-40. Add: Dublin 1915; Rathfarnham 1920. † GI 5, I 1, L 6, RA 25, RHA 156, RSA 2.
KEATINGE, Julia A. Exh. 1884-96
Mrs. R.H. Portrait and landscape painter. Kensington, London 1884; Lynwood, Horsham, Sussex 1896. † D 3, RA 3, RI 2, ROI 1, SWA 1.
KEAY, Harry b. 1914
Painter. Studied Dundee College of Art 1930-37, Hospitalfield, Arbroath 1937-38. Exh. 1936-40. Add: Dundee. † GI 2, RSA 6.
KEAY, L.H. Exh. 1928-33
A Director of Housing, Municipal Buildings, Dale Street, Liverpool. † L 8.
KEBBELL, William Francis Vere Exh. 1915-38
Portrait and still life painter. Studied Byam Shaw and Vicat Cole School of Art. Add: London. † I 2, L 1, RA 9, ROI 6.
KEDSLIE, A.F. Exh. 1885-94
Ryton on Tyne 1885; Edinburgh 1888. † RSA 9, RSW 1.
KEDWARDS, Eric James b. 1905
Painter. b. Bridlington, Yorks. Studied Birmingham College of Art 1924-29. Exh. 1936. Add: 22 Penn House Avenue, Penn, Wolverhampton. † B 1.
KEEBLE-SMITH, Kenneth Exh. 1933-40
Sculptor. 21 Burlington Gardens, Chiswick, London. † GI 1, RA 7.
KEEF, H.W. Exh. 1892-96
60 Castle Street, Liverpool. † L 3.
KEEFFE, Francis Exh. 1899
81 Camberwell New Road, London. † ROI 1.
KEEK, Emil Exh. 1888
Amelien Strasse, Munich, Germany. † L 1.
KEEL, Kathleen Exh. 1938-39
Sculptor. 107 Castellain Mansions, Maida Vale, London. † RA 2.
KEELAN, P.J. Exh. 1884-1921
Pont Aven, Finisterre, France 1884; London 1899. † RHA 6.
KEELEY, Mrs. A.E. Twilton Exh. 1925
16 Hawkesley Mill Lane, Northfield, Birmingham. † B 1.
KEELEY, F.W. Exh. 1883-87
Birmingham. † B 3.
KEELEY, Jane Exh. 1893
Greenwood Villa, Upper Mary Street, Balsall Heath, Birmingham. † B 1.
KEELEY, John d. 1930
Landscape painter. R.B.S.A. 1902. Add: Birmingham 1882 and 1927; Sutton Coldfield, Warwicks. 1926. † B 122, D 2, L 3, RA 1, RBA 2, RI 11.
KEELING, Cecil Exh. 1940
† NEA 2.
KEELING, Miss D.T. Exh. 1914
45 Lansdowne Road, London. † L 1.
KEELING, Gertrude Exh. 1896-1940
Watercolour painter and etcher. London. † B 7, GI 5, L 18, NEA 1, RA 2, RI 10, SWA 12.
KEELING, R.L. Exh. 1905
c/o Messrs H. Graves & Co., 6 Pall Mall, London. † RA 1.
KEELING, William Exh. 1891-1908
Landscape painter. Sheffield 1891; Chesterfield 1908. † B 2, M 2, RA 6.
KEELING, William Knight 1807-1886
Watercolour figure painter. Founder of the Manchester Academy of Fine Arts and President from 1864-77. A.R.I. 1840, R.I. 1841. Add: Laburnam Cottage, Barton-on-Irewell 1880. † L 1, M 1, RI 5.
KEELY, Mrs. E.G. Exh. 1881
Bird painter. 2 Regent Street, Nottingham. † N 2.
KEELY, Edith S. Exh. 1895-96
London. † RBA 2, ROI 1.
KEEN, Arthur 1860-1938
Architect. London 1883; Snatts, Limpsfield, Surrey 1933. † GI 2, RA 24.
KEEN, Dorothy A. Exh. 1930-36
† L 1, RCA 1.
KEEN, Doris M. Exh. 1929
24 Alverston Avenue, Claughton, Birkenhead. † L 2.
KEEN, Miss H. Cornock Exh. 1930-31
Birmingham. † B 4.
KEEN, Miss M.E. Exh. 1915-17
Birkdale, Kidderpore Avenue, Hampstead, London. † I 4, RA 1, RI 2.
KEEN, Paul W. Exh. 1926
† M 2.
KEEN, R.W. Exh. 1916
Knowle, Bristol. † L 1, RA 1.
KEENE, Mrs. Annie Exh. 1921-33
Flower and landscape painter. 99 Uttoxeter New Road, Derby 1921; Littleover, Derbys. 1933. † B 3, N 16.
KEENE, A. Jack Exh. 1889-1924
Flower, landscape and figure painter. Irongate, Derby 1889; 99 Uttoxeter New Road, Derby 1919. † B 2, L 1, N 13, RBA 2.
KEENE, Charles Samuel 1823-1891
Humerous artist and illustrator. On staff of "Punch", R.E. 1881. "Self Portrait" purchased by Chantrey Bequest 1922. Exh. 1891. † FIN 251.
KEENE, Elmer Exh. 1895
Landscape painter. Park Terrace, St. Saviour's Road, Leicester. † RA 1.
KEENE, W.C. Exh. 1880-91
Watercolour landscape painter. London. † D 2, RA 6, RBA 7, RI 2.
KEEPING, Miss D.G. Exh. 1929-32
Chilgrove, Fecitt Brow, Intack, Blackburn. † L 2.
KEEPING, Miss G.D. Exh. 1916-17
12 Southsea Terrace, Southsea, Portsmouth. † L 4.
KEES, Miss M.I. Exh. 1912-30
10 Alleyn Park, West Dulwich, London. † L 2, RBA 2, RI 9, SWA 14.
KEESEY, Walter Monckton b. 1887
Watercolour painter, etcher, architect and designer of bank notes. Studied Tonbridge and Woolwich Art Schools and Royal College of Art (travelling scholarship in architecture). Served R.E. 1914-19. Art master A.A. 1913-25. H.M. Inspector for Board of Education. A.R.E. 1914. Exh. 1912-37. Add: London. † L 18, RA 16, RE 23, RSA 1.
KEET, Miss A. Exh. 1886-88
3 Cairns Street, Liverpool. † L 2.
KEET, Emmy G.M. Exh. 1934-40
Painter, designer and illustrator. Grays, Essex 1934; Wisbech, Cambs. 1939. † RA 8.
KEEVER, J.S.H. Exh. 1937
Figure painter. † CON 1.
KEEY, G.E. Exh. 1923-35
Birmingham. † B 6.
KEFFORD, John A.C. Exh. 1928
Flower painter. † AB 1.
KEHOE, Chris J. Exh. 1919-36
Everton, Liverpool. † L 9, RSA 3.
KEIGHLEY, Mabel Exh. 1898-1907
Plymouth. † B 1, L 1, RA 1, RMS 1.
KEILLER, Mrs. D. Phil-Morris Exh. 1914-15
London 1914; Ballater, Aberdeenshire 1915. † RSA 2.
KEILLER, Eric B. Exh. 1913
South Lodge, Cobham, Surrey. † LS 3.
KEILOR, Bertha Exh. 1896-97
Landscape and coastal painter. 27 Warwick Gardens, London. † RA 1, SWA 1.
KEILY, S.M. Rosemary Exh. 1916
Reservoir Road, Prenton, Birkenhead. † L 3.
KEIR, Bridget Exh. 1910-40
Watercolour landscape painter. Studied under Claude Hayes in Paris. Taught in Summer School at Rye. Commissioned by Countess Haig in 1937 to do drawing of Earl Haig's Grave in Dryburgh Abbey, which led to a series of studies of the old Abbeys of Melrose, Kelso and Jedburgh. Travelled on the Continent and the Middle East. Cousin of the Fripp Bros. A.S.W.A. 1919. Add: London. † D 6, GI 9, RHA 1, RI 3, RSA 11, RSW 19, SWA 25, WG 536.

KEIR, Elizabeth E. Exh. 1929-36
Mrs. J.C. 16 Milton Avenue, Cambuslang. † GI 1, RSA 1.

KEIR, Harry Exh. 1933-40
161 Shamrock Street, Glasgow. † GI 6, RSA 2.

KEIR, James C. Exh. 1919-36
Glasgow 1919; Rutherglen 1922; 16 Milton Avenue, Cambuslang 1936. † GI 2, RSA 2.

KEIR, Mrs. J.L. Exh. 1895-96
14 Cavendish Place, London. † SWA 2.

KEIR, W.I. Exh. 1924
Architect. Writers Buildings, Calcutta, India. † RA 1.

KEITH, Allan Exh. 1880
Landscape painter. 57 Wood Lane, London. † D 1.

KEITH, David B. Exh. 1937-40
The Cottage, Thurso. † RSA 4, RSW 1.

KEITH, Elizabeth b. 1887
Etcher and wood cut artist. b. Scotland. Spent 9 years in Japan, China and Korea. Exh. 1923-40. Add: London and Tokyo. † BA 80, L 16, RA 3, RI 1, TOO 2.

KEITH, Letitia Margaret Exh. 1880-1919
Mrs. D. nee Parsons. Flower painter. Add: Frome, Somerset 1880; London 1889; Penge, Kent 1906. † D 2, G 2, M 2, NG 5, RA 14, RI 7, ROI 9.

KEITH, O Exh. 1881
8 Upper Camden Street, London. † RHA 3.

KEITH, William* Exh. 1898-1907
London. † NG 2, RA 2.

KELK, Miss K.H. Exh. 1926
44 Park Road, Southport, Lancs. † L 1.

KELL, Ellen Exh. 1880-81
Flower and still life painter. Lupton Villas, 104 Carleton Road, Tufnell Park, London. † SWA 2.

KELL, Frederick John Exh. 1909-34
West Hill, Sydenham, London. † LS 6, RA 1, RI 17, ROI 9.

KELL, Thomas Exh. 1880
Architect. 40 King Street, Covent Garden, London. † RA 2.

KELL, Miss V.B. Exh. 1909-12
Watercolour painter. 68 Chatsworth Gardens, Acton Hill, London. † L 2, RA 2, RI 1.

KELLAR, Kenneth W. Exh. 1938
6 West End Park Street, Glasgow. † GI 2.

KELLER, Mrs. Evelyn R. Exh. 1892-1921
Miniature and portrait painter. R.M.S. 1896. Add: Walton on Thames 1892; Woking, Surrey 1913. † LS 3, RA 16, RMS 6, SWA 1.

KELLER, Fanny H.M. Exh. 1883-92
Miniature portrait painter. Newman Street, Oxford Street, London. † GI 1, RA 12.

KELLER, Johan Exh. 1898-1915
Glasgow 1898; London 1914; Helensburgh, N.B. 1915. † GI 40, L 4, RA 7, RSA 5.

KELLER, P.W. Exh. 1884
c/o Grundy and Smith, Manchester. † M 1.

KELLMAN, Anita Exh. 1923
† G 1.

KELLOCK, David Taylor b. 1913
Watercolour painter. Studied Edinburgh College of Art 1932-36. Exh. 1937. Add: Woodlea, Carnock Road, Dumfermline. † RSA 3.

KELLOW, Kate Exh. 1893-98
Miniature portrait painter. 100 Elgin Crescent, London. † RA 1, RI 2.

KELLY, Miss Exh. 1904
2 Avenue Montague, Paris. † RHA 1.

KELLY, Anna Exh. 1934-38
Painter and linocut artist. School of Art, Dublin 1934, Fairview, Dublin 1938. † RHA 4.

KELLY, Mrs. A. Elizabeth Exh. 1931-40
Portrait painter. c/o Bourlet and Sons Ltd., Nassau Street, London. † P 3, RA 6, RCA 3, ROI 2, RSA 2, SWA 3, WG 26.

KELLY, Mrs. A.M. Exh. 1894
12 Peel Street, Liverpool. † L 1.

KELLY, C. Exh. 1912-15
11 Raleigh Gardens, Brixton Hill, London. † RA 3.

KELLY, Cecil F. Exh. 1934-38
New Zealand landscape painter. c/o J. Bourlet and Sons, Nassau Street, London. † RA 3, RBA 1, RCA 1, RSA 1.

KELLY, Frances Exh. 1899-1908
Liverpool 1899; Wimbledon 1902. † L 6.

KELLY, Frances Exh. 1929-37
Figure and portrait painter. Dublin 1929 and 1934; Paris 1933; Dundrum, Co. Dublin 1936. † RHA 29.

KELLY, Gerald Festus* 1879-1972
Portrait, figure and landscape painter. Studied in Paris. A.R.A. 1922, R.A. 1930, A.R.H.A. 1908, R.H.A. 1914, R.P. 1926. "The Jester (W. Somerset Maugham)" (1911) purchased by Chantrey Bequest 1933 and "A Vicar in his Study" (1912) purchased in 1959. Exh. from 1905. Add: London. † BAR 2, CG 5, COO 2, G 13, GI 27, GOU 30, I 41, L 96, LS 11, M 8, NEA 2, NG 1, P 18, RA 115, RHA 110, RSA 3.

KELLY, H. Hilland Exh. 1881-85
Tullarone, Co. Kilkenny. † RHA 3.

KELLY, Irene Exh. 1927
Deanfield, Londonderry. † RHA 1.

KELLY, John Exh. 1886
Architect. 5 Westminster Chambers, London. † RA 1.

KELLY, James Exh. 1886
58 Gt. Hamilton Street, Glasgow. † GI 2.

KELLY, Joseph Exh. 1895
24 George Street, Moss Side, Manchester. † M 1.

KELLY, Joseph Exh. 1931
Buchanan Street, Dunfermline. † RSA 1.

KELLY, John Turner Exh. 1890-1907
Edinburgh. † GI 2, RSA 27.

KELLY, Muriel Exh. 1911-15
15 Curzon Road, Birkenhead. † L 3.

KELLY, Rose Exh. 1911
Claude Road, Drumcondra. † RHA 1.

KELLY, Capt. Richard Barrett Talbot 1896-1971
Painter, pastel, pen and ink artist and modeller. b. Birkenhead. R.I. 1925. Son of Robert Talbot and grandson of Robert George K. q.v. Exh. from 1921. Add: London. † BK 68, GI 1, L 18, RA 5, RI 73, ROI 1.

KELLY, Robert George Exh. 1881-1907
Landscape painter. Father of Robert George Talbot and grandfather of Richard B.T.K. q.v. Add: Liverpool and Birkenhead 1881; Parkgate, Cheshire 1901. † B 2, L 52, RA 1, RHA 17.

KELLY, Robert George Talbot 1861-1934
Landscape painter. b. Birkenhead. Son of Robert George and father of Richard B.T.K. q.v. Travelled extensively in the Middle East and Burma. R.B.A. 1893, R.I. 1907. Add: Birkenhead 1882; Liverpool 1893; London 1903. † B 17, FIN 239, GI 3, L 105, LEI 167, M 10, RA 12, RBA 63, RHA 8, RI 100, ROI 4, RSA 1.

KELLY, Tom Exh. 1888-9
Landscape painter. Denston Park, Newmarket, Suffolk 1888; London 1901; Bedford 1892. † NG 8.

KELLY, Thomas Meikle b. 186
Painter and etcher. Studied Glasgow School of Art. Exh. 1893-1940. Add: Glasgow 1893; Milngavie, Dumbartonshire 1925. † GI 11, L 3, M 1, RSA 6, RSW 14.

KELLY, Vincent Exh. 193
Architect. 87 Merrion Square, Dublin. † RHA 4.

KELLY, Violet G. Exh. 189
49 Leigh Road, Highbury, London. † GI 2.

KELLY, William 1861-194
Architect. Exh. 1894-1926. Add: Aberdeen. † GI 3, RSA 15.

KELMAN, Janet Harvey Exh. 190
29 Dick Place, Edinburgh. † RSA 2.

KELSALL, Miss L.E. Exh. 188
Mayfield, Alexandra Road, Waterloo, Liverpool. † L 1.

KELSEY, A. Exh. 190
Springwood, Winchester Avenue, Leicester. † N 1.

KELSEY, Charles J. Exh. 1912-4
Landscape painter. Bristol 1912; Tickenham, Somerset 1933. † B 4, GI 2, L 1, RA 2, RCA 8, RHA 3, ROI 1, RSA 4.

KELSEY, Charles W. Exh. 192
Stained glass designer. 125 Muswell Hill, London. † RA 1.

KELSEY, Frank Exh. 1887-193
Marine and flower painter. London 1887, Ballinger, Great Missenden, Bucks. 1919. † L 1, RA 28, RBA 24, RI 3, RID 68, ROI 7, TOO 9.

KELSO, Roberta Exh. 194
16 Woodland Avenue, Paisley. † GI 1.

KEMM, Robert* Exh. 1882-91
Genre painter. London. † B 2, GI 1, L 6, M 2, RBA 5, RHA 1.

KEMP, Ada Exh. 1890-91
17 Portland Road, Edgbaston, Birmingham. † B 2.

KEMP, Agnes Exh. 1892-1910
Landscape, fruit, flower and figure painter. Edinburgh 1892; London 1899. † GI 4, RBA 2, RI 1, RID 28, RSA 1, SWA 2.

KEMP, Arthur C. Exh. 1936-40
Landscape painter. The Cottage, 75 Middleton Hall Road, King's Norton, Birmingham. † B 10, RA 1.

KEMP, Amy K.P. Exh. 1889-90
Landscape painter. Sussex Cottage, 10 Kenninghall Road, Clapton, London. † RBA 2.

KEMP, Amy Paget Exh. 1895-1919
32 Cumberland Park, Acton, London. † I 1, RI 2.

KEMP, Emily G. Exh. 1893-1913
Landscape painter. London. † ALP 9, L 1, SWA 2.

KEMP, George C.C. Exh. 1935-37
23 Petersfield Road, Hall Green, Birmingham. † B 4.

KEMP, Miss Jeka Exh. 1905-21
London 1905 and 1908; Glasgow 1906, 1909 and 1921; Paris 1920. † GI 9, I 3, L 16, RA 1, RSA 2.

KEMP, Mrs. Jessie Exh. 1910
Daneham, Hough Green, Widnes, Lancs. † L 1.

KEMP, John Exh. 1907-11
20 Lansdowne Crescent, Glasgow. † GI 2.

KEMP, Kenneth d. c.1918
Exh. 1914-18. London. † L 1, LS 3, RA 2, RBA 10.

KEMP, Marjorie Exh. 1921-40
Stained glass artist. b. Blairgowrie, Perthshire. Studied Glasgow School of Art. Add: Edinburgh. † GI 3, RA 6, RSA 13.

KEMP, Robert Exh. 1922-32
87 Willows Crescent, Cannon Hill Park, Birmingham. † B 5, RI 1.

KEMP, T.J.C. Exh. 1882
Newpark, Nuthurst, Horsham, Sussex. † RSA 1.

KEMP, Violet I. Exh. 1940
Elm Lodge, Dalkeith. † RSA 1.

KEMP, W.A. Exh. 1927-28
4 Eleanor Road, London. † RI 2.

KEMP, W.G. Exh. 1880-85
Edinburgh. † GI 1, RSA 4.

KEMP, Walter M. Exh. 1887-95
Sculptor. Surbiton, Surrey 1887; Eastcote, Nr. Pinner, Middlesex 1888. † L 1, RA 3.

KEMPE, Miss C. Exh. 1906-7
14 Montague Place, London. † RA 1, SWA 3.

KEMPE, Harriet Exh. 1880-93
Genre painter. London. † B 14, D 9, GI 1, L 10, M 8, RA 14, RBA 5, RHA 14, RI 1, SWA 3.

KEMPLEN, Alfred R. Exh. 1897-1907
Paris. † D 1, RA 1.

KEMPSON, Frederick R. Exh. 1881-1905
Architect. Hereford 1881; Chelsea, London 1893; Cardiff 1905. † RA 4.

KEMPSON, George Exh. 1893
15 Ladypool Road, Sparkbrook, Birmingham. † B 1.

KEMPSON, Miss M. Freeman Exh. 1880-1911
Landscape, coastal and figure painter. S.W.A. 1880. Add: Perth Villa, Wellesley Grove, Croydon, Surrey. † L 2, RBA 4, SWA 213.

KEMPTHORNE, Helen Mary Exh. 1900-19
Miniature portrait painter. A.R.M.S. 1907, R.M.S. 1910. Add: London 1900; Newquay, Cornwall 1919. † L 8, NG 11, RA 12, RMS 37.

KEMP-WELCH, Edith M. Exh. 1898-1939
Miniature painter. R.M.S. 1900. Sister of Lucy E. K-W, q.v. Add: Bushey, Herts. † B 3, L 2, M 2, RA 25, RI 1, RMS 27, SWA 14.

KEMP-WELCH, Lucy Elizabeth* 1869-1958
Animal painter. b. Bournemouth. Studied Herkomers, Bushey, Herts. Principal of Kemp-Welch School of Painting, Bushey. Sister of Edith M. K-W, q.v. R.B.A. 1902, R.I. 1907. "Colt Hunting in the New Forest" purchased by Chantrey Bequest 1897 and "Forward the Guns" in 1917. Exh. 1895-1940. Add: Hythe, Kent 1895; Bushey, Herts. 1896 and 1923; London 1922. † AR 71, B 4, D 19, FIN 63, GI 17, L 23, M 6, NG 3, RA 61, RBA 16, RCA 53, RHA 2, RI 36, ROI 4, RSA 3, SWA 3.

KEMP-WELCH, Margaret Exh. 1898-1940
Landscape and portrait painter, etcher and engraver. Head of Art Training College, Clapham High School. A.R.E. 1901. Add: Godstone, Surrey 1898; London 1901 and 1910; Wimbledon, Surrey 1904; Croyde, Devon 1936. † L 7, RA 14, RBA 1, RE 104, RI 8, RID 63, SWA 1.

KENDA, Arthur D. Exh. 1889
† RID 1.

KENDALL, Donald Exh. 1886-1927
Liverpool 1886; Egremont, Cheshire 1890; Liscard, Cheshire 1894; Higher Bebington, Cheshire 1902; Llanbedr, Tal-y-Cafn, Wales 1913; Rock Ferry, Cheshire 1919. † L 74, M 1, RA 2, RCA 30.

KENDALL, Ethel M.L. Exh. 1898-1939
Miniature and landscape painter. A.R.M.S. 1938. Add: London 1898 and 1914; Beckenham, Kent 1904 and 1920. † BG 2, L 3, RA 8, RMS 11, ROI 1, SWA 2.

KENDALL, Isabel Exh. 1900-9
Lancelyn, Rock Ferry, Cheshire. † L 12, RMS 1.

KENDALL, John David 1893-1936
Architect. 1 Paternoster Row, London. † RA 1.

KENDALL, Miss M.L. Exh. 1914
Ashburnham Road, Chelsea, London. † SWA 2.

KENDALL, Sergeant Exh. 1892
12 Rue de Seine, Paris. † NEA 1.

KENDALL, Thomas H. Exh. 1898-1900
Wood carver. Warwick. † RA 3.

KENDELL, William Clement Exh. 1888
Yorks. † D 2.

KENDERDINE, Augustus Exh. 1901
Landscape painter. b. Manchester. Add: 90 Church Street, Blackpool. Emigrated to Canada. † L 1, RA 1.

KENDON, Frank Exh. 1924
Miniature painter. 29 Hogarth Road, Earl's Court, London. † RA 1.

KENDRICK, A. Exh. 1906
Fulthorpe Studios, 3E Warwick Avenue, Maida Hill, London. † RA 1.

KENDRICK, Alicia J.E. Exh. 1899-1901
Old Dromore, Mallow, Co. Cork. † RHA 5.

KENDRICK, Flora Exh. 1910-27
Watercolour painter, modeller and sculptor. Studied Royal College of Art. Add: London. † GI 1, I 3, L 5, M 1, RA 12, RSA 2.

KENDRICK, Sydney* Exh. 1903-15
Figure painter. 3C Warwick Road, Maida Hill, London. † RA 4.

KENEALY, Noel Byron Exh. 1886-93
Engraver: Bushey Grove, Watford, Herts. † RA 3, RBA 1.

KENISON, I. Exh. 1884
38 Fenton Street, Rochdale, Lancs. † L 1.

KENMORE, F. Exh. 1890
Landscape painter. 18 Roderick Road, London. † RBA 1.

KENNARD, H. Exh. 1906-9
Architect. 13 Railway Approach, London Bridge, and 23 Devereux Court, Strand, London. † RA 3.

KENNARD, J. Moir Exh. 1904-18
Architect. 13 Railway Approach, London Bridge, London. † RA 3.

KENNAWAY, C.G. Exh. 1891-1918
Landscape and figure painter. London 1891 and 1901; Glasgow 1898; Lenzie, N.B. 1899. † DOW 42, GI 11, I 4, L 3, NG 1, RA 3, RI 1, RSW 2.

KENNAWAY, May Exh. 1911-16
St. Helens, Teignmouth, Devon. † L 6, RHA 4.

KENNEDY, Cecil* b. 1905
Portrait and flower painter. Brother of Thomas K. q.v. Exh. 1925-38. Add: Clifton House, Church Road, Leyton, Essex. † RA 1, RHA 1, RSA 3.

KENNEDY, Cedric J. b. 1898
Landscape and portrait painter. Studied R.A. Schools. Prisoner of war World War 1. Drawing master Rugby School. Exh. 1926-38. Add: Watford, Herts. 1926; London 1928; Painswick, Glos. 1935. † COO 3, NEA 3, RA 5, WG 177.

KENNEDY, Miss C.M. Exh. 1940
21 Westbourne Terrace, London. † ROI 3.

KENNEDY, Charles Napier 1852-1898
Portrait, genre and mythological painter. Studied Slade School. Married Lucy K. q.v. A.R.H.A. 1896, R.O.I. 1883. Add: London. † B 7, G 4, GI 9, L 12, M 3, NG 8, P 7, RA 18, RBA 3, RHA 10, ROI 27.

KENNEDY, D. Exh. 1886
30 Steven Street, Glasgow. † GI 3.

KENNEDY, David Exh. 1895
Architect. 18 Maddox Street, London. † RA 1.

KENNEDY, Mrs. E.K.O. Exh. 1916
23 Stephen's Road, Tunbridge Wells, Kent. † RHA 1.

KENNEDY, Edward Sherard* Exh. 1880-95
Genre painter. Married Florence S.K. q.v. Add: London 1880; Edenbridge, Kent 1895. † B 10, D 3, GI 2, L 9, M 1, RA 3, RBA 3, RI 4, ROI 6.

KENNEDY, Edward W. Exh. 1892-1919
Merchiston, N.B. 1892; Edinburgh 1898. † GI 6, L 1, RSA 10.

KENNEDY, Florence S. Exh. 1880-93
nee Laing. Figure, domestic and landscape painter. Married Edward Sherard K. q.v. Add: London 1880 and 1885; Exmouth, Devon 1884. † B 10, D 2, G 1, L 5, M 1, RA 4, RBA 1, ROI 4.

KENNEDY, Hazel see ARMOUR

KENNEDY, Miss H.C. Exh. 1891-93
Low Nook, Ambleside. † B 1, L 1.

KENNEDY, Joseph Exh. 1883-88
Figure and domestic painter. Barnstaple, Devon. † RA 1, RBA 4, RHA 1.

KENNEDY, James Duncan Exh. 1922-38
Figure painter. 147 King Henry Road, London. † D 1, I 2, L 3, RA 1, RBA 3.

KENNEDY, John Davies Exh. 1920-37
Selkirk 1920; Edinburgh 1921; Cramond Bridge 1931. † GI 1, L 3, RSA 22, RSW 10.

KENNEDY, J.L. Exh. 1899
104 Hartley Road, Nottingham. † N 1.

KENNEDY, Kathleen C. Exh. 1916-40
Landscape painter. Mariner's Rectory, Kingstown, Dublin 1916; Sisters Residence, New Barracks, Fermoy 1917; Ranelagh, Dublin 1940. † RHA 5.

KENNEDY, Lucy Exh. 1884-97
nee Marwood. Figure and domestic painter. Married Charles Napier K. q.v. Add: London. † B 1, GI 6, L 3, M 1, NG 10, RI 4, RHA 1.

KENNEDY, L.F. Exh. 1899
Abbey Road, Stirling. † GI 1.

KENNEDY, Marcus Exh. 1919-20
Belfast. † RHA 3.

KENNEDY, Magnus A. Exh. 1909-16
Dumfries, N.B. 1909; Liverpool 1915. † GI 3, L 3.

KENNEDY, R. Exh. 1914
47 Chaussee d'Ixelles, Brussels. † RA 1.

KENNEDY, Robert A. Exh. 1892-1940
Glasgow 1892; Dundee 1899; Edinburgh 1905; Liberton, Nr. Edinburgh 1937. † GI 14, L 1, RSA 14.

KENNEDY, S. Exh. 1885
† GI 1.

KENNEDY, Mrs. Sara Exh. 1896-99
Watercolour painter. London. † RA 1, RBA 1, RI 4, SWA 2.

KENNEDY, Thomas b. 1900
Landscape and portrait painter. Brother of Cecil K. q.v. Add: Clifton House, Church Road, Leyton. Essex. † RA 2, RSA 5.

KENNEDY, T.B. Exh. 1886
Bolton Studios, London. † ROI 1.

KENNEDY, Mrs. W. Exh. 1900-16
Stirling 1900; Glasgow 1901; Tangier, Morocco 1913. † GI 29, L 7, RSA 1.

KENNEDY, William* 1859-1918
Landscape, animal and military painter. Studied Paris 1880-85. Add: Paris 1882; Glasgow 1885 and 1900; Stirling 1897; Tangier, Morocco 1913. † GI 74, L 11, NEA 1, RA 1, ROI 8, RSA 18, RSW 2.

KENNEDY, W.J. Exh. 1887-1914
Glasgow 1887; Edinburgh 1914. † GI 1, RSA 1.

KENNEDY, W.R. Exh. 1890
55 St. George's Road, London. † D 2.

KENNELL, W.H. Exh. 1880-91
Hornton Cottage, Campden Hill, London. † D 3.

KENNEP, A. Exh. 1885
4 Montgomery Street, Edinburgh. † RSA 1.

KENNET, see SCOTT, Lady Kathleen

KENNEY, Mrs. Asta Exh. 1936
Sculptor. Shirley Place, Upper Shirley, Surrey. † RA 1.

KENNINGTON, Carrie Exh. 1895
12 Red Lion Street, Boston, Lincs. † RBA 1.

KENNINGTON, Eric Henri 1888-1960
Painter, draughtsman, pastel artist and sculptor. Studied St. Paul's Art School, Lambeth and Kennington Art Schools. Son of Thomas B.K. q.v. A collection of his work is in the Tate Gallery. Exh. 1908-33. Add: London. † ALP 105, BA 1, CHE 1, FIN 6, GOU 90, I 11, L 16, LEI 192, P 6, RA 2, ROI 10.

KENNINGTON, Thomas Benjamin* 1856-1916
Portrait and genre painter. b. Grimsby. Father of Eric Henri K. q.v. N.E.A. 1886 (Hon. Sec. 1886-88), R.B.A. 1888, R.O.I. 1889, V.P.R.O.I. 1908, R.P. 1891. Add: London. † B 19, G 3, GI 7, L 61, M 20, NEA 1, NG 1, P 55, RA 72, RBA 16, RE 2, RHA 1, RI 4, ROI 92, RSA 1.

KENNION, Miss Exh. 1884
Painter. 22 Upper Montague Street, London. † SWA 1.

KENNION, Mary Exh. 1898
Southborough, Kent. † D 2.

KENNY, Desmond Courtney Exh. 1934-40
Portrait and flower painter. London. † RA 1, ROI 2.

KENRICK, Dorothy b. 1887
Miniature painter. b. Reigate. Add: London 1921; Brighton, Sussex 1937. † RA 12.

KENT, H.R.H. the Duchess of 1906-1968
Princess Marina, daughter of Prince Nicolas of Greece. Exh. 1936-38. Add: Belgrave Square, London. † GI 2, SWA 4.

KENT, Adrian Arnold Exh. 1928-31
Landscape painter. † AG 2, NEA 1.

KENT, Beatrice Exh. 1923-29
Southport, Lancs. † L 14.

KENT, Cynthia Exh. 1927
c/o St. George's Gallery, London. † RHA 1.

KENT, Ethel A. Exh. 1896-98
Watercolour portrait painter. Cliftonville, Margate, Kent 1896; Sydenham, London 1898. † RA 1, SWA 1.

KENT, James S. Exh. 1900
212 St. Vincent Street, Glasgow. † GI 2.

KENT, Leslie b. 1890
Coastal, landscape, sky and seascape painter. Studied under Fred Milner at St. Ives 1918-20. Travelled throughout the world. A.R.B.A. 1939. R.B.A. 1940. Exh. 1929-40. Add: Bonds Cay, Radlett, Herts. † GOU 2, NEA 3, RA 4, RBA 28, ROI 24, RSA 3, WG 97.

KENT, Mary b. 1915
Mrs. G. Kent Harrison. nee Marryat. Studied Kingston School of Art 1933-35 and R.A. Schools 1937-38. Exh. 1940. Add: 27 Mecklenburgh Square, London. † RA 1.

KENT, Peter Exh. 1940
Architect. 16C Chesham Road, Brighton, Sussex. † RA 1.

KENT, Miss Ursula S. Exh. 1935
Portrait painter. Greys, Radlett, Herts. † RA 1, RBA 1.

KENT-BIDDLECOMBE, Jessica Doreen b. 1898
Portrait and flower painter. b. Burnham on Sea. Studied Slade School. Exh. 1924-29. Add: 46 Beulah Hill, Upper Norwood, London. † RA 1, ROI 6.

KENWORTHY, Esther Exh. 1881-82
Watercolour flower painter. Kerrison Lodge, Ealing, London. † L 1, RA 2, RBA 1.

KENWORTHY, John Dalzell 1858-1954
Portrait and rustic painter. Add: St. Bees, Cumberland 1895 and 1915; Whitehaven 1908. † L 9, RA 1, RCA 36.

KENWORTHY-BROWNE, Faith b. 1882
Portrait and landscape painter and poster artist. b. Bournemouth. Studied at Sir Arthur Cope's School and London School of Art. Art teacher at St. Albans College, Prince Albert, Saskatchewan, Canada. Exh. 1924-40. Add: London. † COO 4, GOU 1, NEA 1, RA 1, RBA 1, ROI 6, SWA 3.

KENYON, Arthur W. Exh. 1914-40
Architect. London. † RA 4.

KENYON, Miss E.G. Exh. 1903-14
Twickenham, Middlesex. † B 1, GI 1, L 5, RA 1, RMS 1, RSA 1.

KENYON, George Exh. 1893-96
Architect. 35 New Bond Street, London. † RA 4.

KENYON, John Dyke Exh. 1937
Conway, Wales. † RCA 1.

KENYON, May Exh. 1929
Linden, Rock Hill, Woolton, Liverpool. † L 2.

KENYON, W. Ernest Exh. 1906-11
Leeds. † L 2, RA 1, RCA 4.

KEOGH, Alice Exh. 1891-1903
Chiswick, London 1891; Roxborough Park, Harrow, Middlesex 1897. † M 2, RHA 4, SWA 4.

KEPPIE, Miss Jessie d. 1951
Watercolour flower painter. Studied Glasgow School of Art. R.S.W. 1934. Exh. 1892-1940. Add: Glasgow. † BG 2, GI 57, L 5, RSA 13, RSW 36.

KEPPIE, John Exh. 1888-1940
A.R.S.A. 1920, R.S.A. 1940. Add: Glasgow 1888; Prestwick, Ayrshire 1940. † GI 62, L 1, RSA 35, RSW 6.

KER, B. Exh. 1910-14
London 1910; Bristol 1914. † B 1, RA 3.

KER, Joan Exh. 1931-38
Landscape painter. Ledaig, Argyll 1931; Strathbane 1934; Rye, Sussex 1937. † NEA 4, RA 1, RBA 4, RSA 3, SWA 1.

KER, Margaret Exh. 1889-1919
Liverpool. † B 2, L 15.

KERBY, Fred J. Exh. 1904-9
Landscape painter. Reading, Berks. † RA 1, RCA 1.

KERCKHOVE, de see D

KERMACK, Agnes M. Exh. 1891-97
Edinburgh. † GI 5, RSA 2.

KERMODE, E.W. Exh. 1930
Linocut artist. † RED 3.

KERMODE, J.J. Exh. 1883
3 Borough Road, Birkenhead. † L 1.

KERNOFF, Harry Aaron* b. 1900
Portrait, landscape and decorative painter. b. London. Studied Metropolitan School of Art, Dublin (Taylor scholarship). A.R.H.A. 1935, R.H.A. 1935. Exh. 1926-40. Add: 13 Stamer Street, Dublin. † RA 1, RHA 81.

KERNOT, Mrs. Exh. 1880-87
Landscape painter. Granville House, Hornsey Rise, London. † SWA 9.

KERR, Annie S. Exh. 1914
48 Orrell Lane, Aintree, Liverpool. † L 1.

KERR, Barbara Exh. 1912
2 The Boltons, London. † L 1.

KERR, Mrs. Beatrice Exh. 1925
14 Duke Street, Hawick. † RSA 1.

KERR, Charles Henry Malcolm 1858-1907
Portrait, landscape and coastal painter. R.B.A. 1890. Add: London. † L 6, M 1, NEA 1, RA 28, RBA 13, RHA 1, RI 1, ROI 12.

KERR, Mrs. Esther Barbara Nicloux Exh. 1927-35
Flower and interior painter. London. † ALP 1, AR 12, L 7, RA 2, RBA 1, RCA 4, RHA 2, RID 3, ROI 5, RSA 1, SWA 3.

KERR, Mrs. E. Lamorna Exh. 1939
Coastal painter. Treens Bungalow, Mousehole, nr. Penzance, Cornwall. † RA 1.

KERR, Edith M. Exh. 1930
The Anchorage, Loch Ranza, Isle of Arran. † GI 2.

KERR, Frederick B. Exh. 1915-31
Watercolour landscape painter. Leeds 1915; London 1930. † AB 36, B 12, RA 2, RI 1.

KERR, Frederick James b. 1853
Landscape painter and art master. Studied Swansea School of Art and Royal College of Art. Exh. 1904-16. Add: Twynceri, Colcot, Barry, S. Wales. † L 3, NG 2, RA 1, RCA 6, RI 4.

KERR, George Cochrane Exh. 1880-1907
Marine painter. London 1880 and 1882; Ramsgate, Kent 1881; Gillingham, Kent 1890; Rochester, Kent 1896. † B 1, FIN 50, GI 5, L 14, M 2, RA 12, RBA 15, RHA 1, RI 18, ROI 10, RSA 3, RSW 2.

KERR, Grace M. Exh. 1890
194 Bath Street, Glasgow. † GI 1.

KERR, Henry Francis Exh. 1883-1937
Edinburgh. † GI 3, RSA 18.

KERR, Henry Wright 1857-1936
Portrait and figure painter. A.R.S.A. 1893, R.S.A. 1909, R.S.W. 1891. Add: Edinburgh. † DOW 1, GI 26, L 12, RA 8, RI 1, RSA 159, RSW 70.

KERR, James H. Exh. 1880-98
Glasgow 1880; Dalry Road, Edinburgh 1885. † GI 14, RSA 5.

KERR, Miss K. Exh. 1896
13 Rue Washington, Champs Elysees, Paris. † B 1, L 1.

KERR, Maree Exh. 1937-38
The Cairns, Carlisle Road, Hamilton. † GI 3.

KERR, Margaret Exh. 1880-85
Figure and domestic painter. Glyn Cottage, Park Vale East, London. † SWA 5.

KERR, Nesta Exh. 1886-94
Glasgow. † GI 5.

KERR, Peter Exh. 1889-1906
Greenock. † GI 17, RHA 7, RSA 4.

KERR, R.W. Graham Exh. 1931
9 The University, Glasgow. † GI 1.

KERRAWAY, May Exh. 1912
St. Helens, Teignmouth, S. Devon. † RHA 1.

KERRIDGE, H.K. Exh. 1886-1920
Liverpool 1886; Seacombe 1891; Liscard, Cheshire 1896; New Brighton, Cheshire 1908. † L 19, M 1, RA 1, RCA 2.

KERRIDGE, W.W. Exh. 1885
Alderley Edge, nr. Manchester. † M 1.

KERRISON, Mrs. Jessie Exh. 1898
Burlingham House, Norwich. † SWA 1.

KERRISON, Mary Exh. 1910-23
200 Seaview Road, Liscard, Cheshire. † L 3, RCA 1.

KERR-LAWSON, James 1864-1939
Figure, portrait and landscape painter, mural decorator and lithographer. b. Anstruther, Fife. Went to Canada in his early childhood. Studied in Rome and Paris. Add: Pittenween, Fife 1890; Kirkintilloch, N.B. 1892; Glasgow 1894; London 1903. † ALP 12, B 1, BA 39, DOW 50, G 1, GI 10, I 13, L 8, M 8, P 2, RBA 1, ROI 1.

KERRY, A.R. Exh. 1914-33
Landscape painter. 2 Melton Grove, West Bridgford, Notts. 1914; Nottingham 1930. † N 19.

KERRY, M. Beatrice Exh. 1900
Moor Park Avenue, Preston, Lancs. † M 1.

KERRY, Stanley C. Exh. 1925-30
Figure and landscape painter. West Bridgford, Notts. 1925; Nottingham 1929. † N 5.

KERRY, William L. Exh. 1882-93
Landscape painter. Gallery of Art, Royal Institution, Liverpool 1882; Waterloo, Liverpool 1892. † L 13.

KERSHAW, Agnes Exh. 1898-1902
Figure painter. 28 Blakeney Road, Crookes, Sheffield. † RA 1, SWA 2.

KERSHAW, Miss E. Exh. 1905
† SWA 1.

KERSHAW, J.F. Exh. 1911-14
London 1911; Sandside, nr. Milnthorpe, Westmorland 1914. † I 1, L 1, RA 3.

KERSHAW, Lilian Exh. 1924-26
Watercolour painter. 95 Central Avenue, New Basford, Nottingham. † N 3.

KERSHAW, Mary E. Exh. 1901-28
A.R.E. 1902. Add: 7 Westcliffe Road, Birkdale. † B 1, GI 2, L 9, RA 2, RE 27, RSA 1.

KERSHAW, M. Lilian Exh. 1907
51 West Parade, Huddersfield. † L 2.

KERVILY, de see D

KESS, Miss M.I. Exh. 1927
10 Alleyn Park, London. † RBA 1.

KESSEY, Walter M. Exh. 1924
24 Bedford Square, London. † GI 1.

KESSISOGLU, Esther Exh. 1891-92
Flower painter. 27 Notting Hill Terrace, Holland Park, London. † RBA 2.

KESTELMAN, Morris b. 1905
Painter, lithographer and designer. Studied at Central School of Arts and Crafts and Royal College of Art. Exh. 1928-32. Add: London 1928; Old Marston, Oxon. 1929; Oxford 1930. † NEA 4.

KESTEVEN, Mary Exh. 1925-27
Hernwood, nr. Sevenoaks, Kent. † L 1, NEA 2.

KESWICK, James D.T. Exh. 1940
† NEA 1.

KETCHLEE, Nellie M. Exh. 1891-92
Figure painter. London 1891; Wadhurst, Sussex 1892. † RBA 2.

KETCHLEY, Miss H.S. Exh. 1913-14
Barton le Street, Malton, Yorks. 1913; Pickering, Yorks. 1914. † L 3, RA 1.

KETTLE, Sir Rupert 1817-1894
Painter. Clay-y-Don, Fowyn, N. Wales 1882; Wolverhampton 1884. † B 2, RI 1.

KETTON, F.G. Exh. 1888
8 West Kensington Terrace, London. † RI 2.

KEVER, Jacob Simon Hendrik* 1854-1922
Dutch painter. Exh. 1885-86. Add: Amsterdam. † GI 1, M 1.

KEWELL, John E. Exh. 1925-29
Architect. 290 Oxford Road, Manchester. † RA 2.

KEWLEY, George Exh. 1915-24
New Brighton, Cheshire 1915; Liverpool 1922. † L 7.

KEWNEY, Gertrude Exh. 1888
15 Bassett Road, North Kensington, London. † RSA 1.

KEY, Mrs. Exh. 1919
27A Church Street, London. † SWA 1.

KEY, Henry Exh. 1883-86
West Pershore, Worcs. † B 3.

KEY, John E. Exh. 1931-35
26 Gray's Inn Road, London. † ROI 2.

KEY, Sam Exh. 1888-99
West Kensington Park, London 1888; Richmond, Surrey 1891; Croydon, Surrey 1899. † D 29, L 1, M 1.

KEYES, Diana Exh. 1935
Portrait and animal painter. † WG 8.

KEYES, K. Exh. 1935
Painter. † WG 9.

KEYES, Phyllis Exh. 1908-11
Portrait painter and lithographer. Hampton Court Palace, London. † L 3, WG 12.

KEYES, Major P. Hubert Exh. 1922-26
Architect. Add: P.O. Architect (P.W.D.) Collyer Quay, Singapore 1922; Aldwych, London 1926. † RA 6.

KEYMEULEN, E.A. Exh. 1881
Brussels. † GI 2.

KEYON, Arthur W. Exh. 1934
Architect. 21 Bedford Square, London. † RA 2.

KEYS, Frances Exh. 1880-81
Landscape painter. 20 Duppas Hill Terrace, Croydon, Surrey. † SWA 9.

KEYS, G.F. Exh. 1890-93
Landscape painter. London. † RA 2, RBA 4.

KEYSER, de see D

KEYSER, E. Exh. 1884
c/o 38 Queen Street, Cheapside, London. † L 1.

KEYTE, H.W. Exh. 1914
27 Cedar Road, Northampton. † RHA 1.

KEYWORTH, William Day junr. b. 1843
Sculptor. b. Hull. Son of William Day K. sen. (1817-1897). Exh. 1880-96. Add: London. † RA 9.

KHNOPFF, Fernand* 1858-1921
Belgian painter. Exh. 1891-1921. Add: Brussels. † FIN 3, GI 1, I 2, L 11, NG 15, P 5, RSA 1.

KIBBLER, Dudley Exh. 1915-20
Figure painter. Ashcroft, Ringmer, Sussex. † RA 2.

KIBBLER, W. Ambrose Exh. 1891-97
Landscape painter. 134 Mare Street, Hackney, London. † RI 4.

KIBBLEWHITE, Diana Exh. 1922-23
67 Frith Street, London. † NEA 2.

KIDD, Anne Elsie Exh. 1926
nee Roberts. Portrait and landscape painter. b. Liverpool. Add: 62 Shrewsbury Road, Birkenhead. † L 1.

KIDD, Eleanor Exh. 1881-84
Fruit and still life painter. Mount Vernon, Nottingham. † N 4.

KIDD, William A.T. Exh. 1940
Painter. c/o Bourlet and Sons Ltd. 17 Nassau Street, London. † RHA 1, RSA 1.

KIDDALL, Helen D. Exh. 1921-40
Figure painter. A.S.W.A. 1935. Add: London 1921 and 1931; Alford, Lincs. 1927; Felixstowe, Suffolk 1932. † G 7, L 1, M 1, RA 9, RBA 1, SWA 16.

KIDDEY, Robert P. Exh. 1923-40
Painter and sculptor. A.N.S.A. 1932. Add: Nottingham 1923; Newark, Notts. 1931. † N 24, RA 4, RCA 2.

KIDDIER, Miss Alice Exh. 1914-40
Figure painter. A.N.S.A. 1917, N.S.A. 1927. Add: Nottingham 1914; Woodthorpe, Notts. 1938. † I 8, L 1, N 6, ROI 1, SWA 8.

KIDDIER, Ernest Exh. 1908-10
Landscape painter. A.N.S.A. 1908, N.S.A. 1909. Add: 12 South Parade, Nottingham. † N 3.

KIDDIER, William 1859-1934
Painter, etcher and writer. N.S.A. 1892, (Hon. Sec. 1893) V.P.N.S.A. 1908-17. Add: Nottingham 1888; Woodthorpe, Notts. 1929. † FIN 43, GI 3, L 13, N 65, RA 3, RHA 2, RSA 3.

KIDDS, D. Gordon Exh. 1939
23 Charlotte Square, Edinburgh. † RSA 1.

KIDGER, Clarence W. Exh. 1924-38
Figure, landscape and still life painter. Sutton in Ashfield, Notts. † N 9.

KIDMAN, Hilda Elizabeth b. 1891
Mrs. M. Tomson. Portrait, flower, animal and still life painter. Studied Slade School, Calderon's School of Animal painting and St. John's Wood School. A.S.W.A. 1934. Exh. 1911-40. Add: Hitchin, Herts. † L 6, P 1, RA 10, RCA 1, RSA 4, SWA 25.

KIDNER, William Exh. 1888
Architect. 23 Old Broad Street, London. † RA 1.

KIDSON, Frank Exh. 1884-89
128 Burley Road, Leeds 1884 and 1889; Liverpool 1886. † L 4.

KIDSON, H.E. Exh. 1887-1909
4 Beech Terrace, Beech Street, Liverpool. † L 31, RI 2.

KIDSTON, Annabel Exh. 1922-37
Wood engraver. Glasgow 1922; Hedcliffe, Helensburgh 1930. † GI 20, RA 1, RSA 16.

KIEFFER, Joseph Exh. 1907
Aston Lower Grounds, Birmingham. † B 4.

KIEFFER, William J. Exh. 1920-35
Architect. 83 Pall Mall, London 1920; Bourne End, Bucks. 1935. † RA 13.

KIEHL, Miss W.J.L. Exh. 1890
85 Bezinderhout, The Hague, Holland. † M 1.

KIESEL, Professor Exh. 1890
c/o Baron von Hoevel, Asgard, Ampthill Square, London. † G 1.

KIKUCHI, Sohseki Exh. 1936
Watercolour painter. 73 Harcourt Terrace, London. † RA 1.

KILBURN, Joyce b. 1884
Mrs. D. nee Collier. Miniature portrait painter. Daughter of Hon. John Collier q.v. Studied Slade School. A.R.M.S. 1937, R.M.S. 1938, A.S.W.A. 1940. Exh. 1905-40. Add: London. † AR 21, P 4, RA 7, RMS 16.

KILBURNE, George Goodwin, sen.* 1839-1924
Genre painter, and engraver. Studied for 5 years with the Dalziel Bros. A.R.I. 1866, R.I. 1868, R.M.S. 1898, R.O.I. 1883. Father of George Goodwin K. jun. q.v. Exh. 1880-1923. Add: London. † AG 16, B 18, DOW 1, GI 3, L 28, M 7, RA 37, RBA 1, RI 106, RMS 3, ROI 52, TOO 3.

KILBURNE, George Goodwin, junr.* 1863-1938
Figure and domestic painter. Son of George Goodwin K. sen. q.v. R.B.A. 1889. Add: London 1882; Horsham, Sussex 1900; Ashhurst, Kent 1905; Carshalton, Surrey 1912. † L 4, M 3, RA 24, RBA 47, RI 4, ROI 18.

KILBURNE, Miss M. Exh. 1918
4 Castlenau Mansions, Barnes, London. † RA 2.

KILGOUR, A. Wilkie 1868-1930
Exh. 1908-9. b. Kirkcaldy, Scotland. d. Montreal, Canada. Add: 8 Fitzroy Street, London. † LS 5.

KILGOUR, Belle M. Exh. 1925-36
Edinburgh. † RSA 4.

KILGOUR, J. Noel Exh. 1938
Painter. 242 Gloucester Terrace, London. † RA 2.

KILLICK, Kate Exh. 1906
Townfield House, Altrincham, Cheshire. † M 1.

KILLIN, G. Goldie Exh. 1920
Claremont, 7 Stewarton Drive, Cambuslang, Lanarks. † L 1.

KILLMISTER, C. Gordon Exh. 1889-99
Architect and architectural painter. Westminster, London 1889; St. Ives, Cornwall 1897. † L 1, RA 1, RI 1, RHA 3.

KILPACK, Sarah Louisa Exh. 1880-1909
Landscape painter. London. † SWA 58.

KILPATRICK, J.A. Exh. 1888
28 Arlington Street, Glasgow. † GI 1.

KILPATRICK, Renie Exh. 1927
3 Eldon Villas, Mount Florida, Glasgow. † GI 1.

KILPATRICK, Robert Exh. 1935-39
153 Garthland Drive, Glasgow. † B 2, GI 3, RSW 4.

KILPIN, Legh Mulhall* 1853-1919
Painter. b. Ryde, I.O.W. Exh. 1882-1911. Add: London. d. Montreal, Canada. † L 3, RA 3, RHA 2, RI 1, ROI 1.

KILROY, R. Exh. 1924
Portrait painter. Upper Broughton, Melton Mowbray, Leics. † N 1.

KILROY, Robert A. Exh. 1929
Watercolour landscape painter. 43 Kensington Park Gardens, London. † AB 4, NEA 1, RA 1.

KILROY, Miss Winifrede Exh. 1924
Landscape painter. Upper Broughton, Melton Mowbray, Leics. † N 3.

KIMBALL, Katharine Exh. 1906-24
Etcher, pencil and pen and ink artist. b. New Hampshire, U.S.A. Studied National Academy of Design, New York and Royal College of Art, London. A.R.E. 1909. Add: 9 Glendower Place, South Kensington, London 1906; c/o Brown, Shipley and Co., Pall Mall, London 1907. † I 4, L 15, RA 15, RE 20.

KIMBER, S. Virginia May Exh. 1916-39
A.R.M.S. 1916, R.M.S. 1919. Add: Chelston, Torquay, S. Devon 1916; London 1920. † B 2, L 9, RMS 25, SWA 3.

KIMM, A.K. Exh. 1916-23
Kirkcudbright 1916; Mount Florida, Glasgow 1917; Brampton, Carlisle 1921. † GI 8, RSA 2.

KIMPTON, Miss C.E. Exh. 1920
The Red House, Addlestone, Surrey. † SWA 1.

KIMURA, Ryoichi Exh. 1918
8 Eton Street, Regent's Park, London. † RI 1.

KINCAIRD-PITCAIRN, Mary Mabel b. 1875
nee Thorne. Watercolour miniature flower painter. Studied at Colarossi's, Paris. Exh. 1931-39. Add: 80 Finnart Street, Greenock. † L 4, RI 23, RSA 8.

KIND, August Exh. 1894
Ville des Spains, Nancy, France. † GI 1.

KINDER, Miss E.L. Exh. 1887
St. Margarets. Babbacombe, Torquay. † B 1.

KINDERSLEY, Fanny K. Exh. 1883-85
Figure painter. London 1883; Dorchester 1884. † RI 3.

KINDLEBERGER, D. Exh. 1901
c/o J. McLure Hamilton, Murestead, 6 Grove End Road, London. † I 1.

KINDON, Mary Evelina Exh. 1881-1919
Portrait, landscape and domestic genre painter. Croydon, Surrey 1881; London 1883; Watford, Herts. 1899. † B 5, GI 3, L 8, LS 5, M 1, RA 28, RBA 20, RHA 1, RI 12, ROI 13, SWA 44.

KING, Mrs. Exh. 1929
Flower painter. † FIN 1.

KING, Miss A. Exh. 1892
7 Mellifont Avenue, Kingstown, Ireland. † RHA 1.

KING, Alice Exh. 1891-1940
nee Knowles. Landscape painter. Married William Joseph K. q.v. Add: Birmingham. † B 131, RCA 5.

KING, A. Armstrong Exh. 1891-92
18 De Pary's Avenue, Bedford. † M 2.

KING, Agnes Gardner Exh. 1880-1902
Landscape, figure and flower painter. A.S.W.A. 1889. Sister of Elizabeth Thomson K. q.v. Add: Florence 1880; London 1882; Newbury, Berks. 1902. † B 13, D 3, GI 22, L 7, RA 8, RBA 10, RI 16, RMS 2, RSA 1, SWA 50.

KING, Alice Price Exh. 1907-22
Landscape and flower painter. London 1907; Bedford 1918. † BG 4, LS 9, SWA 1, WG 36.

KING, Miss A.R. Exh. 1931
London. † RCA 1.

KING, Baragwanath Exh. 1903-14
Landscape painter. Studio, 55 Connaught Avenue, Plymouth. † BG 48, RI 1.

KING, Bertha Exh. 1900-1
Sevenoaks, Kent 1900; Redland, Bristol 1901. † RA 1, RBA 1.

KING, Ben B. Exh. 1880-1904
Glasgow. † GI 20.

KING, Cecil 1881-1942
Marine and landscape painter. Studied Westminster School of Art and Ecole des Beaux Arts, Paris. R.B.A. 1910, R.I. 1924, R.O.I. 1932. Exh. 1906-35. Add: London. † B 4, CHE 2, FIN 37, GOU 3, I 13, L 6, M 3, RA 18, RBA 55, RI 40, ROI 12.

KING, Clarence E. Exh. 1913-18
Argenteuil, France 1913; Colombes, Seine, France 1914; Luton, Beds. 1917. † LS 12.

KING, C.H. Exh. 1909-11
122 Goldsmith Street, Nottingham. † N 4.

KING, Charles Robert Baker Exh. 1885-95
Architect. London. † RA 3.

KING, Dorothy Exh. 1937-40
Portrait and figure painter. London. † GOU 2, NEA 3, RA 4, RBA 2, SWA 1.

KING, Edith Exh. 1927-34
Watercolour landscape and still life painter. 51 Hartington Grove, Cambridge. † AB 3, RA 1, RI 2, SWA 9.

KING, Elizabeth Exh. 1892-1939
Flower painter. Studied Ealing Art School and under C.E. Tomson. Add: London. † L 1, RA 9, RI 18, ROI 14, SWA 2.

KING, Mrs. Emilie Exh. 1903-40
Miniature portrait painter. A.R.M.S. 1909. Married John W. K. q.v. Add: Oxford 1903; Holywell, St. Ives, Hunts. 1908; Scarborough, Yorks. 1919; Snainton, Yorks. 1928. † B 3, L 22, RA 12, RHA 1, RMS 61.

KING, Eric Exh. 1936
Engraver. † RED 3.

KING, E.G. Exh. 1891
Sculptor. 57 Elizabeth Street, Pimlico, London. † NEA 1.

KING, E. Lewis Exh. 1930
Flower painter. † FIN 1.

KING, Edward R.* Exh. 1884-1924
Portrait, figure and landscape painter. N.E.A. 1888. Brother of Gunning K. q.v. Add: London 1884 and 1908; South Harting, Petersfield, Hants. 1886; St. Ives, Cornwall 1895; Fordingbridge, Hants. 1897; Broadstone, Dorset 1898; Parkstone, Dorset 1906; East Molesey, Surrey 1916. † B 3, FIN 3, G 1, L 19, M 5, NEA 6, RA 54, RBA 4, ROI 7.

KING, Ethel Slade See GASCOYNE

KING, Elizabeth Thomson Exh. 1880-1901
Landscape and figure painter. Sister of Agnes Gardner. Add: Florence 1880; London 1882; Newbury, Berks. 1902. † D 4, G 1, GI 18, RA 4, RBA 4, RI 2, ROI 1, RSA 3, SWA 7.

KING, Frank Exh. 1893-1914
Landscape painter. 24 Gt. Titchfield Street, London 1898; Winslow, Bucks. 1901. † L 1, LS 3, P 1, RA 4, RBA 3.

KING, Fred Exh. 1891
Landscape painter. Upper Lambourne, Berks. † RBA 1.

KING, F.J. Exh. 1881
South View Lodge, Clontarf, Ireland. † RHA 2.

KING, Gunning 1859-1940
Painter, etcher and illustrator. Studied South Kensington and R.A. Schools. N.E.A. 1887. Brother of Edward R.K. q.v. Add: London 1880; South Harting, Petersfield, Hants. 1887. † B 3, BA 1, G 6, GI 8, L 39, M 8, NEA 1, NG 2, P 7, RA 47, RBA 2, RI 1, ROI 2, RSA 3.

KING, Haynes* 1831-1904
Landscape and genre painter. b. Barbados. Came to London in 1854. Studied at Leigh's Academy. R.B.A. 1864. Exh. 1880-1903. Add: London. † B 7, GI 12, L 33, M 7, RA 30, RBA 120, RI 4, ROI 15, RSA 1, TOO 4.

KING, Henry John Yeend* 1855-1924
Landscape and rustic genre painter. Worked for 3 years in a glass works. Studied under William Bromley and in Paris. R.B.A. 1879, R.I. 1887, V.P.R.I. 1901, R.O.I. 1888. "Milking Time" purchased by Chantrey Bequest 1898. Exh. 1880-1924. Add: London. † B 13, BG 1, D 3, DOW 53, FIN 2, G 6, GI 2, L 29, M 27, RA 87, RBA 92, RHA 2, RI 161, ROI 102.

KING, J. Arthur Exh. 1881-85
Figure painter. 4 Swiss Terrace, Hampstead, London. † RA 2, RBA 1.

KING, J.C. Exh. 1930-33
Urban landscape painter. † LEF 2.

KING, J.J. Exh. 1885
Sauchiehall Street, Glasgow. † GI 2.

KING, John Loxwood Exh. 1880
Architect. 18 North Road, Surbiton, Surrey. † RA 1.

KING, Jessie Marion Exh. 1901-40
Painter, etcher and illustrator. b. New Kilpatrick, Scotland. Studied Glasgow School of Art. A.S.W.A. 1925. Married Ernest Archibald Taylor q.v. Add: Glasgow 1901; Pendleton, Manchester 1909; Paris 1911; Kirkcudbright 1916. † BG 1, BRU 72, GI 85, L 22, LS 3, RHA 1, RSA 48, RSW 4, SWA 4.

KING, John W. Exh. 1893-1924
Figure and domestic painter. Married Emilie K. q.v. Add: London 1893; Oxford 1901; Holywell, St. Ives, Hunts. 1908; Huntingdon 1918; Scarborough 1924. † B 4, L 11, RA 6, RBA 6, RHA 1, RI 6, RMS 1, ROI 9, RSA 1.

KING, Miss K.G. Exh. 1919-20
Miniature portrait painter. Bristol 1919; London 1920. † RA 2.

KING, Lydia B. Exh. 1886-90
Flower, figure, portrait and landscape painter. 23 Highbury Park, London. † L 1, RA 2, RBA 1, RI 2, ROI 1, SWA 9.

KING, Lilian Yeend b. 1882
Mrs. Hatton Fraenkl. Landscape painter. Studied Heatherleys. Daughter of H.J. Yeend King q.v. Exh. 1904-27. Add: London 1904 and 1914; Wolverhampton 1908; Lancaster 1910; West Wittering, Sussex 1925. † L 3, M 1, RA 2, RI 22, ROI 8.

KING, Mabel Exh. 1899
Hall Green, Birmingham. † B 2.

KING, Mlle. Marie Exh. 1882
11 Boulevard de Clichy, Paris. † GI 1.

KING, Mrs. M. Maitland Exh. 1896-98
Bampton, Oxon 1896; Ripley, Surrey 1897. † GI 1, RHA 2, RSA 1.

KING, Petah Exh. 1937-39
2 Canning Place, London. † GOU 2, NEA 1, RBA 1.

KING, Mrs. Ralda Exh. 1936-37
21 Church Street, London. † SWA 2.

KING, Stamford Exh. 1901
39 Darenth Road, Stamford Hill, London. † RI 1.

KING, Susan Exh. 1902
7 Cambridge Park, Redland, Bristol. † B 1.

KING, Mrs. Violet M. Exh. 1928-32
Flower painter. Battersea Park, London 1928; Windlesham, Surrey 1932. † RA 3.

KING, Mrs. Wilson Exh. 1921-28
19 Highfield Road, Edgbaston, Birmingham. † B 6.

KING, Winifred Exh. 1930-33
Collaborated with Mildred Murphy q.v. Add: The Studio, Old Palace Yard, Earl Street, Coventry. † B 11.

KING, William Charles Holland b. 1884
Sculptor. b. Cheltenham. Studied R.A. Schools. Exh. 1910-40. Add: London 1910 and 1918; Berwick on Tweed 1917. † GI 13, L 20, RA 46, RI 2, RSA 5.

KING, W.J. Exh. 1922
Leaf pictures. † WG 33.

KING, William John Exh. 1912-13
Government Lymph Establishment, Colindale Avenue, The Hyde, London. † LS 5.

KING, William Joseph b. 1857
Landscape and marine painter and black and white artist. Married Alice K. q.v. Exh. 1885-1940. Add: Birmingham. † B 233, L 6, RSA 1.

KINGDON, Walter Exh. 1887
Figure painter. 29 Auriol Road, Kensington, London. † G 1.

KINGDON, William P. Exh. 1890-1930
Seacombe 1890; Birkenhead 1894. † L 4, RCA 1.

KINGDON-ELLIS, Edith Exh. 1896-99
Portrait painter. Westgate, Peterborough 1896; Nottingham 1899. † B 3, N 3, RA 1, RI 1.

KING-FARLOW, Hazel Exh. 1937-39
Flower, still life, figure and landscape painter. London. † COO 30, GOU 1, RED 2, SWA 1.

KINGHAM, Sylvia Sarah Exh. 1925-27
nee Wynn. Sculptor. b. Reading, Berks. Studied Central School of Arts and Crafts. Add: London. † GI 2, L 3, RA 1.

KINGHORN, Dorothy Exh. 1933-35
Llandudno. † RCA 2.

KINGSFORD, Florence Exh. 1899-1900
Figure and domestic painter. London. † RA 3.

KINGSFORD, Herbert Exh. 1895-1906
London. † D 6.

KINGSFORD, Miss V. Exh. 1913-15
73 Cathcart Studios, 45 Redcliffe Road, London. † I 1, RA 1, SWA 2.

KINGSLEY, F.J. Exh. 1911
Combe Grange, Monkton Combe, Bath. † L 1.

KINGSLEY, H.R. Exh. 1930-36
46 Anson Road, Tufnell Park, London. † RI 2.

KINGSLEY, J.M. Exh. 1885
Victoria Park, Manchester. † M 1.

KINGSLEY, Lydia Exh. 1890-98
Fruit, still life and figure painter. London. † RA 4, RBA 4, RI 3, RSW 1.

KINGSTON, Eliza A. Exh. 1909
Addlestone, Surrey. † SWA 1.

KINGSTON, Gertrude Angela d. 1937
Mrs. Silver. nee Konstam (changed her name to Kingston c. 1887). Painter, decorative artist and actress. Studied under Carolus Duran in Paris. Exh. 1883-87. Add: 64 Gloucester Place, Portman Square, London. † RBA 1, ROI 2.

KINGSTON, James A. Exh. 1890
Landscape painter. Witham House, South Windsor Road, Ealing, London. † RBA 1.

KINGWELL, Miss M.A. Exh. 1914-23
Whetcombe, North Huish, South Devon 1914; Plymouth 1923. † L 2, RA 1.

KININMONTH, Mrs. Caroline Exh. 1940
46A Dick Place, Edinburgh. † RSA 1.

KINKEAD, Alice S. Exh. 1897-1926
Forster House, Galway 1897; London 1898. † GI 1, L 18, LS 3, P 2, RA 1, RCA 1, RHA 7, SWA 2.

KINLOCH, George Washington Andrew Exh. 1880-87
Sculptor. 32 Drummond Place, Edinburgh. † RA 3, RSA 11.

KINLOCH, M.W. Exh. 1890-94
Glasgow. † GI 4.

KINNAIRD, Elizabeth Holmes b. 1897
Portrait, landscape and miniature painter and teacher. Studied Municipal College of Technology, Belfast. Exh. 1922-36. Add: Dunmurry, Co. Antrim 1922; Belfast 1928. † RA 3, RHA 3, RMS 4.

KINNAIRD, F.G.* Exh. 1881-82
Landscape painter. 77 Newman Street, Oxford Street, London. † RA 1, RHA 5.

KINNAIRD, Henry John* Exh. 1880-1908
Landscape painter. London 1880; Chingford, Essex 1887; Arundel, Sussex 1908. † B 9, RA 8, RBA 8, ROI 2.

KINNAIRD, Wiggs Exh. 1894-1911
London 1894; Boscastle, Cornwall 1902; Wellingborough, Northants. 1903; Gillingham, Kent 1904. † B 32, D 6, GI 4, L 1, M 1, RBA 2.

KINNEAR, Mrs. Anthoula Exh. 1925
College of Art, Edinburgh. † RSA 1.

KINNEAR, Harry Exh. 1882
4 Sydney Street, Glasgow. † GI 1.

KINNEAR, James Exh. 1880-1917
Landscape painter. Edinburgh. † GI 18, M 2, RA 7, RI 1, RSA 80.

KINNEAR, Leslie Gordon b. 1901
Painter, and etcher. Studied Ecole d'Industrie, Bordeaux. Exh. 1929-40. Add: Dundee. † RSA 23, RSW 4.

KINNEIR, Vera Exh. 1918-19
52 Pulteney Street, Bath. † I 2, SWA 2.

KINNEY, Troy b. 1871
American etcher. Exh. 1924-26. † FIN 8.

KINNISON, James Exh. 1898
1 Westifeld Avenue, Dundee. † RSA 1.

KINROSS, Elizabeth Exh. 1935
12 North Parade, Grantham, Lincs. † N 2.

KINROSS, John 1855-1931
Architect. A.R.S.A. 1893, R.S.A. 1905. Exh. 1895-1926. Add: Edinburgh. † RSA 19.

KINSELLA, Katharine Exh. 1905
38A St. George's Road, Eccleston Square, London. † I 1.

KINSELLA, Thomas Exh. 1908-20
Landscape painter. London. † RA 6.

KINSEY, Vera M. Exh. 1909
Carlton House, Moorland Road, Bournemouth. † L 1.

KINSLEY, Albert b. 1852
Landscape painter. b. Hull. R.B.A. 1889, R.I. 1896 (Hon. Retd. 1937). Exh. 1881-1940. Add: Tufnell Park, London 1881 and 1883; Leeds 1882. † B 12, D 12, GI 9, L 13, M 6, NG 20, RA 23, RBA 97, RCA 85, RHA 8, RI 217, ROI 6, RSA 1, WG 45.

KINSLEY, H.R. Exh. 1912-36
Son of Albert K. q.v. Add: Tufnell Park, London. † RCA 16, RI 15.

KINTON, Florence Exh. 1884
Watercolour painter. The Mount, Great Malvern, Worcs. † RA 1.

KIRBY, Mrs. C.W. Exh. 1908-33
Park Gate, Chester. † L 4.

KIRBY, Edmund Exh. 1888-1919
Architect. Liverpool 1888; Oxton, Birkenhead 1908. † L 4, RA 3.

KIRBY, Mrs. E.J. Exh. 1934-40
London. † SWA 2.

KIRBY, Ernest W. Exh. 1931-38
Landscape painter. London. † RA 2.

KIRBY, John Kynnersley Exh. 1914-39
Figure painter. Studied Slade School. N.E.A. 1930, A.N.S.A. 1916, N.S.A. 1918, R.O.I. 1937. Add: Cotgrave, Notts. 1914; Nottingham 1917; London 1924; Stansted, Essex 1929. † CHE 3, GOU 2, L 1, M 2, N 29, NEA 37, RA 5, ROI 6.

KIRBY, Reginald G. Exh. 1901
Architect. 37 Fawcett Street, Sunderland. † RA 1.

KIRBY, Stuart C. Exh. 1926
Architect. 35 Bedford Square, London. † RA 1.

KIRCHMAYR, Professor Cherubino Exh. 1886-1902
Figure painter. R.B.A. 1902, R.M.S. 1900. Add: London 1886 and 1889; Liverpool 1888. † B 2, L 5, M 3, RA 6, RBA 5, RMS 8.

KIRCHNER, Raphael d. 1917
American painter. b. Vienna. Exh. 1915. † BRU 23.

KIRK, Mrs. C. (Alex) Exh. 1905-39
Landscape, portrait and miniature painter. Keston, Kent 1905; Tunbridge Wells, Kent 1913; Wimborne, Dorset 1939. † RA 11, RBA 1, WG 113.

KIRK, Ann E Exh. 1896
Orchard Road, Erdington, Birmingham. † B 1.

KIRK, Arthur Nevill Exh. 1923-26
Enameller, jeweller and silversmith. Studied Central School of Arts and Crafts, London. Teacher of Enamelling at Central School of Arts and Crafts. R.M.S. 1924. Add: The Willow Studio, 54 Willow Road, Hampstead, London. † L 3, RMS 7.

KIRK, David Exh. 1884-1900
Glasgow. † GI 12, RSA 5.

KIRK, Miss E. Exh. 1885
New Street, Altrincham, Cheshire. † M 1.

KIRK, Eve* 1900-1969
Landscape painter. Exh. 1924-39. Add: Harlow, Essex 1924; London 1926. † BA 1, BK 1, NEA 10, RED 1, TOO 31.

KIRK, F.P. Exh. 1896-1937
Flower and decorative painter. West Bridgford, Notts. † N 26.

KIRK, Mrs. H.S. Exh. 1922
Mrs. Bertram Baker. Add: 7 Esme Road, Sparkhill, Birmingham. † B 1.

KIRK, James Exh. 1923-32
28 Burlington Road, Withington, Manchester. † L 2.

KIRK, Miss Janet Exh. 1910-38
28 Burlington Road, Withington, Manchester. † B 1, L 8, M 3, RCA 22.

KIRK, J.L. Exh. 1921
46 Lady Bay Road, West Bridgford, Nottingham. Landscape painter. † N 1.

KIRK, Miss K. Joyce Exh. 1936-38
Flower painter. 28 William Road, West Bridgford, Nottingham. † N 2.

KIRKBY, Gertrude Caroline Exh. 1909-11
Watercolour landscape painter. Lodsworth Common, Petworth, Sussex. † BG 2, LS 9.

KIRKBY, R.G. Exh. 1906-10
Pietermaritzburg, Natal, South Africa 1906; Town Hall, Bradford 1910. † RA 3.

KIRKBY, William A. Exh. 1938-39
Sculptor. 80 Albert Street, Newark, Notts. † N 3.

KIRKE, Miss H.V. Exh. 1918-26
Markham, Maori Road, Guildford, Surrey. † B 4, RHA 1, RI 2, SWA 1.

KIRKHAM, Miss N. Exh. 1920
Gladwyn, Stoke-on-Trent. Staffs. † B 1.

KIRKMAN, Miss C.M. Exh. 1907
19 Dartmouth Park Hill, London. † L 4.

KIRKMAN, Dorothy G. Exh. 1919-36
Miniature portrait painter. 4 Woodlands Terrace, Swansea 1919 and 1922; Kings Heath, Birmingham 1920. † B 2, RA 3, RSA 3.

KIRKMAN, Miss K. Exh. 1909-19
London 1909; Bexhill, Sussex 1919. † SWA 4.

KIRKMAN, Mary Exh. 1898
19 Mount Road, Clive Vale, Hastings, Sussex. † L 2.

KIRKPATRICK, A. Exh. 1916
34 Manor Avenue, Great Crosby, Liverpool. † L 1.

KIRKPATRICK, Edith Exh. 1904
Watercolour landscape painter. † FIN 1.

KIRKPATRICK, Ethel Exh. 1890-1934
Painter and colour wood cut artist. Studied R.A. Schools and Central School of Arts and Crafts, London. Sister of Ida Marion K. q.v. Add: London 1890; Harrow-on-the-Hill, Middlesex 1892. † ALP 42, BA 2, GI 2, I 1, LS 5, M 1, RA 15, RBA 11, RI 9, SWA 19.

KIRKPATRICK, Ella McL. Exh. 1912-37
Flower and landscape painter. 73 Penkett Road, Liscard, Cheshire. † COO 11, L 5, RCA 4.

KIRKPATRICK, Ida Marion Exh. 1888-1927
Watercolour landscape and flower painter. Studied Royal Female School of Art and Juliens, Paris. Sister of Ethel K. q.v. Add: London 1888; Harrow-on-the-Hill, Middlesex 1892. † ALP 36, D 8, I 9, RA 6, RBA 16, RI 5, ROI 1, SWA 25.

KIRKPATRICK, Irene N. Exh. 1900
23 Lower Baggot Street, Dublin. † RHA 1.

KIRKPATRICK, J. Exh. 1881
148 Bellfield Street, Glasgow. † GI 1.

KIRKPATRICK, Joseph Exh. 1891-1928
Painter and etcher. Fairfield 1891; Birkenhead 1893; Liverpool 1897; Curdridge, Hants. 1905; London 1916; Arundel, Sussex 1928. † B 6, L 78, RA 13, RCA 6, RI 3.

KIRKPATRICK, Lily Exh. 1894-1902
Figure painter. St. Ives, Cornwall. † B 8, L 3, M 1, RA 3, RHA 8.

KIRKPATRICK, Susan Louise Exh. 1940
21 Lesnuir Drive, Scotston, Perthshire. † GI 1.

KIRKPATRICK, Miss T. Exh. 1905-22
Mrs. Hermann Silberbach. Add: Liscard, Cheshire 1905; Birkenhead 1910; Manchester 1922. † L 12.

KIRK-SMITH, G. Exh. 1932
† L 1.

KIRKWOOD, Alexander Exh. 1880-1903
St. James Square, Edinburgh. † RSA 4.

KIRKWOOD, Miss Bobbie Exh. 1924
The Homestead, Cabra. † RHA 1.

KIRKWOOD, Constance R.B. Exh. 1916-19
Designer and pottery artist. Studied Edinburgh College of Art, Dublin and Camden. London. Add: Edinburgh. † RSA 6.

KIRKWOOD, Miss D.M. Exh. 1914-29
Glasgow 1914; Edinburgh 1929. † GI 8, L 3, RSA 1.

KIRKWOOD, Elizabeth H. Exh. 1909-23
Enameller. Edinburgh. † B 1, GI 3, L 11, RA 3, RMS 1, RSA 9.

KIRKWOOD, Mrs. Harriet Exh. 1920-37
Landscape and still life painter. Baily, Howth, Ireland 1920; Collinstown Park, Clondalkin, Ireland 1928. † RHA 9.

KIRKWOOD, Mary K. Exh. 1897-1900
18 Melville Street, Portobello, N.B. † RSA 6.

KIRKWOOD, Robert Exh. 1880-83
37 London Street, Edinburgh. † RSA 3.

KIRKWOOD, T. Exh. 1889
9 Hampden Terrace, Mount Florida, Glasgow. † GI 2.

KIRLEW, Mrs. Doris E. Exh. 1938
Portrait and landscape painter. Abbey House, Castle Gate, Grantham, Lincs. † N 4.

KIRLEW, Miss M.K. Exh. 1934
14 Finkin Street, Grantham, Lincs. † N 1.

KIRMSE, Persis Exh. 1929
Animal painter. † WG 62.

KIRNIG, Paul Exh. 1929
Kunstgewerbeschule, Vienna. † RSA 1.

KIRSCH, Joanna Exh. 1885
† GI 1.

KIRSCH, Ulrica Exh. 1922
Watercolour painter. 21 Hyde Park Mansions, London. † RA 1.

KIRTON, Miss Kathleen Exh. 1935
Sculptor. Church Hill, Honiton, Devon. † RA 1.

KISLING, Moise* 1891-1953
Painter. b. Cracow. Studied Ecole des Beaux Arts, Paris. Exh. 1929. Add: Paris. † GI 1.

KISSLING, Richard 1848-1919
Swiss sculptor. 31 Harewood Road, Gunnersbury, London 1887. † RA 1.

KITCH, Alice Exh. 1930-37
Figure, landscape and animal painter. Beeston, Notts. † N 15.

KITCHEN, Miss E.M. Exh. 1906-13
St. Bees, Cumberland 1906; London 1912. † L 5, RA 1.

KITCHEN, James Exh. 1880-85
Leith 1880; Dumbarton 1885. † RSA 2.

KITCHEN, John 1928
32 Gordon Road, London. † NEA 1.

KITCHENER, Bessie Maud b. 1886
Mrs. Elliot K. nee MacIver. Watercolour landscape and flower painter. b. Liverpool. Studied Guildford School of Art. Exh. 1924-40. Add: Iomhar, Abbotswood, Guildford, Surrey. † AR 2, COO 2, L 2, RI 6, WG 30.

KITCHENER, Mrs. F.W. Exh. 1890
c/o Mrs. Fenton, Pennington Lodge, Lymington, Hants. † M 1.

KITCHENER, Madge Exh. 1921-29
Medalist and portrait painter. Born Kasauli, India. Studied Slade School. Add: The Little Gallery, Ashstead, Surrey. † L 5, RA 3, RID 3, RMS 4.

KITCHIN, Kathleen Exh. 1906-40
Leeds 1906; Scarborough 1921. † L 1, RA 1, RCA 23, SWA 5.

KITCHIN, R.H.W. Exh. 1931
† NEA 1.

KITCHINER, Robert Montague b. 1907
Painter, pen and pencil and linocut artist. Studied Slade School 1928-31. Exh. 1929. Add: Factory House, Wilton, Salisbury, Wilts. † NEA 1.

KITCHINGMAN, Joseph Exh. 1889-1914
Egremont, Cheshire 1889; Liscard, Cheshire 1901. † L 30, LS 6, RCA 2.

KITE, Joseph Milner* c.1864-1946
Figure, domestic and landscape painter. Exh. 1884-1908. Add: London 1884; Paris 1886. † B 12, D 2, GOU 1, L 14, P 1, RA 4, RBA 11, ROI 2.

KITSELL, Thomas R. Exh. 1898-1910
Architect. Plymouth. † RA 7.

KITSON, Catherine M. Exh. 1886-92
Watercolour figure and flower painter. London. † RA 1, RBA 1, RI 1, SWA 2.

KITSON, H. Exh. 1911-14
London 1911; Limpsfield, Surrey 1912. † RA 1, RHA 3.

KITSON, R.H. Exh. 1920-40
Watercolour landscape painter. A.R.B.A. 1921, R.B.A. 1925. Add: Casa Casani, Taormina, Sicily 1920; Stonegates, Meanwood, Leeds 1929. † RA 1, FIN 68, GI 8, GOU 13, L 2, RA 7, RBA 45, RED 48.

KITSON, Robert L. Exh. 1889-91
Figure painter. Birch Mount, Berry Brow, Huddersfield. † B 1, L 1, RA 3.

KITSON, S. Exh. 1880
Sculptor. 10 Via dei Greci, Rome. † RA 1.

KITSON, Sydney Decimus 1871-1937
Architect. Leeds. † RA 3.

KITTON, Frederick George 1856-1904
Engraver and writer. b. Norwich. d. St. Albans. Add: London 1880. † RBA 1.

KIVERSTEIN, Louis Exh. 1940
Landscape painter. 79 Kendal Road, Gladstone Park, London. † RA 1.

KIWCHENKS, A. Exh. 1883
5 Schutzenstrasse, Munich. † M 1.

KLANG, Mayer Exh. 1902-39
Portrait and figure painter. London. † L 7, RA 5, RBA 13, ROI 1.

KLEIN, Miss A. Exh. 1887
Flower painter. c/o B. Lyons, 6a Camden Road, London. † RA 1.

KLEIN, Adrian B. Exh. 1914-18
London. † I 4, LEI 3, LS 3, NEA 1.

KLEIN, Maud Exh. 1929
Wood engraver. 72 Carlton Hill, London. † RA 1.

KLEIN, Professor Max Exh. 1902-5
Sculptor. Warmbrunnerstrasse 8, Grunewald, Berlin. † GI 1, L 1, RA 2.

KLEINWORT, Lady Alex Exh. 1909-14
London. † LS 17.

KLEINWORT, Miss H. Exh. 1907-8
Champion Hill, London. † SWA 4.

KLEINWORT, Lily Exh. 1924
45 Belgrave Square, London. † SWA 1.

KLERK, de see D

KLEUDGEN, Von see V

KLIMSCH, Eugen* 1839-1896
German domestic painter. Exh. 1890. Add: Bleichstrasse 66A, Frankfurt am Maine, Germany. † RA 1.

KLIMSCH, Fritz Exh. 1904
† I 1.

KLIN, Leo b. 1887
Painter. b. Russia. Studied at the Imperial Academy of Fine Arts, St. Petersburg. Exh. 1940. Add: 66 Hamilton Terrace, London. † RA 2.

KLINDWORTH, Charles Exh. 1903-9
2 Dale Street, Liverpool. † L 5.

KLINGENDER, L.W.H. Exh. 1883-94
Dusseldorf, Germany. † L 2.

KLINGER, Professor Max 1857-1920
German painter, sculptor and etcher. Exh. 1901-12. Add: Dresden 1901; Leipzig 1912. † I 32, RSA 1.

KLINGHOFFER, Clara 1900-1972
Portrait painter. b. Poland. Came to London as a child. Studied London Central School of Arts and Crafts and Slade School. "The Old Troubadour" (1926) purchased by Chantrey Bequest 1933. Exh. 1921-38. Add: London 1921 and 1938; Holland 1934. † BK 2, G 6, GI 4, GOU 87, LEI 87, NEA 30, RA 2, RED 89, TOO 2.

KLINKENBERG, Karel 1852-1924
Dutch painter. Exh. 1895. Add: c/o Boussod, Valadon and Co., 5 Regent Street, London. † RA 1.

KLITGAARD, Christiane Brix See MAY

KLOTZ, Hermann Exh. 1891
Sculptor. Vienna. † RA 2.

KLUMPKE, Anna Elizabeth b. 1856
American artist. Exh. 1889-1902. Add: Paris 1889; Thomery, Seine et Marne, France 1902. † L 4.

KLUSKA, Sylvain b. 1911
Painter, leather engraver and writer. b. Paris. Naturalised British. Studied St. Martins School of Art and Royal College of Art. Exh. 1929-36. Add: 19 Little Turner Street, London. † RA 4.

KNAGGS, Nancy Exh. 1887-95
Landscape, figure and flower painter. London. † M 1, RA 1, RBA 13, RI 3, SWA 2.

KNAPP-FISHER, Arthur Bedford b. 1888
Architect and painter. Studied A.A. Professor of Architecture Royal College of Art 1934. Exh. 1914-29. Add: London. † RA 2, RED 17, RID 4.

KNAPPING, Edith M. Exh. 1880-89
Flower and landscape painter. Sister of Margaret Helen K. q.v. Add: Swiss Cottage, Blackheath, London. † SWA 8.

KNAPPING, Helen d. 1935
Flower and landscape painter. Studied under E. Aubrey Hunt in England, France and Belgium. Sister of Edith M.K. q.v. Add: Blackheath Park, London 1880; St. Ives, Cornwall 1911. † B 3, D 4, G 1, GI 3, GOU 2, L 6, LS 6, M 3, RA 3, RBA 9, RHA 4, RI 3, RSA 5, SWA 30.

KNAPTON, Miss E. Mayo Exh. 1907
Grafton House, Evesham, Worcs. † L 1.

KNEE, Howard b. 1899
Watercolour painter. Studied Dublin Metropolitan School of Art. Exh. 1916-40. Add: Clovelly, Mount Tallan Avenue, Terenure, Dublin. † RA 1, RHA 40.

KNEEN, E.W. b. 1866
Landscape painter. Garston, Liverpool 1913; Hale, Liverpool 1925. † L 6.

KNEEN, William 1862-1921
Landscape painter. b. Isle of Man. Art master at Westminster School of Art for 37 years. N.E.A. 1899, R.B.A. 1899. Add: London 1886; Richmond, Surrey 1918. † GOU 17, I 4, L 27, LS 19, M 7, NEA 28, P 1, RA 4, RBA 75, RI 1.

KNEESHAW, Cecily Margaret b. 1883
nee Lever. Watercolour painter. Exh. 1905-39. Add: Montpellier Lodge, Harrogate 1905; Penmaenmawr 1907; Abergele 1930; Lyndhurst, Hants. 1932. † B 6, L 1, RCA 20, RI 8, RSA 1.

KNELLAR, Frank b. 1914
Exh. 1939-40. Add: London. † RCA 1, RSW 1.

KNEWSTUB, Walter John 1831-1906
Genre painter, watercolourist and caricaturist. Studio assistant to Rossetti 1862. Father in law of Sir William Rotherstein q.v. Worked on Manchester Town Hall Frescoes 1878-93. Add: London. † B 1, M 1, NEA 4, NG 1, RBA 2.

KNEWSTUB, W. Holmes Exh. 1882-86
Landscape painter. London. † B 3, D 3, M 1, ROI 1.

KNEWSTUBBS, Miss K. Exh. 1930-33
Latham Street, Preston, Lancs. † L 2.

KNIBB, Miss M. Exh. 1926
265 Normanton Road, Derby. † N 1.

KNIGHT, Adah Exh. 1887-1928
Miniature painter. R.M.S. 1901. † B 3, FIN 2, RA 42, RMS 4.

KNIGHT, Adam d. 1930
Watercolour landscape painter. Frequent visitor to the South of France. N.S.A. 1881, V.P.N.S.A. 1908-11, 1914-17 and 1927. Acting P.N.S.A. 1912. Add: Nottingham 1880; West Bridgford, Notts. 1892. † B 6, L 21, M 12, N 272, RA 2, RBA 2, RCA 9, RI 2, WG 244.

KNIGHT, Annie Exh. 1889-98
Figure painter and mezzotint engraver. Askgreen, Musselburgh. † FIN 3, RSA 3.

KNIGHT, Arnold b. 1906
Painter and colour printer. Studied Poole School of Art and under Walter Stritch Hutton. Exh. 1930-37. Add: 10 Alton Road, Parkstone, Dorset. † L 1, RA 3.

KNIGHT, Aston b. 1873
Landscape painter. 1 Woronzow Road, Studios, St. John's Wood, London. † RA 2.

KNIGHT, A.B. Exh. 1907
c/o Messrs. Staples, 208 West End Lane, London. † RA 1.

KNIGHT, Arthur W. Exh. 1900
Landscape painter. c/o S. Jennings, 15 Duke Street, Manchester Square, London. † RA 1.

KNIGHT, Charles Exh. 1880-1913
Landscape painter. N.S.A. 1895. Add: Nottingham 1880; Colwick, Notts. 1884; West Bridgford, Notts. 1894; Stanton on the Wold, Notts. 1907. † L 1, M 2, N 112, RA 2.

KNIGHT, Charles* b. 1901
Landscape and figure painter and etcher. b. Hove, Sussex. Studied Brighton School of Art and R.A. Schools (Landseer scholarship and Turner Gold Medal for landscape). R.O.I. 1933, A.R.W.S. 1933, R.W.S. 1935. Exh. 1925-40. Add: Brighton 1925; Ditchling, Sussex 1935. † FIN 7, L 2, RA 31, ROI 11, RWS 73.

KNIGHT, Clara Exh. 1880-1940
Landscape painter. Daughter of Joseph Knight R.I., R.E., q.v. Married Frank Beswick q.v. Studied Manchester School of Art. Add: Bettws-y-Coed, Wales 1880; London 1886; Wallingford, Berks. 1889; Chester 1892; Streatley on Thames 1895; Llandudno, 1901; Deganwy, N. Wales 1902. † B 1, D 1, L 18, M 7, RA 6, RBA 7, RCA 100, RI 5, ROI 5.

KNIGHT, Charles Neil b. 1865
Landscape and figure painter. Studied Juliens Paris and under Hubert Vos. Exh. 1892-1920. Add: London 1892; Moved to Bath, Somerset c.1925. † L 5, RA 4, RBA 2, ROI 12.

KNIGHT, Charles Parsons, 1829-1897
Landscape and marine painter. b. Bristol, went to sea before studying at Bristol Academy. Exh. 1882-96. Add: Tiverton, Devon 1882; St. John's Wood, London 1888. † L 15, M 13, NG 14, RA 8, ROI 4.

KNIGHT, Mrs. D. Exh. 1924
65 Albany Mansions, Battersea Park, London. † L 5.

KNIGHT, Doreen Exh. 1940
Watercolour painter. 78 Cambridge Road, Seven Kings, Ilford, Essex. † RA 1.

KNIGHT, Daniel Ridgway 1839-1924
Landscape, flower and figure painter. b. U.S.A. Exh. 1882-1906. Add: Place de l'Eglise, Poissy, Seine et Oise, France. † RA 3, TOO 7.

KNIGHT, Miss E. Exh. 1882
Figure painter. 73 Cambridge Terrace, Hyde Park, London. † RBA 1.

KNIGHT, Emma Exh. 1890-93
Painter of stained glass windows. Add: Northcote, Landsdowne, Bath. † RA 4.

KNIGHT, Ethel see HOLE

KNIGHT, Miss E.L. Exh. 1902
8 Belgrave Square, Nottingham. † N 1.

KNIGHT, Edward Loxton b. 1905
Landscape painter, poster and woodcut artist. b. Long Eaton, Derbys. Studied Nottingham School of Art. R.B.A. 1935. Exh. 1924-39. Add: Long Eaton, Derbys. 1924 and 1934; London 1929. † BK 46, CON 1, FIN 1, N 6, RA 4, RBA 23, RED 1, RI 4, ROI 6.

KNIGHT, Edith M. Exh. 1935
363 Chester Road, Erdington, Birmingham. † B 1.

KNIGHT, Fred G. Exh. 1889-92
Architect. 6 Gt. College Street, Westminster, London. † RA 4.

KNIGHT, Harold* 1874-1961
Landscape, portrait, flower and figure painter. Son of William Knight (architect) q.v. Married Laura K. q.v. Studied Nottingham Art School and L'Ecole des Beaux Arts, Paris. N.S.A. 1908, P.N.S.A. 1937, A.R.A. 1928, R.A. 1937, R.O.I. 1906, R.P. 1925. "A Student" purchased by Chantrey Bequest 1938. Add: Nottingham 1890; London 1904 and 1917; Staithes, Yorks. 1905; Newlyn, Penzance 1908; Paul, Penzance 1911; St. Buryan, Penzance 1914. † B 11, BG 3, G 38, GI 15, GOU 6, I 12, L 12, LEI 78, M 6, N 29, NEA 1, P 11, RA 107, RHA 4, ROI 27, RSA 1.

KNIGHT, Henry Hall Exh. 1889-1908
Landscape painter. The Cottage, Leatherhead, Surrey. † B 15, GI 1, RBA 4, RI 4, ROI 6.

KNIGHT, Horace Henry Exh. 1912-18
A.N.S.A. 1914-20. Add: 29 Millicent Road, West Bridgford, Notts. 1912 and 1918; A.P.C., R.40, B.E.F. 1917. † N 14.

KNIGHT, John Exh. 1884-1928
Landscape painter. Nottingham. † N 63.

KNIGHT, Joseph b. 1870
Landscape painter and etcher. b. Bolton. Studied Paris. Headmaster Bury School of Art. Exh. 1891-1930. Add: Bury, Lancs. † L 9, M 3, RA 8, RCA 8.

KNIGHT, Joseph* 1837-1909
Landscape painter. b. Manchester. Self taught. Father of Clara K. q.v. R.E. 1883, R.I. 1882, R.O.I. 1883. "A Tidal River" purchased by Chantrey Bequest 1877. Add: Bettws-y-Coed, Wales 1880; Chelsea, London 1886; Llan Rhos, nr. Llandudno 1892; Tywyn, nr. Llandudno 1893; Bryn Glas, Conway, Wales 1902. † B 7, D 8, DOW 1, FIN 3, GI 3, L 88, M 62, RA 38, RBA 1, RCA 146, RE 90, RI 142, ROI 40.

KNIGHT, John William Buxton* 1843-1908
Landscape painter and watercolourist. Studied R.A. Schools. R.B.A. 1875, R.E. 1881. "Old December's Bareness Everywhere" purchased by Chantrey Bequest 1908. Add: Sevenoaks, Kent 1880; London 1881, 1899 and 1907; West Drayton, Middlesex 1894; Chorley Wood, Herts. 1897 and 1902. † AG 2, B 7, D 9, G 16, GI 8, GOU 71, I 2, L 17, LEI 2, M 17, NEA 50, NG 11, RA 50, RBA 16, RCA 2, RE 12, RI 1, ROI 1.

KNIGHT, Dame Laura* 1877-1970
nee Johnson. Landscape, figure, portrait painter and etcher. b. Long Eaton, Derbys. Studied Nottingham School of Art. Married Harold K. q.v. N.S.A. 1908, A.R.A. 1927, R.A. 1936, A.R.E. 1924, R.E. 1932, A.R.W.S. 1909, R.W.S. 1928, S.W.A. 1933, D.B.E. 1929. "Spring" (1916-20) purchased by Chantrey Bequest 1935 and "The Gypsy" in 1939. Add: Nottingham 1895; Staithes, Yorks. 1905; Newlyn, Penzance 1908; Paul, Penzance 1911; St. Buryan, Cornwall 1914; London 1919. † AG 3, ALP 136, B 4, BG 3, CG 1, CON 29, FIN 32, G 9, GI 31, GOU 35, I 44, L 112, LEI 348, M 62, N 31, RA 112, RE 19, RHA 8, ROI 2, RSA 20, RWS 103, SWA 31.

KNIGHT, Lawrence John d. 1950
Watercolour painter and illustrator. Studied Leicester College of Art 1926-37. Exh. 1937-39. Add: May Villa, 23 Norwood Road, Leicester. † N 8.

KNIGHT, Miss M. Exh. 1902
12 Queen Street, Edinburgh. † RSA 1.

KNIGHT, Miss Madge Exh. 1911-31
Watercolour landscape and figure painter. A.N.S.A. 1920. Add: West Bridgford, Notts. 1911; London 1922. † G 2, I 2, L 1, N 29, NEA 4, RA 4, RI 1, WG 21.

KNIGHT, Mrs. Menie Exh. 1922-36
Landscape painter. London 1922; Pulborough, Sussex 1936. † AB 3, COO 1, RA 1, RCA 2, RI 1, ROI 1, SWA 5.

KNIGHT, P. Exh. 1934
Figure painter. c/o Cambridge & Co., Dublin. † RHA 3.

KNIGHT, Paul Exh. 1883-1904
Landscape and figure painter and engraver. Bettws-y-Coed, Wales 1883 and 1890; Chelsea, London 1886 and 1903; Llan Rhos, Carnarvonshire 1891; Manchester 1894; Conway, Wales 1898. † L 3, M 7, RA 3, RBA 1, RCA 61, ROI 2.

KNIGHT, R.W. Exh. 1882
† FIN 1.

KNIGHT, William Exh. 1888-1912
Architect. Father of Harold K. q.v. Add: Nottingham. † N 25.

KNIGHT, William b. 1872
Landscape and genre painter. Designer and teacher. Studied Leicester College of Art and Heatherleys. Exh. 1897-1940. Add: Leicester. † B 8, BG 1, L 1, N 22, RA 14, RBA 1, RI 2.

KNIGHT, William George d. 1938
Portrait and landscape painter. Studied Royal College of Art. Master at Weston Super Mare School of Art. R.B.A. 1898. Exh. 1896-1924. Add: Weston Super Mare. † RA 4, RBA 24.

KNIGHTLEY, Thomas E. Exh. 1880
Architect. 106 Cannon Street, London. † RA 1.

KNIGHTON, Kathleen A. Exh. 1909-10
51 Hawley Square, Margate, Kent. † B 2.

KNILL-BARTLETT, Dorothy G. Exh. 1925
† RMS 1.

KNOBLOCK, Gertrude Exh. 1906-40
Sculptor. b. New York. Studied at the Art League of New York, Juliens, Paris and Royal College of Art, 1902-7. Add: London. † B 1, I 2, L 1, RA 10, RSA 2, SWA 3.

KNOCH, S.G. Exh. 1911
11 Gilpin Avenue, East Sheen, London. † RA 1.

KNOECHL, Hans Exh. 1894
Painter. 25 Kellett Road, Brixton, London. † RA 1.

KNOFF, Albert L. Exh. 1922-23
Landscape Painter. 12 Tavistock Place, London. † GOU 2, NEA 2, RA 1.

KNOTT, Ada Exh. 1931-39
Miniature painter. Brookside Cottage, Prestbury, Nr. Macclesfield. † L 6, RA 4, RMS 4, RSA 4.

KNOTT, A.S. Exh. 1927
Architect. 45 Bloomsbury Square, London. † RA 1.

KNOTT, J.W. Exh. 1885
2 North View, Mersey Road, Ashton on Mersey. † M 1.

KNOTT, Ralph c. 1878-1929
Architect (London County Hall). Exh. 1899-1913. Add: London. † RA 5, RSA 2.

KNOTT, Tavernor Exh. 1880-89
York Place, Edinburgh. † GI 2, RSA 16.

KNOTTESFORD-FORTESCUE, Mrs. Alice Margaretta Exh. 1909-14
45 Banbury Road, Oxford. † LS 11.

KNOTTESFORD-FORTESCUE, Miss Joan Exh. 1909-11
45 Banbury Road, Oxford. † LS 3.

KNOWLAND, D.G. Exh. 1939
† NEA 1.

KNOWLES, A. Exh. 1928-33
Liverpool. † L 3.

KNOWLES, Annie L. Exh. 1890-1926
106 Devonshire Street, Higher Broughton, Manchester. † L 2, M 1, RI 1.

KNOWLES, Davidson* Exh. 1880-98
Landscape and figure painter. R.B.A. 1890. Add: London. † B 1, GI 13, L 5, M 8, NEA 3, NG 1, P 1, RA 14, RBA 47, ROI 16.

KNOWLES, Edgar Exh. 1904-5
26 Sir Thomas Street, Liverpool. † L 2.

KNOWLES, Eleanor Exh. 1895-1903
8 King Street, Manchester. † L 5, M 7.

KNOWLES, Esther Exh. 1888
32 Capel Street, Dublin. † RHA 1.

KNOWLES, Ethel M. Exh. 1905-33
St. Helens, Lancs. 1905; Bradford, Yorks. 1907; Blackburn, Lancs. 1933. † L 4.

KNOWLES, Frederick J.* b. 1874
Landscape and figure painter. Studied Cavendish School of Art. Probably brother of George Sheridan and Juliet K. q.v. Exh. 1890-1933. Add: Moss Lane, Moss Side, Manchester 1890; Chorlton cum Hardy 1895; Manchester 1898. † L 3, M 14, RA 1, RCA 19, RI 48.

KNOWLES, Farquar McGillivray 1859-1932
Landscape painter. Born U.S.A. Died Toronto, Canada. Exh. 1892-93. Add: 67 Cricketfield Road, Clapton, London. † RBA 1, ROI 1.

KNOWLES, George Sheridan 1863-1931
Painter. R.B.A. 1890, R.I. 1892, R.O.I. 1901. Probably brother of Frederick J.K. and Juliet K. q.v. Add: Moss Lane, Moss Side, Manchester 1883; London 1885. † B 5, GI 3, L 28, LEI 1, M 32, RA 28, RBA 39, RCA 42, RHA 1, RI 108, ROI 91.

KNOWLES, Joseph Exh. 1926
† M 2.

KNOWLES, Miss Juliet Exh. 1883-1901
Fruit and watercolour painter. Probably sister of Frederick J. and George Sheridan K. q.v. Add: 117 Moss Lane, Moss Side, Manchester 1883; Chorlton cum Hardy, 1895; Manchester 1898. † L 3, M 18, RA 1, RI 3.

KNOWLES, L.S. Exh. 1926
Lonsdale, Laurel Road, St. Helens, Lancs. † L 1.

KNOWLES, Marie Exh. 1925
166 Lord Street, Southport, Lancs. † L 2.

KNOWLES, Margaret Exh. 1906-31
Flower painter. Flixton Place, Ballymena, Ireland 1906; Ballycastle, Co. Antrim 1931. † RHA 23.

KNOWLES, Violet Exh. 1909
† LS 1.

KNOWLES, William H. Exh. 1901-18
Architect. Newcastle on Tyne. † RA 5, RSA 3.

KNOWLES, William Pitcairn Exh. 1882-92
Landscape and figure painter. Christchurch, Hants. † L 2, NG 2, RA 2, RBA 5, RI 5.

KNOX, Archibald Exh. 1895
Watercolour landscape painter and art master. 70 Athole Street, Douglas, I.O.M. † RBA 1.

KNOX, Miss E.A. Exh. 1893-1901
Bridge of Allan, N.B. 1893, Woodend, by Callander, N.B. 1901. † GI 2.

KNOX, Mrs. Godfrey Exh. 1912-14
51 Northumberland Road, Dublin. † RHA 2.

KNOX, G.J. Exh. 1881
Plymouth, Devon. † RHA 2.

KNOX, Mrs. Hilda Exh. 1913
Landscape painter. † ALP 1.

KNOX, Isobel Mary b. 1895
Mrs. Huffman. Miniature and portrait painter. b. Toronto, Canada. Studied Toronto, Slade School, Dublin School of Art, Colarossi's, Paris and Rome. Exh. 1924-30. Add: London. † RI 7, RMS 1.

KNOX, John* Exh. 1930-32
Glasgow. † GI 1, RSA 2.

KNOX, Madeline Exh. 1910-19
Landscape, flower and figure painter. London. † CAR 29, LS 9, NEA 7.

KNOX, Mrs. R. (M). Exh. 1884-94
Landscape painter. The Holt, nr. Farnham, Surrey. † SWA 4.

KNUPFFER, Daisy b. 1908
Portrait and landscape painter and mural decorator. Studied Slade School. Exh. 1926-40. Add: London. † NEA 1, RA 4, ROI 1.

KNUTTON, S. Exh. 1921-23
Landscape painter. Springfield, New Sawley, Derbys. † N 3.

KNYVETT, Major J.S. Exh. 1939
Watercolour landscape painter. † AR 1.

KOBERWEIN, Georgina see TERRELL

KOBERWEIN, Rosa Exh. 1880-84
Portrait and genre painter. Daughter of Georg K. (1820-1876), and sister of Georgina Terrell q.v. Add: London 1880; Fordingbridge, Hants. 1883; Downton, nr. Salisbury, Wilts. 1884. † D 5, G 3, L 2, M 1, RA 2, RHA 2, RI 2.

KOCH, Alexander Exh. 1890-1910
Architect. London. † GI 2, RA 9.

KOCH, Christine Exh. 1929-38
Langley, Broughton Park, Manchester. † L 1, RCA 6.

KOCH, Elisa* Exh. 1887-90
Painter. 36 Boulevard Clichy, Paris. † GI 3.

KOCH, G. Exh. 1883
Painter. † FIN 1.

KOCH, Walter Exh. 1893-94
Figure painter. Prinsholme, Bushey, Herts. † RBA 1, ROI 2.

KOE, Hilda Exh. 1895-1901
Decorative designer. Kensington, London. † L 1, RA 2.

KOE, Laurence Exh. 1888-1908
Portrait painter and sculptor. Brighton 1888 and 1891; London 1889 and 1892. † B 3, L 9, P 3, RA 22, RBA 1, RI 1, ROI 11.

KOE, Winifred Exh. 1888-1909
Landscape, flower and portrait painter. 15 Bennett Park, Blackheath, London. † RBA 1, SWA 2, WG 47.

KOEKKOEK, Willem* 1839-1895
Dutch artist. Exh. 1884. Add: 72 Piccadilly, London. † L 1, M 1.

KOELLER, Mrs. Jeannie L. Exh. 1935-36
Landscape and flower painter. Studied Belfast School of Art. Add: 48 Grasmere Road, London. † ROI 1, WG 32.

KOENEMANN, Hermann Exh. 1903-4
German artist. Wiesbaden, Germany 1903; Stargard in Micklenburg, Germany 1904. † GI 2, L 1, RSA 2.

KOHLER, Elsie Exh. 1920-40
Portrait and landscape painter. b. Bath. Studied Clifton School of Art, Bristol and Paris. Art teacher at Cheltenham Ladies College and Eastbourne School of Arts and Crafts. Add: Bristol. † L 1, RCA 1, RSA 1.

KOK, J. Exh. 1936
† RSA 3.

KOLBE, Georg 1877-1947
German sculptor. Exh. 1936. † RSA 4.

KOLDEWEY, B.H. Exh. 1889
Dordrecht, Holland. † ROI 1.

KOLDEWEY, B.J. Exh. 1936
† RSA 1.

KOLLE, Marjorie Exh. 1927-40
Watercolour landscape painter. Saint Hill, Alphington, Exeter. † AB 1, COO 2, M 1, RBA 2, RCA 4, RSA 5, SWA 2.

KOLLWITZ, Kathe 1867-1945
nee Schmidt. German painter, etcher and sculptor. Exh. 1921. † G 2.

KOMAI, Gonnoske Exh. 1936
Landscape and flower painter. 73 Harcourt Terrace, London. † RA 2.

KOMAROMY, Istvan Exh. 1939
† RMS 2.

KOMJATI, Julius d.1958
Etcher. A.R.E. 1931. Exh. 1930-40. Add: 44 Redcliffe Gardens, London. † RA 9.

KONARSHKA, Tanina Exh. 1935
Wood engraver. † RED 2.

KONDRUP, Katinka Exh. 1880-86
Sculptor. London. † RA 2.

KONEKAMP, Frederick Rudolph b.1897
Landscape painter, author and lecturer. Exh. 1939. † BK 31.

KONEN, Exh. 1932
Woodcut artist. † BA 2.

KONODY, Pauline Evelyn Exh. 1926-36
Watercolour painter. Daughter of art critic Paul George K. Studied Royal College of Art. Add: London 1926; Whistler's Wood, Woldingham, Surrey 1929. † CG 3, COO 9, FIN 2, GOU 29, RA 8, RHA 1, SWA 1, WG 4.

KONSTAM, Gertrude A. see KINGSTON

KOOP, Charles R. Exh. 1912-23
Married Mary K. q.v. Add: London. † I 1, L 6.

KOOP, Mary Exh. 1909-31
nee Bredall. Landscape and portrait painter. Studied Croydon School of Art and London School of Art. Married Charles K. q.v. A.S.W.A. 1928. Add: Croydon, Surrey 1909; London 1912. † L 6, LS 12, M 2, NEA 1, P 2, RA 3, ROI 7, SWA 13.

KOOPMAN, Augustus 1869-1914
Landscape and figure painter. b. U.S.A. Exh. 1899-1910. Add: Paris 1899; London 1903; Etaples, Pas de Calais, France 1907. † FIN 5, GI 7, GOU 2, I 5, LS 8, M 1, P 1, RA 1.

KOPPEN, Theodor Exh. 1882
Munich. † RSA 1.

KOPPERS, Miss K. Exh. 1889
c/o Chapman Bros. 251 King's Road, Chelsea, London. † M 1.

KOPTA, Emery Exh. 1910
American sculptor. Add: c/o Allied Artists Assn., 67 Chancery Lane, London. † LS 2.

KOREN, Exh. 1939
† GOU 1.

KORMIS, Fred J. b.1894
Sculptor. Born and Studied in Frankfurt. Exh. 1935-40. Add: London. † RA 2.

KORNBLUTH, Nathaniel Exh. 1937
Etcher. 56 High Street, Whitechapel, London. † RA 2.

KORSHAW, M. Lilian Exh. 1907
51 West Parade, Huddersfield. † L 2.

KORTRIGHT, Guy b.1877
Landscape and decorative painter. b. Clifton Glos. Spent part of his early life in Canada. Studied St. Ives, Penzance, Cornwall. Exh. 1901-39. Add: St. Ives, Cornwall 1901; Pen-y-Wern, Flints. 1911; London 1913. † BA 41, BAR 3, L 9, M 1, RA 33, RCA 1, ROI 2.

KORTRIGHT, Henry Somers 1870-1942
Landscape and portrait painter. b. Southampton. Studied Lambeth School of Art and Herkomers, Bushey, Herts. Married Primrose Margaret K. q.v. R.B.A. 1909. Add: London 1899 and 1918; Bexhill on Sea, Sussex 1908. † B 3, D 1, GI 3, L 9, M 1, RA 20, RBA 60.

KORTRIGHT, Primrose Margaret Exh. 1909-11
nee Hervey. Miniature portrait painter. Married Henry Somers K. q.v. Add: Grenville Lodge, Bexhill on Sea, Sussex. † RA 3.

KOSMINSKI, Mrs. Bushka Exh. 1921-26
Sculptor. London. † GI 6, L 11, RA 7.

KOSSAK, de see D

KOSTER, Miss Exh. 1914
Painter. † WG 36.

KOTASZ, Karl b.1872
Hungarian painter. Exh. 1928. † AB 52.

KOTERA, Jan Exh. 1900
Architect. Rudolovo Nabrezi, 6 Prague. † RA 4.

KOTSCHENREITER, Hugo* 1854-1908
German painter. Exh. 1882. Add: Manchester. † M 1.

KOUSNETZOFF, C. Exh. 1904
Paris. † I 1.

KOVACS, Frank Exh. 1938-39
Portrait medalist. 48 Robson Avenue, London. † RA 2, RMS 3.

KOZAKIEWICZ, Anton* b. 1841
Polish painter. Exh. 1883. Add: c/o Graphic, 190 Strand, London. † FIN 1, M 1.

KOZNIEWSKA, Miss M. Exh. 1905
Stubben Edge, Ashover, Chesterfield. † RA 1.

KRABBE, H.M. Exh. 1912-13
Laren, Holland. † RA 2.

KRAFTMEIER, Miss Murta Exh. 1899-1901
Portrait painter. London. † NG 1, RA 3, RHA 2, RMS 2.

KRAMER, Fritz b.1905
Portrait painter. b. Vienna. Studied Vienna School of Fine Arts, and Berlin and Dresden Academies. Add: Wimslow, Bucks. 1938; London 1940. † RA 1, ROI 2.

KRAMER, Jacob 1892-1962
Portrait painter. Member London Group 1914. Exh. 1914-38. Add: London 1914; Leeds 1919. † GOU 1, L 1, LS 6, M 1, NEA 5, RSA 1.

KRAMER, M. Exh. 1891
Hagdstradt, Schiedam, Holland. † GI 2.

KRAMSTYK, Romain b.1885
c/o Galerie Zak, 16 Rue de l'Abbaye, Paris. † GI 1.

KRAUSE, Mrs. Exh. 1903-9
Comberton Hall, Kidderminster. † B 7.

KRAUSE, Emil A. Exh. 1891-1914
42 Liverpool Road, Birkdale, Southport, Lancs. 1891; Glasfry, Conway 1893; Bryn Tawel, Conway 1898; Southport, Lancs. 1901 and 1910; Tywyn, N. Wales 1906. † L 14, M 3, RCA 20.

KRAUSE, Frances Exh. 1882-91
42 Liverpool Road, Birkdale, Southport, Lancs. † L 1, M 4.

KRAUSS, Amy Eliza Exh. 1907-15
Watercolour painter and pottery artist. Bristol. † I 10, L 6, LS 8, NEA 1, RA 1, ROI 1.

KREIGER, Fritz Exh. 1912
c/o J.G. Bauer, Augsburg, Germany. † L 2.

KREIGER, Wilhelm Exh. 1912-14
Munich 1912, c/o Fritz Kreigner, Elsinore, Dalton Road, Liscard, Cheshire 1913. † GI 4, L 9, RA 3, RHA 4, RSA 5.

KRELL, E. Beatrice Exh. 1898-1910
Liverpool. † L 22.

KRETZINGER, Clara Josephine b.1883
American artist. Exh. 1909-11. Add: 59 Avenue de Saxe, Paris. † L 1, RA 1.

KRICHELDORF, Carl* Exh. 1892-1900
Figure and landscape painter. Tetbury, Glos. † RA 9, RBA 2.

KRISHNA, Roop Exh. 1929
Watercolour painter. Royal College of Art, South Kensington, London. † RA 2.

KRISTIAN, Ronald Exh. 1915
Wood cut artist. 9 Malden Crescent, London. † NEA 1.

KROHG, Per Lasson* b.1889
Norwegian painter, sculptor, and teacher. Studied under his father Christian K. at Colarossi's Paris and under Henri Matisse. Exh. 1913-14. Add: Bragvei Christiana, Norway. † LS 5.

KRONBERG, Louis Exh. 1898-1909
49 Boulevard du Montparnasse, Paris 1898; 9 Bolton Studios, Redcliffe Road, London 1909. † GI 1, GOU 1, LS 3.

KRONER, Christian* Exh. 1883
Landscape painter. † FIN 1.

KRONSTRAND, B. Exh. 1903
8 Alexandra Terrace, Penzance, Cornwall. † B 1.

KROPHOLLER, A.J. Exh. 1936
† RSA 2.

KROSTEWITZ, F. Exh. 1905
c/o A. Lucas, 38 Baker Street, London. † RA 1.

KROUPA, B. Exh. 1880
Fettes College, Edinburgh. † RSA 1.

KRUGER, G.E. von W. Exh. 1905-18
Painter. London. † GI 2, L 5, M 1, NG 13, RA 13.

KRUMLEIN, H. Exh. 1882
Camden Town, London. † RHA 1.

KRZYZANOWSKI, Konrad Exh. 1908-9
16 Koszykowa, Warsaw, Poland. † LS 7.

KUCHL, Professor K. Exh. 1893
77 Gabelsberger strasse, Munich. † GI 1.

KUCK, Mrs. May Seddon Exh. 1920
† RMS 1.

KUEHL, Professor Gotthardt Johann* c.1850-1915
German artist. 9 Rue Chaptal, Paris 1884; Royal Academy, Dresden 1901. † GI 1, I 9, M 1, RSA 1.

KUGGE, Gaston J. Exh. 1925
Miniature painter. 314 Rue des Pyrenees, Paris. † RA 1.

KUHL, J.E. Exh. 1911
Lisburn Street, Alnwick, Northumberland. † RA 1.

KUHN, Miss C. Exh. 1910-15
c/o C.H. West, 117 Finchley Road, London. † I 1, RA 1.

KUHN, Friedrich Exh. 1884
Sculptor. Schiller Strasse, Munich. † RA 1.

KUHN, Walt* 1880-1949
American painter. Exh. 1925. † CHE 2.

KUHNERT, Wilhelm* 1865-1926
German animal painter and etcher. Exh. 1911-26. † FIN 520.

KUKLA, Charles Exh. 1937
† M 1.

KUMMER, Von See V

KUMMER, Paul Exh. 1882-1913
Sculptor. London. † L 2, RA 5.

KURIHARA, Chuji Exh. 1916-27
Watercolour landscape painter. Add: London. A.R.B.A. 1919. † COO 15, GOU 2, I 4, L 1, RBA 52, RI 2.

KURNATOWSKA, de See D

KUSEL, de See D

KUSSNER, Amalia Exh. 1896-1905
Mrs. Coudert. Miniature portrait painter. London. † RA 5.

KUSTNER, Carl b. 1861
German artist. Exh. 1904. Add: Munich. † GI 1.

KUWASSEG, Charles Euphraise Exh. 1887
French painter. Boulevard Courcelles, Paris. † RHA 1.

KUZMIK, de See D

KYD, James Exh. 1885
Figure painter. 45 Portland Road, Notting Hill, London. † B 1.

KYLBERG, Regina Exh. 1884-85
Watercolour painter, c/o H. Wilkinson, Esq., Winton House, Ealing, London. † L 1, M 1, RBA 5.

KYLBERG, Miss V. Exh. 1885
c/o H. Wilkinson, Esq., Winton House, Ealing, London. † L 1.

KYLE, Mrs. Agnes Exh. 1925-36
Radlett, Herts. 1925; 58 Makepeace Mansions, Highgate, London 1935. † RI 2, SWA 1.

KYLE, Georgina Moutray Exh. 1921-39
Landscape, figure and portrait painter. Studied Colarossi's, Paris. Add: 5 West Elmwood, Lisburn Road, Belfast. † GI 13, L 3, RHA 16, ROI 6, RSA 3, SWA 1.

KYLE, T. Exh. 1885
10 Derby Place, Broughty Ferry, Edinburgh. † RSA 1.

KYNASTON, Arthur Exh. 1904-16
Landscape and portrait painter. Guildford 1904; Pulborough, Sussex 1914. † GOU 23, L 4, RA 15.

KYNASTON, Mrs. Helena S. Exh. 1903-9
Fruit and flower painter. Fulven's Farm, Abinger Hammer, Dorking, Surrey 1903; Guildford 1909. † GOU 2, RA 1.

KYNOCH, M. Exh. 1897-1912
8 Airlie Place, Dundee. † GI 2, RSA 2.

KYRKE-SMITH, Grace Exh. 1903-33
Kirkstone, Waterloo, Liverpool 1903; Hawkshead, Lancs. 1933. † L 3.

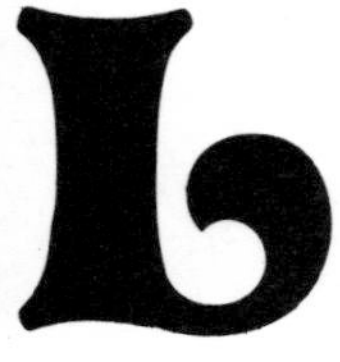

LABILLIERE, de see D
LABORDE, Ernest Exh. 1913
Watercolour painter. † FIN 3.
LABOUCHERE, Norna Exh. 1905-25
Landscape, figure and still life painter. 23 Chapel Street, London. † GI 1, GOU 27, I 8, L 4, LS 4, NEA 3, P 2, RA 5.
LABOUGLE, Mme. R.M.L. Exh. 1911
40 Rue Desrenaudes, Paris. † L 1.
LABROUSSE, Jeanne A. Exh. 1919-24
Miniature painter and pen and ink artist. A.S.W.A. 1920. Add: Colnbrook, Middlesex 1919; Tottenham, London 1922. † RA 4, SWA 5.
LACAZETTE, Miss A. Exh. 1883
Painter. Great Western Hotel, London. † RBA 1.
LACEY, Constance Mary b. 1884
Painter, designer, illuminator and embroiderer. b. Cotes, Leics. Studied Sir Arthur Cope's School of Painting and Royal College of Art. Assistant at Ipswich School of Art, Assistant Derby School of Art, and Examiner in Embroidery for the Union of Lancs. and Cheshire Institutes. Exh. 1935. Add: 72 St. Chad's Road, Derby. † N 1.
LACEY, Mrs. Eleanor Exh. 1940
Etcher. 37 Hampstead Lane, London. † RA 1.
LACEY, Elias Exh. 1929
Landscape and flower painter. Byron Studio, Hucknall, Notts. † N 3.
LACEY, Enid Exh. 1932-39
Figure painter. 117 Herbert Road, Woolwich, London. † NEA 1, RA 1.
LACEY, Edward Hill b. 1892
Sculptor and etcher. Exh. 1924-38. Add: London. † BA 1, CG 1, CON 2, GI 1, I 1, L 3, RA 14, RBA 2.
LACEY, Frederick W. Exh. 1885-86
Painter and architect. Brentwood, Essex 1885; London 1886. † RA 2.
LACEY, Joseph Exh. 1931
Figure painter. 4 Napier Avenue, Hurlingham, London. † RA 1.
LACK, Henry Martyn Exh. 1934-40
Etcher. A.R.E. 1934. Add: School House, Bozeat, Northants. 1934; Christ's Hospital, Horsham, Sussex 1938. † RA 6, RE 17.
LACK, Katherine O. Exh. 1918-19
61 Adelaide Road, Brockley, London. † I 2, RA 1.
LACK, Miss M.K. Exh. 1919-35
Woodcut artist. 11 Christchurch Road, London. † COO 2, SWA 1.
LACK, Miss Z. Exh. 1905-10
Surbiton, Surrey 1905; Woolton, Liverpool 1909; Southsea, Hants. 1910. † L 8, RA 1, RMS 1.
LACON, Jessie Exh. 1903
28 Broughton Road, Handsworth, Birmingham. † B 1.
LACOSTE, Gerald Exh. 1935
Architect. Calder House, Dover Street, London. † RA 1.
LACOUR, Octave L. Exh. 1887-91
Etcher. Teddington, Middlesex 1887; London 1891. † RA 4.
LACRETELLE, Jean Edouard 1817-1900
Portrait painter. 8 Little Stanhope Street, Mayfair, London. † RA 1.
LACROIX, de see D
LACY, de see D
LACY, George J.J. Exh. 1897-1905
Decorative architect. London. † RA 5.
LADDS, John Exh. 1886
Architect. 4 Chapel Street, Bedford Row, London. † RA 3.
LADEFOGED, Miss M. Exh. 1913
Eton Avenue, London. † SWA 1.
LADELL, Rev. A.R. Exh. 1931
† WG 1.
LADELL, Edward* Exh. 1880-96
Still life painter. Married Ellen L. q.v. Add: Exeter 1880 and 1885; Manchester 1883. † M 1, RA 3, ROI 3, TOO 16.
LADELL, Ellen* Exh. 1886-98
Still life painter. Married Edward L. q.v. † TOO 6.
LAENEN, Gerard Exh. 1938
Landscape and flower painter. † BK 34.
LAERMANS, Eugene* 1864-1940
Belgian painter. Exh. 1915. † I 1.
LAEVERENZ, Gustave* Exh. 1882
Figure painter. 40A Barclay Road, Walham Green, London. † RA 1, RSA 1.
LAFAGE, G.L. Exh. 1934
† BA 1.
LAFAURIE, Mme. Exh. 1925
8 Rue Royale, Paris. † RSA 1.
LAFONTAINE, de see D
LAFONTINELLA, de see D
LAFORGE, Mme. Marie Exh. 1903-21
A.R.M.S. 1908, R.M.S. 1909. Add: Paris 1903; Braisne Aisne, France 1921. † L 6, NG 3, RMS 9.
LAGAE, Jules b. 1862
Sculptor. Exh. 1914-31. Add: 8 Avenue Michael Ange, Brussels. † GI 1, L 3, RSA 8.
LAGARE, Eugene Exh. 1911
9 Rue Duguay Tronin, Paris. † RSA 2.
LAGLENNE, Jean Francis b. 1898
French painter. Exh. 1933-35. Add: Paris. † LEF 25, ROI 1.
LAGOS, B. Exh. 1880-81
16 Avenue Trudaine, Paris. † RHA 2.
LAGUILLERMIE, Frederic b. 1841
French etcher. Exh. 1889. Add: 4 Rue Robert Estienne, Paris. † RA 1.
LA HAYE, Alexis Exh. 1893
French painter. Ecole des Beaux Arts, Nismes, France. † RA 1.
LAHEY, Miss Vida b. 1882
Australian artist. Exh. 1928. † NEA 1.
LAIB, Erik Exh. 1925-27
Painter. 9 St. Albans Studios, Kensington, London. † GOU 1, RA 1.
LAIDLAW, A. Exh. 1882-86
72 Solway Street, Liverpool. † L 3.
LAIDLAW, Elise Gerloff Exh. 1908-12
30 Lansdowne Crescent, London. † LS 16.
LAIDLAW, Grace Exh. 1904
35 Albert Road, Manchester. † L 1.
LAIDLAW, Jessie Exh. 1888-96
Linda Villa, Goven. † GI 5.
LAIDLAW, Nicol b. 1886
Portrait and landscape painter, etcher and illustrator. b. Edinburgh. Studied Edinburgh College of Art (medal, life class 1909), also Paris and Spain. Exh. 1915-29. Add: London 1915; Edinburgh 1917. † GI 8, L 5, RA 4, RSA 19, RSW 5.
LAIDLAW, Thomas H. Exh. 1882-1905
Hawick, N.B. † RSA 3.
LAIDLAW, William C. Exh. 1902
4 York Buildings, Edinburgh. † RSA 1.
LAIDLAY, Lucy Exh. 1891-94
Flower painter. Deans Court, Wimborne, Dorset. † ROI 4.
LAIDLAY, Thurston Shoosmith Exh. 1905
30 Billing Road, Northampton. † L 1.
LAIDLAY, William James 1846-1912
Landscape painter. Studied in Paris 1879-85, with Carolus Duran and Bouguereau. Founder member N.E.A. 1886. R.B.A. 1903. Add: London. † G 3, GI 26, GOU 5, L 29, LS 7, M 8, NEA 13, NG 19, RA 19, RBA 40, ROI 1, RSA 1.
LAIDMAN, Edith A. Exh. 1904-34
Miniature painter, sculptor and potter. Sister of Ida Frances L. q.v. Add: Bushey, Herts. 1904; Milford, Surrey 1908. † ALP 1, GI 1, L 4, RA 22.
LAIDMAN, Ida Frances Exh. 1905-39
Portrait and miniature painter. b. India. Studied Bushey, Herts. Travelled frequently on the continent, America and Canada. Sister of Edith A.L. q.v. A.R.M.S. 1919. Add: Bushey, Herts. 1905; Milford, Surrey 1907; London 1921. † L 8, RA 22, RMS 48, SWA 2.
LAINAS, Miss A.G. Exh. 1933
35 Stoneby Drive, Wallasey, Cheshire. † L 1.
LAING, A. Exh. 1886
Castlehead, Paisley. † RSA 1.
LAING, Annie Rose Exh. 1898-1927
nee Low. Figure painter. Married James Garden L. q.v. Add: Glasgow 1898; Frascati, Italy 1926; London 1927. † GI 63, L 8, M 1, RA 3, RSA 10.
LAING, E. Exh. 1888
24 Napiershall Street, Glasgow. † GI 2.
LAING, Mrs. Ethel Exh. 1932
Boscombe, Hants. † RCA 1.
LAING, Elsie E. Exh. 1926-30
46 Park Road, Wigan, Lancs. † L 6.
LAING, Mrs. E. Janet Exh. 1936-37
† RMS 2.
LAING, Frank b. 1862
Landscape painter. b. Tayport. A.R.E. 1892. Add: Paris 1891; Tayport, N.B. 1894 and 1897; Dundee 1896. † GI 6, RA 3, RE 33, RSA 6, RSW 1.
LAING, Miss Georgina Exh. 1882-1922
Landscape and portrait painter. A.R.M.S. 1913. Add: 9 The Temple, Dale Street, Liverpool 1882; Anfield, Liverpool 1919. † B 2, L 80, RA 3, RMS 11.
LAING, Iris Exh. 1932-36
1 West House, 118 Campden Hill Road, London. † RBA 1, SWA 3.
LAING, Miss J. Exh. 1908-12
East Croydon, Surrey. † SWA 9.
LAING, James Garden 1852-1915
Landscape painter. b. Aberdeen. R.S.W. 1885. Married Annie Rose L. q.v. Add: Glasgow. † DOW 5, FIN 61, G 40, GI 80, L 13, M 9, RA 21, RBA 1, RI 6, RSA 55, RSW 114.
LAING, J. Marian Exh. 1929-33
Landscape painter. Culverlands, Farnham, Surrey. † COO 1, WG 1.
LAING, Margaret J. Exh. 1925-40
Edinburgh. † RSA 3.
LAING, Tomson* Exh. 1890-1904
Partick, Glasgow. † GI 4, L 4, RSA 1.
LAING, William Exh. 1880-85
Edinburgh. † RSA 14.
LAING, William Wardlaw Exh. 1882-1922
Figure and landscape painter. 8 The Temple, Dale Street, Liverpool. † B 1, GI 2, L 69, M 4, RA 9, RI 2.
LAING-SCOTT, Vera see FIDGEON
LAINSON, Thomas G. Exh. 1891
Architect. 104 Lansdown Place, Hove, Sussex. RA 1.

LAIRD, Alicia H. Exh. 1881-97
Landscape painter. Richmond, U.S.A. † SWA 10.

LAIRD, Arthur Robert 1881-c.1957
Lithographer. Studied Camberwell School of Arts and Crafts and Westminster School of Art. Exh. 1914-21. Add: Ivy Cottage, London Road, Ewell, Surrey. † LS 12.

LAIRD, Miss E.M. Exh. 1896
19 Park Road, Southborough, Tunbridge Wells, Kent. † ROI 1.

LAIRD, James Austen Exh. 1903-30
131 West Regent Street, Glasgow. † GI 5.

LAIRD-CLOWES, Lady Exh. 1907-8
4 Connaught Avenue, East Sheen, London. † L 4.

LAISTER, John Walter b. 1869
Landscape and still life painter. Studied under Stanley Royle at Sheffield. Exh. 1928. Add: 1 Winter Street, Sheffield. † L 2, RA 2.

LAKE, Alice R. Exh. 1934-40
Merchiston, Edinburgh 1934; Colinton 1940. † RSA 2.

LAKE, Evelyn Frances Coote Exh. 1937-40
Animal and bird painter. Studied Camden and Hornsey Schools of Art and on the continent. Add: Heage House, Crouch Hill, London. † COO 1, NEA 1, RBA 2, RI 2, ROI 1.

LAKE, Flora Exh. 1905
Ashcroft, Shalford, Guildford. † L 1.

LAKE, Gertrude Exh. 1891-1926
Landscape painter. Liverpool 1891 and 1898; Manchester 1893 and 1900; Carig, Hadnock Road, Monmouth 1923. † B 1, D 2, L 18, M 5, NG 1, RA 1, RI 1.

LAKE, John Gascoyne b. 1903
Painter. Studied Eastbourne School of Art, 1918-25 and Royal College of Art 1925-29. Exh. 1931-37. † NEA 3.

LAKE, Miss M.H. Exh. 1907-9
Mrs. C.P. Blatchley. Miniature portrait painter. Add: Sutton, Surrey 1907; Golder's Green, London 1909. † RA 2.

LAKEMAN, W. Stuart Exh. 1919
† I 3.

LAKIN, Miss Exh. 1897
Guy's Cliff Road, Warwick. † B 2.

LALAING, de see D

LALANDE, Edith see PATTERSON

LALANNE, Louise Exh. 1882-86
17 Boulevard Suchet, Passey, Paris. † GI 5.

LALANNE, Maxime 1827-1886
French etcher. Exh. 1882-84. Add: 74 Rue de Lafayette, Paris. † GI 6.

LALAUZE, Adolphe 1838-1905
French artist. Exh. 1882. Add: 15 Quai Bourbon, Paris. † GI 2.

LALHAM, T.N. Exh. 1888
4 Benson Street, Liverpool. † L 1.

LALL, Diana Metford b. 1886
nee Read. Painter, wood engraver and illustrator. b. Bridgwater, Somerset. Studied Crystal Palace Art School, Slade School, St. John's Wood, R.A. Schools and British School at Rome. Lived in Italy and India. Lecturer in art University of Birmingham. Exh. 1921-24. Add: Birmingham. † B 5.

LALLY, J. Exh. 1939
46 Whitworth Road, Ilkeston, Derbys. † N 1.

LAMAISON, Evelyn Exh. 1904-11
St. Ives, Cornwall. † LS 6, SWA 1.

LAMB, Adrian b. 1901
American artist. Exh. 1930. Add: 42a Easton Terrace, London. † RBA 1.

LAMB, Alfred Exh. 1910
Redclyffe, St. Anne's-on-Sea, Lancs. † L 1.

LAMB, Charles Vincent 1893-1965
Figure and landscape painter. b. Armagh, Ireland. Studied Metropolitan School of Art, Dublin (gold and silver medal). A.R.H.A. 1922, R.H.A. 1938. Add: School of Art, Dublin 1919; Carraroe, Co. Galway 1929. † RA 1, RHA 62.

LAMB, Eliza Exh. 1880
Figure painter. 29 Dartmouth Park Road, Highgate, London. † SWA 1.

LAMB, Edward Beckitt Exh. 1893-1901
Architect. London. † RA 6.

LAMB, Florence E. Exh. 1899
70 Norwood Grove, Newsham Park, Liverpool. † L 3.

LAMB, G.F. Exh. 1898-1908
London. † D 35.

LAMB, Henry* 1883-1960
Portrait, figure and landscape painter and draughtsman. b. Australia. Brought up in Manchester and studied medicine before taking up art. Studied under Francis Dodd and Augustus John, London and Paris. A.R.A. 1940. "The Artist's Wife" purchased by Chantrey Bequest 1934, "Death of a Peasant" (1911) in 1944, "Lytton Strachey" (1914) in 1957 and "The Artist's Family" (1940-d.1944) in 1961. Add: London 1906, 1927 and 1935; Poole, Dorset 1922; Coombe Bassett, Salisbury, Wilts. 1933. † ALP 70, CAR 5, CHE 3, G 3, GI 1, GOU 22, L 4, LEI 418, LS 5, M 4, NEA 23, RA 15, RED 1, RSA 5.

LAMB, Helen Adelaide Exh. 1913-39
Illuminator and pencil artist. Studied Glasgow School of Art (travelling bursary). Art teacher St. Colombas School, Kilmacolm. Add: Bryanston, Dunblane 1913 and 1923; Glasgow 1920. † GI 5, L 2, RSA 4.

LAMB, John d. 1909
Exh. 1889-1909. Add: 3 Churchfield Road, East Acton, London. † D 59.

LAMB, Lynton b. 1907
Painter, designer and wood engraver, lithographer and illustrator. b. India. Studied Central School of Arts and Crafts 1928-30. Instructor School of Book Production, Central School of Arts and Crafts 1935-39. Member London Group 1939. Exh. 1930-40. † COO 1, LEI 1, RED 1.

LAMB, Mildred R. Exh. 1930-37
Bryanston, Dunblane. † GI 1, RSA 2.

LAMB, Margaret Thurlow b. c.1873
nee Thurlow. Sculptor. Studied Wimbledon College of Art (1892), South Kensington and R.A. Schools. Add: Wimbledon 1892, Didsbury, Manchester 1897; Prestwich, Manchester 1898; Bowden, Cheshire 1920; Southport, Lancs. 1934. † B 3, L 14, LS 3, M 3, RA 1, RCA 3, RHA 5.

LAMB, P.A. Exh. 1912
13 John Street, Adelphi, London. † RA 3.

LAMB, Philip Agnew b. 1897
R.P. 1939. Exh. 1936-38. † P 6.

LAMB, Sylvia A. Exh. 1930
† L 1.

LAMB, William Exh. 1925-40
Sculptor. A.R.S.A. 1932. Add: Edinburgh 1925; London 1931; Montrose, Angus 1934. † GI 18, L 1, RA 2, RSA 58, RSW 3.

LAMBART, Alfred b. 1902
Portrait painter, poster artist and illustrator. b. Darlington. Studied Allan Fraser College, Arbroath. Exh. 1927-32. Add: London. † RA 4.

LAMBE, Barbara Ann Exh. 1931-32
† RMS 2.

LAMBERT, Adeline Exh. 1923
Linnerlie, Belvedere Park, Liverpool. † L 1.

LAMBERT, Alice M. Exh. 1890-95
Leece Lodge, Heaton Chapel, Manchester. † L 1, M 5.

LAMBERT, Cecil Exh. 1885
c/o Mr. Price, Dresden House, Soho Hill, Birmingham. † B 1.

LAMBERT, Clement 1854-1924
Landscape and figure painter. Exh. 1883-1901. Add: Brighton. † D 5, G 1, GI 1, NG 1, RA 8, RBA 20, RI 13, ROI 8.

LAMBERT, Edwin J. Exh. 1881-1928
Landscape and animal painter. London. † AG 2, L 6, RA 11, RBA 3, RHA 3, RI 4, ROI 3.

LAMBERT, Felix Borne Exh. 1911
Landscape painter. † BRU 1.

LAMBERT, George Washington* 1873-1930
Portrait painter. Born in Russia the son of an American father and English mother. Came to England 1878. Went to Australia 1891. Studied Sydney School of Art. Won a 3 year scholarship to Paris. Took up teaching at the London School of Art 1910. Returned to Australia c.1928. Father of Maurice L. q.v. A.R.A. 1922. Exh. from 1904. † FIN 2, G 1, GI 5, GOU 11, I 65, L 6, NEA 12, RA 28, RHA 5, ROI 1, RSA 5.

LAMBERT, J. Exh. 1892
57 Eccles Street, Dublin. † RHA 1.

LAMBERT, Miss L. Exh. 1885
Ringmore House, Teignmouth, Devon. † L 1.

LAMBERT, Louisa Exh. 1880
68 Amiens Street, Dublin. † RHA 2.

LAMBERT, Louis Eugene* 1825-1900
French painter. Exh. 1883-93. Add: 204 Rue de Courcelles, Paris. † FIN 1, RI 1.

LAMBERT, Maurice b. 1901
Sculptor. b. Paris. Son of George Washington L. q.v. Studied under Derwent Wood. Member London Group 1930. A.R.A. 1941. "Head of a Woman" purchased by Chantrey Bequest 1938. Exh. 1933-38. Add: 1A Logan Studios, Logan Place, London. † GI 2, L 2, RA 1, RSA 3.

LAMBERT, Thomas Exh. 1881-82
Watercolour landscape painter. 81 Sherwood Street, Nottingham. † N 4.

LAMBERT, Terence Henry b. 1891
Etcher and black and white artist. Exh. 1925-40. Add: Ealing, London. † L 1, RA 9, RBA 3, RI 2.

LAMBOURNE, Nigel b. 1919
Etcher and lithographer. b. Nottingham. Studied Central School of Arts and Crafts, Regent Street Polytechnic and Royal College of Art. Exh. 1940. Add: 5 Redcliffe Gardens, London. † RA 1.

LAMBRICK, Mrs. Dulcie Exh. 1935-39
Portrait painter. Wembley, Middlesex 1935; London 1937. † BK 23, RA 3.

LAMI, Stanislas b. 1858
Sculptor. Exh. 1904. Add: 51 Rue Scheffer, Paris. † L 2.

LAMMING, H. Exh. 1898
Miniature portrait painter. 33 Kenilworth Road, Ealing, London. † RA 1.

LAMMINI, Miss Exh. 1886
Watercolour flower painter. Eridge House, Fulham Park, Fulham, London. † RBA 1.

LAMOND, Henry Exh. 1889-1915
Glasgow. † GI 5.

LAMOND, William B.* c.1858-1925
Landscape painter. R.B.A. 1904. Add: Dundee 1889 and 1906; Tayport, Fife 1905. † GI 25, RA 1, RBA 8, RSA 16.

LAMONT, Miss C.I.J. Exh. 1913-23
62 Hartington Road, Sefton Park, Liverpool. † L 6.

LAMONT, Elsie Exh. 1926-40
Watercolour landscape painter. Travelled widely. Add: 2 Carlise Place, London 1926; Seaport, Elie, Fife 1936. † D 2, GI 1, RI 1, RSA 1, RSW 5, SWA 1, WG 76.

LAMONT, John Charles 1894-1948
Painter. Studied Glasgow School of Art. Add: Glasgow 1922, Kirkcudbright 1938. † GI 8, L 1, RSA 6.

LAMONT, J.R. Exh. 1881-90
19 North Bank, Regent's Park, London. † B 1, GI 1.

LAMONT, Lelia Exh. 1880-89
53 Rue Renneguin, Paris 1880; c/o 159 Queen Street, Glasgow 1888. † GI 7, RSA 4.

LAMONT, Ramsay Exh. 1891-99
Seine, France 1891; 9 Marine Parade, North Berwick 1897; Somme, France 1899. † GI 8.

LAMONT, Thomas Reynolds 1826-1898
Genre painter and watercolourist. Studied in Paris. A.R.W.S. 1866. Add: St. John's Wood, London. † AG 1, GI 2, L 7, RA 1, RSA 1, RWS 18.

LAMOTTE, Alphonse Exh. 1888-93
Engraver. 6 Rue Hippolyte Lebas, Paris 1888 and 1891; London 1889. † RA 4.

LAMOY, Florence Exh. 1921
88 Lyncombe Hill, Bath. † L 2.

LAMPLOUGH, Augustus Osborne 1877-1930
Landscape and architectural painter. b. Manchester. Studied Chester School of Art. Travelled on the continent, Middle East and North Africa. Teacher and lecturer at Leeds School of Art. Add: Mold, Flints 1904; Rhyl, N. Wales 1912; Ruthin 1914; Dolwyddelan, Carnarvonshire 1921; Abergele 1925. † FIN 64, L 12, RA 1, RCA 2.

LANAM, Susie Exh. 1913
Rose Cottage, Dulwich Village, London. † L 1.

LANCASTER, A. Exh. 1884
62½ George Street, Nottingham. † N 1.

LANCASTER, Alfred Dobree Exh. 1882-1905
Figure painter. London. † L 5, M 1, RA 8, ROI 2.

LANCASTER, Clara Bracebridge Exh. 1924-40
nee Manger. Portrait, still life and landscape painter. b. Hong Kong. Studied in Brussels, Byam Shaw and Vicat Cole School and under Algernon Talmage at St. Ives, Cornwall. Add: London. † RA 1, RBA 1, ROI 5, SWA 6.

LANCASTER, Miss E.M. Exh. 1907-11
Coventry. † SWA 5.

LANCASTER, Edward Purser 1911-1954
Painter and poster artist and designer. Studied Southport Art School, Liverpool, City School of Art and Chelsea Art School. Exh. 1939. † GOU 2.

LANCASTER, Miss H.M. Exh. 1916
198 Gloucester Terrace, Hyde Park, London. † RA 1.

LANCASTER, John Exh. 1882-84
Landscape and figure painter. London. † RBA 3.

LANCASTER, J.C. Exh. 1924-25
Landscape painter. 10 Churchville, Hartley Road, Nottingham. † N 6.

LANCASTER, J.C. Exh. 1887-88
Portrait painter. 5 Churchfield Lane, Radford, Notts. † N 2.

LANCASTER, Lilian Exh. 1911-39
Figure and flower painter. Studied Westminster School of Art and Slade School. Life mistress at Brighton and Eastbourne Art Schools. m. Alfred Clive Gardiner q.v. Add: London. † COO 3, GOU 55, I 5, L 1, LS 9, NEA 31, P 11, RA 7, SWA 1.

LANCASTER, Percy* 1878-1951
Landscape, painter and etcher. b. Manchester. Studied Southport School of Art. R.B.A. 1914, A.R.E. 1912, R.I. 1921. Add: Southport, Lancs. 1901 and 1923; London 1918. † B 8, D 1, FIN 12, G 3, GI 6, I 3, L 123, M 7, NEA 1, RA 20, RBA 104, RCA 69, RE 60, RHA 1, RI 110, ROI 1, RSA 2, WG 99.

LANCASTER, Mrs. V. Exh. 1910
14B Ladbroke Terrace, London. † RA 1.

LANCE, Eveline Exh. 1891-1907
Landscape painter. London. † L 1, NG 3, RBA 3, RI 6, SWA 3.

LANCE, Marjorie b. 1900
Mrs. C. Webb. Landscape, portrait and figure painter. Studied Slade School 1920-23. Exh. 1923-40. Add: London 1923 and 1927; Scarborough, Yorks. 1924. † GOU 12, NEA 6, RSA 1.

LANCE, William Exh. 1887-1906
Figure painter. Chelsea, London. † L 1, NG 1, RA 1, RBA 1, RI 3, ROI 1.

LANCE, Wilmot Exh. 1893-94
Flower painter. Hillside, Christchurch Street, Ipswich, Suffolk. † RA 1, RBA 2.

LANCE, William B. Exh. 1882-91
Domestic painter. Chiswick, London. † B 1, L 1, RBA 1.

LANCHESTER, Mary b. 1864
Painter and colour print artist. Studied Brighton School of Art. Exh. 1896-1910. Add: London 1896; Ripley Villa, New Malden, Surrey 1900. † B 1, BG 8, RA 1, RBA 2, RI 1, SWA 7.

LANCHESTER, R.V. Exh. 1910
47 Bedford Square, London. † RSA 3.

LANCHESTER, Waldo S. Exh. 1937
St. Ann's Pottery, Malvern, Worcs. † B 1.

LANCHIOR, H. Exh. 1884
21 Park Village, Regent's Park, London. † L 1.

LANCON, Auguste 1836-1885
French artist. Exh. 1881. Add: 68 Rue Vandamme, Paris. † RE 6.

LAND, Mrs. Edith Exh. 1926-38
Miniature painter. 41 Bullingham Mansions, Church Street, London. † L 2, RA 1, RI 14, RMS 3, SWA 4.

LANDALE, The Misses Exh. 1911
Watercolour painter. † WG 57.

LANDAU, Dorothea Exh. 1903-27
Mrs. Da Fano. Painter, draughtsman and sculptor. A.R.B.A. 1923, R.O.I. 1904. Add: London 1903 and 1922; Hughenden, Bucks. 1912. † BA 2, BG 1, I 12, L 5, NEA 2, NG 2, RA 10, RBA 20, ROI 38, RSA 1.

LANDELLE, Charles* 1821-1908
French artist. Exh. 1884-1901. Add: 21 Quai Voltaire, Paris. † GI 3, L 1.

LANDER, C.J. Exh. 1895-96
3 St. Helen's Terrace, Richmond, Surrey. † GI 2, RBA 2.

LANDER, Capt. Edgar b. 1883
Watercolour painter and etcher. Exh. 1920-36. Add: London 1920; Chinnor, Oxford 1934. † GI 5, L 6, LS 3, RA 4, RSA 1.

LANDER, Harold C. Exh. 1902-6
Architect. 1 Arundel Street, London. † L 1, RA 4.

LANDER, Henry Longley Exh. 1881-1903
Landscape painter. London. † D 3, M 2, RA 1, RI 1, ROI 1.

LANDER, John St. Helier 1869-1944
Portrait painter. b. Jersey, C.I. Studied Calderon's School of Animal Painting, R.A. Schools and Juliens, Paris. R.O.I. 1916. Add: Jersey 1895 and 1905: London 1898 and 1906. † FIN 8, GI 1, I 2, L 5, P 21, RA 30, ROI 57.

LANDER, Wills Exh. 1887-90
Landscape painter and sculptor. 128 Gower Street, London. † NG 1, RA 2, RBA 1, ROI 1.

LANDI, Aristodemo Exh. 1881
Flower painter. 45 Brompton Square, London. † RA 1.

LANDLESS, J. Exh. 1883-93
2 Elliott Street, Hillhead, Glasgow. † GI 2.

LANDLESS, W. Exh. 1880-84
227 West George Street, Glasgow. † GI 6.

LANDON, Mrs. Brenda Exh. 1932
Figure painter. 97 Ennerdale Road, Richmond, Surrey. † RA 1.

LANDON, Perceval Exh. 1908-9
5 Pall Mall Place, London. † LS 8.

LANDOWSKI, Paul Maximilien b. 1875
French sculptor. Exh. 1911. Add: 12 Rue Moissons-Desroches, Boulogne, Seine, France. † RSA 3.

LANDRE, de see D

LANDRE, Louise A. Exh. 1882-87
Painter. 233 Faubourg St. Honore, Paris. † GI 3, SWA 1.

LANDREMONT, Charles Exh. 1911
Landscape painter. † BRU 2.

LANDSEER, Miss Exh. 1880
Landscape painter. H.S.W.A. 1880. Add: 6 Kensington Park Gardens, London. † SWA 2.

LANE, Mrs. Exh. 1881
86 Upper George Street, Kingstown, Ireland. † RHA 2,

LANE, Constance Exh. 1919-40
Landscape painter. Hemel Hempstead, Herts. 1923; London 1925. † BA 51, CHE 1, GOU 3, I 4, NEA 4, RA 3, ROI 2.

LANE, Cyril Exh. 1938-39
Landscape painter. 24 Wimbledon Road, Nottingham. † N 3.

LANE, C.J. Exh. 1887
Little Caddesden, Berkhamsted, Herts. † D 2.

LANE, Dorothy M. Exh. 1913
42 Newburgh Road, Acton, London. † L 1.

LANE, Edith Exh. 1890
Heaton Lodge, Heaton Mersey, Lancs. † M 1.

LANE, Emily Exh. 1880-84
Flower and landscape painter. 19 Gloucester Terrace, Campden Hill, London. † SWA 7.

LANE, E. Tudor Exh. 1902-3
The Tower House, Boscastle, North Cornwall. † B 1, L 1, M 2.

LANE, Georgina A.J. Exh. 1926-31
Lancaster House, Portland Place, Leamington, Warwicks. † B 3, L 2.

LANE, James B. Exh. 1939-40
† NEA 2.

LANE, J.Q. Exh. 1885-89
82 Alfred Terrace, Mount Pottinger, Belfast. † L 1, RHA 2.
LANE, Margaret R. Exh. 1909-38
Edinburgh. † RSA 19.
LANE, Mary S. Exh. 1899-1930
Flower painter. Fairy Hill, Monkstown, Cork 1899; Vernon Mount, Cork 1914; London 1929. † RHA 17.
LANE, Marian U.M. Exh. 1932
† RMS 2.
LANE, Miss N.A. Exh. 1910-12
Devonshire House, Beeston, Notts. † N 5.
LANE, Walter Exh. 1880-81
Architect. 55 Cowcross Street, London. † RA 3.
LANFANT de Metz, Francois Louis* 1814-1892
French artist. Exh. 1880-82. Add: 16 Avenue Trudaine, Paris. † RHA 23.
LANFEAR, Bertha Exh. 1884
Watercolour flower painter. Gay Lodge, Eastbourne. † SWA 1.
LANG, A. Exh. 1885-87
Mont Castleland, Paisley. † GI 1, L 2.
LANG, Emily A. Exh. 1904-8
Landscape painter. 50 Park Hill Road, Hampstead, London. † I 1, RA 2, ROI 1.
LANG, George Ernest b. 1902
Painter and illustrator. Self taught. Exh. 1937-38. Add: Clapham, London. † RBA 1, RI 2.
LANG, Jessie M. Exh. 1881-83
Royal Bank House, Port Glasgow. † GI 2.
LANG, J. Ramsay Exh. 1897-1917
Rutherglen, N.B. 1897 and 1917; Glasgow 1906. † GI 4, RSA 1, RSW 2.
LANG, Lila Exh. 1907
Langwell, Ayr. † GI 1.
LANG, Leslie W. Exh. 1909-37
Portrait and landscape painter. R.B.A. 1911. Add: London 1909 and 1923; Exeter 1922. † GOU 41, L 4, RA 1, RBA 42, WG 47.
LANG, Marion C. Exh. 1897-1913
Milnbank House, Milnbank. † GI 3, L 1.
LANG, Naomi Exh. 1927
Rosary Gardens, London. † SWA 1.
LANG, Mrs. Philip Exh. 1933-35
19 Wetherby Gardens, London. † RI 16.
LANGDALE, Alice M. Exh. 1912
Pennant Lodge, Queen's Park, Brighton. † GI 1.
LANGDALE, Miss I.S.R. Exh. 1937-39
Ashford House, Cheltenham, Glos. 1937, c/o C.H. West, 117 Finchley Road, London 1939. † RBA 2, RSA 1.
LANGDALE, Marmaduke* d. 1905
Landscape painter. Studied R.A. Schools (Turner gold medal). Add: Staines, Middlesex 1880; Brighton 1901. † D 2, RA 13, RBA 5, ROI 1.
LANGDALE, Stella Exh. 1912-24
Studied Brighton School of Art and Glasgow School of Art. Add: Pennant Lodge, Queen's Park, Brighton. † B 3, GI 4, L 6, M 4, RSA 2.
LANGDON, Beatrice Exh. 1924-40
Landscape painter. Studied Byam Shaw and Vicat Cole School. Add: London. † B 1, CON 4, GI 2, L 2, M 1, NEA 4, RA 3, RBA 5, ROI 4.
LANGDON, Edith A. Exh. 1922-23
Portrait and miniature painter. Glynde, Hersham Road, Walton-on-Thames, Surrey. † RA 2.
LANGDON, Edith A. Exh. 1898-1903
The Park, Nottingham. † B 1, D 2, L 3, M 1, N 16, RA 1, RCA 4, SWA 8.
LANGDON, Edgar Mortimer b. 1892
Painter and lecturer. Exh. 1934. Add: 6 Disabled Officers Garden Homes, Leavesden, Watford, Herts. † RBA 1.
LANGDON, John Exh. 1936-38
Watercolour painter. † WG 6.
LANGDON, Mary Exh. 1911-15
15 Kremlin Drive, Stoneycroft, Liverpool. † L 3.
LANGDON-DOWN, Elspie Exh. 1934-35
Mrs. A.R. Cusden. Landscape painter. Add: Glenside, Oxted, Surrey. † RA 2, RBA 3.
LANGE, Helen Exh. 1911
† M 2.
LANGE, Otto b. 1879
German artist. Exh. 1906. Add: 246 Munchener Strasse, Munich. † RA 1.
LANGFIELD, Miss M. Exh. 1902-3
9 Asken Road, Shepherds Bush, London. † SWA 3.
LANGFORD, Miss E. Exh. 1883
17 Bristol Road, Birmingham. † B 1.
LANGFORD, Lady Margaret Exh. 1940
51 South Street, Park Lane, London. † SWA 2.
LANGHAM, Hon. Mrs. Exh. 1882
50 Ebury Street, London. † G 1.
LANGHAM, John Exh. 1882-90
Architectural painter. Manchester. † RA 3.
LANGHORNE, Miss Exh. 1910-12
Harrogate, Yorks. † SWA 3.
LANGHORNE, Miss C. Exh. 1912-21
London. † L 2, SWA 2.
LANGHORNE, J.A. Exh. 1938-40
Cookham, Berks. 1938; Four Oaks, Birmingham 1940. † B 4.
LANGHORNE, Miss K.L. Exh. 1880-81
Domestic painter. 45 Scarsdale Villas, Kensington, London. † RSA 1, SWA 2.
LANGLADE, Pierre Exh. 1882-90
Lothian Place, Bonnyrigg, Edinburgh. † GI 1, RSA 1.
LANGLANDS, Alexander Exh. 1922-36
Glasgow. † GI 2, RSA 1.
LANGLANDS, George A. Nasmyth d.1940
Landscape and portrait painter. Studied Edinburgh and Antwerp. R.S.W. 1896. Exh. 1882-1938. Add: Edinburgh. † AR 2, GI 35, L 4, M 1, RA 6, RSA 88, RSW 113.
LANGLEY, Ed Exh. 1904-8
Morley, Leeds. † RCA 3.
LANGLEY, Mrs. Elizabeth Exh. 1927-29
Ellesmere, Bridget Street, Rugby. † L 4.
LANGLEY, Helen Exh. 1897-1939
Sculptor. London. † I 1, L 11, LS 6, RA 19, RMS 3, SWA 20.
LANGLEY, Nina Scott Exh. 1928
Animal painter. † WG 72.
LANGLEY, Walter* 1852-1922
Genre painter. b. Birmingham. Studied South Kensington 1873-75. R.B.S.A. 1884, R.I. 1883. Add: Birmingham 1880 and 1887; Newlyn, Penzance 1888. † B 57, D 4, DOW 17, FIN 72, GI 10, L 26, LEI 2. M 9, RA 30, RBA 3, RHA 1, RI 80, ROI 8, RSW 2.
LANGLEY, Walter George b. 1885
Landscape and still life painter. b. Marlow, Bucks. Exh. 1925-39. Add: Marlow, Bucks. 1925; London 1926. † RI 16, ROI 19.
LANGLIN, Victoriano Codina Exh. 1880-1909
Figure painter. London. † RA 7, RBA 1.
LANGLOIS, H.A. Exh. 1888-89
31 St. Mary Avenue, London. † M 2.
LANGMAID, Rowland Exh. 1924-30
Watercolour marine painter and etcher. 62 Clifton Hill, London. † AB 95, L 3, RA 1.
LANGREN, F.H. Exh. 1882
New York. † GI 1.
LANGRIDGE, Miss F. Exh. 1901
4 Callow Street, South Kensington, London. † SWA 1.
LANGRIDGE, Mrs. G. Exh. 1939
26 Scarsdale Avenue, Allestree, Nr. Derby. † N 1.
LANGRIDGE, W.S. Exh. 1937-39
Figure and portrait painter. Vaud Studio, 72 St. James Street, Nottingham. † N 11.
LANGRISH, Miss E.M.L. Exh. 1907
Heath End, Farnham, Surrey. † L 1.
LANGRISH, Miss M. Exh. 1915-23
Rathfarnham, Dublin 1915; Ballsbridge, Dublin 1918; Dublin 1921. † RHA 6.
LANGRISHE, May Exh. 1902
12 North Frederick Street, Dublin. † RHA 1.
LANGSFORD, William C. Exh. 1899
Stained glass artist. 33 Goring Road, New Southgate, London. † RA 1.
LANGSTON, A.J. Exh. 1886
Newhall Chambers, 8 Newhall Street, Birmingham. † B 1.
LANGSTON, Horace Exh. 1938
† M 1.
LANGSTONE, T.R. Exh. 1892-1903
Birmingham. † B 8.
LANGTON, H.C. Exh. 1894
7 Durham Villas, Campden Hill, London. † RI 1.
LANGTON, Mary Exh. 1935-39
119 Church Street, London. † GOU 1, P 1, SWA 2.
LANGTON, St. John Exh. 1929-33
Landscape painter. Highfield, South Benfleet, Essex. † L 1, RA 1, ROI 1.
LANGTREE, Edna E. Exh. 1937
158 Franklin Road, King's Norton, Birmingham. † B 1.
LANNES, Gustave Exh. 1911
210 Avenue Daumesnil, Paris. † L 1.
LANNOY, de see D
LANSDELL, Mark J. Exh. 1884-85
Architect. Bedford Row House, London. † RA 3.
LANSDOWN, Beatrice Exh. 1891-1916
Fruit and still life painter. London. † M 1, RA 3, ROI 1.
LANSDOWN, George H. Exh. 1897-1900
Architect. London. † RA 3.
LANSYER, Emmannuel* 1835-1895
French painter. Exh. 1884. Add: 29 Quai Bourbon, Paris. † GI 2.
LANTERI, Edouard 1848-1917
Sculptor. Assistant to Sir Edgar Boehm for nearly 20 years. Succeeded Dalou as sculpture master at Royal College of Art. "The Sacristan" purchased by Chantrey Bequest 1917. † B 2, GI 9, I 4, L 4, NG 2, RA 70, RSA 4.
LANTIER, Lucien L. Exh. 1913
5 Rue des Beaux Arts, Paris. † L 1.
LANTOUR, A. Exh. 1924
12 Woburn Square, London. † L 1.
LANYON, G.P. Exh. 1937-38
St. Ives, Cornwall. † ROI 2.
LANYON, John Exh. 1880
1 Alexander Chambers, Lombard Street, Belfast. † RHA 1.
LANYON, Mrs. K. Exh. 1933-40
Strangeways, Limpsfield, Surrey 1933; Stapleton, Dorset 1939. † RI 6, SWA 2.
LAPINE, Andre C.G. Exh. 1933
Canadian artist. b. Russia. † RSW 1.
LAPRADE, Pierre* 1875-1932
French painter. Exh. 1921-28. † GOU 11.

LA PRIMAUDAYE, Idonea Exh. 1905-37
Flower and figure painter. London. † GOU 6, LS 8, P 4, RA 7.

LAPTHORN, Miss M. Dickenson Exh. 1913-26
London. † I 2, RA 2, RI 2.

LAPWORTH, Joan M. Exh. 1933-39
Sutton, Surrey. † GOU 1, SWA 1.

LAPWORTH, William Exh. 1891
Landscape painter. Orme Studios, St. Petersburg Place, Bayswater, London. † RI 1.

LARA, Percy Leslie b. 1870
Landscape painter. b. Worcester. Exh. 1922-29. Add: 44 Edith Road, Kensington, London. † RA 1, ROI 2.

LARBALESTIER, Thomas Charles Exh. 1908
13 Beresford Street, St.Helier, Jersey, C.I. † LS 4.

LARGE, Maude Exh. 1907-8
Manchester 1907; London 1908. † M 2.

LARK, Tremayne Exh. 1882-84
Figure painter. 9 Pembridge Place, Bayswater, London and 30 Rue Chaptal, Paris. † L 1, M 2, RA 2.

LARKIN, Charles H. Exh. 1932-36
Landscape painter. 14 Longland Road, Eastbourne, Sussex. † RA 3.

LARKING, Louisa Margaret b. 1898
Etcher. b. Melbourne, Australia. Studied Slade School, L.C.C. Central School and Royal College of Art. Add: London 1924; Christmas Common, Nr. Warlington, Oxon. 1929. † L 3, NEA 1.

LARKING, Patrick Lambert b. 1907
Painter. Studied R.A. Schools 1923. Exh. 1939. Add: 45 Rowland Gardens, London. † RA 1.

LARKINS, Dora Exh. 1902-8
Vesey Road, Wylde Green, Birmingham. † B 4.

LARKINS, E. Exh. 1910
45 Glenmore Road, Hampstead, London. † RA 1.

LARKINS, William Martin b. 1901
Painter and etcher. A.R.E. 1925. Visiting instructor of etching at Croydon School of Art. Exh. 1922-31. Add: London. † GI 1, L 1, M 1, NEA 1, RA 4, RE 7.

LAROCHENOIRE, M. Exh. 1882
16 Avenue Trudaine, Paris. † RHA 1.

LAROCQUE, G. Exh. 1884-85
5 Rue Martin, Les Ternes, Paris. † GI 2.

LARRIEU, O. Exh. 1910
48 Rue Lecourbe, Paris. † L 1.

LARRIVE, Jean Exh. 1911
6 Rue du Val de Grace, Paris. † RHA 2.

LARSON, Virginia Exh. 1880
Interior painter. 90 Carleton Road, Tufnell Park, London. † RBA 1.

LARSSON, Carl* 1853-1919
Swedish painter. Exh. 1885-1905. Add: Grezpar-Nemours, France 1885; Sundbern, Sweden 1905. † I 2, RI 2.

LARY, Roland Exh. 1892-97
98 Wynstraat, Dordrecht, Holland. † RHA 7.

LASCELLES, Charles b. 1890
Watercolour landscape painter. b. London. Exh. 1925. Add: The Grange, Weston, Bath. † B 2.

LASCELLES, Thomas W. Exh. 1885-1914
Figure and domestic painter and etcher. Cookham Dean, Berks. 1886; London 1891. † RA 7, RBA 2.

LASELLAY Exh. 1888
74 Rue d'Amsterdam, Paris. † M 1.

LASEMANN, Mrs. K. Exh. 1908-14
Colwyn Bay, Wales. † RCA 9.

LASENBY, Nommie Exh. 1930
10 Hammersmith Terrace. London. † NEA 1.

LASHMAR, Mrs. D. Exh. 1933
Woodruff, Hinderton Road, Neston. † L 2.

LASKER, Joseph Exh. 1924
158 Islington, Liverpool. † L 2.

LASSAM, Susie b. 1875
Miniature painter. Studied Lambeth School of Art, Royal College of Art and L.C.C. School of Arts and Crafts. S.W.A. 1938. Exh. 1908-37. † GI 2, L 7, RA 8, RI 35, RMS 10.

LASSENCE, de See D

LAST, Ethel M. Exh. 1929-35
Watercolour portrait and animal painter. Add: 8 St. Augustin's Road, Bournemouth. † RI 13.

LASZLO, de See D

LATCHFORD, Alice d. c.1925
Miniature painter. R.M.S. 1897. Exh. 1895-1912. Add: London. † L 1, NG 1, RA 1, RI 3, RMS 44, SWA 9.

LATENAY, de See D

LATHAM, A.G. Exh. 1907
5A Temple Row, Birmingham. † RA 1.

LATHAM, B.M. Exh. 1887
Sculptor. Add: 3 Primrose Hill Studios, London. † RBA 1, ROI 1.

LATHAM, Frances P. Exh. 1887-89
Landscape painter. Add: London. † D 5, RI 1.

LATHAM, Miss G.M. Exh. 1920-21
62 Maiden Lane, Clubmoor, Liverpool. † L 2.

LATHAM, Harold Exh. 1922-40
Watercolour landscape and coastal painter. R.I. 1939. Add: Arundel, Sussex 1922; Martyr Worthy, Winchester 1924; Amberley, Sussex 1928. † CON 43, COO 52, L 1, NEA 5, RA 9, RBA 7, RI 10, ROI 3.

LATHAM, Hilda Exh. 1928
The Hollins, Hoghton, Preston, Lancs. † L 1.

LATHAM, H.M. Exh. 1889
Landscape painter. Add: Florence Villa, Torquay. † RID 1.

LATHAM, John Exh. 1926
c/o W. Knip, Summerfield, West Derby, Liverpool. † L 1.

LATHAM, J.E. Exh. 1883
4 Benson Street, Liverpool. † L 1.

LATHAM, Miss M.J. Exh. 1928
226 Hagley Road, Birmingham. † B 1.

LATHAM, T.N. Exh. 1904
38 Melville Place, Liverpool. † L 1.

LA THANGUE, Henry Herbert* 1859-1929
Landscape and rustic painter. Studied at South Kensington, Lambeth, R.A. Schools and Ecole des Beaux Arts, Paris (3 years). N.E.A. 1886, A.R.A. 1898, R.A. 1912, R.O.I. 1883. "The Man with the Scythe" purchased by Chantrey Bequest 1896. Add: London 1880 and 1923; Bradford 1885; Bosham, Chichester 1891; Graffham, Petworth, Sussex 1897; Runeton, Chichester 1926. † B 3, G 8, GI 20, I 3, L 25, LEI 42, M 22, NG 17, RA 127, RCA 1, RHA 1, ROI 3, RSA 2.

LATIMER, Alice M. Exh. 1892-1919
Dublin. † L 1, RHA 30.

LATIMER, Elizabeth Osborne Exh. 1899-1940
Morningside Place, Edinburgh. † GI 8, RSA 18, RSW 1.

LATIMER, R.R. Exh. 1913-14
Palazzo Barbaro, Venice, Italy. † RA 2.

LATOIX, Gaspard* Exh. 1882-1903
Landscape, figure and interior painter. Add: Leamington, Warwicks 1882; London 1896; Basingstoke, Hants. 1902. † B 8, GI 5, L 1, RA 7, RBA 2.

LA TOUCHE, Gaston* 1854-1913
French painter. Exh. 1889-1913. Add: St. Cloud, France. † FIN 51, GI 2, GOU 1, I 8, L 2, RSA 4.

LATOUR, de See D

LATTER, Miss B. Exh. 1897-1903
East Liss, Hants. 1897; Bromley, Kent 1903. † RI 1, SWA 2.

LATTER, F.C. Exh. 1913
16 Ewart Grove, Wood Green, London. † L 1, RA 1.

LATTER, Ruth Exh. 1906-37
Mrs. Cecil L. Flower, landscape and portrait painter. Add: 44 York Mansions, Battersea, London. † B 1, BG 30, L 6, LS 7, RA 16, SWA 1.

LATZARUS, Edith M. Exh. 1890-99
Flower and interior painter. Add: London. † L 2, M 1, RA 2, RBA 4, RHA 4.

LAUDER, Charles J. d. 1920
Watercolour landscape painter. R.S.W. 1899. Add: Glasgow 1880 and 1904; Richmond, Surrey 1889 and 1894; London 1892; Thorntonhall, Lanarks 1910. † DOW 3, GI 86, L 15, M 7, RBA 6, RI 4, RSA 23, RSW 85.

LAUDER, Gertrude Annie d. 1918
nee Ashton. Flower painter. Married Charles J.L. q.v. Add: Streatham, London 1886; Glasgow 1904; Thorntonhall, Lanarks 1914. † GI 23, L 3, M 1, RSA 3, RSW 2, SWA 1.

LAUDER, Isabella S. Exh. 1884-90
25 Merchiston Avenue, Edinburgh. † GI 1, RSA 9.

LAUDER, J. Exh. 1907
Still life painter. † GOU 1.

LAUDER, Nancy b. 1880
Flower and landscape painter. Exh. 1907-36. Add: Kilmarnock, N.B. † GI 28, RA 1, RSA 5, RSW 4.

LAUGEE, Desiree Francois 1823-1896
French miniature painter. Exh. 1883-87. Add: Boulevard Lannes, Passy, Paris. † GI 1, M 2.

LAUGEE, Georges* b. 1853
French painter. Exh. 1883 and 1904. Add: Paris. † L 1, ROI 1.

LAUGHTON, Miss M.L. Exh. 1889-98
Portrait and landscape painter. Add: 130 Sinclair Road, West Kensington Park, London. † RID 21.

LAUGHTON, Mary L. Exh. 1929
Landscape painter. Add: 7 Hansley Grove, East Molesey, Surrey. † RID 3.

LAUNDY, George Albert Exh. 1882-94
Landscape painter. Add: London. † RA 1, RI 1, ROI 5.

LAUNDY, Rev. S.R. Exh. 1935
20 Knighton Road, Woodthorpe, Nottingham. † N 1.

LAUPHEIMER, Anton b. 1846
German figure painter. Exh. 1883-87. Add: London. † M 1, RA 1, RBA 1.

LAURENCE, Frederick Exh. 1906
Charnwood, Beresford Road, Pokesdown, Bournemouth. † L 1.

LAURENCE, Kathleen G. Exh. 1904-40
Figure and landscape painter. Add: Reading 1904; Wimborne, Dorset 1912; East Grinstead, Sussex 1926; London 1940. † B 3, COO 2, GI 1, L 4, RA 4, RHA 1, RI 1.

LAURENCE, Lydia Exh. 1889-1905
Painter and decorative artist. Add: 44 Westbourne Terrace, Bayswater, London. † RID 11.

LAURENCE, Samuel* 1812-1884
Portrait painter and chalk artist. Add: 6 Wells Street, Oxford Street, London. † G 1, RA 1, RSA 1.

LAURENCE, Sydney Mortimer b. 1865
Landscape painter. b. U.S.A. R.B.A. 1895. Exh. 1890-1902. Add: St. Ives, Cornwall 1890; Tonbridge, Kent 1902. † DOW 2, GI 1, L 2, M 3, RA 2, RBA 20, RHA 5.

LAURENCIN, Marie* 1885-1956
French painter, etcher and lithographer. Exh. 1925-38. † BA 2, CHE 2, GOU 2, RED 8, SWA 3.

LAURENS, Jean Paul* 1838-1921
French painter. Taught at L'Ecole des Beaux Arts, Paris. H.F.R.A. Exh. 1907-11. Add: Paris. † L 2, RA 1.

LAURENS, Paul Albert b. 1870
French painter. Exh. 1925. † CHE 1.

LAURENT, C. Sabon Exh. 1899-1901
Landscape painter. c/o C. Robertson and Co., 99 Long Acre, London. † RA 4.

LAURENT, Ernest* 1859-1929
French painter. Exh. 1907. † GOU 1.

LAURENT, Henry Exh. 1902
7 Villa Michel Ange, Rue Bastien Lepage, Paris. † L 1.

LAURENT, Lea Exh. 1921-22
Painter. Add: 4 Nottingham Place, London. † GOU 2, P 1, RA 1, ROI 3.

LAURIE, David Exh. 1890-92
152 Cromwell Road, London. † L 1, RSA 1.

LAURIE, John b. 1916
Painter. b. Shrewsbury. Studied Glasgow School of Art 1933-36 and Hospitalfield, Arbroath 1938-40 (Carnegie travelling scholarship 1939). Exh. 1937-40. † GI 3, RSA 3.

LAURIE, Jessie S. Exh. 1881
11 Percy Terrace, Glasgow. † GI 2.

LAVENDER, W.D. Exh. 1937
2 Clifford Street. Dudley, Worcs. † B 1.

LAVENDER, William R. Exh. 1899-1901
Figure painter. Add: 128 Manchester Road, Southport, Lancs. † B 2, M 1, RA 4, RCA 1.

LAVENSTEIN, Cyril b. 1891
Landscape painter. b. Birmingham. Studied Birmingham School of Arts and Crafts (scholarship, silver and bronze medals). Second master Kidderminster School of Art. Exh. 1921-40. Add: Kidderminster 1921 and 1928; Brighton, Sussex 1927. † B 47, L 1, NEA 2, RA 15, RSA 3.

LAVER, John H. Exh. 1938
Landscape painter. Add: 182 Cemetery Road, Sheffield. † RA 1.

LAVEROCK, Miss F.H. Exh. 1902-15
Warrington, Lancs. † L 9.

LAVERS, Arthur C. Exh. 1900-1
Stained glass artist. Add: 14 Heathfields Gardens, Chiswick, London. † RA 4.

LAVERS, Arthur E. Exh. 1882
Landscape painter. Add: 22 Endell Street, Long Acre, London. † L 1, RBA 1.

LAVERTY, Miss A. Sorel Exh. 1881-97
Watercolour flower painter. Add: Ryde, I.O.W. 1881; Caversham, Reading, Berks. 1885 and 1892; Totton, Hants. 1891. † B 6, D 5, GI 2, L 3, M 3, RBA 6, RI 3, SWA 4.

LAVERY, Lady Hazel d. 1935
nee Martyn. Portrait painter. Second wife of Sir John Lavery q.v. Exh. 1903-23. † ALP 30, CHE 1, I 3, L 1, P 3.

LAVERY, Sir John* 1856-1941
Portrait and landscape painter. b. Belfast. Studied Glasgow, London and Juliens, Paris. Married Hazel L. q.v. N.E.A. 1887, A.R.A. 1911, R.A. 1921, A.R.H.A. 1906, R.H.A. 1907, H.R.O.I. 1910, R.P. 1893, A.R.S.A. 1893, R.S.A. 1896. Knighted 1918. "The Jockey's Dressing Room at Ascot" purchased by Chantrey Bequest 1924 and "The Chess Players" in 1930. † AG 4, ALP 51, B 3, BAR 1, BG 2, CG 84, CHE 3, FIN 3, G 40, GI 125, GOU 115, I 74, L 92, LEI 71, LS 2, M 11, NEA 5, NG 17, P 140, RA 154, RBA 4, RED 2, RHA 53, ROI 33, RSA 97, RSW 2.

LA VILLETTEE, Mme Exh. 1886
St. Denis, Seine, France. † M 1.

LAVRIN, Mrs. Nora Exh. 1930-31
Painter and etcher. Add: Mapperley, Nottingham 1930; London 1931. † RA 3, RHA 1.

LAVRUT, L. Exh. 1905.
c/o A.M. Pourriere, 6 Castle Street, Liverpool. † L 1.

LAW, Andrew* Exh. 1895-1940
Portraitt, animal and urban landscape painter. b. Ayrshire. Studied Kilmarnock, Glasgow School of Art and Academie Delecluse, Paris. Add: Kilmarnock 1895; Glasgow 1909. † GI 93, L 9, RSA 30.

LAW, Annie Exh. 1880-88
Watercolour landscape painter. Daughter of David L. q.v. Add: 9 Regent's Park Terrace, London. † RBA 16, RHA 14, SWA 5.

LAW, Arthur E. Exh. 1926-36
Landscape painter. Add: 14 Fetteresso Terrace, Stonehaven, Kincardineshire 1926; Dundee 1936. † ALP 1, L 3, RA 8, RSA 14.

LAW, A.M. Exh. 1880-90
Glasgow. † GI 13, RSA 1.

LAW, Alexander McCallum Exh. 1922
21 Ravenswood Drive, Shawlands. † GI 1.

LAW, Beatrice Exh. 1883-88
Watercolour landscape painter. Daughter of David L. q.v. Add: 9 Regent's Park Terrace, London. † RBA 6, RHA 4, SWA 6.

LAW, C. Orlando Exh. 1896
Architect. Add: Dacre House, Arundel Street, London. † RA 1.

LAW, David 1831-1902
Landscape painter and etcher. b. Edinburgh. Studied Trustees Academy, Edinburgh 1845-50. Father of Annie and Beatrice L. q.v. R.B.A. 1884, H.R.B.A. 1893, R.E. 1881. Add: 9 Regent's Park Terrace, London. † AG 3, B 1, D 4, DOW 66, FIN 14, GI 9, L 4, M 2, RA 42, RBA 28, RE 41, RHA 10, RI 1, RSW 9.

LAW, D. M'Kay Exh. 1933-40
Edinburgh 1933; Leith 1939. † RSA 3.

LAW, Edward Exh. 1880-85
Watercolour landscape painter. Add: 7 Danes Inn, Strand, London. † D 5, DOW 5, L 3, RBA 3.

LAW, Edward Exh. 1901
4 Dulka Road, Clapham Common, London. † RCA 2.

LAW, Ernest Exh. 1891-1900
Coastal, landscape and figure painter. Add: 147 Osbaldeston Road, Stoke Newington, London. † RA 1, RBA 11.

LAW, Freda Graves Exh. 1903
10 Salisbury Road, Edinburgh. † RSA 1.

LAW, Helen Exh. 1890
Pastel artist. Add: Glenval, Pollokshields, Nr. Glasgow. † NEA 1.

LAW, Mrs. Jean Exh. 1927
14 Fetteresso Terrace, Stonehaven, Kincardineshire. † RSA 2.

LAW, John Exh. 1882-84
Edinburgh. † RSA 4.

LAW, L. Pauline Exh. 1909-11
64 Cambridge Road, Southport, Lancs. † L 2.

LAW, Mrs. M. Exh. 1912
15 Rossetti Garden Mansions, Chelsea, London. † D 1.

LAW, Mrs. M.I. Exh. 1905
Eaton Hall Hotel, Pretoria, South Africa. † RA 1.

LAW, Oliver b. 1900
Architect. Studied Bartlett School of Architecture under Prof. Richardson. Exh. 1930-40. Add: 6 Pump Court, Temple, London. † RA 11.

LAW, Walter E. Exh. 1904
Landscape painter. Add: 115 Fleet Street, London. † RA 1.

LAWES, Charles
See LAWES-WITTEWRONGE

LAWES, Harold Exh. 1892
31 Chalcot Crescent, Primrose Hill, London. † B 1.

LAWES-WITTEWRONGE, Sir Charles Bennet, Bt. 1843-1911
Sculptor. Add: London. † L 2, RA 8, RBA 4, ROI1.

LAWFORD, C.H. Exh. 1897-98
Aylestone Park, Leicester. † N 2.

LAWFORD, Edgar C. Exh. 1883-93
Etcher. Add: Thames Ditton, Surrey 1883; London 1893. † D 1, RA 2, RE 3.

LAWFORD, Mrs. Rowland Exh. 1880-82
Flower and figure painter. Add: 4 Gayton Crescent, Hampstead, London. † D 2.

LAWLER, E.K. Exh. 1930-33
14 Bromley Road, Wallasey, Cheshire. † L 2.

LAWLER, J.J. Exh. 1911
4 Kimberley Avenue, Gt. Crosby, Liverpool. † L 3.

LAWLESS, Miss E. Exh. 1888
Moel View, Dolgelly, North Wales. † B 1.

LAWLESS, Mrs. F.P. Exh. 1907-15
Add: London 1907; Budleigh Salterton, South Devon 1910; Exmouth, South Devon 1911; Twickenham, Middlesex 1915. † L 4, RA 5, RMS 2.

LAWLOR, Miss G. Exh. 1922
17 Brewster Gardens, North Kensington, London. † RHA 2.

LAWLOR, John 1820-1901
Sculptor. b. Dublin. Studied with the Dublin Society and R.A. Schools (1847). Came to England 1845 and assisted John Thomas (1813-1862) with the Statuary for the Houses of Parliament. Also among his works is the Group "Mechanics" for the Albert Memorial. Went to the U.S.A. 1886-88. A.R.H.A. 1861. Exh. 1880-87. Add: Stanhope Street, Hampstead Road, London. † RBA 4, RHA 9.

LAWLOR, Michael Exh. 1880-1913
Sculptor. Add: London. † G 1, RA 5, RHA 3.

LAWLOR, Miss M.C. Exh. 1883
3 Lower Abbey Street, Dublin. † L 1, RHA 1.

LAWRANCE, Mrs. Marguerite E. Exh. 1903-19
Portrait painter and etcher. Add: West Kensington, London 1903; Wimslow, Bucks. 1905; Stokeley, Nr. Kingsbridge, Devon 1909. † I 1, L 3, LS 4, P 5, RA 3, RHA 2, ROI,1.

LAWRELL, Mrs. Emma C. Exh. 1898-1901
115 Ashley Gardens, London. † RMS 3.

LAWRENCE, Miss Exh. 1919
Ramornie, Esher, Surrey. † LS 3.

LAWRENCE, Alfred Kingsley b. 1893
Painter and mural decorator. Studied Royal College of Art. Prix de Rome Scholar 1923. A.R.A. 1930, R.A. 1938. Exh. 1929-40. Add: London. † RA 34.

LAWRENCE, Bessie Exh. 1905
12 Morley Road, Southport, Lancs. † L 1.

LAWRENCE, Bringhurst B. Exh. 1881-89
Animal painter. Add: 12 Colville Houses, Bayswater, London. † DOW 1, M 1, RBA 1.

LAWRENCE, Charlotte Exh. 1923-24
† GOU 3.

LAWRENCE, Mrs. Clara Exh. 1917-19
Ramornie, Esher, Surrey. † LS 3, SWA 3.

LAWRENCE, Edith Exh. 1884-86
Flower painter. Add: 9 Fitzroy Street, Fitzroy Square, London. † L 1, M 3, RBA 9.

LAWRENCE, Elizabeth A. Exh. 1919-21
164A Aigburth Road, Liverpool. † L 2.

LAWRENCE, Edith Mary b. 1890
Landscape and portrait painter. b. Surrey. Studied Slade School (Wilson Steer special painting prize). Exh. 1916-38. Add: London. † L 3, LS 3, NEA 3, RA 1, RED 28, ROI 1, RSA 1, SWA 3.

LAWRENCE, F. Exh. 1906-7
London. † L 3, RA 1.

LAWRENCE, F.O. Exh. 1912-28
Architect. Add: Liverpool. † L 6.

LAWRENCE, Georgina Exh. 1886-88
Still life and figure painter. Add: 62 Burton Crescent, London. † RBA 2.

LAWRENCE, Henry Exh. 1880-1907
Figure painter. Add: Fulham, London. † B 15, L 7, M 2, RA 1, RBA 5, RHA 6.

LAWRENCE, Henry Spencer Exh. 1926-34
Architect. Add: 7 Gray's Inn Place, London. † RA 7.

LAWRENCE, John C.* Exh. 1880-88
Figure and landscape painter. Add: London. † G 1, M 1, RA 4, RBA 5, ROI 3.

LAWRENCE, John Smellie Exh. 1929
Jasmin Cottage, Sapperton, Cirencester, Glos. † GI 1.

LAWRENCE, Leonard E. Exh. 1880-97
Figure painter. Add: London. † L 2, P 1, RA 6, RBA 1, ROI 2.

LAWRENCE, Miss L.M. Exh. 1919
52 Pulteney Street, Bath. † SWA 1.

LAWRENCE, Miss M. Exh. 1922
Stained glass artist. Add: 44 Grafton Road, Handsworth, Birmingham. † RA 1.

LAWRENCE, Mervyn b. 1868
Painter and sculptor. b. Dublin. Studied Royal College of Art. Exh. 1894-1931. Add: London 1894 and 1898; Dublin 1897. † GI 12, GOU 14, I 8, L 7, LS 30, M 1, NG 2, RA 23, RHA 9, RI 1, ROI 1.

LAWRENCE, Miss S. Exh. 1917-19
Cliff House, Black Rock, Brighton. † I 3, RA 1.

LAWRENSON, Charlotte Mary b. 1883
nee Thompson. Portrait painter and mural decorator. b. Dublin. Studied Slade School and Byam Shaw School. Married Edward Louis L. q.v. Exh. 1908-39. Add: London 1908; Hadlow Downs, Uckfield, Sussex and London 1919. † FIN 2, GI 1, I 8, L 6, LS 7, NEA 3, P 5, RA 12, RHA 38, ROI 3, RSA 4, SWA 4.

LAWRENSON, Dorothy A. Exh. 1935-40
Figure and portrait painter. Add: Ayton School, Gt. Ayton, Yorks. 1935; Seaford, Sussex 1939. † RA 7.

LAWRENSON, Edward Louis b. 1868
Painter and etcher. b. Dublin. Studied Old School of Design, Dublin (at age 10), Royal College of Art and in Paris and Holland. Married Charlotte Mary L. q.v. Exh. 1900-34. Add: Dublin 1900; London 1903; Hadlow Down, Uckfield, Sussex and London 1915. † ALP 13, CHE 2, FIN 98, GI 9, I 11, L 24, LS 1, NEA 9, RA 23, RCA 2, RHA 36, RSA 1.

LAWRIE, Miss C.A. Exh. 1887-88
Nairne Lodge, Duddengstone, N.B. † RSA 4.

LAWRIE, Mary H.S. Exh. 1887
23 Saxe Coburg Place, Edinburgh. † RSA 1.

LAWS, Eric J. Exh. 1924-39
Painter, sculptor and black and white artist. Add: School House, Gotham, Derby 1924; Sherwood, Nottingham 1931. † L 1, N 26.

LAWS, John L. Exh. 1926-35
Watercolour painter and black and white artist. Add: School House, Gotham, Derby 1926; Sherwood, Nottingham 1932. † N 11.

LAWS, Lilian Exh. 1923-38
Sculptor. A.N.S.A. 1923. Add: Draycott, Derby 1923; Goodmayes, Essex 1938. † N 3, RA 1.

LAWSON, Alexander Exh. 1886-1920
Landscape painter. Add: Wolverhampton 1886 and 1895; London 1891 and 1915; Leamington, Warwicks 1894. † B 40, D 3, GI 1, L 6, RA 17, ROI 2.

LAWSON, Bernard Exh. 1897
4 Starbank Place, Trinity, Edinburgh. † RSA 1.

LAWSON, Constance B. Exh. 1880-1903
nee Philip. Flower painter. Married Cecil Gordon L. q.v. S.W.A. 1886-1903. Add: Heathedge, Haslemere, Surrey. † B 23, D 11, FIN 6, G 14, GI 4, L 13, M 19, NG 7, RA 11, RBA 3, RI 13, ROI 1, SWA 6.

LAWSON, Cecil C.P. Exh. 1913-23
Paris 1913; London 1922. † G 1, GI 1, I 4, L 3, RA 1, ROI 1.

LAWSON, Cecil Gordon* 1851-1882
Landscape painter. b. Shropshire. Son of Elizabeth R. and brother of Francis Wilfred L. q.v. Married Constance B. L. q.v. Add: Heathedge, Haslemere, Surrey. † G 5, GI 4, RA 4.

LAWSON, Dorothy Exh. 1932-39
London. † NEA 4, RBA 1, RI 1, ROI 1, SWA 11.

LAWSON, E. Exh. 1888
13 Elm Row, Edinburgh. † L 1.

LAWSON, Edith M. Exh. 1891
Interior painter. Add: 19 Eardley Crescent, London. † RBA 1.

LAWSON, Edwin M. Exh. 1938
Architect. Add: Barras Buildings, Barras Bridge, Newcastle on Tyne. † RA 1.

LAWSON, Elizabeth R. Exh. 1882-94
Mrs. William L. nee Stone. Figure and flower painter. Mother of Francis Wilfred and Cecil Gordon L. q.v. Add: Chelsea, London 1882; Bedford 1894. † G 6, GI 2, L 1, M 2, NG 1, RBA 1, RHA 2.

LAWSON, Florence Exh. 1922
30 Alva Street, Edinburgh. † RSA 1.

LAWSON, Frederick b. 1888
Watercolour painter, etcher and wood engraver. b. Yeadon, Nr. Leeds. Studied Leeds School of Art. Exh. 1913-39. Add: Castle Bolton, Redmire, Yorks. † COO 9, GI 8, L 23, RA 9, RI 12, WG 5.

LAWSON, Florence G. Exh. 1897-1902
Edinburgh 1897; Carlisle 1902. † GI 1, RSA 5.

LAWSON, Francis Wilfred 1842-1935
Painter and illustrator. b. Shropshire. Son of Elizabeth R.L. q.v. and brother of Cecil Gordon L. q.v. Exh. 1880-1913. Add: London 1880; Crowhurst, Buxton 1913. † B 2, G 1, GI 5, L 4, M 2, NEA 1, RA 4, RBA 1, ROI 2, RSA 2.

LAWSON, George Anderson 1832-1904
Sculptor. b. Edinburgh. Studied under Alexander Ritchie. R.S.A. Schools and Rome. H.R.S.A. 1884. Add: London 1880; Richmond, Surrey 1901. † GI 8, RA 17, RBA 1, RI 2, RSA 7.

LAWSON, Gladys M. Exh. 1926-28
San Carlos, St. Helens Road, Ormskirk, Lancs. † L 2.

LAWSON, George S. Exh. 1881-97
Henfield, Sussex 1881; Edinburgh 1886. † GI 2, RSA 2.

LAWSON, Henry Exh. 1880-82
4 Coate's Place, Edinburgh. † GI 2, RSA 5.

LAWSON, Isabel Exh. 1894-98
Edinburgh. † GI 1, RSA 2.

LAWSON, J. Exh. 1899-1902
Atholl Crescent, Edinburgh. † GI 3, RSA 8.

LAWSON, Jeannie Exh. 1901
34 Darlington Street, Wolverhampton. † RBA 1.

LAWSON, Sir John, Bt. Exh. 1910
Father of William L. q.v. Add: Whitby, Yorks. † L 3.

LAWSON, John Exh. 1935
c/o W.J. Lawson, North Gate, Crawley. † ROI 1.

LAWSON, John d. 1909
Landscape painter. Add: Strathbungo 1882; Glasgow 1883. 1885 and 1897; Sheffield 1892; Girvan, N.B. 1896. † B 1, GI 55, L 4, M 1, RI 1, RSA 16.

LAWSON, Miss J.B. Exh. 1888
241 West George Street, Glasgow. † GI 1.

LAWSON, Jessie L. Exh. 1920-21
Dornoch, Cambuslang. † GI 1, RSA 1.

LAWSON, Miss J.M. Exh. 1910-15
London. † GI 1, L 5, RA 10, RSA 4.

LAWSON, Lizzie Exh. 1884-1902
Mrs. R. Mack. Figure painter. Italian Villa, Hurlingham Lane, Fulham, London. † D 1, RA 4, RSA 1.

LAWSON, Margaret Exh. 1927-31
Portrait painter. Add: 3 Town Hill, Lingfield, Surrey. † GOU 1, RA 1, SWA 2.

LAWSON, Marion Exh. 1886
Figure painter. Add: Tooting, London. † ROI 1.

LAWSON, Miss M.C. Exh. 1916-17
6 Addison Mansions, West Kensington, London. † I 1, RI 1.

LAWSON, Margaret E. Exh. 1935
160 Onslow Drive, Glasgow. † RSA 1.

LAWSON, T. Exh. 1894
13 Moray Place, Edinburgh. † GI 1.

LAWSON, Vivien Sherwood b. 1905
Painter. Studied Chelsea Polytechnic and Royal College of Art. Exh. 1930-31. Add: 13 Ovington Gardens, London. † NEA 1, RA 1.

LAWSON, William Exh. 1911-13
London. † LS 8.

LAWSON, William b. 1893
Stained glass designer, decorative and watercolour painter. b. Whitby, Yorks. Son of Sir John L. q.v. Studied Scarborough and Camberwell. Exh. 1923-36. Add: London 1923; St. Albans, Herts 1928. † RA 7.

LAWSON, William Rawson b. 1900
Studied Edinburgh College of Art and under Robert Burns. Exh. 1920-35. Add: Edinburgh. † GI 1, L 1, RSA 13, RSW 2.

LAWTON, Barbara Exh. 1916
Mrs. Joseph L. Add: 339 Wavertree Nook Road, Wavertree, Liverpool. † L 1.

LAWTON, Joseph Exh. 1911-16
Liverpool. † L 8.

LAWTON, Kitty Exh. 1930
† L 1.

LAWTON, Miss M.F. Exh. 1907
1 High Street, Macclesfield, Cheshire. † RCA 1.

LAX, Olive Exh. 1936-39
Moorlands, Alwoodley Lane, Harrogate Road, Leeds. † B 5, RCA 1.

LAY, Cecil Howard Exh. 1913-40
Painter and writer. Self taught. Add: Aldringham, Leiston, Suffolk. † GI 1, LS 6, NEA 2, RA 5, RBA 1, RCA 2, RHA 3, RI 1, RSA 1.

LAYARD, Major Arthur Exh. 1892-1911
Watercolour painter and illustrator. 88 Brook Green, Hammersmith, London. † BRU 69, NEA 2.

LAYARD, Barbara Exh. 1881
Watercolour landscape painter. 26 Courtfield Gardens, South Kensington, London. † SWA 3.

LAYCOCK, E.P. Exh. 1906
4 Bloomsbury Place, London. † RA 1.

LAYCOCK, R.A. Exh. 1929
343 Manchester Road, Hollinwood, Oldham, Lancs. † L 1.

LAYCOCK, R. Turner Exh. 1928-29
Roxburgh, Stuart Road, Liverpool. † L 2.

LAYNG, Mabel Exh. 1916-28
Landscape and figure painter. London. † GI 2, GOU 3, I 7, L 8, LS 3, RA 5, ROI 1, WG 25.

LAYTON, Eva Exh. 1914-21
Landscape painter. 4 Bloomfield Terrace, London. † RA 1, RI 1, SWA 4.

LAYTON, Henry Exh. 1900-1
2 Morgan Street, Grove Road, London. † L 1, RBA 4.

LAZELL, Mrs. Exh. 1934
Watercolour coastal painter. † COO 1.

LAZZERINI, A. Exh. 1912-14
Sculptor. 18 Castle Boulevard, Nottingham. † N 4.

LEA, Anita Exh. 1902-32
Liverpool. † L 43.

LEA, Eric Exh. 1930-34
London. † B 3, RBA 6.

LEA, Lily Exh. 1891-1929
Liverpool. † L 94.

LEACH, Mrs. Exh. 1927
19 Albert Road, Birkdale, Southport, Lancs. † RSA 2.

LEACH, Alice J. Exh. 1882-87
Landscape painter. The Castle, Devizes, Wilts. 1882; c/o Chapman Bros., King's Road, London 1887. † M 1, SWA 1.

LEACH, A. Moorhouse Exh. 1934
Watercolour still life painter. 34 Park Avenue, Wood Green, London. † RI 1.

LEACH, Bernard Howell b. 1887
Painter, draughtsman, etcher, potter, writer and designer. b. Hong Kong. Studied Slade School and London School of Art. Lived and worked in Japan for ten years. Owner-manager of the Leach Pottery, St. Ives, Cornwall. Exh. 1925-27. Add: St. Ives, Cornwall. † L 46, NEA 1.

LEACH, Claude Pemberton Exh. 1893-1909
Architect. London. † RA 2.

LEACH, Ellen M. Exh. 1910-32
20 Maple Avenue, Chorlton-cum-Hardy, Manchester. † L 3.

LEACH, Frederick Exh. 1912
22 Albert Street, Douglas, I.o.M. † L 1.

LEACH, Vera Exh. 1925
29 Palace Gate, London. † SWA 1.

LEACHWOOD, E. Exh. 1892
10 Rue Longue, Bergerbout, Antwerp. † L 1.

LEADAM, Mrs. J.C. Exh. 1903-4
36 Addison Gardens, Kensington, London. † B 8.

LEADBETTER, M.M. Exh. 1885-91
Waterhouse, Gillsland Road, Edinburgh. † GI 2, RSA 8.

LEADBETTER, Thomas Exh. 1885-96
Architect. Edinburgh. † GI 8, RA 2, RSA 18.

LEADBITTER, Margaret Fletcher Exh. 1908-40
nee Fletcher. Landscape and figure painter. b. Dumans, Argyllshire. Studied Paris, London and Italy. Add: Newton-le-Willows, Lancs. 1908; Harrogate, Yorks. 1920 and 1930; London 1922. † CHE 1, I 2, L 5, LS 5, P 1, RA 1, RCA 2, RHA 1, RSA 9.

LEADER, Benjamin Eastlake d. 1916
Landscape painter. Son of Benjamin Williams and Mary Eastlake L. q.v. Killed World War I. Add: Gomshall, Guildford, Surrey 1900; St. Buryan, Cornwall 1911. † GI 4, RA 26, ROI 16, RSA 1, TOO 8.

LEADER, Benjamin Williams* 1831-1923
Landscape and coastal painter. Born Benjamin Williams but took the surname Leader to distinguish himself from the Williams family to whom he was not related. Married Mary Eastlake L. q.v. and father of Benjamin Eastlake L. q.v. A.R.A. 1883, R.A. 1898. Add: Whittington, Worcs. 1880; Gomshall, Guildford, Surrey 1890. † AG 1, B 6, CAR 1, L 10, M 11, RA 158, RCA 1, RHA 1, ROI 2, TOO 193.

LEADER, Mary Eastlake Exh. 1883-1905
nee Eastlake. Flower painter. Married Benjamin Williams L. q.v. and mother of Benjamin Eastlake L. q.v. Add: Whittington, Worcs. 1883; Gomshall, Guildford 1890. † RA 7, RI 3, ROI 1.

LEADER, Violet Eustace V. b. 1903
Mrs. Delmege. Miniature and landscape painter. b. Co. Cork, Ireland. Exh. 1923. Add: Barr's Lodge, Loch Etive, Tayniult, Argyll. † RA 1.

LEAF, Mary d. 1914
Landscape painter. Exh. from 1895. Add: London. † RID 38.

LEAHY, Lilian Exh. 1930-34
Landscape painter. † LEF 7.

LEAKE, Gerald F. b. 1885
Landscape painter. R.B.A. 1914. Exh. 1908-14. Add: Amberley, Sussex 1909; London 1914. † GOU 1, RA 4, RBA 9.

LEAKE, Stafford Exh. 1914-34
Landscape painter. Studied Camden School of Art. Travelled in France and East Africa. R.B.A. 1915. Add: London. † FIN 54, L 2, NEA 1, RA 5, RBA 107.

LEAN, Mrs. C. Exh. 1920-25
The Cottage, Hook Hill, Sanderstead, Surrey. † SWA 3.

LEAN, Miss Edith M. Exh. 1924
The Cottage, Hook Hill, Sanderstead, Surrey. † SWA 1.

LEANDRE, Charles Lucien* 1862-1934
French artist. Exh. 1911-13. Add: 59 Rue Lepic, Paris. † I 8, L 2.

LEARED, Mrs. J.W. Exh. 1887-89
New Ross, Ireland. † RHA 4, RSA 2.

LEARED, Mrs. L. Exh. 1904
Miniature portrait painter. 12 St. Augustines Road, Birmingham. † RA 1.

LEASK, Henry Exh. 1883
6 Summerhall Square, Edinburgh. † RSA 1.

LEAT, James H. Exh. 1910-11
Glasgow. † L 4.

LEATHAM, Kenneth. Exh. 1934-36
Landscape painter. 1 St. Mary's Place, Stamford, Lincs. † RA 2.

LEATHART, Julian R. Exh. 1924-40
Architect. London. † GI 1, RA 5.

LEATHER, Amy H. see FOSTER

LEATHER, Dorothy H. Exh. 1924
Holywood, Sandown Park, Wavertree, Liverpool. † L 1.

LEATHERBARROW, Mrs. K.E.C. Exh. 1916-20
Miniature portrait painter. 14 Rye Hill Park, Peckham Rye, London. † RA 2.

LEAVERS, Lucy A. Exh. 1881-1905
Figure and domestic painter. N.S.A. 1885-1910. Add: Wilford Grove, Nottingham. † L 9, M 4, N 41, RA 8.

LEAVEY, Kathleen Exh. 1930
Witley Lodge, Up Hatherley, Cheltenham, Glos. † B 1.

LE BAS, Edward 1904-1966
Painter. Studied Royal College of Art. Brother of Molly Le B. q.v. Member London Group 1940. "Saloon Bar" purchased by Chantrey Bequest 1940. Exh. 1928-40. Add: London. † GOU 2, M 1, NEA 16, P 13, RA 7, RED 4, TOO 2.

LE BAS, Molly b. 1903
Sculptor. Studied in Paris. Exh. 1925-31. Sister of Edward Le B. q.v. Add: London. † GI 1, L 3, RA 6.

LEBASQUE, Henri* b. 1865
French painter. Exh. 1907-28. † GOU 15.

LE BLANT, Julien b. 1851
French artist. Exh. 1883. Add: Paris. † GI 1.

LEBLING, Max Exh. 1883
Painter. c/o Graphic, 190 Strand, London. † FIN 1, M 1.

LEBOURG, Albert* 1849-1928
French painter. Exh. 1881-1926. † GOU 10, RHA 1.

LE BRETON, Louis Exh. 1939
Landscape painter. † GOU 51.

LE BROCQUY, Louis M. b. 1916
Painter. b. Dublin. Self taught. Add: 51 Kenilworth Square, Rathgar, Dublin 1937; Menton, France 1939; Dublin 1940. † RHA 6.

LE BROCQUY, Miss Melanie Exh. 1938-39
Sculptor. 51 Kenilworth Square, Rathgar, Dublin. † RHA 3.

LE BRUN, Rene de l'Hopital Exh. 1903
82 Earl's Court Road, Kensington, London. † NG 2.

LE CHEVALIER, Mlle. Madeline Exh. 1907
16 Rue de Parc Royal, Paris. † L 1.

LECHMERE, K. Exh. 1913
59 Longridge Road, Earl's Court, London. † LS 3.

LECK, William Exh. 1888
Architect. 22 Wakehurst Road, Wandsworth Common, London. † RA 1.

LECKEY, Susan Exh. 1880-92
Flower painter. London. † FIN 1, M 4, RHA 5, SWA 7.

LECKIE-EWING, J.G. Exh. 1920
Maxwell Bank, St. Andrews. † GI 1.

LECLAIR, Victor 1830-1885
French artist. Exh. 1885. Add: Paris. † GI 2.

LECLERQ, Louis Antoine Exh. 1924
Equihen, par Outreau, Pas de Calais, France. † L 1.

LE COCQ, Doris Roosmale Exh. 1930-36
Sculptor and potter. b. Blackheath. Spent part of her childhood in Canada. Studied Central School of Arts and Crafts and Royal College of Art. Pottery Instructor Camden Hill Technical Institute and Provincial Institute of Technology and Art, Calgary, Alberta, Canada. A.R.M.S. 1935. Add: London 1930; Alberta, Canada 1936. † GI 1, RA 2, RMS 11.

LECOMPTE, Paul* 1842-1920
French painter. Exh. 1887-1912. Add: c/o H. Duval, 44 Inverness Terrace, Bayswater, London. † GOU 3, L 1, RHA 2, RI 1, ROI 2.

LECOMPTE, Paul Emile* b. 1877
French watercolour painter. Exh. 1938. † WG 53.

LECOMPTE, Victor b. 1856
French artist. Exh. 1912. Add: 91 Quai de la Varenne, La Varenne, St. Hilaire, Seine, France. † L 1.

LE CONTE, John Exh. 1880-86
5 Glanville Place, Edinburgh. † RSA 10.

LE COSTE, Mrs. Exh. 1904
Oxney Court, nr. Dover, Kent. † SWA 1.

LECOURTIER, Prosper b. 1850
French sculptor. Exh. 1904. Add: Rue Dareau, Paris. † L 1.

LE COUTEUX, Lionel Aristide 1847-1909
French etcher. Exh. 1881-94. Add: Paris. † RA 1, RE 3.

LECREUX, Gaston Exh. 1912-13
19 Rue de Vintimille, Paris. † L 1, RSA 1.

LEDBROOK, Emily Exh. 1886-1932
Flower painter. Leamington, Warwicks. † B 51, L 29, RA 5.

LEDEBUR, Eugen Exh. 1937
Animal painter. † RED 3.

LEDERES, John Exh. 1889
43 Trinity Road, Bootle, Lancs. † L 1.

LEDGER, Marion Exh. 1893
Mrs. E. Sculptor. 18 Chester Terrace, Regent's Park, London. † RA 1.

LEDGER, Mildred Mai Exh. 1901-37
Miniature portrait painter and commercial artist. Studied St. John's Wood and R.A. Schools. Add: Hampstead, London 1901; Ipswich, Suffolk 1934. † L 4, RA 15, RI 11, RMS 2, SWA 4.

LEDINGHAM, James Exh. 1892
Architect. District Bank Chambers, Bradford. † RA 1.

LEDINGHAM, Margaret Exh. 1909
216 Woodlands Road, Glasgow † GI 1.

LEDINGHAM, William Exh. 1891-93
68 Northern Grove, Didsbury. † M 2.

LEDOUX, Philippe Exh. 1930-36
Portrait painter. London. † GI 2, L 4, RA 8, ROI 2.

LE DOUX, Picart* Exh. 1913-29
c/o Allied Artists Association, Chancery Lane, London 1913; Paris 1929. † GI 1, GOU 2, LS 6.

LEDSAM, M. Exh. 1880
Painter. Westbank Cottage, Woodland Road, Norwood, London. † D 1.

LEDWARD, Gilbert 1888-1960
Sculptor. Son of Richard Arthur L. q.v. Studied Royal College of Art, R.A. Schools and British School at Rome (1914). A.R.A. 1932, R.A. 1937. "Monolith" purchased by Chantrey Bequest 1936. Add: London 1911 and 1915; Rome 1914. † G 1, GI 3, L 2, LEI 3, RA 57, RSA 6.

LEDWARD, John Ashworth b. 1903
Painter and pastel artist. b. Altrincham, Cheshire. Studied Slade School and Westminster Art School. Exh. 1925-31. Add: London. † GOU 11, L 1, M 1, NEA 6.

LEDWARD, Richard Arthur 1857-1890
Sculptor. Studied South Kensington. Father of Gilbert L. q.v. N.E.A. 1887. Add: London. † NG 4, RA 12.

LEDWICH, Miss S. Exh. 1882-97
Dublin 1882; Moy Valley, Co. Kildare 1897. † RHA 7.

LEE, Mrs. Exh. 1913
13 Crescentwood Road, Sydenham Hill, Surrey. † L 1.

LEE, Agnes Exh. 1891-99
Figure painter. 1 Park Road, Haverstock Hill, London. † L 5, RA 1.

LEE, Annie Exh. 1891
Flower painter. 229 Elgin Avenue, Maida Vale, London. † RBA 1.

LEE, Arthur Exh. 1909
34 Brooklyn Road, Coventry. † B 1.

LEE, Augusta Exh. 1886-98
Edinburgh. † GI 1, RSA 4, RSW 1.

LEE, Auriol Exh. 1880-94
Landscape painter. Savile Lodge, Surbiton Hill, Surrey 1880; Hampstead, London 1893. † SWA 5.

LEE, Anna Frances Exh. 1909
† LS 3.

LEE, Mrs. A.H. Exh. 1885
Blairhoyle, Stirling. † RSA 1.

LEE, Alfred L. Exh. 1912-13
Birmingham. † LS 6.

LEE, Miss B.M.A. Exh. 1910-11
St. Leonards, Sussex. † SWA 4.

LEE, Bremner P. Exh. 1884
8 The College, Glasgow. † GI 1.

LEE, Mrs. C.E. Exh. 1890
Dullington Park, Ilminster. † SWA 1.

LEE, Constance L. Exh. 1900-39
Watercolour painter. A.R.M.S. 1935. Add: London. † RA 1, RMS 20, SWA 17, WG 44.

LEE, David Exh. 1902-7
Hogarth House, Maidenhead, Berks. † RI 7.

LEE, D.A. Beveridge Exh. 1922
36 Dale Street, Liverpool. † L 1.

LEE, David T. Exh. 1880-89
Figure and portrait painter. 1 Elm Tree Road, St. John's Wood, London. † G 1, L 4, M 3, RA 3, RI 1, ROI 1.

LEE, E. Exh. 1908
13 Marcus Street, Lenton, Nottingham. † N 1.

LEE, Mrs. E. Exh. 1918-19
London 1918; Holme Lacey Vicarage, Hereford 1919. † RA 1, SWA 1.

LEE, Miss E. Exh. 1907-15
Liverpool 1907 and 1910; Bootle, Lancs. 1908. † L 9.

LEE, Emily Exh. 1882-83
Landscape painter. Downside, Leatherhead, Surrey. † RBA 1, RI 1.

LEE, Erica Exh. 1920-40
Sculptor. b. Manchester. Studied under E. Whitney-Smith and W. Reid Dick. Add: London. † GI 7, L 5, RA 26, RSA 4, SWA 2.

LEE, Ernest Claude Exh. 1882-87
Architect. 30 Great James Street, Bedford Row, London. † RA 8.

LEE, Miss E.K. Exh. 1914-22
Rokeby, Hanworth Road, Feltham, Middlesex. † SWA 5.

LEE, Frances A. Exh. 1894-1905
Landscape painter. Torquay 1894; London 1902. † RA 3, SWA 3.

LEE, Frederick Walter Exh. 1894-1938
Painter and miniature portrait painter. R.M.S. 1897. Add: London 1894; Radford, Notts. 1919; Nottingham 1935. † B 2, L 2, M 1, N 9, NG 2, RA 2, RHA 2, RMS 6.

LEE, G. Exh. 1884-87
Landscape painter. 15 Duke Street, Basford, Notts. † N 2.

LEE, George Exh. 1923-33
Landscape painter. Self taught. Add: 5 Scott Avenue, Chorlton-cum-Hardy, Manchester. † GOU 4, L 13, RCA 1.

LEE, G.E. Exh. 1911-37
London 1911; Woking, Surrey 1929; Sidcup, Kent 1931. † L 1, M 2, RI 8.

LEE, H. Exh. 1906
Hogarth House, St. Luke's Road, Maidenhead, Berks. † RA 1.

LEE, Helen Edith Exh. 1884
Landscape painter. † SWA 1.

LEE, Henry John St. F. Exh. 1914-32
Landscape, figure and decorative printer. Warlingham, Surrey 1914; London 1923. † CHE 1, L 1, LS 2, NEA 2, RA 5.

LEE, John Exh. 1889-1900
Figure painter. Fulham, London 1889; Middleton-on-Teesdale, Darlington 1900. † RA 1, RBA 1, ROI 2.

LEE, Janet A. Exh. 1902
64 Northumberland Street, Edinburgh. † RSA 1.

LEE, James B. Exh. 1913
43 Bromwich Road, Sheffield. † L 1.

LEE, John Ingle Exh. 1880
Figure painter. Sunnycote, Hampstead Hill Gardens, London. † RA 1.

LEE, James N. Exh. 1881-1911
Figure and domestic painter. Hilmartin Road, Camden Road, London. † RA 8, RI 2, ROI 4.

LEE, J.R. Exh. 1894-98
171 Moseley Road, Birmingham. † B 7, RHA 6.

LEE, John S. Exh. 1899-1911
Architect. London. † RA 4.

LEE, John Thomas Exh. 1887-1916
Architect. Egremont, Cheshire 1887; London 1890. † L 1, RA 11.

LEE, J.W. Exh. 1883-87
Aberdeen. † RSA 5.

LEE, Lilian Exh. 1933-39
Landscape painter. Wollaton Park, Nottingham. † N 13.

LEE, Lawrence S. Exh. 1937
Portrait painter. 52 Albemarle Gardens, New Malden, Surrey. † RA 1.

LEE, Myrtle Exh. 1934-36
Watercolour landscape and figure painter. Five Winds, Bovey Tracey, Devon. † COO 73, RI 2.

LEE, May Bridges Exh. 1905-39
Lady Stott. Portrait and miniature painter. b. Lahore, India. Studied Lambeth School of Art. R.M.S. 1920, A.S.W.A. 1922, S.W.A. 1924. Add: London. † G 3, L 29, P 1, RA 28, RI 29, RMS 66, RSA 9, SWA 5.

LEE, Mary H. Exh. 1889-1923
Liverpool 1889; Bootle, Lancs. 1908; Birkenhead 1916. † L 29.

LEE, M.L. Gwendoline Exh. 1892-94
Figure painter. 148 York Road, Lambeth, London. † ROI 3.

LEE, Mrs. Olive Exh. 1903-37
Portrait and figure painter. London. † P 6, RA 2, RCA 2, RHA 1, RMS 1, RSA 4.

LEE, Oswin A.J. Exh. 1897-98
Edinburgh. † RSA 2.

LEE, Pattie Exh. 1901
Cop House, Saltney Ferry, nr. Chester. † L 1.

LEE, Rachael Exh. 1882
Flower painter. Ravenswood, West Hill, Putney Heath, London. † RBA 1.

LEE, Rupert Exh. 1919-39
Figure and portrait painter. Member London Group 1922. Add: London. † COO 5, G 4, LEI 1, LS 2, NEA 7.

LEE, R.A. Exh. 1901-4
54 Northumberland Street, Edinburgh. † RSA 2.

LEE, Sydney 1866-1949
Painter, etcher and wood engraver. b. Manchester. Studied Manchester and Paris. N.E.A. 1906, A.R.A. 1922, R.A. 1930, R.B.A. 1904, A.R.E. 1905, R.E. 1915. Member of the Society of 25 Artists. "Amongst the Dolomites" purchased by Chantrey Bequest 1924. Add: Prestwich, Manchester 1886; London 1893. † B 1, BAR 1, CG 148, FIN 1, G 2, GI 18, GOU 3, I 45, L 47, LEI 1, LS 1, M 6, NEA 95, NG 6, RA 49, RBA 7, RE 98, RHA 7, RSA 5.

LEE, Sydney Williams Exh. 1880-88
Figure and domestic painter. London. † B 1, L 2, RA 8, RBA 2, ROI 2.

LEE, Thomas Stirling 1856-1916
Painter and sculptor. N.E.A. 1887. Add: London. † FIN 15, G 6, GI 13, I 19, L 12, M 1, NEA 10, NG 9, P 2, RA 26, RBA 3, RHA 4, ROI 1, RSA 2.

LEE, Walter Exh. 1928-39
Figure, portrait, still life and landscape painter. Grantham, Lincs. † N 23.

LEECH, Beatrice Mary Seccombe b. 1880
Watercolour landscape and genre painter. b. Eccles, Lancs. Studied under W.H. Wilkinson in Manchester. Exh. 1913-19. Add: Manchester. † AR 111, L 5, M 3, RCA 2, RHA 6, RSA 1.

LEECH, Mrs. George Exh. 1887
Erdington, Birmingham. † B 2.

LEECH, Gwendoline Exh. 1898
1 Witherby Gardens, London. † SWA 1.

LEECH, George William 1894-c.1971
Painter and etcher. Studied Lambeth and Putney Schools of Art. R.I. 1935. Exh. 1924-40. Add: London 1924 and 1936; Weybridge 1925. † AR 1, D 1, FIN 1, L 9, M 2, P 3, RA 13, RBA 2, RI 35, ROI 3.

LEECH, John Exh. 1934-38
Architect. Stansted, Essex 1934; Watford, Herts. 1937. † RA 4.

LEECH, Mrs. M. Turner Exh. 1925
Embroiderer. Hillsboro, Duffield Road, Derby. † N 1.

LEECH, Mrs. W.J. Exh. 1914
16 Eardley Crescent, Earls Court, London. † RHA 3.

LEECH, William John 1881-1968
Figure and landscape painter. Studied Juliens, Paris. Add: Dublin 1899; Paris 1903; Concarneau, Finisterre, France 1905; London 1912. † B 2, BG 43, FIN 5, GI 1, GOU 68, I 2, L 3, LS 12, M 1, NEA 6, P 5, RA 8, RHA 216, ROI 16.

LEECHMAN, James Exh. 1888-90
Glasgow. † GI 3.

LEEDER, Nan Exh. 1930
Wood engraver. † RED 1.

LEEDHAM, E. Exh. 1932
45 Thomas Street, West Bromwich. † B 1.

LEEDS, Miss M. Exh. 1909-12
Miniature portrait painter. Haslemere, Surrey. † RA 4.

LEE-HANKEY, Edith Mary see GARNER

LEE-HANKEY, Mabel Emily d. 1943
nee Hobson. Miniature painter. First wife of William L.-H. q.v. R.B.A. 1905, R.M.S. 1896, S.W.A. 1918. Exh. 1889-1939. Add: London. † D 1, L 9, NG 3, RA 82, RBA 11, RI 6, RMS 109, ROI 2, SWA 3.

LEE-HANKEY, William* 1869-1952
Portrait and landscape painter and colour engraver. Studied Chester School of Art, Royal College of Art and in Paris. Served with Artists Rifles 1915-19. Married first Mabel Emily L.-H. q.v. and second Edith Mary Garner q.v. R.B.A. 1896, A.R.E. 1909, R.E. 1911, R.I. 1896 (resigned 1906, re-elected 1918, resigned 1924), R.M.S. 1896, R.O.I. 1901 (Hon. Ret. 1940), A.R.W.S. 1925, R.W.S. 1936. Member of the Society of 25 Artists. Add: Chester 1893; London 1895 and 1931; Etaples, France 1923. † B 1, CG 1, CON 40, D 1, DOW 2, FIN 150, G 1, GI 18, GOU 3, I 9, L 104, LEF 113, LEI 359, M 2, NG 5, RA 74, RBA 43, RE 80, RHA 2, RI 42, RID 4, RMS 11, ROI 69, RSA 5, RWS 125, TOO 42, WG 33.

LEE-HOLLAND, Mrs. Hetty Exh. 1926-27
21 Gt. Peter Street, London. † NEA 2.

LEEKE, F.S. Exh. 1936-37
29 Hallewell Road, Birmingham. † B 3.

LEEKE, P. Dorothy Exh. 1908
9 Hertford Street, Mayfair, London. † RCA 1.

LEEMING, M. Rodway Exh. 1923-27
276 Gt. Cheetham Street, Higher Broughton, Manchester. † L 5, M 3.

LEEMING, S.J.R. Exh. 1932
† L 2.

LEEMPATTEN, Van See V

LEEMPOELS, Jef b. 1867
Belgian artist. Exh. 1909-1913. Add: 176 Rue Americaine, Brussels. † L 3.

LEEMPUTTEN, Van See V

LEEPER, Reginald Mervyn Charles b. 1897
Painter and etcher. b. Kesh, Co. Fermanagh. Studied Chelsea Polytechnic and Academie de la Grande Chaumiere, Paris. Exh. 1925-32. Add: Chrome Cottage, Benenden, Kent. † CHE 1, CON 2, L 1, NEA 1, RA 8, RHA 5.

LEES, Ada Exh. 1900-1
35 Mecklenburgh Square, London. † SWA 2.

LEES, Alice M. Exh. 1902
19 Pembroke Road, Kensington, London. † B 1.

LEES, Charles* 1800-1880
Portrait, landscape and genre painter. Studied under Raeburn. R.S.A. 1829, Treasurer R.S.A. 1868-80. Add: 19 Scotland Street, Edinburgh. † GI 1.

LEES, Derwent* 1885-1931
Landscape painter. b. Australia. Studied Manchester School of Art, Slade School and Paris. Painted extensively on the continent. N.E.A. 1911, Add: London. † ALP 1, BK 2, CHE 23, GOU 11, L 6, NEA 72, RED 3.

LEES, Dorothy M. Exh. 1923
† SWA 1.

LEES, Mrs. E.S. Exh. 1916
Ivy Cottage, Bushey Grove Road, Watford, Herts. † RA 1.

LEES, Frederick Exh. 1894
Architect. 20 Victoria Street, Westminster, London. † RA 1.

LEES, G. Exh. 1915
27 Duke Street, New Basford, Nottingham. † N 1.

LEES, Ida d. 1928
Painter of moonlight and night effects and black and white and pencil artist. b. Ryde I.O.W. A.R.B.A. 1925. Add: Ryde, I.O.W. 1891; Pembury, Kent 1895; Kingston by Sea, Nr. Brighton 1911. † DOW 62, L 5, LS 33, RA 2, RBA 20.

LEES, Miss L.C. Exh. 1899-1904
Miniature portrait painter. 40 Pembroke Road, Kensington, London. † RA 3, SWA 3.

LEES, Mrs. Madge Exh. 1889
113 St. Georges Road, Glasgow. † GI 1.

LEES, Mary C.M. b. 1876
Watercolour painter and miniaturist. Studied Calderon's School of Animal Painting. Exh. 1923-40. Add: 33 Pembroke Road, Kensington, London. † RA 4, RI 11, SWA 1.

LEES, Robert Exh. 1926
1 Vesta Place, Blackrock Road, Cork. † RHA 1.

LEESE, A.S.M. Exh. 1937-38
Watercolour painter. † WG 5.

LEESE, Gertrude Exh. 1902-11
9 Moss Hall Crescent, North Finchley, London. † GI 1, L 3, LS 10, RA 2.

LEESE, Spencer Exh. 1882-92
Landscape painter. Hampstead, London 1882, Birkdale, Southport. Lancs. 1883. † L 3, M 17, RBA 1.

LEESMITH, Mary Lascelles See HARCOURT

LEESON, Dorothy Exh. 1931-33
Landscape painter. London. † RA 2.

LEESON, Miss E.M. Exh. 1911
Clifdon House, Twickenham, Middlesex. † RA 1.

LEESON, John A. Exh. 1930
† L 1.

LEESON, Miss O. Exh. 1907-11
Collingham House, Cromwell Road, London. † NG 1, RA 3.

LEET, Gerald McK. Exh. 1935
Portrait painter. 35 York Grove, London. † RA 1.

LEEUW, de See D

LE FANU, Miss E.C. Exh. 1909-27
Ballymorris, Bray, Co. Wicklow 1909 and 1921; London 1912. † LS 18, M 1, RA 1, RHA 9.

LE FANU, G. Brinsley Exh. 1881-1916
Landscape painter. London. † D 1, M 1, RA 5, RBA 7, RHA 3, RI 1.

LE FAUCONNIER, Henri* 1881-1945
French painter. Studied at Juliens, Paris. Exh. 1922. † GOU 3.

LEFEBVRE, Charles Exh. 1891
Landscape painter. c/o T. MacLean, 7 Haymarket, London. † RA 1.

LEFEBVRE, Mme. C. Delarue Exh. 1909
204 Boulevard Raspail, Paris. † L 1.

LEFEBVRE, Hippolyte b. 1863
French sculptor. Exh. 1913. Add: 112 Rue du Cherche Midi, Paris. † GI 1.

LE FEBVRE, Jules c. 1835-c. 1912
French painter. Exh. 1892-93. † P 2.

LEFEVRE, Carlos b. 1875
French artist. Exh. 1903. Add: 4 Rue Aumont-Thieville, Paris. † L 1.

LE FLEMING, George H. Exh. 1905-26
Leek, Staffs. 1905; Hatherton Hall, Cannock, Staffs. 1906; Springthorpe, Cheltenham, Glos. 1926. † L 9.

LE FLEMING, Mildred Exh. 1884-91
Landscape painter. Rydal Hall, Ambleside. † RI 3.

LEFORT, Jean Louis b. 1875
French artist. Exh. 1908. Add: 5 Rue de Bagneaux, Paris. † L 1.

LEFRANC, Raymond Exh. 1902
15 Quai d'Anjou, Paris. † L 1.

LEFROY, Frances J. Exh. 1896-99
123 Blenheim Crescent, London. † RI 1, SWA 4.

LEFROY, Phoebe Exh. 1939
Landscape painter. Gortmore, Dundrum, Co. Dublin. † RHA 1.

LEFTWICH, Florence Exh. 1889
94 Barry Road, East Dulwich, London. † B 2.

LEFTWICH, George Rober Exh. 1880-1911
Figure and domestic painter. London 1880; Wealdstone, Middlesex 1908. † D 1, M 1, LS 8.

LEFTWICH, Peter b. 1913
Figure painter and fresco artist. b. London. Studied Durban School of Art 1931 and University of Cape Town, South Africa 1932-36. Exh. 1939. Add: Cheyne Walk, London. † RA 2.

LE GALLIENNE, Gwen Exh. 1935-36
1 Adelaide Street, London. † SWA 2.

LEGER, Miss E. Exh. 1905
† SWA 2.

LEGG, Albert T. Exh. 1919
Symonsbury, Bridport, Dorset. † LS 3.

LEGG, Miss C.M. Exh. 1912-15
45 Kingston Road, New Malden, Surrey. † L 1, RA 3, SWA 2.

LEGG, Miss D.B. Exh. 1920
56 The Pavement, Penge, Kent. † SWA 2.

LEGG, Isabel S. Exh. 1898-1913
Watercolour landscape painter. 27 Madeley Road, Ealing, London. † SWA 3, WG 66.

LEGGAT, James Exh. 1909
52 Hawkhill Avenue, Ayr. † GI 1.

LEGGATT, William B. Exh. 1930
Wood engraver. 49 East Sheen Avenue, East Sheen, London. † RA 1, RBA 1.

LEGGE, Arthur J. Exh. 1883-1920
Figure and landscape painter. R.B.A. 1892. Father of Phyllis Mary L. q.v. Add: Glasgow 1883; Derby 1886; London 1887 and 1889; Doncaster 1888; Buckhurst Hill, Essex 1896; West Ham Technical Institute, Stratford, E. London 1903; Woodford, Essex 1905; Forest Gate, East London 1912. † GI 1, L 1, RA 17, RBA 72, RI 3.

LEGGE, A.K. Exh. 1895-1905
37 Sloane Gardens, London. † D 13.

LEGGE, Emily Exh. 1914
19 Alderley Avenue, Claughton, Birkenhead. † L 1.

LEGGE, Margaret M. Exh. 1902-3
Flower painter. † BG 6.

LEGGE, Phyllis Mary Exh. 1919-38
Watercolour painter, enameller and etcher. Daughter of Arthur J.L. q.v. Studied West Ham School of Art and Royal College of Art. Art mistress Borough Polytechnic and West Ham School of Art. A.R.M.S. 1921, R.M.S. 1930. Add: East London. † L 2, RA 10, RMS 22.

LEGGETT, Alex* Exh. 1880-84
Leith Walk, Edinburgh. † RSA 9.

LEGGETT, Mrs. A. Doris Exh. 1927-30
Kia Ora, Heather Lane, Little Sutton, Birkenhead. † L 5.

LEGGETT, Dora Exh. 1884
3 King's Place, Leith Walk, Edinburgh. † RSA 2.

LEGGETT, Miss K. Exh. 1903
The Haven, Spa Hill, Upper Norwood, London. † SWA 1.

LEGGETT, Miss Rowley Exh. 1904-19
Landscape and figure painter. A.S.W.A. 1910. Add: Ockley, Surrey 1904; Ewhurst, Surrey 1907; Peaslake, Surrey 1909; Fittleworth, Sussex 1919. † B 3, GOU 1, I 4, L 4, LS 14, NEA 3, RCA 3, RID 22, ROI 8, SWA 16.

LE GOUT-GERALD, Fernand Marie Eugene* 1856-1924
French artist. Exh. 1901-9. Add: Paris. † L 10, LS 3.

LEGRAND, A. Exh. 1882
14 Quai Bourbon, Paris. † GI 1.

LEGRAND, L. Exh. 1891
Sydbrook House, Nr. Ross, Herefords. † L 2.

LEGRAND, Louis* Exh. 1904-22
11 Rue le Peletier, Paris. † I 97, L 5, M 2, RSA 2.

LEGRAND, Louise Exh. 1891
Miniature portrait painter. 4 Woodford Villas, Mannamead, Plymouth. † RA 1.

LEGRAND, Maud Exh. 1919-23
Miniature portrait painter. London. † L 1, RA 3.

LEGROS, Professor Alphonse 1837-1911
Painter, etcher, lithographer, sculptor and medal designer. b. Dijon. Studied Ecole des Beaux Arts and under Lecoq de Boisbaudran. Came to England 1863, Teacher of Etching South Kensington School of Art, Professor of Fine Art Slade School, University College London 1876-92. R.E. 1880, H.R.S.A. 1911. A collection of his works are in the Tate Gallery. † CAR 15, CON 2, FIN 30, G 20, GI 4, M 14, NG 36, P 12, RA 8, RE 100, RSA 3.

LE HAY, John Exh. 1897
189 Adelaide Road, London. † RBA 1.

LEHEUTRE, Gustave b. 1861
French etcher. A.R.E. 1908. Exh. 1908-13. Add: 41 Rue de la Tour d'Auvergne, Paris. † L 11, RE 12.

LEHMAN, H.G. Exh. 1880-96
Landscape painter. Cromwell Street, Nottingham. † N 4.

LEHMANN, Olga Exh. 1932-33
Slade School of Art, Gower Street, London. † RBA 1, SWA 1.

LEHMANN, Rudolph* 1819-1905
Portrait painter. London 1880; Bushey, Herts. 1904. † B 2, G 24, L 11, M 5, NG 21, P 2, RA 45, RHA 1.

LEIBIEDZKI, Edward Exh. 1910
Wohllebengasse 5, Vienna. † L 1.

LEICESTER, Emily Exh. 1907-32
Portrait and miniature painter. The Gables, Church Road, Northwich, Cheshire. † L 44, M 2, RCA 1.

LEICESTER, E.C. Exh. 1882
18 Charles Street, Bath, Leicester. † M 1.

LEIFCHILD, Henry Stormouth 1823-1884
Sculptor. Studied at the British Museum and R.A. Schools 1844 and Rome 1848. Exh. 1882. Add: 15 Kirkstall Road, Streatham Hill, London. † RA 1.

LEIGH, Dora B. Exh. 1902-3
Portrait and figure painter. 7 Rue Leopold Robert, Boulevard Raspail, Paris. † RA 2.

LEIGH, Ethel D. Exh. 1910-34
Landscape painter. Saltburn by the Sea, Yorks. 1910; London 1913 and 1934; Bowden, Cheshire 1925. † CHE 1, L 7, NEA 3, RA 1, RCA 2, RSA 1, SWA 1.

LEIGH, G.G. Exh. 1909
Architect. Craigleith, Mukleneuk, Pretoria, S. Africa. † RA 1.

LEIGH, George Leonard b. 1857
Landscape painter. b. Forest Hill. Direct of the Birmingham School of Landscape painting. Exh. 1886-1939. Add: Birmingham 1886 and 1920; Hampton in Arden 1888. † B 92, L 1, RA 1.

LEIGH, Mrs. Ina Exh. 1927
Watercolour painter. Rob Roy House, Burns Street, Nottingham. † N 1.

LEIGH, Katharine Exh. 1920
Sculptor. 68 Grand Parade, Brighton. † RA 1.

LEIGH, Leila Exh. 1937-40
Portrait painter. Muswell Hill, London. † COO 1, GOU 1, NEA 5, RA 1.

LEIGH, Mrs. Muriel G. Exh. 1932
Bindon House, Nr. Wellington, Somerset. † ROI 1.

LEIGH, Roger Exh. 1887-1907
Landscape painter. London. † I 1, L 1, NG 1, ROI 3.

LEIGH, Rose J. Exh. 1883-1912
Landscape painter. Antwerp 1883; Rosgarland, Co. Wexford, Ireland and London 1888-99; London 1900. † B 5, GI 2, L 16, LS 12, M 4, NEA 1, RA 6, RBA 2, RHA 29, ROI 1, SWA 2.

LEIGH, Mrs. T. Exh. 1909
Northgate, Naybank, Stoke on Trent, Staffs. † L 2.

LEIGH, William Robinson* b. 1866
American artist. Exh. 1891. Add: Royal Academy of Fine Arts, Munich. † GI 1.

LEIGH-PEMBERTON, E. Exh. 1922
† SWA 5.

LEIGH-PEMBERTON, John Exh. 1934-38
Figure painter. R.O.I. 1936. Add: 3 Callow Street, London. † NEA 3, RA 2, RCA 2, ROI 15.

LEIGH-PEMBERTON, Katharine Exh. 1924-36
52 Lower Sloane Street, London. † GOU 3, NEA 7.

LEIGHTON, Alfred Crocker b. 1901
Landscape painter. A.R.B.A. 1927, R.B.A. 1930. Exh. 1926-34. Add: Mountfield, St. Helens Crescent, Hastings. † NEA 2, RA 6, RBA 43, RI 1, RID 3.

LEIGHTON, A.G. Exh. 1914
225 Long Lane, Bermondsey, London. † RA 1.

LEIGHTON, Miss C.D. Exh. 1906
† P 1.

LEIGHTON, Clare Veronica Hope b. 1900
Portrait painter and wood engraver. Studied Brighton School of Art and Slade School. A.R.E. 1930, R.E. 1934. Exh. 1921-40. Add: London. † GI 3, L 3, NEA 12, RA 1, RE 37, RED 15, RHA 4, RSA 3.

LEIGHTON, David Exh. 1909
† LS 1.

LEIGHTON, Edmund Blair* 1853-1923
Historical genre painter. Son of Charles Blair L. (1823-1855). Father of J. Blair L. q.v. R.O.I. 1887, Add: London. † B 4, DOW 2, GI 2, L 8, M 5, RA 65, RBA 2, ROI 32, TOO 16.

LEIGHTON, Lord Frederic* 1830-1896
Baron Leighton of Stretton. Historical and mythological painter, sculptor and engraver. b. Scarborough. Studied in Florence and Rome. A.R.A. 1864, R.A. 1868, P.R.A. 1878, R.B.A. 1870, H.R.S.A. 1878, R.W.S. 1888. Knighted 1878. Made Baronet 1886. Raised to peerage 1896 (the only English artist to have been accorded this honour). His house in Holland Park Road, London is now a museum. "The Bath of Psyche" purchased by Chantrey Bequest 1890, and "An Athlete Wrestling with a Python" in 1877. † AG 1, B 9, FIN 20, G 4, GI 4, L 16, M 24, P 4, RA 77, RBA 44, RCA 8, RHA 11, RSA 5, TOO 8.

LEIGHTON, Frederick Exh. 1903
Designer. 122 Upper Tulse Hill, London. † RA 1.

LEIGHTON, Frederick Exh. 1926
Landscape painter. 13 Knollys Road, Streatham, London. † RA 1.

LEIGHTON, John 1822-1912
Figure and landscape painter. London 1882; Swallowfield, Berks. 1898. † L 12.

EIGHTON, J. Blair Exh. 1914-39
Portrait and landscape painter. Son of Edmond B. L. q.v. R.B.A. 1931, R.P. 1936. Add: London. † CHE 1, GOU 2, I 6, L 1, P 20, RA 22, RBA 4, RED 50.

LEIGHTON, Kathleen M. Exh. 1940
Watercolour painter. Southside, The Park, Hull. † RA 1.

LEIGHTON, Mrs. Kathryn Woodman b. 1876
American portrait painter. Exh. 1929. † AB 9.

LEIGHTON, Miss M. Exh. 1884
34 Princess Road, Edgbaston, Birmingham. † B 1.

LEIGHTON, Sarah Exh. 1883-85
Flower painter. London. † L 2, RI 1.

LEINQUE, Mme. B. Exh. 1901
Miniature portrait painter. 34 Oakley Street, Chelsea, London. † RA 1.

LEIPER, William 1839-1916
Architect. A.R.S.A. 1892, R.S.A. 1896 (Hon. Ret. 1914). Add: Terpersie, Helensburgh, and Glasgow. † GI 18, RA 1, RSA 26, RSW 3.

LEIPNER, Helen Exh. 1893
38 Hampton Park, Redland, Bristol. † B 2.

LEIPOLD, Carl b. 1864
German painter. Exh. 1908. † GOU 2.

LEISENRING, Alice Exh. 1933-40
Painter and pencil artist. b. Sandyrun, U.S.A. Studied Slade School. Add: Great Bealings, Nr. Woodbridge, Suffolk. † NEA 5, RA 1, RSA 2.

LEIST, Fred Exh. 1910-30
Portrait and figure painter. R.B.A. 1913, R.O.I. 1916. Add: London. † CHE 1, GOU 1, I 2, L 1, P 6, RA 14, RBA 8, ROI 27.

LEISTIKOW, Walter* 1865-1908
German landscape painter. Exh. 1901-7. Add: Berlin. † I 6.

LEITCH, Annie Mary Exh. 1901-18
Landscape painter and teacher. Studied Glasgow. Add: 1 Finnart Terrace, Greenock, N.B. † GI 10, L 1, M 1, RSA 1.

LEITCH, George W. Exh. 1933
Watercolour landscape painter. † FIN 1.

LEITCH, Kitty M. Exh. 1916-21
Cathcart, Glasgow 1916; c/o H. Cowles, Colon 11.20 Vigo, Spain 1920; Chelsea, London 1921. † GI 6.

LEITCH, Lilian O. Exh. 1938-39
1 Gordon Terrace, Edinburgh. † RSA 3.

LEITCH, William Leighton* 1804-1883
Watercolour landscape painter. b. Glasgow. Studied in Italy. Scenery painter at the Theatre Royal, Glasgow, before coming to London. Teacher of drawing and watercolour painting to Queen Victoria and the Royal Family for 22 years. R.I. 1862 (V.P. for many years), R.W.S. 1862. † DOW 2, RI 13.

LEITH, A.L. Exh. 1882
Comrie, Perthshire. † RSA 1.

LEITH, Hay Exh. 1936-37
Hon. Mrs. Henrietta. Add: Leith Hall, Kennethmont. † GI 4.

LEITH, James Exh. 1886-1901
Glasgow. † GI 2.

LE JEUNE, Henry L.* 1819-1904
Genre painter. Studied R.A. Schools. Drawing master at the R.A. 1845, Curator R.A. 1848, A.R.A. 1863. Add: London. † RA 23.

LEKEGIAN, Gabriel Exh. 1883-85
Watercolour figure painter. Constantinople. † RA 3.

LELEUX, Mrs. Doris A.E. Exh. 1929-39
Miniature flower painter. A.R.M.S. 1933, R.M.S. 1939. Add: London. † L 3, RA 8, RMS 34.

LELUK, Mme. J.F. Exh. 1910
57 Rue de Cherche-Midi, Paris. † L 1.

LEMAIRE, Georges Exh. 1903
Sculptor. 22 Rue Tourlogue, Paris. † RA 1.

LE MAISTRE, Francis William Synge 1859-1940
Landscape and marine painter. b. Jersey, C.I. R.O.I. 1917. Add: London 1888; St. Aubin, Jersey, C.I. 1908. † LS 11, RA 3, RBA 4, ROI 79.

LEMAITRE, Albert Exh. 1921
Landscape painter. † GOU 4.

LE MAITRE, W. Courtney Exh. 1910-29
Architect. London. † RA 2.

LEMAN, Alicia J. Exh. 1891
Sporting painter. 2 Ravenna Road, Putney, London. † RA 1.

LEMAN, G.H. Exh. 1926
26 Crammer Street, Nottingham. † N 1.

LEMAN, Miss P. Exh. 1904
22 Westbourne Terrace, London. † SWA 1.

LEMANN, E.A. Exh. 1881-85
Landscape painter. Home Lodge, Bathampton, Bath. † SWA 5.

LEMATTE, Fernand J.F. b. 1850
French artist. Exh. 1883-1909. Add: Neuilly sur Seine, France 1883; St. Remy sur Avre, France 1909. † L 2, M 1.

LE MESURIER, Miss E. Exh. 1892
Portrait painter. † FIN 1.

LEMEUNIER, Basile Exh. 1911
Villecresnes, Seine et Oise, France. † L 1.

LEMMERS, F.G. Exh. 1909
26 Rue de Martaens, Brussels. † I 1.

LEMON, Arthur* 1850-1912
Painter of genre and Italian pastoral scenes. b. Isle of Man. Spent his youth in Rome. Was a cowboy for ten years in California. Returned to Europe and studied under Carolus Duran in Paris. Married Blanche L. q.v. "An Encampment" purchased by Chantrey Bequest 1913. Add: Florence 1880; London 1881 and 1905; Betchworth, Surrey 1893. † BG 1, G 12, GI 10, GOU 153, L 14, M 23, NG 25, RA 47, ROI 6.

LEMON, Blanche Exh. 1888-91
Figure and portrait painter. Married Arthur L. q.v. Add: London. † NG 2, RA 1.

LEMON, Miss E. Exh. 1907
Kensington, London. † SWA 1.

LEMON, M. Exh. 1922
† SWA 1.

LEMONIUS, Miss A.M. Exh. 1892-1910
Stonehouse, Allerton, Nr. Liverpool 1892; 128 Piccadilly, London 1905. † L 11.

LENANTON, Carola Exh. 1922
85 Cadogan Gardens, London. † L 1.

LENBACH, von See V

LENCH, H. Exh. 1929-30
Blackheath, Birmingham. † B 2.

LENCHARS, Edgar Exh. 1893
† D 2.

LENDIS, H. Exh. 1926-27
19 Greenside, Kendal, Westmorland. † B 2, L 4, RCA 2.

LENDON, Warwick William b. 1883
Painter, etcher and illustrator. Exh. 1918-21. Add: Cresthill, Lansdowne, Bath. † P 2, ROI 1.

LENDRUM, Florence Exh. 1893-1901
Landscape painter. Huddersfield 1893; Flamborough, Yorks 1900. † L 4, M 1, RA 3, RMS 1.

LENEY, Miss K.E.M. Exh. 1894-1903
Bray, Co. Wicklow, Ireland. † L 1, RHA 7.

LENFESTEY, Giffard Hocart b. 1872
Landscape and interior painter. Studied Royal College of Art and under Raphael Collin in Paris. R.B.A. 1898. Exh. 1895-1938. Add: London. † BG 1, D 1, GOU 2, I 1, M 2, RA 22, RBA 203, RI 5, RID 50, ROI 1.

LENNARD, Miss H. Exh. 1910
8 Lansdowne Road, Holland Park, London. † RA 1.

LENNIE, John Exh. 1880-1902
2 Napier Road, Edinburgh. † GI 2, L 1, RSA 14, RSW 2.

LENNOX, Annie Exh. 1881
Watercolour figure painter. † SWA 1.

LEO, Ansel Exh. 1884-85
Sculptor. 448 Edgware Road Studios, London. † RA 2.

LEON, Edouard b. 1873
French artist. Exh. 1906-7. Add: 19 Rue Edouard Jacques, Paris. † L 2.

LEON, Herman c. 1838-1907
French animal painter. Exh. 1883. Add: c/o Graphic, 190 Strand, London. † FIN 1, M 1.

LEONARD, Mrs. Claire Exh. 1929-38
Miniature portrait painter. Oxhey Cottage, Oxhey Woods, Northwood, Middlesex. † RA 2, RHA 2, RSA 4.

LEONARD, George Henry b. 1868
American artist. Exh. 1901-8. Add: 17 Rue Boissonade, Paris. † GI 1, LS 4.

LEONARD, John Henry 1834-1904
Landscape and architectural painter. Studied under William Moore at York. Travelled on the continent. Exh. 1880-95. Add: London. † B 6, D 10, L 3, M 4, RA 1.

LEONARD, Mrs. S.H. (E.M.) Exh. 1896-1903
London. † SWA 15.

LEONHARDT, Johanne D. Exh. 1911
Rainsfield, Maidenhead, Berks. † LS 3.

LEOPOLD, Mrs. J.F. Exh. 1905
31 Ashdale Road, Elm Hall Drive, Wavertree, Liverpool. † L 1.

LEOTARD, Alice Exh. 1904-7
33 Rue des Deux Englises, Brussels. † GI 2.

LEOWE, Arthur Exh. 1930
† L 1.

LEPERE, Auguste* 1849-1919
French etcher and engraver. H.R.E. 1915. Exh. 1883-1913. Add: Paris. † I 16, L 27, RSA 3.

LE PETIT, Ferdinand Exh. 1882-97
Animal painter. London 1882; Stoke Newington, London 1897. † RA 3.

LE PETTIT, H. Exh. 1881-82
Animal and figure painter. 7 Queensbury Street, Essex Road, Islington, London. † RBA 2.

LEPINE, A. Exh. 1883-84
Landscape painter. 1A Old Bond Street, London. † G 2, GI 2.

LEPINE, Joseph Louis Francois Exh. 1908-9
203 Boulevard Raspail, Paris. † LS 8.

LEPLAT, Rene Exh. 1931
Landscape painter. † GOU 22.

LE POITEVEN, Louis 1849-1909
Landscape painter. 23 Piet Hein Straat, L'Hague, Holland. † BRU 1, GI 1.

LEPROVOST, Odette Exh. 1928-29
13 Ely Place, Dublin. † L 1, RHA 2.

LE QUESNE, Fernard b. 1856
French artist. Exh. 1912-18. Add: 34A Onslow Gardens, London. † RA 3.

LE QUESNE, Rose Exh. 1886-95
Painter and sculptor. London 1886 and 1891; Jersey, C.I. 1890. † L 6, NEA 1, RA 8, RBA 1.

LEQUEUX, Emile Exh. 1907-8
119 Rue de Grenelle, Paris. † L 1, LS 5.

LE RAT, Paul Exh. 1888-91
Etcher. Paris. † RA 2.

LERCHE, H.S. Exh. 1910
c/o M.A. Hebrard, 8 Rue Royale, Paris. † L 1.

LE RESCHE, S. Exh. 1885
48 Preston Street, Kirkham, Lancs. † L 1.

LE RICHE, Henri Exh. 1908
198 Rue de Courcelles, Paris. † L 1.

LERMITTE, Mrs. E.W. Exh. 1880
Painter. Muswell Hill, London. † SWA 1.

LEROLF, Exh. 1892
18 Avenue de Villiers, Paris. † RHA 1.

LE ROLLE, Miss H. Exh. 1910
20 Avenue Duquesne, Paris. † L 1.

LE ROSSIGNOL, Miss C.E. Exh. 1907
14 Vicarage Gate, Kensington, London. † RA 1.

LEROUX, Auguste J.M. b. 1871
French artist. Exh. 1909-11. Add: Paris. † L 2.

LEROUX, Louis* Exh. 1880-83
96 St. Donat's Road, New Cross, Kent. † B 3, M 1, RHA 10.

LE ROY, Aimee C. Exh. 1910-29
Landscape and portrait painter. b. Paris. Educated in England. Wrote books and articles under the name of Esme Stuart. Add: Witham Lodge, Winchester. † B 1, BG 20, D 5, L 2, M 1, P 3, RCA 2, RI 2, SWA 2.

LEROY, Miss H.F. Exh. 1883-85
Figure and domestic painter. 31 Woburn Place, Russell Square, London. † B 2, L 1, M 2, RBA 1.

LEROY, Paul A.A. Exh. 1906
25 Avenue de Wagram, Paris. † L 1.

LE ROYDE, Miss M. Exh. 1901
36 Queen's Road, Bayswater, London. † L 1.

LE ROY d'ETIOLLES, Mme. H. Exh. 1913
40 Rue Lauriston, Paris. † L 1.

LERRA, E. Exh. 1881
33 Avenue de l'Opera, Paris. † RHA 1.

LERROLLE, Henry Exh. 1906
† P 2.

LESAGE, Clara Exh. 1892-1909
Landscape and miniature painter. London. † RA 1, ROI 3.

LESHNICK, E.R. Exh. 1924
269 Litherland Road, Bootle, Lancs. † L 1.

LE SIDANER, Henri Eugene 1862-1939
French painter. Studied at the Tate Gallery and Museums in London, Paris, Rome, Amsterdam, Brussels, Dublin, Cardiff and Pittsburg. Exh. from 1901. † CHE 1, GI 16, GOU 70, I 9, L 16, RHA 1.

LESLEY, Miss M.W. Exh. 1884
1008 Clinton Street, Philadelphia, U.S.A. † L 1.

LESLIE, Alexander J. 1873-1930
Sculptor. "Dolce Far Niente" purchased by Chantrey Bequest 1911. Add: London. † GI 6, L 11, RA 42, RSA 4, RSW 1.

LESLIE, Cecil Exh. 1904-13
Landscape and figure painter. Little Sark, C.I. † RA 2, RI 6.

LESLIE, Miss Cecil b. 1900
Painter, aquatinter, sculptor and furniture designer. Exh. 1923-39. Add: London 1923; West Byfleet, Sussex 1933. † GI 9, L 11, M 2, NEA 1, RA 17, RBA 1, RCA 2, ROI 1, RSA 32, SWA 2.

LESLIE, Miss F. Exh. 1885
6 Walpole Road, Brighton. † M 1.

LESLIE, Frank Exh. 1880-92
180 West Regent Street, Glasgow. † GI 3.

LESLIE, Miss F.M. Exh. 1893
Westbrook House, Aston Village, Birmingham. † B 1.

LESLIE, F.S. Exh. 1892
Whitehall, London. † D 2.

LESLIE, George Dunlop* 1835-1921
Landscape and genre painter. Studied under his father Charles Robert L. (1794-1859) and at R.A. Schools. A.R.A. 1868, R.A. 1876. "The Deserted Mill" purchased by Chantrey Bequest 1906. Father of Peter L. q.v. Add: London 1880; Wallingford, Berks. 1884; Linfield, Hayward's Heath, Sussex 1907. † AG 4, B 1, FIN 7, G 3, GI 2, L 6, M 6, NG 1, RA 64.

LESLIE, Harry Exh. 1880-81
176 Alexandra Road, St. John's Wood, London. † D 2.

LESLIE, Hugh Exh. 1908
Bramble Hill, Heswall, Cheshire. † L 1.

LESLIE, Sir John Exh. 1882-1937
Landscape and portrait painter. H.R.H.A. Add: London 1882; Glasslough, Co. Monaghan, Ireland 1926. † G 3, RHA 6.

LESLIE, Mrs. J.H. Exh. 1880-81
Landscape painter. 23 Upper Montague Street, Montague Square, London. † SWA 4.

LESLIE, J.T. Exh. 1892
49 Park Street, Stoke Newington, London. † RHA 2.

LESLIE, Lionel Exh. 1934-35
Sculptor. 5 Avenue Studios, 76 Fulham Road, London and Glasslough, Co. Monaghan, Ireland. † RA 1, RHA 2.

LESLIE, Mary Exh. 1885-87
Flower painter. Brighton. † B 2, SWA 1.

LESLIE, Peter b. 1877
Landscape, figure and portrait painter. Son of George Dunlop L. q.v. Studied Herkomer's, Bushey, Herts. Exh. 1899-1924. Add: Bushey, Herts. 1899, 1903 and 1909; Wallingford, Berks. 1900 and 1905; Lindfield, Haywards Heath 1907 and 1918. † D 3, FIN 1, L 4, M 1, NG 2, P 3, RA 43, RHA 1, RI 9, ROI 2.

LESLIE, Robert C. Exh. 1880-87
Marine, portrait and genre painter. Eldest son of Charles Robert L. (1794-1859). Brother of George Dunlop L. q.v. Add: 6 Moira Place, Southampton. † RA 4.

LESLIE, Robert M. Exh. 1913-14
Annfield Plain, Co. Durham 1913; Clanfield, Oxon 1914. † LS 4.

LESREL, Adolphe Alexandre* Exh. 1890-1912
French artist. Paris. † L 11, TOO 17.

LESSELS, James Exh. 1881-1904
Edinburgh 1881 and 1902; Kirkcaldy 1883; Montrose, N.B. 1890; Leith 1903. † RSA 16.

LESSELLS, Jay Exh. 1927
Surma, West Kilbride. † GI 1.

LESSEPS, de See D

LESSI, Tito Exh. 1911-12
c/o 7 Haymarket, London. † L 3, RSA 1.

LESSORE, Frederick 1879-1951
Sculptor and painter. b. Brighton. Son of Jules L. q.v. Studied Paris and London (medalist R.A. Schools 1906). Exh. 1903-33. Add: London. † B 2, BA 5, GI 2, I 4, L 4, M 1, RA 15.

LESSORE, Jules* 1849-1892
Landscape, portrait, genre and architectural painter. b. Paris. Studied under his father Emile Aubert L. (1805-1876) and F.J. Barrias. Father of Frederick L. q.v. R.I. 1888. Add: Southwick, Sussex 1880; Rotherfield, Sussex 1887. † D 5, G 4, GI 18, L 1, M 10, RA 9, RBA 21, RI 28, ROI 4.

LESSORE, Therese d. 1945
Landscape, portrait and figure painter. Second wife of Walter R. Sickert q.v. Founder member London Group 1913. Exh. 1913-40. Add: London. † BA 18, G 1, GOU 6, LEF 39, LS 18, NEA 1, RSA 1, SWA 1.

LE STALKER, Frederic Exh. 1940
Landscape painter. 36 Cedar Lawn Avenue, Barnet, Herts. † RA 1.

LE SUEUR, Miss C.M. Exh. 1909
Miniature portrait painter. 7 Forburg Road, Stamford Hill, London. † RA 1.

LESUR, Henry Exh. 1898
31 Boulevard Buthier, Paris. † L 1.

LE TALL, Charles McL. Exh. 1883-87
Landscape painter. 24 Bridge Road, West Battersea, London. † RA 2, ROI 2.

LETHABY, William Richard 1857-1931
Landscape painter and architect. Architect to Westminster Abbey, from 1906. Exh. 1881-90. Add: London. † RA 9.

LETHAM, Jane C. Exh. 1889
3 Tennant Street, St. Rollox. † GI 2.

LETHEM, Lady Exh. 1940
1a Ramsey Garden, Edinburgh. † GI 1.

LETHBRIDGE, James M. Exh. 1903
Architect. 9 Cholmeley Villas, Highgate, London. † RA 1.

LETHEN, J.B. Exh. 1883-87
41 John Dalton Street, Manchester. † M 7.

LETHERBROW, John H. Exh. 1882
Akademie der Bilden Kunste, Munich. † M 1.

LETHERBROW, Lila Exh. 1889-97
Hazel Grove, Nr. Stockport, Lancs. 1889; Alderley Edge, Manchester 1897. † M 2.

LETHING, May Exh. 1909
13 Lavender Gardens, London. † GI 1.

LETNIKNOFF, Miss Lubor Exh. 1916-19
Landscape painter. 43 Gwendwr Road, Kensington, London. † NEA 2, SWA 2.

LE TOURNIER, J. Exh. 1938
† BA 2.

LETT-HAINES, Exh. 1919
Church Street Studios, Newlyn, Penzance, Cornwall. † LS 3.

LETTS, Charles Hubert b. 1874
Painter. Studied Slade School and R.A. Schools. Governing Director of the Fine Arts Publishing Co. Ltd. Exh. 1909-36. Add: Warlingham, Surrey. † RA 3.

LETTS, Miss F.I. Exh. 1896
St. Ann's Vicarage, Stamford Hill, London. † RBA 1.

LEUCHARS, E. Exh. 1914
Whitmore Vale House, Hindhead, Surrey. † RA 1.

LEUDET, Jacques T. Exh. 1909-10
c/o Allied Artists Assn. 67 Chancery Lane, London. † LS 6.

LEURS, J. Exh. 1916
Painter. † CON 1.

LEUVILLE, de See D

LEVASSEUR, Henri L. Exh. 1898-1911
Paris. † L 4.

LEVE, Frederick Louis Exh. 1906
Landscape painter. 8 Boulevard d'Argenson, Neuilly sur Seine, France. † L 2.

LEVEILLE, Andre* b. 1880
French artist. Exh. 1913-14. Add: 18 Boulevard Magenta, Paris. † LS 6.

LEVEN, Miss Exh. 1880-82
26 Saxe Coburg Place, Edinburgh. † RSA 4.

LEVENE, Miss F. Exh. 1920-21
136B Upper Parliament Street, Liverpool. † L 2.

LEVENTON, Herbert Exh. 1907-15
Liverpool 1907; Huyton, Lancs. 1908. † L 4.

LEVER, Cecily Margaret See KNEESHAW

LEVER, F.W. Exh. 1903-6
Montpellier Lodge, Harrogate. † RCA 2, RSA 4.

LEVER, Richard Hayley* b. 1876
Landscape painter. b. Adelaide, Australia. R.B.A. 1908. Exh. 1902-13. Add: St. Ives, Cornwall. † L 4, NEA 1, RA 6, RBA 21, RHA 1, ROI 3.

LEVER, Ward Exh. 1920-40
Sway, Hants 1920; Lyndhurst, Hants. 1922; Anthog, Merioneth 1934. † B 3, RCA 1, RHA 2, ROI 6.

LEVERING, Ida Exh. 1893
† RBA 1.

LEVERITT, Winifred Exh. 1930-40
Sculptor. London. † GI 4, RA 11.

LEVERKUS, Elsie Exh. 1917-27
Flower painter. London 1917; Harrow, Middlesex 1927. † RA 2.

LEVERKUS, Gertrude W.M. Exh. 1928
Architect. 5 Gower Street, London. † RA 1.

LEVESON, Dorothy Exh. 1896
Portrait painter. Cluny, Anerley, London. † RA 5.

LEVESON, Mary E. Exh. 1899-1908
Portrait painter. London. † RA 3.

LEVETT-PRINSEP, Miss G.M. Exh. 1925-32
Overstowe, Lichfield, Staffs. † B 3.

LEVETUS, Celia A. Exh. 1895
23 Carpenter Road, Edgbaston, Birmingham. † B 2.

LEVEY, H. Gabrielle Exh. 1932
Mrs. A. Michael Robinson. Portrait and flower painter. Studio 12, Phillimore Terrace, Allen Street, London. † COO 53.

LEVICK, Richard 1864-1917
Figure painter. b. Philadelphia, U.S.A. Exh. 1898. Add: St. Ives, Cornwall. † RA 1, ROI 1.

LEVICK, Ruby Winifred See BAILEY

LEVIN, Victoria Exh. 1884-86
Landscape and architectural painter. London. † RBA 1, SWA 1.

LEVIS, Maurice* Exh. 1903-13
Landscape painter. London 1903; Paris 1908. † L 1, RA 4, RHA 2.

LEVY, Ada Goodman Exh. 1907-15
29 Cumberland Terrace, Regent's Park, London. † L 1, RA 3, RHA 2, RMS 1, RSA 4.

LEVY, Emanuel b. 1900
Portrait and figure painter. Studied Manchester School of Art and St. Martin's School of Art. Instructor in drawing and painting Manchester University. Exh. 1925-38. Add: Manchester 1925; West Hampstead, London 1938. † L 5, M 1, NEA 2, RBA 2.

LEVY, Fanny Exh. 1882-85
Figure painter. Konigsberg, Prussia. † SWA 2.

LEVY, J. Exh. 1896-99
Liverpool. † L 7.

LEVY, Mlle. Jeanne Exh. 1909-13
59 Rue Condorcet, Paris. † L 4.

LEVY, Julia M. Exh. 1883-88
Figure and decorative painter. London. † G 1, RA 4, ROI 1.

LEVY, Lucien Exh. 1895
Watercolour painter. 46 Rue Larochefoucauld, Paris. † RA 1.

LEVY, Miss L.M. Exh. 1883
4 Victoria Street, Nottingham. † RHA 1.

LEVY, Mabel Exh. 1896-1907
Miniature portrait painter. London. † RA 4, RMS 1.

LEVY, Mabel Annie Exh. 1911-38
Watercolour painter, dry point artist and etcher. Studied Nottingham School of Art and Belgium. A.N.S.A. 1922. Add: 76 Muster's Road, West Bridgford, Notts. † L 3, N 73, RBA 2, RCA 6.

LEVY, Mary G. Exh. 1939
Figure painter. 27 Bishopsthorpe Road, Sydenham, London. † RA 1.

LEVY, Netta Exh. 1898
Flower painter. 85 Mitcham Lane, Streatham, London. † RA 1.

LEVY-ENGELMAN, Mlle. Yvonne Exh. 1932-34
124 Rue de Tocqueville, Paris. † RI 12.

LEWES, Maud Exh. 1922
Figure painter. St. Catherine's, Broxbourne, Herts. † RA 1.

LEWIN, Stephen* Exh. 1890-1908
Figure painter. London. † B 5, RA 5, ROI 4, TOO 1.

LEWINGTON, Margaret Exh. 1925
57 Church Road, St. Leonards on Sea, Sussex. † L 2.

LEWIS, A. Exh. 1885-86
River View, Cheyne Walk, Chelsea, London. † B 1, RI 1.

LEWIS, Avery Exh. 1899
Mizpah House, Military Road, Rye, Sussex. † RA 1.

LEWIS, Alfred E. Exh. 1893-1903
Sculptor. London. † L 11, RA 3.

LEWIS, Arthur James 1825-1901
Landscape and portrait painter. London. † G 2, L 1, M 2, NG 4, RA 2.

LEWIS, Aletta M. b. 1904
Mrs. D.C. Dunlop. Painter. b. Orpington. Studied Slade School. Teacher at Sydney Art School, Australia. Exh. 1924-31. † GOU 2, NEA 1.

LEWIS, Anne Madeline Exh. 1880-1922
Landscape and flower painter. A.S.W.A. 1908. Add: Sevenoaks, Kent 1880; Sittingbourne, Kent 1889; London 1893; Petworth, Sussex 1901; Pulborough, Sussex 1921. † B 18, BG 2, D 6, L 17, NG 1, RA 5, RBA 15, RI 4, SWA 86.

LEWIS, Alfred Neville 1895-1972
Portrait, figure and landscape painter. b. Cape Town, S. Africa. Studied Slade School 1912-14. Active Service World War I in France, Belgium and Italy. Toured South Africa in 1924. N.E.A. 1920, R.P. 1935. Exh. 1915-39. Add: London 1915 and 1924; Winchfield, Hants. 1920; Peasmarsh, Nr. Rye, Sussex 1937. † CG 2, G 11, GOU 144, I 4, LEI 46, M 3, NEA 58, P 14, RA 10, RED 12, RSA 1, TOO 4.

LEWIS, Amy Vernon Exh. 1903-37
London 1903; Henfield, Sussex 1918 and 1935; Hayes Common, Kent 1924. † L 2, NEA 1, NG 1, SWA 2.

LEWIS, Arthur Wellesley Noyes Exh. 1900-11
Figure painter. Southsea, Hants. 1900; London 1903. † BRU 3, RA 3, RI 1.

LEWIS, Benjamin Archibald Exh. 1892-1938
Landscape painter. Morfa House, Carmarthen. † B 9, L 6, LS 18, RA 1, RCA 14.

LEWIS, B. Bannatyne Exh. 1938-40
Architect. London. † RA 3.

LEWIS, Charles James* 1830-1892
Landscape and figure painter. R.I. 1882, R.O.I. 1883. Add: London. † AG 3, B 31, D 7, GI 30, L 26, M 11, NG 1, RA 9, RBA 8, RHA 14, RI 72, ROI 26, TOO 8.

LEWIS, C.W. Mansel Exh. 1880-1905
Painter and etcher. R.E. 1881-1920. Add: Llanelly, Carmarthenshire 1880 and 1882; London 1881. † RA 4, RBA 1, RE 6.

LEWIS, Dione Tyrrell b. 1903
Landscape painter and illustrator. Studied Chelsea and Regent Street Polytechnic and Central School of Arts and Crafts. Exh. 1924-40. Add: London. † BK 26, NEA 2, RA 2, RBA 2, RI 6, SWA 11.

LEWIS, Eveleen Exh. 1880-96
Landscape painter. London. † L 9, RBA 10, RID 11.

LEWIS, Elizabeth E. Exh. 1885
9 Lidlington Place, Ampthill Square, London. † RHA 1.

LEWIS, Eileen I. Exh. 1937-38
12 Barnsley Road, Edgbaston, Birmingham. † B 1, NEA 1.

LEWIS, Edward Morland 1903-1943
Landscape, figure and coastal painter. b. Carmarthen, Wales. Studied St. Johns Wood and R.A. Schools. Member London Group 1932. Exh. 1929-40. Add: London. Died in Tunisia World War II. † AG 3, BK 1, COO 34, LEI 4, NEA 3, RCA 2.

LEWIS, E. Wansley Exh. 1932-39
Architect. London 1930; Weymouth 1937. † RA 5.

LEWIS, Miss F. Exh. 1896-1904
4 Blucher Street, Waterloo, Liverpool. † L 21.

LEWIS, Florence Exh. 1881
Miniature flower painter. 9 Stockwell Park Road, London. † RA 1.

LEWIS, Florence d. c.1917
Flower painter. A.S.W.A. 1914. Exh. 1902-17. Add: Fox Hill, Selsdon Road, South Croydon, Surrey. † B 5, BG 8, D 24, L 2, RA 1, RWS 1, SWA 36.

LEWIS, Mrs. Florence Exh. 1934
Flower painter. Wingfield, Bray, Co. Wicklow. † RHA 1.

LEWIS, Frederick Exh. 1882-99
Liverpool. † L 26, TOO 3.

LEWIS, Furley Exh. 1893-94
Charcoal landscape artist. Standard Hill, Nottingham. † N 3.

LEWIS, Miss G.M. Exh. 1892
Longton House, Rainhill, Lancs. † L 1.

LEWIS, Grace R. Exh. 1900
Miniature portrait painter. 46 Brixton Hill, London and 148 Rue de Vaugirard, Paris. † RA 4.

LEWIS, H.M. Exh. 1893
2 Connaught Square, London. † L 1.

LEWIS, Helen Vaughan b.1879
American artist. Exh. 1913. Add: Bryn Fedw, Irvington on Hudson, New York, U.S.A. † RA 2.

LEWIS, Isabel Exh. 1906-29
163 Selsdon Road, South Croydon, Surrey. † D 20, SWA 22.

LEWIS, Miss J. Exh. 1889-93
Flower painter. 17 Walpole Street, London. † SWA 2.

LEWIS, James Exh. 1923-26
Manchester. † RCA 2.

LEWIS, Janet Exh. 1891-94
Landscape painter. Chelsea, London 1891; Chelmsford, Essex 1892. † L 1, RI 2.

LEWIS, Mrs. Joseph Exh. 1887
Ivanhoe, 27 Carlyle Road, Edgbaston, Birmingham. † B 1.

LEWIS, J.A. Exh. 1885
Miniature portrait painter. 9 Lidlington Place, London. † RA 1.

LEWIS, John Hardwicke* 1840-1927
Portrait and landscape painter. b. India. Studied under his father and in Paris. Add: London 1880 and 1888; Hastings 1884; Guildford, Surrey 1885; Bromley, Kent 1897. † ALP 4, D 5, L 2, M 3, RA 13, RBA 5, RHA 5, ROI 2, WG 295.

LEWIS, John R. Exh. 1921-40
Watercolour landscape painter. b. Lincoln. Studied Lincoln School of Art and Bolton. Add: Conway, Wales. † B 11, L 5, RCA 90.

LEWIS, Lennard 1826-1913
Landscape and architectural painter. London. † B 18, D 7, G 1, GI 1, L 13, M 12, NG 11, RA 13, RBA 13, RHA 3, RI 8, ROI 2.

LEWIS, Mrs. Lennard Exh. 1880-90
Landscape painter. London. † SWA 6.

LEWIS, Miss M. Exh. 1891-97
9 Yewtree Road, Edgbaston, Birmingham. † B 4.

LEWIS, Mrs. M. Exh. 1908-9
The Manse, Blackwell, Nr. Alfreton, Notts. † N 3.

LEWIS, Mary Exh. 1894-1901
Miniature portrait painter. R.M.S. 1896. Add: London. † L 2, P 3, RA 7, RMS 12.

LEWIS, M.A. Exh. 1880
Landscape painter. 10 North Road, Clapham Park, London. † RBA 1.

LEWIS, Miss May Hardwicke Exh. 1907-24
Mrs. Redman. Landscape and figure painter. Daughter of John Hardwicke q.v. Add: Veyteaux, Vaud, Switzerland. † ALP 25, B 3. WG 135.

LEWIS, Mabel Terry Exh. 1896-1925
Mrs. Batley. Miniature portrait painter. Add: London 1896; Corscombe, Dorchester 1913; Zeals, Wilts. 1918; Hemel Hempstead, Herts. 1925. † NG 9, P 3, RA 6, RMS 3.

LEWIS, Percy Wyndham* 1884-1957
Painter, etcher and writer. Born on his father's yacht off Nova Scotia. Studied Slade School. Travelled with Spencer Gore on the continent 1902-8. Founder Member London Group 1913 and a founder of the Rebel Art Centre. Edited and contributed to "Blast". A collection of his works are in the Tate Gallery. Exh. 1904-39. Add: London. † BA 15, CAR 5, G 1, GOU 57, LEF 70, LEI 44, LS 7, M 1, RED 1.

LEWIS, Reginald Augustus b. 1901
Sculptor, portrait painter, modeller, stone and wood carver and teacher. b. Birmingham. Studied Birmingham Central School of Arts and Crafts (John Henry Chamberland medal for sculpture and design). Exh. 1932-40. Add: Sutton Coldfield 1932; London 1933 and 1937; Water Orton 1936. † B 4, RA 3.

LEWIS, Shelton Exh. 1880-83
Landscape painter. 2 Upper Cheyne Row, Chelsea, London. † GI 1, RBA 1.

LEWIS, Sydney b. 1883
Watercolour landscape and figure painter, pastellier and designer. b. Wiveliscombe, Som. Exh. 1913-25. Add: 68 York Avenue, Whalley Range, Manchester. † L 3, M 3, RCA 1, RI 1.

LEWIS, Stanley Cornwell b. 1905
Portrait painter and mural decorator. b. Cardiff. Studied Newport School of Art and Royal College of Art. Assistant master Newport School of Arts and Crafts. Exh. 1932-40. Add: Llwyn-On, Croes-y-Ceilog, nr. Newport, Mon. † RA 8.

LEWIS, Sylvia C. Exh. 1890
Landscape painter. Westhays, Putney Hill, London. † L 1, RBA 2.

LEWIS, Mrs. Theo Exh. 1919
3 Colchester Street, Pimlico, London. † NEA 2.

LEWIS, Tobias d.1916
Painter and etcher. Second master Brighton School of Art. Exh. 1911-14. Add: London 1911; Brighton 1913. † RA 2, RE 1.

LEWIS, Mrs. Tyrrell Exh. 1897-1907
11 Elvaston Place, Queen's Gate, London. † NG 6, RMS 1.

LEWIS, Tom Noyes Exh. 1898-1904
Landscape painter. High Barnet 1898; Lincoln's Inn, London 1904. † RA 3.

LEWIS, Mrs. Violet Exh. 1906
96 Sinclair Road, West Kensington, London. † RHA 1.

LEWIS, W. Exh. 1882-84
165 Balsall Heath Road, Birmingham. † B 2, M 1.

LEWIS, William George Blackmore Exh. 1883-95
Architect. Hackney, London. † L 5, RA 5.

LEWIS, William Lander Exh. 1903-10
Loxwood, Totteridge, Herts. 1903; Muswell Hill, London 1904; New Barnet, Herts. 1905. † D 15, LS 6.

LEY, A.S.R. Exh. 1911
214 Bishopsgate, London. † RA 1.

LEY, Beatrice Exh. 1907-14
c/o Messrs. Ireland, 21 Sheen Road, Richmond, Surrey. † LS 23, RA 1.

LEY, Margaret Exh. 1904-18
Mrs. Sewell. Miniature portrait painter. Add: Surbiton, Surrey 1906; Bushey, Herts. 1911 and 1918; Harrow Weald, Middlesex 1913. † RA 10, RMS 1.

LEY, Sophie Exh. 1899
c/o Mrs. Frank Trier, 6 The Terrace, Champion Hill, London. † SWA 2.

LEYCESTER, R. Neville Exh. 1883
Fruit and still life painter. 53 Warwick Road, South Kensington, London. † RBA 2.

LEYDE, Marion E. Exh. 1893-1902
17 St. Bernard's Crescent, Edinburgh. † RSA 15, RSW 3.

LEYDE, Otto Theodore* 1835-1897
Portrait painter and engraver. b. Wehlau, Prussia. Moved to Edinburgh as a youth and employed as a lithographic artist. R.E. 1881, A.R.S.A. 1870, R.S.A. 1880 (Librarian 1886-96) R.S.W. Add: 3 Douglas Crescent, Edinburgh 1880; 17 St. Bernard's Crescent, Edinburgh 1890. † DOW 6, GI 13, M 3, RA 2, RE 9, RSA 119, RSW 45.

LEYDEN, Ernst 1892-1969
Landscape painter. Exh. 1936. Add: 105 Charlotte Street, London. † RA 1.

LEZCANO, Carlos Exh. 1908-9
Alcaron 5, Madrid, Spain. † LS 4.

LHERMITTE, Leon Augustin* 1844-1925
Figure and landscape painter and etcher. R.E. 1881-89. Add: London 1880; Paris 1884. † GI 5, GOU 2, L 3, RA 3, RE 5.

LHOTE, Andre* 1885-1962
French painter. Exh. 1914. † ALP 1.

LHULLIER, Victor Exh. 1883-88
Etcher. London. † RA 2.

LIAS, James W. Exh. 1918-19
Illuminator. Newton Abbot, Devon 1918; Truro, Cornwall 1919. † RA 2.

LIBERTY, Octavia Exh. 1881-82
Flower painter. 2 Cranmore Street, Nottingham. † G 2, L 2, N 8.

LICHTENSTEIN, G. Exh. 1889
22 India Street. Edinburgh. † RSA 2.

LIDBETTER, Hubert Exh. 1923-37
Architect. London. † RA 22, RSA 1.

LIDDELL, D.E. Exh. 1926
† GOU 1.

LIDDELL, G.G. Exh. 1893
Binfield, Berks. † D 3.

LIDDELL, Mary Exh. 1940
97 Eaton Place, London. † NEA 1, SWA 1.

LIDDELL, Mary Francis Exh. 1892
Apsley Place, Glasgow. † GI 1.

LIDDELL, Thomas Hodgson 1860-1925
Landscape painter. R.B.A. 1905. Travelled widely. Add: Edinburgh 1882; London 1887, 1903 and 1911; Holywell, St. Ives, Hunts. 1890; Beer, Devon 1896; Pershore, Worcs. 1899 and 1908; Chepstow, Somerset 1922. † B 10, GI 1, L 3, LS 2, M 4, RA 17, RBA 46, RI 1, ROI 3, RSA 14, WG 83.

LIDDELL, William F. Exh. 1905-27
Watercolour painter. 105 Victoria Mansions, South Lambert Road, London. † L 18, RA 3, RI 4.

LIDDERDALE, Charles Sillem* 1831-1895
Genre painter. R.B.A. 1875. Add: London. † B 5, D 4, L 6, M 1, RA 3, RBA 3, TOO 1.

LIDDLE, Miss M. Exh. 1933
57a Barlow Moor Road, Didsbury, Manchester. † L 1.

LIE, Emil b. 1897
Norwegian sculptor. Studied Ecole des Beaux Arts, Paris 1916-19, and Rome. Exh. 1933. Add: Kunstuernes Hus, Oslo. † RSA 2.

LIEBERMANN, Professor Max* 1847-1935
German painter. Exh. 1900-11. Add: Berlin. † GI 2, I 13, M 3, P 1.

LIEBERT, E.M. Exh. 1899
Capellstrasse 6, Dusseldorf, Germany. † L 1.

LIEDTKE, Minnie Marie Exh. 1909
† LS 3.

LIEPMANN, Louisa Exh. 1890
40 Lexham Gardens, London. † GI 1.

LIERRES, de see D

LIEVIN-BAUWENS, M. Felicia Exh. 1934-40
Landscape and figure painter. London 1934; Amberley, Sussex 1940. † NEA 3, RA 2, RBA 4, ROI 2.

LIFTON, Walter Exh. 1883
4 Regent Street, Gloucester. † B 2.

LIGAT, J. Exh. 1888
Myrtle Bank, Rutherglen, N.B. † GI 1.

LIGER, Miss E.S. Exh. 1903
11 Durham Terrace, London. † SWA 1.

LIGERON, J. Rene Exh. 1910
10 Place d'Italie, Paris. † L 1.

LIGHT, Ernest W. Exh. 1932
13 St. John Street, Hanley, Stoke on Trent, Staffs. † B 1.

LIGHTBODY, Alex Exh. 1891
Braidwood, Carluke, N.B. † L 1.

LIGHTBODY, Robert Exh. 1883-89
Landscape painter. Elmsley Road, Mossley Hill, Liverpool. † B 1, D 1, L 2, M 4, RI 1.

LIGHTFOOT, Harold H. Exh. 1915-22
Engine Inn, St. Helens, Lancs. † L 4.

LIGHTFOOT, Maxwell Gordon 1886-1911
Portrait, figure and landscape painter. Exh. 1907-10. Add: 3 Dovedale Road, Mossley Hill, Liverpool. † CAR 4, L 4, NEA 3.

LIGHTFOOT, Robert Exh. 1921
55 Halkyn Road, Hoole, Chester. † L 2.

LIGHTFOOT, Thomas E. Exh. 1930-31
Watercolour painter. 6 Gainsborough Studios, Bedford Park, London. † RA 2.

LIGHTON, Sir Christopher Robert, Bt. Exh. 1891-93
Watercolour painter. 9 Codrington Place, Brighton. † D 1, L 3, RI 1.

LIGHTOWLER, Frank Exh. 1909-26
8 Heywood Street, Moss Side, Manchester. † M 1, L 1.

LIGHTOWLER, Mrs. Nellie Exh. 1929
2 Park Road, Whalley Range, Manchester. † L 1.

LILEY, Ethel Exh. 1926
Derwent House, Roby, Liverpool. † L 1.

LILEY, Henry G. Exh. 1880-91
Decorative architect. London. † RA 7.

LILEY, W. Exh. 1921
† NEA 1.

LILJEFORS, Bruno* b.1860
Swedish landscape and animal painter. Exh. 1905. Add: Morki, Sweden. † I 1.

LILLEY, Albert E.V. Exh. 1892-1940
Landscape painter. Birmingham 1892; Municipal School of Art, Wolverhampton 1898; Municipal School of Art, Leamington 1911; School of Arts and Crafts, Dudley 1916; School of Arts and Crafts, Sheffield 1922; Leamington Spa, Warwicks. 1930. † B 119, RA 13, RI 1.

LILLEY, Constance Exh. 1889-96
Sefton Park, Liverpool. † L 2.

LILLEY, Catherine A. Exh. 1887-1910
Flower painter. Moseley, Birmingham 1887; Thorpe le Soken, Essex 1899; Weeley, Essex 1906. † B 40, BG 3, RA 4.

LILLEY, Elizabeth A. Exh. 1885-1907
Figure painter. 7 Canterbury Road, Brixton, London. † RA 5, RBA 3, RI 3, SWA 3.

LILLEY, H.R. Exh. 1914-22
Belfast. † GI 3, L 10, RHA 41, RSA 5.

LILLEY, Miss R.S. Exh. 1907
Brixton, London. † SWA 1.

LILLIE, A. Exh. 1888
67 Wynnstay Gardens, Kensington, London. † D 1.

LILLIE, Charles T. Exh. 1882
Landscape and flower painter. 3 Wynchcombe Studios, Haverstock Hill, London. † RBA 2.

LILLIE, Nesta Exh. 1913
Tynecote, Bushey, Herts. † L 1.

LILLIE, Robert Exh. 1892-1940
Painter. London 1892; Milngavie 1919. † GI 21, L 8, RA 2, RI 5, ROI 4, RSA 5.

LILLINGSTON, G.B.P. Exh. 1880-99
Watercolour landscape and marine painter. Leamington, Warwicks 1880; Edgbaston, Birmingham 1882; Exmouth 1883; Cheltenham, Glos. 1887; Penzance 1898. † B 3, D 10, L 3, RA 1, RBA 2.

LILLY, Marjorie Exh. 1919-40
Painter and linocut artist. London. † BG 25, LS 3, NEA 1, RBA 2, RED 1, ROI 3, WG 19.

LIM, Kae Keong Exh. 1926
Miniature painter. 4 Briardale Gardens, Hampstead, London. † RA 1.

LIMBURG, Ir. junr. Exh. 1936
† RSA 1.

LIMONT, M. Evangeline Exh. 1921-24
133 St. Julian's Farm Road, West Norwood, London. † D 10, L 1, LS 3.

LIMRICK, Mary Frances Rose b.1890
Painter, and linocut artist. b. Liverpool. A.N.S.A. 1929. Exh. 1920-29. Add: Wallasey, Cheshire 1920; Carlton, Notts. 1929. † L 3, N 1.

LIN, Clifton Exh. 1884-87
Flower painter. Studied under Whistler. Add: London. † G 3, RBA 10.

LINCOLN, F.W. Exh. 1935
30 Hooking Green, North Harrow, Middlesex. † RBA 1.

LIND, Inez M. Exh. 1924-28
Rockwood, Sandown Park, Wavertree, Liverpool. † L 3.

LINDAY, Agnes A. Exh. 1935-38
Mrs. Waldmeyer. Landscape painter. Green Meadow, Broadgate, Beeston, Notts. † N 7.

LINDEMAN, Agnes Exh. 1928-32
Acocks Green, Birmingham. † B 13, GOU 2.

LINDEN, E.V.D. Exh. 1881
Sculptor. 50 Upper Marylebone Street, Portland Place, London. † RA 1.

LINDEN, Florence Exh. 1907
49 St. Paul's Road, Camden Square, London. † ROI 1.

LINDEN, G. Exh. 1890-91
Latimer House, Church Street, Chiswick, London. † B 2, ROI 2.

LINDER, Miss P. Exh. 1885
Watercolour figure painter. c/o Mr. J. Grierson, 5 Rathbone Place, London. † RA 1.

LINDHE, Ivan Exh. 1904-14
Portrait painter. 65 Glebe Place, Chelsea, London. † D 4, L 2, LS 8, RA 5, RI 4.

LINDLEY, Alice Exh. 1908-22
Sculptor. Godley, Cheshire 1908; Mottram in Longendale, Manchester 1914; London 1922. † L 2, M 1, RA 2, RCA 3.

LINDLEY, Charles Exh. 1936-37
Landscape and coastal painter. 60 Bromham Road, Bedford. † RA 1, RI 1.

LINDLEY, Edgar Exh. 1898
46 Rue Jouffroy, Paris. † B 2, M 1.

LINDLEY, Helenor Exh. 1886-96
Watercolour flower and still life painter. Redcliffe, Mapperley Road, Nottingham. † N 9.

LINDLEY, Maude Exh. 1907-27
London 1907; Guildford, Surrey 1921. † L 3, RA 4, RMS 1.

LINDLEY, Max Exh. 1896
Ye Hutte, Cookham Dene, Berks. † L 1.

LINDNER, Augusta Baird Exh. 1898-1933
nee Smith. Landscape and flower painter. Married Moffat Peter L. q.v. Add: St. Ives, Cornwall. † B 1, RA 2, RBA 2.

LINDNER, Daphne b. 1912
Painter and etcher. b. Charlton, Glos. Studied Cheltenham School of Art and Royal College of Art (scholarship, Robert Austin Prizeman and silver medalist). A.R.E. 1935. Exh. 1934-37. Add: Ravensgate, Charlton Lane, Cheltenham and Chelsea, London. † RA 3, RE 12.

LINDNER, Doris L.M. Exh. 1927
Sculptor. Poplar Cottage, Addlestone, Surrey. † RA 1.

LINDNER, G.M. Exh. 1887-89
Landscape painter. London 1887; Steyning, Sussex 1888. † D 10.

LINDNER, Moffat Peter* 1852-1949
Landscape and marine painter. b. Birmingham. Studied Slade School and Heatherleys. Married Augusta Baird L. q.v. N.E.A. 1889, R.B.A. 1888, R.I. 1906, R.O.I. 1903, A.R.W.S. 1917. Add: London and St. Ives, Cornwall. † ALP 1, B 37, D 3, FIN 63, G 7, GI 22, GOU 6, I 4, L 70, LS 4, M 31, NEA 73, NG 24, RA 68, RBA 12, RHA 13, RI 35, RID 75, ROI 52, RSA 1, RWS 165, TOO 12.

LINDQUIST, Miss E. Exh. 1901-3
Sculptor. 28 Langdon Park Road, Highgate, London. † RA 1, SWA 5.

LINDSAY, Lady Blanche (of Balcarres) d. 1912
nee Fitzroy. Watercolour painter. Married Sir Coutts L. Bt. q.v. R.I. 1879. Exh. 1880-1903. Add: London. † B 2, FIN 2, G 20, GI 1, L 4, M 6, NG 8, RHA 1, RI 37, ROI 1, RSA 1, SWA 1.

LINDSAY, Sir Coutts, Bt. 1824-1907
Painter and watercolourist. Founder of the Grosvenor Gallery in 1878. The separation from his wife Blanche L. q.v. led to its closure in 1890 and the founding of the New Gallery. R.I. 1879. Exh. 1880-98. Add: London. † G 18, GI 2, L 2, M 5, RI 5, ROI 2.

LINDSAY, Daryl* b. 1891
Landscape painter. b. Creswick, Victoria, Australia. Probably brother of Lionel and Norman L. q.v. Studied Slade School. Director National Gallery of Victoria 1939-41, A.R.W.S. 1938. Exh. 1933-40. Add: c/o Chapman Bros. Kings Road, London. † CG 41, RWS 18, TOO 34.

LINDSAY, George Exh. 1886
5 Airlee Terrace, Dundee. † RSA 1.

LINDSAY, Gertrude Exh. 1902-35
Watercolour figure and miniature painter and illustrator. Studied R.A. Schools (3 silver medals). Add: Rugby 1902; London 1924. † B 4, L 27, RA 9.

LINDSAY, Helen Exh. 1931-33
Cleland, nr. Glasgow 1931; Wishaw, nr. Glasgow 1933. † GI 2.

LINDSAY, Ian Gordon b. 1906
Architect. Studied at Cambridge Architectural School. Exh. 1939. Add: 21 Alva Street, Edinburgh. † RSA 2.

LINDSAY, James Exh. 1881-1906
Glasgow 1881; Largs, N.B. 1906. † GI 19.

LINDSAY, J. Seymour Exh. 1940
46 Dover Street, London. † RI 1.

LINDSAY, Lionel* b. 1874
Watercolour painter, etcher and drypoint artist. b. Creswick, Victoria, Australia. Probably brother of Daryl and Norman L. q.v. Exh. 1927-37. Add: c/o Colnaghi and Co. New Bond Street, London. † AB 19, BA 6, CG 122, CON 4, FIN 3, GI 2, RA 3, RHA 6.

LINDSAY, Hon. Mrs. Lloyd Exh. 1883
Lady Wantage. Painter. 2 Carlton Gardens, London. † D 2.

LINDSAY, Mrs. N. Exh. 1913
5 Leighton Studios, 38 Redcliffe Road, London. † RA 1.

LINDSAY, Norman* b. 1879
Etcher and watercolour painter. b. Creswick, Victoria, Australia. Probably brother of Daryl and Lionel L. q.v. Exh. 1925-28. † AB 4, LEI 52.

LINDSAY, Mrs. Ruth Exh. 1880-87
Fruit and flower painter. Married Thomas M.L. q.v. Add: Art Museum, Rugby. † B 1, D 1, L 2, M 2, RHA 1, SWA 1.

LINDSAY, Tom b. 1882
Animal and life painter, etcher and photographer. Studied Glasgow School of Art. Exh. 1908-40. Add: Busby, N.B. 1908; Clarkston, nr. Glasgow 1914. † GI 10, RSA 2.

LINDSAY, Thomas M. Exh. 1880-1910
Landscape painter. Married Ruth L. q.v. Add: Art Museum, Rugby 1880; Blundellsands, Liverpool 1909. † B 13, L 19, M 10, RA 9, RHA 3, RI 1.

LINDSAY, Violet see RUTLAND

LINDSAY, W. Caird Exh. 1893-98
5 Glenavon Terrace, Partick. † GI 3.

LINDSAY, William K. Exh. 1936-39
2 Boswall Terrace, Edinburgh. † RSA 2.

LINDSELL, Violet Thorpe Exh. 1912-27
Watercolour painter. Oundle, Northants. 1912; Dunchurch, Rugby 1916. † L 1, SWA 6, WG 49.

LINDSEY, S. Arthur Exh. 1902-40
Miniature painter. R.M.S. 1907, V.P.R.M.S. from 1919. Hon. Treas. R.M.S. from 1920, H.R.M.S. 1929. Add: Southbourne, Hants. 1902; Bournemouth 1918; London 1920. † L 31, NG 2, RA 33, RI 3, RMS 140.

LINDSLEY-SIMS, Mrs. Elsie Mary Exh. 1922-24
nee Davey. Watercolour landscape and portrait painter, modeller, metal and leather worker, embroiderer and lecturer. Studied Royal College of Art and Leeds, Wolverhampton, and Taunton Schools of Art. Add: Park House, Wellington, Salop. † B 1, L 1, RCA 2, SWA 1.

LINDSTROM, Arvid M. Exh. 1882-87
Landscape painter. London. † B 3, L 4, M 2, RA 6, RBA 1, ROI 1.

LINEHAM, J. Exh. 1914
108 Palewell Park, East Sheen, London. † L 1, RA 1.

LINEHAM, Wilfred J. Exh. 1905-15
21 Newstead Road, Lee, London. † LS 20, RA 4, RI 1.

LINES, Miss F.A. Exh. 1918
Yoxford, Suffolk. † SWA 1.

LINES, Gladys b. 1894
nee Entwistle. b. Adlington, Lancs. Studied St. Anne's on Sea School of Art. Teacher of art Colwyn Bay, Wales. Exh. 1920-27. Add: Colwyn Bay, Wales. † RCA 2.

LINES, Henry Harris* 1801-1889
Landscape painter and teacher. Studied under David Cox. Add: 7 Albany Terrace, Worcester. † B 8.

LINES, Vincent 1909-1968
Painter, lithographer and etcher. Studied Central School of Arts and Crafts and Royal College of Art (travelling scholarship 1932). A.R.W.S. 1939. Add: London. † LEI 1, NEA 3, RA 5, RSA 3, RWS 14.

LINFORD, John E. Exh. 1931-33
16 Beauchamp Avenue, Leamington Spa, Warwicks. † B 4.

LINGARD, Henry Exh. 1884
Landscape painter. 3 Ealing Terrace, Ealing, London. † RA 1.

LINGSTROM, Freda b.1893
Poster designer and decorative landscape painter. Studied Central School of Arts and Crafts and Heatherleys. Commissioned by Norwegian and Swedish Governments to do drawings in Scandinavia for English travel propaganda. Exh. 1931. Add: London. † RBA 1.

LINGWOOD, Edna Exh. 1931
Etcher. 38 Clonmel Road, Teddington, Middlesex. † RA 2.

LINGWOOD, Edward J. Exh. 1884-1907
Landscape painter. Needham Market, Suffolk 1884; Dunwich, Suffolk 1894; Westleton, Suffolk 1906. † L 1, M 6, RA 21, RBA 1, RHA 2, ROI 1.

LINGWOOD, Mrs. Mildred Exh. 1907-9
Bedford Park, London. † B 5, GI 1, L 3, M 1, RA 1.

LINKLATER, Rev. M.H. Exh. 1887-88
Watercolour landscape painter and architect. Sneinton, Nottingham. † N 5.

LINN, M. Exh. 1880
Pollokshields, Glasgow. † GI 1.

LINNELL, Mrs. Edith Madeline Exh. 1902-32
Designer and worker in precious metals. A.R.M.S. 1927. Add: Moseley, Birmingham 1902; London 1926. † B 2, L 591, LS 13.

LINNELL, John* 1792-1882
Landscape and portrait painter and engraver. Studied under John Varley and at R.A. Schools 1805. H.R.S.A. 1871, R.W.S. 1812. A Collection of his works are in the Tate Gallery. Father of James Thomas, Thomas G. and William L. q.v. Add: Redhill, Surrey. † GI 2, RA 1.

LINNELL, James Thomas* 1820-1905
Landscape painter. Second son of John L. q.v. Exh. 1882-88. Add: Redhill, Surrey. † M 1, RA 5, ROI 1.

LINNELL, Laurence G. Exh. 1909-26
Watercolour landscape painter and pastelier. West House, St. Stephen's Road, Leicester. † FIN 60, N 2, WG 79.

LINNELL, Miss M. Exh. 1908
60 St. Stephens Road, Leicester. † N 3.

LINNELL, Margaret Exh. 1906-25
Watercolour painter of gardens. Add: Hampstead, London. † SWA 4, WG 72.

LINNELL, Thomas George* c.1836-1911
Landscape painter. Youngest son of John L. q.v. Exh. 1881-84. Add: Tonbridge, Kent 1881; Redhill, Surrey 1882. † D 2, GI 2, L 1, RA 2, RBA 2, RI 1, ROI 2.

LINNELL, William* 1826-1906
Landscape and rustic genre painter. Eldest son of John L. q.v. Exh. 1880-93. Add: Redhill, Surrey 1880; London 1883. † GI 1, L 4, M 2, RA 11.

LINNEY, E. Exh. 1904
13 Norton Lees Road, Sheffield. † L 1.

LINO, Selvatico Exh. 1905
Alla Maddalena, Venice. † I 1.

LINSLEY, W.D. Exh. 1904
Landscape and coastal painter. 84 Serpentine Road, Liscard, Cheshire. † L 1.

LINTON, John Exh. 1940
Muirhead of Liff, Angus. † RSA 1.

LINTON, Sir James Dromgole* 1840-1916
Figure, portrait and historical painter and lithographer. Studied at J.M. Leigh's Art School. A.R.I. 1867, R.I. 1870, P.R.I. 1884-99 and 1909-16, H.R.M.S. 1896, H.P.R.M.S. 1910, R.O.I. 1883, P.R.O.I. 1883, R.S.W. 1884. Knighted 1885. Father of Violet L. q.v. Add: London. † AG 9, B 7, BG 1, D 1, FIN 72, G 3, GI 7, L 21, LEI 2, M 15, NG 17, P 2, RA 19, RCA 2, RHA 1, RI 72, RMS 3, ROI 39, RSW 14.

LINTON, James W.R. Exh. 1890-1909
Figure painter. London. † L 1, M 1, RBA 1, RI 9, ROI 5.

LINTON, Muriel Exh. 1911-16
Potter. b. Hay, N.S.W. Australia. Studied Grosvenor School and Slade School. Add: 37 St. Margaret's Road, Oxford. † L 4, RA 4.

LINTON, Thomas Exh. 1911-12
8 Albyn Place, Edinburgh. † RSA 2.

LINTON, Thomas McCracken Exh. 1938
Landscape painter. 27 Ravensdene Park, Belfast. † RHA 1.

LINTON, Violet Exh. 1899-1940
Mrs. T.J. Cheater. Painter and miniaturist. Daughter of Sir James D.L. q.v. Studied Royal College of Art and the Royal Drawing Society. Add: London. † L 51, NG 1, RA 11, RI 49, RMS 11, ROI 24, SWA 8.

LINTON, William Evans b. 1878
Landscape and animal painter and author. b. Portishead, Somerset. Assistant art master Clifton College. Exh. 1909-32. Add: Bushey, Herts. 1909; Oxhey, Watford, Herts. 1911; Clifton, Bristol 1913. † RA 6, RCA 12, RI 1, ROI 3.

LINTOTT, Mrs. Audrey Exh. 1933-40
Lived at the same addresses in Edinburgh as Henry L. q.v. † GI 2, RSA 10.

LINTOTT, Edith Exh. 1908-19
Lived at the same addresses in Edinburgh as Henry L. q.v. † B 2, RSA 11.

LINTOTT, Edward Bernard b. 1875
Portrait and landscape painter and author. b. London. Studied at Juliens, and Ecole des Beaux Arts and the Sorbonne, Paris. Exh. 1910-35. Add: Fittleworth, Sussex 1910; London 1912 and 1918; Greenford, Middlesex 1916; Weybridge, Surrey 1935. † CG 1, CHE 50, FIN 2, G 9, GI 16, GOU 38, I 31, L 12, LEF 37, LEI 64, M 2, NEA 19, P 4, RA 21.

LINTOTT, Henry b. 1877
Painter. A.R.S.A. 1916, R.S.A. 1923. Exh. 1904-40. Lived at various addresses in Edinburgh with Audrey and Edith L. q.v. † B 2, GI 56, I 2, L 25, RA 13, RI 1, RSA 87, RSW 3.

LINTOTT, Harry Chanen 1880-1918
Miniature portrait painter. A.R.M.S. 1907, R.M.S. 1909. Died of wounds received on the Western Front whilst serving with Artists Rifles World War I. Exh. 1900-18. Add: London. † L 8, NG 1, RA 7, RMS 25.

LINTOTT, Miss K. Exh. 1889
Flower painter. Parkfield, Horsham, Sussex. † SWA 1.

LINTZ, Ernest Exh. 1880-91
Figure and portrait painter. London 1880 and 1884, Huddersfield 1883. † B 1, G 2, GI1, L 2, P 1, RA 3, RBA 6, RHA 1, ROI 4.

LINYARD, A. Exh. 1932
† L 1.

LINYARD, Joseph b.1897
Sculptor. b. Keighley, Yorks. Studied Liverpool City School of Art. Exh. 1925-27. Add: Ro-Brandt, Milner Road, Heswall Hills, Cheshire. † L 5.

LINZELL, Dorothy M. Exh. 1923
Stanley House, Orwell Road, Felixstowe. † L 1.

LION, Flora 1876-1958
Portrait, figure and landscape painter. Studied R.A. Schools and Juliens, Paris. R.O.I. 1909, R.P. 1913. Exh. 1899-1937. Add: London. † B 1, BAR 53, BRU 2, CHE 1, FIN 41, G 4, GI 5, GOU 2, I 17, L 24, LS 3, NG 2, P 83, RA 51, RBA 1, ROI 32, SWA 8.

LIPCZINSKI, Albert Exh. 1906-13
Liverpool. † L 15.

LIPSCOMBE, Edith Mabel Exh. 1909-29
Landscape painter. Studied at Colarossi's Paris and under Norman Garstin. Add: Bolton, Lancs. 1909; Boxmoor, Herts. 1926, St. Albans, Herts. 1927. † ALP 5, D 13, G 1, LS 12, RA 9.

LIPSCOMBE, Guy Exh. 1908-37
Painter. London. † AB 7, D 2, L 6, LS 5, RA 4, ROI 6.

LIPSCOMBE, Jessie b. 1861
Mrs. Elborne. Sculptor. Studied in London and Paris. Exh. 1885-87. Add: Peterborough. † RA 3.

LIPSON, Mollie Exh. 1924
Lowwood, Queen's Drive, Moseley Hill, Liverpool. † L 1.

LISHMAN, Frank Exh. 1911-38
Watercolour architectural painter. London 1911; North Curry, Taunton, Somerset 1926; Burnham, Somerset 1928. † L 1, RA 4, WG 82.

LISLE, de see D

LISLE, Alice F. Exh. 1909-14
Collaborated with Blanche Waldron, q.v. Add: 7 Alma Road, Portswood, Southampton. † L 99.

LISLE, B. Exh. 1909-12
Architect. 43 Devereux Road, London. † RA 2.

LISLE, Harold Exh. 1911-40
Miniature portrait painter. London. † RA 9, RMS 2.

LISLE, John W. Exh. 1904-20
Stained glass and bookplate designer, West Ealing, London. † RA 7.

LISMORE, William b. 1886
Watercolour miniature painter, illuminator and etcher. Studied Kensington School of Art, Bristol and Royal College of Art. Assistant art master St. Albans School of Art. Exh. 1919-38. Add: St. Albans, Herts. † RA 2, RI 1.

LISSMORE, Charles Exh. 1883
Painter. 7 Harley Street, London. † ROI 2.

LISTER, Hon. Beatrix Exh. 1881
† G 1.

LISTER, Elizabeth Exh. 1929-32
Landscape and portrait painter. 39 Sloane Street, London. † BA 54, WG 1.

LISTER, Lady Evelyn Exh. 1907
64 Cadogan Square, London. † NG 1.

LISTER, Edward D'Arcy b. 1911
Painter and colour print artist. Studied Leeds College of Art 1928-33 and Royal College of Art 1933-37. Add: London 1935, Horsforth, Leeds 1939. † RA 2.

LISTER, E.M. Exh. 1882-1911
Watercolour landscape and flower painter. Leytonstone, Essex 1882. † BG 3, D 1, RBA 1.

LISTER, Fanny Dove Hamel b. 1864
Mrs. Calder. Painter and illustrator and stained glass, bookplate and frieze designer. b. Liverpool. Studied Liverpool School of Architecture and Applied Art under Anning Bell, Augustus John and David Muirhead. Exh. 1903-22. † BK 34, L 1.

LISTER, George Exh. 1881-82
Painter. Arts Club, Hanover Square, London. † RBA 2.

LISTER, Henrietta b. 1895
Landscape painter. Studied Byam Shaw and Vicat Cole School 1912-14. Exh. 1939. Add: Redmire, Leyburn, Yorks. † RA 2.

LISTER, May Exh. 1893-1920
Miniature portrait painter. R.M.S. 1897. Add: London. † L 1, RA 5, RHA 1, RMS 7.

LISTER, Miss M.M. Exh. 1905
38 Pembridge Villas, Bayswater, London. † RA 1.

LISTER, Sir Villiers Exh. 1899-1900
64 Cadogan Square, London. † M 1, NG 1.

LISTER, Walter Llewellyn 1876-1951
Watercolour painter and colour print artist. Studied Westminster School of Art and St. Martins School of Art (1900-4). Exh. 1894-1933. Add: London. † M 1, RBA 1, ROI 1.

LITCHFIELD, Dorothy Fraser Exh. 1917-21
Portrait painter. R.P. 1920. Add: 73 Bedford Gardens, Campden Hill, London. † GI 3, I 3, L 4, NEA 1, P 8, RA 4, SWA 2.

LITHERLAND, Ida Exh. 1900
191 Malmesbury Road, Bow, London. † RBA 3.

LITHERLAND, Roland H. Exh. 1938
† M 1.

LITHIBY, Beatrice Ethel b. 1889
Landscape and figure painter. Studied R.A. Schools. R.B.A. 1930. Exh. 1920-39. Add: London. † L 2, M 2, RA 5, RBA 53, RI 2, SWA 21, WG 66.

LITTEN, Sydney Mackenzie b. 1887
Painter, etcher, engraver and mezzotint artist. Studied St. Martin's School of Art and Royal College of Art. Exh. 1915-40. Add: London. † AB 1, BK 3, CG 56, GOU 1, I 1, NEA 5, RA 10, RBA 6, RHA 1, WG 42.

LITTLE, Mrs. B. Winifred Exh. 1924
Miniature portrait painter. 2 Templeton Place, Earl's Court, London. † RA 1.

LITTLE, Miss C.V.F. Exh. 1908
Coburg House, Millbrook, Plymouth. † RA 1.

LITTLE, Emily Exh. 1883-1902
Figure and portrait painter. London. † B 2, L 5, NG 8, RA 3.

LITTLE, Elspeth A. Exh. 1926-31
53 Ledbury Road, London. † NEA 3.

LITTLE, Edith J. Exh. 1881-88
34 Palmerston Place, Edinburgh. † GI 7, RSA 5.

LITTLE, G. Leon Exh. 1884-1926
Landscape and portrait painter. London 1884; Rudgwick, nr. Horsham, Sussex 1888; Kingswood, Reigate, Surrey 1900. † GOU 13, L 4, NEA 1, RA 3, RBA 7.

LITTLE, Helen Exh. 1905-10
17 Keir Street, Edinburgh. † RSA 3.

LITTLE, James Exh. 1880-1910
14 West Laureston Place, Edinburgh 1880; 34 St. Andrew Square, Edinburgh 1885; 17 Keir Street, Edinburgh 1899. † GI 4, RSA 58.

LITTLE, J. Raymond Exh. 1930
† L 1.

LITTLE, John W. Exh. 1922-30
The Cedars, Tonbridge, Kent. † GOU 1, RCA 3.

LITTLE, L.S. Exh. 1881
Kirkcaldy. † RSA 1.

LITTLE, N. Exh. 1907-9
12 The Boltons Studios, South Kensington, London. † LS 3, RA 1.

LITTLE, Owen C. Exh. 1921-22
Architect. London. † RA 2.

LITTLE, Robert 1854-1944
Painter and lithographer. b. Greenock. Studied Glasgow University, R.S.A. Schools 1876-81, British Academy, Rome and under Dagnan Bouveret in Paris 1886. R.O.I. 1901, R.S.W. 1885 (resigned 1904, re-elected 1910) H.R.S.W. 1936, A.R.W.S. 1892, R.W.S. 1899, V.P.R.W.S. 1913-16. Add: Edinburgh 1880; London 1890; St. Ives, Cornwall 1919; East Grinstead, Sussex 1926. † AR 1, B 7, D 5, DOW 6, FIN 68, GI 69, GOU 14, L 32, LEI 72, LS 1, M 13, NG 5, RA 15, RI 8, ROI 30, RSA 74, RSW 128, RWS 288, WG 35.

LITTLEBOY, M. Clare Exh. 1935
Wrexham. † RCA 2.

LITTLEBURY, M. Alma Exh. 1913-29
Mrs. Shilllito. London 1913; Purley, Surrey 1921; Birkenhead 1929. † L 5, RA 4,

LITTLEBY, Miss A.E. Exh. 1911-13
The Woodlands, Saltburn by the Sea, Yorks. † D 3.

LITTLEDALE, Miss E.P. Exh. 1916-20
187 Upper Parliament Street, Liverpool. † L 3.

LITTLEDALE, Henry A.P. Exh. 1933-40
Miniature portrait painter and enamellist A.R.M.S. 1938. Add: Crab Tree, Streatley on Thames, Berks. † B 16, RA 1, RMS 11.

LITTLEDALE, Mrs. Mildred Exh. 1939
Crab Tree, Streatley on Thames, nr. Reading, Berks. † B 1.

LITTLEJOHN, Henry E. Exh. 1901
3 Warrender Park Terrace, Edinburgh. † RSA 1.

LITTLEJOHNS, Mrs. Idalia Blanche Exh. 1922-36
Painter, writer and lecturer. Married John L. q.v. Add: 4 Brook Green Studios, London. † D 11, ROI 3, SWA 1, WG 40.

LITTLEJOHNS, John b. 1874
Painter, illustrator, lecturer and writer. b. Orchard Hill, nr. Bideford, Devon. Pupil-teacher of drawing at Bideford School of Art at age 16. Married Idalia Blanch L. q.v. R.B.A. 1919, R.I. 1931. Exh. 1911-40. Add: London. † D 12, FIN 61, G 1, I 2, L 1, RA 6, RBA 163, RCA 16, RI 51, RID 4, ROI 2, WG 66.

LITTLER, Emily Exh. 1900-11
Miniature portrait painter. Jocelyns, Sawbridgeworth, Herts. † RA 3, RMS 2.

LITTLER, Frank E. Exh. 1887-88
Architect. 12 Storey's Gate, London. † RA 2.

LITTLER, H. Exh. 1906
16 Ribblesdale Place, Preston, Lancs. † RA 1.

LITTLER, Joseph Exh. 1885
Watercolour illustrative painter. † RBA 1.

LITTLER, William Farran* Exh. 1887-92
Portrait painter. Pimlico, London. † RA 1, ROI 1.

LITTLETON, Miss L.A. Exh. 1880-83
Chidcock, nr. Bridport, Dorset. † GI 2.

LITTLEWOOD, James Exh. 1887
Flower painter. 25 Bramham Gardens, Witherley Road, South Kensington, London. † RBA 1.

LITTLEWOOD, W.H. Exh. 1882-1913
Manchester. † L 3, M 13, RA 1.

LIVEN, Francis Exh. 1933
6 Porthmeor Studios, St. Ives, Cornwall. † RBA 2.

LIVENS, Amie S. Exh. 1927
Sculptor. Manor House, East End Road, Finchley, London. † RA 1.

LIVENS, Miss Dora B. Exh. 1892-94
Figure painter. Mansfield, West Croydon, Surrey. † RBA 7.

LIVENS, Horace Mann* 1862-1936
Landscape, flower and poultry painter, etcher and engraver. R.B.A. 1895. Member of Society of 25 Artists. Add: Mansfield, Croydon, Surrey 1888; Sutton, Surrey 1903; Hatch End, Middlesex 1912. † ALP 1, B 1, BA 14, BG 13, CG 5, CHE 2, G 77, GI 13, GOU 244, I 182, L 21, M 1, NEA 7, P 14, RA 26, RBA 94, RHA 3, RI 9, ROI 18, RSA 10, RSW 3.

LIVERTON, Thomas Alfred b. 1907
Painter, designer, black and white and commercial artist. b. Barnstaple. Studied at Bromley and Beckenham Schools of Art 1924-28, and Royal College of Art 1928-32. Exh. 1935-37. Add: Bromley, Kent 1935; Park Langley, Beckenham, Kent 1937. † RA 2.

LIVESAY, Miss F. Exh. 1880-1914
Watercolour landscape painter. Sandrock Spring, Chale, I.O.W. † D 29, L 1, LS 3, RA 2, RSA 5, SWA 2.

LIVESAY, F.T.B. Exh. 1933-34
35 St. George's Road, London. † SWA 2.

LIVESAY, G.A. Bligh Exh. 1899-1913
Architect. Boscombe, Hants. 1899; Parkstone, Dorset 1913. † RA 3.

LIVESAY, Rose M. Exh. 1897
Mural designer. 27 Bramham Gardens, Earl's Court, London. † RA 2.

LIVESAY, William Exh. 1882-84
Sudbury, Derby. † L 2, RE 2.

LIVESEY, Miss P. Exh. 1900-1
5 York Villas, Anfield, Liverpool. † L 3.

LIVETT, Ursula Exh. 1928-31
Painter and etcher. Reigate 1928; Canterbury 1931. † NEA 5, RA 2.

LIVINGSTONE, Miss E.G. Exh. 1893
7 St. German's Place, Blackheath, London. † L 1.

LIVINGSTONE, Isobel T. Exh. 1905-7
Westfield, Shawlands, N.B. † GI 3.

LIVINGSTONE, Jessie M. Exh. 1892-1910
7 St. German's Place, Blackheath, London 1892; Spring Grove, Isleworth, Middlesex 1909. † B 3, GI 1, L 3, LS 6.

LIVINGSTONE, Jessie W.S. Exh. 1888-1913
17 Hill Street, Wishaw, N.B. † GI 4, RSA 5.

LIVINGSTONE, Mrs. Nan C. Exh. 1900-40
3 St. Bernard's Crescent, Edinburgh. † B 7, GI 4, L 5, RSA 17, RSW 3.

LIVOCK, Stanley G. Exh. 1932-39
Architect. 21 Bedford Square, London. † RA 4.

LIVSEY, Gwyneth M. Exh. 1923-36
Liverpool 1923; London 1930. † L 9, P 2, ROI 9.

LLEWELLYN, Bernard H. Exh. 1933-36
29 Shaftmoor Lane, Acocks Green, Birmingham. † B 8.

LLEWELLYN, Frederick A. Exh. 1921-40
Architect. H.M. Office of Works, King Charles Street, Westminster 1921; H.M. Office of Works, Storey's Gate, London 1932. † RA 33, RSA 1.

LLEWELLYN, Marion Exh. 1896-1913
nee Meates. Miniature portrait painter. R.M.S. 1900. Married William H.S.L. q.v. Add: London. † GI 2, L 4, NG 24, RA 24, RMS 5.

LLEWELLYN, Sir William Samuel Henry* c.1860-1941
Portrait and landscape painter. b. Cirencester. Studied Royal College of Art 1879-80 and under J. Lefebvre and G. Ferrier in Paris. Married Marion L. q.v. N.E.A. 1887, A.R.A. 1912, R.A. 1920, P.R.A. 1928-38, R.B.A. 1888, R.E. 1929, R.I. 1918, H.R.M.S. 1930, R.O.I. 1898, H.R.O.I. 1929, R.P. 1891. Member of Society of 25 Artists. Knighted c. 1918. "Sailing at Blakeney" purchased by Chantrey Bequest 1938. Add: London. † B 10, G 11, GI 8, I 2, L 48, M 7, NEA 2, NG 50, P 46, RA 169, RBA 22, RE 2, RHA 2, RI 5, ROI 45.

LLEWELLYN, Victor Exh. 1937-39
Cardiff. † RCA 3.

LLEWELYN, Miss L.C.D. Exh. 1898-99
118 Earl's Court Road, London. † SWA 2.

LLIMONA, Rafael Exh. 1937
Landscape and figure painter. † BA 2.

LLOYD, Miss Exh. 1917
† P 1.

LLOYD, Mrs. Alin Exh. 1912
Painter and etcher. Manor House, Sudborough, nr. Thrapston, Northants. † ALP 17.

LLOYD, Andrew Exh. 1881
Landscape painter. 28 Oakley Crescent, Chelsea, London. † RBA 1.

LLOYD, A.D. Exh. 1928
Otterspool Bank, Aigburth Vale, Liverpool. † L 1.

LLOYD, Miss Alwen M. Exh. 1909
Penzance, Cornwall. † SWA 1.

LLOYD, A.V. Exh. 1907-8
42 Arnold Street, Princes Road, Liverpool. † L 2.

LLOYD, Arthur Wynell b. 1883
Political cartoonist, illustrator (Essence of Parliament) in "Punch" and cartoonist to "News of the World". Exh. 1934. † COO 115.

LLOYD, Beatrice Exh. 1899-1900
24 Carlyle Mansions, Cheyne Walk, London. † SWA 2.

LLOYD, Benjamin b. 1868
Sculptor. b. Rhayader. Studied Guernsey and City and Guilds of London Institute. Worked with W.S. Frith for 5 years. Exh. 1896-1938. Add: London 1896; Rhayader, Radnorshire 1928. † L 6, LS 9, M 1, RA 5, RCA 3.

LLOYD, Miss C. Exh. 1904
† I 1.

LLOYD, Clara Exh. 1903
85 Trafalgar Road, Moseley, Birmingham. † B 1.

LLOYD, Dorothy b. 1891
Miniature and small landscape painter in watercolour. b. Bridgwater, Somerset. Studied Heatherley's and South Kensington School of Art. Exh. 1921-27. Add: Wisborough, Forest Road, Broadwater, Worthing, Sussex. † RI 7, RMS 1.

LLOYD, E. Exh. 1885-91
Crumpsall, Manchester 1885; Withington, Manchester 1895. † M 3

LLOYD, Miss Edith Exh. 1893
Watercolour flower painter. Home Cottage, 119 Brook Green, Hammersmith, London. † RI 1.

LLOYD, Mrs. Edith Exh. 1930
nee Boyce. Watercolour painter and black and white artist. 94 Wildwood Road, N.W. London. † RBA 3.

LLOYD, Eleanor Exh. 1891-1913
Landscape painter. Weybridge, Surrey 1891; Crowborough, Sussex 1908. † RID 12.

LLOYD, Esme Exh. 1938
† P 1.

LLOYD, Ethel A. Exh. 1893-1916
Portrait and figure painter. Warwick 1893 and 1916; London 1898; Bonchurch, I.O.W. 1899; Newlyn, Penzance 1914. † B 5, L 4, P 1, RA 7, RBA 1, RHA 2, RMS 2, ROI 1.

LLOYD, Miss E.B. Exh. 1894-98
124 Lexham Gardens, London. † SWA 3.

LLOYD, Ernest H.D. Exh. 1895-1909
Miniature painter. London. † GI 1, L 4, RA 8, RI 1.

LLOYD, E. Llewellyn Exh. 1909-12
57 Tempest Road, Beeston Hill, Leeds. † RCA 5.

LLOYD, Geraldine Exh. 1889-1907
Married Arthur Stewart q.v. Add: Dublin 1889; London 1891. † B 3, GI 3, L 3, M 2, P 1, RHA 11.

LLOYD, Captain G.W. Exh. 1889-90
Figure and landscape painter. Rome. † RID 4.

LLOYD, Miss H. Exh. 1923
Cathcart Studios, 33 Redcliffe Road, London. † NEA 1.

LLOYD, Henrietta B. Exh. 1897-1907
Oxton, Cheshire 1897; Liverpool 1901. † L 8, RMS 1.

LLOYD, Julia Exh. 1935-38
2 Kingsmead Close, Selly Oak, Birmingham. † B 2.

LLOYD, Julianna Exh. 1880-93
Still life, flower, figure and landscape painter. London. † D 1, RHA 1, SWA 10.

LLOYD, J. Andrew Exh. 1888-1911
Landscape painter. Fulham, London 1888; Marlborough, Wilts. 1891. † G 1, L 1, RA 1, RHA 2, ROI 2.

LLOYD, Katharine Constance Exh. 1923-40
Portrait and flower painter and pastelier. Studied Slade School. Add: London and Hartley Wintney, Hants. † AB 2, COO 47, NEA 1, P 5, RA 5, SWA 1.

LLOYD, Miss L. Exh. 1890
c/o Charles Soar, 1 Sussex Villas, Kensington, London. † B 1.

LLOYD, Leonard Exh. 1892-1903
Landscape painter. 48 Park Road, Lenton, Notts. † N 24.

LLOYD, Lucy Ella Exh. 1887
Painter. 71 Maida Vale, London. † SWA 1.

LLOYD, Maud Exh. 1897-1916
West Kensington, London 1897; Rathmines, Dublin 1912. † RHA 9.

LLOYD, M. Constance Exh. 1908-12
Figure, still life, flower and landscape painter. Paris. † ALP 9, LS 5.

LLOYD, Miss Margaret E. Exh. 1905-11
Liverpool. † L 7.

LLOYD, Mrs. Margaret E. Exh. 1933-40
Landscape and figure painter. Mucklowe House, Strand on the Green, London 1933; Westhumble, Dorking, Surrey 1940. † RA 8.

LLOYD, Mary L. Exh. 1908-14
Rydal Mount, Marlborough Road, Liverpool. † I 1, L 5.

LLOYD, Norman b. 1895
Landscape painter. b. Hamilton, Australia. Studied Sydney Art School, France and Italy. R.O.I. 1935. Exh. 1927-40. Add: London. † AR 2, L 2, RA 10, ROI 28.

LLOYD, Olwyn M. Exh. 1909-13
Mrs. G. Ballance. Add: Claremont, Cheadle Hume, Cheshire. † L 2, M 1, RA 3, RCA 2.

LLOYD, Mrs. P. Exh. 1920
Bryn Olwyn, Waterpark Road, Prenton, Birkenhead. † L 1.

LLOYD, Percy Exh. 1934
Watercolour landscape painter. 145 The Avenue, Newcastle, Staffs. † RA 1.

LLOYD, R. Malcolm Exh. 1880-99
Landscape and marine painter. London. † D 23, GI 3, L 3, RA 11, RBA 31, RI 6, ROI 3.

LLOYD, Stanley Exh. 1922
Watercolour painter. 42 Hamilton Gardens, St. John's Wood, London. † RA 1.

LLOYD, Titus Exh. 1938
Newport, Pembrokeshire. † RCA 1.

LLOYD, Thomas James* 1849-1910
Landscape, genre and marine painter. R.O.I. 1883, A.R.W.S. 1878, R.W.S. 1886. Add: London 1880; Yapton, Sussex 1894; Littlehampton, Sussex 1910. † B 13, FIN 3, GI 10, L 19, LEI 1, M 5, RA 36, RBA 7, ROI 9, RSA 3, RWS 85, TOO 3.

LLOYD, Mrs. Walter Exh. 1890-92
Landscape painter. Walpole House, Chiswick Mall, London. † RID 5.

LLOYD, Winifred Edith Exh. 1897-1904
Miniature painter. R.M.S. 1898. Add: London 1897; Sutton, Surrey 1902. † RA 1, RMS 10.

LLOYD, W. Stuart Exh. 1880-1924
Landscape and marine painter. R.B.A. 1879. Add: London 1880, Barnham Junction, Sussex 1900; Brighton 1909. † B 10, D 2, FIN 1, G 3, GI 3, L 10, M 16, RA 40, RBA 168, RI 56, ROI 22, RSA 1, TOO 1.

LLOYD, W.W. Exh. 1888-95
Cork, Ireland. † D 21.

LLOYD-BOWEN, A. Exh. 1926
79 Francis Road, Edgbaston, Birmingham. † B 3.

LLOYD-JONES, Lydia Exh. 1898-99
Landscape and coastal painter. 53 Drayton Gardens, South Kensington, London. † RA 1, SWA 2.

LLUELLYN, Mrs. Exh. 1889
10 St. Alban's Road, Kensington, London. † ROI 2.

LOACH, Eve Exh. 1919-23
Stained glass artist. Londonderry Lane, Smethwick, Birmingham. † RA 6, RSA 1.

LOADAN, W.M. Exh. 1885
55 Park Road, West Dulwich, London. † G 1.

LOANE, Cecilia Exh. 1925
11 Upper Columba's Road, Drumcondra. † RHA 1.

LOBLEY, James* 1829-1888
Figure and landscape painter. Brighouse, Yorks. 1880; Bradford, Yorks. 1884. † RA 3.

LOBLEY, John Hodgson b. 1878
Portrait, figure and landscape painter. b. Huddersfield. Studied Royal College of Art, Slade School and R.A. Schools (Turner Gold medal and scholarship for landscape painting 1903 and 2 silver medals). Official war artist World War I. A.R.B.A. 1926, R.B.A. 1927. Exh. 1901-39. Add: London. † ALP 1, CHE 1, GI 1, GOU 19, I 2, L 1, LS 9, M 2, RA 15, RBA 52, RI 1, RID 4, ROI 1.

LOBRE, Maurice* b. 1862
French artist. N.E.A. 1888. Exh. 1889-93. Add: 36 Rue de Lourcine, Paris. † GI 1, ROI 1.

LOCH, Alice Helen Exh. 1882-88
Watercolour landscape painter. Bishopsgate Cottage, Englefield Green, London. † D 8, RBA 1, RI 2.

LOCHHEAD, Alfred G. Exh. 1926-40
Glasgow. † GI 5, RSA 1.

LOCHHEAD, Edwin H. Exh. 1931-35
29 Havelock Street, Glasgow. † GI 2.

LOCHHEAD, James Exh. 1891
24 St. Vincent Crescent, Glasgow. † GI 1.

LOCHHEAD, James Exh. 1930
115 Cadzow Street, Hamilton. † GI 1.

LOCHHEAD, John* d. 1921
Figure painter. R.B.A. 1911. Add: Edinburgh 1882; Craigmill, Stirling 1891; Campsie Glen, Stirling 1894; Glasgow 1898; Abinger, West Kilbride, Ayrshire 1900. † GI 75, L 22, M 14, NG 2, RA 3, RBA 56, ROI 1, RSA 77, RSW 5.

LOCHHEAD, Mary Exh. 1898-1901
Edinburgh 1898; Abinger, West Kilbride, Ayrshire 1900. † GI 2, RSA 2.

LOCK, Anton b. 1893
Painter, etcher, wood engraver and illustrator. Studied Westminster School of Art 1910-12, School of Lithography, Bolt Court 1912-14. Exh. 1927-35. Add: 14 Lancaster Road, Wimbledon Common, London. † CHE 3, RA 2, RBA 2, ROI 5.

LOCK, Helen R. Exh. 1912-38
Watercolour landscape and flower painter. South Croydon, Surrey. † ALP 1, B 2, G 4, GI 9, GOU 6, I 13, L 18, NEA 24, RA 17, RCA 6, RI 14, RID 13, SWA 3, WG 89.

LOCK, Norah F. Exh. 1901
c/o Messrs. R. Jackson and Sons, 3 Slater Street, Liverpool. † L 1.

LOCK, Susan Beatrice see FRIPP

LOCKE, Miss Exh. 1930
The Bungalow, Manor Road, Richmond, Surrey. † RI 1.

LOCKE, Agnes Exh. 1918-19
The Priory, Frensham, Surrey. † RI 2.

LOCKE, Mabel Renee b. 1883
Sculptor, painter and pencil artist. b. Selkirk. Studied in Edinburgh. Exh. 1905-40. Add: Edinburgh and Hawick, N.B. † GI 20, L 3, RSA 16, RSW 1.

LOCKERBIE, Ethel Exh. 1913-14
13 Windsor Terrace, Glasgow. † GI 2.

LOCKHARD, A.M. Exh. 1891
9 Chamberlain Road, Edinburgh. † RSA 2.

LOCKHART, John Exh. 1881-84
Glasgow. † GI 1, RSA 3.

LOCKHART, J.H. Bruce Exh. 1929-40
Watercolour landscape painter. Rugby 1929; Cramond Bridge 1931; School House, Sedbergh 1939. † RA 1, RI 2, RSA 3, RSW 7.

LOCKHART, Stephen Exh. 1937
Landscape painter. † BA 39.

LOCKHART, William Ewart* 1846-1900
Painter of genre, landscapes, Spanish subjects, Scottish historical subjects and portraits. b. Annan, Dumfrieshire. Studied under J.B. Macdonald in Edinburgh at age 15. Went to Australia in 1863 for his health. Returned to Edinburgh and in 1867 made his first trip to Spain. Commissioned by Queen Victoria to paint "The Jubilee Ceremony in Westminster Abbey" in 1887. R.E. 1881, R.P. 1897, A.R.S.A. 1871, R.S.A. 1878, A.R.W.S. 1878. Add: Edinburgh 1880; Kensington, London 1891. † B 2, G 2, GI 24, L 7, M 7, NG 1, P 6, RA 25, RHA 2, RSA 54, RSW 15, RWS 22.

LOCKHART, W.M. Exh. 1912
151 Sword Street, Glasgow. † GI 1.

LOCKING, Kate Exh. 1881-82
Watercolour landscape and figure painter. Virginia Villa, Chertsey, Surrey. † RBA 3.

LOCKING, Kitty Exh. 1880-81
Painter. 3 Norfolk Square, London. † SWA 3.

LOCKING, Nora Exh. 1886-95
Landscape, flower, figure and portrait painter. London. † L 2, M 1, P 1, RA 3, RBA 2, RID 2, ROI 3, SWA 9.

LOCKLEY, Doris Exh. 1933-36
Skokholm Island, Pembrokeshire. † RCA 5.

LOCKLEY, H.J. Exh. 1887-1920
Sunnyside, Tettenhall, Wolverhampton. † B 13.

LOCKTON, C.L. Exh. 1910
Teeton, Warlingham, Surrey. † B 2.

LOCKWOOD, Mrs. D.M. Exh. 1939
25 Chesterwood Road, Kings Heath, Birmingham. † B 1.

LOCKWOOD, Florence E. see MURRAY

LOCKWOOD, Frank T. Exh. 1935-40
15 Dalston Road, Acocks Green, Birmingham. † B 7.

LOCKWOOD, Lucy Exh. 1927
The Priory, Melrose. † RSA 1.

LOCKWOOD, T.M. Exh. 1884-92
Architect. 80 Foregate Street, Chester. † L 10, RA 10.

LOCKWOOD-BUNCE, Ada Exh. 1937-40
33 Princes Avenue, Liverpool. † GI 2, RCA 5, RSA 1.

LOCKYER, D. Exh. 1936-38
186 Colonial Road, Bordesley Green, Birmingham. † B 4.

LOCKYER, Florence A. Exh. 1886
Watercolour painter. 33 Freegrove Road, Holloway, London. † RBA 1.

LOCKYER, Isabel de B. Exh. 1914-39
Painter, lino and woodcut artist. London. † AR 2, BA 2, COO 4, D 16, GI 1, GOU 1, L 2, RED 5, RSA 5, SWA 1.

LODDER, Charles junr. Exh. 1880-1902
Largs, N.B. † GI 18, RHA 2, RSA 24, RSW 1.

LODDER, Capt. Charles A., R.N. Exh. 1880-85
Marine painter. Edinburgh 1880; Largs, N.B. 1881. † D 1, GI 5, L 2, RBA 2, RHA 9, RSA 17.

LODDIGES, Laelia Exh. 1897-98
Castlenau, Barnes, South London. † SWA 3.

LODGE, Christopher E. Exh. 1885-1908
Dublin. † RHA 23.

LODGE, C.H. Exh. 1887
Castlehill Cottage, Kenilworth, Warwicks. † B 1.

LODGE, Carron O. Exh. 1906-10
Figure and landscape painter. Father of Francis Graham L. q.v. Add: London. † B 1, L 1, LS 6, NEA 3, RA 2.

LODGE, Miss E.C. Exh. 1883-90
Spring Side, Prestwick, Manchester. † M 5, RA 1.

LODGE, Edward Howitt Exh. 1889-93
Landscape and coastal painter. London. † B 15, L 7, M 4, RA 2, RBA 3, RI 1, ROI 1.

LODGE, Miss Florence F. Exh. 1889
Watercolour flower painter. 1 Micheldever Road, Lee, Kent. † RA 1.

LODGE, Francis Graham b. 1908
Black and white artist. b. Burton on Trent. Son of Carron O.L. q.v. Self taught. Artist with "Everyman" and the "Observer". Exh. 1933. Add: 2 Rochester Terrace, Camden Road, London. † RA 1.
LODGE, George Edward* Exh. 1881-1917
Figure and landscape painter. London. † B 1, I 3, L 3, M 1, RA 12, RBA 3, ROI 7.
LODGE, Miss G.B. Exh. 1918-19
422 Fulham Road, London. † L 1, RA 2.
LODGE, Joan O. Exh. 1930
School of Art, Glasgow. † GI 1.
LODGE, Oliver W.F. Exh. 1928
3 Cathcart Studios, Redcliffe Road, London. † GOU 1, NEA 1.
LODGE, Reginald B. Exh. 1881-92
Landscape painter. London 1881; Enfield, Middlesex 1890. † RA 7, RBA 1.
LOE, Vera Exh. 1940
Portrait painter. 33 Towton Road, West Norwood, London. † RA 2.
LOEWENTAL, Arthur J. Exh. 1936-40
Intaglio and medal artist. Elm Tree Road, N.W. London. † RA 6, RMS 3.
LOEWENTHAL, Joan E. Exh. 1937-40
Painter. London 1937; 20 Howard Street, Belfast 1940. † RHA 2, SWA 1.
LOFTHOUSE, Irene Margaret see SLATER
LOFTHOUSE, James A.E. Exh. 1899-1929
Architect. Middlesborough. † RA 5.
LOFTHOUSE, Mary see FORSTER
LOFTHOUSE, Roger Exh. 1901
62 Albert Road, Middlesborough. † RA 1.
LOFTHOUSE, Samuel H.S. Exh. 1880-82
Landscape painter. Married Mary Forster q.v. Add: 50 Pall Mall, London. † D 2.
LOFTHOUSE, T.W. Exh. 1887
2 Victoria Street, Manchester. † M 1.
LOFTUS, Mrs. Dorothy Exh. 1913-14
26 Southgreen, Southwold, Suffolk. † LS 4.
LOFTUS, Miss T.E. Exh. 1896
Addiscombe, Croydon, Surrey. † SWA 2.
LOGAN, Mrs. Carleton Exh. 1909
† LS 3.
LOGAN, Miss E. Exh. 1906
59 London Road, St. Albans, Herts. † B 1.
LOGAN, Mrs. E. Exh. 1929-32
65 Castle Street, Edinburgh. † GI 2.
LOGAN, Frances Exh. 1926
Hocrom, Bridgnorth, Salop. † L 3.
LOGAN, Gladys see BARRON
LOGAN, George B. Exh. 1898-1904
Greenock. † GI 6.
LOGAN, John Garth b. 1877
Painter, sculptor and commercial artist. Studied Gray's School of Art. Exh. 1922. Add: 46 Elm Bank Terrace, Aberdeen. † RSA 1.
LOGAN, Mabel F. Exh. 1910
Braham, Bray Park Avenue, Maidenhead, Berks. † LS 2.
LOGAN, Paul Exh. 1931
Linocut artist. † RED 1.
LOGAN, Pauline Exh. 1936-37
Engraver. † RED 1, SWA 3.
LOGAN, R.F. Exh. 1881-85
Painter. 4 Picardy Place, Edinburgh. † RI 1, RSA 4.
LOGAN, Thomas Exh. 1893-1906
Glasgow. † GI 2.
LOGAN, William Exh. 1894-96
327 St. Vincent Street, Glasgow. † GI 1, RSW 1.
LOGAN, William P. Exh. 1922
4 Canaan Lane, Edinburgh. † RSA 1.

LOGIE, Harrison Exh. 1919-23
100 St. John's Street, Craighall Road, Glasgow. † GI 2.
LOGIN, Helen M. Exh. 1891-1905
Edinburgh. † RSA 7.
LOGSDAIL, Miss Marian Exh. 1882-1909
Figure and architectural landscape painter, N.E.A. 1886. The Close, Lincoln 1883; Ramsbury, Hungerford, Berks. 1909. † B 5, L 1, RA 12.
LOGSDAIL, William* 1859-1944
Portrait, architectural, figure and landscape painter. Studied Lincoln School of Art and L'Academie des Beaux Arts, Antwerp. Worked in Antwerp, Venice, Cairo and Sicily. N.E.A. 1886. R.P. 1913. "St. Martins in the Fields" purchased by Chantrey Bequest 1888. Add: The Close, Lincoln 1880; London 1888 and 1903; Venice 1892; Noke, nr. Islip, Oxon 1923. † B 29, FIN 147, G 7, GI 19, L 32, M 24, NG 35, P 43, RA 88, RBA 2, ROI 9, TOO 6.
LOISEAU, Exh. 1901
c/o Messrs Durand Ruel, 16 Rue Lafitte, Paris. † I 1.
LOISEAU, Georges Exh. 1925
Painter. † CHE 1.
LOISEAU, Gustave* 1865-1935
French painter. † GOU 14.
LOISEAU-ROUSSEAU, Pául Louis Emile 1861-1927
French sculptor. Exh. 1906-9. Add: 28 Rue Notre Dame des Champs, Paris. † L 3.
LOLE, Mrs. Jeanie Exh. 1921-39
Watercolour flower painter. Sherwood, Willes Road, Leamington Spa, Warwicks. 1921; Purley, Surrey 1933. † L 6, RA 1, RI 2, SWA 5.
LOMAS, Miss H.W. Exh. 1923-40
Wood Green, Wednesbury 1923; Langley 1925; Sheffield 1936. † B 32.
LOMAS, J.A. Mease Exh. 1912-19
R.B.A. 1912. Add: London. † L 2, RBA 10.
LOMAS, J.L. Exh. 1882-83
Sutton Road, Erdington, Birmingham. † B 2.
LOMAS, William Exh. 1880-89
Figure and portrait painter. Kensington, London. † L 2, M 5, RA 6, RHA 2.
LOMAX, Cyril Exh. 1938
Watercolour painter. † WG 4.
LOMAX, Conrad Hope b. 1885
Painter, etcher, illustrator, decorative designer and poster artist. Studied Lambeth and St. Martins Schools of Art. Despatch rider in East Africa World War I. Proprietor Press Art Studio and instructor in figure composition at St. Martins School of Art. Exh. 1925. Add: London and Wraysbury, Bucks. † RA 2.
LOMAX, Miss F. Exh. 1886
Dun Edin, Talbot Road, Old Trafford. † M 1.
LOMAX, Fanny C. Exh. 1914
Les Vagues, Pontac, Jersey, C.I. † LS 3.
LOMAX, Jane Exh. 1900-39
Landscape and flower painter. Southport, Lancs. 1900; London 1908; Welwyn Garden City, Herts. 1932. † L 10, RA 13.
LOMAX, John Arthur* 1857-1926
Genre painter. b. Manchester. Studied at Munich Academy. R.B.A. 1891, R.O.I. 1893. Add: Didsbury 1880; Heaton Chapel 1882; Manchester 1887; London 1888. † B 1, L 11, M 29, RA 56, RBA 33, ROI 27.

LOMAX, John Chadwick Exh. 1889-96
Landscape painter. London 1889; Yoxford, Suffolk 1891. † M 3, NG 1, RA 3.
LOMAX, L. Exh. 1883
Watercolour painter. c/o F. Healey Esq., Savoy Theatre, Strand, London. † RBA 2.
LOMAX, O'Bryen Exh. 1880
Watercolour landscape painter. Thomond Villa, 6 Buckingham Road, Brighton, Sussex. † RBA 1.
LOMBARD, Mrs. Exh. 1887
South Hill, Rathmines, Dublin. † RHA 1.
LOMBARD, Rev. B.S. Exh. 1926-38
Landscape painter. Cound Rectory, Cressage, Salop. † AB 4, B 2, WG 17.
LOMBARDI, Eugenio Exh. 1888
Sculptor. c/o Bellman and Ivey, 37 Piccadilly, London. † RA 1.
LOMNITZ, Mabel Exh. 1932
8 Little Stanhope Street, London. † ROI 1.
LOND, Mrs. Margaret Exh. 1923
98 Selly Oak Lane, Selly Oak, Birmingham. † L 1.
LONERGAN, E.F. Exh. 1929-33
5 Water Street, Port Sunlight, Cheshire. † L 4.
LONES, Thomas Sutton Exh. 1889-97
Etcher. Smethwick, Birmingham 1889; Stafford 1896. † B 4, RA 2.
LONG, Miss C.L. Exh. 1885-1900
Godalming, Surrey 1885; Dublin 1900. † RHA 11.
LONG, Charles William b. 1888
Architect. Studied A.A. Exh. 1928-37. Add: London and Cambridge. † RA 2, RSA 1.
LONG, Edwin* 1829-1891
Portrait, historical and biblical painter. b. Bath. Studied under John Phillip. A.R.A. 1876, R.A. 1881. Add: London. † B 1, GI 1, L 4, M 3, RA 45, ROI 1, TOO 9.
LONG, Mrs. Effie Exh. 1929
454 Aigburth Boulevard, Liverpool. † L 2.
LONG, Emily L. Exh. 1890-1905
Landscape and figure painter. Portsmouth 1890; London 1892. † L 1, RA 3, RBA 2, SWA 6.
LONG, Hilda M. Exh. 1925-26
Police Residence, Moseley Street, Birmingham. † B 4.
LONG, John P. d. 1882
Watercolour landscape and coastal painter. R.S.W. Add: 2 Blandford Place, Regent's Park, London. † D 9, RA 2, RSW 1.
LONG, Miss L. Exh. 1885-1908
Liverpool. † L 29.
LONG, Miss Noel Exh. 1934-39
Watercolour portrait and miniature painter. Coombe Lea, Bovey Tracey, Devon. † RA 1, RI 1, RMS 1.
LONG, R.J. Exh. 1914
1 High Street, Galway. † RHA 2.
LONG, Sydney* Exh. 1913-30
Painter and etcher. A.R.E. 1921. Add: London 1913; Willoughby, Australia 1930. † AB 15, GI 9, L 4, RA 8, RE 19, RSA 1.
LONGBOTTOM, Miss M. Exh. 1915-17
Osborne Grange, Wilderton Road, Branksome, Bournemouth. † RA 3.
LONGBOTTOM, Mrs. P.H. Exh. 1940
Trefriw, Wales. † RCA 1.
LONGBOTTOM, W.W. Exh. 1938-40
Trefriw, Wales. † RCA 4.
LONGDEN, Alfred A. Exh. 1901-8
Landscape painter. Exhibition organiser and lecturer. Studied Royal College of Art. Add: London 1901; Aberdeen 1908. † NG 7, RA 2, RI 2.

LONGDEN, D. Exh. 1911
The Bungalow, Cleeve Hill, Cheltenham, Glos. † RA 1.

LONGDEN, J. Exh. 1926-29
11 Drumry Road, Clydebank, Glasgow. † GI 2.

LONGDEN, R.T. Exh. 1909
Architect. Market Place, Burslem, Staffs. † RA 1.

LONGE, Miss Blanche A. Douglas Exh. 1900-1
The Barracks, Hounslow, Middlesex 1900; Spixworth Park, Norwich 1901. † L 1, RHA 2.

LONGE, Mrs. Douglas Exh. 1900-3
The Barracks, Hounslow 1900; Spixworth Park, Norwich 1903. † L 2, RHA 1.

LONGE, Miss J.G. Exh. 1920
Victoria Club for Ladies, 36 Grosvenor Place, London. † † SWA 2.

LONGE, L.R. Exh. 1884
Watercolour landscape painter. 13 Copt Hall Place, Folkestone, Kent. † SWA 1.

LONGFIELD, Joanna Exh. 1881-1937
Watercolour landscape, flower and figure painter. Mallow, Ireland 1881; Mauchline, N.B. 1902; Venice 1913. † BG 1, GI 1, RHA 6, RSW 9, SWA 2.

LONGHURST, Joseph d. 1922
Landscape painter. Hove, Sussex 1902; Brighton 1904; London 1907; Cranleigh, Surrey 1920. † L 3, LS 5, RA 10, ROI 6.

LONGLAND, Miss A. Exh. 1889
Figure painter. Headington Quarry Vicarage, nr. Oxford. † SWA 2.

LONGLEY, Stanislaus Soutten 1894-c.1967
Watercolour landscape and decorative figure painter. Studied Regent Street, Polytechnic. A.R.B.A. 1924, R.B.A. 1925, R.I. 1932. Add: Aylesbury 1924, London 1928. † FIN 76, GI 4, L 4, RA 15, RBA 88, RI 29.

LONGMAID, William Exh. 1886-1909
Painter and sculptor. Southport, Lancs. † B 5, GI 1, L 12, M 10, RA 2, RCA 3, RHA 2.

LONGMAN, Eleanor D. Exh. 1880-1901
Watercolour landscape and flower painter. London. † D 1, RBA 1, SWA 7.

LONGMAN, Helen Exh. 1901-3
Watercolour painter. London. † FIN 1, SWA 8.

LONGMAN, Mildred Exh. 1931-34
Painter. London 1931; Bromley, Kent 1934. † RA 1, ROI 2, RSA 1.

LONGMATE, Ernest Exh. 1916-34
Landscape and figure painter. London. † RA 4, RI 5.

LONGMIRE, George Exh. 1916
21 Brookland Road, Stoneycroft, Liverpool. † L 2.

LONGMIRE, Mabel M. Exh. 1927-35
Liverpool. † I 12, L 6.

LONGMIRE, R.O. Exh. 1914-23
Liverpool. † L 5.

LONGMORE, A.H. Exh. 1927-31
59 Markley Road, Winson Green, Birmingham. † B 4.

LONGMUIR, A. Exh. 1933-37
2 Queen's Road, Sheffield. † B 1, L 1.

LONGMUIR, A.D. Exh. 1880-86
Landscape painter and etcher. Sherborne, Dorset. † D 1, RE 2, RSA 1.

LONGSDON, David Exh. 1890-1904
Landscape painter. London. † L 9, M 3, NG 3, RA 6, RBA 5, ROI 10.

LONGSHAW, Frank W. d. 1915
Landscape painter. Exh. 1884-1915. Add: Deganwy, nr. Conway, Wales. † L 31, M 18, RA 1, RBA 1, RCA 117, RI 6.

LONGSTAFF, Mrs. Edytha M. Exh. 1914-19
Miniature portrait painter. Crawley Hill, Camberley 1914; Bexhill, Sussex 1918. † RA 5.

LONGSTAFF, Mrs. G.B. Exh. 1889-98
Landscape painter. Southfield Grange, Wandsworth, London. † RID 8.

LONGSTAFF, John* Exh. 1891-1920
Portrait painter. R.P. 1915. Add: Paris 1891; London 1894. † L 1, NG 1, P 9, RA 29.

LONGSTAFF, Leonard W. Exh. 1910-14
13 Butler Avenue, Harrow, Middlesex. † LS 9.

LONGSTAFF, Mrs. R. Exh. 1923
† SWA 1.

LONGSTAFF, Ralph Exh. 1924-35
Figure and portrait painter. London. † RA 6.

LONGSTAFF, Will Francis* Exh. 1919
Watercolour landscape painter. 87 Clifton Hill, St. John's Wood, London. † RA 1.

LONGSTAFFE, Edgar Exh. 1884-89
Landscape painter. Newport, Essex 1884; Liphook, Hants. 1888. † B 1, RA 6, RHA 1.

LONGSTAFFE, E.J. Exh. 1889
Tower View, Ormskirk, Lancs. † L 1.

LONGWORTH, Olive Exh. 1930-38
Old Colwyn, Wales. † RCA 11.

LONIE, Alexander S. Exh. 1907
21 Adelphi, Aberdeen. † RSA 1.

LONSDALE, Horatio Walter Exh. 1886
Architect. 26 Bedford Row, London. † RA 1.

LONZA, Antonio* Exh. 1890
Figure painter. 157 New Bond Street, London. † RA 1.

LOO, van der see V

LOOMIS, Chester Exh. 1882-85
Historical and figure painter. London 1882; Paris 1885. † GI 5, ROI 1.

LOOSELY, George Frederick Exh. 1900-19
Figure and portrait painter. London 1900; Campden, Glos. 1903; High Stakesby Hall, nr. Whitby, Yorks. 1908; Chipperfield, Kings Langley, Herts. 1912. † B 1, L 2, LS 12, P 1, RA 6.

LOPPE, Gabriel Exh. 1891
Landscape painter. † FIN 76.

LORAINE, Nevison Arthur Exh. 1889-1908
Figure and landscape painter. R.B.A. 1893. Add: Chiswick, London 1889; Esher, Surrey 1908. † GOU 1, L 5, RA 8, RBA 15, ROI 8.

LORD, A.B. Exh. 1889
Heathercroft, Balham Hill, London. † B 1.

LORD, Charles Exh. 1882
Bridge Street, Hungerford, Berks. † B 1, GI 1.

LORD, Elyse Exh. 1915-39
Watercolour painter and colourprint artist. R.I. 1922. Add: Sidcup, Kent 1915; Foots Cray, Kent 1922; Bexley, Kent 1935. † B 7, BK 9, FIN 3, GI 2, GOU 2, L 21, LEF 83, RA 2, RCA 2, RED 1, RI 20, RSA 17.

LORD, G.W. Exh. 1908-11
The Red House, Pendleton, Manchester 1908, Port Sudan, Red Sea 1911. † RA 2.

LORD, H. Exh. 1885
Manchester. † M 1.

LORD, Hilda Exh. 1912
Todmarden, Yorks. † M 3.

LORD, J.C. Exh. 1882
67 Manchester Road, Southport, Lancs. † L 4.

LORD, Lillian Rose b. 1900
Miniature and watercolour portrait painter. 130 Trundley's Road, New Cross, London. † RA 4, RMS 2.

LORD, W. Turner Exh. 1908
3 Holland Lane, Melbury Road, London. † LS 3.

LOREIN, Victor Exh. 1918
115 Charlotte Street, London. † LS 3.

LORENZ, Johannes Exh. 1880-84
Medalist. Hamburg 1880, c/o Hung, 84 King's Street, West Hammersmith, London. † RA 4.

LORENZI, Pierre Exh. 1907
21 Rue Racine, Paris. † L 2.

LORIMER, Ann D. Exh. 1901-7
Edinburgh. † RSA 6.

LORIMER, Freida Exh. 1929-30
22 Gt. King Street, Edinburgh. † GI 2.

LORIMER, John Henry 1856-1936
Portrait, figure, landscape and flower painter. Studied R.S.A. Schools and Edinburgh University. R.O.I. 1890, R.P. 1892, A.R.S.A. 1882, R.S.A. 1900, R.S.W. 1885, A.R.W.S. 1908, R.W.S. 1934. Brother of Sir Robert S.L. q.v. "Sir Robert Lorimer, A.R.A. as a Boy" (1875) purchased by Chantrey Bequest 1930. Add: Edinburgh 1880 and 1900; London 1885. † AG 2, B 1, BG 2, DOW 2, G 2, GI 59, GOU 1, L 32, M 6, NG 6, P 81, RA 43, RHA 2, RI 2, ROI 8, RSA 123, RSW 33, RWS 88.

LORIMER, Henry Exh. 1890-91
Loriotlea, Cathcart, Glasgow. † GI 2.

LORIMER, Hew Exh. 1936
11 Belford Mews, Edinburgh. † RSA 1.

LORIMER, Sir Robert Stodart 1864-1929
Architect. Brother of John Henry L. q.v. A.R.A. 1920, A.R.S.A. 1903, R.S.A. 1921. Knighted 1911. Add: Edinburgh. † GI 16, L 4, P 3, RA 12, RSA 84, RWS 1.

LORING, Francis William 1838-1905
Landscape and figure painter. b. Boston, U.S.A. Exh. 1886-93. Add: Florence, Italy. † RA 4.

LORIOZ, de see D

LORME, de see D

LORNE, Francis Exh. 1937-39
Architect. 1 Montague Place, Bedford Square, London. † GI 2, RSA 2.

LORNE, Marchioness of
see LOUISE, H.R.H. Princess

LOS, Naum b. 1882
Sculptor. Exh. 1923. Add: 22 Via Margutta, Rome. † RA 1.

LOTIRON, Robert* b. 1886
French landscape painter. Exh. 1922-23. † GOU 3.

LOTT, Frederick Tully Exh. 1881-90
Landscape painter. 119 Alexander Road, St. John's Wood, London 1881, c/o Palmer and Howe, Manchester 1888. † M 4, RHA 4.

LOTZ, Henry J. Exh. 1912-34
Landscape painter. Sutton, Surrey 1912; London 1914. † G 1, GOU 3, LEI 3, LS 8, NEA 4, RA 4, ROI 2.

LOTZ, Miss M. Exh. 1899
2 Kensington Gardens Square, Bayswater, London. † L 1.

LOUD, Arthur Bertram 1863-1930
Portrait and landscape painter. Add: London 1884; Teddington, Middlesex 1925; Kingstone on Thames 1927. B 4, RA 3, RCA 52.

LOUD, Mrs. Margaret Exh. 1930-32
30 Willow Road, Bournville, Birmingham. † B 7.

LOUDAN, Dorothy Exh. 1904
30 Bryanston Square, London. † L 1.

LOUDAN, William Mouat* 1868-1925
Portrait and genre painter. Studied R.A. Schools (gold medal and travelling studentship), and in Paris under Bouguereau. N.E.A. 1886, R.P. 1891. Exh. from 1883. Add: London. † B 3, BA 1, BG 5, G 5, GI 22, I 1, L 32, M 20, NEA 2, NG 3, P 37, RA 67, RBA 17, ROI 6.

LOUDON, John Exh. 1893-1900
Blantyre, N.B. and Hamilton, N.B. † GI 5, RSA 1, RSW 1.

LOUDON, Jean B.M. Exh. 1940
Miniature portrait painter. 54 Westbourne Road, Southport, Lancs. † RA 1.

LOUDON, Laura J. Exh. 1892-1938
Mrs. John L. nee Bennie. Add: Glasgow 1892; Hamilton, N.B. 1903; Ayr 1909. † GI 5, L 1, P 1, RSA 9.

LOUDON, Miss Noni Exh. 1925-28
Moorlands, Bellevale, Ayr. † RSA 2, RSW 1.

LOUDON, Terence Exh. 1921-40
Flower painter. London. † CON 10, FIN 2, P 1, RA 10.

LOUISE, H.R.H. The Princess 1848-1939
Marchioness of Lorne and Duchess of Argyll. Painter and sculptor (Queen Victoria in Kensington Gardens). Daughter of Queen Victoria. Studied under Edgar Boehm. H.R.E. 1897, R.M.S. 1897, R.S.W. 1884, H.R.W.S. † AR 1, D 1, G 4, GI 2, L 8, M 1, NG 1, RMS 1, RSW 16, RWS 14.

LOUKOMSKI, Georges b. 1881
Russian painter. Exh. 1939. † FIN 46.

LOUP, Eugenie b. 1867
French artist. Exh. 1910-12. Add: 25 Rue Vaneau, Paris. † L 2.

LOUSADA, Anthony Exh. 1930
33 Phillimore Gardens, London. † NEA 1.

LOUSADA, Mrs. Julian (Maude) Exh. 1911-27
Figure and landscape painter. London. † GOU 8, LS 6, NEA 10.

LOUSADA, Julian G. Exh. 1938
Landscape painter. 11 Campden Hill Square, London. † RA 1.

LOUTEN, Leon Vanden Exh. 1915
c/o Mrs. Sarolea, 21 Royal Terrace, Edinburgh. † RSA 1.

LOVATELLI, Filippo Exh. 1924
Sculptor. Via Maria Christina 5, Rome 10, Italy. † L 1, RA 1.

LOVATT, James A. Exh. 1927
6 Ludwall Road, Normacot, Longton, Stoke on Trent, Staffs. † ROI 1.

LOVATTI, Augusto Exh. 1888
Painter. c/o Mrs. H. Beerr, 23 Eaton Place, London. † NG 1.

LOVATTI, Matteo Exh. 1885-1917
Military painter. 25 Bedford Street, Strand, London. † FIN 69, RSA 1.

LOVE, Andrew Exh. 1896-1919
Newmills, N.B. † GI 4, RSA 2, RSW 3.

LOVE, Henry Exh. 1915-23
2 Seapoint Terrace, Monkstown, Dublin. † RHA 17.

LOVE, Janet M. Exh. 1901-2
21 St. James Street, Paisley, N.B. † GI 2, L 1.

LOVE, Lillian Exh. 1888
Geilsland, Leith, N.B. † GI 1.

LOVE, Mrs. Margaret Joyce Exh. 1940
122 Queen's Drive, Glasgow. † GI 1.

LOVE, Mrs. Vera Exh. 1930
Landscape painter. Three Sevens, Broughton, Stockbridge, Hants. † RA 1.

LOVEDAY, Dorothy Exh. 1929-38
Sculptor. 22 Cheniston Gardens, London 1929; Bloxham, Banbury, Oxon 1938. † L 1, RA 4, RSA 1.

LOVEDAY, R.W. Exh. 1938
110 Colwyn Road, Northampton. † B 1.

LOVEGROVE, Beatrice V. Exh. 1887-89
Watercolour landscape painter. Nottingham. † N 3.

LOVEGROVE, Mildred Exh. 1903-25
18 Foxgrove Road, Beckenham, Kent 1903; Ruthin School, Ruthin, Wales 1925. † B 4, RA 2, RCA 1, ROI 1, SWA 9.

LOVEL, Charles Edward Exh. 1890-92
Figure painter. Studio, 151 Gloucester Road, South Kensington, London. † NG 1, ROI 2.

LOVELACE, The Countess of Exh. 1895
Wentworth House, Swan Walk, Chelsea, London. † M 1, NG 2.

LOVELL, Miss E. Exh. 1887
Eton Villa, Weston super Mare, Somerset. † B 1.

LOVELL, Elizabeth M. Exh. 1880-84
Landscape and flower painter. London. † L 1, RBA 1, RHA 1, RI 1, SWA 1.

LOVELL, J.F. Exh. 1917
92 Trinity Road, Upper Tooting, London. † RA 1.

LOVELL, Mary Exh. 1895-96
The Studio, Church Walk, Hampstead, London. † RBA 2.

LOVELL, Margaret J. Exh. 1899-1931
Landscape and coastal painter. Hampstead Lane, Highgate, London. † L 1, RA 1, RBA 1, RI 1, SWA 10.

LOVELL, Martha S. Exh. 1880
Flower painter. 48 Oakley Road, Canonbury, London. † SWA 1.

LOVELL, P. Exh. 1916
26 Portland Road, Southall, Middlesex. † L 1, RA 1.

LOVELL, Richard J. Exh. 1891-1907
Architect. 46 Queen Victoria Street, London. † RA 6.

LOVELL, Robert S. Exh. 1889-90
Portrait painter. 45 Cornwall Road, Bayswater, London. † RA 2.

LOVELL, Miss S. Exh. 1890
48 Oakley Road, Canonbury, London. † SWA 2.

LOVERING, Ida Exh. 1881-1915
Landscape, portrait and figure painter. A.S.W.A. 1886. Add: London. † B 32, D 2, GI 2, L 17, M 4, P 1, RA 14, RBA 3, RHA 15, RI 4, RID 48, ROI 10, SWA 39.

LOVETT, A.C. Exh. 1899-1901
Horfield, Bristol 1899; c/o W.J. Jenkins, 570 Fulham Road, London 1901. † RBA 1, RI 1.

LOVETT, W.G. Exh. 1933-35
109 Castle Road, Quinton. † B 3.

LOVIBOND, Phyllis Ellen see BICKNELL

LOW, A.R. Exh. 1894-98
Glasgow. † GI 7, RSA 2, RSW 1.

LOW, Annie Rose see LAING

LOW, Charles* Exh. 1881-1905
Landscape and cattle painter. R.B.A. 1897. Add: Hungerford, Berks. 1881 and 1899; Witley, Surrey 1896. † B 1, L 1, RA 17, RBA 61, RHA 11, RI 21, ROI 3, RSA 2.

LOW, Charlotte E. Exh. 1880-85
Flower painter. 90 Grove Lane, Denmark Hill, London. † D 1, RBA 1, SWA 8.

LOW, Diana b. 1911
Painter and textile designer. Studied Slade School and Academie Ranson. Exh. 1934-38. Add: 42 South Moulton Street, London. † NEA 1, RBA 1.

LOW, D. Paton Exh. 1880-83
209 Hope Street, Glasgow. † GI 2.

LOW, Henry Charles Exh. 1939-40
Landscape painter and pencil artist. 68 West Borough, Wimborne, Dorset. † AR 126, GOU 1, RSA 2.

LOW, Marie Exh. 1895-96
Watercolour flower painter. The Studio, 293 Oxford Street, London. † B 1, RA 2, RBA 2, SWA 3.

LOW, Mabel Bruce Exh. 1906-40
Watercolour landscape painter and woodcut artist. b. Edinburgh. Studied Edinburgh College of Art, Westminster School of Art, and London School of Art. A.R.B.A. 1919, R.B.A. 1924, S.W.A. 1932. Add: London 1906; Bournemouth 1937. † COO 2, I 3, L 4, NEA 1, P 1, RA 18, RBA 133, RI 3, RSA 17, SWA 17.

LOW, Mrs. Mabel Warren Exh. 1910-37
Watercolour flower painter. Harley Street, London. † I 1, L 3, LS 3, RA 7, RI 23.

LOW, W.R. Exh. 1916
10 Basinghall Street, London. † RA 1.

LOWCOCK, Charles Frederick Exh. 1880-1917
Genre painter. R.B.A. 1897. Add: Headingley, Leeds 1881; Huddersfield 1882; Leeds 1883; Chalk, Kent 1890; South Woodford, Essex 1900; Wanstead, Essex 1907. † GI 3, L 3, M 3, RA 26, RBA 36, RHA 2, RSA 5.

LOWE, Alfred Exh. 1926
Portrait and landscape painter. † AB 62.

LOWE, Arthur Exh. 1896-1939
Landscape painter. N.S.A. 1898. Add: Nottingham 1896; Keyworth, Notts. 1903; Kinoulton, Notts. 1908. † B 5, L 4, N 99, RA 2, RCA 2.

LOWE, Annie Exh. 1904-10
Figure and miniature portrait painter. London. † L 2, RA 8, RMS 1.

LOWE, A.T. Exh. 1898-1918
Nottingham 1898; West Bridgford, Notts. 1912. † N 15.

LOWE, Ella Exh. 1889
Watercolour flower painter. Woodcote, Inner Park Road, Wimbledon, London. † RA 1.

LOWE, Miss E.L. Exh. 1904-8
Birmingham. † B 5, RA 1.

LOWE, Edward S. Exh. 1893-1928
Landscape painter. Buckhurst Hill, Essex 1893; Kingstown, Dublin 1916; c/o Bourlet and Co., Nassau Street, London 1925. † GOU 3, I 2, L 3, LS 3, RA 1, RBA 3, RHA 17, RI 1, ROI 5.

LOWE, Mrs. Frances M.A. Exh. 1909
† LS 1.

LOWE, George Theodore b. 1858
Landscape painter and black and white artist. b. Leeds. Studied Leeds, Liverpool, Huddersfield and R.A. Schools. Exh. 1926. Add: 74 New North Road, Huddersfield. † L 1, RA 1.

LOWE, Mrs. H.C. Exh. 1933
31 Church Street, Southport, Lancs. † L 3.

LOWE, H.J.R. Exh. 1884
67 Elsham Road, Kensington, London. † D 1.

LOWE, Isabella Wylie Exh. 1896-1921
Perth. † GI 12, RSA 5.

LOWE, Miss J.C. Exh. 1933
31 Church Street, Southport, Lancs. † L 1.

LOWE, Miss M.A. Exh. 1901-3
Bluebell Villa, Gt. Barr, Birmingham. † B 3.

LOWE, Miss M.B.E. Exh. 1928-32
81 Larkhill Lane, Liverpool. † L 5.

LOWE, Mary C. Exh. 1886-96
Figure and landscape painter. London 1886; Abbots Bromley, Staffs. 1888; Royston, Herts. 1892. † B 2, L 3, RA 2, ROI 2, SWA 3.

LOWE, Robert Allensmore b. 1873
Watercolour painter and black and white artist. Exh. 1902. Add: 36 Alma Road, Birkdale, Southport, Lancs. † L 1.

LOWE, R.D. Exh. 1881
20 Mortimer Street, Regent's Park, London. † RHA 1.

LOWENADLER, Karin Exh. 1937
† NEA 1.

LOWENGRUND, Margaret Exh. 1930
American etcher. † FIN 25.

LOWENSTAM, Leopold d. 1898
Etcher. London 1880; Three Bridges, Sussex 1897. † L 3, M 2, RA 18, RI 2.

LOWENTHAL, Bertha Exh. 1888-1919
Architectural landscape painter. London. † D 3, L 4, RA 17, RBA 2, RHA 1, RI 5, ROI 1, RSA 1, SWA 4.

LOWENTHAL, E. Exh. 1882-83
Figure painter. 33 Via Margutta, Rome. † M 1, RA 1, RHA 1.

LOWINGS, Albert Exh. 1940
Aquatint artist, 29 Blawith Road, Harrow, Middlesex. † RA 1.

LOWINSKY, Thomas Esmond 1892-1947
Painter and illustrator. Studied Slade School. Served with the Scots Guards in France World War I. N.E.A. 1926. "Mrs. James Mackie" (1935) purchased by Chantrey Bequest 1939. Add: Sunninghill, Berks. 1914; 41 Kensington Square, London 1920. † CHE 1, G 1, I 1, L 2, LEI 31, NEA 20, RA 1.

LOWITH, Wilhelm b. 1861
Austrian artist. Exh. 1885-99. Add: 72 Schwanthalstrasse, Munich. † GI 1, TOO 1.

LOWNDES, Miss C. Exh. 1928
Dilhorne, Barnt Green, Birmingham. † B 1.

LOWNDES, Miss D.L. Exh. 1899
The Mount, New Brighton, Cheshire. † L 1.

LOWNDES, Mrs. Katherine M. Exh. 1921-23
Corbys, Hoylake, Cheshire. † L 3.

LOWNDES, Mrs. Margaret Exh. 1908-9
North Western Hotel, Lime Street, Liverpool. † L 3.

LOWNDES, Mary S. Exh. 1884-88
Landscape and figure painter. London. † L 1, M 2, RBA 1, SWA 2.

LOWRY, Mrs. Agnes B. Exh. 1908-13
Beeches, Poplar Road, Oxton, Cheshire. † L 4.

LOWRY, Mrs. B. (F.E.) Exh. 1926-31
Dartans, Penrhyn Bay, nr. Llandudno. † L 2, RCA 7.

LOWRY, Miss D. Exh. 1926-38
Dartans, Penrhyn Bay, nr. Llandudno. † RCA 14.

LOWRY, Laurence Stephen* 1887-1976
Painter of figures and industrial landscapes. b. Manchester. Studied Manchester School of Art and Salford School of Art. R.B.A. 1935. Several of his works are in the Tate Gallery. Exh. 1926-40. Add: 117 Station Road, Pendlebury, Manchester. † B 1, L 8, LEF 26, M 5, NEA 12, RA 7, RBA 34, RHA 4, ROI 7, RSA 8.

LOWRY, Robert Exh. 1920-35
Architect. London. † RA 6.

LOWRY, Ruth Exh. 1914-16
Portrait painter. 11 Ladbroke Terrace, London. † NEA 1, RA 2.

LOWTH, Olive Exh. 1922-25
Black and white portrait artist. 6 St. John's Street, Mansfield, Notts. † N 5.

LOWTHER, Miss E.H. Exh. 1911
† RHA 1.

LOWTHER, Jessie Exh. 1899
Alexandra House, Kensington Gore, London. † L 1.

LOWTHER, Hon. Mrs. W. Exh. 1889
Kensington Gore, London. † D 2.

LOY, Mina Exh. 1910
Portrait painter. 48 Costa san Georgio, Florence. † NEA 1.

LOYD, Mrs. Exh. 1893
Northampton. † D 1.

LOYNES, Reginald Jesse b. 1902
Miniature portrait painter. Add: 14 Featherstone Buildings, High Holborn, London 1928. † RA 1.

LOZOFF, Abraham Exh. 1934-35
Sculptor. 109A Oxford Gardens, London. † RA 2.

LOZOWICK, Louis b. 1892
American etcher. b. Russia. Exh. 1930. † FIN 10.

LUARD, Miss L. Exh. 1898-1908
Flower painter. The Lodge, Witham, Essex. † L 2, RA 1, RI 1, SWA 5.

LUARD, Lowes Dalbac d. 1944
Landscape, figure and animal painter and etcher. R.B.A. 1937. Add: Harrow, Middlesex 1898; London 1900 and 1934; Paris 1911 and 1927; Chipperfield, Kings Langley, Herts. 1923. † FIN 189, GI 3, GOU 18, L 2, LS 10, NEA 4, NG 9, P 1, RA 4, RBA 9, RHA 1, RSA 2.

LUBBERS, Holger Exh. 1882
Landscape painter. 537 Caledonian Road, Holloway, London. † RA 1.

LUCAS, Alfred Exh. 1883-86
Etcher. Acton, London. † RA 2.

LUCAS, Arthur Exh. 1934-35
Stained glass designer. 132 Bravington Road, London. † RA 3.

LUCAS, Arthur Exh. 1883-1909
Landscape painter. Hanover Square, London 1883; 27 Bruton Street, London 1889. † D 1, G 6, L 3, M 4, NG 51, RA 1, RI 3, ROI 1.

LUCAS, Mrs. Arthur Exh. 1903-9
27 Bruton Street, London. † NG 14.

LUCAS, Albert Durer* 1829-1919
Flower painter. Son of Richard Cockle L. q.v. Exh. 1880-1909. Add: Chilworth, Romsey, Hants. 1880; Southampton 1890. † L 2, LS 3, M 1, RHA 1, RSA 1.

LUCAS, Miss A.M. Exh. 1886
Landscape painter. Rose Cottage, Hitchin, Herts. † SWA 2.

LUCAS, A.P. Exh. 1896
Painter. 221 Boulevard Rsapail, Paris. † RA 1.

LUCAS, Bernard 1853-1910
Landscape painter and illustrator. Add: London 1885; Bramber, Sussex 1907. † G 8, L 3, M 4, NG 11, WG 91.

LUCAS, Caroline Byng Exh. 1939
Painter. † LEI 23.

LUCAS, Desire* Exh. 1900-6
Landscape painter. † TOO 3.

LUCAS, Mrs. Dorothy Exh. 1920-34
Portrait, figure, flower and still life painter. A.S.W.A. 1922. Add: Epping, Essex and London. † P 1, RBA 3, RID 4, ROI 4, SWA 17.

LUCAS, Edith Evelyn Exh. 1900-4
Portrait and figure painter. 10 Marlborough Hill, London. † RA 2.

LUCAS, Edward George Handel* 1861-1936
Landscape, portrait, figure and still life painter, lecturer and teacher. Studied Heatherleys, R.A. Schools, St. John's Wood and British Academy, Rome (1888-89). Add: Sutton, Surrey 1880; Croydon, Surrey 1881 and 1896; Rome 1888; West Norwood 1891; Brighton 1911; Streatham 1919. † G 2, L 5, M 1, RA 14, RBA 7, ROI 14.

LUCAS, E.V. Exh. 1925
Lord Roberts Memorial Workshops, 122 Brompton Road, London. † L 35.

LUCAS, Florence See BREWER

LUCAS, Fred Exh. 1911
Painter. † BRU 1.

LUCAS, F.J. Exh. 1909
Architect. Ingram House, Stockwell, London. † RA 1.

LUCAS, Geoffrey Exh. 1899-1929
Architect. Hitchin, Herts 1899; London 1902. † RA 15.

LUCAS, George Exh. 1880-99
Landscape and figure painter. Essex Villa, The Avenue, Acton, London. † B 3, G 1, GI 8, L 6, M 10, RA 17, RBA 7, RI 16, ROI 1.

LUCAS, Hannah Exh. 1885-94
Landscape and figure painter. 55 Oxford Gardens, Notting Hill, London. † L 2, RI 1, SWA 3.

LUCAS, H.F. Exh. 1885-86
Albert Street, Rugby. † B 2.

LUCAS, J. Archibald Exh. 1928
Architect. Alexandra House, Denmark Road, Exeter, Devon. † RA 2.

LUCAS, John Seymour* 1849-1923
Genre and historical painter. Married Marie Cornelissen q.v. and cousin of John Templeton and William L. q.v. A.R.A. 1886, R.A. 1898, A.R.I. 1876, R.I. 1877, R.O.I. 1883. "After Culloden, Rebel Hunting" purchased by Chantrey Bequest 1884. Add: London. † AG 1, B 6, GI 3, L 11, M 1, P, 1, RA 187, RBA 1, RCA 1, RHA 2, RI 5, ROI 10, RSA 1, TOO 15.

LUCAS, Mrs. John Seymour
See CORNELISSEN, Marie

LUCAS, John Templeton* 1836-1880
Landscape and genre painter. Son of John L. (1807-1874), cousin of John Seymour L. q.v. and brother of William L. q.v. Exh. 1880. Add: London. † GI 1.

LUCAS, Miss J.V. Exh. 1910
27 Bruton Street, London. † RA 1.

LUCAS, Marjorie A. b. 1911
Painter, illustrator, wood and line engraver. Studied Royal College of Art. Married Murray M. Tod, q.v. Add: Highgate, London 1933; Haugh of Urr, Castle Douglas, Kirkcudbright 1937. † GI 7, RA 2, RSA 11.

LUCAS, M. Ellen Seymour Exh. 1903-28
Miniature painter. London 1903; The Priory, Blythburgh, Suffolk 1928. † L 1, RA 4.

LUCAS, May Lancaster Exh. 1888-1910
Portrait painter. London. † B 5, G 1, GI 4, L 10, LS 3, M 1, P 1, RA 9, RHA 2, SWA 21.

LUCAS, O.F. Exh. 1930
King's Road, Chelsea, London. † SWA 1.

LUCAS, Richard Cockle 1800-1883
Sculptor. Studied R.A. Schools 1828. Father of Albert Durer L. q.v. Exh. 1883. Add: Chilworth, Romsey, Hants. † L 1.

LUCAS, Richard McD. Exh. 1901
Architect. Bar Gate Chambers, Southampton. † RA 1.

LUCAS, S. Bright Exh. 1883-91
Landscape painter. London. † RBA 2, RI 1.

LUCAS, Sydney Seymour Exh. 1909-40
Portrait painter and illustrator. Add: Bushey, Herts. 1909; London 1934; Blythburgh, Suffolk 1936. † P 3, RA 12, RSA 2.

LUCAS, Thomas G. Exh. 1896-1908
Architect. Add: Hitchin, Herts. 1896; London 1904. † RA 8.

LUCAS, Veronica Exh. 1924-30
Landscape painter. Studied Westminster School of Art. Add: 81 Elm Park Gardens, London. † FIN 1, GOU 6, RSA 2.

LUCAS, William 1840-1895
Watercolour portrait and figure painter and lithographer. Son of John L. (1807-1874), brother of John Templeton L. q.v. and cousin of John Seymour L. q.v. A.R.I. 1864. Exh. 1884. Add: 92 Clifton Hill, St. John's Wood, London. † GI 1.

LUCAS, William b. 1860
Architect. b. Melbourne, Australia. Studied Melbourne (Australia) School of Art and Cheltenham School of Art. Exh. 1928. Add: 19 Lansdown Street, East Melbourne, Australia. † RA 1.

LUCAS, William James b. 1888
Painter and etcher. Exh. 1924-30. Add: Port Sunlight, Cheshire. † L 16.

LUCAS, William Louis c. 1866-1929
Architect. Exh. 1896-1911. Add: London. † RA 4.

LUCAS-ROBIQUET, Mme. Marie Andrea b. 1864
French artist. Exh. 1904. Add: Chez M. Pollard, 28 Rue du Bassano, Paris. † L 1.

LUCCHESI, Andrea Carlo 1860-1925
Sculptor. b. Italy. Studied 5 years at R.A. Schools. Exh. from 1881. Add: London. † GI 20, L 35, NG 17, RA 73, RI 1, ROI 2, RSA 3.

LUCCHESI, E. Exh. 1921
9 Preston Park Avenue, Brighton. † RA 1.

LUCCHESI, Giorgio Exh. 1883-94
Painter. Add: Lucca, Italy 1883; c/o Messrs. Smith and Upland, Mortimer Street, London 1893. † B 1, GI 1, RBA 1.

LUCCHESI, Professor U. Exh. 1882
Sculptor. c/o Loughi, 27 New Broad Street, London. † RA 1.

LUCE, Maximillian* 1858-1941
French painter. Exh. 1911-21 † GOU 8, M 1.

LUCEY, Mrs. Florence Exh. 1934-40
Flower painter. Haslemere, Hemingford Grey, St. Ives, Hunts. † RA 1, RBA 1, RSA 2.

LUCK, K. Exh. 1930
† L 1.

LUCK, Mrs. Mabel Exh. 1910-21
120 St. James Court, Buckingham Gate, London. † LS 19, RA 1.

LUCK, Mrs. Marion F. Exh. 1903-8
nee Horn. Landscape painter. Add: Harbeston, Totnes, Devon 1903; Camberley, Surrey 1904; St. Ives, Cornwall 1905. † L 2, LS 2, RA 5, RCA 2, ROI 1.

LUCY, Mrs. A.S. Exh. 1894-97
Mrs. Charles Hampden L. Add: Hampton Bishop, Hereford 1894; 78 Elgin Crescent, London 1896. † B 4, L 1, M 2, RHA 7.

LUCY, Charles Hampden Exh. 1884-1902
Landscape, figure and decorative painter. Son of Charles L. (1814-1873). Add: London 1884; Hampton Bishop, Hereford 1890; 78 Elgin Crescent, London 1897; Bristol 1902. † B 8, GI 2, L 1, M 2, RA 3, RBA 1, RHA 4, ROI 2.

LUCY, Edward Falkland c. 1852-1908
Landscape painter. London. † AG 2, B 3, GI 2, L 3, M 4, NG 1, RA 2, RHA 3, RI 2, ROI 2, RSA 1.

LUCY, Hubert A. Exh. 1901-11
Landscape painter. London. † BRU 1, RBA 1, RHA 2, RI 1.

LUDBY, Mrs. H.C. Exh. 1895-1918
Mrs. Max L. Add: St. Ives, Cornwall 1895; Guildford, Surrey 1916. † RI 5, ROI 1.

LUDBY, Max 1858-1943
Landscape, genre painter and engraver. Studied in Antwerp 1882-84. R.B.A. 1886, R.I. 1891. Add: Tufnell Park, London 1880; Cookham Dean, Berks. 1881; Carbis Bay, Lelant, Cornwall 1897; Guildford, Surrey 1911. † AG 18, D 6, DOW 91, FIN 1, G 3, GI 1, L 16, LS 3, M 4, RA 7, RBA 49, RI 229, ROI 11.

LUDDINGTON, Mrs. Leila Tansley Exh. 1932-40
Walton's Park, Ashdon, Saffron Walden, Essex. † NEA 2, RBA 5, RSA 1, RSW 1, SWA 8.

LUDGATE, Patricia K. Exh. 1916-39
Sculptor. London. † L 3, RA 4, RBA 1.

LUDLOW, E. Exh. 1888-89
Blyborough, Kirton Lindsay, Lincs. 1888; Tiverton, Devon 1889. † L 2, RSA 3.

LUDLOW, Henry Stephen (Hal) b. 1861
Portrait painter and illustrator ("Illustrated London News", "Sketch" etc). Studied Heatherleys and Highgate College. Exh. 1888-1928. Add: London. † GI 2, L 8, RA 35, RI 10.

LUDLOW, Mary Sophia Exh. 1908-9
90 Rue d'Assas, Paris. † LS 8.

LUDOVICI, Albert, Senr.* 1820-1894
Genre painter. Father of Albert junr. and Marguerite C.L. q.v. R.B.A. 1867. Add: London. † B 5, D 3, G 1, GI 14, L 6, M 6, RBA 117, RHA 4, RI 8, ROI 3.

LUDOVICI, Albert Junr. 1852-1932
Figure and landscape painter. b. Prague. Son of Albert L. sen. q.v. N.E.A. 1891, R.B.A. 1881. Add: London. † B 1, RA 3, DOW 150, FIN 1, G 4, GI 13, GOU 53, I 64, L 17, M 12, NEA 17, RA 15, RBA 79, RHA 1, RI 1, ROI 4.

LUDOVICI, Marguerite Exh. 1880-1920
Mme. E. Cathelin. Flower, landscape and miniature portrait painter. Daughter of Albert L. sen. q.v. Add: London. † B 13, BG 1, D 4, GI 8, L 5, M 13, RA 8, RBA 48, RHA 4, ROI 6, SWA 6.

LUGARD, Charlotte E. See HOWARD

LUHRIG, Georg b. 1868
German artist. Exh. 1911. † M 1.

LUIGINI, Ferdinand Jean* b. 1870
French painter. Exh. 1904-13. Add: Paris. † FIN 6, I 7, L 2.

LUKE, Flora Exh. 1906-16
London 1906; Worthing, Sussex 1916. † L 1. RA 2.

LUKE, Fred Exh. 1884-1915
Rathmines, Dublin. † RHA 22.

LUKE, John b. 1906
Landscape and still life painter. Studied Belfast College of Art 1923-27, Slade School 1927-30 and Westminster School of Art 1930-31. Exh. 1937-39. Add: 4 Lewis Street, Belfast. † RHA 4.

LUKE, Mrs. Nellie Exh. 1892
Netherby, Broughty Ferry, N.B. † RSA 1.

LUKE, Miss R.W. Exh. 1908
Broom Villa, Sale, Manchester. † M 3.

LUKE, Miss V. Exh. 1920
9 Evelyn Gardens, Kensington, London. † L 2.

LUKER, A. Exh. 1885
Landscape painter. 34 Chestnut Road, Merton, Surrey. † RA 1.

LUKER, Mrs. Ada Exh. 1900-1
Landscape and figure painter. 22 Campden Hill Square, London. † RA 3, ROI 1.

LUKER, Mrs. Frances Exh. 1933-40
Miniature portrait painter. Moseley, Birmingham. † B 18, RA 1, RMS 1.

LUKER, Mrs. F. Helen Exh. 1938-40
22 High Street, Petersfield, Hants. † RI 2.

LUKER, G. Lewis Exh. 1880-1901
Architect and painter. Add: London 1880 and 1900; Milford, Surrey 1887. † B 7, D 10, GI 1, L 5, M 2, RA 3, RBA 6, RI 7, TOO 1.

LUKER, Louise H. Exh. 1901-24
Mrs. Louise Burrell. Miniature portrait painter. A.R.M.S. 1912. Add: Bushey, Herts. 1901; London 1904. † L 2, RA 15, RMS 8.

LUKER, Miss U. Exh. 1940
Shortheath, Farnham, Surrey. † RI 2.

LUKER, William Senr.* Exh. 1880-1900
Portrait, genre, animal and landscape painter. Father of William L. junr. q.v. Add: London. † B 22, D 1, GI 1, L 8, M 15, RA 6, RBA 24, RHA 29, RI 1, ROI 6, TOO 29.

LUKER, William Junr. b. 1867
Figure, animal, landscape and portrait painter and illustrator. Son of William L. Senr. q.v. R.B.A. 1896. Exh. 1885-1939. Add: London 1885, 1906; Stanford le Hope, Essex 1893; Gravesend, Kent 1903; Pulborough, Sussex 1915; Amberley, Sussex and London 1919. † B 9, GOU 2, L 1, LS 5, M 4, NEA 2, RA 7, RBA 358, RHA 2, RI 5, ROI 6.

LULING, Peter Exh. 1938
Painter and etcher. † RED 1.

LUMB, Florence Emily Exh. 1897-1901
Liverpool. † L 3.

LUMB, Levi Exh. 1918-32
26 Moore Street, South Shore, Blackpool. † L 1, RCA 1.

LUMBY, H. O. Exh. 1937-40
44 Erasmus Road, Sparkbrook, Birmingham. † B 7.

LUMLEY, Augustus Savile Exh. 1880-99
Genre and portrait painter. London. † L 1, RA 1, RBA 1, RSA 1.

LUMLEY, Edith Exh. 1901-6
Figure painter. London. † L 1, P 3, RA 4.

LUMLEY-ELLIS, Mrs. Hilda Exh. 1925-28
Figure painter. Littlefield Manor, Worplesdon, Surrey. † RA 1, SWA 2.

LUMSDAINE, Amy Exh. 1891-93
Edrom, N.B. † D 4.

LUMSDEN, Mrs. Barbara Exh. 1933-38
Landscape painter. Springfield, Lyme Regis, Dorset. † RA 1, RBA 1, SWA 1.

LUMSDEN, D.A. Exh. 1908
13 South Bank, Oxton, Birkenhead. † L 1.

LUMSDEN, Mrs. E.F. Exh. 1905
† SWA 1.

LUMSDEN, Ernest S. b. 1883
Landscape and portrait painter, etcher and writer. Studied Reading School of Art, Juliens Paris and Edinburgh College of Art (1908). Travelled widely in India and the East. A.R.E. 1909, R.E. 1915, A.R.S.A. 1923, R.S.A. 1934. Exh. 1906-40. Add: Reading 1906; Edinburgh 1908. † BA 2, FIN 41, G 2, GI 14, L 63, RA 2, RE 58, RSA 97, RSW 2.

LUNAN, Alice M.M. Exh. 1933-35
40 Belmont Gardens, Glasgow. † GI 1, RSA 1.

LUNAN, T. Melville Exh. 1906
1 Beaumont Gate, Dowanhill, N.B. † GI 1.

LUNBERG, F.A. Exh. 1912
Hoylake, Cheshire. † L 1.

LUND, Alice R. Exh. 1919
Sculptor. 15 Springfield Terrace, Lancaster. † RA 1.

LUND, Kenneth F. Exh. 1907
8 Collingham Road, South Kensington, London. † L 1.

LUND, Niels Moller 1863-1916
Landscape painter and etcher. b. Denmark. Moved to Newcastle on Tyne at age 4. Studied Newcastle on Tyne, St. John's Wood, R.A. Schools and Paris. R.B.A. 1896, A.R.E. 1915-16, R.O.I. 1897. Add: London. † B 3, GI 3, L 20, M 3, RA 43, RBA 1, RE 9, RHA 1, RID 9, ROI 36.

LUNDIE, J.M. Exn. 1910-11
138 Finborough Road, Earl's Court, London. † L 2.

LUNDQUIST, John b. 1882
Swedish artist. Exh. 1933. Add: Klippgatan 13, Stockholm. † RSA 3.

LUNGLEY, Dorothy Exh. 1928-35
Colour woodcut and pottery artist, embroiderer and designer. Studied at the Royal College of Art. Add: 125 Coleherne Court, Earl's Court, London. † COO 3, L 4.

LUNGLEY, Edith Exh. 1928-39
Stained glass artist. Studied Royal College of Art (diploma in design 1913). A.R.M.S. 1928. Add: 10 Thurloe Court, London. † L 1, RA 20, SWA 5.

LUNGREN, Ferdinand 1859-1932
American painter. Exh. 1900-1. Add: Devon Lodge, Edwardes Square, Kensington, London. † I 1, L 4, RA 2.

LUNN, Dora E. Exh. 1915-27
London. † L 9.

LUNN, H. Augustus Exh. 1936-40
Figure painter. † COO 2, NEA 5.

LUNOIS, Alexandre 1863-1916
French artist. Exh. 1887-1911. Add: Paris. † GI 2, I 3, M 2.

LUNT, F. Gladys Exh. 1901
The Grove, Montague Road, Edgbaston, Birmingham. † B 1.

LUNT, Wilmot Exh. 1900-17
Painter. b. Warrington, Lancs. Studied Juliens and Ecole des Beaux Arts, Paris. Add: Warrington 1900; London 1906; Boreham, Elstree, Herts. 1907. † L 2, RA 4, RI 5.

LUNTLEY, James Exh. 1881-86
Portrait painter. Beeston, Notts. † N 8.

LUPTON, Edith D. Exh. 1880-93
Domestic painter. London. † D 1. RBA 5.

LUPTON, Miss E.J. Exh. 1937
30 Evesham Place, Stratford on Avon, Warwicks. † B 1.

LUPTON, Lewis F. b. 1909
Landscape painter and designer. Studied Sheffield College of Art 1923-30 and Westminster School of Art. Exh. 1940. Add: 23 Grove Park Gardens, London. † RA 3.

LUPTON, Mary A. Exh. 1887-93
Landscape painter. Add: London 1887; Baden, Germany 1893. † SWA 3.

LUPTON, Norman Exh. 1934-38
Chalmington, Dorset. † NEA 2, RBA 3.

LURCAT, Jean* 1892-1966
French painter, lithographer and tapestry designer. Exh. 1933-36. † L 1, LEF 21.

LURSEN, J.B. Exh. 1936
† RSA 2.

LURSSEN, Eduard Exh. 1883
Sculptor. Bausakademie, Berlin. † RA 2.

LUSH, H. Exh. 1906
4 Hopwood Terrace, Church Road, Teddington, Middlesex. † RA 1.

LUSH, Mary E. Exh. 1939
39 Welldon Crescent, Harrow, Middlesex. † SWA 1.

LUSY, Marino M. b. 1880
French artist. Exh. 1913. † CG 1.

LUTIGER, Frank b. 1871
Sculptor. Studied Ecole des Arts Industriels, Geneva and Academie Menn, Paris. Exh. 1896-1931. Add: London. † GI 2, I 2, L 13, RA 29, RMS 9.

LUTSCHER, Exh. 1892
18 Avenue de Villiers, Paris. † RHA 1.

LUTTEROTH, Professor A. Exh. 1891
Landscape painter. Uhlenhorst, Hamburg, Germany. † RI 3.

LUTTRELL, Mary Exh. 1924-28
Watercolour landscape painter. Studied under Wallace Rimington. † WG 123.

LUTYENS, Charles Augustus Henry* 1829-1915
Portrait, animal and sporting painter. Father of Edwin Landseer L. q.v. Exh. 1880-1903. Add: 16 Onslow Square, London. † D 1, G 1, M 1, RA 13, RHA 7, RI 1.

LUTYENS, Eadred J.T. Exh. 1927
Architect. 7 Buckingham Street, Adelphi, London. † RA 1.

LUTYENS, Sir Edwin Landseer 1869-1944
Architect (e.g. Cenotaph, Whitehall). Son of Charles Augustus Henry L. q.v. and father of Robert L. q.v. A.R.A. 1913, R.A. 1920. P.R.A. 1938-44. Knighted c.1918. Add: London. † GI 3, L 7, RA 66, RSA 10.

LUTYENS, F.M. Exh. 1889-99
Figure painter. Onslow Square, London. † G 1, L 1, M 1, P 1.

LUTYENS, Robert Exh. 1936-39
Architect. Son of Edwin Landseer L. q.v. Add: 5 Eaton Gate, London. † RA 3.

LUTZNER, W.T. Exh. 1910
Walworn, Haslington, Crewe. † L 1.

LUXMOORE, Arthur C.H. Exh. 1880-90
Watercolour landscape painter and etcher. A.R.E. 1888-91. Add: Kilburn, London 1880; Herne Bay, Kent 1886. † D 4, GI 1, RA 4, RE 9, RHA 1.

LUXMOORE, Kate F. Exh. 1880
Mrs. Arthur C.H.L. Figure painter. Add: 2a Brondesbury Road, Kilburn, London. † D 1.

LUXMORE, Myra E. d. 1919
Portrait and figure painter. A.R.M.S. 1910, R.M.S. 1911, A.S.W.A. 1908. Exh. from 1887. Add: London and Somerford, Newton Abbot, Devon. † B 13, L 19, M 11, P 9, RA 19, RBA 1, RID 53, RMS 23, SWA 12.

LUXTON, Alice E. Exh. 1897
14 Ardgowan Square, Greenock. † GI 1.

LUYTEN, Henry Exh. 1909
† LS 2,

LUZ, Julius Marsden Exh. 1883-91
Figure and domestic painter. London. † B 1, GI 1, L 2, M 4, RA 5, RBA 2.

LYALL, Gill Exh. 1931
† NEA 1.

LYALL, Miss M. Exh. 1895
18 Queen's Gate, London. † NG 1.

LYBAERT, Theophile Exh. 1901-12
Figure painter. 8 Place St. Michel, Ghent, Belgium. † L 5, RA 7.

LYCETT, Miss G. Exh. 1906-11
London 1906; Bourne End, Bucks. 1911. † L 3, RA 1.

LYCETT, Miss I. Exh. 1923-24
Castle Hill, Wolverley, Kidderminster. † B 3.

LYDDON, Albert Exh. 1899-1901
5 Gloucester Road, Brownswood Park, London. † RBA 3, RI 1.

LYDIS, Mariette* Exh. 1935-39
Painter, etcher and lithographer. London. † CG 49, RED 3, SWA 2.

LYE, Len Exh. 1933-34
Painter. † LEI 9.

LYLE, Peter Exh. 1927
Watercolour landscape painter. The Bungalow, Bluebell Inn, Attenborough, Notts. † N 2.

LYLE, Thomas Byron Exh. 1880-91
Figure and domestic painter. Add: Glasgow 1880 and 1889; London 1887. † GI 23, L 4, RA 1, RSA 10.

LYLE, W. Claud Exh. 1939-40
Eaglescliffe, Durham. † RSW 4.

LYMAN, E. Exh. 1909-11
A.N.S.A. 1912. Add: Croyland, Beeston, Notts. † N 7.

LYMN, Mrs. G.A. Exh. 1914
53 Hampstead Way, Golder's Green, London. † RA 1.

LYNAS, J. Langtry b. 1879
Sculptor and painter. Studied London and Paris. Exh. 1940. Add: 12 Bloomfield Gardens, Belfast. † RHA 2.

LYNAS-GRAY, John Abernethy b. 1869
Landscape, figure and genre painter. b. Oxton, Cheshire. Studied Liverpool and London. Exh. 1897-1928. Add Liverpool 1897; New Brighton, Cheshire 1901; Aysgarth, Yorks. 1907; Nant Peris, Carnarvonshire 1923. † B 1, L 2, M 1, RCA 4, RHA 1, RI 2.

LYNCH, Mrs. Exh. 1900
90 Oakley Street, Chelsea, London. † SWA 1.

LYNCH, Albert* Exh. 1893
Portrait painter. † P 1.

LYNCH, D.D. Exh. 1933
18 Clavell Road, Liverpool. † L 1.

LYNCH, Mrs. F. Exh. 1897-98
Ardley, Romford, Essex. † SWA 2.

LYNCH, Frank Exh. 1931-38
Sculptor. c/o Australia House, Strand, London. † RA 2.

LYNCH, Henrietta Exh. 1882-1919
61 Merrion Square, Dublin. † M 1, RHA 7, SWA 1.

LYNCH, Ibery Exh. 1913
Painter and illustrator. † FIN 38.

LYNCH, Marie L. Exh. 1917-20
Merrion, Dublin 1917; Kingstown, Ireland 1919. † RHA 7.

LYNCH, Rose Exh. 1899-1925
Mount Verdon, Summer Hill, Cork. † RHA 14.

LYNDE, Francis G. Exh. 1903
Figure painter. Fairseat, Wrotham, Kent. † RA 1.

LYNDE, Raymond Exh. 1899
Miniature portrait painter. 10 Porchester Gardens, London. † RA 1.

LYNDEN, de See D

LYNDON, Herbert Exh. 1880-1921
Landscape painter. London. † B 2, G 1, L 13, M 7, NG 1, RA 10, RBA 14, RHA 4, RI 9, ROI 12, RSA 1.

LYNE, Mrs. Amy Exh. 1922-29
nee Squire. Watercolour painter. Studied St. John's Wood and St. Martins Schools of Art. Add: London 1922; Broadfield, Warrent Street, Nr. Lenham, Kent 1928. † L 5, RA 1, RI 3, SWA 3.

LYNES, G.G. Exh. 1904-11
Dublin. † RHA 3.

LYNN, Miss E.C. Exh. 1913-19
1 Church Street, Grantham, Lincs. † N 3.

LYNN, William H. d. 1916
Architect. A.R.H.A. 1865, R.H.A. 1872. Exh. 1880-96. Add: Callendar Street, Belfast. † RHA 7.

LYNNE, Miss I. Exh. 1917
2 Craven Terrace, Settle, Yorks. † RA 1.

LYNTON, Cranford Exh. 1927
† D 3.

LYON, Alice Exh. 1882-91
Animal painter. 16 Inverness Terrace, Hyde Park, London 1882; Windlesham, Bagshot, Surrey 1887. † B 2, RA 1, RSA 12.

LYON, Charles E. Exh. 1889
Flower painter. 38 Ovington Square, London. † RA 1.

LYON, Emma Exh. 1892
Landscape painter. Hayes Lodge, Morley, Derby. † RID 1.

LYON, Edith F. Exh. 1885-90
Figure painter. 16 Inverness Terrace, Hyde Park, London 1885; Windlesham, Bagshot, Surrey 1887. † B 2, RBA 1, ROI 1, RSA 7.

LYON, George P. Exh. 1881-90
Landscape painter. Add: Glasgow 1881; Thornhill, by Stirling 1886. † GI 20, RA 1.

LYON, Henry J. Exh. 1897-1933
Landscape painter. St. Helens, Lancs. † L 70, RCA 26, RI 1.

LYON, Mrs. Hilda M. Exh. 1920-23
Miniature portrait painter. A.R.M.S. 1918. Add: Pontefract, Yorks. 1920; Atherstone, Leics. 1923. † RA 2.

LYON, John Howard d. 1921
Painter. Add: Edinburgh 1902; Strathyre 1914. † GI 6, RSA 18, RSW 2.

LYON, Kenneth Exh. 1934-35
49 Holland Park, London. † RBA 2.

LYON, Lucy S. Exh. 1884-1901
Flower painter. London. † GI 2, M 5, RBA 1, SWA 1.

LYON, Maurice b. 1887
Architect, painter and etcher. b. Rainhill, Lancs. Studied Birkenhead School of Art, Liverpool University and R.A. Schools. Served R.N.A.S. and R.A.F. (1915-19). Exh. 1927. Add: State Buildings Dept., Public Works Ministry, Cairo. † RA 1.

LYON, Robert b. 1894
Painter and decorative designer. Studied Liverpool School of Art, Royal College of Art and British School at Rome. R.O.I. 1932. Exh. 1915-40. Add: Liverpool 1915; London 1929; Corbridge on Tyne 1933. † L 9, RA 10.

LYON, Robert Exh. 1935-40
Castleview, Dollar 1935; Dumfries 1938; Art Department, The Academy, Dumfries 1940. † GI 4, RSA 6.

LYON, Rose Exh. 1900
21 Rotton Park Road, Edgbaston, Birmingham. † B 1.

LYON, Thomas Bonar b. 1873
Painter and etcher. Studied Glasgow School of Art, Royal College of Art, France, Belgium and Holland. Art master Royal Academy, Irvine and supervisor of Art in Schools, Ayrshire Education Authority. Exh. 1905-40. Add: Irvine, Ayrshire 1905; Mosside, Ayr 1911. † GI 80, RSA 22, RSW 2.

LYON, Thomas H. Exh. 1897-1923
Architect. Add: London 1897; University School of Architecture, Cambridge 1920. † RA 6.

LYON, W.F. Exh. 1887
50 Lincoln's Inn Fields, London. † RSA 1.

LYONCOURT, de See D

LYONS, Arthur J. Exh. 1911-21
Landscape painter. 39 Bis, Rue de la Grande, Chaumiere, Paris 1911; 14 Chepstow Place, London 1920. † L 3, RA 4.

LYONS, A. Wesley Exh. 1902-3
22 Lady Lawson Street, Edinburgh. † RSA 2.

LYONS, Andrew W. Exh. 1923-25
12 Melville Place, Edinburgh. † RSA 4.

LYONS, Edward Exh. 1926
40 Henderson Road, Forest Gate, London. † B 2.

LYSAGHT, Alfred Exh. 1890-93
Fair View, Tywyn, Conway, Wales. † RCA 9.

LYSONS, Gen. Sir Daniel Exh. 1893
22 Warwick Square, London. † D 2.

LYSONS, Ida Exh. 1935-39
London. † NEA 2, RBA 1, ROI 1, SWA 2.

LYSTER, Dorothea Exh. 1916-20
Sculptor. 6 Orme Square, Bayswater, London. † I 2, L 1, RA 2.

LYSTER, F.L. Exh. 1902
14 Olive Street, Liverpool. † L 1.

LYSTON, Mary Wenstead Exh. 1895
Grassendale, Liverpool. † L 1.

LYTTON, The Hon. Mrs. Exh. 1910
Animal painter. † CAR 9.

LYTTON, Hon. Neville 1879-1951
Portrait and landscape painter and fresco artist. b. Calcutta, India. Studied Ecole des Beaux Arts, Paris 1898. Exh. 1900-40. Add: London. † AG 1, ALP 185, BA 115, CAR 144, DOW 2, GOU 4, L 2, NEA 2, NG 1, P 19, RA 5.

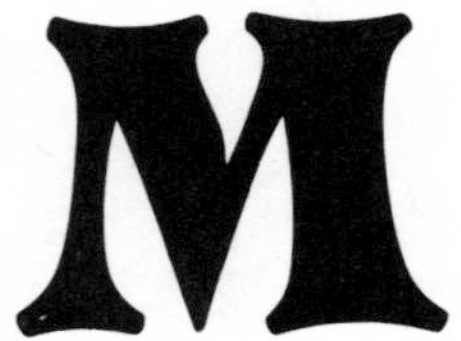

MAAN, Alex Exh. 1887-88
136 Wellington Street, Glasgow. † RSA 2.

MAARELS, Van der See V.

MAAS, Edith Exh. 1890-1909
Miniature painter. R.M.S. 1896. Add: London. † L 3, LS 3, NG 5, RA 27, RMS 14.

MABEY, Charles H. Exh. 1880-89
Sculptor. Prince's Street, Storey's Gate, London. † RA 5.

McADAM, B.J. Exh. 1914
10 New Square, Lincoln's Inn, London. † RA 1.

McADAM, Mrs. J. Exh. 1892-93
18 Percy Street, Liverpool. † L 2.

McADAM, Miss M. Exh. 1883
2 Adelaide Street, Kingstown, Ireland. † RHA 5.

MACADAM, Margaret Exh. 1923
† SWA 2.

McADAM, Walter 1866-1935
Painter. R.S.W. 1894. Add: Glasgow. † G 1, GI 115, RA 3, RSA 3, RSW 48, RWS 2.

M'ALDOWIE, J. Exh. 1885-1913
Edinburgh. † GI 4, RSA 16, RSW 2.

M'ALISTER, Beith Exh. 1916
47 Old Bond Street, London. † GI 2.

MacALISTER, Helen Exh. 1936-38
The Laurels, Buxton, Derbys. † RI 2.

McALLISTER, John A. Exh. 1919
12 Milewater Road, Belfast. † RHA 1.

M'ALLISTER, Stewart Exh. 1935-37
Glenholm, Wishaw. † GI 1, RSA 2.

MACALLUM, Hamilton* 1841-1896
Watercolour landscape, coastal and figure painter. Studied R.A. Schools. R.I. 1882. R.O.I. 1883, R.S.W. Add: London. † AG 16, D 3, G 7, GI 11, L 12, M 7, NG 10, RA 7, RI 39, ROI 25, TOO 21.

McALPINE, Helen Emmeline Exh. 1903-32
Mrs. Bacon. Watercolour landscape painter. b. London. Studied Lambeth, Glasgow and Edinburgh Schools of Art. Travelled on the continent. Add: Copack, Inverness. † B 9, D 7, L 1, LS 7, RSW 7, WG 54.

McALPINE, Mrs. Nellie Exh. 1924
25 Kenyon Road, Wavertree, Liverpool. † L 1.

McANALLY, Rachel Exh. 1935
3 Pembroke Villas, London. † SWA 1.

MacANDREW, Miss Exh. 1906
Harrow, Middlesex. † SWA 1.

MACANDREW, Ernest Henry b. 1877
Painter and etcher. b. Lima, Peru. Studied St. John's Wood and Slade School. Exh. 1905-38. Add: Dudley Lodge, Harrow, Middlesex. † G 1, I 1, L 3, M 1, P 2, RA 11, RID 37, ROI 7.

MacANTSIONNAIGH, S. Exh. 1925-27
128 Thorold Road, Ilford, Essex. † NEA 2, M 1.

MACARA, J. Exh. 1925
Portrait painter. Add: 66 Nottingham Road, Mansfield, Notts. † N 1.

M'ARA, Miss J.M. Exh. 1913
26 Lunedoch Street, Glasgow. † GI 1.

McARDLE, Miss F. Exh. 1883
Killeneg Villa, Egremont, Liverpool. † L 1.

MACARDLE, James Exh. 1930
† L 1.

MACAREE, Henry Exh. 1932
Watercolour urban landscape painter. Add: 29 Minerva Street, Hackney Road, London. † RA 1.

MACARTHUR, Agnes M. Exh. 1880-1902
Landscape painter. Add: 1 Darnaway Street, Edinburgh. † RSA 12, SWA 1.

MACARTHUR, Blanche F.* Exh. 1880-1903
Genre and portrait painter. Add: 30 John Street, Bedford Row, London. † B 28, D 7, GI 15, L 15, M 12, RA 3, RBA 14, RHA 40, RSA 20, SWA 20.

MACARTHUR, Donald M. Exh. 1940
18 Wellington Street, Edinburgh. † RSA 1.

MACARTHUR, Jane S. Exh. 1880-1903
Flower painter. Add: Darnaway Street, Edinburgh. † RSA 22, SWA 1.

McARTHUR, Lindsay G. Exh. 1886-1940
Figure and landscape painter. Add: Oban, Argyllshire 1886; Willersey, Glos. 1898; Broadway, Worcs. 1899; Winchcombe, Glos. 1911; London 1935. † L 17, M 1, NG 4, RA 34, ROI 3, RSA 4.

MACARTHUR, Mary Exh. 1880-98
Domestic painter. Add: 30 John Street, Bedford Row, London. † B 13, GI 14, M 3, RA 2, RBA 1, RHA 18, ROI 1, RSA 5, SWA 5.

MACARTNEY, Beatrix S. Exh. 1928-36
Landscape painter. Add: London. † COO 61, SWA 1.

MACARTNEY, Carlile Henry Hayes 1842-1924
Landscape painter. Travelled on the continent and in the Middle East. Add: London 1880; Edenbridge, Kent 1893; Crookham, Nr. Newbury, Berks. 1897. † D 8, G 1, L 4, M 2, RA 22.

MACARTNEY, Mervyn Ed. Exh. 1882-1927
Architect. Surveyor and architect to St. Paul's Cathedral, London. Add: London. † GI 2, RA 15.

MACARTNEY, Robin H. Exh. 1934
Watercolour landscape painter. Add: 13 Upper Hornsey Rise, London. † RA 1.

MACARTNEY, Sylvia Carlile Exh. 1940
Painter. Studied Chelsea Polytechnic and Colarossi's, Paris. † NEA 2.

MACAULAY, Kate Exh. 1880-96
Coastal and harbour painter. R.S.W. 1879 (resigned 1898)., A.S.W.A. 1880, S.W.A. 1890. Add: Capel Curig, North Wales. † D 24, DOW 4, GI 19, L 3, RA 5, RBA 6, RI 1, RSA 7, RSW 43, SWA 72.

MACAULAY, William John b. 1912
Painter, mosaic and stained glass artist. Studied Edinburgh College of Art 1930-35 and British School of Archaelogy 1935-36. Exh. 1937. Add: 80 Pilrig Street, Edinburgh. † RSA 1.

McAULEY, Charles J. Exh. 1933-39
Landscape painter. Add: Greenvalley, Cushendall, Co. Antrim. † RHA 5.

MACBEAN, Major General W. Forbes Exh. 1880
Val Rive, Dinan, France. † D 1.

MACBETH, Ann Exh. 1902-16
Glasgow 1902 and 1907; St. Anne's on Sea, Lancs. 1906. † GI 7, L 6.

MACBETH, James 1847-1891
Landscape painter. Add: London 1880 and 1884; Glasgow 1881; Churt, Surrey 1890. † G 3, GI 11, L 2, M 7, RA 4, RBA 1, RI 9, ROI 6, RSA 8.

MACBETH, L. Exh. 1886
Portrait painter. c/o Aitken and Dott, Edinburgh. † RA 1.

MACBETH, Norman* 1821-1888
Portrait painter. b. Aberdeen. Studied Engraving in Glasgow and later studied at R.A. Schools and in Paris. Father of Robert Macbeth q.v. and Henry Macbeth--Raeburn q.v. A.R.S.A. 1870, R.S.A. 1880. Died in London. Add: Edinburgh 1880; Hampstead, London 1886. † GI 17, RA 8, ROI 2, RSA 39.

MACBETH, Robert Walker* 1848-1910
Pastoral landscape and rustic genre painter and etcher. b. Glasgow. Son of Norman M. q.v. Studied in London. Worked for the "Graphic". A.R.A. 1883, R.A. 1903, R.E. 1880, H.R.E. 1909, R.I. 1882, R.O.I. 1883, A.R.W.S. 1871, R.W.S. 1901. "The Cast Shoe" purchased by Chantrey Bequest 1890. Add: London 1880; 1887 and 1898; Edinburgh 1886; Washford, Taunton, Somerset 1896. † AG 1, B 3, BG 2, CAR 2, DOW 5, FIN 5, G 13, GI 10, L 15, LEI 1, M 9, NG 13, P 4, RA 127, RE 49, RI 4, ROI 4, RSA 2, RWS 16.

MACBETH-RAEBURN, Henry 1860-1947
Painter and etcher. b. Helensburgh. Son of Norman M. q.v. Studied R.S.A. Schools and Juliens, Paris. A.R.A. 1921, R.A. 1933, R.E. 1899 and 1920. Add: Edinburgh 1880; Glasgow 1882; London 1883 and 1898; Walkingford, Berks. 1897; Newbury, Berks. 1925. † CON 3, GI 5, L 15, M 3, P 1, RA 143, RBA 1, RE 39, RI 4, ROI 8, RSA 24, WG 28.

McBEY, James* 1884-1959
Painter and etcher. b. Newburgh, Aberdeenshire. Travelled to Holland, Spain and Morocco 1913. Official artist to Egyptian Expeditionary Force 1917-18. Add: Aberdeen 1906; London 1912. † AB 3, AG 9, BA 11, BAR 1, CG 199, COO 2, FIN 144, G 119, GI 35, L 74, LEF 84, M 4, NEA 2, RA 15, RSA 12.

McBIRNEY, S. Exh. 1885
4 Cowper Road, Upper Rathmines, Dublin. † RHA 1.

MacBRAYNE, A. Madge Exh. 1914-38
Landscape painter. Add: Auchenteil, Helensburgh, Dumbartonshire. † GI 29, RA 1, RSA 18, RSW 2.

McBRAYNE, D.R. Exh. 1888
4 Lilybank Terrace, Glasgow. † GI 1.

MacBRAYNE, M. Exh. 1887
4 Lilybank Terrace, Glasgow. † GI 1.

McBRIDE, Aggie Exh. 1888-90
Tollcross, Glasgow. † GI 4.

MacBRIDE, Alexander 1859-1955
Watercolour painter. Studied Glasgow University and Juliens, Paris. R.I. 1899, R.S.W. 1887. Add: Glasgow. † AR 1, DOW 2, GI 145, L 5, M 2, RA 1, RI 147, RSA 9, RSW 141.

MacBRIDE, Alice Exh. 1914
Sunnyside House, Cathcart, Glasgow. † RI 1.

McBRIDE, Charles Exh. 1880-1902
Sculptor. Add: 7 Hope Street, Edinburgh. † GI 5, RA 2, RSA 40.

MacBRIDE, Mrs. John Exh. 1891-93
1 Colebrooke Place, Glasgow. † GI 2.

MacBRIDE, John Alexander Paterson 1819-1890
Sculptor. Studied under William Spence and under Samuel Joseph to whom he later became chief assistant. Exh. 1882-87. Add: London. † L 5.

McBRIDE, M. Hunter Exh. 1890-92
Tollcross, Glasgow. † GI 4.

McBRIDE, M. Wilson Exh. 1900
1 Colebrooke Place, Glasgow. † GI 1.
MacBRIDE, Nina Exh. 1928-39
33 Carpenter Road, Edgbaston, Birmingham. † B 13.
McBRIDE, Miss N. Rowan Exh. 1930
† P 1.
MacBRIDE, William* Exh. 1909-40
Stained glass artist, mural decorator, portrait and landscape painter. b. Ballymena, Ireland. Studied Royal College of Art and Dublin. Add: Belfast 1909; Dublin 1915. † RHA 35.
MacBRIDE, William d. 1913
Landscape painter. Add: Glasgow 1880, 1889 and 1896; Paris 1888; Edinburgh 1895. † GI 79, L 12, M 2, RA 5, RSA 25, RSW 3.
McBRYDE, J. Exh. 1890
Cowley Hill, St. Helens, Liverpool. † L 1.
McBRYDE, Nellie Exh. 1901
Miniature painter. Add: St. Andrews House, Mortimer Street, London. † RA 2.
McBRYDE, Robert* b. 1913
Studied Glasgow School of Art and France and Italy 1937-39. Exh. 1940. Add: Maybole, Ayrshire. † RSA 1.
McCAIG, Isobel Exh. 1938
Wimaisia, Abercromby Street, Helensburgh. † GI 1.
MacCALL, Mrs. A. St. John Exh. 1904-10
Grange Hill Lodge, South Norwood, London. † B 9.
MacCALL, Archibald St. John Exh. 1911-31
Landscape painter. R.B.A. 1913. Add: London 1911; Burnham on Crouch, Essex 1930. † GI,1, L 10, RA 4, RBA 104, RI 5.
McCALL, Charles James b. 1907
Painter and pastellier. Studied Edinburgh College of Art. Exh. 1932-40. Add: Edinburgh 1932; London 1938. † NEA 2, RA 1, RSA 14.
McCALL, F.W. Exh. 1929
72 Bold Street, Liverpool. † L 1.
McCALL, Gertrude S. Exh. 1887
Fruit painter. Add: Manor House, Newton Harcourt, Nr. Leicester. † RBA 2.
McCALL, Lizzie C. Exh. 1900
The Manse, Ardrossan, N.B. GI 1.
McCALL, Miss M. Exh. 1886
Ardrossan. † GI 1.
McCALLIEN, William J. Exh. 1899-1913
Tarbert, Loch Fyne. † GI 8, RSA 2.
McCALLUM, Mrs. Alice Exh. 1886
6 Leamington Street, Blackburn, Lancs. † M 1.
MacCALLUM, Andrew* 1821-1902
Landscape painter. b. Nottingham. H.N.S.A. 1885. Add: Nottingham 1881; 47 Bedford Gardens, Kensington, London 1882. † AG 4, B 21, G 1, L 17, M 17, N 1, RA 4.
McCALLUM, Philip Exh. 1891-94
Link Common, Malvern, Worcs. † B 7, M 1.
McCALMONT, Ethel E. Exh. 1883
Watercolour landscape painter. Hampton Court, London. † RA 1.
McCALMONT, H.B. Exh. 1881
Watercolour landscape painter. Add: Hampton Court, London. † RBA 1.
McCAMMOND, David Exh. 1891-95
8 Margaret Street, Greenock. † GI 6, L 1.
McCANN, Edith A. Exh. 1899-1900
3 College Park, East Belfast. † GI 3, RHA 2.
McCANN, L.E. Exh. 1894
† GI 1.
McCANN, Miss M. Exh. 1915
Slainte Studios, Anhalt Road, Albert Bridge, London. † L 1, RA 1.
McCANN, R. Greville Exh. 1924
Landscape painter. c/o Bank of Australasia, 4 Threadneedle Street, London. † L 1, RA 1.
MacCANN, Samuel Exh. 1922
† G 2.
MacCANN, Somhairle Exh. 1935
Landscape, figure and religious painter. Add: 3 Mill Street, Galway. † RHA 6.
McCANNELL, Ursula Vivian b. 1923
Figure and portrait painter and illustrator. Daughter of William Otway McC. q.v. and Winifred Cooper q.v. Exh. 1937-40. Add: Farnham, Surrey. † GOU 1, NEA 4, P 3, RA 1, RED 39, ROI 1, SWA 2.
McCANNELL, Mrs. Winifred See COOPER
McCANNELL, William Otway 1883-c.1971
Figure and landscape painter. b. Wallasey. Changed his name from Cannell to McCannell c. 1919. Studied Bournemouth Art School, Royal College of Art, France and Italy. Married Winifred Cooper q.v. Father of Ursula Vivian McC. q.v. Life instructor and lecturer of Art for the L.C.C. Principal of Farnham Art School. A.R.B.A. 1919, R.B.A. 1921, A.R.M.S. 1916, R.M.S. 1917. Exh. 1912-40. Add: London 1912 and 1918; St. Albans, Herts. 1915; Farnham, Surrey 1929. † COO 1, G 1, GI 28, GOU 4, L 17, NEA 2, P 2, RA 13, RBA 141, RHA 10, RI 9, RMS 6, ROI 4, RSA 2.
MACCARI, Cesare 1840-1919
Italian painter. Exh. 1880. Add: 536 Via Margretta, Rome. † D 1.
McCARTAN, Nora Exh. 1936-40
Flower, figure and landscape painter. Studied Metropolitan School of Art, Dublin. Add: Dublin. † RHA 6.
McCARTHY, Clara J. See CHRISTIAN
MacCARTHY, Desmond Exh. 1936
Still-life painter. Add: Sandymount Avenue, Dublin. † RHA 1.
McCARTHY, Emily Exh. 1899-1920
Dublin. † RHA 3.
MACCARTHY, E.B. Exh. 1919-21
Mrs. J. Redwood Anderson. Add: 41 Deringham Street, Springbank, Hull. † LS 6.
McCARTHY, G.M. Exh. 1936
Landscape painter. † LEF 1.
MacCARTHY, Hamilton P. b. 1847
Sculptor. Exh. 1880-84. Add: London. † RA 4.
MacCARTHY, John F. Exh. 1935-40
Landscape painter. Add: Mardyke, Cork 1935; Dublin 1940. † RHA 2.
McCARTHY, John James d. 1882
Architect. A.R.H.A. 1851, R.H.A. 1860. Add: London. † RHA 1.
McCARTHY, John S. Exh. 1885
Sculptor. Add: 32 Newman Street, London. † RA 1.
MacCARTHY, M. Exh. 1897
13 Batoun Gardens, West Kensington Park, London. † RBA 1.
McCARTHY, Madeline Exh. 1895
54 Glebe Studios, Glebe Place, Chelsea, London. † NG 1.
McCARTHY, M.D. Exh. 1932
Painter. Add: Buckleigh Road, Streatham, London. † RHA 1.
McCARTHY-MOR, W. Norman Exh. 1913-20
Miniature portrait painter. Add: Lancing, Sussex 1913; Horley, Surrey 1920. † RA 3.
McCAUL, Meta W. Exh. 1884
Marine painter. Add: Creggandarroch, Chislehurst, Kent. † RBA 1.
MacCAUL, Miss V. Exh. 1894-95
Abbey Institute, Nuneaton, Warwicks. † SWA 2.
McCAUSLAND, Charlotte Katherine Exh. 1884-1909
Landscape, portrait, figure and flower painter. Add: London. † D 2, G 1, GI 1, L 7, LS 3, M 1, NEA 1, P 1, RA 7, RBA 9, ROI 10, SWA 1.
McCAUSLAND, H.M. Exh. 1880-82
Add: Dublin 1880; Garvagh, Ireland 1882. † RHA 2, RSA 1.
McCAW, Terence J. Exh. 1935-36
Barclays Bank, 111 St. Martins Lane, London. † RBA 2, ROI 2.
McCAY, Edith Exh. 1926-28
32 Bentley Road, Liverpool. † L 3.
McCHEANE, A. Exh. 1938
† WG 2.
MacCHESNEY, Clara Taggart 1860-1928
American artist. Exh. 1905-6. Add: 27 West 33rd Street, New York, U.S.A. † RA 2, SWA 1.
M'CHEYNE, J.R. Murray b. 1911
Sculptor. Studied Edinburgh College of Art 1930-35, Copenhagen 1936-37 and Athens and Florence 1937-38. Exh. 1935-40. Add: Leslie 1935; Fair Mile Head 1935; Kings College, Newcastle on Tyne 1940. † RSA 9.
McCHLEARY, David Exh. 1924-30
45 Danes Drive, Scotstoun. † GI 8.
McCLATCHIE, Florence Exh. 1886-1905
Boothwick Hill, Bath, 1886; London 1900. † L 5, RA 1, RSA 1.
McCLEAN, Anna Exh. 1901-37
Landscape and seascape painter. b. Tunbridge Wells, Kent. Studied in London. Add: Tunbridge Wells, Kent 1901; Isle of Barra 1937. † L 3, NG 3, RA 5, RBA 1, RCA 1, ROI 2, SWA 2.
McCLEARY, Nelson Exh. 1929
c/o C. Candell, 5 Tottenham Street, London. † RI 2.
McCLEERY, Robert C. Exh. 1887-92
Landscape painter. Paint Room, Gaiety Theatre, London 1887; Camden Square, London 1892. † RI 4.
McCLELLAN, Miss E. Exh. 1908
35 Alexandra Road, London. † LS 2.
McCLELLAND, Miss L. Exh. 1894
Elmfield, Freshfield, Lancs. † L 2.
McCLELLAND, Miss P.J. Exh. 1920
The Manor House, Berkswell, Nr. Coventry. † B 2.
McCLINTOCK, Mary Howard (Maidhi) b. 1888
nee Elphinstone. Painter, modeller and woodcut artist. b. Bagshot, Surrey. Studied Slade School. Exh. 1925-34. Add: Edinburgh 1925; Godstone, Surrey 1934. † CON 40, D 7, GOU 2, L 1, RA 2, RBA 4, RI 3, RSA 10, RSW 6, SWA 2.
McCLOSKEY, A. Binford Exh. 1893
Flower painter. Add: 58 Rue Notre Dame de Lorette, Paris. † RBA 1.
M'CLOSKEY, William J. Exh. 1892-93
Painter. Add: 81 Charlotte Street, Fitzroy Square, London. † RBA 1, RI 1, ROI 3.
McCLOY, Samuel* Exh. 1880-91
Figure painter. Add: Belfast 1880; Clapham, London 1886. † RBA 6, RHA 6, RI 1, RSA 2.
McCLURE, Alick Exh. 1935-37
Portrait painter. Add: London 1935; Millard, Sussex 1936. † GI 3, P 2, RA 1.

McCLURE, Joseph Crosland Exh. 1900-14
Sculptor. Add: Hayton Quarry, Nr. Liverpool 1900; The Newarke, Leicester 1905; London 1913. † GI 7, L 11, RA 18.

McCLYMONT, John I. Exh. 1880-98
Figure painter. Add: Edinburgh. † GI 16, L 1, RA 2, RSA 36.

MacCOLL, Dugald Sutherland 1859-1949
Watercolour painter. b. Glasgow. Studied Westminster School. N.E.A. 1896, R.S.W. 1938. "Crock and Cottage Loaf No. 2" (1931) purchased by Chantrey Bequest 1940. Add: London. † AG 26, BG 1, CAR 47, CG 3, DOW 1, FIN 9, G 11, GI 10, GOU 107, L 3, M 7, NEA 162, RA 2, RSA 10, RSW 3.

M'COLL, Mrs. Kathleen Exh. 1940
Helensburgh, Dumbartonshire. † GI 1.

McCOLL, Samuel Exh. 1939
† RSA 1.

McCOMAS, Francis* Exh. 1908
Watercolour landscape painter. † CAR 22.

McCOMAS, Miss J.L. Exh. 1899
The Grange, Monkstown, Co. Dublin. † RHA 1.

McCOMB, Mary Exh. 1895
7 India Street, Glasgow. † GI 1.

McCOMBIE, Miss R. Exh. 1887
Aberdeen. † RSA 1.

McCOMISKEY, Miss J.E. Exh. 1896-97
Baymount Lodge, Booterstown. † RHA 2.

McCONCHIE, John Exh. 1892-94
West Kilbride, Ayrshire 1892 and 1894; Paris 1893. † GI 4.

McCONNACHIE, Margaret Exh. 1921
St. Rule, Prenton Lane, Prenton, Cheshire. † L 1.

McCONNELL, Miss D. Exh. 1889
Flower painter. Add: 6 Petersham Terrace, South Kensington, London. † SWA 1.

MacCONNELL, Jessie Exh. 1909
Figure and landscape painter. † GOU 2.

McCONNELL, Jeannie Margaret Exh. 1924-35
Miniature portrait painter. A.R.M.S. 1924. Add: Banbury, Oxon 1924; Oxford 1925; Dowlais, Glam. 1935. † L 1, RA 6, RMS 7.

MacCONVILLE, Charles Exh. 1938-40
Rankin Drive, Largs. † GI 3.

McCORD, Mary Rose Exh. 1934-40
Landscape painter. Add: Enniskerry, Co. Wicklow. † RHA 6.

McCORKINDALE, Flora Exh. 1908-37
Craiginan Lodge, Dollar, N.B. 1908; Birnam, Perthshire 1937. † GI 3, RSA 1.

MacCORMACK, Katherine Exh. 1929
Dun Emer, Dundrum, Ireland. † RHA 1.

McCORMACK, William W. Exh. 1911-18
Anchorage, Helensburgh, N.B. 1911; Lurgan 1914. † GI 2, RSA 5.

McCORMICK, Arthur David* 1860-1943
Landscape and figure painter. b. Colgraine, Ireland. Studied Royal College of Art. R.B.A. 1897, R.I. 1906, R.O.I. 1905. Add: London. † ALP 88, B 2, BK 21, GI 2, L 12, RA 49, RBA 24, RHA 7, RI 91, ROI 33.

McCORMICK, Miss M.A. Exh. 1920-21
Landscape and coastal painter. c/o Mrs. Malam, 17 Jameson Street, Hull. † RA 1, RSW 1.

McCORMICK, Mrs. Nettie J. Exh. 1906-32
Landscape painter. Add: Dublin 1906; London 1923. † GOU 2, L 9, RA 1, RHA 46, SWA 1.

McCOWEN, Doris M. Exh. 1921-39
Painter and wood cut artist. Add: London. † CHE 1, COO 4, GOU 4, L 7, M 2, NEA 5, RA 1, RSA 1.

McCOY, Miss M.H. Exh. 1926
Leoville, Waterford, Ireland. † RHA 1.

McCRACKEN, Cynthia G.S. Exh. 1918-40
Ochter House, Elie, Fife. † GI 1, RSA 1, RSW 1.

M'CRACKEN, Francis Exh. 1922-39
10 Forth Street, Edinburgh. † GI 3, L 3, RSA 30, RSW 5.

McCRACKEN, Katharine 1844-c.1930
Landscape painter and illustrator. Studied under Sir James Linton and at the British Museum. A.S.W.A. 1904. Add: London 1880; Perugia, Italy 1905. † B 18, D 1, GI 2, L 11, M 5, NG 16, RA 6, RI 28, SWA 83.

McCREA, Evelyn J. Exh. 1934-35
Painter. Add: c/o Bourlet and Sons, 17 Nassau Street, London. † RHA 1, ROI 2, SWA 1.

McCREA, N. Exh. 1928
Heathfield, Denmark Road, Gloucester. † L 1.

McCREADY, Mrs. Nellie B. Exh. 1927-30
Flower and landscape painter. Add: 20 College Gardens, Belfast. † FIN 1, RHA 9.

M'CRINDLE, A.D.A. Exh. 1928-33
Gowanbrae, Girvan, Ayrshire. † GI 2, L 2, RSA 2, RSW 1.

McCROSSAN, Jessie Exh. 1926
Colaborated with Miss E. Waddington, q.v. The Craft Room, West Mersea, Mersea Island, Essex. † L 7.

McCROSSAN, Mary d. 1934
Landscape, figure and flower painter. b. Liverpool. Studied Liverpool School of Art and Academie Delecluse, Paris. A.R.B.A. 1926, R.B.A. 1927. Add: Liverpool 1886; London 1911; St. Ives, Cornwall 1931. † AB 3, BA 58, BG 93, CHE 5, GI 10, GOU 59, I 11, L 113, LS 34, M 7, NEA 30, RA 22, RBA 67, RHA 1, RI 4, ROI 7, RSA 2, SWA 8.

McCRUM, Joseph Pierce Exh. 1929-38
Landscape painter. Add: Edgware, Middlesex 1929; London 1938. † NEA 1, RA 1.

McCRUM, W.S. Exh. 1921-22
Feddans, Marlborough Park, Central Belfast. † L 1, RHA 4.

MACCULLOCH, Andrew A. Exh. 1917-27
Public Works Office, Edinburgh. † RSA 2.

McCULLOCH, D.R. Exh. 1888
50 West Clyde Street, Helensburgh. † GI 1.

McCULLOCH, Elizabeth M. Exh. 1886
2 Alfred Place, Newington. † RSA 1.

McCULLOCH, George Exh. 1880-1901
Landscape and figure painter and sculptor. Add: London 1880; Logan, Stranraer 1901. † D 2, G 1, GI 7, M 2, RA 20, RBA 1, ROI 1.

McCULLOCH, Herbert Graham b. 1883
Landscape painter. Studied Chester School of Art. Exh. 1925-39. Add: Glenside, Talybont, Talycafn, N. Wales. † RCA 11.

MacCULLOCH, James d. 1915
Landscape painter. R.B.A. 1884, R.S.W. 1885. Add: London. † D 15, DOW 4, G 1, GI 23, L 4, M 5, RA 1, RBA 120, RI 24, ROI 1, RSA 1, RSW 68.

McCULLOCH, Joseph Ridley Ratcliffe b. 1893
Watercolour painter and etcher. b. Leeds. Studied Leeds College of Art and Royal College of Art. Painting master and visiting master in Life Drawing at Ipswich School of Art. R.B.A. 1935. Exh. 1921-40. Add: Leeds 1921; Ipswich 1923; London 1927. † CHE 3, LEI 3, M 1, NEA 10, RA 18, RBA 9, RED 6, RI 1.

McCULLOCH, Mary Miller Exh. 1900-10
Kilmarnock, N.B. † GI 8, L 6, RA 1, RSA 1.

McCULLOCH, Margaret Nicholas b. 1881
Landscape and figure painter. Studied Liverpool School of Art. Exh. 1911. Add: 10 Heald Street, Garston, Liverpool. † L 1.

McCURDY, Mrs. Louise M. Exh. 1905-7
36 Steele's Road, Haverstock Hill, London. † B 4.

McCUTCHION, John Exh. 1935-40
3 Lothian Gardens, Glasgow. † GI 3, RSW 2.

McDERMOTT, Edith K.M. Exh. 1923
22 Wellington Place, Belfast. † L 14.

McDERMOTT, Norman Exh. 1916
162 Chatham Street, Liverpool. † L 9.

MACDERMOTT, Miss N.A. Exh. 1912-16
86 Singleton Avenue, Prenton, Birkenhead. † L 29.

McDERMOTT, W.K. Exh. 1913
Boro Green, Kent. † RA 1.

McDONALD, Alexander Exh. 1893-1913
Portrait painter. Add: Aberdeen, Bushey, Herts. 1893; Winchester, Hants. 1901. † B 1, L 2, RA 11, RSA 1.

MACDONALD, Alfred Exh. 1881-1920
Landscape painter. Add: Oxford 1881; Watford, Herts. 1894. † D 1, L 6, RA 16, RI 2.

MACDONALD, Alice Exh. 1897-1902
4 Marine Terrace, Aberdeen. † GI 2.

MACDONALD, Arthur Exh. 1897-1940
65 West Regent Street, Glasgow 1897; Pittenweem, Fife 1902. † GI 95, L 3, M 2, RSA 29, RSW 3.

MacDONALD, A.F. Exh. 1931
Landscape painter. Add: 79 Newton Avenue, Blackrock, Co. Dublin. † RHA 1.

MacDONALD, A.G. Exh. 1885
38 Warrender Park Terrace, Edinburgh. † RSA 1.

MacDONALD, Alister G. Exh. 1932
Architect. Add: 13 Queen Anne's Gate, London. † RA 1.

MACDONALD, A.M. Exh. 1880-88
Edinburgh. † RSA 27.

MACDONALD, Archibald W. Exh. 1930-33
Glasgow 1930; Coventry 1932. † B 3, RSA 1.

MACDONALD, Biddy Exh. 1895-1938
Portrait painter. Married Alexander Jamieson q.v. Add: London. † B 1, CHE 2, GI 1, I 2, L 3, LS 8, P 12, ROI 1, RSA 2, SWA 4.

MACDONALD, Miss C. Exh. 1894
Church Street, Egremont, Cheshire. † L 2.

MACDONALD, Mrs. E. Exh. 1914
Streatham Hill, London. † SWA 1.

MACDONALD, Edith Exh. 1911-12
103 Upper Richmond Road, Putney, London. † D 3.

MacDONALD, Evan Exh. 1928
14 Bedford Place, London. † ROI 2.

MacDONALD, Mrs. E.B. Exh. 1928-33
Flower painter. Add: 7 Netherton Grove, London. † FIN 1, ROI 1, WG 45.

MACDONALD, E.M. Exh. 1888
3 Gt. King Street, Edinburgh. † RSA 1.

MACDONALD, Freda Exh. 1908-9
9 St. Paul's Studios, West Kensington, London. † LS 7.

MACDONALD, Fred A. Exh. 1910-14
15 Heathfield Road, Tenenure, Co. Dublin. † RHA 12.

MACDONALD, Frances E. Exh. 1893-98
9 Windsor Terrace, Glasgow. † GI 2, L 3, RSW 1.

MACDONALD, Mrs. Gertrude Exh. 1912-28
Mrs. J.A. Figure and interior painter. Add: Neatherlea, Ilkeston, Derbys. † N 23, RA 1.

MACDONALD, Hugh Exh. 1906-20
Glasgow. † GI 15, RA 1.

MACDONALD, Ione Exh. 1904-28
Mrs. Burrows. Watercolour landscape and miniature painter. Add: London. † L 1, RA 2, WG 153.

MACDONALD, Irene Exh. 1889-90
Portrait painter. Add: Casa Coraggie, Bordighera. † RID 4.

MacDONALD, J. Exh. 1885
8 Leslie Place, Edinburgh. † RSA 2.

MacDONALD, Miss J. Exh. 1926-29
25 Campden Street, London. † ROI 1, SWA 1.

McDONALD, James Exh. 1885
19 Belgrave Road, Rathmines, Dublin. † RHA 1.

MACDONALD, James Exh. 1936
368 Main Street, High Blantyre, Lanarks. † GI 1.

McDONALD, Jessie Exh. 1880-89
Edinburgh 1880; Pollokshields 1881. † GI 6, RSA 3.

McDONALD, John Blake* 1829-1901
Landscape and historical genre painter. A.R.S.A. 1862, R.S.A. 1877. Add: Edinburgh. † RSA 76.

MACDONALD, J.C. Exh. 1938
† M 1.

MACDONALD, J.H. Exh. 1898
4 St. Peter's Place, Edinburgh. † RSA 1.

MacDONALD, J.L. Exh. 1882
16 Greenside Street, Edinburgh. † RSA 1.

McDONALD, Miss J.M. Exh. 1882-89
Stonehaven 1882; Edinburgh 1889. † RSA 6.

MACDONALD, J.T. Exh. 1889-1919
Liverpool 1889; London 1898. † L 27.

MACDONALD, L.A. Exh. 1880
Southannan, Fairlie. † GI 1.

MACDONALD, Lucy Winifred b. 1872
nee Cary. Miniature painter, restorer and manageress of the Arlington Galleries Ltd. R.M.S. 1897 (Sec. from 1918). Exh. 1896-1940. Add: London. † L 4, NG 1, RA 16, RMS 26.

MACDONALD, Murray Exh. 1889-95
Edinburgh. † RSA 7.

McDONALD, Madeline M. Exh. 1896-1936
Portrait and landscape painter. A.S.W.A 1930. Add: London. † I 10, L 1, P 2, RA 17, SWA 8.

MACDONALD, Margaret M. Exh. 1880-1922
R.S.W. 1898 (resigned 1923). Married Charles Rennie Mackintosh q.v. Add: Glasgow 1880; London 1921. † GI 14, I 3, L 4, RSA 1, RSW 21.

MACDONALD, Dr. Ronald Annandale b. 1899
Etcher. Studied Edinburgh College of Art. Exh. 1928-31. Add: 69 Merchiston Crescent, Edinburgh. † RSA 3.

MacDONALD, Robina Murray Exh. 1898
95 Bristol Street, Manchester. † L 1.

McDONALD, Robert Nevil Exh. 1887-88
Galston. † GI 3.

MACDONALD, Somerled Exh. 1891-1939
Portrait painter. Add: Armadale, Skye 1891; Edinburgh 1900; Inverness 1939. † GI 3, L 1, LS 3, RA 1, RSA 16.

MacDONALD, Mrs. Ursula Exh. 1936
Watercolour architectural painter. Add: 8 Lansdowne Crescent, Worcester. † RA 1.

MACDONALD, William Exh. 1884-1938
Landscape painter. Married Beatrice Huntingdon q.v. Add: London 1884; Bushey, Herts. 1905; Edinburgh 1911. † B 1, D 2, GI 4, LS 2, RA 4, RBA 3, ROI 3, RSA 24.

MACDONALD, W. Alister Exh. 1935-36
Watercolour landscape painter. † AR 244.

MacDONNELL, Miss H.J. Exh. 1907
Liverpool. † SWA 1.

McDONNELL, James Exh. 1880-89
19 Belgrave Road, Rathmines, Dublin. † RHA 9.

MACDONNELL, Laurence A. Exh. 1881-93
Architect. Dublin. † RA 1, RHA 3.

MacDONNELL, Violet Exh. 1916-21
65 Dartmouth Square, Leeson Park, Dublin. † RHA 4.

McDOUGAL, John Exh. 1880-1934
Landscape and coastal painter. Add: Liverpool 1880; Cemaes, Nr. Amlwch, Anglesea 1900. † B 8, FIN 1, GI 7, L 117, M 7, RA 26, RBA 4, RCA 88, RI 6, RSA 2, RSW 7.

McDOUGAL, Miss N. Exh. 1882-99
Liverpool. † L 40.

MACDOUGALD, George Duncan Exh. 1910-36
Sculptor and painter. Add: London 1910 and 1936; Beaconsfield, Bucks. 1918. † GI 3, L 3, RA 10, RSA 3.

MACDOUGALL, Agnes Exh. 1894
Sghor Bheann, Bullwood, Dunoon. † GI 1.

MACDOUGALL, Allan* Exh. 1880-89
Hillside House, Partickhill Road, Glasgow. † GI 3, RSA 1.

McDOUGALL, Archibald Exh. 1900
18 Randolph Gardens, Partick, Glasgow. † GI 1.

MacDOUGALL, Colquhoun Exh. 1938
Flower and landscape painter. † BK 29.

MACDOUGALL, Jessie Exh. 1910-16
Mrs. Ronald L. Add: Drumleck, Baily, Howth, Ireland 1910; The Park, Ealing, London 1916. † LS 10, RHA 7.

MacDOUGALL, Lily M.M. Exh. 1900-40
Bonnyrigg, Midlothian 1900; Edinburgh 1909. † GI 3, RSA 16, RSW 7.

MacDOUGALL, M.O. Exh. 1931-32
6 Barington Drive, Glasgow. † GI 2.

McDOUGALL, Norman M. Exh. 1880-1927
Landscape painter. Add: Glasgow 1880 and 1889; London 1881. † D 1, GI 47, L 27, M 1, RA 7, RBA 11, RI 4, RSA 13, RSW 3.

McDOUGALL, Mrs. Violet Exh. 1926-40
Landscape painter. Add: Icknield, Tring, Herts. † B 1, COO 38, M 1, NEA 2, RA 1, RBA 2, RCA 5, ROI 12, RSA 4, SWA 5.

MACDOUGALL, William Brown d. 1936
Painter, black and white artist, etcher and wood engraver. Studied Julians, Paris. N.E.A. 1890. Add: Glasgow 1887; Loughton, Essex 1926. † GI 9, L 1, M 1, NEA 6, RA 2, RSA 6.

M'DOWAL, Jessie Exh. 1921-24
Miniature painter. Add: Sketty Park, Sketty, Glamorgan. † B 1, L 2, RA 1, RSA 3.

M'DOWALL, Mrs. Flora Exh. 1915-17
Carrondale, Larbert, N.B. † GI 2, RSA 2.

MacDOWALL, J. Stuart Exh. 1915
27 Main Street, Kilbirnie, N.B. † GI 1.

McDOWALL, Mary Exh. 1916-39
Painter, lino and woodcut artist. Add: Broadmayne, Dorset 1916; Chelsea, London 1928. † COO 2, GOU 5, L 2, NEA 4, RA 1, RED 4.

McDOWALL, William Exh. 1938
c/o Black, 262 Bath Street, Glasgow. † RSA 1.

McDOWALL, William b. 1905
Landscape painter. b. Girvan, Ayrshire. Studied Edinburgh College of Art. Exh. 1931-40. Add: Edinburgh 1931; London 1938. † RSA 9.

M'DOWELL, C. Exh. 1925
10 Belgrave Road, Rathmines, Dublin. † RHA 3.

McDOWELL, G. Moore Exh. 1882-86
Stained glass artist. London. † L 1, RA 3.

McDOWELL, Mrs. Hilda Exh. 1934-37
Winchester, Hants. † SWA 3.

McDOWELL, William Exh. 1919-28
Painter. Add: Barrow in Furness 1919; Wallasey, Cheshire 1927. † L 5, RA 1.

MACE, John Edmund b. 1889
Landscape, flower and marine painter. Official artist in France 1918-19. R.B.A. 1934. Exh. 1920-38. Add: 179 Queen Victoria Street, London. † G 2, L 4, LS 3, RA 7, RBA 23, RI 9, RMS 1, ROI 6.

MacEGAN, Darius J. (The) Exh. 1881-1939
Landscape, figure and interior painter. Add: Dublin 1881; Dunlaoghaire 1936. † RHA 85.

McELDOWNEY, Miss Iva Exh. 1925
c/o Reeves and Son, 161 High Street, Kensington, London. † ROI 1.

McELWEE, Bessie S. Exh. 1910-22
93 Hope Street, Glasgow. † L 53.

MacELWEE, Henry Kennedy d. c.1971
Painter and draughtsman. b. Rathmelton, Co. Donegal. Studied Westminster School of Art 1912, Royal College of Art 1913, and Slade School 1923-27. † CHE 1, GOU 1.

McENTEE, Jervis 1828-1891
American painter. Exh. 1880. Add: 51 West Tenth Street, New York, U.S.A. † RA 1.

McENVOY, William Exh. 1880
Landscape painter. Add: Minerva Villa, The Newlands, Peckham Rye, London. † RSA 3.

M'ERLEAN, John F. Exh. 1930
126 Castle Street, Glasgow. † GI 1.

McEUNE, R.E. Exh. 1913
36 St. Albans Terrace, Gatehead on Tyne. † RI 1.

McEVOY, A. Ambrose* 1878-1927
Portrait, landscape and figure painter. b. Crudwell, Wilts. Studied Slade School 1893. Visited the continent and New York (1920). Served with the Royal Navy World War I. Married Mary McE. q.v. N.E.A. 1902, A.R.A. 1924, R.P. 1925. "Michael McEvoy" (1919) purchased by Chantrey Bequest 1939. Add: London 1900 and 1906; Shrivenham, Berks. 1903. Died of pneumonia in London. † AG 1, CHE 4, G 23, GI 2, GOU 4, I 69, L 14, LEI 109, LS 3, M 2, NEA 105, P 11, RA 12, RHA 4, RSA 6, RSW 1, RWS 4.

McEVOY, Christopher C. Exh. 1937-38
Figure and landscape painter and pencil artist. Add: Abbotsleigh Cottage, Freshford, Bath. † RA 3.

McEVOY, Mary 1870-1940
nee Edwards. Portrait, interior and flower painter. Married A. Ambrose McE. q.v. Add: Freshford, Bath 1899; London 1902 and 1906; Shrivenham, Berks. 1904. † AG 1, FIN 6, GOU 4, LS 4, M 1, NEA 26, RA 13, SWA 1.

McEWAN, Agnes Exh. 1899-1906
Alva, N.B. † GI 4, RSA 3.

McEWAN, A.D. Exh. 1896-1905
Crosshill, N.B. 1896; Cathcart, N.B. 1901; Glasgow 1905. † GI 3.
McEWAN, Daniel Exh. 1885-1907
Glasgow 1885; 3 Albert Drive, Crosshill 1887; 1 Gray Street, Shettleston, 1906. † GI 5.
McEWAN, James Exh. 1894-97
Hazelwood, Grange, West Lothian 1894; Edinburgh 1897. † RSA 2.
McEWAN, M. Exh. 1890-91
Glasgow. † GI 3.
McEWAN, Miss M.G. Exh. 1898
28 Chalk Hill, New Bushey, Herts. † RSA 1.
McEWAN, Peter Exh. 1888-89
3 Albert Drive, Crosshill, Glasgow. † GI 2.
McEWAN, Thomas* 1861-1914
Figure painter. R.S.W. 1883. Add: Glasgow 1880, 1886 and 1903; Helensburgh 1885; Strathbungo 1900; Gourock 1913. † DOW 2, GI 97, L 1, M 2, RA 1, RSA 2, RSW 49.
McEWAN, Walter Exh. 1902
11 Place Pigalle, Paris. †, L 1.
MacEWAN, Winnie Exh. 1906-34
Painter. Add: London. † LS 5, M 1, RA 3, SWA 1.
McEWEN, Charles Exh. 1880-92
Landscape painter. Add: West Regent Street, Glasgow. † GI 42, L 1, RA 2, RBA 1, RSA 2.
McEWEN, Frank Exh. 1931
† GOU 2.
McEWEN, Francis J Exh. 1936
† NEA 1.
MacEWEN, Helen B. Exh. 1889
8 Rosslyn Terrace, Kelvinside, Glasgow. † GI 2.
MacEWEN, J. Exh. 1891
79 High Street, Lochee, N.B. † RSA 1.
McEWEN, Kate Exh. 1881
Hill of Drip, Nr. Stirling. † GI 1, RSA 1.
MacEWEN, Molly Exh. 1935
Inverness. † RSW 1.
McEWEN, Miss M. Poyntz Exh. 1899-1905
Figure painter. Add: Inverness, N.B. † RA 2, RI 1, RSA 1, SWA 2.
McEWEN, Robert d. 1882
Landscape painter. Exh. 1881. Add: Glasgow. † GI 1.
MACEY, Miss F.M. Exh. 1925-26
Willow Studio, Willow Road, Hampstead, London. † L 8.
McFADDEN, Frank Exh. 1881-92
Landscape and architectural painter. Add: Avenue Road, Southampton 1881 and 1884; Bushey, Herts. 1883. † D 2, FIN 1, L 2, RA 3, RE 3, ROI 1.
McFADDEN, Rowland Exh. 1907-8
Landscape and architectural painter. Add: Avenue Road, Southampton. † RA 3.
MACFALL, Major C. Haldane 1860-1928
Figure, landscape and military painter. Exh. 1891-1923. Add: London. † I 4, RA 3.
MacFARLAN, Amy J.L. Exh. 1894
Invermay, Lake Road, Wimbledon, London. † GI 1.
MacFARLAN, Miss H.A. Exh. 1918-19
Invermay, Lake Road, Wimbledon, London. † RA 1, SWA 1.
McFARLANE, A. Exh. 1897
7 Scott Street, Garnett Hill, Glasgow. † RSA 1.
MACFARLANE, Alasdair Exh. 1932-37
24 Ibrox Street, Glasgow. † GI 6, RSA 1.
MACFARLANE, Miss Anne Exh. 1932-38
Woodlea, 5 Fox Street, Greenock. † RSA 2.
MACFARLANE, Mrs. Anne Exh. 1909-13
68 Lauriston Place, Edinburgh. †, RSA 1, RSW 2.
MacFARLANE, D. Exh. 1931-34
433 Strand, London. † RI 3, ROI 2.
MacFARLANE, Frances Exh. 1920-22
College of Art, Edinburgh 1920; Lugton, St. Andrews 1922. † GI 2, RSA 1.
MacFARLANE, George G. Exh. 1928-29
Architect. Add: 41 Acacia Road, London. † RA 1, RSA 1.
MACFARLANE, Mrs. H.E. Exh. 1906
33 Granville Road, Fallowfield, Manchester. † M 1.
McFARLANE, Hilda J. Exh. 1909-10
3 Princes Terrace, Dowanhill, N.B. † GI 2.
McFARLANE, John Exh. 1910-11
Thistlebank, Ashgrove Street, Ayr. † GI 2.
MACFARLANE, Mrs. John P. Exh. 1900
Sylvan Grove, C. on M., Manchester. † M 1.
MACFARLANE, J.R. Exh. 1882-1905
Glasgow 1882; Partick, Glasgow 1904. † GI 5.
MacFARLANE, T.D. Exh. 1894-97
12 Dalhousie Street, Glasgow. † GI 2.
MACFARLANE, W.W. Exh. 1883-1909
Edinburgh. † RSA 4.
MacFARLAYNE, D. Exh. 1914
70 Barry Road, East Dulwich, London. † LS 3.
MACFEE, John Exh. 1887
176 Commercial Road, London. † RI 1.
MACFIE, Barbara E. Exh. 1939
17 Westercoates Terrace, Edinburgh. † RSA 1.
McGAREL-HOGG, Hon. A. Exh. 1910-17
36 Lincoln's Inn Fields, London. † RA 2.
McGAVIGAN, Anna Exh. 1901
Jessieville, Lenzie, N.B. † GI 1.
McGAW, John Thorburn 1872-1952
Watercolour painter. Studied under F.E. Andrews. A.R.B.A. 1940, R.I. 1940. Exh. 1920-40. Add: St. Leonards Forest, Horsham, Sussex. † B 7, COO 2, L 6, RBA 6, RCA 19, RID 4, RWS 3.
MACGEAGH, John Exh. 1938
Architect. Add: 23 Ocean Buildings, Donegall Square, Belfast. † RA 1.
McGECHAN, David Exh. 1885
7 Clunebraefoot, Port Glasgow. † RSA 1.
McGECHAN, M.M. Exh. 1893-1903
Paisley, Glasgow. † GI 12, RSA 1.
McGEE, Mary A. Exh. 1880-96
Drumcondra 1880; Dublin 1885. † RHA 12.
McGEEHAN, Aniza b. 1874
Mrs. V. Murphy. Sculptor. Studied Glasgow School of Art, Colarossi's, Paris. Exh. 1894-1931. Add: Rawyards, Airdrie 1894; Glasgow 1897; Liverpool 1902 and 1927; London 1904. † GI 17, L 11, RA 8, RSA 3.
McGEEHAN, Jessie M. Exh. 1892-1913
Rawyards, Airdrie 1892; 134 Bath Street, Glasgow 1897. † GI 34, L 29, RA 1, RSA 11.
McGEOCH, Anderson James b. 1913
Painter, draughtsman and sculptor. Studied Glasgow School of Art 1932-37. Exh. 1938. Add: 53 Underwood Road, Paisley, Glasgow. † RSA 1.
MacGEORGE, Mrs. M.V. Exh. 1919-40
nee Monro. Watercolour painter. R.S.W. 1930. Add: Edinburgh 1919; Bield, Gifford, East Lothian 1931. † AR 2, GI 4, RSA 41, RSW 44.
MacGEORGE, William Stewart* 1861-1931
Portrait and landscape painter. b. Castle Douglas. Studied R.S.A. Schools. Travelled in Italy. A.R.S.A. 1898, R.S.A. 1910. Add: Castle Douglas 1885; Edinburgh 1888 and 1913; Kirkcudbright 1909 and 1918. † GI 56, L 8, M 8, RA 8, RHA 3, RSA 148.
McGHIE, John* b. 1867
Painter and etcher. Studied Glasgow School of Art, R.A. Schools and Juliens, Paris. Exh. 1891-1940. Add: Hamilton, N.B. 1891; Glasgow 1892. † GI 114, L 5, RA 8, RSA 18, RSW 2.
M'GHIE, John N. Exh. 1936
Bellfield, 49 Muir Street, Lanarkshire. † RSA 1.
McGIBBON, Alexander Exh. 1886-91
Architect. Add: Glasgow. † GI 3, RA 1.
MacGIBBON, Andrew Exh. 1901
Walberswick, Southwold, Suffolk. † M 2.
McGIBBON, Bell C. Exh. 1901-12
23 Learmouth Terrace, Edinburgh. † RSA 3.
McGIBBON, Jessie R. Exh. 1896-1910
23 Learmouth Terrace, Edinburgh. † GI 2, RSA 3.
McGIBBON, W.F. Exh. 1885-1902
221 West George Street, Glasgow. † GI 13.
McGILL, David Exh. 1889-1927
Sculptor. Studied South Kensington and R.A. Schools. Add: London 1889; West Moors, Dorset 1919. † B 1, GI 8, I 13, L 3, M 2, NG 1, RA 45, RI 1.
McGILL, David Exh. 1938
68 London Road, Kilmarnock. † RSA 1.
McGILL, Elizabeth Exh. 1908-12
7A Strathmore Gardens, Kensington, London. † GI 1, LS 8.
M'GILL, James Exh. 1924-38
Glasgow. † GI 12, L 1, RSA 5.
McGILL, Marjorie R. Exh. 1929-36
Figure painter. Royal College of Art, London 1929; Bexhill on Sea, Sussex 1936. † RA 2.
McGILL, Mrs. W.M. Exh. 1882-88
6 Clarendon Road, Putney, London 1882; Richmond, Surrey 1888. † RA 1, RHA 1.
McGILL, William Murdoch Exh. 1882
6 Clarendon Road, Putney, London. † D 1, M 3.
McGILLIVRAY, F. Exh. 1887-88
Glasgow. † GI 6.
McGILLIVRAY Florence Helena b. 1864
Canadian artist. Exh. 1933. † RSW 2.
MACGILLIVRAY, James Pittendrigh 1856-1938
Sculptor, painter and architectural artist. b. Inverurie, Aberdeenshire. Worked for 7 years in studio of William Brodie. His Majesty's Sculptor for Scotland 1921. A.R.S.A. 1892, R.S.A. 1901. Add: Glasgow 1882; Edinburgh 1895. † G 5, GI 56, L 2, M 1, NEA 2, RA 3, RSA 137.
McGILLWRAY, Miss H.M. Exh. 1890
5 Livingstone Avenue, Sefton Park, Liverpool. † L 1.
McGINITY, Miss K. Exh. 1911
11 Marine Crescent, Waterloo, Liverpool. † L 1.
McGINN, Francis A. Exh. 1895
118 Stow Hill, Newport, Mon. † RHA 1.
McGLASHAM, J.S. Exh. 1912
33 Grosvenor Street, Liscard, Cheshire. † L 1.
McGLASHAN, Archibald A. b. 1888
Portrait and figure painter. Studied Glasgow School of Art. A.R.S.A. 1936, R.S.A. 1939. Exh. 1909-40. Add: Paisley 1909; Glasgow 1919; London 1938. † GI 38, L 11, LEF 6, RA 3, RSA 35.

McGLASHAN, D.A. Exh. 1904
68 Buccleuch Street, Glasgow. † GI 1.

McGLASHAN, Violet Exh. 1894-96
Glasgow 1894; Kirkintilloch, N.B. 1896. † GI,4.

McGLOUGHLIN, A.J. Exh. 1883
48 Gt. Brunswick Street, Dublin. † RHA 1.

M'GOLDRICK, H.V. Exh. 1918
59 Brighton Road, Rathgar, Dublin. † RHA 4.

McGONIGAL, Maurice J.* Exh. 1924-40
Landscape, coastal and figure painter. A.R.H.A. 1932, R.H.A. 1936. Add: National College of Art, Kildare Street, Dublin. † RHA 93.

McGOOGAN, A. Exh. 1888-1929
Dublin. † RHA 54.

MacGOUN, Hannah Clarke Preston 1864-1913
Figure and domestic painter. R.S.W. 1903. Add: Edinburgh. † GI 28, L 13, M 4, RA 2, RHA 2, RSA 68, RSW 37.

McGOVERN, Mrs. Jessie Exh. 1927
61 Portland Street, Southport, Lancs. † L 2.

McGOWAN, William J. Exh. 1902-19
Miniature portrait painter. Add: London. † RA 4, RHA 7, RSA 1.

McGRATH, Carrie Exh. 1936
† B 1.

McGRATH, Edward F. Exh. 1930-37
Allerton Road, Liverpool. † L 6, RCA 2.

McGRATH, James P. Exh. 1897
14 South Circular Road, Portobello, Dublin. † RHA 1.

MACGREGOR, Dr. Exh. 1938
c/o Eton College, Berks. † ROI 2.

MACGREGOR, Miss A. Exh. 1912-13
290 Hagley Road, Birmingham. † L 2, RA 1.

MACGREGOR, Annie Exh. 1897
Stamford Brook House, Hammersmith, London. † M 1.

MACGREGOR, Archie G. Exh. 1884-1905
Painter and sculptor. Add: London. † L 12, M 2, NG 3, RA 14, RHA 1, RI 2, ROI 1.

McGREGOR, A.R. Exh. 1882-83
113 Breadalbane Terrace, Glasgow. † GI 3.

M'GREGOR, Miss Chris Exh. 1921-25
113 West Regent Street, Glasgow. † GI 7, L 1, RSA 1.

McGREGOR, Douglas Exh. 1899
7 Rue Belloni, Paris. † GI 1.

McGREGOR, Edith Exh. 1905
Plaish House, Christchurch, Hants. † RHA 1.

MacGREGOR, G.S. Exh. 1891
5 Huntley Gardens, Kelvinside, Glasgow. † RSA 3.

MacGREGOR, Harry Exh. 1894-1934
Edinburgh 1894 and 1929; Glasgow 1900; Peebles 1909; Loanhead 1916. † GI 22, RSA 83, RSW 5.

McGREGOR, John Exh. 1900
7 New Broughton, Edinburgh. † RSA 1.

MacGREGOR, Jessie* d. 1919
Genre, historical and portrait painter. A.S.W.A. 1886, S.W.A. 1887. Add: London. † B 10, GI 10, L 39, M 8, RA 32, ROI 1, SWA 6.

MacGREGOR, John Douglas d. 1951
Watercolour painter. Exh. 1932-40. Add: Glasgow. † GI 2, RSA 7, RSW 4.

MACGREGOR, Miss J.M. Exh. 1888
Glengyle Lodge, Bruntsfield Place, Edinburgh. † RSA 2.

MACGREGOR, Marie S. Exh. 1886-1901
Garnet Hill, Glasgow. † GI 3, RSA 2.

MACGREGOR, P. Exh. 1886
2 Danube Street, Edinburgh. † RSA 1.

MacGREGOR, Miss P. Exh. 1885-89
113 Breadalbane Terrace, Garnet Hill, Glasgow. † GI 5.

MacGREGOR, Patrick Exh. 1897-98
3 Carfin Street, Glasgow. † GI 1, L 1.

McGREGOR Robert* 1847-1922
Figure painter. A.R.S.A. 1882, R.S.A. 1889. Add: Edinburgh. † B 2, D 12, G 1, GI 100, L 17, M 8, RA 15, RHA 3, ROI 1, RSA 169.

McGREGOR, Sara Exh. 1898-1919
Edinburgh 1898 and 1915; Joppa 1904; Portobello, N.B. 1905. † GI 13, L 1, RA 2, RSA 30.

McGREGOR, Sarah Exh. 1880-1914
Flower Painter. Add: London. † RBA 2, SWA 9.

MACGREGOR, Walker Exh. 1937
13 Durcombe Street, Glasgow. † GI 1.

MacGREGOR, William F. Exh. 1921-24
51 Albany Street, Edinburgh. † GI 1, RSA 4.

MacGREGOR, William Yorke* 1855-1923
Landscape painter. Studied under James Docharty and at the Slade School. Visited South Africa 1888-90 because of ill health. N.E.A. 1892, A.R.S.A. 1898, R.S.A. 1921, R.S.W. 1885. Add: Glasgow 1880; Bridge of Allan 1892. † AG 1, CON 5, DOW 5, GI 45, L 3, M 1, NEA 27, RA 2, RSA 48, RSW 19.

McGRIGOR, Miss Douglas C. Exh. 1903-6
Figure painter. Add: 8 King's Mansions, Chelsea, London. † RA 1, SWA 2.

McGUINNESS, Katherine Exh. 1898
80 Upper Beechwood Avenue, Dublin. † RHA 1.

McGUINNESS, Norah* Exh. 1924-40
Watercolour painter, illustrator and costume designer. Studied Metropolitan School of Art, Dublin (1923 medal, Tailteann competition, Royal Dublin Society medal). Add: Dublin 1924 and 1940; Wicklow 1928. † LEI 2, RHA 5.

McGUINNESS, William Bingham d. 1928
Watercolour landscape painter. A.R.H.A. 1882, R.H.A. 1884. Add: Dublin 1880; London 1902. † AG 2, B 4, D 8, L 10, RHA 132, RI 11.

McGUSTY, H.A. Exh. 1897
2 Rue Melebranche, Paris. † RHA 2.

McHANDY, Miss E.A. Exh. 1884-89
Edinburgh. † GI 1, RSA 5.

McHARDY, Edith Exh. 1911
Sunnyside, Ayr. † GI 1.

McHARDY, M.A. Exh. 1910
Sunnyside, Ayr. † GI 1.

McHATTIE, T. Exh. 1920-23
Harpenden, Herts. † D 3, L 2.

MACHELL, Reginald* Exh. 1881-1900
Flower, figure and landscape painter. R.B.A. 1894. Add: London. † G 2, L 4, RA 5, RBA 57, RHA 1, RI 1, ROI 3.

MACHEN, Drusilla Exh. 1913
108 Middlewood Road, Sheffield, Yorks. † L 1.

MACHIN, Arnold b. 1911
Sculptor. Exh. 1940. Add: 5 Stamford Bridge Studios, London. † RA 1.

MACHIN, E.W. Exh. 1883
6 Ranelagh Road, Dublin. † RHA 1.

MACHIN, John Exh. 1935-38
31 St. Andrews Street, Glasgow. † GI 7.

MACHIN, Mary V. Exh. 1938
Sculptor. Add: Gateford Hill, Nr. Worksop, Notts. † N 1.

MACHKOFF, Ilia Exh. 1911-12
c/o Allied Artists Association, 67 Chancery Lane, London. † LS 6.

MACHONOCHIE, Leonore G. Exh. 1936
c/o Green and Stone Ltd., 258 Kings Road, London. † RBA 1.

MacHUTCHEON, John C. Exh. 1907
212 West Regent Street, Glasgow. † GI 1.

MACIAS, Joaquin b. 1906
Painter and etcher. Studied Royal College of Art. Exh. 1931. Add: Harding House, Harding Terrace, Stoke on Trent, Staffs. † RA 1.

MacILROY, Maude G. Exh. 1915-23
Glasgow 1915; Turnberry, Ayrshire 1920. † GI 14, L 3, RSA 12.

McILWAINE, John Bedell Stanford 1857-1945
Landscape painter. A.R.H.A. 1893, R.H.A. 1911. Add: Dublin 1880; Caledon, Co. Tyrone 1926. † RA 1, RBA 2, RHA 102.

M'ILWRAITH, Agnes Exh. 1919-20
Mrs. C.F. Fyfe. Add: 21 Bruce Road, Pollokshields. † GI 2.

McILWRAITH, Madeline Exh. 1927
Glebe Place, Chelsea, London. † SWA 1.

MACINNES, Colin Exh. 1940
Painter. † LEF 3.

McINNES, J. Exh. 1881-82
22 Home Street, Edinburgh. † RSA 2.

McINNES, William Exh. 1913
The Waits, St. Ives, Hunts. † ROI 1.

McINNES, William Beckwith* b. 1889
Australian portrait painter. Exh. 1928-33. Add: National Gallery, Melbourne, Australia 1928; c/o Australia House, Strand, London 1933. † RA 2.

McINROY, Patricia Exh. 1886-96
Landscape painter. Add: The Birkenward, Skelmorlie. † FIN 1, GI 3, RSA 2.

MACINTOSH, John Exh. 1888-1914
Strath Cottage, Galston. † GI 1, LS 8.

MACINTOSH, John M. 1847-1913
Landscape painter. R.B.A. 1890. Add: London and Woolhampton, Reading, Berks. † B 1, D 19, DOW 54, FIN 3, G 7, GI 3, L 12, NG 1, RA 28, RBA 116, RI 25, RID 70, ROI 6.

MACINTOSH, R. Exh. 1935-37
94 Pepys Road, London. † RI 3.

MacINTOSH, R. Exh. 1909-10
Etcher. Add: 147 Jerningham Road, New Cross, London. † RA 2, RSA 1.

MACINTYRE, Donald Edward b. 1900
Painter, etcher and jeweller. Studied Edinburgh College of Art. Assistant art master George Watson's Boys College, Edinburgh and Edinburgh College of Art (evening classes). Exh. 1923-28. Add: 33 Montpellier Park, Edinburgh. † GI 1, RSA 7.

MACINTYRE, Edith A. Exh. 1929-36
Landscape painter. Add: Vinebank, Broughty Ferry, Forfarshire. † L 1, RSA 4.

MACINTYRE, James Exh. 1938-39
Ord House, Isleornsay, Skye. † B 3.

McINTYRE, James* Exh. 1880-1909
Figure and domestic painter. Add: London 1880; Giffen by Beith, N.B. 1909. † B 2, GI 1, L 1, M 1, RA 4, RBA 1, RHA 8.

McINTYRE, Jean Exh. 1910-14
Urban landscape painter. Add: London. † LS 11, NEA 4.

McINTYRE, John Exh. 1908-11
28 North Bridge Street, Edinburgh. † RSA 4.

McINTYRE, Jessie E. See HEASON

McINTYRE, John H. Exh. 1896-1904
Landscape painter. Add: East View, Vale of Health, Hampstead, London. † RA 2.
McINTYRE, Joseph Wrightson* Exh. 1880-94
Marine and landscape painter. Add: 2 Market Place, Sheffield. † B 1, L 4, M 3, RA 1, RBA 7, RHA 23.
MACINTYRE, Maggie Exh. 1889-90
139 Greenhead Street, Glasgow. † GI 2.
MACINTYRE, Mary Exh. 1880-81
Landscape painter. Add: London. † SWA 2.
McINTYRE, Raymond Exh. 1880-1931
Portrait, figure and landscape painter. Studied under William Nicholson and Walter Sickert. Art critic for "The Architectural Review". Add: London. † G 1, GI 3, GOU 27, I 1, L 2, LS 5, M 1, NEA 1, RA 3, RBA 3, RHA 11, ROI 1.
MACIRONE, Emily Exh. 1880-81
Landscape, architectural and figure painter. Add: 5 Park Village West, London. † SWA 4.
M'ISAAC, James N * Exh. 1934-38
13 West Brighton Crescent, Portobello, Edinburgh. † RSA 2.
MacIVER, Agnes Edith Exh. 1910-11
Glendower, Farquhar Road, Upper Norwood, London. † LS 6.
MacIVER, C. Maud Exh. 1910
Riverbank, Grassendale, Liverpool. † L 1.
McIVOR, E.G. Exh. 1901
11 Caroline Place, Birkenhead. † L 1.
MacIVOR, Monica Exh. 1903-34
Portrait, miniature, landscape and figure painter. b. Bushire, Persia. Studied Juliens, Paris. Married Frank Freyburg q.v. Add: Golden Grove, Roscrea 1903; St. Ives, Cornwall 1911; London 1914. † B 4, L 1, P 4, RA 12, RHA 11, ROI 15, SWA 3.
MACK, Dolly Exh. 1895
21 Abercromby Square, Liverpool. † L 1.
MACK, Hilda Muriel See WATKINSON
MACK, Mary Hamilton b. 1903
Portrait and landscape painter and woodcut artist. Studied Slade School (Slade scholarship Melville Nettleship scholarship). Worked in Sydney, N.S.W. and West Australia 1924-27. Exh. 1922-33. Add: London 1922; Ewell, Surrey 1931. † GOU 2, NEA 1, RA 2, RSW 1, SWA 1.
MACKAY, Miss A. Exh. 1902-3
London. † RI 2.
MACKAY, A. Exh. 1918-39
Landscape and portrait painter. A.N.S.A. 1918, N.S.A. 1927. Add: 182 Harrington Drive, Lenton, Nottingham 1927. † N 41.
MACKAY, A.G. Exh. 1895
Figure painter. † RID 1.
MACKAY, Alasdair G.D. Exh. 1913-37
Glasgow. † GI 6, RSA 18.
MACKAY, Alexander S. Exh. 1880-89
13 Cornwall Street, Edinburgh. † RSA 11.
MACKAY, Arthur Stewart b. 1909
Painter and poster artist and art master. Studied Regent Street Polytechnic and Hornsey School of Arts and Crafts (bronze medal). Exh. 1931-38. Add: London. † RA 3, RBA 2, ROI 2.
MACKAY, Charles b. 1868
Watercolour, landscape painter and furniture designer. Studied Glasgow School of Art and Academie Delecluse, Paris. Exh. 1900-40. Add: Glasgow and Finnart, Cambuslang. † GI 20, L 5, RSA 2, RSW 13.
MACKAY, C. Melville Exh. 1890-94
Birkenhead 1890; Stoke on Trent 1891; Heswall, Cheshire 1894. † L 4.
McKAY, Miss Dalziel Exh. 1892-1933
30 Shrewsbury Road, Birkenhead. † L 42, LS 18.
MACKAY, David B. Exh. 1883-99
High Street, Crail, Fifeshire and Kilmarnock. † GI 8, L 1, RSA 13, RSW 2.
MACKAY, Mrs. D.E. Exh. 1886-90
Cleobury Mortimer 1886; Brockley, Northants. 1890. † L 2.
McKAY, Elizabeth Exh. 1935-36
Portrait and figure painter. Add: 9 Kevins Park, Dartry Road, Dublin. † RHA 5.
MACKAY, Florence Agnes Exh. 1896
Landscape and flower painter. Studied Gray's School of Art, Aberdeen, France and Belgium. Art mistress Peterhead Academy and Aberdeen High School. Add: 256 Gt. Western Road, Aberdeen. † RSA 1.
McKAY, Georgina Exh. 1907-9
Flower painter. Add: Stanley Studios, Park Walk, Chelsea, London. † GOU 1, L 2, LS 8, RHA 1, SWA 2.
MACKAY, G.D. Exh. 1925
11 Boswell Quadrant, Wardie. † RSA 1.
MACKAY, H. Exh. 1902-6
West Prince's Street, Glasgow. † GI,5.
MACKAY, Helen Victoria b. 1897
Sculptor. b. Cardiff. Studied Regent Street Polytechnic School of Art (gold, silver and bronze medals). Exh. 1922-40. Add: London. † ALP 1, GI 1, RA 12, RSA 4, SWA 1.
McKAY, Isabella Exh. 1889-1934
17 Gloucester Road, Regent's Park, London 1889; 143 Cherryhinton Road, Cambridge 1934. † L 1, RI 4.
MACKAY, Jessie Exh. 1910
2 Woodland Drive, New Brighton, Cheshire. † L 2.
MACKAY, John Exh. 1930-40
Edinburgh. † RSA 13.
MACKAY, James M. Exh. 1880-1904
Edinburgh. † RSA 32.
M'KAY, J.R. Exh. 1925-38
4 Melville Street, Edinburgh. † RSA 5.
MACKAY, Rose Exh. 1890-99
Figure and portrait painter. Add: London. † L 1, NEA 1, P 2, RA 2, RBA 2, SWA 2.
MACKAY, Thomas Exh. 1893-1912
Add: Liverpool 1893; Chester 1911. † L 28, RA 3.
MACKAY, Thomas Exh. 1940
Mossmorran, Belmont Road, Juniper Green, Edinburgh. † RSA 1.
McKAY, Thomas H. Exh. 1907-23
Glasgow. † GI 22, RA 2, RSA 1, RSW 3.
McKAY, William Darling* 1844-1924
Painter. A.R.S.A. 1877, R.S.A. 1883. Librarian 1896-1907 and Secretary 1907-24. Add: Edinburgh. † G 2, GI 46, M 3, RHA 2, RSA 160.
MacKEACHAN, D Exh. 1895
Garmoyle, Langbank, N.B. † GI 2.
MacKEAN, Mrs. Muir Exh. 1889-93
Oakshaw, Paisley. † GI 9.
MacKEAN, Robert Exh. 1925-26
Boydston, Barfillan Drive, Cardonald. † GI 3.
McKEAN, R. McGillivray Exh. 1910
6 Calder Street, Glasgow. † GI 1.
McKEAND, Clara Exh. 1885-88
24 Royal Crescent, Glasgow. † GI 5.
McKEAND, Lucy Exh. 1885-96
24 Royal Crescent, Glasgow 1885; Kelvinside, Glasgow 1896. † GI 3, RSA 3.
McKECHNIE, Alexander Balfour 1860-1930
Watercolour painter. Studied Glasgow School of Art. R.S.W. 1900. Add: Glasgow. † GI 87, L 4, M 1, RA 1, RI 9, RSA 13, RSW 84.
MACKECHNIE, Robert Exh. 1934
4 Stafford Mansions, London. † RSA 1.
MACKECHNIE, R.G.S. Exh. 1921-38
R.B.A. * 1930. Add: School of Art, Glasgow 1921; London 1929; Rye, Sussex 1935. † GI 1, RBA 55, RSA 1.
M'KEE, George H. Exh. 1932-35
99 Claythorn Street, Glasgow. † GI 2.
MACKEI, B. Jessopp Exh. 1889-90
Painter. Add: 41 Lambton Road, Hornsey Rise, London. † L 1, RBA 2.
McKELLAR, Archibald Exh. 1887-88
Kenmore Street, Aberfeldy. † GI 3.
MACKELLAR, Agnes C Exh. 1909
c/o Henderson and Reid, 258 West George Street, Glasgow. † GI 1.
MACKELLAR, Duncan* c. 1848-1908
Figure painter and watercolourist. R S.W. 1885. Add: Glasgow. † DOW 1, G 1, GI 76, L 11, RA 2, RI 2, RSA 33, RSW 75.
McKELLAR, John C. Exh. 1905-7
Glasgow. † GI 5.
McKELLAR, J.E. Exh. 1890
112 Bath Street, Glasgow. † GI 2.
McKELVEY, Frank* b. 1895
Landscape, portrait and genre painter. Studied Belfast Municipal School of Art (Fitzpatrick prize for figure drawing 1913-14, Sir Charles Brett prize for figure drawing 1911-12) Exh. 1918-40. Add: Belfast. † FIN 2, GI 23, RHA 137.
MACKELVIE, Mary Baillie Exh. 1933-38
Edinburgh. † GI 2, RSA 2, RSW 1.
M'KENDRICK, Andrew Exh. 1936-38
150 Morningside Street, Glasgow. † GI 2.
McKENNA, F.S. Exh. 1928-35
Straffan House, Co. Kildare 1928; The Hollies, Droitwich Spa, Worcs. 1935. † B 1, RHA 3.
McKENNA, Hugh Exh. 1936-39
40 Midcroft Avenue, Glasgow. † GI 5, RSA 1.
MACKENNAL, Sir Bertram 1863-1931
Sculptor and coin designer. b. Australia. Came to England 1883 and studied at the British Museum, R.A. Schools and in Paris. Won competition for the decoration of Government House, Victoria in 1889 and returned to Australia to carry out the work. A.R.A. 1909, R.A. 1922, H.R.S.A. 1920. Knighted c. 1922. "The Earth and the Elements" purchased by Chantrey Bequest 1907 and "Diana Wounded" 1908. Add: Madeley, Salop 1886; London 1894; Watcombe, Torquay 1928. † FIN 29, GI 11, ! 3, L 10, RA 75, RI 2, RSA 12.
McKENZIE, Andrew b. 1886
Watercolour painter and architect. Studied Glasgow School of Art and Glasgow School of Architecture. Exh. 1920-32. Add: Glasgow. † GI 5, L 3, RSA 1, RSW 8.
MACKENZIE, Miss A.F Exh. 1939
Ballone, 37 Buckston Terrace, Edinburgh. † RSA 1.
MACKENZIE, Alexander G.R. 1879-c.1970
Architect. b. Aberdeen. In partnership with Alexander Marshall M. q.v. Exh. 1921-25. Add: 75 Victoria Street, London. † L 1, RA 4, RSA 8.

MACKENZIE, Alexander Marshall 1848-1933
Architect and landscape painter. A.R.S.A. 1893, R.S.A. 1918. In partnership with Alexander G.R.M. q.v. Add: Aberdeen. † GI 7, RA 4, RSA 53.

MACKENZIE, C. Douglas Exh. 1895-1926
Liverpool. † L 56.

MACKENZIE, Clarence V. 1889-1949
Landscape painter. Studied Brighton School of Art and Regent Street Polytechnic. Curator Dudley Art Gallery 1933. Exh. 1924-38. Add: Pedmor, Nr. Stourbridge, Worcs. 1924; Halesowen, Nr. Birmingham 1935. † B 44, RA 1, RSW 2.

MacKENZIE, Constance V. Exh. 1924-28
Landscape painter. Add: 13 Palliser Road, Baron's Court, London. † RA 1, SWA 1.

MacKENZIE, Dorothy Exh. 1917-24
New Park, St. Andrews 1917; London 1923. † P 2, RSA 2, SWA 3.

MACKENZIE, Esme Exh. 1928-35
Linocut artist. Add: 3 Carlton Hill, London. † NEA 2, RBA 5, RED 2.

MACKENZIE, Frank J. Exh. 1891-93
Landscape painter. London and Godalming, Surrey. † B 1, L 3, M 1, RA 4, RBA 3.

MACKENZIE, Frederick W. Exh. 1939-40
Architect. 29 St. George Street, Hanover Square, London. † RA 5.

MacKENZIE, G.A. Exh. 1884-98
Liverpool. † L 23, M 1.

McKENZIE, George F. Exh. 1921-40
Edinburgh. † RSA 7, RSW 1.

McKENZIE, George J. Exh. 1892
Bombay. † GI 1.

MACKENZIE, G. Ord Exh. 1885
Figure painter. 37 Belsize Park Gardens, London. † SWA 1.

MACKENZIE, H.A.O. Exh. 1891
Painter. 20 Westbourne Park Crescent, London. † RBA 1.

MACKENZIE, Helen Margaret Exh. 1905-39
Painter and etcher. b. Elgin. Studied Royal College of Art. Married Herbert Ashwin Budd q.v. R.O.I. 1923, A.S.W.A. 1918, S.W.A. 1923. Add: London. † CHE 1, COO 1, GI 7, L 1, M 2, P 4, RA 22, ROI 46, SWA 38.

MACKENZIE, Isabel Exh. 1936
36 Gt. Ormond Street, London. † SWA 1.

MACKENZIE, Commander Ivor, R.N. b. 1880
Watercolour painter. b. Grasmere. Self taught. Exh. 1940. Add: Bournemouth. †, RI 2.

MACKENZIE, John Exh. 1931-40
Glasgow 1931; Arbroath, Angus 1940. † GI 2, RSA 2.

MACKENZIE, J.C. Exh. 1882-98
Edinburgh 1882; Glasgow 1898. † GI 4, RSA 11.

MACKENZIE, John D. Exh. 1886-91
Painter and black and white artist. London 1886; Newlyn, Penzance 1889. † RA 3, RBA 1.

MACKENZIE, James Hamilton* 1875-1926
Painter and etcher. Studied Glasgow School of Art (travelling scholarship to Italy). Sketched in East Africa World War I. A.R.S.A. 1923, A.R.E. 1910, R.S.W. 1910. Add: Glasgow. † GI 75, L 17, M 10, RE 26, RSA 49, RSW 57.

McKENZIE, J.S. Exh. 1883-88
Glasgow. † GI 4.

M'KENZIE, James Scarth Exh. 1929-38
Edinburgh. † GI 3, L 1, RSA 2.

MACKENZIE, James Wilson Exh. 1882-92
Portrait and figure painter. 28 Falkner Street, Liverpool. † GI 2, L 33, M 3, RA 3, RSA 3.

MACKENZIE, Mrs. Katherine Exh. 1934-36
Hayley Green, Halesowen, Birmingham. † B 5.

McKENZIE, Kenneth Exh. 1884-99
Landscape painter. Holyhead, North Wales 1884; Carradale, Argyle 1893; Kilchrenan 1896; Forres, N.B. 1897. † B 11, GI 4, L 14, M 4, N 4, RA 37, RBA 1, RHA 13, ROI 14.

MACKENZIE, Mary Exh. 1880
Magdalen Yard Road, Dundee. † RSA 1.

MACKENZIE, Mary Exh. 1936-40
88 Bedford Place, Aberdeen. † RSA 4.

MACKENZIE, Molly Exh. 1935
74 Deanston Drive, Glasgow. † RSA 1.

MacKENZIE, M.A. Exh. 1884
44 Warrender Park Road, Edinburgh. † RSA 2.

MACKENZIE, Muriel Alison Exh. 1918-38
Sculptor and engraver. London. † GI 5, LS 3, RA 3, RED 1, ROI 2, RSA 2, SWA 4.

MACKENZIE, N.M. Exh. 1913
Landscape painter. † ALP 2.

MACKENZIE, Mrs. Philippe Exh. 1889-90
Landscape painter. 19 Wimpole Street, London. † SWA 3.

MACKENZIE, Roderick D. Exh. 1908
31 Boulevard de Port Royal, Paris. † LS 4.

McKENZIE, Robert Tait 1867-1938
Sculptor. b. Ontario, Canada. Add: Montreal, Canada 1903; Philadelphia, U.S.A. 1907; London 1929. † L 2, RA 6.

MACKENZIE, Thomas Exh. 1928-36
Painter and etcher. Old Thatches, Rushden, Buntingford, Herts. † BA 1, RA 1.

MacKENZIE, Violet L. Exh. 1927-33
42 Craighouse Avenue, Edinburgh. † RSA 6.

MACKENZIE, William G. d. 1925
Portrait painter. A.R.H.A. 1914. Add: London 1894; Belfast 1906. † RA 3, RHA 22.

McKENZIE, Miss W.J.M. Exh. 1886-1917
Edinburgh 1886; London 1896. † L 1, M 1, RBA 8, RI 2, ROI 1, RSA 1, SWA 7.

MACKENZIE, W.M. Exh. 1880-1908
Edinburgh. † GI 14, L 5, RSA 54, RSW 2.

McKENZIE, Winifred M. Exh. 1926-38
Engraver and woodcut artist. Mount Ida, Kilmacolm. † GI 14, L 2, RED 2, RSA 2.

MacKENZIE-SMITH, Barbara Exh. 1925-39
Landscape painter. London. † GOU 1, LEI 2, NEA 3, RA 1, TOO 2.

M'KERRACHER, Robert Exh. 1923
2 Heriot Gardens, Burntisland. † RSA 2.

M'KERRELL, Duncan Exh. 1931-33
3 Pine Street, Greenock. † GI 3, RSA 3.

McKERROW, J.D. Exh. 1901-2
Craigandoran, Crieff, N.B. † GI 1, RSA 1.

MACKESON, George P. Exh. 1929-34
Painter. 1 Eldon Road, London. † RBA 1, WG 2.

MACKEY, Mrs. Flory Exh. 1926-29
Portrait and flower painter. Daughter of Peter Paul Pugin, q.v. Studied Birmingham Art School and in Paris under B. Fleetwood-Walker. Add: 16 Highfield Road, Edgbaston, Birmingham. † B 6, SWA 1.

MACKEY, Haydn Reynolds b. 1883
Painter and illustrator. Studied Slade School. Life master Waltham School of Art and official war artist World War I. Exh. 1913-39. Add: London. † D 1, RA 2, RHA 4, ROI 1.

McKIBBEN, Mary Exh. 1937-39
† P 3.

McKIBBIN, J. Exh. 1932
† L 1.

MACKIE, Annie Exh. 1887-1934
Flower painter. Sister of Charles Hodge M. q.v. Add: London 1887 and 1892; Portobello, N.B. 1890; Edinburgh 1903. † B 4, L 1, RA 5, RBA 1, RI 1, RSA 22, RSW 9.

MACKIE, Charles Hodge* 1862-1920
Landscape and figure painter. A.R.S.A. 1902. R.S.A. 1917, R.S.W. 1901. Brother of Annie M. q.v. Add: Portobello N.B. and Edinburgh 1880; Murrayfield N.B. 1896. † AG 1, CON 4, GI 1, GI 35, L 14, M 4, NEA 1, RA 6, RHA 16, RSA 126, RSW 52.

MACKIE, Donald M. Exh. 1932-33
Son of Charles Hodge M. q.v. Coltbridge Studio, Murrayfield, N.B. † RSA 2.

McKIE, Mrs. Edith Exh. 1923-24
Castle Bank, Bangor, Wales. † L 1, RCA 1.

MACKIE, Miss E.D. Exh. 1932
11 High Street, Montrose. † RSA 2.

MACKIE, Mrs. Esmee M. Exh. 1934-37
Miniature portrait painter. Redlands, Cheam Road, Sutton, Surrey. † RA 2, RMS 1.

MACKIE, Helen Madeleine Exh. 1921-36
Painter and illustrator. Studied Lambeth School of Art. On staff of "Bystander". Add: 8 Jubilee Place, Chelsea, London. † RHA 1, SWA 3, WG 114.

MACKIE, Isobel Exh. 1939
Woodside, Rothiemay. † RSA 1.

MACKIE, Mrs. Kathleen Isabella b. 1899
nee Metcalfe. Portrait and landscape painter. Studied R.A. Schools and Belfast School of Art (Ardilaun scholarship, Taylor Bequest 1922 and British Institute scholarship for 2 years). Exh. 1926-27. Add: Knock, Belfast. † RHA 7.

MACKIE, M. Exh. 1921
32 Hermosilla, Madrid. † L 1, RA 1.

MACKIE, Mary Exh. 1940
Moor Croft, Milngavie. † GI 1.

MACKIE, Muriel Exh. 1932-40
Edinburgh. † RSA 12.

MACKIE, Peter Robert Macleod d. 1959
Painter and pastellier. Studied Edinburgh and Paris. A.R.S.A. 1933. Add: Leith 1890; Dunfermline 1892; Culsors, Fife 1924; c/o Doig, Wilson and Wheatley, Edinburgh 1930. † GI 16, L 1, M 1, RSA 96.

MACKIE, Thomas Callender Campbell b. 1886
Interior architect and decorator, and designer. Studied Glasgow School of Art and Architecture. Head of design section of Glasgow School of Art. Exh. 1904-40. Add: Helensburgh 1904; School of Art, Glasgow 1925; Milngavie 1934. † GI 35, RA 1, RSA 48.

MACKILL, Isa Exh. 1896-1900
Dunoon, N.B. 1896; Glasgow 1897. † GI 6, RHA 1.

McKILLIP, Mrs. Day Exh. 1910-34
Landscape painter. The Cottage, Victoria Park, Londonderry..† L 2, RA 2.

McKILLOP, John b. 1888
Watercolour landscape and seascape painter. Studied Glasgow School of Art. Exh. 1940. Add: 6 Regent Moray Street, Glasgow. † GI 2.

McKINLAY, D. Exh. 1888-1901
Glasgow 1888 and 1901; Gt. Malvern, Worcs. 1898. † GI 4.

MacKINLAY, Duncan Exh. 1880-91
Glasgow. † GI 13, RSA 1.

McKINLAY, D. McKenzie Exh. 1882-92
Grandsable, Polmont. † GI 3, L 1, RSA 10.

MACKINLAY, Georgia A.E. Exh. 1898-1926
Painter and miniaturist and teacher. Studied Royal College of Art and Clapham School of Art. Add: London. † L 7, RA 10, RBA 1, RHA 1, RI 2, RMS 7, RSA 1, SWA 1.

McKINLAY, Kate Exh. 1887–93
Glasgow. † GI 4.

MACKINLAY, Miguel b. 1895
Landscape, portrait and figure painter. b. Guadalajara, Spain. Spent his early life in Spain and Australia. Self taught. Exh. 1921-39. Add: London 1921; Bushey, Herts. 1930. † GI 1, L 2, M 1, RA 10.

McKINLAY, Mary C.S. Exh. 1937
Alexandra House, Carmyle. † GI 1.

McKINLEY, A. Exh. 1937
Painter. † RED 1.

McKINLEY, Agnes Exh. 1897-1901
2 Woodside Crescent, Glasgow. † GI 2.

MACKINLEY, Miss L.M. Exh. 1911
West Norwood, London. † SWA 1.

McKINNA, Edward Burns Exh. 1927-35
Painter and etcher. Add: Glasgow. † GI 6, RA 1, RSA 6.

McKINNA, Mary E. Tait Exh. 1932-40
150 Locksley Avenue, Glasgow. † GI 16, RSA 11

MACKINNON, Aileen Robertson b. 1901
Painter and musician. b. Perth. Studied Regent Street Polytechnic. Exh. 1926-30. Add: Shrewsbury Road, Birkenhead. † ALP 1, GI 1, L 6, RA 1.

MACKINNON, Esther Blaikie Exh. 1913-30
Painter, etcher, lithographer and illustrator. Add: Aberdeen 1913 and 1923; Bath 1920. † AB 2, GI 4, GOU 6, I 3, L 4, LS 18, P 4, RSA 10, SWA 4.

MACKINNON, Finlay Exh. 1891-1930
Landscape painter. b. Poolewe, Rossshire. Studied South Kensington, Paris and Italy. Add: London and Poolewe, Rossshire. † AG 5, BRU 85, D 1, FIN 130, L 16, M 1, NG 16, RA 19, RI 23, RSA 1, WG 74.

McKINNON, J.H. Exh. 1890
334 Scotland Street, Glasgow. † GI 1.

MacKINNON, M. Allan Exh. 1900-1
139 Greenhead Street, Glasgow. † GI 2.

McKINNON, Margaret C. Exh. 1897-1903
Greenock, N.B. † GI 2, RHA 2, RSA 2.

MACKINNON, Robert Exh. 1896-1907
Govan, N.B. † GI 11, RSW 1.

MACKINNON, Sine b. 1901
Landscape and figure painter. b. Newcastle, Co. Down. Studied Slade School. Add: London 1922; and 1940; Paris 1932. † CG 4, FIN 21, G 6, GI 1, GOU 65, LEF 48, LEI 1, M 5, NEA 19, RED 52, RHA 1, SWA 2, TOO 41.

MacKINTOSH, Alexander Exh. 1918
55 Bible House, Astor Place, New York. † RSA 1.

MACKINTOSH, Anne F. Exh. 1932
Western House, 108A University Avenue, Glasgow. † RSA 1.

MACKINTOSH, Colin J. d. 1910
Landscape and figure painter. Exh. 1896-1907. Add: Inverness. † RSA 3.

MACKINTOSH, Charles Rennie* 1868-1928
Architect. Designer of Glasgow School of Art. Married Margaret Macdonald q.v. Exh. 1891-1923. Add: Dennistoun 1891; Glasgow 1892. † GI 21, GOU 2, RSW 2.

MACKINTOSH, F.H. Exh. 1934
Hythe, Station Road, Wylde Green, Birmingham. † B 1.

MACKINTOSH, George Exh. 1908
7 Molesworth Street, Dublin. † RHA 2.

MACKINTOSH, James Exh. 1882-84
42 Queen Street, Edinburgh. † RSA 3.

MACKINTOSH, John S. Exh. 1924-38
Edinburgh. † GI 3, RSA 5.

MACKINTOSH, Margaret M. See MACDONALD

MACKINTOSH, T.A. Exh. 1906
17 Golden Square, Aberdeen. † GI 1.

MACKLEY, George Exh. 1932-40
Painter and wood engraver. Add: Purley, Surrey. † RA 10.

MACKLIN, Thomas Eyre* c. 1867-1943
Landscape and portrait painter, sculptor and illustrator. R.B.A. 1902. Add: Newcastle 1882 and 1897; London 1889 and 1914. † L 1, RA 17, RBA 3, RSA 1.

McKNIGHT, Alice S. Exh. 1912-13
29 Arundel Avenue, Sefton Park, Liverpool. † L 5.

MACKNIGHT, W. Dodge Exh. 1891
Landscape painter. Add: c/o R.L. Stannard, 30 Gt. Russell Street, London. † NEA 2.

MACKRETH, Caroline E. Exh. 1886
Painter. † SWA 2.

MACKROW, Elsie M. See HARVEY

MACKUBIN, Florence 1861-1918
American miniature painter. Add: Manchester 1889; N. Baltimore, Maryland, U.S.A. 1901. † M 1, RA 2, RMS 2.

MacKUSICK, Ivy Exh. 1921-29
117 Charlotte Street, London. † NEA 3.

MACKWORTH, Audley Exh. 1884-1909
Painter. Add: London 1884 and 1887; Teddington, Middlesex 1886; Leighton Buzzard, Beds. 1909. † D 2, L 3, RA 7, ROI 2.

MACKWORTH, Miss T. Exh. 1886
Painter. Add: Sunnybank, Teddington, Middlesex. † RI 1.

MACKY, Gordon Exh. 1884
Lochcarron, Ross-shire. † RSA 1.

McLACHLAN, Aileen Exh. 1887-99
Landscape painter. Add: London. † NEA 2, NG 1, ROI 11, SWA 1.

McLACHLAN, Miss E. Hope Exh. 1881-1912
Still life painter. Add: London 1881 and 1899; Weybridge, Surrey 1896. † RBA 2, ROI 17, SWA 1.

McLACHLAN, James Exh. 1908-30
Edinburgh. † GI 1, RSA 8.

McLACHLAN, John* Exh. 1881-92
29 York Buildings, York Place, Edinburgh. † RSA 11.

McLACHLAN, James M. Exh. 1938-39
36 Plewlands Gardens, Edinburgh. † RSA 1, RSW 1.

MacLACHLAN, J.O. Exh. 1890
20 Fitzroy Street, London. † G 2.

McLACHLAN, Kate Exh. 1887
Helensburgh, N.B. † GI 1.

MACLACHLAN, Miss M.C.. Exh. 1912
Olga, Springvale, I.O.W. † RHA 1.

McLACHLAN, N. French Exh. 1920-37
Landscape and portrait painter. Add: Dublin. † L 1, RHA 16.

McLACHLAN, Thomas Hope 1845-1897
Landscape painter. b. Darlington. N.E.A. 1887, R.I. 1897, R.O.I. 1890. Add: Weybridge, Surrey 1880; London 1882. † B 1, BG 2, G 16, GI 1, L 13, M 9, NEA 10, NG 18, RA 36, RE 7, RI 7, RID 9, ROI 29.

McLACHLAN, W.F. Exh. 1920-21
1 Terenure Park, Dublin. † RHA 3.

MACLAGAN, Mrs. Dorothea F. b. 1895
Painter. b. Greenock. Studied Byam Shaw School 1914-17. Exh. 1935-40. Add: 56 Elgin Crescent, London. † COO 3, RA 5.

MACLAGAN, Miss M.L. Exh. 1881-1901
5 Eton Terrace, Edinburgh. † RSA 3.

MACLAGAN, Philip Douglas b. 1901
Figure, portrait and landscape painter. b. Swatow, China. Exh. 1922-34. Add: New Barnet, Herts 1922; London 1929. † ALP 1, L 2, M 1, NEA 8, P 3, RA 14, RBA 6, ROI 10.

MacLAGAN, Sheila Exh. 1924
Sculptor. Add: 12 Berwick Road, Bournemouth. † RA 1.

McLAGHLAN, W.W. Exh. 1897
11 Saxe Coburg Place, Edinburgh. † RSA 3.

McLANDSBOROUGH, Arthur Waite b. 1884
Watercolour landscape painter, stained glass artist and mural decorator. b. Otley, Yorks. Studied Manchester School of Art. Exh. 1924-34. Add: 11 St. Margaret's Road, Horsforth, Leeds. † L 7, RA 4, RCA 2, RSA 1.

McLAREN, Charlotte G. Exh. 1895-1932
Mrs. O'Flaherty. Miniature and portrait painter. b. Glasgow. Studied Glasgow School of Art, Slade School, Munich and Paris. Add: Glasgow 1895 and 1911; Edinburgh 1904; Millport 1927. † BG 4, GI 18, L 15, RA 11, RHA 2, RMS 1, RSA 23, RSW 2.

McLAREN, Dora Exh. 1912-25
Wood engraver. Add: London. † I 1, L 4, RA 1.

MacLAREN, Donald Graeme 1886-1917
Landscape and portrait painter. Add: London. † CAR 17, GOU 3, I 1, NEA 16.

MACLAREN, Helen Exh. 1925-38
Landscape and figure painter. b. Port Augustus, N.B. Studied under Bernard Adams. R.O.I. 1933, A.S.W.A. 1927. Married Hylton Waymouth q.v. Add: London 1925 and 1937; Bishops Stortford, Herts. 1934. † AB 3, COO 2, RA 1, ROI 31, SWA 23.

MACLAREN, James Exh. 1881-1917
Edinburgh 1881; Dennistoun, N.B. 1903. † GI 10, RSA 17.

MACLAREN, John Exh. 1885-88
Edinburgh. † GI 2, L 1, RSA 1.

MacLAREN, James M. Exh. 1887-90
Architect. London. † RA 4, RSA 1.

MACLAREN, John Stewart b. 1860
Landscape painter. Studied R.S.A. Schools and Paris. Exh. 1890-1922. Add: Edinburgh 1890; Moffat 1895 and 1904; London 1900. † GI 25, L 7, RA 6, RBA 2, RSA 26, RSW 1.

McLAREN, M.A. Exh. 1880-81
15 Elgin Grove Place, Glasgow. † GI 4.

McLAREN, M.C.G. Exh. 1906-9
† P 2.

MacLAREN, Miss Ottilie See WALLACE

M'LAREN, Peter Exh. 1932-36
48 Leys Park Road, Dunfermline. † RSA 4.

MacLAREN, Thomas Exh. 1885-92
Architect. Add: London. † RA 9, RSA 1.

MacLAREN, Thomas Exh. 1918-20
320 Hagerman Buildings, Colorado, U.S.A. † RSA 5.

MacLAREN, Walter Exh. 1881-1909
Landscape and figure painter. Add: London and Capri, Italy 1881; Worthing 1896; Torquay 1909. † B 1, G 8, GI 8, L 4, NG 19, RA 3, RI 1, ROI 8.

McLARNEY, Mrs. E.J. Exh. 1887-1900
Banagher, Co. Galway. † RHA 2.

MacLAUCHLAN, D. Exh. 1888
30 Carnarvon Street, Glasgow. † GI 1.

McLAUCHLAN, William Exh. 1896-99
Paisley, Glasgow. † GI 2.

MacLAUCHLAN, W.H. Exh. 1900
14 Hill Street, Edinburgh. † RSA 1.

MacLAUGHLAN, Donald Shaw b. 1876
American etcher. N.E.A. 1912. Exh. 1901-36. Add: London 1901; Asolo, Prov. di Treviso, Italy 1912; Paris 1930. † FIN 233, I 18, LEI 40, NEA 13, RA 2.

McLAURIN, Duncan* 1848-1921
R.S.W. 1878. Add: Bloomfield, Lomond Street, Helensburgh. † GI 55, L 1, RSA 4, RSW 4.

McLAURIN, James N. Exh. 1890-1906
Kelvin Cottage, Bothwell 1890; Leith, N.B. 1906. † GI 12, RSW 4.

MACLAURIN, Robert Exh. 1900-4
39 Caldercuilt Road, Maryhill, N.B. 1900; Glasgow 1904. † GI 3.

MACLAURIN, Robert Exh. 1940
Homesteads, Stirling. † GI 1.

McLAY, Helen Exh. 1897-1919
Birkenhead 1897 and 1912; Liverpool 1900. † B 2, L 42.

McLEA, D.F. Exh. 1884-86
43 Eleanor Street, South Shields. † RSA 2.

MACLEAN, Mrs. Exh. 1881
Watercolour painter. Add: Compton House, Torquay, Devon. † SWA 1.

MACLEAN, Alexander 1867-1940
Moonlight, marine and landscape painter. R.B.A. 1900, V.P.R.B.A. 1918. Add: London. † B 6, L 6, M 6, RA 16, RBA 229, RI 4, ROI 10.

McLEAN, Allan Exh. 1880
18 Markland Terrace, Hillhead, Glasgow. † GI 2, RSA 1.

M'LEAN, Arthur Exh. 1913-15
Ivy Lodge, Drumcondra, Ireland. † RHA 4.

McLEAN, Dorothy Exh. 1925-29
Norwood, Denton's Green, St. Helens, Lancs. † L 12.

McLEAN, Mrs. Douglas Exh. 1933
Miss Mary Rocke. Watercolour landscape and flower painter. † WG 52.

MACLEAN, Edith Exh. 1897-99
London. † SWA 5.

MACLEAN, G.D. Exh. 1900
Langsdale, Gourock. † RSA 2.

MACLEAN, Hector Exh. 1880
Watercolour landscape painter. Add: 45 Park Crescent, Brighton. † RBA 1.

McLEAN, James Exh. 1880-1910
Glasgow. † GI 13, RSA 6.

M'LEAN, John Exh. 1933-38
Glasgow. † RSA 5.

M'LEAN, James C. Exh. 1931
295 High Street, Linlithgow. † RSA 1.

McLEAN, James W.L. b. 1878
Portrait and landscape painter. b. Stranraer. Studied Glasgow School of Art. Exh. 1906-28. Add: Glasgow 1906; Wavertree, Liverpool 1920. † GI 1, L 10, RCA 1.

MacLEAN, Miss K.D. Exh. 1922-23
13 Hillside Road, Mossley Hill, Liverpool. † L 2.

MacLEAN, Mrs. Sara Exh. 1902-34
Landscape and coastal painter. Add: London 1902; Fowey, Cornwall 1914; Rochdale, Lancs. 1923. † L 2, RA 1, RCA 1, SWA 3.

McLEAN, Thomas Exh. 1935
Blackburn, Lancs. † RCA 1.

MACLEAN, Thomas Nelson 1845-1894
Sculptor. R.B.A. 1876. Add: London. † G 26, GI 9, L 1, NG 1, RA 18, RBA 16, RI 1, ROI 1.

M'LEAN, Tom W. Exh. 1933
† RSW 1.

MACLEAN, Miss W. Exh. 1926
5 Brunel Terrace, Derby Road, Nottingham. † N 2.

McLEAN, William H. Exh. 1919
Architect. Add: c/o G.L. Pepler Esq., Local Government Board, Whitehall, London. † RA 2.

McLEAN, William J. Exh. 1895-1913
Sculptor. Add: Fallowfield, Manchester 1895; London 1897. † L 4, M 9, NG 1, RA 13.

MACLEAR, Arthur Exh. 1900
Miniature portrait painter. Add: 190 Foster Hill Road, Bedford. † L 1, RA 1.

MacLEAY, Alex Exh. 1920
Sandon Studio, School Lane, Liverpool. † L 1.

MACLEAY, Alex G. Exh. 1896
Portrait painter. Add: 21 Queen's Gate Place, London. † RID 1.

MACLEAY, Miss M.R. Exh. 1919
† L 1.

McLEISH, John Exh. 1904
Edinburgh. † RSA 1.

McLEISH, Phoebe G. Exh. 1903
99 Westminster Road, Kirkdale, Liverpool. † L 1.

McLELLAN, Alexander Matheson 1872-1957
Painter of portraits, historical figures and mural panels and stained glass artist. Studied R.A. Schools and Ecole des Beaux Arts, Paris. R.B.A. 1910, R.S.W. 1910. Add: Glasgow. † AR 2, GI 18, LS 5, RA 2, RBA 12, RSA 9, ROI 1, RSW 66.

McLELLAN, Annie S. Exh. 1887-94
Haghill House, Dennistoun, Glasgow. † GI 6, RSA 2.

MACLELLAN, Mrs. Eva Exh. 1922
† RMS 1.

M'LELLAN, Janet Exh. 1936-40
Middleton, Friockheim, by Arbroath. † RSA 1, RSW 3.

McLELLAN, John Barland Exh. 1938-39
15 Parkend Cottages, Saltcoats, Ayr. † GI 1, RSA 1.

MACLELLAN, Malcolm Exh. 1937-40
127 Montford Avenue, King's Park, Glasgow. † GI 5, RSA 1.

McLELLAN, Neil Exh. 1896-97
183 King's Road, Chelsea, London. † GI 2.

McLELLAN, Sadie F. Exh. 1940
14 Ferguson Avenue, Milngavie. † RSA 2.

McLENNAN, J. Forbes Exh. 1902-5
Edinburgh. † RSA 2.

McLENNAN, Kate Exh. 1903
20 Heriot Row, Edinburgh. † RSA 1.

MACLENNAN, Miss K.C. Exh. 1912
Archnacloich, Amulree, Dunkeld, Perthshire. † L 1.

MACLENNAN, T. Forbes Exh. 1931
7 South Charlotte Street, Edinburgh. † RSA 1.

McLENNON, W.D. Exh. 1898-1900
Paisley, Glasgow. † GI 3.

MACLEOD, Miss Exh. 1881
Landscape painter. Add: 12 Passage Serviez, Pau, France. † SWA 1.

McLEOD, Edith Exh. 1916
5 Bratton Road, Birkenhead. † L 1.

MacLEOD, John Exh. 1882
160 Hope Street, Glasgow. † GI 1.

MACLEOD, Mrs. M. Exh. 1940
17A Gerald Road, London. † SWA 1.

MacLEOD, R. Exh. 1883-87
Liverpool. † L 2.

McLEOD, Sophie H. Exh. 1899
Fionary, Shandon. † GI 1.

MACLEOD, Mrs. W. Douglas Exh. 1930
Kilmichael, Milngavie. † GI 1.

MACLEOD, William Douglas b. 1892
Cartoonist and etcher. Studied Glasgow School of Art. Exh. 1921-40. Add: Glasgow and Milngavie. † AB 1, FIN 22, GI 37, L 2, RSA 5.

McLINTOCK, A.H. Exh. 1937-39
Etcher. London. † RA 1, RSA 1.

McLINTOCK, John Exh. 1888
81 Eglinton Street, Glasgow. † GI 1.

M'LOUGHLIN, Michael Exh. 1923-25
5 Russell Street, Dublin. † RHA 5.

MACLUCKIE, Ella R. Exh. 1912-13
Braeside, Falkirk, N.B. † GI 1, L 2, RSA 1.

MACLURE, Andrew Exh. 1880-82
Landscape painter. Add: 14 Ladbroke Grove, London. † GI 1, RA 2.

MACLURE, C. Exh. 1885-86
Manchester. † M 2.

MACLURE, D.G.L. Exh. 1888
32 Granville Street, West Glasgow. † GI 1.

McLURE, H.J. Exh. 1882-89
London. † G 1, M 3.

M'MANUS, Philip E.J. Exh. 1934
College of Art, Edinburgh. † RSA 1.

McMASTER, B. Exh. 1885-1904
Liverpool 1885; Sulby, I.O.M. 1904. † L 4.

McMASTER, Miss E.M. Exh. 1910-20
22 Lorne Road, Birkenhead. † L 4.

MacMASTER, James d. 1913
Landscape painter. R.B.A. 1890, R.S.W. 1885. Add: Glasgow 1880; St. Monance, N.B. 1890; Ayr 1895. † D 39, DOW 3, GI 75, L 2, RA 8, RBA 19, RI 3, RSA 14, RSW 39.

McMEEKAN, John Exh. 1880-97
Glasgow. † GI 7, RSA 8.

MacMILLAN, Ethel d. c.1971
Painter. b. Richmond, Surrey. Studied R.A. Schools. Exh. 1939-40. Add: Edenbridge, Kent. † RBA 4.

McMILLAN, Emmeline S.A. Exh. 1885-1927
Figure and landscape painter. Add: London 1885 and 1927; Wimbledon, Surrey 1895. † B 18, L 6, M 2, RA 2, RI 2.

MacMILLAN, Hamilton Exh. 1880-1906
Helensburgh. † GI 29, RHA 43, RSA 15.

McMILLAN, Hamilton J. Exh. 1886-1908
Landscape painter. Add: Edinburgh. † GI 21, RA 1, RHA 26, RSA 21.

MACMILLAN, Mary E. Exh. 1901-32
Painter and etcher. b. South Africa. Studied under Robert MacGregor, R.S.A. Schools and Paris. Add: 12 Chalmers Crescent, Edinburgh. † GI 6, L 5, RSA 7.

McMILLAN, Mrs. P. Schmidt Exh. 1894-95
123 Schneider Terrace, Barrow in Furness. † L 1, M 1.

McMILLAN, William b. 1887
Sculptor. b. Aberdeen. A.R.A. 1925, R.A. 1933. "The Birth of Venus" purchased by Chantrey Bequest 1931. Exh. 1917-40. Add: London. † GI 14, I 1, L 7, RA 61, ROI 2, RSA 15.

MacMILLAN, Winifred Exh. 1880-85
Greenock. † GI 7, RSA 3.

MacMONNIES, Mrs. Exh. 1902
Figure painter. Add: c/o 137 Gower Street, London. † NEA 2.

MacMONNIES, Frederick Exh. 1902
Painter. Add: Giverny, Eure, France. † RA 1.

MacMORLAND, Arthur Exh. 1925-40
Dunfermline 1925; Troon 1936. † GI 6, RSA 10, RSW 20.

MacMORRAN, Donald H. Exh. 1933-37
Architect. Add: Harrow on the Hill, Middlesex 1933; London 1937. † RA 2.

MacMORRAN, Miss M.L. Exh. 1935-40
London. † GOU 1, RBA 3, RI 4, ROI 3, RSA 1.

McMORRINE, H. Exh. 1893-97
Glasgow. † GI 3.

McMORRINE, Miss H.M. Exh. 1883
36 Harrowby Street, Liverpool. † L 1.

MACMULDROW, Miss E.N. Exh. 1888-95
Liverpool. † L 6.

McMULLAN, Mary Exh. 1927-40
Figure, flower and still life painter. Add: London. † COO 34, RA 3, SWA 1.

McMULLAN, Mary S. Exh. 1898-1902
Dunvarna, Adelaide Park, Belfast. † GI 1, SWA 2.

MACMUNN, Lettice Ann Exh. 1908-9
1 Bloomfield Terrace, St. Leonards on Sea, Sussex. † LS 7.

McNAB, Allan b. 1901
Watercolour painter, copper and wood engraver. b. Southampton. Exh. 1924-35. Add: London. † AB 1, BA 2, CHE 1, FIN 10, GI 9, GOU 3, L 11, NEA 7, RA 5, RSA 1.

MACNAB, Mrs. Fiona Exh. 1940
10 Hamilton Drive, Glasgow. † GI 1.

MACNAB, Iain 1890-c.1970
Painter and engraver. b. Iloilo, Philippine Islands. Studied Glasgow School of Art and Heatherleys. Joint Principal Heatherleys School of Art 1919-25. Principal Heatherleys School of Art 1925-40. A.R.E. 1923, R.E. 1934, R.O.I. 1932. Add: London. † GI 28, GOU 6, L 11, M 3, NEA 7, RA 12, RCA 2, RE 40, RED 9, ROI 27, RSA 24.

M'NAB, Mrs. James Exh. 1929-33
121 West George Street, Glasgow. † GI 4.

McNAB, John Exh. 1889-91
Landscape painter. Add: 9 Harrington Gardens, South Kensington, London. † GI 2, L 3, ROI 2.

McNAB, John S. Exh. 1880-87
Glasgow. † GI 3, RSA 1.

MACNAB, Peter* d. 1900
Landscape and rustic genre painter. R.B.A. 1879. Add: London 1880; Woking, Surrey 1894. † B 5, FIN 1, GI 16, L 7, M 2, RA 6, RBA 9, RI 37, ROI 6.

McNAB, Robert Allan b. 1865
Painter. b. Preston. Exh. 1925-33. Add: Preston 1925; c/o Fine Art Society, New Bond Street, London 1934. † L 1, RA 4.

McNAB, William Hunter Exh. 1902-29
121 West George Street, Glasgow. † GI 12, RSA 6.

MacNAGHTEN, Brigid Exh. 1924-25
28 Campden House Court, Kensington, London. † GOU 2, NEA 4.

M'NAIR, Charles J. Exh. 1932
112 Bath Street, Glasgow. † GI 1.

MACNAIR, Mrs. Frances Exh. 1908-11
Watercolour painter. Add: Old Blue Coat School, Liverpool. † BG 11, LS 8.

MacNAIR, Grace Exh. 1925-27
Landscape and figure painter. † CHE 2, M 1.

MACNAIR, Grove Exh. 1931-38
Flower painter. Add: Near Okehampton, Devon 1931; London 1934. † GOU 2, NEA 1, P 2, RA 3, RBA 13, RCA 1, ROI 1.

McNAIR, J. Herbert Exh. 1894-1911
Watercolour painter and illustrator. Add: Glasgow 1894; Liverpool 1907. † BG 23, GI 4, L 3, LS 5, RSA 2.

McNAIRN, Arthur Stuart Exh. 1900-2
Stained glass artist. Add: 12 Hart Street, Edinburgh. † RA 1, RSA 3.

M'NAIRN, John Exh. 1933-40
7 Gladstone Street, Hawick. † RSA 2.

McNALLY, Frederick A. Exh. 1914-19
Landscape painter. Add: Sawrey Vicarage, Windermere. † L 2, RA 3.

M'NALTY, Major Irvine d. 1920
Exh. 1914. Add: Kingscourt, North Circular Road, Dublin. † RHA 3.

McNALTY, Kathleen Exh. 1902-4
Miniature painter. Add: London. † RA 1, RMS 1, RHA 1.

MACNAMARA, Grace Exh. 1900-34
Miniature painter. Add: Mallow, Co. Cork 1900; Fermoy, Co. Cork 1910; Dublin 1914 and 1928; London 1927 and 1933. † D 2, L 2, RA 1, RHA 33.

M'NAMARA, May Exh. 1928
Priory House, Fairfield, Cork. † RHA 3.

MACNAMARA, Nicolette Exh. 1935-40
Watercolour painter. † COO 19, NEA 1.

McNAUGHT, A. Exh. 1883
4 Culverland Road, Exeter. † L 1.

McNAUGHT, Elsie Exh. 1910-20
Landscape painter. Add: London. † NEA 16.

M'NAUGHT, James Exh. 1940
48 Craigpark Drive, Glasgow. † GI 1.

McNAUGHT, R. Exh. 1882
282 Bath Crescent, Glasgow. † GI 1.

MacNAUGHTON, Alan G. Exh. 1935-40
Glasgow. † GI 12, RSA 5, RSW 2.

MacNAUGHTON, Colin Exh. 1928-33
Painter. Studied Edinburgh College of Art. Add: 39 Braid Road, Edinburgh. † RSA 3.

McNAUGHTON, D. Exh. 1887-1905
Glasgow. † GI 3.

MACNAUGHTON, Jessie Exh. 1900-2
3 Hope Terrace, Edinburgh. † RSA 2.

MACNEAL, Margaret O. Exh. 1940
Painter. Add: 74 Marina Street, Leonards on Sea, Sussex. † RA 1.

MACNEE, Sir Daniel* 1806-1882
Portrait painter. b. Fintry, Stirlingshire. Studied under John Knox in Glasgow and at the Trustees Academy, Edinburgh. R.S.A. 1829, P.R.S.A. 1876-1882. Knighted 1876. Add: Edinburgh 1880. † GI 10, RA 4, RSA 9.

McNEE, John Exh. 1902
33 Montpellier Park, Edinburgh. † RSA 1.

McNEE, Mary Exh. 1894
Craigmill, Stirling. † RSA 1.

MACNEE, Margaret B. Exh. 1901
20 Caledonia Street, Paisley. † GI 1.

McNEE, Patricia Exh. 1886
6 Leamouth Terrace, Edinburgh. † RSA 1.

MACNEE, Robert Russell* Exh. 1884-1940
Landscape and figure painter. b. Milngavie, Dumbartonshire. Studied Glasgow School of Art. Add: Glasgow 1884 and 1896; Edinburgh 1887; Longforgan, near Dundee 1895; Birham, Dalkeld 1923; Angus 1929. † GI 115, L 1, M 1, RA 3, RHA 1, RSA 35, RSW 3.

McNEE, Thomas W. Exh. 1886-94
6 Learmouth Terrace, Edinburgh. † GI 2, RSA 2.

MACNEIL, Alexander Exh. 1913-4
Painter. Add: Glasgow. † GI 29, L 1 RSA 14, RSW 2.

McNEIL, George Exh. 192
5 Arthur Street, Paisley, Glasgow. † GI 1

McNEIL, Miss M. Exh. 189
130 Belgrave Road, London. † SWA 1.

M'NEIL, Norman S. Exh. 1934-4
56 Newark Drive, Pollokshields, Glasgow † GI 2, RSA 4.

McNEILL, Miss A.M. Exh. 193
Glendun Lodge, Cushenden, Co. Antrim † B 1.

McNEILL, Flora Exh. 188
57 Westbourne Terrace, London † RSA 1.

McNEILL, Ida Exh. 189
Cushenden House, Co. Antrim, Ireland † B 1.

McNEILL, Robert C. Exh. 193
875 Mosspark Drive, Cardonald, Glasgow † RSA 1.

McNEILL, W.D. Exh. 1911-1
Liverpool. † L 5.

MacNICOL, Bessie 1869-190
Figure and domestic painter. Studie Glasgow School of Art and Paris. Add Glasgow. † GI 22, I 2, L 4, M 3, P 1 RA 1, RSA 5, RSW 1.

McNICOL, Ian Exh. 1928-3
Son of John McN. q.v. Add: Kilmarnock N.B. † GI 16, RSW 2.

McNICOL, John b. 186
Landscape painter and master-gilder. b Partick, Glasgow. Father of Ian McN. q.v Exh. 1895-1940. Add: Kilmarnock. † B 1 GI 34, L 3.

M'NICOL, R.A. Exh. 193
8 Dunure Drive, Kilmarnock. † GI 1.

McNICOLL, Helen Exh. 1913-1
R.B.A. 1913. Add: 3 Fulthorpe Studios Warwick Avenue, London. † RBA 11.

MacNIVEN, D.P. Exh. 1881-8
Figure painter. Add: London. † RBA 2

MacNIVEN, John d. 189
Landscape painter. Add: Glasgow † GI 35, L 1, RA 4, RSA 5, RSW 4.

McOWEN, Doris Exh. 192
115 Gower Street, London. † L 2.

MACPHAIL, Alex Exh. 189
13 Ann Street, Hillhead, Glasgow † RSW 1.

McPHAIL, John Exh. 1881
9 West Princes Street, Glasgow. † GI 1.

MacPHERSON, Alexander d. 197
Watercolour landscape painter. R.S.W. 1932. Add: Paisley, Glasgow 1926 and 1935; Wembley, Middlesex 1934. † AR 2, GI 34, L 1, RA 1, RSA 21, RSW 37.

MACPHERSON, Archibald Exh. 1882-190
Architect. Edinburgh. † GI 3, RSA 13.

MACPHERSON, Annie W. Exh. 1894
Towershiel, Lenzie, N.B. † GI 1.

MACPHERSON, Barbara H. Exh. 1881-190
Watercolour painter. Add: London 1881, Glasgow 1906. † GI 2, L 2, RBA 2, RI 5, RSA 3.

MACPHERSON, Constance M. Exh. 1898
Flower painter. Add: Invergyle, Conyers Road, Streatham, London. † RID 1.

M'PHERSON, Donald Exh. 1924-34
Figure and landscape painter. Add: Belfast. † FIN 3, RHA 18.

MACPHERSON, Douglas b. 1871
Illustrator. b. Abridge, Essex. Son of John M. q.v. Studied Westminster School of Art. On staff of the "Daily Graphic" and "Graphic" 1890-1913, and the "Sphere" from 1913. Exh. 1907. Add: London. † RA 1.

McPHERSON, D. Reid Exh. 1895
57 Dalhousie Street, Glasgow. † GI 1.
MACPHERSON, Miss E. Exh. 1911-13
23 High Street, Elgin, N.B. † GI 2, L 5.
M'PHERSON, Henry Exh. 1913-23
57 Rolland Street, Maryhill, Glasgow. † GI 2.
MACPHERSON, John Exh. 1881-84
Watercolour landscape painter. Father of Douglas M. q.v. Add: St. Andrews 1881; London 1882. † RBA 1, RHA 1, RI 1, RSA 1.
MACPHERSON, Mrs. J.L. Exh. 1917
Barrogill, Bothwell. † RSW 1.
MACPHERSON, Margaret Campbell Exh. 1885-1904
Figure painter. Add: St. Johns, Newfoundland 1885; Edinburgh 1888; Paris 1901. † GI 17, L 5, RA 1, RSA 33.
MacPHERSON, Margaret R. Exh. 1913-19
Flower and still life painter. A.S.W.A. 1916. Add: London 1913 and 1916; Bonmahon, Co. Waterford 1915; Pentewan, Cornwall 1917. † L 4, NEA 12, RA 4, SWA 9.
MACPHERSON, Nora Exh. 1883
31 Melville Street, Edinburgh. † RSA 1.
MACPHERSON, R. Exh. 1923-26
Portrait painter. Add: 34 Magdala Road, Nottingham. † N 5.
McPHERSON, William b. 1905
Landscape and portrait painter and decorative figure composition artist. Studied Glasgow School of Art (landscape prize). Exh. 1925-40. Add: Glasgow. † GI 1, RA 3, RSA 7, RSW 3.
McQUAID, Miss D. Exh. 1923
† SWA 2.
MACQUARRIE, Donald Exh. 1896-1932
Add: Greenock 1896; Glasgow 1902; Maybole, Ayrshire 1903; Gladsmuir, Kilmacolm 1920. † GI 8, L 2, RSA 2, RSW 1.
MACQUEEN, Alison Exh. 1917-19
2 Danube Street, Edinbuigh. † RSW 2.
MACQUEEN, Jane Una Exh. 1905-8
Landscape painter. Add: Fae-me-Well, Cothal, Aberdeenshire. † B 3, RSA 1.
MacQUEEN, Kenneth* Exh. 1929-31
Landscape painter. Add: 146 High Street, London. † NEA 1, RA 2, RI 2.
McQUIE, Miss B.M. Exh. 1889
4 Acton Terrace, Rock Ferry, Cheshire. † L 1.
MACQUOID, Percy 1852-1925
Genre painter, watercolourist, theatrical costume designer, illustrator for the "Daily Graphic" and "Graphic" Son of Thomas Robert M. q.v. R.I. 1882, R.O.I. 1883. Add: London. † B 3, D 2, FIN 37, G 2, GI 1, L 4, M 4, RA 4, RI 35, ROI 7.
MACQUOID, Thomas Robert 1820-1912
Architectural painter, watercolourist and illustrator. On staff of the "Graphic" and "Illustrated London News". R.I. 1882, R.O.I. 1883. Father of Percy M. q.v. Add: London. † D 15, GI 12, L 29, M 19, RA 1, RI 169, ROI 7, RSW 1.
McQUOID, Winston Exh. 1936
Still life painter. Add: 8 Balham Park Road, London. † RA 1.
MACRAE, Barbara Exh. 1932-36
Mrs. Mayne. Add: 17a Herkomer Road, Bushey, Herts. † RCA 4, RSA 1.
MacRAE, Ebenezer James Exh. 1915-40
Edinburgh. † RSA 12.
MACRAE, Grace Exh. 1891-98
Edinburgh. † GI 1, RI 1, RSA 2.
MACRAE, John Exh. 1880-83
Edinburgh. † RSA 3.
MACRAE, L.C. Exh. 1894-99
Landscape and figure painter. Add: Edinburgh 1894; London 1898. † GI 10, RA 2, RI 1, ROI 4, RSA 9.
MacRAE, Mary See WHITE
McRAEBURN, Agnes Exh. 1901
1 Hillhead Street, Glasgow. † RSA 1.
MacRITCHIE, Alexina Exh. 1885-1932
Portrait painter. Studied Slade School and Juliens, Paris. Add: London 1885, 1889 and 1903; Edinburgh 1888 and 1898; Paris 1892. † B 1, GI 5, L 4, P 4, RA 3, RSA 12.
McROBERTS, Edward C. Exh. 1899-1923
Pollokshields, Glasgow 1899; Dumbreck 1922. † GI 6.
MACRORY, Anna A. Exh. 1895-1904
Mrs. Clifford. Figure painter. Add: Dalkey, Co. Dublin 1895; Florence, Italy 1900; Kilmessan, Co. Meath 1904. † RA 2, RHA 1.
McSHANNON, Miss A. Exh. 1894
7 Scott Street, Off Sauchiehall Street, Glasgow. † L 1.
M'SKIMMING, Elizabeth E. Exh. 1915
12 Campden Drive, Bearsden, Glasgow. † GI 1.
McSWEENEY, Mrs. M.A. Exh. 1922
7 The Ropewalk, Nottingham. † N 1.
McSWINEY, Eugene Joseph b. 1866
Portrait and landscape painter and decorator. Assistant master Municipal School of Art, Cork. Exh. 1892-1930. Add: Cork 1892; London 1897. † RA 4, RHA 35.
MacSYMON, John b. 1876
Painter and black and white artist and critic. b. Greenock. Exh. 1911-29. Add: Birkenhead. † L 14, RCA 2.
McTAGGART, William 1835-1910
Landscape and coastal painter. Studied Trustees Academy, Edinburgh 1852-59. A.R.S.A. 1859, R.S.A. 1870, R.S.W. 1878. Grandfather of William M. q.v. "Harvest Moon" (1899) purchased by Chantrey Bequest 1933. Add: Edinburgh † AG 1, DOW 1, GI 30, L 10, NEA 3, RHA 3, RSA 74, RSW 11.
MacTAGGART, William* b. 1903
Painter. Grandson of William M. q.v. Studied Edinburgh College of Art. A.R.S.A. 1937. Exh. 1920-40. Add: Loanhead, Midlothian 1920; Edinburgh 1925. † G 1, GI 12, L 6, LEF 1, RSA 38, RSW 28.
MACTAGGERT, Betty Exh. 1933-36
Dean Park, Bonnyrigg. † GI 1, RSW 2.
McTAGUE, George Exh. 1940
7 Chancelot Terrace, Edinburgh. † RSA 1.
McTAVISH, A. Exh. 1880
74 George Street, Edinburgh. † RSA 1.
MACVEAN, Mrs. H.E. Exh. 1934
Kilchrenar by Taynuilt, Argyll. † RSW 1.
MACVIE, A. Exh. 1891
Temple Rhydding, Baildon, Shipley, Yorks. † L 1.
MACWHEEDLE, John Exh. 1909
Painter. Add: c/o Chenil and Co., Town Hall, Chelsea, London. † GOU 1, NEA 1.
MACWHIRTER, Agnes E. Exh. 1880
6 Marlborough Road, London. † GI 1.
MACWHIRTER, John* 1839-1911
Landscape painter. Travelled widely on the continent and America. A.R.A. 1879, R.A. 1893, R.E. 1881, R.I. 1882, H.R.M.S. 1902, A.R.S.A. 1867, H.R.S.A. 1882. "June in the Austrian Tyrol" purchased by Chantrey Bequest 1892. Add: St. John's Wood, London. † AG 31, B 7, BG 5, CAR 1, FIN 229, G 5, GI 26, L 26, LEI 70, M 22, NG 18, RA 126, RE 3, RHA 10, RI 10, RMS 2, ROI 9, RSA 20, RSW 9, TOO 15.
MacWHITE, Mrs. Paula Exh. 1927-28
43 Quai Wilson, Geneva. † M 1, RHA 1.
McWHOR, Alice Fergusson Exh. 1925-28
4 Frankby Road, Gt. Meols, Cheshire. † L 8.
M'WILLIAM, John A. Exh. 1934
115 Hanover Street, Edinburgh. † RSA 1.
McWILLIAMS, H.H. Exh. 1929
Black and white artist. Add: 52 Thurloe Square, London. † RA 1.
M'WILLIAMS, Joseph Exh. 1922
3 Hampstead, Cavehill Road, Belfast. † RHA 3.
MacWILSON, John Exh. 1906-7
133 Cheyne Walk, Chelsea, London. † ROI 3.
MADAN, Mrs. Nigel (E.H.) Exh. 1887-1914
Landscape painter. Add: West Halham Rectory, Derby 1887; Plumtree Rectory, Nottingham 1908; Bleasby Rectory, Notts. 1914. † D 5, N 14.
MADDAMS, Arthur Exh. 1939
Sculptor. Add: 123 St. Georges Road, London. † RA 1.
MADDINGTON, M. Exh. 1886
Landscape painter. † SWA 1.
MADDISON, John Exh. 1896-1901
Still life painter. Add: 149 Grange Road East, Middlesborough. † L 1, RA 5.
MADDOCK, S. Exh. 1908
Main Street, Frodsham, Cheshire. † L 2.
MADDOX, Eric Exh. 1923
11 Willis Street, Warrington, Cheshire. † L 1.
MADDOX, Richard Willes b. 1851
Stained glass artist and painter. b. Scutari, Constantinople. Studied Slade School. Exh. 1882-1919. Add: London. † B 4, D 2, L 8, NG 1, RA 23, RBA 1, RI 3, ROI 3.
MADDOX, Walter Exh. 1921
136 Benedict Street, Bootle, Lancs. † L 1.
MADELEY, Lucy Exh. 1903-39
Painter, miniaturist, art teacher and lecturer on history of Art. A.R.M.S. 1911, R.M.S. 1919. Add: London. † B 16, L 28, M 2, RA 8, RBA 1, RI 7, RMS 69.
MADELEY, Mrs. M. Exh. 1922-28
78 Thornhill Road, Handsworth, Birmingham. † B 9.
MADELINE, Paul* 1864-1921
French painter. Exh. 1911. † BRU 2.
MADET, Oswald R. Exh. 1912
21 Rue de Bourgogne, Paris. † L 1.
MADGE, Miss A. Exh. 1889-90
51 Walter's Road, Swansea. † L 2.
MADGE, Helen Exh. 1928
Landscape painter. † AB 3.
MADGE, J. Annie Exh. 1887-1911
Miniature portrait painter. Add: Swansea 1887; Liverpool 1899. † GI 3, L 12, RA 3.
MADGE, Miss Victoria Exh. 1910
Bushey, Gt. North Road, Whetstone, London. † L 6.
MADGWICK, Mary Exh. 1880
Landscape painter. Add: Andover, Hants. † SWA 2.
MADIEU, Arthur Leon Exh. 1912
7 Rue de L'Hotel de Ville, Neuilly sur Seine, France. † RSA 1.
MADRASSI, Luca Exh. 1903
French sculptor. Add: 49 Boulevard du Montparnasse, Paris. † L 4.
MADRAZO, R. Exh. 1884
† GI 1.

MAETERLINCK, Louis b. 1846
Belgian artist. Exh. 1886 and 1896. Add: Manchester 1886; Ghent, Belgium 1896. † GI 1, M 1.

MAGAHEY, William H. Exh. 1916-17
Mount Temple Lodge, Clontarf, Dublin. † RHA 2.

MAGEE, Claude Exh. 1908-9
Liver Sketch Club, 11 Dale Street, Liverpool. † L 3.

MAGEE, T.R. Exh. 1931-37
Chesterfield 1931; Bangor 1935. † B 1, GI 1, RCA 5.

MAGER, Ernest J. Exh. 1903
Landscape painter. Add: 28 Carleton Road, Tufnell Park, London. † RA 1.

MAGER, Frederick b. 1882
Painter. Studied Southampton School of Art 1927-31. Worked with F. Fedden in France 1924-25 and with B. Nicholls 1935-37. Exh. 1938-40. Add: Brockenhurst, Hants. † NEA 1, RI 4, ROI 2, RSA 1.

MAGGI, Cesare* Exh. 1911-13
Landscape painter. † ALP 8.

MAGGS, Miss C.M. Exh. 1906
25 Upperton Gardens, Eastbourne. † B 1, NG 1.

MAGGS, Miss C.M.Y. Exh. 1915-18
35 Elm Park Mansions, Park Walk, London. † RI 2.

MAGILL, Miss E. Exh. 1900-31
London. † L 1, ROI 2, SWA 11.

MAGILL, L. Exh. 1891
Painter. Add: 7 Strathmore Gardens, Kensington, London. † RBA 1.

MAGILL, Miss L. Exh. 1882-84
Mullantine, Stewartstown, Co. Tyrone. † L 1, RHA 5.

MAGINNIS, Mrs. M.A. Exh. 1880-1910
nee Geare. Landscape painter. Add: London. † D 2, RA 1, SWA 3.

MAGNIAC, Hon. Mrs. Exh. 1887
Landscape painter. Add: 16 Charles Street, Berkeley Square, London. † SWA 1.

MAGNIAC, C. Exh. 1882-86
Manchester 1882; Chorlton upon Medlock, Manchester 1885. † M 11.

MAGNIEU, C. Exh. 1899
c/o Miss Gregory, 77 Hampden Street, Bolton, Lancs. † L 1.

MAGNUS, Emma b. 1856
Figure, flower and still life painter. Studied Manchester School of Art and Slade School. Sister of Rose and Herman M. q.v. Exh. 1882-1926. Add: Fallowfield, Manchester. † L 11, M 43, RA 12, RBA 19, RCA 19, ROI 4.

MAGNUS, Herman Exh. 1882-1902
Brother of Emma and Rose M. q.v. Add: Fallowfield, Manchester. † M 8. NG 1, RHA 1.

MAGNUS, Rose Exh. 1882-99
Flower painter. Sister of Emma and Herman M. q.v. Add: Fallowfield, Manchester 1882; and 1889; Bournemouth 1889; Llanfairfechan, N. Wales 1897. † GI 1, L 10, M 38, P 7, RBA 10, RCA 4, RHA 3, ROI 7, SWA 2.

MAGNUSSON, Kristjan H. b. 1903
Landscape painter. b. Iceland. Exh. 1931-36. † COO 39, FIN 60.

MAGOWAN, James Exh. 1921-22
6 Maryville Park, Belfast. † RHA 2.

MAGRATH, Miss Carrie Exh. 1933-35
19 Tennyson Road, Small Heath, Birmingham. † B 2.

MAGRATH, William* 1838-1918
Landscape and figure painter. Add: London 1880; Cork, Ireland 1891. Died in New York. † D 2, GI 2, L 5, M 3, RA 6, RBA 5, RHA 2, RI 10, ROI 2.

MAGUIRE, Bertha Exh. 1881-1904
Watercolour flower painter. Daughter of Thomas Herbert M. q.v. Add: 6 Bloomfield Crescent, Westbourne Terrace, London. † B 1, FIN 1, RA 4, RI 8, SWA 13.

MAGUIRE, Edith Exh. 1884-92
Dublin. † L 1, RHA 1.

MAGUIRE, Helena J. Exh. 1880-1904
Figure and domestic painter. Daughter of Thomas Herbert M. q.v. Add: 6 Bloomfield Crescent, Westbourne Terrace, London. † B 22, D 2, DOW 1, L 23, M 2, RA 13, RBA 4, RHA 3, RI 25, SWA 12.

MAGUIRE, J.E. Exh. 1914
Mansefield, Eaglesham. † GI 1.

MAGUIRE, John T. Exh. 1934-36
8 Wilton Street, Glasgow. † GI 4.

MAGUIRE, May Exh. 1886-1916
Dublin. † RHA 3.

MAGUIRE, Mollie Exh. 1926-32
Painter and stained glass artist. Studied Metropolitan School of Art, Dublin. Add: Dublin 1926; London 1932. † RHA 13.

MAGUIRE, M.J. Exh. 1885
21 Upper Wilmot Street, Hulme, Manchester. † M 1.

MAGUIRE, P. Exh. 1885-95
Dublin. † RHA 6.

MAGUIRE, Robert Exh. 1925
38 Harcourt Street, Dublin. † RHA 1.

MAGUIRE, Sidney Calton Exh. 1880-82
Portrait and miniature painter. Son of Thomas Herbert M. Add: 6 Bloomfield Crescent, Westbourne Terrace, London. † B 2, D 1, L 3, RA 4, RBA 2.

MAGUIRE, Thomas Herbert 1821-1895
Portrait, genre and historical painter and lithographer. Lithographer to Queen Victoria. Father of Bertha, Helena J. and Sidney Calton M. q.v. Add: 6 Bloomfield Crescent, Westbourne Terrace, London. † B 1, L 6, RA 7, RHA 1.

MAHALM, Cecilia Exh. 1925
114 Pembroke Road, Dublin. † RHA 1.

MAHLER, Elsie Exh. 1900
Rothemburg Am Tauber, Germany. † SWA 2.

MAHLER, Henry Exh. 1908-40
Add: New Brighton, Cheshire 1908; Ludlow 1912; Y Ffrwd, Tal-y-Cafn, Wales 1918; Conway, Wales 1930. † L 4, RA 3, RCA 87.

MAHLER, Mrs. Mary Exh. 1918-22
Y Ffrwd, Tal-y-Cafn, Wales. † L 1, RCA 6.

MAHON, Gilbert Exh. 1937
Lyndhurst, Hants. † RCA 1.

MAHON, G.J. Exh. 1913-15
161 Rake Lane, Liscard, Cheshire. † L 3.

MAHON, Luke Exh. 1936-40
Landscape painter. Add: Castlegar, Ahascragh, Co. Galway. † RHA 6.

MAHON, Lilian G. Exh. 1905-10
Add: Liverpool 1905; Liscard, Cheshire 1907. † L 4.

MAHON, Ursula Exh. 1927-29
Castlegar, Ahascragh, Co. Galway. † RHA 6.

MAHONEY, Cyril Exh. 1928-36
1 Kensington Crescent, London. † NEA 4.

MAHONY, Miss A. Exh. 1881
4 Camden Quay, Cork. † RHA 1.

MAHONY, Martin F. Exh. 1913-29
Lota Beg, Co. Cork 1913; Dublin 1925. † RHA 24.

MAHOOD, Mrs. W. Exh. 1883
18 Low Hill, Liverpool. † L 1.

MAIDEN, Sydney J.F. Exh. 1927-36
Landscape painter. Add: London 1927; Chipstead, near Sevenoaks, Kent 1934. † GOU 2, NEA 11, RA 3.

MAIDES, F. Exh. 1928
Landscape painter. † AB 1.

MAIDMAN, Edward C.H. Exh. 1897-1915
Edinburgh 1897; Sherborne, Dorset 1915. † RA 1, RSA 16.

MAIDMENT, Mrs. Kathleen Exh. 1908-26
Dublin 1908; Dundrum, Ireland 1917; Dalkey 1924. † RHA 12.

MAIDMENT, Thomas b. 1871
Landscape painter. Studied Royal College of Art (travelling scholarship). Exh. 1905-38. Add: Ilford, Essex 1905; Newlyn, Penzance 1910; St. Ives, Cornwall 1932. † L 2, LS 6, M 1, RA 12, RSA 1.

MAILE, Alfred Exh. 1882-89
Landscape and architectural painter. Add: Langdale, Windermere 1882; Durham 1888. † L 3, RA 3.

MAILLARD, Auguste Exh. 1928
112 Boulevard Malesherbes, Paris. † L 1, RSA 2.

MAILLARD, Emile* Exh. 1911
Marine painter. † BRU 1.

MAILLART, Diogene Ulysee Napoleon 1845-1908
French painter. Exh. 1889. Add: 6 Rue de Furstenberg, Paris. † L 3.

MAILLAUD, Fernand* b. 1863
French painter. Exh. 1938. † COO 53.

MAILLOL, Aristide* 1861-1944
French sculptor. Exh. 1935. † RSA 1.

MAILLOS, Andre Jean Marie b. 1871
French painter. Exh. 1909-10. Add: c/o Allied Artists Association, Chancery Lane, London. † LS 6.

MAIMON, Moses Exh. 1907-8
115 Malvern Road, Kilburn, London. † LS 1, RA 2.

MAIN, De See D

MAIN, John P. Exh. 1893-1928
Add: Govan 1893; Glasgow 1896; Pollokshields 1901; Clarkston, Busby 1909. † GI 24, L 1, LS 1, RSA 9, RSW 4.

MAIN, Robert Hall Exh. 1934
Watercolour painter. † WG 1.

MAIN, William Exh. 1933-38
Painter. Northampton. † RA 1, RSA 6.

MAINDS, Allan Douglass 1881-1945
Painter and designer of costumes and posters. Son of William Reid M. q.v. Studied Glasgow School of Art (travelling scholarship). Lecturer at Glasgow School of Art and Professor of Fine Art, Durham University. A.R.S.A. 1929. Add: Glasgow 1909 and 1925; Old Kilpatrick 1921; Ponteland, Northumberland 1931. † GI 58, L 2, RA 1, RSA 38, RSW 1.

MAINDS, William Reid Exh. 1885
Painter. Father of Allan Douglass M. q.v. Add: 2 Iona Terrace, Helensburgh. † GI 1, RSA 1.

MAINE, de See D

MAINELLA, R. Exh. 1904
Watercolour painter. † FIN 1.

MAINETTY, Joseph M. Exh. 1909
† LS 3.

MAINMAN, Elizabeth S.H. Exh. 1928-29
81 Canning Street, Liverpool. † L 2.

MAINWARING, Mrs. W.G. Exh. 1884
Watercolour painter. Add: Bowls, Chigwell, Essex. † SWA 1.

MAIR, Alex Exh. 1937
20 Wellington Square, Ayr. † GI 2.

MAIR, Miss Maud See EASTMAN

MAIRET, Mrs. Ethel Mary 1872-1952
nee Partridge. Handloom weaver and dyer. b. Barnstaple. Exh. 1929. Add: Gospels, Ditchling, Sussex. † L 4.

MAIS, Dorothy Exh. 1932
Chalk artist. Add: 4 Stratford Studios, Stratford Road, London. † RA 1.

MAISTRE, le See L

MAITLAND, Alister Exh. 1930-36
13 Stephen Drive, Linthouse, Glasgow. † GI 9, RSA 3.

MAITLAND, Ann Emma Exh. 1890-1940
Flower painter. Add: Sevenoaks 1890; Glasgow 1893; Bexley, Kent 1896; London 1902. † BG 92, GI 12, L 11, M 1, RA 9, RBA 3, RI 8, ROI 1, SWA 20, WG 51.

MAITLAND, Capt. Alex Fuller Exh. 1887-1922
Landscape and marine painter. Add: Belfast 1887; Garth, Breconshire 1888; Newbury, Berks. 1896; Hove, Sussex 1902. † FIN 92, L 2, M 1, RA 18, RHA 5, ROI 2.

MAITLAND, Mrs Edith A. Exh. 1913-18
1 Chatsworth Villas, Cheltenham, Glos. † L 8, LS 14, RA 1.

MAITLAND, Edward Fuller Exh. 1911-26
Landscape painter. Married Gertrude M. q.v. Add: Wood Rising, Rye, Sussex. † RA 1, WG 64.

MAITLAND, Florence Exh. 1920-39
Miniature portrait painter. Add: 38 Cheyne Walk, Chelsea, London. † L 1, RA 1, RMS 5.

MAITLAND, Mrs. F.J. Exh. 1897
Craighead, Tollcross, N.B.† GI 1.

MAITLAND, Gertrude Exh. 1909-30
Landscape painter. Married Edward Fuller M. q.v. Add: Wood Rising, Rye, Sussex. † L 1, RA 1, RCA 1, RID 3, SWA 14, WG 56.

MAITLAND, The Viscountess Gwendoline Luce Exh. 1899-1907
Miniature portrait painter. Add: 14 Lower Sloane Street, London. † L 1, NG 4, RA 19.

MAITLAND, J.E. Exh. 1882
Landscape painter. Add: 10 Chester Place, Hyde Park, London. † D 1.

MAITLAND, Lorna Exh. 1930-39
Miniature painter. A.R.M.S. 1935. Add: 26 Palace Mansions, London. † L 1, RA 3, RMS 18, WG 33.

MAITLAND, Paul Fordyce* 1863-1909
Landscape painter. Studied Royal College of Art and under Theodore Roussell. Taught drawing at South Kensington. N.E.A. 1888. Add: London. † BG 7, GI 20, GOU 6, L 1, M 3, NEA 13, RBA 2.

MAITLAND, R.E. Fuller Exh. 1904-24
Figure and portrait painter. Add: Stansted Hall, Essex 1904; London 1924. † P 1, RA 4.

MAITLAND, The Hon. Mrs. W.F. Exh. 1898
Essex. † D 1.

MAITRE, le See L

MAJOLI, Luigi Exh. 1880
Sculptor. Add: 11 Via degli Incurabili, Rome. † RA 1.

MAJOR, Florence Talfourd Exh. 1894-1905
Landscape painter. Add: 13 Somerset Terrace, Upper Woburn Place, London. † RID 10.

MAJOR, Geraldine Exh. 1922-30
c/o Bank of Montreal, 47 Threadneedle Street, London. † L 6, RI 1, SWA 2.

MAJOR, Rev. Talfourd N. Exh. 1893-99
Landscape and figure painter. Add: London. † RID 13.

MAJORELLE, Jacques Exh. 1938
French painter and illustrator. † COO 25.

MAK, Paul Exh. 1929
Painter. Add: c/o Leicester Galleries, Leicester Square, London. † RA 2.

MAKIN, Hannah L. Exh. 1909
57 Crawford Avenue, Sefton Park, Liverpool. † L 2.

MAKIN, J.K. Exh. 1882-1906
Colwyn Bay, N. Wales. † L 10, M 20, RCA 5.

MAKIN, Lilian J. Exh. 1907-8
46 Hamilton Square, Birkenhead. † L 2.

MAKIN, Stanley Exh. 1923
30 Cantsfield Street, Liverpool. † L 1.

MAKINS, F. Exh. 1928
Champflower, Bruton, Somerset. † D 1.

MALAM, Beatrice E. Exh. 1916-33
Miniature portrait painter. m. Sutherland Rollinson q.v. Add: Hull 1916; Cottingham, E. Yorks. 1927. † L 3, RA 14.

MALBURN, May Exh. 1914-34
Miniature portrait painter. A.R.M.S. 1917. Add: London 1914 and 1918; Marple, Cheshire 1917; East Runton, Norfolk 1919; Northampton 1923; Stockport 1934. † L 4, RA 7, RMS 5.

MALCHUS, P.P. Exh. 1882
Munich. † RSA 1.

MALCOLM, A.N. Exh. 1938
Education Offices, Spittal Street, Stirling. † GI 1.

MALCOLM, Beatrice Exh. 1892-1906
Portrait and figure painter. Add: London. † M 1, P 6, NEA 20, ROI 1, SWA 2.

MALCOLM, Jessie Pescod Exh. 1900-33
Liverpool 1900, 1906 and 1913; New Brighton, Cheshire 1901 and 1912; Wallasey, Cheshire 1932. † B 3, GOU 5, L 47, M 3, RI 2.

MALCOLM, Thalia Exh. 1930
Rake Manor, Milford, Surrey. † NEA 1.

MALCOLM, Thomas Exh. 1888
1 Salmond Place, Edinburgh. † GI 1.

MALCOLMSON, Miss B. Exh. 1907-13
Minella, Clonmel, Co. Tipperary. † RHA 3.

MALCOLMSON, James C. Exh. 1932
3 Lounsdale Drive, Paisley. † GI 1.

MALCOLMSON, Lizzie Exh. 1912-13
Minella, Clonmel, Co. Tipperary. † RHA 5.

MALDEN, Agnes Exh. 1889
Painter. Add: 109 Comeragh Road, West Kensington, London. † RID 1.

MALDEN, Miss E. Scott Exh. 1920
Painter. Add: Windlesham House, Southern Cross, near Brighton. † RA 1.

MALEMPRE, Leo* Exh. 1885-1909
Portrait, figure and domestic painter. Add: London. † GI 1, L 6, NG 3, RA 13, ROI 7.

MALET, Guy S. Warre b. 1900
Painter and wood engraver. Studied Regent Street Polytechnic and Grosvenor School of Art. R.B.A. 1936. Add: London. † RA 9, RBA 19, RED 14.

MALET, P. Exh. 1881
Portland Place, London. † GI 1.

MALI, Christian Friedrich 1832-1906
Landscape painter. Exh. 1881-87. Add: 46 Landwehrtstrasse, Munich. † FIN 1, M 1, RHA 7.

MALIM, J.J. Exh. 1938-39
86 Union Street, Torquay, Devon. † RCA 2, RI 2.

MALIN, Mrs. Frank H. Exh. 1904
Painter. Add: 7 Sherwood Rise, Nottingham. † N 1.

MALIPHANT, William Exh. 1887-1909
Landscape and figure painter. Add: Wood Green, London. † RA 3, RBA 3, RI 7, ROI 1.

MALISSARD, Georges Exh. 1930
Sculptor. Add: 12 bis Rue Pergolese, Paris. † RA 1.

MALLALIEU, Harold Exh. 1936-40
Portrait painter. Add: 402A Kings Road, London. † P 2, RA 1, ROI 2.

MALLAM, Beatrice Exh. 1901-18
Painter and illustrator. Add: London. † L 1, RA 2, RMS 2, SWA 2.

MALLAM, Ellen Exh. 1884-98
Figure painter. Add: 13 Gilston Road, London. † SWA 6.

MALLET, Harriette Exh. 1882
Flower painter. Add: 33 Sister's Avenue, Clapham, London. † D 3.

MALLET, Miss L.A. Exh. 1910-20
A.N.S.A. 1912-28. Add: Mapperley, Nottingham 1910; Fiskerton, Notts. 1911; Nottingham 1919. † N 21.

MALLET, Pierre Exh. 1887-96
Etcher. Add: Brighton 1887; London 1889. † RA 9.

MALLET, Stephen P. Exh. 1895-98
Landscape painter. Add: Tiltham, Godalming 1896; London 1898. † NEA 6, ROI 2.

MALLETT, Maud Constance Exh. 1911
The Haven, Northwood, Middlesex. † LS 3.

MALLINSON, Mrs. Edyth Exh. 1927-33
Miniature portrait painter. Add: Greystones, Wilmslow, Cheshire. † RA 2.

MALLINSON, Ethel M. Exh. 1917-40
Fairleigh, Ilkley, Yorks. † GI 27, L 4, RSA 6, RSW 2.

MALLINSON, W.E. Exh. 1903-4
Decorative painter. Add: Dunkirk, Notts. 1903; New Chilwell, Notts. 1904. † N 2.

MALLOCH, Stirling Exh. 1897-1901
33 Albany Street, Edinburgh. † GI 1, L 3, RSA 11, RSW 1.

MALLOL, Miss A. Exh. 1930-37
245 Bristol Road, Birmingham. † B 6.

MALLORIE, Mrs. Margaret E.M. Exh. 1911-33
nee Trinder. Watercolour landscape painter. Studied Westminster and Lambeth Schools of Art and under A.W. Rich and Sickert. Add: London 1911; Barham Rectory, Canterbury 1933. † RA 4.

MALLOWS, Charles Edward Exh. 1888-1915
Architect. Add: London 1888 and 1907; Bedford 1895. † RA 33.

MALONE, Blondelle E. Exh. 1911-15
Painter. Add: London 1911; United Arts Club, Dublin 1915. † NEA 1, RHA 5, SWA 1.

MALONE, Miss R. Exh. 1919
Painter. Add: Norfolk House, Twickenham, Middlesex. † SWA 1.

MALONY, F. Exh. 1910
Clare Cottage, West Byfleet, Surrey. † L 1.

MALPASS, J.C.L. Exh. 1926-38
The Studio, Greenhall Farm, Atherton. † L 3, M 3.

MALRIC, Charles L. Exh. 1907
37 Villa d'Alesia, Paris. † L 1.

MALTBY, E.H. Exh. 1926-32
Wednesbury 1926; West Bromwich 1932. † B 5.

MALTBY, Mrs. Emily M. Exh. 1900-28
nee Worsfold. Miniature portrait painter. Add: Feltham, Middlesex 1900; Brighton 1926. † RA 11, RMS 3.

MALTBY, F.C. Exh. 1886
Landscape painter. Add: c/o 293 Oxford Street, London. † SWA 1.

MALTBY, Kathleen H. See GUTHRIE

MALTESE, Signora Exh. 1921-22
c/o Mrs. Musgrave, 1 South Parks Road, Oxford. † B 6.

MALTHOUSE, E.J. Exh. 1932-40
Add: Erdington, Birmingham 1932; Shipley, Yorks. 1940. † B 3.

MALTWOOD, Mrs. Katherine Exh. 1911-19
Sculptor. Studied Slade School. Add: Tadworth, Surrey 1911; London 1917; Bridgwater, Som. 1919. † L 1, LS 8, RA 1, RID 1.

MANASSE, Emanuel Exh. 1940
Sculptor. Add: 120 Adelaide Road, London. † RA 1.

MANBY, Eleanor E. Exh. 1889
38 Park Road, London. † D 2.

MANCINI, Antonio* 1852-1930
Italian portrait and figure painter. N.E.A. 1910. Exh. 1893-1921. Add: London. † G 12, GOU 3, I 5, L 2, LS 4, NEA 4, NG 1, P 14, RA 3, RSA 4.

MANCINI, F. Exh. 1926-27
Sculptor. Add: 7 Roman Road, Cheltenham, Glos. † L 1, RA 1.

MANCOE, Hubert Exh. 1884-85
Sparkbrook, Birmingham. † B 2.

MANDER, Eileen Exh. 1934-37
Landscape painter. Add: Spon House, Coventry. † B 2, RA 1.

MANDER, Miss F.L. Exh. 1915-16
14 Derby Road, Liscard, Cheshire. † L 4.

MANDER, William Henry* Exh. 1882-1914
Landscape painter. Add: Birmingham 1882 and 1907; Dolgelly, N. Wales 1899; Lincoln 1904; Sheffield 1905. † B 66, RCA 7, RHA 14.

MANENTI, Mrs. Bushka Exh. 1930-36
Sculptor. Add: 416 Fulham Road, London. † RA 5, RSA 1.

MANENTI, Mario Exh. 1923-25
Sculptor. Add: 416 Fulham Road, London. † L 1, RA 3.

MANGAN, Wilfrid C. Exh. 1933
Architect. Add: 36 Southampton Street, Strand, London. † RA 1.

MANGIN, Mrs. Con W. Exh. 1884
Catstackburn, Selkirk. † RSA 1.

MANGLES, Alice Exh. 1881
Littleworth, Longham, Surrey. † D 1.

MANGUIN, Henri* b. 1874
French painter. Exh. 1921-28. † GOU 11.

MANIS, John P. Exh. 1897
Cardowan Road, Stepps, Glasgow. † L 1.

MANLEY, Agnes P. Exh. 1893
196 Hagley Road, Egbaston, Birmingham. † B 1.

MANLEY, C. Macdonald 1855-1924
Landscape painter. b. Surrey. Exh. 1882-89. Add: Dublin 1882; London 1883. Died in Canada. † L 2, M 1, RBA 2, RHA 3, RI 2.

MANLEY, Mrs. Edna b. 1900
nee Swithenbank. Sculptor. Studied Regent Street Polytechnic and St. Martins School of Art. Member London Group 1930. Exh. 1938. Add: Kingston, Jamaica. † RSA 1.

MANLY, Alice Elfrida Exh. 1880-1917
Landscape painter. Sister of Eleanor E. and Sarah M. q.v. Add: Hampstead, London. † B 10, D 56, L 6, M 5, RA 16, RBA 2, RI 5, ROI 1, SWA 16.

MANLY, Eleanor E. Exh. 1880-98
Figure and genre painter. Sister of Alice E. and Sarah M. q.v. Add: Hampstead, London. † B 2, D 5, L 5, M 8, RA 11, RBA 2, ROI 3, SWA 10.

MANLY, Miss F.M. Exh. 1901-4
Glenthorne, 157 Highbury New Park, London. † SWA 7.

MANLY, Sarah Exh. 1880-90
Flower painter. Sister of Alice E. and Eleanor E.M. q.v. Add: Park Road, Haverstock Hill, London. † B 3, L 2, RA 1, RI 3, SWA 15.

MANN, Alexander* 1853-1908
Landscape and genre painter. Studied under Carolus Duran. Travelled on the continent and North Africa. N.E.A. 1886, R.O.I. 1893. Father of Mary Gow M. q.v. Add: Glasgow 1880; Hagbourne, near Didcot 1888; London 1890. † B 18, FIN 1, GI 69, L 47, M 12, NEA 11, NG 1, RA 24, RBA 18, RHA 2, RID 15, ROI 48, RSA 11.

MANN, Bessie Exh. 1904
Flower painter. Add: 13 Dairy House Road, Derby. † N 1.

MANN, Bertha A. Exh. 1921-23
Flower painter. Add: "Woodside", 53 Alfred Street, Ripley, Derbys. † N 2.

MANN, Catherine Exh. 1904
Narrabei, Cole Park, Twickenham, Middlesex. † RI 1.

MANN, Cathleen d. 1959
The Marchioness of Queensberry. Portrait, still life, and flower painter. Daughter of Harrington and Florence Sabine M. q.v. Studied Slade School and in Paris. R.O.I. 1935, R.P. 1931, S.W.A. 1932. Exh. 1924-40. Add: London. † GI 7, GOU 49, I 5, L 1, LEF 37, LEI 28, M 2, NEA 12, P 34, RA 23, RED 1, ROI 4, RSA 2, SWA 8, TOO 4.

MANN, Mrs. C.M.A. Exh. 1922-23
41 Castle Street, Liverpool. † L 3.

MANN, Dora Exh. 1898-1907
Miniature portrait painter. Add: Weybridge, Surrey 1898; Surbiton Hill, Surrey 1899; Walton on Thames 1903; London 1907. † L 4, RA 4, RMS 5.

MANN, Ellen Exh. 1885-86
Watercolour landscape painter. Add: 76 Queensboro Terrace, London. † SWA 3.

MANN, Ed. H. Exh. 1936-38
Lydiate Avenue, Bromsgrove, Birmingham. † B 10.

MANN, Miss Florence Exh. 1883-95
Flower and figure painter. Add: London. † B 3, RA 2, RBA 4, SWA 4.

MANN, Florence Sabine Exh. 1895-1923
nee Pasley. Painter. 1st wife of Harrington and mother of Cathleen M. q.v. Add: Duncryne, Alexandria, Dumbartonshire 1895; London 1902. † G 1, GI 2, I 1, NG 7, P 1.

MANN, Frank W. Exh. 1888-93
Watercolour painter. Add: 49 Merrow Street, Walworth, London. † RA 3.

MANN, Harrington 1864-1937
Portrait painter. b. Glasgow. Studied Slade School (travelling scholarship). Married Florence Sabine and father of Cathleen M. q.v. R.E. 1885-91, R.P. 1900. Add: Glasgow 1882 and 1889; Rome 1888; London 1896 and 1899; Alexandria, Dumbartonshire 1897. Died on a visit to New York. † AG 31, B 1, D 3, G 9, GI 60, GOU 7, I 31, L 27, LEI 23, M 4, NEA 8, NG 12, P 87, RA 46, RBA 1, RE 1, RI 1, ROI 1, RSA 27.

MANN, Horace E. Exh. 1929-34
Landscape painter. Add: New House, Potters Bar, Middlesex. † RA 2.

MANN, James Exh. 1936
67 Croftfoot Road, Glasgow. † GI 1.

MANN, Julia A. Exh. 1891-1903
Hillhead, Glasgow 1891; Aberdeen 1896. † GI 8.

MANN, Joshua Hargrave Sams* Exh. 1880-85
Genre painter. R.B.A. 1875. Add: London. † B 7, GI 2, L 4, RA 6, RBA 46, RHA 1, RI 2, ROI 3, RSA 1.

MANN, James Scrimgeour* 1883-1946
Marine painter and poster artist. b. Dundee. Studied Liverpool School of Art. R.I. 1932. Add: Liscard, Cheshire 1910; Liverpool 1913. † B 1, GI 1, L 49, M 1, RA 2, RBA 4, RCA 27, RI 55.

MANN, Kathleen Exh. 1935
3 Park Terrace, Glasgow. † GI 2.

MANN, Mabel Exh. 1938
Colwyn Bay, Wales. † RCA 1.

MANN, Merby Exh. 1936
† SWA 1.

MANN, Mary Gow b. 1888
Watercolour painter. Studied Goldsmith's College and under Norman Garstin (1923). Daughter of Alexander M. q.v. Exh. 1927. Add: Ledard, Henley on Thames, Oxon. † RA 1.

MANN, Miss Merlyn K.D. Exh. 1935
Painter and illustrator. Add: 36 Colville Terrace, London. † RA 2.

MANN, Mabel M. Exh. 1885
Flower painter. Add: 51 Hamilton Terrace, London. † RBA 1.

MANN, Robert* Exh. 1882-92
Birmingham. † B 23.

MANN, Samuel Exh. 1909
3 Moscow Drive, Stoneycroft, Liverpool. † L 1.

MANN-DIERKS, Mrs. Catarina Exh. 1899
c/o Mrs. Adeline Trier, 6 The Terrace, Champion Hill, London. † SWA 1.

MANNERS, Lady Marjorie Exh. 1906
16 Arlington Street, London. † RA 1.

MANNERS, Norman Egmont b. 1905
Landscape, portrait painter and lithographer. b. Shoreham, Kent. Studied Chelsea School of Art 1921-24. Scholarship to Allan Fraser Art College, Arbroath 1921-27. Exh. 1928-36. Add: London 1928; Harrow, Middlesex 1936. † RA 6.

MANNERS, Lady Victoria Exh. 1899-1916
Watercolour painter. Add: 3 Cambridge Gate, Regents Park, London. † FIN 88, NG 14, SWA 1.

MANNERS, Mrs. Violet See RUTLAND

MANNERS, William* Exh. 1885-1904
Landscape painter. R.B.A. 1893. Add: Bradford 1885; Otley, Yorks. 1890; Shipley, Yorks. 1892; Crosshills, near Keighley, Yorks. 1899; Sutton Coldfield 1904. † B 10, L 18, M 2, RA 3, RBA 41, RSA 2.

MANNEVILLE, Andre Exh. 1911
192 Rue de Vaugirard, Paris. † RSA 1.

MANNFELD, Conrad Exh. 1880-1901
Flower and landscape painter. Add: London. † G 2, M 1, RA 2, RBA 4, ROI 10.

MANNING, Eliza F. Exh. 1880-90
Figure and flower painter. Add: St. Leonards Villa, Victoria Road, Surbiton, Surrey. † D 3, M 2, RA 2, RI 1, SWA 16.

MANNING, J.A. Exh. 1921
Vine Cottage, Station Road, Monmouth. † RA 1.

MANNING, Lilian Exh. 1901-3
Miniature portrait painter. Add: 27 Perryn Road, East Acton, London. † L 2, RA 2, RMS 1.

MANNING, May R. Exh. 1880-92
Flower painter. Add: Dublin 1880 and 1892; Hampstead, London 1889. † B 1, L 1, RHA 4.

MANNING, William Westley* b. 1868
Landscape painter and etcher. Studied University College School and Julians, Paris. R.B.A. 1901, A.R.E. 1917, R.O.I. 1916. Exh. 1889-1940. Add: London. † B 9, BG 57, CHE 6, FIN 4, GI 42, GOU 17, I 29, L 28, LS 8, M 8, NEA 8, NG 12, P 3, RA 33, RBA 222, RE 44, RHA 11, RI 23, ROI 74, RSA 18.

MANNING-SANDERS, Joan Exh. 1928-35
Figure painter. R.O.I. 1931. Add: Sennen Cove, Penzance, Cornwall. † L 2, NEA 2, RA 7, ROI 10, RSA 1, SWA 1.

MANNIX, Mary Exh. 1882
10 South Frederick Street, Dublin. † RHA 1.

MANNIX, Robert Exh. 1880-98
Dublin 1880; Glasgow 1898. † GI 2, RSA 34.

MANNIX, R. Junr. Exh. 1882-1901
10 South Frederick Street, Dublin. † RHA 3.

MANNOCH, Sydney Exh. 1900-17
Landscape and coastal painter. Add: London 1900; Falmouth, Cornwall 1911. † LS 18, RA 5, RI 6.

MANNUCCI, Professor Cipriano Exh. 1922
Painter. Add: Italian House, 30 Wigmore Street, London. † RA 1, RSA 1.

MANSBRIDGE, John Exh. 1927-40
Portrait painter. Add: London. † GOU 6, M 1, NEA 1, P 1, RA 1, RBA 1.

MANSEL, Miss H.C. Exh. 1883
Flakedale, Hamilton, N.B. † RSA 2.

MANSELL, Mrs. Arthur Exh. 1900
Dorchester. † D 2.

MANSELL, Marianne Exh. 1885-1909
Flower and landscape painter. Add: London. † L 3, RA 8, RBA 3, SWA 1.

MANSFIELD, F.E. Exh. 1901-5
Bracknell, Berks. 1901; Wokingham, Surrey 1905. † B 1, D 3.

MANSFIELD, H.E. Exh. 1908-37
London. † RA 2, RI 1.

MANSFIELD, Leslie Exh. 1908-26
Etcher. Add: Bickley, Kent 1908; London 1915. † BA 30, RA 11, RSA 1.

MANSFIELD, W. Exh. 1913-20
31 Ogden Street, Heaton Park, Manchester. † L 4, M 3.

MANSON, Miss B. Exh. 1890
11 Templeton Place, Earls Court, London. † SWA 1.

MANSON, James Bolivar* 1879-1945
Portrait, landscape and flower painter and writer. Studied Heatherleys, Lambeth School of Art and Julians, Paris. Critic for "The Outlook" and "Daily Herald". Director of the Tate Gallery 1930-38. N.E.A. 1926, Founder Member London Group 1913. Add: London. † AG 2, BA 2, CAR 8, CHE 4, G 1, GOU 36, I 1, L 1, LEF 1, LEI 30, LS 9, NEA 16, RA 5, RED 8, ROI 3, RSA 1.

MANSON, J. Wellwood Exh. 1930-38
103 Greenock Road, Paisley, Glasgow. † GI 3.

MANSON, Ruth Exh. 1909
Fruit painter. Add: Cambridge House, The Grove, Blackheath, London. † NEA 1.

MANSUY, Rene Exh. 1909
41 Quai des Grands Augustins, Paris. † L 1.

MANTLE, G.H. Exh. 1921-22
37 Park Road, Moseley, Birmingham. † B 2.

MANTON, E.L. Exh. 1939
† GOU 1.

MANTON, G. Grenville* 1855-1932
Portrait painter and illustrator. R.B.A. 1899. Add: London 1880; Bushey, Herts. 1895. † B 1, L 2, P 1, RA 39, RBA 19, ROI 3.

MANUEL, John Exh. 1900-4
Edinburgh 1900 and 1904; Hawick, N.B. 1901. † RSA 4.

MANUEL, J. Wright T. d. 1899
R.B.A. 1896. Exh. from 1896. Add: London. † RBA 17, ROI 5.

MANWARING, Edward E. Exh. 1901-4
Landscape painter. Add: Holmbury Street, Botolphs Road, Worthing, Sussex. † L 2, RA 2, ROI 3.

MANWELL, James Barr Exh. 1937
5 Grays Crescent, Paisley. † GI 1.

MANZANA-PISSARRO, Georges* Exh. 1908
A Medan par Villennes, Seine et Oise, France. † LS 5.

MANZINI, G. Exh. 1885
Sculptor. Add: c/o G.C. McCracken, 38 Queen Street, London. † RA 1.

MANZONI, Carlo Exh. 1894
c/o Conrad Dressler, 34 Hamilton Square, Birkenhead. † L 1.

MANZONI, D. Exh. 1882
c/o Dowdeswell, 133 New Bond Street, London. † GI 1.

MANZONI, G.C. Exh. 1905-6
3 Clifton Road, Birkenhead. † L 4.

MAPLESTONE, Miss Florence E. Exh. 1880-1902
Watercolour figure and illustrative painter. Add: 1 Richmond Gardens, Uxbridge Road, London 1880; Clapham Common 1900. † B 1, M 1, RBA 3, RI 1, SWA 3.

MAPLESTONE, Henry d. 1884
Watercolour landscape painter. A.R.I. 1841. Add: 1 Richmond Gardens, Uxbridge Road, London. † M 3, RI 11.

MAPPIN, Douglas Exh. 1911
Snapbrook, Hollingbourne, Kent. † RA 1.

MARAIS, Adolf Exh. 1885
Landscape painter. Add: Sefton Place, Warning Camp, Arundel, Sussex. † RA 1.

MARC, E. Exh. 1921
Still life painter. † GOU 1.

MARC, Maxim Exh. 1932
Flower painter. Add: 9 Gayton Crescent, London. † RA 1.

MARCEL-BERONNEAU, Pierre b. 1869
French artist. Exh. 1911-24. Add: 11 Impasse Ronsin, Paris. † L 2.

MARCEL-CLEMENT, Amedée Julien* Exh. 1913-14
Coastal painter, 14 Homeau Boileau, 38 Rue Boileau, Paris. † L 1, RSA 1.

MARCELLY, de See D

MARCETTE, Alexandre b. 1853
Belgian artist. Exh. 1913-15. Add: Goupil Gallery, 5 Regent Street, London. † FIN 7, GI 1, L 4, RA 1, RI 1.

MARCH, Miss Elsie Exh. 1912-39
Sculptor. A.R.B.A. 1923, R.B.A. 1932. Add: Goddendene, Farnborough, Kent. † GI 2, L 4, RA 8, RBA 97, RMS 4.

MARCH, Sydney Exh. 1901-35
Sculptor. Add: Goddendene, Farnborough, Kent and London. † L 5, NEA 1, RA 25, ROI 3.

MARCH, Vernon Exh. 1891-1915
Sculptor. Add: Goddendene, Farnborough, Kent and London. † GI 2, L 4, RA 9, TOO 2.

MARCHAND, F. Exh. 1915-37
Portrait and landscape painter. † BA 1, CAR 43, RSA 1.

MARCHAND, Jean* b. 1883
French painter. Exh. 1914-39. Add: c/o Independent Gallery, 7 Grafton Street, London. † ALP 5, BA 2, GI 4, L 1, RSA 1.

MARCHANT, Mrs. H.S. Exh. 1880-81
Landscape painter. Add: The Laurels, Tabor Grove, Wimbledon, London. † SWA 3.

MARCHANT, Robert Exh. 1898-1937
Architect. Add: Sutton at Stone, Sussex 1898; London 1905. † RA 7.

MARCHE, Ernest b. 1864
French artist. Exh. 1907. Add: 109 Boulevard Richard, Lenoir, Paris. † L 1.

MARCHETTI, G. Exh. 1895-1912
Figure and portrait painter. Add: 12 Pembroke Studios, Kensington, London. † L 1, NG 1, RA 4.

MARCHINGTON, Kate Exh. 1906-13
Northendon, Cheshire 1906; Salcombe, Devon 1913. † L 2, M 4.

MARCHMENT, Wallace Exh. 1934-35
Architect. Add: 11 Stanley House, Larkhall, London. † RA 2.

MARCKE, Van See V

MARCKS, Gerhard b. 1889
German sculptor. Exh. 1936. † RSA 3.

MARCOTTE, Mlle. M.A. Exh. 1910
184 Rue de la Province Sud, Antwerp. † L 1.

MARCUCCI, Dominico Exh. 1890
Watercolour painter and designer. Add: Allervale, Newton Abbot, Devon. † RBA 1.

MARCUS, Miss H. Exh. 1882-92
2 Endsleigh Gardens, London. † L 13, RSA 1.

MARCUS, Miss L. Exh. 1915
25 Mount Pleasant Villas, Crouch Hill, London. † L 1.

MARCUSE, Rudolf Exh. 1907
13 Faranenstrasse, Charlottenburg, Berlin. † L 1.

MARDER, Ed Exh. 1911-14
Lyme Regis, Dorset. † LS 11.

MARE, Mrs. Florence Exh. 1936-40
284 Stoney Lane, Yardley, Birmingham. † B 2, RCA 1.

MARECHALL, J. Exh. 1882
57 Frederick Street, Edinburgh. † RSA 1.

MARESCAUX, Mrs. Kathleen Exh. 1912-36
Flower painter. Add: Sheerness, Kent 1912; Inchikolohan, Killkenny, Ireland 1918. † FIN 1, RA 1, RHA 7.

MARGETSON, Colleen Exh. 1938-39
37 Hollycroft Avenue, London. † ROI 5.

MARGETSON, Mrs. Ellen M. Exh. 1908-11
18 Albert Hall Mansions, London. † L 4, LS 6, RA 3.

MARGETSON, Miss Hester Exh. 1914-36
Daughter of William Henry and Helen Howard M. q.v. Add: Blewbury by Didcot, Berks. 1914; Wallingford, Berks. 1927; Oxford 1936. † RI 7, ROI 1.

MARGETSON, Helen Howard b. 1860
nee Hatton. Pastel and watercolour artist. b. Bristol. Studied R.A. Schools and Colarossi's, Paris. Married William Henry and mother of Hester M. q.v. Exh. 1880-1939. Add: London 1882; Blewbury by Didcot, Berks. 1904; Wallingford, Berks. 1924. † B 3, FIN 2, G 3, L 18, M 9, NG 2, RA 10, RI 32, ROI 28.

MARGETSON, H.J. Exh. 1893
Sculptor. Add: Upper Cheyne Row, Chelsea, London. † RA 1.

MARGETSON, William Henry 1861-1940
Painter, illustrator and designer. Studied South Kensington and R.A. Schools. Drawing instructor at L.C.C. Central School. R.I. 1909, R.M.S. 1896, R.O.I. 1901. Married Helen Howard and father of Hester M. q.v. Add: London 1881; Blewbury by Didcot, Berks. 1903; Wallingford, Berks. 1930. † B 3, G 6, GI 5, L 24, M 4, RA 50, RBA 2, RI 80, ROI 94.

MARGETTS, Mrs. Mary d. 1886
Watercolour painter. R.I. 1842. Add: Barby Lodge, Lillington Road, Leamington, Warwicks. † RI 3.

MARGITSON, Maria* Exh. 1880-85
Fruit painter. Add: Ketts Castle Villa, Mousehold Heath, Norwich. † SWA 3.

MARIA, Marius Exh. 1887
Rome. † G 2, L 1.

MARIE, Adrien 1848-1891
French painter. Add: Paris and c/o "Graphic", 190 Strand, London. † AG 1, FIN 1, M 3.

MARIE, Paul Exh. 1911
Painter. † BRU 1.

MARIENTREU, Von See V

MARIN, Ricardo Exh. 1923-35
Painter and illustrator. † FIN 249.

MARION, Jean Exh. 1911-13
16A Albemarle Street, London. † LS 9.

MARION, Jules Exh. 1887
5 Ormond Street, Queens Square, London. † GI 1.

MARIS, Jacob* 1837-1899
Dutch painter. Brother of Matthew and William M. q.v. Add: The Hague, Holland. † B 1, FIN 1, G 1, GI 7, GOU 58, M 1, NG 1, RA 1, RSA 3, RSW 1, TOO 1.

MARIS, Matthew* 1839-1917
Dutch painter, and etcher. Brother of Jacob and William M. q.v. Add: The Hague, Holland. † FIN 4, GI 4, GOU 5, I 9, L 1, RSA 9.

MARIS, William* 1844-1910
Dutch painter. Brother of Jacob and Matthew M. q.v. Add: The Hague, Holland. † BRU 2. GOU 14, M 4, RSA 2.

MARJORIBANKS-HAY, T. Exh. 1891
Watercolour landscape painter. Add: 41 Charlotte Street, Edinburgh. † RA 2.

MARK, Mrs. Elsie Pardoe Exh. 1900
Ivy Cottage, Blakebrook, Kidderminster. † B 1.

MARK, Lucy E. Exh. 1885-1923
Figure painter. Add: London. † L 3, RA 2, RE 1, RI 2, SWA 6.

MARKBY, L. Exh. 1881
Watercolour landscape painter. Add: Headington Hill, Oxford. † SWA 1.

MARKBY, Mary Exh. 1933
Brighton, Sussex. † RCA 1.

MARKHAM, Cecil Exh. 1913
Morland, Penrith. † L 1.

MARKHAM, Mrs. Charles Exh. 1903
Frodsham Vicarage, Cheshire. † NG 1.

MARKHAM, John Hatton b. 1882
Architect. b. Ventnor, I.O.W. Studied A.A. Schools. Ashipitel Prize 1905, Arthur Cates Prize 1906, Grissnell Gold Medal 1908. Exh. 1923-36. Add: H.M. Office of Works, Storey's Gate, London. † RA 19.

MARKHAM, Miss Mabel F. Exh. 1904
Morland, Penrith, Cumberland. † D 1.

MARKHAM, Sybil Exh. 1936-37
Painter. Add: 71 St. Helens Road, Booterstown, Ireland. † RHA 2.

MARKIEWICZ, Comte Casimir Dunin b. 1874
b. Russia. Married Constance Gore Booth q.v. Exh. 1905-9. Add: St. Mary's, Frankfort Avenue, Rathgar, Dublin. † RHA 11.

MARKIEWICZ, Comtesse see BOOTH, Constance Gore

MARKIEWICZ, Herbert Otto b. 1900
Painter and etcher. b. Berlin. Studied Berlin and Rome. Exh. 1940. Add: Hurtmore Farmhouse, Godalming, Surrey. † RA 2.

MARKINO, Yoshio Exh. 1904-28
London. † G 1, I 2, L 5.

MARKS, Anne Exh. 1893-1924
Miniature painter. Add: London. † L 3, LS 19, RA 5, RCA 25, SWA 1.

MARKS, Barnett Samuel 1827-1916
Portrait painter. b. Cardiff. Add: London from 1880. † G 1, M 1, RA 9, RCA 27.

MARKS, Claude* Exh. 1899-1915
Add: London 1899 and 1915; Paris 1908. † L 5, LS 8, RA 1, ROI 2.

MARKS, Mrs. D. Exh. 1927
28 Lawrie Park Road, Sydenham, Kent. † L 1, RI 1.

MARKS, Ellis C. Exh. 1898-1904
London. † NG 4.

MARKS, Florence Exh. 1889-1918
Portrait and figure painter. Add: London. † L 1, P 11, RA 6, ROI 1, SWA 6.

MARKS, George Exh. 1880-1938
Landscape painter. Add: Penge, Kent 1880; High Wycombe, Bucks. 1883; Greenwich, London 1885; Shere, Guildford, Surrey 1887; Ross, Herefords. 1927. † B 19, D 152, DOW 70, L 77, M 23, NG 1, RA 77, RBA 33, RCA 2, RI 36, ROI 10.

MARKS, Gertrude Exh. 1897-1903
London. † RCA 5, SWA 1.

MARKS, Gilbert L. Exh. 1899-1903
Metal worker. Add: The Quest, Hazeldean Road, Croydon, Surrey. † GI 10, L 14, RA 1.

MARKS, Henry Stacey 1829-1898
Genre painter, watercolourist and illustrator. Studied under J.M. Leigh and under Picot in Paris. Married Mary Harriet M. q.v. A.R.A. 1871, R.A. 1878, H.R.E. 1881, A.R.W.S. 1871, R.W.S. 1883. Add: London. † AG 18, B 6, FIN 197, GI 5, L 19, M 13, RA 41, RCA 8, ROI 4, RWS 32.

MARKS J. Exh. 1897
67 Smallbrook Street, Birmingham. † B 1.

MARKS, Marguerite Exh. 1923-33
Miniature painter. Add: London. † L 8, RI 27.

MARKS, Mary Harriet Exh. 1894-1901
nee Kempe. Figure and portrait painter. Married Henry Stacey M. q.v. Add: London. † GI 4, L 1, M 1, RA 2, SWA 2.

MARKS, Mrs. Stella Lewis b. 1889
Miniature and portrait painter. b. Melbourne, Australia. Studied National Gallery School of Art, Melbourne. A.R.M.S. 1917, R.M.S. 1922. Exh. 1921-40. Add: New York, U.S.A. 1921; St. Leonards, near Tring, Herts. 1935. † RA 10, RMS 30.

MARKWICK, Harold Exh. 1935-39
Filchin, Crowhill, Plymouth, Devon. † B 5, RBA 1, RCA 1, RI 3, RSA 1.

MARLAND, Mrs. J. Exh. 1910
110 Derby Road, Long Eaton, Notts. † N 1.

MARLES, Dorothy M. Exh. 1924
Figure and urban landscape painter. Add: Coddington Hall, Newark on Trent, Notts. † N 4.

MARLIN, Mrs. Hilda G. Exh. 1933
Painter and lithographer. Add: 21 Upper Mount Street, Dublin. † RHA 6.

MARLOW, Albert Exh. 1884-88
7 Broad Street Corner, Birmingham. † B 10.

MARLOW, F. Exh. 1912
Nashaty-bey-houses, Choubra Road, Cairo, Egypt. † RA 1.

MARLOWE, Florence Exh. 1883-88
Figure and still life painter. Add: Sutton, Surrey 1883; Hammersmith, London 1886. † B 1, RBA 4, ROI 1.

MARNI, Leo Exh. 1911
Painter. † BRU 1.

MARNY, Paul c. 1834-1914
French painter. Add: Scarborough 1882; Wembley, Middlesex 1890. Died at Scarborough. † B 1, GI 1, RA 1.

MAROLDA, Emilio Exh. 1882
Landscape and coastal painter. Add: Hogarth Studios, 64 Charlotte Street, London. † RBA 2.

MARPLES, George 1869-1939
Painter and etcher. Studied Royal College of Art, Ecole des Beaux Arts, Paris and Ecole des Arts Decoratifs, Geneva. Principal of Hull and Huddersfield Schools of Art and Liverpool City School of Art. A.R.E. 1918. Add: Derby 1895; Meols, Cheshire 1917; Liverpool 1920. † GI 38, L 4, N 2, RA 15, RCA 2, RE 29, RHA 1, RSA 9.

MARQUAND, Emily R. Exh. 1903-4
Miniature portrait painter. Add: 42 Craven Park Road, Willesden, London. † RA 2.

MARQUESTE, Laurent Honore 1848-1920
French sculptor. Exh. 1898-1911. Add: Paris. † RA 1, RSA 2.

MARQUET, Albert* 1875-1947
French painter. Exh. 1912-38. † GOU 7, RED 1, RSA 1.

MARQUET, Miss C.A. Exh. 1916-17
67 Herbert Road, Sherwood Rise, Nottingham. † N 2.

MARQUIS, Alice Exh. 1930-32
† L 2.

MARQUIS, J. Richard d. 188?
Landscape painter. A.R.H.A. 1861, R.H.A. 1861. Add: London. † L 3, RHA 25, ROI 1.

MARR, F. Exh. 1889
20 Church Street, Liverpool. † L 1.

MARR, Jessie Exh. 1881-83
Oxhill Villa, Dumbarton. † GI 6.

MARR, J.W. Hamilton Exh. 1881-1913
Landscape painter. Married Sophie M. q.v. Add: Birmingham 1881; Hockley Heath, Warwicks 1885; Edgbaston, Birmingham 1895; Stratford on Avon, Warwicks. 1899. † B 77, G 1, GI 4, L 21, M 11, RCA 177, RHA 35, ROI 2, RSA 2.

MARR, Sophie d. 1901
Painter. Married J.W. Hamilton M. q.v. Add: Hockley Heath, Warwicks. 1884; Edgbaston, Birmingham 1895; Stratford on Avon, Warwicks. 1899. † B 29, GI 4, L 7, M 7, RCA 2, RHA 17, ROI 2.

MARRABLE, Miss Exh. 1882
42 Ladbroke Road, Notting Hill, London. † M 1.

MARRABLE, Cecil Charles Exh. 1910-27
25 Onslow Square, London. † D 15.

MARRABLE, Edith See FERGUSON

MARRABLE, Madeline d. 1916
nee Cockburn. Landscape and figure painter. S.W.A. 1880. President S.W.A. Add: London. † ALP 8, B 5, D 11, G 5, L 11, LS 5, M 14, NG 3, RA 6, RBA 10, RI 3, SWA 215.

MARRABLE, Miss T.R. Exh. 1903-21
A.S.W.A. 1910. Add: 25 Onslow Square, London. † SWA 17.

MARRET, Henri b. 1878
French artist. Exh. 1910. Add: 28 Rue Chaptal, Paris. † L 1.

MARRIAN, F.T. Exh. 1882-83
123 Gt. Hampton Street, Birmingham. † B 1, RSA 1.

MARRIOTT, E.T. Exh. 1899
Architect. Add: 3 Cliffords Inn, Temple, London. † RA 1.

MARRIOTT, Frederick 1860-1941
Portrait and landscape painter and etcher. b. Stoke-on-Trent. Studied Royal College of Art. Headmaster Goldsmith's College of Art 1895-1925. A.R.E. 1909, R.E. 1924. Exh. from 1882. Add: London. † B 4, BA 2, CHE 2, CON 35, GI 3, L 23, M 1, NG 8, P 4, RA 42, RE 53, ROI 5.

MARRIOTT, Miss K.A. Exh. 1896-98
11 Gill Street, Nottingham. † N 5.

MARRIOTT, Pickford Exh. 1898-1908
Decorative sculptor. London 1898; Port Elizabeth School of Art, Cape Colony, S. Africa 1907. † B 1, L 1, NG 2, RA 6, RSA 1.

MARRIOTT, R.S. Exh. 1889-92
9 Conduit Street, London. † B 4, RHA 2.

MARRIOTT, Richard W. Exh. 1926-35
Landscape painter. Burpham, Nr. Arundel, Sussex 1931. † FIN 71, NEA 2, ROI 1.

MARRIS, Miss J.R. Exh. 1900-5
Kidderminster 1900, Bedford 1905. † B 4.

MARRIS, Rose Exh. 1882
7 Arthur Road, Edgbaston, Birmingham. † B 1.

MARRIS, Miss S. Exh. 1889
4 Victoria Road, Leamington, Warwicks. † B 1.

MARR-JOHNSON, Patrick Exh. 1931
Etcher. Station House, Deepcut, Blackdown. † RA 1.

MARSDEN, Mrs. H.B. Exh. 1918-25
London. † GI 1, L 1, RA 2.

MARSDEN, J.B. Exh. 1908
Cheapside Bottoms, Morley, Leeds. † RA 1.

MARSDEN, Sydney Exh. 1914
39 Khartoum Road, Sheffield. † L 2.

MARSDEN, W. Exh. 1889-90
12 Fort William, Douglas, I.o.M. † M 2.

MARSDEN, Walter Exh. 1915-40
Sculptor. London. † GI 1, L 2, M 2, RA 19.

MARSEILLE, Pierre Exh. 1935-36
Landscape and still-life painter. Rue Sainte, Marseilles, France. † RA 3.

MARSH, Arthur H. 1842-1909
Genre painter and watercolourist. R.B.A. 1882, A.R.W.S. 1870. Add: London 1880; Alnmouth, Northumberland 1886; Cullercoats, Northumberland 1891; Newcastle-on-Tyne 1900. † B 2, FIN 1. L 9, M 16, RA 7, RBA 1, RWS 46.

MARSH, Clare Exh. 1899-1922
Raheen, Clondalkin and Dublin. † L 4, LS 3, RHA 69, SWA 1.

MARSH, Charles F. Exh. 1892-1901
Figure and landscape painter. East Grinstead, Sussex 1892; Ludham, Nr. Norwich 1893; Sudbury, Suffolk 1896; Dedham, Colchester 1899. † M 3, RA 1, RBA 2.

MARSH, Charles J. Exh. 1895
145 Tachbrook Street, London. † ROI 1.

MARSH, Dorothy Eleanora Chisenhale Exh. 1909-13
London. † L 4, LS 6.

MARSH, Mrs. E. Exh. 1915
Sandford Manor House, Stanley Bridge, Fulham, London. † RA 1.

MARSH, Eva Exh. 1895-1925
Watercolour landscape painter. b. Redhill Studied Crystal Palace Art School and R.A. Schools (Landseer scholarship). Add: Winchester 1895; Worthing, Sussex 1905; Croydon, Surrey 1910; London 1917; Warbleton, Sussex 1925. † B 1, RA 2, SWA 7.

MARSH, Edwin W. Exh. 1915-39
Landscape and portrait painter. A.N.S.A. 1922. Add: Mapperley, Notts. 1915; Nottingham 1924. † N 57, RCA 1.

MARSH, Miss G. Exh. 1923
† SWA 1.

MARSH, Lucy F. Exh. 1904-11
73 Mulgrave Street, Liverpool. † L 15.

MARSH, Mary C. Exh. 1912-30
36 The King's Gap, Hoylake, Cheshire. † L 5.

MARSH, Mrs. R.M. see BOWYER, Ellen

MARSH, S.A.H. Exh. 1884-97
† TOO 2.

MARSHALL, Mrs. A. Exh. 1901-13
Chilwell, Notts. 1901; Nottingham 1912; Lockington Derby 1913. † N 3.

MARSHALL, Annie Exh. 1880-1903
1 Park Grove Terrace, Edinburgh. † GI 2, RMS 1.

MARSHALL, Arthur Exh. 1889-1914
Painter and architect. N.S.A. 1890. Add: Nottingham. † N 21, RA 1.

MARSHALL, Alexander J. Exh. 1920-39
Sculptor and painter. West Bridgford, Notts. 1920; London 1933. † N 3, RA 7.

MARSHALL, Charles* 1806-1890
Landscape and theatrical scenery painter. Father of Charles junr. and Roberto Angelo Kittermaster M. q.v. Add: London. † B 2, D 2, FIN 1, RA 2, RI 1.

MARSHALL, Charles, junr. Exh. 1881-86
Landscape painter. Son of Charles M. q.v. Add: London. † B 2, D 1, M 1, RI 1.

MARSHALL, C. Beresford Exh. 1936
Architect. 9 New Cavendish Street, London. † RA 1.

MARSHALL, Clemency Christian Sinclair b. 1900
Painter, miniaturist and black and white artist. b. St. Andrews, Fife. A.R.M.S. 1926, R.M.S. 1930. Exh. 1924-33. Add: London. † L 9, RA 3, RI 1, RMS 42, SWA 2.

MARSHALL, Charles Edward Exh. 1880-1920
Portrait and figure painter. R.B.A. 1890. Add: London. † B 2, GI 3, L 24, M 6, RA 30, RBA 42, RHA 1, ROI 17, RSA 1.

MARSHALL, Charles H. Exh. 1889-91
Figure, portrait and historical painter. N.S.A. 1890-91. Add: Retford, Notts. † N 5.

MARSHALL, Dorothy Exh. 1890-95
Figure painter. † RID 7.

MARSHALL, Mrs. Emily K. Exh. 1921-30
Landscape painter. London. † ALP 1, M 2, NEA 1, RA 1, RI 1, SWA 4.

MARSHALL, E. Newell Exh. 1907-21
Landscape and figure painter. Add: Lowell, Mass., U.S.A. † BG 39, FIN 42, G 1, GOU 103.

MARSHALL, Ernest W. Exh. 1903-17
Architect. 139 Oxford Street, London. † RA 3.

MARSHALL, Frank Exh. 1889-1910
Landscape painter. Nottingham. † N 4.

MARSHALL, Miss F. Exh. 1885
12 Gorsey Road, Nottingham. † N 2.

MARSHALL, George Exh. 1904
23 Stanley Street, Brighouse, Yorks. † RCA 1.

MARSHALL, Gertrude Exh. 1893
Eastbourn, Prospect Road, Moseley, Birmingham. † B 1.

MARSHALL, G.D. Exh. 1887
73 Elderslee Street, Glasgow. † GI 1.

MARSHALL, George Fred Exh. 1899
Kenmare, Victoria Road, Headingley, Leeds. † RBA 3.

MARSHALL, Henry J. Exh. 1880
Figure painter. 5 Acacia Road, St. Johns Wood, London. † RBA 1.

MARSHALL, Herbert Menzies* 1841-1913
Landscape painter, watercolourist and architect. b. Leeds. Studied under the French architect Questel. Professor of landscape painting at Queens College, London. R.E. 1881-99, R.O.I. 1901, A.R.W.S. 1879, R.W.S. 1883. Add: London. † AG 2, B 1, D 15, FIN 386, L 21, LEI 190, M 13, NEA 1, NG 10, RA 10, RE 37, ROI 14, RWS 235.

MARSHALL, Helen Ray Exh. 1929-36
Landscape painter. London. † COO 4, NEA 1, WG 4.

MARSHALL, John d. 1896
Genre, still-life and animal painter. Father of John Fitz M. q.v. Add: The Hollies, Broad Green Avenue, Croydon. † B 13, NG 2, RA 22, RHA 2, ROI 7.

MARSHALL, John Exh. 1935-40
123 Kingsheath Avenue, Rutherglen. † GI 7, RSA 3.

MARSHALL, John Exh. 1905-40
Edinburgh 1905 and 1929; St. Quinox by Ayr 1919; Glasgow 1929. † GI 4, RSA 13, RSW 3.

MARSHALL, John B. Exh. 1898-1932
Edinburgh 1898; Colington, Midlothian 1919. † GI 3, RSA 35, RSW 6.

MARSHALL, J.C. Exh. 1883-99
Liverpool 1883; Bowgreave, Nr. Garstang 1888; Bolton-le-Sands, Nr. Carnforth 1891. † L 8.

MARSHALL, J.D. Exh. 1880-89
Edinburgh 1880; Glasgow 1889. † GI 2, RSA 4.

MARSHALL, John Eric Exh. 1932-38
2 The Green, Bromborough Pool, Cheshire. † L 2, RCA 4.

MARSHALL, J.F. Exh. 1884-1920
A.N.S.A. 1908. Add: Nottingham. † N 9.

MARSHALL, J. Fitz 1859-1932
Landscape, animal and flower painter. Son of John M. q.v. R.B.A. 1896. Add: Croydon, Surrey 1880 and 1904; Epsom, Surrey 1894; Shipton-under-Wychwood, Oxon. 1920. † B 47, D 4, GI 13, M 3, NG 44, RA 11, RBA 186, RHA 12, ROI 13.

MARSHALL, John Miller Exh. 1881-1927
Landscape painter. Liverpool 1881; Norwich 1884; Teignmouth, Devon 1894; Clifton, Bristol 1901; London 1927. † GI 6, L 11, M 2, RA 4, RBA 1, RI 5.

MARSHALL, Miss L.E. Exh. 1912-14
The Beaches, Long Eaton, Notts. † N 5.

MARSHALL, Mrs. Lenore Fairfax Exh. 1903-32
Flower painter. Patterdale Hall, Penrith. † B 8, RA 1, RCA 8, RI 1.

MARSHALL, L.H. Exh. 1937
Landscape painter. 11 Woodstock Avenue, Radford, Notts. † N 1.

MARSHALL, Mervyn Exh. 1903
11 Alhambra Road, Southsea, Hants. † RCA 2.

MARSHALL, Miss M.C. Exh. 1904
29 Colville Terrace, Bayswater, London. † SWA 1.

MARSHALL, Margaret E. Exh. 1928-39
Landscape, portrait and flower painter. Feldafing, Rickmansworth, Herts. † AR 2, L 1, NEA 2, RA 4.

MARSHALL, Mary E. Exh. 1899-1900
56 New Street, Huddersfield. † L 2.

MARSHALL, Mrs. Maude G. Exh. 1926-40
Mrs. R.J. Wilson M. Add: Little Turnberry, by Givan, Ayrshire. † GI 10, RSA 2.

MARSHALL, Mrs. Philippa Exh. 1880
Watercolour flower painter. c/o W.A. Ingram, 65 Warwick Road, Maida Vale, London. † RBA 1.

MARSHALL, Mrs. Rose Exh. 1880-1910
Flower, fruit, figure and landscape painter. Leeds 1880; Edinburgh 1883. † G 2, GI 2, RA 10, RBA 14, ROI 6, RSA 19.

MARSHALL, Roberto Angelo Kittermaster b. 1849
Landscape painter. Studied under his father Charles M. q.v. Exh. 1880-1912. Add: London 1880; Herstmonceux, Sussex 1902 † AG 6, D 70, DOW 3, L 3, M 10, RA 7, RI 10.

MARSHALL, Rosamund C. Exh. 1907
Priorsgate, St. Andrews, N.B. † RSA 1.

MARSHALL, T.E. Exh. 1905
City Bank Chambers, James St. Harrogate, Yorks. † RA 1.

MARSHALL, T. William Exh. 1908-13
Paris. † LS 20.

MARSHALL, Violet Exh. 1925-29
Watercolour landscape painter. 34 Peak Hill, Sydenham, Kent. † AB 2, SWA 2.

MARSHALL Vera E. Exh. 1925-27
36 Leyland Road, Southport, Lancs. † L 3.

MARSHALL, W. Exh. 1880-83
Sculptor. London. † RA 4.

MARSHALL, Walter Exh. 1903-8
Leeds. † RA 1, RCA 2.

MARSHALL, Wilhelmina Exh. 1890-91
Figure painter. 10 Orme Square, Bayswater, London. † RA 2, ROI 1.

MARSHALL, William b. 1885
Stained glass artist. Head artist at Pearce and Cutler Ltd., Birmingham. Headmaster Birchfields School of Art and visiting art master Birmingham. Exh. 1929-30. Add: 94 Holly Lane, West Smethwick. † RA 4.

MARSHALL, Winifred Exh. 1898-1919
Miniature portrait painter. London. † RA 15

MARSHALL, William Calder 1813-1894
Sculptor. b. Edinburgh. Studied Trustees Academy, Edinburgh, under Francis Chantrey, Edward Baily, R.A. Schools (silver medal) and Rome 1836-39. A.R.A. 1844, R.A. 1852, A.R.S.A. 1840, H.R.S.A. 1861. "The Prodigal Son" purchased by Chantrey Bequest 1881. Add: London. † B 1, GI 3, M 1, RA 19, RSA 13.

MARSHALL, William Elstob Exh. 1800-84
Figure, landscape and animal painter. London. † B 1, L 1, RA 1, RBA 1.

MARSON, Guy Exh. 1937
Landscape painter. † LEF 20.

MARSON, Thomas Exh. 1890-1927
Landscape painter. Crick, Rugby. † B 7, M 3, RA 6, ROI 1.

MARSON, W., junr. Exh. 1886
189 Gt. Alfred Street Central, Nottingham. † N 1.

MARSTON, E.C. Exh. 1929
Old Castle Buildings, Preeson's Row, Liverpool. † L 1.

MARSTON, Miss E.M. Exh. 1923
9 Wrottesley Road, Harlesden, London. † L 2.

MARSTON Freda 1895-1949
nee Clulow. Figure and landscape painter and etcher. Studied Regent St. Polytechnic 1916-20. Married Reginald St. Clair M. q.v. A.R.B.A. 1924, R.B.A. 1926, R.O.I. 1931. Add: London 1919 and 1929; Houghton, nr. Arundel, Sussex 1923; Amberley, Sussex 1927; Dedham, Essex 1937. † B 4, BK 2, CON 5, FIN 41, GI 9, M 1, RA 27, RBA 52, RI 4, ROI 52, SWA 2.

MARSTON, George E. Exh. 1919-23
A.R.B.A. 1919. Add: Oakshott Hanger, Hawkley, Hants. † G 2, RBA 7.

MARSTON, Mabel Exh. 1885-1931
Flower and portrait painter. London. † B 4, G 1, M 2, RA 9, RBA 8, RID 15, ROI 7, SWA 1.

MARSTON, Reginald St. Clair 1886-1943
Landscape painter. b. Wittenhall, Staffs. Married Freda M. q.v. A.R.B.A. 1923, R.B.A. 1924, R.O.I. 1924. Add: Wolverhampton 1921, Houghton, nr. Arundel, Sussex 1923; Dedham, Essex 1931. † B 6, CON 5, FIN 40, G 2, GI 5, M 1, RA 20, RBA 92, RI 1, ROI 35.

MART, Frank Griffiths Exh. 1894-1922
Landscape painter. London. † B 1, D 2, L 1, NEA 1, RA 20, RBA 1, RI 4.

MARTELLI, U. Exh. 1916
c/o A. Stiles and Sons, 617 Fulham Road, London. † GI 1.

MARTELLO, Joseph Exh. 1884-86
2 Upper Wilmot Street, Manchester. † RHA 3.

MARTEN, Elliot H. Exh. 1886-1901
Landscape painter. Hawick, Scotland. † D 5, RA 1.

MARTEN, Jessie Exh. 1904
29 Greenway, Uxbridge, Middlesex. † L 1.

MARTEN, William J. Exh. 1882-1903
Still life painter. London 1882; 34 Grosvenor Street, West Hartlepool 1903. † M 1, RA 1.

MARTENS, Willie b. 1856
Dutch artist. Exh. 1894-1908. Add: 2 Statenlaan, The Hague, Holland. † GI 2.

MARTHY, David Exh. 1916
25 Frederick Street, Edinburgh. † RSA 2.

MARTIN, A. Exh. 1933
49A Boulevard Britannique A Gand, Belgium. † L 3.

MARTIN, Ada Exh. 1881
Watercolour flower painter. † SWA 1.

MARTIN, Adele Exh. 1922-40
Flower and figure painter. London. † GOU 4, L 1, P 2, RA 8, ROI 1.

MARTIN, Alex Exh. 1893-1917
Glasgow. † GI 14, RSW 1.

MARTIN, Gen. Sir Alfred, K.G.B. Exh. 1921
Watercolour painter. † WG 28.

MARTIN, Mrs. Annie Exh. 1893-1906
Swaylands, Crowborough, Sussex. † I 1, L 2, M 1, RI 1, SWA 6.

MARTIN, Arthur C. Exh. 1899-1921
Architect. London. † RA 9.

MARTIN, Arthur Edmund d. 1932
Painter and mural decorator. Examiner in drawing. University of London. Exh. 1905-26. Add: London 1905; Rickmansworth, Herts. 1926. † RA 4.

MARTIN, Agnes Fulton b. 1904
Urban landscape and figure painter. Studied Glasgow School of Art. Exh. 1931-39. Add: Glasgow 1931; Cove, Dumbartonshire 1937; Epsom, Surrey 1938. † GI 4, GOU 2, NEA 5, RBA 2, RCA 1, ROI 2, RSA 4, SWA 3.

MARTIN, Alf L. Exh. 1883
39 Raymourd, Paris. † GI 1.

MARTIN, Anmora M. Exh. 1894-1900
London and Upton on Severn. † L 4, NG 6, SWA 1.

MARTIN, Alfred R. Exh. 1901-28
Liverpool 1901; London 1907; Natal, S. Africa 1928. † L 15, RA 3.

MARTIN, Beatrice Exh. 1900-6
Sculptor. 11 Rathbone Place, London. † L 5, NG 1, RA 1.

MARTIN, Beatrix b. 1876
Watercolour painter. b. Sevenoaks. Studied Sevenoaks and South Kensington. Sister of Ethel M. q.v. Exh. 1901-38. Add: Sevenoaks, Kent 1901 and 1906; London 1904 and 1915; Dormans Land, Surrey 1907. † BG 20, L 1, RA 3, RI 3, RSW 2, SWA 4.

MARTIN, Charles 1820-1906
Portrait painter. Son of John Martin (1789-1854). Add: London 1883; Liverpool 1903. † L 6, RA 7, RBA 1, RI 2, ROI 1.

MARTIN, Cicely Bridget Exh. 1899-1914
A.S.W.A. 1904. Add: Bromley, Kent 1899; Purley Surrey 1900; Wallington, Surrey 1902; London 1910. † B 8, L 2, LS 19, RBA 3, SWA 35.

MARTIN, Miss C.E. Exh. 1901
27 Brompton Avenue, Liverpool. † L 2.

MARTIN, C.F. Exh. 1911
5 Newcastle Road, Wavertree, Liverpool. † L 1.

MARTIN, Miss C. Hargrave Exh. 1912-19
London. † SWA 26.

MARTIN, Miss D. Exh. 1917-18
Burgh Heath, Surrey. † RA 1, RI 1, SWA 1.

MARTIN, David Exh. 1887-1935
Landscape painter. Glasgow. † GI 33, RI 1, RSA 6, RSW 4.

MARTIN, Dorothy Burt b. 1882
Watercolour painter, etcher, pottery worker, embroiderer and illuminator. Studied Wolverhampton Municipal School of Art and Royal College of Art. Assistant teacher at Wolverhampton School of Art, art teacher Leeds and Wood Green Training Colleges, Head of Art Dept. Rodean School, Brighton, teacher of etching at Brighton Municipal School of art, painter to the Royal Horticultural Society. Exh. 1902-32. Add: Wolverhampton 1902; Stafford 1908; London 1914; Brighton 1917. † B 2, RA 9, RI 1.

MARTIN, D.D. Exh. 1883
26 Carrington Street, Glasgow. † GI 1.

MARTIN, Mrs. Dorothy Freeborn b. 1886
nee Roberts. Watercolour landscape, portrait and miniature painter. Studied Slade School. R.B.A. 1912, A.R.M.S. 1911. Exh. 1909-38. Add: London 1909, 1914; Aston on Clun, Salop. 1913; Weybridge, Surrey 1933. † L 5, NEA 6, P 3, RA 24, RBA 17, RMS 8.

MARTIN, D. Kay Exh. 1907-8
Crieff, N.B. 1907; Cardwell Bay, Gourock 1908. † GI 2.

MARTIN, D.O. Exh. 1884-86
Glasgow. † GI 3.

MARTIN, Edwin Exh. 1913-38
Portrait and landscape painter. b. Forfar, Angus. Studied Glasgow School of Art. Add: London. † COO 4, GI 6, L 5, M 1, NEA 1, P 3, RA 10, RI 1, RSA 7, WG 4.

MARTIN, Ellis Exh. 1916
Denshott, Dorking, Surrey. † RA 1.

MARTIN, Enid Exh. 1928-32
Linocut artist. † BA 1, NEA 1.

MARTIN, Ethel Exh. 1894-1938
Mrs. Fridlander. Landscape and figure painter. Sister of Beatrix M. q.v. Add: Sevenoaks, Kent 1894 and 1899; Coventry 1895; Liverpool 1902; London 1911. † B 13, BG 17, GI 8, L 13, M 1, NG 1, P 4, RA 8, RBA 3, RI 1, SWA 4.

MARTIN, Eugenie Exh. 1908-31
Mrs. A. Anderson. Portrait painter. b. St. Petersburg. Studied St. Petersburg, Dresden and Paris. Add: London. † RA 4, SWA 4.

MARTIN, Mrs. Edith E. b. 1875
nee Dunkley. Painter. Studied Croydon School of Art, Spenlove School of Painting and Germany. Exh. 1921-28. Add: Croydon, Surrey 1921; London 1928. † RA 1, SWA 3.

MARTIN, Elizabeth H. Exh. 1940
Etcher. 1 Huyton Lane, Prescot, Lancs. † RA 1.

MARTIN, Ethel R. Exh. 1919-39
4 Sussex Square, Brighton. † L 4, RBA 1, RI 3.

MARTIN, Ethel S. Exh. 1920-35
Watercolour painter. b. London. Art mistress Liverpool City School of Art. Add: Liverpool 1920; Hoylake, Cheshire 1923. † L 15, RA 7.

MARTIN, Ernest W. Exh. 1903
Station House, Mitcham, Surrey. † ROI 1.

MARTIN, Mrs. Florence Exh. 1880-93
Figure and domestic painter. 66 St. George's Square, London. † B 1, GI 1, L 5, M 1, NG 1, RA 3, RBA 7.

MARTIN, F.H. Exh. 1898-1900
6 Balmoral Grove, Colwick Vale, nr. Nottingham. † N 3.

MARTIN, Franc P. b. 1883
Genre painter. b. Austruther. Studied Glasgow School of Art. Exh. 1912-40. Add: Glasgow. † GI 35, L 3, RSA 26.

MARTIN, George D. Exh. 1899-1900
Architect. 3 Pall Mall, London. † RA 2.

MARTIN, George H. Exh. 1905
8 Selborne Terrace, Bradford, Yorks. † L 1.

MARTIN, Gerald Trice 1893-1961
Portrait and still life painter. b. Clifton. Studied R.A. Schools. Exh. 1933-35. Add: London. † RA 2.

MARTIN, Hannah Exh. 1925-35
Liverpool 1925; Darwen, Lancs. 1926; Manchester 1935. † I 4, L 6.

MARTIN, Henri* 1860-1943
French painter. Exh. 1907-30. Add: Paris. † GI 1, GOU 10, L 3, RSA 2.

MARTIN, Henry* Exh. 1880-94
Landscape and coastal painter. St. Paul's Penzance, Cornwall 1880 and 1883; Sidcup, Kent 1882; Plymouth 1884 and 1886; London 1885; Saltash, Cornwall 1894. † G 1, L 6, M 2, RA 10, RBA 8, RI 2.

MARTIN, Helen Alice b. 1889
Landscape and portrait painter, etcher and poster designer. Studied Sheffield, Eastbourne and Cheltenham Schools of Art. Exh. 1923-29. Add: Cheltenham. † AB 2, B 5, L 4.

MARTIN, H.D. Exh. 1885
Landscape painter. 42 Rue Gambette, Honfleur, Calvados, France. † RBA 1.

MARTIN, H.F. Exh. 1884-89
19 Broompark Drive, Dennistoun, Glasgow. † GI 7.

MARTIN, Miss I.V. Exh. 1917
40 Elibank Road, Well Hall, Eltham, Kent. † RA 1.

MARTIN, J. Exh. 1912-14
13 Clareville Road, Rathgar, Ireland. † RHA 4.

MARTIN, J. Bruce Exh. 1880-1905
Edinburgh 1880 and 1903; Glasgow 1882. † GI 6, RSA 4.

MARTIN, J.G. Exh. 1910-14
55 Cathles Road, Balham Hill, London. † RA 2, RI 2, ROI 1.

MARTIN, Miss J.H. Exh. 1912-15
Paris 1912; Carrigtwohill, Co. Cork 1915. † RA 2.

MARTIN, J.L. Exh. 1892-99
Dublin. † RHA 6.

MARTIN, J. Shower Exh. 1905
54 St. George's Road, Leyton, Essex. † D 2.

MARTIN, Kenneth b. 1905
Painter and sculptor. Studied Sheffield School of Art and Royal College of Art. Exh. 1936-40. † COO 2, LEI 1, NEA 3.

MARTIN, Mrs. K.M. Exh. 1927
† D 1.

MARTIN, Leonard Exh. 1912-29
Architect. Waterloo Place, London. † RA 4.

MARTIN, Leslie Exh. 1925-27
Urban landscape painter. 8 Collington Street, Beeston, Notts. † N 5.

MARTIN, Louise Exh. 1901
† RMS 1.

MARTIN, Leon F. Exh. 1882
37 Rue Berchmans, St. Giles, Brussels. † GI 1.

MARTIN, Maude Exh. 1896
Flower painter. Clevelands, London Road, Croydon, Surrey. † RA 1.

MARTIN, Max Exh. 1916-27
Portrait and figure painter. London 1916; Kinsale 1927. † L 1, NEA 1, RA 2, RBA 1, RHA 1.

MARTIN, Merian Exh. 1899-1909
Miniature painter. West Kensington, London. † L 4, RA 4, RBA 1, RMS 1, SWA 3.

MARTIN, Mary D. Exh. 1880-82
Landscape and coastal painter. London. † D 4, RA 1, RBA 1.

MARTIN, Miss M.E. Exh. 1883-86
Rectory House, Killeshander, Co. Cavan. † D 1, RHA 5.

MARTIN, Mabel, I.L. b. 1887
Portrait and miniature painter, lithographer and teacher. b. Dover. Studied Westminster School of Art, Regent Street Polytechnic and Paris. Exh. 1920-37. Add: London. † L 1, RA 5.

MARTIN, Robert c. 1843-1923
Potter and modeller. Studied Lambeth School of Art. Exh. 1888. Add: Southall, Middlesex. † RA 2.

MARTIN, Miss R.M.L. Exh. 1937
Glenmore, 54 Valley Road, Sheldon, Birmingham. † B 1.

MARTIN, Rosa Plant Exh. 1899-1913
Miniature painter. R.M.S. 1902. Add: London 1899; Shiplake on Thames 1904. † L 1, NG 3, RA 1, RMS 37.

MARTIN, Mrs. Sam Exh. 1923-34
Watercolour portrait painter. 4 Bedford Park, Croydon, Surrey. † COO 2, RI 2.

MARTIN, Sylvester Exh. 1886
Brook Cottage, Hall Green, Birmingham. † B 1.

MARTIN, Thomas Mower* 1839-1934
b. London. Exh. 1906-7. Add: Kew Gardens, London. Died in Canada. † D 1, L 1.

MARTIN, Violet Freda Exh. 1934-38
Landscape painter. Add: Fidelis, Strathcona Avenue, Little Bookham, Surrey. † NEA 2, RA 6.

MARTIN, W Exh. 1882
14 Anfield Road, Woolton, Liverpool. † L 1.

MARTIN, W. Exh. 1909-16
Teversal Avenue, Lenton Sands, Nottingham. † N 13.

MARTIN, William Exh. 1888-89
Edinburgh 1888; Walton 1889. † L 1, RSA 1.

MARTIN, William Exh. 1927
† M 1.

MARTIN, William Alison Exh. 1901-33
Painter, etcher and lithographer. Studied Liverpool School of Art (gold medal for drawing and travelling studentship to Paris). Add: Liverpool. † BG 36, GI 10, L 103, LS 23, M 1, RA 5, RCA 1, RSA 4.

MARTIN, Mrs. W.F. Exh. 1909
Redcourt, Champion Hill, London. † RI 1, SWA 1.

MARTINDALE, Blanche Exh. 1882-1909
Miniature painter. Paris 1882; Dresden 1884; London 1904. † B 3, L 2, M 2, RA 1.

MARTINDALE, Percy Henry 1869-1943
Mezzotint engraver and lecturer on engraving. Studied under J.B. Pratt. Add: London 1892; Harpenden Herts. 1900 and 1918; Marple, Cheshire 1908. † L 9, RA 2.

MARTINEAU, Mrs. Basil (Clara) Exh. 1881-1906
Portrait, figure and flower painter. 3 Eldon Road, Hampstead, London. † L 2, M 1, RA 6, RBA 1.

MARTINEAU, Edith 1842-1909
Landscape, genre and portrait painter and watercolourist. A.R.W.S. 1888. Sister of Gertrude M. q.v. Add: London. † AG 19, B 56, BG 2, D 28, FIN 1, G 1, GI 2, L 63, M 36, RA 9, RBA 1, RHA 8, RI 14, RSA 4, RSW 1, RWS 101, SWA 15.

MARTINEAU, Edward Henry Exh. 1891
Architect. 30 Weymouth Street, Portland Place, London. † RA 1.

MARTINEAU, Gertrude Exh. 1880-1911
Genre and animal painter. Sister of Edith M. q.v. Add: London. † AG 5, B 45, D 77, GI 2, L 22, M 21, RA 4, RBA 3, RHA 19, RI 5, ROI 1, RSA 2.

MARTINEAU, Lucy Exh. 1898-1900
Painter. 4 South Road, Clapham Park, London. † RA 2.

MARTINET, Marguerite Exh. 1904-9
Paris. † L 2.

MARTINETTI, A. Exh. 1880
Figure painter. 1 Fitzroy Square, London. † RBA 1.

MARTIN-HARVEY, M. Exh. 1940
Rowstock Cottage, Didcot, Berks. † RI 1.

MARTINO, Anna Blunden b. 1829
nee Blunden. Figure and landscape painter. Exh. 1882-1911. Add: Edgbaston, Birmingham. † B 30, LS 3, M 4, NG 1.

MARTINO, de see D

MARTINS, W.S. Exh. 1887
c/o L. Alma Tadema, R.A., 17 Grove End Road, London. † G 1.

MARTIN-SMITH, Donald F. Exh. 1925-36
Architect. London. † RA 4.

MARTLEW, T. Edward Exh. 1926
86 North Road, Bloomfield, Belfast. † RHA 2.

MARTLEW, W. Exh. 1929
85A Berkley Street, Liverpool. † L 1.

MARTYN, Anne S. Exh. 1914-24
24 Killisea Avenue, Streatham Hill, London. † GI 1, RI 3, SWA 4.

MARTYN, Dora Exh. 1883-1914
Landscape and figure painter. Kimbolton, Manchester 1883; London 1893; Uckfield, Sussex 1907. † B 3, GI 5, L 4, LS 12, M 5, RA 1, RBA 2, SWA 4.

MARTYN, Emily C. Exh. 1889-94
Landscape and figure painter. Add: 9 Kensington Gate, London. † RID 22.

MARTYN, Ethel King Exh. 1886-1923
Painter and etcher. A.R.E. 1898, R.E. 1902-23. Add: London 1886 and 1906; Penn, Amersham, Bucks. 1894; Chiselhurst, Kent. 1895. † B 1, L 1, NG 1, RA 12, RBA 2, RE 75, ROI 1.

MARTYN, Hazel See LAVERY

MARTYN, Sir Henry Linnington b. 1888
Watercolour painter and etcher. Exh. 1927. Add: Windsor, Berks. † D 2.

MARTYN, Mary P.K. Exh. 1938-40
Sculptor. Add: London. † RA 2.

MARTYR, J. Greville Exh. 1886-87
Figure painter. Add: Rhine Villa, Upper Norwood, London. † RA 1, RBA 1.

MARVAL, Exh. 1912-23
Painter. † GOU 3.

MARVIN, Phillip J. Exh. 1880-1924
Architect. London. † RA 12.

MARWICK, Thomas R. Exh. 1901-2
43 York Place, Edinburgh. † RSA 3.

MARWICK, Thomas W. Exh. 1938
† RSA 1.

MARWOOD, D. Exh. 1888-91
Landscape painter. Add: Halford House, Richmond, Surrey. † RI 2, ROI 4.

MARY, Jules Fernand Exh. 1903
Chandebee en Caux, Seine Inferieure, France. † L 1.

MARYON, Herbert J. Exh. 1904-27
A.R.B.A. 1926. Add: School of Industrial Arts, Keswick 1904; Grange over Sands 1906; University College, Reading, 1910. † L 11, RA 1, RBA 4.

MARYON, L. Edith C. Exh. 1900-12
Sculptor. Add: South Hanningfield, Essex 1900; London 1901. † GI 3, L 16, NG 1, RA 21, RE 2.

MASEY, Francis Exh. 1887-89
Architect. Add: 18 Gordon Street, Gordon Square, London. † RA 3.

MASEY, Philip E. Exh. 1889
Architect. Add: Hope Villa, Harold Street, London. † RA 1.

MASHEDER, Mrs. Exh. 1907
All Saints Rectory, Heaton Norris, Stockport, Lancs. † NG 1.

MASON, Miss A. Exh. 1921
37 Oakley Crescent, Chelsea, London. † RA 1.

MASON, Albert E. Exh. 1936-39
Landscape painter. Add: c/o Bourlet and Sons, Nassau Street, London. † RA 1, ROI 4.

MASON, Arnold H. 1885-1963
Portrait and landscape painter. Studied Royal College of Art and Slade School. A.R.A. 1940, R.P. 1935. Add: Oswestry 1905; London 1908 and 1918; Ludlow 1913. † CHE 6, GI 1, GOU 7, I 1, L 5, LEI 11, LS 6, M 2, NEA 16, P 35, RA 38, ROI 3.

MASON, Agnes M.M. Exh. 1899-1903
Fern Tower, Kelvinside, Glasgow. † GI 2, RSA 3.

MASON, Adrienne V. Exh. 1927-40
Portrait and landscape painter and wood engraver. Add: London 1927; Oxleys, Dean's Hill, Stafford 1935. † AB 8, NEA 2, P 2, RA 1, SWA 3.

MASON, Alfred William 1848-1933
Figure and landscape painter. Studied St. Martins School of Art and Royal College of Art. Headmaster Birkbeck College School of Art and Headmaster St. Martins School of Art. Exh. 1881-82. Add: London. † D 1, RBA 1.

MASON, Blossom Exh. 1881-85
Flower painter. Add: London 1881; Uxbridge, Middlesex 1885. † RBA 2.

MASON, Charles Exh. 1880
Landscape painter. Add: 3½ Weekday Cross, Nottingham. † N 2.

MASON, Charles Exh. 1884
Sculptor. Add: 26 Tedworth Square, Chelsea, London. † RA 1.

MASON, Clement S. Exh. 1933-38
89 Loughborough Road, Belgrave, Leicester. † B 7, N 3.

MASON, Miss D. Exh. 1910-12
Manor House, Sproughton, Ipswich, Suffolk. † L 4, RA 1.

MASON, Miss E. Exh. 1900
Whissendire, Cumberland Road, Kew. † B 1, GI 1, L 1.

MASON, Miss E. Exh. 1891-1907
Add: Leamington, Warwicks. 1891; Taunton, Somerset 1900; Liscard, Cheshire 1905. † B 5, L 2.

MASON, Edgar Exh. 1883
86 New Street, Birmingham. † B 1.

MASON, Mrs. Evelyn Exh. 1884-1909
Miniature and flower painter. Add: London 1884; Farnham, Surrey 1898. † L 4, NG 11, RA 8, RBA 2, RMS 5.

MASON, Ernold A. Exh. 1883
Figure painter. Add: 38 Beamont Street, Portland Place, London. † RA 1.

MASON, Emily Florence b. 1870
Portrait painter and teacher. b. Birmingham. Studied Royal College of Art. Exh. 1920. Add: 21 Cambridge Gardens, Notting Hill, London. † L 1.

MASON, Edith Mary See HINCHLEY

MASON, Ethel M. Exh. 1905-6
Cranbrook, Buxton, Derbyshire. † L 2, M 2.

MASON, Ethel M. Exh. 1923
† RMS 1

MASON, Ernest R. Exh. 1917-33
Watercolour landscape and figure painter. Add: 1 Cranleigh Villas, Annett Road, Walton on Thames. † L 5, RA 4.

MASON, Miss F. Exh. 1892-95
Leamington, Warwicks. † B 3.

MASON, F. Bateson b. 1910
Painter. b. Bradford. Studied Bradford College of Art 1927-32, under H. Butler 1932-35 and under Sir W. Rothenstein. Exh. 1936-37. † NEA 2.

MASON, Frank Henry* 1876-1965
Painter, etcher, illustrator and poster designer. R.B.A. 1904, R.I. 1929. Add: Birmingham 1893; Taunton, Somerset 1897; Scarborough, Yorks. 1900; London 1930. † B 3, GI 1, L 4, M 1, RA 8, RBA 29, RHA 1, RI 40.

MASON, Gilbert Exh. 1935
Etcher. Add: 5 Caerau Road, Newport, Mon. † RA 1.

MASON, Miss G.F. Exh. 1913-18
Nottingham. † N 4.

MASON, G. Heather Exh. 1907-11
Add: London 1907; Reading, Berks. 1908. † L 1, LS 2, RA 3.

MASON, G.W. Exh. 1926
2 Gayton Avenue, New Brighton, Cheshire. † L 1.

MASON, Josephine Exh. 1902-40
Painter, miniaturist and etcher. Add: London. † CHE 2, G 2, GOU 4, LS 3, NEA 21, RA 6, RED 4.

MASON, Jessie M. Exh. 1908
Cranbrook, St. John's Road, Buxton, Derbys. † L 1.

MASON, Mabel Exh. 1904
Sculptor. Add: 20th Century Club, Stanley Gardens, London. † RA 1.

MASON, Mary Exh. 1881-1908
Landscape, figure and interior painter. Add: Clarendon House, Putney, London. † D 12, LS 5, M 1, RI 4, SWA 9.

MASON, Miles B. Exh. 1880-86
Landscape and figure painter. Add: London. † B 1, L 1, RA 1, RBA 7.

MASON, Mary May Exh. 1904-17
Miniature portrait painter. Add: London. † RA 3.

MASON, Miss M. Watts Exh. 1893-94
Figure painter. Add: 12 Bolton Studios, Redcliffe Road, London. † ROI 2.

MASON, O. Exh. 1916
Gainsborough Cottage, Garrison Lane, Felixstowe, Suffolk. † RA 1.

MASON, Olga E. Exh. 1932
4 Sherbourne Road, Acocks Green, Birmingham. † B 1.

MASON, Oscar W. Exh. 1933-34
10 Cedar Grove, Fallowfield, Manchester. † L 1, RCA 1.

MASON, W.H. Exh. 1899
Dalhousie Road, Esbank, N.B. † RSA 1.

MASON, W.H. Exh. 1880-1911
Morton Hall, East Retford, Notts. † D 7, L 3, N 9, RI 1.

MASON, W.H. Exh. 1880-88
Marine painter. Add: Malvern Lodge, Worthing, Sussex. † D 10, L 2, RA 1.

MASSA, Nina Exh. 1884
499 Via del Corso, Rome. † RHA 2.

MASSANI, Pompeo* 1850-1920
Italian figure painter. Exh. 1884-86. Add: 133 New Bond Street, London. † M 3.

MASSARD, F. Victor Exh. 1912-23
Studio, Quarry Hall Terrace, Hamilton, N.B. † GI 1, RI 1, RSW 1.

MASSE, Pierre Augustin Exh. 1888-92
Etcher. London. † RA 2.

MASSEY, Delia V. Exh. 1940
Landscape painter. † COO 1.

MASSEY, Mrs. Eleanor E. Exh. 1908-14
Bamford Hall, nr. Rochdale, Lancs. † L 2, LS 4, SWA 1.

MASSEY, E. Martin Exh. 1885-1921
Landscape painter. Add: Hilton House, Hilton, nr. Derby. † N 13, RA 1, RBA 4.

MASSEY, Frederick Exh. 1892-93
Marine painter. Add: Penryn, Cornwall. † L 1, RBA 1, RI 1.

MASSEY, Mrs. Gertrude b. 1868
nee Seth. Portrait, decorative, landscape and miniature painter. Married Henry Gibbs M. q.v. R.M.S. 1904. Exh. 1898-1918. Add: London. † FIN 22, L 2, NG 8, P 2, RA 23, RMS 29.

MASSEY, Henry Gibbs 1860-1934
Painter and etcher. Studied London, Bushey, Herts and Paris. Principal of Heatherleys School of Fine Art. A.R.E. 1894-1900. Married Gertrude M. q.v. Add: London 1884 and 1906; Bushey, Herts. 1894. † B 9, CHE 1, FIN 2, GOU 4, L 11, M 6, RA 8, RBA 1, RE 12, RI 9.

MASSEY, Kenneth W. Exh. 1928
Students School of Dental Surgery, Liverpool. † L 2.

MASSEY, Miss S. Exh. 1882-84
Fairlawn, Sale, Manchester. † M 4.

MASSIE, Mary Exh. 1920-21
615 Stratford Road, Birmingham. † B 3, RMS 1.

MASSON, Alexander Exh. 1911
Painter. † BRU 1.

MASSON, Cecilia Exh. 1888-96
Oakshaw Side, Paisley. † GI 4.

MASSY, Lord Exh. 1893
Rathfarnham, Co. Dublin. † D 1.

MASSY-BAKER, G.H. Exh. 1888-91
Portrait painter. London. † D 1, ROI 1.

MAST, Edith M. Exh. 1900
89 Hills Road, Cambridge. † B 1.

MASTENBROCK, van See V

MASTERS, Edwin Exh. 1916-35
Miniature painter. Add: Tooting Bec Common, London 1916; Crowthorne, Berks. 1935. † RA 5, RI 20.

MASTERS, Mrs. George E.F. Exh. 1884
Landscape painter. Add: Sylvabelle, Lansdown Road, Bournemouth. † SWA 1.

MASTERS, William E. Exh. 1930-38
Architect. London. † GI 1, RA 5.

MASTIN, John Exh. 1898-1903
Portrait, figure and landscape painter and illustrator. R.B.A. 1899. Add: Sheffield. † B 5, L 3, M 1, RA 1, RBA 14.

MASURE, Jules b. 1819
French artist. Exh. 1884. Add: 34 Bis, Rue de Brancas, Sevres, France. † GI 1.

MATANIA, Fortunio* b. 1881
Painter and illustrator. b. Naples. Joined staff of the "Graphic" at age 19 and the "Sphere" at age 22. Official war artist World War I. R.I. 1917. Exh. 1908-40. Add: London. † L 1, RA 10, RI 27.

MATANIA, Ugo Exh. 1909-18
Figure painter. Add: 47 Sutherland Avenue, London. † L 1, RA 4.

MATCHWICK, Beryl Alice b. 1907
Still life and flower painter. Studied Reigate Art School. Exh. 1931-40. Add: Greencroft, Reigate, Surrey. † RA 2, RI 18, RMS 4, RSA 1.

MATEAR, Huon Arthur Exh. 1883-1920
Architect. Add: Liverpool 1883 and 1920; London 1915. † L 16, RA 8.

MATESDORF, T. Exh. 1886-89
Portrait and figure painter. Add: London. † M 1, RA 2.

MATHER, Elizabeth M. Exh. 1904
Miniature portrait painter. Add: 27 Forest Drive West, Leytonstone, Essex. † RA 2.

MATHER, Harold Exh. 1915
c/o J. Pearce, 1 Cross Hall Street, Liverpool. † L 1.

MATHER, Mary A. Exh. 1882
Tudor Lodge, Radbourne Street, Derby. † N 1.

MATHERS, David S. Exh. 1938-40
19 Buckingham Terrace, Edinburgh 1938; Castle Hill, Cumberland 1940. † RSA 4.

MATHERS, Helen Mann Exh. 1910
31 Snowdown Place, Stirling. † GI 1.

MATHERS, Miss M.A. Exh. 1911-19
Figure and still life painter. Add: London 1911 and 1919; Chichester, Sussex 1916; Southsea, Hants. 1917. † I 2, LS 9, NEA 8, RA 1.

MATHESON, Gertrude A. Exh. 1937-40
Landscape,figure and animal painter. Add: 41 George Square, Edinburgh. † COO 21, RSA 3, RSW 1.

MATHESON, Margaret Exh. 1889-93
Landscape and portrait painter. Add: 46 Clarendon Road, Notting Hill, London. † RID 8.

MATHESON, R.M. Exh. 1885
19 Northumberland Street, Edinburgh. † RSA 1.

MATHET, Louis D. Exh. 1909
24 Rue Edouard Jacques, Paris. † L 1.

MATHEW, Kathleen Exh. 1913-29
Portrait painter. Add: Lee House, Dovercourt, Essex. † RA 2.

MATHEW, J.F. Exh. 1886
c/o R.T. Kelly, Glasnevin, Ball's Road, Claughton. † L 1.

MATHEWES, Blanche Exh. 1888-1906
Portrait and figure painter. Add: Camilla Lodge, Sutton, Surrey 1888; London 1906. † RA 6.

MATHEWS, Miss A.E. Exh. 1914
47 Marlborough Crescent, Bedford Park, London. † RA 1.

MATHEWS, Dorothy Margaret Exh. 1925-38
Mrs. Palmer Allen. Watercolour portrait and miniature painter. b. Belfast. Add: Belfast. † L 1, RA 3, RHA 3.

MATHEWS, Ethel A. Exh. 1926-38
Horsley, Streetly 1926; Birmingham 1930; Walsall 1937. † B 15, RCA 9.

MATHEWS, Mrs. F.C. Exh. 1888-96
Landscape painter. Add: Sevenoaks, Kent 1888; London 1892. † RI 4, ROI 1, SWA 3.

MATHEWS, John Chester Exh. 1884-1900
Painter of horses. Add: London. † G 1, L 4, RBA 2, ROI 1.

MATHEWS, Janet D. Exh. 1907-12
Ethel Hall, Lancaster 1907; Zeals House, Wilts. 1912. † L 11, NG 1, RA 1.

MATHEWS, Minnie Exh. 1886-94
Flower and landscape painter. Add: London. † NG 1, RA 2, SWA 1.

MATHEWS, Morton b. 1866
Etcher, aquatinter and art teacher. Exh. 1907-27. Add: Pickwick House, Halstead, Essex. † FIN 1, GOU 19, L 1, RA 8.

MATHEWS, M.C. Exh. 1926
† M 4.

MATHEWS, Mrs. M.J. Exh. 1935
New Park, Brockenhurst, Hants. † B 2.

MATHEWSON, Davina Exh. 1907-11
London. † D 4.

MATHEY, Armand Exh. 1902
Etcher. Add: c/o Dowdeswells Ltd., 160 New Bond Street, London. † RA 1.

MATHEY, S. Exh. 1904
22 Rue Pinel, St. Denis, Seine, France. † L 1.

MATHIAS, Mrs. Alfred Exh. 1884
Watercolour landscape painter. Add: Lamphey, Bridgnorth, Salop. † SWA 1.

MATHIAS, Betty Exh. 1937-38
† NEA 2.

MATHIAS, Mrs. E. Exh. 1908
15 Montagu Square, London. † RA 1.

MATHIE, Emily Exh. 1890
15 South Park Terrace, Hillhead, Glasgow. † GI 1.

MATHIE, James Exh. 1897-1938
Add: Newmills 1897; Kilmarnock, N.B. 1906. † GI 25, L 1, RSA 3.

MATHIESON, John George Exh. 1918-40
Painter and etcher. Add: Allan Park, Stirling. † GI 18, L 3, RA 1, RSA 21, RSW 1, WG 101.

MATHIESON, James Muir Exh. 1892-1922
Bridge of Allan, N.B. 1892; Glasgow 1905. † GI 10, L 9, M 1, RA 3, RSA 4.

MATHIEU, Pol Exh. 1931
c/o Messrs Aitken, Dott and Son, 26 Castle Street, Edinburgh. † RSA 1.

MATHISON, Miss K. Exh. 1906-38
Edgbaston, Birmingham 1906; Kings Norton, Birmingham 1910; Walsall 1938. † B 5.

MATHON, E. Exh. 1885
1A Old Bond Street, London. † GI 2.

MATIGNON, Albert b. 1869
French painter. Exh. 1902. Add: 17 Rue de Tournon, Paris. † L 1.

MATISSE, Auguste Exh. 1923-29
Rue Cassini, Paris. † L 2, RSA 1

MATISSE, Henri* 1869-1954
French painter. Exh. 1921-38. † CHE 1, GOU 4, RED 1.

MATKIN, Susanna Exh. 1884
Landscape painter. Add: Stamford, Lincs. † RI 1.

MATROD-DESMURS, Mme. B. Exh. 1903-7
46 Rue Lafitte, Paris. † L 2.

MATSON, Mrs. William Exh. 1908-9
19 Alverstone Road, Sefton Park, Liverpool. † L 2.

MATSUYAMA, R. Chuzo Exh. 1916-39
Watercolour painter. London. † I 4, L 6, RA 6, RI 1, RSA 1.

MATTE, Mrs. R. Exh. 1921
Villa Torrossa, Fiesole, Florence. † RA 1.

MATTEY, Sidney B. Exh. 1937-40
Watercolour landscape painter. Add: London 1937; Sevenoaks, Kent 1940. † RA 2.

MATTHEW, Jessie Exh. 1901-4
Edinburgh. † RSA 2.

MATTHEW, John F. Exh. 1935
17 Gt. Stuart Street, Edinburgh. † RSA 3.

MATTHEW, Robert H. Exh. 1932
Edinburgh College of Art, Edinburgh. † RSA 1.

MATTHEWMAN, F. Exh. 1884-85
Fernleigh, Cambridge Road, Huddersfield. † RHA 3.

MATTHEWMAN, John W. Exh. 1938
Seascape painter. Add: Treen, Porthcurno, Cornwall. † RA 1.

MATTHEWS, Miss A. Exh. 1905-6
Kensington Gore, London 1905; Tunbridge Wells, Kent 1906. † SWA 3.

MATTHEWS, Dora Exh. 1932-38
34 Peak Hill, London. † RI 6.

MATTHEWS, Edith Exh. 1900-1
Figure and portrait painter. Add: 4 Roseleigh Avenue, Highbury Park, London. † L 3, RA 1.

MATTHEWS, Edith E. Exh. 1908-39
Birmingham. † B 25, RA 1.

MATTHEWS, Grace Exh. 1928-40
Landscape and portrait painter. Add: 22 Harcourt Terrace, London. † COO 2, NEA 2, RA 1, RBA 1, ROI 2, SWA 2.

MATTHEWS, Miss H.H. Exh. 1908-10
14 Teville Road, Worthing. † L 8.

MATTHEWS, Herbert W. Exh. 1919
Architect. Add: London Aerodrome, Hendon. † RA 1.

MATTHEWS, J. Exh. 1882
Market Place, Newark, Notts. † N 1

MATTHEWS, J. Exh. 1893
† TOO 1.

MATTHEWS, Julia Beatrice d. 194?
Figure painter. R.I. 1912 (resigned 1922). Add: Richmond Hill, Surrey 1893; Newquay, Cornwall 1904. † L 3, RA 2, RBA 1, RHA 2, RI 22.

MATTHEWS, Lydia B. Exh. 1894-1900
Flower painter. Add: Richmond, Surrey 1894; London 1898. † RA 1, RBA 1, SWA 5.

MATTHEWS, Mrs. Laura E. Exh. 1932-40
20 Chantry Road, Moseley, Birmingham. † B 6.

MATTHEWS, Percy G. Exh. 1928
Portrait painter. Add: 8 Madeira Grove, Woodford Green, Essex. † RA 1.

MATTHEWS, R. Exh. 1914
Pearl Buildings, Portsmouth. † RA 1.

MATTHEWS, Miss R.A. Exh. 1891-97
Ashwell, Earls Colne, Essex. † RBA 1, RI 1.

MATTHEWS, Robert Wilson b. 1895
Illustrator and commerical designer. Studied Edinburgh College of Art, R.S.A. Schools. (Carnegie Travelling Scholarship 1922, Chalmers Bursary 1922). Exh. 1920-22. Add: Edinburgh. † RSA 3.

MATTHEWS, William Exh. 1914-40
Landscape painter. London. † NEA 1, RA 14, ROI 27.

MATTHEWS, Winifred Exh. 1894
Painter. Add: 41 Mentholme Road, Wandsworth Common, London. † NEA 1.

MATTHEY, Mrs. Constance Exh. 1888
97 Belgrave Road, London. † B 1, D 1.

MATTHIAS, W.C. Exh. 1913
76 Battersea Rise, London. † RA 1.

MATTHISON, William Exh. 1883-1923
Landscape painter. Add: Banbury, Oxon 1883; Oxford 1905; Heddington, Oxon 1918. † B 37, D 5, FIN 21, GI 2, L 9, LS 3, M 4, RA 2, RBA 25, RI 8.

MATTOCK, Miss F. Exh. 1919
15 Gloucester Road, South Ealing, London. † SWA 2.

MATTOCKS, Edith Exh. 1900-18
Flower painter. Add: Nottingham. † N 13.

MATTON, Ida b. 1863
Sculptor. b. Sweden. Exh. 1891-1932. Add: Paris. † RA 3.

MATTOS, de See D

MAUCHLEN, Robert Exh. 1929
Architect. Add: 2 Collingwood Street, Newcastle on Tyne. † RA 1.

MAUD, W.T. d. 1903
Portrait painter. London. † RA 1, ROI 2.

MAUDE, Agnes Exh. 1884
Watercolour landscape painter. Add: Thorncroft, Bromley Park, Kent. † SWA 2.

MAUDE, Hon. Alice C. b. 1879
Sculptor, etcher, watercolour painter and black and white artist. b. Horsmonden. Studied Chelsea, Lambeth, Hammersmith and Central School (silver medal for etching). Exh. 1914-19. Add: Cheyne Walk, London. † RA 2, SWA 3.

MAUDE, Kathleen Exh. 1938
† RMS 2.

MAUDE, Sybil Exh. 1909-25
Landscape painter. Add: Eastbourne 1909; Finchampstead, Berks. 1924. † RHA 2, SWA 4, WG 80.

MAUDE, W. Exh. 1901
32 Alwyne Road, Canonbury, London. † L 1.

MAUDE-ROXBY, Jean Exh. 1940
Sculptor. Add: Burwash, Sussex. † RA 1.

MAUDSLAY, Queenie Exh. 1913-25
Miniature painter. A.R.M.S. 1919. Add: Parkstone, Dorset 1913; Bournemouth 1920. † RA 10, RMS 15.

MAUDSLEY, H. Exh. 1905
16 Harwood Road, Fulham, London. † RA 1.

MAUFE, Edward Brantwood b. 1883
Architect and examiner in design Cambridge and Liverpool Universities. Studied A.A. A.R.A. 1938. Exh. 1922-40. Add: London. † RA 36, RSA 8.

MAUGER, Roland Exh. 1938-40
Portrait painter. Add: London 1938; St. Peter Port, Guernsey 1940. † RA 5.

MAUGHAM, Arthur Ernest Exh. 1908
12 Springfield Road, Millhouses, nr. Sheffield. † L 1.

MAUGHAM, Miss D. Exh. 1921
5 The Avenue Studio, 76 Fulham Road, London. † SWA 1.

MAUGHAM, Miss M.S. Exh. 1908-9
24 Baker Street, Nottingham. † N 2.

MAUGHELING, Miss A. Exh. 1920
The Cottage, Ham Road, Worthing Sussex. † SWA 2.

MAUGHLIN, Annie Exh. 1917-19
Eastwood, Wanstead Place, London. † LS 13.

MAUGIN, Mrs. C.W. Exh. 1886
Catslackburn, Yarrow, Selkirk. † RSA 1.

MAUL, Berta Exh. 1901-3
Miniature portrait painter. Add: Cheltenham. † RA 2.

MAULE, Hugh P.G. c. 1873-1940
Architect. Exh. 1926-39. Add: London. † RA 13.

MAUNDRELL, Charles Gilder 1860-c. 1924
Landscape and figure painter. "Le Chateau d'O" purchased by Chantrey Bequest 1899. Add: London 1884 and 1888; Premiere, France 1886. † B 2, D 1, L 2, M 6, RA 18, RBA 3, RI 8, ROI 3.

MAUNSELL, Mrs. Geraldine b. 1896
nee Mockler. Coloured woodcut engraver. b. Bahmo, Burma. Studied Glasgow and Edinburgh Schools of Art. Exh. 1926-27. Add: Lanark. † GI 4, L 4, RSA 1.

MAUPRAT, Henri Exh. 1910
c/o Allied Artists Association, 67 Chancery Lane, London. † LS 3.

MAUR, W.C. Exh. 1881
Landscape painter. Add: 9 Fitzroy Square, London. † RBA 2.

MAURER, Alfred H.* 1868-1932
American painter. Exh. 1904-14. Add: 9 Rue Falguiere, Paris. † I 1, LS 8.

MAURICE, Constance Exh. 1895-1928
Painter. London. † GOU 9, I 1, L 1, LS 2, RA 1, RBA 1, RHA 1.

MAURIER, du See D

MAURINGNY, de See D

MAURY, Louise M. Exh. 1896-1914
Liverpool 1896; London 1913. † L 3, LS 6.

MAUVE, Anton* 1838-1888
Dutch painter and etcher. Exh. 1882-86. Add: The Hague, Holland. † GI 2, M 4, RSA 2.

MAVROGORDATO, Alex J. Exh. 1892-1933
Landscape and figure painter. London. † FIN 26, GI 1, L 3, M 9, NG 6, RA 31, RHA 3, RI 23, RID 85, ROI 4.

MAVROGORDATO, Elsie Exh. 1919
† I 1.

MAVROGORDATO, John Exh. 1925-26
† GOU 4.

MAVROGORDATO, Julia Exh. 1932-38
Lino-cut artist and wood engraver. † BA 1, RED 15.

MAVROJANI, Mary Exh. 1929-35
Portrait painter of horses. Add: Clyro Court, Clyro, Hereford. † B 4, RCA 3, WG 8.

MAW, Cecilia Exh. 1903-29
Miniature portrait painter. London. † B 3, L 3, RA 11.

MAWDSLEY, Henry b. 1878
Portrait painter and teacher. b. Halifax. Studied Royal College of Art and Academie de la Grande Chaumiere, Paris. Exh. 1919-37. Add: 137 Eglinton Hill, London. † L 1, P 2, RA 3.

MAWDSLEY, Miss J.G. Exh. 1903-4
c/o Mrs. Gibbons, Canning Chambers, St. Johns Street, Liverpool. † L 2.

MAWE, Annie Louisa Exh. 1890-192
Watercolour painter. Add: Chislehurs Kent 1891; Blackheath, London 190 † B 4, L 1, RBA 1, RI 1, SWA 2, WG 11

MAWSON, Clarence Exh. 1919-2
Clevancy, High Cliffe, Warrington, Lanc † L 7.

MAWSON, Miss C. Hermione Exh. 1919-2
School of Art, Museum Street, Warringto 1919; Clevancy, High Cliffe, Warringto 1924. † L 5.

MAWSON, Elizabeth Cameron Exh. 1881-9
Flower and landscape painter. Add Ashfield, Gateshead on Tyne. † B 2, D 1 L 6, RA 2, RBA 1, RI 7, ROI 1, RSA 1 RSW 1, SWA 3.

MAWSON, Edward Prentice b. 188
Architect and town planner. b. Win ermere. Son of Thomas H.M. q.v. Studie A.A. and Ecole des Beaux Arts, Paris. Ex 1915-18. Add: High Street House, Lar caster. † RA 3.

MAWSON, Miss R.M. Exh. 1920-3
School of Art, Museum Street, Warring ton. † L 4.

MAWSON, Sidney G. d. 194
Landscape painter and lecturer in textil design at the Slade School. Add: Mar chester 1882; Richmond, Surrey 190 † L 1, M 1, NEA 3.

MAWSON, Thomas H. c. 1861-193
Architect and Town Planner. Father o Edward Prentice M. q.v. Add: Windermer 1900; London 1903; High Street House Lancaster 1915. † RA 27.

MAX, Gabriel* 1840-191
Austrian painter. Exh. 1886. † TOO 1.

MAXENCE, Edgard Henri Marie* b. 187
French painter. Exh. 1903-25. Add: Paris † CHE 1, L 3.

MAXFIELD, Mrs. Margaret Exh. 1927-4
78 Brandwood Road, King's Heath Birmingham. † B 5.

MAXIMOS, Mrs. Exh. 188
Watercolour painter. Add: 43 Condui Street, Regent's Street, London. † RA 1

MAXSE, Mrs. Exh. 189
Landscape painter. Add: c/o Stannard an Co., 30 Gt. Russell Street, London † ROI 2.

MAXTON, H. Exh. 189
Hogarth House, Sandwich, Kent † RBA 3.

MAXTON, John K. Exh. 193
39 Marchmont Road, Edinburgh † RSA 1.

MAXWELL, Lady Exh. 1938-3
A.R.M.S. 1938. Add: 1 Brampton Court Hendon. † RMS 10.

MAXWELL, Alexander Exh. 1901
Douglas Gardens, Bearsden, N.B. † GI 1

MAXWELL, Mrs. Constance Exh. 1926-3
Watercolour landscape and portrai painter. Add: 3 The Green, Wimbledor Common, London. † RI 2, WG 28.

MAXWELL, Donald 1877-193
Painter, illustrator and writer. Studie South Kensington and Slade School 1897 Official artist to the Admiralty World Wa I. Add: Twickenham, Middlesex 1908 Rochester, Kent 1910; Maidstone, Ken 1936. † L 1, M 2, RA 14.

MAXWELL, Hamilton 1830-1923
Watercolour landscape painter. R.S.W. 1885. Add: Luss, Loch Lomond 1883 Glasgow 1886. † GI 100, L 6, RA 1, RI 2, RSA 6, RSW 133.

MAXWELL, John 1905-1962
Landscape painter. Teacher Edinburgh College of Art 1936-46. Exh. 1937-40. Add: Edinburgh. † RSA 2.

MAXWELL, John A. Exh. 1935
Landscape painter. Add: 8 Rosslyn Mansions, 21 Goldhurst Terrace, London. † RA 2.

MAXWELL, Sir John Stirling 1866-1956
Trustee Wallace Collection and National Galleries of Scotland. R.S.W. 1936, H.R.W.S. 1938. Exh. 1914-40. Add: Pollokshaws, Glasgow. † GI 4, RSW 10, RWS 1.

MAXWELL, Kathleen Exh. 1887-1913
Dublin. † RHA 19.

MAXWELL, Marcia Exh. 1897-1900
16 Beaufort Road, Edgbaston, Birmingham. † B 3.

MAXWELL, Marion M. Exh. 1900
10 Northpark Street, Glasgow. † GI 1.

MAXWELL, Tom d. 1937
Etcher. Add: Glasgow 1906 and 1928; Kilbridge, Ayrshire 1917. † CON 3, GI 36, L 13.

MAXWELL, W. Hall Exh. 1880-86
Add: Edinburgh 1880 and 1885; Barbizon, France 1884. † GI 10, RSA 15.

MAY, Alfred Exh. 1898-1900
Landscape painter. Add: 26 Medhurst Road, Bow, London. † RA 1, RBA 2, ROI 1.

MAY, Arthur Dampier Exh. 1882-1910
Genre and portrait painter. R.M.S. 1896 (Hon. Treas. 1897-98). Add: London. † D 1, G 3, GI 2, L 4, M 2, NG 4, P 4, RA 31, RBA 3, RHA 6, RI 4. RMS 20, ROI 6, TOO 1.

MAY, Arthur J. Exh. 1933
Architect. Add: 77 Attimore Road, Welwyn Garden City, Herts. † RA 1.

MAY, Arthur Powell Exh. 1880-99
Landscape painter. Add: Bexley Heath, Kent 1880; Littlehampton, Sussex 1888. † D 63, L 6, RA 1, RBA 10, RI 10, ROI 5.

MAY, Mrs. A.S. Exh. 1887-97
Landscape painter. Add: 13 Sandall Road, Camden Road, London. † G 2, M 4, NG 4, RA 1, RBA 1.

MAY, A.W. Exh. 1882-91
Landscape painter. Add: Kensington, London. † B 1, ROI 2, RSA 1.

MAY, Charles Exh. 1933
Etcher. Add: 45 Cartwright Gardens, London. † RA 1.

MAY, Charles Exh. 1896
The Studio, Penn House, Rudall Crescent, London. † NG 2.

MAY, Clementina Exh. 1884-93
Mrs. Frank M. Landscape painter. Add: The Grange, Elstree, Herts. † L 1, RBA 3, ROI 2, SWA 1.

MAY, Christiane Brix Kittgaard 1876-1954
Mrs. J.J. May. Portrait, figure, landscape and miniature painter. b. British Honduras. Studied Antwerp, Dresden and Royal Danish Academy at Copenhagen. Add: Bournemouth 1922; London 1926; Thames Ditton, Surrey 1931; Hurlingham, London 1935. † L 1, P 1, RA 1, RCA 1, RI 32, RMS 3, ROI 2.

MAY, Elizabeth A. Exh. 1892-95
Raven's Cliff, Oxford Road, Moseley, Birmingham. † B 4.

MAY, Mrs. Emma A. Exh. 1930-40
London. † GOU 1, RBA 2, RCA 1, ROI 3.

MAY, Edward John Exh. 1881-1929
Architect. London. † G 2, GI 2, RA 42, RSA 2.

MAY, Frank Exh. 1882-95
Birmingham. † B 6, L 1.

MAY, F.S. Exh. 1912
St. Margaret's, Hampstead Heath, London. † RA 1.

MAY, Gwen Exh. 1938-40
Watercolour painter, etcher and wood engraver. Studied Hornsey School of Art. Painter of Heraldry at the College of Arms, London 1930. Add: London. † RA 2.

MAY, Gertrude Brooke Exh. 1887-96
Flower painter. London. † G 3, L 1, NEA 3, NG 7, RA 2, RBA 3.

MAY, H. Goulton Exh. 1884-87
Figure and domestic painter. London. † D 1, RBA 1, RI 2.

MAY, J.C. Exh. 1906
Woodbourne, Partickhill, Glasgow. † GI 1.

MAY, Kate Exh. 1881-83
Figure and flower painter. Add: Alcombe, Dunster, Somerset. † L 2, RA 2.

MAY, Margery Exh. 1880-85
Figure painter. Add: 26 Warwick Gardens, Kensington, London. † B 2, RA 1, ROI 2, SWA 1.

MAY, Miss M.F. Exh. 1902-3
10 The Green, Marlborough, Wilts. † SWA 3.

MAY, Phil 1864-1903
Portrait painter, black and white artist and illustrator. Worked for "Punch". N.E.A. 1894, R.I. 1897, R.P. 1896. Several of his works are in the Tate Gallery. Add: London. † FIN 8, GI 1, RA 1.

MAY, William Charles 1853-1931
Sculptor and painter. Exh. 1880-96. Add: London. † L 1, NG 5, RA 13.

MAY, William Holmes Exh. 1880-1910
Painter and etcher. R.E. 1883. Add: London. † L 3, RBA 1. RE 105.

MAY, Walter William* 1831-1896
Marine painter and watercolourist. A.R.I. 1871, R.I. 1873, R.O.I. 1883. Add: London. † AG 4, B 1, DOW 134, FIN 2, L 10, M 2, RA 2, RI 113, ROI 36, TOO 4.

MAYAN, Theo Orgon Exh. 1904-6
Bouches du Rhone, France. † L 3.

MAYBANK, Thomas Exh. 1898-1912
Illustrative painter. Add: Beckenham, Kent 1898; Bromley, Kent 1906; Esher, Surrey 1909. † BG 2, RA 5, RBA 3, RHA 1, ROI 1.

MAYBEE, E.D. Exh. 1910
115 Rue Notre Dame des Champs, Paris. † RA 1.

MAYBERY, Edgar James b. 1887
Painter and etcher. Exh. 1922-29. Add: Newport, Mon. † L 2, RCA 18, RHA 1.

MAYCOCK, Mary C. Exh. 1893-95
229 Hagley Road, Edgbaston, Birmingham. † B 3.

MAYER, Ethel Exh. 1925
Mrs. William Murray. Flower and still life painter. Self taught. † WG 41.

MAYER, F. Katherine Exh. 1907-26
Portrait and figure painter. Add: Twickenham, Middlesex 1907; Chelsea, London 1917. † GI 1, GOU 43, I 3, RA 4.

MAYER, H.M. Exh. 1933
Maldon, South Drive, Upton, Wirral, Cheshire. † L 1.

MAYER, Mrs. Lilian M. Exh. 1919-39
Miniature painter. A.R.M.S. 1928, A.S.W.A. 1932. Add: London. † GOU 17, L 20, RA 4, RI 39, RMS 51.

MAYER, Millicent Phelps See PHELPS

MAYER, R.S. Exh. 1911-30
Urmston, Manchester. † L 8, M 2, RCA 13.

MAYERS, Miss A.R. Exh. 1913
Sutton, Surrey. † SWA 1.

MAYERS, W.A. Exh. 1925-27
36 Kickmansholme Lane, Longsight, Manchester. † B 3, RCA 2.

MAYERS, Zoe Exh. 1909
† LS 3.

MAYFIELD, F. Exh. 1888
Landscape painter. Add: 27 Sabina Street, Nottingham. † N 1.

MAYGOR, Mrs. Louie E. Exh. 1898-1909
Llandudno, Wales. † L 4, RCA 4.

MAYNARD, Miss E.F. Exh. 1911
East Durrants, Havant, Hants. † RA 1.

MAYNARD, Harriette Exh. 1885
Illustrative painter. Add: 4 Brunswick Square, Bloomsbury, London. † RBA 1.

MAYNARD, Miss H.M. Exh. 1895
70 Lillieshall Road, Clapham, London. † SWA 1.

MAYNARD, Miss L. Exh. 1894
11 Lansdowne Circus, Leamington, Warwicks. † B 1.

MAYNARD, Robert Ashwin b. 1888
Painter and wood engraver. Studied Westminster and Paris. Exh. 1933. † COO 3.

MAYNE, Mrs. Alice Exh. 1889-94
Mountainville Lodge, Dundrum, Co. Dublin. † B 2, RHA 2.

MAYNE, Arthur Exh. 1892
56 Bruntsfield Place, Edinburgh. † RSA 1.

MAYNE, Annie E. Exh. 1880
William's Park, Rathmines, Dublin. † RHA 1.

MAYNE, Arthur Jocelyn d. 1893
A.R.H.A. 1870, R.H.A. 1873. Add: Dublin. † L 4, RHA 36.

MAYNE, Hamilton Exh. 1898
8 Kensington Gardens Square, London. † RHA 1.

MAYNE, S. Kate Exh. 1883
Lisburne Villas, Birchfield, Birmingham. † B 1.

MAYNE, W.F.N. Exh. 1938
Painter. Add: Glenrosa, Sutton, Co. Dublin. † RHA 1.

MAYO, Daphne Exh. 1925
Sculptor. Add: c/o Mrs. Bateman, The Web, Reigate Heath, Surrey. † RA 1.

MAYO, Eileen Exh. 1930-38
Painter, lithographer, lino-cut artist, and writer. b. Norwich. Studied Slade School. † BA 1, RED 8.

MAYO, Frederick Harrison Exh. 1907-8
32 Kilton Street, Battersea Park, London. † LS 5, RA 1.

MAYOR, Fred 1865-1916
Figure, landscape and coastal painter. Married Hannah M. q.v. Add: London 1888, 1897 and 1914; Amberley, Sussex 1894; Montreuil, Pas de Calais 1905; Aylesbury, Bucks. 1910. † BG 1, GI 2, GOU 19, I 9, L 5, LEI 100, LS 5, M 1, NEA 16, RA 11, RBA 5, RSA 4.

MAYOR, Hannah b. 1871
nee Hoyland. Flower and still life painter. b. Heeley, Staffs. Studied Royal Female School of Art and Westminster. Married Fred M. q.v. Exh. 1896-1940. Add: London 1896 and 1914; France 1903; Whitchurch, Aylesbury, Bucks. 1910; Betchworth, Surrey 1935. † BG 2, GOU 9, NEA 5, RA 7, RBA 1, RI 2, SWA 4.

MAYOR, Pattie Exh. 1894-1913
Ashton on Ribble, nr. Preston, Lancs. † L 8, LS 6.

MAYS, Douglas Lionel b. 1900
Painter and illustrator. Studied at Goldsmith's College. Exh. 1938. Add: Chalfont Street, Giles, Bucks. † RA 1.

MAYSTON, A.R. Exh. 1904-5
Architect. Add: 11 Gt. James Street, Bedford Row, London. † RA 2.

MAZE, Paul Lucien* b. 1887
Painter. b. Havre of French parents. Went to school in Southampton at age of twelve. Joined British Army 1914. Exh. 1923-39. † AG 2, GOU 1, LEI 77, RSA 2, TOO 2.

MAZZAROLI, T. Exh. 1886
6 Carter Street, Liverpool. † L 2.

MEACHAM, Charles S. b. 1900
Illuminator, poster artist and designer. b. Catford, Kent. Studied Birmingham Central School of Arts and Crafts. Part time teacher at Bournville School of Art and Wolverhampton School of Arts and Crafts. Exh. 1924-33. Add: Hildenborough 1924; Rustington, Sussex 1925; Lichfield, Staffs. 1930. † B 7, L 1, RCA 1, ROI 1.

MEAD, Mrs. Exh. 1934
Watercolour landscape painter. † COO 1.

MEAD, Alec O. Exh. 1926-27
Royal College of Arts, South Kensington, London. † L 2.

MEAD, Larkin G. Exh. 1891
Medallionist. Add: 4 bis Via delle Officine, Florence, Italy. † RA 1.

MEAD, Marion Grace d. c.1933
Miniaturist. A.R.M.S. 1924. Exh. from 1906. Add: London. † L 10, RA 9, RI 3, RMS 58.

MEAD, Mary P. Exh. 1880-83
Watercolour landscape painter. London. † D 1, RBA 3, SWA 1.

MEAD, Roderick Exh. 1936
Engraver. † RED 1.

MEAD, Rose Exh. 1896-1938
Portrait and figure painter. Add: Bury St. Eds. 1896 and 1899; London 1897. † P 2, RA 6, RCA 2, SWA 3.

MEADE, Arthur Exh. 1888-1939
Landscape and figure painter. R.B.A. 1895, R.O.I. 1909. Add: London 1888; St. Ives, Cornwall 1891; Blackwater, Hants. 1933; Lelant, Cornwall 1934. † B 13, L 7, M 18, NG 1, RA 63, RBA 12, ROI 92.

MEADE, Cyril M. Exh. 1923
† NEA 1.

MEADE, Hope Exh. 1904-9
Figure painter. Add: The Woodlands, Dulwich Common, London. † RA 4, RMS 1.

MEADE, John M. Exh. 1937-40
Landscape painter. Add: 71 Surbiton Hill Park, Surbiton, Surrey. † NEA 2, RA 3.

MEADE, Mark Exh. 1926-33
Watercolour landscape painter. Add: Norbury, London 1926; 71 Surbiton Hill Park, Surbiton, Surrey 1933. † RA 2.

MEADOWCROFT, J.H. Exh. 1933
15 Queens Terrace, Morecambe, Lancs. † L 1.

MEADOWS, Arthur Joseph* 1843-1907
Marine painter. Son of James M. (1798-1864) and brother of James Edwin M. q.v. Add: London. † RBA 4, TOO 3.

MEADOWS, Chris Exh. 1883-1901
Glasgow 1883; Johnstone 1897; Saltcoats 1901. † GI 15.

MEADOWS, James Edwin* 1828-1888
Marine painter. Son of James M. (1798-1864) and brother of Arthur Joseph M. q.v. Add: London. † B 7, L 2, M 3, RHA 12.

MEADOWS, Miss L.M. Exh. 1920-22
Kilmona, Sandford Road, Dublin. † RHA 2.

MEADOWS, Robert Exh. 1888-96
Glasgow. † GI 4.

MEADOWS, Samuel Douglas Exh. 1925-38
Architect. Municipal Architect's Offices, Singapore 1925; Whitehall, London 1938. † RA 3.

MEARNS, Fanny Exh. 1880-88
Landscape and figure painter. London. † B 1, RBA 4.

MEARNS, Lois M. Exh. 1880-85
Landscape and figure painter. London. † B 1, RBA 1.

MEARS, Frank Charles 1880-1953
A.R.S.A. 1937. Exh. 1909-40. Add: Edinburgh. † GI 3, RSA 28.

MEARS, J. Exh. 1933
10 Perrain Road, Allerton, Liverpool. † L 1.

MEASE, Miss R.T. Exh. 1905-13
26 Christchurch Road, Streatham Hill, London. † L 4, RA 4, RI 3, SWA 6.

MEASHAM, Henry 1844-1922
Landscape and portrait painter. Add: Manchester 1880, 1889 and 1910; Tal-y-bont, Conway 1883; Tal-y-Cafn, Wales 1898. † L 10, M 17, RA 3, RCA 75, RI 1.

MEASOM, Allen Exh. 1898
45 Lessar Avenue, Clapham Common, London. † RI 1.

MEASOM, William Frederick b. 1875
Figure, portrait and landscape painter. b. New Jersey, U.S.A. Exh. 1898-1934. Add: London 1898 and 1910; Pulborough, Sussex 1908. † D 2, RA 14, RBA 38, RI 10.

MEASOR, Ellen M. Exh. 1903-10
Glenthorne, Elmfield Road, Bromley, Kent. † L 1, SWA 10.

MEASURES, Harry B. Exh. 1896
Architect. Add: 16 Gt. George Street, Westminster, London. † RA 1.

MEATS, Muriel b. 1904
Silversmith, enameller and engraver. Studied Central Art School, Birmingham. Exh. 1930-33. Add: Coventry. † B 9.

MECHELEN, Van See V

MECKEL, Von See V

MECREDY, Seymour Exh. 1904-10
Landscape painter. Add: Bushey, Herts. 1904; Headingley, Leeds 1907. † RA 5.

MEDCALF, T. Exh. 1882-86
Liverpool 1882; Aughton, nr. Ormskirk, Lancs. 1886. † L 3.

MEDCALF, William J. Exh. 1901-30
Aughton, nr. Ormskirk 1901 and 1911; Liverpool 1909 and 1921. † L 32.

MEDD, Henry A.N. Exh. 1928-34
Architect. Add: 2 Bedford Square, London. † RA 3.

MEDLAND, John Exh. 1883-1902
Landscape, interior and architectural painter. London. † GI 5, RA 1, RBA 1, RI 5.

MEDLEN, Louise Exh. 1895-96
48 Manor Park, Lee, London. † RI 2.

MEDLEY, Robert b. 1905
Painter. Member London Group 1937. Exh. 1927-38. † AG 1, COO 21, GOU 11, LEI 3, M 1.

MEDLYCOTT, Sir Hubert J. Bt. b. 1841
Landscape and architectural painter. Exh. 1880-1930. Add: Milborne Port, Somerset 1880; Hill, Glos. 1883; London 1887. † B 1, D 102, G 3, L 14, M 2, RBA 22, RI 20, WG 140.

MEDWIN, Leslie Exh. 1892-95
Landscape painter. Add: c/o Cole Bros., 2 Percy Street, London. † ROI 4.

MEDWORTH, Frank Charles b. 1892
Painter, etcher and engraver. Studied Camberwell City and Guild of London Institute, Dover, Royal College of Art and Westminster. Served in France and East Africa 1914-19. Visiting master Westminster and Hammersmith Schools of Art. R.B.A. 1931. Exh. 1921-38. Add: London. † BA 2, G 2, GI 4, GOU 25, L 2, NEA 13, RA 13, RBA 36, RED 2, RHA 1, RSA 1.

MEE, Miss A.E. Exh. 1885-1904
Landscape painter. Add: Nottingham 1885; Carrington, Notts. 1904. † N 2.

MEE, Frank W. Exh. 1887-96
Architect. Add: 100 King Street, Manchester. † M 3, RA 2.

MEE, H. Exh. 1932
† L 1.

MEE, Miss P.S.A. Exh. 1923
694 Chester Road, Erdington, Birmingham. † B 1.

MEEDY, W.W. Exh. 1915-16
43 St. Leonard's Road, Poplar, London. † RA 2.

MEEKLEY, Frederick George Exh. 1927-38
Watercolour landscape painter. Add: Carlisle. † GI 1, L 4, RA 8, RSA 5.

MEEKYN, George Exh. 1882-92
Figure painter. Add: 1 Raglan Street, Nottingham. † N 4.

MEERE, Matthew C. Exh. 1923
Landscape painter. Add: 195 Ham Park Road, Forest Gate, London. † GI 1, RA 2.

MEERES, Theodora Exh. 1926-28
Forder House, Moreton Hampstead, Devon. † NEA 2.

MEERS, Mrs. Exh. 1906
Arundel Gardens, London. † SWA 1.

MEESON, Dora d. 1956
Mrs. George Coates. Portrait, landscape figure and flower painter. b. Melbourne, Australia. Studied Melbourne National Gallery and Julians, Paris. R.O.I. 1920. Add: London 1907 and 1911; Poole, Dorset 1910. † BG 2, CHE 3, GOU 1, I 4, L 8, LS 13, P 8, RA 4, RI 3, ROI 82, RSA 2, SWA 4.

MEESTER, de See D

MEG, G. Exh. 1931
† GOU 1.

MEGE, Louise Exh. 1885-97
Figure and portrait painter. London. † L 1, RMS 1, SWA 2.

MEGGETT, John C.H. Exh. 1896-1934
Birmingham 1896; Solihull, Warwicks. 1933. † B 9.

MEGGITT, Marjorie b. 1906
Sculptor. b. Sheffield. Studied Sheffield College of Art and R.A. Schools (gold medal and travelling scholarship 1930, Prix de Rome for sculpture 1932-35). Exh. 1930-40. Add: Sheffield 1930; London 1932. † GI 1, RA 11.

MEGINN, F. Exh. 1885-1905
Liverpool. † L 33.

MEGRET, L.N. Adolph 1829-1911
French sculptor. Exh. 1901. Add: Paris. † RA 1.

MEGSON, A.L. Exh. 1926-30
Bow Green, Bowdon, Cheshire. † RCA 4.

MEGSON, M.B. Exh. 1886
32 Fairfield Road, Bradford, Yorks. † RSA 1.
MEGSON, W. Exh. 1885-86
32 Fairfield Road, Bradford, Yorks. † B 1, M 1, RSA 1.
MEIHE, Winifrede A. Exh. 1900
Miniature painter. Add: Limathburg, Ambleside Avenue, Streatham, London. † RA 1.
MEIKLEJOHN, Mrs. D. Exh. 1882-83
Lasswade 1882, Mount Lothian, Dalkeith 1883. † RSA 2.
MEIN, Margaret J. d. c.1897
Painter. Add: 12 Glencairn Crescent, Edinburgh. † GI 13, L 4, M 1, RA 1, RBA 1, RI 1, RSA 10, RSW 2.
MEIN, Thomas Exh. 1880-85
Edinburgh. † RSA 6.
MEIN, Will G. Exh. 1886-1912
Figure painter. Add: Kelson 1886; Edinburgh 1894; London 1903. † GI 2, RA 1, RI 2, RSA 3.
MEINEL, Erna Exh. 1940
Urban landscape painter. Add: 23B Clifton Gardens, London. † RA 1.
MEISEL, Jules Exh. 1909-10
c/o Allied Artists Assn., 67 Chancery Lane, London. † LS 6.
MEISSNER, Erich Exh. 1939
Figure and portrait painter. † GOU 26.
MEISSONIER, Jean Louis Ernest* 1815-1891
French painter. H.R.I. 1867. Exh. 1881. † RE 2.
MELCHERS, F.M. Exh. 1926
Portrait and theatrical painter. † GOU 93.
MELCHERS, Gari 1860-1932
American painter. Exh. 1912. † P 1.
MELDRUM, David G. Exh. 1884
Kirkaldy. † RSA 1.
MELDRUM, George William Exh. 1917-40
Sculptor. Add: Dennistoun, Glasgow 1917; Rutherglen 1925; Hampstead, London 1931. † GI 9, RA 1, RSA 1, RSW 1.
MELDRUM, R. Exh. 1909
373 Mansfield Road, Nottingham. † N 2.
MELDRUM, Roy Exh. 1925-27
Landscape painter. † CHE 2.
MELDRUM, Thomas Exh. 1881-96
Landscape painter. N.S.A. 1886-98. Add: Nottingham. † N 68, RA 6.
MELEYARD, Sydney Exh. 1907
Historical painter. † FIN 1.
MELHUISH, Miss G. Exh. 1905-16
London. † RA 5, SWA 1.
MELKA, Vincent Exh. 1880
83 Ranelagh Road, Dublin. † RHA 2.
MELLAND, Sylvia Exh. 1940
Portrait painter. † COO 1.
MELLANVILLE, de See D
MELLERSH, Evelyn Exh. 1928-40
Flower painter. Add: Fir Grove, Godalming, Surrey 1928; London 1938. † COO 4, D 3, L 1, RBA 2, RI 5, SWA 4.
MELLERSH, Miss Mayne Exh. 1934-38
London. † RMS 3, SWA 2.
MELLIAR, Gladys Foster Exh. 1910-21
London and Ipswich. † L 4, RA 3.
MELLIAR-SMITH, Peggy Exh. 1936
Watercolour painter. Add: Lynton Lodge, West Street, Reigate, Surrey. † RA 1.
MELLIN, Emily C.P. Exh. 1912
11 Onslow Road, Fairfield, Liverpool. † L 1.
MELLING, Sydney Exh. 1902-4
78 Cropper's Hill, St. Helens, Lancs. † L 2.
MELLIS, Margaret Nairne Exh. 1934-38
Landscape painter. Add: Edinburgh 1934; Gullane, East Lothian 1935. † LEF 2, RSA 3.
MELLODEW, W. Turner Exh. 1912
65 Hawthorne Road, Deane, Bolton, Lancs. † L 2.
MELLON, Campbell b. 1876
Landscape and coastal painter. Studied under Sir Arnesby Brown 1918-21. A.R.B.A. 1938, R.B.A. 1939, R.O.I. 1938. Exh. 1924-40. Add: Upper Cliff Road, Gorleston on Sea, Norfolk. † FIN 6, GI 1, L 2, RA 18, RBA 13, ROI 11.
MELLON, C.A. Exh. 1908-15
A.N.S.A. 1908-15. Add: West Bridgford, Notts. 1908; Nottingham 1911. † N 32.
MELLON, E. Leo Exh. 1899-1902
38 George Street, Manchester. † M 2.
MELLOR, Jessie Exh. 1898-99
Greville Villa, Dickenson Road, Rusholme, Manchester. † L 1, M 1.
MELLOR, J.P. Exh. 1906-8
1 Embankment Gardens, Chelsea, London. † RA 2.
MELLOR, Kate Exh. 1893
Arley House, Withington, Manchester. † L 1.
MELLOR, William* 1851-1931
Landscape painter. Add: Laurel Bank, Brighton Grove, Rusholme 1887; Chorlton cum Hardy, Manchester 1908. † L 5, M 4.
MELLORS, E.L. Exh. 1929
Landscape painter. Add: Sherwood Hall Estate, Clipstone Road, Mansfield, Notts. † N 2.
MELLY, Dorothy H. Exh. 1919
† L 1.
MELLY, Miss E. Exh. 1885-1910
90 Chatham Street, Liverpool. † L 6.
MELOY, H. Exh. 1929
72 Bold Street, Liverpool. † L 1.
MELROSE, W.B. Exh. 1887-96
Edinburgh. † GI 12, L 1, RSA 22, TOO 1.
MELTZER, Mrs. Charlotte Reinmann Exh. 1911-12
51 Cambridge Street, Eccleston Square, London. † LS 3, SWA 1.
MELVILL, Edith Exh. 1886
Figure painter. Add: 84 Church Street, Fulham Road, London. † SWA 1.
MELVILL, Miss H. Exh. 1918
South Hampstead, London. † SWA 2.
MELVILLE, Exh. 1886
21 Sutton Court Road, Chiswick, London. † L 1.
MELVILLE, Mrs. Alexander Exh. 1880-83
Eliza Anne Smallbone. Figure painter. London. † D 2, GI 1, L 4, SWA 1.
MELVILLE, Arthur* 1858-1904
Watercolour genre and figure painter. Studied in Paris and at R.S.A. Schools. R.P. 1891, A.R.S.A. 1886, A.R.W.S. 1888, R.W.S. 1899. Add: Edinburgh 1880 and 1883; Cairo, Egypt 1882; London 1889. † B 3, DOW 1, G 3, GI 18, L 29, M 5, NG 4, P 3, RA 15, RI 8, RSA 66, RSW 1, RWS 24.
MELVILLE, E.A.L. Exh. 1894-95
† TOO 2.
MELVILLE, Frank 1832-1916
American etcher. Exh. 1910-15. Add: New York. † GI 8, L 5, LS 2, RSA 1.
MELVILLE, Miss F.A. Exh. 1886
41 Townsend Place, Kirkcaldy. † RSA 1.
MELVILLE, Harden Sidney Exh. 1882
Animal and figure painter. Add: 2 Percy Street, London. † B 1.
MELVILLE, Mary Exh. 1883-86
Glasgow. † GI 5.
MELVILLE, Rosa Frances Exh. 1881
Figure painter. Add: 34 Gloucester Road, London. † SWA 1.
MELVILLE, Miss V. Exh. 1904
8 Argyll Road, Kensington, London. † SWA 1.
MELVIN, J.W. Exh. 1892
43 Peddie Street, Dundee. † GI 1.
MEMBER, Ter Exh. 1886
148 New Bond Street, London. † M 2.
MEMISON, Rolfe Exh. 1938
Watercolour figure painter. Add: 22 Jubilee Place, London. † RA 1.
MENARD, E.R. Exh. 1905-28
Paris. † I 1, L 6.
MENARD, Victor Exh. 1911
Figure painter. † BRU 1.
MENART, Charles J. Exh. 1908-21
Perth 1908; Glasgow 1911. † GI 5, RSA 1.
MENCIA, A.G. Exh. 1906
c/o 118 New Bond Street, London. † RA 1.
MENDHAM, Edith Exh. 1888-1911
Figure and illustrative painter. Add: Clifton, Bristol 1888; Stroud, Glos. 1893; Clevedon, Somerset 1911. † B 2, L 6, M 2, RI 1, SWA 14.
MENDHAM, John B. Exh. 1929-38
Architect. London. † RA 3.
MENDILAHARZU, G. Exh. 1884-85
29 Boulevard des Batignolles, Paris. † GI 2.
MENDOZA, A.M. Exh. 1887
Painter. Add: The Lodge, 319A Mile End Road, London. † RA 1.
MENDOZA, Philip Exh. 1939
Figure painter. Add: 35 Creswick Road, West Acton, London. † RA 1.
MENDS, Brig. Horatio Reginald b. 1851
Painter. Exh. 1918-21. Add: Morton House, York. † RA 1, RI 1.
MENELAW, W. Brown Exh. 1927-39
Monkwood, Colinton, Edinburgh. † RSA 10, RSW 23.
MENELAWS, William Exh. 1901-3
3 Tantallon Place, Edinburgh. † GI 1, M 1, RSA 4.
MENGARINI, Fausta V. Exh. 1921-27
Sculptor. Add: 8 Wentworth Studios, Manresa Road, London. † RA 4.
MENGIN, A. Exh. 1886
† M 1.
MENGUE, Jean M. Exh. 1904-11
Paris. † L 2.
MENIER, A.G. Exh. 1880
16 Avenue Trudaine, Paris. † RHA 1.
MENINSKY, Bernard* 1891-1950
Landscape and portrait painter. b. Russia. Studied Liverpool, London and Paris. Teacher of drawing and painting at Central School of Arts and Crafts and Westminster School. N.E.A. 1923. Member London Group 1919. Add: Liverpool 1910; London 1914. † AG 7, ALP 1, CHE 4, COO 9, G 1, GOU 71, I 6, L 14, LEF 2, LEI 2, M 3, NEA 42, RED 2, RSA 2.
MENNELL, M. Exh. 1902-3
Flower and portrait painter. † BG 4.
MENPES, Mortimer* 1860-1938
Painter and etcher. b. Australia. Studied under Whistler. Artist-war correspondent in South Africa. N.E.A. 1886, R.B.A. 1885, R.E. 1881, R.I. 1897, R.O.I. 1899. Add: London. † BG 3, D 8, DOW 618, FIN 296, GI 9, L 21, LEI 140, NG 1, RA 42, RE 94, RI 18, ROI 3.
MENTA, Edouard Exh. 1882-1905
Landscape painter. Add: 32 Castlenau Villas, Barnes, Surrey 1882; Nice, France 1891. † L 5, RA 3.

MENZEL, Adolph* 1815-1905
German painter. Exh. 1882-99 Add: Berlin. † G 1, NEA 3, RWS 2.

MENZIES, Miss Exh. 1886
8 Jarratt Street, Hull. † RI 1.

MENZIES, Anne Exh. 1928
Painter. † AB 1.

MENZIES, Beryl Exh. 1908-11
56 St. George's Terrace, Jesmond, Newcastle on Tyne. † L 4.

MENZIES, D.P. Exh. 1891
53 Bentinck Street, Glasgow. † GI 1.

MENZIES, Mrs. E.M. Exh. 1916
395 Lower Addiscombe Road, Croydon, Surrey. † RA 1.

MENZIES, Miss F.M. Exh. 1886
Landscape painter. † SWA 1.

MENZIES, John Exh. 1880-1938
Landscape painter. Add: 8 Jarratt Street, Hull 1880; Edinburgh 1897. † D 3, GI 10, L 1, M 1, RA 4, RI 1, RSA 46.

MENZIES, Mrs. John (Maria) Exh. 1880-1900
Landscape painter. Add: 8 Jarratt Street, Hull 1880; Edinburgh 1899. † GI 1, RA 3, RI 3, RSA 3.

MENZIES, William A. Exh. 1886-1911
Figure painter. London. † D 1, L 3, RA 18, RI 2.

MENZIES, W.C. Exh. 1929
22 Braeside Avenue, Rutherglen. † GI 1.

MENZIES-JONES, Llewelyn Frederick b. 1889
Painter and potter. Studied Slade School. Art master Eton College. Exh. 1929-36. Add: Eton College, Windsor, Berks. † COO 7, RI 1, WG 3.

MEO, Gaetano d. 1925
Landscape painter and mosaic artist. Assistant to Sir W.B. Richmond in the decoration of St. Paul's dome. Exh. 1880-1917. Add: London. † L 6, NG 45, RA 3, RBA 4.

MEO, Innes Exh. 1910-27
Landscape painter. Add: London 1910; Stoner Hill, nr. Petersfield, Hants. 1926. † NEA 5.

MERANT, E. Exh. 1888
c/o Mrs. Davies, 186 Villa Street, Birmingham. † B 1.

MERBITZ, de See D

MERCER, Eleanor L. Exh. 1897-99
Sculptor. Add: 12 Rathbone Place, Oxford Street, London. † RA 5.

MERCER, E. Stanley Exh. 1913-32
Portrait and landscape painter. R.O.I. 1927, R.P. 1920. Add: London. † GI 2, P 38, RA 3, ROI 7.

MERCER, Frederick Exh. 1881-1937
Figure painter. R.B.S.A. 1925. Add: Birmingham 1881; Abbots Bromley, Rugeley, Staffs. 1883. † B 38, D 7, L 7, RA 3, RBA 1, RHA 1, RI 5.

MERCER, Fletcher J. Exh. 1901-22
Landscape, flower and portrait painter. Add: London 1901; Gainsborough, Lincs. 1907; Edinburgh 1920. † I 6, NEA 32, P 1, RSA 1, RSW 1.

MERCER, John Exh. 1888
Oxford Street, St. Helens, Lancs. † L 1.

MERCER, J.S.A. Exh. 1890-91
1 Arkles Road, Anfield. † L 2.

MERCER, Lewis Exh. 1904
Landscape painter. Add: Regents Chambers, Long Row, Nottingham. † N 1.

MERCER, M.J. Exh. 1909
Flower painter. † BG 2.

MERCER, Thomas Exh. 1882
51 South John Street, Liverpool. † L 1.

MERCHANT, Henry Exh. 1893-1940
Figure, animal, landscape and still life painter. Studied at Liverpool and Southport. Art master King George V School, Southport. Add: Southport, Lancs. 1893; and 1912; Liverpool 1906; Bridgnorth, Salop 1908. † B 12, GI 1, L 49, RA 1, RCA 32, ROI 1, RSA 1.

MERCIE, Fernand Exh. 1935
Architectural landscape painter. Add: 12 Rue Victor Considerant, Paris. † RA 2.

MERCIER, Miss F. Exh. 1882
102 Upper Huskisson Street, Liverpool. † L 1.

MERCIER, Mlle. Ruth Exh. 1882-1913
Flower and landscape painter. Add: Cannes, France 1882; Paris 1902; London 1905. † G 2, M 1, RA 4, RI 1, RSA 1, WG 52.

MERCULIANO, Jacques Exh. 1909
† LS 3.

MEREDITH, Arthur Exh. 1936
82 Hazlewood Road, Acocks Green, Birmingham. † B 1.

MEREDITH, Eric Norman Exh. 1935-36
Painter and illustrator. b. Liverpool. Studied Liverpool College of Art, Royal College of Art, Italy, France, Germany and Holland. Add: London. † ROI 2.

MEREDITH, Joyce Exh. 1913-36
St. Margaret's Home, Upper Parliament Street, Liverpool 1913; House of Prayer, Burnham, Bucks. 1936. † L 3, RSA 2.

MEREDITH, Sophie D'Ouseley Exh. 1889-90
Mrs. William M. nee D'Ouseley. Watercolour painter. b. Waterford. Studied at Penzance and Heatherleys. Add: 96 Lansdowne Road, Bayswater, London 1889; lived at Nailsworth, Glos. c.1913 and Burton on Trent, Staffs. c.1927. † RI 1, SWA 2.

MEREDITH, William b. 1851
Exh. 1882-1926. Add: Manchester 1882 and 1886; Conway 1885. † L 3, M 8, RCA 1.

MERIC, de See D

MERLIN, C.E.P. Exh. 1880
Figure painter. Add: Athens, Greece. † RA 1.

MERONTI, Marius Exh. 1927
Painter. Add: 60 Central Hill, Upper Norwood, London. † RA 2.

MERRETT, Walter Exh. 1881-1911
Sculptor. London. † L 4, M 1, RA 26, RBA 4.

MERRICK, Emily M. b. 1842
Portrait, figure and domestic painter. Exh. 1880-1902. Add: London. † B 11, G 3, GI 4, L 6, M 8, P 2, RA 10, RBA 12, RHA 18, RSA 1, SWA 19.

MERRICK, Jessie Exh. 1904-5
120 Bedford Street, Liverpool. † L 2.

MERRICK, Marianne Agnes Exh. 1902-11
Miniature portrait painter. Add: 5 Carlisle Street, Edgware Road, London. † RA 6, RMS 3.

MERRIFIELD, Leonard Stamford b. 1880
Sculptor. b. Wyck, Rissington, Glos. Studied Cheltenham Art School, City and Guilds of London and R.A. Schools. A.R.B.A. 1919, R.B.A. 1921, A.R.M.S. 1922, R.M.S. 1924. Exh. 1906-40. Add: London. † GI 5, L 7, P 2, RA 65, RBA 4, RMS 9, RSA 8.

MERRILLS, Sydney Exh. 1922-34
Edinburgh 1922; Liverpool 1923. † L 24, RSA 3.

MERRIMAN, Fred S. Exh. 1898-1931
Land and seascape painter. N.S.A. 1908. Add: Nottingham. † N 105, RA 1.

MERRIMAN, H.I. Exh. 191
4 Newman's Row, Lincoln's Inn Field London. † RA 1.

MERRIMAN, Owen Exh. 1891-190
Landscape painter. Add: 78 Derby Roa Nottingham. † N 8.

MERRIOTT, Jack 1901-196
Landscape and portrait painter. Studie Croydon School of Art and St. Marti School of Art. Add: Addiscombe, Surre 1930; Shirley, Surrey 1935. † L 1, RA RI 4, ROI 7.

MERRISON, Charles Redford Exh. 1910-2
Painter. Add: Stoke Newington, Londo † LS 8, RA 1.

MERRITT, Mrs. Anna Lea 1844-193
nee Lea. Portrait and genre painter an etcher. b. Philadelphia, U.S.A. R.B.A 1903, R.P. 1891, A.R.E. 1887-92 an 1905-19, A.S.W.A. 1886. "Love locke out" (1884) purchased by Chantre Bequest 1890. Add: London 188 Philadelphia, U.S.A. 1903; Hurstbourn Tarrant, nr. Andover, Hants. 1904. † B GI 1, L 10, M 10, NG 6, P 12, RA 2 RBA 14, RE 30, ROI 8, SWA 1.

MERRITT, Henry Samuel Exh. 1908-3
Watercolour landscape painter. Ad Chingford, Essex 1908; Kent 1927; c/ Pope and Son, London 1934. † LS M 1, RA 5.

MERRITT, William J. Exh. 1886-9
Marine painter. London. † B 1, GI 4, L RA 5, RBA 3, RI 3, ROI 5.

MERRY, Godfrey Exh. 1883-191
Figure and landscape painter. Londo † B 9, FIN 1, G 1, GI 3, L 1, LS 3, RA RBA 8, ROI 6.

MERRY, Mabel Exh. 189
6 Rosebery Terrace, Kelvin Bridg Glasgow. † GI 1.

MERRY, Mrs. W.J.C. Exh. 191
Watercolour pastoral painter. † WG 31.

MERRYLEES, Miss Exh. 189
1 Lennox Street, Edinburgh. † RSW 1.

MERRYLEES, Annie R. Exh. 1894-193
Miniature painter. Married Reginald E Arnold q.v. R.M.S. 1900. Add: Londo † GI 6, L 3, NG 1, P 1, RA 46, RI 21 RMS 16, RSA 1.

MERRYLEES, A. Russell Exh. 189
Studio, Albert Hall, Edinburgh. † RSA 1

MERTENS, Adolphe Exh. 192
Sculptor. Add: 43 Dreve de Lorraine Brussels. † RA 1.

MERTON, Owen 1885-193
Watercolour painter. b. Christchurch, New Zealand. Studied London and Paris and under P. Tudor-Hart 1911-14. R.B.A 1910. Exh. 1910-28. Add: London † L 2, LEI 61, NEA 1, RBA 12.

MERVYN, A. Sonia Exh. 1935-4
Painter and teacher. London. † P 3, RA 5 RBA 1, ROI 1.

MERVYN, R. Grahame Exh. 1930-3
Landscape painter. Add: 2 Parkhi Studios, London. † COO 2, GOU 1 ROI 1.

MERWART, Paul Exh. 1885-8
13 Avenue Frochot, Paris. † GI 2.

MERY, Eugene Exh. 188
136 Wellington Street, Glasgow. † GI 1

MERY, Paul Exh. 190
15 Rue Hegesippe Moreau, Paris. † L 1.

MESDAG, Mme. c. 1834-190
nee Van Houten. Landscape and flowe painter. Add: The Hague, Holland † AG 2, BG 1, GI 6.

ESDAG, Hendrik William* 1831-1915
Dutch landscape painter. Add: The Hague, Holland. † D 4, G 2, GI 34, I 5, L 10, M 6, NG 2, RA 7.

ESDAG, Jaco Exh. 1887-92
The Hague, Holland 1887; Scheveningen 1889. † GI 5.

ESHAM, J.B. Exh. 1931
Linocut artist. † RED 1.

ESLE, Joseph Paul 1885-1927
French artist. Exh. 1912-13. Add: Par la Forte sous Jouarre, Champigny. † RSA 2.

ESS, N. Exh. 1891
Sculptor. Add: Scheveningen, Holland. † L 1, RA 1.

ESSELL, Oliver b. 1905
Painter and theatre and ballet designer. Studied Slade School. Exh. 1938. † LEI 37, RED 4.

ESSER, A.A. Exh. 1909-10
Architect. Add: 5 The Broadway, Woking, Surrey. † RA 2.

ESSER, Mabel B. Exh. 1910-40
Miniature portrait and flower painter. London. † AB 1, LS 9, RA 5, RI 14, RMS 1, SWA 1.

ESSINESI, Aristides A. b. 1891
Maker of tapestry brocades and rugs. b. Patras, Greece. Studied Byam Shaw School, Polytechnic Central School of Arts and Crafts, Slade School, R.C.A. (for short periods 1910-22), Luther Hooper Weaving Studios (1923-26). Exh. 1928. Add: Staplands Neston, Cheshire. † L 4.

ESTRE, de See D

ESTROVIC, Ivan 1883-1962
Sculptor. b. Otavice, Jugoslavia. Apprenticed at age 15 to a master mason in Split, went to Vienna a year later where he obtained an appointment with Helmer. Studied Vienna Academy of Arts. Exh. 1915-20. Add: Cromwell Court Hotel, Cromwell Road, South Kensington, London. † GI 9, GOU 1, RSA 22.

MESURIER, le See L

METCALF, Miss Exh. 1909
Leamington, Warwicks. † SWA 1.

METCALF, Mrs. Exh. 1920
135 Fellowes Road, London. † SWA 2.

METCALF, Elizabeth M. Exh. 1921-24
Holmcrest, Lyndhurst Road, Wallasey. † L 5.

METCALF, Sophia J. Exh. 1925-27
Holmcrest, Lyndhurst Road, Wallasey. † L 3.

METCALFE, Florence Exh. 1895-1910
The Elms, Ringwood, Hants. † LS 9, SWA 6.

METCALFE, Gerald Fenwick Exh. 1894-1929
Portrait painter, miniaturist, mural painter, pen and ink illustrator and modeller. b. Landour, N.W.P. India. Studied South Kensington, St. John's Wood School and R.A. Schools. Add: London 1894; Southampton 1908; Albury, Guildford, Surrey 1910. † L 4, NEA 1, NG 2, RA 21, RBA 1, RMS,1, RSA 1.

METCALFE, H.M. Exh. 1881
5 Rathmines Road, Dublin. † RHA 1.

METCALFE, Kathleen Isabella See MACKIE

METCALFE, Muriel Exh. 1932
Castle Bolton, Redmire, Yorks. † GI 2.

METCALFE, Percy Exh. 1921-38
Sculptor and medalist. Add: Barnes, Surrey. † GI 4, RA 6.

METCHIM, Donald Bridgman Exh. 1909-14
Courtlands, Nightingale Lane, Clapham Common, London. † LS 19.

METEYARD, Sidney Harold 1868-1947
Decorative painter and stained glass artist. b. Stourbridge. Studied Birmingham School of Art. R.B.S.A. 1908. Add: Birmingham. † B 34, L 7, NG 2, RA 20.

METEYARD, T.B. Exh. 1922-29
Watercolour landscape painter. † D 1, FIN 71.

METGE, Geraldine Exh. 1909-23
Killinure, Athlone. † L 2, RHA 4.

METHERINGHAM, A. Exh. 1910-11
The Limes, Chilwell, Notts. † N 3.

METHLING, Louis Exh. 1885
50 Rue Perronnet, Seine, France. † GI 2.

METHUEN, Lord b. 1886
4th Baron, Paul Ayshford. Landscape and figure painter. Trustee National Gallery and Tate Gallery 1938-45. R.B.A. 1938. Add: Melksham, Wilts. 1929; London 1931; Corsham Court, Wilts. 1939. † CG 38, LEI 37, NEA 6, RA 19, RBA 13, RED 3.

METHUEN, C.W. Exh. 1883
80 Union Street, Greenock. † GI 1.

METHUEN, Miss E. Exh. 1889-93
Portrait and figure painter. London. † RID 15, SWA 2.

METHUEN, Florence Exh. 1897-1902
Miniature portrait painter. Add: East Ham, Essex 1897; Maida Vale, London 1902. † RA 1, RI 1.

METSON, J.C. Exh. 1929-38
Birmingham. † B 23.

METZ, de See D

METZMACHER, Emile Exh. 1883
Figure painter. Add: 6 Penywern Road, London. † RA 1.

MEUGENS, Sibyl Exh. 1917-37
Painter. London. † GOU 2, I 5, L 6, RA 1, SWA 2.

MEULEN, Francois Pieter Ter* b. 1843
Dutch painter. Exh. 1882-1912. Add: The Hague, Holland. † FIN 2, GI 2, M 2.

MEUNIER, Mme. C. Exh. 1885-1901
Paris 1885; Brussels 1901. † GI 2, I 1.

MEUNIER, Henri Exh. 1907
33 Rue Claude Bernard, Paris. † L 1.

MEUNIER, Marc Henry Exh. 1908
13 Rue de la Levure, Ixelles, Brussels. † LS 6.

MEUTE, C. Exh. 1881
54 Bedford Gardens, Kensington, London. † D 1.

MEVILL, Harold Exh. 1924
† D 1.

MEW, Anne Exh. 1908-19
Flower and miniature portrait painter. Add: 6 Hogarth Studios, 64 Charlotte Street, Fitzroy Square, London. † L 4, RA 3.

MEW, Leonard Exh. 1929
Watercolour landscape painter. "Engadine", Rufford Road, Sherwood, Nottingham. † N 2.

MEWTON, I.R. Exh. 1933
Liverpool. † RCA 2.

MEWTON, Mrs. Zita Exh. 1932-33
Liverpool. † L 1, RCA 1.

MEY, Van der See V

MEYBURG, H. van der Kloot Exh. 1936
† RSA 1.

MEYER, Astrid Exh. 1930-31
Linocut artist. † RED 2.

MEYER, Adolph C. Exh. 1888-1918
Etcher. A.R.E. 1899-1919. Add: New Brighton, Cheshire 1888; Liverpool 1893; Conway, N. Wales 1896. † B 19, L 71, RA 11, RCA 94, RE 25, RI 1, ROI 1.

MEYER, Beatrice Exh. 1880-99
Historical and figure painter. Add: London. † B 1, L 3, M 3, RA 1, RBA 17, RHA 1, RI 5, ROI 7.

MEYER, Constance Exh. 1882-84
Flower painter. Add: London. † D 2.

MEYER, Mrs. Cornelia Exh. 1894-1902
Miniature portrait painter. Add: Hampton Wick 1894; and 1901; Fairfield, Liverpool 1899. † L 1, RA 2, RMS 1.

MEYER, Miss Connie H.E. Exh. 1899-1901
Miniature portrait painter. Add: Parkside, Hampton Wick. † RA 1, RMS 1.

MEYER, F.W. Exh. 1880-95
Landscape and coastal painter. Add: London. † M 2, RA 1, RBA 16, ROI 3.

MEYER, Hans 1846-1919
German etcher. R.E. 1881. Exh. 1881. † RE 3.

MEYER, Julia Exh. 1893-1907
Figure painter. Add: London. † L 3, M 2, RA 5, RBA 4, ROI 4, SWA 9.

MEYER, Louis Exh. 1907
3 Pakenham Road, Edgbaston, Birmingham. † B 1.

MEYER, Mrs. Louise Exh. 1936-37
† RMS 2.

MEYER, Margaret Exh. 1883-86
Flower and figure painter. Add: 3 Princes Gardens, Clapham Common, London. † RA 1, RBA 1, ROI 1.

MEYER, Mary H. Exh. 1882-85
Flower painter. Add: 3 Princes Gardens, Clapham Common, London. † RBA 1, ROI 1.

MEYER, Sylvia Exh. 1914-1916
Figure and portrait painter. Add: 25 Cheyne Walk, London. † NEA 4.

MEYERHEIM, Paul* 1842-1915
German painter. Add: Berlin. † B 1, FIN 1, L 1, M 1, NG 1, RI 2.

MEYERHEIM, Robert Gustave 1847-1920
German landscape painter. Studied under H. Gude and Oswald Achenbach. Settled in England 1876. R.I. 1898. Add: London 1880; Cookham Dean, Berks. 1881; Hastings 1882; Guildford, Surrey 1887; Horsham, Sussex 1889. † BG 1, GI 3, L 26, M 1, RA 41, RBA 6, RE 2, RI 71, ROI 3.

MEYEROWITZ, William b. 1889
Etcher. b. Russia. Exh. 1930. † FIN 9.

MEYNIAC, Mrs. C. Egan Exh. 1924
Clare Cottage, Limerick, Ireland. † RHA 2.

MEYRICK, Arthur Exh. 1903-14
Add: Wargrave, Berks. 1903; Hartfield, Sussex 1908. † D 52.

MEYRICK, Myra Exh. 1886-91
Watercolour landscape painter. Add: Blickling Rectory, Aylsham, Norfolk. † L 1, RA 1, RHA 1, RI 3.

MEZZARA, Charles Exh. 1886-1890
Portrait painter. Add: 19 Quai St. Michel, Paris. † GI 1, RA 1.

MEZZARA, Francois Exh. 1883
4 Rue de Grands Degres, Paris. † GI 1.

MICALI, Giuseppe Exh. 1889-1907
Add: Rome 1889; Liverpool 1907. † L 3.

MICH, Jean Exh. 1924
Sculptor. Add: 39 Route d'Orleans, Arcueil, Seine, France. † GI 1, L 1, RA 1.

MICHAEL, A.C. Exh. 1905-9
Painter and etcher. Add: 37 Bath Road, Bedford Park, London. † RA 11, RI 1.

MICHAEL, Frederick Howard Exh. 1892-1929
Landscape and portrait painter. Add: London. † L 3, LS 3, M 1, RA 19, RBA 1, RMS 4, ROI 4.

MICHAEL, Max Exh. 1882
27 Grosvenor Road, London. † RSA 1.

MICHAEL, W.A. Exh. 1887-94
Landscape painter. Add: 14 Bramham Gardens, South Kensington, London. † ROI 6.

MICHAELSON, Assur Exh. 1895-1913
Painter. R.B.A. 1905. Add: London. † P 1, RA 4, RBA 26.

MICHEL, Charles Exh. 1910-11
6 Rue Jacques Jordaens, Brussels. † L 3, RA 1.

MICHEL, Marius Exh. 1884
148 New Bond Street, London. † M 1.

MICHELL, E. Gabriel Exh. 1896
Poplar Avenue, Edgbaston, Birmingham. † B 1.

MICHEL-LEVY, Henri Exh. 1901
42 Rue de Bougainvilliers, Paris. † L 1.

MICHELMORE, Arthur Cecil Exh. 1900
Congowes Wood College, Sallins. † RHA 1.

MICHETTI, Francesco Paolo 1851-1929
Italian artist. Exh. 1882. Add: 117 New Bond Street, London. † L 1.

MICHIE, James Coutts 1861-1919
Landscape and portrait painter. Studied in Edinburgh, Rome and Paris. Brother of Mary M. q.v. R.O.I. 1901, A.R.S.A. 1893. Add: Edinburgh 1880; Aberdeen 1888; London 1895; Haslemere, Surrey 1912. † B 2, FIN 21, G 3, GI 27, L 27, LEI 10, M 14, NG 29, P 4, RA 45, RBA 2, ROI 18, RSA 99.

MICHIE, John D. Exh. 1880-92
Landscape painter. Add: Edinburgh. † GI 8, RSA 42.

MICHIE, Mrs. John D. Exh. 1880
Figure painter. Add: 8 St. Peters Place, Viewforth, Edinburgh. † SWA 1.

MICHIE, Mary Coutts Exh. 1890-97
Flower painter. Add: Aberdeen 1890; London 1897. † GI 1, L 1, RA 1, RSA 2.

MICHIE, T.S. Exh. 1880-81
Cudzow Street, Hamilton. † GI 2.

MICHL, Ferdinand Exh. 1906-8
18 Boulevard Edgar Quinet, Paris. † I 3, L 2.

MICHOLLS, Mrs. Ada Montefiore Exh. 1903-23
nee Beddington. Portrait and landscape painter. Studied Royal College of Art (3 silver and bronze medals). Add: London. † G 4, RA 5, RI 1, SWA 2.

MICKLETHWAITE, John Thomas. c.1843-1906
Architect to Westminster Abbey. Exh. 1881. Add: 6 Delahay Street, Great George Street, London. † RA 1.

MICOCCI, G. Exh. 1887
8 St. Martins Place, Trafalgar Square, London. † G 1.

MICOCCI, Joseph Exh. 1911-13
Landscape painter. † ALP 9.

MIDDLECOAT, George Keith de Blois b. 1896
Portrait, landscape, still life painter and poster artist. b. Herne Hill. Studied London School of Art and R.A. Schools. Exh. 1928. Add: 31 Queen Anne's Grove, Bedford Park, London. † RA 1.

MIDDLEDITCH, Frank Exh. 1933-34
Landscape painter. Add: 218 Adelaide Road, Hampstead, London. † NEA 1, RA 1.

MIDDLEMAS, A. Exh. 1895-1902
2 St. Peters Place, Viewforth, N.B. † RSA 3.

MIDDLEMORE, Miss S. Exh. 1909-19
Barnsley Hall, Bromsgrove, Worcs. † L 6, RSA 2.

MIDDLETON, A. Exh. 1918-20
167 Georgory Boulevard, Nottingham. † N 6.

MIDDLETON, Blanche Exh. 1897-1900
Sister of Nellie and May M. q.v. Add: 116 Belgrave Road, Edgbaston, Birmingham. † B 4.

MIDDLETON, Colin Exh. 1938-40
Landscape painter. Add: 28 Chichester Avenue, Antrim Road, Belfast. † RHA 5.

MIDDLETON, Mrs. E. Exh. 1884
6 Villa Road, Handsworth, Birmingham. † B 1.

MIDDLETON, Etta Exh. 1909-11
Miniature portrat painter. Add: Hoby, Leicester 1909; St. Albans, Herts. 1911. † L 1, RA 2, RMS 1.

MIDDLETON, Fanny Exh. 1881-97
Watercolour landscape painter. Sister of Mary E. M. q.v. Add: York 1881 and 1886; Maida Vale, London 1884. † B 3, D 3, DOW 1, L 1, M 1, RBA 1, RI 1, SWA 11.

MIDDLETON, F. Warren Exh. 1893
67 Finchley Road, London. † L 1.

MIDDLETON, Mrs. F. Warren Exh. 1893
67 Finchley Road, London. † B 1.

MIDDLETON, George Exh. 1899-1911
Add: Leeds 1899 and 1903; Wainfleet, Lincs. 1902. † B 5, L 4, M 6, RBA 5, RCA 3, RHA 3, RSA 2.

MIDDLETON, H. Exh. 1910-28
Figure painter. Add: 57 Mandalay Street, Basford, Nottingham. † N 6.

MIDDLETON, Horace Exh. 1902-19
Portrait and figure painter. R.B.A. 1911. Add: Withington, Manchester 1902; London 1904 and 1919; Southend on Sea, Essex 1917. † B 2, L 3, M 3, RA 5, RBA 39.

MIDDLETON, Miss H.E.E. Exh. 1906-8
Twickenham 1906; Stanwell, nr. Staines 1907. † B 2, L 1, RMS 2,.

MIDDLETON, H.O. Exh. 1920-26
Landscape painter. Add: 98 Queens Road, Beeston, Notts. † N 11.

MIDDLETON, Helen Regina Exh. 1911-29
Still life, flower and landscape painter. Add: Kensington Park Road, London. † LS 9, NEA 13, RA 2.

MIDDLETON, James Exh. 1893
8 Grosvenor Crescent, Edinburgh. † RSA 1.

MIDDLETON, Janet Exh. 1906
Manorhead, Stow, Midlothian. † GI 1.

MIDDLETON, James C. b. 1894
Painter, engraver, metal worker, jeweller, and art master. b. Redruth. Studied Royal College of Art, Redruth School of Art and Birmingham School of Art. Exh. 1933-38. Add: Wallington, Surrey. † RA 1, ROI 1.

MIDDLETON, John Henry 1846-1896
Architect. Slade professor of Fine Art, Cambridge 1886. Director Fitzwilliam Museum, Cambridge 1889-92 and art director South Kensington Museum 1892-96. Exh. 1882. Add: 48 Storey's Gate, St. James Park, London. † RA 1.

MIDDLETON, James Raeburn b. 1855
Portrait and landscape painter. Travelled widely. Exh. 1887-1928. Add: Glasgow. † B 1, GI 57, GOU 2, L 5, M 1, RA 6, RBA 1, RSA 4, RSW 2.

MIDDLETON, Katherine Exh. 1890-91
Landscape painter. Add: 26 North Street, Wandsworth, London. † RBA 2.

MIDDLETON, Kathleen Joy Exh. 1925-36
Scarborough 1925; West Ayton, Yorks. 1929. † NEA 1, RCA 7.

MIDDLETON, May Exh. 1895-97
Sister of Blanche and Nellie M. q.v. Add: 116 Belgrave Road, Birmingham. † B 3.

MIDDLETON, Mary E. Exh. 1881-97
Watercolour landscape painter. Sister of Fanny M. q.v. Add: York 1881 and 1886; London 1884. † B 1, D 4, DOW 1, M 1, RA 1, RBA 2, RI 1, SWA 12.

MIDDLETON, Nellie Exh. 1894-97
Sister of Blanche and May M. q.v. Add: 116 Belgrave Road, Edgbaston, Birmingham. † B 5.

MIDDLETON, O. Exh. 1912
7 Standard Bank Buildings, Port Elizabeth, S. Africa. † RA 1.

MIDDLETON, Miss W. Exh. 1918
Queens Gate, London. † SWA 1.

MIDFORTH, Charles Henry Exh. 1884-91
Painter. Add: London. † RA 5, RBA 1, ROI 3.

MIDGLEY, A. Exh. 1907
46 Leicester Street, Hunslet, Leeds. † RA 1.

MIDGLEY, J.H. Exh. 1883
18 Hope Terrace, Edinburgh. † RSA 1.

MIDGLEY, J.T. Exh. 1916
Brambleshaw, Harrogate, Yorks. † RA 1.

MIDGLEY, William d. 1933
Painter and sculptor. Headmaster of Aston School of Art. R.B.S.A. 1906. Add: Birmingham 1899; Aston 1902; Sutton Coldfield 1905. † B 16, RA 2.

MIDWOOD, Alfred Exh. 1911-25
Ditchfield Road, Hough Green, nr. Widnes. † L 7.

MIDWOOD, Florence Exh. 1901-12
Mrs. Fleming. Animal painter. Add: Holmgarth, Henfield, Sussex. † L 1, M 3, WG 7.

MIDWOOD, F. Toft Exh. 1893-98
Knutsford, Cheshire. † L 1, M 4.

MIDWOOD, Miss Lilly Exh. 1897
Sculptor. Add: Brierwood, Knutsford, Cheshire. † RA 1.

MIDWOOD, Miss M. Exh. 1884-88
Cheadle, Cheshire. † M 10.

MIDY, Arthur b. 1877
French artist. Exh. 1912. Add: 68 Rue de L'Assumption, Paris. † L 1, RA 2.

MIELICH, Alphonse Exh.. 1891-93
Figure painter. Add: Paris 1891; Vienna 1893. † RA 2, RBA 1.

MIETHER, Antonie Exh. 1884-85
Painter. Add: 89 Wilberforce Road, Finsbury Park, London. † SWA 2.

MIEVILLE, Mrs. Emma Exh. 1933
Watercolour painter. Add: Cudlow House, Rustington, Sussex. † RA 1.

MIGL, de See D

MIGNON, A. Exh. 1908
c/o Frost and Reed, 8 Clare Street, Bristol. † RA 1.

MIGNOT, V. Exh. 1911
30 Avenue d'Orleans, Paris. † L 1.

MILBANKE, Mark Richard 1875-1927
Portrait painter. London. † B 2, L 23, M 2, P 3, RA 21, RHA 3, RSA 1.

MILCENDEAU, C. Exh. 1901-11
Add: Paris 1901; Vendee, France 1905. † I 15.

MILCH, Dr. Eugen Exh. 1927
Landscape painter. † AB 141.

MILDMAY, Miss C.E. Exh. 1893
4 Rosary Gardens, London. † D 1.

MILDMAY, C. St. John Exh. 1880-87
Watercolour landscape painter. Add: London. † D 9, L 2, RBA 2.

MILDMAY, Mabel St. John Exh. 1901-32
Mrs. Walter M. Watercolour landscape painter. Studied at Antwerp Academy and London. Add: Painswick, Glos. 1901; Dursley, Glos. 1905. † B 1, COO 2, D 21, RI 5, SWA 6, WG 189.

MILDMAY, Walter St. John Exh. 1899-1905
Figure painter. Add: Compton, Guildford, Surrey 1899; Painswick, Glos. 1901. † B 3, D 5, RA 1.

MILEHAM, Charles Henry Money Exh. 1882-1906
Architect. London. † RA 16.

MILEHAM, Harry Robert b. 1873
Portrait and historical figure painter and decorative painter for churches. Studied Lambeth Art School and R.A. Schools (gold medal and travelling studentship for historical painting 1895). Exh. 1896-1934. Add: London 1896 and 1906; Beckenham, Kent 1898; Hove, Sussex 1918. † GI 1, L 16, M 1, NG 13, RA 16, RCA 3.

MILEHAM, Mary L. Exh. 1899-1905
Miniature portrait painter. Add: London. † L 2, NG 2, RA 3.

MILES, Agnes Exh. 1933-39
Cardiff. † RCA 7.

MILES, Arthur Exh. 1880-83
Portrait and genre painter. Add: 18 Patshull Road, Kentish Town, London. † RBA 2, TOO 1.

MILES, Annie Stewart Exh. 1888-1907
Mme. Albert. Landscape and flower painter. Add: London. † L 1, RA 16, RBA 2, RSA 2, SWA 3.

MILES, Clarina Exh. 1907
59 Egerton Gardens, London. † SWA 2.

MILES, C. Isadore Exh. 1904
Miniature portrait painter. Add: Enmore, Burnt Ash Hill, Lee, Kent. † RA 1.

MILES, F. Exh. 1880
Bingham, Notts. † N 1.

MILES, George Francis (Frank) 1852-1891
Portrait, genre and marine painter. Add: Llangraviog, Cardiganshire 1880; Chelsea, London 1882. † BG 1, G 2, M 7, RA 14.

MILES, Helen Jane Arundel Exh. 1883
Watercolour illustrative painter. Add: 54 South Lambeth Road, Clapham, London. † M 1.

MILES, J.T. Exh. 1897
30 Lower Mount Street, Dublin. † RHA 1.

MILES, Leonidas Clint Exh. 1880-83
Landscape and architectural painter. 24 Marquis Road, Camden Square, London. † RA 1, RBA 4.

MILES, Maurice A. Exh. 1931
Painter. 6 St. Johns Wood Studios, London. † RA 1.

MILES, Miss R.H. Exh. 1892-1910
Dublin 1892; Sandycove 1894. † RHA 55.

MILES, T.G.H. Exh. 1881-82
Flower, figure and landscape painter. 79 Newman Street, London. † RBA 1, RHA 1.

MILES, Thomas Rose* Exh. 1880-1906
Landscape and coastal painter. London 1880 and 1905; Dublin 1895. † RA 5, RBA 2, RHA 8, TOO 1.

MILESI, Alessandro* b.1856
Italian painter. Exh. 1890-1905. Add: Ognissanti 1450, Venice. † GI 2, RA 1.

MILEY, R. Exh. 1881-88
Dublin. † RHA 14.

MILL, Alex George Exh. 1904
121 St. Vincent Street, Glasgow. † GI 1,

MILLAIS, Everett Exh. 1888-89
Sculptor. 31 Grosvenor Road, Westminster, London. † NG 2.

MILLAIS, H. Raoul* Exh. 1928-36
Landscape, animal and sporting painter. † FIN 101.

MILLAIS, Sir John Everett 1829-1896
Painter, watercolourist and illustrator. Studied under Henry Sass from 1838 and R.A. Schools from 1840. Exhibited his first work at the R.A. in 1846 at age 16. Member of the Pre-Raphaelite Brotherhood. R.P. 1893, A.R.A. 1853, R.A. 1863, P.R.A. 1896, H.R.I. 1896, H.R.S.A. 1866. In 1885 became the first British artist to be made a Baronet. "Speak! Speak!" purchased by Chantrey Bequest 1895 and "Hearts are Trumps" (1872) purchased in 1945. Add: London. † AG 5, B 8, FIN 1, G 19, GI 3, L 6, M 35, NG 7, P 16, RA 70, RCA 1, RHA 6, RSA 13, TOO 5.

MILLAIS, John Guille 1865-1931
Painter, sculptor and author. † FIN 112.

MILLAIS, William Henry* 1828-1899
Landscape painter and watercolourist. Brother of John Everett M q.v. Add: Wardhill, Farnham, Surrey. † AG 5, D 1, FIN 5, M 1, RA 4, RI 10, TOO 2.

MILLAR, Alice J Exh. 1897
8 Garway Road, Westbourne Grove, London. † RMS 1.

MILLAR, E.C. Frenes Exh. 1938
Tollcross, Glasgow. † GI 1.

MILLAR, Fred Exh. 1915-23
Etcher. 32 Museum Street, London. † RA 2.

MILLAR, F.H.C. Exh. 1893
The Bryn, Trevone, Padstow, Cornwall. † L 1.

MILLAR, Mrs. G.D. Exh. 1928-31
Portrait and landscape painter. 56 Belmont Avenue, Donnybrook, Dublin. † RHA 6.

MILLAR, Harold R Exh. 1892-1903
Painter and illustrator. Upper Tooting, London. † RA 3.

MILLAR, James H.C. Exh. 1884-1903
Landscape and marine painter. London. † B 1, L 3, M 1, RA 5, ROI 1, RSA 1.

MILLAR, J.N. Exh. 1884
8 St. David's Road, Carnarvon. † B 1.

MILLAR, L. Roger Exh. 1893-96
7 Albert Drive, Queen's Park, Glasgow. † GI 3.

MILLAR, M.G. Exh. 1902
Brook Lawn, Blackrock, Dublin. † RHA 2.

MILLAR, Mrs. Nevinson Exh. 1918-19
Killarney Wood, Bray. † RHA 4.

MILLAR, Robins Exh. 1918
67 Hope Street, Glasgow. † GI 2.

MILLAR, Mrs. R.C. Exh. 1899
Brook Lawn, Blackrock, Dublin. † RHA 1.

MILLAR, T. Andrew Exh. 1904-19
Glasgow. † GI 3.

MILLARD, Elsie M. Exh. 1893-1916
Mrs. O'Keefe. Landscape and miniature portrait painter. London 1893; Rathmines, Dublin 1904. † L 3, NG 1, RA 5, RBA 1, RHA 19, RI 1, SWA 2.

MILLARD, Fred* Exh.1882-1910
Genre painter. R.B.A. 1893. Add: London 1882 and 1892; Newlyn, Penzance, Cornwall 1885; Falmouth, Cornwall 1904. † B 4, DOW 3, L 1, M 1, RA 4, RBA 56, ROI 7.

MILLARD, Patrick Ferguson b. 1902
Animal and landscape painter. b. Aspatria. Studied Liverpool School of Art and R.A. Schools (R.A. gold medallist and Edwin Stott travelling scholarship). Principal St. Johns Wood Art Schools. R.B.A. 1928. Exh. 1924-38. Add: Cold Norton, Chelmsford, Essex 1924; London 1928. † BA 2, BK 74, L 1, RA 2, RBA 75.

MILLARD, Walter J.N. Exh. 1881-1920
Architect. London 1881; Hitchen, Herts. 1920. † D 1, RA 10.

MILLER, Alec b. 1879
Sculptor. b. Glasgow. Teacher of drawing and sculpture Campden School of Arts and Crafts 1902-14, and Oxford City School of Art 1912-23. A.R.M.S. 1921. Exh. 1920-35. Add: The Studio, Campden, Glos. † B 10, GI 4, L 5, RA 12, RMS 3, RSA 2.

MILLER, Alfred Exh. 1898-1909
115 Mulberry Street, Liverpool. † L 3.

MILLER, Alfred A. Exh. 1923-35
107 Gough Road, edgbaston, Birmingham. † B 3.

MILLER, Arch. E. Haswell b.1887
Painter. Studied Glasgow School of Art 1906-9 and Munich 1909-10. Keeper of the National Galleries of Scotland 1930. Married Josephine Heswell M. q.v. R.S.W. 1924. Exh. 1906-34. Add: Glasgow. † AR 2, GI 18, L 6, RA 5, RSA 23, RSW 26.

MILLER, Alexander G Exh. 1885-95
Bettws-y-Coed, Wales 1885; London 1890. † M 4, RA 1.

MILLER, Albert J. Exh. 1922-32
Sculptor. c/o Miss Simonson, 129 Queen's Gate, London. † RA 8, RI 2.

MILLER, Bernard A. Exh. 1929-33
Architect. School of Architecture, Liverpool University. † L 8.

MILLER, Mrs. B. Bell Exh. 1913
Pembroke Square, London. † SWA 1.

MILLER, Miss B.M. Exh. 1907-16
Sunnycroft, Snakes Lane, Woodford Green, Essex. † L 1, RA 7, RI 3, SWA 2.

MILLER, Catherine Exh. 1926-33
4 Erskine Hill, London. † L 23, RMS 4.

MILLER, Capt. C.K. Exh. 1888
Glasgow. † RSA 1.

MILLER, C.R. Leslie Exh. 1907-8
26 Dean Terrace, Kilmarnock, N.B. † GI 3.

MILLER, Charles S Exh. 1883-91
Coastal painter. c/o Hill, 151 Essex Road, London. † B 8, L 5, M 7, RA 7, RBA 12, RI 3, ROI 3.

MILLER, Dorothy Exh. 1910-13
Hollywood, Carrickmines, Co. Dublin. † RHA 4.

MILLER, Drew Exh. 1928-29
Landscape painter. c/o A.C. Stewart, 3 Gunter Hall, Gunter Grove, London. † AB 3, RBA 3.

MILLER, Ethel G, Exh. 1922-26
c/o Miss Clark, York Chambers, King Street, Nottingham. † N 3.

MILLER, E.J. Exh. 1891
Landscape painter. 19 Appach Road, Brixton Hill, London. † RI 1.

MILLER, E.M. Exh. 1906
3 Millbank Street, Westminster, London. † D 1.

MILLER, Francis Exh. 1886
Landscape painter. Barnsbury, London. † ROI 1.

MILLER, Fred Exh. 1886-97
Engraver. London. † RA 5.

MILLER, Frederick Exh. 1880-92
Marine painter. Father of William Ongley M. q.v. Add: West Brighton 1880; Burgess Hill, Sussex 1882; Haywards Heath, Sussex 1884. † L 4, RA 1, RBA 1, RI 3.

MILLER, Frederick Exh. 1939
Tolesa, Lymington, Hants. † RI 1.

MILLER, F.J.W. Exh. 1884
Architect. London. † L 2.

MILLER, Felix Martin Exh. 1880
Sculptor. 16 Victoria Grove, Fulham Road, London. † RA 1.

MILLER, George Exh. 1889-98
Hillhead, Glasgow. † GI 9, RSA 5.

MILLER, Guy Exh. 1911-37
Painter and stained glass artist. Curator of the South London Art Gallery. Add: London. † P 1, RA 18.

MILLER, George M. Exh. 1880-81
3 Osborne Terrace, Govan. † GI 2.

MILLER, G.W. Exh. 1890-96
Flower painter. Whitehouse, Chislehurst, Kent. † RA 2, RBA 5.

MILLER, H. Exh. 1928
Landscape painter. † AB 2.

MILLER, Harrison Exh. 1889-1933
Figure and domestic painter. R.M.S. 1903. Add: Clifton Hampden, Abingdon, Berks. 1891; Bray 1895; London 1903; Chertsey, Surrey 1911; Cold Waltham, Pulborough, Sussex 1928. † B 1, L 3, NG 1, RA 9, RBA 7, RHA 5, RI 2, RMS 26, ROI 5.

MILLER, Henrietta Exh. 1880-1907
Flower, figure and landscape painter. A.S.W.A. 1889. Add: London. † G 1, L 1, RA 1, RBA 2, RI 2, SWA 34.

MILLER, H.A. Exh. 1909-17
Sculptor. 1 Thorpe Dene, Norwich. † RA 4.

MILLER, Miss H.I. Exh. 1918
† SWA 2.

MILLER, Mrs. Hilda T. Exh. 1918-21
Painter. Lindean, Harpenden, Herts. † RA 1, RSA 6.

MILLER, Miss J. Exh. 1883
23 South Tay Street, Dundee. † RSA 2.

MILLER, James b. 1860
Architect. A.R.S.A. 1906, R.S.A. 1931. Exh. 1887-1938. Add: Edinburgh 1887; Glasgow 1893. † GI 25, RA 3, RSA 50.

MILLER, James b. 1893
Painter. Studied Glasgow School of Art. R.S.W. 1934. Exh. 1922-40. Add: Glasgow. † GI 24, RSA 25, RSW 32.

MILLER, John Exh. 1880-1909
Figure and landscape painter. 40 West Nile Street, Glasgow. † B 1, G 1, GI 64, L 1, RA 2.

MILLER, J.C. Exh. 1887
43 Abingdon Villas, Kensington, London. † D 1.

MILLER, John D. Exh. 1882-1903
Engraver. London 1882; Barnet, Herts. 1893. † RA 16.

MILLER, J. Hutcheson Exh. 1880-93
Hamilton 1880; Glasgow 1890. † GI 5, RSA 1.

MILLER, Josephine Haswell b. 1890
Painter, etcher and teacher of etching. Studied Glasgow School of Art. A.R.S.A. 1939. Married Arch. E. Haswell M. q.v. Exh. 1919-39. Add: Glasgow. † GI 16, L 3, M 1, RA 3, RSA 26, RSW 3.

MILLER, J. Jerome Exh. 1912-15
73 Westoe Road, South Shields. † GI 1, L 3, RA 1, RSA 1.

MILLER, James J. Exh. 1905
1A Hawthorn Terrace, Birmingham. † B 1.

MILLER, Jessie J.A.J. Exh. 1882-88
Miniature painter. London. † RA 6, RSA 1.

MILLER, J. Nina b. 1895
Painter and black and white artist, and teacher. Studied Glasgow School of Art, France and Italy. Married Charles Lamb Davidson q.v. Exh. 1922-35. Add: Glasgow. † GI 10, RSA 4, RSW 1.

MILLER, J.R. Exh. 1880-1912
Glasgow. † GI 18.

MILLER, John William Exh. 1936-40
Edinburgh. † RSA 2, RSW 1.

MILLER, Keith Exh. 1935-36
Bangor, Wales. † RCA 3.

MILLER, Kathleen Helen b. 1904
Flower and landscape painter. Studied Ipswich School of Art. Exh. 1925-35. Add: Woodbridge, Suffolk 1925; Martlesham, Suffolk 1928; Ipswich 1931; Kesgrave, Suffolk 1935. † RA 4.

MILLER, Linden Exh. 1938
Watercolour landscape painter. 38 Hogarth Road, London. † RA 1.

MILLER, Lucy Exh. 1892-99
London 1892; Spring Hill, Rugby 1893. † D 11, L 1, RHA 4, SWA 5.

MILLER, Lila W. Exh. 1915-40
Edinburgh. † GI 4, L 1, RSA 7, RSW 1.

MILLER, Maggie Exh. 1884
2 Ettrick Terrace, Kelvinside, Glasgow. † GI 1.

MILLER, Mrs. Marjorie Exh. 1935
53 Grosvenor Gardens, Woodford Green, Essex. † RI 1.

MILLER, Marmaduke b. 1900
Etcher, wood engraver and watercolour painter. Studied Skipton School of Art. Exh. 1938. Add: Arncliffe, nr. Skipton in Craven. † RA 1.

MILLER, Mary Backhouse Exh. 1880-96
nee Blackhouse, Figure painter. A.S.W.A. 1880. Married William E.M. q.v. Add: London. † B 17, L 2, M 1, RA 6, RBA 6, ROI 8, SWA 11.

MILLER, N.A.L. Exh. 1931-36
Watercolour painter. † WG 7.

MILLER, Philippa Exh. 1924
Old Mill House, Oulton Broad, Suffolk. † L 2.

MILLER, Miss P. Graham Exh. 1932
21 Lennox Street, Edinburgh. † RSA 1.

MILLER, Philip Homan d. 1928
Painter of genre, portraits and literary subjects. A.R.H.A. 1890. Married Mrs. Sophia M. q.v. Add: London 1880 and 1891; Dublin 1887. † B 2, L 8, LS 7, M 3, RA 9, RBA 6, RHA 59.

MILLER, Richard Exh. 1912
16 Rue Boissonade, Paris. † RSA 1.

MILLER, Robert Exh. 1897
24 Broughton Place, Edinburgh. † GI 1.

MILLER, Robert A. Exh. 1902
Stained glass artist. Studio, 26 Pilgrim Street, Newcastle on Tyne. † RA 1.

MILLER, Miss R. Binnie Exh. 1937
Crossford, Dunfermline. † GI 1.

MILLER, Robert R. Exh. 1934-40
3 Beaconsfield Terrace, Hawick. † RSA 6.

MILLER, Mrs. Sophia Exh. 1892-1928
Flower painter. Married Philip Homan M. q.v. Add: London. † BG 5, GI 1, L 6, M 1, RA 6, RBA 5, RHA 31, RI 5.

MILLER, Miss Sophia Exh. 1895-1929
Liverpool. † L 34.

MILLER, Stanley Exh. 1940
11 Kellie Place, Alloa. † GI 1.

MILLER, Sylvia Exh. 1929-30
Landscape painter. London. † AB 3, SWA 2.

MILLER, Sarah Alice Exh. 1881-97
Landscape and figure painter. London 1884 and 1896; Bishops Stortford, Herts. 1888. † RA 2, RBA 14, ROI 2, SWA 7.

MILLER, S. Houghton Exh. 1911-30
Edinburgh. † RSA 10.

MILLER, T. Henderson Exh. 1901
4 Harcourt Avenue, Seacombe, Cheshire. † L 1.

MILLER, T.M. Exh. 1886-99
New Brighton 1886; Liverpool 1889. † L 17.

MILLER, Major W. Exh. 1882
67 George Street, Edinburgh. † RSA 1.

MILLER, Walter Exh. 1894-1940
Kilmarnock, N.B. 1894; Glasgow 1895. † GI 67, RSA 1, RSW 3.

MILLER, William 1796-1882
Engraver and watercolour painter. A.R.S.A. 1826 (one of the 9 artists who withdrew after the first meeting). H.R.S.A. 1862. Exh. 1881. Add: Edinburgh. † RSA 1.

MILLER, William Exh. 1880-1932
Glasgow 1880; Bridge of Allan 1907; Edinburgh 1924; Prestwich 1929. † GI 62, RSA 6, RSW 8.

MILLER, William Exh. 1883-1906
Landscape painter. Glasgow 1883 and 1906; Milngavie 1900. † GI 27, L 3, RA 1, RSA 3.

MILLER, William E. Exh. 1880-1909
Portrait painter. Married Mary Backhouse M. q.v. Add: London. † B 1, G 2, L 1, NG 1, RA 18, RSA 2.

MILLER, William G. Exh. 1891-1908
Painter. Sandyford, Glasgow 1891 and 1902; London 1901. † GI 16, L 1, RA 6, RI 7.

MILLER, W. Muir Exh. 1892-94
Uddington 1892; Glasgow 1893. † GI 3.

MILLER, William Ongley b. 1883
Landscape and figure painter and architect. b. Haywards Heath, Sussex. Son of Frederick M. q.v. Studied Brighton School of Art and Royal College of Art (travelling scholarship in architecture 1908 and Owen Jones travelling studentship 1910), Manchester School of Art 1920-24. Headmaster Gravesend School of Art from 1924, design master Sheffield School of Art 1911-20. Exh. 1923-30. † L 1, M 2, RA 4.

MILLERS, Emma Townley Exh. 1901-39
Landscape painter. b. Northenden, Cheshire. Studied Slade School and Spenlove School of Painting. Add: West Didsbury, Manchester 1901; Tunbridge Wells, Kent 1924. † B 11, GI 1, L 8, LS 3, M 5, P 1, RA 1, RCA 15, SWA 6.

MILLES, Professor Carl 1875-1955
Swedish sculptor. Exh. 1927-39. Add: Lidingo Villastad, Sweden. † GI 1, RSA 1.

MILLET, Francis David* 1846-1912
American portrait, genre and fresco painter and illustrator. Studied under J. Van Lerins and N. de Keyser in Antwerp. R.O.I. 1885. "Between Two Fires" purchased by Chantrey Bequest 1892. Add: London 1883; Broadway, Worcs. 1891. Died in the sinking of the "Titanic". † B 1, L 12, M 2, NG 3, P 1, RA 20, ROI 13.

MILLETT, Lucy Constance Marian Exh. 1909-14
Portrait, landscape and figure painter, commercial artist, modeller and teacher. Studied Lambeth School of Art, South Kensington, R.A. Schools, France and Belgium. Add: Hampton Wick. † LS 12, SWA 5.

MILLEZ, Margaret Exh. 1900
Figure painter. Widdington, Newport, Essex. † NEA 2.

MILLHAM, Mary L. Exh. 1899
Hillcrest, West Hill, Sydenham, Kent. † L 1.

MILLICAN, Alice Lindley Exh. 1926
† M 1.

MILLIER, Herbert L. Exh. 1933-34
166 St. Paul's Road, Balsall Heath, Birmingham. † B 2.

MILLIER, James Exh. 1899
Architect. 9 Abbey Gardens, St. John's Wood, London. † RA 1.

MILLIGAN, A.F.M. Exh. 1900-6
Wallasey, Cheshire 1900; Liverpool 1901. † L 4.

MILLIGAN, Miss E.H. Exh. 1928
20 Village Road, Oxton, Birkenhead. † L 1.

MILLIGAN, Grace Exh. 1901
30 Hillside Road, Wallasey, Cheshire. † L 1.

MILLIGAN, Robert F. Exh. 1910-17
58 Bain Street East, Glasgow. † GI 5.

MILLIGAN, Thomas R. Exh. 1882-1902
Glasgow 1882; Greenock 1902. † GI 9, RSW 1.

MILLIKEN, J.W. Exh. 1887-1930
Liverpool. † L 50, RA 1, RCA 3.

MILLINGTON, Miss C.A. Exh. 1882-94
School Lane, Heaton Chapel, Stockport, Lancs. † L 2, M 16.

MILLIS, Edward Exh. 1897
41A Cathcart Road, South Kensington, London. † L 4.

MILLIS, Miss Eileen C.A. Exh. 1926-27
Sculptor. 84 Gregory Boulevard, Nottingham. † N 2.

MILLIS, Walter Exh. 1926-28
Portrait and miniature painter. 84 Gregory Boulevard, Nottingham. † N 8.

MILLMAKER, J. Exh. 1885
43 Gibson Street, Hillhead, Glasgow. † M 1.

MILLNER, William Edward 1849-1895
Genre and animal painter. Son of William M. (1818-1870). Add: Gainsborough, Lincs. † RA 8.

MILLONS, Thomas b. 1859
Marine and architectural painter and sailor. Exh. 1885-1927. Add: Edinburgh 1885; Tal-y-Cafn, Wales 1919; Lasswade, Midlothian 1927. † BG 2, L 1, RA 1, RCA 6, RSA 2, RSW 1.

MILLOR, Lizzie R. Exh. 1891
7 Albert Drive, Crosshill, Glasgow. † GI 1.

MILLS, A.H. Exh. 1905
33 Brazenose Street, Manchester. † RA 1.

MILLS, Arthur J. Exh. 1899-1909
Sculptor. London. † L 4, M 1, NG 3, RA 6, RHA 1, RSA 1.

MILLS, Miss A.S. Exh. 1889
15 Fitzroy Street, Fitzroy Square, London. † L 2.

MILLS, Arthur Stewart Hunt 1897-c.1971
Wood engraver, etcher and art master. Studied Goldsmiths College School of Art. A.R.E. 1934. Exh. 1933-39. Add: London. † RA 4, RE 14.

MILLS, Arthur Wallis 1878-1940
Illustrator. On staff of "Punch". Exh. 1895-99. Add: Long Bennington, Grantham, Lincs. 1895; London 1899. † N 1, RA 1.

MILLS, Charles A. d. 1922
A.R.H.A. 1913. Add: Dublin. † RHA 38.

MILLS, Dorothy G.H. Exh. 1919
Miniature portrait painter. Glen View, Harphill, Battledown, Cheltenham. † RA 1.

MILLS, Edward* Exh. 1882-1918
Landscape painter. Rome 1882; Edinburgh 1883; London 1890. † AG 1, B 7, L 3, M 4, P 1, RA 13, RI 2, ROI 1, RSA 3.

MILLS, Mrs. Ernestine d. 1959
nee Bell. Metalworker and enameller. Studied Slade School and Finsbury Central Technical School. A.S.W.A. 1919, S.W.A. 1920. Exh. 1900-40. Add: London. † L 63, RA 4, RMS 2, RSA 2, SWA 5.

MILLS, Elsie J.L. b. 1887
Wood carver and leather worker. Exh. 1925-29. Add: 22 Denmark Road, Southport, Lancs. † L 8.

MILLS, Emily S. Exh. 1882
17 Tennyson Street, Nottingham. † N 2.

MILLS, Fred C. Exh. 1884-91
Sculptor. London. † RA 2.

MILLS, Gordon Exh. 1933
Barry, Glamorgan. † RCA 2.

MILLS, H. Exh. 1893-97
19 Richmond Place, North Circular Road, Dublin. † RHA 4.

MILLS, John Exh. 1907
50 Kent Road, Glasgow. † GI 2.

MILLS, J.D. Exh. 1919
10 Tay Square, Dundee. † RSA 1.

MILLS, Miss Louie Exh. 1885-89
Landscape painter. Chester 1885; Blackheath, London 1889. † M 1, RI 1.

MILLS, Miss L.M. Exh. 1905-9
Coniston, Hale, Altrincham, Cheshire. † RCA 4.

MILLS, Reginald Exh. 1921-38
Portrait, landscape and coastal painter. R.B.A. 1930. Add: Cavendish Mansions, Mill Lane, West Hampstead, London. † RA 8, RBA 31, RI 2.

MILLS, Stewart Exh. 1930
Wood engraver. 3 Baxter Avenue, Southend-on-Sea, Essex. † L 1, RA 1.

MILLS, S.F. d. 1882
Watercolour painter. 27 Marylebone Road, London. † D 2, RA 1, RBA 3.

MILLS, William* Exh. 1882-88
Landscape painter. Birmingham and London. † B 10, RA 2, RBA 2, ROI 2.

MILLS, Walter C. Exh. 1880-84
Dublin. † RHA 6.

MILLSON, Frederick Exh. 1885-88
Landscape and figure painter. London 1885; Teddington, Middlesex 1888. † RA 1, RBA 2.

MILLWARD, A. Exh. 1887
Clifton, Ashbourne, Derbys. † GI 2.

MILMAN, Helen Exh. 1904
Mrs. Caldwell Crofton. Watercolour painter of landscapes and gardens. † FIN 55.

MILMAN, Sylvia Frances Exh. 1906-31
Mrs. J. Mills Witham. Painter, wood engraver, etcher and bookbinder. Studied R.A. Schools. Add: London. † ALP 11, GOU 8, I 1, LS 20, M 1, NEA 3, RA 3.

MILMINE, F.W. Exh. 1900-3
Black and white artist. N.S.W. 1908. Add: 8 King John's Chambers, Nottingham. † N 4.

MILMINE, Miss R. Exh. 1939
14 Teesdale Road, Sherwood, Nottingham. † N 1.

MILNE, Ada Dora see BURNE

MILNE, Arthur E. Exh. 1914-18
Edinburgh. † RSA 2.

MILNE, Miss A.N. Exh. 1896-1910
London. † B 2, RA 1, SWA 10.

MILNE, Catherine W. Exh. 1937
Park Terrace, 269 Blackness Road, Dundee. † RSA 1.

MILNE, Miss D.E.G. Exh. 1921-23
12 Gunter Grove, Chelsea, London. † L 5, RA 1.

MILNE, Dorothy S. Exh. 1935
42 Northway, London. † SWA 1.

MILNE, Ellis R. Exh. 1934-40
Edinburgh. † RSA 5.

MILNE, H.D. Exh. 1881
Fruit, flower and still life painter. Crayford. Kent. † RBA 1.

MILNE, Hilda L. Exh. 1906-40
Flower and still life painter. Sister of Malcolm M. q.v. Add: Cheadle, Cheshire 1906; London 1913; Henfield, Sussex 1934. † COO 1, L 2, M 10, NEA 7, RA 2.

MILNE, James d. 1918
Exh. 1913. 70 Beechgrove Terrace, Aberdeen. † RSA 1.

MILNE, Jean Exh. 1904-17
Sculptor. London. † GI 3, I 11, L 9, M 1, RA 5, RSA 6.

MILNE, Joe Exh. 1905-8
London. † L 2, RA 1, RI 1.

MILNE, Joseph Exh. 1880-1903
Landscape painter. Edinburgh. † GI 45, L 5, M 1, RA 6, RSA 81.

MILNE, Miss J.J. Exh. 1925-27
33 Frederick Street, Edgbaston, Birmingham. † B 3.

MILNE, John Maclauchlan d. 1957
Landscape painter. A.R.S.A. 1934, R.S.A. 1938. Exh. 1912-40. Add: Dundee. † GI 28, L 1, RSA 47.

MILNE, J.T. Exh. 1920
2 Perth Street, Edinburgh. † RSA 2.

MILNE, Malcolm 1887-1954
Flower, landscape and portrait painter. N.E.A. 1919. Brother of Hilda L.M. q.v. Add: London 1912; Henfield, Sussex 1934. † BA 2, CG 1, CHE 2, COO 1, FIN 1, G 3, GOU 3, I 5, M 4, NEA 69, RA 5, RED 1, TOO 1.

MILNE, Mary G. Exh. 1939
Wood engraver. Pannal, Harrogate, Yorks. † RA 1.

MILNE, N.M. Exh. 1917-19
Painter. 12 Edith Grove, Chelsea, London. † NEA 3.

MILNE, O. Exh. 1929
Watercolour coastal painter. † AB 2.

MILNE, Oswald Partridge b. 1881
Architect. Son of William O.M. q.v. Exh. 1903-38. Add: London 1903; Pulborough, Sussex 1918. † RA 10, RSA 5.

MILNE, Samuel F. Exh. 1938
437 Duke Street, Glasgow. † GI 1.

MILNE, William Exh. 1883-1907
Edinburgh 1883; St. Monan's, Fife 1906. † GI 18, L 1, RSA 27.

MILNE, William Exh. 1895
7 St. John's Terrace, Clontarf. † RHA 1.

MILNE, William Oswald Exh. 1887
Architect. Father of Oswald P.M. q.v. Add: 44 Great Marlboro Street, London. † RA 1.

MILNE, William W. Exh. 1927-34
St. Ives, Hunts. † M 1, RCA 1.

MILNE, William Watt Exh. 1908-15
Cambuskenneth, Stirling. † GI 14, RSA 2.

MILNER, Miss Exh. 1885
Flower painter. Bishopsthorpe, Yorks. † SWA 1.

MILNER, Miss A.E. Exh. 1906-9
Liverpool. † L 5.

MILNER, Donald Ewart b. 1898
Painter, stained glass artist and book decorator. b. Huddersfield. Studied Camberwell School of Arts and Crafts and Royal College of Art 1919-23. Headmaster Aston School of Arts and Crafts, Birmingham, Principal Gloucester Municipal School of Arts and Crafts. Exh. 1922-39. Add: Gloucester 1922; Bristol 1936. † COO 3, NEA 4, RA 13.

MILNER, Elizabeth Eleanor Exh. 1887-1929
Painter and engraver. Studied Lambeth and St. John's Wood. Add: London 1887; Bushey, Herts. 1889. † B 1, L 41, RA 14, ROI 5, SWA 5.

MILNER, Miss E.M. Exh. 1892
Painter. † FIN 1.

MILNER, Florence Exh. 1884-86
Ellesmere Park, Eccles, Manchester. † M 4.

MILNER, Fred d. 1939
Landscape painter. R.B.A. 1896. Add: Cheltenham, Glos. 1887; St. Ives, Cornwall 1898. † AB 1, B 12, FIN 1, GI 5, I 1, M 1, RA 30, RBA 85, ROI 1.

MILNER, H.V. Exh. 1896-1913
Stained glass artist. 47 Park Road, Haverstock Hill, London. † RA 4.

MILNER, Jessie Exh. 1893-1915
Miniature painter. Lawn House, Atkins Road, Clapham Park, London. † RA 11, RMS 6, SWA 1.

MILNER, John 1876-1951
Painter. Studied Nottingham School of Art 1897-1905. A.N.S.A. 1914, N.S.A. 1930. Father of Vernon M. q.v. Add: Nottingham 1901; 93 Trent Boulevard, West Bridgford, Notts. 1925. † N 71, RCA 1.

MILNER, Joseph b. 1888
Watercolour painter and designer. b. Chorlton-cum-Hardy. Studied Manchester School of Art. Exh. 1921-38. Add: London. † GI 1, L 7, M 1, RA 4, RBA 1.

MILNER, James Hiley b. 1869
Painter, etcher and colour woodcut artist. b. Huddersfield. Studied Huddersfield, Manchester and Colarossi's, Paris. Exh. 1931-35. Add: Lewisham, London. † NEA 2, RA 3.

MILNER, Mrs. Mildred G. Exh. 1932-34
Landscape painter. School of Art, Brunswick Road, Gloucester. † RA 1, SWA 1.

MILNER, T. Stuart b. 1909
Painter and designer of interior decoration. Studied Central School of Art and Regent Street Polytechnic 1926-29. R.B.A. 1935. Exh. 1933-38. Add: Woodford Green, Essex 1933; London 1938. † RA 7, RHA 1, RI 5, RSA 1.

MILNER, Vernon Exh. 1926-32
Portrait, figure and landscape painter. A.N.S.A. 1926. Son of John M. q.v. Add: 93 Trent Boulevard, West Bridgford, Nottingham. † N 16.

MILNER, William* Exh. 1924-31
Flower, still life and figure painter. London. † AB 28, ALP 10, AR 15, RA 5.

MILNES, Annie Exh. 1892-1910
Figure painter. Bradford, Yorks. 1892; Bushey, Herts. 1910. † L 1, NG 1, RA 2, ROI 2, SWA 1.

MILNES, Lady Celia Exh. 1906
Crewe House, Curzon Street, London. † NG 1.

MILNES, Sibyl b. 1902
Painter and black and white artist. b. Gislingham, Suffolk. Studied Derby School of Art, Regent Street Polytechnic and Clapham School of Art. Exh. 1930-40. Add: Clapham, London. † RA 6, SWA 1.

MILNES, William Henry b. 1865
Painter and etcher. b. Wakefield. Studied Antwerp and South Kensington. R.B.A. 1906, A.R.E. 1899. Exh. 1898-1938. Add: London 1898; Coventry 1905; Polstead, Colchester 1927; Oxted, Surrey 1935. † L 2, RA 7, RBA 62, RE 17.

MILSTED, Frisby Exh. 1896
Black and white artist. 45 Rosenau Road, Albert Bridge, London. † RA 1.

MILWARD, Clementina B. Exh. 1889-95
Landscape painter. London. † B 5, RHA 1, ROI 2, SWA 3.

MILWARD, J. Humphreys Exh. 1909-11
49 Harrow Road, Anfield, Liverpool. † L 2.

MILWARD, Mrs. Marguerite Exh. 1931-36
Sculptor. London. † B 1, GI 3, RA 2, SWA 1.

MILWARD, Mary Exh. 1880-81
Landscape and figure painter. The Holt, Farnham, Surrey. † RBA 1, SWA 6.

MILWARD, W.J. Exh. 1918-26
Sculptor. Station Road, Ruddington, Notts. † N 3.

MILWOOD, F. Exh. 1892
c/o R. Jeffreys, 88 Bold Street, Liverpool. † L 1.

MIMPRISS, Miss V. Baber Exh. 1914-30
Portrait and figure painter. Studied R.A. Schools (Landseer scholarship and Hacker silver portrait medal). Add: London. † GI 1, GOU 2, I 2, L 2, M 1, RA 7, RBA 4, RHA 1, RSA 2.

MINARD, Lilian J. Exh. 1921-25
Landscape, portrait and domestic painter. 116 Kingswood Road, Brixton Hill, London. † RA 7.

MINCHIN, Mrs. A. Exh. 1916
The Grange, Binfield, Berks. † RA 1.

MINCHIN, Hamilton Exh. 1882
Still life painter. 23 Newman Street, Oxford Street, London. † RBA 1.

MINCHIN, N. Exh. 1940
35 Elmsleigh Road, Wandsworth, London. † SWA 1.

MINETT, C.E. Exh. 1931-38
127 King's Avenue, London. † ROI 6.

MINETT, Charles W. Exh. 1933
Architect. Fairmead, Bridgefield Road, Tankerton, Kent. † RA 1.

MINETT, Miss M. Exh. 1900-6
London 1900; Tenbury, Worcs. 1906. † B 2, SWA 4.

MINN, Kathleen Exh. 1930-33
St. Hilda's Lodge, Bushey, Herts. † B 5, RCA 1.

MINNE, George b. 1866
Sculptor. Exh. 1915-31. Add: Llanidloes, Wales 1919; Belgium 1932. † GI 1, I 1, RA 1, RSA 2.

MINNS, B.E. Exh. 1895-1913
London. † GI 1, L 1, RA 3, RI 2.

MINNS, Fanny M. Exh. 1881-1905
Flower and landscape painter. Glen Cottages, Newport, I.o.W. † B 11, L 2, RBA 2, SWA 10.

MINNS, Horace Exh. 1925-26
60 Oakwood Road, Golder's Green, London. † L 9.

MINNS, James Exh. 1897
Sculptor. 11 Mariner's Lane, Norwich. † RA 1.

MINOPRIO, Anthony Exh. 1932-33
Architect. 18 Seymour Street, London. † RA 3.

MINOR, Mrs. Helen Exh. 1908
Avonmore, Alderley Edge, Cheshire. † M 2.

MINOR, Robert C. Exh. 1880-81
Landscape painter. 5 Stratford Avenue, Stratford Road, Kensington, London. † G 2, RA 4, RHA 1.

MINSHALL, Miss M.W. Exh. 1886
Castle View, Oswestry, Salop. † RI 1.

MINSHULL, R.T. Exh. 1880-1902
Genre painter. Liverpool. † L 22, RA 5, RBA 1.

MINTER, Bertha Exh. 1903
Interior painter. 12 Lorne Terrace, Darlington, Co. Durham. † RA 1.

MINTER, Muriel H. Exh. 1929-35
Mrs. G.A. Cooper. Painter and etcher. London. † NEA 2, RA 8.

MINTO, James Exh. 1884-86
Ivy Cottage, Ivy Terrace, Edinburgh. † RSA 4.

MINTON, H.A. Exh. 1891-1920
Whalley Range, Manchester 1891; Abergele 1912; Beaumaris, N. Wales 1914; Exmouth, Devon 1917; Mousehole, Cornwall 1920. † B 1, L 2, M 3, RCA 9.

MINTON, John W. Exh. 1884-92
Sculptor and medalist. London. † RA 3.

MINTY, E. Arden Exh. 1898-1910
London. † GI 1, RA 1.

MINTY, James A. Exh. 1899-1904
Architect. London. † L 1, RA 4.

MINTY, R.J. Hugh Exh. 1938
Architect. 93 Park Lane, London. † RA 1.

MIR, Joaquin Exh. 1937
Landscape painter. † BA 2.

MIREMONDE, Madeleine Exh. 1889
Barnsley, Yorks. † M 1.

MIRFIELD, Sarah A. Exh. 1904
Coastal painter. Queen Anne's Chambers, Sunbridge Road, Bradford, Yorks. † RA 1.

MIRMONT, de see D

MIRO, Joan* b. 1893
Spanish painter. Exh. 1926-36. † CHE 6, LEF 3.

MIROUX, Clement Elie Exh. 1912
15 Rue Mazagram, Paris. † RSA 2.

MIRYLEES, Rita Exh. 1921-27
Torphine, 8 Victoria Avenue, Church End, Finchley, London. † D 2, SWA 1.

MISCHEF, Mrs. P. Exh. 1910
51 Queen's Gate, London. † RA 1.

MITCHELL, Alfred Exh. 1894-1904
Marine and landscape painter. Lipson, Plymouth 1894; Mullion, Cornwall 1897; Yelverton, Devon 1904. † RA 4.

MITCHELL, Annie Exh. 1889
1 Glentham Road, Barnes, Surrey. † B 1.

MITCHELL, Arnold Bidlake 1863-1944
Architect. Add: Heaton Moor, Yorks. 1882; London 1885 and 1887; Withington, Manchester 1886. † M 4, RA 57, RHA 6.

MITCHELL, Arthur Croft b. 1872
Landscape and figure painter. Studied Slade School. Married Molly Ware M. q.v. Exh. 1903-31. Add: London. † B 4, I 2, L 4, LS 8, NEA 5, RA 5, RI 1, RID 4.

MITCHELL, Miss A.M. Exh. 1889-93
Flower painter. 8 Nassington Road, Hampstead, London. † SWA 3.

MITCHELL, Colin C. Exh. 1933-40
Germiston Road, Edinburgh. † GI 1, RSA 2, RSW 12.

MITCHELL, Colin G. d. c.1938
Glasgow 1894 and 1936; Tunbridge Wells, Kent 1934. † GI 15, L 3, M 1, RA 3, RSA 6, RSW 3.

MITCHELL, C.L. d. 1918
Painter. Dundee 1892; Tayport, N.B. 1908. † GI 16, RSA 3.

MITCHELL, Charles William Exh. 1881-94
Portrait and figure painter. London. † G 3, L 4, M 1, NG 3, RA 5.

MITCHELL, David H. Exh. 1938
3 Saffron Hall Crescent, Hamilton. † RSA 1.

MITCHELL, Mrs. Dorothy H. Exh. 1935
St. Albans, Herts. † RCA 1.

MITCHELL, Edith Exh. 1905-40
Mrs. Edwin M. Landscape and coastal painter. A.S.W.A. 1927, S.W.A. 1930. Add: London 1905 and 1939; Amersham, Bucks. 1924. † GOU 1, L 1, LS 8, RA 2, RBA 3, RI 3, SWA 49.

MITCHELL, Elspeth Exh. 1940
Mrs. Alan Cuthbert. Add: 7 Grosvenor Crescent, Glasgow. † GI 1.

MITCHELL, Emily Exh. 1887
Figure painter. 109 Park Street, Grosvenor Square, London. † SWA 1.

MITCHELL, Ernest Exh. 1927-28
Riverholme, Sandy Lane, Chester. † L 2.

MITCHELL, Eleanor B. Exh. 1903
Figure painter. Portrans Villas, Farnborough Green, Farnborough, Hants. † RA 2.

MITCHELL, Mrs. Enid B. Exh. 1920-30
Painter and linocut artist. 4 Westminster Road, Handsworth, Birmingham. † B 6, RED 2.

MITCHELL, E. Grace see HENRY

MITCHELL, Ernest Gabriel b. 1859
Landscape painter. Self taught. R.B.S.A. 1898. Exh. 1885-1933. Add: Birmingham 1885; Dumbleton, Nr. Broadway, Worcs. 1902; Chipping Norton, Oxon. 1906; Knowle 1909; Tamworth-in-Arden 1924. † B 59.

MITCHELL, Mrs. E. McFarlane Exh. 1901
† RMS 1.

MITCHELL, Mrs. Evelyn V. Exh. 1937
Landscape painter. 32 Mallord Street, London. † RA 1.

MITCHELL, Mrs. Frank Johnstone
Exh. 1880-1910
Landscape and coastal painter. H.S.W.A. 1880. Add: Caerlon 1880; Newport, Mon. 1899. † SWA 21.

MITCHELL, Frederick James b. 1902
Painter, black and white artist and calligrapher. Studied Willesden School of Art 1917-20 and Royal College of Art 1920-24. Head of Department Painting and Publicity Design, Keighley, Yorks. 1925-32. Head of Department Book and Publicity Design Hornsey School of Art from 1932. Exh. 1924-40. Add: London. † GI 1, L 1, NEA 2, RA 4.

MITCHELL, Gertrude A. Exh. 1901-21
Woolton, Liverpool 1901; Huyton, Liverpool 1905. † GI 1, L 24.

MITCHELL, Gladys Dorothy Alexandra
Exh. 1921-31
Watercolour landscape painter. Studied Cheltenham School of Art. Add: Cheltenham 1921, Charlton Kings, Glos. 1929. † RA 2, RHA 1, RI 2, RSA 1, SWA 4.

MITCHELL, George J. Exh. 1921
Braeside, Lawside Road, Dundee. † RSA 1.

MITCHELL, Henry Exh. 1931
Landscape painter. 18 Burgoyne Road, London. † RA 1.

MITCHELL, Henry Exh. 1882-1902
Rock Ferry, Cheshire 1882; Whiteinch 1893; Glasgow 1896. † GI 10, L 9.

MITCHELL, Hutton Exh. 1920
"Pueblo", Tarraway Road, Preston, Paignton, Devon. † L 2.

MITCHELL, Miss H.A. Exh. 1882
1 Craven Terrace, Sale, Manchester. † M 1.

MITCHELL, Helen H. Exh. 1899-1904
Edinburgh. † GI 4, RSA 8.

MITCHELL, James Exh. 1885-1902
Edinburgh 1885; Prestonpans, N.B. 1900. † RSA 17.

MITCHELL, Jean Exh. 1897-1936
Figure painter. Married Frank Saltfleet q.v. Add: Sheffield. † RA 6, RI 1, SWA 3.

MITCHELL, Jeanie Exh. 1891
Haslewood, Langside, Glasgow. † GI 1.

MITCHELL, John c.1837-1926
Landscape painter. Exh. 1880-1908. Add: 10 Gladstone Place, Queen's Cross, Aberdeen. † GI 2, RA 5, RSA 34.

MITCHELL, John Exh. 1886-90
Edinburgh. † GI 4, RSA 5.

MITCHELL, James B. Exh. 1883
Painter. Teusleys, Hampstead Green, London. † RI 1.

MITCHELL, Mrs. James B. Exh. 1882-83
Flower painter. Paris 1882; London 1883. † G 3, L 1.

MITCHELL, John Campbell 1865-1922
Landscape and seascape painter. A.R.S.A. 1904, R.S.A. 1919. Add: Edinburgh 1891; Corstorphine 1903. † BG 27, GI 67, L 3, M 7, RA 8, RSA 99, RSW 2.

MITCHELL, J.E. Exh. 1893-95
15 Castle Street, Dundee 1893; Edinburgh 1895. † RSA 3, RSW 1.

MITCHELL, J. Edgar d. 1922
Figure painter. Newcastle-on-Tyne. † GI 1, RA 4, RI 1, RSA 1.

MITCHELL, Jessey Rosetta Exh. 1908-16
Wadhurst, Sussex 1908; London 1916. † LS 16.

MITCHELL, J.S. Exh. 1889
15 The Avenue, Southampton. † B 1.

MITCHELL, Canon John T. Exh. 1929-38
Landscape painter. † AB 2, WG 7.

MITCHELL, Jemima W. Exh. 1899-1900
31 Alva Street, Edinburgh. † RSA 2.

MITCHELL, Lucy Exh. 1883-84
Still life painter. The Acre, Stroud, Glos. † RA 2.

MITCHELL, Miss L.C. Exh. 1899-1908
Stirling. † GI 7, RHA 1.

MITCHELL, Laura M.D. Exh. 1929-37
† RMS 3.

MITCHELL, Miss M. Exh. 1885
The Bays, Sandown, I.O.W. † GI 1.

MITCHELL, Miss M. Exh. 1896
6 Penywern Road, London. † SWA 1.

MITCHELL, Mrs. Mary Exh. 1887-1912
Miniature portrait painter. R.M.S. 1898. Add: London 1887 and 1894; Bickley, Kent 1889. † D 2, RA 9, RMS 8, SWA 1.

MITCHELL, Miss M.D. Exh. 1881-89
Flower painter. Regent's Park, London. † D 3, G 6.

MITCHELL, Miss M.E. Exh. 1891
Devon House, Leamington Spa, Warwicks. † B 1.

MITCHELL, Maggie Richardson
Exh. 1907-40
Mrs. George J. nee Richardson. Sculptor. A.R.B.A. 1927, R.B.A. 1931, S.W.A. 1932. Add: London 1907; Southport, Lancs. 1915; Montacute, Somerset 1922; Preston Plucknett, Somerset 1925; Norton-sub-Hamden, Somerset 1936. † GI 1, L 4, RA 23, RBA 17, RSA 7, SWA 7.

MITCHELL, Mrs. Molly Ware
Exh. 1927-29
Landscape painter. Married Arthur Croft M. q.v. Add: 32 Mallord Street, London. † RID 3, SWA 4.

MITCHELL, Madge Y. Exh. 1930-38
Bieldside, by Aberdeen 1930; Ferryhill, Aberdeen 1932. † GI 3, RSA 11, RSW 1.

MITCHELL, Percy Exh. 1886
Landscape painter. Bolton Studios, London. † ROI 1.

MITCHELL, Philip 1814-1896
Landscape painter. A.R.I. 1854, R.I. 1879. Add: Plymouth. † M 8, RBA 2, RI 114.

MITCHELL, Dr. P. Chalmers Exh. 1917
Zoological Society, London. † LS 3.

MITCHELL, Peter McDowall b.1879
Painter and etcher. b. Galashiels. Studied Glasgow School of Art (travelling scholarship in painting). Exh. 1922-39. Add: 84 Mossgiel Road, Yewlands, Glasgow. † GI 5, L 8, RSA 4, RSW 16.

MITCHELL, S. Exh. 1884
Manchester Road, Bradford, Yorks. † L 1.

MITCHELL, Sophia Exh. 1893-1913
Landscape and portrait painter. Studied at Kensington; under Mrs. Spenlove, and at Grosvenor School of Art. Add: London. † B 2, RA 1, RHA 1.

MITCHELL, Sydney Exh. 1883-88
Architect. Edinburgh. † RA 3, RSA 9.

MITCHELL, Thomas Exh. 1881-85
21 Drury Street, Glasgow. † GI 1, RSA 1.

MITCHELL, Tom Exh. 1885-1906
Landscape and flower painter. Eccles Hill, nr. Bradford 1885; Bingley, Yorks 1906. † G 1, L 5, M 1, RA 4.

MITCHELL, Vyvyan b.1879
Landscape painter. b. Bexley, Kent. Studied Goldsmiths College, Regent Street Polytechnic and with W.T. Wood. Exh. 1912-35. Add: Chorley Wood, Herts. 1912; London 1925; Gt. Missenden, Bucks. 1933. † GOU 7, LS 3, RA 5, RI 2, ROI 2.

MITCHELL, W. Exh. 1919
Church Gate, Cheshunt, Herts. † RSA 1.

MITCHELL, William Exh. 1880-1903
18 Kew Terrace, Glasgow. † GI 11.

MITCHELL, W.B. Exh. 1884-1902
St. George's Free Church, Stafford Street, Edinburgh. † GI 1, RSA 5.

MITCHELL, William G. Exh. 1903-4
Architect. Royal Engineer Office, nr. Aldershot, Hants. † RA 2.

MITCHELL, William Mansfield
d.1910
Architect. A.R.H.A. 1889, R.H.A. 1890. Exh. 1881-1903. Add: 10 Leinster Street, Dublin. † RHA 19.

MNISZECH, Count Andre Exh. 1880
† G 1.

MOAT, Edna Howard Exh. 1935-37
Painter, linocut artist and fabric designer. Carlyle House, 18 Burns Street, Nottingham. † N 5.

MOBERLY, Major Alfred Exh. 1882-84
Flower painter. Tynwald, Hythe, Kent. † B 2, D 1.

MOBERLY, Arthur Hamilton b. 1886
Architect. Studied Kings College, Cambridge. Exh. 1925. Add: 45 Berners Street, London. † GI 2, RA 1.

MOBERLY, Mrs. Mariquita Jenny b. 1855 nee Phillips. Portrait, figure, landscape, flower and miniature painter. Studied in Germany under Bertha Froriep and in Paris under Carolus Duran. A.S.W.A. 1902. exh. 1881-1935. Add: Epsom, Surrey 1881; London 1884; Mitcham, Surrey 1899. † B 30, D 135, G 1, GI 14, L 24, M 12, NG 2, RA 19, RBA 3, RHA 19, RI 28, RID 6, ROI 19, RSW 1, SWA 77, WG 90.

MOCATTA, G. Exh. 1885
Watercolour coastal painter. 54 Cleveland Square, Hyde Park, London. † SWA 1.

MOCATTA, Miss L. Exh. 1887-89
Flower painter. London. † B 2, RI 1, SWA 1.

MOCATTA, Maria Exh. 1883
Figure painter. 58 Kensington Gardens Square, London. † ROI 1.

MOCATTA, Rebecca Exh. 1882-1912
Figure painter. London 1882; Sussex 1907. † GOU 1, RBA 2, SWA 2.

MOCKLER, Nellie Exh. 188?
Denby Vicarage, Derbys. † N 1.

MOCKRIDGE, Gertrude Eileen Exh. 1914-26
Portrait and miniature painter. Add: Bristol 1914; Parkstone, Dorset 1925. † L 2, RA 9.

MOES, Wally P.C.* Exh. 1885-95
Figure painter. Amsterdam. † RA 1, RBA 3.

MOFFAT, Arthur Elwell Exh. 1880-98
Landscape painter. Edinburgh 1880 and 1889; London 1887. † GI 4, RA 1, RHA 2, RI 3, RSA 24, RSW 1.

MOFFAT, Betsy B. Exh. 1930-38
Milngavie 1930; Glasgow 1937. † GI 3, RSA 12, RSW 3.

MOFFAT, C.B. Exh. 1929-30
London. † NEA 4.

MOFFAT, Isobel Exh. 1930
Clairinch, Milngavie. † RSA 1.

MOFFAT, J. Fred Exh. 1880-88
Edinburgh. † GI 5, RSA 34.

MOFFAT, Muirhead Exh. 1916
134 Douglas Street, Glasgow. † GI 1.

MOFFAT, Miss Nan Muirhead Exh. 1930-31
11 Dungoyne Gardens, Glasgow. † GI 3.

MOFFATT, John S. Exh. 1900-6
Larbert, N.B.† GI 2, RSA 1.

MOFFETT, W. Noel Exh. 1940
Urban landscape painter. 25 Lower Baggot Street, Dublin. † RHA 1.

MOGFORD, John* 1821-1885
Landscape and coastal painter. Studied Government School of Design at Somerset House. A.R.I. 1866, R.I. 1867, R.O.I. 1883. Add: 17 Park Road, Haverstock Hill, London. † B 6, DOW 80, L 11, M 7, RA 1, RI 47, ROI 9, TOO 1.

MOGGRIDGE, Miss G. Exh. 1912-14
47 Stanley Gardens, Hampstead, London. † LS 3, ROI 1, RSA 1, SWA 1.

MOGGRIDGE, Mrs. Helen Exh. 1938
Landscape painter. 19 Croftdown Road, London. † NEA 1, RA 1.

MOHOLY-NAGY, Lazlo* 1895-1946
Painter and sculptor. b. Hungary. d. Chicago, U.S.A. Exh. 1936. Add: London. † LEF 2.

MOHR, J.M. Exh. 1881
Sculptor. 18 Weber Strasse, Bonn, Germany. † RA 1.

MOIR, Frank Exh. 1930
† L 1.

MOIR, Mrs. James Exh. 1902
16 Hamilton Drive, Pollokshields, Glasgow. † GI 3.

MOIR, John Exh. 1884-87
4 Selbourne Terrace, Wolldands Road, Glasgow. † GI 3.

MOIR, Mrs. Jessie K. Exh. 1927-40
Landscape and still life painter. Sancreed, Penzance, Cornwall 1927; Chard, Somerset 1932. † GOU 1, L 2, NEA 1, RA 3, RSA 4.

MOIRA, Miss Exh. 1917
Philbeach Gardens, London. † SWA 1.

MOIRA, Edward d.1887
Miniature painter to Queen Victoria. Father of Gerald Edward M. q.v. Add: London. † L 2, RA 17, RI 2.

MOIRA, Gerald Edward 1867-1959
Portrait, figure and landscape painter and lithographer. Professor at the Royal College of Art. Collaborated with Frank Lynn Jenkins q.v. Son of Edward M. q.v. R.O.I. 1932; V.P.R.O.I. 1935; R.W.S. 1917. "Washing Day" purchased by Chantrey Bequest 1938. Exh. from 1891. Add: London. † BA 8, FIN 4, G 1, GI 29, GOU 6, I 7, L 28, LS 5, NG,1, P 1, RA 47, ROI 31, RSA 11, RSW 2, RWS 102.

MOISAND, Maurice Exh. 1894-96
Figure and domestic painter. Rue Bara 6, Paris. † L 1, RA 4.

MOLD, Cecil Allen b.1905
Watercolour painter. Exh. 1938-40. Add: 45 Ridgmount Gardens, London. † RI 5, ROI 1.

MOLE, Clara Exh. 1880-87
Flower painter. 7 Guildford Place, Russell Square, London. † RI 3, SWA 4.

MOLE, Charles J. Exh. 1932-33
Architect. H.M. Office of Works, Storey's Gate, London. † RA 5.

MOLE, F. Exh, 1923-33
488 Fishponds Road, Bristol. † L 7, RCA 9.

MOLE, John Henry* 1814-1886
Landscape and miniature painter and watercolourist. b. Alnwick. A.R.I. 1847, R.I. 1848, V.P.R.I. 1884, R.O.I. 1883. Add: London. † DOW 2, GI 5, L 9, RBA 5, RI 60, ROI 12, TOO 1.

MOLESWORTH, Mary N. Exh. 1928
6 Boltons Studios, Redcliffe Road, London. † L 1.

MOLESWORTH, Mollie R. b. 1907
Watercolour landscape painter. b. India. Studied for 3 years at Wimbledon Polytechnic. Returned to India for 2 years. Travelled Kashmir, Tibet and the Punjab. Exh. 1930. † WG 67.

MOLEYNS, de see D

MOLIERE, Professor M.J. Grapre Exh. 1936
† RSA 3.

MOLIN, Carl Hjalmar Valentin b.1868
Swedish painter, etcher and architect. Studied Academy of Fine Arts, Stockholm. A.R.E. 1904-28. Exh. 1904-26. Add: Stockholm 1904; Ostergotland, Sweden 1926. † L 5, P 1, RE 14.

MOLINEUX, M. Exh. 1888
Landscape painter. London. † RA 1.

MOLINEUX, Muriel Normand Exh. 1906-30
Painter and modeller. Hessle, East Yorks. † L 14, RA 10.

MOLL, Everet Exh. 1905-6
74 Finborough Road, London. † I 1, RA 2, RI 1.

MOLLAN, Poppy Exh. 1927-40
Arnsban, Glastonbury Avenue, Belfast. † RHA 6.

MOLLER, Miss M. Exh. 1898-1902
20 The Ropewalk, Nottingham. † N 11.

MOLLER, Muriel Exh. 1908
Broad Leys Cottage, Widdington, Newport, Essex. † LS 3.

MOLLIET, Mme. C. Exh. 1904
119 Avenue de Clichy, Paris. † L 1.

MOLLISON, M.T. Exh. 1887
4 Windsor Terrace, Glasgow. † GI 1.

MOLLOY, O.F. Exh. 1899
Glenoir, Taylor's HIll, Galway. † RHA 5.

MOLONY, Miss F. Exh. 1899-1911
Painter and etcher. Married Edward Millington Synge, q.v. Add: London 1899; Clare Cottage, West Byfleet, Surrey 1908. † CON 5, GI 4, L 5, RHA 4, SWA 6.

MOLS, Robert Exh. 1886
Landscape painter. 41 Rue des Martyrs, Paris. † L 1.

MOLYNEAUX, Edward Exh. 1899-1909
Landscape painter. London. † RA 7.

MOLYNEAUX, Elizabeth Gowanlock d.1969
Watercolour painter. R.S.W. 1923.Exh. from 1915. Add: Edinburgh. † AR 2, GI 22, RSA 60, RSW 76, SWA 2.

MOMMEN, F. Exh. 1895
31 Rue de la Charite, Brussels. † B 1.

MOMPOU, Jose b.1888
Spanish painter. Studied Barcelona and Paris. Exh. 1937-38. † BA 7.

MONAGHAN, George C. Exh. 1913
79 Regent Street, Glasgow. † GI 1, RSW 1.

MONAGHAN, Robert J. Exh. 1935-39
34 Brighton Street, Glasgow. † GI 1, RSA 7.

MONAHAN, Rev. William B. Exh. 1927-36
Landscape painter. † AB 3, WG 9.

MONARD, De see D

MONCKTON, Emily Exh. 1881-82
Mrs. G. Figure painter. 21 Westbourne Park, Bayswater, London. † L 1, SWA 1.

MONCKTON, Mrs. Lancelot Exh. 1927
Watercolour painter. † WG 39.

MONCKTON, Mrs. May S. Exh. 1928-37
Maidstone, Kent. † RBA 6, RI 2, ROI 1.

MONCRIEFF, Col. Alexander Exh. 1883-86
Landscape painter. 15 Vicarage Gate, Kensington, London. † RI 1, ROI 1, RSA 1.

MONCRIEFF, Mary M. Exh. 1911
13 Dean Park Crescent, Edinburgh. † RA 1.

MONCRIEFF, W.W.S. Exh. 1921
28 Old Burlington St. London. † RA 1.

MONCUR, Jane Exh. 1918-30
London. † NEA 3.

MOND, May Exh. 1929
Sculptor. 22 Hyde Park Square, London. † RA 2.

MONDINEAU, J.G.E. Exh. 1911
44 Rue Notre Dame de Lorette, Paris. † L 1.

MONDRIAN, Piet* 1872-1944
Painter. b. Amsterdam. d. New York. Exh. 1936. Add: London. † LEF 3.

MONET, Claude* 1840-1926
French painter. Exh. 1887-1925. Add: Giverny, Eure, France 1887; Brookieknowe, nr. Edinburgh 1900; Paris 1908. † CHE 1, GOU 3, I 4, L 1, NEA 7, RBA 4.

MONEY, Cuthbert Exh. 1935-39
Painter. "Colthamby", St. John's Avenue, Chaddesden, Derby. † N 5.

MONEY-COUTTS, Hon. Godfrey B. Exh. 1929-35
Portrait, landscape painter, etcher and wood engraver. London 1930; Adisham, nr. Canterbury, Kent 1935. † COO 23, RA 3, WG 20.

MONGER, Arthur P. Exh. 1889-98
Sculptor. Ewell, Surrey 1889; Crouch End, London, 1898. † RA 3.

MONGIN, Augustin d. 1911
French etcher. Ech. 1880. Add: Paris. † RA 1.

MONGREDIEN, Miss A. Exh. 1886-1909
Sister of Miss J.M. q.v. Add: Forest Hill, London. † B 23, L 1, RHA 3, SWA 1.

MONGREDIEN, Miss H. Exh. 1886-1904
Sister of Miss A.M. q.v. Add: Forest Hill, London. † B 20, M 1, RHA 6, ROI 1, SWA 3.

MONIER-WILLIAMS, Mrs. Stanley (C. Mary) Exh. 1891-1915
Landscape, portrait and figure painter. Walton on the Hill, Surrey 1891 and 1910; Southwold, Suffolk 1907; London 1914. † D 3, I 1, L 1, RA 1, RID 26, SWA 3.

MONIGOT, de see D

MONK, Jessie M. Exh. 1925
35 High Street, Alton, Hants. † SWA 1.

MONK, William 1863-1937
Painter, etcher and wood engraver. b. Chester. Studied Chester and Antwerp Academy. Founded and worked with "The London Almanack" for 35 years. A.R.E. 1894, R.E. 1899. Add: Chester 1889; London 1894 and 1913, Amersham, Bucks. 1905. † AB 2, BG 1, FIN 14, G 2, GI 1, I 29, L 3, M 2, RA 25, RE 134, RI 1, WG 175.

MONKHOUSE, Miss B. Exh. 1911
5 Greencroft Gardens, Hampstead, London. † RA 1.

MONKHOUSE, G. Exh. 1940
3 Dinmore Avenue, Northfield, Birmingham. † B 2.

MONKHOUSE, Mary F. Exh. 1882-1938
Landscape and figure painter. Manchester 1882 and 1887; Knutsford, Cheshire 1885; Disley, Cheshire 1899. † L 11, M 23, NEA 1, NG 2, RA 2.

MONKHOUSE, Victoria Exh. 1918-20
18 Rosebery Gardens, Ealing, London. † SWA 6.

MONKS, J.A.S. Exh. 1884
c/o Cassells, Ludgate Hill, London. † L 1.

MONKSWELL, Lord see COLLIER, Sir Robert

MONNINGTON, Walter Thomas 1903-1976
Painter and mural decorator. Studied Slade School 1918-23, Rome Scholar in decorative painting 1923-26. Assistant drawing master Royal College of Art and assistant master of drawing and painting R.A. Schools. N.E.A. 1929, A.R.A. 1931, R.A. 1938 (P.R.A. from 1966). Add: London. † AG 2, GI 2, L 1, LEI 3, NEA 2, RA 27.

MONOD, Lucien M. Exh. 1904-39
Portrait and figure artist in crayons. † DOW 51, GOU 3.

MONREL, de see D

MONRO, Charles C. Binning Exh. 1880-1910
Landscape, coastal and marine painter. London 1880 and 1890; Abingdon, Berks. 1889. † B 2, GI 4, L 7, RA 8, RBA 1, RHA 1, RSA 14.

MONRO, Eleanor J. Exh. 1880
Landscape painter. 4 Wyndham Place, Bryanston Square, London. † SWA 2.

MONRO, Hugh Exh. 1915-28
16 Picardy Place, Edinburgh. † RSA 20, RSW 2.

MONRO, James M. Exh. 1893
28 Bath Street, Glasgow. † GI 1.

MONRO, Miss M.V. see MacGEORGE

MONSELL, Elinor Mary see DARWIN

MONT, de see D

MONT, du see D

MONTADOR, Catherine Exh. 1929
37 Upton Road, Birkenhead. † L 2.

MONTAGU, Ella Exh. 1901-7
London. † L 1, NG 4, RA 1, RMS 1.

MONTAGUE, Alfred* Exh. 1880-88
Landscape and coastal painter. R.B.A. 1843. Add: London 1880; Birmingham 1885. † B 3, D 2, GI 1, L 1, RBA 4, ROI 1, TOO 2.

MONTAGUE, Clifford* Exh. 1885-93
Birmingham 1885; Penkridge 1891. † B 19, L 2, M 2, RHA 1, RSA 1.

MONTAGUE, Ellen Exh. 1886-94
Figure painter. London 1886 and 1888; Limerick 1887. † B 2, RA 1, RHA 2.

MONTAGUE, H. Exh. 1915
370 Moseley Road, Birmingham. † RHA 3.

MONTAGUE, Helen Exh. 1893
5B Kensington Studio, Kelso Place, Kensington, London. † B 1.

MONTAGUE, H. Irving Exh. 1880-83
Figure painter. London. † B 2, D 2, RBA 1.

MONTAIGNE, William John d. 1902
Portrait, landscape and historical painter. Studied R.A. Schools. Exh. 1882-90. Add: London. † RA 4, RBA 2.

MONTALBA, Anthony Exh. 1880-84
Landscape painter. Probably brother of Clara, Ellen, Hilda and Henrietta Skerret M. q.v. Add: 20 Stanley Crescent, Kensington Park Gardens, London. † B 2, GI 3, L 1, M 1, RA 3.

MONTALBA, Clara* 1842-1929
Landscape and marine painter. b. Cheltenham. Studied under Eugene Isabey in Paris for 4 years. Sister of Ellen, Hilda and Henrietta Skerrett M. q.v. and probably of Anthony M. q.v. A.R.W.S. 1874, R.W.S. 1892. Died in Venice. Add: London 1880 and 1897; Venice 1894, 1901 and 1923; Brussels 1921. † AG 3, B 28, FIN 25, G 6, GI 49, L 62, M 45, NG 14, RA 11, RBA 2, RSA 3, RSW 2, RWS 196, SWA 8, TOO 2.

MONTALBA, Ellen Exh. 1881-1901
Portrait, landscape and genre painter. b. Bath. Studied South Kensington. Sister of Clara, Hilda and Henrietta Skerrett M. q.v. and probably of Anthony M. q.v. Add: London 1881; Venice 1894. † B 4, GI 6, L 8, M 3, RA 9, RBA 1, SWA 1.

MONTALBA, Hilda d. 1919
Landscape and genre painter. Sister of Clara, Ellen and Henrietta Skerrett M. q.v. and probably of Anthony M. q.v. Add: London 1880 and 1895; Venice 1894 and 1903. † B 33, BG 1, FIN 1, G 16, GI 39, L 38, M 30, NG 24, RA 34, RSA 17, ROI 13, SWA 13.

MONTALBA, Henrietta Skerrett 1856-1893
Sculptor. Sister of Clara, Ellen and Hilda M. q.v. and probably of Anthony M. q.v. Add: London. † B2. G 10, GI 5, L 1, NG 3, RA 14.

MONTALD, Constantin Camille b. 1862
Belgian portrait painter, sculptor and decorative artist. Studied L'Ecole Industrielle and Academie de Dessin, Ghent and in Paris. Travelled in Italy and Egypt. Exh. 1925. Add: Brussels. † RSW 1.

MONTBARD, Georges 1841-1905
Landscape and figure painter and black and white artist. London. † L 2, M 9, RA 3, RBA 6, RI 7, ROI 7.

MONTBARD, Miss M.L. 1904-15
London. † RI 5.

MONTEATH, Miss C. Exh. 1881-98
Glenhead Cottage, Dunblane. † GI 2, RSA 12.

MONTEFIORE, Edward Brice Stanley Exh. 1880-1909
Landscape and genre painter. London 1880; Newnham, Glos. 1909. † M 3, RA 9, ROI 3.

MONTEFIORE, E.L. Exh. 1881
Etcher. † RE 3.

MONTEITH, John A. Exh. 1880-1903
Glasgow. † GI 34, L 1, RSA 6.

MONTEITH, William Exh. 1893
Springdale, Langside, N.B. † GI 1.

MONTENEGRO, Alberto Exh. 1914
Portrait and figure painter. † FIN 2.

MONTEVERDE, Luigi Exh. 1884-86
Lugano. † GI 4, L 3.

MONTEZIN, Alfred Pierre Exh. 1894-1909
Painter. Nottingham. † N 7.

MONTEZIN, E. or A. Exh. 1937-38
Landscape painter. c/o Bourlet & Son, London. † RA 2.

MONTEZIN, Pierre Eugene* b. 1874
French painter. Exh. 1906. Add: 42 Boulevard Magenta, Paris. † L 1.

MONTFORD, Horace Exh. 1880-1911
Sculptor. Worked in Manchester under John Banks. Architectural sculptor on the restorations to Manchester Cathedral. Assistant to Matthew Noble and then C.B. Birch. Appointed First Curator of the new Sculture School at the R.A. 1881. Father of Paul Raphael M. q.v. Add: London. † GI 19, L 21, RA 39, RBA 1.

MONTFORD, Marian Alice b.1882
nee Dibdin. Painter, miniaturist and pencil artist. Studied Chelsea Polytechnic and R.A. Schools 1891-1905. Married Paul Raphael M. q.v. Exh. 1904-20. Add: Sutton, Surrey 1904; Purley, Surrey 1907; London 1912. † M 1, RA 13, RBA 4.

MONTFORD, Paul Raphael 1868-1938
Sculptor and painter. Studied Lambeth and R.A. Schools. Appointed modelling master Chelsea Ploytechnic 1898. R.B.A. 1904. Son of Horace M. q.v. Married Marian Alice M. q.v. Add: London 1892; Melbourne, Australia 1934. † GI 8, L 15, RA 59, RBA 46, RI 1.

MONTGOMERIE, Miss A Exh. 1917
Guildford, Surrey. † SWA 1.

MONTGOMERIE, Mary M. Exh. 1904-6
Miniature portrait painter. East Harling, Norfolk 1904; London 1906. † NG 1, P 1, RA 1.

MONTGOMERIE, W.C. Exh. 1928
Etcher. † AB 2.

MONTGOMERY, A.A.G. Exh. 1880-84
Stobo Castle, N.B. † RSA 8.

MONTGOMERY, C. Exh. 1926
Etcher. † FIN 1.

MONTGOMERY, Elizabeth Exh. 1923-24
Painter, illustrator and designer. 424 Fulham Road, London. † RA 1, SWA 1.

MONTGOMERY, Lucy Exh. 1900
1 Chesham Street, Belgrave Square, London. † RMS 2.

MONTGOMERY, Lily M. Exh. 1896
Fairholme, Grange Road, Bushey, Herts. † L 2.

MONTGOMERY, Robert Exh. 1881-92
Landscape painter. 22 Rue Mozart, Antwerp. † B 1, L 1, RA 2, RHA 2.

MONTGOMERY, Miss Snookie Exh. 1932
8 St. Bernards Crescent, Edinburgh. † RSA 1.

MONTHOLON, de see D

MONTIGNY, Jules* 1847-1899
Belgian artist. Exh. 1884-89. Add: Terveuren, Brussels. † GI 6.

MONTMORENCY, de see D

MONTRAVEL, de see D

MONVEL, de see D

MONYPENNY, Miss E.L. Exh. 1907
13 Barton Street, Westminster, London. † NG 1.

MONZIES, Louis Exh. 1890-96
Etcher. A.R.E. 1894-99. Add: Paris 1890; Sarthe, France 1896. † RA 1, RE 9.

MOODIE, Donald Exh. 1919-40
Portobello 1919; Edinburgh 1925; Ratho Station, Midlothian 1929. † GI 1, L 2, RSA 41.

MOODIE, Helen C. Exh. 1894
256 Gt. Western Road, Glasgow. † GI 1.

MOODY, Albert Exh. 1928-29
Portrait painter. 1 Chartham Terrace, Ramsgate. † L 1, RA 2.

MOODY, Edward G. Exh. 1884-90
Landscape and portrait painter. London. † L 1, RA 1, RBA 1, ROI 1.

MOODY, Fannie b.1861
Mrs. Gilbert King. Animal painter and miniaturist. Daughter of Francis Wollaston M. (1824-1886). Studied under J.T. Nettleship. A.S.W.A. 1886, S.W.A. 1887. Exh. 1880-1940. Add: London. † B 10, D 3, L 50, LS 6, M 1, RA 38, RBA 10, RMS 3, ROI 6, SWA 15.

MOODY, John Charles 1884-1962
Figure and landscape painter and etcher. Studied London, Paris, Antwerp and Italy. Principal Hornsey School of Art. A.R.E. 1922, R.I. 1931. Add: London. † GI 3, I 2, L 4, RA 29, RE 43, RI 39, ROI 1.

MOODY, Victor Hume b. 1896
Painter. Studied Battersea Polytechnic. Head of Malvern School of Art since 1935. Exh. 1931-40. Add: Mitcham, Surrey 1931; Malvern Worcs. 1935. † B 1, COO 2, GOU 33, NEA 1, RA 8, RSA 1.

MOON, Alan George Tennant b. 1914
Painter, pencil and chalk artist. Studied Cardiff School of Art 1929-33 and Royal College of Art. Exh. 1936-39. Add: Penarth, Glam. † RA 5.

MOON, Cicily Exh. 1893
Pengrael, Llanymynech. † L 1.

MOON, Ethel Exh. 1904
50 Green Street, Park Lane, London. † D 2.

MOON, Emmeline M. Exh. 1887-90
Flower painter. Charlwood House, Horsham, Sussex. † RBA 1, SWA 4.

MOON, Henry George 1857-1905
Landscape painter. London 1880; St. Albans, Herts. 1893. † D 1, M 1, NEA 2, RA 9, RBA 8, RI 1, ROI 1.

MOON, William H.B. Exh. 1889
Watercolour fruit painter. 2 Belgrave Crescent, Scarborough. † RA 1.

MOONEY, Edmund Exh. 1938
Painter. Beaumont, Blackrock, Co. Dublin. † RHA 1.

MOONEY, E. Hartley Exh. 1926-32
124 Droylesden Road, Newton Heath, Manchester. † L 1, M 3, RCA 4.

MOONIE, Mrs. Janet Exh. 1940
78 Newbattle Terrace, Edinburgh. † GI 1, RSA 3.

MOONY, Mrs. A. Enraght Exh. 1893-95
The Doon, Athlone. † RHA 5.

MOONY, Robert James Enraght 1879-1946
Painter and illustrator. b. The Doon, Athlone. Studied Juliens, Paris. R.B.A. 1912. Exh. from 1900. Add: London. † B 6, BA 49, FIN 2, GI 2, L 14, M 2, NEA 20, RA 24, RBA 55, RI 1.

MOOR, Dora E. Exh. 1897
193 Goldhawk Road, Shepherds Bush, London. † RBA 1.

MOOR, E.M. Exh. 1885-86
Thornleigh, Woolston, Southampton. † L 2.

MOOR, Janet Exh. 1885-90
Bolton le Moors. † L 1, M 4.

MOORE, Mrs. Anne Exh. 1928
Addlestone, Surrey. † SWA 1.

MOORE, A.E. Exh. 1926-29
Landscape painter. Basford, Notts. 1926; Nottingham 1929. † N 7.

MOORE, Agnes E.C. Exh. 1881-85
Flower painter. 4 Sheffield Terrace, Kensington, London. † D 4, G 1, RI 1.

MOORE, A.H. Exh. 1923
Somerleyton Road, London. † L 2.

MOORE, Arthur H. Exh. 1902
Architect. London. † RA 1.

MOORE, A. Harvey d. 1905
Landscape and marine painter. Married Florence M. q.v. Add: Barnes, Surrey 1882; Putney 1892; Leigh, Essex 1894. † M 1, NG 10, RA 32, RBA 6.

MOORE, Albert Joseph* 1841-1893
Painter, black and white and pastel artist. Son of William M. (1790-1851) and brother of Edwin, Henry, John Collingham and William junr. M. q.v. A.R.W.S. 1884. Add: London. † B 1, CG 1, DOW 1, FIN 3, G 16, GI 10, L 9, M 3, NEA 1, NG 3, P 1, RA 10, RI 1, RWS 10, TOO 1.

MOORE, Alfred J. Howell Exh. 1899-1910
Figure and landscape painter. Walthamstow 1899; Wallington, Surrey 1903. † RA 9, RI 3.

MOORE, Annie Osborne Exh. 1888-1923
Flower painter. London 1888; Twickenham, Middlesex 1914. † B 1, LS 3, RA 1, ROI 1, SWA 5.

MOORE, A.W. Exh. 1915-16
18 Gloucester Road, Kew, Surrey. † RA 2.

MOORE, A.W. Exh. 1908-9
9 Mount Hooton, Nottingham. † N 6.

MOORE, Miss Benson Exh. 1929
† RMS 1.

MOORE, Bertha Exh. 1889-93
Mrs. W.E. Gordon. Landscape and flower painter. London. † D 4, RBA 1, SWA 2.

MOORE, Mrs. Betty Exh. 1938-40
Landscape and flower painter. 6 Crofton Mansions, Dun Laoghaire. † RHA 3.

MOORE, Brenda Exh. 1930-39
Painter and sculptor. Brighton 1930; Hamstead, London 1936. † RA 5.

MOORE, Miss B.A. Exh. 1896
6 Oakley Flats, Chelsea, London. † L 1.

MOORE, Colin Ansdell Exh. 1884-1904
Nottingham 1884; New Lenton, Notts. 1900. † N 4.

MOORE, C.H. Exh. 1884
Landscape painter. c/o Farrer, Queen Anne House, Primrose Hill, London. † RA 1.

MOORE, C. Rupert b. 1904
Painter and stained glass artist. Studied Sheffield School of Art and Royal College of Art. Exh. 1929-40. Add: London. † AR 2, RA 9.

MOORE, Claude T. Stanfield* d. c.1901
Marine painter. N.S.A. 1881. Add: Nottingham. † M 1, N 80, RBA 1.

MOORE, Dora Maxwell Exh. 1909
† LS 3.

MOORE, Dorothy Winifred b. 1897
Portrait and landscape painter and teacher. b. Cork. Studied Edinburgh College of Art. Exh. 1919-31. Add: 24 Buccleuch Place, Edinburgh. † ALP 1, L 9, RA 1, RHA 11, RSA 4, RSW 3.

MOORE, Edith Exh. 1898-1900
Llandaff Hall, Merrion, Co. Dublin. † RHA 3.

MOORE, Edwin 1813-1893
Watercolour painter and teacher. Studied under David Cox the Etcher and Samuel Prout. Son of William M. (1790-1851) and brother of Albert Joseph, Henry, John Collingham and William junr. M. q.v. Add: York. † B 2, D 4, L 2, RI 2.

MOORE, Eleanor Exh. 1909-40
Married Dr. Robert Cecil Robertson q.v. Add: Newmilns, Ayr 1909; Kilmarnock 1934. † GI 14, L 1, RSA 7.

MOORE, Ella Exh. 1904
1 Fullwood Park, Liverpool. † L 1.

MOORE, Ernest 1865-1940
Portrait painter. b. Barnsley, Yorks. Studied London and Paris. Add: Barnsley, Yorks. 1886; Sheffield 1896; London 1916. † B 5, L 7, M 4, P 9, RA 9, RBA 1, ROI 2, WG 78.

MOORE, Ethel Exh. 1937-39
Beachwood, Cookham Dean, Berks. † NEA 1, SWA 2.

MOORE, Evelyn Exh. 1909-13
Watercolour landscape painter. West Runton House, Nr. Cromer, Norfolk. † RA 1, WG 33.

MOORE, Elizabeth A. Exh. 1884-87
Interior painter. Winchester Street, Sherwood, Notts. † N 8.

MOORE, E.M. Exh. 1904-10
Belfast 1904; Strandstown, Co. Down 1910. † RHA 5.

MOORE, Esther M. Exh. 1890-1911
Sculptor. Bedford Park, London 1890 and 1911; Tunbridge Wells, Kent 1909. † L 9, NG 14, RA 18, RSA 2, SWA 3.

MOORE, Mrs. Florence Exh. 1898-1907
Landscape painter. Married A. Harvey M. q.v. Add: Leigh, Essex 1898; West Kensington, London 1906. † NG 8, RA 3.

MOORE, Frank b. 1876
Watercolour painter and etcher. Studied University College, London. Exh. 1910-39. Add: Winkleigh, North Devon 1910; St. Ives, Cornwall 1914 and 1922; Five Ashes, Sussex 1920; Bosham, Sussex 1925; Woodchurch, Kent 1930; Uffculme, Devon 1935. † D 4, LS 8, RA 1, RCA 54.

MOORE, Miss Florence A. Exh. 1896
Avonside, Tewksbury. † B 1.

MOORE, Miss F.M. Exh. 1888-1900
Liverpool. † L 4.

MOORE, Fred W. Exh. 1882
Sculptor. Hammond House, Thames Ditton, Surrey. † RA 1.

MOORE, Gwendolen Exh. 1905-39
Landscape and flower painter. Liverpool. † AR 2, B 2, L 23, RCA 1.

MOORE, H. Exh. 1920-23
Landscape painter. Derby Sketching Club, Derwent St. Derby. † B 1, N 5.

MOORE, Henry* 1831-1895
Marine and landscape painter and watercolourist. Studied under his father William M. (1790-1851) York School of Design and R.A. Schools. A.R.A. 1885, R.A. 1893, R.O.I. 1883, R.W.S. 1880. "Cats Paws off the Land" purchased by Chantrey Bequest 1885. Add: London. † AG 3, B 24, BG 2, D 8, FIN 102, G 20, GI 18, L 28, LEI 99, M 31, NG 13, RA 44, RBA 2, RHA 5, ROI 13, RSA 1, RWS 60, TOO 6.

MOORE, Miss Hogarth Exh. 1900-4
Avonside, Tewkesbury 1900; London 1902. † B 7.

MOORE, Harry Humphrey 1844-1926
American painter. Exh. 1891-96. Add: Paris. † RA 2.

MOORE, Helen N.S. Exh. 1923-26
Kilternan Grange, Kilternan, Co. Dublin. † RHA 3.

MOORE, Henry Spencer* b. 1898
Sculptor and painter. b. Castleford, Yorks. Studied Leeds College of Art 1919-21, Royal College of Art 1921-25 (travelling scholarship), Instructor at Royal College of Art, School of Sculpture. Member London Group 1930. A number of his works are in the Tate Gallery. Exh. 1935. Add: London. † RSA 1.

MOORE, H. Wilkinson Exh. 1882-90
Architect. 6 Beaumont Street, Oxford. † RA 6.

MOORE, James Exh. 1880-83
H.R.H.A. 7 Chichester Street, Belfast. † RHA 10, RSA 3.

MOORE, James Exh. 1885-1904
Figure painter. Sheffield. † L 1, M 1, RA 1.

MOORE, James Exh. 1908-9
N.S.A. 1908. Add: 9 Mount Hooton, Nottingham. † N 3.

MOORE, James Exh. 1923
† D 1.

MOORE, Jennie Exh. 1880-1918
Painter of domestic genre and scriptural subjects. Godalming, Surrey 1880; Eastbourne 1882; Leeds 1883; Sutton, Surrey 1885; London 1890 and 1914; Birmingham 1910. † B 1, D 7, L 4, RA 7, RBA 2, RI 4, SWA 5.

MOORE, John Exh. 1910-36
Landscape painter. Kew, Surrey 1910; London 1936. † RA 3.

MOORE, John Exh. 1935-40
Painter. 60 Regent Road, Handsworth, Birmingham. † B 8, WG 14.

MOORE, Joan A.M. Exh. 1939
Interior painter. 16 Varndell Street, London. † RA 1.

MOORE, J.C. Exh. 1891
20 Rifle Crescent, Aston, Birmingham. † B 2.

MOORE, John Collingham 1829-1880
Portrait, landscape and genre painter. Studied R.A. Schools 1850. Son of William M. (1790-1851) and brother of Albert, Joseph, Edwin, Henry and William junr. M. q.v. Add: London. † D 4, G 5, RA 1.

MOORE, John D. Exh. 1931
Australian painter. † NEA 1.

MOORE, J.E. Exh. 1914-19
Clarence House, Clapham Park, London. † LS 12.

MOORE, J.E.S. Exh. 1935
Watercolour landscape painter. † WG 9.

MOORE, J.H. Exh. 1903
† P 2.

MOORE, John W. Exh. 1897-99
Landscape painter. Birmingham. † L 1, RA 2, RI 1.

MOORE, J. White Exh. 1897
61 York Road, West Hartlepool. † GI 1.

MOORE, Miss K. Exh. 1916
c/o Miss H. Clark, York House, King Street, Nottingham. † N 1.

MOORE, Miss K.N. Exh. 1914-23
4 Knoclaid Road, West Derby, Liverpool. † L 21.

MOORE, Leslie Exh. 1920
Architect. 3 Raymond Buildings, Gray's Inn, London. † RA 1.

MOORE, Miss Leslie Exh. 1903-8
Miniature portrait painter. Bushey, Herts. 1903; Salcombe, Devon 1904. † L 1, RA 1, RMS 1.

MOORE, Letitia A. Exh. 1890-93
Uladh Tower, Dalmuir, N.B. † GI 3.

MOORE, Miss M. Exh. 1927
24 Buccleuch Place, Edinburgh. † RHA 1.

MOORE, Madena Exh. 1880-87
Mrs. Seddon-Moore. Portrait, figure and fruit painter. London 1880; Eastbourne 1887. † RA 3, RBA 2, RI 1, SWA 2.

MOORE, Marian Exh. 1888-96
Upper Merrion Street, Dublin. † RHA 3.

MOORE, Marjorie Exh. 1922-37
Liverpool 1922; Sutton Coldfield 1930. † B 1, L 1, RCA 2, SWA 4.

MOORE, Mark Exh. 1887
Decorative painter. 54 Upper Talbot Street, Nottingham. † N 1.

MOORE, Mary Exh. 1902
15 Heath Bank Road, Birkenhead. † L 1.

MOORE, Miss M. Fowler Exh. 1921
Anglesea House, Ipswich, Suffolk. † L 1.

MOORE, Mary Temple Exh. 1912-14
Daughter of Temple L.M. q.v. Add: 46 Well Walk, Hampstead, London. † L 5.

MOORE, Norman Exh. 1929-30
19 Wordsworth Avenue, Rock Ferry, Birkenhead. † L 3.

MOORE, Mrs. Norman Exh. 1881-84
Watercolour flower painter. The College, St. Bartholemew's Hospital, London. † SWA 4.

MOORE, Olive Exh. 1914-16
17 White Lion Street, Norwich. † LS 4.

MOORE, Percival 1886-1964
Painter. b. Oakworth, Yorks. Studied Royal College of Art. Principal Wakefield School of Art 1920-27. Principal Southampton School of Arts and Crafts from 1928. Exh. 1914. Add: Upper Norwood, London. † RA 1.

MOORE, Rubens Arthur Exh. 1881-1920
Landscape painter. N.S.A. 1893. Add: Nottingham 1881; New Lenton, Notts. 1908, Mansfield, Notts. 1911. † N 111.

MOORE, R.D. Exh. 1928
Ethington Road, Fire Station, Birmingham. † B 1.

MOORE, R.H. Exh. 1885
Painter. 74 St. John's Road, Highgate Archway, London. † RBA 1.

MOORE, Sidney Exh. 1880-1906
Landscape painter. London 1880 and 1890; Wallington, Surrey 1888; Thornton Heath, Surrey 1893. † M 3, NG 14, RA 6, RBA 40, ROI 17.

MOORE, Sidney Exh. 1937-39
Norwich. † RBA 1, ROI 2.

MOORE, Mrs. Sylvia Exh. 1923-24
4 Aigburth Drive, Liverpool. † L 2, RCA 1.

MOORE, Miss Theo b. 1879
Landscape painter. b. Birmingham. Studied St. Ives, Spenlove School of Art, Paris and under Sir Alfred East and Terrick Williams. Principal Cathcart School of Modern Painting. Exh. 1911-29. Add: Wallington, Surrey. † AB 2, RI 2, ROI 2, SWA 9.

MOORE, Thomas Cooper Exh. 1880-99
Painter. Nottingham. † N 26.

MOORE, Thomas F. Exh. 1937-38
40 Rankin Street, Dundee. † RSA 2.

MOORE, Temple L. Exh. 1897-1918
Architect. Father of Mary Temple M. q.v. Add: London. † L 3, RA 45, RSA 3.

MOORE, Thomas Sturge 1870-1944
Illustrator, wood engraver and poet. Studied Lambeth School of Art and wood engraving under Charles Roberts. Exh. 1914. † RSA 3.

MOORE, William Junr. 1817-1909
Landscape painter and teacher. Son of William M. (1790-1851) and brother of Albert Joseph, Edwin, Henry and John Collingham M. q.v. Add: 24 Bruton Lane, York. † D 10, L 1, RI 8.

MOORE, W.D. Exh. 1931-32
Landscape painter. 55 Heanor Road, Shipley End, Ilkeston, Derbys. † N 3.

MOORE, W.H. Exh. 1886
18 Rue d'Aumaille, 10 Passage Doisy, Ternes, Paris. † M 2.

MOORE, William J. Exh. 1885-92
Figure and watercolour portrait painter. London. † RA 3.

MOORE, W. Leslie P. Exh. 1936
Engraver. † RED 1.

MOOREHEAD, Ada Exh. 1925-32
Painter. 13 Charville Road, Rathmines. † RHA 4.

MOORHEAD, Ethel Exh. 1901-20
Painter. Dundee, 1901; London 1916; Dublin 1918. † GI 4, L 1, NEA 1, RSA 8.

MOORHOUSE, Blanche b. 1885
nee Ellis. Watercolour painter and pastel artist. Studied Leeds School of Art. Married George Mortram M. q.v. Exh. 1923-30. Add: Morland, Nr. Penrith 1923; Helsington, Kendal 1926. † L 4, RCA 7, RHA 1, RSA 3.

MOORHOUSE, Ethel Exh. 1894
Sunnyside, Freshfield, Lancs. † L 1.

MOORHOUSE, George Mortram b. 1882
Figure painter. Studied under Frank Brangwyn, J.M. Swan, Orpen and Augustus John. Married Blanche M. q.v. Exh. 1908-30. Add: Arnside, Westmorland 1908; Morland, Nr. Penrith 1922; Helsington, Kendal 1926. † L 9, RA 1, RCA 10, RHA 1, RSA 8.

MOORSEL, van see V

MOORWOOD, Ruth F. Exh. 1927-37
Mrs. Graham Munro. 10 Moray Place, Edinburgh. † RSA 4.

MOPPETT-PERKINS, J. Exh. 1898-1927
Landscape painter. London. † I 3, M 1, NEA 1, RA 5, RI 1, ROI 8.

MORA, Francis Luis* b. 1874
American figure painter. Exh. 1909. Add: London. † L 1, RA 1.

MORAHAN, Michael Joseph b. 1875
Sculptor. Teacher of modelling and carving at Bow Polytechnic and Arts and Crafts, Ireland. Exh. 1908-32. Add: London. † GI 2, RA 9.

MORAN, Miss A. Exh. 1915
58 Everton Road, Liverpool. † L 1.

MORAN, A.G. Exh. 1892
6 Russell Street, Dublin. † RHA 1.

MORAN, J.P. Exh. 1881-93
Paris 1881; Dublin 1885. † RHA 19.

MORAN, Mrs. Mary Nimmo 1842-1899
Etcher. b. Scotland. Married Thomas M. q.v. d. New York. R.E. 1881. Exh. 1881-84. Add: New York. † L 1, RE 7.

MORAN, Peter* 1841-1914
American artist. b. Bolton, Lancs. Brother of Thomas M. q.v. Exh. 1884. Add: c/o Cassells, Ludgate Hill, London. † L 1.

MORAN, Thomas* 1837-1926
American painter and etcher. Brother of Peter M. q.v. Married Mary Nimmo M. q.v. R.E. 1881-87. Exh. 1881-1905. Add: New York, U.S.A. 1881; London 1905. † L 1, RA 1, RE 13.

MORAN, William Exh. 1938
Landscape painter. National College of Art, Kildare Street, Dublin. † RHA 2.

MORANI, A. Exh. 1889
Figure painter. c/o Mr. Squire, 293 Oxford Street, London. † NG 1.

MORANT, Charles Harbord Exh. 1886-93
Figure and interior painter. London. † RA 1, ROI 2.

MORBY, Walter J. Exh. 1883-90
Landscape painter. South Hackney, London 1883; Sunbury-on-Thames 1884. † B 4, D 1, M 1, RA 2, RBA 12, RHA 1, RI 1.

MORCH, Miss S. Exh. 1891
17 Rock Park, Rock Ferry, Cheshire. † L 2.

MORCOM, Isobel Exh. 1924
Sculptor. The Clock House, Bromsgrove, Worcs. † RA 1.

MORCOM, Joseph Herbert b. 1871
Sculptor. New Ferry, Cheshire 1899; Liverpool 1906; Leicester 1911. † L 23, RA 6, RCA 5.

MORDAUNT, Caroline Exh. 1901
Hampton Lucy, Warwick. † B 1.

MORDAUNT, Miss E. Exh. 1927
11 Elm Park Road, Wallasey, Cheshire. † L 1.

MORDECAI, Joseph 1851-1940
Portrait and landscape painter. Studied Heatherleys, and R.A. Schools. Add: London. † L 4, RA 20, RCA 1, ROI 6.

MORDIN, Herbert Exh. 1938
† M 1.

MOREAU, Charles b. 1830
French painter. Exh. 1886. Add: Paris. † M 1.

MOREL, H. Exh. 1911
c/o R. Murray, 21 Mincing Lane, London. † LS 3.

MOREL, Vaar Zon Exh. 1911
Landscape painter. † BRU 1.

MORELL, D'Arcy Exh. 1880-82
Landscape and coastal painter. London. † G 1, M 1.

MORELLE, John P. Exh. 1884-86
Figure painter. Parkstone Villa, High Road, Chiswick, London. † RA 1, RBA 1, RI 1.

MORENO, Manuel Exh. 1928
Portrait, figure and landscape painter. † BA 62.

MORENO, Matias Exh. 1881
Figure painter. 89 Rue de Rennes, Paris. † RA 1.

MORETON, Margaret Exh. 1909
Hill Grove, Bembridge, I.o.W. † RCA 1.

MORETON, Samuel H. Exh. 1911-14
198 Oxford Terrace, Christchurch, New Zealand. † LS 8.

MOREWOOD, George N. Exh. 1926-40
Sculptor. 3 Radnor Studios, Radnor Street, London. † RA 10.

MORGAN, de see D

MORGAN, Alfred* Exh. 1880-1917
Still life, fruit, flower, portrait, landscape and historical painter. Father of Alfred Kedington, Baxter and Ethel M. q.v. Add: London. † G 16, L 3, M 2, NG 2, RA 26, RBA 6, ROI 4.

MORGAN, Annie Exh. 1900-40
Edinburgh. † GI 23, RSA 60, RSW 1.

MORGAN, Miss A.B. Exh. 1884-97
Edgbaston, Birmingham 1884; Winchester, Hants. 1897. † B 6.

MORGAN, Alfred George Exh. 1896-1919
Still life and fruit painter. 4 Elgin Street, Whitby, Yorks. † B 4, L 1, RA 10.

MORGAN, Mrs. A.K. see HAYES Gertrude Ellen

MORGAN, Alfred Kedington 1868-1928
Portrait and landscape painter and etcher. Art master Rugby School. Son of Alfred M. q.v. Married Gertrude Ellen Hayes q.v. A.R.E. 1901. Exh. 1899-1906. Add: London. † RA 2, RE 6.

MORGAN, A.O. Exh. 1914
50 Ladbroke Road, London. † LS 3.

MORGAN, Barbara Exh. 1930
Wood engraver. † RED 1.

MORGAN, Baxter Exh. 1905-32
Son of Alfred M. q.v. Add: 30 Palewell Park, East Sheen, London. † L 1, ROI 1.

MORGAN, Brenda A.R. Exh. 1923-27
12 Cheyne Gardens, London. † ROI 2, SWA 1.

MORGAN, Charles Exh. 1882-1912
Coastal painter. Handsworth, Birmingham. † B 33, M 1, RBA 4.

MORGAN, Miss D. Exh. 1903
68 Grosvenor Street, London. † SWA 1.

MORGAN, Miss D. Exh. 1914
Wallington. † SWA 2.

MORGAN, Mrs. Dorothy Exh. 1928-29
3 Princes Gate East, Liverpool. † L 5.

MORGAN, Miss D.B. Carey Exh. 1909-39
Painter and pastel artist. Add: London. † B 2, I 2, L 13, RA 3, RI 1, RSA 3.

MORGAN, Major D.N. Exh. 1918-36
Watercolour painter. Travelled in India. Add: Rostrevor, Seaford, Sussex. † ROI 1, WG 145.

MORGAN, Miss E. Exh. 1911-14
9 Rue Campagne Premiere, Paris. † L 1, RA 3.

MORGAN, Miss E.A. Exh. 1929
Carlton, Ford Road, Upton, Wirral, Cheshire. † L 3.

MORGAN, Edwin Ernest b. 1881
Portrait and miniature painter and teacher. Studied Paris, America, Lambeth School of Art and Heatherleys. A.R.M.S. 1909, R.M.S. 1911. Exh. 1908-40. Add: London 1908; Torquay 1927. † GI 1, L 1, RA 30, RMS 54.

MORGAN, Edith F. Exh. 1898-1908
London. † L 3, RA 2, RMS 2, SWA 3.

MORGAN, E.J. Exh. 1937
Flower painter. † COO 4.

MORGAN, Ethel M. d. 1927
Miniature portrait painter. A.R.M.S. 1923. A.S.W.A. 1918. Daughter of Alfred M. q.v. Add: London 1900 and 1911; Paris 1907. † L 8, RA 24, RI 7, RMS 29, SWA 9.

MORGAN, E.P. Exh. 1883-89
Landscape painter. Add: London 1883; Killiney, Co. Dublin 1889. † B 1, D 1, RBA 1.

MORGAN, Frederick* 1856-1927
Animal, portrait, child and domestic genre painter. Married Alice Mary Havers q.v. R.O.I. 1883. Add: London 1880; Broadstairs, Kent 1904. † B 24, FIN 1, GI 20, L 27, M 36, RA 50, RBA 1, RI 2, ROI 64, TOO 6.

MORGAN, Frank Somerville Exh. 1883-8
Figure painter. Add: London. † D 3 RBA 5, RI 5.

MORGAN, Fred W. Exh. 191
29 Chandos Road, Cricklewood, London † L 2.

MORGAN, George Exh. 1880-81
Medalist and sculptor. Add: Philadelphia U.S.A. and London. † RA 2.

MORGAN, Grace Exh. 1900-1
London. † B 5, L 3, SWA 16.

MORGAN, Gwenda b. 190
Wood engraver and illustrator. Studie Goldsmiths College and Grosvenor Schoo of Modern Art. Exh. 1936. Add: Pet worth, Sussex. † RA 1, RED 1.

MORGAN, Gwynydd Ruth b. 190
Painter, etcher and wood engraver. b Ascension Island. Studied Chelsea Poly technic, Maidstone School of Art an Birmingham School of Art. Exh. 1938-40 Add: Birmingham 1938; Worcester 1940 † B 3.

MORGAN, G.T. Exh. 192
Philadelphia, U.S.A. † B 2.

MORGAN, Mrs. G. Valentine Exh. 1914-3
Figure painter. Add: London 1914 Holford House, Baldock, Herts. 1930. † L 1, RA 1.

MORGAN, Miss H.G. Exh. 1889
Flower painter. Add: 8 Pelham Place, Seaford, Sussex. † SWA 1.

MORGAN, Hugh T. Exh. 1923-24
Architect. Add: 14 Gray's Inn Square London. † RA 2.

MORGAN, Jane Exh. 1884
Figure painter. Add: 32 Briennerstrasse, Munich. † SWA 2.

MORGAN, John Exh. 1889
27 Strand Street, Liverpool. † L 1.

MORGAN, John* 1823-1886
Figure and domestic painter. R.B.A. 1875. Add: Guildford, Surrey 1880; Hastings 1882. † B 8, GI 9, L 7, M 12, RA 13, RBA 39, ROI 7, RSA 2.

MORGAN, John C.B. Exh. 1906
20 Minerva Street, Glasgow. † GI 1.

MORGAN, Kate Exh. 1882-99
Watercolour figure painter and black and white artist. Add: London 1882 and 1895; Bingham, Notts. 1894. † G 1, NG 1, RA 9, RHA 6.

MORGAN, Mrs. L. Louisa Exh. 1883-1905
Portrait painter. Add: Manchester 1883; The Hut, Fairlie, Ayr and London 1899. † M 6, NG 2, RA 1, SWA 5.

MORGAN, Miss M. Exh. 1884-86
Carron, South Norwood Park, London. † L 1, RE 3.

MORGAN, M. Alice Exh. 1889-1900
Milford Haven, S. Wales. † D 28, SWA 1.

MORGAN, Maude A. Exh. 1934-39
42 Harold Road, Cliftonville, Margate. † ROI 3.

MORGAN, Mary E.T. Exh. 1896-99
Figure painter. Add: c/o Mr. E.T. Perrott, Cartref, Sutton, Surrey. † RA 1, RCA 2, RHA 1.

MORGAN, M.L. Exh. 1888
Landscape painter. Add: Woodbine House, North End Road, Fulham, London. † RI 1.

MORGAN, Mary Vernon Exh. 1880-1927
nee Vernon. Fruit, flower and landscape painter. Studied under her father William H. Vernon, q.v. Married Walter Jenks M. q.v. Add: Handsworth, Birmingham. † B 72, D 1, L 5, RA 8, RBA 20, WG 27.

MORGAN, Olga Exh. 1897-1906
Miniature portrait painter. London. † B 1, RA 7, RMS 3.

MORGAN, Owen Exh. 1898-1907
Landscape painter. London. † RA 3, RBA 2.

MORGAN, Rendle Exh. 1936
School of Art, Brighton. † RBA 2.

MORGAN, S.H. Exh. 1938
Architect. Add: 34 King Street, South Rochdale, Lancs. † RA 1.

MORGAN, T.H. Exh. 1884
Simla Villa, Waverley Street, Nottingham. † N 1.

MORGAN, Mrs. Violet M. Exh. 1938
Portrait painter. Add: The Bell House, Fetcham, Leatherhead. † RA 1.

MORGAN, William Exh. 1898-1900
61 Jane Street, Glasgow. † GI 3.

MORGAN, Miss Woodbine Exh. 1940
Figure painter. Add: 15 Roland Gardens, London. † RA 1.

MORGAN, William Evan Charles b. 1903
Line engraver and etcher. Studied Slade School (Prix de Rome Scholarship 1924). Travelled in Italy. Exh. 1928-36. Add: c/o Beaux Arts Galleries, Bruton Place, London 1928; Craigblea, Ardtornich, Morvern, Argyll 1935. † BA 41, CON 4, FIN 11, L 7, RA 11.

MORGAN, Walter Jenks 1847-1924
Genre painter and illustrator. Studied Birmingham School of Art and South Kensington. Worked for the "Graphic", "Illustrated London News" and Messrs. Cassell and Co. R.B.A. 1884, R.B.S.A. 1888. Married Mary Vernon M. q.v. Add: London 1880; Handsworth, Birmingham 1889. † B 94, L 24, RA 7, RBA 127, RI 4, WG 65.

MORGARI, R. Exh. 1885
Turin. † RSA 1.

MORHAM, R. Exh. 1884
11 Royal Exchange, Edinburgh. † RSA 1.

MORICE, Miss A.A. Exh. 1881-85
Watercolour landscape painter. Add: Matfield Green, Brenchley, Kent. † RA 2, RBA 5.

MORICE, A.F. Exh. 1884-89
Watercolour landscape painter. Add: Sandfels, Reigate. † SWA 4.

MORIER, Mrs. Catherine Exh. 1913
65 Hamilton Terrace, London. † LS 2.

MORIES, Fred G. Exh. 1905-37
Watercolour portrait painter and charcoal artist. Add: Greenock 1905; Glasgow 1909; London 1937. † GI 10, RA 2, RBA 1, RSA 5.

MORISON, C. Graham Exh. 1880
27 Park Terrace, Stirling. † GI 1.

MORISON, John Exh. 1880-1912
Copewood, Kilmalcolm. † GI 14, RSA 2.

MORISON, J.R.M. Exh. 1905
33 Craiglea Drive, Morningside, Edinburgh. † RSA 2.

MORISON, Margaret Heron Exh. 1936-39
Newmiln, Perth. † RCA 3, RSA 3.

MORISON, Rosie J. Exh. 1889-1904
Edinburgh. † GI 13, RSA 38.

MORISOT, Berthe* 1841-1895
French painter. Exh. 1893. † NEA 1.

MORLAND, James Smith d. 1921
South African landscape painter and teacher. Exh. 1882-1910. Add: Liverpool 1882; Trefriw, N. Wales 1884; c/o E. Aughton, Seacombe, Lancs. 1890; c/o H.T. Doble, Tavistock, Devon 1893; c/o Chapman Bros. Kings Road, London 1910. † B 1, L 13, RA 7.

MORLEY, Elinor Exh. 1938
† NEA 1.

MORLEY, E. Beryl Exh. 1937-38
† P 2.

MORLEY, F. Exh. 1884
Byard's Leap, nr. Sleaford, Lincs. † N 1.

MORLEY, Florence Exh. 1881-88
Watercolour painter. Add: Temple Brewer, Wellingore, Grantham, Lincs. † N 5.

MORLEY, Harry* 1881-1943
Portrait, figure, landscape painter and engraver. b. Leicester. Trained as an architect. Studied Leicester School of Art, Royal College of Art (travelling scholarship in architecture), Paris and Italy. A.R.A. 1936, A.R.B.A. 1923, R.B.A. 1924, A.R.E. 1929, R.P. 1937, A.R.W.S. 1927, R.W.S. 1931. "Apollo and Marsyas" purchased by Chantrey Bequest 1924. Add: London 1905 and 1910; Groby, Leics. 1908. † AG 6, BA 142, CG 3, CHE 2, FIN 6, G 5, GI 6, GOU 4, I 18, L 16, M 3, NEA 10, P 17, RA 83, RBA 22, RHA 5, RE 32, RI 1, ROI 1, RSA 4, RWS 161, TOO 1.

MORLEY, Henry 1869-1937
Painter, etcher and pastelier. b. Nottingham. Studied Nottingham School of Art and Juliens, Paris. Married Isabel M. q.v. Add: Nottingham 1891; Cambuskenneth, Stirling 1894; Whins of Milton, Stirling 1902; St. Ninians, Stirling 1910. † GI 77, GOU 2, I 2, L 12, M 3, N 10, RSA 48, RSW 4.

MORLEY, Henry Charles Exh. 1892-1900
Landscape painter. Add: 71 Hunger Hill Road, Nottingham. † N 7.

MORLEY, H.S.. Collinson Exh. 1923-25
Etcher. † FIN 5.

MORLEY, Mrs. Ida Exh. 1897-1907
Landscape painter. Add: Hampstead, London. † B 4, RA 7.

MORLEY, Isabel Exh. 1902-16
Married Henry M. q.v. Add: Whins of Milton, Stirling 1902; St. Ninians, Stirling 1910. † GI 17, L 1.

MORLEY, Julia Exh. 1937
† NEA 1.

MORLEY, J.C. Exh. 1891
Goyt Place, Whaley Bridge, Derbys. † M 2.

MORLEY, Mrs. Lilias Exh. 1922-35
Portrait painter. Add: 4 Pembroke Road, London. † RA 1, SWA 2.

MORLEY, Mabel Exh. 1904-6
96 Sinclair Road, West Kensington, London. † RHA 3.

MORLEY, Mary D. Exh. 1930
† P 1.

MORLEY, Robert* 1857-1941
Figure, animal and landscape painter. Studied Slade School, Munich and Rome. R.B.A. 1889. Add: London 1880; Farnham, Surrey 1892; Frensham, Surrey 1904; Lechlade, Glos. 1926. † B 35, D 2, FIN 6, L 52, M 14, NG 2, RA 14, RBA 310, RHA 19, ROI 26, RSA 2.

MORLEY, Ruth Exh. 1913-27
Sculptor. Studied Neuchatel College. Add: Paris 1913 and 1916; London 1914 and 1920. † B 2, GI 5, I 1, L 28, LS 6, RA 2, RBA 3, RCA 2, RSA 2.

MORLEY, T.W. Exh. 1906-27
Bromley, Kent 1906; c/o A.A. Bailey, 188 Brompton Road, London 1927. † RA 5, RI 9, ROI 7.

MORLEY, Walter J. Exh. 1882-83
Animal painter. Add: 104 Victoria Park Road, London. † M 1, RBA 1.

MORLON, Antoine P.E.* Exh. 1891-92
Marine painter. Add: c/o C.C. Barton, 6 Lowndes Square, London. † RA 2.

MORLOT, Alphonse Alexis 1838-1918
French artist. Exh. 1883. Add: 18 Rue de Chabrol, Paris. † GI 1.

MORO, Mrs. Arthur Exh. 1903-5
Landscape painter. Add: 87 Gloucester Terrace, Hyde Park, London. † BG 1, NG 7.

MOROSOFF, Vera Exh. 1939
c/o Leicester Galleries, Leicester Square, London. † SWA 1.

MOROT, Aime 1850-1913
French artist. Exh. 1903. Add: 11 Rue Weber, Paris. † GI 1.

MORPHEW, Reginald Exh. 1901-8
Architect. London. † RA 4.

MORREY, P. Exh. 1930
Architect. Add: New Oxford House, Hart Street, London. † RA 1.

MORRICE, James Wilson* 1865-1924
Canadian figure and landscape painter. Add: Montreal 1897; Paris 1901. † GI 2, GOU 14, L 2.

MORRIER, Molly Gartside Exh. 1925
116 Maida Vale, London. † SWA 1.

MORRILL, Elizabeth Exh. 1880
Flower and bird painter. Add: Pocklington, Yorks. † SWA 2.

MORRIS, Alice Exh. 1882-1900
Flower painter. Add: Manchester 1882; Coalville, nr. Leicester 1896. † B 1, L 3, M 6, N 5, RI 4.

MORRIS, Andrew Exh. 1887
Etcher. Add: Wyndham Villa, Cambridge Road, Bevois Mt., Southampton. † RA 2.

MORRIS, Mrs. Ann Exh. 1939
Flower painter. Add: Ash, Aldershot. † RA 1.

MORRIS, Mrs. Annie Exh. 1918
64 Morningside Road, Edinburgh. † GI 1.

MORRIS, Miss A.R. Exh. 1904
Inversnaid, Southcote Road, Reading, Berks. † D 1, RHA 1.

MORRIS, Bettie Exh. 1910-24
25 Moss Grove, Birkenhead. † L 13.

MORRIS, Miss B.E. Exh. 1914-18
5 Ashley Avenue, Cheriton, Folkestone. † RA 1, RHA 2.

MORRIS, C. Exh. 1913
Florence House, Newlyn, Penzance. † RA 1.

MORRIS, C. Exh. 1937-40
Harefield, Ridgemount Road, St. Albans, Herts. † RI 4.

MORRIS, Carey Exh. 1909-17
London 1909; Sandown, I.O.W. 1915; c/o Bourlet and Sons, London 1917. † B 2, GI 1, LS 11, P 2, RA 4.

MORRIS, Cedric b. 1889
Landscape, still life, flower and bird painter. b. Wales. Studied Paris, Rome and Berlin. Member London Group 1927. Exh. 1919-37. Add: Newlyn, Penzance, Cornwall 1919; Higham, Colchester 1935. † BA 2, CON 1, FIN 3, GI 1, LEI 47, LS 6, NEA 2, RCA 4, RED 8, TOO 71.

MORRIS, Charles Alfred b. 1898
Portrait and landscape painter. b. Portsmouth. Studied Brighton College of Art and R.A . Schools. Life master Liverpool School of Art. Head of Drawing and Painting Department, Brighton College of Art. Married Muriel M. q.v. Exh. 1925-39. Add: Liverpool 1925; Sompting, nr. Worthing 1930. † GOU 1, L 6, RA 8, ROI 2.

MORRIS, Charles F. Exh. 1932
16 King Alfred Street, Barrow in Furness. † RSA 2.

MORRIS, Charles Greville b. 1861
Landscape painter. b. Lancashire. Studied in Paris. R.B.A. 1896. Exh. 1882-1921. Add: Eccles, Manchester 1882; St. Ives, Cornwall 1893; Wareham, Dorset 1905. † B 3, DOW 2, FIN 4, GI 2, L 11, LS 5, M 10, NG 2, RA 25, RBA 6, RHA 1, ROI 5.

MORRIS, Daphne Wingate Exh. 1935-38
Northwood, Middlesex. † SWA 5.

MORRIS, Edith Exh. 1903-4
Miniature painter. Add: c/o G. Kelbe Esq., Westholm, Avondale Road, South Croydon, Surrey. † RA 3.

MORRIS, Miss E.E. Exh. 1907-11
8 West Hoe Terrace, Plymouth. † RA 2.

MORRIS, Miss E.F.E. Exh. 1904-5
Inversnaid, Southcote Road, Reading. † D 1, GI 1, RHA 1.

MORRIS, Mrs. E.G. (M) Exh. 1912
45 Newhall Street, Birmingham. † RA 1.

MORRIS, Ethel R. Exh. 1933-34
Sculptor. Add: 17B Holland Park Road, London. † RA 2.

MORRIS, F. Exh. 1884
Percy Villa, Cricklefield Road, Clapton. † RHA 1.

MORRIS, Miss F. Exh. 1882
Pembroke Place, Bolton, Lancs. † M 1.

MORRIS, Frank Exh. 1911-18
Minehead, Somerset 1911; London 1918. † LS 20.

MORRIS, Fred Exh. 1930-31
Earlstown, Lancs. † L 1, RCA 1.

MORRIS, Frances M. Exh. 1927
Hill Crest, Glossop, nr. Manchester. † L 2.

MORRIS, Miss G. Exh. 1887-1911
Birmingham. † B 5, L 1, LS 3, RA 1.

MORRIS, Mrs. G. Exh. 1924
182 Cromwell Road, London. † SWA 1.

MORRIS, Miss G.G. Exh. 1905
† SWA 1.

MORRIS, G.H. Exh. 1880-98
Landscape painter. N.S.A. 1898. Add: Nottingham. † N 6.

MORRIS, G. Llewelyn Exh. 1891-98
Architect. London. † RA 5.

MORRIS, Helen Exh. 1890-1928
Gloucester 1890 and 1928; Hove 1913. † I 1, L 2, RI 4.

MORRIS, Hilda Gertrude Exh. 1928-30
Watercolour painter, wood engraver and linocut artist. Studied Slade School and Tudor Hart's Studio in Paris. Add: Bishops Stortford, Herts. † AB 6, SWA 4.

MORRIS, James Archibald 1857-1942
Architect. Studied Slade School and R.A. Schools. A.R.S.A. 1916, R.S.A. 1932. Add: Ayr. † GI 18, RA 1, RSA 42.

MORRIS, Mrs. Kathleen* Exh. 1939
c/o Charles H. West, 117 Finchley Road, London. † SWA 2.

MORRIS, Lillian N. Exh. 1900
Sculptor. Add: 25 Ifield Road, Fulham, London. † RA 2.

MORRIS, M. Exh. 1915
Stockingford, nr. Nuneaton. † RA 1.

MORRIS, Margaret b. 1891
Miniature painter. b. Lisbon, Portugal. Studied Manchester Municipal School of Art. Exh. 1916-19. Add: London. † LS 8.

MORRIS, Marion Exh. 1883-92
3 Columbia Road, Oxton, Cheshire. † L 2.

MORRIS, Mary Exh. 1893-1938
Glasgow 1893 and 1914; Pollockshields, N.B. 1909. † GI 50, L 1.

MORRIS, Mary Exh. 1937
Painter. Add: Castlefield, Clonmel. † RHA 1.

MORRIS, Max Exh. 1916-17
Etcher. Add: 54 Blenheim Gardens, Cricklewood, London. † NEA 1, RA 1, RSA 1.

MORRIS, May Exh. 1896-1908
8 Hammersmith Terrace, London. † NG 1, SWA 1.

MORRIS, Mittie Exh. 1882-94
Mrs. T. Wilson M. Painter, etcher and Christmas card designer. Add: London. † M 1, RA 5, RBA 1.

MORRIS, Mrs. Muriel Exh. 1927-28
nee Drummond. Married Charles Alfred M. q.v. Add: Aigburth, Liverpool. † L 3.

MORRIS, M.H. Exh. 1928
Landscape painter. † AB 3.

MORRIS, Marjorie V.O. Exh. 1931-35
Portrait and figure painter. Add: London 1931; Epsom, Surrey 1935. † RA 3.

MORRIS, Nancy G. Exh. 1907-14
London. † B 2, L 8, RA 5.

MORRIS, Oliver Exh. 1883-92
Watercolour landscape painter. Add: 18 Haydn Park Road, Shepherds Bush, London. † RI 2.

MORRIS, Peter Exh. 1926
Landscape and portrait painter. † ALP 62.

MORRIS, Philip Richard* 1836-1902
Portrait and genre painter. b. Davenport. Studied R.A. Schools 1855 (gold and silver medals and travelling studentship). Visited France and Italy. A.R.A. 1877. Add: London. † B 17, BG 3, FIN 1, G 19, GI 9, L 28, M 29, P 6, RA 72, RHA 5, ROI 7, TOO 4.

MORRIS, Roy Exh. 1910-40
Painter and etcher. Studied Chester School of Art, Slade School and Central School of Arts and Crafts. Teacher at Derby School of Art from 1920. Add: Chester 1910; Derby 1920. † L 13, M 2, NEA 6, RA 10, RBA 5.

MORRIS, R.V. Exh. 1939
Bleasby, Nottingham. † N 1.

MORRIS, S. Exh. 1908
36 Cambridge Street, London. † RA 1.

MORRIS, Shelagh C.M. Exh. 1930-35
120 Birchfield Road, Handsworth, Birmingham. † B 3.

MORRIS, William 1834-1896
Painter, stained glass, tapestry and wall paper designer and poet. Founder of the Kelmscott Press in 1890. "Figure of Guinevere" (c. 1858) purchased by Chantrey Bequest 1940, and 2 cartoons for stained glass "Guinevere and Elaine" and "Angel of the Resurrection". Exh. 1886. Add: London. † L 1.

MORRIS, William Bright b. 1844
Portrait, genre and landscape painter. R.O.I. 1883. Exh. 1880-1905. Add: London. † B 4, G 2, GI 2, L 7, M 41, NG 4, RA 18, RBA 3, ROI 23, TOO 2.

MORRIS, W.V. Exh. 1907
13 George Street, Edinburgh. † RSA 1.

MORRISET, F.H. Exh. 1903-10
15 Rue Lemercier, Paris. † L 2.

MORRISH, Sydney S. Exh. 1881-94
Genre, landscape and portrait painter. Add: Clare House, Torquay. † L 2, M 5, RA 13.

MORRISH, W.S. Exh. 1880-1903
Watercolour landscape painter. Add: Chagford, Devon. † D 9, RA 1, RBA 3, RI 2.

MORRISON, Albert b. 1872
Etcher. Studied Glasgow School of Art. Registrar of Glasgow University. Exh. 1929-31. Add: 12 Austen Road, Jordanhill, Glasgow. † GI 3.

MORRISON, Alexander Exh. 1880-8
Elgin 1880; Glasgow 1888. † GI 1
RSA 9.

MORRISON, Mrs. Graham Exh. 192
31 Grange Road, Southport, Lancs. † L 2

MORRISON, Joseph Albert Colquhoun b. 188
Painter and black and white artist. Studie
Trinity Hall, Cambridge 1901-4 and Nev
Art School. R.B.A. 1931. Exh. 1923-40
Add: Chalford, Stroud, Glos. † CHE 2
GOU 5, M 1, NEA 7, RA 3, RBA 8.

MORRISON, J.C. Exh. 188
Banff. † RSA 1.

MORRISON, Mrs. Jessie M. Exh. 193
Paris, Ashton under Hill, nr. Evesham
Worcs. † B 1.

MORRISON, Kenneth Maciver Exh. 1898-193
Painter. b. Claygate, Surrey. Studie
Juliens, and Colarossi's, Paris. Membe
London Group 1924. Add: Paris 1898
London 1920. † BA 56, CHE 3, GOU 2
L 3, P 2, RA 3, RED 31.

MORRISON, Marjorie Exh. 1931-3
4 Belford Road, Edinburgh. † RSA 2.

MORRISON, Mary Exh. 192
Via Giovanni Prati 23, Florence, Italy
† GI 1, L 1.

MORRISON, Mary E. Exh. 191
London. † M 1, RI 1.

MORRISON, Nina d. 1904
Exh. 1902-4. Add: 21 Ivanhoe Road
Sefton Park, Liverpool. † L 3.

MORRISON, R. Boyd b. 189
Painter, designer, modeller and teacher. b
Belfast. Studied Belfast School of Art and
Slade School. Exh. 1923-40. Add: London
1923; Bangor, Ireland 1940. † GOU 1
RA 1, RHA 1.

MORRISON, Robert Edward 1852-1925
Portrait and genre painter. b. Peel, I.O.M.
Add: Liverpool from 1882. † B 1, GI 4
L 191, M 3, RA 41, RBA 2, RCA 53
RI 2, ROI 5.

MORRISON, W. McIvor Exh. 1880-93
Rathmines, Dublin 1880; Rothesay, Isle of Bute 1884. † GI 3, RSA 16.

MORRISON, W.W. Exh. 1885
Painter. Add: 2 Daphne Terrace, Chiswick, London. † ROI 1.

MORROCCO, Alberto Exh. 1939
35 Causewayend, Aberdeen. † RSA 2.

MORROW, Albert 1863-1927
Watercolour painter and black and white artist. b. Belfast. Brother of George and Edwin M. q.v. Contributer to "Punch". Add: London 1890; Eastbourne 1917. † M 2, RA 9.

MORROW, Edwin A. Exh. 1903-9
Landscape painter. Brother of Albert and George M. q.v. Add: London. † RA 3.

MORROW, George 1870-1955
Artist with "Punch" from 1906. b. Belfast. Brother of Albert and Edwin M. q.v. Exh. 1897-1904. Add: London. † RA 1, RBA 1.

MORROW, Jack Exh. 1912-16
15 D'Olier Street, Dublin. † RHA 3.

MORSE, Miss F.L. Exh. 1904-11
Hove, Sussex. † L 3, LS 3.

MORSE, Miss H.W. Exh. 1896
57 Bedford Gardens, London. † SWA 1.

MORSE, Mrs. Margery Exh. 1929-34
Barton on Sea, Hants. 1929; New Milton, Hants. 1934. † B 3, L 1, RCA 4, SWA 1.

MORSE, Mary Enid Exh. 1928-34
Landscape painter. † COO 1, NEA 1.

MORSE, W. Exh. 1889-90
Poplar Lodge, Yardley, Staffs. † B 2.

MORSE-RUMMEL, Frank b. 1884
German painter. Exh. 1923-35. † ALP 46, FIN 65.

MORSHEAD, Arminell Exh. 1916-28
Painter and etcher. b. Tavistock, Devon. Studied Slade School and Royal College of Art. Add: Bushey, Herts. 1916; Guildford, Surrey. 1920. † I 1, P 5, RA 3, RCA 7, RI 1, ROI 2, SWA 1.

MORSTADT, Anna Exh. 1910-12
4 Rue Cochin de Passage a Alger, Paris. † L 1, RSA 1.

MORT, F.G. Exh. 1892
22 Carleton Road, Tufnell Park West, London. † RI 1.

MORT, J.D. Exh. 1884-86
Belle Vue Hotel, Trefriw, North Wales. † L 2.

MORT, Marjorie Exh. 1932-38
† L 1, M 2.

MORTEN, Miss E.E. Exh. 1914-15
High Peak Hotel, Forest Road West, Nottingham. † N 2.

MORTEN, Jessie Exh. 1903-5
Miniature portrait painter. Add: Uxbridge, Middlesex 1903; London 1905. † RA 2.

MORTEN, Jane Wells Exh. 1886-1928
Flower and landscape painter. Add: London 1886; Nottingham 1913. † N 22, RI 1, SWA 2.

MORTIMER, Alex Exh. 1885-88
London. † GI 1, L 1, RSA 1, TOO 7.

MORTIMER, Constance Exh. 1899
Miniature portrait painter. Add: 78 Eccleston Square, London. † RA 1.

MORTIMER, John Exh. 1933
56 Croftburn Drive, Kings Park, Glasgow. † RSA 1.

MORTIMER, Miss J.D. Exh. 1896
5 Brunswick Place, London. † SWA 1.

MORTIMER, Miss M.A. Exh. 1933
Cardiff. † RCA 1.

MORTIMER, Robert Exh. 1891
Architect. Add: 6 Delahay Street, Westminster, London. † RA 1.

MORTIMORE, Annie Exh. 1887
Landscape painter. Add: Belgrave Square, Nottingham. † N 1.

MORTLOCK, Ethel d. 1928
Portrait painter. Exh. 1880-1904. Add: London. † G 2, L 1, M 1, RA 27.

MORTON, A. Exh. 1905
52 Pembroke Road, Kensington, London. † RA 1.

MORTON, Alastair Exh. 1939
Painter. † LEF 7.

MORTON, Arthur Exh. 1927-34
109 Aylesford Road, Handsworth, Birmingham. † B 5.

MORTON, Annie Wilhelmina b. 1878
Painter. Studied Edinburgh School of Art, Julians, Paris and Edinburgh College of Art. Assistant design teacher, Edinburgh College of Art. Exh. 1912-40. Add: 29 Polwarth Gardens, Edinburgh. † GI 6, L 2, RSA 26, RSW 9.

MORTON, Cavendish Junr. b. 1911
Painter, colour woodcut artist and theatrical designer. b. Edinburgh. Studied under his father. Exh. 1930-36. Add: Alverstoke, Hants. 1930; Bembridge, I.O.W. 1933. † RA 4.

MORTON, Constance Exh. 1937
61 Marlborough Place, London. † ROI 1.

MORTON, Charles F. Exh. 1907-34
Birmingham. † B 19.

MORTON, Miss D.C. Exh. 1916-33
8 Hawarden Avenue, Sefton Park, Liverpool. † L 36.

MORTON, Edgar Exh. 1885-86
Landscape painter. Add: 26 Francis Street, Tottenham Court Road, London. † RBA 2, ROI 1.

MORTON, Mrs. Ellen Exh. 1894
Miniature portrait painter. Add: 8 Tower Street, York. † RA 1.

MORTON, George Exh. 1883-1904
Portrait and genre painter. N.E.A. 1887. Add: London. † B 5, L 18, M 12, NEA 4, RA 18, RBA 8, RHA 9, RI 8, ROI 31.

MORTON, G.E. Exh. 1926
5 Grove Park, Liverpool. † L 1.

MORTON, H. Exh. 1937
Painter. † RED 1.

MORTON, James B. Exh. 1904
15 Pitt Street, Edinburgh. † RSA 1.

MORTON, James H. 1881-1918
London 1907; Darwen, Lancs. 1911. † I 1, L 16, RA 2.

MORTON, Miss M. Exh. 1919-25
London. † SWA 4.

MORTON, Margaret Exh. 1908
Hill Grove, Bembridge, I.O.W. † RSA 2.

MORTON, Mary Exh. 1908-40
Sculptor and watercolour painter. Studied Bristol School of Art and Royal College of Art, modelling school 1911-13. A.S.W.A. 1925. Add: Clifton, Bristol 1908; London 1913. † D 4, GI 11, L 32, M 2, P 6, RA 26, RBA 1, RI 5, RMS 7, RSA 15, SWA 5, WG 54.

MORTON, May Exh. 1919-33
Watercolour painter. Add: West Kirby, Birkenhead. † L 22, RCA 8.

MORTON, Nellie I. Exh. 1912-13
59 Balliol Road, Bootle, Lancs. † L 2.

MORTON, Robert Harold Exh. 1924-40
Edinburgh 1924; Corstorphine 1927. † GI 7, RSA 21.

MORTON, Robert Scott Exh. 1932-36
Edinburgh. † RSA 5.

MORTON, S.C. Exh. 1892-1904
Glasgow. † L 3.

MORTON, Thomas Exh. 1883-1911
Partick, Glasgow. † GI 12, RSW 1.

MORTON, Thomas Corsan 1859-1928
Painter and pastelier. Keeper of the National Galleries of Scotland and Curator of Kirkcaldy Museum and Art Gallery. Add: Glasgow 1880; Edinburgh 1908; Kirkcaldy 1926. † G 3, GI 102, I 4, L 4, M 10, NEA 1, RBA 1, RSA 47, RSW 2.

MORTON, W. Exh. 1883-94
Manchester. † GI 2, L 3, M 24.

MORTON, William Exh. 1910-19
9 Glyn Road, Liscard, Cheshire. † L 11, M 1, RA 2.

MORTON, W.G. Exh. 1896-1940
Glasgow. † GI 40, RSA 2, RSW 3.

MORTON, William Scott Exh. 1881-1902
Architectural painter. Add: Edinburgh 1881; London 1894. † RA 2, RSA 9.

MORTON-SALE, J. Exh. 1940
Edge Moor, Mortonhampstead, Devon. † RI 1.

MOSCHELES, Felix 1833-1917
Portrait, genre and landscape painter. Studied under Jacob van Lerius at the Antwerp Academy. Travelled on the continent, Spain and Algiers. Married Margaret M. q.v. Add: London. † B 4, G 13, GI 2, L 8, LEI 61, LS 8, M 14, NG 1, P 6, RA 6, RHA 5, ROI 12.

MOSCHELES, Margaret Exh. 1893-1924
Landscape and flower painter. Married Felix M. q.v. Add: London. † BA 23, BG 2, GI 12, I 6, L 11, LS 11, M 12, RA 2, ROI 10, SWA 18.

MOSCHOWITZ, Paul Exh. 1898
26 Rue Servandori, Paris. † B 1.

MOSEDALE, G.W.T. Exh. 1926-37
54 Riversley Road, Nuneaton. † B 13.

MOSELEY, Doris H. Exh. 1926
127 Union Road, Maidstone, Kent. † L 3.

MOSELEY, R.S. Exh. 1880-93
Genre and animal painter. London. † B 4, L 1, M 1, RA 1, RBA 1, ROI 3.

MOSER, Mrs. Amy Exh. 1931-32
Landscape painter. Add: Lyceum Club, 138 Piccadilly, London. † RA 3.

MOSER, Charles Exh. 1923
c/o Dante, 1 Bolzano, Alto Adige, Italy. † L 14.

MOSER, Oswald b. 1874
Painter and illustrator. Studied St. John's Wood Art School. R.I. 1909, R.O.I. 1908. Exh. 1904-40. Add: London 1904; Bournemouth 1928; Rye, Sussex 1929. † GI 4, L 27, RA 37, RI 70, RSA 2.

MOSER, Robert James Exh. 1884-93
Watercolour landscape painter. Add: London. † RA 3, RI 8, RBA 1.

MOSHKOWITZ, Sara Exh. 1930
Portrait painter. Add: 30 Templars Avenue, London. † L 1, RA 1.

MOSLER, Henry 1841-1920
American painter. Exh. 1892. Add: Paris. † RA 2.

MOSLEY, Leslie W. Exh. 1909-17
Sherwood, Notts. 1909; Beeston, Notts. 1916. † N 10.

MOSLEY, W.R. Exh. 1915
Central Chambers, Slough, Bucks. † RA 1.

MOSS, Rev. A. Miles Exh. 1911-19
Helm, Windermere. † L 2.

MOSS, Ella Exh. 1900
12 The Waldrons, Croydon, Surrey. † SWA 2.

MOSS, Mrs. Elizabeth Campbell Exh. 1935-38
Watercolour flower and landscape painter. Studied Glasgow School of Art. † WG 79.

MOSS, G. Lawton Exh. 1934-37
The Firs, Kenilworth. † B 3.

MOSS, Henry William Exh. 1885-1938
Landscape painter. Studied Dublin Metropolitan School of Art, R.H.A. Schools, under Stanhope Forbes at Newlyn, Penzance and at Heatherleys. Travelled on the continent. Add: Sandyford, Co. Dublin 1885; Milltown, Co. Dublin 1904; Howth, Co. Dublin 1918. † B 3, RHA 54.

MOSS, John H.B. Exh. 1892
Black and white artist. Add: 33 Parliament Street, Gloucester. † RA 1.

MOSS, Philipson Exh. 1934
Waterolour painter. † COO 1.

MOSS, Phyllis Exh. 1927-33
10 Hillside Road, Wallasey, Cheshire. † L 2.

MOSS, R.W. Exh. 1911
61 Whitworth Road, Dublin. † RHA 1.

MOSS, Sidney Dennant 1884-1946
Landscape and figure painter. b. Ipswich. Travelled in the Middle East. A.R.B.A. 1926, R.B.A. 1935. Add: London 1912; Tunbridge Wells, Kent 1920. † BA 25, FIN 58, GI 3, L 21, RA 18, RBA 32, RI 17, ROI 6.

MOSS, Thomas Exh. 1913
The School House, Scorton, nr. Garstang. † L 1.

MOSS, W. Exh. 1904
49 Lower Clapton Road, London. † RI 1.

MOSS, W.H. Exh. 1883
3 Summer Terrace, Onslow Square, London. † RE 1.

MOSSMAN, David Exh. 1883-90
Figure and miniature painter. Add: 4 Brook Street, Hanover Square, London. † RA 2, RBA 3, RHA 1, RI 7.

MOSSMAN, John 1817-1890
Sculptor. Studied under his father William M. (1793-1851). H.R.S.A. 1885. Add: Glasgow. † GI 20, RSA 3.

MOSSMAN, Mary S. Exh. 1880
2 Chatham Place, Glasgow. † GI 1.

MOSSMAN, William d. 1884
Sculptor. Glasgow. † GI 6.

MOSSOP, Harold Exh. 1918-19
14 Ampthill Square, London. † L 1, RA 1.

MOSTYN, C.S. Exh. 1939
† NEA 2.

MOSTYN, Dorothy Exh. 1916-25
Landscape painter. Daughter of Tom M. q.v. Add: London 1916; Crookham, Torquay 1920. † L 3, RA 2, RCA 3.

MOSTYN, The Hon. Harold P.Exh. 1892-98
London 1892; Rome 1898. † M 1, NG 2.

MOSTYN, Ida Exh. 1907-37
Flower and interior painter. Daughter of Tom M. q.v. Add: London. † COO 1, I 1, L 7, NEA 1, P 4, RA 10, RMS 1, ROI 2, SWA 10.

MOSTYN, Marjorie b. 1893
Portrait, flower and interior painter. Daughter of Tom M. q.v. Studied St. John's Wood School of Art and R.A. Schools 1912-15. Exh. 1916-21. Add: London 1916; Crookham, Torquay 1921. † RA 2.

MOSTYN, Tom (Thomas Edwin)1864-1930
Landscape, figure, flower and garden painter. b. Liverpool. Father of Dorothy, Ida and Marjorie M. q.v. R.B.A. 1897, R.O.I. 1917. Add: Manchester 1885; Stockport, Cheshire 1891; Bushey, Herts. 1893; Chorlton cum Hardy, Manchester 1895; London 1904; Crookham, Torquay 1919. † B 3, COO 99, DOW 2, FIN 223, G 1, GI 4, GOU 4, L 58, M 38, NG 3, P 2, RA 36, RCA 19, RHA 4, ROI 16.

MOTE, George William* 1832-1909
Landscape painter. Self taught. Exh. 1882. Add: London. † RSA 1.

MOTHANS, Alfred Exh. 1883
Watercolour landscape painter. Add: 17 Nassau Street, Oxford Street, London. † RI 1.

MOTHERSOLE, Jessie Exh. 1901-14
Landscape and miniature portrait painter. Add: 141 Willesden Lane, London. † L 1, LS 8, RA 5, WG 35.

MOTLEY, Exh. 1938
Painter. † RED 8.

MOTLEY, David Exh. 1898
c/o Mrs. Uplar, 45 Buccleuch Street, Glasgow. † GI 1.

MOTLEY, Joan Exh. 1936
Sculptor. Add: Nuneham, Riverside, Staines. † RA 1.

MOTT, Alice M. Exh. 1880-1908
Still life and miniature portrait painter. A.R.M.S. 1896. Add: Walton on Thames 1880; London 1891. † L 3, RA 30, RBA 1, RMS 12, ROI 1.

MOTT, Miss H.W. Exh. 1894
94 Redcliffe Gardens, London. † SWA 1.

MOTT, Laura Exh. 1892-1940
Portrait painter. London. † RA 7, RMS 3.

MOTT, Miss P. Exh. 1924
25 Nottingham Place, London. † B 1.

MOTT, Rosalind D. Exh. 1885-86
Flower painter. Add: Crichley Hill, nr. Gloucester. † SWA 2.

MOTT, Miss W. Exh. 1900
Detmore, Cheltenham, Glos. † RI 2.

MOTTE, E. Exh. 1915
41 Glebe Place, Chelsea, London. † RA 1.

MOTTE, Henri* 1846-1922
French painter. Exh. 1882-1905. Add: 21 Grande rue, Bourg la Reine, Seine, France. † L 1, NG 2, RA 2.

MOTTRAM, Alfred Exh. 1883-86
Landscape painter. Add: East Somerton, Yarmouth 1883; London 1886. † M 1, RI 1.

MOTTRAM, Charles Sim Exh. 1880-1919
Coastal and landscape painter. R.B.A. 1890. Add: London 1880; 1892 and 1904; Weymouth, Surrey 1891; St. Ives, Cornwall 1900. † B 4, D 5, FIN 1, L 11, M 12, RA 57, RBA 63, RI 32, ROI 4.

MOTTRAM, Miss E. Exh. 1908-10
Etcher. Add: West Brompton, London. † L 1, RA 4.

MOTTRAM, J.M. Exh. 1888
Painter. Add: 17 Nassau Street, London. † RI 1.

MOTT-SMITH, H. Exh. 1910
26 Wellington Road, Nantwich, Cheshire. † RCA 1.

MOULD, F.A. Exh. 1920-23
Figure painter. Add: 13 Poynters Avenue, Thorneywood, Nottingham. † N 7.

MOULD, Phyllis A. Exh. 1936
Engraver. † NEA 1, RED 1.

MOULES, George Frederic b. 1918
Wood engraver, watercolour painter and designer. Studied Glasgow School of Art. Exh. 1936-40. Add: Glasgow 1936; Eaglesham, Renfrewshire 1939; London 1940. † GI 7, RA 1, RSA 5.

MOULIN, Eugene Emile Exh. 1911
7 Rue Belloni, Paris. † RSA 1.

MOULLE, Albert Exh. 1907
21 Rue de Constantinople, Paris. † L 1.

MOULT, Mrs. E. Exh. 1885-90
Sale, Manchester. † M 4.

MOULT, Eileen M. Exh. 1936-38
Painter and mural designer. Add: North Villa, 89 Derby Road, Long Eaton, Notts. † N 6.

MOULT, Emily R. Exh. 1894-1912
60 King Street, Manchester. † L 1, M 9.

MOULTRAY, J. Douglas Exh. 1880-83
130 George Street, Edinburgh. † M 2, RSA 11.

MOULTRIE, Mabel P. Exh. 1882-94
Figure painter. Add: London 1882; Aldeburgh, Suffolk 1884; Walton, Surrey 1889; Milford, nr. Godalming, Surrey 1890. † B 13, M 7, SWA 14.

MOUNCEY, William d. 1902
Add: Kirkcudbright from 1881. † B 1, GI 26, I 1, L 3, M 1, RSA 37.

MOUNSEY, Michael Exh. 1927-34
Landscape painter and wood engraver. Add: London 1927; West Hendon House, Sunderland 1934. † RA 4, RI 3, ROI 1.

MOUNSEY, R.K. Exh. 1885-87
Figure painter. Add: 71 Dickenson Road, Risholm, Manchester. † GI 3, M 1, ROI 2.

MOUNSEY-WOOD, M. Exh. 1940
† NEA 1.

MOUNTAIN, William Exh. 1882-83
Figure and landscape painter. Add: 151 Kennington Road, London. † RBA 2.

MOUNTFORD, Edward William 1855-1908
Architect (Central Criminal Court). b. Shipston on Stour. Add: London from 1885. † RA 51.

MOUNTFORD, Horace Exh. 1892
Winders Road, Battersea, London. † L 1.

MOUNTFORD, P.R. Exh. 1892
Winders Road, Battersea, London. † L 2.

MOUNTFORT, Arnold b. 1878
Portrait and landscape painter. Exh. 1892-1916. Add: Birmingham 1892; London 1899. † B 8, L 1, P 5, RA 9.

MOUNTFORT, Enid Exh. 1930-40
Portrait, flower and miniature painter. Add: London. † BA 22, NEA 2, P 1, RA 6, RMS 3.

MOURANT, E. Exh. 1882-83
Landscape painter. Add: 72 Baker Street, London. † B 2, RI 1.

MOURANT, Elsie Exh. 1940
Painter. Add: 27 Idrone Terrace, Blackrock, Co. Dublin. † RHA 1.

MOUSHIBARA, Yoshigiro Exh. 1937
Painter. Add: c/o Waddington's Galleries, St. Anne Street, Dublin. † RHA 3.

MOWBRAY, A. Mardon Exh. 1882-90
Architect. Add: Eastbourne 1882; Oxford 1890. † RA 2.

MOWBRAY, H.S. Exh. 1882
† TOO 1.

MOWELS, John Herniman b. 1889
Designer and sculptor. Studied Brighton School of Art. Principal Southport School of Art; Curator Atkinson Art Gallery; examiner to the Lancashire and Cheshire Institutes; Lecturer and writer on art; art critic to "Manchester Guardian". Exh. 1923. Add: Sale, Cheshire. † L 1.

MOWLL, Mrs. D. Exh. 1927-35
Cantaar, Temple Ewell, nr. Dover. † L 1, RBA 2, RI 3.

MOWLL, Dorothy N. Exh. 1915-23
Liverpool. † L 4.

MOXHAM, G. Exh. 1909-10
Architect. Add: 39 Castle Street, Swansea. † RA 2.

MOXON, J. Exh. 1880
Figure and rustic painter. Add: 3 Kilgraston Road, Edinburgh. † RBA 2.

MOYE, Joseph S. Exh. 1880
Architect. Add: 3 Southwick Street, Hyde Park Square, London. † RA 1.

MOYES, F. Exh. 1881
Landscape painter. Add: c/o J. Schenhauser, 184 Aldersgate Road, Stoke Newington, London. † RBA 1.

MOYES, Muriel Exh. 1926
Sculptor. Add: 20 Upper Montague Street, London. † RA 1.

MOYNAN, Richard Thomas d. 1906
A.R.H.A. 1889, R.H.A. 1890. Add: Dublin 1880 and 1887; Paris 1886. † L 12, RHA 87.

MOYNIHAN, Rodrigo b. 1910
Portrait, figure and landscape painter. b. Canary Islands. Studied Slade School. Member London Group 1933. Exh. 1937-40. Add: London. † COO 1, LEI 3, RA 1, RED 34.

MOYNIHAN, Ursula b. 1912
Painter. Studied Royal College of Art. Exh. 1932. Add: Wolverhampton. † B 2.

MUCKE, Karl Anton Heinrich 1806-1891
German painter. Exh. 1883-87. Add: London. † L 1, M 1, RA 1.

MUCKLE, Mrs. Mary Jeanie Exh. 1909-28
Miniature portrait painter. A.R.M.S. 1914. Add: Kings Langley, Herts. 1909; London 1911; Gedgrave, nr. Orford, Suffolk 1928. † L 8, RA 10, RMS 10.

MUCKLEY, Angelo Fairfax Exh. 1886-95
Landscape and portrait painter and etcher. Add: London 1886; Wraysbury, Bucks. 1895. † B 2, G 1, M 5, RA 3, RBA 1, ROI 2.

MUCKLEY, Louis Fairfax Exh. 1889-1914
Painter and etcher. Studied Birmingham School of Art. Add: Stourbridge, Worcs. 1889; London 1901. † B 1, NG 2, RA 5.

MUCKLEY, William Jabez 1837-1905
Flower, figure and still life painter. b. Audnam Worcs. Studied Birmingham, London and Paris. Worked as a teacher at the Government Schools in Wolverhampton and Manchester. R.B.A. 1876, R.B.S.A. 1892. Add: Withington, Manchester 1880; London 1882; Loweswater, Cumberland 1889; Witham, Essex 1896. † B 28, DOW 5, G 19, GI 1, M 4, RA 31, RBA 9, RI 4, ROI 2.

MUCKLEY, W.R. Exh. 1885-91
Add: Sale, Manchester 1885; School of Art, Castle Green, Hereford 1889. † B 1, L 1, M 10.

MUDD, James Exh. 1882-93
Richmond Hill, Bowdon, Cheshire. † L 3, M 11.

MUDGE, A. Exh. 1885
2 Eton Terrace, Richmond, Surrey. † B 1.

MUDGE, B.G. Exh. 1929
Painter. † AB 1.

MUDIE, Arthur T. Exh. 1888-1919
Liverpool 1883; Barnes, Surrey 1901; Gerrard's Cross, Bucks. 1908; Freshfield, Lancs. 1911. † L 25, RA 3.

MUDIE-COOKE, Olive Exh. 1914-22
22 Queen's Road, London. † D 6.

MUE, Del See D

MUENIER, Jules Alexis b. 1863
French artist. Exh. 1902-8. Add: Paris. † L 2.

MUFF, E. Brantwood Exh. 1903-9
Architect. Add: London 1903; Bexley Heath, Kent 1909. † RA 2.

MUHLENBERG, G.E. Exh. 1910
38 Rue Falguiere, Paris. † L 1.

MUHRMAN, Henry 1854-1916
American painter. N.E.A. 1887. Add: London 1884; Saxony 1904; c/o Goupil Gallery, Regent Street, London 1908. † DOW 40, FIN 1, G 10, GI 32, GOU 59, I 44, L 12, M 1, NEA 18, RBA 8, RI 1, RSA 8.

MUIR, Ada Exh. 1902-13
Miniature portrait painter. Add: 56 Kyverdale Road, Stamford Hill, London. † GI 3, RA 6, SWA 2.

MUIR, Anne Davidson d. 1951
Painter of flower and head studies. b. Hawick. Studied Edinburgh School of Art and Heriot-Wall College Art School, Edinburgh. R.S.W. 1915. Add: Edinburgh 1899; Glasgow 1905. † AR 2, BG 16, GI 79, L 7, RA 2, RSA 30, RSW 72.

MUIR, David Exh. 1881-88
Painter and engraver. Add: London. † RA 1, RBA 1, RSA 4.

MUIR, G.R. Exh. 1881-83
49 Cowper Street, Leith. † RSA 5.

MUIR, Jessie Exh. 1884
Watercolour painter. Add: 89 Mildmay Park, London. † RI 1.

MUIR, Mrs. John Exh. 1935-39
B. Ames. Add: 27 Merchiston Crescent, Edinburgh. † RSW 5.

MUIR, Mrs. Jean Seaton Exh. 1904
nee Chapman. Flower and landscape painter. b. London. Studied in Paris and Scotland. Add: 22 Caledonian Road, Edinburgh. † RSA 1.

MUIR, Lily Exh. 1915-39
Portrait painter. Add: London 1915; Broad Campden, Glos. 1922; Evesham, Worcs. 1925. † B 18, I 3, P 1, RA 1, ROI 3, SWA 1.

MUIR, Maria Exh. 1889
18 Monteith Row, Glasgow. † GI 1.

MUIR, W. Temple Exh. 1883-1907
Landscape painter. Add: Girvan, Ayr 1883; London 1884 and 1891; Burnham, Bucks. 1885. † GI 2, L 1, RA 5, RHA 2, RI 2, ROI 1, RSA 3.

MUIRHEAD, Miss A. Exh. 1890-98
Liverpool. † L 8.

MUIRHEAD, Charles Exh. 1882-1933
Landscape and figure painter. Add: Liverpool 1882 and 1911; New Brighton, Cheshire 1902; Formby, Lancs. 1923. † B 7, GI 1, L 74, M 9, RA 12, RCA 12, RI 1, ROI 1.

MUIRHEAD, David 1867-1930
Landscape painter. b. Edinburgh. Studied R.S.A. Schools and Westminster School of Art. N.E.A. 1900, A.R.A. 1928, A.R.W.S. 1924. Member of the Society of 25 Artists. Brother of John M. q.v. Add: Edinburgh 1889; London 1896. † AG 2, BA 1, CG 77, CHE 2, FIN 4, G 87, GI 22, GOU 20, I 1, L 14, LEI 2, M 5, NEA 274, P 1, RA 10, RBA 2, RHA 39, RI 1, RSA 25, RSW 1, RWS 47, TOO 1, WG 9.

MUIRHEAD, John* 1863-1927
Landscape painter. b. Edinburgh. R.B.A. 1904. R.S.W . 1892. Brother of David M. q.v. Add: Edinburgh 1881; London 1898. † GI 76, L 11, RA 10, RBA 223, ROI 13, RSA 85, RSW 112.

MUIRHEAD, John B. Exh. 1880-95
Glasgow. † GI 7, RSA 4.

MUIRHEAD, J.R. Exh. 1884-88
Edinburgh. † RSA 3.

MUIRHEAD, Katie Campbell Exh. 1914-24
Edinburgh. † GI 4, RSA 12

MUIRHEAD, Lionel Exh. 1884
Watercolour landscape painter. Add: 8 Gt. Marylebone Street, London. † RI 2.

MUIRWOOD, Helen Exh. 1888-92
17 Rosslyn Terrace, Kelvinside, Glasgow. † GI 3.

MUKERJI, K.K. Exh. 1916
Southmead, Formby, Lancs. † L 3.

MULEN, F.P. Exh. 1885
224 Kanaal, The Hague, Holland. † RSA 3.

MULHOFER, Elizabeth Exh. 1929
† RMS 1.

MULLARD, Joseph Albert b. 1868
Landscape and portrait painter. Studied Bradford, London and Paris. Exh. 1913-40. Add: Horton, Tadworth 1913; Sydenham, London 1923. † RA 5.

MULLEN, Rory b. 1900
Figure painter. b. Dublin. Studied Ecole Nationale des Beaux Arts, Paris, Florence and Rome. Exh. 1928. † GOU 2.

MULLER, Adele R.B. Exh. 1891-1906
Manchester. † M 9.

MULLER, Miss H. Exh. 1894
49 Garnet Street, Saltburn on Sea. † SWA 1.

MULLER, Louis Exh. 1909
15 Rue de L'Estrapade, Paris. † L 1.

MULLER, Prof. Leopold Carl 1834-1892
German sculptor and painter. Add: London 1884 and 1889; Dusseldorf, Germany 1888. † G 3, M 1, RA 4.

MULLER, Paul Exh. 1881
Landscape painter. Add: c/o J. Ichenhausser, 184 Aldersgate Street, London. † RA 1.

MULLER, Peter Paul Exh. 1891-92
Linprunn Strasse, Munich. † GI 2.

MULLER, R. Exh. 1882
c/o McNair, Dudley Gallery, London. † L 1, RHA 2.

MULLER, Robert Antoine Exh. 1881
Portrait painter. Add: Kensington Villa, 11 Notting Hill Terrace, London. † RA 3.

MULLER, R.G. Exh. 1889
† TOO 1.

MULLETT, F.T. Exh. 1917
Downing House, Cambridge. † RA 1.

MULLIGAN, J.A. Exh. 1899
Shore View, Rhyl. † RCA 1.

MULLIGAN, W.A. d. 1919
Painter and teacher. Add: Malvern, Worcs. 1888; Crawford Municipal School of Art, Cork 1892. † B 5, RHA 31.

MULLIN, J.C. Exh. 1882-84
1 Ormond Terrace, Rathmines, Dublin. † RHA 5

MULLINER, Miss M. Exh. 1915
Dallington, Northampton. † RA 1.

MULLINS, C.P. Exh. 1914
54 Broomwood Road, Wandsworth Common, London. † RA 1.

MULLINS, Edwin Roscoe 1848-1907
Sculptor. Studied Lambeth School of Art and R.A. Schools. Add: London. † D 1, GI 6, L 6, M 7, NG 30, RA 26, RBA 1.

MULLINS, Monica Exh. 1896-1917
London. † B 1, I 2, L 3, LS 3, RA 2, RI 7, ROI 2, SWA 4.

MULLINS, T.P. Exh. 1881
Landscape painter. Add: 1 Tudor Lodge Studios, Albert Street Regents Park, London. † RBA 2.

MULLORD, Henry Exh. 1915
105 Lynwood Avenue, Darwen. † L 1.

MULOCK, Emily Cole Exh. 1899-1903
Kilnagarna, Athlone. † RHA 3.

MULOCK, Frederick d. 1932
Landscape and figure painter. Studied at Brussels and under Herkomer at Bushey. Add: London 1887; 1900 and 1922; Gt. Marlow, Bucks. 1895; Instow, N. Devon 1908. † B 3, CHE 1, G 1, I 5, L 3, M 1, NEA 1, P 5, RA 11, RHA 20, RI 2, ROI 1, RSA 1, WG 133.

MULOCK, Lily Exh. 1899
Kilnagarna, Athlone. † RHA 1.

MULREADY, Augustus E.* d. 1886
Genre painter. Add: London. † AG 2, M 1, RA 1, ROI 1, TOO 3.

MULRONEY, Miss M. Exh. 1888
Hazlewood, Dundrum, Dublin. † RHA 1.

MULVEY, Mrs. Matilda Exh. 1931-39
Portrait and flower painter. Studied Heatherleys. R.B.A. 1937. Add: London. † GI 3, L 1, P 8, RA 6, RBA 22, ROI 8, RSA 4, SWA 17.

MUMFORD, Miss J.J. Exh. 1911-14
125 Boulevard Montparnasse, Paris. † RA 2.

MUMFORD, Robert T. Exh. 1895-1939
Figure painter and teacher. Add: Dover 1895; London 1908. † NEA 2, RA 3, RBA 6, RI 5, ROI 14.

MUMMERY, Mrs. H. Exh. 1884-86
Coastal painter. Add: 1 Holly Terrace, Highgate, London. † D 1, SWA 2.

MUMMERY, Horace Exh. 1888-93
Landscape painter. Add: Rainalds, Pellatt Grove, Wood Green, London. † RA 1, RI 1, RBA 10.

MUMMERY, J. Howard Exh. 1881-83
Landscape painter. Add: 1 Holly Terrace, Highgate, London. † RE 5.

MUMMERY, W.S. Exh. 1930
Landscape painter. † LEF 2.

MUNBY, Alan Edward b. 1870
Architect. b. Manchester. Studied Durham University, Heidelberg University and Cambridge University. Exh. 1911-33. Add: London. † RA 3.

MUNCASTER, Claude* b. 1903
Marine and landscape painter, etcher, illustrator, lecturer and writer. Son of Oliver Hall, q.v. R.O.I. 1932, A.R.W.S. 1931, R.W.S. 1936. Exh. 1923-39. Add: London 1923; Pulborough, Sussex 1926; Petworth, Sussex 1934. † AR 2, BA 8, BAR 64, FIN 263, GI 7, L 11, M 2, NEA 2, RA 41, RHA 1, ROI 7, RWS 111, WG 11.

MUNCE, Iza Exh. 1915-25
Belfast. † RHA 5.

MUNCE, Miss M. Exh. 1917
182 Clifton Park Avenue, Belfast. † RHA 2.

MUNCH, Constance Exh. 1894-1911
Countess Hohenwart. Watercolour flower painter. Add: Austria 1894; Nice, France 1911. † RA 1, RI 1.

MUNDAY, John Exh. 1890-1902
Stoke on Trent. † B 4.

MUNDEN, P.J. Exh. 1932-33
Architect. Add: 28 South Frederick Street, Dublin. † RHA 4.

MUNDY, Ethel Frances b. 1876
Wax portrait artist. b. Syracuse, New York. Studied Art Students League of New York, Rochester Mechanics Institute and Syracuse University. A.R.M.S. 1913. Exh. 1913-24. Add: 121 College Place, Syracuse, New York. † RMS 9.

MUNDY, Louis Exh. 1913
c/o J. Pearce, Royal Insurance Buildings, Liverpool. † L 4.

MUNGALL, John B. Exh. 1936
31 Garnethill Street, Glasgow. † RSA 2.

MUNGER, Gilbert* 1836-1903
American landscape painter. Exh. 1880-85. Add: London. † FIN 12, RA 4, RBA 1, RE 1, RHA 3.

MUNK, E. Exh. 1900-16
Landscape painter. A.N.S.A. 1908-36. Add: Beeston, Notts. † N 14.

MUNK, Eugenie Exh. 1903
Figure painter. Add: 18 Aberdare Gardens, Hampstead, London. † L 2, RA 1.

MUNKACSY, de See D

MUNN, George Frederick 1852-1907
American flower and landscape painter and sculptor. Studied under Charles Calverly; the National Academy, New York and South Kensington, London. R.B.A. 1884. Exh. 1880-86. Add: London. † B 5, G 6, GI 2, L 5, M 8, RA 8, RBA 8, ROI 2.

MUNNING, Miss E. Exh. 1900
St. Leonard's Villa, Victoria Road, Surbiton. † RI 1.

MUNNINGS, Alfred J.* 1878-1959
Sporting painter. b. Mendham, Suffolk. Studied Norwich School of Art and Paris. A.R.A. 1919, R.A. 1925, R.I. 1905 (resigned 1911), R.P. 1925, A.R.W.S. 1921. "Epsom Downs — City and Suburban Day" purchased by Chantrey Bequest 1920, "From my Bedroom Window" in 1930 and "Their Majesties Return from Ascot" (1925) in 1937. Add: Norwich 1899; Harleston, Norfolk 1900; Swainsthorpe, Norwich 1907; Lamorna, Penzance 1913; Dedham, Essex 1920; London 1930. † ALP 41, B 6, CG 3, CON 12, FIN 24, G 5, GI 47, I 55, L 43, LEI 56, M 5, P 6, RA 178, RI 60, ROI 2, RSA 9, RSW 2, RWS 31.

MUNNINGS, Mrs. E.F. Exh. 1913-14
Lamorna, Penzance, Cornwall. † L 1, LS 3, RA 2.

MUNNOCH, John d. 1915
Exh. 1912-15. Add: 24 York Place, Edinburgh. Killed in action World War I. † GI 1, RSA 8.

MUNNS, Bernard d. 1942
Portrait and landscape painter. Son of Henry Turner and father of Una M. q.v. Studied Birmingham School of Art and Graphic School. R.B.S.A. 1923. Exh. 1898-1940. Add: Birmingham. † B 99, CHE 1, P 5, RA 8, RCA 1, ROI 6.

MUNNS, Henry Turner Exh. 1882-97
Portrait, landscape and figure painter. Father of Bernard M. q.v. Add: Birmingham. † B 47, GI 1, L 7, M 5, RA 5.

MUNNS, Una b. 1900
Portrait painter and jeweller. Daughter of Bernard M. q.v. Studied Birmingham Central School of Art. A.S.W.A. 1927. Exh. 1921-38. Add: Edgbaston, Birmingham. † B 68, L 45, RCA 1, SWA 3.

MUNRO, Alexander Graham Exh. 1923-40
Corstorphine 1923; Edinburgh 1931. † GI 1, RSA 28, RSW 3.

MUNRO, Andrew Oswald Exh. 1904
3 Victoria Terrace, Mount Florida, N.B. † GI 1.

MUNRO, Alexander R. Exh. 1937-40
2 Harbour Road, Musselburgh. † RSA 3.

MUNRO, Mrs. Campbell Exh. 1888
Painter. Add: 27 Eaton Place, London. † G 1.

MUNRO, D.R. Exh. 1888
5 Westbank Quadrant, Hillhead, Glasgow. † GI 1.

MUNRO, E. Exh. 1885
† TOO 2.

MUNRO, Hugh b. 1873
Painter and black and white artist. Exh. 1913-37. Add: Glasgow. † GI 60, RSA 5.

MUNRO, Ian Exh. 1936-37
13 Crescent Grove, Clapham Common, London. † GI 2, RBA 1.

MUNRO, Minnie Exh. 1885-94
Glasgow. † GI 11, L 3, RSA 4.

MUNRO, Nora Exh. 1911-12
Painter and etcher. Add: London. † L 1, NEA 4.

MUNRO, Olive Exh. 1900-1
27 Eaton Place, London. † L 2, NG 2.

MUNRO, Robert Exh. 1880-1907
Related to Thomas M. q.v. Add: Glasgow. † GI 35, L 2, RSA 11.

MUNRO, Robert Henry b. 1886
Painter. b. Belfast. Studied Edinburgh College of Art and R.S.A. School of Painting. Exh. 1914-25. Add: Edinburgh. † GI 2, RSA 4, RSW 3.

MUNRO, Thomas Exh. 1880-1904
Related to Robert M. q.v. Add: Glasgow. † GI 30, L 1, RSA 5, RSW 5.

MUNRO, William Exh. 1919-20
21 Macdonald Road, Edinburgh. † GI 2, RSA 12.

MUNTHE, Ludwig* 1841-1896
Landscape painter. Exh. 1880-81. Add: London. † RA 2.

MUNTZ, Elizabeth b. 1894
Sculptor, painter and pencil artist. b. Toronto, Canada. Studied Ontario College of Art, L'Academie de la Grande Chaumiere, Paris and under Frank Dobson. Member London Group 1927. Exh. 1938-39. Add: London. † COO 4.

MUNTZ, Julie Exh. 1914
The Studio, Thurloe Square, London. † RHA 1.

MUNTZ, Jessie E. Exh. 1903-24
Park Walk, Chelsea, London 1903; The Studio, Thurloe Square, London 1904. † B 4, L 2, LS 31, SWA 4.

MUNTZ, Mrs. J. Oscar Exh. 1921
Animal painter. † WG 18.

MUNTZ, Mrs. K.B. Exh. 1911-14
Avonmore, Killiney, Dublin. † RA 3, RMS 1.

MUNTZ, Mrs. L. Exh. 1899
9 Rue des Fourneaux, Paris. † GI 1.

MUNTZ, R. Exh. 1896
Aylett, Umberslade, nr. Birmingham. † B 1.

MURA, Charlotte Exh. 1894-1905
Domestic painter. Married Frank M. q.v. Add: London 1894; Dunmow, Essex 1901. † L 1, NG 1, P 1, RA 5, ROI 3.

MURA, Frank* b. 1861
Landscape and figure painter. b. Alsace. Went to America as a child. Returned to Europe at age 20. Studied at Munich and the Hague. Exh. 1894-1913. Add: London 1894; Dunmow, Essex 1904. † CG 13, GI 3, I 23, NEA 2, RA 5, ROI 3.

MURANYI, Gyula Julius b. 1881
Hungarian artist. Exh. 1913. Add: 6 Rosetti Studios, Chelsea, London. † RA 1.

MURCH, Mrs. Arthur (Edith) Exh. 1880-90
nee Edenborough. Figure and landscape painter. Married 2nd Matthew Ridley Corbet q.v. Add: Rome 1880; Chelsea, London 1886. † G 20, L 2, M 3, NG 6, ROI 1.

MURCH, Arthur J. Exh. 1939
Portrait painter. Add: 320 Earls Court, London. † RA 1.

MURCHIESON, Ruth Exh. 1914
Volendam, Holland. † LS 3.

MURCHLAND, D. Exh. 1928
Painter. † AB 1.

MURDOCH, Agnes A. Exh. 1887-89
9 Newton Place, Glasgow. † GI 3.

MURDOCH, Ada M. Exh. 1902-7
New York, U.S.A. 1902; c/o Datt & Co., 26 Castle Street, Edinburgh 1903. † B 1, GI 1, L 4.

MURDOCH, Alice M. Exh. 1906
187 Goldhurst Terrace, South Hampstead, London. † RA 2.

MURDOCH, Miss D. Burn Exh. 1905
Charlotte Square, Edinburgh. † RSA 1.

MURDOCH, John Exh. 1900-6
Shrewsbury House, Stafford. † B 2, GI 1, RBA 1, RCA 4.

MURDOCH, J.A. Exh. 1881-85
Antigua Villa, Cambuslang. † GI 1, RSA 1.

MURDOCH, Morag Burn Exh. 1887-1916
Edinburgh 1887 and 1902; Paris 1901. † GI 8, I 1, RSA 10, RSW 1.

MURDOCH, Miss M.E. Exh. 1927
A.S.W.A. 1936. Add: Lawrence Lane, Burford, Oxford. † L 4.

MURDOCH, Robert W. Exh. 1902
34 Victoria Street, South Circular Road, Dublin. † RHA 2.

MURDOCH, William Duff Exh. 1899-1923
Portrait, landscape and still life painter. Chalk and pencil artist. b. Dumfriesshire. Studied Regent Street Polytechnic, Slade School and the British Museum. Add: Sanguhar, Dumfriesshire 1899; London 1901. † I 1, L 3, RA 4, RSA 1.

MURDOCH, W.G. Burn Exh. 1882-1919
Painter, lithographer, etcher and writer, Studied under Verlat at the Antwerp Academy, under Carolus Duran in Paris, Madrid, Florence and Naples. Add: Edinburgh. † GI 6, L 6, NG 2, RA 3, RSA 55.

MURDOCK, G. Stewart Exh. 1922-27
Walsall, Staffs. † B 6.
MURGATROYD, E. Winifred Exh. 1926-29
Painter. Married Tom Gentleman, q.v. Add: Glasgow 1926; London 1929. † GI 3, RSA 1, WG 4.
MURIEL, Mrs. Ernest Exh. 1935
Watercolour landscape painter. Visited Burma. † WG 1.
MURIEL, Miss N.R. Exh. 1926-27
Liverpool. † L 3.
MURPHY, Bailey S. Exh. 1908
28 North Bridge, Edinburgh. † RSA 1.
MURPHY, Diana Exh. 1930-40
Watercolour painter and illustrator and embroiderer. Studied Clapham School of Art and Royal College of Art. Add: London. † COO 1, NEA 10, RA 1, SWA 1.
MURPHY, Elizabeth Exh. 1923-29
28 Princes Avenue, Liverpool. † L 18, RCA 1.
MURPHY, Emily Exh. 1909-13
13 Merrion Square, Dublin. † RHA 2.
MURPHY, E. Benley Exh. 1905
36 MacLaren Road, Edinburgh. † RSA 1.
MURPHY, Eva M. Exh. 1902-4
Dartry, Upper Rathmines, Dublin. † RHA 2.
MURPHY, F.A. Exh. 1891-92
225 Manchester Street, Werneth, Oldham. † M 4.
MURPHY, H. Dudley Exh. 1936
c/o Bourlet, London. † RCA 1.
MURPHY, Harry George Exh. 1923
† RMS 1.
MURPHY, Mrs. I. Exh. 1883
Leinster Terrace, Kingstown, Ireland. † RHA 1.
MURPHY, James Exh. 1923-26
61 Esher Road, Kensington, Liverpool. † L 3.
MURPHY, Mrs. Joan Exh. 1928-31
Painter. Add: Denford, Stoke Green, Coventry. † B 5, L 1, RA 2.
MURPHY, J. Ross Exh. 1880-84
10 Ellis Quay, Dublin. † RHA 6.
MURPHY, Michael Exh. 1890-94
Sculptor. Father of Thomas Joseph M. q.v. Add: Chelsea, London. † RA 3.
MURPHY, Mildred Exh. 1930-31
Collaborated with Winifred King q.v. Add: The Studio, Old Palace Yard, Earl Street, Coventry. † B 7.
MURPHY, Muriel Exh. 1911
Carrigmore, Cork. † RHA 1.
MURPHY, Mary E. Exh. 1938
Painter. Add: Cloughdun, Crookstown, Co. Cork. † RHA 1.
MURPHY, Patrick Exh. 1930-34
Landscape painter. † LEF 4.
MURPHY, Rose Exh. 1925-28
18 Somerville Grove, Waterloo, Liverpool. † L 3.
MURPHY, Seanus Exh. 1935-40
Sculptor. Add: 149 Sun Row, Dillons Cross, Cork. † RHA 8.
MURPHY, S.T. Exh. 1883-84
School of Art, Waterford. † RHA 2.
MURPHY, Thomas Joseph b. 1881
Sculptor, and painter. b. Cork. Son of Michael M. q.v. Studied Kennington and R.A. Schools. Exh. 1911-27. Add: London 1911; Winkfield, Windsor, Berks. 1926. † RA 4.
MURPHY, W.H. Exh. 1887
18 Redcross Street, Liverpool. † L 1.
MURPRAT, Henri Exh. 1909
† LS 3.

MURRAY, Mrs. A. Exh. 1902-4
The Manor House, Dunstable, Beds. † SWA 3.
MURRAY, Mrs. Alastair Exh. 1898-1901
21 Grosvenor Street, Edinburgh. † D 2, RSA 1, RSW 1.
MURRAY, Andrew b. 1865
Etcher and engraver. Studied Glasgow School of Art and the British Museum. Exh. 1931-32. Add: Rambling Bridge, Kinrosshire. † GI 1, RSA 2.
MURRAY, Archibald Exh. 1912-38
Landscape and figure painter and pencil artist. Add: Glasgow 1912; Dundrennan, Kirkcudbright 1919; London 1922. † GI 8, L 9, RA 5, RI 1, RSA 2, RSW 1.
MURRAY, Miss A.B. Exh. 1884-1904
17 Cumin Place, Edinburgh. † RSA 5.
MURRAY, Albert E. c. 1850-1924
Architect. Professor of Architecture R.H.A. A.R.H.A. 1893, R.H.A. 1910. Add: Dublin. † RHA 23.
MURRAY, A.F. Exh. 1881
25 High Street, London. † GI 1.
MURRAY, Alexander Henry Hallam 1854-1934
Watercolour painter and decorative designer. Studied Slade School. Travelled widely in Europe, N. Africa, India, Australia and New Zealand. Add: London 1881; Hythe, Kent 1915. † D 3, FIN 59, RA 25, RBA 2, RI 7, RID 48.
MURRAY, A. McE. Exh. 1923-26
74 Cairns Road, Cambuslang. † GI 2.
MURRAY, Charles 1894-1954
Painter, etcher and wood engraver. b. Aberdeen. Studied and taught at Glasgow School of Art. Exh. 1919-38. Add: Glasgow. † GI 7, L 1, RSA 6.
MURRAY, Charles Fairfax* 1849-1919
Figure painter. Studied under Dante G. Rossetti. Worked for Morris and Co. Exh. 1880-90. Add: Florence, Italy 1880 and 1884; London 1882 and 1887. † G 12, M 1, NG 6.
MURRAY, Charles Oliver 1842-1924
Painter and etcher. R.E. 1881. Add: London. † FIN 3, L 13, M 1, RA 67, RE 153, RSA 7.
MURRAY, Sir David* 1849-1933
Landscape painter. b. Glasgow. A.R.A. 1891, R.A. 1905, R.I. 1916, P.R.I. 1917, H.R.M.S. 1919, R.O.I. 1886, H.R.O.I. 1919, A.R.S.A. 1881, H.R.S.A., R.S.W. 1878, H.R.S.W., R.W.S. 1886. Knighted c. 1916. "My Love has gone a-sailing" purchased by Chantrey Bequest 1884 and "In the Country of Constable" in 1903. Add: Glasgow 1880; London 1884. † AG 2, B 32, BG 1, CAR 1, DOW 4, FIN 133, G 24, GI 26, L 77, M 40, NG 14, RA 248, RHA 3, RI 68, ROI 39, RSA 83, RSW 60, RWS 45, TOO 5.
MURRAY, D.S. Exh. 1892
Morgan Academy, Dundee. † RSA 1.
MURRAY, Hon. Lady Edith Exh. 1880-89
Landscape painter. Add: Oaklands Hall, West End Lane, London. † RBA 1, SWA 7.
MURRAY, Edward Exh. 1932-35
Portrait painter. Add: 33 Tite Street, Chelsea, London. † L 1, P 1, RA 1.
MURRAY, Eileen b. 1885
Mrs. Stewart M., nee Chester. Portrait, figure and genre painter. b. Templemere, Cork. Studied under Stanhope Forbes at Newlyn, Penzance. Exh. 1923-29. Add: Mosstown House, Co. Longford. † RHA 21.

MURRAY, Elizabeth 1815-1882
Mrs. Henry John M. nee Heaphy. Painter of portraits, genre and oriental subjects. Studied under her father Thomas Heaphy (1775-1835). Travelled widely. R.I. 1861. Add: Florence 1880. † RI 5.
MURRAY, Mrs. Elsie Exh. 1926-38
Glenbracken, Oak Bank Avenue, Blackley, Manchester. † L 1, RCA 14.
MURRAY, Mrs. Ethel Exh. 1899-1902
Kilemore, Eton Avenue, South Hampstead, London. † SWA 9.
MURRAY, Ethel Exh. 1931
Painter. † WG 18.
MURRAY, Mrs. Ethelred Exh. 1880-1906
Figure painter. A.S.W.A. 1903. Add: London. † RA 1, RBA 3, SWA 5.
MURRAY, Mrs. E.D. Exh. 1880
Figure and landscape painter. Add: c/o Burke, St. Stephens Avenue, Shepherds Bush, London. † SWA 2.
MURRAY, Elizabeth Emily Exh. 1888-98
Figure and still life painter. Add: London. † GI 1, RI 4, SWA 6.
MURRAY, E. Hay Exh. 1880-81
Landscape and interior painter. Add: Godington Park, Ashford, Kent. † SWA 5.
MURRAY, Eben H. Exh. 1880-86
Edinburgh 1880 and 1885; Musselburgh 1883. † GI 5, L 2, RSA 20.
MURRAY, Edward M. Exh. 1923-24
Flower and still life painter. Add: The Old Palace, Oxford. † RA 2.
MURRAY, Frank* Exh. 1880-99
Landscape and figure painter and decorative artist. Add: London. † L 2, M 2, RA 18, RBA 8, RI 5, ROI 4, TOO 1.
MURRAY, Florence E. Exh. 1889-1929
Mrs. Lockwood. Landscape painter. Add: Plymouth 1889; London 1890; Linthwaite, Huddersfield 1903. † RBA 1, RID 51, SWA 4.
MURRAY, F. Waldo Exh. 1910-16
R.P. 1913. Add: 33 Tite Street, Chelsea, London. † L 1, P 9, RA 2
MURRAY, Frances Wynne Exh. 1919-39
Mrs. M.R. nee Johnson. Portrait, landscape and flower painter. b. Chichester. Studied Spenlove School of Art and Kensington and Chelsea Polytechnic. Add: London. † B 2, COO 5, D 2, GI 2, L 1, RCA 6, ROI 1, RSW 3, SWA 4, WG 28.
MURRAY, George Exh. 1883-1922
Painter and decorative designer. Add: Glasgow 1883; London 1899 and 1903; Blairgowrie, N.B. 1902. † BG 2, GI 3, L 4, RA 25, RI 3, RSA 4.
MURRAY, G.N. Exh. 1926-29
32 Kible Street, Ince, nr. Wigan. † L 3.
MURRAY, John Exh. 1903-19
Architect. Add: London. † RA 4.
MURRAY, John C.T. Exh. 1881-1909
Add: Glasgow 1881; Westminster, London 1909. † GI 2.
MURRAY, James G. d. 1906
Portrait painter. A.R.E. 1895. Add: Aberdeen 1886; Glasgow 1893 and 1900; Stirling 1896. † GI 15, L 3, RA 2, RE 25, RSA 11, RSW 1.
MURRAY, John Reid* Exh. 1880-1906
Landscape painter. Add: Helensburgh 1880; Glasgow 1887. † GI 50, I 2, L 2, M 2, RA 1, RHA 7, RSA 43.
MURRAY, James T. d. 1931
R.S.W. 1927. Exh. from 1888. Add: Edinburgh. † GI 16, RSA 52, RSW 9.
MURRAY, Kathleen Exh. 1932-38
Flower painter. † LEF 7.
MURRAY, Keith Exh. 1928
Architectural pencil artist. † LEF 28.

MURRAY, Kenneth L. Exh. 1938-40
Architect. Add: Martin Street, Stafford. † GI 2, RA 4.

MURRAY, Lizzie Exh. 1900-6
Primrose Bank, High Carriage Hill, Paisley. † GI 3.

MURRAY, M. Exh. 1880
27 Victoria Place, Stirling. † GI 1.

MURRAY, Margot Exh. 1930-31
95 Cadogan Gardens, London. † GOU 2, NEA 1.

MURRAY, M.A. Exh. 1885
Dollerie, Crieff. † RSA 1.

MURRAY, Mary M. Exh. 1931
5 Pembroke Street, Glasgow. † GI 1.

MURRAY, Robert Exh. 1915-16
College of Art, Edinburgh. † GI 2, RSA 1.

MURRAY, Robert C. Exh. 1893
Architect. Add: 1 Racquet Court, Fleet Street, London. † RA 1.

MURRAY, Ronald James Exh. 1908
72 Cathcart Studios, Redcliffe Road, London. † LS 5.

MURRAY, Mrs. S. Exh. 1880-1908
22 Mortimer Street, Regent Street, London 1880; Ballygears, Mullingar 1908. † RHA 5.

MURRAY, T.E. Exh. 1890
13 North John Street, Liverpool. † L 2.

MURRAY, T.G.B. Exh. 1886
12 Woodburn Terrace, Edinburgh. † RSA 1.

MURRAY, William Exh. 1884
1 Rosslyn Crescent, Edinburgh. † RSA 1.

MURRAY, William Grant 1877-1950
Landscape and figure painter. b. Portsoy. Studied Edinburgh School of Art, Royal College of Art and Julian's, Paris. Principal Swansea School of Arts and Crafts. Add: London 1901; Swansea 1927. † RA 4, RCA 2, RI 1.

MURRAY, W. Hay Exh. 1880-96
Architect. Add: Hastings, Sussex. † RA 4.

MURRAY, William Miller Graham b. 1907
Landscape painter, etcher and wood engraver. b. Langside. Studied Glasgow School of Art, Paris and Istanbul. Exh. 1928-40. Add: 5 Stewarton Drive, Cambuslang, Glasgow. † GI 14, L 2, LEF 21, RA 2, RSA 7, RSW 2.

MURRAY, William Staite b. 1881
Painter and potter. Instructor in pottery. Royal College of Art. Exh. 1927-35. Add: London and Bray, Berks. † BA 2, L 18, LEF 32, LEI 1.

MURRAY-JARDINE, Katherine Exh. 1911-27
Sculptor. Add: London 1911 and 1925; Moffat, N.B. 1915. † GI 1, L 3, RA 6.

MURRELL, Miss L.M. Exh. 1902-5
7 Thurlow Park, West Dulwich, London. † SWA 8.

MURRY, Richard b. 1902
Landscape, figure and genre painter. Studied Central School of Arts and Crafts 1922 and Slade School 1925. Assistant drawing master at the A.A. Exh. 1925-40. Add: London. † GOU 21, M 1, NEA 14.

MUSCHAMP, Francis Exh. 1880-85
Landscape painter. Add: 52 Fitzroy Road, Regents Park, London. † RBA 2, RHA 10.

MUSCHAMP, F. Sydney* d. 1929
Landscape and figure painter. R.B.A. 1893. Add: London. † B 8, D 1, L 5, M 2, RA 14, RBA 74, RHA 7, RI 7, ROI 13.

MUSGRAVE, A.F. Exh. 1911
Coates, Fittleworth, Sussex. † RA 3.

MUSGRAVE, Alex J. Exh. 1913-14
School of Art, Winnipeg, Manitoba, Canada. † GI 1, RSA 1.

MUSGRAVE, G.A. Exh. 1887
45 Holland Park, London. † D 1.

MUSGRAVE, Harry Exh. 1884-1910
Marine painter. Add: London. † D 1, FIN 1, GI 3, L 1, RA 17, RBA 2, ROI 2, TOO 2.

MUSGROVE, A.J. Exh. 1913-33
79 West Regent Street, Glasgow. † RA 1, RSW 1.

MUSGROVE, W. Exh. 1881-83
Edinburgh. † RSA 2.

MUSIN, Auguste* b. 1852
Belgian painter. Exh. 1880-94. Add: 114 Rue de la Limite, Brussels. † B 1, GI 3, L 2, M 9, RHA 9.

MUSIN, Francois* 1820-1888
Belgian painter. Add: 114 Rue de la Limite, Brussels. † GI 2, M 4, RHA 9.

MUSKETT, Winifred Alice Exh. 1921-24
2 Powis Square, London. † RA 1, RMS 2.

MUSMAN, Ernest B. Exh. 1930-37
Architect. Add: 7 Carteret Street, London. † RA 4.

MUSMANN, E. Exh. 1912
61 Frognal, Hampstead, London. † RA 1.

MUSPRATT, Aimee Exh. 1901-19
Miniature portrait painter. A.R.M.S. 1905. R.M.S. 1917. Add: Cley, Norfolk 1901; Christchurch, Hants. 1905; Paris 1906; London 1909; Woking, Surrey 1915. † B 4, I 6, L 17, LS 3, RA 6, RMS 16, SWA 3.

MUSPRATT, Alicia Frances Exh. 1922-36
Portrait and flower painter. b. Freshfield, Lancs. Studied Liverpool School of Art and under Garnet Wolseley. Add: Liverpool 1922; Enfield, Middlesex 1934. † COO 30. G 1, L 3, RA 1, RCA 1, ROI 1.

MUSPRATT, Hildegarde Exh. 1893-95
Seaforth Hall, Seaforth, Lancs. † L 4.

MUSSELWHITE, Miss N. Exh. 1896
79 Brigstock Road, Surrey. † SWA 1.

MUSSINI, Professor Luigi Exh. 1882
Director of Fine Arts, Siena, Italy. † M 2.

MUSSON, Miss F.K. Exh. 1908
16 Upper Charles Street, Leicester. † N 1.

MUSSON, Miss Georgie Exh. 1912-13
Sandhurst, Sefton Park, Liverpool. † L 3.

MUSTERS, Mrs. L.C. Exh. 1902
Wiverton, Bingham, Notts. † N 3.

MUSTO, Frederick Exh. 1900
Landscape painter. Add: Greek Street Chambers, Park Row, Leeds. † RA 1.

MUTCH, George Kirkton b. 1877
Painter, etcher and teacher. b. Stricken, Aberdeenshire. Studied Grays School of Art, Aberdeen. Exh. 1906-32. Add: Hamilton 1906; Edinburgh 1919. † GI 4, L 1, RSA 8, RSW 1.

MUTERMILCH, Mrs. M. Exh. 1910-1'
130 Boulevard Montparnasse, Paris. † L 1, LS 2, RSA 1.

MUTRIE, Annie Feray* 1826-1893
Flower and fruit painter. b. Manchester. Studied Manchester School of Design. Sister of Martha Darley M. q.v. Add: 36 Palace Gardens Terrace, Kensington, London. † B 2, GI 1, RA 2, RI 2.

MUTRIE, Martha Darley 1824-1885
Flower painter. Studied at the Manchester School of Design. Sister of Annie Feray M. q.v. Add: 36 Palace Gardens Terrace, Kensington, London. † RI 1.

MUTTLEBURY, Mrs. C.A. Exh. 1907
Westbourne Crescent, London. † SWA 1.

MYDDELTON, Mrs. Exh. 1933
18 Carlton House Terrace, London. † SWA 1.

MYDDELTON, A. Biddulph Exh. 1901
2 Turners Studios, Glebe Place, Chelsea, London. † NG 1.

MYER, Hyam b. 1904
Portrait, landscape and flower painter. Studied Slade School and Paris. Member London Group 1930. Exh. 1924-32. † AG 4, ALP 45, GOU 34, LEF 87.

MYER, Val Exh. 1904
Architect. Add: 157 Sutherland Avenue, London. † RA 1.

MYERS, Mrs. Annette M. Exh. 1889-94
York Road, Edgbaston, Birmingham. † B 2, L 1, M 1.

MYERS, Christina Exh. 1926-32
27 Broad Oak Road, Worsley, Manchester. † L 5, M 2.

MYERS, Hannah Exh. 1893-1920
Miniature and portrait painter. R.M.S. 1904. Add: London. † B 1, BG 38, GI 4, I 4, L 6, LS 5, NEA 1, RA 24, RMS 24, ROI 1, RSA 3, SWA 2.

MYERS, J. Exh. 1910
10 Grays Inn Square, London. † RA 1.

MYERS, Jane Exh. 1881-1907
Bervie, Kincardine 1881; Montrose 1885; Edinburgh 1898. † GI 1, RSA 9.

MYERS, John* Exh. 1882-89
Figure painter. Add: London. † B 2, L 2, M 1, RA 3, RHA 1.

MYERS, Minnie Exh. 1899
Sculptor. Add: 49 College Road, Haverstock Hill, London. † P 1, RA 1.

MYERS, William Exh. 1910-26
28 Nelson Road, Victoria Avenue, Higher Blackley, Manchester. † L 1, M 1.

MYERSCOUGH, C. Exh. 1938
† P 1.

MYERSCOUGH, Peggy Exh. 1935-40
Still life painter. Add: Clonard, Dundrum. † RHA 2.

MYERSCOUGH, Winifred Exh. 1936
Landscape painter. Add: Clonard, Dundrum. † RHA 1.

MYERSLOUGH-WALKER, Herbert Raymond b. 1908
Architect and illustrator. Studied at the A.A. Exh. 1933-40. Add: London. † RA 5.

MYHLENPHORT, Isa Exh. 1910
13 June Street, Battersea Park, London. † LS 3.

MYILL, L. Exh. 1893
7A Strathmore Gardens, Kensington, London. † M 1.

MYLES, W.S. Exh. 1886-89
Forfar 1886; Dundee 1889. † RSA 2.

MYLIUS, Mlle. Agnes Exh. 1888
Milan, Italy. † RHA 3.

MYLNE, Hannah Exh. 1880-84
Landscape painter. Add: Amwell, Ware, Herts. † SWA 6.

MYLNE, J.M. Exh. 1884-89
Portrait painter. Add: London. † SWA 4.

MYLNE, John M. Exh. 1886-1919
Glasgow. † GI 30, RSA 3.

MYNORS, Stella Exh. 1904
Tixall Hall, Stafford. † B 4.

MYRES, C.J.H. Exh. 1935
Liverpool. † RCA 1.

MYRES, T. Harrison Exh. 1896
Architect. Add: 19 Railway Approach, London Bridge, London. † RA 1.

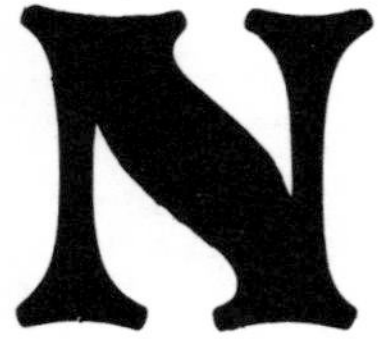

NACHSHEN, Donia Esther b. 1903
Portrait painter and illustrator. b. Ghitomir, Russia. Studied Slade School Exh. 1924-33. Add: London. † RA 3, ROI 2, SWA 4.

NACCIARONE, Gustave Exh. 1884
Figure painter, 34 Kensington Square, London. † RBA 1.

NADIN, Mrs. Harold B. Exh. 1889-90
Painter. Ashby Road, Burton-on-Trent. † SWA 3.

NAEGLEY, Henry Exh. 1893
Painter. c/o Messrs. Uppard and Smith, 77 Mortimer Street, London. † RA 1.

NAFTEL, Mrs. Isabel Exh. 1880-91
nee Oakley. Landscape, flower, portrait and genre painter. b. Guernsey. Daughter of Octavius Oakley (1800-1867). 2nd wife of Paul Jacob and mother of Maude N. q.v. S.W.A. 1880. Add: London. † B 5, D 3, G 7, GI 7, L 7, M 3, NG 4, RA 4, RI 9, SWA 39.

NAFTEL, Maud 1856-1890
Flower and landscape painter. Daughter of Paul Jacob and Isabel N. q.v. Studied Slade School and under Carolus Duran in Paris. A.R.W.S. 1887, A.S.W.A. 1885, S.W.A. 1886. Add: London. † B 4, D 6, FIN 3, G 7, GI 9, L 2, M 2, NG 3, RA 7, RI 5, RWS 10, SWA 31.

NAFTEL, Percy H. Exh. 1904-5
18 Earlston Road, Liscard, Cheshire. † L 2.

NAFTEL, Paul Jacob* 1817-1891
Landscape painter and teacher. b. Guernsey. Self taught. Married Isabel and father of Maud N. q.v. A.R.W.S. 1850, R.W.S. 1859. Add: London. † B 5, FIN 70, GI 3, L 4, M 2, RWS 76, TOO 1.

NAGHI BEY, Mohamed 1888-1956
Figure, portrait and landscape painter. Exh. 1936. † BA 45.

NAGLE, Minnie Exh. 1910-12
Artist and teacher. Cork 1910; Newry 1912. † RHA 5.

NAGY, de see D

NAHEBIDIAN, Rita Exh. 1918-19
29 Compagne Gardens, London. † I 1, NEA 2.

NAIRN, Andrew Exh. 1924-40
Glasgow. † GI 10, RSA 4.

NAIRN, Frederick C. Exh. 1884-1905
Glasgow. † GI 7.

NAIRN, George J. Exh. 1934-36
Landscape, figure and still life painter. 361 Clontarf Road, Dublin. † RHA 3.

NAIRN, George N. Exh. 1880-83
51 Denzille Street, Dublin. † RHA 6.

NAIRN, J. Gilbert Exh. 1910
117 Stephens Green, Dublin. † RHA 2.

NAIRN, James M. Exh. 1880-90
Landscape painter. Glasgow. † GI 23, NEA 1, RSA 4.

NAIRN, Peter Exh. 1888-1910
Liverpool. † L 4.

NAIRNE, Lieut. Col. Sylvester Exh. 1939
Watercolour landscape painter. Plover Hill, Compton, Winchester, Hants. † RA 1.

NAISH, Charles Exh. 1896
Painter and illustrator. 114 College Place, Camden Town, London.† RA 1.

NAISH, John George* 1824-1905
Figure, genre, landscape and marine painter. Studied R.A. Schools, Paris, Bruges and Antwerp. Add: Ilfracombe, Devon 1880; c/o C. Gatehouse Westwood, Noctorum, Cheshire 1899. † B 1, L 9, RA 5, RHA 1.

NAISH, Richard E. Exh. 1930-40
Portrait, landscape and still life painter. London and Oxfordshire. † COO 7, L 1, NEA 4, RA 2.

NAISMITH, Margery H. Exh. 1933-39
12 Albert Gate, Glasgow. † GI 1, RSA 1, RSW 2.

NAJERA, Miguel H. Exh. 1911
c/o M. Blanchet, 38 Rue Bonapoarte, Paris. † L 1.

NAKANO, Hideto b. 1890
Landscape painter. b. Japan. Exh. 1928. Add: 86 Clarendon Road, Putney, London. † RA 1.

NAKESKA, Eleanora Exh. 1900-2
11 Dundas Street, Edinburgh. † RSA 5.

NAKKEN, Willem Carel* Exh. 1888-90
Landscape and figure painter. Huygenstraats 22, The Hague, Holland. † FIN 2, M 2.

NALDER, James H. Exh. 1880-81
Portrait and genre painter. 159 High Street, Notting Hill, London. † RBA 2.

NAMUR, Paul F. Exh. 1913-14
68 Rue Spontini, Paris. † LS 3.

NANCE, Armorel Mary Exh. 1924-29
Sculptor, painter, designer and engraver. Studied Slade School, Royal College of Art, Rome and British School at Athens. Add: Pentowan, Carbis Bay, Cornwall. † L 3, RA 1.

NANCE, Robert Morton Exh. 1895-1909
Painter, illustrator and ship modeller. Add: Bushey, Herts. 1895; Penarth, South Wales 1903; Nanchedrea, Nr. Penzance, 1909. † L 1, NG 5, RA 3.

NANKIVELL, Frank Arthur b. 1869
Painter, etcher, humorous and satirical illustrator. b. Australia. Studied New York, London, Japan and China. Contributor to "Punch". Exh. 1930. † FIN 9.

NANKIVELL, Helen L. Exh. 1892-94
Landscape painter. London. † M 1, RBA 3.

NANNINI, Raffaello Exh. 1897
Sculptor. Via S. Niccolo No. 1, Florence. † L 1. RA 1.

NAPER, Charles W.S. Exh. 1910-33
Landscape painter. Married Ella N. q.v. Add: Looe, Cornwall 1910; St. Buryan, Cornwall 1929. † L 1, RA 5.

NAPER, Ella b. 1887
nee Steel. Jeweller and potter. Studied London University and New Cross and Camberwell Schools of Arts and Crafts. Married Charles W.S.N. q.v. Collaborated with Dame Laura Knight q.v. Exh. 1919-34. Add: St. Buryan, Cornwall. † I 5, L 21, RBA 2.

NAPIER of Magdala, Lady Exh. 1892-1906
Painter. Add: London. † RA 3, ROI 4.

NAPIER, Charles b. 1889
Watercolour painter and painter of pottery. b. Edinburgh. Studied Edinburgh College of Art. R.S.W. 1914. Exh. 1908-40. Add: Edinburgh 1908; London 1932. † AR 2, GI 46, L 11, M 4, RBA 4, RSA 62, RSW 59.

NAPIER, Caroline M. Exh. 1899
5 Morningside Drive, Edinburgh. † RSA 1.

NAPIER, Mrs. Eva Exh. 1885-89
Landscape painter. Add: 8 Seville Street, Lowndes Square, London. † RA 1, RBA 1, ROI 1.

NAPIER, James Exh. 1887-97
Shawlands, Glasgow 1887; Strathbungo 1890. † GI 7.

NAPIER, John Exh. 1885-98
Edinburgh 1885 and 1890; Greenock 1886. † RSA 6, RSW 1.

NAPIER, James Brand Exh. 1884-85
Painter and teacher. Father of James Harold N. q.v. Add: Edinburgh. † RSA 3.

NAPIER, James Harold Exh. 1912-26
Painter, writer and art critic. b. Edinburgh. Son of James Brand N. q.v. Studied Edinburgh University. Add: London. † GOU 2, LS 3, RI 6.

NAPIER, J. Macvicar Exh. 1885-93
Landscape painter. Add: Dungowan, Gourock 1885; Birdston, Kirkintilloch 1890. † GI 14, L 2, RA 2, RSA 4.

NAPIER, N.S. Exh. 1892
Omaha, Helensburgh. † GI 1.

NAPIER, Robert Exh. 1880-1906
Dennistown, Glasgow 1880; Shawlands, Glasgow 1889; Strathbungo 1890; Glasgow 1906. † GI 10, L 1, RSA 1.

NAPIER, Miss V. Exh. 1901
Laurel Cottage, Bushey Heath, Herts. † SWA 1.

NAPPER, Harry Exh. 1890-1916
Landscape painter. Add: London. † BG 10, RA 6, RBA 3.

NAPPER, Mrs. Heda Exh. 1936-37
Landscape painter. Add: Ecclestone Studio, High Street, London. † RA 2.

NARBETH, William Arthur b. 1893
Painter and etcher. Studied Goldsmiths College School of Art. Exh. 1926-35. Add: Rosemary Cottage, Heathfield Road, Seaford, Sussex. † BA 2, GI 2, RA 12.

NARDI, Enrico Exh. 1906-26
Portrait painter. Add: 48 Via Margutta, Rome 1906; c/o Mrs. T.A. Emmet, 66 Grosvenor Street, London 1926. † L 2, RA 1, RSA 1.

NARDONNET, Charles Eugene Exh. 1912
8 Rue Adolphe Focillon, Paris. † RSA 2.

NARRACOTT, Elizabeth Exh. 1915-28
Liverpool. † L 26.

NARRACOTT, H.R. Exh. 1912-14
14 Adderley Street, Liverpool. † L 3.

NASH, Albert Exh. 1906-22
Birmingham. † B 12.

NASH, Adrienne A. Exh. 1922-40
Watercolour figure painter. Add: London. † RA 5, RI 21.

NASH, Donald Exh. 1931-39
Flower and landscape painter. Add: Bexley Heath, Kent 1931; Horsham, Sussex 1934; Harrow, Middlesex 1939. † RA 4.

NASH, Mrs. Ethel See HOWELL

NASH, Eustace P.E. b. 1886
Painter and lithographer. b. Bournemouth. Studied Drummond School of Art. Exh. 1912-39. Add: Bournemouth. † L 4, RA 5.

NASH, John Northcote* b. 1893
Painter, illustrator and wood engraver. Self taught. Official war artist World War I. Assistant master Ruskin School of Drawing. Teacher of Design Royal College of Art. Brother of Paul N. q.v. N.E.A. 1919, A.R.A. 1940. Founder Member London Group 1913. "A Suffolk Landscape" (c.1936-37) purchased by Chantrey Bequest 1939. Add: Iver Heath, Bucks. 1913; Gerrards Cross, Bucks. 1920; Meadle, nr. Princes Risborough 1922. † AG 16, BA 1, COO 2, FIN 11, GI 5, GOU 310, L 6, LEF 4, LEI 4, M 5, NEA 52, RA 5, RED 26, RSA 4, TOO 6.

NASH, Joseph Junr.* d. 1922
Marine, landscape, interior and historical painter. Son of Joseph N. (1808-1878). R.I. 1886 (resigned 1907). Exh. 1883-97. Add: 36 The Avenue, Bedford Park, London. † B 1, GI 1, L 7, M 5, RA 2, RHA 2, RI 20, ROI 1.

NASH, J.O. Exh. 1891-97
Watercolour landscape and coastal painter. Add: 3 Seymour Terrace, Plymouth. † M 2, RA 1, RI 2.

NASH, Mrs. Kathleen Exh. 1916-26
nee Sparrow. Still life painter. b. Plymouth. Add: London. † B 2, L 1, LS 3, ROI 7, SWA 3.

NASH, Marjorie Exh. 1905-16
Taplow, Bucks. 1908; London 1912. † L 6, RA 1, SWA 2.

NASH, Paul* 1889-1946
Painter, engraver and theatrical designer. Studied Chelsea Polytechnic and Slade School 1909-10. Joined Artists Rifles and was wounded in France 1917. Became an official war artist on the Western Front. Brother of John Northcote N. q.v. N.E.A. 1919. Member London Group 1914. Several examples of his works are in the Tate Gallery. Add: Iver Heath, Bucks. 1913; London 1915 and 1929; Dymchurch, Kent 1922. † AG 7, BA 2, BK 2, CHE 3, FIN 9, L 6, LEF 4, LEI 226, LS 3, M 3, NEA 54, P 1, RED 128, RSA 4, RSW 1, TOO 38.

NASH, Thomas Exh. 1921-38
Painter of figures and biblical subjects. Add: Pangbourne, Dorset 1921; London 1928. † GOU 1, NEA 15, RA 1, RED 54.

NASH, William F. Exh. 1930
117 Cato Street, Saltley. † B 2.

NASH, Walter Hilton c.1850-1927
Architect. Add: London. † RA 3.

NASMITH, Mrs. Mary F. Exh. 1938-40
Portrait painter. Add: Heaton Mersey, Manchester. † M 1, RA 1.

NASMYTH, Jean Burns Exh. 1912
18 Mayfield Gardens, Edinburgh. † GI 1.

NATHAN, Adelaide A. Burnett Exh. 1881-87
Figure and architectural painter. Add: London. † B 2, L 1, RBA 4, SWA 1.

NATHAN, Annette M. Exh. 1885-88
Figure painter. Add: London 1885; Edgbaston, Birmingham 1888. † B 3, RBA 3, SWA 2.

NATHAN, Estelle Exh. 1898-1928
Mrs. G.E. Portrait and figure painter. Mother of Pamela d'Avigdor N. q.v. Worked in China for 3 years. Add: London. † G 1, I 21, LS 12, NEA 2, NG 5, P 8, RA 4.

NATHAN, Fanny Exh. 1890-97
Landscape painter. Add: London and Richmond, Surrey. † B 6, L 2, M 1, RA 2, RHA 2, ROI 5, RSA 1, SWA 2.

NATHAN, Louise Exh. 1913
3 Avenue Road, Regents Park, London. † LS 4.

NATHAN, M.H. Exh. 1885-86
21 Bedford Square, London. † L 1, RHA 1.

NATHAN, Pamela d'Avigdor b. 1905
Painter and wood engraver. Daughter of Estelle N. q.v. Studied Slade School. Exh. 1930-33. Add: London. † L 1, RA 3, RED 1, RMS 1, SWA 1.

NATHAN, Robert F. Exh. 1930-34
Watercolour landscape painter. Travelled widely in Europe, North Africa and the Mediterranean. † WG 153.

NATHUSENS, de See D

NATHUSIUS, von See V

NATORP, Gustave Exh. 1884-1906
Sculptor. Did not take up sculpture until he was over 40. Studied at Slade School and under Rodin in Paris 1881-83. Add: London. † GI 2, L 9, M 3, NG 3, RA 14.

NATTRESS, George Exh. 1881-89
Flower, landscape and architectural painter. Add: London. † D 1, L 3, NG 2, RA 12, RI 6.

NAUGHTEN, Elizabeth Exh. 1880-81
Figure and landscape painter. Add: 32 Charlotte Street, Fitzroy Square, London. † D 3, SWA 3.

NAUGHTON, Miss E. Exh. 1882-85
Edinburgh. † RSA 5.

NAVELLIER, Edouard Exh. 1925-30
4 Rue Royer Collard, Paris. † GI 5, RSA 4.

NAVIASKY, Philip b. 1894
Pastel and watercolour landscape and portrait painter. Studied Leeds School of Art and Royal College of Art. Exh. 1914-40. Add: London and Leeds. † ALP 1, GI 1, GOU 8, I 1, L 8, M 3, NEA 5, P 12, RA 8, RHA 3, ROI 1, RSA 15.

NAVONE, Edouardo P. Exh. 1891
Painter. Add: 1 St. Andrews Square, Surbiton, Surrey. † RA 1.

NAWIASKY, Mechthild Exh. 1939
† GOU 1.

NAYLOR, Mrs. Alice M. Exh. 1927-30
26 Wentworth Road, Harborne, Birmingham. † B 6.

NAYLOR, Miss G.M.C. Exh. 1928
14 Derwent Drive, Wallasey, Cheshire. † L 1.

NAYLOR, James J.S. Exh. 1908-26
Architect. Add: 19 Hanover Square, London. † L 2, RA 7.

NAYLOR, Marie J. Exh. 1883-1904
Fruit, flower, figure and portrait painter. Add: Barnes, Surrey and London 1883; Paris 1896. † L 2, M 2, RA 12, RBA 9, RHA 8, ROI 5, RSA 1, SWA 3.

NAYLOR, William Exh. 1922
c/o W. Doubleday, 67 Colmore Row, Birmingham. † B 1.

NEAL, David Exh. 1892
† GI 1.

NEAL, George Exh. 1926-36
Painter. b. Boston Fen, Lincs. Studied Leicester School of Art. Add: Leicester 1926; Birstall, Leics. 1936. † L 3, N 13, RA 1, RCA 3.

NEAL, James H.P. b. 1918
Landscape and portrait painter. Studied St. Martins School of Art 1932-35, and Royal College of Art 1935-39. Exh. 1937-40. Add: 23 Pleasant Place, Islington, London. † RA 3.

NEAL, Jabez N. Exh. 1932
Flower painter. Add: 40 Sykefield Avenue, Leicester. † RA 1.

NEALE, Edward Exh. 1880-98
Bird and animal painter. Add: London. † B 3, D 12, L 2, RA 1.

NEALE, Edward J. Exh. 1886-1915
Landscape painter. Add: London 1886; Kew, Surrey 1898; Ashingdon, Essex 1904; Hockley, Essex 1913. † RBA 3, RHA 11.

NEALE, George Hall Exh. 1883-1935
Portrait and genre painter. Studied Liverpool School of Art and Juliens, Paris. Married Maud Hall N. q.v. Add: Liverpool 1883 and London 1910. † B 1, GI 1, L 129, M 4, P 10, RA 60, RCA 14, ROI 9.

NEALE, James Exh. 1881-96
Architect. Add: 10 Bloomsbury Square, London. † RA 17.

NEALE, Maud Hall Exh. 1889-1940
nee Rutherford. Portrait painter. Studied Liverpool, and Paris under Delecluse. Married George Hall N. q.v. A.S.W.A. 1910, S.W.A. 1911. Add: Liverpool 1889 and Liverpool and London 1910. † L 100, P 9, RA 42, ROI 13, SWA 89

NEAME, Ellen A. Exh. 1929-35
Mrs. J. Armstrong N. Watercolour landscape and flower painter. b. New Zealand. Studied in Florence. † WG 108.

NEAME, J. Armstrong Exh. 1929-35
Watercolour landscape and flower painter and etcher. † WG 91.

NEAME, Miss M.M. Exh. 1913-17
Kyle, Herkomer Road, Bushey, Herts. † L 1, RA 4, ROI 1.

NEATBY, Edward Mossforth 1888-1949
Portrait and landscape painter. b. Leeds. Son of William James N. q.v. Studied Royal College of Art and Slade School A.R.M.S. 1912, R.M.S. 1913. Add: Birkenhead 1911; London 1917 and 1922; High Wycombe, Bucks. 1921; Ipswich, Suffolk 1932. † B 2, FIN 5, I 3, L 43, P 12, RA 6, RBA 2, RI 1, RMS 41, RSA 2.

NEATBY, William James 1860-1910
Miniature painter. b. Barnsley. Father of Edward Mossforth N. q.v. A.R.M.S. 1906; R.M.S. 1907. Add: London. † L 11, NG 2, RA 3, RMS 20.

NEATE, Margaret Exh. 1934
Pastel portrait artist. Studied under Mme. Debillemont-Chardon. † WG 33.

NEAVE, Alice Headley b. 1903
Painter. b. Hastings. Studied Slade School and R.A. Schools. Exh. 1936-39. Add: London. † GI 1, RA 1.

NEAVE, David S. Exh. 1903-36
Landscape painter and etcher. Add: London 1903; Topsham, Devon 1911. † AB 24, FIN 1, GI 8, GOU 37, I 3, L 1, LS 3, NEA 6, RA 3, RSA 1.

NEED, Edith M. Exh. 1908
Lygon Pharmacy, Malvern, Worcs. † B 2.

NEEDELL, Philip G. Exh. 1910-28
Sunningfields Road, Hendon, London. † L 2, ROI 1.

NEEDHAM, A. Exh. 1936
Painter. † WG 2.

NEEDHAM, F. Exh. 1884
† TOO 1.

NEEDHAM, Miss F.M. Exh. 1902-12
Add: Woburn Sands, Beds. 1902; London 1911. † L 6, RA 1, RCA 2.

NEEDHAM, J.A. Exh. 1918-20
Ilkeston, Derbys. † N 5.

NEEDHAM, Kathleen R. Exh. 1930
Upper Colwyn Bay, Wales. † RCA 1.

NEEDHAM, Mary Exh. 1901-13
Westwood, Ainsdale, nr. Southport, Lancs. † L 2, RCA 9.

NEEDHAM, Mrs. V. Exh. 1912-15
London 1912; Colchester 1914. † RA 3.
NEER, de See D
NEFF, James Exh. 1935-36
Landscape painter. Add: Cork Art Club, 25 Patrick Street, Cork. † RHA 5.
NEHER, Dora Exh. 1909
† LS 3.
NEIGHBOUR, Sydney W. Exh. 1899
Architect. Add: 8 Martin's Place, London. † RA 1.
NEIL, George Exh. 1888-1930
Glasgow. † GI 8.
NEIL, H. Exh. 1910-15
30 Shakespeare Villas, Shakespeare Street, Nottingham. † N 10.
NEIL, Thomas Exh. 1881-82
42 Bath Street, Glasgow. † GI 2.
NEILD, Agnes L. Exh. 1906-7
Lyndale, Westminster Road, Eccles. † M 4.
NEILD, Edward Exh. 1912
Ellesmere Park, Eccles. † M 1.
NEILD, Julie Exh. 1936-40
Landscape and flower painter. † COO 9, NEA 2.
NEILL, C.O. Exh. 1890
9 Gresford Avenue, Sefton Park, Liverpool. † L 3.
NEILL, David Exh. 1916-17
5 Caddlehill Terrace, Greenock. † RSA 3.
NEILL, Henry Echlin b. 1888
Landscape, seascape and figure painter. Studied Belfast School of Art. Exh. 1929-38. Add: Belfast. † RHA 17.
NEILSEN, Kay d. 1957
Painter and illustrator. Exh. 1913. † M 4.
NEILSON, Miss A. Exh. 1881
10 Somerville Place, Glasgow. † RSA 2.
NEILSON, Angus M. Exh. 1934
Eastfield House, Joppa. † RSA 1.
NEILSON, Mrs. Dorothy Exh. 1910-11
Plovers Moss, Sandiway, Cheshire. † L 2.
NEILSON, Duncan H. Exh. 1907
Roselea, Renfrew Road, Paisley. † GI 3.
NEILSON, Miss E. Exh. 1883-92
Still life painter. Add: 61 Bessborough Street, London. † L 3, RBA 1.
NEILSON, Elmer M. Exh. 1897
The Studio, Burpham, nr. Arundel, Sussex. † RSA 1.
NEILSON, Harry B. Exh. 1895-1900
Airliewood, Forest Road, Claughton, Birkenhead. † L 5.
NEILSON, Henry Ivan Exh. 1900-9
Kirkcudbright, N.B. 1900 and 1909; Edinburgh 1908. † GI 9, L 5, M 2, RSA 17.
NEILSON, James Exh. 1917
Eastwood, Mount Vernon, Glasgow. † GI 1.
NEILSON, Jennie L. Exh. 1908-12
Springburn, N.B. 1908; Glasgow 1911. † GI 5, L 2.
NELDER, Norah Margaret Exh. 1925-27
18 Monmouth Road, Wallasey, Cheshire. † L 4.
NELSON, A. Kerr Exh. 1881
Painter. Add: 37 Bolsover Street, Portland Road, London. † SWA 1.
NELSON, Amy Margaret See WARD
NELSON, Ben Exh. 1911
Landscape painter. Add: 21 Sutherland Avenue, Maida Vale, London. † NEA 1.
NELSON, C. Mabel Exh. 1924
Watercolour painter. Add: Hillside, Ockbrook, Derby. † N 1.
NELSON, Mrs. Essington Exh. 1886-90
Landscape painter. Add: Cheltenham 1886; South Kensington, London 1890. † B 5, GI 1, L 3, M 3, SWA 7.
NELSON, E.C. (C.C.) Exh. 1916
Still life painter. Add: 7 Henniker Mews, Elm Park Road, Chelsea, London. † NEA 1.
NELSON, Edmund Hugh b. 1910
Portrait and landscape painter and illustrator. Studied Goldsmiths College 1927-30. Exh. 1938. Add: 352 Pickhurst Rise, West Wickham, Kent. † P 1, RBA 2.
NELSON, Mrs. E.M. Exh. 1890
2 Myrtle Villas, New Malden, Surrey. † SWA 1.
NELSON, George d. 1921
Painter. Add: London 1895; Whitehaven 1896. † RBA 1, RI 1.
NELSON, Geoffrey C. Exh. 1914-31
Landscape and portrait painter. Add: London. † NEA 8, RA 2.
NELSON, Gwen W. Exh. 1934-38
Landscape and flower painter. Add: London. † BK 48, SWA 3.
NELSON, Harold E.H. b. 1871
Painter, etcher, illustrator, designer and advertising artist. b. Dorchester. Studied Lambeth School of Art and Central School of Arts and Crafts. Exh. 1899-1928. Add: London 1899 and 1907; Carshalton, Surrey 1902. † L 1, RA 8, RI 3, RMS 1.
NELSON, Ida Exh. 1926-39
Mrs. Bond. Sculptor. Studied Manchester School of Art and Slade School. Add: London 1926 and 1929; Manchester 1928; Harrow on the Hill, Middlesex 1939. † L 6, M 2, RA 3, RSA 1.
NELSON, J.P. Exh. 1933
Arden House, Henley in Arden. † B 2.
NELSON, Katherine Boyd b. 1897
Portrait and landscape painter and pencil artist. Studied Goldsmiths College. Exh. 1918-28. Add: 24 Ulundi Road, Blackheath, London. † NEA 2, P 3, RA 1, SWA 1.
NELSON, Raphael b. 1898
Painter, black and white caricaturist and linocut artist. Exh. 1924-28. Add: London. † AB 1, GOU 2.
NELSON, William J. Exh. 1883
Painter. Add: 18 Dorchester Place, Blandford Square, London. † RA 1.
NERET, Adrien Moreau Exh. 1886
Painter. Add: 6 Rue de Seine, Paris. † RI 1.
NERUDA, L. Norman Exh. 1886
6 Bedford Gardens, Kensington, London. † G,1.
NERUDA-NORMAN, Wilma Exh. 1913
Landscape painter. † ALP 3.
NESBIT, G.W. Exh. 1909-10
Figure painter. Add: 6 Wentworth Studios, Manresa Road, London. † L 1, RA 1.
NESBIT, John J. Exh. 1934-39
Landscape and portrait painter. Add: 84 London Road, Leicester. † N 13.
NESBIT, Wilson Exh. 1917-33
Portrait painter. Add: Bournemouth 1917; London 1923. † RA 6.
NESBITT, Frances E. c.1864-1934
Landscape, coastal and figure painter. A.S.W.A. 1899. Add: London 1886 and 1906; Ilfracombe, Devon 1900; Louth, Lincs. 1901; Kings Langley, Herts. 1926. † D 61, L 12, NG 1, RA 3, RBA 25, RHA 39, RI 10, ROI 2, SWA 171.
NESBITT, John* 1831-1904
Landscape and marine painter. Add: Edinburgh. † GI 1, RHA 2, RSA 18, RSW 1, TOO 1.
NESBITT, S. Exh. 1881
Kingston Villa, Lewisham. † RHA 1.
NESFIELD, Dorothy Exh. 1900
Speldhurst, Tunbridge Wells, Kent. † NG 1.
NESS, Anne W.K. Exh. 1933
7 South Gray Street, Edinburgh. † RSA 1.
NESS, Helen L. Exh. 1921
Watercolour painter. Add: 18 Bridgford Road, Nottingham. † N 1.
NESS, James Exh. 1901-10
Paisley, 1901; Perth 1909; London 1910. † GI 8, L 1, RSA 4.
NESS, John Alexander d. 1931
Watercolour landscape painter and etcher. b. Glasgow. N.S.A. 1908; V.P.N.S.A. 1920, A.R.E. 1903. Exh. from 1903. Add: 18 Bridgford Road, Nottingham. † FIN 5, GI 3, N 80, RE 30.
NETHERWOOD, Arthur* d. 1930
Landscape painter. b. Huddersfield. Married Edith Mary Dyas q.v. Add: Deganwy, Llandudno, Wales 1893; Conway, Wales 1910; Huddersfield 1922; Shrewsbury 1925. † B 1, GI 1, L 15, M 3, RA 3, RCA 115, RI 3.
NETHERWOOD, Edith Mary See DYAS
NETHERWOOD, Norman Exh. 1903-38
Deganwy, Landudno 1903; and 1921; Conway 1910. † L 11, RCA 120
NETTERVILLE, Dolly Exh. 1905
c/o Mrs. Synnott, Furness, Naas, Co. Kildare. † RHA 1.
NETTERVILLE, Pauline Exh. 1922-26
Park House, Killiney. † RHA 3, RMS 1.
NETTLESHIP, Ida d. 1907
Studied Slade School 1892-98 (scholarship 1895). Daughter of John T.N. q.v. Married Augustus John q.v. Mother of Edwin John q.v. Exh. 1898-1900. Add: 58 Wigmore Street, London. † NG 2.
NETTLESHIP, John Trivett* 1841-1902
Animal and genre painter, illustrator and author. b. Kettering. Studied Heatherleys and Slade School and the Zoological Gardens. Visited India. Father of Ida N. q.v. R.O.I. 1894. Add: London. † BG 1, GI 1, L 19, M 7, NG 21, RA 24, RHA 3, RI 3, ROI 28.
NEUHUYS, Albert* 1844-1914
Dutch domestic and figure painter. Add: London and Amsterdam. † AG 1, G 1, GI 5, M 3, RA 4, RSA 2.
NEUMANS, Alphonse Exh. 1885-89
Figure and landscape painter. Add: Scarborough 1885; South Hampstead, London 1889. † RA 1, RBA 1.
NEUMEGAN, Florence A. Exh. 1892-1906
Mrs. C. Engelbach. Figure painter. Add: London 1892; Newcastle on Tyne 1903. † B 2, L 1, P 1, RA 1, RBA 1, ROI 3.
NEUVILLE, de See D
NEUWIRTH, Miss W.L. Exh. 1899-1914
Add: Manchester 1899; London 1907. † LS 12, M 3, RA 2.
NEVE, Arthur Exh. 1911
Landscape painter. † ALP 1.
NEVE, A. Augustus Exh. 1888-96
Figure painter. Add: London. † RA 3, ROI 1.
NEVE, A.G. Exh. 1903
5 Jeypore Road, Wandsworth, London. † L 1.
NEVE, Marion Exh. 1896-1911
Benenden, Cranbrook, Kent. † B 3, RBA 1, SWA 3.
NEVE, William West Exh. 1880-1902
Architect. Add: 5 Bloomsbury Square, London. † RA 7.
NEVELL, Miss F.L. Exh. 1912-13
Stoke Newington, London. † SWA 3.

NEVEN, Du Mont Exh. 1900
7 Cromwell Place, Chelsea, London. † GI 2.

NEVILL, Miss D. Exh. 1889-93
c/o Mrs. Haill, 10A Church Alley, Church Street, Liverpool. † L 8.

NEVILL, Miss E. Exh. 1918
† I 2.

NEVILL, Mrs. Isobel Exh. 1913-40
Landscape, fruit and flower painter. Add: Chislehurst, Kent 1923; London 1928; Ringwood, Hants. 1937. † ALP 6, B 5, GOU 12, I 1, LS 6, P 1, ROI 9, RSA 3.

NEVILL, Ralph Exh. 1886-89
Architect. Add: London. † RA 5.

NEVILL, Walter b. 1878
Watercolour painter. Exh. 1927. Add: Paris. † WG 46.

NEVILLE, Amy Exh. 1924-39
Sister of E. Kate N. q.v. Add: 7 Mulberry Walk, London. † RI 2, SWA 2.

NEVILLE, A. Munro Exh. 1923-39
Dumbreck, Glasgow 1923; Drumchapel, Dumbartonshire 1937. † GI 4, RSA 1, RSW 3.

NEVILLE, E. Kate Exh. 1938
Sister of Amy N. q.v. Add: 7 Mulberry Walk, London. † RI 1.

NEVILLE, G.F. Exh. 1884
5 Regent's Park Terrace, London. † GI 2.

NEVILLE, H. Exh. 1913-15
Grassington, Skipton, Yorks. † RA 1, RI 5.

NEVILLE, Herbert W. Exh. 1900-35
Landscape painter and teacher. Add: Newcastle on Tyne 1900; Cornhill on Tweed 1902; Lymington, Hants. 1915; Birlingham, Worcs. 1932. † B 2, L 3, M 1, RA 3, RBA 1, RI 3, ROI 2.

NEVILLE, Louis Exh. 1887-1914
Watercolour landscape painter. Add: South Queensferry N.B. 1887; Sutton, Co. Dublin 1907; Infantry Barracks, Ballinrobe, Co. Mayo 1910. † L 10, NG 1, RHA 4, RSA 1, WG 70.

NEVILLE, Margaret Exh. 1918-20
Mill Street House, Galway. † RHA 5.

NEVILLE, Maud Exh. 1915-26
Blackburn, Lancs. † L 3.

NEVILLE, P.C.M. Exh. 1915-18
Weston, Enniskerry, Co. Wicklow. † RHA 3.

NEVILLE, Winifred Exh. 1932
41 Mosspark Drive, Glasgow. † GI 1.

NEVINS, W. Probyn Exh. 1885
Figure painter. Add: 121 Portsdown Road, London. † ROI 1.

NEVINSON, Christopher Richard Wynne* 1889-1946
Watercolour painter, etcher and lithographer. Studied St. John's Wood School of Art, Slade School 1908-12 and Juliens, Paris 1912-13. Official artist World War I. N.E.A. 1929, A.R.A. 1939, R.B.A. 1931, R.O.I. 1932. Founder Member London Group 1913. "A Star Shell" (Exh. 1916) purchased by Chantrey Bequest 1962. Add: London. † AG 7, AR 4, BAR 42, BK 3, CHE 5, COO 51, FIN 14, G 5, GI 4, L 13, LEI 12, LS 18, NEA 85, RA 18, RBA 48, RED 50, RHA 1, ROI 26, RSA 2.

NEVINSON, E.S. Exh. 1889-96
13 Lyndhurst Road, Hampstead, London. † B 9, RHA 7.

NEW, Edmund Hort 1871-1931
Etcher, illustrator and lecturer. b. Evesham. Studied and taught at Birmingham School of Art. Add: Evesham 1898; Oxford 1905. † B 3, FIN 4, RA 3.

NEW, J.C. Exh. 1911
29 Santos Road, East Putney, London. † LS 3.

NEWALL, Lina Exh. 1895-1908
Add: Wavertree, Liverpool 1895; London 1903. † L 5, SWA 10.

NEWBERRY, Miss C.B. Exh. 1903
Stafford House, Broxbourne, Herts. † SWA 1.

NEWBERRY, John E. Exh. 1889-1902
Architect. Add: London. † RA 4.

NEWBERY, Francis H. Exh. 1890-1940
Painter and teacher. b. Membury, Devon. Studied Bridport and South Kensington Schools of Art. Married Jessie Rowat N. q.v. Add: School of Art, Glasgow 1890; Corfe Castle, Dorset 1919. † GI 68, I 40, L 21, M 3, NEA 4, P 6, RA 10, RBA 1, RSA 46, RSW 4.

NEWBERY, Jessie Rowat Exh. 1892-1900
Mrs. Francis H. Add: Glasgow. † GI 8, RSA 1, RSW 3.

NEWBERY, Maud Exh. 1892
Watercolour fruit painter. Add: 1 Mount Lebanon Villas, Westcombe Park, Blackheath, London. † RA 1.

NEWBOLD, Annie Exh. 1892-94
Landscape painter. Add: 9 Claro Terrace, Richmond Road, South Kensington, London. † ROI 3.

NEWBOLT, Mrs. Exh. 1929
3 Lansdowne Crescent, London. † WG 4.

NEWBOLT, Sir Francis George 1863-1940
Etcher. b. Bilston. Studied Slade School, Oxford and under Ruskin and Herkomer. A.R.E. 1889. Knighted c.1921. Add: Weybridge, Surrey 1897; London 1905. † BA 6, I 1, RA 17, RE 62.

NEWBOULD, Frank 1887-1951
Painter, poster and black and white artist. Studied Bradford College of Art. Exh. 1925. Add: London. † CHE 2.

NEWBURY, Mary See STURROCK

NEWBY, Alfred T. Exh. 1885-90
Landscape painter. Add: Leicester. † RI 2.

NEWCOMB, R. Exh. 1911-13
The Lodge, Heckington, Lincs. † N 4.

NEWCOMBE, A.E. Exh. 1907
31 Munster Square, Regents Park, London. † RA 1.

NEWCOMBE, Beatrice Exh. 1926
† GOU 3.

NEWCOMBE, Bertha Exh. 1880-1908
Figure, landscape, portrait and flower painter. N.E.A. 1888. Add: Croydon, Surrey and London. † D 4, FIN 1, L 15, LS 5, M 4, NEA 4, RA 13, RBA 8, RI 1, ROI 4, SWA 14.

NEWBOMBE, Frederick Clive 1847-1894
Landscape painter and watercolourist. b. Frederick Harrison Suker but adopted Newcombe to distinguish him from his brother Arthur Suker q.v. and father William S. Studied at Mount Street School of Art under John Finnie. Add: Keswick, Cumberland 1880; Coniston, Lancs. 1893. † B 1, L 2, M 1, RA 3, RSA 1.

NEWCOMBE, S. Exh. 1911-15
2a Pembroke Road, Kensington, London. † L 1, RA 4.

NEWELL, F. Exh. 1912-33
96 Ongar Road, Brentwood, Essex. † B 1, D 3, RA 1.

NEWELL, Leonard Exh. 1910
Llanbeth Lodge, Tal-y-bont, Tal-y-Cafn, North Wales. † L 1.

NEWELL, L.M. Exh. 1910
22 Fenwick Street, Liverpool. † L 1.

NEWEY, Erle Foster b. 1888
Marine painter and illuminator. Son of Harry Foster and husband of Gertrude N. q.v. Studied Birmingham School of Art. Exh. 1927-32. Add: 14 New Street, Birmingham. † B 9.

NEWEY, Gertrude Exh. 1931-34
nee Follows. Married Erle Foster N. q.v. Add: 14 New Street, Birmingham. † B 5.

NEWEY, Harry Foster 1858-1933
Landscape painter and illuminator. Studied Birmingham School of Art. Father of Erle Foster N. q.v. R.B.S.A. 1927. Add: Birmingham 1882; 1896 and 1928; Hampton in Arden 1892; Tunstall, Staffs. 1897; Sutton Coldfield 1920. † B 86.

NEWHAM, Theodore Exh. 1930
† P 1.

NEWILL, Miss D. Exh. 1907
61 Haworth Road, Gorton, Manchester. † M 3.

NEWILL, Mary J. Exh. 1884-1912
Painter, illustrator, black and white artist and embroiderer. Studied Birmingham School of Art. Add: Wellington, Salop 1884; Edgbaston, Birmingham 1892. † B 9, FIN 4.

NEWLAND, Hugh B. Exh. 1934
Oakside, Oxley Bank, Bushbury, Wolverhampton. † B 1.

NEWLANDS, Hunter Exh. 1934-35
7 Carlyle Gardens, Haddington. † RSW 2.

NEWLING Exh. 1920
† P 1.

NEWLING, Miss A. Exh. 1883-90
Add: Liverpool 1883; Sheffield 1885; Ambleside 1889. † GI 1, L 3.

NEWMAN, A. Exh. 192[illegible]-32
26 Bentley Road, Liverpool. † L 4.

NEWMAN, Adelaide C. Exh. 1900-7
Mrs. Philip A. Miniature portrait painter. Add: 2 Woburn Square, London 1900; Hatch End, Middlesex 1907. † RA 4.

NEWMAN, Constance Exh. 1911-15
Newlyn, Penzance 1911; Topsham, Devon 1913. † B 1, L 3, RA 1.

NEWMAN, Mrs. Charlotte J. Exh. 1882
Decorative artist. Add: 6 Grand Hotel Buildings, Trafalgar Square, London. † RA 1.

NEWMAN, Catherine M. Exh. 1889-99
Watercolour flower painter. Add: London. † RA 2, RI 4, SWA 16.

NEWMAN, Dudley Exh. 1892-1911
Architect. Add: London. † RA 3.

NEWMAN, Mrs. E. Exh. 1912-14
Casalini, Moseley, Birmingham. † L 20.

NEWMAN, Mrs. Ethel Exh. 1937-38
6 The Avenue, Craigendoran. † GI 1. RSA 1.

NEWMAN, Florence Exh. 1890-1929
Coloured wax miniaturist and sculptor. Studied Slade School. Married Frederick Thomas Callcott, q.v. A.R.M.S. 1911, Add: London. † ALP 12, B 2, GI 7, I 1, L 38, LS 10, NG 2, RA 30, RBA 1, RMS 29, RSA 6.

NEWMAN, Frank Exh. 1904
Architect. Add: 4 Bouverie Square, Folkestone. † RA 1.

NEWMAN, F. Winton Exh. 1899
Architect. Add: 48 Buckley Road, Brondesbury, London. † RA 1.

NEWMAN, Henry R. Exh. 1881-99
Landscape and architectural painter. Add: 1 Piazza de Rossi, Florence. † FIN 15, G 2.

NEWMAN, Paul Exh. 1892-97
Sculptor. Add: 61 Vanbrugh Park, Blackheath, London. † GI 1, L 1, RA 4.

NEWMAN, Philip Harry 1840-1927
Painter and stained glass designer. R.B.A. 1897. Add: London. † L 1, M 1, RA 27, RBA 93.

NEWMAN Samuel J. Exh. 1882-86
Architect. Add: 32 Alington Street, Northampton. † RA 3.

NEWMAN, Theodore Exh. 1916
† LEI 1.

NEWMAN, William A. Exh. 1885-95
Landscape painter. Add: Hyson Green, Nottingham. † N 15.

NEWMARCH, Ethel M. Exh. 1903-14
Miniature portrait painter. Add: Howden Lodge, Clarendon Road, Southsea, Hants. † RA 7, RMS 1.

NEWMARCH, Marguerite H. Exh. 1924-27
Bold, Widnes 1924; Leigh on Sea 1926; London 1927. † L 3, M 1.

NEWNUM, Eric G. Exh. 1932
Architect. Add: State Buildings Dept., Ministry of Public Works, Cairo, Egypt. † RA 1.

NEWNS, C.A. Exh. 1907
4 Breech Road, Anfield, Liverpool. † L 2.

NEWSOME, Amelia Exh. 1895
36 St. Aubyn's, Brighton. † B 1.

NEWSOME, Dorothy Exh. 1916-26
Painter, illustrator and poster artist. Daughter of Lucy Ann N. q.v. Add: The Crescent, Coventry. † B 8.

NEWSOME, Mrs. Lucy Ann Exh. 1895
Landscape painter and teacher. Studied at Coventry, London and Italy. Principal Crescent Art School, Coventry. Mother of Dorothy N. q.v. Add: Coventry. † B 1.

NEWSTEAD, Miss K.M. Exh. 1889-94
Add: New Brighton, Cheshire 1889; Liverpool 1893. † L 4.

NEWTON, Algernon* 1880-1968
Landscape painter. Studied Calderon's School of Animal painting and London School of Art. A.R.A. 1936, R.A. 1943. "The Surrey Canal, Camberwell" (1935) purchased by Chantrey Bequest 1940. Father of Nigel N. q.v. Add: London 1903 and 1921; Berkhamsted, Herts. 1911; St. Buryan, Cornwall 1918. † CG 10, GI 1, I 4, L 8, LEI 58, M 1, NEA 9, RA 44.

NEWTON, Alfred E. Exh. 1899-1921
Add: Liverpool 1899 and 1915; Seacombe, Cheshire 1913. † I 12, L 10.

NEWTON, Alfred Pizzey 1830-1883
Watercolour landscape painter. b. Rayleigh, Essex of Italian descent. Self taught. A.R.W.S. 1858, R.W.S. 1879. Add: 44 Maddox Street, Regent Street, London. † GI 3, L 2, M 1, RA 1, RWS 37.

NEWTON, Charles M. Exh. 1885-99
Portrait painter. Add: London. † L 7, NG 2, P 2, RA 5.

NEWTON, Edward Exh. 1909-29
Add: Bedford 1909; Lichfield 1911. † D 20.

NEWTON, Elizabeth Exh. 1904-18
London. † B 2, L 6, LS 3, NG 4.

NEWTON, Eric b. 1893
Decorative painter and mosaic artist. Art critic with the "Manchester Guardian". Exh. 1932-34. Add: Manchester and London. † RA 2.

NEWTON, Ernest 1856-1922
Architect. A.R.A. 1911, R.A. 1919. Father of William Godfrey N. q.v. Add: London. † GI 13, RA 77, RSA 6.

NEWTON, Ernest E. Exh. 1927-40
Painter, etcher and wood engraver. Add: London. † ALP 1, RA 4.

NEWTON, E.G. Exh. 1891
Flower painter. Add: 138 Woodborough Road, Nottingham. † N 2.

NEWTON, Edith Nicola Exh. 1885
Watercolour landscape painter. Add: Osbourne Villa, Princes Road, Weybridge, Surrey. † SWA 1.

NEWTON, Francis b. 1873
American painter. Exh. 1935. Add: Fulling Mill Farm, East Hampton, London Island, U.S.A. † RA 1.

NEWTON, F.G. Exh. 1909
Watercolour landscape painter. Add: 8 Clifford's Inn, London. † RA 1.

NEWTON, Frances Harriet Exh. 1881-1911
Watercolour flower painter. Add: London. † D 4, SWA 2.

NEWTON, Miss G.A. Exh. 1901-38
Miniature painter. Add: 49 Ravenscourt Gardens, Ravenscourt Park, London. † D 4, RA 3, SWA 6.

NEWTON, Herbert H. 1881-1959
Landscape painter. Exh. 1924-40. Add: London. † ALP 70, GOU 48, L 5, M 2, NEA 13, RA 3, TOO 29.

NEWTON, H.R. Exh. 1881-86
202 Gt. Brunswick Street, Dublin. † RHA 5.

NEWTON, Isabel T. Exh. 1935
42 Redcliffe Square, London. † SWA 1.

NEWTON, John Edward Exh. 1881-84
Fruit and landscape painter. Add: Kingston on Thomas 1881; Norbiton 1884. † L 4, RA 1, RI 1.

NEWTON, Katharine Townsend Exh. 1908-12
45 Hornton Court, Kensington, London. † L 1, LS 7, RA 1.

NEWTON, Nigel Ramsey b. 1903
Landscape and still life painter. Studied St. John's Wood School of Art 1922-23. Son of Algernon N. q.v. Add: Dublin 1933; Falmouth, Cornwall 1940. † RA 2, RHA 2.

NEWTON, Percy E. Exh. 1895-1900
Architect. Add: London. † RA 4.

NEWTON, Violet Exh. 1908
32 Randolph Gardens, Maida Vale, London. † LS 3.

NEWTON, William Exh. 1935-37
Landscape painter. Add: 32 Winstanley Drive, Leicester. † N 8.

NEWTON, William Godfrey 1885-1949
Architect. Son of Ernest N. q.v. Studied Royal College of Art. Professor of architecture Royal College of Art and editor of the "Architectural Review". Add: London and Marlborough, Wilts. † GI 2, RA 13.

NIAS, Miss Exh. 1880
Landscape painter. Add: 56 Montague Square, London. † SWA 1.

NIBBS, Richard Henry* c.1816-1893
Marine and landscape painter. Add: Brighton. †,D 4, L 1, RA 6, RBA 8.

NIBLETT, F.D. Exh. 1882-84
Edinburgh. † RSA 2.

NICCOLE, Cannici Exh. 1883
60 Bedford Gardens, Campden Hill, London. † M 1.

NICHOL, Alfred Exh. 1910
161 Elsley Road, Lavender Hill, London. † LS 3.

NICHOL, Bessie Exh. 1890-94
Figure and landscape painter. Add: Kensington, London. † B 2, L 1, M 1, RA 1, RBA 1, ROI 4.

NICHOL, Edwin Exh. 1880-91
Landscape, coastal and figure painter. Add: London. † GI 1, L 6, M 1, RA 14, RBA 12, ROI 1, RSA 2.

NICHOL, Regi Exh. 1933
† RSW 2.

NICHOL, T.W. Exh. 1885
4 Stratford Road, Kensington, London. † L 1.

NICHOLAS, Graham S. Exh. 1897-99
Architect. Add: 2 South Square, Gray's Inn, London. † RA 3.

NICHOLAS, John Exh. 1938
2 Arundel Street, London. † RBA 2.

NICHOLAS, J.B. Exh. 1935
Painter. † AR 1.

NICHOLAS, J.M. Exh. 1884-85
Watercolour landscape painter. Add: West Molesey Vicarage, Surrey. † SWA 4.

NICHOLAS, Kathleen L. Exh. 1922
† G 1.

NICHOLAS, Isabel Exh. 1934
Watercolour flower painter. † RED 16.

NICHOLL, Andrew* 1804-1886
Landscape painter and illustrator. b. Belfast. Studied in London. Teacher of painting and drawing at Colombo Academy, Ceylon 1849. A.R.H.A. 1837, R.H.A. 1860. Add: London. † RHA 9.

NICHOLL, Agnes Rose b. 1842
nee Bouvier. Flower and genre painter. b. London of French descent. Travelled frequently. Married Samuel Joseph N. q.v. Exh. 1880-92. Add: 1 Caversham Road, Kentish Town, London. † B 1, D 1, GI 4, L 1, RA 7, RBA 10, RI 14, SWA 9.

NICHOLL, Mrs. Ilted Exh. 1887-90
Landscape painter. Add: 32 Lancaster Gate, Hyde Park, London. † SWA 2.

NICHOLL, J.L. Exh. 1904
98 Marchmont Crescent, Edinburgh. † RSA 1.

NICHOLL, Mary Anne H. Exh. 1893
82 Denmark Road, Camberwell, London. † RHA 1.

NICHOLL, Samuel Joseph Exh. 1880-88
Architect. Married Agnes Rose N. q.v. Add: 1 Caversham Road, Kentish Town, London. † RA 6.

NICHOLLS, Mrs. A.L. Exh. 1890
79 Newman Street, London. † L 1.

NICHOLLS, Bertram* b. 1883
Landscape painter and teacher. b. Didsbury. Studied Slade School, Madrid, Italy and France. R.B.A. 1931, P.R.B.A. c.1932, R.O.I. 1931. "Drying the Sails" purchased by Chantrey Bequest 1921. Exh. 1905-40. Add: Sale, Cheshire 1905; London and Steyning, Sussex 1912. † BAR 124, CG 1, FIN 264, G 2, GI 19, L 11, M 35, P 1, RA 36, RBA 53, ROI 16, RSA 9.

NICHOLLS, B.H. Exh. 1882
Port Aven, Finistere, France. † M 1.

NICHOLLS, Claude Exh. 1932-33
16 Abberley Street, Rotton Park, Birmingham. † B 2.

NICHOLLS, Charles Wynne* 1831-1903
Landscape, historical and genre painter. b. Dublin. Studied Royal Dublin Society Schools and R.H.A. Schools. A.R.H.A. 1861, R.H.A. 1869. Add: London 1880. † L 2, RA 1, RBA 1, RHA 15, ROI 2.

NICHOLLS, Denys Exh. 1937
† NEA 1.

NICHOLLS, D.A. Exh. 1937-40
85 Spring Lane, Erdington, Birmingham. † B 6.

NICHOLLS, Ethel Exh. 1907
57 New Camp Road, Leeds. † RCA 1.

NICHOLLS, Edward Exh. 1885-89
Sculptor. Add: London. † RA 2.

NICHOLLS, George F. Exh. 1885-1937
Watercolour landscape and flower painter. Add: Liverpool 1885; Liscard, Cheshire 1894; Rock Ferry, Cheshire 1899; Evesham, Worcs. 1906; Oxford 1912; Horsepath, Oxon 1923. † B 17, BG 4, GOU 3, L 51, M 3, RA 10, RBA 1, RCA 32, RI 20, WG 142.

NICHOLLS, John E. Exh. 1923-38
Painter and etcher. Add: London. † NEA 6, RA 6, RED 2.

NICHOLLS, M.I.M. Exh. 1930-31
67 South Hill Park, Hampstead, London. † NEA 2.

NICHOLLS, Muriel M. Exh. 1914-16
Woodside, Christleton, Chester. † L 5.

NICHOLLS, Margaret S. Exh. 1908-32
Prestwick, Manchester. † L 6, M 1.

NICHOLLS, Mrs. Rhoda Holmes 1854-1930
American landscape painter. Exh. 1884. Add: c/o Fine Art Society, New Bond Street, London. † FIN 1, RA 1.

NICHOLLS, R.K. Exh. 1939
213 Spring Grove Road, Isleworth, London. † RSA 1.

NICHOLLS, W.S. Exh. 1919
10A Haldow Road, Wandsworth, London. † LS 3.

NICHOLS, Bowyer Exh. 1894-1905
Painter. Add: London. † NEA 2, RA 1.

NICHOLS, Catherine Maude c.1848-1923
Painter and etcher. R.E. 1882 (1st woman member). Add: Surrey Street, Norwich. † B 1, D 1, L 9, LS 18, M 2, NG 1, RA 8, RBA 4, RE 109, SWA 10.

NICHOLS, Kate Edith Exh. 1880-1918
Watercolour landscape painter. Add: 12 Clanricarde Gardens, London. † SWA 68.

NICHOLS, Laura R. Exh. 1915
12 Clanricarde Gardens, London. † D 2.

NICHOLS, Miss M. Dyce Exh. 1906
Cornwall Gardens, London. † SWA 1.

NICHOLS, W.P. Exh. 1885-1913
Watercolour landscape painter. Add: Little Cheverell Rectory, Devizes, Wilts. † D 60, RI 2.

NICHOLSON, Albert Exh. 1882-89
62 Fountain Street, Manchester. † M 3.

NICHOLSON, Alexander Exh. 1884
Watercolour landscape painter. Add: Reigate Road, Sutton, Surrey. † RI 1.

NICHOLSON, Alice Hogarth Exh. 1899-1940
Figure painter. Studied Manchester School of Art and Colarossi's, Paris. A.S.W.A. 1916. Add: Wilmslow, Cheshire 1899; St. Ives, Cornwall 1911; Gerrards Cross, Bucks. 1915; Hindhead, Surrey 1923. † D 4, GI 7, L 12, M 3, RA 7. ROI 2, SWA 42.

NICHOLSON, Alice M. Exh. 1880-90
Fruit, flower and still life painter. Add: 9 St. Thomas Square, Newcastle upon Tyne. † L 8, RA 2, RBA 1, RHA 2, RI 1, RSA 13, SWA 10.

NICHOLSON, Ben* b. 1894
Painter. b. Denham, Bucks. Son of Sir William and Mabel N. q.v. Studied Tours, Milan and Madeira 1911-14, Pasadena, U.S.A. 1917-18 and Slade School. Married first Winifred N. q.v. and second Barbara Hepworth q.v. "Le Quotidien" (1932) purchased by Chantrey Bequest 1965. Exh. 1919-40. Add: London. † BA 19, G 2, I 6, L 2, LEF 102, LEI 26, LS 3, NEA 1, RED 1, TOO 33.

NICHOLSON, Sir Charles A. Exh. 1894-1923
Architect. Add: London. † RA 30.

NICHOLSON, Doris Exh. 1924
Painter. Add: Western House, The Park, Nottingham. † N 1.

NICHOLSON, E. Exh. 1930
Wood engraver. † RED 2.

NICHOLSON, Ellen D. Exh. 1913-28
Landscape painter. Add: London 1913 and 1917; Gosport, Hants. 1914. † LS 11, NEA 3, RA 1, SWA 1.

NICHOLSON, Fanny Exh. 1890
Salmon's Cross, Reigate, Surrey. † B 2.

NICHOLSON, Mrs. F.T. Exh. 1916-17
14 Eastern Road, Brockley, London. † RA 2.

NICHOLSON, George Exh. 1928-37
Painter. Add: London. † RBA 1, RED 84.

NICHOLSON, Greer Exh. 1916-40
Landscape, seascape and flower painter. Studied South Kensington Art School. Add: Waterloo, Liverpool. † L 21, RA 1, RCA 28, RI 1.

NICHOLSON, G.M. Exh. 1903
Salmon's Cross, Reigate, Surrey. † L 2.

NICHOLSON, G.T. Exh. 1927-36
Blackgrove Farmhouse, Lingfield, Surrey. † M 1, RBA 1.

NICHOLSON, Hugh Exh. 1893-1914
Miniature portrait painter. R.B.A. 1904, R.M.S. 1896. Add: London 1893 and 1908; Baltimore, U.S.A. 1904. † L 1, NG 3, RA 17, RBA 4, RMS 30.

NICHOLSON, John M. Exh. 1880-88
Landscape painter. Add: 2 St. Thomas Walk, Douglas, I.O.M. † B 2, G 7, M 9, RI 1.

NICHOLSON, Mabel d. c.1920
nee Pryde. Figure and portrait painter. 1st wife of Sir William and mother of Ben N. q.v., and sister of James Ferrier Pryde q.v. Exh. 1910-20. Add: London. † GI 3, GOU 2, I 6, L 4, NEA 3.

NICHOLSON, Margaret Dorothy Exh. 1920-40
Portrait and figure painter. Add: 4 Derby Villas, Forest Hill, London. † AB 2, G 1, GOU 2, NEA 13, P 2, RA 10, RBA 4, SWA 2.

NICHOLSON, Nellie Exh. 1893
Newark on Trent. † D 1.

NICHOLSON, Miss P.E. Exh. 1914-15
5 Appleton Road, Borrowash, nr. Derby. † N 3.

NICHOLSON, P.W. Exh. 1883-85
Albert Studio, Shandwick Place, Edinburgh. † GI 2, RSA 12.

NICHOLSON, Richard E. Exh. 1882-88
Watercolour bird painter. Add: Halifax. † L 2, RA 2, RI 1.

NICHOLSON, Reginald P. Exh. 1933
Watercolour landscape painter. † RED 1.

NICHOLSON, Lady Sarah Elizabeth Exh. 1880
Figure painter. Add: The Grange, Totteridge, Herts. † RA 1.

NICHOLSON, S.G. Exh. 1914
Augra Bank, Waterloo, nr. Liverpool. † L 1.

NICHOLSON, Sir William* 1872-1949
Painter and poster artist. b. Newark on Trent. Studied Juliens, Paris. Worked with his brother in law James Ferrier Pryde, q.v. as the Beggarstaff Brothers. Husband of Mabel and father of Ben N. q.v. R.P. 1909. Knighted c.1936. Several of his works are in Tate Gallery. Add: Newark on Trent 1892; Uxbridge, Middlesex 1895; Woodstock, Oxon 1901; London 1905. † AG 4, BA 193, BAR 13, BK 2, CHE 8, CG 1, FIN 2, G 5, GI 34, GOU 159, I 70, L 29, LEI 114, M 2, NEA 11, P 19, RED 1, RHA 4, ROI 1, RSA 18, RSW 3.

NICHOLSON, Winifred* b. 1893
nee Roberts. Painter. b. Oxford. Studied Byam Shaw School of Art, India and Italy. Granddaughter of George Howard 9th Earl of Carlisle q.v. 1st wife of Ben Nicholson q.v. N.E.A. 1937. Exh. 1927-39. Add: Low Row, Cumberland 1933. † BA 56, L 2, LEF 35, LEI 89, NEA 6, RED 6, RSA 1, TOO 2.

NICKAL, John Exh. 1909-14
Landscape painter. R.B.A. 1913. Add: Radlett, Herts. 1910; London 1913. † GOU 2, LS 3, NEA 4, RBA 7.

NICKALLS, Beatrice Exh. 1908
Walton on Thames. † ROI 1.

NICKALLS, Grace Exh. 1926
Watercolour landscape painter. Add: Boxley Abbey, Maidstone, Kent. † RA 1.

NICKALLS, Maud Exh. 1904-31
Add: Redhill, Surrey 1904; Boxley Abbey, Maidstone, Kent 1910. † ROI 8, SWA 2.

NICKALLS, Roger S. Exh. 1937
Landscape painter. Add: 66 London Street, Chertsey. † RA 1.

NICKALLS, Miss W. Exh. 1895
Fallowfield, Chiselhurst, Kent. † ROI 1.

NICKELS, May Exh. 1907-8
Chenotric, Noctorum, Birkenhead. † L 2.

NICKLIN, Miss Jessie M. Exh. 1904-21
Summer Hill House, Smethwick, Birmingham 1904; Ashton under Hill, Glos. 1921. † B 10, L 2.

NICKLIN, Mrs. Mary Exh. 1902-8
Summer Hill House, Smethwick, Birmingham. † B 2.

NICKOLLS, William Exh. 1882
32 Larches Street, Birmingham. † B 1.

NICKSON, Miss F.K. Exh. 1886
Painter. Add: The Lindens, Nightingale Lane, Balham. † RBA 1.

NICKSON, R.S. Exh. 1934
Architect. Add: Conway, Wales. † RCA 1.

NICKSON, T. Marriott Exh. 1932-35
496 City Road, Edgbaston, Birmingham. † B 4.

NICKSON, William Exh. 1908
32 Clifton Road, Birkenhead. † L 2.

NICOL, Ada Exh. 1880
10 Leamington Road Villas, Westbourne Park, London. † RSA 1.

NICOL, Erskine* 1825-1904
Genre painter. b. Leith. Studied at the Trustees Academy Edinburgh 1838. A.R.A. 1866, A.R.S.A 1855, R.S.A. 1859 (Hon. Ret. 1896). Father of Erskine E. and John Watson N. q.v. Add: London 1880; Colinton, Midlothian 1885; Feltham, Middlesex 1895. † AG 1, GI 12, RA 4, RSA 27, TOO 4.

NICOL, Erskine E. d. 1926
Landscape painter. Son of Erskine and brother of John Watson N. q.v. Travelled widely. Add: Colinton, Midlothian 1886; London 1892 and 1906; Feltham, Middlesex 1897. † B 7, GI 4, GOU 1, L 1, RA 7, ROI 2, RSA 16, RSW 1.

NICOL, George Salway 1878-1930
Architect and decorative designer. b. London. Son of J. Coulson N. q.v. Studied Birmingham University and A.A. Schools. Architect to the Imperial War Graves Commission. Exh. 1920-30. Add: 117 Colmore Row, Birmingham. † B 19, RA 1.

NICOL, J. Coulson Exh. 1921
Architect. Father of George Salway N. q.v. Add: 117 Colmore Row, Birmingham. † B 2.

NICOL, John Watson* 1856-1926
Genre, portrait and historical painter. Son of Erskine and brother of Erskine E. N. q.v. R.O.I. 1888. Add: London. † B 16, GI 2, L 7, M 9, RA 45, ROI 19, RSA 8.

NICOL, Miss M.D. Exh. 1907
Drayton Gardens, London. † SWA 1.

NICOLET, Gabriel* 1856-1921
Portrait and figure painter. R.O.I. 1898, R.P. 1897. Add: London. † GI 4, L 15, LEI 52, P 37, RA 25, RHA 3, RI 2, ROI 17.

NICOLET, Theo Exh. 1926
c/o Miss S. Nicolet, West Malvern, Worcs. † RHA 3.

NICOLI, C. Exh. 1881
Sculptor. Add: c/o Aristide Fontana Esq., 180 Buckingham Palace Road, London. † RBA 1.

NICOLL, Archibald Frank b. 1886
Portrait and landscape painter. b. Christchurch, New Zealand. Exh. 1912-30. Add: Glasgow 1912; Kew, Surrey 1913; c/o Aitken Dott and Sons, Edinburgh 1917; c/o Chapman Bros., London 1930. † GI 2, L 1, RA 2, RSA 3, RSW 1.

NICOLL, Lady Catherine Robertson
Exh. 1889-1931
nee Pollard. Watercolour painter, and black and white artist. b. High Down, Hitchin, Herts. Add: High Down, Hitchin, Herts. 1889; The Old Manse, Lumsden, Aberdeenshire 1925. † GI 2, L 6, RBA 6, RI 5.

NICOLL, Gordon William b. 1888
Painter. Studied Hornsey School of Art. R.I. 1934. Exh. 1921-40. Add: London 1921; West Byfleet, Surrey 1934. † AR 2, GI 1, RA 4, RI 29.

NICOLL, James Craig 1846-1918
American artist. Exh. 1882-84. Add: 51 West Tenth Street, New York and c/o Cassells, Ludgate Hill, London. † L 1, RE 2.

NICOLL, Leonard G. Exh. 1919-20
Miniature portrait painter. Add: 19 Bergholt Crescent, Stamford Hill, London. † RA 4.

NICOLL, Maggie Exh. 1897-1937
Painter. Studied Glasgow School of Art. Add: Greenock. † GI 9, RSA 1.

NICOLSON, John 1891-1951
Painter, etcher and illustrator. Studied St. Martin's School of Art. A.R.B.A. 1927, R.B.A. 1929, A.R.E. 1923, R.S.W. 1930. Add: London. †, AR 1, CHE 2, GI 5, L 8, NEA 1, P 10, RA 12, RBA 29, RE 36, RHA 13, ROI 2, RSA 20, RSW 33.

NICOLSON, John P. Exh. 1885-1909
Landscape painter. Add: Leith and Edinburgh. † GI 9, L 2, M 2, RA 7, RBA 2, RHA 3, RSA 41, RSW 1.

NICOLSON, J.W. Exh. 1914-21
3 Beresford Road, Hornsey, London. † RA 3.

NICOLSON, William Campbell
Exh. 1930-38
181 Mosspark Drive, Glasgow. † GI 9, RSA 2, RSW 2.

NICOLSON, Winifred Ursula b. 1881
Mrs. Wightman. Miniature painter. b. St. Petersburg, Russia Studied Edinburgh. Painted miniatures at the Russian Court 1901-8. A.R.M.S. 1907, R.M.S. 1909. Exh. 1906-31. Add: Marple, Cheshire 1906; London 1910. † GI 1, L 1, M 6, NG 2, RA 5, RMS 19, RSA 5, RSW 1.

NIELSEN, Mme. Anne Marie Carl b. 1863
Danish sculptor. Exh. 1911. Add: Copenhagen. † RA 1, RSA 1.

NIELSEN, Miss Bodil Exh. 1936
Sculptor. Add: Copenhagen, Denmark. † RA 1.

NIELSSEN, Clemence Exh. 1884
Painter. Add: 36 Hesse Strasse, Munich. † SWA 1.

NIEMANN, E.H. Exh. 1884-87
London. † RHA 3.

NIETSCHE, Paul Exh. 1930
Still life painter. Add: 411 Lisburn Road, Belfast. † RHA 2.

NIEUWENKAMP b. 1874
Etcher. Exh. 1913. † FIN 6.

NIGHTINGALE, Agnes Exh. 1881-85
Landscape painter. Married Leonard Charles N. q.v. Add: 52 Lansdown Gardens, South Lambeth, London. † B 3, RA 3, RBA 1.

NIGHTINGALE, Charles Thrupp
Exh. 1922-27
Wood engraver and illustrator. Add: The Old Cottage, Biggin Hill; Upper Norwood, London. † B 2, L 4, RA 5, RSA 4.

NIGHTINGALE, Florence Exh. 1905
76 Magazine Lane, New Brighton, Cheshire. † L 1.

NIGHTINGALE, Frederick C. Exh. 1880-89
Landscape painter. Add: London. † D 21, L 1.

NIGHTINGALE, Leonard Charles*
Exh. 1880-1913
Figure and landscape painter. Married Agnes N. q.v. Add: South Lambeth, London. † B 7, D 1, L 18, LS 3, M 5, RA 22, RBA 6, RI 1, ROI 2.

NILLET, Germain David 1861-1932
French sculptor. Exh. 1906-10. Add: 218 Faubourg St. Antoine, Paris. † L 2, RHA 1.

NIMMO, Harry Exh. 1939-40
16 Craigs Avenue, Corstorphine. † RSA 2, RSW 5.

NIMMO, James Exh. 1881-98
Edinburgh. † GI 5, RSA 6.

NINNES, Bernard b. 1899
Painter. b. Reigate, Surrey. Studied Slade School 1927-30. R.B.A. 1934, R.O.I. 1934. Add: St. Ives, Cornwall 1933 and 1940; Dublin 1938; Guildford, Surrey 1939. † RA 4, RBA 36, ROI 22.

NISBET, Miss A.H. Exh. 1890-91
Mavisbank, Partick Hill, N.B. † GI 2.

NISBET, E. Exh. 1889
1 Park Road Studios, Park Road, Haverstock Hill, London. † GI 1.

NISBET, Ethel C. Exh. 1882-1916
Watercolour flower painter. Add: London 1882 and 1902; Harrow on the Hill, Middlesex 1899. † L 6, RA 9, RBA 6, RI 17, ROI 1, SWA 9.

NISBET, H. Exh. 1885
Marine painter. Add: Redcliffe Road, South Kensington, London. † RBA 1.

NISBET, Hume 1849-1923
Painter, and author. Travelled widely. Exh. 1880-85. Add: Edinburgh. † GI 1, RSA 4, RHA 4.

NISBET, Mrs. Helen A. Exh. 1928-29
Landscape painter. Add: 7 Bedford Gardens, Campden Hill, London. † RA 2.

NISBET, H. Crockett Exh. 1898
2 Western Terrace, Murrayfield, Edinburgh. † RSA 1.

NISBET, Jane Exh. 1881-1900
Hillhead, Glasgow. † GI 30, L 3, RSA 21.

NISBET, John Exh. 1903-40
Glasgow 1903; Edinburgh 1938. † GI 9, L 4, RSA 6, RSW 4.

NISBET, James D. Exh. 1932-37
57 Victoria Park Drive South, Glasgow. † GI 1, RSA 2, RSW 3.

NISBET, Lucy Exh. 1882
3 Old Cavendish Street, London. † RSA 1.

NISBET, Margaret Dempster
Exh. 1886-1932
nee Dempster. Portrait and miniature painter. Studied Royal Institution Edinburgh and Paris. Married Robert Buchan N. q.v. Add: Edinburgh 1886; Comrie, Perthshire 1898; Crieff 1904. † GI 16, L 5, LS 4, NG 1, RA 1, RBA 1, RI 7, RSA 37.

NISBET, Miss M.H. Exh. 1908-9
Painter. Add: 6 Albert Studios, Albert Bridge Road, Battersea, London. † RA 2.

NISBET, Noel Laura* b. 1887
Painter and black and white artist. Daughter of Hume N. q.v. Studied South Kensington 1910. Married Harry Bush q.v. R.I. 1925. Exh. 1914-40. Add: London 1914 and 1921; Newbury, Berks. 1920. † GI 1, L 10, RA 25, RI 62, ROI 13.

NISBET, Pollok Sinclair* 1848-1922
Landscape, architectural and coastal painter. Travelled in Italy, Morocco, Tunis, Algeria and Spain. Brother of Robert Buchan N. q.v. A.R.S.A. 1892, R.S.W. 1881. Add: Edinburgh. † B 2, DOW 3, GI 69, L 7, M 3, RHA 3, RI 2, RSA 165, RSW 119, TOO 3.

NISBET, Robert Buchan* 1857-1942
Landscape painter. Studied Board of Manufacturers School Edinburgh, R.S.A. Life Class 1882-85 and under Bouguereau in Paris. Brother of Pollok Sinclair and husband of Margaret Dempster N. q.v. R.B.A. 1890, R.I. 1892 (resigned 1907), A.R.S.A. 1893, R.S.A. 1902, R.S.W. 1887, H.R.S.W. 1934. "Evening Stillness" purchased by Chantrey Bequest 1890. Add: Edinburgh 1880; Crieff 1904. † AG 1, CON 6, FIN 70, G 2, GI 125, L 39, LS 8, M 5, RA 22, RBA 25, RHA 10, RI 100, RSA 214, RSW 185.

NISBET, Scott Exh. 1935-40
Figure and portrait painter. Add: London. † RA 6, RBA 1.

NISBET, Thomas Exh. 1935-40
Landscape painter. Add: Dublin. † RHA 18.

NISBETT, Hamilton More Exh. 1901-20
122 George Street, Edinburgh. † RSA 5.

NISH, Alexander Exh. 1911
Landscape painter. † BRU 2.

NISSEN, Mrs. Sylvia Exh. 1937-40
Crookham, Hants. † SWA 4.

NISSL, Rudolf* b. 1870
German painter. Exh. 1898-1900. Add: 77 Gabelsbergen Strasse, Munich. † GI 2.

NITTIS, de See D

NIVEN, David P.M. Exh. 1880
Landscape painter. Add: 20 Huntley Street, Bedford Square, London. † RBA 1.

NIVEN, Forrest Exh. 1888-1911
Add: Edinburgh 1888; Glasgow 1889; Pollokshields 1911. † GI 6.

NIVEN, Jean Exh. 1933-36
4 Fox Street, Greenock. † GI 2, RSA 1.

NIVEN, Katherine Exh. 1893
71 Hill Street, Glasgow. † GI 1.

NIVEN, Margaret Graeme b. 1906
Landscape, flower and portrait painter. Daughter of William N. q.v. Studied Heatherleys. R.O.I. 1936. Exh. 1923-39. Add: Piper's Field, Winchester. † COO 2, M 1, P 8, RED 1, ROI 21, SWA 3.

NIVEN, William Exh. 1881-1911
Etcher. A.R.E. 1887-1921. Father of Margaret Graeme N. q.v. Add: Epsom, Surrey 1881; Teddington, Middlesex 1883; London 1885; Faringdon, Berks. 1891; Gt. Marlow, Bucks. 1902. † L 4, RA 1, RE 38.

NIVEN, William Exh. 1926
Herald Office, 65 Buchanan Street, Manchester. † GI 1.

NIX, Ethel Exh. 1924
Miniature portrait painter. Add: Hopkinson House, Vincent Square, London. † RA 1.

NIXON, A.J. Exh. 1881
501 Lawnmarket, Edinburgh. † RSA 1.

NIXON, A.W. Exh. 1933
Zigeuner Cottage, Ash Green, Trentham, Staffs. † L 1.

NIXON, Bessie Exh. 1910
Ellerslie, Grassendale, Liverpool. † L 1.

NIXON, C. Exh. 1910
3 Trentham Avenue, Wavertree, Liverpool. † L 1.

NIXON, Job 1891-1938
Painter and etcher. b. Stoke on Trent. Studied Royal College of Art, Slade School (studentship in engraving at British School in Rome 1923). Assistant teacher of etching at South Kensington. N.E.A. 1936, A.R.E. 1923, A.R.W.S. 1928, R.W.S. 1934. Add: London 1915 and 1935; Lamorna, Penzance 1932; St. Ives, Cornwall 1933. † AG 3, BA 2, CHE 2, CG 95, FIN 31 G 1, GI 2, L 19, LEI 3, M 1, NEA 77, RA 36, RE 38, RSA 4, RSW 1, RSW 93.

NIXON, Miss K.J. Exh. 1920-26
Birmingham 1920; Coventry 1922. † B 7.

NIXON, Lucy Exh. 1909
12 Queen Street, Leek, Staffs. † L 1.

NIXON, Mima Exh. 1894-1918
Watercolour landscape painter. Add: Ballybrack 1894; Wimbledon, Surrey 1896; London 1907. † B 9, BG 54, D 23, FIN 135, L 10, LS 7, M 2, RA 10, RHA 13, RI 11, SWA 18.

NIXON, William Charles Exh. 1897
104 Seville Place, Dublin. † RHA 1

NOAD, R. Mervyn Exh. 1933-35
261 West George Street, Glasgow. † GI 3, RSA 3.

NOAKES, Charles G. Exh. 1885-88
Flower painter. Add: 1 Carlton Terrace, Sydenham, Kent. † RI 2.

NOAR, Eva Exh. 1906-40
Watercolour landscape painter and miniaturist. b. Swinton, Lancs. A.R.M.S. 1909. Add: Manchester. † B 11, GI 3, L 35, M 20, RA 32, RHA 3, RMS 86, RSA 4.

NOBBS, Percy E. Exh. 1918-35
Montreal, Canada. † RSA 3.

NOBES, Miss M.L. Exh. 1901-3
120 Tulse Hill, London. † SWA 3.

NOBLE, Charlotte M. Exh. 1880-97
Domestic genre painter. Add: London. † B 12, RBA 20.

NOBLE, David Exh. 1882-90
6 Comely Green Place, Edinburgh. † RSA 21.

NOBLE, Edwin Exh. 1898-1930
Animal painter. Married Beatrice Greenwood q.v. and sister of Florence K. N. q.v. R.B.A. 1907. Add: London 1898 and 1906; Guildford, Surrey 1904; Milford on Sea, Hants. 1922. † BG 2, FIN 35, GI 4, L 7, RA 13, RBA 45, ROI 2, RSA 5.

NOBLE, Florence Exh. 1898-1907
Animal painter. Sister of Edwin N. q.v. Add: London. † RA 3, RBA 1, RI 5, ROI 1, SWA 2.

NOBLE, F.W. Exh. 1880
Landscape painter. Add: 30 Grafton Street, Tottenham Court Road, London. † RBA 1

NOBLE, Helen Exh. 1916-30
Miniature portrait painter. Add: Leicester 1916; Nottingham 1928. † N 5, RA 3.

NOBLE, Inglis Exh. 1884-1906
6 Comely Green Place, Edinburgh. † RSA 11.

NOBLE, John* Exh. 1915-18
Landscape painter. Add: 61 Earl's Court Square, London. † I 5, LS 2, NEA 1.

NOBLE, James Campbell* 1846-1913
Landscape, coastal, figure and portrait painter. Studied R.S.A. Schools. Cousin of Robert N. q.v. A.R.S.A. 1879, R.S.A. 1892. Add: Edinburgh 1880, 1887 and 1900; Shere, nr. Guildford, Surrey 1881; Coldingham, Berwickshire 1885; Corstorphine 1896. † G,1, GI 20, L 19, M 17, RA 11, RBA 1, RHA 1, RSA 160, RSW 1.

NOBLE, John Sargeant* 1848-1896
Animal and sporting painter. Studied R.A. Schools and was a pupil of Landseer. R.B.A. 1872. Add: London 1880; New Malden, Surrey 1890. † B 10, FIN 1, GI 5, L 7, M 6, RA 35, RBA 51, RI 1, ROI 1, TOO 10.

NOBLE, Leonard M. Exh. 1903-8
Landscape painter. Add: London. † B 2, RA 2, RI 1.

NOBLE, Marion Exh. 1883-84
Figure painter. Add: 2 Dean Road, Willesden Gardens, London. † M 2, RA 1, ROI 1.

NOBLE, Robert* 1857-1917
Landscape and genre painter. Studied under his cousin James Campbell N. q.v. at the Trustees School and the R.S.A. Life Class 1879-84 and under Carolus Duran in Paris. R.O.I. 1897, A.R.S.A. 1892, R.S.A. 1903. Add: Edinburgh 1880; Preston Kirk, Haddington 1890. † FIN 1, G 3, GI 37, L 7, M 7, NG 1, RA 20, RHA 4, ROI 18, RSA 134, RSW 1, TOO 1.

NOBLE, R.F. Exh. 1934-39
Watercolour landscape painter. † AR 1, COO 2.

NOBLE, T.C. Exh. 1929
56 Cliffe Street, Rishton, Blackburn. † L 1.

NOCI, Arturo b. 1874
Portrait painter. b. Rome. Exh. 1929. Add: 15 West 67th Street, New York, U.S.A. † RA 1.

NOCQ, Henri b. 1868
French sculptor. Exh. 1909. Add: 29 Quai Bourbon, Paris. † RA 1.

NOEK, E. Exh. 1892
Thorn Studio, Chagford, South Devon. † B 2.

NOEL, Charlotte Exh. 1913
Watercolour garden painter. † WG 32.

NOEL, J. Exh. 1881
16 Avenue Trudaine, Paris. † RHA 1.

NOEL, John Bates Exh. 1893-1909
Landscape painter. Add: Birmingham 1893; Sutton Coldfield 1894; Moseley, Birmingham 1899; West Malvern, Worcs. 1901. † B 18, L 1, LS 4, M 1, NG 2, RA 5.

NOKES, Mrs. H. Langley Exh. 1920
Cragnant, Acocks Green, Birmingham. † B 1.

NOLAN OF CASTLEKNOCK, Exh. 1910-1
Landscape painter. Add: 15 Yeoman Row, London. † NEA 2, ROI 1.

NOLAN, Gladys Exh. 1925-3
Landscape and still life painter. Add Sunday's Well, Cork. † RHA 5.

NOLAN, John Exh. 1938-3
Painter. Add: 22 Urquhart Street, Dundee † RA 1, RSA 1.

NOLTENIUS, Marie T. Exh. 1938-3
21 The Ridgeway, London. † SWA 2.

NONCLERQ, C.E. Exh. 191
c/o M. Dupain, 152 Boulevard d Montparnasse, Paris. † L 1.

NONNENMACHER, Hermann Exh. 194
Sculptor. Add: 163 Cunder Road London. † GI 1, RA 2.

NOOTH, W. Wright Exh. 1887-9
Etcher. Add: 42 St. John's Wood Road London. † RA 9.

NORBLIN, S.N. de la Gourdaine Exh. 1937
Portrait painter. Add: Mazowiecka 1 Warsaw, Poland. † RA 1.

NORBURY, The Countess of Exh. 1934
Watercolour landscape painter. † COO 1.

NORBURY, Edwin Arthur 1849-1918
Painter. One of the founders of the Royal Cumbria Academy. Add: Rhyl 1881; Liverpool 1892; London 1907. † D 1, L 6, M 2, RA 1, RCA 77, RHA 10, RI 1, ROI 2.

NORBURY, E. Meta Exh. 1901-26
Liverpool. † L 6, RCA 3.

NORBURY, F.H. Exh. 1888-1913
Liverpool 1888; Wallasey, Cheshire 1912. † L 24.

NORBURY, Laura Exh. 1881-1924
Watercolour figure painter. Add: Liverpool 1883; New Brighton, Cheshire 1902; Basingstoke, Hants. 1908; Liscard, Cheshire 1911. † L 23, RCA 22, SWA 2.

NORBURY, Miss M.A. Exh. 1889-90
Landscape and interior painter. Add: 32 Gordon Square, London. † RBA 2, RI 1.

NORBURY, Richard* 1815-1886
Portrait and historical painter, illustrator engraver and sculptor. b. Macclesfield. Assistant master to the Schools of Design at Somerset House and Liverpool. Add: Liverpool 1883. † L 7.

NORCROSS, Mrs. Kathleen M. Exh. 1935
Blackburn, Lancs. † RCA 2.

NORDFELDT, Bror Julius Olsson b. 1878
Portrait painter. b. Sweden. Exh. 1901. Add: 68 London Street, Reading. † RA 1.

NORDGREN, Anna 1847-1916
Figure and landscape painter. b. Finland. Exh. 1885-1901. Add: London. Died Sweden. † B 17, GI 1, L 18, NEA 1, NG 5, P 2, RA 18, RBA 2, RI 5, SWA 7.

NORDHAGEN, Johann Exh. 1903-6
A.R.E. 1903. Add: Torvet 9, Christiania, Norway. † RE 10.

NORDHOFF, R.F. Exh. 1895
58 Glebe Place, Chelsea, London. † RBA 1.

NORDLING, A. Exh. 1886
Coastal painter. Add: 20 Stanley Crescent, London. † RBA 2.

NORFIELD, Edgar Exh. 1936
Painter and illustrator. Studied Cambridge, London and Paris. Add: London. † RI 1.

NORGATE, Miss Ethel Exh. 1935
c/o New Park, Buckfastleigh, South Devon. † RBA 1.

NORGATE, Miss E.M. Exh. 1937
122 Cheyne Walk, London. † RI 1.

NORGATE, Mrs. E.M. Exh. 1905-15
Add: Beckenham, Kent 1905; Shortlands, Kent 1911. † B 1, I 1, L 3, RA 1, SWA 3.

NORIE, M.L.J. Exh. 1885-89
Coltbridge Hall, Murrayfield. † RSA 7, RSW 8.

NORIE, Orlando* 1832-1901
Battle and military painter. Add: London. † M 2, RA 2, RI 2.

NORIENA, Corienne Exh. 1913-16
Add: Liverpool 1913; Hamm Common, Surrey 1916. † L 4.

NORMAN, Miss Exh 1934
Watercolour landscape painter. † COO 2.

NORMAN, A.E. Exh. 1928-29
4 Barrack Place, Coventry. † B 2.

NORMAN, C.C. Exh. 1930
44A Sidney Road, St. Margarets on Thames. † RI 1.

NORMAN, Mrs. Caroline H. Exh. 1880-91
Watercolour flower and bird painter. Add: Ker Street, Devonport, Devon. † L 2, RA 9, RBA 3, RI 19.

NORMAN, Dorothy Exh. 1936
Mrs. Hodgkinson. Add: 99 Hagley Road, Edgbaston, Birmingham. † B 2.

NORMAN, Eileen Exh. 1935
The Cowdray Club, 20 Cavendish Square, London. † RI 6.

NORMAN, Mrs. E.M. Exh. 1922-37
Sutton Coldfield. † B 11.

NORMAN, Florence Exh. 1914-33
Landscape painter. Add: Brighton 1914; Steyning, Sussex 1929. † I 1, L 2, LS 3, P 1, RA 2, RBA 1, ROI 3.

NORMAN, Miss G. Exh. 1887
4 Regents Park Road, London. † ROI 1.

NORMAN, Ivy E. Exh. 1927-29
Landscape, animal and figure painter. Add: Radstock Road, Thorneywood, Nottingham. † N 7.

NORMAN, John Exh. 1937-38
Landscape painter. Add: 40 Church Drive, Carrington, Nottingham. † N 4.

NORMAN, John Henry b. 1896
Landscape painter. b. Nottingham. Studied Coventry School of Art. Served in Army 1915-19. R.O.I. 1935. Add: Coventry. † B 17, RA 1, RBA 10, ROI 6.

NORMAN, Mrs. de Loria b. 1872
American artist. Exh. 1913-14. Add: The Studio, Campden House Mews, London. † LS 5, SWA 1.

NORMAN, Marion Exh. 1917-20
164 Melton Road, West Bridgford, Notts. † N 4.

NORMAN, N.V. Exh. 1908-14
27 Flanders Road, Bedford Park, Chiswick, London. † LS 16.

NORMAN, Parsons Exh. 1881-97
Landscape and coastal painter. Add: Lowestoft, Suffolk 1881; Thorpe St. Andrews, Norwich 1897. † B 1, RA 3, RBA 1.

NORMAN, Philip c. 1843-1931
Watercolour landscape painter. Studied Slade School. Add: London. † D 21, L 8, M 8, NEA 2, NG 67, RA 48, RBA 2, RI 23, ROI 2.

NORMAN, Miss W. Exh. 1934-37
Rettendon Rectory, Wickford, Essex. † RI 5, ROI 1.

NORMAN, William H. Exh. 1930-38
Watercolour portrait, landscape and interior painter. Add: 805 Commercial Road, Limehouse, London. † RA 5.

NORMAND, Mrs. Ernest
See RAE, Henrietta

NORMAND, Ernest* 1857-1923
Historical, genre and portrait painter. Studied R.A. Schools 1880-83 and Ecole des Beaux Arts, Paris. Married Henrietta Rae q.v. Exh. 1881-1909. Add: London. † B 8, GI 3, L 16, M 11, NG 6, RA 29, RHA 3, ROI 1, TOO 1

NORMANN, A. Exh. 1885-1911
Landscape painter. Add: Dusseldorf 1885; 157 New Bond Street, London 1886; Charlottenburg, Berlin 1911. † GI 1, M 5, RA 6, TOO 1.

NORMINTON, Miss E. Exh. 1919-29
4 Edgeley Gardens, Orrell Park, Liverpool. † L 4.

NORRIE, Daisy M. b. 1899
Etcher, aquatinter and dry point artist. b. Fraserburgh. Studied Aberdeen Art School (travelling scholarship). Exh. 1924-25. Add: 28 Cross Street, Fraserburgh. † GI 1, RSA 3.

NORRIS, Arthur b. 1888
Portrait and landscape painter and teacher. Son of William Foxley N. q.v. Studied Slade School 1907-10. Exh. 1929-39. Add: London. † FIN 52, NEA 1, P 3, RA 8.

NORRIS, C.N. Exh. 1912
18 Allfarthing Lane, Wandsworth, London. † RA 1.

NORRIS, Miss E.A. Exh. 1928-34
120 Portland Road, Nottingham. † N 2.

NORRIS, Francis Edward b. 1905
Designer and illustrator. Studied Birmingham Central School of Art 1923-30. Exh. 1928-29. Add: 50 Middleton Hall Road, Kings Norton. † B 2.

NORRIS, G. Milton Exh. 1928-29
69 Elgin Crescent, Notting Hill, London. † ROI 2.

NORRIS, Helen Bramwell Exh. 1891-94
Flower painter. Add: 13 Matham Grove, East Dulwich, London. † M 2, ROI 2.

NORRIS, Hugh L. c. 1863-1942
Landscape and flower painter and watercolourist. Probably brother of William Foxley N. q.v. Add: London 1888; Fordingbridge, Hants. 1900; Romsey, Hants. 1921. † B 10, BG 4, DOW 4, FIN 335, L 1, LEI 2, RA 27, RBA 2, RI 5, RID 46, ROI 1, TOO 1.

NORRIS, J. Exh. 1898-99
6 Argyle Street, Kettering, Northants. † L 1, RBA 1.

NORRIS, Laurence Exh. 1933-36
Figure painter. Add: 60 Upper Elmers End Road, Beckenham, Kent. † L 1, RA 2.

NORRIS, Mrs. Mary C. Exh. 1923-38
Figure and flower painter. Add: Guildford 1923; Charlton Kings, Glos. 1924. † B 4, RA 3, RHA 3, ROI 3.

NORRIS, Percy Exh. 1892
2 Fullwood Terrace, Old Trafford, Manchester. † M 1.

NORRIS, Miss R. Exh. 1935
Talycafn, Denbighshire. † RCA 1.

NORRIS, William b. 1857
Painter and mural decorator. b. Gloucester. Studied Gloucester School of Art and Royal College of Art. Art master Royal College of Art for 4 years and Freehand Examiner Board of Education for 18 years. Exh. 1885-1926. Add: London. † B 4, L 2, NEA 1, RA 4, RBA 6, RI 3, ROI 5.

NORRIS, William Foxley b. 1859
Dean of Westminster. Watercolour landscape painter. Add: Eton, Windsor, Berks. 1884; Chatham, Kent 1886; Tetsworth, Oxford 1887; Huddersfield 1894; London 1916 and 1926; York 1923. † AB 95, B 1, FIN 3, L 3, RA 13, RBA 2, RI 29, RID 2, WG 18.

NORRISS, Bess 1887-1939
Mrs. Tait. Watercolour painter and miniaturist. b. Melbourne, Australia. Studied Melbourne Art Gallery School and Slade School. Mother of Gilbert J. N. Tait q.v. A.R.M.S. 1906, R.M.S. 1908. Add: London. † G 9, GOU 13, I 10, L 17, NG 6, P 16, RA 22, RBA 6, RCA 9, RMS 120, SWA 5, WG 138.

NORST, Miss Elan Exh. 1932
2 Kensington Gate, Glasgow. † RSW 1.

NORSTEDT, Reinhold* Exh. 1911
Landscape painter. † L 1.

NORSWORTHY, Harold Milford d. 1917
Add: London 1908 and 1912; Liverpool 1911. Killed in action World War I. † L 11, LS 3, NEA 1, RA 2, ROI 1.

NORSWORTHY, Ina Exh. 1921-29
Wendy Cottage, France Lynch, nr. Stroud, Glos. † GOU 2, NEA 3.

NORTCLIFFE, Frank Exh. 1937
Landscape painter. † RED 1.

NORTH, Arthur William Exh. 1882-87
Figure painter. Add: Antwerp 1882; Huddersfield 1884; Newlyn, Penzance 1885. † L 2, RA 2, RBA 5, TOO 1.

NORTH, Frederick Exh. 1936
c/o Y.M.C.A. Dale End, Birmingham. † B 1.

NORTH, Mrs. Fred Exh. 1888-95
New Brighton, Cheshire. † L 4.

NORTH, Herbert L. Exh. 1898-1912
Architect. Add: London 1898; Conway 1902; Llanfairfechan 1906. † RA 2, RCA 19.

NORTH, Mrs. Jane A. Exh. 1880-1900
Mrs. S.W. Miniature portrait painter. Add: London. † L 3, RA 23.

NORTH, Dr. Janet Grey Exh. 1914
1 Cockspur Street, London. † LS 3.

NORTH, John William* 1841-1924
Landscape and genre painter, illustrator and wood engraver. Studied Marlborough House School of Art. Employed by Dalziel Bros. 1862-66. A.R.A. 1893, A.R.W.S. 1897, R.W.S. 1883. "The Winter Sun" purchased by Chantrey Bequest 1891. Add: London 1880; Washford, Taunton, Somerset 1887. † AG 8, B 3, CAR 1, FIN 4, G 10, GI 2, L 8, M 11, NG 13, RA 43, RHA 1, RSW 7, RWS 48, TOO 2, WG 6.

NORTH, Kennedy S. Exh. 1921
Flat 5, Bassett Road, London. † G 1.

NORTH, Lucy E. Exh. 1893
High Street, Tewkesbury. † B 3.

NORTH, M. Helen Exh. 1884-89
Painter. Add: Nottingham. † N 11.

NORTH, Mrs. M.S. See HOLMES

NORTH, Robert O'B. Exh. 1899
Architect. Add: 44 Ethelburga Street, Battersea, London. † RA 2.

NORTH, Sidney Vincent b. 1873
Painter and architect. Exh. 1918-37. Add: London. † L 1, RA 17, ROI 11.

NORTHBOURNE, Lord
See JAMES, Walter John

NORTHCOTE, P.B. Exh. 1890
Landscape painter. † DOW 1.

NORTHEY, Mrs. Elma b. 1876
nee Thomson. Watercolour landscape painter. b. Glasgow. Exh. 1900-40. Add: Strathdoon, Ayr 1900; Callander 1936. † GI 3, L 2, LS 3, RI 5, RSA 4, RSW 1.

NORTHEY, Miss G. Exh. 1914
Woodcote House, Epsom. † RA 1.

NORTHING, C.W. Exh. 1920-35
Bowling, Bradford 1920; Romiley, Cheshire 1933. † L 7, RCA 2.

NORTHING, Mrs. Pat Exh. 1935
Romiley, Cheshire. † RCA 2.

NORTON, Miss Exh. 1885
Watercolour landscape painter. Add: Heath Lodge, Ranelagh Road, Ealing, London. † SWA 1.

NORTON, C.H. Exh. 1909
Architect. Add: 14 Bedford Row, London. † RA 1.

NORTON, Charles William c. 1870-1946
Figure and landscape painter. R.I. 1935. Exh. 1912-40. Add: London. † AR 3, GI 1, M 1, RA 11, RCA 5, RI 30.

NORTON, Miss F.E. Exh. 1901-2
21 Camden Road, London. † ROI 2.

NORTON, Miss F.M. Exh. 1898
Figure painter. Add: 13 Hillgrove Road, South Hampstead, London. † RA 1.

NORTON, F. Montgomery Exh. 1928
Landscape painter. † AB 2.

NORTON, Marjorie Exh. 1928
20 Dalkeith Street, Joppa. † RSA 1.

NORTON, Peter Exh. 1939-40
c/o Rowley Gallery, 140/2 Kensington Church Street, London. † NEA 1, RBA 1.

NORTON, Phyllis Exh. 1929-35
nee Spence. Watercolour landscape painter. Daughter of Percy Spence q.v. Spent 10 years in India after her marriage. Add: London 1929-35. † RA 9, WG 62.

NORTON, R.D. Exh. 1904-29
Watercolour landscape and coastal painter. Travelled widely. Add: 97 Cheyne Walk, Chelsea, London. † D 1, FIN 57.

NORTON, Wilfred b. 1880
Potter, sculptor and designer. b. Oakengates Salop. Studied Royal College of Art and under Rudolf Steiner in Switzerland. Exh. 1914-40. Add: London. † GI 1, RA 7.

NORTON, William Edward* 1843-1916
American marine painter. Exh. 1882-1901. Add: 23 Camden Road, London. † B 3, G 3, GI 1, L 19, M 3, NEA 1, RA 31, RBA 3, RI 5, ROI 7.

NORWAY, Carlo b. 1886
Painter, architectural sculptor, portrait and decorative artist. Studied Colarossi's, Paris, and Royal Academy of Art Dresden. Travelled in Italy, Germany and Scandinavia. Exh. 1916-27. † I 2, LS 3, M 1.

NORWOOD, Arthur Harding Exh. 1889-93
Landscape painter. Add: 144 Woodvale, Forest Hill, London. † RBA 4, ROI 1.

NORWOOD, Miss E.J.G. Exh. 1912-13
404 Goldhawk Road, Chiswick, London. † L 5.

NOSKE, A. Exh. 1932
Woodcut artist. † BA 2.

NOTT, Alice B. Exh. 1913
37 Kremlin Drive, Stoneycroft, Liverpool. † L 3.

NOTT, G. Exh. 1912-13
London. † RA 2.

NOTT, Mrs. K. Exh. 1907-8
95 Moscow Drive, Liverpool. † L 2.

NOTT, Rhoda Exh. 1931-39
Sculptor. Add: Edgbaston, Birmingham 1931; Brockweir, nr. Chepstow, Mon. 1939. † B 2, RA 1.

NOTTELLE, Mme Exh. 1882
42 George Road, Edgbaston, Birmingham. † B 1.

NOUFFLARD, Anne Exh. 1900-4
20 Milner Street, Cadogan Square, London. † L 1, NG 3.

NOURIGAT, E. Exh. 1913
15 Rue Payenne, Paris. † LS 3.

NOURSE, Elizabeth b. 1860
American figure and landscape painter. Exh. 1891-1913. Add: 11 Chelsea Gardens, London 1891; Paris 1909. † L 4, RA 3, RI 1, ROI 2.

NOUVEAU, Louis H. Exh. 1936-37
Landscape and still life painter. Add: 54 Rue Paradis, Marseilles, France. † RA 2.

NOVO, Stefano* b. 1862
Italian painter. Exh. 1890-1900. Add: Venice 1890 and 1893; London 1892. † GI 7, RA 1, RSA 1.

NOVRA, Mrs. H.G. Exh. 1884
7 Cromwell Grove, West Kensington Park, London. † B 2.

NOWELL, Arthur Trevethin 1862-1940
Portrait, landscape and genre painter. b. Garndiffith, Wales. Studied Manchester School of Art, R.A. Schools and Paris. R.I. 1913, R.O.I. 1903, R.P. 1914. Add: Runcorn, Cheshire 1881; London 1884 and 1890; New Mills, nr. Stockport 1887. † B 11, FIN 1, GI 3, L 60, M 33, NG 15, P 22, RA 95, RI 129, RID 3, ROI 11, RSA 4.

NOWILL, Miss K.B. Exh. 1923
Old Manor House, Shirehampton, Bristol. † SWA 1.

NOWLAN, Carlotta d. 1929
Miniature painter of portraits, animals and flowers, and watercolourist. Daughter of Frank and sister of Pauline N. q.v. R.M.S. 1897. Add: London 1885; North Cheam, Surrey 1892. † L 16, NG 3, RA 17, RI 3, RMS 112.

NOWLAN, Frank c. 1835-1919
Portrait and genre painter and miniature restorer. b. Co. Dublin. Came to London 1857 and studied at Leigh's School and the Langham School of Art Father of Carlotta and Pauline N. q.v. Add: London. † RA 1 RBA 1, RMS 1.

NOWLAN, Pauline L. Exh. 1900-21
Daughter of Frank and sister of Carlotta N. q.v. Add: The Elms, North Cheam, Surrey. † P 1, RA 1, RMS 7.

NOYCE, W. Exh. 1904
Architect. Add: 70 Great Percy Street, London. † RA 1.

NOYES, Dora Exh. 1883-1907
Genre, landscape and portrait painter. Add: London 1883; Milston, Salisbury, Wilts. 1895; Torquay, Devon 1903; Upton Lovel, Wilts. 1907. † B 2, G 1, L 15, M 8, NEA 1, NG 2, RA 26, RBA 11 RI 3, SWA 7.

NOYES, H.J. Exh. 1886-87
1 Cheyne Road, Chester. † L 2.

NOYES, Mary Exh. 1883-97
Figure painter. Add: London 1893; Milston, Salisbury, Wilts. 1897. † RBA 3, RI 1, SWA 5.

NOYES, Theodora Exh. 1887
Landscape painter. Add: 2 Trafalgar Studios, Manresa Road, Chelsea, London. † RA 1.

NOYES-LEWIS, T. Exh. 1892-94
Figure painter. Add: Stanford Lodge, Monken Hadley, Barnet, Herts. † ROI 3.

NOZAL, Alexandre* 1852-1913
French landscape painter. Exh. 1913. † ALP 3.

NUGENT, Miss F. Exh. 1883
Wimbledon, London. † L 1.

NUGENT, Mary Helen Elizabeth
See CARMICHAEL, Lady Gibson

NUNN, Arabella Exh. 1903-4
Manchester. † M 2.

NUNN, G.L. Exh. 1913
153 Lisburn Lane, The Brook, Liverpool. † L 2.

NUTT, Elizabeth Styring d. 1946
Landscape and miniature portrait painter. Studied Sheffield School of Art; under Professor Simi of Florence; France, and with Stanhope Forbes at Newlyn. Head teacher Firshill Branch Art School, Sheffield, and teacher of art Training College and University Sheffield. Principal Nova Scotia College of Art from 1927. Add: Sheffield 1905; Halifax, Nova Scotia 1927. † RA 5, RBA 1.

NUTT, Mrs. Gertrude I. Exh. 1907-22
Mrs. Walter. Portrait and figure painter. Add: Singapore 1907; London 1909. † BG 28, L 1, RA 7.

NUTT, Mark Exh. 1888-1908
Birkenhead. † L 3.

NUTT, Miss M.P. Exh. 1890
1 Via Tornabuoni, Florence. † SWA 1.

NUTTALL, Muriel V.C. Exh. 1913-27
Miniature portrait painter. Add: 15 Maxella Gardens, North Kensington, London. † L 13, RA 9, RMS 1.

NUTTER, Katherine M. Exh. 1883-90
Watercolour flower painter. Add: 42 Regents Park Road, London. † B 1, L 1, RA 5, RBA 1, RI 2, SWA 6.

NUTTGENS, Joseph E. Exh. 1915-34
Architect. Add: Harrow, Middlesex 1915; High Wycombe, Bucks. 1930. † RA 20, RSA 1.

NUTTING, A.H. Exh. 1933-36
† WG 5.

NYAN, B.A. Exh. 1928
34 Paultons Square, London. † L 1.

NYBERG, Henning Exh. 1925
Landscape painter. Add: 26 Culmington Road, Ealing, London. † RA 1.

NYE, Elsie L. Exh. 1898-1936
Miniature portrait painter. Add: Camperdown, Wallington, Surrey. † AB 2, RA 6, RMS 1.

NYE, George F. Exh. 1882
77 Brighton Street, Robin Hood's Chase, Nottingham. † N 1.

NYE, Herbert Exh. 1885-1927
Sculptor and painter. Add: London 1885; Walton on Thames 1895 and 1902; Pulborough, Sussex 1923. † L 5, RA 17, RI 3, ROI 3.

NYE, Maud Exh. 1900
Miniature portrait painter. Add: 16 Colville Terrace, Kensington Park, London. † RA 1.

NYREN, Miss A. Exh. 1882-85
London. † B 1, GI 1, L 1.

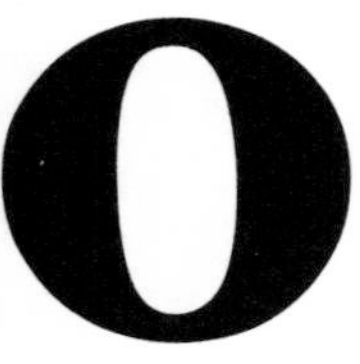

OADES, Emily Exh. 1889
Flower painter. Add: 77 Upper Tulse Hill, London. † SWA 2.

OAKE, Herbert Walter Exh. 1922-31
Painter and teacher. Studied Edinburgh College of Art, R.S.A. Schools and Royal College of Art. Add: College of Art, Edinburgh 1922; Kings Lynn, Norfolk 1931. † RA 1, RSA 5, RSW 2.

OAKES, Colin St. Clair Exh. 1934-35
Architect. Add: Crofters, Amersham, Bucks. † RA 2.

OAKES, Miss J.G. Exh. 1915-18
Felecy Priory, Jacksdale, Nottingham. † N 3.

OAKES, John Wright* 1820-1887
Landscape painter. A.R.A. 1876, A.R.I. 1874, H.R.S.A. 1883. Add: Kensington, London. † GI 5, L 1, M 3, RA 24, RSA 8, TOO 3.

OAKES, L. Rycroft Exh. 1898
Architect. Add: Queen's Chambers, John Dalton Street, Manchester. † RA 1.

OAKESHOTT, George J. Exh. 1887-1923
Architect. Add: London. † RA 3.

OAKESHOTT, Miss V. Exh. 1893
81 Parchmore Road, Thornton Heath, Surrey. † SWA 1.

OAKEY, Miss H. Exh. 1923-24
Mayfield, Christchurch Park, Sutton, Surrey. † SWA 2.

OAKLEY, Alfred James 1880-1959
Sculptor. b. High Wycombe. Visiting Professor, The City Company's School and The Art Wood Carving School. "Mamua" purchased by Chantrey Bequest 1926. Add: London. † GI 10, L 2, M 1, RA 27, RSA 12.

OAKLEY, Constance Exh. 1893-95
53 Soho Hill, Birmingham. † B 3.

OAKLEY, E.M. Exh. 1923
4 Gracewell, 262 Wake Green Road, Moseley, Birmingham. † B 1.

OAKLEY, E.W. Exh. 1888
10 Huntingdon Street, Barnsbury, London. † B 1.

OAKLEY, Edward W. Exh. 1933
Sculptor. Add: 4 The Orchard, Blackheath, London. † RA 1.

OAKLEY, F.P. Exh. 1901
Architect. Add: Haworth's Buildings, Cross Street, Manchester. † RA 1.

OAKLEY, Harold Exh. 1912-29
Watercolour painter. Studied Slade School. Add: London. † LS 3, WG 105.

OAKLEY, Harry Lawrence b. 1882
Silhouette worker. b. York. Studied Royal College of Art. Exh. 1935. Add: London. †, AR 4.

OAKLEY, Rosemary Exh. 1936-40
Landscape painter. Add: Eynsham, Oxon 1936; c/o Rowley Galleries, Kensington Church Street, London 1939. † RA 1, SWA 7.

OAKLEY, William Harold Exh. 1881-88
Architect and landscape painter. Add: 30 Maiden Lane, Strand, London. † RA 4, RBA 1, RI 1.

OAKMAN, Josephine M. Exh. 1929-34
Painter and etcher. Add: London. † AB 2, SWA 2.

OATES, Dorothy Exh. 1913-33
London. † L 7.

OBBARD, Catherine Exh. 1880
Flower painter. Add: Grove Park Lodge, Chiswick, London. † SWA 1.

OBERTEUFFER, George b. 1878
American artist. Exh. 1914-37. Add: 17 Rue Boissonade, Paris. † GI 1, I 1, RSA 3.

O'BRIEN, Mrs. Brendan Exh. 1938-39
Landscape painter. Add: 65 Fitzwilliam Square, Dublin. † RHA 10.

O'BRIEN, Brigid Exh. 1928-29
Mrs. Ganly. Landscape and portrait painter. A.R.H.A. 1936. Daughter of Dermod O'B. q.v. Add: Dublin. † RHA 48.

O'BRIEN, Dermod* 1865-1945
Portrait, landscape and animal painter. b. Foynes, Co. Limerick. Studied Antwerp, Paris and Slade School. Trustee and governor National Gallery of Ireland. H.R.A. 1912, H.R.B.A. 1919, A.R.H.A. 1905, R.H.A. 1907, P.R.H.A. 1910-45, H.R.S.A. 1914. Father of Brigid O'B. q.v. Add: London 1894; Dublin 1901 and 1913; Ardagh, Co. Limerick 1908. † FIN 8, L 9, NEA 7, NG 1, P 2, RA 26, RBA 5, RHA 212, RSA 4.

O'BRIEN, Mrs. Donough Exh. 1935-38
Animal painter. Add: 74 O'Connell Street, Limerick. † RHA 5.

O'BRIEN, Mrs. Dorothy Exh. 1937
Landscape painter. Add: Portmore, Carrickfergus, Co. Antrim. † RHA 2.

O'BRIEN, Geraldine Exh. 1940
Flower painter. Add: 74 O'Connell Street, Limerick. † RHA 1.

O'BRIEN, Katharine Frances See CLAUSEN

O'BRIEN, Lucy Exh. 1940
Interior painter. Add: Ray House, Ray, Co. Donegal. † RHA 1.

O'BRIEN, Lucius Richard* 1832-1899
Canadian landscape and coastal painter. Exh. 1887-92. Add: c/o R. Dolman, 6 New Compton Street, London and Toronto, Canada. † D 8, G 1, RA 1, RBA 2, RHA 4, RI 3.

O'BRIEN, Miss M. Exh. 1908-9
Miniature portrait painter. Add: Caritas, Bushey, Herts. † RA 2.

O'BRIEN, Nelly Exh. 1896-1922
Dublin. † RHA 44.

O'BRIEN, Peter Exh. 1932-38
14 Woodstock Avenue, Reddish, Stockport. † L 3, M 1.

O'BRIEN, Seumas b. 1880
Sculptor Studied Metropolitan School of Art, Dublin. Exh. 1912-14. Add: Dublin. † RHA 3.

OBUTHELL, M. Exh. 1913
Ye Arts and Crafts Studio, Baxtergate, Whitby, Yorks. † L 1.

O'CALLAGHAN, Jerome Exh. 1940
Landscape painter. National College of Art, Kildare Street, Dublin. † RHA 3.

O'CALLAGHAN, J.J. Exh. 1883-88
Dublin. † RHA 9.

O'CALLAGHAN, Lucius d. 1954
Architect. Professor of architecture. R.H.A., A.R.H.A. 1921, R.H.A. 1923. Exh. 1901-9. Add: Dublin. † RHA 3.

OCHTERLONY, Sir Matthew M. Bart Exh. 1915-33
A.R.S.A. 1939. Add: Colinton, Midlothian 1915; Edinburgh 1932. † GI 1, RSA 9.

O'CONNOR, Aileen Exh. 1929-31
Miniature painter. Add: 7 Highfield Avenue, Cork. † RHA 3.

O'CONNOR, Andrew 1874-1941
Sculptor. Exh. 1907. Add: 84 Boulevard Garibaldi, Paris. † RHA 4.

O'CONNOR, Andrew Exh. 1933-39
Architect. Add: Glebe Place, Chelsea, London. † RA 1, RSA 2.

O'CONNOR, Aloysius Patrick Exh. 1932-34
39 Mellor Street, Gorse Hill, Manchester. † B 1, RCA 2.

O'CONNOR, Dominic M. Exh. 1908
25 Suffolk Street, Dublin. † RHA 1.

O'CONNOR, E. Exh. 1881
51 Upper Sackville Street, Dublin. † RHA 1.

O'CONNOR, Miss E.B. Exh. 1907
4 Clarence Parade, Southsea, Hants. † RA 1.

O'CONNOR, Edward Dominic 1896-1958
Painter and etcher. Studied Leicester College of Art and Leicester School of Architecture. Exh. 1939. Add: Desford, Leics. † RHA 2.

O'CONNOR, Francis H. Exh. 1895
52 Glebe Place, Chelsea, London. † P 1.

O'CONNOR, George L. Exh. 1896-1938
Architect. Add: Dublin. † RHA 19.

O'CONNOR, John* 1830-1889
Landscape painter. b. Co. Derry, Ireland. Worked in Dublin and Belfast as a painter of theatrical scenery. Went to London 1848. R.I. 1887, A.R.H.A. 1883. Add: 28 Abercorn Place, St. John's Wood, London 1880 and 1889; Blackwater, Hants. 1888. † D 9, G 20, GI 3, L 9, M 8, RA 8, RHA 17, RI 12, ROI 6, RSA 1.

O'CONNOR, John Scorror b. 1913
Painter, wood engraver and lithographer. Studied Leicester College of Art 1930-33 and Royal College of Art 1933-37. Instructor Birmingham College of Art 1937-38 and Bristol College of Art 1938-40. Exh. 1935-40. † RA 2, RED 4.

O'CONNOR, Patrick Exh. 1930-40
Portrait and figure painter. Add: Paris 1930; Dublin 1940. † GI 1, RHA 2.

O'CONOR, Roderic* 1860-1940
Figure painter. b. Roscommon, Ireland. Member London Group 1923. Lived in Paris for many years. † CHE 4, G 2, LS 5, NEA 1, RHA 7.

ODDIE, Mrs. Exh. 1884-87
Watercolour painter. Add: 6 Campden Grove, Kensington, London. † SWA 7.

ODDIE, J.W. Exh. 1882-86
Syzwick Hall, Keswick, Cumberland. † L 1, M 1.

ODDIE, Mrs. Mary E. Exh. 1931-37
Painter. Add: Broadview, Uckfield, Sussex. † COO 1, RCA 2, ROI 8.

ODDIE, Maude G. Exh. 1897-1904
Portrait painter. Add: Watford, Herts. † RA 2.

ODDY, Henry Raphael Exh. 1882-1907
Landscape painter. Add: Halifax, Yorks. † B 1, L 4, RA 8, RI 1.

O'DEA, Eric Exh. 1934-36
Landscape and flower painter. † RED 45.

ODGERS, Alice M. Exh. 1906-11
North Finchley, London. † L 2, RA 1.

ODGERS, W. Ernest Exh. 1905
Adrum, Devonport. † L 1.

O'DICEY, E.M. Exh. 1925
c/o St. George's Gallery, 32A George Street, London. † GI 1.

ODLE, Allan Elsden Exh. 1914
Designer of the Grotesque and illustrator. Studied Sidney Cooper School of Art, Canterbury and St. John's Wood Art Schools. Add: 32 Queen's Terrace, St. John's Wood, London. † RSA 2.

O'DOHERTY, Angela Exh. 1926
Metropolitan School of Art, Dublin. † RHA 2.

O'DONEL, Miss Nuala Exh. 1898-1900
Kensington Gore, London 1898; Dublin 1899. † RHA 3.

O'DONNELL, Eleanor Exh. 1937-38
Landscape painter. Add: 34 Fitzwilliam Square, Dublin. † RHA 2.

O'DONNELL, Helena Exh. 1909
Figure and flower painter. Add: 24 Alma Road, Clifton, Bristol. † BG 1, L 1, RA 1.

O'DONNELL, Henry C. Exh. 1926-38
Landscape painter. Add: London 1932; Dublin 1938. † CG 1, GOU 2, RA 1, RBA 1, RHA 1.

O'DONNELL, Kittie Exh. 1927
23 Chelmsford Road, Dublin. † RHA 1.

O'DONOHOE, Francis d. 1912
A.R.H.A. 1912. Killed in a motor accident. Exh. 1899-1911. Add: Dublin. † RHA 26.

O'DOWD, Freda Exh. 1921-22
Add: Newhaven, Mersey Avenue, Aigburth, Liverpool. † L 2.

O'DRISCOLL, Patrick J. Exh. 1935
Landscape painter. Add: Cork Art Club, 25 Patrick Street, Cork. † RHA 1.

O'FAGAN, George Exh. 1907
Add: Astagob, Clonsilla, Co. Dublin. † RHA 1.

O'FARRELL, Miss B. Exh. 1897-1908
Bray, Co. Wicklow. † RHA 18.

O'FARRELL, Fergus Exh. 1938
Watercolour landscape painter. Add: 61 Dollymount Avenue, Clontarf. † RHA 1.

O'FEELY, Mary S. Exh. 1914-32
Liver Sketching Club, 11 Dale Street, Liverpool. † L 18.

OFFERMANS, T. Exh. 1886
Dutch painter. Add: 117 New Bond Street, London. † M 2.

OFFICER, E.C. Exh. 1896-1904
R.B.A. 1900. Add: Etaples, Pas de Calais 1896; Paris 1898; Finistere, France 1900. † RBA 11, ROI 2.

OFFOR, Beatrice Exh. 1887-1917
Figure painter. Add: London. † B 2, RA 14, SWA 1.

OFFORD, Gertrude E. Exh. 1894-1915
Watercolour flower painter. Add: St. Giles, Norwich. † RA 8.

OFFORD, John James Exh. 1886
Figure painter. Add: 193 Euston Road, London. † RA 1.

OFFORD, Mary H. Exh. 1886-1900
Landscape painter. Add: 193 Euston Road, London. † RA 2.

OFFORD, Miss M.S. Exh. 1901
6 Oval Road, Gloucester Gate, London. † SWA 1.

O'FLAHERTY, Charlotte Gordon
See McLAREN

O'FLYNN, Miss G.M. Exh. 1916-19
13 Northumberland Road, Dublin. † RHA 3.

OGDEN, Agnew J.T. b. 1868
Painter, black and white artist and designer. b. York. Studied York, London and Paris. Senior assistant York School of Arts and Crafts, Headmaster Wellington Art and Technical School and headmaster Tiverton School of Arts and Crafts. Exh. 1914. Add: Tiverton, Devon. † LS 3.

OGDEN, Jane Exh. 1880-82
Watercolour flower painter. Add: London 1880; Eccles, Lancs. 1882. † D 4, RA 5, RBA 1.

OGDEN, Joseph d. 1925
Architect and teacher. Exh. 1900-14. Add: Canterbury, Kent. † RA 4.

OGE, Pierre 1849-1912
French sculptor. Exh. 1880. † RA 1.

OGER, F. Exh. 1924
221 Rue de la Convention, Paris. † L 1.

OGG, James Exh. 1936
11 Springbank Terrace, Aberdeen. † RSA 1.

OGG, Miss M. Braid Exh. 1909-15
Mrs. S.H. Williams. Add: 17 Hadassah Grove, Sefton Park, Liverpool. † L 10.

OGG, Mary Lyle Exh. 1910-28
17 Hadassah Grove, Sefton Park, Liverpool. † L 13.

OGG, Robert A. Exh. 1927
26 Stanley Street, Aberdeen. † RSA 1.

OGILVIE, Miss C. Exh. 1911-29
Add: Harrogate, Yorks. 1911; The Three Arts Club, 19A Marylebone Road, London 1929. † RA 1, RI 3.

OGILVIE, Charles H.E. Exh. 1903-28
Add: Glasgow 1903; Saltcoats 1928. † GI 11, L 1, RSA 2.

OGILVIE, Mrs. Clare Mary Exh. 1930-38
† RMS 7.

OGILVIE, Frederick D Exh. 1886-1917
Watercolour landscape and coastal painter. Add: Edinburgh 1886; Bonhill 1887; Glasgow 1891; Helensburgh 1893; Harrogate, Yorks 1901; Dunster, Somerset 1914. † G 12, GI 10, L 4, RA 1, RHA 1, RI 4, RSA 9, RSW 7.

OGILVIE, Frederick F. Exh. 1907-20
Watercolour landscape painter. Travelled in the Middle East. Add: London. † RA 1, RSA 2, WG 106.

OGILVIE, Frank S. Exh. 1885-1915
Portrait, landscape and figure painter. Add: London 1885, 1891 and 1905; Bushey, Herts. 1888; North Shields 1899; Newcastle on Tyne 1900; Letchworth, Herts. 1912. † B 6, FIN 2, GI 4, L 2, RA 10, RBA 7, RI 1, ROI 2, RSA 4.

OGILVIE, J.D. Exh. 1885
Watercolour landscape painter. Add: 1 Bellhaven Terrace, Edinburgh. † RA 1.

OGILVIE, J.M. Exh. 1907
1 Inverleith Row, Edinburgh. † RSA 1.

OGILVIE, Miss J.M. Exh. 1916-40
Add: 16 Coltbridge Terrace, Murrayfield, Edinburgh 1916; 14 Campbell Avenue, Edinburgh 1934. † GI 2, RSA 5, RSW 4.

OGILVIE, Lilian L. Exh. 1924-40
Add: 16 Coltbridge Terrace, Murrayfield 1924; 14 Campbell Avenue, Edinburgh 1936. † GI 6, RSA 10.

OGILVIE, M. Exh. 1912-14
16 Bramerton Street, Chelsea, London. † LS 7.

OGILVIE, R. Exh. 1933
16 Coltbridge Terrace, Edinburgh. † RSA 1.

OGILVIE, Sophia J. Exh. 1908-17
London. † B 4, LS 19.

OGILVIE, William Exh. 1919-24
10 Cameron Park, Edinburgh. † RSA 3.

OGILVIE, W.A. Exh. 1933
† RSW 4.

OGILVY, Gilbert Exh. 1937
Winton, East Lothian. † RSA 1.

OGILVY, James S. Exh. 1893-1909
Landscape painter. Add: 5 Kensington Park Road, London. † D 21, NG 4, ROI 2.

OGILVY, Miss N. Exh. 1904
Baldovan, Dundee. † RSA 2.

OGILVY, Violet Exh. 1888-1900
Add: Inchture, N.B. 1888; Strathmartine, N.B. 1900. † RSA 2, RSW 1.

OGLE, Frances M. Exh. 1934-39
Watercolour landscape painter. † AR 1, COO 1.

OGLE, Mary A. Exh. 1928
Landscape painter. † AB 2.

OGLE, Richard B. Exh. 1920-29
Portrait painter. Add: 56 Huron Road, Balham, London. † D 1, RA 1.

O'GORMAN, John Exh. 1933-39
Landscape painter. Add: Glenart Avenue, Blackrock, Co. Dublin. † RHA 6.

O'HALLORAN, Miss F. Exh. 1923
53 Wellington Road, Dublin. † RHA 1.

O'HALLORAN, Mrs. Fogarty Exh. 1927-34
Dwelly, Edenbridge, Kent. † RHA 2, ROI 4, SWA 2.

O'HALLORAN, J. Exh. 1924-25
53 Wellington Road, Dublin. † RHA 3.

O'HANLON, Judge Exh. 1882
31 Lower Abbey Street, Dublin. † RHA 1.

O'HANRAHAN, Joseph Exh. 1923-38
149 North Strand, Dublin. † RHA 4.

O'HARA, A. Exh. 1895-97
Mrs. Geoffrie. Landscape painter. Add: 10 Grenville Place, London. † RID 2.

O'HARA, Eliot b. 1890
American watercolour landscape painter. Exh. 1930. † WG 51.

O'HARA, Helen Exh. 1881-1908
Watercolour painter. Add: Portstewart, Co. Derry 1881; Lismore 1899. † D 28, L 1, M 1, RHA 15, RI 13, SWA 63.

O'HLY, William F.C. Exh. 1935-37
Sculptor. Add: London. † GI 1, RA 3.

O'KEEFE, Mrs. Elsie See MILLARD

O'KEEFE, Margaret Exh. 1916-21
Add: Dublin 1916; Wexford 1917. † RHA 8.

O'KEEFE, Stephen Exh. 1912-29
Liverpool. † L 18.

O'KELLY, Mrs. Exh. 1884
Add: 73 Brighton Square, Rathgar, Dublin. † RHA 2.

O'KELLY, Aloysius C.* b. 1850
Landscape and genre painter. b. Dublin. Studied under Bonnat and Gerome in Paris. Travelled in the Middle East. Exh. 1880-95. Add: London 1880 and 1886; Co. Galway 1881; Yalding, Kent 1885. † L 2, M 4, RA 18, RBA 16, RHA 35, RI 4, ROI 7.

O'KELLY, Norah M. Exh. 1912-20
Templeogue, Co. Dublin 1912; Dublin 1916. † RHA 8.

O'KENNEDY, Eleanor K. Exh. 1918-19
Miniature portrait painter. Add: Tunbridge Wells, Kent 1918; Southborough, Kent 1919. † RA 2, RHA 1.

OKEY, Mabel L. Exh. 1895-99
3 Park Road Studios, Haverstock Hill, London. † L 3.

OLDACRE, R. Samuel Exh. 1900
Architect. Add: 14 Temple Street, Birmingham. † RA 1.

OLDEN, Henry Exh. 1883-85
Stoneycroft, Liverpool. † L 2.

OLDEWELT, F. Exh. 1885
99 P.C. Hooftshoot, Amsterdam. † GI 1.

OLDFIELD, A. Exh. 1922
† SWA 1.

OLDFIELD, J. Reffitt Exh. 1890-1903
Landscape painter. N.E.A. 1891. Add: Harrogate, Yorks. 1890; c/o James Newman, Soho Square, London 1891; c/o Madderton & Co., Loughton, Essex 1898; Braunton, Devon 1903. † GI 4, L 2, NEA 10, NG 4.

OLDFIELD, Mrs. Millicent Exh. 1904-6
Miniature portrait painter. Add: Preston, Lancs. 1904; Clifton, Bristol 1906. † RA 2.

OLDFIELD, Mrs. Violet E. Exh. 1911
The Bank, Scunthorpe, Lincs. † RCA 1.

OLDHAM, Dorothy Blanche Exh. 1910-12
Kensington, London. † LS 9.

OLDHAM, Emma Exh. 1890-1901
Miniature portrait painter. Add: North Wingfield Rectory, Chesterfield 1890; Lyme Regis, Dorset 1900. † D 3, L 2, RA 3.

OLDHAM, Frank Exh. 1930
Portrait painter. Add: 9 Hillway, Highgate, London. † RA 1.

OLDHAM, F.H. Exh. 1882-84
Architect. Add: 23 John Dalton Street, Manchester. † RA 3

OLDHAM, Roger Exh. 1909-14
Add: Timperley, Cheshire 1909; Manchester 1910. † L 7, M 8.

OLDHAM, Richard C. Exh. 1890-94
Landscape painter. Add: 275 Friern Road, Dulwich, London. † M 1, RA 1.

OLDOFREDI, Count S. Exh. 1880
Sculptor. † RA 2.

OLDREY, Clarence Exh. 1913
22 Prescot Street, New Brighton, Cheshire. † L 3.

OLDRIDGE, Margaret Exh. 1918-39
Miniature portrait painter. Add: Kew Gardens, Surrey 1918; London 1928. † RA 7, RMS 6.

OLDRIEVE, William Thomas 1853-1922
Architect. His Majesty's Principal Architect for Scotland. H.R.S.A. 1914. Exh. 1913. Add: H.M. Office of Works, Edinburgh. † RSA 3.

OLIPHANT, Alexander G. Exh. 1934-36
25 Marshall Street, Grangemouth. † RSA 2.

OLIPHANT, F.K. Exh. 1905
Houghton, Hunts. † RA 1.

OLIPHANT, Janet Mary Exh. 1895
† NG 1.

OLIPHANT, Kinsley Exh. 1890
Architect. 33 Finsbury Circus, London. † RA 1.

OLIVA, E. Exh. 1884-1900
† TOO 6.

OLIVE, Frances Exh. 1884-90
Figure and miniature portrait painter. Add: London. † RA 1, SWA 4.

OLIVER, Mrs. Exh. 1893
Winchfield, Hants. † SWA 2.

OLIVER, Alfred Exh. 1886-1921
Landscape painter. N.S.A. 1895. Probably father of Capt. T.A.O. q.v. Add: Ruddington, Notts. 1886; Capel Curig, N. Wales 1902. † L 8, N 27, RA 7.

OLIVER, A.D. Exh. 1887-88
38 Grove End Road, London. † L 2.

OLIVER, Basil Exh. 1910-29
Architect. Studied Bury St. Edmunds School of Architecture, Liverpool University, R.A. Schools and Central School of Arts and Crafts, London. Teacher with the Architecture and Building Crafts Section L.C.C. Central School of Arts and Crafts. Add: London and Sudbury, Suffolk. † RA 10.

OLIVER, Catherine Exh. 1927
Argyll. † M 1.

OLIVER, Constance Exh. 1925-39
Watercolour portrait and landscape painter. Studied Slade School. Add: London. † BK 38, NEA 3, P 3, RA 2, RBA 5, ROI 1, SWA 3.

OLIVER, Dorothy Exh. 1905-14
Liberton House, Midlothian. † GI 1, L 4, RSA 3.

OLIVER, Dora M. Exh. 1886-90
Moston Terrace, Mayfield, Edinburgh. † RSA 2.

OLIVER, Edith Exh. 1911-38
Miniature portrait painter. b. Newcastle. Studied at the Praga School, Kensington. Add: Cullercoats, Northumberland 1911; Kew, Surrey 1937. † L 8, RA 11.

OLIVER, Evelyn Exh. 1932-33
Painter. Add: Lamorna, Sidcup, Kent. † RA 1, ROI 1.

OLIVER, E.A. (Lizzie) Exh. 1896-1902
Glasgow. † GI 5.

OLIVER, Mrs. Edmund G. Exh. 1913
Landscape painter. † ALP 3.

OLIVER, G. Exh. 1928
81 Royal Avenue, Lowestoft, Suffolk. † L 2.

OLIVER, George D. Exh. 1885-87
Architect. Add: Carlisle. † RA 3.

OLIVER, Miss L. Campbell Exh. 1900-1
Olive Lodge, Polwarth Terrace, Edinburgh. † RSA 2.

OLIVER, Margery Exh. 1938
Landscape painter. Add: 104 Cheyne Walk, London. † RA 2.

OLIVER, M.C. Exh. 1920-33
13 Hampstead Gardens, London. † L 3, RMS 1.

OLIVER, Robert Dudley c. 1857-1923
Portrait and figure painter and architect. Exh. 1883-1908. Add: London. † L 3, RA 16.

OLIVER, Torfrida See SWANN

OLIVER, Capt. T.A. d. c.1919
Landscape painter. Probably son of Alfred O. q.v. Exh. 1913-19. Add: The Studio, Capel Curig, N. Wales. † RA 3.

OLIVER, Mrs. Violet Exh. 1911
Landscape painter. † ALP 2.

OLIVER, William* Exh. 1881-97
Portrait and figure painter. Add: London. † B 4, L 1, M 4, RA 3.

OLIVER, Mrs. William 1819-1885
Miss Emma Eburne. Landscape painter and watercolourist. Studied under her first husbank William O. (1804-1853). R.I. 1849. Add: Watford, Herts. 1880; Gt. Berkhamsted, Herts. 1884. † GI 1, L 3, RI 28, SWA 6.

OLIVER, William Thomas b. 1877
Landscape and seascape painter. Exh. 1924. Add: 66 Kingston Road, Ilford, Essex. † RA 1.

OLIVIE, Leon c. 1832-1901
French artist. Exh. 1882-85. Add: Paris. † RHA 5.

OLIVIER, Ferdinand Exh. 1908-9
6 Square Delambre, Paris. † LS 8.

OLIVIER, Herbert Arnould 1861-1952
Portrait, figure and landscape painter. b. Battle, Sussex. Studied R.A. Schools (Creswick Prize 1882). R.B.A. 1887, R.I. 1929, R.P. 1894. Add: London. † B 10, FIN 66, G 1, GI 1, L 34, M 1, NG 16, P 114, RA 86, RBA 26, RCA 1, RHA 5, RI 29, RID 32, RSA 1.

OLIVIER, Rene Exh. 1908-9
8 Rue Garanciere, Paris. † LS 7.

OLLEY, Nellie Exh. 1908-15
Liverpool. † L 3.

OLLIVANT, Miss K.F. Exh. 1904-14
Add: Elliott's, Nuthurst, Horsham, Sussex. † D 15, L 3, RHA 2, SWA 9.

O'LOAN, J.C. Exh. 1887-88
39 Ritson Street, Liverpool. † L 2.

OLORENSHAW, May Exh. 1924-29
Oaklands, Crabmill Lane, Hollywood. † B 4.

OLSON, Anders Exh. 1906-13
Add: Bruges, Belgium 1906 and 1908; London 1907; Kristianstad, Sweden 1912; Malmo, Sweden 1913. † GI 11, L 1, LS 5, RA 4, RSA 6.

OLSSON, Julius* 1864-1942
Landscape and coastal painter. b. London of a Swedish father and English mother. N.E.A. 1891, A.R.A. 1914, R.A. 1920, R.B.A. 1890, H.R.M.S. 1926, R.O.I. 1897, P.R.O.I. 1920. "Moonlit Shore" purchased by Chantrey Bequest 1911. Add: Purley, Surrey 1888 and 1894; St. Ives, Cornwall 1889; London 1912. † B 23, BA 33, DOW 2, FIN 41, G 4, GI 43, L 55, M 29, NEA 7, NG 7, RA 175, RBA 35, RHA 21, RI 7, RID 40, ROI 126, RSA 2, WG 40.

OLSSON, Muriel Exh. 1912
9 Edith Road, West Kensington, London. † ROI 1.

OLVER, Kate Elizabeth d. 1960
Mrs. Higgins. Portrait, landscape and figure painter, and illustrator. Studied R.A. Schools. A.S.W.A. 1935. Exh. 1907-40. Add: London. † GI 1, L 3, P 4, RA 29, RSA 1, SWA 11.

OLYETT, Bertha Exh. 1936-39
Painter. Add: Ilford, Essex. † RA 1, ROI 2.

O'MAHONEY, Florence Exh. 1882-85
Figure painter. Add: 22 Mortimer Street, London. † RA 1, RHA 1.

O'MALLEY, Rev. F. Exh. 1933
Add: Ratcliffe College, Leicester. † N 4.

O'MALLEY, James Exh. 1881-83
Add: Newport, Co. Mayo 1881; Paisley 1883. † GI 1, RHA 2.

O'MALLEY, Power b. 1870
Landscape and figure painter. b. Co. Waterford. Exh. 1939. † BA 45.

OMAN, C.M.A. Exh. 1921-22
Frewin Hall, Oxford. † L 1, RCA 1.

O'MEARA, Frank 1853-1888
Landscape painter. Add: Seine et Marne, France and Dublin Street, Carlow, Ireland. † FIN 1, G 2, GI 4, L 4.

O'MEARA, Teresa M. Exh. 1904-10
45 Lower Mount Street, Dublin. † RHA 6.

OMMANNEY, George Exh. 1912-17
Figure and landscape painter. Add: 16 Warwick Gardens, London. † LS 12, NEA 1, P 1, RA 1.

O'MURCHADHA, Seamus Exh. 1931
Sculptor. Add: 149 Sun Row, Dillons Cross, Cork. † RHA 1.

O'MURNAGHAN, Art Exh. 1929-35
Painter. Add: 15 Brighton Square, Dublin. † RHA 6.

O'NEILL, Charles Exh. 1883-1924
Lived in and around Liverpool. † L 80, RA 3.

O'NEILL, George Bernard* 1828-1917
Genre painter. b. Dublin. Add: Young Street, Kensington, London 1880. † L 1, RA 14, TOO 28.

O'NEILL, Harry Exh. 1914-15
7 Commercial Buildings, Clontarf, Dublin. † RHA 3.

O'NEILL, Hon. Henrietta Exh. 1906
Shane's Castle, Antrim. † RHA 2.

O'NEILL, Mary Exh. 1935
Painter and black and white artist. b. Carisbrooke, I.O.W. Studied Slade School and R.A. Schools. Add: 54 King Henry''s Road, Hampstead, London. † RBA 1.

O'NEILL, Peggy Exh. 1939
† P 1.

O'NEILL, W.G. Exh. 1884-90
Add: Brussels 1884; Penge, S.E. London 1888. † B 3, RHA 2.

ONION, Harley Exh. 1935-39
Landscape painter. A.N.S.A. 1936. Add: Nottingham 1935; Sherwood, Nottingham 1939. † N 9.

ONIONS, Miss M.A. Exh. 1895-96
The Grange, Tysley, Birmingham. † B 3.

OPFFER, Ivan Exh. 1931
Portrait painter. Add: Allegade 6, Copenhagen, Denmark. † RA 1.

OPIE, Edward 1810-1894
Genre and portrait painter. Studied under H.P. Briggs. Add: 5 Braidwood Terrace, Plymouth 1880-86. † RA 9.

OPPENHEIMER, Charles* 1875-1961
Landscape painter. Studied Manchester School of Art and Italy. A.R.S.A. 1927, R.S.A. 1935, R.S.W. 1912. Add: Manchester 1894; Kirkcudbright 1909. † AR 1, FIN 84, GI 74, L 17, M 22, RA 46, RHA 5, RSA 83, RSW 98.

OPPENHEIMER, Joseph Exh. 1903-39
Portrait and figure painter. Add: London. † GOU 3, I 6, L 6, M 1, P 2, RA 8.

OPPENHEIMER, L.J. Exh. 1906-7
8 Manley Road, Alexandra Park, Manchester. † RA 2.

OPPENHEIMER, Mary Exh. 1923-26
8 Clarendon Road West, Chorlton cum Hardy, Manchester. † GI 3, M 3.

OPPENOORTH, Willem J.* Exh. 1890-95
Landscape and figure painter. Add: London. † L 1, RBA 2, ROI 3.

OPPLER, Alex Exh. 1904-5
15 Boulevard Berthier, Paris. † I 3.

OPPLER, Ernest 1867-1927
Landscape and figure painter. Add: London 1894; Sluis, Holland 1904. † B 2, G 2, GI 4, GOU 1, I 3, L 7, M 3, NEA 2, P 5, RA 2.

OPSOMER, Isadore* b. 1878
Belgian landscape painter. Exh. 1915-25. Add: London. † GI 2, I 2, L 8.

ORAM, Janet Exh. 1920-36
Painter. Add: 1 Bolingbroke Grove, Wandsworth Common, London. † RA 5.

ORCHAR, James Exh. 1880-91
Angus Lodge, Broughton Ferry, Dundee. † RSA 9.

ORCHARD, Miss A.G. Exh. 1892-94
120 Shepherd's Bush Road, London. † ROI 3.

ORCHARD, Gertrude Exh. 1896-1904
Miniature portrait painter. Add: Calvados, France 1896; London 1897; Eastbourne 1904. † NEA 1, RA 5, RBA 1, RI 4, RMS 1.

ORCHARDSON, Charles M.Q.* 1873-1917
Portrait and landscape painter. Son of William O. q.v. R.B.A. 1902, R.O.I. 1907. Add: London. Died of wounds in the Middle East, World War I. † B 4, GI 4, L 13, NG 1, P 6, RA 30, RBA 6, ROI 15.

ORCHARDSON, Sir William Quiller* 1832-1910
Portrait and genre painter. b. Edinburgh. Studied under R.S. Lauder. A.R.A. 1868, R.A. 1877, H.R.M.S. 1900, R.P. 1897, H.R.S.A. 1871. "Napoleon on Board the Bellerophon" purchased by Chantrey Bequest 1880. Add: London and Westgate, Thanet. † AG 2, B 6, BG 1, G 3, GI 19, I 1, L 15, NG 2, P 14, RA 67, RHA 3, RSA 23, TOO 2.

ORCZY, Baroness Emmuska Exh. 1888-94
Figure painter. Add: London. † L 5, M 3, RA 4, RBA 3, SWA 1.

ORDE, Alice (Mrs. J.) Exh. 1895-1913
Miniature portrait painter. Add: London 1895; Woking, Surrey 1896; Tongham, Surrey 1899; Bromley, Kent 1913. † RA 5, RMS 4, SWA 2.

ORDE, Cuthbert b. 1888
Portrait, landscape and still life painter. Exh. 1921-39. Add: London. † ALP 40, CHE 1, GOU 6, L 1, P 15, RA 10, ROI 4.

ORDE, Eileen Rosalind Exh. 1917-29
Painter. Add: London 1917; Marlborough 1929. † NEA 5.

ORDE, Miss M.L. Exh. 1896-97
21 Cadogan Gardens, London. † SWA, 2.

ORDE-WARDE, C.M. Exh. 1928
Landscape painter. † AB 2.

O'REILLY, Denis Exh. 1924
Add: Clare Villa, Claremorris, Co. Mayo. † RHA 1.

O'REILLY, Joseph* d. 1893
Figure and domestic painter. A.R.H.A. 1892. Add: 61 Upper Grangegorman, Dublin. † RHA 11.

O'REILLY, Maud (Mrs. J.F.) Exh. 1926
Sculptor. Add: Overseas Club, Vernon House, St. James's, London. † RA 1.

O'REILLY, Patrick J. Exh. 1880-82
7 North Earl Street, Dublin. † RHA 4.

O'REILLY, Mrs. Veronica Exh. 1930
Landscape painter. Add: Rathnestin, Ardee, Co. Louth. † RHA 1.

ORETON, Florence Exh. 1902-5
Walford Hall, Hampden in Arden. † B 4.

O'RINN, Liam Exh. 1939
Landscape painter. Add: Bothar Ghort na Mara, Cluain Tairib. † RHA 1.

ORLOFF, Nina Exh. 1932-40
Watercolour flower painter. Add: London. † RA 4.

ORME, Alfred Exh. 1881-1900
Miniature portrait painter. Add: Liverpool 1881; Manchester 1894; Altrincham, Cheshire 1896; Rusholme, nr. Manchester 1898; Southport, Lancs. 1900. † L 15, RA 12.

ORMEROD, Edith Exh. 1926
North Bank, Blackburn, Lancs. † L 4.

ORMOND, Mrs. Kate Exh. 1900-1
Overton, Kilmalcolm, N.B.† GI 1, RSA 3.

ORMOND, Reine Exh. 1923-27
21 Mulberry Walk, London. † NEA 2.

ORMROD, Frank Exh. 1922-38
Watercolour landscape painter. Add: London 1922; Dunsmoor, nr. Wendover, Bucks. 1931. † NEA 7, RA 6.

ORMSBY, V. Exh. 1880-86
Figure painter. Add: St. John's Wood, London. † GI 1, RA 4.

O'RORKE, Brian Exh. 1935-40
Architect. Add: London. † RA 2.

O'ROURKE, H.T. Exh. 1908
10 Glentworth Street, Limerick. † RHA 3.

OROVIDA, See PISSARRO, Miss Camille

ORPEN, Bea b. 1913
Painter. Studied R.H.A. Life School 1932-35, and Slade School 1935-39. Exh. 1934-40. Add: Lisheens, Carrickmines, Co. Dublin. † RHA 17.

ORPEN, Diana Exh. 1933-39
Painter. † COO 1, NEA 1.

ORPEN, Dickie Exh. 1937
Painter. † COO 2.

ORPEN, Miss D.E. Exh. 1940
Pencil artist. Add: 5 Church Street, London. † RA 1.

ORPEN, Richard Caulfield 1863-1938
Architect and watercolourist. Brother of Sir William O. q.v. A Governor and guardian of the National Gallery of Ireland and visitor to R.H.A. Life School. A.R.H.A. 1911, R.H.A. 1912. Add: Dublin. † NEA 1, RHA 104.

ORPEN, Sir William* 1878-1931
Portrait painter. b. Stillorgan, Co. Dublin. Studied Metropolitan School of Art, Dublin and Slade School 1897-99. Official artist World War I. Brother of Richard Caulfield O. q.v. N.E.A. 1900, A.R.A. 1910, R.A. 1919, A.R.H.A. 1904, R.H.A. 1907, H.R.H.A. 1930, R.I. 1919, H.R.O.I. 1929, R.P. 1905. Knighted 1918. "Sir William McCormick" purchased by Chantrey Bequest 1921. Exh. from 1899. Add: London. † AG 127, ALP 3, B 1, BA 34, CAR 23, CG 4, CHE 15, COO 6, FIN 2, G 12, GI 24, GOU 102, I 19, L 98, LEI 2, LS 1, M 4, NEA 119, P 51.

ORPHEUS, W. Exh. 1902
Painter. Add: 2 Rue Berckmans, Brussels. † RA 1.

ORPHOOT, Burnett Napier Henderson b. 1880
Architect and etcher. b. Peebles. Studied Edinburgh and Paris. A.R.S.A. 1936. Exh. 1912-39. Add: Edinburgh. † GI 6, L 8, RSA 10.

ORPHOOT, Miss M.J.C. Exh. 1907-9
Greenhithe, North Berwick. † L 1, RSA 2.

ORPIN, Isabel Exh. 1901-4
24 Elgin Road, Dublin. † RHA 5.

ORR, Alex Exh. 1940
15 Blythswood Square, Glasgow. † GI 1.

ORR, Arthur Anselm b. 1868
Stained glass, ecclesiastical, metal and wood craftsman. Studied Birmingham, Westminster and the Royal College of Art. Exh. 1898-1938. Add: Harrow, Middlesex. † RA 40.

ORR, A.W. Exh. 1889
Secrora, Killiney. † RHA 1.

ORR, Ina R. Exh. 1883-87
136 Wellington Street, Glasgow. † GI 6, RHA 2.

ORR, Jack Exh. 1909-40
Add: Rutherglen 1909; Glasgow 1911; Moffat 1925; Edinburgh 1940. † GI 20, L 1, RA 1, RSA 7, RSW 11.

ORR, Miss J.F. Exh. 1888-90
Langside, Glasgow. † GI 3.

ORR, James R. Wallace Exh. 1930-40
Engraver. Add: Glasgow 1930; Kirkcudbright 1933; Helensburgh 1936. † GI 2, RA 1, RSA 11.

ORR, J.T. Herbert Exh. 1922
15 Sandymount Green, Dublin. † RHA 1.

ORR, Miss K. Exh. 1881
Greenwood, Blackrock, Ireland. † RHA 1.

ORR, Monro Scott b. 1874
Painter, etcher and illustrator. Studied Glasgow School of Art. Brother of Stewart O. q.v. Exh. 1900-27. Add: Glasgow 1900; Hatch End, Middlesex 1924. † GI 28, L 9, RSA 2, RSW 3.

ORR, Patrick W. Exh. 1889-1932
Painter. Add: Glasgow. † GI 58, L 5, M 1, RA 2, RSA 4, RSW 1.

ORR, Stewart 1872-1944
Watercolour painter and illustrator. Studied Glasgow School of Art. Brother of Monro Scotto, q.v. R.S.W. 1925. Add: Woodford Green, Essex 1901; Dumbreck 1902; Glasgow 1903; Corrie, Isle of Arran 1920. † AR 2, CON 65, GI 68, L 20, RA 2, RI 6, RSA 36, RSW 44.

ORR, W.E.A. Exh. 1938
Old Aucherdrane, Bearsden, Glasgow. † RSW 1.

ORRIDGE, Caroline E. Exh. 1890-91
Painter. Add: London. † GI 1, RBA 1, SWA 1.

ORRIDGE, John Exh. 1936
Stained glass artist. Add: 15 Warner Road, London. † RA 1.

ORROCK, James* 1829-1913
Landscape painter and watercolourist. b. Edinburgh. Qualified as a dentist and practised in Nottingham. Worked at Nottingham School of Design and later studied under James Ferguson, John Burgess, Stewart Smith and W.L. Leitch. Went to London 1866. A.R.I. 1871, R.I. 1875, R.O.I. 1883. Add: London. † AG 22, B 13, DOW 51, FIN 102, G 12, GI 1, L 18, LEI 1, M 8, NG 24, RA 3, RI 123, ROI 57, RSW 1, TOO 17.

ORSI, Carlo Exh. 1881-93
Painter and sculptor. Add: Toscana, Italy 1881; Florence 1893. † AG 3, RA 1, RHA 2.

ORTLIEB, Friedrich* 1839-1909
German painter. Exh. 1881. Add: Munich, Bavaria. † RSA 1.

ORTMAN, Miss L.A. Exh. 1914
Hellerup 189, Strandvei, Denmark. † LS 4.

ORTON, Gladys Exh. 1914-29
Miniature painter. Add: Gordon Road, Borrowash, nr. Derby. † N 84.

ORTWEILER, Winifred b. 1905
Painter. Add: The End House, Christchurch Avenue, Brondesbury, London. † D 2, ROI 1.

O'RYAN, Fergus* b. 1911
Painter and illustrator. Exh. 1938-40. Add: National College of Art, Kildare Street, Dublin. † RHA 8.

OSBORN, Evelyn Exh. 1892
Draycott Terrace, St. Ives, Cornwall. † L 1, M 3.

OSBORN, Emily Mary* b. 1834
Genre painter. Studied at Dickinson's Academy in Maddox Street. S.W.A. 1893. Exh. 1880-1913. Add: London. † B 22, D 1, G 7, GI 16, L 3, M 9, NG 16, P 7, RA 3, RBA 1, RHA 6, ROI 1, SWA 58.

OSBORN, J.R. Exh. 1935
Sidelands, North Leigh, Oxon. † RI 2.

OSBORN, Will E. Exh. 1886-1902
Landscape painter. Add: Rochdale 1886; Higher Broughton, Manchester 1893; St. Ives, Cornwall 1894; Exmouth, Devon 1898; Ludlow, Salop 1902. † L 4, M 5, RA 2, RBA 4, ROI 1.

OSBORNE, Arthur Exh. 1899
Sculptor. Add: 49 East Street, Faversham, Kent. † RA 3.

OSBORNE, A.B. Exh. 1905
19 Alfred Road, Birkenhead. † L 1.

OSBORNE, Mrs. Cherrie Exh. 1936
The Manse, Cockenzie. † RSA 1.

OSBORNE, Cecil Exh. 1930-38
Landscape and figure painter. † LEF 23, M 1, NEA 1.

OSBORNE, Mrs. Emily McEwen Exh. 1933
40 Warwick Avenue, London. † B 4.

OSBORNE, Frederick
See OSBORNE, Walter Frederick

OSBORNE, Mrs. Gladys Exh. 1937
Nottingham Street, London. † SWA 1.

OSBORNE, James Thomas Armour b. 1907
Painter, etcher, wood engraver and illustrator. Studied Hastings and Sussex Art School 1922-25, Royal College of Art 1925-30, and Rome 1931-32. Exh. 1936-40. Add: St. Leonards on Sea, Sussex. † RA 4, RBA 1.

OSBORNE, Kathleen M. Faussett Exh. 1930-40
Figure painter. Member London Group 1940. Add: Queendown Warren, nr. Sittingbourne, Kent 1930. † COO 1, NEA 1.

OSBORNE, Malcolm b. 1880
Etcher and engraver. b. Frome, Somerset. Studied Queens School of Art, Bristol and Royal College of Art. A.R.A. 1918, R.A. 1926, A.R.E. 1905, R.E. 1909, P.R.E. 1938. Exh. 1905-40. Add: London. † AB 2, BA 4, CHE 2, FIN 1, GI 10, I 1, L 19, LEI 6, RA 94, RE 116, RID 27, RSA 2.

OSBORNE, Margaret Exh. 1915-25
Hinton Firs, Manor Road, Bournemouth. † L 12, RA 2, RMS 1.

OSBORNE, Rex Exh. 1899-1920
Painter. Add: London. † RA 3.

OSBORNE, William* 1823-1901
Animal and portrait painter. Studied R.H.A. Schools 1845. Father of Walter F.O. q.v. A.R.H.A. 1854, R.H.A. 1868. Add: 5 Castlewood Avenue, Rathmines, Dublin. † B 29, GI 1, L 12, RHA 115.

OSBORNE, Walter Frederick 1859-1903
Landscape and portrait painter. Studied R.H.A. Schools and Antwerp Academy under Verlat. Son of William O. q.v. N.E.A. 1887, A.R.H.A. 1883, R.H.A. 1886, R.O.I. 1891. "Life in the Streets: Hard Times" purchased by Chantrey Bequest 1892. Add: Dublin 1880 and 1886; Wherwell, nr. Andover, Hants. 1885. † B 16, FIN 2, G 1, I 1, L 31, NEA 10, NG 2, RA 46, RHA 146, ROI 33, TOO 4.

OSCROFT, Grace Exh. 1930-34
Landscape painter. † LEF 16.

OSCROFT, Samuel William 1834-1924
Landscape painter and watercolourist. N.S.A. 1884 (Treas. 1881-98 and Hon. Sec. 1882-89). Add: Nottingham. † B 2, D 4, L 4, N 195, RA 4, RI 16.

O'SHEE, Miss G.P. Exh. 1891-99
Add: Piltown, Ireland 1891; Portlaw, Co. Waterford 1899. † B 3, L 3, M 2, NG 1, RHA 2.

OSKOTSKY, Isaac J. Exh. 1931
Pencil artist. Add: 350 Commercial Road, London. † RA 1.

OSLER, Frank Exh. 1930
Architect. Add: 28 Queensborough Terrace, London. † RA 2.

OSLUND, Elis Exh. 1906-7
London. † L 1, RA 2.

OSMAN, George F. Exh. 1930
63 Lottie Road, Selly Oak, Birmingham. † B 2.

OSMOND, Arthur James Exh. 1886
Sculptor. Add: 79 Clifton Street, Finsbury, London. † RBA 1.

OSMOND, Mrs. Constance M. Exh. 1930
Sculptor. Married to Edward O. q.v. Add: White Cottage, Highview, Pinner, Middlex. † RA 2.

OSMOND, Edward b. 1900
Painter and illustrator. b. Suffolk. Teacher Regent Street Polytechnic. Married Constance M.O. q.v. A.R.B.A. 1926. Exh. 1924-28. Add: London. † L 1, RA 4, RBA 6.

OSMOND, John Exh. 1881
Landscape painter. Add: The Priory, Lee Road, London. † RBA 1.

OSMOND, Robert b. 1874
Portrait painter, etcher, engraver, illustrator and teacher. Exh. 1922-40. Add: London. † RA 25.

OSMOND, Sandals F.G. Exh. 1938
Sculptor. Add: 75 Idmiston Square, Worcester Park. † GI 1, RA 1.

OSOSKI, Gerald Judah b. 1903
Portrait, landscape and decorative painter and teacher. b. London. Studied St. Martins School of Art and Royal College of Art. Exh. 1926-29. Add: London. † GOU 5, NEA 3.

OSPALAK, Alfred A. Exh. 1936-37
Architect. Add: 13 Old Queen Street, London. † RA 2.

OSPALAK, David Exh. 1936-37
Architect. Add: 13 Old Queen Street, London. † RA 2.

OSPOVAT, Henry 1877-1909
Portrait painter, caricaturist and black and white artist. Add: London. † BG 189, I 1, NEA 2.

OSPREY, Gerard Exh. 1913
26 Rue Geoffrey L'Asnier, Paris. † LS 3.

OSS, Van See V

OSSANI, Allesandro* Exh. 1880-88
Portrait and genre painter. Add: London. † G 1, RA 7, RBA 2.

OSTELL, Mary M. Exh. 1893-1901
Painter. Add: London. † RI 3, SWA 7.

OSTERLIND, Allan* Exh. 1906
Figure painter. Add: 21 Boulevard du Chateau, Neuilly sur Seine, France. † L 1.

OSTERMAN, Bernhard b. 1870
Swedish artist. Exh. 1912-25. Add: Paris 1912; Stockholm 1925. † L 2.

OSTERMAN, Emil b. 1870
Swedish artist. Exh. 1912. Add: Fredrikshofg 4, Stockholm. † RA 1.

OSTREHAN, Mrs. E. Exh. 1906
97 Kenilworth Court, Putney, London. † RA 2.

OSTREHAN, George Exh. 1890-1903
Painter and stained glass artist. Add: London 1890; Sunbury on Thames, Middlesex 1899. † DOW 1, M 1, RA 6, RBA 1.

O'SULLIVAN, Mrs. Amy Exh. 1905-26
Married to Patrick O'S. q.v. Add: Dublin. † RHA 16.

O'SULLIVAN, Col. G.H.W. Exh. 1919-21
7 Adam Street, Adelphi, London. † LS 6.

O'SULLIVAN, James Exh. 1923-27
29 Leinster Road, Rathmines, Dublin. † RHA 5.

O'SULLIVAN, John or Jack A. Exh. 1924-36
Portrait and still life painter and pastellier. Add: Dublin 1924; Walmer, Sutton 1933. † RHA 17.

O'SULLIVAN, Michael Exh. 1933
Sculptor. Add: 15 Hartlands Road, Cork. † RHA 1.

O'SULLIVAN, Patrick Exh. 1900-14
Married to Amy O'S. q.v. Add: London 1900; Dublin 1905. † RHA 13.

O'SULLIVAN, Sean* d. 1964
Portrait painter and teacher at the School of Art, Dublin. A.R.H.A. 1928, R.H.A. 1931. Exh. 1926-40. Add: Dublin. † RHA 106, RSA 1.

OSWALD, C.W. Exh. 1892
258 Whitefield Road, Liverpool. † L 1.

OSWALD, John H.* Exh. 1880-99
Landscape painter. Add: 28 London Street, Edinburgh. † GI 32, L 5, M 7, RA 5, RHA 6, RI 2, ROI 1, RSA 82, RSW 1.

OSWALD, Miss Mary Exh. 1888-1905
28 London Street, Edinburgh. † GI 9, RSA 41.

OSWALD, Margaret M. Exh. 1930-37
Prestatyn, Wales. † RCA 11.

OTTEWELL, Benjamin John d. 1937
Watercolour landscape painter. H.R.I. 1895. Add: Wimbledon 1884 and 1891; East Burnham, Slough, Bucks. 1890. † G 2, L 1, NG 10, RA 4, RBA 1, RHA 1, RI 21.

OTTMANN, Miss Exh. 1896
Hopetown House, N.B. † SWA 1.

OTTMANN, Henri* 1877-1927
French painter. Exh. 1924-25. † GOU 4.

OTTOLINI, Mrs. Raquel Exh. 1936
† SWA 2.

OTWAY, J. Exh. 1888
Figure painter. Add: Waterford, Cork. † G 1.

OUDERAA, van der See V

OUGH, Ellenor S. Exh. 1906-10
428 High Road, Streatham Common, London. † L 2, SWA 4.

OULD, E.A. Exh. 1883
Architect. Add: 24 Newgate Street, Chester. † RA 1.

OULD, F. Exh. 1891
31 Grange Mount, Birkenhead. † L 3.

OULESS, Catherine b. 1879
Landscape and portrait painter. Studied R.A. Schools. Daughter of Walter W.O. q.v. A.S.W.A. 1906. Exh. 1902-37. Add: London. † B 4, L 5, M 1, RA 56, SWA 5, WG 215.

OULESS, Walter William 1848-1933
Portrait and figure painter. b. St. Helier, Jersey. Son of Philip J.O. (1817-1885). Father of Catherine O. q.v. Studied R.A. Schools 1865-69. A.R.A. 1877, R.A. 1881. Add: London. † AG 1, B 8, GI 6, L 3, M 6, P 6, RA 197, RSA 3.

OULETT, Jessie J. Exh. 1887
Figure painter. Add: 1 Norfolk Terrace, Willesden, London. † ROI 1.

OULSNAM, Howard Exh. 1915-16
Add: 57 Oakwood Road, Hampstead Garden Suburb, London. † L 1, RSA 1.

OULTON, W.H.S. Exh. 1899
5 West Albert Road, Liverpool. † L 1.

OUSEY, Buckley d. 1889
Coastal and figure painter. Add: Conway, Wales 1884; Kensington, London 1889. † L 9, M 3, RA 1, RBA 1, RCA 12, ROI 1.

OUSTON, Miss E.M. Exh. 1935-37
6 Berwyn Road, Richmond, Surrey † NEA 1, RBA 2.

OUTHWAITE, Ida Rentoul Exh. 1920
Figure and imaginative artist. † FIN 66.

OUTLAW, Arthur Exh. 1920
† P 1.

OUTRAM, George Exh. 1907
253 Crookesmoor Road, Sheffield. † L 1.

OUTRAM, W.H. Exh. 1884-1903
Add: Formby, Lancs. 1884; Huyton, Lancs. 1890; Freshfield, Liverpool 1892. † B 1, L 28, RCA 1.

OUTRIM, Emily Alice Exh. 1885-1912
Landscape painter. Add: Tunbridge Wells, Kent. † LS 6, SWA 3.

OVENDEN, Rev. Charles T. Exh. 1882-1902
Add: Dublin 1882; Enniskillen 1888. † RHA 16.

OVENS, W. Roberts Exh. 1927-40
Add: Knowle. Blackhall 1927; Edinburgh 1938. † RSA 1, RSW 3.

OVEREND, William Heysham 1851-1898
Marine painter. Worked for the Illustrated London News. R.O.I. 1886. Add: London. † D 1, GI 2, L 1, RA 9, ROI 5.

OVERTON, Dorothea G. Exh. 1927-28
408 London Road, Lowestoft, Suffolk. † L 5.

OVERWEG, Lily Exh. 1897-98
Portrait painter. Add: 9 Rue Campagne, Paris. † RA 2.

OVEY, Ada Exh. 1890-93
49 Halliwell Lane, Cheetham Hill, Manchester. † M 5.

OVEY, Margaret Exh. 1937
Landscape and figure painter. † COO 3.

OVINGTON-JONES, Miss M. Exh. 1916-23
Cleadon Lodge, Park Road, Hampton Hill. † RA 2, RI 1.

OWDEN, Mrs. Exh. 1923
Sandpits, Powick, Worcs. † B 1.

OWEN, Arthur Exh. 1912
40 Cavendish Street, All Saints, Manchester. † L 1.

OWEN, Miss A.H. Exh. 1895-1910
Add: Oxton, Birkenhead 1895; Liverpool 1901; London 1908. † L 10, M 1, RA 1.

OWEN, Barbara Exh. 1934
Miniature portrait painter. Add: 20 Wren Avenue, Cricklewood, London. † RA 1.

OWEN, Bernard b. 1886
Miniature painter and pastel artist. Studied Crystal Palace. Exh. 1916-35. Add: London 1916; Brighton 1932; Hove 1935. † RA 9, RHA 1.

OWEN, C.A. Exh. 1901
29 Molesworth Street, Dublin. † RHA 1.

OWEN, D.G. Exh. 1885-92
The Polygon, Eccles, Lancs. † M 2.

OWEN, Gladys Exh. 1924-29
Watercolour landscape painter. Add: London 1924; Kettering, Northants. 1927. † L 4, RI 1, SWA 6, WG 44.

OWEN, G. Elmslie 1899-1964
Painter and engraver. Studied Edinburgh College of Art 1921-23, L'Academie Moderne, Paris 1923-25. R.B.A. 1934. Add: London. † GI 3, NEA 2, RA 1, RBA 19, RHA 1, RSA 3.

OWEN, G.J. Exh. 1887
107 Buchanan Street, Glasgow. † GI 1.

OWEN, G.O. Exh. 1887-1912
R.B.S.A. 1898. Add: Birmingham 1887; Ashton under Hill, Tewkesbury 1899; Old Trafford, Manchester 1910. † B 43, L 2, RI 1.

OWEN, Harold Exh. 1931-33
Figure painter. Add: Reading, Berks. 1931; Ipsden, Oxford 1933. † RA 2.

OWEN, Helen D. Exh. 1935-36
46 Lavender Avenue, London. † SWA 2.

OWEN, H.J. Exh. 1928
Watercolour painter. † AB 20.

OWEN, H.W. Exh. 1916
39 Red Post Hill, Herne Hill, London. † RA 1.

OWEN, Joseph Exh. 1927-33
71 Urban Road, Sale, Cheshire. † L 1, RCA 3.

OWEN, John Carter Exh. 1920
The Old Hall, Halkyn, Holywell, N. Wales. † RCA 1.

OWEN, John J. Exh. 1883-84
10 Corunna Street, Glasgow. † GI 2.

OWEN, K. Exh. 1884
Painter. Add: c/o 203 Albany Street, London. † SWA 1.

OWEN, Mona Exh. 1919
† L 2.

OWEN, Muriel Ethel b. 1906
Painter. Studied at Liverpool University. Exh. 1925-32. Add: 41 Arundel Avenue, Liverpool. † L 10.

OWEN, Rowland Exh. 1938
Landscape painter. Add: 18 Derby Road, Borrowash, Derbys. † N 3.

OWEN, R. Wynn Exh. 1901-2
Liverpool. † L 2.

OWEN, Sam Exh. 1937
Marine painter. † CON 1.

OWEN, Mrs. Susan H.R.
Edgbaston Vicarage, Birmingham. † B 3.

OWEN, Will 1869-1957
Black and white and poster artist and illustrater. b. Malta. Studied Lambeth School of Art. Add: Richmond, Surrey 1907; London 1923. † BK 100, RCA 12.

OWEN, William Exh. 1891-93
Architect. Add: Cairo Street Chambers, Warrington, Lancs. † L 3, RA 1.

OWEN, W.H. Exh. 1929
51 Belmont Road, Anfield, Liverpool. † L 1.

OWENS, Mrs. Exh. 1914
Worcester Park, Surrey. † SWA 1.

OWER, Charles Exh. 1938-39
Add: Dundee 1938; Lochee 1939. † RSA 2.

OWLES, Alice J. Exh. 1904
Penshurst, Kent and London. † B 2, SWA 2.

OWTRAM, Robert Lancelot
Exh. 1892-1913
Portrait, figure and flower painter. Add: Beckenham, Kent 1892; London 1901; Woking, Surrey 1906. † B 3, FIN 1, RA 10.

OXENFORD, Caroline Exh. 1910-12
16 Westbourne Gardens, Hove, Sussex. † LS 9.

OXLEY, Freda K. Exh. 1909-11
4 High Street, Windsor, Berks. † L 1, LS 6.

OXLEY, Hylton R. Exh. 1933
Architect. Add: 196 Hedge Lane, Palmers Green, London. † RA 1.

OXLEY, Miss M.E. Exh. 1920-25
9 Montrell Road, Streatham Hill, London. † RI 4, SWA 5.

OXLEY, Thomas D. Exh. 1935
Architect. Add: 10 Bishopsthorpe Road, Sydenham, Kent. † RA 1.

OXTON, Florence Exh. 1904-32
Liverpool. † L 9.

OXTON, Harris Exh. 1886-1930
Add: Liverpool 1886; Birkenhead 1926. † L 23, RCA 3.

OYENS, David 1842-1902
Exh. 1886. Add: 116 New Bond Street, London. † M 2.

OYLER, Mrs. Elsa G. Exh. 1929
Flower painter. Add: Woodgreen, Salisbury, Wilts. † RA 1.

OYLER, Judith Audrey Allenby
Exh. 1936-38
Watercolour painter. b. Wynchbold, Worcs. Studied Grimsby School of Art and Leicester College of Art. Add: Lincoln 1936; Kingskerwell, Devon 1937. † RI 3, SWA 3.

OYSTON, George Exh. 1891-97
Landscape painter. Add: London 1891; Shepperton on Thames 1897. † RBA 1, RI 1.

OYSTON, G. Dean Exh. 1925-37
106 Wychall Lane, Kings Norton, Birmingham. † B 7.

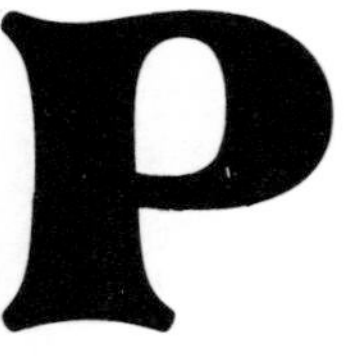

PACANOWSKA, Felicta Exh. 1935-38
Figure and portrait artist. † RED 6.

PACE, Ion Exh. 1880-96
Stained glass artist. Add: 2 Duke Street, Adelphi, London. † RA 12.

PACE, Percy Currall Exh. 1898-1936
Landscape, portrait and still life painter. b. Sutton, Surrey. Studied Antwerp Academy. Add: Loxwood, nr. Billingshurst, Sussex 1898; Steyning, Sussex 1926. † GOU 1, L 3, LS 6, RA 8, RBA 3, ROI 2.

PACEY, Doris E. Exh. 1922-33
9 Cranmer Grove, Nottingham. † L 1, N 2.

PACEY, Jean E. Exh. 1937
Landscape painter. Add: c/o T.R. Smith, 16 Bottle Lane, Nottingham. † N 1.

PACEY, Philip H.P. Exh. 1920
36 Shirley Road, Acocks Green, Birmingham. † B 2.

PACKARD, Sir Edward b. 1843
Painter. b. Saxmundham, Suffolk. Studied British Museum and Ipswich School of Art. Exh. 1880. Add: Ipswich. † D 1.

PACKARD, Sylvia E. Exh. 1909-28
Landscape painter. Daughter of Sir Edward P. q.v. Add: London 1909; Godalming, Surrey 1910; Bath 1916; Bramford, nr. Ipswich, Suffolk 1920. † I 3, NEA 7, SWA 5.

PACKE, Mary Exh. 1929-35
Mrs. William P. Add: Bromley Common, Kent. † RMS 2, SWA 2.

PACKER, Elizabeth Exh. 1888-89
Portrait painter. Add: 2 Goodwin Street, Nottingham. † N 2.

PACKER, H. Exh. 1900
Castle Chambers, Hounds Gate, Nottingham. † N 2.

PACKER, L. Exh. 1928
Landscape painter. † AB 2.

PADBURY, Miss J. Exh. 1908
Streatham, London. † SWA 1.

PADDAY, Alice Exh. 1909-25
Add: London 1909; Bexhill, Sussex 1922. † B 3, L 6, LS 6, ROI 2, SWA 12.

PADDAY, Charles Murray* Exh. 1890-1937
Landscape, coastal and marine painter. R.I. 1929, R.O.I. 1906. Add: London 1890; Bosham, Sussex 1895; Hayling Island, Hants 1908; Hythe, Kent 1919; Folkestone, Kent 1928. † L 7, RA 33, RBA 8, RI 6, ROI 2.

PADDISON, Lucy Exh. 1900
Newton on Trent, Newark, Notts. † SWA 1.

PADDOCK, William Exh. 1892-1920
Flower painter. Add: Glasgow. † BG 5, GI 14, P 1, RA 3, RSA 2, RSW 3.

PADGETT, Horace Exh. 1908
18 Royds Hall Terrace, Whitehall, Leeds. † RA 1.

PADGETT, William 1851-1904
Landscape painter. Add: Twickenham, Middlesex 1881; London 1882. † G 8, GI 15, I 1, L 27, M 11 NG 50, RA 14, RBA 8, RID 22, ROI 18.

PADWICK, Philip Hugh* b. 1876
Landscape painter. b. Horsham, Sussex. Studied Slade School. R.B.A. 1908, R.O.I. 1927. Exh. 1908-40. Add: Fittleworth, Sussex. † BAR 42, CHE 2, FIN 51, I 15, NEA 6, RA 35, RBA 104, RCA 2, RID 16, RHA 13, ROI 43, RSA 11, WG 41.

PAGANI, Luigi Exh. 1880
Sculptor. Add: Milan. † RA 1.

PAGE, Alfred H. Exh. 1930-31
† RMS 2.

PAGE, Amy M. Exh. 1895-1902
Add: Edgbaston, Birmingham 1895; Pershore, Worcs. 1902. † B 2.

PAGE, A.P. Exh. 1916
Rose Cottage, Park Road, Chilwell, Notts. † N 1.

PAGE, C.W. Exh. 1934-39
Add: Luton, Beds. 1934; Harpenden, Herts. 1936. † B 8.

PAGE, Eleanor B. Exh. 1892-1926
Landscape and flower painter and teacher. Add: Liverpool. † L 27.

PAGE, Florence W. Exh. 1927
Mrs. Green. Painter and etcher. Add: Holmbury, Stoneham Common, Bassett, Southampton. † RA 1.

PAGE, Grace Exh. 1934
London. † RCA 1.

PAGE, George Gordon Exh. 1880
Architect. Add: 4 Gt. James Street, Bedford Row, London. † RA 1.

PAGE, Graham Seaton Dudley b. 1905
Portrait and landscape painter. Engraver and humorous illustrator. Studied Slade School. Exh. 1936-40. Add: Gaywood Road, Kings Lynn, Norfolk. † RA 2.

PAGE, Henry Exh. 1881-92
Painter and sculptor. Add: London. † D 3, L 2, RA 11, RBA 2.

PAGE, Mrs. Helen Alice b. 1886
nee Holderness. Painter and decorative artist. b. Eastbourne. Studied Slade School (Frederick Ward Prizeman and Nettleship Prizeman). Exh. 1933-35. Add: 134 Harley Street, London. † RA 1, RBA 5.

PAGE, Henry Maurice* Exh. 1880-95
Landscape and animal painter. Add: London 1880; West Croydon 1887; Sandwich, Kent 1893. † M 7, RA 10, RBA 50, ROI 3, TOO 5.

PAGE, Henry W. Exh. 1902-13
Medalist. Add: London. † L 1, RA 5.

PAGE, Jane L. Exh. 1889
2 Royal Terrace, Portobello, Edinburgh. † RSA 1.

PAGE, L. Exh. 1919-23
162 Mansfield Street, Sherwood, Nottingham. † N 9.

PAGE, Margaret Exh. 1904
Painter. Add: 4 Garden Studios, Manresa Road, Chelsea, London. † RA 1.

PAGE, Pearl Exh. 1921-33
2 Kings Mount, Oxton, Birkenhead. † L 29, RCA 11.

PAGE, Robert Exh. 1881-90
Landscape and rustic genre painter. Add: Gt. Clacton, Essex. † L 9, RA 11, RBA 3, ROI 5.

PAGE, Richard Charles 1849-1883
Architect. Exh. 1880. Add: London. † RA 1.

PAGE, Sara Exh. 1892-1935
Portrait and figure painter. Add: Wolverhampton and Paris 1892; Neuilly, Seine, France 1901 and 1921; Purley, Surrey 1915. † B 7, L 15, RA 10.

PAGE, Theodore Exh. 1882
Greenfield Road, Birmingham. † B 1.

PAGE, William M. Exh. 1900-1
7 Hermand Terrace, Edinburgh. † RSA 2.

PAGET, Arthur Exh. 1896
58 Queen Anne Street, London. † NG 1.

PAGET, Claude Exh. 1890
1 Sherwood Place, London. † D 1.

PAGET, Elise Exh. 1880-89
Watercolour landscape and figure painter. Add: Pinner, Middlesex 1880; Westbourne Park, London 1885. † B 5, D 2, FIN 1, G 1, GI 1, L 5, RA 1, RBA 7, RHA 2, RI 6, SWA 4.

PAGET, Harry Exh. 1922-23
† G 2.

PAGET, Commander H.E.C. Exh. 1922
Watercolour landscape painter. † FIN 53.

PAGET, Mrs. H.M. Exh. 1882-1907
Figure painter. Add: London. † B 1, G 2, GI 4, L 2, RA 3.

PAGET, Henry Marriott 1856-1936
Portrait and figure painter and illustrator. Brother of Sidney and Walter Stanley P. q.v R.B.A. 1889. Add: London. † B 2, FIN 1, G 3, GI 9, L 6, M 4, RA 24, RBA 1, ROI 1.

PAGET, Sidney* 1861-1908
Painter and illustrator. On staff of the 'Illustrated London News' and the 'Sphere'. Illustrated "Sherlock Holmes". Brother of Henry Marriott and Walter Stanley P. q.v. Add: London 1880 and 1902; Chipperfield, Kings Langley, Herts. 1899. † D 1, L 8, M 2, NG 1, RA 17, RBA 2, ROI 7.

PAGET, Thomas Humphrey b. 1893
Sculptor and medallist. b. Croxley Green, Herts. Son of Walter Stanley P. q.v. Studied R.A. Schools (Landseer scholarship). Teacher of modelling at the L.C.C. Central School of Arts and Crafts from 1913. Exh. 1920-40. Add: London. † G 1, L 1, RA 14.

PAGET, Walter Stanley 1863-1935
Painter and illustrator. Brother of Henry Marriott and Sidney and father of Thomas Humphrey P. q.v. Add: London. † G 5, L 1, M 2, NG 3, RA 5, RBA 1, ROI 1.

PAGET-KEMP, Miss L.G. Exh. 1903
35 Cranwick Road, Stamford Hill, London. † SWA 1.

PAGUENEAU, Jean Exh. 1904
c/o Col. W. Rainsford, St. Catherine's, Borstal Road, Rochester, Kent. † D 1.

PAICE, Bowes A. Exh. 1883
Architect. Add: 9 George Street, Hanover Square London. † RA 1.

PAICE, George Exh. 1881-97
Landscape figure and still life painter. Father of Philip Stuart P. q.v. Add: Pimlico, London 1881; Croydon, Surrey 1892. † RA 7, RBA 4.

PAICE, Philip Stuart 1884-1940
Painter. b. London. Son of George P. q.v. Studied Heatherleys and R.A. Schools 1905-10 (Landseer scholarship). Art master Denver Colorado U.S.A. and art master Birkenhead Institute. Exh. 1922-38. Add: Birkenhead. † L 20, RA 1, RCA 23.

PAIGE, C. Willis Exh. 1933-37
Etcher. Add: Bristol. † RA 4.

PAILLARD, Henri 1844-1912
French artist. Exh. 1910. Add: 13 Avenue Frochot, Paris. † L 1.

PAIN, F.G. Exh 1908
120 Holland Road, Brixton, London. † RA 1.

PAIN, Mrs. H.E.S. Exh. 1913
Ryll Court, Exmouth. † RA 1.

PAINE, Miss Beatrice Exh. 1901-14
A.S.W.A. 1910. Add: 30 Farquhar Road, Upper Norwood, London. † B 7, D 4, RI 1, SWA 30.

PAINE, C. Exh. 1916
11 North View, Brentham, Ealing, London. † RA 1.

PAINE, Edith A. Exh. 1883-85
Landscape painter. Add: 36 Gloucester Crescent, Hyde Park London. † G 2.

PAINE, G.H. Exh. 1916
62 Moorgate Street, London. † RA 1.

PAINE, Mrs. Mary M. Exh. 1906-20
30 Farquahar Road, Upper Norwood, London. † B 1, SWA 14.

PAINE, Ruth Iwerne Exh. 1900
c/o A. Frampton, 3 Copthall Buildings, London. † RBA 1.

PAINTER, Elizabeth Exh. 1937
† P 1.

PAIRMAN, J.R. Exh. 1884
Samiston Lodge, Portobello, Edinburgh. † RSA 1.

PAIRPONT, Nellie M. Exh. 1897-1914
Animal painter. Add: 139 Stockwell Park Road, Brixton, London 1897; Croydon, Surre, 1913. † LS 6, RA 2.

PAKENHAM, E. Joy Exh 1924-40
Portrait, landscape and flower painter. b. Chelmsford. Studied Birmingham and under Stanhope Forbes. Add: Eccleshall, Staffs. 1924; Lichfield, Staffs. 1939. † B 14, COO 5, RA 3, RBA 2, RI 6.

PAKINGTON, E.N.F. Exh. 1884
6 Eaton Terrace, London. † D 1.

PAKINGTON, Hon. H.P.M. Exh. 1888-91
Landscape painter. Add: 76 Elm Park Gardens, London. † B 1, RA 3.

PALETHORPE, Mary Cox Exh. 1887-1916
Figure and landscape painter. Add: Liverpool. † B 16, L 63, M 3, RA 2.

PALHAM, T.K. Exh. 1889
14 St. Peter's Square, Hammersmith, London. † B 1.

PALIN, Mrs. M. Exh. 1896
No. 1 Studio, Campden Hill Road, London. † L 1.

PALIN, William Mainwaring b. 1862
Painter and decorator. b. Hanley, Staffs. Worked 5 years with Wedgwood and Son before studying at the Royal College of Art, Italy and Paris. R.B.A. 1905, V.P.R.B.A. 1914 (Hon. Sec. 1911-13). Add: Burslem, Staffs. 1887; London 1889 and 1896; Milford, Surrey 1892. † I 3, L 7, LS 1, P 4, RA 44, RBA 63, ROI 2.

PALLANDRE, A. Exh. 1910
5 Bis Rue Saint Sophie, Versailles, France. † L 1.

PALLIS, Andrea Exh. 1928
Neston, nr. Birkenhead. † L 5.

PALLISER, Herbert William b. 1883
Sculptor. b. Northallerton, Yorks. Studied Slade School. Exh. 1921-40. Add: London. † GI 1, L 1, NEA 1, RA 10.

PALMER, A. Exh. 1934
18 Prince of Wales Terrace, London. † SWA 1.

PALMER, Alfred 1877-1951
Painter, sculptor and illustrator. Studied R.A. Schools and Juliens, Paris. R.B.A. 1912, R.O.I. 1922. Add: Sandwich, Kent 1903; London 1904; Fordwich, nr. Canterbury, Kent 1911. † L 12, NEA 1, RA 7, RBA 31, RHA 2, RI 6, ROI 52.

PALMER, Ada M. Exh. 1884-87
Sculptor. Add: Turnour's Hall, Chigwell, Essex. † RA 4, RBA 1.

PALMER, C.A. Exh. 1908-13
Sculptor. Add: 14A Cheyne Row, London. † I 1, L 1, LS 5, RA 9, RSA 1.

PALMER, Dorothea Exh. 1884-87
Landscape and flower painter. Add: The Avenue, Datchet, Windsor, Berks. † L 1, SWA 5.

PALMER, Mrs. Eleanor Annie b. 1867
nee Sharpin Watercolour portrait painter and miniaturist. b. Bedford. Studied Slade School. A.R.M.S. 1906, R.M.S. 1910. Mother of Joan P. q.v. Add: Bedford 1887 and 1917; Altrincham, Cheshire 1902; Bowden, Cheshire 1920. † D 3, L 11, M 16, NG 1, RA 22 RMS 80.

PALMER, Mrs. Emmeline A. Exh. 1900-11
Miniature portrait painter. Add: Watford, Herts. 1900; Bushey, Herts. 1911. † RA 3.

PALMER, Mrs. Ellen B. Exh. 1935-40
Alkerton House, Leamington, Warwicks. † B 6.

PALMER, Fred A.H. Exh. 1913-14
3 Marlborough Studios, Finchley Road, London. † LS 2.

PALMER, Gerald Exh. 1909-27
Watercolour landscape painter. Add: Corbridge on Tyne 1911; London 1927. † LS 1, RA 3, RBA 2, WG 53.

PALMER, Gertrude Exh. 1884-85
Landscape painter. Add: 4 Merridale Lane, Wolverhampton. † B 2, M 1, RBA 1, SWA 1.

PALMER, H. Maurice Exh. 1922-24
20 Speedwell Road, Claughton, Birkenhead. † L 4.

PALMER, Harry Sutton* 1854-1933
Landscape painter and watercolourist. b. Plymouth. R.B.A. 1892, R.I. 1920. Add: London. † AG 5, BK 5, CON 2, D 1, DOW 382, FIN 517, G 1, L 19, LEI 303, M 30, RA 33, RBA 15, RI 25, WG 6.

PALMER, H.W.H. Exh. 1911
The Outer Temple, 222 Strand, London. † RA 2.

PALMER, Miss Joan Exh. 1927
Daughter of Eleanor Annie P. q.v. Add: The Lymes, Priory Road, Bowden, Cheshire. † L 1.

PALMER, John Exh. 1887
Interior painter. Add: Holbrook Villa, 33 Finchley Road, London. † RA 1.

PALMER, John W. Exh. 1899
Figure painter. Add: 23 Cressida Road, Highgate London. † RA 2.

PALMER, Lynwood* Exh. 1910-17
Animal and portrait painter. b. Linwood, Lincs. R.O.I. 1917. Add: Heston, Middlesex. † L 3, ROI 2.

PALMER, Miss L.R. Exh. 1896-1912
6 Second Avenue, Sherwood Rise, Nottingham. † N 32.

PALMER, Miss M. Exh. 1920
Sullington Rectory, Pulborough, Sussex. † SWA 2.

PALMER, Maud C. See FORBES

PALMER, Nancy Felix Exh. 1903-16
Add: Datchet, nr. Windsor, Berks. 1903 and 1916; Wareham, Dorset 1910. † B 1, RI 6, SWA 14.

PALMER, Philip Evans b. 1898
Architect, furniture designer and interior decorator. b. Kettering, Northants. Studied Eastbourne and London. Exh. 1929-32. Add: Welwyn Garden City, Herts. † RA 4.

PALMER, R. Exh. 1929-30
Landscape painter. Add: Ilkeston, Derbys. † N 3.

PALMER, Richard Alfred Field Exh. 1908-11
c/o Allied Artists Association, 67 Chancery Lane, London. † LS 9.

PALMER, Samuel* 1805-1881
Landscape painter, etcher and illustrator. A.R.W.S. 1843, R.W.S. 1854. Add: Redhill, Surrey 1880. † FIN 13, RWS 3.

PALMER, Susan b. 1912
Figure painter and stage designer. Exh. 1935-38. † BA 1, COO 20.

PALMER, William Exh. 1883-89
Landscape painter. Add: 49 Wellington Road, St. John's Wood, London. † L 2, RA 2.

PALMER, William James Exh. 1882-94
Landscape and genre painter. Add: London 1882; Farnborough, Kent 1894. † D 2, RA 2, RI 6.

PALMER-JONES, William John b. 1887
Painter and architect. b. Hartford, Hunts. Studied A.A. and Central School of Arts and Crafts. Exh. 1912-38. Add: London. † L 3, RA 16.

PALSER, Albert Exh. 1911
Architect. Add: The White House, Cannon Road, Southgate, London. † RA 1.

PANATI, Carlo Exh. 1887-95
Sculptor. Add: London 1887; Rome 1895. † RA 2.

PANE, J.G. Exh. 1884
47 Addison Road, Kensington, London. † D 1.

PANERAI, R. Exh. 1884
6 Haymarket, London. † M 1.

PANKHURST, E. Sylvia Exh. 1903-4
Painter. Add: 30 King Street, Manchester. † L 1, M 1.

PANN, Abel* b. 1883
Painter and lithographer. b. Russia. Exh. 1935-38. † FIN 153.

PANNELL, Charles L.W. Exh. 1927-40
Landscape painter. Add: Birmingham. † B 31, RA 1.

PANNELL, Lillie Exh. 1906-22
Miniature portrait painter. Add: Tooting Common, London. † L 1, P 2, RA 11.

PANT, Miss K. Exh. 1938
28 Elvetham Road, Edgbaston, Birmingham. † B 1.

PANT, van der See V

PANTON, Alexander Exh. 1880-88
Landscape painter. Add: Fitzroy Street, London. † B 1, L 1, RA 5, RBA 10.

PANTON, Lawrence A.C. 1894-1954
Painter. b. Egremont, Cheshire. Studied Ontario College of Art, Canada. Exh. 1933. † RSW 4.

PANUNZI, S. Exh. 1894
c/o M. Ciardiello, 53 Moscow Road, Pembridge Square, London. † M 1.

PAOLETTI, Antonio Ermolao* 1834-1912
Italian painter. Exh. 1886-1901. Add: Venice. † L 6, M 3, RA 4, RBA 1, RI 1, ROI 3.

PAOLETTI, Rodolfo b. 1866
Italian painter. Exh. 1891 † DOW 1.

PAOLETTI, Silvio N. Exh. 1890-92
Add: 25 Queen Anne Street, London 1890; c/o R. Blakeston, 5 Midland Terrace, nr. Liverpool. † M 1, RI 1, ROI 1.

PAPE, Frank Cheyne Exh. 1908
78 Deodar Road, Putney, London. † L 1.

PAPE, William Exh. 1892
Architect. Add: Air Street, Leeds. † RA 4.

PAPENDRECHT, Van See V

PAPILLON, J.W. Exh. 1899
Manor House, Kingscliffe, Wansford. † L 1.

PAPPERITZ, Georg* 1846-1918
German portrait painter. Exh. 1886-88. Add: c/o H. Frank 2 Vere Street, London 1886; Munich, Germany 1888. † RA 2.

PAPWORTH, A.W. Exh. 1910
Town Hall Chambers, Old Street, London. † RA 1

PAPWORTH, Edgar George junr. b. 1832
Sculptor. Son of Edgar George P. senr. (1809-1866). Studied R.A. Schools 1848. Exh. 1880-89. Add: London 1880; Manchester 1884. † G 1, M 8, RA 1.

PARBURY, Oliver b. 1887
Painter and gilder. b. Pembroke. Studied Crewe, Warrington and Holland. Exh. 1924. Add: 1 Grant Street, Farnworth, Bolton, Lancs. † RCA 1.

PARDOE, Elsie E. Exh. 1893-97
Woodlands, Rookery Road, Handsworth, Birmingham. † B 6.

PARE, David b. 1911
Landscape and portrait painter. Studied Nottingham College of Art 1932-36 and Slade School 1936-38. Exh. 1933-39. Add: 8 Premier Road, Nottingham. † N 20, NEA 1, RA 3, ROI 1.

PAREDES, Vicenta Exh. 1886
Historical painter. Add: 74 Rue D'Amsterdam, Paris. † L 3.

PARFITT, T.W. Exh. 1914-15
104 Belmont Street, Haverstock Hill, London. † RA 3.

PARGETER, Mrs. Constance Exh. 1925-32
Sculptor. Add: 12 Kensington Park Road, London. † RA 5, WG 3.

PARIS, de See D

PARIS, Alexander Exh. 1932
10 Provost Road, Linlithgow. † RSA 2.

PARIS, Auguste Exh. 1905
122 Avenue d'Orleans, Paris. † L 1.

PARIS, Walter Exh. 1880-91
Watercolour landscape painter. Travelled widely. Add: Bloomsbury, London 1880; Woolwich 1887; Blackheath 1888. † D 5, NG 1, RBA 6, RI 7.

PARISANI, Count Napoleone b. 1854
Italian landscape painter. Exh. 1890-1906. Add: Rome. † NG 8.

PARISH, Ada Exh. 1887
Painter. Add: 66 Grove Lane, Camberwell, London. † SWA 1.

PARISH, Eleanor Exh. 1880-81
Carlton Villa, Barclay Road, Fulham, London. † RHA 4.

PARISH, Emmie Frances Exh. 1899-1928
The Hollies, Halesowen, Cheshire. † B 8.

PARISH, Miss L.J. Exh. 1902
Nether Exe, 10 Denmark Road, Reading, Berks. † SWA 1.

PARK, Andrew Exh. 1909
152 George Street, Paisley. † L 2.

PARK, Carlon Moore b. 1876
Painter and illustrator. Studied Glasgow School of Art. R.B.A. 1902. Exh. 1897-1910. Add: Glasgow 1897; Chelsea, London 1901. † BG 91, GI 4, I 4, L 2, NEA 1, RA 1, RBA 15.

PARK, Charles R. Exh. 1897
Miniature portrait painter. Add: 159 Haverstock Hill, London. † RA,1.

PARK, D.S. Exh. 1886
101 St. Vincent Street, Glasgow. † GI 1.

PARK, Francis E. Exh. 1937
Loseberry, Elie, Fife. † RSA 1.

PARK, George H. Exh. 1881-87
6 Shandwick Place, Edinburgh. † GI 3, RHA 1, RSA 17.

PARK, H. Morley Exh. 1884-95
Colombrano, 19 Clarendon Road, Redland, Bristol. † B 1, GI 2.

PARK, John d. 1919
Etcher. A.R.E. 1898. Exh. 1885. Add: 7 Waterville Terrace, South Shields. † RA 1.

PARK, John Anthony 188-1962
Landscape and marine painter. b. Preston, Lancs. Studied Paris under Julius Olsson. R.B.A. 1934, R.O.I. 1923. "Snow Falls on Exmoor" purchased by Chantrey Bequest 1940. Add: Preston 1901 and 1919; St. Ives, Cornwall 1905, 1923 and 1939; London 1934; Dedham, Essex 1937. † G 1, L 10, M 2, NEA 1, RA 48, RBA 27, RHA 1, ROI 63.

PARK, James Chalmers b. 1858
Painter and etcher. b. Wetherby, Yorks. Studied Leeds School of Art. Exh. 1910 and 1930. Add: Leeds. † B 2, L 2.

PARK, J.R.S. Exh. 1915-39
Landscape and coastal painter. A.N.S.A. 1915, N.S.A. 1917, V.P.N.S.A. 1918-19. Chairman of Council N.S.A. 1920-23. Add: Nottingham 1915; Goathland, Yorks. 1929; Lincoln 1936. † L 1, N 50.

PARK, Mary Exh. 1885-89
Add: Dunedin, New Zealand 1885; Paris 1889. † GI 1, RSA 3.

PARK, M. Alexander Exh. 1902-4
Greenburn, Helensburgh. † GI 2.

PARK, Stuart* 1862-1933
Flower and portrait painter. b. Kidderminster. Studied Glasgow School of Art and Paris. Add: Glasgow 1883; Kilmarnock 1904. † BG 6, CON 4, G 2, GI 116, I 11, L 27, M 2, RA 1, RSA 29, RSW 2.

PARK, W. Mason Exh. 1905
65 Kelvindale Street, Glasgow. † GI 1.

PARKER, Alfred b. 1887
Landscape painter. Assistant Curator City of Nottingham Art Museum. A.N.S.A. 1924, N.S.A. 1929 (Hon. Sec. from 1931). Exh. 1909-30. Add: Nottingham 1909; Attenborough, Notts. 1922. † N 42.

PARKER, Alfred Exh. 1935-40
Etcher and wood engraver. Add: Stratford on Avon, Warwicks. † B 2, RA 2, RCA 2.

PARKER, Alice Exh. 1904
50 Sandwell Road, West Bromwich. † B 3.

PARKER, Amy Exh. 1903-8
Carleton Hill, Penrith. † B 2, RCA 9.

PARKER, A.H. Exh. 1905
5 Foregate Street, Worcester. † RA 1.

PARKER, Agnes Miller b. 1895
Painter and wood engraver. b. Ayrshire. Studied Glasgow School of Art 1914-19. A.R.E. 1940. Exh. 1930-40. † RE 4, RED 10, RSA 1.

PARKER, Miss B. Exh. 1920
7 Priory Gardens, Highgate, London. † SWA 1.

PARKER, Barry Exh. 1913-23
Architect. Add: Letchworth, Herts. † RA 4.

PARKER, Beatrice Exh. 1887
Painter. Add: Claxby Rectory, Alford, Lincs. † SWA 1.

PARKER, Bessie Exh. 1924-25
School of Arts and Crafts, Lowestoft, Suffolk. † L 2.

PARKER, Brynhild Exh. 1930-38
Landscape and figure painter. † GOU 3, LEF 76, NEA 1.

PARKER, Barbara M. Exh. 1938
Craft worker. Add: 23 Westminster Road, Handsworth, Birmingham. † B 1.

PARKER, B. Nelson Exh. 1936
Painter. † LEF 1.

PARKER, Miss C. Exh. 1914-15
1 Northwick Terrace, London. † RA 2.

PARKER, Cicely Exh. 1898
19 Pembroke Gardens, Kensington, London. † RBA 1.

PARKER, Cushla Exh. 1921
9 Ann Street, Edinburgh. † RSA 2.

PARKER, C.J. Exh. 1927
Landscape painter. Add: 105 Noel Street, Nottingham. † N 2.

PARKER, Caroline Maude Exh. 1919
Landscape and flower painter and teacher. b. London. Studied Sheffield School of Art. † L 1.

PARKER, E.D. Exh. 1927
Farnborough, Kent. † M 1.

PARKER, Ellen Grace Exh. 1880-1903
Flower and figure painter. Probably daughter of John P. q.v. Add: St. John's Wood, London. † B 34, D 7, GI 4, L 5, M 1, NG 1, RA 5, RBA 16, ROI 2.

PARKER, Ethel N. Exh. 1889-1907
Landscape, portrait and miniature painter. Add: London. † P 3, RA 7, RBA 3, RHA 4, RID 2, SWA 3.

PARKER, Elizabeth Rose Exh. 1897-1940
Landscape and miniature portrait painter and teacher. b. Renfrewshire. Studied Glasgow School of Art, Paris, London and Edinburgh. A.R.M.S. 1907. Add: Partick 1897; Glasgow 1902. † AR 2, GI 32, L 1, NG 1, RA 3, RMS 34, RSA 12.

PARKER, Frederick H.A. d. 1904
Landscape and figure painter. N.E.A. 1887, R.B.A. 1890. Add: London. † GI 2, L 10, M 2, NEA 1, P 2, RA 14, RBA 57, ROI 6.

PARKER, Harold b. 1873
Sculptor. b. Australia. Studied South London Art School and City and Guilds of London. "Ariadne" purchased by Chantrey Bequest 1908. Exh. 1903-29. Add: London. † B 1, GI 6, I 2, L 1, RA 32, RI 1, ROI 1, RSA 1.

PARKER, H.C. Exh. 1918-19
Beech Cliff, Matlock Bath, Derbys. † N 5.

PARKER, Harold Wilson b. 1896
Sculptor. Exh. 1925-40. Add: London. † GI 1, L 3, RA 9, RMS 4.

PARKER, John 1839-1915
Landscape and figure painter. b. and studied Birmingham. R.B.S.A. 1891, R.O.I. 1883, A.R.W.S. 1876, R.W.S. 1881. Probably father of Ellen Grace P. q.v. Add: St. John's Wood, London. † B 68, FIN 2, G 6, GI 30, L 38, M 32, NG 35, RA 5, RCA 44, RHA 7, ROI 16, RWS 157.

PARKER, Lady Katherine Exh. 1888
31 Princes Gardens, London. † D 2.

PARKER, Louise Exh. 1892-93
Figure painter. Add: Boa Vista, Earlsfield Road, Wandsworth, London. † RBA 2.

PARKER, Lilian G. See WELLS

PARKER, Laura Margarita b. 1904
Portrait and landscape painter. b. Montevideo. Studied Royal College of Art. Exh. 1931. Add: 21 Joubert Mansions, Jubilee Place, London. † RA 1.

PARKER, Mabel Exh. 1907
Beguley House, Timperley, Cheshire. † L 1.

PARKER, Maude Exh. 1904-32
Watercolour landscape and coastal painter. Add: Maidenhead, Berks. 1904; Bourne End, Bucks. 1915; Sennen, Cornwall 1924. † BA 32, D 2, FIN 78, NEA 2, RA 2, RI 1, SWA 1.

PARKER, Mordaunt M. Exh. 1925-40
Watercolour landscape painter. Travelled widely. Add: London. † AR 36, RA 1, RHA 1, RI 6.

PARKER, Mary W. Exh. 1925
11 Taviton Street, Gordon Square, London. † NEA 2.

PARKER, Mrs. N. Exh. 1910
Netherton, Torquay. † RA 1.

PARKER, Nellie Exh. 1895-99
170 Rotton Park Road, Edgbaston, Birmingham. † B 4.

PARKER, Mrs. Neta Exh. 1901
† RMS 1.

PARKER, Nevillia Exh. 1882-88
Landscape and figure painter. Add: London. † L 1, RA 1, RBA 2, RHA 1, SWA 1.

PARKER, Olive Exh. 1936
High Wycombe, Bucks. † SWA 2.

PARKER, Phoebe Exh. 1882-86
Painter. Add: Waddington Parsonage, Clitheroe, Lancs. † L 1, RA 2.

PARKER, Phyllis M. Exh. 1906-10
15 George Street, Edinburgh. † RSA 4.

PARKER, R. Barry Exh. 1896-97
Architect. Add: Buxton, Derbys. † RA 2.

PARKER, Richard Henry 1881-1930
Painter, etcher, sculptor and author. b. Dewsbury. Studied Royal College of Art and British School at Rome. Principal Harrogate School of Art, lecturer Royal College of Art and Leeds Training College, and Principal Plymouth School of Art. Exh. 1912. Add: Leeds. † L 1.

PARKER, Miss R.M. Exh. 1900-2
London. † RBA 1, RI 1, SWA 2.

PARKER, Sheelah Exh. 1933-37
Figure and landscape painter. Add: 12 Fortfield Terrace, Dartry, Dublin. † RHA 8.

PARKER, Sybil C. b. 1860
Figure painter. Add: Clitheroe, Lancs. 1880; Lewisham, London 1893. † L 2, M 1, RA 4, RBA 1, SWA 2.

PARKER, W.N. Exh. 1933
43 The Avenue, Kew Gardens, Surrey. † ROI 2.

PARKES, Anne Exh. 1887-97
Landscape painter. Add: 8 Grove Road, Surbiton, Surrey. † SWA 7.

PARKES, G.A. Exh. 1931
1 Albert Street, Birmingham. † B 1.

PARKES, Jane Exh. 1937
7 Westwood Avenue, Giffnock, Glasgow. † GI 1.

PARKES, Miss N.W.A. Exh. 1907
Holmesdale, Riverhead, Sevenoaks, Kent. † L 1.

PARKES, Robert Bowyer Exh. 1883
Engraver. Add: 14 Upper Tollington Park, Finsbury Park, London. † RA 1.

PARKES, Thomas N. Exh. 1922-24
139 Colwyn Road, West Hartlepool. † ROI 2.

PARKES, U. Winifred A. Exh. 1897-1913
Add: London 1897 and 1912; Wittersham Rectory, Ashford, Kent 1898. † I 2, L 2, RA 1, ROI 1, SWA 7.

PARKES, W. Theodore Exh. 1880-83
12 Fleet Street, Dublin. † RHA 19.

PARKHOUSE, Bentley Exh. 1909-10
2 Queen's Gate Terrace, Plymouth. † LS 6.

PARKIN, A. Daisy Exh. 1924-39
Landscape painter. Sister of Lucy P. q.v. Add: Nottingham. † N 35.

PARKIN, C. Exh. 1922-26
Still life, landscape and flower painter. Add: 6 Newstead Colliery, Notts. † N 7.

PARKIN, Hubert Exh. 1932-37
Portrait painter. Add: Boscombe, Bournemouth 1932; Chelsea, London 1935. † P 2, RA 1, RBA 5.

PARKIN, Lucy O. Exh. 1926-38
Landscape painter. Sister of A. Daisy P. q v. Add: Nottingham. † N 14.

PARKIN, Mary A. Exh. 1915-19
Flower painter. Add: The Limes, 5 Sherwood Rise, Nottingham. † N 5.

PARKINS, Miss M.E. Exh. 1915
2 Shaftesbury Road Walthamstow, Essex. † RA 1.

PARKINSON, Mrs. Edith A. Exh. 1927
Plaster worker. Add: 62 Pierrepont Road, West Bridgford, Nottingham. † N 1.

PARKINSON, Miss Florence Exh. 1940
Landscape painter. Add: Durford Wood, Petersfield, Hants. † RA 1.

PARKINSON, Mrs. Florence Exh. 1890-1918
Painter, sculptor and miniaturist. Married William P. q.v. Add: London. † L 2, RA 16, RID 2.

PARKINSON, Mrs. Francis U. Exh. 1902
† RMS 1.

PARKINSON, G.L. Exh. 1908
Church Walk, Eastwood, Notts. † N 1.

PARKINSON, Isabel Exh. 1897
Yewbarrow House, Grange over Sands, Lancs. † L 1.

PARKINSON, John W. Exh. 1880-81
Figure painter. Add: 4 St. Thomas Street, Portsmouth. † RA 1, RE 2.

PARKINSON, Leslie Ernest b. 1903
Landscape and flower painter. Add: 30 Freegrove Road, Holloway, London. † L 4, RA 3, ROI 4.

PARKINSON, Mrs. M. Exh. 1887
11 Reedale Crescent, Hampstead, London. † L 2.

PARKINSON, Miss M.E. Exh. 1930
† L 1.

PARKINSON, William Exh. 1882-95
Figure and landscape painter. Married Florence P. q.v. Add: London. † RA 6, RBA 5, RID 4.

PARKINSON, William Exh. 1931-38
1 Dale Street, Coventry. † B 8.

PARKINSON, William H. Exh. 1892-98
Landscape and figure painter. Add: Bradford, Yorks. † RA 7, RBA 1.

PARKS, Frederick Exh. 1900-27
Watercolour landscape painter. Add: Forest Hill, London 1900; Mertsham, Surrey 1908. † B 4, D 101, L 1, RA 5, RI 7.

PARKS, J. Gower Exh. 1926
† NEA 1.

PARKYN, John Herbert b. 1864
Painter, modeller and designer. b. Cumberland. Studied Clifton School of Art, Royal College of Art and Juliens, Paris. Head of Kingston upon Hull School of Art for 11 years. Headmaster Academy, Ayr. Add: Bristol 1883; Kingston upon Hull 1902; Dalry, Galloway 1915. † L 2, M 1, RA 7, RI 1.

PARKYN, William Samuel b. 1875
Landscape painter. b. London. Studied Newquay and St. Ives, Cornwall. Exh. 1899-1940. Add: Newquay, Cornwall 1899; London 1900; Sandwich, Kent 1906; St. Ives, Cornwall 1908. † B 13, D 37, L 4, LS 6, RA 3, RCA 188, RI 14, ROI 5.

PARLBY, D. Exh. 1923-27
Bedford Park, London. † SWA 3.

PARLBY, George c. 1856-1944
Stained glass artist. Add: London. † AR 1, RA 44.

PARMENTER, Miss A.M. Exh. 1914
Flower painter. Add: Mount House, Braintree, Essex. † NEA 1.

PARMENTER, Mabel Exh. 1908
104 Rue D'Assas, Paris. † LS 2.

PARNELL, Miss A.M. Exh. 1926
† RMS 2.

PARNELL, Gwendolen Exh. 1923-31
S.W.A. 1922. † RMS 10.

PARNELL-BAILEY, Eva Exh. 1938-40
Landscape and interior painter. Studied under Harold Workman. Add: 82 Lavington Road, London. † NEA 2, RA 2, ROI 2, SWA 1.

PARR, Agnes R. Exh. 1885-95
Miniature portrait painter. Add: Gravesend, Kent 1885; Greenhythe, Kent 1887; South Norwood, London 1892. † RA 5, RI 1.

PARR, George Exh. 1888-1912
Landscape painter. Probably brother of Samuel P. q.v. Add: Nottingham 1888 and 1895; Edwalton, Notts. 1894. † N 90.

PARR, Harry b. 1882
Sculptor and potter. b. Wolstanton, Staffs. Studied Royal College of Art. Exh. 1910-40. Add: London. † B 1, GI 1, I 4, L 3, RA 31.

PARR, Miss M.L. Exh. 1933
Carrick House, Stafford Road, Eccles, Lancs. † L 1.

PARR, Samuel d. 1921
Landscape painter. N.S.A. 1890. Secretary and Treasurer 1908-13. V.P.N.S.A. 1914-17. Probably brother of George P. q.v. Exh. from 1886. Add: Nottingham. † N 161, RA 2.

PARRATT, Helen L. Exh. 1882
17 Nassau Street, London. † B 1.

PARRISH, Charles Exh. 1885
Architect. Add: Carlton Chambers, Regent Street, London. † RA 1.

PARRISH, Miss C.W. Exh. 1911
c/o Chapman Bros., 241 Kings Road, Chelsea, London. † L 1, RA 1.

PARRISH, Maxfield* b. 1870
American painter and illustrator. Exh. 1903-9. Add: c/o John Lane, The Albany, London. † GI 4, NG 1.

PARRISH, Stephen* b. 1846
American etcher. R.E. 1881-86. Exh. 1881-82. Add: Philadelphia, U.S.A. † RE 21.

PARROTT, C.M. Exh. 1906-13
Miniature painter. Add: Wolverhampton 1906; Dulwich, London 1909; Paignton, Devon 1911. † B 2, LS 9, RA 3.

PARROTT, Mrs. Isabella Exh. 1905
50 Priar's Stile Road, Richmond. † B 1.

PARRY, Charles James Exh. 1881-1900
Landscape painter. Add: Herne Hill 1881; London 1886. † B 1, M 1, RA 5, RBA 1, ROI 2, TOO 4.

PARRY, David H. Exh. 1891-95
Watercolour landscape painter. Add: Stoke Newington, London. † D 3, GI 1, L 3, RA 2, ROI 1.

PARRY, E. Exh. 1930
Wood engraver. † RED 2.

PARRY, Geo. H. Exh. 1911-16
30 Buckingham Road, The Brook, Liverpool. † L 22.

PARRY, G.M. Exh. 1933
85 South End Road, London. † L 2.

PARRY, J. Jarrett Exh. 1922-23
Caerau, Nevin. † L 5.

PARRY, Morris Exh. 1933
Llangefri, Anglesey. † RCA 1.

PARRY, Muriel Exh. 1919-20
38 Belvidere Road, Liverpool. † L 2.

PARRY, Ruby Exh. 1911-16
Rhuddlan, N. Wales 1911; Kensington, London 1914. † GI 1, L 10, RA 1, RSA 2.

PARRY, Thomas P. Jones Exh. 1884-88
Watercolour landscape painter. Add: Ellesmere 1884; Wrexham 1888. † RI 3.

PARRY, W.K. Exh. 1880-96
Dublin. † RHA 11.

PARSONS, Alfred* 1847-1920
Landscape painter watercolourist and illustrater. Studied South Kensington Art School. N.E.A. 1886, A.R.A. 1897, R.A. 1911, R.I. 1882 (res. 1898), H.R.M.S. 1919, R.O.I. 1883, R.S.W. 1917, A.R.W.S. 1899, R.W.S. 1905, P.R.W.S. 1913. "When Nature Painted all Things Gay" purchased by Chantrey Bequest 1887. Add: London. † AG 1, B 18, CAR 1, D 10, DOW 2, FIN 341, G 10, GI 19, L 48, LEI 78, M 28, NEA 4, NG 35, RA 90, RHA 1, RI 34, ROI 10, RSW 3, RWS 3, RWS 79, TOO 5, WG 4.

PARSONS, A. Maude Exh. 1918-40
A.S.W.A. 1940. Add: 33A Priory Terrace, West Hampstead, London. † SWA 9.

PARSONS, Arthur Wilde* d. 1931
Landscape and marine painter. Exh. 1882-1922. Add: Bristol. † B 11, GI 4, L 6, M 1, RA 23, RBA 13, RI 12.

PARSONS, Beatrice 1870-1955
Portrait, figure, landscape and flower painter. Studied R.A. Schools. Add: Peckham, London 1889; Hampstead, London 1901; Watford, Herts. 1907. † AB 2, DOW 183, GI 1, L 12, NG 2, RA 9, RI 2, ROI 1, SWA 1.

PARSONS, Miss C. Exh. 1912-14
51 Mornington Road, Regent's Park, London. † LS 3, SWA 2.

PARSONS, Charlotte M. Exh. 1891
Sculptor. Add: Melbourne House, Blackheath, London. † RA 1.

PARSONS, Miss E.K. Exh. 1906
Hampstead, London. † SWA 1.

PARSONS, Mrs. Florence Exh. 1915
86 Bidston Road, Birkenhead. † L 1.

PARSONS, Grace Exh. 1938-39
† GOU 1, NEA 1.

PARSONS, Mrs. Gladys A. Exh. 1929-37
Watercolour flower painter. Add: Langley, Bredon, Newbury, Berks. † RA 1, RI 5.

PARSONS, G.W. Exh. 1891-94
River House, Burton on Trent, Staffs. † B 3.

PARSONS, G.W.L. Exh. 1935-39
Landscape painter. Add: 31 Wiverton Road, Sherwood Rise, Nottingham. † N 7.

PARSONS, Miss J.E. Exh. 1929
Ware, Herts. † SWA 1.

PARSONS, John F. Exh. 1883-88
Add: Birmingham 1883; Redland, Bristol 1886. † B 2, L 1.

PARSONS, J.R. c. 1826-1909
Figure painter. Exh. 1883. Add: 9 Cornwall Residences, Regent's Park, London. † G 1.

PARSONS, J.V.R. Exh. 1891-1914
Portrait and figure painter. Add: Liverpool. † B 10, L 59, RA 5, RCA 2, RI 6.

PARSONS, J.W. Exh. 1895-96
Largs, Ayrshire 1895; Glasgow 1896. † GI 3, RI 1, RSA 1.

PARSONS, John Whitehill* b. 1859
Landscape, seascape, portrait and miniature painter. b. Greenock. Studied R.S.A. Schools and Academie Delecluse, Paris. R.B.A. 1896, R.M.S. 1897. Exh. 1885-1936. Add: Edinburgh 1885; Bedminster, Dorset 1894; Glasgow 1896; Pulborough, Sussex 1904. † GI 31, L 2, RA 3, RBA 87, RHA 2, RI 1, RMS 18, RSA 33, RSW 3.

PARSONS, Karl 1884-1934
Stained glass artist. Add: London. † COO 3, RA 2.

PARSONS, Mrs. K.C. Exh. 1908
Said House, The Mall, Chiswick, London. † RA 2.

PARSONS, Letitia Margaret See KEITH

PARSONS, Owen P. Exh. 1904-33
Architect. Add: Birmingham. † B 2, RA 5.

PARSONS, Phyllis Exh. 1907-11
Painter. Add: Garston, Frome, Somerset. † L 1, NG 1, RA 3.

PARSONS, S.F. Exh. 1906
Milton Chambers, Milton Street, Nottingham. † RA 1.

PARSONS, Winifred Exh. 1939
Landscape painter. Studied Paris. Travelled 2 years in East Africa. † WG 49.

PARTING, Alice Exh. 1882-86
Flower, figure and still life painter. Add: 6 Florence Terrace, Ealing, London. † M 2, SWA 5.

PARTING, Florence Exh. 1882-86
Flower, fruit and still life painter. Add: 5 Florence Terrace, Ealing, London. † L 2, ROI 1, SWA 7.

PARTINGTON, Miss A. Exh. 1891
The Limes, Sydenham Park, London. † M 1.

PARTINGTON, H. Exh. 1889-90
23 Market Place, Heywood, Manchester. † M 2.

PARTINGTON, Harold Exh. 1912-22
Brambles, Highbury Road, St. Annes on Sea, Lancs. † RCA 5.

PARTINGTON, J.H.E. b. 1843
Portrait, figure and marine painter. b. Manchester. Probably father of Richard Lantry P. q.v. Exh. 1880-92. Add: Manchester 1880; Ramsey, I.O.M. 1885; Stockport 1887; Oakland, San Francisco, U.S.A. 1892. † G 5, L 2, M 24, RA 9, RI 1.

PARTINGTON, Richard Lantry 1868-1928
b. Stockport. Probably son of J.H.E.P. q.v. Exh. 1886-92. Add: Ramsey, I.O.M. 1886; Stockport 1888; Oakland, San Francisco, U.S.A. 1892. † M 9.

PARTINGTON, Walter Exh. 1906-19
Painter. Add: Hounslow, London. † L 1, RA 2.

PARTON, Ernest* 1845-1933
Landscape painter. b. Hudson, New York, U.S.A. Studied under his elder brother Arthur P. (1842-1914). Came to England 1873. R.O.I. 1883. Also brother of Henry Woodbridge P. q.v. Exh. from 1880. Add: London. † ALP 1, B 17, DOW 52, FIN 1, G 16, GI 21, L 44, M 40, NEA 1, NG 27, RA 80, RBA 12, RHA 3, RI 42, ROI 101, TOO 26.

PARTON, Frank Exh. 1886
Maidstone, Kent. † ROI 1.

PARTON, George Exh. 1886-93
Birmingham. † B 4.

PARTON, Henry Woodbridge 1858-1933
Flower painter. Brother of Ernest P. q.v. Exh. 1885. Add: 8 Elm Tree Road, St. John's Wood, London. † RA 1.

PARTRIDGE, Ann St. John Exh. 1888-1935
Landscape and flower painter. Studied Paris. A.R.B.A. 1924, R.B.A. 1926, R.I. 1935, S.W.A. 1936. Add: London. † BA 1, BG 1, CHE 5, FIN 2, GI 6, GOU 3, I 65, L 7, LS 7, RA 15, RBA 57, RHA 23, RI 7, RID 4, ROI 7, RSA 4, RSW 3, SWA 5.

PARTRIDGE, Sir Bernard 1861-1945
Painter, illustrater, stained glass artist and decorative painter. Joined staff of "Punch" 1891. N.E.A. 1893, R.I. 1896 (res. 1906). Add: London. † FIN 112, GI 3, L 12, LEI 44, NEA 2, RA 18, RI 3.

PARTRIDGE, Edith Exh. 1902-4
Landscape painter. Add: The Limes, Burton Joyce, Notts. † N 2.

PARTRIDGE, Edward Exh. 1880-96
Landscape painter. Add: Alexander Road, Birmingham. † B 10.

PARTRIDGE, Ellen Exh. 1880-94
Landscape, figure and miniature portrait painter. S.W.A. 1880. Add: London. † RA 5, SWA 33.

PARTRIDGE, Mrs. Hart Exh. 1908
Heathdale, Harborne, Birmingham. † B 1.

PARTRIDGE, Lilian May Exh. 1917-24
A.R.M.S. 1917. Add: London 1917; Hove, Sussex 1921. † L 1, RMS 5.

PARTRIDGE, Roy b. 1888
American artist. Exh. 1913-14. Add: 5 Rue Nouvelle Stanislas, Paris. † L 6.

PARTRIDGE, Miss S. Exh. 1913-14
83 Pendle Road, Streatham, London. † RA 2.

PARTRIDGE, W.L. Exh. 1889-90
Metchley Lane, Edgbaston, Birmingham. † B 2.

PARTRIDGE, William Ordway 1861-1930
American sculptor. Exh. 1891-92. Add: Paris. † RA 2.

PASCAL, Jean Louis 1837-1920
French architect. H.R.S.A. 1911. Exh. 1911-12. Add: 8 Boulevard Street, Denis, Paris. † RSA 6.

PASCHKOFF, Olga Exh. 1927-39
A.R.M.S. 1937. Add: La Chaudronnerie, Zouy en Zosas, Seine et Oise, France. † RMS 14.

PASCOE, William Exh. 1905-12
Landscape painter. Add: 6 Wellington Terrace, Penzance. † L 2, LS 3, M 1, WG 44.

PASERUTTI, A. Exh. 1888
c/o L. Dondy, 6 Carter Street, Liverpool. † L 1.

PASH, Florence Exh. 1886-1924
Mrs. A.A. Humphrey. Portrait and figure painter. Add: London. † G 2, L 6, LS 8, M 2, NEA 13, NG 1, P 5, RA 12, RBA 15, RI 3, ROI 9, SWA 23.

PASLEY, Louisa M.S. Exh. 1880-84
Sculptor. Add: Moorhill, Shedfield Botley, Southampton. † RA 2.

PASLEY, Nancy A. Sabine Exh. 1886-95
Figure and flower painter. Add: London. † GI 6, RBA 1, ROI 11, SWA 3.

PASMORE, Alfred Exh. 1929-37
Watford, Herts. † D 1, RCA 1.

PASMORE, Daniel junr.* Exh. 1880-91
Portrait and genre painter. R.B.A. 1862. Related to Emily and F.G.P. q.v. Add: London. † RBA 28, RI 2.

PASMORE, Emily Exh. 1881-84
Fruit and flower painter. Related to Daniel and F.G.P. q.v. Add: 54 Crowndale Road, Camden Town, London. † RBA 4.

PASMORE, E.J. Victor Exh. 1929
Watercolour painter. Add: 18 Dewhurst Road, Brook Green, London. † RA 1.

PASMORE, F.G. junr.* Exh. 1880-84
Animal and figure painter. Related to Daniel and Emily P. q.v. Add: 54 Crowndale Road, Camden Town, London. † RBA 4.

PASMORE, G.W. Exh. 1940
Painter. † COO 2.

PASMORE, Victor* b. 1908
Figure, flower and landscape painter. b. Chelsham, Surrey. Founder and leading teacher of the Euston Road School of Painting and Drawing 1937. Member London Group 1934. Exh. 1933-40. Add: London. † AG 1, BA 3, COO 14, LEF 1, LEI 4, RA 1.

PASQUOLL, R.D. Exh. 1904-26
Glasgow. † GI 9, L 3, RSA 2.

PASS, Harry Exh. 1883-99
Add: Liverpool 1883; Rock Ferry, Cheshire 1899. † L 3.

PASS, Miss Jenny Exh. 1898-1909
345 Old Chester Road, Rock Ferry, Cheshire. † B 1, L 6.

PASSEY, Charles Henry* Exh. 1883-85
Landscape painter. Add: London. † RHA 4, ROI 1.

PASSINGHAM, Leila M.A. Exh. 1895-1906
Portrait painter. Add: London. † L 2, RA 2, SWA 1.

PASSINI, Ludwig* 1832-1903
Watercolour portrait painter. H.R.I. 1883. Add: Venice. † RA 2, RI 2.

PASTEUR, Mme Charles Exh. 1913
65 Rue d'Anjou, Paris. † LS 3.

PASTORE, Victor Raphael Exh. 1934
Manchester. † RCA 1.

PASTOUKHOFF, Boris Exh. 1935-38
Portrait, landscape and flower painter. Add: 20 Boulevard Flandrin, Paris. † BK 49, RA 1.

PATALONO, Enrico Exh. 1880-90
Portrait painter. Add: Glasgow 1880; London 1890. † GI 13, RA 1, RSA 2.

PATERSON, Agnes Exh. 1897
5 Leamington Terrace, Edinburgh. † RSA 1.

PATERSON, Alexander Exh. 1937
8179 Hudson Avenue, Vancouver, Canada. † RSA 1.

PATERSON, Andrew Exh. 1883
2 Buchanan Terrace, Paisley. † GI 1.

PATERSON, A.A. Exh. 1915
30 Hartington Place, Edinburgh. † RSA 1.

PATERSON, Annie M. Exh. 1888-1925
Figure and landscape painter. Add: Glasgow 1888; London 1910; Edinburgh 1912. † BG 40, GI 15, L 19, RA 1, RSA 13, RSW 2, SWA 1.

PATERSON, Alexander Nesbitt 1862-1947
Painter and architect. A.R.S.A. 1911, R.S.W. 1916. Husband of Maggie and father of Mary Viola P. q.v. Add: Glasgow 1882 and 1892; London 1890; The Long Croft, Helensburgh 1916. † AR 2, GI 101, L 1, NEA 1, RA 1, RI 1, RSA 105, RSW 108.

PATERSON, Caroline Exh. 1880-99
Figure painter. Married Sutton Sharpe q.v. Add: Hampstead, London. † AG 16, B 6, D 7, DOW 3, L 3, M 24, RI 6, SWA 19.

PATERSON, C.M. Exh. 1885
6 Merchiston Crescent, Edinburgh. † RSA 1.

PATERSON, Catherine W. Exh. 1920-30
Add: London 1920; Glasgow 1930. † L 1, RSA 1, SWA 1.

PATERSON, David Exh. 1937-40
36 Napier Place, Falkirk. † RSA 1, RSW 2.

PATERSON, E.A. Exh. 1889
Colonnade House, Blackheath, London. † L 1.

PATERSON, Emily Murray 1855-1934
Landscape and flower painter. b. Edinburgh. Studied in Edinburgh and Paris. R.S.W. 1904, A.S.W.A. 1910. Travelled widely. Add: Edinburgh 1880; London 1922. † AB 1, AR 2, BAR 51, COO 2, GI 57, GOU 5, I 4, L 8, M 9, NG 4, RA 17, RBA 4, RHA 2, RI 24, RMS 12, RSA 91, RSW 108, SWA 68, WG 83.

PATERSON, Frederick Exh. 1909
† LS 3.

PATERSON, Gavin Exh. 1897-1906
19 Cadzow Street, Hamilton, N.B. † GI 4.

PATERSON, George Andrew Exh. 1899
Architect. Father of G.W. Lennox P. q.v. Add: Dalmuir, N.B. † GI 2.

PATERSON, George M. Exh. 1880-1904
Painter. Add: Edinburgh 1880; Portobello 1891; Blackhall, Midlothian 1900; Slateford 1903; Liverton, Midlothian 1904. † GI 11, L 6, M 2 RA 2, RSA 28.

PATERSON, G.W. Lennox b. 1915
Painter and wood engraver. Studied Glasgow School of Art. Son of George Andrew P. q.v. Exh. 1938-40. Add: Glasgow. † GI 6, RSA 6.

PATERSON, H. Exh. 1884
† TOO 1.

PATERSON, Hamish C. Exh. 1912-40
Portrait and landscape painter. Add: Edinburgh. † GI 19, L 4, RA 3, RHA 1, RSA 56, RSW 10.

PATERSON, James Exh. 1885-1904
Ancrum Manse, Ancrum, Edinburgh. † L 1, RSA 1.

PATERSON, James* 1854-1932
Landscape and portrait painter. Studied Glasgow and Paris. N.E.A. 1887, A.R.S.A. 1896, R.S .A. 1910, R.S.W. 1885, P.R.S.W 1923, A.R.W.S. 1898, R.W.S. 1908. Add: Parris 1880; Glasgow 1882; Edinburgh and Moniaivie, Dumfries 1885. † AG 3, AR 2, B 2, BG 3, D 1, DOW 4, FIN 2, G 4, GI 130, GOU 2, I 5, L 57, M 31, NEA 12, NG 2, P 1, RA 29, RBA 5, RHA 2, RSA 177, RSW 152, RWS 193, TOO 5.

PATERSON, Jentie Exh. 1904
2 Windsor Quadrant, Kelvinside, Glasgow. † GI 1.

PATERSON, John Exh. 1884
Newlands, Ayr. † GI 1.

PATERSON, J.C. Exh. 1917-18
17 India Street, Edinburgh. † RSA 2, RSW 1, RWS 3.

PATERSON, James C. Exh. 1885-1904
Glasgow. † GI 2.

PATERSON, John Ford Exh. 1880-83
Edinburgh. † GI 1, RSA 9.

PATERSON, Miss J.J. Exh. 1907-12
Add: Bradstones, West Derby, Liverpool. † L 16, RA 1.

PATERSON, James Phillips Exh. 1902-5
31 High Street, Dunfermline, N.B. † RSA 3.

PATERSON, J.S. Exh. 1896
Whitehill, New Deer, Aberdeenshire. † GI 1.

PATERSON, Kate W. Exh. 1898
25 University Gardens, Glasgow. † GI 2, RSA 1.

PATERSON, Miss L. Exh. 1887-88
1 Athole Gardens Place, Hillhead, Glasgow. † GI 3.

PATERSON, Mrs. Leslie Exh. 1921-27
The Vicarage, Speke, nr. Liverpool. † L 4.

PATERSON, Mary Exh. 1887-90
193 Rendrew Street, Glasgow. † GI 4.

PATERSON, Maggie Exh. 1889-1940
nee Hamilton. Still life and figure painter. Wife of Alexander Nesbitt and mother of Mary Viola P. q.v. Add: Helensburgh, N.B. † GI 92, L 4, RA 4, RSA 47.

PATERSON, Maggie C. Exh. 1890
Cordoba, Bothwell. † GI 1.

PATERSON, Mary Stewart Exh. 1892
† RSA 1.

PATERSON, Mary Viola b. 1899
Painter and lithographer. Studied Glasgow School of Art 1919-21, Academie de la Grande Chaumiere and Academie L'Hote. Daughter of Alexander Nesbitt and Maggie P. q.v. Exh. 1920-40. Add: The Long Croft, Helensburgh, N.B. † GI 15, RA 3, RED 7, RSA 10, RSW 1.

PATERSON, Oscar Exh. 1895-96
118 West Regent Street, Glasgow. † GI 2.

PATERSON, O.M. Exh. 1887
Laurieville, Crosshill, Glasgow. † GI 1.

PATERSON, Reginald Exh. 1936
† RI 2.

PATERSON, Rex Exh. 1919
† LS 3.

PATERSON, Robert Exh. 1887-89
Engraver. Add: London. † RA 4.

PATERSON, Robert E. Stirling Exh. 1889-1940
Landscape and coastal painter. Add: Edinburgh. † D 1, GI 8, L 1, RA 2, RSA 33, RSW 11.

PATERSON, Robert Tod Gow b. 1866
Painter and pencil portrait artist. Studied Edinburgh. Travelled widely. Exh. 1927-31. Add: 6 Morningside Park, Edinburgh. † RSA 3.

PATERSON, T. Exh. 1919
196 St. Vincent Street, Glasgow. † GI 2, RSA 2.

PATERSON, Thomas T. Exh. 1896-1904
5 York Place, Edinburgh. † RSA 9.

PATERSON, Violet Exh. 1932
Colour woodcut artist. † BA 2.

PATERSON, W. Exh. 1900
Landscape painter. Add: 61 Chancery Lane, London. † RA 1.

PATERSON, William Exh. 1884-1939
Add: Glasgow 1884 and 1907; Edinburgh 1891 and 1912. † GI 9, L 1, RSA 16.

PATEY, Ethel J. Exh. 1892-94
Portrait painter. Add: Meadowcroft, Bexley, Kent. † RBA 3, ROI 3.

PATMORE, Bertha G. Exh. 1880-1903
Figure and landscape painter. Add: Hastings 1880; Lymington, Hants. 1903. † RA 5.

PATON, Archibald G. Exh. 1880-1939
Etcher. Add: 257 West George Street, Glasgow. † GI 21, L 1, RA 2, RSA 8.

PATON, Agatha Waller Exh. 1895
4 George Square, Edinburgh. † RSA 1.

PATON, C. Exh. 1885
94 Edith Road, West Kensington, London. † RSA 1.

PATON, David Exh. 1883-92
Add: Johnstone, Glasgow 1883; Pittenween, Fife 1892. † GI 2, RSA 1.

PATON, Donald Exh. 1897-1906
Add: Corrie, Arran, N.B. 1897 and 1904; Edinburgh 1903. † GI 4, RSA 1.

PATON, Dorothy Exh. 1916-32
Painter and etcher. Add: London 1916; Walton on the Naze, Essex 1918; Romford, Essex 1921. † I 1, L 2, RA 4, RI 2, SWA 1.

PATON, David William Exh. 1891-1925
Edinburgh. † RSA 10.

PATON, Eliza L.M. Exh. 1940
Midfield, Lasswade, Midlothian. † GI 1.

ATON, Frank* 1856-1909
Figure and animal painter and illustrator. Add: London 1880; Ditton, nr. Maidstone, Kent 1883; Herongate, nr. Brentwood, Essex 1887; Morton, nr. Ongar, Essex 1890. † FIN 1, L 1, RA 16.

ATON, Hugh 1853-1927
Painter, etcher, pastellier and author. b. Glasgow. A.R.E. 1887. Add: Manchester and Ardenadam, Marple, Cheshire. † L 26, M 4, RA 1, RCA 1, RE 112.

PATON, J.C. Exh. 1890
157 New Bond Street, London. † M 1.

PATON, James Fraser Exh. 1903-12
52 Eldon Street, Greenock. † GI 1, LS 11, RSA 2.

PATON, Jessie G. Exh. 1905
Mrs. D.N. Rolls. Add: 3 Yarrow Gardens, Kelvinside, Glasgow. † GI 1.

PATON, Sir Joseph Noel* 1821-1901
Religious, historical, mythical and allegorical painter. b. Dunfermline. Studied R.A. Schools 1843. Appointed H.M. Limner for Scotland and knighted 1866. Brother of Waller Hugh P. q.v. and probably father of Ranald Noel P. q.v. A.R.S.A. 1846, R.S.A. 1850. Add: Edinburgh. † G 3, GI 5, L 1, RSA 18.

PATON, Lilian Exh. 1926
† M 1.

PATON, M. Exh. 1888-92
Probably son of Waller Hugh P. q.v. Add: 14 George Square, Edinburgh. † RSA 6.

PATON, Mrs. M.C. Exh. 1919
Blackburn, Dulwich Wood Park, London. † SWA 3.

PATON, Ranald Noel Exh. 1890-95
Portrait painter. Probably son of Sir Joseph Noel P. q.v. Add: 33 George Square, Edinburgh. † RA 1, RSA 4.

PATON, Mrs. Waller Exh. 1882
14 George Square, Edinburgh. † RSA 1.

PATON, Waller Hugh* 1828-1895
Landscape painter. b. Dunfermline. Studied under John Houston. Brother of Sir Joseph Noel and probably father of M. and W. Hubert P. q.v. A.R.S.A. 1857, R.S.A. 1865, R.S.W. Add: Edinburgh. † AG 1, D 8, DOW 2, GI 30, L 5, M 3, NG 2, RA 1, RHA 9, RI 4, RSA 111, RSW 33.

PATON, W. Hubert Exh. 1885-1932
Probably son of Waller Hugh P. q.v. Add: Edinburgh. † GI 5, L 1, RSA 67.

PATRI, Carlo Exh. 1911
Painter. † BRU 2.

PATRICK, Elizabeth Exh. 1880-92
Glasgow. † GI 14.

PATRICK, James Exh. 1880-1905
Add: Wemyssfield, Kirkaldy 1880; Edinburgh 1881. Clearly related to John and John Rutherford P. q.v. as the Edinburgh addresses are the same. † GI 1, RSA 25.

PATRICK, John Exh. 1880-86
Add: Wemyssfield, Kirkaldy 1880; Edinburgh 1885. Clearly related to James and John Rutherford P. qv. as the Edinburgh addresses are the same. † GI 4, RSA 19.

PATRICK, J.B. Exh. 1884
17 Barony Street, Edinburgh. † RSA 2.

PATRICK, Jessie G. Exh. 1902-3
59 Bath Street, Glasgow. † GI 1, L 2.

PATRICK, James McIntosh* b. 1907
Painter and etcher. Studied Glasgow School of Art. A.R.E. 1932. "Winter in Angus" purchased by Chantrey Bequest 1935. Exh. 1926-40. Add: Glasgow 1926; Dundee 1930. † FIN 6, GI 3, L 1, LEI 1, M 2, RA 14, RBA 1, RE 8, RSA 18.

PATRICK, John Rutherford Exh. 1882-1904
Painter. Add: Edinburgh 1882 and 1893; Prestonkirk, Haddingtonshire 1891. Clearly related to John and James P. q.v. as the Edinburgh addresses are the same. † GI 6, RA 1, RSA 23.

PATRICKSON, George Exh. 1904-11
Add: Cumberland Lodge, Westgate Road, Beckenham, Kent. † B 6, L 5, RA 2, RCA 2, RI 1, ROI 6.

PATRICOT, Jean Exh. 1906
4 Avenue du Chateau, Neuilly sur Seine, France. † L 1.

PATRY, Edward 1856-1940
Portrait and figure painter. Studied Royal College of Art 1879-82, and under Herr Frisch in Germany. R.B.A. 1908. Add: Sydenham Hill 1882; Kensington, London 1891; Battle, Sussex 1931. † B 14, L 27, M 4, P 4, RA 34, RBA 57, RHA 6.

PATRY, James H. Exh. 1923-26
c/o Lloyds Bank, Cheltenham 1923; c/o Rowley Gallery, Church Street, London 1926. † L 4.

PATTEN, Alfred Fowler* b. 1829
Genre painter. Son of George P. (1801-1865). R.B.A. 1874. Exh. 1880-1895. Add: London 1880 and 1894; Brighton 1882. † B 18, M 2, RBA 34, RHA 8.

PATTEN, Leonard Exh. 1889
57 Moray Road, Finsbury Park, London. † RA 1.

PATTENDEN, Miss M.W. Exh. 1902-15
Streatham, London 1902; Purley, Surrey 1915. † RA 1, SWA 3.

PATTERSON, Mrs. E.B. (R) Exh. 1914-17
The Rectory, Deal, Kent. † D 4, L 2, RA 1, RI 2, SWA 2.

PATTERSON, Mrs. Edith Lalande Exh. 1914-24
nee Lalande. Landscape painter. Add: London. † L 4, RA 10.

PATTERSON, George Malcolm b. 1873
Pencil artist and etcher. b. Twickenham. Exh. 1921-38. Add: Dauphin Hill, St. Andrews, Fife. † L 8, RA 7, RSA 27.

PATTERSON, Ida M.F. Exh. 1900-2
11 Burlington Gardens, Acton, London. † L 3.

PATTERSON, Miss J. Exh. 1903-5
3 Seaview Terrace, Donnybrook. † RHA 3.

PATTERSON, Kate M. Exh. 1882-1911
Miniature painter. A.R.M.S. 1897. Add: London. † B 2, GI 2, L 3, M 1, RA 4, RI 3, SWA 2.

PATTERSON, Matthew Exh. 1889-90
Rockhill, Dennistoun. † GI 2.

PATTERSON, Miss M.S. Exh. 1888
28 Rutland Street, Edinburgh. † RSA 1.

PATTERSON, Margaret W. Exh. 1909-25
Landscape and figure painter. Add: Corner Cottage, Pyrford, Woking 1922. † BG 5, L 1, RA 2.

PATTERSON, Thomas R. Exh. 1899
5 Atholl Place, Edinburgh. † RSA 1.

PATTERSON, William J. Exh. 1937-38
Portrait and figure painter. Add: 16 Wharfedale Street, London. † RA 2.

PATTINSON, Annie Exh. 1899-1904
Mrs. O'Halloran. Miniature painter. Add: 49 Buckland Crescent, Hampstead, London. † L 1, RA 6, RMS 3.

PATTINSON, K. Alex Exh. 1911
51 Parkfield Road, Liverpool. † L 1.

PATTISON, Charles T. (Carl) Exh. 1880-84
Landscape and coastal painter. Add: Dusseldorf and London. † B 2, RA 1, RBA 3, ROI 2.

PATTISON, Mrs. Eunice Exh. 1900-14
Miniature portrait painter. Add: Market Harborough, Leics. † RA 4.

PATTISON, Edgar L. b. 1872
Painter, etcher and designer. Studied Lambeth Art School. Exh. 1906-35. Add: London. † AB 69, CHE 1, GI 1, L 3, LEI 15, NEA 1, RA 20, RI 3, ROI 7.

PATTISON, George Exh. 1884
† GI 2.

PATTISON, Thomas W. Exh. 1930-40
Watercolour landscape painter. Add: Chester le Street, Co. Durham 1930; Newcastle on Tyne 1934. † RA 3, RSA 4.

PATTON, Emily H. Exh. 1903-26
Landscape painter. Add: Ryde, I.O.W. 1903; Oakley, Surrey 1905; London 1916. † AB 2, B 2, D 16, RI 1.

PATTON, Kathleen A. Exh. 1895-1901
24 Hatch Street, Dublin. † RHA 6.

PATTON, Mrs. Mary Frances Exh. 1896-1935
Figure and animal painter. Add: Collinstown, Westmeath 1896; Kilbarrack, Sutton 1935. † L 4, RA 3, RHA 33, SWA 2.

PAUL, Mrs. Exh. 1896-97
Knighton Drive, Leicester. † L 2.

PAUL, Annie Exh. 1906
Flower painter. † BG 1.

PAUL, A. Balfour Exh. 1899
21 St. Andrew Square, Edinburgh. † RSA 1.

PAUL, A.L. Exh. 1882-85
Landscape and coastal painter. Add: 47 Addison Road, Kensington, London. † D 2, GI 2, RBA 6.

PAUL, Miss A.M. Exh. 1907-9
c/o G.F. Hill, 10 Kensington Mansions, Earls Court, London. † B 1, D 3, L 1, LS 3.

PAUL, Clara Exh. 1880
Coastal painter. Add: Regents Road, Leicester. † RBA 1.

PAUL, Elizabeth Exh. 1940
13 Dunlop Crescent, Bothwell. † GI 1.

PAUL, Florence Exh. 1886-1909
Landscape painter. Add: Waltham House, Waltham Cross. † BG 39, RBA 1, ROI 2.

PAUL, Florens A.J. Exh. 1922-35
Landscape and flower painter. † WG 133.

PAUL, G. Exh. 1883
† TOO 1.

PAUL, Gen. Exh. 1936
Flower and fruit painter. † RED 1.

PAUL, Miss H.R. Exh. 1912-16
36 Napier Court, Hurlingham. † L 2, RA 2.

PAUL, H.S. Exh. 1887-88
Kirkton, Dumbarton. † GI 2.

PAUL, J.B. Exh. 1891
96 Buchanan Street, Glasgow. † RSA 1.

PAUL, J.G. Exh. 1880-84
Landscape and marine painter. Add: Glasgow and Kensington, London. † GI 1, RBA 3.

PAUL, Mrs. May Exh. 1925
11 Trafalgar Studios, Chelsea, London. † ROI 1.

PAUL, McLean Exh. 1889
Figure painter. Add: 9 Charlton Crescent, Islington, London. † RI 1.

PAUL, Paul Exh. 1899-1932
Landscape painter. R.B.A. 1903. Add: Bushey, Herts. 1899; Kersal, nr. Manchester 1901 and 1904; London 1902 and 1918. † B 4, GI 1, GOU 1, L 27, M 18, RA 10, RBA 27, ROI 9.

PAUL, R. Exh. 1916
9 Princes Buildings, Clifton, Bristol. † RA 1.

PAUL, Roland W. Exh. 1887-1911
Architect. Add: London. † RA 17.

PAUL, W. Phyllis Exh. 1900
Broomhill, Drumcondra, Dublin. † RHA 1.

PAULDEN, Charles A. Exh. 1911-31
Landscape and coastal painter. A.N.S.A. 1921, N.S.A. 1927. Add: Carlton, Notts. † L 2, N 62.

PAULDEN, H. Alfred Exh. 1887-1913
Manchester 1887; Bramhall, Cheshire 1913. † M 5.

PAULDEN, Lily A. Exh. 1918-26
Mrs. C.A. Landscape painter. Add: Carlton, Notts. † N 6.

PAULDEN, R.W. Exh. 1908-25
Landscape and marine painter. A.N.S.A. 1917. Add: Carlton, Notts. † N 46.

PAULIN, George Henry b. 1888
Sculptor. b. Muckhart. Studied Edinburgh College of Art, Italy and France. Brother of Jeanie Wright Ellis q.v. H.R.I. 1935, A.R.S.A. 1920. Exh. 1909-40. Add: Edinburgh 1909; Florence 1913; Glasgow 1917; London 1926. † GI 46, L 7, RA 27, RI 16, RSA 61.

PAULIN, Jeanie Wright See ELLIS

PAULL, Mrs. Edith C. Exh. 1888-1909
Landscape and figure painter. Add: London. † LS 8, NEA 4, RBA 2.

PAULL, Vera Exh. 1927
596 Lord Street, Southport, Lancs. † L 1.

PAULUS, Francis Petrus 1862-1933
American etcher. Exh. 1908-9. Add: 21 Rue du Sablon, Bruges, Belgium. † LS 8.

PAUNCEFOTE, Clara Exh. 1897-1910
Miniature painter. R.M.S. 1898. Add: Folkestone 1897; London 1900. † L 2, NG 2, RA 4, RMS 19.

PAUVERT, Mlle. L.M.H. Exh. 1910-12
139 Rue du Cherche-Midi, Paris. † L 3.

PAVIERE, Sydney Herbert 1891-c. 1970
Painter and etcher. Studied at Oxford and Paris. Assistant to Secretary of Oxford University Museum 1905-12. Assistant Curator Maidstone Museum and Art Gallery 1912-16. Assistant curator Lady Lever Art Gallery, Port Sunlight 1922-23. Curator and art advisor to Lord Leverhulme 1923-25. Exh. 1926-32. Add: Preston. † L 3, RCA 2.

PAVY, Eugene* Exh. 1880-1902
Figure painter. Add: Langham Chambers, Portland Place, London 1880 and 1883; Lynmouth, North Devon 1882. † BG 1, G 1, RA 2, RBA 5.

PAVY, Philip* Exh. 1880-89
Figure and landscape painter. Add: 1 Langham Chambers, Portland Place, London. † L 1, RA 2, RBA 16.

PAWLE, Miss E. Exh. 1916
Widford, Ware, Herts. † RI 1..

PAWLEY, Charles James Chirney d. 1922
Architect. Exh. 1896-1903. Add: Victoria Street, London. † RA 7.

PAWSEY, Jane E. Exh. 1913-34
Landscape and figure painter. Add: 126 Palewell Park, East Sheen, London. † ALP 3, I 1, RA 1, SWA 7.

PAXTON, Josephine Exh. 1928
60 Gordon Mansions, Francis Street, London. † NEA 1.

PAXTON, Phillis K. Exh. 1939
Watercolour landscape painter. † AR 2.

PAXTON, Robert B.M. Exh. 1911-23
Portrait painter. Add: London. † GI 3, RA 1.

PAYEN, Emily Exh. 1911
Figure painter. † BRU 1.

PAYNE, A.E. Exh. 1912
44 Hammerfield Avenue, Aberdeen. † RA 1.

PAYNE, Arthur Frederick Exh. 1880-84
Etcher. Add: London. † G 3, RI 1.

PAYNE, Alice M. Exh. 1880
11 The Crescent, King Street, Leicester. † N 1.

PAYNE, Miss B.H. Exh. 1932
Windyridge, Daybrook Vale, Sherwood, Nottingham. † N 1.

PAYNE, C.E. Exh. 1938
24 Frederick Road, Wylde Green, Birmingham. † B 1.

PAYNE, David* Exh. 1882-91
Landscape painter. Add: Barrow on Trent 1882; Duffield 1884; Derby 1888. † B 11, N 2.

PAYNE, Edith Exh. 1914-36
Flower painter. Married Henry Albert P. q.v. Add: Amberley, Glos. † B 3, FIN 13, NEA 5, RA 4.

PAYNE, E. Harding Exh. 1903-5
Architect. Add: 11 John Street, Bedford Row, London. † RA 3.

PAYNE, Edward Raymond b. 1906
Painter and stained glass artist. Studied Royal College of Art 1924-27 and stained glass under his father Henry Albert P. q.v. Exh. 1936-39. Add: Box, Minchinhampton, Glos. † COO 3, RA 1.

PAYNE, E.W. Exh. 1882
Solihull, Birmingham. † B 1.

PAYNE, Florence Exh. 1883-86
Flower painter. Add: 31 Broad Street, Oxford. † L 1, M 4, RA 1, RI 1.

PAYNE, Frances E. Exh. 1903
39 King's Mount, Birkenhead. † L 1.

PAYNE, Frederic W. Exh. 1924-36
Northampton 1924; London 1933. † RI 9.

PAYNE, G.E. Exh. 1913
45 Calais Gate, Myatt's Park, London. † RA 1.

PAYNE, G.R. Exh. 1932
† L 2.

PAYNE, Harriet Ada Exh. 1881-85
Landscape, flower and bird painter. Add: London. † L 2, RBA 3, SWA 4.

PAYNE, Henry Albert* c. 1868-1940
Portrait and landscape painter and stained glass artist. Husband of Edith and father of Edward Raymond P. q.v. R.B.S.A. 1909, A.R.W.S. 1912, R.W.S. 1920. Add: Municipal School of Art, Birmingham 1898; Amberley, Glos. 1912. † B 8, FIN 45, GI 2, L 6, M 6, NG 1, P 3, RA 22, RSW 3, RWS 124, WG 9.

PAYNE, James Exh. 1896
24 Gt. Titchfield Street, London. † ROI 1.

PAYNE, Miss J. Exh. 1914
4 Rue de Chevreuse, Paris. † RA 2.

PAYNE, Miss Mary Exh. 1938
Beckenham, Kent. † SWA 1.

PAYNE, Mrs. M.B. Exh. 1918
97 Lennard Road, Beckenham, Kent. † RA 1.

PAYNE, Miss M.H. Exh. 1911
The Rest, Dartmouth, South Devon. † RA 1.

PAYNE, Sylvia Exh. 1917-19
London. † LS 9.

PAYNE, Vera Irene Exh. 1927-36
Miniature painter. A.R.M.S. 1930. Add: Northwood, Middlesex 1927; Chesterfield 1930. † L 9, RA 6, RSA 2, RMS 37.

PAYNE, W. Exh. 1934
Landscape painter. † AG 1.

PAYNE, Miss W. Exh. 1919
611 Fulham Road, London. † SWA 2.

PAYNTER, David Exh. 1923-40
Portrait and figure painter. Add: London. † COO 1, L 2, NEA 4, RA 19.

PAYO, T. Exh. 1920
† P 1.

PAYTEN, Peggy Exh. 1934-35
Shirley, Fullarton Drive, Troon. † RSA 2.

PAYTON, Miss S.A. Exh. 1887
Penshurst, Richmond Hill Road, Edgbaston, Birmingham. † B 2.

PAZOLT, Alfred J. Exh. 1901-12
Landscape painter. Add: Seaforth, St. Ives, Cornwall. † L 3, LS 2, RA 4, ROI 1.

PAZZINI, Norbeto Exh. 1900
Via del Babuino N 22, Pi, Rome. † NG 2.

PEACAN, John Philip Exh. 1880-99
Landscape painter. Add: London 1880 and 1889; Dublin 1884; Roundstone, Co. Galloway 1891. † B 1, L 4, RA 1, RBA 3, RHA 37.

PEACE, W.G. Exh. 1897
37 Albany Road, Sheffield. † RI 2.

PEACEY, Mrs. J. Lawson Exh. 1920-38
Sculptor. A.S.W.A. 1923, S.W.A. 1927. Add: London. † GI 5, L 2, P 2, RA 15, RSA 7, SWA 16.

PEACH, Catherine Exh. 1936-40
Sculptor. Add: Chapel Lane, Knighton, Leics. † N 5, RA 3.

PEACH, Charles Stanley c.1858-1934
Architect. Add: London. † RA 6.

PEACH, Henry Exh. 1894-1928
Painter. Add: Derby 1894; Ambergate, Derbys. 1897. † B 2, N 1.

PEACHE, G. Alan Exh. 1898
Architect. Add: Broad Sanctuary Chambers, Westminster, London. † RA 1.

PEACHEY, Mary Ellen Exh. 1904-23
Add: Eastbourne 1904; London 1908. † B 1, L 3, LS 8, NG 1, SWA 2.

PEACOCK, Miss A. Exh. 1892-94
Landscape painter. Add: 10 Grenville Place, London. † RID 7.

PEACOCK, Alex Exh. 1880
48 Obernewton Square, Glasgow. † GI 1.

PEACOCK, A.W. Exh. 1885
9 McLaren Road, Edinburgh. † RSA 1.

PEACOCK, Christine Lorna b. 1904
Painter and wood engraver. Studied London. Exh. 1936-40. Add: London 1936; Weybridge, Surrey 1940. † SWA 5.

PEACOCK, Miss E. Exh. 1910
Dixon House, Tipton, Staffs. † B 1.

PEACOCK, J. Neil Exh. 1935-37
279 Mosspark Drive, Glasgow. † GI 3.

PEACOCK, Kenneth Exh. 1940
Architect. Add: 213A Ebury Street, London. † RA 1.

PEACOCK, Mabel Redington Exh. 1911-24
Painter and illustrator. Studied Hornsey School of Art, Kings College and R.A. Schools. Married Clarence A.B. White q.v. Add: London. † L 2, RA 7, RI 1, ROI 1, SWA 3.

PEACOCK, Ralph* 1868-1946
Portrait and landscape painter and illustrator. Studied Lambeth School of Art 1882, St. Johns Wood and R.A. Schools 1887 (gold medal and Creswick prize). Teacher at St. Johns Wood Art School. "Ethel" purchased by Chantrey Bequest 1898. Add: London. † B 6, G 1, GI 2, L 27, M 4, NG 4, P 1, RA 93, RBA 5, RCA 1, ROI 9.

PEACOCK, Mrs. Sarah Catharine Exh. 1923-35
Watercolour landscape painter and miniaturist. b. Huntingdon. Studied Bedford, Germany and Paris. Lived for 10 years in British Columbia. Add: Manchester. † L 8, RA 4.

PEACOCK, T.R. Exh. 1896-97
34 St. Andrew Square, Edinburgh. † RSA 2.

PEACOCK, Thomas Reid Exh. 1935
81 St. Peter's Street, Quebec, Canada. † RSA 1.

PEAKE, Audrey Exh. 1912
The Red Cottage, Wrington, Somerset. † L 1.

PEAKE, Mrs. Ada E. Exh. 1919-35
Miniature painter. Add: Beckenham, Kent 1919; Birchington, Kent 1923. † RA 2, RI 8.

PEAKE, Miss A.K. Exh. 1880
Miniature portrait painter. Add: Spring Grove, Isleworth, Middlesex. † SWA 1.

PEAKE, Mrs. Carol Exh. 1937-39
8 Birdwell Croft, Wheeler's Lane, Kings Heath, Birmingham. † B 3.

PEAKE, Emma Exh. 1884
5 Cathcart Road, South Kensington, London. † D 1.

PEAKE, Miss E.M. Exh. 1882-86
Sleaford, Lincs. † N 5.

PEAKE, Harry Exh. 1910
The Little House, Sidley, Sussex. † ROI 1.

PEAKE, John N. Exh. 1890
Figure and landscape painter. Add: Chapel House, Congleton, Cheshire. † M 1, RBA 2.

PEAKE, Kathleen Exh. 1904-6
Figure painter. Add: 9 The Green, Twickenham, Middlesex. † RA 2.

PEAKE, Mary Exh. 1937
St. Anns Pottery, Malvern, Worcs. † B 1.

PEAKE, Mervyn* b. 1911
Painter and theatrical designer. b. Kuling, Central China. Studied Croydon School of Art and R.A. Schools. Exh. 1931-39. Add: 55 Woodcote Road, Wallington, Surrey. † LEI 46, RA 1, RBA 2.

PEAKE, Miss M.A. Exh. 1881-84
Landscape and bird painter. Add: Sleaford, Lincs. † N 8.

PEAKE, Miss R.K. Exh. 1922
20 The Green, Twickenham, Middlesex. † RI 1.

PEARCE, Mrs. A. Exh. 1916-21
London. † RA 5.

PEARCE, Ada Exh. 1882
8 The Ferns, Crosby, Liverpool. † L 1.

PEARCE, Arthur E. Exh. 1882-1906
Landscape painter. Add: London. † RA 1, RBA 1, RI 3.

PEARCE, Alfred W. Exh. 1931-39
Watercolour painter. Add: London 1931; Eastbourne 1939. † RA 1, RI 1.

PEARCE, Christina Exh. 1881
Figure painter. Add: Heatherley Lane, Cheltenham, Glos. † D 1.

PEARCE, Cyril C. b. 1882
Painter. Studied Barnstaple and Reading. Teacher of design and composition Reading University. A.R.B.A. 1919, R.B.A. 1921. Exh. 1914-38. Add: Reading. † I 2, RA 1, RBA 83.

PEARCE, Charles Maresco b. c.1878
Painter and etcher. Studied Chelsea Art School, under John and Orpen and Jacques Blanche in Paris and Walter Sickert. N.E.A. 1912. Member London Group 1929. Exh. 1902-39. Add: London. † BA 3, CAR 52, CHE 6, COO 3, GOU 55, I 4, L 8, LEI 59, LS 8, M 5, NEA 150, RA 1, RED,1, RHA 6, RSA 1, RSW 1.

PEARCE, Charles Sprague* 1851-1914
American figure painter. Exh. 1882-84. Add: London. Died in Paris. † RBA 1, TOO 1.

PEARCE, Elizabeth Exh. 1880-92
Landscape and figure painter. Add: London and Hauxton, nr. Cambridge. † B 5, RBA 1, RHA 1, SWA 2.

PEARCE, Edward Holroyd b. 1901
Landscape painter. R.B.A. 1940. Add: London. † NEA 2, RA 3, RBA 8, ROI 11.

PEARCE, Miss E.I. Exh. 1920
School of Art Museum, Warrington, Lancs. † L 1.

PEARCE, E. Vernon Exh. 1915
The Studio, Camden Lane, York Road, Camden Town, London. † RSA 1.

PEARCE, Mrs. Fay T. Exh. 1923-40
Painter. Add: 51 Alexandra Road, Basingstoke, Hants. † CG 1, D 2, L 1, M 1.

PEARCE, Ivy T. Exh. 1938-39
Trevarthian, 24 Edgecombe Gardens, Newquay, Cornwall. † SWA 2.

PEARCE, John Exh. 1935-37
Landscape painter. Add: Dublin. † RHA 4.

PEARCE, Joseph Exh. 1908-30
c/o Pearce and Lloyd, Royal Insurance Buildings, Liverpool. † L 20.

PEARCE, J.A. Exh. 1890-95
Municipal School of Art, West Bromwich. † B 1, P 1.

PEARCE, Lydia K. Exh. 1912-20
Miniature portrait painter. Add: London 1912; Stony Stratford, Beds. 1915. † L 3, RA 8, RMS 1.

PEARCE, Mrs. M. Thekla Exh. 1890-98
School of Art, West Bromwich. † B 5.

PEARCE, Miss P.M. Exh. 1923-40
Watercolour landscape painter. Add: Priest's Mere, Tadworth, Surrey. † AR 2, COO 1, RI 2, SWA 4.

PEARCE, Rosa A. Exh. 1926-35
Enfield Chase, Middlesex. † RMS 1, SWA 1.

PEARCE, Stephen 1819-1904
Portrait and equestrian painter. Studied at Sass's Academy, R.A. Schools 1840 and became a pupil of Sir Martin Archer Shee 1841. Add: 54 Queen Anne Street, Cavendish Square, London. † RA 6.

PEARCE, S. Dominic F. Tring d. c.1933
A.R.M.S. 1928. Add: Hythe, Kent 1928; Tunbridge Wells, Kent 1930; London 1931. † L 5, RMS 31.

PEARCE, Susan J. Exh. 1890-94
Landscape painter. Add: Nottingham. † M 1, N 8.

PEARCE, S. Tring Exh. 1880-95
Figure, historical and landscape painter. Add: Kensington, London 1880; Margate 1881 and 1895; Torquay 1894. † D 2, RA 2, RBA 1.

PEARCE, Thirkell Exh. 1929
18 Clarendon Road, Putney, London. † RCA 1.

PEARCE, William Exh. 1883-85
Figure painter. Add: 19 Chesham Terrace, Brighton. † B 1, RHA 3, ROI 1.

PEARCE, Walter J. Exh. 1926
† M 1.

PEARCE, William T. Exh. 1895-97
Portrait painter. Add: London. † RA 3.

PEARCEY, Eileen Exh. 1936-40
Painter and pen and chalk artist. Add: London. † RA 1, SWA 4.

PEARCEY, Frederick Murray b. 1897
Painter and mural decorator and illustrator. Studied Goldsmiths College, R.A. Schools and Bristol University. Artist to the Canadian Exhibition Commission. Exh. 1927-29. Add: London. † L 1, RA 1.

PEARD, Frances M. Exh. 1884-91
Landscape painter. Add: Sparnon, Torquay. † B 1, L 1, RI 3.

PEARMAN, T. Gregory Exh. 1937-40
Horndon on the Hill, Essex. † RI 4.

PEARS, Augusta Exh. 1893
10 Western Road, Hove. † NG 1.

PEARS, Agnes M. Exh. 1930
Royal College of Art, Exhibition Road, South Kensington, London. † NEA 1.

PEARS, Arthur W.H. Exh. 1936
36 Chancer Grove, Greenwood Avenue, Acocks Green, Birmingham. † B 2.

PEARS, Charles 1873-1958
Painter and lithographer. b. Pontefract. Official Naval Artist 1914-18 and 1940. Exh. 1904-39. Add: London. † CHE 1, CON 1, FIN 6, I 8, L 3, NEA 1, RA 9, RI 1, ROI 52.

PEARS, Evelyn Exh. 1900
Eastmere House, Mere, Lincoln. † B 1.

PEARS, Miss F. Exh. 1895
Mere, Lincoln. † SWA 1.

PEARSALL, Phyllis Exh. 1929-40
nee Cross. Painter and etcher. Married Richard M.S.P. q.v. Add: London 1929 and 1940; Peasmarsh, Sussex 1930. † GOU 47, RA 3, SWA 3.

PEARSALL, Richard Montague Stack b.1891
Painter and etcher. b. Dublin. Son of W. Booth and husband of Phyllis P. q.v. Studied Juliens, Paris and Slade School. Exh. 1929-39. Add: London 1929 and 1936; Peasmarsh, Sussex 1930. † L 2, RA 8, RHA 2, RSA 4.

PEARSALL, W. Booth Exh. 1880-1912
H.R.H.A. Father of Richard M.S.P. q.v. Add: Dublin 1880; London 1904. † RHA 55.

PEARSE, Alfred c. 1854-1933
Painter, black and white artist and illustrator. Exh. 1880-1900. Add: London. † RA 1, RBA 1.

PEARSE, Mrs. Annette Exh. 1932-40
Woodend, Dullator, Dunbartonshire. † GI 16.

PEARSE, F. Mabelle See UNWIN

PEARSE, Lilian G. Exh. 1914-33
Miniature portrait painter. Add: London 1914; Liverpool 1933. † L 2, RA 9.

PEARSE, Norah Exh. 1929-40
Watercolour painter, aquatinter and linocut artist. Studied Exeter School of Art. Add: Exeter. † AR 2, COO 5, RBA 3, RCA 2, RHA 1, RSA 5, SWA 4.

PEARSE, Susan B. Exh. 1910-37
Watercolour painter. Add: London 1910; Blewbury, Berks. 1926. † RA 10, RI 3, SWA 21.

PEARSE, William J. Exh. 1909-13
Cullenswood House, Oakley Road, Rathmines, Dublin. † RHA 7.

PEARSON, Arthur Exh. 1881
Landscape painter. † N 1.

PEARSON, C. Exh. 1892-1905
Higher Tranmere, Cheshire 1892; New Brighton, Cheshire 1899. † L 8.

PEARSON, Cornelius 1805-1891
Watercolour landscape painter and engraver. b. Boston, Lincs. Collaborated with Thomas Francis Wainewright q.v. Add: 15 Harper Street, Bloomsbury, London. † AG 2, D 3, RBA 17, RI 8, TOO 2.

PEARSON, Charles B. Exh. 1920-30
Architect. Add: Wallasey, Cheshire 1920; Lancaster 1921. † L 1, RA 9.

PEARSON, Mrs. C.D. Exh. 1920
The Studio, Bolton Abbey, Yorks. † L 1.

PEARSON, Dorothy Exh. 1938-40
16 Learmouth Terrace, Edinburgh. † RSW 3.

PEARSON, E. Exh. 1884
6 Milton Villas, Bearwood Road, Birmingham. † B 1.

PEARSON, E.M. Exh. 1904
Still life painter. Add: 72 Camberwell Road, London. † N 1.

PEARSON, Eleanor W. Exh. 1899
Miniature portrait painter. Add: Greyside, Muswell Hill, London. † RA 1.

PEARSON, Frank L. Exh. 1892-1919
Architect. Add: 13 Mansfield Street, Portland Place, London. † RA 22.

PEARSON, Florence M. Exh. 1904-7
Ealing, London 1904; East Grinstead, Sussex 1907. † L 2.

PEARSON, Guy Exh. 1903
Landscape painter. Add: 24 Lynn Road, Wisbech, Cambs. † RA 1.

PEARSON, Hilda Exh. 1910-31
Painter and etcher. Add: Gainsborough, Lincs. 1910; Send, Surrey 1913; Worth, Sussex 1926. † GOU 1, LS 9, RCA 1, ROI 1, WG 55.

PEARSON, Harry John 1872-1933
Portrait painter. R.B.A. 1915. Add: London. † D 2, FIN 2, GOU 3, I 3, L 3, P 4, RA 7, RBA 147, ROI 19.

PEARSON, Jenny Exh. 1901
4 Rock Park, Rock Ferry, Cheshire. † L 1.

PEARSON, John Exh. 1880-1907
Watercolour landscape painter. Add: Mold Green, Huddersfield. † L 10, M 1, RA 2, RBA 6, RHA 6.

PEARSON, John K.L. Exh. 1936
Coastal painter. Add: Norwood Lane, Meopham, Kent. † RA 1.

PEARSON, John Loughborough 1817-1897
Architect. A.R.A. 1874, R.A. 1880. Add: London. † RA 22.

PEARSON, Kathleen Margaret 1898-1961
Portrait and equestrian painter. b. Knutsford. Studied Slade School 1920, R.A. Schools 1921-26. Add: Llandudno 1923; London 1924; Lymington, Hants. 1933; Broadway, Worcs. 1937. † COO 2, I 1, L 3, M 1, P 8, RA 3, RBA 1, RCA 6, RHA 3, ROI 9, RSA 4, SWA 2.

PEARSON, L.O. Exh. 1926
Chescot, Greenfield Street, Old Lenton, Nottingham. † N 2.

PEARSON, Mary A. Exh. 1889-99
Landscape and portrait painter. Add: London. † P 2, RA 1, RHA 2, SWA 7.

PEARSON, Miss M.G. Exh. 1913
Spennithorne, Barrow in Furness. † L 3.

PEARSON, Robert Exh. 1892-1909
Painter. Add: 97 Falsgrove Road, Scarborough. † B 1, L 1, RA 2, RHA 1.

PEARSON, Walter Buckley b. 1878
Landscape painter. b. Dukinfield. Studied Ashton under Lyne School of Art and Royal College of Art. Head of Life Department Leeds School of Art 1905-21. Headmaster Halifax School of Art from 1921. Exh. 1916-33. Add: Headingley, Leeds 1916; Halifax 1933. † NEA 3, RA 2.

PEARSON-RIGHETTI, Lydia Exh. 1931
Painter. Member London Group 1922. † LEI 1.

PEART, Frederick Exh. 1901
5 St. Leonards Road, Ealing, London. † RBA 2.

PEART, Herbert E. Exh. 1907-32
Landscape painter. Add: London 1907; Salisbury 1911; Cheltenham 1922; c/o Bourlet, Nassau Street, London 1930. † M 1, NEA 18, RA 3, RED 8.

PEART, Capt. J.B. Exh. 1937-38
Oxford House, Mill Hill Lane, Derby. † B 3.

PEART, Mary Exh. 1938
† M 1.

PEART, Miss M.A. Exh. 1933-38
Mrs. Vance. Landscape and decorative painter and illustrator. Add: 2 Grove House, Gedling Grove, Nottingham. † N 17.

PEASE, Miss A. Exh. 1908-10
Sculptor. Add: 19 Vesta Road, Brockley, London. † RA 3.

PEASE, Humphrey Exh. 1932-36
Landscape and figure painter. Add: London. † RA 2, RCA 1, ROI 2, RSA 1.

PEASE, W. Exh. 1934-38
Landscape painter. Add: 68 Mona Road, West Bridgford, Nottingham. † N 2.

PEASTON, Nancy Exh. 1930-35
79 South Street, Greenock. † GI 7, RSA 3.

PEAT, A. Nolan Exh. 1884-92
Flower painter. Add: Holly Cottages, Lenton Sands, Notts. † N 17.

PEATAIN, Sean ua Exh. 1930
Sculptor. Add: 39 Harcourt Street, Dublin. † RHA 1.

PECK, Orrin 1860-1921
American painter. Exh. 1906-7. Add: The White House, 35 Tite Street, Chelsea, London. † B 1, NEA 1, RA 3.

PECK, Miss W. Somerville Exh. 1888-91
Southport, Lancs. 1888; Wigan, Lancs. 1889. † L 7.

PECKER, Alec Maurice b. 1893
Etcher, dry point and pencil artist. Studied St. Martins School of Art and Central School of Art. Exh. 1929-38. Add: London. † RA 4.

PECKITT, Thomas Exh. 1880-1926
Painter and copyist. Studied Westminster School, Goldsmiths College, National Gallery and Tate Gallery. Add: London. † B 2, GOU 2, RA 2, RBA 2, ROI 1.

PECQUEREAU, Alphonse Exh. 1883
66 Rue du Marteau, Brussels. † GI 1.

PEDDER, Anne Exh. 1885-1914
Painter. Add: 13 Somerset Place, Bath. † B 15, D 8, L 3, LS 12, RCA 22, RI 2, SWA 32.

PEDDER, Beatrice Stella b. 1875
Portrait and landscape painter. Studied Westminster School of Art. Exh. 1911-39. Add: London 1911 and 1925; Cleveden, Somerset 1920. † AR 45, COO 1, GOU 15, I 17, L 1, NEA 2, P 9, RA 5, RBA 2, RI 1, ROI 5, SWA 4.

PEDDER, John 1850-1929
Landscape, figure and animal painter and watercolourist. Born and studied in Liverpool. Add: Liverpool 1881; London 1882; Maidenhead 1886. † AG 2, B 13, D 4, G 1, L 50, M 5, RA 35, RBA 4, RI 149, ROI 3.

PEDDIE, Barbara S. Exh. 1881-1908
Landscape and flower painter. Add: Edinburgh. † BG 1, GI 11, RI 1, RSA 40, SWA 2.

PEDDIE, Christian Exh. 1892-1937
Married J.A. Henderson Tarbet q.v. Add: Edinburgh. † GI 4, RSA 35, RSW 13.

PEDDIE, James Dick Exh. 1885-191
Landscape painter. Add: Edinburgh 188 and 1905; London 1898 and 191 † GI 4, L 2, M 2, NG 2, RA 5, RSA 3 RSW 2.

PEDDIE, John Dick 1824-189
Architect. A.R.S.A. 1868, R.S.A. 187 (Sec. 1870-76). Add: Edinburgh. † L 1 RSA 12.

PEDLEY, Mrs. Ada E. Exh. 192
Halcyon Club, 2 Cork Street, London † L 3.

PEDRICK, F.T. Exh. 1915-1
11 Westbury Terrace, North Road Plymouth. † L 1, RA 2, RI 1.

PEEBLES, Alexander M. d. 189
Architect. Add: London. † RA 4.

PEEBLES, Mrs. Eleanor Exh. 192
The Manse, Uddingston, Lanark † RSA 1.

PEEL, Amy Exh. 1880-8
Landscape painter. Probably daughter of James P. q.v. Add: Arden Lea, The Drive Walthamstow, Essex. † RBA 11.

PEEL, Annie Exh. 1882-9
Painter. Add: Clitheroe, Lancs. 1882 Lancaster 1894. † D 1, SWA 1.

PEEL, C. Bertha Exh. 1883-8
Landscape painter. Add: Knowlmere Clitheroe, Lancs. † D 1, L 1, RI 1.

PEEL, Cicely M. Exh. 194
Painter. Add: Rathmore, Raheny, Co Dublin. † RHA 1.

PEEL, Gertrude Exh. 1886-191
Watercolour landscape and flower painter Add: London. † BG 4, D 9, RI 3, SWA 9

PEEL, James* 1811-190
Landscape painter. b. Newcastle. R.B.A. 1871. Probably father of Amy P. q.v. Add: Walthamstow, Essex 1880; Barnet Herts. 1890; Beaconsfield, Bucks. 1895 Reading, Berks. 1901. † GI 4, L 2, M 4 RA 4, RBA 178, RHA 2, ROI 6, TOO 13

PEEL, J. Maud Exh. 1880-190
Landscape and flower painter. Add Clitheroe, Lancs. 1880; London 1893 Winchelsea, Sussex 1903. † D 44, FIN 1 L 5, RA 2, RBA 3, RHA 1, RI 2, SWA 5

PEEL, Phyllis Neville Exh. 1933-3
Painter. † COO 4.

PEEL, Ruth Morton Exh. 1920-2
St. Margaret's, Eton Grove, Swansea † L 1, RA 1, RSA 4.

PEELE, John Thomas* 1822-189
Landscape, portrait and genre painter. b Peterborough. Emigrated to U.S.A. at ag 12. Studied New York. Returned t London c.1851. R.B.A. 1872. Add London 1880 and 1888; Bexley Heath Kent 1885. † B 3, GI 11, RA 5, RBA 59

PEERS, C.R. Exh. 1895-9
Landscape painter. Add: London † RID 4.

PEERS, Gertrude K. Exh. 1900-
Mrs. C.R. Landscape and flower painter Add: London. † RID 6.

PEES, Sophia Exh. 188
Flower painter. Add: 15 Herbert Street Haverstock Hill, London. † SWA 1.

PEGG, W.H. Exh. 1937-3
Watercolour landscape painter. Add Caythorpe, Notts. † N 6.

PEGGS, Wallace Exh. 188
Painter. Add: 9 Welbeck Mansions Cadogan Terrace, London. † RI 1.

PEGRAM, A. Bertram d. 194
Sculptor. Married Mary Buzzard q.v. Exh from 1895. Add: London. † GI 15, I 1 L 10, M 5, RA 50, RI 1, ROI 1.

EGRAM, Frederick 1870-1937
Portrait, figure and landscape painter and illustrator. R.I. 1925. Add: London 1889; Chichester, Sussex 1904. † CHE 1, CON 8, GI 14, I 1, L 4, P 4, RA 8, RI 45.

EGRAM, Henry Alfred 1863-1937
Sculptor. Studied R.A. Schools. A.R.A. 1904, R.A. 1922. "Ignis Fatuus" purchased by Chantrey Bequest 1889 and "Sibylla Fatidica" in 1904. Add: London. † GI 4, L 14, NG 12, P 1, RA 168, RSA 2.

EGRAM, Mary C. See BUZZARD

EHRSON, Miss Ulrika Exh. 1919-21
Kincraig, Chislehurst, Kent. † L 2, SWA 5.

EILE, Edith M. Exh. 1906-19
Sporting painter. Add: London. † BG 3, GOU 1, NEA 1, RA 4, ROI 5, SWA 3.

EILL, Octavia Exh. 1895
30 Tite Street, Chelsea, London. † P 1.

EIRCE, Florence M. Exh. 1895
18 Endymon Road, Finsbury Park, London. † RBA 1.

EISER, V. Exh. 1936
† NEA 2.

ELECIER, M.C. Exh. 1902
15 Rue Bourgeois, Paris. † L 1.

ELEGRIN, Mariano Exh. 1898-1904
3 Jesmond High Terrace, Newcastle on Tyne. † L 2, RBA 3, RI 1.

ELHAM, Miss E.H. Exh. 1882-83
19 Queen's Road, Everton, Liverpool. † L 2.

ELHAM, James 1840-1906
Watercolour landscape and figure painter. b. Saffron Walden. Son of James P. (1800-1874). Add: Liverpool. † D 1, L 25, M 2, RA 1.

ELHAM, Maude Exh. 1884
Painter. Add: 26 Belsize Square, London. † SWA 1.

ELHAM, Thomas Kent* Exh. 1880-92
Figure and landscape painter. Add: London 1880 and 1888; Brockley, Kent 1885. † B 10, D 1, GI 2, L 4, M 10, RA 4, RBA 9, TOO 1.

ELISSIER, F.S. Exh. 1886-89
Landscape painter. Add: London. † G 1, GOU 4, RA 1, RBA 3, RI 1.

ELL, John Exh. 1883-84
27 Dame Street, Dublin. † RHA 3.

ELLEREAU, Mrs. Emily Exh. 1898-1908
Flower painter. Add: c/o F.J. Brown, 32 Charlotte Street, Fitzroy Square, London. † B 4, BG 1, M 1.

ELLEW, Claughton b. 1890
Painter, etcher and engraver. b. Redruth, Cornwall. Studied Slade School. Married Marie P. q.v. Exh. 1921-30. Add: The Pightle, Overstrand, Norfolk. † GI 5, GOU 64, NEA 1, RHA 1, RSA 1.

ELLEW, Marie Exh. 1921
nee Tennent. Married Claughton P. q.v. Add: The Pightle, Overstrand, Norfolk. † GOU 59, NEA 1.

PELLICER, Charles Exh. 1909-11
c/o R. Collinge, Piercefield, Freshfield, Liverpool. † L 2.

PELLIGRINI, Carlo 1838-1889
Caricaturist. Known as "Ape". Exh. 1880-83. Add: London. † G 7, GI 1, L 2.

PELLING, Mrs. Lucy Exh. 1922
Watercolour painter of India. † WG 75.

PELLING-HALL, Miss L. Exh. 1896-1902
c/o Chapman Bros., King's Road, Chelsea, London. † B 2, GI,1, L 5.

PELLY, Cecily S. Exh. 1925-26
Watercolour landscape and figure painter. Add: The Lodge, Witham, Essex. † L 2.

PELLY, F.I. Clare Exh. 1914-30
The Priory, Yetbury, Glos. † L 3, RCA 2.

PELOUSE, Leon Germain* 1838-1891
French painter. Exh. 1883. Add: Cernay la Ville, Seine et Oise, France. † GI 1.

PELTON, Dorothy Gendle Exh. 1921
† RMS 1.

PEMBER, Winifred Exh. 1898
Portrait painter. Add: 8 Bryanston Square, London. † RA 2.

PEMBERTON, Florence S. Exh. 1907-31
Leeds. † B 2, L 7, LS 18, RA 4, RCA 2, SWA 1.

PEMBERTON, Hilda Mary Exh. 1897-1940
Painter, etcher and decorative designer. Studied Goldsmiths College and Royal College of Art (silver and bronze medals). Married E. Marsden Wilson q.v. A.S.W.A. 1922. Add: London. † RA 10, RCA 9, RSA 6, SWA 24.

PEMBERTON, John Exh. 1940
Pen and chalk artist. Add: 11A Curzon Street, London. † RA 1.

PEMBERTON, Max W. Exh. 1911-21
Claughton, Birkenhead 1911; Rock Ferry, Cheshire 1921. † L 7, RCA 2.

PEMBERTON, Sophie T. Exh. 1897-1910
Mrs. Beanlands. Figure, portrait and landscape painter. Studied South Kensington, Westminster and Julians, Paris. Settled in Victoria, British Columbia. Add: London 1897; Orpington, Kent 1910. † B 3, L 1, M 1, RA 6, SWA 4.

PEMBERTON, Walter Exh. 1919
† L 1.

PEMBERTON, Mrs. Wykeham Leigh Exh. 1885
Figure painter. Add: 19 Cadogan Place, London. † G 1.

PEMBERTON-LONGMAN, Joanne b. 1918
Painter. Studied Byam Shaw School 1934-38. Exh. 1939-40. Add: 25 Palace Court, London. † GOU 2, NEA 2, RA 1, RBA 1, RI 2.

PEMBERTON-LONGMAN, Sybil Exh. 1939
25 Palace Court, London. † GOU 1, ROI 1, SWA 1.

PEMSEL, Oliver Exh. 1935-36
Landscape painter. Add: Cleckheaton, Yorks. 1935; Harrogate, Yorks. 1936. † RA 2.

PENA, de la See D

PENBERTHY, K. Exh. 1933
Courtleigh Gardens, London. † SWA 2.

PENDER, W. Exh. 1885
6A Salisbury Street, Edinburgh. † RSA 1.

PENDER, Walter L. Exh. 1904
10 Grantly Street, Shawlands, Glasgow. † GI 1.

PENDER-CRICHTON, A. Exh. 1934
24 Gibson Street, Glasgow. † RSA 3.

PENDINI, Ugo Exh. 1889-90
Figure painter. Add: 25 Queen Anne Street, London. † L 2, ROI 1.

PENDLETON, Clara Exh. 1894-95
43 St. Peter's Road, Hansworth, Birmingham. † B 3.

PENDRED, Bruce Exh. 1936-37
Portrait painter. Add: London. † P 1, RA 1.

PENFOLD, Frank C. Exh. 1881-83
Figure painter. Add: Pont Aven, Finisterre, France. † RBA 1, ROI 1.

PENFOLD, Mrs. M.C. Exh. 1885-94
Flower painter. Add: 1 Dorville Crescent, Hammersmith, London. † SWA 3.

PENGELLY, Kitty Exh. 1910-12
Holly Bank, Green Lane, Stoneycroft, Liverpool. † L 2.

PENHALE, R.H. Exh. 1920
42 Bute Avenue, Lenton Sands, Nottingham. † N 1.

PENLEY, E.A. Exh. 1881
† RHA 2.

PENLLYN-JONES, Miss C.H. Exh. 1933
Old Colwyn, Wales. † RCA 1.

PENN, Prudence E. Exh. 1927-38
Sculptor. Add: London. † RA 3, RBA 3, RMS 1.

PENN, William Charles* b. 1877
Portrait and figure painter. Studied R.A. Schools and Ecole des Beaux Arts, Paris. R.O.I. 1910. Exh. 1904-38. Add: London 1904; School of Art, Liverpool 1911, Birkenhead, Cheshire 1922. † GI 3, L 74, M 9, P 5, RA 36, ROI 74, WG 47.

PENN, Walter E. Exh. 1912-29
Watercolour landscape painter. Add: The Whym, Bosham, nr. Chichester, Sussex. † RA 3, RCA 2.

PENNACCHINI, O.P. Exh. 1885
Sculptor. Add: 4 Rendal Road, North Kensington, London. † RA 2.

PENNE, de See D

PENNEFATHER, Lady Exh. 1912
Pastel landscape artist. † GOU 2.

PENNEFATHER, G.C. Exh. 1913
Pastel landscape artist. † GOU 3.

PENNEFATHER, George R.S. Exh. 1940
Landscape painter. Add: The Caravan, c/o Transit Ltd., 10 Union Quay, Cork. † RHA 2.

PENNEFATHER, Helen Exh. 1940
Landscape painter. Add: The Caravan, c/o Transit Ltd., 10 Union Quay, Cork. † RHA 2.

PENNELL, Eugene H. Exh. 1882-90
Landscape painter. Add: St. John's Wood, London. † RA 3, RBA 1.

PENNELL, Harry* Exh. 1899-1900
Marine studio, Llanfairfechan, Wales. † RCA 7.

PENNELL, Joseph 1860-1926
American watercolour painter, etcher, lithographer and illustrator. R.E. 1882-88. Add: Philadelphia, U.S.A. 1882; London 1885. † ALP 3, FIN 244, G 6, GI 28, I 87, L 103, LEI 2, NEA 9, RSA 7.

PENNELL, Lucila Exh. 1903-5
Mount Garden, Lanfairfechan, Wales. † RCA 3.

PENNETHORNE, Roddice b. 1881
Mrs. Constable. Landscape and miniature portrait painter, and lithographer. Studied Clapham, Lambeth and London Schools of Art. Exh. 1909-28. Add: London. † L 1, LS 12, RA 2.

PENNEY, Andrew M. Exh. 1880-1907
Edinburgh. † RSA 18, RSW 1.

PENNEY, Victor E. b.1909
Painter, illustrator, black and white and commercial artist. Studied Dublin College of Art. Exh. 1930-33. Add: 7 Sandford Terrace, Clonskea, Ireland. † RHA 4.

PENNINGTON, Miss E.L. Exh. 1909-17
Miniature painter. Add: Rowledge, Farnham, Surrey. † RA 5.

PENNINGTON, Frederick Exh. 1893-94
Architect. Add: London. † RA 2.

PENNINGTON, Harper 1854-1920
American portrait painter. N.E.A. 1886. Exh. 1885-87. Add: Chelsea, London. † B 1, M 1, RA 1, RBA 12.

PENNINGTON, Kate Exh. 1925
36 Gidlow Avenue, Wigan, Lancs. † L 1.

PENNINGTON, Oliver Exh. 1929
Crosby Road, Waterloo, Liverpool. † L 1.

PENNOYER, Mrs. C. Ellen Exh. 1893-94 Miniature portrait painter. Add: 42 Clovelly Mansions, Gray's Inn Road, London. † RA 3.

PENNY, Gwenneth Exh. 1909-18 Miniature painter. A.R.M.S. 1916. Add: 3 Park Hill, Ealing, London. † L 4, RA 6, RMS 5.

PENNY, Miss M. Exh. 1912-13 3 Winchester Road, South Hampstead, London. † RA 1, RI 1.

PENNY, William Exh. 1884 99 Park Road, Hockley, Birmingham. † B 2.

PENNY, William Daniel* 1834-1924 Marine painter. Exh. 1882. Add: Hull, Yorks. † RHA 3.

PENROSE, Francis Cranmer 1817-1903 Architect. Exh. 1881. Add: 68 St. Paul's Churchyard, London. † RA 2.

PENROSE, James Doyle* 1862-1932 Portrait and landscape painter. b. Michelstown, Co. Dublin. Studied South Kensington, St. John's Wood and R.A. Schools. A.R.H.A. 1901, R.H.A. 1904. Add: London 1886; Bushey, Herts. 1908. † B 2, G 1, L 13, RA 19, RHA 52, ROI 2.

PENROSE-QUICK, Miss Exh. 1902-4 Wanderersruh, Merry Mount, Bushey, Herts. † SWA 3.

PENSON, Frederick T. Exh. 1891-1934 Landscape and figure painter. Add: Stoke on Trent 1891; London 1929. † RA 4.

PENSON, James Exh. 1883 7 Boon's Place, Plymouth. † L 1.

PENSON, R. Kyrke 1815-1886 Architect and coastal and architectural painter. R.I. 1836. Add: Dinham House, Ludlow, Salop. † L 1, RI 14

PENSON, Miss S. Exh. 1880 Still life painter. Add: 5 Rue de Boulogne, Paris. † SWA 1.

PENSTONE, Edward Exh. 1880-1906 Landscape and genre painter. Add: London 1880 and 1906; Headcorn, Ashford, Kent 1894. † B 2, D 37, L 7, M 1, RA 3, RBA 3, RE 1, RHA 3.

PENSTONE, John Jewell Exh. 1881-95 Landscape and figure painter. Add: London. † RA 1, RE 2, RI 1.

PENSTONE, William Exh. 1880 Architect. Add: 22 Great James Street, Bedford Row, London. † RA 1.

PENTLAND, J. Howard Exh. 1889-1908 Architect. A.R.H.A. 1894, R.H.A. 1895. Add: Office of Public Works, Dublin. † RHA 5.

PENTY, Arthur Joseph 1875-1937 Architect. Exh. 1902-3. Add: Effingham House, Arundel Street, London. † RA 4.

PENWARDEN, Ernest Exh. 1899-1901 13 Vicarage Road, Camberwell, London. † RI 3.

PEPLOE, Denis Exh. 1938-40 13 India Street, Edinburgh. † GI 1, RSA 2.

PEPLOE, Fitzgerald Cornwall 1861-1906 Sculptor. Add: Weobley, Herefords. 1887; 6 Albermarle Street, Piccadilly, London 1889. † RA 3.

PEPLOE, Mrs. Margaret Exh. 1935 13 India Street, Edinburgh. † RSA 1.

PEPLOE, Samuel John* 1871-1935 Flower, figure, still life and landscape painter. Studied Edinburgh School of Art, and Julians, Paris 1890-93. A.R.S.A. 1918, R.S.A. 1927. Add: Edinburgh 1896 and 1912; Paris 1911. † AG 1, BA 7, BAR 14, BG 62, CG 1, G 5, GI 43, GOU 20, I 6, L 21, LEF 2, LEI 35, LS 5, RED 1, RSA 82, TOO 2.

PEPLOE, W.W. Exh. 1910-40 Edinburgh. † RSA 14.

PEPPER, Annie M. Exh. 1924 Watercolour painter. Add: 1 Noel Street, Nottingham. † N 1.

PEPPERCORN, Arthur Douglas 1847-1924 Landscape painter. Studied Ecole des Beaux Arts, Paris 1870. N.E.A. 1887, R.I. 1897 (resigned 1903), R.O.I. 1896. Add: Leatherhead, Surrey 1880; and 1898; London 1895; Ashtead, Kent 1917. † AG 2, B 2, BA 2, D 2, FIN 3, G 2, GI 6, GOU 92, I 30, L 12, LEI 122, M 17, NEA 2, NG 25, RA 19, RBA 10, RI 7, ROI 19.

PEPPERCORNE, Isabel C. Exh. 1933-40 Miniature portrait painter. Add: London. † RA 5.

PERALTO, F. Exh. 1883 c/o Mendye, King Street, St. James, London. † M 1.

PERBOYRE, Paul Emile Leon* Exh. 1882-94 French military painter. Add: Paris. † G 1, GI 5.

PERCEVAL, Marjory Exh. 1909 Painter. Add: Guns Green, Wimbledon, Surrey. † NEA 1.

PERCEVAL, Rachel M. Exh. 1940 Watercolour painter of Kenya. † WG 24.

PERCEVAL-CLARK, Evelyn Exh. 1899-1910 Watercolour landscape painter. Add: 9 Queen Anne's Gardens, Bedford Park, London. † B 1, BG 36, NG 1.

PERCIVAL, A.F. Exh. 1894-97 Alma Place, Shawlands, Glasgow. † GI 3.

PERCIVAL, Bessie See JOHNSON

PERCIVAL, Constance M. Exh. 1920-26 70 Yew Tree Road, Walton, Liverpool. † L 2.

PERCIVAL, E.D. Exh. 1891-1905 Tunbridge Wells, Kent 1891; Ilfracombe, Devon 1901. † B 3, GI 1.

PERCIVAL, Edith M. Exh. 1897-1914 Minster Close, Peterborough, Lincs. † SWA 15.

PERCIVAL, Harold 1868-1914 A.R.E. 1905. Add: Seaford 1905; Steyning, 1908. † GI 2, L 5, LS 3, RE 32, RSA 2.

PERCIVAL, J. Exh. 1889 8 Middleton Road, Wandsworth Common, London. † B 1.

PERCIVAL, Walter Exh. 1892 Architect. Add: 65 Caroline Street, Longton, Staffs. † RA 1.

PERCY, Miss A.B. Exh. 1885-86 Shaftesbury Lodge, Brandenburg Road, Gunnersley, London. † B 2, L 1.

PERCY, Amy Dora Exh. 1883-86 Landscape painter. Youngest daughter of Sidney Richard P. q.v. Add: Woodseat, Sutton, Surrey. † D 1, RA 1, RBA 3, SWA 2.

PERCY, Miss B.W. Exh. 1939 Mrs. Allen Purvis. Add: 191 Ember Lane, East Molesey, Surrey. † RI 1.

PERCY, Henry Exh. 1894 18 Laurel Road, Fairfield, Lancs. † L 1.

PERCY, Herbert Sidney Exh. 1880-1903 Landscape painter and picture restorer. Son of Sidney Richard P. q.v. Add: Woodseat, Sutton, Surrey 1880; London 1889. † D 1, L 2, M 2, NG 2, RA 1, RBA 8, ROI 1.

PERCY, Ida See NELSON

PERCY, Mrs. Lilian Snow Exh. 1885-92 Flower and still life painter. Eastbourne 1885; Twickenham 1886; South Croydon, Surrey 1892. † L 1, RBA 1, SWA 2.

PERCY, Sidney Richard* 1821-18 Landscape painter. 5th son of Edwa "Old" Williams (1782-1855). Changed name to avoid confusion with oth members of the family. Father of An Dora and Herbert Sidney P. q.v. Ad Woodseat, Sutton, Surrey. † L 5, M RA 8, RBA 2, TOO 5.

PERCY, Thomas Exh. 18 5 Camden Street, Oakley Square, Londo † RHA 1.

PERCY, William 1820-19 Portrait painter. Pupil of William Bradle Add: Manchester. † M 18.

PERCY, W.S. Exh. 1931- c/o J.B. Bennett and Son, Glasgo † RSA 6.

PEREDA, Raimondo 1840-19 Sculptor. Exh. 1880. Add: Via Montebel 3, Rome. † RA 1.

PERGOLA, Luigi Exh. 191 Landscape painter. † BRU 1.

PERIGAL, Arthur* 1816-18 Landscape painter. A.R.S.A. 1841, R.S. 1868 (Treas. 1880-84). Add: Edinburg † GI 15, M 2, RSA 31, RSW 18.

PERILLARD, Jules Exh. 191 134 Rue Broca, Paris. † RSA 1.

PERIN, Bradford Exh. 192 † NEA 1.

PERKEN, Stella Louise See WILSO

PERKIN, Mrs. Isabell L. Exh. 1888-192 Flower painter. Tiverton, Devon 188 Oxford 1928. † B 9, RA 3.

PERKINS, Arthur E. Exh. 1889-9 Architect. East Finchley, London † RA

PERKINS, Athelina Lois Gwendoline b.189 Painter, modeller, illuminator and pewt worker. Studied Central School of Ar Birmingham and Slade School. Ex 1920-24. Add: Countisbury, Belveder Road, Coventry. † B 6, L 2, RA 4, RMS 3

PERKINS, Christopher b. 189 Landscape and portrait painter. b. Pete borough. Studied Slade School. Ex 1914-40. Add: London 1914 and 193 Sudbury, Suffolk 1919; St. Aubin, Jersey C.I. 1929; Southwold, Suffolk 1940 † LS 4, P 1, RA 2, ROI 1.

PERKINS, Charles P. Exh. 1880-8 Miniature portrait painter. Stockwel London 1880; Brighton, Sussex 188 † RA 3.

PERKINS, F.J. Exh. 194 51 Kimbolton Road, Bedford. † RI 1.

PERKINS, Emily Exh. 1884-9 Watercolour landscape painter. St. Paul Square, York. † SWA 14.

PERKINS, George Exh. 1881-9 Landscape painter, 21 Kennedy Stree Manchester. † M 22, RA 1, REA 1.

PERKINS, Mrs. Zilla Temple Exh. 1899-190 4 Dean's Yard, Westminster, Londo † LS 3, N 3, RI 1, SWA 1.

PERKS, Mrs. J. Exh. 189 64 Castletown Road, London. † SWA 1

PERKS, Sydney d. 194 Architect and surveyor to Corporation o the City of London 1904-31. Exh 1897-1929. Add: London. † RA 16.

PERKS, W.A. Exh. 192 670 Stratford Road, Sparkhill, Birming ham. † B 1.

PERKS, W.G. Exh. 1930-3 Trefriw, Caerns. † RCA 5.

PERLMUTTER, Isaac 1866-193 Hungarian artist. Exh. 1914. Add: Hun gary. † RSA 1.

PERLZWEIG, Hyman W. Exh. 1938-40
Watercolour figure and landscape painter. 29 Endersleigh Gardens, Hendon, London. † RA 3.

PERMAIN, Miss E.M. Exh. 1896
36 Brunswick Square, London. † SWA 3.

PERMAN, Miss F. Bassingham Exh. 1929
Miniature flower painter. 48 Meadway, Old Southgate, London. † RA 1.

PERMAN, Louise d. 1921
Mrs. Torrance. Flower painter. Exh. from 1884. Add: Glasgow. † BG 4, GI 79, L 24, M 3, NG 8, RA 6, RHA 10, ROI 1, RSA 28, SWA 8.

PERMEKE, Constant* 1886-1952
Belgian painter. Exh. 1918. † I 2.

PERNA, Charles Exh. 1896-98
Landscape painter. Kensington, London. † RA 5.

PERNOT, A. Exh. 1910-11
12 Rue du Parc de Mont Souris, Paris. † L 2.

PERRAULT, Leon 1832-1908
French artist. Exh. 1902. Add: 43 Boulevard Lannes, Paris. † L 1.

PERRAULT-HARRY, E. Exh. 1908
10 Rue Herran, Paris. † L 1.

PERRET, Aime* 1847-1927
French figure painter. Exh. 1882-1904. Add: Paris. † L 1, RHA 1.

PERRETT, Mrs. Edith L. Exh. 1910-21
Birmingham. † B 3.

PERRETT, Rev. John Exh. 1929-38
Religious painter. † AB 6, WG 8.

PERRETT, J.E. Exh. 1934-37
45 Leithcote Gardens, London. † RI 4.

PERRETT, L. Everett Exh. 1927
† D 1.

PERRETT, Miss M.E. Exh. 1930
22 Beaufort Road, Edgbaston, Birmingham. † B 1.

PERRIMAN, G.S. Exh. 1924-29
Ambleside, Ashingdon, nr. Rochford, Lancs. † L 4.

PERRIN, Alfred Feyen d. 1918
Landscape painter. Paris 1883; Conway, Wales 1884. † B 26, GI 1, L 4, M 1, RA 1, RCA 177.

PERRIN, Clara Caroline Exh. 1897-1918
Married George Edward Collins, q.v. Add: Glan Conway, North Wales. † B 5, L 1, RCA 34.

PERRIN, Ida Southwell b. 1860
nee Robins. Painter and manager of the De Morgan Pottery Works, Bushey. Daughter of Edward C. Robins q.v. Exh. 1884-1925. Add: Hampstead 1884; Bushey, Herts. 1918. † RA 8, RBA 2, ROI 3, SWA 2.

PERRIN, Jacques 1847-1915
French sculptor. Exh. 1892. Add: Paris. † RSA 1.

PERRIN, John W. Exh. 1884-1909
Miniature painter. Add: London. † B 1, RA 9, RBA 8, RHA 10, RI 2, ROI 14.

PERRIN, Mary M. Exh. 1881-1916
Watercolour painter. Add: Portfields House, Terenure, Dublin. † L 1, RA 9, RI 13, SWA 2.

PERRIN, Ross Exh. 1891
Painter. Add: 56A Harold Street, Camberwell, London. † RA 1.

PERRINS, John H. Exh. 1935
71 Python Hill Road, Rainworth, Mansfield, Notts. † N 1.

PERRINS, Rosa Exh. 1884-94
Birmingham. † B 12.

PERROT, Albert Exh. 1900
43 Courtfield Road, London. † L 2.

PERROT, Patty Exh. 1935
8 Wild Hatch, London. † SWA 1.

PERROTT, Freda Exh. 1899-1940
Flower painter. Add: Belmont Avenue, Donnybrook. † RHA 74.

PERROTT, Maria Exh. 1881-87
Dublin. † RHA 5.

PERROTT, Mary Exh. 1905-30
Miniature painter. Studied Brighton School of Art, Camden School of Art and Regent Street Polytechnic. A.R.M.S. 1923, A.S.W.A. 1924, S.W.A. 1928. Add: London. † L 9, LS 3, RA 2, RI 10, RMS 26, SWA 13.

PERRY, A. Exh. 1909-13
Maun Vale, Brunt Street, Mansfield, Notts. † N 4.

PERRY, Albert Exh. 1933-39
Painter. Add: 113 Franciscan Road, London. † AR 45, ROI 6, RSA 2.

PERRY, Alfred Exh. 1880-84
Landscape, animal and genre painter.. Add: Plumstead, Kent. † D 2, L 1.

PERRY, Alice See FLOWER

PERRY, Arthur W. Exh. 1908
Prospect House, Seaton, Devon. † B 2.

PERRY, Dorothy M. Exh. 1912
School Lane, Bidston, Cheshire. † L 1.

PERRY, Ernest B. Exh. 1923-39
Landscape, coastal and river painter. A.N.S.A. 1927, N.S.A. 1929. Add: Sherwood, Notts. † N 53.

PERRY, Ernest Thomas b. 1908
Portrait painter. Studied Heatherleys and R.A. Schools. Assistant teacher, Heatherleys. Joint principal of St. John's Wood Art School. Exh. 1936. Add: London. † P 1.

PERRY, H.J. Exh. 1922-32
Birmingham. † B 14, NEA 1.

PERRY, John Tavenor Exh. 1880-1905
Architect. Add: London. † RA 3.

PERRY, Mrs. Lilla Exh. 1909-30
Landscape painter. Add: Bird Hill, Clonmel. † LS 3, RHA 5.

PERRY, Miss L.M. Exh. 1886
Mount Hill, Springfield, Chelmsford, Essex. † M 1.

PERRY, S.R. Exh. 1887-90
† TOO 4.

PERRY, Will Exh. 1902-18
Figure and landscape painter. Add: London. † L 1, LS 8, M 1, RA 6.

PERRY, W.J.M. Exh. 1886-1912
Dublin. † L 3, RHA 53, RSA 1.

PERRY-COSTE, Mrs. Maud Exh. 1898-1901
Warren Cottage, Polperro, Cornwall. † B 3.

PERTWEE, R. Exh. 1907
12 Trafalgar Studios, Manresa Road, London. † RA 1.

PERTZ, Anne J. Exh. 1880-1911
Still life, figure and portrait painter. Add: Florence 1880 and 1886; London 1884; Cambridge 1889. † ALP 2, D 1, G 2, L 1, M 1, RA 8, SWA 2.

PERTZ, Emma Exh. 1893-96
4 Finchley Road, St. John's Wood, London. † L 1, M 2.

PERUGINI, Charles Edward* 1839-1919
Portrait and genre painter. b. Naples. Came to England 1863. Married Kate P. q.v. Add: London. † B 9, FIN 2, GI 2, L 30, M 10, NG 22, P 1, RA 50, RSA 1.

PERUGINI, Kate 1839-1929
Genre and portrait painter. Daughter of Charles Dickens. Married 1st Charles Allston Collins (1828-1873), 2nd Charles Edward P. q.v. S.W.A. 1886. Exh. 1880-1908. Add: London. † B 2, G 3, GI 1, L 20, M 2, NG 28, P 1, RA 33, RI 3, SWA 13.

PERUGINI, Laurence Exh. 1935-37
Painter. Add: 11 Market Street, Rye, Sussex. † COO 4, RA 1, RI 2.

PERY-KNOX-GORE, Miss I. Exh. 1938
Menai Bridge, Anglesey. † RCA 1.

PESENTI, D. Exh. 1882
Interior painter. Add: c/o Loughi, 27 New Broad Street, London. † RA 1.

PESKETT, Greta Exh. 1934-38
Miniature portrait painter. Add: 96 Malthouse Road, Crawley, Sussex. † RA 2.

PETCH, J.B. Exh. 1911
5 Baronsmead Road, Barnes, Surrey. † RA 1.

PETER, Robert Charles b. 1888
Painter, etcher and mezzotint engraver. Studied L.C.C. School, Bolt Court. A.R.E. 1921. Exh. 1907-40. Add: London. † AB 1, CHE 2, GOU 1, L 8, RA 22, RE 28, RID 4.

PETERS, Clinton b. 1865
American portrait painter. Exh. 1894. Add: 10 Rue Lecourbe, Paris. † RA 1.

PETERS, Mrs. Frances Exh. 1896
† SWA 1.

PETERS, T. Exh. 1919-30
Landscape painter. Add: 21 Washington Road, Sheffield. † L 4, RA 1.

PETERS, William Exh. 1895-97
Painter. Add: London. † L 1, RA 2.

PETERS, William Exh. 1897
101 Bath Street, Glasgow. † GI 1.

PETERSEN, Prof. Hans 1850-1914
German artist. Exh. 1901. Add: Schwanthaler Strasse G. Munchen, Germany. † I 2.

PETERSEN, Lilian Exh. 1923
Miniature portrait painter. Add: 48 Markham Square, Chelsea, London. † RA 1.

PETERSON, Bridget Exh. 1938-40
Flower and portrait painter. Add: 40A Halima Park Road, South Croydon, Surrey. † RA 5.

PETHERBRIDGE, Albert George 1882-c. 1934
Painter, etcher and pastellier. Add: Bushey, Herts. 1920; Brockenhurst, Hants. 1924. † AB 61, L 9, RA 6, RCA 2, RI 3.

PETHERICK, Edith M. Exh. 1889-1929
Painter and etcher. Add: London 1889; Exeter 1890. † AB 3, B 2, D 5, I 4, L 4, RA 2, ROI 2, SWA 8.

PETHERICK, Horace William 1839-1919
Painter and black and white artist. Worked for the "Illustrated London News". Add: Addiscombe, Surrey 1891; Croydon, Surrey 1901. † L 1, RA 3.

PETHERICK, L. Bonney Exh. 1937
Flower painter. † COO 1.

PETHYBRIDGE, Grace Exh. 1928-33
Mrs. E. Bulmer. Watercolour landscape painter. Add: Launceston, Cornwall 1928; Hereford 1933. † RA 6.

PETHYBRIDGE, J. Ley Exh. 1885-93
Figure and landscape painter. Add: Lyndhurst, Hants. 1885; Launceston, Cornwall 1889. † L 4, RA 2, RBA 4.

PETIT, le See L

PETITJEAN, Francois d. 1933
Etcher. b. Charelles, France. Studied Colarossi's, Paris. Exh. 1894-1918. Add: Chiswick, London. † RA 3.

PETMAN, H.C. Bevan Exh. 1919-39
Portrait painter. Add: London. † I 2, RHA 1.

PETO, Gladys Emma b. 1890
Mrs. Emmerson. Watercolour painter and black and white artist. b. Maidenhead. Studied Maidenhead School of Art and London School of Art. On staff of "Sketch" 1915-26. Lived in Malta, Cyprus and Egypt 1924-28. Exh. 1929. † AB 40.

PETO, Morton K. Exh. 1881-84
Figure painter. Add: Eastcote House, Pinner, Middlesex. † B 1, M 1, RA 1, RHA 1, ROI 1.

PETO, Mrs. Ralph Exh. 1914-16
Painter. Add: 24 Manchester Square, London. † LS 4, NEA 1.

PETRIE, Elizabeth C. Exh. 1880-1902
Watercolour landscape painter. Sister of Graham P. q.v. Add: London. † B 5, D 1, L 5, M 2, RBA 10, RI 4, SWA 18.

PETRIE, Graham 1859-1940
Landscape painter, poster designer and author. Brother of Elizabeth P. q.v. R.I. 1903 (Hon. Retd. 1937), R.O.I. 1920 (Hon. Retd. 1939). Travelled widely. Add: London. † B 2, CHE 2, DOW 2, FIN 79, G 1, GI 4, L 7, LEI 79, M 5, NEA 4, NG 14, RA 39, RBA 10, RHA 6, RI 100, RID 72, ROI 35.

PETRIE, Mrs. Maria b. 1887
nee Zimmern. Painter and sculptor. b. Frankfurt, Germany. Studied Frankfurt College of Art and under Aristide Maillol, Maurice Denis, Theo von Rysselberghe and Paul Serusier in Paris. Exh. 1926-37. Add: Ilkley, Yorks. 1926; London 1937. † L 2, RA 1, RSA 1.

PETRIE, W.M. Exh. 1892-1916
Teacher Glasgow School of Art. Add: 248 West George Street, Glasgow. † GI 44, M 1, RSA 8, RSW 5.

PETRIE, William P. Exh. 1914
54 Shandwick Place, Edinburgh. † GI 1.

PETTAFOR, Charles R. Exh. 1880-1900
Landscape painter. Add: Elsie Bank, Victoria Road, Eltham, Kent. † D 8, RA 15, RBA 5, RI 2, ROI 1.

PETTAFOR, Mabel M. Exh. 1903-12
Miniature painter. Add: 32 Park Road, Southborough, Tunbridge Wells, Kent. † L 1, RA 5.

PETTIE, John* 1839-1893
Historical and portrait painter and illustrator. b. Edinburgh. Studied at the Trustees Academy, Edinburgh at age 16. Moved to London 1862. A.R.A. 1866, R.A. 1873, H.R.S.A. 1871. "The Vigil" purchased by Chantrey Bequest 1884. † B 9, G 7, GI 17, L 20, M 12, P 5, RA 65, RHA 1, ROI 3, RSA 27, TOO 6.

PETTIGREW, Hettie Exh. 1893-1909
London. † GI 8, L 2, LS 3.

PETTINGER, John Frederick Exh. 1904-34
Landscape painter. Add: London 1904; Leicester 1916. † B 3, N 13, NEA 4, RA 12.

PETTITT, Edwin Alfred* 1840-1912
Landscape painter. Add: Bettws-y-Coed, Wales 1880; Birmingham 1883. † L 3, RA 1.

PETTITT, Wilfred Stanley b. 1904
Landscape painter and commercial artist. Studied Gt. Yarmouth and Norwich Schools of Art. Exh. 1928-32. Add: Camphill, Reedham, Norfolk. † RA 2.

PETTIWARD, Roger d. 1942
Painter. Artist with "Punch" 1936-40. (Signed work Paul Crum.) Exh. 1935-39. Add: London. † LEI 1, M 1, NEA 3, P 3, RBA 1.

PETTMAN, Mrs. Clara Exh. 1903-5
Flower painter. Add: 125 Alexandra Road, St. John's Wood, London. † L 2, RA 1, SWA 2.

PETTS, R. John Exh. 1936
Llanllechid, Caerns. † RCA 1.

PETTY, W.R. Exh. 1886-99
Figure painter. Add: London 1886; East Barnet, Herts. 1899. † L 2, RA 2, RI 6, ROI 3.

PETYT, Emily Exh. 1885
Watercolour landscape painter. Add: Bolton Abbey, Skipton, Yorks. † RSA 1, SWA 1.

PETZET, Hermann Exh. 1899
14 Jahnstrasse, Carlsruhe, Baden, Germany. † GI 1.

PEUCKERT, Edward A. Exh. 1893-94
Coastal painter. Add: 20 Bryantwood Road, Highbury, London. † RA 3.

PEYMAN, J. Esdaile Exh. 1937-40
Windward, Sidmouth, Devon. † NEA 5, SWA 1.

PEYROL, Francois A.H. 1856-1929
French sculptor. Exh. 1905. Add: 76 Rue Borgheses, Neuilly sur Seine, France. † L 1.

PEYTON, Barbara Exh. 1934
Wood engraver. Add: Burlings, Pondfield Road, Hayes, Kent. † RA 1.

PEYTON, Emily M. Exh. 1903-11
Mrs. J.W. Add: London. † LS 14, RA 3, SWA 1.

PEZANT, Aymar* b. 1846
French landscape painter. Exh. 1907. Add: 15 Rue Hegesippe Moreau, Paris. † L 1.

PFEIFER, Miss C.M. Exh. 1905
10 Rue Campagne, Paris. † RA 1.

PFEIFFER, Mrs. Emily Exh. 1880-84
Flower painter. Add: Mayfield, West Hill, Putney. † D 3, RA 1.

PFEIFFER, Miss E.M. Exh. 1895-96
33 Glazbury Road, London. † SWA 2.

PFLAUM, Nance Exh. 1911-35
Landscape painter, pastelier and aquatinter. Add: Ashlar House, Chapel Allerton, Leeds. † BG 1, L 7, LS 6, RA 2, RSA 4, SWA 4.

PHELPS, Miss A.T. Exh. 1896-99
62 Onslow Gardens, London. † SWA 3.

PHELPS, Millicent Exh. 1890-1921
Mrs. Mayer. Portrait and flower painter. Add: London. † L 1, P 1, RA 10, ROI 5.

PHIBBS, Harry Exh. 1902
Architect. Add: William Street, Brierley Hill, Staffs. † RA 1.

PHILBRICK, Miss M. Exh. 1905
† SWA 1.

PHILIP, Alex A. Exh. 1937
Brackendale Road, Bournemouth. † RSA 1.

PHILIP, Constance B. See LAWSON

PHILIP, M. Exh. 1892-96
296 Gt. Western Road, Glasgow. † GI 3.

PHILIP, M. Exh. 1938
† RED 2.

PHILIPP, W. Exh. 1932
Woodcut artist. † BA 2.

PHILIPS, Herman Exh. 1887-95
† TOO 5.

PHILIPSON, Miss A. Exh. 1896-1902
77 Lancaster Gate, London. † SWA 5.

PHILLIMORE, Alice Exh. 1881
Watercolour painter. Add: 5 Arlington Street, London. † SWA 2.

PHILLIMORE, Cordelia M. Exh. 1880-81
Still life painter. Add: Hill House, Sneinton, Notts. † N 3.

PHILLIMORE, Catherine Mary Exh. 1881
Painter. Add: 5 Arlington Street, London. † SWA 1.

PHILLIMORE, Lucy Exh. 1927-37
Landscape painter. Add: Queen's Gate, London. † AB 1, SWA 5.

PHILLIMORE, Reginald P. b. 1855
Painter, etcher and black and white artist. Studied Nottingham and Oxford. Exh. 1886-1923. Add: Chiswick, London 1886; Rockstowes, North Berwick 1918. † B 1, N 1, RA 1, RI 2, RSA 10.

PHILLIP, Albert Exh. 1939-40
Etcher. Add: 21 Edith Grove, London. † RA 3.

PHILLIP, Colin Bent 1855-1932
Watercolour landscape painter. Son of John Phillip (1817-1867). Studied Lambeth School of Art, Edinburgh, and under David Farquharson. R.S.W. 1890 (res. 1907), A.R.W.S. 1886, R.W.S. 1898. Add: Lynton, North Devon 1882; London 1883; Lynmouth, Devon 1915; Braunton, Devon 1928. † B 1, D 5, DOW 1, FIN 1, GI 2, L 11, M 4, RA 15, RHA 1, RI 9, RSW 20, RWS 114.

PHILLIPPE, L.H. Exh. 1912
20 Rue Littre, Paris. † RSA 1.

PHILLIPS, Miss Exh. 1881
Watercolour landscape painter. Add: London. † SWA 1.

PHILLIPS, Arthur Exh. 1887-92
Flower and landscape painter. Add: Nottingham. † B 2, N 14, RA 1.

PHILLIPS, A. Gertrude Exh. 1928
Landscape painter. † AB 1.

PHILLIPS, A.M. Exh. 1880-81
Landscape and figure painter. Add: Shere, nr. Guildford, Surrey 1880; Redhill, Surrey 1881. † RBA 3.

PHILLIPS, Alfred P.* Exh. 1880-96
Landscape and figure painter. Add: London 1880; New Maldon 1903. † M 2, RA 6, RBA 2.

PHILLIPS, Arthur T. Exh. 1933
Architect. Add: 45 Lower Belgrave Street, London. † RA 1.

PHILLIPS, Bessie Exh. 1881
Watercolour landscape painter. Add: The Crab Trees, Sutton, Chester. † SWA 1.

PHILLIPS, Miss B.E. Exh. 1888
The Vicarage, Lye, nr. Stourbridge, Worcs. † B 1.

PHILLIPS, Charles E.S. Exh. 1924-38
Landscape painter. Add: Castle House, Shooters Hill, London. † RA 2, ROI 17.

PHILLIPS, Charles Gustav Louis b. 1863
Painter and etcher. b. Montevideo. Exh. 1891-1932. Add: Dundee. † GI 9, RSA 22.

PHILLIPS, Mrs. Dubois Exh. 1899
Gt. Crosby, Liverpool. † L 1.

PHILLIPS, Elizabeth Exh. 1935
Linocut artist. † RED 2.

PHILLIPS, Mrs. E.K.M. Exh. 1892-1900
Chaceley, nr. Tewkesbury 1892; Cheltenham 1894. † B 4, RBA 1.

PHILLIPS, G. Exh. 1914
20 Buckingham Street, Adelphi, London. † RA 1.

PHILLIPS, Georgina Exh. 1903-4
Portrait painter. Add: Bhundara, Chingford Hall Road, Chingford, Essex. † RA 1, SWA 1.

PHILLIPS, Helen Exh. 1889-1900
Landscape painter. Add: Dorney House, 25 Disraeli Road, Putney, London. † B 2, L 5, M 1, RA 1, RBA 4, RI 2, SWA 6, TOO 1.

PHILLIPS, H.E. Exh. 1892
Langleigh, West Worthing, Sussex. † B 2.

PHILLIPS, H. Graham Exh. 1915-18
Dublin. † RCA 1, RHA 2.

PHILLIPS, H. Raines Exh. 1940
Sculptor. Add: Tiverton, Devon. † RA 1.

PHILLIPS, J. Exh. 1910-11
St. George's Studio, 1 Back Canning Street, Liverpool. † L 1.

PHILLIPS, J.L. Exh. 1895
7 Barton Street, Baron's Court, London. † NG 1.

PHILLIPS, Miss L. Exh. 1896
18 Stockwell Street, Leek, Staffs. † M 1.

PHILLIPS, Lawrence Barnett 1842-1922
Painter and etcher. A.R.E. 1887. Add: London. † DOW 1, GI 3, L 29, M 6, RA 10, RBA 3, RE 77. ROI 4, WG 65.

PHILLIPS, May Exh. 1893-1911
South London. † B 1, RHA 3.

PHILLIPS, Mariquita Jenny See MOBERLY

PHILLIPS, Mary S. Exh. 1880-81
Landscape, coastal and figure painter. Add: 13 Kildare Gardens, London. † SWA 3.

PHILLIPS, Mrs. Philip Exh. 1881
Miss Elizabeth Rous. Married Philip P. (d.1864) Landscape painter. Add: 20 Stockwell Green, Stockwell. † SWA 1.

PHILLIPS, Patrick Edward b. 1907
Portrait and landscape painter. Studied Byam Shaw School 1926-30. Principal Byam Shaw Art School. Add: London 1931 and 1935; Godalming, Surrey 1932. † COO 9, NEA 2, P 3, RA 8.

PHILLIPS, Mrs. Stephen Exh. 1887-98
Add: Edgbaston, Birmingham 1887; Winslow, Bucks. 1888; Dudley, Worcs. 1897. † B 5.

PHILLIPS, Sarah Catharine b. 1867
Miniature painter. Exh. 1908-11. Add: Middlegate, Northwood, Middlesex. † RA 4.

PHILLIPS, S. Henry Exh. 1924-25
134 Muirhead Avenue, West Derby, Liverpool. † L 2.

PHILLIPS, Thomas Exh. 1886-1913
Add: Liverpool 1886; Seacombe 1894; Liscard, Cheshire 1904. † I 1, L 54, RCA 11.

PHILLIPS, Thomas Exh. 1880-88
Landscape painter. Add: Nottingham 1880; Carlton, Notts. 1884. † N 11.

PHILLIPS, William Exh. 1890-1909
Landscape painter. Add: London. † L 8, RA 3, RBA 4, ROI 4.

PHILLIPS, Winifred Exh. 1909-15
Flower, figure and landscape painter. Add: Liverpool 1909; London 1911. † NEA 17.

PHILLIPS, Mrs. W.E. Exh. 1924
Figure and flower painter. Add: Hilton Road, Mapperley, Nottingham. † N 2.

PHILLIPS, William J. Exh. 1898-99
9 Kingsley Road, Willesden Lane, London. † RBA 3.

PHILLIPS, Walter Joseph* b. 1884
Watercolour painter, wood engraver and teacher. Studied Birmingham Municipal School of Art. Exh. 1912-33. Add: Salisbury 1912; Canada 1924. † COO 52, GI 1, RA 1, RSA 2, RSW 4.

PHILLIPSON, Barbara Exh. 1930
Portrait artist. Add: College House, Dollis Avenue, Finchley, London. † RA 1.

PHILLIPSON, Charles Exh. 1926-28
Pensilva, Wythenshaw Road, Sale Moor, Cheshire. † L 1, M 1.

PHILLOTT, Constance 1842-1931
Watercolour painter. Studied R.A. Schools. A.R.W.S. 1882. Add: London. † B 1, L 10, LEI 1, M 5, NG 3, RA 1, RSA 2, RWS 69.

PHILLP, Laura E. Exh. 1882-87
Landscape painter. Add: Falmouth House, Hagley Road, Edgbaston, Birmingham. † B 8, L 1, SWA 5.

PHILLPOTTS, Miss C.M. Exh. 1904
Walkern Rectory, Stevenage, Herts. † SWA 1.

PHILLPOTTS, Maude S. Exh. 1896-1900
Miniature portrait painter. Add: School House, Bedford. † B 5, RA 2.

PHILP, Miss Avis N. Exh. 1891-1913
Add: London 1891; Wallasey, Cheshire 1913. † L 2.

PHILP, Mrs. A. Nickels Exh. 1897-1910
132 Falkner Street, Liverpool. † B 3, L 19, M 3, RCA 2.

PHILP, James George 1816-1885
Landscape and coastal painter and watercolourist. b. Falmouth. A.R.I. 1856, R.I. 1863, R.O.I. 1883. Add: Falmouth 1880. † D 1, L 4, RI 43, ROI 3.

PHILPOT, Mrs. Exh. 1925
Watercolour painter. † WG 49.

PHILPOT, Glyn Warren* 1884-1937
Portrait and figure painter. Studied Lambeth School of Art: under Jean Paul Laurens in Paris; Spain and Italy. A.R.A. 1915, R.A. 1923, R.O.I. 1909, H.R.O.I. 1925, R.P. 1925. "A Young Breton" purchased by Chantrey Bequest 1917 and "Mrs. Gerard Simpson" in 1937. Add: London. † BG 59, CG 2, CHE 2, FIN 7, G 3, GI 4, GOU 8, I 30, L 15, LEI 77, LS 5, P 11, RA 54, RED 76, ROI 13, RSA 9.

PHILPOT, Leonard Daniel b. 1877
Flower painter. Studied Architecture at South Kensington. Practised architecture in London, China and America, also furniture design and interior decoration before taking up painting. Exh. 1928-40. Add: Fittleworth, Sussex 1928; Bognor Regis 1932; West Moors, Dorset 1940. † FIN 1, GI 1, L 12, RA 10, RI 2.

PHILPOT, T.D. Exh. 1905
23 Gresham Road, Brixton, London. † RA 1.

PHINNEY, Emma E. Exh. 1880
c/o J. Edmorton, 12 Gt. Winchester Street, London. † G 1.

PHIPPS, C.A. Gayer
See DAKIN, Rose Mabel

PHIPPS, Edmund Exh. 1884-1915
Landscape painter. Add: Breeze Hill, Liverpool 1884; Glan Conway, Wales 1910; Seacombe 1915. † B 1, L 50, RCA 4. RI 1.

PHIPPS, Miss Lizzie G. Exh. 1887-1902
Breeze Hill, Bootle, Liverpool. † L 4.

PHIPPS, Miss M.E. Exh. 1907
Towcester, Northants. † SWA 1.

PHIPPS, Paul Exh. 1927-28
Architect. Add: 2 Boyle Street, Savile Row, London. † RA 2.

PHIPSON, A. Exh. 1897
The Langdales, Worcester. † B 1.

PHIPSON, Edith S. Exh. 1882-84
Metchley Lane, Birmingham. † B 3.

PHOENIX, George Exh. 1886-1935
Figure and landscape painter. Add: Wolverhampton 1886 and 1891; Bournemouth 1889. † B 12, L 2, NG 3, RA 13.

PHOTAS, G.C. Exh. 1908-9
Greek Church, Moscow Road, London. † LS 1, RA 1.

PHYSICK, Robert Sen. b. 1815
Sculptor. Studied R.A. Schools 1837 (silver medal). Father of Thomas and William P. q.v. Add: 20 Carlton Street, Kentish Town, London. † RBA 4.

PHYSICK, Sidney H. Exh. 1890-96
Sculptor. 136 Marylebone Road, London. † L 2, M 1, RA 3.

PHYSICK, Thomas Exh. 1881
Painter and sculptor. Son of Robert P. sen. q.v. Add: 20 Carlton Street, Kentish Town, London. † RBA 1.

PHYSICK, William Exh. 1890
Sculptor. Son of Robert P. sen. q.v. Add: 11 Warrender Road, Tufnell Park Road, London. † RBA 1.

PHYTHIAN, W. Exh. 1938
† P 1.

PIBWORTH, Charles James b. 1878
Sculptor and painter. b. Bristol. Studied Bristol School of Art, Royal College of Art and R.A. Schools (2 gold, silver and bronze medals). Exh. 1900-39. Add: London. † GI 4, L 7, LS 5, NG 1, RA 42, RBA 2, RI 3, ROI 2.

PICABIA, Francis* 1879-1953
French painter. Exh. 1925. † CHE 1.

PICARD, Robert Exh. 1895
Brussels. † P 1.

PICART-le-DOUX Exh. 1928
† GOU 2.

PICASSO, Pablo* 1881-1973
Spanish painter. Exh. 1922-38. † CHE 4, GOU 1, L 1, RED 6, RSA 1.

PICCINI, C. Exh. 1888
c/o L. Dondy, Carter Street, Liverpool. † L 1.

PICKARD, Alison Exh. 1938
Sculptor. 107 Chesil Court, London. † RA 1.

PICKARD, Louise 1865-1928
Landscape, still life and flower painter. b. Hull. Studied Slade School. N.E.A. 1928. "Still life by a Window" (c.1916) purchased by Chantrey Bequest 1941. Add: London. † BA 2, CHE 2, FIN 1, G 3, GI 2, GOU 52, I 4, L 1, LS 24, M 2, NEA 48, RA 8, RED 1.

PICKERILL, F.R. Exh. 1894-1921
Landscape painter. A.N.S.A. 1908-22. Add: Nottingham and Sherwood, Notts. † N 17.

PICKERILL, Miss Jessy Exh. 1919-22
33 Dame Agnes Street, Nottingham. † N 5.

PICKERING, Charles Exh. 1886
Painter. 51 Rathbone Place, London. † RI 1.

PICKERING, Evelyn 1855-1919
Painter. Studied under her uncle John Roddam Spencer Stanhope and at Slade School 1873. Married William de Morgan (1839-1917). Add: London. † BG 1, FIN 10, G 17, L 19, M 7, NG 13, RI 3, ROI 5.

PICKERING, Ferdinand Exh. 1881-82
Genre and historical painter. 28 High Street, Camden Town, London. † RBA 2.

PICKERING, Joseph Langsdale* 1845-1912
Painter of romantic landscapes. b. Wakefield. Trained as a civil engineer. Worked in Italy and Peru. Gave up engineering on his return to England and took up painting. R.B.A. 1890, R.O.I. 1889. Add: London. † B 30, GI 26, L 22, LS 1, M 19, NG 22, RA 36, RBA 30, RHA 14, ROI 32, RSA 1, TOO 11.

PICKERING, Ruby Exh. 1892-93
20 Montgomerie Quadrant, Glasgow. † GI 3.

PICKERING, W.V. Exh. 1928-33
22 Stafford Road, Handsworth, Birmingham. † B 3.

PICKERSGILL, Frederick Richard* 1820-1900
Historical genre painter. Studied under his uncle W.F. Witherington. A.R.A. 1847, R.A. 1857. Exh. 1882. Add: Yarmouth, I.O.W. † M 6.

PICKERSGILL, Mrs. Rose M.* Exh. 1889-92
Figure painter. Hayes, Middlesex 1889; Redmarley d'Abitot, Glos. 1891. † B 1, RA 1.

PICKETT, Albert R. Exh. 1909-10
67 Broadway, Bexley Heath, Kent. † LS 6.

PICKETT, Mary S. Exh. 1892-1909
Figure and miniature portrait painter. London 1892; Worplesdon, Guildford, Surrey 1909. † RA 6, RI 5, RMS 1.

PICKFORD, E.W. Exh. 1921
Ecclesbourne, Clifton Street, Stourbridge, Worcs. † B 1.

PICKFORD, William L. Exh. 1924
Wrought iron gate designer. 108 Fernside Road, Wandsworth Common, London. † RA 1.

PICKHARD, Mrs. Maud Florence Sutton Exh. 1914-20
R.B.A. 1915. Add: Onslow Hotel, Queen's Gate, London. † L 11, RA 2, RBA 15.

PICKLES, John Exh. 1883-86
3 Angela Street, Liverpool. † L 3.

PICKNELL, William Lamb 1854-1897
Landscape and marine painter. b. Boston, Mass. Studied under George Inness in Rome 1874-76 and under Gerome in Paris. R.B.A. 1884. Add: Ealing, London 1884 and 1890; Brockenhurst, Hants. 1888. † B 2, L 4, M 7, RA 8, RBA 6.

PICKSTONE, Mrs. Grace Exh. 1933-40
Flower painter. 64 Alexandra Road, London. † RA 1, SWA 1.

PICKTON, Marie Exh. 1927
7 Springfield Street, Warrington, Lancs. † L 1.

PICKTON, William H. Exh. 1884
11 Dale Street, Liverpool. † L 1.

PICOT, Miss A.M. Exh. 1916-21
St. Heliers, Grove Park, Wanstead, Essex. † L 2, RA 2, SWA 1.

PICTON-WARLOW, Tod Exh. 1935
Flower painter. London. † LEF 1, RCA 2.

PIDCOCK, Katherine M. Exh. 1887
Painter. Sprucer House, Eastbourne. † SWA 1.

PIDDUCK, Mrs. Gertrude Exh. 1910
81 Whitefield Road, Stockton Heath, Warrington, Lancs. † L 2.

PIDGEON, Henry Clark 1807-1880
Landscape, architectural and portrait painter, engraver, lithographer and teacher. Professor of drawing Liverpool Institute 1847. Add: 39 Fitzroy Road, Regent's Park, London 1880. † RI 2.

PIELOU, Mrs. Florence G. Exh. 1914-37
Landscape and figure painter. Annandale, Sandford Road, Dublin. † RHA 34.

PIENKOWSKI, de See D

PIENNE, Georges Exh. 1891-92
Landscape painter. London. † RA 3.

PIEPHO, Carl Exh. 1904
Munich. † GI 1.

PIERCE, Charles E. b. 1908
Painter, etcher and wood engraver. Studied Edinburgh College of Art and R.S.A. Schools. Exh. 1927-33. Add: Edinburgh. † RSA 4.

PIERCE, Evelyn G. Exh. 1903-8
Chiltern House, Thornton Heath, Surrey. † L 1, RA 4, RI 3, SWA 1.

PIERCE, Mrs. E.L. Exh. 1884
Philadelphia, U.S.A. † L 8.

PIERCE, Ethel M. Exh. 1931-39
Portrait and figure painter. London. † P 2, RA 4, ROI 3.

PIERCE, Lucy Elizabeth d. 1950
Watercolour painter and Limoges enameller. A.R.B.A. 1926, A.R.M.S. 1921, R.M.S. 1937, A.S.W.A. 1925. Exh. 1910-40. Add: Enfield, Middlesex. † D 14, GI 5, L 25, LS 6, M 1, RA 13, RBA 8, RI 19, ROI 2, RMS 63, RSA 3, SWA 17, WG 54.

PIERCE, Robert 1884-c.1970
Architect. Studied University College of Wales, Bangor and A.A. 1905-10. Exh. 1915-38. Add: Colwyn Bay, Wales. † RCA 15.

PIERCY, Frederick Exh. 1880-82
Portrait, landscape and genre painter. 534 Caledonian Road, Holloway, London. † RA 1, RBA 1.

PIERCY, Frederick Hawkins junr. Exh. 1880-83
Sculptor. 534 Caledonian Road, Holloway, London. † RA 1, RBA 3.

PIERIS, Justin Exh. 1937
Figure painter. † RED 1.

PIERPONT, Herbert Exh. 1922
Terrace Studio, Swiss Cottage, London. † RI 1.

PIERPONT, Stanley Exh. 1904-15
Painter. Beulah Villa, Barnard's Green, Gt. Malvern, Worcs. † LS 1, RA 3.

PIERRE, G. Exh. 1912
Painter. † GOU 1.

PIERREPONT, C. Constance Exh. 1880
Flower painter. 1 St. James Terrace, Caledonian Road, London. † SWA 3.

PIERREPONT, Mrs. Marie-Louise R. Exh. 1922-38
Landscape, figure and interior painter. London. † G 2, RA 3, RHA 1, SWA 2.

PIERS, Hubert Exh. 1914
247 Hampstead Road, London. † LS 3.

PIERSON, Mrs. L.J. Exh. 1927-35
Rodmarton, Cirencester, Glos. † B 7.

PIERSON, Nellie Exh. 1890
Miniature portrait painter. Old Road, Gravesend, Kent. † RA 1.

PIET, Fernand* Exh. 1902
Figure painter. 38 Rue Rochechouart, Paris. † L 1.

PIETERS, Evert* 1856-1932
Dutch painter. Exh. 1913. Add: Blaricum, Holland. † RSA 1.

PIETERSEN, Jacqueline Exh. 1921-39
Figure painter. London. † NEA 7, RA 1, SWA 1.

PIFFARD, Harold H. Exh. 1895-99
Military painter. London. † B 1, L 2, RA 4.

PIGGFORD, Effie Exh. 1901-4
Portrait and miniature painter. Teversal Grange, Mansfield, Notts. † N 14.

PIGGOTT, John Exh. 1882
Landscape painter. Gainsborough House, Brunswick Street, Leamington, Warwicks. † RA 1.

PIGGOTT, Marjorie Exh. 1928
Landscape painter. † AB 3.

PIGGOTT, Miss M.H.C. Exh. 1907-9
Miniature portrait painter. Hartsholme, Seaford, Sussex. † RA 2.

PIGOTT, Barbara L. Exh. 1934
Sculptor. 4 Mecklenburgh Street, London. † RA 1.

PIGOTT, Charles Exh. 1888-98
Landscape painter. Sharrow, Sheffield. † RBA 4, RI 3.

PIGOTT, F.T. Exh. 1880
Architect. 11 Chester Terrace, Eaton Square, London. † RA 1.

PIGOTT, Lucy E.R. Exh. 1937
Landscape painter. St. John's, Kimmage Road, Terenure, Dublin. † RHA 2.

PIGOTT, W.H.* d. 1901
Watercolour landscape painter. Sharrow, Sheffield. † AG 6, L 1, RA 1, RBA 1, RI 7.

PIGUENIT, William Charles Exh. 1894-1910
Landscape painter. Hunter's Hill, Sydney, N.S.W. † LS 3, M 1.

PIJNEN, Francoise I. Exh. 1924
20 Brookdale Road, Liverpool. † L 3.

PIKE, Miss A.G. Exh. 1889
Landscape painter. 4 The Grove, Highgate, London. † B 3, RBA 4.

PIKE, Bernard Tozer b. 1908
Painter and pencil artist. Studied and taught at Byam Shaw School. Exh. 1931-39. Add: London. † COO 4, P 1, RA 4.

PIKE, Clement E. Exh. 1880-84
Figure painter. Sparrow Hill House, Loughborough, Leics. † RBA 1, ROI 2.

PIKE, C.W. Exh. 1909-16
Architect and painter. 28 Theobald's Road, London. † LEI 3, RA 1.

PIKE, Florence E. Exh. 1882
Villa Road, Handsworth, Birmingham. † B 1.

PIKE, John Exh. 1902
191 Stockport Road, Manchester. † L 1.

PIKE, Joseph Exh. 1888-90
Landscape and coastal painter. Addison Studios, West Kensington, London. † RA 1, RBA 4.

PIKE, Leonard W. 1887-1959
Painter, mural painter and designer. Studied Worcester School of Arts and Crafts. Exh. 1934-40. Add: Worcester. † B 7, RA 1, RBA 1, RCA 2, RI 1.

PIKE, Miss N. Exh. 1926
20 Barrack Lane, Nottingham. † N 1.

PIKE, N.H. Exh. 1889
Landscape painter. 66 Park Road, Haverstock Hill, London. † RA 1.

PIKE, Olive See SNELL

PIKE, Sidney* Exh. 1880-1907
Landscape and genre painter. Brixton 1880; Taplow, Bucks. 1882; Christchurch, Hants. 1889; Polesdown, Hants. 1896; London 1899. † M 1, RA 22, RBA 13, ROI 12.

PIKE, W.H.* b. 1846
Landscape painter. R.B.A. 1889, R.O.I. 1890. Exh. 1880-1907. Add: London. † L 4, RA 2, RBA 39, RHA 3, RI 15, ROI 37.

PIKE, Mrs. W.H. Exh. 1909
St. Ronans, 66 Park Road, Haverstock Hill, London. † RI 1.

PILCHER, Dr. Cecil Westland b. 1870
Watercolour painter and etcher. Exh 1923-32. Add: Boston, Lincs. † NEA 1 RA 5.

PILCHER, Kathleen M. Exh. 1908
12 Milner Street, Cadogan Square, London. † LS 5.

PILCHER, Miss M. Exh. 1887
Nursery Terrace, Hunters Lane, Handsworth, Birmingham. † M 1.

PILCHER, Mrs. T.D. Exh. 1896-97
14 Ely Place, Dublin. † RHA 2.

PILCHER, Thomas Dodson b. 1908
Watercolour painter. Studied City and Guilds of London School of Art and Heatherleys. Exh. 1936. Add: Lambeth Palace Road, London. † RA 1.

PILCHER-CLARK, D. Exh. 1936-38
7 Osborne Place, The Hoe, Plymouth. † B 1, NEA 1, RBA 1.

PILE, Albert Thomas b. 1882
Painter, etcher, lithographer and illustrator. Studied Central School of Art, Camberwell School of Art, Goldsmiths College and Bournemouth College of Art. Exh. 1929-40. Add: London. † D 5, RHA 1, RSA 1.

PILICHO, Mrs. Lena Exh. 1908-9
123 Boulevard St. Michel, Paris. † LS 6.

PILICHOWSKI, Leopold 1869-1933
Portrait and landscape painter. Studied in Paris under Benjamin Constant. Add: Paris 1908; London 1915. † GOU 104, I 1, L 3, LS 7, RA 6.

PILKINGTON, Charles Exh. 1911
Landscape painter. † ALP 1.

PILKINGTON, Flora Exh. 1887-1918
Landscape painter of old world gardens. Add: London. † B 2, RHA 1, RI 1, SWA 1.

PILKINGTON, F.T. Exh. 1882
Architect. 2 Hill Street, Edinburgh. † RSA 1.

PILKINGTON, G.W. Exh. 1932-37
Painter. Cape Town, South Africa. † RA 1, RBA 2, RCA 2, ROI 1.

PILKINGTON, H.W. Exh. 1895
The Hazels, Prescot, Lancs. † L 1.

PILKINGTON, Jackson C. d'O Exh. 1938
12 Church Lane, Edinburgh. † RBA 2.

PILKINGTON, Miss L.D. Exh. 1901-9
192 Queen's Gate, London. † SWA 6.

PILKINGTON, Margaret Exh. 1916-20
Painter and wood engraver. Studied Slade School and Central School of Arts and Crafts. Add: Firwood, Alderley Edge, Cheshire. † NEA 3.

PILKINGTON, Miss M.D. Exh. 1901-4
192 Queen's Gate, London. † SWA 6.

PILKINGTON, Maude E. Exh. 1888-1923
Mrs. H. Price. Figure and miniature portrait painter. R.M.S. 1899. Add: London. † M 1, RA 22, RBA 9, RI 2, RMS 8, RSA 1.

PILKINGTON, Sydney Exh. 1898-1905
Landscape painter. The Hazels, Prescot, Lancs. † L 5, NEA 11.

PILL, Martha Exh. 1884-85
Watercolour landscape painter. 279 High Street, Lewisham. † RBA 2.

PILLE, William Exh. 1880
Landscape painter. 48 Stockwell Park Road, London. † D 1.

PILLEAU, F. Startin Exh. 1882-92
Watercolour painter. London 1882; Dorking, Surrey 1886. † D 1, RI 8.

PILLEAU, Henry 1813-1899
Landscape painter. Spent many years in the Army Medical Corps and became Deputy Inspector General of Hospitals. Died in Brighton. R.I. 1882, R.O.I. 1883. † D 10, L 6, M 3, RA 1, RBA 1, RI 112, ROI 40, RSA 1.

PILLET, M.L. Exh. 1912
7 Rue Coetlogon, Paris. † RSA 1.

PILLITZ, Hedwig Esther Exh. 1924-40
Portrait, landscape and flower painter. b. London. Studied Byam Shaw and Vicat Cole Schools of Art. Add: London. † COO 1, L 3, P 6, RA 4, RBA 7, RHA 4, ROI 6, RSA 12, WG 4.

PILSBURY, Elizabeth Exh. 1880-81
Watercolour painter. Knighton Park Road, Leicester. † RA 3.

PILSBURY, E.H. Exh. 1907
Hazel Copse, Godalming, Surrey. † RA 1.

PILSBURY, Harry Clifford b. 1870
Portrait and landscape painter and teacher. Son of Wilmot P. q.v. Exh. 1899-1925. Add: Whittlesey, nr. Peterborough 1899; Leicester 1916. † B 2, L 15, N 1, RA 15, RI 1.

PILSBURY, Miss K. Exh. 1926-29
Collaborated with Miss M.R. Brace, q.v. Add: London. † L 8.

PILSBURY, Wilmot 1840-1908
Landscape and figure painter. b. Dorking, Surrey. Studied Birmingham School of Art and South Kensington. Headmaster of Leicester School of Art. Father of Harry Clifford P. q.v. R.B.S.A. 1890, A.R.W.S. 1881, R.W.S. 1898. Add: Leicester 1880; Bossington, nr. Minehead, Somerset 1890; Taunton 1891; Shere, nr. Guildford, Surrey 1892; Dorking, Surrey 1898. † B 39, D 4, FIN 68, L 12, LEI 2, M 8, RA 6, RWS 250, TOO 4.

PILSON, Miss A.A. Exh. 1904-5
Malvern Wells 1904; Chelsea, London 1905. † SWA 2.

PIMLOTT, E. Philip Exh. 1893-1940
Painter and etcher. A.R.E. 1901-11. Add: London 1893 and 1901; Aylesbury, Bucks. 1897. † NEA 9, RA 3, RE 22.

PIMLOTT, John b. 1905
Painter and illustrator. Studied Goldsmiths College. Exh. 1925-40. Add: London 1925 and 1940; Bromley, Kent 1932; Shortlands, Kent 1935. † RA 8.

PIMM, Joseph Frank b. 1900
Watercolour painter and etcher. Studied Birmingham College of Art. Exh. 1936-38. Add: Birmingham. † B 3, RA 1.

PIMM, L. (Mrs. T.) Exh. 1907
Clarence House, Broomfield Road, Kew Gardens, Surrey. † RA 1.

PIMM, William E. Exh. 1890-1910
Figure and animal painter. London. † D 4, RA 3, RBA 5, RI 1, ROI 3.

PINCHES, Miss E. Exh. 1902-4
1 Nevern Road, London. † SWA 2.

PINCHES, Frederick Exh. 1886
Architect. 5 John Street, Adelphi, London. † RA 1.

PINCHES, John Robert b. 1885
Landscape painter, medallist and sculptor of sports cups and trophies. Studied Slade School and Paris. Exh. 1902-23. Add: 21 Albert Embankment, London. † L 5, NEA 2, RA 6, RSA 4.

PINCKNEY, Roger A.P. Exh. 1931
Architect. 7 Gray's Inn Square, London. † RA 1.

PINDER, Edith Harriet Exh. 1908-9
90 Edridge Road, Croydon, Surrey. † LS 8.

PINDER, G.A. Exh. 1931
Sculptor. Glenthorne, Redhill, Arnold, Notts. † N 1.

PINGEL, Gustav Exh. 1884
Sculptor. 5 Torrington Square, Bloomsbury, London. † RA 1.

PINION, Arthur Hyde Exh. 1908-13
Painter. 22 Pembridge Villas, London. † LS 5, RA 2.

PINKERTON, Eustace Exh. 1890-1921
Landscape and figure painter. 87 Vanburgh Park, Blackheath, London. † RID 5.

PINKERTON, Mary H. Exh. 1892-93
14 East Claremont Street, Edinburgh. † GI 1, RSA 1.

PINKERTON, W.E. Exh. 1885
Architect. 212 Liverpool Road, London. † RA 2.

PINKS, Gladys A. b. 1890
Portrait painter. Studied at the Grosvenor Studio under Walter Donne 1909-12 and in Paris under Lucien Simon 1912-13. Exh. 1930-40. Add: London 1930; Lindsell, Chelmsford, Essex 1938. † RA 1, RI 4, SWA 6.

PINKS, R. Arthur Exh. 1910-15
9 Joubert Mansions, Chelsea, London. † M 1, RA 2.

PINOT, Albert Exh. 1908-9
45 Rue Royale, Brussels. † L 1, LS 5.

PINTNER, D. Exh. 1918
20 Ruthven Street, Hillhead, Glasgow. † GI 2.

PINTO, Angelo Exh. 1930
Etcher. † FIN 15.

PINTO, J.J. de Souza Exh. 1882-1902
Portrait painter. Paris. † L 2, RA 1.

PINTO, Salvatore Exh. 1930
Etcher. † FIN 15.

PINYON, William Exh. 1935
Watercolour painter. 37 Martin's Road, Shortlands, Kent. † RA 1.

PIOT, Antoine Exh. 1886
French painter. 21 Quai Malaquais, Paris. † GI 1.

PIPER, Edith Exh. 1910
117 West Green Road, South Tottenham, London. † L 1.

PIPER, Elizabeth Exh. 1892-1932
Painter and etcher. Studied Clifton School of Art, Bristol; Royal College of Art; Belgium and Paris. A.R.E. 1892. Add: Chelsea, London 1892; Stanmore, Middlesex 1913. † L 3, RA 4, RE 52.

PIPER, Herbert William Exh. 1884-1911
Portrait, landscape and genre painter. London. † ROI 5, WG 59.

PIPER, John* b. 1903
Landscape painter. b. Epsom, Surrey. Studied Richmond School of Art, Royal College of Art and Slade School. Exh. 1934-40. † COO 1, LEF 5, LEI 44.

PIPER, Mabel Exh. 1928
Painter. † AB 1.

PIPPET, Elphege J. Exh. 1925-32
Herbert Road, Solihull, Warwicks. † B 4.

PIPPET, G. Exh. 1939
Vine House, Uffington, Berks. † B 1.

PIPPET, Gabriel J. Exh. 1915
Decorative designer. † FIN 3.

PIPPET, Oswald C. Exh. 1894-1935
Solihull, Warwicks. † B 4.

PIPPET, Raphael J. Exh. 1898
Solihull, Warwicks. † B 1.

PIPPITT, W.E. Exh. 1904
47 Huskisson Street, Liverpool. † L 1.

PIPRELL, Mary G. Exh. 1937
Portrait painter. London. † RA 1, SWA 1.

PIRET, Fernand Exh. 1911-35
c/o Allied Artists Association, 67 Chancery Lane, London 1911; Edgbaston, Birmingham 1933. † B 4, LS 2.

PIRIE, Miss A.A. Exh. 1889-93
Aberdeen. † GI 2, RSA 1.

PIRIE, Sir George* 1863-1946
Painter of figures, animals and farmyard scenes. b. Campbeltown, Argyllshire. Studied Glasgow. H.R.A. 1934, A.R.S.A. 1913, R.S.A. 1923, P.R.S.A. 1933-44, H.R.S.W. 1934. Knighted 1937. "Mother Duck" (Exh. 1932) purchased by Chantrey Bequest 1940. Add: Glasgow 1884; Wardend, Torrance, Nr. Glasgow 1901 and 1909; Midhurst, Surrey 1904. † FIN 2, G 4, GI 120, L 18, M 2, RA 21, RSA 86.

PIRIE, John B. Exh. 1885
123 Union Street, Aberdeen. † RSA 1.

PIRIE, Miss J.M. Exh. 1933
6 Devonshire Road, Princes Park, Liverpool. † L 1.

PIRNIE, Jackson G. Exh. 1899
10 North Street, David Street, Edinburgh. † RSA 1.

PIRRETT, John Exh. 1933-40
37 Eastside, Kirkintilloch. † GI 1, RSA 6.

PISA, Alberto Exh. 1892-1919
Watercolour landscape and figure painter. London 1892; Holmwood, Surrey 1913. † FIN 500, L 8, M 1, RA 25, RI 8, ROI 2.

PISANI, Nerina Exh. 1895
Florence. † ROI 1.

PISSARRO, Lucien* 1863-1944
Landscape painter and engraver. b. Paris. Studied under his father Camille P. (1831-1903). Came to England in 1890 and became a naturalized British subject in 1916. Father of Orovida P. q.v. N.E.A. 1906. "April, Epping" (1894) and "All Saints Church, Hastings: Sun and Mist" (1918) purchased by Chantrey Bequest 1934, "Ivy Cottage, Coldharbour: Sun and Snow" (1916) purchased in 1943. Add: The Brook, Stamford Brook Road, London. † BAR 2, BK 2, CAR 44, CHE 4, GI 1, GOU 136, I 17, L 8, LEI 208, LS 17, NEA 229, RA 15, RHA 3, RED 10, RSA 1.

PISSARRO, Orovida* 1893-c.1970
Painter, etcher and panel decorator. b. Epping, Essex. Studied under her father Lucien P. q.v. Add: The Brook, Stamford Brook Road, London. † GI 15, GOU 7, L 3, LEI 18, LS 2, M 1, NEA 28, RA 12, RED 104, RSA 2.

PISSARRO, Paul Emile* Exh. 1914-20
Painter and wood engraver. The Brook, Stamford Brook Road, London. † GOU 115, LS 9, NEA 11.

PITCAIRN, Constance Exh. 1881-1901
Landscape, flower and portrait painter. Add: London and Eccles Vicarage, nr. Manchester 1881; Shottermill, Haslemere, Surrey 1901. † D 2, L 2, M 10, RA 3, RBA 1, RHA 1, ROI 1, SWA 1.

PITCHER, Albert J. Exh. 1935
Architect. London and Edinburgh. † RA 1, RSA 1.

PITCHER, F.M. Sotheby Exh. 1935
Playden, nr. Rye, Sussex. † SWA 1.

PITCHER, Neville Sotheby Exh. 1907-39
Landscape, seascape and figure painter. London 1907; Rye, Sussex 1925. † RA 10, RI 1, ROI 1.

PITCHER, William John Charles 1858-1925
Painter and stage designer. Known also as "C. Wilhelm". R.I. 1920. Exh. from 1903. Add: London. † BG 4, L 1, RI 16.

PITCHFORD, Ethel S. Exh. 1925
13 Elaine Street, Warrington, Lancs. † L 2.

PITCHFORTH, Roland Vivian b. 1895
Painter, etcher and wood engraver. Studied Royal College of Art. Member London Group 1929. "Night Transport" purchased by Chantrey Bequest 1940. Exh. 1922-39. Add: Wakefield 1922; London 1929. † AG 2, BK 3, CHE 1, COO 7, GOU 3, L 5, LEI 4, M 3, NEA 5, RA 3, RED 33, RHA 2.

PITE, Arthur Beresford 1861-1934
Architect. Studied South Kensington. Professor of architecture Royal College of Art 1900-23, and director of architecture L.C.C. School of Building, Brixton 1905-28. Brother of William Alfred P. q.v. Add: London. † L 2, RA 58, RSA 1.

PITE, William Alfred Exh. 1887-1920
Architect. Brother of Arthur Beresford P. q.v. Add: London. † GI 4, RA 32.

PITFIELD, Thomas Baron b. 1903
Painter and linocut artist. b. Bolton. Studied Municipal School of Art, Bolton. Exh. 1936. Add: 88 The Crescent, Tettenhall Wood, Compton, nr. Wolverhampton. † B 1.

PITHAWALLA, M.L. Exh. 1906
† P 1.

PITMAN, Edith Exh. 1887
Landscape painter. Solihull, Warwicks. † ROI 1.

PITMAN, Janetta R.A. d. 1903
Flower, still life and figure painter and decorative designer. N.S.A. 1885. Add: Basford Vicarage, nr. Nottingham. † D 5, G 1, L 2, M 4, N 102, RA 18, RBA 2, RI 9.

PITMAN, Rosie M.M. Exh. 1883-1905
Painter and illustrator. Brooklands, Manchester 1883; Mellor, nr. Stockport 1886; Withington 1890; London 1894. † GI 1, L 5, M 8, RA 7, RSA 2.

PITT, Charles Peter Exh. 1880-95
Edgbaston, Birmingham. † B 19, GI 1, L 1, M 13, RHA 10, RSA 1.

PITT, Miss E.K. Exh. 1909-18
Miniature painter. 107 Whiteladies Road, Clifton, Bristol. † L 2, RA 2.

PITT, E.W. Exh. 1899
† P 1.

PITT, Edgar W. Exh. 1927-40
A.N.S.A. 1938. Add: Birmingham 1927; Nottingham 1939; London 1940. † B 22, N 5, RBA 2, RSA 1.

PITT, Henry Exh. 1936
Architect. Holtspur Lane, Woodburn Green, Bucks. † RA 1.

PITT, Lynn d. 1921
Exh. 1908. Add: The White Studio, St. Ives, Cornwall. † LS 2.

PITT, William* Exh. 1880-99
Landscape painter. London 1880; Edgbaston, Birmingham 1886. † B 19, D 1, M 3, RA 1, RBA 2, RI 1.

PITTAR, J.F. Barry b. 1880
Painter, architect, plastic artist, etcher, poster artist and ceramist. Studied St. Johns Wood and Royal College of Art. A.R.B.A. 1919, R.B.A. 1920. Exh. 1919-39. Add: London 1919; Dunstable, Beds. 1924. † AB 1, FIN 65, G 3, GI 1, RBA 143, ROI 1, RSA 10.

PITTARA, Charles Exh. 1888
22 Rue de Douai, Paris. † GI 1.

PITTARD, Charles William Exh. 1880-1911
Still life and figure painter. London 1880; Twickenham, Middlesex 1901. † B 2, L 15, RA 12, RBA 4, RHA 2.

PITTARD, Mrs. Maria Exh. 1925
12 Lebanon Park, Twickenham, Middlesex. † RI 1.

PITTMAN, Osmund b. 1874
Landscape painter. Studied South Kensington. R.O.I. 1916. Exh. 1901-40. Add: London 1901 and 1920; Newbury, Berks. 1905; Ludlow 1911. † CON 1, GI 18, I 1, L 10, RA 46, RI 4, RID 4, ROI 76.

PITTS, Frederick Exh. 1882
Figure painter. 29 Bolsover Street, Fitzroy Square, London. † M 1, RA 1.

PITTS, Mary Exh. 1893-1929
Miniature portrait painter. A.R.M.S. 1907. Add: London. † L 18, NG 4, RA 28, RMS 18, SWA 1.

PITTS, Marcus W. Exh. 1886-1919
Figure painter. London. † B 19, RA 1, ROI 3.

PITT-TAYLOR, Mrs. W.W. (D.) Exh. 1933
Watercolour landscape painter. Cholderton House, nr. Salisbury, Wilts. † RA 1.

PITTUCK, Douglas b. 1911
Landscape painter. Studied Ruskin School of Drawing, Oxford 1931-39. Exh. 1936. † COO 3.

PIXTON, Amy Exh. 1927-31
3 Brownlow Road, Ellesmere, Salop. † L 1, RCA 4.

PIXTON, Florence Exh. 1927
17 Bouverie Street, Chester. † L 1.

PIXTON, Miss K. Exh. 1930-33
39 Birch Road, Oxton, Birkenhead. † L 4.

PIZEY, Emma G. Exh. 1924
Morven, Grove Park Road, Weston Super Mare, Somerset. † L 1.

PIZIO, Orestes Exh. 1904
4 Rue de Paradis, Paris. † L 1.

PIZZO, Giuseppe Exh. 1933
Sculptor. Via Andrea Appiani 15, Milan, Italy. † RA 1.

PLACE, P. Currall Exh. 1911
Landscape painter. † BRU 1.

PLACE, Rosa Exh. 1880-81
Landscape and flower painter. 42 Warwick Road, Maida Hill, London. † SWA 2.

PLAISTOWE, J.H. Exh. 1935-37
Landscape and flower painter. 43 Markham Square, Chelsea, London. † RA 3.

PLANCK, W. Exh. 1911
16 Blandfields Street, Nightingale Lane, Clapham, London. † RA 1.

PLANQUETTE, Felix* b. 1873
French painter. Exh. 1904. Add: 33 Rue Lamarck, Paris. † L 1.

PLANT, Esther M. Exh. 1915-33
Mrs. Reeves. Miniature portrait painter. A.R.M.S. 1919, R.M.S. 1926. Add: Bournemouth 1915; London 1919; Wolvercote, Oxford 1921; Harlow, Essex 1924; Broadstone, Dorset 1929. † I 3, L 11, RA 9, RMS 45.

PLANT, Miss F.E. Exh. 1883-84
182 Hagley Road, Edgbaston, Birmingham. † B 2.

PLANT, Nellie M. Exh. 1882-83
182 Hagley Road, Edgbaston, Birmingham. † B 5.

PLANT, R. Exh. 1902-9
112 Lodge Road, Birmingham. † B 2, LS 2.

PLASSE, Georges Exh. 1911
15 Rue Hegesippe Moreau, Paris. † L 1.

PLATER, Gilbert E. Exh. 1935
Miniature portrait painter. Ash Lodge, The Green, London. † RA 1.

PLATT, Miss A. Exh. 1897
Beak Heys, 18 Grosvenor Road, Birkdale, Lancs. † L 1.

PLATT, Miss A.E. Exh. 1911-27
New Brighton, Cheshire 1911; Wallasey, Cheshire 1927. † L 17.

PLATT, Charles Adams 1861-1933
American architect and artist. R.E. 1882-89. Exh. 1882-86. Add: New York 1882; Paris 1883. † L 1, RE 13.

PLATT, Miss E. Exh. 1933
Riber, Granville Park, Aughton, Lancs. † L 2.

PLATT, Eric Warhurst b. 1915
Painter and etcher. b. Yorkshire. Studied Royal College of Art 1937-40. Exh. 1939-40. Add: London. † RA 3.

PLATT, Joyce Exh. 1939-40
8 Park Drive, Heaton, Bradford. † GOU 2, SWA 1.

PLATT, John Edgar 1886-1967
Colour woodcut artist. b. Leek, Staffs. Studied Royal College of Art. Principal Leicester College of Arts and Crafts. Principal Blackheath School of Art. Father of Michael P. q.v. Add: Leek, Staffs. 1913; College of Art, Edinburgh 1918; Leicester 1924; Blackheath, London 1929. † BA 4, GI 16, I 5, L 5, NEA 24, RA 23, RED 3, RSA 6.

PLATT, John Gerald b. 1892
Painter, etcher and wood engraver. b. Bolton, Lancs. Studied Newcastle Armstrong College, Leicester School of Art and Royal College of Art. Drawing master Kingston School of Art and master of book illustration and wood engraving Goldsmiths College. A.R.E. 1924. Exh. 1921-32. Add: London 1921; Twickenham, Middlesex 1929; Kenton, Middlesex 1931. † L 4, RA 11, RE 10.

PLATT, Mrs. K. Eileen Exh. 1922-40
Bickley, Kent 1922; Chislehurst 1928. † ROI 4, SWA 15.

PLATT, Michael b. 1914
Painter. b. Leek, Staffs. Son of John Edgar P. q.v. Studied Blackheath School of Art and Royal College of Art. Exh. 1937-38. Add: Blackheath, London. † NEA 1, RA 1.

PLATTEN, Una Exh. 1930-39
Birmingham. † B 4.

PLATTS, Elsie M. Exh. 1919-39
Landscape and figure painter. 71 Gladstone Street, Derby. † N 7.

PLAYER, F. da Ponte Exh. 1880-82
Landscape and marine painter. 4 Langham Chambers, Portland Place, London. † D 2, RBA 6, RHA 3.

PLAYER, William H. Exh. 1883-84
Landscape painter. 4 Lauder Terrace, Wood Green, Essex. † RA 1, RI 1.

PLAYFAIR, J.C. Exh. 1904
† TOO 1.

PLAYFAIR, Vere D.M. Exh. 1934
Lithographer. 28 Stanley Gardens, Belsize Park, London. † RA 1.

PLAYNE, Anne Exh. 1925
2 Brunswick Square, London. † SWA 1.

PLAYNE, Caroline E. Exh. 1919
Watercolour landscape painter. † ALP 18.

PLEHN, Alice Exh. 1903-6
8 bis Rue Campagne Premiere, Paris. † ROI 2.

PLENDERLEITH, Mungo Exh. 1881-1918
Glasgow 1881 and 1912; Edinburgh 1901. † GI 37, RI 2, RSA 6, RSW 1.

PLENNELL, J. Exh. 1912
American painter and lithographer. † FIN 35.

PLESSIS, du See D

PLESTER, W.A. Exh. 1914
The Gables, Forester Road, Thorneywood, Nottingham. † N 1.

PLEWS, Helen M. Exh. 1887-1908
Landscape painter. London. † RA 4, RI 2, ROI 6, SWA 1.

PLIMPTON, Constance See SMITH

PLIMSOLL, Fanny Grace Exh. 1907-14
Cromwell Road, London. † RMS 2, SWA 2.

PLINSTON, E. Exh. 1910
21 Stafford Road, Warrington, Lancs. † L 1.

PLOCKHORST, Bernhard 1825-1907
German painter. Exh. 1881. Add: Berlin. † RA 1.

PLOWDEN, Edith R. Exh. 1885-89
Interior and figure painter. London. † RA 1, RBA 1.

PLOWDEN, Lucy Exh. 1935-36
14 Bywater Street, London. † SWA 2.

PLOWMAN, Miss E. Exh. 1912
32 Mote Road, Maidstone, Kent. † RA 1.

PLOWMAN, George Taylor 1869-1932
American etcher. b. Minnesota. Studied Royal College of Art and Paris. Exh. 1912-23. Add: London. † L 1, RA 3.

PLOWRIGHT, Rosamund M.J. Exh. 1939
Watercolour figure painter. Weston Park, Thames Ditton, Surrey. † RA 1.

PLUM, R. Bagshaw Exh. 1886-92
Landscape painter. Worcester. † B 4, L 1, ROI 1.

PLUMBE, Charles Conway b. 1881
Landscape painter. b. Mansfield, Notts. Exh. 1926-27. Add: Totley Rise, nr. Sheffield. † RA 3.

PLUMBE, Rowland Exh. 1881-1911
Architect. 13 Fitzroy Square, London. † RA 8.

PLUMPTON, Irene Exh. 1922
Flower painter. 17 Kew Gardens, Kew, Surrey. † RA 1.

PLUMRIDGE, Mab Exh. 1918-19
1 Perham Crescent, West Kensington, London. † I 1, RA 1.

PLUMTREE, Miss R. Exh. 1896
18 Peel Street, Nottingham. † N 2.

PLUNKET, Lord Exh. 1937
† P 1.

PLUNKET, Hon. Gertrude Exh. 1881-85
Watercolour landscape painter. 64 Eaton Place, London. † SWA 5.

PLUNKET, Hon. H. Exh. 1886
Landscape painter. 64 Eaton Place, London. † SWA 1.

PLUNKET, Hon. Katharine Exh. 1881-86
Watercolour landscape painter. 64 Eaton Place, London. † SWA 9.

PLUNKETT, Lt. Col. G.T. Exh. 1897
Science and Art Museum, Dublin. † NG 1.

PLUNKETT, Mrs. Joseph Exh. 1940
Architect. 11 Nassau Street, Dublin. † RHA 1.

POCKLINGTON, Daphne Exh. 1929-33
Miniature portrait painter. A.R.M.S. 1930. Add: London 1929; Capel St. Mary, Ipswich, Suffolk 1930. † RA 2, RMS 17.

POCKLINGTON, F.C. Exh. 1884
Landscape painter. Ashley Course, Woburn, Beds. † G 1.

POCOCK, Alfred Lyndhurst b. 1881
Watercolour painter, gem sculptor, potter and metal worker. Son of Lexden Lewis P. q.v. Studied R.A. Schools. Gem sculptor to the Russian Court Jewellers. R.M.S. 1919. Exh. 1909-39. Add: London 1909; Slinfold, Sussex 1925. † L 12, RA 8, RMS 74.

POCOCK, Fania Exh. 1937
Sculptor. 6 The Pheasantry, 132 Kings Road, London. † RA 1.

POCOCK, Geoffrey Buckingham b. 1879
Painter, etcher and pastelier. Studied Slade School. Married Anna Airy q.v. Life master and teacher of etching Battersea Polytechnic School of Art and Life master at L.C.C. School of Photo-Engraving and Lithography, Bolt Court. Exh. 1908-36. Add: London 1908; Playford, Nr. Ipswich 1935. † L 10, NEA 6, RA 18, RI 2, ROI 6.

POCOCK, Henry Childe 1854-1934
Watercolour painter. b. East Grinstead, Sussex. Studied St. Martin's School of Art, Heatherleys and under Sir James Linton. Professor of drawing and painting from life at Birkbeck College. R.B.A. 1899. Add: London. † L 2, RA 2. RBA 40, RI 8, ROI 4, RSW 1.

POCOCK, Hilda Joyce b. 1892
Mrs. John H. Stewart. Miniature painter, craftworker and ecclesiastical designer. Daughter of Lexden Lewis P. q.v. Studied Regent Street, Polytechnic. R.M.S. 1916. Exh. 1911-38. Add: London 1911; Saskatchewan, Canada 1921. † L 8, RA 12, RMS 5.

POCOCK, Julia Exh. 1883-1903
Watercolour portrait painter and sculptor. London. † B 1, RA 1.

POCOCK, Lilian Josephine Exh. 1908-38
Stained glass artist, watercolour painter and illustrator. Daughter of Lexden Lewis P. q.v. Studied Regent Street Polytechnic and Central School of Arts and Crafts. A.S.W.A. 1909. Add: London. † D 2, L 16, RA 25, RI 2, RSA 5, SWA 12.

POCOCK, Lexden Lewis 1850-1919
Landscape and figure painter. Studied at Slade School, R.A. Schools and Rome. Father of Alfred Lyndhurst, Hilda Joyce and Lilian Josephine P. q.v. Add: London. † B 16, BG 2, D 151, FIN 1, GI 2, L 19, M 7, RA 51, RBA 9, RHA 8, RI 19, ROI 4.

POCOCK, Margaret Exh. 1883
Painter of miniature portraits on ivory. 45 Edith Grove, Chelsea, London. † RA 1.

POCOCK, Margaret E. Exh. 1931-35
Watercolour landscape painter. 34 Lewin Road, Streatham, London. † RA 2.

POCOCK, Maurice H. Exh. 1881-1912
Architect. Westminster, London 1881; Chiddingfold, Surrey 1907. † RA 11.

PODE, Miss B.C. Exh. 1902-3
Slade Tag Bridge. † SWA 4.

POEHLMANN, Charlotte Exh. 1887-94
Portrait and figure painter. Nottingham 1887; London 1893. † B 2, L 2, M 2, N 2, RA 1, ROI 2.

POER, Miss Exh. 1896
26 Russell Square, London. † SWA 1.

POGGENBEEK, Georges* 1853-1903
Dutch painter. Exh. 1885. Add: 41 Ruysdallkade, Amsterdam. † GI 1.

POGLIANI, Miss M.A. Exh. 1914
Comelio, Celso 8, Rome. † LS 6.

POGSON, Miss H.C. Exh. 1915-22
Flower painter. Nottingham. † N 6.

POINGDESTRE, Charles H.* d. 1905
Painter of Italian landscapes and genre. President of the British Academy in Rome. Add: Jersey, C.I. 1880; London 1889. † B 13, G 1, GI 2, L 13, M 7, NG 2, RA 18, RHA 25, RI 9, ROI 10, RSA 1.

POINTELIN, Auguste 1839-1933
French artist. Exh. 1894-1912. Add: Paris. † RHA 1, RSA 1.

POINTER, G. Henry Exh. 1896-99
Portrait painter and black and white artist. 3 The Mall, Park Road, Haverstock Hill, London. † RA 4.

POIRE, Emmanuel c.1857-1909
Caricaturist who used the name Caran d'Ache. Exh. 1898. † FIN 177.

POIRET, Lucien J. Exh. 1909
Ste. Menhould, Marne, France. † L 1.

POIROT, E. Exh. 1892
18 Avenue de Villiers, Paris. † RHA 2.

POISSON, M. Exh. 1930
18 Rue de Moulin de Beaue, Paris. † RSA 2.

POISSON, Pierre Marie b. 1876
French sculptor. Exh. 1911. Add: 23 Boulevard Pasteur, Paris. † RSA 2.

POITEVEN de la Croix, le See L

POIX, de See D

POL, W. Jilts Exh. 1932-38
Landscape, figure and still life painter. † BA 70.

POLEY, Edward William Exh. 1883-1908
Architect. Strand, London. † RA 4.

POLHILL, G.J. Exh. 1884
12 Wakefield Road, Brighton. † B 1.

POLIVANOVA, Magda Exh. 1924-25
† GOU 2.

POLLARD, Mrs. Ann Exh. 1927-39
A.R.M.S. 1932. Add: Marsh House, Crabtree, Plympton, South Devon. † L 16, RI 5, RMS 34.

POLLARD, A. Read Exh. 1884-85
Figure painter. Worthing, Sussex. † ROI 2.

POLLARD, Miss Haynford Exh. 1899
Norwich. † B 4.

POLLARD, J.E. Exh. 1909
4 Winston Gardens, Headingley, Leeds. † L 1.

POLLARD, Kattern
See NICOL, Lady Catherine Robertson

POLLARD, Marion Exh. 1902
20 Handon Road, Lee, London. † RE 1.

POLLARD, Mary A. Exh. 1904
Willowside, Lower Tooting, London. † L 1.

POLLARD, Renira Exh. 1887-1912
Fruit, flower and landscape painter. London. † L 1, RA 3, RBA 2, RI 7, ROI 1, SWA 1.

POLLARD, William J. Exh. 1920-28
Aquatinter. Add: School of Arts and Crafts, Torquay. † GI 1, RA 1, RCA 1.

POLLEN, Arthur J. Exh. 1924-39
Sculptor. Member London Group 1929. Add: London. † GI 1, NEA 5, RA 7.

POLLEN, John Hungerford* 1820-1902
Painter, architect and critic. London. † G 6, RA 3.

POLLEN, Zalman Exh. 1918
39 Hackney Road, London. † LS 3.

POLLENTINE, Alfred* Exh. 1880
Painter of Venetian scenes. 34 Fonthill Road, Holloway, London. † RBA 1.

POLLEXFEN, J. Exh. 1882
Painter. c/o John Varley Esq., 6 William Street, London. † RBA 1.

POLLITT, Albert Exh. 1885-1926
Manchester 1885; Warrington 1892; North Wales 1911. † L 7, M 31.

POLLITT, C. Stanley Exh. 1915-26
6 Parkhill Road, Hampstead, London. † L 1, M 2, RA 2, ROI 1.

POLLITT, Harold Exh. 1897
Rock House, Croft, nr. Warrington, Lancs. † NG 1.

POLLITT, Jessie Exh. 1881-86
54 Grosvenor Road, Charlton upon Medlock, Manchester. † GI 1, M 4.

POLLITT, Mary Exh. 1927-40
Landscape painter. Studied London and Paris. Travelled in Europe, Spain and Morocco. Add: Edinburgh. † GI 1, RSA 9, RSW 17, SWA 2, WG 55.

POLLOCK, Andrew D. Exh. 1930-33
5 West Montgomery Place, Edinburgh. † RSA 8.

POLLOCK, Beatrice M. Exh. 1896
Watercolour landscape painter. 61 Cadogan Place, London. † RA 1.

POLLOCK, Courtenay 1877-1943
Sculptor, author and inventor. b. Birmingham. Studied Birmingham School of Art and Royal College of Art. R.B.A. 1905. Add: London 1906; Northfield Grange, Worcs. 1911; Ilfracombe, Devon 1920. † BRU 1, GI 2, L 3, LS 4, RA 6, RBA 30, RSA 1.

POLLOCK, Dorothy Exh. 1940
Portrait painter. Great Bookham, Surrey. † RA 1.

POLLOCK, Mrs. Isabella Exh. 1932
Harefield, Chaucer Road, Cambridge. † RSA 1.

POLLOCK, Mrs. J.C. Exh. 1914-1/
43 Wellington Road, Bournemouth. † LS 9.

POLLOCK, Jackson N.* 1912-1956
Painter. Exh. 1939. Add: Medway Bank, Gylenuir Road, Edinburgh. † RSA 1.

POLLOCK, Maurice Exh. 1882-89
Landscape painter. London. † G 3, L 1, M 2, NG 3, RA 1, RBA 1.

POLLOCK, Sir Montague Exh. 1911-30
Landscape painter. Bussock Wood, Newbury, Berks. 1911; London 1918; Headington Hill, Oxford 1926. † NEA 12.

POLLOCK, Muriel Exh. 1922
† G 1.

POLLOCK, Miss M.A. Exh. 1919
20 York Terrace, London. † SWA 1.

POLLOCK, Millicent E. Exh. 1930
† L 2.

POLLOK, Netta Exh. 1929-31
Langside, Glasgow 1929; Rutherglen 1931. † GI 3.

POLOWETSKI, Charles T. Exh. 1909-14
c/o Allied Artists Association, 67 Chancery Lane, London 1909; Paris 1913. † LS 18.

POLUNIN, Elizabeth b. 1887
nee Hart. Portrait painter and stage designer. b. Ashford, Kent. Studied Colarossi's, Lucien Simon's School, and Ecole des Beaux Arts, Paris and Leon Bakst's School at St. Petersburg. Scene parter to Diaghileff's Russian Ballet. Married Vladimir P. q.v. Exh. 1917-40. Add: Reading, Berks. 1917; London 1924. † BA 3, GI 1, GOU 2, L 2, NEA 9, P 16, RA 8, RBA 2, RED 2, SWA 2.

POLUNIN, Vladimir b. 1880
Decorative and stage designer. b. Moscow. Studied St. Petersburg, Munich and Paris. Designer for Diaghileff's Russian Ballet and Sir. T. Beecham's Opera. Teacher at Slade School. Married Elizabeth P. q.v. Exh. 1937-38. † BA 1, RED 1.

POLWALSKI, J. Exh. 1881
The Hague, Holland. † RHA 1.

POMERANCE, Mrs. Fay b. 1912
Painter. Studied Birmingham School of Art. Exh. 1939-40. Add: Sheffield. † B 3, SWA 2.

POMEROY, Frederick William 1856-1924
Sculptor. Studied Lambeth and R.A. Schools (gold medal and travelling studentship), Paris and Italy. Won competition for the commission for the Centenary Statue of Robert Burns for Paisley. A.R.A. 1906, R.A. 1917. "The Nymph of Loch Awe" purchased by Chantrey Bequest 1897. Add: London. † GI 27, I 2, L 45, NG 15, RA 99, RBA 1, RI 14, ROI 5, RSA 11.

POMEROY, Hon. Mrs. M. Katherine Exh. 1940
Painter. 56 Onslow Gardens, London. † RA 1.

POMEROY, Rosamund Exh. 1938-39
Flower painter. 56 Onslow Gardens, London. † NEA 2, RA 1.

POMEROY, Thomas Exh. 1886
87 Chippenham Road, Harrow Road, London. † GI 1.

POMPON, M. Exh. 1930
3 Rue Campagne Premiere, Paris. † RSA 4.

PONCHIN, Antoine 1872-1934
French artist. Exh. 1911-13. Add: Paris. † L 2, RA 1.

PONCY, Alfred Verier Exh. 1880-90
Landscape and figure painter. Balham, London. † D 3, RA 2, RBA 3, RE 1.

PONDER, James R. Exh. 1880-84
Figure painter. 5 Elizabeth Street, Hans Place, London. † B 1, D 2, RA 1, RBA 1.

PONSON, E. Debat Exh. 1890
Elms Cottage, Harrow Weald, Middlesex. † GI 1.

PONSONBY, Arthur Exh. 1905
Watercolour landscape painter. † CAR 32.

PONT, du See D

PONTET, du See D

PONTIN, George Exh. 1898-1916
Landscape and marine painter and etcher. b. Sussex. Studied for 15 years in Melbourne, Australia. Add: Yapton, Arundel, Sussex 1898; Shirley, Southampton 1903; Gloucester 1914. † LS 5, M 1, RA 7, RBA 1, RCA 10.

PONTIN, Sophie E. Exh. 1910
55 Millbrook Road, Southampton. † RCA 1.

PONTING, Charles E. Exh. 1892-1911
Architect. Marlborough, Wilts. † RA 17.

PONTON, James Exh. 1898
13 Harrington Street, Liverpool. † L 1.

POOL, Agnes Exh. 1903-5
Erdington, Birmingham. † B 2, L 2, RA 1.

POOL, Lily Exh. 1916
9 White Street, Derby. † L 2.

POOLE, A. Exh. 1892
Painter. † FIN 2.

POOLE, A.G. Exh. 1909
3 Bilbie Street, Nottingham. † N 1.

POOLE, A.H. Exh. 1921-40
9 Gordon Road, Harborne, Birmingham. † B 4.

POOLE, Christopher Exh. 1882-91
Watercolour landscape painter. London 1882; Poole, Dorset 1889; Teignmouth, Devon 1891. † D 2, M 1, RA 5, RBA 25, RI 9.

POOLE, C.P. Exh. 1926-28
1 Rice Lane, Wallasey, Cheshire. † L 3.

POOLE, Dunbar Exh. 1894-96
59 Bank Street, Hillhead, Glasgow. † G 1, GI 2, RSW 1.

POOLE, F. Leonard Exh. 1924
Architect. 29 New Bridge Street, London. † RA 1.

POOLE, Frederick Victor Exh. 1890-1910
Figure and landscape painter. Southampton 1890; London 1901. † I 1, L 3, NEA 3, RA 4, RI 1, ROI 1.

POOLE, George Augustus Exh. 1881-1926
Portrait painter. Nottingham 1881; West Bridgford, Notts. 1910. † N 19.

POOLE, Henry 1873-1928
Sculptor. Studied Lambeth School of Art and R.A. Schools. Brother of Samuel P. q.v. A.R.A. 1920, R.A. 1927. "The Little Apple" (Exh. 1927) purchased by Chantrey Bequest 1929. Add: London. † G 1, GI 7, L 1, NG 4, P 3, RA 46, RI 1, ROI 2, RSA 2.

POOLE, Samuel b. 1870
Landscape painter and illuminator. Studied Heatherleys. Designer for 25 years with Cedric Chivers Ltd. of Bath. Brother of Henry P. q.v. Add: London 1892; Bath 1906. † RA 8, RBA 7, RI 5, ROI 4.

POOLE, Vera Ellen Exh. 1916-22
Landscape painter. The Vale, Hampstead, London 1916; Oxford 1917. † NEA 10.

POORE, Miss Exh. 1910
Ryde, I.O.W. † SWA 1.

POORE, M.E. Exh. 1922-23
† SWA 2.

POORE, Phyllis Exh. 1921-27
Highfield, Andover. † D 4, L 1.

POORTENAAR, Jan b. 1886
Dutch watercolour painter, etcher and lithographer. Exh. 1916-21. Add: 151 King Henry's Road, London. † B 1, FIN 14, GI 2, GOU 2, L 6, M 1, NEA 2.

"POP" See HART, George Overbury

POPE, Annie Exh. 1906-39
Weybridge, Surrey. † RA 1, RI 2.

POPE, Arthur Edward Exh. 1884-87
17 Newington Grove, London. † L 1, RHA 1, ROI 2.

POPE, Arthur Wybrow b. 1877
Painter. b. Nottingham. Studied Nottingham School of Art and Royal College of Art. Second master Harrogate School of Art and head of Life and Painting Dept. Leeds College of Art. Exh. 1898-1928. Add: Nottingham 1898; Leeds 1928. † N 12, RA 1.

POPE, Miss F. Exh. 1912
Highbury, London. † SWA 1.

POPE, Gustav* Exh. 1880-95
Genre, historical and portrait painter. London. † B 10, GI 11, L 15, M 8, RA 15, RBA 5, ROI 2.

POPE, Henry Exh. 1882-1907
Landscape painter. 90 New Street, Birmingham. † B 83, L 4, RI 2.

POPE, John Russell Exh. 1914-31
527 Fifth Avenue, New York, U.S.A. † RA 1, RSA 12.

POPE, Miss M. Exh. 1900
c/o Mrs. Snell, 18 Castle Gate, Nottingham. † N 1.

POPE, M.I. Exh. 1922
† SWA 1.

POPE, Samuel junr. Exh. 1881-1940
Aberdeen. † GI 1, RHA 1, RSA 1.

POPE, Theodora P. Exh. 1894
7 Kilburn Square, London. † NG 1.

POPE, W.L. Exh. 1896
13 Sarsfield Street, Berkeley Road, Dublin. † RHA 1.

POPERT, Charlotte Exh. 1883-1911
Painter and etcher. London 1883; Rome 1910. † BG 82, D 1, L 6, M 1, RI 4.

POPHAM, C.V. Exh. 1885
22 Oxford Street, Weston Super Mare, Somerset. † M 1.

POPHAM, James Kidwell b. 1884
Landscape and figure painter. Exh. 1929-39. Add: Witham, Essex 1929; Little Baddow, Essex 1931. † RID 4, ROI 17.

POPHAM, Mary Exh. 1935-37
A.R.M.S. 1932, A.S.W.A. 1935. Add: The Brambles, West Wickham, Kent. † RMS 11.

POPOVITCH, Sava Exh. 1918-26
Member London Group 1922. Add: Westminster College, Cambridge 1918. † GOU 3, LS 3.

POPPLE, Edward Exh. 1919
Sunnymead, Berkhamsted, Herts. † RSA 1.

POPPLETON, Albert H. Exh. 1928
108 Princess Road, Manchester. † RCA 2.

POPPLEWELL, F. Exh. 1885
87 Mosley Street, Manchester. † M 1.

PORCHERON, Miss A.E. Exh. 1902
11 Madeira Road, Streatham, London. † SWA 1.

PORTAELS, Jean Francois* 1818-1895
Belgian painter. Exh. 1880-93. Add: Brussels. † P 1, RSA 3.

PORTE, Gabriel William Church b. 1900
Architect, black and white artist and sculptor. Studied Belfast School of Art 1917-20. Exh. 1922-31. Add: Belfast. † RA 3, RHA 17.

PORTEOUS, Jessie G. Exh. 1898
6 Mansfield Place, Edinburgh. † RSA 1.

PORTEOUS, William Exh. 1880-1882
5 Kerr Street, Stockbridge. † RSA 13.

PORTER, Arthur Bowmar Exh. 1898-1934
Landscape and figure painter and teacher. b. Jersey. Studied Reading University and Royal College of Art. Add: Reading 1898; London 1902; Chingford, Essex 1915; Woodford Green, Essex 1919. † GI 2, I 9, L 7, LS 8, P 3, RA 3, RI 1, ROI 3.

PORTER, Alfred Thomas Exh. 1882-1919
Figure and historical painter. London. † B 10, L 2, LS 6, RA 10, ROI 2.

PORTER, Miss B. Exh. 1905
49 Pembroke Road, Dublin. † RHA 1.

PORTER, Barbara Exh. 1899
The Well Cottage, Chilworth, Surrey. † B 1.

PORTER, Mrs. C.K. Exh. 1895
Designer of Christmas Cards. Add: 9 Oval Road, Regents Park, London. † RA 1.

PORTER, Daniel Exh. 1888-1901
Figure, portrait and landscape painter. London. † L 1, M 4, RA 9, RBA 7, ROI 5.

PORTER, E. Exh. 1938
Carrickmines, Co. Dublin. † RCA 1.

PORTER, Ethel Exh. 1899-1911
Portrait and miniature painter. R.M.S. 1901. Add: London. † RA 5, RMS 6, ROI 1, WG 37.

PORTER, Miss E.C. Exh. 1895
12 Lysias Road, Balham, London. † ROI 2.

PORTER, Edward P. Exh. 1892-1900
Landscape painter. London. † L 2, RA 2, ROI 8.

PORTER, Frank Exh. 1888-94
Landscape painter. Stourbridge, Worcs. 1888; Twickenham, Middlesex 1893. † B 2, RA 1.

PORTER, Frederick J. Exh. 1901-37
Earnhope, Comrie, N.B. 1901; Morningside Road, Edinburgh 1908. † G 4, GI 1, LS 14, RSA 7, RSW 1.

PORTER, Frederick James 1883-1944
Landscape and flower painter. b. New Zealand. Studied Julians, Paris. Member London Group 1920. Add: London. † AG 20, BK 1, CHE 9, COO 6, GOU 16, L 1, LEF 1, LEI 24, NEA 3, RED 2.

PORTER, Mrs. Hetty Exh. 1918-19
167 Hampstead Way, Hendon, London. † LS 3, SWA 4.

PORTER, Hilda Exh. 1894-1925
Figure painter. Foxrock, Co. Dublin 1894; London 1899 and 1922; Falkirk 1919; Kippen, Stirlingshire 1924. † GI 1, L 7, RA 2, RCA 1, RHA 22, ROI 2, SWA 4.

PORTER, Horsbrugh Exh. 1926-28
151 Gloucester Road, London. † RHA 3.

PORTER, Ida Exh. 1885-87
Watercolour flower painter. 16 Russell Square, London. † L 1, RBA 1, RI 1.

PORTER, Miss Margery Exh. 1940
65 Morningside Road, Edinburgh. † RSA 1.

PORTER, Maud Exh. 1888-1905
Portrait and figure painter. London. † L 6, M 1, NG 1, P 14, RA 19, RI 5, ROI 3, SWA 2.

PORTER, Mary E. Exh. 1911
Landscape painter. † BRU 1.

PORTER, Marjorie I. Exh. 1935-40
Pensthorpe, Fakenham, Norfolk. † B 11, RCA 3, RI 1, SWA 1.

PORTER, Percy C. Exh. 1880-86
Landscape painter. London. † D 1, RBA 5.

PORTER, Major T.C. Exh. 1890
The Carabineers, Birmingham. † B 1.

PORTEUS, Edgar* Exh. 1885
Figure painter. 331 Strand, London. † B 2.

PORTIELJIE, Gerard* b. 1856
Belgian painter. Exh. 1883. Add: Antwerp. † ROI 1.

PORTLOCK, Mary Exh. 1928
Landscape painter. † AB 1.

PORTSMOUTH, Percy Herbert b. 1874
Sculptor. b. Reading. Studied University College of Reading and Royal College of Art. Head of sculpture Dept. Edinburgh College of Art. A.R.S.A. 1906, R.S.A. 1923. Add: London 1902; Edinburgh 1904; Buntingford, Herts. 1929. † GI 49, L 6, P 1, RA 35, RMS 1, RSA 101.

POSENER, May Exh. 1902-4
The Cottage, Bolton Studios, Redcliffe Road, London. † B 3, M 2, RCA 2.

POSNETT, Miss D.M. Exh. 1922
The Mount, Runcorn, Cheshire. † L 8.

POSSOZ, Milly b. 1896
Drypoint artist. b. Lisbon, Portugal. Exh. 1930. † FIN 42.

POST, E.C. Exh. 1880
104 Maida Vale, London. † RHA 1.

POSTHUMA, Mrs. M. Exh. 1911-12
c/o A. Lemon, 104 Beaufort Mansions, Chelsea, London. † RA 2.

POSTLETHWAITE, Elinor b. 1866
Painter, illustrator and colour woodcut artist. b. Hall Thwaites, Cumberland. Studied Calderons and Westminster. Sister of Mary Emily P. q.v. Exh. 1889-1901. Add: Kilburn, London. † B 4, GI 2, L 1, RA 1, RBA 2.

POSTLETHWAITE, Mary Emily Exh. 1882-1903
Landscape and figure painter. Sister of Elinor P. q.v. Add: Broughton in Furness 1882; Kilburn, London 1883. † B 8, GI 4, M 1, RA 2, RBA 5, SWA 1.

POSTMA, G. Exh. 1880-87
Haarlem, Holland. † RSA 2.

POSTON, G.G. Exh. 1933
The Chalet, Upton Road, Moreton, Cheshire. † L 2.

POTCHETT, Caroline See FOX

POTCHETT, Emily Exh. 1880-84
Landscape painter. Sister of Caroline Fox q.v. Add: 70 Belsize Road, South Hampstead, London. † RBA 1, SWA 4.

POTHECARY, Mrs. Madeline Exh. 1931-39
Watercolour landscape painter. Barberries, Sevenoaks, Kent. † COO 2, RA 3, RBA 2, RI 5, SWA 9.

POTHER, W.H. Exh. 1911
Avondale, Warescot Road, Brentwood, Essex. † D 2.

POTT, de See D

POTT, Avril Corbould Exh. 1926-39
† NEA 1, RMS 1.

POTT, Charles L.* Exh. 1886-90
Landscape painter. London. † L 2, RBA 2, ROI 1, TOO 2.

POTT, Constance Mary b. 1862
Etcher. A.R.E. 1894, R.E. 1898. Exh. 1893-1927. Add: London. † FIN 2, L 3, RA 22, RE 106, RID 62, SWA 5.

POTT, Laslett John* 1837-1898
Historical genre painter. b. Newark, Notts. Studied under Alexander Johnston. R.B.A. 1890. Add: St. John's Wood, London. † BG 1, L 2, RA 19, RBA 2, TOO 4.

POTT, Prunella C. Exh. 1932-40
Portrait painter. 11 Scarsdale Villas, London. † COO 12, NEA 2, P 1, RC 12.

POTTEN, Christopher Exh. 1880
Landscape painter. The Studio, Ash Church Grove, Shepherds Bush, London. † RBA 1.

POTTER, Arthur Exh. 1882-92
Figure and fruit painter. Related to Sydney P. q.v. Add: High Road, Chiswick, London. † RA 3, RBA 3, ROI 3.

POTTER, Charles Exh. 1934-35
Etcher. 285 Brettenham Road, Walthamstow, London. † RA 3.

POTTER, Charles Exh. 1880-1902
Landscape painter. Llanbedr Lodge, Taly-Bont, nr. Conway. † L 5, M 16, RA 5, RCA 90, RI 2.

POTTER, C. Wyte Exh. 1905-10
40 Humberstone Gate, Leicester. † B 3, LS 3.

POTTER, Miss E. Exh. 1911-12
Taenen, Buckingham Road, Harrow, Middlesex. † L 2, RA 3.

POTTER, Frank b. 1885
Painter and etcher. Studied Julians, Paris 1910. Exh. 1912-40. Add: London. † ALP 39, B 1, I 4, L 2, LS 6, NEA 3, RA 6, RCA 1, RI 1, ROI 1, RSA 1.

POTTER, Frank Huddlestone 1845-1887
Genre painter. Studied Heatherleys and R.A. Schools. R.B.A. 1879. Add: London. † GI 1, L 2, RA 1, RBA 3, ROI 3.

POTTER, F. Tennant Exh. 1887-1926
Seacombe 1887; New Brighton, Cheshire 1888; Egremont, Cheshire 1897; Liverpool 1902. † L 12, RA 1.

POTTER, Miss H.B. Exh. 1896
2 Bolton Gardens, London. † SWA 3.

POTTER, James Exh. 1882
Stretford, Manchester. † M 1.

POTTER, Leonard G.F. Exh. 1925-38
Stained glass artist. London. † RA 1, RSA 1.

POTTER, Mary* b. 1900
Flower and landscape painter. Studied Beckenham School of Art and Slade School. Member London Group 1940. Exh. 1924-40. Add: London. † COO 1, LEI 1, NEA 4, RED 26, RI 2, TOO 34.

POTTER, Miss M.J.T. Exh. 1917-19
134 Widmore Road, Bromley, Kent. † SWA 3.

POTTER, Mary Kynaston
See WATTS-JONES

POTTER, Maud M. Exh. 1889
Ringley Parsonage, Stoneclough, nr. Manchester. † M 1.

POTTER, Percy C. Exh. 1885
Watercolour coastal painter. † RBA 1.

POTTER, Robert Exh. 1940
Architect. 75 New Street, Salisbury, Wilts. † RA 2.

POTTER, Sydney Exh. 1883-89
Landscape painter. Related to Arthur P. q.v. Add: High Road, Chiswick, London. † RA 3, RBA 3, ROI 3.

POTTER, W.A. Exh. 1928-29
Landscape painter. † AB 2.

POTTER, Walter B. Exh. 1894-1905
Landscape painter. 2 Bolton Gardens, London. † L 6, RA 13, RSA 14.

POTTER, William H. Exh. 1905-31
Painter. Watford, Herts. 1905; Maldon, Essex 1907; Forest Hill, London 1931. † D 30, L 3, M 1, RA 6.

POTTER, W.J. Exh. 1912-14
Piazza Studio, St. Ives, Cornwall. † LS 3, ROI 2.

POTTINGER, John Exh. 1915
2 Berbice Road, Mossley Hill, Liverpool. † L 1.

POTTS, Arthur Exh. 1904
Figure painter. Bushey, Herts. † RA 1.

POTTS, C.L. Exh. 1905-6
Cae Gwyn, Caernarvon, Wales. † RCA 2.

POTTS, Dulcie H. Exh. 1912-15
Glanrye, Dewey Avenue, Aintree, Liverpool. † L 5.

POTTS, J.J. Exh. 1887-89
West Jesmond, Newcastle on Tyne. † L 2.

POTTS, Mrs. M. Exh. 1939
Rectory Cottage, Lapworth. † B 1.

POTTS, Walter Exh. 1911-38
Stockport, Lancs. 1911; Godley, Cheshire 1925. † L 11, M 5, RA 1, RBA 1, RCA 2, RMS 1.

POULTER, Annie Exh. 1884
18 Ardgowan Square, Greenock. † GI 1.

POULTER, Briant A. b. 1881
Architect, watercolour painter and black and white artist. Travelled in Canada and U.S.A. Brother of H. Reginald P. q.v. Exh. 1905-36. Add: London and Camberley, Surrey. † RA 29, RSA 1.

POULTER, Harry Exh. 1887-93
Figure painter and black and white artist. London. † RA 5.

POULTER, H. Reginald Exh. 1915-33
Architect. Brother of Briant A.P. q.v. Add: Camberley, Surrey and London. † RA 15.

POULTER, J.A. 1825-1921
Landscape painter. Exh. 1882-87. Add: The Home Close, Bury, Hunts. † GI 1, L 1, RE 5.

POULTER, Miss L.S. Exh. 1881
The Limes, Handsworth, Birmingham. † RSA 1.

POULTNEY, Richard Curzon Exh. 1894-97
Miniature portrait painter. 3 North Terrace, Alexander Square, South Kensington, London. † RA 5, RMS 1.

POULTON, Lily S. Exh. 1883-92
Watercolour painter. Great Malvern, Worcs. † B 4, L 2, M 6, SWA 3.

POULTON, Richard Exh. 1927
80 High Street, Rutherglen. † GI 1.

POULTON, T.L. Exh. 1914-15
Figure painter. 27 Fitzroy Square, London. † NEA 2.

POULTON, Mrs. W.M. Exh. 1940
Petersfield, Hants. † RI 2.

POUPELET, Jeanne 1878-1932
French sculptor, and pencil artist. Exh. 1925. † CHE 7.

POW, Thomas Exh. 1929
62 South Street, Armadale. † RSA 1.

POWELL, Aelfreda Exh. 1901-2
Miniature portrait painter. 43 Sutherland Avenue, London. † L 1, RA 2.

POWELL, Alfred Exh. 1880-1913
Landscape painter. Acacia Road, St. John's Wood, London. † AG 39, B 37, D 12, DOW 3, FIN 40, GI 2, L 15, LEI 33, M 19, RA 9, RBA 17, RI 45.

POWELL, Alfred and Louise Exh. 1925-26
40 Mecklenburgh Square, London. † L 10.

POWELL, A.H. Exh. 1925
Watercolour architectural painter. † BA 1.

POWELL, Alfred H. Exh. 1890-91
Architectural artist. 18 Selwood Place, Onslow Gardens, London. † RA 3.

POWELL, Miss A.M. Exh. 1888-95
Aston, Birmingham 1888; Droitwich 1895. † B 4.

POWELL, Blanche H. Exh. 1928-38
Miniature portrait painter. Roseleigh, Alverton, Penzance. † L 3, RA 7, RSA 4.

POWELL, C. Exh. 1883
Watercolour landscape painter. The Elms, Dixton, Monmouth. † RBA 1.

POWELL, Charles Edward Exh. 1882
Architect. 89 Chancery Lane, London. † RA 1.

POWELL, Miss D.V. Exh. 1909-11
Miniature painter. 40 Lebanon Park, Twickenham, Middlesex. † RA 4.

POWELL, Elizabeth Exh. 1928
† NEA 1.

POWELL, E.F. Exh. 1927
15 Tothill Street, Ebbw Vale, Monmouth. † B 2.

POWELL, Miss E. Folliott Exh. 1887-1908
Portrait and figure painter. 5 Notting Hill Square, Campden Hill, London. † M 1, RA 3, RBA 2, RID 23, ROI 1, SWA 6.

POWELL, Edward G. Exh. 1939
34 Falkland Mansions, Hyndland, Glasgow. † RSA 1.

POWELL, Edward Turner Exh. 1892-1922
Architect. London. † RA 11.

POWELL, Eric Walter 1886-1933
Watercolour landscape painter. Studied Julian's, Paris. Drawing master at Eton College. Killed with 3 other Eton masters in the Alps. Exh. from 1913. Add: Eton College, Windsor, Berks. † RI 2, WG 665.

POWELL, Sir Francis 1833-1914
Watercolour landscape and coastal painter. b. Pendleton, Manchester. Studied Manchester School of Art. Founder Member of R.S.W. 1878 and first President R.S.W. A.R.W.S. 1867, R.W.S. 1876. Knighted 1893. Add: Dunoon, Argyllshire. † AG 12, D 1, DOW 4, FIN 9, GI 2, L 6, M 2, RSA 2, RSW 51, RWS 62, TOO 2.

POWELL, Frederick Atkinson
Exh. 1882-1935
Watercolour landscape painter. Kennington Road, London. † RBA 4, RI 4.

POWELL, George S. Exh. 1920
Architect. 1 Raymond Buildings, Gray's Inn, London. † RA 1.

POWELL, Hugh Peter Exh. 1887
Landscape painter. Isleworth, Middlesex. † ROI 1.

POWELL, Mrs. J. Exh. 1883
Flower painter. † DOW 1.

POWELL, Miss J. Exh. 1938
The Priory, Kenilworth, Worcs. † B 1.

POWELL, John A. b. 1911
Portrait and landscape painter and etcher. Studied Nottingham College of Art 1932-35 and Royal College of Art 1935-39. Add: Nottingham 1932; Sutton, Surrey 1940. † N 21, RA 2.

POWELL, Joseph A. Exh. 1901-14
London. † B 10, D 57, RA 1, RI 4.

POWELL, J. Crofts d. 1914
Stained glass artist. Exh. 1901. Add: Whitefriars Glass Works. † RA 1.

POWELL, James C. Exh. 1882-84
Landscape and cattle painter. 27 Thurloe Place, London. † D 2, DOW 1.

POWELL, Kate Exh. 1885-88
3 Bright's Crescent, Edinburgh. † RSA 4.

POWELL, L.L. Exh. 1909
Architect. 7 High Street, Marlow, Bucks. † RA 1.

POWELL, Leonard Marlborough
Exh. 1883-1916
Landscape and coastal painter. Hertford and London. † B 4, D 7, L 11, LS 6, NG 3, RA 9, RBA 2, RI 7, ROI 3.

POWELL, Mary Exh. 1900-25
Birmingham. † B 9.

POWELL, Mrs. Margaret Exh. 1894-95
Wake Green Road, Moseley, Birmingham. † B 2.

POWELL, Mrs. Moila Exh. 1915-39
10 Cambridge Terrace, Leeson Park, Dublin. † GOU 1, RHA 2.

POWELL, Minnie E. Exh. 1893-1900
2 Whitelady's Road, Clifton, Bristol. † GI 7.

POWELL, Olive M. Exh. 1919
† L 1.

POWELL, Miss Q.F. Exh. 1914
Addison Court Gardens, London. † SWA 1.

POWELL, Samuel K. Exh. 1884-1901
Figure painter. Hammersmith 1884; Isleworth, Middlesex 1901. † RBA 1, RI 1.

POWELL, Violet M. Exh. 1913-35
Sculptor. Westminster, London 1913; Dublin 1935. † LS 6, RHA 2.

POWELL, William Henry Exh. 1883-89
Architect. London. † RA 4.

POWER, Albert George 1883-1945
Sculptor. A.R.H.A. 1911, R.H.A. 1919. Add: Dublin. † RHA 67.

POWER, Cyril Edward Exh. 1896-1938
Architect, watercolour painter, etcher, drypoint artist and author. A.R.B.A. 1927, R.B.A. 1930. Add: London. † GOU 2, GI 1, L 2, RA 7, RBA 30, RED 50.

POWER, Mrs. Emma Exh. 1890-1901
Richmond, Surrey 1890; Eastbourne 1891. † M 1, SWA 12.

POWER, F. Exh. 1880-82
Merrion Square, Dublin. † RHA 3.

POWER, Henry H. Exh. 1882-1902
Erdington, nr. Birmingham 1882; Knowle, Birmingham 1885; Dunsford, Exeter 1899. † B 8, RA 2.

POWER, Helen le Poer Exh. 1881-87
Landscape painter. Ham Common, Surrey. † SWA 5.

POWER, Harold Septimus* Exh. 1908-35
Painter. R.I. 1925, R.O.I. 1916. Add: London 1908; Bushey, Herts. 1920. † AR 53, CHE 1, GI 1, I 2, L 1, LS 11, P 3, RA 33, RHA 4 RI 11, ROI 31, RSA 1.

POWER, John Exh. 1925-37
Painter. Cork. † RHA 13.

POWER, James P. Exh. 1924-38
Landscape painter. R.B.A. 1930. Add: Haarlem, Holland 1930; Warmond. Holland 1938. † CON 5, D 3, RA 1, RBA 6.

POWER, J.W. Exh. 1919-31
Member London Group 1923. † I 2, LS 3, TOO 1.

POWER, Lucy Exh 1893-98
Portrait and figure painter. 37A Great Cumberland Place, Hyde Park, London. † RA 3, RBA 1.

POWER, May Exh. 1933-40
Sculptor. 18 Geraldine Street, Dublin. † RHA 8.

POWER, Molly Exh. 1904-32
Miniature portrait painter and wood engraver. R.M.S. 1916, H.R.M.S. 1934, A.S.W.A. 1920. Add: Greenhithe, Kent 1904; East Molesey, Surrey 1910; London 1918, Wells, Somerset 1926. † B 1, GI 1, I 1, L 17, NG 1, RA 14, RHA 11, RMS 54, RSA 7, SWA 5.

POWER, Ronald Exh. 1932-39
Painter. London. † GI 1, NEA 2, RA 2.

POWERS, Longworth d. 1904
American sculptor. Son of Hiram P. (1805-1873) and brother of Preston P. q.v. Exh. 1886. Add: 11 Via Dante da Castiglione, Florence. † RA 1.

POWERS, Marion Exh. 1905-6
Pension Tarbary, Rue Montreuil, France 1905; Hampstead, London 1906. † L 1, RA 2.

POWERS, Preston b. 1843
American sculptor. Son of Hiram P. (1805-1873) and brother of Longworth P. q.v. Exh. 1882. Add: c/o Mr. J. Spiers, 56 Bloomsbury Street, London. † RA 1.

POWIS, Mary Exh. 1895-1904
18 Hunters Road, Handsworth, Birmingham. † B 14.

POWLES, Lewis Charles 1860-1942
Landscape painter. R.B.A. 1903. Add: London 1894 and 1928; Rye, Sussex 1918. † BG 3, L 2, LEI 2, M 1, NEA 1, NG 1, RA 7, RBA 173.

POWNALL, Ellen Louise Exh. 1888-90
Miniature portrait painter. 20 Harcourt Terrace, South Kensington, London. † RA 3.

POWNALL, G. Exh. 1899
c/o Messrs Shepherd Bros., Angel Row, Nottingham. † N 2.

POWNALL, Gilbert A. Exh. 1903-38
Portrait and figure painter. Twickenham, Middlesex 1903; Burstall, Suffolk 1911; London 1919. † L 8, RA 14.

POWNALL, Leonard A. Exh. 1897-1913
Painter and stained glass artist. London 1897; Northwood, Middlesex 1901; Falmouth 1911. † RA 17.

POWNALL, Mary
See BROMET, Mary Pownall

POXON, Ethel Exh 1931
Landscape painter. 43 Norfolk Road, Thornton Heath Surrey. † RA 2.

POYNTER, Sir Ambrose Macdonald 1868-1923
Architect. Son of Sir Edward John P. q.v. Add: London 1893 and 1913; Buenos Aires, Argentina 1912. † NG 4, RA 17.

POYNTER, Sir Edward John* 1836-1919
Painter, illustrator and medallist. b. Paris. Studied with Leigh and W.C.T. Dobson and at R.A. Schools. Lived in Paris for several years. Appointed Slade Professor and Director of Art at the South Kensington Museum. Director of the National Gallery 1894-1906. A.R.A. 1869, R.A. 1876, P.R.A. 1896-1918, H.R.B.A. 1897, R.E. 1881, R.M.S. 1896, H.R.M.S. 1897, H.R.O.I. 1898, R.P. 1912, H.R.S.A. 1896, R.W.S. 1883. Father of Ambrose M.P. q.v. "A Visit to Aesculapius" purchased by Chantrey Bequest 1880. Add: London. † AG 4, B 4, CAR 1, D 1, DOW 2, FIN 166, G 12, GI 5, I 1, L 17, M 17, NG 15, P 2, RA 147, RE 1, RHA 4, RMS 2, RSA 3, RWS 35.

POYNTER, Fred G. Exh. 1919-40
Fernside, Ledgers Road, Slough, Bucks. † RBA 2 ROI 5.

POYNZ, Geo Exh. 1911
68 David Street, Liverpool. † L 1.

POYSER, John Rigby Exh. 1902-15
Architect. Queen's Chambers, King Street, Nottingham. † N 12.

POYSER, T.J. Exh. 1885
101 Nottingham Road, New Basford, Notts. † N 1.

POZZO, da See D.

PRADEZ, Edith Exh. 1882
Watercolour landscape painter. 24 Rue Nysten Liege, Belgium. † RBA 2.

PRAED, Mrs. Exh. 1887
Landscape painter. 11 Pont Street, Belgrave Square, London. † SWA 2.

PRAEGER, Sophia Rosamond b. 1867
Sculptor, and illustrator. b. Holywood, Co. Down. Studied Belfast School of Art and Slade School. H.R.H.A. 1927. Exh. 1891-1940. Add: Holywood, Co. Down. † L 8 RA 9, RHA 47.

PRAETORIUS, Charles Exh. 1888-1914
Painter and illustrator. London. † L 1, M 1, RA 14, ROI 1.

PRAETORIUS, Mrs. Minnie Exh. 1924
Miniature portrait painter. Selsey, Chichester. † RA 1.

PRAGA, Alfred Exh. 1887-1939
Portrait painter, miniaturist and pastelier. b. Liverpool. Studied London, Paris and Antwerp. R.B.A. 1911. Add: London. † D 5, GI 1, L 10, LS 5, NG 1, P 3, RA 25, RBA 79, RI 69, ROI 9.

PRAGNELL, Kate Exh. 1898
164 Sloane Street, London. † SWA 5.

PRALESI, G. Exh. 1886
c/o P. Marchiafava, 28 Duke Street, London. † L 1.

PRANCE, Bertram b. 1889
Painter, black and white, humerous sketch and "Punch" artist. b. Bideford, Devon. Exh. 1934-35. Add: Chudleigh, Rudgwick, Sussex. † AR 3, RA 1.

PRANGLEY, Alice E. Exh. 1893-1905
Bedington, Cheshire 1893; Formby, Lancs. 1902. † L 5, SWA 1.

PRASAD, V.N. Exh. 1934
19 Esplanade Terrace, Joppa. † RSA 1.

PRAT, Arthur Exh. 1911
Portrait and landscape painter. † BRU 44.

PRAT, Loys J. Exh. 1907
151 bis Rue de Grenelle, Paris. † L 1.

PRATER, Ernest Exh. 1897-1914
Painter and illustrator. On staff of "Black and White", "Sphere" and "Graphic". Add: London. † RA 7.

PRATER, Harry Exh. 1923-28
Wood engraver. Crantock, Church Road, Harold Wood, Essex. † RA 2.

PRATER, Joseph Exh. 1928-29
Wood engraver. 18 Beresford Road, Highbury, London. † RA 2.

PRATT, A. Epps Exh. 1880-86
Landscape and coastal painter. Shottermill, Haslemere, Surrey 1880; London 1881; Bournemouth 1885. † B 1, RHA 1, SWA 7.

PRATT, Annie E. Exh. 1884-1900
Figure and landscape painter. Nottingham 1884; Ruddington, Notts. 1899. † N 11.

PRATT, Claude* b. 1860
Genre painter and watercolourist. b Leicester. Son of Jonathan P. q.v. Studied Birmingham School of Art, Antwerp and Paris. R.B.S.A. 1888. Exh. 1882-1935. Add: Birmingham 1882, 1884 and 1920; Paris 1883; Broadway, Worcs. 1894. † B 167, L 17, RI 3, RMS 1, ROI 4.

PRATT, Rev. C.E. Exh. 1929-34
Painter. † AB 4, WG 11.

PRATT, D. Camden Exh. 1896-1940
14 Shaftesbury Terrace, Glasgow. † GI 5, RSW 1.

PRATT, Derrick Edward Henry b. 1895
Painter and etcher. b. Walsall. Studied Leeds School of Art and Royal College of Art. Principal Llanelly School of Art. Son of Edward Derrick P. q.v. Exh. 1935. Add: Llanelly, Carmarthenshire. † RA 1.

PRATT, Edward Exh. 1880-81
Figure painter. c/o Mr. Scott, 78 Princes Street, Edinburgh. † RA 1, RSA 1.

PRATT, Miss E. Exh. 1903
52 Aubert Park, Highbury, London. † SWA 2.

PRATT, Edith Exh. 1904
12 North Side, Clapham Common, London. † M 1.

PRATT, Edward Derrick Exh. 1908-11
Father of Derrick E.H.P. q.v. South Ealing, London 1908; Leeds 1911. † L 1, RA 2.

PRATT, Emily E. Exh. 1890
Landscape painter. 56 Castle Gate, Nottingham. † N 1.
PRATT, Mrs. Gertrude Exh. 1890
19 Greenfield Crescent, Edgbaston, Birmingham. † B 1.
PRATT, Mrs. H. Exh. 1899
† P 1.
PRATT, Mrs H.A. Exh. 1900
71 Osborne Road, Newcastle. † NG 1.
PRATT, James Exh. 1880
103 Renfrew Street, Glasgow. † GI 1.
PRATT, John Exh. 1892
High Street, Crail, Fife. † GI 1.
PRATT, John Exh. 1882-1911
Flower and still life painter. Related to Ralph P. q.v. Add: Leeds. † L 4, RA 12.
PRATT, Jonathan* 1835-1911
Genre painter. Father of Claude P. q.v. Add: Edgbaston, Birmingham. † B 101, GI 1, L 18, M 2, RA 8, RBA 3, ROI 7.
PRATT, Joseph Bishop 1854-1910
Engraver. London 1880; Harpenden, Herts. 1897. † RA 38.
PRATT, Mabel Exh. 1914-38
Miniature portrait painter. Leeds. † L 9, M 1, RA 6.
PRATT, N.H. Exh. 1914
Meadow Lane, Nottingham. † N 1.
PRATT, Ralph Exh. 1881-93
Still life painter. Related to John P. q.v. Add: 49 Portland Crescent, Leeds. † L 1, M 1, RA 9.
PRATT, S.C. junr. Exh. 1905
Carlton House, Harpenden, Herts. † RA 1.
PRATT, Thomas M. Exh. 1883-98
Glasgow. † GI 9, RSA 1.
PRATT, Victoria Exh. 1922-32
Margaret Road, Harborne, Birmingham. † B 25.
PRATT, William* b. 1855
Figure and marine painter. Studied Glasgow School of Art and Julians, Paris. Exh. 1880-1936. Add: Glasgow 1880; Kirkintilloch 1888; Lenzie 1911. † GI 161, L 23, M 2, NG 1, RA 6, RSA 64, RSW 7.
PRATT, William B. Exh. 1883
Wrought iron gate designer. 69 Rendlesham Road, Clapton, London. † RA 1.
PRATT, W.H. Exh. 1923-32
London 1923; Edinburgh 1932. † RSA 3.
PRATTEN, M.A. Exh. 1881-86
Watercolour flower and fruit painter. Haslemere, Surrey. † SWA 7.
PRATTER, Miss M. Exh. 1885
12 Abbey Street, Bethnal Green Road, London. † M 1.
PREAN, Amy Exh. 1899-1903
123 Bridge Road, Battersea, London. † SWA 3.
PREDG, A. Exh. 1889
74 Rue d'Amsterdam, Paris. † M 2.
PREECE, Patricia b. 1900
Flower and figure painter. Studied Slade School and Paris. Married Stanley Spencer q.v. Exh. 1936-40. Add: Moss Thatch, Cookham, Berks. † AG 1, COO 1, GI 1, GOU 1, LEF 8, NEA 8, RBA 3.
PREHN, William Exh. 1880-90
Sculptor. London. † G 2, L 1, RA 2.
PREINDLSBERGER, Marianne
See STOKES
PRELL, Herman 1854-1922
German painter. Exh. 1889. Add: Handelstrasse, Berlin. † RA 1.
PRENDERGAST, John Exh. 1908-11
Etaples, pas de Calais, France 1908; London 1911. † LS 6.

PRENDERGAST, W.M. Exh. 1898-1902
15 Cheyne Court, Chelsea, London. † D 12.
PRENTICE, Andrew Noble b. 1866
Architect. b. Greenock. Exh. 1892-1940. Add: London. † GI 17, RA 51, RSA 7.
PRENTICE, Kate Exh. 1880-97
Landscape painter. Kensington, London. † B 5, D 3, G 1, L 4, M 1, RA 1, RI 3, SWA 18.
PRENTICE, Marie Y. Exh. 1905-13
Albany Chambers, Charing Cross, Glasgow. † GI 13, RA 1.
PRENTIS, Valerie E.G. Exh. 1921-32
London. † G 2, GOU 1, NEA 5, RBA 4, SWA 1.
PRESALE, de See D
PRESCOTT, Miss Claude Exh. 1922-31
Flower and portrait painter. London. † RA 1, SWA 2.
PRESCOTT, Charles Barrow 1870-1932
Portrait and landscape painter and etcher. b. Wilmslow, Cheshire. Studied Calderons, St. Johns Wood, Voss's and Julians, Paris. Travelled widely in Europe and the north coast of Africa. Add: London. † AB 69, GOU 2, L 4, LS 6, M 1, P 1, RA 4, RI 3, ROI 2, WG 142.
PRESCOTT, C. Trevor Exh. 1892-97
Painter. 71 Upper Stanhope Street, Liverpool. † B 1, L 8, RA 1.
PRESCOTT, Miss E.W. Exh. 1920-23
Swanpool Lane, Aughton, Ormskirk. † L 4.
PRESCOTT, Mrs. Katherine Exh. 1899
Sculptor. Boston, Mass. U.S.A. † NG 2.
PRESCOTT-DAVIES, Daphne Exh. 1913
219 Maida Vale, London. † RI 1.
PRESCOTT-DAVIES, Norman 1862-1915
Flower, portrait and miniature painter. b. Isleworth, Middlesex. R.B.A. 1893. Add: Isleworth 1880; Hampstead, London 1890. † B 8, D 2, G 1, L 17, M 2, NG 1, RA 12, RBA 93, RCA 82, RHA 1, RI 9, ROI 9.
PRESS, Henry Exh. 1909
† LS 3.
PRESSLAND, Annie L. Exh. 1892-1923
Watercolour flower painter. 32 Knoll Road, Wandsworth, London. † B 5, BG 2, L 3, LS 12, M 2, RI 5, SWA 12.
PREST, Oswald E. Exh. 1904
Stained glass artist. Clarence House, 47 Haverstock Hill, London. † RA 1.
PRESTON, A.C. Exh. 1882-1906
Landscape painter. Abbot's Grange, Chester. † D 2, L 4, RI 1, RCA 1.
PRESTON, Edward b. 1851
Profile carver in ivory from photographs. Studied Liverpool Institute. Exh. 1925-29. Add: 18 Burdett Street, St. Michael's, Liverpool. † L 1 RCA 2.
PRESTON, E. Carter Exh. 1909-38
Landscape and figure painter, watercolourist and wood engraver. A.R.M.S. 1928, R.M.S. 1929. Add: Liverpool. † AB 4, CAR 20, FIN 50, L 29, NEA 5 RMS 13, RSA 1.
PRESTON, G.H. Exh. 1938
Watercolour painter. † WG 3.
PRESTON, Henry Exh. 1898-1901
520 Hornsey Road, London. † D 4.
PRESTON, Josephine Exh. 1888-1905
Painter. London. † L 2, LS 4, P 1, RBA 1, ROI 1.
PRESTON, Lawrence Exh. 1936-38
Watercolour landscape painter. 73 Springfield Road, Brighton. † RA 3.

PRESTON, Maud B. Exh. 1914-23
Painter. Thongsbridge, nr. Huddersfield 1914; Southport, Lancs. 1920. † B 2, L 14, RA 2.
PRESTON, Robert H.J. Exh. 1929-30
Sculptor. c/o J. Varley Esq., 11 Stanley Gardens, London. † GI 1, L 3, RA 1, RCA 1, RSA 1.
PRESTON, W.B. Exh. 1923
1 Doon Street, Kirkdale, Liverpool. † L 1.
PRESTON-ROSEVEAR, Mrs. Nan
Exh. 1936
10 Lansdowne Circus, Leamington Spa, Warwicks. † B 1.
PRESTWICH, Mrs. R.T. Exh. 1909
Holmeleigh, Park Lane, Higher Broughton, Manchester. † L 1.
PREUSCHER, von See V
PREWETT, Miss E. Exh. 1893
Miles House, Horsham, Sussex. † SWA 1.
PRICE, Miss Exh. 1886
Landscape painter. 14 Woodlands Villa, Blackheath, London. † SWA 1.
PRICE, Miss A. d. 1922
Exh. 1920-21. Add: 10 The Grove, Villa Road, Handsworth, Birmingham. † B 4.
PRICE, Alice Exh. 1881
Figure painter. 159 Winston Road, Stoke Newington, London. † RBA 1.
PRICE, A.S. Exh. 1923
Liverpool. † L 1.
PRICE, Miss A.S. Exh. 1883
Afton, Waterloo Park, Liverpool. † L 1.
PRICE, Claude b. 1892
Landscape and still life painter and decorative designer. Studied Nottingham School of Art and London. A.N.S.A. 1920, N.S.A. 1927. Exh. 1922-39. Add: 407 Alfreton Road, Nottingham. † N 29, RA 2, RBA 2.
PRICE, Miss C. Exh. 1885
5 Pakenham Road, Birmingham. † B 1.
PRICE, Miss C. Exh. 1895
Chepstow House, Hereford. † SWA 1.
PRICE, Coverley A.V. Exh. 1940
42 White Lands House, Cheltenham Terrace, London. † RBA 2.
PRICE, Mrs. Doris Exh. 1930-35
39D North Side, Clapham Common, London. † RI 10, RMS 2, ROI 2.
PRICE, E. Exh. 1884
† N 2.
PRICE, Elizabeth Exh. 1926-27
Moss Bank, 2 Woodley Park, Rock Ferry, Birkenhead. † L 2.
PRICE, Ernest Exh. 1916
89 Hampden Street, Bolton, Lancs. † L 2.
PRICE, Mrs. E.M. Exh. 1923
† SWA 1.
PRICE, Edmund N. Exh. 1888-89
Stained glass artist. 4 Grove Cottages, Manor Street, Chelsea, London. † RA 2.
PRICE, Frank Corbyn b. 1862
Landscape painter. R.B.A. 1895. Married Lydia Jemima P. q.v. Exh. 1888-1933. Add: London 1888; Billingshurst, Sussex 1891; Pulborough, Sussex 1919. † DOW 1, L 22, RA 10, RBA 158, RCA 6, RI 3.
PRICE, Miss G. Exh. 1911
46 Warwick Road, London. † RA 1.
PRICE, Geo Exh. 1889
47 Croydon Grove, Croydon, Surrey. † B 2.
PRICE, Henry Exh. 1901-5
Sculptor. Onslow Studios, 183 Kings Road, London. † GI 2, L 1, NG 1 RA 5.
PRICE, Isabella Exh. 1886-87
London. † G 1, L 1.

PRICE, Ivor S. Exh. 1894-99
Architect. St. Leonard's on Sea, Sussex 1894; London 1899. † RA 2.
PRICE, James M. Exh. 1896-1902
Liverpool. † L 2.
PRICE, Julius Mendes* 1857-1924
Figure and landscape painter. London. † B 4, G 3, L 2, M 2, RA 6, RBA 4, RHA 2, ROI 6.
PRICE, J.W. Exh. 1884
2 The Albany, Liverpool. † L 1.
PRICE, Mrs. Laura Exh. 1891-92
26 Watergate Row, Chester. † L 2.
PRICE, Leslie b. 1915
Portrait painter, commercial artist and designer. Studied Birmingham College of Art 1930-34. Exh. 1935-40. Add: Birmingham. † B 5.
PRICE, Lydia Jemima Exh. 1890-99
nee Jeal. Watercolour flower and figure painter. Married Frank Corbyn P. q.v. Add: London 1890; Billingshurst, Sussex 1891. † L 6, RA 6, RBA 2, RI 8, RSW 1.
PRICE, May Exh. 1882
5 Fairholme Road, Crosby, Liverpool. † L 1.
PRICE, Miss M.C. Blackwood Exh. 1885-1903
Portrait painter. London 1885; Downpatrick, Ireland 1891. † B 1, G 2, L 1, RHA 2.
PRICE, M. Zandria Exh. 1929
28 Burlington Street, Blackburn, Lancs. † L 2.
PRICE, Miss N.G.P. Exh. 1911
124 Castle Hill, Reading, Berks. † L 1,
PRICE, N.M. Exh. 1905
Carlton Studio, 180 Fleet Street, London. † RA 1.
PRICE, Reginald Exh. 1929
62 Cavan Road, Clubmoor, West Derby, Liverpool. † L 2.
PRICE, T. Walmsley Exh. 1885-87
Chester. † L 3, M 3.
PRICE, Mrs. T.W. Exh. 1887
26 Watergate Row, Chester. † L 1.
PRICE, W. Frederick Exh. 1880-1905
Landscape painter. Crosby, Liverpool. † L 20, RBA 1.
PRICE, Walter G. Exh. 1910-33
Etcher. Birmingham. † B 8, RA 1.
PRICE-HUGHES, Barbara b. 1908
Portrait painter. b. Cape of Good Hope. Studied Slade School, R.A. Schools and Italy. Exh. 1930-35. Add: Redlands, Shalford, Guildford, Surrey. † L 1, P 4, RA 1, SWA 1.
PRICHARD, Miss G.M. Exh. 1913
7 Brockenhurst Road, Ramsgate, Kent. † L 1.
PRICHARD, W.S. Exh. 1884
27 Redcliffe Road, South Kensington, London. † D 1.
PRICKETT, Dorothy See DAVIES
PRICKETT, M. Exh. 1923
9 Greenhill Place, Edinburgh. † RSA 1.
PRIDE, James Exh. 1937
Portrait painter. † RED 1.
PRIDE, John b. 1877
Painter, black and white artist, etcher and engraver. Studied Liverpool School of Art. Exh. 1903-32. Add: Liverpool. † L 21.
PRIDE, Miss P.E. Exh. 1939-40
† P 1, ROI 1.
PRIDE, Samuel Exh. 1882-1912
Liverpool 1882; Wallasey, Cheshire 1899. † L 64.
PRIDEAUX-BRUNE, Gertrude R. Exh. 1880-1909
Landscape and coastal painter. Padstow, Cornwall 1880 and 1890; London 1886; Guildford, Surrey 1908. † L 2, LS 8, RA 1, RBA 4, ROI 26.
PRIDHAM, Dorothy Anne Exh. 1916-19
Miniature portrait painter. 21 St. Johns Road, Harrow, Middlesex. † RA 2, SWA 1.
PRIEST, Alfred* 1874-1929
Painter, etcher, black and white artist and tapestry designer. b. Harborne, Birmingham. Studied R.A. Schools 1892-97 (Turner gold medal and travelling studentship) and Julians, Paris 1898. On staff of "Daily Chronicle" 1904-5. R.P. 1917. Add: London 1898 and 1900; Edgbaston, Birmingham 1899. † B 27, GI 1, GOU 2, I 4, L 13, LS 4. P 21, RA 22, RI 3, ROI 7.
PRIEST, Mrs. Martin Exh. 1923-31
Miniature portrait painter. Fir Cottage, Lamorbey, Sidcup, Kent. † RA 4, RMS 1.
PRIESTLEY, Mrs. F. Exh. 1898
71 Colmore Row, Birmingham. † B 1.
PRIESTLEY, Philip Collingwood b. 1901
Painter, black and white artist and cartoonist. Studied Leicester College of Arts and Crafts 1915-20. Exh. 1934. Add: 22 Hazlewood Road, Leicester. † N 3.
PRIESTLEY-SMITH, Hugh Exh. 1922-29
Dingle Hill, Bradfield, Berks. † L 142.
PRIESTMAN, Arnold 1854-1925
Landscape painter. R.B.A. 1891. Add: London 1883; Bradford, 1885. † B 22, D 1, G 9, GI 16, GOU 7, I 1, L 44, M 29, NG 29, RA 38, RBA 31, RHA 8, RSA 6.
PRIESTMAN, Bertram* 1868-1951
Landscape, coastal, cattle and portrait painter. b. Bradford. Studied Slade School. Travelled widely on the continent. N.E.A. 1896, A.R.A. 1916, R.A. 1923, R.B.A. 1894, R.O.I. 1910. Member of the Society of 25 Artists. Add: Bradford 1888; London 1889 and 1924; Skipton 1918; Walberswick, Suffolk 1919. † AG 1, B 2, BG 28, BK 1, FIN 2, G 4, GI 22, GOU 13, I 14, L 39, M 11, NEA 18, NG 11, RA 140, RBA 22, RHA 3, ROI 27.
PRIESTMAN, Gertrude Exh. 1921-36
Watercolour landscape painter. Hillfoot, Ben Rhydding, nr. Leeds. † GI 2, L 1.
PRIESTMAN, John B. Exh. 1934
Cromwell Hall, East Grinstead, Sussex. † RBA 1.
PRIM, J.M. Exh. 1937
Painter. † BA 1.
PRIMAUDAYE, la See L
PRIME, Eva M. Exh. 1892-93
Hagley Road, Edgbaston, Birmingham. † B 3.
PRIMMER, Kathleen M.F. Exh. 1935
Portrait painter. 85 Prince of Wales Road, London. † RA 1.
PRINCE, Miss Exh. 1903
The Study, Bonsall, Matlock, Derbys. † SWA 1.
PRINCE, Annie Exh. 1880
Painter. 85 Gower Street, London. † SWA 1.
PRINCE, Constance H. Exh. 1889-1911
Manchester. † M 5.
PRINCE, Harry b. 1879
Architect. b. Lucknow, India. Studied Kings College and Victoria and Albert Museum. Exh. 1913-19. Add: London. † RA 2.
PRINCE, Louis S.M. Exh. 1923-40
Watercolour landscape painter. Leigh, Lancs. 1923; London 1926 and 1930; Stanway, nr. Colchester, Essex 1928; Sudbury, Suffolk 1935. † L 1, NEA 1, RA 17.
PRINCE, Nora Exh. 1891-93
Park Villa, West Bromwich. † B 2.
PRINCE, Walter Exh. 1886-1900
Manchester. † M 4.
PRINCEP, Amy Elise Exh. 1933
Watercolour painter, etcher, designer, jewellery worker and embroiderer. Studied Kensington School of Art, Clifton and Royal College of Art (c.1904-9). Add: Clifton, Bristol. † RCA 1.
PRINCEPS, Lilian Exh. 1893
36 Route de Lyons, Geneva. † M 2, SWA 1.
PRINET, Rene Xavier b. 1861
French painter. Exh. 1907-13. Add: Paris. † GOU 1, L 1.
PRING, Miss E.M. Exh. 1898-1922
Marton Vicarage, Chelford, Cheshire 1898; London 1903. † B 5, L 1, M 4, RA 1, SWA 8.
PRING, Miss N. Gratton Exh. 1921-26
Purley Rectory, nr. Reading 1921; Streatham, London 1926. † L 1, SWA 3.
PRINGLE, Agnes Exh. 1884-1911
Figure, portrait and landscape painter. 58 St. Oswald's Road, West Brompton, London. † B 10, L 6, LS 14, M 2, RA 5, RBA 2, RI 2, SWA 4.
PRINGLE, Alexander Exh. 1880-82
32 Fountainbridge, Edinburgh. † RSA 2.
PRINGLE, Elizabeth A. Exh. 1887-93
58 St. Oswald's Road, West Brompton, London. † B 2.
PRINGLE, Elizabeth S. Exh. 1935-38
31 Craiglockhart Crescent, Edinburgh. † RSA 4, RSW 1.
PRINGLE, Helen Exh. 1881-88
Corstorphine 1881; Edinburgh 1888. † RSA 2.
PRINGLE, J. Connell Exh. 1930
120 Polwarth Terrace, Edinburgh. † RSW 1.
PRINGLE, John J. Exh. 1896-98
788 London Road, Glasgow. † GI 5.
PRINGLE, Kate Exh. 1897-1900
7 Fettes Row, Edinburgh. † GI 2, RSA 7.
PRINGLE, Lydia See ELLIS
PRINGLE, Mary Exh. 1897-1930
Miniature portrait painter. b. Gotha, Thuringia. Studied Royal Academia, Milan and Atelier Mosler, Paris. Add: London. 1897; Brighton 1909. † L 4, RA 5, RI 2, RMS 1.
PRINGLE, S.B. Exh. 1932
† L 1.
PRINS, Pierre Exh. 1912
French pastelier. 35 Rue Rousselet, Paris. † RSA 2.
PRINSEP, Katie B. Exh. 1919-29
Mrs. Muntz. Miniature portrait painter. London 1919; Wokingham, Surrey 1929. † L 2, RA 2.
PRINSEP, Valentine Cameron* 1838-1904
Portrait, historical and genre painter. b. Calcutta, India. Studied under G.F. Watts. Travelled on the continent and was commissioned by the Indian Government to paint Lord Lytton's Durbar to proclaim Queen Victoria Empress of India. Professor of Painting at the R.A. from 1901. A.R.A. 1879, R.A. 1894, H.R.M.S. 1900. "Ayesha" purchased by Chantrey Bequest 1887. Add: London. † B 11, G 13, GI 2, L 15, M 18, NG 4, RA 57, RHA 2, TOO 1.

PRIOLO, Paolo* Exh. 1880-90
Historical, biblical and genre painter. 64 Stockwell Park Road, London. † RBA 5.

PRIOR, Edward Schroder 1852-1932
Architect, modeller, author and lecturer. Slade professor of Fine Art at Cambridge from 1912. A.R.A. 1914. Add: London, Cambridge and Chichester. † RA 15.

PRIOU, Louis b. 1845
French artist. Exh. 1883. Add: 10 Rue Clauzel, Paris. † GI 1.

PRITCHARD, E.F. Exh. 1884
Stanfield, Dean Park, Bournemouth. † D 1.

PRITCHARD, George Exh. 1912-16
Oaklands, Grove Avenue, Yeovil, Somerset. † LS 12.

PRITCHARD, G.H. Exh. 1900
Painter. c/o F. Foster, 11 Carlyle Square, Chelsea, London. † NEA 2.

PRITCHARD, Ivor Mervyn d. 1948
Architect and etcher. b. Beaumaris, Isle of Anglesey. Studied North Wales University; A.A. and R.A. Schools. Exh. 1925-33. Add: 12 Calais Gate, London and Beaumaris, Isle of Anglesey. † B 6, D 1, L 8, RCA 62.

PRITCHARD, J.C. Exh. 1882
Castlefield, Knot Mill, Manchester. † M 2.

PRITCHARD, Marion Exh. 1908-29
Aintree, Liverpool. † L 45.

PRITCHARD, Mary E. Exh. 1893-1913
Flower and fruit painter. Hyde Park, London 1893; Beckesbourne, Canterbury 1913. † RA 4, RBA 1, SWA 1.

PRITCHARD, Stanger Exh. 1905-18
Watercolour painter. London. † GI 1, M 1, RA 5, WG 73.

PRITCHARD, T. Henry Exh. 1902
Landscape painter. West Park Street, Dewsbury, Yorks. † NEA 2.

PRITCHARD, Walter b. 1905
Painter and stained glass artist. b. Dundee. Studied Dundee School of Art (scholarship and travelling scholarship). Stained glass instructor Edinburgh College of Art. Exh. 1931-32. Add: College of Art, Lauriston Place, Edinburgh. † RA 2.

PRITCHARD, Zarh Exh. 1930
Painter of coral, fish, and underwater scenes. † AR 45.

PRITCHARD-BARRETT, S. Exh. 1938
Painter. Park Farm House, Barnstone, Notts. † N 3.

PRITCHETT, Dora C. b. 1878
Miniature portrait painter. b. Folkestone. Studied Goldsmiths College, Camberwell School of Art and Redhill School of Art. Exh. 1903-40. Add: London 1903; Horley, Surrey 1908; Mousehole, Cornwall 1940. † L 1, RA 2, SWA 1.

PRITT, Henry Exh. 1882-88
Landscape painter. 18 Ribblesdale Place, Preston, Lancs. † L 1, RI 1.

PRITT, William Exh. 1915-33
Landscape painter. 52 Frenchwood Street, Preston, Lancs. † GI 2, L 9, RA 1, RCA 1.

PRITTIE, Edward d. 1882
Painter. A.R.H.A. 1871. Add: Dublin. † RHA 8, RSA 2.

PRITZELWITZ, von See V

PROBST, Carl* b. 1854
Austrian figure painter. Exh. 1898-1901. Add: 23B Theresianumgasse, Vienna. † L 2, M 3, RA 3.

PROCHNOWNNICK, Mabel L. Exh. 1918-29
Avenue House, Hendon, London. † GI 1, RI 7.

PROCTER, Albert Exh. 1885-1904
Coastal painter. Liverpool. † L 36, RA 2, RCA 2.

PROCTER, Mrs. Dod* b. 1891
Painter. Studied Newlyn, Penzance and Paris. Spent a year in Rangoon after World War I decorating the Royal Palace with her husband Ernest P. q.v. N.E.A. 1929, A.R.A. 1934, R.A. 1942. "Kitchen at Myrtle Cottage" purchased by Chantrey Bequest 1935 and "The Orchard" (1934) purchased in 1937. Exh. 1913-40. Add: Newlyn, Penzance and London. † BAR 2, BK 1, COO 1, FIN 20, G 5, GI 4, I 1, L 2, LEI 67, M 1, NEA 13, RA 58, RSA 1, SWA 9.

PROCTER, Ernest* 1886-1935
Painter and designer. b. Northumberland. Studied Newlyn and Paris. Spent a year in Rangoon after World War I decorating the Royal Palace with his wife Dod P. q.v. N.E.A. 1929, A.R.A. 1932. "The Zodiac" (1925) purchased by Chantrey Bequest 1936. Add: Newlyn, Penzance 1906 and 1916; Ben Rhydding, Yorks. 1907; London 1929. † BAR 30, CG 1, FIN 40, GI 3, GOU 4, I 5, L 9, LEI 99, NEA 27, P 1, RA 49, RHA 1.

PROCTER, Janet Exh. 1910-33
Painter. Huttons Ambo, York. † I 1, L 4, RA 2, SWA 1.

PROCTER, Miss M.L. Exh. 1904-9
Ben Rhydding, Yorks. † L 2, SWA 1.

PROCTOR, Adam Edwin* 1864-1913
Landscape and figure painter. Studied Lambeth School of Art, Langham Life Class and Westminster School of Art. Travelled on the continent and North Africa. R.B.A. 1890, R.I. 1909, R.O.I. 1907. Add: Brixton 1882; Albury, nr. Guildford, Surrey 1900. † B 5, L 5, RA 34, RBA 241, RI 21, ROI 53, RSA 1.

PROCTOR, Mrs. Cecile A. b. 1897
Painter, pen and ink and pastel artist. Studied Chelsea, St. John's Wood and Byam Shaw School. Exh. 1935-37. Add: London. † RBA 1, RI 2, ROI 1, RSW 1.

PROCTOR, Edward J. Exh. 1896-1930
Stained glass artist. Tufnell Park, London 1896; Wembley, Middlesex 1898. † G 2, P 1, RA 4.

PROCTOR, Irene Exh. 1902-5
Miniature portrait painter. Twickenham Park, Middlesex 1902; Westcliffe on Sea, Essex 1905. † L 1, RA 8.

PROCTOR, John Exh. 1880-83
Landscape painter. 73 Wiltshire Road, Brixton, London. † RBA 2.

PROCTOR, Miss M. Exh. 1923
21 Upper Mount Street, Dublin. † RHA 1.

PROCTOR, Thea Exh. 1907-19
Figure and landscape painter. Chelsea, London. † GOU 59, I 8, L 2, LS 5, NEA 13, RA 4, RID 6.

PROFEIT, Mrs. Eleanor Harrison Exh. 1908-11
22D Ebury Street, Grosvenor Gardens, London. † LS 8.

PROFFIT, Isabella H. Exh. 1924
13 Prenton Road East, Birkenhead. † L 1.

PROFFITT, J.T. Exh. 1911
Central Buildings, Walkden, Manchester. † RA 1.

PROOST, A. Exh. 1918
22 Thomas Street, Oxford Street, London. † I 3, RA 1.

PROPERT, John Lumsden Exh. 1880-82
Etcher. 100 Gloucester Place, Portman Square, London. † DOW 1, RA 5, RE 1.

PROPHET, J.R.H. Exh. 1937-38
Watercolour painter. † WG 5.

PROSCHWITZKY, Frank Exh. 1883-89
Watercolour still life painter. 178 Ladbroke Grove Road, London. † RA 2.

PROSPERI, L. Exh. 1891
24 North John Street, Liverpool. † L 2.

PROSSER, Clara Exh. 1899
36 Thicket Road, Anerley, London. † ROI 1.

PROSSER, James Stanley b. 1887
Watercolour painter and black and white artist. b. Manchester. Studied Belfast School of Art. Exh. 1923-27. Add: St. Colum's, Haddington Gardens, Belfast. † RHA 14.

PROSSER, William Henry Exh. 1887-99
Sculptor. London. † L 5, RA 9, RBA 2.

PROTHERO, Rev. Canon Exh. 1888
Landscape painter. Cloisters, Westminster Abbey, London. † RBA 1.

PROTHERO, Henry A. Exh. 1891
Architect. 13 Promenade, Cheltenham, Glos. † RA 1.

PROTHERO, Mrs. Rowland See HAMLEY, Barbara

PROTHEROE, Thomas Exh. 1904
12 Northwick Terrace, St. John's Wood, London. † RCA 2.

PROUDFOOT, Alexander 1878-1957
Sculptor. b. Liverpool. Head of Sculpture Dept., Glasgow School of Art 1912-28. A.R.S.A. 1920, R.S.A. 1933. Exh. from 1910. Add: Glasgow. † GI 51, L 4, RA 6, RSA 39, RSW 2.

PROUDFOOT, James b. 1908
Portrait painter and black and white artist. b. Perth. Studied Heatherleys, Goldsmith's and in Paris. R.O.I. 1934. Exh. 1933-40. Add: London 1933 and 1938; Perth 1936. † NEA 6, P 6, RA 5, ROI 11, RSA 3.

PROUDFOOT, William Exh. 1880-1900
Perth. † GI 2, RSA 33.

PROUT, Edith Mary b. 1862
Seascape painter. Exh. 1906-27. Add: Plymouth 1908; Newquay, Cornwall 1922. † B 8, LS 3, SWA 1.

PROUT, Marjorie Exh. 1909
† LS 3.

PROUT, Mrs. Margaret Fisher* 1875-1963
nee Fisher. Animal, figure and landscape painter. Studied under her father Mark Fisher q.v. and at Slade School. N.E.A. 1925, R.O.I. 1936, S.W.A. 1935, A.R.W.S. 1938. Add: Newport, Essex 1897; Harlow, Essex 1906 and 1915; London 1908 and 1920; Sawbridgworth, Herts. 1909; East Grinstead, Sussex 1933. † ALP 1, BA 7, BK 1, CHE 2, FIN 1, GI 1, I 5, L 5, NEA 115, P 2, RA 37, RED 38, RHA 12, ROI 15, RSA 1, SWA 16, TOO 5.

PROUT, Victor Exh. 1888
Watercolour painter. † GOU 1.

PROVAN, Mrs. Elizabeth G. Exh. 1880-1912
Flower painter. Glasgow. † GI 62, L 1, RA 4, RSA 14, RSW 1.

PROVAN, G.W. Exh. 1911-12
6 Wester Craigs, Dennistoun, N.B. † GI 2.

PROVIS, Alfred* Exh. 1883-86
Figure and interior painter. Thornton House, Kingstone Lisle, Wantage, Berks. † RBA 4.

PROWDE, Emily Exh. 1908
Kilburn Vicarage, York. † NG 1.

PROWETT, J.C. Exh. 1890-1925
Stirling. † GI 55, L 3, RHA 1, RSA 10, RSW 2.

PROWSE, Miss A. Exh. 1885
29 Cavendish Road, Liverpool. † L 1.

PROWSE, N. Exh. 1884
Painter. c/o 2 Endsleigh Gardens, N.W. London. † SWA 1.

PROWSE, Ruth* Exh. 1938
Landscape painter. South Africa House, Trafalgar Square, London. † RA 1.

PROWSE, Mrs. W. Exh. 1889
29 Carisbrooke Road, Walton, Liverpool. † L 1.

PRUNA, Pedro* b. 1904
Spanish painter. Exh. 1926-38. † BA 36, CHE 9.

PRUSMAN, W.R. Exh. 1885-89
Claremont Villa, Heaton Road, Withington, Manchester. † L 1, M 10.

PRUST, Alfred J. Exh. 1924-37
Ilford, Essex 1924; Leigh Sinton, nr. Malvern, Worcs. 1937. † ROI 2.

PRUST, Edward C. Exh. 1925
Wood engraver. 397 Ley Street, Ilford, Essex. † RA 1.

PRYCE, Thomas Edward Exh. 1882-1900
Architect. 9 Argyll Street, Regent Street, London. † RA 8.

PRYDE, James Ferrierr* 1866-1941
Painter, poster artist and theatrical designer. b. Scotland. Studied R.S.A. Schools. Brother of Mabel Nicholson q.v. Worked with his brother in law Sir William N. q.v. as the Beggarstaff Brothers. H.R.O.I. 1934. "The Doctor" (Exh. 1909) purchased by Chantrey Bequest 1940. Add: Edinburgh 1884; Bushey, Herts. 1891; London 1894. † AG 1, ALP 2, BA 4, BG 33, CHE 5, G 2, GI 8, GOU 65, I 26, L 4, LS 4, NEA 2, RHA 1, RSA 8.

PRYNNE, Edward A. Fellowes 1854-1921
Painter. R.B.A. 1896. Add: London. † G 1, L 3, NG 1, RA 4, RBA 14.

PRYNNE, George H. Fellowes Exh. 1880-1923
Architect. London. † RA 36.

PRYOR, Alvin R. Exh. 1915-40
Drypoint artist. Blundellsands, Liverpool 1915; London 1940. † L 11, RA 1.

PRYOR, Mrs. Ethel Exh. 1915
Agnes Road, Blundellsands, Liverpool. † L 3.

PRYOR, Margaret Ethne Exh. 1921-29
Landscape painter. Lannock Manor, Stevenage, Herts. † NEA 4, RID 4.

PRYTHERCH, T. Exh. 1901-16
Landscape painter. Wroxeter, Shrewsbury. † L 1, RA 3.

PUCKETT, Egmont Sinclair Exh. 1910-11
15 Grosvenor Road, Watford, Herts. † LS 4.

PUCKLE, Ethel M. Exh. 1885
Flower painter. The Grennell, Sutton, Surrey. † RA 1.

PUCKLE, Mrs. William Exh. 1885
Landscape painter. South Hill House, Tunbridge Wells, Kent. † SWA 1.

PUECH, Denys b. 1854
French sculptor. Exh. 1912-13. Add: 163 Rue de l'Université, Paris. † GI 2, RSA 1.

PUELMA, Alfredo Valenzuela Exh. 1908
Portrait, figure and landscape painter. † BK 8.

PUGH, Agnes Exh. 1896-1901
St. Albans, Herts. 1896; Potters Bar, Herts. 1901. † B 3, RI 4, SWA 1.

PUGH, E. Exh. 1883-88
Grove Street, Liverpool. † L 9.

PUGH, Gwynneth M. Exh. 1931-32
67 Merridale Road, Wolverhampton. † B 3.

PUGH, H.W. Exh. 1887-88
58 Grove Street, Liverpool. † L 4.

PUGH, R. Segar Exh. 1901-32
Edgbaston, Birmingham 1901; Harlech, N. Wales 1928. † B 5, L 2, RCA 4.

PUGHE, Buddig Anwylini b. 1857
Landscape and portrait painter. Studied Liverpool School of Art, Paris and Rome. Exh. 1882-1938. Add: Liverpool 1882 and 1938; Towyn, Wales 1900; Aberdovey, Wales 1905; Llwyngwril, Wales 1932; Merioneth 1935; Aberystwyth 1937. † B 9, L 108, LS 15, M 2, RA 9, RCA 32, RHA 17, RI 5, SWA 2.

PUGIN, Peter Paul Exh. 1892
Landscape painter. 111 Victoria Street, Westminster, London. † GI 1.

PUJOL, Clement* Exh. 1901-8
18 Rue Boissonade, Paris. † L 10.

PULINCKX, Lod Exh. 1882
Forest Road, Loughton, Essex. † L 2.

PULLAN, Richard Popplewell Exh. 1882-85
Architect. 15 Buckingham Street, Strand, London. † L 5, RA 1.

PULLAR, Ayrion Exh. 1887
c/o G.A. Musgrave, 45 Holland Park, London. † D 1.

PULLAR, Howard Exh. 1897-98
Landscape painter. 4 Albemarle Street, London. † L 1, RA 2.

PULLEE, Ernest E. Exh. 1931-38
Landscape painter. School of Art, St. Margaret Road, Cheltenham 1931; Gloucester 1937. † COO 3, NEA 1, RA 5.

PULLEE, Margaret Exh. 1936
Landscape painter. † COO 3.

PULLER, Louisa Exh. 1913-40
Landscape painter. Elsecar, nr. Barnsley, 1913; London 1940. † COO 2, L 4, RA 1.

PULLING, Edward W. Exh. 1914
14 St. James Place, Pall Mall, London. † LS 3.

PULLING, Phyllis Mary 1892-1951
Painter and poster artist. Studied London School of Art, St. Johns Wood and Royal College of Art. Add: London 1919; Whitestone, nr. Exeter 1927. † GOU 5, I 2, L 1, RA 1, RI 5, ROI 1, SWA 7.

PULLINGER, Diana B.L. Exh. 1932-37
Landscape painter. London. † RA 2, RBA 1, RI 1, ROI 1.

PULLON, B. Exh. 1902-8
Nottingham. † N 2.

PULSFORD, Charles Denis Exh. 1938-40
22 Gt. King Street, Edinburgh. † RSA 3, RSW 2.

PULVERMACHER, Anna Exh. 1882-88
Figure and still life painter. London. † B 3, L 4, RA 2, RBA 3, RHA 5, ROI 4.

PURCELL, Agnes Talbot Exh. 1909-16
Wem, Salop. † LS 21.

PURCHAS, Mrs. Rosena (Langhorne) Exh. 1889-90
Landscape painter. Gosport, Hants. 1889; South Kensington, London 1890. † D 5, SWA 1.

PURCHAS, Thomas J. Exh. 1880-94
Landscape painter. Guildford, Surrey 1880 and 1883; Surbiton, Surrey 1881. † D 1, L 1, RA 3, RBA 1, ROI 5.

PURCHASE, Alfred Exh. 1889
Landscape painter. Park Street, Fishguard, Wales. † RA 1.

PURCHASE, E. Keynes Exh. 1884
Architect. 3 Mecklenburgh Street, Foundling Hospital, London. † RA 1.

PURCHASE, Miss S. Exh. 1903-5
Hillandale, Chorleywood, Herts. † SWA 5.

PURDEY, Peter Exh. 1939
Theatrical designer. † BK 38.

PURDIE, J. Exh. 1881
Aberdour, Fife. † RSA 1.

PURDOM, Dorothy Exh. 1918-19
Langheugh, Hawick. † RSA 2.

PURDY, James Exh. 1939
Watercolour landscape painter. 52 Marlborough Street, Oldham, Lancs. † RA 2.

PURKISS, Alice B. Exh. 1881
Watercolour flower painter. 37 Lansdown Road, Clapham, London. † SWA 1.

PURNELL, Alfred Exh. 1907-9
25 Carlingford Road, Hampstead Heath, London. † D 13.

PURSELL, Mrs. M.C. Exh. 1880
Landscape painter. 8 St. Marks Square, Dalston. † RBA 1.

PURSER, Elinor F. Exh. 1916
12 Palmerston Road, Dublin. † RHA 2.

PURSER, Sarah H.* 1848-1943
Portrait painter. Established a crafts school in Dublin for the manufacture of stained and painted glass. H.R.H.A. 1890, A.R.H.A. 1923, R.H.A. 1924. Add: Dublin. † FIN 2, G 1, L 2, NG 3, RA 2, RHA 137.

PURSER, W. Exh. 1912
Landscape painter. † AG 1.

PURTSCHER, Alfons b. 1885
Animal, figure, landscape and portrait painter. b. Klagenfurt, Austria. Studied Academy of Munich. Exh. 1927-40. Add: 37 Arundel Gardens, London. † COO 21, NEA 4.

PURVES, James M. Exh. 1932
22 Wilton Drive, Glasgow. † GI 1.

PURVES, Robert Exh. 1934
9 Walmer Terrace, Ibrox, Glasgow. † RSA 1.

PURVIS, Fanny Exh. 1885-87
Flower painter. London. † G 1, L 1, SWA 1.

PURVIS, John Milne Exh. 1909-37
Painter. Perth 1909; Technical College, School of Art, Bell Street, Dundee 1911. † GI 3, L 5, RA 1, RSA 9, RSW 5.

PURVIS, T.G. Exh. 1900-10
Cardiff 1900; Greenwich 1910. † B 2, RHA 1.

PURY, de See D

PUSHMAN, Housep* b. 1877
American painter. Exh. 1937. Add: Park Central Hotel, 7th Avenue, New York, U.S.A. † RA 1.

PUSINELLI, Mrs. Doris Exh. 1918-40
Portrait and flower painter. R.I. 1934, S.W.A. 1939. Add: London. † AR 23, GI 1, LS 1, P 13, RA 3, RBA 6, RI 35, SWA 5.

PUTT, Hilda Exh. 1898
Figure painter. Studio, Gas Office Chambers, Grainger Street, Newcastle. † RA 1.

PUTTERILL, Winifred Exh. 1923-35
Miniature portrait painter. 24 St. Mary's Grove, Grove Park, London. † L 1, RA 5.

PUY, Exh. 1921
Landscape painter. † GOU 1.

PUYVALLEE, de Bengy See D

PUZEY, Ada C. Exh. 1907-38
London. † I 2, L 3, LS 6, ROI 2, SWA 2.

PYATT, Miss H.E. Exh. 1929
9 Livingston Avenue, Sefton Park, Liverpool. † L 1.

PYBUS, Mrs. A. Nellie Exh. 1926-40
Watercolour painter. Ashdowne, Malvern Wells. † B 4, L 4, NEA 2, RA 2, RBA 5, RI 9.

PYE, D.W. Exh. 1934
Watercolour landscape painter. † COO 2.

PYE, James B. Exh. 1904
Architect. Woodfield, St. Annes on Sea. † RA 1.

PYE, Lucy J. Exh. 1899-1908
London 1899; Chester 1902. † B 2, L 11, RMS 1.

PYE, Miss N.E. Exh. 1910-12
Painter. Priest Hill, Limpsfield, Surrey. † ALP 3, RSA 1.

PYE, Randall Howell Exh. 1908-9
Chantry House, 32 Matlock Lane, Ealing, London. † LS 6.

PYE, William Exh. 1881-1908
Landscape painter. Hadleigh, Essex 1881; Weymouth 1882. † B 7, D 7 L 11, M 11, RA 3, RBA 16, RHA 13, RI 4, ROI 4.

PYE-SMITH, Miss N. Exh. 1934
Watercolour landscape painter. † COO 2.

PYKE, Mary Exh. 1888
Painter. 19 Phillimore Gardens, Campden Hill, London. † G 1.

PYKE-NOTT, Evelyn E.C. Exh. 1891-99
Portrait, figure and miniature painter. London. † GI 1, L 2, RA 12, ROI 2.

PYKE-NOTT, Mrs. Geo Exh. 1899
4 St. Edmund's Terrace, Regent's Park, London. † GI 1.

PYKE-NOTT, Isabel C. Exh. 1894-1914
Figure painter. R.M.S. 1900. Add: London. † GI 1, L 2, RA 12, RBA 1, RI 1, RMS 2, ROI 1.

PYKE-NOTT, James S. Exh. 1897-1936
Painter. London 1897; Woldingham, Surrey 1932. † COO 3, M 1, RA 2.

PYM, Jessie Exh. 1900-37
Doods, Reigate, Surrey. † L 2, RBA 1, RI 2, SWA 5.

PYM, Roland Exh. 1935-38
Painter. † LEI 1, RED 1.

PYMAN, Joan Exh. 1921-38
Mrs. Stewart. Sculptor. Hampstead, London. † GI 3, L 3, RA 9, SWA 4.

PYNE, Annie C. Exh. 1886-92
Flower and landscape painter. Daughter of Thomas P. q.v. Add: London 1886; Dedham, nr. Colchester 1892. † RBA 5, RI 8.

PYNE, Charles Exh. 1880
Watercolour landscape painter. 2 Clarendon Road, Lewisham. † RBA 1.

PYNE, Eva E. Exh. 1886-1933
Mrs. A. Warden. Landscape, flower and miniature painter. Daughter of Thomas P. q.v. Add: London 1886 and 1899; Dedham, nr. Colchester 1892. † L 2, RA 24, RBA 8, RI 13, RMS 6.

PYNE, Thomas 1843-193
Landscape painter and watercolourist Studied under his father James Baker P (1800-1870). Father of Annie C. and Eva E.P. q.v. R.B.A. 1883, R.I. 1885, H.R.I 1916. Add: London 1880; Dedham, nr Colchester 1892. † AG 10, B 11, D 9 FIN 2, L 15, M 12, RA 10, RBA 27 RHA 1, RI 224, ROI 24.

PYNEN, Frances Irene Exh. 1923-2
20 Brookdale Road, Liverpool. † L 12 RCA 2.

PYPER, Miss A.E. Exh. 188
New Radford Vicarage, Nottingham † N 1.

PYPER, Mrs. Theodosia Exh. 188
New Radford Vicarage, Nottingham † N 2.

PYRDE, James Exh. 1924-2
3 Lansdowne House, Lansdowne Road Holland Park, London. † GI 1, RSA 5.

PYRSE, G. Spencer Exh. 1930-3
c/o Twenty-One Gallery, Glasgow. † GI 7

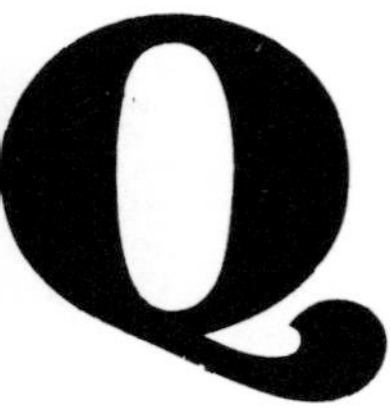

QUADRONE, Jean B. Exh. 1887
Painter. c/o T. Agnew & Sons, 39B Old Bond Street, London. † RA 1.

QUAIL, Ethelwynne May b. 1903
Mrs. Borne. Sculptor. b. Johannesburg. Exh. 1929-33. Add: London. † L 2, RA 2.

QUANCE, R. Exh. 1885-86
Penzance, Cornwall. † L 4, RHA 1.

QUARMBY, George 1883-1957
Painter. Studied Holmfirth and Huddersfield Art Schools, Paris, Italy and South Africa. H.M. Inspector of Art, Ministry of Education, 1930-46. Exh. 1915-31. Add: London. † M 2, P 3, RA 3, RBA 6, ROI 6.

QUARRIE, Miss J. McG. Exh. 1913-14
43 Holly Terrace, Hensingham, Whitehaven, Cumberland. † D 3, SWA 2.

QUARTLEY, Arthur* 1839-1886
Landscape painter. Exh. 1884. Add: 8 Elm Tree Road, London. † ROI 1.

QUARTREMAINE, G.W. Exh. 1881-84
Painter. Stratford on Avon. † D 6.

QUARTREMAINE, William Exh. 1906-8
9 Church Street, Stratford on Avon. † NG 3.

QUAYLE, E. Christian Exh. 1894-1921
Douglas, I.O.M. 1894; Liverpool 1898; Port Erin, I.O.M. 1921. † L 4.

QUAYLE, Henry Exh. 1914-22
Leicester 1914; Stourbridge, Worcs. 1922. † B 1, L 1.

QUAYLE, Mrs. Lucy G. Exh. 1922-40
Stourbridge 1922; Worcester 1935. † B 3, ROI 3, SWA 4.

QUAYLE, W. Exh. 1933-34
A.N.S.A. 1933. Add: c/o 5 Hamilton Drive, The Park, Nottingham. † N 5.

QUEENSBERRY, The Marchioness of
See MANN, Cathleen

QUENARD, A. Exh. 1910
83 Boulevard Richard le Noir, Paris. † L 1.

QUENNELL, Charles H.B. Exh. 1898-1914
Architect. London. † GI 4, RA 8.

QUENNELL, Mrs. Marjorie b. 1883
Painter, black and white artist and author. b. Bromley, Kent. Studied Crystal Palace Studio, Technical Art School, Vincent Square. Exh. 1905-19. Add: London 1905; Bickley, Kent 1906; Birkhamstead, Herts. 1919. † L 4, NG 3, RA 3, SWA 1.

QUENNEVILLE, Chantal Exh. 1928
Painter. Member London Group 1926. † RED 1.

QUERENA, Luigi Exh. 1882
Landscape painter. † FIN 1.

QUESNE, le See L

QUESTED, George R. Exh. 1895-99
Bookplate designer. London 1895 and 1899; Edgbaston, Birmingham 1897. † RA 7.

QUIBELL, Alexander G. Exh. 1897
Architect. 27 Burgoyne Road, Harringay, London. † RA 1.

QUICK, Edith P. Exh. 1900
Landscape painter. The Lynches, Shalford, Guildford, Surrey. † RA 1.

QUICK, Miss F. Exh. 1913-17
32 Banbury Road, Oxford. † L 1, LS 3, RA 3, RI 2.

QUICK, Grace M. b. 1898
Watercolour painter. Exh. 1927. Add: 54 Stokenchurch Street, Fulham, London. † L 1, RA 1.

QUICK, Hilda Exh. 1930-36
Wood engraver. c/o St. George's Galleries, London. † NEA 1, RED 4, RHA 1.

QUICK, Horace Edward Exh. 1913-29
Streatham, London. † P 2, RA 1, RI 1.

QUICK, Richard* Exh. 1882-1889
Painter. b. Bristol. Studied South Kensington School of Art (4 years) and Munich Academy (4 years). Curator Bristol Art Gallery and curator Russell-Cotes Art Gallery and Museum, Bournemouth 1921-32. Add: London and Munich 1882; Wolverhampton 1889. † B 6, GI 4, L 2, RBA 2, RHA 6, RSA 1.

QUIGGIN, Audrey Exh. 1912-14
The Tower House, Freshfield, Lancs. † L 3.

QUIGLEY, Arthur Grainger
Exh. 1894-1933
Landscape painter. Studied Birkenhead School of Art and Liverpool School of Art. Add: Birkenhead 1894; Little Sutton, Cheshire 1932. † L 4.

QUIGLEY, Jane Exh. 1929
22 Trafalgar Square, London. † SWA 1.

QUIGLY, Ethel Exh. 1918
5 Clareville Road, Rathgar, Dublin. † RHA 2.

QUIGLY, Kathleen Exh. 1921-34
Stained glass artist, wood engraver and illuminator. Studied Dublin and London. Add: Dublin. † RHA 11.

QUILTER, Miss E. Exh. 1890-93
Landscape and still life painter. 8 Duke Street Mansions, London. † RID 11.

QUILTER, Harry d. 1907
Landscape painter. Exh. 1884-92. Add: London. † ROI 11.

QUINLAN, Mrs. Eve Exh. 1939-40
Painter. London 1939; Lower Shiplake in Henley, Oxon 1940. † RA 2.

QUINN, Mrs. Blanche Exh. 1919-20
nee Guernier. Married to James Peter and mother of Rene Robert Q. q.v. Add: 109 New King's Road, Fulham, London. † ROI 2, SWA 1.

QUINN, James Peter* b. 1871
Portrait painter. b. Melbourne, Australia. Studied Melbourne National Gallery 1895 (3 year travelling scholarship), Julians and Ecole des Beaux Arts, Paris. Official artist Australian Military Forces 1917-18 and official artist Canadian War Records. R.O.I. 1908, R.P. 1917. Married to Blanche and father of Rene Q. q.v. Exh. 1900-36. Add: Paris 1900; London 1904. † CHE 3, G 1, GI 1, I 11, L 16, M 1, P 62, RA 26, ROI 85, RSA 1.

QUINN, Rene Robert d. 1934
Son of James Peter and Blanche Q. q.v. Exh. 1920-31. Add: Fulham, London 1920; Twickenham Park, Middlesex 1931. † P 3, ROI 6.

QUINNELL, Mrs. Anita Exh. 1934-38
† RMS 4.

QUINNELL, Cecil Watson d. 1932
Miniature painter. R.B.A. 1904, R.M.S. 1896 (Hon. Sec. 1897-1916), H.R.M.S. 1922. Add: London. † L 9, NG 3, RA 1, RBA 24, RI 3, RMS 94.

QUINTIN, Irma Exh. 1929
Landscape painter. 20 Ennerdale Road, Richmond, Surrey. † RA 1.

QUINTON, Alfred Robert b. 1853
Watercolour landscape painter and black and white artist. Studied Heatherleys. Exh. 1880-1919. Add: London. † B 11, D 4, DOW 4, G 1, GI 2, L 16, M 3, RA 19, RBA 9, RHA 10, RI 18, ROI 1.

QUINTON, G. Gertrude Exh. 1940
Still life painter. 42 Bishopric Court, Horsham, Sussex. † RA 1.

QUIRK, Phyllis M. See BLUNDELL

QUISTGAARD, J.W. b. 1877
Miniature painter. b. Denmark. Exh. 1908-24. Add: Paris. † L 2, RA 1.

QUITTNER, Rudolf 1872-1910
Austrian artist. Exh. 1907. Add: 47 Quai Francois Joseph, Vienna. † L 1.

QUIZET, Leon Alphonse* b. 1885
French painter. Exh. 1927-38. † BA 2, GOU 1.

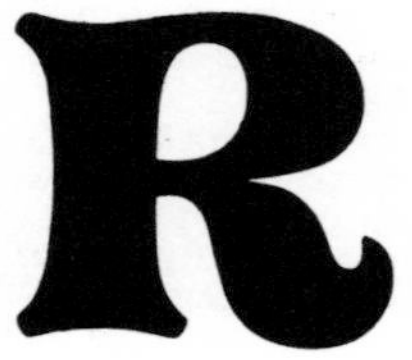

RAAB, Ada Watson Exh. 1903-40
nee Watson. Painter and black and white artist. Studied Slade School and under Alice Fanner. Add: London 1903; New York, U.S.A. 1913; Richmond, Surrey 1928 and 1937; Twickenham, Middlesex 1931. † B 7, BG 1, FIN 1, L 2, LS 8, NEA 3, RA 9, RHA 3, ROI 1, SWA 4.

RAALTE, Van See V

RABEUF, Hippolyte Exh. 1893
Black and white figure artist. 32 Newman Street, London. † RA 1.

RABY, Mrs. Henry Exh. 1881
Landscape painter. 8 Clarence Parade, Southsea, Hants. † SWA 1.

RACHEL, Mme. Exh. 1886
Figure painter. Villa Pernice, 13 Via Casani, Milan. † RI 1.

RACKHAM, Arthur* 1867-1939
Watercolour painter, black and white artist and illustrator. Studied Lambeth School of Art 1884. Married Edyth Starkie R. q.v. A.R.W.S. 1902, R.W.S. 1908. Add: London 1887; Houghton, Arundel, Sussex 1921; Limpsfield, Surrey 1930. † B 4, BG 1, FIN 12, GI 3, I 2, L 17, LEI 837, P 4, RA 23, RBA 4, RI 3, RID 3, ROI 1, RSA 2, RSW 1, RWS 152.

RACKHAM, Edyth Starkie Exh. 1895-1925
nee Starkie. Painter. Married Arthur R. q.v. Add: London 1895; Houghton, Arundel, Sussex 1921; Limpsfield, Surrey 1925. † I 5, L 8, P 2, RA 8, RSA 1, RWS 1.

RADCLIFFE, Mrs. C.A. Exh. 1919
† P 1.

RADCLIFFE, Eva Exh. 1880-81
Figure painter. 46 Cambridge Gardens, Notting Hill, London. † SWA 3.

RADCLIFFE, Miss G. Exh. 1916
Willmount, Kells, Ireland. † RHA 2.

RADCLIFFE, J.C. Exh. 1885-86
65 Ranelagh Road, Dublin. † RHA 2.

RADCLIFFE, Mabel Delme Exh. 1902-35
Birmingham. † B 6.

RADCLIFFE, Radcliffe W. Exh. 1881-95
Landscape painter. Holmbury, St. Mary, nr. Dorking, Surrey 1881; Petersfield, Hants. 1883; London 1890. † B 1, D 14, FIN 1, GI 1, L 8, M 1, RA 28, RBA 23, RI 9, ROI 10.

RADCLIFFE-WILSON, H. Exh. 1911-14
Boston Spa, Yorks. 1911; Hampsthwaite, via Leeds, Yorks. 1914. † L 1, RI 3.

RADCLYFFE, Charles Walter 1817-1903
Landscape painter. Birmingham. † B 69, D 2, RA 1, RI 5, ROI 3.

RADFORD, E. Exh. 1930
Black and white artist. 136 Coventry Road, Bulwell, Notts. † N 1.

RADFORD, Edward* 1831-1920
Genre painter and watercolourist. A.R.W.S. 1875. Add: London 1880; Maidenhead, Berks. 1899; Crowborough, Sussex 1900. † AG 2, B 10, L 8, M 4, RA 1, ROI 1, RWS 34, TOO 1.

RADFORD, Hester Maitland b. 1887
Painter and lacquer screen worker. Studied Slade School. Exh. 1913-36. Add: London 1913; Stroud, Glos. and London 1928. † COO 3, I 11, L 4, NEA 4, RI 2.

RADFORD, Mrs. Mary W. Exh. 1932
Watercolour landscape painter. Wattlesyke, Melrosegate, Haworth, Yorks. † RA 2, SWA 2.

RADOVANI, Franco Angeli Exh. 1916-19
Painter and sculptor. London. † FIN 57, RA 1, ROI 1.

RAE, Cecil W. Exh. 1892-99
52 Beaufort Street, Chelsea, London. † L 2, ROI 2.

RAE, Edna M.W. Exh. 1933
93 St. Andrews Drive, Glasgow. † RSA 1.

RAE, Henrietta* 1859-1928
Mrs. Normand. Painter of classical and literary subjects, portraits and genre. Studied Heatherleys and R.A. Schools. Married Ernest Normand q.v. S.W.A. 1906. Add: London. † B 5, G 2, GI 2, L 24, M 8, NG 18, RA 36, RBA 5, RHA 1, ROI 4, SWA 3, TOO 1.

RAE, Isa Exh. 1890-1907
Painter. London 1890; Etaples, Pas de Calais, France 1897. † GI 1, RBA 7, ROI 5, SWA 2.

RAE, Mrs. Margaret Exh. 1914-21
Liverpool 1914; Carlisle 1921. † L 3, RA 1.

RAE, Mary Exh. 1883-87
Watercolour portrait painter. 32 Phillimore Gardens, Kensington, London. † RA 1, RI 1, RSA 5.

RAEBURN, Agnes Middleton d. 1955
Landscape and flower painter. Studied Glasgow School of Art. R.S.W. 1901. Exh. from 1893. Add: Glasgow. † AR 2, BG 6, GI 98, L 13, RSA 35, RSW 144.

RAEBURN, Ethel Exh. 1892-1940
Edinburgh. † G 1, GI 14, I 6, L 5, LS 10, RI 2, RSA 40, RSW 27.

RAEBURN, Elizabeth A. Exh. 1937
33 Heriot Row, Edinburgh. † RSA 1.

RAEMAEKERS, John Adrien d. 1894
Sculptor. 22 Bloomfield Terrace, Pimlico, London. † L 1, M 3, RA 14, RBA 11.

RAEMAEKERS, Louis 1869-1956
Dutch painter and war cartoonist. H.R.M.S. 1916. Exh. 1915-20. † FIN 550.

RAEMCESTER, Exh. 1886
148 New Bond Street, London. † M 1.

RAFFAELLI, Jean Francois* 1850-1924
French painter. Exh. 1892-1912. Add: Paris. † GI 8, GOU 1, I 5, L 5, LS 5, NEA 1, RSA 1.

RAFFAELLI, O. Exh. 1909
c/o M. Georges Petit, 8 Rue de Seze, Paris. † L 1.

RAFFAN, George Exh. 1937-40
Painter. Crawley, Sussex 1937; London 1940. † NEA 4, P 1, RA 1, RBA 3, ROI 4.

RAFFE, Walter George b. 1888
Wood engraver, author, lecturer and critic. b. Bradford. Studied Halifax Technical College, Leeds School of Art and Royal College of Art. Principal Lucknow Government School of Art and Lecturer Calcutta University and City of London College. Exh. 1916-20. Add: London. † L 8, RA 1.

RAFFLES, W. Hargreaves Exh. 1894-1919
Architect. London. † L 1, RA 3.

RAFTER, Francis M. Exh. 1884
Portrait and figure painter. 29 Lower Talbot Street, Nottingham. † N 1.

RAGG, Isabel Mary b. 1901
Portrait painter. b. Birkenhead. Studied Liverpool School of Art, R.A. Schools and Pennsylvania Academy. Exh. 1923-33. Add: Caldy, Cheshire 1923 and 1933; London 1931. † L 14, NEA 1, RA 1, SWA 1.

RAGG, Archdeacon Lonsdale Exh. 1931-39
Painter of trees. † FIN 62, RMS 1, WG 443.

RAGGI, Mario 1821-1907
Sculptor. b. Italy. Add: London. † RA 11.

RAGON, Adolphe* d. 1924
Marine painter. Studied under Lionel B. Constable. Add: London 1880 and 1912; Leigh on Sea, Essex 1909. † D 2, LS 1, M 1, RA 5, RBA 1, RI 16, ROI 17.

RAHBULA, Mabel See EDWARDS

RAHILLY, Richard H. Exh. 1907-8
Listowel, Co. Kerry. † LS 5, RHA 2.

RAILTON, Betty Exh. 1932
Etcher. Orchard Lea, Windsor Forest, Berks. † RA 1.

RAIMBACH, David Lewis Exh. 1887-1912
Miniature portrait painter. R.M.S. 1899. Add: Birmingham 1887; Bromsgrove, Worcs. 1894; London 1899. † B 6, RA 3, RI 1, RMS 11.

RAIMBACH, Louis Exh. 1882-94
Miniature portrait painter. London 1882; Birmingham 1886; Bromsgrove, Worcs. 1894. † B 3, RA 3.

RAINBIRD, Victor Noble b. 1888
Painter, stained glass artist and illustrator. Studied Armstrong College (University of Durham) and R.A. Schools. (Landseer studentship). Exh. 1926-30. Add: Richmond, Yorks. 1926; Newcastle on Tyne 1930. † L 1, RA 2.

RAINBOW, W.C. Exh. 1883-84
Landscape painter. London 1883; Byrnealog, Frefrin, N. Wales 1884. † L 1, RI 1.

RAINE, Alfred O. Exh. 1913-14
4 Merton Avenue, Chiswick, London. † LS 4.

RAINE, Herbert Exh. 1900-5
Architect. London. † RA 5.

RAINE, H. Keyworth Exh. 1896-1910
Miniature portrait painter. London. † LS 6, NG 2, RA 1.

RAINES, J. Exh. 1891
61 Pigott Street, Birmingham. † B 1.

RAINEY, Mrs. Elizabeth Exh. 1934
10 Harbeton Drive, Belfast. † RSA 1.

RAINEY, H. Exh. 1905-6
4 Steele's Studios, Haverstock Hill, London. † RA 2.

RAINEY, Tristram b. 1910
Landscape and portrait painter. Studied Slade School 1921-28. A.R.B.A. 1939. Exh. 1938-40. Add: London 1938; Kingsbridge, Devon 1939; Westerham, Kent 1940. † P 3, RA 1, RBA 11, RED 33.

RAINEY, William 1852-1936
Landscape and figure painter, watercolourist and illustrator. Studied Royal College of Art and R.A. Schools. R.I. 1891, H.R.I. 1930, R.O.I. 1892. Add: London 1880 and 1909; Shoreham, Kent 1887; Chichester, Sussex 1891; Emsworth, Hants. 1913; Eastbourne 1922. † GI 2, L 16, M 5, RA 23, RBA 4, RI 150, ROI 6.

RAINGER, Gus Exh. 1883-85
Painter. Liverpool. † L 2, RE 2.

RAINSFORD, Mabel Exh. 1928-30
Watercolour landscape painter. b. Ireland. Studied in Dresden. Lived some years in Bermuda after World War I. Add: Exmouth, Devon. † RHA 9, WG 209.

RAINY, Anne Exh. 1925
Rosevalley, Croy, Inverness-shire. † GI 2.

RAISSIGNIER, P. Emile Exh. 1905
2 Rue d'Areueil, Paris. † NG 2.

RAJON, Paul Adolphe 1842-1888
French etcher. Exh. 1883-87. Add: Seine et Oise, France. † L 2, M 5, RA 2, ROI 1.

RAKE, Mrs. Clare Exh. 1928-40
23 Lawn Crescent, Kew Gardens, London. † RI 1, SWA 4.

RAKOCZI, Basil Exh. 1939-40
Painter. Garde Cottage, Leenare, Connemara, Ireland. † COO 1, RBA 3.

RALEIGH, Mrs. Walter (Lucie) Exh. 1890-92
Portrait painter. Liverpool. † RID 2.

RALFE, Mrs. E. Exh. 1892
Landscape painter. 26 Queen Anne's Street, Cavendish Square, London. † RBA 2.

RALLI, H. Exh. 1882-83
Figure painter. London. † G 2.

RALLI, Theodore Jacques* 1852-1909
Figure painter. Paris 1880 and 1884; London 1881. † GI 2, L 9, M 6, RA 4.

RALLI-SCARAMANGA, Th. Exh. 1908
24 Rue Bonaparte, Paris. † LS 5.

RALPH, Mrs. E.R. (L) Exh. 1910-11
London. † RA 2.

RALPH, Kate Exh. 1898
28 Charleville Road, West Kensington, London. † ROI 1.

RALSTON, J. Mc. L. Exh. 1889
Watercolour painter. † DOW 2.

RALSTON, William d. 1911
Black and white artist. Glasgow 1902; London 1910. † GI 2.

RAM, Jane Adye Exh. 1893-1918
Painter and sculptor. London. † B 2, BG 1, L 1, M 1, RA 9, RBA 2, ROI 5.

RAMAGE, J. Exh. 1888
17 Torphichen Street, Edinburgh. † RSA 1.

RAMAGE, Peter Exh. 1914-15
181 Shamrock Street, Glasgow. † GI 2.

RAMBAUT, Anna Beatrice Exh. 1921-27
Painter and writer. Templeville, Killiney, Co. Dublin. † RHA 11.

RAMEAU, Claude Exh. 1924-25
† GOU 3.

RAMIE, C.W. Exh. 1885-88
Landscape painter. New Maldon, Surrey. † RA 3, RBA 3.

RAMIE, Marian Exh. 1886-1904
Flower painter. New Maldon, Surrey 1886; Northwood, Middlesex 1904. † L 1, RBA 2.

RAMMELL, John Exh. 1932
St. Albans, Herts. † RCA 1.

RAMOND, Paul Exh. 1913-14
3 Place Interieur St. Michel, Toulouse, Garonne, France. † LS 4.

RAMPLING, R.E. c. 1836-1909
Watercolour painter. Exh. 1885-86. Add: Lancaster. † L 2.

RAMSAY, Miss Alice Exh. 1926-28
Old Manse, Kilbarchan. † GI 1, RSA 1.

RAMSAY, Allan* Exh. 1880-87
Portrait painter. Dundee. † RSA 9.

RAMSAY, A. Edgell Exh. 1889-1900
Brechin, N.B. † GI 4, RSA 10.

RAMSAY, Catherine Exh. 1885-90
Landscape painter. Sister of Emily K.R. q.v. Add: 13 Upper Park Place, Richmond, Surrey. † SWA 5.

RAMSAY, Colin Cameron Exh. 1918-28
Glasgow. † GI 1, L 2, RSA 2.

RAMSAY, David b. 1869
Watercolour landscape painter. b. Ayr. Studied Glasgow School of Art. Art master Greenock Academy. Exh. 1909-40. Add: Greenock 1909; Glasgow 1937. † GI 9, L 1, RSA 6, RSW 13.

RAMSAY, David P. Exh. 1923-39
Portrait and figure painter. Perth 1923; Dunkeld 1933. † GI 13, L 5, RA 3, RSA 16.

RAMSAY, Eilbert Exh. 1904
Elenlee, Kilmalcolm, N.B. † GI 1.

RAMSAY, Eleanor Exh. 1888-1921
Landscape painter. A.S.W.A. 1916. Sister of Elizabeth E. and Frances L.M. and probably daughter of Mrs. E.G.R. q.v. Add: Beaumaris, Wales 1888; London 1898; Chipping Camden, Glos. 1918. † L 1, RA 2, RID 81, SWA 40.

RAMSAY, Elizabeth E. Exh. 1884-1908
Flower and landscape painter. Sister of Eleanor and Frances L.M. and probably daughter of Mrs. E.G.R. q.v. Add: London 1884; and 1894; Beaumaris, Wales 1886. † L 3, RA 1, RHA 1, RI 2, ROI 3, RSA 1, SWA 9.

RAMSAY, Mrs. E.G. Exh. 1885
Probably Mother of Eleanor, Elizabeth E. and Frances L.M.R. q.v. Add: 7 Victoria Terrace, Beaumaris, Wales. † L 1.

RAMSAY, Emily K. Exh. 1885-90
Landscape painter. Sister of Catherine R. q.v. Add: 13 Upper Park Place, Richmond, Surrey. † SWA 6.

RAMSAY, Frances L.M. Exh. 1885-1921
Portrait and landscape painter. A.S.W.A. 1909. Sister of Eleanor and Elizabeth E. and probably daughter of Mrs. E.G.R. q.v. Add: Beaumaris, N. Wales 1885; London 1893; Chipping Camden, Glos. 1918. † GI 1, L 1, P 4, RA 1, RID 80, ROI 6, RSA 1, SWA 66.

RAMSAY, Gilbert c. 1880-1915
c/o W. Leiper, Sun Buildings, Glasgow 1902. † GI 1.

RAMSAY, Gladys C. Exh. 1937-39
18 West Castle Road, Edinburgh. † RSA 1, RSW 1.

RAMSAY, Hugh McD. Exh. 1938-40
101 Clarence Drive, Glasgow. † GI 1, RSA 1.

RAMSAY, James Exh. 1911-12
Old Manse, Kilbarchan, N.B. † GI 2, L 1.

RAMSAY, James A. Exh. 1919-40
Edinburgh. † RSA 11, RSW 11.

RAMSAY, Owen Gustave Exh. 1923-37
Miniature portrait painter. Dulwich, London. † RA 6, RMS 1.

RAMSAY, Lady Patricia 1886-1974
H.R.H. Princess Victoria Patricia of Connaught. Granddaughter of Queen Victoria. Flower and landscape painter. N.E.A. 1931, H.R.I. R.S.W. 1932, A.R.W.S. 1940. Add: Clarence House, St. James, London. † AR 1, FIN 2, GOU 113, LEF 8, NEA 50, NG 3, RA 3, RHA 2, RWS 4, SWA 3.

RAMSAY, Susan E. Exh. 1914-15
Drumore, Blairgowrie, Perthshire. † L 3.

RAMSAY, Wilfred Exh. 1939-40
Landscape and coastal painter. Bridles, Worth Matravers, Swanage, Dorset. † RBA 1, RHA 1, RSA 1.

RAMSBOTHAM, Jane F. Exh. 1936-40
Woodhouse, Milnthorpe, Westmorland. † P 2, SWA 2.

RAMSBOTTOM, Emma Exh. 1893
14 Ridgefield, John Dalton Street, Manchester. † M 1.

RAMSDEN, Elizabeth Exh. 1929
13 Philbeach Gardens, London. † SWA 1.

RAMSDEN, Frederick F. Exh. 1926-33
Nailsworth, Glos. † GOU 2, RCA 1.

RAMSDEN, F.P. Exh. 1914
Pen'rallt, Penmaenmawr, Wales. † RCA 1.

RAMSDEN, Omar 1873-1939
Gold and silversmith. b. Sheffield. Studied Royal College of Art. R.M.S. 1921. Add: London. † L 81, RA 6, RMS 95.

RAMSDEN, Richard H. Exh. 1883-84
Miniature portrait painter. 3 Park Cottage, Ravenscourt Park, Hammersmith, London. † RA 3.

RAMSDEN, Thomas Exh. 1883-1933
Landscape painter. Leeds 1883 and 1891; London 1888; Stainburn, nr. Otley, Yorks. 1910; Wigan 1928. † L 8, M 1, RA 2, RBA 10, RCA 1.

RAMSEY, George S. Exh. 1896-1921
Landscape painter. Buxton, Derbys. 1896; Leicester 1908. † N 13, RA 5.

RAMSEY, J. Exh. 1887
Coastal painter. 5 Hereford Gardens, London. † RBA 1.

RAMSEY, Stanley C. Exh. 1930-35
Architect. 46 Gt. Russell Street, London. † RA 3.

RAMSEY, William Exh. 1910-18
London 1910; Dorking, Surrey 1918. † RI 5.

RANDAL, Charles Exh. 1892
Landscape and miniature portrait painter. 13 Gt. Western Road, London. † RA 2.

RANDAL, Frank Exh. 1887-1901
Watercolour landscape painter. London. † L 1, NG 2, RA 3, RI 3.

RANDALL, Mrs. A. Maud Exh. 1904-40
Landscape painter. London 1904; Epsom, Surrey 1923; Storrington, Sussex 1932. † L 1, RA 2, RI 5, ROI 9, SWA 2.

RANDALL, Maurice Exh. 1899-1919
Netherleigh, Blandford, Dorset 1899; London 1900; Claygate, Surrey 1918. † B 1, D 2, GI 1, L 6, RA 3, RI 3.

RANDALL, Richard J. Exh. 1895-1907
Landscape painter. Raynham Road, Hertford. † RA 2.

RANDALL, Stella Exh. 1924-25
11 Flanders Road, London. † L 14.

RANDALL, W. Exh. 1920
36 Bayswater Road, Birchfield, Birmingham. † B 2.

RANDALL, William Frederick Exh. 1886-94
Architect. 31 Stowe Road, Shepherds Bush, London. † RA 5.

RANDANINI, Carlo d. 1884
Italian figure painter. Exh. 1883. Add: 42 Via Margutta, Rome and 53 Weymouth Street, Portland Place, London. † RA 1.

RANDLE, Florence Exh. 1880
200 Union Street, Plymouth. † D 1.

RANDLE, Katrina M. Exh. 1929
Portrait painter. 396 Derby Road, Lenton, Nottingham. † N 3.

RANDOLPH, Doris May Exh. 1923
Miniature portrait painter. 1 Tennison Road, South Norwood, London. † RA 2.

RANDOLPH, John Exh. 1882
18 Albert Street, Merthyr Tydfil. † L 1.

RANDOLPH, Mrs. Vera Exh. 1903-25
London. † LS 13, SWA 2.

RANDS, Lilian Exh. 1895-1905
Northampton 1895; Bristol 1905. † B 1, SWA 1.

RANDS, Sarah E. Exh. 1896-1902
Portrait and figure painter. Northampton. † RA 4.

RANFURLY, Countess Exh. 1880
Landscape painter. Dungannon Park, Co. Tyrone. † SWA 2.

RANGER, Edgar Exh. 1927-29
Architect. 9 Grays Inn Square, London. † RA 2.

RANGER, Henry Ward* 1858-1916
American painter. Exh. 1903. Add: 228 West 44th Street, New York, U.S.A. † RA 1.

RANKEN, Mrs. A. Exh. 1914-21
London 1914; Oxford 1919. † LS 15.

RANKEN, William Bruce Ellis 1881-1941
Portrait, interior, flower and landscape painter and decorator. b. Edinburgh. Studied Slade School. R.I. 1915, R.O.I. 1910, V.P.R.O.I. 1920, R.P. 1916. Add: London 1901; Edinburgh 1908; Dumfries and London 1914; Eversley, Hants. 1929. † AG 1, CAR 35, G 5, GI 4, GOU 140, I 39, L 28, NEA 2, P 102, RA 22, RED 1, RI 99, ROI 60, RSA 22.

RANKIN, Arabella Louisa b. 1871
Painter and colour woodcut artist. b. Muthill, Perthshire. Exh. 1889-1935. Add: Muthill, Perthshire 1889; Edinburgh 1903; London 1905 and 1922; Abbotsbrae, Crieff 1913. † COO 3, GI 18, I 4, L 8, RI 1, RSA 24, RSW 3, SWA 6.

RANKIN, Andrew Scott b. 1868
Animal painter. b. Aberfeldy. Studied Edinburgh (Manufacturers School, Royal Institute and Life School). On staff of "Idler" and "Today". Exh. 1891-1940. Add: Edinburgh 1891; Aberfeldy 1894; Strathay, Perthshire 1900; Pitlochrie, Perthshire 1916. † GI 5, L 7, M 3, RA 3, RCA 1, RSA 27, RSW 2.

RANKIN, Catherine Geraldine Exh. 1913-37
Portrait and landscape painter. Studied South Kensington. Add: Manchester. † LS 3, RCA 4.

RANKIN, Miss J.M. Exh. 1928-29
The Shrubbery, Walmley. † B 5.

RANKIN, Renee H.M. Exh. 1923-29
Watercolour painter. Broughton Tower, Broughton in Furness. † L 10, RA 1, RI 2.

RANKINE, John P. Exh. 1922-28
Hamilton. † GI 2.

RANKINE, Walter D. Exh. 1883-95
Glasgow 1883; Hamilton 1895. † GI 3.

RANN, Edith Chirm Exh. 1895
Painter. 66 Musters Road, West Bridgford, Notts. † N 1.

RANN, F.O. Exh. 1923
Parkdale, Sedgley, Dudley, Worcs. † B 1.

RANNIE, H.A. Exh. 1888-97
11 Nelson Terrace, Hillhead, Glasgow. † GI 4.

RANSOM, Frank b. 1874
Sculptor and wood engraver. Studied Lambeth School of Art and R.A. Schools (Landseer scholarship and Armitage prize). Instructor at Clerkenwell and Hammersmith Art Schools and assistant to Sir George Frampton. Exh. 1901-32. Add: London. † GI 2, L 1, RA 33.

RANSOM, George Exh. 1899-1915
Flower and landscape painter. Fairfield, Farnham, Surrey. † L 1, RA 7, ROI 2.

RANSOME, E.E. Exh. 1940
20 Warwick Road, Coulsdon, Surrey. † RI 1.

RANSOME, James Exh. 1895-1919
Architect. London. † RA 8.

RANSOME, S. Exh. 1928
Painter of Gardens. † AB 3.

RAPHAEL, Mrs. Arthur (Mary F.)* Exh. 1889-1917
Figure painter. A.S.W.A. 1906. Add: London. † GI 1, I 9, L 21, LS 9, NG 2, P 5, RA 18, ROI 10, SWA 7.

RAPHAEL, Mrs. Herbert Exh. 1899-1900
23 Berkley Square, London. † SWA 3.

RAPPARD, Clara 1862-1912
Figure and portrait painter. Exh. 1880-87. Add: 3 Cromwell Crescent, South Kensington, London. † M 1, RA 3.

RAPPARD, Josine Exh. 1886-1920
Watercolour painter and miniature portrait painter. London 1886; Woldingham, Surrey 1898. † M 1, RA 16, RI 17, RMS 3, ROI 3, SWA 18.

RAPPART, Mrs. Alice Exh. 1907-10
Liscard, Cheshire 1907; West Kirkby, Cheshire 1909. † L 4.

RASCH, Heinrich* 1840-1913
German painter. Exh. 1890. † TOO 3.

RASCOVICH, Roberto 1857-1904
American artist. b. Austria. Exh. 1883. Add: c/o Dowdeswells, New Bond Street, London. † RI 1.

RASINELLI, Roberto Exh. 1881
Italian painter. Add: Rome and Harris and Co., 67 Lower Thames Street, London. † D 1.

RASMUSSEN, A. Exh. 1880-1913
London 1880; Puddletown, Dorset 1913. † LS 3, RHA 1.

RASMUSSEN, Osborne Exh. 1936
26 Highbury, Jesmond, Newcastle on Tyne. † RSA 1.

RASMUSSEN, Wilhelm Exh. 1933
Kunstuernes Hus, Oslo. † RSA 2.

RASPONI, Mlle. A. Exh. 1899-1904
Painter of children's subjects. † FIN 32.

RASSENFOSSE, Andre Exh. 1862-1934
Belgian artist. Exh. 1916. Add: c/o P. Lambotte, Browns Hotel, Dover Street, London. † L 1.

RAT, le See L

RATCLIFFE, Mabel M. Exh. 1904-29
Didsbury, nr. Manchester 1904; Bidston, Cheshire 1919; Birkenhead 1927. † L 20.

RATCLIFFE, Miss R. Exh. 1933
117 Holly Lodge Mansions, Highgate, London. † L 1.

RATCLIFFE, William* 1870-1955
Landscape, still life and figure painter. b. Kings Lynn. Studied Manchester and Slade School. Founder member London Group 1913. Add: Letchworth, Herts. 1911; London 1912; Farholt, Sweden 1913; London 1914. † CAR 7, GI 1, GOU 2, LS 12, M 2, NEA 2, RED 1.

RATCLIFFE, W.A. Exh. 1889-96
Stockport, Lancs. † M 6.

RATE, Lettice M. Exh. 1928-29
Milton Court, Dorking, Surrey. † NEA 4.

RATHBONE, Mrs. Alice Exh. 1913
Elwy, Llandudno, Wales. † L 1.

RATHBONE, E. Exh. 1891-1914
Edinburgh 1891; Liverpool 1894. † L 3, RSA 1.

RATHBONE, Harold Steward b. 1858
Portrait and figure painter. Exh. 1882-1921. Add: Liverpool 1882 and 1907; London 1890; Birkenhead 1900; Llandudno 1908; Port St. Mary, I.O.M. 1916. † G 6, GI 4, L 118, M 12, NG 2, RCA 3, ROI 1.

RATHBONE, Mrs. M. Exh. 1924-29
Ovoca, Abbotsford Road, Blundellsands, Liverpool. † L 3.

RATHBONE, Miss M.C. Exh. 1898-99
22 Onslow Road, Fairfield, Liverpool. † L 2.

RATHBONE, William b. 1884
Portrait and figure painter and bronze miniaturist. b. Sunderland. Studied Sunderland School of Art. Second master Darlington School of Art 1905-9, and Preston School of Art 1909-14. Headmaster Preston School of Art from 1914. A.R.M.S. 1929. Exh. 1916-39. Add: Preston, Lancs. † L 9, RA 2, RMS 19.

RATHJENS, William 1842-1882
Flower painter. Exh. 1881. Add: Claremont Villa, Heaton Road, Withington, Manchester. † RA 1.

RATHSACK, Svend b. 1885
Swedish artist. Exh. 1934. Add: Mathilde Fibigersvej 3, Copenhagen. † RSA 3.

RATMAN, Dora Exh. 1933
Watercolour flower painter. 36 Warriner Gardens, Battersea Park, London. † RA 1.

RATMAN, Romeo b. 1880
Sculptor and modeller. b. Trieste, Italy. Studied under Senator G. Monteverde in Rome. Exh. 1925-32. Add: London. † ALP 1, RA 6.

RATTRAY, John Exh. 1880-88
45 Cumberland Street, Edinburgh. † RSA 10.

RATTRAY, Wellwood* 1849-1902
Landscape painter and watercolourist. N.E.A. 1887, A.R.S.A. 1896, R.S.W. 1885. Add: Glasgow 1880 and 1886; London 1884. † B 3, DOW 3, G 5, GI 58, L 14, M 8, NEA 1, RA 23, RHA 2, RI 2, RSA 66, RSW 37.

RAUBER, W. Exh. 1884
39 Rue Chaptal, Paris. † M 2.

RAUDNITZ, Albert Exh. 1883-84
Portrait and landscape painter. 1 Queens Road Studios, St. John's Wood, London. † B 1, G 1, L 2, RA 1, RBA 1.

RAVANNE, Leon Gustave 1854-1904
French artist. Exh. 1892. Add: 3 Rue Cauchois, Paris. † GI 1.

RAVEL, E. Exh. 1884
Manchester. † M 1.

RAVEL, Jules Exh. 1880-84
Portrait and figure painter. Rue de Lisbonne, Paris. † GI 1, RBA 1.

RAVELLI, Federigo Exh. 1924-34
Painter. London. † RA 1, ROI 10.

RAVENHILL, Anna Exh. 1883-84
Watercolour interior painter. Clapham Common, London. † D 1, RBA 1.

RAVENHILL, Holmes Exh. 1937-40
Landscape and portrait painter. 17 Cheyne Walk Gardens, London. † COO 73, RA 1.

RAVEN-HILL, Leonard 1867-1942
Painter and illustrator. "Punch" artist 1895-1935. Add: London 1887 and 1911; Bromham, Wilts. 1898. † FIN 192, G 3, GI 2, I 1, L 4, LEI 172, NEA 3, RA 8, RBA 6, RI 5, ROI 9, RSA 2.

RAVENHILL, Margaret F. Exh. 1880-1902
Watercolour landscape painter. London 1880; Iver, Bucks. 1894; Ealing 1897. † B 3, G 1, GI 1, L 6, M 1, RA 3, RBA 3, SWA 5.

RAVENSCOURT, G. Exh. 1914-17
12 Westcroft Square, London. † LS 9, RA 1.

RAVENSCROFT, Frederick E. Exh. 1899-1902
Architect. Reading, Berks. † RA 3.

RAVENSCROFT, William Exh. 1892-98
Architect. Reading, Berks. † RA 3.

RAVENSHAW, Dorothy Exh. 1936-37
Southwoods, Surrendon Road, Brighton, Sussex. † RI 1, SWA 1.

RAVENSHAW, Edith L. Exh. 1896-1900
Watercolour landscape painter. 70 Mount Ararat Road, Richmond, Surrey. † RA 1, SWA 1.

RAVERAT, Mrs. Gwendolen b. 1885
nee Darwin. Wood engraver. Studied Slade School. A.R.E. 1920. Exh. 1912-40. Add: Cambridge 1912; Royston, Herts. 1913; Stevenage, Herts. 1916; France 1923; London 1925; Harlton, nr. Cambridge 1933. † ALP 8, GI 4, L 3, NEA 17, RE 60, RED 19, RHA 6, RSA 4.

RAVILIOUS, Eric William 1903-1942
Painter and engraver. b. London. Studied Eastbourne and Royal College of Art (travelling scholarship). Exh. 1930-39. † LEI 1, RED 5, TOO 28.

RAVINCOURT, Von See V

RAWDON, Mrs. Henry G. Exh. 1883-97
42 Rodney Street, Liverpool. † L 10.

RAWES, Miss A.M. Exh. 1896-1900
Beckenham, Kent. † B 3, L 1, RBA 3, ROI 2, SWA 4.

RAWLE, John S. Exh. 1882-87
Landscape painter and watercolourist. Teacher at School of Design, Nottingham. Add: London. † L 2, RA 3, RBA 1, RI 3.

RAWLENCE, Fred A. Exh. 1886-1905
Watercolour landscape painter. Bulbridge House, Wilton, Salisbury, Wilts. † B 2, FIN 123, L 4, NG 3, RA 1, ROI 1, RSA 1.

RAWLIN, Mrs. Alexander Exh. 1909
Dumfries. † SWA 1.

RAWLINGS, Ada Exh. 1881
Watercolour painter. 5 Albert Villas, Sydenham Hill, London. † RBA 1.

RAWLINGS, Alfred b. 1855
Painter, illustrator and teacher. Exh. 1900-29. Add: Reading. † B 1, D 2, RA 1.

RAWLINS, Darsie b. 1912
Sculptor. Studied Royal College of Art 1930-34. Exh. 1938. Add: Kings Lane, Gt. Missenden, Bucks. † RA 1.

RAWLINS, Ethel Louise Exh. 1900-40
Landscape, flower and interior painter. Studied Slade School and Newlyn, Penzance. Add: Gt. Houghton Hall, Northants. 1900 and 1916; London 1915; Hassocks, Sussex 1921; Ditchling, Sussex 1933. † BK 23, I 12, L 3, RA 8, RBA 14, RE 1, RHA 1, RI 4, ROI 6, SWA 29.

RAWLINS, G.E.H. Exh. 1902-10
Collaborated with his wife. Add: Waterloo, Liverpool 1902; Windermere 1906; Kent Mere, Westmorland 1910. † L 65.

RAWLINS, Mrs. G.E.H. Exh. 1906-10
Collaborated with her husband. Add: Low Skelgill, Windermere 1906; Kent Mere, Westmorland 1910. † L 26.

RAWLINS, Monica b 1903
Portrait and figure painter and wood-engraver. Studied Central School of Arts and Crafts and under Leon Underwood. Exh. 1925-30. Add: London. † RED 2, SWA 2.

RAWLINS, Miss O.B.E. Exh. 1906-10
Waterloo, Liverpool. † L 3.

RAWLINS, Mrs. V. Alex Exh. 1904-12
Architectural painter. Dumfries, N.B. † B 2, GOU 1, L 8, RA 1.

RAWLINSON, Ethel B. Exh. 1911-33
29 Windsor Road, The Brook, Liverpool. † L 7.

RAWLINSON, Kathleen Exh. 1934-37
Mural decorator, and portrait painter. The Chantry, Nottingham Lane, Eltham, London. † ROI 3.

RAWLINSON, William T. Exh. 1932-38
Wood-engraver. Liverpool. † L 4, RA 1, RCA 3.

RAWNSLEY, Edith Exh. 1882-84
Mrs. H.D. Watercolour landscape painter. Wray Vicarage, Ambleside 1882; Crosthwaite Vicarage, Keswick 1884. † D 4, RA 1, RI 2.

RAWNSLEY, Una Exh. 1923
Sculptor. 6 Stanley Gardens, Kensington Park Road, London. † RA 2.

RAWORTH, Miss Exh. 1905
Leicester. † SWA 1.

RAWORTH, Mrs. A. Exh. 1904
Fairholm, Uppingham Road, Leicester. † SWA 2.

RAWSON, William Exh. 1913-14
321 Chesterfield Road, Meersbrook, Sheffield. † L 2.

RAY, Betty Exh. 1932
20 Palatine Road, Withington, Manchester. † RSA 1.

RAY, Miss C. Exh. 1900
5 Holmesdale Road, Kew Gardens, London. † SWA 1.

RAY, Mlle. G.C. Exh. 1912-14
27 Rue Corbeau, Paris. † L 1, RA 1.

RAY, Jean Exh. 1911
Portrait artist. † GOU 4.

RAY, Maurice Exh. 1904
Painter. 16 Rue de Vienne, Paris. † L 1, RA 1.

RAY, Stuart Exh. 1940
Painter, etcher and engraver. Studied Royal College of Art. Add: 8 Winterbourne Road, Thornton Heath, Surrey. † RA 2.

RAY, W. David Exh. 1883-85
Landscape painter. 13 Cornwall Residences, Clarence Gate, London. † RBA 3.

RAY-JONES, Raymond b. 1886
Portrait painter and etcher. b. Ashton under Lyne. Studied Royal College of Art and Julians, Paris. A.R.E. 1914, R.E. 1926. Exh. 1913-38. Add: London 1913; Maldon, Essex 1930; Carbis Bay, Cornwall 1936. † CHE 1, FIN 6, L 10, NEA 1, RA 19, RE 20.

RAYMENT, Robert Exh. 1883-85
Landscape painter. 79 The Chase, Clapham Common, London. † D 1, RI 1, ROI 1.

RAYMOND, Francis Exh. 1920
The Green Studio, St. Ives, Cornwall. † RCA 2.

RAYMOND, Maud Exh. 1890
Sculptor. 14 Morden Road, Blackheath, London. † RA 1.

RAYNE, Miss D. Exh. 1909-18
Miniature painter. Pond House, Teddington, Middlesex. † RA 8.

RAYNE, Lilian M.R. Exh. 1909-19
Miniature painter. Pond House, Teddington, Middlesex. † L 4, RA 13, RMS 1.

RAYNER, Mrs. A.B. Exh. 1929
7 Monks Way, West Kirby, Liverpool. † L 2.

RAYNER, D.L. Exh. 1932
† L 1.

RAYNER, Louise* 1829-1924
Landscape and architectural painter and watercolourist. Sister of Margaret R. q.v. Add: Ash Grove, Chester. † B 21, D 3, L 31, M 9, RA 3, RBA 1, RHA 1, RI 22, SWA 30.

RAYNER, Margaret Exh. 1880-95
Watercolour landscape and architectural painter. Sister of Louise R. q.v. S.W.A. 1880. Add: London. † B 1, RI 1, SWA 36.

RAYNER, Miss M.L. Exh. 1903
Tiviotdale, Stockport. † ROI 1.

RAYNER, Prebble b. 1886
Landscape painter and decorative designer. Exh. 1918-28. Add: London. † GI 2, L 5, NEA 1.

RAYNER, Mrs. Rosa Exh. 1884-85
Watercolour painter. London. † RA 1, SWA 2.

RAYNER, William F. Exh. 1932-40
Maitlandfield, Haddington 1932; Edinburgh 1939. † RSA 4.

RAYNOR, Miss M. Exh. 1934
Holm Royd, Trent Boulevard, West Bridgford, Notts. † N 1.

RAYSON, Thomas Exh. 1940
Watercolour landscape painter. 35 Beaumont Street, Oxford. † RA 1.

REA, Mrs. Betty Exh. 1939
Sculptor. 3 Penn House, London. † RA 1.

REA, Cecil* 1860-1935
Figure and portrait painter. Studied Paris and R.A. Schools. Head of Art Section L.C.C. School of Lithography. Married Constance R. q.v. R.O.I. 1899. Member of Society of 25 Artists. Add: London. † FIN 3, GI 7, L 6, NG 3, RA 11, RBA 1, RHA 1, RID 34, ROI 12.

REA, Constance Exh. 1891-1935
nee Halford. Figure and portrait painter. Married Cecil R. q.v. Member of Society of 25 Artists. Add: London. † BG 54, FIN 27, G 1, GI 5, GOU 6, I 28, L 10, P 6, RA 27, RBA 1, RID 19, ROI 5, SWA 2.

REA, Herbert F. Exh. 1933
Architect. 8 High Street, Totnes, Devon. † RA 1.

READ, A. Everard Exh. 1899-1919
Landscape painter. Nottingham 1899; London 1914. † B 4, L 7, M 3, N 10, NG 1, RA 2, RCA 7, RHA 14, RSA 3.

READ, Mrs. Alice J. Exh. 1924
57 Joyce Avenue, Sherwood, Nottingham. † N 1.

READ, Arthur Rigden b. 1879
Colour woodcut artist. Exh. 1923-40. Add: The Dower House, Winchelsea, Sussex. † BA 6, GI 16, L 8, RA 9, RED 1, RSW 1.

READ, Charles Exh. 1935-39
Architect. Rickmansworth, Herts. 1935; Chorley Woods, Herts. 1939. † RA 4.

READ, Constance Exh. 1897-1908
Liverpool. † L 13.

READ, Charles Carter Exh. 1882-1907
Landscape painter. R.B.S.A. 1905. Add: Birmingham 1882 and 1905; Fladbury, nr. Pershore 1895. † B 82, L 8, NG 1, RA 3, RBA 4.

READ, Edward Harry Handley b. 1870
Portrait and landscape painter, black and white illustrator. Studied Kensington and Westminster Schools of Art and R.A. Schools (Creswick prize). R.B.A. 1895. Add: London 1890 and 1918; Harrowby Camp, Grantham, Lincs. 1916; Storrington, Sussex 1927; Salisbury, Wilts. 1932. † CHE 2, FIN 30, GI 1, GOU 1, L 9, LEI 122, M 1, RA 17, RBA 123, RI 21, ROI 14.

READ, Frank H. Exh. 1927-36
St. Margaret on Thames 1927; Teddington, Middlesex 1934. † RBA 6.

READ, G.W. Exh. 1885
14 Trafalgar Studios, Kings Road, Chelsea, London. † M 1.

READ, Herbert Exh. 1886
Architect. 88 Brook Green, London. † RA 1.

READ, Henry Exh. 1882
Castletown, I.O.M. † L 1.

READ, Herbert H. Exh. 1917
B.E.F. France. † LS 1.

READ, H. Hope Exh. 1907-28
Figure painter. London. † ALP 1, M 2, NEA 2, RA 1.

READ, Samuel* c. 1815-1883
Watercolour coastal and architectural painter. b. Needham Market, Suffolk. Studied under W. Collingwood Smith. Contributor to the "Illustrated London News" from 1844-83. A.R.W.S. 1857, R.W.S. 1880. Add: Bromley, Kent 1880. Died at Sidmouth, South Devon. † L 1, RWS 8.

READ, S.F. Exh. 1914
15 Charnwood Grove, West Bridgford, Notts. † N 2.

READ, Stanley L. Exh. 1922
Figure painter. 107 Saltram Cross, Paddington, London. † RA 3.

READ, W.F. Exh. 1914-27
32 Brookdale Road, Sefton Park, Liverpool. † L 4.

READ, Miss W.M. Exh. 1916
Cadbyrie, Castlebar Hill, Ealing, London. † L 1.

READE, Albert Vincent b. 1864
Portrait, landscape and still life painter. Studied Manchester Academy of Fine Arts and Colarossi's, Paris. Exh. 1901-33. Add: Manchester. † M 3.

READE, F.G. Exh. 1932
† L 1.

READE, Mrs. H.V. Exh. 1913
Landscape painter. † ALP 1.

READE, Mary Exh. 1892-1933
Watercolour landscape painter. Daughter of Thomas Mellard R. q.v. Studied Liverpool School of Art. Add: Blundellsands, Liverpool. † L 42.

READE, Thomas Mellard Exh. 1884-93
Architect. Father of Mary R. q.v. Add: Liverpool. † L 3.

READER, E.K. Exh. 1928
Painter. † AB 2.

READER, F.W. Exh. 1889
171 Hemingford Road, London. † B 1.

READING, Beatrice Exh. 1902-3
Miniature portrait painter. 142 Abbey Road, West Hampstead, London. † RA 2.

READMAN, W.R. Exh. 1920
Freeland, Bishopbriggs. † GI 2.

READSHAW, Emily S. Exh. 1883-93
Flower painter. Dusseldorf, Germany 1883; Sutton Coldfield 1885. † B 15, RA 1.

REAM, Carducius Plantagenet*
Exh. 1892-98
Fruit painter. Balham, London 1892; Maidstone, Kent 1898. † RA 3.

REAN, William H. Exh. 1937
Flower and decorative painter. Burwalls, Morley Road, Farnham, Surrey. † RA 3.

REASON, Florence* Exh. 1881-1914
Landscape, figure and flower painter. London. † B 1, L 7, M 3, RA 17, RBA 2, RI 3, SWA 7.

REASON, Robert G. Exh. 1897-1902
Etcher. St. Ives, Cornwall 1897; Salterton, Devon 1902. † L 3, RA 4.

REASON, S.R. Exh. 1923-39
Landscape, coastal and still life painter. A.N.S.A. 1928. Add: Nottingham. † N 49.

REAVELL, G. jnr. Exh. 1907
Alnwick, Northumberland. † RA 1.

RECKITT, Francis William 1860-1932
Landscape painter. Hampstead 1899; Rickmansworth, Herts. 1913. † L 5, M 1, NG 9, RA 7, ROI 6.

RECKITT, Rachel B. Exh. 1935-40
Painter and engraver. Roadwater, West Somerset. † COO 2, NEA 3, RED 4, SWA 1.

RECKNELL, H.J. Exh. 1917
19 Canonbury Grove, London. † RA 1.

REDDIE, Arthur W.L. Exh. 1882-85
Landscape and flower painter. 5 Pagoda Villas, Brandram Road, Lee, Kent. † RA 2, RBA 1.

REDDISH, Christine Exh. 1938
Portrait painter. Beacon Lodge, Grantham, Lincs. † N 1.

REDDROP, Miss J.A. Exh. 1915-17
London 1915; Lancaster 1917. † RA 2.

REDFEARN, Elsie M. Exh. 1927-28
Manchester 1927; Northampton 1928. † RSA 3.

REDFERN, Harry Exh. 1894-1905
Architect. London. † RA 4.

REDFERN, Richard Exh. 1880-1913
Watercolour landscape painter. Manchester 1880; Stockport 1885; Lancaster 1906. † AG 2, L 2, M 7, RA 6, RI 1.

REDFERN, Mrs. S.A. Exh. 1911
The Laurels, Top Road, Calow, nr. Chesterfield. † N 2.

REDFIELD, Edward Willis* b. 1869
American painter. Exh. 1925. † CHE 1.

REDFORD, Anthony Exh. 1940
Painter. 16 Heytesbury Lane, Dublin. † RHA 2.

REDFORD, Miss C.N. Exh. 1901-10
Liverpool. † L 7.

REDFORD, Mrs. Daisy A.S. Exh. 1907
62 Prescot Street, New Brighton, Cheshire. † L 1.

REDFORD, George Exh. 1883-85
Portrait painter. Cricklewood, London. † G 5.

REDGATE, Annie E. Exh. 1884
227 Lenton Sands, Nottingham. † N 1.

REDGATE, Arthur W.* Exh. 1880-1906
Landscape and figure painter. N.S.A. 1881. Add: Nottingham 1880; Castle Donnington, nr. Derby 1886; West Bridgford, Notts. 1893. † B 4, L 1, M 1, N 95, RA 28, RBA 2.

REDGATE, H.L. Exh. 1886
10 Angel Row, Nottingham. † N 2.

REDGATE, J.S. Exh. 1908-14
Woodborough Road, Nottingham. † N 4.

REDGATE, Sylvanus Exh. 1880-1900
Portrait painter. N.S.A. 1884. Add: Nottingham. † N 30.

REDGRAVE, Evelyn Leslie Exh. 1880-88
Watercolour landscape painter. Daughter of Richard R. q.v. Add: Hyde Park Gate, Kensington, London. † D 3, M 2, RA 7, RBA 1, RI 7.

REDGRAVE, Frances M. Exh. 1882
Landscape and figure painter. Daughter of Richard R. q.v. Add: Hyde Park Gate South, Kensington, London. † RA 1.

REDGRAVE, J.T. Exh. 1890-93
Eltham. † D 8.

REDGRAVE, Richard* 1804-1888
Landscape and genre painter. Studied R.A. Schools 1926. First keeper of Paintings at the South Kensington Museums and Inspector of the Queen's Pictures. Coauthor with his brother Samuel of "A Century of Painting". Father of Evelyn Leslie and Frances M.R. q.v. A.R.A. 1840, R.A. 1851. Add: Hyde Park Gate, South Kensington, London. † RA 3. RE 1.

REDGRAVE, William Exh. 1937
Portrait and landscape painter. 24 York Road, London. † ROI 1.

REDMAN, Mrs. M. Hardwicke
See LEWIS, May Hardwicke

REDMAN, W.A. Exh. 1892-98
Liverpool. † L 3.

REDMAYNE, Mrs. Nessy I.
Exh. 1894-1913
Black and white portrait artist. London. † RA 7.

REDMOND, Mary Exh. 1880-87
Dublin 1880; Florence 1887. † L 2, RHA 12.

REDMOND, W.A. Exh. 1882
Osborne House, Bold Street, Liverpool. † L 1.

REDMORE, Henry* 1820-1887
Marine painter. c/o J. Jackson, Esq., Junior Reform Club, Manchester 1885. † M 1.

REDPATH, Anne* 1895-1965
Mrs. J.B. Michie. Painter. Studied Edinburgh College of Art 1913-19. Add: Calais 1919; Hawick 1935. † GI 4, RSA 14, RSW 8.

REDRUP, Sidney Exh. 1887
Etcher. 8 Park Street, Windsor, Berks. † RA 1.

REDWORTH, William b. 1873
Landscape painter. b. Slough. Studied Chelsea Art School. Exh. 1907-38. Add: Slough, Bucks. † GI 12, I 14, L 1, RA 12, RI 12, RID 3, ROI 19, RSA 1, WG 34.

REED, Annie L. Exh. 1888
Miniature portrait painter. 46 Colby Road, Gipsy Hill, London. † RA 2.

REED, Dorothy Exh. 1906
Watcombe, St. Mary Church, Devon. † L 1, NG 1.

REED, Eleanor Exh. 1890-94
6 Woodside, Sunderland. † M 10.

REED, Edward Tennyson c. 1860-1933
Caricaturist and "Punch" artist. Exh. 1885-1914. Add: London. † D 3, FIN 197, GI 1, LEI 142, NG 8, RID 6, ROI 1.

REED, Fred H. Exh. 1884
Architect. 9 John Street, Adelphi, London. † RA 1.

REED, George A. Norris Exh. 1922-38
Watercolour landscape painter. London 1922; Blackburn, Lancs. 1932. † L 3, M 1, RA 13.

REED, Hilda Exh. 1895-1906
Mrs. B. Miniature portrait painter. Hexham, Northumberland 1895; Exeter 1906. † RA 4, RMS 1.

REED, Kate Exh. 1880-82
Portrait, flower, figure and still life painter. London. † RBA 4, SWA 2.

REED, Lillie Exh. 1904-10
Sculptor. Hastings 1904; London 1905. † L 3, RA 5.

REED, Louis Exh. 1914-23
Liverpool 1914; London 1923. † L 3, NEA 2.

REED, Margaret Exh. 1919-21
London. † L 2, SWA 1.

REED, Mary Exh. 1880-98
Landscape, flower and miniature portrait painter. London. † B 1, L 1, RA 3, RBA 9, RI 1, ROI 1, SWA 2.

REED, M. Blanchard Exh. 1882-88
Painter. Horsham, Sussex 1882; London 1885. † B 2, SWA 1.

REED, Stanley b. 1908
Portrait, landscape, still life and figure painter. Studied Liverpool College of Art 1926-32. Travelling scholarship to Italy 1932. Exh. 1928-38. Add: Liverpool. † GI 1, L 12, M 2, RA 7.

REED, Selina G.C. Exh. 1910
15 Princes Avenue, Liverpool. † L 1.

REED, Trelawney Dayrell Exh. 1913-15
Landscape painter. 183A Kings Road, Chelsea, London. † CHE 42, NEA 2.

REED, T.E. Exh. 1895
3 St. Pauls Studios, West Kensington, London. † NG 1.

REED, William Schoolar Exh. 1910
c/o Allied Artists Association, 67 Chancery Lane, London. † LS 3.

REED, William Thomas d. 1881
Landscape painter. Englefield Green, Egham 1880; Hastings 1881. † RBA 4.

REEKIE, William Maxwell b. 1869
Painter. b. Manchester. Studied under Tom Mostyn and Walter Sickert. Exh. 1893-1933. Add: Manchester. † L 2, M 10.

REEKS, May Exh. 1909-10
Derrymount, Bransgore, nr. Christchurch, Hants. † B 1, LS 3.

REERINK, Mrs. M. Exh. 1910
44 Leicester Square, London. † ROI 1.

REES, A. Exh. 1892
33 Hoxhill Street, Liverpool. † L 1, RHA 1.

REES, A.J. Exh. 1892-94
SS. Kildare, City of Dublin Steam Packet Co., North Wall, Dublin. † RHA 2.

REES, Dilys A. Exh. 1938
47 Three Shires, Oak Road, Bearwood. † B 1.

REES, Gladys Mary b. 1898
Mrs. Teesdale. Watercolour painter, etcher, illustrator and poster artist. Studied and taught at Chelsea School of Art. A.S.W.A. 1927, S.W.A. 1939. Exh. 1923-40. Add: London 1923; Uffingham, nr. Stamford, Lincs. 1930. † RA 2, SWA 21.

REES, H.T. Exh. 1915
25 Nimrod Road, Streatham, London. † RA 1.

REES, John Exh. 1880-94
Landscape painter. Sunbury on Thames, Middlesex. † B 10, M 1, RHA 7.

REES, Mary Exh. 1903-4
Annandale, Warwick Road, Redhill, Surrey. † L 1, SWA 1.

REES, Muriel Exh. 1902
143 Upper Parliament Street, Liverpool. † L 2.

REES, T. Taliesin Exh. 1903-26
Liverpool. † L 13.

REES, Verner O. Exh. 1934-39
Architect. London. † RA 6, RSA 1.

REES, W.B. Exh. 1905
3 Dumfries Place, Cardiff. † RA 1.

REEVE, Alfred L. Exh. 1933-38
Watercolour landscape painter. Riverslea, Four Elms Hill, Rochester, Kent. † RA 4.

REEVE, Eileen Exh. 1938-40
Watercolour flower painter. 9 Prebend Mansions, Chiswick High Road, London. † RA 3.

REEVE, Herbert b. 1870
Etcher. Exh. 1919-30. Add: London 1919; Croydon, Surrey 1927. † L 12, RA 4.

REEVE, Hope Exh. 1880-81
Landscape painter. 62 Rutland Gate, London. † SWA 3.

REEVE, Miss H.M. Exh. 1920
Dare's Dyke, Redditch, Worcs. † B 1.

REEVE, J. Arthur Exh. 1887-91
Architect. London. † RA 3.

REEVE, J.E. Exh. 1883
23 Church Street, Liverpool. † L 5.

REEVE, Mary Strange Exh. 1917-26
Miniature painter, illustrator (book covers and wrappers) and commercial artist. Studied Regent Street Polytechnic. On staff of Oxford University Press. Add: Walthamstow, Essex 1917; Chingford, Essex 1926. † RA 7.

REEVE, Russell Sidney 1895-c. 1970
Painter, etcher, illustrator, writer and teacher. b. Hethersett, Norfolk. Studied Norwich School of Art, Slade School 1919-22 and Royal College of Art. R.B.A. 1932. Add: London. † GOU 11, NEA 16, P 8, RA 4, RBA 50, RED 1.

REEVE-FOWKES, Mrs. Amy C. b. 1886
Watercolour flower painter. Studied Bournemouth School of Art. Exh. 1929-40. Add: Eastbourne. † AR 49, FIN 3, RA 5, RBA 5, RCA 1, RI 18, SWA 1, WG 70.

REEVES, A. Seymour Exh. 1910
Garthmere, Solihull, Birmingham. † B 1.

REEVES, C. Exh. 1891
† TOO 2.

REEVES, Carey K. Exh. 1906-9
Northbrooks, The Beach, Shoreham, Sussex. † L 2, LS 5.

REEVES, C.W. Exh. 1905
3 Gray's Inn Square, London. † RA 1.

REEVES, Edith M. Exh. 1895-1900
Mrs. B.A. Miniature portrait painter. Emsworth, Hants. 1895; London 1897. † L 2, NG 1, RA 4, RMS 1.

REEVES, George H. Exh. 1881-1911
Landscape painter. A.N.S.A. 1908-10. Add: Leicester. † L 1, N 10, RA 2, RBA 1.

REEVES, Mary Exh. 1880-1906
Landscape and coastal painter. Tramore, Douglas, Cork. † D 6, L 1, RBA 1, RHA 7, RI 3, SWA 1.

REEVES, Miss Phoze Exh. 1880-86
Landscape painter. Tierwarna, St. Johns Road East, Putney Hill, London. † SWA 7.

REEVES, P. Oswald Exh. 1904-9
Sculptor and teacher. Metropolitan School of Art, Dublin. † L 1, RA 3, RHA 2.

REEVES, Miss Rhoy Exh. 1886
Tiervarna, St. Johns Road, Putney Hill, London. † B 1, L 1.

REEVES, Thomas Exh. 1884
145 Finlay Drive, Dennistoun, Glasgow. † GI 1.

REEVES, Walter* Exh. 1882-1900
73 St. Peters Road, Handsworth, Birmingham. † B 38, L 1.

REEVES, William Exh. 1935
Landscape painter. 17 Eardley Crescent, London. † RA 1.

REHFISCH, Alison Exh. 1936
36 Gt. Ormond Street, London. † ROI 1, SWA 1.

REIACH, Alan Exh. 1929-31
Etcher and pencil artist. Edinburgh. † RA 2, RSA 15.

REICHARDT, Miss M.N. Exh. 1894
Ewell, Surrey. † SWA 1.

REICHENBACH, Von See V

REICHSRITTER, Hugo von Bouvard Exh. 1930
Vienna and c/o Mrs. J.S. Fraser, 50 Melville Street, Edinburgh. † RSA 2.

REID, A. Exh. 1880
66 Pembroke Road, Dublin. † RHA 1.

REID, A. Exh. 1881
103 St. Vincents Street, Glasgow. † RSA 1.

REID, Andrew Exh. 1881-1932
Edinburgh 1882 and 1932; Paisley 1908. † GI 24, L 23, RSA 26.

REID, Annie Exh. 1925-38
Heathfield, Campbeltown. † RSA 1, RSW 5.

REID, Allan Douglas b. 1898
Architect. 5 Verulam Buildings, Grays Inn, London. † RA 1.

REID, Archibald David* 1844-1908
Landscape painter. Studied R.S.A. Schools and Paris. Brother of Sir George and Samuel R. q.v. Travelled on the continent. R.O.I. 1898, A.R.S.A. 1892, R.S.W. 1883. Add: Aberdeen 1880 and 1883; Edinburgh 1881. † D 2, DOW 2. GI 29, L 9, M 3, NEA 1, RA 3, ROI 4, RSA 70, RSW 42.

REID, Agnes L. b. 1902
Mrs. James Jardine. Portrait and figure painter in oil, watercolour landscape painter and etcher. Exh. 1925-35. Add: Slateford, Midlothian 1925; Edinburgh 1935. † RSA 6.

REID, Augusta M. Exh. 1885
Watercolour landscape painter. 12 Fielding Road, West Kensington Park, London. † SWA 1.

REID, Alexander W.D. Exh. 1932
Architect. 1 Lincolns Inn Fields, London. † RA 1.

REID, Mrs. Beryl Exh. 1916-30
Edinburgh. † GI 1, L 2, RSA 11, RSW 2.

REID, Claud B. Exh. 1922
Fairhill, Camberley, Surrey. Architect. † RA 1.

REID, Edith M. Exh. 1880
Watercolour painter. 3 Fenchurch Buildings, London. † D 1, RBA 1.

REID, E.M.W. Exh. 1915
c/o Cole Bros., 2 Percy Street, Tottenham Court Road, London. † RA 1.

REID, Mrs. Emily Payton Exh. 1916-36
nee Smith. Married Robert Payton R. q.v. Add: Hemingford Abbots, St. Ives, Hunts. 1916; Felpham, Sussex 1928; Edinburgh 1936. † RSA 3.

REID, Florence A. Exh. 1917
Craigpark House, Thorntonhall, Lanarks. † GI 1.

REID, Flora Macdonald Exh. 1880-1938
Landscape and figure painter. b. London. Studied R.S.A. Schools and under her brother John Robertson R. q.v. Sister of Lizzie R. q.v. Add: Ashington, Sussex 1880; London 1881 and 1914; Polperro, Cornwall 1904. † B 25, FIN 1, G 9, GI 87, L 81, LEI 3, M 45, NG 45, RA 83, RBA 50, RCA 2, RHA 2, RI 26, ROI 39, RSA 16, SWA 5.

REID, Sir George* 1841-1913
Portrait painter and illustrator. Studied Edinburgh, Utrecht and Paris. Brother of Archibald David and Samuel R. q.v. H.R.M.S. 1906, H.R.O.I. 1898, A.R.S.A. 1870, R.S.A. 1877, P.R.S.A. 1891-1902, H.R.S.A. 1903, R.S.W. 1892. Knighted 1891. Add: Aberdeen 1880 and 1892; Edinburgh 1888 and 1912; Oak Hill, Somerset 1910. † B 1, FIN 1, GI 30, L 10, M 4, NG 20, P 2, RA 17, RHA 6, ROI 7, RSA 125.

REID, G.A. Exh. 1913-33
c/o F.E. Galbraith Studio, 29 Notting Hill Gate, London. † RA 1, RSW 2.

REID, George Ogilvy* 1851-1928
Historical genre and landscape painter and engraver. b. Leith. A.R.S.A. 1888, R.S.A. 1898. Add: Edinburgh. † B 1, G 1, GI 80, L 33, M 11, RA 69, RHA 1, RSA 237, RSW 1.

REID, Henry J. Macphail Exh. 1931
4 Finnieston Quay, Glasgow. † GI 1.

REID, Isabella E. Exh. 1880-1936
Miniature portrait painter. Aberdeen 1880 and 1897; London 1891. † GI 1, RA 7, RI 6, RSA 6.
REID, J. Exh. 1883
24 Oxford Road, Ranelagh, Ireland. † RHA 1.
REID, J. Exh. 1901
49 Queen Mary Avenue, Crosshill, Glasgow. † GI 1.
REID, Janet Exh. 1912-27
Edinburgh. † RSA 2, RSW 8.
REID, John Exh. 1880-82
10 Nicholson Street, Edinburgh. † RSA 6.
REID, John A. Exh. 1935
233 West Regent Street, Glasgow. † GI 1.
REID, James Campbell Exh. 1906-11
209 St. Vincent Street, Glasgow. † GI 3.
REID, J.E. Exh. 1888-89
19 Picardy Place, Edinburgh. † GI 1, RSA 3.
REID, James Eadie Exh. 1908-17
Paris 1908; Kew Gardens, London 1917. † LS 7.
REID, J.F. Rennie Exh. 1880-96
Edinburgh. † RSA 16.
REID, John G. Exh. 1896-1903
The Manse, Hurlford, N.B. 1896; Glasgow 1903. † GI 1, RSA 1.
REID, John J. Exh. 1880
21 Broughton Place, Edinburgh. † RSA 1.
REID, John Robertson* 1851-1925
Landscape, coastal and genre painter. Studied under G.P. Chalmers and W. MacTaggart. Brother of Flora Macdonald and Lizzie R. q.v. R.B.A. 1880, R.I. 1897, R.O.I. 1883. "Toil and Pleasure" purchased by Chantrey Bequest 1879. Add: Hampstead, London 1880 and 1907; Polperro, Cornwall 1904. † B 20, BG 1, DOW 1, FIN 61, G 23, GI 68, I 2, L 85, LEI 67, M 68, NEA 6, NG 34, RA 98, RBA 59, RHA 4, RI 163, ROI 140, RSA 39, TOO 1.
REID, J.T. Exh. 1881-84
Murthly, Perthshire. † RSA 2.
REID, J. Watson Exh. 1897-1901
Glasgow. † GI 3.
REID, Katherine M. Exh. 1887-91
Glasgow. † GI 5.
REID, Lizzie Exh. 1880-1918
Figure painter. Sister of Flora Macdonald and John Robertson R. q.v. Add: Ashington, Sussex 1880; Hampstead, London 1881. † G 9, GI 2, L 4, M 5, NG 1, RA 5, RBA 16, ROI 4, RSA 6.
REID, Leslie F.N. Exh. 1935
Manchester. † RCA 1.
REID, Mrs. Marell Exh. 1935
Uplands, Bearsden. † GI 1.
REID, Marion Exh. 1885-1925
Landscape, figure, miniature and decorative panel painter. Altrincham, Cheshire 1885; London 1887; Cheam, Surrey 1923. † L 3, M 1, RA 6, ROI,2.
REID, Mary H. 1854-1921
Exh. 1912-13. Add: c/o Allied Artists Association, 67 Chancery Lane, London 1912; Toronto, Canada 1913. † LS 6.
REID, Nano Exh. 1925-37
Landscape and figure painter. Dublin 1925; Drogheda, Co. Louth 1931. † RHA 32.
REID, Nina Winder b. 1891
Landscape and marine painter. b. Hove. Studied St. Johns Wood Art School. Exh. 1911-40. Add: London 1911 and 1933; Cheam, Surrey 1932. † AR 106, B 1, L 1, RBA 5, RCA 3, RHA 1, ROI 8, RSA 3, SWA 2, WG 37.
REID, Pattie Exh. 1897
3 Cart Street, Paisley. † GI 1.
REID, R. Cecil Exh. 1920-21
3 Gundall Place, St. Bees. † RCA 4.
REID, Robert Payton b. 1859
Painter and illustrator. Studied R.S.A. Schools, Munich and Paris. Married Emily Payton R. q.v. A.R.S.A. 1896. Exh. 1880-1940. Add: Edinburgh 1880, 1889 and 1933; Munich 1888; Queensferry 1894 and 1920; Hemingford Abbots, St. Ives, Hunts. 1916; Felpham, Sussex 1932. † GI 30, L 3, M 5, RA 2, RHA 7, ROI 2, RSA 181.
REID, R.S. Exh. 1880-81
Edinburgh 1880; Leith 1881. † RSA 1.
REID, Samuel* 1854-1919
Watercolour landscape painter. Brother of Archibald David and Sir George R. q.v. R.S.W. 1885. Add: Aberdeen 1880; Glasgow 1882; Alloa 1888; Stirling 1891; Pinner, Middlesex 1896; Chorley Wood, Herts. 1904. † DOW 1, GI 69, L 6, LS 5, NEA 2, NG 2, RA 16, RSA 48, RSW 22.
REID, Stephen 1873-1940
Decorative, historical and portrait painter and illustrator. b. Aberdeen. Studied Gray's School of Art, R.S.A. Schools. R.B.A. 1906. Add: Edinburgh 1895; London 1899 and 1917; Chesham, Bucks. 1910; Northwood, Middlesex 1914. † L 10, M 1, RA 24, RBA 19, RI 2, RSA 2.
REID, Stuart Exh. 1914
79 West Regent Street, Glasgow. † GI 1, RSW 3.
REID, Sylvia Exh. 1939
Portrait and theatrical portrait painter. † COO 27.
REID, Savile G. Exh. 1889-1905
Honiton, Devon 1889; Yalding, Kent 1905. † D 15.
REID, Violet Exh. 1889-1917
Figure painter. Hanworth, Middlesex 1889; Withycombe, Exmouth 1914. † LS 6, RID 5, SWA 1.
REID, William Exh. 1891-1906
Hamilton, N.B. 1891; Glasgow 1904. † GI 4, RSA 1.
REID, William A. Exh. 1903
Etcher. 16 Crouch Hill, London. † RA 1.
REID, William B. Exh. 1916-38
Landscape and figure painter. Edinburgh 1916; London 1938. † GI 3, L 2, RA 3, RSA 12, RSW 1.
REID, William E. Exh. 1940
13 Duke Street, Edinburgh. † RSA 1, RSW 2.
REIDPATH, Miss M.I. Exh. 1896
49 Harvard Road, London. † SWA 1.
REIFFEL, C. Exh. 1900-1
Brooklyn House, Gedling, Notts. † N 6.
REIGH, J. Exh. 1880
Richmond House, Inchicore, Dublin. † RHA 4.
REILLY, Charles Exh. 1902
Architect. 23 St. Swithins Lane, London. † RA 1.
REILLY, C.A. Exh. 1906
49 Chesilton Road, Fulham, London. † RA 1.
REILLY, Charles H. Exh. 1902-29
Architect. Professor of Architecture, Liverpool University. Add: London 1902; Liverpool 1905. † L 4, RA 15, RSA 3.
REILLY, Fred Exh. 1890-1903
Landscape painter. Staines 1890; France 1898; Pinner, Middlesex 1900; London 1903. † NG 1, P 1, ROI 2.
REILLY, Michael b. 1898
Landscape painter and commercial designer. Studied Central School of Arts and Crafts, Birmingham 1923-26. Exh. 1934-40. Add: Four Oaks, Birmingham 1934; London 1940. † B 10, RA 2.
REILLY, Mrs. Nell P. Exh. 1904
Miniature portrait painter. Moss Lane, Pinner, Middlesex. † RA 1.
REILLY, Nora Trouse Exh. 1890-95
Landscape painter. Bognor 1890; London 1891. † B 1, RBA 2, RI 1.
REILY, Alice L. Exh. 1899-1910
16 Weston Road, Handsworth, Birmingham. † B 8.
REILY, Francis Exh. 1884-1919
Miniature portrait painter and teacher. London 1884; School of Art, Southport 1890. † B 3, L 4, RA 1.
REINCKE, Miss A.M. Exh. 1911
Denmark Hill, London. † SWA 2.
REINHART. Charles Stanley 1844-1896
American painter. Exh. 1883. Add: 147 Avenue de Villiers, Paris. † L 1, RI 1.
REINHART, H. Exh. 1881
Figure painter. c/o Baron de Biegehben, Austrian Embassy, Belgrave Square, London. † D 1, RA 1.
REISS, Fritz Exh. 1912
Kirchgarten, Freiberg, Baden, Germany. † L 2.
REISS, George Francis b. 1893
Wood-engraver. Exh. 1926-40. Add: Market Place, Kendal, Westmorland. † AB 3, B 4, GI 1, L 10, N 19, RA 2, RCA 27, RED 1, RHA 15, RSA 7.
REISS, Miss S. Exh. 1882
7 Selborne Grove, Bradford. † M 3.
REITLINGER, Gerald b. 1900
Painter. b. London. Studied Slade School. Exh. 1924-28. † GOU 3, NEA 1, RED 1.
RELF, Douglas Exh. 1935-38
Portrait, landscape and figure painter. London 1935; Hatfield Peverel, Essex 1936. † RA 6, RBA 1, ROI 2.
REMANDAS, Mme Lily Exh. 1889-95
Watercolour figure and miniature portrait painter. London. † RA 7.
REMBOWSKI, Jan Exh. 1913-14
Rue Nowotarsko No. 11, Lakopane, Austria. † LS 6.
REMINGTON, A.W. Exh. 1883-96
Weston super Mare, Somerset 1883; London 1896. † B 2, L 1.
REMINGTON, Frederic 1861-1909
American sculptor and painter. Exh. 1897. Add: 301 Webster Avenue, New Rochelle, Westchester, New York, U.S.A. † RA 1.
REMINGTON, Mary Exh. 1935-40
Painter. London. † RA 2, ROI 2.
REMMETT, F.C. Exh. 1886
197 Bristol Street, Birmingham. † B 1.
REMNANT, Mrs. Marjorie Exh. 1940
† RI 1.
REMOND, Jean 1872-1913
French artist. Exh. 1906. Add: 95 Rue de Vaugirard, Paris. † L 1.
RENANDIN, Alfred Exh. 1900
6 Rue Cyffle, a Luneville, France. † L 1.
RENARD, Antonin Roux Exh. 1911
Figure and portrait painter. † BRU 2.
RENARD, E. Exh. 1900-1
Cartergate, Newark, Notts. † N 6.
RENARD, Edward* Exh. 1880-1909
Watercolour landscape painter. Add: National Art Schools, South Kensington, London 1880; Saltaire, nr. Bradford 1885; Leeds 1891; School of Art, Shipley, Yorks. 1896; London 1909; Eastbourne 1910. † B 1, L 3, LS 14, RA 4, RBA 5, RI 1.

RENARD, Emile 1850-1930
French artist. Exh. 1904-12. Add: Paris. † L 2.

RENAUDOT, Paul 1871-1920
French artist. Exh. 1907. Add: 1 Rue Cassini, Paris. † L 1.

RENAULT, de see D

RENAULT, Victor Exh. 1883
30 Rue Richard, Versailles. † GI 1.

RENCOULE, Marcel Armand Exh. 1923-26
b. Paris. Naturalised British 1919. Proprietor of the Regent Gallery, Glasgow. Add: Glasgow. † GI 2, L 2, RSA 1.

RENDALL, Arthur D.* Exh. 1887-1913
Landscape and portrait painter. London. † B 1, L 9, RA 6, RBA 1, RID 53.

RENDALL, Bessie Exh. 1896-1906
Portrait painter. Dulwich Common, London 1896; Godalming, Surrey 1904. † RA 3.

RENDALL, Mabel E. Exh. 1913-14
The Hill, Sutton Coldfield, Warwicks. † RHA 2.

RENDELL, Mrs. E.M. Exh. 1917-22
South Norwood, London 1917; Thornton Heath, Surrey 1922. † RCA 2, ROI 3.

RENDELL, Joseph Frederick Percy 1872-1955
Marine, figure and landscape painter, clay modeller and potter. Studied under Walter Wallis and Julius Olssen. Chief of Staff Croydon School of Art 1897-1932. A.R.B.A. 1926. Add: South Norwood and Croydon. † D 12, GI 1, GOU 2, L 2, LS 14, M 1, RA 6, RBA 3, RCA 13, RI 3, ROI 17, RSA 1.

RENDERS, Maurice* b. 1877
French still life painter. Exh. 1906-13. Add: 19 Rue Francoeur, Paris. † L 6.

RENDLE, Miss G.E. Exh. 1927-29
Godalming, Surrey. † L 11.

RENDLE, Morgan 1889-1952
Painter and illustrator. b. Bideford. Studied Bideford School of Art, Brighton School of Art and Royal College of Art. Art master and Vice Principal Brighton School of Art from 1924. R.B.A. 1937, R.I. 1938. Add: Brighton 1928; Hove 1930. † RA 14, RBA 15, RI 23, ROI 3.

RENESSE, von see V

RENIE, J.E. Exh. 1883
29 Rue Singer, Paris. † RHA 2.

RENISON, William Exh. 1893-1938
Painter, etcher and engraver. b. Glasgow. Add: Glasgow 1893, 1898 and 1903; Dublin 1896; Withington, Manchester 1901; London 1917; Auchterarder, Perthshire 1931. † FIN 4, GI 39, L 2, M 5, RA 2, RHA 9, RSA 4.

RENKIN, Leo W. Exh. 1927-28
12 Brattan Road, Birkenhead. † L 2.

RENNELL, Phoebe b.1883
Script and illuminating artist. b. London. Studied Clapham Art School. Exh. 1916. Add: Huttoft Grange, Alford, Lincs. † L 3.

RENNIE, Miss I. Exh. 1920
Moreby Park, York. † SWA 1.

RENNIE, Miss J. Exh. 1911
74 Falkland Road, Egremont, Cheshire. † L 1.

RENNIE, James G. Exh. 1929
3 Lauriston Place, Edinburgh. † RSA 1.

RENNIE, John O. Exh. 1930-31
Flower painter. Seamore Court, Seamore Place, London. † RA 2.

RENNIE, Louisa K. Exh. 1898
49 Queen's Gate, London. † RI 1.

RENNIE, W.J. Exh. 1885-86
8 Douglas Terrace, Broughty Ferry, Edinburgh. † GI 1, RSA 4.

RENOIR, Pierre Auguste* 1841-1919
French painter. Exh. 1897-1910. Add: Paris. † GOU 2, NEA 3.

RENOUARD, Charles Paul 1845-1924
French painter and etcher. R.E. 1881. Exh. 1881-1907. Add: "The Graphic", Strand, London 1894; Paris 1907. † L 1, NEA 1, P 1, RE 2.

RENOUF, Mrs. Exh. 1883
Still life and interior painter. 13 Old Cavendish Street, London. † RBA 2.

RENSHAW, Alice Exh. 1881-92
Figure and landscape painter. Chelsea, London. † B 13, GI 1, L 8, M 1, RBA 1, RHA 1.

RENSHAW, J. Exh. 1886-94
85 Howard Street, Eccles New Road, Salford, Lancs. † M 8.

RENTON, D.S. Stewart Exh. 1933
106 Thirlstone Road, Edinburgh. † RSW 1.

RENTON, J.D. Exh. 1907-10
Miniature portrait painter. Clare House, Tiverton, Devon. † I 6, L 5, RA 4.

RENWICK, Mrs. Emily Exh. 1887
The Terrace, Gartcosh, Glasgow. † GI 1.

REPIN, Ilya 1844-1930
Russian painter, and black and white artist, Exh. 1881. Add: Palazzo Rezzonico, Venice. † RSA 1.

RESCHE, le see L

RESTALL, Miss C. Exh. 1891
Acocks Green, Worcs. † B 1.

RESTON, Arthur Exh. 1884-85
Park House, Stretford, Manchester. † L 1, M 2.

RETTIGAN, Rita Exh. 1895-99
London 1895; Dublin 1899. † RHA 3.

REUSS, Albert Exh. 1939
We Two, St. Mawes, Cornwall. † RBA 1.

REUSS, Lilly Exh. 1890-1908
Miniature painter. Carlton Studios, St. Ann's Street, Manchester. † M 9, RA 1, RMS 1.

REVEL, John Daniel b. 1884
Painter and decorative designer. b. Dundee. Studied Royal College of Art 1906-12 (travelling scholarship). Director Chelsea School of Art 1913-25 and Director Glasgow School of Art 1925-32. Married to Lucy R. q.v. R.O.I. 1923, R.P. 1924. Exh. 1910-40. Add: London 1910; Glasgow 1926; Mullion, Cornwall 1935; Blewbury, Berks. 1938. † CHE 3, D 3, G 3, GI 2, I 21, L 1, P 19, RA 6, ROI 6, RSA 11.

REVEL, Mrs. Lucy E.B. Exh. 1915-40
Figure and flower painter. S.W.A. 1922. Married to John Daniel R. q.v. Add: London 1915; Glasgow 1925; Mullion, Cornwall 1936; Blewbury, Berks. 1938. † GI 1, I 1, L 1, RA 4, RSA 5, SWA 40.

REVERTERA, Countess Helfenberg Exh. 1913
Austria. † SWA 2.

REVILL, Miss E.M. Exh. 1930
Flower painter. Brook Lane, Green Hillocks, Ripley, nr. Derby. † N 1.

REVILLE, H. Whittaker Exh. 1881-1903
Figure painter. London. † B 5, L 4, RA 2, RBA 4, RHA 5, ROI 1.

REVILLE, James Exh. 1932-40
Watercolour painter. Dundee. † RA 3, RSA 12.

REW, Charles Henry Exh. 1880-84
Architect. London. † RA 3.

REW, Miss E. Exh. 1901-4
15 Dean Road, Willesden Green, London. † SWA 4.

REY, Loris Exh. 1934-39
Sculptor. Bridge of Weir 1934; London 1937. † GI 1, RA 2, RSA 3.

REYERS, W.L. Exh. 1931
Linocut artist. † RED 2.

REYMAN, Teodora Exh. 1887
Watercolour painter. 72 Via Sistina, Rome. † L 3.

REYMOND, Carlos* Exh. 1909
Painter. † LS 3.

REYNELL, Miss G. Exh. 1914-16
London. † L 1, RA 3.

REYNERS, Joseph F. Exh. 1890
Medallionist. 25 Delancy Street, London. † RA 1.

REYNOLD, C. Exh. 1936-37
Still life and landscape painter. Glen View, Victoria Crescent, Private Road, Nottingham. † N 3.

REYNOLDS, Apollonia Exh. 1882
Watercolour painter. Blenheim Lodge, Guildford, Surrey. † D 1, RBA 1.

REYNOLDS, Mrs. A.M. Exh. 1912
4 Haarlem Road, Brook Green, London. † L 2, RA 1.

REYNOLDS, Caroline Jeannie Exh. 1898-1937
Miniature portrait painter. R.M.S. 1902. Add: Alton, Hants. 1898; Sunbury on Thames 1902; Kew, Surrey 1907; Richmond, Surrey 1933. † L 2, NG 2, RA 8, RI 2, RMS 44.

REYNOLDS, Elizabeth Exh. 1931
Flower painter. 13a Summer Place, London. † RHA 2.

REYNOLDS, E.A. Exh. 1912
29 St. Peters Road, South Croydon, Surrey. † RA 1.

REYNOLDS, Edith C. Exh. 1909-37
Leamington, Warwicks. 1909; Petworth, Sussex 1931. † L 6, ROI 21, SWA 7.

REYNOLDS, Edwin F. Exh. 1898-1931
Architect. R.B.S.A. 1923. Add: Birmingham. † B 1, RA 2.

REYNOLDS, Ethel M. Exh. 1907
Wharfedale, The Driffold, Sutton Coldfield, Warwicks. † B 1.

REYNOLDS, Frank b. 1876
Watercolour painter, black and white artist and illustrator (e.g. Dickens). Studied Heatherleys. On staff of "Illustrated London News" and "Sketch"; Art editor of "Punch" 1922-32. R.I. 1903 (resigned 1933). Exh. 1903-30. Add: London. † D 1, L 3, RI 20, WG 184.

REYNOLDS, Frederick George 1828-1921
Landscape and figure painter, and watercolourist. Related to Walter R. q.v. Add: London. † L 5, RA 4, ROI 2.

REYNOLDS, F.S. Exh. 1910
3 New Street, Birmingham. † B 1.

REYNOLDS, George A. Exh. 1883-1905
52 St. Peters Road, Handsworth, Birmingham. † B 8.

REYNOLDS, H. Exh. 1882-86
189 Clifton Road, Aston, Birmingham. † B 5.

REYNOLDS, Henry Joseph Exh. 1918
67 Albion Grove, Barnsbury, London. † LS 3.

REYNOLDS, Mrs. H. Tangye Exh. 1914-34
Landscape and flower painter. b. Redruth, Cornwall. Married Reginald Francis R. q.v. Add: London 1914, and 1918; St. Ives, Cornwall 1916. † B 9, CHE 1, D 4, LS 1, RA 3, RBA 1, RID 2, ROI 17, RSA 2, SWA 4, WG 21.

REYNOLDS, Mrs. J.P. Exh. 1882-89
Latchford, nr. Warrington, Lancs. † B 3, M 3.

REYNOLDS, Lilian Exh. 1928
Painter. Studied in Paris. Add: 30A Northampton Park, Canonbury, London. † RI 1.

REYNOLDS, Lyn Exh. 1926-32
School of Art, Glasgow 1926; Hyde, Cheshire 1932. † L 1, RSA 1.

REYNOLDS, Lilian Mary Exh. 1884-1914
Mrs. J.F.J. nee Etherington. Portrait painter. Studied Ridleys Art School and in Brussels. Add: London. † L 3, RA 7, RBA 2, RID 62, ROI 2, RMS 1, SWA 2.

REYNOLDS, Mrs. Margaret Exh. 1906-36
nee Haley. Miniature portrait painter. Manchester 1906; Liverpool 1909; Liscard, Cheshire 1913; Willaston, Cheshire 1916; Barry, Glam. 1936. † L 16, RA 6, RCA 2.

REYNOLDS, Margaret K. Exh. 1930-40
A.S.W.A. 1940. Add: Glasgow 1930; Renfrewshire 1938. † GI 2, L 1, RSA 3.

REYNOLDS, Owen B. Exh. 1927-38
Landscape painter. London 1927; Long Melford, Suffolk 1933. † AR 61, B 1, L 2, RA 6, RBA 4, ROI 7.

REYNOLDS, P.T. Exh. 1914
37 Greenham Road, Muswell Hill, London. † RA 1.

REYNOLDS, Reginald Francis d. 1936
Landscape and coastal painter. Married H. Tangye R. q.v. A.R.B.A. 1919, R.B.A. 1922. Add: Barnes, Surrey 1902; London 1920. † B 4, CHE 1, D 11, GOU 1, L 1, LS 3, RA 7, RBA 79, RCA 4, RHA 1, RI 1, ROI 1, RSA 1, WG 30.

REYNOLDS, V. Exh. 1906-8
Farnham, Surrey 1906; Paris 1908. † I 1, RA 2.

REYNOLDS, Walter Exh. 1880-85
Landscape painter. Related to Frederick George R. q.v. Add: Enfield, Middlesex 1880; London 1885. † M 2, RA 4, RBA 8, RI 5.

REYNOLDS, Warwick 1880-1926
Animal painter and black and white artist. R.S.W. 1924. Exh. from 1920. Add: Glasgow. † GI 36, L 15, RA 8, RSA 18, RSW 8.

REYNOLDS, William F. Exh. 1931
† NEA 1.

REYNOLDS-STEPHENS, Annie 1896-1925
nee Ridpath. Married Sir William R-S q.v. Add: St. Johns Wood, London. † GI 2, L 3, NG 1, SWA 1.

REYNOLDS-STEPHENS, Sir William 1862-1943
Sculptor, painter and metalworker. b. Detroit U.S.A. of British parents. Studied R.A. Schools. Married Annie R-S q.v. H.R.I. 1922. Knighted 1931. "The Royal Game" purchased by Chantrey Bequest 1911. Add: London. † G 1, GI 8, L 24, NG 4, RA 81, RBA 2, RI 8, ROI 1, RSA 5.

RHEAD, George Woolliscroft 1855-1920
Painter, etcher and stained glass artist and illustrator. R.E. 1883. Add: Chelsea, London 1880; Putney 1894. † D 3, GI 2, I 2, L 16, LS 6, NG 2, RA 19, RBA 3, RE 75, RI 2.

RHEAM, Henry Meynell 1859-1920
Watercolour painter. R.I. 1895. Add: Claughton, Birkenhead 1886 and 1903; Newlyn, Penzance 1891 and 1904. † B 10, D 2, DOW 1, FIN 1, GI 4, L 46, M 12, NG 1, RA 20, RBA 2, RCA 1, RI 77, RSW 2.

RHIND, Alexander Exh. 1935
45 Belford Road, Edinburgh. † RSA 1.

RHIND, Alexander Exh. 1930-39
Dunfermline 1930 and 1936; Falkirk 1935. † GI 2, RSA 15.

RHIND, Douglas H. Exh. 1902-4
Edinburgh. † RSA 3.

RHIND, Ethel Exh. 1913
69 Lower Mount Street, Dublin. † RHA 1.

RHIND, John 1828-1892
Sculptor. A.R.S.A. 1892 (died a few days after election). Father of John Massey and William Birnie R. q.v. Add: Edinburgh. † GI 5, RA 1, RSA 27.

RHIND, Jessie A. Exh. 1894
9 Mardale Crescent, Edinburgh. † RSA 1.

RHIND, John Massey 1868-1936
Sculptor. b. Edinburgh. Son of John R. q.v. Studied R.A. Schools. Spent some time in the U.S.A. A.R.S.A. 1932, R.S.A. 1935. Add: London 1886; Edinburgh 1888 and 1930; Glasgow 1889. † GI 3, RA 3, RSA 19.

RHIND, J.S. Exh. 1880-1920
Edinburgh. † GI 12, RSA 49.

RHIND, Sir Thomas Duncan 1871-1927
Architect and etcher. Edinburgh. † GI 1, L 4, RSA 23.

RHIND, William Birnie 1853-1933
Sculptor. Studied under his father John R. q.v. and in Paris. A.R.S.A. 1893; R.S.A. 1905. Add: Edinburgh. † GI 41, L 8, RA 10, RHA 3, RSA 133.

RHIND, W.J. Exh. 1883-84
30 Kemp Place, Edinburgh. † RSA 3.

RHOADES, Geoffrey b. 1898
Landscape painter. Exh. 1923-39. Add: London. † GOU 8, NEA 3, RA 1, ROI 1.

RHODES, Angela Exh. 1893-96
21 Pembridge Crescent, London. † B 2, P 1.

RHODES, Bertha Exh. 1905-12
Southport, Lancs. 1905; Liversedge, Yorks. 1907. † L 8, RA 2, RCA 2.

RHODES, Cecil W. Exh. 1919-20
Painter. 50 Sydenham Park, London. † I 2, RA 2.

RHODES, Mrs. E.J. Exh. 1882-87
Sculptor. Kensington, London. † RA 1, RBA 2.

RHODES, E. Millicent Exh. 1926-32
Sculptor. Roslyn, Warwick Drive, Hale, Cheshire. † L 9, M 3, RA 1, RCA 2.

RHODES, Henry Exh. 1884
Hogarth Club, Hanover Square, London. † D 2.

RHODES, H. Douglas Exh. 1905-14
19 Buckingham Gate, London. † D 23.

RHODES, Henry J. Exh. 1882-84
Watercolour landscape painter. 7 Eden Villas, Knight's Hill, Norwood, London. † D 1, RA 1.

RHODES, John William Exh. 1899-1908
Architect. Mitre Court Chambers, Temple, London. † LS 3, RA 2.

RHODES, Marion b. 1907
Painter, etcher and teacher. Studied Huddersfield School of Art, Leeds School of Art 1925-29 and Central School of Arts, London 1934-39. Exh. 1934-40. Add: Huddersfield 1934; London 1936. † RA 7, RSA 2.

RHODES, Miss M.P. Exh. 1902
Whiston Grange, Rotherham, Yorks. † SWA 3.

RHODES, O.V. Exh. 1915
9 Shirburn Avenue, Mansfield, Notts. † N 5.

RHODES, Rowland Exh. 1886-89
Sculptor. Preston, Lancs. 1886; Newcastle, Staffs. 1889. † L 1, RA 2.

RHODES, Mrs. S. Wynfield Exh. 1910-15
Prestwick, Lancs. † L 3, M 2, RCA 6.

RHODES, T.H. Exh. 1910
Highfield, Northwood, Middlesex. † RA 1.

RHYS, Oliver* Exh. 1880-97
Landscape and genre painter. London. † B 3, G 2, GI 3, L 3, RA 8, RBA 1, ROI 1, TOO 2.

RIACH, May J. Exh. 1933-34
74 Beaufort Mansions, London. † RSA 3, SWA 1.

RIBARZ, Rudolf* Exh. 1886
Landscape painter. 17 Rue Duperre, Paris. † GI 2.

RIBBANS, Albert Charles b. 1903
Mural and watercolour painter. Studied Ipswich School of Arts and Crafts. Exh. 1931-40. Add: Ipswich 1931; Rushmere, nr. Ipswich 1936. † GI 1, RA 12, RI 2.

RIBOLT, T. Exh. 1881
Kt. of Legion of Honour, 33 Avenue de l'Opera, Paris. † RHA 2.

RIBOT, Germane* Exh. 1882
Painter. 16 Avenue Trudaine, Paris. † RHA 1.

RIBOT, M. Exh. 1900
† P 1.

RIBOT, T. Exh. 1922-26
Painter. † GOU 3.

RIBY, Edwin Exh. 1923
34 Carleton Street, Keighley, Yorks. † RCA 2.

RICARDO, Halsey Ralph 1854-1928
Architect. Exh. 1883-1907. Add: 13 Bedford Street, Bedford Square, London. † RA 13.

RICCARDI, E. Exh. 1923
Sculptor. 18 Chepstow Villas, London. † RA 1.

RICCI, de See D

RICCI, Alfred Exh. 1889
Painter. c/o G. Squire, 193 Oxford Street, London. † NG 1.

RICCI, Paolo Exh. 1884-88
Florence and c/o Burns and Oates, Orchard Street, London. † D 2, G 1.

RICE, Anne Estelle Exh. 1911-27
Landscape, coastal, portrait and figure painter. Paris. † BG 71, G 1, GOU 1, LS 12, M 2.

RICE, Bernard b. 1900
Painter, wood engraver, etcher, poster artist and furniture designer. b. Innsbruck. Son of Bernard G. q.v. Studied Royal College of Art, Westminster School of Art and R.A. Schools. Exh. 1925-30. Add: Hastings. † CHE 2, RED 2.

RICE, Bernard G. Exh. 1920-27
Stained glass artist. Father of Bernard R. q.v. Add: London 1920; Birmingham 1924. † B 1, GI 1, RA 2.

RICE, E.E. Exh. 1934-37
St. Ives, Cornwall. † SWA 2.

RICE, Mrs. E. Garrett Exh. 1920-29
Coventry. † B 3, L 6.

RICE, E.J. Exh. 1936-38
Birmingham. † B 4.

RICE, Frederick A. Exh. 1893
Black and white artist. 5 East Street, Chelsea, London. † RA 1.

RICE, Florence M. Exh. 1897-1929
Figure painter. Northampton 1897; Bushey, Herts. 1903; Bournemouth 1916; Coventry 1921; London 1924. † B 1, I 1, L 3, RA 2, RI 1, SWA 2.

RICE, Miss J.M.P. Exh. 1929
55 Chester Terrace, London. † SWA 1.

RICE, Mary Exh. 1940
Flower painter. 55 Chester Row, London. † RA 1.

RICE, M.P. Exh. 1939
339 Eachelhurst Road, Walmley, Birmingham. † B 1.

RICH, Alfred William 1856-1921
Watercolour landscape painter. Studied Slade School 1890-96 and at Westminster. N.E.A. 1898. Add: Croydon, Surrey 1894 and 1913; Hassocks, Sussex 1902, 1907 and 1920; Hurstpierpoint, Sussex 1903 and 1916; Amersham, Bucks. 1910; London 1912; St. Albans, Herts. 1914. † AG 2, ALP 430, BA 1, CAR 72, DOW 2, FIN 81, GI 1, GOU 22, I 23, L 27, LEI 76, M 4, NEA 181, RBA 1, RHA 4, RSA 4, RSW 1, WG 102.

RICH, William George Exh. 1881-97
Landscape and figure painter. London 1881; Brentford, Essex 1884. † GI 2, RA 1, RBA 3, TOO 5.

RICHARD, Dorothy Exh. 1926
Kirkton, Carmyle. † GI 1.

RICHARD, Mlle. M.L. Exh. 1905
32 Place Carriere, Nancy, France. † L 1.

RICHARD-PUTZ, Michel Exh. 1908
15 Rue Hegesippe Moreau, Paris. † L 1.

RICHARDS, Anna Exh. 1898-1902
Figure and landscape painter. London. † B 1, RA 4, RMS 3.

RICHARDS, Annie Exh. 1897-1900
Burton on Trent 1897; School of Art, Birmingham 1899. † B 4.

RICHARDS, Aimee G. Exh. 1893-95
Painter. London. † M 1, RA 2, RI 1.

RICHARDS, Mrs. Alice S. Exh. 1892-93
Figure painter. 23 Romola Road, Herne Hill. † RBA 2.

RICHARDS, Ceri* 1903-1971
Painter and black and white artist. b. Dunvant, nr. Swansea. Studied Swansea School of Art and Royal College of Art. Member London Group 1938. Exh. 1938-39. † COO 3, LEI 1.

RICHARDS, Charles A. Exh. 1903-39
Figure painter. A.N.S.A. 1908. N.S.A. 1910. Add: Thorneywood, Notts. 1903; Mapperley, Notts. 1913; Sherwood, Notts. 1916 and 1937; Nottingham 1920. † N 35.

RICHARDS, Miss D. Exh. 1914
32 Elm Avenue, Nottingham. † N 2.

RICHARDS, Miss Evelyne Exh. 1899-1905
Comyn House, Leamington, Warwicks. † B 3.

RICHARDS, Edith M. Exh. 1909-29
Epsom, Surrey 1909; Edgbaston, Birmingham 1910; Penzance 1911; London 1924. † B 1, GOU 1, L 15, RCA 1, SWA 1.

RICHARDS, Eugenie M.K. Exh. 1900-20
Portrait painter. Nottingham. † I 6, L 1, N 57, RA 9.

RICHARDS, Fanny Exh. 1897-99
Flower painter. 39 Claremont Road, Highgate, London. † L 1, RA 1, RI 1, ROI 1.

RICHARDS, Frank Exh. 1883-1925
Landscape and figure painter. R.B.A. 1921. Add: Birmingham 1883 and 1887; Lulworth, Dorset 1885; Newlyn, Penzance 1892; London 1897; Wareham, Dorset 1902; Bournemouth 1917. † B 9, DOW 5, L 3, M 4, RA 3, RBA 2, ROI 1.

RICHARDS, Florence A. Exh. 1907
64 Longmore Street, Birmingham. † B 1.

RICHARDS, Frederick Charles 1879-1932
Etcher and drypoint artist. b. Newport, Mon. Studied Royal College of Art. A.R.E. 1913, R.E. 1921. Add: London. † CG 92, CHE 2, CON 5, FIN 2, GI 9, I 1, L 9, RA 37, RE 49, RSA 1.

RICHARDS, George Exh. 1883
Figure painter. 168 New Bond Street, London. † ROI 1.

RICHARDS, George Exh. 1900
53 Victoria Buildings, Manchester. † L 1.

RICHARDS, Helena Exh. 1892
Landscape painter. 11 Garden Studios, Manresa Road, Chelsea, London. † RBA 1.

RICHARDS, Hetty Exh. 1903-15
Wolverton, Bucks. 1903; Kingston, Surrey 1914; Hythe, nr. Southampton 1915. † B 1, RA 8, RCA 9, SWA 9.

RICHARDS, Mme. Hortense Exh. 1903
162 Boulevard du Montparnasse, Paris. † L 1.

RICHARDS, J. Cruwys Exh. 1919-22
Stained glass artist. 22 Beech Road, Bourneville, Birmingham. † B 5, RA 1.

RICHARDS, L. Exh. 1940
Architect. 41 Hayes Way, Beckenham, Kent. † RA 1.

RICHARDS, Mrs. L. Exh. 1898-1907
Comyn House, Leamington Spa, Warwicks. † B 2, SWA 3.

RICHARDS, Mary Exh. 1893-1925
Manchester 1893; London 1914. † L 26, M 50, RA 1, RCA 12.

RICHARDS, Marjorie M. Exh. 1924-26
Watercolour painter. 5 Burns Street, Nottingham. † N 2.

RICHARDS, Phyllis M. Exh. 1933
3 Vicarage Road, Wood Green, Wednesbury. † B 1.

RICHARDS, Samuel Exh. 1895-1901
Landscape painter. Castle Street, Sneinton, Notts. † N 9.

RICHARDS, Sylvia M. Exh. 1908-16
179 Gloucester Terrace, London. † B 5, L 3, RA 2, RSA 1, SWA 7.

RICHARDS, Thomas Robert Exh. 1884
Architect. 17 King Street, Cheapside, London. † RA 1.

RICHARDS, W. senr. Exh. 1884-94
Birmingham. † B 12.

RICHARDS, W. junr. Exh. 1882-84
Birmingham. † B 4.

RICHARDS, Walter Exh. 1923
Etcher. † FIN 1.

RICHARDS, W.H. Exh. 1892-1916
40 North John Street, Liverpool. † L 13.

RICHARDS, William Trost* 1833-1905
American landscape and marine painter. b. Philadelphia. Exh. 1880-1903. Add: Notting Hill Gate, London. † B 1, D 5, G 2, L 3, M 3, RA 9, TOO 1.

RICHARDSON, Mrs. Exh. 1902
Portrait painter. 28 Roland Gardens, London. † NEA 1.

RICHARDSON, Arthur Exh. 1887-1919
Landscape painter. R.B.A. 1904. Add: Peckham, London 1887; Newcastle on Tyne 1890; Cheltenham, Glos. 1904; Dawlish, Devon 1920. † L 5, M 1, RA 3, RBA 30.

RICHARDSON, A. Constance Exh. 1927-38
Flower and portrait painter. Studied under Seymour Lucas and George Harcourt and at Byam Shaw and Vicat Cole School and Regent Street Polytechnic. Add: London. † AB 1, P 1, RA 3, ROI 2.

RICHARDSON, Adelaide E. Exh. 1927-40
Landscape painter. Ladbroke Grove, London. † RA 1, RI 2, ROI 1, SWA 3.

RICHARDSON, Ada E. Exh. 1902-35
Miniature portrait painter. London. † L 5, P 5, RA 27, RI 3, RMS 5.

RICHARDSON, Agnes E. Exh. 1894-1902
Landscape painter. Hawkes Point, Lelant, Cornwall. † L 3, M 3, RA 2, RMS 1.

RICHARDSON, Albert E. b. 1880
Architect. Professor of Architecture University of London from 1919, and at the R.A. A.R.A. 1936. Exh. 1906-40. Add: London 1906 and 1936; St. Albans, Herts. 1910. † GI 2, RA 24.

RICHARDSON, Alice G. Exh. 1895-1902
Painter. 13 Barn Hill, Stamford, Lincs. † N 8.

RICHARDSON, Mrs. Anna M. Exh. 1908
85 Rue Notre Dame des Champs, Paris. † LS 5.

RICHARDSON, C. Exh. 1922-26
Landscape painter. Arnold, Notts. 1922; Nottingham 1923. † N 5.

RICHARDSON, Miss C. Exh. 1883-94
Sutton Coldfield, Birmingham 1883; Liscard, Cheshire 1886. † B 1, L 14.

RICHARDSON, Miss Car Exh. 1910-40
Landscape painter. Tithe Barn, Chesham Bois, Bucks. † ALP 9, NEA 4, RA 3, RBA 6.

RICHARDSON, Charles Exh. 1880-1901
Landscape painter and watercolourist. Son of Thomas Miles R. sen. (1784-1848) and brother of John Isaac and Thomas Miles R. junr. q.v. Add: London 1880; Petersfield, Hants. 1899. † D 7, L 3, RA 14, RI 2.

RICHARDSON, Caroline B. Exh. 1905-11
9 Cranbourne Court, Albert Bridge, London. † L 9.

RICHARDSON, C. Douglas Exh. 1884-88
Painter and sculptor. London. † RA 3, RBA 1, ROI 1.

RICHARDSON, Charles E. Exh. 1897-1909
Painter. Kirklevington Hall, Yarm, Yorks. † RA 11.

RICHARDSON, Dudley 1862-1929
Watercolour architectural and landscape painter. b. Darlington. Travelled on the continent. Exh. 1926-28. Add: Blackwell Manor, Darlington. † L 3, RA 1.

RICHARDSON, Douglas W. Exh. 1932
Architect. 10 Dingwall Road, Croydon, Surrey. † RA 1.

RICHARDSON, Edith b. 1867
Painter, decorator, illustrator, and writer. b. Newcastle on Tyne. Studied Paris. Add: Newcastle on Tyne 1899; Bushey, Herts. 1900; Tolmere, nr. Hertford 1913. † B 2, GI 1, L 26, LS 9, P 2, RA 4, RBA 1, RI 9, ROI 1.

RICHARDSON, Ellen Exh. 1884-99
Painter. c/o Mrs. Smith, Coldharbour, nr. Dorking, Surrey. † L 1, RBA 2, ROI 1.

RICHARDSON, Edward H. Exh. 1930-33
138 Cecil Street, Whitworth Park, Manchester. † L 2, M 3, RCA 1.

RICHARDSON, Frank Exh. 1907
Portrait pencil artist. † BG 13.

RICHARDSON, Frederic Stuart 1855-1934
Landscape painter. b. Clifton, Bristol. Studied under Carolus Duran in Paris. R.I. 1897, R.O.I. 1901, R.S.W. 1894. Add: Sandy Rectory, Beds. 1883, 1885 and 1889; Abinger, Surrey 1884; London 1888; Long Ashton, Bristol 1917. † B 7, GI 8, L 15, M 5, NG 2, RA 49, RBA 5, RI 156, ROI 51, RSW 80.

RICHARDSON, Miss F.S.A. Exh. 1883
Chipping Vicarage, nr. Preston, Lancs. † L 2.

RICHARDSON, F.W. Exh. 1881-83
Architectural artist. 25 Stratford Place, Camden Square, London. † RA 2.

RICHARDSON, Harry Linley b. 1878
Portrait, figure and landscape painter, illustrator, etcher and draughtsman. Studied Goldsmiths School of Art, Westminster and Julians, Paris. R.B.A. 1905. Exh. 1900-39. Add: Dulwich, London 1900 and 1907; Dorking, Surrey 1905; Wellington Technical College, New Zealand 1914. † B 1, L 2, RA 3, RBA 66, RCA 1.

RICHARDSON, Irene Exh. 1938-40
Watercolour flower and miniature portrait painter. 31 St. Dunstans Avenue, London. † RA 3.

RICHARDSON, John F. Exh. 1933
Landscape painter. 117 Wells Street, Camberwell, London. † RA 1.

RICHARDSON, John Isaac 1836-1913
Landscape and figure painter and watercolourist. Son of Thomas Miles R. sen. (1784-1848) and brother of Charles and Thomas Miles R. junr. q.v. R.I. 1882 (Hon. Retd. 1907), R.O.I. 1883. Add: London. † B 12, D 7, L 6, M 4, RA 2, RI 69, ROI 9.

RICHARDSON, Joseph Kent d. 1972
Watercolour landscape painter. R.S.W. 1917. Add: Edinburgh. † AR 2, GI 17, RA 1, RSA 37, RSW 94.

RICHARDSON, J.S. Exh. 1906-19
Liverpool 1906; Edinburgh 1910. † L 5, RSA 11.

RICHARDSON, John Thomas Exh. 1900-9
Landscape painter. Etaples, France. † LS 1, RA 1.

RICHARDSON, Kathleen See HYETT

RICHARDSON, Lilian Exh. 1928-29
White Lodge, Woolhampton, Berks. † NEA 2.

RICHARDSON, Marjorie Exh. 1937-40
Painter. College Lane, Hurstpierpoint, Sussex. † RA 1, SWA 1.

RICHARDSON, Miss M.A. Exh. 1894
The Hawthorns, Wordsley, nr. Stourbridge. † B 2.

RICHARDSON, Maggie R. See MITCHELL

RICHARDSON, Miss N. Exh. 1914
The Barn, Walberswick, Suffolk. † RA 1.

RICHARDSON, Miss P. Exh. 1923
Annandale, Lowmoor Road, East Kirkby, Notts. † N 1.

RICHARDSON, R. Exh. 1887-91
Watercolour landscape painter. Southover Rectory, Lewes 1887; Sidmouth, Devon 1890. † D 6, RI 1.

RICHARDSON, Rosemary Exh. 1929
† NEA 1.

RICHARDSON, R. Esdaile Exh. 1897
Landscape painter. Norlington Brading, I.O.W. † RA 1.

RICHARDSON, Ralph J. Exh. 1900
Painter and illustrator. c/o E. Lander, 22 Joubert Mansions, Jubilee Place, Chelsea, London. † RA 1.

RICHARDSON, Robert J. Exh. 1907-19
Medalist. London 1907; Edgware, Middlesex 1909. † RA 4.

RICHARDSON, Thomas Miles junr.* 1813-1890
Watercolour landscape painter. Son of T.M. R. sen. (1784-1848) and brother of Charles and John Isaac R. q.v. A.R.W.S. 1843, R.W.S. 1851. Add: London. † AG 4, L 5, M 3, RWS 61, TOO 4.

RICHARDSON, Miss V. Exh. 1912
Cheniston Gardens, London. † SWA 2.

RICHARDSON, William Exh. 1882
25 Stratford Place, Camden Square, London. † L 1.

RICHARDSON, W.F. Exh. 1896-1902
81 Burton Road, Derby. † B 1, L 1.

RICHARD-TRONCY, Mme. Laura
See BELL, Laura Anning

RICHE, le See L

RICHE, Louis b. 1887
French sculptor. Exh. 1907-10. Add: 1 Rue Leclere, Paris † L 2.

RICHES, Charles M. Exh. 1904
Painter. 122 Fleet Street, London. † RA 1.

RICHES, Kate Winifred b. 1891
Miniature and portrait painter and illustrator. Studied Clapham School of Art and City and Guilds Technical Institute. Exh. 1920-34. Add: London. † RI 2, RMS 3.

RICHETON, Leon 1854-1934
Etcher. R.E. 1881. Exh. 1881-88. Add: London. † RA 5, RE 4.

RICHEY, Mary E. Exh. 1927-38
Painter. Edinburgh 1927; Polperro, Cornwall 1932; Bridport, Dorset 1935. † RA 1, RSW 1, SWA 10.

RICHFORD, Dorothy Ella Exh. 1920-23
Miniature portrait painter. Summer Hill, Headcorn, Kent. † RA 2.

RICHIR, Herman b. 1866
Portrait, figure and landscape painter. b. Brussels. Studied Academie des Beaux Arts, Brussels. Exh. 1894-1924. Add: Brussels 1894 and 1925; London 1922. † L 7, M 1, RA 2, RI 1.

RICHMOND, Andrew Exh. 1880-99
St. Vincent Street, Glasgow. † GI 34, RSA 1.

RICHMOND, A.E. Exh. 1882-85
Collingham, Newark, Notts. † N 5.

RICHMOND, Ethel M. Exh. 1896-1901
London. † RBA 1, SWA 1.

RICHMOND, George* 1809-1896
Portrait and miniature painter, watercolourist and sculptor. Studied R.A. Schools. Father of Sir William Blake R. q.v. A.R.A. 1857, R.A. 1866, H.R.B.A. 1880. Add: London. † RA 6, RBA 1.

RICHMOND, Miss H. Exh. 1923
84 Ilkeston Road, Nottingham. † N 1.

RICHMOND, John Exh. 1898
Architect. 7 Gt. College Street, Westminster, London. † RA 1.

RICHMOND, Leonard* Exh. 1912-40
Landscape and figure painter and teacher. Studied Taunton School of Art. R.B.A. 1914, R.O.I. 1919. Add: Brentford, Middlesex 1912; Southall, Middlesex 1914; London 1919; Guildford, Surrey 1935. † AR 3, COO 38, FIN 56, GI 1, GOU 22, I 21, L 3, NEA 2, RA 20, RBA 171, RI 9, RID 4, ROI 47, WG 40.

RICHMOND, Sir William Blake* 1842-1921
Painter, sculptor and medalist. Son of George R. q.v. Studied under Ruskin and at R.A. Schools 1857. Decorated the dome of St. Pauls Cathedral. A.R.A. 1888, R.A. 1895, H.R.B.A. 1898, P.R.M.S. 1899-1907, Hon. P.R.M.S. 1908-9. Add: London. † B 106, BG 1, CAR 3, FIN 153, GI 5, L 21, M 23, NG 38, RA 72, RBA 9, RCA 1, RMS 3.

RICHTER, Charles Augustus b. 1867
Painter, interior decorator and furniture designer. b. Ovingdean, Sussex. Studied Bath School of Art, London School of Art and Heatherleys. Brother of Herbert Davis R. q.v. Exh. 1926-39. Add: Bathwick Hill House, Bath. † L 1, RA 2, RI 4.

RICHTER, E. Exh. 1887
16 Rue de la Tour d'Auvergne, Paris. † GI 1.

RICHTER, Gertrude b. 1879
nee Barber. Bead craftsman. b. Birmingham. Studied under her busband Herbert Davis R. q.v. A.S.W.A. 1918, S.W.A. 1920. Exh. 1908-27. Add: London. † L 44, SWA 2.

RICHTER, Herbert Davis* 1874-1955
Flower painter, decorative artist, furnishings designer, lecturer. b. Brighton. Studied under J.M. Swan and Frank Brangwyn, 1895-1906. Brother of Charles Augustus and husband of Gertrude R. q.v. R.B.A. 1910, R.I. 1920, R.O.I. 1917, R.S.W. 1937. Add: Bath 1906; London 1907. † B 11, BA 7, CG 1, CHE 2, FIN 9, G 3, GI 45, GOU 37, I 18, L 33, LEI 37, RA 67, RBA 64, RHA 40, RI 105, RID 12, ROI 102, RSA 43, RSW 15.

RICHTER, Irma 1876-1956
Landscape and portrait painter. b. Paris. Studied Slade School and Paris. Teacher of Art at Rosemary Hall, Greenwich, Connecticut, U.S.A. Exh. 1909-28. Add: 20 Gordon Place, Campden Hill, London. † BA 18, GOU 3, I 4, NEA 2.

RICHTER, John Exh. 1907
288 New City Road, Glasgow. † B 1, M 1.

RICHTER, Otto Exh. 1885
2 Ailsa Terrace, Hillhead, Glasgow. † RSA 1.

RICKARD, J.H. Kingston Exh. 1938-39
Tongham, Farnham, Surrey. † RBA 4.

RICKARD, Stephen Exh. 1940
Sculptor. 72 Randolphe Avenue, London. † RA 2.

RICKARDS, Helena Exh. 1890-98
Portrait and landscape painter. Harberton Lodge, Upper Tooting, London. † D 1, L 1, RID 12, SWA 1.

RICKATSON, Annie E. Exh. 1895
Overstone, Ashton on Mersey. † M 2.

RICKATSON, Octavius Exh. 1880-93
Landscape painter. R.B.A. 1890. Add: London. † AG 3, D 5, DOW 66, FIN 1, G 2, L 8, M 8, NG 2, RA 25, RBA 30, RHA 1, RI 8, ROI 5.

RICKENBACH, Frieda Exh. 1898-1901
Airlie Cottage, Mayfield, Sussex. † D 5, RA 2, SWA 4.

RICKETTS, Amy Exh. 1889-90
Miniature portrait painter. 26 Grosvenor, Bath. † RA 2.

RICKETTS, Charles* 1866-1931
Painter, wood engraver, illustrator and theatrical designer. b. Geneva. Studied Lambeth School of Art. A.R.A. 1922, R.A. 1928. Add: London. † AG 1, CAR 19, CG 2, FIN 1, G 5, GI 2, I 42, L 8, M 18, RA 24, RBA 1, RI 2, ROI 2, RSA 4.

RICKETTS, William C. Exh. 1900-6
Flower painter. Barbourne, Worcs. † B 2, RA 2.

RICKEY, Jane Exh. 1933
Clarendon, Helensburgh. † GI 1.

RICKMAN, Philip Exh. 1936
Watercolour painter of game birds and wildfowl. † CON 41.

RICKS, James Exh. 1880-94
Figure painter. 120 Adelaide Road, London. † B 11, L 1, RBA 5, RHA 3.

RIDAL, Miss P.A. Exh. 1885-91
Landscape painter. Rock Lynn, Mapperley Road, Nottingham. † N 2.

RIDDALL, Walter Exh. 1898
St. Ives, Cornwall. † ROI 1.

RIDDEL, Daisy Exh. 1901-2
Corklaw, Cockburnspath, N.B. † RSA 2.

RIDDEL, James 1858-1928
Landscape, portrait and genre painter. Born and studied in Glasgow. Headmaster Heriot Watt College Art Department. A.R.S.A. 1919, R.S.W. 1905. Add: Forfar 1882; Edinburgh 1887; Colinton 1888; Mauchline, Ayrshire 1922; Balvonic, Balerno, Midlothian 1924. † GI 100, L 11, M 6, RA 7, RHA 2, RSA 128, RSW 51.

RIDDELL, Lady Buchanan Exh. 1885
Coastal painter. 50 Queen's Gate, London. † RI 1.

RIDDELL, William F. Exh. 1913
105 Victoria Mansions, South Lambeth Road, London. † RI 1.

RIDDETT, Leonard Charles Exh. 1893-95
Watercolour painter. 30 Bedford Row, London. † RBA 1, RI 1.

RIDDLE, Hugh Joseph b. 1912
Painter. b. Beaconsfield. Studied Slade School and Byam Shaw School. Exh. 1938. Add: 43 Roland Gardens, London. † RA 1.

RIDDLE, John Exh. 1903-34
Landscape painter. Welling, Kent 1903; Blackheath, London 1915. † CHE 4, I 35, NEA 1, RA 6, ROI 4.

RIDEL, Louis Marie Joseph b. 1866
French artist. Exh. 1901. Add: 65 Boulevard Arago, Paris. † L 1.

RIDEOUT, Miss E. Exh. 1887
Woodlands, Winton, Patricroft. † M 1.

RIDER, Haywood Exh. 1899-1911
Landscape painter and teacher. 1 Ashwood Terrace, Headingley, Leeds. † M 1, RA 2.

RIDER, Mrs. Helen K. Exh. 1919
† L 2.

RIDER, Urban Exh. 1883-86
Watercolour landscape painter. Dover 1883; Folkestone 1884. † RI 4.

RIDGE, Alfred Monday Exh. 1880-83
Architect. 123-124 Newgate Street, London. † RA 2.

RIDGERS, E. Lawrence Exh. 1905-6
8 Uplands Road, Handsworth, Birmingham. † B 2.

RIDGEWAY, Ann Exh. 1931
Landscape painter. 42 Adair House, Oakley Street, London. † RA 1.

RIDGWAY, Ellen Exh. 1881
Flower painter. Fernbrook, Penmaenmawr, North Wales. † SWA 2.

RIDGWAY, Ernest Frederick b. 1886
Painter, commercial and scientific artist. b. Hale, Cheshire. Studied Manchester School of Art and Royal College of Art. Art master at St. Mary's Training College, Cheltenham and at Denbighshire Technical Institute, Wrexham. Exh. 1925-30. Add: Cheltenham 1925; Wrexham 1930. † B 2.

RIDGWAY, G. Winifred Exh. 1907
Wildersmoor, Lymm, Cheshire. † L 1.

RIDGWAY, Rose Exh. 1906
Westray, Harvey Road, Cambridge. † RCA 1.

RIDGWAY, Miss S.E.B. Exh. 1902-5
Haughton Park, Ampthill, Beds. † B 3, D 4, RCA 6, SWA 1.

RIDGWAY, William Exh. 1880-1916
Engraver. Ealing, London. † L 1, RA 8, RCA 2, RI 1.

RIDING, Harold Exh. 1926-33
Painter. Studied Manchester School of Art. Add: 37 Bury New Road, Prestwich, Manchester. † L 4, M 1.

RIDING, Jessie M. Exh. 1908-26
Married Frederick E.C. Gardner q.v. Add: Liverpool 1908; Barnes, Surrey 1912; Leicester 1920. † L 21, RA 6.

RIDLEY, Ada Paul Exh. 1908
Widdington, Essex. † LS 4.

RIDLEY, Mrs. Charles Exh. 1897
Witchfield, Hants. † SWA 1.

RIDLEY, Dorothy Exh. 1907-13
Painter. † RID 6.

RIDLEY, Edward b. 1883
Portrait and figure painter. Art master Central School of Arts and Crafts, Birmingham and art critic to "Birmingham Mail". Exh. 1912-37. Add: Birmingham 1912; Rednal, nr. Birmingham 1930. † B 17, RA 5.

RIDLEY, Frank Exh. 1929
2 Agnes Place, Levenshulme, Manchester. † L 1.

RIDLEY, Joy Exh. 1932
27 Young Street, London. † SWA 1.

RIDLEY, Miss M.E. Exh. 1912
Oxted, Surrey. † SWA 1.

RIDLEY, Matthew White* 1837-1888
Landscape, portrait and genre painter. b. Newcastle on Tyne. Studied R.A. Schools and under Smirke and Dobson. Add: London 1880. † G 1, GI 2, RA 5, RI 1.

RIDLEY, Viscountess Rosamund Exh. 1913-29
Sculptor. London 1913; Dorking, Surrey 1929. † I 5, L 1, RA 4.

RIDLEY-SMITH, Mrs. Exh. 1920-22
309 Yardley Road, South Yardley, Birmingham. † B 3.

RIDPATH, Mrs. Exh. 1896
12 West Kensington Gardens, London. † SWA 3.

RIDSDALE, E.S. Exh. 1905
4 Albert Road, Evesham, Worcs. † B 2.

RIEDER, Marcel b. 1852
French artist. Exh. 1901-11. Add: Paris. † L 3.

RIEGELHUTH, Miss D. Exh. 1918
Three Arts Club, 19A Marylebone Road, London. † RA 1.

RIEU, Charles Exh. 1899
5 St. Johns Wood Studios, London. † L 1.

RIGBY, A.B. Exh. 1902-26
Liscard, Cheshire 1902; New Brighton, Cheshire 1916. † L 6.

RIGBY, Cuthbert 1850-1935
Landscape painter and watercolourist. b. Liverpool. Studied under W.J. Bishop. A.R.W.S. 1877. Add: Broughton in Furness, Lancs. 1880; Southport, Lancs. 1882; Seascale via Carnforth 1884; Kendal 1900; Windermere 1901; Ambleside 1906. † B 12, DOW 2, L 95, M 16, RA 2, RHA 3, ROI 1, RWS 299..

RIGBY, George Exh. 1883
8 Minster Buildings, Church Street, Liverpool. † L 1.

RIGBY, Helen Exh. 1923-27
Portrait painter. London 1923; Blackpool 1926. † L 3, M 1, RA 1.

RIGBY, Harold Ainsworth Exh. 1904-15
Decorative painter and teacher. b. Preston. Studied Royal College of Art. Add: Preston, Lancs. 1904; London 1906; Christs Hospital, Horsham, Sussex 1913. † L 1, RA 5.

RIGBY, Honora M. Exh. 1888-1915
Sculptor. Abbots Heyes, Chester. † B 12, GI 9, L 59, M 14, NG 1, RA 8, RBA 3, RHA 17, RSA 7.

RIGBY, May Exh. 1913-14
77 Hallan Street, Portland Place, London. † L 7, RA 1.

RIGG, Alfred Exh. 1895-97
Landscape painter. 44 Kirkgate, Bradford. † RA 6.

RIGG, Arthur H. Exh. 1882-1906
Landscape painter. Bradford. † B 3, G 3, GI 2, L 7, M 9, NG 4, RA 2, RBA 3, RHA 1.

RIGG, Ernest Higgins* Exh. 1897-1923
Portrait, landscape and animal painter. b. Bradford, Yorks. Studied Juliens, Paris. Add: Hinderwell, Yorks. 1897; 1904 and 1909; Bradford 1900 and 1917; Catsfield, Sussex 1908; Shipley, Yorks. 1918; Richmond, Yorks. 1919. † L 6, M 1, RA 20, RBA 1.

RIGG, J.E. Exh. 1882-84
39 Inverleith Row, Edinburgh. † RSA 2.

RIGG, William Exh. 1907
79 West Regent Street, Glasgow. † GI 1.

RIGGALL, L. Exh. 1911-14
Nottingham. † N 4.

RIGHTON, Katherine H. Exh. 1897-1935
Figure painter. London 1897 and 1921; Hockley Heath, Warwicks. 1910. † B 2, GI 1, L 3, RA 3, RHA 1, ROI 1, SWA 2.

RILEY, A. Muriel Exh. 1900
30 Clarendon Square, Leamington Spa, Warwicks. † B 2.

RILEY, Mrs. C. Exh. 1924
Painter. 11 Caunton Avenue, Mapperley, Notts. † N 1.

RILEY, F. Exh. 1921
Watercolour painter. 87 Kingsway, Ilkeston, Derbys. † N 1.

RILEY, Harry b. 1895
Watercolour painter and commercial artist. Studied Bolt Court 1910-15 and St. Martins School of Art. R.I. 1940. Exh. 1932-40. Add: London. † AR 3, RA 3, RBA 6, RI 8, ROI 1.

RILEY, Jessie Exh. 1888
6 Royal Terrace, Crosshill, Glasgow. † GI 1.

RILEY, James A.H. Exh. 1930
36 Florence Road, West Bromwich. † B 1.

RILEY, Miss K. Exh. 1885
School Lane, Heaton Chapel, Manchester. † M 1.

RILEY, Kate E. Exh. 1910-29
Mrs. Turner. Collaborated with R. Turner q.v. Add: London. † B 2, L 294, RCA 1.

RILEY, Laura C. Newton Exh. 1899
10 Belgrave Terrace, Huddersfield. † RMS 1.

RILEY, Lizzie L. Exh. 1892-98
Landscape painter. 18 Belgrave Square, Nottingham. † N 6.

RILEY, Reginald R. b. 1895
Landscape painter. Studied St. Albans Art School. Exh. 1934-40. Add: London. † RI 4.

RILEY, Thomas Exh. 1880-92
Painter and etcher. Chelsea, London. † G 5, L 17, M 4, NG 4, RA 19, RBA 5, RE 5, RI 4, ROI 6.

RILEY, William Edward 1852-1937
Landscape painter and architect. R.B.A. 1906. Exh. from 1906. Add: London. † GI 1, RA 4, RBA 208.

RILLIE, A. Exh. 1900-1
Fenwickland, Ayr. N.B. † GI 2.

RIME, M. Exh. 1918
7 Rue Periere Annecy, Haute Savoie, France. † RA 1.

RIMELL, Miss D.M. Exh. 1929-34
Mrs. D. Haydon. Add: Wold's End, Campden, Glos. † B 5, SWA 3.

RIMER, William Exh. 1888
Portrait and figure painter. 80 Newman Street, Oxford Street, London. † RBA 1.

RIMINGTON, Alexander Wallace d. 1918
Watercolour painter. R.B.A. 1903, A.R.E. 1887. Married Evelyn Jane R. q.v. Add: Weston super Mare 1880 and 1883; London 1882, 1884 and 1887; Meran, South Austria 1886. † FIN 681, G 1, LEI 1, NG 2, RA 34, RBA 41, RE 32, RI 6, ROI 2.

RIMINGTON, Evelyn Jane Exh. 1897-1939
nee Whyley. Watercolour landscape painter and architect. A.S.W.A. 1904, S.W.A. 1918. Married Alexander Wallace R. q.v. Add: Alton Vicarage, Hants. 1897; London 1905. † FIN 108, L 3, RA 2, RI 1, SWA 109, WG 66.

RIMMER, Alfred 1829-1893
Painter, illustrator and author. Add: Chester 1882. † L 3, M 2.

RIMMER, Miss D. Exh. 1892-1926
Woolton, Liverpool 1892; Malpas, Cheshire 1922. † L 18.

RIMMER, Edward Exh. 1926-37
Architect. Liverpool 1926; Rock Ferry, Cheshire 1927. † L 3, RA 4.

RIMMER, Heber Exh. 1891-92
Architect. 6 Abbey Square, Chester. † L 1, RA 1.

RIMMER, Isabel Exh. 1928-29
Strathmore, Freshfield, nr. Liverpool. † L 2.

RIMMER, John Exh. 1910
2 Frost Street, Liverpool. † L 1.

RIMMER, Kate Exh. 1905
21 Welbeck Road, Birkdale, Southport, Lancs. † L 1.

RIMMER, Ned Exh. 1905-10
30 Rock Lane East, Rock Ferry, Cheshire. † L 2.

RIMMER, Oswald Exh. 1905-33
Liverpool. † L 3.

RIMMER, Mrs. Percy E.
See WILSON, Miss A.

RIMMINGTON, Frank Exh. 1908-33
Architect and architectural perspective and watercolour painter. b. Epworth, Lincs. Studied Liverpool. Add: Liverpool. † L 24, RA 1.

RIMMINGTON, Miss F.M. Exh. 1907-16
London. † L 2, LS 12, RA 1.

RIMMINGTON, L. Exh. 1927
Eardley Road, London. † SWA 1.

RINALDI, Claudio* Exh. 1881-97
Figure painter. Florence. † M 1, RHA 1.

RING, Ethel S. Exh. 1884
Portrait artist. 10 Fitzroy Street, Fitzroy Square, London. † RA 1.

RINGEL, Daniel Exh. 1886
Medallionist. 29 Cite d'Autin, Paris. † RA 1.

RINGER, Mrs. Frederica A. Exh. 1913

RINTOUL, Alexander Exh. 1884
27 Elder Street, Edinburgh. † RSA 1.

RINTOUL, David Exh. 1892-1919
Tollcross 1892; Glasgow 1902; Renfrew, N.B. 1904. † GI 9.

RINZI, Ernest c.1829-1902
Miniature painter. R.M.S. 1896. Add: London. † RA 44, RMS 24.

RIOS, da See D

RIOU, Louis Exh. 1924-25
† GOU 3.

RIPLEY, Miss O.C. Exh. 1915-16
5 St. Mary Abbott's Terrace, High Street, Kensington, London. † RI 3, ROI 1.

RIPLEY, W.G. Exh. 1921-29
Landscape painter. 198 Wilford Road, Nottingham. † N 31.

RIPPIN, Dorothy C. Exh. 1931
Hughenden, Lenzie, Glasgow. † RSA 1.

RIPPIN, Miss Everilde Exh. 1934
Hughenden, Lenzie, Glasgow. † RSA 1.

RIPPON, Dorette Exh. 1937
Flower painter. † COO 7.

RISCHGITZ, Alice 1856-1936
Landscape and miniature portrait painter and teacher. Daughter of Edouard R. q.v. Exh. 1880-1900. Add: London. † D 2, RA 1, RBA 2.

RISCHGITZ, Edouard 1828-1909
Landscape and figure painter. b. Ghent, Belgium. Father of Alice and Mary R. q.v. R.E. 1881. Add: London. † RE 10.

RISCHGITZ, Mary Exh. 1883-1906
Flower painter. Daughter of Edouard R. q.v. Add: London. † B 6, L 3, M 1, RA 7, RBA 7, ROI 2, SWA 2.

RISING, Alice Exh. 1883
1 Park Place, Regents Park, London. † L 1.

RISK, Kathleen Exh. 1929
Gozarbank House, Corstorphine. † RSA 1.

RISOS, Mme. W.A. Exh. 1891
c/o Bourlet, 17 Nassau Street, London. † B 1.

RISSBROOK, C.W. Exh. 1927-30
70 Wheelwright Road, Erdington, Birmingham. † B 5.

RISSIK, Albert W.M. Exh. 1922-29
Watercolour portrait painter, etcher, wood engraver and teacher. Studied Slade School. Add: 11 Warwick Mansions, London. † D 2, P 2, NEA 1, WG 28.

RITCHARD, Edgar Exh. 1931-38
Theatrical designer. † GOU 1, RED 5.

RITCHIE, Adeline Exh. 1907-9
Mrs. Thackeray. London. † L 3, NG 4, P 3.

RITCHIE, Charles E. Exh. 1897-1918
Portrait and landscape painter. R.O.I. 1902. Add: London and Stonehaven, N.B. † FIN 32, GI 4, L 12, NG 11, RA 23, RBA 1, RI 2, ROI 27, RSA 3.

RITCHIE, Duncan S. Exh. 1888
13 Rosslyn Terrace, Kelvinside, Glasgow. † GI 1.

RITCHIE of DUNDEE Exh. 1929
Landscape and coastal painter. 18A Collingham Gardens, London. † RID 4.

RITCHIE, Eleanora Exh. 1880-84
Figure painter. 5 Denbigh Road, Bayswater, London. † L 3, RBA 1, SWA 1.

RITCHIE, Miss E.C. Exh. 1927-30
Walsall, Staffs. 1927 and 1930; Montrose 1928. † B 3, L 2, RSA 1.

RITCHIE, Fullarton Exh. 1880
3 Gladstone Place, London. † RSA 1.

RITCHIE, F. Mure Exh. 1928
Landscape painter. † AB 2.

RITCHIE, G.W.H. Exh. 1883
109 Liberty Street, New York City, U.S.A. † RE 2.

RITCHIE, H. Exh. 1880
9 Gardner's Crescent, London. † RSA 1.

RITCHIE, Hannah Exh. 1926-32
† L 1, M 1.

RITCHIE, Hope K. Exh. 1920-39
2 Ormidale Terrace, Edinburgh. † GI 2, RSA 1, RSW 4.

RITCHIE, Prof. James Exh. 1938-40
31 Mortonhall Road, Edinburgh. † RSA 2.

RITCHIE, M.E. Exh. 1934
29 Stanley Gardens, London. † SWA 2.

RITCHIE, M.J.G. Exh. 1918
† I 2.

RITCHIE, Trekkie b. 1902
Landscape and portrait painter. b. Natal. Studied Slade School. Married Peter Brooker q.v. Exh. 1926-38. Add: London. † GOU 8, NEA 10.

RITSCHEL, William Fredrik b. 1864
Marine and figure painter. b. Nueremberg, Bavaria. Studied Royal Academy, Munich. Exh. 1925-37. Add: Carmel Highlands, California, U.S.A. † RA 1, RSA 1.

RITTER, Lorenz Exh. 1881-86
Landscape painter. c/o Todd, 2 Connaught Square, London. † D 2, G 2, RA 1.

RITTER, Louis* 1854-1892
Portrait painter. 10 Park Road, Regents Park, London. † RA 1.

RIVA-MUNOZ, de la See D

RIVAZ, Claude F. Exh. 1895
Painter. The Old Courthouse, Knutsford, Cheshire. † M 3, RA 1.

RIVAZ, Richard Charles b. 1908
Painter, illustrator and woodcut artist. b. Shillong, India. Studied Winchester School of Art, and Royal College of Art. Exh. 1933-36. Add: London. † RA 3.

RIVERS, A.M. Exh. 1910-12
10 Redston Road, Hornsey, London. † M 1, RA 2, RI 1.

RIVERS, Elizabeth J. b. 1903
Painter and wood engraver. Studied Goldsmiths College 1921-24, R.A. Schools 1925-30 and Paris 1931-34. S.W.A. 1940 Exh. 1928-39. Add: London 1928; Kilmurry 1936; Sawbridge, Herts. 1939. † AB 1, RA 5, RHA 7, SWA 3.

RIVERS, Leopold* 1850-1905
Landscape painter. Studied under his father William Joseph R. R.B.A. 1890. "Stormy Weather" purchased by Chantrey Bequest 1892. † B 11, GI 2, L 7, M 10, RA 55, RBA 188, RI 31, ROI 24.

RIVERS, Richard Godfrey Exh. 1880-84
Landscape painter. 11 Palmeira Square, Brighton. † L 1, RA 1, RBA 1.

RIVERS-WILSON, Lady Exh. 1896
Scultpr. 16 Wilton Street, Belgravia, London. † RA 1.

RIVETT-CARNAC, Mrs. E. Exh. 1905-18
London 1905; Swefling Rectory, Saxmundham, Suffolk 1912; The Rectory, Woldingham, Surrey. 1916. † RA 5.

RIVIERE, Annette L. Exh. 1880-87
Miniature portrait painter. London. † D 4, RA 3, RI 1.

RIVIERE, Briton* 1840-1920
Genre and animal painter. Studied under his father William R. and under J. Pettie and W. Orchardson. Nephew of Henry Parsons and father of Hugh Goldwin R. q.v. A.R.A. 1878, R.A. 1880, R.E. 1881 (only), H.R.M.S. 1900. "Beyond Man's Footsteps" burchased by Chantrey Bequest 1894. Add: London. † AG 2, B 8, CAR 1, FIN 160, G 2, GI 5, L 25, LEI 1, M 12, NG 1, RA 105, RCA 1, RHA 3, ROI 1, RMS 1, RSA 4, TOO 7.

RIVIERE, Mrs. Briton Exh. 1927
† D 2.

RIVIERE, Charles Exh. 1913
24 Boulevard Richard Lenoir, Paris. † RSA 1.

RIVIERE, Hugh Goldwin 1869-1956
Portrait painter. b. Bromley, Kent. Son of Briton R. q.v. Studied R.A. Schools. R.O.I. 1907, R.P. 1900. Add: London. † B 6, FIN 1, GI 4, L 24, M 2, NG 6, P 96, RA 90, RHA 1, RID 6, ROI 2, RSA 1.

RIVIERE, Henry Parsons* 1811-1888
Genre landscape and portrait painter and watercolourist. Uncle of Briton R. q.v. R.I. 1834 (resigned 1850). A.R.W.S. 1852. Add: Rome and London. † AG 3, B 11, L 10, M 2, RA 2, RBA 3, RWS 42.

RIVINGTON, Margaretta Agnes Exh. 1884-1904
Flower painter. London. † GI 1, SWA 11.

RIX, Miss F.C. Exh. 1911
Lewisham. † SWA 1.

RIX-NICHOLAS, E. Hilda Exh. 1916-32
Landscape and figure painter. b. Australia. Add: Paris and London. † BA 69, I 1, L 1, P 2, RA 2, RBA 1, RHA 4, ROI 1, SWA 1.

RIXON, Laura Exh. 1886
Still life painter. 57 St. Charles Square, London. † RBA 1, ROI 1.

RIXON, William Augustus Exh. 1880-1936
Landscape painter. R.B.A. 1884. Add: Cookham Dean, Berks. 1880; London 1889; Bridgwater, Somerset 1899; North Leach, Glos. 1918. † AG 1, COO 2, D 2, DOW 3, G 1, L 3, NEA 2, RA 10, RBA 17, RI 7, ROI 3.

RIZO, T. Exh. 1882
27 Boulevard Courcelles, Paris. † L 1.

ROACH, Addie Exh. 1931-32
Birmingham. † B 2.

ROASE, R. William Arthur Exh. 1887
6 Wells Street, Oxford Street, London. † RI 2.

ROBB, Alexander B. Exh. 1897
Architect. 3 Stockwell Park Walk, Brixton, London. † RA 1.

ROBB, Edith Exh. 1889
Flower painter. 10 Woodberry Grove, Finsbury Park, London. † SWA 1.

ROBB, Emma Exh. 1886-96
Busby House, Busby, Glasgow. † GI 10, RSA 3.

ROBB, Mrs. E.M. Exh. 1934
17 Nassau Street, London. † RSA 1.

ROBB, G.M. Exh. 1880-81
Landscape painter. Mistley, Manningtree, Essex. † RA 1, RBA 1.

ROBB, John Exh. 1901
34 St. Enoch Square, Glasgow. † GI 1.

ROBB, William George 1872-1940
Landscape and figure painter. b. Ilfracombe. Studied Aberdeen School of Art and under Bouguereau in Paris. Add: London 1900 and 1937; Limpsfield, Surrey 1908. † BG 80, CHE 1, FIN 171, L 1, M 1, RA 10.

ROBBE, L. Exh. 1883
Painter. † FIN 1.

ROBBE, Manuel Exh. 1909
c/o M. Georges Petit, 8 Rue de Seze, Paris. † L 1.

ROBBINS, Anna Exh. 1881-85
Flower and fruit painter. Shropham Vicarage, Thetford, Norfolk 1881; c/o S. Jennings, 16 Duke Street, Manchester Square, London 1885. † L 1, SWA 5.

ROBBINS, Miss M. Exh. 1887-1900
Birmingham. † B 2.

ROBBINS, Miss M.C. Exh. 1920
Arthur House, Wellington Road, Edgbaston, Birmingham. † B 1.

ROBBINS, Rose H. Exh. 1882-1902
Wellington Road, Edgbaston, Birmingham. † B 15, L 1, RHA 4.

ROBECK, de see D

ROBERT, Caroline Exh. 1884-93
Flower and fruit painter. Sutton, Surrey 1884; Sidcup, Kent 1893. † RA 1, SWA 9.

ROBERT, H. Lucien Exh. 1913
97 Rue Perronet, Neuilly sur Seine, France. † L 1.

ROBERT, P. Exh. 1882
3 Boulevard de Clichy, Paris. † GI 1.

ROBERT, Theophile b. 1879
French artist. Exh. 1923. † GOU 3.

ROBERTON, Alfred J. Exh. 1883-86
Landscape painter. 42 Oakfield Road, Kentish Town, London. † RBA 6.

ROBERTON, Jean Exh. 1939
Nuneaton, Warwicks. † RCA 2.

ROBERTS, Annie Exh. 1880-1910
Watercolour landscape painter. London 1880; West Bromwich 1905; Erdington, Birmingham 1910. † B 2, RBA 7.

ROBERTS, A.B. Llewelyn Exh. 1923-35
Architect. London. † RA 6, RSA 2.

ROBERTS, Austin Crompton Exh. 1928-40
Liverpool 1928; Teddington-on-Thames 1940. † GI 1, L 3.

ROBERTS, A.J. Rooker Exh. 1928-40
London 1928; Pewsey, Wilts. 1939. † RBA 2, RI 3.

ROBERTS, A. Leonard Exh. 1932-35
Architect. The Castle, Winchester, Hants. † RA 2.

ROBERTS, Ada M. Exh. 1899-1909
Broadway, Worcs. 1899 and 1909; Birmingham 1904. † B 11, L 1.

ROBERTS, A.T. Exh. 1900-14
Leicester. † N 5.

ROBERTS, Bertha Exh. 1929-31
Landscape painter. 11 Julian Road, West Bridgford, Nottingham. † N 2.

ROBERTS, Beryl Exh. 1928
2 Well Street, Ruthin, North Wales. † RCA 1.

ROBERTS, Bessie Exh. 1909
Ivinghoe, Tring, Herts. † D 2.

ROBERTS, Bruce b. 1918
Painter, illustrator and designer. Studied Liverpool School of Art 1936-38, St. Martin School of Art and Chelsea Polytechnic 1938-39. Exh. 1939. † GOU 1.

ROBERTS, C. Exh. 1921
Landscape painter. "Journal", Nottingham. † N 1.

ROBERTS, Mrs. Chandler Exh. 1885
Watercolour flower painter. The Royal Mint, London. † RI 1.

ROBERTS, Cyril 1871-1949
Portrait and landscape painter and black and white artist. Studied Royal College of Art 1889-92, Slade School 1892-94 and Julian's, Paris 1894-96. R.B.A. 1904. Add: London 1889; Langley, Bucks. 1936. † B 4, CHE 1, I 2, L 14, LS 3, M 2, P 7, RA 6, RBA 174, RI 6, ROI 3, WG 176.

ROBERTS, Charles H. Exh. 1926
Architect. 58 Frith Street, London. † RA 1.

ROBERTS, Miss Dorothy Freeborn see MARTIN

ROBERTS, Mrs. Dorothy M. Exh. 1935-40
Figure and flower painter. Way High, Speldhurst, Tunbridge Wells, Kent. † NEA 2, RA 4, ROI 2.

ROBERTS, Edwin* Exh. 1881-86
Genre painter. London. † RA 3, RBA 17.

ROBERTS, Mrs. Etienne Exh. 1892-93
Flower painter. 11 Belgrave Road, South Norwood, London. † RBA 1, ROI 1.

ROBERTS, Enid Chidlam Exh. 1924-30
Painter. Aberdovey, North Wales. † L 5, RCA 1.

ROBERTS, Edith H. Exh. 1897-1905
Liscard, Cheshire 1897; New Brighton, Cheshire 1905. † L 7.

ROBERTS, Ellis William 1860-1930
Portrait and china painter. b. Burslem, Staffs. Studied Royal College of Art 1882-83 (Travelling scholarship, Prix de Rome 1884-85) and Julian's, Paris 1887-88. R.P. 1893. Add: London. † G 1, GI 1, L 12, P 98, RA 16.

ROBERTS, F.A. Exh. 1933
Architect. Mold, Flints. † RCA 5.

ROBERTS, George Exh. 1884
130 Princes Street, Manchester. † M 1.

ROBERTS, G.H. Exh. 1894
35 Bull Street, Birmingham. † B 1.

ROBERTS, Gwyneth M. Exh. 1925-26
Eryl, College Road North, Blundellsands, Liverpool. † L 2.

ROBERTS, H. Exh. 1884-95
† TOO 2.

ROBERTS, H. Exh. 1919-30
St. Helens, Lancs. † L 9.

ROBERTS, Hilda Exh. 1922-40
Portrait and figure painter. London 1922; Milltown, Co. Dublin 1927; Bray 1931; Newtown School, Waterford 1933. † RHA 35.

ROBERTS, Henry Benjamin 1832-1915
Genre painter. b. Liverpool. R.B.A. 1878. A.R.I. 1867, R.I. 1870 (resigned 1884). Add: London 1880; Leyton, Essex 1883 and 1897; Ness, Cheshire 1890; Trefriw, North Wales 1895. † B 1, L 18, RI 22.

ROBERTS, H. George Exh. 1919
458 City Road Park, Sheffield. † ROI 1.

ROBERTS, Herbert H. Exh. 1887-1912
Figure painter. London. † RA 2.

ROBERTS, Helen S.S. Exh. 1884
Painter. 106 Cazenove Road, Upper Clapton, London. † SWA 1.

ROBERTS, Henry William Exh. 1885-86
Watercolour landscape painter. Leicester. † RI 2.

ROBERTS, Ivy Exh. 1920-22
103 Garmoyle Road, Sefton Park, Liverpool. † L 7.

ROBERTS, Mrs. Irene M. Exh. 1929
82 Holmefield Road, Aigburth, Liverpool. † L 2.

ROBERTS, John Exh. 1882-1930
Liverpool 1882; Edinburgh 1889; Stirling 1891; Glasgow 1896; Dunblane 1897; Callander 1906. † GI 38, L 3, RSA 17, RSW 4.

ROBERTS, J. Eric Exh. 1922-29
Wolverhampton. † B 5.

ROBERTS, J.W. Exh. 1906-14
Leamington Spa, Warwicks. 1906; Gloucester 1914. † B 1, LS 6.

ROBERTS, Mrs. Kittie Exh. 1928-34
Painter. A.S.W.A. 1933. London. † RA 1, ROI 2, SWA 10.

ROBERTS, Katharine M. Exh. 1897-1939
Painter and etcher. Liverpool 1897; Shrewsbury 1904; London 1913; Painswick, Glos. 1931; Cheltenham 1939. † B 2, L 10, RA 9.

ROBERTS, Lancelot Exh. 1912-29
Painter. Old Trafford, Manchester. † B 5, L 7, M 1, RA 1, RCA 105.

ROBERTS, Leonora E.O. Exh. 1920-30
Animal painter. 32 Marlborough Road, Donnybrook, Ireland. † RHA 7.

ROBERTS, Margaret Exh. 1885-98
Flower painter. † SWA 3.

ROBERTS, Marion Exh. 1885-86
Watercolour painter. 14 The Grove, Clapham Common, London. † RBA 1, RI 2.

ROBERTS, Mary Exh. 1935-39
Llandudno, Wales. † RCA 2.

ROBERTS, Morley Exh. 1929
Watercolour landscape painter. † AB 52.

ROBERTS, Mildred Crompton Exh. 1892-1937
Watercolour flower painter. London. † COO 3, RI 4, SWA 3.

ROBERTS, M. Hope Exh. 1894-96
22 Lower Dominick Street, Dublin. † RHA 8.

ROBERTS, Mrs. Maud M. Exh. 1916-30
Miniature portrait painter. Blackheath, London. † RA 3.

ROBERTS, Major P. Exh. 1880-81
Little Grange, Droghede. † RHA 3.

ROBERTS, Rachel b. 1908
Wood engraver. Studied Swindon Art School and Royal College of Art, 1930-33. Exh. 1937-39. Add: St. Leonards-on-Sea, Sussex. † RA 2.

ROBERTS, R.B. Exh. 1894
c/o Messrs. R. Jackson and Sons, 3 Slater Street, Liverpool. † L 4.

ROBERTS, Miss R.E.F. Exh. 1890
Holland Road, Brixton. † SWA 1.

ROBERTS, R.J. Exh. 1898-1907
Stirling 1898; Dollar, N.B. 1899. † GI 4, L 2, RSA 5.

ROBERTS, Mrs. R.J. Exh. 1933
Portrait painter. 148 Albert Palace Mansions, London. † RA 1.

ROBERTS, R.P. Exh. 1905-28
Liverpool. † L 19.

ROBERTS, R. Stanley Exh. 1929
4 Brentford Street, Wallasey, Cheshire. † L 1.

ROBERTS, Miss R.W. Exh. 1916-20
London. † L 1, RA 2, RI 1.

ROBERTS, Tom 1856-1931
Landscape and figure painter. b. Dorchester. Travelled on the continent and spent some time in Australia. Exh. 1893-1921. Add: Sydney, Australia 1893; London 1904. † NEA 2, NG 2, P 4, RA 8, ROI 7, WG 50.

ROBERTS, Thomas Edward 1820-1901
Portrait, genre and historical painter and engraver. R.B.A. 1855. Exh. 1880-99. Add: Kentish Town, London 1880; Tufnell Park Road, London 1882. † GI 2, L 1, M 2, RA 2, RBA 66, ROI 5.

ROBERTS, T.P. Exh. 1883-90
3 Hardy Street, Liverpool. † L 2.

ROBERTS, Violet M. Exh. 1903-4
Miniature portrait painter. Claremont, St. Helier, Jersey, C.I. † RA 1, SWA 1.

ROBERTS, Miss W. Exh. 1914
1 Palace Green, Kensington, London. † RA 1.

ROBERTS, William Exh. 1884
6 Tower View, Seacombe, Liverpool. † L 1.

ROBERTS, William Patrick b. 1895
Painter. Studied Slade School and St. Martins School of Art. Official War Artist World War I. Member London Group 1914. Exh. 1913-39. Add: London. † AG 2, ALP 1, CHE 8, COO 42, GOU 6, L 1, LEF 80, LEI 26, NEA 10, RED 1, RSA 5, TOO 2.

ROBERTS, W. Pierce Exh. 1902-38
Sculptor. Hoole, Chester 1902; Chester 1908; Prestatyn 1914; London 1924; Arnold, Notts. 1935. † L 4, LS 2, M 2, N 9, RCA 1.

ROBERTS, Winifred Russell Exh. 1893-1907
Watercolour landscape painter. London. † DOW 129, RBA 4, RI 3, SWA 5.

ROBERTS, W.T.B. Exh. 1880-94
Landscape painter. A.R.E. 1892 (ceased 1896). Add: Winchester, Hants. † RA 1, RE 25.

ROBERTSON, A. Exh. 1918
† GI 1.

ROBERTSON, Alice Exh. 1888-1902
Clonkskeagh, Dublin 1888; Harrow-on-the-Hill, Middlesex 1902. † B 1, RHA 5.

ROBERTSON, Arthur d. 1911
Landscape painter. A.R.E. 1888. Add: Surbiton, Surrey 1882; London 1887; Godalming 1898. † L 13, M 2, P 1, RA 9, RBA 15, RE 50, RI 12, ROI 1, TOO 1.

ROBERTSON, A.D. Exh. 1881
48 Dundas Street, Glasgow. † RSA 1.

ROBERTSON, Miss A. Hope Exh. 1904
Penlee, Canterbury. † D 2.

ROBERTSON, Canon A.J. Exh. 1934-38
Watercolour painter. † WG 12.

ROBERTSON, Miss A.K. Exh. 1908-14
London 1908; Edinburgh 1914. † GI 1, M 1, RA 2, RSA 1.

ROBERTSON, Agnes Muir Exh. 1898
U.P. Manse, North Berwick. † RSA 1.

ROBERTSON, Miss A.S. Exh. 1927-28
27 Victoria Park, Wavertree, Liverpool. † L 2.

ROBERTSON, A. Struan Exh. 1903-18
Glasgow 1903; Eaglesham, near Glasgow 1914. † GI 14.

ROBERTSON, Barbara Exh. 1935-37
Landscape and portrait painter. 10 Raglan Road, Dublin. † RHA 5.

ROBERTSON, Bessie M. Exh. 1897-1922
Edinburgh. † RSA 27.

ROBERTSON, Cecile see WALTON

ROBERTSON, Charles* 1844-1891
Landscape and genre painter and engraver. R.E. 1885, A.R.W.S. 1885, R.W.S. 1891. Father of Percy R. q.v. Add: Walton-on-Thames 1880; Godalming, Surrey 1881. † AG 27, D 15, DOW 201, FIN 132, GI 1, L 11, M 2, RA 10, RE 16, RI 1, ROI 1, RWS 25.

ROBERTSON, C.C. Exh. 1886
Painter. London. † SWA 1.

ROBERTSON, Charles F. Exh. 1888-91
Romford, Essex. † RE 3.

ROBERTSON, Mrs. C.K. (Jane) Exh. 1885-1923
Edinburgh 1885; Carshalton, Surrey 1898; Chelsea, London 1899. † RA 10, RSA 1, SWA 1.

ROBERTSON, Charles Kay Exh. 1888-1931
Portrait, figure and flower painter. Edinburgh 1888; London 1901. † GI 9, L 1, P 1, RA 14, RSA 57.

ROBERTSON, David 1834-1925
Architect. A.R.S.A. 1893. Add: Edinburgh. † RSA 16.

ROBERTSON, David Exh. 1897-1901
Kilmarnock. † GI 2, RSA 1.

ROBERTSON, David b. 1885
Etcher and architect. b. Strathblane. Studied Glasgow School of Art. Served with Artists Rifles World War I. Exh. 1936. † FIN 3.

ROBERTSON, Delphine Exh. 1927
Miniature portrait painter. Sandhurst, St. Georges Road, St. Margarets-on-Thames. † RA 1.

ROBERTSON, David M. Exh. 1883-94
Landscape painter. Edinburgh 1883; School of Art, Douglas, I.o.M. 1885. † GI 2, L 1, RA 1, RSA 9.

ROBERTSON, Elspeth Exh. 1927-30
Wood engraver. c/o St. Georges Gallery, 32A George Street, London. † GI 1, RED 1.

ROBERTSON, Eric b. 188
Portrait, landscape and figure painter. b. Dumfries. Studied Edinburgh College of Art. Exh. 1908-33. Add: Edinburgh 190 Liverpool 1925. † G 1, GI 12, GOU I 3, L 39, M 1, RA 2, RSA 47, RSW 3.

ROBERTSON, Ewan B. Exh. 1911-1
8 Murrayfield Drive, Edinburgh. † L RSA 5.

ROBERTSON, Emily C. Exh. 189
Naparina, Cambuslang. † RSW 2.

ROBERTSON, Elsa D. Exh. 190
205 Newhaven Road, Edinburgh † RSA 1.

ROBERTSON, Eva H. Exh. 1931-3
Edinburgh. † RSA 5.

ROBERTSON, E.L. Exh. 1885-8
Painter. 35 Park Road, Haverstock Hill London. † SWA 2.

ROBERTSON, Elsie L. Exh. 1927-4
Mrs. David R. Still life, portrait and landscape painter. 3 Upper Cheyne Row London. † NEA 2, RA 9, SWA 2.

ROBERTSON, Mrs. Ethel Lily Exh. 1915-3
Miniature portrait painter. London † NEA 1, RA 8, RMS 2.

ROBERTSON, Ellen McT. Exh. 1901-1
Edinburgh. † D 1, RSA 7, RSW 1.

ROBERTSON, Edith S. Exh. 192
52 Beech Hill Road, Sheffield. † L 2.

ROBERTSON, Florence G. Exh. 1923-2
Miniature painter. 8 Cartwright Gardens London. † L 1, RA 1, RMS 1.

ROBERTSON, Mrs. F.M. Exh. 1936-4
24 Clarendon Avenue, Leamington Spa Warwicks. † B 4.

ROBERTSON, G. Exh. 1887-9
Leatherhead, Surrey. † RE 2.

ROBERTSON, George Edward* b. 186
Portrait, figure, historical and landscape painter. Studied St. Martins School of Art and under his father William R. Exh 1883-1926. Add: Battersea, London † GI 2, L 5, M 1, RA 29, RBA 3, ROI 3

ROBERTSON, Henry Exh. 1885-98
Landscape painter. A.R.E. 1896. Add: Ipswich 1885; Tonbridge, Kent 1896 Norwich 1898. † D 5, M 1, NG 2, RA 3, RE 9.

ROBERTSON, Howard b. 1888
Architect. b. U.S.A. Studied A.A. London and Ecole des Beaux Arts, Paris. Exh. 1935. Add: 54 Bedford Square, London. † RA 1.

ROBERTSON, Helen H. Exh. 1890-92
Painter. Dowan Hill Gardens, Glasgow. † FIN 1, GI 1.

ROBERTSON, Mrs. H.J. Exh. 1880-99
Hillhead, Glasgow. † GI 26, L 13, RSA 21.

ROBERTSON, Henry Robert 1839-1921
Landscape, figure and portrait painter, etcher and engraver. R.E. 1881, R.M.S. 1896, H.R.M.S. 1911. Father of Janet S.R. q.v. Add: 1 Steele's Studios, Haverstock Hill, London. † B 2, GI 1, L 22, M 2, NG 2, RA 36, RBA 4, RE 69, RI 8, RMS 36, ROI 2.

ROBERTSON, Isobel Exh. 1897
17 Nottingham Place, London. † SWA 1.

ROBERTSON, J. Exh. 1909
† TOO 1.

ROBERTSON, James Exh. 1888
16 Carlingford Road, Drumcondra, Dublin. † RHA 2.

ROBERTSON, John Exh. 1885
Architect. Inverness. † RSA 2.

ROBERTSON, John Exh. 1883-91
Dunfermline 1883; Edinburgh 1891. † RSA 5.

ROBERTSON, J.B. Exh. 1926-36
Glasgow. † GI 8, RSA 3.

ROBERTSON, James G. Exh. 1880-86
Edinburgh. † RSA 8.

ROBERTSON, J. Murray Exh. 1885-98
Architect. Edinburgh 1885; Dundee 1897. † GI 1, RA 1, RSA 2.

ROBERTSON, Janet S. b. 1880
Watercolour portrait, miniature and landscape painter. Daughter of Henry Robert R. q.v. Studied Royal College of Art. A.R.M.S. 1909, R.M.S. 1911. Exh. 1902-30. Add: Elworthy Terrace, Hampstead, London. † GI 1, L 7, M 1, RA 40, RMS 41.

ROBERTSON, Joan Souter Exh. 1936-37
Flower and portrait painter. † NEA 2, RED 2.

ROBERTSON, Mrs. L. Murray Exh. 1902-7
Figure painter. London. † BG 4, SWA 1.

ROBERTSON, Miss M. Exh. 1920-27
10 Grafton Square, Glasgow. † GI 2, L 2.

ROBERTSON, M'Culloch Exh. 1905-16
Muckart by Dollar, N.B. 1905; Dunkeld 1912; London 1913. † GI 1, L 6, LS 2, RI 12.

ROBERTSON, Minnie B. Exh. 1909
Bellarina, Ayr. † GI 1.

ROBERTSON, Mrs. Mabel C. Exh. 1924
Landscape and portrait painter. The Rosary, East Leake, near Loughborough, Leics. † N 2.

ROBERTSON, Margaret Jean Exh. 1936
Stratford Road, London. † SWA 2.

ROBERTSON, Margaret M. Exh. 1899-1905
18 North Road, West Kirby, Cheshire. † L 5.

ROBERTSON, Mrs. Nora Murray Exh. 1908-9
Dublin 1908; London 1909. † LS 3, RHA 1.

ROBERTSON, Percy b. 1869
Watercolour landscape painter and etcher. b. Ballagio, Italy. Son of Charles R. q.v. A.R.E. 1887, R.E. 1908. Exh. 1885-1930. Add: Godalming, Surrey 1885; London 1901 and 1916; Maidenhead, Berks. 1906. † AG 7, L 20, M 1, RA 33, RE 166, RI 15.

ROBERTSON, R.C. d. 1910
Painter. Exh. from 1894. Add: 15 Shandwick Place, Edinburgh. † B 1, GI 4, L 5, M 1, RHA 2, RSA 16.

ROBERTSON, Mrs. R.C. see MOORE, Eleanor

ROBERTSON, R. Currie Exh. 1911-14
59 Dean Street, Kilmarnock, N.B. and Glasgow. † GI 3.

ROBERTSON, Robert Cantley Exh. 1927-40
Edinburgh. † GI 2, RSA 16.

ROBERTSON, Dr. Robert Cecil Exh. 1932-40
Landscape painter. Married Eleanor Moore, q.v. Add: Kilmarnock and Edinburgh. † GI 9, RA 1, RSA 5.

ROBERTSON, Richard Ross b. 1914
Sculptor. Studied Glasgow 1932 and under T.B. Huxley-Jones in Aberdeen 1933-38. Exh. 1938. † RSA 1.

ROBERTSON, Stewart Exh. 1912-20
London. † GI 2, L 2, M 1, RSA 2.

ROBERTSON, Mrs. Stewart Exh. 1920-22
124 Cheyne Walk, Chelsea, London. † L 3.

ROBERTSON, Miss Struan Exh. 1938
149 Warrender Park Road, Edinburgh. † RSA 1.

ROBERTSON, T. Exh. 1890-96
178 George Street, Glasgow. † GI 3.

ROBERTSON, Thomas Exh. 1880
15 Haymarket Terrace, Edinburgh. † RSA 3.

ROBERTSON, Tom* b. 1850
Landscape and marine painter. Studied Glasgow School of Art and under Benjamin Constant in Paris. R.B.A. 1896, R.O.I. 1912 (Hon. Retd. 1937). Exh. 1880-1935. Add: Uddington 1880; Glasgow 1885; London 1899; Eastbourne 1935. † FIN 77, G 1, GI 92, GOU 70, I 4, L 11, LEI 59, M 2, NG 2, RA 15, RBA 52, RHA 1, RI 2, ROI 51, RSA 7, RSW 4.

ROBERTSON, T.S. Exh. 1893
† GI 4.

ROBERTSON, Thomas W. Exh. 1906-12
74 Norse Road, Scotstoun, N.B. † GI 2.

ROBERTSON, Victor John Exh. 1892-1909
Painter and illustrator. London. † L 3, RA 10.

ROBERTSON, W. Exh. 1931-33
41 Northumberland Street, Workington. † B 2.

ROBERTSON, William Exh. 1924
67 Connaught Road, Liverpool. † L 1.

ROBERTSON, Walford Graham* b. 1867
Portrait and landscape painter, illustrator, stage costume designer and playwright. Studied South Kensington and under Albert Moore. N.E.A. 1891, R.B.A. 1896, R.O.I. 1910, R.P. 1912. Exh. 1889-1933. Add: London. † B 16, BG 5, CAR 61, G 1, GI 9, GOU 13, L 27, LS 2, M 6, NEA 6, NG 24, P 23, RA 1, RBA 43, ROI 5.

ROBERTSON, Miss W.J. Exh. 1907
11 Thurlow Road, Hampstead, London. † RA 1.

ROBERTSON, W.T. Exh. 1909-27
Liverpool. † L 22.

ROBERTSON, W.W. Exh. 1890-91
3 Parliament Square, Edinburgh. † RSA 2.

ROBERTSON-RAMSEY, Miss Eden Exh. 1905
Cooling Castle, Rochester. † L 1, ROI 1, SWA 1.

ROBERTSON-REID, Doris Exh. 1928-37
Landscape painter. 1 Cathcart Road, Epsom, Surrey. † AB 3, SWA 1.

ROBEY, Eileen Exh. 1931
Portrait painter. Studied R.A. Schools. Add: London. † RED 1.

ROBEY, H.J. Exh. 1885
62 Dorset Street, Hulme, Manchester. † M 1.

ROBILLIARD, Miss M.H. Exh. 1908-20
Painter. Shortlands, Kent 1908; London 1911. † L 2, RA 7.

ROBIN, Miss G.F. Exh. 1911
Woodchurch Rectory, Birkenhead. † L 1.

ROBINET, Paul 1845-1932
French painter. Exh. 1883-85. Add: London 1883; Poissy, Seine et Oise, France 1885. † GI 1, RBA 1.

ROBINS, Edward C. Exh. 1880-90
Architect. Father of Ida Southwell Perrin, q.v. Add: London. † RA 3.

ROBINS, Gertrude M. Exh. 1887
Watercolour portrait painter. 149 Fellowes Road, Hampstead, London. † RA 1.

ROBINS, Ida Southwell See PERRIN

ROBINS, Mrs. L. Exh. 1900
Belmont, Darlaston. † B 1.

ROBINS, Mrs. M.L. Exh. 1915
Hop Springs, London Road, Knebworth, Herts. † RA 1.

ROBINS, Miss O. Exh. 1932-33
Purley, Caldy, Cheshire. † L 2.

ROBINS, Susan Exh. 1903-4
London. † D 6.

ROBINS, T.S. Exh. 1900-1
† TOO 2.

ROBINS, William Palmer b. 1882
Painter and etcher. Studied St. Martins School of Art, Goldsmiths College and Royal College of Art. Head of Etching Dept. L.C.C. Central School of Arts and Crafts. A.R.E. 1913, R.E. 1917. Exh. 1912-40. Add: Knebworth, Herts. 1912; Welwyn, Herts. 1916; Artists Rifles, Romford, Essex 1917; Bromley, Kent 1919; Sutton, Surrey 1926; London 1931. † CG 15, FIN 108, G 54, GI 9, I 2, L 21, LEI 15, NEA 11, RA 50, RCA 4, RE 96, RHA 3, RSA 16.

ROBINSON, Amy Exh. 1926-31
Sculptor. 16 Tyson Road, Forest Hill, London. † L 1, RA 3.

ROBINSON, Alexander Charles b. 1867
American artist. Braunton, North Devon 1900; Bruges, Belgium 1905. † GI 1, I 1, LS 3.

ROBINSON, A. Julius Exh. 1897-1930
London. † B 6, L 2, LS 7, RHA 5.

ROBINSON, Annie Louisa See SWYNNERTON

ROBINSON, Miss A.M. Exh. 1914-17
Wenden, Saffron Walden, Essex. † RA 3.

ROBINSON, Alan Marshall b. 1915
Figure painter. b. Toronto, Canada. Studied Bournemouth School of Art. Exh. 1940. Add: 14 Guildhall Road, Bournemouth. † RA 1.

ROBINSON, Anne Marjorie 1858-1924
Miniature portrait painter. A.R.M.S. 1912, A.S.W.A. 1918. Add: London 1911; Belfast 1917. † L 20, RA 10, RHA 16, RI 1, RMS 25, SWA 5.

ROBINSON, Arthur P. Exh. 1890-1900
Landscape painter. London 1890; Winchelsea, Sussex 1900. † B 1, RA 1, RHA 1.

ROBINSON, Barbara Cayley Exh. 1928-39
Painter. 1 Lansdown House, Lansdown Road, London. † GOU 1, NEA 2, RA 1, RID 2.

ROBINSON, Miss B.E. Exh. 1899
34 Addison Street, Nottingham. † N 1.

ROBINSON, Charles 1870-1937
Watercolour painter and illustrator. R.I. 1932. Add: London 1898; Chesham, Bucks. 1931. † AR 3, BK 90, GI 2, L 2, RA 10, RI 32.

ROBINSON, Constance C. McLean Exh. 1900-33
Figure painter. Liverpool. † L 17, RA 1, RMS 1.

ROBINSON, Charles F. d. 1896
Landscape painter and engraver. A.R.E. 1890. Add: London and Rainham, nr. Romford, Essex. † D 14, L 1, RA 3, RBA 8, RE 3, RI 1.

ROBINSON, Daisy Exh. 1896
Netterleigh, Chesterfield. † RI 1.

ROBINSON, Diana Exh. 1931
Flower painter. Stone Cottage, Nevells Road, Letchworth Garden City, Herts. † RA 1.

ROBINSON, Mrs. Dolly Exh. 1936
Painter. Sorrento Cottage, Dalkey, Co. Dublin. † RHA 1.

ROBINSON, Douglas Exh. 1939
Architect. 14 Hanover Square, London. † RA 1.

ROBINSON, Dorothy A.F. Exh. 1904-18
Southport, Lancs. 1904; Bromley, Kent 1918. † L 1, M 2, RA 2.

ROBINSON, Douglas F. 1864-1937
Landscape and figure painter. N.E.A. 1897. Add: Paris 1890; London 1897; Fernhurst, Sussex 1930. † FIN 56, GI 3, I 22, M 1, NEA 13, P 2, RA 5, RBA 3, ROI 1, RSA 8.

ROBINSON, Edith Exh. 1883
Winwood, Tunbridge Wells, Kent. † L 1.

ROBINSON, Eleanor Exh. 1895
Lamancha, Langside, Glasgow. † GI 1.

ROBINSON, Emily Exh. 1880-85
Fruit painter. 427 Kings Road, Chelsea, London. † SWA 4.

ROBINSON, Ernest Exh. 1890
Landscape painter. 8 Tadema Road, Chelsea, London. † RA 1.

ROBINSON, Edith Brearey Exh. 1889-93
Landscape, figure and flower painter. West Bank, Westbourne Grove, Scarborough, Yorks. † NEA 2, RA 2, RBA 3, RI 4.

ROBINSON, Evelyn Fothergill* Exh. 1908-18
Landscape painter. London. † BG 41, GOU 1, LS 9, NEA 3, SWA 6.

ROBINSON, Miss E.H. Exh. 1904-6
4 Aynhoe Mansions, Brook Green, London. † D 3, SWA 2.

ROBINSON, E. Julia Exh. 1881-1905
Landscape and figure painter. Travelled widely. Add: Hopedene, Dorking, Surrey. † B 10, FIN 115, G 2, L 1, RI 11, SWA 1.

ROBINSON, Miss F. Exh. 1920-24
27 Beaumont Street, Oxford. † SWA 10.

ROBINSON, Mrs. Frances Exh. 1939
Watercolour landscape painter. Abingdon, Berks. † RA 1.

ROBINSON, Frederick Cayley* 1862-1927
Painter, decorator, illustrator, poster artist and theatrical designer. Studied St. Johns Wood School of Art, R.A. Schools and Julians, Paris 1890-92. Professor of figure composition and decoration Glasgow School of Art 1914-24. N.E.A. 1912, A.R.A. 1921, R.B.A. 1890, R.O.I. 1906, A.R.W.S. 1911, R.W.S. 1918. "Pastoral" purchased by Chantrey Bequest 1924. Add: London 1887 and 1901; Florence 1900. † CAR 40, GI 16, GOU 2, I 1, L 21, LEI 95, LS 7, M 4, NEA 6, NG 1, RA 14, RBA 37, ROI 7, RSA 4, RSW 1, RWS 30.

ROBINSON, Mrs. F.G. Exh. 1924
Portrait and landscape painter. Wandesley Lodge, Ilkeston, Derby. † N 3.

ROBINSON, F.S. Exh. 1890-95
London. † B 6.

ROBINSON, Francis Stanislaus b. 1885
Landscape painter. b. Manchester. Studied Liverpool. Exh. 1926. Add: 133 Seabank Road, Wallasey, Cheshire. † RCA 1.

ROBINSON, Gerald Exh. 1883-1901
Engraver. A.R.E. 1892. Related to Sir John Charles R. q.v. Add: London 1883; Leatherhead, Surrey 1888; Swanage, Dorset 1897. † B 2, G 1, RA 10.

ROBINSON, Grace Exh. 1922
† I 3.

ROBINSON, Gregory Exh. 1907-34
Marine painter. b. Plymouth. Studied R.A. Schools. Spent 4 years at sea World War I. Add: Southampton 1907; Hamble, Hants. 1910. † L 1, RA 1, WG 91.

ROBINSON, George Crosland d. 1930
Portrait painter. Paris 1882; London 1884. † L 4, M 2, NG 1, P 3, RA 11, RBA 1, RHA 2, ROI 4.

ROBINSON, Geoffrey Favatt Exh. 1931-37
† NEA 2.

ROBINSON, George Gidley b. 1854
Landscape painter. b. Howrah, Bengal. Exh. 1911. † BG 4.

ROBINSON, Mrs. Gidley M.E. Exh. 1892-1914
Landscape and figure painter. Godalming, Surrey 1892; St. Leonards on Sea 1908; Newbury, Berks. 1912. † RID 49.

ROBINSON, G.V. Exh. 1906
28 Pellatt Grove, Wood Green, London. † NG 1.

ROBINSON, G.W. Exh. 1881
Lavant, Chichester. † RHA 1.

ROBINSON, Miss H. Exh. 1885
Woodlands, New Brighton, Cheshire. † L 1, M 4.

ROBINSON, Henry Exh. 1892
High Croft, Calder Bridge, Carnforth, Lancs. † L 1.

ROBINSON, Helen Dora Exh. 1911-38
Painter, black and white artist and wood engraver. b. Higham, Suffolk. Studied Byam Shaw and Vicat Cole School. A.R.B.A. 1926. Add: Taunton, Somerset 1911; Winchester 1912 and 1919; East Grinstead, Sussex 1914; Newbury, Berks. 1925. † CHE 1, GOU 3, I 4, L 1, LS 3, M 2, NEA 14, RA 11, RBA 2, SWA 1, WG 2.

ROBINSON, Henry Harewood Exh. 1884-1904
Figure, landscape and coastal painter. Married Maria D.R. q.v. Add: Finistere, France 1884; St. Ives, Cornwall 1886. † B 15, DOW 2, G 1, GI 9, L 13, M 9, RA 13, RBA 9, RHA 11, ROI 5.

ROBINSON, H.L. Exh. 1905-30
The Cottage, Hutton, Berwickshire. † L 1, RSA 1.

ROBINSON, Harry W. Exh. 1897-1934
Glasgow 1897 and 1900; Bridge of Weir, N.B. 1899. † GI 50, LS 12, M 2, RSA 5, RSW 3.

ROBINSON, H. Walter Exh. 1889-1918
Landscape painter. London. † L 1, RA 10, RI 2, ROI 4.

ROBINSON, James Exh. 1910-28
Liverpool. † L 21, RCA 1.

ROBINSON, John Exh. 1885
Architect. 5 Whitehall Gardens, London. † RA 1.

ROBINSON, Joseph Exh. 1882-83
Watercolour landscape painter. 112 Leighton Road, Kentish Town, London. † D 1, RI 1.

ROBINSON, John A. Exh. 1920-40
Landscape painter. London. † I 1, L 1, NEA 1, RA 9, ROI 1.

ROBINSON, J. Carleton Exh. 1893
Landscape painter. Blackheath, London. † D 1.

ROBINSON, Sir John Charles 1824-1913
Landscape painter. Surveyor of Her Majesty's Pictures. 1st Superintendent of the Victoria and Albert Museum Art collection. R.E. 1893. Add: London 1894; Newton Manor, Swanage, Dorset 1902. † L 5, RE 39.

ROBINSON, John H. Exh. 1882
7 Zoar Place, Beeston Hill, Leeds. † L 2.

ROBINSON, J.L. Exh. 1927
33 Marine Parade, Dover. † RI 2.

ROBINSON, John Loftus d. 1894
Architect. A.R.H.A. 1886, R.H.A. 1892. Add: 198 Gt. Brunswick Street, Dublin. † RHA 19.

ROBINSON, John N. Exh. 1928
12 Davidson Road, Liverpool. † L 1.

ROBINSON, J.W. Exh. 1909-13
Helstonleigh, Holme Road, West Bridgford, Notts. † N 9.

ROBINSON, Lucy Gwladys b. 1900
Portrait and landscape painter and etcher. b. Leicester. Studied Cheltenham School of Art, R.A. Schools and Royal College of Art. Exh. 1924-26. Add: Sevenoaks, Kent. † L 3, RA 2.

ROBINSON, M. Exh. 1923
14 Lyra Road, Waterloo, Liverpool. † L 1.

ROBINSON, Miss M. Exh. 1887
Lignhales, Knighton, Herefords. † B 1.

ROBINSON, Miss M. Exh. 1921-22
Western House, Coventry Street, Kidderminster. † B 2.

ROBINSON, Marian Exh. 1893-1913
Watercolour painter. 13 Great Underbank, Stockport, Lancs. † BG 5, GOU 7, M 1.

ROBINSON, Mathias Exh. 1881-85
Genre painter. 427 Kings Road, Chelsea, London. † M 2, RBA 2.

ROBINSON, Maud Exh. 1880-81
Painter. Eastbury, Leighton Court Road, Streatham, London. † SWA 2.

ROBINSON, Mildred Exh. 1899-1901
Miniature portrait painter. Hampton Wick 1899; Dublin 1901. † L 2, RA 2, RHA 5.

ROBINSON, Mabel Catherine b. 1875
Mrs. Barnes. Watercolour painter and etcher. Studied Lambeth Art School and R.A. Schools. A.R.E. 1908. Exh. 1901-28. Add: London. † AB 2, BG 27, I 1, L 13, RA 25, RE 42, RSA 1, SWA 5, WG 19.

ROBINSON, Maria D. Exh. 1881-1910
nee Webb. Figure, landscape and flower painter. Married Henry Harewood R. q.v. Add: Dublin 1881; Finistere, France 1884; St. Ives, Cornwall 1886. † B 10, DOW 2, L 19, LS 1, M 12, RA 13, RBA 3, RHA 71, ROI 5.

ROBINSON, Mary E. Exh. 1931-33
Bookbinder. b. South Shields. Studied London and Paris. Add: London. † B 3, L 2.

ROBINSON, Miss M.H. Exh. 1885-86
16 Greenside Place, Edinburgh. † RSA 2.

ROBINSON, Mary Stewart Exh. 1890-1940
Portrait and animal painter. Cambridge 1890, 1914 and 1940; Dover 1913; London 1916. † LS 21, SWA 5.

ROBINSON, Nellie Exh. 1889-90
Landscape painter. West Bank, Scarborough. † L 2, NEA 2, RA 1.

ROBINSON, Penelope Exh. 1922
Landscape painter. † BK 4.

ROBINSON, Percy Exh. 1903-33
Leeds. † L 2, RA 3.

ROBINSON, Phyllis Exh. 1933-38
Colwyn Bay, Wales. † P 1, RCA 8.

ROBINSON, T. Exh. 1899-1900
Marine painter. London. † RA 2.

ROBINSON, Thomas Osborne b. 1904
Landscape painter, commercial artist and theatrical designer. b. Northampton. Exh. 1931-40. Add: Northampton. † RA 3, RSA 12.

ROBINSON, Vera Exh. 1916-22
Miniature portrait painter. The Hut, Westfield Road, Western Park, Leicester. † N 2, RA 5.

ROBINSON, W. Exh. 1886
The Ferns, Frodsham. † L 1.

ROBINSON, William 1835-1895
Landscape painter. Manchester. † AG 1, L 3, M 15, RA 1, RI 4, RSA 2.

ROBINSON, Wilfrid Harold b. 1876
Architect. Exh. 1905. Add: 2 New Court, Carey Street, London. † RA 1.

ROBINSON, William Heath* 1872-1944
Humorous painter, black and white artist and illustrator. b. Hornsey. Studied R.A. Schools. Add: Maidstone, Kent 1927. † FIN 84, RA 1.

ROBINSON, William Howard Exh. 1902-1917
Portrait and figure painter. b. Inverness-shire. Studied Slade School and under Sir S.J. Solomon. Add: London. † L 2, NG 4, P 4, RA 1.

ROBINSON, Winifred L. Exh. 1938
Sculptor. 56 Albyn Road, London. † RA 1.

ROBINSON, Marion C. Exh. 1916-37
Ecclesiastical artist and gilder. Queens College, Paradise Street, Birmingham. † B 22, I 1, L 3, SWA 3.

ROBLIN, Mme. M.E. Exh. 1903-4
4 Rue Treilhard, Paris. † L 3.

ROBOTHAM, Mrs. Frances C. Exh. 1893-99
Painter. Kensington, London. † B 3, RA 1, RBA 1.

ROBOTHAM, Mrs. K. Exh. 1928-36
4 Milford Road, Harborne, Birmingham. † B 4.

ROBOTHAM, Lilian A. Exh. 1900-6
Pennhurst, Aston Lane, Perry Bar, Birmingham. † B 4.

ROBOTHAM, Rose A. Exh. 1903-6
Aston Lane, Perry Bar, Birmingham. † B 5.

ROBOTTOM, Mrs. C.H. Exh. 1920
Phoenix Lodge, Varna Road, Edgbaston, Birmingham. † B 1.

ROBSON, A.H. Exh. 1933
† RSW 1.

ROBSON, Mrs. Edith A. Exh. 1929
45 Shore Road, Ainsdale, Southport, Lancs. † L 1.

ROBSON, Mrs. Elsie May Exh. 1920-38
nee Dawson. Flower and landscape painter and still life miniaturist. Studied Leeds Art School and under Owen Bowen. Add: Leeds 1920; Hurstwood, Sussex 1927. † ALP 1, B 1, FIN 11, L 20, RA 6, RCA 15, RHA 1, SWA 3.

ROBSON, Edward Robert 1835-1917
Architect. Westminster, London. † NG 12, RA 13.

ROBSON, Featherstone b. 1880
Landscape painter. b. Hexham. Studied South Shields School of Art. Exh. 1918-23. Add: High Barnet, Herts. † RA 1, ROI 2.

ROBSON, Forster Exh. 1888-1906
Liverpool. † L 18, RCA 3.

ROBSON, Frederick C. Exh. 1926
Architect. Gate Cottage, Fordcombe, nr. Tunbridge Wells, Kent. † RA 1.

ROBSON, Gertrude Exh. 1893-99
Architectural painter. 10 Fielding Road, Kensington, London. † RBA 4.

ROBSON, Rev. G.B. Exh. 1924
30 Somerset Road, Handsworth Wood, Birmingham. † B 1.

ROBSON, Guy Coburn b. 1888
Watercolour painter and black and white artist. Deputy Keeper, Dept. of Zoology, British Museum of Natural History. Exh. 1914-21. Add: London. † I 2, LS 3, NEA 2.

ROBSON, Mrs. G.E. Exh. 1921
Fernhurst, West End Terrace, Stockton on Tees. † B 1.

ROBSON, Henrietta Exh. 1880-88
Flower and still life painter. Woodlands, New Brighton, Cheshire. † L 12, M 6, RA 2.

ROBSON, Hannah B. Exh. 1881-96
Birkenhead 1881; Woodlands, New Brighton, Cheshire 1882; Liscard Vale, Cheshire 1894. † GI 1, L 8, M 3.

ROBSON, J.J. Exh. 1916
17 Burch Road, Rosherville, Gravesend, Kent. † RA 1.

ROBSON, Miss J.M.A. Exh. 1882-83
2 Brighton Terrace, Seacombe, Cheshire. † L 2.

ROBSON, Maggie Exh. 1880-81
14 Royal Crescent, Glasgow. † GI 4.

ROBSON, Phillip A. Exh. 1899
Architect. 9 Bridge Street, Westminster, London. † RA 1.

ROBSON, S. Barnes Exh. 1929
5 Ebor Street, Bishopthorpe Road, York. † RCA 1.

ROBSON, William Exh. 1882-1938
Painter and pastel artist. Studied Paris and Florence. Add: Edinburgh 1882; Kirkcudbright 1904. † GI 18, L 7, RA 5, RSA 64.

ROBUS, Mabel Exh. 1936-38
Bromley, Kent. † SWA 4.

ROC-B'HIAN, de See D

ROCHDALE, A. Exh. 1888
Painter. 12 Douro Place, Victoria Road, London. † ROI 1.

ROCHE, Alexander Ignatius 1861-1921
Landscape and portrait painter. b. Glasgow. Studied Glasgow School of Art and Julians, Paris. Visited Italy (1890s) and America. N.E.A. 1891, R.P. 1898, A.R.S.A. 1893, R.S.A. 1900. Add: Glasgow 1881; Edinburgh 1897. † AG 1, G 2, GI 72, I 7, L 15, M 6, NEA 14, P 1, RA 10, RHA 2, ROI 1, RSA 82, RSW 1.

ROCHE, Miss D. Exh. 1910
2 Emperor's Gate, London. † RI 1.

ROCHE, Mrs. Eily Exh. 1937-40
Sculptor. London. † RA 3.

ROCHE, L.F. Exh. 1884
15 North Mall, Cork. † RHA 1.

ROCHE, Mark Exh. 1881-87
Sculptor. Camden Square, London. † L 1, RA 6.

ROCHE, Pierre 1885-1922
French sculptor. Exh. 1913. Add: 25 Rue Vanneau, Paris. † RSA 1.

ROCHE, Walter Exh. 1881-1911
Sculptor. Camden Square, London 1881; Norwich 1910. † L 2, LS 5, RA 19.

ROCHEGROSSE, Georges Marie* b. 1859
French painter. Exh. 1924. Add: Djenan Meryem El Rias, pres Alger, Algeria. † L 1.

ROCHFORT, Constance Exh. 1896-1914
Brussels 1896; Dunlavin, Wicklow 1900; Greystones, Co. Wicklow 1911. † RHA 7, SWA 3.

ROCK, Helen Frazer d. 1932
Sculptor and potter. Studied R.A. Schools. A.R.M.S. 1929. Exh. from 1909. Add: London. † B 1, I 3, RA 11, RMS 27.

ROCK, S.C. Exh. 1911
32 Holly Lane, West Smethwick, Birmingham. † B 1.

RODA, Leonarda Exh. 1911
Landscape painter. † ALP 1.

RODBARD, Miss C.A. Exh. 1901
22 Manville Road, Balham, London. † RI 1.

RODD, Frances Exh. 1901-11
29 Beaufort Gardens, London. † B 5, D 10, L 4, P 1, RA 1, SWA 2.

RODD, Lady Lilian G. Exh. 1904-5
Sculptor. 17 Stratford Place, Oxford Street, London. † RA 2.

RODDIS, Alfred J. Exh. 1903-10
Architect. London. † RA 2.

RODECK, Carl* Exh. 1880-81
Landscape painter. 94 Koppel, Hamburg, Germany and 26 Maida Vale, London. † RA 2.

RODECK, Pieter Exh. 1899
Architect. 449 Edgware Road, London. † RA 1.

RODEN, Mary Exh. 1882-1937
Birmingham. † B 20.

RODEN, W.F. Exh. 1882-1900
Birmingham 1882; Manchester 1893. † B 2, GI 2, M 4.

RODEN, William Thomas 1817-1892
Engraver and portrait painter. Birmingham. 1882. † B 5.

RODENHURST, Ellen B. Exh. 1908-23
Painter and colour woodcut artist. Studied Newlyn and Paris. Add: Newlyn, Penzance 1908; Shrewsbury 1909; Reading, Berks. 1923. † B 1, L 2, RCA 1.

RODERICK, D. Exh. 1886
110 Moscow Drive, Liverpool. † L 3, M 1.

RODGER, George Exh. 1890-93
Braiffauld, Tollcross, N.B. † GI 2.

RODGERS, Miss Barbara H. Exh. 1889-94
Watercolour interior painter. Edwinstowe, Newark, Notts. † N 11.

RODGERS, Joseph Exh. 1884-90
Watercolour landscape painter. Edwinstowe, Newark, Notts. † L 1, RA 1, RSA 3.

RODGERS, Marjorie Exh. 1917-40
Flower, figure, portrait and miniature painter. Married F. Douglas Wray q.v. Add: Balham, London 1917; Edgware, Middlesex 1931. † RA 12, RI 1, ROI 3.

RODGERS, Maud Mary Exh. 1885
4 Tennyson Street, Nottingham. † N 1.

RODGERS, Robert Exh. 1890
Sculptor. Ravenscraig, Honeywell Road, Wandsworth, London. † RA 2.

RODGERSON, Walter L. Exh. 1929
85 Church Street, Westhoughton, nr. Bolton, Lancs. † L 1.

RODIN, August* 1840-1917
French sculptor and black and white artist. R.E. 1882-89. H.R.S.A. 1907. Add: Paris 1882 and 1891; London 1884. † G 3, GI 8, I 79, L 8, M 1, RA 2, RBA 3, RE 2, RSA 38.

RODIN, T. Exh. 1898
† P 1.

RODO, Ludovic Exh. 1908-20
Painter, etcher and wood engraver. Paris 1908 and 1913; London 1909; Ashford, Middlesex 1914. † BG 2, GOU 32, LS 23, NEA 14.

RODOCANACHI, Hypatia Exh. 1904
Sculptor. 2 Clarendon Place, Hyde Park Gardens, London. † RA 1.

RODWAY, Mrs. Philip Exh. 1937-40
3 Speedwell Road, Edgbaston, Birmingham. † B 3.

ROE, Clarence* d. 1909
Landscape painter. Exh. 1887. Add: 9 South Crescent, Tottenham Court Road, London. † RHA 2.

ROE, C.E. Exh. 1913-16
6 Alfred Road, Brighton. † RA 3.

ROE, Fred 1865-1947
Portrait, landscape, historical and battle painter. Son of Robert Henry R. (1793-1880). Studied Heatherleys and under J. Seymour Lucas. R.B.A. 1895, R.I. 1909. Add: London. † B 19, L 41, M 16, RA 72, RBA 18, RI 130, ROI 24.

ROE, Laurence Exh. 1899
2 Turner Studios, Glebe Place, Chelsea, London. † L 1.

ROE, May D.H. Exh. 1926-27
Flower painter. 6 Annersley Grove, Addison Street, Nottingham. † N 3.

ROE, Richard M. Exh. 1880-1913
Watercolour architectural landscape painter. London 1880; Twickenham, Middlesex 1912. † LS 6, RBA 3.

ROE, Walter Herbert Exh. 1882-1909
Genre painter. London. † B 5, GI 1, L 1, LS 3, RA 5, RBA 12, RI 2, ROI 12, TOO 1.

ROEBECK, Lady Exh. 1937
London. † RCA 1.

ROEDER, Miss Malley Exh. 1889-98
Ernsee Cottage, Amhurst Street, Fallowfield, Manchester. † L 2, M 10.

ROEKNAGEL, Otto Exh. 1883
Painter. c/o Graphic, Strand, London. † FIN 1, M 1.

ROELOFS, Albert* Exh. 1908-12
Allied Artists Association, 67 Chancery Lane, London. † LS 5.

ROELOFS, Willem E. junr. Exh. 1884-1910
Watercolour painter. Brussels 1884; The Hague, Holland 1892. † FIN 12, GI 5, GOU 1, LS 5, M 4.

ROEMMELLE, Mrs. Exh. 1906
34 Kelvinside Gardens, Glasgow. † GI 1.

ROERICH, Nicholas Konstantin b. 1874
Painter. b. Leningrad. Exh. 1920. † GOU 198.

ROFF, Miss L.R. Exh. 1906-13
Sculptor. 121 Cheyne Walk, Chelsea, London. † GI 2, L 9, NG 1, RA 5.

ROFFE, Alfred Exh. 1883
Painter. c/o Thames Side, Windsor, Berks. † ROI 3.

ROFFE, Robert Exh. 1881
Watercolour landscape painter. † AG 2.

ROFFE, Miss S. Exh. 1889
13 Parolles Road, Highgate, London. † M 1.

ROFFE, William John Exh. 1880-89
Landscape and coastal painter. London. † RA 1, RBA 3.

ROGANEAU, F.M. Exh. 1914
9 Rue Falguiere, Paris. † RSA 2.

ROGER, Charles Exh. 1914
3 Villa Eugene, Comombes, Seine, France. † RSA 1.

ROGER, Louis Exh. 1925
Rue Notre Dame des Champs 73, Paris. † L 1.

ROGERS, A. Exh. 1918
186 Goldhawk Road, Shepherds Bush, London. † RA 1.

ROGERS, Arthur Lee Exh. 1882-89
Watercolour landscape painter. 125 Bedford Street, Liverpool. † L 19, M 2, RA 10, RBA 1, RI 1, ROI 1.

ROGERS, Mrs. Alice N. Exh. 1894-1918
London. † RHA 11, SWA 8.

ROGERS, Arnold T. Exh. 1936-37
39 Carless Avenue, Harborne, Birmingham. † B 3.

ROGERS, Claude* b. 1907
Landscape portrait and figure painter. Studied Slade School. Founder member with Graham Bell, Victor Pasmore and William Coldstream of the Euston Road School 1937. Member London Group 1938. "Mrs. Richard Chilver" (1937-38) purchased by Chantrey Bequest 1940. Exh. 1928-40. Add: London. † AG 4, CG 1, COO 4, L 3, LEI 34, NEA 5.

ROGERS, Charles H. Exh. 1903
Landscape painter. Abbeywood, Croydon Road, Anerley, London. † RA 1.

ROGERS, Miss E. Exh. 1882-83
16 Merton Road, Bootle Lane, Liverpool. † L 3.

ROGERS, Ethel Exh. 1894-1907
Miniature portrait painter. London 1894; Paignton, Devon 1896; Wanstead, Essex 1907. † RA 1, RI 2, RMS 2, SWA 1.

ROGERS, Eric b. 1902
Sculptor. Studied Leeds School of Art and Royal College of Art. Art master City of Leeds School and modelling, carving and pottery instructor West Bromwich School of Art. Exh. 1930-31. Add: 4 Coventry Place, Leeds. † B 2.

ROGERS, Evelyn E. Exh. 1889-1900
Miniature portrait painter. R.M.S. 1897. Add: Kingston Hill, Surrey 1889; Teignmouth, Devon 1894; Ryde, I.O.W. 1895; Ealing, London 1896. † RA 5, RI 4, RMS 10.

ROGERS, Edward James b. 1872
Portrait, landscape and miniature painter. Son of James Edward R. q.v. Studied Heatherleys. Exh. 1903-36. Add: London 1903 and 1926; Dublin 1908; Glenbrook, Co. Cork 1929; Kingstown 1932; Laoghaire 1934. † L 1, RA 2, RHA 44, RMS 2, ROI 1.

ROGERS, Frederick Exh. 1889-95
Sculptor. London. † RA 3.

ROGERS, Frances Clare b. 1890
nee Woodhouse. Painter and illustrator. b. Southport, Lancs. Studied Birmingham School of Art, Florence and Goldsmiths. Signs work "Frank Rogers". Mother of G. Cedric H.R. q.v. Exh. 1922. Add: 29 Sydenham Hill, London. † RA 1.

ROGERS, Gilbert Exh. 1905-15
Portrait painter. Liverpool. † L 22, RA 4.

ROGERS, Grace Exh. 1900-29
Watercolour flower and landscape painter. b. South Wales. Add: Forest Row, Sussex 1900; London 1905. † AB 2, GOU 7, I 2, NEA 1, RBA 5, RI 7, SWA 6.

ROGERS, G. Cedric H. Exh. 1939
Painter. Son of Frances Clare R. q.v. Add: 29 Sydenham Hill, London. † RA 1.

ROGERS, Gina J. Exh. 1886-89
Watercolour landscape painter. London. † RI 2, SWA 3.

ROGERS, Miss H. Exh. 1902-7
8 Denning Road, Hampstead, London. † SWA 8.

ROGERS, Henrietta Exh. 1930
Etcher. Middleham, Ringmer, Sussex. † L 1, RA 1.

ROGERS, James Edward 1838-1896
Watercolour landscape, architectural and marine painter, illustrator and architect. b. Dublin. Father of Edward James R. q.v. A.R.H.A. 1871. Moved to London 1876. † D 13, L 5, RA 4, RE 1, RHA 32, RI 22, ROI 1.

ROGERS, Miss J.M. Exh. 1882
56 Berners Street, London. † L 1.

ROGERS, Kate Exh. 1884-85
Watercolour flower painter. 17 Tadema Road, Chelsea, London. † RBA 1, RI 1.

ROGERS, Lalla Exh. 1914-33
21 Grove Park, Liverpool. † L 2.

ROGERS, L.N. Norris Exh. 1938
34 Hinstock Road, Handsworth, Birmingham. † B 1.

ROGERS, Marie Exh. 1905-6
Rue de Paris, Villeneuve St. George, Seine et Oise, France. † L 4.

ROGERS, Mark 1848-1933
Sculptor, wood carver and illustrator. Add: London. † L 17, RA 26.

ROGERS, Mrs. M.J. Exh. 1901
The Vicarage, Pendeen, Cornwall. † D 1, RI 1.

ROGERS, Nina Exh. 1936
Cardiff, Wales. † RCA 2.

ROGERS, Rose Exh. 1889-1901
c/o Kemp and Co., Pimlico, London. † D 16.

ROGERS, Miss R.S. Exh. 1912-14
Gt. Yarmouth, Norfolk. † SWA 4.

ROGERS, Mrs. Winterfold Exh. 1918
Hampstead Way, London. † SWA 3.

ROGERS, W.G. Exh. 1885
7A Dunville Avenue, Rathmines, Dublin. † RHA 2.

ROGERS, W.H. Exh. 1911-14
Liverpool. † L 3, RA 1.

ROGERS, W.P. Exh. 1883
2 Rugby Road, Ranelagh, Dublin. † RHA 1.

ROGER-SMITH, Mrs. D. Exh. 1932
Capel, Surrey. † SWA 1.

ROGERSON, John Exh. 1920-21
202 Hope Street, Glasgow. † GI 2.

ROGERSON, Joseph Exh. 1884-1903
Liverpool. † L 8.

ROGERSON, Miles Exh. 1882
172 Islington, Liverpool. † L 1.

ROGET, Isabel Exh. 1897-1923
5 Randolphe Crescent, London. † SWA 7.

ROGGEN, van See V

ROGIER, John M. Exh. 1884-1903
Landscape and figure painter. Hastings 1884; London 1885. † L 1, RA 8.

ROHL, Mme. Frieda Exh. 1880-86
Glasgow. † GI 15, RHA 8, RSA 11.

ROHRS, H.H. Exh. 1914
13 Ashleigh, Anfield, Liverpool. † L 1.

ROILOS, G. Exh. 1905-7
Liverpool. † L 5, M 2, RA 1.

ROLAND, B. Exh. 1931
London. † RCA 2.

ROLASON, Miss K. Exh. 1916-25
2 Radnor Road, Handsworth, Birmingham. † B 3, L 1, RA 1, RMS 1.

ROLFE, Henry Leonidas* Exh. 1881
Painter of fishing subjects. Add: 31 Nicholas Lane, City, London. † RBA 1

ROLFE, Miss L.S. Exh. 1916
35A Kingsland Road, Birkenhead. † L 1.

ROLL, Alfred Philippe 1847-1919
French painter. Exh. 1883-1912. Add: Brompton, London 1883; Paris 1893. † GOU 1, L 1, P 2.

ROLL, Marcel Exh. 1908
145 Avenue de Villiers, Paris. † LS 4.

ROLLAND, Helen M. Exh. 1923-35
Watercolour landscape painter. Peebles 1923; Edinburgh 1930. † AB 2, GI 3, RSA 5, RSW 12, SWA 4.

ROLLASON, Ena M. Exh. 1927
Mount Park Road London. † SWA 1.

ROLLASON, Mary Exh. 1893
85 Colmore Chambers, Newhall Street, Birmingham. † B 1.

ROLLASON, Mark Arthur Exh. 1903
Swiss Cottage, Olton, Warwicks. † B 2

ROLLASON, W.A. Exh. 1884-99
Landscape painter and teacher. Birmingham 1884 and 1893; Cornwall 1891; Truro, Cornwall 1898. † B 25, M 1, ROI 2.

ROLLE, le See L

ROLLE, Mlle. Marie Exh. 1912
3 Elfenstrasse, Berne, Switzerland. † L 1.

ROLLE, Miss S.L. Exh. 1902
17 Silverdale Road, Oxton, Birkenhead. † L 1.

ROLLER, Mrs. Exh. 1891-93
8 Alma Square, Abbey Road, London. † BG 2.

ROLLER, George b. 1858
Portrait painter. Studied Lambeth and under Bougereau and Fleury in Paris. Sporting advertisement designer to Burberrys for 30 years and picture restorer to R.A. for 20 years. R.E. 1885. Exh. 1884-1906. Add: London 1884; Tadley, nr. Basingstoke, Hants. 1889. † FIN 49, L 2, RA 3, RBA 4, RE 20, ROI 2.

ROLLESTON, Lady E. Exh. 1907-18
54 Curzon Street, London. † RA 3, RMS 2.

ROLLESTON, Lucy Exh. 1888
Figure painter. 26 St. Anne's Terrace, St. Johns Wood, London. † ROI 1.

ROLLESTON, Miss L.E. Exh. 1890
Lower Sloane Street, London. † SWA 1.

ROLLET, Henry Exh. 1886-1916
West Kirby, Cheshire 1886; Wallasey, 1887; Ludlow, Salop 1889; Liscard 1892; Birkenhead 1912. † L 8.

ROLLETT, George Exh. 1929-39
165 Heathfield Road, Handsworth, Birmingham. † B 6.

ROLLETT, Herbert 1872-1932
Landscape painter. b. Gainsborough. A.R.B.A. 1926, R.B.A. 1930. Father of I. Kathleen R. q.v. Add: Grimsby 1904; Gt. Coastes, Lincs. 1931. † B 18, L 8, RA 8, RBA 33, RCA 3, ROI 1, RSA 7.

ROLLETT, I. Kathleen b. 1898
Watercolour painter. b. Grimsby. Daughter of Herbert R. q.v. Exh. 1921-34. Add: Grimsby 1921; Gt. Coates, Lincs. 1931; Nottingham 1932. † B 7, GI 1, L 5, N 10, RA 1, RSA 2.

ROLLINCE, Mlle. Jeanne Exh. 1904
6 Rue Casimir Perier, Paris. † L 1.

ROLLINS, John Wenlock Exh. 1887-1913
Sculptor. Studied Birmingham School of Art and R.A. Schools till 1890. Visited Italy. Executed the carving and sculpture of Croydon Town Hall c. 1894 and a series of colossal Statues for the New General Hospital, Birmingham c. 1896. Add: London. † B 3, GI 3, L 8, NG 2, RA 20, RI 1, ROI 1.

ROLLINSON, Sunderland b. 1872
Painter, lithographer and etcher. b. Knaresborough. Studied Scarborough School of Art and Royal College of Art. Married Beatrice Malam q.v. Exh. 1901-36. Add: London 1901; Edinburgh 1905; Scarborough 1907; School of Art, Kingston upon Hull 1912; Cottingham, Yorks. 1913. † GI 1, L 12, RA 1, RBA 1, RI 2, RSA 3.

ROLLO, Alex Exh. 1914
9 Carlton Gardens, Glasgow. † GI 2.

ROLLO, Mrs Freda Exh. 1929-31
Sculptor. Highmoor, Wigton, Cumberland. † L 3, RA 1.

ROLLS, Daisy K. Exh. 1912-13
29 Redcliffe Square, London. † LS 3.

ROLLS, Florence Exh. 1888-89
Figure and portrait painter. Hampden Mount, Caterham Valley, Surrey. † M 1, RA 1.

ROLLS, Frances A. Dudley Exh. 1893-1906
Medallionist. Surbiton, Surrey 1893; Eastbourne 1901. † RA 9.

ROLSHOVEN, Julius 1858-1930
American portrait and landscape painter. Exh. 1892-1911. Add: London 1892 and 1896; Paris 1895. † BRU 1, I 1, L 2, M 1, NG 3, P 2, RA 8, RBA 1, RID 10.

ROLT, Vivian 1874-1933
Landscape painter and watercolourist. b. Stow on the Wold. Studied Slade School, St. Johns Wood, Bushey and Heatherleys. R.B.A. 1913. Add: London 1893 and 1912; Storrington, nr. Pulborough, Sussex 1904; Watersfield, nr. Pulborough, Sussex 1918. † CHE 1, D 46, L 14, M 1, RA 13, RBA 142, RI 15.

ROMAINE-WALKER, Winefride Exh. 1924-32
Figure and animal modeller. Daughter of William Henry R. q.v. Studied Royal College of Art Add: London. † L 5, RA 8.

ROMAINE-WALKER, William Henry Exh. 1881
Architect. Father of Winefride R-W. q.v. Add: 19 Buckingham Street, Adelphi, London. † RA 1.

ROMANES, Margaret C. Exh. 1935-40
3 Whitehouse Terrace, Edinburgh. † RSA 11.

ROMBAUX, Egide 1865-1942
Belgian sculptor. Studied Ecole des Beaux Arts, Brussels. Son of Felix R. (sculptor). Add: Brussels 1914 and 1923; London 1915. † GI 4, I 4, L 1, RA 1, RSA 7.

ROME, L. Exh. 1940
Abbey Gate, Bangor on Dee, North Wales. † SWA 2.

ROME, N.L. Exh. 1939
28 Cheniston Gardens, London. † SWA 2.

ROMEIN, Bernard Exh. 1939
Painter. 75 Merrion Square, Dublin. † RHA 3.

ROMER, de See D

ROMER, George A. Exh. 1907
28 Reginald Road, Bearwood, Smethwick, Birmingham. † B 1.

ROMLEY, Lester Exh. 1936-38
Painter. 7 Pembroke Walk, London. † NEA 2, P 1, RA 1.

ROMMEL, Miss A. Exh. 1907
Herne Hill, London. † SWA 1.

ROMMEL, Miss E.L. Exh. 1907
Denmark Hill, London. † SWA 2.

RONALD, Alan Ian b. 1899
Painter. Studied Edinburgh College of Art. R.S.W. 1935. Exh. 1920-40. Add: Edinburgh 1920 and 1934; Markinch 1925; Dunfermline, 1926 and 1933. † GI 12, L 7, RSA 28, RSW 37.

RONALDSON, Heriot Mary Barker Exh. 1910-12
London. † LS 9.

RONALDSON, Thomas Martine b. 1881
Portrait painter. b. Edinburgh. Exh. 1905-40. Add: Edinburgh 1905; London 1908. † CG 2, G 7, GI 2, I 2, L 13, LS 5, P 18, RA 26, ROI 1, RSA 42.

RONDEL, Georgette Exh. 1940
Painter. 25 Lower Baggot Street, Dublin. † RHA 1.

RONDEL, H. Exh. 1893-38
Portrait and figure painter. † COO 1, P 1.

RONDENAY, Mlle. M.A. Exh. 1907
165 Avenue Rouget de l'Isle, Vitry sur Seine, France. † L 1.

RONDIE, E. Exh. 1886
30 Gt. Russell Street, London. † M 2.

RONGIER, Mlle. Jeanne Exh. 1880-82
42 Rue Fontaine, St. Georges, Paris. † M 1, RHA 5.

RONIG, Hugo Exh. 1891
Munich. † GI 2.

RONNER, Alfred Exh. 1880-95
51 Chaussee de Fleurgart, Brussels. † GI 15.

RONNER, Alice* Exh. 1880-1918
Still life painter. 51 Chaussee de Fleurgart, Brussels 1880; London 1918. † GI 12, L 2, NEA 1.

RONNER, Edward Exh. 1882
51 Chaussee de Fleurgart, Brussels. † GI 2.

RONNER, Emma b.1857
Exh. 1888-96. Add: 51 Chaussee de Fleurgart, Brussels. † GI 3.

RONNER, Mme. Henriette* 1821-1909
Animal painter. R.I. 1894. Add: 51 Chaussee de Fleurgart, Brussels. † B 2, FIN 115, GI 38, GOU 31, L 4, M 10, NG 2, RA 16, RI 16, ROI 13, RSA 24, RSW 1, SWA 1.

RONNIGER, Mme. M.J. Exh. 1883
1 Abingdon Villas, Kensington, London. † M 1.

ROODENBURG, Henry E. Exh. 1923
Etcher. Van den Boschstraat 209, The Hague, Holland. † RA 1.

ROOK, Mrs. Clarence Exh. 1921
41 Cathcart Road, London. † L 1.

ROOKE, Barnard Exh. 1885-88
Painter. Sittingbourne, Kent. † RA 4.

ROOKE, Caroline Mary b.1848
Watercolour painter. Exh. 1904-15. Add: Embleton, Christonbank, Northumberland and London. † D 20, SWA 3.

ROOKE, Henri Exh. 1895
Painter. 5 Avenue Philippe Leboucher, Neuilly sur Seine, Paris. † RA 1.

ROOKE, Herbert Kerr b. 1872
Marine painter and poster designer. Studied Royal College of Art and Slade School. R.B.A. 1899. Exh. 1894-1927. Add: Ealing, London 1894; Sutton, Surrey 1900; Wimbledon 1915. † GOU 1, L 2, M 1, RA 25, RBA 108, RI 1.

ROOKE, Madeline Exh. 1902
20 Brighton Square, Rathgar, Dublin. † RHA 2.

ROOKE, Noel 1881-1953
Painter, engraver, book decorator and poster designer. Studied Slade School and L.C.C. Central School of Arts and Crafts. Head of School of Book Production Central School of Arts and Crafts, London. Son of Thomas Matthews R. q.v. A.R.E. 1920. Add: London. † NEA 6, RE 10, RHA 1.

ROOKE, Thomas Matthews* 1842-1942
Landscape, architectural, portrait and biblical painter. Studied Royal College of Art and R.A. Schools. Worked as assistant to Burne-Jones for many years and from 1878-93 worked for Ruskin on drawings of continental cathedrals and buildings. Father of Noel R. q.v. A.R.W.S. 1891 R.W.S. 1903. "The Story of Ruth" purchased by Chantrey Bequest 1877. Add: 7 Queen Anne's Gardens, Bedford Park, London. † B 47, FIN 1, G 12, GI 14, L 27, M 30, NG 26, RA 16, RBA 1, RHA 10, RI 3, RWS 263.

ROOME, Mrs. Lilian Exh. 1929-40
Watercolour landscape painter. Weybridge, Surrey. † NEA 2, RA 9, RI 3.

ROOME, Winifred Exh. 1900-18
Kensington, London 1905 and 1918; Hassocks, Sussex 1915. † B 1, L 3, LS 27, RHA 1, ROI 5, SWA 24.

ROONEY, Lucas Exh. 1906
36 Fairview Strand, Fairview, Dublin. † RHA 2.

ROONEY, Pat Exh. 1931-32
c/o Mr. R. Kennedy, Patrick Thomson Ltd., North Bridge, Edinburgh. † RSA 2.

ROOPMAN, A. Exh. 1905
153 Church Street, Chelsea, London. † ROI 1.

ROOS, Eva* b. 1872
Portrait and figure painter and black and white illustrator for childrens books. b. London. Studied Colarossi's and Delecluse's Paris. Married S.H. Vedder q.v. Exh. 1898-1928. Add: London. † B 1 BG 3, L 3, M 1, RA 16, ROI 5.

ROOSE, Mrs. Cecily M. Exh. 1928
37 Castleton Mansions, Barnes, London. † RCA 2.

ROOSENBOOM, Marguerite* Exh. 1889-90
Watercolour flower painter. † FIN 48.

ROOTH, Hilda M. Exh. 1904
Landscape painter. The Cliff, Dronfield, nr. Sheffield. † N 1.

ROOTS, Gertrude Exh. 1898-1912
Figure painter. Canterbury 1898; Margate 1912. † RA 1, SWA 1.

ROPE, Dorothy Aldrich A. Exh. 1903-18
Sculptor. Sister of Ellen Mary and George Thomas R. q.v. Add: London. † L 1, RA 3, SWA 2.

ROPE, Ellen Mary 1855-1934
Sculptor, modeller and plaster designer. b. Blaxhall, Suffolk. Studied Slade School and the British Museum. Sister of Dorothy A.A. and George Thomas R. q.v. Add: London and Blaxhall, Suffolk. † G 13, GI 8, L 37, M 8, NG 8, RA 41, RBA 1, RMS 6.

ROPE, George Thomas 1845-1929
Painter and pencil artist. Brother of Dorothy A.A. and Ellen Mary R. q.v. Add: Blaxhall, Wickham Market, Suffolk. † L 3, RA 2.

ROPER, Cecil B. Exh. 1888-94
Architect. Elm View, Shaw Hill, Halifax. † RA 6.

ROPER, Miss F.M. Exh. 1916-30
Flower painter. Belvoir Hill, Sneinton, Nottingham. † N 16.

ROPER, Frederick William Exh. 1881
Architect. 9 Adam Street, Adelphi, London. † RA 1.

ROPER-CALDBECK, Mrs. Marion Exh. 1939
London. † RCA 1.

ROPS, Felicien Exh. 1893
Painter and illustrator. 1 Place Boiledieu, Paris. † NEA 2.

ROQUES, Casimir Exh. 1880-86
16 George Street, Edinburgh. † RSA 11.

RORVAL, R.W.A. Exh. 1891
4 Newgate Street, London. † RSA 1.

ROSA, de la see D

ROSA, Frederick A. Exh. 1884-88
40 Frederick Street, Edinburgh. † RSA 7.

ROSA, Mme. R. Exh. 1894-1905
Liverpool 1894; Manchester 1895. † L 4, M 7.

ROSALES, de see D

ROSATI, Giulo Exh. 1889-90
Painter. 25 Queen Anne Street, London. † B 2.

ROSCOE, Cicely Exh. 1921
Watercolour landscape painter. † WG 25.

ROSCOE, Frank Exh. 1939
Architect. 90 Fulham Road, London. † RA 1.

ROSCOE, Frank junr. Exh. 1925
Watercolour landscape painter. Brownlea, Berkhampstead, Herts. † RA 1.

ROSCOE, H. Gordon Exh. 1927-40
Hampton in Arden, Warwicks 1927; Shirley, Warwicks 1928. † B 17.

ROSCOE, S.G.W. Exh. 1880-1914
Watercolour landscape painter. Topsham, Devon and Kentish Town, London. † D 141, DOW 12, L 5, M 6, RA 3, RBA 14, RI 10.

ROSCOE, Mrs. Theodora Exh. 1935-38
Painter and writer. Studied Spenlove School of Painting. Add: Horn Hill Court, Chalfont St. Peter, Bucks. † P 1, RBA 1, RSA 1.

ROSE, Mrs. Adele Exh. 1918-34
Landscape painter. 37 Kingscourt Road Streatham, London. † D 1, RA 3, RMS 4.

ROSE, Alison Helen b. 1900
Landscape painter. b. Edinburgh. Studied Heatherleys. Exh. 1924-39. Add: Penzance, Cornwall. † GOU 5, NEA 1, RA 6, RSA 1, SWA 3.

ROSE, A.W. Exh. 1908-12
London. † RA 7.

ROSE, Mrs. Beatrix Exh. 1898
49 Onslow Gardens, London. † RMS 1.

ROSE, C. Stuart Exh. 1935
78 Thames Eyot, Twickenham, Middlesex. † RI 1.

ROSE, David T. Exh. 1915-38
Watercolour painter, black and white artist and etcher. Goodwick, nr. Fishguard, Wales 1915; Pateley Bridge, Yorks. 1923; Brighton 1938. † ALP 1, L 1, RA 5, RI 7.

ROSE, Miss E. Exh. 1915
6 Bath Parade, Cheltenham, Glos. † RA 1.

ROSE, Edna Exh. 1926-38
Sculptor. Hoylake, Cheshire. † L 9, M 1, RA 1.

ROSE, E.H. Exh. 1910
6 Parkside Gardens, Wimbledon. † RA 1.

ROSE, Gwendolen Exh. 1924
Mrs. Smith. Watercolour painter. 31 Bracken Gardens, Barnes, Surrey. † RA 1.

ROSE, George Herbert 1882-1955
Landscape painter and etcher. b. Chipping Ongar, Essex. Studied Regent Street, Polytechnic. Add: London. † ALP 1, CG 20, GI 1, L 2, NEA 4, RA 27, RI 3, RSA 3.

ROSE, G.V. Exh. 1914
c/o Miss Harold, 33 Regents Square, London. † RA 2.

ROSE, Henry Exh. 1893-97
Architect. 6 Staple Inn, Holborn, London. † RA 3.

ROSE, Herbert* Exh. 1932-34
Landscape painter. London. † RA 2.

ROSE, H. Ethel Exh. 1881-90
Portrait and genre painter. London. † B 1, D 1, L 1, M 3, RA 5, RBA 4, RHA 2, RI 5, ROI 6, SWA 2.

ROSE, H. Randolph Exh. 1880-1907
Landscape, portrait and genre painter. London 1880 and 1907; Algiers 1906. † B 4, D 5, G 1, L 9, NG 4, RA 11, RBA 10, RI 9, ROI 12.

ROSE, Isabella Exh. 1893-1926
Liverpool. † L 2.

ROSE, Jeannie Morrison Exh. 1890-1903
Newcastle on Tyne. † B 1, GI 1, L 2, RBA 2, RMS 1.

ROSE, Mrs. Katherine Exh. 1916
20 Princes Square, Bayswater, London. † LS 3.

ROSE, Kenneth Exh. 1936-40
Flower painter. Wadhouse, Bewdley, Worcs. † B 2, RA 2.

ROSE, Lily Exh. 1885-1914
Mrs. Charles R. Later Lady Rose (1910). Portrait painter and sculptor. London 1885; Hardwick House, nr. Reading, Berks. 1898. † NG 2, P 1, RA 4, RID 20.

ROSE, Marian Exh. 1892-1900
Edinburgh. † RSA 2.

ROSE, Margaret Exh. 1898
Torquay, Devon. † D 2.

ROSE, Peggy Exh. 1937
† NEA 1.

ROSE, Richard H. Exh. 1881-95
Figure painter. 23 Gaisford Street, Kentish Town, London. † D 1, RBA 2, RI 8, ROI 3.

ROSE, Robert Traill b. 1863
Painter, engraver, lithographer and designer b. Newcastle on Tyne. Studied Edinburgh School of Art. Exh. 1898-1926. Add: Edinburgh 1898; Tweedsmuir, Peebleshire 1918. † GI 3, L 7, RSA 29, RSW 7.

ROSE, Miss W. Exh. 1888-89
Loweswater House, Loweswater, Cockermouth. † B 2, M 1.

ROSE, W.G. Exh. 1901
8 Adam Street, Liverpool. † L 1.

ROSEBLADE, Mrs. M.W. Exh. 1920
17 Westwood Avenue, Timperley, Cheshire. † L 4.

ROSEBLADE, William b. 1882
Watercolour landscape painter. b. Leicester. Exh. 1912-37. Add: Coventry 1912; Leicester 1936. † B 20, FIN 2, N 2, RA 1.

ROSEBURGH, William Exh. 1907
Loanhead, Midlothian. † RSA 1.

ROSELIEB, L. Fritz see ROSLYN

ROSELLE, Percy Exh. 1886
59 Lillie Road, London. † B 1.

ROSELLO, Francisco Exh. 1896
Landscape painter. 8 Ormonde Terrace, Regents Park, London. † RA 1.

ROSEN, G.D. Exh. 1911
c/o Allied Artists Association, 67 Chancery Lane, London. † LS 3.

ROSENAUER, Michael Exh. 1934
Architect. 1 Upper George Street, London. † RA 1.

ROSENBERG, Ethel J. Exh. 1883-1909
Portrait, figure and miniature painter. London. † L 7, LS 3, NG 17, RA 30, RMS 3.

ROSENBERG, G.L. Exh. 1926
Etcher. † FIN 10.

ROSENBERG, Miss G.M. Exh. 1908-12
St. Ives, Cornwall 1908; London 1911. † GI 2, RA 2, ROI 3.

ROSENBERG, Henry M. b. 1858
American artist. Exh. 1882. Add: c/o Reitmeyer, Piazza St. Mark, Venice. † RE 1.

ROSENBERG, Isaac 1890-1918
Painter and pencil artist. London 1912; Military Hospital, Bury St. Edmunds, Suffolk 1915. † NEA 4.

ROSENBERG, Louis Conrad b. 1890
Etcher. b. Portland, Oregon, U.S.A. Practised in London under Malcolm Osborne at the Royal College of Art. A.R.E. 1926. Exh. 1925-40. Add: London and New York. † CON 6, FIN 32, RA 10, RE 24.

ROSENBERG, William George Home Exh. 1882-84
Miniature painter. London. † L 2, RA 1.

ROSENBURGH-FLECK, H. Exh. 1935
Sculptor. c/o Mrs. Herriman, 89 Kingsley Way, London. † RA 1.

ROSENKRANTZ, Baron Arild b. 1870
Painter, stained glass artist and sculptor. b. Fredriksborg, Denmark. Studied Julians, Paris. Exh. 1908-38. Add: London. † AB 78, BA 48, BG 37, COO 218, GI 2, L 2, NG 4.

ROSENTHAL, Louis Chattel b. 1887
Sculptor. b. Lithuania. A.R.M.S. 1923. Exh. 1922-31. Add: 2300 Whittier Avenue, Baltimore, U.S.A. † RMS 10.

ROSENTHAL, Toby Edward 1848-1917
Portrait painter. b. U.S.A. Died in Berlin. Exh. 1881. Add: 2 Maximilian Street, Munich, Bavaria. † RA 1.

ROSENVINGE, Odin Exh. 1913-33
4 Browning Avenue, Rock Ferry, Cheshire. † L 8.

ROSHER, Charles Exh. 1906-7
2 The Orchard Studios, Brook Green, London. † D 1, ROI 1.

ROSHER, Grace Exh. 1926-38
Portrait and miniature painter. London. † RA 4.

ROSHER, Mrs. G.B. Exh. 1881-95
Figure and domestic painter. London 1881; Gravesend, Kent 1889. † M 5, RA 6, RBA 7, ROI 5.

ROSIER, Jean Guillaume b. 1858
Belgian portrait and figure painter. Exh. 1890-1928. Add: Anvers 1890; Antwerp 1892; Malines, Belgium 1898; London 1915. † B 1, L 8, M 1, RA 6.

ROSKELL-REYNOLDS, W.F. Exh. 1937-39
Flower painter. London. † RA 1, RBA 2.

ROSKILL, Elizabeth Exh. 1939
† GOU 2.

ROSKILL, N. Exh. 1881
1B Warwick Road, Kensington, London. † RHA 1.

ROSKILL, Sybil Exh. 1930
† GOU 1.

ROSKRUGE, Miss E. Exh. 1910
Hollybank, Yelverton, South Devon. † RA 1.

ROSLYN, Louis Frederick b. 1878
Sculptor. b. London. Studied City and Guilds of London ana R.A. Schools (Landseer scholarship and travelling studentship). Also exhibited under the name of L. Fritz Roselieb. Exh. 1904-40. Add: London. † L 13, M 1, RA 42, RHA 3, RMS 1.

ROSS, Mrs. Exh. 1880-91
Edinburgh. † GI 3, RSA 5.

ROSS, Miss Exh. 1882
Kersdale, High Broughton, Manchester. † M 1.

ROSS, Mrs. Adelaide Exh. 1902-14
18 Upper Westbourne Terrace, Paddington, London. † L 1, LS 13, RA 1, SWA 2.

ROSS, Alice E. Exh. 1886-1937
Watercolour figure and portrait painter. Edinburgh 1886 and 1899; Alloa 1888. † GI 29, L 13, M 1, RA 2, RSA 55, RSW 6.

ROSS, Miss A.F. Exh. 1921-28
Liverpool. † L 12.

ROSS, Aitken M. Exh. 1890-93
114 West Campbell Street, Glasgow. † GI 2.

ROSS, Albert Randolph Exh. 1911
16 East 42nd Street, New York City, U.S.A. † RSA 4.

ROSS, Lady Blanche of Bladensburg Exh. 1910-14
36 Upper Merrion Street, Dublin. † RHA 3.

ROSS, Miss C. Exh. 1932
Burnham House, Elm Bank, Nottingham. † N 1.

ROSS, Catherine Henderson Exh. 1913
Riverfield, Inverness. † RSA 1.

ROSS, Cyril J. Exh. 1938-40
Landscape and figure painter. 146 Woodland Drive, Hove, Sussex. † COO 23, RA 1.

ROSS, Mrs. Campbell M.L. Exh. 1934
A.N.S.A. 1932. Add: Burnham House, Elm Bank, Nottingham. † N 1.

ROSS, Christina Paterson 1843-1906
Watercolour landscape and figure painter. Daughter of Robert Thorburn R. (1816-1876) and sister of Joseph Thorburn R. q.v. R.S.W. 1800. Add: Edinburgh. † DOW 4, GI 31, L 32, M 1, RA 1, RBA 2, RHA 1, RI 7, RSA 77, RSW 66.

ROSS, Miss D. Exh. 1912
1 Princess Park, Liverpool. † L 1.

ROSS, Edward Exh. 1880
15 South Eaton Place, London. † RSA 1.

ROSS, Ellie Exh. 1902
Riverfield, Inverness. † RSA 1.

ROSS, Eleanor M. Exh. 1880-1919
Miniature painter. Edinburgh 1880; London 1911. † GI 9, L 3, RA 4, RSA 35.

ROSS, Mrs. Frances Exh. 1892
nee Trufitt. Add: 6 Salisbury Place, Newington Road, Edinburgh. † RSA 1.

ROSS, Florence A. Exh. 1929-38
Landscape painter. Greystones, Co. Wicklow, 1929; Enniskerry 1934; Dublin 1935. † RHA 8.

ROSS, Henry Exh. 1886
Architect. Accrington, Lancs. † RA 1.

ROSS, Helena M. Exh. 1902
† RMS 2.

ROSS, J. Exh. 1883
Etcher. c/o T. Brown, 32 Charlotte Street, Fitzroy Square, London. † RA 1.

ROSS, Mrs. Jane Exh. 1880-1900
Landscape and figure painter. London. † B 1, RA 2, RBA 5, RHA 3, SWA 2.

ROSS, John E. Exh. 1886-1930
Glasgow 1886; Birkenhead 1910. † GI 10, L 8.

ROSS, John Ferguson Exh. 1927-37
Glasgow. † GI 12, RSA 10.

ROSS, Joseph Halford b. 1866
Painter and teacher. b. Ross, Scotland. Studied Wolverhampton, Leicester, Nottingham and London. Exh. 1892-1909. Add: Nottingham 1892; West Bridgford, Notts. 1909. † N 3.

ROSS, Jessie S. Exh. 1884-96
Edinburgh 1884; Ballagan, Strathblane 1896. † GI 1, L 1, RSW 2.

ROSS, Joseph Thorburn 1849-1903
Landscape and figure painter. Son of Robert Thorburn R. (1816-1876) and brother of Christina Paterson R. q.v. A.R.S.A. 1896. Add: Edinburgh. † GI 36, L 23, M 3, RA 5, RHA 3, RI 1, RSA 64, RSW 5.

ROSS, Jane W. Exh. 1883-97
26 Huntley Gardens, Glasgow. † GI 11, RSA 3.

ROSS, Launcelot Hugh b. 1885
Architect. b. Aberdeen. Studied Gray's School of Art, Aberdeen, and London University. Assistant to Sir John James Burnet. Exh. 1914-40. Add: Glasgow. † GI 17, RSA 2.

ROSS, Mrs. Madge Exh. 1890-1921
Portrait painter. Paris 1890; London 1891; Helensburgh 1893; Glasgow 1909. † GI 7, RA 2.

ROSS, Margaret Exh. 1911-23
Montrose, N.B. 1911; Glasgow 1923. † GI 2, L 2, RSA 1.

ROSS, Michael Exh. 1926-39
Painter and etcher. London. † AB 1, BA 2, NEA 4, P 1, RA 2, RED 1, ROI 1, TOO 1.

ROSS, Miss M.J.T. Exh. 1882
17 Clarinda Park, Kingstown, Ireland. † RHA 1.

ROSS, Oriel Exh. 1937
Watercolour painter. † RED 2.

ROSS, Miss R. Exh. 1885
28 Walker Street, Edinburgh. † RSA 1.

ROSS, Robert Exh. 1880-90
Edinburgh and Musselburgh. † GI 1, L 2, RSA 37.

ROSS, R.C.S. Exh. 1908-37
Landscape painter. West Bridgford, Notts. † N 18.

ROSS, Robert Henry Alison Exh. 1898-1940
Edinburgh. † GI 12, L 2, RCA 1, RSA 36.

ROSS, R. McAllister Exh. 1927-37
Glasgow. † GI 5.

ROSS, Tom Exh. 1915-40
Birkhill, Lochee, Dundee. † GI 5, L 4, RSA 3.

ROSS, Vera Exh. 1923-36
Mrs. Weekley. Landscape and figure painter. Studied Slade School 1920-24. Add: Woking, Surrey 1923; London 1924. † BA 1, GOU 21, NEA 11, RHA 2.

ROSS, Mrs. W. Exh. 1889
14 Vezey Place, Kingstown, Ireland. † RHA 1.

ROSS, William Exh. 1938
189 Pitt Street, Glasgow. † GI 2.

ROSS, William A. Exh. 1937
Architect. War Office, Whitehall, London. † RA 3.

ROSS, William H.A. Exh. 1883-91
Edinburgh. † RSA 3.

ROSS, William Leighton Exh. 1907-8
18 Glenorchy Terrace, Edinburgh. † GI 2, RSA 3.

ROSSELL, Henry Exh. 1891
Landscape painter. Birch House, Alfreton Road, Nottingham. † N 1.

ROSSELL, Miss M. Exh. 1908-9
Church Street, Sandiacre, Notts. † N 3.

ROSSER, Dulce V. Exh. 1923-28
Rosslyn, Western Drive, Grassendale, Liverpool. † L 5.

ROSSET-GRANGER, Edouard Exh. 1906
45 Avenue de Villiers, Paris. † L 1.

ROSSI, A.H. Exh. 1884
Landscape painter. 39 Clifton Gardens, Maida Vale, London. † RA 1.

ROSSI, Alexander M.* Exh. 1880-1905
Portrait and genre painter. London. † B 19, FIN 1, GI 8, L 36, M 7, RA 49, RBA 34, RI 23, ROI 10, RSA 6.

ROSSI, E. Exh. 1902-8
12 Piazza Vittoria, Naples. † NG 5, RA 2.

ROSSI, L. Exh. 1884
5 Haymarket, London. † M 1.

ROSSI, Mary H. Exh. 1894-97
Figure painter. Hampstead, London. † B 2, RA 1, RBA 1, RI 1.

ROSSI, Silvio A. Exh. 1936-40
Airdrie. † RSA 6.

ROSSIGNOL, le see L

ROSSI-SCOTTI, Count Lemmi Exh. 1890-1903
Figure painter. Rome 1890; Perugia, Italy 1900. † L 3, NG 4.

ROSSITER, Mrs. Bettina Exh. 1913-15
59 Victoria Road, Chingford, Essex. † L 4.

ROSSITER, Charles* b. 1827
Genre painter. Married Frances and father of Frances A.R. q.v. Exh. 1880-90. Add: Uppingham, Rutland. † L 3, M 1, RA 5, RBA 1.

ROSSITER, Miss E.A. Exh. 1932-38
Coventry. † B 6.

ROSSITER, Frances Exh. 1882-98
nee Sears. Genre and bird painter and watercolourist. Studied under Leigh and her husband Charles R. q.v. Mother of Frances A.R. q.v. Add: Uppingham, Rutland. † B 1, D 2, L 11, M 10, RA 1, RI 5.

ROSSITER, Frances A. Exh. 1880-1914
Bird painter. Exh. 1880-1914. Daughter of Charles and Frances R. q.v. Add: London 1880; Uppingham, Rutland 1883; Warrington, Lancs. 1914. † L 4, M 2, RBA 1.

ROSSITER, Henry Exh. 1885
Watercolour landscape painter. 4 Princes Road, Notting Hill, London. † RI 1.

ROSSITER, Walter b. 1871
Landscape and architectural painter. b. Bath. Studied Bath, Rouen and Paris. Exh. 1928-29. Add: Bromley, Kent. † L 1, RI 1.

ROST, Amelia Exh. 1884
Flower painter. 21 Dresdner Strasse, Leipzig. † SWA 1.

ROST, Adolph E.L. Exh. 1892-93
Sculptor. 126 Haverstock Hill, London. † RA 2.

ROSTROM, Miss E. Exh. 1892
Sparthbank House, Heaton, Stockport, Lancs. † M 1.

ROSTRON, Ralph H. Exh. 1914
85 Portland Street, Southport, Lancs. † L 2.

ROTCH, Arthur Exh. 1880
Landscape painter. c/o R. Phene, Spier Square, Regent Street, London. † D 1.

ROTH, Mrs. Constance Exh. 1894
Watercolour landscape painter. 8 Bedford Place, London. † RA 1.

ROTH, P.R. Exh. 1911
30 Place Denfert, Rochereau, Paris. † L 2.

ROTHENSTEIN, Albert Daniel see RUTHERSTON

ROTHENSTEIN, Mrs. Betty Exh. 1932-40
nee Fitzgerald. Painter and sculptor. Married Michael R. q.v. S.W.A. 1939. Add: London. † GI 1, RA 3, SWA 8.

ROTHENSTEIN, Michael b. 1908
Landscape, still life, figure and flower painter. Studied Chelsea Polytechnic and Central School of Arts and Crafts. Son of Sir William and Betty R. q.v. A.R.B.A. 1940. Add: London. † AG 2, COO 1, LEI 38, NEA 3, RA 7, RBA 2.

ROTHENSTEIN, Sir William* 1872-1945
Painter, draughtsman, lithographer, and writer. b. Bradford. Studied Slade School 1888 and Julians, Paris 1889-93. Professor of Civic Art, University of Sheffield 1917-26. Official war artist 1917-18 and to the Canadian Army of Occupation 1919. Principal Royal College of Art 1920-35. Trustee of Tate Gallery 1927-33. Son in law of Walter John Knewstub q.v. Father of Michael R. q.v. and brother of Albert Rutherston q.v. Visited India 1910. N.E.A. 1894, R.P. 1897, Knighted 1931. "The Princess Badroulbadour" (1908) purchased by Chantrey Bequest 1924 and "Barnett Freedman" (1925) purchased in 1943. Add: London. † AG 84, ALP 7, B 7, BAR 1, CAR 92, CG 2, CHE 89, COO 2, FIN 7, G 14, GI 8, GOU 156, I 4, L 16, LEF 3, LEI 173, M 56, NEA 142, P 50, RA 15, RED 1, RHA 2, RSA 11, RSW 1.

ROTHERAN, Miss M.C. Exh. 1897
Bellevue, Crossakiel, Co. Meath. † RHA 1.

ROTHNEY, Nina Exh. 1904-8
Pembury, 1 Tudor Road, Upper Norwood, London. † SWA 10.

ROTHSCHILD, Edith Exh. 1896-97
25 Pershore Road, Edgbaston, Birmingham. † B 2.

ROTHWELL, Adah Exh. 1935-39
Miniature portrait painter. 40 Roland Gardens, London. † RA 4, RMS 2, SWA 3.

ROTHWELL, Elizabeth Exh. 1928-30
Figure painter. Married William Dring q.v. Add: London. † NEA 3, RA 1.

ROTHWELL, J.H. Exh. 1884
58 Gilda Brook Road, Eccles, Manchester. † M 1.

ROTHWELL, L. Exh. 1928
366 Radford Road, Nottingham. † N 1.

ROTHWELL, Margarita R. Exh. 1881-87
Painter. Hampstead, London 1881; Belfast 1882. † B 5, L 1, RHA 12, SWA 1.

ROTHWELL, R.E. Exh. 1890
20 Callender Street, Ramsbottom, nr. Bury, Lancs. † M 1.

ROTHWELL, Selim 1815-1881
Etcher. India Buildings, 14 Cross Street, Manchester. † RA 1.

ROTHWELL, T.H. Exh. 1908
Ash Grove, Llanfairfechan, North Wales. † L 11.

ROTIG, Georges Frederic b. 1873
French artist. Exh. 1909. Add: 9 Rue Bochard de Saron, Paris. † L 1.

ROTINOFF, Margarita Exh. 1930-40
Portrait painter. 36 Queen's Gate, London. † L 1, NEA 1, P 7, RA 3.

ROTTA, Silvio Guilio 1853-1913
Italian painter. Liverpool 1881; Venice 1905. † I 1, RA 1.

ROTTESMAN, M. Exh. 1926
† M 1.

ROTTON, Rev. H.F.A. Exh. 1928-33
Painter. † AB 3, WG 1.

ROTY, Georges Exh. 1930
Sculptor. 58 Rue de Vaugirard, Paris. † RA 1.

ROUAULT, Georges* 1871-1958
French painter. Exh. 1925-38. † CHE 4, RED 1.

ROUGH, Helen M. Exh. 1888
35 Kersland Terrace, Hillhead, Glasgow. † GI 1.

ROUGH, James Johnston Exh. 1920-40
Edinburgh. † B 1, GI 7, RSA 9, RSW 3.

ROUGH, Miss Toussa Exh. 1909-14
8 Sheffield Terrace, Campden Hill, London. † LS 6, P 1, SWA 2.

ROUGH, W. Ednie Exh. 1926-35
Edinburgh 1926; Corstorphine 1932. † GI 3, RSA 7, RSW 10.

ROUGHLEY, Edward Exh. 1933
Architect. Prestatyn, Wales. † RCA 1.

ROUGHTON, Mrs. E.M. Exh. 1889-1920
Architectural painter, mainly in watercolour. London 1889; Shrewsbury 1906; Liverpool 1912; Caerwys, Flints. 1913; Heswell, Cheshire 1919. † B 1, BG 29, L 13, RBA 5.

ROUGVIE, Walter Exh. 1930-36
136 High Street, Leslie, Scotland. † RSA 4, RSW 4.

ROULAND, Orlando b. 1871
American artist. Exh. 1909. Add: 130 West 57th Street, New York, U.S.A. † GI 1.

ROULLET, Gaston Exh. 1903
Landscape painter. 34 Rue de Lille, Paris. † L 1.

ROUMSCHIJSKY, Mme. B. Exh. 1914
5 Rue Pajou, Passy, Paris. † RA 2.

ROUND, Cecil M. Exh. 1884-98
Landscape and figure painter. Bridport, Dorset 1884; London 1886; Ockley, Surrey 1889; Teignmouth, Devon 1898. † B 4, GI 1, M 4, NG 2, RA 8, RBA 4, ROI 3.

ROUND, D.G. Exh. 1910-12
Adelphi Terrace House, Strand, London. † RA 2.

ROUND, Frank H. Exh. 1913-38
Portrait painter. Godalming, Surrey 1913; London 1920. † B 5, L 2, RA 6.

ROUND, Miss S.A. Exh. 1882
114 Hadley Road, Birmingham. † B 1.

ROUNDEBUSH, John Heywood Exh. 1901
Giverny, Vernon, Eure, France. † NG 1.

ROUNTHWAITE, Bertha Exh. 1936-39
14 Oakhill Road, London. † ROI 6.

ROUS, J. Exh. 1887-88
6 Sandon Street, Liverpool. † L 5.

ROUSE, F.B. Exh. 1883-1904
Watercolour landscape painter. London. † GI 1, L 1, RBA 1, RI 3.

ROUSE, Fred J.C.V. Exh. 1888-93
Landscape painter. London. † RA 8, RBA 6.

ROUSE, Robert William Arthur Exh. 1883-1927
Landscape painter and etcher. R.B.A. 1889. Add: London 1883 and 1898; Merton, Surrey 1896; Long Crendon, Bucks. 1925; Thame, Oxon 1927. † GI 1, L 15, M 2, RA 45, RBA 64, RHA 6, RI 6, ROI 13, RSA 3.

ROUSEAU, Loiseau Exh. 1894
28 Rue Notre Dame des Champs, Paris. † GI 2.

ROUSEL, Jules H.R. Exh. 1929-38
Portrait painter and etcher. London. † FIN 1, P 2, RA 2.

ROUSSADO, de see D

ROUSSE, Charles Exh. 1882-85
214 Ladywood Road, Birmingham. † B 6.

ROUSSE, Frank Exh. 1897-1915
Watercolour landscape painter. Ilford, Essex 1897; Hadley, Herts. 1915. † RA 2, RI 3.

ROUSSEAU, Emile Exh. 1909
14 Rue de Chabrol, Paris. † L 3.

ROUSSEAU, H.E. Exh. 1911
15 Rue Hegesippe Moreau, Paris. † L 1.

ROUSSEAU, J.J. Exh. 1901-9
Painter. Paris. † GOU 4, L 1, ROI 1.

ROUSSEAU, Victor b. 1865
Sculptor. Exh. 1931. Add: 187 Avenue Van Volxem, Forest, Brussels. † RSA 4.

ROUSSEL, Ker Xavier* b. 1867
French painter. Exh. 1921. † GOU 1.

ROUSSEL, Raphael T. Exh. 1908-29
Painter and etcher. London. † BG 1, GOU 9, L 2, RA 1, RSA 2.

ROUSSEL, Theodore* 1847-1926
Painter and etcher. N.E.A. 1887, R.B.A. 1887, A.R.E. 1921. Add: London. † BG 1, CHE 63, CON 34, DOW 1, G 1, GI 22, GOU 14, I 10, L 13, LS 6, M 1, NEA 10, NG 19, P 6, RBA 7, RE 8, RHA 2, RI 1, RID 1, RSA 1.

ROUSSOFF, Alexandre N. Exh. 1880-1911
Landscape painter. London 1880; Venice 1881. † D 4, FIN 346, GI 1, M 3, RA 5, RI 1.

ROUSTEAUX-DARBOUR, Mme. E. Exh. 1902
Villa Apoloni, Chemin St., Charles, Carabacel, Nice, France. † L 1.

ROUTCHINE, Mlle. Sonia Exh. 1912-14
Paris 1912; London 1914. † GI 4, L 1, RSA 4.

ROUTH, Mrs. Exh. 1887
c/o W.P. Buckham, 14 Bedford Row, London. † D 2.
ROUTH, A.L. Exh. 1889
Sibford, Banbury, Oxon. † B 1.
ROUTLEDGE, Bessie Exh. 1887
Still life painter. Yarra Yarra, Eastbourne. † SWA 1.
ROUTLEDGE, F.B. Exh. 1916
108 Seabank Road, Wallasey, Cheshire. † L 1.
ROUX, Paul Exh. 1885
21 Rue Pigalle, Paris. † GI 1.
ROVEREDO, Mlle. Yvonne Ripa Exh. 1908-9
4 Rue Girodet, Paris. † LS 8.
ROWAN, William G. Exh. 1891-1903
Architect. 234 West George Street, Glasgow. † GI 20, RA 3.
ROWAN-ROBINSON, Mrs. Evelyn Russell Exh. 1929
Landscape painter. b. Ireland. Studied Dresden and under William Wood. Add: 8 Evelyn Mansions, Carlisle Place, London. † RID 4.
ROWAND, M. Exh. 1893
227 West George Street, Glasgow. † GI 1.
ROWANTREE, Frederick Exh. 1898-1903
Glasgow 1898; London 1903. † GI 3.
ROWAT, James Exh. 1889-1923
Watercolour landscape painter. Glasgow. † GI 31, L 2, RA 1, RSA 3, RSW 1.
ROWAT, Mary Exh. 1892
Warriston, Paisley, Glasgow. † GI 1.
ROWBOTHAM, Miss B. Exh. 1916
15 Finchley Way, Church End, Finchley, London. † RI 1.
ROWBOTHAM, Charles* Exh. 1881-1913
Landscape painter. Son of Thomas C.L.R. (1823-1875). Add: London 1881; Brighton 1899; Croydon, Surrey 1913. † B 3, D 6, GI 4, L 2, M 1, RBA 2, RHA 1, RI 4.
ROWBOTHAM, Claude H. Exh. 1900-12
Watercolour landscape painter. Wallingford, Berks. † D 1, WG 121.
ROWBOTHAM, Mrs. Frances C. Exh. 1896-98
24 Russell Road, Kensington, London. † B 2.
ROWBOTHAM, G.H. Exh. 1885
10 Langworthy Road, Manchester. † M 3.
ROWBOTHAM, Sir Walter Exh. 1909-13
Artist and teacher. Jamsetjee Jejeebhoy School of Art, Bombay 1909; Colwyn Bay, Wales 1913. † LS 7.
ROWBOTTOM, Percy Exh. 1884-89
Landscape painter. Idridgehay, Derbys. † N 13.
ROWDEN, Jessie Exh. 1891
Landscape painter. 15 St. Giles, Oxford. † RI 1.
ROWDEN, Thomas 1842-1926
Painter. Exh. 1883. Add: c/o Slade Bros. 169 Gt. Portland Street, London. Moved to Exeter c.1890. † RHA 2.
ROWE, Ashley b. 1882
Woodcut and aquatint artist and etcher. b. Plymouth. Exh. 1927-29. Add: Chacot Studio, Mount Hawke, Truro, Cornwall. † L 3.
ROWE, Constance Exh. 1929-31
Painter. East End Way, Pinner, Middlesex. † NEA 2, RA 1.
ROWE, E. Arthur d. 1922
Landscape and garden painter. London 1885; Tunbridge Wells, Kent 1902. † B 3, D 1, DOW 543, GOU 5, L 21, LS 3, M 13, NG 14, RA 26, RBA 24, RI 22, ROI 4.
ROWE, Edith D'Oyley Exh. 1889-1922
Flower painter. 27 Hilmarten Road, London. † B 3, L 3, RBA 1, RI 3, SWA 8.
ROWE, Elsie Hugo Exh. 1913-40
Mrs. Rhys Thomas. Landscape, still life, figure and interior painter. b. Halifax. Studied Slade School, Paris and under Bertram Priestman. Add: London 1913 and 1918; Datchet, Bucks. 1914; Birmingham 1934. † B 5, G 4, GOU 2, I 4, L 3, LS 19, M 2, NEA 3, RA 5, ROI 3, SWA 6.
ROWE, Gertrude Exh. 1895-96
Trecarrel, Redruth, Cornwall. † RBA 2.
ROWE, Gwendoline Exh. 1900-5
St. Laurence's Rectory, Denton, nr. Manchester. † L 1, M 1.
ROWE, Hadley Exh. 1929-30
Painter. 21 Limeston Road, London. † NEA 2, RA 1.
ROWE, Hooper Exh. 1928-32
Painter and linocut artist. † GOU 20, RED 5.
ROWE, Mrs. I.S. Exh. 1917-22
Angle House, St. Austell, Cornwall. † SWA 6.
ROWE, John Exh. 1888
Taunton, Somerset. † RHA 1.
ROWE, Mary J. Exh. 1922-29
Crabwell, Talbot Road, Birkenhead. † L 6.
ROWE, Miss R.M. Exh. 1894-98
Southborough, Tunbridge Wells, Kent. † L 2, RBA 1, RI 1.
ROWE, S. Exh. 1885
250 High Holborn, London. † M 1.
ROWE, Sidney Grant 1861-1928
Landscape painter. Studied St. Martins School of Art. R.B.A. 1897, R.O.I. 1908. Add: London 1880 and 1897; Rickmansworth, Herts. 1895; Warlingham, Surrey 1896. † B 6, L 1, RA 11, RBA 109, RE 22, RI 24, ROI 91.
ROWE, Tom Trythall b. 1856
Landscape painter. N.E.A. 1886, N.S.A. 1886. Exh. 1882-1915. Add: London 1882; Cookham Dene, Berks. 1891; Rotherham, Yorks. 1896; Nottingham 1909. † D 2, DOW 1, L 7, M 3, N 94, NEA 7, RA 22, RBA 16, RHA 5, RI 6, ROI 18.
ROWE, W. Exh. 1900-17
Landscape painter. London. † RA 2.
ROWE, William J. Monkhouse Exh. 1883-91
Painter and etcher. London. † RA 3.
ROWE, W.P. Exh. 1914
Wilmington, Hendon Lane, Finchley, London. † RA 1.
ROWED, Marion Exh. 1910-15
Eccleston Park, Prescot, Lancs. † L 9.
ROWELL, John Exh. 1936-40
Landscape painter. London. † GI 3, RA 2, RHA 1, ROI 3.
ROWE-THOMAS, Mrs. Beatrice Exh. 1915-26
Flower and garden painter. 15 Finchley Way, Church End, London. † AB 4, RI 2.
ROWLAND, Miss A.M. Exh. 1898
15 Pond Place, Fulham Road, London. † RI 1.
ROWLAND, Edith Exh. 1901-40
Portrait, landscape, figure painter and miniaturist. Studied Heatherleys, National Gallery London and the Louvre, Paris. Add: Eversleigh, Derby Road, Woodford, Essex. † L 5, NG 1, RA 2, RCA 10, RHA 19, RSA 30, SWA 3.
ROWLAND, Mrs. Evelyn Graham Exh. 1930-31
Glasgow. † GI 2, L 1, RSA 2.
ROWLAND, Miss M.A. Exh. 1901
191 Revidge Road, Blackburn, Lancs. † L 2.
ROWLANDS, A. Exh. 1932
† L 2.
ROWLANDS, Mrs. Constance Ethel b. 1891
nee Hutchinson. Painter and illustrator. b. Fukuoka, Japan. Studied Regent Street Polytechnic and Kensington School of Art Bristol. Exh. 1928-30. Add: Winscombe, Somerset. † L 4, RA 2.
ROWLANDS, J.V. Exh. 1887-88
24 Slater Street, Liverpool. † L 2.
ROWLANDS, Tom Exh. 1886
8 Woodfield Villa, St. Paul's Road, Sparkbrook, Birmingham. † B 1.
ROWLANDSON, Miss E. Exh. 1891-93
Clare House, Tiverton, North Devon. † M 2.
ROWLANDSON, George Derville* b. 1861
b. India. Studied Gloucester, Westminster and Paris. Exh. 1911-18. Add: 22 Priory Road, Bedford Park, London. † RI 4.
ROWLES, Lilian May Bevis Exh. 1914-18
nee Hall. Commercial artist and illustrator. b. Newport, Mon. Studied West Bromwich Municipal School of Art. Married Stanley Charles R. q.v. Add: Congleton, Cheshire 1914; London 1915. † L 2, RA 5.
ROWLES, Marjorie Kathleen Exh. 1923-39
Landscape, seascape and figure painter. b. Gloucester. Studied Slade School. Add: London. † GOU 39, NEA 28, RA 5, RCA 3, RED 2, RHA 7, RSA 7, SWA 5.
ROWLES, Stanley Charles b. 1887
Commercial artist. Studied Royal College of Art 1905-11, Putney School of Art and Battersea Polytechnic School of Art. Headmaster West Bromwich Municipal School of Art. Married Lilian M.B.R. q.v. Add: West Bromwich 1914; Surbiton Hill, Surrey 1917. † L 1, RA 2.
ROWLEY, Alice B.C. Exh. 1909-10
Painter. 30 Rossetti Mansions, Chelsea, London. † NEA 2.
ROWLEY, A.J. Exh. 1915-28
Decorative inlaid wood panel artist. The Rowley Gallery, 140 Church Street, Kensington, London. † L 10.
ROWLEY, Blanche Exh. 1916-22
Landscape painter. 11 Cheyne Walk, London. † I 1, NEA 10.
ROWLEY, Mrs. Francis Exh. 1893
6 Wentworth Studios, Manresa Road, Chelsea, London. † L 1, NG 1.
ROWLEY, J. Sydney R. Exh. 1907
218 Cloncliffe Road, Drumcondra, Dublin. † RHA 2.
ROWLEY, Mrs. M. Exh. 1905
Meanwood, Leeds. † RA 1.
ROWLEY-SMART Exh. 1912
Manchester. † M 1.
ROWLING, Dorothy M. Exh. 1938-40
Miniature portrait painter. 1 Stanley Place, London. † RA 2.
ROWLING, Eileen Marjorie b. 1906
Portrait and miniature painter. Exh. 1926-30. Add: 159 Hainault Road, Leytonstone, Essex. † L 6, RA 4, RSA 1.
ROWLINSON, Miss M.H. Exh. 1928-29
The Homestead, Broome Edge, Lymm, Cheshire. † L 4.
ROWNEY, Lilian Exh. 1893-1934
Mrs. Harley. Landscape, figure and miniature portrait painter. Hampstead, London 1893, Northwood, Middlesex 1918; Harrow, Middlesex 1930. † L 7, LS 8, M 4, NEA 1, RA 19, RBA 1, RI 17, RMS 3, ROI 1, SWA 16.
ROWNEY, Mary Exh. 1892-95
Co. Galway, Ireland 1892; Cambridge 1895. † GI 1, RHA 1.

ROWNEY, Margaret E. Exh. 1933-38
Watercolour landscape painter. Hampstead, London. † NEA 3, RA 2, RI 3.
ROWNTREE, Fred Exh. 1904-7
11 Hammersmith Terrace, London. † GI 7, L 1.
ROWNTREE, Irma T. Exh. 1912
32 King Street West, Manchester. † M 2.
ROWNTREE, Kenneth b. 1915
Painter and designer. b. Scarborough. Studied Ruskin School of Drawing, Oxford and Slade School. Exh. 1936-40. † COO 9, GOU 2, LEF 2, LEI 1, NEA 7.
ROWORTH, Edward* b. 1880
Portrait painter. Studied Slade School. Exh. 1902-28. Add: Heaton Moor, nr. Southport, Lancs. 1902; Manchester 1904; Donnybrook, Ireland 1928. † B 2, GI 1, L 1, M 1, RHA 1.
ROWSE, Herbert J. Exh. 1931-38
Architect. Liverpool. † L 3, RA 5.
ROWSELL, Rev. T. Norman Exh. 1889-1928
Landscape painter. Eltham, Kent 1889; London 1903. † AB 6, D 3, RI 2.
ROWSON, Walter S. Exh. 1883-90
Macclesfield 1883; Stretford, nr. Manchester 1885; Urmston, Lancs. 1890. † L 1, M 4.
ROWSTORNE, Edwin Exh. 1891
Figure painter. 2 Station Terrace, New Southgate, London. † RA 1.
ROWTON, Miss G.M.E. Exh. 1903
The Close, Bradfield, Reading, Berks. † SWA 1.
ROWTON, Miss K. Exh. 1882
Gloucester Street, Coventry. † L 1.
ROX, Henry Exh. 1937-38
Sculptor. 17 Lancaster Road, London. † GI 1. RA 2.
ROXBURG, William Exh. 1906
Loanhead, Midlothian. † GI 1.
ROXBURGH, Ebenezer B. Exh. 1880-97
Edinburgh. † RSA 28.
ROXBURGH, Mrs. E.G. Exh. 1909-11
Miniature painter. 3 The Serpentine, Grassendale, Liverpool. † L 2, RA 1.
ROXBURGH, Josephine M. Exh. 1881-82
Newington Lodge, Edinburgh. † GI 2, RSA 1.
ROXBY, C.W. Exh. 1880-1910
Watercolour landscape and figure painter. London 1880; Alverstoke, Hants. 1899. † B 4, D 15, L 4, M 1, RBA 17.
ROXBY, Evelyn Florence Exh. 1898-99
Sherborne, Dorset. † D 2.
ROXBY, Genevieve Exh. 1895-1902
† D 3.
ROXBY, Irene Sibyl Exh. 1898
Sherborne, Dorest. † D 1.
ROXLEY, Carus Wilson Exh. 1909
† LS 3.
ROY, le see L
ROY, Van see V
ROY, Abani Exh. 1931-36
Landscape painter. London. † RA 4, RSA 1.
ROY, J.B. Exh. 1900
† TOO 2.
ROY, K. Chandra Exh. 1933
Sculptor. Royal College of Art, South Kensington, London. † RA 1.
ROY, Marius b. 1833
French artist. Exh. 1883-85. Add: Rue de Lavel, Paris. † GI 2.
ROYBET, Ferdinand* 1840-1920
French figure and portrait painter. Exh. 1892-1915. Add: Paris. † I 1, L 1, P 2.
ROYDE, le See L
ROYDS, A.F. Exh. 1910
29B Lincoln's Inn Fields, London. † RA 1.
ROYDS, J.I. Exh. 1913-14
1 Clifton Hill Studios, St. Johns Wood, London. † L 2, RA 2.
ROYDS, Mabel A. Exh. 1899-1940
Mrs. E.S. Lumsden. Add: London 1899; Edinburgh 1909. † GI 1, I 1, L 6, RHA 1, RSA 45, SWA 1.
ROYDS, Norah Exh. 1881
Watercolour painter. Coddington Rectory, Chester. † SWA 1.
ROYER, Henri b. 1869
French artist. Exh. 1913-23. Add: 63 Boulevard Berthier, Paris. † GI 1, L 1, RSA 3.
ROYLE, Mrs. C. Mary Exh. 1881
Landscape painter. 26 Pier Road, Rosherville, Kent. † SWA 1.
ROYLE, Edith Exh. 1898
Adswood House, Stockport, Lancs. † M 1.
ROYLE, Herbert* Exh. 1892-1940
Landscape and figure painter. b. Manchester. Studied under J. Buxton Knight. Add: Stockport, Lancs. 1892; Ilkley, Yorks. 1919. † B 25, GI 10, I 3, L 118, M 5, NEA 1, RA 18, RBA 1, RCA 11, ROI 8, RSA 4.
ROYLE, Stanley 1888-1961
Landscape painter. b. Stalybridge, Lancs. Studied Sheffield Technical School of Art. A.R.B.A. 1919, R.B.A. 1921. Add: Sheffield 1911; Nova Scotia College of Art, Halifax, Nova Scotia 1932. † GI 26, L 27, RA 39, RBA 21, RI 2, ROI 6, RSA 9.
ROZIER, Dominique 1840-1901
French artist. Exh. 1881. Add: 16 Avenue Trudaine, Paris. † RHA 1.
ROZSNYAY, de See D
RUAULD, Maud See HILLIARD
RUBEN, Franz* Exh. 1882-92
Landscape painter. Venice 1882 and 1886; London 1884. † L 10, RA 2.
RUBERY, Miss E.H. Exh. 1885-86
15 Highfield Road, Birmingham. † B 2.
RUBIN Exh. 1938
† TOO 32.
RUBIN, M.J. Exh. 1911
270 Elgin Avenue, Maida Vale, London. † RA 1.
RUBY, Richard J. Exh. 1930
Wesley Street, Bradley, Bilston, Wolverhampton. † B 1.
RUCK, Berta Exh. 1903
Watercolour painter. † BG 1.
RUDD, Agnes J. Exh. 1888-1938
Landscape painter. Bournemouth. † B 5, D 74, L 3, RA 14, RBA 4, RI 28.
RUDD, David Heylin b. 1894
Painter, wood engraver, etcher and engraver. Studied Glasgow, London, Basle, Paris and Zurich. Assistant curator Glasgow Corporation Art Gallery. Exh. 1928-31. Add: 48 Clifford Street, Glasgow. † GI 4, L 4, RSA 2.
RUDD, Susan D. Exh. 1895-1911
Clonhaston, Enniscorthy, Co. Wexford. † RHA 6.
RUDDER, de See D
RUDDLE, W.H. Exh. 1916
49 Elgin Road, Croydon, Surrey. † ROI 2.
RUDDOCK, Oliver L. Exh. 1880
Sculptor. 5 West Street, Pimlico, London. † RA 1.
RUDDOCK, Samuel Exh. 1880-92
Sculptor. 5 West Street, Pimlico, London. † RA 2.
RUDGE, Bradford* Exh. 1880-84
Landscape painter and lithographer. Bedford. † D 1, L 2, RBA 3, RSA 1.
RUDGE, Carlotta Exh. 1927
Redrigg, Exmouth, Devon. † L 1.
RUDGE, C.D. Exh. 1920-21
135 Bath Row, Birmingham. † B 3.
RUDGE, Margaret M. Exh. 1913-29
Etcher, 16 Trinity Road, Wandsworth Common, London. † RA 2, SWA 2.
RUDKIN, Arthur E. Exh. 1920-37
Landscape painter. Leicester. † N 7.
RUET, Louis Exh. 1896-1913
Etcher. London 1896 and 1909; Paris 1903. † RA 5, RMS 6.
RUFF, George Junr. Exh. 1880
Landscape and still life painter. 164 Gt. Titchfield Street, Portland Place, London. † RBA 1.
RUFF, George sen. Exh. 1880-86
Watercolour landscape and figure painter. 45 Queen's Road, Brighton. † RA 1, RBA 3, RI 2, ROI 2.
RUFFLE, Emma M. Exh. 1908-35
London 1908; Weston super Mare, Somerset 1933. † L 3, RI 12.
RUGER, Curt Exh. 1904
Munich. † GI 1.
RUILLE, de See D
RUITH, Van See V
RUL, Henri b. 1862
Belgian landscape painter. Exh. 1890. Add: Merkem, Antwerp. † RA 1.
RULLAN, Ayrton Exh. 1883
St. Ann's Mount, Polton, Midlothian. † RSA 1.
RUMBLELOW, Edith Exh. 1900
33 Penn Road Villas, Camden Road, London. † SWA 1.
RUMMELHOFF, C. Exh. 1888
† D 3.
RUMNEY, Nora Rowland Exh. 1933-39
Warrington, Lancs. † RCA 7.
RUMSCHISKY, Mme. B. Exh. 1915-16
London 1915; Reading, Berks. 1916. † L 3, RA 2.
RUNACRES, Frank b. 1904
Landscape painter. Studied St. Martins School of Art, Slade School and Royal College of Art 1930-33. Exh. 1927-40. Add: London 1927 and 1940; Westerham, Kent 1939. † M 1, RA 4.
RUNCIMAN, Kate Exh. 1903
Miniature portrait painter. 105 Bridge Street, Battersea, London. † RA 1.
RUNTZ, Ernest Exh. 1891-99
Architect. London. † RA 8.
RUSDEN, A. Exh. 1926
† M 1.
RUSHBURY, Mrs. Florence Exh. 1919-27
nee Layzell. Landscape painter. Married Henry R. q.v. Add: London. † NEA 4, RA 1.
RUSHBURY, Sir Henry 1889-1968
Watercolour painter and etcher. b. Harborne, Birmingham. Studied Birmingham College of Art and Slade School. Married Florence R. q.v. N.E.A. 1917, A.R.A. 1927, R.A. 1936, A.R.E. 1921, R.E. 1922, A.R.W.S. 1922, R.W.S. 1926. "St. Paul's" purchased by Chantrey Bequest 1931. Add: London 1912, 1925 and 1938; Petworth, Sussex 1923; Stoke by Nayland, Essex 1933. † AB 3, AG 3, BA 16, BAR 4, BK 3, CON 92, CG 2, CHE 5, FIN 24, G 134, GI 11, GOU 5, L 50, LEI 3, M 5, NEA 75, RA 77, RE 39, RHA 6, RSA 4, RWS 64.
RUSHER, R. Eaton Exh. 1886
29 Alfred Place, London. † ROI 1.

RUSHFORTH, G. Exh. 1885-86
Engineer's Office, General Station, Liverpool. † L 2.

RUSHTON, Alfred Josiah b. 1864
Portrait, figure and landscape painter. b. Worcester. Studied Birmingham School and Art and Royal College of Art. 2nd master Leeds School of Art. Principal of West Hartlepool School of Art. Exh. 1880-1908. Add: Worcester 1880; Cheltenham, Glos. 1881; Leeds 1905; West Hartlepool 1908. † B 8, RA 3, RBA 2.

RUSHTON, Desmond Exh. 1931-33
Portrait and figure painter. 30 Upper Ely Place, Dublin. † RHA 4.

RUSHTON, Dorothy Marion b. 1884
Painter, mural decorator, etcher and teacher. Studied at Cope's, R.A. Schools and Hanover. Exh. 1909-22. Add: London. † L 9, RHA 2, SWA 4.

RUSHTON, George Robert Exh. 1894-1940
Watercolour painter and decorative artist. b. Birmingham. Studied Birmingham and London. A.R.B.A. 1922, R.B.A. 1938, R.B.S.A. 1925, R.I. 1929. Add: Birmingham 1894; Newcastle on Tyne 1896; Pyton on Tyne 1902; Ipswich, Suffolk 1911; Blewbury, Berks. 1928; Dedham, Essex 1937. † B 80, D 2, FIN 45, GI 2, L 10, RA 25, RBA 79, RCA 1, RI 71.

RUSHTON, Kate A. Exh. 1892
Flower painter. 32 Lordship Park, Stoke Newington, London. † RBA 1.

RUSHTON, William C. d. 1921
Cambuslang 1904; Edinburgh 1908; Bingley, Yorks. 1909. † GI 5, L 9.

RUSHWELL, W.W. Exh. 1885
13 Uverdale Road, Chelsea, London. † L 1.

RUSHWORTH, Miss E. Exh. 1905
Church Hill, Royston, Barnsley. † RCA 1.

RUSHWORTH, W. Maynard Exh. 1891-1929
Studied Liverpool School of Art and School of Architecture, Liverpool University. Add: Liverpool. † L 17.

RUSINOL, Santiago* 1861-1931
Spanish painter. Exh. 1912-21. Add: Barcelona, Spain. † L 2.

RUSKIN, John* 1819-1900
Writer, critic and artist. Studied under Copley Fielding and J.D. Harding. Rede lecturer at Cambridge 1867, Slade Professor at Oxford 1869-84. H.R.W.S. 1873. Add: Brantwood, Coniston, Lancs. 1881. † D 3, RHA 1, RWS 4.

RUSS, Annie L.R. Exh. 1896-1904
Pollokshields. † GI 3, RSA 1, RSW 1.

RUSSELBERGHE, van See V

RUSSELL, Amanda J. Exh. 1893-1906
39 Mountjoy Square, Dublin. † RHA 5.

RUSSELL, Agatha L. Exh. 1892
Victoria Road, Barnstaple, Devon. † B 1.

RUSSELL, Alexander L. Exh. 1929
School of Art, Dundee. † RSA 1.

RUSSELL, A.W. Exh. 1919
81 Balgreen Road, Murrayfield, Edinburgh. † RSA 1.

RUSSELL, Bertha A. Exh. 1888-94
Painter. London. † L 1, RA 2, ROI 3.

RUSSELL, Charles d. 1910
Painter. A.R.H.A. 1891, R.H.A. 1893. Exh. from 1880. Add: Dublin. † B 1, L 2, RA 1, RHA 86.

RUSSELL, Daisy Exh. 1928
11 Ardgowan Square, Greenock. † GI 1.

RUSSELL, Miss Dhuie Exh. 1894-97
Spey Cottage, Fochabers, Scotland. † RHA 2.

RUSSELL, Mrs. Dorothy Exh. 1927
Miniature portrait painter. Restharrow, Marks Road, Warlingham, Surrey. † RA 1.

RUSSELL, Edith Exh. 1915
17 Cheltenham Avenue, Sefton Park, Liverpool. † L 1.

RUSSELL, Edwin Exh. 1898
Figure painter. Flat 2, 65 High Street, Fulham, London. † RA 1.

RUSSELL, Elsie E. Exh. 1908-9
Castle Bromwich 1908; Gravelly Hill, Birmingham 1909. † B 2.

RUSSELL, Miss E.F. Exh. 1904
Fairham, Paignton, Devon. † SWA 1.

RUSSELL, Miss E.M. Exh. 1912-14
Upper Dicker Vicarage, Sussex. † L 4, RHA 3.

RUSSELL, Mrs. E. Rose Exh. 1912
Beaminster, Dorset. † L 1.

RUSSELL, Francis Exh. 1936
80 Peel Street, London. † ROI 2.

RUSSELL, Miss F.R. Exh. 1900
Stanley Lodge, Burgoyne Road, Southsea, Hants. † SWA 1.

RUSSELL, Gyrth 1892-c. 1971
Landscape, painter, etcher, poster artist and illustrator. b. Dartmouth, Nova Scotia. Studied Julians, Paris. Official war artist with Canadian Army World War I. Add: Rye, Sussex 1916; Thorverton, Devon 1918; London 1928. † GI 1, RBA 12, ROI 3.

RUSSELL, G.R. Exh. 1923-26
4 Belsize Park Gardens, Hampstead, London. † GOU 3, ROI 1.

RUSSELL, George William (A.E.) 1867-1935
Painter. Dublin. † FIN 3, LS 8, RHA 3.

RUSSELL, H. Exh. 1916
Millstreet, Co. Cork. † RHA 3.

RUSSELL, Capt. Harald Alain b. 1893
Painter of landscapes, seascapes, fish and insect life. b. Belle-Ile-en-Mer, France. Son of John Peter R. q.v. Exh. 1924-25. Add: Kilninver, Oban 1924; Vaux, France 1925. † GI 2, RSA 1, RSW 2.

RUSSELL, Hilda Gertrude b. 1890
Landscape painter, woodcut artist, embroiderer and teacher. Studied Camberwell School of Art. Exh. 1932-36. Add: Brockley, London. † RA 1, RBA 1, RI 1.

RUSSELL, James Exh. 1887
Painter. 14 Panton Street, Haymarket, London. † ROI 1.

RUSSELL, Jessie Exh. 1906-10
81 Victoria Road, Victoria Park, Rusholme, Manchester. † L 1, M 5.

RUSSELL, Joan Exh. 1923-38
Portrait, landscape and miniature painter. London. † B 3, COO 2, G 1, L 3, NEA 1, P 2, RA 3, RBA 1, RMS 1, ROI 1, RSA 7.

RUSSELL, John Exh. 1880
90 George Street, Edinburgh. † RSA 1.

RUSSELL, John Exh. 1907-39
Paris 1907; Neuilly sur Seine, France 1908; Streatham, London 1916. † LS 11, NEA 2, RA 1.

RUSSELL, J.A. Exh. 1886
Spey Cottage, Fochabers, Scotland. † RHA 1.

RUSSELL, Jehanne A. Exh. 1922
† I 1.

RUSSELL, Janette Catherine Exh. 1884-94
Figure and portrait painter. The Priory, Surbiton, Surrey. † B 1, L 1, M 1, RA 5, SWA 4.

RUSSELL, J. Elgar Exh. 1899-1907
Westcott's Quay, St. Ives, Cornwall. † L 1, RA 1.

RUSSELL, J.H. Exh. 1899-1922
Salthill, Galway 1899; Templemore, Co. Tipperary 1900; Millstreet, Co. Cork 1915; Mitchelstown, Co. Cork 1919. † RHA 23.

RUSSELL, J.M. Exh. 1889
9 Hextol Terrace, Hexham, Northumberland. † L 1.

RUSSELL, John Peter* Exh. 1891
Painter. Father of Harald Alain R. q.v. Add: c/o Stannard, Gt. Russell Street, London and Belle Ile, Morbihan, France. † NEA 4.

RUSSELL, J.R.E. Exh. 1915-16
Porthmeor Studios, St. Ives, Cornwall. † ROI 2.

RUSSELL, Lilian Exh. 1884-98
43 Catherine Street, Liverpool. † L 28, SWA 4.

RUSSELL, Miss M. Exh. 1901
Landscape painter. Pennington House, Ravenglass, Cumberland. † RA 1.

RUSSELL, Marie Exh. 1910
Cleveden, Kelvinside, Glasgow. † GI 1.

RUSSELL, Miss M.K. Exh. 1916
68 Madeley Road, Ealing, London. † L 1.

RUSSELL, Neil Exh. 1938
Blairburn, Culross. † RSA 1.

RUSSELL, Paul Exh. 1920
13 Trigon Road, Fentiman Road, London. † L 1.

RUSSELL, Reg Exh. 1926-30
39A South Castle Street, Liverpool. † L 5.

RUSSELL, Robert Exh. 1880
7 Panmure Place, Edinburgh. † RSA 1.

RUSSELL, Robert Exh. 1925-35
Landscape painter. Higher Coombe, Buckfastleigh, Devon. † GOU 1, NEA 3, RED 1.

RUSSELL, Rachel A. Exh. 1911-12
Painter. Stubbers, North Ockendon, Essex. † LS 3, NEA 1.

RUSSELL, Rose A. Exh. 1884
The Priory, Surbiton, Surrey. † B 1.

RUSSELL, R. Ramsey Exh. 1884-1912
Edinburgh 1884; Glasgow 1912. † GI 1, RSA 3.

RUSSELL, Robert T. Exh. 1922-23
Architect. Raisina, Delhi, India. † RA 4.

RUSSELL, Samuel B. Exh. 1889-1915
Architect. London. † RA 7.

RUSSELL, T. Stuart Exh. 1895-1903
St. Johns, Wakefield, Yorks. † RBA 1, RHA 3, RI 5.

RUSSELL, Wallace Exh. 1887-97
Figure painter. Glasgow. † GI 4, L 1, RA 1, RSA 1.

RUSSELL, William Exh. 1934
Wood engraver. Upway, Hinksey Hill, Oxford. † RA 1.

RUSSELL, W.T. Exh. 1926-34
Couthiche, Carstairs, Lanarks. † GI 2, L 5, RSA 4.

RUSSELL, Sir Walter Westley* 1867-1949
Painter, illustrator and etcher. b. Epping. Studied Westminster School of Art. Painting and Drawing Teacher Slade School 1895-1927. Served with the Camouflage Corps 1916-19. Keeper of the R.A. 1927-42. N.E.A. 1895, A.R.A. 1920, R.A. 1926, R.P. 1907, A.R.W.S. 1921, R.W.S. 1930. Member of the Society of 25 Artists. Knighted c. 1930. "The Blue Dress" (1911) purchased by Chantrey Bequest 1925, "Cordelia" purchased 1930, "The Farmyard" 1934, "High Tide. Blakeney" 1938 and "Carting Sand" (Exh. 1910) purchased in 1940. Add: London. † AG 5, BA 2, BAR 2, CHE 5, D 1, G 20, GI 26, GOU 204, I 25, L 43, LEI 74, M 2, NEA 168, P 12, RA 109, RHA 8, RSW 3, RWS 67, WG 3.

RUSSELL-BIGGS, Ursula Exh. 1940
Stanhope Court Hotel, London. † RBA 1.

RUSSELL-ROBERTS, Ethel Marguerite Exh. 1895-1923
Landscape painter. London. † RI 4, SWA 9.

RUST, Beatrice Agnes Exh. 1883-1901
Portrait and figure painter. London. † D 1, L 6, M 3, RA 10, RBA 5, RHA 6, RI 3, SWA 6.

RUST, Miss C. Exh. 1915-16
Lyceum Club, Piccadilly, London. † L 1, RA 1.

RUST, Lancelot D. Exh. 1927-32
Painter. Science and Art School, Market Road, Chelmsford, Essex 1932. † GOU 1, RA 1.

RUSTI-HOECK, Miss F. Exh. 1897
c/o Mr. F.J. Brown, 32 Charlotte Street, Fitzroy Square, London. † RBA 1.

RUSTON, George Exh. 1891
Watercolour landscape painter. 63 Cauden Road, Clapham, London. † RI 1.

RUTER, Franz Exh. 1886
Landscape painter. 70 Rio Terrace, Catecumerie, Venice. † G 1.

RUTHERFORD, Miss A.C. Exh. 1881
The Scaurs, Jedburgh. † RSA 1.

RUTHERFORD, Doris A. Exh. 1929
2 Harboro Terrace, Waterloo, nr. Liverpool. † L 1.

RUTHERFORD, Enid Exh. 1902-8
Flower painter. Heathfield, Wavertree, Liverpool. † BG 1, GI 1, L 13.

RUTHERFORD, George Junr. Exh. 1932
12 Watt Street, Greenock. † GI 1.

RUTHERFORD, Harry* b. 1903
Landscape painter. Exh. 1930-39. Add: Romiley, Cheshire 1930; London 1932; Enfield, Middlesex 1937. † L 2, M 1, NEA 1, RA 15, RBA 1.

RUTHERFORD, Helen Copeland Exh. 1910-29
Ardnadam, Argyllshire 1910; London 1916 and 1926; Edinburgh 1918 and 1927. † L 2, RA 1, RI 7, RSA 6.

RUTHERFORD, H.M. Exh. 1910
Blundellsands, Liverpool. † L 1.

RUTHERFORD, J. Exh. 1908
Architect. H.M. Office of Works, Westminster, London. † RA 1.

RUTHERFORD, Mrs. James Exh. 1894
2 Ailsa Terrace, Hillhead, Glasgow. † GI 1.

RUTHERFORD, J.H. Exh. 1914
39 Bootham, Yorks. † RA 1.

RUTHERFORD, Joyce Watson Exh. 1923-40
Mrs. Neil R. nee Watson. Add: Rhu, Dunbarton 1933; Huelva, Spain 1935. † GI 2, RSA 2, RSW 6.

RUTHERFORD, Miss L.L. Exh. 1902-3
Broxmore, Dorking, Surrey. † L 2, M 1.

RUTHERFORD, Miss M. Exh. 1894
Pulborough, Sussex. † SWA 1.

RUTHERFORD, Maud
See NEALE, Maud Hall

RUTHERFORD, Maggie A. Exh. 1908-12
Govanhill, Glasgow. † GI 4, RSA 1.

RUTHERFORD, Mary W. Exh. 1895-1920
Edinburgh. † GI 8, L 4, RSA 21.

RUTHERFORD, Peggy Exh. 1931-39
Flower and figure painter. New Malden, Surrey 1934; London 1936; Chelmsford, Essex 1937. † GOU 1, RA 2, RED 1, SWA 1.

RUTHERFORD, Patrick J. Exh. 1889-91
Edinburgh. † GI 1, L 1.

RUTHERFORD, Rosemary Exh. 1937-38
† NEA 2.

RUTHERFORD, R.H. Exh. 1883-97
12 St. Albans Road, Bootle, Lancs. † L 16.

RUTHERFORD, Stewart Exh. 1927-38
Glasgow. † GI 3, NEA 2.

RUTHERFORD, Miss W. Exh. 1910
11 Melville Place, Edinburgh. † L 1.

RUTHERSTON, Albert Daniel* 1881-1953
Painter and stage designer. b. Bradford, Yorks. Brother of Sir William Rothenstein q.v. Studied Slade School 1898-1902. Visiting teacher of Painting and Drawing L.C.C. Camberwell School of Arts and Crafts. Ruskin Master of Drawing, Oxford University from 1929. N.E.A. 1905, A.R.W.S. 1934, R.W.S. 1941. Add: London 1900; Bisley, nr. Stroud, Glos. 1929. † AG 3, CAR 71, COO 1, FIN 3, G 3, GOU 13, I 3, L 1, LEI 168, LS 5, M 1, NEA 153, RSA 1, RWS 24.

RUTLAND, Charles 1859-1943
Sculptor. b. Cheltenham. Studied Kennington Art School. Add: London. † GI 4, L 3, RA 10, ROI 2.

RUTLAND, Violet, Duchess of 1856-1937
Marchioness of Granby, Mrs. Manners, nee Lindsay. Pencil and watercolour portrait artist and sculptor. b. Wigan, Lancs. S.W.A. 1932. Add: Wantage, Berks. 1880; London 1883. † BA 3, D 5, FIN 100, G 20, GI 11, I 2, L 7, NG 42, P 12, RA 17, RMS 1, SWA 6.

RUTLEDGE, William Exh. 1881-1900
Painter. Sunderland 1881; East Acton, London 1892. † RA 1, RBA 2, ROI 7.

RUTLEY, Frank Exh. 1883-84
22 Fairholme Road, West Kensington, London. † D 4.

RUTLEY, Maude Exh. 1895-98
Miniature portrait painter. London. † RA 5.

RUTTER, Edward Exh. 1880-82
Painter. London. † D 2.

RUTTER, Mrs. Frank Exh. 1913
7 Westfield Terrace, Chapel Allerton, Leeds. † LS 1.

RUTTER, Mabel S. Exh. 1912
81 Erpingham Road, Putney, London. † LS 3.

RUTTER, Thomas William b. 1874
Landscape painter, etcher and wood engraver. b. Nr. Richmond, Yorks. Studied Liverpool, Burnley and Royal College of Art. Assistant master Northampton School of Arts and Crafts. Exh. 1921-33. Add: 38 Albany Road, Northampton. † N 1, RA 6, RCA 1, ROI 2.

RUXTON, Charles C. Exh. 1933
18 Glover Street, Arbroath. † RSA 1.

RUYTER, de See D.

RYALL, F. Exh. 1913
65 Coniger Road, Fulham, London. † RA 1.

RYAN, Cathleen b. 1900
Landscape painter and teacher. b. Athlone. Studied under R. Cresswell Boaks in Belfast. Exh. 1928. Add: Murrisk, Westport, Co. Mayo. † RHA 2.

RYAN, Claude Exh. 1880-85
Flower and landscape painter. London. † RBA 5, RI 1.

RYAN, Charles J. Exh. 1885-92
Landscape and figure painter. Ventnor, I.O.W. 1880 and 1892; Bushey, Herts. 1890. † RA 2, RI 1.

RYAN, Sally Exh. 1935-38
Sculptor. London. † RA 1, RSA 4.

RYAN, T.E. Exh. 1881
London. † RHA 1.

RYAN, Thomas F. Exh. 1936
Architect. Add: School of Architecture, University College, Dublin. † RHA 1.

RYAN, Vivian D. Exh. 1915-31
Landscape painter. A.R.B.A. 1926. Add: Hintlesham Hall, Ipswich 1915; London 1916. † GOU 3, L 8, P 4, RA 8, RBA 5, ROI 2.

RYAN, W.P. Exh. 1909
1 Metal Exchange Buildings, Whittington Avenue, Leadenhall Street, London. † RHA 1.

RYDE, Florence Exh. 1894
Miniature portrait painter. 9 Upper Winchester Road, Catford, London. † RA 1.

RYDER, C.F. Exh. 1906
Etaples, Pas de Calais, France. † ROI 1.

RYDER, Frances Elizabeth b. 1886
nee Leigh. Potter and etcher. b. Stoke on Trent. Studied Burslem. Married George R. q.v. A.S.W.A. 1927. Exh. 1932-40. Add: London. † SWA 17.

RYDER, George b. 1887
Painter and teacher. b. Hanley, Stoke on Trent. Studied Hanley School of Art, Royal College of Art and Victoria and Albert Museum. Married Frances Elizabeth R. q.v. Exh. 1927-40. Add: London. † AB 1, NEA 5, RA 1, RBA 1, RI 3.

RYDER, Harriet E. Exh. 1889-1904
Miniature portrait painter. London. † B 8, GI 1, L 5, RA 12, RHA 1, RI 12, RMS 4, ROI 3.

RYDER, Lady Isobel Exh. 1934
Miniature animal portrait painter. Heyday, Links Road, Parkstone, Dorset. † RA 1.

RYDING, George Exh. 1926-27
5 Wingate Road, Heaton Chapel, Manchester. † L 1, M 2, RCA 1.

RYLAND, Mrs. A. Mary Exh. 1923-26
Elstree House, Asbourne Road, Windsor, Berks. † D 7, GOU 3, L 2.

RYLAND, Alfred Samuel Exh. 1935-40
Silversmith, jeweller and watercolour landscape painter. Studied Royal College of Art. Head master Preston School of Art and principal Maidstone School of Arts and Crafts. Add: La Bonhaye, Loose, nr. Maidstone, Kent. † RA 4.

RYLAND, Henry 1856-1924
Painter, watercolourist, decorator and designer. R.I. 1898. Add: London. † B 1, G 3, GI 18, L 57, M 22, NG 24, RA 33, RBA 4, RHA 1, RI 137, ROI 4, RSW 2.

RYLAND, Irene Exh. 1911-40
Figure, interior, landscape, flower and still life painter. Studied Grosvenor Life School and London School of Art. A.R.B.A. 1923, R.B.A. 1925, R.O.I. 1936, S.W.A. 1931. Add: London. † GI 10, I 1, L 20, NEA 4, RA 14, RBA 114, RI 5, ROI 13, RSA 5, SWA 43.

RYLAND, Lesley Exh. 1939
Still life painter. Sea Lawn, Sutton, Co. Dublin. † RHA 1.

RYLAND, William Exh. 1884
Landscape painter. Ashland Road, Sheffield. † RBA 1.

RYLE, Arthur Johnston 1857-1915
Landscape painter. R.B.A. 1893. Add: Christchurch, Hants. 1888; The Studio, Thurloe Square, London 1889. † B 6, L 40, M 15, NG 33. RA 9, RBA 130, ROI 4.

RYLE, H. Exh. 1896
7 Gloucester Road, Birkdale, Southport, Lancs. † L 2.

RYLE, Miss R.A. Exh. 1889
54 Catherine Street, Liverpool. † L 1.

RYMER, Winifred Anne Exh. 1929-36
Figure painter. † COO 3, NEA 1.

RYND, Edith Exh. 1892-1901
Watercolour painter. Kensington Gore, London 1892; Oxford 1893. † RBA 1, RI 5.

RYND, Meliora Exh. 1909
Sutzow Ufer 38, Berlin. † RHA 1.

RYND, Winifred L. Exh. 1908-14
Brasted Rectory, Kent 1908; London 1914. † B 1, I 1, LS 8.

RYOTT, Sylvia Exh. 1929-39
Otley, Yorks. † SWA 8.

RYSWYCH, von see V

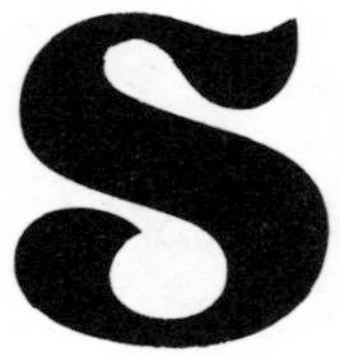

SABATTE, Fernand* b. 1874
French painter. Exh. 1913. Add: 35 Rue Gros, Paris. † L 1.

SABIN, J.F. Exh. 1883
New York and 43 Wellington Street, Strand, London. † RE 1.

SACCAGGI, Cesare Exh. 1903
235 Rue du Faubourg St. Honore, Paris. † L 1.

SACCHETO, Attilio Exh. 1908
Black and white artist. † GOU 18.

SACHELL, Theo Exh. 1886
286 Upper Richmond Road, Putney, London. † RHA 1.

SACHEZ, de See D

SACHS, Edwin O. Exh. 1902
Architect. 3 Waterloo Place, Pall Mall, London. † RA 1.

SACHS, Mrs. Jessie W. Exh. 1899-1906
Miniature painter. 32 Whitehead's Grove, Chelsea, London. † RA 3, RMS 2.

SACHSE, Edward J. Exh. 1884-98
Landscape painter. South Norwood, London 1884; Sutton, Surrey 1893; Winchelsea, Sussex 1896. † D 10, NEA 1, RA 10, RBA 3, RI 4.

SACHY, de See D

SADDLER, John 1813-1892
Engraver. Studied under George Cooke. Engraved many of Turners paintings. Add: London 1880; Wokingham, Berks. 1883. † RA 3.

SADEE, A. Exh. 1884-86
New Bond Street, London. † M 3.

SADEE, Philippe* 1837-1904
Dutch painter. Exh. 1882-93. Add: The Hague, Holland. † FIN 4, GI 3.

SADLER, Miss A. Exh. 1896
25 Clapton Common, London. † SWA 2.

SADLER, George Exh. 1880-84
Figure painter. London. † B 2, D 1, GI 2, L 1, M 1, RBA 3.

SADLER, Kate Exh. 1880-94
Flower painter and watercolourist. Horsham, Sussex. † B 10, DOW 7, FIN 5, L 12, M 9, RA 8, RBA 6, RI 24, ROI 2, RSW 1, SWA 1.

SADLER, R. Exh. 1920-29
Edgbaston, Birmingham. † B 9.

SALDER, Thomas Exh. 1881-86
Flower and figure painter. London. † B 1, RA 1, RBA 2.

SADLER, William Exh. 1889
Sculptor. 2 White Lodge Terrace, Cleveland Road, Barnes, Surrey. † RA 1.

SADLER, Walter Dendy* 1854-1923
Genre painter. b. Dorking, Surrey. Studied Heatherleys and with W. Simmler in Dusseldorf. R.B.A. 1880, R.O.I. 1883. Add: London 1880; Hemingford Grey, St. Ives, Hunts. 1897. † B 7, D 1, G 3, GI 6, L 15, M 8, RA 51, RBA 14, RHA 1, ROI 14, RSA 1, TOO 8.

SADLER, W.W. Exh. 1885-88
Maghull, Liverpool. † L 4.

SAEDELEER, de See D

SAEGHER, de See D

SAGA, Paolo Exh. 1892
Queen Insurance Buildings, 10 Dale Street, Liverpool. † L 1.

SAGE, Mrs. Faith K. Exh. 1918-23
† G 5, I 4, P 3.

SAIN, Paul Exh. 1883
33 Rue du Dragon, Paris. † GI 1.

SAINSBURY, Everton 1849-1885
Genre painter. London. † G 1, GI 1, L 6, M 4, RA 14, RBA 3, ROI 3, TOO 3.

SAINSBURY, Grace E. Exh. 1888-1917
Landscape and figure painter. London. † L 10, M 1, RA 16, RBA 6, ROI 8, SWA 3.

SAINSBURY, Mrs. Maria Tuke Exh. 1885-1911
nee Tuke. Landscape and flower painter. Sister of Henry Scott Tuke q.v. Add: London. † G 1, NEA 1, RA 4, RI 3.

SAINSBURY, S. Fox Exh. 1888-97
Figure painter. 50 Larkhill Rise, Clapham, London. † L 2, RA 1, RBA 2, RI 1.

ST. AUBERT, Leroy Exh. 1885
Paris. † RHA 1.

ST. AUBYN, James Piers Exh. 1886
Architect. Lamb Buildings, Temple, London. † RA 1.

ST. CLAIR, H.J. Exh. 1885
41 Hautland Street, Edinburgh. † RSA 1.

ST. CROIX, de See D

ST. DALMAS, de See D

ST. GAUDENS, Augustus 1848-1907
American sculptor. b. Ireland. Exh. 1894. † NG 1.

ST. GEORGE, Clare Exh. 1909-14
Dublin. † RHA 6.

ST. GEORGE, Sylvia Exh. 1905-40
Landscape painter. Edinburgh 1905; Colchester, Essex 1915. † COO 1, G 1, GOU 3, NEA 6, RA 6, RSA 5.

SAINTHILL, Loudon* Exh. 1939
Painter and designer. † RED 55.

ST. LEGER, Mrs. Exh. 1900
c/o Spence, Westmoreland Street, Dublin. † RHA 1.

ST. LEGER, Mrs. Thea Exh. 1932
8 Gray's Inn Square, London. † ROI 1.

ST. MARCEAUX, de See D

SAINTON, Charles Prosper 1861-1914
Portrait, figure and landscape painter and silver point artist. R.I. 1897, R.M.S. 1904. Add: London 1885 and 1910; Godalming, Surrey 1901. † B 1, BK 33, BRU 2, DOW 87, FIN 52, G 3, GI 1, L 14, M 1, P 5, RA 5, RI 36, RMS 4, ROI 1.

ST. VIDAL, Mme. Exh. 1881
123 Rue de la Course, Bordeaux. † RHA 1.

SALA, Braitou Exh. 1923-26
9 Rue Alfred Stevens, Paris. † L 1, ROI 1, RSA 1.

SALAMAN, Isabella J. Exh. 1889
Sculptor. 20 Pembridge Crescent, Bayswater, London. † RA 1.

SALAMAN, Mrs. Marie Exh. 1923-40
Miniature portrait painter. A.R.M.S. 1937. S.W.A. 1932. Add: 6 Regents Court Park Road, London. † RA 16, RMS 17, RSA 1.

SALAMAN, Malcolm Charles 1855-1940
Artist and writer. Art Critic for "Sunday Times", 1883-94. H.R.E. 1921. Exh. 1932. Add: 4 Colville Gardens, London. † NEA 1.

SALAMAN, Michael H. Exh. 1901-5
Landscape and portrait painter. Fitzroy Square, London. † NEA 3.

SALAMAN, Ruth Exh. 1930
8 St. Edmunds Terrace, London. † NEA 1.

SALANSON, Eugenie Exh. 1892-1905
Figure painter. c/o Hollender and Cremetti, Hanover Gallery, 47 New Bond Street, London. † RA 2.

SALANTI, A. Exh. 1888
Ville Albese Brianza, Italy. † RSA 1.

SALE, Miss E.E. Exh. 1919-22
Taunton, Somerset 1919; Woodchester, Glos. 1921; Tewkesbury 1922. † ROI 4.

SALE, Lucy Exh. 1890
42 Dover Street, Chorlton on Medlock, Manchester. † M 1.

SALE, Margaret Exh. 1923
† SWA 1.

SALES, J.H. Exh. 1919-27
Landscape painter. Birkin Avenue, Nottingham. † N 11.

SALINELLES, de See D

SALIS, Jose Exh. 1908-9
Irun, Spain. † LS 5.

SALISBURY, C. Roma Exh. 1936
c/o Bourlet, 17 Nassau Street, London. † ROI 1.

SALISBURY, Frank Owen b. 1874
Historical and ceremonial portrait and landscape painter. Studied Heatherleys, R.A. Schools and Italy. R.B.A. 1905, R.I. 1936 (res. 1945), R.O.I. 1909, R.P. 1917. Exh. 1899-1939. Add: London 1899 and 1910; Harpenden, Herts. 1901. † B 4, FIN 92, GI 5, L 56, P 76, RA 78, RBA 40, RHA 1, RI 11, ROI 10.

SALKELD, Cecil ffrench* 1908-1968
Painter, pencil and dry point artist and wood engraver. b. Karimganj, Assam. Studied Metropolitan School of Art, Dublin and Royal and Imperial Kumstakademie, Cassel. Exh. 1929-39. Add: Enniskerry, Co. Wicklow 1929; Dublin 1939. † RHA 2.

SALLITT, Lily Exh. 1891
Watercolour painter. Hawthornden, Ilkley, Yorks. † RA 1.

SALMON, Charles Edgar Exh. 1903-16
Architect. Reigate, Surrey. † L 2, LS 16, RA 3.

SALMON, Dorothy Exh. 1911
Training College, Swansea, Wales. † RCA 1.

SALMON, Emeline Exh. 1904
Painter. 70 Kenninghall Road, Clapton, London. † RA 1.

SALMON, Miss E.F. Exh. 1896-1906
Brimpton, Reading 1896; Goring on Thames 1906. † B 1, ROI 3, SWA 4.

SALMON, Helen R. Exh. 1881-91
Flower and figure painter. Glasgow 1881; Gairlockhead, Dunbarton 1890. † GI 23, L 4, RA 6, RSA 6.

SALMON, James Exh. 1895-1916
Architect. Glasgow. † GI 13.

SALMON, John Exh. 1884
c/o Raynor, 26 Francis Street, London. † RHA 1.

SALMON, John Cuthbert 1844-1917
Landscape painter. Liverpool 1881 and 1884; Tal-y-bont, Conway, Wales 1882 and 1887; Deganwy, Llandudno, Wales 1894. † B 3, L 86, M 4, RA 14, RCA 235, RI 4, ROI 1.

SALMON, J. Marchbank b. 1916
Painter, pen and ink artist, potter and lithographer. Studied Edinburgh College of Art and Berlin. Exh. 1936-40. Add: Murraybank, Murrayfield. † RSA 2, RSW 2.

SALMON, Louisa Russell Exh. 1913-21
Painter. b. Alverstoke, Hants. Studied under Martin Snape and Charles Hannaford. Add: Mona House, Okehampton, Devon. † LS 21.

SALMON, Maud Exh. 1894-1918
Landscape painter. Deganwy, Llandudno, Wales. † L 18, RA 1, RCA 40.

SALMON, Miss M.C. Exh. 1885
Watercolour painter. Blenheim House, York Road, Montpelier, Bristol. † SWA 2.

SALMON, William Forrest Exh. 1892-96
197 St. Vincent Street, Glasgow. † GI 5.

SALMOND, Gwendolen d. 1958
Figure painter. Studied Slade School for 4 years. Married Matthew Smith q.v. Add: London 1902; Alfreston, Notts. 1910. † LS 5, NEA 3, RA 1, RSA 1.

SALMOND, Isa M. Exh. 1884-1900
Paris. † GI 4.

SALMOND, Mary A. Exh. 1927-40
7 St. Margarets Road, Edinburgh. † RSW 6.

SALMSON, Hugo 1843-1894
Swedish artist. Exh. 1885-91. Add: Paris. † GI 1, TOO 4.

SALOME, Mlle. Jeanne Exh. 1911
10 Rue Tour Gambette, Louviers (Eure) France. † L 1.

SALOMON, Adam Exh. 1880
French sculptor. 99 Rue de la Faissanderie, Paris. † RA 1.

SALOMON, Herman Exh. 1907
Boscombe, Bournemouth. † L 1.

SALOMONS, E. Exh. 1880-1905
Landscape and architectural painter and architect. 78 King Street, Manchester. † AG 2, G 5, M 29, NG 41, RA 3.

SALSBURY, Robert Exh. 1883-90
Landscape painter. London 1883; Maidstone, Kent 1890. † L 2, RA 1, RBA 8, ROI 9.

SALT, Miss S.A. Exh. 1884
Watercolour landscape painter. 29 Gordon Square, London. † D 1, SWA 1.

SALTER, Anne G. Exh. 1880-85
Bird and still life painter. Binswood Lodge, Leamington, Warwicks. 1880; Bushey, Herts. 1885. † ROI 2, SWA 5.

SALTER, P. King Exh. 1880
Villa Speranza, Cannes, France. † G 1.

SALTER, Lieut. R.J. Exh. 1917
Northumberland Brigade H.Q. Catterick, Yorks. † RA 1.

SALTFLEET, Frank c. 1860-1937
Watercolour landscape and river painter. Married Jean Mitchell q.v. Add: Sheffield. † FIN 71, L 1, RI 1.

SALTFLEET, Jean M. See MITCHELL, Jean

SALTMARSHE, Ernest Exh. 1903-20
Landscape painter. Junior Carlton Club, Pall Mall, London. † LEI 2, RA 5.

SALTMER, Florence A. Exh. 1882-1908
Landscape and genre painter. London 1882; Redhill, Surrey 1887; Guildford, Surrey 1891; Shoreham, Sussex 1899; Cranleigh, Surrey 1905; Gomshall, Surrey 1907. † B 9, G 1, L 2, NG 1, RA 20, RBA 1, RI 1, ROI 15, SWA 2, TOO 5.

SALTOFT, Edward Exh. 1920
Lithographer. † ALP 67.

SALUSBURY, Theodora Exh. 1920-28
Stained glass artist. London. † L 4, RA 3.

SALVESEN, G.W. Exh. 1921-26
Edinburgh. † GI 1, RSA 5.

SALVETTI, Antonio Exh. 1894
Landscape painter. Colle Val d'Elsa, Sienna, Italy. † RA 1.

SALWEY, J.P. Exh. 1908-9
Landscape painter. Stokesay, Salop 1908; Reading, Berks. 1909. † L 4, NEA 2.

SAMARAN, U.M. Exh. 1907
64 Rue Cortambert, Paris. † L 1.

SAMBERGER, Leo b. 1861
German artist. Exh. 1906. Add: Munich. † I 1.

SAMBOURNE, Edward Linley 1844-1910
Designer and illustrator. Artist with "Punch" for many years. Add: 18 Stafford Terrace, Kensington, London. † FIN 367, GI 1, L 1, RA 45.

SAMORA, Maria Exh. 1939-40
Figure painter. 29 Notting Hill Gate, London. † RA 2.

SAMPSON, Miss B. Exh. 1905
Eperstone, Fleet, Hants. † RA 1.

SAMPSON, Dr. Basil Exh. 1923-28
London. † NEA 1, ROI 4.

SAMPSON, Fanny C. Exh. 1912-13
Sole Oak, Gt. Bookham. † LS 7.

SAMPSON, Helen Exh. 1937-39
† NEA 4.

SAMPSON, J.E. Exh. 1933
† RSW 1.

SAMPSON, L. Exh. 1889-90
Landscape painter. 37 Choumert Road, Peckham, London. † ROI 2.

SAMPSON, Lila Exh. 1904-22
Portrait painter. The Cedars, Tibshelf, Derbys. † N 30, RA 2.

SAMPSON, Robert W. Exh. 1889-1919
Landscape painter and architect. Stoke Newington, London 1889; Sidmouth, Devon 1899 and 1919; Ottery St. Mary, Devon 1916. † RA 7.

SAMPSON, S.M. Exh. 1907-9
Myrtle Cottage, Newlyn, Penzance, Cornwall. † L 3.

SAMSON, Alfred G.L. Exh. 1932
Lyon Court, Edinburgh. † RSA 1.

SAMUEL, Charles b. 1862
Sculptor and medallist. b. Brussels. Studied Academie Royale des Beaux Arts, Brussels. Exh. 1914-23. Add: 36 Rue Washington, Brussels. † GI 2, L 2, RSA 4.

SAMUEL, S.R. Exh. 1903-10
21 Torrington Square, London. † B 2, RA 2.

SAMUELS, E.P.P. Exh. 1912-14
Town Hall, Conway, Wales. † RCA 4.

SAMUELS, F. Carol Exh. 1923-26
Bryn-y-Coed, Llanbedr, Tal-y-cafn, Wales. † RCA 5.

SAMUELS, Miss M.K. Exh. 1886
275 Gt. Clowes Street, Manchester. † M 1.

SAMUELSON, Miss J. Exh. 1940
54 Elsworthy Road, London. † RI 1.

SANCHA, F. Exh. 1916
† LS 1.

SANCHEZ-PERRIER, Emilio* 1853-1907
Spanish painter. Exh. 1880. Add: c/o Mr. Hews, 96 Gracechurch Street, London. † RSA 1.

SANCTIS, de See D

SANCTUARY, Mrs. Maysie T. Exh. 1935
Landscape and portrait painter. Granville House, Bridport, Dorset. † RHA 2.

SANDBERG, Mrs. Alexandra Forbes Exh. 1933-39
Flower painter. A.R.M.S. 1933. Add: Crockham Hill, nr. Edenbridge, Kent 1933; London 1936. † L 3, RA 1, RMS 19, RSA 1.

SANDEMAN, Archibald Exh. 1930-40
Watercolour landscape painter. Lochend Farm, Bearsden. † GI 14, L 1, RSW 16, WG 72.

SANDEMAN, Miss Margot Exh. 1940
Lochend, Bearsden. † GI 2.

SANDEMAN, Mary (Mrs. B.) Exh. 1884-86
Painter. 44 Kensington Park Gardens, London. † RA 3.

SANDEMAN, Phyllis Exh. 1937
Landscape and still life painter. † COO 14.

SANDEMAN, T. Exh. 1883-1901
29 Earls Court Square, London. † D 4.

SANDERCOCK, Esme V. Exh. 1930
Wood engraver and dry point artist. Royal College of Art. South Kensington, London. † RA 1, RED 1.

SANDERCOCK, Henry Ardmore Exh. 1882-84
Watercolour landscape and coastal painter. Northam, Bideford, Devon. † D 3, L 3, RA 2, RI 1.

SANDERS, Alfred J. Exh. 1895-98
2 Willow Terrace Road, Leeds. † GI 1, M 1, RI 1.

SANDERS, Christopher Cavania b. 1905
Painter and illustrator. Studied Wakefield School of Art 1922-24, Leeds School of Art 1924-26 and Royal College of Art 1926-29. Exh. 1933-40. Add: Osterley, Middlesex 1933; Heston, Middlesex 1935; Cranford, Middlesex 1940. † NEA 1, RA 8.

SANDERS, D.A. Exh. 1939
Braeside, Douglas Road, Long Eaton, Derbys. † N 1.

SANDERS, Edward Exh. 1914
Eastleigh, Church Road, Hanwell, Middlesex. † LS 3.

SANDERS, Ernest Exh. 1908-36
Watercolour landscape painter. Slough, Bucks. 1908; West Drayton, Middlesex 1914; Aylesbury, Bucks. 1936. † LS 5, RA 1, RI 2.

SANDERS, Gertrude E. Exh. 1881-1922
Edinburgh. † GI 4, RSA 16.

SANDERS, John Exh. 1893-1914
Liverpool. † L 3.

SANDERS, J.M. Exh. 1903
c/o F.W. Crane, 56 Byron Road, West Bridgford, Notts. † N 1.

SANDERS, J.M. Exh. 1900-32
Wallasey, Cheshire 1900; Sutton Courtney, Bucks. 1932. † L 31, RCA 1, RI 1.

SANDERS, Mabel Exh. 1890
West Mount, Edgbaston, Birmingham. † B 1.

SANDERS, Margery Beverly b. 1891
Miniature and french watercolour portrait painter. Studied Brussels, Paris and London. A.R.M.S. 1912. Exh. 1912-21. Add: London 1912; Burnham, Somerset 1916; Bath 1920. † L 10, RA 6, RMS 18.

SANDERS, T. Hale Exh. 1880-1906
Painter of landscapes and river scenes. Add: Balham, London. † B 21, GI 5, L 13, M 12, RA 10, RBA 13, RI 2.

SANDERS, Violet b. 1904
Painter, wood engraver, clay modeller and heraldic illuminator. b. Mexico City. Studied Blackheath School of Art 1922-23, Harrow Technical School 1923-25, Willesden Polytechnic 1925-28 and Willesden Technical College 1931. Exh. 1937-39. Add: 54 Moss Lane, Pinner, Middlesex. † RA 2.

SANDERS, Walter G. Exh. 1882-92
Flower painter. London. † L 4, RA 13, RBA 6, ROI 2.

SANDERSON, Archibald Exh. 1928-39
Landscape painter. London. † RA 10.

SANDERSON, Miss A.E. Exh. 1890
38 Gough Street, Edgbaston, Birmingham. † B 1.

SANDERSON, C.E. Exh. 1894-95
4 Wychcombe Studios, Englands Lane, London. † L 2.

SANDERSON, Edith (Mrs. T.) Exh. 1893-1908
Liverpool 1893; Dublin 1908. † L 8, RHA 1.

SANDERSON, Frank S. Exh. 1932
2 Paternoster Row, Carlisle. † RSA 1.

SANDERSON, G. Gordon Exh. 1923
44 Gladstone Road, Chester. † L 1.

SANDERSON, H. Exh. 1924-36
Landscape painter and linocut artist. Sutton in Ashfield, Notts. † N 5.

SANDERSON, J. Exh. 1908-37
Landscape, figure and portrait painter. Sutton in Ashfield, Notts. † N 39.

SANDERSON, Joan Exh. 1880-82
Forest Road, Edinburgh. † RSA 2.

SANDERSON, John Exh. 1890
Landscape painter. Glentworth, Lincoln. † RBA 2.

SANDERSON, Julia Exh. 1881-83
Figure, flower and landscape painter. London. † RBA 4, RSA 1, SWA 1.

SANDERSON, Robert Exh. 1880-1903
Forest Road, Edinburgh. † GI 17, L 1, RSA 49, RSW 1.

SANDERSON, Miss S.M. Exh. 1891
Landscape painter. 64 Mallinson Road, Wandsworth Common, London. † RA 1.

SANDERSON, Thomas Exh. 1892-98
63 Netherfield Road South, Liverpool. † L 2.

SANDFORD, Hilda Exh. 1902
Hill House, Blackwell, nr. Bromsgrove. † B 1.

SANDFORD, Mrs. Katherine Exh. 1908-10
14 Mount Street, Cromer, Norfolk. † B 3, SWA 1.

SANDHAM, Henry* 1842-1910
Painter. b. Montreal, Canada. Exh. 1905-8. Add: London. † B 2, L 2, RA 4, RI 1.

SANDHEIM, Mrs. Amy Exh. 1919-29
130 High Street, Notting Hill Gate, London. † L 81, SWA 3.

SANDILANDS, Hon. Alison M. Exh. 1909
Calder House, Mid Calder, N.B.. † L 1.

SANDILANDS, Miss G. Exh. 1901
† P 1.

SANDILANDS, George Somerville b. 1889
Painter and etcher. Art critic with "Daily Herald" 1928-39. Registrar Royal College of Art 1939. Exh. 1940. Add: Kingswood Way, Sanderstead. † RA 2.

SANDILANDS, Mlle. Yolande Exh. 1908
148 Boulevard Raspail, Paris. † LS 2.

SANDLANDS, Jillian Exh. 1936-38
Landscape painter. 77 Bedford Gardens, London. † RA 2, RED 1.

SANDOE, Ernest H. Exh. 1934
Etcher. 4 Aldermary Road, Bromley, Kent. † RA 1.

SANDON, Ella Exh. 1919
Kenilworth Court Hotel, Eastbourne. † LS 3.

SANDOZ, Edouard M. Exh. 1910-39
Sculptor. Paris. † L 8, RA 1, RSA 4.

SANDS, Ethel* 1873-1962
Still life, figure, interior and flower painter. b. Newport, U.S.A. Studied Paris. Founder member London Group 1913. Add: London 1905; Wallingford, Berks. 1913. † AG 1, BA 2, CAR 21, COO 1, G 5, GOU 56, I 1, LEI 1, LS 19, NEA 3, NG 2, RA 1, SWA 1.

SANDS, H.H. Exh. 1886-1906
Birmingham. † B 32, L 1, M 1.

SANDS, Henry S. Exh. 1933-37
Figure painter. 47 Wynford Road, Acocks Green, Birmingham. † B 7, RA 3.

SANDS, Irving Exh. 1882-89
Landscape painter. 11 Glebe Street, London Road, Nottingham. † N 7.

SANDS, Mary B. Exh. 1935-38
Miniature portrait painter. Belvoir Cottage, Caythorpe, Nottingham. † N 5.

SANDS, Sarah Ann Exh. 1882
Flower painter. Clumber Road North, The Park, Nottingham. † N 2.

SANDWITH, Miss E.L. Exh. 1901-5
12 Maidstone Road, Rochester, Kent. † B 1, RI 1, SWA 1.

SANDWITH, Miss H.S. Exh. 1901
12 Maidstone Road, Rochester, Kent. † SWA 1.

SANDY-BROWN, Mrs. J.A. Exh. 1940
Stronsaule, Connel, Argyll. † RSA 1.

SANDYS, Frederick* 1832-1904
Figure and portrait painter, woodcut artist and illustrator. b. Norwich. Studied R.A. Schools. H.R.O.I. 1898. Add: London. † FIN 1, L 14, NG 2, P 12, RA 9.

SANDYS, Winifred Exh. 1903-14
A.R.M.S. 1913. Add: London. † GI 5, L 10, NG 4, P 2, RA 5, RMS 7.

SANDYS-LUMSDALE, Amy Exh. 1891-02
Blanerne, Edrom, N.B. † B 2.

SANER, Carrie Exh. 1889-91
Painter. Whitefriars, West Hampstead, London. † L 3, SWA 1.

SANER, Evelyn M. Exh. 1938-39
Painter. Westwood Lodge, Beverley, East Yorks. † RA 2, RSA 1.

SANFORD, Honora A. Exh. 1932
Flower painter. The Court, Broadway, Worcs. † RA 1.

SANFORD, S. Ellen Exh. 1886-1921
Figure, portrait and landscape painter. A.S.W.A. 1902. Add: London 1886; Carshalton, Surrey 1900; Abingdon, Berks. 1904; Ascot, Berks. 1911; Redhill, Surrey 1913 and 1919; Horsham, Sussex 1914. † L 15, M 1, RA 7, RI 15, RID 39, SWA 52.

SANG, Rev. A.M. Exh. 1885
High Church Manse, Castlehead, Paisley. † RSA 1.

SANG, Frederick J. Exh. 1884-1908
Landscape painter and architect. London. † RA 12, RBA 5.

SANG, Geraldine Exh. 1926-31
Watercolour painter and wood engraver. Westbrook, Balerno, Midlothian. † RSA 1, RSW 2.

SANGER, Mrs. Percy Exh. 1921
Seal Hollow, Sevenoaks, Kent. † L 1.

SANGSTER, Alfred Exh. 1904-14
Portrait and figure painter. London 1904 and 1914; Thanet, Kent 1906. † L 1, RA 7.

SANGUINETTI, Edgardo Exh. 1880-89
Sculptor. Florence, Italy 1880; London 1885. † G 1, RA 2, RBA 5, RI 2, ROI 1.

SANGY, Louis Exh. 1898
Landscape painter. 40 Rue de la Poste, Berne, Switzerland. † RA 1.

SANKEY, Mrs. Alice M. Exh. 1912
63 Merrion Square, Dublin. † RHA 1.

SANKEY, Miss K.M.O. Exh. 1925
Boreatton Park, Baschurch, Salop. † B 1.

SANKEY, Millicent B. Exh. 1924-27
Landscape painter. Kenilworth Road, The Park, Nottingham. † N 8.

SANKEY, Miss M.M. Exh. 1921-29
Watercolour landscape painter. Westwards, Sidmouth, Devon. † SWA 1, WG 43.

SANKEY, Mrs. M.M. Exh. 1903
19 Herbert Road, Sherwood Rise, Nottingham. † N 1.

SANSALVADORE, Piero 1892-1955
Landscape painter, etcher and draughtsman. b. Turin. Self taught. Add: 91a Peel Street, London 1932. † CON 84, FIN 114, GI 6.

SANSOM, Nellie Exh. 1894-193
Portrait painter. Studied Royal College o Art. R.M.S. 1896. Add: Kensingtor London. † B 2, GI 1, L 9, M 1, RA 1 RBA 8, RCA 1, RI 15, RMS 19, SWA 6

SANT, H.R. Exh. 189
Landscape painter. 43 Grove End Roac London. † ROI 1.

SANT, James* 1820-191
Portrait, figure and genre painter. Studie under John Varley and A.W. Callcot Appointed Portrait painter to Quee Victoria 1872. A.R.A. 1861, R.A. 1869 "Miss Martineau's Garden" (1873) pu chased by Chantrey Bequest 1922. Add 43 Lancaster Gate, Hyde Park, London † B 18, CAR 2, D 2, G 4, GI 5, L 39 M 13, P 2, RA 160, ROI 2.

SANTER, Rudolf H. Exh. 192
c/o Grove Lodge, The Grove, London † L 1.

SANTESSON, Mrs. Ninnan Exh. 193
Sculptor. 21 Ladbroke Square, London † RA 1.

SANTORO, F.R. Exh. 1883-9
Lewes, Sussex 1883; Rome 1884 an 1897; Bristol 1889. † GI 2, L 1, M 3 RSA 3.

SANZEA, J. David Exh. 188
19 Rue d'Sevres, Ville d'Avray, Seine e Oise, France. † GI 1.

SAPWORTH, Mary Exh. 1896-9
Woodford Green, Essex. † D 5.

SARASIN, Regnault Exh. 191
64 Rue de la Victoire, Paris. † LS 3.

SARAWAK, H.H. The Ranee of Exh. 1900-
Redbourne, Malmesbury 1900; Greyfriars Ascot 1902. † L 14, NG 5.

SARE, Hilda Mary b. 187
nee Farhall. Portrait and miniature painte and black and white illustrator. b Hitchen, Herts. Studied Westminster Lambeth and Regent Street Polytechnic Exh. 1905-28. Add: London. † L 1 RA 7, RMS 1.

SARGANT, Francis William 1870-196
Sculptor. Brother of Mary Florence q.v Add: London 1912 and 1920; Burford Oxon 1919; Florence, Italy 1924. † I 3 LS 1, RA 13.

SARGANT, Miss Mary See FLORENCE

SARGEANT, Edith Exh. 1927
† D 1.

SARGENT, Emily Exh. 1891
Landscape painter. c/o J.S. Sargent, 33 Tite Street, London. † NEA 1.

SARGENT, H. Garton Exh. 1889-90
Landscape painter. London. † RA 2.

SARGENT, John Singer* 1856-1925
Painter and watercolourist. b. Florence. Son of a Philadelphia doctor. Studied Rome, Florence and with Carolus Duran in Paris 1874. Travelled often in Europe, North Africa, the Middle East and America. N.E.A. 1886, A.R.A. 1894, R.A. 1897, H.R.O.I. 1898, R.P. 1903, H.R.S.A. 1906, R.S.W. 1917, A.R.W.S. 1904, R.W.S. 1908. "Carnation, Lily, Lily, Rose" purchased by Chantrey Bequest 1887. Add: Paris 1882; 31 Tite Street, Chelsea, London 1887. † AG 2, B 8, CAR 128, FIN 8, G 17, GI 20, I 10, L 103, M 5, NEA 63, NG 37, P 17, RA 145, RHA 18, ROI 4, RSA 31, RSW 5, RWS 28.

SARGENT, Katharine Evelyn Exh. 1918-29
nee Clayton. Flower and fruit painter. b. nr. Bilston, Staffs. Married Louis A.S. q.v. Add: London. † BA 2, I 11, RA 8, SWA 1.

SARGENT, Kathleen P. Exh. 1912
38 Elm Grove, Birkenhead. † L 1.

SARGENT, Louis Augustus b. 1881
Painter and sculptor. Married Katharine Evelyn S. q.v. Exh. 1906-27. R.O.I. 1913. Add: London 1906 and 1919; St. Ives, Cornwall 1910 and 1916. † BG 19, CHE 1, GOU 19, I 21, LEI 51, LS 5, NEA 10, RA 1, ROI 19.

SARGINT, Mrs. Kate Exh. 1901-27
Landscape painter. Bootle and Liverpool 1901; Clonmer over Sands 1926. † L 28, LS 5, M 2, NEA 7.

SARGISSON, Ralph M. Exh. 1929-37
R.B.S.A. 1935. Add: 33 Broad Road, Acocks Green, Birmingham. † B 15.

SARREBOURSE, Mlle. J. de Enghien Exh. 1887
Seine et Oise, France. † GI 1.

SARSFIELD, Miss A. Exh. 1893
Doughcloyne, Cork. † RHA 1.

SARSON, G. Exh. 1910-36
Landscape painter. 96 Pool Road, Leicester. † N 40.

SARTAIN, William 1843-1924
American artist. Exh. 1919. † RE 1.

SARTIN, Mrs. H.F. Exh. 1939-40
Watford, Herts. † RCA 2.

SARTORARI, Matilde Exh. 1939
† GOU 2.

SARTORIO, Guilio Aristide 1861-1932
Italian painter, sculptor, engraver and writer. b. Rome. Travelled widely in Europe and Middle East. Exh. 1915-25. † FIN 72.

SASSOON, Lady A. Exh. 1905-8
25 Park Lane, London. † L 3, RA 1.

SASSOON, Alfred Exh. 1890-92
London. † L 3, ROI 1.

SASSOON, David b. 1888
Landscape painter. b. Walton on Thames. Exh. 1912-34. Add: Walton on Thames 1912; Kirkcudbridge 1925. † L 1, LS 21, RSA 2.

SASSOON, Mrs. Dulcie Exh. 1919-27
Painter and wax modeller. Add: 51 Westbourne Terrace, London. † RA 3.

SASSOON, Theresa Exh. 1889-97
Mrs. Alfred S. Painter. London. † NG 1, RA 1.

SATCHELL, Theodore Exh. 1883-90
Landscape and coastal painter. 268 Upper Richmond Road, Putney, London. † L 3, RA 2, RBA 5, RI 2, ROI 1.

SATO, Takezo Exh. 1915-38
Watercolour landscape, flower and bird painter. London. † I 7, RA 3, RI 12.

SATTERLEE, Walter 1844-1908
American painter. Exh. 1892. Add: 3 Stanhope Place, Marble Arch, London. † RA 1.

SATTERTHWAITE, Birket N. Exh. 1920-30
Portrait painter and dry point artist. Bury 1920; London 1924; East Grinstead, Sussex 1927. † I 1, L 6, P 2, RA 3, ROI 1.

SATUR, de See D

SAUBER, George Exh. 1894
10 Airlie Gardens, London. † B 1.

SAUBER, Robert 1868-1936
Genre and portrait painter and illustrator. Studied Juliens, Paris. R.B.A. 1891. R.M.S. 1896, V.P.R.M.S. 1896-98. Add: London. † B 8, BA 1, L 3, NG 2, RA 6, RBA 39, RMS 6, ROI 7.

SAUBES, Daniel 1855-1922
French artist. Exh. 1905-21. Add: Paris. † L 2.

SAUGY, L. Exh. 1905
Leonardstrasse 21, Basle, Switzerland. † RA 2.

SAUL, George H. Exh. 1880-87
Sculptor. Carlisle 1880; London 1887. † G 4, RA 2.

SAUL, George P.D. Exh. 1891
Ecclesiastical designer. Add: 11 Sellwood Place, South Kensington, London. † RA 1.

SAUL, Henry A. Exh. 1910-23
Architect. Studied A.A., R.A. Schools and on the continent. Add: 10 Gray's Inn Square, London. † RA 2.

SAUL, Isabel Florrie b. 1895
Illuminator, illustrator, etcher, potter and stained glass artist. Studied Bournemouth Municipal College of Art. Exh. 1926-40. Add: Southbourne on Sea, Bournemouth. † RA 14.

SAUL, Millie Exh. 1892-96
Hornsey, London 1892; Teignmouth, Devon 1894; Chelsea, London 1896. † B 1, RHA 2.

SAUL, Stanley Exh. 1914-15
15 Hardwick Street, Liverpool. † L 2.

SAULLES, de See D

SAUMAREZ, Christine Exh. 1936
Landscape, figure and flower painter. † BA 19.

SAUMAREZ, Hon. Marion Exh. 1906-8
43 Grosvenor Place, London. † LS 3, NG 1.

SAUMAREZ, Veronica Exh. 1936
Landscape, portrait and flower painter. † BA 22.

SAUNDERS, Alick Boyd Exh. 1887-94
Sculptor. London. † L 1, NG 3, RA 3, RSA 1.

SAUNDERS, Bernard F. Roy Exh. 1933
Cardiff, Wales. † RCA 1.

SAUNDERS, Beatrice H. Exh. 1918-40
Figure painter. London. † NEA 1, RA 2.

SAUNDERS, Charles L. d. 1915
Landscape and seascape painter. Add: Liverpool and Conway, North Wales 1881; Chester 1883; Tranmere 1886; Oxton 1889; Tal-y-Bont, nr. Conway 1894; Castle Douglas 1902; Birkenhead 1907. † L 64, RA 7, RCA 1.

SAUNDERS, Edith Exh. 1926-32
Painter. Clova, Mayfield Road, Sutton, Surrey. † GOU 1, P 2, RA 2, RBA 1, RSA 1.

SAUNDERS, Edith A. Exh. 1882-1902
Tal-y-bont, Conway, Wales 1889; Wolverhampton 1902. † B 1, L 1.

SAUNDERS, Helen 1885-1963
Painter. Studied Slade School 1906-7. Add: Castlebar Park 1912; Liss, Hants. 1913. † LS 5.

SAUNDERS, Henry Exh. 1881
Sculptor. 6 St. Marks Grove, Fulham Park, West Brompton, London. † RBA 1.

SAUNDERS, Miss L. Exh. 1889-91
Endwood House, Holly Walk, Leamington, Warwicks. † B 3.

SAUNDERS, Margaret E. Exh. 1904-18
Dublin 1904; London 1918. † RHA 45.

SAUNDERS, Margaret E.D. Exh. 1933-35
Crewe, Cheshire. † RCA 5.

SAUNDERS, Mrs. Nora Exh. 1918-22
Portrait painter. Glasgow. † GI 4, L 2, RA 1, RSA 3.

SAUNDERS, Ruth H. Exh. 1935-36
Miniature painter of flowers and butterflies. 3 Bowden Lodge, Grove Road, London. † RA 3, RMS 1.

SAUNDERSON, Mrs. Alice Exh. 1919
Landscape painter. 22 Ladbroke Square, London. † ALP 3.

SAUNDERSON, Bridget Exh. 1937
† NEA 1.

SAURIN, E.K. Exh. 1911-13
Painter. † GOU 5.

SAUSMAREZ, de See D

SAUTER, Georg 1866-1937
Portrait painter. Father of Rudolf S. q.v. R.P. 1898. Add: London. † B 1, GI 5, GOU 4, I 28, L 23, M 1, NEA 1, P 24, RA 1, RHA 4, RSA 5.

SAUTER, Rudolf b. 1895
Portrait and landscape painter, illustrator, lithographer and etcher. Son of Georg S. q.v. Studied London and Munich. Exh. 1920-40. Add: London 1920; Bury, nr. Pulborough, Sussex 1927; Wittersham, Kent 1934. † AR 47, GI 1, I 1, L 5, LEF 58, NEA 5, P 8, RA 9, RBA 9, RHA 5, RI 3, ROI 6, RSA 12.

SAUTY, de See D

SAVAGE, Aldan b. 1901
Portrait painter. b. Stratton on the Fosse, Somerset. Exh. 1924-31. Add: London 1924; Wealdstone, Harrow, Middlesex 1931. † L 2, P 2, RA 3.

SAVAGE, F.J. Exh. 1938-39
66 Audley Road, London. † ROI 3.

SAVAGE, James H. Exh. 1905-7
London 1905; Romsey, Hants. 1906; School of Art, Bury St. Edmunds, Suffolk 1907. † D 6.

SAVAGE, Reginald Exh. 1886-1902
Figure and portrait painter. London. † BG 1, NG 2, RA 1, RBA 2, RI 6, ROI 1.

SAVAGE, Rupert Exh. 1901-26
Architect. Studied London and abroad. Add: Birmingham 1901; London 1926. † RA 2.

SAVAGE, Wilfrid Exh. 1929-30
23 Parkfield Avenue, Birkenhead. † L 3.

SAVAGE, William Beck Exh. 1906-14
Figure, landscape and decorative painter. London. † NEA 5, RA 1, RI 1.

SAVEZ, R. Exh. 1933
Landscape painter. † RED 1.

SAVIDGE, Joseph T. Exh. 1900
Fruit painter. Newington, London. † RA 1.

SAVIDGE, W. Brandreth Exh. 1893-1901
Painter and architect. Nottingham. † N 3.

SAVILL, Mrs. Exh. 1882
289 Brixton Road, London. † D 1.

SAVILL, Edith See BERKELEY

SAVILL, Gertrude Mary Exh. 1891-1936
Portrait painter. 22 Alexandra Villas, Brighton. † FIN 1, L 1, P 12, RA 9, RBA 2, ROI 1, SWA 8.

SAVILL, Joseph S. Exh. 1884
Wrenthorpe, nr. Wakefield, Yorks. † M 1.

SAVILLE, Emma M. Exh. 1923-40
Landscape and flower painter. 63 Clarke Grove Road, Sheffield. † AR 59, L 4, RCA 2, ROI 1, RSA 2, RSW 2.

SAVILLE, Josephine Exh. 1880-1906
Figure and flower painter. London 1880; Clacton, Essex 1906. † G 1, L 1, M 2, ROI 1, SWA 10.

SAVORY, Ernest b. 1861
Painter. b. Cirencester. Self taught. Exh. 1910-29. Add: Bristol. † L 5, RCA 1, ROI 4.

SAVORY, Eva Exh. 1920-37
Watercolour flower painter. Sandgates, Chertsey, Surrey. † AR 46, D 10, G 2, L 9, RA 2, RCA 8, RHA 5, RI 22, SWA 9.

SAVRY, Hendrick* 1823-1907
Dutch painter. Exh. 1888-91. † TOO 4.

SAWERS, T.L. Exh. 1881-94
Edinburgh. † GI 2, RSA 37.
SAWKINS, Harold 1888-1957
Painter. Exh. 1936. Add: Harrow, Middlesex. † RI 2.
SAWYER, Amy Exh. 1887-1909
Figure and decorative painter. A.S.W.A. 1901. Add: Bushey, Herts. 1887; Ditchling, Sussex 1902. † B 6, FIN 8, L 2, M 1, RA 16, ROI 5, SWA 11.
SAWYER, Dorothy K. Exh. 1911-29
Animal and landscape painter. † D 2, WG 30.
SAWYER, Mrs. Ethel Exh. 1898-1900
Portrait painter. Haverstock Cottage, Bushey Heath, Herts. † RA 2.
SAWYER, E.W. Exh. 1915
Biddenden, Kent. † RA 2.
SAWYER, Fred Exh. 1934-35
Draughtsman and pen and ink artist. Studied Leicester College of Art. Add: 96 Berners Street, Leicester. † N 4.
SAWYER, Rowena B. Exh. 1927-40
Abergele, North Wales. † D 1, RI 2, RCA 7.
SAWYER, R.D. Exh. 1886
Landscape painter. 7 Avenue Gourgand, Paris. † RA 1.
SAWYERS, Lilian D. Exh. 1928-34
Landscape painter. 38 Springfield Road, Brighton. † RA 5.
SAXBY, Miss K. Exh. 1912
8 bis Rue Campagne Premiere, Paris. † RA 1.
SAXON, George Exh. 1880-85
Figure and flower painter. Parklands, Broughton, Somerset. † D 5, L 2, RA 1.
SAXON, Sydney Exh. 1911
1 Sheel Road, Liverpool. † L 1.
SAXTON, Donald D. Exh. 1936-38
908 Sauchiehall Street, Glasgow. † GI 4, RSA 1.
SAYCE, Rev. Arthur B. Exh. 1928-31
Landscape painter. † AB 2, WG 2.
SAYER, Charles E. Exh. 1895-1903
Architect. 17 Soho Square, London. † RA 2.
SAYER, Harold Exh. 1940
Etcher. 66 Finchley Court, London. † RA 2.
SAYER, Harold Wilfred b. 1913
Etcher. A.R.E. 1937. Exh. 1935-40. Add: 49 Hartham Road, Isleworth, Middlesex. † RA 7, RE 3.
SAYER, Jessie C. Exh. 1887-1911
Watercolour flower painter. London. † LS 3, RA 1, RBA 2, RI 1.
SAYERS, Freda Irene b. 1902
Watercolour painter and sculptor. b. Norfolk. Studied Ipswich Art School and Regent Street, Polytechnic. Exh. 1929-39. Add: London. † L 2, RA 3.
SAYERS, Richard Exh. 1936-40
Landscape painter. Beanacres, Peasmarsh, Sussex. † RA 4, RBA 4.
SAYLE, Miss A.H. Exh. 1913
44 King Street, Egremont, Cheshire. † L 1.
SAYNOR, Mary Exh. 1931-32
Deganwy, Wales. † RCA 2.
SAYWELL, E.P. Exh. 1909-10
Brougham Chambers, Wheeler Gate, Nottingham. † N 2.
SAYWELL, Mrs. P. Exh. 1915
33 Bingham Road, Sherwood, Notts. † N 1.
SCADDING, Rev. Norris A. Exh. 1936-39
Watercolour painter. Dover College, Dover. † GOU 3, RI 3, WG 2.
SCALE, Betty Lilian Exh. 1938
Farnham, Surrey. † SWA 2.
SCALE, Kathleen Muriel Exh. 1933-38
Figure, flower and landscape painter. Clutha, Lower Bourne, Farnham, Surrey. † NEA 2, RA 7, RBA 3, SWA 1.
SCALES, Edith Marion b. 1892
Watercolour painter. b. Newark, Notts. Studied Nottingham School of Art. Exh. 1914-39. Add: Newark, Notts. 1914; London 1923; New Malden, Surrey 1937. † GI 1, L 3, N 1, P 2, RA 1, RI 5, ROI 2 RSA 5.
SCALES, Miss F. Exh. 1911
9 Queen Anne's Gardens, Bedford Park, London. † RA 1.
SCALLAN, F.C. Exh. 1920
c/o Bourlet and Sons, 18 Nassau Street, London. † RSA 1.
SCALLY, Mrs. Caroline M. Exh. 1915-39
Painter. Bailey, Co. Dublin 1915; Raheny, Co. Dublin 1938. † RHA 13.
SCALTOLA, F. Exh. 1906-7
c/o Sir W.B. Richmond, R.A., Hammersmith, London. † L 2, NG 4.
SCALY, A.C. Exh. 1892
Hogarth Club, 36 Dover Street, London. † M 1.
SCAMPTON, Mary Exh. 1881-83
Flower painter. Highbury Terrace, Coventry. † B 1, RBA 3.
SCANES, Miss Agnes Exh. 1880-1901
Flower, portrait, figure and landscape painter. London. † B 10, L 3, M 2, RA 2, RBA 4, RI 5, ROI 8.
SCANES, Edwin L. Exh. 1882-1905
Figure painter. London. † B 2, L 1, M 3, RA 3, RBA 2, RHA 2, ROI 2.
SCANLON, Mrs. Carrie L. Exh. 1903
Still life painter. St. Ives, Hunts. † L 1, RA 1, SWA 1.
SCANLON, Robert Joseph Exh. 1927
1 Hornby Street, Birkenhead. † L 1.
SCANNELL, Edith M.S. Exh. 1880-1921
Figure painter. Kensington, London † B 3, L 10, M 6, NG 1, P 1, RA 14, RBA 3, RHA 9, RMS 4, ROI 4, RSA 1, SWA 54.
SCANTLEBURY, Edith A. Exh. 1901-9
187 Willesden Lane, London. † L 5, RA 1, RCA 2, SWA 9.
SCAPPA, E.C. Exh. 1880
Landscape painter. 17 Nassau Street, London. † D 1.
SCAPPA, G.A. Exh. 1886-87
Landscape, coastal and river painter. London. † B 1, RBA 1.
SCARBOROUGH, F.W. Exh. 1896-1939
Coastal and landscape painter. Ayr, N.B. 1896; London 1900; Folkingham, Lincs. 1908; Grantham, Lincs. 1931. † B 2, GI 4, N 9.
SCARBOROUGH, Miss G. Exh. 1905-17
Alyn Bank, Crescent Road, Crouch End, London. † RA 2, SWA 3.
SCARBOROUGH, M.H. Exh. 1911-30
3 Willowdale Road, Mossley Hill, Liverpool. † L 3.
SCARFE, Lawrence b. 1914
Painter, miniaturist, black and white artist and lithographer. b. Idle, Yorks. Studied Royal College of Art 1933-37. Lecturer Bromley School of Art 1937-39. Exh. 1938-40. Add: London. † RA 1, RED 1.
SCARGILL, Dr. Lionel Walter Kennedy b. 1871
Painter. Beaufort, Kerry 1921; Kidderminster 1922; Whitby, Yorks. 1925; Guildford 1934. † B 16, COO 1.
SCARLETT, Miss Exh. 1893
The Rocks, Uckfield, Sussex. † SWA 1.
SCARLETT, Frank Exh. 1927
6 Mount Street Crescent, Dublin. † RHA 4.
SCARTH, Bertha Exh. 1898
Bearsted, Maidstone, Kent. † SWA 1.
SCARVELL, Jessie E. Exh. 1899
Commercial Bank of Sydney, 18 Birchin Lane, London. † ROI 1.
SCARVELLI, S. Exh. 1906-7
Spiro, Corfu, Ionian Islands. † D 13.
SCATTERGOOD, E. Exh. 1902
60 St. James Street, Nottingham. † N 1.
SCATTERGOOD, Miss Offlow Exh. 1899-1908
Central School of Art, Birmingham. † B 8.
SCEVOLA, Lucien V. Exh. 1909-25
Paris. † L 2.
SCHACK-SOMMER, Miss F. Exh. 1913-14
10C Hyde Park Mansions, London. † LS 6.
SCHADOW, Hans Exh. 1894-98
7 Hill Road, Abbey Road, London. † B 1, P 1.
SCHAEFFER, Phil Otto Exh. 1904
Munich. † GI 1.
SCHAEKEN, Leo Exh. 1905
Saint Gilles, Brussels. † L 1.
SCHAFER, Henry Thomas* b. 1854
Figure, still life and flower painter and sculptor R.B.A. 1890. Exh. 1880-1917. Add: London. † B 43, G 3, GI 17, I 2, L 34, LS 29, M 8, NG 1, P 1, RA 39, RBA 47, RI 1, ROI 14, RSA 1.
SCHALK, Charles F. Exh. 1912-13
c/o Allied Artists Association, 67 Chancery Lane, London. † LS 6.
SCHAMPHELEER, de see D
SCHARNER, T.T. Exh. 1885
Furness, Belgium. † GI 1.
SCHARPF, Joseph Exh. 1892-93
Landscape painter. Brookland, Romney Marsh, Kent. † L 1, RBA 10.
SCHAUFELBERG, Ernest Exh. 1932
Architect. 106 Jermyn Street, London. † RA 1.
SCHEBSMAN, Betia Exh. 1908-12
87 Victoria Road, Kilburn, London. † LS 17, SWA 2.
SCHEIBE, Richard b. 1879
German artist. Exh. 1936. † RSA 1.
SCHELL, Anton Exh. 1894
Miniature painter. 6 Albert Road, Brighton. † RA 1.
SCHELL, Lily Exh. 1880-85
Flower, figure and miniature painter. London. † RA 1, RBA 5.
SCHENCK, G. Exh. 1910
Nursery Road, Mitcham, Surrey. † LS 3.
SCHENHAUSER, Mrs. N. Exh. 1895
1 Langham Chambers, Portland Place, London. † SWA 1.
SCHENK, Mrs. Agnes Exh. 1880-89
Fruit, flower, figure and landscape painter. London. † D 3, GI 1, L 9, M 1, RA 1, RBA 5, RHA 1, ROI 3, RSA 4, SWA 6.
SCHENK, Frederick E.E. Exh. 1886-1907
Sculptor. Stoke on Trent 1886; London 1889. † GI 8, L 4, RA 25, RSA 2.
SCHERREWITZ, Johan* b. 1868
Dutch painter. Exh. 1907-11. Add: Hilversum, Holland and c/o 120 Pall Mall, London. † L 3, RA 1.
SCHIESS, F. Exh. 1930-34
Watercolour painter. Nottingham. † N 6.
SCHILL, Adrian Exh. 1881
16 Avenue Trudaine, Paris. † RHA 1.
SCHILSKY, Eric Exh. 1923-40
Sculptor. 32A Queen's Road, St. Johns Wood, London. † GI 3, L 1, RA 10.

SCHIOLL, Nic Exh. 1933
Kunstuernes Hus, Oslo. † RSA 2.

SCHIRMACHER, M. Dora Exh. 1884-89
Landscape painter. Liverpool 1884; Upper Norwood, London 1889. † L 4, RA 2.

SCHJERFBECK, Helene* Exh. 1887-90
Landscape and figure painter. St. Ives, Cornwall. † DOW 1, ROI 3.

SCHLAPP, Otto Exh. 1904-32
Fisherrow, N.B. 1904; Edinburgh 1909. † RSA 5.

SCHLEGEL, Hans Exh. 1909
† LS 3.

SCHLESINGER, Hans Exh. 1908
15 Via Maria Christina, Rome. † LS 4.

SCHLESINGER, Henri Guillaume* c. 1813-1893
Portrait painter. b. Frankfurt. Exh. 1883. Add: 15 Rue Treilhare, Paris. † RHA 1.

SCHLESWIG-HOLSTEIN, H.H. Princess Augusta 1846-1923
Daughter of Queen Victoria and mother of Princess Marie Louise S-H q.v. Exh. 1905-8. Add: 21 Queensbury Place, London. † NG 3.

SCHLESWIG-HOLSTEIN, H.H. Princess Marie Louise 1872-1956
Daughter of Princess Augusta S-H q.v. Exh. 1913. Add: 21 Queensbury Place, London. † RA 1.

SCHLOBLACH, Willy Exh. 1894-1910
Brussels 1894; London 1895; Rhode, St. Genese 1910. † L 2, P 1.

SCHLOESSER, Carl* b. 1836
Landscape painter. Exh. 1880-1913. Add: London. † B 16, FIN 1, G 5, GI 14, L 29, M 11, RA 28, RHA 3.

SCHLOESSER, Maud Exh. 1895-1914
Landscape painter. London 1895; Paddocks, Gt. Bookham, Surrey 1899. † B 1, L 6, LS 13, RA 2, SWA 17.

SCHLOSS, Hubert D. Exh. 1913-14
Landscape painter. 18 Horton Court, Kensington, London. † NEA 2.

SCHLOSS, Sigismund Exh. 1908
15 Stanhope Gardens, London. † LS 2.

SCHMALZ, Herbert Gustave* 1856-1935
Painter of portraits, landscapes, flowers, religious and classical subjects. b. Ryton on Tyne. Studied South Kensington, R.A. Schools and Antwerp. After 1918 exhibited under the name of Carmichael (his mother's maiden name). Exh. from 1880. Add: London. † B 14, D 1, DOW 1, FIN 41, G 26, GI 8, L 43, LEI 28, M 13, NG 34, P 1, RA 45, RHA 6.

SCHMEID, Francois Louis b. 1873
Painter and illustrator. Exh. 1896-1938. Add: Paris 1906. † COO 5, L 1.

SCHMID, F. Exh. 1930
c/o National City Bank of New York, 86 Bishopsgate, London. † NEA 1.

SCHMIDT, Dorothea Charlotte Exh. 1909
† LS 1.

SCHMIDT, Miss E. Exh. 1898
17 Seely Road, Nottingham. † N 1.

SCHMIDT, Fred W Exh. 1905-30
Miniature painter. Manchester. † L 8, M 6, RA 1.

SCHMIDT, H. Exh. 1935
Woodcut artist. † RED 1.

SCHMIDT, J. Exh. 1926
Miniature portrait painter. The Studio, 26 Victoria Street, Manchester. † RA 1.

SCHMIDT, Margaret R. b. 1899
Sculptor. Studied Goldsmiths College of Art. Exh. 1926-28. Add: Southacre, Sydenham, Kent. † L 1, RA 1, RSA 1.

SCHMIDT, Theo Exh. 1891-94
Munich. † GI 2.

SCHMIDT, William Exh. 1881
Ottersberg, Bremen, Germany. † RSA 1.

SCHMIECHEN, Hermann Exh. 1884-95
Portrait painter. London. † D 2, G 1, L 5, M 4, RA 7, RHA 5.

SCHMIECHER, Miss Hene Exh. 1882
54 Parliament Street, London. † M 1.

SCHMITT, Guido* Exh. 1881-88
Portrait and figure painter. 291 Regent Street, London. † B 8, GI 1, L 1, M 3, RA 1, RBA 1, RSA 1.

SCHMITT, Mlle. Noemie Exh. 1904-12
Paris 1904; Fontenay aux Roses (Seine) France. † L 2.

SCHMOLLE, Stella Exh. 1938-40
Lithographer, London. † RA 2.

SCHMUTZER, Ferdinand* 1870-1928
Austrian etcher. Exh. 1908-13. † BG 29, CG 1.

SCHNABEL, Marie Exh. 1888-89
Figure painter. 42 Oakford Road, London. † RBA 2.

SCHNEGG, Gaston Exh. 1905-13
French sculptor. Paris. † I 3, L 1.

SCHNEGG, Lucien Exh. 1905-9
2 Rue Dutot, Paris. † I 6.

SCHNEIDER, Honore Exh. 1912
59 bis Rue Popincourt, Paris. † RSA 1.

SCHNEIDER, M. Exh. 1888
Bramfels, Lahn, Germany. † D 1.

SCHNEIDER-LANG, Mme. G. Exh. 1913
Basle, Switzerland. † LS 3.

SCHNELL, Van see V

SCHOFIELD, Miss A. Exh. 1891-92
Whitefield, Manchester. † M 2.

SCHOFIELD, Arthur Exh. 1916-35
Painter. School of Arts and Crafts, Beckenham, Kent 1916; Hayes, Kent 1935. † RA 2.

SCHOFIELD, Miss D. Exh. 1914-16
The Heys, Westbourne Road, Birkdale, Southport, Lancs. † L 1, RCA 1.

SCHOFIELD, Miss E.L. Exh. 1929-33
Shaw House, Rochdale, Lancs. † L 5.

SCHOFIELD, Mrs. Joan Exh. 1940
Miniature portrait painter. 91c Linden Gardens, London. † RA 2.

SCHOFIELD, John d. c.1931
Exh. from 1882. Add: Rochdale, Lancs. † B 2, M 3, RCA 1.

SCHOFIELD, John William d. 1944
Landscape, portrait and flower painter. R.B.A. 1903, R.I. 1917 (Hon. Retd. 1938). Add: Halifax, Yorks. 1889; Combe Martin, Devon 1892; Lynton, Devon 1899; London 1903 and 1910; Saunton Sands, Devon 1906. † AR 10, B 9, GI 3, L 15, LS 1, M 5, P 3, RA 29, RBA 138, RI 84, ROI 6.

SCHOFIELD, Kershaw Exh. 1900-38
Landscape painter. Bradford, Yorks. † B 1, L 4, M 4, RA 10.

SCHOFIELD, Nellie Exh. 1893-1904
Seafield, Waterloo, Liverpool. † L 4.

SCHOFIELD, Miss Saranna Exh. 1890-97
Thornfield, Old Trafford, Manchester. † D 3, M 8.

SCHOFIELD, Winifred Exh. 1938-40
Landscape painter. 61 Waters Road, Salisbury, Wilts. † RA 1, SWA 5.

SCHOFIELD, Walter Elmer 1867-1944
American landscape and marine painter. R.B.A. 1907, R.O.I. 1910. Add: St. Ives, Cornwall 1906; Ingleton, Yorks. 1908; London 1923; Ipswich, Suffolk 1936. † L 2, RA 3, RBA 5, ROI 1, RSA 1.

SCHOLDERER, Otto* 1834-1902
German still life, portrait and genre painter. Studied Frankfurt State Institute 1849-52. Exh. 1880-98. Add: Putney, London 1880; Kensington, London 1889-98. † B 16, G 2, GI 11, L 4, M 4, NEA 4, P 4, RA 32, RBA 3, ROI 6.

SCHOLES, Margaret Exh. 1930
6 Lydgate Road, Coventry. † B 1.

SCHOLFIELD, Margaret Exh. 1928-32
105 Philbeach Gardens, London. † SWA 4.

SCHOLTZE, Miss B. Exh. 1915-16
22 St. Anne's Villas, Royal Crescent, Holland Park, London. † RA 3, RI 1.

SCHOLZ, Carlo Exh. 1914
34 Warren Street, London. † LS 3.

SCHOMMER, F. Exh. 1904
83 Boulevard Bineau, Neuilly sur Seine, France. † L 1.

SCHON, Otto b. 1893
German painter. Exh. 1936. Add: c/o A. Allinson, 87A Clifton Hill, London. † RA 1.

SCHONBERG, John Exh. 1895
Figure painter, and black and white artist. Add: 77 Loughborough Park, Brixton, London. † RA 2.

SCHONLEBER, Gustav* 1851-1917
Dutch painter. Exh. 1906. Add: 18 Johnstrasse, Karlsruhe, Germany. † L 1.

SCHOONJANS, Adolphe Exh. 1882-84
Sculptor. London. † RA 2.

SCHORR, P.A. Exh. 1905
† I 1.

SCHORR, Raoh Exh. 1937-38
Animal sculptor, and pencil artist. 17 The Boltons, Redcliffe Road, London. † RA 3, RED 20.

SCHOTS, Louis Exh. 1891-99
Sculptor. London 1891; Manchester 1899. † L 3, RA 1.

SCHOTT, Cecil Exh. 1887
Painter. Little Holland House, Melbury Road, Kensington, London. † RA 1.

SCHOTT, Max Exh. 1910
235 Faubourg St. Honore, Paris. † L 1.

SCHOTZ, Benno b. 1891
Sculptor. b. Esthonia. Studied Technical University, Darmstadt and Royal Technical College, Glasgow. A.R.S.A. 1934 R.S.A. 1938. Exh. 1920-40. Add: Glasgow. † GI 51, L 9, RA 13, RSA 56.

SCHOVE, Miss L. Exh. 1913-16
Clevelands, Eldon Park, South Norwood, London. † L 8, RA 3.

SCHRADER, Julius 1815-1900
German portrait painter. Exh. 1880. Add: 135 Friedrichstrasse, Berlin. † RA 1.

SCHREGEL, Bernard Exh. 1906
Watercolour landscape painter. † FIN 12.

SCHREINER, Julia F. Exh. 1896-1902
† P 6.

SCHREYER, A. Exh. 1909-10
Painter. † GOU 2.

SCHRODER, Enid Exh. 1904-15
Miniature portrait painter. Hampstead, London. † L 2, RA 3.

SCHRODER, Hubert Exh. 1891-1924
Etcher and teacher. A.R.E. 1893. Add: London 1891 and 1911; Bournemouth 1898; Southampton 1901; Kew, Surrey 1903. † L 17, LS 5, RA 26, RBA 1, RE 57, RI 1.

SCHRODER, Walter G. Exh. 1885-1932
Landscape painter. Teacher Chester School of Art. Add: Chester. † L 26, LS 1, M 3, RA 6, RBA 7, RCA 8, RI 5, ROI 1.

SCHROEDER, Heinrich Exh. 1938
Pencil landscape artist. c/o A.P. Allison, 87A Clifton Hill, London. † RA 1.

SCHROTTKY, Baroness Hilda Exh. 1936
16 Pelham Place, London. † SWA 1.

SCHRYVER, Louis Exh. 1882-99
Paris. † L 2.

SCHRYVER, Miss R.M. Exh. 1933-36
Eastside House, Kew Green, Surrey. † ROI 2, SWA 6.

SCHULHOF, S. Edith Exh. 1890-92
Painter. London. † L 1, RBA 1, ROI 1.

SCHULMANN, Leon Exh. 1909
248 Boulevard Raspail, Paris. † L 2.

SCHULTZ, C.S. Exh. 1930
Etcher. † FIN 1.

SCHULTZ, Miss E.T. Exh. 1928
Flower painter. † ALP 1.

SCHULTZ, Robert Weir Exh. 1885-1910
Architect. London 1885 and 1891; British Schools, Athens 1890. † RA 18, RSA 2.

SCHULTZE, Carl Exh. 1882-87
London. † L 1, M 1, RSA 1.

SCHULZ, Ila E. b. 1894
Portrait, flower and landscape painter. b. Hungary. Studied Royal Academy Budapest and R.A. Schools. Exh. 1927-39. Add: London. † BK 60, RA 2, SWA 2.

SCHUMACHER, Bernard Exh. 1897-1900
Etcher. A.R.E. 1897-1903. Add: Hampstead, London 1897; Lewisham 1899. † RA 3, RE 19.

SCHUMACHER, Vera Exh. 1912-13
London. † LS 6.

SCHUPPNER, Robert* Exh. 1938
Watercolour painter. † RED 20.

SCHURIG, Felix Exh. 1880
Strehlnerstrasse 7, Dresden. † RSA 1.

SCHUSTER-WOLDAN, Raffael b. 1870
German artist. Exh. 1905. Add: 38 Franz Josef Strasse, Munich. † I 1.

SCHUTZE, Angela Exh. 1884-85
Painter. Southampton 1884; Brockenhurst, Hants. 1885. † RBA 1, RSA 1.

SCHUTZE, Lizzie Exh. 1880
Painter. 3 Pelham Crescent, South Kensington, London. † SWA 1.

SCHWAB, Carlos b. 1866
German artist. Exh. 1908. Add: 150 Rue Perronet, Neuilly sur Seine, France. † LS 5.

SCHWABE, Mrs. E.H.M. Exh. 1903-6
26 Lennox Gardens, London. † L 4, M 2.

SCHWABE, G.A.E. Exh. 1909-23
Architect. Manchester 1909; Braunton, North Devon 1923. † RA 3, RCA 1.

SCHWABE, H. Thackeray Exh. 1883-93
Pendleton 1883; Manchester 1885; London 1893. † L 1, M 4.

SCHWABE, Miss Maude Exh. 1903-7
26 Lennox Gardens, London. † L 1, NG 7.

SCHWABE, Randolph 1885-1948
Painter and etcher. b. Manchester. Studied Slade School 1900-5; Julians, Paris 1906. Slade Professor of Fine Arts, University of London 1930. N.E.A. 1917, A.R.W.S. 1938, R.W.S. 1942. Member London Group 1915. Add: London 1909; Oxford 1940. † BA 8, BAR 23, CAR 2, CHE 5, COO 2, FIN 10, G 3, GI 2, GOU 60, I 2, L 12, LEI 2, M 1, NEA 151, RSA 3, RWS 15.

SCHWABEN, Hans W. Exh. 1894-1914
Edinburgh 1894; London 1911. † GI 1, L 1, LS 11.

SCHWABE-SOTHERN, Miss E.H. Maude Exh. 1918-20
Sculptor. London. † RA 3.

SCHWAGER, Franz J. Exh. 1906-15
Bavaria 1906; Bournemouth 1910; Blackheath, London 1913. † B 1, LS 6, RA 2.

SCHWANN, Miss Ismena Exh. 1926
Society of Handloom Weavers, Melville Chambers, Lord Street, Liverpool. † L 1.

SCHWARTZ, A. Exh. 1882
28 Vignor Street, Cheetham, Manchester. † L 1.

SCHWARTZ, Raphael Exh. 1908
15 Rue Hegesippe Moreau, Paris. † L 1.

SCHWARTZE, Theresa 1852-1918
Dutch portrait and figure painter. Add: Amsterdam and London. † L 1, M 2, P 4, RA 1, RBA 1, RHA 2, SWA 3.

SCHWEIGER, Hans Exh. 1884
Painter. c/o Boehm, 72 Fulham Road, London. † G 2.

SCIORTINO, Prof. Antonio b. 1883
Sculptor and architect. b. Malta. Studied Rome Royal Institute of Fine Arts and Paris. Travelled widely. Director of the British Academy of Arts in Rome. Exh. 1925. Add: Rome. † RA 1.

SCLANDERS, Margaret H. Exh. 1924-40
Mrs. Kirkpatrick. Portrait and flower painter. Add: London 1924; Wimborne, Dorset 1932. † NEA 2, RA 4, RSA 1, SWA 1.

SCOFFIN, G.R. Exh. 1928-37
Watercolour portrait painter. Grantham, Lincs. † N 8.

SCORER, Frederick Exh. 1895-1903
Landscape painter. Kent Hatch, Edenbridge, Kent. † RA 4, RI 1.

SCORER, George O. Exh. 1894-1912
Architect. London. † RA 13.

SCORGONI, Alessandro Exh. 1884
Painter. 40A Barclay Road, Walham Green, London. † ROI 1.

SCORGONI, T. Exh. 1883
Pastel artist. c/o Tolfrey, 40A Barclay Road, Walham Green, London. † M 1, RA 1.

SCOTLAND, Isabel G. Exh. 1930-36
Biggarton, Airdrie. † GI 3, RSA 6.

SCOTLAND, John Thomas Exh. 1880-84
Banff 1880; Edinburgh 1884. † RSA 4.

SCOTLAND, T.M. Exh. 1910
Tolcross, Glasgow. † GI 1.

SCOTT, Ada Exh. 1900-7
Landscape painter. Ventnor, I.o.W. 1900; Edinburgh 1907. † GI 1, RA 1.

SCOTT, Agnes Exh. 1906-8
Portland, Linnet Lane, Sefton Park, Liverpool. † L 3.

SCOTT, Alban Exh. 1940
Architect. 30 Bouverie Street, London. † RA 1.

SCOTT, Alexander d. c.1932
Landscape painter. Travelled throughout the world. † FIN 140, LS 3.

SCOTT, Alfred Exh. 1882
26 York Street, Heywood, Lancs. † M 1.

SCOTT, Alice Exh. 1881-87
Watercolour flower painter. Abbeyfield, Bickley, Kent. † SWA 6.

SCOTT, Lady Alice Exh. 1933-35
Watercolour landscape painter. Visited Kenya. † WG 107.

SCOTT, Mrs. Alma Exh. 1888
Flower painter. 5 Guildford Place, Russell Square, London. † RA 1.

SCOTT, Amy Exh. 1881-1905
Figure, landscape and still life painter. London and Brighton. † M 2, RA 3, RBA 4, RI 4, ROI 3, SWA 11.

SCOTT, Arthur Exh. 1880-84
Edinburgh 1880; Islay 1884. † L 2, RSA 10.

SCOTT, Arthur b. 1881
Painter and etcher. Studied Royal College of Art 1907-13. Painting master Cambridge School of Arts and Crafts 1913-16. Headmaster Watford School of Art. A.R.B.A. 1925, R.B.A. 1930. Exh. 1905-39. Add: Burslem 1905; Cambridge 1914; Watford, Herts. 1922. † L 7, RA 2, RBA 29.

SCOTT, Major Gen. Sir Arthur Exh. 1933-39
44 Iverna Court, London. † RBA 6, RI 6.

SCOTT, Mrs. A.E. St. Clair Exh. 1896-1905
R.M.S. 1899. Add: London. † L 1, RMS 17.

SCOTT, A. Gilbert Exh. 1906-38
Architect. London. † GI 1, RA 14.

SCOTT, A. Hamilton Exh. 1900-26
Paisley, Glasgow 1900; Shawlands, Glasgow 1917. † GI 7, L 5, RSA 1.

SCOTT, Alice M. Exh. 1880-89
Portrait and figure painter and sculptor. Church Row, Hampstead, London. † D 2, L 2, M 4, RA 7, SWA 5.

SCOTT, A.R. Exh. 1885
10 Primrose Terrace, Slateford Road, Edinburgh. † RSA 1.

SCOTT, Bessie Dundas Exh. 1904
Landscape painter. 25 Inverleith Row, Edinburgh. † RSA 1.

SCOTT, Catherine Exh. 1888
Watercolour landscape painter. 43 Inverness Terrace, London. † B 1, RI 1.

SCOTT, Mrs. Claud Exh. 1890-1921
Landscape and figure painter. London 1890; Chorley Wood, Herts. 1908. † RID 34.

SCOTT, Charles Hepburn Exh. 1907-12
Edinburgh 1907; Glasgow 1910. † GI 3, RSA 3.

SCOTT, C.M. Oldrid Exh. 1903-27
Architect. Oxted, Surrey 1903; Westminster, London 1917. † RA 4.

SCOTT, Dorothy Exh. 1915-25
15 College Street, Belfast. † RHA 5.

SCOTT, Miss D.H. Exh. 1907
173 Newport Road, Cardiff. † RCA 1.

SCOTT, Edith Exh. 1882
Figure painter. 90 Charlotte Street, Fitzroy Square, London. † RBA 1.

SCOTT, Edith Exh. 1882-99
Birmingham. † B 10.

SCOTT, Edith Exh. 1925-26
The Liverpool Society of Handloom Weavers, 50A Lord Street, Liverpool. † L 4.

SCOTT, Edwin Exh. 1914
17 Rue Boissonade, Paris. † RSA 1.

SCOTT, Emile Exh. 1927-30
49 Lethbridge Road, Southport, Lancs. † L 4.

SCOTT, Emily Exh. 1900
2 Clarence Villas, Penfields, Wolverhampton. † B 1.

SCOTT, Ellen Annie Exh. 1907-8
13 Upper Grosvenor Road, Tunbridge Wells, Kent. † B 2, LS 4, RA 1.

SCOTT, Ernest C. Exh. 1929
Watercolour landscape painter. 5 Vigo Street, London. † RA 1.

SCOTT, E. May Exh. 1921-28
Liverpool. † L 15.

SCOTT, Esther P. Exh. 1893-1908
Landscape and seascape painter. North End House, West Kensington, London. † RBA 1, SWA 2.

SCOTT, Eric R. Exh. 1935
Watercolour landscape painter. 4a Lownds Avenue, Bromley, Kent. † RA 2.

SCOTT, Mrs. Effie Welsh Exh. 1914-40
Grafton House, Chorley Old Road, Bolton, Lancs. † L 17, RMS 3, RSA 17.

SCOTT, Frank Exh. 1917-21
Miniature portrait painter. A.R.M.S. 1917. Add: The Studio, 14 Jubilee Place, Chelsea, London. † L 9, RA 1, RMS 15.

SCOTT, Frieda Exh. 1932
24 Redcliffe Square, London. † SWA 1.

SCOTT, Fanny C. Exh. 1880-1900
Painter. Hammersmith, London 1880; Albury, Surrey 1900. † RBA 1, SWA 1.

SCOTT, Gavin Exh. 1889-1909
Glasgow 1889; Uddingston, N.B. 1898; Edinburgh 1903. † GI 16, L 3, RSA 12.

SCOTT, Lady George Exh. 1940
Bank End Farm, St. Lawrence, I.o.W. † SWA 1.

SCOTT, Georges* b. 1873
French painter. Exh. 1909-12. Add: 83 Rue Denfert Rochereau, Paris. † L 1, RA 1.

SCOTT, Gladys Exh. 1925-29
Cork. † RHA 8.

SCOTT, Guild Exh. 1909
Hillside House, Gourock, N.B. † GI 1.

SCOTT, Miss G.A.C. Exh. 1882-98
Manchester 1882; London 1898. † M 3, ROI 1.

SCOTT, George Gilbert Exh. 1883-84
Architect. London. † RA 2.

SCOTT, Sir Giles Gilbert 1880-1960
Architect. A.R.A. 1918, R.A. 1922. Knighted 1924. Add: London. † GI 3, L 4, RA 30, RSA 17.

SCOTT, Gertrude H. Exh. 1889-1900
Portrait and landscape painter. † RID 7.

SCOTT, H.B. Exh. 1893
Madeline Cottage, Warton, near Kirkham. † L 1.

SCOTT, Henrietta S. Exh. 1891-92
Landscape painter. 20 Torrington Square, London. † B 4, M 2, RBA 1.

SCOTT, Isabel Exh. 1883-84
18 Nelson Street, Chorlton-upon-Medlock. † M 3.

SCOTT, Isobel Maclagan b. 1900
Mrs. Chalmers. Etcher and designer. Studied Glasgow School of Art. Exh. 1925. Add: 25 Hamilton Drive, Glasgow. † GI 1, RSA 1.

SCOTT, James Exh. 1881-89
Engraver. Middle Lane, Hornsey, London. † RA 5.

SCOTT, Jan Exh. 1939
44 Old Park Road, Palmers Green, London. † RBA 1.

SCOTT, Jessie Exh. 1881
Watercolour tree painter. Abbeyfield, Bickley, Kent. † SWA 1.

SCOTT, John Exh. 1883-84
41 Burlington Road, London. † B 1, RHA 1.

SCOTT, John Exh. 1908
52 Dalry Road, Edinburgh. † RSA 1.

SCOTT, John* 1850-1918
Genre, literary and historical painter. R.B.A. 1882, R.I. 1885, R.O.I. 1883. Add: London. † B 5, D 1, FIN 2, G 2, GI 10, L 36, M 16, NG 1, RA 20, RBA 19, RHA 2, RI 96, ROI 61.

SCOTT, Mrs. John Exh. 1886
27 Thurlow Hall, Hampstead, London. † D 1.

SCOTT, Jonathan Exh. 1938
† NEA 1.

SCOTT, J. Beattie Exh. 1891-1917
Landscape painter. Aberdeen. † D 3, L 13, RA 2, RHA 12, RSA 2.

SCOTT, James B. Exh. 1920
Architect. 18 Maddox Street, London. † RA 1, RHA 1.

SCOTT, John Douglas* Exh. 1880-82
Landscape painter. 24 George Street, Edinburgh. † G 1, GI 3, RA 2, RSA 7.

SCOTT, James Fraser 1878-1932
Portrait and landscape painter. b. New Zealand. Studied Julians, Paris, and Munich Academy. Official artist to Australian Imperial Forces. A.R.B.A. 1919. Add: London 1919 and 1926; Weybridge, Surrey 1922. † L 1, RA 4, RBA 14, ROI 2.

SCOTT, Joan Gilbert Exh. 1938-39
Painter. Bourne End, Bucks. † NEA 1, RA 1, SWA 2.

SCOTT, Miss J.H. Exh. 1915-16
Shanagoblan, Bray, Co. Wicklow. † RHA 5.

SCOTT, John H. Exh. 1884-89
Watercolour landscape painter. Brighton 1884; Edinburgh 1889. † RA 1, RI 3 RSA 2.

SCOTT, James Maxwell Exh. 1929-35
Orchard Cottage, Ringsend, Ruislip, Middlesex. † RSA 9.

SCOTT, J. Mary Exh. 1896-1939
Mrs. H.W. Finch. Miniature painter. A.R.M.S. 1906, R.M.S. 1916. Add: Wimbledon 1896; London 1903; West Byfleet, Surrey 1919; Burgess Hill, Sussex 1928. † GI 1, L 18, LS 3, NG 3, RA 14, RMS 71.

SCOTT, John Oldrid 1842-1913
Architect. London. † L 2, RA 26.

SCOTT, James V. Exh. 1880-92
Landscape painter. Dublin 1880; Edinburgh 1884. † D 2, GI 8, RA 2, RI 10, RSA 19.

SCOTT, Katherine Exh. 1880-1929
Flower, fruit and architectural painter. Streatham, London. † D 7, L 7, RA 3, RBA 3, RI 15, RID 28.

SCOTT, Lady Kathleen 1878-1947
nee Bruce. Married 1st Capt. Scott (of the Antarctic), 2nd Sir E. Hilton Young, Lord Kennett of the Dene. Sculptor. Studied Florence and Paris. Travelled widely. Mother of Peter S. q.v. Add: London. † G 2, GI 3, I 13, L 22, NG 2, P 2, RA 29, RCA 1, RHA 3, RMS 6, SWA 1.

SCOTT, Kathleen M. Exh. 1904
Woodstock, St. Anne's on Sea, Lancs. † L 1.

SCOTT, Laura Exh. 1887-88
Edinburgh. † GI 1, RSA 1.

SCOTT, Laurence* Exh. 1883-98
Landscape, flower and genre painter. Cheltenham, Glos. 1883 and 1897; Dewsbury, Yorks. 1888; St. Ives, Cornwall 1890; Scarborough, Yorks. 1893. † DOW 1, GI 2, L 2, M 7, RA 13, RBA 1, ROI 9.

SCOTT, Lena Exh. 1890-91
1 St. Thomas Place, Newcastle on Tyne. † GI 2.

SCOTT, Lilian Exh. 1926
Society of Handloom Weavers, Melville Chambers, Lord Street, Liverpool. † L 1.

SCOTT, Lucy Exh. 1928-34
Figure and still life painter. London. † RBA 2, RID 2, ROI 3, SWA 11.

SCOTT, Miss L.D. Exh. 1899-1908
6 Cavendish Road, Birkenhead. † L 6.

SCOTT, Mary Exh. 1940
Ardchoile, Aberfoyle. † RSA 1.

SCOTT, Michael Exh. 1937-39
Architect. South Frederick Street, Dublin. † RHA 6.

SCOTT, Muriel Exh. 1920
† RMS 1.

SCOTT, Mackay H. Baillie Exh. 1894-1939
Architect. Douglas, I.O.M. 1894; Bedford 1902; London 1914. † RA 27, RSA 2.

SCOTT, Mary J. Exh. 1898
2 Teviot Terrace, Glasgow. † RSW 1.

SCOTT, Michael Muir Exh. 1882-1934
Edinburgh. † GI 1, RSA 1.

SCOTT, Lady Nora Exh. 1913-23
17 Cowley Street, Westminster, London. † L 9.

SCOTT, Miss Nora Exh. 1887
27 Thurloe Road, Hampstead, London. † D 1.

SCOTT, Peter* b. 1909
Painter, illustrator and naturalist. Son of Kathleen S. q.v. Studied Munich State Academy and R.A. Schools. Exh. 1933-37. Add: London. † COO 1, RA 6.

SCOTT, Richard Exh. 1883
Watercolour landscape painter. Merle Bank, Beulah Hill, Norwood, Middlesex. † RI 1.

SCOTT, Robert Bagge Exh. 1886-96
Landscape painter. London 1886; Norwich, Norfolk 1889. † L 4, RA 8.

SCOTT, Mrs. R.F. Exh. 1912
174 Buckingham Palace Road, London. † L 7.

SCOTT, Hon. Robert Hepburne Exh. 1893-1919
Watercolour landscape painter. Cambridge 1893; St. Boswells, N.B. 1899; Edinburgh 1918. † BG 48, D 2, RSA 2, RSW 2.

SCOTT, Miss R.P. Exh. 1908-14
Gortaglanna, Kilbrittan, Co. Cork. † RHA 11.

SCOTT, Stanley Exh. 1897-99
R.M.S. 1898. Add: London. † RMS 8.

SCOTT, Sydney Exh. 1880-1908
Ulverston 1880; Windermere 1902. † GI 3, M 1, RCA 1, RHA 5.

SCOTT, Septimus Edwin* b. 1879
Landscape painter and poster designer. b. Sunderland. Studied Royal College of Art. A.R.B.A. 1919, R.I. 1927 (res. 1932), R.O.I. 1920. Add: Sunderland 1900; London 1902 and 1916; Slinfold, Sussex 1915. † B 1, L 1, RA 27, RBA 12, RI 3, ROI 9.

SCOTT, Selina L. Exh. 1925-36
Etcher. 10 Springfield Avenue, Muswell Hill, London. † AB 1, D 1, L 1, RED 1, RMS 5, RSA 2.

SCOTT, Selina S. Exh. 1906
Hornsey, London. † SWA 1.

SCOTT, Thomas 1854-1927
Landscape painter. A.R.S.A. 1888, R.S.A 1902. Add: Edinburgh and Earlston, Berwickshire 1880; Selkirk 1902. † D 1, DOW 1, GI 3, L 1, RA 3, RI 1, RSA 151, RSW 11.

SCOTT, Thora Exh. 1902
3 Montpelier Parade, Monkstown, Co. Dublin. † RHA 1.

SCOTT, Tom Exh. 1912-15
Sandymount, Dublin 1912; Romily, Cheshire 1915. † RHA 23.

SCOTT, Thomas D. Exh. 1889-94
Miniature portrait painter. 30 Gloucester Road, Peckham Grove, London. † RA 8.

SCOTT, Thomas E. Exh. 1939
Architect. 2 Gray's Inn Square, London. † RA 1.

SCOTT, T.M. Exh. 1915
24 Robinson Street, Sunderland. † RA 1.

SCOTT, T. Mary Exh. 1897-1900
12 Homefield Road, Wimbledon. † RI 1, SWA 1.

SCOTT, Thomas T. Exh. 1904
Architect. 43 Lowther Street, Carlisle. † RA 1.

SCOTT, Walter Exh. 1899-1938
Watercolour landscape painter and etcher. Studied and lived in Edinburgh. † GI 4, L 2, RCA 2, RSA 9, RSW 7.

SCOTT, Rev. Walter Exh. 1937
Colwyn Bay, Wales. † RCA 1.

SCOTT, William Exh. 1880-97
Painter and etcher. R.E. 1881. Add: London 1880; Rome 1882; Venice 1884; Bordighera, Italy 1896. † B 4, GI 1, M 3, RA 8, RBA 3, RE 16, ROI 4.

SCOTT, W.A. d. 1921
Architect. A.R.H.A. 1910. Add: Drogheda 1899; Dublin 1904. † RHA 52.

SCOTT, W.B. Exh. 1899
13 Dalrymple Crescent, Edinburgh. † GI 1.

SCOTT, William G. Exh. 1896-1910
Architect. 25 Bedford Row, London. † RA 2.

SCOTT, William G. Exh. 1936
Biblical painter. Mousehole, nr. Penzance, Cornwall. † RA 1.

SCOTT, Walter S. b. 1906
Exh. 1934. Add: Broomlands, Kelso. † RSA 1.

SCOTT, W.T. Exh. 1925
356 Umbilo Road, Durban, S. Africa. † RSA 1.

SCOTT-MONCRIEFF, William Exh. 1922
† NEA 1.

SCOTT-SMITH, Jessie Exh. 1883-1903
Miniature painter. R.M.S. 1896. Add: London. † B 3, GI 1, L 5, M 1, RA 13, RI 4, RMS 23.

SCOTT-SNELL, Mrs. K. Exh. 1905
Wimbledon Park, London. † SWA 1.

SCOULAR, W.G. Exh. 1925
40 West Preston Street, Edinburgh. † RSA 1.

SCOVIL, Mrs. M.A. Exh. 1893
73 Dyke Road, Brighton. † B 1.

SCRIVEN, J.W. Exh. 1890-93
Sculptor. 10 Napier Road, Kensington, London. † RA 2.

SCRIVENER, Miss M. Exh. 1907-17
London. † RA 1, RI 1.

SCRIVENER, W.H. Exh. 1912
12 Salcott Road, Wandsworth Common, London. † RA 1.

SCROGGIE, Edward b. 1906
Figure and portrait painter and woodcut artist. Studied Eastbourne. Exh. 1928-31. Add: Paignton, Motcombe Road, Eastbourne. † NEA 2.

SCRUBY, Cecil Exh. 1905
Norfolk House, Bishops Stortford, Herts. † D 2.

SCRUBY, George 1868-1937
Heraldic artist. Exh. 1923-26. Add: London. † L 2.

SCULL, Doris Exh. 1929
Durham Wharf, Hammersmith Terrace, London. † L 2.

SCULL, Mrs. Gertrude L. Exh. 1914
Hotel Huss, Vevez, Switzerland. † LS 3.

SCULL, Max L. Exh. 1908-14
Paris 1908; Vevez, Switzerland 1914. † LS 20.

SCULL, W.D. Exh. 1886-90
Painter. 2 Langland Gardens, Frognal, Hampstead, London. † D 2, RBA 1, RID 11.

SCULLY, Harry d. 1935
Landscape painter. A.R.H.A. 1900, R.H.A. 1906. Add: London 1887; Cork 1892; Orpington, Kent 1931. † RA 3, RHA 101, RI 6.

SCULTHORPE, Agnes Exh. 1934-38
43 Albert Road, Tamworth, Staffs. † B 2.

SCUOTTO, Nicola Exh. 1903
Sculptor. 38 St. Oswald's Road, West Brompton, London. † RA 1.

SCUTT, Walter Exh. 1907-9
Etcher. Barnstaple, Devon 1907; Exeter 1909. † L 2, RA 2.

SEABROOKE, Elliott 1886-1950
Landscape painter. Member London Group 1920. Add: London, Buckhurst Hill and Gt. Langdale, Ambleside, Westmorland. † AG 2, CAR 82, COO 1, GOU 104, L 3, LEI 2, LS 5, M 2, NEA 23.

SEABY, Allen W. 1867-1953
Painter and colour woodcut artist. Studied Reading. Professor University of Reading 1920-33. Exh. from 1904. Add: Reading. † BA 5, FIN 6, GI 11, I 37, L 2, M 2, RSA 2.

SEAGO, Edward Brian* b. 1912
Portrait, and animal painter. Studied under Bertram Priestman. Exh. 1930-39. Add: Brooke Lodge, Norfolk. † RA 5, RCA 2, RHA 1, ROI 8, RSA 1.

SEAGRAVE, Miss Exh. 1890
Steephill Road, Ventnor, I.O.W. † SWA 1.

SEAGRIM, Francis S. Exh. 1936
Architect. Shorton Road, Paignton, Devon. † RA 1.

SEALE, Barney Exh. 1936-37
Sculptor. R.B.A. 1938. Add: London. † RA 2, RBA 5, RCA 2, RSA 4.

SEALY, Allen Culpeper* Exh. 1880-90
Landscape and genre painter. London. † B 16, FIN 1, L 3, M 9, RA 9, RBA 9, RHA 2, ROI 4.

SEALY, A.H. Exh. 1882
6 Lower Fitzwilliam Street, Dublin. † RHA 2.

SEALY, Colin Exh. 1925-40
Painter. Fawkham, Kent 1925; London 1940. † NEA 1, RA 1.

SEALY, Miss E. Exh. 1905-6
Oak Hill House, Weybridge, Surrey. † RA 2.

SEARLE, A.H. Exh. 1888
Painter. 31 Hilldrop Crescent, Camden Road, London. † RBA 1.

SEARLE, Emma E. Exh. 1897
Architectural painter. 40 Burnley Street, Greenwich, London. † RA 1.

SEARLE, Mrs. Kate Exh. 1933-40
Figure and landscape painter. London. † P 2, RA 2.

SEARLE, W.J. Exh. 1935-36
Southcote, Mangotsfield, nr. Bristol. † ROI 2.

SEARLES-WOOD, H.D. Exh. 1895
Architect. 157 Wood Exchange, London. † RA 2.

SEARS, Dorothy Exh. 1927-29
48 Jermyn Street, Princes Park, Liverpool. † L 3.

SEARS, E. Exh. 1920-23
Painter and illustrator. Nottingham 1920; West Bridgford, Notts. 1922; Hyson Green, Notts. 1923. † N 6.

SEARS, Francis b. 1873
Landscape and seascape painter. Studied Birmingham School of Art. Exh. 1907-32. Add: Ombersley Road, Sparkbrook 1905 and 1920; Scarborough, Yorks. 1910; Balsall Heath, Birmingham 1911. † B 35.

SEARS, Philip Shelton b. 1867
American sculptor. b. Boston, U.S.A. Studied Boston. Exh. 1931. Add: 260 Heath Street, Brooklyn, Mass., U.S.A. † RA 1.

SEATON, Miss A.E. Exh. 1886
Painter. 59 Albert Road, Heeley, Sheffield. † G 1.

SEATON, Mrs. E.J. Exh. 1922
29 Oakley Street, Chelsea, London. † L 2.

SEATON, M. Catherine Exh. 1912
Lawn Park, Boxmoor, Herts. † D 3.

SEATON, Miss R.M. Exh. 1922
29 Oakley Street, Chelsea, London. † I 1, L 3.

SEATON-WHITE, A. Exh. 1936
Painter. † COO 3.

SEATREE, Evelyn Exh. 1909-16
Liverpool. † L 11.

SEBRIGHT, R. Exh. 1911
230 Bath Road, Worcester. † RA 1.

SEBRY, Mrs. H.L. Exh. 1933
9 Balfour Road, Highbury, London. † L 2.

SECCOMBE, Henry E. Exh. 1933-35
Architect. H.M. Office of Works, Storey's Gate, London. † RA 7.

SECCOMBE, Lt. Col. F.S. Exh. 1883-85
Military painter. 2 Ellerside Villas, Shooter's Hill, London. † L 1, RBA 4, RI 2, ROI 1.

SECKENDORF, Count d. 1910
Watercolour painter. H.R.I. 1886. Add: c/o Graphic, London 1883; Berlin 1890. † FIN 100, M 3, RI 63.

SECKHAM, Violet Thorne Exh. 1909-23
Lichfield, Staffs. 1909; London 1913; Rugeley, Staffs. 1923. † B 1, L 2, LS 18.

SECRETAN, Miss D. Exh. 1913-19
Crawley, Sussex 1913; Horsham, Sussex 1919. † L 1, SWA 1.

SECRETAN, Joan Exh. 1936
Portrait painter. Swaynes, Rudgwick, Sussex. † RA 1.

SEDCOLE, Herbert b. 1864
Etcher, mezzotint and stipple engraver. Studied South Kensington Museum and under Joseph Bishop Pratt. Exh. 1889-1931. Add: London 1889; Knebworth, Herts. 1899; Much Hadham, Herts. 1931. † RA 14, RBA 1.

SEDDING, Edmund H. Exh. 1886-1905
Architect. London 1886; Plymouth, Devon 1892. † RA 5.

SEDDING, John Dando 1838-1891
Architect. London. † GI 1, RA 27.

SEDDON, Helen Exh. 1930
Landscape, seascape and architectural painter in watercolour and still painter in oils. b. Shropshire. Studied Edinburgh and Paris. Add: St. Ives, Cornwall. † SWA 1.

SEDDON, John Pollard 1827-1906
Architect. Westminster, London. † RA 2.

SEDDON, Maude Exh. 1890-99
Mrs. Birch. Portrait painter. London 1890 and 1896; Heswall, Cheshire 1893; Walton le dale, Preston, Lancs. 1899. † L 1, NG 1, RA 2, SWA 1.

SEDDON, Richard Exh. 1902-32
St. Helens, Lancs. 1902; Eccleston Park, nr. Prescot 1916. † L 26, RCA 2.

SEDGEFIELD, Isabel M. Exh. 1885-91
Flower painter. Kent House, Lower Mall, Hammersmith, London. † RA 1, RBA 4, SWA 2.

SEDGER, George Exh. 1886-1905
Architect. London. † RA 5.

SEDGWICK, Mary M. Exh. 1880-81
Flower and bird painter. 25 Gloucester Street, London. † SWA 3.

SEDGWICK, Winifred Exh. 1919-39
A.N.S.A. 1916. Add: Grantham House, Grantham, Lincs. † N 5.
SEDLEY, A.O.L. Exh. 1882
39 Graham Terrace, Dublin. † RHA 2.
SEEBOECK, Ferdinand Exh. 1894
Sculptor. 118 Via Margutta, Rome and 14 Hall Road, London. † NG 1, RA 1.
SEED, Miss F. Exh. 1891
4 Avenue Terrace, Preston, Lancs. † L 1.
SEELEY, Ellen Exh. 1880-88
Miniature painter. Richmond Hill, Surrey 1880; Littlehampton 1888. † RA 7.
SEELEY, Miss E.L. Exh. 1880
Figure painter. 50 Hilldrop Crescent, Camden Road, London. † SWA 1.
SEFI, Mrs. B.Z. Exh. 1887-88
7 West Cromwell Road, South Kensington, London. † L 2.
SEFTON, Edith L. Exh. 1910
7 Fairfield Avenue, Fairfield, Manchester. † L 2.
SEFTON, Mabel P. Exh. 1907-10
Sculptor. 7 Fairfield Avenue, Fairfield, Manchester. † L 8, RA 1.
SEGANTINI, Giovanni* 1858-1899
Italian painter and sculptor. Add: Milan. † GI 2, L 6.
SEGER, Ernst Exh. 1926-30
Sculptor. Hubertusallu 21, Grunevald, Berlin. † RA 4.
SEGNI, Bartolome Exh. 1930
† L 2.
SEGONZAC, Dunoyer de See DUNOYER
SEGRAIS, de See D
SEIGNAC, Guillaume* Exh. 1938
French painter. † COO 1.
SEILER, Carl* 1846-1921
German painter. Exh. 1899-1905. Add: Munich. † GI 1, L 1.
SELB, Orpheus Victor W. Exh. 1898
Painter. Brook House, Bosham, nr. Chichester. † RA 1.
SELBY, Miss D.L. Exh. 1912
The Precinct, Rochester, Kent. † RA 1.
SELBY, Edgar H. Exh. 1890
Architect. 26 Craven Street, Strand, London. † RA 1.
SELBY, Emma Margaret Exh. 1903-27
Portrait painter and miniaturist. Studied Royal College of Art. Add: London. † L 3, RA 9.
SELBY, F. Exh. 1899
Architect. 44 Chancery Lane, London. † RA 1.
SELBY, Rose E. Exh. 1885
Watercolour flower painter. † SWA 1.
SELBY, R.R. Exh. 1925
Landscape painter. 30 Chaucer Street, Leicester. † N 2.
SELCRAIG, J.K. Exh. 1895
10 Montgomerie Terrace, Glasgow. † RSA 1.
SELIGMAN, Edgar Exh. 1911-34
Landscape, figure and coastal painter. London. † FIN 52, RA 2.
SELIGMAN, Hilda M. Exh. 1939
51 Parkside, Wimbledon, London. † SWA 1.
SELL, Charles Exh. 1880-84
Painter. London. † GI 2, L 2, RA 1, TOO 1.
SELL, Frederick J. Exh. 1897
Waterloo House, Salisbury Road, Plymouth, Devon. † B 1.
SELLAR, Charles A. d. 1926
Portrait painter and watercolourist. R.S.W. 1893. Add: Edinburgh 1880; Leuchars, Fife 1892 and 1897; Dundee 1896; Perth 1901. † GI 20, L 7, RA 2, RBA 1, RHA 2, RI 1, RSA 73, RSW 63.
SELLARS, D.R. Exh. 1885-90
Edinburgh 1885; Lauriston, N.B. 1888; Dundee 1889. † GI 2, RSA 18.
SELLARS, Jeannie A. Exh. 1907
13 Loudon Terrace, Kelvinside, Glasgow. † GI 2.
SELLARS, W.W. Exh. 1885-89
28 Long Wynd, Dundee. † RSA 3.
SELLER, Christine Exh. 1924-29
Watercolour figure painter and commercial artist. Studied Regent Street Polytechnic. Add: London 1924; The Copse, Beaconsfield, Bucks. 1927. † RI 1, SWA 3.
SELLER, Sage Exh. 1889-90
1 Carter Street, Liverpool. † L 2.
SELLERS, James Henry Exh. 1891-1938
Architect. York 1891; Carlisle 1896; Manchester 1908. † L 1, RA 13.
SELLERS, Mrs. Kate R. Exh. 1907-30
Miniature portrait painter. London. † LS 6, RA 3, SWA 2.
SELLON, William Exh. 1882
12 Bold Place, Liverpool. † L 3.
SELLS, Violet E. Exh. 1903-4
Painter. Whitehall, Guildford. † B 1, RA 1, SWA 2.
SELOUS, Miss C. Exh. 1883
24 Gloucester Road, Regents Park, London. † L 1, RHA 2.
SELOUS, Dorothea Exh. 1908-38
Portrait painter, miniaturist and potter. Studied R.A. Schools and Paris. Married R. Kirkland Jamieson q.v. Add: London 1908, and 1927; Hove, Sussex 1909. † BRU 1, L 1, NEA 2, P 3, RA 7, RBA 56, RI 1, SWA 10.
SELOUS, Henry Courtney 1811-1890
(formerly Slous). Genre, portrait, landscape, historical and literary painter, lithographer, illustrator and author. Studied under John Martin and R.A. Schools c. 1818. Add: 28 Gloucester Road, London 1885. † RA 1.
"SEM" See GOURSAT, George
SEMBACH, Marguerite Exh. 1884
Watercolour painter. 2 Weesperryde, Amsterdam. † SWA 2.
SEMENOWSKY, Eisman Exh. 1900-5
Polish landscape, portrait and figure painter. 15 Trinity Road, Tulse Hill, London. † L 3, RA 4, RI 1.
SEMPLE, William Exh. 1927-38
Glasgow. † GI 14.
SEN, Lalit M. Exh. 1930-31
American Indian artist. 48 Penywern Road, London. † RA 2.
SENGEL, Helen Exh. 1911-26
Watercolour landscape painter. London 1911; Ockley, Surrey 1919. † AB 3, L 2, RA 1, RI 7, SWA 3.
SENIOR, Mark* 1864-1927
Landscape painter. Ossett, Yorks. 1892; Leeds 1896. † B 1, GI 1, GOU 3, I 4, L 1, M 1, RA 37, RSA 1.
SENIOR, Oliver b. 1880
Portrait, figure and landscape painter, etcher, colour printer and mural painter. b. Nottingham. Studied Manchester School of Art 1896-1903, Royal College of Art 1903-7, France and Belgium. Painting master Sheffield School of Art 1908-17. Life drawing and painting master Eastbourne School of Art from 1919. Exh. 1927-28. Add: The Studio, 1 Gildredge Road, Eastbourne. † L 1, RA 2.
SEPHTON, George Harcourt* Exh. 1885-1923
Landscape, portrait and figure painter. Sevenoaks, Kent 1885; London 1886. † M 1, NG 2, P 1, RA 10, RBA 2, RMS 1, ROI 3.
SERCOLD, Lucy Pearce Exh. 1884-90
Watercolour landscape painter. Taplow Hill, Maidenhead, Berks. † SWA 2.
SERGEANT, L. Exh. 1932
98 Bordesley Park Road, Smallheath, Birmingham. † B 1.
SERGEANT, Mrs. Mary Exh. 1927-40
Miniature painter. Kirkham, Lancs. 1927; Wallingford, Berks. 1928. † L 6, RA 1.
SERJEANT, Helen Marguerite b. 1901
Painter and teacher. Exh. 1920-28. Add: Liverpool. † L 14.
SEROFF, M. Exh. 1907
† P 1.
SERRA, Juan Exh. 1937
Still life painter. † BA 1.
SERRES, Antony* Exh. 1880-86
Figure painter. London 1880; France 1882. † GI 5, M 1, RHA 2.
SERSHALL, G.J. Exh. 1882-93
Birmingham. † B 6.
SERSHALL, H.J. Exh. 1890-96
Birmingham 1890; Science Art and Technical School, Plymouth 1896. † B 5.
SERT, Jose-Maria 1876-1945
Spanish decorative artist and mural painter. Exh. 1915-16. † AG 5.
SERUSIER, Paul* 1863-1927
Landscape figure and still life painter. Exh. 1921-26. † GOU 3.
SERVAIS, Miss S.F. Exh. 1888
Holly Lea, Livingston Drive, Sefton Park, Liverpool. † L 1.
SERVANT, A. Exh. 1882
49 Boulevard de Rochechonart, Paris. † GI 1.
SETH, Florence Exh. 1908-37
Miniature portrait and landscape painter, illustrator and designer on pottery and china. Studied South Kensington, Heatherleys and Paris. Add: London. † RA 13.
SETH-ARTHUR, N. Exh. 1897
Marsh Maldon, New Oxford. † ROI 1.
SETH-SMITH, William Howard Exh. 1885-1904
Architect. 46 Lincoln's Inn Fields, London. † L 1, RA 17.
SETON, Charles C. Exh. 1881-94
Landscape, genre, historical and literary painter. London. † B 5, FIN 3, G 2, L 6, M 10, RA 12, RBA 3, ROI 2, RSA 1 TOO 1.
SETON, Isabel Margaret Exh. 1898-1915
Edinburgh. † GI 5, L 2, RSA 6.
SETON, Miss M. Exh. 1893
16 Randolphe Road, Maida Hill, London. † SWA 1.
SETON, Mary E. Exh. 1923-34
Watercolour painter. Dirleton, East Lothian 1923; Gullane, East Lothian 1928. † RI 1, RSA 1, RSW 8.
SETTLE, W. Moss Exh. 1903
Architect. Ramsden Square, Barrow in Furness. † RA 1.
SEVAN, C.E. Exh. 1908
21 Camden Road Studios, London. † RI 1.
SEVERINI, Gino* 1883-1966
Urban landscape and figure painter. Exh. 1917. † LS 2.
SEVERN, Arthur* 1848-1931
Landscape and marine painter mainly in watercolour. Son of Joseph S. (1793-1879). Studied Paris and Rome. Married Ruskin's niece. R.I. 1882, R.O.I. 1883. Add: Herne Hill and Brantwood, Coniston, Lancs. 1880; 9 Warwick Square, London 1909. † D 22, FIN 249, G 5, L 20, LEI 125, M 1, RA 8, RI 122, ROI 63.

SEVERN, Miss A.W. Exh. 1916
63 Hounds Gate, Nottingham. † N 1.

SEVERN, Miss Christian Exh. 1893-1903
Daughter of Walter S. q.v. Add: 9 Earls Court Square, London. † D 28, SWA 1.

SEVERN, Cecil A. Exh. 1905-14
Son of Walter S. q.v. Add: 9 Earls Court Square, London 1905; Dockyard Cottage, Sheerness, Kent 1913. † D 8.

SEVERN, Nigel B. Exh. 1883-1907
Son of Walter S. q.v. Add: 9 Earls Court Square, London. † D 140, L 1.

SEVERN, Walter* 1830-1904
Landscape painter mainly in watercolour. Son of Joseph S. (1793-1879) and father of Christian, Cecil and Nigel S. q.v. One of the founders of the Dudley Gallery. Add: 9 Earls Court Square, South Kensington, London. † AG 1, D 67, G 2, L 10, RBA 1, RCA 11.

SEVEROTTI, Julian Exh. 1881
Sculptor. London. † RA 1.

SEVIER, Michael Exh. 1922-27
Painter. † COO 13, G 3, GOU 3.

SEVILLE, Marianne Exh. 1913-14
72 Lansdowne Road, West Didsbury, Manchester. † M 2.

SEWARD, Edwin d. 1924
Architect. Exh. 1888-95. Add: Cardiff. † L 1, RA 1, RCA 19.

SEWARD, Edith Jessie Exh. 1889-91
Landscape painter. Married to Edwin S. q.v. Add: 55 Newport Road, Cardiff. † L 2, RA 2.

SEWARD, Mrs. Marion Exh. 1913-23
Cambridge. † L 3.

SEWARD, Miss M.W. Exh. 1939-40
8 Bembridge Crescent, Southsea, Hants. † RI 3.

SEWELL, Miss C.E. Exh. 1903
12 Denmark Avenue, Wimbledon, Surrey. † SWA 1.

SEWELL, Mrs. Margaret See LEY

SEXTON, Mrs. Hilda Benjamin Exh. 1928-36
Landscape painter. London. † NEA 2, RA 1.

SEXTON, James E. Exh. 1927-37
Landscape painter. Chiswick, London. † AB 1, NEA 5, RA 2.

SEXTON, Joan M. Exh. 1940
Sculptor. 90 Hanley Road, Stroud Green, London. † RA 1.

SEXTON, Lloyd Exh. 1938
Painter. c/o Bourlet, London. † RA 1.

SEXTON, Leo L. Exh. 1936
Painter. London. † RA 1.

SEYMOUR, Mrs. Exh. 1882-83
207A Parliament Street, Liverpool. † L 5.

SEYMOUR, Mrs. Exh. 1884
Landscape painter. Salisbury Vicarage, Southampton. † SWA 2.

SEYMOUR, Christina Exh. 1881
† GI 1.

SEYMOUR, Emily Exh. 1883
Lower Church Street, Warwick. † B 1.

SEYMOUR, Miss Ely Exh. 1914
63 Lower Mount Street, Dublin. † RHA 1.

SEYMOUR, George L.* Exh. 1883-1916
Figure and animal painter. London and Dieppe. † CON 2, FIN 1, L 1, M 4, RI 1, ROI 2, TOO 11.

SEYMOUR, Henry Exh. 1880-1903
Landscape painter. N.S.A. 1881. Add: Nottingham. † N 44.

SEYMOUR, Harriette A. Exh. 1880-1906
Landscape painter. S.W.A. 1880. Add: Beacon Crag, Porthleven, Cornwall 1880 and 1893; Kensington, London 1889. † RID 10, SWA 34.

SEYMOUR, Miss Romilly Exh. 1939-40
Landscape and figure painter. 13 Belgrave Road, Rathmines, Dublin. † RHA 3.

SEYMOUR, R.E. Exh. 1926-27
Argyll House, Manor Road, St. Albans, Herts. † RI 5.

SEYMOUR, Robert G. Exh. 1880-85
Dublin 1880; Bristol 1881 and 1884; Bangor, N. Wales 1883. † RHA 12.

SEYMOUR, Walter Exh. 1888-1914
Landscape and figure painter. London. † L 3, RA 10, RBA 2, ROI 3.

SEYSSES, F.A. Exh. 1909
Sculptor. 4 Rue Brea, Paris. † L 2.

SHACKLE, George H. Exh. 1897-1900
Architect. Rosedale, Stanford Road, New Southgate, London. † RA 2.

SHACKLETON, H. Exh. 1889
23 Watt Street, Harpurhey, Manchester. † M 1.

SHACKLETON, Kathleen Exh. 1923
81 Westbourne Terrace, London. † L 1.

SHACKLETON, Katherine R. Exh. 1937
Beech Park Clonsilla, Co. Dublin. † B 1, RCA 2.

SHACKLETON, Mrs. Pattie Exh. 1923-24
65 Northampton Street, Bradford. † L 1 RCA 4.

SHACKLETON, Miss R.H. Exh. 1923
Annaliffey House, Lucan. † RHA 5.

SHACKLETON, William* 1872-1933
Figure, landscape and portrait painter. b. Bradford. Studied Bradford Technical College, Royal College of Art, Paris and Italy. Married Marian Elizabeth Furniss q.v. N.E.A. 1909. Add: London 1893 and 1899; Amberley, Sussex 1898. † B 2, BAR 52, G 1, GI 7, GOU 99, I 3, L 31, LEI 22, LS 4, M 3, NEA 156, NG 7, RA 12, RBA 1, RHA 10, RI 5 ROI 5.

SHACKLETON, W.A. Exh. 1885-1926
Liverpool 1885; West Kirby, Cheshire 1916; Freshfield, Liverpool 1923. † L 7.

SHACKLOCK, G. Exh. 1938
Linocut artist. Lulworth Cottage, Church Hill, Kirkby in Ashfield, Notts. † N 1.

SHADE, William Exh. 1887
Figure painter. c/o W.B. Richmond, 6 Holland Park Road, London. † G 1, L 1.

SHADLOCK, F. Exh. 1913
87 Burton Road Lincoln. † N 1.

SHAER, Maurice M. Exh. 1935
Painter. † LEF 2.

SHAFTO, Phyllis Exh. 1931-40
London. † RBA 1, RI 5.

SHAKERLEY, Georgiana H. Exh. 1880-85
Watercolour landscape and figure painter. Travelled widely. Add: Somerford Park, Congleton, Cheshire. † SWA 8.

SHAKERLEY, Irene Exh. 1920-22
Stained glass artist. Somerford Park, Congleton, Cheshire. † RA 2.

SHAKESHAFT, J. Mildred Exh. 1914
9 Chester Road, Lower Walton, Warrington, Lancs. † L 1.

SHAKESPEARE, Percy b. 1906
Portrait and figure painter. Studied and taught Birmingham Central School of Art. Exh. 1934-40. Add: 12 Maple Road, Priory, Dudley, Worcs. † B 13 RA 5.

SHALES, Miss S.J. Exh. 1896-1904
8 Clarendon Gardens, Maida Hill, London. † L 3, P 1, RMS 2.

SHALLCROSS, Thomas M. Exh. 1904-5
Architect. 6 Dale Street, Liverpool. † RA 2.

SHAND, Christine R. Exh. 1884-1903
Flower painter. Studio, Gas Company's Chambers, Newcastle on Tyne. † B 1, L 3, RA 3, SWA 3.

SHAND, Edward A. Exh. 1884-85
Croftan High Gardens, Edinburgh. † RSA 2.

SHAND, Mrs. Valerie Exh. 1937
Sculptor. 13 Macaulay Road, London. † RA 1.

SHANKLAND, Jennie C. Exh. 1892-96
The Craigs, Newark Street, Greenock. † GI 2, RHA 1, RSA 2.

SHANKS, Alexander Exh. 1940
7 Kirkwood Street, Glasgow. † GI 1.

SHANKS, Miss E. Exh. 1916-18
10 Addison Crescent, London. † RA 3.

SHANKS, Mary Exh. 1909
† LS 3.

SHANKS, William Somerville d. 1951
Watercolour landscape painter. A.R.S.A. 1923, R.S.A. 1934, R.S.W. 1925. Exh. from 1892. Add: Glasgow. † AR 2, GI 122, L 9, M 2, RA 6, RSA 74, RSW 36.

SHANNAN, Archibald McFarlane 1850-1915
Sculptor. A.R.S.A. 1902. Add: Glasgow. † GI 37, RA 4, RSA 33.

SHANNAN, Louise E. Exh. 1895-1910
Mrs. A. McF. Add: Glasgow. † GI 15.

SHANNON, Charles Hazelwood* 1863-1937
Figure and portrait painter, illustrator and lithographer. b. Quarrington, Lincs. Studied wood engraving Lambeth School of Art 1882, A.R.A. 1911, R.A. 1920, R.E. 1891, R.P. 1898. "The Lady with the Amethyst" purchased by Chantrey Bequest 1916. Add: London 1885 and 1904; Richmond, Surrey 1898; Kew, Surrey 1930. † AG 2, BA 1, BAR 63, CAR 10, CG 73, FIN 1, G 10, GI 16, GOU 10, I 35, L 54, LEI 46, M 6, NEA 12, NG 2, P 27, RA 51, RBA 3, RE 4, RHA 3, RI 5, ROI 5, RSA 5.

SHANNON, Mrs. Eva Exh. 1915-26
1 Brighton Avenue, Rathgar, Dublin. † RHA 15.

SHANNON, Mrs. H.M.L. Exh. 1933
Kemmel, Storeton Road, Barnston, Wirral. † L 1.

SHANNON, Sir James Jebusa 1862-1923
Figure and portrait painter. b. Auburn, New York, U.S.A. of Irish parents and came to London 1878. Studied Royal College of Art 1878-91. Founder member N.E.A. 1886. A.R.A. 1897, R.A. 1909, R.B.A. 1888, A.R.H.A. 1907, H.R.M.S., R.O.I. 1889, R.P. 1891, P.R.P. 1910-23. Knighted 1922. "The Flower Girl" purchased by Chantrey Bequest 1901 and "Phil May" (1902) purchased 1923. Add: London. † AG 1, B 3, G 10, GI 11, I 5, L 51, LEI 31, M 5, NEA 10, NG 62, P 54, RA 157, RBA 10, RHA 9, ROI 15, RSA 6.

SHANNON, Kitty Exh. 1919-26
Mrs. W.S. Keigwin. Figure painter. Add: 37 Ovington Square, London. † P 17, RA 1.

SHAPLAND, Mrs. A.F. Terrell Exh. 1890
Watercolour painter. 70 Grand Parade, Brighton. † RA 1.

SHAPLAND, Miss Ellen Exh. 1883-89
Watercolour fish and flower painter. 70 Grand Parade, Brighton. † RA 4.

SHAPLAND, John* d. 1929
Painter. Headmaster Exeter School of Art 1899-1913. Exh. 1901-14. Add: 8 Topsham Road, Exeter, Devon. † FIN 1, L 2, NG 1 RA 5, RI 1.

SHAPLEY, Miss A.F. Exh. 1905
Regent Studios, Clifton Grove, Bristol. † L 1.

SHARD, J.H. Exh. 1880
4 Downe Terrace, North Woodside, Glasgow. † GI 2.

SHARDLOW, William M. Exh. 1901-4
Landscape painter. 19 Albert Road, Nottingham. † N 6.
SHARLAND, E.W. Exh. 1911-25
Etcher. Bristol. † L 1, RA 3.
SHARLAND, Miss L.A. Exh. 1880-86
Figure painter. London † B 7, M 2, RHA 17, RSA 2.
SHARP, Arthur D. Exh. 1903
Architect. 3 Caroline Place, London. † RA 1.
SHARP, Arnold Haigh b. 1891
Sculptor. b. Halifax. Studied Royal College of Art, Italy and France. Principal, Darlington School of Art and Wakefield School of Arts and Crafts. Exh. 1917. Add: Royal College of Art, South Kensington, London. † RA 1.
SHARP, C.J. Exh. 1902
45 Roland Gardens, South Kensington, London. † GI 1.
SHARP, Dorothea* 1874-1955
Landscape, figure and flower painter. Studied Regent Street Polytechnic and Paris. R.B.A. 1906, R.O.I. 1923, A.S.W.A. 1903, S.W.A. 1908. Add: London 1901 and 1909; Beaconsfield, Bucks. 1908. † CHE 1, CON 34, FIN 2, G 1, GI 11, I 1, L 1, RA 54, RBA 154, RHA 7 ROI 44, RSA 1, SWA 107.
SHARP, Edward Exh. 1919
† L 3.
SHARP, E.H. Adelina Exh. 1881
Landscape painter. Jesmond Villa, Downs Road, Clapton, London. † SWA 1.
SHARP, John Exh. 1916-26
Sculptor. Duns, Berwickshire 1916; Glasgow 1921. † GI 14.
SHARP, Joseph Exh. 1880-1910
Glasgow. † GI 42, M 1.
SHARP, J.S. Exh. 1903-6
Laburnum Cottage, Epworth, Doncaster. † RCA 3.
SHARP, Mrs. L.E. Exh. 1906
Banchory, nr. Aberdeen. † GI 1.
SHARP, Mary Exh. 1927
27 Vernon Road, Southport, Lancs. † L 1.
SHARP, Mary Exh. 1883-91
Landscape painter. Upton Court Reading, Berks. † B 1 D 4, G 5, L 3, SWA 2.
SHARP, Miles Balmford b. 1897
Painter, etcher, wood engraver and lithographer. b. Brighouse. Studied Bradford School of Art, Leeds School of Art, Royal College of Art and London Central School of Arts and Crafts. Principal Nuneaton School of Arts and Crafts. Exh. 1929-40. Add: Morley, Hinckley Road, Nuneaton. † B 23, L 1 RA 5, RBA 1, ROI 3
SHARP, Maud F. Exh. 1931-40
Etcher. Bickley, Kent 1931; Chiselhurst, Kent 1940. † RA 2.
SHARP, Miss M.O. Exh. 1910
5 Vanbrugh Terrace, Blackheath, London. † RA 1.
SHARP, Nancy Exh. 1940
Portrait and flower painter. 16 South Leinster Street, Dublin. † COO 2, RHA 1.
SHARP, Nellie H. Exh. 1887
4 Doune Terrace, Hillhead, Glasgow. † GI 1.
SHARP, P.A. Exh. 1924-27
Landscape painter. Ilkeston, Derbys † N 2.
SHARP, R.S.W. Exh. 1927
585 Argyle Street, Glasgow. † GI 1.
SHARPE, Mrs. Exh. 1881
Dublin. † RHA 1.
SHARPE, Rev Alfred Bowyer Exh. 1908
Cottesbrooke Grange, Northampton. † LS 5.
SHARPE, Miss A.M. Exh. 1896
Leckhampton, nr. Cheltenham, Glos. † SWA 1.
SHARPE, Miss A.M. Exh. 1928
c/o U. Baxter, Northcliff, Alderley Edge, Cheshire. † L 1.
SHARPE, Mrs. C. Exh. 1923-28
12 Pakenham Road, Edgbaston, Birmingham. † B 2.
SHARPE, Mrs. Caroline See PATERSON
SHARPE, C.W. Exh 1881
Etcher. † RA 1
SHARPE, Charles William* d. 1955
Landscape and figure painter. Studied Liverpool. Principal Laird School of Art 1930-46. Exh. from 1901. Add: Liverpool. † L 69, M 1, RA 7, RCA 47, RI 2.
SHARPE, Edith Exh. 1887-1916
Painter. Croydon, Surrey 1887; Queen's Gate, London 1903; Leatherhead, Surrey 1907. † LEI 2, SWA 50.
SHARPE, Miss E.A. Exh. 1889-91
21 East Cliff, Dover, Kent. † L 4, RI 1.
SHARPE, Mary Exh. 1880
Figure painter. London. † D 2.
SHARPE, Mrs. Phyllis Exh. 1934-39
Watercolour landscape painter. Limpsfield, Surrey 1934; Lilliput, Parkstone, Dorset 1939. † AR 1, COO 2, RHA 1, RI 1, SWA 1.
SHARPE, R. Exh. 1924
Landscape painter. 23 Sincil Street, Lincoln. † N 1.
SHARPE, Sutton Exh. 1882
Etcher. Married Caroline Paterson q.v. Add: The Grove, Hampstead, London. † L 2.
SHARPIN, Miss Eleanor Annie See PALMER
SHARPLES, Elsie Exh. 1908-11
Sefton Park, Liverpool. † L 4.
SHARPLES, George Exh. 1897
48 Cambridge Road, Seaforth, Lancs. † L 1.
SHARPLES, Miss K.A. Exh. 1882-90
15 Brompton Avenue, Liverpool. † L 4.
SHARPLES, R. Exh. 1929
Etcher. † BA 2.
SHARPLEY, Reginald b. 1879
Watercolour painter and etcher. Studied Heatherleys. Exh. 1924-40. Add: Campden, Glos. 1924; Minchinhampton, Glos. 1937. † B 16, COO 2, L 1, NEA 1, RA 9, RI 4, WG 61.
SHARWOOD-SMITH, Iris Exh. 1938-40
Painter. 6 Keats Grove, London. † NEA 1, RA 1.
SHAW, Miss Exh. 1887
24 Clarinda Park, West Kensington, London. † RHA 1.
SHAW, Miss A. Exh. 1898
Mount Saville, Terenure, Ireland. † SWA 1.
SHAW, Ann Exh. 1902
† RMS 1.
SHAW, Althea Glynne Exh. 1926
† M 3.
SHAW, Alice Mary Exh. 1909-19
Miniature portrait painter. Langleybury Vicarage, Kings Langley, Herts. † LS 3, RA 10.
SHAW, Arthur Winter b. 1869
Landscape, figure and cattle painter. Studied Westminster and Slade School. R.I. 1900. Exh. 1891-1936. Add: London 1891 and 1897; Beckenham, Kent 1895; Amberley, Sussex 1905; Barham, Canterbury, Kent 1930. † B 2, GI 8, GOU 20, L 2, M 11, NG 1, RA 15, RBA 2, RHA 12, RI 118, ROI 1, WG 4.
SHAW, A. Wilson Exh. 1911-15
Dennistoun, Glasgow. † GI 1, L 8.
SHAW, Byam* 1872-1919
Painter, decorator, illustrator and teacher. b. Madras, India. Studied R.A. Schools. R.I. 1898, R.O.I. 1899, A.R.W.S. 1913. Married Evelyn S. q.v. Add: London. † B 11, DOW 97, GI 8, L 32, LS 5, M 2, NG 8, RA 37, RI 4, ROI 5, RSA 1, RWS 7.
SHAW, Betty E. Exh. 1929
2 Stoneleigh, Grassendale Road, Liverpool. † L 2.
SHAW, C. Exh. 1891-92
112 Bath Street, Glasgow. † GI 1, RSA 1.
SHAW, Crawford Exh. 1892-99
Glasgow. † GI 14, L 4, RSA 4.
SHAW, Charles E. Exh. 1884-99
Landscape and figure painter. Preston 1884; Wonersh, nr. Guildford, Surrey 1891. † B 2, L 3, M 3, RA 3, RBA 1, RI 2, ROI 12.
SHAW, Charles L.* Exh. 1880-98
Landscape painter. N.S.A. 1881. Add: Gelding, Notts. 1880; Mapperley, Notts. 1884; Nottingham 1889. † N 33.
SHAW, Miss C.R. Exh. 1887
Ellerslie, Sefton Park Liverpool. † L 2.
SHAW, D.K. Exh. 1918
† NEA 1.
SHAW, Miss D.L. Exh. 1920-21
Leeds 1920; Dewsbury 1921. † L 2.
SHAW, D.M. Exh. 1906-7
Myrtle Cottage, Newlyn, Penzance, Cornwall. † L 3.
SHAW, Eva Exh. 1923
51 Acresfield Road, Pendleton, Manchester. † L 1.
SHAW, Everton Exh. 1937
Sculptor. 177 Cliffords Inn, London. † RA 1.
SHAW, Mrs. Evelyn Byam Exh. 1900-36
Miniature portrait painter. S.W.A. 1924. Married to Byam S. q.v. Add: London 1900; Woldingham, Surrey 1936. † GI 1, L 2, RA 47, SWA 1.
SHAW, Miss E.J. Exh. 1884
West End Chambers, Broad Street Corner, Birmingham. † B 2.
SHAW, Miss E.K. Exh. 1939
9 Alma Terrace, Nottingham. † N 1.
SHAW, Mrs. Eunice M. Exh. 1907-8
Oak Hill, St. Buryan, Cornwall. † L 3.
SHAW, Mrs. Ellen S. Exh. 1938-39
† RMS 2.
SHAW, E. Sylvia Exh. 1899-1924
Portrait and figure painter. Highgate, London. † L 3, RA 9, RBA 1, RI 5, ROI 11, SWA 21.
SHAW, Ernest Wilson Exh. 1915-17
4 Greenfield Road, Stoneycroft, Liverpool. † L 4.
SHAW, Frederick d. 1923
Landscape painter. Exh. from 1880. Add: Liverpool. † B 4, L 143, M 6, RA 2, RI 2.
SHAW, F.K. Exh. 1891-1908
Ardwick, Manchester 1891; Lancaster 1908. † L 1, M 1.
SHAW, F.W. Exh. 1925-26
Landscape painter. 29 East Street, Ilkeston, Derbys. † N 6.
SHAW, Mrs. G. Exh. 1897
Raby Drive, Bromborough. † L 1.
SHAW, Gerard T. Exh. 1910-11
Lamorna, Penzance 1910; Paul, Penzance 1911. † B 3, L 4.

SHAW, Henry Exh. 1880-81
Architect. 39 Clapton Square, Clapton, London. † RA 2.

SHAW, Hugh George* Exh. 1880-95
Genre painter, Barnes, Surrey 1880; Bell Busk, via Leeds 1886; Totteridge, Herts. 1887; London 1892; Youlgrave, nr. Bakewell 1894. † B 12, L 9, M 16, RBA 17, ROI 1.

SHAW, Helen Kathleen Exh. 1886-91
Painter. London 1886; Totteridge, Herts. 1888. † B 2, L 1, M 9, RA 1, RBA 8.

SHAW, James Exh. 1883-1901
Edinburgh. † GI 7, L 1, RSA 24.

SHAW, John Bruce b. 1912
Painter and lithographer. R.I. 1942. Add: 17 Park Way, Friern, Barnet, Herts. † RA 4, RI 6.

SHAW, J.C. Exh. 1887-90
Glasgow. † GI 11, RSA 1.

SHAW, John J. Exh. 1885-1904
Architect. London. † RA 11.

SHAW, Kathleen T. Exh. 1886-1914
Sculptor and medallionist. Dublin 1886; London 1889 and 1893; Rome 1891. † B 2, GI 9, L 15, M 4, NG 11, RA 16, RHA 44, RSA 16.

SHAW, Leonard J. Exh. 1925-28
Black and white landscape artist. West Bridgford, Notts. 1925; Nottingham 1927. † N 5.

SHAW, Miss M. Exh. 1937
121 Warwick Road, Olton. † B 1.

SHAW, Mary Exh. 1909-10
35 Church Road, Urmston, nr. Manchester. † L 5.

SHAW, Margaret Exh. 1921-28
Eccles, Lancs. 1921; Barton on Irwell, Manchester 1927. † L 6.

SHAW, Michael Exh. 1885
7 Campbell Street, Riccarton, Kilmarnock. † RSA 2.

SHAW, Mary Helen Exh. 1896-1911
Landscape and flower painter. Beverley, Yorks. and Hull. † ALP 2, BG 1, L 4, LS 3, M 2, RA 11.

SHAW, Neville Exh. 1938-40
Etcher. Kemsing, Kent. † RA 5.

SHAW, Peggy Exh. 1936-37
Portrait painter. Crossways, Temple Sheen, London. † RA 3.

SHAW, Rita Exh. 1932-34
17 Balmeg Avenue, Giffnock, Glasgow. † GI 2, RSA 1.

SHAW, Richard Norman 1831-1912
Architect. b. Edinburgh. A.R.A. 1872, R.A. 1877, H.R.S.A. 1911. Add: London. † L 1, RA 22, RSA 4.

SHAW, Winifred Exh. 1920-23
Watercolour painter. Studied under Henry Pope. Add: Edgbaston, Birmingham 1920; West Southbourne 1923. † L 3.

SHAW, Walter James* 1851-1933
Marine, coastal and landscape painter. Salcombe, Devon. † D 1, FIN 1, GI 1, L 5, RA 20, ROI 1, TOO 7.

SHAYER, William J. junr.* b. 1811
Animal and landscape painter. Son and imitator of his father William S. (1788-1879) Exh. 1885. Add: 191 Regent Street, London. † L 2, RA 1, ROI 2.

SHEARD, Mrs. Mabel Exh. 1903-8
4 Holland Park Road Studios, Kensington, London. † SWA 5.

SHEARD, Thomas Frederick Mason* 1866-1921
Landscape and figure painter. Professor of Art, Queens College London. R.B.A. 1897. Add: Paris 1891; Oxford 1892; London 1895. † B 10, GI 1, L 6, LS 5, M 5, NEA 1, RA 27, RBA 199, RHA 8, RI 7, RMS 5, ROI 3.

SHEARER, James Exh. 1882-1940
Dunfermline. † RSA 15.

SHEARER, James Elliot b. 1858
Watercolour painter. b. Stirling. Exh. 1881-1940. Add: Benview, Stirling 1881; Manchester 1891; Edinburgh 1895. † GI 16, L 1, M 1, RA 1, RSA 76, RSW 22.

SHEARER, Robert Exh. 1899
79 Ruskin Street, Kirkdale, Lancs. † L 1.

SHEARER, Rosa L. Exh. 1899-1912
Benview, Stirling 1899 and 1902; 79 Ruskin Street, Kirkdale, Liverpool 1901. † GI 10, L 1, RSA 1.

SHEARER, R.S. Exh. 1909-13
Bootle, Liverpool 1909; Cheltenham, Glos. 1911. † L 1, RA 3.

SHEARER, T. Smith Exh. 1912-25
Morton Lodge, Dunfermline. † RSA 3.

SHEARIM, Arnold W. Exh. 1898-1906
Liverpool. † L 6.

SHEARLEY, F.H. Exh. 1921
1 Featherstone Buildings, High Holborn, London. † RA 2.

SHEARMAN, G.T. Exh. 1913-25
Watercolour landscape painter and designer. Collaborated with F.H. Ball q.v. Add: 21 Bentinck Road, Nottingham. † N 8.

SHEARNE, Miss G.A. Exh. 1939
126 Musters Road, West Bridgford, Nottingham. † N 1.

SHEBBEARE, H.V. Exh. 1940
2 Southwood Lane, Highgate, London. † NEA 1, RBA 2, RI 1.

SHEEHAN, Charles A. Exh. 1901-26
Portrait, figure and biblical painter. London. † D 3, L 1, NEA 3, RA 5, RMS 1.

SHEEHAN, William Exh. 1916-17
86 Gt. William O'Brien Street, Cork † RHA 3.

SHEELER, Charles* b. 1883
American landscape and still life painter. Exh. 1925. † CHE 2.

SHEEN, E. Exh. 1912
5 Lessing Street, Honor Oak Park, London. † L 1.

SHEFFIELD, George 1839-1892
Landscape painter. Douglas, I.O.M. 1882; Manchester 1888. † L 5, M 17, RBA 1.

SHEFFIELD, Margaret A. Exh 1887-96
Landscape painter. 9 Dartmouth Row, Blackheath, London 1887; Sidcup, Kent 1891. † B 5, L 4, M 2, RA 2, RBA 11.

SHEFFIELD, Mary J. Exh. 1887-98
Flower painter. 9 Dartmouth Row, Blackheath, London 1887; Sidcup, Kent 1892. † B 8, L 5, M 2, RA 7, RBA 16, ROI 2, SWA 2.

SHEFFIELD, T. Percy Exh. 1883
Landscape painter. Crown Inn, Farnham Royal, Bucks. † RA 1

SHEILDS, Miss A. Wentworth Exh. 1890
4 Vanbrugh Park Road, London. † SWA 1.

SHELDON, Miss Exh. 1899
5K Hyde Park Mansions, London. † SWA 2.

SHELDON, Mrs. Agnes Exh. 1933
Landscape painter. 4 Yeomans Row, London. † RA 1.

SHELDON, Mrs. Eileen M. Exh. 1939
Flower painter. Three Ways, Westwood Court, Leeds. † RA 1.

SHELDON, F. Kedward Exh. 1909-25
Birmingham. † L 68.

SHELDON, Frederick S. Exh. 1885-86
Sculptor. 11 Cheyne Gardens, Chelsea, London. † L 1, RA 1, RSA 1.

SHELDON, Mrs. L.K. Brown Exh. 1896-1902
Birmingham. † B 3.

SHELDON, Pearl Exh. 1925-33
Painter. London. † GI 1, L 1, RBA 1, RCA 1, RHA 1, ROI 1, RSA 1, WG 40.

SHELDON-WILLIAMS, Mrs. Ina Exh. 1908-38
nee Thomson. Landscape, figure and flower painter. Studied Slade School and Paris. Travelled widely. Add: Stroud, Glos. 1908; Sharnbrook, Beds. 1934. † LS 5, NEA 1, RA 3, RMS 1, WG 168.

SHELDON-WILLIAMS, Inglis Exh. 1902-39
Military figure and landscape painter and illustrator. Studied Belgium, Paris, Slade School and under Sir Thomas Brock. Spent 6 years in South Africa and served as a trooper in the Boer War. Add: London 1902 and 1911; Stroud, Glos. 1908; Italy 1928; Sharnbrook, Beds. 1934. † B 1, FIN 97, GI 3, GOU 2, L 1, LS 9, NEA 1, RA 18, RI 2, RID 21, ROI 21, WG 36.

SHELLARD, Doris Exh. 1922
St. Mellon's, nr. Cardiff. † RCA 2.

SHELLARD, Henry Walter Exh. 1899-1937
Cardiff 1899; St. Mellon's, nr. Cardiff 1922. † L 2, RCA 10.

SHELLEY, Mrs. E. Mary Exh. 1922-28
nee Webb. Etcher and dry point artist. b. Ironbridge, Salop. Add: London. † WG 123.

SHELLEY, Frank Exh. 1895-1924
Portrait painter. London. † RA 3, RBA 1, RI 1.

SHELLEY, Frederick b. 1865
Landscape painter, modeller and designer. b. Hanley, Staffs. Studied Hanley School of Art, Royal College of Art, Italy, France and Belgium. Principal Plymouth School of Art. Exh. 1890-1926. Add: London 1890 and 1926; Plymouth, Devon 1899. † RA 8.

SHELLEY, John Exh. 1884
Redhill Lodge, Petworth, Sussex. † RHA 1.

SHELLEY, Maud Exh. 1919-36
Miniature painter. Woking, Surrey 1919; London 1936. † LS 2, RA 1.

SHELLEY-ROLLS, Sir John Exh. 1935-40
Marine painter. South Lodge, Knightsbridge, London. † RI 2, ROI 1, WG 50.

SHELLSHEAR, Alicia J. Exh. 1882-87
Watercolour portrait painter. London. † M 3, RA 2.

SHELLY, Arthur 1841-1902
Landscape painter. b. Yarmouth. Add: Chislehurst 1880; London 1881; Hampton on Thames 1886. Died Plymouth. † D 3, RA 5, RBA 2, RI 2, ROI 1.

SHELMERDINE, T. junr. Exh. 1885
Municipal Office, Dale Street, Liverpool. † L 1.

SHELTON, Esther Exh. 1901-29
Miniature portrait painter. London. † L 1, RA 20, RI 1, RMS 1.

SHELTON, Harold Exh. 1939-40
Etcher. Royal College of Art. London. † RA 4, RE 5.

SHELTON, Sidney Exh. 1881-89
Landscape painter. London 1881; Eastbourne 1889. † RA 2, RBA 2.

SHENORKIAN, M. Exh. 1910
3 Hamilton Gardens, St. Johns Wood, London. † RA 1.

SHENTON, Annie F. Exh. 1904-6
Miniature portrait painter. 54 Greyhound Road Mansions, West Kensington, London. † RA 2.

SHEPARD, Ernest Howard 1879-1976
Painter and illustrator (e.g. Winnie the Pooh). Studied Heatherleys and R.A. Schools (Landseer Scholar 1899 and British Institute Scholar 1900). On staff of "Punch". Married Florence Eleanor S. q v. Add: London 1901; Shamley Green, Guildford, Surrey 1905. † B 1, GI 1, L 2, M 1, RA 16.

SHEPARD, Florence Eleanor Exh. 1901-26
nee Chaplin. Painter. Studied R.A. Schools. Married Ernest Howard S. q.v. Add: London 1901; Shamley Green, nr. Guildford, Surrey 1912. † RA 7.

SHEPARD, Frank Newton Exh. 1888-1911
Portrait, figure and landscape painter. London 1890; Amberley, Sussex 1904. † FIN 9, NEA 1, NG 1, RA 2, RBA 4, RID 21.

SHEPARD, Henry Dunkin Exh. 1885-99
Watercolour figure and landscape painter. Married Jessie S. q.v. Add: London. † B 7, D 2, L 6, M 7, NG 3, RA 5, RBA 1, RHA 4, RI 22.

SHEPARD, Mrs. Jessie Exh. 1888
Still life painter. Married Henry Dunkin S. q.v. Add: 10 Kent Terrace, Hanover Gate, London. † RA 1.

SHEPARD, R.W. Exh. 1913
9 Proby Square, Blackrock, Dublin. † RHA 1.

SHEPARD, Thomas Exh. 1908
Broad Green, Wellingborough, Northants. † NG 1.

SHEPARD, Major Thomas Exh. 1909-14
Office of Arms, Dublin Castle, Dublin. † RHA 16.

SHEPHARD, E. Courtnay Exh. 1901-9
Landscape painter. London 1901; Brentwood, Essex 1909. † L 1, RA 1, RBA 1.

SHEPHARD, Rupert b. 1909
Painter and teacher. Studied Slade School 1926-29. Exh. 1930-40. † COO 20, GOU 2, LEF 1, LEI 4, NEA 3.

SHEPHERD, Annie M. Exh. 1913-16
4 Priory Gardens, Highgate, London. † LS 4.

SHEPHERD, Eric Anders d. 1937
Landscape painter. b. Chile, South America. Add: Torquay, Devon 1886; Bray, Co. Wicklow 1894. † RA 1, RHA 2.

SHEPHERD, F.H.S. b. 1877
Landscape, portrait and figure painter. b. Stoke under Ham, nr. Yeovil, Studied Slade School 1898-1902. N.E.A. 1912. Exh. 1902-38. Add: London. † BA 75, BG 1, CG 29, CHE 65, COO 2, G 5, GOU 117, I 8, L 14, LS 5, M 2, NEA 143, P 6, RA 14, RBA 1, RHA 8, RSA 1.

SHEPHERD, Gertrude K. Exh. 1894-99
Flower and portrait painter. 3 Warwick Square, London. † RID 10.

SHEPHERD, Herbert C. Exh. 1888-99
Landscape painter. Cardigan 1888; Bridge End, Wales 1890; Penarth, Glam. 1895; Flushing, nr. Falmouth, Cornwall 1897. † L 2, RA 4.

SHEPHERD, J. Exh. 1884
Whiley Street, Longsight, Manchester. † M 1.

SHEPHERD, J.A. Exh. 1909-31
Painter. † BG 4, GI 1.

SHEPHERD, Julia C. Exh. 1883-92
Manchester. † M 6.

SHEPHERD, Mrs. Kate Exh. 1888-1916
Mrs. F.H. nee Hammond. Portrait and figure painter. Add: Nottingham 1888; London 1908; Amberley, Sussex 1916. † LS 5, N 16, RA 2.

SHEPHERD, Mary Exh. 1927
Brookside, Hale Barnes, Cheshire. † L 2.

SHEPHERD, M.G. Exh. 1891-92
8 St. Stephens Crescent, Westbourne Park, London. † B 2.

SHEPHERD, S. d'Horne b. 1909
Painter and lithographer. b. Dundee. Studied Glasgow School of Art 1927-30. Teacher of painting Glasgow School of Art 1929-31. Exh. 1932-33. Add: Glasgow. † GI 1, RSA 1.

SHEPHERD, Stanley Raymond b. 1906
Painter, etcher and engraver. Studied Harrow School of Art and Royal College of Art. Exh. 1925-36. Add: 96 Sussex Road, Harrow, Middlesex. † ALP 1, RA 4.

SHEPHERD, Violet Edgecombe see JENKINS

SHEPLEY, Clifford Exh. 1932
11 Restalrig Avenue, Edinburgh. † RSA 1.

SHEPLEY, Eleanor M. Exh. 1919-39
Miniature portrait painter. London 1919; Hastings, Sussex 1937; Bramber, Sussex 1939. † P 1, RA 1 RI 1, RMS 1, SWA 1.

SHEPPARD, Arthur Exh. 1923
Still life painter. 7A Campden Street, Kensington, London. † RA 1.

SHEPPARD, Ammie Exh. 1926
† M 2.

SHEPPARD, B. Exh. 1905-6
5 Wentworth Studios, Manresa Road, Chelsea, London. † GI 1, NG 3, RA 3.

SHEPPARD, Miss B. Exh. 1922
† SWA 4.

SHEPPARD, Charlotte Lillian d. 1925
Animal and figure painter and watercolourist. Exh. from 1885. Add: London. † B 10, D 3, I 6, L 4, LS 34, RBA 1, RHA 3, RI 2, ROI 1, SWA 10.

SHEPPARD, Emma Exh. 1885-1900
Flower painter. 1 York Road, Northampton. † L 3, RA 4, SWA 3.

SHEPPARD, Faith T. Exh. 1938-39
Landscape painter. 4 Kings House, 396 Kings Road, London. † RA 1, ROI 2.

SHEPPARD, Guy Exh. 1939
Caricaturist. † COO 41.

SHEPPARD, Kathleen M. Exh. 1930-31
Wood engraver. Beechwood, The Broadwalk, Winchmore Hill, London. † RBA 1, RED 1.

SHEPPARD, Mrs. Nancy b. 1890
nee Huntly. Watercolour landscape painter and black and white portrait artist. b. Nusseerabad. Studied Edinburgh, Kunstgewerbe Schule, Dusseldorf and R.A. Schools. Exh. 1913-37. Add: London 1913 and 1937; Welwyn Garden City, Herts. 1933. † L 1, P 1, RA 7.

SHEPPARD, Oliver 1865-1941
Sculptor. b. Tyrone, Ireland. Studied Royal College of Art (travelling scholarship). A.R.H.A. 1895, R.H.A. 1901. Add: London 1886; Nottingham 1894 and 1901; Dublin 1897 and 1903. † GI 1, N 7, RA 14, RHA 109.

SHEPPARD, O.S. Exh. 1913
Seymour Place, Fulham Road, London. † RHA 2.

SHEPPARD, Reuben Exh. 1894-1914
Sculptor. Drumcondra, Dublin 1894; London 1901. † L 1, M 1, RA 11, RHA 2, RI 2.

SHEPPERSON, Claude A. 1867-1921
Watercolour painter, pen and ink artist, illustrator and lithographer. b. Beckenham, Kent. Studied Heatherleys, and Paris. Contributor to "Punch". A.R.A. 1919, A.R.E. 19, R.I. 1900, R.M.S. 1900, A.R.W.S. 1910. Add: London. † AB 2, FIN 13, G 1, GI 16, I 1, L 17, LEI 256, LS 5, M 4, RA 39, RI 8, RID 68, RMS 1, RSA 1, RWS 38.

SHEPPEY, J.E. d. 1924
Exh. from 1915. Add: 18 Amberley Street, Liverpool. † L 11, RCA 4.

SHERAR, Robert Exh. 1885-1903
Edinburgh. † RSA 5.

SHERATT, Thomas Exh. 1880
Engraver. 10 Basinghall Street, London. † RA 1.

SHERBORN, Miss A. Exh. 1893
540 Kings Road, Chelsea, London. † L 2.

SHERBORN, Charles William 1831-1912
Painter and etcher. R.E. 1881. Add: London. † L 11, RA 39, RE 120.

SHERBOURNE, James Exh. 1938
Wigan, Lancs. † RCA 1.

SHERIDAN, Clare 1885-1970
Sculptor. Studied South Kensington, Add: London. † I 11, RA 1.

SHERIDAN, Christina D. Exh. 1933
School of Art, Glasgow. † RSA 2.

SHERIDAN, George P. Exh. 1897
Commercial Buildings, Dublin. † RHA 1.

SHERIFF, Flora Exh. 1913-14
Carronvale, Larbert, Stirlingshire. † RSA 3.

SHERIFF, G.V. Exh. 1882-90
Liverpool. † L 22.

SHERIFF, William Exh. 1883-90
5 Minard Terrace, Partickhill, Glasgow. † GI 3.

SHERINGHAM, George 1884-1937
Landscape and decorative painter, illustrator, poster and fan artist, theatrical and textile designer. Studied Slade School and Paris. Add: London. † BK 85, CHE 3, FIN 61, GOU 29, I 11, L 9, LEI 54, M 5, RA 2, RED 2, RID 9, RMS 1, ROI 1, RSA 1, WG 7.

SHERLOCK, A. Marjorie b. 1897
Mrs. Barrett. Painter and engraver. Studied Slade School, Westminster, Royal College of Art and Paris. Exh. 1916-37. Add: The Limes, Mill Road, Cambridge. † GOU 41, I 4, LS 2, NEA 17, RA 4.

SHERLOCK, John A. Exh. 1884-94
Figure painter. La Bossiere, pres Neuphle le Chateau, Seine et Oise, France 1884; Eton, Berks. 1887; Windsor, Berks. 1889; London 1890. † B 7, M 1, RBA 1.

SHERLOCK, Mrs. Madge Exh. 1913-26
Ross, Summerfield, Dalkey, Ireland. † RHA 5.

SHERNOVITCH, B. Exh. 1929
71 Leopold Street, Leeds. † L 2.

SHERRARD, Florence E. Exh. 1884-95
Landscape, coastal and figure painter. 7 Oxford Square, London. † B 1, DOW 1, L 6, M 3, RA 8, RBA 7, ROI 1, SWA 16.

SHERRATT, Lily Exh. 1935-38
Bowdon, Cheshire. † RCA 5.

SHERRATT, Mrs. V. Exh. 1886
35 Wyndcliffe Road, Small Heath, Birmingham. † B 1.

SHERRIFF, Mrs. Annie Exh. 1885-88
Figure and flower painter. London 1885; Pale Corwen, North Wales 1887. † RA 4, RBA 1, ROI 2.

SHERRIFFS, John Exh. 1888-1905
Aberdeen 1888; Greenwich 1905. † RSA 3.

SHERRIN, David* b. 1868
Landscape and coastal painter. Exh. 1898-1900. Add: c/o J.J. Wroe, 4 St. Ann's Place, Manchester. † M 2.
SHERRIN, George Exh. 1880-89
Architect. London. † RA 11.
SHERRIN, John 1819-1896
Still life and animal painter, mainly in watercolour. Studied under W.H. Hunt. A.R.I. 1866, R.I. 1879. Add: 3 Codrington Villas, Ramsgate, Kent. † B 2, GI 2, L 22, M 13, RA 13, RI 52, RSA 3, RWS 9, TOO 2.
SHERVIL, Alfred H. Exh. 1896-1902
Miniature painter. R.M.S. 1898. Add: London. † RA 4, RMS 12.
SHERWIN, Frank b. 1896
Watercolour painter. Studied Derby School of Art and Heatherleys 1920. Son of Samuel S. q.v. Exh. 1926-40. Add: London. † AR 2, L 2, RA 2, RBA 3, RI 19.
SHERWIN, Mrs. Kate Exh. 1896
Landscape painter. 4 Portman Mansions, London. † RA 1.
SHERWIN, Samuel Exh. 1884-99
Landscape painter. Father of Frank S. q.v. Add: Derby. † B 1, N 11.
SHERWOOD, A. Exh. 1939
Watercolour painter. † AG 2.
SHERWOOD, F. Exh. 1905-11
Brayton House, Selby, Yorks. † RCA 3.
SHERWOOD, Fred Exh. 1886-1900
Landscape painter. Mansfield, Notts. † N 18.
SHERWOOD, Mrs. Maud Exh. 1932
Watercolour landscape painter. 4 Porta Pinciana, Rome, Italy. † RA 2.
SHERWOOD, Miss R.C. Exh 1932
Derrymore, Rectory Road, Sutton Coldfield. † B 2.
SHERWOOD, William b. 1855
Figure and flower painter. Exh. 1901-40. Add: Birmingham. † B 57, NEA 1, RA 2, RBA 1, RCA 2, RI 1, ROI 3.
SHIACH, James Alex Exh. 1898
7 Duddingstone Crescent, Portobello, Edinburgh. † RSW 1.
SHIACH, John S. Exh. 1939-40
Aberdeen. † RSA 3.
SHIELD, Jane Hunter Exh. 1886-93
Watercolour painter. R.S.W. 1885 (res. 1903). Add: Edinburgh. † DOW 3, RSA 9, RSW 4.
SHIELDS, D. Gordon d. 1940
Portrait painter. London 1910; Perth 1915; Edinburgh 1918. † GI 23, L 1, RA 1, RSA 50.
SHIELDS, Frederick James* 1833-1911
Painter, watercolourist, decorator, illustrator and mural decorator. A.R.W.S. 1865. Add: St. Johns Wood, London 1880; Merton, Surrey 1902. † AG 1, ALP 213, L 2, M 10, NG 2, RWS 13.
SHIELDS, Henry Exh. 1885
Landscape and coastal painter. Perth 1885 and 1891; Glasgow 1887; Tighnabruaich, Argyleshire 1904. † GI 25, RBA 3, RSA 2.
SHIELDS, Harry G. 1859-1935
Landscape painter. R.B.A. 1898. Add: East Barnet, Herts. 1888; Perth 1894; Inverkeithing 1896; Dalmeny 1900; Farnham, Slough 1907; Abernethy 1909; St. Andrews 1932. † GI 2, RA 8, RBA 62, ROI 10, RSA 13.
SHIELDS, H.R. Exh. 1903-4
Palace Garden Mansions, Kensington, London. † D 5.
SHIELDS, John Exh. 1901-5
Manchester. † M 3.
SHIELDS, Thomas W.* 1850-1920
Figure painter. b. Scotland. Exh. 1880. Add: Paris. Died in America. † RA 1.
SHIELLS, Peter Exh. 1880-83
20 Tobago Street, Edinburgh. † RSA 5.
SHIELLS, W. Thornton Exh. 1898-1938
Landscape painter. Willesden Green, London 1898; Longley Road, Wealdstone, Middlesex 1907. † D 1, GI 1, L 18, RA 8, RI 3, RSA 1, RSW 4.
SHIELS, Nicholas Exh. 1884-89
Edinburgh 1884; Rye, Sussex 1889. † RSA 4.
SHIFFNER, Eleanor Barbara Georgina b. 1896
Animal, landscape and portrait painter. b. Rossington, Yorks. Studied Byam Shaw School and R.A. Schools. (Landseer scholarship, silver and bronze medals). Exh. 1922-36. Add: London 1922 and 1924; Bawtry, Yorks. 1923. † CHE 5, L 6, M 1, NEA 1, RA 11.
SHILLABEER, Mrs. Mary Exh. 1931-36
Landscape painter. 9 Kent Gardens, Ealing, London. † RA 2.
SHILLAKER, Mrs. Annie Exh. 1918-33
Miniature portrait painter. The Austerby, Bourne, Lincs. † RA 4, RI 14.
SHILLAKER, Elsie Exh. 1939
Figure painter. 123 High Road, Woodford Green, Essex. † RA 1.
SHILLINGLAW, Miss P. Exh. 1928
St. Agnes, Cornwall. † L 6.
SHILLITO, M. Alma see LITTLEBURY
SHILSTON, C.E. Exh. 1914
84 Charlotte Street, Fitzroy Square, London. † RA 1.
SHILTON, Mary Exh. 1934-35
Conway, Wales. † RCA 2.
SHILTON, Thomas Exh. 1907-14
Stoke Golding, Nuneaton, Warwicks. † B 1, N 9.
SHINDLER, Florence A. Exh. 1888
Watercolour painter. 15 Queenstown Road, Lower Clapton, London. † GI 2, RA 1.
SHINER, Cyril J. Exh. 1930-39
59 Kathleen Road, South Yardley, Birmingham. † B 21.
SHINER, Christopher M. Exh. 1892-1903
Architect. London. † RA 7.
SHINGLER, David Exh. 1937
Swansea. † RCA 2.
SHINGLER, Kathleen Exh. 1937-39
Painter. 11 Edith Road, London. † RA 2.
SHINGLER, Mrs. Mildred Exh. 1937-38
† RMS 2.
SHINKWIN, Alice Staveley Exh. 1895-99
Altcar Camp, Hightown, nr. Liverpool. † L 3.
SHIPLEY, Miss B. Exh. 1928-34
Nottingham. † N 2.
SHIPLEY, W.A. Exh. 1924
Watercolour painter. 64 Lawrence Street, Long Eaton, Notts. † N 1.
SHIPWAY, John Exh. 1926-31
Birmingham 1926; Cheltenham, Glos. 1929. † B 9.
SHIPWRIGHT, Emily A. Exh. 1893-1904
Still life and miniature portrait painter. London. † RA 3, RBA 1, RMS 1.
SHIRLAW, Walter 1838-1910
Landscape and figure painter. b. Paisley. 1st President of the Society of American Artists. Died in Madrid, Spain. Exh. 1881-91. Add: London. † RA 3.
SHIRLEY, Elizabeth Exh. 1890-91
Watercolour painter. 35 York Terrace, Regents Park, London. † RI 3.
SHIRLEY-FOX, Ada R. see HOLLAND
SHIRLEY-FOX, John d. 1939
Portrait painter. Studied Ecole des Beaux Arts, Paris. Married Ada R. Holland q.v. R.B.A. 1902. Add: Liverpool 1889; London 1890. † L 3, M 2, NG 16, P 2, RA 15, RBA 49, RI 4, ROI 1.
SHIRREFFS, John Exh. 1890-1937
Figure and interior painter and watercolourist. A.R.S.W. 1895 (written off 1909). Add: Aberdeen and Greenwich. † GI 6, L 2, RA 4, RBA 11, RHA 1, RI 5, RSA 18, RSW 5.
SHIRREFFS, William Exh. 1883-1900
Glasgow. † GI 18, RSA 2.
SHIVAS, James Exh. 1886
46 Queen Street, Peterhead. † RSA 1.
SHOESMITH, Kenneth Denton 1890-1939
Painter, poster and decorative artist. b. Yorks. R.I. 1925. Add: Golders Green, London. † GI 3, L 13, RA 2, RI 52.
SHOOSMITH, Arthur G. Exh. 1933-37
Architect. Crawley, Sussex 1933; London 1937. † RA 3.
SHOOSMITH, Fanny V. Exh. 1919-25
Landscape, still life and figure painter. Becket House, Northampton. † I 1, RA 4, RI 1.
SHOOSMITH, Thurston Laidlaw 1865-1933
Landscape painter. R.B.A. 1919. Add: Northampton. † B 7, BG 49, G 5, GOU 3, I 22, L 10, LS 5, RA 4, RBA 77, RHA 5, RI 9, RID 12, RSA 1, WG 17.
SHOOSMITH, W.B. Exh. 1894
Ivy Tower, Northampton. † RI 1.
SHONE, Mary E. Exh. 1900
18 Maison Dieu Road, Dover, Kent. † B 1.
SHONE, Margaret W. Exh. 1923-29
Red Gables, Hoylake, Cheshire. † L 6.
SHOPPEE, Charles Herbert Exh. 1890
Architect. 22 John Street, Bedford Row, London. † RA 1.
SHORE, Agatha Catherine b. 1878
nee Hall. Portrait, interior and landscape painter. Studied Slade School 1898-1901. Exh. 1905-40. Add: London 1905; Cambridge 1909. † B 1, I 2, LS 6, NEA 2, P 2, ROI 1, SWA 14.
SHORE, Bertha Emma Louisa Exh. 1891-1914
Landscape painter. London 1891 and 1904; Cambuskenneth, Stirling 1900. † GI 3, I 2, L 4, LS 20, RBA 1.
SHORE, Capt. the Hon. F.W.J. Exh. 1880-88
Landscape painter. Edinburgh 1880; Gibraltar 1882; London 1883; Clonmel, Ireland 1888. † D 3, RA 2, RBA 1, ROI 4, RSA 9.
SHORE, Hon. Henry Noel 1847-1925
Lord Teignmouth. Watercolour painter. Studied under Legros. Add: Edinburgh 1880 and 1888; London 1883; Greenock 1884; Thomastown, Co. Kilkenny 1921. † GI 4, RHA 6, RI 2, RSA 5.
SHORE, Priscilla T. Exh. 1938
47a Priory Road, London. † SWA 1.
SHORE, Robert S. Exh. 1892-1922
Marine and landscape painter. A.R.H.A. 1894, R.H.A. 1895. Keeper to the R.H.A. Add: Dublin. † RA 2, RHA 174.
SHORE, Walter Exh. 1905-12
Liverpool. † L 10.
SHORES, Mrs. A.M. Exh. 1905
The Nook, Claygate, Esher, Surrey. † RA 1.
SHORT, Mrs. C. Exh. 1909-11
Chesterfield. † N 4.

SHORT, E. Exh. 1907
R.E. Office, Bulford Camp, Salisbury, Wilts. † RA 1.

SHORT, Mrs. E.J. Exh. 1925-33
84 Handsworth Wood Road, Birmingham. † B 7.

SHORT, Sir Frank (Francis Job) 1857-1945
Painter, etcher and engraver. b. Worcester. Studied South Kensington and Westminster. Teacher of engraving, Royal College of Art. N.E.A. 1888, A.R.A. 1906, R.A. 1911, R.E. 1885, P.R.E. 1910, R.I. 1917, H.R.M.S. 1912. Knighted c.1911. Add: London. † CON 1, FIN 290, GI 5, GOU 5, L 47, NEA 5, RA 100, RBA 3, RE 174, RHA 37, RI 16, RSA 17.

SHORT, Frederick Golden* Exh. 1882-1908
Landscape painter. Lyndhurst, Hants. † L 4, NG 30, RA 4, RBA 5, ROI 20, TOO 9.

SHORT, George Howard Exh. 1900-23
Painter. Acton, London 1900; New Maldon, Surrey 1911; Orpington, Kent 1923. † L 1, RA 6.

SHORT, M. Dudley Exh. 1929-38
Painter and linocut artist. 43 Regents Park Road, London. † AB 6, RED 2, SWA 7.

SHORT, Percy Exh. 1888-94
Figure and portrait painter. London. † RA 4, RBA 1, ROI 2.

SHORT, Richard 1841-1916
Coastal and landscape painter. Cardiff, Wales. † B 11, D 1, G 2, L 9, M 4, RA 14, RBA 2, RCA 10, RHA 3, ROI 4.

SHORT, Terry Exh. 1936
Birmingham. † SWA 2.

SHORT, William* 1827-1921
Exh. 1914. Add: Hillside, Eye, Suffolk. † RA 1.

SHORTALL, Michael J. Exh. 1899
15 Berkeley Road, Dublin. † RHA 1.

SHORTHOUSE, Arthur Charles 1870-1953
Portrait and landscape painter. Studied Birmingham College of Art. R.B.S.A. 1928. Add: Birmingham. † AB 1, B 61, RA 5.

SHORTHOUSE, Mrs. Florence M. Exh. 1908
74 Alexandra Road, Edgbaston, Birmingham. † B 1.

SHORTHOUSE, Stella H. Exh. 1887-90
Flower painter. South Croydon, Surrey 1887; London 1888. † L 2, RA 2.

SHORTLAND, Mrs. Julia M. Exh. 1911-21
St. Helens Parade, Southsea, Hants. 1911; Purley, Surrey 1913. † LS 20.

SHORTT, Mrs. Georgina Hastings Exh. 1908-24
Painter of miniatures and church pictures. Southwick, Sunderland. † B 2, L 18, LS 9, RCA 5, RSA 4.

SHOWELL, C. Exh. 1882-1932
Solihull, Birmingham 1882; Minchinhampton, Glos. 1924; Cheltenham, Glos. 1926. † B 10.

SHREAD, Evelyn Exh. 1905
Glenhurst, Hampstead Road, Handsworth, Birmingham. † B 1.

SHRIMPTON, Ada M. Exh. 1889-1925
Mrs. Giles. Portrait, flower and figure painter. A.S.W.A. 1902. Add: London. † B 19, GI 2, L 12, LS 7, M 10, RA 16, RBA 14, RI 12, RSA 2, SWA 28.

SHRING, Margaret S. Exh. 1880
The School House, Uppingham, Rutland. † D 1.

SHRUBSOLE, W.G. Exh. 1881-89
Landscape painter. Maidstone, Kent 1881; Bangor, Wales 1882; Manchester 1888. † B 6, L 2, M 5, RA 5, RCA 6.

SHTETININ, Mme. V. Exh. 1929
9 St. Mary's Street, Manchester. † L 3.

SHUBRICK, Louisa Exh. 1937
Givons Grove, Fleet, Hants. † RI 1.

SHUBROOK, Emma L. see HARDMAN

SHUBROOK, Laura A. Exh. 1889-98
Flower painter. Sister of Minnie Jane Hardman q.v. and Emma L. Hardman q.v. Add: London. † L 1, RA 5, RBA 11, RHA 2, ROI 8.

SHUBROOK, Minnie Jane see HARDMAN

SHUCKARD, Frederick P. Exh. 1880-1901
Flower painter. London. † RA 5.

SHUFFREY, James Allen b. 1859
Watercolour, architectural and landscape painter. Exh. 1912-23. Add: 99 Woodstock Road, Oxford. † D 15, LS 6.

SHUFFREY, Leonard A. Exh. 1889
Architect. 38 Welbeck Street, London. † RA 1.

SHULDHAM, E.B. Exh. 1884-1906
Flower painter. London. † RBA 5, ROI 1.

SHURROCK, Francis A. Exh. 1934-39
Sculptor. 18 Hagley Street. Riccarton, Christchurch, New Zealand. † RA 4.

SHUTE, Mrs. E. Exh. 1883-89
Watercolour painter. 7 Onslow Square, London. † D 1, G 1, L 2, RHA 8, RI 2, SWA 7.

SHUTER, Agnes Exh. 1881-84
Sculptor. London. † RA 3.

SHUTTLEWORTH, Alfred Exh. 1898
Painter and teacher. 24 Villa Road, Handsworth, Staffs. † RA 1.

SHUTTLEWORTH, Gwen Exh. 1926
† GOU 2.

SHUTTLEWORTH, H.F. Exh. 1932
† L 1.

SHUTTLEWORTH, T.B. Exh. 1904
9 Golgotha Road, Bowerham, Lancaster. † L 1.

SHUTTLEWORTH, T.O. Exh. 1889
11 Deane Road, Fairfield, Liverpool. † L 1.

SHUTTLEWORTH, William Thomas Exh. 1921
Lynwood, Skipton, Yorks. † LS 3.

SIBBINGS, Robert Exh. 1926
c/o St.. George's Gallery, 32a George Street, London. † GI 1.

SIBLEY, David C.G. Exh. 1938-40
King Edward VIII School, Sheffield 1938; Ballater, Aberdeenshire 1940. † B 1, RBA 2, RSA 1.

SIBLEY, Mrs. F.T. Exh. 1898-1904
Gwfnfryn Junction, Conway 1898; Marl Park, Conway 1904. † RCA 10.

SIBLEY, Frederick T. Exh. 1882-1903
Coastal and landscape painter. Southport, Lancs. 1882; London 1890; Gwfnfryn Junction, Conway, Wales 1898. † B 2, L 11, M 6, NG 1, RA 1, RBA 1, RCA 69.

SIBREE, Miss M.C. Exh. 1887
11 Claremont Road, Birmingham. † B 1.

SICARD, Bernard Exh. 1901
9 Rochesterr Road, Camden Town, London. † B 1.

SICARD, Francois 1862-1934
French sculptor. Exh. 1930. Add: Paris. † RSA 2.

SICARD, N. Exh. 1911
32 Cours Morand, Lyon, France. † L 1.

SICHEL, Ernest Leopold 1862-1941
Portrait and figure painter. N.E.A. 1891. Add: Bradford, Yorks. † L 12, NEA 3, NG 14, RA 10.

SICHEL, May Exh. 1928-29
The Nest, Greenhill Road, Otford, Kent. † NEA 2.

SICKERT, Bernard* 1863-1932
Landscape, portrait, figure and coastal painter and pastel artist. Son of Oswald and brother of Walter Richard S. q.v. N.E.A. 1888. Add: London. † G 2, GI 12, GOU 7, L 8, LS 17, M 5, NEA 138, NG 4, RA 2, RBA 10, ROI 3.

SICKERT, Oswald Exh. 1881-83
Landscape and figure painter. Father of Bernard and Walter Richard S. q.v. Add: 12 Pembroke Gardens, Kensington, London. † G 2, RA 1.

SICKERT, Walter Richard* 1860-1942
Painter of street scenes, genre, interiors and portraits and illustrator. b. Munich. Son of Oswald S. q.v. Came to England 1868. Studied Slade School 1881 and under Whistler. N.E.A. 1888, A.R.A. 1924, R.A. 1934 (res. 1935), R.B.A. 1928, R.E. 1887-92 re-elected A.R.E. 1925. Member London Group 1916. One of the founders of the Camden Town Group. Married Therese Lessore q.v. "Harold Gilman" (1912) purchased by Chantrey Bequest 1957. Add: London 1884 and 1906; Dieppe, France 1900. † AG 90, BA 182, BAR 5, BG 4, BK 5, CAR 287, CHE 1, G 4, GI 15, GOU 65, I 9, L 21, LEF 7, LEI 391, LS 13, M 5, NEA 117, RA 24, RBA 23, RE 21, RED 171, RHA 1, RI 1, ROI 4, RSA 14, TOO 12.

SIDANER, le see L

SIDDALL, Margaret Exh. 1908-28
Chester. † I 1, L 36.

SIDEBOTHAM, Emma Exh. 1899
c/o B.B. Dickinson Esq., Bloxham House, Rugby. † L 2.

SIDEBOTHAM, F. Nevill Exh. 1902
The Hall Cottage, Cheadle Hulme, Cheshire. † L 1, M 1.

SIDEBOTHAM, Jessie Exh. 1922-29
Heaton Moor, nr. Stockport, Lancs. 1922; Babbacombe, Torquay, Devon 1929. † L 79, M 3.

SIDEBOTTOM, G.J. Exh. 1886
67 Albert Road, Southport, Lancs. † M 1.

SIDEBOTTOM, N. Exh. 1914
143 Warrender Park Road, Edinburgh. † RA 1, RSA 1.

SIDES, Hilda Mary b. 1871
Watercolour landscape and garden painter. Studied St. Johns Wood School of Art, London, Dresden and Atelier Delecluse, Paris. Travelled widely. Exh. 1908-34. Add: Dresden 1908; London 1925. † B 3, L 1, LS 3, RI 1, RSA 2, WG 164.

SIDLEY, Albert Exh. 1881
Watercolour landscape painter. 8 Victoria Road, Kensington, London. † RBA 1.

SIDLEY, Samuel* 1829-1896
Portrait, genre and literary painter. b. York. Studied Manchester School of Art and R.A. Schools. R.B.A. 1890. Add: 8 Victoria Road, Kensington, London. † G 6, L 6, M 7, RA 10, RBA 15, RCA 9, ROI 4.

SIDNEY, Herbert d. 1923
Figure painter. Exh. from 1881. Add: London. † B 1, L 5, RA 1, RCA 8, RHA 1, ROI 1, TOO 4.

SIEDLECKA, de see D

SIEFERT, Emanuela Exh. 1893
17 Theresienhohe, Munich, Bavaria. † L 1.

SIEFFERT, L.E. Exh. 1911
36 Rue de Brances, Sevres, France. † L 1.

SIEVEKING, Ella Exh. 1886-87
Landscape painter. 17 Manchester Square, London. † SWA 3.

SIEVEKING, Natalie Exh. 1938
40 Carlyle Square, London. † RBA 1.
SIEVWRIGHT, Helena Exh. 1899-1901
London. † NG 3.
SIGMUND, Benjamin D. Exh. 1880-1904
Genre and landscape painter. London, Maidenhead, Berks. and Lynmouth, Devon 1830; Slough, Bucks. 1899. † B 6, D 5, DOW 15, L 17, M 2, RA 31, RBA 25, RHA 19, RI 34, RSW 1.
SIGNAC, Paul* 1863-1935
French painter and black and white artist. Exh. 1920-28. † GOU 22.
SIGNORINI, Giuseppe* 1857-1933
Italian watercolour painter. Exh. 1885-1911. Add: Bloomsbury, London 1885; Paris 1904. † L 5.
SIGNORINI, Telemaco* 1835-1901
Italian painter. Exh. 1882-85. Add: 60 Bedford Gardens, Campden Hill, London. † G 4, M 2, RA 1.
SIGRIST, Charles Exh. 1929-39
Portrait painter and etcher. 5 Highbury Terrace, London. † GI 1, RA 8.
SIKES, F.H. Exh. 1927
† D 2.
SIKES, Miss H.M. Exh. 1899-1900
Almondbury, Huddersfield. † L 3.
SILAS, Ellis Exh. 1916-35
Marine painter. Travelled widely. Add: London. † AR 1, I 1, RA 2, RI 1, ROI 3.
SILBURN, A. Exh. 1885
Landscape painter. 22 Eyot Gardens, Chiswick Mall, London. † RA 1.
SILCOCK, Arnold 1889-1952
Architect. b. Bath. Son of T.B.S. q.v. Studied Bath School of Art and A.A. Architect to Provincial Government, Szehuan, China 1921-25. Exh. 1927-36. Add: London. † RA 9.
SILCOCK, T.B. Exh. 1895
Architect and surveyor. Father of Arnold S. q.v. Add: Octagon Chambers, Milson Street, Bath. † RA 2.
SILCOCK, William Exh. 1932-34
41 Carron Road, Falkirk. † RSA 2.
SILK, Henry Exh. 1930-37
Landscape, figure, architectural and interior painter. † AG 4, LEF 47.
SILK, Oliver Exh. 1882-1928
Liverpool. † L 59.
SILLARS, D. Exh. 1886-1900
Glasgow. † GI 6, RSA 2.
SILLARS, William K. Exh. 1929-31
33 London Road, Kilmarnock. † GI 2.
SILLEM, Charles Exh. 1883-91
Animal and dead game painter. London. † L 4, M 1, RA 3, RBA 3.
SILLINCE, William Exh. 1931
Dry point artist. 47 Melody Road, Wandsworth, London. † RA 1.
SILLIVAN, Mrs. Florence J. Exh. 1909
63 Promenade, Southport, Lancs. † L 1.
SILVA, de see D
SILVA, Mrs. Maria de Jesus Conciaco Exh. 1930
† RMS 1.
SILVA, William Posey b. 1859
American painter. Exh. 1922. † FIN 33.
SILVER, Mrs. Exh. 1890
Beechcroft, Oaklands Park, London. † D 1.
SILVER, Arthur Exh. 1891-94
Designer of wallpaper and textiles. 84 Brook Green, London. † NEA 5.
SILVER, Rosa H. Exh. 1913
Landscape painter. † ALP 2.
SILVESTER, Jessie M. Exh. 1903-15
Portrait and figure painter. London. † RA 4.
SIM, Agnes M. Exh. 1912-40
Watercolour painter. R.S.W. 1927. Add: Paris 1912; Lochside, Montrose 1913. † AR 2, GI 5, RSA 26, RSW 46.
SIM, Edwin Lionel Exh. 1935
Douglas, I.O.M. † RCA 1.
SIM, James Exh. 1880-95
Landscape and genre painter. Chelsea, London 1880; Edinburgh 1895. † RA 4, RI 2, RSA 1.
SIM, Mary E. Exh. 1906-10
c/o Mrs. Crawford, 36 Willowbank Street, Glasgow. † GI 2.
SIM, Nan Exh. 1926
Lochside, Montrose. † RSW 1.
SIM, Stewart Exh. 1929
16 Melville Terrace, Edinburgh. † RSA 1.
SIMCOCK, Miss A.H. Exh. 1926-29
Longsight, Manchester 1926; Rhyl, Wales 1927. † L 4.
SIMCOCK, Leonora M. Exh. 1930-33
3 Gladstone Buildings, Rhyl, Wales. † L 4.
SIMCOCK, Norah b. 1906
Painter. decorative artist and cretonne designer. Studied Manchester School of Art. Exh. 1929-39. Add: Stoneleigh, Heaton Moor, Manchester. † RA 1, RCA 14, SWA 1.
SIMCOX, Albert Exh. 1914-16
13 Finsbury Market, London. † LS 6.
SIME, John R. Exh. 1935
30 Hereford Road, Nottingham. † N 1.
SIME, Sidney Herbert c. 1865-1941
Portrait and black and white artist and illustrator. Add: Liverpool 1889; London 1896; Worplesden, Guildford 1900. † BG 18, L 1, RBA 15.
SIMEON, Eunice Exh. 1928-40
Landscape painter. 83 West Side, Clapham Common, London. † NEA 4, RA 11, RSA 10, SWA 2.
SIMKIN, Beatrice T. Exh. 1899-1911
Sister of Louisa S. q.v. Add: 2 Canning Place, Kensington Gate, London. † SWA 11.
SIMKIN, Louisa Exh. 1881-1902
Landscape painter. Sister of Beatrice T.S. q.v. Add: London. † RHA 1, SWA 14.
SIMKINS, Edith A. Exh. 1896-1913
Figure painter. Nottingham 1896; Castle Conington 1902; Loughborough, Leics. 1908. † N 25.
SIMKINS, J.G. Exh. 1889
Architectural painter. Lowdham Lodge, Notts. † N 1.
SIMKINSON, Winefred Exh. 1923
† SWA 2.
SIMM, Franz* b. 1853
Austrian painter. Exh. 1899. Add: 11 Werneckstrasse, Munich. † GI 2.
SIMM, Henry Exh. 1894-1914
Portico, nr. Preston, Lancs. and Liverpool. † B 3, L 14.
SIMM, William Norris Exh. 1927-38
Harris Museum and Art Gallery, Preston, Lancs. † GI 4, L 5, RSA 2.
SIMMANCE, Miss E. Exh. 1906
17 Ravenscourt Park, London. † RI 1.
SIMMINGTON, Mrs. Robert Exh. 1921
16 Finglas Road, Dublin. † RHA 1.
SIMMONDS, Fred A. Exh. 1892-1936
Painter and teacher. Derby 1892 and 1936; Alvaston, nr. Derby 1900; Littleover, Derby 1910. † B 11, N 1.
SIMMONDS, Thomas C. Exh. 1881-99
Landscape painter and teacher. Derby. † B 6, RA 1.
SIMMONDS, William George b. 1876
Sculptor, wood carver and painter. b. Constantinople. Studied Royal College of Art and R.A. Schools. "Seeds of Love" purchased by Chantrey Bequest 1907 and "Old Horse" purchased in 1937. Exh. 1903-37. Add: London 1903; Stroud, Glos. 1933. † B 1, GI 1, L 5, RA 13.
SIMMONS, Mrs. Anna Exh. 1908-9
32 Randolph Gardens, London. † LS 3.
SIMMONS, C. Evelyn Exh. 1923-24
Architect. Palace Chambers, Westminster, London. † RA 4.
SIMMONS, D. Exh. 1886
† TOO 1.
SIMMONS, Eyres Exh. 1902-14
Cardisland, Herefords 1902; Ruan Minor, Cornwall 1913. † D 8, L 1.
SIMMONS, Edward E. Exh. 1881-91
Landscape, coastal and figure painter. Married Vesta S.S. q.v. Add: Paris 1881; Concarneau, Finistere, France 1882; London 1886; St. Ives, Cornwall 1887. † DOW 2, G 1, GI 3, L 4, M 2, RA 6, RBA 3, ROI 2.
SIMMONS, Graham C. Exh. 1916-19
† I 3.
SIMMONS, John* b. 1871
Landscape painter. Exh. 1925-40. Add: Chilterns, Amersham Common, Bucks. † GOU 3, L 2, NEA 2, P 1, RA 4, RBA 11, ROI 33.
SIMMONS, J. Deane Exh. 1882-89
Landscape and rustic genre painter. Dorking 1882; Henley on Thames 1884; London 1886. † B 1, D 2, L 1, RA 7, RBA 13, RI 12, ROI 12.
SIMMONS, Percy Exh. 1920-26
Painter and craft worker. Studied Stafford School of Art. Peripatetic art master for Salop County Council. Add: 27 Victoria Road, Bridgnorth, Salop. † B 5, L 6.
SIMMONS, S. Noel Exh. 1909-38
Painter. London. † L 5, M 1, NEA 7.
SIMMONS, Mrs. Vesta S. Exh. 1889-90
Figure painter. Married Edward E.S. q.v. Add: St. Ives, Cornwall. † DOW 2, G 1, ROI 1.
SIMMONS, William Henry 1811-1882
Mezzotint engraver. 247 Hampstead Road, London. † RA 1.
SIMMONS, W. St. Clair Exh. 1880-1917
Portrait, landscape and genre painter. London 1880 and 1885; Hemel Hempstead, Herts. 1883. † B 2, D 5, GI 6, L 6, M 3, NEA 113, NG 5, P 2, RA 11, RBA 4, RI 11, RID 20, ROI 6.
SIMMS, C. Exh. 1895
Black and white artist. Add: 2 Penywern Road, Earl's Court, London. † RA 1.
SIMMS, Kate Exh. 1902
109 Walford Road, Sparkbrook, Birmingham. † B 1.
SIMMS, Maude Exh. 1908-22
Torquay, Devon. † GOU 1, RA 1.
SIMNETT, R.J. Exh. 1932-37
60 Hinstock Road, Birmingham. † B 4.
SIMON, Alfred P. Exh. 1916-38
Lymdale, West Didsbury, Manchester. † GOU 1, I 5, LS 3, M 1.
SIMON, Eva Exh. 1892-1905
London. † L 1, RA 1, ROI 3, SWA 1.
SIMON, Frank W. Exh. 1883-98
Moseley, Birmingham 1883; Edinburgh 1885. † B 1, GI 3, RSA 17.
SIMON, Gwladys M. Exh. 1907-9
Northover, Marple, Cheshire. † RCA 4.
SIMON, J. Georges Exh. 1940
Watercolour figure painter. 5 Chelsea Studio, London. † RA 2.

SIMON, Mme. Jeanne Lucien Exh. 1912-24 3 bis Rue Cassini, Paris. † GI 5, L 2, RSA 12, RWS 2.

SIMON, Lucien* b. 1861 French watercolour painter. R.B.A. 1930. Exh. 1901-38. Add: 3 bis Rue Cassini, Paris. † BAR 1, FIN 3, GI 6, GOU 2, I 6, L 5, M 2, P 2, RA 9, RHA 1, RI 4, RSA 9, RWS 1.

SIMON, Naomi B. Exh. 1898-1936 Portrait, figure and landscape painter, black and white and lettering artist and miniaturist. b. Sydney, Australia. Studied Kings College for Women, Hammersmith and Byam Shaw and Vicat Cole School of Art. Add: London. † COO 8, D 3, G 1, I 1, L 2, M 1, RA 3, RID 4, ROI 3, SWA 8, WG 4.

SIMON, Miss S. Exh. 1932 23 Herbert Road, Sherwood Rise, Nottingham. † N 1.

SIMON, T. Francois Exh. 1907-26 Etcher. A.R.E. 1910. Add: Paris 1907; Austria 1914. † FIN 22, L 14, RE 26.

SIMONAU, Mrs. Louise Exh. 1897-98 Landscape painter. 1 Stratford Studios, Kensington, London. † B 2, RA 1, RBA 1.

SIMONDS, George b. 1843 Sculptor. Lived in Rome from c.1865-77. Among his works "The Falconer" stands in Central Park, New York; Her Majesty Queen Victoria at Reading, and the memorial to Sir Joseph Bazalgette on the Thames Embankment. Exh. 1880-1903. Add: London. † D 1, G 1, L 13, M 2, NG 13, RA 24.

SIMONE, Edgardo b. 1890 American sculptor. Exh. 1931. Add: 33 West 67th Street, New York, U.S.A. † RA 1.

SIMONET, Exh. 1880 16 Avenue Trudaine, Paris. † RHA 1.

SIMONETTI, Exh. 1880 Watercolour painter. † AG 1.

SIMONI, Gustavo b. 1846 Watercolour figure painter. Exh. 1880-87. Add: London 1880; Paris 1885. † AG 2, L 5, M 5, RA 1.

SIMONI, Sapione Exh. 1885-86 c/o A. Brabant, 74 Rue d'Amsterdam, Paris. † M 3.

SIMONIDY, Michel 1871-1933 Rumanian artist. Exh. 1925. † GOU 1.

SIMONS, Miss A.C. Exh. 1896-98 71 Abingdon Villas, London. † SWA 2.

SIMONS, Gertrude C. Exh. 1919-27 13 South Exchange Place, Glasgow. † GI 3, I 2, L 2, RSA 1, RSW 3.

SIMONS, J. Franz Exh. 1882 Brasschart, Antwerp. † L 1.

SIMONS, Marcius* Exh. 1885-91 Figure painter. c/o H. Mansfield, Cliftonville, Northampton. † RA 1, TOO 1.

SIMONSON, Anna Exh. 1895-1923 Figure, portrait and flower painter. 129 Queen's Gate, London. † NG 1, P 2, RA 5, RBA 1, ROI 12.

SIMPKINS, Edith A. Exh. 1914 Painter. Elmley Island, Sittingbourne, Kent. † LS 3.

SIMPSON, Alexander Brantingham Exh. 1904-31 Painter and dry point artist. R.I. 1917 (ret. 1932). R.O.I. 1912. Add: London 1904; Horstead Keynes, Sussex 1930. † I 2, RA 15, RI 76, ROI 31.

SIMPSON, A.C. Exh. 1937 7 Vallance Road, London. † RBA 1.

SIMPSON, Annie L. Exh. 1894-1913 Figure and miniature portrait painter. Halifax 1894; Etaples, Pas de Calais, France 1909. † B 11, GI 4, GOU 1, L 8, LS 12, M 1, RA 1, RBA 5, ROI 2, RSA 1.

SIMPSON, Alice M. Exh. 1885-98 Flower painter. London. † RBA 1, SWA 4.

SIMPSON, Miss A.V. Exh. 1932-33 Dalmore, Blundellsands. † L 4.

SIMPSON, Constance Mary Exh. 1923-25 Watercolour painter and illustrative painter. 41 Forest Road, Nottingham. † L 1, N 11.

SIMPSON, Christine T. Exh. 1937 Landscape painter. Papplewicke Locke, Notts. † N 5.

SIMPSON, Charles Walter* b. 1885 Landscape, marine, bird and animal painter and illustrator. Studied Bushey, Herts. and Juliens, Paris. R.B.A. 1914, R.I. 1914, R.O.I. 1923. Married Ruth S. q.v. Exh. 1907-40. Add: Penzance, Cornwall 1907, 1911 and 1933, Farnborough, Hants. 1908; London 1925. † ALP 50, BG 46, FIN 317, GI 20, I 8, L 12, NEA 1, RA 40, RBA 34, RCA 1, RHA 26, RI 110, ROI 13, RSA 1.

SIMPSON, E. Exh. 1884-85 † TOO 3.

SIMPSON, Edgar Exh. 1898-1903 Jeweller, Nottingham. † N 19.

SIMPSON, Edgar Exh. 1921-22 14 Mersey View, Blundellsands, Liverpool. † L 61.

SIMPSON, Mrs. Edith Exh. 1935-38 22 Strathearn Road, Edinburgh. † RSA 3.

SIMPSON, Elspeth Exh. 1927-29 Bromley, Kent. † SWA 2.

SIMPSON, Eugenie Exh. 1883-88 Flower and fruit painter. London. † B 2, L 2, RA 7, RBA 2, ROI 4, SWA 3.

SIMPSON, Ethel H. Exh. 1890 Eastwood, Ferry Road, Edinburgh. † RSA 1.

SIMPSON, Edith M. Exh. 1886-93 Flower and figure painter. 95 Darenth Road, Stamford Hill, London. † SWA 3.

SIMPSON, Evelyn M. Exh. 1931-37 Flower and portrait painter. Park End, Willow Grove, Chislehurst, Kent. † RA 3.

SIMPSON, Frederick Moore Exh. 1888-1924 Architect. Professor of Architecture, Liverpool University College and London University College. Add: London 1888 and 1904; Liverpool 1901. † RA 18, RSA 1.

SIMPSON, Gwen Exh. 1927 98 Cholmley Gardens, London. † RBA 1.

SIMPSON, George G. Exh. 1883-1908 Flower and figure painter. London 1883; Bishops Stortford, Herts. 1905. † BG 4, L 1, RA 4.

SIMPSON, H. Exh. 1880 c/o Dr. Simpson, Eastwood, Bonnington, Sussex. † RA 1.

SIMPSON, H. Exh. 1891 4 York Place, Halliwell Lane, Cheetham Hill, Manchester. † M 2.

SIMPSON, Henry 1853-1921 Landscape, coastal, architectural and figure painter. b. Nacton, Suffolk. N.E.A. 1887. Add: London. † D 6, FIN 2, G 4, GI 7, L 13, LEI 63, M 4, NEA 8, NG 1, RA 4, RBA 7, RHA 1, RI 10, ROI 4.

SIMPSON, Henry Exh. 1909-40 Aberdeen 1909 and 1940; Ayr 1922. † RSA 3.

SIMPSON, Harold A. Exh. 1913-40 Flower painter. Crewe. † GI 1, L 11, RA 17, RCA 1.

SIMPSON, H.D. Exh. 1909 9 Kemp Street, Hamilton, N.B. † RSW 1.

SIMPSON, Henry Graham Exh. 1882-1913 Watercolour and miniature portrait painter. Liverpool 1882 and 1889; London 1886 and 1892; Penrith, Cumberland 1891; Carlisle 1908. † L 7, LS 4, RA 3, RI 3, RSA 1, RSW 1.

SIMPSON, H. Hardey Exh. 1882-1902 Portrait and figure painter. Bowdon, Cheshire 1882; Conway, Wales 1902. † B 1, L 9, M 17, RA 2, RBA 2, RCA 1, RHA 1.

SIMPSON, Herbert W. Exh. 1899-1933 Painter and etcher. London 1899; Birstall, Leicester 1932. † GI 1, L 5, RA 9, RBA 2, ROI 1.

SIMPSON, Ida Mackintosh Exh. 1928-32 Portrait, figure and flower painter. b. Ackworth, Yorks. Studied Byam Shaw School, Westminster and R.A. Schools. Add: London. † GOU 10, NEA 2, RA 2.

SIMPSON, Joseph b. 1879 Painter, etcher and caricaturist. b. Carlisle. Studied Edinburgh. R.B.A. 1909. Exh. 1898-1927. Add: Edinburgh 1898; London 1908; Kirkcudbright 1926; Glasgow 1927. † BG 19, BK 1, GI 4, I 2, L 4, LEI 38, LS 8, RBA 20, RSA 8, RSW 1.

SIMPSON, J.A. Exh. 1894-1900 London. † L 1, NG 4.

SIMPSON, J.A. Exh. 1923 21 Gambier Terrace, Liverpool. † L 1.

SIMPSON, John Godfrey Exh. 1935-36 Wood engraver. 8 Mansion Place, Queen's Gate, London. † RA 2, RED 2.

SIMPSON, J.H. Exh. 1890 c/o John Spiers, 136 Wellington Street, Glasgow. † GI 2.

SIMPSON, James L. Exh. 1931-37 Architect. Unilever House, London. † GI 1, RA 1.

SIMPSON, Janet S.C. Exh. 1904-38 Watercolour painter and etcher. Studied Lambeth and Royal College of Art (1 silver and 2 bronze medals). A.R.E. 1910. Add: Bromley, Kent 1904; Brenchley, Kent 1926. † AB 54, G 1, L 19, RA 29, RE 49, RSA 7.

SIMPSON, John W. Exh. 1881-1904 Architect. London. † GI 2, RA 8.

SIMPSON, Kate Exh. 1910 Thoresby, Shortlands, Kent. † LS 3.

SIMPSON, Katherine Exh. 1880-93 Mrs. T.W. Landscape, marine and figure painter. Ruswarp, Whitby. † RBA 3, SWA 4.

SIMPSON, L. Gibson Exh. 1929 27 Botanic Road, Edge Hill, Liverpool. † L 1.

SIMPSON, Lizzie J. Exh. 1883 22 London Street, Edinburgh. † RSA 1.

SIMPSON, Mrs. M. Exh. 1921 15 Grove Park, Liverpool. † L 1.

SIMPSON, Mary Exh. 1888 2 Moredun Crescent, Edinburgh. † RSA 1.

SIMPSON, Mrs. Magdalene D. Exh. 1927 11 The Common, Ealing, London. † L 1.

SIMPSON, Maria E. Exh. 1880-99 nee Burt. Miniature portrait painter. Married William S. q.v. Add: 19 Church Road, Willesden, London. † RA 6, RI 7, RMS 6.

SIMPSON, Mary Goudie d. 1934
Watercolour painter, craftworker, designer and teacher. Studied Lambeth School of Art. R.B.A. 1915, A.S.W.A. 1908, S.W.A. 1910. Exh. from 1893. Add: London 1893; Bromley, Kent 1903; Keston, Kent 1925; Benenden, Kent 1931. † B 4, BG 21, D 20, L 30, NG 1, RBA 104, RCA 5, RHA 2, RI 8, RSA 1, SWA 89.

SIMPSON, Margaret H.A. Exh. 1880-96
Portrait, figure and landscape painter. London. † D 2, GI 1, L 3, RA 3, RBA 7, RSA 1, SWA 8.

SIMPSON, M. Lilian Exh. 1896
Sculptor. 37 Elsham Road, Kensington, London. † L 2, RA 2.

SIMPSON, Miss May Marshall Exh. 1921
15 Grove Park, Liverpool. † L 1.

SIMPSON, Ruth Exh. 1918-23
nee Alison. Married Charles Walter S. q.v. Add: The Shore Studio, St. Ives, Cornwall. † I 3, SWA 4.

SIMPSON, Thomas Exh. 1887-1926
Landscape painter. London 1887; Kelvedon, Essex 1910. † D 1, GI 2, L 1, LS 18, NEA 9, RA 2, RBA 4, WG 79.

SIMPSON, William* 1823-1899
Painter, engraver and illustrator. b. Glasgow. Made sketches of the Crimean War. Travelled in India, Kashmir and Tibet 1859-62. Also visited China, Russia and Afghanistan. Married Maria E.S. q.v. A.R.I. 1874, R.I. 1879, R.O.I. 1883. Add: 19 Church Road, Willesden, London. † GI 4, L 5, RI 36, ROI 5.

SIMPSON, William Exh. 1880-87
Edinburgh. † GI 1, RSA 12.

SIMPSON, William Bank Exh. 1884-85
Figure painter. Lyndhurst, Hants. † RBA 1, RSA 2.

SIMPSON, W. Graham Exh. 1880-98
Miniature portrait and figure painter. London. † NG 1, RA 6, RBA 1, RMS 1.

SIMPSON, W.H. Exh. 1880
Landscape painter. 145 Lancaster Road, Notting Hill, London. † D 1.

SIMS, Charles* 1873-1928
Portrait, landscape and decorative painter and illustrator. Studied South Kensington, Julians, Paris 1891 and R.A. Schools 1893. A.R.A. 1908, R.A. 1915. Keeper of the R.A. 1920-26 (resigned due to mental illness). R.O.I. 1904, R.S.W. 1926, A.R.W.S. 1911, R.W.S. 1914. "The Fountain" purchased by Chantrey Bequest 1908 and "The Wood Beyond the World" purchased in 1913. Add: London 1893; 1901 and 1912; Southminster, Essex 1899; Paris 1903; Petworth, Sussex 1908 and 1914. Committed suicide. † AG 1, B 3, BAR 42, CG 1, CHE 1, FIN 5, GI 23, GOU 4, I 4, L 30, LEI 95, M 3, NEA 7, RA 116, RCA 1, RI 2, ROI 10, RSA 12, RSW 1, RWS 35.

SIMS, William A. Exh. 1911
Bushey, Herts. † M 1.

SIMSON, E.R. Exh. 1886
Bedrule, Jedburgh. † RSA 1.

SIMSON, Miss F.K. Exh. 1886-88
25 Nile Grove, Morningside, Edinburgh. † RSA 3.

SIMSON, G.W. Exh. 1889
Broomieknowe, Lasswade, N.B. † RSA 1.

SIMSON, John Aberdein Exh. 1905
9 Eton Terrace, Edinburgh. † RSA 1.

SIMSON, T. Exh. 1896
Black and white landscape artist. Blackmoor, Liss, Hants. † NG 5, RA 1.

SINANIDES, Constance Exh. 1882
5 Rue Cambon, Paris. † RHA 3.

SINCLAIR, Alfred b. 1866
Exh. 1899-1902. Add: Dolgelly, North Wales. † B 2, L 2.

SINCLAIR, Andrew Exh. 1937
† RSA 1.

SINCLAIR, Alexander Garden 1859-1930
Landscape and portrait painter. Edinburgh. † CON 4, GI 5, L 2, M 1, RSA 74, RSW 2.

SINCLAIR, Beryl Maude b. 1901
nee Bowker. Landscape painter. Studied Bath School of Art and Royal College of Art. Exh. 1928-40. Add: Upper Gloucester Place, London. † COO 1, GOU 1, LEI 3, NEA 12, RA 10, SWA 4.

SINCLAIR, E.D. Exh. 1938
246 Sarehole Road, Hall Green, Birmingham. † B 1.

SINCLAIR, Mrs. Fannie Exh. 1909
Loughoreen, Hill of Howth, Co. Dublin. † RHA 1.

SINCLAIR, George Exh. 1899
95 Bath Street, Glasgow. † GI 1.

SINCLAIR, Mrs. Gertrude Exh. 1928
c/o 97a Gt. Georges Street, Liverpool. † L 1.

SINCLAIR, Helen M. Exh. 1912-17
Landscape and miniature painter, black and white artist and illustrator. London. † L 3, RA 8, WG 47.

SINCLAIR, Isabel Exh. 1919-30
Miniature portrait painter. 22 Cartwright Gardens, London. † L 3, RA 1.

SINCLAIR, Jessie Exh. 1888-1905
Oxton, Cheshire 1881; Liverpool 1894; Birkenhead 1905. † L 3.

SINCLAIR, John Exh. 1881-1923
Landscape painter. Liverpool 1881; Birkenhead 1899. † D 1, L 82, RA 1, RCA 1, RI 2.

SINCLAIR, James R. Exh. 1896
29 Queen Street, Edinburgh. † RSA 1.

SINCLAIR, Mrs. L.H. Exh. 1920
18 Ann Street, Edinburgh. † RSA 1.

SINCLAIR, Miss M. Exh. 1916
42 Blessington Road, Anfield, Liverpool. † L 1.

SINCLAIR, Mary Exh. 1886
3 Gloucester Place, Edinburgh. † RSA 3.

SINCLAIR, Mrs. Sophia M. Exh. 1881-89
16 Hart Street, Edinburgh. † RSA 13.

SINCLAIR, W. Braxton Exh. 1924-27
Architect. 8 Buckingham Street, Adelphi, London. † RA 5.

SINDICI, Mrs. Francesca Stuart Exh. 1892-93
Military/ painter. 6 William Street, Lowndes Square, London. † B 3, L 2, M 3, RA 2.

SINDING, Otto* 1842-1909
Norwegian painter. Exh. 1890. Add: 11a Hanover Street, Edinburgh. † RI 1.

SINDING, Stephan 1846-1922
Norwegian sculptor. Exh. 1892. Add: Copenhagen. † GI 1.

SINET, Andre Exh. 1893
Portrait, figure and landscape painter. † GOU 85.

SINET, E. Exh. 1910
151 Stanhope Street, London. † RA 1.

SINET, F. Exh. 1907
28 Robert Street, Hampstead, London. † L 1, RA 1.

SING, Justine Kong Exh. 1911-19
219 Kings Road, Chelsea, London. † I 1, L 3, RA 3.

SING, Theodora (Dora) Exh. 1890-1903
Portrait and landscape painter. Kelton, Aigburth, Liverpool. † L 6, RID 4.

SINGER, Miss Amy M. Exh. 1882-89
Sculptor. Frome, Somerset. † L 1, NG 1, RA 9.

SINGER, Edgar Ratcliffe Exh. 1918-31
Sculptor and designer. Studied Frome and South Kensington. Add: Knoll House, Frome, Somerset. † RA 5.

SINGH, Sushila Exh. 1936
Engraver. Married to Arthur H. Andrews q.v. † RED 1.

SINGLEHURST, Mrs. J. Exh. 1933
Rosslare Park West, Heswall, Cheshire. † L 1.

SINGLETON, Jeannie Exh. 1913
27 Carless Avenue, Harborne, Birmingham. † RA 1.

SINGTON, Miss G. Exh. 1893
12 Scardale Villas, Kensington, London. † SWA 1.

SINS, Miss Lindsley Exh 1924
† D 1.

SINTEMIS, Renee b. 1888
German sculptor. Exh. 1936. † RSA 4.

SINTRAM, H.S.R. Exh. 1880
Painter. 24 Gt. Russell Street, London. † G 1.

SIODIA, Rustem Exh. 1911
Architectural landscape painter. 109 Gower Street, London. † NEA 1.

SIPMAN, Frances E. Exh. 1888-91
Flower, landscape and figure painter. 18 Corporation Oaks, Nottingham. † N 6.

SIRR, Harry Exh. 1902
Architect. 50 Twisden Road, Highgate Road, London. † RA 1.

SISQUELLA, Alfredo b. 1900
Spanish painter. Studied Escuela de Bellas, Artes de Barcelona. Exh. 1937. † BA 3.

SISSMORE, Charles Exh. 1885-86
Landscape painter. 4 Yerbury Road, Tufnell Park, London. † RA 1, ROI 3.

SISSON, Marshall b. 1897
Architect. Studied R.I.B.A. Jarvis student, British School at Rome 1924, student of the British School of Archaeology at Athens. Exh. 1937. Add: 3 Staple Inn, London. † RA 1.

SISSONS, Hilda H. Exh. 1901
North Ferriby, Brough, Yorks. † L 2.

SISSONS, Miss M. Exh. 1910-16
Villa des Reves, Mentone, France. † RA 10.

SISTERE, de See D

SITCH, T. Exh. 1920
205 Brunswick Road, Sparkbrook, Birmingham. † B 1.

SIVELL, Robert Exh. 1909-40
Painter. Studied Glasgow School of Art (Guthrie award and Torrance award). A.R.S.A. 1937. Add: Paisley 1909; Glasgow 1916; Kirkcudbright 1924. † GI 33, L 7, RA 1, RSA 34.

SKEAPING, Mrs. Barbara See HEPWORTH

SKEAPING, Mrs. Emily J. Exh. 1908-16
173 Upper Parliament Street, Liverpool 1908; Eccleston Park, Prescot, Lancs. 1910. † L 9.

SKEAPING, John Exh. 1889-1939
Figure and landscape painter and lithographer. Studied Liverpool School of Art and on the continent. Brother of Lily Skeaping Kaufmann q.v. Headmaster St. Helens School of Art, Lancs. Member London Group 1930. Add: Liverpool 1889; Prescot, Lancs. 1909. † BA 47, BK 1, L 56.

SKEAPING, John Rattenbury b. 1901
Sculptor. b. Woodford, Essex. Son of Kenneth Mathieson S. q.v. Studied R.A. Schools (gold medal and travelling studentship, Prix de Rome Sculpture scholarship). Married Barbara Hepworth q.v. Exh. 1922-34. Add: Bexley Heath, Kent 1922; London 1927. † RA 1, RSA 2.

SKEAPING, Kenneth Mathieson Exh. 1883-1920
Painter. Father of John Rattenbury S. q.v. Add: Liverpool 1883 and 1905; London 1889; South Woodford, Essex 1897; Bexley Heath, Kent 1909. † L 34, M 2.

SKEAPING, Lily See KAUFMANN

SKEATS, Frank G. Exh. 1880-87
Watercolour landscape painter. Father of Leonard Frank S. q.v. Add: Erene, The Polygon, Southampton. † RBA 1, RI 2.

SKEATS, Leonard Frank* 1874-1943
Portrait and figure painter. b. Southampton. Son of Frank G.S. q.v. Studied Hartley University College School of Art, Southampton and Julians, Paris. Add: Southampton 1901; Croydon, Surrey 1904; London 1909; Mere, Wilts. 1914; Bath c.1927. † LS 3, M 3, RA 6, RI 1, ROI 1, WG 44.

SKEATS, Thomas Exh. 1880-82
Watercolour landscape, flower and figure painter. 7 Evan's Terrace Avenue, Southampton. † D 3, RBA 5.

SKEEN, E. Exh. 1928
Landscape painter. † AB 1.

SKELDON, H.B. Exh. 1905
60 Albany Road, Lowhill, Liverpool. † L 2.

SKELSEY, Maud Exh. 1920-23
Greenhayes, Hillside Gardens, Wallington, Surrey. † D 1, SWA 2.

SKELTON, Miss E.M. Exh. 1907
The Hermitage of Braid, N.B. † RSA 1.

SKELTON, Frances Emily Exh. 1909
† LS 3.

SKELTON, George Exh. 1912-15
Abbey Park Road, Grimsby, Lincs. † ROI 2.

SKELTON, Joseph Ratcliffe Exh. 1888-1927
Figure painter and black and white illustrator. b. Newcastle on Tyne. Add: Newcastle on Tyne 1888; Hinckley, Leics. 1891; Bristol 1893; Sundridge, nr. Sevenoaks, Kent 1911; London 1925. † M 2, P 1, RA 2, RI 1, ROI 6.

SKELTON, Leslie James 1848-1929
American/Canadian landscape painter. Add: Colorado, U.S.A. 1901; Montreal, Canada 1904. † L 1, RA 2.

SKELTON, Ralph Fisher b. 1899
Portrait painter. b. Port Byron, Illinois. Studied Chicago Art Institute, R.A. Schools and Slade School. Exh. 1926. Add: 17a British Grove, Hammersmith, London. † P 1, RA 1.

SKENE, Ruth Exh. 1914
21 Ovington Square, London. † LS 3.

SKERRITT, F.G. Exh. 1908
62 Hucknall Road, Nottingham. † N 1.

SKIDMORE, Emily Exh. 1899-1913
Streatham, London 1899; Isleworth, Middlesex 1913. † RCA 1, SWA 4.

SKIDMORE, Harriet Exh. 1884-1909
Landscape painter. London. † B 13, D 49, GI 1, M 3, RA 1, RBA 4, RHA 12, SWA 7.

SKILBECK, Clement O. Exh. 1884-1901
Figure and illustrative painter. London. † GI 1, L 1, NG 5, RA 3, RBA 1, RI 2, ROI 4.

SKILL, Frederick John 1824-1881
Landscape and rustic genre painter, illustrator and engraver. A.R.I. 1871, R.I. 1876. Add: London. † RI 3.

SKINNER, Constance M. Exh. 1911-19
Sculptor. London. † RA 2.

SKINNER, E.A. Exh. 1883-88
Prescot Road, Fairfield, Liverpool. † L 4, M 3.

SKINNER, Edward F. Exh. 1888-1919
Portrait and landscape painter. London 1888; Lewes, Sussex 1891. † L 1, RA 2, RBA 2.

SKINNER, F. Exh. 1899
Clevedon, Somerset. † L 2.

SKINNER, Frank b. 1896
Landscape and portrait painter and etcher. Studied Municipal School of Art, Bristol. Teacher of Art Bristol University. Exh. 1919-20. Add: Bristol. † L 6.

SKINNER, H.F.C. Exh. 1915
Cronkould, Anerley Road, Anerley, London. † RA 1, RI 1.

SKINNER, William Exh. 1892-1903
Edinburgh. † GI 5, RSA 23, RSW 1.

SKINNER, W.G. Exh. 1911
19 Queen's Road, Richmond Hill, Surrey. † RA 1.

SKIPPER, Charles F. Exh. 1925-33
Architect. 64 St. Andrews Street, Cambridge. † RA 9.

SKIPPER, George John Exh. 1906-32
Architect, watercolour painter, pastel and pen and ink artist. Add: Norwich 1906; London 1932. † RA 8.

SKIPTON, Mrs. Theo E. Exh. 1912-14
Dublin. † RHA 2.

SKIPWORTH, Arthur Henry Exh. 1889-1907
Architect. 5 Staple Inn, Holborn, London. † RA 35, RSA 2.

SKIPWORTH, Frank Markham* d. 1929
Portrait, genre and historical painter. R.O.I. 1909, R.P. 1891. Exh. from 1882. Add: London. † B 29, BG 1, CHE 1, DOW 4, FIN 1, G 13, GI 16, L 50, M 23, NG 34, P 83, RA 43, RBA 11, RI 4, ROI 54.

SKIPWORTH, J. Exh. 1901
Vicers Street, Nottingham. † N 2.

SKIRVING, Alexander Exh. 1880-1913
Architect. Glasgow. † GI 24, RSA 1.

SKIRVING, Christina A. Exh. 1896-1903
Croys, Dalbeattie, N.B. † D 2, RSA 2. RSW 2.

SKOULDING-CANN, Miss E. Exh. 1924-29
Flower painter. † AB 2, D 5.

SKREDSVIG, Christian Exh. 1883
Norwegian landscape painter. † FIN 1.

SKRIMSHIRE, Alfred J. Exh. 1899-1901
Engraver. 31 Ryde Vale Road, Tooting Common, London. † RA 2.

SLACK, Mrs. M. Exh. 1933-38
Cliff Cottage, Winchelsea, Sussex. † RI 3.

SLACK, Miss M.E. Exh. 1887
Figure painter. 26 Winchester Street, Warwick Square, London. † ROI 1.

SLADDIN, Capt. Thomas A. Exh. 1919
Architect. 60 Tufton Street, Westminster, London. † RA 1.

SLADE, Adam b. 1875
Landscape painter. Exh. 1914-35. Add: Rye Sussex 1914; London 1915; Battle, Sussex 1935. † BA 2, G 1, GOU 15, NEA 8, RA 3.

SLADE, Anthony b. 1908
Landscape painter. Studied Brighton School of Art. Exh. 1931-37. † GOU 3, LEI 35, RED 35.

SLADE, Arthur Exh. 1931
Landscape painter. † CG 1.

SLADE, Basil A. Exh. 1895-1911
Architect. London. † RA 2.

SLADE, C.A. Exh. 1910-13
Etaples, Pas de Calais, France 1910; Paris 1911. † L 8, LS 5.

SLADE, Emily Exh. 1880-81
Landscape painter. 6 Apsley Terrace, Acton, London. † SWA 2.

SLADE, Edgar A. Exh. 1904-25
Portrait and landscape painter. London. † CHE 1, LS 3, NEA 6.

SLADE, Frank Exh. 1909-14
Ashford, Kent 1909; Rye, Sussex 1913; Chiswick, London 1914. † D 2, LS 9.

SLADE, Madeline Exh. 1923
† SWA 2.

SLADE, Patricia Exh. 1939
Portrait painter. † COO 34.

SLADE, Roland L. Exh. 1932
113 Beauchamp Road, Kings Heath, Birmingham. † B 2.

SLADE, Sydney Exh. 1908-19
Miniature portrait painter. 1 Westcliff, Seaton, South Devon. † RA 11.

SLADEN, Alice Amelia Exh. 1897-1912
Rhydoldog, Rhayader, Radnorshire. † D 1, LS 9, SWA 2.

SLADER, Samuel Ernest Exh. 1880
Watercolour flower painter. 9 Magdala Terrace, Dulwich, London. † D 1.

SLAGG, Petty Exh. 1933-38
Painter, etcher and dry point artist. 71 Campden Street, London. † P 1, RA 2, RBA 2, ROI 3.

SLANEY, M. Noel b. 1915
Mrs. G.F. Moules. Painter. Studied Glasgow School of Art. Exh. 1938-40. Add: Glasgow, London and Eaglesham, Renfrewshire. † RA 1, RSA 4, RSW 3.

SLATER, Dorothy Exh. 1908-13
Cheadle Hulme, nr. Stockport 1908; Hazel Grove, Cheshire 1912. † L 3, M 2, RCA 3.

SLATER, Eric Exh. 1928-37
Colour woodcut artist. Winchelsea, Sussex 1928; Seaford, Sussex 1929. † BA 5, GI 12, L 4.

SLATER, Frank S. Exh. 1930-40
Portrait painter. Rowfant Mill, nr. Crawley, Sussex. † P 3, RA 1.

SLATER, H.A. Exh. 1911-14
19 Bowers Avenue, Nottingham. † N 6.

SLATER, Herbert G. b. 1892
Watercolour painter and etcher. Studied Sheffield School of Art. Exh. 1921-26. Add: Sheffield. † L 4.

SLATER, Irene Margaret Exh. 1916-32
Mrs. Lofthouse. Watercolour painter and miniaturist. Southport, Lancs. 1916; London 1923. † B 1, L 7, RA 2, RCA 2, RI 1.

SLATER, John Exh. 1880
Langley Mill, Notts. † N 3.

SLATER, John Exh. 1920
12 Craigmellar Park, Edinburgh. † RSA 1.

SLATER, J. Atwood Exh. 1883-1906
Architect. London 1883; Bristol 1902; St. Buryan, Cornwall 1906. † RA 13, RI 1.

SLATER, John Falconar* b. 1857
Landscape, seascape and portrait painter and etcher. Exh. 1885-1936. Add: Ashton under Lyne 1885; Forest Hall, Northumberland 1889; Newcastle on Tyne 1899; Whitley Bay 1911. † L 5, M 1, RA 22.

SLATER, Walter James 1845-1923
Landscape painter. Manchester 1880; Deganwy, Llandudno 1891; Conway 1897. † M 9, RA 9, RCA 98, RI 1.

SLEATH, William Exh. 1895-1907
Landscape painter. London. † B 1, M 1, NG 15, RA 1, RBA 2, RI 6, ROI 8.

SLEATOR, James Sinton d. 1950
Portrait, still life and landscape painter. b. Co. Armagh. Studied London, Dublin and Florence. A.R.H.A. 1917, R.H.A. 1917. Exh. from 1915. Add: Dublin 1915; Belfast 1924; London 1931. † FIN 2, GI 1, P 4, RA 2, RHA 41.

SLEE, Katie C. Exh. 1915-16
Helmerley, Langdale Road, New Brighton, Cheshire. † L 3.

SLEE, Mary Exh. 1898-1935
Miniature painter. b. Carlisle. Studied Royal College of Art and Heatherleys. Teacher Carlisle School of Art. Add: Carlisle. † L 15, NG 1, RA 5, RHA 6, RMS 3, RSA 7.

SLEIGH, Bernard b. 1872
Watercolour painter, wood engraver, stained glass artist and mural decorator and teacher. R.B.S.A. 1928. Exh. 1898-1938. Add: Birmingham 1898 and 1909; Chesham, Bucks. 1908; Campden, Glos. 1937. † B 85, FIN 4, GI 4, L 23, NG 6, RA 3.

SLEIGH, Mrs. Warner(Phill) Exh. 1880-83
Sculptor and painter. London. † RA 2, SWA 2.

SLEIGHT, Arthur b. 1883
Landscape and flower painter. b. Wath-on-Dearne, Yorks. Studied Rotherham and Bournemouth Schools of Art. Exh. 1919-38. Add: Grange over Sands, Lancs. 1919; Bournemouth 1925. † L 9, RA 10, RBA 1.

SLESSOR, Maud Exh. 1919
Pekin Cottage, Rottingdean, Sussex. † LS 3.

SLIGHT, Daisy Exh. 1906
North Mains, Ormiston, N.B. † GI 1.

SLINGER, Edith C. Exh. 1902-34
Miniature portrait painter. Urmston, nr. Manchester 1902; Brooklands, Cheshire 1923; Sale, Cheshire 1928. † L 1, M 4, RA 2, RCA 18.

SLINGO, O.W. Exh. 1910
Broad Green, Liverpool. † L 2.

SLINN, Walter Exh. 1930-31
28 Harland Road, Sheffield. † B 2.

SLIWINSKI, S.T. Exh. 1936
Landscape and illustrative painter and designer. c/o 14 St. Kevins Park, Dublin. † RHA 3.

SLOAN, Chrissie S.P. Exh. 1912-40
2 Crown Circus, Dowanhill, N.B. † GI 4, RSA 1, RSW 5.

SLOAN, Ethel R. Exh. 1912-29
Birkenhead. † L 6.

SLOANE, Constance Exh. 1902-4
Moore, nr. Warrington, Lancs. † L 3.

SLOANE, George* Exh. 1901
Figure painter. † TOO 1.

SLOANE, James Fullarton Exh. 1886-1940
Figure, landscape and still life painter, illustrator and poster artist. Add: Glasgow. † GI 49, L 3, RA 1, RSA 7, RSW 9.

SLOANE, Marianna Exh. 1905
c/o A. Ward, 34 Craven Street, Strand, London. † B 2, RA 1.

SLOANE, Mary A. Exh. 1889-1938
Painter, engraver, etcher, illustrator and mezzotint artist. b. Leicester. Studied Herkomers and Royal College of Art. A.R.E. 1900, A.S.W.A. 1902, S.W.A. 1905. Add: London 1889 and 1896; Bushey, Herts. 1891; Leicester 1892. † ALP 22, B 3, D 50, FIN 1, I 2, L 2, M 2, N 2, P 4, RA 26, RBA 5, RE 52, RI 12, RID 66, SWA 61.

SLOBBE, A.G.W. Exh. 1915
424 Fulham Road, London. † RA 1.

SLOCOCK, Mabel Exh. 1898-1911
Landscape and miniature portrait painter. Visited Cyprus and India. Add: London. † L 3, NG 3, RA 3, WG 36.

SLOCOCK, Mrs. S. Exh. 1922-34
Landscape painter. † COO 2, SWA 1.

SLOCOMBE, Alfred Exh. 1881-95
Painter and etcher. Brother of Charles Philip, Edward and Frederick Albert S. q.v. Father of Miss J. and Shirley Charles Llewellyn S. q.v. Add: Hampstead, London. † RA 3, RCA 81, RE 3, RI 1, ROI 1.

SLOCOMBE, Charles Philip 1832-1895
Watercolour painter and etcher. Teacher at the National Art Training School. Brother of Alfred, Edward and Frederick Albert S. q.v. A.R.E. 1881. Add: 10 Rockall's Terrace, Cricklewood, London. † D 2, RA 10, RE 8, RHA 2.

SLOCOMBE, Edward d. 1915
Painter and etcher. R.E. 1883. Brother of Alfred, Charles Philip and Frederick Albert S. q.v. Exh. from 1883. Add: Watford, Herts. † FIN 6, L 8, LS 10, NG 3, RA 35, RE 171, RHA 13.

SLOCOMBE, Frederick Albert 1847-1920
Painter and etcher. R.E. 1881. Brother of Alfred, Charles Philip and Edward S. q.v. Add: Cricklewood, London 1880; Hendon, London 1884. † B 27, D 3, L 27, M 1, RA 34, RBA 15, RE 91, RHA 6, RI 4, ROI 3.

SLOCOMBE, Miss J. Exh. 1898
Daughter of Alfred S. q.v. Add: Cumberland House, West Hampstead, London. † RCA 1.

SLOCOMBE, Shirley Charles Llewellyn Exh. 1887-1916
Painter and etcher. Son of Alfred S. q.v. Add: London. † L 2, LS 3, M 1, RA 9, RCA 12, RI 5, ROI 1.

SLOOVERE, de See D

SLOTHOUWER, Professor D.F. Exh. 1936
† RSA 1.

SLOTT-MOLLER, Mme. Agnes Exh. 1897
Painter. 13 Ny Vestergade, Copenhagen. † RA 1.

SLOUS, Henry Courtney See SELOUS

SLOUS, James George Exh. 1909
† LS 3.

SLUITER, Willy* Exh. 1906-24
Dutch watercolour painter. London 1906; Katwijr ann Zee, Holland 1909; Laren, Holland 1911; The Hague, Holland 1924. † FIN 12, GI 7, L 4, NG 3.

SMAIL, Betty C. Exh. 1936
1 Grange Terrace, Edinburgh. † RSA 2.

SMAIL, Christine Exh. 1931
Portrait pencil artist. 37 Foxley Lane, Purley, Surrey. † RA 1.

SMAIL, Elizabeth M.H. Exh. 1881-86
40 Coates Gardens, Edinburgh. † GI 1, RSA 1.

SMALE, Christine Exh. 1936-38
Landscape painter. 68 Edburton Street, Brighton. † RA 3.

SMALE, Phyllis M. b. 1897
Landscape painter. b. Darlington. Studied Darlington School of Art and Regent Street Polytechnic. On staff of the Regent Street Polytechnic School of Art. A.S.W.A. 1940. Exh. 1925-40. Add: London. † NEA 1, RA 3, ROI 22, SWA 11.

SMALL, Alexander G. Exh. 1900-22
Painter, miniaturist and sculptor. London. † GI 1, L 3, RA 10, RSA 2.

SMALL, Miss B. Exh. 1891
† P 1.

SMALL, Barbara H. Exh. 1919
Miniature portrait painter. 33 Woodlands, Golders Green Road, London. † L 1, RA 2.

SMALL, Catherine E. (Kate) Exh. 1914-40
10 Braid Crescent, Edinburgh. † GI 10, L 1, RSA 25, RSW 21.

SMALL, C. Percival Exh. 1901-12
Landscape painter. London. † NEA 1, ROI 2.

SMALL, David Exh. 1887-96
Glasgow 1887; Dundee 1891. † GI 16, RSA 2, RSW 1.

SMALL, Mrs. Evan Exh. 1890-91
Interior painter. 11 Arthur Street, Nottingham. † N 3.

SMALL, Florence
See HARDY, Mrs. Florence Deric

SMALL, Frank O. b. 1860
American painter and illustrator. Exh. 1909. Add: 28 March Avenue, West Roxbury, Boston, Mass. U.S.A. † L 1.

SMALL, J. Exh. 1894
88 Albion Street, Aberdeen. † RSA 1.

SMALL, James E. Exh. 1880
6 Washington Place, Edinburgh. † RSA 1.

SMALL, John W. Exh. 1880-83
Architect. 56 George Street, Edinburgh. † RSA 8.

SMALL, McKenzie Exh. 1894
Rose Villa, Ibrox, Glasgow. † GI 1.

SMALL, Miss T. Exh. 1917
Wadham Gardens, London. † SWA 1.

SMALL, Tunstall Exh. 1938
Watercolour painter. Studied Royal College of Art. † WG 40.

SMALL, William* 1843-1931
Painter, lithographer and illustrator. b. Edinburgh. Studied R.S.A. Schools. A.R.I. 1870, R.I. 1883, H.R.S.A. 1917. "The Last Match" purchased by Chantrey Bequest 1887. Add: London 1880; Worcester 1915. † AG 1, B 3, FIN 2, GI 6, L 7, M 10, RA 22, RHA 3, RI 10, ROI 9, RSA 15.

SMALLEY, A. Exh. 1928
51 North Road, West Bridgford, Notts. † N 1.

SMALLEY, Miss E.M. Exh. 1934
8 Freehold Street, Shepshed, nr. Loughborough, Leics. † N 2.

SMALLFIELD, Beatrice C. Exh. 1886-1920
Figure and miniature portrait painter. R.M.S. 1901. Daughter of Frederick S. q.v. Add: London. † D 8, GI 3, L 5, NG 1, P 2, RA 20, RMS 36, SWA 8.

SMALLFIELD, Frederick* 1829-1915
Genre painter and watercolourist. Studied R.A. Schools. A.R.W.S. 1860. Father of Beatrice, Philip and Rosalind S. q.v. Add: London. † B 1, G 5, GI 3, L 12, M 19, RA 2, RI 2, ROI 2, RWS 139.

SMALFIELD, Philip C. Exh. 1882-1907
Portrait and figure painter. Son of Frederick S. q.v. Add: London. † B 1, D 19, GOU 1, L 5, RA 6, RBA 2, RI 2, ROI 2.

SMALLFIELD, Rosalind C. Exh. 1885-1914
Landscape painter. Daughter of Frederick S. q.v. Add: London. † RA 1, SWA 5.

SMALLPIECE, Mrs. Exh. 1922
† SWA 1.

SMALLWOOD, Miss Exh. 1881
Watercolour figure painter. 21 Sussex Gardens, London. † SWA 3.

SMALLWOOD, Miss E. Exh. 1911
142 St. Albans Road, Arnold, Nottingham. † N 1.

SMALLWOOD, R.W. Exh. 1904-10
Liverpool. † L 3.

SMART, Miss A.E. Exh. 1897
The Orchard, Zulla Road, Nottingham. † N 1.

SMART, Bessie Exh. 1889
Balgreen, Hamilton, N.B. † GI 1.

SMART, Capt. B. Neville Exh. 1919
Architect. The Barracks, Reading, Berks. † RA 1.

SMART, Charles J. Exh. 1890
Watercolour landscape and still life painter. 1 Elwell Road, Larkhall Lane, Clapham, London. † RI 2.

SMART, Dorothy Agnes b. 1879
Portrait and landscape painter and miniaturist on Ivory. b. Tresco, Scilly Isles. Studied at Sir Arthur Cope's School. A.R.M.S. 1909. Exh. 1909-14. Add: Bideford, Devon 1909; Westward Ho!, Devon 1910; Ross on Wye 1912. † L 2, RA 3, RMS 18.

SMART, Douglas I. b. 1879
Watercolour painter and etcher. A.R.E. 1905, R.E. 1922. Exh. 1907-39. Add: London. † CG 42, CHE 2, CON 1, FIN 3, GI 7, I 6, L 41, RA 48, RE 66, RI 2.

SMART, Mrs. E. Hodgson Exh. 1898
Jubilee House, Alnwick. † B 1.

SMART, Edmund Hodgson b. 1873
Portrait and allegorical painter. b. Alnwick. Studied Antwerp Academy, Julians, Paris and Herkomers, Bushey. Exh. 1902-34. Add: London. Went to America. † L 1, LS 8, P 2, RA 3, RSA 1.

SMART, Edward J. Exh. 1909-15
Old Trafford, Manchester. † L 3.

SMART, Edgar Rowley 1887-1934
Watercolour landscape painter. b. Manchester. Studied Liverpool and Paris. Add: Manchester 1910; London 1925. † ALP 60, BA 5, GOU 2, L 11, M 1, RA 1.

SMART, Mrs. F. Exh. 1921
Polesworth, Tamworth, Staffs. † B 1.

SMART, Hilda E. Exh. 1919-39
Landscape painter. A.N.S.A. 1924, N.S.A. 1930. Add: West Bridgford, Nottingham. † L 6, N 46.

SMART, John* 1838-1899
Landscape painter. b. Leith. Studied under H. McCulloch. R.B.A. 1878, A.R.S.A. 1871, R.S.A. 1877, R.S.W. 1878. Add: Edinburgh. † B 5, D 9, DOW 2, G 8, GI 53, L 8, M 3, RA 12, RBA 6, RHA 3, RI 4, ROI 2, RSA 129, RSW 61, TOO 2.

SMART, J. Gordon Exh. 1897-98
Probably son of John S. q.v. Add: 13 Brunswick Street, Hillside, Edinburgh. † RSA 5.

SMART, K.J. Exh. 1934
29 Vyner Road, Acton, London. † RBA 1.

SMART, M. Exh. 1880-81
Landscape painter. Church Road, Tunbridge Wells, Kent. † SWA 3.

SMART, R. Borlase 1881-1947
Painter, etcher and poster designer. b Kingsbridge, Devon. Studied Plymouth Art School 1896, Royal College of Art 1899 and under Julius Olsson 1913. Artist and art critic to the Western Morning News Co. of Plymouth. R.B.A. 1919, R.O.I. 1922. Add: Plymouth 1908; Grantham, Lincs. 1918; St. Ives, Cornwall 1919 and 1928; Salcombe, Devon 1925. † CHE 2, FIN 38, L 18, LS 5, RA 16, RBA 37, RCA 8, RHA 6, RI 2, ROI 57, RSA 18.

SMART, Thomas H. Exh. 1905-13
London 1905; Birkenhead 1913. † D 1, L 1.

SMART, Violet Exh. 1933-40
Miniature portrait painter. 95 Overhill Road, London. † RA 2, RI 9.

SMARTT, Kathleen Exh. 1888-95
54 Parade, Leamington, Warwicks. † B 4.

SMAWLEY, George A. Exh. 1922-32
20 Osbourne Road, Handworth, Birmingham. † B 9.

SMEAL, R.W. Exh. 1924
Pembury, Kent. † RSW 1.

SMEALL, Miss E.M. Exh. 1932
5 Nile Grove, Edinburgh. † RSA 1.

SMEALL, James E. Exh. 1882
5 Newton Terrace, East Tynecastle, Edinburgh. † RSA 2.

SMEDLEY, Alice V. Exh. 1880-1903
Landscape painter. 34 St. George's Road, Abbey Road, London. † L 2, SWA 3.

SMEDLEY, Ethel Exh. 1898-99
25 Hooley Range, Heaton Moor, Stockport, Lancs. † M 2.

SMEDLEY, H.E.H. Exh. 1927
27 Grand Parade, Brighton. † L 2.

SMEDLEY, W.H. Exh. 1920
245a Ormaston Road, Derby. † N 1

SMEE, F.E. Exh. 1909-12
Architect. Southend on Sea 1909; London 1912. † RA 2.

SMEE, Sylvia Exh. 1924-40
Painter, etcher and aquatinter. London. † GI 3, L 4, NEA 3, RA 6, RCA 7, RMS 3, RSA 12, SWA 6.

SMELLIE, John* d. 1925
Exh. from 1909. Add: Glasgow. † GI 22, RSA 9, RSW 5.

SMELLIE, Robert Exh. 1880-1908
Edinburgh. † GI 7, RSA 31.

SMELLIE, Mrs. S.M. Exh. 1895
13 Union Street, Edinburgh. † RSA 1.

SMELLIE, Thomas Exh. 1934
46 Portland Road, Kilmarnock. † GI 1.

SMET, de See D

SMETHAM-JONES, G.W. Exh. 1887-93
Figure painter. London 1887; Stroud, Glos. 1889; Coniston, Lancs. 1890. † B 1, L 5, RA 1, RBA 1, RI 4.

SMIETON, Mrs. J.P. Exh. 1880
Panmure Villa, Broughty Ferry, N.B. † RSA 2.

SMIETON, T.A. Exh. 1883
Panmure Villa, Broughty Ferry, N.B. † RSA 1.

SMILES, Miss J. Exh. 1900
Fairoak, Overberry Avenue, Beckenham, Kent. † SWA 1.

SMILES, Leon Exh. 1933
Bexley, Kent. † RCA 1.

SMILEY, John McA. Exh. 1913-21
Belfast. † GI 1, L 6, RHA 30.

SMILLIE, George Henry* 1840-1921
American painter. Exh. 1884. Add: c/o Cassell and Co., Ludgate Hill, London. † L 1.

SMILLIE, James David 1833-1909
American painter and etcher. R.E. 1881-87. Exh. 1881-84. Add: New York, U.S.A. † L 1, RE 6.

SMIRKE, Dorothy Exh. 1901-36
Mrs. Biggar. Painter and miniaturist. Teddington, Middlesex 1901; Richmond, Surrey 1903; Hastings, Sussex 1921; Crowborough, Sussex 1936. † B 2, L 7, RA 13, RI 9.

SMITH, Mrs. Exh. 1890
c/o Weir and Clyde, 463 Eglinton Street, Glasgow. † GI 1.

SMITH, A. Exh. 1912
17 Penyston Road, Maidenhead, Berks. † RA 1.

SMITH, Agneta Exh. 1899-1914
Royston, Herts. † SWA 17.

SMITH, Alan Exh. 1911-33
Seacombe, Cheshire 1911; Wallasey, Cheshire 1927. † L 12, RCA 7.

SMITH, Albert Exh. 1921
Watercolour architectural painter. 45 Colwick Vale, Colwick, Notts. † N 1.

SMITH, Alexander Exh. 1885
11 Albany Street, Edinburgh. † RSA 1.

SMITH, Mrs. Alfred Exh. 1901-7
Landscape painter. Lynwood, Swinburne Street, Derby. † N 6, RCA 1.

SMITH, Alison Exh. 1937
Figure painter. 38 Osmond Road, Hove, Sussex. † RA 1.

SMITH, Annie Exh. 1880
Landscape and figure painter. c/o C. Meileham, 114 Gower Street, London. † RA 1.

SMITH, Arthur Exh. 1880-85
Landscape, coastal and figure painter. London 1880; Hurstpierpoint, Sussex 1884. † RA 2, RBA 7.

SMITH, Annie Bliss Exh. 1925-33
Landscape painter and wood engraver. London. † L 16.

SMITH, Augusta Baird See LINDNER

SMITH, A.C. Exh. 1889
103 Lord Street, Greenheys, Manchester. † L 1.

SMITH, Albert C. Exh. 1889
Landscape painter. 144 Holland Road, Kensington, London. † RA 2.

SMITH, Arthur C. Morgan Exh. 1905
Llanbadarn, 80 Trinity Road, Bridlington, Yorks. † M 1.

SMITH, Albert D. Exh. 1888-91
Architect. Westminster, London. † RA 5.

SMITH, Arnold D. Exh. 1925
Architect. 6 Queen Square, London. † RA 1.

SMITH, A.F. Exh. 1899
St. Albans Road, Leicester. † N 1.

SMITH, A. Freeman Exh. 1882-1924
Birmingham 1882; Toronto, Canada 1923. † B 8.

SMITH, Ada G. Exh. 1887-89
3 Vernon Terrace, Booterstown. † RHA 3.

SMITH, A. Guy Exh. 1898-1901
Figure painter. The Mall, Park Hill Road, Hampstead, London. † L 2, M 1, RA 1.

SMITH, A. Harold Exh. 1900-20
Metal worker. London 1900; Stirling 1915; Glasgow 1920. † GI 9, L 2, RA 4, RSA 11.

SMITH, A.J. Exh. 1940
6 Wall Street, Camelon, Falkirk. † GI 1, RSA 1.

SMITH, Arthur J. Exh. 1939
Landscape painter. 14 Didsbury Road, Tewkesbury. † RA 1.

SMITH, Arthur John Exh. 1880-1917
Sculptor. London. † GI 1, L 4, NG 2, RA 8, RBA 6.

SMITH, A. Leslie Exh. 1926-28
Landscape painter. Broughton House, 405 Mansfield Road, Sherwood, Nottingham. † N 11.

SMITH, Anna Leigh Exh. 1880-86
Painter. London. † B 1, D 3, G 1, RI 1.

SMITH, Archer L. Exh. 1912-20
Rock Ferry, Cheshire. † L 5.

SMITH, A. Martin Exh. 1924
† D 2.

SMITH, Alexander Monro 1860-1933
Painter, black and white artist, and illustrator. b. Falkirk. Studied Glasgow School of Art. Worked in London 1884-1915. Add: Edinburgh 1917 and 1920; Glasgow 1919. † L 3, RSA 7, RSW 2.

SMITH, Arthur Reginald 1872-1934
Watercolour landscape and figure painter. b. Skipton in Craven. R.S.W. 1926, A.R.W.S. 1917, R.W.S. 1925. Add: London 1900; Grassington, Yorks. 1918. Drowned in the River Wharfe near Bolton Abbey. † AR 2, B 1, BA 1, FIN 409, G 3, GI 22, GOU 2, L 11, M 2, RA 30, RI 7, RSW 37, RWS 160, WG 35.

SMITH, Alan Verner b. 1908
Painter. b. Southampton. Studied Bournemouth School of Art and Westminster. Assistant teacher A.A. School of Architecture. Exh. 1929-35. Add: Southbourne, Hants. 1929; London 1932. † NEA 2, RA 1, RBA 1.

SMITH, Mrs. Barbara Exh. 1882-85
12 Sandyford Street, Glasgow. † GI 6, L 1.

SMITH, Bernard Exh. 1880-94
Architect. Gibraltar 1880; London 1881. † RA 10.

SMITH, Berta Exh. 1899-1908
Dunblane, N.B. 1899; Jedburgh, N.B. 1907. † GI 5, RSA 18.

SMITH, Miss B.A. Exh. 1903
Painter. 31 Chenies Chambers, Bloomsbury, London. † NEA 1.

SMITH, Mrs. Beatrice A. Exh. 1926
Miniature painter. The Lodge, Old Catton, Norwich. † RA 1.

SMITH, B. Gordon Exh. 1935-40
Landscape painter. 50 Chepstow Place, London. † RA 1, RBA 2.

SMITH, Miss B.M. Exh. 1928
358 Gravelly Lane, Erdington, Birmingham. † B 1.

SMITH, Bessie N.W. Exh. 1898
Portrait painter. 28 Viale Regina Vittoria, Florence. † RA 1.

SMITH, B.S. Exh. 1903-10
Nottingham 1903; Woodthorpe, Notts. 1909. † N 3.

SMITH, B.W. Exh. 1932
† L 1.

SMITH, Mrs. C. Exh. 1889
Northcote House, Devises, Wilts. † B 2.

SMITH, Catherine b. 1874
Painter, etcher, designer and teacher. Studied Royal College of Art. Travelled in Italy. Exh. 1898-1911. Add: London. † RA 6.

SMITH, Chadwell Exh. 1886-96
Coastal painter. Rye, Sussex 1886; London 1894. † L 5, RA 3, RHA 1, ROI 7.

SMITH, Charles* Exh. 1880-1918
Landscape painter. London. † B 39, BG 1, D 4, GI 11, L 10, M 15, RA 28, RBA 49, RHA 17, RI 6, ROI 21, RSA 2, TOO 15.

SMITH, Cicely Exh. 1933-39
Portrait painter. Chelsea, London. † RA 2.

SMITH, Clarence Exh. 1890
Marton Vicarage, Rugby. † B 1.

SMITH, Coke Exh. 1881
Painter. † G 2.

SMITH, Mrs. Cuthbert Exh. 1898-1904
Liverpool. † L 4.

SMITH, Carlton Alfred* 1853-1946
Portrait and genre painter and watercolourist. Studied Slade School (gold and silver medals). Visited India 1916-23. R.B.A. 1879, R.I. 1889, R.O.I. 1892. Add: London 1880 and 1904; Witley, Surrey 1897. † B 15, D 5, GI 13, L 47, M 14, RA 57, RBA 116, RHA 4, RI 138, ROI 74.

SMITH, Mrs. Carlton Alfred Exh. 1883-1907
Miss Martha Sarah King. Landscape, coastal and figure painter. London 1883 and 1907; Witley, Surrey 1898. † L 2, RA 2, RBA 18, ROI 6.

SMITH, Christian A. Exh. 1929-37
40 Blacket Place, Edinburgh. † RSA 3.

SMITH, C. Christopher Exh. 1888
Landscape painter. 36 Penmartin Road, Brockley, London. † RA 1.

SMITH, Charlotte Elizabeth Exh. 1911-16
Landscape and flower painter and etcher. Studied Royal College of Art, Glasgow School of Art, France and Holland. Art teacher Peterhead Academy. Add: London 1911; Peterhead 1912. † RA 1, RSA 1.

SMITH, Miss C.E. Freeman Exh. 1923
38 Ernescliffe, Wellesley Street, Toronto, Canada. † B 1.

SMITH, Carl Frithjof b. 1868
American painter. Exh. 1889. Add: 20 Brienner strasse, Munich. † RA 1.

SMITH, C.F.O. Exh. 1912-33
Eskbank, N.B. 1912; Edinburgh 1918. † GI 1, RA 1, ROI 1, RSA 5.

SMITH, Miss Constance I. Exh. 1890-93
Miniature portrait painter. Weston Lodge, Weston Road, Bath. † RA 2.

SMITH, Miss C.K. Exh. 1903
Green Lane, Belper, Derbys. † N 2.

SMITH, Campbell Lindsay d. 1915
Portrait and figure painter. London 1901; Aberdeen 1903. † GI 5, L 1, RA 6, RSA 6.

SMITH, C.P. Exh. 1908
The Chalet, Friars Hill, Guestling, Hastings. † RA 1.

SMITH, Mrs. Constance P. Exh. 1884-1900
nee Plimpton. Figure, portrait, flower and animal painter. London 1884; Greyshott, Hants. 1897. † L 12, RA 24, RBA 11, RI 1, ROI 4.

SMITH, C. Ruth Exh. 1918
Studio, Belfast House, Jervis Place, Bournemouth. † LS 3.

SMITH, Charles S. Exh. 1885-1913
Architect. 164 Friar Street, Reading, Berks. † RA 7.

SMITH, C. Snodgrass Exh. 1882-98
Meadow Row, Lenzie, Glasgow. † GI 4.

SMITH, Miss Constance T. Exh. 1898
13 Royal Crescent, Crosshill, Glasgow. † GI 1, RSW 1.

SMITH, C. Welby Exh. 1885
Landscape and marine painter, and watercolourist. 62 Talfourd Road, Peckham, London. † RA 1, RWS 7.

SMITH, Cyril Wontner 1877-1952
Architect. Exh. 1915-27. 2 Grays Inn Square, London; Hadley Wood, Herts.; Broadwater, Sussex. † RA 5. Cousin of W.C. Wontner (q.v.).

SMITH, Cyril W. Exh. 1904-15
Architect. London 1904; Halifax 1915. † RA 5.

SMITH, D. Exh. 1903
Ivy House, Bourne, Cambridge. † NG 1.

SMITH, Miss Daisy Exh. 1930-37
Miniature painter. Northampton. † RA 4, RSA 4.

SMITH, Mrs. Daisy Exh. 1923-40
Flower painter. London 1923; Hull 1930. † GI 2, L 3, M 2, RA 14.

SMITH, David Exh. 1891-92
Fern Cottage, Newport, Fife. † RSA 11.

SMITH, David Exh. 1909
† LS 3.

SMITH, David Exh. 1919
Mossgiel, Wormit on Tay. † RSA 1.

SMITH, David Exh. 1938-39
Wilson Studio, 53 Frederick Street, Edinburgh. † RSA 2.

SMITH, D. Atherton Exh. 1911-12
Landscape painter. Paris. † L 2, RSA 2.

SMITH, D.J. Exh. 1932
26 Dunbar Avenue, Rutherglen. † GI 1.

SMITH, Miss D.M. Exh. 1938
45 Goldsmith Road, Kings Heath, Birmingham. † B 1.

SMITH, David Murray b. 1865
Landscape painter and etcher. Studied Edinburgh School of Art and R.S.A. Schools. R.B.A. 1905, R.S.W. 1934 (res. 1940), A.R.W.S. 1916, R.W.S. 1934. Add: Edinburgh 1886; London 1893 and 1906; Farnham Common, Bucks. 1916; Thame, Oxon 1924; Gomshall, Guildford, Surrey 1932; Sutton Abinger, Dorking, Surrey 1936. † CG 1, COO 1, FIN 62, G 1, GI 27, GOU 1, I 6, L 28, LEI 52, M 1, NEA 5, RA 19, RBA 118, RI 3, ROI 6, RSA 18, RSW 16, RWS 199, WG 18.

SMITH, Dorothea N. Exh. 1932-40
35 Heriot Row, Edinburgh. † GI 9, RSA 6.

SMITH, E. Exh. 1932
9 Kingsley Road, Sneinton, Nottingham. † N 1.

SMITH, Miss E. Exh. 1894
12 Eliot Place, Blackheath, London. † SWA 2.

SMITH, Edward Exh. 1904-23
Seacombe, Cheshire 1904; Liverpool 1909. † L 11.

SMITH, Eleanor Exh. 1940
38 Redcliffe Road, London. † RSA 1.

SMITH, Elsie Exh. 1920
6 Gregory Street, Ilkeston, Derbys. † N 1.

SMITH, Erik Exh. 1940
Engraver. 39 Kildare Terrace, London. † RA 2.

SMITH, Ernest Exh. 1882-1908
Landscape painter. Shottermill, Hazlemere, Surrey 1882; London 1885. † RA 3, RBA 2.

SMITH, Ernest Exh. 1932
Sculptor. 304 Fulham Palace Road, London. † RA 1.

SMITH, Edith A. Exh. 1899
Hughenden, Chester Road, Erdington, Birmingham. † B 1.

SMITH, E.B. Exh. 1928-31
Sculptor. 27 Hogarth Street, Off Carlton Road, Nottingham. † N 2.

SMITH, Miss E.B. Exh. 1912
7 Bay View, Northam, North Devon. † RA 1

SMITH, Miss E. Bass Exh. 1912-21
Muswell Hill, London 1912; Horley, Surrey 1920. † SWA 6.

SMITH, E. Bellingham Exh. 1940
Painter. † COO 1.

SMITH, Edward Blount d. 1899
Landscape painter. London 1881 and 1885; Rome 1884. † B 1, D 3, G 4, GI 6, L 11, NG 5, RA 7, RBA 11, RHA 3, RI 9, ROI 10, RSW 3.

SMITH, E. Christie Exh. 1927
Greystoke, Ormaston Road, Prenton, Birkenhead. † L 1.

SMITH, Eveleen Cathcart Exh. 1909
† LS 2.

SMITH, Miss E.D. Exh. 1924-27
34 St. Mary's Crescent, Leamington Spa, Warwicks. † L 5.

SMITH, E. Fenton Exh. 1915-22
Keynsham, Bristol 1915; Harting, Petersfield, Hants 1919. † B 1, L 3.

SMITH, E. Findlay Exh. 1916
† LEI 2.

SMITH, E.G. Exh. 1936
Penarth, Glamorgan. † RCA 1.

SMITH, Ethel G. Exh. 1895-1904
9 Haynes Road, Beckenham, Kent. † RBA 1, ROI 2, SWA 3.

SMITH, Mrs. E.H. Exh. 1917
2 Oakley Crescent, London. † RA 1.

SMITH, Edith Heckstall Exh. 1884-90
Landscape and figure painter and watercolourist. Beckenham, Kent 1884; London 1886. † B 6, D 2, RA 4, RBA 6, RI 3, ROI 2, SWA 9.

SMITH, Edwin J. Exh. 1934-35
7 Guthrie Terrace, Broughty Ferry, Angus. † GI 2.

SMITH, Miss E. Lawrence Exh. 1914-21
London. † L 6, RA 2, RI 1, SWA 1.

SMITH, E.M. Exh. 1881-96
Painter. London. † SWA 3.

SMITH, Miss Ethel M. Exh. 1899-1933
Landscape painter. Bramcote Hall, Notts. 1899; Linby, Notts. 1918; Kegworth, Derby 1928. † N 46.

SMITH, Mrs. Ethel M. Exh. 1934-37
Watercolour landscape, figure and flower painter. Add: Dinas, Gordon Avenue, Stafford. † RA 6.

SMITH, Eveline M. Exh. 1916-21
Sculptor. Southport, Lancs. 1916; Barnes, Surrey 1919. † L 1, RA 2.

SMITH, Miss E.N. Exh. 1907-13
Landscape painter. The Crossways, Totteridge, Herts. † BG 4, LS 6, M 1, NEA 1, RA 2.

SMITH, Elizabeth P. Exh. 1906
Pentland, The Knowe, Kilbarchan, N.B. † GI 1.

SMITH, E. Toulmin Exh. 1882
Wood Lane, Highgate, London. † L 1.

SMITH, Effie U. Exh. 1923
† SWA 1.

SMITH, Edwin Whitney 1880-1952
Sculptor. b. Bath. Studied Bath and Bristol. "The Irishman" (1900-10) purchased by Chantrey Bequest 1940. Add: London. † G 3, GI 14, I 1, L 17, M 1, NG 2, RA 49, RI 2, ROI 4, RSA 6.

SMITH, Eleanor Whyte Exh. 1935-37
38 Redcliffe Road, London. † SWA 5.

SMITH, Freda Exh. 1913-25
Painter and etcher. 2 Clarence Terrace, Regents Park, London. † G 2, L 4, RI 1, SWA 2, WG 73.

SMITH, Faith Blomfield Exh. 1928-35
Miniature portrait painter. Lindula, Chigwell Road, Bournemouth. † RA 8.

SMITH, F.C. Exh. 1912
10 Downe Terrace, Richmond, Surrey. † LS 3.

SMITH, F. Denner Exh. 1901-8
Landscape painter. The Studios, Edith Terrace, Chelsea, London. † LS 5, RA 1.

SMITH, F. Ella Exh. 1916
A.N.S.A. 1910-16. Add: 27 Fox Road, West Bridgford, Notts. † N 1.

SMITH, F. Gilbert Exh. 1933
Rhyl, Wales. † RCA 1.

SMITH, Frederick G. Exh. 1889
Stained glass artist. 19 Wolmersley Road, Stroud Green, London. † RA 1.

SMITH, Fred Hargreaves Exh. 1896-1901
Painter. London 1896; Liverpool 1897 and 1900; Birkenhead 1899. † GI 2, L 4, RA 2, RBA 1.

SMITH, Miss F.M. Exh. 1921
Studio, 1 Newhall Street, Birmingham. † B 2.

SMITH, Frederick M. Bell 1846-1923
Landscape painter. b. London. Exh. 1888. Add: c/o Dolman and Son, 6 New Compton Street, Soho, London. Moved to Canada. † RA 1, RBA 1.

SMITH, F. Newland Exh. 1926
† M 3.

SMITH, Frederick Richard b. 1876
Watercolour painter and leatherworker. b. Harascombe. Studied Birmingham (2 silver medals). Assistant at Lydney School of Art and Wolverhampton School of Art. Exh. 1924-28. Add: The Cottage, Hampton in Arden, Warwicks. † B 3.

SMITH, Frederick Sydney b. 1888
Watercolour landscape and mural painter, etcher and designer. b. Pensnett, Dudley. Studied Ryland Memorial School of Art, West Bromwich and Royal College of Art (travelling scholarship). Assistant master Newport School of Arts and Crafts and assistant master Ryland Memorial School of Art, West Bromwich. Exh. 1931-40. Add: Stourbridge, Worcs. † B 10, RA 3.

SMITH, Frances Tysoe Exh. 1891-1921
Landscape painter. Banbury, Oxon 1891; Eastbourne 1898; Llandrindod Wells, Wales 1900. † B 19, L 8, LS 18, RA 1.

SMITH, Fred T. Exh. 1906
11 Forths Green Avenue, Muswell Hill, London. † D 5.

SMITH, F.W. Exh. 1925-26
Landscape painter. 9 Wallett Avenue, Beeston, Notts. † N 3.

SMITH, Frederick Yorke Exh. 1901-3
11 Eccleston Square, London. † L 2, RI 1.

SMITH, G. Exh. 1908
6 Derby Terrace, The Park, Nottingham. † N 1.

SMITH, Gabell Exh. 1903-30
Landscape painter. London 1903; Chudleigh, Lewes, Sussex 1919. † BG 4, I 3, NEA 2, NG 1, RA 10, ROI 5, SWA 15.

SMITH, Garrett Exh. 1911
Landscape painter. † ALP 2.

SMITH, George 1829-1901
Genre painter. Studied R.A. Schools and under C.W. Cope. Add: Shotter Mill, Haslemere, Surrey 1880; London 1883. † B 19, L 8, M 8, RA 14, RBA 1, RI 5, ROI 8, TOO 1.

SMITH, George 1870-1934
Animal and landscape painter. b. Mid Calder, Midlothian. Studied George Watson's College, Edinburgh and Antwerp. A.R.S.A. 1908, R.S.A. 1921. Add: Edinburgh. † GI 87, L 9, M 6, RA 5, RHA 3, RSA 128.

SMITH, George Exh. 1884-85
29 East Gate Row, Chester. † L 4.

SMITH, Gertrude See BAYES

SMITH, Rear-Admiral Gordon Exh. 1922-23
Watercolour marine painter. † WG 73.

SMITH, Gordon Exh. 1930-38
Watercolour landscape painter. Bromley, Kent 1930; London 1938. † RA 1, RSA 1.

SMITH, Mrs. Graham Exh. 1891-1920
Portrait painter. London. † NG 4, P 1, RA 2.

SMITH, Grainger b. 1892
Painter, etcher and teacher. b. Hull. Studied Liverpool School of Art. Exh. 1914-40. Add: Liscard, Cheshire 1914; Liverpool 1923. † FIN 2, GI 9, L 53, M 1, RA 7, RCA 34, RSA 20.

SMITH, G. Comrie Exh. 1900-12
The Studio, Giffnock, nr. Glasgow. † GI 15, L 2, RSA 4.

SMITH, G. Connor Exh. 1925
37 Warrington Crescent, London. † SWA 1.

SMITH, Miss G.E. Exh. 1880-1918
London 1880; Birchington on Sea, Kent 1918. † B 2, D 1, RA 1, SWA 3.

SMITH, George E. Exh. 1880-1903
Watercolour landscape and coastal painter. London. † RA 1, RBA 1, RI 3.

SMITH, G.G. Exh. 1933
169 The Grove Street, Liverpool. † L 1.

SMITH, Garden Grant 1860-1913
Watercolour painter. R.S.W. 1890. Add: Edinburgh 1881 and 1888; Aberdeen 1882; London 1894. † DOW 5, GI 11, L 3, M 2, RA 3, RBA 5, RI 5, RSA 41, RSW 12.

SMITH, George G. Exh. 1894
Miniature portrait painter. 38 Springfield Road, St. Johns Wood, London. † RA 1.

SMITH, G. Hill Exh. 1886-1918
Watercolour painter and humorous pen and ink sporting artist. Hill House, Herne Hill. † D 1, WG 67.

SMITH, Gerald J. Exh. 1916-29
Edinburgh. † GI 2, RSA 8, RSW 1.

SMITH, Grace Kyrhe Exh. 1911-19
Liverpool. † L 9, RA 2.

SMITH, G.L. Carson Exh. 1893
Bath Terrace, Portrush. † RHA 1.

SMITH, G.M. Exh. 1881
27 Lander Road, Edinburgh. † RSA 2.

SMITH, G.R. Exh. 1883-86
London. † L 2, RE 4.

SMITH, Harold Exh. 1903-6
Byculla, Malden, Surrey. † D 5.

SMITH, Harold Exh. 1938
Decorative artist. 92 Tennal Road, Harborne, Birmingham. † RA 1.

SMITH, Herbert Exh. 1907-13
Liverpool. † L 10, LS 1.

SMITH, Hely Augustus Morton* b. 1862
Portrait, marine and flower painter. b. Wambrook, Dorset. Studied Lincoln School of Art and Antwerp Academy. R.B.A. 1902. Exh. 1887-1940. Add: Market Rasen, Lincs. 1887; Looe, Cornwall 1890; London 1899. † B 41, D 39, GI 1, L 14, RA 21, RBA 305, RHA 6, RI 35, ROI 12, RSA 3.

SMITH, Hugh Bellingham 1866-1922
Landscape painter. Studied Slade School and under Benjamin Constant in Paris. N.E.A. 1893. Add: London 1881; East Grinstead, Sussex 1918; Burwash Common, Sussex 1919; Hailsham, Sussex 1920. † GI 1, GOU 19, I 7, L 5, M 6, NEA 107, RA 5, RBA 10, RID 45, ROI 2, RSA 2, WG 3.

SMITH, H.D. Exh. 1884
Lingfield Lodge, Wimbledon, London. † D 2.

SMITH, Mrs. Hannah Elizabeth
Exh. 1888-1916
Miniature portrait painter. R.M.S. 1897. Add: London. † B 1, RA 9, RMS 23.

SMITH, Harry F. Exh. 1886
Watercolour landscape painter. 22 Lacton Street, Bow, London. † RBA 1.

SMITH, Harry J.E. Exh. 1929
Sculptor. 76 Sloane Avenue, Chelsea, London. † RA 1.

SMITH, Heather K.S. Oswald Exh. 1931-35
Miniature portrait painter. The Lawn, Roundham Road, Paignton, Devon. † RA 1, RMS 1.

SMITH, Henry Lawson b. 1894
Portrait and sepia watercolour painter and miniaturist. b. Wymondham, Norfolk. Exh. 1928. Add: 26 Fletcher Road, Ipswich, Suffolk. † RA 1.

SMITH, Helen M. Exh. 1880-87
Landscape painter. London. † SWA 5.

SMITH, Herbert Tyson b. 1883
Sculptor. Studied Liverpool University. Exh. 1923-31. Add: 269 Grove Street, Liverpool. † L 9, RA 1.

SMITH, Hope Toulmin See DOUGLAS

SMITH, H.V. Crawfurth Exh. 1898
Architect. 2 Westbourne Villas, Hove, Sussex. † RA 1.

SMITH, H. Watson Exh. 1921-37
R.B.S.A. 1938. Add: Stourbridge, Worcs. 1921; London 1925; Birmingham 1931. † B 8, L 37.

SMITH, Ida Bernard Exh. 1923-27
27 Sefton Drive, Sefton Park, Liverpool. † L 5.

SMITH, Iris S. Exh. 1939
Coastal painter. Hermitage, Berks. † RA 1.

SMITH, Jacob Exh. 1885
Amsterdam. † GI 1.

SMITH, James Exh. 1885-1901
Montrose 1885; Glasgow 1901. † GI 1, RSA 5.

SMITH, Hon. Mrs. Jervoise Exh. 1884-1914
Watercolour painter. London. † D 4, SWA 3.

SMITH, John Exh. 1880-86
Aberdeen and Edinburgh. † RSA 6.

SMITH, John Exh. 1933
Warwick. † L 2.

SMITH, John Exh. 1929-33
Portrait and chalk artist. Abbeys, Hurstpierpoint, Sussex. † NEA 1, RA 1.

SMITH, Mrs. John Exh. 1881
12 Sandyford Place, Glasgow. † GI 1.

SMITH, Joseph Exh. 1913-17
307 New City Road, Glasgow. † GI 2.

SMITH, Joshua* Exh. 1918-26
R.B.A. 1919. Add: London 1918. Moved to Canada c. 1920. † RBA 13, RI 1.

SMITH, Joyce Exh. 1914-28
Painter. A.S.W.A. 1918. Add: London and Erdington, Birmingham. † B 7, RA 10, SWA 6.

SMITH, Julia Exh. 1897
5 Blythswood Square, Glasgow. † GI 1.

SMITH, Miss J.B. Exh. 1909
Miniature painter. 14 Ryletts Crescent, Shepherds Bush, London. † RA 1.

SMITH, James Burrell* Exh. 1881
Landscape painter and watercolourist. Add: 26 Scarsdale Villas, Kensington, London. † RBA 1.

SMITH, John Brandon* Exh. 1880-91
Landscape painter. London 1881; Granthams, Chiddingfold, Surrey 1882. † B 2, L 4, M 4, RBA 2, RHA 1, RSA 4, TOO 22.

SMITH, J. Caldwell Exh. 1887-93
Bray 1887; Motherwell 1893. † GI 1, RHA 1.

SMITH, J. Connor Exh. 1929
† NEA 1.

SMITH, Julia Cecilia Exh. 1880-81
Portrait and figure painter. 60 Beaumont Street, Portland Place, London. † RBA 1, SWA 2.

SMITH, James F. Exh. 1912-15
Birkenhead. † L 2.

SMITH, J. Francis b. 1888
Painter, etcher and commercial artist. Studied Liverpool School of Art. Exh. 1909-34. Add: Liverpool. † L 36, RCA 11.

SMITH, John Guthrie Spence 1880-1951
Landscape painter. Studied Edinburgh School of Arts and R.S.A. Schools. A.R.S.A. 1931, R.S.A. 1940. Add: Glasgow 1909; Edinburgh 1930. † GI 44, L 11, RA 1, RSA 83, RSW 3.

SMITH, Miss J.H. Exh. 1881
27 Raeburn Place, Edinburgh. † RSA 1.

SMITH, J. Hatchard Exh. 1895-1917
Architect. London. † RA 11.

SMITH, John H. Exh. 1924
The Laurels, Gravelly Hill, Birmingham. † B 1.

SMITH, John Henry Exh. 1880-1915
Figure and animal painter. London 1880; Holmrock, Carnforth, Lancs. 1900. † B 12, L 24, M 2, RA 14, RBA 18, ROI 8.

SMITH, Joseph Linden* b. 1862
American painter. Exh. 1885-97. Add: c/o American Exchange, Lime Street, London 1885; c/o J. Rankin, 22 Bank Street, Galashiels, N.B. 1897. † L 1, RSA 1.

SMITH, J. Morrison Exh. 1937-40
146 Park Road, Glasgow. † GI 3.

SMITH, J. Moyr Exh. 1888-1923
Watercolour painter. London 1888; Richmond, Surrey 1896; Kilcreggan, Firth of Clyde 1911; Liverpool 1912. † B 3, GI 3, L 9, RA 3, RBA 3, RSA 1, RSW 2.

SMITH, J. Myrtle Exh. 1891-99
Montrose 1891; Edinburgh 1899. † RSA 4.

SMITH, J.M.D. Exh. 1891
Fraserburgh. † RSA 1.

SMITH, Jane N. Exh. 1890
10 Learmouth Terrace, Edinburgh. † RSA 1.

SMITH, J. Newton Exh. 1926
72 Westdale Road, Wavertree, Liverpool. † L 1.

SMITH, John R. Exh. 1894-97
Engraver, London. † RA 3.

SMITH, J. Raymond Exh. 1894-95
246a Marylebone Road, London. † RBA 2.

SMITH, Mrs. J.R. Donald Exh. 1929
71 Shrewsbury Road, Oxton, Birkenhead. † L 3.

SMITH, J.R. Hunter Exh. 1934
14 Stirling Avenue, Westerton, Glasgow. † RSA 2.

SMITH, J.S. Exh. 1892
2 Hill Street, Edinburgh. † L 1.

SMITH, Miss J. Thompson Exh. 1910
45 Catharine Street, Liverpool. † L 1.

SMITH, J.W. Exh. 1935
Landscape painter. Delamere, St. Johns Road, Sandymount, Dublin. † RHA 1.

SMITH, James Whittet Exh. 1880-86
Landscape painter. London. † D 7, RA 1, RI 5.

SMITH, James W.G. Exh. 1930
Architect. 28 Elthiron Road, Fulham, London. † RA 1.

SMITH, James William Garrett Exh. 1880-87
Landscape and coastal painter. 30 Abercorn Place, Hamilton Terrace, St. Johns Wood, London. † RA 8, RBA 4, RHA 2, RI 1.

SMITH, Kate Alice Exh. 1893-1909
Miniature portrait painter. R.M.S. 1897. Add: London 1893; Missenden, Bucks. 1909. † RA 3, SWA 2.

SMITH, Miss K.S. Exh. 1899
Alvaston House, nr. Derby. † N 1.

SMITH, Kate Sydney Exh. 1893-98
Fernbank, Ashley Road, Epsom, Surrey. † B 3, SWA 7.

SMITH, Miss L. Exh. 1887
Hillside House, Robert Road, Handsworth, Birmingham. † B 1.

SMITH, L. Exh. 1899-1902
49 Laurel Street, Sycamore Road, Nottingham. † N 3.

SMITH, Mrs. L. Exh. 1901
49 Laurel Street, Nottingham. † N 1.

SMITH, Louisa Exh. 1881-84
Watercolour flower painter. Chesham House, Croydon, Surrey. † M 2, SWA 4.

SMITH, Leonora B. Exh. 1889-95
London 1889; Glasgow 1890. † GI 10, RSA 7.

SMITH, Mrs. Lucy Bentley Exh. 1881-1914
Miniature painter. Devonport 1881; London 1884 and 1889; Hastings, Sussex 1886. † GI 1, L 2, RA 14, RBA 2, RI 5, RMS 4, SWA 1.

SMITH, Miss L.F. Exh. 1926
c/o 151 Gregory Boulevard, Nottingham. † N 1.

SMITH, Leonard John b. 1885
Etcher. b. Aberdeen. Studied Toronto, Canada and New York, U.S.A. Exh. 1928-39. Add: London 1928; Seaford, Sussex 1939. † L 3, RSA 2.

SMITH, Leslie J. Exh. 1924-39
Portrait painter. London. † P 3, RA 1, RBA 1.

SMITH, Lesley N. Exh. 1912-30
Linocut artist. Ellenbank, Bridge of Allan, N.B. † GI 1, RED 1.

SMITH, L.R. Poole Exh. 1908-26
Landscape painter. Episy-pres-Moret, Seine et Marne, France. † L 1, LS 8, RA 4.

SMITH, L. Sommers Exh. 1916
20 Sommerville Road, St. Andrews Park, Bristol. † L 1.

SMITH, M. Exh. 1886
131 Anfield Street, Denistoun, Glasgow. † RSA 2.

SMITH, Mabel Exh. 1930
Sculptor. The Studio, 16 King Street, Reading, Berks. † RA 1.

SMITH, Malcolm Exh. 1909
The Hut, St. Levan, Treen, Cornwall. † L 8.

SMITH, Marcella Exh. 1916-40
Landscape and flower painter. b. East Molesey, Surrey. Studied U.S.A. and Paris. A.R.B.A. 1919, R.B.A. 1920, S.W.A. 1922. Add: St. Ives, Cornwall 1916 and 1940; London 1922. † I 11, L 2, M 1, NEA 1, RA 9, RBA 159, RCA 2, RI 19, ROI 3, SWA 66.

SMITH, Margaret Exh. 1896-1938
Landscape, flower and portrait painter. London 1896 and 1928; Winchcombe, Glos. 1906. † GI 1, L 3, LS 3, NEA 8, RA 28, SWA 4.

SMITH, Marjorie Exh. 1925-26
Sherwood Rise School, Nottingham. † N 2.

SMITH, Mary b. 1901
Portrait and landscape painter. Studied Slade School. Exh. 1922-27. Add: London 1922; Paris 1927. † M 2, NEA 7.

SMITH, Sir Matthew* 1879-1959
Landscape, figure, flower and still life painter. b. Halifax. Studied Manchester School of Art, Slade School and under Matissen in Paris. Married Gwendolen Salmond q.v. Member London Group 1920. "Nude, Fitzroy Street, No. 1" (1916) purchased by Chantrey Bequest 1952. Exh. 1921-40. Add: London and Brittany. † AG 5, BA 4, CHE 5, COO 1, G 4, GI 2, GOU 4, L 7, LEF 9, LEI 30, M 2, RED 17, TOO 116.

SMITH, Miller Exh. 1882-1919
Figure and landscape painter. R.B.A. 1902. Probably father of W. Miller S. q.v. Add: Norwich 1882; Rochester, Kent 1917; Gt. Yarmouth 1919. † B 1, L 3, M 3, RA 11, RBA 18, RI 8, ROI 1.

SMITH, Millicent Exh. 1895
Painter. Forest Grove, 5 Hardy Street, Nottingham. † N 1.

SMITH, Mrs. Milliken Exh. 1888-91
Glenthorne, Wake Green Road, Moseley, Birmingham. † B 2, D 6.

SMITH, May Aimee Exh. 1930-36
Wood engraver. c/o Lloyds Bank, School Road, Sale, Cheshire. † L 4, RED 4.

SMITH, Maud C. Exh. 1891
Painter. Northgate House, Devizes, Wilts. † NEA 1.

SMITH, M. Cannon Exh. 1918
15 Cheltenham Road, Hampton, Evesham, Worcs. † LS 3.

SMITH, Miss M. Conway Exh. 1901
25 Upper Bridge Road, Red Hill, Surrey. † SWA 2.

SMITH, Muriel Constance b. 1903
Portrait and miniature painter. b. Gunthorpe, Notts. Studied Nottingham School of Art. A.N.S.A. 1927, N.S.A. 1929. Exh. 1923-39. Add: 9 Mount Hooton, Forest Road, Nottingham. † L 4, N 70, RA 8, RMS 14, WG 33.

SMITH, Margaret E. Exh. 1908-38
Miniature portrait painter. York 1908; Birmingham 1915. † B 1, L 8, RA 3.

SMITH, M. Eleanor Exh. 1897-1901
Charlton Lodge, Hayne Road, Beckenham, Kent. † RBA 3, SWA 2.

SMITH, Miss M.F. Colvin Exh. 1889-1921
Landscape painter. London. † RID 36.

SMITH, Madelaine G. Exh. 1911
35 Park Crescent, Southport, Lancs. † L 2.

SMITH, Mrs. Mary H. Exh. 1884-1900
Edinburgh. † RSA 8.

SMITH, Mary I. Exh. 1883
11 St. George's Road, Regent's Park, London. † RHA 1.

SMITH, Mrs. M.I. Hamblin Exh. 1914-29
A.S.W.A. 1918. Add: Cambridge. † B 8, L 7, LS 14, RA 1, SWA 17.

SMITH, Maxwell M. Exh. 1892
Architect. 2 York Villas, Campden Hill, London. † RA 1.

SMITH, Marion Newland Exh. 1887-1905
Birmingham. † B 7.

SMITH, Marjorie R. Exh. 1931-38
22 Inverleith Gardens, Edinburgh. † RSA 6.

SMITH, Margaret W. Exh. 1927-35
Fulford, Gt. Crosby, nr. Liverpool. † L 2, NEA 1.

SMITH, Mary W. Exh. 1934
Figure and landscape painter. Studied Slade School 1923-26. † BA 12.

SMITH, Nellie Exh. 1880-81
Painter. The Warren, Royston, Herts. † SWA 3.

SMITH, Noel Exh. 1889-1900
Watercolour landscape painter. London. † L 1, RA 5, RI 2.

SMITH, Nora Exh. 1940
38 Redcliffe Road, London. † GI 1.

SMITH, O. Exh. 1883
42 Duke Street, Liverpool. † L 2.

SMITH, O.S. Exh. 1891
Meadow View, Lenzie, Glasgow. † GI 1.

SMITH, Olive Wheeler Exh. 1880-89
Watercolour flower and bird painter. 8 Elgin Road, Addiscombe, Surrey. † B 1, D 1, GI 1, L 5, RA 2, RBA 1, SWA 2.

SMITH, Peter Exh. 1888
2 Queen's Street, Edinburgh. † RSA 1.

SMITH, Peter b. 1902
Watercolour landscape painter, architect and designer. Studied Architecture at Cambridge University. Add: Blundellsands, Liverpool 1921; London 1929. † L 2.

SMITH, Phyllis Exh. 1927
30 Alva Street, Edinburgh. † RSA 1.

SMITH, Pamela Coleman Exh. 1905-17
Painter. London. † BG 42, I 1, SWA 3.

SMITH, Philip C. Exh. 1910-15
Landscape and interior painter. 1 Merton Road, South Hampstead, London. † I 2, LS 3, NEA 3.

SMITH, P.E. Exh. 1932
55 Shakespeare Street, Nottingham. † N 1.

SMITH, Percy John d. 1948
Painter and etcher. Exh. 1904-12. Add: 108 Friern Road, East Dulwich, London. † L 6, RI 1.

SMITH, Phillip J. Exh. 1912-32
Landscape and coastal painter. A.N.S.A. 1913, N.S.A. 1917. Add: Nottingham 1912; Woodthorpe, Notts. 1913; Aylestone, Leics. 1915; Leicester 1919. † N 55.

SMITH, Peggy L. Exh. 1938
View Park, East Newport, Fife. † RSA 1.

SMITH, Phil W. Exh. 1892-1907
Fairfax Road, Prestwich, Manchester 1892; Chorlton on Medlock, Manchester 1893; Manchester 1900. † M 11.

SMITH, R. Exh. 1922
5 Greys Road, Woodthorpe, Notts. † N 1.

SMITH, R. Exh. 1914
13 Alfred Place, South Kensington, London. † RA 1.

SMITH, Reginald Exh. 1940
Landscape painter. 34 Park Road, London. † RA 1.

SMITH, Reginald 1855-1925
Landscape painter. R.B.A. 1895. Add: Bristol. † B 29, L 16, M 4, RA 19, RBA 71, RCA 60, RI 8.

SMITH, Ronald Exh. 1934-37
Rustic painter. 137 Dunstan's Road, East Dulwich, London. † RA 3.

SMITH, Rosa Exh. 1893
Painter. Ivy Cottage, Brighton Road, South Croydon, Surrey. † RBA 1.

SMITH, Ruby Exh. 1899
Miniature portrait painter. 78 Eastgate Street, Winchester, Hants. † L 3, RA 1.

SMITH, Mrs. R.A. Exh. 1881-85
27 Raeburn Place, Edinburgh. † RSA 8.

SMITH, Mrs. R. Beatrice Lawrence Exh. 1890-1938
Watercolour painter. London 1890; Challock, nr. Ashford, Kent 1926. † D 2, L 14, NG 4, RA 16, RCA 8, RI 14, ROI 1, RSA 2, SWA 8, WG 43.

SMITH, Robert Catterson Exh. 1880-90
Figure and landscape painter. London. † D 2, L 3, M 2, RA 7, RBA 6, RHA 5, RI 1.

SMITH, R. Chipchase Exh. 1887
Painter. Orleans Lodge, Woodfield Avenue, Streatham, London. † RI 1.

SMITH, R. Christie Exh. 1904-27
Birkenhead. † L 5, RCA 8.

SMITH, R.F. Exh. 1891
Artists Club, Eberle Street, Liverpool. † L 1.

SMITH, R.G. Edington Exh. 1893-1937
Glasgow 1893 and 1906; Dumfries 1900. † GI 5, L 1, RSA 3.

SMITH, Robert Henry Exh. 1906-9
Painter, black and white artist, etcher and illustrator. Studied Lambeth Art School (silver medal). Add: Greenwich and London. Later moved to Dorset and Cornwall. † D 5, L 1, RA 1.

SMITH, R.J. Exh. 1890
92 Littledale Road, Seacombe, Cheshire. † L 1.

SMITH, Raymond Maynard Exh. 1893
7 Ashton Place, Dowanhill, Glasgow. † GI 1.

SMITH, Rosa M. Exh. 1883-93
Flower painter. London. † M 1, RA 1, RBA 4.

SMITH, Samuel b. 1888
Painter and etcher. b. Glasgow. Studied Glasgow School of Art. Exh. 1918-36. Add: Glasgow. † GI 6, L 2, RA 1, RSA 8.

SMITH, Sidney Exh. 1885
10 Smith Street, Hillhead, Glasgow. † RSA 1.

SMITH, Stanley b. 1893
Landscape painter. b. Halifax. Studied Halifax School of Art, 1908-13 and Royal College of Art 1913-19. Exh. 1927-38. Add: Stafford. † FIN 2, L 1, RA 10.

SMITH, Stephen Exh. 1883
Watercolour landscape painter. Morden Road, Blackheath Park, London. † RI 1.

SMITH, Mrs. Stewart Exh. 1880-87
Landscape painter. Edinburgh. † GI 1, RSA 6, SWA 7.

SMITH, Miss S.A. Exh. 1881
10 Duncan Street, Drummond Place, Edinburgh. † RSA 1.

SMITH, Sarah Burrell Exh. 1880
Landscape painter. 26 Scarsdale Villas, Kensington, London. † SWA 1.

SMITH, S.B.E. Exh. 1889-90
47 Inverleith Row, Edinburgh. † RSA 2.

SMITH, Stephen Catterson 1849-1912
Portrait painter. Studied under his father Stephen Catterson S. (1806-1872). A.R.H.A. 1876, R.H.A. 1879. Secretary R.H.A. for 20 years. Add: Dublin. † B 1, GI 5, L 9, RHA 152, RSA 1.

SMITH, Sidney Dallas Exh. 1934-38
Watercolour painter. † WG 13.

SMITH, S.F. Exh. 1914
123 Hurlingham Road, Fulham, London. † RA 2.

SMITH, Sidney Herbert Exh. 1909
† LS 3.

SMITH, Sydney N.S. Exh. 1938-40
Painter. Belfast. † RBA 2, RHA 2.

SMITH, Sidney R. James 1857-1913
Architect. Exh. 1888-1905. Add: 15 York Buildings, Adelphi, London. † RA 9.

SMITH, S. Theobald Exh. 1891
Landscape painter. Sartor Lodge, West Hill, Wandsworth, London. † RI 1.

SMITH, Sydney Ure* Exh. 1928
Australian landscape painter. † AB 11.

SMITH, Thomas Exh. 1912-19
152 St. Vincent Lane, Glasgow. † GI 3, L 5.

SMITH, Tom Exh. 1882-85
8 Bancroft Road, Mile End, London. † B 2, GI 4, L 1, RHA 5.

SMITH, Tom Exh. 1914-35
Edinburgh. † I 2, RSA 5, RSW 7.

SMITH, T.B. Exh. 1918-37
9 Sandholes, Paisley 1918; Cardonald, Glasgow 1936. † GI 4, L 4, RSA 4.

SMITH, T. Capel Exh. 1922-38
South Yardley 1922 and 1936; Kings Heath, Birmingham 1930. † B 21.

SMITH, T.E. Exh. 1924
Watercolour painter. 11 Bruce Grove Meadows, Nottingham. † N 2.

SMITH, Thomas Henry Exh. 1887-96
Architect. London. † B 4, L 1, RA 5.

SMITH, Thomas Moore Exh. 1915-37
Watercolour landscape painter. London. † RA 4, RI 4.

SMITH, T.R. Exh. 1881
12 Thistle Grove, Kensington, London. † D 1.

SMITH, Thomas Roger d. 1903
Architect. Exh. 1881-94. Add: London. † RA 2.

SMITH, T. Strethill Exh. 1892-1905
Architect. London. † GI 1, RA 1.

SMITH, T.W. Exh. 1889
Hawthorne Grove, Heaton Moor, Manchester. † M 2.

SMITH, V. Exh. 1912-14
Hanworth House, Holt, Norfolk. † RA 2, RI 1.

SMITH, Vincent Exh. 1913-16
35 Uxbridge Street, Liverpool. † L 2.

SMITH, Vera Crichton Exh. 1907-29
Miniature portrait painter. Dudley, Worcs. 1907; London 1924. † B 5, L 8, RA 15, RMS 4.

SMITH, Vernon H. Exh. 1901-7
Chorlton cum Hardy, Manchester 1901; Higher Broughton, Manchester 1903; Heaton Moor, nr. Stockport, Lancs. 1907. † L 7.

SMITH, Violet Mary Exh. 1912-40
Painter. London. † LS 9, RA 1, SWA 3.

SMITH, Capt. V.N. Exh. 1915
Beechcroft, Kilmington, Devon. † RA 2.

SMITH, Mrs. W. Exh. 1886
Landscape painter. 44 Hanley Road, Crouch Hill, London. † SWA 1.

SMITH, William Exh. 1889-1919
Edinburgh 1889; Aberdeen 1896. † GI 3, RA,1, RSA 15.

SMITH, William Exh. 1901
55 Ormskirk Street, St. Helens, Lancs. † L 1.

SMITH, W.A. Exh. 1885-92
Landscape painter. London 1885; Houghton, nr. Arundel, Sussex 1890. † B 1, G 3, NG 4, RBA 3.

SMITH, William Alex Exh. 1885-87
Landscape painter. Balderton, Newark, Notts. 1885; Nottingham 1887. † N 3.

SMITH, W. Bassett Exh. 1887
Architect. 10 John Street, Adelphi, London. † RA 1.

SMITH, W. Boase Exh. 1884
10 Trelawney Road, Falmouth, Cornwall. † B 1.

SMITH, William Collingwood* 1815-1887
Landscape painter and watercolourist and teacher. b. Greenwich. Studied under J.D. Harding. Farther of W. Harding S. q.v. A.R.W.S. 1843, R.W.S. 1851. Add: Brixton Hill, London. † L 3, RWS 60.

SMITH, W.H. Exh. 1883-99
77 Rylands Road, Edgbaston, Birmingham. † B 10.

SMITH, W.H. Exh. 1933
St. Helens, Lancs. † RCA 1.

SMITH, W. Hammond Exh. 1913-14
Sidney College Lodge, Cambridge 1913; Chiswick, London 1914. † LS 6.

SMITH, W. Harding 1848-1922
Landscape, genre and historical painter. Studied under his father William Collingwood S. q.v. R.B.A. 1890. Add: Brixton Hill, London. † D 4, L 3, RBA 187, RI 8.

SMITH, W.J. Exh. 1899
21 St. James Road, London Road, Leicester. † ROI 1.

SMITH, William James Exh. 1920-37
Architect. Glasgow. † GI 6, RSA 1.

SMITH, W. Miller Exh. 1923-27
Portrait and figure painter. Probably son of Miller S. q.v. Add: 98 Hamilton Road, Newtown, Gt. Yarmouth, Norfolk. † P 2, RA 1.

SMITH, Mrs. W.P. Exh. 1919-26
11 Cwyder Crescent, Swansea, Wales. † B 3, GI 2, RHA 3, RSA 1.

SMITH, W.R. Exh. 1888
† D 4.

SMITH, W. Thomas b. 1862
Portrait, figure and historical painter. Exh. 1890-1925. Add: London 1890; Canada 1925. † CHE 2, L 1, M 1, P 1, RA 3, RBA 1, RI 1.

SMITH, Zoe Gordon Exh. 1907-8
5 Oakhill Road, Putney, London. † L 3.

SMITHARD, G.R. d. 1919
Landscape painter. Visited South Africa. Exh. 1906-7. Add: 20 Birchington Road, West Hampstead, London. † BG 21, ROI 1.

SMITHERS, Alec b. 1878
Architect. Studied R.A. Schools and A.A. Exh. 1924-40. Add: London and Gt. Hallingbury, Bishops Stortford, Herts. † RA 6.

SMITHERS, Collier Exh. 1892-1936
Portrait, figure and rustic painter. London. † B 4, L 11, M 1, NG 20, RA 7, RHA 1.

SMITHETT, Agnes L. Exh. 1893
Landscape painter. 45 Highbury Hill, London. † RBA 1.

SMITH-HALD, F. Exh. 1885-92
Paris 1885; Bergen, Norway 1892. † GI 1, RSA 1.

SMITHIES, James Exh. 1895
Aldenbank, Water Lane, Wilmslow, Cheshire. † M 1.

SMITHSON, Miss M. Stuart Exh. 1926-40
Flower painter. London 1926; Dublin 1940. † B 1, FIN 1, L 2, RHA 1, ROI 4, WG 45.

SMITHYES, Arthur W. Exh. 1883
Landscape painter. † ROI 1.

SMITS, Jakob* 1855-1928
Dutch painter. Exh. 1911. Add: Malvina Nof, Aghterbosch Moll, Belgium. † RSA 1.

SMORENBERG, Dirk Exh. 1915
14 Ayr Terrace, St. Ives, Cornwall. † L 2.

SMOURS, de See D

SMYLIE, Ernest K. Exh. 1912-13
591 Alexandra Parade, Dennistoun, N.B. † GI 3.

SMYLY, Eileen Exh. 1905
58 Merrion Square, Dublin. † RHA 1.

SMYTH, Agnes E. Exh. 1895-98
Lauragh, Portarlington. † RHA 4.

SMYTH, Clive C. Exh. 1918
† I 1.

SMYTH, Dora Exh. 1899
Hillside, Tettenhall, Wolverhampton. † B 1.

SMYTH, Dorothy Carleton Exh. 1904-23
Painter. Sister of Olive Carleton S. q.v. Add: Cambuslang, Glasgow. † GI 10, L 3, RA 1, RSA 1.

SMYTH, Elizabeth Exh. 1913
13A Margaret Street, Cavendish Square, London. † RHA 2.

SMYTH, Miss E.M.J. Exh. 1913
Stroud, Glos. † SWA 2.

SMYTH, Miss E.Z. Exh. 1913
Stroud, Glos. † SWA 2.

SMYTH, George Exh. 1880
5 Blessington Street, Dublin. † RHA 2.

SMYTH, James Exh. 1920-30
Landscape painter. Assistant design master Edinburgh College of Art. Add: Edinburgh. † L 5, RSA 9, RSW 10.

SMYTH, Mary Exh. 1884-87
Birmingham. † B 4.

SMYTH, Maud Exh. 1897
New Barnet, Herts. † SWA 1.

SMYTH, Montague Exh. 1890-1939
Landscape painter. Studied Westminster and on the continent. R.B.A. 1894, R.O.I. 1904, Member Society of 25 Artists. Add: London. † AR 1, B 3, BA 1, BG 60, D 12, DOW 116, FIN 43, G 2, GOU 8, I 6, L 3, LEI 13, M 3, NEA 3, NG 17, RA 29, RBA 86, RI 24, ROI 128, RSW 2.

SMYTH, Mrs. Montague Exh. 1905-7
nee Bell. Add: 56 Abbey Road, London. † NG 3.

SMYTH, Max L. Exh. 1907-35
Watercolour landscape painter. Studied under Frank Burridge at Liverpool. Lived in Florence for many years. Add: Liverpool 1907; Bishops Stortford, Herts. 1909. † L 8, LS 13, RA 1, WG 21.

SMYTH, Nora L. Exh. 1906-8
Barrowmore, Chester. † L 3.

SMYTH, Olive Carleton b. 1882
Fresco artist, illuminator and decorator. Studied Glasgow School of Art. Sister of Dorothy Carleton S. q.v. Add: Cambuslang, Glasgow. † GI 19, I 5, L 11, RA 9, RHA 3, RI 1, RSA 9, RSW 3.

SMYTH, P.C. Exh. 1913
161 Brecknock Road, London. † RA 1.

SMYTH, R. O'B. Exh. 1883-85
2 Kenilworth Square, Dublin. † RHA 4.

SMYTHE, Miss L. Exh. 1922
34 Camp Hill, Birmingham. † B 1, RSA 1.

SMYTHE, Lionel Percy* 1839-1918
Landscape and rustic genre painter. Studied Heatherleys Art School. A.R.A. 1898, R.A. 1911, R.I. 1880, R.O.I. 1883, A.R.W.S. 1892, R.W.S. 1894. Father of Minnie S. q.v. Add: London 1880; Chateau d'Honvault, par Wimille, Pas de Calais, France 1894. † B 1, D 2, DOW 2, FIN 1, GI 7, L 15, M 4, RA 50, RBA 18, RI 19, ROI 4, RWS 31.

SMYTHE, Minnie Exh. 1896-1939
Watercolour painter. A.R.W.S. 1901. Daughter of Lionel Percy S. q.v. Add: Chateau d'Honvault, par Wimille, Pas de Calais, France 1896; London 1920. † FIN 1, L 11, LEI 2, M 2, RA 21, RHA 2, RSW 1, RWS 61, SWA 1.

SMYTHE, Richard b. 1863
Portrait painter, mezzotint engraver and etcher. b. Cromford, Derbys. Studied Manchester School of Art. Exh. 1888-1930. Add: London 1888; Hampton Hill, Middlesex 1911. † L 2, LS 9, RA 9.

SMYTHSON, Marcus Exh. 1883-84
Painter. 1 Harpur Street, Bloomsbury, London. † L 1, RA 1, ROI 3.

SNAGGE, Leonard Exh. 1901
12 Bolton Studios, Redcliffe Road, London. † RHA 1.

SNAPE, Harold Exh. 1939-40
Birmingham. † B 2.

SNAPE, J.G. Exh. 1891
21 Aston Lane, Perry Barr, nr. Birmingham. † B 1.

SNAPE, Martin Exh. 1881-1905
Bird, animal and landscape painter. Spring Garden Cottage, Forton, Gosport, Hants. † G 2, L 3, RA 17, RE 7.

SNAPE, Winifred Exh. 1926-29
6 Pickering Road, Wallasey, Cheshire. † L 3.

SNAPE, William H.* Exh. 1885-89
Painter and etcher. Spring Garden Cottage, Forton, Gosport, Hants. † L 1, RA 3, RE 4.

SNELL, Henry Saxon 1829-1904
Architect. Exh. 1880-83. Add: 22 Southampton Buildings, London. † RA 2.

SNELL, James Herbert* 1861-1935
Landscape painter. Studied Heatherleys, Paris and Amsterdam. R.B.A. 1890, R.O.I. 1909. Add: London 1880, 1889 and 1903; Glasgow 1887; Tonbridge, Kent 1900; Burnham, Bucks. 1902. † B 5, G 7, GI 20, GOU 19, I 7, L 5, M 5, NG 16, RA 45, RBA 47, RCA 3, RHA 1, RI 16, RID 12, ROI 118, RSA 10.

SNELL, May Exh. 1901-2
Flower painter. Needham Market, Suffolk 1901; Ipswich 1902. † RA 1, SWA 2.

SNELL, Olive Exh. 1910-40
Mrs. Pike. Portrait painter. b. Durban, South Africa. Studied under Boris Anrep and Augustus John. Add: London 1918; Petersfield, Hants. 1935. † FIN 50, G 3, GOU 9, I 5, NEA 2, P 5, RA 3, RED 57, ROI 6, SWA 2.

SNELL, Robert Exh. 1923
Stell, Kirkcudbridge. † L 1.

SNEYD, Eleanor F. Exh. 1892-93
Miniature portrait painter. 55 Portland Place, London. † RA 5.

SNEYD, Sarah M. Exh. 1895
Watercolour landscape painter. 24 Nottinghill Terrace, London. † RA 1.

SNODGRASS, J.B. Exh. 1940
148 Saracen Street, Glasgow. † GI 1.

SNODGRASS, R. Nesbet Exh. 1927-39
Glasgow. † GI 13, RSA 10.

SNOECK, Jac Exh. 1908-10
13 Teignmouth Road, Brondesbury, London. † GI 3.

SNOW, Bertha Exh. 1928
49 Hilberry Avenue, Tue Brook, Liverpool. † L 2.

SNOW, Miss Chris Exh. 1913
14 Belsize Park Gardens, London. † RHA 1.

SNOW, Dorothy M. Exh. 1926-36
Landscape painter. 111 St. George's Square, London. † L 2, RA 5, RI 3, RID 4, SWA 5.

SNOW, Fanny Exh. 1921
† LS 2.

SNOW, Miss L.B. Exh. 1915
Braxfield, Queen's Park Gardens, Bournemouth. † L 1, RA 1.

SNOW, Miss L.I. Exh. 1907
Redcliffe Road, London. † SWA 1.

SNOW, Miss M. Exh. 1897-1900
61 Westbourne Terrace, London. † SWA 4.

SNOWBALL, Joseph Exh. 1909-19
L'Atelier 16, Lorigstone Road, Furzedown Park, Streatham, London. † LS 4.

SNOWDEN, Alice Exh. 1925-28
Port Sunlight 1925; The Orthopoedic Hospital, Gobowen, nr. Oswestry 1928. † L 4.

SNOWDEN, Ernest Exh. 1925-28
Bridge Cottage, Port Sunlight. † L 3.

SNOWDEN, John Exh. 1883
1 Blenheim Road, Bradford, Yorks. † RSA 1.

SNOWDON, Douglas Exh. 1919
Watercolour interior painter. Interlaken, Tregonwell Road, Bournemouth. † RA 1.

SNOWDON, Margaret Kemplay Exh. 1918-38
Painter. Studied R.A. Schools. Add: St. Lawrence, Cheltenham, Glos. † COO 1, RA 1, ROI 2.

SNOWMAN, Isaac* Exh. 1892-1919
Figure and portrait painter. London. † B 1, L 4, RA 32, ROI 2.

SNUSHALL, Miss M. Exh. 1915-16
A.N.S.A. 1913-18. Add: The Mount, Burns Street, Nottingham. † N 6.

SOAMES, Harold Exh. 1910
Landscape painter. † BG 19.

SOBBE, von See V

SODEN, John E. Exh. 1880-87
Genre painter. London. † RBA 17, ROI 1.

SODEN, Susannah Exh. 1880-90
Flower painter. London. † RA 2, RBA 1, RI 1, SWA 3.

SODINI, Dante 1858-1935
Italian sculptor. Exh. 1895-1909. Add: 15 Viale Regina Vittoria, Florence, Italy. † RA 2.

SOEBORG, Knud Exh. 1895-97
Portrait painter. Glasgow 1895; South Kensington, London 1897. † GI 2, RA 1.

SOEST, van See V

SOHNS, Frederick Exh. 1880-1901
Nahant Villa, Juniper Green, Edinburgh. † GI 1, RSA 34.

SOILLEUX, F. Exh. 1884
60 Southgate Road, Islington, London. † RHA 2.

SOISSONS, de See D

SOLANA, Jose Gutierez b. 1886
Spanish artist. Exh. 1921. Add: 5 Santa Feliciana, Madrid. † L 1.

SOLE, Mrs. V. Exh. 1939-40
† RCA 1, RI 1, RSW 1.

SOLLAS, E.H. Exh. 1916
89 Mayow Road, Sydenham, London. † RA 1.

SOLLAS, E.W. Exh. 1901
Saker's Mead, Reigate, Surrey. † ROI 1.

SOLLY, Evelyn W. Exh. 1895-1903
Painter. Married Alfred Soord q.v. Add: Bristol 1895; Bushey, Herts. 1897. † L 1, RA 4, ROI 3.

SOLLY, N. Neal Exh. 1882-94
Landscape painter. Birmingham and Hampstead, London. † B 10, RI 1.

SOLOMON, Carrie Exh. 1909-12
Highfield, Bishops Road, Sutton Coldfield. † B 4, LS 3.

SOLOMON, E. Exh. 1894
31 South King Street, Manchester. † L 1.

SOLOMON, Enid M. b. 1910
Painter and teacher. Studied Paris, St. Johns Wood and R.A. Schools. Married Paul Drury q.v. Exh. 1936-40. † NEA 5.

SOLOMON, Gilbert Bernard 1890-1955
Portrait and figure painter. Studied Slade School 1907-11 and Paris under Renee Prinet 1913-14. A.R.B.A. 1923, R.B.A. 1926. Add: Kensington, London. † CHE 1, P 3, RA 4, RBA 92.

SOLOMON, Mrs. Gwladys Gladstone Exh. 1910
98 Sumatra Road, West Hampstead, London. † LS 3.

SOLOMON, Mrs. Maria Exh. 1920
† NEA 1.

SOLOMON, Miss R. Exh. 1893-1913
London. † B 4, P 1, RA 2, RBA 1, RMS 2, SWA 3.

SOLOMON, Solomon Joseph* 1860-1927
Portrait and figure painter. Studied R.A. Schools, Ecole des Beaux Arts Paris and under Rev. S. Singer. Camouflage artist World War I. Brother of Lily Delissa Joseph q.v. N.E.A. 1886, A.R.A. 1896, R.A. 1906, R.B.A. 1919, P.R.B.A. 1919, R.O.I. 1887, R.P. 1891. Add: London. † AG 1, B 6, BG 1, CAR 2, G 3, GI 3, L 34, M 5, NEA 4, NG 1, P 27, RA 141, RBA 32, RHA 3, ROI 16.

SOLOMON, William E. Gladstone Exh. 1903-40
Figure and portrait painter. b. Sea Point, Cape Town, South Africa. Studied under Sir Arthur Cope and Watson Nicol, and R.A. Schools (gold medal and travelling studentship). Served with Artists Rifles World War I. Spent 17 years in India after the war. Principal Bombay School of Art. Add: London 1903-18 and 1938-40. † L 3, LS 13, RA 10, RBA 1, RCA 2, RI 1, ROI 3, WG 111.

SOLOMONS, Estella Frances 1882-c. 1968
Landscape and portrait painter. A.R.H.A. 1925. Add: Dublin 1905 and 1940; Rathfarnham 1927. † GI 1, RHA 174.

SOLON, Leon Victor b. 1872
Sculptor. R.B.A. 1899. Exh. 1897-1905. Add: Stoke on Trent. Moved to U.S.A. † B 2, L 3, RA 7, RBA 3.

SOMEREN, van See V

SOMERS, Kate Exh. 1904-10
London. † L 3.

SOMERSCALES, John W. Exh. 1893-1910
Sculptor. London 1893; Hull 1896. † B 13, L 3, RA 2, RHA 1.

SOMERSCALES, Marjorie I. Exh. 1921-37
Landscape painter. Withernwick, Yorks. 1921; Chislehurst, Kent 1922; Nottingham 1929. † NEA 6, RA 2.

SOMERSCALES, R. Exh. 1917
Romford Lodge, Garden City, Huntingdon. † RA 1.

SOMERSCALES, Thomas Jaques* 1842-1927
Marine painter. b. Hull. Teacher in the Navy. Lived in Chile 1865-1892. Father of Thomas J.S. q.v. "Off Valparaiso" purchased by Chantrey Bequest 1899. Add: London 1893; Hull 1896. † B 9, L 10, M 2, RA 25, ROI 2.

SOMERSCALES, Thomas J. junr.* Exh. 1900-38
Landscape painter. Son of Thomas Jaques S. q.v. Add: Hull 1900 and 1926; Scunthorpe, Lincs. 1916; Brough, East Yorks. 1933. † B 1, L 1, M 1, RA 10.

SOMERSET, Frank Exh. 1882-83
Figure and illustrative painter. 57 Bedford Gardens, Kensington, London. † RA 1, RBA 1.

SOMERSET, G. Exh. 1898
25 Framfield Road, Highbury Fields, London. † L 1.

SOMERSET, Jane Exh. 1888-97
Landscape and coastal painter. London. † RA 1, RBA 1, ROI 3, SWA 1.

SOMERSET, J.H. Exh. 1910-12
Manchester 1910; London 1912. † RA 2.

SOMERSET, Nina Evelyn Mary Exh. 1920-28
Decorative painter, ecclesiastical artist and illuminator. Add: Bournemouth 1920; London 1925. † RI 1, RMS 9, SWA 3.

SOMERSET, Richard Gay 1848-1928
Landscape painter. b. Manchester. R.O.I. 1898. Add: Manchester 1880; Llanrwst, Wales 1890; Bettws-y-Coed, Wales 1891. † B 1, G 2, L 25, M 84, NG 19, RA 18, RBA 8, RCA 133, ROI 63.

SOMERVELL, Theodore Howard Exh. 1917-36
Watercolour landscape painter. Visited France, India, Kashmir and Tibet. Add: Brantfield, Kendal 1917. † ALP 101, NEA 3.

SOMERVILLE, Alex Exh. 1898
32 Hillside Street, Edinburgh. † RSA 1.

SOMERVILLE, Alec P. Exh. 1936-40
40 Langside Drive, Glasgow. † GI 1, RSW 1.

SOMERVILLE, Charles b. 1870
Landscape, figure and portrait painter, and teacher. b. Falkirk, Stirlingshire. Father of Stuart Scott S. q.v. Exh. 1908-29. Add: Doncaster, Yorks. 1908; Ashford, Middlesex 1928. † FIN 1, RHA 2.

SOMERVILLE, Edith (OE) Exh. 1888-1927
Landscape painter, black and white artist and illustrator. Studied Academies Colarossi and Delecluse, Paris. Add: Drishane, Skibbereen, Co. Cork. † D 2, FIN 3, GOU 99, L 1, RHA 8, SWA 2, WG 209.

SOMERVILLE, Howard Exh. 1910-40
Portrait, figure, interior and still life painter and etcher. Born and studied in Dundee. R.P.E. 1917. Add: London. † ALP 1, B 1, CHE 5, COO 4, G 8, GI 28, GOU 9, I 14, L 17, LS 14, NEA 6, P 70, RA 14, RSA 8.

SOMERVILLE, John W. Exh. 1902-15
Glasgow 1902; Dalkeith 1911; Edinburgh 1912; Heriot, N.B. 1915. † GI 1, RA 2, RSA 10, RSW 2.

SOMERVILLE, Mary Exh. 1916-19
68 Narrow Street, Limehouse, London. † RI 4, SWA 2.

SOMERVILLE, Margaret S. Exh. 1929
The Old Ford Farm, Ashford, Middlesex. † ROI 2.

SOMERVILLE, Peggy Exh. 1937
Fox House, Wigginton, nr. Tring, Herts. † ROI 2.

SOMERVILLE, Stuart Scott b. 1908
Landscape, interior, still life and flower painter. b. Arksey, nr. Doncaster. Son of Charles S. q.v. Exh. 1925-36. Add: Ashford, Middlesex 1925; Dickling, Sussex 1933; Haywards Heath, Sussex 1935; London 1936. † ALP 1, FIN 4, L 2, RA 10, RHA 4, ROI 12, RSA 1.

SOMERVILLE, William Exh. 1940
29 Lawnmoor Street, Glasgow. † GI 1.

SOMES, Miss E.M. Exh. 1909-24
Bushey, Herts. 1909; London 1913. † D 3, LS 3, RI 1, SWA 12.

SOMMERVILLE, Isabella Exh. 1901
Mossfield, Maxwell Park, Glasgow. † GI 2.

SONNIS, Alexander b. 1905
Painter, lithographer and designer. Studied Central School of Arts and Crafts and Royal College of Art, 1929-32. Exh. 1940. Add: c/o Mrs. Heatley, Bisham, Bucks. † RA 1.

SONREL, Elizabeth Exh. 1924-25
53 Rue de Chenaux, Sceaux, Seine, France. † L 4.

SOORD, Alfred U. 1868-1915
Landscape, portrait and figure painter. Married Evelyn W. Solly q.v. Add: Bushey, Herts. † B 2, FIN 3, GI 3, L 6, NG 1, RA 26, RI 10, ROI 3.

SOPER, Eileen Alice b. 1905
Painter and etcher. Studied under her father George S. q.v. Exh. 1921-30. Add: Harmer Green, Welwyn, Herts. † AB 50, ALP 1, CON 3, FIN 26, GI 4, M 2, RA 10, RSA 9.

SOPER, George b. 1870
Watercolour painter, etcher and wood engraver. Father of Eileen Alice S. q.v. A.R.E. 1918, R.E. 1920. Exh. 1890-1940. Add: London 1890; Harmer Green, Welwyn, Herts. 1911. † ALP 1, FIN 4, GI 14, I 1, L 3, NEA 1, RA 48, RBA 3, RE 80, RHA 6, RI 3, RSA 18.

SOPER, Harold C.W. Exh. 1900
Miniature portrait painter. 14 Rectory Grove, Clapham, London. † RA 1.

SOPER, Thomas James* Exh. 1880-92
Landscape painter. London 1880; Milton, Steventon, Berks. 1884. † B 13, D 9, GI 1, L 8, M 4, RA 2, RBA 13, RHA 6, RI 15, ROI 2.

SOPER, William Exh. 1882-1903
Enameller of miniature portraits on copper. London. † RA 3.

SORBY, John Henry Exh. 1896-1916
37 Aldred Road, Steel Bank, Sheffield. † RA 1, RHA 1.

SORBY, Miss M. Exh. 1905
Orgreave, Queen's Drive, Colwyn Bay, Wales. † RCA 1.

SORLEY, Miss Exh. 1900
32 Onslow Square, London. † SWA 1.

SOROLLA-y-BASTIDA, Joaquin* 1862-1923
Spanish painter. Madrid. Exh. 1897-1906. † I 1, RA 3.

SORRELL, Alan b. 1904
Painter, illustrator and lithographer. Studied Southend School of Art, Royal College of Art, 1924-27, and British School at Rome 1928-31. Senior assistant instructor at Royal College of Art 1931-48. A.R.W.S. 1937, R.W.S. 1942. Exh. 1931-40. Add: London. † GOU 2, NEA 3, RA 6, RWS 21, WG 46.

SORSBIE, Gertrude J. Exh. 1893-1932
Artist and teacher. Clare Vicarage, Suffolk 1893; Colchester 1911; c/o Mrs. Fridlauder, 6 Prince Arthur Road, London 1932. † GI 2, LS 3, RI 2.

SORTINI, Saverio Exh. 1901
Sculptor. London. † RA 2.

SOTHEBY, Mrs. C. Barbara Exh. 1930
† P 1.

SOTHERS, Dorothy M. Exh. 1915-19
Miniature painter. 2 The Grove, Muswell Hill, London. † RA 2.

SOUDEN, Miss E.B. Exh. 1929
Mount Rideau, North Berwick. † RSW 1.

SOUKOP, Willi b. 1907
Sculptor. Exh. 1935-38. Add: Studio, Summerhouse, Dartington Hall, Totnes, S. Devon. † GI 1, RA 3.

SOUMARAKOV-ELSTON, Countess Elen Exh. 1919-25
A.S.W.A. 1925. Add: London 1919; Cannes, France 1922. † I 3, SWA 6.

SOUSTER, E.G.W. Exh. 1927
Architect. 3 St. James Street, London. † RA 1.

SOUTAR, Charles G. Exh. 1921-40
Dundee. † GI 2, RSA 8.

SOUTAR, Hilda M. Exh. 1940
85 Magdalen Yard Road, Dundee. † RSA 1.

SOUTER, George Exh. 1887-1908
Elgin, N.B. † L 2, RSA 6.

SOUTER, John B. Exh. 1914-40
Painter and etcher. Aberdeen 1914; London 1922. † CHE 1, FIN 3, GI 21, I 1, L 3, RA 18, RED 5, RSA 6.

SOUTH, Annie M. Exh. 1880-1911
Mrs. Henry J. Watercolour landscape painter. Richmond, Surrey 1880; London 1910. † D 1, LS 9, SWA 14.

SOUTHALL, Joseph Edward 1861-1944
Painter and engraver. b. Nottingham. Articled to an architect 1878-1882. Visited Italy 1883 and 1897. N.E.A. 1926, R.B.S.A. 1902, A.R.W.S. 1925, R.W.S. 1931. Add: 13 Charlotte Road, Edgbaston, Birmingham. † ALP 77, B 110, BAR 1, D 2, FIN 41, G 2, GI 3, L 28, LEI 116, M 3, NEA 100, NG 28, RA 18, RWS 88.

SOUTHALL, Mary L. Exh. 1887
The Craig, Ross, Herefords. † B 1.

SOUTHAMPTON, Lady Exh. 1893-1936
Hilda Mary Dundas. Watercolour landscape painter. Studied drawing and watercolour painting after her marriage to Lord Southampton in 1892. Add: London. † GOU 19, RHA 1, RSA 1, RSW 4, WG 39.

SOUTHBY, E.H. Exh. 1922
† SWA 2.

SOUTHBY, E. Mabel Exh. 1906-15
Aldern Bridge House, Newbury, Berks. † RI 2, SWA 3.

SOUTHBY, Vera H. Exh. 1922-40
Figure, portrait and landscape painter. Visited China. Add: London 1922; Gerrards Cross, Bucks. 1930. † ALP 59, GI 1, GOU 1, L 6, M 1, NEA 1, RA 12, SWA 4.

SOUTHERN, J.M. Exh. 1880-92
Landscape painter. Liverpool 1880 and 1887; Trefrin, Wales 1883. † AG 1, L 23, RA 7, RCA 6.

SOUTHERN, Miss L. Exh. 1887
Bescot, Walsall, Staffs. † B 1.

SOUTHGATE, Arthur C. Exh. 1938
Watercolour landscape painter. 58 Roseberry Road, Ipswich, Suffolk. † RA 2.

SOUTHGATE, Elsie Exh. 1880-87
Landscape painter. 107A Long Acre, London. † RA 3, RBA 5, ROI 1, SWA 1.

SOUTHGATE, Frank d. 1916
R.B.A. 1905. Died in France. Add: Conway, Wales 1904; Wells, Norfolk 1910. † L 7, RA 3, RCA 3, RBA 23.

SOUTHORN, Gertrude B. Exh. 1908-10
3 Euston Grove, Claughton, Birkenhead. † L 2.

SOUTHWICK, Alfred b. 1875
Sculptor and watercolour painter. Studied Armstrong College, Newcastle on Tyne and Wolverhampton and City and Guilds of London. Exh. 1919-33. Add: London. † GOU 1, LS 3, RA 1, ROI 4.

SOUTINE, Chaim* 1893-1943
Landscape, figure and portrait painter. Exh. 1938. † BA 1, RED 3.

SOUTTAR, Anna Exh. 1896-1901
Bushey, Herts. 1896; East Grinstead, Sussex 1898. † D 2, GI 1, RSA 1, SWA 2.

SOUTTEN, Dora Exh. 1905-32
Portrait and miniature painter. Studied St. Johns Wood and Westminster Schools of Art, British Museum and Victoria and Albert Museum. A.R.M.S. 1916, R.M.S. 1919. Add: London. † L 13, RA 18, RMS 31.

SOUTTER, Miss E. Exh. 1914-19
133 Park Road, Regents Park, London. † LS 12, SWA 2.

SOUTTER, Rose Stanley Exh. 1892-93
Church Lane, Kirkcaldy. † GI 4.

SOWDEN, John b. 1838
Landscape painter. Exh. 1883-1913. Add: 1 Blenheim Road, Bradford, Yorks. † B 1, D 2, G 1, L 6, M 4, NG 1, RA 5, RI 1, RSW 1.

SOWERBY, Miss C.E. Exh. 1889-97
Painter. London. † RHA 1, SWA 3.

SOWERBY, John G.* Exh. 1880-1914
Landscape, flower and domestic painter. Father of Millicent S. q.v. Add: Ravenshill, Gateshead 1880; Wall on Tyne, Northumberland 1894; Boxted House, nr. Colchester, Essex 1898; Slaggyford, Carlisle 1901; Reigate, Surrey 1903; Abingdon, Berks. 1904; Ross on Wye 1910. † B 5, BG 33, BRU 65, D 7, GI 4, L 2, M 1, RA 20, RI 2, RSA 4.

SOWERBY, Jessie M. Exh. 1880
Painter. 12 Rokeby Road, New Cross, London. † SWA 2.

SOWERBY, Kate Exh. 1883-1900
Painter and sculptor. London. † L 1, RA 4, SWA 3.

SOWERBY, Laurence P. Exh. 1908-25
Landscape painter. 14 Gauntley Street, Nottingham. † N 18.

SOWERBY, Millicent Exh. 1900-9
Watercolour painter and illustrator. Daughter of John G.S. q.v. Add: Boxted House, nr. Colchester 1900; Slaggyford, Carlisle 1901; London 1903; Sutton Courtenay, Abingdon, Berks. 1904. † BG 35, L 1, RI 8.

SOYER, Paul* 1823-1903
French painter. 26 Maida Vale, London 1880. † AG 5, GI 1, RHA 1, TOO 4.

SOZONOV, Vsevold Exh. 1924-39
Landscape and figure painter. London. † BA 2, GOU 17, NEA 7, RED 33, TOO 2.

SPACKMAN, Cyril Saunders b. 1887
Painter, etcher, sculptor and architect. b. Cleveland, Ohio, U.S.A. Architectural draughts man in Cleveland 1905-10. R.B.A. 1919, R.M.S. 1916. Exh. 1913-40. Add: London 1913; East Croydon, Surrey 1922. † AB 2, I 2, L 15, RA 3, RBA 147, RCA 2, RMS 10, ROI 1.

SPACKMAN, Mary A. Exh. 1889-98
Watercolour flower painter. London 1889; Bedford 1898. † B 1, RA 1, RBA 1, RI 1, SWA 4.

SPACKMAN, P.G. Exh. 1923
c/o Bourlet and Sons, 17 Nassau Street, London. † ROI 1.

SPAIGHT, Mrs. G. Exh. 1910
5 Harcourt Road, Boscombe, Hants. † RA 1.

SPAIN, John E.D. Exh. 1900-17
Architect. London. † RA 12.

SPAIN, John Henry Exh. 1889-98
Architectural painter. London. † RA 1, RBA 2, RI 1.

SPALDING, Mrs. Anne Exh. 1933-36
Painter. Oxford. † COO 7, SWA 1.

SPANIEL, Otaker Exh. 1908
Sculptor. 93 Rue de Vaugirard, Paris. † LS 4.

SPANTON, H. Margaret Exh. 1901-5
Portrait and figure painter. Greencroft, Hadley Wood, Barnet, Herts. † NEA 3.

SPANTON, Mabel Mary b. 1874
Watercolour landscape painter. Studied under J.S. Cartlidge and at Newlyn, Penzance under Stanhope Forbes. Lived mostly abroad. Exh. 1921-40. Add: Hastings 1921; Bexhill-on-Sea 1923; c/o Bourlet and Sons, Nassau Street, London 1932. † AB 2, B 7, D 7, GI 2, GOU 1, L 5, RA 1, RBA 3, RCA 14, RHA 13, RI 2, RSA 1, RSW 1, SWA 8, WG 190.

SPARE, Austin Osman* 1888-1956
Portrait, imaginary figure and decorative painter, illustrator and etcher. Studied Lambeth and Royal College of Art. Add: London. † BG 111, BRU 114, LEF 114, RA 3.

SPARK, Adelaide Louise Exh. 1906-39
Landscape and flower painter in watercolour and portrait and miniature painter in oils. Studied Lambeth School of Art. A.R.B.A. 1926. Add: London. † D 6, L 5, RA 17, RBA 6, RI 8, SWA 11.

SPARKE, Frank S. Exh. 1928-34
Edinburgh 1928; Colinton 1930. † RSA 7, RSW 1.

SPARKES, Catherine Adelaide b. 1842
Mrs. John S. nee Edwards. Genre painter and illustrator. Worked as a tile painter and designer for the Lambeth Pottery. Exh. 1880-92. Add: London 1880; Ewhurst, Guildford, Surrey 1884. † D 2, G 1, L 2, M 1, RA 4, RI 6, ROI 5.

SPARKES, James Exh. 1921-32
Birmingham. † B 17.

SPARKES, Lucy Exh. 1886
Painter. 8 Observatory Avenue, Campden Hill, London. † SWA 1.

SPARKS, Ellen Exh. 1894-97
40 Rossetti Mansions, Chelsea, London. † RBA 1, SWA 4.

SPARKS, Henry Exh. 1893
14 The Crescent, Bromsgrove. † B 1.

SPARKS, Herbert Blande Exh. 1892-93
Miniature portrait painter. 50 Woodsome Road, Highgate Road, London. † L 1, RA 1.

SPARKS, J. Exh. 1917
41 St. Leonards Road, Exeter, Devon. † RA 2.

SPARKS, Nathaniel b. 1880
Watercolour painter and engraver. Studied Bristol and Royal College of Art. A.R.E. 1905, R.E. 1910. Exh. 1905-37. Add: London. † CHE 2, CON 29, GI 3, L 9, RA 38, RE 86, RI 1.

SPARLING, Constance Exh. 1932-39
Chipping Campden, Glos. † B 1, RCA 9.

SPARROW, Clodagh H.K. Exh. 1938
Painter. 21 Royal Crescent, London. † RA 1.

SPARROW, Evelyn Exh. 1895-1914
Liverpool 1895; Ross, Herefords. 1906. † B 1, GI 1, L 10.

SPARROW, Nellie Exh. 1903
Roleston House, Fallowfield, Manchester. † M 1.

SPARROW, Thomas Exh. 1880
15 Dryden Street, Nottingham. † N 1.

SPARROW, W.S. Exh. 1882-87
Brussels 1882 and 1885; Wrexham 1883. † GI 2, L 8, M 1.

SPAULL, Leslie Charles b. 1914
Painter black and white artist, illustrator and teacher. Studied Richmond School of Art, St. Johns Wood and R.A. Schools. Exh. 1936-38. Add: 27 Denehurst Gardens, Richmond, Surrey. † RA 2.

SPAWFORTH, Gladys K. Exh. 1923
Stained glass artist. Studio, 6a Gunter Grove, Chelsea, London. † RA 2.

SPEAIGHT, Alice Langford Exh. 1897-1924
nee Cundy. Miniature painter. London 1897; Beaconsfield, Bucks. 1911. † RA 25, RMS 10.

SPEAR, A.J. Ruskin* b. 1911
Portrait and figure painter. Studied Hammersmith School of Art and Royal College of Art. Exh. 1932-40. Add: London † RA 6.

SPEAR, Francis H. Exh. 1923-37
Stained glass artist. London 1923; Edgware, Middlesex 1936. † RA 4.

SPECK, E. Blanche Exh. 1911-12
Wesley Manse, Airdrie, N.B. † GI 2.

SPEDDING, Joan Exh. 1936
Flower painter. 6 Cambridge Road, West Bridgford, Notts. † N 1.

SPEDDING, Mary Exh. 1934
Jessamine House, Bishop Auckland, Co. Durham. † RSA 1.

SPEDDING, Sidney b. 1916
Sculptor. b. Ashington, Northumberland. Studied Armstrong College, Durham University 1932-36 and Edinburgh College of Art 1936-39. Exh. 1939. Add: Edinburgh. † RSA 1.

SPEED, Mrs. Exh. 1893
15 Devonshire Place, London. † D 4.

SPEED, Harold* 1872-1957
Landscape and portrait painter. Studied Royal College of Art 1887, R.A. Schools 1890, Paris, Vienna and Rome. R.P. 1897. "The Alcantara, Toledo, by Moonlight" (1894) purchased by Chantrey Bequest 1905. Add: London. † B 11, BA 5, CHE 7, FIN 137, GI 23, I 4, L 36, LEI 62, LS 8, M 12, NEA 3, NG 37, P 166, RA 83, RBA 5, RCA 1, RHA 1, RID 10, ROI 5, RSA 1.

SPEED, Katherine G. Exh. 1888-1901
Figure painter. London. † G 1, RA 3.

SPEEDWELL, Miss J.H. Exh. 1883-85
c/o Scott, 78 Princes Street, Edinburgh. † GI 2, L 1, RSA 1.

SPEELMAN, Isidore Exh. 1933
Still life painter. 75b Grand Parade, Harringay, London. † RA 1.

SPEIGHT, Clifford Exh. 1935
Birkenshaw, Yorks. † RCA 1.

SPEIGHT, Henry Exh. 1936-38
Sculptor. 29 East Road, Egremont, Cheshire. † RA 2.

SPEIGHT, Thomas Exh. 1885-1903
Landscape and figure painter. London. † L 4, RA 2, RHA 1.

SPEIR, Guy Exh. 1925-28
Painter. The Abbey, North Berwick. † RSA 2, WG 86.

SPEIR, Miss S. Exh. 1937
Cardiff, Wales. † RCA 2.

SPEIRS, John Exh. 1885-88
Glasgow. † GI 4, L 1, RSA 4.

SPEIRS, Robert Exh. 1909
34 High Street, Paisley. † GI 2, L 1.

SPEIRS, William Exh. 1906-12
Glasgow. † GI 2.

SPEIRS-ALEXANDER, Sheila Exh. 1937-38
2 Welbeck House, Welbeck Street, London. † ROI 2.

SPELLING, F.C. Exh. 1933-35
Landscape painter. † LEF 2.

SPENCE, Elizabeth Exh. 1889
Mount Pleasant, Sale, Manchester. † M 1.

SPENCE, Ernest Exh. 1884-1913
Figure and portrait painter. Probably father of Miss R.A.S. q.v. Add: London 1884; Guildford, Surrey 1899. † L 5, RA 12, RI 1, ROI 2.

SPENCE, Harry Exh. 1882-1928
Landscape painter. N.E.A. 1887, R.B.A. 1909. Add: London 1882 and 1905; Bushey, Herts. 1884; Glasgow 1885. † B 1, FIN 2, G 1, GI 63, I 1, L 16, M 8, NEA 1, RA 11, RBA 38, RCA 1, ROI 3, RSA 21, RSW 3.

SPENCE, John Simpson Exh. 1919-36
Leith 1919; Edinburgh 1936. † RSA 6.

SPENCE, Mrs. Mary Exh. 1891
The Woods, Bowdon, Cheshire. † M 2.

SPENCE, Matheson Exh. 1936
Watercolour painter. 74 Sterndale Road, Brook Green, London. † RI 1, WG 1.

SPENCE, Philip Exh. 1902-12
Landscape painter. Possibly brother of Robert S. q.v. Add: Kensington, London 1909; North Shields 1905; Gosforth, Newcastle on Tyne 1906. † L 6, RA 7.

SPENCE, Phyllis Exh. 1918-19
Figure and portrait painter. Probably daughter of Percy F.S.S. q.v. Add: 4 Edwardes Square Studios, London. † RID 7.

SPENCE, Percy F.W. b. 1868
Landscape painter. b. Sydney, N.S.W. Probably father of Phyllis S. q.v. Exh. 1896-1916. Add: London. † B 1, D 2, L 5, NG 1, RA 7.

SPENCE, Robert b. 1871
Painter and etcher. b. Tynemouth. Possibly brother of Philip S. q.v Studied Newcastle School of Art, Slade School 1892-95 and Paris. A.R.E. 1897, R.E. 1902. Exh. 1896-1940. Add: London 1896; and 1900; North Shields 1897. † FIN 4, I 2, L 22, NEA 1, RA 24, RE 112.

SPENCE, Miss R.A. Exh. 1920
Probably daughter of Ernest S. q.v. Add: One Tree Corner, Guildford, Surrey. † SWA 1.

SPENCE, Mrs. T.R. Exh. 1893
45 Rathbone Place, London. † B 1.

SPENCE, Thomas Ralph* Exh. 1882-1916
Landscape and figure painter. Newcastle on Tyne 1882; London 1890; Beckenham, Kent 1913. † B 4, BG 2, FIN 36, G 1, GI 2, L 27, M 7, NG 5, RA 11, RBA 1, RSA 1.

SPENCE, Williamina Exh. 1882
109 Cork Street, Dublin. † RHA 1.

SPENCE, W. Naylor Exh. 1899
38 Westmoreland Street, Dublin. † RHA 1.

SPENCELAYH, Charles* 1865-1958
Figure, portrait and miniature painter and etcher. b. Rochester, Kent. Studied Kensington School of Art. Father of Vernon S. q.v. R.B.S.A. 1928, R.M.S. 1897. Add: Chatham, Kent 1887; London 1894 and 1936; Olney, Bucks. 1918; West Didsbury, Manchester 1922; Hollingbourne, Kent 1933. † ALP 1, B 68, GI 2, L 83, M 5, NG 3, RA 30, RCA 10, RHA 2, RI 3, RMS 129, ROI 16.

SPENCELAYH, Vernon b. 1891
Painter and ivory miniaturist. Studied under his father Charles S. q.v. Exh. 1921-30. Add: Olney, Bucks. 1921; London 1923. † L 13, RI 3, RMS 5.

SPENCELY, H.G.C. Exh. 1933
8 Dudley Gardens, Westmoreland Street, London. † L 2.

SPENCER, Augustus 1866-1924
Principal Royal College of Art 1900-20. Add: Coalbrookdale, Salop 1888; London 1900. † B 1, L 1, RA 1.

SPENCER, Blanche Exh. 1882-84
Painter. 5 St. Augustine's Road, Camden Square, London. † G 1, GI 1, RBA 5, RI 1, ROI 1.

SPENCER, Charles Exh. 1909
† LS 3.

SPENCER, Charles H. Exh. 1935-38
Painter and etcher. A.R.E. 1935. Add: Dunolly, Southfield Park, Harrow, Middlesex. † RA 2, RE 8.

SPENCER, C. Neame Exh. 1896-1917
Painter. Beckenham, Kent 1896; London 1898; Tatsfield, Surrey 1906. † B 2, GI 1, M 1, NG 1, RA 4, RBA 1, ROI 2, RSA 2.

SPENCER, Mrs. Doris Exh. 1923-40
Portrait, figure, flower and miniature portrait painter. A.R.M.S. 1932. Add: London. † NEA 6, P 7, RA 9, RBA 4, RI 2, RMS 29, SWA 4.

SPENCER, Edward d. 1938
Metal worker. Probably brother of Ethel S. q.v. Add: Odsey Grange, Ashwell, Herts. 1901; London 1904. † I 1, L 17.

SPENCER, Elsie Exh. 1899
The Sycamores, Blackburn, Lancs. † L 1.

SPENCER, Ethel Exh. 1895-1921
Probably sister of Edward S. q.v. Add: Odsey Grange, Ashwell, Herts. 1895 and 1906; London 1901. † L 16, M 1, RA 3, ROI 1, SWA 21.

SPENCER, Florence Exh. 1885
Watercolour flower painter. 5 Lansdown Place, Clifton, Bristol. † SWA 1.

SPENCER, Fred Exh. 1891-1924
Fruit and still life painter. London. † B 12, D 5, L 13, RA 16, RI 19, ROI 10.

SPENCER, Gilbert* b. 1892
Portrait, figure and landscape painter. b. Cookham, Berks. Studied Camberwell School of Arts and Crafts, Slade School 1913-15 and 1919-20. Professor of painting Royal College of Art from 1932. Brother of Stanley S. q.v. N.E.A. 1919. "A Cotswold Farm" purchased by Chantrey Bequest 1932. Add: Cookham, Berks. 1915; London 1920 and 1932; Caversham, Reading, Berks. 1921; Oxford 1925 and 1935; Basildon, Berks. 1937; Shaftesbury, Dorset 1940. † AG 13, BA 1, CHE 2, G 3, GOU 270, I 2, L 3, LEI 84, M 5, NEA 30, RA 10, RED 3, RSA 1, TOO 13.

SPENCER, H. Exh. 1918
27 Blenheim Road, St. Johns Wood, London. † RA 1.

SPENCER, Mrs. Henry Exh. 1935
Balham, London. † SWA 2.

SPENCER, H. Hammond Exh. 1939-40
4 Collingham Road, London. † RI 3.

SPENCER, J.H. Exh. 1929
Enamelled plaster worker. 57 Yorke Street, Mansfield Woodhouse, Notts. † N 1.

SPENCER, Leonard Exh. 1908
Waitknowe Terrace, Galashiels, N.B. † RSA 1.

SPENCER, Margaret Exh. 1925-33
Liverpool. † L 8.

SPENCER, Marianne Exh. 1885
Flower painter. † SWA 2.

SPENCER, Marjorie See BREND

SPENCER, Noel b. 1900
Etcher, engraver and stained glass artist. b. Nuneaton, Warwicks. Studied Ashton School of Art, Manchester School of Art and Royal College of Art. Drawing master at Birmingham Central School of Arts and Crafts. Exh. 1926-38. Add: Ashton-under-Lyne 1926, Birmingham 1930, Sheffield 1933, Huddersfield 1935. † B 16, L 1, NEA 6, RA 9.

SPENCER, Sam Exh. 1931-40
Painter. A.R.B.A. 1939. Add: 6 Ripplevale Grove, Barnsbury, London. † RBA 16, RI 10, WG 9.

SPENCER, Sir Stanley* 1891-1959
Landscape, figure, biblical, decorative and mural painter. b. Cookham, Berks. Studied Slade School 1909-12. Travelled in Italy, Yugoslavia and Switzerland. Brother of Gilbert S. q.v. Married 1st Hilda Carline q.v. and 2nd Patricia Preece q.v. N.E.A. 1919, A.R.A. 1932. Knited 1959. "The Roundabout" (1923) purchased by Chantrey Bequest 1944, "Study for Joachim among the Shepherds" (1912) purchased 1955, "The Centurion's Servant" (1914) purchased 1960, "Mending Cowls, Cookham" (1914) purchased 1962 and "St. Francis and the Birds" (1935) purchased 1967. Add: Cookham, Berks. 1912 and 1935; Bourne End, Bucks. 1921; Petersfield, Hants. 1922; London 1924. † AB 4, BA 1, G 2, GI 1, GOU 113, L 3, LEI 1, M 1, NEA 21, RA 9, RED 1, RHA 1, RSA 2, TOO 38.

SPENCER-PRYSE, Gerald 1881-1956
Watercolour painter, lithographer and poster artist. Studied London and Paris. R.B.A. 1914. Add: London. † ALP 100, CHE 1, G 7, GI 18, I 23, L 21, LEI 24, RA 3, RBA 4, RSA 12.

SPENDER, Humphrey b. 1910
Landscape painter. Studied A.A. Exh. 1936-37. † RED 8.

SPENDLER, J.E. Exh. 1890
15 Leopold Place, Edinburgh. † GI 1.

SPENLOVE, Francis R. Exh. 1924-28
Wharf Studio, St. Ives, Cornwall. † L 1, P 4, ROI 1.

SPENLOVE-SPENLOVE, Frank* 1868-1933
Figure and landscape painter. b. Bridge of Allan, Stirling. Studied London, Paris and Antwerp. Founder and principal of the Spenlove School of Painting (The Yellow Door Studio) from 1896. R.B.A. 1895, R.I. 1907, R.O.I. 1910. Add: Shortlands, Kent 1885; Beckenham, Kent 1888; London 1892. † B 9, GI 21, GOU 2, I 1, L 38, M 18, NG 18, RA 79, RBA 144, RCA 42, RHA 5, RI 106, ROI 91, WG 2.

SPENTON, Miss M.M. Exh. 1934-38
c/o Bourlet and Son, Nassau St., London. † RCA 5.

SPERO, Claude Exh. 1901
35 Cranbourne Street, London. † L 1.

SPEYBROUCH, Van see V

SPICER, Charles Exh. 1885
Figure painter. 112 Gt. Portland Street, London. † RA 1.

SPICER, Miss E.L. Exh. 1910-32
Liverpool. † L 10.

SPICER, Edward Vincent Exh. 1935
Spalding, Lincs. † RCA 1.

SPICER, Miss H.L. Exh. 1905-10
London. † L 7.

SPICER, Peter Exh. 1905
14 Leam Terrace East, Leamington, Warwicks. † B 3.

SPICER-SIMSON, Margaret b. 1874
Mrs. Theodore S-S. Miniature portrait painter. b. Washington, D.C., U.S.A. Exh. 1900-1. Add Paris 1900; Hampstead, London 1901. † RA 3.

SPICER-SIMSON, Theodore F. b. 1871
Sculptor. b. France. A.R.M.S. 1937. Exh. 1900-39. Add: Paris 1900; London 1913; Bourron, Seine et Marne, France 1937. † L 2, NG 2, RA 15, RMS 5, RSA 1.

SPIELMEYER, Wilhelm Exh. 1894
Black and white artist. 90 Chancery Lane, London. † RA 2.

SPIERS, Miss A. Exh. 1885-86
28 Tavistock Road, Westbourne Park, London. † M 4.

SPIERS, Bessie J. Exh. 1880-1901
Landscape painter. A.S.W.A. 1893. Sister of Charlotte H.S. q.v. Add: London. † B 9, DOW 5, FIN 1, L 11, M 8, NG 4, RA 4, RBA 3, RHA 1, RI 16, SWA 59.

SPIERS, Benjamin Walter Exh. 1880-93
Genre and still life painter. London. † B 2, D 6, L 13, M 12, RA 14, RBA 19, RHA 1, RI 19.

SPIERS, Charlotte H. Exh. 1880-1914
Landscape, fruit and flower painter. Sister of Bessie J.S. q.v. A.S.W.A. 1893. Add: London. † B 8, D 6, DOW 2, FIN 1, G 1, L 15, LEI 1, M 6, NG 8, RA 5, RBA 7, RHA 1, RI 20, SWA 112.

SPIERS, Elizabeth Exh. 1883-95
Birmingham. † B 25.

SPIERS, Harry Exh. 1899-1900
Toronto, Canada and c/o Mrs. Goldsmith, Hammelson Road, Bromley, Kent. † RBA 2.

SPIERS, John A. Exh. 1880-97
Glasgow. † GI 10, L 2.

SPIERS, Richard Phene 1838-1916
Watercolour landscape and architectural painter. London. † D 16, DOW 2, FIN 2, G 7, GI 23, L 5, LEI 1, M 15, NG 9, RA 54, RBA 15, RHA 8, RI 30.

SPILHAUS, Nita* Exh. 1909-13
Etcher. c/o Findlay, Durham and Brodie, 110 Cannon Street, London. † RA 3.

SPILLER, Miss B. Exh. 1896
10 Tanza Road, London. † SWA 1.

SPILLER, Ernest W. Exh. 1937
Architect. 4A Fredericks Place, London. † RA 1.

SPILLER, Miss J.R. Exh. 1905-13
2 Lindfield Gardens, Hampstead, London. † RA 4.

SPILLER, W.H. Exh. 1884-86
Painter. Hampstead Hill Gardens, London. † ROI 3.

SPINDLER, Jane Elizabeth Exh. 1880-1903
Edinburgh 1880, 1888 and 1901; Dundee 1882; Blairgowrie, N.B. 1890. † GI 8, RSA 29.

SPINDLER, James G.H. Exh. 1880-1907
Landscape painter. Dundee. † GI 11, L 1, RA 1, RSA 17.

SPINDLER, Walter E. Exh. 1892-96
Portrait and figure painter. 59 Avenue de Saxe, Paris and Old Park, Ventnor, I.o.W. † L 2, M 1, NG 1, P 2, RA 4.

SPINELLI, Raffaele Exh. 1894
Engraver. c/o Messrs. Graves, 7 Pall Mall, London. † RA 1.

SPINETTI, Mario* Exh. 1902
Landscape painter. c/o E. Rosenberg Esq., 45 Belsize Square, London. † RA 1.

SPINKS, Thomas* Exh. 1880-1907
Landscape painter. London 1880; Bettws-y-Coed, Wales 1899. † L 2, M 1, RA 4.

SPIRIDON, J. Exh. 1884-85
† TOO 2.

SPITTLE, William M. Exh. 1885-1912
Figure painter. R.B.A. 1902, R.B.S.A. 1898. Add: Birmingham. † B 28, L 9, M 1, RA 2, RBA 7.

SPOFFORTH, Miss D.V. Exh. 1934-36
4 Stratford Studios, Stratford Road, London. † RBA 3, RI 2.

SPONG, Annie E. Exh. 1892-1909
Figure, portrait and animal painter. A.S.W.A. 1905. Add: London 1896; Ditchling, Sussex 1908. † B 2, FIN 1, GI 1, LS 5, P 1, RA 9, SWA 12.

SPONG, Walter Brookes Exh. 1881-1914
Watercolour landscape painter. London. † L 1, RA 8, RI 9, WG 66.

SPOONER, Arthur* Exh. 1890-1940
Landscape and portrait painter. N.S.A. 1908, V.P.N.S.A. 1924 and 1938, A.R.B.A. 1919, R.B.A. 1920. Add: Nottingham. † B 3, COO 34, L 15, N 144, RA 15, RBA 83.

SPOONER, A de S Exh. 1890
130 Princess Street, Manchester. † L 1.

SPOONER, Charles Sydney 1862-1938
Architect. Instructor in woodwork at L.C.C. Central School of Arts and Crafts. Married Minnie Dibden S. q.v. Add: London. † RA 15.

SPOONER, Miss E. Exh. 1918
1a Southey Street, Nottingham. † N 2.

SPOONER, Minnie Dibden Exh. 1893-1927
nee Davison. Portrait painter and etcher. Married Charles Sydney S. q.v. R.M.S. 1901. Add: London. † L 1, NG 1, RA 17, RHA 1, RMS 7.

SPOONER-LILLINGSTON, G.B. Percy Exh. 1894-1930
Penzance, Cornwall 1894; Plymouth 1922. † B 11.

SPOWERS, Ethel Exh. 1930-38
Lincocut artist. † RED 6.

SPRADBERY, Walter Ernest b. 1889
Landscape painter, and decorative landscape poster designer. Studied Walthamstow School of Art. Exh. 1921-40. Add: Walthamstow 1921; Buckhurst Hill, Essex 1929. † ALP 1, CHE 3, D 25, FIN 1, L 15, RA 11, RCA 1, RHA 2, RI 12, RSA 2.

SPRAGUE, Edith Exh. 1883-1933
Landscape, portrait and figure painter. R.M.S. 1896. Add: London 1883; South Woodford, Essex 1902; Maidstone, Kent 1919. † B 15, L 3, RA 32, RBA 2, RID 44, RMS 5, ROI 21, SWA 3, WG 3.

SPRAGUE, Hilda G. Vaughan Exh. 1895-97
29 Buckingham Terrace, Edinburgh. † RSA 2.

SPREAD, Miss A. Exh. 1880
27 Pembridge Crescent, Bayswater, London. † RHA 1.

SPREAD, William d. 1909
Landscape and architectural painter and engraver. Studied under Verlat in Antwerp. R.E. 1881. Add: 27 Pembridge Crescent, Bayswater, London. † L 2, RA 15, RBA 2, RE 7, RI 2.

SPRECKLEY, Annie M. Exh. 1884-1926
Painter. Nottingham 1884; Hoveringham, Notts. 1925. † N 6.

SPRENGER, Charles Exh. 1888-1906
Glasgow 1888; Lenzie, N.B. 1906. † GI 7.

SPRIGGS, Mabel Exh. 1893
Chad Mont, Augustus Road, Edgbaston, Birmingham. † B 1.

SPRINCHORN, Carl* b. 1887
American painter. b. Sweden. Exh. 1932. † RED2.

SPRINCK, Emilie M. Exh. 1908-35
Miniature portrait painter. London. † L 1, RA 4, RI 10.

SPRINCK, Leon Exh. 1893-1903
Portrait painter. Portland Place, London. † L 2, RA 1, RHA 1.

SPRING, A. Exh. 1883
Glasgow. † GI 1.

SPRING, Mrs. E.M. Exh. 1924-32
Studio, 2a Cathcart Studios, Recliffe Road, London. † RBA 1, SWA 3.

SPRINGER, Miss E. Exh. 1912
4 Rue de Chevreuse, Paris. † RA 1.

SPRINGETT, Miss B. Exh. 1902
Ashfield, Hawkhurst, Kent. † SWA 1.

SPRING-SMITH, Effie Exh. 1930-40
Figure, portrait and landscape painter. b. Woodbridge, Suffolk. Studied Ipswich School of Art and Slade School. R.B.A. 1940. Add: London. † GI 2, L 5, NEA 4, P 1, RA 7, RBA 15, ROI 6, RSA 1, SWA 1.

SPRINKSMANN, M.C. Exh. 1905-14
Etaples, Pas de Calais, France 1905; Paris 1911; South Kensington, London 1914. † GI 1, I 2, L 10, LS 4, RA 1.

SPROAT, W. Edwardes Exh. 1900-6
Glasgow 1900; Liverpool 1906. † GI 1, L 1.

SPRUCE, E.C. Exh. 1887-1915
Beermantoft's Pottery, Leeds 1887; 48 Back Cowper Street, Leeds 1906. † L 3, RA 5.

SPRULES, A. Crossingham Exh. 1915-18
Trelawne, Sutton, Surrey. † L 1, RA 2, ROI 4.

SPURGEON, Rev. Thomas Exh. 1909
Watercolour painter. † WG 180.

SPURLING, Alys Exh. 1891-92
Watercolour figure painter. Greys Cottage, Kelvedon, Essex. † RI 2.

SPURLING, Celia see BAY

SPURLING, Christine Exh. 1940
Portrait painter. Clatford Park Farm, Marlborough, Wilts. † RA 1.

SPURNAY, C. Aimee Exh. 1914
21 Wilton Street, London. † LS 3.

SPURR, Miss B. Exh. 1914
Dowlands, Hitchin, Herts. † RA 1.

SPURR, Elizabeth Exh. 1937-40
Sculptor and wood engraver. London. † RA 2, RED 22.

SPURR, Gertrude E. Exh. 1888-90
Landscape, flower and fruit painter. 17 Keildon Road, New Wandsworth, London. † RBA 3, SWA 6.

SPURRIER, Mabel Annie Exh. 1920-40
Watercolour painter. b. Moseley, Birmingham. Studied Birmingham College of Art. R.I. 1934. Add: Eton, Windsor, Berks. 1920; Birmingham 1921; London 1937. † B54, RA 1, RI 29, SWA 1.

SPURRIER, Steven 1878-1961
Painter, black and white artist and poster designer. Studied Lambeth and Heatherleys. R.B.A. 1934, R.O.I. 1912. "Yellow Wash-Stand" purchased by Chantrey Beuqest 1940. Add: London 1905, 1919 and 1930; Hull 1917; Glasgow 1918; West Wittering, Chichester, Sussex 1928. † G 1, GI 5, GOU 3, I 12, L 6, M 1, RA 24, RBA 24, RHA 1, RI 8, ROI 29, RSA 8.

SPURWAY, Miss C.A. Exh. 1910-19
Witton Street, London. † SWA 5.

SPURWAY, Mrs. E.A. Exh. 1920-30
106 College Road, Moseley, Birmingham. † B 9.

"SPY" see WARD, Sir Leslie

"SPY JUNIOR" see UDVARDY, Imre Laszlo

SPYKES, J.A.L. Exh. 1888-90
Luscombe Villa, Woodfield Road, Kings Heath, Birmingham. † B 4.

SQUIRE, Alice 1840-1936
Landscape and genre painter and watercolourist. Sister of Emma S. q.v. R.I. 1888, A.S.W.A. 1886. Add: 28 Tavistock Road, Westbourne Park, London. † D 13, L 9, M 4, RA 21, RBA 3, RI 117, RSW 2, SWA 27, TOO 1.

SQUIRE, Amy see LYNE

SQUIRE, Ellis Exh. 1884
Landscape painter. † FIN 1.

SQUIRE, Emma Exh. 1880-1916
Genre and still life painter. Sister of Alice S. q.v. Add: 28 Tavistock Road, Westbourne Park, London. † L 4, M 2, RA 12, RI 1, ROI 1, SWA 6.

SQUIRE, Harold Exh. 1911-27
Landscape painter. N.E.A. 1919. Founder member London Group 1913. Add: London 1911 and 1920; Graylingwell War Hospital, Chichester, Sussex 1916. † GOU 4, L 1, NEA 33, RHA 5.

SQUIRE, Helen Exh. 1889-1905
Figure painter. London. † B 1, L 2, M 3, RA 4, RI 5, ROI 4, SWA 2.

SQUIRE, John Exh. 1880-96
Landscape painter mainly in watercolour. Ross, Hereford 1880; Exeter, Devon 1881; Swansea, Wales 1883; London 1895. † D 3, L 3, M 1, RA 2, RBA 6, RI 1.

SQUIRE, Louisa A. Exh. 1893
60 Hogarth Road, Cromwell Road, London. † L 1.

SQUIRE, L.E. Exh. 1885
Moss Fern, Stoneycroft. † L 1.

SQUIRE, Maud Hunt b. 1873
American artist. Exh. 1908-9. Add: 39 Boulevard St. Jaques, Paris. † GI 3, L 4, LS 4.

SQUIRRELL, Mrs. A.M. Exh. 1926-28
Melrose Avenue, Beeston, Notts. † N 4.

SQUIRRELL, Leonard Russell b. 1893
Watercolour painter, etcher and engraver. b. Ipswich. Studied Ipswich School of Art and Slade School (gold and silver medals and British Institute Scholarship in engraving 1915). A.R.E. 1917, R.E. 1919, R.I. 1931, A.R.W.S. 1935, R.W.S. 1941. Exh. 1913-40. Add: Ipswich, Suffolk. † AB 1, CON 1, FIN 89, GI 21, L 7, M 2, NEA 1, RA 51, RE 68, RHA 3, RI 68, RSA 7.

SRAWLEY, Langsford George b. 1905
Painter, illustrator, black and white artist and designer. Studied Birmingham Municipal School of Art (Louisa Ryland scholarship). Exh. 1925-37. Add: 35 Ombersley Road, Balsall Heath, Birmingham. † B 5.

SRIGLEY, W.H. Exh. 1913-28
Liverpool. † L 5.

STAACKMANN, H.M. Exh. 1888
† TOO 2.

STAATEN, Van see V

STABB, Charles T. Exh. 1899-1936
Landscape, portrait and figure painter. 28 Campden Hill Gardens, London. † G 1, GI 17, I 1, NEA 32, RHA 2.

STABB, Mrs. H. Sparke (Janetta) Exh. 1893-97
Watercolour landscape painter. Add: Liphook, Hants. † L 1, RA 2, RI 1.

STABELL, Harold Exh. 1899-1901
Landscape painter. London. †RA 1, RBA 2.

STABLE, Fanny Exh. 1880-97
Landscape painter. 152 Finborough Road, London. † B 11, RA 5, RBA 3, RI 2, ROI 3.

STABLER, Harold 1872-1945
Enameller, jeweller, silver worker, glazed sculptor and potter (inventor of "Pyrex") b. Levens, Westmorland. Instructor at Royal College of Art and Head of Art Dept., Sir John Cass Technical Institute. Married Pheobe S. q.v. Add: London. † GI 6, L 36, LS 2, NG 4, RA 11, RMS 1.

STABLER, Phoebe d. 1955
Sculptor. Studied Liverpool University and Royal College of Art (travelling scholarship). Married Harold S. q.v. A.R.M.S. 1911, R.M.S. 1913, S.W.A. 1922. Exh. from 1908. Add: London. † B 2, G 1, GI 40, I 2, L 52, NG 4, P 2, RA 23, RBA 2, RHA 1, RID 1, RMS 13, SWA 7.

STABLES, O.W. Exh. 1898-1919
New Brighton, Cheshire 1898; Tal-y-Cafn, Wales 1916. † L 17, RCA 3.

STABLES, T.G. Exh. 1884-86
Landscape painter. Lake Road, Ambleside. † D 1, L 3, RI 1, RSA 1.

STABLES, Theresa J. Exh. 1880-85
Landscape painter. Church Street, Lancaster. † RBA 4, SWA 5.

STACE, Mrs. Walter Exh. 1886
Landscape painter. 23 St. Phillips Road, Surbiton, Surrey. † SWA 1.

STACEY, Doris Marion Exh. 1918-36
Flower and figure painter and dry point artist. Studied Royal College of Art and R.A. Schools. Add: St. Peters, The Beeches, Carshalton, Surrey. † I 1, NEA 1, P 2, RA 5.

STACEY, Hugh Ex. 1923-27
Landscape painter. Netherfield, Notts. 1923; Gedling, Notts. 1926. † N 5.

STACEY, H.E. 1838-1915
Exh. 1890-1900. Add: Bristol. † B 3.

STACEY, Mary D. Exh. 1911
Landscape painter. † WG 31.

STACEY, Thomas Exh. 1890-91
28 Varna Road, Edgbaston, Birmingham. † B 2.

STACEY, Walter Sydney 1846-1929
Landscape painter in watercolour; figure painter in oil, decorative designer and illustrator. Studied R.A. School. R.B.A. 1881, R.O.I. 1883. Add: London 1880; New Milton, Hants. 1906; Tiverton, Devon 1911 and 1913; St. Buryan, Cornwall 1912; Newton Abbot, Devon 1915. † D 97, L 18, LS 9, M 1, NEA 1, RA 26, RBA 24, RI 13, ROI 6.

STACK, A.J.S. Exh. 1889
Mitfield, Redhill, Surrey. † RHA 1.

STACK, Blanche Exh. 1900-8
Dublin. † RA 3, RHA 18.

STACPOOLE, Frederick 1813-1907
Engraver. A.R.A. 1880. Add: 6 Theresa Terrace, Hammersmith Road, London. † RA 20.

STACPOOLE, Mary Constance Exh. 1887-1924
Portrait, figure and flower painter. London. † G 1, M 1, RA 7, RBA 1, RI 2, ROI 2, SWA 3.

STACQUET, Henri 1838-1906
Belgian artist. Exh. 1880-84. † GI 3.

STAFFORD, C.E. Exh. 1917
19A Marylebone Road, London. † LS 3.

STAFFORD, John Phillips Exh. 1886
Painter. 6 Tournay Road, Walham Green, London. † RA 1.

STAFFORD-BAKER, C. Exh. 1939
Watercolour landscape painter. 77 Thames Drive, Leigh-on-Sea, Essex. † RA 1.

STAFFORD-BAKER, Julius B. Exh. 1933-40
Coastal and landscape painter. Hockley, Essex 1933; Leigh-on-Sea, Essex 1935. † GI 1, RA 10, RBA 8, RI 7, ROI 1.

STAGG, H.W. Exh. 1912
46 Woodbury, The Avenue, Beckenham, Kent. † RA 2.

STAGG, Mrs. Jessie A. Exh. 1907-11
Sculptor. Atrincham, Cheshire 1907; Rusholme, Manchester 1910; Sunderland 1911. † L 2, LS 2, M 1.

STAGG, Miss V.D. Exh. 1906
111 Jermyn Street, London. † NG 1.

STAGG, William d. 1928
Watercolour landscape painter. Exh. 1923-24. Add: The Vicarage, Brislington, Bristol. † L 2.

STAHL, Mrs. G. Exh. 1891
21 Clarendon Road, College Park, Lewisham. † M 1.

STAINER, F. Exh. 1891
Bangor Terrace, Ash Lane, Pe y Barr, Birmingham. † B 1.

STAINFORTH, Martin F.* Exh. 1895-1931
Engraver and painter. London. † RA 12.

STAINTON, E.S. Exh. 1925
4 Nansen Road, Sparkhill, Birmingham. † B 1.

STAINTON, George* Exh. 1882-99
Marine and landscape painter. Birmingham. † B 40, L 3.

STAITE, Harriet Exh. 1895-1903
Landscape painter. Catford, London 1895; Southsea, Hants. 1903. † RA 1, RBA 1, ROI 2, SWA 1.

STAKHOWSKY, K. Exh. 1919
† I 4.

STALKER, Colin J. Exh. 1885-1925
Edinburgh. † RSA 6, RSW 2.

STALKER, le See L

STALLAERT, Joseph 1825-1903
Belgian artist. Exh. 1882-84. Add: 20 Rue des Chevaliers Ixelles, Brussels. † GI 2, RHA 2.

STAMMERS, Harry J. Exh. 1933-39
Landscape painter and stained glass artist. Add: 37 Coleraine Road, Blackheath, London. † RA 5.

STAMP, Ernest 1869-1942
Portrait painter and mezzotint engraver. b. Sowerby, Yorks. Studied under Herkomer at Bushey. A.R.E. 1894. Add: Bushey, Herts. 1892; Manchester 1895; Hampstead, London 1905. † L 6, M 1, RA 8.

STAMP, Winifred L. Exh. 1899-1911
Miniature portrait and figury painter. London. † RA 4, RMS 2.

STAMPA, George Loraine b. 1875
Illustrator and pen and ink artist. Studied Heatherleys c. 1892 and R.A. Schools 1895-1900. Exh. 1898-1909. Add: London. † RA 3, WG 104.

STAMPER, James William b. 1873
Landscape and still life painter. b. Birmingham. Studied Manchester School of Art. Exh. 1906-37. Add: Conway 1906; Manchester 1911 and 1923; Betws-y-Coed, 1922; Amlwch, Anglesey 1931. † B 2, L 4, M 2, RCA 112.

STAMPS, Walter, J. Exh. 1901-3
Landscape painter and teacher. London 1901; West Bromwich 1903. † B 3, RA 1.

STANBURY, Kathlene R. Exh. 1933
Chalk portrait artist. 90 West Hill, London. † RA 1.

STANDEN, Miss E.R. Exh. 1907
40 Courtfield Gardens, South Kensington, London. † RA 1.

STANDEN, Frances Exh. 1890-91
Fruit painter. Sutton in Ashfield, Notts. † N 2.

STANDEN, Miss Grace P. Exh. 1903-15
Lindfield, Sussex 1903; Romsey, Hants. 1915. † D 21.

STANDEN, R.S. Exh. 1893-1915
London 1893; Lindfield, Sussex 1903; Romsey, Hants. 1914. † D 103.

STANDING, Robert Exh. 1909-10
103 George Street, Cheetham Hill, Manchester. † L 3.

STANDISH, Albert E. Exh. 1929-32
Watercolour flower painter. 25 Alexandra Road, Swiss Cottage, London.

STANDRING, Arthur Exh. 1884-91
Landscape painter. Manchester. † M 3, RA 1.

STANFELD, W.A. Exh. 1894
Crompton, Eshott Hall, Shipley, Yorks. † L 1.

STANFIELD, Charles Exh. 1882-95
Landscape painter, Apperley Bridge, nr. Leeds 1882; Yeadon, nr. Leeds 1890; Ilkley, Yorks. 1895. † L 8, M 9, RA 2, ROI 1.

STANFIELD, Miss G. Exh. 1903-13
A.N.S.A. 1913-15. Lincoln Circus, The Park, Nottingham. † N 23.

STANFIELD, Marion Willis d. 1965
Sculptor and decorative worker in chromium plating. Studied Goldsmiths College and Paris. Assistant art lecturer Whitelands Training College, Putney. Add: Bickley, Kent 1922; London 1925. † GI 8, L 10, RA 2.

STANFORD, Guy D. Exh. 1933
Watercolour landscape painter. 10 Wilbraham Place, London. † RA 1.

STANGA, V. Exh. 1916
c/o A. Stiles and Sons, 617 Fulham Road, London. † GI 1.

STANHOPE, Miss G. Spencer Exh. 1886-1909
London 1886; Canon Hall, Barnsley 1896; Villa Nuti, Bellagarda, Florence, Italy 1908. † B 1, GI 2, L 7, M 1, NG 1.

STANHOPE, John Roddam Spencer* 1829-1908
Mythological, allegorical and fresco painter. Studied under G.F. Watts. R.I. 1883. Add: London 1880; Villa Nuti, Bellagarda, Florence, Italy 1882. † CAR 8, G 9, L 11, M 5, NG 10, RA 2, RI 6.

STANHOPE, Miss W.J. Spencer Exh. 1885-99
Sculptor. London. † G 1, NG 2, RBA 1.

STANIER, Henry Exh. 1884
Landscape, flower and historical genre painter. Lived in Birmingham. Was for a while Vice-Consul in Granada, Spain. Add: Granada, Spain. † B 1.

STANIER, May Exh. 1913-14
London. † LS 6.

STANILAND, Charles Joseph* 1838-1916
Genre and historical painter and illustrator. b. Kingston-upon-Hull. Studied Birmingham School of Art, Heatherleys, South Kensington Schools and R.A. Schools 1961. Contributed to "The Illustrated London News" and "The Graphic". A.R.I. 1875, R.I. 1879, R.O.I. 1883. Add: London 1880; Chingford, Essex 1893. † B 5, FIN 1, GI 1, L 13, M 9, RA 1, RI 26.

STANILAND, L.N. Exh. 1935
19 Vicarage Hill, Kingsteignton, South Devon. † RI 1.

STANLEY, Arthur Exh. 1891-1913
Landscape painter. A.N.S.A. 1908. Add: Beeston, Notts. 1891; Nottingham 1908. † L 1, N 9.

STANLEY, Miss A.L. Exh. 1885
143 Denmark Hill, London. † B 1.

STANLEY, Diana b. 1909
Landscape and animal painter. Studied Byam Shaw School of Art 1929-34. Exh. 1935-36. Add: 1 Radnor Place, London. † COO 2, RA 1.

STANLEY, Dora Exh. 1928
Pastel portrait artist. 20 Abercorn Place, St. Johns Wood, London. † RA 1.

STANLEY, Lady Dorothy 1855-1926
nee Tennant. Portrait and genre painter and illustrator. Studied Slade School and with Henner in Paris. Married the African explorer Sir Henry Stanley. R.E. 1881 only. Add: Richmond Terrace, Whitehall, London. † BG 1, D 3, FIN 1, G 19, L 33, M 4, NG 25, RA 9, RE 1, RHA 2, RID 1, ROI 2.

STANLEY, Miss E.M. Exh. 1882-85
Newstead, Hagley Road, Birmingham. † B 4.

STANLEY, Frank John Exh. 1921-32
Miniature portrait painter. A.R.M.S. 1922. Add: 56 Halesworth Road, London. † ALP 1, L 11, RA 7, RMS 44.

STANLEY, J. Exh. 1883-85
Nuneaton, 1883; London 1885. † B 5.

STANLEY, James H. Exh. 1906-14
Architect. Banstead Road, Purley, Surrey. † RA 5.

STANLEY, Kate Exh. 1880-96
Landscape painter. Sister of Maria S. q.v. Add: London. † GI 1, RBA 2, ROI 21, SWA 6.

STANLEY, Maria Exh. 1884-89
Watercolour painter. Sister of Kate S. q.v. Add: 116 Adelaide Road, London. † SWA 7.

STANLEY, Maud Exh. 1924-35
Landscape painter. Nottingham. † N 7.

STANLEY, Sara Exh. 1895-1902
Landscape painter. Hastings 1895; London 1900. † B 6, L 2, M 4, RA 2, RBA 1, ROI 4.

STANLEY, Sidney Walter 1890-1956
Mural painter, interior decorator, illustrator, toy designer and scale model maker. Studied Clapham Art School and Heatherleys. Add: London. † GI 1, I 1, L 2, RA 3, RI 3.

STANLEY, William Exh. 1880-91
Landscape painter. N.S.A. 1881. Add: Nottingham 1880; Beeston, Notts. 1885. † N 12.

STANLEY-CREEK, Braida b. 1910
Painter and mural decorator. Studied Farnham School of Art, Guildford School of Art and Slade School. Exh. 1930-40. Add: Farnham, Surrey 1930; London 1935; Rottingdean, Brighton, Sussex 1938; Mousehole, Cornwall 1940. † NEA 3, RA 14, RBA 5, RSA 1.

STANNARD, Alexander Molyneux 1878-1975
Landscape painter. Son of Henry J.S. q.v. Add: Bedford 1900; Wolverton, Bucks. 1901; Wellingborough, Northants. 1909; Biddenham, Bedford 1914. † D 1, RA 8, RBA 2, RI 1.

STANNARD, Emily* 1875-1907
Landscape painter. Daughter of Henry J.S.q.v. Add: Bedford 1896; Woburn Sands, Beds. 1904. † B 1, D 1, RA 7, RBA 3, RCA 1, RI 4.

STANNARD, Eloise Harriet* c.1838-1915
Still life painter. Eldest daughter of Alfred S. (1806-1889). S.W.A. 1880. Add: Norwich. † L 1, M 1, RA 1, ROI 2, SWA 28.

STANNARD, H.F.D. Exh. 1929
Black and white artist. The Elms, Daybrook, Nottingham. † N 1.

STANNARD, Henry J. 1844-1920
Landscape painter. Father of Alexander Molyneux, Emily, Harry Sylvester, Ivy and Lilian S. q.v. R.B.A. 1894. Add: Harpur Place, Bedford. † B 2, D 9, L 2, M 3, RA 15, RBA 182, RCA 3, RI 4.

STANNARD, Harry Sylvester 1870-1951
Landscape and garden painter. Studied South Kensington School of Art. Son of Henry J.S. q.v. and father of Theresa Sylvester S. q.v. R.B.A. 1896. Add: Bedford 1892 and 1921; St. Albans 1893; Flitwick, Beds. 1895; Buckden, Hunts. 1917. † AB 10, B 6, D 90, L 13, LS 4, M 8, NG 5, RA 35, RBA 70, RCA 1, RHA 1, RI 29.

STANNARD, Ivy 1881-1968
Mrs. Oswald Horn. Daughter of Henry J.S.q.v. Add: Harpur Place, Bedford 1908. † D 2, RA 2, RCA 3.

STANNARD, Lilian 1877-1944
Mrs. Silas. Landscape and garden painter. Daughter of Henry J.S. q.v. Add: Bedford 1898 and 1919; London 1910 and 1930; Lancing, Sussex 1918. † B 1, D 27, L 2, RA 27, RBA 1, RCA 1, RI 7, SWA 3.

STANNARD, Theresa Sylvester 1898-1947
Mrs. Dyer. Watercolour painter of gardens, flowers and cottages. b. Flitwick, Beds. Daughter of Harry Sylvester S. q.v. Add: Flitwick, Beds. 1910; Buckden, Hunts. 1911; Bedford 1923. † L 1, RA 2, RI 32, RMS 2, SWA 3, WG 55.

STANNUS, Antony Carey* Exh. 1880-1910
Marine, landscape and genre painter. London 1880 and 1900; Brighton 1897. † D 1, L 1, LS 5, RA 5, RBA 1, RHA 4.

STANNUS, Caroline Exh. 1880
Watercolour flower painter. 38 Upper Brook Street, London. † RBA 1.

STANNUS, Hugh Exh. 1886
Architect. 61 Larkhall Rise, Clapham, London. † RA 1.

STANNUS, L.G. Exh. 1912
23 Earls Court Square, London. † LS 1.

STANSBURY, Edith Exh. 1898-1906
London 1898; Ottery St. Mary, Devon 1905. † L 4, SWA 1.

STANSFIELD, Ellen Louisa Exh. 1902-35
Portrait painter and miniaturist. b. India. Add: Bedford 1902; London 1926; Boscombe, Hants. 1929; Bournemouth 1934. † L 7, RA 3, RI 10, SWA 2.

STANSFIELD, Miss F.M. Exh. 1919-23
Horbury, nr. Wakefield 1919; Wakefield 1923. † L 21.

STANSFIELD, H.H. Exh. 1911
Witnesham, Suffolk. † LS 3.

STANT, J. Lewis Exh. 1931-39
Landscape painter. Walsall 1931; St. Ives, Cornwall 1935; Birmingham 1936. † B 19, RBA 2, RCA 8, RHA 3, RSA 2.

STANTON, Clark* 1832-1894
Sculptor and painter. b. Birmingham. Curator. R.S.A. Life School, A.R.S.A. 1862, R.S.A. 1885. Add: 1 Ramsay Lane, Edinburgh. † B 2, GI 16, L 4, M 3, RSA 68, RSW 2.

STANTON, Ethel S.M. Exh. 1900-4
Toddington Vicarage, Winchcombe, Glos. † B 1, SWA 2.

STANTON, H.E. Exh. 1923
18 London Road, Newcastle, Staffs. † NEA 2.

STANTON, Horace Hale Exh. 1880-84
Watercolour landscape painter. Oxton, nr. Birkenhead 1880; New Brighton, Cheshire 1882. † D 1, L 6, RA 1.

STANTON, John G. Exh. 1883-86
1 Ramsay Lane, Edinburgh. † RSA 3.

STANTON, Rose Emily Exh. 1880-1905
Watercolour flower, animal, bird and fruit painter. Upfield, Stroud. Glos. † D 6, RA 16, RI 6.

STANTON, Sandys Exh. 1893-1911
Flower painter. Leicester. † B 1, N 4, RI 1, SWA 2.

STANTON, Stephen J.B. Exh. 1909-20
Architect. 47 Cavendish Road, Brondesbury, London. † RA 5.

STAPLEDON, May Exh. 1909
10 Banks Avenue, Meols, Cheshire. † L 1.

STAPLES, Frederick A. Exh. 1936-39
Miniature portrait painter. 114 Queen's Road, Finsbury Park, London. † RA 1, RMS 2.

STAPLES, John C. Exh. 1880
Landscape painter. Brighton, Sussex. † D 1.

STAPLES, Mary Ellen see EDWARDS

STAPLES, Owen b. 1866
Canadian artist. b. Somerset. Exh. 1937. † RSW 1.

STAPLES, Sir Robert Ponsonby 1853-1943
12th Bt. Portrait, genre and landscape painter. Studied Louvain Academy 1865-70 and Brussels Academy 1872-74. Visited Australia 1879-80. R.B.A. 1898. Add: London 1880; Knock, Belfast 1906; Cooktown, Co. Tyrone 1913. † B 6, G 13, GI 2, L 4, M 10, NEA 1, WG 14, P 15, RA 10, RBA 17, RHA 24, ROI 11.

STAPLETON, Mrs. George Exh. 1880-85
Painter. 4 Sumner Terrace, Onslow Square, London. † D 3, L 1, RHA 4, RI 1.

STAPPEN, van der see V

STARFORTH, John Exh. 1887
37 York Place, Edinburgh. † RSA 1.

STARFORTH, Robert M. Exh. 1897
37 York Place, Edinburgh. † RSA 1.

STARK, Mrs. A.J. (R. Isabella) Exh. 1899
Painter. Nutfield, Redhill, Surrey. † RI 1.

STARK, Arthur James* 1831-1902
Landscape and animal painter. Studied under his father James S. (1794-1859), under Edmund Bristow and at R.A. Schools. Add: London 1880; Redhill, Surrey 1887. † B 12, D 4, GI 1, L 1, M 3, RA 1, RBA 2, RHA 8, RI 4, ROI 3.

STARK, Mrs. Flora M. Exh. 1892-97
Figure and landscape painter. Married to Robert S. q.v. Add: Chagford, Devon 1892; Torquay, Devon 1893. † RA 2, RBA 2.

STARK, James Exh. 1933-37
Burngreen, Kilsyth. † L 1, RSA 1.

STARK, James D. Exh. 1915
6 East Savile Road, Edinburgh. † RSA 1.

STARK, Lizzie J.R. Exh. 1888
3 Northampton Villas, Seven Sisters Road, London. † GI 1.

STARK, Malcolm Exh 1880-92
167 St. Vincent Street, Glasgow. † GI 11, RSA 1.

STARK, Mina Exh. 1883
3 Northampton Villa, Seven Sisters Road, London. † GI 1.

STARK, Miss M.B. Exh. 1919-21
6 Warrender Park Crescent, Edinburgh. † RSA 2.

STARK, Philippa Exh. 1938
† P 2.

STARK, Robert 1853-1931
Sculptor, and painter. Studied South Kensington and Florence. Married Flora S. q.v. "Indian Rhonoceros" (1887) purchased by Chantrey Bequest 1892. Add: London 1883; Chagford, Devon 1889; Farnham, Surrey 1901; Liverpool 1916. † I 1, L 19, NEA 1, RA 16, RBA 1.

STARK, W.S. Exh. 1933-37
Woodstock Drive, Newlands, Glasgow. † GI 2, L 1.

STARKENBURGH, von see V

STARKEY, Annie Exh. 1902-14
80 Rathmines Road, Dublin. † RHA 15.

STARKEY, A.P. Exh. 1910
Pemberley Avenue, Bedford. † RA 1.

STARKEY, Frank Exh. 1928
The Sedges, Delamere Road, Kingsley, Cheshire. † RCA 1.

STARKEY, Sara Exh. 1887
Penrhyn House, Stanmore Road, Edgbaston, Birmingham. † B 1.

STARKEY, Winifred Exh. 1912-29
Miniature and landscape painter. Penmaen, Hampton Wick, Middlesex. † L 6, LS 9, RA 2.

STARKEY, W.H. Exh. 1882-1909
Birmingham. † B 31.

STARKEY, Mrs. W.H. Exh. 1883
Meadow Road, Edgbaston, Birmingham. † B 1.

STARKIE, Cecily Exh. 1923-26
Figure painter. 76 Gloucester Street, London. † NEA 1, RA 1.

STARKIE, Edyth see RACKHAM

STARLING, Albert Exh. 1880-1913
Portrait, marine and genre painter. Widmerpool, Grove Road, Sutton, Surrey 1880 and 1895; London 1886. † B 28, L 5, M 1, RA 16, RBA 7, RI 1, ROI 8.

STARLING, Dora Exh. 1898-1902
London. † GI 1, NG 2, RMS 5.

STARLING, Eric F. Exh. 1940
Architect. 3 Addiscombe Road, Croydon, Surrey. † RA 1.

STARLING, Elsie M. Exh. 1931-40
Wood engraver. Briar Close, Hosey Hill, Westerham, Kent. † RA 9, RED 1, RHA 11.

STARLING, Henry J. Exh. 1935-40
Etcher. 3 Carrow Hill, Norwich, Norfolk. † RA 3.

STARLING, Miss M. Exh. 1920
24 Malvern Road, Wallasey, Cheshire. † L 1.

STARLING, May Exh. 1901-2
Lynwood, Coleraine Road, Westcombe Park, Blackheath, London. † RBA 1, SWA 2.

STARLING, Marion A. Exh. 1883
Painter. Beresford Lodge, Brighton, Sussex. † RA 1.

STARLING, S.W. Exh. 1929-33
138 Yardley Wood Road, Moseley, Birmingham. † B 4.

STARMER, Walter Percival Exh. 1928-40
Mural painter and stained glass artist. b. Teignmouth. Studied Norwich School of Art and Birmingham School of Art. Add: Edgware, Middlesex 1928, Bushey, Herts. 1939. † RA 5. RBA 1.

STARR, Louisa 1845-1909
Mme. Canziani. Portrait and figure painter. Mother of Estella Canziani q.v. S.W.A. 1894. Add: London. † FIN 1, G 5, GI 1, L 17, M 7, NG 6, P 2, RA 44, SWA 20.

STARR, Sidney 1857-1925
Portrait, genre, landscape and decorative painter. b. Kingston-upon-Hull. N.E.A. 1886, R.B.A. 1886. Add: London 1880. Went to New York c.1890. † D 3, G 1, GI 1, GOU 12, L 5, M 4, NEA 11, RA 6, RBA 38, RI 1, ROI 3.

STATHAM, Edith Exh. 1897
33 Rectory Road, Crumpsall, Manchester. † M 1.

STATHAM, Henry Heathcote 1839-1924
Architect. Editor of "The Builder" 1883-1908. Add: London. † GI 4, RA 18.

STATHAM, Mildred Ellinor Exh. 1911 38
Embroiderer and handicraftsman. Studied South Kensington. Add: London 1911 and 1927; Sutton, Surrey 1924; Dorking Surrey 1928. † L 18, SWA 3.

STAVELEY, Amy D. Exh. 1900-16
Miniature portrait painter London. † D 4, L 2, RA 3, RMS 1, SWA 1.

STAYNES, George Exh. 1880
Catherine Villas, 9 Dame Agnes Street, Nottingham. † N 1.

STAYNES, Percy Angelo b. 1875
R.I. 1935, R.O.I. 1916. Exh. 1915-40. Add: Bedford Park, London. † GI 1, RI 16, ROI 39.

STAYNES, Miss R. Exh. 1915
Avenue House, Avenue Road, Leicester. † N 1.

STEAD, Ella M. Exh. 1894-95
Miniature painter. Red Barns, Formby, Lancs. † L 3, RA 1.

STEAD, Frederick b. 1863
Portrait, figure and landscape painter. b. Shipley, Yorks. Studied Shipley School of Art and Royal College of Art (travelling scholarship and gold and silver medals). Instructor of Life Drawing Bradford School of Art. Married May S. q.v. Exh. 1889-1930. Add: Shipley, Yorks. 1889; Bradford 1892. † B 1, L 10, M 1, P 1, RA 32.

STEAD, Leslie L. Exh. 1931
34 Thurslestone Road, London. † RBA 1.

STEAD, May Exh. 1900-34
nee Greening. Flower, landscape and miniature painter. b. Bradford. Studied Shipley School of Art and London. Art teacher, Bradford Girls Grammar School. Married Frederick S. q.v. Add: Shipley, Yorks. 1900; Bradford 1930. † L 2, RA 3, RI 1, RMS 1.

STEAD, Miss M. Cecil Exh. 1896-1901
Red Barns, Formby, Liverpool. † L 3, RMS 1.

STEAD, P.H. Exh. 1911-12
15 St. Julians Farm Road, West Norwood, London. † L 1 RA 1.

STEADMAN, J.T. Exh. 1884-1911
Figure, interior, landscape and coastal painter. Liverpool 1884; Wolverhampton 1903. † B 9, L 44, M 4, RBA 3, RCA 1.

STEAN, Maria J. Exh. 1902
† RMS 3.

STEANE, Howard N. Exh. 1889-91
43 St. Margaret's Road, Brockley, Kent. † D 5.

STEARN, Henrietta M. Exh. 1887
Strathmore Lodge, Bushhill Park, Enfield, Middlesex. † RHA 1.

STEAVENSON, C. Herbert Exh. 1893
Yorkshire. † D 1.

STEBBING, Mrs. E.P. Exh. 1910
c/o King and Co., 9 Pall Mall, London. † LS 3.

STECCHI, Fabio Exh. 1891
Medallionist. c/o Mrs. Le Poer Wynne, 85 Carlisle Mansions, Victoria Street, London. † RA 1.

STECHAN, Louis Exh. 1885-86
13 Elm Row, Edinburgh. † RSA 7.

STEDMAN, A.J. Exh. 1911-13
South Street, Farnham, Surrey 1911; London 1913. † RA 2.

STEEDMAN, A. Exh. 1900
11 Greenhill Gardens, Edinburgh. † GI 2.

STEEDMAN, Miss C.L. Exh. 1903
Ravenhough, Selkirk. † SWA 2.

STEEDMAN, Miss E.M. Exh. 1921-39
2 Heriot Row, Edinburgh. † GI 2, L 2, RSA 19, RSW 27.

STEEDMAN, Mary Exh. 1898
11 Greenhill Gardens, Edinburgh. † B 1.

STEEGMAN, Philip b. 1903
Figure and portrait painter and sculptor. Studied Slade School and Rome University. Exh. 1926-33. Add: London. † NEA 1, ROI 1.

STEEL, F.S. Exh. 1909
Landscape painter. 1 Rosemount Place, Perth. † RA 1.

STEEL, Geo. Hammond 1900-1960
Landscape painter. Studied Sheffield, Birmingham and London. Add: Sheffield. † B 3, GI 5, L 18, RA 10, RBA 1 RI 2.

STEEL, Helen Exh. 1888
66 South Portland Street, Glasgow. † GI 1.

STEEL, Mrs. H. Eadie Exh 1910-11
142 Cambridge Drive, Kelvinside, Glasgow. † GI 2.

STEEL, John Exh. 1902-35
Architect. Studied Glasgow School of Art and R.A. Schools. Add: Wishaw, N.B. † GI 2, RSA 2.

STEEL, John Sydney 1863-1932
Animal and sporting painter. b. Perth. Studied Slade School. Add: London 1886; Perth 1895. † G 3, GI 1, L 2, RA 6, RBA 9, RE 2, ROI 7, RSA 8.

STEEL, Kenneth b. 1906
Landscape painter, line engraver and designer. Studied Sheffield School of Art. R.B.A. 1935. Add: Sheffield. † BK 5, CON 51, FIN 39, L 3, RA 4, RBA 20, RHA 24.

STEEL, Hon. Mrs. Maud Exh. 1934
Portrait painter. 8 Cranley Place, London. † RA 1.

STEEL, Margaret R. Exh. 1901
3 Dowan Hill Terrace, Partick, Glasgow. † GI 1.

STEELE, Alice A. Exh. 1883
55 Albany Street, Edinburgh. † RSA 1.

STEELE, Miss E. Exh. 1919
96 Holland Road, London. † SWA 1.

STEELE. Elizabeth A. Exh. 1918-34
Portrait painter. London. † RA 12, RMS 2.

STEELE, Florence H. Exh. 1896-1918
Sculptor and metal worker. London. † L 6, NG 1, RA 34.

STEELE, Miss F.M. Exh. 1892
Painter. † FIN 1.

STEELE, Grace Exh. 1892-93
Polquhirter, New Cumnock, N.B. † GI 2.

STEELE, Louis J. Exh. 1880-86
Etcher. 101 Clarendon Road, Notting Hill, London. † DOW 2, RA 9.

STEELE, Mary b. 1880
Portrait and landscape painter. b. Oxford. Studied Ruskin School of Drawing, Oxford. Exh. 1929. Add: 6 Roden Terrace, Woodstock Road, Belfast. † RHA 1.

STEELE, S. Emily Exh. 1891
Enniskillen, Ireland. † D 2.

STEELINK, William* b. 1856
Dutch landscape painter. Exh. 1899-1925. Add: The Hague, Holland 1899; Voorburg, Holland 1925. † GI 1, RA 1, TOO 10.

STEELL, David George* 1856-1930
Animal and bird painter. Studied Edinburgh School of Art and R.S.A. Schools. Son of Gourlay S. q.v. A.R.SA. 1885. Add: Edinburgh. †, G 1, GI 15, L 4, M 6, RA 1, RSA 202.

STEELL, Gourlay 1819-1894
Animal painter. Studied Trustees Academy, Edinburgh and under R.S. Lauder. Appointed painter to the Highland and Agricultural Society, also appointed animal painter for Scotland by Queen Victoria and Curator National Gallery of Scotland. Brother of Sir John and father of David George and Goulay S. junr. q.v. A.R.S.A. 1846, R.S.A. 1859. Add: Edinburgh. † L 2, M 2, RA 1, RSA 53.

STEELL, Gourlay junr. Exh. 1880
Son of Gourlay S. q.v. Add: 25 Haddington Place, Edinburgh. † RSA 1.

STEELL, Sir John 1804-1891
Sculptor. b. Aberdeen. Studied Trustees Academy Edinburgh and Rome. Appointed sculptor in Ordinary for Scotland by Queen Victoria. Among his works is the seated figure of Sir Walter Scott in Princes Street Edinburgh. Brother of Gourlay S. q.v. R.S.A. 1829. Knighted 1876. Add: Edinburgh. † RSA 2.

STEEN, Annie Exh. 1890-1926
Birmingham. † B 17, L 33.

STEEN-HERTEL, Mrs. Exh. 1913-14
Copenhagen, Denmark. † LS 9.

STEEPLE, John* d. 1887
Landscape and coastal painter. London. † AG 6, B 5, D 2, DOW 3, FIN 1, RI 7, RSA 2.

STEEPLE, Miss R.M. Exh. 1933
Wolverton, The Mall, Newport, I.O.W. † B 1.

STEEPLES, Nellie Exh. 1922-26
Painter. Codnor, Derbys. † N 6.

STEER, Henry Reynolds* 1858-1928
Portrait, historical and literary painter, illustrator and lithographer. Studied Heatherleys 1879-86. R.I. 1884, R.M.S. 1896. Add: London 1880; Hinckley, Leics. 1891; Leicester 1897. † B 15, D 9, DOW 4, L 46, M 13, N 34, RA 4, RBA 23, RHA 1, RI 215, RMS 4, ROI 9.

STEER, Philip Wilson* 1860-1942
Landscape, coastal, portrait and genre painter. b. Birkenhead. Studied Gloucester School of Art, Ecole des Beaux Arts and Julians, Paris 1882. Teacher of painting Slade School from 1895. N.E.A. 1886. "Mrs. Raynes" purchased by Chantrey Bequest 1922, "Paddlers" purchased 1930 and "Bird-nesting, Ludlow" (1898) purchased 1937. Add; Gloucester 1883; Bournemouth 1884; London 1885. † AG 17, BA 12, BAR 202, CAR 32, CG 1, CHE 1, FIN 13, G 5, GI 18, GOU 224, I 6, L 44, LEI 2, LS 3, M 30, NEA 284, P 2, RA 6, RBA 4, RED 13, RHA 6, ROI 1, RSA 14, RSW 4, TOO 6.

STEERE, A.E. Exh. 1925-26
Landscape painter. 32 Warwick Road, Nottingham. † N 2.

STEFAN, Miss E. Exh. 1917-20
London. † SWA 8.

STEFANICZ, Z. Exh. 1905
23 Rue Boissonade, Paris. † L 1.

STEFANO, Novo Exh. 1892
3936 Sn. Pantaleone, Venice. † GI 1.

STEFFECK, C. Exh. 1883
Painter. † FIN 1.

STEFFELAAR, Nico Exh. 1885
Figure painter. c/o C. Robertson and Co., 99 Long Acre, London. † RBA 3.

STEGGLES, Harold Exh. 1930-38
Landscape painter. † AG 1, BK 1, LEF 65, M 2, TOO 1.

STEGGLES, Robert J. Exh. 1899-1903
Stained glass artist. London. † RA 4.

STEGGLES, W.J. Exh. 1930-38
Landscape painter. † AG 1, LEF 79, M 1, TOO 1.

STEICHEN, Edward J. b. 1879
American artist. Exh. 1905. Add: 291 Fifth Avenue, New York, U.S.A. † I 2.

STEIGER, de See D

STEIN, Miss C.M. Exh. 1913-14
Woodview, Blackrock, Co. Dublin. † RHA 6.

STEIN, Lillie Exh. 1900-27
Flower and miniature painter. London. † L 8, RA 2, RI 8, RMS 6.

STEIN, Nettie H. Exh. 1936-40
Edinburgh. † RSA 1, RSW 2.

STEINFORTH, Laura Exh. 1913-33
Portrait, fairytale and imaginary painter and decorative illustrator. Studied Liverpool School of Art. Add: Liverpool. † L 16.

STEINHAL, Mrs. Edith Exh. 1900-3
Ingleside, Knutsford, Cheshire. † M 4.

STEINHARDT, F.O. Exh. 1889
c/o Smith and Uppard, 77 Mortimer Street, London. † B 1.

STEINHEIL, Adolph Charles Edouard d. 1908
French artist. Exh. 1883. Add: 152 Rue de Vaugirard, Paris. † GI 2.

STEINLEN, Alexandre Theophile* 1859-1923
French etcher and illustrator. H.R.E. 1919. † BG 4, RE 10.

STEINMETZ, John Henry Exh. 1882-84
Painter. Heathfield, Bushey Heath, Herts. † D 1, RI 1.

STEINTHAL, Mrs. Bertha Noel Exh. 1925-33
Portrait, landscape and figure painter. 37 Alan Road, Withington, Manchester. † L 2, M 3.

STEINTHAL, Egbert Exh. 1889-1933
Manchester 1889; 37 Alan Road, Withington, Manchester 1914. † L 3, M 2.

STEINTHAL, Mrs. Emmeline P. Exh. 1890-1905
Sculptor. Ilkley, Yorks. † L 3, RA 4.

STEINTHAL, H. Exh. 1932
† L 2.

STEINTHAL, Maria Zimmern Exh. 1914
42 South Street, Durham. † LS 6.

STELFOX, Clifford Exh. 1915-16
Craigmore, Over, Cheshire. † L 2.

STELFOX, Dora Exh. 1893
Oakfield, Ormeau Park, Belfast. † RHA 1.

STELL, Florence Exh. 1925
Watercolour painter. Poplars, Marston Road, Sneinton Hill, Nottingham. † N 3.

STELLETZKY, D. Exh. 1910
15 Rue Boissonade, Paris. † L 1.

STELSON, Charles Walter Exh. 1899
c/o Mrs. Maurice Macmillan, 52 Cadogan Place, London. † NG 1.

STENHOUSE, Charles b. 1878
Landscape painter. b. Dundee. Studied Glasgow School of Art. Father of Kathleen S. q.v. Exh. 1906-37. Add: Glasgow. † GI 28, L 3, RSA 9.

STENHOUSE, J. Armstrong Exh. 1888-1901
Architect. London 1888; Bickley, Kent 1901. † RA 7.

STENHOUSE, Kathleen Exh. 1937
Daughter of Charles S. q.v. Add: 653 Shields Road, Glasgow. † GI 1.

STENHOUSE, May Exh. 1900-1
Lothian Vale, Holyrood, Edinburgh. † RSA 3.

STENLAKE, G. Exh. 1934-37
Felix House, Valletort Road, Stoke, Plymouth. † RMS 4.

STENNING, Amy Maud Exh. 1905-25
Watercolour portrait painter and miniaturist. Beckenham, Kent. † L 5, RA 7, RMS 1.

STENNING, Alexander Rose Exh. 1884-1906
Architect. 121 Cannon Street, London. † RA 5.

STENNING, Kathleen Exh. 1931
Landscape painter. 13 Portland Road, Holland Park, London. † RA 1.

STEPHEN, Agnes M. Exh. 1932-38
Invergare, Rhu, Dumbartonshire. † GI 5, RSA 1.

STEPHEN, Eleanor Exh. 1905-7
London. † GI 2, L 3, RA 1.

STEPHEN, Stephen D. Exh. 1935-38
Sculptor. 8 Hesketh Road, Southport, Lancs. † RA 3.

STEPHEN, T. Exh. 1920-22
6 Hillside Place, Springburn, Glasgow. † GI 4, RSA 1.

STEPHEN, Vanessa See BELL

STEPHENS, A.G. Exh. 1923-28
Figure and portrait painter. Elm Hill, Barrowby Road, Grantham, Lincs. † N 8.

STEPHENS, Charles William Exh. 1886
Architect. 47 Hans Place, London. † RA 2.

STEPHENS, Daisy B. Exh. 1903
Flower painter. 85 Ridge Road, Stroud Green, London. † RA 1.

STEPHENS, Miss E.B. Exh. 1909-16
Kingsettle, Paignton, South Devon. † L 3.

STEPHENS, Edward Bowring 1815-1882
Sculptor. b. Exeter. Studied R.A Schools 1836 and 1842. Visited Italy 1839-41. A.R.A. 1864. Add: 110 Buckingham Palace Road, London. † RA 4.

STEPHENS, Emily H. Exh. 1880-1910
Landscape painter. London 1880 and 1903; Bournemouth 1891; Richmond, Surrey 1898. † B 6, G 3, M 1, NEA 2, NG 8, SWA 3.

STEPHENS, Elizabeth L. Exh. 1906-8
18 Nassau Street, Dublin. † RHA 6.

STEPHENS, E.W.J. Exh. 1911
6 Franklin Road, Gillingham, Kent. † B 1, RA 1.

STEPHENS, G. Exh. 1930
Landscape painter. 27 Fitzwilliam Square, Dublin. † RHA 1.

STEPHENS, Mrs. George Exh. 1924
Painter. † WG 40.

STEPHENS, H. Channing Exh. 1898-1917
Woodthorpe, Purley, Surrey. † P 1, ROI 1.

STEPHENS, Helen E. Exh. 1892
Portrait painter. 21 Woburn Place, Russell Square, London. † RBA 1.

STEPHENS, Jessica Walker Exh. 1904-32
nee Walker. Painter, critic and writer. b. Arizona, U.S.A. Studied Liverpool School of Art (travelling scholarship to Italy), Paris and Florence. Correspondent for "Studio". Add: Liverpool. † L 23, LS 12, M 1, RCA 1.

STEPHENS, Miss L. Exh. 1896-1905
Studio, 15 Leinster Street, Dublin. † RHA 19.

STEPHENS, Lettice Exh. 1890-92
Figure and landscape painter. Tyringham, Beckenham, Kent. † RBA 2.

STEPHENS, Olive Bertha Exh. 1910-27
Watercolour painter, etcher and teacher. Studied Queens Road School of Art, Bristol, Central School of Arts and Crafts, London. Add: Bristol. † L 12, RA 4, RCA 3, RHA 2.

STEPHENS, Violet M. Exh. 1922-23
Badgeworth Court, nr. Cheltenham, Glos. † L 1, SWA 1.

STEPHENSON, Dorothy Exh. 1910
Newburgh, N.B. † L 3.

STEPHENSON, David R. Exh. 1919
Still life painter. 70 Eltham Road, Lee Green, London. † RA 1.

STEPHENSON, George Exh. 1882-85
R.P.E. 1881-88. Add: 12 Waterloo Street, Glasgow. † L 1, RE 6.

STEPHENSON, George Exh. 1939
Sculptor. London. † RA 1.

STEPHENSON, G. Terrance Exh. 1906-14
Landscape painter. Pont Aven, Finistere, France and London 1906; Betchworth, Surrey 1914. † B 1, GI 3, L 1, NEA 2, RA 4, RHA 1, RI 2, RSA 1.

STEPHENSON, Henry Exh. 1889
25 New Street, Huddersfield. † L 1.

STEPHENSON, Isabel H. Exh. 1883-91
Flower painter. London. † B 5, GI 11, L 1, M 1, RBA 6, RHA 1, ROI 1, SWA 5.

STEPHENSON, James 1828-1886
Engraver. 29 Dartmouth Park Road, London. † RA 1.

STEPHENSON, John Cecil 1889-1965
Painter, gold and silversmith and enamel worker. Studied Leeds School of Art, Royal College of Art and Slade School. Exh. 1934-39. † LEF 5, LEI 2.

STEPHENSON, Miss L. Exh. 1893
29 Morehampton Road, Dublin. † RHA 2.

STEPHENSON, Margaret E. Exh. 1904-14
Shalford, Surrey 1904; Guildford, Surrey 1914. † B 3, L 2.

STEPHENSON, Mrs. Marie E. Exh. 1934-39
Flower and landscape painter. 20 Courtfield Gardens, London. † P 2, RA 3, ROI 5, SWA 1.

STEPHENSON, Norman Exh. 1923-24
42 Teviot Street, Poplar, London. † RI 1, ROI 1.

STEPHENSON, Philippa Anna Frederica Exh. 1896-1937
Mrs. Theodore S. nee Watson. Watercolour landscape painter. Travelled widely. Add: Fermoy 1896; Warley, Essex 1899; London 1913. † ALP 105, COO 2, D 4, RA 6, SWA 1, WG 71.

STEPHENSON, T.A. Exh. 1922
4 Treford Road, Aberystwyth, Wales. † B 1.

STEPHENSON, T.H. Exh. 1910-12
Mount Cottage, Coniston, Lancs. † LS 6, RA 1.

STEPHENSON, Willie Exh. 1893-1938
Landscape painter. Studied Huddersfield Technical College. Add: Huddersfield 1893; Deganwy, Llandudno 1896; Conway 1899; Rhos on Sea 1912; Wem, Salop 1933. † B 2, L 77, M 1, RA 11, RCA 246, RI 2.

STERLING, Frances Exh. 1882-99
Figure painter. 18 Sheffield Terrace, Kensington, London. † L 1, RA 4.

STERLING, H. Exh. 1881-82
The Crag, Falmouth, Cornwall. † D 4.

STERLING, Mrs. John L. Exh. 1893
26 Albion Crescent, Dowanhill, Glasgow. † GI 2.

STERN, Professor Ernest Exh. 1938-39
Painter and stage designer. † NEA 4, RED 5.

STERN, Florence Exh. 1902-23
Birmingham. † B 6, L 48.

STERN, Irma* Exh. 1937
Portrait, figure and flower painter of African and Eastern subjects. † COO 60.

STERN, Laura Exh. 1914-27
Upton Manor, Birkenhead, Cheshire. † L 2.

STERN, Susie Exh. 1936
Still life painter. 55 Queen's Road, London. † RA 1.

STERN, Sophia T. Exh. 1894-1906
Mrs. S.T. Gaynor. Portrait and figure painter. 5 Clifton Road, Brighton, Sussex. † L 2, P 4, RA 3, SWA 1.

STERNBERG, Frank Exh. 1881-1904
Painter and engraver. A.R.E. 1891, R.E. 1892. Add: Leeds 1881; Bushey, Herts. 1887; London 1904. † FIN 3, L 2, RA 11, RE 1, RSA 3.

STERNBERG, Sylvia Exh. 1923
† G 1.

STERNDALE, O.J. Exh. 1881
Landscape painter. 10 Berkeley Row, Tunbridge Wells, Kent. † RBA 1.

STERNE, Maurice* 1878-1957
Painter and sculptor. Studied National Academy of Design, New York, Paris and Italy. Exh. 1925. † CHE 2.

STERNER, Albert 1863-1946
American painter and etcher. b. London. Exh. 1905-30. Add: New York 1905. † FIN 19, I 1.

STERRY, Eva Exh. 1930-40
Llandudno, Wales. † RCA 13.

STERRY, Eleanor S. Exh. 1897-1910
Miniature portrait painter. Croydon, Surrey. † RA 11, RMS 2.

STERRY, Ida S. Exh. 1892-97
Landscape painter. 3 Bedford Place, Croydon, Surrey. † RBA 1, RI 1.

STETTEN, von See V

STEUART, Alice M. Gow Exh. 1886-1906
Painter and etcher. London 1886 and 1901; Paris 1898; Hawkhurst, Kent 1900. † B 2, RA 2, SWA 6.

STEUART, James Exh. 1897-1900
Landscape painter. 52 Northumberland Street, Edinburgh. † RSA 7, RSW 1.

STEUART, Kathleen Exh. 1919
† I 2.

STEVEN, Helen M. Exh. 1888-91
34 Berkeley Terrace, Glasgow. † GI 4, RSA 1.

STEVEN, Jane Exh. 1893
44 Granby Terrace, Hillhead, Glasgow. † GI 1.

STEVEN, Maria G. Exh. 1886-91
Edinburgh. † RSA 2.

STEVENS, Albert Exh. 1923
The Manse Studio, Malvern Wells, Worcs. † L 2.

STEVENS, Albert Exh. 1880-1907
Landscape painter and watercolourist. Married Mary S. q.v. Add: London. † AG 16, B 19, D 82, G 2, GI 8, L 22, LEI 37, M 12, RA 9, RBA 38, RE 1, RHA 31, RI 9, ROI 3, RSA 2.

STEVENS, Alfred* 1828-1906
Belgian painter. Grand Officer of the Order of Leopold of Belgium, Commander of the Legion of Honour etc. R.B.A. 1887. Add: Paris. † P 2, RBA 5.

STEVENS, Agnes D. Exh. 1903-21
Liverpool. † L 16.

STEVENS, Albert G. Exh. 1903-22
Figure painter. Barnard Castle, Durham 1903; Whitby, Yorks. 1906. † I 1, L 3, RA 9, RI 4.

STEVENS, Christopher T. Exh. 1910-11
Newland House, Old Town, Eastbourne. † LS 5.

STEVENS, Dorothy Exh. 1910-13
Figure and landscape painter. London. † NEA 7.

STEVENS, Miss D.M. Exh. 1935-40
Dalehead, Stocksfield, Northumberland. † RBA 2, RI 1, SWA 3.

STEVENS, Frederick W. Exh. 1880
Architect. Cumballa Hill, Bombay. † RA 1.

STEVENS, Geoffrey Howard b. 1899
Painter, engraver, and illustrator. Studied Chelsea School of Art and Goldsmiths College. R.B.A. 1936. Exh. 1929-40. Add: Broxbourne, Herts. 1929; Maes-y-pwll, New Quay, Cardiganshire. † NEA 1, RBA 11, RSA 3.

STEVENS, Harold Exh. 1902-4
25 High Park Street, Liverpool. † L 2.

STEVENS, Henry P. Exh. 1919-37
Watercolour landscape painter. Bickley, Kent 1919; Croydon, Surrey 1930. † G 3, RA 1, RED 2, RI 1.

STEVENS, Joane Exh. 1918
White House, Eynsham, Oxon. † LS 3.

STEVENS, Joseph Herbert b. 1847
Landscape painter. Exh. 1882-1930. Add: Liverpool. † L 59, RA 2.

STEVENS, Kate Exh. 1891-98
Flower painter. Osmaston Road, Derby. † L 1, RA 4.

STEVENS, Miss K.B. Exh. 1891
Limetree House, Macclesfield, Cheshire. † M 3.

STEVENS, Mary Exh. 1886-1924
Flower and bird painter. Married Albert S. q.v. London. † B 2, D 48, GI 1, L 11, LEI 64, M 10, RA 5, RBA 1, RHA 4, RI 1, SWA 11.

STEVENS, Miss M.J. Exh. 1925
The Nunnery, Penryn, Cornwall. † B 1.

STEVENS, Miss M.V. Exh. 1913
12 Stanley Gardens, Cricklewood, London. † RA 1.

STEVENS, Susanna Exh. 1898
5 Loudon Road, London. † NG 1.

STEVENS, Thomas Exh. 1891-93
Landscape painter. Weston Green, Thames Ditton. † RA 1, RBA 1, RI 1.

STEVENS, T.G. Exh. 1928-34
8 Upper Wimpole Street, London. † RI 6.

STEVENS, Vera Exh. 1934-37
Landscape painter. 73 Sutton Court Road, Chiswick, London. † RA 1, ROI 2.

STEVENS, W.C. Exh. 1895-1903
London 1895; Shipley, Yorks. 1900. † L 1, M 4, NG 1, RBA 1.

STEVENS, W.H. Exh. 1921
Portrait painter. 30 Sitwell Street, Derby. † N 1.

STEVENS, W.K. Exh. 1881-1908
Figure and landscape painter. 336 Clapham Road, London. † B 18, D 8, L 11, M 3, RA 10, RBA 8, RI 7, ROI 1.

STEVENS, Walter Rupert Exh. 1883-93
Landscape painter. London. † D 61, FIN 1, GI 11, L 2, RA 5, RBA 12, RHA 7, RI 4, ROI 4.

STEVENSON, Ada Exh. 1893-1900
The Manse, Rutherglen, N.B. † GI 4.

STEVENSON, A.H. Exh. 1940
3 Chivelston, Parkside, London. † RBA 2.

STEVENSON, Christina R. Exh. 1887-88
Wardend, Milliken Park, Glasgow. † GI 2.

STEVENSON, David Watson 1842-1904
Sculptor. Studied under William Brodie and at R.S.A. Schools. Brother of William Grant S. q.v. A.R.S.A. 1877, R.S.A. 1886. Add: Edinburgh. † GI 26, L 6, NG 7, RA 9, RHA 2, RSA 106.

STEVENSON, E.A. Exh. 1911
16 Delamare Terrace, London. † LS 3.

STEVENSON, E.L. Exh. 1914-21
Glasgow. † L 5.

STEVENSON, Effie M. Exh. 1929-31
Stained glass artist. 70a Campden Street, London. † RA 5.

STEVENSON, F. Exh. 1885
Rosewood Villa, Crosshill, Glasgow. † RSA 1.

STEVENSON, F.G. Exh. 1910
10 Kohat Road, Wimbledon, London. † L 1.

STEVENSON, George Exh. 1881
Landscape painter. c/o Mr. Kiddiers, 25 Sneinton Street, Nottingham. † N 1.

STEVENSON, George Exh. 1919
Birmingham. † RE 2.

STEVENSON, G.C. Exh. 1919-37
Edinburgh 1919; Hamilton 1932; Airdrie 1934. † RSA 8, RSW 1.

STEVENSON, George H. Exh. 1901
Architect. Newland, Northampton. † RA 1.

STEVENSON, Miss G.M. Exh. 1899
Holmden, Burns Street, Nottingham. † N 1.

STEVENSON, George V. Exh. 1940
36 Woodlands Drive, Glasgow. † GI 2, RSA 1.

STEVENSON, Helen G. Exh. 1923-35
Colour woodcut artist. Studied Edinburgh College of Art 1923. Add: Edinburgh. † BA 6, GI 15, L 10, RSA 14.

STEVENSON, H.P. Exh. 1883
57 Chepstow Place, Pembridge Square, London. † L 1.

STEVENSON, Ida Exh. 1891
Landscape painter. Spean House, Broadhurst Gardens, West Hampstead, London. † RBA 1.

STEVENSON, Mrs. J. Exh. 1886-1937
Edinburgh. † GI 31, RSA 47, RSW 1.

STEVENSON, John junr. Exh. 1940
4 Gray Street, Glasgow. † GI 1.

STEVENSON, James Alexander 1881-1937
Sculptor. b. Chester. Studied Royal College of Art (travelling scholarship) and R.A. Schools. (Landseer scholarship). Signs work "Myrander Sc." Add: London. † D 1, GI 3, I 1, L 3, RA 65, RMS 1, RSA 1.

STEVENSON, John James Exh. 1880-1906
Architect. London. † GI 7, RA 25, RSA 1.

STEVENSON, Patric b. 1909
Painter. b. Wadhurst, Sussex. Studied Belfast School of Art 1926-28, and Slade School. Exh. 1938-40. Add: The Deanery, Waterford 1938; Dublin 1940. † RHA 3.

STEVENSON, Robert Alan Mowbray 1847-1900
Landscape painter and critic. Studied Edinburgh, Antwerp and Paris. Professor of Fine Art Liverpool University College 1880-93 and Art Critic to "Pall Mall Gazette" 1893-1900. Add: London. † M 1, RA 4, RBA 1, ROI 3, RSA 1.

STEVENSON, Richard Macaulay* 1854-1952
Landscape painter. R.S.W. 1906 (struck off 1913). Add: Glasgow 1881 and 1887; Fairlie, Ayrshire 1885; Milngavie 1897, 1915 and 1926; Montreuil sur Mer, France 1913 and 1924; Kirkcudbright 1932. † B 1, BRU 30, GI 75, I 3, L 14, M 3, RA 2, RSA 17, RSW 1.

STEVENSON, Mrs. R. Macaulay Exh. 1896-1900
Glasgow 1896; Robinsfield by Milngavie 1897. † GI 6.

STEVENSON, Stanmore Dean Exh. 1903-4
Robinsfield by Milngavie, Glasgow. † GI 2.

STEVENSON, Mrs. Stanmore Dean Exh. 1905-30
Robinsfield by Milngavie, Glasgow. † GI 11.

STEVENSON, Walter Exh. 1880-83
Figure, portrait and landscape painter. London 1880; Iver Heath, Bucks. 1881. † M 1, RA 2, RBA 3.

STEVENSON, William Exh. 1882-1900
Edinburgh 1882; Leith 1888. † GI 4, RSA 18.

STEVENSON, William Grant 1849-1919
Sculptor and animal painter. Studied Royal Institution Edinburgh and R.S.A. Life School. Brother of David Watson S. q.v. A.R.S.A. 1885, R.S.A. 1896. Add: Edinburgh. † GI 66, L 3, M 1, RA 7, RBA 1, RHA 2, RSA 121, RSW 9.

STEVENSON, W.L. b. 1911
Painter. b. Liverpool. Exh. 1930-32. † L 2.

STEWARD, H.S.R. Exh. 1881
Painter. 24 Gt. Russell Street, London. † G 2.

STEWART, Mrs. A. Exh. 1887
6 Percy Street, Paisley Road, Glasgow. † GI 1.

STEWART, Alexander Exh. 1897-1938
Glasgow 1897; Cardonald, N.B. 1917; Bucklyvie 1923; Paisley 1930. † GI 21.

STEWART, Allan 1865-1951
Landscape, figure and portrait painter and illustrator. Studied Edinburgh Institution and R.S.A. Schools (Maclaine-Walters medal, Stuart prize and Chalmers prize), Paris and Spain. On staff of "Illustrated London News". Add: Edinburgh 1888; London 1896. † CON 2, FIN 1, GI 8, L 6, M 5, RA 9, RSA 27, RSW 1.

STEWART, Amy Exh. 1889-1901
Painter. London and Edinburgh. † GI 2, L 1, RA 3, RBA 3, RSA 9, RSW 1.

STEWART, Arthur Exh. 1899-1937
Landscape painter. R.B.A. 1900. London. † L 1, LS 6, RBA 138, ROI 1.

STEWART, Mrs. Arthur
See LLOYD, Geraldine

STEWART, Amy Eleanor Exh. 1922-29
nee Boal. Metal worker. b. Halifax. Studied Leeds School of Art. Collaborated with her son Kenneth and husband Tom S. q.v. Add: Northwich, Cheshire 1922; Hartford, Cheshire 1925. † L 87.

STEWART, Alice M. Exh. 1899
164 Sloane Street, London. † SWA 3.

STEWART, B. Exh. 1897
Balshagray House, Partick, Glasgow. † GI 1.

STEWART, Col. B.H. Shaw Exh. 1928-38
Speanbridge, Inverness-shire 1928; Glasgow 1938. † GI 6, RSA 1, RSW 1.

STEWART, Barnett M. Exh. 1899
67 Ashburnham Road, Bedford. † D 3.

STEWART, Miss Cumbrae Exh. 1923-36
Watercolour painter and pastel artist. Studied at Melbourne National Gallery. Travelled in Europe. Add: Melbourne, Australia 1923; London 1924. † BA 184, GI 3, L 1, RA 4, ROI 3, SWA 5, WG 111.

STEWART, Charles Edward* Exh. 1887-1938
Painter. b. Glasgow. Studied R.A. Schools and Julians, Paris. Add: Glasgow 1887; London 1890 and 1892; Dunning, Perthshire 1891; Little Kimble, Bucks. 1922. † FIN 2, GI 19, L 2, M 7, NG 12, RA 37, RHA 2, ROI 3, RSA 3.

STEWART, D. Gordon Exh. 1936-39
Dundee. † RSA 5.

STEWART, Dora M. Exh. 1882-86
Watercolour flower painter. 44 West Cromwell Road, London. † B 1, L 1, M 1, RBA 5, RI 5, SWA 4.

STEWART, Ethel d. 1924
Etcher. Hon. Ret. A.R.E. 1906. Add: Bebington 1904; Huntspill, nr. Highbridge, Somerset 1911. † GI 1, L 22, RA 3. RE 33, RSA 1.

STEWART, Eunice Exh. 1884
Watercolour painter. 44 Holland Street, Kensington, London. † RBA 1.

STEWART, Elizabeth D. Exh. 1907
10 Salisbury Road, Edinburgh. † RSA 2.

STEWART, Edith F. Exh. 1926-31
Burley, Hants. 1926; Brockenhurst, Hants. 1931. † L 5.

STEWART, Elizabeth M. Exh. 1910-14
10 Arthur Street, Belfast. † RHA 12.

STEWART, Florence Exh. 1884-86
Flower painter. London. † G 2, RA 1.

STEWART, F. Craik Exh. 1923-31
Etcher. Cathcart, Glasgow 1923; Blackhall, Midlothian 1926. † GI 17, L 1, RSA 3.

STEWART, Frances E. Exh. 1939-40
41 Orleans Avenue, Glasgow. † GI 1, RSA 2.

STEWART, George Exh. 1880-85
Landscape painter. 180 Marylebone Road, London. † RA 1, RBA 3.

STEWART, George A. Exh. 1891-1900
Eastbourne. † B 2.

STEWART, Gilbert P. Exh. 1925-39
Landscape painter. Sale, Manchester 1925; Brooklands, Cheshire 1929. † GI 4, L 11, RA 8.

STEWART, Helen Exh. 1899-1938
Landscape and miniature painter. Bushey, Herts. 1899 and 1917; London 1910. † B 2, D 2, GI 3, L 11, RA 15, RI 2, SWA 2.

STEWART, Henry b. 1897
Watercolour painter and etcher. Exh. 1923-37. Add: Glasgow 1923; Bridge of Weir 1927. † GI 2, L 2, RSA 2, RSW 3.

STEWART, Hilda Joyce See POCOCK

STEWART, Miss H.M. Exh. 1924
132 Newport Road, Middlesborough. † L 1.

STEWART, Ian Exh. 1923-35
Portrait, flower and still life painter. Newlands, Glasgow 1923; Whitley Bay, Northumberland 1931; London 1935. † GI 4, L 1, RA 3, RSA 1.

STEWART, Isabel Exh. 1917-18
49 Polwarth Gardens, Hyndland, Glasgow. † GI 1, RSA 1.

STEWART, Ida Strother Exh. 1919-25
nee Taylor. Add: Newcastle on Tyne 1919; London 1925. † RI 1, SWA 2.

STEWART, John Exh. 1884-1901
Greenock and Kilmalcolm, N.B. † GI 9, RSA 2.

STEWART, Mrs. John Exh. 1896-1908
12 Garscube Terrace, Murrayfield, N.B. † RSA 4.

STEWART, J.A. Exh. 1883-93
Dundee 1883 and 1887; Edinburgh 1886. † GI 1, RSA 10.

STEWART, J.B. Exh. 1889
Architect. Glasgow. † GI 1.

STEWART, Janie B. Exh. 1893
Craigard, Pollokshields. † GI 1.

STEWART, Mrs. Jane Gertrude Exh. 1891-1908
Twynholm, Kirkcudbright, 1891; Edinburgh 1907. † GI 1, L 1, RSA 3.

STEWART, James Lawson* Exh. 1883-1905
Figure and landscape painter. London. † L 1, P 1, RA 3, RBA 2, RI 3, ROI 1.

STEWART, Julius L.* 1855-1920
American painter. Exh. 1882-85. Died in Paris. † TOO 4.

STEWART, J. Malcolm Exh. 1880-97
Landscape and coastal painter. Glasgow 1880 and 1897; London 1883. † GI 5, RA 1, RBA 1, RSA 8.

STEWART, J. Oswald Exh. 1880-85
Fordyce Castle, Portsoy 1880; Edinburgh 1885. † RSA 13.

STEWART, J. Smith Exh. 1938
53 Holehouse Road, Kilmarnock. † GI 1.

STEWART, James Scott Exh. 1880-1919
Glasgow. † GI 1, L 1, RSA 6, RSW 1.

STEWART, J. Tytler Exh. 1905
Craigend, Cardross, N.B. † GI 1.

STEWART, Katherine Exh. 1887-1917
Landscape and portrait painter and miniaturist. London. † L 2, M 1, NG 3, P 3, RA 19, RBA 4, RMS 1.

STEWART, Kenneth Exh. 1923
Collaborated with his parents Amy and Tom S. q.v. Add: 28 The Crescent, Northwich, Cheshire. † L 9.

STEWART, M. Exh. 1897
The School House, Roseneath, N.B. † GI 1.

STEWART, Miss M. Exh. 1923
31 Flanders Road, Bedford Park, London. † L 9.

STEWART, Marjorie Exh. 1936
166 Cromwell Road, London. † SWA 1.

STEWART, Mrs. Mary Exh. 1888-1907
Miniature portrait painter. London. † RA 10.

STEWART, Mary Exh. 1910-35
Miniature painter. b. Sandal, nr. Wakefield. Studied under Gilbert Foster, Stanhope Forbes and Alfred Praga. Add: London 1913 and 1935; Harrogate, Yorks. 1910 and 1918; Brighton 1914; Bournemouth 1923. † LS 3, RI 29, SWA 5.

STEWART, Marguerite F. Exh. 1926-35
Woodcut artist. Bistern Lodge, Burley, Hants. † COO 4, L 8.

STEWART, Maggie P. Exh. 1893-98
Kelvindale, Maryhill, Glasgow. † GI 4, RSW 1.

STEWART, Minnie R. Exh. 1888-1918
Glasgow. † GI 9.

STEWART, Miss M.W. Exh. 1915-28
Waterloo, Liverpool 1915; Middlesborough 1928. † L 3.

STEWART, Nellie Exh. 1900-35
Landscape and garden painter. Kirkaldy, N.B. 1900; Edinburgh 1923. † GI 2, L 1, RSA 2, RSW 10.

STEWART, Nina Exh. 1894
218 The Grove, Hammersmith, London. † RBA 1.

STEWART, R. Exh. 1900
Coastal painter. 29 Maddox Street, London. † RA 1.

STEWART, R.H. Exh. 1910
46 Gunter Grove, Chelsea, London. † RSA 1.

STEWART, R. Lees Exh. 1906-16
Glasgow. † GI 5.

STEWART, Robert Wright Exh. 1905-40
Painter and etcher. Studied Edinburgh School of Art, London and Paris. A.R.E. 1911. Add: Edinburgh 1905; London 1906. † ALP 1, CHE 2, GI 6, I 8, L 12, P 6, RA 21, RE 31, ROI 3, RSA 5.

STEWART, Sara Exh. 1884
7 Loudoun Terrace, Kelvinside, Glasgow. † GI 2, RSA 1.

STEWART, Sydney B. Exh. 1938
128 Queen's Street, Peterhead. † RSA 1.

STEWART, Susan C. Exh. 1886-1901
Greenock 1886; Skelmorlie 1894. † RSA 7.

STEWART, Thomas Exh. 1890
45 Brougham Street, Greenock, N.B. † GI 1.

STEWART, Tom Exh. 1922-29
Metalworker. b. Leeds. Studied Leeds University. Collaborated with his wife Amy Eleanor and son Kenneth S. q.v. Add: Northwich, Cheshire 1922; Hartford, Cheshire 1925. † L 80.

STEWART, W. Exh. 1890
Urban landscape painter. 5 Sherwin Street, Nottingham. † N 2.

STEWART, William Exh. 1880-94
Glasgow 1880 and 1887; Girvan 1882; Greenock 1888. † B 1, GI 19, L 1, RSA 11.

STEWART, William Exh. 1909
Architect. 4/5 Aldgate High Street, London. † RA 1.

STEWART, William b. 1886
Painter, illustrator and theatrical designer. Studied Lambeth School of Art. R.B.A. 1926. Exh. 1912-26. Add: Paisley 1912; London 1922. † GI 8, L 3, RA 1, RBA 4, RSA 2.

STEWART, William A. b. 1882
Painter. b. Ilkley, Yorks. Visited the Middle East. Exh. 1907-38. Add: The Loft Arts Club, Bradford 1907; Bedford 1938. † L 6, LS 3, RA 1.

STEWART, Wood E. Exh. 1885
44 Holland Street, Kensington, London. † GI 1.

STEWART-JONES, Elizabeth E. Exh. 1934-38
Landscape painter. London. † NEA 1, P 1, RA 1, RBA 1, ROI 2, SWA 3.

STEYN, Stella Exh. 1927-30
Landscape and figure painter. Metropolitan School of Art, Dublin 1927; Dublin 1928. † M 1, NEA 2, RHA 19.

STICKLAND, Elizabeth Exh. 1935
Figure painter. 2 Hamilton Road, Ealing, London. † RA 1.

STICKLAND, Mary Exh. 1923
† SWA 2.

STICKS, G.B.* Exh. 1882-86
Landscape painter. 200 Westgate Road, Newcastle. † RSA 2.

STICKS, Harry* Exh. 1894-1911
Landscape painter. Heaton, Newcastle 1894; Newcastle upon Tyne 1911. † B 3, RI 1, RSA 1.

STIEBEL, Henry H. Exh. 1910
8 Upper College Street, Nottingham. † GI 1.

STIEBEL, Helen M. Exh. 1904-25
Landscape, coastal and portrait painter. A.N.S.A. 1913, N.S.A. 1924-29. Add: 8 Upper College Street, Nottingham. † L 1, N 39.

STIFF, W. Eden Exh. 1890-92
Edgbaston, Birmingham 1890 and 1892; South Kensington, London 1891. † B 7.

STIFFE, C.E. Exh. 1882-1901
Landscape painter. London. † RA 3, RBA 1, ROI 1.

STIFFE, John Gilbee Exh. 1888
Landscape painter. 154 Alexander Road, South Hampstead, London. † RA 1.

STIFFE, Katherine Exh. 1904-39
Flower painter. Folkestone 1904; Lelant, Cornwall 1913; Launceston, Cornwall 1927; Uckfield 1928; Horsham 1932. † B 2, L 9, RI 2.

STIGAND, Helen M. Exh. 1880-84
Landscape painter. c/o Biggs and Co., 7 Maddox Street, Regent Street, London. † D 1, M 2, RSA 3, SWA 3.

STIKEMAN, Annie Exh. 1880-86
Watercolour flower painter. 15 Kidbrooke Park Road, Blackheath, London. † M 1, RBA 2, RI 2, SWA 7.

STILES, Sybella K. Exh. 1937
Landscape painter. Barnet Wood, Bromley Common. † COO 1, GI 2, RA 2.

STILL, Miss E.A. Exh. 1917-23
Steadham, nr. Midhurst, Sussex 1917; Parkstone, Dorset 1921; c/o The Art Gallery, Park Lane, Croydon, Surrey 1922. † D 6, L 1, SWA 6.

STILLINGFLEET, Hilda Exh. 1935
55 Grove Park Road, London. † SWA 1.

STILLMAN, Cecil G. Exh. 1935
Architect. West Sussex County Council, North Street, Chichester. † RA 1.

STILLMAN, Effie Exh. 1892-1907
Sculptor and medallionist. Daughter of Marie S. q.v. Add: Rome 1892; London 1897. † L 2, NG 35, P 1, RA 2.

STILLMAN, Lisa R. Exh. 1888-1909
Portrait painter. Daughter of Marie S. q.v. Add: London 1888 and 1893; Rome 1890. † NEA 1, NG 64, P 3, RA 1.

STILLMAN, Marie 1844-1927
Mrs. William J.S. nee Spartali. Painter. Studied under Ford Madox Brown. Mother of Effie and Lisa S. q.v. Add: Florence, Italy 1880; London 1881, 1898 and 1908; Rome 1890 and 1897. † B 3, G 13, L 17, M 4, NG 46, RA 1, RI 2.

STILWELL, Miss N.G. Exh. 1923
† SWA 1.

STINTON, Walter Exh. 1896
Shucknall Hill, Hereford. † B 1.

STIRLING, Evangeline Exh. 1880-94
Sculptor. London 1880; Stoneycroft, Liverpool 1885; Cheltenham, Glos. 1888 and 1894. † L 4, RA 4.

STIRLING, Florence Hutcheson Exh. 1882-95
4 Laverock Bank Road, London. † GI 5, RSA 5.

STIRLING, Mary Exh. 1898-1913
Hampton Court Palace, London. † D 4.

STIRLING, Nina Exh. 1884-92
Flower and still life painter. London 1884; Dalkey 1892. † B 1, L 3, M 3, RA 2, RBA 2, RHA 1, ROI 1.

STIRLING, T.L. Exh. 1884
280A Kings Road, Chelsea, London. † L 2.

STIRLING, W. Exh. 1880-97
Dublin. † RHA 13.

STIRLING, William Exh. 1885-94
Architect. London. † RA 8, RSA 1.

STIRLING, William Exh. 1935-39
Sculptor. 84 Rodney Court, Maida Vale, London. † GOU 1, RA 2.

STIRRAT, Eliza B. Exh. 1887-98
11 Derby Crescent, Kelvinside, Glasgow. † GI 5.

STIRRUP, Gertrude I. Exh. 1926
34 Wellington Street, St. Johns, Blackburn, Lancs. † L 1.

STITT, Fanny H. Exh. 1886
Woodburn, Dalkeith. † RSA 1.

STJERNSTEDT, Mme. S. Exh. 1882
Landscape painter. c/o Brown, 32 Charlotte Street, London. † RA 1.

STOBART, Miss A. Exh. 1886
Pepper Arden, Northallerton, Yorks. † M 2.

STOBART, Adela Exh. 1921-29
Watercolour painter. b. Etherley, Durham. Add: Hassocks, Sussex 1921; London 1923. † AR 2, COO 2, D 2, L 1, RCA 15, RI 1, SWA 3.

STOBIE, E. Exh. 1885
36 Old Exchange Arcade, Manchester. † L 1, M 1.

STOCK, Cicely Exh. 1916-39
Landscape and flower painter. Member London Group 1920. Add: London. † COO 2, G 1, GOU 3, LEI 2, LS 12.

STOCK, Ernest Exh. 1929
American landscape painter. Visited France and the Channel Islands. † BA 41.

STOCK, Edith A. Exh. 1880-1929
Landscape, portrait and flower painter. Richmond, Surrey 1880; Rotherham, Yorks. 1885; Kimberworth, Yorks 1890; London 1900; Petersham, Surrey 1903; Sandown, I.O.W. 1905. † BG 3, L 8, M 2, RA 4, RBA 4, RI 1, RID 46, ROI 2, SWA 12.

STOCK, Emile A. Exh. 1921
10a Hoghton Street, Southport, Lancs. † L 1.

STOCK, Francis R. Exh. 1880-84
Fruit and genre painter. Stanhope Studios, Delancy Street, London. † D 3, GI 5, L 1, M 1, RA 4, RBA 3.

STOCK, Henry Exh. 1886-87
Architect. 9 Denham Street, London Bridge, London. † RA 3.

STOCK, Henry John* 1853-1930
Portrait, genre and imaginary subject painter. Studied R.A. Schools. R.I. 1880, R.O.I. 1883. Add: London 1880; Bognor, Sussex 1910. † DOW 3, FIN 1, L 7, LEI 1, M 5, RA 30, RI 131, ROI 76.

STOCK, Vaughan Exh. 1928
14 St. James Terrace, London. † NEA 1.

STOCKDALE, Christine Exh. 1930
Sculptor. Stoke Prior, Bromsgrove. † RA 1.

STOCKDALE, Miss C.M. Exh. 1921
41 Powis Square, London. † RA 1.

STOCKELBACH, Lavonia Exh. 1937
Painter of Canadian birds. † WG 90.

STOCKER, Ethel Exh. 1903-40
Handsworth, Birmingham 1903; Cornwall 1906. † B 1, GOU 1, SWA 2.

STOCKER, Florence A. Exh. 1884-89
Watercolour landscape and flower painter. Burnham, Maidenhead, Berks. † L 2, RI 2, SWA 4.

STOCKHAM, Mrs. Leah Minnie Exh. 1897-1904
Birmingham. † B 5.

STOCKS, Arthur* 1846-1889
Genre and portrait painter. Studied under his father Lumb S. q.v. and at R.A. Schools. R.I. 1882. Add: 29 Hanley Road, Hornsey Rise, London. † B 12, D 3, GI 12, L 16, M 9, RA 22, RHA 2, RI 16, ROI 6.

STOCKS, Bernard O. Exh. 1881-99
Still life painter. Son of Lumb S. q.v. Add: London 1881; Enfield, Middlesex 1899. † L 1, RA 3, RI 3.

STOCKS, E. Exh. 1896-97
136 Wellington Street, Glasgow. † GI 2.

STOCKS, Ernest Exh. 1936
Wood engraver. 20 Cooper Street, Doncaster, Yorks. † RA 1.

STOCKS, Joseph Exh. 1933-39
Landscape painter. 20 Cooper Street, Hyde Park, Doncaster, Yorks. † RA 3.

STOCKS, Miss J. Christian Exh. 1934
Osborn House, Kirkcaldy. † RSW 1.

STOCKS, Katharine Exh. 1880-89
Flower and still life painter. Daughter of Lumb S. q.v. Add: 9 Richmond Villas, Seven Sisters Road, London. † D 11, GI 2, L 2, M 4, RA 6, RI 10, SWA 7.

STOCKS, Lumb 1812-1892
Engraver. Father of Arthur, Bernard O., Katharine and Walter Fryer S. q.v. A.R A. 1853, R.A. 1871. Add: 9 Richmond Villas, Seven Sisters Road, London. † RA 11.

STOCKS, Miss Minna Exh. 1882
c/o Paschen, 25 Faulkner Street, Manchester. † M 1.

STOCKS, R. Bremner Exh. 1885
Portrait painter. † G 1.

STOCKS, Walter Fryer Exh. 1880-1903
Landscape and still life painter. Son of Lumb S. q.v. Add: London 1880; Essenden, nr. Hatfield, Herts. 1884; Stratford sub Castle, Salisbury, Wilts. 1892; St. Asaph 1903. † B 8, D 14, GI 5, L 12, M 12, RA 43, RE 5, RHA 5, RI 21, ROI 2.

STODART, Grace Exh. 1889-1922
Landscape and figure painter. b. Chesterhall, Lanarks. Studied with Christina Ross at Edinburgh, Colarossi's Paris, and Edinburgh College of Art. Add: Plaistow, Kent 1889; Winton Hill, Pencaitland 1893; Upper Keith, N.B. 1911; Humbie, N.B. 1913. † GI 4, L 8, M 2, RSA 38, RSW 1, SWA 2.

STODART, George J. Exh. 1884-91
Engraver. Godstone, Surrey 1884; Gt. Yarmouth 1891. † RA 4.

STODART, Mary T. Oliver Exh. 1897-1901
Tweedsmuir, Peebleshire 1897; Edinburgh 1900. † GI 1, RSA 2.

STODDARD, Edith E.J. Exh. 1903-4
† RMS 2.

STODDARD, Florence Enid Exh. 1903-28
Miniature portrait painter. A.R.M.S. 1912. Add: London 1903; Pulborough, Sussex 1928. † L 4, NG 2, RA 20, RMS 8.

STODDARD, J. Exh. 1936
4 Hamilton Drive, The Park, Nottingham. † N 1.

STODDART, Andrew Exh. 1901-30
Stained glass artist. Father of Maureen S. q.v. Add: Nottingham 1901; Lenton, Notts. 1927. † N 55, RA 9.

STODDART, Christina M. Exh. 1893-1914
Painter. Edinburgh 1893; London 1910. † GI 3, L 4, LS 3, RA 1, RSA 14.

STODDART, David McKay Exh. 1899-1922
Kelvinside, N.B. 1899; Glasgow 1921. † GI 2, RSA 4.

STODDART, Maureen Exh. 1928-29
Stained glass artist. Daughter of Andrew S. q.v. Add: 54 Park Road, Lenton, Notts. † N 3.

STODDART, Margaret O. Exh. 1899-1906
Landscape painter. London 1899; St. Ives, Cornwall 1906. † B 2, BG 40, RA 1, RBA 4, RI 1, SWA 2.

STODDART, R.W. Exh. 1922
Architect. 27a Bush Lane, London. † RA 1.

STODDART, Sarah C. Exh. 1893
16 Lansdowne Crescent, Glasgow. † GI 1.

STODE, Miss E.A. Exh. 1900
13 York Place, Portman Square, London. † SWA 1.

STOHWASSER, Rosina Exh. 1882-85
Watercolour landscape painter. 7 Marlborough Road, St. Johns Wood, London. † D 2, L 1, RI 1, SWA 4.

STOKER, Matilda Exh. 1880-84
Dublin and London. † RHA 7.

STOKES, Adrian* 1854-1935
Landscape, portrait, genre, historical and literary painter. Studied R.A. Schools 1872-75 and in Paris under Dagnan Bouveret 1885-86. Brother of Leonard and husband of Marianne S. q.v. N.E.A. 1887, A.R.A. 1910, R.A. 1919, R.O.I. 1888, A.R.W.S. 1920, R.W.S. 1926, V.P.R.W.S. 1933. Travelled widely in Europe. "Uplands and Sky" purchased by Chantrey Bequest 1888 and "Autumn in the Moutains" purchased 1903. Add: London 1880 and 1891; St. Ives, Cornwall 1890. † B 15, D 1, DOW 5, FIN 51, G 11, GI 16, GOU 2, L 49, LEF 10, LEI 64, M 23, NEA 1, NG 35, RA 125, RBA 5, RHA 3, RI 2, RID 11, ROI 20, RSA 2, RSW 2, RWS 47, TOO 5.

STOKES, Miss A.J. Exh. 1887-1908
Cheltenham, Glos. 1887; London 1904. † D 15, RI 1.

STOKES, Mrs. Beth Exh. 1925
† RMS 1.

STOKES, Miss C.E. Exh. 1902-9
The Rectory, Aughnacloy, Ireland. † RHA 4.

STOKES, Miss E. Exh. 1940
Atlantis, Looe, Cornwall. † RI 2.

STOKES, Ernest E. Exh. 1923-24
Marl Park Studio, Victoria Drive, Llandudno Junction, Wales. † RCA 2.

STOKES, Miss E.S. Exh. 1911-12
Sunderland. † L 2.

STOKES, Folliott d. 1939
Landscape painter. Exh. 1892-98. Add: St. Ives, Cornwall. † NG 1, RA 4, RBA 3.

STOKES, Frank Wilbert Exh. 1927
American painter. 3 Washington Square, New York, U.S.A. † L 1, RA 1.

STOKES, George Vernon 1873-1954
Landscape and animal painter and etcher. A.R.B.A. 1923, R.B.A. 1930, R.M.S. 1896. Add: London 1895 and 1923; Emsworth, Hants. 1907; Crosby upon Eden, Cumberland 1911; Irthington, nr. Carlisle 1914; Gt. Mongeham, nr. Deal 1930. † FIN 3, NG 1, RA 13, RBA 88, RI 2, RMS 17.

STOKES, Leonard 1858-1925
Architect. Brother of Adrian S. q.v. Add: London. † GI 4, L 2, RA 60, RSA 1.

STOKES, Margaret Exh. 1895
Carrig Brac, Howth. † RHA 5.

STOKES, Margaret Exh. 1938-40
Painter. 32 Upper Pembroke Street, Dublin. † RHA 2.

STOKES, Marianne* 1855-1927
nee Preindlsberger. Portrait, genre and biblical painter. b. Southern Austria. Studied under Lindenschmidt in Munich. Married Adrian S. q.v. N.E.A. 1887, A.R W.S. 1923, A.S.W.A. 1887. Add: London. † B 4, DOW 1, FIN 34, G 2, GI 6, L 33, LEI 2, M 3, NEA 2, NG 23, RA 35, RBA 3, RID 5, ROI 11, RWS 23, SWA 2.

STOKOE, Charles John Exh. 1907-14
East Bergholt, Suffolk 1907; Chelmsford, Essex 1914. † LS 12, RA 2.

STOLL, Juan Exh. 1936-40
Landscape, flower and animal painter. 84 Charlotte Street, London. † BA 31, NEA 5, RA 3.

STOLTERFOHT, Mrs. Caroline R. Exh. 1902-8
Holly Bank, Mossley Hill, Liverpool. † L 12.

STONE, Ada Exh. 1884-1916
Miniature portrait, still life and figure painter. London. † L 4, RA 13, RBA 2, ROI 1.

STONE, Coutts Exh. 1881
Architect. 16 Gt. Marlborough Street, London. † RA 1.

STONE, Cyril Exh. 1935-39
Landscape painter. 90 Edward Street, Brighton. † RA 4.

STONE, Celine E. Exh. 1887
Flower painter. 22 The Terrace, Yorktown, Farnborough, Hants. † SWA 1.

STONE, Mrs. Dora Exh. 1927
Miniature painter on ivory. 31 Denning Road, Hampstead, London. † RA 1.

STONE, Ethel E. Exh. 1895
92 Ryland Road, Edgbaston, Birmingham. † B 2.

STONE, E.H. Exh. 1928
Landscape painter. † AB 3.

STONE, E. Joyce Exh. 1939-40
Etcher. 33 Warley Road, Bristol. † RA 3.

STONE, F. Exh. 1911
133 Cheyne Walk, London. † RA 1.

STONE, Miss H. Exh. 1900
† P 3.

STONE, Henry Exh. 1882-86
Architect. 31 John Street, Bedford Row, London. † RA 2.

STONE, H. Mulready Exh. 1905-36
Etcher. London 1905; Salcombe, South Devon 1912. † FIN 63, I 5, L 12, LS 4, NEA 1, RA 6.

STONE, Jean Exh. 1928
Canal and river landscape painter. † AB 2.

STONE, Louisa Exh. 1881
Watercolour landscape painter. Precincts, Canterbury. † SWA 4.

STONE, Marcus* 1840-1921
Historical genre painter and illustrator. Studied under his Father Frank S. (1800-1859). A.R.A. 1877, R.A. 1886, R.O.I. 1883. "Il y en a toujours un autre" purchased by Chantrey Bequest 1882. Add: 8 Melbury Road, Kensington Road, London. † AG 1, B 4, FIN 1, GI 3, L 6, M 4, RA 49, TOO 18.

STONE, Melicent Exh. 1895-1921
Sculptor. Thursley, Godalming, Surrey 1895; London 1897. † B 2, I 1, L 7, NG 9, P 1, RA 3, RSA 2, RMS 3.

STONE, Percy Goddard Exh. 1883-98
Architect. 16 Gt. Marlborough Street, London. † RA 2.

STONE, Reynolds Exh. 1936
Engraver. † RED 1.

STONE, Richard Exh. 1906-9
London. † L 1, LS 8, M 1, NG 2.

STONELAKE, Francis P. Exh. 1902
School of Animal Painting, Rathmines Road, Dublin. † RHA 4.

STONES, Emily R. Exh. 1882-1925
Landscape, figure and flower painter. A.S.W.A . 1914. Add: London. † D 5, GI 1, L 7, M 5, RA 6, RBA 12, RHA 1, RI 13, ROI 1, RSA 1, SWA 65, WG 48.

STONES, G.C. Exh. 1903
Ash Field, Matlock Bath, Derbys. † N 2.

STONES, G.E. Exh. 1910
Needham Market, Suffolk. † RA 1.

STONES, Sam Exh. 1890-91
Stamford Street, Ashton under Lyne. † M 2.

STONEY, Charles Butler Exh. 1880-1908
Landscape, flower, portrait and architectural painter. London 1880 and 1908; Malmesbury, Wilts. 1887 and 1891; Newton Abbot, Devon 1890; Parkestone, Dorset 1893. † B 9, GI 1, L 11, M 8, NG 2, RA 21, RBA 2, ROI 8.

STONEY, Gertrude B. Exh. 1898-1901
London. † RHA 2.

STONEY, Naomi Exh. 1929-3
Painter. Polegate, Sussex 1929; Londo 1931. † L 1, RHA 1.

STONEY, Thomas Butler Exh. 1899-191
Marine and coastal painter. London 189 and 1912; Portland, Co. Tipperary 191 † B 1, D 2, I 2, L 3, NEA 4, P 2, RA 4 RHA 3.

STONHAM, Miss M. Exh. 190
Meadowcroft, Downview Road, Worthing Sussex. † SWA 1.

STONOR, Winifred M. Exh. 1918-2
Ealing, London 1918; Glasgow 1929 † GI 1, SWA 3.

STOOK, Annie Exh. 193
Artist and teacher. Taunton, Somerset † RI 1.

STOPFORD, Charlotte C. Exh. 1887-191
Dublin 1887 and 1903; Mallow, Co. Cork 1898 and 1909; Kinsale, Co. Cork 1906 † RHA 27.

STOPFORD, Ethel Exh. 191
34 Ashdale Road, Terenure, Dublin † RHA 3.

STOPFORD, Robert L. Exh. 188
1 Hardwick Street, Patricks Hill, Cork † RHA 1.

STOPFORD, William Henry 1842-189
Landscape painter. Add: School of Art Halifax 1880. † L 1, M 1, RA 1.

STOPFORD-BROOK, Rev. Exh. 190
1 Manchester Square, London. † NG 3.

STOPFORD-DIXON, E. Exh. 192
Landscape painter. † AB 1.

STOPPOLONI, Auguste G. Exh. 1893-1911
Figure and portrait painter. London † B 4, D 2, GI 4, L 4, P 1, RA 16, RBA 3 RI 1, ROI 5.

STOREY, Annie Exh. 192
Portrait painter and modeller. b. Pendleton. Studied Salford Technica College and Manchester School of Art. Art mistress Stockport School of Arts and Crafts. † M 1.

STOREY, Ada M. Exh. 1921-23
Dublin 1921; Hilleshandra, Co. Cavan 1923. † RHA 4.

STOREY, George Adolphus* 1834-1919
Portrait and genre painter. Studied under Dulong. Professor of Perspective at R.A. Schools. A.R.A. 1876, R.A. 1914. Add: London. † AG 1, B 1, D 3, GI 1, L 14, M 10, RA 116, RI 1, ROI 8, RSA 1.

STOREY, Harold Exh. 1912-40
Landscape painter. Glasgow 1912 and 1926; Newton Mearns, Renfrewshire 1919 and 1934. † GI 43, L 9, RA 7, RSA 21, RSW 1.

STOREY, T.G. Exh. 1917
Brooklyn House, Altham Terrace, Lincoln. † RA 1.

STORIE, Andrew Exh. 1911-19
Edinburgh. † RSA 5.

STORK, Mrs. Jennie Exh. 1913-15
47 Millfield Road, York. † RCA 3.

STORLENBECKER, P. Exh. 1886
133 New Bond Street, London. † M 2.

STORMONT, Howard Gull Exh. 1884-1923
Landscape painter. West Brighton, Sussex 1884; London 1886; Richmond, Surrey 1896; Rye, Sussex 1900. † B 3, BRU 12, D 30, GI 1, L 7, RA 17, RBA 9, RHA 3, RI 12, RID 79, ROI 3.

STORMONT, Mary Exh. 1899-1940
Mrs. Howard Gull S. Watercolour landscape painter. Ypres Studio, Rye, Sussex. † BRU 19, D 18, GI 1, L 5, NG 1, RA 26, RBA 1, RI 6, RID 56.

STORR, Milton Exh. 1890-91
Landscape painter. Haslemere, Surrey. † GI 1, L 2, RA 1, RBA 1.

STORR, Sidney Exh. 1890
40 Brondesbury Road, Kilburn, London. † GI 2.

STORRAR, David Exh. 1880-86
Kirkaldy. † GI 1, RSA 6.

STORROW, George O. Exh. 1932
126 Botchergate, Carlisle. † RSA 1.

STORTZ, Philip G. Exh. 1882
19 Kings Road, Brighton, Sussex. † L 1.

STORY, Blanche Exh. 1880-88
Flower and still life painter. The Forest, Nottingham. † G 9, N 18.

STORY, Elma Exh. 1880-1940
Glasgow. † GI 30, L 1, RSA 5, RSW 1.

STORY, Mrs. Elizabeth Jessie Exh. 1924-36
Painter and etcher. b. Oxford. Studied Slade School. Add: London. † ALP 17, L 3, NEA 2, RA 2, RSW 1, SWA 2.

STORY, Gordon Exh. 1902-22
Edinburgh. † GI 1, L 1, RSA 3.

STORY, Julian* 1857-1919
Portrait painter. b. England, son of Waldo W.S. q.v. R.P. 1897. Add: London 1882; Paris 1883. Went to America. † G 12, GI 2, L 6, M 2, NG 6, P 4, RA 4.

STORY, John James d. 1900
Landscape and figure painter. Nottingham. † N 15.

STORY, Mary S. Exh. 1880-88
Flower painter. The Forest, Nottingham. † G 5, N 20, RA 2.

STORY, Winifred Exh. 1912
19 Pennsylvania, Exeter, Devon. † L 1.

STORY, Waldo W. Exh. 1882-90
Sculptor. Father of Julian S. q.v. R.B.A. 1887. Add: Rome. † G 12, L 3, RA 1, RBA 1.

STOTT, Miss A.E. Exh. 1912
Parkside, The Haulgh, Bolton, Lancs. † RA 1.

STOTT, Edward* 1859-1918
Landscape and rustic genre painter. b. Rochdale. Studied in Paris under Carolus Duran and Cabanel. N.E.A. 1886, A.R.A. 1906, "Changing Pastures" (1893) purchased by Chantrey Bequest 1922. Add: Paris 1883; Littletons, nr. Evesham, Worcs. 1884; Wherwell, nr. Andover, Hants. 1885; Higher Broughton, Manchester 1888; Amberley, Sussex 1889. † B 8, G 4, GI 8, GOU 2, L 51, M 43, NEA 16, NG 43, RA 49, RHA 4, ROI 3, RSA 8.

STOTT, John Exh. 1881
Painter. 4 Passage Dulac, Rue de Vaugirard, Paris. † G 1.

STOTT, William Exh. 1884
Ravenglass, Cumberland. † M 1.

STOTT, William (of Oldham) * 1857-1900
Landscape, portrait and figure painter. b. Oldham, nr. Manchester. Studied in Paris under Gerome 1879. N.E.A. 1890, R.B.A. 1885. Add: Paris 1881; London 1890. † B 5, D 4, FIN 3, G 3, GI 22, L 26, M 18, NEA 1, NG 1, P 4, RA 13, RBA 21, RSW 1.

STOTT, William R.S. Exh. 1905-34
Landscape and portrait painter. London 1905 and 1910; Aberdeen 1909. † GI 4, L 1, LS 3, RA 22, RHA 1.

STOUGHTON, Mrs. K. Exh. 1915-19
London. † RA 1, SWA 3.

STOUPE, Seamus b. 1872
Watercolour painter, sculptor and lithographer. Studied Belfast Model School. Modelling master Belfast Municipal Technical College. Exh. 1905-31. Add: Belfast. † RHA 69.

STOURTON, Everard Exh. 1891-97
Sculptor. London. † GI 2, NG 6, RA 1.

STOW, Mary Florence Exh. 1933-38
Woodcut artist. Newport 1933; Maidenhead 1937. † COO 3, RCA 10.

STOWELL, Louisa Exh. 1895-1912
R.M.S. 1898. Add: Birkenhead 1895; Liverpool 1909. † L 25, M 1, RMS 3.

STOWERS, T. Gordon Exh. 1881-94
Portrait and figure painter. 76 Newman Street, Oxford Street, London. † L 1, RA 3, RBA 1.

STOYE, Walter Exh. 1924
Architect. c/o Barkentin and Krall, 291 Regent Street, London. † RA 2.

STRACEY, Miss C.M. Exh. 1922
† NEA 1.

STRACHAN, Alexander Exh. 1929-35
Stained glass artist. 5a Balcarres Street, Edinburgh. † L 3, RSA 2.

STRACHAN, Arthur Claude b. 1865
Watercolour painter of landscape and English cottages. b. Edinburgh. Studied Liverpool. Exh. 1885-1932. Add: Liverpool 1885 and 1896; Warwick 1895; Evesham, Worcs. 1903; New Brighton, Cheshire 1914; Glasgow 1929. † B 4, L 64, RA 4, RI 1.

STRACHAN, Arthur W. Exh. 1920
Miniature portrait painter. Netherley, Dollar, N.B. † RA 1.

STRACHAN, Douglas b. 1875
Portrait, figure, decorative and mural painter and stained glass artist. b. Aberdeen. Studied R.S.A. Life School, France, Italy and Spain. H.R.S.A. 1920. Exh. 1900-27. Add: Aberdeen 1900; Edinburgh 1910. † GI 1, RSA 8.

STRACHAN, F.G. Exh. 1915-16
London. † RA 2.

STRACHEY, Henry b. 1863
Landscape and figure painter. Studied Slade School. Art critic to "Spectator" 1896-1922. Exh. 1888-1923. Add: London 1888; Pensford, Bristol 1891; Clutton, Bristol 1903. † B 4, G 1, L 2, LS 8, NEA 1, NG 3, RA 10.

STRADLING, A.R. Exh. 1929-37
Watercolour painter. Studied in Paris. Travelled widely in Europe, Africa and the East. † WG 258.

STRAHAN, Col. Geoffrey d. 1916
Landscape painter. R.B.A. 1906. Add: London 1900; Tatsfield, Surrey 1912. † FIN 40, I 3, L 3, M 1, NEA 6, NG 5, RA 1, RBA 4, RI 7, ROI 9, RSA 1.

STRAIN, Hilary 1884-1960
Portrait painter. b. Alloway. Studied Baden and Glasgow School of Art. Add: Maybole, Ayrshire. † GI 17, L 3, P 1, RA 1, RCA 1, RSA 9.

STRAIN, Pamela Exh. 1937-38
† NEA 2.

STRAKER, Harry Exh. 1906-27
Painter. Primrose Hill Studios, Fitzroy Road, London. † L 1, RA 7.

STRANG, David b. 1887
Etcher. b. Dumbarton. Son of William S. q.v. Studied Glasgow University. Exh. 1923-25. Add: London. † CHE 1, FIN 3, I 1, RA 1.

STRANG, Miss H.M. Exh. 1916
19 Hartington Road, Liverpool. † L 2.

STRANG, Ian 1886-1952
Painter and etcher. Studied Slade School 1902-6 and Julians, Paris 1906-18. Son of William S. q.v. A.R.E. 1926, R.E. 1930. Add: London. † AB 1, BA 3, CHE 77, FIN 18, GI 3, GOU 18, I 4, L 5, LEI 42, M 9, NEA 59, RA 36, RE 47, RHA 1, RSA 8.

STRANG, James Exh. 1897-1902
Westwood, Busby, N.B. † GI 3, RSA 1.

STRANG, Maggie Exh. 1888
Craignairn House, Cross Hill, Glasgow. † GI 1.

STRANG, Margaret Kippen Exh. 1904-5
Bosfield, East Kilbride, Glasgow. † GI 2.

STRANG, Mrs. Norma Exh. 1936-39
Surrey Cottage, Ruxley, Claygate, Surrey. † RSA 3.

STRANG, William* 1859-1921
Painter and etcher. b. Dumbarton. Studied Slade School. Father of David and Ian S. q.v. A.R.A. 1906, R.A. 1921, R.E. 1881, R.P. 1904. "Self-Portrait" (1919) purchased by Chantrey Bequest 1921. Add: London. † AG 3, CG 1, CON 57, FIN 410, G 101, GI 18, GOU 11, I 73, L 32, LEI 84, M 56, NEA 11, P 15, RA 69, RE 181, RHA 3, RSA 18.

STRANGE, Albert G. Exh. 1882-97
Landscape, coastal and genre painter. Teacher Scarborough School of Art. Add: Scarborough, Yorks. † L 5, RA 10, RBA 2, RI 5, ROI 1.

STRANGE, Albert V. Exh. 1894
130 Embden Street, Hulme, Cheshire. † M 1.

STRANGE, Christopher William Exh. 1902-31
Landscape, flower and still life painter. Padworth, nr. Reading 1902 and 1914; Brimpton, Berks. 1913. † L 2, LS 6, M 2, NEA 8, RA 7.

STRANGEMAN, Clive Venn b. 1888
Landscape painter and commercial artist. Teacher of design L.C.C. School of Photo-engraving and lithography. Exh. 1922-38. Add: Wimbledon 1922; Belmont, Surrey 1938. † RA 2, RI 1.

STRANGEWAYS, R. Fox Exh. 1927
Flower painter. † WG 97.

STRANGMAN, Miss A.L. Exh. 1905-11
London. † L 2, RA 2.

STRANGWAYS, Juliet Exh. 1913
56 Holland Road, Kensington, London. † RHA 1.

STRAPP, M. George Exh. 1886
Painter. 50 Broadhurst Gardens, London. † RBA 1.

STRASSER, Roland Exh. 1934
Australian landscape painter. c/o Arkeden, Bishops Avenue, Finchley, London. † RA 2.

STRATHERN, A.S. Exh. 1907-11
Glasgow 1907; Giffnock, Renfrewshire 1911. † GI 2.

STRATHIE, Thomas J. Exh. 1897
2 Lansdowne Place, Shawlands, N.B. † GI 2.

STRATTEN, Lucy A. Exh. 1890-1912
Portrait and miniature painter. R.M.S. 1899. Add: Hessle, Yorks. 1890; London 1905. † GI 2, L 8, NG 3, RA 29, RMS 50, SWA 3.

STRATTON, Arthur J. Exh. 1900-13
Architect. East Sheen, Surrey 1900; London 1904. † RA 3.

STRATTON, Fred Exh. 1898-1932
Landscape and figure painter. London 1898 and 1928; Amberley, Sussex 1905. † BRU 34, CG 1, DOW 39, G 3, GI 1, GOU 13, I 2, L 1, M,1, NEA 1, NG 2, P 2, RA 10, RI 2, RID 37, ROI 7, TOO 5, WG 7.

STRATTON, Helen Exh. 1892-1924
Portrait, figure and landscape painter. London. † BG 2, I 1, L 3, LS 3, RA 4, RBA 2, RHA 2, RI 2, RID 4, SWA 17.

STRATTON, Hilary Exh. 1940
Sculptor. 11 The Boltons, London. † RA 1.

STRATTON, Hilda Exh. 1927 Flower painter. † TOO 1.

STRATTON, Janet Exh. 1893-1924 S.W.A. 1927. Add: London. † D 4, RBA 1, SWA 17.

STRATTON, Mrs. Lilian Exh. 1934 Wilmington, Polegate, Sussex. † RI 1.

STRATTON, Mrs. Wallace See JOHNSON, Barbara

STRAUBE, Miss N.M. Exh. 1912-14 3 Wynchcombe Studios, Englands Lane, London. † L 5, RA 1.

STRAUSS, Anne Exh. 1938 Sculptor. 25 Cheyne Walk, London. † RA 1, RBA 2.

STRAW, Miss O. Exh. 1916-17 c/o Miss H. Clark, York Chambers, King Street, Nottingham. † N 2.

STREATFIELD, Granville Edward Stewart b. 1869 Architect. b. Howick, Northumberland. Exh. 1899-1920. Add: London. † L 1, RA 3, RI 1.

STREATFIELD, Josephine b. 1882 Painter and etcher. A.S.W.A. 1909. Exh. 1907-9. Add: Wynthorpe, Longton Avenue, Sydenham, Kent. † L 2, P 2, RA 5, SWA 2.

STREATFIELD, James Philip S. Exh. 1901-15 Portrait, figure and landscape painter. London. † L 5, P 1, RA 9, RHA 2, RI 2, ROI 3, WG 132.

STREATFIELD, Kathleen Exh. 1906-27 Portrait painter. A.S.W.A. 1909. Add: Wynthorpe, Longton Avenue, Sydenham, Kent. † P 13, RA 2, SWA 40.

STREATFIELD, Ruth See GERVIS

STREATFIELD, Roland H. Exh. 1933-38 Watercolour painter. † WG 10.

STRECKER, Constance Exh. 1882 54 Theresica Strasse, Munich. † GI 1.

STRECKER, J. Exh. 1880 Landscape painter. 35 Parliament Street, London. † RA 1.

STREET, Arthur Edmund Exh. 1886-98 Architect. London. † RA 16.

STREET, Florence McK. Exh. 1925-26 5 Blackburne Place, Hope Street, Liverpool. † L 4.

STREET, Florence N. Exh. 1884 Watercolour painter. 114 Ledbury Road, Bayswater, London. † SWA 1.

STREET, George Edmund 1824-1881 Architect (e.g. Royal Courts of Justice). A.R.A . 1866, R.A. 1871. Add: London. † RA 8.

STREET, Kate Exh. 1880-1915 Flower, bird, figure and decorative painter. Add: London. † D 4, L 11, M 1, RA 21, RBA 6, RI 13, ROI 3, SWA 2.

STREET, Miss S.A. Exh. 1890 Sutton Manor House, Guildford, Surrey. † SWA 1.

STREETER, Rosalie Ethel Exh. 1893-95 Painter. Brighton 1893; London 1895. † ROI 3.

STREETER, Walter Exh. 1936-38 133 Hartham Road, Isleworth, Middlesex. † RBA 2.

STREETON, Arthur* 1867-1943 Landscape painter. b. Australia. Travelled widely. R.B.A. 1909, R.O.I. 1910. Add: London. † ALP 48, B 1, BG 49, GI 10, GOU 5, I 1, L 8, M 1, NEA 9, NG 6, RA 29, RBA 5, RHA 10, ROI 13, RSA 2.

STREKALOVSKY, Veevold Exh. 1935 Watercolour figure and portrait painter. 2 Alma Studios, Stratford Road, London. † RA 2.

STRELLETT, Ephraim Exh. 1900-35 Miniature painter. London. † L 5, LS 3, NEA 1, RA 3, RBA 1, RI 37, RMS 2, ROI 2.

STRETCH, M. Exh. 1880 148 Strand, London. † RHA 1.

STRETTON, Emilia Dorothea Maria See DUDGEON

STRETTON, Hesba D. Exh. 1884-86 Watercolour flower and interior painter. London. † L 1, RA 1, RBA 1.

STRETTON, Miss M.T. Exh. 1901 Artist and teacher. 91 Manor Road, Brockley, London. † RBA 1, SWA 1.

STRETTON, Philip Eustace* Exh. 1884-1915 Animal, sporting and genre painter. R.O.I. 1904. Add: London 1884 and 1886; Wellington, Salop 1885; Cranbrook, Kent 1901; Farncombe, Surrey 1911. † B 5, D 2, GI 2, L 12, NG 19, RA 32, RBA 3, RI 1, ROI 40, RSA 3, TOO 4.

STREUVE, de See D

STRICKLAND, Helen Exh. 1927-28 Watercolour flower painter and illustrator. Studied Westminster School of Art. Add: 76 Dartford Road, Dartford, Kent. † NEA 1, RA 1.

STRICKLAND, Mary Exh. 1921 Cattistock, Dorset. † SWA 1.

STRINGER, Agnes Exh. 1900-6 Sunbury on Thames 1900; Putney 1906. † RBA 2, SWA 3.

STRINGER, Miss E. Exh. 1928 Painter. 2 Cheniston Gardens Studios, Kensington, London. † RA 1.

STRINGER, Noelle Exh. 1939 Sculptor. Turlough, 68 Terenure Road, East Dublin. † RHA 1.

STRINGER, Mrs. Randolph Exh. 1914-17 22 Coleherne Road, London. † LS 6.

STRINGER, Mrs. Wyn Exh. 1937 Flower painter. Riverside, Mortlake, London. † RA 1.

STROBENTZ, Fritz b. 1856 Hungarian artist. Exh. 1898-99. Add: 77 Gabelsberger Strasse, Munich. † GI 2.

STROBL, de See D

STRONACH, Ancell b. 1901 Painter of portraits and subject pictures, and church decorator. b. Dundee. Studied Glasgow School of Art (Guthrie award, travelling scholarship and Torrance Memorial Prize). A.R.S.A. 1935. Exh. 1920-40. Add: Glasgow. † GI 20, L 5, RA 2, RSA 25, RSW 3.

STRONACH, George Exh. 1880 11 Torphichen Street, Edinburgh. † RSA 1.

STRONG, C. Gordon Exh. 1905 69 Montpelier Park, Edinburgh. † RSA 1.

STRONG, Isabel G. See WHITE

STRONG, J. Exh. 1888 Watercolour painter. Bedford Hill, Balham, London. † RI 1.

STRONG, James Exh. 1885-1900 Architect. Liverpool. † L 2, RA 1.

STRONG, William Exh. 1883 Black and white artist. c/o Stewart, 51 Rathbone Place, Oxford Street, London. † RA 1.

STRONGMAN, B. Exh. 1883-84 56 Hill Street, Garnet Hill, Glasgow. † GI 2, RSA 1.

STRONGMAN, William Exh. 1891 School of Art, Dunbarton. † GI 1.

STROUD, Maud See WHEELWRIGHT

STROUDLEY, Leonard James Exh. 1927-39 Figure and landscape painter. R.B.A. 1934. Add: London. † GOU 3, L 1, NEA 2, RA 3, RBA 22.

STRUBEN, Edith F.M. Exh. 1914-33 Flower painter. Luncarty, Claremont Cape Province, South Africa. † M 6 RA 1.

STRUCK, Hermann Exh. 1902-14 Portrait painter and etcher. A.R.E 1904-14. Add: Berlin 1902; London 1903 † RA 1, RE 41.

STRUDWICK, John Melhuish* 1849-1937 Painter. Studied South Kensington and R.A. Schools. Worked as studio assistant for Spencer Stanhope and Burne-Jones "A Golden Thread" purchased by Chantrey Bequest 1885. Add: London † B 5, G 9, L 19, M 1, NG 23.

STRUTHERS, A. Exh. 1891 287 Duke Street, Glasgow. † GI 2.

STRUTHERS, Agnes J. Exh. 1901 2 Kelvingrove Terrace, Glasgow. † GI 1

STRUTHERS, Anna S. Exh. 1881 5 Oakfield Terrace, Glasgow. † GI 1.

STRUTHERS, M. Fleming Exh. 1901-10 Glencairn, Craigmill, Stirling, N.B. † GI 2, L 1, RHA 1, RSA 1.

STRUTHERS, T.R. Margaret Exh. 1881 5 Oakfield Terrace, Glasgow. † GI 1.

STRUTT, Arthur Edward Exh. 1886-1914 Landscape painter. Gravesend, Kent † B 15, GI 2, L 3, M 5, RA 4, RI 8.

STRUTT, Alfred William* 1856-1924 Animal, genre and portrait painter and etcher. b. Tanaraki, New Zealand. Studied under his father William S. q.v. and South Kensington School of Art. Accompanied King Edward VII on a hunting trip to Scandinavia. R.B.A. 1888, A.R.E. 1889. Add: Molynden, nr. Staplehurst, Kent 1880; London 1883; Wadhurst, Sussex 1891. † B 1, BG 1, CON 12, FIN 1, L 43, LS 7, M 10, RA 51, RBA 50, RCA 70, RE 31, RHA 1, RI 28, ROI 9, RSA 1, TOO 1.

STRUTT, Margaret J. Exh. 1925 37 Queens Road, Kingston Hill, Surrey. † RCA 2.

STRUTT, Nellie M. Exh. 1921-25 Wadhurst, Sussex 1921; Kingston Hill, Surrey 1925. † RCA 8.

STRUTT, Rosa J. Exh. 1884 Landscape painter. † ROI 1.

STRUTT, William* 1826-1915 Genre, animal and portrait painter. Son of William Thomas S. (1777-1850) and father of Alfred William S. q.v. Studied Ecole des Beaux Art, Paris. Went to Australia 1850; New Zealand 1856, and returned to England 1862. R.B.A. 1890. Add: London 1884; Wadhurst, Sussex 1890 and 1904; Tunbridge Wells, Kent 1901. † L 3, LS 2, M 7, RA 16, RBA 56, ROI 1.

STRYDONCK, van See V

STUART, A. Exh. 1893 11 Kersland Terrace, Hillhead, Glasgow. † GI 1.

STUART, A. Burnett Exh. 1883-95 Watercolour painter. Mellifont Wells, Somerset. † D 11, GI 1, L 3, RA 1, RI 2, RSA 2.

STUART, Barbara Exh. 1939 Engraver. 48 Delamare Road, Liverpool. † RA 1..

STUART, Charles* Exh. 1880-1904 Still life, landscape and marine painter. Married Jane Maria Bowkett q.v. and probably father of C.E. Gordon S. q.v. Add: London 1880; Pinner, Middlesex 1904. † B 26, G 1, GI 8, L 33, M 25, NG 1, RA 36, RBA 25, RHA 50, RI 4, ROI 9, RSA 10, TOO 10.

STUART, C.E. Gordon Exh. 1882-96
Figure painter. Probably son of Charles S. q.v. Add: London. † B 14, L 3, M 3, RBA 1, RHA 13, ROI 1.

STUART, Edward Exh. 1928
9 Melrose Road, Kirkdale, Liverpool. † L 1.

STUART, Ernest Exh. 1889-1915
Landscape and coastal painter. London. † L 1, RA 1, RBA 1, RI 1.

STUART, Gertrude Villiers Exh. 1903-10
Dromana, Cappoquin, Ireland 1903; London 1905. † D 1, RHA 3, SWA 10.

STUART, Isa Exh. 1885-97
Edinburgh 1885; Glasgow 1897. † GI 1, RSA 1.

STUART, John Exh. 1886
Douglas Terrace, Largs. † GI 1.

STUART, John Exh. 1880
91 North Hanover Street, Glasgow. † GI 1.

STUART, K.G. Exh. 1929
Old Parsonage, Dalkeith. † RSW 1.

STUART, Leila Exh. 1882
18 Mildmay Road, Kensington, London. † B 2.

STUART, Morton G. Exh. 1899-1900
2 Bedford Park, Edinburgh. † RSA 2.

STUART, Robert Easton Exh. 1890-1940
Landscape painter. Studied R.S.A. Schools. Add: Edinburgh. † GI 14, L 6, RSA 51.

STUART, Mrs. Sheila 1905-1949
Painter. Studied Edinburgh College of Art and Paris. Add: Levenhall, Midlothian 1927; The Old Parsonage, Dalkeith 1930. † RSA 13, RSW 12.

STUART-HILL, A. Exh. 1918-37
Portrait and landscape painter. R.P. 1931. Add: 41 Glebe Place, Chelsea, London. † G 3, GI 2, I 6, L 8, NEA 3, P 12, RA 28, RED 23, RSA 3.

STUART-MENTEATH, Evelyn O. Exh. 1909
† LS 3.

STUBB, C.E. Exh. 1920
25 Cunningham Road, Doncaster. † L 1.

STUBBING, Marjorie B. Exh. 1924
c/o 94 High Street, Lowestoft, Suffolk. † L 1.

STUBBINGS, Fred Exh. 1927
Coleshill, Amersham, Bucks. † ROI 1.

STUBBINGTON, Joan Exh. 1935
Selly Oak, Birmingham. † SWA 1.

STUBBINGTON, Mrs. Mabel Exh. 1936-38
54 Charlotte Road, Edgbaston, Birmingham. † B 2.

STUBBS, Charles E. Exh. 1919
† L 2.

STUBBS, E.J. Exh. 1905
30 Craven Street, Charing Cross, London. † RA 2.

STUBBS, Florence Exh. 1900
Fort William, Finglas, Co. Dublin. † RHA 1.

STUBBS, Ida Exh. 1905
Braunston, Sandford Road, Moseley, Birmingham. † B 1.

STUBBS, J. Woodhouse Exh. 1893-1908
Watercolour painter and teacher. Add: Government School of Art, Sunderland 1893; Norwich 1904. † B 9, L 7, RA 10, RI 1.

STUBBS, Kathleen Exh. 1932-37
29 George Road, Solihull, Birmingham. † B 2.

STUBBS, Lucas P. Exh. 1890-1913
Mount Road, New Brighton, Cheshire. † L 5.

STUBBS, Miss M.E. Exh. 1928-32
Dunmore, Willaston, Birkenhead. † L 4, RCA 3.

STUBINGTON, George H. Exh. 1902-22
Landscape painter. N.S.A. 1908. Chairman of Council N.S.A. 1914. V.P.N.S.A. 1916. Add: Nottingham. † B 1, N 60.

STUBINGTON, R.J. Exh. 1902-20
Birmingham. † B 6, NEA 1.

STUCHLIK, Camill Exh. 1890
Figure painter. 1420 Floreazgasse, Prague. † RA 1.

STUCK, Prof. Franz* 1863-1928
German painter. Exh. 1899-1907. Add: Munich. † GI 2, I 8.

STUDD, Arthur Haythorne 1864-1919
Landscape painter. Worked with Whistler. Add: London. † GOU 17, I 2, L 5, NEA 13, NG 1.

STUDD, Leonard Exh. 1922-23
Etcher. 21 Limerston Road, Chelsea, London. † RA 3.

STUDDERT, Rev. G. Exh. 1891-1905
Landscape painter. Edwardstone Vicarage, Boxford, Colchester, Essex 1891; London 1905. † RA 1, RHA 1, ROI 5.

STURDEE, Percy Exh. 1885-1939
Figure, portrait, flower and still life painter. London 1885; Edinburgh 1902; Colyford, Devon 1909; Georgeham, Devon 1922; Little Clacton, Essex 1924; Wilmington, Sussex 1934. † GI 2, L 2, M 1, NG 1, RA 12, RBA 1, RI 1, RSA 1.

STURGE, Anne Matilda Exh. 1880
Painter. 20 The Waldrons, Croydon, Surrey. † SWA 1.

STURGE, F.W. Exh. 1895-1904
Landscape painter. Tintagel, Cornwall. † GI 2, RID 2.

STURGEON, Kate Exh. 1881-95
Watercolour painter. 53 Doddington Grove, London. † GI 2, L 6, RA 5, RBA 8, RI 9, SWA 5.

STURGES, W.H. Campbell Exh. 1915
Blenheim Crescent, South Croydon, Surrey. † RA 1.

STURGESS, E. Exh. 1883
34 Bloom Street, Liverpool. † L 1.

STURGESS, John* Exh. 1880-84
Sporting and animal painter. 148 Strand, London. † RBA 1, RHA 3.

STURGESS, William Exh. 1886-92
New Brighton, Cheshire 1886; Liscard, Cheshire 1889. † L 6.

STURGIS, Mrs. H. Exh. 1913
47 York Place, Edinburgh. † D 1.

STURM, Mrs. W. Exh. 1885-86
43 Hyde Grove, Manchester. † M 2.

STURMER, von See V

STURROCK, Angus P. Exh. 1935
14 Marshall Street, Lochee, Dundee. † RSA 1.

STURROCK, Alick Riddell 1885-1953
Landscape painter. Studied Edinburgh School of Art and R.S.A. Life School. Married Mary Newbury S. q.v. A.R.S.A. 1929, R.S.A. 1938. Add: Edinburgh 1909 and 1930; Gatehouse of Fleet 1919. † GI 38, L 8, RA 4, RSA 78, RSW 3.

STURROCK, David Woodburn Exh. 1887-1909
Glasgow. † GI 11.

STURROCK, Mary Newbury Exh. 1911-40
nee Newbury. Married Alick Riddell S. q.v. Add: Glasgow 1911; Edinburgh and Gatehouse of Fleet 1920. † GI 18, L 2, RSA 21, RSW 6.

STURT, Barbara Exh. 1907-11
Horner Grange, Sydenham, Kent. † B 2, ROI 2, SWA 4.

STURT, Florence M. Exh. 1897-98
Miniature portrait painter. Treherne, Bushey, Herts. † RA 1, RMS 1.

STURT, M.C. Exh. 1930
Mrs. Pigache. Add: Cheltenham, Glos. † SWA 1.

STURTON, A. Isabel Exh. 1896
Holbeach, Lincs. † B 1.

STUTFIELD, Mrs. Exh. 1888
21 First Avnue, Brighton, Sussex. † B 1.

STUTTIG, F. Exh. 1899
Sculptor. 149 Wardour Street, London. † RA 1.

STYAN, Miss K.E. Exh. 1890
23 Upper Bedford Place, London. † SWA 1.

STYKA, Tade b. 1889
Exh. 1923. Villa Tade, A'Garches, Seine et Oise. France. † L 1.

STYLE, Amy Exh. 1903-28
Miniature portrait painter. London 1903 and 1924; Richmond, Surrey 1904. † L 3, RA 6, RMS 1, SWA 3.

STYLE, Mrs. Anne b. 1873
nee Gough. Watercolour dog portrait, landscape, flower and miniature painter. b. Peshawar, India. A.R.M.S. 1930. Exh. 1922-39. Add: London. † L 6, RA 1, RHA 1, RI 5, RMS 35, RSA 1, SWA 1, WG 158.

STYLE, J.M. Exh. 1882
35 South Hill Road, Liverpool. † L 1.

STYLES, George C. Exh. 1920
Architect. Elmleigh, The Crescent, Bromsgrove, Worcs. † RA 1.

STYRING, Mrs. Elizabeth Exh. 1911-38
Landscape and architectural painter and teacher. Studied under W.E. Tindall. Add: Sheffield. † B 13, L 9, ROI 4, SWA 1.

STYTCH, B. Exh. 1924-27
6 Augustus Road, Acocks Green, Birmingham. † B 3.

SUAR, du, de la Croix See D

SUCH, May C. Exh. 1914-34
Mrs. C.W. Harvey, later Mrs. H.E.R. Besant. Miniature portrait and watercolour painter. Add: Ealing, London 1914; Ickenham, Uxbridge, Middlesex 1933. † RA 7, RI 1.

SUDBURY, E.A. Exh. 1910-12
Low Pavement, Nottingham. † N 1, RA 1.

SUDBURY, J.W. Exh. 1910
Frankfurt, Vesey Road, Wylde Green, Birmingham. † B 1.

SUDDABY, Rowland* b. 1912
Landscape, flower, still life and figure painter. Studied Sheffield College of Art. Exh. 1936-38. † BK 3, GOU 1, M 3, NEA 1, RED 159, TOO 1.

SUDDABY, William D. Exh. 1932
Watercolour interior painter. London. † RA 1.

SUDDARDS, Frank 1864-1938
Watercolour painter. Studied under T.R. Ablett at Bradford. Inspector of Arts with the Board of Education. Exh. 1881. Add: 4 Fir Grove, Bournemouth. † RI 1.

SUDRE, R. Exh. 1908
68 Rue d'Assas, Paris. † L 1.

SUEUR, le See L

SUGARS, Fanny Exh. 1882-1926
Flower painter. Didsbury 1882; Manchester 1885; Huyton, Lancs. 1899. † L 33, M 22, RA 5.

SUGDEN, A. Exh. 1933
17 Kelso Road, Liverpool. † L 4.

SUGDEN, E. Exh. 1936
Watercolour painter. † WG 2.

SUGDEN, Howard D. Exh. 1938
Architect. 102 Fitzjohns Avenue, London. † RA 1.

SUGDEN, Larner Exh. 1897
Architect. Leek, Staffs. † RA 1.
SUGGATE, F.W. Exh. 1883
Flower and landscape painter. 35 Acacia Road, St. Johns Wood, London. † D 3.
SUHRLAND, C. Exh. 1884-88
Figure painter. London 1884; Leamington, Warwicks. 1886. † B 3, RBA 1.
SUKER, Arthur Exh. 1882-1902
Landscape and coastal painter. Brother of Frederick Clive Newcombe q.v. Add: Chester 1882; Liverpool 1883; Merton, Surrey 1886; Lands End, Cornwall 1890; Teignmouth, Devon 1895; Brixham, Devon 1901. † B 1, D 2, L 12, M 1, RA 1, RI 2.
SUKER, W. Exh. 1883
22 Notting Hill Square, London. † L 1.
SULLIVAN, Daryll Exh. 1926
82 Redcliffe Gardens, London. † NEA 1.
SULLIVAN, Edmund Joseph 1869-1933
Painter, etcher and illustrator. Studied under his father Michael S. On staff of "Graphic" 1889. Examiner in pictorial and industrial art, Board of Education and art examiner for Joint Matriculation Board, Manchester. Brother of James Frank and Leo Sylvester S. q.v. A.R.E. 1925, A.R.W.S. 1903. Add: London 1894 and 1909; Cookham Dene, Berks. 1904. † BA 1, FIN 7, GI 13, I 37, L 56, NEA 9, RA 20, RE 11, RHA 11, RSA 4, RSW 47.
SULLIVAN, F. Exh. 1931
Linocut artist. † RED 3.
SULLIVAN, James Amory Exh. 1908
18 Avenue de Breteuil, Paris. † LS 1.
SULLIVAN, James Frank 1853-1936
Black and white artist and illustrator. Brother of Edmund Joseph and Leo Sylvester S. q.v. Add: London. † FIN 50, RBA 1.
SULLIVAN, Leo Sylvester b. 1878
Architect. Brother of Edmund Joseph and James Frank S. q.v. Exh. 1925-34. Add: London. † RA 6.
SULLIVAN, M.S. Exh. 1913
Pencil artist. † CG 2.
SULLIVAN, Mrs. Timothy Exh. 1919-25
49 Grosvenor Road, Rathgar, Dublin. † RHA 8.
SULLIVAN, William Holmes* d. 1908
Figure painter. London. † B 3, L 1, RCA 12.
SULLY, Frank E. Exh. 1927-28
12 Carlton Mews, Carlton Road, London. † M 2, NEA 1.
SULMAN, Benjamin Arthur Exh. 1908
48 Bullar Road, Bitterne Park, Southampton. † LS 1.
SULMAN, Dora Exh. 1893
Animal painter. Underwood, Church End, Finchley, London. † NEA 1.
SULMAN, John Exh. 1880-85
Architect. 1 Furnivals Inn, Holborn, London. † RA 6.
SUMMER, John Exh. 1889
27 Fitzroy Avenue, Belfast. † RHA 1.
SUMMERFIELD, H. Exh. 1938
261 Sherlock Street, Birmingham. † B 2.
SUMMERFIELD, Miss S. Exh. 1882-93
87 Ryland Road, Edgbaston, Birmingham. † B 16.
SUMMERHAYS, Mrs. Dora 1883-1955
nee Roberts. Watercolour painter and miniaturist. Studied Birmingham College of Art 1932. A.R.M.S. 1938, A.S.W.A. 1939. Add: Tamworth, Staffs. † B 17, RA 6, RMS 12, SWA 2.
SUMMERS, Alick D. Exh. 1929-38
Painter. Portsmouth 1929; Southsea, Hants. 1935. † RA 1, RBA 7.
SUMMERS, Gerald Exh. 1907-38
Landscape painter. London 1907 and 1913; Stalybridge, Cheshire 1909. † CHE 2, L 1, NEA 37, RED 7.
SUMMERS, John Exh. 1932
Linocut artist. † BA 1.
SUMMERS, Mrs. Nora Munro Exh. 1912-22
London. † L 1, NEA 33.
SUMMERS, Rupert F Exh. 1940
Black and white artist. 13 Morton Crescent, London. † RA 1.
SUMNER, Evelyn Exh. 1922-23
Capenhurst, Crosby Road, Waterloo, Liverpool. † L 6.
SUMNER, George Heywood Maunoir 1853-1940
Etcher and archaeologist. Exh. 1880-94. Add: London. † GI 1, RA 2, RE 4.
SUMNER, Henry Exh. 1884-87
Architect. 11 Imperial Buildings, 5 Dale Street, Liverpool. † L 3.
SUMNER, John Exh. 1891-96
Belfast. † RHA 9.
SUMNER, Rev. John A. Exh. 1931-33
† WG 4.
SUMNER, Kathleen Joyce Exh. 1932-38
Etcher. Studied Royal College of Art. Add: London 1932; The Gables, Dorchester 1933. † RA 7.
SUMNER, Miss M. Exh. 1880-85
Landscape painter. Ellesborough Rectory, Tring, Herts. † SWA 4.
SUMNER, Margaret L. Exh. 1882-1913
135 Gower Street, London 1882; Kelbarrow, Grasmere 1898. † D 1, L 4.
SUND, Harold Exh. 1910-14
Landscape and interior painter. Founder member London Group 1913. Add: London. † B 1, LS 8, M 1, NEA 3, RA 6.
SUNDERLAND, Mrs. Frances b. 1866
nee Watson. Watercolour painter and craftworker b. Keighley, Yorks. Studied and taught Keighley Art School. Exh. 1896-1923. Add: Keighley, Yorks. † GI 3, L 3, RCA 2.
SUNGAM, E. Exh. 1905-8
2 George Street, Prestwich, Manchester. † L 1, RCA 1.
SUNLIGHT, Joseph b. 1889
Architect. Liberal M.P. for Shrewsbury. Exh. 1919-24. Add: Manchester 1919; London 1924. † RA 4.
SUPPLE, J.F. Exh. 1882
Fort Pitt, Chatham. † RHA 6.
SURENNE, Mary H. Exh. 1880-84
Artist and teacher. 6 Warreston Crescent, Edinburgh. † RSA 8.
SURGEY, J.B. Exh. 1883
Landscape, architectural and genre painter. Bridge Bourton, Dorset. † RA 1.
SURTEES, John* 1819-1915
Landscape and rustic genre painter. London 1880; Darley Dale, Derbys. 1892. † AG 3, B 4, D 5, L 10, M 5, RA 9, RBA 1, ROI 6, TOO 1.
SURTEES, Mrs. John Exh. 1880-88
Elizabeth Royal. Landscape painter. London. † B 2, D 3, L 3, RBA 1.
SURTEES, Miss M.G. Exh. 1889-93
Figure, landscape and flower painter. 32 Queensborough Terrace, Kensington Gardens, London. † RID 7.
SUSSENS, E. Exh. 1928
Flower painter. † AB 1.
SUTCLIFF, Rosemary b. 1920
Miniature painter. Studied Bideford Art School and under Edwin Morgan. Exh. 1939-40. Add: Yarnscombe, Barnstaple, Devon. † RA 2, RMS 1.
SUTCLIFFE, Alexander K. Exh. 1921-31
Sculptor. Southend on Sea, Essex 1921; Paignton, S. Devon 1931. † RA 12.
SUTCLIFFE, E. Exh. 1901
53 Walterton Road, London. † RI 1.
SUTCLIFFE, Fanny Exh. 1881
8 Canonbury Place, London. † GI 1.
SUTCLIFFE, G.L. Exh. 1910
17 Pall Mall East, London. † RA 1.
SUTCLIFFE, Harriette* Exh. 1881-1907
Sculptor and painter. London 1881 and 1897; Whitby 1896; Harrow, Middlesex 1905. † B 2, GI 1, L 2, M 2, RA 24, ROI 2.
SUTCLIFFE, H.J. Exh. 1884-95
Liverpool. † L 12.
SUTCLIFFE, Irene b. 1883
Miniature painter and woodcut artist. b. Stakesby, nr. Whitby. Exh. 1913-24. Add: Carr Hill, Sleights, Yorks. † RA 2, RSA 3.
SUTCLIFFE, John E. d. 1923
Figure painter. Married E. Earnshaw q.v. R.O.I. 1920. Add: London 1900; Bushey, Herts 1902; Richmond, Surrey 1919. † RA 6, RBA 1, RI 6, ROI 8.
SUTCLIFFE, Mrs. John E.
see EARNSHAW, E.
SUTCLIFFE, Lester Exh. 1880-1930
Landscape painter. Leeds 1880 and 1898; Whitby 1892. † B 6, DOW 2, L 16, M 5, RA 11, RBA 5, RCA 126, WG 14.
SUTCLIFFE, Mrs Lester Exh. 1892-1928
Elizabeth Trevor. Flower painter. Whitby 1892; Leeds 1898. † B 4, L 12, M 4, RA 16, RCA 15, WG 12.
SUTCLIFFE, Mrs. Mollie Exh. 1935-37
Flower painter. 82 Dartmouth Road, Paignton, Devon. † RA 2, SWA 1.
SUTCLIFFE, Millicent M. Exh. 1895-96
193 Gt. Creetham St. Higher Broughton, Manchester. † L 1, M 1.
SUTHER, Mary E. Exh. 1939
3 Lennox Mansions, Southsea, Hants. † SWA 1.
SUTHERLAND, Allan Newton Exh. 1908-15
Aberdeen 1908 and 1915; Glasgow 1913. † GI 8, RSA 2, RSW 2.
SUTHERLAND, Miss C. Exh. 1934
27 Grange Loan, Edinburgh. † RSA 1.
SUTHERLAND, David M. Exh. 1906-40
Figure painter. Married Dorothy Johnstone q.v. A.R.S.A. 1922, R.S.A. 1937. Add: Edinburgh 1906; Grays School of Art, Aberdeen 1930. † GI 19, L 8, RA 1, RSA 110, RSW 1.
SUTHERLAND, Eric A. Exh. 1905-34
96 Renfield Street, Glasgow. † GI 3.
SUTHERLAND, Fanny Exh. 1880-86
Portrait, figure, interior and landscape painter. London. † D 1, L 3, RA 5, RI 1, RSA 2, SWA 2.
SUTHERLAND, Miss F.E. Sinclair Exh. 1940
Lasswade, Midlothian. † GI 1, RSW 1.
SUTHERLAND, Graham* b. 1903
Painter, etcher, engraver and illustrator. Studied Goldsmiths College of Art. Teacher Kingston School of Art and Chelsea School of Art 1927-40. A.R.E. 1925. Member London Group 1937. A collection of his works are in the Tate Gallery. Add: Sutton, Surrey 1923; Farningham, Kent 1928; Eynsford, Kent 1931. † ALP 1, BA 4, CHE 2, GI 3 LEI 33, NEA 3, RA 13, RE 11.

SUTHERLAND, James Exh. 1920-36
Die-cutter. Studied under Alexander Kirkwood of Edinburgh and at Edinburgh College of Art for 8 years. Instructor in Heraldic die-cutting Edinburgh College of Art. Add: 23 Bellevue Road, Edinburgh. † RSA 14.

SUTHERLAND, Jean P. Exh. 1926-27
Portrait and still life painter. c/o Commonwealth Bank of Australia, Australia House, London. † RA 2.

SUTHERLAND, John Robert d. 1933
Designer and heraldic artist. b. Lerwick, Scotland. Studied Heriot Watt College and Edinburgh College of Art. Heraldic artist to the Court of the Lord Lyon, H.M. Register House, Edinburgh. Add: Edinburgh 1898 and 1913; Leith 1911. † L 3, RSA 23, RSW 3.

SUTHERLAND, Mrs. M. Alice Exh. 1929-35
Mrs. H.H. Add: Carron Lodge, St. Andrews. † RSA 1, RSW 3.

SUTHERLAND, Robert Lewis d. 1932
Landscape painter. b. Glasgow. Studied Glasgow School of Art and Academie Delecluse, Paris. Exh. from 1890. Add: Glasgow. † GI 90, L 6, M 1, RSA 13, RSW 6.

SUTHERLAND, Scott b. 1910
Sculptor. b. Wick. Studied Grays School of Art 1928-29, Edinburgh College of Art 1929-33, Ecole des Beaux Arts, Paris 1934. Travelled widely. Exh. 1933-40. Add: Wick, Caithness 1933; Edinburgh 1936; Corstorphine 1939. † RSA 10.

SUTHERS, Leghe* Exh. 1883-1905
Portrait and figure painter. N.E.A. 1887. Add: Southport, Lancs. 1883 and 1895; Newlyn, Penzance 1893; Paul, Penzance 1896; Porlock, Somerset 1900. † B 1, L 6, M 3, RA 12, RSA 1.

SUTHERS, W. Exh 1880-90
Landscape, flower and marine painter. School of Art, South Kensington Museum, London. † D 2, L 7, RA 3, RBA 10.

SUTRO, Mrs. Esther Stella Exh. 1885-1931
nee Isaacs. Painter and pastellier. Studied R.A. Schools. Spent 10 years in Paris. Add: London 1885, 1899 and 1902; Wareham, Dorset 1895; Abingdon, Berks. 1900. † FIN 38, GI 5, GOU 11, I 5, L 37, LEF 24, LEI 47, LS 1, M 6, NG 1, RA 2, RHA 1, ROI 1, SWA 1.

SUTTER, Katherine Eugenie Exh. 1887
6 Bellevue Terrace, Edinburgh. † RSA 1.

SUTTERBY, Herbert Exh. 1901-5
Liscard, Cheshire. † L 3.

SUTTILL, Ada P. Exh. 1889-90
Flower painter. Bridport, Dorset. † RA 2.

SUTTON, A. Exh. 1911
1A Trelawn Avenue, Ash Road, Headingley, Leeds. † RA 1.

SUTTON, Amy Exh. 1916-20
10 Helena Street, Walton, Liverpool. † L 2.

SUTTON, B. Exh. 1910
Market Place Chambers, Reading, Berks. † RA 1

SUTTON, Belle Marian Exh. 1920-24
Watercolour painter and heraldic artist. St. Brelades, Ularian, Glas, Anglesey. † L 3.

SUTTON, Ernest R. Exh. 1902-5
Architect. Bromley House, Nottingham. † RA 3.

SUTTON, Francis C. Exh. 1939
61 Marlborough Place, London. † ROI 1.

SUTTON, G. Exh. 1939
32 Violet Road, West Bridgford, Nottingham. † N 1.

SUTTON, Gordon Exh. 1937-40
14 Kirkley Cliff, Lowestoft, Suffolk. † RI 4, RSW 1.

SUTTON, Helen Constance Pym b. 1882
Mrs. G.H. Edwards. Landscape painter and critic. Studied at St. Ives, Cornwall under Algernon Talmage and Moulton Foweraker 1906-8 and under H. Dawson Barkas at Reading 1909. Add: Wolverhampton 1911; Reading, Berks. 1922. † B 1, SWA 2.

SUTTON, Miss I. Exh. 1900-2
Ruddington, Notts. † N 2.

SUTTON, Isabella M. Exh. 1914-16
Lezayre, Egerton Park, Rock Ferry, Cheshire. † L 3.

SUTTON, J. Exh. 1880-91
Watercolour landscape painter. Edinburgh. † RA 3, RSA 3.

SUTTON, J. Exh. 1893
London Street, Southport, Lancs. † L 1.

SUTTON, Joan Exh. 1934-37
Landscape painter. Rookery Cottage, Shinfield Green, Berks. † COO 5.

SUTTON, Miss N. Exh. 1886
Westbourne House, Barbourne, Worcs. † B 2.

SUTTON, Rev. R.B. Exh. 1935
451 Gillott Road, Birmingham. † B 1.

SUTTON, R. Fran Exh. 1938
Still life painter. Clock House Lane, Ashford, Middlesex. † RA 1.

SVEINBJORNSSON, Miss H. McL. Exh. 1916
94 Thirlestane Road, Edinburgh. † RSA 1.

SVOBODA, Alexander* Exh. 1888
Landscape painter. 143 Ladbroke Grove Road, North Kensington, London. † D 1.

SWABEY, Mrs. Lois Exh. 1932-38
Home Farm House, Ferring, Worthing, Sussex. † RBA 5, SWA 2.

SWAFFIELD, Helena M. Exh. 1891-1906
Portrait, figure, landscape and flower painter. Sevenoaks 1891 and 1902; London 1895. † L 3, P 1, RA 11, RBA 3, ROI 2.

SWAIN, Fred Exh. 1884
c/o Holbrook, 73 New Bridge Street, Manchester. † M 1.

SWAIN, L.L. Exh. 1910-18
London 1910; Ewell, Surrey 1918. † RA 4.

SWAIN, Ned d. 1902
Landscape painter and etcher. R.E. 1882. Add: London 1880 and 1900; Fordwick, Canterbury, Kent 1898. † L 2, RA 5, RBA 5, RE 25, ROI 2.

SWAIN, W.E. Exh. 1921-29
Landscape painter. A.N.S.A. 1921-32. Add: 21 Mansfield Grove, Nottingham. † N 13.

SWAINE, Agnes Kempson b. 1892
Landscape painter, etcher, designer and illustrator. b. Panteg, Mon. Studied Cheltenham and under Stanhope Forbes at Newlyn, Penzance. Exh. 1916-38. Add: Bristol 1916; West Malvern 1929. † B 3, L 4, RI 4.

SWAINE, Mrs. Eva C. Exh. 1895
Eastham, Drogheda. † RHA 2.

SWAINE, Frank A. Exh. 1924-36
Landscape painter. London. † B 1, L 1, RA 1, ROI 1.

SWAINSON, Douglas Exh. 1940
Portrait painter. 85 Church Lane, London. † RA 1.

SWAINSON, Mary Exh. 1884-1913
Sculptor. London 1884, 1892 and 1912; Cheltenham 1891 and 1899; Paris 1906. † G 4, LS 1, NG 3, RA 9 RE 1.

SWAINSON, William Exh. 1884-88
Miniature portrait painter. 29 Beauclerk Road, Hammersmith, London. † L 1, RA 3, RI 1.

SWAINSTON, Laura Exh. 1887-94
Painter and etcher. Add: The Elms, Sunderland. † GI 1, RA 3, RSA 2.

SWAISH, Frederick G. Exh. 1907-29
Portrait and figure painter. Shamley Green, Guildford 1907; Willsbridge, nr. Bristol 1910; Royal West of England Academy, Bristol 1916; Bath 1927. † B 1, L 5, M 1, RA 27, RSA 1.

SWALES, Edward Exh. 1927
8 East Street, Lewes, Sussex. † RBA 1.

SWALLOW, E. Constance Exh. 1884-86
Silverton House, Hill Street, St. Albans, Herts. † D 2.

SWALLOW, J.C. Exh. 1883
6 New Compton Street, Soho, London. † L 1.

SWAN, Alice Macallan d. 1939
Landscape and flower painter and watercolourist, A.R.W.S. 1903. Add: Cork 1882; Lincoln 1884; Glasgow 1887; London 1888. † BA 1, BG 3, GI 4, I 3, L 14, M 1, NEA 1, RA 19, RI 2, RSA 4, RWS 88, SWA 2.

SWAN, Miss B. Exh. 1940
† NEA 1.

SWAN, Cuthbert Edmund* 1870-1931
Wild animal painter. b. Ireland. Studied Seaford College. Teacher of animal drawing for L.C.C. School of Arts and Crafts. Brother of Edwin S. q.v. Add: London. † L 1, M 2, RA 18, RI 20, ROI 25.

SWAN, Edwin b. 1873
Portrait painter. b. Ballyragget, Ireland. Studied Juliens, Paris. Brother of Cuthbert Edmund S. q.v. Exh. 1896-1940. Add: London 1896; 1902 and 1909; Crowborough, Sussex 1900; Bath 1903. † L 4, RA 6, RHA 1, RI 1.

SWAN, Emily R. Exh. 1893
Flower and figure painter. 174 King Street, Hammersmith, London. † L 1, RA 1, RBA 2.

SWAN, Frances I. Exh. 1895-1903
Sculptor. 58 Holland Park, London. † M 2, RA 4.

SWAN, Mrs. H.B. Exh. 1919
† I 2.

SWAN, James Exh. 1906-40
Architect. R.B.S.A. 1932. Add: Birmingham. † B 13, RA 10.

SWAN, James H. Exh. 1908-13
Landscape painter. London 1908; Amersham, Bucks. 1913. † LS 15, NEA 1.

SWAN, John Macallan* 1847-1910
Animal painter and sculptor. Studied Lambeth School of Art, R.A. Schools, and in Paris with Gerome and Fremiet. A.R.A. 1894, R.A. 1905, A.R.W.S. 1896, R.W.S. 1899. "The Prodigal Son" purchased by Chantrey Bequest 1889. Add: Cork 1880; London 1884. † AG 1, B 4, CAR 1, D 4, FIN 217, G 3, GI 19, GOU 2, I 44, L 16, M 1, NG 4, RA 52, RHA 10, RSA 17, RWS 10.

SWAN, Mrs. J.M. (Mary) Exh. 1889-1910
Painter. 3 Acacia Road, London. † B 1, G 1, L 2, NG 3, RA 1, RHA 2.

SWAN, Miss L. Exh. 1890
Indiana, Avondale Road, Croydon, Surrey. † SWA 1.

SWAN, Miss L.B. Exh. 1907-40
Bushey, Herts. 1907; London 1909 and 1912; Haywards Heath, Sussex 1911. † B 1, D 17, L 1, LS 3, RA 1, RI 2, SWA 5.

SWAN, Lilian Bellingham Exh. 1919-21
45 St. Stephens Green, Dublin. † LS 3, RHA 1.

SWAN, Mary A. Exh. 1907-13
Figure painter, London. † GOU 8, RA 3.

SWAN, Mary E. Exh. 1889-98
Flower, fruit and portrait painter. Bromley, Kent 1889; London 1895. † B 2, FIN 2, L 6, NG 1, RA 2, ROI 9.

SWAN, Miss M.W. Exh. 1914
Westbank, Esher, Surrey. † GI 1.

SWAN, Robert John* b. 1888
Portrait and landscape painter. Studied R.A. Schools (Landseer scholarship and British Institute scholarship in painting). Assistant art master at St. Martins School of Art. Exh. 1908-40. Add: London. † CHE 1, D 3, I 5, L 4, P 14, RA 13, RBA 8, RI 2.

SWAN, Thomas Aikman Exh. 1907-39
Architect. Studied Edinburgh. Add: Edinburgh. † RSA 18.

SWANN, Harold Exh. 1940
Painter. 88 Charlotte Street, London. † RA 1.

SWANN, Mrs. Ruth N. Exh. 1934-36
Sculptor. 36 Marryat Road, Wimbledon, London. † RA 2.

SWANN, Mrs. Torfrida Exh. 1919-38
Later Mrs. R.D. Oliver. Watercolour landscape painter. b. Ballarat, Australia. Travelled widely. Add: Witley, Surrey 1919; London 1923. † GI 1, GOU 8, I 1, L 1, RA 1, SWA 1, WG 67.

SWANSON, Margaret Exh. 1899-1903
23 Bellevue Crescent, Ayr, N.B. † GI 2, RSA 1.

SWANSTON, J. Exh. 1902-3
196 High Street, Kirkcaldy, N.B. † GI 2.

SWANWICK, Mrs. Ernest Exh. 1882-84
Lymm, Cheshire. † M 3.

SWANWICK, Harold 1866-1929
Animal, figure and landscape painter. b. Middlewich. Studied Liverpool and Slade School, and Juliens, Paris. Married Lilian Heatley q.v. R.I. 1897, R.O.I. 1909. Add: Winsford, Cheshire 1887; Middlewich, Cheshire 1896; Wilmington, Polegate, Sussex 1909. † B 24, L 119, RA 30, RBA 6, RCA 162, RHA 2, RI 142, ROI 60, RSA 1, WG 102.

SWANWICK, Mrs. Harold
see HEATLEY, Lilian

SWANWICK, J.P. Exh. 1887-89
Winsford, Cheshire. † L 2.

SWANWICK, Miss Kate Exh. 1903-11
Clive House, Middlewich, Cheshire 1903; London 1911. † L 15 RA 1.

SWANWICK, Katharine Exh. 1905
34 Croxteth Road, Liverpool. † L 1.

SWANZY, Mary Exh. 1905-37
Painter, Dublin. † FIN 2, I 2, LEF 20, LS 5, RHA 34, SWA 2.

SWARBRICK, T.F. Exh. 1933
8 Ripon Street, Blackburn, Lancs. † L 1.

SWATKINS, J. Alfred Exh. 1888-1923
Birmingham. † B 14.

SWAYNE, Winifred Exh. 1899-1938
Miniature portrait painter. A.R.M.S. 1916. Add: Bromsgrove 1899; Hereford 1905; Bournemouth 1938. † B 9, L 1, RA 12.

SWEENY, E.F. Exh. 1912
8 Rathdown Road, Dublin. † RHA 2.

SWEET, Ada M. Exh. 1890-91
Figure painter. 15 Albert Square, Clapham Road, London. † RBA 2, ROI 1.

SWEET, Dorothy Exh. 1925-29
Painter and etcher. London. † AB 3, D 3, SWA 1.

SWEET, George Exh. 1885-96
Pollokshields 1885; Hamilton, N.B. 1888. † GI 8.

SWEET, G.L. Exh. 1930
206 Hainault Road, Leytonstone, Essex. † NEA 1.

SWEET, John Exh. 1938-40
Flower and still life painter. 4 Salisbury Road, Birmingham. † B 3, RA 2.

SWEET, Julia M. Exh. 1927
65 London Road, Leicester. † L 7.

SWEETING, J. Exh. 1880
Maylawn, Worthing, Sussex. † RHA 2.

SWEETMAN, Violet Exh. 1929
69 Patrick Street, Cork. † RHA 2.

SWERTSHKOFF, G. Exh. 1908
15 Clifford Street, London. † RA 1.

SWETENHAM, Miss D. Exh. 1890
Moston Hall, Chester. † SWA 1.

SWIFT, Ada E. Exh. 1914-20
Blackrock Hall, Speke, nr. Liverpool. † L 4.

SWIFT, Agnes H. Exh. 1936-37
Figure painter. 54 North View, Pinner, Middlesex. † RA 2, RSA 1.

SWIFT, Fred G. Exh. 1899-1939
Landscape painter. Leicester. † N 16.

SWIFT, Georgiana Exh. 1880
Figure painter. 16 West Cromwell Road, London. † SWA 1.

SWIFT, H. Exh. 1925
Portrait painter. Fern Villa, Heage, nr. Belper, Derbys. † N 1.

SWIFT, Katherine Exh. 1907
Westlands, Compton Road, Wolverhampton. † B 1.

SWIFT, L. Burgess Exh. 1880-85
Animal painter. S.W.A. 1880. Add: 16 West Cromwell Road, London. † SWA 8.

SWINBURN, E. Exh. 1888
† TOO 1.

SWINBURN, Miss V. Exh. 1927
104 West George Street, Glasgow. † L 1.

SWINBURNE, Alice Exh. 1918
† I 2.

SWINBURNE, Hattie Exh. 1893-1914
Landscape painter. Nottingham. † N 23.

SWINBURNE, Thordur J.W. Exh. 1918
94 Thirlestane Road, Edinburgh. † RSA 1.

SWINBURNE, Col. Thomas Robert
Exh. 1917-18
23 Eaton Place, London. † LS 6.

SWINDELLS, Dora M. Exh. 1908
30 Stanley Road, Parkfield, New Ferry, Cheshire. † L 1.

SWINDEN, Elsie C. Exh. 1886-1905
Edgbaston, Birmingham. † B 26.

SWINDEN, F.W. Exh. 1883
Talbot Villa, Merton Road, Bootle, Lancs. † L 1.

SWINDEN, Miss S.A. Exh. 1882-86
Earlsmere, Westfield Road, Birmingham. † B 5.

SWINEY, Agatha M.M. Exh. 1880-1901
Flower and portrait painter. London 1880; Herne Bay 1901. † SWA 9.

SWINEY, C.W. Exh. 1936-39
† GOU 5, NEA 1.

SWINEY, Evelyn Gray Exh. 1913-24
Landscape painter. b. Capetown, South Africa. Add: Crown Hill, Devon 1913; London 1924. † D 1, L 1, RA 1.

SWINGLER, John Frank Exh. 1886-1909
Still life, flower, fruit and fish painter. London. † B 1, L 1, M 2, RA 21, RBA 7, ROI 10.

SWINNERTON, F. Exh. 1887-89
Manchester. † M 3.

SWINNERTON, Jane E. Exh. 1927
18 Town Lane, Woodhey, Rock Ferry, Cheshire. † L 17.

SWINNY, Miss A. Exh. 1919
40 Paultons Square, London. † SWA 1.

SWINNY, E.M.A. Exh. 1884-98
Painter. London 1884; Hadleigh House, Windsor, Berks. 1898. † D 1, SWA 2.

SWINSCOE, Mrs. Marian E. Exh. 1910-38
Portrait and miniature painter. A.N.S.A. 1914, N.S.A. 1921. Add: Bingham, Notts. 1910; West Bridgford, Notts. 1916. † L 8, N 54, RSA 2.

SWINSON, Edward S. Exh. 1893-1936
Portrait and figure painter. London 1893 and 1902; Rugby 1895; Southsea, Hants. 1906; Braunton, Devon 1926; George Nympton, Devon 1930. † B 8, BG 1, L 9, NG 2, RA 12, RBA 3, RSA 2.

SWINSTEAD, Alfred Hillyard Exh. 1881-97
Coastal and figure painter and teacher. Brother of Frank H. and George H.S. and father of A. Lester S. q.v. Add: 70 Jenner Road, Stoke Newington, London. † RA 2, RBA 1.

SWINSTEAD, A. Lester Exh. 1917-39
Painter. Son of Alfred Hillyard S. q.v. Studied R.A. Schools. Add: London 1917; Oswestry, Salop. 1927. † L 1, RA 1, RCA 8.

SWINSTEAD, Charles Exh. 1887
† ROI 2.

SWINSTEAD, Eulalia Hillyard b. 1893
Miniature portrait painter. Daughter of George H.S. q.v. Exh. 1918-32. Add: 14 Kidderpore Avenue, Hampstead, London. † RA 4, RCA 16.

SWINSTEAD, Eliza L. Exh. 1881
Flower painter. 12 St. Marks Square, Dalston. † RBA 2.

SWINSTEAD, Frank Hillyard 1862-1937
Figure and landscape painter. Studied North London School of Art, Royal College of Art and Juliens, Paris. Master North London School of Art 1880-1902. Master Hornsey School of Art 1882-91. Principal Hornsey School of Art 1891-1926. Headmaster Walthamstow School of Art 1882-93 and Headmaster Willesden Polytechnic School of Art 1893-1907. Brother of Alfred H. and George H.S. q.v. R.B.A. 1908. Add: London. † M 5, RA 3, RBA 158.

SWINSTEAD, George Hillyard* 1860-1926
Portrait, genre, landscape and coastal painter. Studied R.A. Schools 1881. Brother of Alfred H. and Frank H. and father of Eulalia H.S. q.v. R.B.A. 1893, R.I. 1907. Add: London. † B 28, D 11, GI 8, L 27, LS 1, M 15, P 6, RA 48, RBA 157, RCA 116, RI 77, ROI 6, RSA 1.

SWINTON, Emily Exh. 1907
Albany Street, Dunfermline. † RSA 1.

SWINTON, Marion Exh. 1905
c/o E. Addison, Esq. 2 Bolton Studios, Redcliffe Road, London. † ROI 1.

SWINTON, Mrs. N. Exh. 1911
Addison Bridge, London. † SWA 1.

SWINY, P.W. Exh. 1935
94 Ebury Street, London. † RBA 1.

SWIRE, John Exh. 1883-87
Watercolour painter and teacher. 5 Westfield Grove, Wakefield, Yorks. † RBA 1, RI 1.

SWOBODA, Rudolf* 1859-1914
Austrian landscape painter. Add: London 1884-92. † B 3, L 4, M 1, RA 3, RBA 8, ROI 1.

SWORN, Miss Alex P. Exh. 1889-90
Flower painter. Lansdowne Road, Bournemouth. † B 2, SWA 2.

SWYNNERTON, Anna Louisa* 1844-1933
nee Robinson. Allegorical, symbolical and portrait painter. b. Kersal, nr. Manchester. Studied Manchester School of Art, Paris and Rome. Married Joseph William S. q.v. N.E.A. 1909, A.R.A. 1922, R.P. 1891, S.W.A. 1887. "New Risen Hope" (1904) purchased by Chantrey Bequest 1924, "The Convalescent" purchased 1929 and "Dame Millicent Fawcett C.B.E., LL.D." purchased 1930. Add: Manchester 1880; London 1882. † B 1, BAR 1, G 9, GI 1, I 1, L 28, M 24, NEA 12, NG 41, P 5, RA 60, RSA 5, SWA 9.

SWYNNERTON, Joseph William 1848-1910
Sculptor. b. Isle of Man. Married Anna Louisa S. q.v. Add: Rome 1883; London 1884. † G 1, L 6, M 4, NG 13, RA 7.

SYANKOWSKI, de see D

SYDALL, Joseph Exh. 1898-1910
Portrait painter. The Studio, Old Whittington, Chesterfield. † RA 4.

SYDENHAM, E.A. Exh. 1938
Watercolour painter. † WG 2.

SYDNEY, John Exh. 1893-94
Figure painter. Fern Villa, High Road, Chiswick, London. † ROI 2.

SYER, John* 1815-1885
Landscape painter. Studied with J. Fisher at Bristol. A.R.I. 1874, R.I. 1875, R.O.I. 1883. Add: London. † L 5, RI 21, ROI 3, TOO 5.

SYER, Percy E. Exh. 1918-24
Watercolour painter. A.R.B.A. 1923. Add: 8th Battalion, East Surrey Regiment, B.E.F. France 1918; London 1919 and 1922; Brighton 1920. † RA 5, RBA 7.

SYERS, Rose Aspinall Exh. 1905-27
Landscape painter. London 1905 and 1922; Worthing 1915. † B 1, GI 2, L 26, LS 8, M 3, RA 5, ROI 7, SWA 2.

SYKES, Mrs. A. Exh. 1890
Edgeley Mount, Stockport, Lancs. † M 1.

SYKES, Angela Exh. 1929-32
Sculptor. Sledmere, Malton, Yorks. † RA 3.

SYKES, Arthur Exh. 1889-1921
Architect. London. † RA 4.

SYKES, A. Bernard Exh. 1893-94
Painter. Perry Hill, Catford, London. † RA 1, RBA 1.

SYKES, Aubrey F. Exh. 1929-40
Watercolour painter. R.I. 1940. Add: Watford, Herts. 1929; Ealing, London 1935. † RA 2, RBA 2, RI 9, ROI 1.

SYKES, Charles Exh. 1911-38
Sculptor. London. † GI 1, L 1, RA 7, RI 2.

SYKES, Dorcie b. 1908
Watercolour flower and figure painter. b. Sheffield. Daughter of John Gutteridge S. q.v. Studied Harvey and Proctor School of Painting. Exh. 1924-40. Add: 2 Church Lane, Newlyn, Penzance, Cornwall. † L 1, RI 9, RSA 8.

SYKES, Mrs. Dorothy Exh. 1937
Sully, Glamorgan. † RCA 2.

SYKES, E.A. Exh. 1885
Painter. Manor Heath, Clapham Common, London. † SWA 2.

SYKES, Ethel Shirley Exh. 1917-19
Holdenhurst Avenue, North Finchley, London. † LS 7.

SYKES, George b. 1863
Watercolour landscape painter and architect. Son of Peace S. q.v. Exh. 1900-29. Add: Estate Buildings, Huddersfield. † L 1, RA 3, RI 10, WG 76.

SYKES, Henry 1855-1921
Landscape and genre painter. R.B.A. 1890. Add: Glasgow 1882; Littleover, nr. Derby 1887; London 1889; Rathmines, Dublin 1901. † GI 1, L 6, M 3, N 2, NG 1, RA 6, RBA 16, RHA 2, RI 4, RSA 2.

SYKES, Josephine Exh. 1927-37
Sculptor. A.S.W.A. 1939. Add: London. † GI 1, RA 4, SWA 2.

SYKES, John A.L. Exh. 1889
Luscombe Villa, Woodfield Road, Kingsheath, nr. Birmingham. † B 1.

SYKES, J.D. Exh. 1926
† M 1.

SYKES, John E. Exh. 1909-14
Huddersfield. † L 6.

SYKES, John Gutteridge b. 1866
Landscape and marine painter. Studied Sheffield School of Art. Father of Dorcie S. q.v. Exh. 1895-1936. Add: Hillsborough, Sheffield 1895; Newlyn, Penzance 1915. † GI 9, L 1, RA 1, RI 8.

SYKES, John W. Exh. 1919-37
Sculptor. 9 Camden Studios, Camden Street, London. † GI 1, I 1, L 6, EA 7.

SYKES, Lilian Exh. 1887-90
Painter. Duppas Hill, Croydon, Surrey. † RI 2, SWA 6.

SYKES, Mrs. M. Exh. 1924
31 Fenton Road, Lockwood, Huddersfield. † L 1.

SYKES, Marianne Exh. 1881-91
Miniature portrait painter. 52 Delancy Street, Gloucester Gate, Regents Park, London. † RA 15.

SYKES, Peace Exh. 1886-1900
Landscape painter. Father of George S. q.v. Add: Huddersfield. † L 2, M 1, RA 3, RI 4.

SYKES, Steven Exh. 1938
22 Gt. King Street, Edinburgh. † RSA 1.

SYLVA, van Damme Exh. 1903
64 Rue Van der Linden, Brussels. † GI 2.

SYLVESTER, John Henry Exh. 1880-94
Portrait, figure, interior and still life painter. London 1880 and 1883; Paris 1882. † B 3, G 1, GI 1, L 1, M 1, P 1, RA 3, RBA 7, RHA 7, ROI 3.

SYM, E.B. Exh. 1910
60 Murrayfield Gardens, Edinburgh. † RSA 1.

SYM, Mary G. Exh. 1927-37
Edinburgh 1927; Colinton 1934. † RSA 2, RSW 10.

SYME, E.W. Exh. 1931
Linocut artist. † RED 2.

SYMES, Edith M. Exh. 1907-8
Painter. Mount Druid, Killiney, Co. Dublin. † NEA 1, RHA 1.

SYMES, Ivor I.J. Exh. 1899-1937
Married to Mabel Gear q.v. Add: Bushey, Herts. 1899; Tadley, Hants. 1934. † RA 2, ROI 10.

SYMINGTON, Lindsay D. Exh. 1891-1903
Landscape and coastal painter. London 1891; Buckfastleigh, Devon 1895; Princetown, Devon 1897. † M 1, RA 2, RBA 4, RI 6.

SYMINGTON, R.S. Exh. 1885-89
Glasgow 1885; Paisley 1888. † GI 4.

SYMONDS, G.H. Exh. 1931
232 Selsey Road, Edgbaston, Birmingham. † B 1.

SYMONDS, P.T. Exh. 1892-93
Belle Vue, Erdington, nr. Birmingham. † L 2.

SYMONDS, S.C. Exh. 1883
Stags End, Hemel Hempstead, Herts. † L 1.

SYMONDS, William Robert 1851-1934
Portrait, figure and landscape painter. b. Yoxford, Suffolk. Studied London and Antwerp. R.P. 1891. Add: Ipswich, Suffolk 1880; London 1881. † B 1, G 3, GI 1, L 31, M 4, NG 27, P43, RA 79, ROI 2.

SYMONS, George Gardiner* 1863-1930
American landscape painter. R.B.A. 1908. Exh. 1899-1913. Add: Oxford 1899; St. Ives, Cornwall 1908; London 1912. † B 1, L 3, RA 7, RBA 8.

SYMONS, James Anthony Exh. 1914
Pastoral landscape painter. 66 Redcliffe Road, South Kensington, London. † NEA 1.

SYMONS, Mark Lancelot 1887-1935
Landscape and figure painter. Son of William Christian S. q.v. Studied Slade School. Add: London 1906 and 1916; Rye, Sussex 1915; Caversham, Reading, Berks. 1925; Wokingham, Berks. 1933. † GOU 3, L 4, LS 6, NEA 12, RA 26.

SYMONS, Rosalie G. Exh. 1918-21
Follett Lodge, Topsham, Devon. † B 6, L 3.

SYMONS, William Christian* 1845-1911
Portrait, genre, landscape, still life, flower and historical painter and decorative and stained glass designer. Studied Lambeth School of Art and R.A. Schools 1866. Father of Mark Lancelot S. q.v. N.E.A. 1891, R.B.A. 1881. Add: Hampstead, London 1880; Mayfield, Sussex 1898; Battle, Sussex 1905; Rye, Sussex 1910. † B 1, BG 2, G 2, GI 4, GOU 9, L 3, M 9, NEA 6, RA 23, RBA 49, RHA 1, RI 1, ROI 4.

SYMS, James J. Exh. 1903
Landscape painter. 30 Ravensbourne Gardens, West Ealing, London. † RA 1.

SYMUND, B.A. Exh. 1883
c/o Cunningham, 52 Cameron Street, London. † L 1.

SYNGE, Edward Millington 1860-1913
Landscape painter and etcher. Self taught. Travelled in France, Spain and Italy. Married F. Molony q.v. A.R.E. 1898. Add: Weybridge, Surrey 1895; London 1901; Byfleet, Surrey 1906. † CON 106, GI 13, GOU 8, L 13, LS 6, RA 11, RE 88, RHA 17, RID 72.

SYNGE, Theodora Exh. 1926
c/o L.M. Synge, Christleton House, nr. Chester. † L 1.

SYNGE-HUTCHINSON, Patrick Exh. 1932-35
Sculptor. London. † RA 4.

SYRETT, Barbara Exh. 1927-28
Miniature painter. 8 Hillcrest Road, Sydenham, Kent. † RA 2.

SYRETT, Miss M. Exh. 1894
113 Ashley Gardens, Westminster, London. † SWA 2.

SZCZEPANOWSKI, Vanda Exh. 1884-86
5 Stanwick Road, West Kensington, London. † L 1, M 1.

SZIRMAI, Tony Exh. 1912
112 Boulevard Malesherbes, Paris. † L 1.

SZNOLLER Exh. 1881
Palazzo Rezzonico, Venice. † RSA 1.

SZONYI, Istvan b. 1884
Hungarian artist. Exh. 1935. † RSA 2.

SZUTS, S. Exh. 1931-35
Watercolour painter. † RED 3.

SZVATEK, Mrs. A.D.C. Exh. 1910
15 Blithfield Street, Kensington, London. † RA 1.

SZYK, Arthur* Exh. 1939
Portrait and figure painter. † AG 89.

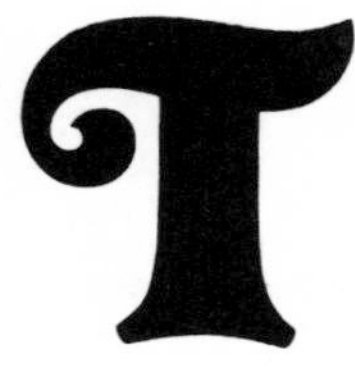

TABLEY, Charles J. Exh. 1914
Painter. † ALP 1.

TA'BOIS, Mrs. Flora Exh. 1911
White House, Harrow Lane, Maidenhead, Berks. † ROI 1.

TABOR, Alan MacKenzie Exh 1938
† M 2.

TABOR, G.H. c.1857-1920
Concarneau, Finistere, France 1889; Teddington, Middlesex 1911. † B 1, LS 10.

TABOR, Helen Exh. 1908-15
Mrs. G.H. Add: The Cottage, Twickenham Road, Teddington, Middlesex. † LS 10.

TABUTEAU, Miss Exh. 1896
54 Eccleston Square, London. † SWA 1.

TACKMAN, Kate Exh. 1889
11 Stoke Newington Road, London. † ROI 1.

TAELEMANS, I.F. Exh. 1909
33 Avenue Brugmann, Brussels. † L 1.

TAFFS, Charles H. Exh. 1896-1905
Black and white artist. London. † RA 4.

TAGGART, Eleanor Exh. 1890
16 Sutherland Drive, Hillhead, Glasgow. † GI 1.

TAIT, Alex Exh. 1888
223 Hope Street, Glasgow. † GI 1.

TAIT, Anne Fraser Exh. 1892-1900
Busby 1892; Glasgow 1898. † GI 7.

TAIT, Adela Seton Exh. 1897-1901
Flower painter. 99 Burnt Ash Road, Lee, London. † RA 3, RBA 4.

TAIT, Mrs. Bess Norriss See NORRISS

TAIT, C.J. Exh. 1911-16
Hampstead Way, Golders Green, London. † RA 2.

TAIT, George Exh. 1886
318 Gala Park Road, Galashiels. † RSA 1.

TAIT, Gilbert J. Norriss Exh. 1936-40
Watercolour landscape painter. Son of Bess Norriss q.v. Add: 137 Church Street, London. † RA 2, WG 15.

TAIT, J.A. Exh. 1894-99
Partick, Glasgow 1894; Dowanhill, N.B. 1897. † GI 5.

TAIT, Mary Exh. 1880-82
Somerset Cottage, Raeburn Place, London. † RSA 3.

TAIT, Margaret E. Exh. 1934
6 Park Terrace, Ayr. † GI 1, RSA 1.

TAIT, Thomas Smith b. 1882
Architect. b. Paisley. Studied Paisley, Glasgow and R.A. Schools (Kings prize for architecture and decorative art). Among his works Adelaide House and Selfridges. Exh. 1928-40. Add: 1 Montague Place, London. † GI 7, RA 7, RSA 13.

TAIT, William N. Exh. 1889
223 Hope Street, Glasgow. † GI 1.

TAKAGI, S. Exh. 1911
165 Finborough Road, London. † ROI 1.

TAKAKI, Haisoni Exh. 1920
7 Stamford Bridge Studios, Chelsea, London. † ROI 1.

TAKE, Sato Exh. 1933-36
Japanese watercolour, silk and lacquer painter. † CON 105.

TAKEKOCHI, Kenzo d. 1930
Japanese etcher. Exh. 1910-19. Add: London. † GI 6, L 5, RA 4.

TALBOT, Miss E. Exh. 1901-10
St. Rhadegund House, New Square, Cambridge. † B 1, L 1.

TALBOT, Mrs. Grosvenor Exh. 1911
Southfield, Burley, Leeds. † L 1.

TALBOT, George Quartus Pine 1853-1888
Landscape and figure painter. Venice 1881; Paris 1882. † B 1, FIN 81, G 2, L 3, RA 4, RHA 1, RI 5.

TALBOT, John Joseph Exh. 1901-2
Architect. Commerce Court, 11 Lord Street, Liverpool. † RA 2.

TALBOT, Lionel A. Exh. 1900
Figure painter. c/o J.P. Jacomb-Hood, 26 Tite Street, Chelsea, London. † RA 1.

TALBOT, May Exh. 1903-5
Mrs. J.E. Landscape and interior painter. 3 Herbert Crescent, London. † CAR 29, D 2.

TALBOT, Rosamond C. Exh. 1884
Watercolour landscape painter. 27 Marloes Road, Kensington, London. † SWA 1.

TALBOT, Tom S. Exh. 1932-33
London 1932; Torquay, Devon 1933. † RBA 3, RI 1.

TALBOT, Viva Exh. 1930
Wood engraver. † RED 1.

TALBOYS, Agnes Augusta Exh. 1908-10
Painter of animals and Persian kittens. 20 Southfield Road, Cotham, Bristol. † B 5.

TALL, le see L

TALLBERG, Axel 1860-1928
Swedish etcher and writer. Studied Royal Academy of Arts, Stockholm, Dusseldorf, Rome and Paris. Lived in England at Burnham, Maidenhead 1881-94. Professor and Principal of the School of Etching and Engraving, Royal Academy of Arts, Stockholm 1908-28. A.R.E. 1891, H.R.E. 1911. Exh. 1891-94. Add: Burnham, Maidenhead, Berks. † RE 18.

TALMAGE, Algernon* 1871-1939
Painter and etcher. Studied with Sir Hubert Herkomer. Official war artist in France for Canada. A.R.A. 1922, R.A. 1929, R.B.A. 1903, H.R.B.A. 1923, R.O.I. 1908, H.R.O.I. 1930. Add: St. Ives, Cornwall 1893 and 1899; Redruth, Cornwall 1896; London 1908 and 1925; Tintagel, Cornwall 1920. † B 1, BAR 1, CHE 4, COO 3, FIN 62, G 8, GI 23, GOU 76, I 6, L 26, LEI 38, LS 1, M 1, NEA 7, P 1, RA 140, RBA 31, RHA 15, RID 14, ROI 30, RSA 3.

TALMAGE, Mrs. G. Exh. 1914-16
14 Draycott Terrace, St. Ives, Cornwall. † RA 2.

TAMBURINI, Arnaldo b. 1863
Italian figure painter. Exh. 1883-89. Add: Paris 1883; London 1889. † GI 1, L 1, M 2.

TAMIRIANTZ, Miss Vartoohy Exh. 1924-26
1 Trafalgar Road, Birkdale, Southport, Lancs. † L 1, RCA 4.

TAMLIN, J. Exh. 1882
Painter. 23 Walpole Street, Chelsea, London. † RBA 1.

TAMLIN, J.H.P. Exh. 1903-11
Landscape painter. Seacombe 1903; Kings Lynn, Norfolk 1909. † L 1, RA 2.

TANGYE, Florence Exh. 1902-31
The Manor House, Knowle, Warwicks. 1902; Hanley Swan, Worcs. 1931. † B 4.

TANGYE, Miss H. see REYNOLDS

TANGYE, L. Exh. 1884
Gilberstone, near Birmingham. † B 1.

TANKERVILLE, the Countess of Exh. 1896
Chillingham Castle, Northumberland. † SWA 2.

TANKERVILLE, The Earl of Exh. 1900
Miniature portrait painter. Chillingham Castle, Northumberland. † RA 4.

TANNER, Arthur Exh. 1896
Newlyn, Penzance, Cornwall. † NG 1.

TANNER, Ethel L. Exh. 1907-19
Kensington, London. † L 2, RA 2, SWA 2.

TANNER, Georgina M. Exh. 1897-1907
Moseley, Birmingham. † B 6.

TANNER, Henry 1849-1935
Architect. London. † RA 11.

TANNER, Miss J.M. Exh. 1893
The Close, Lichfield, Staffs. † B 1.

TANNER, Miss L. Exh. 1910-17
29 Pelham Place, South Kensington, London. † RA 2.

TANNER, Miss L.E. Exh. 1894
Newcote, Wolfington Road, West Norwood, London. † NG 1.

TANNER, Miss M. Exh. 1903
9 Crescent Mansions, Elgin Crescent, London. † SWA 2.

TANNER, Olive Exh. 1922-23
Miniature painter. 4 Whitley Road, Eastbourne. † RA 1, RMS 2.

TANNER, Robin b. 1904
Painter, etcher and teacher. b. Bristol. Studied Goldsmiths College. Exh. 1929-40. Add: Chippenham, Wilts. 1929; Kington Langley, Wilts. 1931. † RA 9, RE 2.

TANOCK, Rachel Marion see de MONTMORENCY

TANOSUKE, Miss Oshena O'gawa Exh. 1909-11
12 Fairfax Road, Hampstead, London. † LS 7.

TANOUX Exh. 1938
Figure painter. † COO 1.

TANQUERAY, Alice F. Exh. 1884-87
Painter. Llangollen, North Wales 1884; Maida Vale, London 1886. † L 3, M 1, RBA 1.

TANZI, Leon Exh. 1905
Pierres, par Maintenon (Eure et Loir), France. † L 1.

TAPIRO, Jose Exh. 1889-1904
Watercolour painter. Tangiers, Morocco 1889; London 1904. † G 1, L 5, NG 1, RA 5, RSA 2.

TAPP, Miss C. Exh. 1889
Watercolour painter. The Gables, Shortlands, Kent. † RI 1.

TAPP, R. Exh. 1919
Woodbridge, Suffolk. † ROI 1.

TAPP, Rosa Exh. 1902-19
A.S.W.A. 1905. Add: The Gables, Shortlands, Kent. † B 1, M 2, RCA 12, SWA 32.

TAPPER, Michael 1886-1963
Architect. Son of Sir Walter John T. q.v. Studied A.A. Exh. 1936-39. Add: London. † RA 2.

TAPPER, Sir Walter John 1861-1935
Ecclesiastic architect. Architect to York Minster and Surveyor of Westminster Abbey. Father of Michael T. q.v. A.R.A. 1926, R.A. 1935. Knighted c.1934. Add: London. † GI 7, L 3, RA 56, RSA 7.

TARBET, J.A. Henderson* d.1938
Landscape painter. Married Christian Peddie q.v. Exh. from 1883. Add: Edinburgh. † GI 31, L 4, RA 4, RHA 1, RSA 108, RSW 25.

TARBOLTON, Harold Ogle b.1869
Architect. Studied R.A. School of Architecture. A.R.S.A. 1931, R.S.A. 1935. Exh. from 1909. Add: Edinburgh. † GI 2, RA 2, RSA 36.

TARBUCK, George Exh. 1924-32
5 Vine Street, Birkenhead. † L 7.

TARBURY, E. Exh. 1938
Figure painter. † COO 1.

TARCY, Alice Exh. 1894
† M 1.

TARDIEU, Victor b. 1870
French artist. Exh. 1906. Add: 3 Rue Chaptal, Paris. † L 1.

TARGETT, Cyril H. Exh. 1935
Architect. 184 Upper Wrotham Road, Gravesend, Kent. † RA 1.

TARLETON, K. Muriel Exh. 1899-1900
Killeigh, Tullamore, Kings Co., Ireland. † RHA 2.

TARN, Miss A.T. Exh. 1908-16
5 Park Avenue, Hull. † L 2.

TARNER, Miss G. Exh. 1893-98
Portrait painter. 3 Park Road Studios, Haverstock Hill, London. † L 2, RA 1.

TARPEY, Miss J.T.K. Exh. 1894-1910
London 1894; Penn, High Wycombe, Bucks. 1910. † M 1, RHA 4.

TARR, James C. b. 1905
Painter. b. Swansea. Studied Cheltenham School of Art 1922-25, Royal College of Art 1925-29. Exh. 1939-40. Add: High Wycombe, Bucks. 1939. † RA 2.

TARRAN, Thomas Exh. 1888
Sculptor. Clyd Villa, Ellerton Road, Surbiton Hill, Surrey. † RBA 1.

TARRANT, B.H. Exh. 1906
65 Hosack Road, Tooting, London. † RA 1.

TARRANT, Margaret Winifred Exh. 1914-34
Watercolour painter and illustrator. Daughter of Percy T. q.v. Studied Clapham School of Art and Heatherleys. Add: The Elms, Gomshall, Surrey. † B 23, COO 2, D 2, L 8, RA 4, SWA 2.

TARRANT, Percy* Exh. 1881-1930
Landscape, coastal and figure painter. Father of Margaret Winifred T. q.v. Add: London 1881 and 1899; Leatherhead, Surrey 1890; Margate 1895; The Elms, Gomshall, Surrey 1916. † B 1, D 4, L 18, RA 22, RBA 1, RI 1, ROI 1.

TARRATT, John Garfield Exh. 1921-24
Landscape and figure painter, decorative, heraldic and stained glass artist and wood carver. Studied Leicester Technical and Art School and Royal College of Art. Art master and Crafts Instructor Warrington School of Art. Add: Warrington, Lancs. † L 3.

TARRING, Joyce Exh. 1916-34
Landscape and figure painter. London. † AB 4, NEA 1, SWA 2.

TARRY, Alice Exh. 1890-96
Domestic painter. Married Frederick Goodall q.v. Add: London. † RA 6.

TARVER, Edward John Exh. 1882-86
Architect. 10 Craig's Court, Charing Cross, London. † RA 2.

TARVER, E.S. Exh. 1922
† SWA 1.

TARVER, Henrietta M. Exh. 1896-1930
Miniature portrait painter. Bushey, Herts. † L 4, NG 2, RA 44, RMS 4.

TARVER, Josephine Exh. 1912-16
The Bungalow, Bushey, Herts. † L 1, RA 2.

TASKER, Francis William Exh. 1881-86
Architect. 2 St. John Street, Bedford Row, London. † RA 2.

TATCHELL, Elizabeth Exh. 1933
Stained glass artist. 14 Langdale Road, Hove, Sussex. † RA 1.

TATCHELL, Phyllis Exh. 1928-40
Stained glass artist. Hove, Sussex 1928; London 1938; West Wittering, Sussex 1940. † RA 5.

TATCHELL, Sydney J. Exh. 1907-21
Architect. Studied under Thomas Henry Watson. Surveyor to Christ's Hospital and consulting architect to St. Martin's in the Fields. Among his works: Eastbourne College. Add: London. † RA 11.

TATE, Barbara Exh. 1895-1900
6 New Court, Lincoln's Inn, London. † RBA 1, SWA 8.

TATE, Eliza Exh. 1883-93
43 Norwood Grove, Liverpool. † L 10.

TATE, Miss I.A. Exh. 1939
Borrowby, near Grantham, Lincs. † N 3.

TATE, Julia Exh. 1882-96
43 Norwood Grove, Liverpool. † L 17.

TATHAM, Agnes Clara b. 1893
Portrait and landscape painter and illustrator. b. Abingdon, Berks. Studied Byam Shaw School of Art and R.A. Schools. R.B.A. 1931. Exh. 1916-40. Add: London 1916 and 1920; Abingdon, Berks. 1919. † ALP 1, COO 9, GI 1, I 1, L 10, M 2, P 13, RA 32, RBA 48, RID 6, WG 5.

TATHAM, Helen S. Exh. 1880-91
Landscape painter. Shanklin, I.o.W. † B 9, D 3, L 5, M 2, N 4, RA 1, RBA 1, SWA 19.

TATLOW, Mrs. Emily Exh. 1927-40
Landscape painter. 31 Templars Avenue, London. † RA 3, RHA 11, RI 3, SWA 6.

TATLOW, Meta L. Exh. 1905-21
London 1905; Dublin 1907. † RHA 44.

TATTERSALL, H. Exh. 1910-20
Artist and teacher. School of Art, Heywood, Lancs. † L 2.

TATTERSALL, J.E. Exh. 1921-24
Red Barns, Victoria Road, Freshfield, near Liverpool. † RCA 3.

TATTERSALL, Lily Exh. 1895-98
Fruit painter. 136 High Street, Putney, London. † RA 1, RHA 2, SWA 6.

TATTERSALL, Margaret H. Exh. 1934
Watercolour portrait painter. Lunsford House, Lunsford Cross, Bexhill, Sussex. † RA 1.

TAUBMAN, Frank Mowbray b. 1868
Sculptor, painter and cartoonist. Studied Finsbury, Lambeth, Paris under Puech and Fremiet and Brussels under Van der Stappen. Visited Canada in 1906. Exh. 1893-1938. Add: Brussels 1893; London 1898, 1910 and 1918; Harrow, Middlesex 1907; Bexley Heath, Kent 1916; Tewkesbury, Worcs. 1933. † B 15, GI 73, I 2, L 20, NEA 1, NG 10, P 1, RA 40, RHA 3, RI 3, ROI 4, RSA 3.

TAUNTON, Donald Battershill 1885-1965
Stained glass artist. b. Birmingham. Studied Birmingham School of Art. Exh. 1926-36. Add: 1 Albemarle Street, Piccadilly, London. † RA 3.

TAVARE, F.L. Exh. 1885
23 Thomas Street, Cheetham Hill, Manchester. † M 1.

TAVERN, Louis Exh. 1896
Rue de Livourne 1, Brussels. † GI 1.

TAVERNER, Annie Exh. 1897-1914
A.S.W.A. 1909. Add: London. † L 1, RBA 5, RI 2, SWA 19.

TAVERNIER, Paul Exh. 1913
38 Rue Royale, Fontainebleau, Paris. † L 1.

TAWSE, H.S. Exh. 1938
c/o Messrs. Tawse and Allan, 10 Bon Accord Square, Aberdeen. † RSA 1.

TAWSE, Sybil Exh. 1925-40
Portrait painter, decorative and poster artist, and illustrator. Studied Lambeth School and Royal College of Art (King's prize scholarship and silver and bronze medal). Add: London 1925; Hythe, Kent 1932. † P 8, RA 4, RI 7.

TAYLER, Albert Chevallier* 1862-1925
Genre, portrait and landscape painter. Studied Heatherleys and R.A. Schools. N.E.A. 1886, R.B.A. 1908, R.O.I. 1890. Add: Newlyn, Penzance, Cornwall 1883; London 1893. † B 13, DOW 1, FIN 90, L 31, M 5, NEA 3, P 1, RA 49, RBA 4, RHA 1, RID 9, ROI 35, TOO 1.

TAYLER, Arnold S. Exh. 1895-1916
Architect. London. † RA 3.

TAYLER, Edward 1828-1906
Figure and miniature portrait painter. R.M.S. 1896. Hon. Treas. R.M.S. 1899-1906. Add: London. † D 8, G 1, L 9, M 10, NG 2, P 1, RA 116, RBA 3, RI 4, RMS 32.

TAYLER, Edward E. Exh. 1935
Portrait painter. 13 Chepstow Villas, London. † RA 1.

TAYLER, Frederick* 1802-1889
Landscape, figure and sporting painter, illustrator, etcher and lithographer. Studied Sass's Academy, R.A. Schools, under Vernet in Paris, and Rome. Father of Norman T. q.v. A.R.W.S. 1831, R.W.S. 1834. Add: London 1880; Brighton 1887. † AG 3, L 5, RCA 4, RWS 20.

TAYLER, Harry Exh. 1882-83
Miniature portrait painter. 26 Haymarket, London. † RA 2.

TAYLER, Ida R. Exh. 1880-96
Portrait, figure, landscape and flower painter. London. † B 7, G 1, L 4, RA 9, RBA 21, RHA 1, ROI 12, SWA 6.

TAYLER, Kate Exh. 1882-1908
Watercolour painter. London 1882 and 1893; Brighton 1887. † D 1, LS 5, NG 1, RA 1, RI 2, SWA 5.

TAYLER, Laurie Exh. 1926
Painter. 31 Carlingford Road, Hampstead, London. † RA 1.

TAYLER, L.B. Exh. 1915-17
London. † L 3, RA 2.

TAYLER, Mrs. M. Exh. 1905-7
London. † RA 3.

TAYLER, Mrs. May Exh. 1919
Miniature portrait painter. Tylehurst, Bexley, Kent. † RA 1.

TAYLER, Minna Exh. 1881-1907
Figure, portrait and landscape painter. London. † B 13, D 1, L 6, M 5, NG 1, RA 18, RBA 6, RE 2, RI 2, ROI 6, SWA 6.

TAYLER, Miss M. Kennerley Exh. 1938
Miniature portrait painter. 23 Old Church Lane, London. † RA 1.

TAYLER, Norman Exh. 1880-1914
Genre, landscape and flower painter. Studied R.A. Schools. Son of Frederick T. q.v. A.R.W.S. 1878. Add: London. † D 1, DOW 1, L 7, M 1, RA 1, RBA 1, RWS 68, TOO 1.

TAYLERSON, John Edward b. 1854
Sculptor and designer. b. Norton, Durham. Studied Faversham, Kennington and Westminster Schools of Art. Teacher of modelling and wood carving Battersea Polytechnic. Exh. 1884-1926. Add: London. † L 5, RA 37.

TAYLOR, Lady Adelaide Exh. 1898
97 Cadogan Gardens, London. † D 1.

TAYLOR, Agnes Exh. 1891-1910
Midfield, Dalkeith 1891; Fernbank, Ayr 1910. † GI 1, RSA 1.

TAYLOR, Alfred Exh. 1880-98
Figure and landscape painter. London 1880; Worthing 1898. † D 1, RA 7, RBA 6.

TAYLOR, Alice Exh. 1881
Watercolour landscape painter. Eastlands, Weybridge, Surrey. † SWA 1.

TAYLOR, Andrew Exh. 1885-1914
Glasgow 1885; London 1906. † GI 11, RA 1.

TAYLOR, Annie Exh. 1891-92
Landscape painter. 18 Cromwell Street, Nottingham. † N 2.

TAYLOR, Annie Anderson Exh. 1906-13
7 Royal Crescent, Edinburgh. † RSA 1, RSW 2.

TAYLOR, Mrs. A. Brenda Exh. 1930
Liverpool. † L 1.

TAYLOR, Ada E. Exh. 1881-82
Fruit painter. 37 Albert Square, Clapham Road, London. † RA 1, RSA 1.

TAYLOR, Arthur J. Exh. 1920-40
Painter,. Glasgow. † GI 17, L 6, RA 1, RSA 13, RSW 3.

TAYLOR, Agatha M. Exh. 1934-40
Miniature portrait painter. Elm Lawn, Dulwich Common, London. † RA 2.

TAYLOR, Andrew Thomas 1850-1937
Architect and watercolour painter. b. Edinburgh. Studied R.A. Schools. Add: London. † RA 4, RSA 11.

TAYLOR, Basil Exh. 1931-33
Painter. † LEI 2.

TAYLOR, Benson Exh. 1917-18
18 Beechwood Drive, Jordanhill, Glasgow. † GI 3.

TAYLOR, Betty Exh. 1926-38
Painter. 15 Holland Park, London. † GI 1, L 2, RA 4 SWA 3.

TAYLOR, Barbara Austin d. 1951
Sculptor. Studied Westminster School of Art, Grosvenor School of Art and Rome. A.S.W.A. 1932. Exh. 1930-37. Add: 7 Oakley Studios, Chelsea, London. † P 2, RA 4, RBA 2.

TAYLOR, Bernard Douglas 1881-1928
Portrait and landscape painter. b. Elland, Yorks. Studied Slade School. Headmaster Royal Technical College Art School, Salford. Add: Manchester. † L 2, M 1.

TAYLOR, Mrs. B.V.W. Exh. 1910-14
Ilford, Essex 1910; Sutton, Surrey 1914. † RA 3.

TAYLOR, Charles junr.* Exh. 1880-91
Marine painter. London and Hastings. † B 10, D 4, L 5, M 1, RBA 2, RHA 17, RI 1.

TAYLOR, Charlotte Exh. 1883-84
Still life painter. 363 Liverpool Road, Islington, London. † RI 2.

TAYLOR, Clara Exh. 1898-1912
Landscape painter. Cowbridge, Glam. 1898; London 1909. † NEA 17, RBA 2.

TAYLOR, C.E. Exh. 1886
85 Everton Road, Longsight, Manchester. † M 1.

TAYLOR, Charles T. Exh. 1901
Architect. 10 Clegg Street, Oldham, Lancs. † RA 1.

TAYLOR, Charles William b. 1878
Wood and copper plate engraver, watercolour painter and teacher. b. Wolverhampton. Studied Wolverhampton and Royal College of Art. A.R.E. 1922, R.E. 1930. Exh. 1912-40. Add: Westcliff on Sea, Essex 1912, Findon, Sussex 1939. † BA 4, GI 13, L 20, RA 36, RE 58, RHA 15, RI 1, RSA 2.

TAYLOR, Daphne Exh. 1929
Portrait and flower painter. Studied Slade School. Add: 30 Tite Street, Chelsea, London. † RA 1.

TAYLOR, Doris Exh. 1925-35
Manchester. † L 4, NEA 8, SWA 1.

TAYLOR, Miss D.M. Exh. 1917
16 St. Andrews Road, Southsea, Hants. † RA 1.

TAYLOR, E. Exh. 1928
39 Gt. Charlotte Street, Liverpool. † L 1.

TAYLOR, Mrs. Edith Exh. 1895-1903
Bushey, Herts. 1895 and 1903; Rye, Sussex 1901. † RBA 1, ROI 5, SWA 3.

TAYLOR, Edwin Exh. 1882-84
Claremont Road, Birmingham. † B 12. L 1.

TAYLOR, Emily Exh. 1896
Philadelphia, U.S.A. † RMS 1.

TAYLOR, Etty Exh. 1888-1905
Landscape painter. 26 Highfield Road, Edgbaston, Birmingham. † B 11, RA 2.

TAYLOR, Miss E.A. Exh. 1925-34
21 Henrietta Street, Bath. † ROI 2.

TAYLOR, Ernest Archibald Exh. 1898-1940
Painter, etcher, interior decorator, furniture designer and stained glass artist. b. Greenock. Married Jessie Marion King q.v. Add: Greenock 1898; Glasgow 1903; Manchester 1907; Paris 1915; Kirkcudbright 1916. † GI 71, L 2, RSA 48, RSW 6.

TAYLOR, E. Constance Exh. 1898
Stanford, Rusholme, Manchester. † M 1.

TAYLOR, Mrs. E.D. Exh. 1880
32 The Terrace, Barnes, Surrey. † RHA 1.

TAYLOR, Ernest E. Exh. 1882-1907
Flower and figure painter. London 1882; East Dunedin, Coleraine 1885; Belfast 1891 and 1896; Bushey, Herts. 1895 and 1907. † B 2, GI 2, L 4, M 1, NG 1, P 1, RBA 1, RHA 20, ROI 1, RSA 6.

TAYLOR, Edward Ingram d. 1923
Landscape painter, etcher and stained glass designer. London. † NEA 1, RA 8, RBA 7, RI 1, ROI 6.

TAYLOR, E.J. Bernard d. 1933
Landscape and portrait painter. Birmingham 1891; Rowington, nr. Warwick 1900; Hockley Heath, Warwicks 1907; Knowle, Warwicks 1911; Lapworth 1930. † B 25, D 1, L 1, RA 4, RHA 1.

TAYLOR, Eileen M. Exh. 1921-32
Liverpool 1921 and 1932; Keynsham, Somerset 1927. † L 3.

TAYLOR, Edward R.* 1838-1912
Portrait, genre, landscape, coastal and biblical painter and potter. b. Hanley, Staffs. Studied Burslem School of Art and Royal College of Art. Headmaster Lincoln School of Art 1863; headmaster Birmingham Municipal School of Art 1876-1903. R.B.S.A. Father of Lizzie T. q.v. Add: 26 Highfield Road, Edgbaston, Birmingham from 1881. † B 55, G 3, L 6, M 5, NG 1, RA 17, RBA 8, RHA 1, RI 1, ROI 2.

TAYLOR, Elizabeth R. Exh. 1906
c/o Miss Bain, 11 Lauriston Place, Edinburgh. † RSA 3.

TAYLOR, Eric Wilfred b. 1909
Painter, etcher and sculptor. Studied Willesden Polytechnic and Royal College of Art 1932-35. Teacher Camberwell School of Art 1936-39. A.R.E. 1935. Exh. 1931-40. Add: London. † NEA 3, RA 9, RE 23, RSA 7.

TAYLOR, E. Zillah Exh. 1891-95
Portrait and figure painter. Nottingham. † N 7.

TAYLOR, Florence Exh. 1928
15 St. Michael's Road, Aigburth, Liverpool. † L 1.

TAYLOR, Francis b. 1899
Painter, black and white and advertising artist, and interior decorator. b. Northampton. Studied Royal College of Art. Exh. 1927. Add: London. † RA 1.

TAYLOR, Frank Exh. 1939-40
Wood engraver, 28 High Street, Skipton, Yorks. † RA 3.

TAYLOR, Fred Exh. 1886
Mount Pleasant, North Malvern, Worcs. † B 1.

TAYLOR, Fred b. 1875
Watercolour painter, poster artist and decorator. Studied Goldsmiths College, R.I. 1917. Exh. 1918-40. Add: London. † AR 1, FIN 2, GI 7, L 15, RA 2, RI 56, RID 3.

TAYLOR, Frederick B. Exh. 1936
4 Roland House, Roland Gardens, London. † ROI 1.

TAYLOR, F.E. Exh. 1908
10 Cobham Road, Kingston Hill, Surrey. † RA 1.

TAYLOR, Frank S. Exh. 1898
Architect. 5 John Street, Bedford Row, London. † RA 1.

TAYLOR, George Exh. 1911-31
Bonnington 1911; Edinburgh 1913. † GI 5, RSA 11, RSW 11.

TAYLOR, George F. Exh. 1925
89 Galton Road, Warley Bearwood, Birmingham. † L 2, RCA 2.

TAYLOR, George Hart* Exh. 1880
Landscape painter. Devoran, Cornwall. † G 2.

TAYLOR, G. Langley Exh. 1936-37
Architect. Beaconsfield, Bucks. and London. † GI 1, RA 2.

TAYLOR, G.S. Exh. 1909-22
Landscape painter. Sneinton Dale, Nottingham. † 1909; Sherwood, Nottingham 1913. † N 7.

TAYLOR, Helen Exh. 1923-30
London and West Clandon. † GOU 7, NEA 4.

TAYLOR, Horace Christopher 1881-1934
Painter and poster artist. Studied R.A. Schools and Royal Academy Munich. Lecturer in commercial art Chelsea School of Art 1931. A.R.B.A. 1919, R.B.A. 1921. † BA 30, I 5, LS 16, RA 2, RBA 16, ROI 1.

TAYLOR, H.E. Exh. 1929
Landscape painter. c/o T.R. Smith, Bottle Lane, Nottingham. † N 1.

TAYLOR, H.J. Exh. 1899
Myrtle Villa, Bernard Street, Carrington, Notts. † N 1.

TAYLOR, H.M.F. Exh. 1921
† NEA 1.

TAYLOR, Henry Ramsay Exh. 1901-13
Edinburgh. † GI 2, RSA 6.

TAYLOR, Hugh S.P. Exh. 1884-87
185 Chesham Place, Kent Road, Glasgow. † GI 3.

TAYLOR, Harold W. Exh. 1922
† D 1.

TAYLOR, J. Exh. 1921
19 Stapleton Hall Road, London. † RA 1.

TAYLOR, James Exh. 1882-87
7 Merchiston Place, Edinburgh. † RSA 11.

TAYLOR, James Exh. 1889
Dewhurst, Rochdale, Lancs. † L 1.

TAYLOR, Joan Exh. 1936-40
Portrait and figure painter. Kemnal Wood, Chislehurst, Kent. † RA 4.

TAYLOR, John Exh. 1880-81
Sculptor, London 1880; Kirkcaldy 1881. † G 2, RA 5.

TAYLOR, John Exh. 1881-92
Glasgow 1881; Edinburgh 1885. † RSA 6.

TAYLOR, John Exh. 1883-94
Llanbedr, nr. Conway, Wales 1883; Dolygarog, Tal-y-bont, Wales 1885. † L 1, M 2, RCA 43.

TAYLOR, John Exh. 1885-96
152 Broad Street, Birmingham. † B 9, L 1.

TAYLOR, J.C. Exh. 1882-85
1 Gladstone Grove, Heaton Chapel, Manchester. † M 7.

TAYLOR, John D. Exh. 1880-1900
Landscape painter. Glasgow. † GI 54, L 1, RA 4, RSA 12.

TAYLOR, J.E. Exh. 1913
Elton Rectory, Nottingham. † N 1.

TAYLOR, James Fraser Exh. 1880-1913
Figure painter. Edinburgh. † AG 4, G 2, GI 6, RSA 64.

TAYLOR, Mrs. Jeannette Forsyth Exh. 1926-38
Sculptor. 46 Home Farm Road, Whitehall, Dublin. † RHA 5.

TAYLOR, Jessie Mary Exh. 1910-12
Mrs. Dahlstrom. Painter. Chester 1910 and 1912; Liverpool 1911. † L 4, RCA 1.

TAYLOR, John Reginald Exh. 1909-14
Haygarth House, Chester 1909; London 1912. † L 21, LS 18.

TAYLOR, John S. Exh. 1932-37
19 Roxburgh Street, Greenock. † GI 3, RSA 4, RSW 2.

TAYLOR, J. Wycliffe Exh. 1881-86
Animal painter. London 1881 and 1884; Surbiton, Surrey 1882. † D 1, G 8, RA 1, ROI 1.

TAYLOR, Kathleen Exh. 1937-39
Douro Lodge, Douro Road, Cheltenham, Glos. † RBA 1, SWA 2.

TAYLOR, Lambert Exh. 1918
64 St. James Street, London. † LS 3.

TAYLOR, Lilian Exh. 1937
Landscape painter. Redgate, Royal George Road, Burgess Hill, Sussex. † RA 1.

TAYLOR, Lizzie Exh. 1883-1904
Interior painter. 26 Highfield Road, Edgbaston, Birmingham. † B 10, RA 3, SWA 5.

TAYLOR, Lorenzo Exh. 1936-37
Watercolour painter. † WG 5.

TAYLOR, Luke 1873-1916
Painter and etcher. Studied Royal College of Art. Instructor in etching and mezzotint Central School of Arts and Crafts. A.R.E. 1902, R.E. 1910. Killed on active service in France. Add: London. † L 2, RA 21, RE 28, RID 24.

TAYLOR, Leonard Campbell* 1874-1963
Figure and portrait painter. b. Oxford. Studied St. Johns Wood School and R.A. Schools. A.R.A. 1923, R.A. 1931, R.O.I. 1906. "The Rehearsal" purchased by Chantrey Bequest 1907. Add: London 1899 and 1926; Hindhead, Surrey 1905; Ewhurst, Surrey 1909; Odiham, nr. Basingstoke, Hants. 1921. † B 3, BAR 1, CG 1, GI 8, GOU 1, I 2, L 28, LEI 38, M 7, NG 6, RA 90, RHA 2, RI 5, ROI 11, RSA 1.

TAYLOR, Mary Exh. 1931
Kirkandrews Rectory, Longtown, Cumberland. † RSA 2.

TAYLOR, Minnie Exh. 1896
Calthorpe House, Islington Row, Edgbaston, Birmingham. † B 1.

TAYLOR, Marjorie Emma b. 1904
Wood engraver, illustrator and teacher. Studied Birmingham University and Central School of Art. Exh. 1927-32. Add: 15 Herbert Road, Handsworth, Birmingham. † B 9.

TAYLOR, Maude E.M. Exh. 1895-96
Flower painter on porcelain. North Circus Street, Nottingham. † N 2.

TAYLOR, M.P. Exh. 1918
5 Oakhill Road, East Putney, London. † RA 1.

TAYLOR, Medland P. Exh. 1880-93
Stained glass artist. 9 Viewforth Terrace, Edinburgh. † GI 2, RA 1, RSA 27.

TAYLOR, Maud W. Exh. 1904-13
Figure painter. London 1904; Wallington 1908. † L 3, RA 2, SWA 1.

TAYLOR, Nora Exh. 1881-85
Flower and landscape painter. 6 Gledhow Gardens, London. † RBA 1, SWA 4.

TAYLOR, Norah Helen b. 1885
Painter and miniaturist. Studied Slade School and under Edwin Morgan. A.R.M.S. 1920, R.M.S. 1922, A.S.W.A. 1929. Exh. 1913-39. Add: London 1913; Stratford on Avon 1934. † B 9, L 27, RA 22, RI 41, RMS 99, RSA 1, SWA 6.

TAYLOR, Olive Exh. 1914-30
A.S.W.A. 1929. Add: London 1914 and 1928; Wallingford, Berks. 1915. † I 3, L 2, LS 3, SWA 5.

TAYLOR, Miss P.C. Exh. 1920-32
37 Wheelwright Road, Gravelly Hill, Birmingham. † B 9, L 1.

TAYLOR, R. Exh. 1934
Watercolour landscape painter. † COO 2.

TAYLOR, S. Exh. 1932
† L 1.

TAYLOR, Stanley Exh. 1938
Painter. 60 Cambridge Mansions, London. † RA 1.

TAYLOR, Sydney Exh. 1938
Cape Town, South Africa. † RI 1.

TAYLOR, Samuel C. Exh. 1896-1936
Still life and landscape painter and teacher. Knock, Belfast 1896; Belfast 1907; Marina, Co. Down 1915; Holywood, Co. Down 1936. † RA 1, RHA 11.

TAYLOR, S.M. Louisa Exh. 1880-87
Figure painter. The Rookery, Headington, Oxford. † G 1, L 1, M 2, RHA 2, SWA 4.

TAYLOR, S. Wilfred Exh. 1901-8
Landscape painter. Sneinton, Notts. 1901; West Bridgford, Notts. 1908. † N 17.

TAYLOR, Tom Exh. 1883-1911
Figure and domestic painter. London. † B 2, D 1, L 6, M 3, RA 6, RBA 9, RHA 2, RI 11, ROI 2.

TAYLOR, Tom Exh. 1938-39
The Mound, Bracknell, Berks. † RCA 4, RSA 1.

TAYLOR, T.E. Exh. 1914-33
Higher Crumpsall, Manchester 1927; Hale, Cheshire 1933. † L 2, M 3.

TAYLOR, T.L. Exh. 1919
212 Bath Street, Glasgow. † GI 1.

TAYLOR, Una E. Exh. 1906-8
London. † RA 4.

TAYLOR, Walter 1875-1943
Landscape and architectural painter and teacher. Studied under Fred Brown 1897 and Royal College of Art 1898. Founder member London Group 1913. Add: London 1898 and 1917; Aylesbury, Bucks. 1911; Brighton 1913. † CAR 25, CHE 1, D 2, GOU 18, LS 23, NEA 22, RA 4, RBA 1.

TAYLOR, Willison Exh. 1934
Whitfield Lodge, Lennoxtown. † GI 1.

TAYLOR, W. Howson b. 1876
Potter. b. Lincoln. Studied Birmingham School of Art. Exh. 1904-30. Add: Ruskin Pottery, Smethwick, Birmingham. † NG 1, L 629, B 1.

TAYLOR, W.J. Exh. 1900-20
Hyson Green, Notts. 1900; Nottingham 1920. † N 4.

TAYLOR, William W. Exh. 1880-96
Sculptor. Kirkcaldy, Fife 1880; Cardiff 1896. † L 1, RA 1.

TCHELITCHEW, Pavel* 1898-1957
Russian portrait and figure painter. Exh. 1933-38. † RED 3, TOO 122.

TCHEREMISSINOF, Elisabeth Exh. 1937-38
Painter and sculptor. 7 Nevern Road, London. † RA 3, RMS 3.

TCHERKASKY, S. Exh. 1882
Barbizon, France. † GI 1.

TEAGUE, G.H. Exh. 1887
64 Elsham Road, Kensington, London. † D 4.

TEAGUE, M.O. Exh. 1916
4 Royal Crescent, Holland Park, London. † L 1, RA 1.

TEAGUE, Violet Exh. 1921-36
Australian painter. Add: London. † RA 1, SWA 2.

TEALDI, Ascanio Exh. 1907-19
Landscape and figure painter. † GOU 3, I 2.

TEALE, Michael b. 1867
Watercolour landscape and coastal painter and black and white artist. b. Leeds. Exh. 1931-38. Add: Clevedon, Somerset. † AR 96, RA 2, RCA 1.

TEALL, Miss E. Exh. 1920
280 Washwood Heath Road, Birmingham. † B 1.

TEAPE, James S. Exh. 1882-1919
Miniature portrait painter. London. † L 5, RA 7.

TEAR, John Exh. 1883-86
Sheffield. † RSA 2.

TEASDALE, Percy Morton b. 1870
Portrait, figure and landscape painter and wallpaper designer. Studied Leeds, Herkomers, Bushey, Herts. and Juliens, Paris. Master at Leeds and Harrogate Art Schools. Exh. 1894-1940. Add: Leeds 1894; London 1915; Bushey, Herts. 1919. † B 2, GOU 2, L 10, LS 6, M 1, RA 17, RCA 36, RI 2, ROI 4, RSA 1.

TEATHER, H.H. Exh. 1929
Painter. 12 Hall Street, Alfreton, Derbys. † N 1.

TEBB, Kathleen Exh. 1926
49 Westbury Road, Bristol. † L 1.

TEBBITT, Frank Exh. 1891
Bolton Studios, Fulham Road, London. † L 1.

TEBBITT, Gertrude Exh. 1885-1908
Landscape and portrait painter. Rome 1885; London 1890. † B 1, RA 3, ROI 1.

TEBBITT, Henri* Exh. 1882-84
Landscape and fish painter. East Molesey, Surrey. † RA 1, RBA 1.

TEBBUTT, Florence H. Exh. 1899
The Hollies, Cheyne Walk, Northampton. † L 1.

TEBBY, Arthur Kemp Exh. 1883-1928
Landscape, figure and flower painter. 36 Lamb's Conduit Street, London 1883; Heybridge, Essex 1928. † RA 4, RBA 6, ROI 4.

TEBBY, Leighton Exh. 1885-88
Landscape painter. 36 Lamb's Conduit Street, London. † RA 1, RBA 3.

TEDDER, Miss M.R. Exh. 1882-91
Landscape painter. Ripley, Woking Station, Surrey 1882; London 1891. † M 1, RI 3.

TEDESCHI, Margherite Exh. 1908
Rue Johnson-Maisons-Laffitte, Seine et Oise, France. † LS 5.

TEE, Hilda Exh. 1914-33
Miniature portrait painter. 4 Esplanade, Waterloo, nr. Liverpool. † L 33, RA 6.

TEED, Eliza W. Exh. 1897-98
188 Camberwell Grove, London. † SWA 3.

TEED, Mrs. Frank J. Exh. 1893
Watercolour flower painter. The Ferns, Grove Park, Denmark Hill, London. † RI 1.

TEED, Henry Samuel 1883-1916
Landscape painter. R.B.A. 1914. Add: London. † B 1, BG 41, GI 2, GOU 16, I 2, L 8, NEA 10, NG 7, RA 3, RBA 26, RHA 2, RID 3, ROI 4.

TEED, Mrs. Isabella Exh. 1898-99
Greenbow, Champion Hill, London. † SWA 5.

TEESDALE, C. Exh. 1883-94
Watercolour landscape painter. London 1883; Coltishall, Norfolk 1894. † RI 6.

TEESDALE, Kenneth J.M. Exh. 1900-13
Landscape painter. Cranleigh, Surrey 1900; Peaslake, Guildford, Surrey 1904. † B 4, LS 3, RA 3, RI 7, ROI 5.

TEESDALE, Miss M.J. Exh. 1883
Whyte House, Chichester. † D 1.

TEGETMEIER, Denis Exh. 1928
† GOU 3.

TEIGNMOUTH, Commander Lord, R.N.
See SHORE, Sir Henry Noel

TEISSIER, de See D

TEKUSCH, Margaret Exh. 1880-88
Miniature portrait painter. Fitzroy Square, London. † RA 26.

TELBIN, Mary Exh. 1884
Painter. 20 Wigmore Street, London. † ROI 1.

TELBIN, William junr. Exh. 1880-81
Landscape and marine painter. Lancaster House, Savoy Street, Strand, London. † RBA 2.

TELFER, C. Exh. 1882
c/o Kegg, Kingston Villa, New Ferry, Liverpool. † L 2.

TELFER, Mrs. C. (J. Buchan)
Exh. 1889-1904
Watercolour painter. London 1889; Beckenham, Kent 1900. † B 1, D 17, RBA 2, RI 1, SWA 1.

TELFER, Henry Monteith Exh. 1880-86
Edinburgh. † GI 4, RSA 28.

TELFER, William Walker b. 1907
Portrait and landscape painter and etcher. Exh. 1935-40. Add: 21 Craigmont Park, Corstorphine. † GI 1, RSA 7, RSW 1.

TELFORD, Jessie R. Exh. 1885
† GI 1.

TELFORD, Percy b. 1895
Painter and advertisement artist. b. Bolton, Lancs. Studied R.A. Schools. Exh. 1938-39. Add: London. † P 1, RA 2, RSA 1.

"TELL" See BUHRER, Albert

TEMPEST, Margaret Exh. 1939
Painter and illustrator (e.g. Little Grey Rabbit). † AR 32.

TEMPEST, Walter Exh. 1913-35
Landscape painter. Halifax, Yorks. † M 1, RA 7, RI 1.

TEMPLAR, H.P. Exh. 1892-1926
Manchester. † L 2, M 10.

TEMPLE, Sir Alfred George 1848-1928
Watercolour painter and writer. H.R.M.S. 1919. Exh. 1881-1921. Add: London. † L 1, RA 2, RBA 2, RI 1.

TEMPLE, Charles H. Exh. 1893-1905
Architect. Ironbridge, Salop. † L 2, RA 5.

TEMPLE, Eleanor S. Exh. 1903-15
Bushey, Herts. 1903 and 1911; Penzance, Cornwall 1906; Kington, Herefords. 1910 and 1915. † L 3, RA 2, SWA 4.

TEMPLE, Isabella L. Exh. 1901
† RMS 1.

TEMPLE, P. Exh. 1938
† M 1.

TEMPLE, Robert Scott Exh. 1880-1905
Landscape painter. Edinburgh 1880; London 1882; Woodford Green, Essex 1905. † L 3, RA 13, RSA 19.

TEMPLE, Vere Exh. 1903-39
Animal, bird and insect painter and etcher. London 1903 and 1928; Warminster, Wilts. 1927. † GOU 6, L 4, NEA 10, RED 38.

TEMPLE-BIRD, Kathleen Emily
Exh. 1930-40
nee Temple. Portrait, and landscape painter. b. Ipswich. Studied Slade School and Florence. Add: London. † L 2, P 2, RA 4, RI 5, ROI 5, SWA 1.

TEMPLETON, Bertha C. Exh. 1927
Stratton House, Parkway, Princes Road, Liverpool. † L 1.

TEMPLETON, J.M. Exh. 1888-89
Glasgow. † GI 3.

TEMPLETON, Rosa Isobel Exh. 1898-1905
Helensburgh, N.B. † GI 2.

TEMPLETOWN, Viscountess Exh. 1906
17 Victoria Street, London. † RI 1.

TEMPRA, Quirino Exh. 1884
Sculptor. c/o Bellman and Tovey, 95 Wigmore Street, London. † RA 1.

TENCH, Miss M.F. Exh. 1885
Valentia Islands, Co. Kerry. † RHA 1.

TENISON, Arthur Heron Ryan 1861-1930
Architect. London. † RA 6.

TENISON, Nell See CUNEO

TENISWOOD, George F. Exh. 1882
Landscape and marine painter. 72 Park Street, Gloucester Square, London. † B 2, L 2.

TEN KATE, Hermann* 1822-1891
Dutch painter. Exh. 1889. † TOO 1.

TEN KATE, Johan Mari Henri* b. 1831
Dutch painter. Exh. 1886-96. Add: 51 Pieta Buth Straat, The Hague, Holland. † GI 1, M 1.

TENNANT, C. Dudley Exh. 1898-1918
Painter. Father of Trevor T. q.v. Add: Liverpool 1898; Purley, Surrey 1913. † L 4, RA 4.

TENNANT, C.H.J. Exh. 1912
2 West Coates, Edinburgh. † RSA 1.

TENNANT, Dorothy See STANLEY

TENNANT, Ernest W.D. Exh. 1910
Oxford House, Ugley, Bishops Stortford, Herts. † LS 3.

TENNANT, Mrs. J. Exh. 1910
† SWA 1.

TENNANT, Miss M. Exh. 1908-13
13 New Bedford Road, Luton, Beds. † D 3, NG 1, RA 3.

TENNANT, Nancy Exh. 1936-39
Portrait painter. 14 Bedford Gardens, London. † GOU 1, RA 1.

TENNANT, Norman b. 1896
Illustrator, etcher and teacher. b. Ilkley. Studied Bradford School of Art and Royal College of Art. Exh. 1921-22. Add: Ilkley, Yorks 1921; London 1922. † L 3, RA 1.

TENNANT, Oscar Exh. 1911
26 Leyton Road, Handsworth, Birmingham. † B 1.

TENNANT, Trevor b. 1900
Landscape and figure painter. Son of C. Dudley T. q.v. Studied R.A. Schools. Exh. 1927-33. Add: Purley, Surrey. † ALP 1, GOU 3, L 3, NEA 2, RA 2, RED 1.

TENNANT, Trevor b. 1906
Sculptor and teacher. Exh. 1938. Add: The Oast, West Peckham, Kent. † RA 1.

TENNANT, Virginia S. Exh. 1888-98
Ayr 1888; Glasgow 1898. † GI 6, RSA 2.

TENNENT, Kechie Exh. 1924-27
Watercolour landscape painter. † GOU 39.

TENNENT, R. Exh. 1880-81
5 Clydeview Terrace, Brighton, Sussex. † GI 2.

TENNENT, Reekie Exh. 1914
Figure painter. Eliot Vale House, Blackheath, London. † NEA 1.

TENNIEL, Sir John* 1820-1914
Painter, illustrator and cartoonist. Self taught. On staff of "Punch" 1851-1901. Illustrator of Lewis Carrol's "Alice in Wonderland" and "Alice Through the Looking Glass". R.I. 1874, H.R.I. 1904. Knighted 1893. Add: London. † FIN 161, L 2, M 14, RA 1, R16, RSA 3.

TERMOTE, A. Exh. 1932
Sculptor. Holland. † RSA 1.

TERNENT, George Exh. 1915
34 Wilton Street, Glasgow. † GI 1, RSA 1.

TERRAIRE, C. Exh. 1913
Landscape painter. † ALP 3.

TERRE, Henry Exh. 1890-92
12 Rue Magellan, Paris. † GI 4.

TERRELL, Georgina Exh. 1880-1905
nee Koberwein. Still life, portrait, genre and fruit painter. Daughter of Georg Koberwein (1820-1876) and sister of Rosa Koberwein q.v. Add: London. † B 3, D 1, L 4, M 8, RA 15, RBA 1, RHA 2, RI 4.

TERRIS, John* 1865-1914
Watercolour landscape painter. R.I. 1912, R.S.W. 1891. Add: Birmingham 1883; Glasgow 1885; Stirling 1897; Bridge of Allan 1901. † B 34, DOW 4, GI 61, L 46, M 14, NG 3, RA 4, RI 13, RSA 34, RSW 68, WG 2.

TERRIS, Mrs. John Exh. 1894-97
4 Ailsa Terrace, Hillhead, Glasgow. † GI 5.

TERRIS, Tom Exh. 1897-1940
Glasgow. † GI 24, L 3, RSA 5.

TERRY, de See D

TERRY, Agnes D. Exh. 1894-1916
Figure and miniature painter. London. † L 16, RA 4, RI 1, RMS 5, SWA 2.

TERRY, Miss A.T. Exh. 1908-11
Beech House, Chestnut Grove, Nottingham. † N 5.

TERRY, Edith Blanche Exh. 1896-1935
Painter, miniaturist and silver point artist. b. Weybridge. Studied under Louise Jopling. Add: London 1896; Bath, Somerset 1914. † LS 15, NEA 1, RI 35, SWA 1.

TERRY, Florence S.S. Exh. 1898-1907
Newcastle on Tyne. † L 4, NG 1.

TERRY, Henry* Exh. 1880-1914
Landscape and figure painter and watercolourist. London 1880; Tetworth, Oxon 1885; Long Sutton, Lincs. 1894; Chesham, Bucks. 1896; Haddenhaur, Bucks. 1898. † B 27, BG 2, D 161, GI 2, L 44, M 15, NG 8, RA 17, RBA 17, RI 21, ROI 9, RSA 1, RSW 1, WG 115.

TERRY, Joseph Alfred b. 1872
Landscape painter. b. York. Studied York School of Art, Juliens, and Colarossi's, Paris. A.R.B.A. 1922, R.B.A. 1924. Exh. 1897-1938. Add: The Firs, Sleights, Yorks. † CAR 38, L 5, LS 8, M 7, RA 3, RBA 89, ROI 6.

TERRY, Miss M.D. Exh. 1900
2 Princes Road, Wimbledon, Surrey. † RI 1.

TERRY, Sarah* Exh. 1880
Painter. 6 Pembroke Villas, Richmond, Surrey. † SWA 2.

TESSIER, Auriol Exh. 1939
Sculptor. Haywards Heath, Sussex. † RA 2.

TESSIER, Kathleen M. Exh. 1933
Miniature painter. 106 High Road, South Woodford, Essex. † RA 1.

TESSIER, Mme. Vieil Noe Exh. 1928
22 Rue Monsieur le Prince, Paris. † L 1, RSA 2.

TESSON, C. Exh. 1899
† TOO 1.

TESTAS, W. Exh. 1884
† GI 1.

TETLEY, Miss A. Exh. 1885-92
Figure painter. Heath Bank, Bingley, Yorks. † FIN 1, M 2.

TETLEY, Ivy L.D. Exh. 1903-33
Miniaturist. Woodville Priory, Honor Oak Rise, London. † L 2, NG 1, RA 2, RI 10, RMS 4.

TEUTEN, Miss A.E. Exh. 1898-1907
London. † B 6, M 1, NG 1, ROI 3.

TEWSLEY, E. Exh. 1929
Etcher. † AB 1.

TEYSSONNIERES, Pierre Exh. 1883
46 Rue des Martyrs, Paris. † GI 1.

THACKER, Samuel T. Exh. 1886-97
Landscape painter. 22 Montague Street, Russell Square, London. † RBA 2, ROI 3.

THACKER, Winifred H. Exh. 1895-96
Miniature portrait painter. Rottingdean, Sussex. † RA 1, RBA 1, RI 2.

THACKERAY, Mrs. C. Exh. 1919-20
53 Albany Mansions, Battersea Park, London. † SWA 2.

THACKERAY, Lance d. 1916
Watercolour figure painter. R.B.A. 1899. Travelled in the Middle East. Exh. from 1899. Add: London. † FIN 60, LEI 72, RA 2, RBA 39, RI 4, WG 112.

THADDEUS, Henry Jones 1859-1929
Portrait painter. A.R.H.A. 1892, R.H.A. 1901. Add: Florence 1883; London 1885 and 1889; Rome 1886. † G 5, L 8, RA 3, RBA 1, RHA 21.

THAGARDH, P. Exh. 1892-94
Landscape painter. 30 Gt. Russell Street, London. † ROI 3.

THANGUE, la See L

THARLE-HUGHES, Elfrida Exh. 1910-39
Landscape painter. Studied Slade School and Paris. Travelled for 2 years in the Far East. Add: London. † BA 1, G 1, I 3, L 1, LS 6, M 1, NEA 2, RED 34.

THARP, Charles Julian b. 1878
Portrait and landscape painter and sculptor. b. Denston Park, Suffolk. Studied Slade School. Exh. 1901-30. Add: London 1901 and 1920; Bushey, Herts. 1919. † COO 51, GI 1, GOU 33, I 5, L 4, M 1, NEA 2, NG 2, P 6, RA 6, RHA 1, ROI 1, RSA 1.

THATCHER, Miss M. Exh. 1911
124 Cromwell Road, Montpelier, Bristol. † RA 1.

THAULOW, Fritz* 1847-1906
Norwegian landscape painter. Add: Montreuil Sur Mer, France 1894; Paris 1899. † CON 1, GI 4, GOU 2, I 32, L 1, M 1, P 1, RA 12.

THEAKER, Harry George* 1873-1954
Painter, designer and illustrator. b. Wolstanton, Staffs. Studied Burslem School of Art and Royal College of Art. Headmaster Regent Street Polytechnic School of Art. A.R.B.A. 1919, R.B.A. 1920. Add: London. † L 8, RA 15, RBA 117, RI 5.

THEAKSTON, Ernest G. Exh. 1908-33
Architect. London 1908; Wendover, Bucks. 1933. † RA 5.

THEARLE, H. Exh. 1928-32
Sandon Studios, School Lane, Liverpool. † L 8.

THEED, E. Frank Exh. 1883-88
Sculptor. Related to William T. q.v. Add: 12A Henrietta Street, Cavendish Square, London. † M 3, RA 6.

THEED, Frank Hilton Exh. 1898
21 The Avenue, Kew Gardens, London. † L 1, NG 1.

THEED, William 1804-1891
Sculptor. Studied R.A. Schools and Florence. Worked for 5 years in studio of E.H. Baily. Commissioned by Queen Victoria to take the death mask of Prince Albert. Son of William T. (1764-1817). Add: 12a Henrietta Street, Cavendish Square, London. † RA 4.

THELWALL, John Augustus Exh. 1883-96
Portrait, landscape and figure painter. London 1883; East Molesey, Surrey 1885; Bournemouth 1896. † L 2, RA 4, RBA 1.

THEOBALD, S.S. Exh. 1885-86
Landscape painter. Putney, London. † RI 3.

THEOBALDS, W. Exh. 1903
Architect. 26 Budge Row, Cannon Street, London. † RA 1.

THEODORE, Frank b. 1892
Marine and landscape painter. Exh. 1925. Add: 34 Clarence Road, Wood Green, London. † RA 1.

THESIGER, Ernest 1879-1961
Painter and actor. Studied Slade School. Exh. 1909-38. † FIN 157, GOU 3.

THESMAR, Fernand Exh. 1906
11 Boulevard Victor Hugo, Neuilly sur Seine, France. † L 2.

THEVENOT, Francois b. 1856
French artist. Exh. 1907. Add: 123 Rue Caulaincourt, Paris. † L 1.

THEW, Mrs. M.R. Exh. 1914-15
Arisaig, Craigendoran, Helensburgh, N.B. † L 13.

THEYRE, Margaret b. 1897
Landscape painter. b. Northants. Exh. 1921-40. Add: London. † B 3, COO 1, D 1, GI 1, L 3, LS 3, RA 2, RBA 2, RCA 18, RHA 3, RI 3, ROI 4, RSA 4, SWA 3, WG 18.

THIBANDEAU, Julien Exh. 1906
85 Rue Notre Dame des Champs, Paris. † L 1.

THICK, Dorothy K. Exh. 1932-40
Landscape painter. 9 Alington Road, Bournemouth. † NEA 4, RA 3.

THIEBAULT, Henri Exh. 1923
113 Avenue de St. Mande, Paris. † RSA 1.

THIEDE, Edwin Adolf Exh. 1882-1908
Miniature portrait painter on ivory. London. † RA 8, ROI 1.

THIEME, Anthony b. 1888
Landscape, coastal and figure painter. b. Rotterdam. Studied Academia Di Belli Arti a Torino. Exh. 1933. Add: 603 Boylston Street, Boston, Mass., U.S.A. † RA 1.

THIRION, Eugene* 1839-1898
French painter. Exh. 1886. † B 1.

THIRKETTLE, R. Frank d. 1916
Exh. 1900. Add: Headingley, Leeds. † L 2.

THIRLBY, Enid M. Exh. 1936
53 Oakfield Road, Birmingham. † B 1.

THIRTLE, John* Exh. 1898-1900
Painter. The Elms, Banstead Road, Ewell, Surrey. † RA 1, RI 1.

THISEWELL, Maud A. Exh. 1901
105 Greencroft Gardens, West Hampstead, London. † RCA 2.

THISTLEWAITE, Miss C.O. Exh. 1905
17 Witham Park, Boston, Lincs. † RA 1.

THOBOIS, A.C. Exh. 1918-19
91 Priory Road, West Hampstead, London. † I 6.

THOLEN, William Bastien* 1860-1931
Dutch landscape painter. Exh. 1883-87. Add: 116 New Bond Street, London 1883; Kampen, Holland 1884; Dieren, Holland 1886. † GI 4, L 2, M 1, RA 1, RBA 1.

THOM, A.A. Exh. 1892
Birkacre, Chorley. † M 2.

THOM, J.C. Exh. 1885
† TOO 1.

THOMA, Hans* 1839-1924
German painter. Exh. 1904-7. Add: Kunstlschule, Karlsruhe. † I 20.

THOMAE, Helen C. Exh. 1929-40
Watford, Herts. 1929; London 1938. † RI 1, SWA 5.

THOMAS, Miss Exh. 1903
The Cleavelands, Wolverhampton. † B 1.

THOMAS, Sir A. Brumwell Exh. 1899-1932
Architect. London. † RA 7.

THOMAS, Albert Gordon 1893-1970
Painter and teacher. Studied Glasgow School of Art. R.S.W. 1936. Add: Glasgow 1921; Milngavie 1935. † GI 20, L 1, RSA 6, RSW 24.

THOMAS, Annie H. Exh. 1883-89
Landscape and coastal painter. London 1883; St. Just, Penzance, Cornwall 1889. † M 1, RBA 2, SWA 1.

THOMAS, Albert J. Exh. 1921-39
Architect. London. † RA 3.

THOMAS, Albert V. Exh. 1904
37 Avenue Montaigne, Paris. † L 1.

THOMAS, Miss A.W. Exh. 1894
36 Mulgrave Street, Liverpool. † L 2.

THOMAS, Bert Exh. 1909
Humorous illustrator. b. Newport, Mon. † LS,3.

THOMAS, Mrs. B.H. Exh. 1924-25
14 Princes Square, Bayswater, London. † SWA 3.

THOMAS, Mrs. B.M. Exh. 1934
Watercolour flower painter. † COO 2.

THOMAS, Mrs. B. Rowe Exh. 1914-21
London. † L 2, RI 2, SWA 2.

THOMAS, Cecil 1885-1967
Sculptor and medallist. A.R.M.S. 1914, R.M.S. 1916. Add: London. † GI 1, L 25, P 2, RA 24, RMS 90.

THOMAS, Charles b. 1883
Painter, etcher, medallist, modeller and silversmith. Studied and taught Birmingham Municipal School of Arts and Crafts. Exh. 1920-38. Add: Birmingham. † B 12, L 15, RA 2.

THOMAS, Clara Exh. 1886
Marine painter. Pencerrig, Builth, Wales. † SWA 1.

THOMAS, Clifton Exh. 1884
Landscape painter. Wilton Road, Salisbury, Wilts. † RA 1.

THOMAS, C.W. Exh. 1889
36 Edith Road, London. † D 3.

THOMAS, Dora Exh. 1886-1922
Painter. Llandudno, Wales. † B 1, GI 1, L 16, LS 12, RCA 10, RI 1, RSW 1.

THOMAS, Dudley Exh. 1881
Landscape painter. Mornington Crescent, Hampstead Road, London. † RBA 2.

THOMAS, David Arthur Exh. 1899-1908
Sculptor. London. † L 2, RA 3.

THOMAS, E. Exh. 1916
Kinfauns Road, Goodmayes, Essex. † RA 3.

THOMAS, Edward Exh. 1884-1930
Llandudno, Wales 1884; Tal-y-Cafn, Wales 1898. † L 1, LS 1, RCA 3.

THOMAS, Elsie Exh. 1911-13
Walden, Tollesbury, Essex. † LS 5.

THOMAS, Ethel Exh. 1899
Tenterfield, Perry Vale, Forest Hill, London. † SWA 1.

THOMAS, Edith E. Exh. 1921-37
Landscape painter. London. † COO 2, G 1, M 1, RA 5, RI 3, ROI 5, SWA 5.

THOMAS, Mrs. Elizabeth E. Exh. 1923-40
Miniature portrait painter. Westcliffe on Sea 1923; Hockley, Essex 1940. † RA 7.

THOMAS, Edgar Herbert Exh. 1888
Portrait painter. Victoria Cottage, Blackweir, Cardiff. † ROI 1.

THOMAS, Eleanor Langford Exh. 1905-1930
Portrait and miniature painter. London 1905 and 1920; Bushey, Herts. 1909; Radlett, Herts. 1914. † RA 10, SWA 1.

THOMAS, Elsie L. Exh. 1931
448 Shaftmoor Lane, Hall Green, Birmingham. † B 1.

THOMAS, Mrs. Emma Louise Osman Exh. 1884-1909
London. † L 2, LS 3.

THOMAS, Mrs. F. Exh. 1885
7 Nelson Street, Manchester. † M 1.

THOMAS, Miss F. Exh. 1902
21A South Grove, Mile End Road, London. † SWA 1.

THOMAS, Francis Exh. 1895
Welling, Kent. † RBA 1.

THOMAS, Frank Exh. 1891-1902
Birmingham. † B 11.

THOMAS, Frederick Exh. 1892-1901
Sculptor. London. † L 1, RA 5.

THOMAS, Frederick Exh. 1940
32 Park Avenue, Portobello, Edinburgh. † RSA 1.

THOMAS, F.C. Exh. 1916
230 Grange Road, Plaistow, London. † RA 1.

THOMAS, F.E. Exh. 1907
29 Melgund Road, Highbury, London. † RA 1.

THOMAS, Fanny E. Exh. 1880
Painter. Brighton and Shortlands, Kent. † G 1, RBA 1.

THOMAS, F. Inigo Exh. 1891-1929
Architect, and black and white artist. A.R.E. 1891. Add: London. † RA 7, RE 18, WG 94.

THOMAS, Francis Wynne b. 1907
Painter. b. Bromley, Kent. Studied Heatherleys 1930-34. Exh. 1936-39. Add: London. † P 4, RA 1, RCA 2, ROI 1, RSA 3.

THOMAS, George A. Exh. 1885
Landscape painter. Coleharbour House, Hildenborough, Kent. † RA 1.

THOMAS, Geraldine B. See BLAKE

THOMAS, G.F. Exh. 1885
3 Steel's Studios, Haverstock Hill, London. † L 1.

THOMAS, George Grosvenor* 1856-1923
Landscape painter. b. Sydney, Australia. Mainly self taught. R.S.W. 1892 (resigned 1908). Member Society of 25 Artists. Add: Glasgow 1889; London 1901. † BG 1, DOW 38, GI 26, I 12, L 6, LS 2, M 3, NG 1, RA 1, RSA 9, RSW 16.

THOMAS, George Havard 1893-1933
Sculptor. b. Sorrento, Italy. Son of James Havard T. q.v. Studied Slade School. Teacher of sculpture at Slade School. Add: London. † L 3, P 1, RA 16, ROI 3.

THOMAS, G.W. Exh. 1911-15
115 Gower Street, London. † D 4, L 3, LS 12, RA 4. RI 3.

THOMAS, Mrs. H Exh. 1917-21
London. † RA 2.

THOMAS, Hubert A. Exh. 1930-33
46 Fenwick Street, Liverpool. † L 5.

THOMAS, Ifor E. Exh. 1934-35
Etcher. Avondale, Cross Hands, Llanelly, South Wales. † RA 2.

THOMAS, Miss I.H. Exh. 1931
65 Bristol Road, Edgbaston, Birmingham. † B 2.

THOMAS, Jessie Exh. 1934
Cardiff, Wales. † RCA 2.

THOMAS, J.A. Exh. 1909
Architect. 60 Haymarket, London. † RA 1.

THOMAS, James Havard 1854-1921
Sculptor. Studied Bristol School of Art and South Kensington. Worked in London 1875-81 then spent 3 years at Ecole des Beaux Arts, Paris. Professor of Sculpture London University. Father of George Havard T. q.v. N.E.A. 1886. "Cardinal Manning" (1876-86) purchased by Chantrey Bequest 1922. Add: London 1880, 1885 and 1906; Paris 1881; Capri, Italy 1890. † CAR 34, G 5, GI 13, GOU 5, I 4, L 4, LS 1, M 9, NEA 6, NG 4, RA 20, RI 1, RSA 3.

THOMAS, Jessie Mary Exh. 1931-36
Painter, designer and lithographer. b. Peterborough. Add: 97 Widmore Road, Bromley, Kent. † RA 2, ROI 2.

THOMAS, Laura b. 1897
Painter. Studied Camberwell and Westminster Schools of Art. Exh. 1926. Add: 41 Farrer Road, Hornsey, London. † RA 1.

THOMAS, Miss L. Exh. 1883-86
Manchester. † L 1, M 4.

THOMAS, M. Exh. 1933
Cardiff, Wales. † RCA 2.

THOMAS, Margaret d. 1929
Portrait painter and sculptor. b. Croydon. Studied under Charles Summers in Australia, R.A. Schools and Rome. Travelled widely. Add: London 1880; Letchworth, Herts. 1909. † LS 3, RBA 1, RHA 1, ROI 2, SWA 2.

THOMAS, Margaret b. 1916
Portrait and still life painter. Studied Sidcup School of Art, Slade School 1936-38 and R.A. Schools 1938-39. Exh. 1938-40. Add: Bexley, Kent. † NEA 1, P 1, RA 2, SWA 1.

THOMAS, May Exh. 1908
Rutherglen, West Derby, Liverpool. † L 1.

THOMAS, Moray Exh. 1926-34
Sundial House, Holly Hill, Hampstead, London. † GOU 1, P 2, RBA 5, ROI 4, RSA 3.

THOMAS, Mrs. Moray Exh. 1928-35
Painter. Sundial House, Holly Hill, Hampstead, London. † L 3, RA 1, RBA 1, ROI 3, RSA 1.

THOMAS, Myfanwy Exh. 1930-38
Bangor, Wales. † RCA 3.

THOMAS, Mary Guest Exh. 1935-39
25 Norfolk Road, London. † RBA 2, ROI 6.

THOMAS, Marjorie Lilian b. 1897
nee Dawes. Painter and illustrator. Studied Birmingham School of Art and Byam Shaw and Vicat Cole School. Exh. 1922-37. Add: Birmingham 1922; Oxford 1937. † B 2, RA 1.

THOMAS, Nancie E. Exh. 1924-29
Miniature painter. 86 Hawthorne Avenue, Uplands, Swansea, Wales. † L 1, RA 2, RSA 2.

THOMAS, Paul b. 1859
French artist. Exh. 1908-9. Add: 6 Rue D'Abbaye, Paris. † L 2.

THOMAS, Percy 1846-1922
Portrait, landscape, genre and architectural painter and etcher. Studied under Whistler, Augusta Delatre and R.A. Schools. R.E. 1881 (Hon. Curator 1906). Add: London. † B 4, D 1, L 15, RA 21, RBA 15, RE 136, ROI 5.

THOMAS, Percy Exh. 1913-39
Architect. Cardiff. † GI 2, L 1, RA 5.

THOMAS, Percy Exh. 1919-31
Medallist. Gt. Pulteney Street, London. † RA 1, RMS 10.

THOMAS, Phoebe Exh. 1935-38
Landscape painter. Pound Green, Buxted, Sussex. † RA 1, RBA 1, SWA 1.

THOMAS, P. Elizabeth F. Exh. 1895-1907
Portrait painter. The Beeches, Uxmaston, Haverfordwest. † GI 3, RA 1, RBA 3, SWA 1.

THOMAS, Richard A. Exh. 1937
Sculptor. 34 Fitzroy Street, London. † GI 1, RA 1.

THOMAS, R.G. Exh. 1882
Fir Grove, Menai Bridge, North Wales. † L 1.

THOMAS, Rose Haig Exh. 1894-1905
Landscape painter. Basildon, Reading 1894; Dorchester 1904. † L 1, NEA 1, NG 7.

THOMAS, Robert Kent Exh. 1880-83
Etcher. R.E. 1881-84. Add: 25 Cloudesley Square, London. † RA 2, RE 6.

THOMAS, R. Lang Exh. 1938-40
215 Oakwood Court, London. † NEA 1, P 1, ROI 1.

THOMAS, Mrs. Sybil Exh. 1889-1900
Miniature portrait painter. London. † D 3, NG 3, RA 1.

THOMAS, Stephen Seymour b. 1868
American portrait painter. c/o H. Vanderspar, 22 George Street, Portman Square, London 1890; Paris 1892. † RA 1, ROI 1.

THOMAS, Thomas Exh. 1882-92
Birmingham. † B 5.

THOMAS, T.H. Exh. 1889-90
45 The Walk, Cardiff, Wales. † RCA 3.

THOMAS, Vernon Exh. 1932
† CG 1.

THOMAS, Walter 1894-1971
Marine painter, poster, pen and ink artist. Studied Liverpool College of Art 1912-13 and London 1913-15. Exh. 1913-15. Liverpool. † L 2.

THOMAS, William Exh. 1889-1900
Liverpool. † L 9.

THOMAS, W.A. Exh. 1908
14 Dale Street, Liverpool. † RA 1.

THOMAS, William B. Exh. 1908
107 High Street, Boston, Lincs. † RCA 1.

THOMAS, William Cave* b. 1820
Genre, historical, literary and biblical painter, etcher and author. Studied R.A. Schools 1838 and Munich Academy. Exh. 1884. Add: 53 Welbeck Street, London. † RI 1.

THOMAS, William F. Exh. 1901
Landscape painter. Lydstep House, Southwold, Suffolk. † RA 1.

THOMAS, William George Exh. 1933-40
Painter and designer. Studied Lambeth School of Art, Westminster School of Art, Royal College of Art, Paris and Fontainebleau. Head of Art Department Battersea Polytechnic and Inspector of Art in Higher Education L.C.C. 1905-19. Add: Minchinhampton, Glos. 1933; Walsall, Staffs. 1939. † NEA 2, RA 1, RBA 2, RCA 3.

THOMAS, William Luson 1830-1900
Watercolour painter and wood engraver. Founder of "The Graphic" in 1869. Worked in Paris, Rome and New York. A.R.I. 1864, R.I. 1875. Add: London 1880; Chertsey, Surrey 1889. † L 3, M 1, RI 35, ROI 4.

THOMAS, W. Murray Exh. 1891
Marine painter. Hollingbourne House, Cobham, Surrey. † RBA 2.

THOMAS, Walker W. Exh. 1882-1910
25 Lord Street, Liverpool. † L 11.

THOMASON, Miss F.A. Exh. 1908
11 Passage Stanislas, Paris. † LS 5.

THOMASON, Mary E. Exh. 1926-29
Waverley, Bryntirion Avenue, Rhyl, Wales. † L 6.

THOMASON, Yeoville Exh. 1886
Architect. 10 John Street, Adelphi, London. † RA 1.

THOMASSET, Miss G. Exh. 1932-40
11 St. Mildred's Road, Lee, London. † RI 6, SWA 4.

THOMASSET, Katherine Exh. 1939
The Barn, Chalfont St. Peter, Bucks. † RI 1.

THOMASSON, J.M. Exh. 1919
† L 1.

THOMASSON, Rowland Exh. 1924-26
87 Mosley Street, Manchester. † L 2, RCA 2.

THOMINET, L.A. Exh. 1918
19 Bridgford Road, West Bridgford, Notts. † N 1.

THOMPSON, Agnes
See HILL, Agnes Thompson

THOMPSON, Anthony Exh. 1936
Landscape painter. † COO 5.

THOMPSON, Annie Bruce Exh. 1889
Clovenford. † RSA 2.

THOMPSON, Miss A.J. Exh. 1880
Flower painter. Waddington Parsonage, Clitheroe, Lancs. † SWA 1.

THOMPSON, Alice J. Exh. 1926-29
Leach Hall, Sutton, St. Helens, Lancs. † L 4.

THOMPSON, Anna M. Exh. 1884-1904
Liverpool. † L 7, SWA 2.

THOMPSON, Miss B.W. Exh. 1924
Painter. 12 Vickers Street, Nottingham. † N 2.

THOMPSON, Mrs. Christiana Exh. 1880-81
Landscape and flower painter. London. † SWA 9.

THOMPSON, C. Broughton Exh. 1933
† WG 2.

THOMPSON, Constance Dutton b. 1882
nee Dutton. Painter, black and white and stained glass artist, lithographer and teacher. b. St. Helens. Studied St. Helens School of Art and Liverpool School of Art. Exh. 1909-40. Add: St. Helens, Lancs. 1909; Liverpool 1914. † L 26, RCA 33.

THOMPSON, Charles H. Exh. 1894-1923
Portrait, landscape and marine painter. Married to Heather T. q.v. Add: Bushey, Herts. 1894; St. Buryan, Cornwall 1903 and 1916; Guildford 1906. † L 2, RA 10.

THOMPSON, Miss C.M. Exh. 1920
Dundonald, Willaston, Birkenhead. † L 1.

THOMPSON, Charlotte Mary
See LAWRENSON

THOMPSON, David Exh. 1889-93
Glasgow. † GI 4.

THOMPSON, Doris Exh. 1931
Colwyn Bay, Wales. † RCA 1.

THOMPSON, Elise d. 1933
Animal painter. Studied Paris, Stirling and Dresden. A.S.W.A. 1904. Add: Godmanchester, Hunts. 1896 and 1904; Craigmill, Stirling 1900 and 1903; Greystones, Co. Wicklow 1902. † BG 2, GI 2, I 2, L 5, LS 3, RA 4, RHA 15, ROI 6, RSA 2, SWA 40.

THOMPSON, Ellen Exh. 1908
Holmwood, Castle Hill, Parkstone, Dorset. † L 1.

THOMPSON, Evelyn Exh. 1909-39
Watercolour painter. 18 Academy Street, Ayr. † AR 1, GI 1.

THOMPSON, Mrs. Edith B. Exh. 1932-33
Interior, landscape and flower painter. 20 Belgrave Square, London. † RA 5.

THOMPSON, Edmund C. Exh. 1928-32
115 Bedford Street, Liverpool. † L 3.

THOMPSON, Miss E.F. Exh. 1910-12
7 St. James Terrace, Regents Park, London. † D 5.

THOMPSON, Mrs. E.H. Exh. 1903
Binstead Vicarage, Alton, Hants. † L 1.

THOMPSON, Ernest Heber Exh. 1924-40
painter, pastelier, black and white artist and etcher. b. Dunedin, New Zealand. Studied Slade School, Royal College of Art and Central School of Arts and Crafts. A.R.E. 1924. Add: 35 Sydenham Avenue, Sefton Park, Liverpool. † L 6, NEA 14, P 6, RA 14, RE 41, RSA 4.

THOMPSON, Ethel Muriel Exh. 1907-40
Flower painter, etcher and teacher. Studied Royal College of Art and Liverpool City School of Art. Add: Birkenhead 1907; Cambridge 1937. † L 23, RA 2.

THOMPSON, E.R. Exh. 1929
Watercolour painter. † AB 2, D 1, NEA 1.

THOMPSON, Frances Exh. 1883-96
Birkenhead. † B 2, L 12, M 3.

THOMPSON, Frank Exh. 1890-1910
Landscape painter. 3 Pimlico, Durham. † GI 2, L 2, RA 4, RBA 1.

THOMPSON, F. Lamoureux Exh. 1907-23
Paul, Penzance 1907; Newlyn, Penzance 1910; Malvern, Worcs. 1921. † G 1, L 3, RA 4.

THOMPSON, Fred S. Exh. 1915
66 Bedford Road, Rock Ferry, Cheshire. † L 2.

THOMPSON, Gabriel Exh. 1889-1908
Portrait, figure, flower and landscape painter. Munich, Germany 1889; Cardiff, Wales 1894; Paris 1907. † GOU 1, L 9, LS 5, M 1, RA 5.

THOMPSON, G.H. Exh. 1885
Landscape painter. 2 Elm Field Villas, Millbrook Road, Freemantle, Southampton. † RA 2.

THOMPSON, Harold Exh. 1927
27 Madelaine Street, Liverpool. † L 1.

THOMPSON, Harri Exh. 1899
Landscape painter. London. † RA 1.

THOMPSON, Heather Exh. 1903-7
nee Sutcliffe. Miniature painter. Married Charles H.T. q.v. Add: St. Buryan, Cornwall 1903; Limnerslease, nr. Guildford 1906. † RA 5.

THOMPSON, Sir Henry 1820-1904
Landscape and still life painter and surgeon. b. Framlingham, Suffolk. Studied under Alfred Elmore and Sir L. Alma-Tadema. Add: 35 Wimpole Street, London. † G 1, RA 4.

THOMPSON, Hilda Beeby Exh. 1927-28
† RMS 2.

THOMPSON, Henry J. Exh. 1904-23
Landscape painter. Melrose, Hampton Road, Teddington, Middlesex. † I 2, RA 4, RI 1.

THOMPSON, H. Raymond Exh. 1892-1914
Portrait, and figure painter and black and white artist. Hampstead, London 1892; Shortlands, Kent 1912. † BG 38, L 8, RA 16, RI 3, ROI 2.

THOMPSON, Harry S. Exh. 1880-84
Landscape painter. Birmingham. † B 4, RBA 1.

THOMPSON, Isa Exh. 1882-1912
Figure painter. Married Robert Jobling q.v. Add: Newcastle on Tyne 1882 and 1890; Cullercoats, Northumberland 1885; Hinderwell, Yorks. 1889; Whitby by Sea, nr. Newcastle 1894. † B 1, GI 3, L 6, M 1, RA 7, RBA 9, RMS 2, RSA 5.

THOMPSON, John Exh. 1892-1933
Chapel House, Rivington, nr. Chorley, Lancs. † L 3.

THOMPSON, Josephine Exh. 1892
Stratton House, Bristol Road, Birmingham. † B 1.

THOMPSON, J. Albert Exh. 1885-1924
Liverpool. † L 13.

THOMPSON, Joyce W. Exh. 1931
Portrait painter. 82 Gloucester Place, London. † RA 1.

THOMPSON, Kate Exh. 1882-83
Figure and landscape painter. Daughter of Sir Henry T. q.v. Add: 35 Wimpole Street, London. † G 1, RA 2.

THOMPSON, Miss K.M. Exh. 1889
25 Sefton Drive, Liverpool. † L 1.

THOMPSON, Miss K.M. Exh. 1889
Flower painter. Kensington Gore, London. † SWA 1.

THOMPSON, Mrs. Lilian Exh. 1928-37
25 Stoneleigh Road, Birchfield. † B 8.

THOMPSON, Lizzie Exh. 1882
Plas Annie, Mold, Flints. † L,1.

THOMPSON, Lucy W. Exh. 1920
52 South Lotts Road, Dublin. † RHA 2.

THOMPSON, Margaret Exh. 1883-1923
Figure, landscape and flower painter. Hitchin, Herts. 1883; Hereford 1915. † B 2, RA 1, RBA 2, RI 6, RSA 9, SWA 2.

THOMPSON, M. D'Arcy Exh. 1930
44 South Street, St. Andrews. † NEA 1.

THOMPSON, Mabel Douglas Exh. 1927-39
Painter. Douglas House, Abergele Road, Colwyn Bay, Wales. † RA 1, RCA 12.

THOMPSON, Matt Raine Exh. 1881-83
Landscape painter. 43 George Street, Portland Square, London. † L 1, RA 1.

THOMPSON, M.W. Exh. 1913
Salters Hall, Sudbury, Suffolk. † RA 1.

THOMPSON, Nelly Exh. 1887-91
Painter. Eastham Ferry, Cheshire 1887; Heswell, Cheshire 1888. † B 3, L 7, M 2, RBA 2.

THOMPSON, Norman Exh. 1934
23 Ransom Road, Erdington, Birmingham. † B 2.

THOMPSON, Stanley b. 1876
Figure and landscape painter. b. Sunderland. Studied Sunderland School of Art and Royal College of Art. Exh. 1899-1926. Add: London 1899; Middleton on Tees, Darlington 1914. † RA 8.

THOMPSON, Mrs. Symes Exh. 1918
Cavendish Square, London. † SWA 1.

THOMPSON, Sydney L. Exh. 1904-23
Painter. Concarneau, Finistere, France 1904; Edinburgh 1923. † RA 2, RSA 1.

THOMPSON, S.P. Exh. 1913-15
Morland, Chislett Road, West Hampstead, London. † L 3, RA 2.

THOMPSON, Professor Silvanus R. Exh. 1884-1913
Landscape painter. University College, Bristol 1884; London 1893. † ALP 13, D 6.

THOMPSON, Theodora Exh. 1908-28
14 Waverley Road, Liverpool. † L 10.

THOMPSON, Ursula Exh. 1938
† NEA 1.

THOMPSON, William A. Exh. 1913-23
Painter. Melrose, Hampton Road, Teddington, Middlesex. † RA 3.

THOMPSON, Walter B. d. 1919
Landscape painter. R.B.A. 1900. Add: London 1890; Leytonstone, Essex 1901. † L 1, RBA 87, ROI 4.

THOMPSON, W. Harding Exh. 1926-27
Architect. 5 Verulam Buildings, Grays Inn, London. † RA 2.

THOMPSON, Wilfred H. Exh. 1884-1901
Landscape, historical and genre painter. A.R.E. 1895 (ceased 1901). Add: Hampstead, London. † B 7, D 3, L 10, P 2, RA 4, RBA 1, RE 14, RHA 7, RI 9, RID 4, ROI 8.

THOMS, Colin E.S. Exh. 1928-40
14 Coates Gardens, Edinburgh. † RSA 13, RSW 1.

THOMS, Kenneth O. Exh. 1932-34
14 Coates Gardens, Edinburgh. † RSA 3.

THOMS, Patrick Exh. 1940
14 Coates Gardens, Edinburgh. † RSA 1.

THOMSON, Lady Exh. 1933
Kynance Mews, London. † SWA 1.

THOMSON, Alex junr. Exh. 1881
Millerston. † GI 1.

THOMSON, Professor Arthur 1858-1935
Watercolour landscape painter. Professor of Anatomy at the Royal Academy from 1900. Add: Edinburgh 1884; Oxford 1888. † RA 4, RSA 5.

THOMSON, Adam Bruce b. 1885
Painter. A.R.S.A. 1938. Exh. 1909-40. Add: Edinburgh. † GI 15, L 9, M 1, RSA 83, RSW 3.

THOMSON, Miss A.E. Exh. 1884-86
Flower painter. Newstead, Forest Hill, London. † RBA 2.

THOMSON, Alex H. Exh. 1938
7 Victoria Place, Airdrie. † GI 1.

THOMSON, Alison H. Exh. 1931
20 Lochend Road, Bearsden. † GI 1.

THOMSON, Alexander P. d. 1962
Watercolour landscape painter. R.S.W. 1922. Exh. from 1906. Add: Glasgow. † AR 2, GI 75, L 60, RA 12, RI 6, RSA 63, RSW 76.

THOMSON, Alfred Reginald b. 1895
Portrait painter, mural decorator and caricaturist. b. Bangalore, India. Studied under John Hassall and C.M.Q. Orchardson. A.R.A. 1938. "Sister Fry" purchased by Chantrey 1940. Exh. 1920-40. Add: London. † CHE 7, I 5, RA 31, ROI 1.

THOMSON, Andrew Ronaldson Exh. 1880-92
Edinburgh 1880; Glasgow 1882. † GI 19, RSA 6.

THOMSON, A.S. Exh. 1881-82
2 West Toll Cross, Edinburgh. † RSA 2.

THOMSON, B. Exh. 1880
Oakfield House, Glasgow. † GI 1, RSA 1.

THOMSON, Bernard Exh. 1919-20
6 Wetherby Place, London. † GI 2, ROI 2.

THOMSON, Bessie Exh. 1883-91
Watercolour flower painter. Glasgow and London. † GI 10, RBA 3, RHA 3, SWA 1.

THOMSON, Beatrice A. Exh. 1895-1908
Landscape painter. Westover, Mount Ephraim, Streatham, London. † RA 3, RBA 1.

THOMSON, Bethia C. Exh. 1880-1908
Glasgow. † GI 4, RSA 2.

THOMSON, Bethia J. Exh. 1932-37
Springfield, Clarkston, Airdrie. † GI 4.

THOMSON, Cecilia Exh. 1885
14 York Place, Edinburgh. † RSA 1.

THOMSON, Connor Exh. 1924
Liberty Buildings, School Lane, Liverpool. † L 1.

THOMSON, Charles Lambert Colyn d. 1926
Watercolour landscape painter. Studied Slade School 1898-1901. Add: Ipswich, Suffolk 1901; London 1904. Died at Woodbridge, Suffolk. † CHE 1, I 2, L 2, LS 5, NEA 8, P 2, RA 1, RHA 2, RSA 2.

THOMSON, Miss C.M. Exh. 1913
Rook's Nest, Stevenage, Herts. † RA 1.

THOMSON, Carl O. Exh. 1922-40
Landscape painter. Sandon Studios, School Lane, Liverpool. † COO 1, L 2.

THOMSON, D.C. Exh. 1880-81
10 Caroline Villas, Willis Road, Prince of Wales Road, London. † RSA 2.

THOMSON, David F. Exh. 1932
7 Infirmary Street, Edinburgh. † RSA 1.

THOMSON, Edith Exh. 1923
† G 1.

THOMSON, Edmond Exh. 1903
1 Studio, 4 Albert Street, Regents Park, London. † ROI 2.

THOMSON, Miss Elma See NORTHEY

THOMSON, Ernest d. 1925
Exh. from 1883. Add: Glasgow. † GI 49, L 3, RSA 1, RSW 5.

THOMSON, Mrs. Ernest Exh. 1897-98
Hillhead, Glasgow. † GI 3.

THOMSON, Emily Gertrude d. 1932
Portrait painter, miniaturist, illustrator and stained glass artist. b. Glasgow. Studied Manchester School of Art. A.R.M.S. 1911, R.M.S. 1912. Add: Manchester 1883; 11 Queens Mansions, Brook Green, London 1908. † GI 1, L 20, M 7, RMS 51.

THOMSON, Mrs. E.M. Exh. 1932
Portrait painter. Samer, Pas de Calais, France. † RA 1.

THOMSON, Elis M. Exh. 1921
Bersham Hall, Wrexham. † L 1.

THOMSON, E.W. Exh. 1881-8
36 George Street, Edinburgh. † RSA 3.

THOMSON, George Exh. 188
2 Roseburn Place, Murrayfield. † RSA 1

THOMSON, George* 1860-193
Portrait, landscape and flower painter N.E.A. 1891. Add: London 1886 an 1934; Samer, Pas de Calais, France 1921 † B 1, CG 34, G 4, GI 8, GOU 125, I 2 L 5, LEI 62, LS 3, M 1, NEA 88, RA 14 RBA 2, RHA 2, RI 1, ROI 1.

THOMSON, G. Douglas Exh. 1927-3
Landscape painter. Moseley, Birmingham 1927; London 1939. † B 2, RA 3.

THOMSON, G.F. Exh. 188
Ruaton and 3 Steel Studios, London † RSA 1.

THOMSON, G.G. Exh. 189
28 Napier Road, Edinburgh. † RSW 1.

THOMSON, Grace Indja Exh. 190
7 Pembroke Studios, Pembroke Gardens Kensington, London. † LS 5.

THOMSON, G. Ramsay Exh. 191
10 Bank Street, Dumfries. † RSA 1.

THOMSON, Horatio Exh. 1884-1906
Glasgow. † GI 10.

THOMSON, Hugh 1860-1920
Watercolour painter, black and white artist and illustrator. b. Coleraine, Co. Derry R.I. 1897. Add: London. † FIN 194, LEI 181, LS 5, WG 32.

THOMSON, Helen P. Exh. 1928
45 Pentland Terrace, Edinburgh. † RSA 1.

THOMSON, Ina See SHELDON-WILLIAMS

THOMSON, J. Exh. 1891-96
Landscape painter. London. † RBA 6.

THOMSON, James Exh. 1902-19
Airdrie, N.B. † GI 11, L 2, RSA 3.

THOMSON, John Exh. 1888-89
121 West Regent Street, Glasgow. † GI 2.

THOMSON, J.B. Exh. 1885
9 Newhall Terrace, Glasgow. † GI 1.

THOMSON, J. Bell Exh. 1934
6 Stair Park Terrace, Girvan. † GI 1.

THOMSON, Jessie Elizabeth Exh. 1897-1934
Painter, miniaturist, black and white and pastel artist. b. Stowmarket, Suffolk. Studied Liverpool School of Art. Add: Liverpool. † L 45, M 2, RCA 9.

THOMSON, J.J. Exh. 1891
2 Doon Terrace, Pollokshields, N.B. † GI 1.

THOMSON, John Knighton (Kinghorn) 1820-1888
Genre and historical painter and teacher. 287 Upper Street, Islington, London. † D 1, RA 2, RBA 6.

THOMSON, James L. Exh. 1882-91
Edinburgh. † GI 1, RSA 6.

THOMSON, J. Leslie 1851-1929
Landscape, and coastal painter. b. Aberdeen. N.E.A. 1887, R.B.A. 1883, R.O.I. 1892, H.R.O.I. 1921, A.R.W.S. 1910, R.W.S. 1912. Add: London. † B 5, D 2, FIN 1, G 12, GI 13, L 27, M 48, NG 25, RA 56, RBA 40, RI 13, ROI 55, RWS 38.

THOMSON, John Murray b. 1885
Animal painter. Studied R.S.A. Schools. (Carnegie travelling scholarship) and Paris. A.R.S.A. 1940, R.S.W. 1917. Exh. 1912-40. Add: Edinburgh. † AR 2, GI 44, L 13, RA 5, RSA 71, RSW 73.

THOMSON, J. Sophie Exh. 1910-37
Ayr 1910; Newlyn, Penzance 1918; London 1919; St. Ives, Cornwall 1925; St. Mawes, Cornwall 1937. † GI 1, L 3, RSA 1, SWA 3.

THOMSON, James Taylor Exh. 1928-33
212 Bath Street, Glasgow. † GI 4, RSA 2.

THOMSON, Kate W. Exh. 1907
Collaborated with W. Armstrong Davidson q.v. Add: 137 West Regent Street, Glasgow. † GI 1, L 3.

THOMSON, Mrs. Lauder Exh. 1895-96
25 Merchiston Avenue, Edinburgh. † RSA 2.

THOMSON, Louisa (Louis) b. 1883
Painter, etcher, lithographer, pen and ink and pencil artist. b. Kandy, Ceylon. Studied under F.E. Jackson and at Rome. Add: London 1907 and 1916; St. Leonards on Sea 1909. † CHE 1, COO 3, D 2, GI 1, GOU 2, I 6, L 25, LS 3, P 3, RA 3, RBA 2, RHA 3, RI 4, RID 4, ROI 10, RSA 6, SWA 16.

THOMSON, Lettice M. Exh. 1925-37
Landscape and flower painter. London. † L 1, RCA 5, ROI 4, WG 93.

THOMSON, Miss M. Exh. 1895-97
61 Greenbank Road, Devonshire Park, Birkenhead. † L 2.

THOMSON, Miller Exh. 1883-84
Park Villa, Rochsolloch, Airdrie. † GI 2, RSA 1.

THOMSON, Mrs. M.E. Exh. 1925-28
New Barnet, Herts. † SWA 2.

THOMSON, Margaret Stanley b. 1891
Watercolour painter, etcher, wood engraver and handcrafts worker. b. Ormskirk. Studied Southport and Eastbourne. Teacher of Embroidery and leatherwork at Southport School of Art. Exh. 1919-33. Add: Southport, Lancs. † L 17, RSA 1.

THOMSON, Nona E. Exh. 1916
† I 2.

THOMSON, R. Exh. 1885
2 Orwell Terrace, Dalry Road, Edinburgh. † RSA 2.

THOMSON, Mrs. Ruby M. Exh. 1928-29
Painter. Fettercairn House, Codnor, Derbys. † N 3.

THOMSON, Susie Anstruther Exh. 1884
Painter. 8 Sydney Place, Onslow Square, London. † SWA 1.

THOMSON, T. Menzies Exh. 1896
Architect. 2 West Regent Street, Glasgow. † GI 1.

THOMSON, William Exh. 1880-94
Landscape, architectural and portrait painter. London. † RA 2, RBA 2.

THOMSON, W. Dawson Exh. 1940
Figure painter. 56 High Street, Amersham, Bucks. † RA 1.

THOMSON, William Hill b. 1882
Portrait painter and miniaturist. b. Edinburgh. A.R.M.S. 1916, R.M.S. 1924. Exh. 1907-40. Add: Edinburgh. † GI 3, L 21, RA 1, RMS 47, RSA 47.

THOMSON, Winifred Hope d. 1944
Portrait painter and miniaturist. R.M.S. 1898. Exh. from 1890. Add: London. † GI 1, L 4, NG 7, RA 43, RMS 23.

THONE, F. Exh. 1886
† TOO 1.

THONGER, G. Exh. 1886-87
High Street, Harborne, Birmingham. † B 5.

THORBURN, Archibald* 1860-1935
Bird and animal painter and illustrator. Son of Robert T. q.v. Add: Kelso 1880; Tunbridge Wells, Kent 1885; London 1887. † D 9, FIN 1, L 1, RA 21, RBA 1.

THORBURN, Catherine Exh. 1897
Watercolour painter. 13 The Lawn, Balham, London. † RA 1.

THORBURN, Miss C.N. Exh. 1904-14
Churchlands, Bebington, Cheshire. † L 6, M 2, RCA 4, RI 1.

THORBURN, Miss D. Exh. 1919-20
Edinburgh. † RSA 5.

THORBURN, Elizabeth Exh. 1926-38
Lady Atkins. Miniature portrait painter. 3 Grosvenor Crescent, London. † L 14, P 1, RA 4, RI 34, RMS 5.

THORBURN, Mrs. Henrietta S.D. Exh. 1930
Portrait painter. 1a Wetherby Studios, London. † L 1, RA 1.

THORBURN, Mrs. Rita Exh. 1932
143 Swan Court, Chelsea, London. † RBA 1.

THORBURN, Robert 1818-1885
Painter and miniaturist. b. Dumfries. A.R.A. 1848, H.R.S.A. 1857. Father of Archibald T. q.v. Add: Kelso 1880; Tunbridge Wells, Kent 1884. † RA 13.

THORELOW, F. Exh. 1885
90 George Street, Edinburgh. † RSA 2.

THORMAN, Frank Exh. 1894
Architect. Tadcaster, Yorks. † RA 1.

THORN, T. Exh. 1887
Painter. 6 Grove Terrace, Highgate Road, London. † RA 1.

THORNBURN, Walter Exh. 1896
7 Culbraid Street, Elgin. † RSA 1.

THORNBURY, J. Exh. 1890
c/o Mr. F. Davis, 3 Steelhouse Lane, Birmingham. † B 1.

THORNBURY, Lily M. Exh. 1904
163 Old Road West, Gravesend, Kent. † RCA 1.

THORNBURY, W.A.* Exh. 1883-1906
Landscape painter. London 1883; Gravesend, Kent 1892. † B 22, RBA 3, RCA 3, RHA 19.

THORNELEY, Charles* Exh. 1880-1902
River, coastal and marine painter. R.B.A. 1886. Add: London 1880; East Moulsey 1888; Eastbourne 1899. † B 9, D 9, G 5, GI 2, L 7, M 1, NG 1, RA 22, RBA 31, RI 9. ROI 29.

THORNELL, Amy Giles Exh. 1900-37
Kings Heath, Birmingham 1900; Knowle, Warwicks. 1937. † B 12.

THORNELY, J.A. Exh. 1881
Watercolour landscape painter. West Brow, Hampstead, London. † SWA 1.

THORNHILL, Miss C. Exh. 1894
13 Gilmore Road, Lewisham, London. † RBA 1, RI 1.

THORNHILL, Emma Exh. 1900-27
Watercolour landscape painter. b. Lowestoft, Suffolk. Studied Dresden and under Herkomer at Bushey. Add: London 1900 and 1911; Beccles, Suffolk 1910; Geldeston, Norfolk 1927. † D 3, L 1, RA 1, SWA 12, WG 69.

THORNHILL, Philip J. Exh. 1895-1912
Flower and allegorical painter. London 1895; Braintree, Essex 1910. † B 5, L 2, NG 4, RA 10.

THORNLEY, Sir Arnold Exh. 1927-33
Architect. Royal Liver Buildings, Liverpool. † L 2, RA 2.

THORNTON, Annie Exh. 1882-83
Lochearnhead, Perthshire 1882; Edinburgh 1883. † RSA 4.

THORNTON, Alfred Henry Robinson 1863-1939
Landscape painter, lecturer and writer. b. Delhi, India. Studied Slade School and Westminster School of Art. Teacher under Walter Sickert 1895-96. N.E.A. 1895. Member London Group 1924. "St. Germans" (1926) purchased by Chantrey Bequest 1930. Add: London 1893; Bath 1905; Painswick, Glos. 1921. † BA 2, COO 4, FIN 49, GOU 7, L 4, LEI 1, LS 12, M 4, NEA 165, RA 2, RBA 5, RED 39, RID 67, RSA 1.

THORNTON, C. Exh. 1882
Colville Street, Nottingham. † N 1.

THORNTON, Catherine Exh. 1880-1901
Interior and architectural painter. Riddings Road, Ilkley, Yorks. † D 13, RI 2, RSA 1, SWA 1.

THORNTON, Edward Exh. 1899-1909
London 1899; Hove, Sussex 1909. † LS 3, ROI 1.

THORNTON, George B. Exh. 1880-89
Edinburgh. † GI 6, RSA 24.

THORNTON, Harold 1892-1958
Painter, pencil artist and poster designer. b. Burnley. Studied Burnley School of Art and Royal College of Art. Art master Burnley Central School and assistant master Plymouth School of Art. Exh. 1933. † CON 4.

THORNTON, Kathleen b. 1901
Portrait, landscape, flower and miniature painter. Studied Heatherleys. Exh. 1924-38. Add: London 1924; Bushey, Herts. c.1930. † L 5, RA 1, RI 17, RMS 2.

THORNTON, Katherine M. Exh. 1909-10
11 Wilbury Avenue, Hove, Sussex. † LS 6.

THORNTON, Lily Exh. 1895-1904
Liverpool. † L 6.

THORNTON, M.J. Exh. 1887
Figure painter. 141 Lexham Gardens, London. † RI 2.

THORNTON, Rev. R.H. Exh. 1940
61 Hamilton Drive, Glasgow. † GI 1.

THORNTON-CLARKE, Emmeline d. 1927
Painter and miniaturist. R.M.S. 1917. Add: Glenleigh, Haringay Park, Crouch End, London. † L 10, NG 2, RA 4, RI 6, RMS 34, SWA 4.

THORNYCROFT, Alyce Exh. 1890-95
Sculptor. Daughter of Mary T. q.v. and Thomas T. (1815-1885). Add: Moreton House, Melbury Road, Kensington, London. † L 1, RA 3.

THORNYCROFT, Alyn M. Exh. 1889
Sculptor and painter. Daughter of Mary T. q.v. and Thomas T. (1815-1885). Add: Moreton House, Melbury Road, Kensington, London. † RA 1

THORNYCROFT, Edith Exh. 1891-92
Bird and insect painter. Eyot Villa, Chiswick Mall, London. † RID 5.

THORNYCROFT, Helen Exh. 1880-1918
Biblical, genre, flower and landscape painter. Daughter of Mary T. q.v. and Thomas T. (1815-1885). A.S.W.A. 1880. Add: London. † B 2, D 20, GI 3, L 3, NG 1, RA 17, RBA 3, RI 3, SWA 122.

THORNYCROFT, Miss J. Exh. 1912
16 Redington Road, Hampstead, London. † RA 1.

THORNYCROFT, Mary 1814-1895
nee Francis. Sculptor. b. Thornham, Norfolk. Studied under her father John Francis (1780-1861). Worked in Rome for several years with her husband Thomas T. (1815-1885). Executed a number of busts of the Royal Family. Mother of Alyn, Alyce, Helen, Theresa G. and William Hamo T. q.v. Add: Moreton House, Melbury Road, Kensington, London. † NG 2.

THORNYCROFT, Theresa G. Exh. 1880-81
Biblical and literary painter. Daughter of Mary T. q.v. and Thomas T. (1815-1885). Add: Moreton House, Melbury Road, Kensington, London. † RA 2, SWA 3.

THORNYCROFT, Sir William Hamo* 1850-1925
Sculptor. Studied under his father Thomas T. (1815-1885) and R.A. Schools. Son of Mary T. q.v. A.R.A. 1881, R.A. 1888. Knighted c.1917. "Teucer" purchased by Chantrey Bequest 1882, and "The Kiss" purchased 1916. † D 3, G 7, GI 14, L 14, M 2, NG 1, P 2, RA 133, RI 6, RSA 5.

THOROGOOD, Stanley b. 1873
Potter. b. Ripley, Surrey. Studied Brighton School of Art and Royal College of Art (travelling scholarship). Superintendent of Art Instruction for Borough of Stoke on Trent. Principal Camberwell School of Arts and Crafts. Exh. 1913 27. Add: Wolstanton, Stoke on Trent, Staffs. 1913; Brighton 1927. † GI 1, L 2, RA 6.

THOROLD, Mary W. Exh. 1939
† GOU 1.

THOROWGOOD, Enid Exh. 1910-12
24 Elm Park Gardens, London. † D 4, LS 3, SWA 1.

THORP, Adelaide C. Exh. 1893
Black and white portrait artist. North Court, Hampstead, London. † RA 1.

THORP, Amy Constance Exh. 1897-98
Miniature portrait painter. 4 Brunswick Square, London. † RA 4.

THORP, Florence Exh. 1904-7
Miniature portrait painter. 7 Hogarth Road, Kensington, London. † NG 1, RA 1.

THORP, Helen Exh. 1913
Landscape painter. 15 Prince of Wales Mansions, Battersea Park, London. † NEA 1.

THORP, Theresa Exh. 1904-11
Miniature portrait painter. A.R.M.S. 1908, R.M.S. 1910. Add: London 1904 and 1907; Preston, Lancs. 1905; Paris 1908. † L 5, M 2, NG 3, RA 3, RI 1, RMS 6, SWA 3.

THORP, William Eric* b. 1901
Landscape painter and designer. Studied R.A. Schools. Exh. 1923. Add: 20 Abinger Road, Bedford Park, London. †,RA 1.

THORP, William Henry b. 1852
Architect, watercolour painter and etcher. Studied Leeds School of Art. Chairman Leeds School of Art 1918-23. Exh. 1884-1902. Add: Leeds. † RA 5.

THORPE, Alice Exh. 1927
Still life painter. The Laurels, Arnot Hill Road, Arnold, Notts. † N 1.

THORPE, Barbara Exh. 1929
13 Upper Redlands Road, Reading, Berks † L 1.

THORPE, Mrs. Florence Exh. 1913
Tyndale, Teignmouth, South Devon. † RI 1.

THORPE, Frederick H. Exh. 1921-28
Malvern, Worcs. 1921; Bournemouth 1928. † L 2.

THORPE, H. Exh. 1906
24 St. James Square, Holland Park, London. † RA 1, RI 1.

THORPE, James b. 1876
Painter and illustrator. Studied Heatherleys. Contributor to "Punch" and first designer of pictorial advertisements to London Press Exchange 1902-22. Exh. 1912-16. Add: Hertford, Herts. † LEI 8, RI 1.

THORPE, John Hall b. 1874
Flower and landscape painter and wood engraver. b. Victoria, Australia. Studied Sydney Art Society, Heatherleys and St. Martin's School of Art. Engraver and artist with the "Sydney Mail". Married Kathleen T. q.v. R.B.A. 1912. Exh. 1912-27. Add: London. † I 2, L 13, RBA 46.

THORPE, Kathleen Hall Exh. 1918-19
nee Clarke. Married to John Hall T. q.v. Add: Redcliffe Square, London. † SWA 3.

THORPE, Leslie Exh. 1932-39
Manchester. † RCA 8.

THORPE, L.T. Exh. 1929
Painter and illustrator. 53 Percival Road, Sherwood, Nottingham. † N 1.

THORPE, Miss T.H. Exh. 1927
Bellevue House, Newlyn, Cornwall. † GI 1.

THORPE, W. Exh. 1897
151 Essex Road, London. † L 1.

THORS, Joseph* Exh. 1883-98
Landscape painter. London 1884; Birmingham 1894. † B 2, RBA 1, ROI 1.

THORS, S. junr. Exh. 1880
Still life painter. 42 Ampthill Square, London. † RBA 1.

THORSEN, O. Exh. 1889
c/o E. Foulger, 32 Fleet Street, London. † M 1.

THRAVES, G.M. Exh. 1883-90
Liscard Road, Egremont, Liverpool. † L 10.

THRING, Annie Exh. 1894-1910
Hemel Hempstead, Herts. 1894; Gt. Dunmow, Essex 1910. † M 1, RCA 1.

THRING, Edmund J. Exh. 1934
Painter. 49 Springfield Road, Brighton, Sussex. † RA 1.

THRING, Miss F. Exh 1903-12
Miniature portrait painter. Cambridge Road, Teddington, Middlesex. † L 2, RA 3.

THROP, John Exh. 1880-86
Sculptor. 54 St. James Street, Leeds. † L 5.

THRUPP, Daisy M.H. Exh. 1940
Sculptor. c/o Miss Goddard, Sevenoaks, Kent. † RA 1.

THRUPP, Frederick 1812-1895
Sculptor and black and white artist. Studied Sass's Academy and R.A. Schools. Exh. 1880. Add: London. † RA 1.

THUMANN, Paul 1834-1908
German figure painter. Exh. 1890-92. Add: 10 Keith Street, Berlin. † RA 1, TOO 2.

THURBER, Mrs. Caroline Exh. 1900-1
Painter. 84 Rue Lauriston, Paris. † L 1, NG 1, RA 1.

THURBURN, Henry M. Exh. 1913-19
Painter. Paris 1913; London 1919. † L 4, RA 1.

THURBURN, Percy C. Exh. 1930-35
Painter. Helford St. Martin, Cornwall. † RA 1, ROI 2.

THURGOOD, Doris Exh. 1931
† GOU 1.

THURLOW, Mrs. Grace Exh. 1929-30
The Lady Thurlow. Add: 2 Livingston Drive North, Liverpool. † L 3.

THURLOW, Leslie J. Exh. 1934-37
Etcher. Frindsbury, Kent 1934; Rochester, Kent 1936. † RA 3.

THURLOW, Margaret See LAMB

THURNALL, Harry J. Exh. 1880-1919
Flower, landscape and still life painter. Royston, Herts. † B 1, D 15, L 1 RA 4, RBA 6, RHA 1, RI 4, RSA 3.

THURNER, Gabriel 1840-1907
French artist. Exh. 1905. Add: 14 Rue des Volontaires, Paris. † L 1.

THURNER, J. Exh. 1886
27 Rue Blomet, Paris. † GI 1.

THURSBY, Ronald Exh 1939
18 Heathfield Avenue, Ashgate Road, Chesterfield. † RSA 1.

THURSTON, John H. Exh. 1899
Marine painter. 4 Albany Terrace, St. Ives, Cornwall. † L 1, RA 1, ROI 1

THURSTON, Rosalie W. Exh. 1932-40
Landscape and architectural painter. Littlecombe, Heathside Park Road Woking, Surrey. † GOU 1, RA 1, RBA 12, RI 6, SWA 6.

THURSTON, Violetta Exh 1930
Dragon Cross, Washford, nr. Minehead, Somerset. † B 1.

THURSTUN, Mrs. Ray (Charlotte) Exh. 1888-95
Landscape painter. Headcorn, Kent 1888; Benenden, Kent 1889. † RA 2, RBA 6, ROI 9.

THYNNE, Catharine Exh. 1910
66 Redcliffe Road, South Kensington, London. † LS 3.

TIBBLE, Geoffrey* 1909-1952
Landscape and figure painter. Studied Reading University and Slade School. Add: London 1928; Reading, Berks. 1929. † LEF 2, NEA 2.

TICHBOURNE, Katie D. Exh. 1887
15 North Great George's Street, Dublin. † RHA 1.

TICKELL, Bertha J. Exh. 1895-1909
Domestic painter. A.S.W.A. 1902, S.W.A. 1905. Add: 20 Cromwell Crescent, South Kensington, London. † L 8, RA 2, RI 2, SWA 42.

TICKELL, Miss L. Exh. 1926-27
Eddystone, Hewlett Road, Cheltenham, Glos. † L 3.

TICKELL, M. Betty Exh. 1901-6
20 Cromwell Crescent, Kensington, London. † L 2, SWA 6.

TIDDEMAN, Florence Exh. 1880-1901
Genre, historical and flower painter. 18 Canterbury Road, Brixton, London. † B 29, D 1, L 1, RA 2, RBA 2, RHA 1, RSA 1, SWA 8.

TIDDEMAN, Letitia E.H. Exh. 1881-1902
Watercolour painter. 18 Canterbury Road, Brixton, London 1881; Hastings 1886. † B 1, GI 1, M 1, RI 7, SWA 1.

TIDDIMAN, Nellie S. Exh. 1888-89
Flower painter. 10 Windsor Terrace, Windsor Street, Nottingham. † N 3.

TIDDIMAN, William Henry Exh. 1890-92
Painter. 48 Castle Gate, Nottingham. † N 3.

TIDEY, Alfred 1808-1892
Miniaturist. Twickenham, Middlesex 1881; Acton, London 1887. † B 1, D 19, L 1, M 3, RA 2, RI 1.

TIDEY, Clara Exh. 1885
Painter. 1 Upper Belsize Terrace, London. † SWA 1.

TIDMARSH, H.E. Exh. 1880-1918
Landscape and figure painter and watercolourist. London. † B 1, D 4, M 1, RA 20, RBA 3, RI 6.

TIDMUS, John A. Exh. 1897
11 Fernley Road, Sparkhill, Birmingham. † B 1.

TIDY, Emmie F. Exh. 1899-1901
29 Bolsover Street, London. † RI 3.

TIDY, Maud Exh. 1934
Seascape painter. 22 Norfolk Road, London. † RA 1.

TIEL, Mrs. Ella Exh. 1927
† D 1.
TIERNEY, Joseph Exh. 1916
Columbian Studios, Westmoreland Street, Dublin. † RHA 1.
TIETJENS, Mrs. Marjorie H. Exh. 1930-31
Nailsworth, Glos. † L 1, RCA 2.
TIGHE, Francis Browne Exh. 1885-1926
Manchester 1885; Bexhill on Sea, Sussex 1908. † LS 4. M 21.
TIGHE, Michael J. Exh. 1895
8 Upper Sherrard Street, Dublin. † RHA 1.
TIJTGAT, Edgard* Exh. 1918
Watercolour painter. † I 5.
TILBROOK, Reginald Exh. 1935-38
Landscape painter. 3 Douglas Mansions, Douglas Road, Hounslow, Middlesex. † COO 31, RA 1, RBA 1, ROI 2.
TILBURN, Geo F. Exh. 1928
Marine and landscape painter. † AB 3.
TILBY, Mrs. M. Exh. 1902
Westerham Road, Keston, Beckenham, Kent. † SWA 1.
TILDEN, Philip A. Exh. 1912-23
Architect. Northwood, Middlesex 1912; Marazion, Cornwall 1913; London 1914 and 1923; Ross on Wye 1917; Maidstone, Kent 1918; Brentor, Devon 1919. † RA 9, RSA 3.
TILL, Professor Exh. 1884-96
† TOO 2.
TILLARD, Katherine Lilian b. 1905
Painter. b. Bolton, Lancs. Studied Slade School. Exh. 1926-33. Add: London. † GOU 2, RBA 1, ROI 1, SWA 1.
TILLARD, Miss L.J. Exh. 1903
The Holme, Godmanchester, Hunts. † SWA 1.
TILLARD, Philip S. Exh. 1924
Painter. 5 Manor Studios, Lower Manor Street, Chelsea, London. † L 1, RA 1.
TILLEY, Henry Exh. 1933
80 Bruin Street, Leicester. † RSA 1.
TILLIER, Paul b. 1834
French artist. Exh. 1888. † TOO 1.
TILNEY, Frederick Colin 1870-1951
Landscape and figure painter, author and illustrator. Studied Westminster c.1908. Add: London 1894; Cheam, Surrey 1909. † L 2, LS 3, RA 10, RI 3, WG 60.
TILT, Mrs. Exh. 1884-87
Watercolour landscape painter. London. † SWA 4.
TILTMAN, A. Hessell Exh. 1883-1909
Architect. London and Guildford, Surrey. † RA 10.
TILY, Eugene b. 1870
Painter, etcher and engraver. b. Walkern, Herts. Studied under Arthur Stock and Walter Williams. Exh. 1913-24. Add: The Rowans, Elgin Road, Sutton, Surrey. † CON 2, GI 1, L 2, RA 1.
TIMBERLAKE, Rev. John A. Exh. 1938-40
Landscape painter. West Looe, Cornwall. † RA 1, ROI 2.
TIMEWELL, Maud A. Exh. 1901-2
105 Greencroft Gardens, West Hampstead, London. † L 1, SWA 4.
TIMMERMANS, Louis* 1846-1910
French painter. Exh. 1885-91. Add: Rue Aumont Thieville, Boulevard Gouvion St. Cyr, Paris. † GI 12.
TIMMINS, S. Dennis W. Exh. 1921-36
Elmhurst, Bloxwich, nr. Walsall, Staffs. † B 5
TIMMINS, William Exh. 1906-40
Glasgow. † GI 10, L 1, RSA 1.
TIMMIS, F. Exh. 1926
3 Harcourt Road, Llandudno, Wales. † RCA 1.
TIMMIS, Mrs. M. Exh. 1925
The Laurels, Park Road East, Birkenhead. † L 1.
TIMMIS, Miss Margaret Exh. 1925-27
The Laurels, Park Road East, Birkenhead. † L 2.
TIMMIS, Robert Exh. 1919-40
Portrait, landscape and decorative painter. b. Leek, Staffs. Studied Allan Fraser Art College, Arbroath. Drawing and Painting master Liverpool City School of Art. Add: Liverpool. † L 8, RA 5.
TIMSON, L.B. Exh. 1913-18
Engadene, Bective Road, Putney, London. † RA 1, RI 1.
TINDAL, Susan A.C. Exh. 1892
Stonehaven, N.B. † RSA 1.
TINDALL, John Empson b. 1885
Architect and aquatinter. Studied London and on the continent. Exh. 1924. Add: Premier Studios, 33 Fleet Street, London. † RA 1.
TINDALL, Rhona Exh. 1906-7
13 Vernon Road, Woodhouse Lane, Leeds, Yorks. † B 2, L 1
TINDALL, William Edwin 1863-1938
Landscape painter. b. Scarborough. R.B.A. 1893. Add: Leeds 1888; Boston Spa, Yorks. 1922. † B 4, L 10, M 3, RA 25, RBA 56, RI 1.
TINKER, Henry A. Exh. 1902
Architect. The Chestnuts, Bridge Street, Andover, Hants. † RA 2.
TINKER, Marion Exh. 1910
211 Withington Road, Whalley Range, Manchester. † L 2.
TINKLER, Emilie Exh. 1906-23
Painter and miniaturist. b. Manchester. Add: Southport, Lancs. 1906; Bolton le Sands, nr. Carnforth, Lancs. 1926. † B 1, GI 5 L 9, LS 20, M 5, RA 1, RMS 1, RSA 2.
TINLING, G.D. Exh. 1880
18 Charlotte Street, Bedford Square, London. † D 1.
TINLING, Rhoda H. Exh. 1895-1907
Gloucester 1895; London 1899; Shere, Guildford 1902. † B 9, L 2 RA 1, SWA 5.
TINNE, Miss E.D. Exh. 1933-40
Landscape and coastal painter. Studied St. Johns Wood School of Art and Holland. Add: Farnham, Surrey 1933; Ambleside, Westmorland 1940. † AR 28, RBA 1, RI 1, WG 28.
TINWORTH, George 1843-1913
Sculptor. Studied Lambeth School 1861 and R.A. Schools 1864. Entered the Doulton Pottery Works 1866. Among his reliefs are a series of 28 panels in the Guards Chapel and works of the same character in York Minster and Wells Cathedral. R.B.A. 1889. Add: London. † G 4, L 7, RA 4, RBA 11.
TIPPIN, Alice Bertha b. 1901
Mrs. Moreton. Sculptor. b. Liverpool. Studied Bootle School of Art, Liverpool School of Art, R.A. Schools 1924-28 (3 silver and 3 bronze medals), Paris and Italy. Exh. 1921 36. Add: Liverpool 1921; Willaston, Wirral, Cheshire 1936. † L 12, RA 3.
TIPPING, Kathleen (Kate) Exh. 1896-1923
Watercolour flower painter. Leamington Spa 1896; London 1908. † BG 2, D 3, I 5, L 11 LS 5, RA 3.
TIPPING, Mrs. Marguerite Exh. 1932-35
Watercolour landscape painter. Sherards, Godalming, Surrey. † COO 1, RBA 1, RI 4.
TIPPINGE, E. Gartside Exh. 1898
† D 2.
TISDALL, Miss B.A. St. C. Exh. 1913-14
Mrs. R.H. Tatton. 55 Addison Way, Golders Green, London. † RA 1, SWA 1.
TISDALL, Henry C. d. 1955
Landscape and figure painter. A.R.H.A. 1892, R.H.A. 1893. Exh. from 1880. Add: Dublin. † B 1, L 4, RHA 254.
TISSOT, James (Jacques Joseph)* 1836-1902
Genre and biblical painter and etcher. b. Nantes. Studied Beaux Arts in Paris. R.E. 1880. "The Ball on Shipboard" (c.1874) purchased by Chantrey Bequest 1937. Add: London 1880 † B 1, DOW 2, FIN 10, GI 5, L 8, M 1, RA 2, RE 11.
TITCOMB, Jessie Ada Exh. 1895-99
nee Morison. Genre painter. Married William Holt Yates T. q.v. Add: London 1895 and 1899; St. Ives, Cornwall 1897. † B 1, M 2, RA 4.
TITCOMB, John Henry 1863-1952
Landscape painter. Studied Slade School. Brother of William Holt Yates T. q.v. Add: St. Ives, Cornwall 1911 and 1921; Clifton, Bristol 1916. † RA 2, RI 1.
TITCOMB, William Holt Yates* 1858-1930
Landscape, figure and flower painter. b. Cambridge. Studied South Kensington, Antwerp under Verlat, Paris under Boulanger and Lefebvre and at Bushey under Herkomer. Brother of John Henry and husband of Jessie Ada T. q.v. R.B.A. 1894. Add: London 1884 and 1899; St. Ives, Cornwall 1894 and 1900; Clifton, Bristol 1910. † B 8, DOW 2, FIN 1, GI 2, L 15, M 6, NEA 7, NG 1, RA 42, RBA 22, RHA 2, RI 5, RID 6, ROI 7, WG 89.
TITLEY, Raymond Exh. 1913-31
Landscape painter. Nottingham. † N 11.
TITO, Ettore* Exh. 1884-92
Domestic painter. London 1884; Venice 1892. † L 2, M 1, RA 1.
TITTENSOR, Harry 1887-1942
Watercolour landscape and figure painter. R.I. 1931. Add: Stoke on Trent, Staffs. † FIN 41, GI 2, L 7, RA 9, RHA 4, RI 42.
TITTLE, Robina Exh 1916
College of Art, Edinburgh. † RSA 1.
TITTLE, Walter b. 1883
American portrait painter, etcher and illustrator. Exh. 1922-32. Add: 123 East 77th Street, New York City, U.S.A. 1932. † LEI 83, RA 1.
TIZARD, Catherine M. (Kate) Exh. 1890-1931
Landscape painter and sculptor. London 1890 and 1916; Paris 1905. † B 1, G 1, GI 3, GOU 12, I 1, L 4, LS 7, NG 3, RA 3, RID 14.
TIZARD, Jenny Exh. 1890
88 Carlton Hill, St. Johns Wood, London. † B 1 SWA 2.
TOBERENTZ, Mrs. Catherine Exh. 1890-92
Sculptor. 20 Cromwell Crescent, South Kensington, London. † NG 1, RA 1.
TOBEY, Mark* b. 1911
American painter. Travelled widely. Exh. 1931. Add: London. † BA 52.
TOBIN, Mrs. Fred (Clare) Exh. 1890
44 Brook Street, London. † G 1.
TOCHER, William E. Exh. 1933-39
Painter, etcher, and sculptor. London. † NEA 1, RA 7.

TOD, David Alex Exh. 1882-1919
Sculptor. Glasgow 1882; London 1885; Edinburgh 1886. † GI 16, RA 1, RSA 25.

TOD, Murray Macpherson b. 1909
Painter, etcher and teacher. Studied Glasgow School of Art, Royal College of Art and British School at Rome. Add: Glasgow 1929; London 1934. † B 2, GI 17, RA 5, RSA 17.

TOD, Richard Exh. 1901-17
Edinburgh 1901; Inverkeithing, N.B. 1913. † RA 1, RSA 8.

TODD, Arthur Exh. 1908-19
Heywood, Lancs. 1908; Lytham, Lancs. 1914. † L 8, RCA 4.

TODD, Arthur Ralph Middleton* 1891-c. 1967
Figure and portrait painter, etcher and engraver. Son of Ralph T. q.v. Studied Central School of Arts and Crafts, Slade School, France, Italy and Holland. A.R.A. 1939, A.R.E. 1923, R.E. 1930, A.R.W.S. 1929, R.W.S. 1937. "The Picture Book" purchased by Chantrey Bequest 1940. Add: Helston, Cornwall 1918; London 1921. † BA 2, BK 3, CHE 1, CG 1, CON 12, FIN 6, GI 1, L 4, NEA 3, RA 41, RE 25, RHA 6, RSW 1, RWS 24.

TODD, Charles T. Exh. 1892
Figure painter. Grosvenor Lodge, Tunbridge Wells, Kent. † RA 1.

TODD, Elizabeth M. Exh. 1890
Landscape painter. 2 Connaught Square, London. † RI 1.

TODD, Edith Ross Exh. 1895-1908
North Great George's Street, Dublin. † RHA 5.

TODD, Mrs. F. Exh. 1903
Westmoreland House, Uckfield, Sussex. † SWA 1.

TODD, G. Exh. 1911-12
Landscape painter. 14 Station Avenue, Gedling, Notts. † N 3.

TODD, H. Exh. 1918
2 Chaucer Villas, Chaucer Street, Nottingham. † N 1.

TODD, H.G. Exh. 1906
73 Wigmore Street, London. † RA 1.

TODD, Henry George* 1847-1898
Still life painter. Croft Street, Ipswich, Suffolk. † D 1, RA 1, RBA 2.

TODD, Miss Ione E. Exh. 1932
Landscape painter. Hotel Crebillon, 4 Rue Crebillon, Paris. † RA 1.

TODD, J.D. Exh. 1886
Aunsby, Sleaford, Lincs. † N 1.

TODD, John George Exh. 1880-92
Flower and figure painter. Econen, Seine et Oise, France 1880; London 1886. † AG 1, RA 8.

TODD, J.H. Exh. 1920-32
Still life and flower painter. Westbarton Place, Bury, Pulborough, Sussex. † GI 2, LEF 25.

TODD, James Henry Exh. 1898-1913
Landscape and flower painter. Glasgow. † GI 6, GOU 9, RSA 2, RSW 1.

TODD, J. Manly Exh. 1887-99
Landscape painter. Belvedere, Kent 1887; London 1899. † B 4, L 5, M 1, RA 2, RHA 3, RI 1, RSA 1.

TODD, Ralph Exh. 1880-1928
Genre and landscape painter. Father of Arthur Ralph Middleton T. q.v. Add: Upper Tooting, London 1880; Newlyn, Penzance, Cornwall 1883; Helston, Cornwall 1912. † B 53, L 11, M 2, RA 3, RBA 10, RI 6, ROI 1.

TODD, Robert Exh. 1893-1905
Glasgow. † GI 10, RSA 2.

TODD, Stanley Exh. 1928-38
Painter and charcoal artist. 45 Stansfield Street, Radford, Nottingham. † N 8.

TODD, William James Walker b. 1884
Architect. Studied Edinburgh College of Art. A.R.S.A. 1932. Exh. 1931-38. Add: 8 Albyn Place, Edinburgh. † RSA 14.

TODD-BROWN, William 1875-1952
Portrait, landscape and decorative painter and etcher. b. Glasgow. Studied Slade School. Principal Redhill School of Art 1922-40. R.O.I. 1935. Add: London 1906 and 1927; Harrow on the Hill, Middlesex 1910; Chesham Bois, Bucks. 1923; Mickleham, Surrey 1934. † GI 1, LS 5, P 1, RA 3, RCA 2, RE 7, RI 5, ROI 23, RSA 4.

TODHUNTER, J.M.H. Exh. 1881-84
Lynn, Cheshire. † RHA 6.

TODT, Max* Exh. 1884
Painter. 116/117 New Bond Street, London. † M 1.

TOFANO, Edouard* Exh. 1888-1900
Portrait painter. London. † L 2, NG 2, RA 5.

TOFT, Albert 1862-1949
Sculptor. b. Birmingham. Studied Stoke on Trent and Royal College of Art. Brother of J. Alfonso T. q.v. "The Bather" purchased by Chantrey Bequest 1915. Add: London. † AR 1, B 32, G 2, GI 39, L 56, NG 59, P 1, RA 98, RBA 3, RI 1, RSA 4.

TOFT, Clifford Exh. 1902-5
Flower painter. Hanley, Staffs. † B 1, L 1, NG 1, RA 3.

TOFT, Edward G. Exh. 1901
69 Byron Road, Small Heath, Birmingham. † B 3.

TOFT, J. Alfonso Exh. 1892-1940
Landscape painter. b. Birmingham. Studied Hanley and Birmingham Schools of Art and Royal College of Art. Brother of Albert T. q.v. R.O.I. 1919 (Hon. Retd. 1939). Add: Trafalgar Studios, Chelsea, London. † B 3, BRU 85, CHE 4, FIN 3, GI 7, GOU 21, L 7, LS 5, M 1, NG 15, P 2, RA 17, RI 13, ROI 55, WG 49.

TOFT, Peter* 1825-1901
Watercolour landscape painter. b. Denmark. Add: 156 Cornwall Road, Notting Hill, London. Died in London. † B 1, D 5, FIN 1, L 2, M 4, RA 2, RBA 11, RI 4.

TOFT, V. Exh. 1913-15
London. † RA 3.

TOFTS, James Exh. 1907-10
12 Norfolk Road, Dalston Lane, London. † B 1, RCA 1, RHA 1.

TOHNO, Yasuhiko Exh. 1932
Flower painter. 37 Clarendon Road, London. † RA 1.

TOLHURST, Edith Exh. 1888-1904
Mrs. Fred J. Gordon. Figure and portrait painter. London 1888; Beckenham, Kent 1903. † P 1, RA 2, ROI 1, SWA 2.

TOLLEMACHE, Hon. Duff Exh. 1883-1932
Marine painter. Studied R.A. Schools and Julians, Paris. Add: London 1883; 1888 and 1901; Peckforton Castle, Tarporley, Cheshire 1886; Alassio, Italy 1897. † B 13, GI 1, L 13, M 9, NG 2, RA 38, RBA 1, RI 8, ROI 10, RSA 2.

TOLLEMACHE, Hon. Mrs. Duff Exh. 1905-8
131 Oakwood Court, Kensington, London. † B 1, L 1.

TOLLEY, Doris Exh. 1937
92 Oakwood Road, Hampstead Garden Suburb, London. † ROI 1.

TOLLEY, Harry Exh. 1880
96 Shakespeare Street, Nottingham. † N 1.

TOLLOCK, B.L. Montague Exh. 1890
Landscape painter. Thurlow, Clapham, London. † RI 1.

TOLSON, M. Dorothy Exh. 1908-13
Oaklands, Dalton, Huddersfield. † L 7, RA 1.

TOLSTOI, Countess Exh. 1912
Moscow, Russia. † SWA 1.

TOM, Jan Bedys* 1813-1894
Dutch animal painter. Exh. 1883. † FIN 1.

TOMASSON, Miss K. Exh. 1916-18
Woodthorpe, Nottingham. † N 3.

TOMBAZIS, G.T. Exh. 1939
Landscape, coastal and figure painter. † BK 41.

TOMBEUR, Lucie H. Exh. 1906-9
Villa Pres, Morray a Spa, Belgium. † GI 1, RSA 1.

TOMBLESON, Christopher Exh. 1936-40
John Watson's School, Belford Road, Edinburgh 1936; Greenlaw, Berwickshire and Russell Hill School, Purley, Surrey 1940. † NEA 2, RBA 2, RSA 7.

TOMKIN, W.S. Exh. 1909
Watercolour coastal painter. 107 Orford Road, Walthamstow, Essex. † RA 1.

TOMKINS, Charles Algernon Exh. 1881-99
Engraver. A.R.E. 1899-1903. Add: London. † RA 12, RE 3.

TOMKINS, Charles John Exh. 1880-94
Portrait and figure painter and black and white artist. London 1880 and 1891; Iver, Bucks. 1884. † RA 11, RE 1.

TOMKINS, Flora Exh. 1910-37
Miniature portrait painter. Cheltenham, Glos. 1910 and 1914; Cowes, I.O.W. 1913. † L 5, RA 20, RMS 12.

TOMKINS, Lawrence Exh. 1925
Sculptor. 4 Marlborough Road, London. † L 1, RA 1.

TOMLIN, Anne D. Exh. 1930-40
Mrs. Lewis T. Add: London 1930; Edinburgh 1936. † GI 1, RSA 1, RSW 7.

TOMLIN, Geoffrey Exh. 1935-36
105 Dulwich Village, London. † ROI 3.

TOMLIN, Robert Exh. 1936
63 Lennox Street, South Circular Road Dublin. † RHA 1.

TOMLINS, E.F. Exh. 1905-8
22 Kilburn Priory, Maida Vale, London. † RA 2.

TOMLINS, J. Exh. 1886-87
5 Gauze Street, Paisley. † GI 1, L 1, RSA 1.

TOMLINSON, Aline Exh. 1927
Bradley Farm, Frodsham, nr. Warrington, Lancs. † L 1.

TOMLINSON, Herbert Exh. 1907
Watercolour painter. b. Wolverhampton. Add: Mariner's View, New Brighton, Cheshire. † L 1.

TOMLINSON, Mabel Exh. 1929-36
Miniature portrait painter. 3 Lancaster Place, Blackburn, Lancs. † L 12, RA 1, RMS 2.

TOMLINSON, Reginald Robert b. 1885
Portrait painter and etcher. b. Overton, Hants. Studied Farnham School of Art, Stoke on Trent School of Art, Hanley School of Art and Royal College of Art, also etching under Frank Short. Travelled on the continent. Master of Life Drawing and Painting, Stoke on Trent School of Art 1913-19, Senior assistant Cheltenham School of Arts and Crafts 1919-22 and Principal 1922-25. A.R.B.A. 1926, R.B.A. 1929. Exh. 1913-40. Add: Stoke on Trent, Staffs. 1913; Cheltenham, Glos. 1922; London 1926. † B 2, COO 1, GOU,1, L 3, LEF 1, NEA 1, P 1, RA 7, RBA 86, ROI 1.

TOMLINSON, T.J. Exh. 1884
Burton Road, Withington, Manchester. † M 1.

TOMMASJ, de See D

TOMPKIN, Alfred P. Exh. 1926
Coastal painter. 13 Parkhill Road, London. † RA 1.

TOMPKINS, Mary Exh. 1931
Painter. † LEI 25.

TOMS, R.G. Exh. 1910-11
7 Windmill Street, Tottenham Court Road, London. † GI 1, L 3.

TOMSON, Arthur 1858-1905
Landscape, genre and animal painter and illustrator. b. Chelmsford, Essex. Studied Dusseldorf. N.E.A. 1890. Add: London 1883; Pinner, Middlesex 1896; Dorchester, Dorset 1901. † B 2, G 5, GI 2, I 4, L 4, M 6, NEA 58, RA 14, RBA 6.

TONELLI, Domenico A. Exh. 1889-1920
Sculptor. Croydon, Surrey 1889; London 1912. † L 3, M 1, RA 8, RSA 1.

TONER, William D. Exh. 1932-35
17 Prospect Avenue, Cambuslang. † GI 1, RSA 1.

TONGE, C. Exh. 1892
Clareville Grove Studios, Brompton, London. † L 1, NG 1.

TONGUE, William Exh. 1885
1 Radcliffe Street, Arkwright Street, Nottingham. † N 2.

TONKOWSKY, Paul N. Exh. 1884
Figure painter. San Frovaso, Venice. † RA 1.

TONKS, Professor Henry* 1862-1937
Landscape and figure painter. b. Solihull, Warwicks. Studied Westminster School of Art. Assistant to Fred Brown at Slade School 1893. Official artist World War I. Professor Slade School 1918-30. N.E.A. 1895. "Spring Days" (1928) purchased by Chantrey Bequest 1931. Add: London. † AG 7, BA 3, BAR 62, CAR 57, G 1, GOU 13, L 2, LS 3, M 1, NEA 170, RA 1, RHA 4, RSA 10.

TONKS, Myles b. 1890
Landscape painter. b. Darley, Warwicks. Studied National Gallery, South Kensington Museum and the Tate Gallery. R.B.A. 1940, R.I. 1938. Add: Manor House, Brompton, Chatham, Kent. † AB 2, B 2, FIN 17, NEA 5, RA 9, RBA 3, RHA 1. RI 27, ROI 6, RSA 1.

TONNEAU, Joseph Exh. 1880-92
Figure painter. London. † B 1, RA 5, RBA 1.

TONNER, William J. Exh. 1893-1912
Glasgow. † GI 29, RSA 4.

TONNESEN, Miss A. Exh. 1889-91
Bergen, Norway. † L 1, RSA 1.

TOOBY, Gerald W. Exh. 1927
Figure and portrait painter. † CHE 2.

TOOGOOD, R.C. Exh. 1936
Landscape painter. 202 Malone Road, Belfast. † RHA 2.

TOOK, William* Exh. 1892
Landscape and portrait painter. 4 Florrie Cottages, Ramsgate, Kent. † RBA 1.

TOOKEY, Olwen b. 1910
Figure painter. 11 Pargeter Road, Bearwood, Birmingham. † B 1, RA 1.

TOOMER, A.J. Exh. 1935
Architect. Park Street, Taunton, Somerset. † RA 1.

TOOROP, J.H. Exh. 1895
c/o E.J. Van Wisselingh, 14 Brook Street, Hanover Square, London. † L 1.

TOOTH, Ann Exh. 1934-38
Landscape, portrait and flower painter. Swaynes Hall, Widdington, Newport, Essex. † COO 32, NEA 7, RA 1.

TOOTH, Miss E.R. Exh. 1928-32
42 Haughton Road Handsworth, Birmingham. † B 9.

TOOTH, Susan K. Exh. 1894-97
Miniature painter. London 1894; Colchester, Essex 1897. † RA 5, RI 2, RMS 2, SWA 1.

TOOVEY, Cecil Wotton 1891-1954
Painter, wood engraver and linocut artist. b. Berkhamsted. Exh. 1931. † RED 1.

TOOVEY, Edwin Exh. 1882-84
Landscape painter and teacher. Father of Richard G.H.T. q.v. Add: Landscape Villa, Leamington, Warwicks. † B 5.

TOOVEY, Mrs. Phyllis M. Exh. 1929-32
Landscape painter. Travelled in Scandinavia and India. Add: c/o J. Bourlet and Sons, 17 Nassau Street, London. † RBA 2, WG 47.

TOOVEY, Richard Gibbs Henry 1861-1927
Landscape, coastal and figure painter and etcher. b. Brussels. Son of Edwin T. q.v. Studied Birmingham School of Art and Paris. R.E. 1885. All art work ceased in 1889 owing to a nervous breakdown followed by partial blindness. Add: Leamington, Warwicks. 1882 and 1885; London 1883. † B 2, D 3, GI 2, L 11, M 2, RA 11, RBA 14, RE 33, RHA 4, RI 3, ROI 4.

TOPARELIAN, Edward Exh. 1937
74 Queensborough Terrace, London. † RI 1.

TOPHAM, Amy Exh. 1902
193 Selhurst Road, South Norwood, London. † B 1.

TOPHAM, Frank William Warwick* 1838-1924
Genre painter and watercolourist. Studied under his father Francis William T. (1808-1877), R.A. Schools and under Gleyre in Paris. R.I. 1879, R.O.I. 1883. Add: London 1880; Ewhurst, Guildford, Surrey 1896. † AG 3, B 36, BA 2, FIN 1, G 14, GI 8, L 54, M 34, NG 37, P 1, RA 55, RHA 3, RI 77, ROI 130, TOO 7.

TOPHAM, Helen M. Exh. 1929
June Cottage, Ewhurst, Guildford, Surrey. † RI 1.

TOPHAM, Inez Exh. 1909-26
Bristol 1909; London 1921. † L 8, RA 4, RHA 1, RI 2.

TOPLIS, J. Exh. 1932
75 Blake Road, West Bridgford, Nottingham. † N 2.

TOPLIS, William A. Exh. 1880-1930
Landscape painter. Bettws-y-Coed, Wales 1880; St. Peters, Jersey, C.I. 1881; Sark, C.I. 1884. † M 3, RA 17.

TORBY, Count Michael Exh. 1929-34
Landscape, still life and flower painter. † WG 134.

TORELLI, Professor Lot Exh. 1880-86
Sculptor. Taylor Institution, Oxford 1880; Florence 1886. † RA 2, RBA 2.

TORINI, P. Exh. 1888
† D 1.

TORPEY, Marguerite Exh. 1904
Figure painter. 120 Gower Street, London. † L 1, RA 1.

TORRANCE, A.H. Exh. 1937
29 Halbeath Road, Dunfermline. † RSA 1.

TORRANCE, James 1859-1916
Painter and illustrator. Glasgow 1898; Torrance 1911; Helensburgh, N.B. 1913. † GI 14.

TORRIE, Alexander Exh. 1906-12
8 Walmer Crescent, Ibrox, Glasgow. † GI 5, L 2.

TORRIE, John J.F. Exh. 1934
c/o Black Tower, Liberton, Edinburgh. † RSW 2.

TORROME, Francisco J. (Frank) Exh. 1890-1908
Landscape, figure and military painter. London. † D 14, L 2, RA 8, RBA 7, RI 5, ROI 3.

TORRY, Rev. Claude Exh. 1927-38
Landscape painter. Streat Rectory, Hassocks, Sussex. † AB 14, RA 1, WG 22.

TORRY, John T. Exh. 1886
Watercolour landscape painter. 64 Frith Street, Soho, London. † RBA 2, RI 2.

TOSO, E. Exh. 1888
c/o L. Dondy, Carter Street, Liverpool. † L 1.

TOTHILL, Mary D. Exh. 1881-85
Landscape painter. Stoke Bishop, Bristol. † D 3, RI 3.

TOTTENHAM, Mrs. W.F. Exh. 1919
64 Grosvenor Road, Rathgar, Dublin. † RHA 1.

TOTTON, Miss M.A. Exh. 1882-97
Landscape painter. Wallington, Carshalton, Surrey. † M 2, SWA 2.

TOUCHE, la See L

TOUDOWZE, Mme. M.A. Exh. 1902
21 Boulevard des Batignolles, Paris. † L 1.

TOUGH, D.J. Exh. 1889
13 North Street, Andrew Street, Edinburgh. † RSA 1.

TOULE, Miss S. (Cissie) Exh. 1903-8
Fruit painter. Burton House, Chestnut Grove, Mapperley Road, Nottingham. † N 3.

TOUNER, William J. Exh. 1898-1900
114 West Campbell Street, Glasgow. † GI 1, RSA 1.

TOUPEY, Alexandre Exh. 1906
32 Rue de la Sante, Paris. † L 1.

TOURNEUR, Louise Exh. 1890
Portrait painter. 22 Rue d'Athenes, Paris. † RA 1.

TOURNIER, le See L

TOURRIER, Alfred Holst* 1838-1892
French historical and genre painter and illustrator. Add: London 1880 and 1888; Herne Hill 1884. † RA 3, RBA 4.

"THE TOUT" Exh. 1931
Racing caricaturist. † WG 128.

TOWELL, Miss I. Exh. 1901
49 Alexandra Road, Southport, Lancs. † L 1.

TOWER, James W. Exh. 1939-40
Landscape painter. Manor House, Cheyre Rock, Sheerness, Kent. † RA 3.

TOWER, Walter Ernest b. 1873
Stained glass artist and architect. Studied architecture at R.A. Schools and stained glass under C.E. Kempe. Exh. 1896. Add: London. † RA 1.

TOWERBY, John Chollerton Exh. 1897
Wall, Northumberland. † B 2.

TOWERS, Alfred Exh. 1892-1928
Married Margaret J.T. q.v. Add: Birmingham 1892; Hatton, Warwick 1906; Knowle, Warwicks. 1907; Radcliffe on Trent, Notts. 1910; Llanbedr, Merioneth 1919. † B 17, N 10, RCA 2.

TOWERS, Daisy Exh. 1929
39 Wellington Avenue, Wavertree, Liverpool. † L 1.

TOWERS, G.H. Exh. 1934-35
9 Carlton Terrace, Ashing Street, Nottingham. † N 2.

TOWERS, Hilton Exh. 1894-96
Albany Chambers, Mawdsley Street, Bolton, Lancs. † L 2.

TOWERS, Miss H.N. Exh. 1916-39
Mrs. H.N. Brazier. Daughter of Samuel T. q.v. Add: Harvington, nr. Evesham, Worcs. † B 1, L 4, RCA 1.

TOWERS, James b. 1853
Landscape painter. Studied Liverpool College School of Art and Liverpool Academy of Art. Exh. 1880-1931. Add: Rock Ferry, Cheshire 1880; Birkenhead 1895; Heaverham, nr. Sevenoaks, Kent 1898; Slough, Bucks. 1904; Gerrards Cross, Bucks. 1911. † B 17, D 1, L 126, LS 18, M 11, RA 17, RBA 7, RCA 105, RHA 2, RI 14, RSA 1.

TOWERS, Mrs. James Exh. 1895-96
Birkenhead. † L 3.

TOWERS, Margaret J. Exh. 1922-33
nee Sutton. Marine painter, lace maker and embroiderer. Married Alfred T. q.v. Add: Llwyn, Llandbedr, Merioneth. † B 12.

TOWERS, Samuel b. 1862
Watercolour painter. b. Bolton. Father of Miss H.N.T. q.v. Add: Bolton 1884; Bolton le Moors 1894; Glan Conway, Wales 1895; Harvington, nr. Evesham, Worcs. 1907. † B 5, L 17 M 3, RA 9, RBA 1, RCA 58, RI 2, RSA 1.

TOWERS, T.E. Exh. 1920-24
Landscape painter. A.N.S.A. 1938. Add: 212 Blue Bell Hill, Nottingham. † N 7.

TOWERS, Walter Exh. 1924
Ardmore, Grangemouth, N.B. † L 2.

TOWGOOD, Mary Y. Exh. 1895-99
Portrait painter. London. † B 1, NG 1, RA 5, ROI 1.

TOWLER, A. Kitson Exh. 1936-38
Painter and engraver. 8 Brnaham Gardens, London. † RBA 2, RED 1, RMS 2.

TOWNDROW, F.H. Exh. 1916-33
London 1916; Lower Bebington 1932. † L 3, RA 1.

TOWNDROW, Sidney Exh. 1925-30
Landscape painter. 11 Kimbolton Avenue, Nottingham. † N 6.

TOWNEND, Miss M. Exh. 1924-25
165 Rustlings Road, Sheffield. † L 13.

TOWNEND, Miss M. Exh. 1897
9 Derby Terrace, Derby Road, Nottingham. † N 1

TOWNER, Donald b. 1903
Landscape and portrait painter. Studied Eastbourne School of Art, Brighton School of Art and Royal College of Art 1923-27. Exh. 1928-40. Add: Hampstead, London. † GOU 1, LEI 29, NEA 15, RA 12.

TOWNLEY, Annie B. Exh. 1881-90
Watercolour landscape painter. Sister of Minnie T. q.v. Add: Birmingham. † B 6, L 2, RBA 1, RI 2, SWA 2.

TOWNLEY, Joyce A. Exh. 1927-29
58 Queen's Drive, Mossley Hill, Liverpool. † L 3.

TOWNLEY, Minnie Exh. 1880-93
Landscape and flower painter. Sister of Annie T. q.v. Add: Birmingham. † B 16, RBA 4, ROI 1, SWA 2.

TOWNROE, Reuben 1835-1911
Sculptor. Exh. 1880. Add: 91 Church Street, Chelsea, London. † RA 1.

TOWNSEND, Miss A. Exh. 1887-96
Pollokshields, N.B. 1887; Hillhead, Glasgow 1888. † GI 10.

TOWNSEND, Alfred O. 1846-1917
Landscape painter. Bristol. † G 1, L 3, NG 2, RA 4, RBA 1, RHA 3, RI 4, ROI 2, RSA 2.

TOWNSEND, Bernard R. Exh. 1924
Borrowdale, Sandal, Wakefield, Yorks. † L 2.

TOWNSEND, Miss C. Exh. 1890
Burleigh Street, London. † SWA 1.

TOWNSEND, C.E. Exh. 1924
Glass House, Fulham, London. † L 1.

TOWNSEND, Charles Harrison 1850-1928
Architect. London. † RA 8.

TOWNSEND, Ernest b. 1880
Portrait and interior painter. b. Derby. Studied Heatherleys and R.A. Schools (Landseer scholarship and Creswick prize). Exh. 1908-37. Add: London 1908; Derby 1913. † B 4, L 2, N 28, P 6, RA 16, RBA 5, ROI 3, RSA 2.

TOWNSEND, Frederick H. 1868-1920
Black and white artist and Art Editor and contributor to "Punch". Add: London. † FIN 138, LEI 19, NEA 2, NG 10 RA 3, RBA 1, RE 4, RSA 1.

TOWNSEND, Joyce Eleanor b. 1900
Architect. b. Bristol. Studied A.A. Exh. 1930-33. Add: 4 Verulam Buildings, Grays Inn, London. † RA 3.

TOWNSEND, Mrs. Jessie M. Exh. 1919
Painter. 8 Gleneldon Road, Streatham, London. † RA 1.

TOWNSEND, Miss K.L. Exh. 1938
The Cedars, Beeches Road, West Bromwich, Birmingham. † B 1.

TOWNSEND, Mrs. Louisa Exh. 1896-1920
Mrs. Frank. Miniature painter. R.M.S. 1896. Add: Barnstaple, North Devon 1896; Bexhill on Sea 1900; London 1911; Hounslow, Middlesex 1918; East Grinstead, Sussex 1920. † LS 8, RA 6, RMS 9.

TOWNSEND, Mrs. M. Exh. 1902-23
London. † SWA 6.

TOWNSEND, May Exh. 1937
Landscape and miniature painter. † COO 4.

TOWNSEND, Miss M. Surtees Exh. 1889
Painter. 4 Grosvenor Terrace, York. † SWA 1.

TOWNSEND, Pattie See JOHNSON

TOWNSEND, Sarah Thompson Exh. 1923-24
Landscape painter. 20 Camden Hill Gardens, London. † RA 2.

TOWNSEND, Theo Exh. 1915-16
Figure and interior painter. London. † NEA 3.

TOWNSEND, Thomas S. Exh. 1894
Sculptor. Atelier Prof. Hildebrand, Maffei Anger, Munich. † RA 1.

TOWNSEND, William b. 1909
Painter and engraver. Studied Slade School 1926-30. Exh. 1936-40. † COO 1, RED 2.

TOWNSEND, W.G. Paulson Exh. 1899-1936
Architect. London. † RA 1, RI 1.

TOWNSHEND, Arthur Louis* Exh. 1880-1912
Sporting and rustic painter. London 1880 and 1907; Newmarket, Suffolk 1884; Paris 1895. † RA 5, ROI 5.

TOWNSHEND, Caroline Exh. 1927-34
Stained glass artist. River Wall, Deodar Road, Putney, London. † L 6, RA 3.

TOWNSHEND, Mrs. Harriet Exh. 1911-35
Portrait painter. Dublin. † RHA 27.

TOWNSHEND, James Exh. 1883-1940
Landscape, figure and portrait painter. R.B.A. 1897. Add: London. † B 17, NG 18, RA 11, RBA 268, RI 8, ROI 10.

TOWNSON, Sophia Exh. 1880-85
Liverpool. † L 1, RHA 7.

TOWSE, Stanley Exh. 1907
8 New Square, Lincoln's Inn, London. † RA 1.

TOWSEY, Basil W. Exh. 1939-40
Painter. 27 Wykeham Road, London. † RA 1, ROI 3.

TOYNBEE, Gertrude Exh. 1898-1902
8 Balcombe Street, Dorset Square, London. † SWA 5.

TOZER, E. Exh. 1909-11
A.N.S.A. 1910. Add: Nottingham 1909; Plumtree, Notts. 1911. † N 3.

TOZER, E.A. Exh. 1892
Cape Cornwall House, St. Just, nr. Penzance, Cornwall. † RHA 1.

TOZER, H.E. Exh. 1933
11 Fernleigh Avenue, Westdale Lane, Mapperley, Nottingham. † N 1.

TOZER, Henry E. Exh. 1889-92
Seascape painter. Penzance, Cornwall. † B 2, RA 1.

TOZER, Marjorie H. Exh. 1940
Mrs. J.F.F. Leefe. Landscape painter. 18 Newlands Avenue, Radlett, Herts. † RA 1.

TOZER, Robert Exh. 1937-40
Hemel Hempstead, Herts. † RCA 8.

TRACY, Arthur J. Exh. 1940
Sculptor. 143 Old Church Street, London. † RA 1.

TRACY, Charles Dunlop Exh. 1908-12
Landscape painter. Shoreham, Sussex 1908; Kingston by Sea, Sussex 1912. † LS 10, RA 2.

TRAFFORD, Major Exh. 1893
Landscape painter. 1 Marlborough Mansions, Victoria Street, London. † RBA 1.

TRAFFORD, Lionel J. Exh. 1899
Figure painter. The Hill, Ross on Wye, Hereford. † RA 1.

TRAILL, Alice M. Exh. 1882-1907
Kirkwall 1882; Edinburgh 1889; Gullane, N.B. 1907. † GI 1, RSA 9, RSW 1.

TRAILL, Cecil G. Exh. 1892-94
Radnor House, Malden, Surrey. † ROI 3.

TRAILL, Miss J.C.A. Exh. 1909-14
Australian etcher. Add: London. † RA 2.

TRANGMAR, Charles Frank b. 1889
Landscape painter and etcher. Studied Brighton School of Art and Royal College of Art. Headmaster Salisbury School of Art and Principal Ealing School of Arts and Crafts. Exh. 1927-32. Add: 39 Cambourne Avenue, London. † RA 2, RBA 11.

TRANTER, Arthur H. Exh. 1937
Sculptor. 56 Warwick Road, Earls Court, London. † B 1.

TRANTOM, Amy Exh. 1910
31 Islington, Liverpool. † L 1.

TRANTOM, Edith Exh. 1893-1912
Birkdale, Lancs. 1893; Seaforth 1897; Liverpool 1900 and 1908; Chester 1903. † B 1, L 17, M 1.

TRANTSCHOLD, Manfred Exh. 1893-94
c/o Mrs. Garrett, 37 High Street, Notting Hill Gate, London. † ROI 2.

TRAPPES, Francis M. Exh. 1880-85
Landscape painter. London 1880; Epping, Essex 1885. † L 1, RA 4, RBA 3.

TRAQUAIR, Phoebe Anna 1852-1936
Mrs. H. Ramsay T. nee Moss. Painter, mural decorator, enameller, embroiderer and illustrator. b. Dublin. Studied Dublin School of Art. Mother of Ramsay T. q.v. H.R.S.A. 1935. Add: Edinburgh 1893; Colinton 1907. † GI 1, L 16, RSA 18.
TRAQUAIR, Ramsay Exh. 1908-12
Son of Phoebe Anna T. q.v. Add: 4 Forres Street, Edinburgh. † RSA 5.
TRASKA, Jan Exh. 1914
8 Wilcra Street, Warsaw, Poland. † LS 3.
TRAVERS, Evelyn R. Exh. 1907-33
London. † B 1, LS 3, RA 1, SWA 1.
TRAVERS, Mrs. Florence Exh. 1889-1902
Rustic painter. Weybridge, Surrey 1889; Horsham, Sussex 1902. † L 1, RBA 9, RI 6.
TRAVERS, F.V. Exh. 1915-21
Kincraigie, Courtmacsherry, Co. Cork. † RHA 13.
TRAVERS, H.M. Exh. 1911-13
3 Priory Road, Bedford Park, London. † RA 4
TRAVERS, Linda Exh. 1925-31
Mrs. Ward. Still life painter. Self taught. Add: Helenslea Ho, Finchley Road, London. † L 7, RA 6, ROI 1, SWA 1.
TRAVERS, Martin Exh. 1915-40
Stained glass artist, and ecclesiastical designer. London. † RA 28, RSA 1.
TRAVERS, Miss N. Exh. 1907-20
Cheam, Surrey. † RA 1, SWA 11.
TRAVERS, Sybil Exh. 1924-38
† GOU 7, NEA 1.
TRAVERS-SMITH, Dorothea Exh. 1934-39
Portrait, flower and cat painter. Studied Regent Street Polytechnic and under Arthur Lindsey. Add: London. † RBA 7, RI 2, SWA 7.
TRAVIS, Mrs. Doris Exh. 1927
25 Ashley Place, London. † NEA 1.
TRAVIS, Miss M.H. Exh. 1928
31 Brookfield Avenue, Gt. Crosby, Liverpool. † L 1.
TRAYER, Jules Baptiste Jules* 1824-1908
French painter. Exh. 1882. Add: c/o Vokins, 14 Gt. Portland Street, London. † RA 2.
TRAYNOR, Elisabeth Exh. 1906-20
15 Kenilworth Square, Dublin. † RHA 12.
TREATT, Chaplin Court Exh. 1909-14
6 Nevern Road, Earls Court Road, London. † L 4, LS 18.
TREBBLE, T. Exh. 1899-1916
Leicester. † N 11.
TREBUCHET, Mme. M. Exh. 1913
Painter. † ALP 3.
TREDINNICK, R.B. Exh. 1927
10 Grange Gardens, Eastbourne. † ROI 1.
TREE, Philip H. Exh. 1887-1908
Architect. 59 London Road, St. Leonards on Sea, Sussex. † RA 9.
TREFUSIS, Hilda Exh. 1925
† GOU 1.
TREGARNETH, Mrs. Anita Exh. 1934-38
Landscape painter. 35 Dover Street, London. † NEA 2, RCA 3, RHA 7, RSA 6, SWA 8.
TREGARTHEN, Kathleen b. 1902
Painter, black and white and commercial artist. Studied Slade School Exh. 1926. Add: 4 Park Road, Woodside, Wimbledon, London. † NEA 1.
TREGENZA, Arthur Exh. 1930-32
Wallasey, Cheshire. † L 2.
TREGLOWN, Ernest d. 1922
Exh. 1891-1916. Add: School of Art, Margaret Street, Birmingham. † B 2, L 1.
TREGO, J.J. William Exh. 1883-99
Landscape painter. London 1883; Coventry 1899. † B 1, RBA 1.
TREHANE, Maude Exh. 1904
6 Alexandra Terrace, Newlyn, Cornwall. † NG 1.
TRELAWNY, F.B.M. Exh. 1889-91
Landscape painter. 13 Lancaster Gate, London. † RID 8.
TRELAWNY, Miss N. Exh. 1891
Shotwick Park, Chester. † L 1.
TREMATOR, Severins Exh. 1927
Morant Studios, 104 Southampton Row, London. † RSA 1.
TREMAYNE, Constance Exh. 1897-98
Miniature portrait painter. Bellefield, Upper Tulse Hill, London. † RA 1, RI 2.
TREMBLAY, Emile Exh. 1898
c/o H.S. Tuke, Lyndon Lodge, Hanwell. † L 1.
TREMEARNE, Rev. Allen Riddle Exh. 1918-29
Landscape painter. London. † AB 15, LS 6.
TREMEL, May Exh. 1907-36
Etcher. b. Bradford, Yorks. Studied Goldsmiths College, Royal College of Art and Frankfurt. Add: Barnes, Surrey 1907; Ivy Hatch, nr. Sevenoaks, Kent 1936. † B 8, L 6, RA 7, RCA 4.
TREMEWAN, M. Exh. 1886
Watercolour landscape painter. 279 High Street, Lewisham. † RBA 1.
TREMLETT, Freda Exh. 1930-38
Painter and wood engraver. Abingdon, Berks. † COO 8, RED 2, SWA 4.
TREMLETT, H.E. Exh. 1938-39
48 Olton Boulevard, Acocks Green, Birmingham. † B 2.
TRENAM, Ruth Exh. 1921
† LS 3.
TRENCH, Lady Chenevix Exh. 1930-40
Watercolour landscape painter. Travelled widely. Add: London. † COO 2, RI 9, WG 116.
TRENCH, Eileen M. le Poer See WYON
TRENCH, Hon. Grace Exh. 1933-34
Landscape painter. Woodlawn, Co. Galway. † RHA 2.
TRENCH, Gilbert Mackenzie Exh. 1935-40
Architect. New Scotland Yard, London. † RA 9.
TRENCH, John A. Exh. 1882-1923
Landscape painter. Oxton Cheshire 1882; Birkenhead 1897; Bettws-y-Coed, Wales 1919. † L 32, M 1, RBA 1, RCA 10.
TRENCH, Marianne L. b. 1888
Landscape painter and teacher. b. Guildford. Studied Slade School and under Bertram Nicholls. A.R.B.A. 1926. Exh. 1920-40. Add: Guildford, Surrey 1920; Steyning, Sussex 1935; Shoreham by Sea, Sussex 1940. † B 21, CG 1, COO 2, D 2, L 13, M 3, RA 10, RBA 46, RCA 25, RHA 18, RI 1, ROI 13, RSA 17, SWA 7.
TRENCH, P.C. Exh. 1880
115 Grafton Street, Dublin. † RHA 1.
TRENT, Newbury Abbot 1885-1953
Sculptor. Studied Royal College of Art. Add: London. † GI 23, L 23, M 1, RA 50, RBA 1.
TRENTACOSTE, Domenico 1856-1933
Italian sculptor. Exh. 1891-93. Add: London 1891; Paris 1893. † L 1, RA 5.
TRESIDDER, H.H. Exh. 1905-12
Painter. 13 Park Terrace, Falmouth, Cornwall. † L 1, M 1, RA 2.
TRESILIAN, Stuart Exh. 1920-22
Pencil and chalk artist. London. † GI 1, RA 3.
TREVAIL, Silvanus 1851-1903
Architect. Truro, Cornwall 1897. † RA 1.
TREVELYAN, Hilda Exh. 1908-28
Landscape painter. 19 Eaton Place, London. † GOU 1, LS 20, NEA 1.
TREVELYAN, Julian* b. 1910
Landscape painter and etcher. Studied in Paris 1930-33. Exh. 1935-40. † LEF 41.
TREVIT, Miss L. Exh. 1883
100 Admiral Street, Liverpool. † L 1.
TREVOR, Edward d. 1885
Landscape painter. b. Conway, Wales. Died in Capri. Add: Conway 1880; Manchester 1882. † L 6, M 11, RA 1, RHA 1.
TREVOR, Miss G.S. Exh. 1892-1915
Bray 1892; Kingstown, Co. Dublin 1915. † RHA 3.
TREVOR, Helen Mabel Exh. 1881-97
Landscape and figure painter. London 1881 and 1886; Concarneau, Finistere, France 1883; Paris 1894. † B 3, L 3, M 4, RA 3, RBA 3, RHA 17, SWA 2.
TREVOR, Miss L. Exh. 1886-90
Tywyn, nr. Conway, Wales. † B 1, L 6, M 5.
TREVOR, Laura Exh. 1900
c/o Mrs. Brooking, 38 Cleveland Gardens, Hyde Park, London. † RMS 1.
TREVOR, Leslie Exh. 1933
† RSW 1.
TREVOR-BATTYE, A. Exh. 1901
2 Whitehall Gardens, London. † RBA 1.
TREVORROW, Mrs. Doris E. Exh. 1932
30 Claremont Street, Glasgow. † GI 1.
TREW, E. Florence Exh. 1887-90
Painter. 6 Brunswick Place, Swansea, Wales. † SWA 2.
TREW, Harold Fletcher b. 1888
Architect, painter and etcher. b. Gloucester. Studied Gloucester and Cheltenham Schools of Art. Architect for reconstruction work and town planning under the Greek Government 1918-20. Exh. 1922-36. Add: Kingsholme, Glos. 1922; Gloucester 1929. † COO 3, NEA 6, RA 4.
TREWBY, Miss E.C. Exh. 1905-10
Langford Lodge, New Park Road, Brixton Hill, London. † RA 4.
TREY, de See D
TREZEL, L.A. Exh. 1903
3 Rue Trezel, Levallois Perret, Seine, France. † L 1.
TRIBE, Barbara Exh. 1940
Sculptor. b. Sydney, Australia. Studied Sydney Technical College 1928-33 (N.S.W. travelling scholarship 1935), Kennington City and Guilds School of Art 1936-37 and Regent Street Polytechnic. Add: 75 Earls Court Road, London. † RA 2.
TRICKETT, Kate W. Exh. 1895-1921
Birmingham 1895 and 1920; London 1907. † B 10, L 3, RA 1.
TRICKETT, Walter Exh. 1892-1907
Birmingham. † B 6.
TRIEBEL, Edith Exh. 1916-36
London. † I 1, ROI 2, SWA 1.
TRIER, Mrs. Adeline Exh. 1880-1916
Flower painter. Champion Hill, London. † B 3, L 2, M 5, RA 11, RBA 4, ROI 2, SWA 10.
TRIER, Hans Exh. 1899-1920
Landscape painter. R.B.A. 1902. Add: Champion Hill, London. † ALP 3, L 1, RA 2, RBA 42, RID 11, ROI 2.
TRIER, Henry A. Exh. 1925-29
Landscape painter. † BAR 36, FIN 125.

TRIGGS, Harry Inigo Exh. 1898-1909
Architect. London 1898; Woking, Surrey 1909. † RA 10.

TRIMNELL, Harold C. Exh. 1900-19
Architect. White Cliff, Woldingham, Surrey. † RA 5.

TRINDER, Margaret E.M. See MALLORIE

TRINGHAM, Holland Exh. 1891-96
Landscape and figure painter. R.B.A. 1894. Add: Streatham, London. † B 1, RA 2, RBA 13.

TRINGHAM, Rev. H.R.P. Exh. 1931-38
Painter. † WG 17.

TRINGHAM, Mrs. Mary E. Exh. 1935
Watercolour flower painter. Fallowfield, Puttenham, Guildford, Surrey. † RA 1.

TRINICK, John B. b. 1890
Stained glass artist. b. Melbourne, Australia. Studied National Gallery of Victoria Art School 1910-15, Byam Shav and Vicat Cole School of Art 1919-20, France and Germany. Exh. 1925-39. Add: London. † RA 7.

TRINQUIER, Louis Exh. 1913
Painter. † ALP 3.

TRIOMFI Signor Exh. 1888
† D 1.

TRIPE, Mary E.R. Exh. 1934-37
Figure painter. c/o Bank of New Zealand, 1 Queen Victoria Street, London. † P 1, RA 1, SWA 5.

TRIPP, Capel N. Exh. 1881
Architect. Eldon Chambers, Gloucester. † RA 1.

TRIPP, Herbert Alker 1883-1954
Painter, poster artist, writer and illustrator. Add: Lee Cottage, Thames Ditton, Surrey. † GI 1, I 1, L 2, RA 9, RI 1, ROI 1.

TRIQUET, Jules Octave b. 1867
French artist. Exh. 1906-12. Add: 110 Boulevard Periere, Paris. † L 8.

TRIST, Beryl Exh. 1936-39
Portrait, landscape and figure painter. Loxton Wrey, Lustleigh, Devon. † GOU 39, P 3, RA 1, RBA 1, RCA 1.

TRISTRAM, Ernest William 1882-1952
Painter. b. Carmarthen, Wales. Studied Royal College of Art. Professor of Design Royal College of Art. Exh. 1912. Add: New Malden, Surrey. † RA 1.

TRITTON, Annette Exh. 1934
Landscape painter. † WG 50.

TRITTON, Miss A.L.A. Exh. 1903-10
London. † SWA 3.

TRITTON, Laura E. Exh. 1898
68 Cromwell Road, London. † D 2.

TRITTON, May Exh. 1923
Watercolour painter. † WG 43.

TRIVETT, Miss B.M. Exh. 1928
81 South Road, West Bridgford, Nottingham. † N 1.

TRIVETT, W. Oram Exh. 1897-99
Landscape painter. N.S.A. 1898. Add: West Gate, Mansfield, Notts. † N 3.

TROBRIDGE, George Exh. 1883-1906
Landscape painter. 2 Mount Pleasant, Belfast. † B 7, RBA 2, RHA 14.

TROBRIDGE, L. Exh. 1880
Landscape painter. 39 South Lambeth Road, London. † D 1.

TROKE, Walter E. Exh. 1940
Architect. 9 Gower Street, London. † RA 1.

TROLLOPE, C.H.B. Exh. 1934-38
Watercolour painter. † WG 9.

TROLLOPE, John E. Exh. 1881-91
Architect. London. † L 2, RA 4.

TROMAN, Clara Exh. 1898-99
The Elms, Solihull, Birmingham. † B 2.

TROMAN, Nancy Exh. 1899-1900
The Elms, Solihull, Birmingham. † B 2.

TROMP, J. Zoetelief* Exh. 1908
Figure painter. Blaricum, Holland. † GI 1.

TRONEL, E.C. Exh. 1882-88
Villa Montmorency, Auteuil, Paris. † GI 9.

TROOD, William Henry Hamilton* 1860-1899
Animal painter and sculptor. 13 Trafalgar Studios, Kings Road, London. † B 4, D 1, G 2, GI 2, L 12, M 6, RA 23, RBA 20, ROI 4, TOO 17.

TROTMAN, Lillias or Lillie Exh. 1881-93
Landscape and figure painter. 55 Lillie Road, Brompton, London. † D 1, L 2, M 1, RA 2, RBA 9, RI 3, SWA 2.

TROTT, John S. Exh. 1890-92
Landscape painter. 25 Addison Terrace, Notting Hill, London. † RA 3.

TROTTER, Miss A.C. Exh. 1908-12
Paris. † L 2.

TROTTER, A.F. Exh. 1887
Elm View, Halifax, Yorks. † M 1.

TROTTER, Alexander Mason d. 1947
Watercolour interior and architectural painter. R.S.W. 1930. Exh. from 1914. Add: Edinburgh. † AR 2, GI 6, L 1, RA 2, RSA 14, RSW 24.

TROTTER, Mrs. A.P. Exh. 1920
Watercolour figure painter. 1 Campdenhill Square, London. † WG 19.

TROTTER, Mrs. Barbara Exh. 1937
16 West Castle Road, Edinburgh. † RSW 2.

TROTTER, James Exh. 1885-1907
Edinburgh. † RSA 3.

TROTTER, Mary Kempton Exh. 1909
† LS 2.

TROUBETZKOY, Prince Paul b. 1866
Sculptor. Brother of Pierre T. q.v. Exh. 1901-24. Add: St. Petersburg 1901; Paris 1907; Neuilly sur Seine, France 1924. † GI 3, I 19, L 4, NG 1, RSA 3.

TROUBETZKOY, Prince Pierre 1864-1936
Landscape and portrait painter and sculptor. b. Milan. Brother of Paul T. q v. R.P. 1896. Exh. 1892-95. Add: Bolton Studios, Redcliffe Road, London. Died in America. † DOW 23, L 2, NEA 1, NG 1, P 6, RA 1, ROI 1.

TROUBRIDGE, Mrs. Una Exh. 1909-16
Sculptor. Commodore's House, Royal Naval Barracks, Chatham, Kent 1909; London 1910. † FIN 4, L 1, RA 5.

TROUP, F. Gordon Exh. 1930
Architect. Amiesmill, Horsham, Sussex. † RA 1.

TROUP, Francis William b. 1859
Architect. b. Huntly, Aberdeenshire. Studied R.A. Schools and R.I.B.A. Consulting architect to the Home Office and supervising architect to the rebuilding of the Bank of England. Exh. 1889-1933. Add: London. † RA 18, RSA 5.

TROUT, John Ridgill b. 1877
Painter, craftworker and teacher Studied Bradford School of Art. Exh. 1911. Add: Bradford. † L 6.

TROUVILLE, Henri Exh. 1882
Barbizon, France. † GI 2.

TROWARD, T. Exh. 1893
137 Gower Street, London. † D 1.

TROWBRIDGE, Geo. Exh. 1907
2 Mount Pleasant, Belfast. † RHA 1.

TROWBRIDGE, Lucy P. Exh. 1897
Miniature portrait painter. 9 Rue Charlet, Paris. † RA 1.

TROY, Mary Exh. 1937-40
Flower and figure painter. 79 Gloucester Street, London. † COO 48, P 1, RA 4, ROI 1.

TRUBNER, Wilhelm* 1851-1917
German portrait, domestic and landscape painter. Exh. 1902-12. † P 2.

TRUCHET, Abel* 1857-1918
French painter. Exh. 1906-8. Add: 4 Rue Caroline, Paris. † L 1, LS 5.

TRUEFITT, George Exh. 1884-86
Architect. 5 Bloomsbury Square, London. † RA 1, RI 1.

TRUELOVE, John Reginald b. 1886
Architect. b. Sheffield. Exh. 1913-29. Add: London 1913; Nottingham 1926. † RA 7, RSA 3.

TRUEMAN, A.J. Exh. 1914
23 Lord Haddon Road, Ilkeston, Derbys. † N 1.

TRUEMAN, Marjorie M. Exh. 1925-26
Figure and landscape painter. 23 Lord Haddon Road, Ilkeston, Derbys. † N 5.

TRUESDELL, Gaylord Sangston* Exh. 1898-99
Landscape painter. London. † B 1, L 1, RA 3.

TRUFFAUT, Fernand Exh. 1913
Watercolour urban landscape painter. † FIN 6.

TRUMAN, Edna Exh. 1923
15 Park Terrace, Nottingham. † N 1.

TRUMAN, Herbert Exh. 1912-33
Landscape painter. St. Ives, Cornwall 1926; London 1912. † AB 3, GI 1, L 1, RA 5.

TRUMAN, Vera Exh. 1921-25
Figure and landscape painter. Park Terrace, Nottingham. † N 11.

TRUNINGER, Mrs. A.C. Exh. 1925-35
The Roundel, Gullane. † RSA 2, RSW 2.

TRUSCOTT, Walter d. 1890
Landscape, marine and figure painter. Falmouth 1882; Kew, Surrey 1885; London 1889. † RBA 26.

TRY, Miss E.L. Exh. 1928-32
28 Grosvenor Street, Wallasey, Cheshire. † L 2.

TRYON, Claude Exh. 1910-11
Landscape painter. † CAR 7.

TRYON, Miss D.M. Exh. 1906
Elmsloe, Tinwell Road, Stamford, Lincs. † RA 1.

TRYON, Wyndham 1883-1942
Landscape painter. N.E.A. 1920. Member London Group 1925. Add: Epsom, Surrey 1909; Watford, Herts. 1923; Cassis, France 1929. † BA 3, CAR 3, GI 1, NEA 67.

TSCHAGGENY, Charles* 1818-1873
Belgian painter. Exh. 1883. † FIN 1.

TSCHANN, J. Rudolf* Exh. 1884-87
Figure painter. Inglewood, Teddington, Middlesex. † RA 1, ROI 1.

TSDHUDI, Lill b. 1911
Swiss painter and linocut artist. Exh. 1930-38. † RED 11, RSA 1.

TUBBS, Miss B. Exh. 1902
113 Darenth Road, Stamford Hill, London. † SWA 2.

TUBERVILLE, Marjorie G. Exh. 1935
161 Stapleton Hall Road, London. † NEA 1.

TUCK, Albert Exh. 1884-1903
Watercolour figure painter. Haverstock Hill, London. † RI 6.

TUCK, Harry Exh. 1880-1906
Genre and landscape painter. Haverstock Hill, London. † B 7, D 6, GI 1, L 14, M 4, RA 2, RBA 21, RI 23, ROI 12.

TUCK, Miss J.M. Exh. 1903
60 Avenue d'Jena, Paris. † L 1.

TUCK, Lucy J. Exh. 1880-88
Figure painter. Uppingham, Rutland 1880; London 1885. † D 4, RI 3, SWA 4.

TUCKER, Mrs. A. Exh. 1884-86
Watercolour landscape painter. Woodlands, Ambleside. † D 1, RSA 2, SWA 1.

TUCKER, Allen b. 1866
American painter. Exh. 1925. † CHE 1.

TUCKER, Arthur 1863-1929
Landscape painter and etcher. b. Bristol. Son of Edward T. q.v. R.B.A. 1896. Add: Ambleside 1882; Windermere 1886. † B 25, D 3, L 75, M 23, RA 37, RBA 184, RHA 4, RI 19, RSA 6, RSW 1.

TUCKER, Ada Eliza Exh. 1881-1928
Figure and domestic painter. A.S.W.A. 1893. Add: Bristol 1881; Stroud, Glos. 1893; Penzance, Cornwall 1910; Tewkesbury 1928. † B 17, L 15, M 12, RA 1, RBA 3, ROI 2, RSA 7, SWA 36.

TUCKER, A.R. Exh. 1913-14
College, Durham. † RA 2.

TUCKER, Rt. Rev. Bishop Alfred R. 1845-1914
Bishop of Uganda. Landscape painter. Exh. 1894. Add: Surbiton, Surrey. † RA 1.

TUCKER, C.C. Exh. 1885-86
Winding Street, Hastings, Sussex. † L 1, RHA 1.

TUCKER, C. Carlyle Exh. 1908
22 Charing Cross Mansions, Glasgow. † GI 1.

TUCKER, Charles E. Exh. 1880-1914
Landscape and figure painter. London 1880 and 1895; Dartmouth 1891; C. on M. Manchester 1894. † D 5, M 1, RA 3, RBA 2, RI 6, ROI 4.

TUCKER, Edward* c. 1846-1909
Landscape and coastal painter. Also exhibited under the name "Edward Arden". Father of Arthur and Frederick T. q.v. Add: Ambleside, Westmorland 1881; Windermere 1886. † B 7, D 7, GI 1, L 24, M 16, RHA 2, RI 7, RSA 2.

TUCKER, Evelyn Alice Exh. 1937
79 Glencairn Drive, Glasgow. † GI 1.

TUCKER, Frederick Exh. 1880-1915
Watercolour landscape painter. Son of Edward T. q.v. Add: Ambleside, Westmorland 1880; Southport, Lancs. 1883; London 1886. † D 2, GI 4, L 5, M 2, NG 2, RA 11, RBA 1, RI 7, RSA 2.

TUCKER, Grace Exh. 1937-40
Landscape painter. † COO 2, NEA 2.

TUCKER, G. Edward Exh. 1898
Architect. 9 Duke Street Mansions, Grosvenor Square, London. † RA 1.

TUCKER, James Walker Exh. 1928-40
Landscape painter. London 1928; Blackfriars, Glos. 1931; Saintbridge, Glos. 1932; Gloucester 1936; Upton St. Leonards, Glos. 1938. † COO 3, L 1, NEA 6, RA 20, RBA 1.

TUCKER, Kate Exh. 1883
Flower painter. Burford Lodge, Horsham, Sussex. † RA 1.

TUCKER, Mildred Exh. 1928
Landscape painter. † AB 1.

TUCKER, M.A. Exh. 1928
Landscape painter. † AB 1.

TUCKER, Raymond Exh. 1882-1903
Landscape, portrait, genre and literary painter. London. † B 2, L 6, M 5, RA 8, RBA 2, RI 1.

TUCKER, Tudor St. George* Exh. 1900-6
Figure and landscape painter. London 1900 and 1906; Hayes, Middlesex 1902. † B 2, L 2, NG 1, RA 6, ROI 1.

TUCKER, Violet H. Exh. 1934-40
14 Northumberland Street, Edinburgh. † RSW 4.

TUCKER, William H. Exh. 1930
Watercolour landscape painter. Lattice House, Sherborne, Dorset. † RA 1.

TUCKERMAN, Stephen Salisbury 1830-1904
Landscape and marine painter. b. Boston, U.S.A. Exh. 1881-85. Add: Kinfore, nr. Stourbridge, Worcs. Died in London. † B 4, RBA 3.

TUCKEY, Elizabeth J. Exh. 1918-25
Cornwall. † D 1, GOU 2, SWA 1.

TUCKWELL, Miss M. Exh. 1940
118 Abbey Road, London. † RI 2.

TUDHOPE, Alice Exh. 1902
28 Lauriston Gardens, Edinburgh. † RSA 1.

TUDHOPE, A.H. Exh. 1885-86
3 Victoria Terrace, Mount Florida, Glasgow. † GI 2, RSA 2.

TUDOR, Miss E. Exh. 1900
Diana Lodge, Gery Street, Bedford. † SWA 1.

TUDOR, Miss M.L.R. Exh. 1910-11
Eastgarston Vicarage, Lambourn, Berks. † B 1, GI 1.

TUDOR-HART, Percyval b. 1873
Painter and sculptor. b. Montreal, Canada. Studied Ecole des Beaux Arts, Paris. Exh. 1909-28. Add: Sevres, France 1909; Paris 1910; London 1914. † L 5, RA 2.

TUDSBURY, W.A. Exh. 1884-88
Landscape painter. Edwinstowe, Newark, Notts. † N 2.

TUELY, Miss E.M. Exh. 1906
Mortimer Lodge, Wimbledon Park, London. † RA 1.

TUGBY, E.G. Exh. 1909
59 Kirkstead Street, Hyson Green, Nottingham. † N 1.

TUGWELL, Emma L. Exh. 1888-89
Painter. 6 Lewisham Road Greenwich, London. † RBA 2.

TUGWELL, Sydney Exh. 1894-1912
Edinburgh 1894; Bournemouth 1911. † L 1, RA 2, RSA 1.

TUITE, T.H. Exh. 1919
† L 1.

TUKE, Henry Scott* 1858-1929
Portrait, figure and marine painter. b. York. Studied Slade School and Florence 1880, and Paris under J.P. Laurens 1881-83. Brother of Maria Tuke Sainsbury q.v. N.E.A. 1886, A.R.A. 1900, R.A. 1914, R.B.A. 1888, A.R.W.S. 1904, R.W.S. 1911. "August Blue" purchased by Chantrey Bequest 1894 and "All Hands to the Pumps" purchased 1889. Add: London 1880; Falmouth 1919. † B 8, BG 1, CAR 2, COO 75, D 2, DOW 59, FIN 3, G 13, GI 13, GOU 7, L 31, M15, NEA 6, NG 14, P 1, RA 142, RBA 9, RHA 3, RI 11 RID 51, ROI 1, RSA 1, RSW 1, RWS 147, TOO 7.

TUKE, Lilian K. Exh. 1905-18
Durham 1905; London 1917. † L 3, P 2, RA 7, RI 1.

TUKE, Maria See SAINSBURY

TUKE, Sydney H. Exh. 1882
Landscape painter. 41 Cochrane Street, St. Johns Wood, London. † RBA 1.

TULK, Augustus Exh. 1880-97
Still life, figure and landscape painter. London. † B 2, D 3, GI 6, L 6, M 3, RA 3, RBA 5, ROI 6.

TULLIS, W. Exh. 1899
5 Harviest Road, North Kensington, London. † ROI 1.

TULLOCK, Frederick H. Exh. 1891-95
Architect. London. † RA 6.

TULLOCH, Geraldine Exh. 1930-36
Portrait and flower painter. London. † P 1, RA 3.

TULLOCH, Mrs. J. Stewart Exh. 1887
Flower painter. St. George's Hill, Bathampton, Bath, Somerset. † SWA 1.

TULLY, Miss Sydney Strickland d. 1911
Watercolour figure painter. b. Toronto. Studied Slade School. Exh. 1896-97. Add: London. † RA 2, SWA 6.

TUN, M. Tha Exh. 1926
Watercolour landscape painter. 138 Fellows Road, London. † RA 1.

TUNN, Miss M. Exh. 1917
† SWA 2.

TUNNARD, John* 1900-1971
Figure, landscape and marine painter. b. Sandy, Beds. Studied Royal College of Art. Member London Group 1934. Add: London. † COO 4, LEF 17, LEI 2, RED 31, RA 3.

TUNNICLIFF, P.H. Exh. 1911-13
Ashby Potters Guild, Woodville, Burton on Trent, Staffs. † LS 3.

TUNNICLIFFE, Charles Frederick* b. 1901
Painter and etcher. b. nr. Macclesfield. Studied Manchester and Macclesfield Schools of Art and Royal College of Art. A.R.E. 1929, R.E. 1933. Exh. 1928-40. Add: Macclesfield. † AB 4, FIN 9, GI 1, L 9, M 1, RA 13, RE 46.

TUNNY Exh. 1902
11 Castle Terrace, Edinburgh. † RSA 1.

TUNSTALL, Eric M. Exh. 1936-39
Portrait and landscape painter. N.S.A. 1934. Add: Elva, Hillside Avenue, Mapperley, Nottingham. † N 15, RI 2.

TUOHY, Patrick Joseph 1894-1930
Portrait and decorative painter. Born and studied in Dublin. Professor of painting at Dublin Metropolitan School of Art. A.R.H.A. 1924, R.H.A. 1925. Add: Dublin. † RA 1, RHA 35.

TUPPER, Margaret E. Exh. 1885-1903
Figure painter. London. † SWA 6.

TUQUET, Marcel Exh. 1888-91
Flower painter. N.S.A. 1890-92. Add: 9 Fox Road, West Bridgford, Nottingham. † N 6.

TURALEY, Henry Exh. 1892
Boldmere, Erdington, Birmingham. † B 2.

TURBAYNE, Albert Angus 1866-1940
American painter and designer. Exh. 1895. Add: London. † RA 1.

TURBERVILLE, M.G. Exh. 1933-36
Engraver. Stroud Green, London. † RED 1, SWA 2.

TURCK, Eliza b. 1832
Portrait, landscape, coastal, architectural, literary and miniature painter. Studied for 6 months at Cary's School then under W. Gale. In 1852 entered the figure class of the Female School of Art in Gower Street and 1859-60 studied in Antwerp. Exh. 1880-1909. Add: London. † D 2, RA 9, RBA 3, SWA 7.

TURLE, Caroline Exh. 1884
177 Cromwell Road, South Kensington, London. † D 1.

TURNBULL, Andrew Watson b. 1874
Painter, etcher and stained glass artist. London 1899; Portobello, N.B. 1903; Edinburgh 1906; Romsey, Hants. 1911; Richmond, Surrey 1923. † FIN 4, GI 7, L 5, RA 9, RSA 8.

TURNBULL, D.L. Exh. 1885
35 South Bridge, Edinburgh. † RSA 1.

TURNBULL, Ellen M. Exh. 1919
47 Ladbroke Square, London. † NEA 1.

TURNBULL, Frederick J. Exh. 1940
18a Morningside Place, Edinburgh. † RSA 1.
TURNBULL, Miss J.P. Exh. 1910
Bramcote House, Old Radford, Nottingham. † N 1.
TURNBULL, Marion See ANCRUM
TURNBULL, Walter Exh. 1892
Sculptor. 6 Esher Street, London. † RA 1.
TURNER, A. Exh. 1933
1 Ash Street, Bryn, nr. Wigan, Lancs. † L 1.
TURNER, Agnes Exh. 1884-1919
Watercolour landscape painter. Roslin Villa, Saltburn by Sea, Yorks. 1884. † D 3, SWA 15, WG 139.
TURNER, Alfred 1874-1940
Sculptor. Studied Lambeth, R.A. Schools and Paris. Father of Winifred T. q.v. A.R.A. 1922, R.A. 1931. "Psyche" (1919) purchased by Chantrey Bequest 1922 and "The Hand" purchased 1936. Add: London. † GI 3, L 2, RA 46, RSA 1.
TURNER, Alice Exh. 1905-7
29 Lady Somerset Road, London. † B 2, ROI 4.
TURNER, Annie Exh. 1882
114 Shenly Road, Camberwell, London. † B 1.
TURNER, Arthur Exh. 1893-1940
Landscape painter. Betchworth, Surrey 1893; Stockport, Lancs. 1913. † B 2, GI 1, L 2, RA 2, RCA 7, ROI 6.
TURNER, Arthur H. Exh. 1934
33 Cranworth Street, Glasgow. † GI 1.
TURNER, Miss A.M. Exh. 1884
20 Bath Street, Stoke on Trent, Staffs. † L 1.
TURNER, Annie M. Exh. 1912
24 Lynedoch Street, Glasgow. † GI 1.
TURNER, Alfred R. Exh. 1923
Landscape painter. 13 Milbourne Grove, The Boltons, London. † RA 1.
TURNER, Arthur R. Exh. 1913-14
29 Lidderdale Road, Sefton Park, Liverpool. † L 2.
TURNER, Arthur W. Exh. 1898-1900
Portrait painter. Hetworth, York. † L 2, RA 2.
TURNER, Barr Exh. 1919
† L 2.
TURNER, Bernhard H. Exh. 1916
39 Nowell Terrace, Leeds, Yorks. † LS 3.
TURNER, Bernard S. Exh. 1921
† LS 1.
TURNER, Claridge Exh. 1882-93
Watercolour landscape painter. Hampstead, London 1882; Yardley 1892; Birmingham 1893. † B 4, D 1, L 2, RBA 1, RI 1.
TURNER, Charles E. Exh. 1912-19
Painter. Heaton Norris, Stockport, Lancs. 1912; South Reddish, nr. Manchester 1913. † L 5, M 2, RA 1.
TURNER, Cora Josephine See GORDON
TURNER, Miss D. Exh. 1929
Almadene, Waverley Road, Sefton Park, Liverpool. † L 2.
TURNER, David C. Exh. 1933-34
Loanhead, Limekilns, Dunfermline. † RSA 3.
TURNER, Ernest Exh. 1890
Architect. 246 Regent Street, London. † RA 1.
TURNER, E.E. Exh. 1939
Cardiff, Wales. † RCA 1.
TURNER, Edgar H. Exh. 1894-1904
Decorative designer. Fitzroy Square, London. † RA 3.
TURNER, E.J. Exh. 1886
c/o George Mountain, Bath Chambers, York Street, Manchester. † M 1.
TURNER, Ethel L. Exh. 1892
The Grange, Sparkhill, Birmingham. † B 1.
TURNER, Ethel M. Exh. 1901-14
London. † LS 12, RBA 1, RMS 1.
TURNER, Edwin Page Exh. 1880-84
Decorative architect. 68 Newman Street, Oxford Street, London. † RA 7.
TURNER, E.R. Horsfall Exh. 1926-31
Llanidloes, 1926; Sutton Coldfield 1931. † B 5, RCA 3.
TURNER, Florence Exh. 1896-98
Sherbourne Lodge, Leamington, Warwicks. † B 2.
TURNER, F.E. Exh. 1905-9
Mrs. T.C. Miniature portrait painter. Add: Regent House, Hull. † RA 5.
TURNER, Miss G. Exh. 1891
35 High Street, Marylebone, London. † L 2, M 2.
TURNER, George* Exh. 1880-1904
Landscape painter. Father of William L. T. q.v. Add: Barrow on Trent, nr. Derby. † B 45, N 45, RBA 3.
TURNER, Geraldine E. d. 1936
nee Martineau. Miniature portrait painter. H.R.M.S. 1920. Exh. from 1913. Add: London. † L 16, LS 3, RA 13, RI 23, RMS 24.
TURNER, Gordon R. Exh. 1933
Wood engraver. 97 Eltham Green Road, London. † RA 1.
TURNER, G.S. Exh. 1901
Sandown, Horsell, Woking, Surrey. † ROI 1.
TURNER, Harry b. 1908
Painter. Studied Halifax and Bradford Art Schools (evening classes). Exh. 1936. Add: 16 Eldreth Road, Savile Park, Halifax, Yorks. † RBA 1.
TURNER, Hawes Exh. 1885-1913
Landscape and figure painter. Married Jessie T. q.v. Add: London. † D 1, L 1, M 2, RA 8, RBA 2, RI 2, ROI 1.
TURNER, Hugh Exh. 1884
7 Polwarth Crescent, Edinburgh. † RSA 1.
TURNER, H.D. Exh. 1885
Painter. 3 Somerset Villa, Parsons Head, Croydon, Surrey. † RA 1.
TURNER, Harry M. b. 1912
Painter. Studied Birmingham College of Art 1929-34. Deputy Principal Wolverhampton College of Art 1938. Exh. 1937-39. Add: Tembani, Lincoln Road, Walsall, Staffs. † B 4.
TURNER, Herbert William John Exh. 1898-1908
Landscape and coastal painter. St. Ives, Cornwall 1898; Carbis Bay, Cornwall 1908. † LS 7, NEA 1.
TURNER, Mrs. Isabella Gibson Exh. 1919-37
Miniature portrait painter. London 1919; Cambridge 1937. † L 3, RA 3, RMS 1.
TURNER, Miss Jessie Exh. 1886-94
Flower and architectural painter. London 1886; Lichfield, Staffs. 1894. † L 2, RBA 1, ROI 2, SWA 2.
TURNER, Mrs. Jessie Exh. 1894-1910
Watercolour landscape painter. Married Hawes T. q.v. Add: London. † M 1, NG 1, RA 3, RI 2.
TURNER, John Exh. 1880
144 Albert Street, Glasgow. † GI 1, RSA 1.
TURNER, J. Doman Exh. 1911-39
Watercolour landscape and coastal painter and pastellier. Brackendale, Downton Avenue, Streatham Hill, London. † CAR 8, I 3, LS 6, NEA 4, RED 2.
TURNER, Miss Jessie G. Exh. 1921
† RMS 1.
TURNER, Katherine Exh. 1900-38
Watercolour flower painter. The Grange, Church Street, Stoke Newington, London 1900; Bournemouth 1933. † BG 47, L 5, NEA 12, RA 1, RI 11, RWS 52, SWA 3.
TURNER, Mrs. K. May J. Exh. 1934-38
Harvey House, 144 Alexandra Road, South Farnborough, Hants. † RMS 6.
TURNER, Mrs. Lizzie Exh. 1881-86
Painter. Horsemoor Green, Langley, Bucks. † SWA 3.
TURNER, Lawrence A. Exh. 1897
Decorative designer of carved wood panels. 56 Doughty Street, London. † RA 1.
TURNER, May Exh. 1930-36
15 Valentine Road, Kings Heath, Birmingham. † B 2.
TURNER, Molly Exh. 1902
5 Upper Leeson Street, Dublin. † RHA 1.
TURNER, Maurice H. Exh. 1931
Portrait painter. 1 Kensington Court, London. † RA 1.
TURNER, Miss M.L. Exh. 1885
Kearsley Moor Vicarage, Stoneclough, Manchester. † M 1.
TURNER, Maud M. Exh. 1891-1908
Watercolour painter. London 1891 and 1901; Wimborne, Dorset 1893. † D 50, RA 1, RI 2, SWA 23.
TURNER, Mrs. Meta P.W. Exh. 1889-92
Flower painter. Ruscombe, Willoughby Road, London. † RBA 1, ROI 1.
TURNER, P. Exh. 1916
13 Kingthorpe Terrace, Dog Lane, Stonebridge Park, London. † RA 1.
TURNER, Peggy Exh. 1940
Painter. † COO 1.
TURNER, P.J. Exh. 1909
Architect. Market Place, Stowmarket, Suffolk. † RA 1.
TURNER, R. Exh. 1920-21
Collaborated with Kate E. Riley q.v. Add: London. † L 48.
TURNER, Stanley Exh. 1933
Canadian painter. † RSW 1.
TURNER, Winifred b. 1903
Sculptor. Daughter of Alfred T. q.v. Studied R.A. Schools (Landseer scholarship). "Thought" purchased by Chantrey Bequest 1933. Exh. 1924-40. Add: London and Solihull, Warwicks. † B 1, GI 3, L 6, RA 18.
TURNER, William B. Exh. 1884-1911
Figure and rustic painter. Antwerp 1884; Trefriw, North Wales 1886; Deganwy, North Wales 1898; Conway 1911. † L 14, M 4, RA 1, RBA 1, RCA 19.
TURNER, William D. Exh. 1902
Portrait painter. Glenavon, Latchett Road, South Woodford, London. † RA 1.
TURNER, W. Eddowes Exh. 1880-88
Cattle and sheep painter. Nottingham. † N 12.
TURNER, W.J. Carpenter Exh. 1940
Architect. 12 Southgate Street, Winchester, Hants. † RA 1.

TURNER, William L. Exh. 1885-1934
Landscape painter. Son of George T. q.v. Studied London. Add: Barrow on Trent, Derbys. 1885; London 1895; Hawkshead, Lancs. 1899; Levens, nr. Milnthorpe, Westmorland 1901; Keswick 1904 and 1911; Madeley, Salop 1907; Leamington, Warwicks. 1925. † B 6, N 81, RA 14, RBA 1, RHA 4.

TURNER, William McAllister b. 1901
Painter and etcher. b. Mold, Flints. Studied Chester School of Art. Exh. 1926-40. Add: Chester 1926; Broughton, Hants. 1937. † L 3, RA 1, RBA 1, RCA 6, RSA 2.

TURPIN, A. Exh. 1930-33
Figure and architectural painter. † LEF 18.

TURPIN, H. Exh. 1933-39
Stamford, Lincs. † N 12.

TURPIN, Samuel Hart Exh. 1882-96
Landscape painter. N.S.A. 1882-98. Add: Nottingham 1882 and 1891; Watford, Herts. 1885. † N 14, RE 2.

TURRELL, Mrs. Adda Exh. 1924
Etcher. Clovelly, Chatsworth Road, Willesden Green, London. † RA 1.

TURRELL, Arthur Exh. 1885-98
Etcher. Father of Arthur James T. q.v. Add: Brondesbury, London. † RA 9.

TURRELL, Arthur James b. 1871
Etcher. Son of Arthur T. q.v. A.R.E. 1916 (resigned 1922). Exh. 1895-1936. Add: London. † GI 1, L 1, RA 35, RE 13.

TURRELL, Charles James 1845-1932
Miniature portrait painter. London 1880-1915. Went to America. † L 5, M 4, RA 133, RMS 2.

TURRELL, Herbert Exh. 1898-1911
Portrait painter. London 1898; Stanmore, Middlesex 1900; Amersham Common, Bucks. 1902; Bellingdon, Bucks. 1904; New Barnet, Herts. 1911. † B 1, L 10, RA 7, RMS 1.

TURTLE, Edward Exh. 1888
Landscape and coastal painter. 23 Union Street, Ryde, I.O.W. † RBA 1.

TURTON, F. Exh. 1913-15
114 Loughborough Road, West Bridgford, Notts. † N 2.

TURVEY, Reginald b. 1882
Landscape and flower painter. b. S. Africa. Add: Carbis Bay, Cornwall 1931; Totnes, Devon 1940. † RA 3, ROI 1.

TUSHINGHAM, Sidney b. 1884
Painter and etcher. b. Burslem, Staffs. Studied Burslem School of Art and Royal College of Art. A.R.E. 1915. Exh. 1905-38. Add: Wolstanton, Staffs. 1905; London 1910. † AB 1, BK 3, CHE 2, CON 38, FIN 3, GI 9, I 13, L 36, RA 26, RE 18, RSA 2.

TUSSAUD, Dora Exh. 1903
† RMS 1.

TUSSAUD, John Theodore b. 1858
Sculptor and modeller in wax. Great grandson of Mme. Tussaud. Succeeded his father as director and artist to the Waxworks Exhibition. Exh. 1891-93. Add: London. † RA 2.

TUSSINERI, H. Danyell Exh. 1901
1 Sussex Villas, Kensington, London. † RI 1.

TUTIN, Miss E. Exh. 1893
Prospect House, Borrowby, Thirsk, Yorks. † L 1, M 2.

TUTTLE, Franklin Exh. 1882-83
Figure painter. 2 Trevor Square, Knightsbridge, London. † RA 1, RBA 2.

TUTTLE, Mrs. J.B. Exh. 1889
Landscape painter. c/o D. Young, William Street, Greenland, Glasgow. † RA 1.

TUXEN, Professor 1843-1927
Danish portrait painter. Exh. 1907. Add: Strandvejen 24, Copenhagen. † L 1.

TUXFORD, A. Exh. 1928
11 Heathcoat Street, Nottingham. † N 1.

TWAMLEY, Miss L. Exh. 1929
8 Manor Road, Bishops Stortford, Herts. † RI 1.

TWAMLEY, R. Exh. 1928
Landscape and architectural painter. † AB 3.

TWEDDLE, Isabel Hunter Exh. 1927-33
Mrs. J. Thornton. Landscape and coastal painter. Travelled widely. Add: Melbourne, Australia and c/o Bourlet, Nassau Street, London. † AR 151, P 1, RBA 1, ROI 1.

TWEED, John 1869-1933
Sculptor. Studied R.A. Schools and Ecole des Beaux Arts under Falguiere. "Lord Clive" (c.1910-12) purchased by Chantrey Bequest 1934. Add: Glasgow 1888; London 1893. † B 2, G 2, GI 49, I 20, L 7, LS 5, NG 10, P 4, RA 64, RI 2, RSA 12.

TWEEDIE, Agnes Exh. 1882-92
Abernyte, Inchture. † RSA 11.

TWEEDIE, Charles Edward Exh. 1899
8 Albyn Place, Edinburgh. † RSA 1.

TWENLOW, Miss B. Exh. 1902-26
Devon Lodge, Alumhurst Road, Bournemouth. † B 1, L 1, M 1.

TWENTYMAN, A. Exh. 1939
Bilbrook Manor, Godsall, Staffs. † B 2.

TWENTYMAN, Betty Exh. 1933-38
Muchall Hall, Penn, Staffs. † B 3.

TWENTYMAN, Hilda M. Exh. 1897-1901
Castlecroft, nr. Wolverhampton, Staffs. † B 5, RCA 1, SWA 5.

TWENTYMAN, Minna Exh. 1886
Landscape painter. Wimbledon Common, London. † SWA 1.

TWIDLE, Arthur 1865-1936
Painter and illustrator. Exh. 1903-13. Add: Sidcup, Kent. † RA 2.

TWIGG, Commander A.G.D. Exh. 1927
Model maker. † AB 5.

TWIGG, Mrs. Alvine Klein Exh. 1881-89
Portrait and flower painter. London. † RA 1, RBA 1.

TWIGG, Joseph Exh. 1884-1912
Watercolour landscape and architectural painter. London 1884; Rugby 1893 and 1906; Walton on Thames 1902; Eastbourne 1903; Northwood, Middlesex 1909. † D 33, RA 2, RI 1.

TWIGGE, Lily Exh. 1898-1910
Liverpool. † L 9.

TWINING, E.W. Exh. 1906
Queen Anne's Chambers, Westminster, London. † RA 1.

TWISS, Miss G.V. Exh. 1937
Landscape painter. Shanagarry, Foxrock, Co. Dublin. † RHA 1.

TWISS, Jane M. Exh. 1901
Sculptor. New Street, Killarney. † RA 1.

TWIST, J.G. Exh. 1918
58 Limerston Street, Kings Road, Chelsea, London. † RA 1.

TWIST, Walter Norman Exh. 1933-37
Architect. Sun Building, Bennetts Hill, Birmingham. † RA 2.

TWORT, Flora C. Exh. 1927-38
Figure and landscape painter. 1 The Square, Petersfield, Hants. † L 1, NEA 1, RA 12, SWA 1.

TWYMAN, E. Exh. 1886
Still life painter. 54 Minford Gardens, West Kensington Park, London. † RBA 1.

TWYMAN, Miriam Exh. 1891-92
Miniature portrait painter. 3 North Villas, Camden Square, London. † RA 2.

TYDEMAN, Miss A. Exh. 1940
† NEA 1.

TYDEMAN, Gretchen Exh. 1930-39
Withington, Manchester 1930; London 1936. † P 3, RBA 2, RCA 1.

TYE, Edith A. Exh. 1892-1907
Flower painter. 57 Tressillian Road, St. Johns, London. † FIN 1, L 3, RA 13, RBA 5, RI 7, ROI 1, SWA 2.

TYLER, Adam A. Exh. 1903-8
Slateford, N.B. 1903; Edinburgh 1905. † GI 1, RSA 4.

TYLER, A.F. Exh. 1917
2 Chelsea Manor Studios, Flood Street, Chelsea, London. † RA 1.

TYLER, Phyllis M. Exh. 1932
Sculptor. Texel, In Harbour, Canal Basin, Gravesend, Kent. † RA 1.

TYLER, William E. Exh. 1889-1917
Bridgnorth, Salop 1889; Carlisle 1907. † B 5, LS 8, RBA 1, ROI 1.

TYLER, William Henry Exh. 1880-93
Sculptor. Kensington, London. † G 19, NG 3, RA 22, RBA 1.

TYNDALE, T. Exh. 1902-11
55 Woodhurst Road, Acton, London. † B 1, D 42, GI 1, L 9.

TYNDALE, Walter Frederick Roofe* 1855-1943
Landscape, architectural, portrait and genre painter and watercolourist. b. Bruges. Studied Antwerp Academy and Paris. Travelled on the continent, Middle East and Japan. R.I. 1911. Add: Bath 1880; London 1882 and 1914; Eltham, Kent 1885; Haslemere, Surrey 1888 and 1894; Bridgnorth, Salop 1893; Venice 1925. † AG 11, B 3, DOW 236, FIN 308, G 2, GI 2, L 10, LEI 276, M 6, NG 2, RA 35, RBA 5, RHA 1, RI 130, ROI 7.

TYNDALL, Donald A. Exh. 1937
Architect. Laurel Lodge, Monkstown, Co. Dublin. † RHA 1.

TYNDALL, Muriel K. Exh. 1932
36 Highfield Road, Edgbaston, Birmingham. † B 1.

TYRE, David Maxwell Exh. 1901
27 Windsor Terrace, Glasgow. † RSA 1.

TYRER, J. Seddon Exh. 1880
Grove Street, Mansfield, Notts. † N 2.

TYRER, Mrs. R. Exh. 1926-27
14 Lanville Road, Mossley Hill, Liverpool. † L 4.

TYRRELL, John Exh. 1894-1911
Landscape painter. A.N.S.A. 1908, N.S.A. 1909. Add: Ilkeston, Derbys. † N 19.

TYRRELL, Norman Exh. 1921-38
Sculptor. London. † GI 1, RA 5.

TYRRELL, Thomas 1857-1928
Sculptor. London. † GI 4, RA 23, RI 2, ROI 2.

TYRWHITT, Rev. Richard St. John 1827-1895
Landscape painter and writer. Vicar of St. Mary Magdalen Oxford 1858-72. Father of Walter Spencer Stanhope T. q.v. Exh. 1880-87. Add: Oxford. † G 1, RA 1.

TYRWHITT, Thomas Exh. 1910-22
Architect. London. † RA 4.

TYRWHITT, Ursula 1878-1966
Watercolour painter. Studied Slade School, Paris and Rome. N.E.A. 1913. Add: London 1901 and 1911; Easton in Gordano, Somerset 1907; Oxford 1922. † ALP 3, BG 2, G 3, I 6, NEA 109.

TYRWHITT, Walter Spencer Stanhope 1859-1932
Watercolour painter. b. Oxford. Son of Richard St. John T. q.v. R.B.A. 1904. Add: Oxford. † BG 53, D 1, M 1, RA 10, RBA 164, RHA 4, RI 13.

TYSON, Alice Exh. 1883-92
Flower painter. Chester. † B 2, L 1, M 4, RA 2.

TYSON, John H. Exh. 1886-1905
Landscape painter. Liverpool 1886 and 1901; Seacombe 1888; Liscard, Cheshire 1898. † L 40, RA 3, RCA 2.

TYSON, Kathleen b. 1898
Landscape and miniature painter. b. Grimsby. Studied Grimsby and Hull Schools of Art. S.W.A. 1939. Exh. 1927-40. Add: Grimsby, Lincs. † B 3, NEA 2, RA 11, RBA 14, ROI 5, SWA 15.

TYTGAT, Edgard* 1879-1957
Belgian painter and engraver. Studied Academy des Beaux Arts in Brussels 1899-1900. Exh. 1919. † NEA 2.

TZIEDEINOFF, Georges Exh. 1936
London and Paris. † RMS 5.

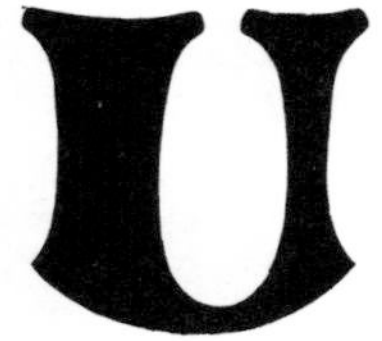

UDEN, Ernest Boye b. 1911
Painter, draughtsman and commercial artist. Studied Camberwell School of Art and Goldsmiths College. Exh. 1933-36. Add: London 1933; Bexley, Kent 1935. † RA 3.
UDVARDY, Imre Laszlo b. 1885
"Spy Junr". Cartoonist and caricaturist. Exh. 1927. Add: Northwood, Middlesex. † AB 31.
UDVARDY, Mrs. Mabel Exh. 1934
Miniature portrait painter. Hill Farm Studio, Potter Street, Northwood, Middlesex. † RA 1.
UFLAND, David Exh. 1940
Portrait pencil artist. 31 Clipstone Street, London. † RA 1.
UGO, Antonio b. 1870
Italian sculptor. Exh. 1907. Add: Via Cavour, Palermo, Sicily. † RHA 1.
UHDE, Von See V
UHLEMANN, Karl Exh. 1915-40
Landscape painter. Dublin 1915 and 1926; Dolphin's Barn, Ireland 1920. † RHA 23.
UHLRICH, Heinrich S. Exh. 1889-1905
Engraver. Brynterion, Chelsfield, Kent. † RA 22.
ULCOQ, Andrew Exh. 1889-97
Landscape painter. 22 Pembridge Gardens, London. † D 2, L 2, RA 2, RI 3, ROI 5.
ULLMAN, Eugene Paul* b. 1897
American painter. Exh. 1907-22. Add: 33 Rue Marboeuf, Paris. † I 2, L 3.
ULLMAN, Raoul Andre b. 1867
French painter. Exh. 1907-12. † GOU 2.
ULLMER, Frederick Exh. 1887-88
Eagle House, Mountford Terrace, Barnsbury, London. † B 1, GI 1.
ULPH, Mrs. J.M. Birt Exh. 1917-18
Bergholt, St. Ives, Hunts. † RA 2.
ULRICH, Charles F. 1858-1908
Figure and domestic painter. Exh. 1889-95. Add: 30F 4, San Barnaba, Venice. † L 1, RA 5, TOO 4.
UMBERS, John Ludford Exh. 1908-21
John Bright Street, Birmingham 1908; Horsebrook Hall, Stretton, Stafford 1921. † B 6.
UNDERHILL, Frederick Thomas Exh. 1880-96
Landscape, fruit, portrait and miniature painter. London. † AG 1, RA 1, RBA 2, RHA 3.
UNDERHILL, Joan E. Exh. 1930
29 Barnbank Gardens, Glasgow. † GI 1.
UNDERWOOD, A. Exh. 1897-99
Landscape painter. London. † L 1, RA 2, RBA 4.
UNDERWOOD, Albert Exh. 1922
Alexandra Stuios, 36 Princes Road, Liverpool. † L 2.
UNDERWOOD, Annie b. 1876
Miniature and portrait painter. Studied under Sir Hubert Herkomer. R.B.A. 1911, A.R.M.S. 1917, R.M.S. 1919. Add: East Grinstead, Sussex. † B 1, L 22, LS 2, RA 35, RBA 74, RI 11, RMS 61.
UNDERWOOD, A.S. Exh. 1885
Watercolour landscape painter. 11 Bedford Square, London. † RI 1.
UNDERWOOD, Mrs. C.J. Exh. 1909
Miniature portrait painter. Hill Crest, Boyne Road, Blackheath, London. † RA 1.
UNDERWOOD, Mrs. Edith M. Exh. 1910
26 Wimpole Street, London. † L 3.
UNDERWOOD, Edgar S. Exh. 1898-1911
Architect. 3/5 Queens Street, Cheapside, London. † RA 7.
UNDERWOOD, F. Exh. 1923-32
Landscape painter. Glenmaye Villa, Marlborough Road, Beeston, Notts. † N 21.
UNDERWOOD, Guy Exh. 1923
Watercolour painter, pastellier and etcher. † ALP 11.
UNDERWOOD, Leon* b. 1890
Sculptor, painter, woodcut artist and engraver. Studied Regent Street Polytechnic 1907-10, Royal College of Art 1910-13 and Slade School 1919-20. Travelled extensively in Russia 1913. Also visited Italy, America and Mexico. "Totem to the Artist" (1925-30) purchased by Chantrey Bequest 1964. Exh. 1916-38. Add: London. † AG 1, ALP 35, BA 29, CHE 87, G 1, GI 2, L 2, LEI 37, M 5, NEA 8, RA 3, RSA 3..
UNDERWOOD, Mrs. Mary Exh. 1939
1 Lovaine Terrace, Berwick on Tweed. † RSA 1.
UNDERWOOD, Robert Exh. 1937-40
Perth 1937; 1 Lovaine Terrace, Berwick on Tweed 1939. † RSA 4.
UNDERWOOD, Mrs. Violet Exh. 1937
8 The Meads, Letchworth, Herts. † B 1.
UNDERWOOD, William S. Exh. 1912
Foxway Rise, Fleet, Hants. † LS 3.
UNITE, Daphne b. 1907
Landscape and flower painter. Studied St. Johns Wood, 1924-26. Exh. 1939. Add: Tenterden Grove, London. † GOU 2, ROI 3.
UNITE, G.W.G. Exh. 1909
60 Chantry Road, Moseley, Birmingham. † RHA 1.
UNNA, Ada Exh. 1890-1905
Flower and landscape painter. London. † L 3, RA 2, RBA 5, ROI 4, SWA 19.
UNSWORTH, William Frederick Exh. 1882-1902
Watercolour and architectural painter. London. † RA 12, RBA 1.
UNTERBERGER, Franz Richard* b. 1838
Swiss painter. Exh. 1889. Add: c/o J.C. Nairn, 51 Denzille Street, Dublin. † RHA 1.
UNTERNHARER, S. Exh. 1880
16 Avenue Trudaine, Paris. † RHA 1.
UNWIN, Frances Mabelle Exh. 1890-1933
Mrs. George U. nee Pearse. Watercolour portrait, figure and flower painter and pastellier. A.S.W.A. 1897, S.W.A. 1899. Add: London 1890 and 1933; Edinburgh 1903; Manchester 1911. † BA 1, L 5, M 6, P 1, RA 2, RBA 3, RSA 4, SWA 53.
UNWIN, Francis Sydney 1885-1925
Landscape and architectural painter and etcher. N.E.A. 1913. Add: London. † BA 2, CAR 4, FIN 2, G 1, GI 5, GOU 1, L 12, NEA 88, RA 1, RHA 15, RSA 1.
UNWIN, Miss G. Exh. 1905
26 St. Albans Road, Bootle, Lancs. † L 1.
UNWIN, Henry Exh. 1927-33
Wigan, Lancs. † L 3.
UNWIN, Ida M. Exh. 1892-94
Figure painter. Chilworth, Surrey. † ROI 3.
UNWIN, Mary L.H. Exh. 1892-1905
Sculptor. Hall Royd, Shipley, Yorks. † L 15, RA 2.
UNWIN, Nora Spicer b. 1907
Wood engraver and illustrator. Studied under Leon Underwood, Kingston School of Art and Royal College of Art. A.R.E. 1935. Exh. 1930-40. Add: Milford, Surrey 1934; London 1939. † RA 9, RE 30, RED 4.
UNWIN, William C. Exh. 1898-1904
Sculptor. Canford Road, Poole, Dorset. † RA 2.
UPCHER, Mrs. A. Exh. 1909-10
Watercolour painter. Halesworth Rectory, Suffolk. † L 3, LS 3, RA 1.
UPCHER, Cecil Exh. 1933
Architect. 8 Upper King Street, Norwich. † RA 1.
UPHILL, Jessie H. Exh. 1896-1904
Sculptor. Blackheath, London. † RA 2.
UPHILL, Wilhelmina Exh. 1887
Painter. Ivy Bank, Kidbrooke Park Road, Blackheath, London. † SWA 1.
UPTON, Mrs. Exh. 1909-16
Coolatore, Moate, Co. Westmeath, Ireland. † RHA 6.
UPTON, A. Exh. 1940
Walter House, Bedford Street, London. † ROI 3.
UPTON, Charles M. Exh. 1937-38
Sculptor. Woodhouse Farm Studio, Tennal Lane, Harborne, Birmingham. † B 3.
UPTON, Florence K. d. 1922
Portrait painter. Paris 1905; London 1909. † FIN 1, I 1, L 3, P 1, RA 9.
UPTON, H. Edith Exh. 1885
Watercolour flower painter. The Grove, Blackheath, London. † SWA 1.
UPTON, John A. Exh. 1881
Portrait painter. 28 Grove Place, Brompton Road, London. † RA 1.
UPTON, R. Exh. 1922
The Manse, Park Road, Coleshill, nr. Birmingham. † L 8.
UPTON, Sydney C. Exh. 1936
Watercolour painter. 27 Blakesware Gardens, London. † RA 1.
UPTON, Thomas Exh. 1883
Minster Buildings, Church Street, Liverpool. † L 1.
URBAN, Herman Exh. 1904
4 Katzmeier Strasse, Munich. † GI 1.
URE, Alan McLymont Exh. 1915-32
Glasgow. † GI 10.
URE, Beth Exh. 1938
Wheatlands, Bonnybridge. † GI 1.
URE, Isa R. Exh. 1881-85
Cairndhu, Helensburgh. † GI 8, RSA 2.
URE, James L. Exh. 1893
45 Queen Square, Strathbungo, Glasgow. † GI 1.
URE, T.H. Exh. 1905
43 Carnegie Street, Dunfermline, N.B. † RSA 1.
U'REN, John C. Exh. 1885-98
Marine painter. Penzance, Cornwall 1885; Plymouth 1898. † RA 2, RI 3.
URGELL, Ricardo Exh. 1921
63 Ballester, San Gervasio, Barcelona, Spain. † L 1.
URIE, Miss O.G. Exh. 1908-12
London 1908; St. Leonards on Sea 1910. † GI 3, L 11, RA 2.
URQUHART, Miss Exh. 1884
Hulan House, Leamington, Warwicks. † B 1.

URQUHART, Annie Mackenzie Exh. 1904-28
Watercolour painter and black and white artist. Studied Glasgow School of Art, Paris and under F.H. Newbury and M. Delville. Add: Bishopton, N.B. 1904; Glasgow 1907; London 1928. † GI 14, L 1, RA 1, RSA 3.

URQUHART, Edith Mary Exh. 1923-40
Portrait, figure and landscape painter. b. Edinburgh. Studied Newlyn and Heatherleys. A.S.W.A. 1930. Add: London. † G 1, P 1, RBA 2, SWA 32.

URQUHART, Helen Exh. 1913
Murray House, Perth. † L 1.

URQUHART, H.H. Exh. 1884
12 Albert Drive, Crosshill, Glasgow. † GI 1.

URQUHART, Maggie Exh. 1880
Langside, Glasgow. † GI 1.

URQUHART, Murray b. 1880
Figure, animal and landscape painter. b. Kirkcudbridgt. Studied Edinburgh School of Art, Slade School, Westminster School of Art, Calderons School of Animal Painting and under J.P. Laurens in Paris. R.B.A. 1914. Exh. 1910-39. Add: London 1910 and 1925; Newbury, Berks. 1914 and 1923; Bridport, Dorset 1919; Meopham, Kent 1928. † LEF 33, GI 4, NEA 1, P 4, RA 16, RBA 152, RHA 5, RI 3, WG 26.

URQUHART, Miss M.C. Exh. 1909
Sculptor. 3 West Street, Leicester. † RA 1.

URQUHART, Thomas C. Exh. 1940
74 Forsyth Street, Greenock. † RSA 1.

URQUHART, W.J. Exh. 1895-1901
Black and white artist. Leicester 1895; London 1899. † RA 5.

URQUHARTSON, C.O. Exh. 1895
Portrait painter. 3 Camden Road Studios, London. † RA 1.

URTIN, Paul Francois Marie Exh. 1909
† LS 3.

URUSHIBARA, Yoshijiro b. 1889
Wood engraver and painter. b. Tokyo, Japan. Exh. 1918-39. Add: London. † AB 44, BA 8, GI 3, I 10, L 14, RA 6, RED 4, RHA 1, RSA 3.

URWICK, Edward Exh. 1898-1905
Blenheim Club, 12 St. James Square, London. † D 7.

URWICK, James Exh. 1881-92
London. † RE 23.

URWICK, Mrs. Margaret Exh. 1920-21
9 Pakenham Road, Edgbaston, Birmingham. † B 3.

URWICK, Sarah E. Exh. 1880
Landscape painter. 49 Belsize Park Gardens, London. † SWA 1.

URWICK, Walter* 1864-1943
Portrait, genre and miniature painter. Studied South Kensington and R.A. Schools. Add: London. † B 2, L 9, M 1, NG 8, RA 30, RHA 2, RI 1, ROI 2.

URWICK, Mrs. W.E. Exh. 1912
Meanwood Lodge, Leeds, Yorks. † L 1.

URWICK, William H. Exh. 1880-1914
Landscape painter and etcher. R.E. 1881 (ceased 1914). Add: Clapham Common, London. † L 6, M 1, RA 7, RE 99, RI 1.

URWIN, Mrs. Jean Foster Exh. 1922
Watercolour painter. Southville, Warkworth, Northumberland. † RA 1.

USHER, A.F. Exh. 1918
45 Finsbury Pavement, London. † RA 1.

USHER, Miss E.F. Exh. 1910-14
Worcester 1910; Kensington, London 1911. † L 5, RA 8.

USSHER, Arland A. Exh. 1881-98
Coastal painter. Dromore, Co. Down and Kingstown, Ireland 1881-93; Newcastle, Co. Down 1895. † D 3, RA 1, RHA 59, RI 3, ROI 6.

USSHER, Isabel Exh. 1895-99
Cappagh, Lismore, Fermoy. † RHA 4.

UTAGAWA, Miss Wakana Exh. 1911
Silk painter. 3 Ormiston Road, Shepherds Bush, London. † BG 40, LS 3.

UTIN, Archie Exh. 1931-38
Landscape painter. 91d Clarendon Road, London. † GOU 1, NEA 1, RA 1.

UTLEY, Annie Exh. 1909
Sefton House, Crosby Green, West Derby, Liverpool. † L 1.

UTLEY, Jane Exh. 1920-30
Deytheur, Llansantffraid, Mon. † L 5.

UTLEY, Jennie Exh. 1903-14
Crosby Green, West Derby, Liverpool 1903 and 1908; Cemaes Bay, Anglesey 1906. † B 2, L 23, RA 3, RHA 1, Fi 1.

UTRILLO, Maurice* 1883-1955
French painter. † BA 1, GI 1, GOU 2, L 1, RED 7, RSA 1.

UTTERSON, Emily Exh. 1880
Painter. Penralt, Bournemouth. † SWA 1.

UTZON-FRANK, Einar Exh. 1934
Royal Academy, Charlottenborg, Copenhagen. † RSA 4.

UYTTERSCHAUT, Victor Exh. 1896
Rue de la Grosse, Tour, Brussels. † GI 2.

UYTVANCK, Van See V

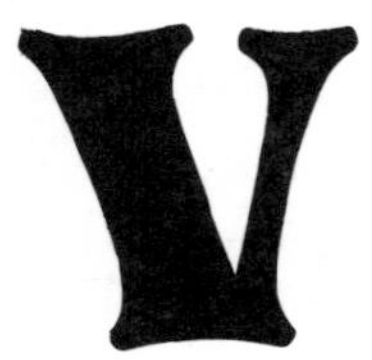

VAA, Dyre Exh. 1933
Kunstuernes, Hus, Oslo. † RSA 2.

VACHER, Charles* 1818-1883
Watercolour landscape painter. Studied R.A. Schools and Rome. Travelled widely on the continent, Middle East and North Africa. A.R.I. 1846, R.I. 1850. Add: The Boltons, South Kensington, London 1880. † RI 18.

VACHER, Miss E. Exh. 1910-15
Birkenhead. † L 12.

VACHER, Sydney 1854-1934
Etcher and architect. Son of Thomas Brittain V. (1805-1880), and nephew of Charles V. q.v. Studied R.A. Schools. Exh. 1882-1914. Add: London. † RA 10.

VAES, Walter* b. 1882
Painter and engraver. b. Antwerp. Exh. 1905-9. Add: Antwerp. † L 3.

VAGA, N.L. Exh. 1940
† RE 4.

VAIL, Eugene b. 1857
American artist. Exh. 1897. Add: Paris. † P 1.

VAILLANT, Emile Exh. 1882
16 Avenue Trudaine, Paris. † RHA 1.

VAL du See D

VALE, Enid Marjorie b. 1890
Mountain, landscape and miniature painter. Studied Wolverhampton and Birmingham Municipal Schools of Art. A.R.M.S. 1919. Exh. 1913-38. Add: The Ferns, Penn Fields, Wolverhampton 1913; Uckfield, Sussex 1937. † B 70, L 27, RA 10, RE 3, RI 1, RMS 54, RSA 15.

VALENTI, Miss Pina Exh. 1919
† L 2.

VALENTINE, Albert Fillmore Exh. 1936-38
Portrait and figure painter. 32 Tavistock Road, London. † RA 2.

VALENTINE, Esther Exh. 1925-26
40 Montpelier Square, London. † L 1, RMS 1.

VALENTINE, Edward B. Exh. 1882-83
Liverpool 1882; Kensington, London 1883. † D 1, L 2.

VALENTINE, J. Exh. 1884
17 Fitzroy Street, London. † ROI 1.

VALENTINE, Leo Exh. 1910-12
10 Warrior Square Terrace, St. Leonards on Sea, Sussex. † LS 8.

VALERO, Maroussia Exh. 1930
22 Redcliffe Street, South Kensington, London. † SWA 1.

VALETTE, Adolphe Exh. 1909-12
Portrait and landscape painter and ecclesiastical decorator. Principal master Manchester School of Art. Add: Manchester. † L 13.

VALKENBURG, Hendrik* 1826-1896
Dutch painter. Exh. 1886. Add: 117 New Bond Street, London. † ,M 3.

VALLANCE, Aymer Exh. 1880
Painter. c/o E. Cox, 144 Cromwell Road, South Kensington, London. † RBA 2.

VALLANCE, David J. Exh. 1880-87
Edinburgh. † GI 1, RSA 21.

VALLANCE, Fanny Exh. 1880-84
Watercolour painter. London. † D 1, SWA 1.

VALLANCE, R.B. Exh. 1885-1901
Edinburgh. † RSA 22.

VALLANCE, Tom Exh. 1897-1929
Glasgow. † GI 8, RSA 3.

VALLANCE, William Fleming* 1827-1904
Marine, portrait and genre painter. b. Paisley. Apprenticed as a carver and gilder to Messrs. Aitken Dott. Studied Trustees Academy and under R.S. Lauder. A.R.S.A. 1875, R.S.A. 1881. Add: Edinburgh. † GI 9, RSA 93, RSW 8.

VALLANCE, Zona Exh. 1888
The Deanery, Stratford, Essex. † B 1.

VALLENTINE, Mrs. Alicia Exh. 1935
Sculptor. 450 Camden Road, London. † RA 1.

VALLET, P. Exh. 1912
26 Alfred Place West, South Kensington, London. † RA 1.

VALLET-BISSON, Mme. F. Exh. 1902
17 Avenue Gourgand, Paris. † L 1.

VALLETTE, Henri Exh. 1911-12
14 Rue Boissonade, Paris. † L 1, RA 2, RSA 3.

VALLOTON, Felix* 1865-1925
French painter. Exh. 1912-23. † GOU 7.

VALMON, Mlle. Leonie Exh. 1886-88
Etcher. 5/6 Haymarket, London. † RA 2.

VALTAT, Louis* 1869-1952
French painter. Exh. 1921. † GOU 3.

VALTER, Miss Eugene M. Exh. 1882-95
Figure painter. 282 Pershore Road, Birmingham. † B 24, GI 1, L 3, M 4, ROI 2.

VALTER, Frederick E. Exh. 1882-1921
Rustic painter. Birmingham. † B 61, GI 2, L 8, M 4, RBA 2, RSA 1.

VALTER, Henry* Exh. 1881-98
Landscape painter. 282 Pershore Road, Birmingham. † B 42, GI 4, L 2, M 5.

VAN ABBE, Joseph Exh. 1922-35
Flower painter. London. † G 1, RA 1, RBA 1.

VAN ABBE, Salomon b. 1883
Painter, etcher and illustrator. b. Amsterdam. Naturalised British. Studied London. R.B.A. 1933, A.R.E. 1928. Exh. 1920-40. Add: London. † AR 5, B 2, CON 3, GI 15, GOU 2, L 13, P 4, RA 16, RBA 36, RE 23, RHA 21, RI 1, ROI 2, RSA 15.

VANAISE, Gustave 1854-1902
Belgian artist. Exh. 1887. Add: Rue Moris, St. Gilles, Brussels. † M 1.

VAN ANGEREN, A. Dirksen Exh. 1913
Etcher. † FIN 10.

VAN ANREP, Boris 1883-1969
Painter and mosaic artist. Member London Group 1919. Exh. 1914-25. Add: London. † G 1, GOU 4, NEA 6.

VAN ANROOY, Anton* b. 1870
Landscape and figure painter. b. Holland. Naturalised British. Studied Hague Academy of Art. Settled in London 1896. R.I. 1918. Exh. 1905-39. Add: London. † B 2, BA 2, DOW 2, GI 15, GOU 11, I 1, L 24, M 1, P 4, RA 32, RI 71, TOO 2.

VAN BAKEL, Mrs. Nellie Exh. 1938-40
Portrait and figure painter. London. † AR 60, B 2, NEA 1, P 1, RBA 3, RCA 3, RSA 2.

VAN BEERS, Jan* b. 1852
Belgian painter. Exh. 1882-1904. Add: Paris 1882 and 1889; London 1884. † DOW 131, FIN 55, G 1, GI 2, L 8, M 10, RA 7.

VAN BEURDEN, Alphonse Exh. 1887-1912
Sculptor. 18 Rue de l'Appell, Antwerp. † L 3, RA 17.

VAN BEVER, de la Quintinie, Mme. M. Exh. 1912
5 Rue de Tournon, Paris. † L 1.

VAN BIESBROECK, Julius J. Exh. 1889
Figure painter. Northbrooke, Catford Hill, London. † RA 1.

VAN BOOSE, Mrs. Bilders Exh. 1895
190 Tasmanstraat, The Hague, Holland. † GI 1.

VAN BUSKIRK, Charlotte Exh. 1903-27
Paris 1903; London 1914; Amersham Common, Bucks. 1927. † B 1, SWA 4.

VAN COUVER, Jan* Exh. 1904-7
Dutch painter. London. † M 1, NG 1, RA 1.

VAN DAMME, G.E. Exh. 1914
10 Ladyewood Road, Liscard, Cheshire. † L 1.

VANDELEUR, Miss M.J.C. Exh. 1922
Kiltennel Rectory, Gorey. † RHA 1.

VANDELEUR, R.S. Exh. 1926
Watercolour landscape painter. † FIN 50.

VAN DEN AUBER, H. Exh. 1880
Figure painter. Pont Aven, Finisterre, France. † RBA 4.

VANDEN BAGARDE, Aime Exh. 1903
291 Bloomsbury Street, Nechells, Birmingham. † B 1.

VAN DEN BERGH, Louise Exh. 1936-37
Dry point and aquatint artist. c/o Mrs. Alston, Cromwell Road, London. † RA 3.

VANDENBERGH, Raymond John b. 1889
Wild animal, animal portrait, figure and landscape painter. Studied Hornsey School of Art and under Arthur Wardle. Exh. 1928-31. Add: 127 Station Road, Church End, London. † RA 1, RI 4.

VAN DER BERGH, A.W. Exh. 1928-29
Landscape painter. † AB 4.

VAN DER BOS, G.P.M. Exh. 1885
39 Rue de Douai, Paris. † GI 1.

VANDER HECHT, G. Exh. 1882
4 Rue de Deausite, Brussels. † GI 1.

VAN DER HECHT, Henri Exh. 1885
Landscape painter. 30 Duke Street, Piccadilly, London. † RBA 1.

VANDERHOOF, Charles A. Exh. 1881
Etcher. 7 Hillmarten Road, London. † RA 2, RE 1.

VAN DER LOO, Marten Exh. 1915-19
Kings Lynn, Norfolk 1915; Twickenham, Middlesex 1917; Antwerp 1919. † GI 7, L 5, RA 3, RSA 6.

VANDERLYN, Nathan Exh. 1897-1937
Watercolour painter, etcher, engraver and black and white artist. Studied Slade School and Royal College of Art. Painting instructor L.C.C. Central School of Arts and Crafts. R.I. 1916. (Name removed 1937). Add: London. † BK 44, L 6, RA 9, RBA 1, RI 63, RMS 2.

VAN DER MAARELS, M. Exh. 1887-88
Gedempte Raamstraat 18, The Hague, Holland. † RSA 2.

VAN DER MEY, M.J. Exh. 1936
† RSA 1.

VAN DER OUDERAA, P. Exh. 1895
Painter. 72 Piccadilly, London. † RA 2.

VAN DER PANT, Antoinette Exh. 1911-14
Dover 1911; Ashford, Kent 1912; Highgate, London 1913. † D 12, LS 12, SWA 1.

VAN DER STAPPEN, Charles 1843-1910
Belgian sculptor. Exh. 1901. Add: Brussels. † I 1.

VAN DER STAPPEN, Pierre C. Exh. 1905-6
15 Joyeuse Entree, Brussels. † GI 4.

VAN DER VEEN, C.W. Exh. 1935-40
The Cottage, Whally Bridge, Cheshire. † B 6, RCA 15.

VAN DER VENNE, Adolf Exh. 1883
Painter. † GI 1.

VAN DER VOORT, H.J. Exh. 1881
20 Mortimer Street, Regent Street, London. † RHA 3.

VANDER VOORT, T. Exh. 1882
440 Keizersgracht, Amsterdam. † RHA 4.

VAN DER WAAY, Nicholas Exh. 1906-13
86 Stadouderskade, Amsterdam. † GI 13, L 7, LS 6.

VAN DER WEYDEN, Harry* b. 1868
Marine and landscape painter. b. Boston, Mass., U.S.A. Studied Slade School, Julians, Paris and under J.P. Laurens. Camouflage officer with the Royal Engineers 1916-18. R.O.I. 1904. Exh. 1880-1936. Add: London 1880 and 1922; Paris 1891; Montrueil-sur-Mer, France 1900; Etaples, Pas de Calais, France 1916. † BA 1, G 2, GI 10, I 3, L 11, NG 5, RA 29, RBA 6, RI 4, ROI 30.

VAN DE WOESTYNE, G. Exh. 1904-19
1 Hill Road, St. Johns Wood, London. † I 2, L 1, RA 1.

VANE, Hon. Mrs. Kathleen Airini b. 1891
nee Mair. Landscape painter. b. New Zealand. Studied London and under Lamorna Birch. Exh. 1924-38. Add: Bovey Tracey, Devon 1924; Virginia Water, Surrey 1938. † L 1, RA 1, RBA 1, RI 2, SWA 1, WG 129.

VAN ELTEN, Kruseman* 1829-1904
American painter. b. Holland. Add: New York 1881; c/o Cassell and Co., Ludgate Hill, London 1884; Paris 1904. † L 2, RE 7.

VAN ESSEN Exh. 1886
117 New Bond Street, London. † M 2.

VAN EVERDINGEN, A. Exh. 1881-87
Landscape painter. Utrecht, Holland. † RA 1, RSA 3.

VAN GOETHEM, Edouard Exh. 1890-1914
Figure painter. Brussels 1898; Parkstone, Dorset 1906. † L 2, LS 15, RA 2, RI 2.

VAN GRUISEN, Florence A. Exh. 1890-1909
Claughton 1890; Oxton, Cheshire 1895. † L 14, LS 8.

VAN HAANEN, Cecil* b. 1844
Figure and domestic painter. R.O.I. 1883 (only). Exh. 1880-1904. Add: London and Venice. † G 3, GI 2, L 3, NG 2, RA 11, ROI 1.

VAN HALL, Miss F. Exh. 1921-22
346 Marsh Lane, Bootle, Liverpool. † L 2.

VAN HALLEN, Henri Exh. 1921
26 Rue de Marteau, Brussels. † RSA 2.

VAN HASSELT, Willem* Exh. 1909
Figure and landscape painter. 20 Alexandra Road, West Kensington, London. † NEA 1.

VAN HAVERMAET, Charles Exh. 1895-1911
Figure painter. Antwerp 1895; London 1901. † GI 2, M 4, RA 12.

VAN HAVERMAET, P. Exh. 1881
Portrait painter. 12 St. James Place, London. † RA 1.

VAN HEDDEGHEM, Alice Exh. 1906-27
Flower painter. 12 Cowley Street, Westminster, London. † AB 93, BG 7, L 3, RA 2.

VAN HEEMSKERCK, Jacoba Exh. 1913
Nassen Tuilensteinstraat 35, The Hague, Holland. † LS 2.

VAN HIER Exh. 1880-81
Landscape painter. 2 New Burlington Street, London. † RBA 2.

VAN HOLDER, Franz Exh. 1909
10 Rue Lausanne, Brussels. † L 1.

VAN HOVE, Edmond* Exh. 1899-1908
Painter. Antwerp 1899; Ghent, Belgium 1902. † GI 9, L 11, M 1, NG 6.

VAN HOYTEMA, T. Exh. 1905
Amsterdam. † I 2.

VAN LEEMPATTEN, E. Exh. 1890
40 Rue Albert de la Tour, Brussels. † L 1.

VAN MASTENBROCK, Johan Hendrik* b. 1875
Dutch painter. Exh. 1896-1910. Add: London 1896; Rotterdam 1905. † AG 1, B 1, GI 1 I 1, L 1, LS 2 M 1, ROI 2.

VAN MECHELEN, A. Exh. 1918
149 Tackbrook Street, London. † RA 2.

VANNET, William Peters b. 1917
Painter and etcher. Studied Dundee College of Art 1935-40. Exh. 1939. Add: 56 Howard Street, Arbroath. † RSA 2.

VANNICOLA, Gaetano Exh. 1887-94
Landscape painter. Rome 1887; London 1894. † G 1, NG 2.

VANNUTELLI, Scipione 1834-1894
Italian sculptor. Exh. 1882-86. Add: Palazzo Pamfili Doria, Rome. † G 2.

VAN OSS, Tom b. 1901
Landscape and portrait painter and satirical illustrator. b. Walberswick, Suffolk. Exh. 1930-39. Add: London 1930 and 1936; Walberswick, Suffolk 1935. † COO 39, P 5, RA 3, ROI 3, WG 49.

VAN PAPENDRECHT, Jan Hoynck* Exh. 1888-1911
Dutch figure and military painter. Rotterdam. † BRU 3, RA 2.

VAN RAALTE, Mrs. C. Exh. 1888
Figure painter. 8 Kensington Palace Gardens, London. † RA 1.

VAN RAALTE, Henri B. Exh. 1901-28
Landscape and figure painter. A.R.E. 1900-7. Add: London. † AB 11, RA 5, RE 2.

VAN ROGGEN, I.M. Grant Exh. 1913
Etcher. † FIN 10

VAN ROY, D. Exh. 1916
26 Harcourt Terrace, West Brompton, London. † RA 1.

VAN RUITH, Horace 1839-1923
Portrait, figure and architectural painter. Bombay, India 1887; Capri, Italy 1888; Rome 1889; Florence 1890; London 1891. † B 5, D 2, L 19, LS 8, M 6, NG 1, P 7, RA 27, RBA 1, RHA 11, ROI 1, RSA 5.

VAN RYSSELBERGHE, Theodore* 1862-1926
Belgian painter. † GOU 4, I 8.

VAN SCHNELL, Gabriel Exh. 1917-34
Etcher. London 1917; Kingston on Thames 1931. † CON 2, NEA 6, RA 3.

VANS GRAVESANDE, Carel Nicolaas Storm 1841-1921
Dutch etcher. R.E. 1881. Add: Brussels 1880 and 1904; Wiesbaden, Germany 1895. † GI 12, I 25, L 1, M 3, RA 3 RE 40, RHA 1, RI 1.

VAN SOEST, Louis W.* b. 1867
Dutch landscape painter. Exh. 1895-1916. Add: c/o Boussod, Valadon and Co., 5 Regent Street, London. † CON 1, RA 1.

VAN SOMEREN, Major Edmund Lawrence b. 1875
Portrait, landscape and figure painter. b. Bangalore, India. Studied R.A. Schools (2 silver medals, Landseer scholarship). R.O.I. 1909 (Hon. Ret. 1929). Exh. 1897-1938. Add: London 1897; Crowborough, Sussex 1915; Melton, Woodbridge, Suffolk 1922. † L 1, NEA 2, NG 2, P 2, RA 3, ROI 62, RSA 2.

VAN SPEYBROUGH, Edward Exh. 1911-12
38 Parvis Street, St. Jacques, Bruges, Belgium. † GI 2, L 2.

VAN STAATEN, L.* Exh. 1908-14
Painter. Wimbledon 1908; Pyrford, Surrey 1914. † RA 3.

VANSTON, Mrs. L. Exh. 1903-21
Willow Bank, Bushey Park Road, Dublin. † RHA 10.

VAN'T HOFF, Adriaan J. Exh. 1926
Watercolour painter. Valkenboschade 562, The Hague, Holland. † L 1, RA 1.

VAN UYTVANCK, B. (of Louvain) Exh. 1917
Eskhaven, Castlemaine Avenue, South Croydon, Surrey. † RA 1.

VAN WART, A. Exh. 1890
Sculptor. 2 South Street, Park Lane, London. † NG 1.

VAN WELIE, Antoon b. 1867
Dutch portrait painter. Exh 1908-9. Add: 1 Rue Juliette Lamber, Paris. † GOU 48, RA 1

VAN ZWANENBERG, Madge Exh. 1935
65 Redlington Road, London. † ROI 1.

VARCOE, Louisa Exh. 1887
Highfield House, Hanley, Staffs. † RSA 1.

VARCOE, Louise Exh. 1916-21
Miniature portrait painter. London. † L 1, RA 1, SWA 5.

VARESHINE, Catherine Exh. 1937
Sculptor. 59 Lancaster Road London. † RA 1.

VARIAN, J.S. Exh. 1915
Garnaville, Stillorgan, Co. Dublin. † RHA 1.

VARLEY, E. Exh. 1930-37
6 Conduit Street, London. † SWA 3.

VARLEY, Edgar John d. 1888
Landscape and architectural painter. Son of Charles Smith V. (1811-1888), and grandson of John V. (1778-1842). Add: London. † G 2, L 1, M 1, RA 2, RBA 4 RI 7.

VARLEY, E.M. Marinto Exh. 1910
Wakefield Road, Huddersfield. † L 3.

VARLEY, Fleetwood Charles Exh. 1896
20 Beaufort Street, Chelsea, London. † L 1.

VARLEY, Capt. Frederick H. Exh. 1919
Landscape painter. 7 The Mall, Parkhill Road, London. † RA 1.

VARLEY, Illingworth Exh. 1901-9
Landscape painter. London 1901; Gt. Malvern, Worcs. 1908. † RA 2

VARLEY, John* 1850-1933
Landscape and oriental painter. Grandson of John V. (1778-1842) and cousin of Edgar John V. q.v. Add: London. † B 1, D 5, DOW 1, G 8, GI 4, GOU 79, L 11, M 6, RA 13, RBA 7, RI 17, ROI 14, TOO 20.

VARLEY, Mrs. John Exh. 1883-87
Landscape and figure painter. 10 Abbey Road, St. Johns Wood, London. † RBA 3, RI 1, SWA 1.

VARLEY, Lucy Exh. 1886-1900
Flower painter. London. † B 1, D 7, L 1, NG 1, RA 3, RBA 1, RI 5, ROI 1, SWA 1.

VARLEY, Mabel Illingworth Exh. 1935-36
Portrait and landscape painter, wood engraver and potter. Studied Malvern School of Art 1924-25, Regent Street Polytechnic 1925-30. Add: Malvern Wells, Worcs. † RCA 2.

VARNEY, Arthur Exh. 1900
Clarendon Terrace, Kenilworth, Warwicks. † B 1.

VASARI, Emilio Exh. 1904
14 Rue Barbes, Courbevoie, Seine, France. † L 1.

VASCONCELLOS, de See D

VASEY, Clary Exh 1891-1923
Watercolour painter. London 1891; Sidmouth, Devon 1921. † RA 1, RI 15, SWA 1.

VASEY, Gladys Exh. 1932-38
† L 1, M 2.

VASS, Elemer b. 1892
Hungarian artist. Exh. 1935. † RSA 1.

VASSELOT, de See D

VAST, William C. Exh. 1927-31
Watercolour painter and etcher. Edinburgh. † RSA 3.

VATLER, Harry Exh. 1897
The Oaklands, Pershore, Edgbaston, Birmingham. † GI 1.

VAUGHAN, A.J. Exh. 1933
2 Faversham Road, London. † L 4.

VAUGHAN, C.E. Exh. 1898
Architect. 25 Lowther Arcade, London. † RA 1.

VAUGHAN, E.M. Bruce Exh. 1897-1903
Architect. Borough Chambers, Cardiff, Wales. † RA 3.

VAUGHAN, Col. H.B. Exh. 1919
103 King Henry's Road, Hampstead, London. † LS 3.

VAUGHAN, J. Exh. 1883
24 Slater Street, Liverpool. † L 1.

VAUGHAN, Miss L. Exh. 1904
Landscape painter. Ardendale, Sherwood Rise, Nottingham. † N 1.

VAUGHAN, Sarah Exh. 1908
6 Stanley Mansions, Park Walk, London. † LS 5.

VAUGHAN-LEE, Elizabeth Exh. 1939
Portrait painter. Kincardine O'Neil, Aberdeenshire. † RA 1.

VAUTHIER, Mme. Exh. 1883
13 Rue Breda, Paris. † GI 1.

VAUTHIER, Pierre Louis* d. 1902
French artist. Exh. 1883-91. Add: Paris 1883; Auteuil, France 1885. † GI 13.

VAUTIER, Benjamin* 1829-1898
German painter. Exh. 1884. † GI 1.

VAWDREY, Elizabeth Glascott
Exh. 1892-1940
Architectural and landscape painter. Studied South Kensington, Heatherleys, Newlyn and Paris. Add: Plymouth, Devon 1892; Paignton, Devon 1902; Falmouth 1903; London 1905; Wookey Hole, Somerset 1940. † B 10, D 7, L 9, M 1, RHA 3, RI 2, SWA 3.

VEACO, John G. Exh. 1883-1919
Liverpool and Derwent House, New Brighton, Cheshire. † L 13.

VEAZEY, David Exh. 1937-38
103 Coburg Road, Camberwell, London. † RI 2.

VEBER, Jean 1864-1928
French caricaturist. Exh. 1908-9. Add: 149 Boulevard Periere, Paris. † L 8.

VEDDER, Elihu* 1836-1923
American painter. Exh. 1899. † DOW 124.

VEDDER, Eva See ROOS

VEDDER, Simon Harmon b. 1866
Portrait, animal and figure painter and silversmith. b. U.S.A. Married Eva Roos, q.v. Exh. 1896-1931. Add: London. † B 1, FIN 1, L 3, RA 15, ROI 1.

VEDER, Hendrik Exh. 1885
Rotterdam, Holland. † GI 1.

VEGA, de See D

VEITCH, Eunice Exh. 1935
Urban landscape painter. † LEF 2.

VEITCH, Kate Exh. 1897-1920
Landscape painter. Edinburgh. † GI 11, M 1, RA 2, RSA 21.

VEITCH, M. Campbell Exh. 1887
18 Drummond Street, Edinburgh. † RSA 1.

VELARDE, Francis X. Exh. 1929-33
Architect. Liverpool. † L 7, RA 1.

VELAY, A.J. Exh. 1882
23 Rue de Cherche Midi, Paris. † G 1.

VELDEN, P.V. Exh. 1885-86
Prizengracht, The Hague, Holland. † M 1, RSA 1.

VELLACK, Miss Exh. 1899
Inglewood, Hale Road, Liscard, Cheshire. † L 1.

VELTEN, W. Exh. 1883-1899
37 Schwanthaler Strasse, Munich. † GI 2, TOO 21.

VENABLES, Alice Exh. 1884
Flower painter. The Precentary, Lincoln. † RBA 1.

VENABLES, Bernard Exh. 1936-38
Painter. 13 Whitworth Road, South Norwood, London. † RA 2.

VENABLES, S. Exh. 1890-91
Glasgow 1890; Liverpool 1891. † GI 1, L 1.

VENESS, Agnes M. Exh. 1895-1916
Flower and figure painter. 28 Malpas Road, Brockley, London. † L 1, RA 12, RBA 1, ROI 1, SWA 3.

VENIS, Miss S.A. Exh. 1905
8 Littledale Road, Egremont, Cheshire. † L 2.

VENNER, V.L. Exh. 1924
25 Walsingham Road, Wallasey, Cheshire. † L 2.

VENNER, W.H.T. Exh. 1886
Sculptor. 53 Comeragh Road, West Kensington, London. † RA 1.

VENNING, Dorothy Mary b. 1885
Sculptor and miniature painter. Exh. 1916-36. Add: London. † RA 12.

VENNING, Sydney J. Exh. 1903
Figure painter. 8 Albert Bridge Road, London. † RA 1.

VENNING, Virginia M. Exh. 1935-37
Sculptor. Kendale Hall, nr. Radlett, Herts. † RA 2.

VENT, Adele Exh. 1881
Flower painter. † SWA 1.

VENTNOR, Arthur Exh. 1896-1926
Domestic painter. Norwich 1896; London 1903. † RA 7.

VENTRESS, Miss E.M. Exh. 1911
65 Vernham Road, Plumstead, Kent. † L 1.

VERA, Paul b. 1882
French artist. Exh. 1908. Add: 72 Rue Blanche, Paris. † LS 2.

VERDAQUER, Dionisio B. Exh. 1898
Painter. 37 Ronda San Pedro, Barcelona, Spain. † RA 1.

VERE, de See D

VERE, P. Exh. 1917
c/o J.P. Brinson, West Woodlands, Reading, Berks. † RA 1.

VERESMITH See WEHRSCHMIDT

VEREY, Arthur* Exh. 1880-1911
Landscape, river and rustic genre painter. Hoddesdon Villa, Cavendish Road, Kilburn, London. † BRU 1, D 7, L 2, M 6, RA 13, RBA 44, RI 5, ROI 8.

VERFLOET, Joseph Exh. 1888
Landscape painter. Palazzo Villa, Florence. † D 3, RI 1.

VERHAEREN, A. Exh. 1909-14
26 Rue d'Edinbourg, Brussels. † L 2, RSA 1.

VERHAERT, Paul Exh. 1880
Figure painter. c/o S. Coombes, 331 Strand, London. † RA 1.

VERHEYDEN, Francois* 1806-1899
Belgian sculptor. London 1881-97. † RA 12.

VERHEYDEN, Isidor* 1846-1905
Belgian artist. Exh. 1894. Add: 78 Rue de la Consolation, Brussels. † GI 2.

VERITY, Edith Exh. 1894
Field Cottage, Kerridge, Macclesfield. † M 1.

VERITY, Francis Thomas d. 1937
Architect. Exh. 1905-28. Add: 17 Sackville Street, London. † LS 5, RA 16, RSA 1.

VERLAT, Professor Charles Exh. 1883-86
Painter. Liverpool 1883; Antwerp 1886. † L 1, RA 1.

VERLET, Raoul Exh. 1913
7 Rue Galvani, Paris. † GI 2.

VERNACHET, J.P. Exh. 1903
Painter. Haut Suet, la Richardais, par Dinard, Ile de Vilaine, France. † RA 1.

VERNEDE, Camille Exh. 1881-1908
Landscape painter. Ealing, London 1881; Brockenhurst, Hants. 1886 and 1900; Poole, Dorset 1890 and 1898; Woolhampton, nr. Reading, Berks. 1893; Wimborne, Dorset 1896; Pulborough, Sussex 1906. † D 1, G 6, L 2, M 2, NG 15, RA 7, RBA 2, ROI 7.

VERNER, Frederick Arthur* 1836-1928
Canadian landscape painter. London 1881-1909. † B 4, D 48, G 2, L 8, M 6, NG 1, RA 7, RBA 3, RHA 6, RI 2.

VERNER, Ida Exh. 1882-1921
Figure and portrait painter. Brighton 1882; London 1884; Hove, Brighton 1917. † G 2, LS 10, NG 1, P 2, RA 8, ROI 1.

VERNEY, John Exh. 1917-19
19 Stafford Road, Wolverton, Bucks. † LS 9.

VERNIER, Emile Louis* 1831-1887
French painter. Exh. 1882-85. Add: 6 Boulevard de Clichy, Paris. † GI 7.

VERNON, Arthur Longley*
Exh. 1880-1917
Figure and portrait painter. St. Johns Wood, London. † B 22, GI 10, L 10, M 7, NG 16, RA 18, RBA 2, RHA 1, ROI 12 TOO 2.

VERNON, Miss C. Exh. 1883
Brabant, Tulse Hill, Surrey. † L 1.

VERNON, Carl Exh. 1909
13 Ratcliffe Road, Sheffield. † RHA 1.

VERNON, Ellen Exh. 1882-1910
Livingstone Road, Birmingham. † B 39, RHA 1.

VERNON, Emile* Exh. 1904
Flower painter. 2 Upstall Street, Camberwell, London. † RA 1.

VERNON, Flo Exh. 1881-1904
The Laurels, Livingstone Road, Birmingham. † B 24, L 2, M 2, RHA 5.

VERNON, George Exh. 1912-27
Architect. London. † RA 2.

VERNON, J. Arthur Exh. 1888
Landscape painter. 16 Park Road, Forest Hill, London. † RA 1
VERNON, Miss M.J. Exh. 1889-1915
Landscape painter. 32 Cheniston Gardens, Kensington, London. † RID 37.
VERNON, Nora Exh. 1891-99
The Laurels, Livingstone Road, Birmingham. † B 9.
VERNON, R. Warren Exh. 1882-1908
Painter and etcher. Winchester 1882; London 1886; Dresden 1903; Ilfracombe, Devon 1905; Southend, Essex 1908. † B 11 D 1, GI 1, L 1, RA 1, RBA 11, RCA 11, RHA 1, RI 2, ROI 1.
VERNON, William H. 1820-1909
Landscape painter. Father of Mary Vernon Morgan q.v. Add: The Laurels, Livingstone Road, Birmingham. † B 105, L 2, RA 2, RBA 1, RHA 14, RSA 2.
VERPILLEUX, Emile Antoine 1888-1964
Portrait and landscape painter, illustrator and engraver. b. London. Studied Academie des Beaux Arts Antwerp. R.B.A. 1914. Add: London 1912; Hadlow Down, Sussex 1920; Danehill, Sussex 1929. † BA 7, CG 9, GOU 7, I 11, L 6, NEA 2, RA 4, RBA 8, RSA 1.
VERRALL, Frederick Exh. 1884
Painter. 2 Cheniston Gardens, London. † ROI 1.
VERRALL, Hugh Exh. 1938-40
Figure and landscape painter. London 1938; Lewes, Sussex 1940. † RA 2.
VERSCHOYLE, Arthur Exh. 1924
41 St. Anne's Road, Drumcondra, Ireland. † RHA 1.
VERSCHOYLE, Mrs. F. Exh. 1927-28
Thendara, Dundrum, Co. Dublin. † RHA 2.
VERSCHOYLE, Rev. G.J.T. Exh. 1919-28
Dundrum, Co. Dublin and Dublin. † RHA 7.
VERSCHOYLE, Miss Kathleen Exh. 1918-32
Portrait painter and sculptor. Dundrum, Co. Dublin and Dublin. † RHA 23.
VERSTRAETE, Theodore 1840-1907
Belgian artist. Exh. 1883-90. Add: 34 Court Rue du Venneau, Antwerp. † GI 1, M 1, RHA 4.
VERT, H. Exh. 1891
2 Queen Anne Villas, Hendon, London. † B 1, M 2.
VERVEER, Elchanon 1826-1900
Dutch artist. Exh. 1884-90. Add: The Hague, Holland. † L 1, M 2.
VERVLOET, Joseph M. Exh. 1889-91
Via del Prato, Florence. † D 8.
VER WEE, C. Exh. 1894
Brussels. † GI 1.
VESCI, de See D
VESEY-HOLT, J. Julia Exh. 1882-87
Landscape and flower painter. The Studio, 1 Phillimore Gardens, London. † D 1, L 1, M 3, RA 1, SWA 2.
VESPER, Deryck Exh. 1936
Watercolour landscape painter. 8 Westfield Road, Beckenham, Kent. † RA 1.
VESQUES, Mlle. Jeanne Exh. 1911
6 Rue des Coutures, St. Gervais, Paris. † L 3.
VETH, Jan 1864-1925
Dutch portrait painter. Exh. 1891. † P 1.
VETTORI, Ernest Exh. 1904
36 Claremont Road, Alexandra Park, Manchester. † L 1.
VEYRASSAT, Jules Jacques* 1828-1893
French artist. Exh. 1881-85. Add: Paris. † GI 3, RHA 1.

VEYRASSAT, Mme. S. Exh. 1913
Landscape painter. † ALP 3.
VEZELAY, Paule b. 1893
Marjorie Watson Williams. Painter, drypoint artist, etcher, wood engraver, lithographer and illustrator. Studied London and Paris. Member London Group 1922. Exh. 1918-35. Add: London and Paris. † I 3, LEF 25, M 1, NEA 2.
VEZIN, Frederick* Exh. 1884-85
Landscape painter. London. † G 1, L 3, M 3, RA 3, ROI 1.
VIALLS, Frederick Jos Exh. 1884-85
Watercolour landscape painter. 16 Carleton Road, Tufnell Park, London. † RI 2.
VIALLS, George Exh. 1889
Architect. 13 Grange Park, Ealing, London. † RA 1.
VIANELLO, Caesare Exh. 1891
St. Trovase Ford Nani 945, Venice. † RSA 1.
VIBERT, Pierre Eugene b. 1875
French artist. Exh. 1908. Add: 12 Rue Morere, Paris. † LS 5.
VICAJI, Dorothy E. Exh. 1915-30
Portrait painter. 17 Holly Mount, Hampstead, London. † BA 16, L 4, P 2, RA 12, RMS 1, SWA 1.
VICAJI, Rustom Exh. 1918-27
Watercolour landscape painter. 17 Holly Mount, Hampstead, London. † FIN 65, RA 1, RI 1.
VICARS, Miss G.A. Exh. 1893
Spring Grove, Isleworth, Middlesex. † SWA 1.
VICARY, Edith M. Exh. 1901-14
Mrs. F. Bulteel. A.S.W.A. 1906, S.W.A. 1910. Add: Chudleigh, Devon 1901; Newton Abbot, Devon 1902; Plymouth, Devon 1913. † D 8, L 1, RA 3, ROI 1, SWA 23.
VICARY, Miss M.M. Exh. 1902-9
Newton Abbot, Devon 1902; Sticklepath, Dartmoor, Devon 1909. † SWA 2.
VICKERS, Emilie Exh. 1899-1911
Dublin 1899; Crosby, nr. Liverpool 1902; London 1911. † L 2, LS 3, RHA 1.
VICKERS, Mrs. Hilda Exh. 1930-31
Landscape and flower painter. Ashwells, Tealing, Chelmsford, Essex. † RA 1, RHA 1.
VICKERS, Izme Exh. 1937-39
11 South Audley Street, London. † ROI 2.
VICKERS, Vincent Cartwright b. 1879
Pen and ink artist. Exh. 1926-31. Add: Royston, Herts. 1926. † AR 54, RA 1.
VICKERY, G.H. Exh. 1907-9
Watercolour painter. Harrowlands, Dorking, Surrey. † RA 3, RI 1.
VICTOR, A. Exh. 1909
Bridge, nr. Canterbury, Kent. † ROI 1.
VIDAL, Eugene* Exh. 1886-1907
Watercolour landscape and figure painter and pencil artist. London 1886; Paris 1896. † L 2, M 2, RA 3.
VIDAL, Vincent 1811-1887
French artist. Exh. 1886. Add: 26 Rue de Laval, Paris. † M 1.
VIDGEN-JENKS, J.C. Exh. 1921-31
Bearwood 1921; London 1923; Stourbridge 1929. † B 8.
VIDGEN-JENKS, Mrs. Lona Exh. 1929-30
17 Clifton Street, Stourbridge, Worcs. † B 2.
VIERGE, Daniel 1851-1904
Painter and etcher. Exh. 1904. Add: 19 Rue Gutemberg, Boulogne sur Seine, France. † I 5.

VIGERS, Allan F. Exh. 1894-1912
Architect. London. † NG 1, RA 8.
VIGERS, Miss E.M. Exh. 1913
Bromley, Kent. † SWA 2.
VIGERS, Frederick Exh. 1884-1904
Landscape and literary painter. Horsham, Sussex 1884; Walton on Thames, Surrey 1886; London 1896. † B 3, L 2, M 2, RA 9, RBA 1, ROI 1.
VIGERS, George Exh. 1881-90
Architect. 4 Frederick's Place, Old Jewry, London. † RA 7.
VIGERS, Margaret Exh. 1920
Etcher. Three Arts Club, 19a Marylebone Road, London. † RA 1.
VIGERS, Marjorie F. Exh. 1928-29
Sevenoaks, Kent. † SWA 3.
VIGNE, de See D
VIGNON, Claude* Exh. 1883
Mme. Rouvier. Sculptor. 152 Rue de la Tour, Passy, Paris. † RA 1.
VIGOR, Charles Exh. 1882-1917
Portrait and domestic painter. London. † B 5, G 4, L 16, M 12, RA 25, ROI 5.
VILENSKY, Mrs. E. Exh. 1922
36 Raymond Street, Dublin. † RHA 1.
VILLANDIERE, Mlle. Ernestine Exh. 1907-9
177 Avenue Gambetta, France. † L 3.
VILLE, de See D
VILLETE, C. Exh. 1914
Landscape painter. † ALP 3.
VILLETTEE, la See L
VILLIERS, E. Exh. 1933
22 Bryanston Street, London. † SWA 1.
VILLIERS, Frederick 1851-1922
Painter. War artist and correspondent with the "Graphic" and "Illustrated London News". Exh. 1882-86. Add: London. † M 2, RA 2, ROI 2.
VILLY, G.H. Exh. 1882-92
Manchester. † M 6.
VINALL, Ella Doreen Exh. 1930-40
Etcher, engraver, fabric printer and illustrator. Daughter of Joseph William Topham V. q.v. Studied Slade School 1924-27. Royal College of Art 1927-30 and Central School of Arts and Crafts, Bolt Court. Add: London. † L 1, RA 2, SWA 7.
VINALL, Joseph William Topham b. 1873
Landscape, figure, portrait, and architectural painter, teacher, writer and examiner. b. Liverpool. Studied Royal College of Art and City and Guilds of London Institution. Brother of Nehemiah R.R. and father of Ella Doreen V. q.v. Exh. 1908-40. Add: London. † AB 96, I 5, L 5, P 1, RA 6, RBA 1, RHA 8, RI 5, ROI 7, RSA 3, WG 94.
VINALL, Nehemiah Row Reeves b. 1879
Portrait painter and teacher. b. Liverpool. Studied Lambeth and Heatherleys. Brother of Joseph William Topham V. q.v. Exh. 1901-32. Add: Ilford, Essex. † L 2, RBA 1.
VINCENT, Arthur E. Exh. 1884-85
66 Chesterton Road, North Kensington, London. † RHA 2.
VINCENT, Miss A.W. Exh. 1906
10 Pembridge Crescent, Kensington, London. † RA 1.
VINCENT, Mrs. Charlotte J. Exh. 1907-8
Montrose, Heatherly Road, Camberley, Surrey. † L 4, M 3, RA 1.
VINCENT, Miss D. Exh. 1893-99
Flower painter. Addlestone, Surrey 1893; Clevedon, Somerset 1899. † L 1, RBA 1.
VINCENT, Miss E.M. Exh. 1889-1901
Landscape and figure painter. London. † B 1, L 1, M 1, RA 1, RI 3, SWA 8.

VINCENT, Henry Exh. 1881-97
Figure and domestic painter. London. † RA 6, RBA 4, ROI 1.
VINCENT, N. Exh. 1913
17 Annesley Road, Aigburth, Liverpool. † L 2.
VINCENT, Nancy Exh. 1927-36
Sculptor. London. † L 1, RA 2.
VINCENT, Spencer Exh. 1882-89
Watercolour landscape painter. R.I. 1882 (Hon. Retd. 1883). Add: 5 Upper Porchester Street, London. † D 4, FIN 1.
VINCOTTE, Thomas Jules b. 1850
Belgian sculptor. Exh. 1881-1923. Add: 101 Rue de la Consolation, Brussels. † RA 2, RSA 4.
VINCZE, Paul Exh. 1940
Sculptor. b. Hungary. Studied Budapest and Rome 1935-37. Add: London. † RA 2.
VINEA, Francesco* 1846-1904
Italian painter. Exh. 1881-83. Add: c/o Mr. Tolfrey, 40A Barclay Road, Fulham, London. † M 1, RA 2.
VINER, Edwin b. 1867
Landscape painter, designer and teacher. b. Birmingham. Studied Liverpool School of Art. Exh. 1895-1933. Add: Liverpool 1895; 38 Birkenhead Road, Hoylake, Cheshire 1910. † L 20, RCA 3.
VINER, Florence J. Exh. 1922-32
38 Birkenhead Road, Hoylake, Cheshire. † L 13, RCA 8.
VINER, Herbert Exh. 1906-27
Cradley Heath, Birmingham. † B 3.
VINING, J.N.R. Exh. 1907-11
89 Chancery Lane, London. † RA 4.
VINNICOMBE, J.E. Exh. 1912
19 Hamilton Road, Dudding Hill, Neasdon, London. † LS 3.
VINOELST, Emanuel Constant Exh. 1881-94
Sculptor London. † L 4, RA 7.
VINSON, Corisande Exh. 1903
Highcroft Hall, Swanley Junction, Kent. † B 2, SWA 2.
VINSON, Mrs. Mary Exh. 1907-12
Highcroft Hall, Swanley Junction, Kent. † M 1, SWA 3.
VINSON, Wilfrid Lawson Exh. 1925-40
Etcher and pen and wash artist. Melbury Avenue, Norwood Green, Southall, Middlesex. † RA 8, RHA 1, RSA 4.
VINTER, Frederick Armstrong Exh. 1880-1915
Portrait, genre and historical painter. Probably son of John Alfred V. q.v. Add: London. † B 4, D 1, M 2, RA 3, RBA 3, RI 1.
VINTER, Harriet Emily Exh. 1880-81
Still life and portrait painter. Probably daughter of John Alfred V. q.v. Add: 29 Monmouth Road, Bayswater, London. † RBA 1, RHA 2.
VINTER, John Alfred 1828-1905
Portrait, genre, literary and historical painter and portrait lithographer. Probably father of Frederick A. and Harriet Emily V. q.v. Add: London. † B 5, D 6, L 2, M 4, RA 8, RBA 2, RHA 2.
VINTRAUT, F.G. Exh. 1906
60 Avenue d'Orleans, Paris. † L 1.
VIPAN, Miss E.N. Exh. 1884-85
Flower painter. Brighton. † RBA 1, ROI 1.
VIRTUE, Ethel M. Exh. 1898-1921
London. † LS 11, NG 1, SWA 3.
VISMARA, E. Exh. 1910
39 Rue Dareau, Paris. † L 2.

VISSER, Cor. Exh. 1938
Landscape, coastal and portrait artist. † COO 95.
VISTED, Svein Exh. 1933
Kunstuernes Hus, Oslo. † RSA 2.
VITALINI, F. Exh. 1901
81 Via Vittoria, Rome. † I 1.
VITELLESCHI, Marchesa Exh. 1894
33 Chapel Street, London. † RSA 1.
VITOFSKI, Henry Exh. 1921-30
Manchester. † L 3, M 2, NEA 2.
VIVIAN, Burton Exh. 1895-1909
London 1895; Hersham on Thames 1896; Paris 1908. † L 2, LS 8.
VIVIAN, Mrs. Comley (Lizzie) 1846-c. 1934
nee Farquhar. Portrait and miniature painter. b. Warwick. R.M.S. 1900, H.R.M.S. 1927. Add: London. † L 9, NEA 1, NG 1, RA 22, RMS 35.
VIVIAN, Mrs. Charlotte A. Exh. 1909-10
c/o Allied Artists Association, 67 Chancery Lane, London. † LS 6.
VIVIAN, Harold Ernest Farquhar Exh. 1909-33
65 Park Road, Chiswick, London. † LS 3, ROI 1.
VIVIAN, Iris Exh. 1932-33
Etcher. 28 Grove Park Gardens, Chiswick, London. † RA 2.
VIVIAN, J. Exh. 1881-88
London 1881; Birmingham 1888. † B 4, L 1, M 2, RHA 7.
VIVIAN, Mrs. Norah Exh. 1937-38
62 Priory Road London. † RI 1, SWA 2.
VIZZOTTO, Guiseppe Exh. 1891-92
Watercolour painter. † DOW 93.
VLAMINCK, de See D
VLOORS, Emile b. 1871
Belgian artist. Exh. 1917-18. Add: 49 Roland Gardens, South Kensington, London. † P 1, RA 1.
VNILLEFROY, G. Exh. 1883
17 Rue St. Augustin, Paris. † GI 1.
VOELCKER, Miss M.E. Exh. 1914
Kensington, London. † SWA 2.
VOGEL, J. Exh. 1882
Harriet Steet, Stretford, Manchester. † M 1.
VOGEL, Karel Exh. 1940
Sculptor. 38 Redcliffe Road, London. † RA 1.
VOGT, C.W. Exh. 1910
577 West Derby Road, Liverpool. † L 2.
VOGTEN, Von See Von
VOIGT, Carel Exh. 1913
Brunswick House, Manchester Road, Southport, Lancs. † L 2.
VOKES, Arthur Ernest b. 1874
Portrait and landscape painter and sculptor. Studied Clifton and Royal College of Art. Exh. 1897-1937. Add: London 1897 and 1919; Northampton 1898. † G 4, GOU 41, I 4, L 12, M 3, P 6, RA 25, WG 13.
VOLCK, Fritz Exh. 1880-81
Watercolour figure painter. 83 Albert Street, Mornington Crescent, London. † D 2.
VOLLET, Henry Exh. 1909
4 Rue Aumont Thieville, Paris. † L 1.
VOLMAR, L. Exh. 1883
† GI 1.
VOLSCHENK, J.E.A. Exh. 1916
c/o High Commissioner for Union of South Africa, 32 Victoria Street London. † ROI 1.
VOLTI, Carl Exh. 1889
77 South Portland Street, Glasgow. † GI 1.

VOLTZ, Professor Freidrich* Exh. 1882
Landscape and cattle painter. Munich. † RSA 1.
VON ANGELI, Heinrich Exh. 1880
Portrait painter. Imperial Kunst Academie, Vienna and Austrian Embassy, Belgrave Square, London. † RA 1.
VON BARTELS, Professor Hans* 1856-1913
German marine painter. H.R.I. 1896, H.R.S.W. 1907. Add: Munich. † GI 9, I 12, L 13, RI 7, RSA 1, RSW 2.
VON BARTELS, Fraulein Wera Exh. 1913
39 Pettenkoferstrasse, Munich. † L 2.
VON BEKERATH, Helene Exh. 1904
65 Boulevard Arago, Paris. † L 1.
VON BERG, Alice Exh. 1883-1921
Landscape painter and aquatinter. Wells, Somerset 1883; Blackheath, London 1892. † B 5, L 4, RA 3, RID 68.
VON BEYERSDORFF, Mathilde Exh. 1907
c/o American Consulate, Florence. † L 2.
VON BORWITZ, Miss R.E. Exh. 1891-92
Landscape painter. Kensington, London. † RA 1, RBA 1.
VON BREUNING, Constanza Exh. 1910
111 Hengasse furst Schwar, Zenberg Garten, Vienna. † L 1.
VON CRAMM, Baroness Helga Exh. 1880-1901
Landscape and flower painter. London 1880; Florence 1885; c/o P. Denniston, Glasgow 1892. † D 2, FIN 1, G 1, GI 1, RI 1, RSA 2, SWA 16.
VON DACKENHAUSEN, Baron Exh. 1932
† RMS 1.
VON EICKEN, Elizabeth Exh. 1896-97
Landscape painter. Berlin 1896; Mecklenburg, Germany 1897. † L 1, RA 1.
VON ELES, Ugo Exh. 1895-98
5 Vigo Street, London. † GI 4.
VON FLOTOW, Baroness Matilde Exh. 1901-9
London. † I 2, L 2, LS 3 NG 1.
VON GEBHARDT, Edouard Exh. 1906-8
c/o E. Schulte, 25 Unter den Linden, Berlin. † I 1, L 1.
VON GLEHN, Jane E. See De GLEHN
VON GLEHN, Oswald Exh. 1880-1908
Painter. London 1880; Betchworth 1901. † NG 21, RA 1.
VON GLEHN, Wilfred Gabriel See De GLEHN
VON GOLDSTEIN, W.B. Exh. 1911-13
Landscape, river, coastal and flower painter. London. † BG 50, RA 3.
VON HERZER, Edith Exh. 1895
Merkurst 5, Baden-Baden, Germany. † M 1.
VON HEYDEN, August 1827-1897
German artist. Exh. 1881. Add: Lutzowplatz 13, Berlin. † RE 1.
VON HEYDEN, Hubert Exh. 1898-99
4 Amalienstrasse, Munich. † GI 3.
VON HOFMANN, Ludwig b. 1861
German pencil artist. Exh. 1906. † CAR 29.
VON KAHLE, Anna Exh. 1885-90
Berlin. † RHA 3.
VON KEMPTZ, F. Exh. 1909-14
Portrait painter. Brighton 1909; Bristol 1911; Hove, Sussex 1913. † I 1, LS 3, RA 4.
VON KLEUDGEN, Baron F. Exh. 1904
Province Porto Maurizio, Italy. † D 5.
VON KUMMER, Miss Exh. 1887
Laurel Bank, Partick. † GI 2.
VON LEEMPUTTEN, Franz* 1850-1914
Belgian painter. Exh. 1893-94. Add: 5 Rue Venus, Antwerp. † L 2.

VON LEMBACH, Professor Franz Ritter 1836-1904
German portrait painter. † P 18, RSA 1.

VON MARIENTREU, Richard Exh. 1938
† P 1.

VON MECKEL, Adolf Exh. 1890
4 Bismarck Strasse, Carlsrhue, Baden, Germany. † GI 1.

VON NATHUSIUS, Mme. Susanne Exh. 1885
Portrait painter. 1 Konisborn, Magdeburg. † G 1.

VONNER, Mme. A.B.N. Exh. 1892
Watercolour portrait painter. 132 Sloane Street, London. † RA 1.

VONNOH, Robert 1857-1933
American portrait painter. Exh. 1908. Add: c/o M.P. Navez, 76 Rue Blanche, Paris. † L 1.

VON PREUSCHEN, Baroness Hermine Exh. 1885
Still life painter. † RA 1.

VON PRITZELWITZ, Mme. S. Exh. 1883-87
Figure and portrait painter. Wilhemstrasse 72, Berlin. † L 1, SWA 2.

VON RAVINCOURT, Mme. J. Exh. 1882
6 Freisinger Gasse, Vienna. † GI 1.

VON REICHENBACH, Count Waldemar Exh. 1881
Painter. Weimar and 39 South Lambeth Road, London. † RA 1.

VON RENESSE, Mrs. M. Exh. 1898-99
3 Peveril Drive, The Park, Nottingham. † N 5.

VON RYSWYCH, Edward Exh. 1908
c/o Mr. Kelk, Sunnybank, Banbury, Oxon. † L 1.

VON SOBBE, Dorothy A. Exh. 1930-33
Woodcroft, Gateacre, Liverpool. † L 5.

VON STARKENBURGH, J.N.T. Exh. 1880
20 Schutzen Strasse, Dusseldorf. † RHA 1.

VON STETTEN, C. Exh. 1895
73 Boulevard Bineau, Paris. † P 1.

VON STRYDONCK, M.V. Exh. 1909
† LS 3.

VON STURMER, Frances Exh. 1880-81
Landscape, figure and interior painter. London. † RHA 1, SWA 2.

VON VOGTEN, M. Exh. 1894
Gorlitz. † GI 1.

VON WEBER, Ada Exh. 1880
Watercolour architectural painter. 54 Park End, Sydenham, Kent. † RBA 1.

VON WERNER, Miss H. Exh. 1901
6 The Terrace, Champion Hill, London. † SWA 1.

VON WILLEWALD, Professor C. Exh. 1885
† GI 1.

VON WILLEWALD, M. junr. Exh. 1885
St. Petersburg. † GI 1.

VOORT, van der See Van

VOS, Hubert b. 1855
Portrait, genre and landscape painter. b. Maastricht. Studied Brussels, Paris and Rome. N.E.A. 1888, R.B.A. 1889, R.P. 1891. Exh. 1888-92. Add: London. Moved to America. † G 2, GI 3, L 2, NEA 3, NG 1, P 9, RA 6, RBA 19, RI 1, ROI 2.

VOSPER, Sydney Curnow 1866-1942
Watercolour painter, etcher and drypoint artist. b. Plymouth. Studied Colarossi's, Paris. A.R.W.S. 1906, R.W.S. 1914. Add: Plymouth, Devon 1896; Morbihan, France 1904; London 1905 and 1930; Okehampton, Devon 1910; Petersfield, Hants. 1911 and 1926; Bude, Cornwall 1914; Plymouth 1925; Oxford 1928. † B 2, CHE 1, L 11, M 20, RA 7, RI 6, RSW 2, RWS 116, WG 6.

VOSS, C.J. Exh. 1910
15 Hagden Lane, Watford, Herts. † RI 1.

VOYSEY, Charles Cowles b. 1889
Architect. Son of Charles F.A.V. q.v. Studied University College London. Exh. 1921-39. Add: London. † RA 24, RSA 1.

VOYSEY, Charles F.A. 1857-1940
Architect, sculptor and designer. Father of Charles Cowles V. q.v. Add: London. † GI 7, RA 22.

VOYSEY, Victor H. Exh. 1929-33
Flower, landscape and portrait painter. Twickenham, Middlesex 1929; Emsworth, Hants. 1932. † NEA 1, RA 4, ROI 2.

VRIES, de See D

VROLYK, Jan Exh. 1886
117 New Bond Street, London. † M 2.

VRY, E. Exh. 1893
Munich. † GI 1.

VUAGNAT, Exh. 1885
† GI 1.

VUILLARD, Edouard* 1868-1940
French painter and lithographer. † I 2, RED 21, RSA 6.

VUILLEFROY, G. Exh. 1884-85
17 Rue St. Augustin, Paris. † GI 2.

VULLIAMY, Anna Maria Exh. 1884
Painter. South Bank, Ipswich, Suffolk. † SWA 1.

VULLIAMY, Miss B.G. Exh. 1898
296 Carlisle Studios, Kings Road, Chelsea, London. † RI 1.

VULLIAMY, Edward Exh. 1913-40
Watercolour pastoral, landscape and marine painter. Cambridge. † BA 2, CHE 4, COO 2, FIN 4, GOU 7, LS 6, NEA 31, WG 153.

VULLIAMY, Wendy Exh. 1936
† NEA 1.

VYBOND, J. Exh. 1908
c/o Frost and Reed, 8 Clare Street, Bristol. † RA 1.

VYCHAN, J.L. Exh. 1886
29 Bolsover Street, London. † B 1.

VYSE, Charles Exh. 1911-27
Sculptor. London. † L 3, RA 28.

VYVYAN, Cristina Exh. 1929-30
Flower and figure painter. Hampstead, London. † AB 2, SWA 3.

VYVYAN, Miss D.M. Exh. 1921-32
Watercolour landscape painter. c/o Bourlet and Sons, 17 Nassau Street, London. † RA 3.

VYVYAN, Mary Caroline Exh. 1881-94
Watercolour painter. London. † D 7, L 3, M 1, RBA 3, RI 2, SWA 5.

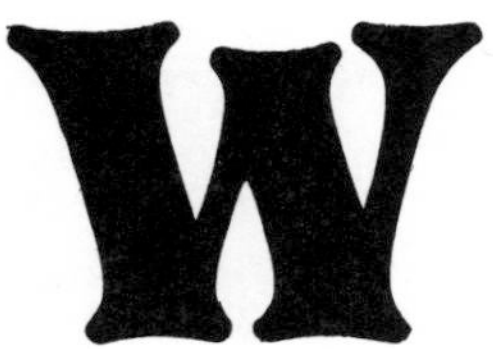

WAALS, P. Exh. 1930
Chalford, Glos. † B 4.
WAAY, van der see V
WACE, Miss J. Exh. 1929
Domestic painter. 44 Addison Avenue, London. † RA 1.
WADDELL, Alex T. Exh. 1926
† M 1.
WADDELL, D. Henderson Exh. 1882
Watercolour landscape painter. 14 Percy Circus, Kings Cross, London. † RA 1.
WADDELL, J.H. Exh. 1886
112 Bath Street, Glasgow. † GI 1.
WADDELL, William Exh. 1880-96
Edinburgh. † GI 2, RSA 22.
WADDILOVE, Agnes M. Exh. 1902-34
Miniature portrait painter. Dormans, Parkstone, Dorset † RA 13.
WADDINGTON, Miss E. Exh. 1926
Collaborated with Jessie McCrossan, q.v. Add: The Craft Room, West Mersea, Mersea Island, Essex. † L 7.
WADDINGTON, Frank Exh. 1927-32
Feniscowles, nr. Blackburn, Lancs. † L 7, RSA 1.
WADDINGTON, Georgina Exh. 1892-98
Landscape and coastal painter. Trafalgar Studios, Chelsea, London. † FIN 2, ROI 1.
WADDINGTON, Maud Exh. 1884-89
Landscape painter. Bagdale, Whitby. † B 6, L 4, M 5, RI 1.
WADDINGTON, Norah Exh. 1931-33
Still life painter. Arnwood, Alcester Road, Stratford on Avon, Warwicks. † B 1, RA 1.
WADDINGTON, Vera b. 1886
Landscape and portrait painter and wood engraver. b. Wiltshire. Studied Slade School. Exh. 1906-40. Add: London 1906 and 1923; Pangbourne, Berks. 1921; Gerrards Cross, Bucks. 1926. † ALP 1, CAR 42, GI 1, GOU 55, M 1, NEA 43, RA 5, RED 2, SWA 1.
WADDINGTON, William H. Exh. 1907-38
Bradford, Yorks. 1907; Windermere, Westmoreland 1936. † NEA 11, RA 1, RSA 2.
WADE, A.C. Exh. 1911
40 Carlyle Road, Manor Park, London. † RA 1.
WADE, Albert Edward Exh. 1911-38
Portrait painter, miniaturist and teacher. Studied Birmingham. A.R.M.S. 1917. Add: Birmingham 1911; London 1917; Dover 1919; School of Art, Sheffield 1921; School of Art, Grimsby 1925. † B 4, L 5, RA 3, RMS 20.
WADE, Arthur Edward b. 1895
Painter. Exh. 1935-37. Add: Cardiff. † RCA 3.
WADE, Charles Exh. 1917-25
Architect. 41 Upton Avenue, Forest Gate, London. † RA 2.
WADE, Doris M. Exh. 1935-38
Portrait and landscape painter. Ruddington, Notts. † N 7.
WADE, Edward Exh. 1882-83
36 Fishergate, Preston, Lancs. † L 1, M 1.
WADE, Fairfax Blomfield Exh. 1889-95
Architect. 2 Princes Mansions, Victoria Street, Westminster, London. † RA 6.
WADE, Gwen Exh. 1937-38
† NEA 2.
WADE, George E. d. 1933
Sculptor. Self taught. Exh. from 1888. Add: London. † G 4, GI 2, L 9, M 3, NG 6, RA 17.
WADE, Miss K. Exh. 1901-17
30 Schubert Road, Putney, London. † SWA 3.
WADE, Mrs. L.M. Exh. 1907-16
London. † L 1, RA 8.
WADE, Mona Exh. 1929
c/o Mr. Best, 67 Upper Leeston Street, Dublin. † RHA 1.
WADE, Percy W. Exh. 1889-99
Landscape painter. Beeston, Notts. 1889; Lenton, Notts. 1899. † N 8.
WADE, R.R. Exh. 1913-14
10 Norton Road, Hove, Sussex. † LS 6.
WADE, Mrs. T. Exh. 1884
Hill Cottage, Windermere. † M 2.
WADE, Thomas 1829-1891
Landscape and rustic genre painter. Self taught. "An Old Mill" purchased by Chantrey Bequest 1879. Add: Hill Cottage, Windermere, 1880 and 1889; Kendal 1886. † L 6, M 11, RA 13.
WADE, Winifred Exh. 1920-37
Still life, flower and landscape painter. Nottingham 1920; West Bridgford, Notts. 1937. † N 31.
WADE-BROWN, E. Exh. 1927-28
Landscape and coastal painter. † AB 8.
WADELY, Zoe M. Exh. 1908-24
Edgbaston, Birmingham. † B 4.
WADEY, Margorie M. Exh. 1931-34
162 Broad Street, Birmingham. † B 4.
WADHAM, B.B. Exh. 1882-98
Landscape painter. Arthog, Wales 1882; Liverpool 1886; Llangollen 1889; Chester 1892. † L 25, RA 1.
WADHAM, Millicent Exh. 1908-19
Sculptor. London. † B 2, GI 1, L 2, RA 6, RMS 1, RSA 1.
WADHAM, M.A. Exh. 1882
1 Vane Street, Bath. † RHA 2.
WADHAM, Percy Exh. 1893-1905
Landscape painter and pen and ink artist. b. Adelaide, Australia. Studied under T.S. Cooper and James Chapman. A.R.E. 1902 (ceased 1910). Add: Windsor, Berks. † FIN 6, RA 4, RE 9.
WADHAM, Sarah Exh. 1880-81
Watercolour portrait painter. 30 Hungerford Road, Notting Hill, London. † GI 1, RBA 2, RHA 2.
WADHAM, W. Joseph* Exh. 1882-1917
Arthog, Wales 1882; Chester 1896; London 1902. † L 4, RA 1, RI 5.
WADHAM-EVANS, Miss F. Exh. 1923-24
53 Fairfax Road, Hampstead, London. † SWA 2.
WADSON, H. Exh. 1884
43 Poland Street, Oxford Street, London. † D 1.
WADSWORTH, Mrs. Exh. 1881-88
Landscape and coastal painter. Nottingham. † N 15.
WADSWORTH, Edward* 1889-1949
Landscape, marine and portrait painter and engraver. b. Cleckheaton, Yorks. Studied Munich 1906-7, Bradford School of Art 1910, Slade School 1910-12 (1st prize for figure painting 1911). Travelled on the continent. N.E.A. 1921, A.R.A 1943. Founder member London Group 1913. "Seaport" (1023) purchased by Chantrey Bequest 1962 and "Deux et Comes 1" (1932) purchased 1969. Add: London. † LEF 10, LEI 94, LS 5, M 1, NEA 4, RED 2, RSA 2, TOO 19.
WADSWORTH, Gertrude Exh. 1898-1903
Jeweller. Nottingham. † N 17.
WADSWORTH, Mrs. W. Exh. 1881
Flower painter. Park Valley, Nottingham. † N 1.
WAEYENBERGE, Van see V
WAGEMANS, Maurice* 1877-1927
Belgian painter. Exh. 1908-18. Add: Brussels, 1908; 10 Jubilee Place, Chelsea, London 1917. † LS 4, NEA 3.
WAGER, Rhoda Exh. 1912
7 West Regent Street, Glasgow. † L 8.
WAGER, William Exh. 1929-36
Painter. Grindleford, nr. Sheffield. † L 2, RA 2.
WAGHORN, Frederick Exh. 1880-98
Landscape painter. London. † RA 3, RBA 1, RI 3.
WAGHORN, Tom 1900-1959
Watercolour landscape painter. Studied Battersea School of Art and Chelsea School of Art. Exh. 1938. Add: Richmond, Surrey. † RA 1.
WAGNER, A. Exh. 1883
Painter. 190 Strand, London. † FIN 1, M 1.
WAGNER, C. Exh. 1910
Kaiserwerth, Rheinland, Germany. † RA 1.
WAGNER, E. Exh. 1888
c/o W. Croft, Esq. 12 Shepherds Bush Road, London. † D 8.
WAGNER, Mrs. Sophie Exh. 1921-36
Still life painter. c/o Charles West, 117 Finchley Road, London. † RA 1, SWA 3.
WAGSTAFF, Constance Exh. 1914
Watercolour painter. † WG 32.
WAGSTAFF, Miss H. Exh. 1920-29
A.S.W.A. 1922. Add: 1 The Square, Petersfield, Hants. † L 8, SWA 1.
WAGSTAFF, M. Exh. 1931
Haslemere, Surrey. † GI 1.
WAGSTAFF, William Exh. 1931
Sculptor. c/o D. Wagstaff, 9 Edith Grove, Chelsea, London. † RA 1.
WAGSTAFF, W.W. Exh. 1910
209 Rutland Street, Hampstead Road, London. † RA 1.
WAHLBERG, Alfred* 1834-1906
Swedish landscape painter. Exh. 1884. † GI 1.
WAIDMANN, P. Exh. 1910-11
103 Avenue de Neuilly, Neuilly sur Seine, France. † GI 1, L 1.
WAIN, Louis* 1860-1939
Painter. Exh. 1889. Add: 3 New Cavendish Street, London. † RBA 1.
WAINEWRIGHT, Thomas Francis* Exh. 1880-99
Landscape painter. Collaborated with Cornelius Pearson q.v. R.B.A. 1852. Add: London. † RBA 22, TOO 2.
WAINWRIGHT, Albert Exh. 1921-24
Monk Fryston, South Milford, Yorks. † GOU 23, L 1.
WAINWRIGHT, Beatrice Exh. 1908-40
Mrs. Roberts. Painter and miniaturist. b. Leicester. Studied Leicester School of Art and Heatherleys. A.S.W.A. 1928, S.W.A. 1933. Add: London. † L 30, RA 17, RMS 10, RSA 1.
WAINWRIGHT, W.E. Exh. 1933-34
Printmash, Priory, Glos. † B 2.

WAINWRIGHT, William John* 1855-1931
Portrait, still life and genre painter, watercolourist and stained glass artist. b. Birmingham. Studied Birmingham School of Art, Antwerp Academy and Colarossi's, Paris. Examiner Birmingham School of Arts and Crafts. R.B.S.A. 1884, P.R.B.S.A., A.R.W.S. 1883, R.W.S. 1905. Add: Paris 1882; London 1884; Birmingham 1888. † B 61, L 4, M 2, RA 1, RBA 2, RCA 1, RWS 67.

WAITCLARK, J. Exh. 1900-5
5 Wake Terrace, Westoe Road, South Shields. † B 1, L 6, RI 3.

WAITE, Alexander Exh. 1930
Watercolour landscape and marine painter. † AR 73.

WAITE, Anita Exh. 1909-24
Painter. A.N.S.A. 1909. Add: Grove House, Peel Street, Nottingham. † N 33.

WAITE, Arthur Exh. 1899
14 Lee Park, Blackheath, London. † RBA 1.

WAITE, Alexander Edward Exh. 1921-25
Etcher. 49 Purley Oaks Road, Sanderstead, Surrey. † CHE 1, RA 1.

WAITE, Charles D. Exh. 1882
Watercolour coastal painter. 4 Westbourne Terrace, Addiscombe, Surrey. † RBA 1.

WAITE, Edward Wilkins* Exh. 1880-1920
Landscape painter. R.B.A. 1893. Add: Blackheath, London 1880 and 1886; Reigate, Surrey 1885; Abinger Hammer, Dorking, Surrey 1892; Guildford 1907; Woolhampton, Berks. 1913; Haselmere, Surrey 1916 and 1920; Fittleworth, Sussex 1919. † B 43, GI 16, L 49, M 18, NG 30, RA 46, RBA 40, RCA 2, RHA 3, ROI 60, RSA 2.

WAITE, Harold Exh. 1893-1939
Landscape painter. Studied R.A. Schools (Creswick prize and Turner gold medal). A.R.B.A. 1924. Add: Blackheath 1893; Bayswater, London 1904; Westgate on Sea, Thanet 1906; Sturry, nr. Canterbury, Kent 1913. † B 4, L 6, M 1, NG 1, RA 18, RBA 93, RI 7, ROI 7.

WAITE, James Clarke* Exh. 1880-85
Genre painter. R.B.A. 1873. Add: 9 Camden Studios, Camden Street, London. † B 2, GI 4, L 4, M 6, RA 4, RBA 49, RHA 1, RI 1, ROI 2.

WAITE, Mrs. Lucretia C. Exh. 1927
Sculptor. Hirondelle, Beech, Alton, Hants. † RA 1.

WAITE, Robert Thorne* 1842-1935
Watercolour landscape and figure painter. b. Cheltenham. Studied South Kensington. R.O.I. 1883, A.R.W.S. 1876, R.W.S. 1884. Add: London 1880; Bournemouth 1914. † AG 15, DOW 154, FIN 71, G 1, L 17, LEI 70, M 17, NG 24, RA 22, RI 3, ROI 27, RWS 496, TOO 9, WG 15.

WAITE, William A. Exh. 1882-97
Landscape and figure painter. Birmingham. † B 24, RI 6.

WAITHMAN, L. Exh. 1897
The Croft, Gomshall, Guildford, Surrey. † GI 1.

WAKE, Margaret Exh. 1893-1903
Still life and portrait painter. London. † RA 1, ROI 3, SWA 3.

WAKE, Reginald Exh. 1926-32
Bridgnorthm Salop. † B 11.

WAKEFIELD, Ethel Exh. 1906-8
Farnagh, Moate 1906; Athboy, Ireland 1907. † RHA 3.

WAKEFIELD, H. Exh. 1923-29
Landscape painter. A.N.S.A. 1925-29. Add: 14 Wellington Square, Nottingham. † N 22.

WAKEFIELD, Miss L. Exh. 1916-21
Hazlewood, Mole Road, Maidstone, Kent. † RA 2.

WAKEFIELD, Leonard Exh. 1912
14 Oakdale Road, Waterloo, Liverpool. † L 1.

WAKEFIELD, Wilfred Robert b. 1885
Watercolour painter and etcher. b. Zanzibar. Studied Liverpool City School of Art. Exh. 1915-33. Add: Waterloo, Liverpool 1915; Gt. Crosby, 1927. † L 22.

WAKEFORD, Mildred N. Exh. 1907-12
Holly Bank, Allerton, Liverpool. † L 2.

WAKEMAN, Mrs. Doris L. Exh. 1929
Watercolour painter. c/o Mrs. R.M. Dixon, Crecy, Redbourn, Herts. † RA 1.

WAKEMAN, Gerald Exh. 1893-1928
Painter. Dublin 1893; London 1928. † RA 1, RHA 51.

WAKLEY, Archibald* Exh. 1902-6
Painter. 76A Monmouth Road, Westbourne Grove, London. † L 1, RA 4.

WAKLEY, Horace M. Exh. 1900-4
Architect. Albion Chambers, 11 Adam Street, London. † RA 3.

WALBANK, A.L. Exh. 1910
20 St. Ann's Terrace, Barnes, London. † RI 1.

WALBOURN, Ernest* Exh. 1895-1920
Landscape painter. Chingford, Essex 1895; Theydon Bois, Essex 1911. † B 12, GI 5, L 6, M 1, RA 9, RBA 1, ROI 9.

WALCOT, William* b. 1874
Watercolour painter, pencil artist and etcher. b. Russia. Studied Paris and Imperial Academy of Art, Petrograd. Visited U.S.A. R.B.A. 1914, A.R.E. 1918, R.E. 1920. Exh. 1908-40. Add: London and Oxford. † BA 182, CHE 5, CON 68, FIN 319, GI 23, L 20, M 2, RA 40, RBA 25, RE 17, RHA 2, RSA 5, RSW 3, WG 3.

WALDEN, de see D

WALDEN, Lionel Exh. 1897-1909
Figure painter. Flushing, nr. Falmouth, 1897; Paris 1908. † LS 5, RA 1.

WALDEN, Margaret F. Exh. 1918-36
Landscape painter. † COO 1, I 4.

WALDMANN, O. Exh. 1898-1913
Paris. † I 1, L 8, RA 5.

WALDMEYER, Agnes A. see LINDAY

WALDRON, Blanche Exh. 1909-11
Collaborated with Alice Lisle q.v. Add: 74 Above Bar, Southampton. † L 58.

WALDRON, Herbert Exh. 1937-38
Watercolour painter. † WG 5.

WALDRON, Isabel M. Exh. 1908-10
Hythe, Southampton 1908; London 1909. † B 3, L 6.

WALDRON, Mary Joan Exh. 1936-38
147 Hartwood Road, London. † SWA 3.

WALE, Joyce I. b. 1900
Mrs. Barton. Portrait, landscape and figure painter. b. Hockley Heath, Warwicks. Studied Birmingham School of Art and Slade School. Exh. 1925-26. Add: The Pound House, Lapworth, Warwicks. † B 3.

WALE, John P. Exh. 1894-1919
Flower painter. Derby. † B 14, N 19, RI 3.

WALE, P. Exh. 1924
Interior painter. 18 Rothesay Avenue, Nottingham. † N 1.

WALENN, Frederick Dudley Exh. 1894-1930
Portrait and child painter. Studied British Museum, R.A. Schools and Juliens, Paris. Principal St. Johns Wood School of Art from 1907. Add: London. † L 8, RA 24, RHA 1, RI 1, ROI 6.

WALES, Douglas b. 1888
Portrait painter. Exh. 1929-40. Add: Lymington, Hants. 1929; London 1939. † L 2, P 2, RA 1, RI 7, ROI 1, RSA 2.

WALEY, Hubert Exh. 1914-17
Painter and lithographer. 13 Hanover Terrace, Ladbroke Road, London. † I 8, NEA 4.

WALEY, Roda R. Exh. 1915
Painter. 14 Dawson Place, London. † NEA 1.

WALFORD, Miss A.C. Exh. 1928-30
86 Eaton Place, London. † SWA 4.

WALFORD, Amy J. Exh. 1883-90
Watercolour landscape painter and teacher. Bushey, Herts. † B 2, FIN 2, RBA 1, RI 3.

WALFORD, Miss A.P. Exh. 1905-15
Landscape painter. 9 Belsize Crescent, South Hampstead, London. † L 5, LS 3, RA 9.

WALFORD, Bettine Christian b. 1905
Mrs. Woodcock. Watercolour painter. Studied Chelsea Polytechnic and under W.T. Wood and John McNab. Exh. 1928-39. Add: London. † GOU 10, L 3, NEA 2, RA 3, RBA 7, RI 1.

WALFORD, H. Louisa Exh. 1891-1904
Flower painter. Bushey, Herts. 1891; Bromsgrove, Worcs. 1904. † RA 2, RI 1.

WALFORD, Miss M.E. Exh. 1914-19
London. † SWA 5.

WALFORD, P.J. Exh. 1923
† D 2.

WALGATE, Mrs. Marion Exh. 1913-32
Sculptor. Studied Gray's School of Art, Aberdeen and Royal College of Art. Add: London 1913; Cape Town, South Africa 1932. † RA 4.

WALHAIN, Charles H.* Exh. 1906-7
50 Rue Perronet, Neuilly sur Seine, France. † L 3.

WALKE, Ann Fearon Exh. 1909-40
nee Fearon. Portrait and figure painter. Studied Chelsea School of Art. London School of Art and under Augustus John, Sir W. Orpen and Sir William Nicholson. Add: London 1909; Polruan, nr. Fowey, Cornwall 1911; St. Hilary, nr. Marazion, Cornwall 1913. † G 3, GOU 3, I 7, L 2, LS 3, NEA 1, P 2, RA 1, ROI 3, SWA 3.

WALKER, A. Exh. 1888
149 Firpark Street, Dennistoun, N.B. † GI 1.

WALKER, Agatha Exh. 1911-39
Sculptor and pottery figure artist. Hoyland, Barnsley 1911; Thame, Oxon 1925; Wimborne, Dorest 1936. † L 4 LS 10, RA 3, RMS 4, RSA 2.

WALKER, Mrs. Aileen b. 1901
nee Holleby. Painter. Studied Byam Shaw and Vicat Cole School of Art. Married Leonard W. q.v. Exh. 1924-36. Add: King Henry's Road, London. † ROI 4.

WALKER, Alexander Exh. 1894-1933
Watercolour painter and etcher. Glasgow 1894; Chislehurst, Kent 1916; Saffron Walden, Essex 1924. † BA 4, GI 20, I 1, M 1, NEA 2, RA 4, RSA 4, RSW 3.

WALKER, Alice Exh. 1893
47 Mount Preston, Leeds. † B 1.

WALKER, Amy Exh. 1885-96
Landscape, flower and domestic painter. London. † L 3, RBA 5, RHA 1, RI 8, ROI 2.

WALKER, Agnes E. Exh. 1887-1900
Figure and portrait painter. London. † L 1, P 2, RA 8, RBA 6, ROI 2.

WALKER, Arthur E. Exh. 1936
Watercolour landscape painter. 138 Stanbeck Lane, Chapel Allerton, Leeds. † RA 1.

WALKER, Arthur George 1861-1939
Painter, sculptor, illuminator and mosaic designer. Studied R.A. Schools and Paris. A.R.A. 1925, R.A. 1936. "Christ at the Whipping Post" purchased by Chantrey Bequest 1925. Add: London 1884; Parkstone, Dorset 1934. † GI 8, I 4, L 20, RA 84, RI 1, RMS 3, ROI 1, RSA 8.

WALKER, Ada Hill Exh. 1927-40
Landscape and portrait painter. b. St. Andrews, Fife. Studied under Mrs. Jopling in London; Glasgow School of Art, and Paris. Add: Dauphin East, St. Andrews, Fife. † RSA 2, RSW 8.

WALKER, Brida Exh. 1889
Painter. 17 Keith Grove, Shepherds Bush, London. † D 1.

WALKER, Miss B.B. Exh. 1883
Mossy Bank, Egremont, Liverpool. † L 1.

WALKER, Bond D. Exh. 1924-25
Belfast. † RHA 5.

WALKER, Bernard Eyre b. 1886
Watercolour painter and etcher. b. Harlow, Essex. Son of William Eyre W. q.v. A.R.E. 1912. Exh. 1909-40. Add: West Byfleet, Surrey 1909; Icomb, nr. Stow on the Wold, Glos. 1922; Boston, Lincs. 1925; Hawkeshead, Ambleside 1927. † AB 1, AR 2, B 10, CON 36, COO 2, GI 1, L 36, M 16, RA 7, RCA 2, RE 58, RSA 5.

WALKER, Bernard Fleetwood b. 1892
Portrait and figure painter, craftworker and modeller. b. Birmingham. Studied Birmingham School of Art, London and Paris. Painting master Aston School of Art and Art Master King Edward Grammar School, Birmingham. R.B.S.A. 1931, R.O.I. 1933. Exh. 1920-40. Add: Birmingham 1920 and 1925; Sutton Coldfield 1922. † B 53, GI 1, L 3, M 2, P 7, RA 20, RHA 5, ROI 12, RWS 53.

WALKER, B.W. Exh. 1887-1914
Watercolour painter. Bayswater, London. † D 14, RI 2.

WALKER, C. Exh. 1929
† D 1.

WALKER, Miss C. Exh. 1884
90 Charlotte Street, Fitzroy Square, London. † M 1, RHA 1.

WALKER, Claude b. 1862
Painter and picture restorer. b. Cheltenham. Studied South Kensington Museum. Exh. 1904-20. Add: London 1904 and 1911; Bushey, Herts. 1910. † L 4, LS 1, RA 3, RI 1, ROI 1.

WALKER, Dr. Cranston Exh. 1931-37
61 Newhall Street, Birmingham. † B 5.

WALKER, Cyril Exh. 1940
† NEA 1.

WALKER, Miss C.A. Exh. 1896-1907
Liverpool. † L 23.

WALKER, Miss C.M. Exh. 1914
Chichester, Sussex. † SWA 1.

WALKER, Constance M. Exh. 1892-96
Painter. 3 Baldry Gardens, Streatham Common. London. † RID 5.

WALKER, C.R. Exh. 1931-33
Sculptor. Bulwell Hall Estate, Notts. 1931; Mansfield, Notts. 1932. † N 3.

WALKER, D. Exh. 1882-92
Stretford, Lancs. 1882 and 1887; Liverpool 1884; Sale, Manchester 1890. † L 10, M 8.

WALKER, Dorothy Exh. 1933-37
Sutton Coldfield 1933; Erdington 1937. † B 3.

WALKER, Dougald Exh. 1929
11 Pitcullen Terrace, Perth. † RSA 1.

WALKER, Dorothy E. Exh. 1906-10
Woodberry, Sydenham Hill, London. † B 1, SWA 3.

WALKER, E. Exh. 1887-91
Glasgow. † GI 1, L 1, RI 1.

WALKER, E. Exh. 1889
Tenterfield House, Putney Hill, London. † L 1.

WALKER, Edward* b. 1879
Landscape painter, poster designer, etcher black and white artist, craftworker and designer. b. Bradford. Studied Bradford College of Art 1895-1900, Royal College of Art 1900-6. Travelled on the continent and North Africa. Head of Design Department Sheffield Technical School of Art 1906-8, Head of Art Department L.C.C. Paddington Technical Institute 1908-11, Director of Art Cheltenham Ladies College 1911-20, Headmaster Scarborough School of Art from 1921. † B 3, GI 1, L 11, RA 28, RBA 6, RCA 1, RI 1.

WALKER, Elizabeth Exh. 1882
Watercolour painter. 6 Thurlow Terrace, Maitland Park, London. † RA 1.

WALKER, Eric Exh. 1936-38
Sculptor. Clenton, 82 Gower Road, Quinton. † B 7.

WALKER, Dame Ethel* 1867-1951
Portrait, figure, landscape and still life painter. b. Edinburgh. Studied Westminster, Slade School and under Sickert and Wyndham Lewis. N.E.A. 1901, A.R.A. 1940, A.R.B.A. 1921, R.B.A. 1931, R.P. 1934. Member London Group 1936. "Miss Jean Warner Laurie" (1927-28) purchased by Chantrey Bequest 1931 and "Seascape: Autumn Morning" (c. 1935) purchased 1939. Add: London. † AB 6, BA 12, BAR 25, BK 4, CG 1, CHE 8, COO 8, FIN 1, G 9, GI 19, GOU 8, I 17, L 8, LEF 187, LEI 46, LS 19, M 9, NEA 192, NG 1, P 25, RA 44, RBA 59, RED 47, RHA 1, RI 1, RSA 11, SWA 20.

WALKER, Eva Allan Exh. 1890-96
Portrait, figure and landscape painter. 3 Baldry Gardens, Streatham Common, London. † RID 8, SWA 1.

WALKER, E. Bent Exh. 1896-1916
Flower, figure and portrait painter. Bushey, Herts. 1896; London 1901. † M 1, P 1, RA 3, ROI 1.

WALKER, Edward B. Exh. 1891-92
Painter. 15 Florist Street, Shaw Heath, Stockport, Lancs. † M 1, RA 1.

WALKER, E.J. Exh. 1882-83
5 Hanover Place, Regents Park, London. † L 4.

WALKER, E.L. Exh. 1912
Barncluith Road, Hamilton, N.B. † GI 1.

WALKER, Mrs. Ella L. Exh. 1929
Bramall, Bothwell. † RSW 1.

WALKER, Miss E.M. Exh. 1906-12
Bromley, Kent 1906; Southampton 1907; Sunningdale, Berks. 1909, c/o Allied Artists Association, London 1912. † LS 1, RA 3.

WALKER, Ethel Margaret Exh. 1915-16
44 Elmwood Avenue, Belfast. † RHA 2.

WALKER, Miss Elmar R. Exh. 1932
St. Leonards, Bearsden, Glasgow. † GI 1, RSA 1.

WALKER, Frank Exh. 1914-16
High Carrons, Shenly, Herts. † L 1, RA 1, RI 1.

WALKER, Mrs. Fred Exh. 1905-11
24 Wellesley Road, Liverpool. † L 6.

WALKER, Frederick A. Exh. 1920-35
Architect. London 1920; Margate, Kent 1935. † RA 4.

WALKER, Miss F.E. Exh. 1914
42 Elsworthy Road, London. † RA 1.

WALKER, Frank H. Exh. 1886-1907
Landscape painter. London 1886; East Burnham Common, Slough, Bucks. 1900. † AG 2, B 1, D 1, L 4, M 1, RA 8, RBA 6, RI 2.

WALKER, Miss F.M. Exh. 1909
Cricklewood, London. † SWA 1.

WALKER, F.P. Exh. 1905-13
London. † L 2, RA 2.

WALKER, Florence Raingill Exh. 1934-37
Landscape and flower painter. Otley Road, Harrogate, Yorks. † RHA 10.

WALKER, Francis S.* 1848-1916
Landscape and genre painter and illustrator. Studied Royal Dublin Society and R.H.A. Schools. Came to London 1868 and worked for the Dalziel Bros. Worked as an illustrator for "The Graphic" and "Illustrated London News". A.R.E. 1890, R.E. 1897, A.R.H.A. 1878, R.H.A. 1879. Add: London. † B 2, GI 2, L 2, M 5, RA 38, RE 86, RHA 107, RI 3, ROI 10.

WALKER, George Exh. 1927
Sculptor. 155 Park Road, Hendon, London. † RA 1.

WALKER, Rev. G.B. Exh. 1884-85
Cruden, Aberdeenshire. † RSA 2.

WALKER, G. Gilbert Exh. 1899-1914
Sculptor. London 1899 and 1911; High Wycombe, Bucks. 1910. † L 3, RA 8.

WALKER, H. Exh. 1890
Teesdale, Birch Grove, Manchester. † L 1.

WALKER, H. Exh. 1914
Roscagh, Kish, Co. Fermanagh, Ireland. † RHA 2.

WALKER, H. Exh. 1935
92 Newlands Road, Glasgow. † GI 1.

WALKER, Harry Exh. 1923-26
Landscape painter. 65 Russell Road, Nottingham. † N 8.

WALKER, Helen see GEORGALA

WALKER, Henry Exh. 1886-1901
Landscape painter. Tunbridge Wells, Kent 1898; North Malvern, Worcs. 1900; London 1901. † RI 2, ROI 1.

WALKER, Hirst b. 1868
Watercolour painter. b. Malton, Yorks. R.B.A. 1919. Exh. 1893-1938. Add: Whitby, Yorks. 1893; Scarborough 1927. † GI 16, GOU 2, L 8, RA 19, RBA 98, RI 10, TOO 9.

WALKER, Horatio* 1858-1938
Canadian landscape painter. R.I. 1901 (resigned 1930). Exh. 1901-22. Add: London and Ile d'Orleans, Canada. † L 3, M 1, NEA 1, NG 1, RA 2, RI 13.

WALKER, Hilda Annetta Exh. 1904-37
Watercolour painter and sculptor. Knowle House, Mirfield, Yorks. † AB 1, B 6, COO 2, L 25, LS 6, RA 1, RI 1, SWA 1, WG 24.

WALKER, H.C. Exh. 1881
Exchange Square, Glasgow. † GI 1.

WALKER, Henry George Exh. 1921-31
Etcher. Birchfield, Birmingham 1921; Torquay, Devon 1931. † B 24.

WALKER, Miss H.M. Exh. 1906-7
Brixton Road, London. † SWA 3.

WALKER, Horace W. Exh. 1884-1935
Landscape painter. A.N.S.A. 1908. Add: Beeston, Notts. † B 2, GI 1, N 134, RHA 5.

WALKER, Miss Isa F. Exh. 1887
Elvetham Lodge, Evetham Road, Edgbaston, Birmingham. † B 1.

WALKER, Jean Exh. 1932
College of Art, Edinburgh. † RSA 1.

WALKER, Jeanette Exh. 1880-83
Edinburgh. † RSA 9.

WALKER, Jessica see STEPHENS

WALKER, J.A. Exh. 1882-86
Painter. 15 Impasse Helene, Paris. † FIN 2, GI 1, TOO 1.

WALKER, Jessie Aitchison Exh. 1910-14
Sister of Wilhelmina W. q.v. Add: North Finchley, London 1910; France 1915. † LS 14.

WALKER, Jenny Bird Exh. 1935-38
St. Leonards, Bearsden. † GI 2, RSW 1.

WALKER, John Beresford b. 1878
Gold and silversmith, teacher and examiner. b. Edinburgh. Studied Edinburgh School of Art and Sheffield School of Art. Exh. 1915-19. Add: Craigielea, Banner Cross Road, Sheffield. † RA 1, RSA 3.

WALKER, John Crampton 1890-1942
Landscape and flower painter and pen and ink artist. Studied Dublin Metropolitan School of Art. A.R.H.A. 1930. Add: Dublin. † FIN 62, RBA 1, RHA 123, ROI 2.

WALKER, John D. Exh. 1902-19
Landscape painter. 13 Parkcliff Mount, Bradford. † L 3, NG 6, RA 16, RI 6.

WALKER, Rev. J.G. Exh. 1931-38
Painter. † WG 12.

WALKER, J. Hanson junr. Exh. 1900-25
Painter and sculptor. London 1900 and 1925; Hadham, Herts. 1905. † L 1, RA 3.

WALKER, John Hanson Exh. 1880-1918
Portrait and genre painter. London. † B 5, D 1, G 10, GI 17, L 29, M 20, NG 1, P 7, RA 62, RBA 7, RHA 1, ROI 10, RSA 10.

WALKER, J.L. Exh. 1926-29
26 Hougoumont Avenue, Waterloo, Liverpool. † L 5.

WALKER, J. Lennox Exh. 1881
Watercolour landscape painter. Edinburgh. † SWA 1.

WALKER, Jessie Margaret Exh. 1908-17
London. † LS 5, RA 1, RI 2.

WALKER, John P.S. Exh. 1933
Watercolour landscape painter. 3 Selbourne Road, Hove, Sussex. † RA 1.

WALKER, J.R. Exh. 1881
63 Hanover Street, Edinburgh. † RSA 1.

WALKER, J.T. Exh. 1882-83
Teasdale, Parbold Hall by Wigan. † L 3.

WALKER, James William 1831-1898
Landscape painter. b. Norwich. Studied Norwich School of Design. Married Pauline W. q.v. Add: 14 York Road, Birkdale, Southport, Lancs. † B 2, D 5, G 8, L 9, NG 8, RA 9, RBA 2, RI 6, RSA 1.

WALKER, Miss K. Exh. 1891
4 Riversdale Road, Seacombe, Cheshire. † M 1.

WALKER, Kate Exh. 1902-40
Miniature portrait painter. Belfast. † L 2, RA 4, RHA 15.

WALKER, Mrs. Kathleen Exh. 1927-28
Landscape painter and etcher. Studied Royal College of Art 1920-23 (travelling scholarship 1924). Add: 222 South Norwood Hill, London. † AB 1, RA 1.

WALKER, Miss Kingston Exh. 1936
Watercolour animal painter. Studied King Edward VII School of Art, Newcastle on Tyne and Byam Shaw and Vicat Cole School. † WG 41.

WALKER, Miss K.B. Exh. 1904-8
39 Kelvin Grove, Liverpool. † L 2.

WALKER, Kate Winifred Exh. 1889-1940
nee Collyer. Miniature portrait painter. b. Leicester. Studied Birmingham School of Art. A.R.M.S. 1909, R.M.S. 1938. Add: Leicester 1889; Erdington, Birmingham 1902. † B 81, GI 1, L 22, N 5, P 6, RA 36, RI 4, RMS 86, RSA 1.

WALKER, Lawrence Exh. 1906-9
Etcher. London. † RA 8.

WALKER, Leonard b. 1877
Painter and stained glass artist. Principal St. Johns Wood School of Art. R.B.A. 1913, R.I. 1915. Exh. 1898-1940. Add: London. † GI 2, L 8, RA 19, RBA 13, RI 103.

WALKER, Miss M. Exh. 1907-14
4 Grosvenor Terrace, York. † RA 3.

WALKER, Miss M. Exh. 1912-14
Blenheim, Gladstone Road, Croydon, Surrey. † RA 2.

WALKER, Mrs. Mabel Exh. 1933-34
29 Barclay Road, Warley Woods. † B 2.

WALKER, Madeline Exh. 1891-1920
Landscape, figure and portrait painter. London. † RID 34, RMS 2.

WALKER, Marcella Exh. 1880-1917
Figure and flower painter. London. † L 4, M 2, RA 21, RHA 1.

WALKER, Margaret Exh. 1908-9
Saltburn, Yorks. 1908; Hinderwell, Yorks. 1909. † L 2.

WALKER, Marion Exh. 1880-81
Figure painter. 66 Margaret Street, Cavendish Square, London. † SWA 3.

WALKER, Mrs. Mary Exh. 1886-1908
Still life painter. Married Philip F.W. q.v. Add: London. † B 2, M 1, NG 19, RBA 1.

WALKER, Maud Exh. 1887-1901
Figure painter. London and Seaton Carew, Durham. † G 1, GI 3, L 1, RA 2, RBA 2, RMS 1, ROI 2, SWA 3.

WALKER, Miss M.A. Exh. 1896-1900
18 Beaconsfield Road, Liverpool. † L 6.

WALKER, Margaret B. Exh. 1936
Watercolour landscape painter. 139 Fellows Road, London. † RA 1.

WALKER, Mildred C. Exh. 1892-1924
Domestic and portrait painter. R.M.S. 1897. Add: 37 Heathfield Park, Willesden Lane, London 1892; Hemel Hempstead, Herts. 1923. † L 5, RA 2, RBA 3, RMS 4.

WALKER, M. Eyre Exh. 1937
Painter. † COO 1.

WALKER, Marian E. Exh. 1897-1901
Liverpool. † L 5.

WALKER, M. Joan W. Exh. 1925
Portrait painter. 6 Dawson Place, London. † RA 1.

WALKER, Mary Scott Exh. 1886-93
22 Derwent Road, Stonycroft. † L 7.

WALKER, Nancy S. Exh. 1928-31
Painter. The Limes, Roehampton Lane, London. † GOU 2, NEA 1, RA 1, SWA 1.

WALKER, P. Exh. 1911-14
Hereford 1911; London 1912. † RA 2, RSA 1.

WALKER, Mrs. Pauline Exh. 1881-84
Still life painter. Married James William W. q.v. Add: 14 York Road, Birkdale, Southport, Lancs. † D 3, L 4.

WALKER, Peggie Exh. 1936-37
Painter, linocut artist and costume designer. 12 Briar Gate, Long Eaton, Notts. † N 5.

WALKER, Phyllis C. Exh. 1939
† NEA 1.

WALKER, Philip F. Exh. 1883-1914
Landscape, coastal and figure painter. Married Mary W. q.v. Add: London. † B 6, L 9, M 8, NG 28, RA 1, RBA 10, RID 32.

WALKER, Robert Exh. 1882
Uppington, Berks. † L 1.

WALKER, Robert Exh. 1883-86
Edinburgh. † L 1, RSA 12.

WALKER, Robert Exh. 1902
Architect. Public Buildings, Windermere. † RA 1.

WALKER, Rosetta Exh. 1939-40
117 Hainton Avenue, Grimsby, Lincs. † RI 3.

WALKER, Mrs. Russell Exh. 1922-30
Watercolour landscape, flower and animal painter. Studied under Mrs. Surtees of Newcastle and Mrs. Langton Barnard. Travelled on the continent. † WG 251.

WALKER, R.E. Exh. 1905-33
Liverpool. † L 30, RA 1.

WALKER, Mrs. R.E. Exh. 1921-29
136 Chatham Street, Liverpool. † L 3.

WALKER, R. Hollands Exh. 1892-1920
Liverpool. † L 7.

WALKER, R.J. Exh. 1892-1938
Glasgow 1892; Bath 1932. † GI 50, RSA 4.

WALKER, R. McAllister b. 1875
Exh. 1912-27. Add: Hamilton, N.B. 1912; Bothwell 1925. † GI 2, L 1, RSA 3, RSW 3.

WALKER, Robert T. Exh. 1895-96
37 Garnethill Street, Glasgow. † GI 2, RSA 3.

WALKER, Seymour Exh. 1887-1903
Landscape and coastal painter. N.E.A. 1889. Add: Stain Cliffe, Seaton Carew, Durham. † NEA 2, RBA 3, ROI 2.

WALKER, Stephen Exh. 1925-29
Landscape painter. Clifton Road West, Ruddington, Notts. † N 11.

WALKER, Sybil Exh. 1936
Landscape painter. † AG 1.

WALKER, S.D. Exh. 1885
Hampden Street, Nottingham. † N 1.

WALKER, Tom Bond Exh. 1924-25
22 Wellington Place, Belfast. † RHA 2.

WALKER, T.H. Exh. 1891
88 Kensington Park Road, London. † M 1.

WALKER, T. Johnson Exh. 1937
427 Queensferry Road, Barnton † RSA 2.

WALKER, W. Exh. 1888
8 Limes Grove, Lewisham, Kent. † ROI 1.

WALKER, Miss W. Exh. 1934
25 Tanya Road, Hampstead, London. † ROI 1.

WALKER, Wilhelmina Exh. 1900-13
Miniature portrait painter. Sister of Jessie Aitchison W. q.v. Add: North Finchley, London 1900; France 1913. † L 2, LS 12, RA 1, RMS 1.

WALKER, William 1878-1961
Painter and etcher. b. Glasgow. Studied Glasgow, London and Paris. Lecturer on history of Art at Chelsea Polytechnic 1919-21, A.R.E. 1914. Add: Greenock 1902; London 1904 and 1907; Stirling 1906 and 1922; Edinburgh 1926; Callendar 1927; Dollar 1933. † CON 77, GI 16, I 3, L 31, NEA 2, RA 7, RE 16, RHA 3, RSA 22.

WALKER, William Exh. 1939
Sculptor. 43 Crayford Road, London. † RA 1.

WALKER, Winifred Exh. 1919-34
Flower painter. Studied Camden School of Art and Ghent. Painter to the Royal Horticultural Society. Add: London. † FIN 1, L 3, RA 3, RI 2, ROI 1, SWA 2.

WALKER, Winston Exh. 1940
Architect. 10 Queen's Gate, Palace Mews, London. † RA 2.

WALKER, William Eyre 1847-1930
Watercolour landscape painter. b. Manchester. Father of Bernard Eyre W. q.v. A.R.W.S. 1800, R.W.S. 1896. Add: Winsford, Cheshire 1880; Hayfield, Derbys. 1881; London 1884; Byfleet, Surrey 1896; Icomb, nr. Stow-on-the-Wold, Glos. 1917; Blandford, Dorset 1923. † AG 2, B 7, D 4, DOW 2, FIN 129, GI 1, L 31 M 35, NG 2, RA 4, RI 1, RSW 1, RWS 335, WG 23.

WALKER, W.H. Exh. 1906-26
Watercolour painter. London. † L 5, RA 1, WG 377.

WALKER, William T. Exh. 1893-1914
Architect. Finsbury Circus, London. † RA 10.

WALKER, William T.C. Exh. 1940
25 Comely Bank Road, Edinburgh. † RSA 1.

WALKEY, R.H. Exh. 1894
c/o Miss B.F. Cresswell, Teignmouth, Devon. † RHA 1.

WALKINSON, Henry Exh. 1886
Holly Bank, Urmston, Lancs. † M 1.

WALKOWITZ, A. Exh. 1930
Etcher. † FIN 7.

WALL, A.J. Exh. 1894
5 Payton Street, Stratford-on-Avon, Warwicks. † B 1.

WALL, A.W. Exh. 1921-22
Painter. Mapperley, Notts. 1921; Sherwood, Notts. 1922. † N 3.

WALL, Emily Wyatt Exh. 1889-1901
Landscape, flower and interior painter. London 1889; Stoke Prior, Bromsgrove, Worcs. 1901. † B 2, RA 1, RBA 2, RSA 1, SWA 1.

WALL, Fred J. Exh. 1919-34
Landscape painter. Long Eaton, Notts. † N 21.

WALL, Helena Exh. 1899-1922
Dublin. † RHA 6.

WALL, Muriel M. Exh. 1928-40
Solihull, Warwicks. 1928; Moseley, Birmingham 1940. † B 2, L 2.

WALL, N. Exh. 1936
116 High Street, Chasetown, Walsall, Staffs. † B 2.

WALL, S.H. Exh. 1925
147 Jockey Road, Sutton Coldfield, Warwicks. † B 1.

WALLACE, Mrs. A. Exh. 1888
4 Newton Place, Glasgow. † GI 1.

WALLACE, A.G. Exh. 1913
7 Deans Yard, Westminster, London. † RA 1.

WALLACE, Ann J. Exh. 1935-37
89 Comeragh Road, Baron's Court, London. † GI 5, RSA 1.

WALLACE, Barbara Exh. 1936
Engraver. † RED 1.

WALLACE, Charles J. Exh. 1898-1903
Gwynedd, Deganwy, North Wales. † RCA 3.

WALLACE, Mrs. Effie Exh. 1921-27
Hamilton House, Perth. † RSW 2.

WALLACE, Ethel Exh. 1900
Quarry Bank, Liscard, Cheshire. † L 1.

WALLACE, H. Exh. 1883-84
26 Francis Street, Tottenham Court Road, London. † RHA 3.

WALLACE, Harry* Exh. 1881-1934
Landscape painter. N.S.A. 1884. Add: Nottingham 1881; Castle Donnington, Derbys. 1884; Leamington, Warwicks. 1887; London 1889 and 1934; Barnsley, Yorks. 1891; Carlisle 1932. † L 1, N 56, RA 5, RSA 3.

WALLACE, Henry Exh. 1897
257 Saracen Street, Possilpark, Glasgow. † GI 1.

WALLACE, Harold Frank b. 1881
Watercolour and black and white artist of landscapes and sporting scenes. Exh. 1932-35. Add: Pelsall, Staffs. and Glen Urquhart, Inverness. † RI 1, RSW 4.

WALLACE, Helen P. Exh. 1907
13 Mayfield Gardens, Edinburgh. † RSA 1.

WALLACE, Isabella Exh. 1896
3 Crown Circus, Glasgow. † GI 1.

WALLACE, J. Exh. 1893
3 Crown Circus, Glasgow. † GI 1.

WALLACE, James d. 1936-37
Exh. from 1900. Add: Berwick-on-Tweed 1900; Paisley 1918. † GI 5, RA 2, RSA 5.

WALLACE, James Exh. 1899-1910
Landscape painter. London. † GI 8, L 2, LS 8, M 3, RA 12, RSA 2.

WALLACE, John Exh. 1880-1902
11 Melbourne Place, Edinburgh. † GI 9, L 9, RSA 33, RSW 2.

WALLACE, John Exh. 1891-97
Architect. Edinburgh. † RSA 4.

WALLACE, John Exh. 1890-1904
Figure painter. Newcastle-on-Tyne. † B 1, RA 3, RSA 1.

WALLACE, J. Milne Exh. 1919
† L 1.

WALLACE, Mary Rowe Exh. 1913-22
Portrait and landscape painter. † BG 31, GOU 22.

WALLACE, Margaret S. Exh. 1880-91
Landscape and figure painter. London. † B 2, D 4, SWA 6.

WALLACE, Mrs. Ottilie b. 1875
nee McLaren. Sculptor. b. Edinburgh. Studied under Rodin in Paris. Exh. 1900-35. Add: Paris 1900; Edinburgh 1901; London 1905. † GI 2, I 7, L 3, RA 4, RMS 1, RSA 11, SWA 1.

WALLACE, Patricia Exh. 1934-40
Landscape painter. Dublin 1934; Rathfarnham, Co. Dublin 1939. † RHA 16.

WALLACE, Robin b. 1897
Painter and etcher. b. Kendal. Studied Byam Shaw and Vicat Cole School of Art. Exh. 1922-40. Add: London 1922 and 1924; Kendal 1923. † BAR 109, CG 2, COO 2, GOU 3, L 6, M 1, NEA 4, RA 23, RBA 1, RI 4, ROI 1.

WALLACE, Robert Bruce Exh. 1885
Watercolour figure painter. 79 Ardwick Green, Manchester. † M 1.

WALLACE, William Exh. 1928
Painter. 168 Ebury Street, London. † RA 1.

WALLACE-WOOD, H. Exh. 1918-21
London. † B 2, GI 4, L 2, RA 1

WALLAN, M.S. Exh. 1883
22 Belsize Square, Belsize Park, London. † L 1.

WALLCOUSINS, Ernest Exh. 1920-28
Watercolour landscape painter. London 1910 and 1916; Toronto, Canada 1913. † ALP 1, L 1, RA 8, RI 5.

WALLER, Arthur B. Exh. 1911-28
Artist and teacher. Add: School of Art, Oswestry 1911; Peel, I.o.M. 1920 and 1923; Liverpool 1921; Sark, C.I. 1924; Wareham, Dorset 1928. † L 31, RCA 4.

WALLER, A. Honeywood Exh. 1884-91
Watercolour landscape painter. Godalming, Surrey. † B 2, D 1, GOU 5, RA 2, RBA 4, RI 4.

WALLER, Rev. Arthur Prettyman b. 1876
Landscape painter. b. Waldringfield, Suffolk. Studied Bridgwater School of Art, Somerset. Exh. 1929. Add: Waldringfield, Suffolk. † AB 4.

WALLER, Frederick Exh. 1894
Architect. Father of Samuel Edward W. q.v. Add: Gloucester. † RA 1.

WALLER, Hilda Exh. 1924
326 London Road, Lowestoft, Suffolk. † L 2.

WALLER, Ivan Exh. 1936-37
Flower and still life painter. 114 Berry Rise, London. † NEA 1, RA 2, RBA 1.

WALLER, Marjory Exh. 1921
Watercolour pastoral painter. † WG 51.

WALLER, Mary Lemon Exh. 1881-1929
nee Fowler. Portrait painter. Studied R.A. Schools. Married Samuel Edmund W. q.v. R.P. 1925. Add: London. † D 2, G 2, L 11, M 1, P 60, RA 46, RE 1, ROI 5, RSA 1, SWA 13.

WALLER, R.E. Exh. 1932-34
42 White Hart Street, Mansfield, Notts. † N 6.

WALLER, Samuel Edmund* 1850-1903
Genre and animal painter. Studied Gloucester School of Art. Worked for a while for his father Frederick W. q.v. Also worked as an illustrator for the "Graphic". Married Mary Lemon W. q.v. R.O.I. 1883. Add: London. † B 2, BG 1, D 1, FIN 1, GI 1, L 6, M 3, RA 19, ROI 14, TOO 15.

WALLET, Philippe Exh. 1913
Landscape painter. † ALP 3.

WALLEY, Miss E.R. Exh. 1940
The Grange, Arley, Coventry. † B 1.

WALLEY, Frank Exh. 1903
Architect. 14 Queen's Road, Chester. † RA 2.

WALLING, A.N. Exh. 1912-21
Black and white landscape artist. Lenton, Notts. 1912; Nottingham 1917. † N 16.

WALLIS, Bernard Exh. 1911
16 Penwerris Terrace, Falmouth. † RA 1.

WALLIS, Charles Alban Exh. 1902-12
Landscape painter. Related to George Herbert and John C.W.q.v. Add: The Willows, Chiswick Mall, London. † L 3, LS 8, M 1, NG 1, RA 8, ROI 2.

WALLIS, Charles F. Exh. 1916
† LEI 1.

WALLIS, Douglas T. Exh. 1929
Architect. 29 Roland Gardens, London. † RA 1.

WALLIS, Emmeline Exh. 1894
Basingstoke, Hants. † SWA 1.

WALLIS, Elsie Jacoba Exh. 1927-39
Mrs. Graham. Portrait and figure painter. Bickley, Kent 1927; Chislehurst, Kent 1930; Sandgate, Kent 1936. † L 5, RA 3, RMS 31.

WALLIS, George Harry 1848-1936
Landscape and coastal painter. Director Nottingham Art Gallery 1878-1929. Hon. Sec. to the Art Union 1884-86. H.N.S.A. 1885. Exh. 1888. Add: The Residence, Nottingham Castle. † N 2.

WALLIS, George Herbert Exh. 1885-88
Landscape painter. Related to Charles Alban and John C.W. q.v. Add: The Willows, Chiswick Mall, London. † G 3.

WALLIS, H. Exh. 1894
Watercolour landscape painter. 10 Meadow Studios, Bushey, Herts. † M 1, RA 2.

WALLIS, Henry* 1830-1916
Historical genre painter. Studied in London and Paris. A.R.W.S. 1878, R.W.S. 1880. Several of his works are in the Tate Gallery. Add: London. † GI 1, L 5, M 1, NG 1, RWS 36.

WALLIS, Hugh Exh. 1899-1922
Flower and figure painter. Altrincham, Cheshire 1899; Bowdon, Cheshire 1909. † GI 1, L 2, M 2, P 2, RA 12.

WALLIS, Henry Charles Exh. 1903-7
Portrait painter. Ryde, I.o.W. 1903; Redruth, Cornwall 1906. † L 1, RA 4, RMS 1.

WALLIS, H.O. Exh. 1910
156 Burwood Road, Nottingham. † N 1.

WALLIS, Miss I. de C. White Exh. 1928-29
Brown House, Sharps Lane, Ruislip, Middlesex. † L 3.

WALLIS, John C. Exh. 1890-1918
Landscape painter. Related to Charles Alban and George Herbert W. q.v. Add: London. † NG 3, RA 6, RBA 1, ROI 1.

WALLIS, Joseph H. Exh. 1880
Landscape painter. 62 Gt. Russell Street, London. † G 2, RA 1.

WALLIS, Joseph H. Exh. 1890
Architect. 8 Adelphi Terrace, London. † RA 1.

WALLIS, Katherine E. Exh. 1897-1914
Sculptor. Chelsea, London 1897 and 1910; Paris 1903. † GI 1, L 11, RA 10.

WALLIS, Miss L.M. Exh. 1896-1900
Bucklebury, Reading, Berks. † B 3, L 1, RHA 5, ROI 4, SWA 2.

WALLIS, Rosa b. 1857
Painter, etcher and enameller on copper. b. Stretton, Staffs. Studied Royal College of Art and Berlin. Travelled widely on the continent. Exh. 1880-1930. Add: London. † B 21, BG 2, FIN 77, L 5, NG 4, RA 10, RBA 23, RI 26, ROI 8, SWA 6, WG 112.

WALLIS, Walter Exh. 1882-93
Figure painter and teacher. Croydon, Surrey. † B 3, L 4, RA 5, RBA 7, ROI 1.

WALLIS, Sir Whitworth Exh. 1884-1925
Painter. Museum of Art Gallery, Birmingham 1884; Stratford-on-Avon, Warwicks. 1921. † B 13, ROI 1.

WALLIS, Walter Cyril Exh. 1929-39
53 Spottiswood Street, Edinburgh. † RSA 2.

WALLIS, William H. Exh. 1890
81 Charlotte Street, Portsmouth. † D 2.

WALLROTH, Catherine E. Exh. 1923-39
Watercolour painter. Westby Road, Boscombe, Hants. † BI 1, RI 1, RCA 10.

WALLS, Arthur Exh. 1909-30
Liverpool. † L 8.

WALLS, James Exh. 1889
18 Queen Anne's Street, Dunfermline. † RSA 2.

WALLS, William 1860-1942
Animal painter. b. Dunfermline. Studied Antwerp Academy and R.S.A. Life School (Keith prize). Teacher of Animal painting at Edinburgh College of Art. A.R.S.A. 1901, R.S.A. 1914, R.S.W. 1906. Add: Edinburgh 1883 and 1888; Dunfermline 1885; Corstorphine, Midlothian 1926. † AB 2, B 1, BG 2, CON 5, GI 98, L 27, M 12, RA 18, RHA 5, RSA 204, RSW 128.

WALLWORK, Amy Exh. 1895
The Oaks, Tatton Road, Heaton Chapel, Manchester. † M 1.

WALLWORK, Mrs. R. Exh. 1910
City School of Art, Liverpool. † L 2.

WALLWORK, Richard Exh. 1909-26
Chelsea, London 1909; City Art School, Mount Street, Liverpool 1910. † L 10, M 1, RA 2.

WALMESLEY-WHITE, Mrs. Jessie Exh. 1937-40
Painter. Ellergarth, Budleigh Salterton, Devon. † RA 1, SWA 5.

WALMSLEY, Alice Exh. 1899
8 Wellesley Terrace, Princes Park, Liverpool. † L 1.

WALMSLEY, H. Exh. 1926
† M 2.

WALMSLEY, H. Exh. 1899-1901
Nottingham 1899; Carlton, Notts. 1901. † N 4.

WALMSLEY, May Exh. 1929-33
189 Branch Road, Blackburn, Lancs. † L 5.

WALMSLEY, Ulric Exh. 1884-1928
85 Redrock Street, Liverpool. † GOU 1, L 3.

WALN, Kathleen J. Exh. 1883-1908
Wallasey, Cheshire 1883; Liscard, Cheshire 1899. † L 5.

WALN, Miss L. Exh. 1885-1905
Wallasey, Cheshire 1885; Liscard, Cheshire 1896. † L 10.

WALN, Zoe Exh. 1891-1908
Massey Park, Liscard, Cheshire. † L 6.

WALPOLE, G. Mary Exh. 1884-1901
Landscape painter. Hampton Court Palace, London. † SWA 9.

WALPOLE, Lucy Gertrude Exh. 1921-40
Portrait and flower painter and watercolour landscape painter. Lancing, Sussex 1921; Brighton 1929; Ufford, nr. Woodbridge, Suffolk 1935. † P 5, RA 2, ROI 5, RSA 1.

WALPOLE, Lady Spencer Exh. 1899
14 Queen's Gate Palace, London, † NG 1.

WALPOLE, Mrs. S.C. Exh. 1886-1905
Landscape painter. Hampton Court Palace, London 1886; Kensington, London 1899. † SWA 11.

WALPOLE, Winifred Exh. 1926-39
Handsworth, Birmingham. † B 13.

WALRAF, Hubertine Exh. 1916-19
Sculptor. 39A Clareville Road, West Kensington, London. † L 1, RA 2.

WALROND, Sir John Bt. Exh. 1884-88
Landscape painter. London. † RI 4.

WALSH, Henry Exh. 1931-32
Painter and linocut artist. School of Art, Dublin. † RHA 9.

WALSH, Janie F. Exh. 1882-88
52 North Circular Road, Dublin. † RHA 7.

WALSH, J.S. Exh. 1940
Valentine Road, Kings Heath, Birmingham. † B 1.

WALSH, Mrs. Lucie E. Exh. 1906-40
Portrait and figure painter. Walton-on-Thames 1907; London 1924; St. Ives, Cornwall 1940. † RA 6, SWA 1.

WALSH, Mary Exh. 1901
8 St. Edward's Terrace, Garfield Avenue, Rathgar Dublin. † RHA 1

WALSH, Robert F. Exh. 1880-92
North Circular Road, Dublin. † RHA 15.

WALSH, T.E.G. Exh. 1885
Painter. 54 Warwick Gardens, London. † RBA 1, ROI 1.

WALSHAM, T.W. Exh. 1886
58 Hamilton Square, Birkenhead. † L 1.

WALSHAW, Charles Moate b. 1884
Landscape and decorative painter and commercial artist. b. Coventry. Exh. 1924-39. Add: Kenilworth, 1924; Westwood Heath, nr. Coventry 1928. † B 13, RA 1, RI 2, RMS 7.

WALSHAW, Thomas W. Exh. 1894
6 South Castle Street, Liverpool. † L 1.

WALSHE, J.C. Exh. 1889-1903
Birmingham. † B 4.

WALTER, Alice Exh. 1882-1915
Berengrave, Rainham, Kent. † D 35 SWA 11.

WALTER, Mrs. Busse Exh. 1885
Portrait painter. c/o Capt. Scott, East Limes, Putney, London. † RBA 1.

WALTER, Clenin Exh. 1926
Painter. † CHE 1.

WALTER, Edmund Exh. 1894
25 Sackville Street, London. † RI 1.

WALTER, Emma Exh. 1880-98
Fruit and still life painter. S.W.A. 1880. Add: London. † B 9, D 12 GI 9, L 2, M 4, RA 1, RI 7, SWA 96.

WALTER, Mrs. Francis Exh. 1901-38
Islip, nr. Oxford 1901; Fareham, Hants. 1938. † D 2, RI 1.

WALTER, Franz Wilfrid Exh. 1908-10
United Arts Club, 10 St. James Street, London. † LS 5.

WALTER, W. Start Exh. 1938-40
Still life, portrait and landscape painter. 24 Makepeace Avenue, London. † RA 3, ROI 1

WALTERS, Amelia J. Exh. 1880-93
Painter and sculptor. London. † L 7, M 5, RA 6, RBA 1, ROI 3.

WALTERS, Miss A.M. Exh. 1902-4
Forthampton Vicarage, Tewksbury. † B 9, L 1.

WALTERS, Mrs. A.M. Exh. 1920
Oakwood, Hoylake, Cheshire. † L 1.

WALTERS, E. Exh. 1882-1911
Birmingham. † B 45.

WALTERS, Evan b. 1893
Portrait and figure painter. b. Wales. Studied Swansea School of Art and R.A. Schools. Exh. 1921-36. Add: Swansea 1921; London 1930. † CHE 2 COO 22, M 1, RA 6, RED 1 RSA 1.

WALTERS, Edward J. Exh. 1933-34
Architect. 28 Gt. Ormond Street, London. † RA 2.

WALTERS, Edith M. Exh. 1908-22
Mrs. Carter. Painter and etcher. Liverpool 1908; Birkdale, Lancs. 1917; St. Ives, Cornwall 1923 † GI 1, I 4 L 8 M 19, RA 3.

WALTERS, Frances Exh. 1930
Miniature portrait painter. 140 Alexandra Road, St. John's Wood, London. † RA 1.

WALTERS, Frank Exh. 1919-20
Miniature portrait painter. c/o Mrs. Barnett, 140 Alexandra Avenue, London. † RA 2

WALTERS, Frederick Arthur Exh. 1890-1909
Architect. Westminster, London. † RA 11.

WALTERS, George Stanfield* 1838-1924
Landscape and marine painter. R.B.A. 1867. Son of Samuel W. q.v. Add: London. † B 6, D 17, G 2, L 19, M 12, RA 19, RBA 408, RI 74, ROI 48, RSW 1, TOO 2.

WALTERS, G.S.H. Exh. 1882
81 Kingsdown Parade, Bristol. † L 1.

WALTERS, Jessica Lloyd Exh. 1905-39
Portrait, figure and landscape painter. Paris 1905; London 1917. † COO 30, L 1, LS 5.

WALTERS, Rt. Hon. Sir J. Tudor Exh. 1925
Architect. 6 Hobart Place, Eaton Square, London. † RA 1.

WALTERS, L. Exh. 1881
Painter. 79 Gower Street, London. † D 1.

WALTERS, Mrs. Lilian Exh. 1893-1916
Croydon, Surrey 1893; Farnham, Surrey 1916. † RI 2.

WALTERS, Phyllis E. Exh. 1923-27
Etcher. London. † RA 3.

WALTERS, Robert Exh. 1899-1924
44 Amhurst Park, Stamford Hill, London. † B 16, D 50, GI 2, LS 12, M 3, RA 1, RCA 15, RI 1, ROI 1.

WALTERS, Samuel* 1811-1882
Marine painter. Self taught. Father of George Stanfield W. q.v. Add: 76 Merton Road, Bootle, Liverpool. † RBA 1.

WALTERS, Mrs. W. Stanisland Exh. 1919
† L 2.

WALTHEW, Miss Louie Exh. 1883-85
Woodhall, Stockport, Lancs. † M 5.

WALTHEW, Susan Fald Exh. 1899
Ardmore, Gatehouse on Fleet † RSA 1.

WALTNER, Charles Albert 1846-1925
French etcher and engraver. Exh. 1880-91. Add: London 1880; Paris 1883. † DOW 4, RA 11.

WALTON, Allan b. 1891-92
Painter and designer. b. Cheadle Hulme, Cheshire. Studied Academie de la Grande Chaumier, Paris; and Westminster School of Art 1918-19. Member London Group 1925. Exh. 1921-38. Add: London. † AG 1, BA 2, BK 3, CHE 1, L 3 LEI 2, NEA 15 RED 12, TOO 41.

WALTON, Carrie Exh. 1880-85
Watercolour flower painter. 11 Paragon, Blackheath, London. † SWA 7.

WALTON, Cecile* 1891-1956
Mrs. Eric Robertson. Painter and sculptor. b. Glasgow, daughter of Edward Arthur W. q.v. Studied London, Edinburgh, Paris and Florence. Add: Edinburgh 1909 and 1934; Cambridge 1929. † D 1, G 1, GI 11, I 4, L 19, RA 6, RBA 1, RSA 46, RSW 5.

WALTON, Constance d. 1960
Mrs. W.H. Ellis. Watercolour flower painter R.S.W. 1887. Add: Hillhead, Glasgow 1883 and 1905; Milngavie 1898. † AR 1, BG 2, DOW 1 GI 98, L 6, M 2, RA 2, RSA 23, RSW 93.

WALTON, Mrs. Catherine R. Exh. 1898-1935
Landscape and figure painter. Newlyn, Cornwall 1898; London 1900. † L 4, LS 11, M 1, NG 1, RA 10, ROI 6, SWA 21.

WALTON, Diana Exh. 1923-27
Portrait, figure and landscape painter. London. † CG 2, G 1, NEA 3, RA 1.

WALTON, Miss D.S. Exh. 1890-92
Flower painter. Holmbury St. Mary, Dorking, Surrey. † B 2, RI 6.

WALTON, Ellen Exh. 1906
7 Bedford Park, Edinburgh. † RSA 1.

WALTON, Miss E.A. Exh. 1928
57 Bayswater Road, Birchfield. † B 1.

WALTON, Edward Arthur* 1860-1922
Landscape and portrait painter. Studied Dusseldorf and Glasgow School of Art. N.E.A. 1887. R.P. 1897, A.R.S.A. 1889, R.S.A. 1905, R.S.W. 1885, P.R.S.W. Father of Cecile W. q.v. Add: Glasgow 1880; London 1895 and 1897; Stow-on-the-Wold, Glos. 1896; Edinburgh 1904. † AG 2 G 2, GI 89, I 32, L 22, M 7, NEA 10, NG 1, P 30, RA 13, RI 3, RSA 100, RSW 61, RWS 2.

WALTON, E. Margaret Exh. 1924-39
Acton, London 1924; Handsworth, Birmingham 1931. † B 26, RBA 1.

WALTON, Frank* 1840-1928
Landscape and coastal painter. R.I. 1882 (Hon. Retd. 1923), H.R.M.S. 1912, R.O.I. 1883, H.R.O.I. 1898. Add: Holmbury St. Mary, Dorking, Surrey. † B 27 FIN 6, D 14, G 7, GI 7, L 28, LEI 1, M 26, NG 34, RA 101, RBA 1, RI 230, ROI 137, TOO 2.

WALTON, F.W. Exh. 1931
Mattishall, Dereham, Norfolk. † B 2.

WALTON, George Exh. 1881-88
Portrait painter. Newcastle-on-Tyne 1881 and 1888; London 1883. † RA 11, RBA 1, RSA 7.

WALTON, George Exh. 1893-99
Glasgow 1893; Bayswater, London 1898. † GI 11.

WALTON, G. Spencer Exh. 1904
† P 1.

WALTON, Miss H. Exh. 1885-86
High Street, Sandloch, Cheshire. † M 2.

WALTON, Hannah Exh. 1899-1906
2 Bothwell Terrace, Hillhead, Glasgow. † GI 3.

WALTON, Helen Exh. 1891-1908
Glasgow 1891; London 1894; Edinburgh 1908. † G 1, GI 8, P 3, RSA 2.

WALTON, Hellene Exh. 1922
Landscape painter. 35 Bedford Gardens, London. † RA 1.

WALTON, Henry D. Exh. 1889-1904
Glasgow. † GI 8.

WALTON, Isabel Exh. 1926-33
Rock Mount, Adelaide Terrace, Blackburn, Lancs. † L 6.

WALTON, Joseph Exh. 1882
23 Stonegate, York. † M 1.

WALTON, Lilian Exh. 1928-40
Cheltenham, Glos. 1928; Guildford, Surrey 1932. † RCA 5, RSA 10.

WALTON, Miss M. Exh. 1888
4 Brunswick Square, London. † L 1.

WALTON, Miss R. Exh. 1889
4 Bath Place, Holywell, Oxford. † B 1.

WALTON, R.T. Exh. 1937-39
St. Aubyn's, Ashfield Avenue, Kings Heath, Birmingham. † B 6.

WALTON, Violet b. 1901
Painter, illuminator, embroiderer, designer and teacher. b. Bootle, Lancs. Studied Liverpool City School of Art. Exh. 1924-33. Add: Bootle, Lancs. 1924; Southport, Lancs. 1933. † L 13.

WALTON, William Exh. 1919
Landscape, architectural and figure painter. † FIN 29.

WALWYN, Percy F. Exh. 1902
Albany Road, Harborne, Birmingham. † B 1.

WAMSLEY, Miss M.W. Exh. 1902
c/o Miss L.H. Wilson, The Home of Rest, Sutton Coldfield, Warwicks. † B 1.

WAND, Helen Exh. 1901
Shepherds Hill, London. † D 1.

WANDSCHNEIDER, Professor Wilhelm Exh. 1907-11
German sculptor. Add: Berlin. † L 2, GI 4, RA 1.

WANE, Ethel Exh. 1900-34
Painter. Daughter of Richard W. q.v. Add: Egremont, Cheshire 1900 and 1934; New Brighton, Wallasey, Cheshire 1924. † B 2, D 5, L 47, LS 3, RCA 14.

WANE, Harold 1879-1900
Painter. Son of Richard W. q.v. Add: 13 Kingslake Road, Egremont, Cheshire. † L 8.

WANE, Richard* 1852-1904
Landscape, coastal and genre painter. Studied with F. Shields and at Manchester Academy. Father of Ethel and Harold W. q.v. Add: Manchester 1881; Conway, Wales 1883; Deganwy, Llandudno, Wales 1887; Dulwich, London 1890; Egremont, Cheshire 1895. † B 2, D 21, G 5, GI 1, L 68, M 32, RA 29, RBA 7, RCA 4, RHA 2, RI 3, ROI 8, RSA 2.

WANEHOPE, Alice Exh. 1898
46 Ashley Gardens, London. † D 2.

WANKLYN, Edith Exh. 1899
St. Andrews, Leatherhead, Surrey. † RMS 1.

WANKLYN, Miss G.M. Exh. 1911-12
Leatherhead, Surrey. † SWA 2

WANSEY, Margaret Raymond Exh. 1913-38
Animal, garden and mountain painter. Studied Clifton Art School and Frank Calderon's School of Animal Painting. Travelled annually in the Alps and Pyranees. Add: London. † ALP 6, L 1, P 2, RA 4, RBA 2 RI 1 RSW 1.

WANT, Randolphe C. Exh. 1893
† D 1.

WANTE, Ernst Exh. 1914
East Downs Road, Bowdon, Cheshire. † M 1.

WANTERS, Emile Exh. 1884
111 Rue Foissart, Brussels. † RHA 1

WAPLINGTON, J. Exh. 1886-87
Landscape painter. 69 Constance Street, New Basford, Notts. † N 2.

WARAKER, Emily Maude Exh. 1908-10
5 Scroop Terrace, Cambridge. † LS 11.

WARBURG, Blanche Exh. 1890-92
Still life and portrait painter. Hampstead, London. † RBA 2.

WARBURG, C.C. Exh. 1940
14 Clarendon Road, London. † SWA 1.

WARBURG, Lily A. Exh. 1895-97
Watercolour painter. 8 Porchester Terrace, London. † L 1, RA 1, RI 2, SWA 2.

WARBURTON, J.R. Exh. 1906
Bosham, Nr. Chichester, Sussex. † L 1.

WARBURTON, Samuel 1874-c.1938
Portrait painter and miniaturist and watercolour landscape painter. b. Douglas, I.o.M. A.R.M.S. 1928, R.M.S. 1930. Add: 22 Queen's Road, Windsor, Berks. † ALP 1, L 6, RA 1, RMS 19

WARD, Alfred Exh. 1880-1929
Portrait, figure and landscape painter and etcher. London. † AR 62, B 8, G 2, GI 1, L 38, LS 5, M 18, P 3, RA 34, RHA 1, ROI 5.

WARD, Annie Exh. 1886-98
Painter. Croydon, Surrey 1886 and 1889; The Hoe, Plymouth, Devon 1888; Kingston-on-Thames 1898. † RA 4.

WARD, Archibald Exh. 1935
Watercolour landscape painter. 27 Gainsborough Road, Ipswich, Suffolk. † RA 1.

WARD, Arthur Exh. 1894
Landscape painter. 1 Palin Street, Hyson Green, Nottingham. † N 1.

WARD, Mrs. A.M. Exh. 1883-1939
Painter and etcher. Birmingham 1883; Warwick 1905. † B 22, WG 42.

WARD, Mrs. Amy Margaret b. 1863
nee Nelson. Horse and flower painter. b. Salmonby, Lincs. Studied Lincoln School of Art and Frank Calderon's School of Animal Painting. Exh. 1916-27. Add: London 1916; Farnham Royal, Bucks. 1927. † LS 9 RI 1, ROI 6, SWA 4.

WARD, Audrey N. Exh. 1937-39
Painter. Guildford, Surrey 1937; Woking, Surrey 1939. † RA 2.

WARD, Beatrice Exh. 1893
Miniature painter and black and white artist. Daughter of Edward Matthew W. (1816-1879) and Henrietta Mary Ada W. q.v. Add: 3 Chester House, Chester Square, London. † L 2.

WARD, Brita Exh. 1909-32
nee de Lagerberg. Painter. Married Orlando W. q.v. Add: London. † RID 1, SWA 4.

WARD, Beryl D. Exh. 1919
† L 2.

WARD, Bernard Evans Exh. 1880-1906
Figure and portrait painter. London. † B 2, L 4, RA 15, RBA 4, ROI 2, RSA 1.

WARD, Miss B.H. Exh. 1921
6 Addison Mansions, London. † SWA 1.

WARD, Cyril 1863-1935
Watercolour landscape and garden painter. b. Oakamoor, Staffs. Add: Glossop, Nr. Manchester 1889; Milford, Godalming, Surrey 1901; Puckeridge, Ware, Herts. 1902; Claygate, Surrey 1908; Birchington, Kent 1919; Alton, Hants. 1925; Southampton 1932. † B 5 D 3 FIN 140, L 39, M 25, RA 27, RBA 11, RCA 163, RHA 36, RI 13.

WARD, Charles A. Exh. 1922-39
Birmingham. † B 9.

WARD, Charlotte Blakeney Exh. 1898-1939
nee Blakeney. Portrait painter. b. Lancs. Studied Royal College of Art and Paris. Married Charles D.W. q.v. Add: London. † D 2, L 3, P 2, RA 27, RID 4, SWA 116.

WARD, Cicely E. Exh. 1889
Landscape painter. Visited North Africa. Add: Hill House, Fryerning, Ingatestone, Essex. † L 1, SWA 2.

WARD, Charles D. b. 1872
Portrait and landscape painter. b. Taunton. Studied Royal College of Art. R.O.I. 1915. Married Charlotte Blakeney W. q.v. Exh. 1895-1938. Add: London 1895; Blewbury, Berks. and London 1931. † CHE 1, D 3, GI 2, L 7 LS 5 NEA 1, P 3, RA 41, RBA 6, RI 6, ROI 86.

WARD, Dorothy Priestley Exh. 1908-36
Mrs. W. Caton Woodville. Watercolour, portrait and miniature painter. b Chislehurst. A.R.M.S. 1910. Add: Sundridge Park, Kent 1908; London 1911 and 1928; Elstree, Herts. 1913. † L 3, RA 37, RMS 44, RSA 5.

WARD, Miss E. Exh. 1905
Moor Allerton House, Leeds. † L 1

WARD, Miss E. Exh. 1932-33
Collingwood, Davenport Park, Stockport, Lancs. † L 2.

WARD, Edith Exh. 1924
Watercolour painter. Glenleigh, The Chase, Nottingham. † N 1.

WARD, Enoch Exh. 1896-1921
Landscape and figure painter. R.B.A. 1898. Add: Northwood, Middlesex 1896; London 1913; Kingston-on-Thames 1917; Hampton Wick 1919. † RA 6, RBA 53, RI 7

WARD, Ethel Exh. 1922
† G 1.

WARD, Eva Exh. 1924
Miniature portrait painter. Summerhill Lodge, Chislehurst, Kent. † RA 1.

WARD, Mrs. E.A. Exh. 1895-99
London. † NG 2, P 1.

WARD, Edward A. Exh. 1885-86
Nottingham. † N 9.

WARD, Edwin Arthur b. 1859
Portrait painter. N.S.A. 1885-88. R.P. 1891. Exh. 1881-1932. Add: London. † B 5, G 12, GI 1, L 10, M 1, N 21, NG 35, P 25, RA 30, RBA 10, RHA 1, ROI 11.

WARD, Effie D. Exh. 1902-3
Hazel Dell, Acocks Green, Birmingham. † B 1, L 8.

WARD, Eliza J. Exh. 1902-8
Linwood, Alcester Road, Kings Heath, Birmingham. † B 6.

WARD, Fanny Exh. 1884-86
Painter. The Firs, Oxford. † B 1, SWA 1.

WARD, Florence Exh. 1900-1
57 Albert Gate Mansions, London. † RMS 2.

WARD, Frank Exh. 1940
Portrait painter. 3 Oakley Studios, Upper Cheyne Row, London. † RA 1.

WARD, F.E. Exh. 1893
Architect. 37 Donegall Place, Belfast. † RA 1.

WARD, Florence Emily Exh. 1907
148 Sheen Road, Richmond, Surrey. † GI 2, RSA 2.

WARD, George Exh. 1904-15
Landscape painter and teacher. Rochester, Kent. † RA 6.

WARD, Greta Exh. 1936
Landscape painter. 63 Bradbourne Vale Road, Sevenoaks, Kent. † RA 1.

WARD, Miss G.D. Exh. 1940
320 Orphanage Road, Birmingham. † B 1.

WARD, Grace F. Exh. 1930-39
Landscape and portrait painter. Studied Regent Street Polytechnic. Add: London. † P 2, RA 5, RBA 1, ROI 4, SWA 10.

WARD, G.H. Exh. 1920-21
Painter. Nottingham. † N 3.

WARD, Gladys H. Exh. 1915
Oak Lawn, Leatherhead, Surrey. † L 1.

WARD, George W. Exh. 1884-1900
Architect. Harlesden 1884; Newcastle-on-Tyne 1900. † RA 5.

WARD, Canon H. Exh. 1928-34
Landscape painter. † AB 12, WG 12.

WARD, Henry Exh. 1900
Architect. 8 Bank Buildings, Hastings. † RA 2.

WARD, Herbert 1863-1919
Painter and sculptor. London 1895; Paris 1910. † L 2, RA 11, TOO 1.

WARD, H.H. Exh. 1920-21
4 Lyncot Road, Aintree, Liverpool. † L 3.

WARD, Henrietta Mary Ada* 1832-1924
Landscape and historical genre painter. Studied under her father George Raphael W. (1797-1879). Married Edward Matthew W. (1816-1879). Mother of Beatrice and Sir Leslie W. q.v. Add: London. † L 2, M 1, RA 10, SWA 2.

WARD, James Exh. 1886-1911
Architectural designer and sculptor. Barnes, Surrey 1886; Macclesfield 1889; Donnybrook, Ireland 1909. † M 2, RA 4, RHA 10.

WARD, Jenny Exh. 1939
† GOU 1.

WARD, Jessie Exh. 1938
Twickenham, Middlesex. † SWA 1.

WARD, Mrs. Katharine M. Exh. 1893-94
Watercolour flower painter. 5 Dordrecht Mansions, Haarlem Road, Brook Green, London. † RA 3.

WARD, Leonard b. 1887
Watercolour painter and etcher. Studied Birmingham College of Art. Exh. 1920-40. Add: Birmingham. † B 68, RA 2.

WARD, Sir Leslie 1851-1922
"Spy". Portrait and architectural painter, caricaturist and engraver. Studied under S. Smirke and at R.A. Schools. Contributed to "Vanity Fair" and the "Graphic". R.P. 1891. Knighted 1917. Son of Edward Matthew W. (1816-1879) and Henrietta Mary Ada W. q.v. Add: London. † DOW 135, G 3, P 42, RA 3, RE 14.

WARD, Lillie Exh. 1924-32
Cheadle Hulme, Cheshire 1924 and 1932; Grasscroft, Nr. Greenfield, Yorks. 1930. † L 5, RCA 3.

WARD, Lydia Exh. 1929
† RMS 1.

WARD, Miss L.M. Exh. 1918-21
London. † SWA 6.

WARD, Leslie Moffat b. 1888
Watercolour painter, etcher and lithographer. Studied and taught at Bournemouth School of Art Exh. 1910-14. Add: 22 Grants Avenue, Bournemouth. † L 21, RA 26, RE 37, RI 8.

WARD, Martha Exh. 1920
314 Baltic Street, Bridgeton. † RSA 1.

WARD, Mary Exh. 1928
31A High Street, Petersfield, Hants. † L 4.

WARD, Melville S. Exh. 1903-11
Architect. London. † RA 2.

WARD, Nellie M. Exh. 1922-39
Stratford-on-Avon, Warwicks. † B 15, RCA 1.

WARD, Orlando Frank Montagu b. 1868
Painter, and picture restorer. b. Rougham. Lived and worked in Italy and Paris for many years. Married Brita W. q.v. Exh. 1890-1927. Add: Hammersmith 1890; Chelsea, London 1922. † NG 1, RA 2, RI 1.

WARD, Mrs. R. Exh. 1884-87
Watercolour painter. 14 Clarendon Gardens, Maida Vale, London. † D 1 SWA 6.

WARD, Thomas Exh. 1884
St. Paul's Close, Clapham, London. † RA 1.

WARD, Thomas Exh. 1938-39
Sheffield. † M 1, RCA 1.

WARD, Vernon* b. 1905
Landscape, portrait, figure and bird painter. Studied Slade School. A.R.B.A. 1926. Exh. 1925-27. Add: 8 South Hill Park Gardens, Hampstead, London. † RBA 5, ROI 1.

WARD, W.C. Exh. 1884-86
Watercolour landscape painter. 2 Church Terrace, Richmond, Surrey. † D 1, DOW 1, L 1.

WARD, W.H. Exh. 1898-1909
Architect. London. † RA 8.

WARD, W.H. Exh. 1920-32
Birmingham. † B 21.

WARDALE, J.J. Exh. 1887
Landscape painter. Barrow-on-Trent, Derby. † N 2.

WARDELL, Ethel M. Exh. 1926-27
Flower painter. 6 Carlyle Studios, Kings Road, London. † NEA 2.

WARDEN, A. Exh. 1889-91
Manchester. † M 5.

WARDEN, Doris G. Exh. 1928-40
Birmingham. † B 27.

WARDEN, Mrs. Eva E. see PYNE

WARDEN, Miss E.J. Exh. 1894
101 Bristol Road, Edgbaston, Birmingham. † B 1.

WARDEN, Mrs. Ethel Mary Exh. 1901-4
Tamworth, Staffs. 1901; Atherstone 1904. † B 6.

WARDEN, Miss G.D. Exh. 1926
Craft Rooms, Queen's College, Birmingham. † B 1.

WARDEN, G.F. Exh. 1905
Birch Grove, Rusholme, Manchester. † RA 1.

WARDEN, Laurence Exh. 1904-13
Rusholme, Manchester 1904; Hessle, East Yorks. 1910. † B 2, L 5, RA 1.

WARDEN, Miss L.M. Exh. 1920
Greta Bridge House, Kirby Lonsdale. † L 1.

WARDEN, Marion Emily Exh. 1921-27
Watercolour painter and teacher. b. Birmingham. Studied Birmingham School of Art. Add: Weston-super-Mare, Somerset. † B 3, D 1.

WARDEN, William b. 1908
Watercolour landscape painter. Studied Liverpool City School of Art. Exh. 1933-40. Add: Liverpool 1933; Tonbridge, Kent 1940. † L 1, NEA 1, RA 1.

WARDLE, Arthur* 1864-1949
Animal painter. R.I. 1922. "Fate" purchased by Chantrey Bequest 1904. Add: London. † AG 1, B 32, D 8, FIN 49, GI 1, L 58, M 17, RA 113, RBA 26, RHA 5, RI 95, ROI 27, RSA 1, RSW 1 TOO 36.

WARDLE, Annie E.L. Exh. 1899
72 Beaufort Road, Edgbaston, Birmingham. † B 1.

WARDLE, B. Exh. 1934
A.N.S.A. 1934. Add: 46 Burns Street, Nottingham. † N 2.

WARDLE, B.A. Exh. 1914
21 Mansfield Road, Nottingham. † N 1.

WARDLE, F. Exh. 1882-89
Landscape painter. London. † D 2, RA 1, RBA 2, ROI 1.

WARDLE, G.E. Exh. 1920-21
Painter. Old Hall, Little Hallam, Ilkeston, Derbys. † N 2.

WARDLE, S.T. Exh. 1910-39
Landscape and flower painter. Ilkeston, Derbys. 1910; Old Hall, Little Hallam, Ilkeston, Derbys. 1920. † N 37.

WARDLE, Thomas Exh. 1929
Painter. † AB 3.

WARDLEY, Mrs. Joan b. 1899
Flower and furniture painter and wall decorator. Studied R.A. Schools. Exh. 1927. Add: 4 Cheyne Court, London. † RA 1.

WARDLOW, Agnes Exh. 1900
† RMS 2.

WARDLOW, Miss Annie Exh. 1887-97
Portrait and miniature painter. Acton and South Norwood, London. † L 2, RA 4, RHA 1, RI 4, SWA 1.

WARDLOW, Alexander Hamilton Exh. 1885-99
Miniature portrait painter. Acton and South Norwood, London. † L 4, RA 12, RHA 2, RI 7.

WARDLOW, Miss Eleanor Francis Exh. 1893-99
Miniature painter. South Norwood, London. † L 1, RI 3.

WARDLOW, Miss Mary Alexandra Exh. 1886-1914
Miniature portrait painter. Acton and South Norwood, London. † L 4, RA 10, RI 5.

WARDMAN, Thomas Exh. 1886
Landscape painter. Hawthorn, Potters Bar, Herts. † ROI 1.

WARDROP, Henry Exh. 1886
19 St. Andrews Square, Edinburgh. † RSA 1.

WARD-WILLIS, S.W. Exh. 1932
4 Belsize Studios, Glenilla Road, Hampstead, London. † RSA 1.

WARE, Mrs. Armyne Exh. 1931-40
Edinburgh. † RSA 15.

WARE, Edmund Exh. 1908-40
Sculptor. London 1908 and 1934; Liverpool 1929. † L 5, RA 5, RSA 1.

WARE, E.T.W. Exh. 1905
36 Gayhurst Road, Dalston, London. † L 3.

WARE, Harry Fabian Exh. 1928-40
Landscape and figure painter. London 1928; Edinburgh 1932. † BA 37, RA 1, RSA 15.

WARING, Miss A.V. Exh. 1917
Oxted, Surrey. † SWA 1.

WARING, C.E.D. Exh. 1882
3 Clarendon Avenue, Altrincham, Cheshire. † M 1.

WARING, Henry Franks Exh. 1900-28
Landscape and architectural painter. London 1900; Bosham, Sussex 1920; Charmouth, Dorset 1925; Ringwould, Kent 1927. † B 3, BG 35, L 5, NEA 1, RA 8, RBA 1 RI 10, ROI 2, WG 77.

WARING, Lily Florence b. 1877
Landscape painter. b. Birkenhead. Studied Manchester School of Art, Cambridge School of Art and in France. Exh. 1906-39. Add: Warrington, Lancs. 1906; Greystones, Ireland 1932; Cambridge 1937. † BA 142, GOU 2, L 1, RBA 1, RCA 2, RHA 4, RI 1, SWA 2.

WARING, W.H. Exh. 1886-1928
Birmingham. † B 22.

WARLEIGH, Norah Exh. 1904-19
Rock Ferry, Cheshire. † L 15.

WARLOW, Mrs. B.R. Exh. 1925-30
10 Hamilton Square, Birkenhead. † L 2.

WARLOW, G.P. Exh. 1901-30
Hamilton Square, Birkenhead 1901 and 1930; Sheffield 1913. † L 3, RA 1.

WARLOW, Miss H. Exh. 1912-32
Ormskirk, Lancs. † L 10.

WARLOW, Herbert Gordon b. 1885
Watercolour painter and etcher. b. Sheffield. Studied Sheffield School of Art. A.R.E. 1916. Exh. 1916-40. Add: London 1916; Sheffield 1917; Weybridge, Surrey 1926. † AB 2, FIN 2, L 5, RA 17, RE 46.

WARLOW, H. Picton Exh. 1933
Painter. † RED 2.

WARMAN, William Exh. 1912-19
Architect and perspective artist. Studied South Kensington, France, Belgium and Italy. Add: London. † RA 4.

WARMBY, Byron Winston b. 1902
Painter. Studied City of Sheffield College of Arts and Crafts, 1920-25. Exh. 1938. Add: 12 Edgedale Road, Sheffield. † B 2.

WARMINGTON, E.S. Exh. 1885
Chapel Terrace, Upper Ranmore Road, Sheffield. † L 1.

WARMINGTON, Margaret Exh. 1894
166 Castle Street, Dudley, Worcs. † B 1.

WARN, Elizabeth Baldwin Exh. 1899-1936
Landscape and miniature portrait painter. Bushey, Herts. 1899; Wirksworth, Derbys. 1905; Marlborough, Wilts. 1914. † D 1, L 8, RA 15, RCA 1, RMS 2, SWA 7.

WARNE, Amy C. Exh. 1894-1933
Fruit and miniature portrait painter. Stamford Hill, London 1900; Bexhill on Sea 1928. † B 2, RA 5, SWA 4.

WARNE, Mrs. Dorothy Hadwen b. 1903
Miniature painter. Studied St. Johns Wood School of Art 1923-25. Exh. 1932-38. Add: 22 The Holt, Alverstoke, Hants. † RA 10, RMS 1.

WARNE, E.J. Exh. 1922
8 Clifford Street, London. † L 1.

WARNER, Compton Exh. 1880
Watercolour landscape painter. The Rookery, Woodford, Essex. † RBA 1.

WARNER, Harry Exh. 1902-4
10 Avondale Road, Mortlake, Surrey. † B 1, D 1, L 3, RCA 1.

WARNER, Howard b. 1881
Watercolour painter. Studied London and Norwich. Exh. 1940. Add: Beecles, Suffolk. † RI 1.

WARNER, John Exh. 1930-39
Birmingham. † B 8.

WARNER, Mrs. L.M. Exh. 1933
Clubhouse, Bidston. † L 1.

WARNER, R. Exh. 1890
10 Fulham Park Gardens, London. † D 3.

WARNES, Herschell F. b. 1891
Painter and craftworker. b. Birmingham. Studied Birmingham School of Art. On teaching staff of Birmingham School of Art for 10 years. Exh. 1921-34. Add: Birmingham. † B 13.

WARNEUKE, Mrs. Amy J. Exh. 1893-1909
Glasgow 1893; Milngavie, N.B. 1904; Hyndland, N.B. 1906. † GI 8.

WARR, G.H. Exh. 1907-33
Sheffield 1907; Liverpool 1921. † L 4, RA 1.

WARRACK, Harriet Exh. 1887-92
Montrose, N.B. 1887; St. Andrews, N.B. 1892. † RSA 2.

WARRE, Miss E.C.F. Exh. 1901-13
Bemerton Rectory, Salisbury, Wilts. † SWA 5.

WARREN, Albert Exh. 1887
Watercolour painter. 20 Vardens Road, Wandsworth Common, London. † RI 1.

WARREN, Benjamin John 1878-1954
Painter, stained glass artist and teacher. Studied Birmingham Municipal School of Art and Heatherleys. Add: Birmingham. † B 25, P 1.

WARREN, Claude Exh. 1887
Landscape painter. c/o R. Mack, 28 St. Pauls Road, Islington, London. † L 2.

WARREN, C.E. Exh. 1884
The Mount House, Shrewsbury. † RHA 1.

WARREN, C. Knighton* Exh. 1880-92
Portrait, genre and historical painter. Married Gertrude M.W. q.v. Add: London. † FIN 1, L 9, M 4, RA 17, RBA 8, RI 7, ROI 1, RSA 1.

WARREN, Mrs. D. Momber Exh. 1936
Landscape painter. 12A Chaplin Road, Wembley, Middlesex. † RA 1.

WARREN, Edward Exh. 1882
16 St. James Street, Liverpool. † L 3.

WARREN, Edward A. Exh. 1928-33
Landscape painter. London 1928; Dublin 1933. † RA 1, RHA 3.

WARREN, Edmund George* 1834-1909
Landscape painter. Son of Henry W. (1794-1879) A.R.I. 1852, R.I. 1856, R.O.I. 1883. Add: London 1888; and 1908; Chudleigh, Devon 1901. † AG 1, DOW 1, FIN 1, L 1, RHA 1, RI 101, ROI 46, TOO 6.

WARREN, E.L. Exh. 1902
14 Borrowdale Road, Sefton Park, Liverpool. † L 1.

WARREN, Emily Mary Bibbens Exh. 1900-39
Landscape and architectural painter. Studied Royal College of Art. A.R.B.A. 1919, R.B.A. 1931. Add: London 1900; West Clandon, Surrey 1927. † B 4, D 50, L7, LS 11, RA 2, RBA 63, RI 5 SWA 29.

WARREN, Edward Prioleau 1856-1937
Architect and architectural painter. London. † RA 42, RID 2.

WARREN, Mrs. Frances Bramley Exh. 1889-1901
Painter. London. † B 11, D 2, GI 3, L 5 M 2, RA 1, RHA 11, SWA 4.

WARREN, G. Exh. 1906
The Studios, Anlaby Road, Teddington, Middlesex. † RA 1.

WARREN, Gerald Exh. 1924-35
Architect. London. † RA 18.

WARREN, Gertrude M. Exh. 1881-98
Painter. Married C. Knighton W. q.v. Add: London. † L 6, M 3, RA 10, RBA 1.

WARREN, H. Broadhurst Exh. 1887-93
Landscape painter. Hillside, Roxbury, Boston, U.S.A. † L 1, M 1, RA 1.

WARREN, Ismena R. Exh. 1926
School of Art, Kildare Street, Dublin. † RHA 1.

WARREN, J.R. Warren Exh. 1888
Watercolour landscape painter. † GOU 2.

WARREN, Miss K.M. Exh. 1881-84
Portrait painter. Lenton Park, Nottingham 1881; Edinburgh 1883. † N 5, RSA 4.

WARREN, Miss L.A. Exh. 1919
25 Westgate Terrace, London. † SWA 2.

WARREN, Nesta Exh. 1909-22
Conway, Wales. † L 2, RCA 19.

WARREN, O.B. Exh. 1930-36
Portrait painter. 119 Dysart Road, Grantham, Lincs. † N 2.

WARREN, Mrs. Roberta Exh. 1913-40
Miniature portrait painter. Kew Gardens, Surrey 1913; Richmond, Surrey 1922. † L 5, RA 7, RI 47, SWA 2.

WARREN, Sarah Exh. 1884
Watercolour landscape painter. † SWA 1.

WARREN, Walter Exh. 1931
Watercolour figure painter. 41 Maplethorpe Road, Thornton Heath, Surrey. † RA 1.

WARREN, W.J. Exh. 1883
Meyrick House, Bournemouth. † D 1

WARREN, William Joseph Exh. 1908-9
The Studio, 34 Anlaby Road, Teddington, Middlesex. † LS 8.

WARREN, William W. Exh. 1885-88
Landscape and coastal painter. Queensborough, nr. Leicester. † N 1, RI 3.

WARRENER, William T. Exh. 1887-99
Figure and landscape painter. R.B.A. 1896. Add: The Moorlands, Bracebridge, Lincoln. † L 4, M 3, NEA 3, RA 8, RBA 15.

WARRICK, F.B. Exh. 1885
21 Avenue de la Gare, Nice, France. † B 2.

WARRINER, Kate E. Exh. 1888
Landscape painter. 39 Burns Street, Nottingham. † N 1.

WARRINGTON, Bishop of Exh. 1928-31
Landscape painter. † AB 4, WG 1.

WARRINGTON, Ellen Exh. 1931-39
Flower painter. London. † L 1, RA 2, ROI 4, SWA 6.

WARRINGTON, E.A. Exh. 1882
Manchester. † M 1.

WARRINGTON, R.W. Exh. 1899-1900
52 Kinglake Street, Liverpool. † L 2.

WARRY, Daniel Robert Exh. 1904-13
Architect. Lewisham 1904; Eltham, Kent 1907. † RA 3.

WARSOP, Albert E. Exh 1882-88
Portrait painter. N.S.A. 1881. Add: Newcastle Chambers, Angel Row, Nottingham. † N 5.

WARSOP, Frederick Exh. 1882-94
Landscape and portrait painter. N.S.A. 1884. Add: Nottingham. † N 5.

WARSOP, H.J. Exh. 1886
76 Queen's Walk, Nottingham. † N 2.

WART, van See V

WARTH, Fanny C. Exh. 1929-38
109 Sandford Road, Moseley, Birmingham. † B 13.

WARTH, Vera S. Exh. 1931
109 Sandford Road, Moseley, Birmingham. † B 1.

WARWICK, E. Exh. 1933
Mill Hill, London. † SWA 1.

WARWICK, M.E. Exh. 1930
Wood engraver. † RED 2.

WARWICK, Septimus Exh. 1904-34
Architect. London. † RA 15.

WARWOOD, Miss M. Exh. 1926
Amberley, Church Stretton, Salop. † B 1.

WASHBROOK, George Exh. 1929-34
Watercolour landscape painter. 10 Cleeve Road, Knowle, Bristol. † RA 3, RBA 2, RI 1

WASHBROOK, M.L. Exh. 1931
Nottingham. † RCA 2.

WASHBROOKE, W.R. Exh. 1925-39
Landscape painter. A.N.S.A. 1926, N.S.A. 1929. Add: Dunkirk, Nottingham 1925; Wollaton Park, Nottingham 1934. † N 60.

WASHINGTON, Miss P. Exh. 1906
13 King Street, Baker Street, London. † RA 1.

WASHINGTON, William 1885-1956
Etcher and engraver. b. Marple. Studied Royal College of Art. Head of Dept. of Arts and Crafts L.C.C. Hammersmith School of Building. A.R.E. 1931. Exh. 1912-40. Add: London. † BA 3, GI 1, I 2, L 3, LS 6, NEA 5, RA 20, RE 20, RHA 1.

WASLEY, Frank* Exh. 1880-1914
Black and white artist. Nottingham 1880; Shrewsbury 1882; Manchester 1895; Whitby, Yorks. 1896; Weston super Mare 1903; Littlehampton 1908; London 1912; Henley on Thames 1914. † B 2, L 2, N 2, RA 3, RI 2.

WASSE, Arthur* Exh. 1882-1910
Flower, figure and landscape painter. Manchester 1882; London 1886; Bavaria 1904; Paris 1910. † GI 5, L 13, M 15, RA 12 RBA 1, RI 1.

WASSE, Emily Exh. 1882-91
Parsonage Road, Flixton, Manchester. † M 8.

WASSERMANN, J.C. Exh. 1880-82
Watercolour painter. 50 Beverly Terrace, Cullercoats, Newcastle. † D 1, GI 1, RA 2, RBA 1, RSA 4.

WATANEBE, Miss Musme Exh. 1923-40
Edinburgh. † GI 8, L 2, RSA 2 RSW 2.

WATELET, Charles J. Exh. 1925
111 Church Street, London. † L 1.

WATELIN, Louis* 1838-1907
French painter. Exh. 1892. † TOO 2.

WATELIN, S. Exh. 1891-95
† TOO 2.

WATERER, Anthony Exh. 1938
Painter. † RED 1.

WATERFIELD, Aubrey Exh. 1911-31
Landscape and flower painter. Laniquiauci, Italy 1911; Florence, Italy 1931. † G 2, NEA 2, RA 1.

WATERFIELD, D.H. Exh. 1936-39
† NEA 4.

WATERFIELD, Geo R. b. 1886
Painter, engraver, wood engraver and illustrator. Studied Birmingham. Exh. 1920-37. Add: Birmingham. † B 41, L 1.

WATERFIELD, Humphrey Exh. 1902-36
Landscape and portrait painter and lithographer. London. † COO 9, NEA 1.

WATERFIELD, Margaret Exh. 1889-1911
Flower painter. A.S.W.A. 1899. Add: Nackington House, Canterbury, Kent. † B 25, D 2, L 5, RBA 3, RI 1, SWA 6.

WATERFIELD, Winifred Exh. 1937
Watercolour painter. Studied in Paris. † WG 38.

WATERFORD, Louise, Marchioness of 1818-1891
The Hon. Miss Stuart. Painter and watercolourist. H.S.W.A. 1887. Add: Ford Castle, Northumberland 1880 and 1888; Christchurch, Hants. 1884 and 1889. † D 2, G 8, M 7, RHA 2, SWA 3.

WATERHOUSE, Alfred 1830-1905
Painter and architect. A.R.A. 1878, R.A. 1885. Add: London. † L 1, M 3, RA 57.

WATERHOUSE, Esther Exh. 1884-1925
Watercolour flower painter. Married John William W. q.v. Add: London. † B 3, L 1, M 3, NG 1, RA 7, RBA 1, RI 6.

WATERHOUSE, G.C. Exh. 1915
c/o H.A. Welch, 7 New Square, Lincolns Inn, London. † RA 1.

WATERHOUSE, Miss G.V. Exh. 1908-13
Dorking, Surrey 1908; Kensington, London 1910. † L 2, RA 3, RI 2.

WATERHOUSE, John William* 1849-1917
Historical genre painter. Studied under his father and at R.A. Schools. Married Esther W. q.v. A.R.A. 1885, R.A. 1895, R.I. 1882, R.O.I. 1885. "The Magic Circle" purchased by Chantrey Bequest 1886. Add: London. † AG 1, B 8, D 4, G 2, GI 9, L 24, M 9, NG 8, P 1, RA 76, RHA 2, RI 2, ROI 4, TOO 3.

WATERHOUSE, Lucy Exh. 1927
Holt Green, Aughton, Ormskirk, Lancs. † L 1.

WATERHOUSE, Michael b. 1888
Architect. Son of Paul W. q.v. Exh. 1921-31. Add: Staple Inn Buildings, Holborn, London. † RA 6.

WATERHOUSE, Paul Exh. 1891-1923
Architect. Father of Michael W. q.v. Add: London. † RA 36, RSA 3.

WATERLOW, Adrian Exh. 1937-38
Painter. 21A Heath Street, Hampstead, London. † RA 2.

WATERLOW, Miss C. Exh. 1893
† SWA 1.

WATERLOW, Sir Ernest Albert* 1850-1919
Landscape and animal painter. Studied at Heidelberg, Lausanne and R.A. Schools (Turner Gold Medal 1873). A.R.A. 1890, R.A. 1903, H.R.M.S. 1898, R.O.I. 1883, H.R.O.I. 1899, R.S.W. 1900, A.R.W.S. 1880, R.W.S. 1894, P.R.W.S. 1897. Knighted 1902. "Galway Gossips" purchased by Chantrey Bequest 1887. Add: London. † AG 1, B 13, D 13, FIN 3, G 13, GI 7, L 37, M 37, NG 4, RA 177, RBA 8, RHA 3, ROI 26, RSW 17, RWS 206, TOO 6, WG 6.

WATERLOW, G.S. Exh. 1916-20
Killinney, Ireland 1916; Dublin 1918. † RHA 18.

WATERLOW, Miss Hinemoa Exh. 1923-34
Miniature portrait painter. London 1923; Edinburgh 1934. † P 1, RA 1, RBA 4, RSA 1, SWA 1.

WATERS, Miss Exh. 1913
35 Cochrane Street, St. Johns Wood, London. † L 1.

WATERS, Arthur Exh. 1928
18 Lockington Road, Battersea, London. † RA 1.

WATERS, Miss Billie b. 1896
Flower, animal and decorative panel painter. b. Richmond, Surrey. Studied Harvey and Proctor School, Newlyn and South Kensington. Exh. 1925-40. Add: London. † GOU 6, L 5, LEI 41, NEA 2, RA 21, ROI 1, SWA 3.

WATERS, Miss C. Exh. 1907
16 Pandora Road, West Hampstead, London. † RA 1.

WATERS, D.B. Exh. 1887-1910
Edinburgh 1887; London 1895. † RA 1, RSA 2.

WATERS, Mrs. Emily Exh. 1887
Landscape painter. 7 Mansfield Street, Portland Place, London. † SWA 1.

WATERS, F. Boyd Exh. 1911-35
Miniature portrait painter. A.R.M.S. 1924, R.M.S. 1928. Add: Paris 1911 and 1924; Weymouth 1919; Cannes, France 1926. † L 7, RA 9, RMS 44.

WATERS, George Exh. 1926-32
Landscape painter. 11 Ophir Gardens, Antrim Road, Belfast. † RHA 6.

WATERS, George Fite b. 1894
Sculptor. b. San Francisco, California, U.S.A. Studied with H. Elwell in New York and Rodin in Paris. Exh. 1927. Add: 33 Rue du Docteur Blanche, Paris. † RA 1.

WATERS, Kate Exh. 1909
Flower painter. † BG 1.

WATERS, Kathleen Exh. 1932
Bolton Studios, Redcliffe Road, London. † ROI 2.

WATERS, Sadie 1869-1900
American landscape painter. Exh. 1897. Add: c/o A. Parsons, 54 Bedford Gardens, Kensington, London. † L 2, RA 1.

WATERS, Mrs. Tolver Exh. 1889-90
Landscape and figure painter. 23 Camperdown, Gt. Yarmouth, Norfolk. † RID 6.

WATERSON, David 1870-1954
Painter, etcher and engraver. A.R.E. 1901. R.E. 1910. Add: Brechin, Scotland. † L 3, RE 89, RSA 14.

WATERSTON, Dorothea Exh. 1914-35
Edinburgh. † RSA 3, RSW 3.

WATERSTON, W. Exh. 1885-86
28 Greyfriars Gate, Edinburgh. † RSA 2.

WATERSTONE, Joshua J. Exh. 1902
10 Claremont Crescent, Edinburgh. † RSA 1.

WATERSTONE, James S. Exh. 1904-10
32 Sanderson Road, Newcastle on Tyne. † L 1, RSA 1.

WATERTON, Albert Edward b. 1896
Portrait, landscape and figure painter. Studied R.A. Schools. Exh. 1925-27. Add: Green Lane, Chalock, nr. Ashford, Kent. † RCA 3.

WATERWORTH, Miss E. Exh. 1923-28
Liverpool. † L 11.

WATERWORTH, Miss M. Exh. 1923-29
Liverpool. † L 14.

WATHERSTON, Evelyn M. d. 1952
Portrait, animal and landscape painter. Studied Paris and R.A. Schools. Sister of Marjorie Violet W. q.v. Exh. from 1901. Add: London. † AR 47, L 8, NG 1, P 2, RA 5, RI 10, ROI 3, SWA 3, WG 41.

WATHERSTON, Marjorie Violet d. c.1970
Mrs. H.L. Geare. Portrait, historical, interior and poster painter. Studied Paris and R.A. Schools. Sister of Evelyn M.W. q.v. Exh. from 1905. Add: London. † AR 33, L 7, P 8, RA 10, RI 1, ROI 10, RSA 3, SWA 2, WG 41.

WATKIN, Isabel Exh. 1895-1940
Landscape and figure painter. London. † G 2, I 1, L 8, RA 9, RBA 1, RI 17, RID 4, SWA 3.

WATKINS, Bartholomew Colles 1833-1891
Landscape painter. A.R.H.A. 1861, R.H.A. 1864. Add: Manchester 1880; Dublin 1884. † RHA 32.

WATKINS, C. Exh. 1888
53 Warwick Road, South Kensington, London. † RHA 1.

WATKINS, Dorothy Exh. 1933-35
21 Bedale Road, Daybrook Vale, Nottingham. † N 3.

WATKINS, Dudley Dexter Exh. 1919-34
Painter. Nottingham. † N 25.

WATKINS, E Stanley Exh. 1898-1914
Stained glass artist. Ealing, London. † RA 9.

WATKINS, Frank Exh. 1880-89
London 1880 and 1866; Wycombe Marsh, Bucks. 1883. † M 1, RHA 8.

WATKINS, G. Exh. 1914
42 Eaton Place, London. † RA 1.

WATKINS, G.A. Exh. 1932
100 Leonard Road, Handsworth, Birmingham. † B 1.

WATKINS, Irene Exh. 1914
7 St. Johns Park, Blackheath, London. † RA 1.

WATKINS, John Exh. 1880-1904
Watercolour painter and etcher. R.E. 1891 (ceased 1908). Add: London and Paris. † B 29, D 2, G 2, L 6, M 1, RA 7, RBA 19, RE 18, RI 11, ROI 2.

WATKINS, Mrs. Kate W. Exh. 1886-88
Landscape painter. The College, Durham. † G 2, RA 2.

WATKINS, L. Clare Exh. 1912-14
Rathmore, Boscombe, Bournemouth. † L 1, LS 3.

WATKINS, Mary K. Exh. 1889
3 Clifton Villas, Maida Hill, London. † RHA 1.

WATKINS, Susan b. 1875
American painter. Exh. 1901. Add: 127 Rue Bourcicaut, Fountenay aux Roses, France. † RA 1.

WATKINS, Samuel W. Exh. 1900
Mayfield, North Circular Road, Dublin. † RHA 1.

WATKINS, T.W. Exh. 1914
23 Old Queen Street, Westminster, London. † RA 1.

WATKINS, William Arthur b. 1885
Landscape painter and etcher. Studied Portsmouth School of Art, Croydon School of Art and City of London School of Art. A.R.B.A. 1926, R.I. 1939. Exh. 1921-40. Add: West Croydon, Surrey. † COO 2, GI 1, RA 3, RBA 2, RI 15, ROI 2.

WATKINSON, Henry Exh. 1884-93
Manchester. † M 10.

WATKINSON, Hilda Muriel b. 1895
Mrs. Mack. Painter and etcher. b. Glasgow. Studied Slade School and Colarossi's, Paris. Exh. 1916-33. Add: Liverpool 1916 and 1920; London 1919. † GOU 2, L 13, NEA 3.

WATMOUGH, Amos Exh. 1884-85
84 High Street, Gt. Horton, nr. Bradford, Yorks. † L 1, M 1.

WATSON, Mrs. Exh. 1881
Watercolour fruit and flower painter. Red House, Witley, Surrey. † RBA 2.

WATSON, Miss Exh. 1926
Liverpool Society of Handloom Weavers, Melville Chambers, Lord Street, Liverpool. † L 1.

WATSON, Miss A. Exh. 1882
Croft Bridge, Cambridge. † B 1

WATSON, Miss Ada See RAAB

WATSON, Alfred Exh. 1898
27 Dora Road, Small Heath, Birmingham. † B 1.

WATSON, Andrew Exh. 1917-25
Ingleside, Woodlands, Falkirk. † GI 1, L 2, RSA 1.

WATSON, Annie Exh. 1884
11 Belmont Crescent, Glasgow. † GI 2.

WATSON, Mrs. A.B.C. Exh. 1898
170 Hammersmith Road, London. † L 1.

WATSON, Mrs. A.E. Lindsay Exh. 1899-1901
Briary Yards, Hawick, N.B. † RSA 2.

WATSON, Annie Gordon Exh. 1888
Flower painter. Wydford House, Ryde, I.O.W. † RBA 1.

WATSON, A.M. Exh. 1905
9 Nottingham Place, London. † RA 1.

WATSON, Albermale P. Exh. 1884-99
Coastal painter. Kingsbridge, Devon 1884; Milverton, Somerset 1899. † B 1, RBA 1.

WATSON, A.R. Exh. 1923
150 Easterhill Street, Tollcross, Glasgow. † GI 1.

WATSON, A.T. Exh. 1883
La Favourita, Guernsey, C.I. † L 1.

WATSON, Barbara See CHRISTIAN

WATSON, Miss B.C. West Exh. 1919
† L 1.

WATSON, Charles John* 1846-1927
Coastal, landscape and figure painter and etcher. Married Minna Bolingbroke q.v. R.E. 1881. Add: All Saints Green, Norwich 1880; London 1889. † AG 1, AR 1, CON 1, D 7, DOW 1, FIN 12, G 3, GI 10, L 15, M 10, NG 1, RA 81, RBA 14, RE 126, RHA 7, RI 13, ROI 2.

WATSON, Constance Stella Exh. 1928
Etcher, sculptor and pottery worker. Studied Goldsmiths College and R.A. Schools. Travelled in New Zealand. Add: 25 Cathcart Road, London. † SWA 2.

WATSON, C. Winifred Exh. 1921-23
Liver Sketching Club, 11 Dale Street, Liverpool. † L 5.

WATSON, D. Exh. 1891
Springside House, Rawtenstall. † L 1.

WATSON, Dan b. 1891
Painter and wood engraver. Studied Leicester College of Art. Exh. 1925-39. Add: 94 Dannett Street, Leicester. † N 36.

WATSON, Rev. David Exh. 1894-99
40 Granby Terrace, Glasgow. † GI 2, RSW 1.

WATSON, Dawson b. 1864
Landscape painter. Llanrwrst, North Wales 1883; London 1889; Conway 1898. Went to U.S.A. † M 4, RA 1, RBA 4, RCA 2, ROI 1.

WATSON, Dora Exh. 1888-1924
Painter. Leeds 1888; Wentbridge, Yorks. 1905; Pontefract, Yorks. 1910; Ranskill, Notts. 1912. † B 3, GI 3, L 2, LS 23, N 2, RHA 3, RSA 1.

WATSON, Mrs. Douglas Exh. 1902-5
A.S.W.A. 1901. Add: 7 Upper Cheyne Road, London. † SWA 2.

WATSON, Dorothea Jane Exh. 1883-96
Figure painter. Model Farm, Tetworth, Oxon. † B 4, SWA 9.

WATSON, Emma Exh. 1880-1904
Painter. Glasgow. † GI 31, L 6, M 1, RA 1, RSA 14, RSW 1.

WATSON, Elizabeth Gill Exh. 1885
Watercolour painter. Gt. Berkhampstead, Berks. † SWA 1.

WATSON, Edith L. Exh. 1914-24
Liverpool 1914 and 1920; London 1919. † L 16, RCA 2, SWA 2.

WATSON, Ethel M. Exh. 1917-21
Miniature portrait painter. 44 Denbigh Road, Ealing, London. † RA 4.

WATSON, E. Vernon Exh. 1938-39
Wardle Crescent, Edinburgh. † RSW 3.

WATSON, Miss Frances See SUNDERLAND

WATSON, F.G. Exh. 1882
Watercolour fruit painter. Red House, Witley, Surrey. † RBA 2.

WATSON, G. Exh. 1929
Etcher. † FIN 2.

WATSON, Lady G. Exh. 1908-11
Watercolour flower painter. 16 Wilton Crescent, London. † B 1, BG 6, LS 14,

WATSON, Geoffrey Exh. 1924-37
Portrait and figure painter. London. † COO 58, GOU 1, M 2, NEA 1, RA 2.

WATSON, Mrs. Gertrude See HENSON

WATSON, George Cuthbert Exh. 1921-40
Edinburgh 1921; Dunfermline 1932. † GI 4, L 1, RSA 23, RSW 1.

WATSON, Grace I. Exh. 1892-96
Painter. 7 Rothschild Gardens, West Norwood, London. † GI 1, L 2, M 2, RA 1, RBA 2, RHA 1, ROI 3, SWA 1.

WATSON, Gabrielle J. Exh. 1936-39
Painter and linocut artist. 94 Dannett Street, Leicester. † N 5.

WATSON, George Mackie Exh. 1901-27
Edinburgh. † GI 2, RSA 8.

WATSON, Mrs. G.P.H.
See AMOUR, Elizabeth Isobel

WATSON, George Patrick Houston
1887-1960
Painter and architect. Studied Edinburgh College of Art. R.S.W. 1938. Married Elizabeth Isobel Amour q.v. Add: Edinburgh 1919 and 1939; Balerno, Midlothian 1934. † GI 18, L 6, RA 1, RSA 24, RSW 19.

WATSON, George Spencer* 1869-1934
Portrait and figure painter. Studied R.A. Schools. A.R.A. 1923, R.A. 1932, R.O.I. 1901, R.P. 1904. "A Lady in Black" (1922) purchased by Chantrey Bequest 1935. Add: London. † FIN 41, G 7, GI 13, I 3, L 4, NEA 2, NG 31, P 77, RA 137, RHA 1, RID 4, ROI 37, RSA 4, RWS 8.

WATSON, Harry 1871-1936
Landscape and figure painter. b. Scarborough. Studied Scarborough School of Art, Royal College of Art, Lambeth School of Art. Life master Regent Street Polytechnic. R.O.I. 1932, A.R.W.S. 1915, R.W.S. 1920. Married Barbara Christian q.v. "Across the River" purchased by Chantrey Bequest 1913. Add: London. † AB 2, B 1, CHE 1, G 2, GI 20, GOU 180, L 31, M 2, NEA 4, RA 81, RBA 4, RI 2, ROI 14, RSA 4, RSW 1, RWS 87, WG 4.

WATSON, Homer* 1855-1936
Canadian landscape painter. Pittenween, Fife 1888; Cookham Dene, Berks. 1890; Maidenhead, Berks. 1897; Hillhead, Glasgow 1898; Doon, Waterloo County, Ontario, Canada 1900. † GI 7, GOU 2, L 2, M 2, NEA 3, NG 6, RA 2, RBA 3, ROI 1.

WATSON, Miss H.B. Exh. 1900-8
Liverpool 1900; Bromborough, Cheshire 1902. † L 10.

WATSON, Henry Weekes Exh. 1895
10 Bolton Studios, Redcliffe Road, London. † L 1.

WATSON, Horace W. Exh. 1930
12½ Pope Street, Birmingham. † B 1.

WATSON, Ida Exh. 1924
Flower painter. 127 Nottingham Road, Langley Mill, Notts. † N 2.

WATSON, James Exh. 1910-32
Watercolour painter. Head of Art Dept. Morgan Academy, Dundee. Add: Dundee. † GI 8, L 5, RA 1, RSA 11.

WATSON, James Exh. 1900
Landscape painter. 5 Nesham Street, Newcastle on Tyne. † RA 1.

WATSON, Jessie Exh. 1891
Wilton Bank, Hawick, N.B. † RSA 1.

WATSON, John Exh. 1888-1901
Kilmarnock. † GI 12.

WATSON, John 1873-1936
Architect. A.R.S.A. 1929. Add: London 1897; Edinburgh 1907; Glasgow 1931. † GI 1, RA 1, RSA 11.

WATSON, John Exh. 1940
1 Kennoway Drive, Glasgow. † GI 1.

WATSON, Joseph Exh. 1902
13 Cromwell Square, Queen's Park, Glasgow. † GI 1.

WATSON, Joyce See RUTHERFORD

WATSON, James A. Exh. 1883-88
Glasgow. † GI 2, RSA 2.

WATSON, J.B. Exh. 1887-89
102 Belgrave Street, Glasgow. † GI 1, RSA 3.

WATSON, John Dawson* 1832-1892
Painter and illustrator. Studied Manchester School of Design and R.A. Schools. Brother of Thomas J.W. q.v. R.B.A. 1882, A.R.W.S. 1865, R.W.S. 1870. Add: London 1880; Conway, Wales 1891. † G 2, GI 9, L 11, M 8, RA 10, RBA 17, RCA 11, RWS 27.

WATSON, J. Hannan Exh. 1892-1908
Glasgow 1892; Houston, Renfrewshire 1899; Gargunoch, Stirling and Glasgow 1900. † GI 28, L 1, RSA 2.

WATSON, J. Hardwick Exh. 1885-88
Edinburgh. † GI 2, RSA 3.

WATSON, Jenny J. Exh. 1894-98
5 Westbourn Terrace, London. † GI 1, RSW 1.

WATSON, Miss J.M. Exh. 1908
14 Cantley Avenue, Clapham Common, London. † RA 1.

WATSON, Mrs. L. Exh. 1886
Leaburn, Hawick, N.B. † RSA 1.

WATSON, Lilian G. See FRECK

WATSON, Leslie Joseph b. 1906
Landscape and figure painter. b. Harrogate. Studied Leeds College of Art 1924-28 and Royal College of Art 1928-32. Exh. 1934-38. Add: London. † NEA 3, RA 5, ROI 1.

WATSON, Lizzie May Exh. 1884-1902
Landscape, figure and portrait painter. Married William Peter W. q.v. Add: London 1884; Pinner, Middlesex 1892. † B 4, L 3, M 2, RA 5, RBA 9, SWA 2.

WATSON, M. Exh. 1887
Tweedie, 49 Grange Road, Edinburgh. † RSA 2.

WATSON, Mary Exh. 1909
Figure painter. † GOU 2.

WATSON, Mary Exh. 1898-1916
North Shields 1898 and 1905; Ben Rhydding, nr. Leeds 1901. † L 10.

WATSON, Michael Exh. 1939
Sculptor. 50 Alderney Street, London. † RA 1.

WATSON, Miss M.B. Exh. 1902
25 Westgate Terrace, Earls Court, London. † SWA 3.

WATSON, Meriel G. Exh. 1921-29
† D 13, LS 1.

WATSON, Mary M. Exh. 1932-35
Blairgowrie House, Blairgowrie. † RSA 1, RSW 2.

WATSON, Miss M.W. Exh. 1908-14
Tooting, London 1908; Glasgow 1911. † GI 2, L 7, SWA 1.

WATSON, O. Exh. 1908
Hambledon House, Thirsk, Yorks. † RA 1.

WATSON, Patrick Exh. 1914
4 Morningside Park, Edinburgh. † GI 1.

WATSON, Paxton Exh. 1897-1933
Architect. Father of R. Paxton W. q.v. Add: London 1897; Worthing, Sussex 1926. † RA 14.

WATSON, P. Fletcher 1842-1907
Watercolour painter. R.B.A. 1903. Add: Manchester 1894; Paignton, Devon 1904. † B 1, D 6, L 1, M 3, NG 1, RA 1, RBA 9, RHA 2.

WATSON, P.G. Exh. 1888
16 Charlotte Square, Edinburgh. † RSA 1.

WATSON, R. Exh. 1881-85
63 Belmont Street, Southport, Lancs. † GI 1, L 2.

WATSON, Rosamund Exh. 1904-8
A.S.W.A. 1886. Add: 17 Canonbury Park, South London. † B 3, LS 5, RA 1, RI 2, ROI 1, SWA 4.

WATSON, Mrs. Ruth L. Exh. 1932
Watercolour flower painter. 17 Pembroke Road, London. † RA 1.

WATSON, Rosalie M. Exh. 1880-87
Landscape, figure and still life painter. A.S.W.A. 1886. Add: London. † B 4, D 7, G 6, L 3, M 4, RA 6, RBA 2, RHA 2, RI 6, ROI 2, SWA 13.

WATSON, R. Paxton Exh. 1937
Architect. Son of Paxton W. q.v. Add: 38 Bell Street, Reigate, Surrey. † RA 1.

WATSON, Samuel Exh. 1895
34 Upper Sackville Street, Dublin. † RHA 1.

WATSON, Mrs. Sissy E.E. Exh. 1892
49 Hanover Road, Woolwich, London. † GI 1.

WATSON, Mrs. S.J. Exh. 1885
Painter. St. Johns Park House, Highgate Road, London. † SWA 1.

WATSON, S. Rowan Exh. 1916-23
34 Upper Sackville Street, Dublin. † RHA 19.

WATSON, Sydney Robert b. 1892
Painter, decorator and etcher. b. Enfield, Middlesex. Studied Royal College of Art 1911-15. Exh. 1921-39. Add: Leicester. † B 7, M 1, N 3, NEA 3, RA 1.

WATSON, Tom Exh. 1892-1907
Bolton, Lancs. † L 1, RA 1.

WATSON, Thomas A. Exh. 1888
St. James Road, Forfar. † GI 1.

WATSON, Thomas Henry Exh. 1884-1904
Architect. 9 Nottingham Place, London. † RA 5.

WATSON, Thomas J. 1847-1912
Painter of landscape, genre and fishing scenes. b. Sedbergh, Yorks. Studied R.A. Schools. Brother of John Dawson W. q.v. and brother in law of Myles Birket Foster q.v. R.B.A. 1882, A.R.W.S. 1880. Add: Witley, Surrey 1880; Cambridge 1883 and 1903; Ilfracombe, Devon 1885; Ripley, Surrey 1887; Leatherhead, Surrey 1892; Steyning, Sussex 1897; Droitwich, Worcs. 1899. † B 4, D 2, GI 1, L 17, M 7, RA 8, RBA 4, RWS 77.

WATSON, Thomas L. Exh. 1882-1911
Architect. Glasgow. † GI 18, RA 6, RSA 2.

WATSON, T.R. Hall Exh. 1890-1914
Glasgow 1890; London 1902. † D 10, GI 6, L 3, LS 11, NG 11, RA 1, RSA 1.

WATSON, Mrs. Thirza S. Exh. 1893-99
Flower painter. Wentworth Villas, 72 Cromwell Street, Nottingham. † N 3.

WATSON, W. Exh. 1883
† TOO 1.

WATSON, W. Exh. 1885-86
1 Wallis Place, Easter Road, Leith, Edinburgh. † RSA 3.

WATSON, William Exh. 1884
Kensington House, Maghull, Liverpool. † L 1.

WATSON, William Exh. 1934-37
Edinburgh. † RSA 5.

WATSON, W.B. Exh. 1903
Architect. Liverpool. † RA 1.

WATSON, William Ferguson b. 1895
Painter and journalist. b. Glasgow. Studied in Leicester. Exh. 1925-35. Add: 15 Harlaxton Street, Leicester. † N 8.

WATSON, W.H. Exh. 1899-1915
Gosforth, Cumberland 1899; Seascale, Cumberland 1904; Braystones, via Carnforth, Cumberland 1907. † GI 4, LS 2, RSA 15.

WATSON, Walter J.* b. 1879
Landscape painter. b. Somerville, Cheshire. Exh. 1910-37. Add: St. Leonards on Sea 1910; Hastings 1912; Bettws-y-Coed, Wales 1923. † L 5, RCA 32.

WATSON, William Peter* d. 1932
Landscape and genre painter and teacher. b. South Shields. Studied South Kensington 1877-81, and Julians, Paris. R.B.A. 1891. Married Lizzie May W. q.v. Add: London 1883; Pinner, Middlesex 1891; Bosham, Sussex 1922. † B 16, L 10, M 2, RA 17, RBA 77, RHA 1, ROI 8.

WATSON, William R.C. Exh. 1890-98
Egremont, Cheshire 1890; Manchester 1898. † L 2, M 1.

WATSON, W.T. Exh. 1883-93
Glasgow. † GI 5.

WATT, Mrs. Amy Exh. 1938-39
Painter of landscape and harbour scenes. St. Ives, Cornwall 1938; Crediton, Devon 1939. † NEA 1, RA 5.

WATT, Mrs. Amy M. Exh. 1929-34
Flower painter. The Studio, Dedham, Essex. † RA 6.

WATT, Daisy Exh. 1939-40
Argyll Cottage, Clackmannan. † RSW 4.

WATT, Doris Exh. 1912-14
Glendarragh, Londonderry. † RHA 3.

WATT, D.Y. Exh. 1923
† P 1.

WATT, Elizabeth Mary Exh. 1922-40
328 Renfrew Street, Glasgow. † GI 16, RSA 2.

WATT, Eva Stuart Exh. 1932-34
Landscape and figure painter. Kilamanjara, Kilmacanogue, Co. Wicklow. † RHA 5.

WATT, George Fiddes 1873-1960
Portrait painter. b. Aberdeen. Studied R.S.A. Schools. R.P. 1926, A.R.S.A. 1910, R.S.A. 1924. "The Artists Mother" (1910) purchased by Chantrey Bequest 1930. Add: Edinburgh and London. † GI 26, L 16, P 45, RA 32, RSA 99.

WATT, James Cromer Exh. 1893-1909
Architect. London 1893; Aberdeen 1896. † NG 1, RA 4, RSA 3.

WATT, James George Exh. 1883-86
Aberdeen. † GI 2, RSA 5.

WATT, John M. Exh. 1936-37
Landscape and flower painter. Trenoweth, St. Ives, Cornwall. † RA 3.

WATT, Katherine K. Exh. 1940
Argyle Cottage, Clackmannan. † RSA 1.

WATT, Linnie Exh. 1880-1907
Landscape, figure and pottery painter. Studied Lambeth School of Art. A.S.W.A. 1880, S.W.A. 1884. Add: London 1880; Dinan, France 1901. † B 2, D 10, DOW 10, GI 16, L 12, M 16, RA 8, RBA 22, RI 3, ROI 3, SWA 44.

WATT, Mary Exh. 1918-20
23 Horsfield Avenue, Aberdeen. † RSA 2.

WATT, Robin Exh. 1926-37
Portrait painter. London 1926; Stowe, Bucks. 1937. † RA 2.

WATT, Victor Robert* Exh. 1937
Painter of watercolour landscapes of Australia. † WG 43.

WATT, Miss W. Felday Exh. 1908
Norwood, London. † SWA 2.

WATTEAU, Miss A. Exh. 1886
c/o Rosenberg, 50 Lime Street, Liverpool. † L 1.

WATTERS, Miss E.F. Exh. 1895
34 Norwich Road, Forest Gate, London. † RBA 1.

WATTERSON, W.R. Exh. 1934-38
Handsworth, Birmingham 1934; Yardley 1938. † B 5.

WATTON, Gwynifrede Dorothy b. 1891
Portrait and landscape painter. b. Llandudno. Studied Chelsea School of Art. A.S.W.A. 1927, S.W.A. 1928. Exh. 1921-39. Add: London. † D 1, L 1, P 4, RA 2, RI 1, ROI 1, SWA 25.

WATTS, Arthur 1883-1935
Poster artist, illustrator and "Punch" artist. b. Chatham, Kent. Studied Slade School, Antwerp, Paris, Moscow and Madrid. A.R.B.A. 1923. Add: 1 Holly Place, Hampstead, London. † FIN 99, RA 1, RBA 4.

WATTS, Alice J. Exh. 1889-90
Landscape painter. 11 Lawn Road, Hampstead, London. † M 2, RBA 2.

WATTS, Mrs. C.H. Exh. 1936
100 Netherby Road, Edinburgh. † RSA 2.

WATTS, Miss C.M. Exh. 1937
St. Asaph. † RCA 2.

WATTS, Mrs. Dorothy Exh. 1938-40
Southwoods, 65 Surrenden Road, Brighton. † RBA 2, RI 4, SWA 3.

WATTS, Dougard Exh. 1901-3
Landscape painter. Boxted, Colchester, Essex. † B 1, L 2, RSA 1.

WATTS, Eileen M. Exh. 1938-40
Landscape and figure painter. 90 Palmerston Road, Buckhurst Hill. † NEA 2, RA 2.

WATTS, George Frederick* 1817-1904
Historical and portrait painter and sculptor (e.g. "Physical Energy" in Kensington Gardens). Apprenticed at age 10 to William Behnes the sculptor. Entered R.A. Schools 1835. Was briefly married to Ellen Terry. A.R.A. 1867, R.A. 1867, R.B.A. 1888, R.P. 1892, H.R.O.I. 1898. Add: London and Guildford. † B 22, FIN 2, G 41, GI 22, L 42, M 24, NG 55, P 40, RA 46, RBA 8, RCA 9, RE 1, RHA 3, ROI 2, RSA 10.

WATTS, H.J. Exh. 1938
15 Eaton Terrace, London. † ROI 1.

WATTS, James Thomas* d. 1930
Landscape painter. b. Birmingham. Studied Birmingham School of Art. R.B.S.A. 1922. Married Louisa Margaret W. q.v. Exh. from 1880. Add: Liverpool. † B 28, D 54, FIN 1, GI 3, L 194, LS 8, M 19, RA 51, RBA 2, RCA 213, RI 58, ROI 6, TOO 2.

WATTS, Leonard Exh. 1892-1927
Portrait painter. Studied R.A. Schools. R.B.A. 1893. Add: London 1892 and 1906; Chichester, Sussex 1904; Barcombe, Sussex 1909; Eastbourne 1911; Wadhurst, Sussex 1917; Worthing, Sussex 1920. † B 7, GI 2, L 2, M 2, RA 19, RBA 44, ROI 1.

WATTS, Louisa Margaret Exh. 1880-1914
nee Hughes. Landscape painter. Married James Thomas W. q.v. Add: London 1880; Liverpool 1884. † B 9, L 90, M 17, RA 7, RCA 10, RI 17, ROI 2, SWA 22.

WATTS, Miss M. Exh. 1900-2
Watertree, Liverpool 1900; Hallam Fields Parsonage, nr. Ilkeston 1902. † L 7.

WATTS, Meryl b. 1910
Painter, modeller and colour woodcut artist. Studied Blackheath School of Art. Exh. 1934-40. Add: Blackheath 1934; Leatherhead, Surrey 1940. † RA 3.

WATTS, Peggy Exh. 1935-37
Portrait and miniature painter. Solihull, Birmingham 1935; London 1937. † RA 2.

WATTS, Peter Exh. 1939
Sculptor. 30 West Cromwell Road, London. † RA 1.

WATTS, Ruth Exh. 1931-32
Painter. 179 Kedleston Road, Derby. † NEA 1, RA 2.

WATTS, W.A. Exh. 1937
St. Asaph. † RCA 2.

WATTS, W.J. Exh. 1904-11
Laird School of Art, Birkenhead 1904; Storey Institute, Lancaster 1909. † L 3.

WATTS-JONES, Mrs. Mary Kynaston Exh. 1897-1932
nee Potter. A.R.M.S. 1914, R.M.S. 1916. Add: Bolton, Lancs. 1897; Preston, Lancs. 1903; Devonport 1912; Bowfell, Windermere 1917. † L 16, M 2, RA 2, RMS 10.

WATTS-JONES, Miss Pamela Exh. 1927
Bowfell, Windermere. † RCA 1.

WAUCHOPE, Alice Exh. 1891-1904
London. † D 6.

WAUD, Reginald L. Exh. 1898-1917
Miniature portrait painter. London 1898; Hoe Benham, nr. Newbury , Berks. 1911. † L 1, NG 1, P 2, RA 3, ROI 2.

WAUGH, Elizabeth J. Exh. 1880-85
Landscape, interior and portrait painter. London 1880; Winchester 1885. † RA 1, SWA 1.

WAUGH, Frederick J.* Exh. 1894-1906
Landscape painter. Sark, C.I. 1894; London 1899. † I 1, L 8, RA 12.

WAUGH, F.W. Exh. 1882
23 Clarence Street, Liverpool. † L 1.

WAUGH, Lilian Exh. 1880
Landscape painter. 24 Tavistock Square, London. † SWA 1.

WAUGH, Nora Exh. 1884-89
Flower and figure painter. London 1884; Kemp Town, Brighton 1887. † RBA 2, RI 1, ROI 3, SWA 5.

WAUTERS, Emile 1845-1933
Portrait and landscape painter. Brussels 1884; Paris 1890. † GI 2, L 4, P 4, RA 9.

WAY, Charles Jones* 1835-1919
Watercolour landscape painter. Studied South Kensington. Visited Canada. Add: London 1880; Lausanne, Switzerland 1908. ALP 17, D 15, GI 2, L 3, LS 3, M 1, RA 4, RI 2.

WAY, Drusilla Exh. 1929
106 Grand Drive, Raynes Park, London. † NEA 1.

WAY, Mrs. Emily C. Exh. 1886-96
Mrs. J.L. Portrait painter. 46 Bedford Gardens, London. † RA 9, RHA 1.

WAY, Fanny b. 1871
Mrs. A. Thacker. Miniature portrait painter. Studied Lausanne and Crystal Palace. R.M.S. 1897. Exh. 1893-1921. Add: London 1893 and 1911; Molesey, Surrey 1903. † L 4, NG 2, RA 23, RI 6, RMS 9.
WAY, Ronald W. Exh. 1937
Landscape painter. 59 Harold Road, London. † RA 1.
WAY, Thomas Robert* c. 1852-1913
Landscape and portrait painter and lithographer. London. † BG 43, L 5, NEA 13, RA 10, RBA 8, RI 13, ROI 13.
WAY, William Cossens 1833-1905
Landscape, genre and still life painter. b. Torquay. Studied South Kensington for 6 years. Art master Newcastle upon Tyne School of Art for 40 years. † B 6, D 1, G 2, L 4, M 2, RA 7, RBA 6, RI 5, RSA 1.
WAYLETT, F. Exh. 1895
Painter. 16 Adamson Road, South Hampstead, London. † NEA 1.
WAYMOUTH, Eleanor See HUGHES
WAYMOUTH, Hylton Exh. 1928-29
Sculptor. Married Helen Maclaren q.v. Add: London. † GI 1, L 1, RA 1.
WAYMOUTH, Mrs. Hylton
See MACLAREN, Helen
WAYMOUTH, W. Charles Exh. 1918-24
Architect. 104 High Holborn, London. † RA 3.
WAYNE, Lilian Sewallis Exh. 1903
Landscape painter. † BG 19.
WAYNE, R.S. Exh. 1880-82
Landscape painter. Aberartro Llanbedr, North Wales. † RBA 3.
WAYTE, Walter Alexander Exh. 1938
Portrait painter. Studied under Edwin Tindall and at Colarossi's Paris. Add: Firbeck Hall, nr. Worksop, Notts. † N 2.
WEAR, Maud Marion b. 1873
Portrait and miniature painter. Studied R.A. Schools 1896-1901. Exh. 1900-40. Add: London 1900; Boscombe, Hants. 1906; Bournemouth 1907; Parkstone, Dorset 1909 and 1916; Brenchley, Kent 1914; Shoreham by Sea 1924; Lancing, Sussex 1925; Beeding, Steyning, Sussex 1927; Buxted, Sussex 1940. † L 14, NEA 1, P 2, RA 37, RMS 3.
WEARNE, Helen Exh. 1882-85
51 York Place, Edinburgh. † RSA 5.
WEATHERBY, Miss C.B. Exh. 1906
Highbury Hill, London. † SWA 1.
WEATHERBY, Richard C. Exh. 1919-40
Landscape and figure painter. Travelled widely. Add: London 1919; La Roquelle sur Giaque, France 1922; Penzance 1930; Curry Cross Lanes, Cornwall 1933. † ALP 49, CHE 1, GI 2, I 2, L 2, P 2, RA 15.
WEATHERBY, William Exh. 1926
† M 3.
WEATHERHEAD, William Harris*
1843-c.1903
Genre painter. R.I. 1885. Add: Kentish Town, London. † B 45, D 4, FIN 2, L 20, M 17, RA 2, RBA 48, RHA 19, RI 99, ROI 15, RSW 3.
WEATHERILL, Mary Exh. 1882
Painter. † FIN 1.
WEATHERILL, R. Exh. 1885
4 Park Terrace, Whitby, Yorks. † B 2.
WEATHERLEY, William Samuel
Exh. 1886-1917
Architect. London. † RA 8.
WEATHERSTONE, Alfred C.
Exh. 1888-1929
Painter and designer. London. † D 2, L 6, M 4, RA 11, RI 2.
WEATHERSTONE, A.J. Exh. 1887
Painter. 137 High Street, Camden Town, London. † SWA 1.
WEAVER, Emily Exh. 1897-1904
Portrait painter. London 1897; Burnham, Somerset 1902. † RA 1, RI 1, SWA 9.
WEAVER, Herbert Parsons d. 1945
Landscape and architectural painter. b. Worcester Studied Royal College of Art. Headmaster Shrewsbury School of Art. R.B.A. 1909. Father of Lydia Mary W. q.v. Add: London 1900; Shrewsbury 1902. † L 4, M 6, RA 15, RBA 112, RCA 169, RI 30
WEAVER, Lydia Mary Exh. 1925-39
Mrs. Clarke. Daughter of Herbert Parsons W. q.v. Add: Hillside House, Lythe Hill, Shrewsbury. † RCA 13.
WEAVERS, Thomas G. Exh. 1896-1922
Birmingham. † B 20.
WEBB, Alfred Exh. 1901-3
58 Arthur Road, London. † ROI 3.
WEBB, Amy Exh. 1886-87
Landscape and coastal painter. 12 Belsize Park Terrace, Hampstead, London. † RBA 1, ROI 1, SWA 3.
WEBB, Archibald Exh. 1886-93
Landscape painter. R.B.A. 1890. Add: London. † B 1, D 30, L 6, M 4, RA 7, RBA 28, RHA 2, RI 6, ROI 5.
WEBB, Sir Aston 1849-1930
Architect. A.R.A. 1899, R.A. 1903, H.R.B.A. 1907, H.R.E. 1919, H.R.M.S. 1919. Knighted c. 1903. Father of Maurice and Philip E.W. q.v. Add: 19 Queen Anne's Gate, London. † GI 4, RA 99, RHA 15, RI 1, RHA 15.
WEBB, Archibald Bertram b. 1887
Watercolour landscape painter, wood engraver, lithographer, illustrator, poster and commercial artist. b. Ashford, Kent. Studied St. Martins School of Art. Art Master Perth Technical College, Perth, Australia. Exh. 1928-34. † AB 9, BA 2, FIN 64.
WEBB, Arthur S. Exh. 1915
Manor House, Newington, Sittingbourne, Kent. † D 2.
WEBB, Bernard H. Exh. 1904
Architect. 14 South Square, Gray's Inn, London. † RA 1.
WEBB, Mrs. Betty T. Exh. 1935
Portrait painter. 72 Eglinton Road, Dublin. † RHA 1.
WEBB, C. Exh. 1887
12 Belsize Park Terrace, London. † RI 1.
WEBB, Miss C. Exh. 1888
Flower painter. Greenfield, Worcester. † RBA 1.
WEBB, Cecilia 1888-1957
Sculptor. b. Stamford, Lincs. Add: 106 Burton Hill, Melton Mowbray, Leics. 1930. † N 8, RMS 1.
WEBB, Clifford C. 1895-1972
Painter, wood engraver and etcher. Drawing master Birmingham School of Art. R.B.A. 1934, A.R.E. 1937. Add: London 1921 and 1928; Birmingham 1925; Abinger Hammer, nr. Dorking, Surrey 1935. † G 1, GI 1, GOU 1, I 1, NEA 5, P 1, RA 1, RBA 37, RE 7, RED 3, RHA 2, ROI 1.
WEBB, Cecil J. Exh. 1908-9
Belluton House, Pensford, Somerset. † LS 6.
WEBB, Dora b. 1888
Miniature painter and sculptor. b. Stamford. Studied Grosvenor School of Art and under Alyn Williams. A.R.M.S. 1916, R.M.S. 1932. Exh. 1908-39. Add: Burton Road, Melton Mowbray, Leics. † L 50, N 72, RA 6, RMS 94, RSA 1.
WEBB, Dora Elizabeth Exh. 1911-37
Painter, craftworker and teacher. Studied Birmingham School of Arts and Crafts. Add: Warwick 1911; Erdinaton, Birmingham 1920. † B 14.
WEBB, D.G. Exh. 1935
North Devon. † SWA 2.
WEBB, Mrs. Eliza Exh. 1890-93
Flower painter. East Combe, Old Charlton, Kent. † B 1, RA 2.
WEBB, Ernest Exh. 1923-40
Sculptor. Nottingham 1923; London 1927. † GI 2, L 2, N 7, RA 13.
WEBB, E. Doran Exh. 1895-97
Architect. 43 High Street, Salisbury, Wilts. † RA 2, RHA 1.
WEBB, Miss E.G. Exh. 1914
c/o Miss Hodgson, 3 Criffel Avenue, Streatham Hill, London. † RA 1.
WEBB, F.B. Exh. 1939
108 Quarry Lane, Northfield, Birmingham. † B 1.
WEBB, Geoffrey Exh. 1919-32
Stained glass and eccliastical designer. Sackville House, East Grinstead, Sussex. † RA 6.
WEBB, George Exh. 1899-1913
Llandudno College, Llandudno 1899; Wellington, Salop. 1913. † I 5, RCA 8.
WEBB, George F. Exh. 1930-34
Architect. 200 High Street, Dudley, Worcs. † RA 4.
WEBB, G.W. Exh. 1890-98
Architect. Reading, Berks. † RA 2.
WEBB, Harry George 1882-1914
Landscape and architectural painter and etcher. London. † D 1, L 6, LS 1, M 2, RA 4, RBA 10, RE 5, ROI 1.
WEBB, Ivy Exh. 1928
Painter. † AB 3.
WEBB, James* 1825-1895
Marine and landscape painter. London. † B 3, D 9, G 1, L 3, M 1, RA 6, RBA 2, RI 7, ROI 10, TOO 36.
WEBB, Joseph 1908-1962
Portrait painter, mural decorator, etcher and engraver. Studied Hospitalfields, Arbroath. Etching master Chiswick Art School and Instructor in painting and sculpture. A.R.E. 1930. Add: London 1929; Harrow, Middlesex 1933 and 1938; Wembley, Middlesex 1934; Farnham Common, Bucks. 1935. † L 1, RA 12, RE 15, RHA 2, RSA 2.
WEBB, Josephine Exh. 1880-1921
Dublin. † RBA 1, RHA 27.
WEBB, John Cother d. 1927
Engraver. Add: 111 Clifton Hill, St. Johns Wood, London. † RA 32.
WEBB, James H. Exh. 1905-6
Dublin. † RHA 3.
WEBB, Kate S. Exh. 1880-96
Watercolour landscape painter. Henley on Thames. † RBA 1, SWA 8.
WEBB, Mrs. L. Exh. 1934
Watercolour landscape painter. † COO 2.
WEBB, Mabel Exh. 1919-28
Etcher. The Maples, Langley Park, Mill Hill, London. † AB 1, L 1, RA 1.
WEBB, Maria D. see ROBINSON
WEBB, Maurice E. Exh. 1908-39
Architect. Son of Sir Aston W. q.v. Add: 19 Queen Anne's Gate, London. † D 2, GI 3, RA 41, RSA 1.

WEBB, Mrs. M.H. Exh. 1911-18
Shepherds Bush Green, London. † B 1, L 1, RA 5.

WEBB, Matthew W. c. 1851-1924
Painter. London 1889; Steventon, Berks. 1909; Oxford 1916. † L 1, LS 6, M 1, NEA 3, RBA 2.

WEBB, Octavius Exh. 1880-89
Animal painter. Shalford, Guildford, Surrey. † B 2, G 1, L 1, RA 5, RBA 12, ROI 4.

WEBB, Osman Exh. 1936
33 Frederick Road, Stechford. † B 1.

WEBB, Philip E. 1886-1916
Architect. Son of Sir Aston W. q.v. Exh. 1914. Add: 19 Queen Anne's Gate, Westminster, London. † RA 1.

WEBB, Roger junr. Exh. 1924
67 Kenilworth Square, Dublin. † RHA 1.

WEBB, Susan Maria Hands Exh. 1908
11 Camden Gardens, Shepherds Bush Green, London. † LS 5.

WEBB, William A. Exh. 1903
Architect. 12 Duchess Street, Portland Place, London. † RA 1.

WEBB, William Edward* 1862-1903
Marine painter. Manchester. † L 6, M 34, RA 3.

WEBB, W.J. Exh. 1882
c/o Stewart, 26 Brazenose Street, Manchester. † M 1.

WEBB, William R. d. 1927/8
Landscape painter. A.N.S.A. 1927. Add: Nottingham 1886; West Bridgford, Notts. 1911. † N 40.

WEBBER, A. Huish Exh. 1898
Miniature portrait painter. The Studio, 59A High Street, Tunbridge Wells, Kent. † RA 1.

WEBBER, Miss Ethel Exh. 1906-9
Miniature painter. Holmwood, Dorking, Surrey. † L 2, RA 3.

WEBBER, Everilda Exh. 1896-97
58 Lower Mount Street, Dublin and Kellyville, Athy. † RHA 2.

WEBBER, Ernest Berry Exh. 1926-36
Architect. London. † RA 12, RSA 4.

WEBBER, Elizabeth Robina Exh. 1933-39
Portrait painter. 2 The Rope Walk, Nottingham. † N 5.

WEBBER, H.S. Exh. 1910
23 Queen Street, Maidenhead, Berks. † RA 1.

WEBBER, Thomas W. Exh. 1889
† D 2.

WEBBER, William John Seward Exh. 1882-91
Sculptor. London 1882; Harrogate, Yorks. 1891. † RA 3.

WEBB-FODDY, T. Exh. 1882
27 St. George's Square, Regent's Park, London. † GI 1.

WEBER, Audrey Exh. 1920-34
Painter. London. † COO 54, I 1, L 2, NEA 1, RA 5, WG 5.

WEBER, Miss A.M. Exh. 1916-18
Hadley Bourne, Barnet, Herts. † L 2, RA 3, SWA 1.

WEBER, Ernest Exh. 1894
Etcher. 1 Wymond Street, Putney, London. † RA 1.

WEBER, Frederick F. Exh. 1908
18 Impasse du Maine, Paris. † LS 3.

WEBER, H. Exh. 1880
† TOO 1.

WEBER, J.D. Exh. 1920-29
152 Ince Avenue, Anfield, Liverpool. † L 4.

WEBER, Lorna Exh. 1937
Watercolour painter of Middle Eastern subjects. † WG 26.

WEBER, L.M. Exh. 1940
22 Lathbury Road, Oxford. † SWA 1.

WEBER, Max* b. 1881
Figure painter. † CHE 1.

WEBER, Otto* 1832-1888
Portrait, animal, genre, landscape and coastal painter. b. Berlin. Studied under Prof. Steffeck. Lived in Paris and Rome. Came to England 1872. R.E. 1881, R.O.I. 1883, A.R.W.S. 1878. Add: London. † B 4, FIN 1, G 2, GI 8, L 6, M 5, RA 15, RE 7, RHA 5, ROI 11, RWS 33.

WEBER, Theodore* 1838-1907
Marine painter. Paris 1883. † GI 1, TOO 15.

WEBER, T.L. Exh. 1884
† TOO 2.

WEBER, von see V

WEBLEY, Sam b. 1877
Painter and decorative panel painter. b. Trowbridge, Wilts. Self taught. Exh. 1900-29. Add: London and Bath. † RA 2, WG 34.

WEBLING, Ethel Exh. 1880-1927
Portrait and miniature painter. R.M.S. 1902. Add: London. † D 2, L 3, RA 34, RMS 4.

WEBSTER, Miss A. Exh. 1919
25 Tedworth Square, London. † SWA 1.

WEBSTER, Alexander Exh. 1880-92
Edinburgh. † RSA 11.

WEBSTER, Alfred A. Exh. 1906-13
Bath Street, Glasgow. † GI 3.

WEBSTER, Alfred George* Exh. 1880-1917
Landscape, architectural and genre painter. On staff Lincoln School of Art. Add: Lincoln. † GOU 6, L 2, NEA 2, RA 22, RBA 1.

WEBSTER, A.H. Exh. 1899
134 St. Vincent Street, Glasgow. † GI 1.

WEBSTER, Miss E.A. Exh. 1894-95
34 The Crescent, Peel Park, Manchester. † M 2.

WEBSTER, Frederick A. Exh. 1907-11
Acock's Green, Birmingham. † B 9.

WEBSTER, George* Exh. 1880-1907
Painter. Edinburgh. † GI 36, RSA 63.

WEBSTER, Miss G.M. Exh. 1914-18
Northampton Road, Addiscombe, Croydon, Surrey. † RA 4, RCA 1.

WEBSTER, Gordon MacWhirter Exh. 1932-38
5 Newton Terrace, Glasgow. † GI 8.

WEBSTER, Henry Exh. 1922-39
Portrait and landscape painter. A.N.S.A. 1938. Add: Sherwood, Notts. 1922; Nottingham 1932; Old Basford, Notts. 1934; Mapperley, Notts. 1935. † N 34.

WEBSTER, Herman Armour b. 1878
Etcher, draughtsman and lithographer. b. New York. Studied Julians, Paris. A.R.E. 1907, R.E. 1914, Exh. 1907-39. Add: London 1907; Paris 1908. † FIN 3, NEA 2, RA 10, RE 48.

WEBSTER, Miss H.V. Exh. 1935-36
44 Thicket Road, Anerley, London. † RBA 2.

WEBSTER, John Dodsley Exh. 1884-86
Architect. 21 Church Street, Sheffield. † RA 2.

WEBSTER, Mary D. Exh. 1882
Sherwood Rise, Nottingham. † N 2.

WEBSTER, Mary E. Exh. 1913-33
Flower painter. Bandon, Co. Cork 1913; Dublin 1926; Blackrock, Co. Cork 1931. † RHA 10.

WEBSTER, Norman Exh. 1925-33
Landscape painter and illustrator. Ripley, Derbys. 1925 and 1933; Croydon, Surrey 1928. † L 1, N 6, NEA 3, RA 1.

WEBSTER, Robert Bruce Exh. 1935-40
Dollar, N.B. 1935; Edinburgh 1938. † RSA 3, RSW 8.

WEBSTER, R. Wellesley Exh. 1887-1903
Landscape painter. Manchester 1887 and 1895; West Anstruther, Fife, N.B. 1894; Southport, Lancs. 1899. † M 16, RA 10, RSA 1.

WEBSTER, Mrs. W. Exh. 1939
Charlwynn, Portland Road, Hucknall, Nottingham. † N 1.

WEBSTER, William Exh. 1884-1902
Landscape painter. Lee, Kent 1884; Blackheath 1899; St. Helens, Lancs. 1902. † L 3, RA 2.

WEBSTER, Walter Ernest 1878-1959
Figure and portrait painter. b. Manchester. Studied Royal College of Art and R.A. Schools. R.I. 1920; R.O.I. 1920; R.P. 1921, V.P.R.P. 1937. Add: London. † B 2, GI 11, L 36, M 1, P 15, RA 43, RCA 1, RI 70, ROI 55.

WEDD, Ada Exh. 1882-90
Flower painter. Manchester 1882; London 1885; Wilmslow, Cheshire 1890. † L 2, M 5, RBA 5.

WEDD, Mary Exh. 1881-1920
Flower painter. Lafford Terrace, Sleaford, Lincs. † L 3, N 5.

WEDDELL, J.W. Exh. 1931
261 West George Street, Glasgow. † GI 2.

WEDDERSPOON, K. Exh. 1892-95
Perth, N.B. 1892; Bridge of Earn, N.B. 1895. † GI 1. RSA 3.

WEDEKIND, Miss H.S. Exh. 1912-28
Shortlands, Kent 1912; London 1927. † RA 2, ROI 2.

WEDEKIND, L. Exh. 1880
Munchen, Germany. † RSA 1.

WEDERKINCH, Holger b. 1886
Danish sculptor. Studied Royal Academy, Copenhagen 1905-8. Exh. 1924-25. Add: Charlottenlund, Copenhagen. † GI 1, RA 5.

WEDGWOOD, Francis Charles B. Exh. 1928-39
Landscape painter. London. † CG 1, NEA 5, RA 12.

WEDGWOOD, Geoffrey Heath b. 1900
Etcher and engraver. Studied Liverpool City School of Art, Royal College of Art and British School at Rome. A.R.E. 1925. Exh. 1923-40. Add: Liverpool 1923 and 1928; London 1924; Rome 1927. † AB 1, FIN 18, GI 1, L 26, NEA 2, RA 29, RE 27, RHA 1.

WEDGWOOD, James Exh. 1925-40
Sculptor. London. † GI 1, L 3, RA 13.

WEE, Ver see V

WEEDON, Augustus Walford* 1838-1908
Watercolour landscape painter. R.B.A. 1883, R.I. 1887. Probably father of Miss M.E.W. q.v. Add: London. † B 21, D 29, DOW 5, FIN 275, GI 3, L 29, LEI 66, M 29, RA 22, RBA 82, RHA 1, RI 153, ROI 18.

WEEDON, Miss M.E. Exh. 1901-3
Probably daughter of Augustus Walford W. q.v. Add: 6 Carlton Mansions, West End Lane, London. † RI 3.

WEEKES, Miss C. Exh. 1914
St. Brides Priory, Milford Haven, Wales. † L 1, RA 1.

WEEKES, Catherine Exh. 1896-1903
82 Margaret Street, London. † GI 2, M 1, NG 3.

WEEKES, Frederick* Exh. 1883-1908
Painter of genre and battle scenes. London. † RA 1, RBA 11, RI 5, ROI 19.

WEEKES, Henry* Exh. 1884-88
Genre painter. Son of sculptor Henry W. (1807-1877), and probably brother of William W. q.v. Add: Harrow Weald, Middlesex 1884; West Hampstead, London 1887. † B 1, GI 1, RA 1, RBA 1, ROI 6, TOO 1.

WEEKES, Joseph Exh. 1931-40
18 Park Circus, Glasgow. † GI 10, RSA 1.

WEEKES, William* Exh. 1881-1909
Genre and animal painter. Probably brother of Henry W. q.v. Add: 21 Oppidans Road, Primrose Hill, London. † B 6, FIN 1, G 1, GI 2, L 15, M 3, RA 37, RBA 1, ROI 8, TOO 3.

WEEKLEY, Barbara Exh. 1928
Landscape painter. † RED 1.

WEEKS, Barbara Exh. 1935-38
Figure and landscape painter. Woodbury, Woodland Way, Kingswood, Surrey. † NEA 1, RA 1.

WEEKS, Miss C.E. Exh. 1906
Regents Park, London. † SWA 1.

WEEKS, Charlotte J. Exh. 1880-91
Historical, literary and genre painter, London. † G 1, GI 12, L 7, M 1, NG 1, RA 8, ROI 3, SWA 9.

WEEKS, Miss D. Exh. 1916
1st London General Hospital, Camberwell, London. † RA 2.

WEEKS, Edwin Lord* 1849-1903
American landscape painter. Add: Paris. † L 1, RA 1, RSA 2, TOO 1.

WEEKS, John Exh. 1924-25
10 Forth Street, Edinburgh. † RSA 4.

WEEKS, Kathleen Exh. 1930
Sculptor. Pine Crest, Winterbourne Earls, Salisbury, Wilts. † RA 1.

WEEKS, Sydney Thomas Charles b. 1878
Painter and commercial artist. Studied Heatherleys. Exh. 1933-39. Add: 7 York House, Highbury Crescent, London. † AR 3, RA 2, RI 1, ROI 8.

WEELE, Van der see V

WEERTS, Jean Joseph 1847-1927
French artist. Add: Paris. † L 5.

WEGMANN, R. or B. Exh. 1891
Portrait painter. The Academy, Copenhagen. † RA 1.

WEGUELIN, John Reinhard* 1849-1927
Genre, classical, biblical and historical painter. Studied Slade School. R.O.I. 1888. A.R.W.S. 1894, R.W.S. 1897. Add: London 1880; Winchelsea, Sussex 1900; Hastings 1910. † B 13, FIN 1, G 16, GI 10, L 17, M 4, NG 12, RA 12, RBA 2, RHA 2, ROI 9, RWS 38.

WEHRSCHMIDT, Daniel Albert 1861-1932
later Veresmith. Portrait painter, mezzotint engraver and lithographer. b. Cleveland, Ohio, U.S.A. Studied Herkomer's, Bushey. Art master at Herkomer's, Bushey for 12 years. R.P. 1915. Add: Bushey, Herts. 1886; London 1900; Doneraile, Co. Cork 1921; North Curry, Taunton, Somerset 1927. † B 3, FIN 17, GI 12, I 14, L 14, LS 9, M 1, NG 4, P 12, RA 39, RHA 2, RSA 8.

WEHRSCHMIDT, Mrs. Daniel A. Exh. 1892
Miss Marie L. Norie. Landscape painter. † FIN 2.

WEHRSCHMIDT, Emil Exh. 1891-99
Mezzotint engraver. Bushey, Herts. 1891; Shepherds Bush, London 1899. † M 1, RA 2.

WEIBEL, Louise Exh. 1905
Geneva and c/o Mrs. West Watson, 7 Grosvenor Crescent, Glasgow. † GI 1.

WEIDMAN, Morris Exh. 1928
† NEA 1.

WEIGALL, Arthur Howes* Exh. 1880-94
Portrait and genre painter. Son of Charles Henry W. (1794-1877). Add: London 1880 and 1889; Campden, Glos. 1887. † G 1, GI 5, L 5, P 1, RA 6, ROI 10, RSA 2.

WEIGALL, Henry junr. 1829-1925
Portrait, genre and miniature portrait painter. Son of Sculptor Henry W. (c. 1800-1883). Add: London 1880; Ramsgate, Kent 1898. † B 2, G 2, L 1, M 6, NG 2, RA 23, RHA 1, RSA 1.

WEIGAND, W.J. Exh. 1882
134 Albany Street, Regents Park, London. † D 1.

WEIGELE, Henri Exh. 1906-13
French sculptor. 2 Rue de Lesseps, Neuilly sur Seine, France. † L 3, RSA 2.

WEIGHT, Carel* b. 1908
Portrait, flower and figure painter. Studied Hammersmith School of Art and Goldsmiths College. R.B.A. 1935. Exh. 1931-40. Add: 5 Shepherds Bush Green, London. † L 1, NEA 2, RA 7, RBA 32.

WEIGHT, Michael Exh. 1938
Theatrical portrait painter. † RED 6.

WEIGHTMAN, John Exh. 1909
43 Bidston Road, Oxton, Birkenhead. † L 1.

WEILAND, J.* Exh. 1916
Painter. † CON 1.

WEINER, Mark Exh. 1913
Painter. 25 Spital Square, Bishopgate, London. † NEA 1.

WEINGARTNER, Louis A. Exh. 1930
Sculptor, metalworker and designer. Collaborated with Walter Gilbert in several works (e.g. the Gates of Buckingham Palace). Add: 10 Kapuzinerioy, Lucerne, Switzerland. † B 1.

WEINGOTT, Victor Marcus* b. 1887
Landscape and figure painter and poster designer. Exh. 1909-38. Add: London. † L 6, M 1, RA 14.

WEIR, Mrs. Archibald (Anne) Exh. 1884-91
Figure and domestic painter. Enfield, Middlesex 1884; Ottery St. Mary, Devon 1891. † GI 1, RA 1, RBA 2, RI 1, ROI 6, SWA 2.

WEIR, Edith D. Exh. 1900
Miniature portrait painter. 58 Trumbull Street, Newhaven, U.S.A. † RA 1.

WEIR, Helen Stuart Exh. 1915-40
Landscape and still life painter and sculptor. b. New York City. Studied in England, Germany and the U.S.A. A.R.B.A. 1926, R.B.A. 1929, R.O.I. 1924, A.S.W.A. 1921. Related to Nina Weir-Lewis q.v. Add: St. Ives, Cornwall 1915; Corston, Bristol 1920; London 1924. † BA 1, GI 9, GOU 48, I 2, L 19, NEA 6, RA 22, RBA 77, RHA 3, RI 2, ROI 70, RSA 20, SWA 58.

WEIR, Harrison William 1824-1906
Animal painter, illustrator and author. b. Lewes. Studied at Camberwell. Worked for "Illustrated London News" and "Graphic; Black and White". A.R.I. 1849, R.I. 1851. Exh. 1880. Add: Brenchley, Kent. † RBA 1.

WEIR, Jessie Exh. 1880-88
Paisley Road, Glasgow. † GI 6.

WEIR, Mary Exh. 1884-96
Paisley Road, Glasgow. † GI 4, RSW 1.

WEIR, P.J. Exh. 1885-88
Landscape painter. Edinburgh. † L 1, RI 1, RSA 2.

WEIR, Robertson Exh. 1923
61 Roslea Drive, Dennistoun, Glasgow. † L 1.

WEIR, R.S. Exh. 1915-24
14 Gray's Inn Square, London. † RA 2, RSA 9.

WEIR, Wilma Exh. 1912-40
Watercolour landscape painter and leather-worker. b. Glasgow. Studied Edinburgh College of Art (travelling scholarship), Italy and Paris. Add: Edinburgh 1912; Glasgow 1921. † GI 6, M 1, RSA 4, RSW 1.

WEIR-LEWIS, Nina (Mrs. W.) Exh. 1915-35
Landscape, still life and figure painter. Related to Helen Stewart Weir q.v. Add: St. Ives, Cornwall 1915; London 1922. † I 1, L 1, RBA 1, RI 2, ROI 11, SWA 6.

WEIRTER, Louis 1873-1932
Painter and etcher. b. Edinburgh. Studied Edinburgh Institute and R.A. Schools. R.B.A. 1905. Add: London 1892; Westcliffe on Sea, Essex 1905 and 1916; Baldock, Herts. 1908. † RA 4, RBA 53, RSA 1.

WEISS, A. Exh. 1881
16 Avenue Trudaine, Paris. † RHA 1.

WEISS, Felix Exh. 1936
Sculptor. 8 The Avenue Studios, 76 Fulham Road, London. † RA 1.

WEISS, Jose* 1859-1929
Landscape painter. Roubaix, France 1887; Amberley, Sussex 1893. † B 3, CON 1, FIN 13, GI 4, GOU 28, L 6, M 5, NG 3, RA 33, RBA 3, RHA 9, ROI 6.

WEISSE, Melanie Exh. 1899-1900
Southam, Warwicks. 1899; Tottington, Thetford, Norfolk 1900. † L 6, RHA 3, RI 8.

WEISSE, M.W. Exh. 1883
68 Eccles Street, Dublin. † RHA 1.

WEISSEN, H. Exh. 1886
117 New Bond Street, London. † M 1.

WEITZEL, Frank Exh. 1930-31
Linocut artist. † RED 7.

WEIZENBERG, G. Exh. 1880-82
Sculptor. 8A Via degli Incurabili, Rome. † RA 2.

WELBANK, J. Exh. 1934
287 Yardley Green Road, Small Heath, Birmingham. † B 1.

WELBOURN, E.S. Exh. 1937-39
Painter. 112 Mansfield Street, Sherwood, Nottingham. † N 2.

WELBURN, Ernest Exh. 1920-40
Small Heath, Birmingham. † B 21.

WELBURN, Mrs. Irene A. Exh. 1936-40
132 Shenley Fields Road, Wesley Hill, Selly Oak, Birmingham. † B 4.

WELBURN, K. Ross Exh. 1930-40
Small Heath, Birmingham 1930; Selly Oak, Birmingham 1936. † B 10.

WELBY, Arthur R. Exh. 1931
Architect. 6 Pump Court, Temple, London. † RA 1.

WELBY, Lady Desiree Exh. 1923-34
nee Copeland-Griffiths. Sculptor. Add: 18 Chester Street, Belgrave Square, London. † G 1, L 6, RA 8, SWA 17.

WELBY, Dorothea Earle Exh. 1933
Portrait painter. † COO 3.

WELBY, E. Exh. 1886
6 Newman Street, London. † RHA 1.

WELBY, Ellen Exh. 1880-1918
Landscape and figure painter. London. † B 5, D 1, L 4, M 5, RA 4, RBA 1, RI 6, RSA 2, SWA 9.

WELBY, Emmeline Mary Elizabeth see CUST

WELBY, G. Exh. 1915
7 Parkhill Studios, Haverstock Hill, London. † RHA 1.

WELBY, Rose E. Exh. 1880-1927
Flower painter. Canterbury 1880; London 1881. † B 3, BG 2, G 1, L 10, M 8, RA 11, RBA 5, RI 4, ROI 11, SWA 7.

WELCH, Denton Exh. 1938-39
Painter. 54 Hadlow Road, Tonbridge, Kent. † NEA 2, RBA 1, RED 1.

WELCH, Emilie Exh. 1914-15
22 Cavendish Gardens, Clapham Park, London. † RA 1, RI 1.

WELCH, Herbert Arthur b. 1884
Architect. b. Seaton, Devon. Studied University College, London. Exh. 1910-28. Add: London. † RA 6.

WELCH, Harry J. Exh. 1881-92
Coastal painter. London. † D 1, DOW 2, L 3, RA 8, RBA 10.

WELCH, Mrs. Mary E. Exh. 1925-33
Blackburn, Lancs. † L 8.

WELCHMAN, Mrs. B. de Vere Exh. 1903-27
Exeter. † B 12, D 19, LS 15, RCA 8, RHA 28.

WELCHMAN, Mrs. Mabel Exh. 1917-19
Miniature portrait painter. 41 Campden House Road, London. † RA 3.

WELCHMAN, Miss Norah Exh. 1917-24
Miniature portrait painter. 41 Campden House Road, Kensington, London. † RA 2.

WELD, Alice K.H. Exh. 1881-1910
Landscape painter. London 1881; Rome 1910. † L 2, NG 2, RA 1, RBA 1, RHA 1, RI 1, SWA 5.

WELD, Mary Izod Exh. 1881-82
Painter. 20 St. George's Road, Regent's Park London. † RHA 2, SWA 1.

WELDON, Evalein Exh. 1899
Forenaghts, Naas, Co. Kildare. † RHA 2.

WELDON, Harriet Exh. 1903-10
Naas, co. Kildare. † RHA 10.

WELHAM, Iris W. Exh. 1925
Painter. Lea-Hurst, Alfreton Road, Sutton in Ashfield, Notts. † N 1.

WELIE, Van see V

WELLAND, S.J. Exh. 1900
108 Pembroke Road, Dublin. † RHA 1.

WELLER, Mrs. Exh. 1907
† P 2.

WELLES, C. Stuart Exh. 1915
32 Upper Hamilton Terrace, London. † RA 1.

WELLESLEY, G.E. Exh. 1893
† P 1.

WELLESLEY, Lady Eileen Exh. 1907
Apsley House, Piccadilly, London. † NG 1.

WELLESLEY, Sir Victor b. 1876
Landscape and portrait painter. b. Petrograd, Russia. Exh. 1932-38. Add: London. † RA 3, ROI 1.

WELLINGS, Alan W. Exh. 1929-30
Wolverhampton 1929; London 1930. † B 2.

WELLINGTON, Miss A.M. Exh. 1909-21
South Hampstead, London. † SWA 2.

WELLINGTON, Hubert Lindsay 1879-1967
Landscape painter. Studied Gloucester School of Art, Birmingham School of Art and Slade School 1899-1900. Lecturer National Gallery 1919-22. Registrar and lecturer Royal College of Art 1932-46. "The Big Barn, Frampton Mansell" (1915) purchased by Chantrey Bequest 1961. Add: London 1901 and 1919; Stafford 1908. † GOU 8, L 2, LS 13, NEA 8.

WELLMAN, E.J. Exh. 1907
Box 1510, Norwich Union Buildings, Fox Street, Johannesburg, S. Africa. † RA 2.

WELLMAN, Mabel Exh. 1920-36
5 The Oval, Stafford. † SWA 7.

WELLS, Archibald b. 1874
Portrait and landscape painter. b. Glasgow. Studied Sydney Art Society, N.S.W. Australia. Exh. 1909-30. Add: Glasgow 1909; Rye, Sussex 1916. † G 1, GI 10, I 3, L 6, NEA 2, RA 1.

WELLS, A.R. Exh. 1914
94 Horsferry Road, Westminster, London. † RA 2.

WELLS, Catherine Colwyn Exh. 1899-1902
London. † M 3, RA 1, SWA 2.

WELLS, Christine M. Exh. 1914
65 High West Street, Dorchester, Dorset. † LS 3.

WELLS, D. (Mrs. S.R.) Exh. 1912
42 Linden Road, Bedford. † RA 1.

WELLS, Denys George b. 1881
Still life and figure painter. b. Bedford. Studied Slade School. R.B.A. 1910. Exh. 1907-40. Add: London 1907, Marlow, Bucks. 1912; New Malden, Surrey 1919. † ALP 1, GI 1, LEI 2, LS 7, NEA 9, RA 10, RBA 173, ROI 6.

WELLS, Edward Francis* Exh. 1897-1938
Portrait and landscape painter. Studied Slade School and R.A. Schools (Creswick Prize 1899). Travelled in Italy, Corsica and Switzerland. Add: London 1897 and 1938; Milton Abbas, Blandford, Dorset 1914. † D 33, L 1, LS 10, RA 8, RHA 3, RI 7, ROI 1, WG 95.

WELLS, E. Kathleen Exh. 1888-89
Portrait painter. Clarendon Road, Waverley Street, Nottingham. † N 2.

WELLS, Frances Exh. 1936-39
45 Draycott Avenue, Kenton, Harrow, Middlesex. † B 4, RCA 5.

WELLS, George Exh. 1880-94
Genre, literary, portrait and landscape painter, London. † L 3, RA 5, RBA 6, RCA 16, RHA 3, RI 3, ROI 1.

WELLS, Henry Tamworth* 1828-1903
Portrait painter and miniaturist. Studied under J.M. Leigh. A.R.A. 1866, R.A. 1870. Add: London and Dorking, Surrey. † B 4, L 6, M 17, P 1, RA 109, ROI 1.

WELLS, John Exh. 1917-35
Portrait and flower painter. London. † I 1, L 1, RA 7, NEA 5.

WELLS, J.C.S. Exh. 1934
Broxtowe House, General Hospital, Nottingham. † N 2.

WELLS, Joseph Robert* Exh. 1880-96
Marine painter. London. † B 2, D 2, GI 6, L 2, M 6, RA 4, RBA 3, RI 18, ROI 3.

WELLS, John Sanderson* b. 1872
Portrait, sporting painter. Studied Slade School and Juliens, Paris. R.B.A. 1896, R.I. 1903. Exh. 1890-1940. Add: Banbury 1890; London 1898. † B 10, FIN 67, L 3, RA 38, RBA 41, RI 138, ROI 14.

WELLS, Mrs. Jane W. see COX

WELLS, Louise Exh. 1921
† LS 3.

WELLS, Miss L.G. Exh. 1908-14
Nottingham 1908; Sherwood, Notts. 1912. † N 10.

WELLS, Lilian G. b. 1880
Mrs. F.W. Parker. Sculptor, watercolour painter and teacher. b. Bolton, Lancs. Studied Royal College of Art. Exh. 1902-27. Add: London. † L 7, RA 5.

WELLS, Leonard Harry b. 1903
Portrait painter. b. Nottingham. Studied Nottingham Municipal School of Art and R.A. Schools. Exh. 1922-31. Add: Nottingham 1922; Sherwood, Notts. 1925; London 1928. † N 5, RA 2.

WELLS, Mary (Mrs. H.W.) Exh. 1886
Figure painter. Whitecross, Wallingford, Berks. † RA 1.

WELLS, Madeline Rachel Exh. 1909-40
nee Holmes. Decorative painter. b. India. Studied Westminster and London Schools of Art. R.B.A. 1915, S.W.A. 1923, Married Robert Douglas W. q.v. Add: St. Albans Studios, Kensington, London. † G 6, GOU 14, I 11, L 3, LS 2, RA 3, RBA 110, RI 7, ROI 1, SWA 34.

WELLS, Nesta Mary Exh. 1911-14
9 Petersham Terrace, South Kensington, London. † LS 9.

WELLS, Robert Douglas b. 1875
Watercolour landscape and still life painter. Studied London School of Art. A.R.B.A. 1926, R.B.A. 1929. Married Madeline Rachel W. q.v. Exh. 1908-40. Add: London. † BG 28, GOU 49, I 3, L 4, NEA 1, RA 1, RBA 78, RI 5.

WELLS, Reginald Fairfax 1877-1951
Sculptor and potter. b. Brazil. Studied Royal College of Art. Exh. 1899-1933. Add: London 1899 and 1910; West Malling, Kent 1905; Storrington, Sussex 1927; Pulborough, Sussex 1933. † G 7, GI 3, I 31, L 3, RA 9, RSA 3.

WELLS, Miss R. Grenville Exh. 1935
57 Fountain Court, London. † ROI 1.

WELLS, T.A. Exh. 1911
The Fold, Wallasley, Cheshire. † RI 1.

WELLS, Mrs. Theodosia Mary Exh. 1908-14
Petersfield, Hants. 1908; London 1913. † LS 23.

WELLS, William* Exh. 1893-1923
Landscape and figure painter. b. Scotland. Studied Slade School, N.S.W. Art Society, Sydney, Australia and Paris. Spent seven years as a theatrical scenic artist at Preston R.B.A. 1906. Add: Richmond 1893; Glasgow 1895; Preston 1898; Lancaster 1904 and 1911; Port St. Mary, I.O.M. 1910 and 1912; Topsham, Devon 1920; Appledore, Devon 1922. † GI 33, L 14, M 1, RA 3, RBA 6, ROI 4, RSA 3, RSW 1.

WELLS-GRAHAM, Mrs. Catherine Exh. 1907
7 Dudley Terrace, Leith. † RSA 1.

WELPLY, Nellie Exh. 1907-15
Floraville, Bandon, Co. Cork. † RHA 14.

WELSFORD, Mildred see HANCOCK

WELSH, Bessie Exh. 1896
3 Dashwood Square, Newton Stewart, N.B. † GI 2, RSW 1.

WELSH, Effie Exh. 1901-31
Mrs. James W. Add: Liberton, N.B. † GI 1, RMS 1, RSA 11, RSW 3.

WELSH, J. Exh. 1881-96
Newton Stewart, N.B. † GI 2, RSA 2.

WELSH, Jane Exh. 1910-13
Painter. 20 Rossetti Garden Mansions, Chelsea, London. † NEA 3, RA 1.

WELSH, J.M. Exh. 1906-14
Mount Florida, Glasgow. † GI 2, RSA 1.

WELSH, Lizzie T. Exh. 1893-94
Newton Stewart, N.B. † GI 3.

WELSH, Miss M.B.C. Exh. 1936
41 York Place, Edinburgh. † RSA 1.

WELSH, William Exh. 1919-29
Landscape and still life painter. Studied Durham University. Add: Harrow on the Hill, Middlesex. † AB 2, GI 1, RA 5, RI 10.

WELSH, William Exh. 1920-32
Hooton, Cheshire 1920; Chester 1927. † L 6.

WELTI, Albert b. 1862
Black and white artist. Exh. 1896. Add: 101 Nymphenburger strasse, Munich. † RA 3.

WEMYSS, Countess of Exh. 1906-8
23 St. James' Place, London. † NG 4.

WEMYSS, Earl of Exh. 1905-7
23 St. James' Place, London. † NG 12, RSA 1.

WEMYSS, M.W. Colchester Exh. 1891-98
Landscape painter. Westbury Court, Newnham, Glos. † RID 2.

WEMYSS, Robert Exh. 1896-1904
Glasgow. † GI 4, RSA 1.

WEMYSS, Zibella Exh. 1895
Durie House, Helensburgh, N.B. † GI 1.

WENCH, Miss M. Selwyn Exh. 1900
40 The Parade, Leamington, Warwicks. † B 1.

WENDEL, T.M. Exh. 1882-86
R.E. 1882 (ceased 1889). † RE 3.

WENDT, William Exh. 1899
Landscape painter. St. Ives, Cornwall. † RA 1.

WENGEL, Jules Exh. 1894-1904
Etaples, Pas de Calais, France 1894; Montreuil sur mer, Pas de Calais, France 1904. † GI 2, I 2.

WENHAM, Arthur T. Exh. 1937-38
41b Lower Teddington Road, Middlesex 1937; Hampton Wick, Kingston on Thames 1938. † NEA 1, RBA 2.

WENHAM, Miss G. Exh. 1900
Wollaton Rectory, Nottingham. † N 3.

WENHAM, Mary Anna Exh. 1884-85
Watercolour landscape painter. The Park, Highgate, London. † D 1, L 1, SWA 3.

WENLOCK, Lady Mary d. 1932
Landscape painter. Exh. from 1899. Add: 26 Portland Place, London. † BA 1, NG 12.

WENNER, Violet B. Exh. 1907
Beechfield, Romiley, Cheshire. † M 2.

WENSLEY, W. Exh. 1907
143 Brecknock Road, London. † RA 1.

WENT, Alfred Exh. 1893
Painter. 11 Nelson Road, Ilkley, Yorks. † RBA 2.

WENT, D.N. Exh. 1913
Riverside, St. Osyth, Colchester, Essex. † LS 3.

WENT, Florence A. Exh. 1924-26
Boundary Road, Bideton Hill, Birkenhead. † L 2.

WENTWORTH, Ida E. Exh. 1925
Chaldon, Bookers Lane, Moseley Hill, Liverpool. † L 4.

WENTWORTH-SHIELDS, Ada Exh. 1891-92
Painter. 4 Vanbrugh Park West, Blackheath, London. † RBA 2.

WENTWORTH-SHIELDS, Pat b. 1906
Painter and commercial artist. b. Goulburn. N.S.W. Australia. Studied Sydney Art School and Grosvenor School of Modern Art. Exh. 1932. Add: 16 Seymour Place, London. † RA 1.

WENYON, H. Exh. 1916-17
9 South Moulton Street, London. † RA 2.

WERENCKJOLD, E. Exh. 1882-83
5 Bloomsbury Mansions, Hart Street, Manchester. † L 1, M 1.

WERGMAN, T. Blake Exh. 1888
24 Dawson Place, London. † ROI 2.

WERLEMANN, Carl Exh. 1908
123 Rue de Livourne, Brussels. † L 2.

WERN, Tom Exh. 1915-31
Landscape painter. Penycaunant, Bettws-y-Coed, North Wales. † L 5, RCA 18.

WERNER, Carl Friedrich Heinrich 1808-1894
German architectural and landscape painter. b. Weimar. Studied Leipzig and Munich. Travelled widely on the Continent, Middle East and England. A.R.I. 1860, R.I. 1860. Add: 1 Lessingstrasse, Leipzig 1880. † RI 4.

WERNER, Louis Exh. 1886
39 Grafton Street, Dublin. † RHA 1.

WERNER, Rinaldo Exh. 1889-98
Painter. London. † D 3, G 1, L 4, M 1, RBA 4, RI 3.

WERNER, Von see V

WERNINCK, Blanche Exh. 1893
Landscape painter. Rose Cottage, Mursley, Winslow, Bucks. † RA 1.

WERNTZ, Carl b. 1874
American painter. Exh. 1935-38. Add: c/o Walker Galleries, London. † RA 1, WG 120.

WERTHEIMER, Eva Exh. 1905
8 Connaught Place, Hyde Park, London. † I 1.

WESLAKE, Charlotte Exh. 1880
Painter. 32 Newcomen Street, Southwark, London. † SWA 1.

WESLAKE, Mary Exh. 1880-81
Painter. 32 Newcomen Street, Southwark, London. † SWA 4.

WESSON, Arthur N. Exh. 1902
Architect. 7 Priestwood Mansions, Highgate, London. † RA 1.

WESSON, Mrs. Emily Exh. 1923
14 St. James Terrace, The Hoe, Plymouth, Devon. † B 1.

WESSON, Madge Exh. 1886
Sherwood, Notts. † N 1.

WEST, Miss A. Exh. 1902
26 The Waldrons, Croydon, Surrey. † SWA 1.

WEST, Alexander Exh. 1880-84
Landscape and coastal painter. London 1880; Manchester 1884. † GI 2, L 1, RA 1, RBA 4.

WEST, Annie Exh. 1929
14 Conniston Avenue, Wallasey, Cheshire. † L 1.

WEST, Anthony Exh. 1921
68 Corringham Road, Golders Green, London. † L 1.

WEST, Alice L. Exh. 1889-1915
Figure and domestic painter. London 1889; Tunbridge Wells, Kent 1900. † L 3, RA 6, RBA 3, RI 3, SWA 5.

WEST, Amy Mary Exh. 1907-13
Bushey, Herts. † LS 9, RA 2, SWA 1.

WEST, A.P. Exh. 1928-29
Liverpool. † L 4.

WEST, Mrs. Belville Exh. 1913
2 Rue Montaigne, Rond Point des Champs Elyssee, Paris. † LS 1.

WEST, Blanche C. Exh. 1882
Still life and figure painter. 37 The Lawn, South Lambeth Road, London. † RA 1.

WEST, Cicely Exh. 1925-29
Illuminator and calligrapher. Collaborated with her father Joseph Walter W. q.v. Studied L.C.C. Central School of Arts and Crafts. Add: The Vane, Northwood, Middlesex. † L 4.

WEST, Charles W. Exh. 1880-82
Portrait and figure painter. London. † RA 1, RBA 4.

WEST, David d. 1936
Watercolour landscape painter. b. Lossiemouth. R.S.W. 1907. Add: Aberdeen 1889; Chilkoot, Lossiemouth, Morayshire 1895. † AR 2, GI 25, L 3, RA 10, RHA 3, RI 2, RSA 94, RSW 97.

WEST, Edith Exh. 1885
Landscape and figure painter. Epsom College, Surrey. † SWA 4.

WEST, Edgar E. Exh. 1881-89
Watercolour landscape painter. London. † B 1, L 2, M 1, RA 1, RBA 3.

WEST, Evangeline M. Exh. 1937-38
† RMS 2.

WEST, Gertrude b. 1872
Flower, landscape and miniature flower painter. b. Birmingham. Studied Hanover and Paris. A.R.M.S. 1924. R.M.S. 1930. Add: Edgbaston, Birmingham 1897; Bromley, Kent 1911; London 1924. † B 6, L 31, RMS 69, SWA 5.

WEST, James Exh. 1883
Architect. 5 Fenchurch Street, London. † RA 1.

WEST, John Exh. 1882
Lilly Cottage, Troutbeck, Windermere. † M 1.

WEST, Joseph b. 1882
Watercolour, landscape and animal painter. b. Farnhill, nr. Keighley, Yorks. Exh. 1913-31. Add: 103 Cavendish Street Studio, Keighley, Yorks. † L 5, RCA 12, RI 2.

WEST, James G. Exh. 1920-32
Architect. H.M. Office of Works, London. RA 2.

WEST, Joan M. Exh. 1913-27
Stroud, Glos. 1913; London 1917. † L 1, M 1, RA 1, SWA 3.

WEST, Joseph Walter 1860-1933
Painter, lithographer and illuminator. b. Hull. Studied St. Johns Wood and R.A. Schools. R.B.A. 1893, A.R.W.S. 1901, R.W.S. 1904. Father of Cicely W. q.v. "Sunshine, Breeze and Blossom, Lake Como" purchased by Chantrey Bequest 1913. Add: Harrow, Middlesex 1885; London 1889; Northwood, Middlesex 1898. † B 3, FIN 1, GI 4, L 44, LEI 1, M 1, NG 2, RA 64, RBA 2, RHA 1, RSW 1, RWS 91, WG 2.

WEST, Katharine Anne (Nan) b. 1904
Painter, decorator and illuminator. Studied Byam Shaw School and Slade School. Exh. 1922-37. Add: 45 Camden House Road, Kensington, London. † CHE 2, GOU 56, M 4, NEA 17.

WEST, L. Exh. 1899
Ravenstead, St. Helens, Lancs. † L 1.

WEST, Lizzie Exh. 1881
Painter. School of Art, Queen's Square, London. † SWA 1.

WEST, Maud Exh. 1901-16
Flower painter. 10 Southfield Road, Tunbridge Wells, Kent. † B 1, RA 3, SWA 2.

WEST, Max Exh. 1903-6
Painter. London. † NEA 7.

WEST, Maud Astley Exh. 1880-90
Watercolour flower painter. London. † D 1, SWA 5.

WEST, Nan see WEST, Katharine Anne

WEST, Reginald Exh. 1903
The Pines, Mudeford, Christchurch, Hants. † D 2.

WEST, Richard Whately 1848-1905
Landscape painter. b. Dublin. Add: London; Alassio, North Italy 1889. † FIN 1, RA 7, RA 25, RHA 5, RI 1, ROI 4.

WEST, Richard William b. 1887
Portrait and landscape painter and etcher. b. Aberdeen. Studied Aberdeen School of Art and Allan Fraser Art College, Arbroath. Principal art master at Forfar Academy. Exh. 1920-22. Add: Aberdeen. † RSA 5.

WEST, Sara Exh. 1898
Station Road, Hayes, Kent. † RMS 2.

WEST, Thomas Alfred Exh. 1912-29
Portrait painter, lithographer and teacher. Born and studied in Manchester. Add: Liverpool 1912 and 1928; Wallasey, Cheshire 1921. † L 15, RA 2, RCA 3, ROI 1.

WEST, Walter J. Exh. 1920-40
Birmingham 1920; Warley, Warwicks. 1928. † B 39.

WESTALL, Robert* Exh. 1880
Watercolour landscape painter. 2 Elm Road, Hampstead, London. † RBA 1.

WESTBROOK, Jessie Duncan Exh. 1906
25 Glengarry Road, East Dulwich, London. † RSA 1.

WESTBROOKE, Elisabeth W. Exh. 1880-87
Portrait and figure painter. London. † B 2, D 1, L 1, M 1, RA 2, ROI 1, SWA 2.

WESTBYE, J.T. Exh. 1909-10
Architect. 1 Princess Road, Primrose Hill, London. † RA 2.

WESTCAR, Mrs. Constance Prescott Exh. 1909-11
c/o Allied Artists Association, 67 Chancery Lane, London. † LS 7.

WESTCOTT, Miss F.A. Exh. 1884-1914
94 Princes Road, Liverpool. † B 3, L 23.

WESTCOTT, Miss L. Exh. 1891
† D 3.

WESTELL, Hubert Exh. 1887
Architect. c/o Thomas & Co., Bolsover Street, London † RA 1.

WESTERN, A. Exh. 1897
Landscape painter. c/o Messrs. Rorke, 104 Fulham Road, London. † RA 1.

WESTERN, Charles Exh. 1884-1900
Landscape painter. London. † M 1, L 2, RA 3, RBA 3, ROI 2.

WESTERN, Henry b. 1877
Miniature and portrait painter. Exh. 1918-25. Add: 37 Nelson Road, Stroud Green, London. † RA 2.

WESTHEAD, G. Reade Exh. 1883
Landscape painter. † ROI 1.

WESTLAKE, Mrs. Exh. 1895-1900
3 Chelsea Embankment, London. † NG 5.

WESTLAKE, Eliza Exh. 1880
Landscape painter. 9 Brunswick Place, Southampton. † SWA 1.

WESTLAKE, Nathaniel Hubert John 1833-1921
Decorative painter of biblical subjects, stained glass artist and writer. b. Romsey. Studied Heatherleys and at Somerset House under Dyce and Herbert. Add: London. † L 1, RA 27, RBA 2, RHA 1.

WESTLAKE, Walter V. Exh. 1922-39
Church Road, Ashford, Middlesex. † D 4, L 1, RCA 14, RI 1.

WESTMACOTT, Bernard Exh. 1902
Landscape painter. 3 Greenhill Park, Harlesden, London. † RA 1.

WESTMACOTT, G.H. Exh. 1883
Crumpshall Grove, Manchester. † M 1.

WESTMACOTT, James Sherwood 1823-1900
Sculptor. Son of sculptor Henry W. (1784-1861). Studied under his uncle Sir Richard W. (1775-1856). Exh. 1880-86. Add: 49 High Street, Eccleston Square London. † RA 6, RI 3.

WESTMINSTER, Dean of see NORRIS, William Foxley

WESTON, Alice E. Exh. 1923-26
Mayfield Studio, Sark, C.I. † L 6.

WESTON, Charles F. Exh. 1882-92
Artist and teacher. Manchester. † L 1, M 3, RHA 1.

WESTON, Charles H.E. Exh. 1910-11
Strode Park, Herne, Kent. † LS 6.

WESTON, Miss D. Exh. 1921
7 High Street, Lyndhurst, Hants. † RA 1.

WESTON, Dorothy Exh. 1905-8
Greenfields, East Sheen, London. † L 4, ROI 2, SWA 2.

WESTON, Doris Hope Exh. 1909-39
Painter. Harborne, Birmingham 1909; London 1913. † B 4, COO 1, P 1, RI 4.

WESTON, Ernest Exh. 1884
Painter. 46 Church Street, Woolwich, London. † RI 1.

WESTON, Mrs. Florence Exh. 1921-39
Architectural, flower, landscape and figure painter. 38 Conniston Road, Earlsdon, Coventry. † B 31.

WESTON, K.V. Exh. 1914
19 Epperstone Road, West Bridgford, Notts. † N 3.

WESTON, W.G. Exh. 1936-39
† GOU 1, NEA 1.

WESTON-WRIGHT, Rev. H. Exh. 1928-38
Architectural painter. † AB 3, WG 13.

WESTRAY, Grace Exh. 1903-18
Landscape, figure and animal painter. London. † I 2, L 2, NEA 16.

WESTROPP, Rosemary O'Callaghan Exh. 1937
Painter. Lismuckane, O'Callaghan's Mills, Co. Clare. † RHA 1.

WESTRUP, E. Kate Exh. 1910-27
A.S.W.A. 1923. Add: New Milton, Hants. 1910; St. Buryan, Cornwall 1911. † D 14, L 13, LS 9, NEA 2, RA 1, SWA 6.

WESTRUP, O.F. Exh. 1887-88
Woodland Grove, Dacre Hill, Cheshire. † L 2.

WESTRUP, Miss P.M. Exh. 1920-25
London. † GI 1, RSA 1.

WESTWATER, Robert H. Exh. 1925-40
Edinburgh 1925 and 1936; London 1931. † GI 2, RSA 12.

WEST-WATSON, C. Maud Exh. 1886-1938
Glasgow. † D 1, GI 19, L 7, RSA 3, RSW 1.

WESTWOOD, Adam Exh. 1881-1901
19 Guildhall Street, Dunfermline. † GI 4, RSA 9.

WESTWOOD, Miss E.M. Exh. 1891-92
Bristol Road, Birmingham. † B 1, M 1.

WESTWOOD, H.R. Exh. 1886-88
8 West Newington Place, Edinburgh. † RSA 3.

WESTWOOD, Miss M.A. Exh. 1920-26
Harborne, Birmingham 1920; Edgbaston, Birmingham 1925. † B 12.

WESTWOOD, Nellie Exh. 1882-87
Rookery Road, Birmingham. † B 6, GI 2.

WESTWOOD, Norman Exh. 1936-39
Watercolour painter and architect. † AR 2, NEA 1.

WESTWOOD, Percy James b. 1878
Painter and architect. Studied at the A.A. Exh. 1915-40. Add: London. † AR 2, COO 2, I 1, L 19, NEA 3, RA 6, RSA 11.

WESTWOOD, William Exh. 1899-1900
Studio, Carnegie Library, Dunfermline. † GI 2.

WESTWORTH, John Exh. 1901-2
Dentonville, St. Helens, Lancs. † L 2.

WETENHALL, Edward B. Exh. 1900-11
Architect. London. † RA 3.

WETHERALL, Miss E.E. Exh. 1928-35
Rugeley, Stafford. † B 1, RI 1.

WETHERBEE, George Faulkener* 1851-1920
Landscape, genre and mythological painter. b. Cincinnati, U.S.A. Studied Antwerp and R.A. Schools. Travelled widely. R.I. 1883 (res. 1909), R.O.I. 1888. Add: London. † AG 12, B 25, D 2, DOW 6, FIN 68, G 3, GI 18, L 44, LEI 53, M 30, NG 35, RA 56, RBA 9, RI 44, ROI 83, RSW 1.

WETHERED, H. Newton Exh. 1902
Coombe Field, Maldon, Surrey. † GI 1.

WETHERED, Maud Llewellyn b. 1898
Sculptor and wood engraver. b. Bury, Sussex. Daughter of Vernon W. q.v. Studied Slade School. Exh. 1925-33. Add: London. † M 2, NEA 3, RA 1.

WETHERED, Margaret M. Exh. 1928-30
Redcourt, Mossley Hill, Liverpool. † L 4.

WETHERED, Vernon 1865-1952
Landscape painter. b. Bristol. Studied Slade School. N.E.A. 1932. Father of Maud Llewellyn W. q.v. Add: Bury, nr. Pulborough, Sussex 1899; London 1908. † BA 6, BAR 4, GOU 3, LS 3, NEA 37, NG 2, RED 57.

WETHERLY, Arthur J. Exh. 1932-36
Landscape painter. † LEF 14.

WETTON, Ernest Exh. 1895-96
Figure painter. 14 Bower Place, Maidstone, Kent. † RA 1, ROI 1.

WETZEL, Pat Exh. 1931
† GOU 3.

WEVILL, Constance H. Exh. 1904
Westbourne, Prenton, Birkenhead. † L 1.

WEVILL, Edward Harding b. 1856
Architect and painter. Studied Liverpool School of Art. Exh. 1893-1928. Add: 417 Old Chester Road, Rock Ferry, Cheshire 1893; Higher Bebington, Cheshire 1922. † L 35, RCA 18.

WEYDEN, can der see V

WEYNS, Jules Exh. 1887
Sculptor. 270 Kings Road, Chelsea, London. † RA 1.

WHAITE, E.W. Exh. 1883
Blackheath, London. † L 1.

WHAITE, Henry Clarence* 1828-1912
Landscape and illustrative painter. b. Manchester. President R.C.A. and President Manchester Academy of Fine Arts. H.R.M.S. 1897, A.R.W.S. 1872, R.W.S. 1882. Add: London 1880; Conway, Wales 1904. † B 21, G 1, GI 1, L 67, M 50, NG 1, RA 24, RCA 143. RMS 3, ROI 6, RSW 3, RWS 135.

WHAITE, James Exh. 1881-1916
Landscape painter. Burton Joyce, Notts. 1881; Liverpool 1882; Seacombe, Cheshire 1896; Liscard, Cheshire 1902. † B 2, GI 2, L 92, M 9, N 4, RA 1, RI 1, RSA 2.

WHAITE, Lilias Exh. 1885
5 Bath Place, Portobello Road, London. † RSA 1.

WHAITE, Lily L.F. Exh. 1894-1914
Mrs. Harries. Flower painter. London 1894; Conway, North Wales 1898. † L 6, RA 1, RCA 21, RI 2.

WHAITE, Thomas sen. Exh. 1880
Burton Joyce, Notts. † N 1.

WHALE, A. Exh. 1914-16
Cheshunt, Herts. 1914; London 1916. † RA 4.

WHALEN, Thomas Exh. 1930-40
A.R.S.A. 1940. Add: Leith and Edinburgh. † GI 15, RSA 26.

WHALEY, Harold Exh. 1914-29
Painter and etcher. Port St. Mary, I.o.M. 1914; Baildon, Yorks. 1916. † L 32, RA 6, RCA 8, RSA 1.
WHALEY, Hubert Exh. 1920
5 Caroline Place, London. † NEA 1.
WHALL, Charles A. Exh. 1882-84
Worksop, Notts. † N 3.
WHALL, Christopher Whitworth d. 1924
Stained glass artist and painter. Father of Veronica W. q.v. Add: Dorking and London. † GI 2, L 1, RA 13.
WHALL, Veronica b. 1887
Stained glass artist and painter. b. Dorking. Daughter of Christopher Whitworth W. q.v. Studied Central School of Arts and Crafts. Exh. 1906-35. Add: London. † L 20, NG 3, RA 10, RHA 2.
WHALLEY, Adolphus Jacob Exh. 1886-91
Painter. London. † L 2, RA 1.
WHALLEY, Lilian M. Exh. 1893
Laurel Cottage, Bushey, Herts. † M 1.
WHALLEY, Percy H. Exh. 1908
33 Park Street, Liscard, Cheshire. † L 1.
WHALLEY-WHALEY, John Exh. 1913
50 Londesboro Road, Scarborough, Yorks. † LS 3.
WHANSHAW, H.W. Exh. 1914
7 Charlwood Terrace, Putney, London. † RA 1.
WHARTON, Amy C. Exh. 1892-1916
Sculptor. Old Chalton, Kent 1892; Ealing Common, London 1916. † L 1, RA 1, RBA 1.
WHARTON, Mary Exh. 1912-25
Dublin. † RHA 5, RSA 1.
WHARTON, Samuel Ernest b. 1900
Painter, designer and draughtsman. b. Beeston, Notts. Studied Nottingham School of Art 1923-27 and Birmingham School of Art 1928-29. Exh. 1925-39. Add: Beeston, Notts. † N 13.
WHATELEY, Miss M. Exh. 1937
1 Mulberry Street, Stratford-on-Avon, Warwicks. † B 1.
WHATELEY, T. Exh. 1919-20
† I 2.
WHATELY, Mrs. . Exh. 1917-25
A.S.W.A. 1918. Add: Pembridge Church Road, Upper Norwood, London. † SWA 23.
WHATELY, Mrs. M. Alice H. Exh. 1892
Watercolour painter. 14 Camden House Road, London. † RA 1.
WHATLEY, Henry* 1842-1901
Watercolour landscape painter. Clifton, Bristol. † B 1, L 1, RI 4.
WHEAT, John William Exh. 1939-40
266 West Bromwich Street, Oldbury. † B 3, RCA 3.
WHEATCROFT, Rachel Exh. 1909-28
Landscape painter. Travelled on the Continent. Add: Eastbourne. † BRU 44, GOU 60, LS 18, SWA 3, WG 41.
WHEATCROFT, Mrs. Cooke Exh. 1890
Watercolour flower painter. Abbey Chambers, Bath. † D 4, RBA 1, SWA 1.
WHEATLEY, Edith Grace 1888-1970
nee Wolfe. Painter. Studied Slade School and Paris. Senior lecturer in Fine Art, University of Cape Town 1925-37. Married John W. q.v. N.E.A. 1921, A.R.M.S. 1910, R.M.S. 1913. Add: London 1904 and 1914; Newquay, Cornwall 1913. † COO 2, G 15, GI 2, L 17, LS 9, NEA 27, P 1, RA 15, RHA 4, RI 4, RMS 13, RSA 1, SWA 6.
WHEATLEY, John 1892-1955
Figure and portrait painter. Studied Slade School. Assistant teacher Slade School 1920-25. Director National Gallery of South Africa and Michaelis Professor of Fine Art and architecture, University of Cape Town. Married Edith Grace W. q.v. N.E.A. 1917, A.R.E. 1921. Add: Newlyn, Penzance 1914; London 1917; Sheffield 1938. † CG 3, COO 2, G 82, GI 1, GOU 1, I 4, L 1, LEI 12, NEA 48, P 1, RA 22, RE 3, RHA 1, RSA 3.
WHEATLEY, Lawrence Exh. 1934-36
Watercolour landscape painter. Bardowie by Milngavie 1934; Burton-on-Trent 1936. † RA 1, RSA 1.
WHEATLEY, Maurice Exh. 1927-33
Etcher. 18 Torrington Park, Finchley, London. † ALP 1, L 6, RA 6.
WHEATLEY, Oliver Exh. 1891-1920
Sculptor. Studied in Paris. Assistant to Thomas Brock. Add: Birmingham 1891; London 1892 and 1898; Paris 1895. † B 4, GI 7, L 10, RA 15, RSA 2.
WHEATLEY, W.C. Exh. 1939
97 Nottingham Road, Arnold, Notts. † N 1.
WHEATLY, Reginald F. Exh. 1932
Architect. Mansion House, Truro, Cornwall. † RA 1.
WHEATON, Miss F.E. Exh. 1911-30
Liverpool. † L 41.
WHEATON, Muriel b. 1902
Watercolour painter. Studied Exeter School of Art, Christchurch, New Zealand; St. Johns Wood School and under Kirkland Jamieson. Exh. 1934-39. Add: Exeter 1934; Wolton, Glos. 1936. † COO 1, RBA 7, SWA 7.
WHEATON, Richard G. Exh. 1899-1921
Sculptor. London. † L 2, LS 6, NG 1, RA 4.
WHEATON, S.W. Exh. 1911-14
17 Rastel Avenue, Streatham Hill, London. † LS 9.
WHEBLE, Mrs. Mary E. Exh. 1927-32
The Little Hermitage, Milverton, Leamington Spa, Warwicks. † B 4, L 1.
WHEELDON, C.D. Exh. 1939
Architect. Elm Avenue, Long Eaton, Nottingham. † N 2.
WHEELER, Miss Exh. 1889-90
Landscape painter. 64 Talgarth Road, West Kensington, London. † RA 1, RI 1.
WHEELER, Miss Annie Exh. 1882-87
Watercolour flower painter. Hackney 1882; Richmond, Surrey 1883; Reigate, Surrey 1887. † RBA 5, RI 3.
WHEELER, Mrs. Amy Eliza Exh. 1890-1908
Miniature portrait painter. London. † LS 3, RA 6.
WHEELER, Miss C. Exh. 1914
Woodhouse Eaves, Loughborough, Leics. † N 2.
WHEELER, Charles 1892-1974
Sculptor. b. Wolverhampton. Studied Royal College of Art. Married Muriel W. q.v. A.R.A. 1934, R.A. 1940, R.B.S.A. 1931. "The Infant Christ" purchased by Chantrey Bequest 1924 and "Spring" in 1930. Add: London. † B 16, CHE 1, GI 12, L 4, LEI 3, P 4, RA 61, ROI 3, RSA 9.
WHEELER, Dorothy Muriel Exh. 1914-34
Watercolour landscape and figure painter. Plumstead, Kent 1914; Esher, Surrey 1920; London 1932. † RA 5, SWA 5.
WHEELER, E. Kathleen Exh. 1906-13
Kewhurst, Tilehurst, nr. Reading, Berks. † L 1, RA 4, RSA 1.
WHEELER, Edwin P. Exh. 1938
Architect. County Hall, London. † RA 1.
WHEELER, Frederick Exh. 1902-3
Architect. London. † RA 2.
WHEELER, Mrs. Fanny G. Exh. 1927-34
Watercolour painter. Rockwood, Greenhill, Hampstead, London. † D 1, RA 1, RI 4.
WHEELER, John Exh. 1938
136 East Dulwich Grove, London. † RBA 1, ROI 1.
WHEELER, Muriel Exh. 1918-40
nee Bourne. Sculptor and painter. Married Charles W. q.v. A.S.W.A. 1934, S.W.A. 1935. Add: London. † B 18, GI 3, L 2, NEA 10, P 12, RA 18, RI 1, RMS 1, ROI 10, SWA 19.
WHEELER, Margaret E. Exh. 1908-14
Edenvale, Dormans Park, Surrey. † LS 18.
WHEELER, Mary E. Exh. 1885-88
Edinburgh 1885; Hillhead, Glasgow 1888. † D 1, RSA 4.
WHEELER, Mildred F. Exh. 1923
† SWA 2.
WHEELER, Marjorie M. Exh. 1940
Miniature portrait painter. 4 Mitchley Avenue, Purley, Surrey. † RA 1.
WHEELER, Nora Constance b. 1892
nee Essex. b. Thrapston. Studied Hastings School of Art. Exh. 1933. Add: London. † RCA 1.
WHEELER, S.A. Exh. 1880
Painter. 90 Abingdon Road, Kensington, London. † SWA 1.
WHEELER, Vera K. Exh. 1927-28
Etcher. 38 Birch Grove, Acton, London. † B 2, RA 1.
WHEELER, William b. 1895
Sculptor, designer, stained glass and ecclesiastical artist. Studied Royal College of Art. Exh. 1924-37. Add: London 1924; St. Albans, Herts. 1932. † RA 3.
WHEELER, W.H. Exh. 1881-95
Landscape painter. Hackney 1881; Richmond, Surrey 1883; Reigate, Surrey 1884. † B 1, D 10, L 10, M 7, RA 1, RBA 11, RHA 1, RI 12, ROI 2, RSA 1.
WHEELER, Mrs. W.H. (Annie) Exh. 1885-86
Watercolour painter. Rosenheath, Reigate, Surrey. † L 3, M 2, RI 3.
WHEELERSMITH, Miss E.V. Exh. 1893
8 Elgin Road, Addiscombe, Surrey. † SWA 1.
WHEELERSMITH, Olive Exh. 1884-86
Watercolour painter. 8 Elgin Road, Addiscombe, Surrey. † RBA 3.
WHEELHOUSE, Mary V. Exh. 1895-1933
Painter and illustrator. Scarborough 1895; London 1900. † BG 54, L 1, M 1, NG 1, RA 2, SWA 2.
WHEELHOUSE, W. Exh. 1923
8 Marshall Street, Sherwood, Nottingham. † N 1.
WHEELWRIGHT, Miss Exh. 1891
47 Upper George Street, Bryanstone Square, London. † B 2.
WHEELWRIGHT, Anna Exh. 1884
Flower painter. 65 Seymour Street, Connaught Square, London. † RBA 1.
WHEELWRIGHT, Mrs. E. Exh. 1908-9
Miniature painter. 9 Ravensbourne Gardens, West Ealing, London. † RA 2.
WHEELWRIGHT, Miss E.W. Exh. 1923
99 Holte Road, Aston, Birmingham. † B 2.
WHEELWRIGHT, Hene Exh. 1880-1903
Painter on ivory. Ewhurst, Hawkhurst, Kent 1880; Bath 1899. † B 7, D 16, GI 20, L 32, M 25, RA 1, RBA 5, RSA 5, SWA 8.

WHEELWRIGHT, Mrs. Jane Elizabeth Exh. 1914-15
Married to Rowland W. q.v. Add: Meadowbrook, Bushey, Herts. † RA 2.

WHEELWRIGHT, Maud (Mrs. W.) Exh. 1892-1912
nee Stroud. Painter and miniaturist. London 1892; Ditchling, Sussex 1909. † L 2, P 1, RA 11, RBA 3, RMS 2, ROI 1.

WHEELWRIGHT, Rowland b. 1870
Painter and illustrator. b. Ipswich, Queensland, Australia. Studied Herkomers, Bushey. R.B.A. 1906. Married Jane Elizabeth W. q.v. Exh. 1893-1938. Add: Watford, Herts. 1893; Bushey, Herts. 1907. † B 3, FIN 3, L 1, P 1, RA 41, RBA 6, RHA 1, RI 1, ROI 30.

WHEELWRIGHT, Mrs. Talbot Exh. 1904
Miniature portrait painter. 5 Little Ealing Lane, South Ealing, London. † RA 1.

WHELAN, Leo 1892-1956
Portrait, figure, landscape and intérior painter. b. Dublin. Studied under William Orpen and at Dublin Metropolitan School of Art. Visiting teacher of painting and drawing R.H.A. Schools. A.R.H.A. 1920, R.H.A. 1924. Add: Dublin. † I 1, P 17, RA 2, RBA 1, RHA 159.

WHELAN, William Exh. 1911-21
Artist and teacher. Dublin. † RHA 27.

WHELLOCK, Robert P. Exh. 1900-3
Architect. 45 Finsbury Pavement, London. † RA 2.

WHELPTON, Miss G.L. Exh. 1913-21
Clive Cottage, Furness Road, Eastbourne. † LS 17.

WHERRETT, J. Ramsey b. 1914
Painter, designer, illustrator and teacher. Studied Birmingham College of Art 1930-36 and Leamington Spa School of Art. Exh. 1940. Add: 23 Emscote Road, Warwick. † RA 1.

WHERRY, Beatrix A. Exh. 1914
5 St. Peters Terrace, Cambridge. † LS 3.

WHETMAN, Dulcie Exh. 1936-40
Daneshill Cottage, Basingstoke, Hants. † RI 6, SWA 1.

WHEWELL, Herbert 1863-1951
Watercolour landscape painter. b. Bolton, Lancs. R.I. 1927. Add: Shere, Surrey 1912; Gomshall, Surrey 1930. † COO 2, L 4, RA 1, RCA 59, RI 75.

WHEWELL, Hilda Exh. 1922-33
51 Lee Crescent, Edgbaston, Birmingham. † L 52.

WHEWELL, Kathleen Exh. 1929-33
Scarsgarth, Alexandra Road, Blackburn, Lancs. † L 2.

WHIBLEY, Alfred T. Exh. 1897-99
Miniature flower painter. Eastbourne 1897; London 1899. † RA 2.

WHICKER, Frederick John Hayes b. 1901
Figure and landscape painter. b. Western Australia. Studied Bristol School of Art. Exh. 1932-35. Add: 19 All Saints Road, Clifton, Bristol. † NEA 1, RA 2, ROI 1.

WHIDBOURNE, Ada F. Exh. 1889-1929
Landscape painter. Travelled on the Continent and in the Middle East. Add: Charante, Torquay, Devon. † D 3, RID 31, SWA 3.

WHIELDON, Miss C.V. Exh. 1905
Eccleshall, Lillington, Leamington, Warwicks. † B 1.

WHIELDON, Eleanor Exh. 1903-7
Eccleshall, Leamington, Warwicks. † B 5.

WHIFFEN, Charles E. Exh. 1889-1916
Sculptor. Cheltenham, Glos. 1889; London 1907. † L 2, RA 8, RBA 1.

WHILE, Mary Ethel Exh. 1912-31
nee Collingwood. Sculptor. b. Mitcham, Surrey. Studied Goldsmiths College. Married Harry Samuel W. q.v. Add: Eltham, Kent 1912; Hampstead, London 1920. † GI 1, RA 12.

WHILE, Harry Samuel b. 1871
Sculptor. b. West Bromwich. Studied Goldsmiths College. Married Mary Ethel W. q.v. Exh. 1911-22. Add: Eltham, Kent 1911; Hampstead, London 1921. † GI 1, RA 6.

WHILES, F. Exh. 1926
22 Wood Street, Alfreton, Derbys. † N 1.

WHINERAY, Miss E.J. Exh. 1899-1933
Watercolour painter. Studied Birkenhead and Liverpool Schools of Art and under Julius Olsson and Arnesby Brown. Add: Hoylake, Cheshire 1899; Dinorben, Heswall, Cheshire 1905. † L 56.

WHINERAY, Miss N. Exh. 1892
West Mead, Liverpool. † L 1.

WHINNERAH, Beatrice H. Exh. 1929
7 Ashbourne Avenue, Blundellsands, Liverpool. † L 1.

WHINNEY, Thomas B. Exh. 1881-1924
Watercolour landscape and architectural painter. London. † RA 7, RBA 1, RI 2.

WHIPP, William Exh. 1915
Standrings, Bagslate, Rochdale, Lancs. † RCA 1.

WHIPPLE, Agnes Exh. 1881-88
Watercolour flower painter. Married to John W. q.v. Add: London. † B 2, D 7, RA 5, RBA 1.

WHIPPLE, John Exh. 1880-1919
Landscape, genre, river and coastal painter. Add: London. † B 23, D 12, G 10, GI 6, L 14, M 11, NG 21, RA 20, RBA 34, RHA 8, RI 15, RID 44, ROI 30.

WHIRLEY, Miss G. Exh. 1933
38 Mortimer Street, London. † L 3.

WHIRTER, Mary Exh. 1928
6 Newport Street, London. † SWA 1.

WHISH, Dorothy Exh. 1900-1
London 1900; Bournemouth 1901. † B 1, SWA 2.

WHISH, Miss M. Scott Exh. 1880
Painter. 16 St. Petersburgh Place, London. † SWA 1.

WHISHAW, Alexander Y. Exh. 1894-1914
New Brighton, Cheshire 1894; Arnside, nr. Carnforth, Lancs. 1903; Steep, nr. Petersfield, Hants. 1913. † B 6, L 35, LS 3, M 6, RA 2.

WHISHAW, Evelyn Exh. 1932
Figure painter. Middle Slewton, Whimple, Devon. † RA 1.

WHISHAW, E.B. Exh. 1926
The Green Frog, Haslemere, Surrey. † L 2.

WHISTLER, James Abbott McNeill* 1834-1903
Painter, etcher and lithographer. b. Lowell, Mass., U.S.A. Studied in Paris 1851. Moved to London 1859. Visited Venice 1879-80. Settled in Paris 1892 and ran his own Art School, the Academie Carmen 1898-1901. R.B.A. 1884, P.R.B.A. 1886-88, R.P. 1892, H.R.S.A. 1902, R.S.W. 1894. A number of his works are in the Tate Gallery. † BG 1, DOW 5, FIN 24, G 11, GI 10, I 8, L 4, LEI 1, M 2, NEA 3, P 17, RBA 52, RSA 7, RSW 1.

WHISTLER, Rex John* 1905-1944
Painter and illustrator and mural painter. Studied Slade School and Rome. Add: Farnham Common, Bucks. 1927; London 1933. † BA 6, BAR 2, GOU 4, L 1, LEI 4, NEA 1, RA 3, TOO 1.

WHITACRE, Rev. Aelred Exh. 1934-37
Sculptor. 24 George Square, Edinburgh. † RA 1, RSA 2.

WHITAKER, Benjamin Exh. 1884
429 Astley Street, Dukinfield, Manchester. † M 1.

WHITAKER, D. Exh. 1892-94
Landscape painter. The White House, Amersham, Bucks. † ROI 3.

WHITAKER, Mrs. D. Exh. 1936-37
Fulmer Road, London. † RBA 1, ROI 1.

WHITAKER, Ethel Exh. 1898
London. † SWA 1.

WHITAKER, Eileen M. Exh. 1931-34
Painter. Highfield, Horsforth, nr. Leeds. † RA 1, RCA 1, SWA 2.

WHITAKER, John Thomas Exh. 1924-28
Chromo-lithographer and designer. Studied Burnley and Manchester Municipal Schools of Art. Art teacher Bath School of Art. Add: 30 Charmouth Road, Bath. † L 6.

WHITAKER, Marston Exh. 1883
Figure and landscape painter. 11 Charles Street, Rutland Gate, London. † RBA 2.

WHITAKER, Mrs. Nellie Exh. 1901
35 Chenies Street Chambers, London. † L 1.

WHITBREAD, Miss F.M. Exh. 1902
111 Belgrave Road, London. † SWA 1.

WHITBY, Mrs. Gladys Exh. 1927
21 Andrews Mansions, Dorset Street, London. † RSA 1.

WHITBY, Mrs. Helen Exh. 1934
Etcher. 22 Melrose Road, East Putney, London. † RA 1.

WHITBY, Miss Lilian Exh. 1923-29
Trinity House, Yeovil, Somerset. † L 10.

WHITBY, W. Exh. 1886
Watercolour landscape painter. Mumbles, South Wales. † RI 1.

WHITCHER, Annie L. Exh. 1886
Landscape painter. 148 Campden Road, London. † SWA 1.

WHITCOMBE, John Exh. 1916
† I 2.

WHITE, Miss Exh. 1907
Portman Square, London. † SWA 1.

WHITE, Miss A. Exh. 1897
The Park House, Whissendine, Leics. † N 1.

WHITE, Agnes Exh. 1885-1915
Landscape painter. London. † L 1, RBA 4, RID 71, SWA 3.

WHITE, Alice Exh. 1880-89
Landscape painter. 9 Campden Hill Gardens, Kensington, London. † D 1, M 3, RA 1, RBA 2, RI 1, SWA 29.

WHITE, Arthur 1865-1953
Landscape and marine painter. b. Sheffield. Studied Sheffield School of Art. Add: St. Ives, Cornwall. † LS 33, ROI 5.

WHITE, Mrs. A.C. Exh. 1884
Watercolour landscape painter. 36 Park Road, Hampstead, London. † SWA 2.

WHITE, Arthur C. Exh. 1898-1924
Sculptor. London. † B 1, GI 8, L 6, RA 24, RSA 1.

WHITE, Albert G. Exh. 1883-87
42 Arundel Gardens, Kensington, London. † L 3, M 4, TOO 2.

WHITE, Miss A.G. Holt Exh. 1921
† SWA 1.

WHITE, Miss Alice H. Exh. 1923
† SWA 1.

WHITE, Arthur R. Exh. 1924-33
Sculptòr. London. † GI 1, L 5, RA 6.

WHITE, B. Exh. 1902
Beauvale Road, Nottingham. † N 1.

WHITE, Mrs. Betty Exh. 1937-40
Painter. 14 Grove Cottages, London. † NEA 2, RA 1.

WHITE, Mrs. B.C. Exh. 1910
39 Newlands Road, Stirchley, Birmingham. † B 1.

WHITE, Beatrice Mary Exh. 1920-26
Painter and chinese lacquer worker. A.S.W.A. 1927. Add: London 1920; Betchworth, Surrey 1923. † L 9, LS 3, SWA 1.

WHITE, Clement Exh. 1889
Landscape painter. 102 Adrian Terrace, West Brompton, London. † RA 1.

WHITE, Clarence Alfred Burke Exh. 1921-39
Portrait painter. Studied R.A. Schools (2 silver medals). Married Mabel Redington Peacock, q.v. Add: 10 Ennismore Avenue, Chiswick, London. † L 1, P 2, RA 7, ROI 2.

WHITE, C.L. Exh. 1938-39
Landscape painter. Easthorpe, Albert Avenue, Carlton Road, Nottingham. † N 4.

WHITE, Clare M.E. Exh. 1929-36
Watercolour landscape painter. Paignton, Devon 1929; Teignmouth, Devon 1936. † GOU 1, RA 1, RBA 9, RI 9, RSW 2, SWA 4.

WHITE, Diana Exh. 1908-22
Landscape painter. London. † GOU 37, LS 5, NEA 4.

WHITE, Dyke d. c.1931
Glasgow 1916; Lenzie, Dumbartonshire 1931. † GI 7, RSA 1.

WHITE, Dorothy Dennett Exh. 1936-40
Watercolour landscape painter. Greenhills, Haslemere, Surrey. † AR 2, RA 1, RI 1.

WHITE, Daniel Thomas Exh. 1882-90
Genre, literary and portrait painter. London. † G 2, RA 1, ROI 1.

WHITE, Mrs. E. Exh. 1905-8
5 Stonor Road, West Kensington, London. † L 1, RA 2.

WHITE, Edward Exh. 1884-86
St. James Street, Edinburgh. † RSA 3.

WHITE, Edward Exh. 1909-13
Architect. 7 Victoria Street, Westminster, London. † RA 3.

WHITE, Ellen Exh. 1905-35
Portrait painter. 13 Albert Street, Regents Park, London. † L 15, RA 3, RI 24, RMS 1.

WHITE, Emilie Exh. 1902-3
Miniature portrait painter. Annaville, Earlswood Road, Strandtown, Belfast. † RA 2, RMS 2.

WHITE, Ethel Exh. 1915
Stopford, 48 Upper Leeston Street, Dublin. †,RHA 1.

WHITE, Ethelbert* 1891-1972
Painter, engraver, poster artist and illustrator. N.E.A. 1921. A.R.W.S. 1933, R.W.S. 1939. Member London Group 1916. Add: 6 The Grove, Hampstead, London. † AG 1, BA 8, BK 1, CHE 4, COO 2, FIN 76, G 5, GI 9, GOU 20, LEF 36, LEI 154, NEA 87, RA 2, RED 82, RSA 2, RSW 1, RWS 51.

WHITE, Evelyn Exh. 1908-12
Cliff House, Croyde Bay, North Devon. † D 9.

WHITE, Edith A. Exh. 1886
35 Carlton Road, Tufnell Park, London. † D 1.

WHITE, Ernest A. Exh. 1901
Portrait painter. Lindum House, Anerly, London. † L 1.

WHITE, E. Fox Exh. 1883
Watercolour landscape painter. 13 King Street, St. James, London. † RI 1.

WHITE, Edgar H. Exh. 1929
Metropolitan School of Art, Dublin. † RHA 2.

WHITE, Erica M. Exh. 1925-38
Sculptor and painter. Studied Slade School, Central Schools of Arts and Crafts and R.A. Schools. Add: London 1925; Kingsdown, nr. Down, Kent 1938. † GI 1. RA 4.

WHITE, Edmund Richard Exh. 1880-1908
Landscape, genre and portrait painter, and watercolourist. 36 Barclay Road, Walham Green, London. † B 16, D 5, L 9, RA 13, RBA 1, RI 7, RSW 2.

WHITE, Flora Exh. 1887-92
Flowe painter. London. † B 1, M 2, RA 1, ROI 2.

WHITE, Florence Exh. 1881-1932
Landscape, flower, portrait and miniature painter. R.M.S. 1904, V.P.R.M.S. 1908-1918 (Hon. Sec. 1917). H.R.M.S. 1920, A.S.W.A. 18923. Add: London 1881; Steyning, Sussex 1925. † B 18, G 1, L 21, M 2, NG 2, P 7, RA 35, RBA 5, RHA 3, RMS 39, ROI 4, SWA 10.

WHITE, Franklin Exh. 1925-29
Landscape and figure painter. b. South Australia. On staff at Slade School. Add: The Reedbeds, Shoreham, Sevenoaks, Kent. † AB 2, M 2, NEA 8.

WHITE, Frances J. Exh. 1883-84
Landscape painter. Dublin 1883; Finglas, Ireland 1884. † RHA 2.

WHITE, G. Exh. 1905
82 Park Road, Burslem, Staffs. † RA 1.

WHITE, Garibaldi Exh. 1882-86
† TOO 6.

WHITE, George Exh. 1884-93
Landscape painter. Heswall, Cheshire 1884; Winchester, Hants. 1891; Windermere 1892. † B 9, GI 2, L 8, M 3, RA 6, RHA 2, ROI 5.

WHITE, Mrs. Grace Exh. 1914-40
Landscape painter, and watercolourist. A.S.W.A. 1921. S.W.A. 1923. Add: Woodlands, West Wickham, Kent. † AB 1, FIN 25, L 4, RA 1, RI 1, ROI 2, RSA 4, SWA 45.

WHITE, Gwendolen B. Exh. 1929-40
Landscape painter and illustrator. b. Exeter. Studied Bournemouth School of Art and Royal College of Art. Add: London. † NEA 1, RA 14.

WHITE, George Harlow* 1817-1888
Landscape and portrait painter. Lived in Canada 1871-80. Add: Charterhouse, London 1883. † RBA 1.

WHITE, Gwendolen Mabel b. 1903
nee Jones. Painter, wood engraver, illuminator and writer. b. Bridgnorth, Salop. Studied Royal College of Art and Kidderminster School of Art. Married Seaton W. q.v. Exh. 1936-38. Add: Pittville Circus Road, Cheltenham, Glos. † COO 4, RA 1.

WHITE, Grace Paterson Exh. 1924-38
nee Paterson. b. Hamilton, Canada. Studied Hamilton Art School and Philadelphia Academy of Fine Arts and Paris. Add: Ellerslie, Galston, Ayrshire. † GI 3, RSA 1, RSW 1.

WHITE, Harold b. 1903
Painter, decorative artist and teacher. Studied Brixton School of Building, Camberwell and Putney Schools of Art and Under H. Davis Richter. Exh. 1925. Add: 112 Engadine Street, Southfields, London. † RA 1.

WHITE, Henry Exh. 1881
Watercolour landscape painter. 9 Campden Hill Gardens, Kensington, London. † RBA 1.

WHITE, Hester E.G. Exh. 1884
Watercolour landscape painter. 42 Cheniston Gardens, Kensington, London. † SWA 2.

WHITE, Herbert H. Exh. 1931-34
Sculptor. London. † RA 2.

WHITE, H. Mabel Exh. 1898-1920
Sculptor and painter. London. † GI 8, I 3, L 11, RA 9, RHA 1, RID 5.

WHITE, Ianthe b. 1901
Mrs. A.V. Goodchild. Miniature painter. Studied Bristol School of Art. Exh. 1937-39. † RMS 3.

WHITE, Isabel G. Exh. 1892-1914
Mrs. Strong. Painter. A.S.W.A. 1898, S.W.A. 1899. Add: Bushey, Herts. 1892; London 1894; Liverpool 1905. † GI 9, L 5, RA 5, RBA 3, RI 2, ROI 2, RSA 1, RSW 1, SWA 45.

WHITE, Mrs. J. Exh. 1934-38
Walmesley, Ellergarth, Budleigh Salterton, Devon. † RI 6.

WHITE, James Exh. 1880
Whitebank, Edinburgh. † GI 1, RSA 3.

WHITE, John Exh. 1915
Portrait painter. 21 Eglinton Road, Bow, London. † NEA 1.

WHITE, John Exh. 1936-38
Landscape painter. Keston, Kent 1936; West Wickham, Kent 1938. † RA 2.

WHITE, John* 1851-1933
Landscape, marine, portrait and rustic genre painter. b. Edinburgh. Spent most of his childhood in Australia. Studied R.S.A. Schools 1871 (Keith Prize for design 1875). R.B.A. 1880, R.I. 1882, R.O.I. 1886. Add: Shere, nr. Guildford, Surrey 1880; London 1883; Axminster, Devon 1891; Heavitree, Exeter 1901; Beer, Devon 1915. † B 14, D 8, FIN 56, G 1, GI 17, L 16, M 15, RA 40, RBA 43, RHA 1, RI 190, ROI 106, RSA 9, TOO 79.

WHITE, Miss J.A. Milburn Exh. 1914-15
Interior and still life painter. Loo, Cornwall and London. † LS 3, NEA 3.

WHITE, J.G. Exh. 1885
9 Fitzroy Place, Glasgow. † GI 1.

WHITE, Jane G. Exh. 1900
55 Alexander Street, Clydebank, N.B. † GI 1.

WHITE, Josephine H.J. Exh. 1887-1940
Landscape and architectural painter. Nottingham 1887; London 1896. † B 11, GI 5, I 6, L 7, LS 11, N 22, RHA 3, RI 4, ROI 9, SWA 3.

WHITE, Josephine M. Exh. 1889-99
Miniature portrait painter. London. † L 3, RA 12, RI 2.

WHITE, J.P. Exh. 1880
79 West Regent Street, Glasgow. † GI 1.

WHITE, J.S. Exh. 1881
Coastal Painter. 10 Drapers Gardens, London. † G 1.

WHITE, J. Talmage* Exh. 1882-93
Landscape, architectural and genre, painter. London 1882; Capri 1886. † D 1, G 4, L 3, M 3, RA 3.

WHITE, Marie Exh. 1933-36
Still life and figure painter. School of Art, Dublin. † RHA 3.

WHITE, Mary F. Exh. 1935
56 Glebe Place, Chelsea, London. † RSA 1.

WHITE, Miss M.H.C. Exh. 1908-9
39 Manningham Lane, Bradford, Yorks. † B 2, L 3, RA 1.

WHITE, M. Mower Exh. 1927-28
112 Harley Street, London. † RBA 6.

WHITE, Mary M. Exh. 1938
Watercolour landscape painter. Milton Street, nr. Polegate, Sussex. † RA 1.

WHITE, Mary Macrae Exh. 1893-1919
Mrs. Martin W. nee Macrae. Figure painter. London 1893 and 1904; Balruddery, nr. Dundee 1900; Edenbridge, Kent 1910. † GI 1, I 2, LS 3, NG 1, RBA 2, RI 2.

WHITE, M.W.G. Exh. 1891
Sudbrook, Pollokshields. † GI 1.

WHITE, Mrs. Olive Exh. 1921-37
Painter. Dublin. † RHA 5.

WHITE, Olive L. Exh. 1903
Sculptor. 170 Queen's Gate, London. † RA 1.

WHITE, Mrs. Olive Russell Exh. 1932
Watercolour figure painter. c/o Standard Bank of South Africa. 9 Northumberland Avenue, London. † RA 1.

WHITE, P. Exh. 1883
† TOO 1.

WHITE, Peter Exh. 1929
9 Falcon Gardens, Edinburgh. † RSW 1.

WHITE, Seaton Exh. 1937
Landscape painter. Married Gwendolen Mabel W. q.v. Pittville, Circus Road, Cheltenham, Glos. † RA 1.

WHITE, Sydney W. Exh. 1892-1917
Landscape and portrait painter. Grimsby 1892; London 1897. † L 1, RA 9, RBA 5, ROI 1.

WHITE, Thomas Exh. 1884
Langham Chambers, London. † D 1.

WHITE, Vera Exh. 1931
Watercolour painter. † LEF 29.

WHITE, W. Exh. 1880-90
Sculptor. Esher, Surrey 1880; London 1881; Birmingham 1890. † B 2, L 2, RA 7.

WHITE, W.B. Exh. 1894-96
Watercolour landscape painter. Nottingham. † N 5.

WHITE, W. Henry Exh. 1901-21
Architect. 14A Cavendish Place, Cavendish Square, London. † RA 24.

WHITE, W.P. Exh. 1882
18 Carlton Terrace, Edinburgh. † RSA 2.

WHITE, W. Tatton Exh. 1898-1901
Landscape painter. R.B.A. 1901. Add: Kildare, Southend-on-Sea, Essex. † RA 2, RBA 11.

WHITE-COOPER, R.C. Exh. 1931
Architect. 9 Woodstock Street, London. † RA 1.

WHITEFORD, Sidney Trefusis
Exh. 1880-81
Still life, genre, bird and flower painter. London. † D 3, RA 4, RBA 2.

WHITEFORD, W.G. Exh. 1932-39
21 Seabank Road, Prestwick, Lancs. † GI 2, RSA 4.

WHITEHEAD, A. Exh. 1890-1901
Artist and teacher. Halifax. † B 3, L 1.

WHITEHEAD, A.R. Exh. 1885
Landscape painter. Maidstone, Kent. † SWA 2.

WHITEHEAD, Christina L. Exh. 1927
15 York Mansions, Battersea Park, London. † L 1.

WHITEHEAD, Edith Exh. 1899
3 Seymour Road, Brook Green, London. † L 1.

WHITEHEAD, Elizabeth Exh. 1880-1922
Flower painter. 5 Landsdown Terrace, Leamington, Warwicks. † B 35, GI 2, L 9, RA 16, RBA 3, RI 3, ROI 2.

WHITEHEAD, Elsie Exh. 1923
Sculptor. Huntingdon Lodge, Benhill Road, Sutton, Surrey. † RA 1.

WHITEHEAD, Edith Hindela Exh. 1922
Mrs. Seldon Parsons. A.R.M.S. 1919. Add: The Westminster, 17th Street, Washington, D.C., U.S.A. † RMS 1.

WHITEHEAD, Miss Frances M.
Exh. 1887-1929
Landscape and coastal painter and etcher. Shustoke Vicarage, Birmingham 1887; London 1903. † B 7, RA 1, RI 2, RID 62, SWA 13.

WHITEHEAD, Frederick William Newton*
1853-1938
Landscape, still life, architectural and portrait painter and etcher. b. Leamington Spa. Studied under John Burgess of Leamington and Juliens, Paris. R.B.A. 1901. Add: Leamington, Warwicks. 1881; London 1893. † B 41, BRU 1, L 8, M 2, NG 4, RA 30, RBA 53, RHA 1, RI 3, ROI 7.

WHITEHEAD, Henry C. Exh. 1890-1921
Landscape and coastal painter. Shustoke Vicarage, Coleshill, Birmingham 1890; London 1903. † B 1, RID 29.

WHITEHEAD, Joseph Exh. 1889-95
Sculptor. The Studios, Vincent Square, Westminster, London. † NG 1, RA 6.

WHITEHEAD, Mrs. Joseph Exh. 1892
Landscape painter. Claremont Terrace, Burton-on-Trent, Notts. † N 1.

WHITEHEAD, J.N. Exh. 1934
Hollydene, Wharncliffe Road, Ilkeston, Derbys. † N 1.

WHITEHEAD, Lilian b. 1894
Painter, etcher and wood engraver. b. Bury, Lancs. Studied Manchester School of Art, Slade School and British School at Rome. A.R.E. 1921. Exh. 1920-34. Add: London 1920 and 1928; Chichester, Sussex 1927. † BA 24, NEA 12, RE 13, RSA 1.

WHITEHEAD, Marjorie Exh. 1924
4 Regent Street, Lancaster. † L 1.

WHITEHEAD, N.R. Exh. 1935-38
Landscape painter. Holydene, Wharncliffe Road, Ilkeston, Derbys. † N 8.

WHITEHEAD, R.H. Exh. 1882-83
Washbrook, Hollinwood, Manchester. † L 1, M 2.

WHITEHEAD, Tom b. 1886
Portrait, landscape painter, etcher and dry point artist. b. Brighouse, Yorks. Studied Halifax School of Art and Royal College of Art. Exh. 1929-38. Add: 29 York Crescent, Halifax. † P 1, RA 1, RSA 3.

WHITEHEAD, Winifred D. Exh. 1936
Landscape painter. 7 Overton Road, Sutton, Surrey. † RA 1.

WHITEHORN, John E. Exh. 1935-38
Watercolour landscape and pencil artist. 26 Chaucer Street, Nottingham. † N 5.

WHITEHOUSE, Arthur E. Exh. 1880-88
Landscape painter. London. † B 1, L 2, M 1, RA 2, RBA 1, ROI 2.

WHITEHOUSE, Daisy Exh. 1903
Lyndon, St. Ives, Cornwall. † GI 1.

WHITEHOUSE, Doris Exh. 1919
Prospect Villa, Laverick Road, Jacksdale, Notts. † N 1.

WHITEHOUSE, Elizabeth Exh. 1924
Lynden, St. Ives, Cornwall. † SWA 1.

WHITEHOUSE, Mrs. Ella C. Exh. 1930-33
171 College Road, Moseley, Birmingham. † B 2.

WHITEHOUSE, Frank Exh. 1906
Victoria Road, Acocks Green, Birmingham. † B 1.

WHITEHOUSE. Sarah E. Exh. 1882-1911
Painter. Leamington, Warwicks. 1882; St. Ives, Cornwall 1891 and 1895; Paris 1893; London 1894. † B 13, L 5, RA 2.

WHITELAW, Alexander N. Exh. 1923-36
Greenholme, Callender 1923; Glasgow 1929. † GI 12, L 1, RSA 5, RSW 7.

WHITELAW, C.H.M. Exh. 1910-11
Edinburgh. † L 1, RSA 2.

WHITELAW, Frederick William Exh. 1881
Watercolour landscape painter. 9 Woronzow Road, St. John's Wood London. † RA 1.

WHITELAW, George Exh. 1912-30
Glasgow 1912; London 1920 † GI 6, L 3.

WHITELAW, Thomas Exh. 1929
8 Craighall Crescent, Leith. † RSA 1.

WHITELEGGE, Edith M. Exh. 1895-98
The Green, Chorlton cum Hardy, nr. Manchester. † M 3.

WHITELEY, John William
Exh. 1882-1916
Watercolour landscape painter. 59 St. Marks Road, Leeds. † FIN 1, L 5, RA 11, RI 5.

WHITEMAN, Leslie W. Exh. 1929
† NEA 1.

WHITEMAN, Moira Exh. 1938
Illuminator. Ashford Road, Maidstone, Kent. † RA 1.

WHITEMAN, V.E. (Mrs. W.) Exh. 1907
Leominster. † SWA 2.

WHITESIDE, H. Exh. 1912
2 Winchester Road, Reading, Berks. † RA 1.

WHITESIDE, Harriott F. Exh. 1908-22
London. † L 7, NG 1, RA 1, RMS 1.

WHITESIDE, H.J. Exh. 1882-1900
Birkenhead 1882; Walton 1886; Liverpool 1894. † L 6.

WHITESIDE, J. Fairfax Exh. 1937
† P 1.

WHITESIDE, R. Cordelia Exh. 1890-1908
Miniature portrait painter. London. † L 23, RA 9.

WHITESIDE, Winifred May Exh. 1920-27
Mrs. Alan M. Bridgman. A.R.M.S. 1920. Add: London. † RMS 14.

WHITEWAY, Miss D. Exh. 1917
30 Lucknow Avenue, Nottingham. † N 2.

WHITFIELD, Clare Exh. 1887
1 Bryanstone Place, Hyde Park, London. † B 2.

WHITFIELD, Mrs. Florence W.
Exh. 1886-1925
Flower painter. Birmingham. † B 20, L 4, RA 3, SWA 1.

WHITFIELD, George Exh. 1910-32
Figure painter, modeller, and art critic with the 'Liverpool Echo'. Add: Liverpool. † L 16.

WHITFIELD, Helen Exh. 1890-1915
Landscape painter. Wimbledon Park, Surrey 1890; London 1914. † LS 3, RA 2, RBA 2, RI 6, ROI 1, SWA 2.

WHITFIELD, Muriel Exh. 1919
31 Cabra Park, North Circular Road, Dublin. † RHA 2.

WHITFORD, Elsie M. Exh. 1937
Stained glass artist. 135 Warwick Road, Birmingham. † RA 1.

WHITHAM, George Exh. 1938
60 Baronscourt Terrace, Edinburgh. † RSA 1.

WHITHAM, Sylvia Mills
See MILMAN, Sylvia Frances

WHITIE, William B. Exh. 1900-15
St. Vincent Street, Glasgow. † GI 9, RA 1, RSA 3.

WHITING, Mrs. Ada Exh. 1900-34
Miniature portrait painter. Melbourne, Australia 1900; c/o Messrs Bourlet, London 1934. † RA 2, RHA 1, RSA 1.

WHITING, Mrs. E. Muir Exh. 1928
Holmrock, Clarence Road, St. Albans, Herts. † B 1.

WHITING, Frederic 1874-1960
Figure and landscape painter and etcher. Studied R.A. Schools and Juliens, Paris. Travelled widely. R.B.A. 1911, R.I. 1918, R.O.I. 1915, R.P. 1914, R.S.W. 1921. Add: London. † AB 1. AR 2. CHE 4, G 5, GI 36, I 4, L 44, LEI 76, P 63, RA 46, RBA 55, RHA 1, RI 33, ROI 4, RSA 8, RSW 41.

WHITING, L.A. Exh. 1911
Brookfield, Bective Road, Putney, London. † RA 1.

WHITING, Miss N. Exh. 1912
West Coker, Somerset. † SWA 1.

WHITING, Onslow Exh. 1895-1937
Sculptor and portrait and animal painter. Studied Slade School and Central School of Arts and Crafts. Master at Central School of Arts and Crafts. Add: London 1895 and 1923; Letchworth, Herts. 1922; Mancannan, nr. Helston, Cornwall 1927. † L 6, M 1, RA 16.

WHITLAW, Nora M. Exh. 1914
Amerden, Taplow, Bucks. † L 1.

WHITLAW, Rosa M. Exh. 1902-14
Watercolour landscape painter. Amerden, Taplow, Bucks. † B 7, D 1, L 4, M 1, RA 5, RI 1, SWA 9.

WHITLAW, S. Frances Exh. 1882-84
Painter. Amerden House, Taplow, Bucks. † RBA 1, SWA 2.

WHITLEY, Mrs. Exh. 1884-85
Eccles 1884; Bolton, Lancs. 1885. † L 2, M 2.

WHITLEY, Elizabeth B. Exh. 1895-1927
Miniature painter. Bury, Lancs. 1895; Whitfield 1903; Prestwich Park, nr. Manchester 1915. † L 10, M 11, RA 1, RMS 1.

WHITLEY, Gladys b. 1886
nee Garner-Watts. Portrait and miniature painter. Studied Heatherleys and Paris. A.R.M.S. 1923, R.M.S. 1930. Exh. 1923-40. Add: Clacton on Sea, Essex 1923; London 1925; Seer Green, Bucks. 1936. † L 18, RA 12, RI 42, RMS 72, SWA 2.

WHITLEY, H. Exh. 1886
63 Cromwell Road, Patricroft. † M 1.

WHITLEY, Kate Mary d. 1920
Still life and flower painter. R.I. 1889. Add: Leicester 1883; South Wigston, nr. Leicester 1886. † B 8, L 4, LEI 1, M 4, N 4, RA 6, RI 56.

WHITLEY, William T. Exh. 1885-1902
Landscape, figure and interior painter. London. † B 3, GI 1, L 1, M 2, RA 9, RBA 5, ROI 4.

WHITLOCK, John b. 1913
Portrait and landscape painter. b. Beaconsfield. Studied Regent Street Polytechnic 1930-32. Exh. 1938-40. Add: 18 Charlotte Street, Bristol. † RA 4.

WHITMORE, Bryan Exh. 1880-97
Landscape and coastal painter. Halliford, Shepperton. † B 6, G 2, L 7, M 3, RA 11, RBA 15, RI 9.

WHITMORE, Herbert Exh. 1931-39
Landscape painter. London. † RA 3.

WHITMORE, Maud M. Exh. 1896-99
Studio, 138 Cromwell Road, London. † B 5, L 2, P 2, SWA 1.

WHITMORE, Mrs. Olive Exh. 1923
Thornton Lodge, Kilsallaghan, Co. Dublin. † RHA 2.

WHITMORE, William R. Exh. 1894
Landscape and figure painter. Newlyn, Penzance, Cornwall. † RA 2.

WHITNALL, Bessie D. Exh. 1919
† L 1.

WHITNALL, W. Exh. 1883-91
Liverpool. † L 9, M 1.

WHITNALL, Walter E. Exh. 1901-10
Liscard, Cheshire. † L 3.

WHITNEY, Blanche M. Exh. 1885-97
Miniature portrait painter. London. † RA 3, RI 3.

WHITNEY, Emma Exh. 1881-84
Portrait painter. Church Road, Albion Road, Hammersmith, London. † G 1, SWA 2.

WHITTAKER, D. Exh. 1891-92
Hillside, Primrose Hill Road, London. † L 2.

WHITTAKER, J. Exh. 1929
Lane Ends, Osbaldeston, nr. Blackburn, Lancs. † RCA 2.

WHITTAKER, Jane Exh. 1939
Burwash, Sussex. † RI 1.

WHITTAKER, Randal Exh. 1925-33
168 Tennall Road, Harborne, Birmingham. † B 3.

WHITTAKER, T.H. Exh. 1910
Sunnywide, Trent Boulevard, West Bridgford, Notts. † N 3.

WHITTALL, Emmy Exh. 1893
83 Lancaster Street, Birmingham. † B 1.

WHITTELL, W.E.R. Exh. 1910-39
Erdington, Birmingham 1910; Wylde Green, Birmingham 1929. † B 19.

WHITTEMORE, William John b. 1860
American artist. Exh. 1910-11. Add: c/o Chapman Bros., Kings Road, Chelsea, London and New York, U.S.A. † L 1, RA 2.

WHITTET, Andrew Exh. 1880-1909
Edinburgh. † L 2, GI 10, M 6, RSA 25.

WHITTET, David Exh. 1903
Architect. 72 Ladbroke Grove, London. † GI 2, RA 1, RSA 1.

WHITTET, Mathew H.W. Exh. 1909-12
Coatbridge, N.B. 1909; Glasgow 1911. † GI 5.

WHITTICK, H.J. Exh. 1926-28
2 Avondale Road, Wolverhampton. † B 3.

WHITTICK, J.R. Exh. 1882-83
8 Railway Street, Altrincham, Cheshire. † M 3.

WHITTINGHAM, Dora Exh. 1912-13
Painter. 28 Shelton Road, Merton Park, London. † NEA 1, RHA 3.

WHITTINGSTALL, Edmund Owen Fearnley b. 1901
Portrait painter. Exh. 1929-32. Add: 7 Stanley Studios, Park Walk, London. † RA 2.

WHITTINGTON, Francis H. Exh. 1931
Landscape painter. Brockenhurst, Hants. † RA 1.

WHITTINGTON, Marjory Exh. 1922-40
nee Hood. Watercolour painter and etcher. R.B.A. 1936. Add: Brockenhurst, Hants. 1922; London 1932. † B 1, FIN 2, G 1, GI 3, GOU 2, L 5, RA 7, RBA 22, ROI 19, RSA 4, SWA 4.

WHITTINGTON, William G. Exh. 1904-14
Landscape painter. Ashford, Middlesex 1904; London 1906. † D 21, RA 2.

WHITTLE, Mrs. Elizabeth Exh. 1880
Fruit painter. Excelsior Villa, Coombe Street, Croydon, Surrey. † SWA 1.

WHITTLE, Florence Exh. 1925-40
Landscape painter. Rock Cottage, Tettenhall, Staffs. † B 36, RA 3, RBA 1, ROI 1.

WHITTLE, Thomas junr.* Exh. 1880-92
Landscape painter. Excelsior Villa, 30 Upper Coombe Street, Croydon, Surrey. † B 6, RBA 3, RHA 6, ROI 1.

WHITTLE, Miss W. Glynn Exh. 1914
Oriel House, Princes Avenue, Liverpool. † L 1.

WHITWELL, E.R. Exh. 1922-23
† SWA 2.

WHITWELL, Francis A. Exh. 1901-8
Architect. 139 Oxford Street, London. † RA 3.

WHITWILL, Miss B.M. Exh. 1919-21
Clifton, Bristol. † M 2.

WHITWILL, Miss E. Exh. 1898
1 Berkeley Square, Clifton, Bristol. † SWA 3.

WHITWORTH, Mrs. Exh. 1886
Belchester, Coldstream. † RSA 1.

WHITWORTH, Charles H. Exh. 1880-1912
Landscape painter and teacher. R.B.S.A. 1892. Add: Birmingham 1880; Newcastle under Lyme, Staffs. 1900; Cheltenham, Glos. 1904. † B 33, DOW 2, L 2, RA 1, RBA 1, ROI 3.

WHITWORTH, S.H. Exh. 1911
22 Seamer Street, Armley, Leeds. † L 1.

WHYATT, George Exh. 1910-23
Worthing 1910; Wolverhampton 1921. † B 2, L 3, M 2, RA 1, RI 2.

WHYDALE, Ernest Herbert b. 1886
Painter and etcher. b. Elland, Yorks. A.R.E. 1920. Add: London 1910; Royston, Herts. 1918 and 1923; Aspley Guise, Beds. 1922. † AB 1, CON 58, FIN 3, G 1, GI 1, I 10, L 1, M 1, RA 34, RE 26, RSA 1.

WHYLEY, Evelyn Jane See RIMINGTON

WHYMPER, Charles 1853-1941
Landscape, bird and animal painter and illustrator. Son of Josiah Wood W. q.v. R.I. 1909. Add: London 1882; Houghton, Hunts. 1915. † ALP 2, B 3, DOW 58, FIN 2, L 14, M 6, NG 21, RA 4, RBA 1, RI 98, RID 4, TOO 36, WG 50.

WHYMPER, Mrs. J.W. Exh. 1883-85
Emily Hepburn. Watercolour landscape and flower painter. Haslemere, Surrey. † L 1, RI 4, SWA 1.

WHYMPER, Josiah Wood 1813-1903
Watercolour landscape painter and engraver. b. Ipswich. Studied under Collingwood Smith. Father of Charles W. q.v. A.R.I. 1854, R.I. 1857. Add: Haslemere, Surrey 1880. † AG 1, L 6, M 1, RI 102, ROI 3.

WHYMPER, W. Exh. 1913
10 Gray's Inn Square, London. † RA 1.

WHYSTRUP, E. Kate Exh. 1922
† D 5.

WHYTE, A.C. Exh. 1890-94
Glasgow. † GI 2.

WHYTE, Catherine Exh. 1921-22
The Weisha, Dundee. † GI 1, RSA 2.

WHYTE. Duncan MacGregor 1866-1953
Portrait, landscape and seascape painter. b. Oban. Studied Glasgow, Paris and Antwerp. Add: Oban, Argyllshire 1898 and 1923; Glasgow 1900 and 1934. † GI 48, L 4, RSA 13, RSW 2.

WHYTE, Edward Towry Exh. 1886-89
Architect. 31 Charing Cross, London. † RA 2.

WHYTE, H.M. Exh. 1911
2 Ashley Road, Hornsey Rise, London. † LS 1.

WHYTE, John B.N. Exh. 1938
2 Battery Terrace, Oban. † GI 1.

WHYTE, John G. Exh. 1880-87
Watercolour landscape painter. Eastwood, Helensburgh. † GI 5, RA 3, RSA 2, RSW 19.

WHYTE, John S. Exh. 1940
Helensfield, Clackmannan. † GI 1, RSA 2.

WHYTE, L. Hester Exh. 1928-30
Trebovir Road, London. † SWA 3.

WHYTE, Margaret M. Exh. 1889-90
North View, Elgin. † RSA 2.

WHYTE, Robert Exh. 1900-21
Helensburgh, N.B. † GI 6, RSA 3.

WHYTE, William Patrick Exh. 1882-1905
Watercolour landscape painter. Edinburgh 1882; Paris 1883; London 1885 and 1897; Little Radfield, nr. Sittingbourne, Kent 1895. † G 1, GI 17, L 4, M 2, RA 3, RI 2, RSA 4.

WIBBERLEY, Miss Dora Mary Exh. 1921-29
Landscape painter. 78 Chaworth Road, West Bridgford, Notts. † N 15.

WIBBERLEY, Herbert Rushton Exh. 1908-39
Landscape painter. A.N.S.A. 1920, N.S.A. 1922, V.P.N.S.A. 1939. Add: Nottingham 1908 and 1927; Sherwood, Notts. 1920. † L 6, N 124, RCA 4.

WICHELHAUS, Miss A. Exh. 1900-1
Sandfield, Egerton Park, Rock Ferry, Cheshire. † L 2.

WICK, Laurie Tamar Blanche Exh. 1906-26
Portrait painter. 3 Stainbeck Lane, Chapel Allerton, Leeds. † L 13, RA 3.

WICKENDEN, Arthur F. Exh. 1918-23
Architect. London. † RA 2.

WICKES, Anne Mary Exh. 1893-1937
Decorative and portrait painter and illustrator. b. Burhampore, Bengal, India. Studied Slade School and British Museum. Add: Northwood, Middlesex 1893; Hampstead, London 1898. † CG 1, I 3, L 2, LS 14, NEA 6, P 3, RA 6, ROI 1, RSA 1.

WICKES, Mrs. E. Ex . 1911-18
West Bromwich 1911; London 1918. † RA 3.

WICKES, Miss E.A.M. Exh. 1896-1923
† G 4, I 3, P 1.

WICKHAM, Alfred Exh. 1910-11
124 Beeches Road, West Bromwich. † B 2.

WICKHAM, Frederick Exh. 1929-37
Landscape painter. Capo di Monte, Judges Walk, Hampstead, London. † RA 3.

WICKHAM, Helen Exh. 1925-29
Potter. b. Batcombe. Add: Studio 12A, Westbere Road, West Hampstead, London. † L 7, RMS 2.

WICKHAM, Michael Exh. 1930-33
Figure painter. R.B.A. 1931. Add: London. † B 1, NEA 3, RA 5, RBA 10.

WICKHAM, Mabel Francis b. 1902
Watercolour landscape painter. Studied Clapham High School Art Training College 1919-23 and under St. Clair Marston. R.I. 1938, A.S.W.A. 1936. Add: Sutton Scotney, Hants. 1930; Sherborne, Dorset 1939. † RA 5, RI 10, SWA 11.

WICKHAM, W.A. Exh. 1906
42 St. Mary's Grove, Chiswick, London. † RCA 2.

WICKS, Adelaide (Mrs. S.) Exh. 1906-34
Miniature portrait painter. Anerley, London 1906; Ashley Lodge, Howard Road, Reigate, Surrey 1909. † RA 27.

WICKSON, Paul G. Exh. 1882-83
Figure painter. 47 Grove Hill Road, Denmark Hill, London. † L 1, RA 1.

WIDDAS, Ernest A. Exh. 1906-23
Portrait, subject and miniature painter. London. † GI 1, L 12, RA 18, RHA 1, RMS 2.

WIDDOWS, Jessie E. Exh. 1921-22
Skewbarrow, Kendal, Westmorland. † L 2.

WIDGERY, Frederick John* 1861-1942
Landscape and coastal painter. Studied Exeter School of Art, under Verlat at Antwerp, and under Herkomer at Bushey. Son of William W. (1822-1893). Magistrate, one time mayor of Exeter and chairman of Exeter Public Art Gallery. Add: Exeter. † L 3, RA 5, RI 3, ROI 6.

WIDMER, John W. Exh. 1931-38
Painter. 3 Ashby Road, Canonbury, London. † COO 5, NEA 2, RA 2.

WIEGELE, Henri Exh. 1910
20 Rue de Lesseps, Neuilly sur Seine, France. † L 1.

WIENHOLT, Miss Abra Exh. 1901
† RMS 3.

WIENS, Stephen (or Siegfried) Makepeace 1871-1956
Portrait and landscape painter and sculptor. b. London. Studied R.A. Schools (Landseer scholarship, Creswick Prize and British Institute scholarship). Add: Sutton, Surrey 1893; London 1896; Hove, Sussex 1928; Worthing 1937. † B 1, GI 2, I 1, L 16, P 2, RA 23, RHA 3.

WIERTER, Lieut. Louis Exh. 1916-22
† G 1, I 1.

WIFFEN, Alfred Kemp b. 1896
Painter, etcher, engraver and dry point artist. Studied Nottingham School of Art. Exh. 1925-39. Add: West Bridgford, Notts. 1925; Meols, Cheshire 1930; Hoylake, Cheshire 1938. † L 6, N 23, RA 1, RCA 2.

WIGAN, Mrs. Exh. 1917
Weybridge, Surrey. † SWA 1.

WIGAN, Bessie Exh. 1894-1939
Mrs. Charles Marriott. Watercolour painter. London. † D 3, GOU 7, LS 3, RBA 1, RHA 8, RI 2, SWA 5, WG 132.

WIGAN, Elizabeth Gertrude Exh. 1909
† LS 3.

WIGAN, Juliet Exh. 1923-25
Figure and portrait painter. 85 Harcourt Terrace, London. † NEA 3, RA 3.

WIGAN, Mabel Exh. 1927
85 Harcourt Terrace, London. † L 1.

WIGG, C.M. Exh. 1915
The Thatched House, Brundall, Norwich. † RA 1.

WIGGIN, John Exh. 1914
Rue Henri van Zuylen Strasse, Uccle, Belgium. † LS 3.

WIGGINS, Carleton* Exh. 1896-97
Landscape painter. St. Ives, Cornwall. † RA 3.

WIGGLESWORTH, Wilfrid P. Exh. 1927-29
Landscape painter. Dirleton, Battlefield Road, St. Albans, Herts. † ALP 1, L 2, RA 1.

WIGHT, Adelaide Exh. 1899-1904
Miniature portrait painter. London 1899; Horley, Surrey 1904. † RA 3.

WIGHT, Ellen Exh. 1881
Watercolour painter. 7 Claydon Terrace, South Lambeth, London. † SWA 1.

WIGHT, Elspeth Exh. 1898-1905
Hawkhill Villa, Lochend Road, Edinburgh. † RSA 11.

WIGHT, Helen Exh. 1886-90
Figure painter. Homeleigh, Loats Road, Clapham, London. † SWA 5.

WIGHT, J.R. Exh. 1883
7 St. Andrews Square, Edinburgh. † RSA 1.

WIGHT, Mrs. N. Exh. 1893
Boscombe Park, Bournemouth. † SWA 1.

WIGHT, Miss W.M. Forbes Exh. 1905-24
Leyton, London 1905; Wallasey, Cheshire 1920. † L 3, RA 1.

WIGHTMAN, Isabel Smaile Exh. 1895-1908
Newcastle on Tyne. † B 2, G 1, GI 1, LS 9, M 2, RA 2, RCA 1, ROI 1.

WIGHTMAN, Minnie A. Exh. 1896
Lovaine Studios, Barras Bridge, Newcastle on Tyne. † GI 1, M,1.

WIGHTMAN, W.E. Exh. 1909
35 Bobbers Mill Road, Nottingham. † N 2.

WIGHTMAN, Mrs. Winifred Ursula
See NICOLSON

WIGLEY, Edith Exh. 1898-1906
The Firns, Olton, Birmingham. † B 9, L 1.

WIGLEY, R.M. Exh. 1938
Solihull Lane, Hampton in Arden, Warwicks. † B 1.

WIGLEY, William Edward b. 1880
Portrait painter and teacher. Studied Birmingham Art School and Royal College of Art. Exh. 1920-40. Add: Erdington, Birmingham 1920; Hampton in Arden, Warwicks. 1922. † B 81, RA 12.

WIGRAM, Miss E. Exh. 1906
Broomfield, Weybridge, Surrey. † RA 1.

WIJBRANDI, Miss Sjouk T. Exh. 1939-40
Sculptor. London. † RA 2.

WILBEE, Christian Mary Exh. 1903-12
Painter, black and white artist and miniaturist. London 1903; Harrow on the Hill, Middlesex 1909. † B 1, RA 6, WG 39.

WILBERFORCE, Ethel Exh. 1901
The Palace, Chichester, Sussex. † D 1.

WILBERFORCE, Mrs. M. Exh. 1919
13 Sunnyside Road, Ealing, London. † SWA 1.

WILBERG, Ch. Exh. 1881
† RE 3.

WILCOCK, R. Exh. 1898
60 Saxon Street, Liverpool. † L 1.

WILCOCKS, F. Exh. 1885
76 St. Stephen's Street, Salford, Lancs. † M 1.

WILCOCKSON, F. Exh. 1887
26 Charleston Road, Dublin. † RHA 1.

WILCOX, Mrs. E.A. Exh. 1901
30 Wellington Street, Long Eaton, Notts. † N 1.

WILCOX, Mrs. Kate Exh. 1920-29
Watercolour painter and writer. London. † D 8, SWA 7.

WILCOXSON, Frederick John b. 1888
Sculptor. Studied Liverpool City School of Art and R.A. Schools (Landseer Scholarship). Pupil and assistant to Francis Derwent Wood. Instructor Royal College of Art School of sculpture 1919-24. Son of William Henry W. q.v. Exh. 1913-40. Add: London. † GI 2, L 15, RA 26.

WILCOXSON, William Henry Exh. 1899
Sculptor. Father of Frederick John W. q.v. Add: 20 Gainsborough Road, Wavertree, Liverpool. † L 1.

WILD, Beatrice Vaughan Exh. 1914
45 Burlington Road, Bayswater, London. † LS 2.

WILD, Mrs. C. Exh. 1909
Carrington Vicarage, Nottingham. † N 1.

WILD, Fred Exh. 1905
37 Dorset Street, Bolton, Lancs. † M 2.

WILD, Frank Percy b. 1861
Portrait and landscape painter. b. Leeds. Studied Royal Academy Antwerp, Paris and Spain. R.B.A. 1901. Add: Thorner, nr. Leeds 1889; Great Marlow, Bucks. 1892. † B 3, GI 1, L 11, M 4, NG 8, RA 19, RBA 52.

WILD, Mrs. Herbert Exh. 1904-12
Landscape painter. Nottingham 1904; Oxford 1912. † D 18, N 4.
WILD, Miss M.E. Exh. 1911
Wayside, Broadstairs, Kent. † RA 1.
WILD, Thomas Exh. 1882
81 Hendham Vale, nr. Manchester. † M 1.
WILD, Thomas Exh. 1882-94
27 Coppice Street, Oldham, Lancs. † M 7.
WILD, Winifred Eveline Exh. 1919-40
Portrait painter, miniaturist and stained glass artist. b. Chalfont St. Giles, Bucks. Studied Central School of Art. Add: Bournemouth 1919; Halstead, Essex 1920; Gt. Yeldham, Essex 1924; Boscombe, Hants. 1924. † L 7, P 3, RA 6, RMS 4, ROI 4.
WILDASH, Frederick Exh. 1892
Landscape painter. 125 Heath Street, Hampstead, London. † RBA 1.
WILDE, Mrs. Amy Exh. 1891
Miniature portrait painter. 57 Grove Street, Liverpool. † L 2.
WILDE, Arthur W. Exh. 1880-93
Landscape painter. Nottingham 1880 and 1892; Carrington, Notts. 1891. † N 18.
WILDE, Charles Exh. 1880-1901
Landscape painter. N.S.A. 1880. Add: Beeston Meadows, Notts. and Nottingham. † N 113.
WILDE, Elizabeth M. Exh. 1897-1938
Landscape painter. London. † L 3, RA 11, RBA 1, ROI 13, SWA 11.
WILDE, Gerald b. 1905
Painter. Exh. 1929-30. Add: 60 Valley Road, London. † NEA 3.
WILDE, William* Exh. 1880-1900
Watercolour landscape painter. N.S.A. 1884. Add: Beeston Meadows, Notts. and Nottingham. † N 82, RBA 1.
WILDEBLOOD, H.S. Exh. 1904
c/o H.S. King and Co., 8 Pall Mall, London. † L 2.
WILDEBLOOD, John Peake Exh. 1926-39
Landscape and figure painter. London 1926; Farnham, Surrey 1930. † AR 147, RA 3, RI 2.
WILDER, Hester Exh. 1937-40
Landscape painter. Twyning Manor, Tewkesbury. † COO 2, N 2, RA 1.
WILDER, H.C. Exh. 1929-38
Landscape painter. † AB 2, WG 5.
WILDING, B.M. Exh. 1927-28
Heimath, Billings Avenue, Blackburn, Lancs. † L 5.
WILDING, Philip Exh. 1939
Landscape and flower painter. † BK 27.
WILDMAN, Anne Exh. 1939
Landscape painter. 37 Aynhoe Road, London. † RA 1.
WILDMAN, William Ainsworth b. 1882
Figure and landscape painter and etcher. b. Manchester. Studied Manchester and London. R.B.A. 1926. Exh. 1906-40. Add: London. † BG 63, CHE 2, G 1, GI 2, GOU 3, I 5, L 7, M 24, NEA 7, P 1, RA 25, RBA 76, RHA 4, ROI 1, RWS 7.
WILDRIDGE, Dorothy Exh. 1919-33
Watercolour flower painter. b. Blackburn. Add: Rimington, nr. Clitheroe, Lancs. 1919; Wilpshire, nr. Blackburn, Lancs. 1921. † L 21, RA 1, RCA 2.
WILDSMITH, Alfred Exh. 1906-27
Watercolour landscape painter. Leeds. † GI 1, L 5, RA 7, RCA 2.
WILENSKI, Reginald Howard 1887-1975
Painter, critic and historian. Studied London and on the continent. Special lecturer in the History of Art at Manchester University 1933-46. Exh. 1910-14. Add: London. † L 3, P 4, ROI 1.

WILES, Bessie Exh. 1909-11
Prenton, Birkenhead. † L 3.
WILES, Francis (Frank) b. 1889
Sculptor. Teacher at Dublin Metropolitan School of Art. Exh. 1911-39. Add: Dublin and Larne, Co. Antrim. † RA 1, RHA 34, RSA 1.
WILES, Frank Exh. 1913-30
Portrait painter. London. † RA 5.
WILES, Irving Ramsay* b. 1861
American painter. Exh. 1906. † I 1.
WILESMITH, Miss E.M. Exh. 1937
Brook Villa, Malvern Link, Worcs. † B 1.
WILHELM, C. See PITCHER, William J.C.
WILKIE, Henry Charles b. 1864
Portrait painter. Studied Brussels; Julians, and Colarossi's, Paris. Exh. 1919-25. Add: Penzance, Cornwall. † L 1, RCA 3, RHA 5, RSA 1.
WILKIE, James b. 1890
Watercolour landscape painter. Studied and taught at Slade School. N.E.A. 1921. Exh. 1920-40. Add: London. † CG 4, CHE 2, FIN 13, G 10, GOU 6, LEI 33, NEA 81, P 2, RA 5, RED 55.
WILKIE, Mary Mein Exh. 1934-40
Wolverhampton 1934; Tettenhall, Staffs. 1939. † B 7.
WILKIE, N. Exh. 1939
453 Berridge Road, West Nottingham. † N 1.
WILKIE, Robert* b. 1888
Landscape and interior painter, lithographer and teacher. b. Sinclairtown, Kirkcaldy. Studied Edinburgh College of Art. Married Mary Ballantine q.v. Exh. 1924-30. Add: Glasgow. † GI 1, L 1, RSA 4.
WILKIN, Mrs. M.H. Exh. 1896
Sydney House, Hampstead, London. † SWA 1.
WILKIN-DAVIES, J.P. Exh. 1910
Holmfield, Morfa, Conway, Wales. † RCA 1.
WILKINS, Amy A. Exh. 1904
Sculptor. 46 Blenheim Crescent, Ladbroke Grove, London. † RA 1.
WILKINS, Elsie Exh. 1929
19 Balmoral Road, Elm Park, Liverpool. † L 2.
WILKINS, Frederick L. Exh. 1895-1938
Birmingham. † B 9.
WILKINS, George Exh. 1880-85
Landscape painter. Derby. † L 1, N 8, RA 1, RBA 4.
WILKINS, Ida Mary Exh. 1935-39
22 Muncaster Road, London. † RMS 1, SWA 1.
WILKINS, Mary A. Exh. 1887
Portrait painter. Cattestock Rectory, Dorchester, Dorset. † RA 1.
WILKINS, Miss S.M. Exh. 1898
44 Onslow Gardens, London. † SWA 1.
WILKINS, Victor Exh. 1912-39
Architect. London. † RA 7.
WILKINS, W. Exh. 1886
12 Reservoir Road, Edgbaston, Birmingham. † B 1.
WILKINS, W.H. Exh. 1916
52 Waldeck Road, Carrington, Nottingham. † N 1.
WILKINSON, A. Exh. 1892-1903
Liverpool. † L 13.
WILKINSON, Miss A.A. Exh. 1910-13
London 1910; Rassen, Lincs. 1912; Tealby, Lincs. 1913. † SWA 3.
WILKINSON, Alfred Ayscough
Exh. 1881-82
Landscape painter. London. † L 2, RBA 2.

WILKINSON, A. Gair Exh. 1932-37
Watercolour landscape painter. San Paolo, Italy 1934; Pulborough, Sussex 1936; c/o Bourlet, Nassau Street, London 1937. † FIN 116, RHA 6.
WILKINSON, Alfred Henry b. 1884
Sculptor. b. Birmingham. Studied Birmingham Central School of Art, L.C.C. Central School of Art and R.A. School of Sculpture (medalist and Landseer Scholarship). Assistant sculptor master L.C.C. Central School of Arts and Crafts. Exh. 1925-39. Add: London. † L 1, RA 9.
WILKINSON, Alfred L. Exh. 1937-38
Architect. 101 Gower Street, London. † RA 5.
WILKINSON, Miss A.R. Exh. 1920-34
Linden House, Anchorage Road, Sutton Coldfield. † B 14, RCA 1.
WILKINSON, Arthur Stanley Exh. 1908
15 Nascot Street, Watford, Herts. † L 5.
WILKINSON, Bertha Exh. 1921-27
68 Maiden Lane, Clubmoor, Liverpool. † L 4.
WILKINSON, Charles A. Exh. 1881-1925
Landscape painter. London 1881; Farnham, Surrey 1916. † G 1, L 7, M 9, RA 11, RBA 19, RHA 1, RI 7, ROI 12, RSA 1.
WILKINSON, Charles Kyle Exh. 1916-26
Painter. London. † NEA 2.
WILKINSON, Charles P. Exh. 1903
H.M. Office of Works, Liverpool. † L 1.
WILKINSON, Ellen Exh. 1882-1901
Sister of Laura W. q.v. Add: Manchester. † L 1, M 9.
WILKINSON, Mrs. Ellis Exh. 1892
2 Percy Street, Rathbone Place, London. † B 1.
WILKINSON, Edward Clegg
Exh. 1882-1910
Landscape, portrait and genre painter. London. † L 6, M 16, NG 2, P 1, RA 10, RBA 6, RI 1, ROI 10.
WILKINSON, Evelyn Harriet b. 1893
nee Mackenzie. Flower painter. b. Wu-King-Fu, Swatow, China. Studied Edinburgh School of Art. Married Norman W. q.v. Exh. 1918-38. Add: London. † RA 2, RI 1, ROI 5, SWA 2.
WILKINSON, Emma Mary b. 1864
Flower, still life, landscape and figure painter. b. Birmingham. Studied Birmingham and Paris. Exh. 1920-38. Add: 84 Hamstead Road, Hansworth, Birmingham. † AR 50, B 9, RA 3, ROI 2, RSA 2, RSW 1.
WILKINSON, Emily S. Exh. 1893-1914
Blackrock, Co. Dublin 1893; Glenageary, Ireland 1912. † RHA 22.
WILKINSON, E.W. Exh. 1881-82
Landscape painter. London Street, Brighton. † B 2, RBA 1.
WILKINSON, Mrs. Frances Exh. 1889-92
Mansfield Chambers, St. Anne's Square, Manchester. † M 4.
WILKINSON, Major F.A. Exh. 1904-37
Landscape painter. London 1904 and 1929; Glasgow 1917; Weybridge, Surrey 1936. † D 6, RHA 4, RI 2, RID 4, RSA 1, RSW,1, WG 99.
WILKINSON, Frances G. Exh. 1929-32
Chelsea Studios H., 416 Fulham Road, London. † NEA 1, SWA 2.
WILKINSON, Lieut. Gen. Fred Green
Exh. 1884
Painter. 19 St. George's Square, London. † RBA 1.
WILKINSON, Gilbert Exh. 1935
Figure painter. † AR 2.

WILKINSON, G. Welby Exh. 1914
7 Parkhill Road Studios, Haverstock Hill, London. † LS 3.

WILKINSON, H. Exh. 1907
† TOO 1.

WILKINSON, Herbert Exh. 1931
† GOU 2.

WILKINSON, Horace Exh. 1903-15
Stained glass artist. Studied Brighton School of Art and Westminster School. Add: London. † G 1, RA 5.

WILKINSON, Hugh Exh. 1880-1921
Landscape painter. Ealing 1880; Cymyran Valley, Anglesey 1890; Brockenhurst, Hants. 1891. † B 3, D 5, G 12, GOU 3, L 6, M 7, NG 12, RA 32, RBA 9, ROI 10.

WILKINSON, Henry Dymoke Exh. 1887-97
Architect. London. † RA 6.

WILKINSON, Henry R. Exh. 1907-8
Teacher Bath School of Art. Add: Conniston, Lancs. 1907; London 1908. † L 2, RA 1.

WILKINSON, Janet Exh. 1907-11
The Haven, Swinton Park, Eccles, Lancs. † L 1, M 1, RCA 4.

WILKINSON, J. Ivor Exh. 1938
9 Grange Road, Dudley, Worcs. † B 1.

WILKINSON, Kate Stanley b. 1883
nee Smith. Landscape and animal painter. Studied Slade School, Heatherleys and under Lucy Kemp-Welch. Married Reginald Charles W. q.v. Exh. 1912-40. Add: Pinner, Middlesex 1912; Winchelsea, Sussex 1917. † D 9, I 2, LS 3, RHA 6, RI 1, ROI 29, SWA 4.

WILKINSON, L. Exh. 1907-12
Ealing, London. † RA 3.

WILKINSON, Laura Exh. 1884-85
Sister of Ellen W. q.v. Add: Manchester. † M 5.

WILKINSON, L.M. Exh. 1881
Watercolour painter. 25 Gordon Street, Gordon Square, London. † D 1.

WILKINSON, Miss L.M. Exh. 1882
Middlethorpe Hall, York. † L 1.

WILKINSON, Mabel Exh. 1910-38
Kensington, London. † LS 2, SWA 1.

WILKINSON, Miss M.E. Exh. 1909
9 Croxteth Grove, Sefton Park, Liverpool. † L 1.

WILKINSON, Maude I. Exh. 1899-1915
Miniature portrait painter. Bushey, Herts. 1899; London 1904. † L 6, NG 3, RA 7, RMS 1.

WILKINSON, Norman 1884-1934
Stage designer. The Hurst, Four Oaks, Sutton Coldfield 1906; London 1912. † B 3, L 6, NG 2.

WILKINSON, Norman* 1878-1971
Marine painter, etcher and poster artist. b. Cambridge. Married Evelyn Harriet W. q.v. R.B.A. 1902, R.I. 1906, P.R.I. 1937, R.O.I. 1908. Add: London. † AB 2, B 3, BA 9, BG 51, CON 2, FIN 155, G 1, GI 9, L 11, LEI 16, NG 1, RA 55, RBA 25, RI 97, ROI 37.

WILKINSON, Sir Nevile Rodwell b. 1869
Watercolour painter, etcher and miniature craft worker. His principal work was "Titania's Palace" which took 15 years to complete and which was opened by Queen Mary in July 1922. A.R.E. 1909, H.R.M.S. 1920, V.P.R.M.S. 1921. Exh. 1907-40. Add: London and Dublin. † L 2, RA 18, RE 7, RHA 47, RMS 54.

WILKINSON, Mrs. P. Exh. 1891
c/o Mrs. Farger, Elm View, Sulbey Glen, I.O.M. † M 1.

WILKINSON, Q.H. Exh. 1884
2 Gower Street, Bedford Square, London. † D 1.

WILKINSON, Reginald Charles b. 1881
Painter. Studied Heatherleys and University College, London. Married Kate Stanley W. q.v. Exh. 1913-35. Add: London 1913; Winchelsea, Sussex 1917. † L 3, LS 3, RA 1, RHA 4, ROI 25.

WILKINSON, R.E. Exh. 1880-82
Landscape painter. N.S.A. 1882. Add: Nottingham. † N 14.

WILKINSON, R. Ellis Exh. 1881-90
Landscape and genre painter. Harrow, Middlesex 1881; Ashburton, Devon 1882; Bath 1885; St. Ives, Cornwall 1887. † AG 1, B 4, D 3, GI 1, L 3, M 4, RA 8, RI 3, ROI 3.

WILKINSON, Robert Stark Exh. 1880-81
Watercolour landscape painter. London. † D 2, RBA 2.

WILKINSON, Scott Exh. 1919-40
Sculptor. London 1919 and 1926; Bromley, Kent 1922; Sutton, Surrey 1931. † RA 14

WILKINSON, Selina Exh. 1895
33 Sydney Avenue, Blackrock, Co. Dublin. † RHA 1.

WILKINSON, Stephen Exh. 1928-39
Architect. b. Stockport, Cheshire. Add: Preston, Lancs. † RA 11.

WILKINSON, W. Exh. 1914
12 Claude Road, Manchester. † M 1.

WILKINSON, W.A. Exh. 1890-91
Liverpool. † L 3.

WILKINSON, Winifred A. Exh. 1895
Oakfield Lodge, Oakfield Road, Selly Park, Birmingham. † B 1.

WILKINSON, W.H. Exh. 1882-1907
Manchester. † L 5, M 12.

WILKINSON, Winifred H. Exh. 1911-40
Hove 1924; Steyning, Sussex 1940. † M 9, RI 1, SWA 3.

WILKS, Miss A.B. Exh. 1899
Uplands, Beckenham, Kent. † SWA 1.

WILKS, Maurice Canning* Exh. 1933-40
Landscape and figure painter. Belfast. † RHA 11.

WILLAERT, Ferdinand b. 1861
Belgian artist. Exh. 1905. Add: 7 Rue Aux Draps, Ghent, Belgium. † L 1.

WILLAN, Miss D. Exh. 1899-1908
Aldenham, Leamington, Warwicks. † B 9.

WILLAN, William S. Exh. 1919
Architect. Duke's Kiln, Gerrard's Cross, Bucks. † RA 1.

WILLARD, Frank Exh. 1886
Painter. 8 Conduit Street, London. † ROI 1.

WILLATS, Mrs. Exh. 1881
Watercolour landscape painter. 71 Queen's Gate, London. † RBA 1.

WILLATS, Percy S. Exh. 1913-36
Painter. London 1913; Bushey, Herts. 1936. † L 1, RA 1.

WILLATS, William E. Exh. 1921-39
Landscape painter. A.R.B.A. 1922, R.B.A. 1925. Add: London 1921; Whitton, Middlesex 1935. † L 12, RA 9, RBA 107.

WILLATT, G. Exh. 1928-37
Landscape painter. 1 Castle Grove, The Park, Nottingham. † N 3.

WILLATT, J. Exh. 1888
Etcher. Elm Bank, Mapperley Road, Nottingham. † N 2.

WILLBOND, W. Gordon Exh. 1934-39
Landscape painter. Nottingham. † N 13.

WILLCOCKS, Conrad Birdwood Exh. 1940
Architect. 11 Friar Street, Reading, Berks. † GI 1, RA 2.

WILLCOCKS, Mabel Exh. 1899-1904
Portrait painter. 5 New Court, Carey Street, London. † M 1, NG 1, RA 3.

WILLCOX, Mrs. Emily Exh. 1887-96
Broxbourne Villa, Park Hill, Moseley, Birmingham. † B 4.

WILLCOX, James N. Exh. 1918
Recess, Co. Galway. † RHA 1.

WILLCOX, Kathleen J. Exh. 1936
Watercolour landscape painter. 1 Manor Place, London. † RA 2.

WILLEMS, Florent* 1823-1905
Belgian painter. Exh. 1884. Add: 7 Rue Chaptal, Paris. † G 2.

WILLES, Clare Exh. 1927
Newbold Comyn, Leamington, Warwicks. † B 1.

WILLES, Edith A. Exh. 1882
Watercolour architectural painter. 13 Bernard Street, Russell Square, London. † RBA 1.

WILLETT, Arthur Exh. 1883-1906
Watercolour landscape and sporting painter. 39 Ship Street, Brighton. † B 2, L 1, RA 7, RBA 3, RHA 4, RI 10, ROI 7, RSA 6.

WILLETT, C. Ida Exh. 1889-91
Painter. Wyke House, Isleworth, Middlesex. † RID 7.

WILLETT, Mrs. J.M. Exh. 1920
c/o Mrs. Grimsdale, Sandycroft, Hoylake, Cheshire. † L 1.

WILLETTE, Adolphe* Exh. 1908
Watercolour painter. † BG 2.

WILLEWALD, von See V

WILLEY, Alfred E. Exh. 1913-14
4 Barlby Road, St. Quintin's Park, North Kensington, London. † LS 6.

WILLIAMS, Albert Exh. 1882-1900
Landscape painter. London. † RBA 4, RI 2.

WILLIAMS, Alexander 1846-1930
Landscape painter. A.R.H.A. 1884, R.H.A. 1891. Add: Dublin. † B 2, D 5, RHA 396.

WILLIAMS, Alfred Exh. 1880 95
Watercolour landscape painter. Churchfield, Salisbury, Wilts. † L 1, NG 1, RA 4.

WILLIAMS, Alfred Exh. 1886-99
Architect. Father of Mary Elizabeth W. q.v. Add: London. † RA 2.

WILLIAMS, Alfred Exh. 1904
15 Cheyney Road, Chester. † L 1.

WILLIAMS, Alice Exh. 1914
74 Rue Mironmesnil, Paris. † LS 3.

WILLIAMS, Alyn 1865-1941
Miniature portrait painter. Studied Slade School and Julians, Paris. R.B.A. 1903. Founder of the R.M.S. 1895. P.R.M.S. 1896-98 and from 1908. V.P.R.M.S. 1899-1907. Add: London 1890; Plumpton, Sussex 1920 and 1933; Baltimore, U.S.A. 1922; Cowes, I.O.W. 1935. † B 9, D 3, DOW 46, L 47, M 3, NG 14, RA 21, RBA 27, RCA 51, RI 9, RMS 196.

WILLIAMS, Mrs. Alyn Exh. 1901
Anna Vernon Dorsey. Add: 62A Grosvenor Street, London. † L 1.

WILLIAMS, Annie Exh. 1887-1916
Painter and etcher. A.R.E. 1893 (ceased 1900). Add: 61 Rowan Road, Hammersmith, London. † B 2, L 6, RA 8, RBA 1, RE 25.

WILLIAMS, Annie Exh. 1895-1907
Walton, Liverpool. † L 4.

WILLIAMS, A. Florence Exh. 1882-1904
Landscape and flower painter. Add: 84 Angel Road, Brixton 1882; 7 New Court, Lincolns Inn, London 1887. † B 5, M 2, RA 5, RBA 5, RI 6.

WILLIAMS, A.H. Exh. 1910-17
23 Loughborough Road, Brixton, London. † L 6, LS 9, RA 2.

WILLIAMS, A.J. Exh. 1922-23
30 Caldy Road, Aintree, Liverpool. † L 4.
WILLIAMS, Miss A.M. Exh. 1901-3
Walcot, Shea Road, East Acton, London. † SWA 2.
WILLIAMS, Alfred Mayhew Exh. 1882
Painter. Thorpe Cottage, Pembroke Road, South Tottenham, London. † RBA 1, RHA 2.
WILLIAMS, Alfred Walter 1824-1905
Landscape painter. Youngest son of Edward "Old" Williams. Add: Redhill, Surrey 1880. † D 3, L 1, M 3, RA 8, RBA 16, RHA 1, RI 4, ROI 13.
WILLIAMS, Benjamin d. 1920
Painter. Art master Aston School of Art, Birmingham. Exh. 1892-1913. Add: Birmingham. † B 10, L 1, RA 3, RCA 2.
WILLIAMS, Betty (Mrs. H.J.) Exh. 1921
Watercolour portrait painter. Melvin Hall, Golders Green Rd., London. † RA 1.
WILLIAMS, Blanche Exh. 1930-33
Bridge Street, Stratford on Avon, Warwicks. † B 3.
WILLIAMS, Benjamin Leader See LEADER
WILLIAMS, Miss B. Moray b. 1911
Wood engraver. b. Petersfield. Studied Winchester School of Art 1929-31 and Royal College of Art. A.R.E. 1936. Exh. 1933-39. Add: London. † GI 1, NEA 3, RA 5, RE 13, RED 2.
WILLIAMS, Caradoc Exh. 1936-38
27 Wood Waye, Oxhey, Herts. † ROI 3.
WILLIAMS, Charles Exh. 1894-95
Birmingham. † B 2.
WILLIAMS, Christopher 1873-1934
Portrait, figure and landscape painter. b. Maesteg. Studied Royal College of Art and R.A. Schools. Travelled in Italy, Spain, Morocco, France and Holland. R.B.A. 1911. Exh. 1902-27. Add: London 1902 and 1906, Maesteg, Glamorgan 1905. † L 2, LS 8, P 4, RA 18, RBA 37, RCA 1.
WILLIAMS, Mrs. Cyprian Exh. 1891-92
Portrait and figure painter. 5 Canfield Gardens, South Hampstead, London. † NEA 5.
WILLIAMS, Miss C.B. Exh. 1910
20 Slatey Road, Birkenhead. † L 2.
WILLIAMS, C.F. Exh. 1906
56 Kenninghall Road, Clapton, London. † RA 1.
WILLIAMS, C.F. Exh. 1914
Heybridge, Essex. † RA 1.
WILLIAMS, Mrs. C.F. Exh. 1888
11 Cathcart Road, London. † D 1.
WILLIAMS, Caroline Fanny 1836-1921
Landscape painter. Daughter of George Augustus W. q.v. Exh. 1880-90. Add: 4 Castlenau Villas, Barnes, Surrey. † B 13, L 2, M 3, RBA 3, RHA 13, ROI 1, SWA 32.
WILLIAMS, Charles Frederick* Exh. 1880
Landscape and coastal painter. Add: Bath Cottage, Bittern, Southampton. † D 1.
WILLIAMS, Charles K. Exh. 1916
Painter. 5 Ancona Road, Highbury, London. † NEA 1.
WILLIAMS, Charles Sneed Exh. 1906-14
Glasgow. † GI 7.
WILLIAMS, David Exh. 1936-37
Dundee. † RCA 4.
WILLIAMS, Dorothy E. Exh. 1936-38
Leatherworker. Stoneleigh, Godsall, Nr. Wolverhampton. † B 4.
WILLIAMS, Dorothy F. Exh. 1924-38
Watercolour flower and landscape painter. Add: Farley Lynches, Luton, Beds. 1924; Harpenden, Herts. 1934. † L 4, RA 6, SWA 9.
WILLIAMS, D.G. Bryn b. 1887
Etcher. Studied Liverpool Institute. Exh. 1927-33. Add: 13 Hallville Road, Mossley Hill, Liverpool. † L 10, RCA 8.
WILLIAMS, Edwin Exh. 1933
Restoration architect. 2 Fitzwilliams Place, Dublin. † RHA 7.
WILLIAMS, Mrs. Emily Exh. 1881-90
Figure painter. London. † B 5, G 8, NG 5, RA 5, ROI 5.
WILLIAMS, Emma Exh. 1895
2 Fulwood Park, Liverpool. † L 1.
WILLIAMS, Enid Exh. 1935-37
Watercolour landscape painter. 17 Pond Place, Chelsea, London. † RA 1, RI 1, SWA 1.
WILLIAMS, Miss E. Edgington Exh. 1885-90
Figure painter. Gravesend, Kent 1885; Kensington, London 1890. † L 1, RA 1.
WILLIAMS, Edith FitzGerald Exh. 1921-24
Painter. b. Newport, Mon. Add: Beachley House, Mill Hill Park, London. † B 2, RCA 6.
WILLIAMS, Mrs. E. Lilian Exh. 1928
Rock Mount, Clifton Road, Birkenhead. † L.
WILLIAMS, Elsie M. Exh. 1919
† L 1.
WILLIAMS, Frederick* Exh. 1891-92
Landscape painter. c/o W.H. King, 1 Holborn Villas, Wollaton Street, Nottingham. † N 2.
WILLIAMS, F. Eirene Exh. 1933
Painter. † COO 1.
WILLIAMS, Frederick Ernest Exh. 1903-7
Architect. London. † RA 4.
WILLIAMS, Francis H. Exh. 1882-1900
Portrait and genre painter. London. † B 1, RA 5, ROI 4.
WILLIAMS, Miss F.I. Exh. 1935
41 Mecklenburgh Square, London. † RBA 1.
WILLIAMS, Garth Exh. 1934-40
Sculptor. London. † RA 5.
WILLIAMS, Grace Exh. 1894
2 Hardman Street, Liverpool. † L 1.
WILLIAMS, George Augustus* 1814-1901
Landscape painter. Third son of Edward "Old" Williams, and father of Caroline Fanny and Walter W. q.v. Exh. 1880-89. Add: 4 Castlenau Cottages, Barnes, Surrey. † B 10, L 1, RA 1, RBA 5, RHA 21.
WILLIAMS, Gertrude Alice d. 1934
nee Williams. Sculptor, decorative painter and stained glass artist. b. Liverpool. Studied School of Architecture and Applied Art, Liverpool and Paris. Married Morris Meredith W. q.v. Add: Liverpool 1900; Paris 1904; Edinburgh 1907; North Tawton, Devon 1933. † ALP 1, GI 4, L 22, RA 7, RSA 37, RSW 3.
WILLIAMS, Geraldine F. Exh. 1915-33
Beachley House, Mill Hill Park, London. † GI 2, L 8, RA 1, RCA 24, RSA 1.
WILLIAMS, Gertrude M. Exh. 1880
Painter. 117 Finchley Road, London. † RBA 1.
WILLIAMS, Gilbert T. Exh. 1919-23
18 Balliol Road, Bootle, Lancs. † L 2.
WILLIAMS, Gladys T. Exh. 1913
5 Dingle Hill, Liverpool. † L 1.
WILLIAMS, G. Vivian Exh. 1936-38
Watercolour painter, pen and ink and linocut artist. Conway House, Red Hill, Nottingham. † N 6.
WILLIAMS, H. Exh. 1912
The Cottage, Roebuck Lane, Buckhurst Hill, Essex. † RA 1, RSA 1.
WILLIAMS, Helen Exh. 1923
12 Lorne Road, Oxton, Cheshire. † L 1.
WILLIAMS, Hugh* Exh. 1898-1919
Painter. London. † LS 3, RA 6, RCA 1, RHA 2, RI 3, ROI 1, RSA 1.
WILLIAMS, Hughes Harry 1892-1953
Painter and teacher. Studied Liverpool School of Art 1909-14, Royal College of Art 1915. Add: Liverpool 1913; Llanerchymedd, Anglesey 1918. † L 3, RCA 66.
WILLIAMS, H.J. Exh. 1885-86
Knutsford, Cheshire 1885; Truro, Cornwall 1886. † M 1, RI 1.
WILLIAMS, Hubert John b. 1905
Portrait, landscape and architectural painter, etcher and illustrator. b. Beckenham. Studied R.A. Schools (Landseer scholarship 1928), St. Martins School of Art and L.C.C. School. Exh. 1926-39. Add: London. † AR 2, COO 2, L 1, NEA 5, RA 9, RI 2, ROI 1, RSA 3.
WILLIAMS, H.L. Exh. 1892-1902
Painter. Woodthorpe, Chichester Road, Croydon, Surrey. † RBA 3, RHA 1, ROI 3.
WILLIAMS, H.M. Exh. 1907
23 Westcroft Square, Ravenscourt Park, London. † L 1, RA 1.
WILLIAMS, Isobel Exh. 1932-33
Lulworth, Margaret Road, Harborne, Birmingham. † B 3.
WILLIAMS, Irene Pownoll Exh. 1922-40
Portrait and landscape painter. Studied Bath School of Arts and Crafts. On staff of Cheltenham School of Art. Daughter of Pownoll T.W. q.v. Add: Cheltenham, Glos. † B 5, COO 3, L 1, NEA 3, RA 7.
WILLIAMS, J. Exh. 1882
Oaklands, Lewisham Park, London. † L 1.
WILLIAMS, J. Exh. 1911
11 Lissenden Mansions, Highgate Road, London. † RA 1.
WILLIAMS, James Exh. 1915-24
Painter. London. † I 2, L 2, RA 4.
WILLIAMS, John Exh. 1891
Painter. Add: The Guild and School of Handicraft. † NEA 1.
WILLIAMS, Judith Exh. 1921-40
Etcher. A.S.W.A. 1930. S.W.A. 1934. Add: Farley Lynches, Luton, Beds. 1921; London 1933. † GOU 2, L 5, M 1, RA 9, RSA 2, SWA 14.
WILLIAMS, James A. Exh. 1882-85
Salford 1882; Bowden, Cheshire 1885. † M 2.
WILLIAMS, James A. Exh. 1913
City Chambers, Edinburgh. † RSA 2.
WILLIAMS, James Besley Exh. 1918
39 Upper Thomas Street, Merthyr Tydvil, Wales. † LS 3.
WILLIAMS, Miss Joan Cyprian Exh. 1912
Painter. Taynton House, Nr. Beerford, Oxon. † NEA 1.
WILLIAMS, Joyce Crawshay Exh. 1906-17
Mrs. L.C. Add: Ashtead, Surrey 1906; St. Johns Wood, London 1909. † NG 3, P 10, RA 5.
WILLIAMS, John Edgar Exh. 1881-83
Portrait and genre painter. 1 St. Edmunds Terrace, North Gate, Regents Park, London. † RA 2.
WILLIAMS, James Leon Exh. 1908
84 Fellows Road, South Hampstead, London. † LS 4.
WILLIAMS, James Leonard Exh. 1897-98
Architect. 3 Staple Inn, Holborn, London. † RA 2.
WILLIAMS, Joyce M. Exh. 1931-32
Landscape and portrait painter. London. † RA 3.

WILLIAMS, Juliet Nora Exh. 1899-1937
Painter of landscapes, flowers, gardens and music subjects. Studied Herkomers, Bushey and Paris. Add: Bushey, Herts. 1899; Hindhead, Surrey 1902; Haslemere, Surrey 1905; Sonning-on-Thames 1908; London 1910. † AR 173, B 2, COO 8, RA 2, RMS 1, ROI 1, SWA 3.

WILLIAMS, Jolan P. Exh. 1938-39
NEA 2.

WILLIAMS, Mrs. J.S. Exh. 1880-83
Landscape painter. Glasgow 1880; Edinburgh 1883. † G 1, GI 5, RSA 3.

WILLIAMS, J.S. Exh. 1921
7 Stanley Studios, Park Walk, London. † RA 1.

WILLIAMS, K.E. Exh. 1890
Painter. 100 Chetwynd Road, Dartmouth Park Hill, London. † RI 1.

WILLIAMS, Mrs. L. Exh. 1910
Hendre, Wrexham. † L 1.

WILLIAMS, Miss L. Exh. 1890
385 Holloway Road, London. † SWA 1.

WILLIAMS, Lily 1874-1940
Portrait painter. A.R.H.A. 1929. Add: Dublin. † RHA 132.

WILLIAMS, L. Gwendolen Exh. 1891-1935
Sculptor and watercolour painter. b. Liverpool. Studied Wimbledon Art College 1893, Royal College of Art and Colarossi's, Paris. Add: Southwall, Notts. 1891; London 1893, 1902 and 1935; Bleasby Vicarage, Nottingham 1901 and 1908; Rome 1910. † B 8, GI 18, I 6, L 42, LS 22, M 13, N 10, NG 3, RA 35, RCA 2, RHA 8, RSA 9, SWA 2.

WILLIAMS, L.J. Exh. 1894
Architect. 6 Staple Inn, Holborn, London. † RA 1.

WILLIAMS, L.L. Exh. 1884
Landscape painter. Rue de Fleurus, 35 bis, Paris. † RBA 1.

WILLIAMS, Margaret Exh. 1914-20
Miniature portrait painter. London. † L 3, RA 2.

WILLIAMS, Dr. Marjorie Exh. 1934-39
Watercolour landscape painter. † AR 2, COO 2.

WILLIAMS, Mary Exh. 1939
Watercolour painter. b. Ottery St. Mary. Studied Exeter School of Art. Add: Verbena, Ottery St. Mary, Devon. † RI 1, SWA 1.

WILLIAMS, Mary Adele Exh. 1903-8
Figure and portrait painter. Chelsea, London 1903; Barnes, Surrey 1904. † LS 5, P 4, RA 8, ROI 1, SWA 2.

WILLIAMS, Melville A. Exh. 1892
65 Bedford Street, Moss Side, Manchester. † M 1.

WILLIAMS, Miss M.B. Exh. 1928
Rose Cottage, Hadassah Grove, Liverpool. † L.

WILLIAMS, Mrs. M.E. Exh. 1894
St. Cross, Weybridge, Surrey. † RI 2.

WILLIAMS, Mary E. Exh. 1909-27
Oxford House, Oswestry. † L 2, RI 2.

WILLIAMS, Mary Elizabeth Exh. 1925-38
Hand weaver. Daughter of Alfred W. q.v. (architect). Add: London. † L 9, SWA 1.

WILLIAMS, Mary Frances Agnes Exh. 1918-33
Portrait and landscape painter. b. Whitchurch, Salop. Studied in Paris. Add: St. Ives, Cornwall. † I 1, RA 1, ROI 3.

WILLIAMS, Mrs. Margaret G.M. Exh. 1937-40
Shelvingstone, Sonning, Berks. † L 1, RCA 3, RSA 1, SWA 1.

WILLIAMS, M. Josephine Exh. 1889-99
Painter. London. † L 1, RBA 1, RI 1, SWA 6.

WILLIAMS, Margaret Lindsay Exh. 1910-39
Portrait and decorative painter. b. Cardiff. Studied at Sir Arthur Cope's School of Painting, R.A. Schools (gold medal and travelling scholarship), Italy and Holland. Add: Barry, South Wales 1910 and 1912; London 1911 and 1928; Dinas Powis, South Wales 1915. † GI 1, L 18, P 1, RA 25, RCA 12.

WILLIAMS, Maud M. Exh. 1905-40
Miniature painter. Croydon, Surrey and London. † L 6, LS 5, RA 15.

WILLIAMS, Morris Meredith b. 1881
Painter, stained glass artist and illustrator. b. Cowbridge, Glamorgan. Studied Slade School Paris and Italy. Married Gertrude Alice M.W. q.v. Exh. 1905-37. Add: Edinburgh 1905; North Tawton, Devon 1929. † GI 2, L 33, P 1, RA 13, RSA 53, RSW 2.

WILLIAMS, Muriel P. Exh. 1922
1 Queens Circus, Cheltenham, Glos. † B 1.

WILLIAMS, Mrs. M.P. Bryn Exh. 1928
15 Hallville Road, Mossley Hill, Liverpool. † L 1.

WILLIAMS, Margaret R. Exh. 1923-27
63 Rowstan Street, New Brighton, Cheshire. † L 2.

WILLIAMS, M.V. Exh. 1935-37
Sherbourne, Dorset. † SWA 1.

WILLIAMS, Marjorie Watson
See VEZELAY, Paule

WILLIAMS, Mrs. Nellie L. Exh. 1913-25
Flower painter. Beeston, Notts. † N 5.

WILLIAMS, O.R. Exh. 1882
46 Bryon Street, Hulme, Manchester. † M 1.

WILLIAMS, Pownoll T. Exh. 1880-97
Landscape and genre painter. Father of Irene Pownoll W. q.v. Add: London. † D 8, G 3, L 2, M 3, RA 8, RBA 6, RI 1, ROI 2.

WILLIAMS, R. Exh. 1889
36 Argyle Street, Birkenhead. † L 1.

WILLIAMS, Richard A. Exh. 1883-91
Still life, figure and landscape painter. London. † RA 1, RBA 3, ROI 1.

WILLIAMS, Richard James b. 1876
Painter and illustrator of childrens books. b. Hereford. Studied Cardiff, Birmingham and London. Head master Worcester School of Arts and Crafts. Exh. 1919-33. Add: 37 Hill Avenue, Worcester. † RCA 80, RI 1.

WILLIAMS, Stella Exh. 1903
Whiston Hall, Albrighton, Wolverhampton. † B 4.

WILLIAMS, Miss S.A. Exh. 1899
2 Hardman Street, Liverpool. † L 1.

WILLIAMS, Sybil V. Exh. 1927-35
Sculptor. 9 Thurlow Park Road, Dulwich, London. † GI 2, L 2, RA 3, RMS 1.

WILLIAMS, Stephen W. Exh. 1887-89
Rhayader, Wales. † RCA 7.

WILLIAMS, Terrick* 1860-1936
Marine and landscape painter. b. Liverpool. Studied Antwerp under Verlat, and Paris. P.N.S.A. 1930, A.R.A. 1924, R.A. 1933, R.B.A. 1894, R.I. 1904, P.R.I. 1934, R.O.I. 1903, V.P.R.O.I. 1933. Member of Society of 25 Artists. Exh. from 1883. Add: London. † B 5, BA 1, BAR 1, CHE 5, D 2, DOW 1, FIN 75, GI 28, L 52, LEI 75, M 3, NEA 3, NG 2, RA 142, RBA 40, RCA 2, RHA 1, RI 130, RID 67, ROI 111, RSA 4.

WILLIAMS, Thomas Exh. 1880-81
136 Wellington Street, Glasgow. † GI 7.

WILLIAMS, T.G. Exh. 1887-92
Architect. 3 Cable Street, Liverpool. † L 4.

WILLIAMS, Violet E. Exh. 1934
Caernarvon. † RCA 1.

WILLIAMS, Dr. W. Exh. 1904
The Old Garden, Hoylake, Cheshire. † L 1.

WILLIAMS, Walter* 1835-1906
Landscape painter. Son of George Augustus W. q.v. Exh. 1880-89. Add: Florence Villa, Lonsdale Road, Barnes, Surrey. Died in Richmond Workhouse. † B 8, M 4, RA 1, RBA 1, RHA 32.

WILLIAMS, Warren Exh. 1901-18
Conway, Wales. † L 7, RCA 95.

WILLIAMS, William Charles Exh. 1891
Flower painter. 56 Balcombe Street, Dorset Square, London. † RBA 1.

WILLIAMS-ELLIS, Mrs. Cecily Exh. 1932
Chwilog, Caern. † RCA 2.

WILLIAMS-ELLIS, Clough b. 1883
Architect. Studied at the A.A. Exh. 1906-31. Add: London. † RA 11, RCA 2.

WILLIAMS-LYOUNS, Herbert Francis b. 1863
Painter and wood engraver. b. Plymouth. Studied in Paris and travelled widely and spent some years in the U.S.A. Exh. 1914-23. Add: Harberton, Devon 1914; Kingsbridge, Devon 1918. † I 2, L 13, RA 2, RCA 2, RHA 1, ROI 3, RSA 2.

WILLIAMSON, Andrew Exh. 1880-84
15 Moray Place, Edinburgh. † RSA 2.

WILLIAMSON, Anne E. Exh. 1911-40
Still life painter. Leeds 1911; London 1919; Seascale, Cumberland 1940. † GOU 2, I 2, L 3, NEA 1, RA 2, RBA 2, ROI 2, SWA 2.

WILLIAMSON, Bertha Exh. 1913
Brigham Hall, Cockermouth, Cumberland. † L 1.

WILLIAMSON, Daniel Alexander 1822-1903
Landscape and genre painter. Son of Daniel W. (1792-1840). Add: Broughton in Furness 1880. † D 6, GI 26, L 7, RI 1, RSW 2.

WILLIAMSON, D.W. Exh. 1888-89
13 Melville Terrace, Edinburgh. † RSA 3.

WILLIAMSON, Mrs. E. Exh. 1884-86
Egerton Road, Fallowfield, Manchester. † M 3.

WILLIAMSON, Ella Exh. 1896-1910
Watercolour flower painter. 28 Rue Washington, Paris. † B 1, BG 8, SWA 5.

WILLIAMSON, Frederick* Exh. 1880-1900
Watercolour landscape painter. Witley Nr. Godalming, Surrey 1880; London 1887. † AG 22, B 4, D 26, DOW 1, FIN 1, G 1, GI 4, L 5, RA 13, RI 17, TOO 3.

WILLIAMSON, Miss F.E. Exh. 1916-18
Blenheim Cottage, Bedford Park, London. † RA 2.

WILLIAMSON, Francis John c. 1833-1920
Sculptor. Exh. 1881-97. Add: Esher, Surrey. † B 1, L 6, RA 30, RBA 2.

WILLIAMSON, Grace Exh. 1899
West Hill, Huddersfield. † L 1.

WILLIAMSON, H. Exh. 1916-18
15 Leeside Crescent, Golders Green, London. † RA 2.

WILLIAMSON, Harold b. 1898
Painter, pencil artist and etcher. b. Manchester. Studied Manchester School of Art. Assistant Life Master Manchester School of Art and painting master Bournemouth School of Art. Artist and designer with Arthur Sanderson and Sons. Exh. 1926-40. Add: Bournemouth. † G 2, L 5, M 4, NEA 2, RA 16.

WILLIAMSON, Miss H.D. Exh. 1891
c/o Mrs. J.W. Williamson, Rock Bank, Monton Road, Eccles, Lancs. † M 2.

WILLIAMSON, Harold Sandys b. 1892
Painter and poster designer. b. Leeds. Studied R.A. Schools (Turner Gold medal). Art master Westminster School and Chelsea School of Art. Member London Group 1933. Exh. 1915-39. Add: London. † COO 1, GOU 11, I 1, LEI 3, M 1, NEA 10, RA 1.

WILLIAMSON, James Exh. 1886-88
Edinburgh 1886; Narni Provincia, d'Umbria, Italy 1887; Netherton, Nr. Liverpool 1888. † L 3, RSA 1.

WILLIAMSON, John* Exh. 1885-95
Portrait and figure painter. Edinburgh 1885; London 1893. † RA 4, RBA 1, RSA 11.

WILLIAMSON, James A. Exh. 1917
City Chambers, Edinburgh. † RSA 3.

WILLIAMSON, J. Anderson Exh. 1894-97
Corstorphine 1894; Edinburgh 1896. † RSA 4.

WILLIAMSON, J.B. Exh. 1880-82
13 Queen's Crescent, Glasgow. † GI 2.

WILLIAMSON, Jessie G. Exh. 1904
West House, St. James Road, Edgbaston, Birmingham. † B 1.

WILLIAMSON, Mrs. Leila K. Exh. 1894-1919
Painter. London 1894 and 1912; Addlestone, Surrey 1895. † D 2, RA 2, RCA 6, RHA 2, RI 7, ROI 11, SWA 2.

WILLIAMSON, R.C. Exh. 1887
6 Admiral Terrace, Edinburgh. † RSA 1.

WILLIAMSON, Sadie H. Exh. 1925-28
Linthouse, Blundellsands, Liverpool. † L 2.

WILLIAMSON, T.F. Exh. 1886
London Road, Dorking, Surrey. † RHA 1.

WILLIAMSON, William Exh. 1898-1923
220 High Street, Kirkcaldy, N.B. † RSA 4.

WILLIAMSON, William Exh. 1919-23
Nottingham. † N 5.

WILLIG, Carl Exh. 1929-30
Portrait artist. c/o Arlington Gallery, 22 Old Bond Street, London. † RA 1, RMS 1.

WILLINCK, Miss H.M. Exh. 1913
Bromley, Kent. † SWA 2.

WILLINGTON, Dorothy Exh. 1915-30
Birkdale, Lancs. † I 1, L 1.

WILLINK, Miss Beatrice Exh. 1912-20
Whitefoot, Burnside, Kendal 1912 and 1920; Liverpool 1915. † L 8.

WILLINK. Mrs. F.N. (A.H.) Exh. 1893-1913
Dingle Park, Liverpool 1893 and 1908; Burnside, Kendal 1901; Oxton, Birkenhead 1913. † L 17.

WILLINK, H.G. Exh. 1886-88
Watercolour landscape painter. 1 Hyde Park Street, London. † RI 2.

WILLIS, Charles Exh. 1919-23
Portrait painter. A.N.S.A. 1908. Add: Rufford Avenue, Mansfield, Notts. † N 38.

WILLIS, Cherry b. 1912
Watercolour painter. Studied Lancaster Art School 1929. Exh. 1933-39. Add: The Laurels, Lancaster. † B 12.

WILLIS, C.E. Exh. 1894-95
43 Elm Park Gardens, London. † M 2, RI 1.

WILLIS, Dorothy S. Exh. 1911-33
Landscape and figure painter. Kensington, London 1914; Newbury, Berks. 1933. † ALP 6, I 2, LS 3, NEA 4, SWA 2.

WILLIS, Evelyn Exh. 1928
14 Belmont Park, Donnybrook, Ireland. † RHA 1.

WILLIS, Ethel Mary b. 1874
Portrait, landscape, flower and miniature painter and drypoint artist. Studied Royal College of Art, Slade School, Academy Delecluse and with Madame Debellemont Chardon, Paris. Teacher of miniature painting Halford House School of Art and Central School Southampton Row and teacher of miniature and pastel painting at the L.C.C. Central School of Arts and Crafts from 1904. A.R.M.S. 1914. Exh. 1900-39. Add: London. † GI 1, L 41, NG 2, RA 13, RI 26, RMS 56, SWA 5.

WILLIS, Frank 1865-1932
Etcher and line engraver. b. Windsor. Assistant in the etching and engraving studios at the Royal Academy Dusseldorf. A.R.E. 1902. Add: Windsor 1892 and 1900; Dusseldorf 1896; Whitstable, Kent 1910. † RA 4, RE 15.

WILLIS, Henry Brittan* 1810-1884
Watercolour landscape and cattle painter and lithographer. b. Bristol. Studied under his father G.W. Willis (Bristol landscape and figure painter and teacher). Visited America 1842. A.R.W.S. 1862, R.W.S. 1863. Add: 12 Palace Gardens Terrace, Kensington, London. † AG 1, B 2, L 2, M 2, RWS 20.

WILLIS, Iris Exh. 1911-14
4 Grange Park, Ealing, London. † L 1, RA 1.

WILLIS, Miss I.A. Exh. 1935
122 Pershore Road, Edgbaston, Birmingham. † B 1.

WILLIS, Janet C.N. Exh. 1926-28
West Kirby, Cheshire. † L 3.

WILLIS, Maj. Gen. John Christopher Temple 1900-1969
Watercolour landscape painter. b. Weymouth. Studied under R. Talbot Kelly and G. Ackerman. Add: London 1925 and 1940; Chatham, Kent 1938. † G 1, L 1, RA 2, RBA 1, RI 7, RSA 2.

WILLIS, John Henry b. 1887
Portrait, figure and landscape painter. b. Tavistock. Studied Armstrong College, Durham and Royal College of Art. R.B.A. 1925. Exh. 1910-40. Add: Stockton-on-Tees 1910; London 1917. † L 3, P 1, RA 21, RBA 104.

WILLIS, Mrs. J.M. Exh. 1905
100 Lower Mount Street, Dublin. † RHA 2.

WILLIS, J.U. Exh. 1919-35
67 Lansdowne Road, Handsworth, Birmingham. † B 4.

WILLIS, Katharina Exh. 1893-98
Portrait painter. London. † RA 5, ROI 2.

WILLIS, Lucy Exh. 1931
c/o H. Foster Newey, Esq. 14 New Street, Birmingham. † B 1.

WILLIS, Richard H.A. Exh. 1880-1905
Painter and sculptor. London 1880 and 1895; School of Art, Cavendish Street, All Saints, Manchester 1889; Killarney, Ireland 1899. † L 2, RA 9, RHA 5.

WILLIS, S. Annie Exh. 1921
† LS 3.

WILLIS, Samuel William Ward b. 1870
Sculptor. Studied West London School of Art and R.A. Schools 1890-95. A.R.M.S. 1914, R.M.S. 1916. Exh. 1894-1935. Add: London. † L 8, LS 6, RA 21, RBA 1, RMS 6.

WILLMER, Arthur W. Exh. 1897-99
24 Village Road, Oxton, Birkenhead. † L 3.

WILLMER, Miss M.L. Exh. 1915-16
Thursley Copse, Haslemere, Surrey. † RA 2.

WILLMORE, Arthur 1814-1888
Engraver. London. † RA 4.

WILLMOT, Lucie Exh. 1906
92 Crompton Road, Handsworth, Birmingham. † B 1.

WILLMOTT, Ernest Exh. 1910-11
1 Raymond Buildings, Gray's Inn, London. † RA 2.

WILLMS, A. Exh. 1884-96
Paris 1884; Birmingham 1885 and 1888; Chennevieres, Marne, France 1887; Worcester 1896. † B 14, G 1, L 1.

WILLOCK, John S. Exh. 1930-35
12 Brocklebank Road, Fallowfield, Manchester. † I 4, L 2, NEA 4.

WILLOCK, Richard Exh. 1893-96
Architect. 5 Eastbourne Road, Stamford Hill, London. † RA 4.

WILLOUGHBY, Althea Exh. 1930
Wood engraver. † RED 1.

WILLOUGHBY, Esther d. 1959
Portrait painter and etcher. b. Croydon. Studied Redhill and Royal College of Art. Exh. 1923-30. Add: London. † L 4, RA 5, SWA 3.

WILLOUGHBY, Ethel Exh. 1908
6 Egerton Gardens, London. † LS 4.

WILLOUGHBY, Mrs. Minnie B. Exh. 1919
Miniature portrait painter. 8 Avenue Mansions, Hampstead, London. † RA 1.

WILLOUGHBY, P. Exh. 1913
5 Tavistock Square, London. † RA 1.

WILLOUGHBY, Mrs. Vera Exh. 1905-19
Watercolour painter, illustrator and decorator. Slindon, Sussex 1911; London 1913. † I 11, L 1, P 2, RI 4.

WILLS, Mrs. Ada M. Exh. 1933
Flower painter. Lady's Grace, Southcott, Nr. Bideford, Devon. † RA 1.

WILLS, Charles Exh. 1923-30
Sculptor. 78 Lenton Boulevard, Nottingham. † B 4, CI 1, L 7, N 26.

WILLS, Edgar Exh. 1881-1907
Landscape painter. London and Brentwood, Essex 1881; Potton, Beds. 1900. † B 1, G 1, GI 8, L 5, M 11, NG 38, RA 7, RBA 6, RHA 2, RI 1, ROI 4.

WILLS, F.G. Exh. 1929
Landscape painter. Ingledene, Barkby Road, Syston, Nr. Leicester. † N 2.

WILLS, Frederick J. Exh. 1933-38
Architect. (e.g. Cumberland Hotel, Marble Arch, London). Add: London. † RA 2.

WILLS, Flora R. Exh. 1909-15
Derby. † B 1, N 2, RA 1.

WILLS, Sir Gilbert Alan Hamilton b. 1880
Sculptor. M.P. for Taunton 1912-18 and for Weston-super-Mare 1918-22. Exh. 1925-26. Add: Batsford Park, Moreton-in-the-Marsh, Glos. † L 1, RA 2.

WILLS, Gerald Berkeley b. 1882
Architect. Studied under Sir Reginald Blomfield. Exh. 1924-40. Add: 7 Stones Buildings, Lincoln's Inn, London. † RA 5.

WILLS, Henry Exh. 1882-85
Sculptor. 9 Regent Street, Cambridge. † RA 2.

WILLS, Mrs. Norah Exh. 1919
c/o Herbert R. Lilley, 11 College Street, North Belfast. † RHA 2.

WILLS, Trenwith b. 1891
Architect. b. Cheshire. Studied University of Liverpool, R.A. Schools (Tite prizeman 1914). Exh. 1922. Add: 24A Yeoman's Row, Brompton Road, London. † RA 1.

WILLS, Thomas Alexander Dodd 1873-1932
Watercolour landscape painter. b. London. Studied Liverpool School of Art. Exh. 1895-1932. Add: Liverpool 1895; Wallasey, Cheshire 1901. † L 36, LS 33, RCA 33, RI 3.

WILLS, Miss W. Exh. 1912
Farnsfield, Notts. † N 1.

WILLS, William German Exh. 1880-81
Painter. The Avenue, 76 Fulham Road, London. † G 3.

WILLS, W.J. Exh. 1889
Garrick Club, London. † NG 1.

WILLSON, E. Dorothy Exh. 1900-2
Landscape painter. Ballamona, Headingley, Leeds. † L 1, RA 1.

WILLSON, John J.* Exh. 1900-2
Landscape painter. Ballamona, Headingley, Leeds. † L 3, RA 1.

WILLSON, Margaret Exh. 1888-97
Flower and landscape painter. Leeds 1888; Headingley, Leeds 1897. † RA 3.

WILLUMSEN, Ian Exh. 1927
Watercolour painter. † FIN 40.

WILLWAY, Alice Mary Exh. 1908-22
Landscape painter. Clifton, Bristol. † BK 30, LS 26.

WILLYAMS, Humphrey J. Exh. 1887-88
Painter. Nauskevala, South Colomb, Cornwall. † L 1, RI 1.

WILMER, John Riley* Exh. 1905-26
Painter. Falmouth, Cornwall. † L 2, M 1, RA 18.

WILMER, Kitty Exh. 1933-35
Portrait and landscape painter. 25 Ailesbury Road, Dublin. † RHA 10.

WILMER, Miss M. Exh. 1906-8
Battle, Sussex 1906; Brede, Sussex 1908. † RA 3.

WILMOT, A. Exh. 1891
Hotel Dorneille, 5 Rue Cornielle, Paris. † B 1.

WILMOT, Miss A.K. Exh. 1885
25 St. Peters Road, Birmingham. † B 1.

WILMOT, Catherine Exh. 1908
19 Hermitage Road, Edgbaston, Birmingham. † B 1.

WILMOT, Constance Exh. 1910-40
Croydon, Surrey 1910; Skipton, Yorks. 1939. † RBA 3, ROI 2, SWA 6.

WILMOT, D.A.T. Exh. 1912
Burnham House, Burnham, Bucks. † RA 1.

WILMOT, Florence Freeman Exh. 1884-1934
Landscape and portrait painter. b. Lea Hall, Staffs. Studied Birmingham School of Art and under Stanhope Forbes. Teacher at Chipping Campden Technical School and Stratford on Avon School of Art. Add: Birmingham 1884 and 1903; Chipping Campden, Glos. 1898; Bettws-y-Coed, Wales 1923; Stratford on Avon, Warwicks. 1934. † B 49, L 3, RA 4, RCA 10, RMS 1, SWA 1.

WILMOT, Miss G. Exh. 1882
Lea Hall, Handsworth, Birmingham. † B 1.

WILMOT, H.E. Exh. 1926
38 Vicarage Road, Yardley, Birmingham. † B 1.

WILMOT, Mary Exh. 1883-84
Lea Hall, Handsworth, Birmingham. † B 2.

WILMOTTE, Simone Exh. 1923
† SWA 1.

WILMSHURST, George C. Exh. 1897-1900
Portrait painter. 136 Camden Road, London. † M 1, RA 3.

WILMURT, Mrs. Addison Exh. 1923-29
Tunbridge Wells, Kent 1923; London 1929. † RI 4.

WILS, Ian Exh. 1936
† RSA 2.

WILSHAW, Miss B.M. Exh. 1907-26
28 Gerard Road, Wallasey, Cheshire. † L 11, RCA 1.

WILSHAW, Miss E.A. Exh. 1913-26
28 Gerard Road, Wallasey, Cheshire. † L 9.

WILSON, A. Exh. 1912
1 Hare Court Temple, London. † RA 1.

WILSON, A. Exh. 1920-22
Landscape painter. 106 Winchester Street, Sherwood, Nottingham. † N 10.

WILSON, A. Exh. 1921
Johannesburg, South Africa. † RA 1.

WILSON, Miss A. Exh. 1887-92
Mrs. Percy E. Rimmer. Add: Liverpool. † L 10.

WILSON, Agnes Exh. 1893-1906
London. † B 2, ROI 1.

WILSON, Alice Exh. 1897-1927
17 Braidburn Terrace, Edinburgh. † GI 1, L 1, RSA 28, RSW 3.

WILSON, Alison Exh. 1901-8
20 Ann Street, Edinburgh. † RSA 5.

WILSON, Alleyne Exh. 1894-97
Alfred House, Alfred Road, Birkenhead. † GI 2, L 2.

WILSON, Alyce Exh. 1902-6
Brentwood, Newcastle on Tyne 1902; Hampstead, London 1906. † RSA 1, SWA 4.

WILSON, Amy Exh. 1884
Watercolour figure painter. 158 Portsdown Road, Maida Vale, London. † SWA 1.

WILSON, A. Aldine Exh. 1911
43 Carlisle Terrace, Manningham, Bradford, Yorks. † L 1.

WILSON, Alice C. Exh. 1892-93
Watercolour flower painter. Heatherbank, Weybridge, Surrey. † RA 1, RI 1.

WILSON, Anna Dove Exh. 1895-99
17 Rubislaw Terrace, Aberdeen. † GI 1, L 1, RSA 1.

WILSON, Annie E. Exh. 1881
Landscape and flower painter. 3 Western Road, Brixton, London. † SWA 2.

WILSON, Annie Heath Exh. 1880-1920
Landscape and figure painter. Eastbourne 1880; Florence 1884; London 1885 and 1908; Genoa, Italy 1888; Tangier, Morocco 1913; Walberswick, Suffolk 1917; Kew, Surrey 1918; Wenhaston, Halesworth, Suffolk 1919. † B 2, D 1, GI 11, L 8, LS 2, RA 5, RBA 20, ROI 3, SWA 14.

WILSON, A.J. Exh. 1924-26
Landscape painter. Stapleford, Notts. 1924; Nottingham 1925; West Bridgford, Notts. 1926. † N 8.

WILSON, Aimee M. Exh. 1895-1910
Oak Hill, Sevenoaks, Kent. † D 2, LS 6, M 2.

WILSON, Ada M.L. Exh. 1909
Painter. 20 Rossetti Garden Mansions, Chelsea, London. † NEA 1.

WILSON, A. Needham Exh. 1886-1906
Architect. Snaresbrook, Essex 1886; Brockley 1888; Leytonstone 1890; Marlborough, Wilts 1892; London 1903. † RA 11.

WILSON, A. Ure Exh. 1895-96
13 Westfield Place, Dundee. † GI 4.

WILSON, A. William Exh. 1893
7 Quadrant, New Brighton, Cheshire. † L 1.

WILSON, B. Exh. 1925-26
Colney Old Hall, Norwich, Norfolk. † L 4.

WILSON, Miss B. Exh. 1926
10 Gardiner's Place, Dublin. † RHA 1.

WILSON, Beatrice J. Exh. 1896-1921
Miniature portrait painter. Teddington, Middlesex 1896; Woking, Surrey 1910; St. Leonards on Sea 1914; Nairn 1917. † RA 10, RMS 3, RSA 2.

WILSON, C. Exh. 1921
Chelsea Arts Club, Church Street, London. † RA 1.

WILSON, Cecil Exh. 1901-13
Portrait painter. London 1901; Cranleigh, Surrey 1911. † L 1, LS 4, NG 1, P 1, RA 4, RBA 1, ROI 1.

WILSON, Clare Exh. 1937-40
Landscape painter. Ravensmere, Kendal Avenue, Epping, Essex. † RA 1, ROI 1, SWA 1.

WILSON, Charles Edward* Exh. 1889-1929
Watercolour painter. b. Whitwell, Notts. Studied Sheffield School of Art. On staff of the French paper "L'Art". Add: Sheffield 1889, 1894 and 1924; London 1893; Milford Heath, Godalming, Surrey 1896; Addiscombe, Surrey 1927. † GI 1, L 15, RA 40, RBA 4, RI 61.

WILSON, Miss C.H. Exh. 1918-21
London 1918; Woldingham, Surrey 1921. † RA 2.

WILSON, Charles Hugh Exh. 1927-34
Painter. 1 Oakhill Road, Stonycroft, Liverpool. † L 7, RA 1.

WILSON, D. Exh. 1880
148 Strand, London. † RHA 1.

WILSON, D. Exh. 1913
41 Leece Street, Liverpool. † L 1.

WILSON, David 1873-1934
Watercolour landscape and flower painter A.R.B.A. 1924, R.B.A. 1926, R.I. 1931. Add: 22 Downton Avenue, Streatham Hill, London. † CHE 2, COO 2, FIN 77, GI 1, GOU 3, L 6, RA 17, RBA 81, RI 19.

WILSON, David Forrester b. 1873
Portrait and decorative painter. b. Glasgow. Studied and taught at Glasgow School of Art. A.R.S.A. 1930, R.S.A. 1933. Exh. 1895-1940. Add: Glasgow 1895, 1904 and 1940; Edinburgh 1904; Milngavie 1913; Islay 1938. † BG 10, GI 79, L 5, M 1, RSA 9, RSW 2.

WILSON, David L. Exh. 1897-1900
3 Maxwell Place, Glasgow. † GI 2.

WILSON, Dora Lynell* Exh. 1923-36
c/o National Bank of Australia and c/o Bourlet & Sons, London. † ROI 14, SWA 1.

WILSON, D.R. Exh. 1880-94
Painter. Glasgow 1881; London 1884; Bushey, Herts. 1886. † GI 4, L 1, RBA 2, ROI 1.

WILSON, Miss E. Exh. 1882-91
Malton, Yorks. 1882; Oldham 1883. † B 1, L 1, M 5.

WILSON, Edgar d. 1918
Painter and illustrator. Exh. from 1886. Add: London. † I 7, RA 2, RI 1.

WILSON, Edith Exh. 1935
51 Dreghorn Loan, Edinburgh. † RSW 1.

WILSON, Ernest Exh. 1882-89
Landscape painter. Heaton Chapel, Stockport 1882; Snaresbrook, Essex 1885; Wanstead, Essex 1888. † DOW 2, M 9, RA 7, RI 4.

WILSON, Dr. Edmund A.* Exh. 1904
Watercolour painter. Exhibited bird and landscape paintings of the "Discovery" Antarctic Expedition. † BRU 287.

WILSON, E. Gertrude Exh. 1903
Flower painter. Blackrock, Southwold, Suffolk. † L 1, RA 1.

WILSON, Edward L. Exh. 1882
13 O'Connell Street, Dublin. † RHA 1.

WILSON, Eli Marsden b. 1877
Etcher and mezzotint engraver. b. Ossett, Yorks. Studied Wakefield School of Art and Royal College of Art. Married Hilda M. Pemberton, q.v. A.R.E. 1907, Exh. 1907-35. Add: London. † L 16, RA 17, RCA 35, RE 40, RSA 13.

WILSON, Francis 1876-1957
Landscape and portrait painter. b. Glasgow. Studied Glasgow School of Art, Rome, Paris and Florence. Add: Glasgow. † GI 75, L 1, M 1, RSA 14, RSW 3.

WILSON, F.G. Bassett Exh. 1923-32
Watercolour landscape painter. † FIN 59, GOU 5, LEF 1.

WILSON, F.S. Exh. 1892-93
Landscape and coastal painter. 48 Bolsover Street, London. † RBA 1, ROI 3.

WILSON, F.S. Exh. 1909
Watercolour figure painter. 51 Hoppers Road, Winchmore Hill, London. † RA 1.

WILSON, G. Exh. 1910
Watercolour painter. † GOU 1.

WILSON, George Exh. 1882-86
Painter. Glasgow 1882; London 1883. † GI 2, L 1, RI 3.

WILSON, George b. 1882
Painter and black and white artist. b. Lille, France. Studied Slade School 1920-22. Exh. 1923-27. Add: 2 Whitehall Court, London. † L 3, NEA 2, P 3, RA 3, ROI 1.

WILSON, Grace Coe Exh. 1926
426 Willow Fields, Burnley Road, Halifax. † L 1.

WILSON, George L. Exh. 1935-38
Architect. c/o C. Ripley, Staple Inn Buildings, High Holborn, London. † RA 2.

WILSON, George Renfrew Exh. 1931-40
27 Stamperland Gardens, Glasgow. † GI 1, RSA 1.

WILSON, George W.J. Exh. 1889-1910
Sculptor. London. † L 3, NG 3, RA 3, ROI 1.

WILSON, Miss H. Exh. 1933
160 Muswell Hill Road, London. † L 2.

WILSON, H. Exh. 1881
Watercolour landscape painter. 7 Neville Street, Onslow Square, London. † SWA 4.

WILSON, Hardy Exh. 1923-28
Pencil artist. London. † RA 2.

WILSON, Harold Exh. 1903-38
Artist and teacher. R.B.S.A. 1929. Add: Birmingham. † B 47, L 3.

WILSON, Mrs. Helen Exh. 1912
Etcher. Burfield, Wimbledon, London. † ALP 22.

WILSON, Henry b. 1864
Architect, sculptor and jeweller. b. Liverpool. Studied Westminster School of Art. Exh. 1888-1927. Add: London 1888; Borough Green, Kent 1904; St. Cloud, Seine et Oise, France 1923. † GI 4, I 13, M 1, NG 4, RA 31, RSA 4.

WILSON, Herbert Exh. 1880
Portrait painter. 167 Cromwell Road, London. † G 1.

WILSON, Hugh Cameron b. 1885
Figure, landscape and portrait painter and teacher. b. Glasgow. Studied Glasgow School of Art. Exh. 1911-40. Add: Glasgow. † GI 52, L 1, RSA 17.

WILSON, Mrs. H.I.T. Exh. 1936
Knaphill, Surrey. † RI 1.

WILSON, H.J. Exh. 1927
Oak Cottage, Hawes Lane, West Wickham, Kent. † RBA 1.

WILSON, Harry M. Exh. 1901-26
Landscape painter. London 1901; St. Albans, Herts. 1904. † B 2, L 3, RA 22, RCA 1, ROI 1.

WILSON, Henry M.D. Exh. 1939-40
142 Harley Street, London. † RI 2.

WILSON, Harry P. Exh. 1895
Watercolour figure painter. 61 Tufnell Park Road, London. † RA 1.

WILSON, Miss Helen Russell Exh. 1908-16
Painter and etcher. R.B.A. 1911. Add: London 1908 and 1916; Tangier, Morocco 1913. † ALP 4, LS 7, RBA 15.

WILSON, Harry Warren Exh. 1924-36
Stained glass artist. London. † RA 3.

WILSON, James Exh. 1880-81
11 Belgrave Terrace, Glasgow. † GI 3.

WILSON, James Exh. 1884
167 Fountains Road, Everton, Liverpool. † L 1.

WILSON, James Exh. 1920-37
11 Sinclaire Drive, Langside, Glasgow 1920 and 1925; New Brighton, Cheshire 1922. † GI 3, L 5.

WILSON, Jessie Exh. 1931-39
Old Colwyn, Wales. † RCA 9.

WILSON, John Exh. 1883-92
Sculptor. London. † G 7, GI 1, L 1, RA 1.

WILSON, John Exh. 1886-1904
Painter. N.S.A. 1903. Add: Nottingham 1886 and 1900; West Bridgford, Notts. 1898; London 1903. † N 19.

WILSON, John Exh. 1907-9
Edinburgh. † RSA 2.

WILSON, John Exh. 1925-28
Landscape painter and designer. b. Halifax. Studied Halifax School of Art. Teacher Liverpool School of Art. Add: Holmleigh, Shawe Green Lane, Broughton, Preston, Lancs. † L 2.

WILSON, Joseph Exh. 1937
200 St. Vincent Street, Glasgow. † GI 3.

WILSON, Judith Exh. 1926-28
80 Waterloo Road, Dublin. † RHA 2.

WILSON, John B. Exh. 1880-1908
Glasgow. † GI 24, RA 1, RSA 4.

WILSON, James C.L. Exh. 1885-1911
Watercolour landscape painter. Hillhead, Glasgow. † GI 3, WG 82.

WILSON, James Frederick b. 1887
Painter, architect, etcher and drypoint artist. Studied at the Art and Technical Institute Newport, and under P.E. Galpin and Cecil Hunt. A.R.B.A. 1919, R.B.A. 1922. Exh. 1919-27. Add: 2 Stanhope Gardens, The Drive, Ilford, Essex. † CHE 1, G 3, GOU 2, RA 3, RBA 36.

WILSON, John G. Exh. 1885-90
Glasgow. † GI 4.

WILSON, Miss J. Ker Exh. 1904
1 Southwood Road, London. † L 1.

WILSON, John L. Exh. 1880
25 Napiershall Street, Glasgow. † GI 1.

WILSON, Miss J.M. Exh. 1882-83
Banknock, Denny, N.B. † L 2.

WILSON, James M. Exh. 1926-38
Architect. London. † RA 10, RHA 1.

WILSON, John McM. Exh. 1927
Flower painter. 30 Brentmead Place, Golders Green, London. † RA 1.

WILSON, J.O. Exh. 1892
† TOO 1.

WILSON, J.T. Exh. 1880-82
Watercolour landscape painter. 9 High Street, Hastings. † RBA 4.

WILSON, J.W. Exh. 1928
Holmcroft, Thurnby, Leics. † N 3.

WILSON, James Watney Exh. 1880-89
Figure painter. London. † B 1, RA 2, RBA 3.

WILSON, Leslie Exh. 1934
67 Harwood Road, London. † RBA 1.

WILSON, Lyons b. 1892
Watercolour landscape painter. b. Leeds. Exh. 1920-40. Add: Aysgarth, Yorks. 1920; Askrigg, Yorks. 1925; Sedbergh, Yorks. 1930 and 1937; London 1932; Tiverton, Devon 1940. † ALP 1, L 8, M 2, NEA 7, RA 11.

WILSON, Mrs. Leonora B. Macgregor Exh. 1905-22
Glasgow 1905 and 1919; Dunoon, N.B. 1907. † GI 17.

WILSON, Miss M. Exh. 1911
Bexhill, Sussex. † SWA 1.

WILSON, Mrs. M. Exh. 1890-97
George Villa, Kilmalcolm, N.B. † GI 5.

WILSON, Margaret Exh. 1902-13
Married J. Hamilton Mackenzie, q.v. Add: Glasgow. † GI 26, L 2, RA 1, RSA 7, RSW 1.

WILSON, Marion Exh. 1889-97
Painter. 3 Beaumont Crescent, London. † SWA 12.

WILSON, Mary Exh. 1899
Easton Court, Chagford, South Devon. † SWA 1.

WILSON, Mary Exh. 1928-33
Landscape painter. The Barn Studio, Langton Mantravers, Dorset. † NEA 1, RA 1, ROI 1.

WILSON, Maurice Exh. 1935
Watercolour marine painter. 57½ Quentin Road, Lee, London. † RA 2.

WILSON, May Exh. 1910-36
Landscape painter. b. nr. Sheffield. Studied under Arnesby Brown. Sister of Violet and Winifred W. q.v. Add: London 1910; Beauchief Abbey, nr. Sheffield 1911; Brooke Priory, Oakham, Rutland 1928. † I 2, L 25, NEA 2, RA 6, ROI 10, SWA 5.

WILSON, Mervyn Exh. 1929-33
Landscape and flower painter. 35 Cochrane Street, London. † AB 4, RBA 1.

WILSON, Montague Exh. 1889
Sculptor. 70 Brompton Road, London. † RA 1.

WILSON, Muriel Exh. 1923-32
Painter. London. † GI 1, GOU 3, L 4, LEF 1, RSA 1, SWA 5.

WILSON, Mrs. M.E. Exh. 1917-18
Pearsonville, Lower Heysham, Lancs. † RA 2, RSA 1.

WILSON, Margaret Elizabeth Exh. 1902-32
Edinburgh. † GI 7, RSA 23, RSW 7.

WILSON, Margaret Evangeline b. 1890
Portrait, miniature and landscape painter and silver point artist. b. Boscombe, Hants. Studied R.A. Schools, Slade School, Westminster, Florence and Paris. A.R.M.S. 1929. Exh. 1919-40. Add: London. † B 3, GI 1, L 11, P 11, RA 3, RBA 2, RCA 2, RMS 6, ROI 10, RSA 11, SWA 8.

WILSON, Maria G. Exh. 1889
Flower painter. 67 Digby Road, Green Lanes, London. † GI 2, RBA 1.

WILSON, Mary G.W. Exh. 1882-1936
Pastelier of landscapes, gardens and flowers. b. Bantaskine, Falkirk. Studied Edinburgh and Paris. Add: Bantaskine, Falkirk and Edinburgh. † BG 5, CON 78, GI 18, L 7, RSA 73, SWA 2, WG 73.

WILSON, Marion H. Exh. 1893-1913
Glasgow. † GI 18, L 4.

WILSON, Mary McIntyre Exh. 1899-1919
2 North Charlotte Street, Edinburgh. † GI 3, RSA 12, RSW 1.

WILSON, Margaret O. Exh. 1893
Etcher. The Crescent, Windsor, Berks. † RA 1.

WILSON, Maggie T. Exh. 1889-1901
Cambuslang, N.B. 1889, Springburn 1892. † GI 14, RSA 3.

WILSON, Miss M.V. Marsh Exh. 1915
91 Belverdere Road, Upper Norwood, London. † RA 1.

WILSON, Mary W. Exh. 1917
50 Melville Street, Glasgow. † RSW 1.

WILSON, Mrs. Nellie Westwood Exh. 1904-11
127 Hampstead Road, Handsworth, Birmingham. † B 9.

WILSON, Oscar* 1867-1930
Genre painter. A.R.B.A. 1926, R.M.S. 1896. Add: London 1886 and 1893; Blackheath 1887; Antwerp 1891. † D 2, GI 2, L 22, M 8, RA 3, RBA 13, RCA 7, RI 2, RMS 1, ROI 25, RSA 3.

WILSON, Patten Exh. 1893-1900
Illustrator, black and white artist and frieze designer. 447 Oxford Street, London 1893; Harrow 1899. † L 1, RA 11.

WILSON, Peggy Exh. 1929
Daughter of David W. q.v. Add: 22 Downtown Avenue, London. † RBA 1.

WILSON, P. Foreshaw Exh. 1938
† M 2.

WILSON, P. Macgregor* d. 1960
Watercolour landscape painter. R.S.W. 1887. Add: Edinburgh 1880; Glasgow 1882, 1900 and 1916; Kilcreggan 1895 and 1904; Blairmore 1903; Crinan 1914. † DOW 2, GI 64, L 9, M 1, RSA 9, RSW 60.

WILSON, Mrs. P. Macgregor Exh. 1898-1901
Kilcreggan, N.B. 1898; Glasgow 1900. † GI 4.

WILSON, Ralph Exh. 1922-39
Painter. A.R.B.A. 1922, R.B.A. 1925. Add: West Wickham, Kent 1922; London 1924; Hayes, Kent 1928. † RA 1, RBA 89, RI 2.

WILSON, Robert Exh. 1895-97
3 Queen Street, Edinburgh. † RSA 3.

WILSON, R.A. Exh. 1911
Hastings House, Maxwell Road, Glasgow. † GI 1.

WILSON, Robert Arthur b. 1884
Painter, etcher and linocut artist. Studied Sunderland College of Art, Royal College of Art 1907-11, and Juliens, Paris 1911-12. Married Stella Louise W. q.v. Exh. 1927-40. Add: London. † LS 3, P 1, RA 5, RBA 1, RED 3.

WILSON, Robert B. Exh. 1935-40
Landscape painter. The Red Cottage, Westergate, nr. Chichester. † RA 1, RCA 2, ROI 1.

WILSON, Robert Francis b. 1890
Modeller, painter, etcher and teacher. b. Nottingham. Studied Nottingham School of Art. Exh. 1914-24. Add: 103 Castle Boulevard, Nottingham. † N 19.

WILSON, Sissie Exh. 1892-93
2 North Charlotte Street, Edinburgh. † GI 2, RSA 1, RSW 1.

WILSON, Stanley Exh. 1880-83
Still life painter. 28A Manchester Street, Manchester Square, London. † D 2, RBA 1.

WILSON, Sydney Ernest b. 1869
Mezzotint engraver. b. Isleworth. Exh. 1906-13. Add: Wynchmore, Harpenden, Herts. † L 13, NG 2, RA 4.

WILSON, Stella Louise Exh. 1921-40
nee Perken. Painter. Studied Camberwell School of Art. Married Robert Arthur W. q.v. Add: London. † AB 2, L 2, RA 4, SWA 8.

WILSON, Stanley R. b. 1890
Painter and engraver. Studied Goldsmiths College. Exh. 1916-37. Add: London. † BA 5, CON 28, GI 6, L 9, RA 1, RSA 1.

WILSON, Thomas Exh. 1880-1915
Edinburgh. † GI 20, L 6, RSA 49, RSW 1.

WILSON, Tryphena Exh. 1889
Cairnview, Kirkintilloch, N.B. † GI 1.

WILSON, T. Butler Exh. 1891
Architect. 12 East Parade, Leeds. † RA 1.

WILSON, T.G. Exh. 1930-38
Painter. Dublin. † RHA 17.

WILSON, Thomas Harrington Exh. 1886
Landscape, genre, portrait, literary and historical painter. 39 Beaufort Street, London. † RI 1, ROI 1.

WILSON, Thomas Millwood b. 1879
Architect. Exh. 1907-36. Add: London. † RA 15.

WILSON, T. Shaw Exh. 1930
3 Scott Street, Glasgow. † GI 2.

WILSON, Thomas Walter* 1851-1912
Landscape and architectural painter and illustrator. A.R.I. 1877, R.I. 1879, R.O.I. 1883. Add: London. † L 13, M 2, RI 16, ROI 8.

WILSON, Violet Exh. 1910-30
Landscape, animal and flower painter. b. Nr. Sheffield. Studied under Arnesby Brown. Sister of May and Winifred W. q.v. Add: Beauchief Abbey, nr. Sheffield 1910; Brooke Priory, Oakham, Rutland 1929. † L 22, RA 11, ROI 11, SWA 8.

WILSON, Vita M. Exh. 1928
2A Church Street, Liverpool. † L 1.

WILSON, Mrs. V. McGlashan Exh. 1897-1904
Cathcart, N.B. 1897; Milngavie, N.B. 1904. † GI 5.

WILSON, Hon. Lady Violet R. Exh. 1903
Sculptor. 21 Pont Street, London. † RA 1.

WILSON, W. Exh. 1884-92
Landscape and coastal painter. Dundee. † GI 4, L 2, RA 4, RSA 17.

WILSON, W. Exh. 1885-86
3 Gt. Avenham Street, Preston, Lancs. † L 3.

WILSON, William Exh. 1881-1916
Kirkaldy 1881; Blantyre 1914. † GI 4, RSA 18.

WILSON, William Exh. 1920
Hallside House, Hallside, Lanarkshire. † L 1.

WILSON, William Exh. 1937-40
Kinchracknie, Milngavie. † GI 2.

WILSON, William d. 1972
Painter, etcher and engraver. A.R.S.A. 1939. Exh. from 1932. Add: Edinburgh. † GI 12, RA 3, RSA 47, RSW 3.

WILSON, Winifred Exh. 1904-27
Painter. Studied under Arnesby Brown. Sister of May and Violet W. q.v. Add: Beauchief Abbey, nr. Sheffield 1904 and 1926; Redmires, nr. Sheffield 1917. † L 10, RA 7, ROI 9, SWA 1.

WILSON, Mrs. Winifred Exh. 1919-40
Landscape and flower and still life painter. Married David W. q.v. A.S.W.A. 1928. Add: London. † L 5, NEA 2, RA 10, RBA 7, RI 3, ROI 3, SWA 24.

WILSON, Mrs. Wright Exh. 1888-99
Birmingham 1888; Cleave Priors 1899. † B 9.

WILSON, W.C. Exh. 1881
13 O'Connell Street, Dublin. † RHA 1.

WILSON, W.C. Exh. 1926
† M 2.

WILSON, W.F. Exh. 1932
The Cottage, Middlefield Lane, Hagley, Worcs. † B 3.

WILSON, W.G. Exh. 1882-84
Glasgow. † GI 2.

WILSON, William George Exh. 1894-1914
Richmond, Surrey 1894; London 1908. † B 4, LS 18, RA 3.

WILSON, William Heath 1849-1927
Landscape and genre painter. b. Glasgow. Studied under his father, Charles Heath W. Headmaster Glasgow School of Art. Add: Florence 1880; London 1885; Betchworth, Surrey 1896; Wenhaston, Suffolk 1908. † B 1, FIN 2, G 1, GI 2, L 4, M 2, NEA 1, RA 16, RBA 15, RID 9, ROI 12. RSA 3.

WILSON, William R. Exh. 1924-29
The High School, Harcourt Street, Dublin. † RHA 8.

WILSON, Mrs. Winifred White Exh. 1938-39
Watercolour painter. Travelled widely. † GOU 54, P 1.

WILSON-HAFFENDEN, Elizabeth Exh. 1928
Watercolour figure painter. 32 Fairdene Road, Coulsdon, Surrey. † RA 1.

WILTHEW, Guy 1876-1913
Figure and portrait painter. R.O.I. 1909. Add: Hatfield, Herts. 1903; London 1905. † L 1, LS 2, NEA 1, NG 1, RA 8, ROI 18.

WILTHEW-SMITH, G. Exh. 1902
The Tree Cottage, Walmer, Kent. † ROI 1.

WILTON, Ellen Exh. 1908
Whatmer Hall, Sturry, Kent. † L 1.

WILTON, Miss K. Exh. 1882-83
127 Broad Street, Birmingham. † B 4.

WILTON, Lois C. Exh. 1931
Studio 3, 5 Church Street, London. † RSA 1.

WILTON, Olive M. Exh. 1904-12
29 St. Johns Wood Park, London. † GI 9, L 7.

WILTSHIRE, Miss D. Exh. 1906-9
Miniature portrait painter. Bushey, Herts. 1906: Frome, Somerset 1907. † L 1, RA 4.

WIMBUSH, Henry B. Exh. 1881-1908
Watercolour landscape painter. London. † AG 1, B 2, D 7, FIN 311, L 3, M 7, RA 4, RI 1.

WIMBUSH, H.M. Exh. 1919
Watercolour landscape painter. Woodcote, Weybridge, Surrey. † RA 1.

WIMBUSH, John L.* d. 1914
Painter and black and white artist. London 1881 and 1889; Addiscombe, Surrey 1881; Penge, Kent 1882; Dartmouth, Devon 1902. † B 1, L 5, M 1, RA 9, RBA 7.

WIMBUSH, Ruth Exh. 1890-91
Painter. Etchington Park, Finchley, London. † RA 1, RBA 1, RI 1.

WIMBUSH, Miss W. Exh. 1911
Saltley Lodge, Broadwater, Worthing, Sussex. † RA 1.

WIMPENNY, G.H. Exh. 1907
209 King Street, Oldham, Lancs. † M 1.

WIMPERIS, Miss D. Exh. 1894-97
38 High Road, Streatham, London. † RBA 2, RI 6.

WIMPERIS, Edmund Exh. 1925-34
Watercolour painter and architectural designer. London. † RI 12, WG 154.

WIMPERIS, Edmund Morison* 1835-1900
Landscape painter and watercolourist and illustrator. b. Chester. Studied Wood engraving under Mason Jackson. Contributed to "Illustrated London News". R.B.A. 1870, A.R.I. 1872, R.I. 1875, V.P.R.I. 1895, R.O.I. 1883. Add: London. † AG 2, B 6, DOW 221, FIN 1, L 10, M 5, NG 13, RBA 2, RI 126, ROI 45, TOO 30.

WIMPERIS, J. Exh. 1880
Landscape painter. Croyde, Barnstaple, Devon. † SWA 1.

WIMPERIS, John T. Exh. 1882-87
Architect. 15 Sackville Street, Piccadilly, London. † RA 4, RI 2.

WIMPY, Charles Exh. 1893
Watercolour portrait painter. 365 Goldhawk Road, London. † RA 1.

WIMSHURST, Miss D.M. Exh. 1912-14
Cintra, Merilocks Road, Blundellsands, Liverpool. † L 5.

WIMSHURST, Vera T. Exh. 1924
10 Palace Gardens Mansions, London. † L 1.

WINAN, Miss G. Exh. 1903
11 Eaton Terrace, Avenue Road, London. † SWA 1.

WINANS, Eva Exh. 1908
Surrenden Park, Pluckley, Kent. † LS 5.

WINANS, Walter Exh. 1894-1920
Sculptor. London 1894 and 1915; Pluckley, Kent 1909. † GI 4, I 1, L 4, LS 6, RA 14.

WINBY, Frederic Charles b. 1875
Painter and etcher. b. Newport, Mon. Studied Slade School and Juliens, Paris. Married Joan W. q.v. Exh. 1909-39. Add: London. † LS 4, RA 1, RI 10.

WINBY, Joan Exh. 1925-34
nee Powell. Watercolour landscape painter. Married Frederic Charles W. q.v. Add: 50 Addison Avenue, London. † RA 1, RI 2, SWA 1.

WINCH, Gertrude D. Exh. 1929
Watercolour landscape painter. † AB 3, NEA 2.

WINCHELSEA, Countess of Exh. 1887
23 Ennismore Gardens, London. † D 2.

WINDASS, Miss Lily Exh. 1913
The Hall, Osbaldwick, Yorks. † RHA 1.

WINDASS, John Exh. 1884-1912
Landscape and coastal painter and teacher. York. † B 1, L 1, M 1, RA 4, RBA 1, RCA 7, RHA 26.

WINDASS, James E. Exh. 1899
13 Priory Street, York. † RHA 1.

WINDER, Miss L. Exh. 1885
Woodgate, Sutton Coldfield, Warwicks. † B 1.

WINDER, W.C. Exh. 1885
Painter. 7 New Street, Covent Gardens, London. † ROI 1.

WINDER, W. Smallwood Exh. 1900-10
Landscape painter. R.B.A. 1903. Add: Carlisle 1900; Kendal 1904. † D 1, L 2, RA 6, RBA 44, RI 2, RSA 1.

WINDHAM, Rachel Exh. 1936-39
Painter. Clifton, Shefford, Beds. † RA 1, RBA 1.

WINDLEY, H.C. Exh. 1921
Cricklade, Wilts. † RA 1.

WINDLEY, Maude R. Exh. 1906-35
Sculptor. London 1906; Leicester 1907. † B 2, L 1, RA 9.

WINDMAIER, Anton* Exh. 1882-95
Landscape painter. Manchester 1882; Paris 1883. † GI 1, M 1, TOO 12.

WINDSOR, Mrs. M.F. Exh. 1937
Cardiff. † RCA 1.

WINDT, G. Exh. 1895
10 Paleisstraat, The Hague, Holland. † GI 1.

WINDT, T. Exh. 1888
Painter. † FIN 1.

WINDUS, William Lindsay* 1822-1907
Painter. Studied under William Daniels and at Liverpool Academy. Exh. 1896-99. Add: London. † NEA 5.

WING, A. Exh. 1903
124 Holme Road, West Bridgford, Notts. † N 1.

WING, Frank F. Exh. 1934
Painter. 116 Stanfell Road, Leicester. † RA 1.

WING, Miss M.L. Exh. 1882-89
Tunbridge Wells, Kent 1882; Liverpool 1889. † L 2.

WING, Miss S.M. Exh. 1895
Brackendene, Upper Tooting, London. † L 1.

WINGATE, Alexander Exh. 1905-6
4 Bowmont Terrace, Glasgow. † GI 2.

WINGATE, Anna M.B. Exh. 1899-1908
Figure and portrait painter. The Manse, Stromness, Orkney 1899; Edinburgh 1902; Colinton, Midlothian 1907. † L 4, RA 3, RSA 6.

WINGATE, Helen Ainslie Exh. 1911-38
Mrs. Thornton. Add: Slateford, N.B. 1911; Edinburgh 1915. † GI 10, L 4, RSA 25, RSW 11.

WINGATE, J. Crawford Paterson
Exh. 1880-1912
Glasgow. † GI 24, L 10, RSA 8.

WINGATE, Mrs. J.C. Paterson
Exh. 1896-1900
Glasgow. † GI 3, RSA 1.

WINGATE, James Lawton* 1846-1924
Landscape, animal and figure painter. A.R.S.A. 1879, R.S.A. 1886, P.R.S.A. 1919-23. Add: Edinburgh 1880 and 1913; Muthill, Perthshire 1887; Colinton 1888; Slateford 1901. † AG 2, BAR 1, GI 31, L 5 M 3, RA 12, RHA 1, RSA 170.

WINGATE, John W. Exh. 1926
† M 1.

WINGFIELD, Hon. Mrs. Exh. 1890
16 Duke Street, Manchester Square, London. † SWA 1.

WINGFIELD, Joan Exh. 1929-32
Caer Rhun, Conway, Wales. † RCA 6.

WINGFIELD, Molly Exh. 1932-34
Watercolour painter. The Castle, Tiverton, Devon. † RA 1, RI 3.

WINKFIELD, Frederick A.*
Exh. 1880-1914
Landscape and coastal painter. 59 Britannia Road, Fulham, London. † B 32, D 2, L 11, M 37, RA 16, RBA 23, RHA 3, RI 6, ROI 8.

WINKLER, John W. b. 1890
Etcher. b. Austria. Exh. 1925. Add: 148 New Bond Street, London. † CON 3, FIN 56, RHA 7.

WINKLES, Mrs. G.M. Exh. 1914
c/o Chapman Bros. 241 Kings Road, Chelsea, London. † RA 2.

WINKLES, Geo M. Exh. 1883-1915
Birmingham 1883; Northwood, Middlesex 1910; c/o Chapman Bros., Kings Road, Chelsea, London 1915. † B 5, RA 1, RCA 1.

WINKLEY, Alice Exh. 1910
11 Gildredge Road, Eastbourne. † RHA 2.

WINDMILL, Charles G. Exh. 1891
Architect. 14 Ham Frith Road, Stratford, London. † RA 1.

WINN, Constance A. Exh. 1939
Aldeburgh, Suffolk. † RBA 1, RI 2.

WINN, Leslie H. Exh. 1907-33
Coombe Cottage, Luton Road, Harpenden, Herts. † RCA 6, RI 2.

WINN, Mrs. Marie Exh. 1901-7
121 King Edward Road, Hackney, London. † L 1, RI 3.

WINN, Susan Exh. 1886
Flower painter. 31 Burnt Ash Lane, Lee, London. † SWA 1.

WINN, Thomas J.R. Exh. 1934-40
Architect. Epsom, Surrey 1934; Sutton, Surrey 1939. † RA 8.

WINNEY, Theodora Exh. 1931
Landscape painter. 19 Tyson Road, Forest Hill, London. † RA 1.

WINNICOTT, Alice Buxton b. 1891
nee Taylor. Painter, potter and modeller. Studied St. John's Wood School of Art and Central School of Art. Principal designer Claverdon Pottery from 1935. Exh. 1933-37. Add: London. † RA 1, RCA 3.

WINSER, Jose Exh. 1923
† SWA 2.

WINSER, Josephine Exh. 1939
Painter. 908 Nell Gwynn House, London. † RA 1.

WINSER, Margaret Exh. 1904-29
Sculptor. London 1904; Ratsberry, Tenterdon, Kent 1909. † GI 1, RA 16.

WINSLOE, Phil Exh. 1908-18
28 Montgomerie Street, Glasgow. † GI 9, L 10, RSA 3.

WINSLOW, Henry* b. 1874
Painter and etcher. b. Boston. Studied Academie des Beaux Arts and Whistler's School, Paris. Married Helen Stirling W. q.v. Exh. 1912-40. Add: London. † FIN 50, GI 1, I 1, L 2, NEA 3, P 8, RA 17, RBA 3, RSA 4.

WINSLOW, Helen Stirling b. 1890
nee Thomas. Painter. Studied in Italy. Married Henry W. q.v. A.S.W.A. 1938, S.W.A. 1939. Exh. 1935-40. Add: London. † RA 1, RBA 5, RI 1, SWA 10.

WINSLOW, Rachel Exh. 1911-16
Landscape painter. London. † L 2, LS 12, NEA 1.

WINSTANLEY, Annie G. Exh. 1926
† M 1.

WINSTON, C.B. Exh. 1929
Painter. † GOU 1.

WINTER, Miss A. Exh. 1893
Flower painter. 124 Christchurch Road, Tulse Hill, London. † RBA 1.

WINTER, Gp. Capt. Alexander Charles
b. 1887
Landscape painter. b. Bradenham. Self taught. Exh. 1938-39. Add: Bramley Grange Hotel, Bramley, Surrey. † GOU 52, RSA 1.

WINTER, Edmund Exh. 1885-1904
Liscard, Cheshire 1885 and 1904; Liverpool 1887; Egremont, Cheshire 1891; Wallasey, Cheshire 1900. † L 10.

WINTER, Eric b. 1905
Painter and illustrator. Studied Hornsey School of Art 1921-29. Exh. 1933. Add: 51 Chalfont Road, Lower Edmonton, London. † RA 1.

WINTER, F. Exh. 1898
20 Mansfield Grove, Addison Street, Nottingham. † N 1.

WINTER, Frederick Exh. 1880-99
Sculptor. London. † L 3, RA 18, RBA 7.

WINTER, Francis J. Exh. 1939-40
Watercolour landscape painter. 70 Langham Gardens, Grange Park, London. † RA 1, RI 3.

WINTER, Miss G.M. Exh. 1905-11
Beechwood, The Park, Hull. † B 2, L 3, M 2.

WINTER, J. Greenwood Exh. 1891-1914
Painter. Chelsea, London. † NEA 3, RA 1, RBA 2, RI 1, ROI 2.

WINTER, Mildred Exh. 1899
17 Reservoir Retreat, Edgbaston, Birmingham. † B 1.

WINTER, Mrs. Marjorie D. Exh. 1909-34
Miniature portrait painter and enamelist. A.R.M.S. 1919. Add: London 1909; Dunmow, Essex 1934. † L 18, RA 12, RMS 18.

WINTER, Miss N. Exh. 1905
Carleton Villas, Penrith, Cumberland. † RI 1.

WINTER, Robert Exh. 1900
Mildenhall, Suffolk. † RI 1.

WINTER, Richard Davidson Exh. 1890-1916
Etcher. London. † L 2, RA 5.

WINTER, William Tatton* 1855-1928
Landscape painter. b. Ashton under Lyne. Studied Manchester Academy of Fine Arts and under Verlat at Antwerp. R.B.A. 1896. Add: Carshalton, Surrey 1885; Reigate, Surrey 1897. † B 23, D 8, FIN 34, GI 15, I 1, L 13, M 14, NG 12, RA 32, RBA 294, RHA 2, RI 43, ROI 16, WG 274.

WINTERBOTHAM, H. Exh. 1935
4 Camelot Crescent, Ruddington, Notts. † N 1.

WINTERBOTTOM, Austin Exh. 1887-1906
Landscape painter. Sheffield. † M 1, RA 4, RBA 1.

WINTERBOTTOM, J. Ernest Exh. 1926
† M 2.

WINTERBOTTOM, W.T. Exh. 1883
64 Lilly Street, Queen's Road, Manchester. † M 1.

WINTER-WILSON, Mrs. Edith M. Exh. 1936
Starwood, Thorntree Drive, Denton, Newcastle on Tyne. † B 1.

WINTHROP, A.G. Exh. 1898
82 Cromwell Road, London. † D 2.

WINTOUR, John Crawford* 1825-1882
Painter. A.R.S.A. 1859. Exh. 1880-81. Add: 30 Hamilton Place, Edinburgh. † GI 6, RSA 14.

WINTOUR, William Sen. Exh. 1883
Hawthornbank, Murrayfield, Edinburgh. † RSA 1.

WINTOUR, William junr. Exh. 1880-84
Edinburgh. † RSA 10.

WINZER, Charles F. b. 1886
Painter and lithographer. b. Warsaw, Poland. Travelled widely. Exh. 1926. † TOO 24.

WIPPELL, E.G. Exh. 1925
The Homestead, Greet, Winchcombe, Glos. † B 1.

WIRE, T. Cyril Exh. 1939
46 Southbrae Drive, Glasgow. † RSA 4.

WIRGMAN, Frances b. 1888
Portrait and landscape painter in oils, watercolour miniaturist, pastelier and teacher. b. Birkenhead. Studied Southport School of Art, London School of Art and Stratford Studios. Exh. 1910-40. Add: Southport, Lancs. † L 25, RCA 6, RSA 2.

WIRGMAN, Theodore Blake* 1848-1925
Portrait, genre, historical and literary painter. R.P. 1891. Add: London 1880, 1886 and 1909; St. Ives, Hunts. 1908. † B 6, BG 2, G 1, GI 20, L 31, M 21, NG 2, P 132, RA 79, RHA 1, RI 6, RID 10, ROI 4.

WIRSING, H. Exh. 1905
72 Schwanthalerstrasse, Munich, Germany. † RA 1.

WISDISH, Wilfred C. Exh. 1936-39
Landscape painter. 129 Devana Road, Leicester. † N 7.

WISE, Constance E. Exh. 1910-39
Miniature portrait painter. London. † RA 49, RMS 5.

WISE, Miss D. Stanton Exh. 1900-13
Sculptor. London. † GI 1, L 8, M 10, RA 3.

WISE, Ernest E. Exh. 1920
Lithographer. 22 Jessamy Road, Weybridge, Surrey. † RA 1.

WISE, Miss E.H. Exh. 1886
Woodside, Colliers Wood, Merton. † B 1.

WISE, Hilda Exh. 1919-21
Miniature portrait painter. 3 Garway Road, Bayswater, London. † L 1, RA 1, SWA 1.

WISE, Henry T. Exh. 1905
5 Craighouse Terrace, Edinburgh. † RSA 1.

WISE, Miss M. Exh. 1915
Windrush, Chapel-en-le-Frith. † L 3.

WISE, Percy Arthur Exh. 1914
Painter and designer for industrial arts. b. Solihull, Warwicks. Studied Birmingham School of Art and Royal College of Art. Principal Darlington, Carmarthen and Poole Schools of Art. Add: 4 Cleveland Terrace, Darlington 1914; Parkstone, Dorset 1927. † RA 1.

WISE, Rosamond Exh. 1928
16 Danvers Street, Chelsea, London. † NEA 1.

WISELY, L. Exh. 1899
56 Argo Road, Waterloo, Liverpool. † L 1.

WISEMAN, S.G. Exh. 1937
† RMS 1.

WISEMAN, Thomas Thorburn Exh. 1888-1913
Hamilton, N.B. 1888; Dublin 1899. † GI 2, RHA 7.

WISH, Louisa Exh. 1902
9 Victoria Terrace, Exeter, Devon. † RI 1.

WISHAAR, Miss G.N. Exh. 1915
49 Boulevard du Montparnasse, Paris. † RA 3.

WISHART, Dora Exh. 1940
South Seafield, 458 Gt. Western Road, Aberdeen. † RSA 1.

WISHART, Peter 1852-1932
Landscape painter. A.R.S.A. 1925. Exh. from 1880. Add: Edinburgh. † GI 25, L 2, M 2, RHA 4, RSA 114, RSW 18.

WISHAW, A.Y. Exh. 1892-1911
New Brighton, Cheshire 1892; Arnside, Westmorland 1911. † B 3, L 1.

WISKIN, Winnifred Steel Exh. 1910-23
Miniature portrait painter. 11 Cedars Road, Beckenham, Kent. † RA 3, RSA 3.

WISSAERT, Paul Exh. 1915-17
Edinburgh 1915; London 1916. † GI 1, L 2, RSA 5.

WITCHELL, Lucy Exh. 1891
Watercolour bird painter. The Acre, Stroud, Glos. † RA 1.

WITCOMBE, John d. 1918
R.B.A. 1912. Exh. from 1909. Add: 10 Edward Street, Bath. † GI 7, I 2, L 7, RBA 38.

WITHAM, Sylvia Mills Exh. 1925
† GOU 2.

WITHAM, Walter Exh. 1894-96
Liverpool. † L 2.

WITHERBY, Miss Exh. 1897
Albury Heath, Guildford, Surrey. † SWA 2.

WITHERBY, Arthur George Exh. 1910-19
Portrait painter. Newton Grange, Newbury, Berks. † LS 6, WG 21.

WITHERBY, Henry Forbes d. 1907
Landscape and flower painter. R.B.A. 1904. Add: Blackheath 1893; Burley, New Forest 1902. † D 35, L 3, M 3, RA 4, RBA 23.

WITHEROP, J. Coburn b. 1906
Painter and engraver. Studied Liverpool City School of Art and Royal College of Art. Exh. 1933-40. Add: 5 Redvers Drive, Liverpool. † GI 1, L 2, M 1, RA 4, RHA 1.

WITHEROW, Mrs. Nina Exh. 1908-20
London. † LS 4, SWA 3.

WITHERS, Alfred 1865-1932
Landscape and architectural painter. Married to Isabelle A. Dods-Withers q.v. R.O.I. 1897. Member of Society of 25 Artists. Add: Bromley, Kent 1881 and 1899; Dorking, Surrey 1886; London 1889 and 1903. † B 3, FIN 3, G 7, GI 4, GOU 1, I 45, L 13, LEI 31, M 6, NG 19, RA 25, RBA 2, RE 5, RID 21, ROI 45, RSA 4.

WITHERS, Annie E.J. Exh. 1890-1908
Painter. Epsom, Surrey 1890; London 1893. † L 2, NG 2, P 4, RA 4, RHA 1, ROI 1.

WITHERS, Henry B. Exh. 1901-24
Landscape painter. A.R.B.A. 1919. Add: Watford, Herts. † D 2, L 5, RA 11, RBA 25, RI 2.

WITHERS, J.B. Mitchell Exh. 1902
Architect. 73 Surrey Street, Sheffield. † RA 2.

WITHERS, Kate Exh. 1889
Salop House, West Smethwick, Birmingham. † B 1.

WITHERS, Miss M. Exh. 1903
Lowlands, West Derby, Liverpool. † L 1.

WITHERS, Maud Exh. 1880-85
Flower painter. London. † D 1, SWA 5.

WITHERS, Mabel H.M. Exh. 1904-10
Benslow Lane, Hitchin, Herts. † RA 1, SWA 4.

WITHERS, Robert Jewell Exh. 1882-83
Architect. 11 Adam Street, Adelphi, London. † RA 5.

WITHERS-LEE, R.W. Exh. 1884-95
Manchester. † L 1, M 3, RHA 4.

WITHERSPOON, Henry Robert Exh. 1909
† LS 2.

WITHEY, B.B. Exh. 1932-37
95 Raglan Road, Smethwick, Birmingham. † B 11.

WITHNALL, A.G.H. Exh. 1921-22
Portrait painter. Ivy Cottage, Burton Road, Gedling, Notts. † N 2.

WITHROW, Eva Exh. 1898-99
Figure painter. 3 Bolton Studios, Redcliffe Road, London. † M 1, NG 1, RA 1.

WITHYCOMBE, Joyce Exh. 1933
Landscape painter. West End Lodge, West End, Southampton. † RA 1.

WITHYCOMBE, John G. Exh. 1909-10
R.B.A. 1909. Add: Dedham, Essex 1909; East Bergholt, Suffolk 1910. † RBA 11.

WITHYCOMBE, Margaret Exh. 1931-32
Sculptor. Southampton. † RA 3.

WITNEY, Alan H. Exh. 1936-39
Portrait painter. London 1936 and 1939; Southampton 1938. † P 1, RA 2, RBA 4.

WITSEN, Willem* 1860-1923
Dutch etcher. Exh. 1885-1913. Add: Utrecht, Holland 1885; Amsterdam 1904. † FIN 13, I 3, L 1.

WITT, de See D

WITT, Miss E.M. Exh. 1904-5
Champion Hill House, Champion Hill, London. † SWA 2.

WITTER, Arthur R. Exh. 1882-1904
Watercolour landscape painter. Liverpool 1882; Danbury, Essex 1904. † B 1, L 22, M 2, RA 4, RBA 1, RI 1.
WITTER, W.G. Exh. 1882-93
Landscape painter. Liverpool. † L 5, M 6, RA 1.
WITTET, G. Exh. 1918
Public Works Dept., Bombay. † RSA 5.
WITTIG, Edward b. 1881
Polish sculptor. Exh. 1906. Add: 62 Rue Barque, Paris. † RA 1.
WITTRUP, J.S. Exh. 1937
P.O. Box 6908, Johannesburg, South Africa. † RBA 1.
WIVELL, Mrs. E.O. Exh. 1933
14 Victoria Mount, Oxton, Birkenhead. † L 1.
WOAKES, Mrs. Maud Exh. 1908
88 Fellowes Road, London. † L 1.
WODEHOUSE, Mrs. F. Exh. 1901-13
Gotham Rectory, Derby. † N 9.
WODEHOUSE, Miss M. Exh. 1910-11
Gotham Rectory, Derby. † N 3.
WOESTYNE, Van de See V
WOHLFORD-HANSON, C.W. Exh. 1932
Etcher. 16 Lower Northdown Road, Margate, Kent. † RA 1.
WOHLMANN, J.B. Exh. 1888-89
Fore Street, Hertford. † B 2.
WOLF, Elizabeth Exh. 1939
Portrait painter. 6 South Drive, Ruislip, Middlesex. † RA 1.
WOLF, Franz Exh. 1922
c/o F. Fawcett, National and Provincial and Union Bank of England, London. † GI 1, I 1.
WOLF, Henry 1852-1916
American wood engraver. Exh. 1905-10. Add: c/o J. Pennell, 14 Buckingham Street, Strand, London. † I 45, L 2.
WOLF, Joseph* 1820-1899
Animal and bird painter, lithographer and illustrator. b. nr. Coblenz, Germany. Apprenticed for 3 years to Brothers Becker, Lithographers of Coblenz. Came to England 1848 and obtained employment at the British Museum. R.I. 1874. Add: 2 Primrose Hill Studios, Fitzroy Road, London 1880. † RI 4.
WOLFE, Edward* b. 189
Landscape, figure and flower painter. b. South Africa. Member London Group 1923. Exh. 1922-39. Add: London. † AG 1, BK 3, CHE 5, COO 23, G 2, GOU 6, L 1, LEF 10, LEI 10, M 5, NEA 1, RED 6.
WOLFE, Miss E.C. Exh. 1898
Kensington Gore, London. † SWA 1.
WOLFE, Edith Grace See WHEATLEY
WOLFE, Mrs. Jessie Exh. 1938
† NEA 2.
WOLFENDEN, Agnes Exh. 1909
Fernsholme, Rainhill. † L 1.
WOLFERS, Marcel b. 1886
Sculptor and lacquer artist. b. Brussels. Studied under J. de Rudder. Exh. 1931. Add: 18 Rue de Pratere, Brussels. † RSA 5.
WOLFF, or WOLFF-FURTH, Mrs. Elizabeth Exh. 1934-40
Sculptor. Berlin Schoenenberg, Germany 1934; Belsize Park Gardens, London 1940. † RA 3.
WOLFF, Gustav b. 1863
Sculptor. b. Germany. Exh. 1936. † RSA 1.
WOLFF-ZAMZOW, P. Exh. 1905
77 Gabelsbergerstrasse, Munich, Germany. † I 1.

WOLINSKI, J. Exh. 1913-15
270 Elgin Avenue, Maida Vale, London. † RA 2.
WOLKOFF, Mrs. Barbara Exh. 1931-38
Painter of flowers and children. † WG 356.
WOLLACOT, G. Exh. 1938
Torquay, Devon. † RCA 1.
WOLLEN, William Barns* 1857-1936
Military, sporting and portrait painter. b. Leipzig. R.I. 1888, R.O.I. 1897, H.R.O.I. 1934. Add: London. † B 5, GI 3, L 16, M 6, RA 35, RHA 2, RI 71, ROI 50, RSA 1.
WOLMARK, Alfred Aaran* 1877-1961
Painter and designer. b. Warsaw. Studied R.A. Schools. Add: London. † ALP 1, B 2, BG 30, CHE 2, COO 34, G 1, GI 4, GOU 19, I 16, L 8, LEF 52, LS 31, M 4, NEA 3, NG,1, P 14, RA 15, RHA 15, ROI 1.
WOLSELEY, Amy L. Exh. 1910-14
London. † LS 6, RA 1.
WOLSELEY, Garnet Ruskin b. 1884
Landscape, figure, portrait and flower painter. Studied Slade School. Exh. 1909-34. Add: Newlyn, Cornwall 1909; Hove 1919; Steyning, Sussex 1920; London 1934. † BA 3, COO 39, FIN 41, G 1, I 2, L 24, NEA 1, RA 11, RHA 4, RI 5, ROI 6.
WOLSEY, Florence Exh. 1893-1910
Figure painter. Shelford Lodge, Peckham Road, Camberwell, London. † RBA 2, RHA 2, SWA 2.
WOLSTENHOLME, Harry Vernon b. 1864
Architect. b. Manchester. Exh. 1912. Add: Billinge-ende, Blackburn, Lancs. † RA 1.
WOLSTENHOLME, Miss M. Exh. 1923-25
Leylands, Bolton le Sands, via Carnforth, Lancs. † L 3.
WOLTZE, Berthold* 1829-1896
German painter. Exh. 1881. Add: c/o F.F. Abbey, Huddersfield. † RA 1.
WONTNER, William Clarke* 1857-1930
Portrait painter. Exh. 1881-1912. Examples of work in the National Portrait Gallery and Glasgow Art Gallery. 1 Edwards Square Studios, Kensington; Ripple, Worcs. † D 3, GI 3, L 13, M 3, NG 29, P 5, RA 32, RBA 1, RI 1, ROI 5, RSA 1. Cousin of SMITH, C. Wontner (q.v.).
WOOD, A. Exh. 1891
Painter. 9 Lenton Avenue, Nottingham. † N 1.
WOOD, Mrs. A. Exh. 1887-88
Liverpool. † B 1, L 2.
WOOD, Mrs. Ada Exh. 1891-92
Highclere, Surbiton Hill Park, Surbiton, Surrey. † B 2.
WOOD, Agatha Exh. 1931
† GOU 3.
WOOD, Miss A.A. Exh. 1896
30 Crescent Road, Bromley, Kent. † ROI 1.
WOOD, A.F. Exh. 1884
25 Glengarry Road, Champion Hill, London. † L 1.
WOOD, Alice Florence Rapley Exh. 1910-37
Landscape, flower and miniature portrait painter. Studied Putney School of Art and Lambeth. A.R.M.S. 1911. Add: London 1910 and 1930; Jaffa, Palestine 1924. † L 6, RA 9, RMS 12, ROI 2, SWA 1, WG 52.
WOOD, Miss A.G. Exh. 1929
47 St. Johns Road, London. † SWA 1.
WOOD, A.J. Carter d. 1915
Landscape painter. Newlyn, Penzance 1907; Paul, Penzance 1908; Ulverston, Lancs. 1910; Silloth, Cumberland 1911. † L 7, RA 5.

WOOD, A.L. Exh. 1928
Arden, Stretton under Fosse, Rugby. † B 5.
WOOD, Mrs. A. Marke Exh. 1924
Walmer Place, Deal, Kent. † L 3.
WOOD, Alice M. Exh. 1915-24
35 Bennetthorpe, Doncaster. † B 2, L 5.
WOOD, Alice M.C. Exh. 1885-86
Keithick, Coupar, Angus. † GI 4, RSA 2.
WOOD, Albert Salisbury Exh. 1896-1928
Landscape painter. Bodlondeb, Conway 1896; Rye, Sussex 1905; Gorsefield, Llanfairfechan 1907; Deganwy, Wales 1911. † L 23, RA 3, RCA 33, ROI 6.
WOOD, Mrs. Annetta T.H. Exh. 1890
Miniature portrait painter. Victoria Cottage, Albert Road, Kensington, London. † RA 1.
WOOD, A. Victor Exh. 1923
Doncrea Lodge, Kilcoll, Co. Wicklow. † RHA 1.
WOOD, Christopher* 1901-1930
Painter and theatrical designer. b. Knowsley, nr. Liverpool. Studied Julians, Paris. Travelled widely in Europe, North Africa, and the Mediterranean. Killed by a train on Salisbury station. † BA 18, GOU 3, TOO 33.
WOOD, Charles Bernard Exh. 1903-34
Painter. Stoke on Trent. † RA 2, RI 1, RCA 11.
WOOD, Charles Haigh* 1856-1927
Genre and portrait painter and etcher. b. Bury, Lancs. Studied R.A. Schools. A.R.E. 1917. Add: London 1880 and 1890; Bury, Lancs. 1881; Taplow, Bucks. 1889. † L 14, M 7, RA 42, RBA 2, RE 12, RI 1, ROI 8.
WOOD, Catherine M. Exh. 1880-1939
Still life, flower and genre painter. Studied Royal Female School of Art. Married Richard Henry Wright q.v. A.S.W.A. 1889, S.W.A. 1893. Add: London. † B 11, BG 1, G 1, GI 32, L 38, M 5, NEA 3, RA 97, RBA 26, RE 2, RHA 7, ROI 32, RSA 12, SWA 35, WG 513.
WOOD, Charles R. Exh. 1899-1929
Liverpool. † L 6.
WOOD, Daniel Exh. 1882
7 Spring Terrace, Cambridge. † L 1.
WOOD, Mrs. Dolly Exh. 1917-19
Miniature portrait painter. Kingston Hill, Surrey. † RA 4.
WOOD, Donald Exh. 1919-39
Portrait, landscape and figure painter. Leeds 1919; Warcop, Westmorland 1922; London 1931. † AR 107, B 1, L 1, P 1, RA 2, RHA 1, RI 8, RMS 1, ROI 3, RSA 1.
WOOD, Douglas Exh. 1930
Architect. 55 Craven Street, Strand, London. † RA 2.
WOOD, D. Frances Exh. 1930
Watercolour landscape painter. 10 Elms Road, Dulwich Village, London. † RA 1.
WOOD, Dorothea M. Exh. 1901
Portrait painter. Monk's Risborough Rectory, Princes Risborough, Bucks. † RA 1.
WOOD, Miss E. Exh. 1890
1 Field Court, Crawley, Sussex. † SWA 1.
WOOD, Miss E. Exh. 1912
West Malling, Surrey. † SWA 1.
WOOD, Edgar Exh. 1895-1934
Architect. 79 Cross Street, Manchester. † RA 24.
WOOD, Elsie Exh. 1893
Landscape painter. Hardwick Road, The Park, Nottingham. † N 1.
WOOD, Eric Exh. 1930
Still life and flower painter. † FIN 2.

WOOD, Eliza Annie Exh. 1887-99
Painter. London. † B 1, RBA 2, ROI 1.

WOOD, Edith F. Carter Exh. 1910
Skimburness, Silloth, Cumberland. † L 1.

WOOD, E.L. Exh. 1891-92
Antwerp. † M 2.

WOOD, Miss E.L. Exh. 1890
23 Stockwell Road, London. † SWA 1.

WOOD, Mrs. E.M. Exh. 1892
3 South Villas, Liscard, Cheshire. † L 1.

WOOD, E. Marshall Exh. 1936-39
London. † SWA 3.

WOOD, Eleanor Stuart Exh. 1882-1910
Fruit, flower and portrait painter. Add: Manchester 1882; Liverpool 1903; Southport, Lancs. 1904. † G 1, GI 2, L 20, M 37, RA 1, RBA 1.

WOOD, Emmie Stewart d. 1937
Landscape painter. Studied Slade School and Juliens, Paris. A.S.W.A. 1887, S.W.A. 1893. Add: London. † B 4, BG 1, D 1, G 10, GI 27, I 2, L 23, LS 11, M 24, NEA 4, NG 23, RA 44, RBA 3, RI 7, ROI 15, RSA 2, SWA 44.

WOOD, Edgar Thomas Exh. 1885-1915
Landscape and architectural painter. London. † B 11, GI 1, L 3, LS 12, M 3, RA 4, RBA 7, RCA 10, RHA 6, RI 2.

WOOD, F. Exh. 1935
Linocut artist. † RED 1.

WOOD, Francis Exh. 1923
Architect. Municipal Offices, Town Hall Street, Blackpool. † RA 1.

WOOD, Frank Exh. 1931-38
Landscape, flower and figure painter. 81 Hastings Street, Sunderland. † NEA 1, RA 9, RSA 5.

WOOD, Francis Derwent 1871-1926
Sculptor. b. Keswick. Studied Royal College of Art 1889-91 and R.A. Schools (travelling scholarship and gold medal 1895). A.R.A. 1910, R.A. 1920. "Henry James" purchased by Chantrey Bequest 1914, "Psyche" purchased 1919, and "Bess Norriss" (1921-22) purchased 1926. Add: Paris 1895; London 1900. † G 10, GI 10, GOU 15, I 10, L 18, NEA 2, NG 19, P 7, RA 106, RHA 1, RI 5, ROI 1, RSA 15.

WOOD, Francis G. Exh. 1906-7
Artist and teacher. Oak Bank, Fairfield, Manchester. † L 1, M 1.

WOOD, Mrs. Fanny M. Russ Exh. 1911-33
Shrewsbury 1911 and 1930; Cheadle Hume, Cheshire 1914; Iffley, Oxford 1932. † B 6, I 1, L 2, M 3, RA 3.

WOOD, Frank Watson 1862-1953
Marine painter. b. Berwick on Tweed. Studied Kensington and Juliens, Paris. Second master Newcastle School of Art 1883-89. Headmaster Hawick School of Art 1889-99. Add: Newcastle on Tyne 1889; Hawick 1898; Berwick on Tweed 1901; Edinburgh 1929. † GI 5, RA 1, RSA 15, RSW 8.

WOOD, Geoffrey Arthur Exh. 1919-20
6 Pelham Street, Ilkeston, Derbys. † N 3.

WOOD, G. Swinford Exh. 1888-1906
Landscape painter. Conway, Wales. † B 1, G 2, L 5, M 2, RA 1, RCA 90, RHA 1.

WOOD, G.T. Exh. 1939
41A Victoria Crescent, London. † ROI 1.

WOOD, Herbert Exh. 1881
Flower and landscape painter. 13 Park Place Villas, Maida Hill, West London. † RBA 1.

WOOD, Herbert Exh. 1888-96
Landscape and figure painter. Nottingham. † N 6.

WOOD, Hortense Exh. 1880
Landscape painter. Munich and c/o Mr. C.E. Austin, 1 Westminster Chambers, London. † RA 1.

WOOD, Henry Harvey Exh. 1923-31
Edinburgh. † RSA 9, RSW 1.

WOOD, Helen Muir Exh. 1890-1901
Glasgow. † GI 9, RSA 1.

WOOD, Henry Roy Exh. 1937-39
Landscape painter. Lenton, Nottingham. † N 13.

WOOD, Miss H.V. Exh. 1908-10
94 Redcliffe Gardens, London. † RA 2.

WOOD, James Exh. 1917-33
Painter. Paisley 1917; Greenock 1927; Kilmalcolm 1929. † GI 6, L 1, LEI 40, RSA 4.

WOOD, John Barlow Exh. 1894-1911
Landscape painter. Oxford 1894; Woodbridge, Suffolk 1897; Ipswich, Suffolk 1905. † B 5, GI 1, L 4, RA 2, RBA 2.

WOOD, James F.R. d. 1920
Miniature painter. R.M.S. 1897. Exh. from 1897. Add: London. † RA 2, RMS 3.

WOOD, John H. Exh. 1921-40
Landscape and still life painter. London. † GOU 6, NEA 2, RA 2.

WOOD, John Warrington 1839-1886
Sculptor. A marble bust of Sir Austen Layard is in the National Gallery. Add: London 1880; Rome 1881. † GI 2, L 2, RA 5.

WOOD, Kate Exh. 1912-27
14 Huntley Road, Fairfield, Liverpool. † L 12.

WOOD, Karl S. Exh. 1930-33
Watercolour landscape painter and black and white artist. Gainsborough, Lincs. † N 14.

WOOD, L. Exh. 1881
3 Chapel Street, Edinburgh. † RSA 1.

WOOD, Lawson 1878-1957
Watercolour painter and illustrator. Son of Lewis Pinhorn W. q.v. Add: London 1904; Bexhill on Sea 1910; Cranleigh, Surrey 1922. † BK 65, D 15, LS 8, RA 1, RI 1, WG 122.

WOOD, Louise Exh. 1888-93
16 Queen Mary Avenue, Crosshill, Glasgow. † GI 2.

WOOD, Lindsay Ingleby Exh. 1900-4
122 George Street, Edinburgh. † RSA 7.

WOOD, L.G. Exh. 1911
† M 2.

WOOD, Lewis John* 1831-1901
Landscape and architectural painter and lithographer. Father of Lewis Pinhorn and grandfather of Lawson W. q.v. A.R.I. 1866, R.I. 1871, R.O.I. 1883. Add: London. † L 2, M 1, RBA 1, RI 30, ROI 8.

WOOD, L. Martina Exh. 1891-92
Black and white artist. 2 Girdler's Road, Brook Green, London. † RA 2.

WOOD, Lewis Pinhorn Exh. 1881-1913
Landscape painter and designer. Son of Lewis John and father of Lawson W. q.v. Add: London 1881 and 1897; Shere, Guildford, Surrey 1884; Pevensey, Sussex 1908. † B 1, D 16, L 1, LS 7, M 4, RA 2, RBA 3, RCA 3, RHA 5, RI 10, ROI 1, WG 6.

WOOD, L.S. Exh. 1910
3 Featherstone Buildings, Holborn, London. † RA 1.

WOOD, Miss M. Exh. 1912
West Malling, Kent. † SWA 1.

WOOD, Margery Exh. 1920
Miniature portrait painter. 35 South Street, Eastbourne. † RA 1.

WOOD, Marguerite Exh. 1907
3 Shardcroft Avenue, Hern Hill. † RA 1.

WOOD, Lady Mary Exh. 1885-88
Flower painter. 34 Hans Place, London. † G 7.

WOOD, Meynella Exh. 1880-81
Watercolour landscape painter. 31 Maryon Road, Charlton. † D 2.

WOOD, Miss M.C. Exh. 1902
Burford, Oxon. † L 1.

WOOD, M. Forrester Exh. 1908
10 Queen's Road, Southport, Lancs. † L 3.

WOOD, Mrs. M. Forrester Exh. 1927
Beaver Grove, Bettws-y-Coed, Wales. † RCA 2.

WOOD, Miss M.G. Exh. 1935-39
70 Wheeleys Road, Edgbaston, Birmingham. † B 8.

WOOD, Margaret H. Exh. 1901-15
Liverpool. † L 2.

WOOD, Mary I. Exh. 1925-40
Edinburgh. † RSA 7.

WOOD, Mary L. Exh. 1912-13
Fairhaven, Sandown, I.O.W. † D 4.

WOOD, Mrs. Norman Exh. 1909-19
2 Olive Vale, Victoria Park, Wavertree, Liverpool. † L 2.

WOOD, Olive Exh. 1933
Miniature portrait painter. Studied Camberwell School of Art and Clapham School of Art. Add: 10 Elms Road, Dulwich Village, London. † RA 1.

WOOD, P. Exh. 1890-92
Painter. 9 Lenton Avenue, The Park, Nottingham. † N 2.

WOOD, Peter MacDonagh b. 1914
Painter and etcher. Studied Southend School of Art, Slade School 1934-36 and Hornsey School of Art 1936-37. Exh. 1936-40. Add: 27 Wenham Drive, Westcliffe on Sea, Essex. † NEA 4, RA 1, RI 1.

WOOD, Robert Exh. 1884-89
Landscape painter. Hedley Terrace, Newcastle on Tyne. † GI 1, L 2, RI 1, RSA 2.

WOOD, Ruth Mary b. 1899
Lettering, illuminating, black and white and decorative artist and illustrator. b. South Shields. Studied Exeter School of Art and the British Museum. Instructor of lettering and illumination Exeter School of Art. Exh. 1934. Add: The Manor House, Weston, Honiton, Devon. † B 1.

WOOD, Robert Sydney Rendle b. 1895
Landscape painter. b. Plymouth. Studied Plymouth School of Art and Edinburgh College of Art. Exh. 1921-30. Add: The Pollock Gallery, Belfast. † GI 1, L 1, RHA 10, RSW 1.

WOOD, Scriven Exh. 1923
† NEA 1.

WOOD, Shakspere 1827-1886
Sculptor and archaeologist. Studied R.A. Schools and Rome. Add: 4 Mornington Street, London 1885. † RI 3.

WOOD, Starr 1870-1944
Humorous draughtsman and illustrator. Self taught. Exh. 1903. Add: Fulham, London. † L 1.

WOOD, Stanley L.* 1866-1928
Military painter and illustrator. London. † L 1, M 1, RA 7, ROI 5.

WOOD, Ursula Exh. 1890-1922
Painter, lithographer, woodcut artist and furniture decorator. Studied St. Johns Wood Art School and R.A. Schools. (Turner gold medal.) Add: London. † GI 1, L 14, M 3, RA 26, ROI 4, RSA 1, SWA 13.

WOOD, Wallace b. 1894
Watercolour painter. Studied Slade School. Exh. 1922-35. Add: London. † GI 2, GOU 9, I 2, L 1, M 2, NEA 1, RI 6, WG 55.

WOOD, William A.C. Exh. 1931-33
Handsworth, Birmingham 1931; Great Barr 1933. † B 7.

WOOD, William Henry Exh. 1881
Architect. 197 Hampstead Road, London. † RA 1.

WOOD, Wilfrid Rene b. 1888
Watercolour painter, poster designer, colour printer and lithographer. Studied Manchester School of Art, Central School of Art, London and Slade School. Exh. 1913-40. Add: Cheadle Hume, Cheshire 1913; Hampstead, London 1925. † CON 51, FIN 3, L 4, M 5, NEA 7, RA 8, RBA 2, RED 3, RI 4, WG 134.

WOOD, William R. Exh. 1889-1902
Landscape painter. Lowestoft, Suffolk 1889; Brandon, Suffolk 1893. † L 3, RA 5, RBA 2, ROI 1.

WOOD, William Thomas b. 1877
Landscape and flower painter. b. Ipswich. Studied Regent Street Polytechnic. Official war artist in the Balkans 1918. R.O.I. 1928, A.R.W.S. 1913, R.W.S. 1918, V.P.R.W.S. 1924-26. Exh. 1900-40. Add: London. † CHE 4, FIN 54, G 2, GI 16, GOU 4, I 4, L 18, LEI 233, M 10, NEA 5, P 2, RA 38, RBA 1, ROI 23, RSW 3, RWS 190, WG 6.

WOODALL, Mary b. 1901
Studied Slade School 1926-28. Exh. 1930. Add: 111 Cheyne Walk, London. † NEA 1.

WOODALL, W.M. Exh. 1910-15
Painter. R.B.A. 1909. Add: Birmingham 1910; St. Ives, Cornwall 1915. † RA 1, RBA 5.

WOODBURN, Clarence Exh. 1935-40
West Bromwich 1935; Handsworth, Birmingham 1936. † B 9, RCA 2, RSA 1.

WOODBURN, T.G. Exh. 1904-5
4 York Avenue, Sefton Park, Liverpool. † L 4.

WOODBURY, Charles Herbert* b. 1864
American painter. Exh. 1908-10. Add: c/o H. Van der Weyden, Montreuil sur Mer, France. † RA 1, ROI 2.

WOODCOCK, Lilian Exh. 1891-1921
Landscape painter. Llandudno, Wales. † B 2, L 3, RBA 2, RCA 19.

WOODCOCK, William J. Exh. 1930
10 Fifth Avenue, Small Heath, Birmingham. † B 1.

WOODFORD, James A. 1893-1976
Sculptor. b. Nottingham. A.R.A. 1937. Exh. 1926-40. Add: London 1926 and 1929; Nottingham 1928. † GI 3, M 1, N 2, RA 34, RSA 8.

WOODFORDE, Millicent Lisle Exh. 1911
Market Drayton, Shropshire. † LS 3.

WOODGATE, Miss G.M. Exh. 1888-97
Crowthorn, Bucks. † B 3.

WOODHALL, G.F. Exh. 1882-83
15 Little Francis Street, Birmingham. † B 3.

WOODHAMS, F.E. Exh. 1916-20
A.N.S.A. 1919-20. Add: Watnall Hall, Notts. 1916; Newthorpe, Notts. 1919; Lincoln 1920. † N 8.

WOODHEAD, Arthur Exh. 1922-36
Wolverhampton. † B 6.

WOODHEAD, Miss B. Exh. 1905-13
South Hampstead, London 1905; Bushey, Herts. 1913. † L 2, RA 2, RI 1, SWA 1.

WOODHOUSE, Alice Exh. 1898-1901
Castle Dale, Chepstow. † D 4.

WOODHOUSE, Basil Exh. 1906-10
Landscape painter. The Grey House, South Parade, Bedford Park, London. † B 1, GI 2, I 1, L 2. RA 5.

WOODHOUSE, Clara Exh. 1938
Painter. 88 Coventry Road, Bulwell, Notts. † N 1.

WOODHOUSE, Miss C.M. Exh. 1901
Langley Furze, Slough, Bucks. † SWA 1.

WOODHOUSE, Dora Exh. 1898-39
Portrait painter. Northampton. † L 1, RA 2, RBA 1, RI 1, RSA 4.

WOODHOUSE, E. Lilian Exh. 1910-14
Liverpool. † L 3.

WOODHOUSE, Col. Harvey Exh. 1888-89
Watercolour painter. East India United Services Club, St. James Square, London. † RI 2.

WOODHOUSE, Isabel H. Exh. 1883-89
Landscape and marine painter. Pinewood, Stoke Poges, Slough, Bucks. † L 1, SWA 3.

WOODHOUSE, John d. 1892
A.R.H.A. 1863. Add: Dublin. † RHA 2.

WOODHOUSE, Ronald Basil Emsley b. 1897
Etcher. b. Morecambe. Studied under his father William W. q.v. Exh. 1924-32. Add: Morecambe, Lancs. † L 2.

WOODHOUSE, Violet E. Exh. 1911-37
Liverpool. † L 48, RCA 4, RMS 1.

WOODHOUSE, Violet M. Exh. 1906-7
The Convent, Lichfield, Staffs. † B 2.

WOODHOUSE, William* 1857-1935
Animal painter. b. Morecambe. Father of Ronald Basil Emsley W. q.v. Add: Morecambe, Lancs. † B 1, L 2, M 1, RA 3, RSA 1.

WOODING, Emily Exh. 1915-31
15 Hartington Road, Sefton Park, Liverpool. † L 17, RCA 6.

WOODLAND, C. Norman Exh. 1925
446 Park Road North, Birkenhead. † L 2.

WOODLAND, Mary Exh. 1897
25A Earls Court Gardens, London. † SWA 3.

WOODLOCK, David 1842-1929
Figure, landscape and garden painter. b. Ireland. Add: Liverpool 1881, 1891 and 1905; Sheffield 1882; Leamington, Warwicks. 1901. † D 1, L 118, M 3, RA 17, RBA 2, RCA 2, RI 8, RSA 3.

WOODMAN, Miss A.L. Exh. 1921-24
Moseley, Birmingham 1921; Gt. Malvern, Worcs. 1924. † B 4.

WOODMAN, Charles Horwell 1823-1888
Watercolour landscape painter. 67 Villes Road, London 1885. † RI 4.

WOODMAN, Miss E.F. Exh. 1919-21
3 Wanstead Road, Bromley, Kent. † SWA 4.

WOODROFFE, Miss Exh. 1884
c/o Mr. Smith, 4 Victoria Street, Nottingham. † N 3.

WOODROFFE, Mrs. Ada Exh. 1922-31
227 Station Road, Wylde Green, Birmingham. † B 8.

WOODROFFE, J. Morris Exh. 1909-15
A.N.S.A. 1908, N.S.A. 1914-15. Add: Nottingham and Shrewsbury, Salop. † N 6, RA 3.

WOODROFFE, Paul b. 1875
Painter and illustrator. b. India. Exh. 1896-1938. Add: London 1896; Campden, Glos. 1904; Bisley, Glos. 1938. † BG 69, FIN 15, GI 2, I 1, NEA 4, RA 9, RHA 1, RMS 1.

WOODROFFE, Walter H. Exh. 1895
Architect. 214 Gt. Denver Street, London. † RA 1.

WOODROFFE-HICKS, Evelyn d. 1930
Figure, portrait, landscape and marine painter. Studied St. Johns Wood and Westminster Schools of Art and under Frank Brangwyn and Max Bohm in France. Travelled widely on the Continent, Middle East and the Mediterranean. Add: London 1902; Langport, Somerset 1921. † L 1, SWA 3.

WOODRUFF, Linda Exh. 1884-1903
Miniature portrait painter. London. † L 2, RA 17, RI 1, RMS 2.

WOODS, Albert Exh. 1892-1937
Landscape painter. Born and lived in Preston, Lancs. † GI 6, L 25, M 1, RA 4, RCA 38, RSA 1.

WOODS, Andrew C. Exh. 1910-13
47 Lorne Street, Fairfield, Liverpool. † L 3.

WOODS, A.E. Exh. 1918-33
Ashwell Street, Netherfield, Notts. † N 3.

WOODS, Ethel Exh. 1901-18
Painter. Cardiff 1901; Cirencester, Glos. 1913. † L 2, RA 4, SWA 2.

WOODS, Ellen M. Exh. 1880-81
Watercolour flower painter. Clifton Park Road, Clifton, Bristol. † D 5, RA 1.

WOODS, Henry* 1846-1921
Landscape and genre painter and illustrator. Born and studied Warrington, Lancs. Worked for the "Graphic". A.R.A. 1882, R.A. 1893, R.O.I. 1883. Add: London 1880; Venice 1881. Died in Venice. † B 4, FIN 3, L 7, M 3, RA 119, ROI 3, TOO 10.

WOODS, Harold James b. 1894
Watercolour painter. b. Sandown, I.O.W. Exh. 1922-33. Add: Sandown, I.O.W. 1922; Porchester, Hants. 1924; Cosham, Hants. 1930. † NEA 5, RA 2, RBA 8.

WOODS, John Goodrich Wemyss Exh. 1889-1934
Watercolour landscape painter. Newbury, Berks. 1889; Burnham, Bucks. 1922; Seaford, Sussex 1927. † ALP 1, RA 7.

WOODS, Kathleen Exh. 1938
Little Hadham, Herts. † SWA 2.

WOODS, Mrs. M.S. Exh. 1909-11
Landscape painter. London 1909; Wallingford, Berks. 1911. † BG 2, LS 1, ROI 1.

WOODS, Patrick J. Exh. 1931-38
Landscape and figure painter. 78 Springfield Road, Belfast. † RHA 18.

WOODS, Sidney W. Exh. 1934-40
Wood engraver and painter. London 1934; Downe, Kent 1940. † RA 3.

WOODS, Wheeldon Exh. 1932-36
Landscape painter. 38 Carrfield Avenue, Long Eaton, Notts. † N 10.

WOODS-HILL, Mrs. Ida Exh. 1936
Landscape painter. Oak Gate, Hayes Way, Beckenham, Kent. † RA 1.

WOODTHORPE, Muriel Exh. 1913-14
Blundellsands, Liverpool. † L 4.

WOODVILLE, Richard Caton* 1856-1927
Military painter and illustrator. Studied in Dusseldorf and Paris. Son of Richard Caton W. (1825-1855) and father of William P. Caton W. q.v. R.I. 1882, R.O.I. 1883. Add: London 1880 and 1910; Farnham, Surrey 1908. † FIN 1, GI 1, L 10, M 3, NG 1, RA 23, RHA 1, RI 1, ROI 4.

WOODVILLE, Mrs. W. Caton
See WARD, Dorothy Priestley

WOODVILLE, William P. Caton b. 1884
Painter and illustrator. Son of Richard Caton W. q.v. Studied Herkomers, Bushey. Exh. 1904-29. Add: Bushey, Herts 1904; Barnes, Surrey 1910; London 1914 and 1929; Elstree, Herts. 1921. † B 6, L 11, RA 6, ROI 2.

WOODWARD, Alice B. Exh. 1885-1909
Watercolour painter and illustrator. 129 Beaufort Street, London. † BG 1, GI 1, I 1, L 1, M 1, NEA 1, RA 5, RBA 9, RI 4, RSW 1.

WOODWARD, A.O. Exh. 1903
47 Temple Row, Birmingham. † B 1.

WOODWARD, A.T. Exh. 1885-86
Ellesmere House, Moseley, Birmingham. † B 2.

WOODWARD, Eliza (Mrs. C.J.) b. 1842
nee Baker. Flower painter. Studied Birmingham and South Kensington. Exh. 1882-1928. Add: Birmingham. † B 41, L 1, RA 2, SWA 4.

WOODWARD, Ellen C. Exh. 1890-95
Painter and black and white artist. Chelsea, London 1890; St. Leonards on Sea, Sussex 1895. † NEA 1, RA 1, RBA 1.

WOODWARD, Mrs. G.M. Exh. 1912
St. Ives, Cornwall. † M 1.

WOODWARD, Miss H. Law Exh. 1896-1910
Miniature portrait painter. London. † I 2, L 1, RA 1.

WOODWARD, J. Exh. 1885-87
30 Stanley Road, Bootle, Lancs. † L 2.

WOODWARD, Law Exh. 1898
14 Ridgefield, Manchester. † L 1.

WOODWARD, Mary Exh. 1890-1914
Painter and miniaturist. London. † B 5, D 3, GI 2, L 10, RA 10, RBA 6, RHA 9, RI 1, RID 5, RMS 2, RSA 3, SWA 19.

WOODWARD, T.J. Exh. 1889
10 Cranhall Lane, Wednesbury. † B 1.

WOODWELL, Joseph R. 1843-1911
American painter. Exh. 1909. Add: c/o Messrs. Chapman Bros., 241 Kings Road, Chelsea, London. † ROI 1.

WOODYATT, Mrs. R.F.H. Exh. 1899-1900
St. John's Vicarage, Over, Cheshire 1899; London 1900. † L 2, M 1, RCA 1.

WOODYATT, Miss V.E. Exh. 1889-92
Market Place, Macclesfield, Cheshire. † B 2, L 2, M 6.

WOOLARD, B.G. Exh. 1898
25 Comley Bank Avenue, Edinburgh. † GI 1.

WOOLARD, William Exh. 1883-1908
Edinburgh. † GI 2, RSA 23, RSW 2.

WOOLCOTT, Wilfred Robert b. 1892
Portrait and landscape painter. b. Cullompton. Studied Tiverton and Southend on Sea. Exh. 1932-33. Add: 3 Clifton Drive, Westcliffe on Sea, Essex. † RA 2.

WOOLER, Blanche Exh. 1929
38 Chetwynd Street, Aigburth, Liverpool. † L 4.

WOOLEY, E. Exh. 1885-86
17 Pembroke Terrace, Cardiff. † RSA 16.

WOOLEY, Harry Exh. 1912
Jesmonde Dene, Water Lane, Brislington, Bristol. † L 2.

WOOLF, Hal b. 1902
Landscape painter. Studied Chelsea Polytechnic 1920-22 and La Grande Chaumiere, Paris. Exh. 1927-39. Add: London. † P 1, RA 2, RED 51, ROI 2.

WOOLF, Sonia Exh. 1927-29
68 Newton Street, Piccadilly, Manchester. † L 5.

WOOLFORD, Charles H. Exh. 1880-1923
Edinburgh. † GI 45, LS 2, M 1, RA 2, RSA 104, RSW 10.

WOOLFORD, Harry Halkerston Russell b. 1905
Artist and picture restorer. b. Edinburgh. Studied Edinburgh R.S.A. Life School (Carnegie travelling scholarship), France and Italy. Exh. 1922-39. Add: Edinburgh. † GI 4, RSA 6, RSW 5.

WOOLHOUSE, E. Margaret Exh. 1895-1905
Flower painter. Tamworth, Staffs. † B 7, RA 4.

WOOLHOUSE, Mary Ellen Exh. 1897
Artist and teacher. Tamworth, Staffs. † B 1.

WOOLL, Charles Fairfield Exh. 1905-8
Liverpool 1905; Paris 1906. † I 2, LS 5.

WOOLLARD, Benjamin Exh. 1890-91
Architect. 18 Alderney Road East, London. † RA 2.

WOOLLARD, Clarence E. Exh. 1910
11 Larkhill Rise, Clapham, London. † L 1.

WOOLLARD, Dorothy E.C. Exh. 1910-39
Etcher. A.R.E. 1916, R.E. 1925. Add: Clifton, Bristol 1910, 1915 and 1921; Westbury on Trym, Bristol 1920; London 1914 and 1922. † CON 2, L 18, RA 30, RE 34, RHA 2.

WOOLLARD, Florence Eliza b. 1878
Landscape painter. Studied Clapham School of Art, Slade School and under Walter Sickert and Beatrice Bland. Exh. 1909-39. Add: 11 Larkhill Rise, Clapham, London. † L 8, LS 6, NEA 2, RA 9.

WOOLLARD, M. Frances Exh. 1916-31
17 Duppas Hill Terrace, Croydon, Surrey 1916. † NEA 6.

WOOLLASTON, Caroline Exh. 1936
† RMS 1.

WOOLLASTON, Leslie b. 1900
Painter. b. Birmingham. Self taught. Exh. 1939-40. Add: Hanwell, Birmingham. † B 1, RBA 1, RCA 1.

WOOLLATT, Amia E. Exh. 1891-92
Landscape painter. Fernville, 42 Mapperley Road, Nottingham. † N 3.

WOOLLATT, Edgar 1871-1931
Landscape and figure painter, illustrator, designer, black and white and commercial artist. b. Nottingham. Studied Nottingham School of Art. N.S.A. 1908, V.P.N.S.A. 1929. Father of Leighton Hall W. q.v. Add: Nottingham. † L 1, N 191, RCA 2.

WOOLLATT, Gertrude Exh. 1891-92
Landscape painter. Fernville, 42 Mapperley Road, Nottingham. † N 3.

WOOLLATT, Leighton Hall b. 1905
Sculptor and decorative painter. b. Nottingham. Son of Edgar W. q.v. Studied Nottingham School of Art. Exh. 1926-34. Add: Nottingham. † N 13, RA 3, ROI 1.

WOOLLER, H. Exh. 1933
18 Wentwood Road, London. † L 1.

WOOLLEY, Alice Mary Exh. 1883-1905
Flower and landscape painter. Collingham, Neward, Notts. 1883; Sheffield 1887; Notting Hill Gate, London 1889. † L 4, M 2, N 4, RA 4, RBA 5, RID 49, SWA 3.

WOOLLEY, H. Exh. 1912-13
Westwood, Bellerton Road, Knowle, Bristol. † RA 1, RMS 1.

WOOLLEY, Marion Exh. 1925-28
Painter. 268 Woodborough Road, Nottingham. † N 6.

WOOLLISCROFT, Annie A. Exh. 1887-89
Watercolour painter. Bath Street, Ilkeston, Notts. † N 3.

WOOLLS, Henry Exh. 1897
Landscape painter. 67 Lancaster Street, Newington Causeway, London. † RA 1.

WOOLMER, Alfred Joseph* 1805-1892
Genre painter. b. Exeter. Studied in Italy. R.B.A. 1841. Add: The Limes, Dartmouth Park Avenue, Upper Holloway, London 1880. † RBA 26.

WOOLMER, Ethel Exh. 1888-1929
Portrait and figure painter and etcher. A.S.W.A. 1907. Add: London. † AB 3, RA 2, RI 8, RID 55, SWA 70.

WOOLNER, Dorothy Exh. 1891-99
Figure and portrait painter. London. † RA 3, RI 1.

WOOLNER, Phyllis Exh. 1897-1924
Painter and pastelier. London. † RMS 1. WG 31.

WOOLNER, Thomas 1825-1892
Sculptor. b. Hadleigh, Suffolk. Studied under William Behnes and at R.A. Schools. Went to Australia 1852-54. Appointed Professor of Sculpture to R.A. 1877 (res. 1879). Member of the Pre-Raphaelite Brotherhood. A.R.A. 1871, R.A. 1874. Add: 29 Welbeck Street, London 1880. † M 1, RA 26.

WOOLNOTH, Alfred Exh. 1880-96
Landscape painter. Edinburgh 1880; London 1889. † D 2, GI 2, L 3, RA 1, RSA 11.

WOOLNOTH, Charles Nicholls d. 1906
Watercolour landscape painter. R.S.W. 1878. Exh. from 1880. Add: Glasgow. † DOW 5, GI 48, RSA 7, RSW 87.

WOOLRICH, E. d. 1916
Painter. Exh. 1908. Add: London. † NG 1.

WOOLRIDGE, Mrs. Margaret A. Exh. 1903
Miniature portrait painter. Belmont, James Street, Stoke on Trent, Staffs. † RA 1.

WOOLWAY, George R. Exh. 1909-27
Watercolour landscape and figure painter and teacher. London. † CHE 5, P 1, RA 2.

WOON, Annie K. Exh. 1880-1907
Artist and teacher. Edinburgh 1880; London 1907. † GI 8, L 2, RSA 12, SWA 1.

WOON, E.A. Exh. 1890-95
4 Walker Street, Edinburgh. † RSA 2.

WOON, Rosa E. Exh. 1881-1914
Edinburgh 1881; London 1904. † BRU 1, GI 1, LS 15, RSA 8, SWA 1.

WOORE, Edward Exh. 1919-36
Painter and stained glass artist. London. † COO 7, RA 14, WG 3.

WOORE, Helen (Mrs. F.) Exh. 1895-1907
Landscape painter. London 1895 and 1907; Ightham, Kent 1903. † RA 2, ROI 4, SWA 4.

WOOTTON, Miss D. Exh. 1938
19 George Street, Tamworth, Staffs. † B 1.

WOOTTON, K.E. Exh. 1912
99 Rodenhurst Road, Clapham Park, London. † RA 1.

WOOTTON, Mary K. Exh. 1890-98
Birmingham. † B 6.

WOOTTON, S. Exh. 1923-26
Landscape painter. Beeston, Notts. 1923; Swarkeston, Derby 1926. † N 9.

WORDEN, Dorothy Exh. 1887-93
Painter. London. † RA 2, RBA 5.

WORES, Theodore* b. 1860
American landscape and figure painter. b. San Francisco, U.S.A. N.E.A. 1891. Exh. 1889-96. Add: London 1889; Yokohama, Japan 1893. † DOW 62, G 1, GI 5, NEA 3, NG 2, RA 2, RBA 1, ROI 3.

WORK, Mrs. G. Orkney Exh. 1913-14
Appletreewick, Skipton, Yorks. † L 2.

WORK, George Orkney d. 1921
Painter. Bridge of Dee, Castle Douglas 1897; Liverpool 1903; Skipton, Yorks. 1913. † GI 2, L 31, RA 1.

WORKMAN, Evelyn Exh. 1900-7
5 Woodside Terrace, Glasgow. † GI 4, RSA 3.

WORKMAN, Gilbert C. Exh. 1936
28 Northfield Road, Harborne, Birmingham. † B 2.

WORKMAN, Harold 1897-1975
Painter and lecturer. b. Oldham. Studied Oldham and Manchester Schools of Art. R.B.A. 1937. Add: Southbourne, Hants. 1932; London 1934. † GI 1, L 2, M 1, NEA 4, RA 11, RBA 26, RCA 1, RI 5, ROI 13.

WORKMAN, Miss J.S. Exh. 1901-3
Figure painter. Craigdarragh, Co. Down, Ireland. † RA 1, SWA 1.

WORKMAN, Nellie Exh. 1900-12
Figure painter. Craigdarragh, Co. Down, Ireland 1900; Glasgow 1912. † GI 2, RA 1, SWA 1.

WORKMAN, R.S. Exh. 1886
Windmill Street, Saltcoats. † RSA 1.

WORLEY, Charles H. Exh. 1901-3
Architect. 62 Welbeck Street, Cavendish Square, London. † RA 2.

WORMLEIGHTON, Francis Exh. 1880-86
Landscape and figure painter. London. † RA 2, RBA RI 1, ROI 1.

WORMS, Jules* 1832-1924
French painter. Exh. 1883. Add: 19 Rue de Navarini, Paris. † RI 1.

WORMSER, Lucie Exh. 1927
† GOU 3.

WORNUM, Catherine A. Exh. 1880-81
Fruit, flower and bird painter. 20 Belsize Square, London. † SWA 5.

WORNUM, George Grey 1888-1957
Architect. Studied Slade School and A.A. Add: London. † RA 4, RSA 3.

WORNUM, Ralph Selden 1847-1910
Architect. London. † RA 12.

WORRALL, A.W. Exh. 1905
Queen's Chambers, North Street, Wolverhampton. † RA 1.

WORRALL, Ella b. 1863
Miniature, garden and landscape painter, and teacher. b. Liverpool. Daughter of J.E. W. q.v. Exh. 1882-1933. Add: Liverpool. † B 5, GI 4, L 130, M 6, RA 4, RMS 4.

WORRALL, Ernest J. Exh. 1929-38
Landscape painter. Ipswich 1929; Royal College of Art, London 1930; Grimsby, Lincs. 1932. † NEA 1, RA 14.

WORRALL, J.E. 1829-1913
Lithographer. Father of Ella W. q.v. Add: Liverpool. † B 14, L 29.

WORRALL, Kate Exh. 1892-94
Landscape painter. Chester Lodge, Gilston Road, London. † ROI 3.

WORSDELL, Clara J. Exh. 1882-99
Watercolour flower painter. King Street, Lancaster. † L 9, M 3, RA 2.

WORSFOLD, Emily M. See MALTBY

WORSFOLD, Kate Exh. 1905
44 Windsor Road, Levenshulme. † M 2.

WORSFOLD, Maud Beatrice Exh. 1894-1938
Portrait painter and miniaturist. Studied R.A. Schools. R.M.S. 1898. Add: Eltham, Kent 1894; London 1896 and 1908; Dover, Kent 1906. † L 1, NG 3, RA 27, RMS 38, WG 74.

WORSLEY, Charles Nathan* Exh. 1886-1922
Landscape painter. R.B.A. 1909. Add: London 1886; Sidmouth, Devon 1891; Bridgnorth, Salop 1892. Went to New Zealand c.1910. † B 10, L 3, M 6, RA 4, RBA 17, RHA 2, RI 3, ROI 6, WG 55.

WORSLEY, Harriet P. Exh. 1884
Watercolour painter. Hovingdean, Yorks. † SWA 2.

WORSLEY-TAYLOR, Miss U. Exh. 1917-25
Moreton, Whalley, Lancs. † L 1, NEA 1, ROI 3.

WORTH, Miss F.C. Exh. 1928
109 Sandford Road, Moseley, Birmingham. † B 2.

WORTH, Laura Exh. 1931-32
Flower painter. The Hut, Finch Lane, Bushey, Herts. † RA 3, ROI 2.

WORTHINGTON, Miss Edith M. Exh. 1899
Broomfield, Alderly Edge, Cheshire. † M 1.

WORTHINGTON, Dr. Harry Edward b. 1867
Painter. b. Worthing. Exh. 1925. Add: The Sycamores, Birchington, Kent. † RI 1.

WORTHINGTON, John Hubert b. 1886
Architect. b. Alderley Edge, Cheshire. Son of Thomas Worthington, Architect. Studied Manchester University School of Architecture, under Sir Edward Lutyens 1911-12 and in Italy. Professor of Architecture Royal College of Art. Exh. 1920-39. Add: 178 Oxford Road, Manchester. † RA 2.

WORTHINGTON, Lena Exh. 1928-39
Landscape painter. Meols, Cheshire 1928; London 1939. † L 1, RA 2.

WORTHINGTON, Percy Scott b. 1864
Architect. b. Crumpshall, nr. Manchester. Son of Thomas Worthington, Architect. Studied R A. Schools. Exh. 1889-1921. Add: Alderley Edge, Cheshire 1889; Manchester 1912. †, M 2, RA 7, RSA 1.

WORTHINGTON, Miss S. Exh. 1892-95
Wilmslow, Cheshire 1892; Stockport, Lancs. 1895. † M 2.

WORTHINGTON, Thomas Locke Exh. 1884-90
Architect. Manchester 1884; London 1889. † M 5, RA 5.

WORTLEY, Archibald James Stuart* 1849-1905
Portrait and sporting painter. Studied under Millais. Founder and President R.P. 1891. Add: London. † D 2, FIN 1, G 37, GI 1, L 5, M 13, NG 4, P 47, RA 21, RSA 1.

WORTLEY, Mary Stuart Exh. 1882-93
Lady Wentworth. Portrait painter. London. † B 1, G 8, M 1, NG 1.

WOTHERSPOON, J. junr. Exh. 1888-91
4 Lynedock Place, Glasgow. † GI 5, RSA 1.

WOTTON, Thomas E. Exh. 1889-90
Glasgow 1889; London 1890. † GI 4.

WOULFE, Viola G. Exh. 1895-1917
Miniature portrait painter. London. † L 6, RA 12, RMS 2.

WOUTERS, Rik* 1882-1916
Belgian painter. Exh. 1914-15. Add: Brussels. † GI 1, L 3, RSA 2.

WOZENCROFT-EVANS, Vyvyan b. 1909
Portrait and still life painter and black and white fashion artist. Studied Old Castle Wharf Studio, Hampton Wick and under Clifford Hall at Richmond. Exh. 1927-28. Add: Hampton on Thames. † GOU 2.

WRAGG, Carl L. Exh. 1936-37
Landscape and portrait painter. 453 Loughborough Road, Birstall, Leics. † N 6.

WRAMPE, Fritz Exh. 1936
† RSA 1.

WRANGEL, Lily See CHRISTIE

WRATESLAW, Miss C.H. Exh. 1900-1
Ringley Hill, Reigate, Surrey. † SWA 4.

WRATHALL, John James Exh. 1885-1911
Stained glass artist. London. † RA 4, RBA 1.

WRATISLAW, Matilda E. Exh. 1882-85
Watercolour interior, architectural and figure painter. Rome. † D 1, L 1, RI 1, SWA 7.

WRAY, F. Douglas Exh. 1922-35
Still life painter. Married Marjorie Rodgers q.v. Add: Harrow, Middlesex 1922; Balham, London 1923; Edgware, Middlesex 1933. † RA 4, RI 3, ROI 10.

WREN, Henry Exh. 1923
† GOU 1.

WREN, John C. Exh. 1883
Watercolour landscape painter. 5 Cornwall Terrace, Penzance, Cornwall. † RI 1.

WREN, Louisa Exh. 1882-1918
Watercolour landscape and miniature portrait painter. London. † D 1, L 4, M 1, RA 5, RI 5, RID 42, ROI 4, SWA 7.

WREN, Thomas Exh. 1914-19
Linkfield Terrace, Mount Sorrel, Loughborough, Leics. † N 6.

WRENCH, Arthur Edwin Exh. 1923-24
165 St. Andrews Road, Pollockshields, Glasgow. † GI 2, L 2.

WRENCH, Marjorie B. Exh. 1932-33
Miniature portrait painter. 147 Mount Road, Wallasey, Cheshire. † L 3, RA 2.

WRENN, J.P. Exh. 1905-8
Dublin. † RHA 2.

WRIGHT, Lady Exh. 1881
Watercolour painter. Hodingham, York. † SWA 1.

WRIGHT, Alan Exh. 1888-97
Landscape and figure painter and designer. London. †, L 1, NEA 5, RA 3, RBA 4, ROI 2.

WRIGHT, A.A. Exh. 1934
Cardiff, Wales. † RCA 2.

WRIGHT, A.C. Exh. 1920
Brandwood House, Birmingham. † B 5.

WRIGHT, Alec E.F. Exh. 1937
West End, Stokesley, North Yorks. † RI 1.

WRIGHT, A.G. Exh. 1900-1
45 Noel Street, Nottingham. † N 5.

WRIGHT, Amy H. Exh. 1895-1932
Artist and teacher. Liverpool. † L 39, RCA 1.

WRIGHT, Miss A.M. Exh. 1893
† SWA 2.

WRIGHT, Alice Maud Exh. 1911-27
Miniature painter and illustrator. b. Hoxton. Studied St. Martins School of Art, under John Parker and under Walter Sickert. Add: Paris 1911; London 1913. † RA 3, RI 4.

WRIGHT, A. Stewart Exh. 1923-32
Mezzotint portrait artist. The Bungalow, Lynton Road, New Maldon, Surrey. † RA 2.

WRIGHT, Mrs. A.T. Exh. 1885-86
Landscape painter. 23 The Avenue, Bedford Park, Chiswick, London. † SWA 3.

WRIGHT, Caroline Exh. 1883-87
Landscape painter. Broughton Rectory, Manchester 1881; London 1887. † L 2, SWA 2.

WRIGHT, C. Barnard Exh. 1911-34
Lockermarsh, Thorne, Yorks. † RCA 1, RHA 1.

WRIGHT, C. Bingham Exh. 1880-1901
Watercolour landscape painter. Related to Nevill W. q.v. N.S.A. 1884. Add: Stapleford Hall, Notts. 1880; Nottingham 1881. † N 22.

WRIGHT, Carrie E. Exh. 1885-86
Painter. 2 Lorne Gardens, Hanover Gate, London. † RBA 2.

WRIGHT, Mrs. Cathleen H.M. Exh. 1913
Kinmouth, Bridge of Earne, N.B. † RSA 1.

WRIGHT, Catherine M. Exh. 1883-91
Landscape and figure painter. A.S.W.A. 1889. Add: Crieff, Perthshire 1883; London 1886. † B 6, G 2, GI 4, L 3, M 7, NG 2, RA 3, RBA 1, ROI 4, RSA 5, SWA 4.

WRIGHT, Charles O. Exh. 1936
Landscape painter. Warwick Road, Bishops Stortford, Herts. † RA 1.

WRIGHT, David Exh. 1911
15 Wilton Road, Edinburgh. † RSA 1.

WRIGHT, Dorothy Kathleen Exh. 1919-40
Miniature portrait painter. London 1919; Croydon, Surrey 1929; Waddon, Surrey 1932. † RA 11, RMS 1, ROI 1.

WRIGHT, Miss E. Exh. 1882
60 King Street, Manchester. † L 1, M 2.

WRIGHT, Edith Exh. 1910
Castlegate, Thirsk, Yorks. † RA 1.

WRIGHT, Edith Exh. 1922-25
Landscape and coastal painter. Devon Lodge, Hartington Road, Sherwood, Nottingham. † N 4.

WRIGHT, Edward Exh. 1883
Watercolour landscape painter. 97 Queen Victoria Street, London. † RBA 1.

WRIGHT, Elsie Exh. 1938-40
Montgomerie Street, Eaglesham. † GI 1, RSW 1.

WRIGHT, Ethel Exh. 1887-1939
Portrait, figure and flower painter. Studied London and Paris. R.B.A. 1912, R.O.I. 1917, A.S.W.A. 1896, S.W.A. 1897. Add: London. † CHE 1, G 3, GOU,1, I 6, L 21, LS 26, M 1, NEA 1, NG 1, P 5, RA 52, RBA 5, ROI 68, SWA 9.

WRIGHT, Miss E.A.J. Exh. 1914-19
8 Grove Road, Leytonstone, London. † SWA 2.

WRIGHT, E.C. Exh. 1885-86
Cliff View Cottage, Polperro, Cornwall. † L 1, RHA 1.

WRIGHT, Edward C.J. Exh. 1887
Watercolour landscape painter. 15 Featherstone Buildings, Holborn, London. † RA 1.

WRIGHT, Miss E.E. Exh. 1905
The Willows, Harlesden, London. † RA 1.

WRIGHT, Edward H. Exh. 1891
Painter. White House, Victoria Crescent, Burton on Trent, Notts. † N 1.

WRIGHT, Miss E.J. Exh. 1880-98
Flower painter. 21 Ledbury Road, Bayswater, London. † SWA 12.

WRIGHT, Miss E.M. Exh. 1905-8
London. † L 1, RA 1.

WRIGHT, Elsie M. Exh. 1893
14 Belhaven Terrace, Kelvinside, Glasgow. † GI 2.

WRIGHT, Mrs. Ethel M. Exh. 1920-28
Flower painter. Stafford. † B 3, L 1, RA 2.

WRIGHT, F. Exh. 1927
13 Milton Road, Waterloo, Liverpool. † L 4.

WRIGHT, Florence Exh. 1894
8 Bolton Studios, London. † P 2.

WRIGHT, Frank Exh. 1901-11
Landscape painter. London. † RA 4.

WRIGHT, Frank Arnold b. 1874
Sculptor. Studied R.A. Schools. Exh. 1903-35. Add: London 1903; East Molesey, Surrey 1930. † GI 3, L 1, RA 25.

WRIGHT, F.P. Exh. 1881-83
Fruit and flower painter. Norfolk Road, Essex Road, Islington, London. † RBA 2, ROI 1.

WRIGHT, G. junr. Exh. 1914-15
73 Ash Grove, Wavertree, Liverpool. † L 2.

WRIGHT, George Exh. 1881-1901
Ednam Street, Annan. † GI 14, RA 1, RSA 33.

WRIGHT, George* 1860-1940
Sporting painter. Leeds 1894; Rugby 1900; Oxford 1908; Richmond, Surrey 1929. † L 6, RA 33.

WRIGHT, Miss G.E. Exh. 1900-24
Manchester. † L 17, M 11, NG 2, RA 2.

WRIGHT, G.H. Exh. 1884
Archibald Road, Lozells, Birmingham. † B 1.

WRIGHT, George H.B. Exh. 1936-40
55 Princes Street, Nonifieth, Angus. † RSA 5.

WRIGHT, Gordon Lorimer Exh. 1910
30 Frederic Street, Edinburgh. † RSA 1.

WRIGHT, G. Rutherford Exh. 1920-26
Rowancliffe, Giffnock 1920; London 1926. † GI 2.

WRIGHT, Gilbert S.* Exh. 1900
Figure painter. 33 St. Germains Road, Forest Hill, London. † RA 1.

WRIGHT, Miss Gytha Warren Exh. 1895
Landscape painter. 8 Wetherby Mansions, Earls Court, London. † RA 1.

WRIGHT, H. Exh. 1940
1 Central Park, Edgware, Middlesex. † RI 2.

WRIGHT, Miss H. Exh. 1909
Green Leas, Halifax, Yorks. † L 2.

WRIGHT, Helen Exh. 1887
Painter. † SWA 1.

WRIGHT, Hilda Exh. 1909-37
Landscape painter. London 1909; Little Roothing, nr. Ongar, Essex 1937. † G 3, GOU 8, I 20, L 9, LS 3, NEA 5, RA 4, SWA 2.

WRIGHT, Helena A. Exh. 1880-91
Painter of flowers, figures and game. Nottingham. † GI 2, M 2, N 30, RBA 1.

WRIGHT, H. Boardman d. 1915
Etcher. A.R.E. 1912. Add: Beckenham, Kent 1910; London 1912. † L 9, RA 8, RE 10.

WRIGHT, Helen B. Exh. 1903-4
Miniature portrait painter. Green Bank, Merton Lane, Highgate, London. † GI 1, RA 1.

WRIGHT, H. Cook Exh. 1917-30
Morven, Helensburgh, N.B. † GI 3.

WRIGHT, Henry Charles Sepping 1850-1937
Painter and war correspondent. Add: Manchester 1882; London 1883. † L 1, M 6, RA 2, RBA 6, RI 1.

WRIGHT, Herbert E. Exh. 1914
132 Derington Road, Upper Tooting, London. † L 1.

WRIGHT, Isabel Exh. 1913-23
Mrs. Calder. Add: Glasgow. † L 49.

WRIGHT, Irene Clara Exh. 1925-28
Miniature painter. Studied Heatherleys. Add: 5 Shoot-up-Hill, Brondesbury, London. † AB 1, RA 3, RMS 1.

WRIGHT, James Exh. 1896-97
Dalblair Villa, Ayr. † GI 1, RSW 1.

WRIGHT, James d. 1947
Landscape and figure painter. R.S.W. 1920. Add: Glasgow 1912; Kilbarchan, Renfrewshire 1916; Garelochhead 1940. † AR 2, GI 57, L 5, RA 3, RSA 36, RSW 82.

WRIGHT, Jessie Exh. 1913
Landscape painter. † ALP 3.

WRIGHT, John Exh. 1894-1929
Watercolour landscape painter and etcher. A.R.E. 1899, R.E. 1917. Add: Sevenoaks, Kent 1894 and 1900; Chipstead, Kent 1896; Robin Hood's Bay, Yorks. 1901; London 1913. † ALP 2, BA 45, BG 50, FIN 5, G 1, GI 1, L 17. RA 24, RE 66, RI 1, RID 5, RSA 1.

WRIGHT, John Exh. 1907
Villa Prima Cruci, Taormina, Italy. † GI 2, RSA 1.

WRIGHT, Joseph* Exh. 1880-1927
Landscape painter. Derby 1880; Lenton, Notts. 1895; Hyson Green, Notts. 1896. † N 35.

WRIGHT, John Buckland b. 1897
Engraver. b. New Zealand. Exh. 1936. † RED 2.

WRIGHT, J.D. d. 1924
Formby, Lancs. 1893; New Ferry, Cheshire 1897; Rock Ferry, 1904 and 1920; Liverpool 1913. † L 22.

WRIGHT, J. Henry Exh. 1882
33 Archibald Road, Birmingham. † B 1.

WRIGHT, Katherine Exh. 1890-93
York Lodge, Kew, Surrey. † D 3, SWA 2.

WRIGHT, Lawrence b. 1906
Architect, painter and etcher. b. Bristol. Studied Liverpool School of Architecture, 1924-29. Exh. 1928-35. Add: Blundellsands, Liverpool 1928; London 1935. † L 4, RA 1.

WRIGHT, Lilian Exh. 1893
Painter. c/o Mr. Jones, 68B Lincoln's Inn Fields, London. † RBA 2.

WRIGHT, Mme. Lois Exh. 1880
Portrait painter. Lamania de Pennedessil, Honfleur. † RA 1.

WRIGHT, Lottie Exh. 1890-92
Flower painter. 9 College Street, Nottingham. † N 3.

WRIGHT, Lilian F. Exh. 1900-30
Flower, figure and miniature portrait painter. London. † L 5, RA 14, RI 1, RMS 4, ROI 1.

WRIGHT, Mrs. Louise W. b. 1875
Mrs. John W. Portrait, landscape and still life painter. b. Philadelphia, U.S.A. Exh. 1924-30. Add: 7 Cheltenham Terrace, London. † BA 42, RA 1.

WRIGHT, Margaret Exh. 1906-40
Mrs. D. Campbell. Add: Glasgow 1906 and 1918; Pollockshaws, N.B. 1912; Gourock 1921. † GI 39, L 3, RSA 23.

WRIGHT, Mary Exh. 1884-87
Landscape and coastal painter. 29 Dawson Place, Bayswater, London. † SWA 5.

WRIGHT, Matvyn Exh. 1939
Painter. † LEF 7.

WRIGHT, Meg Exh. 1886-1929
Landscape and figure painter. Edinburgh. † GI 39, L 2, M 5, RA 3, RBA 3, RHA 2, RSA 83, RSW 7.

WRIGHT, Mrs. Moncrieff Exh. 1904-9
Edinburgh 1904; Milmathort, Kinrossshire 1906; Bridge of Earne, N.B. 1909. † RSA 3.

WRIGHT, Mary E. Exh. 1880
27 Forest Road East, Nottingham. † N 1.

WRIGHT, M.I. Exh. 1888
34 Burbank Gardens, Glasgow. † GI 1.

WRIGHT, Mrs. M.K. Exh. 1928
Bushwood Lodge, Lowsonford, Henley in Arden, Warwicks. † B, 1.

WRIGHT, M. Logan Exh. 1933-34
26 Bina Gardens, London. † SWA 3.

WRIGHT, Mrs. Mary M. Exh. 1887-1923
Landscape painter. Cambridge 1887; London 1909. † D 1, LS 16, RA 2, ROI 1, SWA 5.

WRIGHT, Mrs. M. Walkern Exh. 1937-38
Watercolour and pastel landscape and figure painter. 22 Park Drive, London. † COO 10, RI 2.

WRIGHT, Mrs. Nellie Exh. 1940
Miniature portrait painter. 1 Somerville Gardens, Tunbridge Wells, Kent. † RA 1.

WRIGHT, Nelson Exh. 1925-28
Oldham Road, Newton Heath, Manchester. † L 10, M 2, RCA 1, RI 1, RSA 1.

WRIGHT, Nevill Exh. 1880-97
Landscape and figure painter. Travelled widely. Related to C. Bingham W. q.v. Add: Stapleford Hall, Notts. 1880 and 1890; West Hampstead, London 1885. † N 17, RA 4, RBA 1.

WRIGHT, Nora Exh. 1921-31
Landscape painter. Market Rasen, Lincs. 1921; Horncastle, Lincs. 1930. † GOU 5, I 1, NEA 3, RA 2.

WRIGHT, Percy J. Exh. 1907-14
Wealdstone, Middlesex. † L 10, RA 4.

WRIGHT, R.G. Exh. 1932-40
Bird and landscape painter. Normanton, Stanmore, Middlesex. † COO 101, RI 3.

WRIGHT, Richard Henry* 1857-1930
Architectural and landscape painter. Travelled widely on the Continent and Middle East. Married Catherine M. Wood q.v. Add: London. † ALP 6, L 6, M 1, NEA 1, RA 12, RHA 1, RI 2, ROI 3, WG 430.

WRIGHT, R.J. Exh. 1886
Mayfield, Weston, Southampton. † RHA 1.

WRIGHT, Robert Murdoch Exh. 1889-1902
Landscape painter. London 1889 and 1902; Parkstone, Dorset 1897. † L 1, RA 2, RBA 1, RI 1, RMS 1.

WRIGHT, Mrs. R.T. Exh. 1913-18
103 Cheyne Walk, London. † LS 11.

WRIGHT, Robert W.* Exh. 1880-1900
Domestic painter. London. † L 18, M 9, RA 5, RBA 21.

WRIGHT, Samuel junr. Exh. 1896-97
Cork 1896; Dublin 1897. † RHA 2.

WRIGHT, Miss S.F. Exh. 1893-1911
Portrait painter. London. † B 4, P 1, RA 2, RCA 1, ROI 1, SWA 1.

WRIGHT, Thomas Exh. 1935
Sculptor. 35 Colemeadow Road, Billesley, Birmingham. † RA 2.

WRIGHT, Tom Exh. 1888
31 Queen Mary Avenue, Croshall, Glasgow. † GI 1.

WRIGHT, T.P. Exh. 1886
340 Woodthorpe Rise, Sherwood, Notts. † N 1.

WRIGHT, W. Exh. 1885-86
31 Queen Mary Avenue, Glasgow. † RSA 2.

WRIGHT, William Exh. 1893-95
Medallist. 32 Salcott Road, Wandsworth Common, London. † RA 3.

WRIGHT, William Exh. 1885-95
Landscape and figure painter. London. † M 1, RA 2, RBA 19.

WRIGHT, William Exh. 1896
Marchmont, Falkirk. † RSW 1.

WRIGHT, William Exh. 1921-37
Egremont, Cheshire 1921; Trefriw, Wales 1926; Preston Wynne, nr. Hereford 1927. † RCA 9.

WRIGHT, W.E. Exh. 1930
19 Roseberry Avenue, Gateshead, Co. Durham. † NEA 1.

WRIGHT, Mrs. W.G. Exh. 1923-25
Brentwood, Abbotsford Road, Blundellsands, Liverpool. † L 2.

WRIGHT, W.H. Exh. 1887-88
London 1887; Leicester 1888. † D 5.

WRIGHT, W.H. Exh. 1909
251 Alfred Street Central, Nottingham. † N 1.

WRIGHT, William H. Exh. 1916-38
Sculptor. London 1916; Elam School of Art, Auckland, New Zealand 1931. † GI 2, RA 16.

WRIGHT, Will J. Exh. 1906-29
Glasgow. † GI 3.

WRIGHT, William P. Exh. 1882
Bird painter. 33 Norfolk Road, Essex Road, Islington, London. † RBA 1.

WRIGHT, William T. Exh. 1890-1913
Landscape painter. Kettering, Northampton. † L 1, N 1, RA 1, RI 1, ROI 1.

WRIGHTSON, Ellen Exh. 1905-8
Ockenden, Cuckfield, Haywards Heath, Sussex. † B 1, NG 1, RA 1, RCA 1.

WRIGHTSON, Miss H. Exh. 1912
Brighton. † SWA 2.

WRIGHTSON, Isabel b. 1890
Painter and teacher. b. Croydon. Studied Byam Shaw School and under Stanhope Forbes at Newlyn. Exh. 1919-38. Add: Croydon, Surrey. † L 3, RA 2, RI 12, ROI 9.

WRIGHTSON, Jocelyn Exh. 1922-25
London and Neasham Hall, Darlington, Co. Durham. † SWA 5.

WRIGHTSON, Margaret Exh. 1906-38
Sculptor. S.W.A. 1920. Add: Neasham Hall, Darlington, Co. Durham 1906; London 1913. † L 8, RA 22, SWA 13.

WRIGLEY, Mrs. A.H. Exh. 1916
The Vicarage, Clitheroe, Lancs. † RA 1.

WRIGLEY, Mrs. Mary Exh. 1894-1904
Formby, nr. Liverpool 1894; Northop, North Wales 1904. † B 1, L 1.

WROE, Miss M.A. Exh. 1882-87
Manchester. † L 3, M 6.

WROE, Mary McNicoll Exh. 1882-1930
Watercolour painter and wood engraver. Studied Manchester School of Art. Add: Manchester. † GI 1, L 47, M 18, RA 3, RBA 1, RED 1.

WROOT, Mrs. M. Exh. 1906
R.M.S. 1906. Add: 57 Goldhurst Terrace, South Hampstead, London. † RMS 2.

WROUGHTON, Miss B.C. Exh. 1893
Woolley Park, Wantage, Berks. † SWA 1.

WUNNERBERG, Carl* b. 1850
German figure painter. Exh. 1883. Add: 2 Queen's Road Studios, St. Johns Wood, London. † L 1, RA 1.

WYATT, A.C. Exh. 1883-1908
Watercolour landscape painter. London 1883; Lyndhurst, Hants. 1897. † B 2, D 4, GOU 6, L 4, M 7, NG 3, RA 5, RBA 17, RI 6, WG 51.

WYATT, Miss A.M.B. Exh. 1901
The Manse, Stormness, Orkney, N.B. † RI 1.

WYATT, Colin Exh. 1932-38
Landscape and portrait painter. London. † ALP 89, RBA 1, RED 1.

WYATT, Irene Exh. 1927-39
Portrait, flower and landscape painter. London 1927; Hurstpierpoint, Sussex 1929. † BA 91, GOU 1, NEA 15, RA 7, RED 1.

WYATT, Katharine Montagu Exh. 1889-1929
Landscape and architectural painter and watercolourist. London. † ALP 15, BG 1, D 2, FIN 52, M 3, RA 14, RBA 6, RED 72, RI 12, RSW 1, SWA 2.

WYATT, Mary L. Exh. 1903
† RMS 1.

WYBERGH, E. Exh. 1921-23
City School of Art, Hope Street, Liverpool 1921; Ellesmere, Salop 1922. † L 4.

WYBRANTS, Camilla Exh. 1931
14 Harley House, Upper Harley Street, London. † RBA 1.

WYBRANTS, J.H. Exh. 1910
2 Oakleigh Gardens, Whetstone, London. † RA 1.

WYBURD, Francis John* b. 1826
Genre, literary and historical painter. Studied R.A. Schools. R.B.A. 1879. Exh. 1880-94. Add: 41 Bryanston Street, Portman Square, London. † B 2, L 3, RA 2, RBA 25, ROI 1.

WYBURD, Mrs. Francis John Exh. 1883
Painter. 41 Bryanstone Street, Portman Square, London. † RI 1.

WYBURD, Leonard Exh. 1883-1906
Figure painter. 41 Bryanston Street, Portman Square, London 1883; 1 Cambridge Street, Hyde Park, London 1904. † B 9, L 4, M 1, RA 8, RBA 8, RI 12, ROI 3.

WYDENBRUCK, Countess Nora b. 1894
Painter, woodcut artist, author and journalist. b. London. Studied Frauen-Kunst-Schule, Vienna. Married Alfons Purtscher q.v. Exh. 1927-33. Add: London. † COO 15, RED 1.

WYETH, Paul James Logan b. 1920
Painter and etcher. Studied Royal College of Art. Add: Willesden School of Art. Exh. 1939-40. Add: 123 Portobello Road, London. † RA 4.

WYKES, Henry Exh. 1917-34
Miniature portrait painter. Exeter, Devon. † RA 8.

WYLD, R.S.B. Exh. 1911
31 Bedford Row, London. † RA 1.

WYLD, William* 1806-1889
Landscape painter, watercolourist and lithographer. Studied under Louis Francia. A.R.I. 1849, R.I. 1879. Add: 27 Rue Blanche, Paris 1880. † AG 17, FIN 1, GI 16, RI 18.

WYLDE, Miss D.V. Exh. 1904
19 Palace Gate, London. † SWA 2.

WYLDE, Miss E.M. Exh. 1902
17 The Terrace, St. Ives, Cornwall. † SWA 1.

WYLDE, Geoffrey Spencer b. 1903
Painter and etcher. Studied University of Cape Town, South Africa. Assistant lecturer in drawing and painting University of Cape Town, 1931-35. Exh. 1932-39. † BA 3, NEA 3, P 2.

WYLDE, Theresa (Tressie) V. Exh. 1897-1919
Watercolour figure and miniature portrait painter. London. † L 1, RA 7.

WYLES, Benjamin Exh. 1882-85
54 Nevill Street, Southport, Lancs. † L 2, M 2.

WYLES, Grace Exh. 1916-24
Landscape painter. A.S.W.A. 1920. Add: Chatham, Kent 1916; Rochester, Kent 1919; Tankerton, Kent 1924. † RA 3, SWA 10.

WYLIE, Georgina Mossman Exh. 1880-1918
Mrs. Greenlees. Landscape painter. R.S.W. 1878. Add: Glasgow 1880; Prestwick 1896. † DOW 3, GI 42, RA 1, RSA 18, RSW 89.

WYLIE, James Exh. 1938-40
High Road, Steventon, Ayrshire. † GI 2, RSW 2.

WYLIE, Kate Exh. 1902-40
Flower and portrait painter in oils and watercolour landscape painter. b. Skerlmorlie, Ayrshire. Studied Glasgow School of Art. Add: Homecraig, Skelmorlie. † GI 47, L 1, RA 4, RSA 19.

WYLIE, Michael Exh. 1883-85
Asnieres, nr. Paris 1883; Courbevoie, nr. Paris 1885. † GI 7.

WYLIE, R. Exh. 1889
Architect. Liverpool. † L 2.

WYLLIE, Aileen D. Exh. 1928-29
Figure painter. Tower House, Tower Street, Portsmouth. † L 2, RA 1.

WYLLIE, Barbara Exh. 1913
4 Colquitt Street, Liverpool. † L 1.

WYLLIE, Mrs. C. Exh. 1880-88
Charlotte Major. Figure painter. 3 Earls Court Terrace, Kensington, London. † G 7, L 1, M 5, NG 1.

WYLLIE, Charles William* 1859-1923
Landscape and coastal painter. Son of William Morison and brother of William Lionel W. q.v. R.B.A. 1886, R.O.I. 1888. "Digging for Bait" purchased by Chantrey Bequest 1877. Add: London. † B 6, G 1, GI 15, L 23, M 11, NG 26, RA 55, RBA 34, RI 5, ROI 50, TOO 1.

WYLLIE, G.K. Exh. 1887-90
Glasgow. † GI 7, RSA 2.

WYLLIE, Lt. Col. Harold* b. 1880
Marine painter, pencil artist, etcher and engraver. Studied Cope and Nicholls School and under Sir T.G. Jackson, Edwin Abbey and his father William Lionel W. q.v. Marine painter to the Royal Victoria Yacht Club, Ryde. Exh. 1903-24. Add: Rochester, Kent 1903; Portsmouth 1908. † GI 3, LEI 1, RA 11, RI 2.

WYLLIE, M.A. Exh. 1885
Painter. 11 Melina Place, Grove End, London. † RBA 1.

WYLLIE, William Exh. 1922
9 Dunn Street, Paisley, Glasgow. † RSW 1.

WYLLIE, William Lionel* 1851-1931
Marine and coastal painter, etcher, dry point artist and writer. Studied Heatherleys and R.A. Schools (Turner Gold medal 1869). Son of William Morison and father of Harold W. q.v. Marine painter to the Royal Victoria Yacht Club, Ryde. N.E.A. 1887, A.R.A. 1889, R.A. 1907, R.B.A. 1875, A.R:E. 1903, R.E. 1903, R.I. 1882 (ret. 1894, re-elected 1917). "Toil, Glitter, Grime and Wealth on a Flowing Tide" purchased by Chantrey Bequest 1883 and "The Battle of the Nile" purchased 1899. Add: London 1880; Rochester, Kent 1887; Portsmouth 1907. † AB 107, AG 4, B 5, CAR 1, CON 1, DOW 374, FIN 188, G 6, GI 12, L 33, LEI 150, M 18, NEA 8, RA 180, RBA 26, RE 66, RHA 2, RI 49, ROI 19, RSW 3, TOO 17.

WYLLIE, William Morison* Exh. 1880-91
Genre painter. Father of Charles William and William Lionel W. q.v. Add: London 1880; Les Banques, Guernsey, C.I. 1886; Rochester, Kent 1888. † B 7, G 1, GI 11, L 1, NG 1, RA 5, RBA 5, RHA 1, ROI 6.

WYLSON, Duncan Exh. 1935-39
Architect. 24 Red Lion Square, London. † RA 2.

WYMAN, Florence Exh. 1886-90
Flower painter. 103 King Henry's Road, South Hampstead, London. † B 1, RBA 6, RI 1.

WYMAN, Violet H. Exh. 1888-90
Figure painter. London. † B 1, L 1, M 1, RBA 9, ROI 1, RSA 2, SWA 1.

WYNANTS, Ernest Exh. 1931
273A Chausse de Battel, Malines, Belgium. † RSA 2.

WYNDHAM, Florence Exh. 1889-1917
London. † D 3, LS 3.

WYNDHAM, Hon. Mrs. Percy Scawen Exh. 1898
Madeline Caroline Frances Eden Campbell. Enamelist. 44 Belgrave Square, London. † RA 1.

WYNDHAM, Richard* b. 1896
Landscape and figure painter. b. Canterbury. Exh. 1923-40. Add: London. † BA 1, GOU 48, L 2, LEF 1, LEI 36, M 3, NEA 2, RED 1, RHA 1, TOO 78.

WYNESS, J. Fenton b. 1903
Painter and writer. Studied Grey's School of Art, Aberdeen. Exh. 1938. Add: 45 Salisbury Terrace, Aberdeen. † RSA 1.

WYNFIELD, David Wilkie* 1837-1887
Historical genre painter. Studied with J.M. Leigh. Add: London. † B 4, FIN 1, GI 1, L 4, M 2, RA 7.

WYNN, Edith L. Exh. 1896
Lyfield Lawn, Charlton Kings, Cheltenham. Glos. † B 2.

WYNN, John Exh. 1887
15 Lorne Street, Fairfield. † L 1.

WYNNE, Arthur Exh. 1897
2 Cedar Gardens, Putney, London. † RBA 1.

WYNNE, A.B. Exh. 1881-1906
Kingstown, Ireland 1881; Dublin 1896. † D 76, L 1, RHA 72.

WYNNE, Eironwy Exh. 1939
Landscape painter. Hatfield Peverell, Essex. † RA 1.

WYNNE, E. Kendrick Exh. 1900-26
Watercolour landscape painter. Travelled widely. Add: 62 Queen's Road, Bayswater, London 1900. † L 1, WG 62.

WYNNE, Gladys Exh. 1899
Woodlawn, Killarney. † RHA 2.

WYNNE, Gertrude E. Exh. 1895-1900
25 Bedford Street, Liverpool. † L 3.

WYNNE, Mrs. Nanette Exh. 1903-16
Headley, Hants. 1903; Chiddingfold, Surrey 1916. † B 1, RA 3.

WYNNE, O.J. Exh. 1923-38
† G 1, RI 1.

WYNNE, Mrs. R. Exh. 1930-36
Abergele, Wales. † RCA 5.

WYNNE, R.E. Exh. 1928
8 Wilton Road, Sparkhill, Birmingham. † B 2.

WYNNES, J.C. Exh. 1912
9 Woodburn Terrace, Edinburgh. † RSA 1.

WYNNE-WILLIAMS Exh. 1929
Painter. † AB 4.

WYNNIATT, Maude Exh. 1897
Watercolour portrait painter. The Art College, Wimbledon, Surrey. † RA 1.

WYON, Allan Exh. 1886-1914
Medallist. Father of Allan Gairdner W. q.v. Add: Langham Chambers, Portland Place, London. † L 1, RA 16.

WYON, Alfred Benjamin Exh. 1880-82
Medallist. Langham Chambers, Portland Place, London. † RA 10.

WYON, Allan Gairdner b. 1882
Sculptor and medallist. Studied R.A. Schools. Son of Allan W. q.v. Married Eileen M. W. q.v. A.R.M.S. 1921, R.M.S. 1922, H.R.M.S. 1935. Exh. 1915-39. Add: London 1915; Saltash, Cornwall 1935; Penzance 1939. † GI 15, L 21, RA 45, RHA 1, RMS 26, RSA 18.

WYON, Eileen M. b. 1883
nee Le Poer Trench. Painter, chalk and charcoal artist. Studied Dublin School of Art, R.A. Schools, and under Sir Arthur Cope. Married Allan Gairdner W. q.v. Exh. 1905-28. Add: Dublin 1905; London 1907. † GI 2, RHA 3.

WYPER, Jane Cowan d. 1898
Marine painter. Glasgow. † FIN 5, GI 20, L 2, RSA 7, RSW 2

WYSARD, Tony b. 1907
Caricaturist. b. Pangbourne, Berks. Contributed to "Sphere" and "Daily Dispatch". Travelled on the Continent and South America. Exh. 1936. † WG 100.

WYSE, Henry Taylor b. 1870
Watercolour painter, pastel artist, pottery worker and lecturer. b. Glasgow. Studied Dundee School of Art, Glasgow School of Art, Julians, and Colorassi's, Paris. Exh. 1899-1923. Add: Arbroath 1899; Edinburgh 1906. † GI 3, L 2, LS 6, RSA 8.

WYSMULLER, J.H. Exh. 1880
Landscape painter. 42 Mornington Crescent, Regents Park, London. † RA 1.

WYTSMAN, Juliette Exh. 1894
26 Rue du Berceau, Brussels. † GI 1.

WYTSMAN, R. Exh. 1894-1909
Brussels. † GI 1, I 2, L 1.

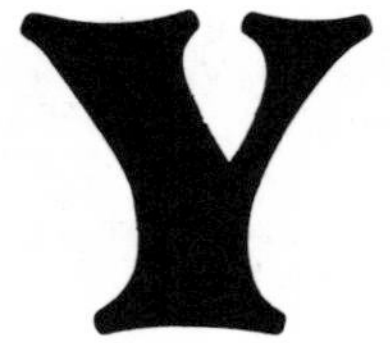

YABSLEY, P. Exh. 1932
417 Chester Road, Erdington, Birmingham. † B 1.

YALLAND, Thomas King 1845-1934
Landscape painter. Fishponds, Bristol. † B 4, L 1, M 1, RSA 1.

YANG, Miss Shoupi Exh. 1937
Bird and flower painter. London. † RA 2.

YARNELL, G.F. Exh. 1911-14
Derby 1911; Nottingham 1912. † N 9.

YARROW, Gwen Exh. 1917-22
Bickley, Kent. † SWA 2.

YARROW-JONES, R. Exh. 1915
† I 2.

YARWOOD, Thomas J. Exh. 1897
c/o Brunner Public Library, Northwich, Cheshire. † M 1.

YATES, Mrs. Ann b. 1897
Watercolour landscape painter. Studied Laird School of Art, Birkenhead. Exh. 1934-40. Add: St. Albans, Herts. 1936; Bedford 1938. † AR 2, COO 1, RBA 1, RI 3.

YATES, Annie Exh. 1907-8
Sale, Cheshire 1907; Altrincham, Cheshire 1908. † M 4.

YATES, Caroline Burland see GOTCH

YATES, Frederic d. 1919
Portrait, landscape and animal painter. Studied Paris, Italy and U.S.A. Travelled in China and Japan. Father of Mary Y. q.v. Add: London 1890, 1896 and 1909; Chislehurst, Kent 1893; Rydal, Ambleside 1907. † B 2, I 2, L 6, M 2, NEA 14, NG 25, P 17, RA 20, WG 88.

YATES, Harold Exh. 1927-40
Landscape painter. St. Michaels, Shinfield, Reading, Berks. † RA 1, RBA 2, RI 5, ROI 4.

YATES, Helen Exh. 1924-31
Portrait and figure painter. Glengeary Lodge, Glengeary, Co. Dublin. † RHA 17.

YATES, Miss I. Exh. 1901-3
Carlton-le-Moorland, Newark on Trent, Notts. † N 4.

YATES, John b. 1885
Landscape painter. Born and lived at Woodhead, Blackburn, Lancs. Exh. 1919-38. † G 1, L 33, M 2, RA 8, RCA 2.

YATES, Miss J.B. Exh. 1913-29
22 St. Helens Road, Ormskirk, Lancs. † L 14.

YATES, Lilian Delves Exh. 1901
35 Gratton Road, Kensington, London. † L 1.

YATES, Margaret Exh. 1909-14
Highfield, Heaton, Bolton, Lancs. † L 4, M 5, RCA 2.

YATES, Mary b. 1891
Pastel landscape artist and sculptor. b. Chislehurst, Kent. Studied under her father Frederic Y. q.v. and in London. Exh. 1918-24. Add: Rydal, Ambleside. † RA 1, RSA 4.

YATES, Miss O. Exh. 1898
Campbell House, Radcliffe, Notts. † N 2.

YATES, Thomas Brown b. 1882
Landscape, figure and portrait painter. b. Croydon. Studied Andre Lhote School, Paris. R.B.A. 1931. Exh. 1925-38. Add: London 1925; Thursley, nr. Godalming, Surrey 1935. † GI 1, NEA 3, P 5, RA 13, RBA 35.

YAXLEY, Miss M.H. Exh. 1938
West Down, Coleshill Road, Marston Green, Birmingham. † B 1.

YEADON, Dick b. 1896
Landscape painter. b. Brierfield, Lancs. Studied Allen Technical School Kendal. Exh. 1926-28. Add: 20 Ann Street, Kendal, Westmorland. † L 3, RA 1.

YEAMES, William Frederick* 1835-1918
Historical genre painter. b. Southern Russia where his father was Consul. Studied in London under G. Scharf and in Italy 1852-58. A.R.A. 1866, R.A. 1878. "Amy Robsart" purchased by Chantrey Bequest 1877. Add: London 1880; Richmond, Surrey 1893; Hanwell, Middlesex 1894; Teignmouth, Devon 1912. † B 6, G 2, GI 3, L 15, M 7, RA 46, RBA 1, RCA 1, RHA 3.

YEARSLEY, Frances Exh. 1928-36
60 North Road, St. Helens, Lancs. † L 3, RCA 4.

YEARSLEY, H. Exh. 1938
† M 1.

YEATES, Alfred Bowman b. 1867
Architect. Exh. 1910-38. Add: London. † RA 23, RI 21.

YEATES, Mrs. Annette V. Exh. 1937-38
Landscape painter. 25 Lower Baggot Street, Dublin. † RHA 5.

YEATES, George A. Exh. 1933-38
Landscape painter. 25 Lower Baggot Street, Dublin. † RHA 5.

YEATES, G.W. Exh. 1884-1931
Landscape painter. Dublin. † RHA 36.

YEATES, R.E. Exh. 1884-89
Dublin. † RHA 4.

YEATMAN, Alice Mary Exh. 1887-1905
Landscape and interior painter and teacher. b. Sutherland. Studied Heatherleys and Royal Drawing Society. Add: Sunderland. † NG 2, RI 1, RSA 1.

YEATS, Elizabeth C. Exh. 1898-99
Blenheim Road, Bedford Park, London. † RHA 4.

YEATS, Jack Butler* 1871-1957
Painter. Son of John Butler Y. q.v. and brother of William Butler Yeats the poet. Studied South Kensington and Westminster. A.R.H.A. 1915, R.H.A. 1916. Hon. Member London Group 1940. Add: Chertsey, Surrey 1895; Strete, nr. Dartmouth, Devon 1898; Greystones, Co. Wicklow 1909; Dublin 1925. † G 3, GOU 9, I 3, L 5, LS 32, RA 1, RHA 91, ROI 2, TOO 72, WG 49.

YEATS, John Butler 1839-1922
Figure and portrait painter. Father of Jack Butler Y. q.v. and William Butler Yeats the poet. A.R.H.A. 1887, R.H.A. 1892. Add: London 1880; Dublin 1881; Greystones, Co. Wicklow 1912. † I 13, L 1, RA 1, RBA 1, RHA 112.

YEATS, Lily Exh. 1898
3 Blenheim Road, Bedford Park, London. † RHA 1.

YEATS, Nellie H. Exh. 1887-1904
Flower painter. Kildare, Manby Road, Gt. Malvern, Worcs. † B 9, RA 1.

YELLAND, John Exh. 1880
24 George Street, Edinburgh. † RSA 1.

YELLI, Professor Exh. 1895
10 Via Mirsilio, Ficino, Florence. † NG 1.

YEMENIZ, Mlle. T. Exh. 1903
11 Rue de L'Universite, Paris. † L 1.

YEMMETT, Miss M.K. Exh. 1906
The Vicarage, Feltham, Middlesex. † RCA 1.

YEO, Imogen Exh. 1931-34
Watercolour landscape painter. Aldsworth House, nr. Emsworth, Hants. † COO 2, RA 1, RBA 1, RI 1.

YEOELL, W.J. Exh. 1886
26 Rosemount Buildings, Edinburgh. † RSA 1.

YEOMANS, Audrey Exh. 1938
Crayon Landscape artist. 3 Cavendish Crescent, The Park, Nottingham. † N 2.

YERINI, Joseph Exh. 1923
† RMS 1.

YETTS, Mrs. Gwendolen Exh. 1914-40
nee Hughes. Landscape, portrait and flower painter. Married Walter Percival Y. q.v. Add: Eastbourne 1914; London 1919. † AB 3, COO 2, L 3, RA 1, RI 2, SWA 7.

YETTS, Walter Percival b. 1878
Painter. b. Reading. Studied London University. Professor of Chinese Art and Archaeology, London University from 1932. Married Gwendolen Y. q.v. Add: London 1912 and 1914; Eastbourne 1913. † L 5, RA 3.

YGLESIAS, Mrs. V.P. Exh. 1890
Flower painter. 14 Grove End Road, St. Johns Wood, London. † RBA 1.

YGLESIAS, Vincent Philip Exh. 1880-1911
Landscape and figure painter. R.B.A. 1888. Add: London. † B 63, BG 1, DOW 1, FIN 1, G 1, GI 34, I 1, L 31, M 16, RA 34, RBA 175, RHA 25, RI 2, ROI 32.

YOCKNEY, K.A. Exh. 1937
Victoria Street, Ryde, I.O.W. † GI 1.

YON, Edmond Charles* 1861-1910
French landscape painter. Exh. 1885. Add: 59 Rue Lepic, Montmartre, Paris. † GI 1.

YONGE, Arthur D. Exh. 1881-90
Landscape painter. Hastings 1881 and 1890; Notting Hill, London 1888. † RA 3.

YONGE, Miss C.L. Exh. 1929-37
Painter and linocut artist. Cranleigh, Surrey 1929 and 1933; Stanmore, Middlesex 1932; London 1935. † B 5, COO 7, L 1, RCA 8, RED 5, RI 2, RSA 2.

YOOLE, Edward Exh. 1910-20
Birkenhead 1919; Liverpool 1920. † L 8.

YORK, F.J. Exh. 1891-92
Liverpool. † L 3.

YORK, Percy H. Exh. 1896-1909
93 Belgrave Road, St. Michaels, Liverpool 1896; Harringay, London 1909. † L 6.

YORKE, Adela Exh. 1929-34
1 Southwick Crescent, London. † RCA 6.

YORKE, H.W. Exh. 1915-35
Black and white landscape artist. Nottingham 1915; Beeston, Notts. 1929. † N 15.

YORKE, Lady Lilian Exh. 1905
22 Queen Anne's Gate, London. † NG 1.

YORKE, R. Exh. 1923
16 Stoney Street, Nottingham. † N 1.

YORKE, Reginald Exh. 1908-20
Liverpool. † L 5.

YORKE, T.F. Exh. 1930-33
Liverpool. † L 2.

YORKE, William Hoard* Exh. 1892-97
Marine painter. 93 Belgrave Road, St. Michael's, Liverpool. † L 3.

YOULE, Mrs. F.L. Exh. 1903
37 Kensington Gardens Square, London. † SWA 2.

YOULE, Mrs. Thes. H. Exh. 1906-7
126 Queen's Road, Bayswater, London. † L 1, RHA 1.

YOUNG, Mrs. Exh. 1934
Watercolour landscape painter. † COO 2.

YOUNG, A. Exh. 1885
18 Morningside Terrace, Edinburgh. † RSA 2.

YOUNG, Miss A. Exh. 1920
100 North Frederick Street, Glasgow. † L 1.

YOUNG, Alexander* Exh. 1883-1920
Landscape painter and teacher. Edinburgh 1883 and 1920; London 1889 and 1898; Pittenween, Fife 1892; South Croydon, Surrey 1919. † GI 1, L 1, RA 8, ROI 2, RSA 10.

YOUNG, Andrew Exh. 1880-1919
Burntisland. † B 2, GI 11, L 8, LS 15, RSA 3.

YOUNG, Arthur Exh. 1882-1917
Architect. London. † M 1, RA 5.

YOUNG, Alexander Ayton Exh. 1925
15 Glebe Terrace, Alloa. † RSA 1.

YOUNG, A. Denoon Exh. 1891-1900
Painter. R.M.S. 1897. Add: London. † RBA 1, RMS 17, RSA 9.

YOUNG, A.M. Exh. 1885
1 Notting Hill Terrace, London. † B 1.

YOUNG, A. Stanley Exh. 1898-1912
Sculptor. Trafalgar Square, Chelsea, London. † RA 8, RI 1.

YOUNG, Aggie Thoms Exh. 1898
15 Kelvingrove Street, Glasgow. † GI 1.

YOUNG, Alexander W. Exh. 1892-1932
Glasgow. † GI 28.

YOUNG, B. Exh. 1886
151 Edmund Street, Birmingham. † B 1.

YOUNG, B. Exh. 1896
481 Mansfield Road, Sherwood, Notts. † N 1.

YOUNG, Blamire* 1865-1935
Landscape painter. A.R.B.A. 1919, R.B.A. 1922, R.I. 1920. Add: Ditchling, Sussex 1914; London 1918; Ropley, Hants. 1921. † FIN 41, I 11, L 2, NEA 1, RA 6, RBA 15, RI 3, RSA 3.

YOUNG, Bessie Innes Exh. 1896-1936
Still life, landscape and garden painter and teacher. b. Glasgow. Studied Glasgow School of Art and Academy Delecluse, Paris. Add: Glasgow. † GI 25, I 1, L 30, NEA 3, RSA 24.

YOUNG, Miss Christian Exh. 1932
Mora, Bonnybridge. † RSA 1.

YOUNG, Christine Exh. 1937-39
† NEA 3.

YOUNG, Clyde Exh. 1901-22
Architect. 6 Lancaster Place, Strand, London. † RA 8.

YOUNG, Mrs. Constance A. Exh. 1902-3
Miniature portrait painter. Eastleigh, London Road, Norbury, London. † RA 2, RMS 1.

YOUNG, Christina E. Exh. 1880-83
Landscape painter. 17 Lexham Gardens, South Kensington, London. † D 2, GI 1, SWA 4.

YOUNG, Miss C.M. Exh. 1934-35
69 Melbourne Road, Leicester. † N 3.

YOUNG, Doris E. Exh. 1936
† RMS 1.

YOUNG, D. Vallance Exh. 1913-21
Abergaveny 1913; Sidmouth, Devon 1921. † RCA 3.

YOUNG, Emma Exh. 1899
11 Adelaide Terrace, Waterloo, nr. Liverpool. † B 1.

YOUNG, Emmeline Exh. 1882-1924
Landscape and figure painter. Huddersfield 1882; Boscombe 1924. † B 1, L 12, RA 3, RBA 2.

YOUNG, Edmund D. Exh. 1908-40
Flower and still life painter. Edinburgh. † GI 16, L 5, RA 5, RSA 48, RSW 1.

YOUNG, Eileen M. Exh. 1937
Flower painter. The Old Rectory, Sanderstead, Surrey. † RA 1.

YOUNG, Evelyn M. Exh. 1912-39
Landscape, flower and miniature portrait painter. Married C. Randle Jackson q.v. Add: Ruislip, Middlesex 1912; Chiswick, London 1916; Croydon, Surrey 1917. † AR 2, L 7, RA 17, SWA 2, WG 39.

YOUNG, Mrs. Flora Exh. 1926-28
Flower painter. 4 St. Peters Street, St. Albans, Herts. † RA 1, RI 1.

YOUNG, Mrs. Filson Exh. 1919
† I 2.

YOUNG, Fannie D. Exh. 1892
The Woodlands, Blossomfield, Solihull, Birmingham. † B 1.

YOUNG, Mrs. Frances E. d. 1938/9
Miniature portrait painter. R.M.S. 1902. Add: Sutton, Surrey 1900; Richmond, Surrey 1912; Thornton Heath, Surrey 1914. † L 5, RA 1, RMS 59.

YOUNG, Miss F.G. Exh. 1911-15
London. † L 3, RA 2.

YOUNG, Godfrey Exh. 1885
Teign Villa, Palace Road, Tulse Hill, London. † RI 1.

YOUNG, Geo P.K. Exh. 1887
42 Tay Street, Perth. † RSA 1.

YOUNG, Harry Exh. 1934-37
Painter. 2 Dalmeny Road, Tufnell Park, London. † RA 2.

YOUNG, H.H. Exh. 1885-86
Carlton Lane, Horsham, Sussex. † G 1, RA 1.

YOUNG, H.P. Exh. 1909-13
28 Clapham Road, Bedford. † D 11.

YOUNG, Ivy Ruth b. 1906
Sculptor, modeller and illuminator. Studied St. Albans School of Art. Exh. 1927. Add: 178 Handside Lane, Welwyn Garden City, Herts. † RA 1.

YOUNG, Jean b. 1914
Painter, black and white artist and illustrator. Studied under McCannell at Farnham, R.A. Schools 1933-38 and Belle Arti Florence 1938. A.S.W.A. 1940. Exh. 1937-40. Eastcote, Ruislip, Middlesex. † RA 1, SWA 3.

YOUNG, Jessie b. 1879
Painter. Studied Beckenham School of Art 1898 and watercolour under L. Burleigh Bruhl 1935-38. Exh. 1936. Add: Watford, Herts. † RCA 1.

YOUNG, John Exh. 1893-1907
Forfar, N.B. 1893; Glasgow 1907. † GI 2.

YOUNG, Julian Exh. 1881
Landscape painter. 7 Charnwood Street, Derby. † N 2.

YOUNG, Juliet Exh. 1926
33 Warwick Square, London. † GI 2, GOU 2.

YOUNG, James A. Exh. 1918
Argyle Street, Glasgow. † GI 1.

YOUNG, Janet B.B. Exh. 1914-23
Glasgow. † GI 6, L 1, RSA 1.

YOUNG, John Henry Exh. 1924-36
Watercolour landscape painter. b. Wellington, New Zealand. Add: National Bank of Australia, 7 Lothbury, London. † D 1, L 2, RA 1, RI 16.

YOUNG, J. Reeve Exh. 1933
Architect. 3 Bedford Square, London. † RA 1.

YOUNG, John William Exh. 1883-85
22 Royal Circus, Edinburgh. † GI 1, RSA 2.

YOUNG, John W.A. Exh. 1928-40
Landscape and figure painter. Visited the Middle East. Add: London. † AR 44, RA 1, RBA 15, RID 4.

YOUNG, Keith Downes Exh. 1892
Architect. 17 Southampton Street, Bloomsbury, London. † RA 1.

YOUNG, Lady Kathleen Hilton
see SCOTT, Lady Kathleen

YOUNG, Keith O.B. Exh. 1891-92
3 Tipperlin Road, Edinburgh. † RSA 4.

YOUNG, Lilian Exh. 1884-90
Portrait, figure and flower painter. London. † B 1, D 13, M 1, RA 5, RBA 4, RI 3, SWA 5.

YOUNG, Lucy Exh. 1923-38
Landscape painter. Stechford 1923; Knowle, Warwicks. 1926. † B 16, RA 1, ROI 4, SWA 2.

YOUNG, Mabel b. 1900
Landscape painter. Studied under Paul Henry in Dublin. Exh. 1928-40. Add: Carrigoona Cottage, Kilmacanogue, Co. Wicklow. † RHA 12.

YOUNG, Monica Exh. 1929
† NEA 1.

YOUNG, Mabel A. Exh. 1918-31
Portrait and landscape painter. 80 Eland Street, Basford, Nottingham. † N 15.

YOUNG, Miss M.E. Exh. 1910
1A Oxford and Cambridge Mansions, London. † L 1.

YOUNG, Maggie F. Exh. 1889-94
Flower painter. London. † L 1, RBA 3, ROI 4, SWA 5.

YOUNG, Margaret H.K. Exh. 1888
110 North Frederick Street, Glasgow. † GI 1.

YOUNG, Mabel J. Exh. 1888-1908
Painter. London. † B 10, L 7, RA 4, RBA 5, SWA 6.

YOUNG, Mary-Rose Exh. 1889-90
Glasgow. † G 1, GI 2, RSA 1.

YOUNG, N.Y. Exh. 1891
Bolton Studios, Redcliffe Road, London. † L 1.

YOUNG, O.A. Exh. 1890-1901
Figure painter. London. † NG 2, ROI 1.

YOUNG, Robert Exh. 1881-98
Glasgow 1881 and 1894; Manchester 1884; Edinburgh 1885. † GI 6, RSA 4.

YOUNG, R. Clouston d. 1929
R.S.W. 1901. Exh. from 1887. Add: Glasgow. † GI 75, L 2, RSA 9, RSW 100.

YOUNG, R.H. Exh. 1885
Landscape painter. 226 Fulham Road, South Kensington, London. † RBA 1.

YOUNG, R.L. Exh. 1933
37 Stirling Road, Edgbaston, Birmingham. † B 1.

YOUNG, Richard L. Exh. 1937-40
Miniature portrait painter. West Cromwell Road, London. † RA 3.

YOUNG, Mrs. Richard L. Exh. 1938
† RMS 1.

YOUNG, R.M. Exh. 1927
Portrait artist. † LEI 1.

YOUNG, Miss R.R.B. Exh. 1910-11
5 Gt. Western Terrace, Glasgow. † GI 2, RA 1.

YOUNG, Stephen Exh. 1887
134 Bath Street, Glasgow. † RSA 1.

YOUNG, Stanley S. Exh. 1890-1904
Figure and portrait painter. London. † L 1, RA 5, ROI 2.

YOUNG, Thomas Exh. 1880-1904
Edinburgh. † RSA 21.

YOUNG, T.P.W. Exh. 1919-38
Glasgow. † GI 13, RSA 5, RSW 1.

YOUNG, T.U. Exh. 1880-88
Terenure, Ireland 1880; Rathmines, Dublin 1881. † RHA 15.

YOUNG, Violet F. Exh. 1930-36
† RMS 2.

YOUNG, Viva M.J. Exh. 1936
Painter. Churton Cottage, Churt, Surrey. † RA 2.

YOUNG, Mrs. Vera R. Exh. 1922-32
Rainworth Lodge, Rainworth, Notts. † N 4.

YOUNG, William Exh. 1881-1900
Architect. 4 Lancaster Place, Strand, London. † GI 1, RA 13.

YOUNG, William d. 1916
Landscape painter. R.S.W. 1880. Exh. from 1880. Add: Glasgow. † DOW 6, GI 101, L 2, RA 4, RSA 34, RSW 88.

YOUNG, W. Drummond Exh. 1880-1920
Edinburgh. † GI 10, RSA 24.

YOUNG, William Maclellan Exh. 1912-26
Glasgow 1912; Bridge of Allen 1921. † GI 8, L 3, RSA 2.

YOUNGER, Edwin B. Exh. 1899
Painter. 5 Worley Road, St. Albans, Herts. † RA 1.

YOUNGER, Jane Exh. 1915-40
Landscape painter. Glasgow 1915; Edinburgh 1919. † AB 1, COO 22, GI 11, L 5, RSA 13, RSW 22, SWA 11.

YOUNGER, Piercy Exh. 1937
31 St. James Square, London. † RBA 1.

YOUNGHUSBAND, R. Exh. 1912
Rosemorran, Woodside Road, Sutton, Surrey. † RA 1.

YOUNGMAN, Annie Mary 1860-1919
Genre, still life and flower painter. Studied under her father John Mallows Y. q.v. R.I. 1887, S.W.A. 1886. Add: London 1880 and 1916; Porton, nr. Salisbury, Wilts. 1902. † B 38, D 4, FIN 1, GI 1, L 1, M 6, RA 6, RBA 8, RHA 39, RI 113, ROI 9, SWA 75.

YOUNGMAN, Harold James b. 1886
Sculptor. b. Bradford. Studied Plymouth School of Art, Royal College of Art 1908-12 and R.A. Schools. Teacher of Sculpture Hornsey School of Arts and Crafts. Exh. 1915-40. Add: London. † GI 3, L 8, RA 26, RSA 6.

YOUNGMAN, John Mallows* 1817-1899
Landscape painter and etcher. Studied under Henry Sass. A.R.I. 1841. Father of Annie Mary Y. q.v. Exh. 1880-82. Add: 1 Notting Hill Terrace, London. † D 1, L 1, M 2, RA 4, RE 3.

YOUNGMAN, Nan b. 1906
Painter. b. Maidstone. Studied Slade School and London Day Training College. Exh. 1939. Add: 3 Penn House, Hampstead, London. † RA 1.

YOUNGS, Lawrence Exh. 1888
Architectural painter. London. † RA 1, RBA 1.

YOUNGS, R.T. Exh. 1930-34
Sculptor. Wilford, Notts. 1930; Nottingham 1934. † N 2.

YOURELLE, T.J. Exh. 1884
38 South Circular Road, Dublin. † RHA 1.

YOURIEVITCH, Serge Exh. 1925
Sculptor. 9 Regent Street, London. † RA 3.

YOXALL, Nora N. Exh. 1937
Stained glass artist. 28 Birchfield Road, Birmingham. † RA 1.

YPRES, Earl of Exh. 1928-39
Watercolour landscape painter. The Ivy House, Hampton Court, London. † GOU 156, RI 5, WG 30.

YRURTIA, Rogelio b. 1879
Sculptor. b. Buenos Aires, Argentina. Exh. 1912. Add: 8 Rue de Gottenberg, Boulogne sur Seine, France. L 2, RSA 2.

YSENBURG, Count C. Exh. 1892
Painter. c/o Dollman and Son, 6 New Compton Street, Soho, London. † RBA 3.

YSERN-y-ALIE, Pierre b. 1876
Spanish artist. Exh. 1909-10. Add: c/o Allied Artists Association, 67 Chancery Lane, London. † LS 6.

YUI, Mme. Shufang Exh. 1939
Watercolour painter. † BA 85.

YUILLE, William Exh. 1885-87
Car Meadow, Hayfield, Derbys. † GI 2, L 1, M 1, RHA 1.

YUILL Helen C. Exh. 1932-34
34 Learmouth Street, Falkirk. † RSA 3.

YUILL, Marion Exh. 1892
26 Palace Gardens, London. † GI 1.

YULE, Winifred see HAYES

YULE, William J. 1868-1900
Portrait painter. Edinburgh 1894; Dundee 1895; London 1897. † GI 6, NEA 1, P 1, RSA 5.

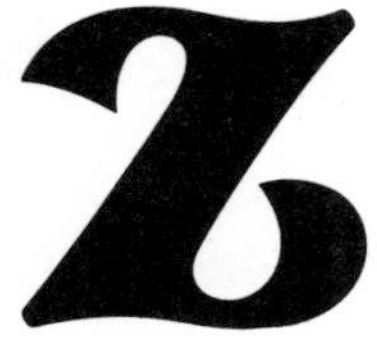

ZACHO, Christian* b. 1843
Danish painter. Exh. 1892. Add: Copenhagen. † RA 1.

ZADKIN, Joe Exh. 1914
35 Rue Rousselet, Paris. † LS 3.

ZADKINE, Ossip* 1890-1967
Gouache painter. Exh. 1928. † TOO 22.

ZAHN, Dorothy Exh. 1939
11 Belsize Grove, London. † SWA 1.

ZAKARIAN, Zachaire Exh. 1905-14
Turkish artist. Add: Paris. † I 1, RSA 1.

ZAMBACO, Mme. M.T. Exh. 1886-88
Sculptor. 6 Clarendon Place, Hyde Park, London. † RA 5.

ZANADO, Exh. 1936
Flower painter. † RED 1.

ZANETTI, Guiseppe Exh. 1891
Fondamente, Soccerso 1585, Venice. † RSA 1.

ZANON, E. Exh. 1924
Watercolour landscape painter. 13 Boulevard les Invalides, Paris. † RA 1.

ZEITLIN, Alexander b. 1872
Sculptor. b. Russia. Exh. 1902-8. Add: London and Paris. † B 3, GI 9, L 5, M 2, NG 13.

ZELL, Beatrice Exh. 1880
Watercolour fruit painter. Fairfax House, Withington, Manchester. † RBA 1.

ZETTWITZ, Christiana Exh. 1900
Bellefield, Alexandra Drive, Aintree, Liverpool. † L 1.

ZEVORT, G. Exh. 1921
Wood engraver. † GOU 7.

ZEVORT, Madeline Exh. 1916
Landscape painter. 1 Mentone Villas, Clarendon Road, Ashford, Middlesex. † NEA 1.

ZEWY, K. Exh. 1890
† TOO 1.

ZEZZOS, Alessandro Exh. 1889-1909
Watercolour figure painter. Edinburgh 1889; Paris 1906. † L 5, LS 5, RA 2, RBA 1, RI 3.

ZIEBLAND, H. Exh. 1890
† TOO 1.

ZIEGLER, Mlle. A. Exh. 1913
Landscape painter. † ALP 3.

ZIEGLER, Archibald b. 1903
Painter, illustrator and mural decorator. Studied L.C.C. Central School of Arts and Crafts 1927-30. Visiting instructor for figure drawing and painting St. Martins School of Art. Exh. 1931. Add: 25 Edith Grove, Chelsea, London. † RA 1.

ZIELINSKA, de see D

ZILCKEN, R. Exh. 1884
The Hague, Holland. † L 1.

ZILEN, A.S. Exh. 1897
Paris. † P 1.

ZILERI, A. Susan Exh. 1887-1923
Portrait, interior and still life painter. b. Scotland. Studied Florence and Paris. Add: London. † B 2, L 3, NEA 2, RA 7, RID 34, ROI 2.

ZIMMERER, F.J. Exh. 1919
The Greengate, Kirkcudbright. † GI 2.

ZIMMERMAN, Amy Mary Exh. 1885-88
Glasgow 1885; Fallowfield, Manchester 1888. † GI 3, L 1.

ZIMMERMAN, Ernest 1852-1901
German painter. Exh. 1881-87. Add: Munich. † RA 2.

ZIMMERMAN, Henry Exh. 1880-98
Landscape painter. R.B.A. 1890. Add: London. † G 1, L 1, RA 3, RBA 72, RHA 3, ROI 2.

ZINGG, Jules Emile* b. 1882
French painter. Exh 1909-28. Add: Paris. † GI 1, GOU 7, L 1.

ZINK, George Frederick Exh. 1882-1915
Figure and miniature portrait painter. London. † GI 2, GOU 5, L 1, RA 38, RBA 5, RI 10, RMS 1, RSA 1.

ZINKEISEN, Anna Katrina* 1901-1976
Portrait, figure and landscape painter and mural decorator. b. Kilereggan, Scotland. Studied R.A. Schools. R.O.I. 1929. Sister of Doris Clare Z. q.v. Exh. 1920-40. Add: Pinner, Middlesex 1920; London 1924. † BA 2, GI 3, I 1, L 12, P 13, RA 24, RBA 1, RED 1, RHA 2, RMS 1, ROI 30, RSA 6, SWA 3.

ZINKEISEN, Doris Clare* Exh. 1918-40
Portrait and landscape painter and theatrical designer. b. Gareloch, Scotland. Sister of Anna Katrina Z. q.v. Add: London. † GI 1, L 8, LEI 29, P 8, RA 19, RED 5, RHA 1, RSA 7, SWA 3.

ZIPLEY, E.D. Exh. 1884
c/o Andrea, Heathfield House, Greenheys, Manchester. † M 2.

ZITTAU, Rudolf Schramm b. 1874
German artist. Exh. 1904-8. Add: Munich. † GI 3.

ZO, Achille* Exh. 1882
Portrait painter. Bayonne, France and c/o A.H. Campbell Johnson, 84 St. Georges Square, London. † RA 1.

ZOETE, Winifred Exh. 1897-98
Chelmsford, Essex. † SWA 4.

ZOIR, Emile b. 1867
Swedish artist. Exh. 1907-8. Add: Paris 1907; Gothenburg, Sweden 1908. † L 1, RA 1.

ZOLLA, V. Exh. 1905-9
Portrait painter. Maidstone, Kent 1905; Torino, Italy 1909. † L 4, RA 1.

ZONA, A. Exh. 1882-85
6 Collingwood Road, South Kensington, London 1882; Via Flaminia, Rome 1883. † M 3, RSA 2.

ZORN, Anders L.* 1860-1920
Swedish portrait and figure painter and etcher. Add: London 1883; Paris 1888; Mora, Sweden 1905. † CG 132, CON 13, D 4, GI 4, I 38, L 41, P 2, RA 12, RI 7, RSA 4.

ZUBER, Jean Henri* 1844-1909
French landscape painter. Exh. 1883-1907. Add: Paris. † GI 2, RA 2.

ZUBLI, Mme. Exh. 1884-85
The Hague, Holland. † L 2.

ZUGEL, Professor Heinrich* b. 1850
German cattle painter. Exh. 1883-99. Add: Munich. † FIN 1, GI 6.

ZULAWSKI, Marek Exh. 1937
Painter. 59 Ladbroke Grove, London. † P 1.

ZULOAGA, Ignacio* 1870-1945
Spanish painter. H.R.B.A. 1919. Add: Eibar, Spain 1893; Paris 1910. † GI 4, I 4, P 2.

ZWANENBERG, Van see V

ZWART, W. Exh. 1905-13
Etcher. Amsterdam. † FIN 8, I 1.

ZWILLER, Marie Augustin* b. 1850
French painter. Exh. 1910-12. Add: 3 Villa Mequille, Neuilly sur Seine, France. † L 3.

ZWINTSCHER, Oscar 1870-1916
German artist. Exh. 1901-4. Add: Dresdener Strasse 33, Meissen, Saxony. † I 2.